CENSUS OF INDIA
1931

CENSUS OF INDIA 1931

WITH COMPLETE SURVEY OF TRIBAL LIFE AND SYSTEMS

IN THREE VOLUMES

VOL. I

J. H. HUTTON

With an Introduction by
K. S. SINGH
Director General, Anthropological Survey of India

GYAN

GYAN PUBLISHING HOUSE

New Delhi 110 002

CENSUS OF INDIA - 1931

Reprint, 2008

ISBN: 81-212-0171-3 (Set)

Gyan Publishing House
4741/23, Main Ansari Road, Darya Ganj,
New Delhi-110002
Phones : 23282060, 23261060
Fax : 011-23285914
E-mail: books@gyanbooks.com
Website: www.gyanbooks.com

Printed at : Vishal Kaushik Printers, Delhi

Foreword

The census report of 1931 was easily the most comprehensive of all such reports complete with maps, statistics, ethnographic accounts and the provinces' reports together with a three-volume all-India report. It has been, therefore, rightly regarded as representing the summit of the series of the census reports that began to be filed since 1881 in the colonial period. The census of 1941 was constrained by the war time economies. The extensive format of the 1931 census inquiry and of its reports could also be explained by the fact that they were drawn up by and under the direction of not an administrator-turned-academician but by an administrator who was formally trained as an anthropologist. J.H. Hutton (1885-1968) brought to bear on his work as the census commissioner the administrative experience of working in the North-east and professionalism of a high order. His major monographs on the Angami and Sema Nagas (1921) and his contributions to J.P. Mills' studies on the Lotha and Ao Nagas were behind him, and many of his ideas on social formations including caste in India, which crystalized in his well-known book, *Caste in India* (1946) were taking shape, of which he gave ample indications in this report. The scope of the census enquiry was widened to include all of the tribes and exterior castes now called the scheduled castes. In laying the foundation of a complete census of these backward communities Hutton was anticipating a great deal by way of the concern that the conditions of these communities would arouse in the constitutional set up that took shape from the mid-1930s. In fact Hutton was one of those administrators who believed that at least the tribals—if not the exterior castes who were as backward-formed a distinct element in the Indian population which was not amenable to normal constitutional processes but which required a strategy of intervention by the government to protect their rights and promote their welfare. He was instrumental in mobilising support for the idea of excluding the primitive tribes from the operation of the constitutional processes, under the Government of India Act of 1935, much to the chagrin of the nationalists who saw in such efforts the shades of the imperial policy of divide and rule. Nor could it be. denied that the exposition of the exterior castes provided grist to the political mill. In retrospect, however, it could be stated that this concern for the welfare of the backward communities was amply reflected later in the Constitution of India with the incorporation in it of the provisions for protection and welfare of the scheduled castes and scheduled tribes.

A merit of this reports is that it gives, for the first time, a reasonably accurate estimate of the numbers and distribution of primitive tribes, based on what was described as a complete census of these people at that time. As Hutton says, no serious attempt had been made from 1891 to arrive at the figures of hill and forest tribes. The 1891 figure of 15 million was incomplete. The 1921 data of 16 million omitted not only' many major tribes but also many small ones. In contrast the 1931 census enumerated all primitive tribes "whatever, their numbers and irrespective of the percentage provison for individual tabulation of caste.' This made it possible to give the accurate number of an identifiable tribal unit, though it was not easy to indicate the extent to which such a unit remained primitive in its habits. While we will revert to this aspect a little later, it would be appropriate to mention that the population of tribe went up steeply to 24.6 million in 1931 in India (including Ceylon and Burma), an increase of nearly 8 million since 1921, out of a population of 352 million, which was 6.9 per cent of the total population. It is necessary to recall that in arriving at this figure Hutton had made all kinds of adjustments. The tribal figure for India (both British and Princely) was rounded off to 27.50 million out of a population of 352 million. Today the population of tribes *i.e.* 51,628,638 (1981) has moved upto 7.76 per cent of the population, and their number from 142 in 1931 to 610 (including sub-tribes).

Similarly, another feature of this report is its first authentic description of all of exterior castes now labelled as the scheduled castes, as mentioned earlier. The new nomenclature in 1931 involved a transition from the concept of the depressed classes in the previous censuses which was considered derogatory, to the term exterior castes which connoted "exclusion but not extrusion". In pursuance of the official policy to generate a better knowledge of the backward and depressed classes and of the problems involved in their present and future welfare, the 1931 census prepared a complete list of the castes that suffered from social disabilities such as denial of access to temples, schools and wells, particularly in the South. The definition of this new category was made rigorous by the inclusion of such parameters as servicing or non-servicing by Brahmins, barbers, water carriers, tailors etc. and pollution by touch and acceptance of water. The 1921 census had estimated the minimum number of the depressed castes at 52.6 million as against 42 million given by the Franchise committee of 1919. The 1931 census identified 277 castes together with the tea garden coolie castes and others (Sudra, Valmiki, Ramdasia etc.) adding up to a population of 50,195,77, which appeared to be a reasonable estimate at that time. This process of identification of the scheduled castes was the first step towards the identification of their problems and of the step to be taken to solve them. Today there are 504 of such communities, nearly double the number of those in the 1931 census, and their population has gone up to 104,754,623 (1981), their proportion to the total population rising from 10.1 in 1931 to 15.57 per cent in 1981.

Contrary to general impression the census of 1931 did not generate data on all castes—as in the case of the primitive tribes and exterior castes—which could be and is supposed to be used by caste lobbies particularly during elections today. In fact the scope of this census in regard to the coverage of castes was rather restricted. The state census officials were told not to tabulate figures for such castes as the state government did not approve of, and the minimum of four rather than two per *mille* (as in 1921) was suggested as the minimal demographic standard for enumeration of castes. This resulted in the enumeration of only a dozen or so of selected castes of wide distribution. The census generated data of such castes by sex ratio, literacy, family-size, fertility, marriage and occupation. This remains a unique feature of the census of 1931, even though it is restricted to selected castes, which were supposed to have served as specimens of the society for all India purposes. Yet another peculiarity of caste enumeration was the reversion to the 1891 census method of grouping castes according to their occupation, even though it was admitted that the matter of occupation was not always a non-contentious issue. Hutton very much hoped to be able to get round the vexatious issue of caste ranking and avoid any semblance of arrangement by order of social precedence. He was critical of Risley's attempt to rank castes which unwillingly made census authorities the dispenser of caste ranking. "All subsequent census officers", he lamented, "must have cursed the day when it occurred to Sir Herbert Risley, no doubt in order to test his admirable theory of the relative nasal index, to attempt to draw up a list of castes according to their rank in society. He failed, but the results of his attempt are almost as troublesome as if he had succeeded, for every census gives rise to a pestiferous deluge of representations, accompanied by highly problematic histories, asking for recognition of some alleged fact or hypothesis of which the census as a department is not legally competent to judge and of which its recognition, if accorded, would be socially valueless. Moreover, as often as no direct action is requested against the corresponding hypothesis of other castes . . . its (the caste's) standing is in fact to be attained by standing upon others rather than with them." Though it is not mentioned in this report, 175 of such claims were registered, out of which 80 were to Kshatriya status, 33 to Brahmin and 15 to Vaisya in the four census regions (of United Provinces, Bengal and Sikkim, Bihar and Orissa, Central Provinces and Berar). Therefore, Hutton pleaded, for the abandonement of the return of caste because it cast an avoidable burden on the census administration. This was done twenty years later in 1951 but not for the same reason. The Constitution of India forbade discrimination on the ground on caste, and enumeration of caste, except that of the social cateogories such as the scheduled castes and the scheduled tribes, was therefore discontinued.

Like other census officials Hutton, too, was prone to describe tribal religion as the "surplus material not yet built into the temple of Hinduism" and to highlight the process of the tribes being swallowed up by this religion. Of the total number of tribes estimated at 24.6 million, 8.28 million, *i.e.* about one-third, was returned as adhering to tribal religions. The majority of the remainder was Hindu; there were also Christians—a growing number—Buddhists and Muslims. This Hinduisation of tribes was ascribed to (*a*) "the energetic" propaganda by the Hindu Mahasabha to return as Hindu every person whose religion could not be found to have originated outside India, that is practically everyone except Muslims, Christians, Parsis and Jews (*b*) agitations by such tribes as Gonds and Oraons to be returned as Hindu and (*c*) action of "overzealous" enumerators mostly Hindus, particularly in the north-east at work among Khasis, Kachari and Miris. While this process of returning tribals as Hindus or Hinduised tribals, which continued to be reported upon in subsequent censuses also, could be related to some of the above mentioned factors, the Hindu Mahasabha was given an importance that it did not deserve. There were other factors, too, of which the census authorities were only dimly aware, namely, the transformation of the tribe into the peasant, as a result of the transfer of technology by and the acceptance by the first of *jati* mores of the latter. Hutton mentions a Korwa telling his census superintendent of the Cenral Provinces, "if we had plough cattle, we should be Hindus", but he could not elaborate on this economic dimension of the process, and instead chose to attribute it to the difficulty of defining Hinduism with its great latitude of religious beliefs and practices, which "makes it possible for a Hindu socially to have a religious belief shared with others who do not regard themselves as members of the same society." It was really not wholly so. The economic dimension which did not fall within the ambit of the census authorities to explore was as important, if not more, than the social.

These trends have persisted since. The number of tribals following their religion declined by 33 per cent between 1921 and 1931. It has fallen from roughly one-third (8.2 million) of the tribal people in 1931 to about 6 per cent now (1981), with Hinduism claiming 87 per cent and Christianity 7 per cent of adherents among tribes. Even so, Hutton and those who have written about this subject seem to have underestimated the autonomy of tribal society and of its religion. Tribal religions have not disappeared as feared even though the censuses continue to return most the tribes as Hindus or Christians. Many elements of tribal religion are as alive, even vigorous, as ever. As studies have recently shown tribal religion has not lost its distinct identity in spite of its long years of interaction with Hinduism and Christianity. It has maintained its system of religious beliefs and practices including propitiation of spirits, magic and witchcraft and the priesthood. Recent trends even suggest revival of many of pristine elements of tribal religion by those who have gone out of its fold. Therefore, the prevalent assumption that the survival of tribal religion is at stake needs to be reconsidered.

Much the same observation may also apply to the status of tribal languages, in spite of the dominance of the languages of various states (called scheduled languages) and increasing incidence of bilingualism among tribes. Hutton's hypotheses that Hinduisation involves loss of tribal languages and that their languages are holding out (for example, Austro-Asiatic languages in Bihar and Orissa) where the tribes are economically independent deserve to be re-examined. The role of economic factor appears to have been over-emphasised and that of acculturation somewhat ignored by him. Today, non-tribals are also turning bilingual, picking up a tribal language or two. Non-tribal languages have emerged as the language of trade, exchange, administration and the underworld of magic and witchcraft. 'Pidginised' languages (such as Desi or Sadani) are the mode of communcation between tribals and non-tribals in parts of middle India. The data on tribal languages over censuses show wide fluctuations. In areas of tribal preponderance tribal languages have survived. The Munda languages still hold sway : their speakers numbered 5.8 million in 1961 as against 4.6 million in 1931. The number of the speakers of Gondi fell slightly from 1.8 to 1.5 million. The Oraons in Madhya Pradesh have regained the linguistic status in 1961 they had lost earlier, but the Bhumij of Orissa have lost theirs. The 1961 census which regrouped tribals' mother tongues estimated at 304 into 101 tribal languages reported 49 per cent of tribals speaking tribal languages, 43 per cent as speakers of non-tribal langugaes and 7.94 per cent as speaking the non-scheduled and non-tribal langugaes. Many tribal movements in recent years have demonstrated renewed interest in their language and script. A literature in tribal languages has developed.

Though like many other census officials, Hutton was prone to describe tribal religion as being inevitably absorbed into Hinduism, unlike them he used the formidable power of his scholarship and rich anthropological imagination, to identify such elements of the tribal material being absorbed into Hinduism as unmistakably bore the impact of primitive religion and the "foreign elements". These were possibly the Negrito reverence for the *pipal* tree and practice of a primitive phallic fertility cult; the Proto-Australoids' totemism; the Mediterraneans' mother goddess and megalithic cultures; the Mundas' theory of life-essence that developed into that of reincarnation; the Aryans' personified deities, practice of sacrificial propitiation and a formalised worship, and institutions such as that of the deva-dasi from Asia Minor (?) and the priestly class. Hutton goes on to describe how the theory of soul-matter influenced fertility cults, the practice of head-hunting, human sacrifice and cannibalism, and the institutions of the memorial to the dead, totemism and witchcraft. These elements are described as the survivals not of "mere vague imaginings of superstitious and untaught minds," as described in the census report of 1911 but as "the debris of a real religious system, a definite philosophy" which testify to "the one time widespread prevalence from Europe to Australia out side India, of a great tribal religion," hagiolatory. Many of the assumptions of this mind-boggling conceptualisation are now open to question, though a few regarding "oceanic instrusions" of people and culture from the Pacific are being explored further.

A lasting significance of Hutton's work thus lies in its highlighting India's prehistoric ties with South-east Asia. It is only now that Indo-Pacific archaeology is coming into its own, and the interaction of the people, particularly the sea-faring communities from the coasts of East and South Africa and Madagascar to the Easter Islands and the South Seas, in terms of migration, exchange of artifacts and languages is beginning to be understood. This new area of archaeology has explored in recent years the modes of dispersal of the Austro Asiatic languages all over North-east India and South-east Asia, possible relationship between their languages and the custom of erecting stone and wooden structures in memory of the dead and in honouring the living, wide diffusion of microlithic tools, etc. Recent anthropological studies have brougnt out the similarities among some sections of the population of South and South-east Asia, particularly those with Negrito or Monogoloid substratums and in terms of the sharing of the Austro-Asiatic languages and lithic cultures, as also the broad similarities of cultural systems of paddy-growing peoples.

Hutton's description of the racial classfication of the Indian population was based on Dr. B.S. Guha's survey, undertaken as part of the 1931 census, which he describes as "easily the most important contribution to the physical anthropology of India since Risley's survey," and to which he added the prehistoric material available from the then finds. Incorporation of such comprehensive data on the physical anthropology of Indian population was a notable feature of the 1931 census report. Herbert Risley's classification was by then being questioned. Risley had taken into account only a limited number of characteristics, confusing linguistic categories (Aryan, Dravidian) with the racial, ignored the Australoids or Kolarian elements or clubbed them with the Dravidian, which was somewhat over-stretched to include the Proto-Australoids, Mediterranean and even the Negrito (?). This scheme was also faulted by Hutton, who, while conceding that nasal index indicates social precedence of a caste, pointed to the fact that Risley had failed to distinguish between the Proto-Australoids, "the true aborigines of India" and the Mediterranean people. However, Hutton's own view that the Proto-Australoids originated in Palestine is now open to question because the present view is that they came from South-east Asia. Hutton was aware of this possibility, if the "recently found remains of Solo man in Java [was] proved to be earlier", which indeed turned out to be so.

The archaeology of North-east India has developed considerably since Hutton discovered the celts from the Naga hills in the 1920s. The North-east has appeared on the archaeological map of India. According to the archaeologists, enough stratigraphical as well as typological data exist in the Garo hills alone for visualising a long stone age sequence, going back to the early paleolithic age in Assam, as in the rest of the country. North-east India has also emerged as a possible nuclear area of plant domestication and early agriculture, as a cradle of fishing-farming communities in the whole of South Asia extending from Assam and Meghalaya to the Philippines in the east and from Yunnan in China to the Indonesian archipelago and as a zone of transition between South and South-east Asia. The North-east could also probably be the homeland of the Proto-Australoid, because the artifacts discovered elsewhere in South-east Asia are reportedly of a later origin. The Garo hills could thus be regraded as a contact zone of India and East Asiatic neolithic traditions, with Chotanagpur—Santal Pargana region serving as another.

Physical anthropology has diversified since Hutton and Guha wrote their reports. Guha's sevenfold classification of Indian population has been now reduced to a fourfold one, the last three categories being subsumed under the Europoids or Caucasoids. There has been a shift away from racial and physical types to "genotypes"among different people. Physical types recognised through the observation of physical features is not considered valid any longer. There has also been a shift from the typological to the statistical approach to the study of population. As a result of this, anthropology today is less concerned with individual racial type and more with populations, their structure, central tendencies and other statistical parameters. Hutton had described the Mediterranean people as those that "contributed most to physical composition of the people of India, and perhaps also to its culture." Such a stress on racial and physical types led anthropologists to indentify the Tamil Brahmins with the Paleo-Mediterraneans and the Sikhs with the Oriental-Mediterraneans. Other census officials and ethnographers also tried to identify castes with racial types. Today serious questions have been raised about such assumptions. The morphological study of castes shows that there is considerable differentiation and heterogeneity among caste groups and that neither *jati* nor *varna* could be identified with a single racial or physical type, and that the correspondence between physical types and social categories is highly problematic. A community cannot be identified with a particular physical type. Further, while human variations or heterogeneity explains how our people have survived through various environmental stresses and deprivations, our likenesses are reportedly more than our differences. The number of genes in which our people differ are fewer in comparison with the vast number of genes which are common. Physical anthropology today, therefore, explores the kaleidoscopic pattern of both heterogeneity and homogeneity of our people.

Hutton strikes a refreshingly contemporary note in his analysis of population growth and birth control. According to 1931 census life expectancy went up, but infant mortality remained high. There were faint stirrings of a movement towards artificial birth control, publicly advocated by a number of medical writers. Mysore led with a number of birth control clinics and Madras boasted of a neo-Malthusian league. Hutton suggested a package of practices comprising a rise in the standard of living, education and culture and "the psychological appreciation of a higher probability of survival". As an orientalist, he too tended to have rather too "spiritual" a view of Indian life, which stood in the way of population control. Modern family welfare programme reflects an awareness of the social factors in their formulation and implementation.

Census and ethnography in India have generally gone together since the census of 1901. The census operation has been consciously used as a tool of generating information of an ethnographic kind about tribes and castes. Ethnographic appendices appeared religiously as part of the census reports, containing first the account of the remote communities in the North-east and in the Islands (the Tabo of North Andaman islands, for example). The 1911 census followed this trend ; the 1921 census briefly turned to economic aspects ; the 1931 census went back the ethnographic tradition and produced a special ethnographic volume (1935) containing interesting material on tribes. The censuses in the post-colonial period have, as mentioned earlier, broken way from the ethnographic tradition of the study of castes but continued with the ethnographic study of scheduled tribes. The social studies, undertaken by the 1961 census, branched off into such areas as village, fairs and festivals and handicrafts. Particularly noteworthy are the ethnographic studies of the scheduled castes who had been neglected by the census ethnography earlier.

The relevance of the 1931 census report lies in the fact that it still remains the source-material not only for the study of the presentday scheduled tribes and scheduled castes but also for a few of widely distributed castes, by scholars and planners. The reprint of this valuable report will serve, it is hoped, a larger clientele today,

K. S. SINGH

OFFICE OF THE

CENSUS COMMISSIONER FOR INDIA.

Simla, the 4th June 1933.

To

The Hon'ble Sir HARRY HAIG, K.C.S.I., C.I.E., I.C.S.,
Member of the Governor-General's Executive Council,
Simla.

Sir,

I have the honour to submit herewith a report on the census of India taken in February 1931. The reports and tables prepared for individual Provinces and States have already been published, since the necessary material is available in detail provincially before it can be compiled for the whole of India. These provincial and state volumes will be found to deal in particular with points which I have been able only to treat in general, and the method I have followed for the most part has been to examine for myself the figures for India as a whole and then to turn to the provincial reports to point a moral or adorn the tale, but the conclusions formed and the opinions expressed are my own.

This India volume consists of five parts, (i) my report (together with that of the actuary, Mr. L. S. Vaidyanathan), (ii) the statistical tables for India, (iii) a collection of papers of ethnographical interest, (iv) the social and linguistic maps for India and the Provinces bound separately and (v) an administrative report, the two latter volumes being intended primarily for departmental use. In submitting it, it is my fortunate duty to bring formally to your notice the able series of the 1931 Census Reports already mentioned, which are numbered indeed after this volume but have appeared before it. I have therefore the honour to recommend with confidence to your perusal not this report but the other twenty-seven, and to be

Sir,

Your most obedient servant,

J. H. HUTTON,

Census Commissioner for India.

TABLE OF CONTENTS.

CHAPTER. PAGE.

PAGE.

DIAGRAMS AND GRAPHS—*contd.*

INTRODUCTION.

At the very outset of this Report I find it incumbent on me to depart from precedent and to begin with acknowledgments, first of all, as is fit, to the people of India themselves whose good sense, good citizenship and general co-operation made the taking of the census possible, but most of all perhaps to that great body of some two million unpaid enumerators by whom the census was actually taken and without whom it could not have been taken, many of whom were out of pocket by the taking and many of whom carried out their work under circumstances of opposition, interference and general unpopularity. The greatest credit is due to them, and that, and a *sanad* of printed paper, is the only reward that most of them have had. The taking of the pecennial census in India involves the co-operation of more than one-sixth of the world's population over an area of nearly two million square miles in a combined response to organised enquiry, and the expense would be prohibitive if all the services rendered were paid. Moreover enumerators' duties were often as onerous physically as they frequently were morally. While city enumerators had generally to take larger blocks than usual since enumerators were harder to come by, those in rural areas often had to cover long distances; in Baluchistan the average enumerator had a block of 836 square miles (in the tribal areas 1,460) in which to find his fifty houses, as a 'village' was often a moving encampment of two or three tents with an average area of 36 square miles to itself.

Acknowledgments are due likewise to the other links in the chain of organisation. Supervisors, Charge Superintendents, District Census Officers, District Magistrates are all part of the necessary machinery and no whit less essential than the enumerator, and in their case the census came as an extra—a piece of gratuitous and troublesome overtime work added to their usual duties in many places already onerous and trying above the ordinary by reason of political agitation. For this census like that of 1921 had the misfortune to coincide with a wave of non-co-operation, and the march of Mr. Gandhi and his *contrabandistas* to invest the salt-pans of Dharasana synchronized with the opening of census operations. The blessing which he gave to the census at the last minute in 1921 was this time wanting, and, though he himself is not known to have issued any advice to boycott the census, it seemed good to some other Congress leaders to do so, as, although they do not seem to have regarded a census as objectionable in itself, the opportunity for harassing government seemed too good to be missed, and January 11th, 1931, was notified by the Congress Committee to be observed as Census Boycott Sunday. This boycott was not, however, taken up with any real enthusiasm and, except in the Gujarat cities of Ahmadabad, Broach and Surat and some smaller municipalities like Ghatkopar and Villaparle, had very little ultimate effect on the taking of the census; but the petty annoyances, resignations and interferences with the preparations for final enumeration very greatly increased the work, the responsibilities and the anxieties of local officers in charge of census work, including as they did not only revenue officers of all grades and village schoolmasters but police, magistrates, paid and honorary, railway officials, forest officers, port officers, ministerial officers in government offices, municipal officers and many others. On the other hand no less trouble was caused in some places by an excess of the zeal on the part of all parties to register as many adherents as possible in view of the possibility of a communal franchise based on the census returns. This was particularly the case in the Punjab, where the exterior castes, badgered first by one party then by another to return themselves as Sikhs, Hindus or Muslims as the case might be, labelled themselves *Ad Dharmi*, or adherents of the original religion, and so added to the number of religions returned in the census schedules. So high did feeling run over the return of religion in the Punjab that disputes as to whether a man was Ad Dharmi or Sikh led to a number of affrays and at least to one homicide. Politics were also troublesome in the borders of Orissa where a pan-Oriya propaganda, carried on to an extent calculated to frustrate its own purposes, engendered a corresponding counter-propaganda, all detrimental to census taking. Special measures were needed in Madras and much additional work caused to the Superintendent of that province and in a less degree also to the Superintendents of

Bengal, Bihar and Orissa and the Central Provinces. Other provinces experienced the usual difficulties that attend census taking in India. In one the Bhils for instance would not have their houses numbered on superstitious grounds, while in Burma householders objected on artistic grounds. In the Shan States the thirteenth and last survivor of a pre-annexation raid happened to occupy the thirteenth house in a block. As the enumerator inconsiderately refused to rearrange the numbers, he decided that his was up indeed, went forth into the jungle and committed harakiri. In less law-abiding places the disposition was rather towards disembowelling the enumerator than the enumerated, while the effacing of census numbers was a minor difficulty that was particularly troublesome in 1931 Here and there wild beasts interfered instead of wild men, and the Administrator of Bastar State, when inspecting census work on the night itself, was attacked by a tiger, which sprang on to the bonnet of his car, but finding the pace and the radiator too hot for him failed to make an end either of the inspector or his inspection.

Difficulties notwithstanding, the census was taken at the appointed time and a complete return was received from all places except Ahmadabad in Gujarat. The returns for some other towns in Gujarat, *e.g.*, Broach and Surat, were probably defective, but, as received from the municipalities concerned, were ostensibly correct. In the case of Ahmadabad the census was not completed and the number actually enumerated was estimated to be some seventy-five to seventy-six thousand short of the real total; according to the census since taken by the Ahmadabad Municipality itself the deficiency was nearly the double of my estimate. In Burma a rebellion broke out between the preliminary and the final enumeration. It interfered with the latter in at least one district but with the former hardly at all. In the Census Abstract published for Parliament I based my estimates of the error caused in the census enumeration by Congress activities on the very carefully estimated error worked out by the Census Superintendent of Bombay for that province which came to ·04 per cent.; this I doubled for the whole of India arriving at a maximum deficiency of ·085 per cent. in the Indian figures. If the Ahmadabad Municipality return be accepted and the deficiency be re-calculated accordingly the error still works out at only ·1 per cent. for the total population of India. This of course refers to any deficiency caused by the clash of politics with the census. Other inaccuracies, whatever the amount, are likely to be fairly constant from census to census; the error in the numerical count has been put at a maximum of one per mille and is probably less. The Census Commissioner in 1921 estimated the percentage of error in recording sex and religion at about one per cent.; I doubt myself if it is nearly as high as this, but otherwise his estimates probably hold good of this census also. Owing to the Sarda Act however there has been a definite decrease of accuracy in the record of civil condition, and I estimate the error in this respect to be not less than ·5 per cent. and probably higher. Fortunately it seems possible to allocate with safety at least the greater part of this error to deliberately inaccurate returns of 'unmarried' instead of 'married' for girls married during 1931 in contravention of the age-limits imposed by the Marriage Restraint Act. Error in classification after the return has been made is quite a different thing from error in record and it is extremely difficult to form any estimate of its extent. The entries in the schedules are copied on to slips, omitting the block, circle and charge numbers and of course the personal names, and are then sorted into sets of labelled pigeon-holes and counted for the figures which constitute the tables. Different colours are used for different religions and each slip is stamped or printed with a symbol to denote sex. These symbols in 1931 were amplified by hand to signify civil condition. It was found quicker to add to the symbol than to have previously marked symbols from which the correct one had to be selected, a course which involved a choice of six according to sex and civil condition for each individual slip. Probably also the practice of altering by hand involves less error than that of selection when the tendency will be for the copyist, who must turn out a minimum number of slips and is paid in part at any rate by outturn, to fill up the wrong slip rather than to waste time by changing it when wrongly selected. In any case there is room for error in slip copying and for error again in sorting, though careful supervision at both stages may keep it down to a very small margin. A certain difficulty and anomaly was also introduced into tabulation by the fact that the Burma figures were tabulated on a different system from that followed in India proper. The method of tabulating by religion has never been found very suitable in Burma and on this occasion was abandoned for tabulation by race in the interests of that province, but at the cost of some inconsistencies in the presentation of the India figures.

This digression on error has led me aside before making my acknowledgments to the census officers of provinces and states, of whom a list will be found in Chapter I. It seemed to me that their work as a whole was admirable. Several had special difficulties Captain Mallam in the North-West Frontier Province, Mr. Turner in the United Provinces, Mr. Porter in Bengal and Mr. Shoobert in the Central Provinces all experienced difficulties in organising their enumeration on account of political agitation; and Khan Sahib Ahmad Hasan Khan in the Punjab had his trouble when the actual enumeration took place; even in Delhi his enumerators found their house numbers obliterated and their movements obstructed. Mr. Dracup in Bombay had to contend with the most difficult and troublesome situations of all on account of the anti-census campaign in Gujarat. Bombay has a bad reputation for breaking the health of her Census Superintendents. The first Superintendent in 1911 broke down after the enumeration was over and the early death of the 1921 Superintendent must be imputed at any rate in part to the strain of that census. Mr. Dracup managed to carry on till the compilation was almost finished and his reports begun (for the Bombay post involved writing two additional reports, one for the Western India States Agency, the other for the Bombay Cities), but his health could not stand it; he suffered the chagrin of being beaten on the post, and had to make over his material to Mr. Sorley. More provinces than usual were handicapped by similar changes. In Bihar and Orissa Mr. Scotland's health broke down very early in the operations and his work was taken over by Mr. Lacey who had a very uphill task indeed to get his census to synchronize, as he came in at a critical stage which found him unfamiliar with the early part of the work and at which the preparations for enumeration had fallen sadly into arrears as the inevitable result of Mr. Scotland's ill-health. In the North-West Frontier Province Captain Mallam lasted like Mr. Dracup till his report was part written; at the earlier stages he was more than once taken away from his census work for administrative ends and but for these diversions would probably have finished single-handed; as it was, Mr. Dundas had like Mr. Sorley the difficult task of writing a report on a census of which he had seen nothing but the materials collected in the course of operations in which he had taken no part at all. Mr. Shoobert in the Central Provinces and Berar was likewise hampered by being abstracted from his census work for administrative necessities for an inconveniently long period at an early stage of the operations and was delayed by illness towards their close. Rai Bahadur Anant Ram in Kashmir had the disadvantage of not having been in charge of the census from the start of operations and Khan Bahadur Gul Muhammad Khan in Baluchistan was taken away before he had finished to be Wazir-i-Azam of Kalat State and had to write his report while performing the onerous duties of his vizierate. Colonel Cole with Rajputana and Ajmer-Merwara, Mr. Porter with Bengal and the City of Calcutta and Khan Sahib Ahmad Hasan Khan with the Punjab and Delhi all had two Reports to write instead of one.

Special difficulties were experienced in Madras and in a lesser degree in Assam and also in Bihar and Orissa and more or less in all provinces as a result of the change in system, which actually took place in 1921 but the full effects of which were not experienced until this census, by which all costs were made debitable to the Central Governments. The local expenses of enumeration, including the travelling allowances of all local officers doing census work in addition to their ordinary duties, and including stationery, stamps and so forth required in mofussil operations, had all been charged hitherto to the expenses of general administration, much the most convenient and economical way of dealing with small items extremely difficult to disentangle from others where no separate organisation existed; and owing to their being merged in general administration no separate record of the expenditure was extant. In 1931 the operations were carried out precisely as before and the methods used by local officers at previous censuses were used again. It was not till afterwards that it was discovered that serious liabilities had been incurred in the matter of travelling allowances to meet which no provision had been made in budgetting. District Officers had little enough time to spare for the census in any case, and the general tendency was in many cases to take the position that this was a central charge, let the central authorities see to it. Moreover, many of the claims were submitted at a date which though admissible for ordinary audit purposes was so long after the journeys had taken place that any check of the claim was made extremely difficult. Mr. Yeatts in Madras received no fewer than 26,000 unanticipated bills for travelling allowances amounting in all to approximately Rs. 3,00,000, many of them claims received during 1932 for journeys undertaken in 1931. Many of these bills contained claims relating to a whole charge or even taluk, and the actual number of personal claims involved was greatly in excess, of course, of the mere total of bills. By subjecting each bill to the strictest personal scrutiny in the light of the actual expenses probably incurred Mr. Yeatts was able to reduce the total actually paid to Rs. 1,30,000, but it was only by ruthlessly cutting down the claims to the amount by which claimants were likely to have been actually out of pocket, a course of action only made possible by the fact that Mr. Yeatts himself had never drawn more than his actual out of pocket expenses when touring, whatever the rules allowed him to draw above that. Both he and Mr. Mullan in Assam must have incurred no little odium in the course of their pruning of travelling allowance bills for the extent and nature of which they were in no way to blame, as they had not even been in a position to prepare their own budgets, since the provincial budgets for the year of enumeration were all prepared by local governments before superintendents took over charge, and there was in any case no separate record of the very considerable sums spent in this way from provincial revenues in 1921.

It was another of the misfortunes of the 1931 census that it coincided with a fall in revenue and a period of economic depression which made the most rigorous economy necessary and which left me no choice but to cut all expenditure as fine as possible and to goad my Census Superintendents unremittingly in an attempt to finish sooner and spend less. Their responses were loyal and whole hearted, and in almost every province the actual cost of the census per head censused has been appreciably reduced, if those items be excluded which never appeared in the accounts of 1921. These items not only included the travelling allowance of local officers, previously debited to general administration and the provincial revenues, as well as stamps, stationery and other items used in district offices and similarly debited, but also included all pay of officers whether Provincial or Imperial who were deputed to the Census Department, as well as their leave pay earned during their census service, passage contributions and so forth. In some cases the budget of this census has even been debited with the leave pay of officers who served the department in 1921 or earlier but not in 1931 at all. Wages had all increased since 1921 and the cost of printing to the census has been enormously enhanced, in some cases by two hundred per cent. or more, as the result of a change in the method of costing. Under the old method the overhead charges were not debited at all to the census when the printing was done, as most of it is, in Government presses. It will be seen at once therefore that a very large part of the increase in the gross cost of the census, approximately Rs. 48,76,000 in 1931 against Rs. 40,00,000 in 1921, is an increase on paper only. As nearly as can be reckoned the actual net expenditure incurred for the 1931 census which is comparable with the expenditure on that of 1921, excluding items not then charged to the census budget, amounts to Rs. 40,13,000, and when this is reduced to the cost per thousand of persons censused, which is the only fair standard of comparison, the 1931 census comes quite creditably through the test having cost only Rs. 12·8 per thousand persons censused as compared to Rs. 14 per thousand in 1921. The cost of the census of England and Wales in 1921 was £9-5-6 per thousand (about Rs. 124 of Indian money) " exclusive of the expenditure on printing, stationery, maps, etc.", the exclusion of which from the costs of the Indian census would reduce the cost per thousand to Rs. 13·3, while the census of Northern Ireland in 1926 cost over £15-6-4 per thousand inclusive of printing, etc., that is Rs. 202 per thousand as compared to India's Rs. 14 inclusive. The census of India therefore is not only by far the most extensive census operation in the world but, besides being one of the quickest, it is probably the cheapest. Even so the cost is no inconsiderable item at a time when the difficulty of restricting expenditure to the limits imposed by dwindling revenue is so difficult that many countries decided to dispense entirely with the census due in 1931 ; and it was therefore necessary to exercise a very parsimonious economy, and I owe to all Census Superintendents and likewise to their administrative, office and compiling staff not only my acknowledgments for their ungrudging co-operation but also my apologies for driving them at a pace which has admitted of closing down the department some seven months earlier than usual, and for cutting down their estimates to the finest possible margin compatible with reasonable efficiency. The work of a provincial census officer in India, all done against time, against expenditure, and without holidays, is far from the pleasant occupation which its interest would make it were the need for speed and economy less exacting.

In spite of this there has been no falling off in the quality of the reports which well maintain the high standard set by past series. The Andamans and Nicobars Report reflects Mr. Bonington's lifelong acquaintance with the forests of those islands and their shy, little-known inhabitants; Colonel Cole brought to the Rajputana volume a knowledge of the Rajputs and their clans acquired not only regimentally but in the course of several years as Recruiting Officer for Rajput battalions; he also showed a commendable despatch and but for his press would have finished even earlier than he did. The other authors of British India Reports are all executive officers in the Imperial or Provincial services and the outlook of the settlement officer is conspicuous among them throughout the series, from Mr. Mullan's lively volume on Assam (also one of the first to be published) to Mr. Turner's exceptionally full and detailed report on the United Provinces. Their several qualities may frequently be inferred from the excerpts given freely in this volume, and where all have reached a high standard it would seem invidious to discriminate. The reports of Messrs. Bonington, Shoobert and Lacey all contain interesting ethnographical material; Mr. Yeatts' particularly well written volume is noticeable for his treatment of infirmities, and Mr. Porter's for a new attack upon the population problem and for an interesting account of the processes of certain decaying rural industries. In Burma and in Bombay Messrs. Bennison and Sorley have brought to the census the experience gained in the study of social and economic questions, and Khan Sahib Ahmad Hasan Khan has opened the volume on Delhi, new to the series, with a conspectus of the capital's historic past. Among the States and Agencies the Rajputana volume has already been mentioned, as also Messrs. Dracup and Sorley's on the Western India States, another new addition to the series, while Mr. Venkatachar has filled in somewhat of a hiatus in the census accounts of the peninsula with his exceptionally interesting report on Central India.

The States that contribute separate volumes pay independently for their own operations and the total cost of their census Owing to this fact I was fortunate enough to be spared the unpleasant task of reducing budgets, but the exigencies of the India work compelled me in some cases to keep hurrying their Census Commissioners during the compilation stage, and my acknowledgments are due to the latter no less than to the Census Superintendents in British India for their efforts to comply with an impatience which they may well have regarded as untimely, and which must certainly have been inconvenient at any rate to Rai Bahadur Anant Ram in Kashmir, who had to finish off his census at a time of political and economic disturbance with a depleted and inadequate staff. Of the other states' Census Commissioners Mr. Ghulam Ahmed Khan in Hyderabad and Mr. Rang Lal in Gwalior have approached their subject from the administrative points of view like most of the Census Superintendents in British India, Mr. Khan incidentally adding to our knowledge of the Chenchus, while Mr. Venkatesa Iyengar in Mysore has given another detailed account of processes of declining industries. Mr. Sankara Menon in Cochin has written a thoughtful report as an educationist, a calling unrepresented in the British series. In Travancore Dr. Pillai has to his credit an admirably produced report embodying not only a brief economic survey of the state but a good deal of fresh information as to the vanishing tribes and disappearing industries of a state which is so advanced that he was able to make a useful experiment in compilation by the employment, as in Cochin, of women as sorters and slip-copyists, and very efficient they proved. The outstanding report among the states is again that of Mr. Mukerjea on Baroda who is to be congratulated not only on his admirable presentation of material but on the extreme rapidity with which he produced so comprehensive a volume. His previous experience in 1921 has been put to the best account and I have myself taken advantage of it, particularly in the arrangement of fertility figures. He is also responsible for an innovation in enumeration by *billets individuels* which may very well bear much fruit at the next census of India.

To Mr. Trousdell and Mr. Golder of the Government of India Press in Simla I owe both acknowledgments for their patience and despatch, and apologies for the inconvenience caused by repeated calls for fresh proofs of altered tables, while I have to thank Mr. Carter of the Government of India Press in Delhi as well as Mr. Golder for much very useful advice and assistance. To Colonel A. J. H. Russell, then Public Health Commissioner, I owe the diagrams of vital statistics and information on several points in Chapter VII. To several others, to more indeed than I can mention here, I owe acknowledgments of some kind for advice, information or criticism. Mr. L. S. Vaidyanathan of the Oriental Government Security Life Assurance Company, Bombay, who has contributed the most comprehensive actuarial examination of the Indian age returns yet attempted and the life tables based on them, Dr. B. S. Guha of the Anthropological Branch of the Zoological Survey of India, who carried out for this census a detailed anthropometrical survey of certain castes and tribes and who has contributed his valuable analysis of their physical characteristics to the volume of ethnographical appendices, Colonel R. B. Seymour Sewell, Director of the same Department, Rai Bahadur Ramaprasad Chanda and Mr. E. J. H. Mackay, both of the Archæological Survey, have all helped me with information and friendly criticism and to Dr. Guha again I owe the drawings of the Bayana, Sialkot and Nal crania that appear in Chapter XII. Mr. Yeatts has added to my obligation to him by his assistance in proof reading.

My final but far from least weighty acknowledgments are due first to my own office, to whose ungrudging co-operation is due the early completion of the report, particularly to the Superintendent Mr. A. R. Chitnis, to whose statistical experience and careful scrutiny of figures must be attributed whatever degree of accuracy their presentation here can claim, to the head compiler, Mr. F. E. Wright and his second Mr. Mulherkar, who are primarily responsible for the compilation of Part II; and then to my predecessors, to Sir Edward Gait in particular, whose work in previous decades has done so much to simplify mine in this. The conception of the social maps was due to a scheme for a population map of India evolved by Colonel Tandy in 1921 and here modified and adapted to suit small scale maps and a high density of population; the idea of the linguistic maps and the record of bilingualism first occurred to me in the course of correspondence with Colonel T. C. Hodson, now Wyse Professor of Anthropology in Cambridge. The German anthropologist, Baron von Eickstedt, suggested a series of maps which would show the population of each village by caste and religion in coloured points of varying shape and size. The system is an admirable one which would if applied to India give a most valuable and interesting record, but the cost of producing series of maps on the large scale necessary to show every village with its inhabitants by castes or tribes was in itself obviously prohibitive, apart from the time and labour involved in compiling the statistics of caste by villages.

A word of apology is due on the contents of this report. The opportunities of a census of India come if at all but once to most of us, and I am only too conscious of opportunity neglected, for I have left undone that which I ought to have done and I have done much less than I should like to have done. *Res angusta civitatis* is my defence; I should be the first to admit it inadequate, but the imperative necessity for a rigid economy made any departure from and still more any enlargement of the known and familiar paths dangerous as well as extremely difficult. As it was, some of the material actually collected in the enumeration schedules had to be left uncopied and unsorted as a measure of retrenchment, and the industrial statistics of 1921 were not attempted; a tally of horsepower, handlooms and mechanical shuttles is hardly a legitimate part of a population census in any case, and the statistics can be just as well collected at another time by the Department of Industries and Labour by means of the circulation of forms unsynchronised with the census schedules. An attempt to collect a return of the educated unemployed on separate schedules was a fiasco, as though large numbers of the schedules were issued very few were received back; the reasons given are various but apathy was probably the prevailing one. Such as they are, both the reasons for the failure and the figures obtained will be found recorded in Chapter IX. The returns of age are probably more accurate than ever before, thanks to the method of treating the figures advocated by Mr. H. G. W. Meikle, as a result of his actuarial examination of the 1921 returns, and adopted for the first time in 1931. On the other hand the figures of urban population in Gujarat and of civil condition must be admitted to be below the previous standard of accuracy, a degeneration due in the one case to Congress activities and in the other primarily to the indirect influence of the Sarda Act, but also perhaps in some degree to the very same change in the method of sorting and compiling which has so much improved the return of age unqualified by other factors. In any case the treatment of sociological features of the population of India is much prejudiced by the absence of any general or compulsory registration of births, deaths or marriages; an absence which would go far to nullify social legislation such as that implied in the Sarda Act itself, and to which attention was drawn by the Age of Consent Committee. The difficulties of introducing compulsory registration are no doubt great, but it is not easy to see how social legislation can be really effective without it. Nevertheless some attempt has been made at this census to collect figures for the fertility of females of different social standing and of various occupations in the hope of throwing some much needed light on the rate of reproduction in India. These are censorious days and there were not wanting articles in newspapers of the baser sort to suggest that the figures of fertility were being collected with a view to defaming the people of India. It is possible therefore that critics may be found who will conceive that they detect in Chapters III to VI, or elsewhere in this report, the cloven slots of a considered cloacinity. It is of course impossible to discuss the growth of population without any reference to its health. Those determined to see ill motives will be deterred by no denials, but to those who are not I would offer an assurance (which I hope is not needed) that nothing has been set down in malice. In the first five chapters, except for a page or two on the population problem, I have allowed myself to depart as little as possible from the statistics to be examined (no haunts for Apollo here); in Chapter VI the social movements and legislation of the decade have called for a short digression before returning to the figures in Chapters VII, VIII and IX. In the last three Chapters I have frankly permitted myself, after examining the relative figures, to venture aside to a more speculative treatment of race and religion. What was for long the orthodox view of the history of race and culture in India was brilliantly propounded by Sir Herbert Risley in the Census Report of 1901; the work that has been done since makes it probable that there has been a far greater degree of continuity in the pre-history of India than was then supposed, and certain that India was not characterised, as Sir Herbert believed, by racial or cultural isolation. Much work has to be done before any views on these subjects can claim finality, but certain hypotheses may fairly be advanced on the material accumulated since that census. With the exceptions mentioned I have stayed by my statistics, a valley of dry bones it may be, very far from Helicon, and I no Ezekiel to clothe them with flesh, content if I have played the part of Joab to hope that I may at least escape the unhappy recompense meted out to that early numberer of peoples. At any rate I have made no naughty omission of Levi and Benjamin on purpose, and if some of the tale have gone untold they must be few indeed when the increase alone since 1921 numbers nearly thirty four millions. For the Father of History is proved right again. 'Ινδῶν δε πλῆθος, he said near twenty-four hundred years ago, πλεῖστόν ἐστι πάντων τῶν ἡμεῖς ἴδμεν ἀνθρώπων and this census has justified him indeed, for it can be once more stated with some confidence that 'of all the nations that we know it is India has the largest population'.

Simla,

June 4th, 1933.

J. H. HUTTON.

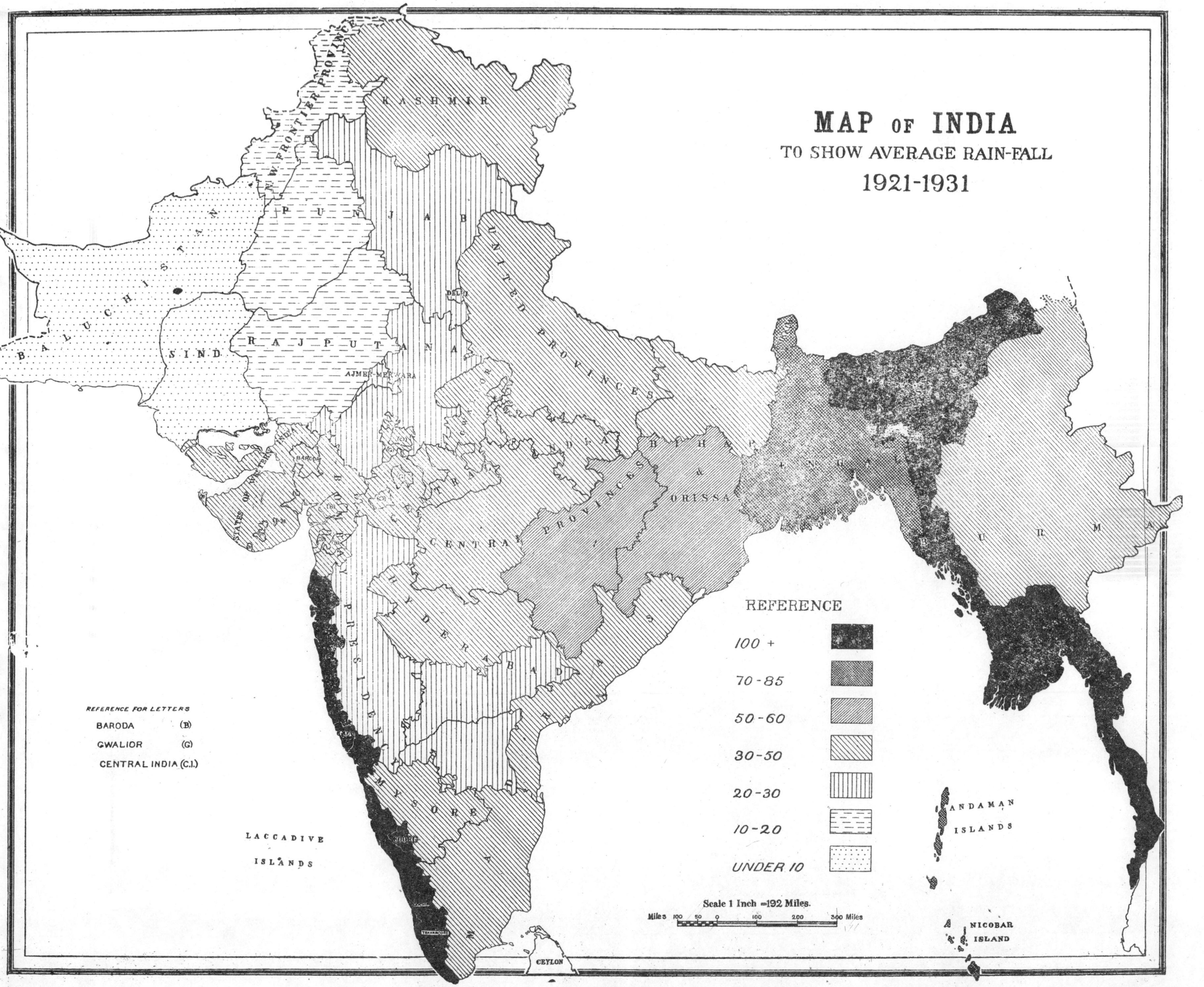
MAP OF INDIA
TO SHOW AVERAGE RAIN-FALL
1921-1931
KASHMIR
N.W. FRONTIER PROVINCE
PUNJAB
BALUCHISTAN
SIND
RAJPUTANA
AJMER-MERWARA
DELHI
UNITED PROVINCES
BIHAR & ORISSA
BENGAL
CENTRAL PROVINCES
CENTRAL INDIA
BARODA
BOMBAY PRESIDENCY
HYDERABAD
MADRAS
MYSORE
COORG
TRAVANCORE
CEYLON
BURMA
ANDAMAN ISLANDS
NICOBAR ISLAND
LACCADIVE ISLANDS
REFERENCE
100 +
70-85
50-60
30-50
20-30
10-20
UNDER 10
REFERENCE FOR LETTERS
BARODA (B)
GWALIOR (G)
CENTRAL INDIA (C.I.)
Scale 1 Inch =192 Miles.
Miles 100 50 0 100 200 300 Miles

REPORT

ON THE

CENSUS OF INDIA, 1931.

CHAPTER I.

Distribution and Movement of Population.

Section i.—Scope of the Report.

Geographical Area.

1. The area covered by the sixth general census of India is approximately identical with that covered by the census of 1921 and differs little from the area of previous occasions from 1881 onwards; 2,308 sq. miles containing some 34,000 inhabitants have been added in Burma and in the north-east of Assam, while on the other hand, six sq. miles have been lost to Nepal. The statistics therefore cover the whole empire of India with Burma and the adjacent islands and islets (exclusive of Ceylon and the Maldives) as well as Aden and Perim Island, but not the Kuria Muria Islands* and Sokotra, which is part of the Aden Protectorate, administered from Aden on behalf of the Colonial Office, and not part of British India. The statistics and the tables do not of course cover those parts of the peninsula which are not parts of the British Empire, that is to say, Afghanistan, Nepal, Bhutan and the French and Portuguese possessions, the area and population of which, together with the rate of increase since 1921 where available, are shown in the marginal table. For the rest the scope of this census extended to the whole of the peninsula of India, forming what is commonly described as a sub-continent between long. 61° and 101° E. and lat. 6° to 37°N. Some information has also been included with regard to natives of India resident permanently or temporarily outside the Indian Empire or serving on the High Seas at the time the census was taken.

Area covered by the census of India.

Year.	Sq. miles.	Increase.
1881	1,382,624	..
1891	1,560,160	177,536
1901	1,766,597	206,437
1911	1,802,657	36,060
1921	1,805,332	2,675
1931	1,808,679	3,347

Changes in external area since 1921.

—	Sq. miles.	Population.
Assam	+908	+15,711
Burma	+1,400	+18,327
United Provinces ..	—6	—130
Total net addition	+2,302	+33,908

—	Area in sq. miles.	Population 1931.	Percentage of Increase since 1921.
Afghanistan	250,000	7,000,000	..
Bhutan ..	20,000	250,000	..
Nepal ..	54,000	5,600,000	..
French India	196	286,410	+6·24
Portuguese India.	1,461	579,969	+5·79

Obviously within an area of such size, part of which is well within the temperate zone while part is almost equatorial, the diversity of condition both of the population and of its environment must be very great indeed. Geologically, while the peninsula is one of the oldest of the world's formations, the Himalayas are one of the most recent. Not unnaturally therefore there is a great variety of physical feature, varying not only from the loftiest mountains of the world to flats salted by every tide, but from sandy deserts with a rainfall of five inches or less in a year in the north-west to thickly wooded evergreen hills which have never less than 100 inches and here and there get 500 inches of rain or even more in the east and south Again in northern India there are extremes of temperature—120° of heat dropping to cold below freezing point, while in the south the temperature is almost static

*The population of these islands remains conjectural, and the only information that can be had about them was obtained in 1920 from the Senior Naval Officer at Aden and it is printed in Part III of this Report, since, although out of date, it appears to be the latest information available. The question of the language of Sokotra formerly perhaps written, but now a spoken language only, is of some interest, as are likewise habits and customs of the populations of these islands some of whom in Sokotra are cave dwellers; it is therefore unfortunate from a scientific point of view that no investigation has ever apparently been made.

in its heat and humidity. As might be expected the physical features of the inhabitants are no less variable than those of their environments. Any haphazard collection of Indians will afford types of very different ethnic groups, though the composition would vary according to the locality. The number of languages, as classified by Sir George Grierson in his *Linguistic Survey of India* and exclusive of dialects, is 225 by the returns of 1931. Creeds may be less numerous, but castes, customs and sects must be no less diverse, and the same applies to social, political and economic conditions. Thus the peoples to be covered by this report present every aspect from that of the latest phase of western civilization to that of the most primitive tribes, which, like the Andamanese or like the Kadar or Uralis of southern India, still exist by hunting and collecting forest produce without ever apparently having reached the stage of agriculture at all. Naturally any report of the census of so large and diversified an area must, if it is to be contained in a volume, be of a superficial nature, leaving the closer examination of the figures and facts revealed by enumeration to the reports severally undertaken for each of the Provinces and larger States.

Serial no. of volume.	Parts contained.	Province, etc., treated.	Author.
Vol. I	(*i*). Report; (*ii*). Tables; (*iii*). Appendix vol.	India	J. H. Hutton.
Vol. II	One	Andamans and Nicobars	M. C. C. Bonington.
Vol. III	(*i*). Report; (*ii*). Tables	Assam	C. S. Mullan.
Vol. IV	One	Baluchistan	Gul Muhammad Khan.
Vol. V	(*i*). Report; (*ii*). Tables	Bengal	A. E. Porter.
Vol. VI	One	City of Calcutta	A. E. Porter.
Vol. VII	(*i*). Report; (*ii*). Tables	Bihar and Orissa	W. G. Lacey.
Vol. VIII	(*i*). Report; (*ii*). Tables;	Bombay (*with Aden*)	A. H. Dracup and H. T. Sorley.
	(*iii*). Aden	*Aden*	D. S. Johnston.
Vol. IX	One	Cities of Bombay	H. T. Sorley.
Vol. X	One	Western India States Agency	A. H. Dracup and H. T. Sorley.
Vol. XI	(*i*). Report; (*ii*). Tables	Burma	J. J. Bennison.
Vol. XII	(*i*). Report; (*ii*). Tables	Central Provinces and Berar	W. H. Shoobert.
Vol. XIII	One	Coorg	M. S. Mandanna.
Vol. XIV	(*i*). Report; (*ii*). Tables	Madras	M. W. M. Yeatts.
Vol. XV	One	North-West Frontier Province.	G. L. Mallam and A. D. F. Dundas.
Vol. XVI	One	Delhi	Ahmad Hasan Khan.
Vol. XVII	(*i*). Report; (*ii*). Tables	Punjab	Ahmad Hasan Khan.
Vol. XVIII	(*i*). Report; (*ii*). Tables	United Provinces of Agra and Oudh.	A. C. Turner.
Vol. XIX	(*i*). Report; (*ii*). Tables	Baroda State	S. V. Mukerjea.
Vol. XX	(*i*). Report; (*ii*). Tables	Central India Agency	C. S. Venkatachar.
Vol. XXI	One	Cochin State	T. K. Sankara Menon.
Vol. XXII	(*i*). Report; (*ii*). Tables	Gwalior State	Rang Lal.
Vol. XXIII	(*i*). Report; (*ii*). Tables	Hyderabad State	Ghulam Ahmad Khan.
Vol. XXIV	(*i*). Report; (*ii*). Tables	Jammu and Kashmir State	Anant Ram.
Vol. XXV	(*i*). Report; (*ii*). Tables	Mysore State	M. Venkatesa Iyengar.
Vol. XXVI	One	Ajmer-Merwara	B. L. Cole.
Vol. XXVII	One	Rajputana Agency	B. L. Cole.
Vol. XXVIII	(*i*). Report; (*ii*). Tables	Travancore State	N. [illegible]unjan Pillai.

Natural and political divisions. 2. At the same time in spite of this great variety the existence for the most part of a uniform system of administration and of a fairly general distribution of the different racial types from which the population is drawn, together with a similar, if perhaps less even distribution of religious and social systems, contribute to give a certain uniformity, if not unity, to the whole, which in spite of local differences is obviously capable of a degree of national consciousness which increases with the spread of education. For the difficulty occasioned by great diversity in treating India as a whole is experienced likewise to a more limited extent in each Province and in most States, since the political boundaries have generally little relation to any other. The difficulty of dealing with the population question by natural divisions is thus greatly enhanced. Obviously the density of the population is in immediate relationship to the conformation of the soil, to the rainfall and to the crops, all of which are inter-dependent, but since the boundaries of administrative units run counter to the divisions of nature, any treatment of the population according to natural divisions is likely to involve the dissipation of figures returned by administrative units into a set of entirely different combinations. This has been attempted for India as a whole on some previous occasions, but the information obtained by such a treatment, however interesting academically, is of little or no administrative value. Demography by natural divisions therefore has been limited to the individual reports of provinces, since in some of the provinces and states the natural divisions are less diverse from divisions political than they are when India is treated as a whole, and within the administrative unit may even be of some practical application.

External population.

3. In addition to the actual population of India some attempt has been made to give information as to Indian nationals in other countries or on the High Seas. These figures are necessarily incomplete, but perhaps go further than they have done on previous occasions by including returns of Indian crews on ocean-going vessels shipped during the eight months or so that preceded the final enumeration. Though not in India at the time of the census, these crews form a permanent part of the population visiting their homes from time to time and in many cases returning agriculture as a subsidiary occupation. Strictly speaking therefore, although the census in intention is one of the *de facto* population that is of the numbers found in India on February 26th, 1931 and not as in the case of the United States, for instance, a *de jure* population, the terms of a census of actual population have not been observed with excessive punctuality. This indeed would have been impossible, since the remoteness of some parts of India, the difficulty of communications and limitations imposed by water, snow and wild animals make a completely synchronous enumeration of the whole peninsula an absolute impossibility.

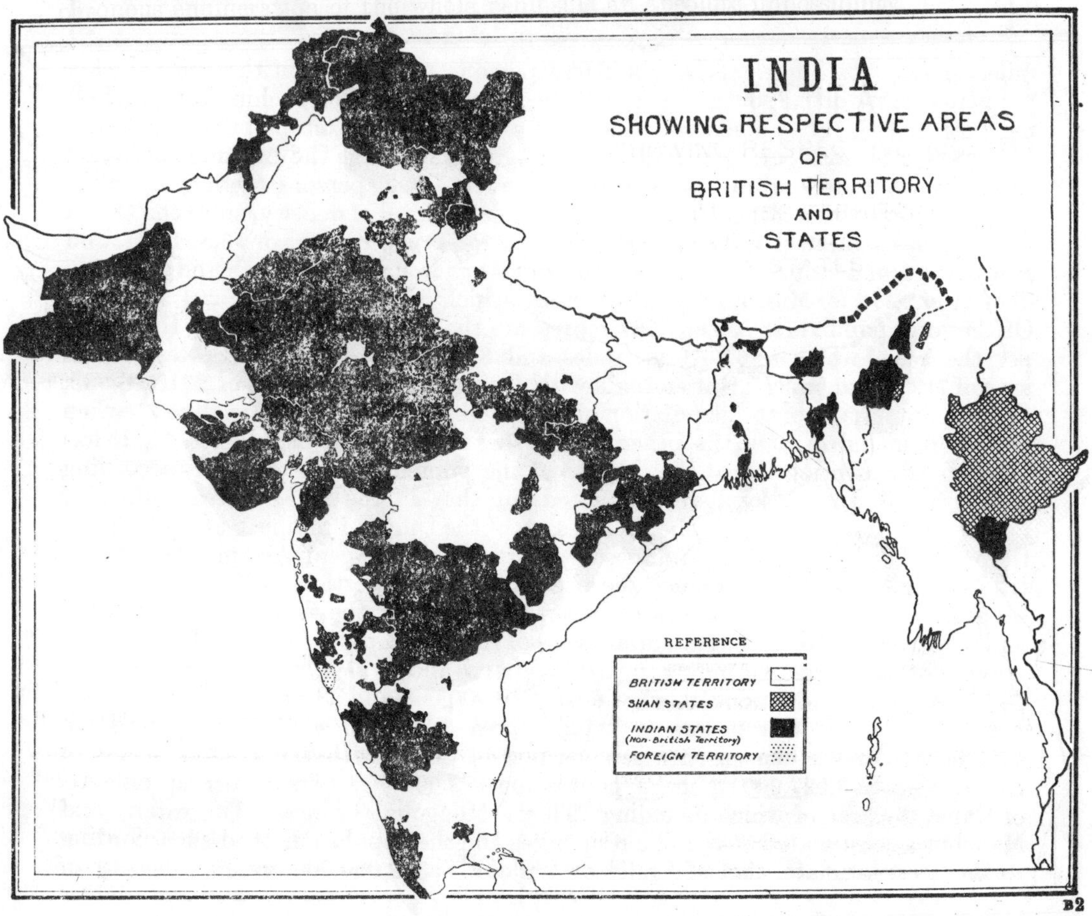

Section ii.—Distribution and Movement.

Area and Population. 4. The total area covered by this census amounts to 18 hundred thousand sq. miles and the population inhabiting it to 353 millions giving a density for the whole area of 195 persons per sq. mile. This density however is a very variable factor appearing at the lowest as 6·5 persons per sq. mile in the mean density of Baluchistan, Chagai District of which has only one person to the square

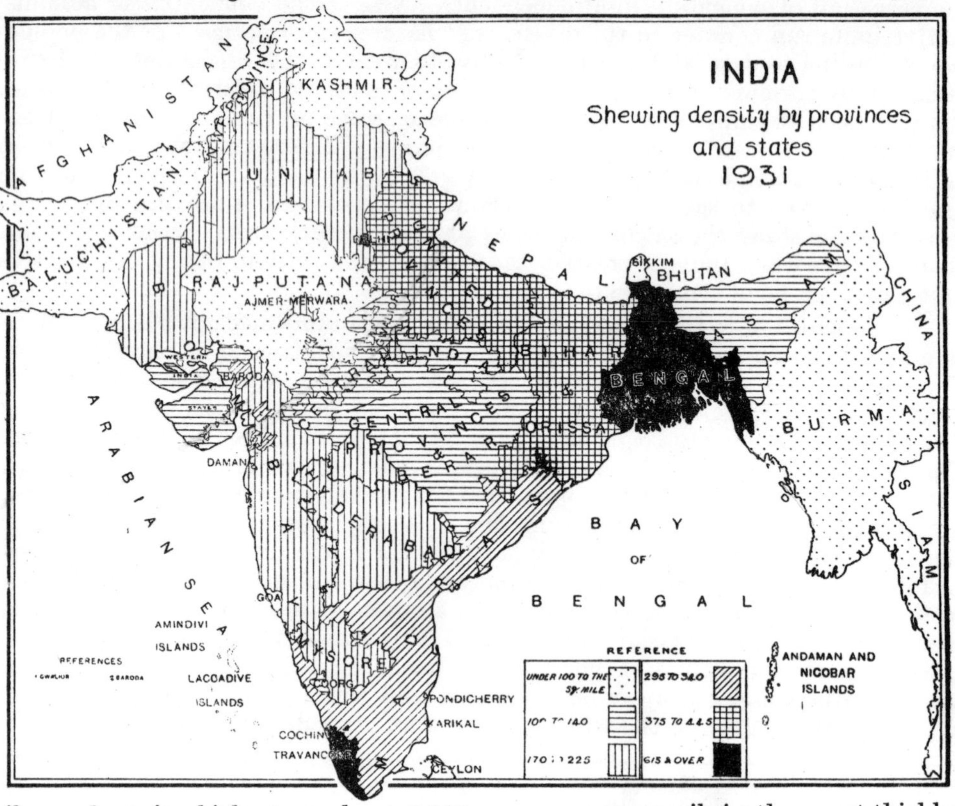

mile, and at its highest at about 2,000 persons per sq. mile in the most thickly populated parts of the south-west coast, the general density of Cochin State, including both the thickly populated coast lands and the almost uninhabited highlands, being 814·2 persons per sq. mile and reaching in one village the amazing maximum found in any purely rural population of over 4,000 persons to the sq. mile. There is, however, in Bengal an even higher general level of density, since the Dacca Division has a mean density of 935 persons for a population of 13,864,104, and reaches a rural density of 3,228 per sq. mile for Lohajang thana, and a mean density of 2,413 for Munshiganj sub-division which has an area of 294 sq. miles. Of the total population 256,859,787 represents the population of British India proper, the area of which is 862,679 sq. miles, and 81,310,845 that of the States with an area of 712,508 sq. miles. British India with Burma has a population of 271,526,933, and the proportion of the population of the States to British India is 23 to 77 when Burma is included. On the other hand if she be excluded it is 24 to 76. It has been already mentioned that the density of the population varies largely according to the rainfall and it may here be pointed out that in the densest areas—those of Cochin, of eastern Bengal, the north-east of the United Provinces and of Bihar, the rainfall is heavier than in any other part of India except Assam, where large tracts of hills and forest reduce the population in proportion to the area, and in southern Burma where there is considerable room for the increase of population and where also there are considerable areas of forest and hills. With India's present population and area we may compare England and Wales with an area of over 58,000 sq. miles and a population of nearly 40,000,000 and a density of 685 persons per sq. mile, or Europe as a whole—area 3,750,000 sq. miles, population 475,000,000, mean density 127 persons per sq. mile, with the United States of America—area 3,027,000 sq. miles, population 123,000,000, persons per sq. mile 41, or China the area of which including Tibet, Mongolia, Chinese Turkestan and Manchuria is estimated at $4\frac{1}{4}$ million sq. miles and the population of which according to the latest estimate, that of Professor Willcox, is 342,000,000 giving a density of

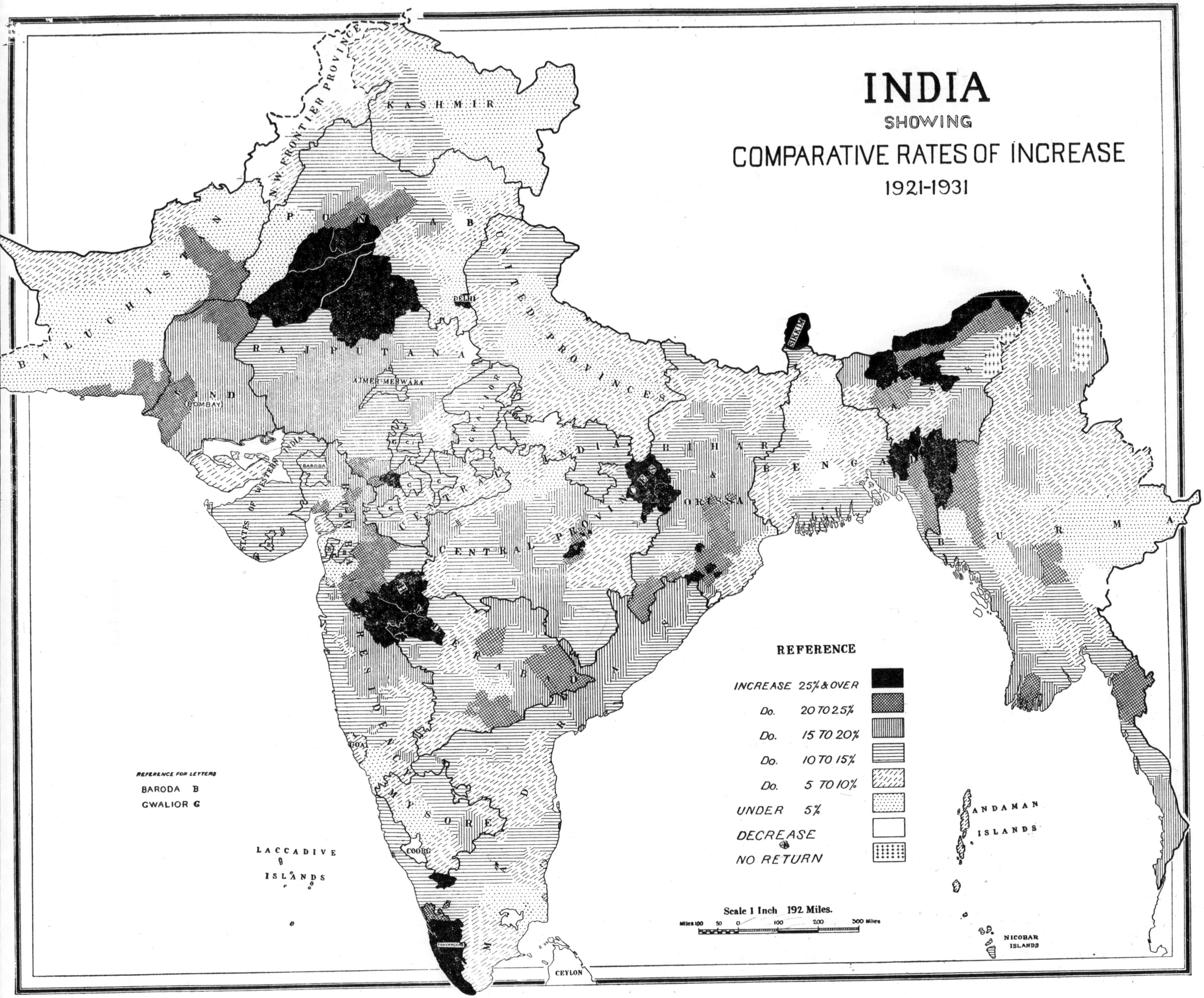

INDIA
SHOWING
COMPARATIVE RATES OF INCREASE
1921-1931
REFERENCE
INCREASE 25% & OVER
Do. 20 TO 25%
Do. 15 TO 20%
Do. 10 TO 15%
Do. 5 TO 10%
UNDER 5%
DECREASE
NO RETURN
Scale 1 Inch 192 Miles.
Miles 100 50 0 100 200 300 Miles
REFERENCE FOR LETTERS
BARODA B
GWALIOR G
KASHMIR
N.W. FRONTIER PROVINCE
PUNJAB
BALUCHISTAN
DELHI
RAJPUTANA
AJMER-MERWARA
SIND
(BOMBAY)
UNITED PROVINCES
SIKKIM
ASSAM
BENGAL
BIHAR & ORISSA
CENTRAL INDIA
CENTRAL PROVINCES
STATES OF WESTERN INDIA
BARODA
BOMBAY PRESIDENCY
HYDERABAD
MADRAS
GOAT
MYSORE
COORG
TRAVANCORE
CEYLON
BURMA
LACCADIVE ISLANDS
ANDAMAN ISLANDS
NICOBAR ISLANDS

80·5 persons per sq. mile, though in the fertile areas it is of course much heavier than this. Indeed a more useful comparison should be with China proper, having an area of about 1½ million sq. miles and a general density of probably 200 to 220 persons per sq. mile. It may be added that the total population of the world is now estimated at about 1,850,000,000, and if this be the fact, the population of India forms almost one-fifth part of that of the whole world. It should be added, as regards area, that the Survey of India is now revising the official figures of the area of districts and provinces which will involve some modification of the figures given in the census reports. Revised figures were not ready in time to be utilised generally at this census, but the necessary changes in area and density are for the most part small and unimportant.

Movement.

5. The actual increase since 1921 is 33,895,298, that is to say, 10·6 per cent. on the population at the last census and 39 per cent. on the population of India fifty years ago and an increase of 12 persons per square mile in 50 years, during which time the increase in area has been principally, if not entirely, confined to comparatively thinly populated areas, and amounts to 426,055 sq. miles. These figures may be compared with an increase in England and Wales since last census of only 5·4 per cent., but of 53·8 per cent. in the last 50 years, with an increase in the United States of 16 per cent. since the last census, with an increase of nearly 18 per cent. in Ceylon and with an increase in Java of 20 per cent. since the last census and of as much as 26 per cent. in the outer islands of the Netherlands Indies. The population of Java is of course not comparable with that of India as a whole on account of its small size and limited area, but having (with Madura) the very high density of 817 persons per square mile it is comparable with the more densely populated parts of India already mentioned. This illustrates the fact that the density in India is so variable that it is impossible to consider the question of movement of the population without going into the question of the distribution and variation of density, for density of population in India depends not on industry, as in the United Kingdom, but on agriculture, and is greatest of course in the most fertile areas. At this census, however, the greatest increase is in the States, where generally speaking the density is lowest, and therefore the increase in the population shown by the figures of this census appears at first sight indicative of pressure upon the margin of cultivation, but while the greatest increase has been in Bikaner (41·9 per cent.) this must be put down largely to the increase of irrigation and to the consequent immigration from outside, and one of next highest increases is that of Travancore in which the density was already among the highest in India. The increase in Hyderabad State again is partly to be attributed to an increase of efficiency in the taking of the census and cannot therefore be safely used as a basis of any comparison of the population as it is now and was then. Obviously the greatest increase in population is to be expected in areas such as that of Burma where the rainfall is above the mean and the density of the population below it. Where the rainfall and the density are at balance, that is, where the population is dense and the rainfall is just adequate as in the southern Punjab, eastern Rajputana, United Provinces, Central India generally and H. E. H. the Nizam's Dominions, irrigation has abated the liability to complete loss of crop, and improved communications have made it possible to prevent heavy loss of life in times of scarcity, thus enabling the population to increase on the margin of subsistence. How high a population can be supported by agriculture when conditions are favourable, is shown by Cochin with areas here and there carrying over 2,000 and in one rural unit actually 4,090 persons to the sq. mile on land producing rice and coconuts, but principally the latter which leaves more room for the erection of buildings and brings in a higher return than rice in actual cash. In such areas, *e.g.* Cochin and Travancore, the increase in the population has been higher than in the sparsely

Census of	Population.	Period.	Increase.	Increase due to Inclusion of new area.	Increase due to Actual increase of population.	Total increase per cent.
1881 ..	253,896,330	1872-81	47,733,970	33,139,081	14,594,889	23·2
1891 ..	287,314,671	1881-91	33,418,341	5,713,902	27,704,439	13·2
1901 ..	294,361,056	1891-01	7,046,385	2,672,077	4,374,308	2·5
1911 ..	315,156,396	1901-11	20,795,340	1,793,365	19,001,975	7·1
1921 ..	318,942,480	1911-21	3,786,084	86,633	3,699,451	1·2
1931 ..	352,837,778	1921-31	33,895,298	35,058	33,860,240	10·6
Total ..	..	1881-31	98,941,448	10,301,035	88,640,413	39·0

populated areas like Baluchistan or Jaisalmer State where there is no general extension of irrigation, although there would appear to be more scope for an extension of cultivation. On the other hand when these thickly populated areas are examined in detail it appears that the actual rate of increase in population is greatest in the less populated, and less fertile, areas. Thus in Travancore, there are three natural divisions the lowland—very fertile, the midland—less so, and the highlands, where the staple crop is tapioca and where irrigation is not practised. Now in these three natural divisions the density in 1921 was 1,403 persons to the sq. mile, 700 persons and 53 respectively, which increased during the decade to 1,743, 892 and 82, that is by 24·2, 27·4 and 54·7 per cent. respectively, showing a vastly higher rate of increase in the area of least density which is also the area of least fertility, though not as great a numerical increase. Similarly in Bengal the greatest rate of increase has been in the Chittagong Hill Tracts, and in Madras in the Nilgiris. Where, therefore, there is a population already dense, there is a clearly perceptible spread towards the less profitable land.

The increase of population has also been dependent in some cases on migration, while, on the other hand, the apparent increase may have depended on the failure to migrate. Thus the increase of 35 per cent. in Ahmadnagar district, a rather barren upland in the Deccan which suffers from recurring famines, is not due so much to a series of good years or to an extension of cultivation on the subsistence margin, as to trade depression, resulting in numbers of the population staying at home instead of migrating to the ports of Bombay and elsewhere where in normal years they are employed during the census months of February and March. Bombay shows a corresponding decrease, probably due, in the particular case of Bombay, largely to the same cause. Other decreases there are which are not so easy to explain.

Migration. 6. Immigration, when India is taken as a whole, influences the population very little. Table VI shows 730,562 persons as born outside India as against 603,526 in 1921, without taking count in either case of persons born in French or Portuguese possessions. The increase is almost entirely in persons born in Asiatic countries. Against this there must be set off on account of emigration about one million persons who are estimated as having emigrated during the decade under review. Migration, however, is of more importance as affecting internal fluctuations of populations, varying in British India from 1,244,249 (net) immigrants into Assam to 15,536 (net) immigrants into the North-West Frontier Province. These figures however include all those whose birth-place was outside the province, and do not refer to the decade 1921-31 only. If we take the actual increase due to immigration during the decade in Assam it is found to be only 121,648,* consequently if a percentage be taken on the increase of population Assam owes only 10·5 per cent. of its increase to immigration, though its immigration figure is the highest among all provinces. Conversely Bihar and Orissa with the greatest loss by emigration shows an increase of 10·8, a little more than that for all India, in spite of the fact that the total loss by emigration is equivalent to almost a third of the actual figure of increase. Migration as between British India and the States has tended in the past to be from the latter to the former, but during the last decade this position has been reversed and the trend of migration on the whole is from British India to the States, where the density is generally lower. Bikaner, where the immigrants total 161,303, *i.e.*, 58 per cent. of its increase in population, is a striking instance ; the greater number of its immigrants (about 54%) come from British India, and while the natural increase of the population of Bikaner State *plus* the normal immigration as recorded in 1921 would have resulted in a general increase of 28 per cent. and thereby brought the population back to the 1891 level merely, the increase at this census is much in excess of that amount, and this excess may be put down entirely to the extension of irrigation.

Mortality. 7. Another factor to be considered is the relation of the birth-rate to the death rate and this factor is far from being the same in different sections of the population. How far the fecundity of different races and castes in India is the result of environment and how far it may have become an inherited racial trait fixed at some period in the past history of the people, and how far it depends on prevailing social practices, is extremely difficult to determine in the light of the existing information, but it is easy to show that there is marked variation in different parts of India and

* *Vide* Assam Census Report, 1931, page 11.

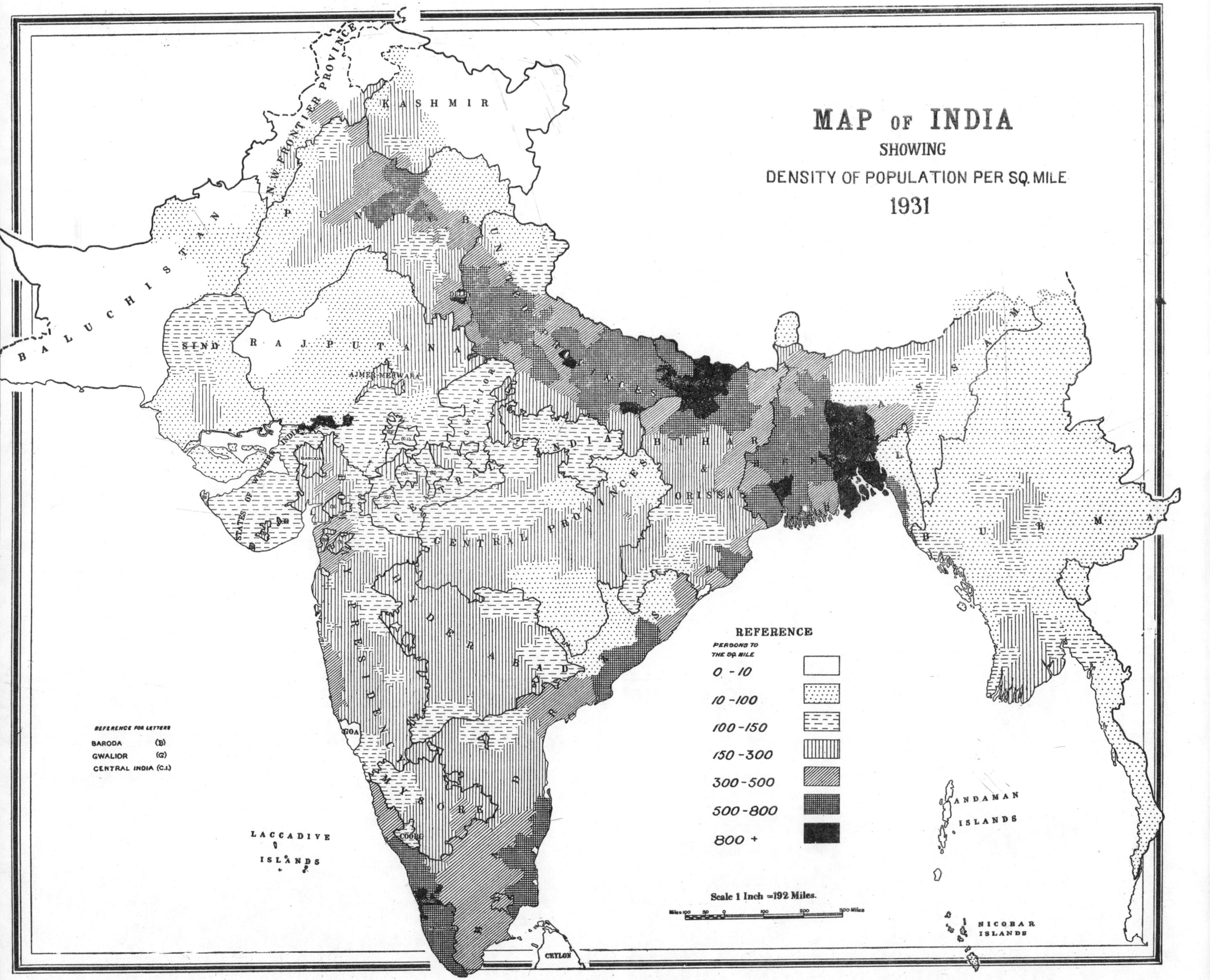

MAP OF INDIA
SHOWING
DENSITY OF POPULATION PER SQ. MILE
1931
REFERENCE
PERSONS TO THE SQ. MILE
0 - 10
10 - 100
100 - 150
150 - 300
300 - 500
500 - 800
800 +
Scale 1 Inch = 192 Miles.
REFERENCE FOR LETTERS
BARODA (B)
GWALIOR (G)
CENTRAL INDIA (C.I.)
KASHMIR
N.W. FRONTIER PROVINCE
BALUCHISTAN
PUNJAB
SIND
RAJPUTANA
AJMER-MERWARA
DELHI
UNITED PROVINCES
CENTRAL INDIA
GWALIOR
BARODA
STATES OF WESTERN INDIA
CENTRAL PROVINCES
BIHAR & ORISSA
BENGAL
ASSAM
BURMA
HYDERABAD
BOMBAY PRESIDENCY
GOA
MYSORE
COORG
MADRAS
CEYLON
LACCADIVE ISLANDS
ANDAMAN ISLANDS
NICOBAR ISLANDS

this question will be reverted to in the chapters on age and sex. Meanwhile it is enough to point out that in India the birth rate is everywhere much higher than in Europe, largely on account of the universality of marriage, the Parsis being perhaps the only Indian community in which late marriage and small families are the rule instead of the exception. The birth-rate is lower among the Hindus than in most of other communities probably to some extent on account of the general disapproval of widow remarriage, resulting in larger numbers of women being unreproductive at the child-bearing age, and to some extent on that of the greater prevalence of immature maternity. On the other hand, the high birth rate of India is largely discounted by a high death rate, particularly among infants as also apparently among women at child-birth. Here again social factors have to be reckoned with, the custom of purdah perhaps exercising its worst effect among the poorer class of Muslims who appear to be more rigid in its observance than the corresponding class of Hindus. This effect is particularly noticeable in crowded urban areas, in which the space available to a woman in purdah and poor circumstances is so small as seriously to affect her health. In the matter of epidemics and of deaths from famine or want, the decade has been particularly favourable to an increase in population. It is true that the influenza epidemic at the end of the previous decade is believed to have fallen most severely on the most reproductive ages and should therefore have had a much more lasting effect than the reduction caused by famine which takes the oldest and the youngest first. There has, however, been no serious famine in the decade under review, and every year sees improved methods of fighting such epidemics as cholera, plague or *kala azar*. Indeed a completely effective treatment for the latter pest has been perfected since the last census, and has made it possible to stamp out the disease. The antimony treatment of *kala azar* was discovered as early as 1913, but the original treatment took three months to apply and therefore did little to prevent the epidemic. The treatment with organic antimony compounds, introduced about 1917, reduced the period of treatment to a month. The improved treatment introduced during the 1921-31 decade however cures the disease in ten days or even less.

Comparison between deduced and enumerated population.

Province (British Territory only).	Variation 1921-1930 according to Vital Statistics (excess of births over deaths+, deficiency —).	Variation 1921-1931 according to Census (excess+, deficiency—)., total population.	Difference Excess or defect of column 3 on column 2.	Population under registration 1921.	Difference per cent. of population under registration.†
1	2	3	4	5	6
Assam	+450,854	+1,163,123	+712,269	6,852,242	+10·39
Bengal	+1,463,484	+3,411,695	+1,948,211	46,522,293	+4·19
Bihar and Orissa ..	+3,254,095	+3,682,158	+428,063	34,004,546	+1·26
*Bombay	+1,728,161	+2,587,404	+859,243	19,165,614	+4·48
Burma	+715,458	+1,454,954	+739,496	10,822,618	+6·83
Central Provinces and Berar.	+1,423,608	+1,594,963	+171,355	13,912,760	+1·23
Delhi	+53,132	+147,794	+94,662	500,539	+18·91
Madras	+4,398,902	+4,421,122	+22,220	41,002,696	+0·05
North-West Frontier Province.	+94,759	+173,736	+78,977	2,135,573	+3·70
Punjab	+2,428,382	+2,895,374	+466,992	20,517,606	+2·28
United Provinces ..	+3,927,768	+3,033,694	—894,074	45,375,787	—1·97
Total ..	+19,938,603	+24,566,017	+4,627,414	240,812,274	+1·92

* Excludes Aden.

† The variation shown in this column would of course be less in the case of excesses or more in the case of deficiency had the population under registration shown in column 5 been annually adjusted by deducting reported deaths and adding reported births.

A brief reference to vital statistics will be found in Section 76 (Chapter IV) below. In view of the admitted inaccuracy of these statistics in many provinces, the discrepancy between the 1931 population as it should have been according to those statistics and as it was found to be by the census is no cause for surprise. The figures are shown in the marginal table, and a calculation of the intercensal population will be found at the end of the chapter in subsidiary Table III, while subsidiary Tables VIII to XI contain additional material with reference to vital statistics.

8. As regards scarcity, improvements in communications, and consequently in ease of distribution, nowadays prevent anything like the famine mortality Economic.

of a century ago, while taking India as a whole the decade ending in 1931 was a prosperous one in the matter of crops, the general economic depression that has supervened having been little apparent outside one or two restricted areas until 1931 itself, so that for a population mainly agricultural the conditions have been very favourable to an increase in population. Nevertheless the decade opened, as it has since closed, in gloom. The frontier was disturbed ; the Moplahs were in rebellion ; there was trouble in the Madras Agency tracts ; the effects of influenza and the bad monsoon of 1920 were still active ; trade was depressed ; prices were high ; finances were embarrassed, and the non-co-operation movement was rampant. From this position there was a rapid recovery ; a series of good harvests followed almost all over India. In Bengal there were floods, it is true, and floods proved to be the principal cause of local distress and scarcity during the decade in India generally, as no province completely escaped the inundation of some portion in the ten years under review. But taking India as a whole the first five years were generally above the average, or little below it. Famines were local and not very serious, though one unfortunate district in Madras had famine declared in it officially in three seasons. Almost to the end of the decade the prices of cotton remained consistently remunerative. The end of the decade showed the most deterioration from this average of agricultural prosperity. Scarcity in some parts, *e.g.*, in the United Provinces, and the heavy fall in the prices of agricultural produce recreated a position not unlike that of the beginning of the decade, but with the additional embarrassment of a population greatly increased by the intervening prosperity. Wages however did not fall as rapidly as prices, and up to the time of the census agricultural prosperity on the whole was greater than ten years before, though the increase in population had diminished the size of holdings. Trade and industry followed much the same course, since the depression, though severely felt by the tea industry as early as 1928, had only just become general by the time of the census. On the other hand much permanent improvement had been carried out in communications everywhere, and a new port for ocean-going steamers had been constructed at Cochin and another begun at Vizagapatam.

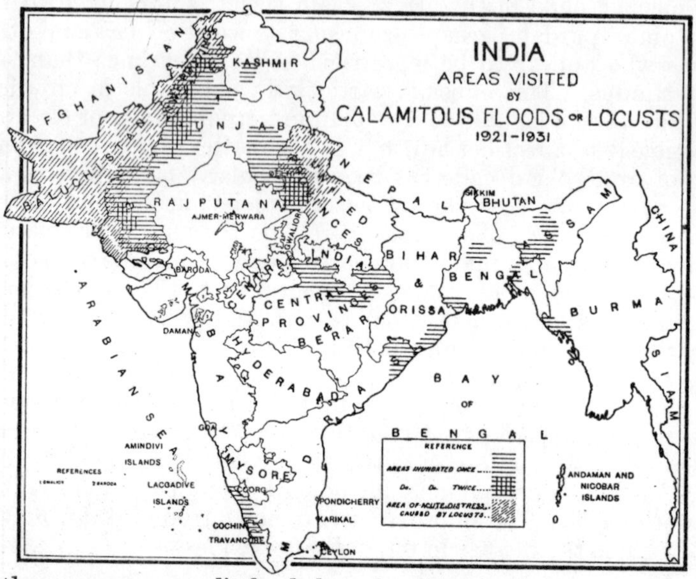

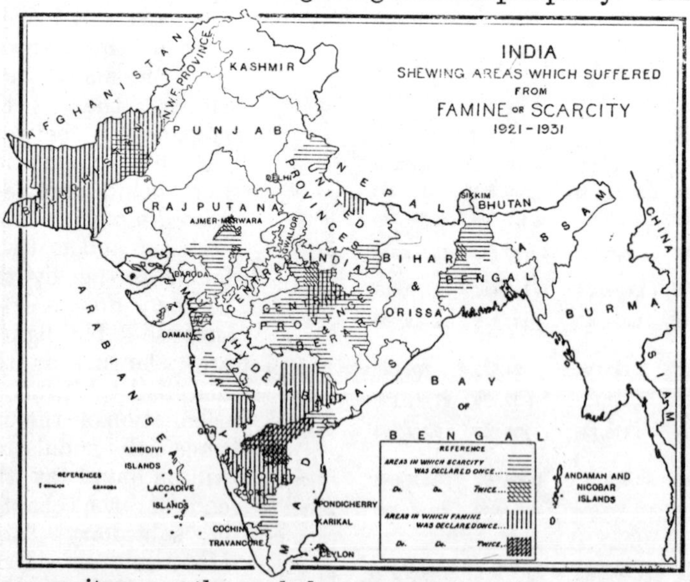

Above all a number of large schemes of irrigation and hydro-electric power development have been completed, particularly in the north-west and south of India. Public health has been exceptionally good during the decade; cholera and plague took much less than their usual toll of life, and *kala-azar* was suppressed by the perfection of an easy cure. The general rise in prosperity throughout the decade is indicated by the comparative deposits in savings banks and state of co-operative societies in 1921 and 1931, tables of which are given in the statements below:—

Post Office Savings Bank Deposits.

Post Office Circle.	No. of Banks.		No. of accounts.		Amount of deposits in rupees.	
	1920-21.	1930-31.	*1920-21.*	1930-31.	*1920-21.*	1930-31.
Bengal and Assam	*2,740*	3,141	*528,427*	615,785	*5,27,34,019*	8,99,83,627
Bihar and Orissa ..	*895*	1,037	*124,361*	158,943	*1,26,42,858*	2,55,71,070
Bombay*	*1,627*	1,823	*375,170*	333,793	*4,85,15,721*	5,66,65,593
Burma	*362*	511	*70,017*	87,246	*72,84,237*	1,26,25,298
Central	*801*	1,234	*95,569*	129,045	*1,27,62,966*	2,10,15,173
Madras	*1,838*	2,279	*207,675*	380,358	*1,40,38,563*	2,56,08,800
Punjab and N.-W. F. P.†	*997*	1,076	*241,494*	358,563	*4,48,87,062*	6,76,83,111
United Provinces ..	*1,453*	1,485	*235,244*	347,269	*3,57,68,516*	5,90,40,642
Sind and Baluchistan ..		260	..	66,611	..	1,20,66,560
Total ..	*10,713*	12,846	*1,877,957*	2,477,613	*22,86,33,942*	37,02,59,874

* *Includes Sind in 1920-21 only.* †*Includes Baluchistan in 1920-21 only.*

The number of Co-operative Societies has more than doubled during the decade, which opened with 47,503 societies and closed with over 100,000, while the number of members of primary societies increased from 1,752,904 to 4,308,262, of whom more than two-thirds are agricultural. Five states which did not appear at all in the statements of 1920-21 have

Five-year Cash Certificates Issue.

Post Office Circle.	Cash price realised from certificates.	
	In 1920-21.	In 1930-31.
	Rs.	Rs.
Bengal and Assam	*13,25,583*	1,69,42,242
Bihar and Orissa	*2,72,753*	39,59,736
Bombay	*13,72,843**	2,79,81,653
Burma	*1,85,628*	24,56,292
Central	*3,01,080*	80,80,370
Madras	*2,90,114*	69,37,890
Punjab and N.-W. F. P.	*7,25,353*†	2,63,83,786
United Provinces	*7,13,908*	1,53,60,699
Sind and Baluchistan	..	97,24,748
Total ..	*51,87,262*	11,78,27,416

*Includes Sind. † Includes Baluchistan.

PROGRESS OF THE CO-OPERATIVE MOVEMENT IN INDIA 1920-21 to 1930-31

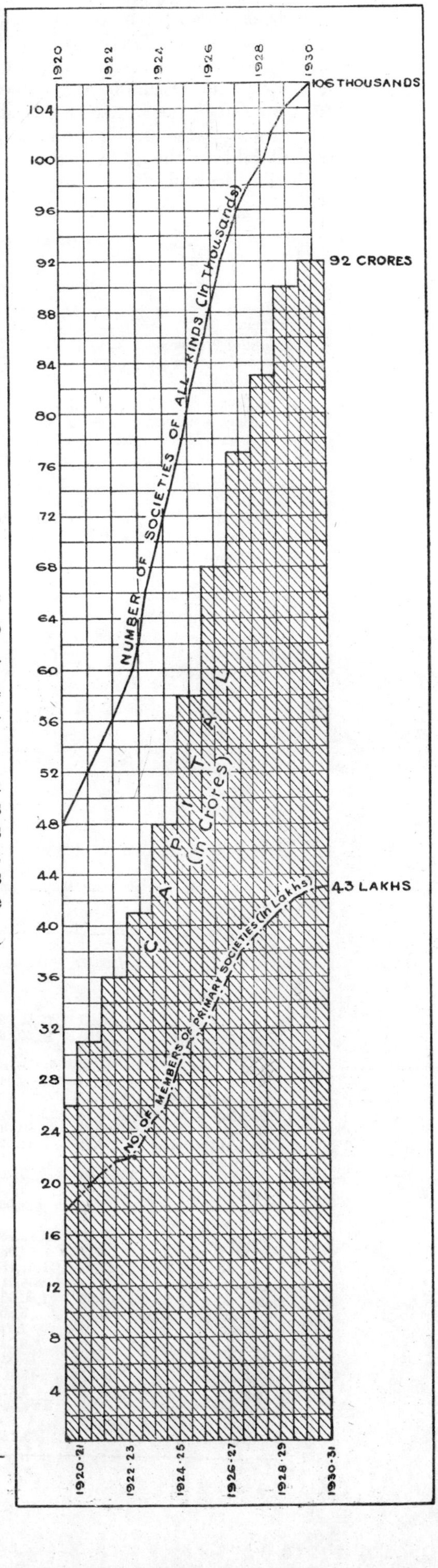

been added to the returns of 1930-31, *viz.*, Cochin, Gwalior, Indore, Jammu and Kashmir and Travancore. It will be seen therefore that inspite of the decline at the end of the decade into a condition of low prices, trade depression non-co-operation and rebellion, this time in Burma, similar to that with which the decade opened if not worse, there still remained at its close many of the economic benefits accumulated during the interval, though they are subject to the greatly enhanced liability of the additional population of approximately 34 millions to the propagation of which the prosperous years had so greatly contributed.

Province or State.	Total no. of societies.		Number of members (primary societies).	
	1920-21.	1930-31.	*1920-21.*	1930-31.
India	47,503	**106,166**	1,752,904	**4,308,262**
British Provinces	43,366	**90,064**	1,600,476	**3,681,300**
Ajmer-Merwara	*522*	654	*17,296*	18,608
Assam	*560*	1,413	*28,084*	69,569
Bengal	*6,366*	23,614	*232,001*	760,812
Bihar and Orissa	*3,580*	9,404	*107,514*	254,462
Bombay	*2,956*	5,896	*265,629*	572,669
Burma	*4,888*	2,972	*125,318*	85,741
C. P. & Berar	*5,011*	4,109	*79,638*	76,615
Coorg	*142*	253	*6,565*	14,037
Delhi	*103*	275	*2,011*	7,795
Hyderabad (*Administered Area*)	*5*	18	*205*	6,173
Madras	*6,287*	14,878	*395,284*	979,745
N.-W. F. P.	..	257	..	7,722
Punjab	*8,453*	20,698	*230,311*	679,616
United Provinces	*4,493*	5,623	*110,620*	147,736
States	4,137	**16,102**	152,428	**626,962**
Baroda	*509*	1,047	*16,932*	37,321
Bhopal	*691*	1,189	*10,446*	20,611
Cochin	..	210	..	24,328
Gwalior	..	4,071	..	70,307
Hyderabad	*1,437*	2,157	*35,293*	53,120
Indore	..	506	..	13,366
Kashmir	..	2,899	..	54,222
Mysore	*1,500*	2,213	*89,757*	134,428
Travancore	..	1,810	..	219,259

(*In thousands of rupees.*)

Province or State.	Share capital paid up.		Loans and deposits held at the end of the year.		Reserve and other Funds.		Total.	
	1920-21.	1930-31.	*1920-21.*	1930-31.	*1920-21.*	1930-31.	*1920-21.*	1930-31.
India	4,05,25	**12,40,83**	20,23,02	**69,18,27**	2,14,66	**10,32,12**	26,42,93	**91,91,22**
British Provinces	3,53,59	**10,60,16**	18,87,90	**63,92,31**	1,99,40	**9,07,08**	24,40,89	**83,59,56**
Ajmer-Merwara	*7,04*	6,73	*32,58*	30,90	*2,85*	9,67	*42,47*	47,30
Assam	*2,36*	8,09	*12,17*	59,94	*2,31*	10,01	*16,84*	78,04
Bengal	*42,28*	1,98,92	*2,64,63*	12,04,27	*26,37*	1,59,32	*3,33,28*	15,62,51
Bihar and Orissa	*10,57*	56,42	*1,02,10*	4,77,60	*10,27*	54,88	*1,22,94*	5,88,90
Bombay	*46,18*	1,77,46	*2,70,62*	11,08,35	*17,77*	1,04,91	*3,34,57*	13,90,72
Burma	*55,23*	88,78	*2,23,25*	1,05,19	*28,42*	75,07	*3,06,90*	2,69,04
Central Provinces and Berar.	*26,49*	34,57	*2,56,87*	4,30,99	*16,14*	66,17	*2,99,50*	5,31,73
Coorg	*99*	2,75	*53*	5,81	*60*	2,47	*212*	11,03
Delhi	*13*	2,59	*82*	20,37	..	2,11	*95*	25,07
Hyderabad (*Administered Area*)	*19*	1,96	*11*	3,10	..	26	*30*	5,32
Madras	*64,87*	2,42,16	*4,07,66*	14,39,78	*18,37*	1,27,94	*4,90,90*	18,09,88
N.-W. F. P.	..	2,08	..	10,44	..	43	..	12,95
Punjab	*69,52*	1,81,15	*2,33,03*	13,72,21	*57,99*	2,50,93	*3,60,54*	18,04,29
United Provinces	*27,74*	56,51	*83,53*	1,23,36	*18,31*	42,91	*1,29,58*	2,22,78
States	51,66	**1,80,66**	1,35,12	**5,25,96**	15,26	**1,25,04**	2,02,04	**8,31,66**
Baroda	*1,85*	5,80	*21,08*	59,45	*2,78*	9,69	*25,71*	74,94
Bhopal	*29*	*1,31*	*11,23*	14,90	*18*	8,36	*11,70*	24,57
Cochin	..	3,03	..	15,15	..	3,06	..	21,24
Gwalior	..	15,03	..	56,06	..	20,53	..	91,62
Hyderabad	*15,17*	45,41	*65,91*	1,39,62	*5,36*	23,12	*86,44*	2,08,15
Indore	..	3,51	..	37,79	..	13,46	..	54,76
Kashmir	..	24,42	..	56,74	..	16,57	..	97,73
Mysore	*34,35*	48,89	*36,90*	1,16,34	*6,94*	24,09	*78,19*	1,89,32
Travancore	..	33,26	..	29,91	..	6,16	..	69,33

Section iii.—Provincial distribution and variation.

Ajmer-Merwara.

9. Ajmer-Merwara is a small province with an area a little less than that of Co. Cork or a little more than that of Devonshire and a population of little more than that of all Connaught or of Midlothian. It is administered by a Commissioner under the Agent to the Governor General in India for Rajputana, by the States of which it is entirely surrounded, and consists of the city and sub-division of Ajmer, the adjacent but detached sub-division of Kekri,

—	Area in sq. miles.	Population.	Density.	Variation of population per cent. 1881 to 1891.	1891 to 1901.	1901 to 1911.	1911 to 1921.	1921 to 1931.	1881 to 1931.
Ajmer-Merwara	**2,711**	**560,292**	**207**	**+17·7**	**—12·1**	**+5·1**	**—1·2**	**+13·1**	**+21·6**
Ajmer and Kekri	2,070	423,918	205	+17·6	—13·0	+3·5	—0·4	+11·9	+18·0
Ajmer City	*17*	*119,524*	*7,031*	*+41·3*	*+7·3*	*+16·8*	*+31·7*	*+5·3*	*+145·3*
Merwara	641	136,374	213	+18·3	—8·8	+10·6	—3·9	+17·2	+34·4

and the tahsils of Merwara, the ancient domain of the Mers, as well as small detached areas which are included in one or other of these units. The population, though the highest yet recorded, only exceeds that of 1891 by less than 18,000 persons. The present census shows an actual increase of 13·1 per cent. for the decade, which probably represents a natural increase of 16·6 per cent. since the 1921 population was swollen by the Khwaja Sahib's *'Urs*. The agricultural produce of Ajmer and Merwara is not enough to support its population and some 360,000 maunds of grain are imported annually. Railway workshops in Ajmer employ many hands.

Andaman and Nicobar Islands.

10. Of the Andaman and Nicobar Islands, which form the charge of a Chief Commissioner directly under the Government of India, the islands of Great Andaman are in the process of development from a penal to a free settlement, the aboriginal population being far on the road to extinction. The density of the Andamans is

Administrative and Natural Division.	Area in square miles.	Population.	Density.	Variation of population per cent. 1881 to 1891.	1891 to 1901.	1901 to 1911.	1911 to 1921.	1921 to 1931.	1901 to 1931.
Andaman and Nicobar Islands.	3,143	29,463	9·37	..	..	+7·3	+2·4	+8·8	+19·5
Andamans	2,508	19,223	7·66	+6·7	+16·2	—2·7	+1·0	+7·9	+6·0
Nicobars	635	10,240	16·1	..	..	+35·4	+5·1	+10·4	+57·3

7·66. Sentinel Island and Little Andaman are still inhabited by Andamanese only, and the Nicobars are likewise occupied almost entirely by Nicobarese except for a few foreign traders, who come to the islands for pearl shell, *bêche-de-mer* and coconuts, by an Assistant Commissioner and by a few police. The density of the Nicobars is 16·1 persons per square mile. The convict population which was and is by far the most numerous element in the population of the Andamans has been much reduced on account of the policy of abolishing transportation to the Andamans. The figures of the foreign population, including convicts and *ex*-convicts, show a steady increase of Burmese and Karens. The climate suits them and they are accustomed to similar surroundings and the indications are that the permanent population of the islands will ultimately be predominately Burmese.

The most striking figures for these islands are those for the indigenous Negrito population which has shown a decrease respectively of 42, 30, 40 and 41 per cent. at each successive census of this century and a total decrease of over 75 per cent. since 1901 alone. If the present rate of decrease continue much longer the Andamanese will be extinct by the end of this century. The Census Superintendent in his report is content to damn with faint praise the policy of civilizing the aborigines and the institution of the ' Andaman Home ', but that policy, now abandoned, resulted in the space of 7 decades in a greater curtailment of human life than the Andamanese themselves are likely to have effected by their more direct methods in as many centuries. In the Nicobars on the other hand, whence the penal settlement was removed in 1888, there has been an increase of 10·4 per cent. since 1921 in spite of the deficiency of females, who are only 881 to every 1,000 males. The ratio of females to males has increased by 112 per mille since 1921 when the ratio was 769 females per 1,000 males, and by 40 per mille during the present century. If Nicobarese of tribal religion alone be examined the increase in the sex ratio is from 866 females per 1,000 males in 1921 to 939 in 1931.

Assam.

11. Assam with a present population of a nine and quarter million shows an increase since 1921 of 15·7 per cent. The decade from the point of view of public health has been " the best in the history of Assam ", and the tea industry, which is, of course, the main industry of the province beyond ordinary agriculture, was on the whole in a flourishing condition, starting the decade with a recovery from the depression of 1919-1921, booming in 1923 and 1924 and remaining prosperous until the end of 1927, when the present depression began to be felt as a result of foreign competition and over-production. The increase in population, in spite of being the highest recorded in Assam, has been mainly due to natural increase and not to an increase by immigration which only formed ten per cent. of the total. The general economic condition of the cultivator does not seem to have deteriorated up to 1929 in spite of a general tendency to decay on the part of the cottage industries. Up to that year the price of agricultural produce had increased and expenditure on luxuries was found by the Assam Banking Enquiry Committee to have increased likewise. The standard of living had gone up, and so also apparently had expenditure on marriage and other ceremonies. This had involved increased indebtedness and " the average agriculturalist has not learned the importance of saving ". The increase in population has extended to the whole province, Hills and Plains districts alike, but is lowest in the Surma Valley, which is the most densely populated part and but little affected by migration. The area of the province has been slightly extended on the frontier towards Burma, but that extension of area has only accounted for 1·25 per cent. of the increase. The area of Assam is 67,334 square miles and its population is 9,247,857 having a mean density of 137 to the square mile. This density, however, is a very variable matter. In the Surma Valley the density is 438 per square mile, and naturally the increase in population has been least in this area. In the Brahmaputra valley it is 171, and it is in this area that immigration is most active; in the Hills, which generally speaking afford a scanty subsistence to scattered villages, the density is only 39. There are no industrial towns in the province of any size or importance. The population is of a very mixed character. In the Brahmaputra valley the indigenous population consists of Bodo and Shan tribes mostly Hinduised, and with an aristocracy of caste Hindus ultimately of foreign extraction but, like the small Muslim population settled in the 17th century, completely identified with the country and the people of the valley by a residence of many generations. The recent immigrants consist either of tea garden coolies, mostly aboriginals from the Madras Agency Tracts, the Central Provinces and Chota Nagpur, who take up land and settle down in the country, and of Muslim cultivators from Maimansingh District in Bengal who have of recent years swarmed into the lower districts of the valley and opened up large areas of waste land. Prolific breeders and industrious cultivators but unruly and uncomfortable neighbours, these immigrants threaten to swamp entirely the indigenous inhabitants and in the course of two or three decades to change the whole nature, language and religion of the Brahmaputra valley and to assimilate it to the Muslim areas of Sylhet, where the population is not Assamese but essentially Bengali, whether Muslim or Hindu. In the other district of the Surma Valley, the plains part of Cachar, the last stronghold of the Kachari kings and once completely Kachari

Provincial and Natural Divisions.	Area in square miles.	Population.	Density.	Variation of population per cent. 1881 to 1891.	1891 to 1901.	1901 to 1911.	1911 to 1921.	1921 to 1931.	1881 to 1931.
Assam ..	**67,334**	**9,247,857**	**137**	**+ 6·8**	**+11·8**	**+15·2**	**+13·2**	**+15·7**	**+ 80·3**
Brahmaputra Valley ..	27,692	4,723,293	171	+10·0	+ 5·8	+18·7	+24·1	+22·5	+109·8
Surma Valley	7,450	3,262,029	438	+11·5	+ 5·3	+10·8	+ 3·3	+ 7·2	+ 44·1
Hills	32,192	1,262,535	39	—22·1	+77·7	+18·5	+ 8·2	+15·6	+105·3

in character, has become a Bengali colony entirely submerging the indigenous Kachari, who has retained his tribal nationality only in the North Cachar Hills. There as in the rest of the Hill districts the indigenous tribes still hold their own, resentful of the intrusion of the plainsmen whether Bengali or Assamese and maintaining their own languages and distinctive cultures and racially belonging for the most part to Burma rather than to India.

Baluchistan.

12. Baluchistan, the most sparsely populated of any province of India, occupies an important strategical position between Afghanistan, India and Persia, while the peninsula and immediate hinterland of Gwadar on its south-west coast is in the possession of the Sultan of Muscat and excluded from the scope of the Census of India. The province consists of British Baluchistan, of Agency Territories, of Tribal areas and of the States of Kalat and Las Bela ; the Agency Territories are grouped with British Territory for administrative purposes and include four tahsils held on lease from the Khan of Kalat. British Baluchistan covers 7 per cent. only of the total area of the province and contains 16 per cent. of the total population, but these figures become 40 and 53 respectively if all the areas under British administration area added to what is strictly British territory. In an area so scattered that the charge of a single enumerator involved the travelling of distances of from 50 to 150 miles, a generally synchronous census was obviously an impossibility, and, the regular synchronized census on the standard schedule covered only 200 square miles and a population mostly alien. The difficulties of obtaining an accurate census are further enhanced by the nomadic character of the population, which is constantly moving from one part of the country to another in search of pasturage or work, and by the periodic movements not only of the local population towards Sind, Afghanistan or Persia in the autumn, but also of foreign nomads from Afghanistan into and through Baluchistan in the winter. These nomads return in the spring, and in the summer Quetta with its cool climate is becoming a seasonal resort from the overbearing heat of Sind. The census therefore of Baluchistan is a census of her winter population and does not necessarily represent with any accuracy the population to be found there in the summer months, which the Census Superintendent estimates at 974,000. The mean density of Baluchistan is 6 persons per square mile, a little more than Tibet with 4 and about the same as Newfoundland exclusive of Labrador ; but this density falls in the Chagai district to 1 person per square mile. The decade started with a period of famine resulting from the drought of 1920-21 and although the years 1923-25 were good the later years were afflicted by locusts and the decade as a whole was below the usual level of prosperity. As a result of famine and scarcity and of the damage done by the invading sands of the Chagai deserts, which bury and lay waste the cultivated areas to the south and east of them and choke both sources and channels of irrigation, the province lost some thousands of its scanty indigenous population by migration. Prices ruled high until 1930 when they fell to a level phenomenally low. Health was poor and to the disease which naturally follows famine conditions were added serious epidemics of cholera, small-pox and measles. A general increase of motor traffic has almost caused the disappearance of animal-drawn vehicles during the decade, and 132 miles have been added to railways. The population increased by 69,000, of which 39,500 represents a natural increase, but the phenomenal increase of 45·5 per cent. in the Tribal Areas is not entirely beyond suspicion, and if the natural population of Baluchistan be alone considered, the 1911 figure has not yet been recovered. The population is far from uniform in character comprising as it does Brahui, Baloch, Lasi and Makrani with their satellite tribes of Loris, Dehwars, Langahs and Naqibs to say nothing of Pathans and Jatts and Persians. The country is of great historical importance

Administrative Unit.	Area in square miles.	Population.	Density per square mile.	Variation of population per cent. 1901 to 1911.	1911 to 1921.	1921 to 1931.	1901 to 1931.
Baluchistan ..	**134,638**	**868,617**	**6**	**+3·0**	**—4·2**	**+8·6**	**+7·1**
British Territory	9,084	136,793	9	+9·3	+1·1	+6·7	+17·7
Agency Territories.	37,864	271,491					
Tribal Areas ..	7,280	55,224	8	+1·3	+6·3	+45·5	+56·7
States ..	80,410	405,109	5	—1·9	—9·8	+6·9	—5·5
Kalat ..	*73,278*	*342,101*	*5*	*—3·6*	*—8·6*	*+4·2*	*—8·2*
Las Bela ..	*7,132*	*63,008*	*9*	*+9·1*	*—17·2*	*+24·3*	*+12·3*

and the researches in recent years of Sir Aurel Stein indicate that Baluchistan was once a fertile country supporting a large population, where it now offers a scanty subsistence steadily dwindling under the encroaching sand.

Bengal.

13. Bengal, ninth of the provinces of India in area, is first in respect of population. The British districts cover 77,521 sq. miles, exclusive of large surfaces of river and estuary, and the Bengal States 5,434. To these for census purposes was added Sikkim State, another 2,818 sq. miles. Thirty sq. miles have been added since 1921 from Bihar and Orissa but changes in calculation of area have increased the size shown in the tables by an additional 678 sq. miles. The total population returned is 51,087,338 for Bengal (of which 50,114,002 were in British and 973,336 in State territory) and 109,808 for Sikkim, the population of Bengal being more than one-sixth of the total for British India. The density in British Bengal is now 646 persons per sq. mile, while that of Sikkim is only 39. Excluding Calcutta the density of Bengal varies from 2,105 in Howrah district to 43 in the Chittagong Hill Tracts, but by far the greater part of the province has a density of over 500 to the sq. mile, and if smaller units are taken a much higher rural density is found in many places, Dacca Division having a mean density of 935, Munshiganj sub-division of 2,413, and Lohajang thana of 3,228 per sq. mile. The rate of increase of population has been 7·3 per cent. since 1921 and that of Sikkim 34·4 per cent. Cooch Behar State is one of the few in India that shows a decrease since 1921. This decrease, 0·27 per cent., is entirely Hindu (—4·76%) and is attributed to the expansion of settled cultivation by Muslims which has the effect of driving the Hinduised tribes, Koch, Mech, Poliya, etc., into the foothills or eastwards into Assam, a process observed likewise in the adjoining Bengal districts. It is also suggested that this decrease is partly due to changes in social custom, such as the abandonment of widow remarriage as part of a campaign of social elevation, and to changes in environment unfavourable to pre-existing adaptations. Tripura State on the other hand, with only 93 persons to the sq. mile, has experienced an increase of 25·6 per cent., and the thinly populated Chittagong Hill Tracts one of 22·9 per cent. Conditions during the decade from the economic standpoint are described as having been “ not entirely unsatisfactory ”. Harvests have been generally good and prices high until 1929, though there have been severe floods in three years, some cyclones and an earthquake. Wages were high till 1930, but their high level was of little benefit to middle class families with fixed incomes, and it was the skilled workman who reaped the most benefit. In industry cotton mills have been prosperous throughout, and jute until 1929 ; tea was prosperous till 1927 ; coal has not been prosperous. Throughout Bengal there seems to have been a general rise in the standard of living, not shown in an improved or more expensive diet, though it is reported that the need for a better balanced dietary is indicated by the fact that an ordinary cultivator is found to improve and gain weight on prison fare, but in minor amenities such as umbrellas and shoes, shirts and coats “ now worn by thousands who would never have dreamt of wearing them ten years ago ”, while the hurricane lantern is almost universally displacing the indigenous oil lamp. In some areas union boards are taking advantage of their powers to tax the union for schemes of village improvement such as the clearing of jungle, maintenance of roads and the excavation of tanks or wells. On the other hand increased earnings have not led to any reduction of the indebtedness of the ryot or labourer. The average debt of an agricultural family seems to be about Rs. 180 and that of a non-agricultural one perhaps a little more, while the average debt of the total population is about Rs. 166 per household. The debts of members of co-operative societies have increased by 3·5 per cent. to which borrowing to forestall the Sarda Act has largely contributed.

Province or State.	Area in sq. miles.	Population.	Density.	Variation of population per cent.					
				1881-1891.	1891-1901.	1901-1911.	1911-1921.	1921-1931.	1881-1931.
Bengal	**82,955**	**51,087,338**	**616**	**+7·5**	**+7·7**	**+8·0**	**+2·8**	**+7·3**	**+38·0**
British Districts ..	77,521	50,114,002	646	+7·6	+7·8	+7·9	+2·7	+7·3	+38·0
Cooch Behar State	1,318	590,886	448	—3·9	—2·1	+4·6	—0·1	—0·3	—1·9
Tripura State ..	4,116	382,450	93	+43·7	+26·1	+32·5	+32·6	+25·6	+299/9
Sikkim	**2,818**	**109,808**	**39**	..	**+93·8**	**+49·0**	**—7·1**	**+34·4***	**+260·5**

* 1891—1931.

In an interesting examination of the population question printed as an appendix to this chapter the Census Superintendent reaches the conclusion that Bengal might have a population of some 53 millions in 1941, and that the maximum population will be from 68 to 74 millions; that the Hindu population has passed the point at which the rate of increase accelerates in successive decades and is approaching a stationary population, whereas the Muslim population has not yet progressed so far along its present cycle of growth but will ultimately be to the Hindu as 4 to 3; and that Bengal could support at the present standard of living nearly double its present population.

14. Bihar and Orissa has a heterogeneous population of 42,329,583 in an area of 111,702 sq. miles giving a mean density of 379 per sq. mile, of which 28,648 sq. miles consist of feudatory States which contain more than 4½ millions of the population. The increase of the province has been 11·5 per cent. since 1921. The population falls naturally into three areas which do not correspond to its administrative divisions, that is into Bihar (exclusive of the Santal Parganas), the Chota Nagpur plateau together with the Santal Parganas and the Feudatory States, and Orissa proper. The mean density gives little indication of its great variation, which is as high as 969 persons per sq. mile in the Muzaffarpur district of Bihar, with a density of 1,073 if calculated on cultivatable area, and as low as 43 in the Feudatory State of Rairakhol. In previous decades the number of emigrants has very greatly exceeded the number of immigrants. This excess has been considerably reduced during the past ten years. **Bihar and Orissa.**

Locality.	Area in sq. miles.	Population.	Density.	Variation of the population per cent.					
				1881-91.	1891-01.	1901-11.	1911-21.	1921-31.	1881-1931.
Bihar and Orissa	111,702	42,329,583	379	+7·5	+1·8	+5·1	—1·2	+11·5	+26·8
Bihar (*excluding Santal Parganas*). ..	36,877	23,676,028	642	+4·7	—1·3	+1·5	—1·3	+ 9·7	+13·6
Orissa (*ex. Angul and Sambalpur*) ..	8,201	4,202,461	512	+6·8	+7·1	+0·9	—4·6	+5·2	+15·8
Chota Nagpur with Santal Parganas, Angul and Sambalpur ..	37,976	9,799,087	258	+10·2	+5·2	+11·8	—0·1	+16·4	+50·6
Feudatory States	28,648	4,652,007	162	+25·6	+9·5	+19·0	+0·4	+17·5	+93·0

But these conditions have been confined to British territory, for in the States there has been in the past an excess of immigrants over emigrants which has been similarly reduced during the past decade. The public health has been exceptionally good throughout the decade, mortality from plague having decreased by about 73 per cent. and from cholera by about 30 per cent. At the same time, though the birth rate has fallen from 41 per mille to 36·5, the survival rate has more than doubled. Earners profited by a general decline in the cost of living, while cultivators also benefited during the greater part of the decade not only by a succession of good harvests but by the fact that the prices of food grains retained a high level after other prices had fallen. There have been heavy investments in post office 5-year cash certificates; in the Post Office Savings Bank the number of depositors has risen since 1921 by 27·8 per cent. and the value of the deposits by 102 per cent. The standard of comfort has everywhere risen among the labouring classes, while an outstanding change in diet is the development of tea-drinking. It has already been pointed out that the population of this province is heterogeneous. That of Bihar is not markedly dissimilar to the population of the east of the United Provinces on the one hand or the west of Bengal on the other, between the populations of which it forms a natural link, and may be regarded as normal Hindustani speaking population of the Ganges valley. In Orissa proper the population is more nearly allied to that of Lower Bengal, but has a distinctive culture of its own. The Chota Nagpur Plateau and the Santal Parganas are primarily the habitat of comparatively primitive Munda speaking tribes and of others speaking Dravidian languages but closely allied to them in race. Sambalpur and Angul are not dissimilar and the inhabitants of the Feudatory States are also of the same kind, though Oriya replaces Hindi on the southern slopes of the plateau as the medium of communication with the more civilised world.

Bombay. 15. Bombay in 1921 included the area which in 1931 was enumerated as the Western India States Agency, and on this occasion therefore its area was reduced to 151,593 square miles (excluding Aden), having a population of 26,347,519 and a mean density of 174. Even with this reduction Bombay remains larger than any province except Burma and Madras. It comprises not only the British districts of the Bombay Presidency proper, but the Bombay States and Agencies and Sind. Aden is separately treated in an individual volume (Vol. VIII, pt. 3), and includes the whole of the Aden Settlement and Perim, but not the Aden Protectorate. An entirely separate volume (IX) deals with the cities of the Bombay Presidency, which is far ahead of any other province in India in the proportion of its urban to rural population, if we exclude Delhi and Ajmer-Merwara, where the principal unit of the province is itself a town.

Locality.	Area in miles.	Popu-la-tion.	Den-sity.	Variation of the population per cent.					
				1881-91.	1891-01.	1901-11.	1911-21.	1921-31.	1881-1931.
Bombay Province	151,673	26,398,997	174	+15·02	—3·6	+6·2	—1·2	+13·7	+32·0
Sind	46,378	3,887,070	84	+19·0	+11·7	+9·4	—6·7	+18·5	+60·8
Presidency ..	77,221	17,992,053	233	+13·7	—4·2	+5·3	—0·8	+12·4	+27·9
Bombay city ..	*24*	*1,161,383*	*48,391*	*+6·3*	*—5·6*	*+26·2*	*+20·1*	*—1·2*	*+50·2*
Bombay States ..	27,994	4,468,396	160	+17·6	—12·0	+7·0	+0·1	+15·5	+28·2
Aden	80	51,478	643	+26·4	—0·2	+5·0	+22·4	—8·9	+47·7

In Bombay City itself the population has actually fallen since 1921, partly probably because the economic depression which had set in by the census of 1931 had driven back to their homes the countrymen who normally come down to Bombay to work during the cold weather and partly no doubt owing to suburban expansion, but every other unit in the confines of the Presidency proper has increased in population during the decade and the general rate of increase, 13·7 per cent., is well above that of India as a whole. In the case of the cities the increase was probably greater than that actually shown, since the municipal authorities did not in all cases co-operate whole-heartedly, while some were definitely obstructive. In Surat, Kaira, Villeparle and Broach at any rate the enumeration was probably defective, and at Ahmadabad it was made impossible to carry it out at all in many parts of the city. For that town therefore an estimate has been made of the numbers not enumerated and added to the actual returns for the purposes of all tables in which details by religion, age, etc., are not required. Aden alone has fallen while the Bombay States and, even more, Sind have increased at a higher rate than the province as a whole, though Sind has been visited by disastrous floods and in 1929-30 revenue to the extent of Rs. 57,71,940 had to be remitted on account of damage by locusts. In marked contrast to all the decades since 1891 no district has suffered from a single very bad season during the whole period under review. Five seasons of the ten were good and five were moderate, and the fact that the prices of food grains fell more slowly than most others while cotton remained exceptionally high was of great benefit to the cultivator. At the same time wages and the demand for labour showed a tendency to rise rather than to fall until 1930, and then did not fall proportionately to the drop in prices. In the towns the decade was also one of prosperity until 1927-28, and in the earlier half of the decade urban labour seems to have reached an unprecedented standard of comfort, but at the end of the period the trade depression, aggravated by the civil disobedience movement, caused much unemployment and discomfort.

Burma. 16. The census of Burma was taken on February 24th two days earlier than that of India proper on account of local festivals which made the 26th an inconvenient date. Though only eighth in order of population figures, Burma is by far the largest of the provinces of the Indian Empire, having an area of 261,610 square miles, of which 233,492 were covered by the census operations of 1931. The population censused is 14,667,146, having increased by 11 per cent. since 1921, part of which increase, as near as can be estimated 320,000* persons, is due to immigration from India. The figures in the marginal table give the variation by "natural" divisions,

Locality.	Area in square miles.	Population.	Density.	Variation of population per cent. 1891-1901.	1901-1911.	1911-1921.	1921-1931.	1891-1931.
Burma ..	**233,492**	**14,667,146**	**63**	**+35·9**	**+15·5**	**+9·1**	**+11·0**	**+89·9**
Burman	156,297	12,856,207	82	+19·5	+14·6	+9·7	+11·7	+67·8
Chin ..	12,278	192,655	16	..	+38·9	—4·9	+20·6	+59·2*
Salween	7,101	111,947	16	..	+31·9	+3·5	—0·8	+35·5*
Shan ..	57,816	1,506,337	26	..	+18·7	+6·3	+5·1	+32·6*

* 1901–1931.

but these divisions are administrative and racial rather than geographical. Thus the Burman Division represents the plains districts of administered Burma in which the population is primarily (94 per cent.) Burmese, though it includes the remnants of the Mons of Pegu, the main bulk of the Karens, who appear also in the Salween and Shan divisions in smaller numbers, and a considerable share of the total number of Chins, Kachins and other indigenous races. It contains nearly all the Chinese other than Yunnanese, that is to say almost two-thirds of the total, and practically all the other foreign or Indo-Burmese population. The Chin division contains for practical purposes Chins and no one else. The Salween division, consisting as it does primarily of the Karenni, the only area in Burma with the status of an Indian State, has a population purely Karen and Tai. The Shan division, constituted by the Northern and Southern Shan States, is of course primarily Tai, but includes a good many Karens and Burmans, almost all the Yunnanese (who make up more than a third of the total Chinese in Burma), almost the whole of the Palaung-Wa branch of the Mon-Khmer race, many Kachins, about half the other indigenous races of Burma, and a few Indians. The immigration of Yunnanese during the decade has been considerable and has added about 10,000 to the population of the Northern Shan States, while Indians, largely Gurkhas from Nepal, have added another 11,000 to the Northern and 5,000 to the Southern Shan States. In the Salween division the population of the Karenni States decreased, and the increase in the rest of that division was largely due to the mines in Salween District. The Chin division has increased not only by the natural growth during a prosperous decade but by the inclusion of previously unadministered country on the Assam border. As far as climatic conditions went the decade was normal and floods and droughts were confined to small areas and involved no widespread calamities comparable with those which befell some parts of India, though the town of Pegu was destroyed by a disastrous earthquake which did damage elsewhere as well. Burma grows more rice than her population consumes, and although cultivable land is not readily capable of extension the area under irrigation was extended by some 317,000 acres during the decade. Industrial expansion, particularly in the production of oil, has been important in some districts and railways have extended by 434 miles. There has been some increase in mining activity in spite of the slump in silver and baser metals. The fall in the price of paddy was perhaps the most serious feature of the decade economically. The marginal table shows the wholesale prices of paddy brought by boat to Rangoon annually from January to March. After a very considerable rise from the 1921 prices, the price fell in 1929 nearly to the 1921 level, in 1930 considerably below it and in 1931 dropped to half. The past decade witnessed a very rapid growth of national feeling in Burma. This feeling tended to take a racial bias and showed itself particularly strong against Indians and Chinese, manifesting itself against the former in the Rangoon riots of May 1930, and against the latter in a riot in January 1931. With these came the rebellion, of which the Burma General Administrative Report for 1930-31 writes :—

Year.	Price in rupees per 100 baskets (46 lbs.)
1921	152
1922	185
1923	178
1924	193
1925	178
1926	185
1927	181
1928	169
1929	159
1930	138
1931	77

"The outbreak of a sudden and prolonged rebellion came as a surprise. It began on 22nd December 1930 in Tharrawaddy (75 miles north of Rangoon), a turbulent district

* *Vide* Chapter I of Burma Census Report, 1931, paragraph 14.

> since Burmese times and in these latter years a favourite resort of political agitators. Military Police were despatched in twenty-four hours, and regular troops followed, but by May 1931 there had been outbreaks in Prome, Yamethin, Pyapon, Henzada, Thayetmyo and attempted outbreaks elsewhere. The rebels were tatooed in order to render them invulnerable, and many wore simple uniform, for the rising was organised. Its object was the overthrow of Government and the enthronement of a jungle king, for in its prime origin it had little to do either with modern politics or with economic stress. It was aggravated by, just as in its turn it proceeded to aggravate, economic stress, but it originated in an outburst of mediæval superstition of a recurrent and recognisable type."

The outbreak coincided, of course, with the census, but luckily the preliminary enumeration could everywhere be completed in undisturbed conditions except in Tharrawaddy District and a small part of Pegu, where there was inevitably some under-enumeration. The rebellion spread to Henzada before the final enumeration, but the preliminary enumeration had already been completed.

Central Provinces.

17. The Central Provinces and Berar, an area totalling 131,095 square miles, include not only the British districts, 82,153 sq. miles, and the fifteen States of the Central Provinces, 31,175 square miles, but the four districts of Berar, 17,767, which are leased in perpetuity from H. E. H. the Nizam. The total area of the province according to the latest revision is 133,050 sq. miles, but this figure was obtained too late for use in the tables. The total population is 17,990,937 with a mean density of 137 per sq. mile, but this density is very variable being exceedingly low in the 20,000 sq. miles still covered by forest. The highest density is that of the Katghora Tahsil which has 492 persons to the sq. mile, and the lowest that of the Ahiri Zamindari with only 16. Famines and epidemics have been responsible for exceptional fluctuations in the past, and the Central Provinces more than any other are marked by recurring alternations between good and bad years. The decade under review opened in conditions of scarcity and high prices, while the effect of the influenza epidemic upon women of the child-bearing ages can be traced in certain age groups at the present census. Up to the end of 1921 public health was bad. Cholera, plague and malaria caused exceptional mortality. In 1922 however the satisfactory monsoons of that and the previous year reduced the death rate from 44 to 29, though the birth-rate also fell from 38 to 36 per 1,000. Good monsoons and healthy years continued until 1926-27, which was marked by serious floods, and 1927-28 saw the beginning of the decline in prosperity. Wheat was attacked by rust and more than half of the crop was lost in the northern districts of the province in that year and health deteriorated. The following year brought the recurrence of non-co-operation, agrarian agitation and general depression, another unsatisfactory agricultural year in the north of the province, and much unhealthiness from cholera, plague, small-pox, influenza and malaria. On the whole, however, the intervening prosperity more than balanced the depression at either end of the decade. The net area cropped increased from 23,585,215 acres to 25,364,376 ; the addition of a thousand miles of irrigation channels added nearly a hundred thousand acres of irrigated land ; a thousand miles of metalled road were added to the existing metalled roads, and many new bridges, and 300 miles of railway. It is significant of the connection between prosperity and population that the growth of the latter was very small in the north of the province which suffered three very bad years at the end of the decade. Elsewhere, as in other provinces, the highest rate of increase was in the most thinly populated areas. The infant mortality rate appears to be higher in the Central Provinces than in India as a whole or in most other parts of India, but the rate of increase at this census has been 12·6% for the province. Both the natural features and the population are very varied. The Narbada valley in the north is a wheat growing tract; the Maratha plain in the west and the Chhattisgarh plain in the east

Locality.	Area in sq. miles.	Population.	Density per sq. mile.	Variation of population per cent.					
				1881 to 1891.	1891 to 1901.	1901 to 1911.	1911 to 1921.	1921 to 1931.	1881 to 1931.
Central Provinces and Berar ..	**131,095**	**17,990,937**	137	+10·7	—7·0	+17·9	—0·3	+12·6	+35·0
British districts	82,153	12,065,885	147	+9·5	—9.2	+17·8	—0·2	+11·3	+30·2
Berar ..	17,767	3,441,838	194	+8·4	—5·0	+11·0	+0·6	+11·9	+28·8
Central Provinces States.	31,175	2,483,214	80	+23·4	—4·8	+29·8	—2·4	+20·1	+79·0

are rice-growing areas ; the Central plateau and the Chota Nagpur p'ateau in the north-east like the States of Bastar and Kanker and the district of Chanda in the south are largely forest. In the open country Marathi is the language of the west and Hindi of the east, but the forest tribes speak Dravidian or Munda languages. In Bastar State, the remotest part of the province, there has been much increase in communication, but the Administrator reports that the increase in traffic is leading to an increase in the consumption of opium and in the case of one tahsil to the substitution for opium of the much more pernicious mercury.

Coorg.

18. Coorg, smallest after Delhi of the provinces of India, is the only one which showed a decrease of population at the census of 1931. It is administered by a Chief Commissioner, who combines this office with that of Resident in Mysore, and has a council of 15 elected and 5 nominated members. Its area is 1,593 square miles (of which 519 are occupied by Reserved Forest) with a population of 163,327—511 less that is than in 1921, and a density of 103 persons per sq. mile. The decrease in population is probably greater than the figures indicate, since there has been a decrease of about 5,000 persons in the natural population most of which is balanced by an increase in immigrants more apparent than real, since it consists mostly of labourers who leave the province for their homes in March. In 1921 many must have already gone when the census was taken but in 1931 the census fell earlier before the exodus had started. The vital statistics showed an excess in deaths over births of 14,000, though it is stated of the average individual in Coorg that his desire " appears to be to have as many children as possible, irrespective of his economic position ". Coffee plantations on an important scale as well as cardamom plantations on the western slopes of the plateau continued to flourish and tea to survive, though plantations of rubber and agave are being abandoned, but the staple crop is rice of which the province produces more than it consumes. Both for rice and coffee the decade was favourable except for the heavy floods in 1924. The fall in prices, steady till 1929, at the end of the decade caused paddy to be sold at exceedingly low rates and the area under rice-cultivation to decrease from 84,587 to 82,822 acres. Urban population has increased and a general increase in the number of occupied houses points to the gradual dissolution of the joint family system prevalent in Coorg.

	Area in Sq. miles.	Population.	Density.	Variation of the population per cent.					
				1881-91.	1891-01.	1901-11.	1911-21.	1921-31.	1881-1931.
Coorg. ..	1,593	163,327	103	—2·9	+4·4	—3·1	—6·4	—0·3	—8·4

Delhi.

19. Delhi is the smallest and most recently constituted of the provinces of India. It came into being as a province on the laying of the foundation stone of New Delhi by His Majesty the King Emperor in December 1911, and as a result of the establishment there of the imperial capital its growth has been phenomenal. It is of course primarily an urban unit and the total area of the province is only 573 sq. miles, but the population is 636,246 persons (722 females per 1,000 males) with a mean density of 1,110 persons per sq. mile. This density varies from 58,273 persons per sq. mile in Old Delhi municipality to 372 in the rural area, where the increase during the decade has been only 3 per cent. as compared with 30·3 per cent. for the province as a whole. This rapid increase is due to the abnormal growth of a newly established capital, and is very largely due to immigration, since the gross balance of migration in Delhi's favour is 189,594 persons, of which the Census Superintendent regards 111,775 as the actual net increase by migration during the decade since 1921. This growth in population has outstripped the rapid building of houses and in the urban area the density per 100 houses has increased from 410 in 1921 to 454 in 1931. The censused population of the urban areas

Locality.	Area in sq. miles.	Population.	Density.	Variation of population per cent.					
				1881 to 1891.	1891 to 1901.	1901 to 1911.	1911 to 1921.	1921 to 1931.	1881 to 1931.
DELHI PROVINCE ..	**573·0**	**636,246**	**1,110**	**+6**	**+9**	**+2**	**+18**	**+30**	**+81**
Urban	65·5	447,442	6,835	+11	+1	+12	+31	+47	+158
Old Delhi Municipality.	*5·96*	*347,539*	*58,273*	*+11*	*+9*	*+11*	*+8*	*+40*	*+104*
New Delhi ..	*48·3*	*73,653*	*1,524*	..	..	..	..	*+95*	..
Rural	507·5	188,804	372	+2	+9	—8	+2	+3	+6

however (447,442) probably falls to about 330,000 in the hot weather, which is likely to be no more and possibly even less than its permanent population at the height of its importance in the reign of Shahjahan.

Madras. **20**. Madras covering 142,277 sq. miles populated by 46,740,107 persons, is second among the major provinces in area, third in population and fifth in density (329), but in rate of increase seventh exceeding only Bengal and the United Provinces the higher population figure of which it is fast overhauling. Its rate of increase for the decade was 10·4 in British territory, a little less than the general rate of the whole Indian Empire. The total irrigated area has increased by some 66,000 acres, that is by 0·90 per cent. only, but important new works are projected. The decrease in the value of the crops raised has been nearly 46 per cent. which indicates not a fall in the quantity of the crop but in the level of prices. At the same time possibilities of agriculture on present methods have more or less reached a maximum and the Presidency can no longer feed itself. The decade was healthy, and not only has it been free from epidemics but the skilled research of Colonel Russell, the Director of Public Health, has made it possible to cope with epidemics when they arise, and in the case of cholera to predict their occurrence and so to forestall their virulence. Cholera, which is endemic in the south of the Presidency, has proved to have a six-year cycle. The vital statistics of Madras are worthy of reference since this province is the only one whose registration of birth and death approaches anything like a satisfactory standard. Even so in 1930 some 62,000 unregistered births and 20,000 unregistered deaths were detected by inspecting officers in the Presidency. In some parts of Madras emigration takes place on a larger scale to Assam, Burma, Ceylon and Malaya, the annual loss being some 13,000, and though the decline in the planting industry has resulted in large numbers of returns, these had not had their full effect by the time the census took place, even from Burma. As in the accuracy of her vital statistics, Madras is ahead of other provinces in the matter of birth control. A tendency is observed by the Census Superintendent for men at any rate to marry later, and contraceptive methods are advocated by influential persons and widely advertised in the press. The Census Superintendent writes "Ten years should show a marked growth in their popularity. Books on the subject are to be found in any bookstall or publisher's list and whether they are read as mild pornography or for serious guidance it is unlikely that they can fail to exert some influence". He adds, as a portent, that contraception of a crude kind has been observed among the Goundans of Salem to prevent large families, the fragmentation of holdings and the weakening of the joint family system.

The external boundaries have not altered. Internally there have been some changes between districts the most important of which has been the re-absorption in the three neighbouring plains districts of the Agency Division, a hilly tract inhabited by Khonds, Sawaras, and similar hill tribes and quite alien to the plains

Province and Natural Divisions.	Area in sq. miles.	Population.	Density.	Variation of the population per cent. 1891-01.	1901-11.	1911-21.	1921-31.	1891-1931.
Madras	**142,277**	**46,740,107**	**329**	**+7·2**	**+8·3**	**+2·2**	**+10·4**	**+31·1**
Agency	19,869	1,763,765	89	+2·4	+16·7	—4·0	+16·5	+33·6
East Coast North	31,532	12,175 530	386	+8·8	+9·8	+3·2	+12·2	+38·5
East Coast Central	32,020	13,349,980	417	+8·9	+7·9	+3·0	+11·3	+34·7
East Coast South*	22,102	10,380,774	470	+5·6	+8·4	+3·0	+5·2	+24·0
West Coast	10,798	5,082,281	471	+6·3	+7·1	+3·3	+13·5	+33·5
Deccan*	25,954	3,994,543	154	+5·5	+3·5	—3·7	+10·3	+16·0

* Excluding States.

districts which have absorbed it. The mean density is 329 but density varies greatly in different areas being only 89 persons to the square mile in the agency tracts and 471 on the west coast, though one district, the plains of Godavari East, on the Coromandel Coast reaches a higher density (660) than Malabar itself with 610. There is a greater tendency to city life in Madras than in any major province but Bombay, but the towns are far less industrial in character than that of the latter province. Nevertheless signs of industrial development are appearing and cotton mills are springing up at small country centres supplied by the cotton growing areas they adjoin. Thus Pollachi, a small town in Coimbatore district, had six mills in 1921 but thirty in 1931. Cheap power from water is a possibility and the use of electricity is steadily advancing in popularity, as the decade has seen many towns with oil lamps or no lamps adopt electric lighting and fans. The standard of living is rising and in ten years the villager has "become accustomed to and takes as necessities what formerly were rather un-looked-for luxuries. The great advance in communications which the motor bus and car has brought has contributed enormously to widening horizons".

North-West Frontier Province.

21. The North-West Frontier Province has an area of 36,356 square miles with a population of 4,684,364 and a mean density of 129 per square mile, but of this area 22,838 square miles constitute the Trans-frontier Agencies, of the population of which 2,212,837 is only estimated and not obtained by enumeration, making a total with those enumerated in trans-frontier posts of 2,259,288 (density 99) and leaving 2,425,076 persons in the five regularly administered districts with an area of 13,518 square miles and a mean density of 179, an area a little greater than that of Holland with a population a little less than that of Denmark. Since 1921 the Malandri tract, 20 square miles, has been added to the administered from the unadministered area and 4 square miles have been transferred from Kohat District to the former. Otherwise there has been no territorial change. The density of population in the administered areas exclusive of urban population varies according to the combined factor of rainfall × irrigable land, decreasing from north to south. The growth of population has depended mainly on the extension of canal irrigation. The Kabul River Canal reached its maximum area of irrigation in 1921 and the Upper Swat Canal in 1929. When the decade opened the agricultural position was bad and the frontier was disturbed, a condition which, however, benefits the inhabitants of the administered districts financially. Both contractors and unskilled labour do well and "to the Pathan of fighting age times of unrest call up memories of a princely pay earned in princely idleness, guarding with a government rifle and the prestige of his race some lonely spot on a winding frontier road". The situation on the frontier improved rapidly, but this improvement was followed by outbreaks of internal disturbance in 1924 and 1927 of a communal nature and in 1929 by revolutionary outbreaks all over the province culminating in the very serious riots of April 1930 in Peshawar with inevitable repercussions among the border tribes, though the situation was restored in time for the census to be taken generally under normal conditions. Agriculturally the decade was satisfactory until 1924, less satisfactory from 1924 to 1928 but improved from 1928 to 1930 when a deficient fall of rain and an excessive fall in prices combined to reduce greatly the area sown for crops. Rs. 22,06,956 of revenue were remitted on account of damage by locusts in the years 1929-30. Public health was bad in the first half of the decade, which the Census Superintendent attributes to the after effects of the influenza epidemic, but the second half was one of "uninterrupted good health" which "restored to the people their normal vitality", and the increase of population in the administered districts since 1921 has been 7·7%. The Co-operative Credit movement was started in 1925, and in 1926 there were 16 societies with a membership of 365 and a working capital of Rs. 39,317. In 1930 there were 166 societies with 5,825 members and a working capital of Rs. 8,92,000. The primary necessity of the province is a settled economic outlook without which an increase in population disproportionate to that in wealth and productive efficiency will involve poverty and discontent and in all probability a destructive agitation and very serious disturbance.

Locality.	Area in sq. miles.	Population.	Density.	Variation of population per cent.					
				1881 to 1891.	1891 to 1901.	1901 to 1911.	1911 to 1921.	1921 to 1931.	1901 to 1931.
N. W. F. P.	**36,356**	**4,684,364**	**129**	..	..	**+79·7**	**+32·9**	**—7·7**	**+120·4**
Administered areas.	13,518	2,425,076	179	+17·9	+9·9	+7·6	+2·5	+7·7	+18·8
Agencies and Tribal areas	22,838	2,259,288	99	..	..	+1,831·9	+74·2	—20·0	+2,590·8

Punjab.

22. The Punjab is the eighth province in India in area, but with the Punjab States Agency fourth in area, sixth in density and fifth in population. It has an area of 136,964 square miles with a mean density of 208, but this includes not only British districts and the Punjab States but also the Punjab States Agency, a separate unit though treated in the same volume. Taken separately British territory has a population of 23,580,852 with a density of 238 over 99,265 square miles. The area appears in the tables as 99,200 the revised figure having been received too late for incorporation, a condition which also explains the appearance of the area 5,820 in Table I as that of the Punjab States instead of the revised area 5,292 square miles with a population of 437,787 and a density of 83. The Punjab States Agency has an area of 32,407 square miles, a population of 4,472,218 and a mean density of 138. The increase in the Punjab population during the last 40 years is well illustrated by the density of Lyallpur district which was 15 per square mile in 1891 and is now 368. The last decade has seen the highest rate of increase yet recorded. It has been a healthy decade, the first half in particular, though in the second half there were plague epidemics in 1924 and 1926, while in 1926 and 1928 there were localized epidemics of cholera. The birth rate, twice that of the United Kingdom, has remained consistently high. Agriculturally the decade has been prosperous. The Sutlej canal system in 1921 fed the Sirhind Canal only; it now irrigates large tracts in Multan, Lahore, Ferozepore and Montgomery districts and in Bahawalpur State, as well as in Bikaner in Rajputana. In the Punjab as a whole canal irrigation has extended by over 19 per cent. and has added 2,000,000 acres of irrigated land during the decade, though a drawback to irrigation has appeared in the tendency towards the rise of the subsoil water level, which forces up from below salts which make the surface soil unfit for cultivation. Agricultural wages remained high until 1928 and have not fallen so rapidly as prices. Agricultural credit has increased its capital from 216·13 lakhs in 1921 to 817·91 in 1931 and its owned capital from 113 to 317 lakhs, and an indication of agricultural prosperity is to be found in the rise by 22 per cent. in the price of agricultural land. There has been a spread of improved varieties of wheat, cotton and sugar-cane and a great advance in the local manufacture of cane mills, ploughs, irrigation wheels and other agricultural implements. In 1921 the Census Superintendent remarked on the noticeable absence of any local manufacture of agricultural implements, but now at Batala, in Gurdaspur, alone there are 21 iron-foundries with an annual output of over 19,000 implements valued at Rs. 537,000. The comparative prosperity and high prices of the earlier part of the decade led to increased interest and activity in the formation of joint stock companies, and factories increased from 297 with 42,428 hands to 526 with 49,549 hands. The extraction of petroleum and the manufacture of cement from limestone have been started in Attock district within the decade, while the Mandi hydro-electric scheme now just completed is likely to hasten the industrialization of the province by the plentiful supply of cheap power. It remains to mention the rural uplift movement started in Gurgaon district in 1931 by Mr. Brayne and taken up elsewhere by the Y. M. C. A. which has also opened in Lahore a broadcasting station which already transmits to 1,500 receivers.

Locality.	Area in sq. miles.	Population.	Density.	Variation in population per cent. 1881 to 1891.	1891 to 1901.	1901 to 1911.	1911 to 1921.	1921 to 1931.	1881 to 1931.
Punjab	136,964	28,490,857	208	+10·2	+6·3	—2·4	+5·5	+13·5	+37·0
British Punjab ..	99,265	23,580,852	238	+10·1	+6·9	—1·8	+5·7	+14·0	+39·2
Punjab States ..	5,292	437,787	83	+8·9	+4·9	+0·1	—1·0	+7·3	+21·5
Punjab States Agency	32,407	4,472,218	138	+10·6	+3·7	—5·3	+5·5	+11·6	+27·7

United Provinces of Agra and Oudh

23. The United Provinces have an area of 112,191 sq. miles of which 5,943 constitute the States of Rampur, Tehri-Garhwal and Benares. The total area is less than that of 1921 by 53 sq. miles on account of 8 sq. miles transferred elsewhere and 45 reduced by fresh surveys. The province (British territory) is a little smaller than the British Isles and has a slightly larger population, while the total population of the province is 49,614,833 with a mean density of 442. Though seventh of the provinces of India in size, it is third in point of population. Eighty per cent.

Locality.	Area in sq. miles.	Population.	Density.	Variation of population per cent. 1881-1891.	1891-1901.	1901-1911.	1911-1921.	1921-1931.	1881-1931.
United Provinces ..	**112,191**	**49,614,833**	**442**	+6·3	+1·7	—1·0	—3·1	+6·7	+10·6
British Territory ..	106,248	48,408,763	456	+6·2	+1·7	—1·1	—3·1	+6·7	+10·6
Agra	*82,094*	*35,613,784*	*434*	*+4·5*	*+1·9*	*—0·7*	*—3·0*	*+7·2*	*+10·0*
Oudh	*24,154*	*12,794,979*	*530*	*+11·1*	*+1·4*	*—2·1*	*—3·1*	*+5·2*	*+12·4*
U. P. States ..	5,943	1,206,070	203	+7·3	—1·4	+2·3	—4·6	+6·3	+9·7

of the earning inhabitants are actively engaged in agriculture. The decade has been a good one in respect of rainfall and crops, in spite of having opened with famine conditions in Gonda and Bahraich, and closing with drought and locusts in certain restricted areas, and with a serious collapse of agricultural prices. The Sarda irrigation canal, on which work was started in 1921, was opened in the main branch, in 1928. The system comprises some 4,000 miles of main channel and distributaries and 1,700 miles of drains over an area of six million acres of which it is anticipated that on an average 1,350,000 will be irrigated annually by its means. New masonry wells to the number of 150,314 have been constructed during the decade, mostly at the expense of the cultivators themselves, but the net cultivated area of the province has not increased and the double-cropped area is also stationary. The principal food crops are rice, millet, wheat, barley and pulse. Sugarcane is very important in the north-west and oilseeds are cultivated often in lines sown through fields of other crops. The condition of livestock during the greater part of the decade was unsatisfactory on account of epidemics. The enquiries made by the Banking Enquiry Committee in 1929 indicated that 46% of tenants and peasant proprietors were then debt-free, and 22% owed less than two years' rent. Of landlords a larger number were in debt and their debts were very much greater. The fragmentation of holdings is a serious disadvantage to the agriculturist, and the reserves built up during the first seven prosperous years of the decade have been exhausted by the collapse at its close.[1] In 1929-31 revenue was remitted to the amount of Rs. 1,68,50,000, and about three times that amount in rents. In industry, of which Cawnpore is the principal centre, the numbers of factories rose by 72·5% from 218 to 376 and of persons employed in them by 33·2% from 69,000 to 92,000, and the increase has been principally in permanent as distinct from seasonal employment. There has been a marked improvement in public health, particularly in the matter of deaths from plague, cholera and small-pox. The increase in population during the decade has been greater in the States than in British territory but amounts over the whole province to 6·7%, the density being greater in the east than in the west. In this connection it is pointed out that the higher castes are predominant in the west of the province, and the lower in the east, or in cases of castes uniformly distributed, the western branches are socially superior. Generally speaking, however, the population of the United Provinces, like its language, is more uniform than that of most provinces in India.

Baroda.

24. Baroda State occupies 8,164 sq. miles in Gujarat and Kathiawar, but is not a compact whole, consisting, as it does, of four major and several minor disconnected areas, with a total population of 2,443,007 and a mean density of 299 per sq. mile. The population has increased by 14·9% since 1921. The natural increase is estimated at 9·4%, and the increase due to immigration was swollen by 26,755 persons who migrated from villages in adjoining British territory for political motives

Locality.	Area in sq. miles.	Population.	Density.	Variation of population per cent. 1881-1891.	1891-1901.	1901-1911.	1911-1921.	1921-1931.	1881-1931.
Baroda State	8,164	2,443,007	299	+10·7	—19·2	+4·1	+4·6	+14·9	+12·0

connected with the Non-co-operation movement. About the size of Württemberg both in area and in population, Baroda is the sixth largest of the Indian States though about sixteenth in area. No epidemics visited the State during the decade, nor were there any calamities claiming a serious toll of lives, but the State suffered severely from floods, frost, locusts and poor seasons and at the end of the decade from the heavy fall in prices. Nevertheless co-operative societies rose in number from 509 in 1921 to 1,047 in 1931, their membership from 16,932 to 37,321 and their capital from 26 to 75 lakhs of rupees. Occupied area increased from 3,780,000 acres to 3,920,000 and the number of permanent irrigation wells increased from 60,433 to 63,775. Medical relief continued to be expanded and child welfare and anti-malarial measures to occupy the State Sanitation Department.

The Central India Agency.

25. The Central India Agency deals with 61 Indian States situated roughly between Rajputana and the Central Provinces and occupying an area of 51,597 sq. miles including the British pargana of Manpur (54 sq. miles) and about 10 sq. miles of States territory under British administration. To them has been added for census purposes Khaniadhana State which is dealt with by the Gwalior Agency and has an area of 68 sq. miles. The total population dealt with is 6,615,120 in the Agency and 17,670 in Khaniadhana with a mean density of 129 per sq. mile. As a result of exchanges of territory with Rajputana and Gwalior there has been a net increase since 1921 of 66 sq. miles. The Agency is not a compact area but consists of " dissimilar tracts with different physical and geographical environment and complex ethnically, culturally and linguistically. Broadly speaking three areas may be recognised. They are Malwa, Bundelkhand and Baghelkhand ". The States with which the Agency deals are described as " bewildering in variety as regards their area, population, income, degree of internal autonomy and their relationship with the paramount power ". Some half dozen or more of these States are compact areas, but the great majority constitute " a medley of interlaced territories and the Agency itself is a mosaic of fragmented sovereignties ". Malwa with its undulating plains and black soil and the fertile Narbada valley, although associated with the inhospitable Vindhya and Satpura hills, contrasts very markedly with the hilly, sandy and stony country of Bundelkhand and Baghelkhand. The west, that is the former, grows cotton, wheat and *jowar*, the latter, the eastern parts, grow rice and *kodon*. The former is a favoured region generally free from seasonal calamities, and the latter though with a higher average rainfall is more subject to drought and scarcity. The decade economically has been

Locality.	Area in sq. miles.	Population.	Density.	Variation of population per cent.					
				1881-91.	1891-1901.	1901-11.	1911-21.	1921-31.	1881-1931.
Central India Agency (*with Khaniadhana State*). ..	**51,597**	**6,632,790**	**129**	..	..	**+12·9**	**—2·1**	**+10·5**	**+22·0***
Manpur Pargana ..	49	6,852	140	..	—8·5	+35·2	—30·9	+50·0	+28·3†
Ali-Rajpur	836	101,963	122	+23·3	—28·4	—44·4	+23·3	+14·0	+79·4
Barwani	1,178	141,110	120	+42·2	—5·1	+42·6	+10·7	+17·4	+150·0
Bhopal	6,902	729,955	106	—0·2	—29·5	+8·7	—6·2	+5·4	—24·4
Dewas, I	449	83,321	186	+11·4	—22·4	+18·5	+16·6	+8·2	+12·7
Dewas, II	419	70,513	168	+2·1	—20·1	+14·3	+5·3	+5·2	+3·4
Dhar	1,784	243,430	136	..	..	+12·0	+19·2	+5·9	+42·0*
Indore	9,518	1,318,237	138	+4·8	—20·8	+16·3	+9·4	+14·5	+21·0
Jhabua	1,336	145,522	109	+28·9	—32·3	+37·2	+11·4	+17·4	+56·6
Jaora	602	100,166	166	..	..	—1·4	+3·9	+16·7	+19·7*
Khilchipur	273	45,583	167	+0·5	—14·2	+28·7	—0·1	+13·8	+26·2
Narsinghgarh ..	734	113,873	155	+3·4	—20·8	+19·3	—7·7	+12·3	+1·3
Rajgarh	962	134,891	140	..	..	+34·1	—9·7	+17·6	+42·4*
Ratlam	693	107,321	155	+2·1	—4·8	—2·9	+3·6	+25·5	+22·9
Sailana	279	35,223	126	+6·0	—18·0	+10·7	—5·0	+29·7	+18·5
Sitamau	202	28,422	141	+8·0	—28·4	+11·0	+0·2	+7·0	—7·8
Other Malwa States ..	526	80,467	153	..	..	+31·1	+8·4	+10·9	+57·7*
Ajaigarh	802	85,895	107	+14·2	—15·9	+11·3	—2·6	+1·3	+5·5
Baoni	121	19,132	158	+8·1	+7·3	+1·7	—1·9	—3·1	+12·2
Bijawar	973	115,852	119	+8·9	—10·5	+13·3	—10·8	+3·7	+2·3
Charkhari	880	120,351	137	+0·1	—13·4	+6·9	—6·9	—2·5	—15·8
Chhatarpur	1,130	161,267	143	+7·5	—9·4	+5·4	—7·4	—3·2	—7·9
Datia	912	158,834	174	+2·1	—6·7	—11·1	—3·8	+6·8	—13·0
Orchha	2,080	314,661	151	+6·9	—3·4	+2·6	—13·7	+10·4	+1·0
Panna	2,596	212,130	82	+5·3	—19·4	+18·6	—13·7	+7·4	—6·7
Samthar	180	33,307	185	—4·9	—17·4	—4·7	+4·1	+0·3	—13·8
Other Bundelkhand States	407	67,586	166	+1·3	—11·0	+4·3	—2·0	—0·4	—8·1
Baraundha	218	16,071	74	+7·6	—15·4	+8·0	—6·3	+1·0	—7·0
Maihar	407	68,991	170	+8·1	—17·6	+14·5	—9·0	+3·7	—3·8
Nagod	501	74,589	149	+5·6	—25·3	+18·8	—8·6	+9·4	—6·3
Rewa	13,000	1,587,445	122	+15·6	—12·0	+14·2	—7·5	+13·3	+21·6
Other Baghelkhand States	580	92,160	159	+15·0	—14·5	+9·8	—6·6	+6·6	+7·4
Khaniadhana ..	68	17,670	260	+10·2	+4·4	+13·2	—5·0	+5·8	+30·9

* 1901—1931. † 1891—1931.

one of comparative prosperity, free from famine or serious scarcity in any large area and from any widespread epidemic. Malwa was short of rain in 1925 and 1929, Bundelkhand and Bagelkhand in 1928 and 1929. The increase in population for the whole agency since 1921 has been 10·5%, ninety-two per cent. of which increase is natural, only eight per cent. of it being due to the favourable balance of migration.

Gwalior.

26. Gwalior State, the dominion of the Scindia family, about the size of the Irish Free State, is the sixth largest of the Indian States in area and

fifth in population, having 3,523,070 inhabitants in an area of 26,367 sq. miles, a density of 134. Thirty-two square miles of area, the status of which is in dispute, have been excluded at this census and 16 square miles not before included have been added, but the total thus arrived at is probably not quite accurate and the latest survey estimate of the area of Gwalior State is 395 sq. miles less than the area here quoted, but the figure has not yet been verified by the State. The increase in population since 1921 has been 10·3% in spite of an adverse migration balance of about —15,000. The State is not a compact area but consists of one large block of contiguous parganas and a number of smaller outlying ones. The Census Commissioner for the State compares the population of India in general and Gwalior in particular to Penelope's web, alternately woven and unpicked; he regards the fluctuation at alternate decades as symptomatic of the normal growth of the population. He concludes that the comparative freedom of the decade from scarcity and epidemics has kept the mortality rate down to normal and that the population which survived the influenza epidemic of the previous decade had a superior biological equipment and a higher survival rate which have been responsible for the exceptional increase experienced.

	Area in sq. miles.	Population.	Density per square mile.	Variation of population per cent. 1881-91.	1891-1901.	1901-11.	1911-21.	1921-31.	1881-1931.
Gwalior State	26,367	3,523,070	134	+13·9	—12·7	+5·3	—1·3	+10·3	+14·0

Hyderabad.

27. His Exalted Highness the Nizam's Dominions, though a little less than Jammu and Kashmir in size, constitute by far the largest of the States in population, containing 14,436,148 persons with a mean density of 175 in an area of 82,698 sq. miles. North of the Godavari and its principal tributary the Manjra the country is rich and highly cultivated, principally in cotton and wheat, while in the south and east the country is more rugged and less fertile, the most valuable crop, at any rate in the east, being rice. The decade was on the whole a good one agriculturally. It opened, it is true, with famine but except for that first year the harvests were either good or moderate and the land under cultivation increased from 38 to 42 million acres. Co-operative Societies increased from 1,437 to 2,157 and their membership from 35,293 to 53,120 and their working capital from eighty-six and a half lakhs to nearly two crores of rupees. Cotton prices fell in 1926, but otherwise the agriculturist benefited by well maintained prices for most of his produce until 1930. The results are seen in the increase in natural population by 14·9%, though part of this may have been due to improved enumeration. In the last 50 years the population of the Marathwara division, the western part of the State, has increased by 28·0% while that of the Telingana, the eastern part, has increased by 69·4%. The north-western part of the State is Maratha by language and population, the south-western is Kanarese and these two areas compose the *Marathwara*; the eastern part of the State (*Telingana*) is Telugu by language and population; both are predominantly Hindu by religion.

Locality.	Area in sq. miles.	Population.	Density.	Variation of population per cent. 1881-91.	1891-1901.	1901-11.	1911-21.	1921-31.	1881-1931.
Hyderabad State ..	**82,698**	**14,436,148**	**175**	**+17·2**	**—3·4**	**+20·0**	**—6·8**	**+15·8**	**+46·6**
Marathwara	41,196	6,881,550	167	+17·0	—10·1	+16·6	—9·0	+14·5	+28·0
Telingana	41,502	7,554,598	182	+17·4	+4·6	+23·6	—4·6	+16·9	+69·4

Jammu and Kashmir.

28. Jammu and Kashmir State is in area the largest of the Indian States but only stands fourth in order of population. Much of the State's surface is occupied by arid desert at a very high elevation unable to sustain any but the scantiest population, and though the fertile valleys of the irrigable country support a high density of population they are too limited in comparison to balance the uninhabitable mountains. The total area is 84,516 sq. miles with a population of

3,646,243, giving a mean density of 43 per sq. mile. This density drops to 5 persons per sq. mile over three quarters of the State in the area of the the semi-Tibetan tracts

Locality.	Area in sq. miles.	Population.	Density.	Variation of population per cent. 1891 to 1901.	1901 to 1911.	1911 to 1921.	1921 to 1931.	1891 to 1931.
Jammu and Kashmir ..	**84,516**	**3,646,243**	**43**	**+14·21**	**+8·7**	**+5·1**	**+9·8**	**+43·3**
Jammu	12,401	1,788,441	144	+5·7	+5·4	+2·7	+9·0	+24·7
Kashmir	8,555	1,569,218	183	+21·9	+11·9	+8·6	+11·5	+65·3
Frontier Districts ..	63,560	288,584	5	+10·2	+14·2	+3·1	+5·6	+80·1

which include the vast deserts of Ladakh at a height of some 16,000 or 17,000 feet above sea level, and the stupendous peaks of the Pamirs and of the Hindu Kush and Karakoram ranges. On the other hand the density for the Jammu and Kashmir provinces by themselves works out at 160·2 persons per sq. mile, while throughout the State most districts carry over 1,000 to the sq. mile of cultivated area, and actually in Ladakh and Gilgit, in the inhospitable mountains, that is, 1,600 is found, the highest density of inhabitants to cultivated land except in the Srinagar District itself. During the decade 136 miles of additional canal have been constructed irrigating an additional area of some 47,000 acres, and great improvements have taken place in road communications. Co-operative societies have increased by about 1,900 and their members by 300 per cent. since 1923, and their working capital amounts to over 97 lakhs. Except for disastrous floods in 1928 the decade has been very prosperous agriculturally, and the volume of both exports and imports has increased by about 25 per cent., though the money value of the exports fell during the last three years of the decade to something below the 1921 value of exports only four-fifths of their present volume. The decennium was also exceptionally healthy. The increase in population over the State as a whole has been 9·8 per cent., increasing the density per sq. mile from 39 to 43. The population is predominantly Muslim, though Ladakh is inhabited by Tibetan Buddhists who keep down the population to a level which their barren mountains can support by a system of polyandry. The other inhabitants of the frontier districts are Muslim including the mongoloid Baltis and the Dards of Gilgit.

Madras States Agency.

29. The Madras States Agency includes five States in the south of India two of which, Cochin and Travancore, in the south-west corner, publish their own

State, etc.	Area in sq. miles.	Population.	Density.	Variation of population per cent. 1881 to 1891.	1891 to 1901.	1901 to 1911.	1911 to 1921.	1921 to 1931.	1881 to 1931.
Madras State Agency ..	**10,698**	**6,754,484**	**631**	**+10·6**	**+13·2**	**+14·9**	**+13·5**	**+23·7**	**+101·9**
Cochin State ..	1,480	1,205,016	814	+20·4	+12·3	+13·1	+6·6	+23·1	+100·7
Travancore ..	7,625	5,095,973	668	+6·5	+15·4	+16·2	+16·8	+27·2	+112·2
Other States ..	1,593	453,495	285	+22·3	+0·93	+9·6	+2·2	—4·6	+32·1

census reports in the India series. The other three, Pudukkottai, Banganapalle and Sandur, are dealt with in the Madras provincial report to which reference must be made for detailed treatment. Figures of the area and population of Pudukkottai, the largest of them, will be found in the supplements to Tables I and II in part (ii), and a separate report has been published by the State, a summary of which forms Appendix VI of Volume XIV (Madras) of this series.

Cochin has an area of 1,480 square miles and a population of 1,205,016 persons, (females exceeding males) showing, over that recorded in 1921, an increase of 23·1 per cent., which the Census Superintendent regards as representing a real increase of 19 per cent. The density is 814 to the square mile, but this is over the whole State, whereas more than a third is mountainous and the area includes the surface of the back waters, long stretches of salt water lagoon cut off from the sea by narrow tongues of land. In the mountainous forests of the Western Ghats the density is very low, as the inhabitants consist only of a few scattered jungle tribes and the forest officials, and if these areas be excluded from the forest taluks, the density of which is 365 to 975 when they are included, the density rises to 1,126, while the density of the coastal taluks excluding the lagoons in a similar manner becomes 2,733, one village, covering an area of 3·8 sq. miles, having the incredible density of 4,090 persons to the sq. mile, for its inhabitants are not an urban population but a rural and agricultural one, the staple crops being coconut and rice, as in the case with most of the taluks of Cochin State.

Travancore is a much larger state than Cochin but otherwise closely resembles it in population and in physical features, though it has a drier strip of coast towards the south running down to Cape Comorin. Its area is 7,625 sq. miles and its population is 5,095,973 with a mean density of 668. Though third in order of population, at least sixteen States in India are larger in size. It falls into three clearly marked natural divisions, the coast, the low hills and the high forest-clad hills. The rainfall varies from 35 inches in the extreme south to nearly 300 in the high hills, but over by far the greater area of the State it varies, as in Cochin, from 100 to 180. The hills have been largely developed and planted with tea and cardamom plantations, but are still thinly inhabited compared to the plains. Except Cochin, Travancore is far more densely populated than any State in India, and is more densely populated than Bengal. In the low hills tapioca is cultivated as a staple food. The net area under cultivation increased by 9·5 per cent. only as compared to an increase of 27·2 per cent. in population between 1921 and 1931, but the food production of the State is inadequate to its needs and Burma rice is purchased with the proceeds of the sale of coconut products, pepper and cardamoms. Wages nearly doubled during the decade and Savings Bank deposits more than doubled. This prosperous position was however being very severely affected by the economic depression in 1931.

Mysore.

30. Mysore State, the centre and main area of the Kanarese speaking population of south India, after Hyderabad the most populous of all the States, and the largest in area after that State and Jammu and Kashmir, has an area of 29,326 square miles, and a population of 6,557,302, with a mean density of 224 persons per square mile. The increase of population since 1921 has been 9·7 per cent., though the increase of natural population alone has been 10·8. This increase has not been evenly distributed, as the State is divided into the Malnad, that is the area of the high hills in the west, where the density falls in one taluk to 66 and where the population is little more than constant, and the Maidan, which is the comparatively level land constituting the plateau which is the main bulk of the State, and in which the increase and density is greater than that of the State as a whole. The highest rural density reached is 457 per square mile in the Narsipur taluk. The State includes the large Civil and Military station of Bangalore which is under British administration. The area under cultivation has increased during

Locality.	Area in sq. miles.	Population.	Density.	Variation of population per cent. 1881-'91.	1891-1901.	1901-'11.	1911-'21.	1921-'31.	1881-1931.
Mysore State	29,326	6,557,302	224	+18·1	+12·1	+4·8	+3·0	+9·7	+56·6
Civil and Military Station, Bangalore.	14	134,113	9,934	+7·0	—10·5	+12·5	+18·0	+12·8	+43·4
Remainder of State ..	29,312	6,423,189	219	+18·3	+12·5	+4·7	+2·7	+9·6	+56·9

the decade by 11·5% while a number of important works has increased the area under irrigation by 25% since 1921. Various improvements in agriculture and cattle breeding are taking place, and the cinema is used for instruction. A Land Mortgage Bank has been established and an Agriculturists' Debt Relief Regulation has been passed by the Legislature. The number of cooperative societies has increased by 713 and their membership by 45,000, making a total membership of 137,615, and the deposits in the Government Savings Bank amounted in 1931 to nearly Rs. 17,000,000, having more than doubled during the decade. Public health was good on the whole throughout the decade, and though prices fell towards its close harvests were good and the cultivator did not suffer severely. The State is importing more cereals for food than it exports, the imports being more than half in husked rice, but it is estimated that some 500,000 more acres can still be brought under irrigation. Rice and *ragi* are the staple crops. Industries are being developed, but it is doubtful if they can be so developed as to keep pace with the needs of the population in periods of normal increase, and the Census Superintendent for the State points out that tabus such as that on marital connection during lactation, or at any rate soon after confinement, which tend to keep down the birth rate, are no longer observed as they used to be, while children are suckled only five or six months instead of until able to consume ordinary food. Meanwhile the Mysore Government has instituted a Birth Control Clinic in the Maternity hospital at Bangalore.

Rajputana. 31. The Rajputana Agency comprises 19 States, 1 Chiefship and 1 Estate grouped together for the purpose of their political relations with the Government of India, which are conducted through the Agent to the Governor-General in Rajputana. It includes also a small area of 6 square miles which is leased from the Sirohi State and is therefore at present under British administration forming the Abu district. The total area of the Agency is 129,059 square miles with a total population of 11,225,712 and a mean density of 87 persons per square mile. That is to say, it is about the same size as Norway with 4 times the population, or considerably larger than the United Kingdom but with one quarter of its population. Density varies very greatly, being 5 only in Jaisalmer and 246 per square mile in Bharatpur State. In the dry western part of the Agency the rainfall is little over 10 inches, whereas in the eastern part it is three times as much. The conditions of the decade have been good and the population has increased by 14·2% since 1921 though this represents an increase of little more than one million on the 1881 figure and the 1931 total is actually less than that returned in 1891, though in that census a considerable number of Bhils were estimated instead of enumerated as in all cases on this occasion. The biggest increase is that of 41·9% in Bikaner State, mostly on account of irrigation and immigration. Bharatpur (—1·9%) is the only State which has actually suffered a loss of population since 1921. Throughout Rajputana there was a general absence of scarcity and epidemic disease throughout the decade and although the prices of grain ruled high the growth of population does not seem to have been adversely affected. The high prices were in some States dealt with by the prohibition of exports and in others by the imposition of a tax on imported food stuffs. Wages were high, particularly in the case of the industrial population.

State or Agency.	Area in sq. miles.	Population.	Density.	Variation of the population per cent. 1881-91.	1891-01.	1901-11.	1911-21.	1921-31.	1881-31.
Rajputana ..	129,059	11,225,712	87	+20·6	—20·5	+6·9	—6·5	+14·2	+9·3
Abu District ..	6	4,532	755	..	+32·2	+5·5	—16·0	+25·7	+47·3*
Alwar ..	3,158	749,751	237	+12·4	+7·9	—4·4	—11·4	+6·9	+9·8
Banswara ..	1,606	225,106	140	+39·2	—17·3	+11·0	+15·0	+18·3	+48·1
Bharatpur ..	1,978	486,954	246	—0·8	—2·1	—10·8	—11·2	—1·9	—24·6
Bikaner ..	23,317	936,218	40	+63·4	—29·7	+19·9	—5·9	+41·9	+83·9
Bundi ..	2,220	216,722	98	+16·1	—42·1	+27·7	—14·5	+15·9	—14·9
Dholpur ..	1,221	254,986	209	+12·1	—3·0	—2·9	—12·7	+10·8	+2·1
Dungarpur ..	1,447	227,544	157	+7·8	—39·5	+59·0	+18·9	+20·2	+48·4
Jaipur ..	15,579	2,631,775	169	+11·7	—5·9	—0·8	—11·3	+12·5	+4·1
Jaisalmer ..	16,062	76,255	5	+7·0	—36·6	+20·4	—23·4	+12·7	—29·5
Jhalawar ..	810	107,890	133	+0·5	—40·3	+6·8	—0·1	+12·2	—28·2
Karauli ..	1,242	140,525	113	+5·3	+0·1	—6·5	—8·8	+5·1	—5·5
Kishangarh ..	858	85,744	100	+11·4	—27·5	—4·2	—10·8	+10·3	—23·9
Kotah ..	5,684	685,804	121	+1·6	—24·2	+17·3	—1·4	+8·8	—3·0
Kushalgarh ..	340	35,564	105	..	+180·9	+35·6	+32·5	+22·0	+515·8
Lawa ..	19	2,790	147	+25·3	—20·5	—4·0	—11·8	+23·3	+4·0
Marwar ..	35,016	2,125,982	61	+43·8	—23·4	+6·3	—10·5	+15·4	+21·0
Mewar ..	12,694	1,566,910	123	+23·5	—44·8	+25·8	+6·7	+14·6	+4·9
Partabgarh ..	886	76,539	86	+10·6	—40·9	+20·5	+7·0	+14·1	—3·8
Shahpura ..	405	54,233	134	+23·0	—32·9	+11·1	+1·5	+12·7	+4·8
Sirohi ..	1,958	216,528	111	+33·5	—19·9	+22·8	+1·0	+16·0	+51·5
Tonk ..	2,553	317,360	124	+12·4	—28·1	+10·9	—5·0	+10·2	—6·1

* 1891—1931.

Western India States. 32. The Western India States Agency, about the size of Hungary with half the population, was constituted as a separate unit in 1924 before which its census returns were incorporated with those of Bombay, with which province its economic conditions have been comparable throughout the decade. Its area is 35,442 sq. miles and its population 3,999,250 with a mean density of 113 per sq. mile. It includes the civil stations of Rajkot and Wadhwan under the administrative control of the Agent to the Governor-General and 202 States and estates, of which 85 have their own rights of jurisdiction, while the others are grouped in thanas each under a thanadar. Of the 85 jurisdictional States 17 are salute States varying greatly in size from Cutch with an area of 8,250 sq. miles to Jafarabad with only 53, while the smallest of the non-jurisdictional estates is only one-third of a square mile in area and has a population of less than 200. The rainfall comes late in the monsoon and varies from moderately good to scanty and deficient, and density therefore varies accordingly from 268 in Rajkot to 59 in the Banas Kantha Agency where it is a wonder " that so many persons can find a livelihood in so little favoured a terrain". On this occasion separate figures have been compiled for 43 units, but complete data for all details for fifty years has proved impossible to obtain and even for some sub-agency groups the changes could not be filled in back to 1881. In the whole Agency there are only 66 towns, 11 of which are in Bhavnagar State ; Bhavnagar itself and Jamnagar in Nawanagar are the only two towns of over 50,000 inhabitants and there are only ten others of over 20,000, is so that it is clear that the Agency, though essentially rural and agricultural, is less so than those of Central India and Rajputana ; and so much of its population is located in towns that its degree of urbanization is just about the same as that of Bombay Presidency.

State or Agency.	Area in sq. miles.	Population.	Density.	Variation of the population per cent. 1881-91.	1891-01.	1901-11.	1911-21.	1921-31.	1881-1931.
W. I. St. Agency	**35,442**	**3,999,250**	**113**	**+15**	**—17**	**+7**	**+0·5**	**+13**	**+17**
Bhavnagar ..	2,961	500,274	169	+17	—12	+7	—3	+17	+25
Cutch ..	8,250	514,307	62	+9	—13	+5	—6	+6	+0·4
Dhrangadhra ..	1,156	88,961	77	+4	—32	+12	+12	+0·6	—11
Dhrol ..	283	27,639	98	+21	—19	+11	—3	+17	+24
Gondal ..	1,024	205,846	201	+19	+1	—1	+3	+23	+52
Jafarabad ..	53	12,083	228	+32	—2	+2	—11	+10	+28
Junagadh ..	3,284	545,152	166	+25	—18	+10	+7	+17	+41
Limbdi ..	344	40,088	117	+12	—35	+8	+5	+13	—7
Morvi ..	870	113,023	130	+17	—17	+3	+1	+24	+26
Nawanagar ..	3,791	409,192	108	+20	—11	+4	—1	+19	+29
Palanpur ..	1,769	264,179	149	+17	—19	+2	+5	+12	+13
Palitana ..	300	62,150	207	+23	—13	+15	—5	+7	+26
Porbandar ..	636	115,673	182	+21	—4	+11	+11	+14	+62
Radhanpur ..	1,150	70,530	61	—0·1	—37	+7	+3	+4	—28
Rajkot ..	282	75,540	268	+7	—0·3	+2	+20	+24	+62
Wadhwan ..	236	42,602	181	—0·1	—18	+3	+6	+12	+0·2
Wankaner ..	417	44,259	106	+29	—30	+19	+13	+20	+45
Banas Kantha Agency ..	3,475	203,553	59	+8·4	—34	—16	+1	—2	—40·5
Eastern Kathiawar Agency	2,764	282,468	102	..	..	..	—2	+12	+10*
Western Kathiawar Agency	2,397	381,731	159	..	..	..	—4	+10	+6*

* 1911—1931.

Other States. 33. The Punjab States Agency and the States in political relation with Provincial Governments are treated with the provinces with which they are associated and Sikkim State with Bengal. Figures of the area and population of the larger States will be found in the supplements to Tables I and II in Part ii of this volume.

Section iv.—Population problem.

Nature of the problem. 34. Attention has already been drawn to the grave increase in the population of this country. The actual figure of the increase alone is little under thirty-four million, a figure approaching equality with that of the total population of France or Italy and appreciably greater than that of such important European powers as Poland and Spain. The population now even exceeds the latest estimate of the population of China, so that India now heads the list of all the countries in the world in the number of her inhabitants. This increase, however, is from most points of view a cause for alarm rather than for satisfaction. The total literate population of India in 1921 was 22,623,651 and is now 28,131,315, so that the mere increase of population during the intervening period has exceeded the former figure by 11 million, that is by 50 per cent., and still exceeds the latter by [illegible] per cent

Even in Travancore State, where the percentage of literacy is much higher than in most parts of India, but where the population has increased by 27 per cent., the

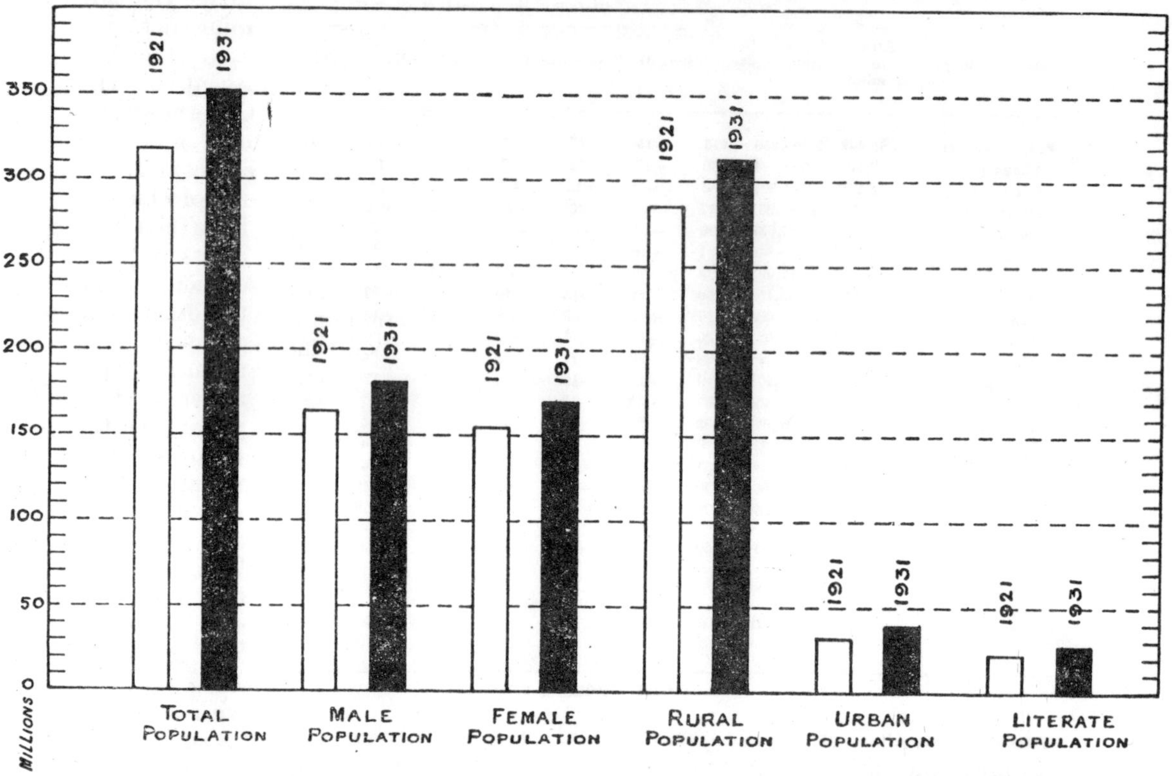

proportion of literacy has fallen from 24·2 per cent. in 1921 to 23·9 per cent. in 1931 though in India as a whole it has risen from 7 per cent. to 8 per cent.

Recent writers on the population question in India, *e.g.*, Wattal and Ranadive, have directed their attention primarily to the question of food production. Their argument is that the population of India is already living permanently on the verge of scarcity and any increase is bound to result in an insufficiency of the food supply. Recent experience, however, throws doubt on this theory ; the general slump in the price of food, and the difficulty found by cultivators in selling their produce, suggest that the danger of a shortage of the food supply is not the most serious aspect of the question. It is not argued that this is not a danger to be reckoned with, and in any case the maximum population possible is very far from identical with the maximum population desirable, since the rise of population on the subsistence margin must reduce the standard of living, but it would seem that the point has not yet been reached at which the ability of the country to feed its occupants is seriously taxed. The position of economists in regard to the west now appears to be that " the devastating torrent of babies " is being reduced to a trickle, and that even if it were swelled again the rapid developments both mechanical and biological that are taking place in the world production of food, would be more than sufficient to cope with the flood, so that it is progressively easier to obtain subsistence. It may be doubted whether either supposition is yet applicable to Indian conditions. In the first place there are as yet no indications of any tendency on the part of the countryman to modify his view of the blessedness of the man who has a quiverful of sons and is not ashamed to meet his enemy in the gate, and, in the second, little sign that agriculture is likely to be appreciably affected during the next decade by means such as those which have so greatly increased wheat production on the American continent. It is however obvious that apart from the law of diminishing returns the ability of agriculture to provide an occupation is limited. In Europe it has been estimated that the maximum population which can be supported by agricultural occupations is 250 to the sq. mile, while an estimate of somewhat higher density has been made in the case of the United States of America, and the island of Porto Rico in the West Indies has an agricultural population of nearly 400 to the sq. mile. The number is as we have seen, very much greater than this in many parts of India, and the rural population which attains the extraordinary density mentioned of parts of Bengal and of the Malabar Coast indicates the extent to which fertile land intensively cultivated together with fish-yielding waters could sustain a population whose material wants are reduced to the minimum by the natural environment of a tropical climate. These, of course, are extreme cases taken from the two most fertile parts of India,* but generally speaking the maximum density of the agricultural population can be far greater in India than in Europe, not only on account of the greater fertility of the land but on account of the diminution in the absolute necessities of life corresponding to a less rigorous climate. The real difficulty is that to cultivate on anything like economic lines the number of individuals that can work on a given area of ground is limited ; and though the food product may be ample for many more than that number, a large increase in the population must either lead to excessive subdivision of the areas cultivated, and so to a diminution in production on account of uneconomic holdings, or on the other hand, to a floating population which is not engaged in agriculture and which has nothing to exchange with the producers for the food which it requires. The employment of this surplus in industrial activity would of course, meet the difficulty for a time, but can only prove a permanent cure if the increase of the population be limited not only to the food producible but also to the saturation point of the demand for industrial labour. When the latter point is passed, as in the United Kingdom, where the increase in population during the last decade was approximately equivalent to the number of unemployed in 1931, unemployment will arise and the fact that the food supply is adequate is to this extent irrelevant. As in some parts of Europe, life on the land as a cultivator is an end in itself rather than a mere means of production of victuals, hence the real danger of a growth of population which must suffer discomfort because this end becomes rapidly more difficult of realisation. The present problem in India would therefore seem to be less the actual total increase of the population, than the increase of that portion of the population, by far the greater part of course, which is occupied in agriculture and allied pursuits, *i.e.*, the population represented by sub-class I of the Occupation Table ; and an additional complication of the problem appears in the fact that the cultivating classes in India generally lack the capital required for the extension of cultivation beyond the existing margin, particularly where the cultivation practised is already dependent on a somewhat problematic rainfall. Mechanical improvements which reduce the need for labour are a doubtful palliative, though no such doubt attaches to biological improvements, enabling a better crop to be obtained from a smaller area. Labour-saving devices will do little for a peasantry whose work takes up part only of the year and certainly they will not enable a greater number of peasants to live on the same area of land where there is neither demand nor market facilities for the minor products of agriculture which contribute to the income of the European small holder or on which, such as poultry, pigs or potatoes, he may principally depend.

35. It appears to be the general opinion of Indian economists who discuss the population problem of this country that the only practical method of limiting the population is by the introduction of artificial methods of birth control, though it is not easy to exaggerate the difficulties of introducing such methods in a country where the vast majority of the population regard the propagation of male offspring as religious duty and the reproach of barrenness as a terrible punishment for crimes committed in a former incarnation. It is justly pointed out by the Census Superintendent of Mysore State that the practice of universal and of early marriage is a social custom and is not, in fact, followed from religious motives, but it is almost always religious arguments which are put forward in opposition to a change in social custom by any society anywhere, and though the religious sanction may be the result rather than the cause of the social custom, this fact only gives the sanction greater force. Nevertheless a definite movement towards artificial birth-control appears to be taking place and is perhaps less hampered by misplaced prudery than in some countries which claim to be more civilized ; thus not only is artificial control publicly advocated by a number of medical writers but Madras can boast a Neo-Malthusian League with two Maharajas, three High Court judges and four or five men very prominent **Remedies.**

* An examination of the population question as regards Bengal by the Census Superintendent of that province is printed as an appendix to this chapter.

in public life as its sponsors. Meanwhile it would appear, in view of the present rate of increase, that efforts to reduce the rate of infantile mortality should be preceded by precautions to reduce the birth-rate, and that if the luxury of 'baby weeks' be permitted they should at least be accompanied by instruction in birth-control. A move in this direction has already been made by the Government of Mysore State, which in 1930 sanctioned the establishment of birth-control clinics in the four principal hospitals of the State.

There are perhaps other methods of checking an excessive increase in population. It has been clearly demonstrated in Europe that a rise of the standard in living is normally accompanied by a fall in the birth-rate, and the same principle no doubt operates in this country; but, even while we must admit the truth of Bacon's aphorism that "Repletion is an Enemy to Generation", a mere superfluity of food supply is not enough, as it only enables the possessor to breed up to the subsistence level again. In order that a higher standard of living may affect the rate of reproduction it is apparent that not only is an increase in education and culture involved, since it seems definitely established that intellectual activity acts as a check upon fertility, but also the psychological appreciation of a higher probability of survival. Recent studies of the population problem in the Pacific by Rivers, Pitt-Rivers, Roberts and others have clearly demonstrated the importance of psychological factors as affecting the increase or decrease of the population, and although the environment is generally entirely different in India, that is no reason for supposing that psychology is any less important here in its action on the rate of reproduction. It is also likely that a changed outlook, in which a greater value was attached to the goods of this world and less regard paid to the speculative possibilities of the next, would operate in the same direction; but it seems doubtful if a materialistic standpoint would commend itself to Indian culture.

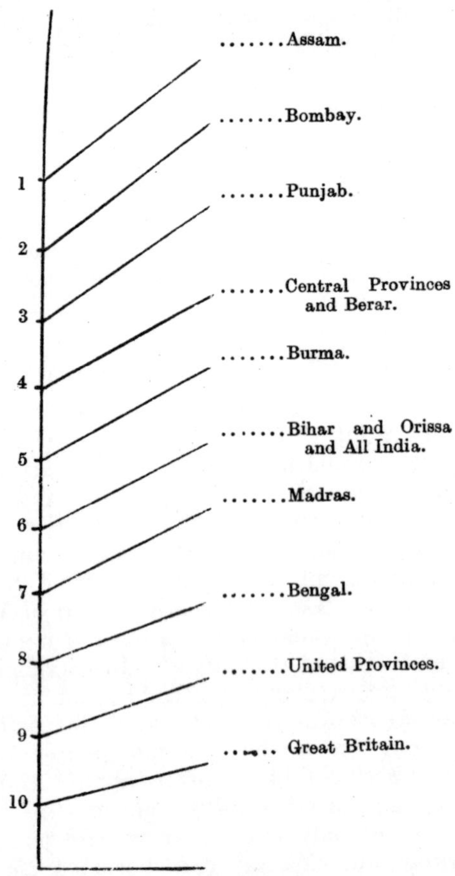

Population Increase 1921-31
(*with acknowledgments to the S. C. O., Madras*).

SUBSIDIARY TABLE I.

Area of India and the Provinces and States.

Province, State or Agency.	Area in Square Miles. 1931.	1921.	1881.	Variation: Increase +, Decrease —. 1921-1931.	1881-1931.
INDIA	**1,808,679**	**1,805,332**	**1,372,588**	**+3,347**	**+436,091**
Provinces	**1,096,171**	**1,094,300**	**911,075**	**+1,871**	..
Ajmer-Merwara	2,711	2,711	2,711	..	..
Andaman and Nicobar Islands	3,143	3,143	..	..	..
Assam	55,014	53,015	*46,341	+1,999	+20,993
Baluchistan (*District and Administered Territories*).	54,228	54,228	..	..	..
Bengal	77,521	76,843	*193,198 (Bengal and Bihar and Orissa)	+678	+1,459 (Bengal and Bihar and Orissa)
Bihar and Orissa	83,054	83,161		—107	
Bombay (*including Aden*)	123,679	123,621	†124,122	+58	..
Aden	*80*	*80*	..	..	..
Burma	233,492	233,707	87,220	—215	+146,272
Central Provinces and Berar	99,920	99,876	102,156	+44	—2,236
Coorg	1,593	1,582	1,583	+11	+10
Madras	142,277	142,260	141,001	+17	+2,869
North-West Frontier Province (*Districts and Administered Territories*).	13,518	13,419	106,632 (North-West Frontier Province, Punjab and Delhi)	+99	+6,659 (North-West Frontier Province, Punjab and Delhi)
Punjab	99,200	99,846		—646	
Delhi	573	593		—20	
United Provinces of Agra and Oudh	106,248	106,295	106,111	—47	+137
States and Agencies	**712,508**	**711,032**	**461,513**	**+1,476**	..
Assam States	12,320	8,456	..	+3,864	..
Baluchistan States	80,410	80,410	..	..	..
Baroda State	8,164	8,127	8,570	+37	—406
Bengal States	5,434	5,434	..	..	..
Bihar and Orissa States	28,648	28,648	..	..	..
Bombay States	27,994	27,982	73,753	+12	—10,317
Central India Agency	51,597	51,531	75,079 (Central India Agency and Gwalior State)	+66	+2,885 (Central India Agency and Gwalior State)
Gwalior State	26,367	26,357		+10	
Central Provinces States	31,175	31,176	28,834	—1	+2,341
Hyderabad State	82,698	82,698	71,771	..	+10,927
Jammu and Kashmir State	84,516	84,258	..	+258	..
Madras States Agency	10,698	10,696	..	+2	..
Cochin State	*1,480*	*1,479*	*1,361*	*+1*	*+119*
Travancore State	*7,625*	*7,625*	*6,730*	..	*+895*
Other Madras States	*1,593*	*1,592*	‡	*+1*	..
Mysore State	29,326	29,475	24,723	—149	+4,603
North-West Frontier Province (*Agencies and Tribal Areas*).	22,838	25,500	35,817 (North-West Frontier Province, Punjab States and Punjab States Agency)	—2,662	+24,082 (North-West Frontier Province, Punjab States and Punjab States Agency)
Punjab States	5,820	5,820		..	
Punjab States Agency	31,241	31,239		+2	
Rajputana Agency	129,059	128,987	129,750	+72	—691
Sikkim State	2,818	2,818	..	..	..
United Provinces States	5,943	5,949	5,125	—6	+818
Western India States Agency	35,442	35,471	§	—29	..

NOTE.—The difference in areas is due in cases to the use of revised survey figures and to corrections for fluvial action and also to inter-provincial transfers, *vide* explanatory notes to Imperial Tables I and II in Part II.

* Inclusive of States; † Excludes Aden; ‡ Included against Madras; § Included against Bombay States.

SUBSIDIARY TABLE II.

The population of India at six Censuses.

	Year	INDIA.	Provinces.	States.
Total Population	1931	**352,837,778**	271,526,933	81,310,845
	1921	**318,942,480**	246,856,191	72,086,289
	1911	**315,156,396**	243,797,647	71,358,749
	1901	**294,361,056**	231,142,489	63,218,567
	1891	**287,314,671**	220,765,285	66,549,386
	1881	**253,896,330**	198,448,631	55,447,699
Males	1931	**181,828,923**	139,931,556	41,897,367
	1921	**163,995,554**	126,798,887	37,196,667
	1911	**161,338,935**	124,641,244	36,697,691
	1901	**149,951,824**	117,426,782	32,525,042
	1891	**146,769,629**	112,335,393	34,434,236
	1881	**129,949,300**	101,119,128	28,830,172
Females	1931	**171,008,855**	131,595,377	39,413,478
	1921	**154,946,926**	120,057,304	34,889,622
	1911	**153,817,461**	119,156,403	34,661,058
	1901	**144,409,232**	113,715,707	30,693,525
	1891	**140,545,042**	108,429,892	32,115,150
	1881	**123,947,030**	97,329,503	26,617,527

The above figures are inclusive of the population of areas newly enumerated at successive censuses as follows:—

	Year	INDIA.	Provinces.	States.
Total population of new areas in	1891	**5,713,902***	3,112,994	2,600,908
	1901	**2,672,077†**	1,654,377	1,017,700
	1911	**1,793,365**	94,495	1,698,870
	1921	**86,633**	86,633	....
	1931	**35,058‡**	35,058	....
Male population of new areas in	1891	**2,872,513**	1,507,043	1,365,470
	1901	**1,362,651**	837,440	525,211
	1911	**945,346**	47,581	897,765
	1921	**43,781**	43,781	....
	1931	**9,746**	9,746	....
Female population of new areas in	1891	**2,793,074**	1,605,951	1,187,123
	1901	**1,283,297**	790,808	492,489
	1911	**848,019**	46,914	801,105
	1921	**42,852**	42,852	....
	1931	**9,601**	9,601	....

NOTE.—The details of the areas newly included at the 1921 and previous censuses will be found on the fly leaf of Table II in the 1921 India Tables Volume. Details of the 1931 figures will be found on the title page to Imperial Table II of the recent tables volume.

* Sex details of 48,315 persons are not available.

† Sex details of 26,129 persons are not available.

‡ Sex details of 15,711 persons are not available.

SUBSIDIARY TABLE III.

Calculated Intercensal Population, 1922-1930.

Year.	1922.	1923.	1924.	1925.	1926.	1927.	1928.	1929.	1930.
Population ..	318,975,613	319,041,879	319,174,412	319,439,478	319,969,610	321,029,873	323,150,400	327,391,454	335,873,562

SUBSIDIARY TABLE IV.

Population distributed by provinces and with variation per cent. in the population and mean density per square mile.

Serial No. Province, State or Agency.	Area in Square Miles.	Population.				Percentage of Variation. Increase+, Decrease—			Mean Density per cent. Square mile.		
		1931.			1921.	1921-31.	1911-21.	1881-1931.	1931.	1921.	1911.
		Persons.	Males.	Females.	Both Sexes.						
1	2	3	4	5	6	7	8	9	10	11	12
INDIA ..	**1,808,679**	**352,837,778**	**181,828,923**	**171,008,855**	**318,942,480**	**+10·6**	**+1·2**	**+39·0**	**195**	**176**	**174**
Provinces ..	**1,096,171**	**271,526,933**	**139,931,556**	**131,595,377**	**246,856,191**	**+10·0**	**+1·3**	**+36·8**	**248**	**225**	**222**
1 Ajmer-Merwara ..	2,711	560,292	296,081	264,211	495,271	+13·1	—1·2	+21·6	207	183	185
2 Andaman and Nicobar Islands.	3,143	29,463	19,702	9,761	27,086	+8·8	+2·4	+101·4	9	9	8
3 Assam	55,014	8,622,251	4,537,206	4,085,045	7,459,128	+15·6	+13·4	+79·2	157	136	120
4 Baluchistan ..	54,228	463,508	270,004	193,504	420,648	+10·2	+1·5	+21·3*	9	8	8
5 Bengal	77,521	50,114,002	26,041,698	24,072,304	46,702,307	+7·3	+2·7	+37·9	646	602	587
6 Bihar and Orissa ..	83,054	37,677,576	18,794,138	18,883,438	33,995,418	+10·8	—1·4	+21·6	454	409	415
7 Bombay Presidency including Aden.	123,679	21,930,601	11,535,903	10,394,698	19,348,219	+13·3	—1·8	+32·8	177	156	159
8 Burma	233,492	14,667,146	7,490,601	7,176,545	13,212,192	+11·0	+9·1	+292·5	63	57	53
9 Central Provinces and Berar.	99,920	15,507,723	7,761,818	7,745,905	13,912,760	+11·5	—0·0	+29·8	155	139	139
10 Coorg	1,593	163,327	90,575	72,752	163,838	—0·3	—6·4	—8·4	103	103	110
11 Delhi	573	636,246	369,497	266,749	488,452	+30·3	+18·0	+81·3	1,110	852	722
12 Madras	142,277	46,740,107	23,082,999	23,657,108	42,318,985	+10·4	+2·2	+51·6	328	297	291
13 North-West Frontier Province (Districts and Administered Territories).	13,518	2,425,076	1,315,818	1,109,258	2,251,340	+7·7	+2·5	+53·9	179	167	163
14 Punjab	99,200	23,580,852	12,880,510	10,700,342	20,685,478	+14·0	+5·7	+39·2	238	209	197
15 United Provinces of Agra and Oudh.	106,248	48,408,763	25,445,006	22,963,757	45,375,069	+6·7	—3·1	+10·6	456	427	440
States and Agencies ..	**712,508**	**81,310,845**	**41,897,367**	**39,413,478**	**72,086,289**	**+12·8**	**+1·0**	**+46·6**	**114**	**101**	**100**
16 Assam States ..	12,320	625,606	306,927	318,679	531,118	+17·8	+10·2	+96·8	51	43	39
17 Baluchistan States ..	80,410	405,109	218,410	186,699	378,977	+6·9	—9·8	—5·5*	5	5	5
18 Baroda State ..	8,164	2,443,007	1,257,817	1,185,190	2,126,522	+14·9	+4·6	+12·0	299	260	249
19 Bengal States ..	5,434	973,336	516,162	457,174	896,926	+8·5	+9·0	+39·4	179	165	151
20 Bihar and Orissa States	28,648	4,652,007	2,288,422	2,363,585	3,959,669	+17·5	+0·4	+93·0	162	138	138
21 Bombay States ..	27,994	4,468,396	2,288,623	2,179,773	3,867,819	+15·5	+0·1	+28·2	160	138	138
22 Central India Agency	51,597	6,632,790	3,405,438	3,227,352	6,002,551	+10·5	—2·1	+22·0*	129	116	119
23 Central Provinces States.	31,175	2,483,214	1,235,385	1,247,829	2,066,900	+20·1	—2·4	+79·0	80	66	68
24 Gwalior State ..	26,367	3,523,070	1,867,031	1,656,039	3,193,176	+10·3	—1·3	+14·6*	134	121	123
25 Hyderabad State ..	82,698	14,436,148	7,370,010	7,066,138	12,471,770	+15·8	—6·8	+46·6	175	151	162
26 Jammu and Kashmir State	84,516	3,646,243	1,938,338	1,707,905	3,320,518	+9·8	+5·1	+43·3†	43	39	37
27 Madras States Agency	10,698	6,754,484	3,373,032	3,381,452	5,460,312	+23·7	+13·5	+101·9	631	510	450
Cochin State ..	*1,480*	*1,205,016*	*589,813*	*615,203*	*979,080*	*+23·1*	*+6·6*	*+100·7*	*814*	*662*	*620*
Travancore State ..	*7,625*	*5,095,973*	*2,565,073*	*2,530,900*	*4,006,062*	*+27·2*	*+16·8*	*+112·2*	*668*	*525*	*450*
Other Madras States	*1,593*	*453,495*	*218,146*	*235,349*	*475,170*	*—4·6*	*+2·2*	*+32·1*	*285*	*298*	*292*
28 Mysore State ..	29,326	6,557,302	3,353,963	3,203,339	5,978,892	+9·7	+3·0	+56·6	224	204	198
29 North-West-Frontier Province (Agencies and Tribal Areas).	22,838	2,259,288	1,212,347	1,046,941	2,825,136	—20·0	+74·2	+2,590·8*	99	124	71
30 Punjab States ..	5,820	437,787	229,290	208,497	408,019	+7·3	—1·0	+21·5	75	70	71
31 Punjab States Agency	31,241	4,472,218	2,451,394	2,020,824	4,008,017	+11·6	+5·5	+27·7	143	128	122
32 Rajputana Agency ..	129,059	11,225,712	5,885,028	5,340,684	9,831,755	+14·2	—6·5	+11·1	87	76	82
33 Sikkim State ..	2,818	109,808	55,825	53,983	81,721	+34·4	—7·1	+260·5†	39	29	31
34 United Provinces States.	5,943	1,206,070	618,171	587,899	1,134,881	+6·3	—4·6	+9·7	203	191	200
35 Western India States Agency.	35,442	3,999,250	2,025,754	1,973,496	3,541,610	+12·9	+0·5	+16·5	113	100	99

* Variation calculated from 1901-1931.

† Variation calculated from 1891-1931.

SUBSIDIARY TABLE V.

Variation in Natural Population 1921—1931.

Province, State or Agency.	Population in 1931. Actual population.	Immi-grants.	Emi-grants.	Natural population.	Population in 1921. Actual population.	Immi-grants.	Emi-grants.	Natural population.	Variation per cent. (1921-1931) in Natural population Increase (+) Decrease(—).
1	2	3	4	5	6	7	8	9	10
INDIA ..	**352,837,778**	**732,204**	**656,709**	**352,763,925**	**318,885,980**	**603,526**	**1,050,951**	**319,333,405**	**+10·5**
Ajmer-Merwara	560,292	106,444	60,909	514,757	495,271	109,890	42,420	427,801	+20·3
Andaman and Nicobar Islands	29,463	14,745	553	15,271	27,086	15,120	316	12,282	+24·3
Assam	9,247,857	1,408,763	74,001	7,913,095	7,990,246	1,290,157	75,978	6,776,067	+16·8
Baluchistan	868,617	90,053	42,771	821,335	799,625	78,387	60,421	781,659	+5·1
Bengal	51,087,338	1,853,708	960,017	50,193,647	47,592,462	1,929,640	697,047	46,359,869	+8·3
Bihar and Orissa ..	42,329,583	509,837	1,758,290	43,578,036	37,961,858	422,244	1,955,048	39,494,662	+10·3
Bombay (*including Aden—1931 figures only*).	26,398,997	1,250,461	601,469	25,750,005	26,701,148	1,081,649	592,009	26,211,508	—1·8
Burma	14,667,146	775,963	24,368	13,915,551	13,212,192	706,725	20,295	12,525,762	+11·1
Central Provinces and Berar	17,990,937	655,574	422,176	17,757,539	15,979,660	609,504	407,294	15,777,450	+12·6
Coorg	163,327	38,718	3,233	127,842	163,838	83,937	2,852	132,753	—0·4
Delhi	636,246	263,188	69,478	442,536	488,188	185,770	69,350	371,768	+19·0
Madras	47,193,602	267,195	1,199,812	48,126,219	42,794,155	209,862	1,756,462	44,340,755	+8·5
North-West Frontier Province ..	4,684,364	159,166	90,892	4,616,090	5,076,476	157,562	84,495	5,003,409	—7·7
Punjab (*including Agency*)	28,490,857	674,152	707,478	28,524,183	25,101,060	627,137	549,429	25,023,352	+14·0
United Provinces of Agra and Oudh.	49,614,833	559,605	1,557,954	50,613,182	46,510,668	480,414	1,402,541	47,432,795	+6·7
Baroda State	2,443,007	324,579	205,202	2,323,630	2,126,522	232,494	221,602	2,115,630	+9·8
Central India Agency ..	6,632,790	600,766	482,564	6,514,588	5,997,023	548,094	486,643	5,935,572	+9·8
Cochin State..	1,205,016	87,417	48,240	1,165,839	979,080	39,759	28,338	967,659	+20·5
Gwalior State	3,523,070	281,550	296,835	3,538,355	3,186,075	290,340	289,029	3,184,764	+11·1
Hyderabad State ..	14,436,148	247,795	332,856	14,521,209	12,471,770	202,781	363,751	12,632,740	+1·5
Jammu and Kashmir State ..	3,646,243	64,196	94,520	3,676,567	3,320,518	63,420	84,291	3,341,389	+10·0
Mysore State	6,557,302	344,592	125,496	6,338,206	5,978,892	314,531	102,104	5,766,465	+9·9
Rajputana Agency ..	11,225,712	330,939	846,866	11,741,639†	9,844,384	243,002	868,117	10,469,499	+12·2
Sikkim State	109,808	15,417	7,213	101,604	81,721	22,978	4,133	62,876	+61·6
Travancore State	5,095,973	135,103	53,336	5,014,206	4,006,062	73,591	30,250	3,962,721	+26·5
Western India States Agency ..	3,999,250	109,674	294,345	4,183,921	*	*	*	*	..

NOTES.—(*i*) The figures for the Provinces are inclusive of the States attached to them except in the case of Madras where they exclude Cochin and Travancore.

(*ii*) The 1921 figures against Bombay exclude details for Aden for which unit no birthplace table was prepared at that census.

(*iii*) *Columns 2 and 6.*—Persons not enumerated by birthplace or whose birthplace was not returned have been included in these columns.

(*iv*) *Column 4.*—The figures against India in this column represent emigrants to foreign countries details of which will be found in subsidiary table 4 to Chapter III.

* Separate figures are not available as this unit was combined with the Bombay States in 1921.

† Includes persons enumerated in the Colonies who returned Ajmer-Merwara as their birthplace.

SUBSIDIARY TABLE VI.

Comparison of Areas and Population of Districts in Main Province.

Province.	Number of districts.	Area and Population of Districts. Average Area.	Average population.	Maximum Area in square miles.		Maximum Population.		Number of districts with population exceeding one million.
Assam	12	4,584·5	718,521	Lushai Hills	8,092	Sylhet	2,724,342	1
Baluchistan	6	9,038	77,251	Chagai	20,036	Quetta-Pishin ..	147,541	*Nil.*
Bengal	28	2,768·6	1,789,786	Mymensingh	6,237	Mymensingh ..	5,130,262	24
Bihar and Orissa ..	21	3,955	179,417	Ranchi	7,102	Darbhanga	3,166,094	16
Bombay (*excluding Aden*)	28	4,414·3	781,397	Thar and Parkar ..	13,636	Ratnagiri	1,302,527	8
Burma	41	5,694·9	357,735	Southern Shan States ..	36,416	Southern Shan States ..	870,230	*Nil.*
Central Provinces and Berar.	22	4,541·8	704,897	Raipur	9,717	Raipur	1,527,573	2
Madras	26	5,472·2	1,797,696	Agency Division ..	19,869	Malabar*	3,533,944	22
North-West Frontier Province.	5	2,703·6	485,015	Dera Ismail Khan ..	3,471	Peshawar	974,321	*Nil.*
Punjab	**29**	**3,420·7**	**813,133**	**Kangra .. ..**	**9,976**	**Lahore .. ..**	**1,378,570**	**6**
United Provinces of Agra and Oudh.	**48**	**2,213·5**	**1,008,516**	**Garhwal .. ..**	**5,612**	**Gorakhpur .. ..**	**3,567,561**	**22**

SUBSIDIARY TABLE VII.

Persons per House and Houses per square mile.

Province, State or Agency.	Average number of Persons per House. 1931.	1921.	1911.	1901.	1891.	Average number of Houses per square mile. 1931.	1921.	1911.	1901.	1891.
INDIA	**5·0**	**4·9**	**4·9**	**5·2**	**5·4**	**39·3**	**36·1**	**35·8**	**31·6**	**33·9**
Ajmer-Merwara	4·6	4·2	4·1	4·4	5·3	45·1	43·3	45·3	39·6	37·5
Andaman and Nicobar Islands ..	5·2	8·2	7·2	..	..	1·8	1·1	1·2	..	..
Assam	4·9	4·7	4·6	4·6	4·8	28·2	27·4	25·0	23·1	22·8
Baluchistan	5·2	5·0	4·9	4·5	..	1·2	1·2	1·3	2·3	..
Bengal	4·7	5·1	5·3	5·2	5·2	131·8	113·6	104·5	100·2	96·0
Bihar and Orissa	5·2	5·1	5·2	5·3	5·7	73·2	67·0	66·5	62·2	71·4
Bombay (*including Aden*) ..	5·1	4·9	4·9	5·1	5·4	34·4	29·3	29·5	26·5	25·6
Aden	*8·4*	*8·3*	..	..	..	*76·6*	*85·5*	..	..	..
Burma	4·7	4·8	4·9	5·0	5·3	13·4	11·7	10·7	8·8	8·3
Central Provinces and Berar ..	5·0	5·0	4·9	4·8	5·0	27·4	24·3	24·8	21·3	22·5
Coorg..	4·8	5·2	5·2	5·9	6·4	21·3	19·8	21·3	19·3	16·9
Delhi	4·6	4·3	*a*	*a*	*a*	242·4	193·4	*a*	*a*	*a*
Madras	5·1	5·1	5·3	5·4	5·3	64·9	58·5	55·0	50·3	47·6
*North-West Frontier Province ..	5·0	5·2	5·0	6·1	6·1	36·0	32·6	32·4	21·3	17·9
Punjab	4·8	4·5	4·5	6·2	6·6	47·5	43·9	43·0	29·7	27·2
United Provinces of Agra and Oudh	4·8	4·6	4·6	5·5	5·7	92·7	90·8	92·3	78·7	74·2
Baroda State	4·3	4·1	4·0	4·0	4·5	68·9	63·1	61·9	60·5	65·5
Central India Agency	4·6	4·5	4·6	5·1	5·2	27·8	25·6	26·4	21·5	25·2
Cochin State	5·8	5·5	5·6	5·6	5·4	140·2	120·5	120·0	107·1	96·1
Gwalior State	4·6	4·5	*b*	*b*	*b*	29·1	27·2	*b*	*b*	*b*
Hyderabad State	4·4	4·6	4·9	4·9	5·0	40·1	32·9	32·8	27·6	27·6
Jammu and Kashmir State ..	5·4	5·5	5·7	6·3	5·7	7·9	7·1	6·6	5·7	5·5
Mysore State	5·0	5·0	5·0	4·9	5·5	44·7	40·6	39·3	37·7	32·0
Punjab States Agency	4·7	4·5	4·4	*a*	*a*	30·6	28·5	28·0	*a*	*a*
Rajputana Agency	4·7	4·3	4·3	5·1	5·5	18·5	17·6	18·9	15·0	16·7
Sikkim State	4·1	5·5	5·3	5·3	..	9·6	5·2	5·9	3·9	
Travancore State	5·5	5·3	5·2	5·1	5·0	122·0	99·9	87·3	81·9	76·8
Western India States Agency ..	4·7	*c*	*c*	*c*	*c*	24·2	*c*	*c*	*c*	*c*

a. Included against Punjab.
b. Included against Central India Agency.
c. Included against Bombay.

* Excludes the Agencies and Tribal Areas where it has not been possible to ascertain the number of occupied houses.

SUBSIDIARY TABLE VIII.

Comparison between Census figures and Vital Statistics.

Province or State.	In 1921-30 total number of Births.	Deaths.	Number per mille of population of 1921 of Births.	Deaths.	Excess (+) or Deficiency (—) of Births over Deaths.	Increase (+) or Decrease (—) of population of 1931 compared with 1921. Natural population.	Actual population.
1	2	3	4	5	6	7	8
Assam	2,079,593	1,628,739	303·5	237·7	+450,854	+892,464	+1,163,123
Bengal	13,255,369	11,791,885	284·9	253·5	+1,463,484	+3,787,656	+3,411,695
Bihar and Orissa	12,347,593	9,093,498	363·1	267·4	+3,254,095	+3,343,122	+3,682,158
Bombay (*excluding Aden*) ..	6,872,564	5,144,403	358·6	268·4	+1,728,161	+2,709,477	+2,587,404
Burma	2,980,296	2,264,838	275·4	209·3	+ 715,458	+1,432,906	+1,454,954
Central Provinces and Berar ..	6,083,012	4,659,404	437·2	334·9	+1,423,608	+1,646,032	+1,594,963
Delhi	217,661	164,529	434·9	328·7	+53,132	+70,768	+147,794
Madras	14,210,900	9,811,998	346·6	239·3	+4,398,902	+3,798,759	+4,421,122
North-West Frontier Province ..	599,824	505,065	280·9	236·5	+94,759	+206,308	+173,736
Punjab	8,658,686	6,230,304	422·0	303·7	+2,428,382	+3,099,356	+2,895,374
United Provinces	15,921,016	11,993,248	350·9	264·3	+3,927,768	+3,102,582	+3,033,694
Baroda State	582,578	446,906	274·0	210·2	+135,672	+207,992	+316,485
Cochin State..	142,516	91,233	145·6	93·2	+51,283	+198,180	+255,936
Hyderabad State	1,143,632	1,279,679	91·7	102·6	—136,047	+1,888,290	+1,964,378
Mysore State	1,125,590	960,862	188·3	160·7	+164,728	+571,662	+578,410
Travancore State	819,173	446,319	204·5	111·4	+372,854	+1,051,485	+1,089,911

SUBSIDIARY TABLE IX.

Reported birth-rate per mille* during the decade 1921-30 in the main Provinces.

Province.	Number of Births (both sexes) per mille in										Average Birth rate per mille during the decade.
	1921.	1922.	1923.	1924.	1925.	1926.	1927.	1928.	1929.	1930.	
1	2	3	4	5	6	7	8	9	10	11	12
Assam	29·6	28·4	28·8	31·0	29·1	30·8	30·3	31·2	32·8	31·4	30·3
Bengal	28·0	27·4	29·9	29·5	29·6	27·4	27·7	29·6	29·3	26·6	28·5
Bihar and Orissa ..	34·6	35·0	37·0	35·7	35·6	37·2	37·6	38·3	35·6	36·2	36·3
Bombay	32·6	32·4	35·6	35·6	34·7	37·1	36·9	38·2	38·3	37·4	35·9
Burma	30·9	30·7	29·5	27·4	25·4	27·6	25·1	25·9	26·4	28·9	27·8
Central Provinces and Berar	37·9	35·8	45·6	44·2	43·9	46·0	45·6	46·5	44·0	47·7	43·7
Delhi	40·6	41·2	42·1	42·4	41·6	41·0	40·5	48·3	47·9	49·3	43·5
Madras	27·0	30·0	33·1	34·9	33·7	36·1	36·5	37·4	37·9	39·8	34·6
North-West Frontier Province	27·3	23·7	27·6	27·0	26·9	30·2	29·3	32·5	30·8	25·6	28·0
Punjab	41·5	39·3	43·2	40·1	40·1	41·6	42·3	46·3	44·5	43·3	42·2
United Provinces	34·4	32·2	36·0	34·7	32·7	34·2	36·7	38·2	34·3	37·3	35·1

* *Calculated on the population figure of 1921.*

SUBSIDIARY TABLE X.

Reported death-rate per mille* during the decade 1921-30 in the main Provinces.

Province.	Number of Deaths (both sexes) per mille in										Average Death-rate per mille during the decade.		
	1921.	1922.	1923.	1924.	1925.	1926.	1927.	1928.	1929.	1930.	Persons.	Males.	Females.
1	2	3	4	5	6	7	8	9	10	11	12	13	14
Assam	26·5	26·9	23·5	27·3	22·5	23·0	23·5	22·2	20·9	21·4	23·8	23·9	23·5
Bengal	30·1	25·2	25·5	25·9	24·9	24·7	25·6	25·5	23·5	22·4	25·3	25·7	25·0
Bihar and Orissa ..	32·8	24·1	25·0	29·1	23·7	25·7	25·1	25·3	26·9	29·6	26·7	28·3	25·1
Bombay	26·0	23·6	25·9	27·6	23·7	28·6	25·7	27·3	30·5	29·5	26·8	26·6	27·1
Burma	21·3	22·2	20·9	21·5	18·8	20·9	19·6	21·3	22·1	20·8	20·9	21·5	20·3
Central Provinces and Berar.	44·0	29·3	30·5	32·6	27·3	34·3	31·3	33·7	34·1	37·8	33·5	35·2	31·7
Madras	20·2	21·0	22·2	24·5	24·4	25·6	24·3	26·4	25·3	25·5	23·9	24·6	23·3
North-West Frontier Province.	31·6	21·7	23·7	31·0	19·8	21·8	22·0	19·3	23·7	21·9	23·7	24·0	23·3
Punjab	30·1	22·1	30·9	43·4	30·0	36·5	27·5	24·7	28·8	29·7	30·4	29·3	31·6
United Provinces ..	39·6	25·0	23·4	28·3	24·8	25·1	22·6	24·2	24·3	27·2	26·4	26·9	25·9

* *Calculated on the population figure of 1921.*

SUBSIDIARY TABLE XI.

Reported deaths from certain diseases per mille in the main Provinces.

Disease.	Actual number of total deaths in 1921.	1922.	1923.	1924.	1925.	1926.	1927.	1928.	1929.	1930.	Total.	Average annual rate per mille.
1	2	3	4	5	6	7	8	9	10	11	12	13
ASSAM.												
Fever ..	107,626	112,094	106,347	113, 98	98,015	93,689	89,324	89,255	83,520	89,772	982,840	14·34
Cholera	12,829	16,219	3,728	19,182	6,233	10,275	15,392	6,915	7,765	6,332	104,870	1·53
Small-pox ..	2,774	2,610	3,213	1,647	2,745	4,840	5,237	8,461	1,648	1,208	34,383	0·50
BENGAL.												
Fever ..	1,070,368	885,268	909,795	912,408	874,228	822,774	789,006	752,003	713,531	705,066	8,434,447	18·61
Cholera ..	80,547	51,712	41,483	48,514	34,276	59,106	118,377	136,245	81,090	54,963	706,313	1·50
Small-pox ..	8,157	7,864	4,236	5,567	17,436	25,548	42,514	43,558	20,407	11,268	186,555	0·39
Plague ..	59	150	98	35	9	..	1	6	..	..	358	0·01
BIHAR AND ORISSA.												
Fever ..	769,871	578,656	599,840	660,635	557,224	584,444	559,360	564,979	602,038	643,518	6,120,565	18·00
Cholera ..	90,688	26,805	8,198	77,480	17,336	27,268	49,022	77,103	104,034	155,215	633,149	1·81
Small-pox ..	7,836	2,560	3,161	6,932	14,382	34,873	34,661	13,567	6,671	7,455	132,098	0·38
Plague ..	16,504	15,066	28,911	10,792	6,788	8,381	6,112	7,627	8,266	4,105	112,552	0·30
BOMBAY.												
Fever ..	226,100	197,888	196,231	214,563	183,764	222,476	183,543	206,356	246,428	223,274	2,100,623	10·98
Cholera ..	3,521	2,768	9,221	8,236	57	73	26,153	6,881	9,084	15,142	81,136	0·42
Small-pox ..	1,771	1,170	2,811	11,152	5,644	3,922	5,091	5,265	10,635	21,341	68,802	0·36
Plague ..	4,672	8,379	33,741	9,214	12,601	9,866	4,076	13,563	18,014	5,026	119,152	0·62
BURMA.												
Fever ..	82,741	82,884	78,629	75,288	68,685	72,790	75,321	76,815	78,546	3,950	775,649	7·14
Cholera ..	3,791	5,047	1,488	8,083	1,932	6,182	4,528	7,209	7,970	661	46,891	0·43
Small-pox ..	987	1,439	2,846	2,501	3,852	2,339	1,704	2,825	1,841	921	21,255	0·20
Plague ...	4,403	7,282	7,606	5,491	4,064	2,906	3,508	4,933	1,867	1,962	44,022	0·41
CENTRAL PROVINCES AND BERAR.												
Fever ..	327,930	237,164	233,575	240,944	204,667	252,609	224,068	259,109	271,054	287,330	2,538,450	18·24
Cholera ..	58,331	64	1,090	9,704	124	4,565	16,311	12,198	6,168	23,250	131,805	0·95
Small-pox ..	1,787	407	275	978	3,145	3,644	2,809	1,399	1,391	4,954	20,789	0·15
Plague ..	5,467	6.149	15,867	11,081	5,223	6,486	3,368	3,770	2,808	871	61,090	0·44
MADRAS.												
Fever ..	316,019	319,688	318,172	322,356	316,406	337,945	321,995	344,683	339,052	330,496	3,266,812	7·99
Cholera ..	27,064	16,502	5,169	51,971	44,815	24,407	35,334	57,677	25,846	18,746	307,531	0·76
Small-pox ..	9,792	22,801	24,434	18,810	20,478	10,957	7,781	7,618	9,708	8,025	140,404	0·33
Plague ..	1,875	9,193	12,110	3,922	2,014	2,143	2,457	2,106	1,801	1,459	49,080	0·12
PUNJAB.												
Fever ..	423,162	306,654	420,398	452,187	401,775	436,156	358,679	316,235	402,429	422,377	3,940,052	19·20
Cholera ..	19,215	128	11	3,351	3,049	87	11,286	2,034	2,309	1,181	42,651	0·21
Small-pox ..	4,575	1,608	2,140	4,040	7,038	17,595	9,920	8,764	7,763	5,341	68,784	0·34
Plague ..	2,553	7,780	50,086	251,261	37,630	108,287	8,452	8,282	2,053	554	476,938	2·32
UNITED PROVINCES.												
Fever ..	1,361,920	909,293	780,049	947,807	875,594	867,939	786,552	765,954	810,583	942,469	9,048,160	19·94
Cholera ..	149,667	2,330	2,591	67,000	7,653	6,166	28,285	44,941	50,924	61,334	420,891	0·93
Small-pox ...	1,439	242	747	2,724	9,373	12,020	7,894	3,012	11,725	11,071	60,247	0·13
Plague ...	24,009	23,291	74,187	56,210	49,091	57,297	15,570	80,943	37,678	10,860	429,136	0·94

APPENDIX TO CHAPTER I.—*By A. E. Porter—The problem of population growth and an estimate of the future population of Bengal.*

Malthus and Doubleday.

Starting with the proposition that population is necessarily limited by the means of subsistence there are in the field two principal rival theories of population growth. That deriving from Malthus has been* stated thus: first that population invariably increased where the means of subsistence increased unless prevented by some very powerful and obvious checks; and secondly that these checks which repress the superior power of population and keep its effects on a level with the means of subsistence are all resolvable into moral restraint, vice and misery. In other words nature having arranged for population to increase at a rate at which it is bound to overtake and pass the means of subsistence periodically redresses the balance by famines, epidemics and other calamities unless human intelligence steps in and prevents the excessive increase either by moral restraint or by measures for limiting the birth rate or for despatching the excess of population. The other theory derives from Thomas Doubleday and gives nature a rather less sinister role. It is that when the existence of a species is endangered " a corresponding effort is invariably made by nature for its preservation and continuance by an increase of fertility, and that this especially takes place whenever such danger arises from a diminution of proper nourishment or food, so that consequently the state of depletion or the deplethoric state is favourable to fertility, and that, on the other hand, the plethoric state or the state of repletion, is unfavourable to fertility in the ratio of the intensity of each state ". It has been thought that this statement lays too much stress upon food and the position has been thus† restated: " In circumstances of ease the birth-rate tends to fall: in circumstances of hardship the birth-rate tends to rise ".

Pell's Law of Births and Deaths.

The recorded census figures of population in Bengal probably cover too short a period to offer clear support to either one of these theories against the other. During the last sixty years the population of Bengal has become nearly half as large again as it was in 1872. There can be no question of intelligence checks having operated, and Bengal has been free from major calamities except in the decade before last when the influenza epidemic from which virtually the whole world suffered operated to reduce the rate of increase during the decade to a figure lower than any in its recorded census history. If the Malthusian doctrine holds, Nature is not yet aware of any need to apply a check to the increase of population in Bengal. If the Darwinian theory holds and " fecundity is in direct relation to the chances of death ", and if the " law " of Doubleday applies, Nature still finds it necessary to maintain in Bengal a high birth-rate in order to keep pace with the high death-rate. In some points at least the Malthusian theory fails to explain the facts. In European countries and America, where most investigation has been carried out, it has been found‡ (*a*) that the birth-rate is negatively correlated with wealth and (*b*) that the indirect psychological and social effect of relative poverty as contrasted with relative wealth express themselves definitely and clearly in the sexual activity of human beings and through sexual activity in birth-rates. On the Malthusian theory in the wealthier classes where the means of subsistence are plentiful the population should increase more rapidly than in the poorer classes where they are less plentiful unless there were some voluntary interference with the rate of birth. The evidence of any such voluntary restriction is not conclusive and the theory generally held is that fertility itself decreases in the higher classes with increasing wealth and culture. The Malthusian doctrine also fails to account for the fact that a high birth-rate and a high death-rate are apparently invariably found together and that conversely where there is a low birth-rate there is also a low death-rate. This fact and the extreme doubtfulness of any evidence to show that conscious limitation of the family can account for the whole or a considerable part of the decrease in the birth-rate where it is low have led to the enunciation of the theory§ that " the net result of the variations of the degree of fertility under the direct action of the environment will bear an inverse proportion to the variations of the capacity for survival." Under this theory variations in the birth-rate are mainly due to the operation of a natural law which adjusts the degree of fertility to suit the death-rate of the race. The theory involves the postulate that the same conditions which lead to a reduction in the death-rate lead also to a decrease in fertility in some manner not yet known. The author of the theory suggests that the hormones assist in regulating the fertility of the germ cells, that the output of hormones by the endocrine glands is regulated by the nervous system which responds to the action of the environment and that the variations in the degree of fertility in response to the direct action of the environment will bear an inverse proportion to the development of nervous energy.

Raymond Pearl's Logistic Curve.

What may be considered to be a development of the second of these two theories is that put forward by ||Raymond Pearl. This theory deduces that populations grow in size according to the same mathematical law that individual animals and plants follow in the growth of their bodies in size, and that human populations grow according to the same law as do experimental populations of lower organisms. The law of growth postulated on these deductions may be expressed by an equation with three constants, and the curve representing this equation is

* *E.g.,* by W. S. Thompson—*Population, A Study in Malthusianism,* 1915.

† By H. Sutherland, see *Proceedings of World Population Conference,* 1927, page 58.

‡ Pearl—*Biology of Population Growth,* 1926.

§ C. E. Pell, *The Law of Births and Deaths,* 1921.

|| R. Pearl, *Studies in Human Biology,* 1924; *The Biology of Population Growth.* 1926.

called by Pearl a "logistic curve". Equations have been worked out and fitted to the populations of fifteen countries of the world, the whole world and the population of certain cities and have been shown to give over the whole recorded census history of each a very reasonable congruity with the recorded facts. Assuming the mathematical form of the curve this theory allows account to be taken of the fact that a population is necessarily confined to a certain area and therefore must have an upper limit of population as well as a lower (which may be nil) and for the fact that population growth takes place in cycles conditioned amongst other factors by cultural achievement. It is possible that over a restricted period the logistic curve may not give so accurate an approximation to the recorded population as a curve of some other form. As a method of predicting future growth also it is liable to the irruption of influences not previously prevalent. Pearl states "predictions of future growth may at any time be altered by the entrance into the situation of new economic or social factors of a different sort to those which have operated during that past period which the equation covers. The population may be stimulated to start upon a new cycle of growth or slighter but still in kind new factors may alter somewhat the upper limiting value of the present cycle". In certain instances however the logistic curve calculated by him gives astonishingly close approximations to the population actually recorded later. For the United States of America in 1930, for instance, a curve worked out before the census of 1920 suggested a population within 5 per 1,000 of that actually enumerated.

The logistic curve applied to Bengal.

Three curves of Pearl's logistic type have been fitted to the census population of Bengal and the population calculated from them .... is compared with the observed population. The first is the equation worked out by Mr. P. J. Griffiths, I.C.S., and it was hoped to give in an appendix brief notes on the method by which it was calculated. Difficulties in setting up the rather complicated mathematical formulæ involved however have prevented this. Briefly however, the method consists in fitting a curve of the required type to three of the recorded census figures and then adjusting it by successive approximations to all the recorded figures. The desired approximation is one in which the algebraic sum of differences between the calculated and the actually recorded populations is nil and the sum of the squares of these differences is a minimum. Mr. Griffiths' curve was worked out for the population actually recorded in Bengal treating the interval between each census count as being exactly ten years and assuming that a negligible error only was introduced by this treatment and by neglecting to make an adjustment for change of area. For the other two calculations the recorded census population was adjusted to represent the estimated population in the area now constituting Bengal on the 1st March of each census year after 1881 and on the 1st March 1871. In making this calculation it was assumed that the population between any two census years changed at a uniform rate and that the rate of change between March 1871 and the date of the census in 1872 was the same as between 1872 and 1881. In arriving at the third equation allowance has been made for a small factor which Mr. Griffiths has noted as being disregarded in his calculation. The equations give a curve of reasonable fit and the last shown is the most accurate approximation for the observations in so far as the algebraic sum and the sum of squares of differences between the observed and calculated population at all census years from 1881 to 1931 is less with this equation than with the other two, whilst for all years including 1871 the sum of the differences is least and the sum of their squares not indeed least but very near to it.

General tendencies of population growth and upper limit of population suggested.

On the first equation the rate of increase was being successively enhanced till 1881 when it began to decline and the maximum population would be about 74 millions, which would be practically attained in 2063 A. D. On the third equation the point of maximum increase was passed in 1872, the rate of growth is also diminishing and a maximum population of about $68\frac{3}{4}$ millions would be expected which would be approximately reached in 2076 A. D. On neither equation is any lower limits of population implied, *i.e.*, the equations do not suggest that the present cycle of population growth began at any definite period, although on the third equation Bengal should have had a population of not less than two millions in 1668 A. D.

The logistic curve applied to the Muslim and Hindu population.

Mr. Griffiths also fitted curves to the population of Muslims and Hindus ....
................The correspondence of these figures, particularly for Hindus, is not so close as is obtained by the equation for the total population, but the Muslim equation gives a reasonable fit for the years 1881 to 1921. The total maximum population towards which the equations suggest that each community is tending would be for Muslims about 32 millions and for Hindus about $23\frac{3}{4}$ millions : in aggregate these figures fall short by 14 to 20 millions of the upper asymptotic population calculated for all communities. The Muslim and Hindu equations imply that the point at which the rate of increase ceased to be successively greater than in previous decades was passed in about 1886 by the Muslims and 1812 by the Hindus who are now approaching a stationary population. In any case the implication is that the Hindu community is further along its present growth cycle than the Muslim : in other words that it is approaching its maximum whilst by comparison the Muslim community is still rapidly growing. It is possible to find a suggested explanation, if this is actually true, in the fact that Muslims live mainly in the healthier regions of Eastern Bengal and Hindus in the less healthy and less progressive portions of West Bengal : but it would be interesting if similar calculations have been made, to know whether the implication arises also in the case of other provinces.

Estimate of population in 1941.

The equations for total populations suggest a population of between 53 and 53¼ millions in 1941. The communal equations appear (and Mr. Griffiths holds them) to be inappropriate. Equations of a more complicated form might give closer correspondence with the observed census figures, but the calculation involves very great labour, they might give no better estimates for the future and in any case they are scarcely worth making in view of the fact that only seven counts are on record. For the future all that can be said is that if the type of equation used is applicable to population growth and if the conditions influencing population growth in Bengal over the period to which it has been applied continue substantially unchanged for the future, the estimates of total population made by use of the equations deduced should represent the population to be expected. The equation themselves suffer however by being fitted to so few observed counts and the conditions influencing population growth cannot be predicted and are difficult to discover if a change in the cycle suggests their existence. Thus after the formation of the German Empire and the institution of the present constitutions in Japan, Pearl found that the cycle of growth was, as it were, speeded up and Germany and Japan starting from the population of that critical time took a leap forward and continued their cycle as if they had been at an earlier stage when growth was more rapid. It is by no means impossible that constitutional change may have a similar effect in Bengal and may affect the different communities to a different degree.

Can Bengal support a larger population.

The prospect or even the possibility of so considerable an increase in a population already one of the densest in the world may lead to apprehension that the population of Bengal is rapidly approaching numbers which cannot be sustained at any reasonable standard of living upon the means of subsistence which Bengal can produce for long. If population actually does increase according to some such law as that illustrated by the logistic curve the fact that considerable increases are inevitable makes the apprehension futile. Pearl himself has pointed out that this inevitable increase need not necessarily increase the misery in the world since first this result has not happened up to the present, secondly " the orderly evolution of human knowledge justifies us in assuming that science will keep pace in discovering means of expanding opportunities of happy human subsistence ", and thirdly the human organism is itself adaptable to an extent not yet imagined. It cannot be denied that a large part of the population of Bengal lives at a very low level of subsistence, and that any increase of population must lead to increased distress unless the potentialities of the province are developed. What is suggested here is that these potentialities are such that pessimism as to the future condition of its population if considerable increase take place is not necessarily justified. Like the rest of India Bengal is notable for its undeveloped resources and the inefficiency with which such resources as it has are exploited. The soil is probably unlikely to deteriorate further and the general opinion about areas such as Bengal, where scanty manuring necessitates small crops, is that a dead level of yield was reached long ago and is conditioned by the rate at which plant food constituents are made available by weathering. The cultivator in Bengal practically never enriches the soil with any manure and the use of manures together with an improvement in the implements of agriculture which would then be rendered possible would probably increase enormously the output of the soil. It has been* estimated that improved methods would result in a reasonable expectation of increased food output of 30 per cent. throughout the whole of India. There is no doubt that any additional labour required under a more intensive form of cultivation could easily be obtained since the agriculturist in Bengal on the whole probably works less than agriculturists in almost any other part of the world. Subsidiary Table I [Bengal Report] also shows that of the total area cultivable only 67 per cent. is now actually under cultivation. If the total cultivable area were brought under cultivation and if improved methods of cultivation yielding an increase of 30 per cent. over the present yield were adopted it is clear from a simple rule of three calculation† that Bengal could support at its present standard of living a population very nearly twice as large as that recorded in 1931. Fresh areas in course of time will be brought under cultivation as lands on the Bay of Bengal accrete and reach a stage suitable for cultivation. Even at present it is clear that by far the majority of the food stuffs consumed in Bengal are locally produced. During 1930-31, taking only grains, pulses and flour, salt, sugar and spices, provisions and oilman's stores Bengal imported goods of the value of Rs. 821 lakhs and exported goods of the value of Rs. 281 lakhs. But the balance of trade during the same year amounted to Rs. 34,52·41 lakhs or more than three times the aggregate export and import trade. The seaborne trade of Calcutta is not confined to goods originating in or meant exclusively for Bengal, but in the year 1930-1931 jute, tea and hides contributed 77¼ per cent. of the total and Bengal contributed all the jutes, nearly all the hides and a very considerable part of the tea. It is consequently clear that the favourable balance of trade to a very small extent only was dissipated outside Bengal and that the balance itself provides sufficiently for an enormously increased importation of food stuffs were it necessary to import them at any time. Not only agriculture but also industry is at present in Bengal practically in its infancy. Reviewing production in India a Bengali writer‡ in 1924 came to the conclusion that the " outstanding feature of the productive system of India

---

* G. Clarke, *Proceedings of the XVIIth Indian Science Conference.*

† $\frac{100}{67} \times \frac{130}{100} = 194.$

‡ Rajani Kanta Das, *Production in India.*

is its inefficiency which is shown by the great wastage of resources on the one hand and the lower productivity of the industries on the other.... It is insufficient production to which is due India's poverty, both absolute and relative.... The lack of capital is partly responsible for the present low productivity....but.... could not .... be regarded as the fundamental cause of insufficient production in India........ Insufficient production is the result of inefficient labour, *i.e.*, lack of capacity on the part of the people to mobilise the physical, intellectual and moral forces of the country and to organise land and capital effectively for national production ". Improvement in methods of production both agricultural and industrial should therefore very easily make possible the subsistence of such an increased population as is suggested by the figures already discussed, and the considerations deduced in this paragraph also make it possible to hope that such an increase of population may be attended with a very considerable increase in the material condition of the people and in the standard of living. It is clear at least that it is not yet time to indulge in gloomy forebodings on the ground that Bengal is over-populated, provided full use is made of the available resources of the country by improved methods.

Extravagant methods of population increase are a practical problem.

A final problem suggested by the growth of population in Bengal concerns the enormous wastage of life with which that growth is achieved. It is clear that what is of importance in population growth is the rate of increment. A high rate of increment can be achieved by a relatively low birth-rate if the death-rate is also low, whilst on the contrary a comparatively low rate of increase results from even a high birth-rate if the death-rate also is high. ....actually both the birth-rate and the death-rate in Bengal are very high and .... there is consequently an appalling wastage of reproductive energy in maintaining the present increase of population. If the logistic theory of population growth is correct a retarded rate of increase is inevitable at the upper stages of the cycle of growth until finally a population is reached which to all intents and purposes is stationary. France in Europe where there is a notoriously low birth-rate probably illustrates this position best but an exhaustive* enquiry into the Arab population of Algiers suggested to Pearl that the retardation of the rate of increase is in general effected at the upper stages of the population growth by decrease both in the birth-rate and in the death-rate. The Arab population of Algiers showed both a decrease in the birth-rate which could not be ascribed to any voluntary measures and a decrease in the death-rate which equally could not be ascribed to improvement in public health measures since the traditional custom of the Arabs offer the utmost possible resistance to any changes in their habits which would improve sanitary conditions. Attempts to effect a retardation of the rate of increase by voluntary limitation of the birth-rate are almost certainly doomed to failure particularly in Bengal. They are repugnant to common sentiment in this country, the methods adopted are so expensive as to be beyond the reach of the great majority of the inhabitants and it is probably true to say that there are as yet none which can be relied upon as being absolutely certain and satisfactory. Figures for the different strata of society .... show that there is no evidence to believe that contraceptive measures are used by the upper classes or those engaged in professions and the liberal arts; and it is certain that they are not practised at all in the lower strata of society. What appears to happen, if the analogy of Western Europe may be accepted, is that a decrease in the death-rate is inevitably followed at some period by a corresponding decrease in the birth-rate. It is clear also that fertility in western countries decreases with the increase of wealth and intellectual interests. It is therefore possible to expect that a reduction of the birth-rate by the adoption of improved measures of public health accompanied by an improvement in the standard of living, an increase in the spread of education and perhaps principally by a further emancipation of women and their introduction to spheres of usefulness and activity from which they are now in Bengal generally debarred by social custom and by the institution of purdah will in due course result in a decrease in the birth-rate corresponding with the decrease in the death-rate which it is the object of public health measures to bring about.

* *Biology of Population Growth.*

CHAPTER II.

Urban and Rural.

Statistics of Urban and Rural Population.

36. The statistics of the urban population are to be found in Imperial Tables I, III, IV and V. Table I gives the territorial distribution of towns and villages and the figures of occupied houses and of the population separately for towns and villages ; Table III shows the population as distributed between villages and towns of different sizes ; Table IV gives the population of towns with the variations for fifty years, and Table V their territorial distribution and their composition by communities of different religions. The floating population which cannot definitely be allotted either to the urban or to the rural totals, that is to say persons enumerated in railway trains, boats or temporary encampments, will be found separately in Table III, and is so small (0·14%) compared to the whole population dealt with that it can be ignored in any consideration of the comparative figures. The total percentage of the population censused as urban was only 11%, showing an increase in its proportion to the whole of 0·8% since 1921. That is to say 6,510,151 or 19·2% of the total increase of the population during the past decade has taken place in towns. This increase is of course partly the natural increase of the pre-existing urban population and partly occasioned by migration from rural areas or by their incorporation into urban ones, while in estimating the growth of the urban population allowance must be made for the expansion of large villages to a size or importance which causes them to be classified as towns, and likewise for the omission of dwindling communities which fall out and are reclassified as rural. The tables therefore which deal with the changes in the urban population do not adhere to the population of the identical sites shown in the corresponding tables of former decades but give the total population enumerated in urban areas at the time of the census, as compared with the similar population ten years previously, the differences due to changing classification as urban or rural being shown in a supplementary table to Table IV. The accompanying table shows the variation in urban and rural populations respectively, and the very small proportion that the urban population bears to the whole is clearly indicated by the close relation between the variation in total population and that of the rural population as contrasted with the general antithesis between the total and the urban variations.

Province.	Variation 1921—31. Increase (+) Decrease (—) Per cent.	Variation in Urban Per cent.	Variation in Rural Per cent.
India	+10·6	+20·0	+9·6
Provinces	*+10·0*	*+18·4*	*+9·0*
1. Ajmer-Merwara	+13·1	+9·4	+15·0
2. Andamans and Nicobars	+8·8	..	+8·8
3. Assam	+15·7	+15·8	+15·2
4. Baluchistan	+10·2	+31·6	+5·9
5. Bengal	+7·3	+15·6	+6·7
6. Bihar and Orissa	+10·8	+20·3	+10·4
7. Bombay	+13·3	+11·6	+13·9
8. Burma	+11·0	+17·7	+10·3
9. Central Provinces and Berar	+11·5	+20·2	+10·4
10. Coorg	—0·3	+11·2	—1·0
11. Delhi	+30·3	+47·0	+2·7
12. Madras	+10·4	+20·1	+9·1
13. North-West Frontier Province	+7·7	+15·0	+6·4
14. Punjab	+14·0	+38·7	+11·0
15. United Provinces of Agra and Oudh	+6·7	+12·9	+5·9
States and Agencies	*+12·8*	*+25·5*	*+11·6*
16. Assam States	+17·8	+17·3	+21·7
17. Baluchistan States	+6·9	+16·0	+6·7
18. Baroda State	+14·9	+18·6	+13·9
19. Bengal States	+8·5	+10·4	+8·5
20. Bihar and Orissa States	+17·5	+29·5	+17·4
21. Bombay States	+15·5	+24·3	+14·3
22. Central India Agency	+10·5	+23·0	+9·3

Province.	Variation 1921—31. Increase (+) Decrease (—) Per cent.	Variation in Urban Per cent.	Variation in Rural Per cent.
23. Central Province States	+20·1	+55·9	+19·3
24. Gwalior State	+10·3	+28·2	+8·7
25. Hyderabad State	+15·8	+36·2	+13·6
26. Jammu and Kashmir State	+9·8	+17·4	+9·1
27. Madras States Agency	+23·7	+50·1	+20·7
Cochin State	*+23·1*	*+62·3*	*+17·2*
Travancore State	*+27·2*	*+36·4*	*+26·2*
Other Madras States	*—4·6*	*+204·1*	*—20·0*
28. Mysore State	+9·7	+21·1	+7·7
29. N. W. F. P. (*Agencies and Tribal Areas*)	—20·0	..	—20·0
30. Punjab States	+7·3	—6·6	+7·8
31. Punjab States Agency	+11·6	+19·1	+10·8
32. Rajputana Agency	+14·2	+18·1	+13·4
33. Sikkim State	+34·4	..	+34·4
34. United Provinces States	+6·3	+9·8	+5·9
35. W. I. States Agency	+12·9	+21·4	+10·7

Definition of Urban Areas.

37. Of a necessity the definition of a town for census purposes has resulted in a distinction which is sometimes arbitrary. Towns of not less than 100,000 inhabitants were to be treated as cities, and also any other towns which the Superintendent decided to treat as cities subject to the sanction of the Local Government. But the Census Code further provided for the treatment as a town of every municipality, all civil lines not included in municipal limits, every cantonment and every other continuous collection of houses, inhabited by not less than 5,000 persons, which the Superintendent of Provincial Census Operations decided to treat as urban. In making this decision the Census Superintendent was instructed to take into consideration the character of the population, the relative density of the dwellings, importance in trade and historic associations, and to avoid treating as towns overgrown villages without urban characteristics. The effect of the latter provision is to be inferred from the marginal statement which shows that of a total of 2,575 places treated as towns in 1931 600, or 23·3%, were places so classified by the Superintendent of Census Operations as (the quotation is from the Jammu and Kashmir State Census Code) "bearing the cachet of urbanity", although not covered by the standard definition and therefore not possessing any urban self-government. On the other hand their inhabitants amount to only 4,122,088, or 10·6 % of the urban population, which indicates the comparatively small size of these towns. There has been inevitably considerable variation in the latitude observed by census superintendents in the exercise of this discretionary power of classification, with the result that the varying degrees of urbanization of different provinces cannot necessarily be taken at their face value. Thus Mysore appears as having a higher proportion of urban population than Madras, but 66 of its 108 towns have a population of less than 5,000, and if such towns be omitted altogether the position of the two units is reversed. Similarly both Bombay and the United Provinces have large proportions of their total urban population represented by the inhabitants of small towns of 5,000 inhabitants or less. In this connection it will be well to bear in mind that the distinction between a small town and a large village as far as the conditions of life or occupation of its inhabitants is concerned is often meaningless, and the treatment of any place as urban rather than rural does not necessarily imply any degree of industrialization and only the minimum degree of a corporate life distinct from that of the ordinary

	Number.		Population.		Percentage of total urban population.	
	1921.	1931.	*1921.*	1931.	*1921.*	1931.
Total Towns	*2,316*	2,575	*32,475,276*	38,985,427	*100*	100
Municipalities, Civil Lines, Notified Areas, Cantonments, etc.	*1,276*	1,975	*25,453,745*	34,863,339	*78*	*89*
Towns arbitrarily classified as such for census purposes ..	*1,040*	600	*7,021,531*	4,122,088	*22*	*11*

village ; to quote the Census Superintendent for Bengal " many of the non-industrial towns................differ but little in their conditions from large villages, except in the provision............of an infrequent lamppost ". A comparison with the figures of last census gives some indication of the spread of local self-government.

The greatest degree of growth has been in the number of towns with a population of from 20,000 to 50,000, the total population of which is now nearly double that of towns of 50,000 to 100,000 and not very much short of that of the 38 towns whose individual populations exceed 100,000. The number of towns has been increased at this census by the treatment of cantonments as separate entities instead of including their figures with that of an adjoining town. Such inclusion may be justified in the case of suburbs, civil lines and notified areas which are more or less dependent for their existence on the proximity of a town, but a cantonment may be and frequently is not only of entirely independent origin and a self-contained unit, but actually indebted to the absence of a large urban population for the site chosen for occupation. Moreover even where it adjoins an old established urban area, the cantonment has a separate organisation and a corporate life of its own. Out of eighty-nine cantonments thirty- four have an elected board and thirteen a nominated board, the administration of the remainder being vested in a corporation sole All of these bodies have an executive officer usually provided in the case of the more important ones by the Cantonment Department. In any case the cantonment depends for its individual and separate existence on causes which are foreign to those governing the growth or decline of cities and towns, and it is therefore desirable to separate the population from that of the urban areas which they so often adjoin. This separation of cantonments has sometimes affected the classification of the town with which it was formerly combined. The figures in the margin indicate how little change there has been in the size of towns during the decade and in urbanization generally.

Class and description of town.	No. of towns in class.		Total population in towns of the class.	
	1921.	1931.	*1921.*	1931.
I. 100,000 and over ..	*35*	38	*8,211,704*	9,674,032
II. 50,000 to 100,000 ..	*54*	65	*3,517,749*	4,572,113
III. 20,000 to 50,000 ..	*200*	268	*5,968,794*	8,091,288
IV. 10,000 to 20,000 ..	*451*	543	*6,220,889*	7,449,402
V. 5,000 to 10,000 ..	*885*	987	*6,223,011*	6,992,832
VI. Under 5,000 ..	*691*	674	*2,333,129*	2,205,760

Urban Population. **38**. The total urban population of India according to the above methods of classification comes to 38,985,427 or 11% of the total population. The distribution of the population between villages and towns is given in subsidiary table I to this chapter, the percentage of the population which is urban ranging from 3·4% of the whole population in Assam to 22·6% in Bombay. Compared to this latter, the most urbanized of the major provinces of India, the proportion of the population classified as urban is 49% in France, 50·8% in Northern Ireland, 53·7% in Canada, 56·2% in the U. S. A. and 80 % in England and Wales.

Distribution of Population in groups of Towns according to size and in Rural Areas, 1891 to 1931.

Class of Places.	1931.		1921.		Per mille of total Population.				
	Places.	Population.	Places.	Population.	1931.	1921.	1911.	1901.	1891.
1	2	3	4	5	6	7	8	9	10
Total Population	699,406	352,837,778	687,981	318,942,480	1,000	1,000	1,000	1,000	1,000
Urban Areas	2,575	38,985,427	2,316	32,475,276	110	102	94	99	95
Towns having—									
I—100,000 and over ..	38	9,674,032	35	8,211,704	27	26	22	22	22
II—50,000 to 100,000 ..	65	4,572,113	54	3,517,749	13	11	9	12	11
III—20,000 to 50,000 ..	268	8,091,288	200	5,968,794	23	19	18	17	16
IV—10,000 to 20,000 ..	543	7,449,402	451	6,220,889	21	19	20	22	19
V—5,000 to 10,000 ..	987	6,992,832	885	6,223,011	20	20	19	20	21
VI—Under 5,000 ..	674	2,205,760	691	2,333,129	6	7	6	6	6
Rural Areas	696,831	313,852,351	685,665	286,467,204	890	898	906	901	905

For reasons of economy in sorting, the available figures of internal migration are less detailed than in 1921, but the returns for twelve cities show that, out of a total population of 3,670,261, as many as 1,746,211 (1,155,543 males and 590,668 females) or 48% of the total population, were born elsewhere, the remainder being the natives of their respective cities. This, of course, does not represent the actual

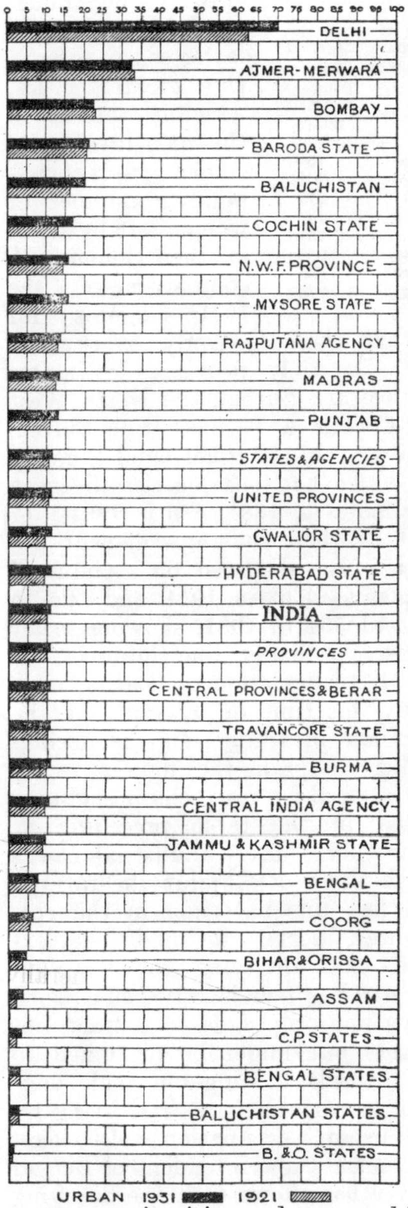

accretion from countries or towns, but indicates the maximum extent to which the population of urban areas is reinforced by immigration as distinct from natural increase. It is, of course, obvious that the composition of the truly urban population is likely to differ from that of the rural population of the surrounding area. It is in the nature of things that the more varied activities of towns should attract a mixed population with less homogeneity than that of the country-side. But beyond this, there appears to be a tendency for the population of towns in general to show different characteristics from those of rural areas in certain definite directions. It is naturally to be expected that the percentage of literacy should be greater in towns, where opportunities for education are more readily available, and accordingly we find that 10% of the total literate population, and 29% of the total literate in English, is to be found in 38 cities, and the ratio of literacy to the total population is 27% in these 38 cities as against 8% in India as a whole. Figures for towns other than cities are not available but would probably much increase the ratio if they were. The corresponding percentages for literacy in English are 10·3 and 1·0%. In the case of infirmities, no separate figures for cities are available but the figures for Bengal go to indicate that those infirmities to record which an attempt is made at the Census are not worse in cities than elsewhere, since the number of insane, for instance, returned from the Rajshahi Division was 6,142 as against 4,245 returned from the Presidency Division. Census figures for infirmities are, however, notoriously unreliable and it is not safe to draw any conclusions.

Urban Sex Proportions.

39. The figures for sex and age in cities have to be considered in the light of the common practice in India by which men leave their families in their homes in villages and go to earn their living as temporary or semi-permanent workers in towns. This naturally results in an excess of males of mature age in cities and towns which is illustrated by the figures in Table I for urban and rural population, where the number of females to every 1,000 males is 815 in urban areas, and 957 in rural as compared to 941 for India as a whole. Similarly the mean age for Calcutta males is 25·8 and that for Bombay males 25·6, years as compared with 23·2 the mean age for males in India, as a whole. This condition does not however apply to the whole of India, as in Rajputana the towns have 913 females per 1,000 males compared to 907 in rural areas*. These towns are not, of course, industrial. The marginal tables show (1) the number of females in the urban population per 1,000 males for each of the main provinces, and (2) for some of the principal cities, not only the number of females per 1,000 males but also the number of married females per 1,000 married males, indicating very

Province (British) or State.	Females per 1,000 males, total popula-tion.	Females per 1,000 males, urban popula-tion.
Madras	1,025	993
Bihar and Orissa	1,005	820
Central Provinces and Berar ..	998	886
Western India States	974	995
Hyderabad State	959	932
Burma	958	681
Central India	948	864
Bengal	924	601
Rajputana	908	913
United Provinces	902	805
Bombay	901	773
Assam	900	577
Ajmer-Merwara	892	823
North West Frontier Province ..	843	642
Punjab	831	699

* For a possible explanation see para. 78.

Sixteen largest cities in order of population.

City (including cantonment).	Females per 1,000 males.	Married females per 1,000 married males.	City (including cantonment).	Females per 1,000 males.	Married females per 1,000 married males.
Calcutta	468	365	Amritsar	666	756
Bombay	554	499	Lucknow..	722	738
Madras	897	936	Karachi ..	688	679
Hyderabad ..	886	822	Howrah ..	550	447
Lahore	565	646	Cawnpore	694	731
Rangoon	477	360	Nagpur ..	848	838
Delhi	694	754	Agra ..	799	865
Ahmadabad ..	717	..	Benares ..	792	776

clearly the unnatural life of the latter sex in some of the greater cities, which in the case of the men involves of course a corresponding number of women left by them in their homes. A comparison of the 1931 figures for the provinces with those of 1921 indicates that there is nearly everywhere a considerable decrease from the 1921 ratio. The only provinces or states in which the urban female ratio shows an increase are Burma, the North West Frontier Province, Baluchistan, Travancore and Cochin, while, excepting Burma, the decrease in the major provinces has been heavy. On the other hand Bombay City which had 664 females to every 1,000 males in 1881, 586 in 1891, 617 in 1901, when the impermanent population was depleted on account of the plague, 530 in 1911 and 525 in 1921 had 554 in 1931, showing a fair increase, probably due however, as in 1901, to depletion of floating male labour, this time on account of the depression in trade. In the accompanying diagram the figures represent the total figures, including suburbs omitted in the table preceding it. In the more purely industrial towns such as those of Gujarat the ratio is much less unequal than in the cosmopolitan ports. It might be expected that decaying towns would show a rising female ratio, since such a town not only fails to attract immigrants but might be presumed to tend towards sending out male emigrants to earn an industrial living by some urban occupation elsewhere. The Census Superintendent of Bengal however has shown that the decaying towns of that province have a falling female ratio, a phenomenon often to be associated with a decline in population in other parts of the world, but not apparently in India generally. In the case of cities which include cantonments allowance must obviously be made for the fact that a disparity in the numbers of the sexes is a necessary concomitant of the concentration of troops. In the main India tables however, that is in Tables III, IV and V, cantonments have been separately shown and are not included in the figures for cities, though in the special tables for cities from Table VI onwards cantonments, etc., are generally included.

City.	Population (including suburbs, cantts., etc.)	Whole rectangle-males; blank area inside-females.	Females per 1,000 males.
Rangoon ..	400,415		477
Calcutta (with Howrah).	1,485,582		490
Bombay ..	1,161,383		554
Lahore ..	429,747		565
Delhi ..	447,442		670
Hyderabad (Deccan).	466,894		886
Madras ..	647,230		897

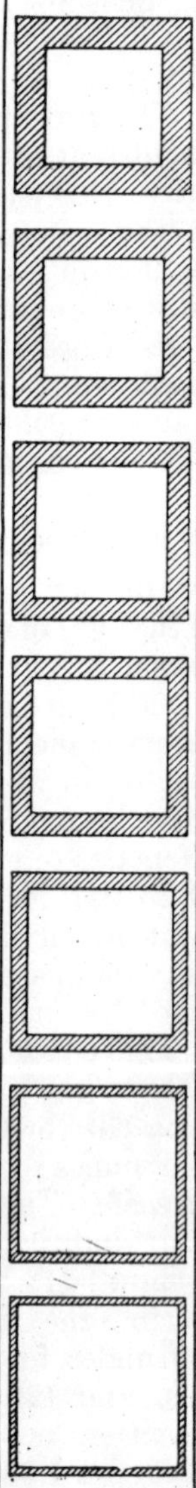

Race and Religion in Towns.

40. It was suggested in the Census Report for 1901 that there were possible connections between race and religion and the practice of congregating in towns.

One of the reasons given for the comparative absence of the urban habit in Bengal was the presumption that its population contained a strong mongoloid element, and it was pointed out that the inhabitants of Assam and Burma, both much more mongoloid than Bengal, were even more markedly rural. It may, however, be questioned whether race has in this case anything to do with the matter, and we should be inclined to account for the phenomenon not by race but by rainfall. The areas of the greatest precipitation in the peninsula are the Malabar Coast, Bengal, Assam and Lower Burma, and if living in cities is unpopular, as it certainly is, in these regions it is perhaps rather on account of the greater degree of discomfort which it involves than on account of the racial composition of the people. The population in at any rate two of these areas has an excessively high density, and one which easily compares with that of drier provinces of greater urbanization ; on the other hand it is spread, where it is thickest, through almost contiguous but rural habitations among coconut groves and rice fields. In northern India it is not impossible to live in a walled village or town and to move about freely on the face of the land during the greater part if not all of the year. In Eastern Bengal or Cochin the heavens are overcast and the land is awash for nearly half the year, and man or beast can only roam in or on the face of the waters, a condition which makes sanitation and evaporation very much more difficult to obtain in closely agglomerated habitations than in scattered homes each in its own demesne. On the other hand in southern India the Tamil as distinct from the Telugu, Kanarese or Malayali does appear to be predisposed towards urban life.

It was further observed in 1901, though no explanation was suggested, that towns attracted population of different religions in varying degrees, and it was pointed out that whereas in Bengal, Baluchistan, Assam and the Punjab the Muslim took less readily to town life than the Hindu, the case was reversed in most other parts of India, particularly in the United Provinces, the Central Provinces and Berar, in Hyderabad, Madras, Mysore and Rajputana. Clearly the reason has nothing to do with religion. Probably it is to be traced to historical causes, and it would appear, as might perhaps be expected, that the intrusive population is that which tends to prevail in the towns. Thus in Rajputana, Bombay, the Central and the United Provinces, and in southern India generally Hindus represent the country stock established before Islam appeared, and it is natural to find that on the land the Hindu still predominates. Conversely in Baluchistan and the North West Frontier Province the Hindu is nowadays intrusive and we find that he tends there to congregate in cities. In the case of Burma both are intrusive, but the Muslim has shown a greater tendency to intermarry with the Burman and to settle locally, while many of the Muslims of Burma (Zerbadis and Yakaing Kalas) are more Burmese than foreign in descent. Consequently we find that the Muslim in Burma shows a greater tendency than the Hindu to leave the towns. The two provinces which at first sight appear to spoil this hypothesis are Bengal and the Punjab. Here, however, the inversion of the usual condition would seem to be due not to a breach of the rule that the intruder clings to the towns but to the fact that the country dwellers have been converted on a much larger scale than elsewhere. The Muslim of East Bengal and of the Surma Valley in Assam seems to be descended for the most part from converted inhabitants, and similarly conversion to Islam was probably imposed on the Punjab with more persistence and efficacy than in parts of India more remote from the course of Muslim invasions and added later to the Mogul dominions. Apart from this the trading classes, which are often racial or religious, naturally tend to be town dwellers, so that Parsis and Jews can hardly be found elsewhere, and Jains, who include large numbers of the Marwari and Kathiawari traders, are more urban than communities of other faiths. Thus too Sikhs who are rural at home are town dwellers elsewhere, whither they go generally as mechanics or artificers of some kind. It remains to be added that the figures of some urban communities in the Punjab may have been slightly affected by intensive propaganda aimed at bringing rustics into the towns on census night to swell if possible the numbers of one electoral community or another, and one or two similar cases occurred in the United Provinces. Where this is alleged to have taken place, however, there seems to have been little or no change in the proportions borne by the community to another.

41. The table below gives a summary of certain information with regard to cities, that is with regard to those which have not less than 100,000 inhabitants. Their figure is moderate enough when compared with those of the west. The United Cities.

Kingdom alone is unfortunate enough to have 56 towns of over this minimum compared to India's 39, while the United States of America have at least 70, though their population is only 123 million, little more than a third of India's. The figures given in column 7 are not all strictly comparable one with another, as the definition of 'foreign born' adopted by different provinces varies. Thus in Calcutta the figure refers to those born outside Bengal, in Hyderabad and Lahore to those born outside the City but in Srinagar to those born outside the State, and in the case of eight other towns to born outside the District.

City.	Total Population.	Density.	Females per 1,000 males.	Literates per 1,000. Males.	Literates per 1,000. Females.	Numbers foreign born per 1,000.	Percentage Variation. 1881 to 1891.	1891 to 1901.	1901 to 1911.	1911 to 1921.	1921 to 1931.	1881 to 1931.
1	2	3	4	5	6	7	8	9	10	11	12	13
1. Calcutta with Howrah ..	1,485,582	24,354	489	430	269	328‖	+12·5	+22·9	+11·0	+4·3	+11·9	+79·2
2. Bombay	1,161,383	48,000	554	291	153	754	+6·3	—5·6	+26·2	+20·0	—1·2	+50·2
3. Madras	647,230	22,249	897	433	170	348	+11·5	+12·6	+1·8	+1·6	+22·8	+59·1
4. Hyderabad with Secunderabad, etc.	466,894	8,809	889	449	118	321	+13·0	+8·0	+12·0	—19·0	+16·0	+27·0
5. Delhi with New Delhi, Shahdara, etc.	447,442	6,835	670	246‡	89‡	483‡	+11·1	+8·3	+11·6	+30·7	47·0	+158·1
6. Lahore	429,747	10,913	565	297	124	513	+12·4	+14·8	+12·7	+23·2	+52·5	+187·7
7. Rangoon	400,415	16,146	477	512	379	351	+34·4	+30·3	+24·9	+16·6	+17·1	+198·4
8. Ahmadabad	313,789	*	853	*	*	*	+16·3	+25·3	+16·6	+26·4	+14·5	+145·9
9. Bangalore with Civil and Military Station.	306,470	11,799	902	405	168	343§	+15·7	—11·8	+19·1	+25·3	+29·0	+96·6
10. Lucknow	274,659	13,272	745	253	43	320	+4·4	—3·3	—1·6	—4·6	+14·2	+8·2
11. Amritsar	264,840	24,844	666	205	69	203	—10·0	+18·8	—6·0	+4·9	+65·3	+74·4
12. Karachi	263,565	6,720	688	286	114	520§	+43·0	+10·9	+30·2	+42·8	+21·5	+258·3
13. Poona	250,187	6,400	811	408	149	363**	+25·8	—4·5	+5·3	+23·9	+16·5	+82·6
14. Cawnpore	243,755	24,756	696	233	62	473	+24·9	+4·5	—12·0	+21·2	+12·6	+56·9
15. Agra	229,764	12,449	813	214	52	306	+5·3	+11·5	—1·4	+0·0	+23·8	+43·4
16. Nagpur	215,165	10,578	848	308	95	302	+19·0	+9·0	—21·0	+43·0	+48·0	+119·0
17. Benares	205,315	25,945	802	300	83	171	+2·2	—4·6	—4·4	—2·6	+3·5	—6·1
18. Allahabad	183,914	12,118	776	347	133	217	+9·4	—1·8	—0·2	—8·4	+17·0	+14·9
19. Madura	182,018	22,555	985	444	94	185	+18·5	+21·2	+26·6	+2·8	+31·0	+146·6
20. Srinagar	173,573	15,779	831	174	14	24§	..	+3·1	+3·0	+12·2	+22·5	+46·0¶
21. Patna	159,690	10,646	731	305	86	193	—3·2	—18·4	+1·0	—11·9	+33·1	—6·42
22. Mandalay	147,932	5,917	905	704†	390†	100§	..	—2·6	—24·8	+7·7	—0·7	—21·7¶
23. Sholapur	144,654	*	885	254†	48†	313†§	+3·4	+21·6	—18·5	+94·9	+21·0	+141·5
24. Jaipur	144,179	48,060	850	218	32	45	+11·4	+0·9	—14·4	—12·3	+19·9	+1·1
25. Bareilly	144,031	17,652	842	227	62	178	+6·7	+8·4	—2·8	—0·0	+11·3	+25·1
26. Trichinopoly	142,843	17,657	957	485	152	217	+7·3	+15·6	+17·9	—2·5	+18·6	+69·1
27. Dacca	138,518	23,086	745	444	261	75‖	+4·1	+10·0	+21·0	+10·0	+16·0	+76·8
28. Meerut	136,709	18,749	750	266	108	267	+19·9	—1·1	—1·6	+5·1	+11·5	+36·8
29. Indore	127,327	14,147	734	348	98	957	..	+4·5	—48·2	+107·1	+36·8	+53·4¶
30. Jubbulpore	124,382	7,897	796	357	109	399§	+11·0	+7·0	+11·0	+8·0	+14·0	+64·0
31. Peshawar	121,866	13,801	607	235†	67†	154†	+5·3	+13·0	+2·9	+6·7	+16·7	+52·4
32. Ajmer	119,524	7,031	811	322	95	435	+41·3	+7·3	+16·8	+31·7	+5·3	+145·2
33. Multan	119,457	9,084	754	200	33	363	+8·6	+17·2	+13·6	—14·5	+40·9	+73·9
34. Rawalpindi	119,284	9,527	570	326	64	617	+39·3	+18·8	—1·4	+16·9	+17·9	+125·2
35. Baroda	112,860	10,964	799	496	184	383	+9·3	—10·8	—4·3	—4·7	+19·2	+6·0
36. Moradabad	110,562	29,020	802	205	75	137	+5·1	+3·0	+8·0	+1·9	+33·7	+59·5
37. Tinnevelly with Palamcottah	109,068	11,314	1,098	458	108	30	+5·5	+84·1	+12·1	+11·9	+8·6	+164·8
38. Mysore	107,142	10,714	887	420	173	169§	÷22·8	+8·0	+4·7	+17·7	+27·6	+77·7
39. Salem	102,179	23,065	973	339	72	67	+33·6	+4·3	—16·2	—11·7	+95·6	+101·7

* Not available. † For municipality only. ‡ For Delhi and New Delhi Cities only. § Born outside the district in which the city lies. ‖ Born outside the province in which the city lies. ¶ 1891—1931. ** For Poona City Taluka.

Only seven of the above cities have more than 400,000 inhabitants, and these will be mentioned severally below. Of the rest it must be pointed out that the figures for Ahmadabad are more or less conjectural. That city determined on a boycott of the census in conformity with the Congress programme and the opposition was so well organised that a complete census could not be taken. Like other cities in Gujarat it consists largely of *pōls*, that is of blind alleys tenanted by a caste community having their own outer gate which affords the only access to the individual houses in that particular block. These *pōls* shut and barred their doors on census night and defied the enumerators to enter. With the aid of police an entry was forced into many of the non-cooperating *pōls*, but even then the obstruction to and interference with the enumerators was continuous and most of the inhabitants remained out of doors in the streets, making the taking of a census impossible in many parts of the city. As it was, the census was carried out effectively in six out of 24 wards. In the other 18 wards the census was partially carried out with varying degrees of incompleteness. The total figures obtained by count were therefore much short of the total population figures given in Table IV, in which the figures formed represent a conservative estimate of the total population by sex, the actual figures obtained by enumeration appearing in Table V.

The Ahmadabad Municipality have since taken a census of their own (in July 1932), and though the result cannot be officially recognized and came too late to make possible a revision of our 1931 estimate, there is no reason to suppose that it is not substantially correct and it is certainly more likely to be accurate than the estimate adopted for the India Tables; the population figure according to the municipal census is 382,768.

Calcutta.

42. The City of Calcutta includes the municipality of Calcutta, with the military area of Fort William, the Port and Calcutta Canal area, the two suburban municipalities of Tollygunge and South Suburban and the municipality of Howrah west of the Hugli river linked to Calcutta by a bridge that has been inadequate now for many decades. In addition to its permanent inhabitants Calcutta City contains by day a temporary population, which comes in to work and returns at night to homes outside, of not less than 26,000 (the number of season tickets in force on local railways on the night of the census) and probably of well over 30,000, for many 'buses serve the municipalities north of Howrah. One of Calcutta's wards, Muchipara, contains a population of over 80,000 and there are nine more with from over 40,000 to over 79,000 inhabitants. The average density of Calcutta municipality is 37,120 persons per square mile, and for the whole of the city east of Hugli it is 19,840, while Howrah has a density of 22,400 per square mile. In the centre of Calcutta the highest density is reached in six wards which have 112,000 per square mile or over, while there are another five with over 100,000. The increase during the decade was 11·1 per cent. in Calcutta proper, 15·2 per cent. in Howrah and 16·3 in the suburban municipalities, figures however which barely reach the half of the increase that took place between 1891 and 1901 in the case of Calcutta and Howrah. Of the city's total population of 1,485,582, 998,656 were born in Bengal; the two provinces contributing most heavily to the immigrant population are Bihar and Orissa, 264,332, and the United Provinces, 143,345, Rajputana coming next with 16,273. The latter immigrants are mainly traders with their dependants. The number of females per 1,000 males for the whole population is 490, but among immigrants taken alone there are only 236 females to every 1,000 males, and there are actually more females (361) per 1,000 males among immigrants from outside India then there are among immigrants from other Indian provinces. In every 10,000 of each sex 4,302 males are literate and 1,213 females, and the corresponding figures for literacy in English are 2,191 and 832. The population of Calcutta City includes

Calcutta.	Area in acres.	Population.	Density per acre.	Variation in Population per cent. 1921 to 1931.	Variation in Population per cent. 1881 to 1931.	Variation in Density per acre. 1921 to 1931.	Variation in Density per acre. 1881 to 1931.
City of Calcutta	**46,655**	**1,485,582**	**32**	**+11·9**	**+179·2**	**+4**	**+14**
Calcutta Municipality	11,954	1,158,044	58	+9·8	+200·5	+6	+25
Fort William and Maidan.	1,283	3,083	2	+11·9	—7·7	..	—1
Port	7,040	33,702	5	+82·7	+12·3	+2	+1
Canals	270	1,905	7	+127·0	—36·6	+4	—4
Suburban	12,617	63,975	6	+16·3	+63·2	+1	+3
Tollygunge	*4,137*	*24,476*	*6*	*+13·1*	*+90·8*	*+1*	*+3*
South Suburban	*8,480*	*39,499*	*5*	*+18·4*	*+49·6*	*+1*	*+2*
Howrah	6,464	224,873	35	+15·2	+245·8	+5	+21

16,234 persons of European race, 746 Armenians, 579 Japanese and 3,046 Chinese. Of those of European race 1,256 are non-British subjects. Anglo-Indians number 18,469.

Bombay.

43. Bombay City includes the main island occupied by the town together with the four islands in the harbour, *viz.*, Cross Island, Middle Ground, Oyster Rock and Butcher Island. Its area has increased by some 415 acres since 1921, as a result of the Back Bay reclamation. The census was taken by the Executive Health Officer, under the general supervision of the Census Superintendent, in circumstances of considerable difficulty on account of the civil disobedience movement, and showed a population of 1,161,383. The Bombay-born population, which was only 16 per cent. in 1921, has gone up according to the figures of birthplace to 24·6 per cent., but there is some doubt as to whether the returns are accurate in this respect. On the other hand an increase was to be expected as a result of the absence of much of the periodic migratory population. Immigrants from Portuguese India number some 39,000, an increase of over 4,500, but Europeans have fallen from 13,544 in 1921 to 8,400 in 1931, 1,009 of whom are non-British subjects. This fall in number is largely but not entirely attributable to a reduction in the number of British troops. A very high proportion of the Bombay population, 20·4 per cent., is drawn from the Ratnagiri District farther down the coast. As in other cities—Rangoon for instance—there is a disproportionate number of persons in the age groups from 20 to 40, and the female ratio, though higher than at any census since 1901, is excessively low, being only 554 females to every 1,000 males, though the ratio in the city-born population is 728. The percentage of literacy has increased from 23 to 24 only, but that of literacy in English from 8 to 11·6. The only industry conducted on any large scale in Bombay is that of cotton textiles; shipping, including both owners and employed, brokers, mariners, boatmen, etc., only accounts for 25 per mille of the total following occupations of all classes. The mean density of the Town and Island in 1931 was 48,000 persons per square mile, a decrease on the density figure of 1921, probably to be accounted for by the absence in certain areas of the floating cold weather population owing to the trade depression. In most parts of the city, however, the density is very much greater than the mean figure. In the Kamathipura quarter it is 385,280 per square mile, in Nagpada II it is 407,040 and in the Kumbharwada quarter 465,280 persons per square mile. At least 36 per cent. of the population of the city suffer from gross overcrowding. Of all tenements 81 per cent. are one-roomed and the average number of persons to each of those rooms is 4·01, but that gives little notion of the congestion at its worst, for 256,379 persons live in rooms occupied by 6 to 9 persons each, 80,133 in rooms of 10 to 19 persons each and 15,490 in rooms occupied by 20 or more persons to each room. These alone comprise between them 30 per cent. of the city's population, and it can hardly be imagined that all those living at the density of less than 6 to one room are free from overcrowding, and 74 per cent. of the city's population—close on 800,000 persons that is, live in one-roomed tenements. Byculla, Sewri, Mazagaon, Parel and Nagpada II are the worst quarters, and 99 per cent. of Byculla's population live in one-roomed tenements; in Mazagaon, where 88 per cent. live thus, the average number per room is 4·95. For the vast majority of Bombay's population the available floor space per head is about six foot square, and while very few of Bombay's population live in tenements of as many as three rooms "there is greater pressure on the floor space of three-roomed tenements than there is on the floor space of one-roomed tenements in London". Bombay is, therefore, to be congratulated that her population has at any rate fallen by 1·2 per cent. since 1921; probably the missing population is to be congratulated likewise.

Figures of housing congestion in Bombay City.

Number of rooms per tenement.	Number of tenements.	Per cent.	Number of occupants.	Per cent. of population.	Average per room.
1 room ..	197,516	81	791,762	74	4·01
2 rooms ..	26,231	11	131,872	12	2·51
3 rooms ..	7,416	3	44,821	4	2·01
4 rooms ..	6,169	2	42,013	4	1·70
5 rooms ..	2,953	1	22,302	2	1·50
6 and over	3,836	2	39,199	4	..

Madras.

44. The growth of the third presidency town has in the past been very much slower than that of Calcutta or Bombay. There was some growth between 1881 and 1901 after which the population increased little during the next two decades.

The last decade however has shown almost double any previous recorded decennial increase. This amounted to 22·8% as compared to 1·6 and 1·8 during the previous decade and the one before that respectively. Industrial development has been marked and the tariffs have enabled the creation of pencil, match and tobacco factories, *biris* being made and exported in some quantity. Communications within the city have been much improved and an extension to the south-west has added a populous and growing suburb of the garden-city type. Nevertheless Madras still has a higher number of persons per occupied house than any other town in the presidency, having 877 persons per 100 occupied census houses, a congestion on one aspect of which the Census Superintendent is quoted in paragraph 51 below. The actual state of congestion varies much between the true city area and the residential suburbs. Two-fifths of Madras' wards have 64,000 persons to the square mile.

45. Hyderabad City, the capital of H. E. H. the Nizam's Dominions, covers an area of some 53 to 54 sq. miles and includes not only the city proper but its suburbs, the Hyderabad Cantonment, the Residency area and the Secunderabad Cantonment with Bolarum and Trimulgherry. The area occupied has doubled since 1901 but the population is now little more than it was at that census, although it was returned as over half a million in 1911. The mean density is 8,809 to the square mile, but rises to 9,956 for the total area within the walled city, while the various wards and suburbs vary from 3,692 persons per sq. mile in the *Berun* ward VII to 65,141 in the *Andarun* ward IV, the three other *Andarun* wards varying from 22,623 per sq. mile to just over 38,000. It may be added that the density of *Andarun* ward IV appears to have decreased by 47% since 1901. The activities of the City Improvement Board and the demand for large buildings for Government offices, colleges, etc., are reported to be causing a great shortage of house accommodation in the city *Andarun*, which is leading to a gradual movement of population from the walled city to the suburbs. During the decade plague has been recurrent in most winters, radiating "from the congested grain markets to the outskirts of the City; cholera, small-pox and the perennial malaria were additional causes of ill-health". The city Improvement Board has cleared away part of the "crowded and insanitary slums" opening out fresh suburban sites on which— **Hyderabad.**

"new roads were laid out, drains constructed and rat-proof houses built and rented to some of the poor who were dishoused. The well-to-do have moved out into the open country round about the City and built houses for themselves. Government very generously advanced loans to its officers for building houses. Thus the City has expanded in area, the continuity of houses in some directions reaching distant villages of certain adjacent taluks. Extension of roads to the new areas, facilitating motor service and improvement of suburban railway communications, have not only brought distant mohallas within easy reach of city dwellers but also helped them to develop urban characteristics. Drainage for carrying sewage and storm water has been laid and numerous disused wells which bred mosquitoes closed down. The health of the City has thereby much improved."

46. Delhi's period of growth starts from 1911 when it became the Capital of India. As a City it must be held to include Old Delhi City and the Notified Area adjoining it, New Delhi, the New Delhi Cantonment and the suburb of Shahdara. The latter suburb is across the Jamna, but is hardly more cut off from the two main urban areas than is the Cantonment, and houses a considerable number of persons whose daily employment is in Delhi proper. The population varies very greatly between winter and summer, and the census was taken when the population was almost at the maximum. An idea of the extent of the seasonal fluctuation in numbers is given by the marginal figures, though there is some change also in those of the Fort and Cantonment and probably too of Shahdara. The congestion in Old Delhi Municipality to which reference has already been made in paragraph 19 (Chapter I) is to some extent relieved during the summer by the migration of appreciable numbers of the inhabitants of the Old Town to the empty quarters in New Delhi whose occupants have moved up to Simla for the hot weather or returned to their homes in other parts of India. The excessive density of Old Delhi Municipality (58,273 persons per sq. mile) has been mentioned; that of New **Delhi.**

Delhi.	Winter Population.	Approximate Summer population.
Old Delhi Municipality .	347,500	300,000
Old Delhi Notified Area .	16,300	10,000
New Delhi . . .	64,900	30,000

Delhi is 1,524 per sq. mile and of Shahdara 6,120. Taking the whole of the city there are 454 persons to every 100 census houses, but this number rises to 473 in Old Delhi Municipality and to 629 in its Churi Walan ward, while the Qarol Bagh ward has 605 and the lowest average is 399 per 100 houses in the Lothian Road ward. Generally speaking the overcrowding is by no means as bad as that in many other cities of India, but partly perhaps as the result of an inadequate water supply the death-rate in a heat wave is serious. The population of Delhi City as a whole has nearly doubled since 1911.

Lahore.

47. The City of Lahore, the capital of the Punjab, includes a municipality and a cantonment covering together an area of over 39 sq. miles and containing a population which has increased by 52·5 per cent. since 1921 and now amounts to 429,747, of which slightly over 400,000 occupy the old walled city and the town and civil station outside it. Inside the walled city there are 176,792 persons living at a density of 198,500 per sq. mile. The increase in population during the last decade has naturally taken place outside the walls, and a chain of dwellings now links the civil station to the cantonment. More than half the inhabitants were born outside the city, and nearly half were born outside Lahore district. Growth has been very rapid since 1881 (187·7%).

Rangoon.

48. The City of Rangoon includes both municipal and cantonment areas and the Port of Rangoon part of which is outside the former. The population has increased from 341,962 in 1921 to 400,415, but part of this increase is due to the extension of the city limits, and the increase since 1921 on the whole area now included is 15·9 per cent. If the adventitious population numbering 22,317 at this census, and including the floating population of the port, inmates of jail, etc., be excluded at both censuses, the decennial increase becomes 17·7 per cent. The density of the city is 16,146 persons to the square mile. The population is largely immigrant with a consequent disproportion in the numbers living at age groups 20 to 40 and in the ratio of females to males. Thus of the Telugus in Rangoon, mostly unskilled labourers, two-thirds are found in age groups 20 to 40, and there are only 20 females per 100 males, an inequality of ratio still more pronounced among Oriyas with 7 and Chittagonians with 2 females to every 100 males. Of every 1,000 persons in Rangoon 509 come from outside Burma of whom more than 450 are Indians, while the total Indian population is 532 per 1,000. Seven and a half per cent. are Chinese and about 4 per cent. European or Anglo-Indian. Nearly one half (496 per mille) were actually born either in India or China and little over a third (351 per mille) in Rangoon itself. Of males alone 633 per mille were born outside Burma, while in the case of females on the other hand 750 per mille were Burma-born. Owing to the small proportion of females to males for the whole population the deaths exceed the births by an amount, according to the vital statistics, of about 46,000, so that the increase of 55,000 during the decade implies an immigration figure of 100,000 during the same period, if the vital statistics can be trusted. The total female ratio has however been rising, being now 48 per 100 males compared to 41 in 1911, and the proportion of foreign born has fallen from 583 per mille in 1911 to the present figure of 509.

Population of Rangoon.

Race.	Numbers.	Females per 100 males.
Burmese	121,998	100
Karens	3,226	100
Other indigenous	2,358	80
Indo-Burmese	12,560	105
Indians	212,929	24
Chinese	30,626	54
Anglo-Indians	9,977	97
Europeans	4,426	53
Others	2,315	71
Total	400,415	48

Rural Population.

49. The distribution between a town and a village however arbitrary is easily effected on a numerical basis, but the definition of the village as a unit is by no means always so easy. As has already been indicated, the thickly populated parts of the Malabar Coast and of Bengal are often occupied by a series of homesteads, which may be grouped in villages for administrative purposes but which do not thereby acquire any of the characteristics of the compact determinate village of Upper India, leaving it difficult to say where one village ends and another begins. The *mauza*, on the other hand, which is the revenue unit, is rather administrative than geographical and may consist of quite separate hamlets or even contain no houses at all. In the hills the conditions are generally the reverse of those in the plains ; that is, where the population is thickest it is found in concentrated villages, as on the N. E. Frontier, whereas when very thin it seems to be spread about in isolated homesteads or scattered hamlets as in the Simla Hills. In Baluchistan, where a large proportion of the population is still more or less migratory, villages are becoming more scattered as the need for defence ceases to be felt. This indeterminate nature of the village unit, which may be a definite residential site, walled or palisaded, or may be an administrative unit containing several residential villages or a number of scattered houses, impairs the significance of the figures of the population as distributed in villages of various sizes. Population, for instance, shown as residing in a village of 2,000 to 5,000 persons may really be the population of a *mauza* containing several small residential villages of less than 500 persons each, whereas a number of villages of less than 500 may really be contiguous hamlets of scattered houses that might just as well be shown as one large village. Generally speaking, however, it may be said that of the total population of India 89 per cent is rural, more than half lives in villages with a population of under 1,000 and nearly one-third (27·6 per cent) lives in villages with a population of under 500 persons.

Houses and Families.

50. Ambiguity has characterised the terms, 'town' and 'village' and it attaches again to the term 'house'. The term 'house' in India covers the greatest diversity of dwellings. The portable screens of bamboo matting carried on a gipsy's ass, or the camel-borne tent of a Bugti nomad are less primitive than the mere foliage wind screens of some of the Andamanese but still hardly conforming to the usual conception of a dwelling-house, though this term can fairly be applied to the conical grass huts of the Chenchu and the Bhil and still more to the thatched and matwalled dwellings, often on piles or in trees, erected in the hills alike of Assam and of Travancore. In Bengal the thatched roof is hogbacked to increase the resistance of the gables to the rooflifting cyclone, while on the west coast the typical Nayar house has picturesquely cocked gables on a very steeply pitched tiled roof the better to resist the torrential rain. Indeed the houses of the well-to-do in Malabar are built round an open *impluvium* on to which a pillared verandah opens giving access to all the rooms, one of which is reserved as in an ancient Roman house for the *lares* and *penates*. In Upper India on the other hand, the mud wall and flat roof of a dry climate prevail, while the rich surround their houses of brick or stone with a walled enclosure and ensure privacy by the greatest economy in windows. Almost everywhere the tendency is apparent towards the replacement of traditional roofing materials by corrugated iron sheeting as ugly as ubiquitous.

If the house may vary from the *chawl* dwelling of a large town to a sprawling *bari* in the country, so too the family is a difficult unit to define in correspondence to the house. Apart from the collective houses of some of the hill tribes which accommodate all the bachelors or spinsters of the village, a Bengal *bari* may house a joint family of several married couples in contrast for instance to the Assam hill custom whereby the elder sons, or in some tribes the elder daughters, set up new houses for themselves or, as in other cases, turn their parents out of the ancestral home to build a house for themselves elsewhere. It was therefore necessary to define the house for census purposes, since a house is far from being a constant unit ; and generally speaking a census house meant the buildings, several, one, or part of one, inhabited by one family, that is by a number of persons living and eating together in one mess with their resident dependants and their servants residing in the house. Even this wide definition proved difficult to apply universally, as it is defeated by the Santal, for instance, whose married sons have entirely separate establishments but resort to their father's house for meals. In the case of town houses it was generally provided that the house for census purposes should be taken as any part of an inhabited building with a separate entrance, which is in practical conformity with the definition of a house given above. The marginal table gives the number of persons per house and houses per sq. mile in India at successive censuses. Figures for the provinces and states are given in subsidiary table VI at the end of

Census.	Persons per house.	Houses per sq. mile.
1881	5·8	31·7
1891	5·4	33·9
1901	5·2	31·6
1911	4·9	35·8
1921	4·9	36·1
1931	5·0	39·3

chapter I. The comparability of the figures of different censuses is to some extent vitiated by changes in the definition of a house, as the structural definition adopted in 1872 has gradually given way to the social one given above, but has not yet been uniformly accepted or rejected by all provinces and states.

Pressure of Population upon Housing.

51. It has already been indicated that city dwelling is not generally congenial to the Indian, and indeed since India is primarily an agricultural country it could hardly be expected that a high proportion of its population would be found in towns. The Census Superintendent for Mysore State quotes a Kanarese proverb "after ruin go to the city", which is sufficiently expressive of the general disposition towards a town life, though it is somewhat typical of the Gujarati and of the Tamil to show a greater inclination towards a town life than most Indian races. It is however to the general absence of such an inclination and to the general absence of industrial activity that the slow growth of urbanization is to be imputed. There are only 39 cities of over 100,000 inhabitants in the whole of the Indian Empire, and the general growth of the urban population has been 20%, while 10% has been that of the rural, although the city of Bombay has actually decreased in population during the decade. On the other hand there has been a very rapid growth in some towns. While Calcutta has increased by 12 per cent., Rangoon by 17 per cent., Madras by 23 per cent., Karachi by 23 per cent. and several other cities by 20 per cent. or a little over, Patna has increased by 33 per cent., Delhi City by 40 per cent., Bangalore City by 45 per cent., Nagpur by 48 per cent., Lahore by 53 per cent. Amritsar by 65 per cent. and Salem by 96 per cent.* The number of occupied houses has not generally increased in proportion to the population though that is not to say that it has not increased proportionately to the number of families, since much of the increase must have been counted in children, while in some cases, *e.g.*, Bangalore Civil and Military Station, houses have increased at a greater rate than the population. At the same time there is very serious congestion in many towns, and the density of urban population is in some cases almost as excessive by western standards as is the density of rural population in the more fertile areas. Thus the density of Belfast County Borough is 17,984 persons per square mile (1926) and the average density of a London County Borough (1931) is 37,568 persons to the square mile, a density which reaches its maximum in Southwark with 97,088 to the square mile. Leith (1931) has 35,000 persons per square mile and the Govan ward of Glasgow, its most densely populated in 1931, has 36,230. With these figures we may compare, the densities of Lahore with 10,913 persons to the square mile, of Peshawar City with 22,830 and of Calcutta with 36,265 ; while half a dozen towns in the United Provinces, including the city of Moradabad, show a municipal density of from 40,000 to 45,000, Bombay has 48,000, Delhi City (Municipality) has 58,273, and Sikandrabad, a small town in the United Provinces, has 63,552 persons per square mile. But if smaller units be taken the densities found are much higher. Two-fifths of the wards of Madras show a density of 64,000 persons to the square mile ; two-thirds of Madura's wards show a density of 64,000 and one ward that of 125,000; three wards of Peshawar have densities of 121,600, 131,840 and 188,800 per sq. mile respectively ; the old walled city of Lahore contains a population of 177,000 persons living at a density of 198,500 per square mile, and although nine-tenths of Lucknow shows a density of under 32,000, parts of the Yahiaganj ward of that town have a density of 423,000 to the square mile. The Kumbharwada quarter of Bombay has 465,280 persons to the square mile. In Cawnpore there is a substantial area with a density of over 100,000 and in Chak No. 95 Talaq Mahal of Anwarganj ward in that city the density of 786,560 persons per square mile is reached.

It is necessary in this connection to consider the size of families and the extent to which they are crowded into single rooms. It must not be forgotten that houses of more than two storeys are probably rather the exception than the rule in Indian urban areas, while even in towns one-storied houses are perhaps even more plentiful than those of two. Thus of the total number of 24,579 structures in Baroda City 10,653 had one storey only, and those with more than two storeys numbered only 3,699, while of the houses in Bombay three in five have only one storey, and in Karachi 77·6%. The definition of a house must likewise be borne in mind, and this in urban areas generally depended on the existence of a separate entrance rather

* In both 1911 and 1921 plague had caused an exodus from Salem.

than of a separate building. The average size of a family is a third important factor. This works out in Lucknow for instance at 4·6 persons but over 14 per cent. of families were found to have 8 or more members. In Travancore the average number of persons in a household is 5·5 and in Rajputana it is 4·7. In Cawnpore the average family consists of 3·5 only, but that is due to the presence of large numbers of industrial workers who leave their wives and children at their homes in villages. Industrial workers form a very small minority of the urban population, and it seems that taking India as a whole the average family contains from four to five individuals. When therefore it is seen that in Delhi, for instance, the average number of persons per 1,000 houses varies according to the ward from 399 to 629 it seems likely that most families get a census house to themselves. Madras on the other hand has 877 persons per 100 houses, Rajahmundry 793, Mangalore 727, Madura 723, Vellore 709 and three more towns more than the maximum average of any ward in Delhi. It is not possible that these figures should represent a distribution of a house per family. Of Madras itself, however, the Census Superintendent writes as follows :—

> " A marked feature of Madras is the street-dweller and squatter. A midnight tour of the central and northern parts of the town any fine night would disclose sleeping persons on every sidewalk. These persons are not all tramps by any means ; the majority indeed are ordinary citizens in everything but the possession of a roof. Such a possession has no great inducement for a population of floating labour in a mild and pleasant climate, in a city where houses are scarce and rents often exorbitant. The figure for Madras may be indicative of a higher number of persons per dwelling than is desirable but before it could be taken as an accurate guide, the street-dwellers and squatters would have to be deducted from the total population used in striking the average. Madura's figure involves to some extent a similar qualification, for to this sacred city of the south wanderers resort in large numbers throughout the year ".

It would be unsafe however to regard this factor as operative in the case of the other towns mentioned, though it is undoubtedly indicative of one factor which distinguishes overcrowding in the east from that in Britain, that is the greater extent to which an open-air life is possible, since weather conditions which compel retreat within doors are very much less prevalent. In Bombay the overcrowding is so great that men have to sleep out wherever possible, and in the monsoon, when the pavement is impossible, verandahs, alley-ways and stairs are all crowded with slumberers.

We have now to return to the census house. This is normally the dwelling of a commensal family, and in towns is usually determined by the existence of a separate entrance, but it very often implies no more than a single room like one of the small compartments provided for servants in the compounds of larger houses. The small size of such rooms may be judged from the density of the population when considered with the absence of lofty houses. A one-roomed tenement in Bombay normally varies from about 10×10 feet to about 12×15 feet, and the average per room is more than four persons, who have therefore each on the average from 5 to 7 square feet of floor space, but in the most congested areas the available space per person is far less than this ; and the following is quoted, with regard to the housing congestion in the Kolar Gold Field, from the Mysore State Census Report :—

Overcrowding in Bombay City.

Number of persons in seven wards living			Percentage of total population living 6 and over per room.
6–9 per room.	10–19 per room.	20 and over per room.	
256,300	79,000	15,500	26·4

> " The standard size of a single room hut is, generally speaking, 9 feet by 9 feet except in Mysore Mine lines where it is 12 feet by 9 feet. In Balaghat, it is 10 feet by 9 feet .... There is a good deal of overcrowding. The following table gives some idea of its extent. It will be seen that there is one instance of three families occupying a single hut and 235 cases of two families living in one hut. One hundred and twenty-five of these huts are the 9 feet ones and the remainder

Total number of huts.	One family.	Two families.	Three families.	Less than four persons.	4 to 6 persons.	6 to 8 persons.	8 to 10 persons.	More than 10 persons.
Single room huts, 6,827	6,591	235	1	3,440	3,522	749	106	10
Single room huts with kitchen or verandah, 1,850	1,734	110	·6	582	668	461	107	32

12 feet by 9 feet. In 42 cases, families of more than ten persons live in one hut with or without kitchen; over 850 single-room huts are occupied by six or more persons per hut".

Matters are even worse elsewhere. Thus the Census Superintendent for the United Provinces :—

" In Lucknow Municipality no less than 670 families of 8 persons or over are living each family in a single room, and...... a further 1,931 families of this size live each in 2 rooms. The corresponding figures for Cawnpore are 323 and 552 respectively. In the margin are given for Lucknow and Cawnpore the distribution of families according to the number of rooms they occupy. The commonest unit of occupation is one room, half the families in Lucknow and nearly two-thirds the families in Cawnpore falling into this group. In Lucknow 90 per cent. of families live in 3 rooms or less, and in Cawnpore this figure reaches 95 per cent ".

Municipality.	Percentage of families who live in— 1 room.	2 rooms.	3 rooms.	4 rooms.	5 or more rooms.
Lucknow . .	50·4	28·9	10·7	5·2	4·8
Cawnpore .. .	62·5	24·8	7·5	2·9	2·3

City.	Percentage of families occupying tenements of— 1 room.	2 rooms.	3 rooms.	4 rooms.	5 or more rooms.
Baroda . .	24·1	27·8	10·6	14·6	22·9

Percentage of families in London administrative county occupying

1 room.	2 rooms.	3 rooms.	4 rooms.	5 or more rooms.
12·2	21·5	25·1	18·4	22·8

Bombay, as we have seen (paragraph 43 above), is far worse still, but Baroda is decidedly better as the marginal figures show. With these figures we may compare the number of rooms occupied by families in the County of London in 1931 figures of which are given in the marginal table. The average family in this case is composed of 3·5 persons, the same size as that of Cawnpore.

By way of contrast to conditions in Bombay, Lucknow and Cawnpore the account of Jamshedpur given by the Census Superintendent for Bihar and Orissa is worth quoting :—

" The industrial city of Jamshedpur is quite unlike any other city or town in the province—or indeed in the whole of India .... To all intents and purposes Jamshedpur is a proprietary town of the Company, owned and administered by them, and its people enjoy the benefits of this highly efficient municipal government without paying any rates whatsoever. The town is administered through a Board of Works, consisting of representatives of the Steel Company and subsidiary companies, with two members of the general public : and the funds required for maintaining the municipal services, such as roads, water-supply, sewage, street lights, hospitals, schools, etc., are contributed by these companies in fixed proportions about Rs. 40,000 by the subsidiary concerns and the rest by Tata's........... Among the more important developments of the last ten years, brief mention may be made of the following. The *pukka* quarters built by the Company for its employees have doubled in number, from 2,756 to 5,483, while the houses and huts constructed by the employees and others have increased from 400 to 8,150. The supply of filtered domestic water is three times as great as it was in 1921, and there are now 60 miles of water-mains and 56 miles of drainage sewers. Provision for medical relief has been extended and improved, and in the main hospital there is at present accommodation for 140 indoor patients as against 42 at the beginning of the decade. In addition to the formerly existing high school and primary schools, three middle English schools and 22 other schools have been opened .... Since the previous census was taken, the population of Jamshedpur has grown from 57,360 to 83,738—an increase of no less than 46 per cent.....................This city furnishes a striking contrast to other urban units of the province. There is no congestion in Jamshedpur, and special care is taken to prevent the growth of slums and unhygienic bazars. Although the number of houses has increased by 100 per cent. since 1921, there are still less than 1,000 houses per square mile, whereas in the other three cities the average is over 2,000. And ....the number of persons occupying each house is exceptionally low in Jamshedpur ".

This however is a solitary case and though there are Improvement Trusts in the larger cities they have much to do before they can do away with congestion. Moreover India differs from Europe in that conditions of overcrowding are probably as bad or worse in villages. The marginal figures for England and Wales in 1921 indicate the difference between urban and rural conditions in the matter of overcrowding in Britain. Northern Ireland, a poorer country, shows rather different figures, but in India "if village densities were calculated on the area of the inhabited site or sites, and not on that of the site *plus* the village lands, they would generally be greater than that of any town". This from the United Provinces report, but the Census Superintendent for Madras says just the same:—

England and Wales, 1921.	Percentage of families occupying				
	1 room.	2 rooms.	3 rooms.	4 rooms.	5 rooms or more.
Urban . .	6·2	13·6	17·7	22·7	39·8
Rural . . .	0·7	6·2	13·3	26·8	53·0

Northern Ireland, 1926.	1 room.	2 rooms.	3 rooms.	4 rooms.	5 rooms or more.
Urban . .	3·1	9·0	12·6	36·9	38·4
Rural . . .	2·3	21·2	24·1	22·3	30·1

"It is by no means sure however that the worst specimens of housing in the presidency do not come from certain rural areas, notably the wealthy delta tracts on the circars coast and in Tanjore. Where land is dear, housing tends to be bad and land fetches a notable value in delta districts where irrigation is assured. Every foot of ground is grudged to the village-site and even a comparatively well-to-do landowner will exist in an almost squalor that surprises the stranger. If this is so with an actual owner of land it can be imagined what is the condition of the farm labourer who in many cases also belongs to the so-called depressed classes. In Tanjore, these last form the backbone of the agricultural labouring population and are even yet little removed from a state of agrestic serfdom. One of the most commendable and valuable activities of the Madras Labour Department during the decade has been the compulsory acquisition of sites on which houses could be built for these people and they be introduced to something approaching decent conditions of livelihood.....................In every country poverty and bad housing go together. This is so in India but a further element enters by the presence of the depressed classes. These people are forced in the villages and often even in towns to live in a hamlet apart. Its site is rarely the most attractive and space is grudged. Little interest is taken in the community and its habitat is rarely visited. A lack of public spirit or ordinary hopefulness is an almost inevitable consequence of such treatment and this added to the other elements tending to produce squalor has the result that the 'paracheris' of this presidency may safely be counted upon to produce its worst examples of housing".

SUBSIDIARY TABLE I.

Distribution of the Population between Towns and Villages.

Province, State or Agency.	Average Population per Town.	Average Population per Village.	Number per mille residing in: Towns.	Number per mille residing in: Villages.	Number per mille of urban population residing in towns with a population of— 20,000 and over.	10,000 to 20,000	5,000 to 10,000	Under 5,000	Number per mille of rural population residing in villages with a population of— 5,000 and over.	2,000 to 5,000	500 to 5,000	Under 500.
1	2	3	4	5	6	7	8	9	10	11	12	13
INDIA ..	**15,140**	**450·4**	**110·5**	**889·5**	**573**	**191**	**179**	**57**	**17**	**123**	**443**	**417**
Provinces ..	**17,466·3**	**484·4**	**109·3**	**890·7**	**618**	**185**	**159**	**38**	**24**	**144**	**485**	**347**
Ajmer-Merwara	36,039·8	508·8	321·6	678·4	939	..	40	21	..	217	482	301
Andaman and Nicobar Islands.	..	123·3	..	1000·0	..	..	..	..	..	135	348	517
Assam	8,218·3	255·8	26·6	973·4	280	289	284	147	2	37	389	572
Baluchistan	7,668·8	260·7	198·5	801·5	655	..	104	241	57	86	419	438
Bengal	26,506	536·0	73·5	926·5	736	171	74	19	49	208	472	271
Bihar and Orissa ..	21,203·0	431·9	43·9	956·1	631	223	143	3	13	70	425	492
Bombay†	22,906·0	637·4	224	776	686	150	145	19	33	189	561	217
Burma	16,522·1	405·9	103·6	896·4	594	147	221	38	10	164	603	223
Central Provinces and Berar	15,075·6	347·6	108·9	891·1	483	268	230	19	2	55	412	531
Coorg	4,913·5	406·1	60·2	939·8	..	..	610	390	..	..	561	438
Delhi	74,573·7	615	703·3	296·7	922	36	42	..	28	120	595	257
Madras	18,639	784·7	135·6	864·4	574	247	173	6	79	328	469	124
North West Frontier Province (*Districts and Administered Territories*).	14,302·9	720·5	159·2	840·8	607	131	249	13	49	292	479	180
Punjab	15,414·4	592·4	130·1	869·9	618	152	183	47	39	167	531	263
United Provinces of Agra and Oudh.	12,300·7	406·9	112·1	887·9	550	167	171	112	6	90	528	376
States and Agencies ..	**10,628·3**	**364·5**	**114·5**	**885·4**	**431**	**210**	**243**	**116**	**10**	**91**	**412**	**487**
Assam States*	85,804	183·7	140·9	859·1	1,000	..	..	..	16	36	436	512
Baluchistan States ..	2,115·4	190·0	26·1	973·9	..	..	..	1,000	..	64	312	624
Baroda State	10,460·1	657·5	214·1	785·9	391	240	273	96	5	206	580	209
Bengal States	5,522	206·4	28·4	971·6	..	429	347	224	27	47	394	532
Bihar and Orissa States ..	6,530·7	237·7	9·8	990·2	..	..	927	73	..	32	265	703
Bombay States	7,499·5	436·9	135·9	864·1	260	196	333	211	18	154	506	322
Central India Agency ..	12,101·3	256·1	102·2	897·8	448	227	236	89	..	57	353	590
Central Provinces States ..	7,506·5	268·8	30·2	969·8	..	519	345	136	..	21	336	643
Gwalior State .. .	9,193·2	288·2	112·2	887·8	391	205	235	169	..	56	398	546
Hyderabad State ..	11,977·6	590·8	112	888	438	212	266	84	79	328	469	124
Jammu and Kashmir State	8,777·3	371·1	93·9	906·1	620	63	81	236	9	71	501	419
Madras States Agency ..	12,137·8	1,256·0	124	876·0	497	237	190	76	§	§	§	§
Cochin State	*17,195*	*3,671·6*	*171·2*	*828·8*	*591*	*264*	*145*	..	*441*	*462*	*95*	*2*
Travancore State ..	*11,995·4*	*1,154·5*	*108·3*	*891·7*	*482*	*241*	*185*	*92*	*111*	*373*	*447*	*69*
Other Madras States ..	*7,216·5*	*743·8*	*175·0*	*825*	*363*	*134*	*337*	*166*	§	§	§	§
Mysore State	9,676·3	334·4	159·4	840·6	519	89	189	203	1	45	460	494
North West Frontier Province (*Agencies and Tribal Areas.*)	..	‡	..	1,000	..	..	..	..	‡	‡	‡	‡
Punjab States	3,633·5	162·2	33·2	966·8	..	..	353	647	..	118	403	479
Punjab States Agency ..	10,219·8	299·8	98·3	901·7	371	302	260	67	11	163	422	404
Rajputana Agency ..	10,733·1	287·0	138·6	861·4	366	239	286	109	3	87	416	494
Sikkim State	..	299·2	..	1,000	..	..	..	..	..	..	330	670
United Provinces States ..	14,015·3	201·4	104·6	895·4	588	99	222	91	..	34	309	657
Western India States Agency	13,390·5	479·6	221	779	472	288	199	41	9	121	527	343

NOTE.—Part of Shillong Town lying in Khasi States has been treated here as lying in British Territory.

* Figures in columns 10—13 relate to Manipur only.

† Excluding Aden.

‡ Figures not available.

§ Included in the British Territory.

SUBSIDIARY TABLE II.

Number per mille of each main religion who live in Towns.

Province, State or Agency.	Number per mille who live in towns.					
	All religions.	Hindu.	Jain.	Zoroastrian.	Muslim.	Christian.
1	2	3	4	5	6	7
INDIA	**111**	**105**	**346**	**891**	**135**	**202**
Provinces	**109**	**106**	**373**	**905**	**121**	**246**
Ajmer-Merwara	322	260	333	997	555	893
Andaman and Nicobar Islands ..	..	..	..	..	..	..
Assam	25	31	334	857	19	17
Baluchistan	199	806	1,000	1,000	107	983
Bengal	74	118	616	888	37	424
Bihar and Orissa	44	40	496	938	88	87
Bombay*	222	203	322	906	249	594
Burma	104	541	831	962	327	217
Central Provinces and Berar ..	109	99	321	934	452	580
Coorg	60	44	602	1,000	178	248
Delhi	703	612	857	1,000	870	655
Madras	136	124	229	957	253	209
North-West Frontier Province .. (*Districts and Administered Territories.*)	159	651	..	1,000	115	934
Punjab	130	178	613	936	122	158
United Provinces of Agra & Oudh	112	79	458	964	289	388
States and Agencies ..	**118**	**101**	**331**	**782**	**224**	**133**
Assam States	164	318	844	1,000	105	105
Baluchistan States	26	90	..	..	24	933
Baroda State	214	191	421	812	444	372
Bengal States	28	35	711	..	14	21
Bihar and Orissa States	10	11	3	..	65	3
Bombay States	136	123	228	264	239	288
Central India Agency	102	80	363	944	475	651
Central Provinces States ..	30	36	495	882	257	27
Gwalior State	112	87	377	933	446	624
Hyderabad State	112	86	285	852	335	173
Jammu and Kashmir State ..	94	135	995	800	83	564
Madras States Agency	124	124	996	938	202	104
Cochin State ..	*171*	*145*	*995*	*1,000*	*210*	*220*
Travancore State	*108*	*113*	*1,000*	*923*	*191*	*81*
Other Madras States ..	*175*	*170*	*1,000*	..	*327*	*83*
Mysore State	159	133	252	976	427	734
North-West Frontier Province .. (*Agencies and Tribal Areas.*)	..	..	..	..	..	..
Punjab States	33	20	507	..	150	44
Punjab States Agency	98	102	488	773	123	252
Rajputana Agency	139	112	308	906	358	572
Sikkim State	..	..	..	..	..	..
United Provinces States ..	105	47	579	..	322	47
Western India States Agency ..	221	174	375	944	442	862

* Excluding Aden.

SUBSIDIARY TABLE III.

Towns classified by Population.

Towns containing a population of :—	India.		Provinces.		States.	
	Number.	Population.	Number.	Population.	Number.	Population.
Total Urban Population ..	**2,575**	**38,985,427**	**1,699**	**29,675,161**	**876**	**9,310,266**
I. 100,000 and over ..	38	9,674,032	29	8,238,808	9	1,435,224
II. 50,000 to 100,000 ..	65	4,572,113	51	3,539,057	14	1,033,056
III. 20,000 to 50,000 ..	268	8,091,288	216	6,551,109	52	1,540,179
IV. 10,000 to 20,000 ..	543	7,449,402	395	5,490,846	148	1,958,556
V. 5,000 to 10,000 ..	987	6,992,832	656	4,733,686	331	2,259,146
VI. Under 5,000 ..	674	2,205,760	352	1,121,655	322	1,084,105

CHAPTER III.

Birth-place and Migration.

Reference to Tables.

52. The first two parts of Table VI, in part ii of this volume, gives details by provinces, states and cities of the number of persons enumerated distributed by their birth-place, and the second part of the same table gives figures of the balance of internal migration. Figures, in so far as they are available in detail, of Indians overseas will be found in the appendix to the same part together with such information as is available of Indians on the high seas at the time the census was taken.

Figures of migration.

53. The figures of migration are generally speaking not of very great importance as affecting the population of the different parts of India, as the fact that the principal occupation of all of India is agriculture militates against any marked movement of population from one part to another. Where the migration figures are high it is generally in the case of small units. Thus Delhi has 41% of immigrants and Ajmer-Merwara 19, while in Ajmer city itself there are nearly as many immigrants as there are native born. In both these cases the migration is the natural result of a movement of labour towards an urban unit, the high rate shown by Delhi being the result of its new growth as a capital city. Two other provinces show a high immigration balance, Assam with 16% and Coorg with 24%. In both these provinces the high rate of immigration is due to the attraction of labourers to plantations of tea in the one case and of coffee in the other. The next highest rate is that of Baluchistan where a large part of the population is naturally migratory. Burma gains 5% by immigrants and Bihar and Orissa loses 4% as emigrants mostly to Assam, after which the percentages fall to about 3% of emigrants in the United Provinces and Madras. It was pointed out by Mr. Jacob in 1921 (*Punjab Census Report,* Chapter III) that it can be shown mathematically that the smaller the unit of population the larger the proportion of persons born elsewhere, and in estimating the significance of migration it is necessary to bear this in mind. India containing nearly one fifth of the world's inhabitants must be expected to show proportionately low figures of migration, and accordingly we find that of the total population enumerated by birthplace, 350½ million odd, less than one million were born elsewhere. Of Indians born in India and found elsewhere at the time of the census no complete figures are of course available, as, though returns of persons of Indian extraction have been obtained from many parts of the British Empire, the number of Indian-born persons resident in foreign countries is unascertainable. It is probable, however, that the number of emigrants from India in other countries at the time of the census amounted to about two and a half millions, the balance of migration being against India.

Proportion of persons born (a) in the province or state where enumerated and (b) elsewhere.

Province, State or Agency.	Number per 10,000 population.	
	Born in province or State where enumerated.	Born elsewhere.
India	9,979	21
Madras	9,943	57
United Provinces	9,887	113
Bihar and Orissa	9,880	120
Hyderabad State	9,828	172
Jammu and Kashmir State	9,824	176
Punjab (including Punjab States Agency)	9,763	237
Travancore State	9,735	265
Western India States Agency	9,726	274
Rajputana Agency	9,705	295
Bengal	9,637	363
Central Provinces and Berar	9,636	364
Bombay (including Aden)	9,525	475
Mysore State	9,474	526
Burma	9,470	530
North-West Frontier Province	9,356	644
Cochin State	9,275	725
Gwalior State	9,201	799
Central India Agency	9,094	906
Baluchistan	8,963	1,037
Baroda State	8,671	1,329
Sikkim State	8,596	1,404
Assam	8,477	1,523
Coorg	7,629	2,371

Nature of migration.

54. Internal migration is of several kinds, for which the following convenient terminology has been used in previous census reports. *Casual* migration, involving minor movements between neighbouring villages, largely by way of marriage, only affects the Indian figures when the boundaries crossed happen to be those of provinces or states. *Temporary* migration is mainly due to the movement in the demand for labour *e.g.* on canals or public buildings, and to pilgrimages and fairs. *Periodic* migration is that caused by recurring seasonal demands, as for harvesters. *Semi-permanent* migration is that of persons who maintain their connection with their pre-migration homes, earning their living elsewhere but ultimately returning and often leaving their wives and families at home during the period of migration. *Permanent* migration is that in which the migrant leaves one place to settle in another for good. It is necessary also at this census to mention an additional form of migration which may be described as *Daily*.

Casual, Periodic and Temporary migration.

55. As already indicated casual migration is largely associated with marriage. It is neatly illustrated by the Census Superintendent for the Punjab and Delhi in the marginal table which shows the exchange of wives between Delhi and neighbouring districts in the Punjab. It might be expected that under the circumstances the volume exchanged by adjoining provinces would balance, but this is not the case since both the low ratio of women to men in the north-west and the practice of hypergamy combined with a decrease in social status from west to east among Hindus of many castes results in a surplus movement of women westwards. Thus whereas the numbers of both sexes born in the United Provinces and enumerated in Bihar and Orissa are of corresponding proportions the numbers born in Bihar and Orissa and enumerated in the United Provinces show a great preponderance of females. Similarly females born in the United Provinces and enumerated in Rajputana greatly outnumber the males. It does not appear, however, that the United Provinces give any excess of females to the Punjab as might be expected. There are possibly historical reasons for this. Periodic migration is particularly heavy at harvest time and also at the changes of season when traders, graziers, herdsmen and labourers from Kabul, Baluchistan, Kashmir and the hills generally move down to the plains for the winter months returning to the hills for the hot weather, when the movement is increased by the addition of plains-dwellers moving up to escape from the heat or to profit by the accumulation of people in hill stations. As regards temporary migration the 1931 census was fortunate in avoiding coincidence with pilgrimages and fairs on a large scale, but the immigration figures of the Central India Agency are probably affected to the extent of a few hundreds by the Khajuraho fair in Chhatarpur State and the Garahet cattle fair in Khilchipur State. In Central India again there was some periodic migration on account of harvesting, which had been begun by the census date, and the same in the case of the Central Provinces. Temporary migration continues throughout the year, and some idea of its volume may be obtained from the figures of encampments in Table III. In the case of Bombay a considerable volume of temporary migration to Baroda State was political in nature and accounted for by raiyats in parts of Bombay adjoining Baroda who made an exodus across the State boundary on account of the Civil Disobedience movement in Gujarat. The number of these *hijratis*, as they were called, amounted to 26,755 persons from 244 villages in Bombay Presidency. Some formed fresh hamlets on Baroda land, some occupied vacant sites in Baroda villages and others stayed as guests in the homes of their acquaintances. Many of them (332 males and 1,339 females) had actually been born in Baroda State, and the distances covered in this *hijra* were of the shortest. The very great majority had returned to their villages in British territory within the year following the census.

Born in Punjab British Territory and enumerated in Delhi Rural Areas.				Born in Delhi Province and enumerated in Gurgaon, Rohtak and Karnal Districts of the Punjab.			
Persons.	Males.	Females.	Females per 1,000 males.	Persons.	Males.	Females.	Females per 1,000 males.
28,205	6,939	21,266	3,065	22,087	6,107	15,980	2,617

Semi-permanent and permanent migration.

56. Semi-permanent and permanent migration are of more importance and are most conveniently examined by those individual provinces where the volume is considerable. The table on page 64 gives the principal figures of the balance of migration as compared with 1921 and they are illustrated graphically in the map opposite it. Of the semi-permanent migration between provinces the most important has been that to Burma from Madras, Bengal and the United Provinces. The non-permanent nature of this movement is shown by the small number of females as compared to males. Before the census actually took place a very large number of the Indians in Burma returned to their own provinces on account of the anti-Indian riots in Rangoon and the general hostility long entertained towards Indians but evinced throughout Burma in 1930 in action as well as in feeling. Even so the census showed in Burma an excess of 751,595 immigrants over emigrants, an increase of 21,000 on the 1921 figure. Of these immigrants

38% come from Madras, Bengal contributing 20%, the next highest quota, and the United Provinces 11%. Of all the immigrants to Burma less than 1 in 5 are women, thus reducing Burma's natural excess of females to a deficiency. Similarly in Assam, but to a far smaller degree, male immigrants reduce the female ratio which is however deficient to start with. This reduction in the case of Assam is slight, since male immigrants are to female immigrants as 4 to 3 only, indicating the much more permanent nature of the movement, which leads to large numbers of tea garden coolies taking up land and settling permanently after leaving the gardens, and which is also in a great degree a migration of Muslim cultivators from Bengal who bring their families with them. Assam's excess of immigrants over emigrants is 1,335,627, of which 41% comes from Bengal, 34 from Bihar and Orissa, 2 of which are from the Bihar and Orissa States, 6 from the Central Provinces, including 1% from the Central Provinces States, 5 from the United Provinces, 4 from Madras (principally from the Agency Tracts) and 2 from Rajputana. No other province has anything approaching this figure of immigration, but Bihar and Orissa have an even larger figure of emigration, the net adverse balance being 1,248,293. The bulk of this goes to Bengal, 65% of the gross emigration, Assam getting 27% and the Bihar and Orissa States over 10%. The United Provinces emigration figure is nearly as high as that of Bihar and Orissa, but the corresponding immigration figure is higher, and the adverse balance is 997,846, Bengal again getting 22%, Bombay 9% and the Punjab 15% of the gross emigration, which is much more evenly distributed between various provinces and states than that of most provinces with a high emigration figure. The same applies to Madras (—868,036 net) once the higher figures of emigration to Burma, 26%, and Mysore, 26%, are excluded; Travancore and Hyderabad come in for the next highest shares of Madras emigration with 9% and 12% respectively. The Punjab has an adverse balance, a considerable proportion of its emigrants going to Bombay. Bengal and Bombay both have high figures of migration, possibly on account of their large Presidency towns, but the balance is in their favour—899,274 in the case of Bengal and 658,267 in that of Bombay. Bengal's immigrants include some 250,000 Nepalis, and 13,557 Europeans 66% of whom were found in Calcutta; Bombay's include 170,085 immigrants from the Nizam's Dominions, 165,477 from Baroda State, nearly 59,000 from Portuguese India, and 16,345 Europeans.

Variation as compared with 1921 in the volume of migration within India.

Province or State.	1931.			1921.			Variation 1921-31.	
	Net gain or loss ±	Immigrants.	Emigrants.	Net gain or loss ±	Immigrants.	Emigrants.	Immigrants.	Emigrants.
1	2	3	4	5	6	7	8	9
PROVINCES OR STATES WHICH GAIN.								
Assam	+1,241,011	1,314,047	73,036	+1,140,752	1,216,661	75,909	+97,386	—2,873
Bengal	+771,936	1,726,370	954,434	+1,132,194	1,817,775	685,581	—91,405	+268,853
Burma	+593,324	617,521	24,197	+553,471	572,530	19,059	+44,991	+5,138
Bombay	+596,707	1,188,901	592,194	+472,023*	1,039,622	567,599	*+256,074	+318,280*
Central Provinces and Berar	+227,003	649,064	422,061	+197,323	603,924	406,601	+45,140	+15,460
Mysore	+215,462	340,700	125,238	+210,064	309,850	99,786	+30,850	+25,452
Delhi	+189,736	259,163	69,427	+113,158	182,485	69,327	+76,678	+100
Baroda	+127,901	333,077	205,176	+10,674	231,880	221,206	+101,197	—16,030
Central India Agency	+115,566	598,102	482,536	+58,056	544,688	486,632	+53,414	—4,096
Travancore	+83,919	133,852	49,933	+49,732	71,973	22,241	+61,879	+27,692
Ajmer-Merwara	+44,029	104,938	60,909	+66,033	108,452	42,419	—3,514	+18,490
Cochin	+41,424	87,214	45,790	+15,792	39,689	23,897	+47,525	+21,893
Coorg	+35,388	38,619	3,231	+30,988	33,838	2,850	+4,781	+381
Baluchistan	+23,779	66,542	42,763	+5,924	66,166	60,242	+376	—17,479
North-West Frontier Province	+21,187	111,868	90,681	+50,835	118,395	67,560	—6,527	+23,121
Andamans and Nicobars	+13,703	14,255	552	+14,080	14,396	316	—141	+236
PROVINCES OR STATES WHICH LOSE.								
Sikkim	—4,782	2,430	7,212	—2,297	1,836	4,133	+594	+3,079
Gwalior	—14,471	281,350	296,821	+632	289,657	289,025	—8,307	+7,796
Jammu and Kashmir	—33,266	61,189	94,455	—22,685	61,561	84,246	—372	+10,209
Punjab†	—67,792	635,025	702,817	+60,940	591,885	530,942	+43,140	+171,875
Hyderabad	—19,788	312,814	332,602	—166,326	197,127	363,453	+115,687	—30,851
Western India States Agency	—186,890	106,795	293,685	Included against Bombay.				
Rajputana	—516,898	329,913	864,811	—625,650	242,243	867,893	+87,670	—21,082
Madras	—888,339	246,892	1,135,231	—718,183	196,609	914,792	+50,283	+220,439
United Provinces	—1,063,143	494,308	1,557,451	—974,642	425,152	1,399,794	+69,156	+157,657
Bihar and Orissa	—1,291,567	466,563	1,758,130	—1,567,968	387,068	1,955,036	+79,495	—196,906

*Includes Western India States Agency. †Includes Punjab States Agency.

NOTE.—The figures for Provinces include those for the States attached to them except in the case of Madras, where they exclude Cochin and Travancore. Migration figures to and from countries from outside British India are excluded.

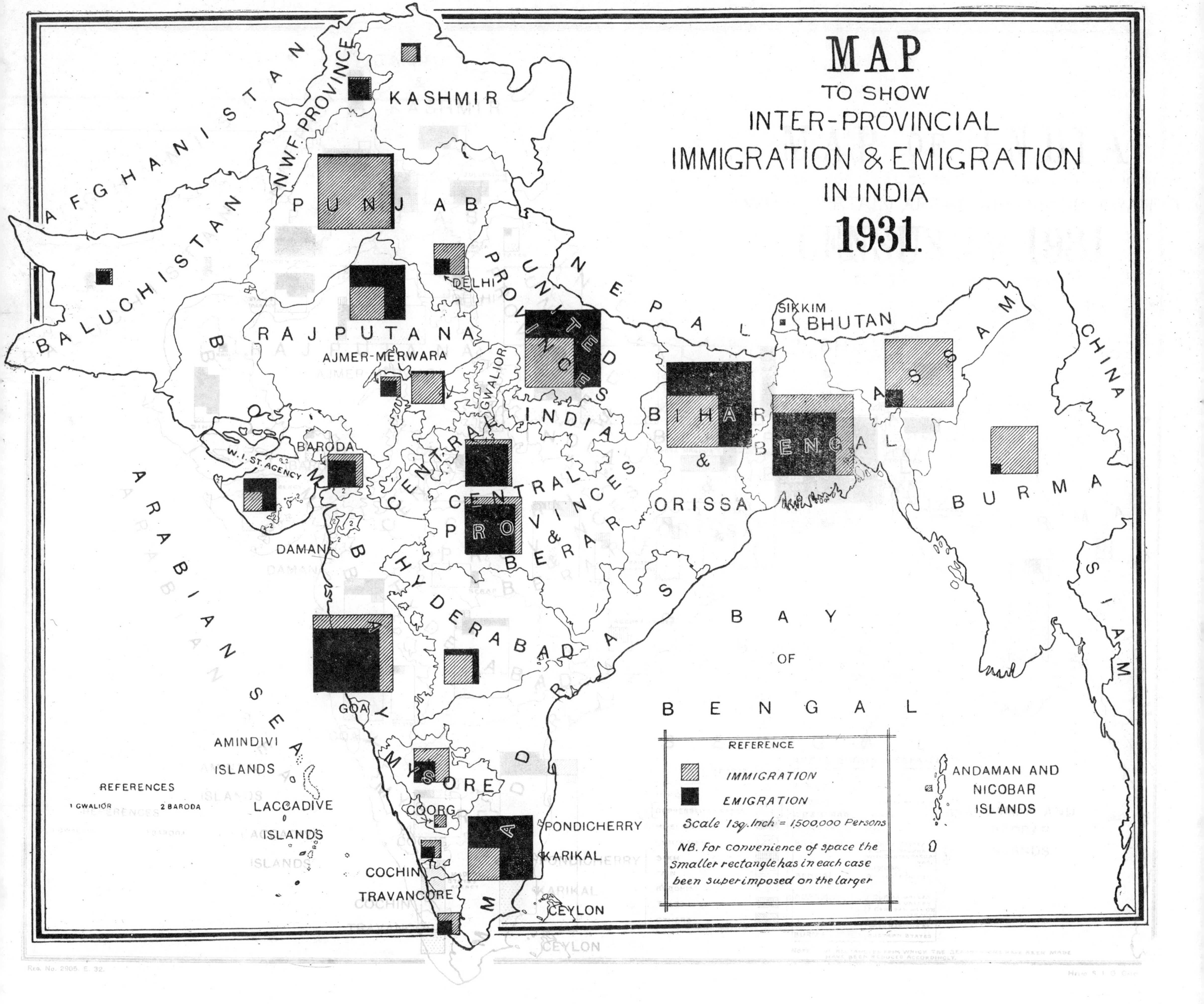
MAP
TO SHOW
INTER-PROVINCIAL
IMMIGRATION & EMIGRATION
IN INDIA
1931.
AFGHANISTAN
BALUCHISTAN
N.W.F. PROVINCE
KASHMIR
PUNJAB
DELHI
UNITED PROVINCES
NEPAL
SIKKIM
BHUTAN
ASSAM
CHINA
RAJPUTANA
AJMER-MERWARA
GWALIOR
CENTRAL INDIA
BIHAR & ORISSA
BENGAL
BURMA
BARODA
W. I. ST. AGENCY
CENTRAL PROVINCES & BERAR
BOMBAY
DAMAN
HYDERABAD
ARABIAN SEA
BAY OF BENGAL
SIAM
GOA
AMINDIVI ISLANDS
LACCADIVE ISLANDS
MYSORE
COORG
MADRAS
PONDICHERRY
KARIKAL
COCHIN
TRAVANCORE
CEYLON
ANDAMAN AND NICOBAR ISLANDS
REFERENCES
1 GWALIOR
2 BARODA
REFERENCE
IMMIGRATION
EMIGRATION
Scale 1 sq. Inch = 1,500,000 Persons
NB. For convenience of space the smaller rectangle has in each case been superimposed on the larger

57. It has been pointed out that Assam's immigration is generally speaking of the permanent type. There have however been some changes and developments since 1921, particularly in respect of the volume of migration from provinces which formerly supplied the tea garden labour. Madras is the only province showing any increase in emigration to Assam, and there has been an extraordinary decrease in emigration from Bihar and Orissa to Assam, though the actual number of persons enumerated on tea gardens has increased by some 60,000. Recruitment to Assam from Bihar and Orissa and elsewhere fell off rapidly after 1921, and in the United Provinces, at any rate, it is stated that emigration to Assam has become unpopular "largely as a result of a deliberate campaign against it by non-co-operators in the early part of the decade". Recruitment from Bihar and Orissa began to revive however in the last half of the decade largely as a result of short-term recruitment under which a cooly is brought up to Assam for a year or so and then sent back to his home. Or to quote the Census Superintendent of Bihar and Orissa, "the increase in the number of emigrants from 1927-28 onwards is attributed largely to the popularity of the system of recruitment for short terms of 6, 9 or 12 months". The introduction of this short-term system assisted by cinema propaganda is clearly changing the permanent nature of migration to the Assam tea gardens. Moreover the need for immigrant labour is less than it was. There has been a steady increase in labour obtained locally and lost by transfer, indicating greater freedom and fluidity. During the last five years adult labour born locally has increased by over 50% and some gardens have taken to sending out motor lorries to bring in labour from the villages. On the other hand the whole complexion of the population of Assam is being altered by the permanent immigrants from Mymensingh in Bengal. This has for years been an obvious and disturbing change to all residents in the Assam Valley and it will be best to quote the Census Superintendent for Assam himself:— **Assam.**

> "Probably the most important event in the province during the last twenty five years—an event, moreover, which seems likely to alter permanently the whole future of Assam and to destroy more surely than did the Burmese invaders of 1820 the whole structure of Assamese culture and civilization—has been the invasion of a vast horde of land-hungry Bengali immigrants, mostly Muslims, from the districts of Eastern Bengal and in particular from Mymensingh. This invasion began sometime before 1911, and the census report of that year is the first report which makes mention of the advancing host. But, as we now know, the Bengali immigrants censused for the first time on the *char* lands of Goalpara in 1911 were merely the advance guard—or rather the scouts—of a huge army following closely at their heels. By 1921 the first army corps had passed into Assam and had practically conquered the district of Goalpara."

The Assam Census Report of 1921 describes Goalpara as inhabited by these settlers to 20% of its population, and Nowgong to 14%; and describes parties of these settlers as invading the Assam Valley by "almost every train and steamer". Since then these settlers have not refrained from breeding and their progeny being born in Assam is not distinguishable in the Census returns, except in so far as it is predominantly Muslim which the indigenous population is not. The rate of increase in the Muslim population of Assam since 1881 is 111%. As to the change at this census the Census Superintendent may again be quoted:—

> "I have already remarked that by 1921 the first army corps of the invaders had conquered Goalpara. The second army corps which followed them in the years 1921-1931 has consolidated their position in that district and has also completed the conquest of Nowgong. The Barpeta sub-division of Kamrup has also fallen to their attack and Darrang is being invaded. Sibsagar has so far escaped completely but the few thousand Mymensinghias in North Lakhimpur are an outpost which may, during the next decade, prove to be a valuable basis of major operations.. ....Where there is waste land thither flock the Mymensinghias. In fact the way in which they have seized upon the vacant areas in the Assam Valley seems almost uncanny. Without fuss, without tumult, without undue trouble to the district revenue staffs, a population which must amount to over half a million has transplanted itself from Bengal to the Assam Valley during the last twenty-five years................the only thing I can compare it to is the mass movement of a large body of ants."

In Goalpara district there is little room left for expansion; in the Kamrup district, where their immigration is new since 1921, there has been an enormous increase of settlers causing the population figures to increase by 69% in Barpeta sub-division since 1921. In Darrang district also they are rapidly taking up any available waste land. In Nowgong district alone Mymensinghias occupied 33,405 acres in 1920-21, and in 1929-30, 102,363 acres, Muslims having 89,078 and Hindus

13,285 acres. In their anxiety to get land these settlers have at one time and another caused a good deal of friction by squatting in Government Reserves or forcibly occupying the land of local people, from which they are not evicted without difficulty. They are however excellent agriculturists and most industrious, and they spend money freely, at any rate on litigation.

"The exact number of these Eastern Bengal settlers (including their children born in Assam) who are at present living in the Assam Valley is a difficult matter to estimate. Mr. Lloyd in 1921 estimated that including children born after their arrival in this province the total number of settlers was at least 300,000 in that year. As far as I can judge the number at present must be over half a million. The number of new immigrants from Mymensingh, alone, has been 140,000 and the old settlers have undoubtedly been increasing and multiplying. As pointed out in the Census Report for 1921 the colonists have settled by families and not singly. This can be seen from the fact that out of the total of 338,000 persons born in Mymensingh and censused in Assam over 152,000 are women. What of the future ? As far as can be foreseen the invasion is by no means complete. . . . . .It is sad but by no means improbable that in another thirty years Sibsagar district will be the only part of Assam in which an Assamese will find himself at home".

There is yet a third class of immigrant in Assam, the Nepali, but the Nepali immigrant is fortunately decreasing in numbers, and the increase of Nepalis at this census has fallen from 89 to 36%. The decrease is attributed to action taken by the Nepal Government to discourage the emigration of its subjects. At the same time they are inconveniently numerous in the Khasia Hills where "in the interests of the Khasi population some measures appear necessary to prevent any further expansion of Nepali colonization".

Bihar and Orissa.

58. Bihar and Orissa is among provinces the antithesis of Assam in the matter of migration. It is typical of the rest of India in the general immobility of its population, and 959 persons in every 1,000 were born in the district in which they were enumerated, while 931 in every 1,000 were enumerated in the district in which they were born; on the other hand it has a higher emigration figure than any other province, from which the general standard of Indian migration, or rather the absence thereof, may fairly be judged. The net loss to the province by emigration is 1,758,000, and if British districts alone be taken the loss is considerably greater as the Feudatory States receive twice as many migrants as they send out, and their immigrants are mostly from the British districts of the same province. As in the case of Assam however a change is taking place and the loss by emigration is considerably less than it was in the previous decade. Emigrants have decreased by 197,000 and immigrants have increased by 79,000, and to this has contributed not only the development of urban and industrial areas within the province and the consequent attraction of settlers from outside, but the economic conditions of the province, which towards the close of the decade compared favourably with the conditions in other provinces more severely affected by the industrial depression. The latter cause has also operated to reduce the periodic emigration from the province, which is of very great volume and importance and is at its highest at the time of the census. The loss sustained by emigration therefore is not by any means a permanent loss of the volume indicated by the figures, since much of it returns when the periodic migration is over at the time of the spring harvest or at the beginning of the monsoon. Over two-thirds of the emigrants from Bihar and Orissa were enumerated in adjacent provinces and perhaps the great majority of these return to their homes later. Of the remainder 95% are found in Assam, and here again the new system of short-term recruitment for tea-gardens involves the inference that recent emigrants belong merely to the semi-permanent class and will ultimately return to their province.

United Provinces.

59. In the case of the United Provinces, which has the next largest volume of emigration, this volume of emigration, in contrast with that from Bihar and Orissa, instead of decreasing has increased by a net balance of 158,000. The emigrants are on the whole comparatively evenly distributed to all parts of northern and eastern India, though Bengal gets three times the share of any other province, Bombay, the Central Provinces and the Punjab standing next, while Rajputana conversely sends back more than it receives; but the bulk of this migration is of the semi-permanent description and is described as a blessing to the province since it relieves the pressure on the soil and will be automatically absorbed within the province by any industrial expansion that takes place.

60. Madras, the third highest province in order of net loss by emigration, is another which calls for some separate treatment, as the bulk of its emigration differs from that of other provinces in being overseas. Here the effect of the worldwide industrial depression is seen in the foreign birthplaces returned in Madras as a result of repatriation. There has been a general increase in the number of persons born in Burma, Ceylon, Mauritius and Natal. Even so the 1931 figure shows a very marked increase in emigration to Malaya as well as in emigration to other parts of India. The overseas migration to Malaya and Ceylon, which is 94 to 95% Madrasi, is treated in another paragraph, but it may be pointed out here that emigration from Madras is not restricted to 'assisted emigration' under the Act of 1922, which controls the departure of any persons from British India who are assisted by any person other than a relative, that is of persons recruited by agencies, but also of a considerable quantity of the natural migration of persons who go and return as they please, and in this connection the Census Superintendent points out that "it is possible for an emigration habit to arise not necessarily connected with financial or seasonal stress at home. This..........undoubtedly exists in South India and the Circars coast touching the emigration movement to Ceylon, Malaya and Burma". The area that supplies Assam and Burma is generally speaking not the same as that from which emigration to Malaya and Ceylon takes place. The latter is a Tamil movement; the emigrants to Burma are Telugus: "the Burmese emigration is largely a Circars phenomenon and......Burmese development has had a profound influence on the Telugu coastal districts". To this the presence of 297,543 Madrasis in Burma at the time of the census testifies in spite of the largely increased number who had returned as a result of the anti-Indian riots in May 1930, after which the volume of return continued so steadily that in May 1931 it was still 40% above that of the year before. Emigration to Assam again is neither Tamil nor Telugu but mainly Sawara from the Vizagapatam Agency tracts, and showed a great increase from 1925-27 as a result of the enforcement in the Sawara maliahs of a policy of forest reservation. Later when the application was mitigated emigration decreased, and recruitment is now of the short-term variety, repatriation after two years being guaranteed. **Madras.**

61. In the Central Provinces the Census Superintendent detects the growth of what may be described as Daily Migration. In England and Wales a column to show the place of work was included in the schedule in 1921, but though such a daily migration is familiar enough in Bombay and in Calcutta where 26,000 living outside the city travel in daily by train alone, to say nothing of those who use cars, buses or trams, in India generally the conditions under which the residence of the worker and the place at which he works are so far apart as to form different census units have hardly yet arisen to an extent to justify a column in the schedule. Nevertheless in some industrial areas it is already becoming a common practice for persons to live outside the place of employment and to visit it every day. This is apparent in Nagpur, for instance, where in some cases clerks live even 25 to 30 miles away at Ramtek and come in by train to their work every morning. Similarly industrial settlements outside the town provide workmen who come in daily. The 'buses run to neighbouring villages for labour by Assam tea gardens have already been mentioned. The Census Commissioner for Travancore State reports that daily migration is now a common feature of important towns like Trivandrum, Nagercoil, Quilon and Alleppey, and the Census Superintendent for Delhi estimates the average volume of daily migration throughout the year between Shahdara and Delhi city, a matter of 3 or 4 miles only, at 1,500 persons. **Daily Migration.**

62. In 1921 the balance of migration as between British and State territory was against the States and in favour of British India, but this position has been reversed during the decade, possibly on account of the increasing pressure on the less thickly populated areas which are mostly in State territory. Whereas the net loss to the states in 1921 was 124,000 (in 1911 it had been 132,000), in 1931 the states gained 490,935 from British India. In spite of this there has been very little change in the direction of migration between the States and British territory, since all those states which gained on the balance in 1921 have continued to do so except Gwalior, where the Census Commissioner of the State attributes "to the dislocation in trade and the general financial stringency" the **British India and States.**

Gain and loss by migration (000's omitted).

States.	Net gain+ or loss—	Receives from British Territory.	Gives to British Territory.
1	2	3	4
States which gain.			
Mysore State ..	+211	331	120
Punjab States and Agency	+187	539	352
Bengal States ..	+155	186	31
C. P. States ..	+135	218	83
B. and O. States ..	+105	225	120
Travancore ..	+87	105	18
Baroda	+77	191	114
Bombay States ..	+69	334	265
Cochin	+37	55	18
Other Madras States	+23	44	21
U. P. States ..	+10	92	82
Gwalior State ..	+7	70	63
N. W. F. Tribal Areas.	+1	29	28
Total gain ..	+1,104	2,419	1,315
States which lose.			
Central India ..	—8	294	302
Jammu and Kashmir	—27	60	87
Hyderabad ..	—88	229	317
W. I. States ..	—148	50	198
Rajputana ..	—326	220	546
Others	—12	13	25
Total loss ..	—609	866	1,475
Net	+495	3,285	2,790

Birthplace of Bikaner population.

Locality of birth.	1921.	1931.	Increase per cent.	Percentage of increase.
Bikaner State ..	*606,398*	*774,915*	*27·8*	*61*
Elsewhere ..	*53,287*	*161,303*	*202·7*	*39*
Rajputana ..	25,874	57,415	121·9	11·3
British Punjab ..	20,852	81,899	292·8	22·2
Punjab States ..	4,318	16,390	279·6	4·3
Elsewhere ..	2,243	5,599	149·6	1·2

choking up of the " migratory streams of business men and labourers " which flowed in former years. On the other hand of those that lost in 1921 only the Central India Agency and Baroda show a gain at this census, though the Bombay States, included in 1921 with what is now the Western India States Agency, a losing unit, show a gain this time treated separately. Indeed the net losses of the Rajputana Agency and Jammu and Kashmir State have considerably increased since 1921, but these increased losses have been far more than balanced by such large net increases as that of the Punjab States which, +84,000 in 1921, were +187,000 in 1931. Although Rajputana as a whole has a migration balance against it, Bikaner State, in which there has been during the decade a great extension of irrigation, has a heavy balance in its favour, since much of its phenomenal increase in population is due to immigration. It will be seen from the marginal table that Bikaner has drawn considerable numbers not only from the other Rajputana States and from British districts of the Punjab, but even from the Punjab States, which otherwise absorb rather than extrude emigrants. Moreover, it is clear that this tendency is not new, though the feature of the decade is the proportion of immigrants drawn from the British Punjab. Whereas much of the emigration from Rajputana generally must be regarded as probably of a semi-permanent nature only, it is clear that the immigration to Bikaner is of a permanent nature. Contrariwise the emigration is largely of the semi-permanent variety, and of the 846,811 persons born in Rajputana and emumerated elsewhere the majority, in all probability, come from Marwar, Bikaner, Jaipur, Jaisalmer and Mewar, but above all from Marwar and Jaipur, and consist of those traders, with their dependants, who are known indiscriminately as Marwaris and play such an ubiquitous and important part in commerce and banking throughout India. One rather unexpected migration item between British territory and the States is the flow of migration to Cochin and Travancore which already have the densest populations in India and the highest natural rate of increase. In Cochin this is probably to be accounted for by the fact that most of the migration is of the ' casual ' type, while in Travancore it consists of Tamil labourers on plantations in the highlands marching with British territory. Here communications with the Tamilnad have in the past been easier than with the coast, but with the opening up of good roads and easy communication between the estates in the hills and the populated plains, it is likely that Travancore State will tend more and more to replace Tamil by indigenous labour.

French and Portuguese India.

63. As between British India and the French and Portuguese settlements the balance of migration is greatly in favour of British India, from which 82,271 persons are received, the very great majority, their figure is estimated at 68,000 at least, from the Portuguese settlements, and the greater part of that going to Bombay. In the case of the French settlements, politics plays a unexpected hand. North Arcot district in Madras was found to contain a remarkable increase in the number of persons born in French India. Enquiry showed that they

represented the party defeated in recent elections in Pondicherry, who found it healthier to withdraw to British territory than to remain at home during the executive arbitrament and jurisdictional domination of their political adversaries.

External Migration.

64. Outside India the balance is the other way, in spite of the fact that circumstances are against emigration from India. Early marriage, which is almost universal, is a great deterrent at one end and immigration restrictions at the other. There are in India altogether 730,546 persons of foreign birth of whom 595,078 are of Asiatic birth, 118,089 of European birth and 17,379 others. Their distribution by origin is shown in the marginal table. On the other hand it has been stated above that there were about 2½ million Indians resident out of India at the census, giving a grand migration balance of –1¾ million. Nearly all of these are resident in other parts of the British Empire, but it should be made clear that this total is intended to include all Indians resident outside India, those who have emigrated during the decade being estimated at 1,000,000 only. A marginal table shows such figures as it has been possible to collect from the different parts of the British Empire. It represents of course the position in 1931, when the repatriation of Indians from Malaya had already taken effect since the depression in rubber production had led to a reduction of wages and employment as early as the end of 1929 both in Malaya and Ceylon ; from the former some 78,000 Indians including infants had been repatriated by the end of 1930, and a further 56,000 followed in 1931, while from Ceylon 11,000 were repatriated in 1931. There are over 75,000 Indians in Fiji, an increase of about 14,500 since 1921, against repatriations to the extent of 11,351 of which 4,435 were Madrasis. Emigrants from the United Provinces, have increased and the increase is still more marked in the case of Punjabis (mostly Sikhs), whose number has quadrupled in the decade—it was 450 in 1921, and of traders from Bombay and the Western India States, whose ratio of increase has been much the same. These were approximately 325 in 1921. Precise numbers are not available as the census due in the Fiji Islands in 1930 did not take place. The Bombay traders travel backwards and forwards more often and bring a higher proportion of women than other immigrants. Probably more than two-thirds of the Indians in the Fiji Islands depend on the sugar industry, holding some 63,000 acres, either as tenants of the sugar company or otherwise, and producing annually cane worth fifty or sixty lakhs of rupees. Demands for repatriation have declined very markedly, having fallen from 1,180 in 1926 to 502 in 1930. During the decade under review Indian emigration has been controlled by the Emigration Act of 1922 under which the emigration of unskilled labour is prohibited except to such countries and under such conditions as may be specified by the Governor-General in Council, whose notification under the Act must be approved by both chambers of the legislature. The quantity of skilled labour which emigrates is very small and is indicated by the partial figures in the accompanying table.

Distribution of Foreign-born by continents.

Born in	1931.	1921.	Variation.
Asia	595,078	472,576	+122,502
Europe	118,089	121,064	—2,975
Africa	11,408	4,719	+6,689
America ..	4,455	3,446	+1,009
Australasia ..	1,516	1,683	—167
Total ..	730,546	603,488	+127,058

Indian Emigration 1921-31.

Destination.	Persons.
Malaya	510,000
Ceylon	365,000
Fiji	15,000
Portuguese East Africa	4,000
United Kingdom	4,000
Elsewhere	12,000
Total ..	1,000,000

Statement showing Skilled Labour Emigrants from the port of Calcutta during the decade 1921--1930.

Embarked for	Profession.					Total.
	Tailoring.	Theatrical Artists.	Brick-laying.	Match-Manufacturing.	Welding.	
Siam (Bangkok)	79	..	..	..	..	79
Mauritius	..	29	18	2	..	49
Sarawak, Malaya and Straits Settlements.	..	..	..	..	2	2
Total ..	79	29	18	2	2	130

The effect of the Emigration Act has been to put an end to the emigration of unskilled labour to any place outside the Indian Empire except Ceylon and Malaya. Even to British Guiana, where the climate is not unlike that of Ceylon, and where the officer (Sir Maharaj Singh) deputed to report on conditions found that the conditions of education, of medical assistance and of the standard of living generally were higher than those of rural India and that no political disabilities of any kind attached to Indian settlers, emigration, stopped on account of mortality on the voyage many years ago, has not been renewed. From South Africa the tendency has been rather for a return to India, which is assisted by the Union Government by a bonus of £20 per adult and £10 per child, with free passage and free railway fares at each end of it. Thus while 791 emigrants from S. Africa returned to Madras and Calcutta in 1930, 1,707 returned to these ports in 1931. The total number of Indians returning from S. Africa to India in 1931 was 1,961 more than half (988) of whom were colonial born. The general position therefore is that in spite of a rapid and heavy increase in population during the decade there has been even less relief by emigration than in previous periods.

Malaya and Ceylon.

65. The two most important countries for Indian emigration at present are Malaya and Ceylon, as indicated above. Recruiting of Indian labour to Malaya was stopped in August 1930 on account of the fall in tin and rubber, and the considerable repatriations have been already mentioned. None the less the 1931 census of British Malaya found 624,009 Indians in that country details of which by sex, by religion and by age are given in the margin. Of this population 222,839 (153,408 males and 69,431 females) were engaged in agricultural pursuits, 30,214 (29,596 males and 618 females) in commercial pursuits and 19,415 (18.280 males and 1,135 females) in industry. The remainder were of miscellaneous, including administrative, personal or professional service (133,898 males and 11,845 females), or of non-productive occupations (85,846 males and 119,952 females). In the case of Ceylon recruitment of Indian labour for rubber estates was stopped in 1930, but otherwise emigration continued, though it appears that the absorption of Indian labour in that country has nearly reached the saturation point. The marginal table shows the net figures of Indian immigration into Ceylon, that is the balance of arrivals over departures, from 1923-1931. A complete census of Ceylon was not taken in 1931, but the figures available show "natives of India" for Colombo, and to these must be added nearly 300 others who are obviously of Indian races including "Afghans", a term used in Ceylòn for Balochis, and about 50 Burmans. Enumeration by religion was likewise incomplete, even for such figures of Indians as we have, but it is easy to allot the different classes of Indians to their main religions with a fair certainty of accuracy, and the result according to religion is shown in the marginal table. The most important Indian elements in Ceylon after the Tamil labour population are Malayalis, of whom Cochin and Travancore States contribute some 2,500 and 4,000 respectively, Nattukottai Chettiyars, Bohras, Baluchis, Mappillas and Memons, about 500 Bengalis, and 200 Parsis, but 95% of the whole Indian population in Ceylon are Tamils, in round numbers 739,000.

Indians in British Malaya in 1931.

Religion.	Persons.	Males.	Females.
Hindu ..	509,202	333,960	175,242
Sikh ..	18,180	13,995	4,185
Muslim ..	56,506	47,962	8,544
Christian ..	36,614	22,699	13,915
Other ..	3,507	2,412	1,095
Age			
0—10 ..	113,791	57,172	56,619
10—20 ..	88,117	52,053	36,064
20—55 ..	413,226	305,557	107,669
55 and over ..	8,875	6,246	2,629

Net emigration India to Ceylon. Excess departures + Excess returns—

1923 ..	+38,530
1924 ..	+97,865
1925 ..	+72,382
1926 ..	+40,481
1927 ..	+71,917
1928 ..	+40,116
1929 ..	+3,867
1930 ..	—7,306
1931 ..	—7,529

Indians in Ceylon 1931.

Religion.	Persons.	Males.	Females.
Hindu ..	743,326	400,743	342,583
Buddhist ..	2,260	1,655	605
Muslim ..	20,778	15,553	5,225
Christian ..	11,428	8,520	2,908
Other ..	378	244	134
Total ..	778,170	426,715	351,455

Some idea of the economic value to India of the emigration to Malaya may be gathered from the fact that land held by Indians in the Straits Settlements alone was estimated as worth Rs. 2,45,01,059; Savings Bank deposits held by Indians in Malaya amounted at the end of 1931 to the equivalent in dollars of Rs. 35,58,614 an average of Rs. 146 per depositor, while remittances by Indians from Malaya to India during 1931 came to a total of Rs. 38,83,065—an average of Rs. 69 per remittance. In Ceylon however the indebtedness of Indian labour is a troublesome problem still unsolved. Emigrants returning in 1929 from Fiji, Mauritius and Trinidad combined brought back a total of Rs. 5,11,147 between 2,174 men, women and children, working out at over Rs. 234 per head, children included.

66. An attempt was made at this census to obtain a return of Indians on the High Seas outside Indian waters through the masters of the vessels on which they were passengers. A census of persons on ships is a familiar undertaking to most masters, and the Port officers at the larger ports were given special forms with instructions to issue them to all vessels shipping crews in Indian ports within the six months before the census, and the masters were requested to return the schedules from the first port touched after February 26th, 1931. The numbers ultimately returned in this way to the ports of Rangoon, Calcutta, Bombay, Karachi and Aden amounted to 12,540 of which 122 represented females. The returns received in Madras proved to come entirely from Indian waters and were therefore not treated separately from the port population. In Bombay and Karachi returns came from outside Indian waters, but were amalgamated in the provincial totals. The majority of the returns were received through Calcutta and Rangoon; they were not amalgamated in the provincial totals and do not appear as part of the population of India but are given separately here together with the returns that came through Bombay, Karachi and Aden, which should, strictly speaking, have likewise been separately treated. These returns will be found in Appendix II to the Tables Volume where they have been arranged in a series of forms corresponding to the Imperial Tables. **Indians on the High Seas.**

The following points are worth notice. Nearly half the Indians enumerated on the High Seas came from Bengal and nearly a quarter from Assam; the remaining quarter or more represented the United Provinces, Bombay, Punjab and other provinces in that order, but as a matter of fact the numbers hailing from French and Portuguese India, mostly of course Goanese, totalled rather more than those who came from the Punjab. Figures for age and civil condition were available only on the Calcutta and Rangoon schedules, and a great majority were naturally aged from 20—40. A majority of them were married, but, as might be expected, even among those over 20 marriage was much less universal than on land. In the matter of occupation they were mostly of course shown under the heading 'Transport by Water', but the large numbers having a subsidiary occupation in cultivation are noteworthy. Most of them, of course, are lascars, who are also cultivators in Bengal or Assam. Well over a quarter of the total are literate, but less than 1 per cent. are literate in English. In languages more than half have Bengali as their mother-tongue and the next most predominant language is Hindustani, and these two languages also predominate among the subsidiary languages spoken. Returns of language, however, are only available, as also in the case of literacy, from the Calcutta and Rangoon schedules. In religion a great majority are Muslims from whatever port the return is obtained. Among Hindus the predominant caste is that of Kharva, a sea-faring caste in Cutch and the neighbourhood.

67. As will be already clear the Indian communities in other parts of the British Empire are no longer reinforced by any emigrants from India except the very small numbers of skilled workmen who come and go to them. Strictly, therefore they are outside the scope of Indian emigration as well as of the India census. But as their numbers are likely to be of interest to their fellow country-men such figures as are available—mostly from British Colonial census returns of 1930 or 1931—have been tabulated in the appendix to the India Tables. In the Union of S. Africa there are about 165,500 Indians of whom 142,979 are found in Natal. In Kenya there are 26,759 Indians; the other overseas Indian communities in order of size are Mauritius, 268,870, Trinidad and Tobago 138,667, British Guiana 130,540, Fiji 75,117, Tanganyika 23,422, Jamaica 17,599, Zanzibar 15,246, Uganda 11,613 and Hong Kong 4,745, no other British colony containing as many as 2,000 Indians. There are about 11,000 Indians scattered in numbers of under 2,000 in various other parts of the British Empire and probably about 9,000 in the British Isles. Ferenczi (*International Migrations*, II page 592) gives 74,000 as the number of Indians in **Indians Overseas.**

England and Wales and 8,000 in Scotland, but it is clear from the Census Report of England and Wales for 1921 that this represents the number of persons born in India—most of them probably British. The increase in that number since 1911, *viz.*, 11,000, though far from being purely Indian is more likely to be indicative of the number of actual Indians, which may conveniently be estimated at 9,243 ; there are reported to be at least 2,000 Indian students alone at different universities in England and Scotland, and the census of England and Wales returned 7,128 Indians of Asiatic origin in those countries in 1931, and one in the Isle of Man. This makes a total for the whole of the Empire outside India of approximately 2,300,000. Outside the Empire there are about 104,000 distributed as follows :—About 5,000 in the U. S. A.; in Surinam (Dutch Guiana) there are probably about 35,000 ; in the Netherlands Indies the number of British Indians is estimated at 25,000, while the French possessions of Madagascar and Réunion contain about 7,500 Indians. There are or were within the decade some 3,900 in Persia, some 5,000 in Portuguese East Africa, 2,362 in Iraq, and at least another 20,000 must be allowed for Afghanistan, the continent of Europe and elsewhere. Apart from students and travellers the Census Commissioner for Baroda State actually reports the presence in Spain of some 200 Bohras from Baroda doing business in Bilbao, Malaga and in other towns. The Imperial Indian Citizenship Association records approximately 20,000 Indians resident outside the British Empire in addition to the foreign countries for which details are given here. It will therefore probably be safe enough to say 20,238 for elsewhere, making a total of Indians resident overseas of approximately 2,404,000, so that a rough statement of two and a half million is not likely to be far from the truth.

Indian resident overseas.

Name of country.	Indian population.	Date of information.*
British Empire.	*2,300,000*	..
Ceylon	778,170	1931
Malaya	624,009	1931
Mauritius	268,870	1931
S. Africa	165,500	1926, 1930
Trinidad, etc. ..	138,667	1931
British Guiana ..	130,540	1931
Fiji	75,117	1930
Kenya	26,759	1931
Tanganyika ..	23,422	1931
Jamaica	17,599	1930
Zanzibar	15,246	1931
Uganda	11,613	1926
England and Wales..	7,128	1931
British Isles (elsewhere)	2,115	..
Hongkong.. ..	4,745	1931
Elsewhere ..	10,500	1911—1931
Foreign territory	*104,000*	..
Dutch East Indies ..	25,000	..
Dutch Guiana ..	35,000	1920
Madagascar, etc. ..	7,500	..
Portuguese East Africa	5,000	1932
U. S. A.	5,000	1921
Persia	3,900	1922
Iraq	2,362	1932
Elsewhere ..	20,238	..

*1931 refers to census figures of that year. The other figures refer to any data available from reports of the Protector of Immigrants, Blue Books, etc., those in round numbers being approximate only, and where no date is given estimated.

Emigration has a perceptible influence socially on Indian emigrants. The Fiji Indians and often the South African are found to have abandoned caste restrictions, and owing to the paucity of women among them inter-caste marriages are frequent, and social relations generally freer than in India.

" Family repatriation is commonest with the Madrasi, who is reported to retain longest his connection with his home country and ancestral lands........Emigration has no observable effect on religion. The Madrasi abroad has sufficient of his own kind around him to be able to continue unaltered in a new country such religious practices as he favours at home........Caste rigidity undoubtedly weakens, but so largely homogeneous are the contributions that here too the effect is less than might be expected. Also no Madrasi emigrant........severs his ties of community with the home country, and on his return he seeks to take a normal place within it........Effects on occupation are less than might be expected. The great mass........go forth to carry out in their new countries the agricultural occupations they inherited at home. The contribution to domestic service is by classes contributing to it in India. The traders are those who in India would probably also have traded........The Madrasi emigrant........ takes his own world with him and sets it down in his new surroundings "

Mutatio loci, non ingenii. Caelum non animum mutant.

SUBSIDIARY TABLE I.

General distribution of the Population of each Province and State by birth-place and place of enumeration.

Province, State or Agency in which enumerated.	Enumerated in Province, State or Agency of Birth-place (000's omitted).			Enumerated in the same province but born elsewhere (000's omitted). Contiguous Provinces.			Non-contiguous Provinces.			Outside India.			Born in the same province but enumerated elsewhere (000's omitted). Contiguous Provinces.			Non-contiguous Provinces.			Outside India.		
	Persons.	Males.	Females.	Persons.	Males.	Females.	Persons.	Males.	Females.	Persons.	Males.	Females.	Persons.	Males.	Females.	Persons.	Males.	Females.	Persons.	Males.	Females.
Ajmer-Merwara ..	543	245	208	101	47	54	3	2	1	1	1	..	33	14	19	27	17	10	..	..	..
Andamans and Nicobars	14	7	7	..	..	..	14	11	3	..	..	..	..	..	..	..	..	..	..	..	..
Assam	7,839	4,025	3,814	582	331	251	731	424	307	94	63	31	67	38	29	5	3	2	..	..	..
Baluchistan ..	778	422	356	48	36	12	17	14	3	23	16	7	39	24	15	2	2	..	..	..	..
Bengal	49,233	25,260	23,973	1,212	848	364	513	369	144	127	80	47	892	547	345	61	35	26	5	4	1
Bihar and Orissa ..	41,819	20,824	20,995	414	207	207	53	35	18	41	16	25	1,260	851	409	497	291	206	..	..	..
Bombay (including Aden).	25,071	13,065	12,006	914	488	426	274	194	80	61	46	15	542	249	293	49	32	17	9	6	3
Burma	13,871	6,847	7,024	461	385	76	156	133	23	158	116	42	11	6	5	12	7	5	..	..	..
Central Provinces and Berar.	17,335	8,651	8,684	553	281	272	95	60	35	6	5	1	283	134	149	138	77	61	..	..	..
Coorg	124	65	59	38	25	13	..	..	..	..	..	..	2	1	1	..	..	..	..	..	..
Delhi	373	215	158	204	118	86	54	33	21	4	3	1	52	19	33	17	12	5	..	..	..
Madras	46,957	23,180	23,777	177	86	91	38	23	15	20	12	8	610	326	284	577	375	202	64	55	9
North West Frontier Province.	2,312	1,239	1,073	93	72	21	18	15	3	47	33	14	65	42	23	25	21	4	..	..	
Punjab	27,816	15,217	12,599	604	297	307	26	14	12	43	32	11	502	283	219	200	145	55	4	4	.
United Provinces ..	49,055	25,812	23,243	439	174	265	54	31	23	65	45	20	873	439	434	684	520	164	..	..	..
Baroda State ..	2,118	1,125	993	288	109	179	34	22	12	1	1	..	200	80	120	5	3	2	..	..	..
Central India Agency	6,032	3,153	2,879	577	237	340	20	13	7	2	2	..	457	190	267	24	14	10	..	..	..
Cochin State ..	1,117	553	564	85	35	50	1	1	..	..	..	..	41	19	22	4	1	3	2	4	..
Gwalior State ..	3,241	1,746	1,495	270	114	156	11	6	5	..	..	..	287	102	185	9	6	3	..	..	..
Hyderabad State ..	14,188	7,203	6,985	214	145	69	27	17	10	4	3	1	323	146	177	8	5	3	..	..	..
Jammu and Kashmir State.	3,582	1,908	1,674	59	27	32	1	1	..	3	2	1	87	53	34	6	5	1	..	..	..
Mysore State ..	6,212	3,163	3,049	327	179	148	13	8	5	3	2	1	117	56	61	7	4	3	..	..	..
Rajputana Agency ..	10,894	5,747	5,147	322	133	189	7	3	4	1	1	..	697	333	364	149	99	50	..	..	..
Sikkim State ..	94	47	47	2	1	1	..	..	..	12	6	6	6	3	3	..	..	..	..	..	..
Travancore State ..	4,960	2,497	2,463	131	66	65	2	1	1	1	1	..	47	22	25	2	2	..	3	3	..
Western India States Agency.	3,889	1,980	1,909	46	19	27	59	24	35	2	1	1	277	137	140	16	11	5	..	..	..

NOTE.—In these Subsidiary Tables the figures for Provinces include those for the States attached to them except in the case of Madras, where they exclude Cochin and Travancore. Figures in columns 5-10 include immigrants (82,271) from French and Portuguese Possessions and those Indians (87,752) whose birth-place was not specified.

Migration between Provinces and

Province, State or Agency in which born.		Province, State or Agency — British Provinces. Assam.	Bengal.	Bihar and Orissa.	Bombay.	W. I. States Agency.	Burma.	C. P. and Berar.	Delhi.	Madras.	N.-W. F. Province.	Punjab (including Agency).	United Provinces.
1		2	3	4	5	6	7	8	9	10	11	12	13
Total	**1931**	**1,408,763**	**1,853,708**	**509,837**	**1,250,461**	**109,674**	**775,963**	**655,574**	**263,188**	**267,195**	**159,166**	**674,152**	**559,605**
	1921	**1,290,157**	**1,929,460**	**422,244**	**1,081,649**		**706,725**	**609,504**	**185,770**	**209,862**	**157,562**	**627,137**	**480,414**
Ajmer-Merwara	1931	77	516	123	20,477	519	24	3,429	777	..	88	931	3,399
	1921	32	1,930	132	7,991		40	1,934	278	445	24	1,536	1,729
Andaman and Nicobar Islands.	1931	4	17	4	81	2	82	96	..	..	2	105	140
	1921	1	32	4	21		128	1	2	2	..	70	33
Assam	1931	..	63,416	2,030	475	2	4,475	587	83	..	80	322	1,169
	1921	..	68,802	949	691		3,018	126	92	51	505	404	904
Baluchistan	1931	245	192	16	35,450	168	115	709	189	..	444	4,065	455
	1921	188	92	47	54,352		31	635	42	147	11	3,567	365
Bengal	1931	575,199	..	157,524	6,005	648	158,098	6,946	6,168	..	795	4,618	30,950
	1921	375,578	..	116,922	7,955		146,087	3,274	2,778	3,181	917	3,172	18,634
Bihar and Orissa	1931	471,786	1,138,850	..	1,504	79	18,732	51,919	715	..	159	1,281	69,733
	1921	570,642	1,227,579	..	3,931		20,616	32,439	246	16,879	129	894	77,693
Bombay (*including Aden*)	1931	6,552	7,797	7,316	..	46,954	8,729	105,013	2,275	..	752	8,611	8,466
Western India States Agency.	1931	..	..	78	198,708	..	8,889	..	..	..	..	..	42
Bombay	1921	1,176	11,223	7,077	..		18,471	107,268	1,236	17,806	2,489	9,987	7,563
Burma	1931	7,787	3,791	298	829	523	..	156	84	3,181	76	2,047	1,388
	1921	7,413	2,361	217	855		..	80	50	1,915	95	1,617	1,380
Central Provinces and Berar.	1931	82,045	45,844	89,317	55,456	657	1,033	..	862	..	338	2,419	15,217
	1921	91,393	54,810	77,323	31,922		1,425	..	329	12,529	92	2,515	11,113
Coorg	1931	1	3	6	144	..	2	254	..	..	..	..	89
	1921	14	6	1	36		3	9	..	345	..	..	30
Delhi	1931	107	2,159	359	5,317	217	503	795	..	..	631	37,119	15,128
	1921	97	1,889	541	4,915		727	781	..	216	1,717	35,165	14,914
Madras	1931	57,469	42,489	40,786*	60,199	381	297,633	13,045*	1,446	..	776	1,601	3,099
	1921	54,536	31,270	35,933	45,592		272,565	6,505	553	..	1,959	1,583	2,220
N.-W. F. Province	1931	593	1,964	1,299	11,686	47	907	1,167	1,758	..	..	52,773	3,562
	1921	318	1,026	329	12,051		1,057	650	616	146	..	34,252	1,893
Punjab (*including Agency*).	1931	6,134	25,084	15,330	90,916	1,161	24,910	15,775	86,612	..	85,146	..	97,908
	1921	3,178	15,826	7,857	57,465		20,938	9,645	64,810	625	97,115	..	84,169
United Provinces	1931	68,126	348,399	126,539	136,847	2,357	86,427	118,753	116,164	..	11,177	232,112	..
	1921	77,048	343,095	115,794	115,029		70,868	102,104	75,084	2,244	7,684	194,155	..
Baroda State	1931	232	350	63	165,477	34,570	342	509	65	..	8	143	326
	1921	125	199	153	215,281		662	393	22	130	228	97	183
Central India Agency	1931	14,887	1,722	2,075	13,898	965	153	176,802	310	..	280	331	109,242
	1921	17,602	941	2,158	19,313		508	194,203	305	..	..	608	82,531
Cochin State	1931	1	23	†	3,035	12	239	..	17	14,820	..	..	..
	1921	4	222	29	479		155	..	3	10,124	17	33	1
Gwalior State	1931	262	1,581	184	2,203	136	90	8,806	1,651	..	156	1,560	47,303
	1921	332	1,788	1,246	1,607		129	2,519	1 457	15	..	1,793	47,600
Hyderabad State	1931	389	849	468	170,085	199	939	91,065	278	58,476	182	797	1,876
	1921	160	389	349	219,252		494	90,930	351	38,916	329	1,115	1,736
Jammu and Kashmir State.	1931	24	209	92	1,285	22	127	273	470	..	8,263	79,691	1,421
	1921	46	169	364	715		149	197	185	33	3,006	75,159	1,404
Mysore State	1931	85	322	403	17,607	88	1,409	711	142	86,485	148	293	525
	1921	234	451	347	14,624		1,640	470	46	66,855	331	258	413
Rajputana Agency	1931	21,780	32,906	20,756	108,472	12,469	1,909	51,621	36,951	..	1,545	199,214	81,794
	1921	15,770	47,865	18,812	156,357		3,418	49,207	33,729	1,415	743	222,173	68,112
Sikkim State	1931	64	6,320	26	724	..	17	12	..	..	..	..	2
	1921	22	4,057	13	2		15	9	..	..	..	..	1
Travancore State	1931	1	8	†	618	3	816	..	4	16,756	..	1	60
	1921	6	532	64	148		319	59	3	8,293	8	6	41
India Unspecified	1931	175	267	1,186	22,311	3,714	28	93	69	51,162	755	842	923
	1921	689	30	282	9,856		8,419	..	225	40	996	1,581	330
French and Portuguese Settlements.	1931	22	1,292	285	59,092	992	893	528	73	16,012	67	33	91
	1921	57	1,181	125	59,182		651	486	43	14,257	..	145	197
Outside India	1931	94,716	127,338	43,274	61,560	2,879	158,442	6,510	4,025	20,303	47,298	43,243	65,297
	1921	73,496	111,865	35,176	42,027		134,195	5,580	3,285	13,253	39,167	35,252	55,262

* Includes figures for Cochin and Travancore.

NOTES.—(*i*) 1921 figures against Bombay include those for the

(*ii*) In this table emigrants to places outside India have not been included.

TABLE II.

States in 1921 and 1931.

in which enumerated.

		Indian States.											
Other Provinces.	Total.	Baroda.	Central India. Agency.	Cochin.	Gwalior.	Hyderabad.	Jammu and Kashmir.	Mysore.	Raj-putana.	Sikkim.	Travan-core.	Total.	Grand Total.
14	15	16	17	18	19	20	21	22	23	24	25	26	27
249,960	**8,737,246**	**324,579**	**600,766**	**87,417**	**281,550**	**247,795**	**64,196**	**344,592**	**330,939**	**15,417**	**135,103**	**2,432,354**	**11,169,600**
237,334	**7,937,998**	**232,494**	**548,094**	**39,759**	**290,340**	**202,781**	**63,420**	**314,531**	**243,002**	**22,978**	**73,591**	**2,030,990**	**9,968,988**
141	**30,501**	529	4,326	..	2,316	1,525	6	183	21,522	..	1	**30,408**	**60,909**
299	**16,370**	110	2,642	..	703	2,946	11	20	19,616	1	..	**26,049**	**42,419**
2	**535**	1	4	..	..	..	..	10	..	..	2	**17**	**552**
1	**295**	2	..	..	2	2	..	15	..	..	..	**21**	**316**
190	**72,829**	11	32	3	2	5	7	12	124	11	..	**207**	**73,036**
176	**75,718**	2	56	..	25	5	2	18	46	23	14	**191**	**75,909**
78	**42,126**	200	162	8	7	21	93	95	51	..	..	**637**	**42,763**
91	**59,568**	232	158	..	25	46	94	63	55	..	1	**674**	**60,242**
1,976	**948,927**	393	844	33	260	313	111	617	1,007	1,707	222	**5,507**	**954,434**
2,322	**680,820**	257	949	9	325	293	105	425	774	1,566	58	**4,761**	**685,581**
769	**1,755,527**	113	985	..	102	564	23	58	452	305	1	**2,603**	**1,758,130**
1,964	**1,953,012**	42	708	..	95	580	32	101	333	128	5	**2,024**	**1,955,036**
7,935	**210,400**	220,659	42,456	291	4,215	68,058	199	31,067	14,332	..	517	**381,794**	**592,194**
539	**208,256**	78,429	2,119	700	355	..	..	210	3,597	..	19	**85,429**	**293,685**
12,842	**197,148**	215,838	45,560	654	3,832	60,700	150	28,583	14,762	1	371	**370,451**	**567,599**
3,071	**23,231**	265	50	31	4	105	29	382	70	..	30	**966**	**24,197**
2,317	**18,300**	88	66	8	4	213	8	322	27	4	19	**759**	**19,095**
1,093	**294,281**	561	100,067	13	9,013	14,289	45	693	2,995	..	14	**127,780**	**422,061**
1,655	**285,016**	565	85,701	55	8,073	25,416	30	823	629	..	203	**121,495**	**406,601**
10	**509**	..	1	2	..	6	..	2,703	2	..	8	**2,722**	**3,231**
13	**457**	..	..	1	..	15	..	2,373	1	..	3	**2,393**	**2,850**
1,929	**64,174**	350	1,113	1	662	949	83	132	1,962	1	..	**5,253**	**69,427**
2,769	**63,731**	159	1,054	..	722	1,112	144	260	2,137	..	8	**5,596**	**69,327**
28,603*	**547,527**	555	736*	54,623	85	132,954	33	294,117	259	..	104,342	**587,704**	**1,135,231**
24,897	**477,613**	264	498	26,388	52	84,149	34	267,305	212	..	58,277	**437,179**	**914,792**
6,870	**82,626**	341	533	2	144	184	6,472	93	279	..	7	**8,055**	**90,681**
6,134	**58,472**	65	367	..	307	237	7,738	44	328	..	2	**9,088**	**67,560**
43,282	**494,258**	1,692	5,352	19	2,896	3,731	53,034	1,196	140,382	164	93	**208,559**	**702,817**
42,092	**403,720**	745	5,420	7	2,541	1,618	52,463	956	63,387	43	42	**127,222**	**530,942**
30,120	**1,277,021**	7,012	145,133	33	50,922	8,038	768	560	67,773	132	59	**280,430**	**1,557,451**
33,548	**1,138,653**	3,932	135,924	7	59,007	6,443	557	585	56,587	58	41	**263,141**	**1,399,794**
112	**202,197**	..	1,620	3	492	37	22	51	745	..	9	**2,979**	**205,176**
262	**217,735**	..	1,471	9	579	198	6	72	862	..	4	**3,471**	**221,206**
2,549	**323,214**	974	..	1	131,333	558	11	110	26,335	..	..	**159,322**	**482,536**
2,080	**320,246**	744	..	..	137,913	195	11	51	27,465	1	6	**166,386**	**486,632**
89	**18,236**	14	..	..	..	31	..	543	2	..	26,964	**27,554**	**45,790**
58	**11,125**	..	25	..	..	14	..	367	..	..	12,366	**12,772**	**23,897**
109	**64,041**	491	184,922	..	..	717	22	26	46,601	..	1	**232,780**	**296,821**
1,991	**60,477**	377	174,753	..	..	316	23	13	53,045	..	21	**228,548**	**289,025**
628	**326,231**	337	1,321	13	232	..	19	4,224	200	..	25	**6,371**	**332,602**
2,429	**356,450**	267	2,697	9	242	..	7	3,335	396	..	50	**7,003**	**363,453**
2,129	**94,006**	30	160	1	39	42	..	73	104	..	..	**449**	**94,455**
2,439	**83,866**	6	40	1	34	12	..	154	133	..	..	**380**	**84,246**
13,202	**121,420**	72	265	127	31	2,869	2	..	72	..	380	**3,818**	**125,238**
10,838	**96,507**	15	51	77	70	2,589	2	..	163	..	312	**3,279**	**99,786**
77,355	**646,772**	8,973	105,405	12	76,480	6,608	64	2,348	..	110	39	**200,039**	**846,811**
70,719	**688,320**	7,473	85,899	11	75,041	8,046	113	2,971	..	11	8	**179,573**	**867,893**
45	**7,210**	..	..	..	..	..	2	..	..	..	..	**2**	**7,212**
14	**4,133**	..	..	..	..	..	..	..	..	..	..	..	**4,133**
39	**18,306**	9	..	31,167	..	28	..	422	1	..	..	**31,627**	**49,933**
47	**9,489**	..	..	12,381	4	10	..	357	..	..	..	**12,752**	**22,241**
1,013	**82,538**	152	136	65	1,743	1,025	127	190	883	..	993	**5,214**	**87,752**
320	**22,768**	72	138	..	..	1,818	15	..	1,140	..	102	**3,285**	**26,053**
476	**79,856**	824	360	66	17	157	17	585	163	..	226	**2,415**	**82,271**
535	**76,859**	625	241	72	61	154	16	**637**	145	..	60	**2,011**	**78,870**
45,606	**700,491**	1,502	2,664	203	200	4,881	3,007	**3,892**	1,026	12,987	1,251	**31,713**	**732,204**
14,482	**563,040**	614	3,406	70	683	5,654	1,859	4,681	759	21,142	1,618	**40,486**	**603,526**

† Included against Madras.
Western India States Agency.
They are shown in Subsidiary Table IV of this Chapter.

SUBSIDIARY

Variation as compared with previous Censuses in the

1	Contiguous — Nepal. 1931.	Nepal. 1921.	Nepal. 1911.	Nepal. 1901.	Afghanistan. 1931.	Afghanistan. 1921.	Afghanistan. 1911.
	2	3	4	5	6	7	8
INDIA	**327,028**	**273,932**	**280,241**	**243,037**	**81,053**	**47,835**	**91,630**
Provinces	**312,438**	**251,432**	**253,248**	**241,452**	**78,408**	**46,939**	**89,679**
1. Ajmer-Merwara	49	34	17	9	65	190	134
2. Andamans and Nicobars	3	10	14	9	..	9	34
3. Assam	88,306	70,344	47,654	21,347	1,346	360	667
4. Baluchistan	3,868	2,455	1,677	6	14,953	5,285	10,625
5. Bengal	98,620	87,283	106,727	161,495	3,837	1,795	2,710
6. Bihar and Orissa	36,586	30,454	35,954		1,423	687	657
7. Bombay*	1,323	1,574	507	213	10,762	4,238	8,237
8. Burma	23,889	13,712	5,997	3,910	132	77	109
9. Central Provinces and Berar	683	88	253	87	834	454	1,064
10. Coorg	..	..	..	3	2	..	..
11. Madras	217	61	18	77	306	77	118
12. North-West Frontier Province	8,051	5,877	5,653	7,711	28,324	22,098	42,480
13. Delhi	427	133	5,430		184	86	21,239
14. Punjab (*including Agency*)	6,922	4,780			14,854	10,603	
15. United Provinces of Agra and Oudh	43,494	34,627	43,347	46,585	1,386	980	1,605
States and Agencies	**14,590**	**22,500**	**26,993**	**1,585**	**2,645**	**896**	**1,951**
16. Baroda State	239	28	49	14	122	78	87
17. Central India Agency	266	191	88	73	216	168	178
18. Gwalior State	56	19			52	44	
19. Cochin State	2	..	..	10	3	..	..
20. Hyderabad State	14	47	19	25	181	125	468
21. Jammu and Kashmir State	974	1,157	1,077	1,384	1,607	329	943
22. Mysore State	25	12	9	8	78	16	24
23. Rajputana Agency	230	170	140	56	260	133	243
24. Sikkim State	12,571	20,876	25,610	†	1	3	2
25. Travancore State	1	..	1	15	24	..	6
26. Western India States Agency	212	..	..	..	101	..	..

1	British Isles. 1911. Persons.	1911. Males.	1911. Females.	1901. Persons.	1901. Males.	1901. Females.	1931.
	24	25	26	27	28	29	30
INDIA	**121,357**	**101,980**	**19,377**	**96,653**	**81,990**	**14,663**	**13,360**
Provinces	**109,483**	**91,860**	**17,623**	**84,933**	**72,222**	**12,711**	**12,200**
1. Ajmer-Merwara	1,223	1,099	124	576	474	102	59
2. Andamans and Nicobars	181	163	18	190	177	13	3
3. Assam	1,427	1,119	308	1,287	1,080	207	187
4. Baluchistan	3,287	2,908	379	2,820	2,636	184	146
5. Bengal	12,179	9,355	2,824	11,886	9,290	2,596	1,334
6. Bihar and Orissa	2,572	1,859	713				399
7. Bombay*	19,682	16,647	8,035	15,753	13,275	2,478	4,964
8. Burma	7,354	6,279	1,075	5,690	5,057	633	897
9. Central Provinces and Berar	4,846	4,275	571	3,537	2,286	1,251	182
10. Coorg	82	58	24	99	62	37	8
11. Madras	6,497	4,908	1,589	5,994	4,874	1,120	1,809
12. North-West Frontier Province	4,836	4,390	446	21,690	19,471	2,219	222
13. Delhi	23,311	19,954	3,357				73
14. Punjab (*including Agency*)							1,435
15. United Provinces of Agra and Oudh	22,006	18,846	3,160	15,411	13,540	1,871	483
States and Agencies	**11,874**	**10,120**	**1,754**	**11,720**	**9,768**	**1,952**	**1,160**
16. Baroda State	55	35	20	22	12	10	16
17. Central India Agency	3,192	2,841	351	3,255	2,767	488	62
18. Gwalior State							13
19. Cochin State	20	14	6	26	16	10	30
20. Hyderabad State	3,790	3,359	431	5,728	4,929	799	460
21. Jammu and Kashmir State	109	69	40	92	45	47	36
22. Mysore State	3,939	3,289	650	2,100	1,661	439	350
23. Rajputana Agency	521	342	179	255	170	85	34
24. Sikkim State	11	11	..	†	†	†	2
25. Travancore State	237	160	77	242	168	74	126
26. Western India States Agency	..	..	..	.	..	..	31

* Figures in the 1931 columns refer to Bombay *plus* Aden.

NOTE.—(*i*) 1901 figures below Afghanistan include those of Yaghistan.

TABLE III.

number of Immigrants from certain foreign countries.

Countries.									Distant Countries.					
	China.				Japan.				British Isles.					
									1931.			1921.		
1901.	1931.	1921.	1911.	1901.	1931.	1921.	1911.	1901.	Persons.	Males.	Females.	Persons.	Males.	Females.
9	10	11	12	13	14	15	16	17	18	19	20	21	22	23
115,908	**120,745**	**108,495**	**80,282**	**46,831**	**2,334**	**1,867**	**1,261**	**353**	**104,729**	**82,363**	**22,366**	**115,606**	**92,602**	**23,004**
112,977	**120,639**	**108,431**	**80,238**	**46,785**	**2,274**	**1,798**	**1,248**	**348**	**96,677**	**75,978**	**20,699**	**104,267**	**83,392**	**20,871**
120	6	9	1	1	..	..	2	1	1,207	1,023	184	1,065	916	149
32	179	428	35	1	135	3	..	..	145	133	12	133	121	12
1,101	640	183	270	134	1	..	..	..	2,341	1,722	619	1,714	1,275	439
3,525	34	7	8	..	1	3	7	..	3,936	3,204	732	4,109	3,620	489
	3,507	3,856	3,087		538	384	146		12,223	8,237	3,986	12,453	9,245	3,208
4,363				2,321				16						
	30	136	20		2	2	9		3,014	2,118	896	3,272	2,354	918
12,513	718	793	513	297	869	813	328	187	11,381	8,369	3,012	20,370	16,386	3,984
253	114,270	102,344	75,365	43,328	570	449	666	100	6,201	4,837	1,364	6,097	4,735	1,362
839	31	16	35	16	18	5	4	7	4,024	3,254	770	3,680	3,050	630
2	1	..	1	1	..	..	..	..	64	36	28	73	48	25
100	95	133	148	42	90	108	30	33	5,716	4,174	1,542	5,435	3,397	2,038
	23	15	8	..	2	..	..		10,336	9,401	935	9,691	8,680	1,011
89,128	29	3		456	2	..		2	3,063	2,357	706	2,835	2,426	409
			595				12							
	963	423			17	3			15,554	12,423	3,131	16,068	13,003	3,065
1,001	113	85	152	188	29	28	44	2	17,472	14,690	2,782	17,272	14,136	3,136
2,931	**106**	**64**	**44**	**46**	**60**	**69**	**13**	**5**	**8,052**	**6,385**	**1,667**	**11,339**	**9,210**	**2,129**
155	3	2	..	11	44	..	..	..	72	55	17	50	29	21
			..		..	2			1,898	1,577	321	2,773	2,440	333
186	36	11		1			4	..						
			..		..	1			43	31	12	551	490	61
2	2	..	..	..	1	..	..	..	38	22	16	27	20	7
886	13	7	..	2	12	31	3	..	2,088	1,944	144	3,395	2,863	532
1,347	5	8	2	15	..	..	..	..	147	64	83	148	68	80
21	25	16	18	12	3	5	4	..	2,812	2,061	751	3,831	2,935	896
308	2	1	8	1	..	..	1	..	406	257	149	347	210	137
†	15	9	15	†	..	..	..	†	3	2	1	8	6	2
26	2	10	1	4	..	30	1	5	377	263	114	209	149	60
..	3	..	..	..	..	..	..	..	168	109	59	..	..	..

Distant Countries.														
Other European Countries.			Africa.				America.				Australasia.			
1921.	1911.	1901.	1931.	1921.	1911.	1901.	1931.	1921.	1911.	1901.	1931.	1921.	1911.	1901.
31	32	33	34	35	36	37	38	39	40	41	42	43	44	45
5,458	**8,546**	**7,930**	**11,408**	**4,719**	**3,767**	**8,293**	**4,455**	**3,446**	**2,750**	**2,069**	**1,516**	**1,683**	**1,266**	**646**
4,785	**7,805**	**7,401**	**8,187**	**4,245**	**3,214**	**8,193**	**4,099**	**3,174**	**2,495**	**1,992**	**1,406**	**1,507**	**1,206**	**610**
45	43	17	40	20	9	3	10	8	9	5	10	4	12	7
6	1	2	3	1	..	1	3	5	3	3	8	15	2	..
46	69	53	76	10	14	15	110	97	58	49	28	37	25	20
32	36	36	29	18	8	15	41	32	37	9	15	16	19	5
903	1,323		112	134	232		393	407	312		143	422	306	
		1,449				170				370				195
197	289		43	17	30		230	179	66		30	40	40	
1,500	2,233	3,070	4,764	2,260	1,503	7,007	999	455	277	340	303	177	149	10
456	983	639	173	70	53	58	489	559	403	211	168	214	205	48
493	286	239	87	75	46	17	279	374	145	93	21	51	60	16
10	13	14	7	2	3	2	5	3	2	2	2	4	2	..
599	1,412	987	1,779	737	893	672	497	261	255	212	149	107	97	92
12	55		46	16	24		44	5	26		38	20	28	
76	595	536	28	63		87	55	24		273	17	13		92
					122				267				107	
205			657	583			319	307			121	136		
205	467	359	343	239	277	146	625	458	635	425	353	251	154	125
673	**741**	**529**	**3,221**	**474**	**553**	**100**	**356**	**272**	**255**	**77**	**110**	**176**	**60**	**36**
14	15	11	938	371	257	23	15	21	12	2	1	..	..	..
55			22	9			88	72			9	11		
	91	113			129	13			89	12			8	8
20			..	8			19	13			..	20		
18	30	7	5	..	..	2	3	3	3	2	2	4	1	..
149	146	101	4	10	98	16	92	48	40	19	21	88	11	..
10	17	18	9	8	6	8	12	8	10	2	17	4	1	2
218	324	206	167	55	46	18	63	77	76	27	30	36	34	16
28	40	23	28	7	16	16	23	26	16	9	11	11	4	6
3	3	†	..	..	..	†	1	..	..	†	1	..	..	†
158	75	50	29	6	1	4	32	4	9	4	16	2	1	4
..	..	..	2,019	..	..	..	8	..	..	..	2	..	..	..

† Included in Bengal.

(*ii*) The figures against Bombay for the years 1901-21 are inclusive of those for the Western Indian States Agency.

SUBSIDIARY TABLE IV.

Number of Indians born in India who were enumerated in Great Britain and the Colonies during the period 1926 to 1931.

Colony where enumerated.		Total Born in India.			Details by Provinces, States and Agencies. Bengal.		Bombay.		Madras.		Punjab.		Other Provinces and States.‡		India Unspecified.		Number of Natives of India in Colony irrespective of Birth-place.		
		Persons.	Males.	Females.	Males.	Females.	Males.	Females.	Males.	Females.	Males.	Females.	Males.	Females.	Males.	Females.	Persons.	Males.	Females.
	1	2	3	4	5	6	7	8	9	10	11	12	13	14	15	16	17	18	19
	Total ..	**656,709***	**477,465**	**178,911**	**4,627**	**952**	**6,518**	**2,679**	**54,744**	**9,608**	**4,357**	**304**	**8,656**	**855**	**398,563**	**164,513**	**1,304,400**	**813,143**	**491,257**
Europe	England and Wales	7,129	6,844	285	2,189	40	851	78	342	40	1,062	26	1,779	88	621	13	7,129†	6,844	285
	Gibraltar	56	56	..	..	..	56	..	..	..	..	..	..	..	..	..	56†	56	..
	Irish Free State	1,989	919	1,070	..	..	..	..	..	..	..	..	..	..	919	1,070	1,989†	919	1,070
	Malta..	40	37	3	..	..	..	..	..	..	..	..	..	..	37	3	43	38	5
	Northern Ireland	1,003	485	518	..	..	..	..	..	..	..	..	..	..	485	518	1,003†	485	518
	Scotland	2,003	1,986	17	614	1	257	4	79	5	374	..	353	4	309	3	2,003†	1,986	17
Asia	Ceylon	71,165	61,022	10,143	77	15	644	210	53,179	8,999	107	25	6,237	723	778	171	80,721	66,141	14,580
	Cyprus	3	3	..	1	..	..	..	..	..	2	..	..	..	..	..	4	3	1
	Hong Kong	3,823	3,553	270	46	5	80	18	5	2	2,495	154	169	3	758	88	4,745	3,989	756
	Malaya (British)	492,504	352,634	139,870	..	..	..	..	..	..	..	..	..	..	352,634	139,870	624,009	421,028	202,981
	North Borneo	610	538	72	13	..	15	3	93	21	225	28	31	2	161	18	1,206	843	363
	Palestine	40	25	15	..	..	..	..	..	..	..	..	..	..	25	15	60	34	26
Africa	Egypt	539	465	74	..	..	..	..	..	..	..	..	..	..	465	74	821	623	198
	Gold Coast Colony	56	56	..	..	..	52	..	1	..	1	..	..	..	2	..	56†	56	..
	Mauritius	6,829	4,557	2,272	1,684	891	568	248	1,008	533	..	..	..	..	1,297	600	268,870	139,668	129,202
	Nigeria	32	32	..	..	..	..	..	..	..	..	..	..	..	32	..	32†	32	..
	North Rhodesia	127	116	11	..	..	94	9	12	1	2	1	2	..	6	..	171	139	32
	Nyasaland	1,405	1,252	153	..	..	..	..	..	..	..	..	..	..	1,252	153	1,509	1,306	203
	Seychelles	333	..	..	4		78		229		..	..	8		14		503	398	105
	Sierra Leone	19	19	..	..	..	19	..	..	..	..	..	..	..	..	..	25	22	3
	Somaliland	234	166	68	2	..	44	17	18	6	18	10	84	35	..	..	520	310	210
	Sudan	421	316	105	..	..	..	..	..	..	..	..	..	..	316	105	525	368	157
	Tanganyika	13,742	9,242	4,500	..	..	..	..	..	..	..	..	..	..	9,242	4,500	23,422	14,177	9,245
	Zanzibar	6,050	3,899	2,151	..	..	3,828	2,091	..	..	71	60	..	..	..	..	15,246	9,955	5,291
America	British Guiana	23,236	14,447	8,789	..	..	..	..	..	..	..	..	..	..	14,447	8,789	130,540	69,729	60,811
	British Honduras	45	39	6	..	..	..	..	..	..	..	..	..	..	39	6	497	266	231
	Trinidad	23,255	14,738	8,517	..	..	..	..	..	..	..	..	..	..	14,738	8,517	138,667	73,704	64,963
Australasia	Fanning Islands	2	2	..	..	..	1	..	1	..	..	..	..	..	..	..	4	4	..
	Gilbert Islands	1	1	..	1	..	..	..	..	..	..	..	..	..	..	..	1†	1	..
	Tongan Islands	18	16	2	..	..	9	1	6	1	..	..	1	..	..	..	23	19	4

*The details in columns 3 and 4 do not work up to the total in column 2, as the sex details of emigrants to Seychelles are not available.

No information as to the number of persons born in India and enumerated in Colonies not scheduled in this table is available.

† (Columns 17—19).—In the absence of detailed information the figures in columns 2—4 have been repeated.

‡ (Columns 13 and 14).—Includes Andamans and Nicobars (1), Assam (965), Baluchistan (8), Bihar and Orissa (160), Burma (171), C. P. and Berar (115), Coorg (2), Delhi (51), N.-W. F. Province (211), United Provinces (503), Baroda (26), Central India (28), Cochin (2,450), Gwalior (14), Hyderabad (254), Jammu and Kashmir (65), Mysore (258), Rajputana and Ajmer-Merwara (55), Sikkim (1), Travancore (3,403) and the Western India States Agency (660).

SUBSIDIARY TABLE V.

Number of Emigrants to Colonies, etc., who were registered at the ports of Calcutta, Madras, Bombay and Karachi during the decade 1921 to 1930.

Colony, etc.	Emigrants who embarked on the various Colonies from				Emigrants who returned from the various Colonies to			
	Calcutta.	Bombay.	Madras.	Karachi.	Calcutta.	Bombay.	Madras.	Karachi.
Ceylon ..	..	..	1,159,010	..	..	..	703,715	..
Fiji ..	..	..	..	..	13,214	..	3,459	..
British Guiana	..	..	..	..	4,478	..	314	..
Jamaica ..	..	..	..	..	2,765	..	177	..
Malaya and Strait Settlements	..	..	721,959	..	..	..	133,343	..
Mauritius ..	1,428	..	..	..	944	1,292	642	..
Natal ..	..	..	..	..	3,735	..	10,027	..
Sarawak ..	2	..	..	..	..	..	..	..
Siam (Bangkok)	79	..	..	..	102	..	..	..
Surinam ..	..	..	..	..	1,101	..	..	..
Trinidad ..	..	..	..	..	8,947	..	644	..
Other Ports	..	5,595	225,025	1,638	16	4,996	238,091	46
Total ..	1,509	5,595	2,105,994	1,638	35,302	6,288	1,090,412	46

Principal birth districts of Emigrants from Calcutta and Madras.

District	Number	District	Number
Madras			
Trichinopoly	267,053	Tinnevelly ..	26,134
Salem ..	156,200	Coimbatore ..	25,845
North Arcot	153,147	Chittoor ..	21,042
Tanjore ..	105,573	Vizagapatam	14,674
Madura ..	84,219	Nellore ..	5,013
South Arcot	72,914	South Kanara	1,791
Chingleput ..	59,055	Guntur ..	1,617
Ramnad ..	50,383	Kistna ..	1,598
Malabar ..	38,445	Godavari ..	1,112
Pudukottai State ..		.. ..	42,597
Travancore ..		.. ..	2,501
Bengal ..		.. ..	1,676*
Mysore ..		.. ..	1,383

*Includes certain persons who did not embark owing to sickness or other causes.

SUBSIDIARY TABLE VI.

Actual and Natural Populations.

Province, State or Agency.	Actual Population at Census.	Immigrants (Persons born elsewhere but enumerated in Province or State).	Persons born in Province but enumerated in other Parts of India.	Persons born in Province or State but enumerated outside India.	Natural Population (Persons born in Province or State irrespective of the place of emigration).
1	2	3	4	5	6
INDIA	352,837,778	730,562	..	656,709*	352,763,925
Ajmer-Merwara	560,292	106,444	60,909	†	514,757
Andamans and Nicobars	29,463	14,745	552	1	15,271
Assam	9,247,857	1,408,763	73,036	965	7,913,095
Baluchistan	868,617	90,053	42,763	8	821,335
Bengal	51,087,338	1,853,708	954,434	5,583	50,193,647
Bihar and Orissa	42,329,583	509,837	1,758,130	160	43,578,036
Bombay (*including Aden*) ..	26,398,997	1,250,461	592,194	9,275	25,750,005
Burma	14,667,146	775,963	24,197	171	13,915,551
Central Provinces and Berar ..	17,990,937	655,574	422,061	115	17,757,539
Coorg	163,327	38,718	3,231	2	127,842
Delhi	636,246	263,188	69,427	51	442,536
Madras	47,193,602	267,195	1,135,231	64,581	48,126,219
North-West Frontier Province ..	4,684,364	159,166	90,681	211	4,616,090
Punjab (*including Agency*) ..	28,490,857	674,152	702,817	4,661	28,524,183
United Provinces..	49,614,833	559,605	1,557,451	503	50,613,182
Baroda State	2,443,007	324,579	205,176	26	2,323,630
Central India Agency	6,632,790	600,766	482,536	28	6,514,588
Cochin State	1,205,016	87,417	45,790	2,450	1,165,839
Gwalior State	3,523,070	281,550	296,821	14	3,538,355
Hyderabad State	14,436,148	247,795	332,602	254	14,521,209
Jammu and Kashmir State ..	3,646,243	64,196	94,455	65	3,676,567
Mysore State	6,557,302	344,592	125,238	258	6,338,206
Rajputana Agency	11,225,712	330,939	846,811	55	11,741,639
Sikkim State	109,808	15,417	7,212	1	101,604
Travancore State..	5,095,973	135,103	49,933	3,403	5,014,206
Western India States Agency ..	3,999,250	109,674	293,685	660	4,183,921

*Includes 563,208 persons who failed to make the return of birth place.
† Included in Rajputana.

CHAPTER IV.

Age.

The return of age.

68. The returns of age will be found tabulated by sex and civil condition in Tables VII and VIII of part II of this volume. Table VII gives particulars for the whole population by annual groups from 0 to 5 and thereafter in quinquennial groups for India and for provinces and states separately, followed by tables for cities in decennial groups. Table VIII gives returns for selected castes as first sorted into alternate ternary and septenary groups without the adjustment applied to the ages in Table VII. The enumerators at the 1931 census were instructed to record age not as hitherto in terms of the number of years completed but as age at the nearest birth-day. The discrepancy which on the face of it would be involved between the figures of the 1931 and all previous censuses is more theoretical than real. Ignorance of precise age is almost universal in India and the probability is that the returns of age given at the 1921 and the previous censuses were just as nearly the returns of age for the nearest birth-day as the returns of completed years. In fact it is the belief that the age obtained by the enquiries made at previous censuses is more likely to have represented age to the nearest birth-day than the number of completed years, that has caused the change in the instructions to enumerators. In any case the Indian age returns are admitted on all hands to be extremely inaccurate, and even if the practice of recording as *nil* the ages of infants under six months, which the return of age at the nearest birth-day involves, be regarded as an absurdity, it is certainly no worse than the conflicting instructions of previous censuses under which (1) all children under one year were returned as infants and (2) all children whose names could not be stated were likewise returned as infants. A taboo on children's names is a common thing in India, but it is by no means one which ceases when the child reaches one year of age and the result at previous censuses has been, whether or no caused by this instruction, greatly to swell the numbers of infants under one year of age at the expense of infants over one year, an inflation which is liable to be increased by the addition of the survivors of births occurring between the preliminary and final enumeration, a space of time which may vary from a day or two to as much as a couple of months. This latter inflation is, however, a recurrent feature of the Indian census and the comparative value of the figures from 0–1 is not affected. The misstatement of the age of infants naturally appears at its maximum in the ages from 1–2, as indeed would appear to have been the case in 1911 in the United Kingdom also, while there is comparatively little understatement of the ages of children of 2–3 years, and from three to five the tendency seems to be rather to overstate than understate the age. In pointing out this tendency the Census Commissioner of Gwalior State says that it was brought first to his notice when dealing with the fertility and fecundity schedules, in the returns on which it was common to find women who said they had been married four years but had three children whose ages they gave as 5, 3 and 1 year. Further the abovementioned taboo would not be merely on uttering the name. It would much more often than not, in all probability, be unlucky for an infant to be shown to a strange enumerator, who may therefore have as his only guide the statement of a mother whose ideas of the passage of time are of the vaguest possible. Another attitude is illustrated by the Madras Census Superintendent :—

> " A Salem ...... father, challenged about the absence from his account of persons present of any indication of a very recent arrival, said with some surprise : 'It is but now born ! Do you count it ?' ".

He continues " When one reflects on conditions in India it is difficult to place any serious value on the change and I could detect among supervisors a not infrequent wonder that it should be thought worth while to particularize on the day of birth at all when in the vast majority of cases the month is unknown and in most cases the year, while the lustrum and even the decade must frequently be a guess .... A peculiar difficulty arose from the fact that in parts of Malabar the equivalent Malayalam in common use for both 'nearest' and 'next' was the same. This was met by special instructions but illustrates well the difficulties of a polyglot census."

Misstatements of Age.

69. Apart from ignorance there are many reasons which appear to operate towards a deliberate misstatement of age at the census return. This is particularly the case with unmarried girls who have reached puberty. It is invariably found that the age-period of girls from 10–15 is defective in numbers and this is no doubt justly put down in part at any rate to the unwillingness of better caste Hindus, particularly Brahmans, to admit to having unmarried daughters already pubescent, who should therefore be already married in accordance with the injunctions or at least the strong recommendations of the Smritis. It may, however, be also due to short enumeration as a result of secrecy, and indeed the actuary who examined the 1921 census returns felt so convinced of actual shortage of enumeration, as distinct from misstatement of age, at the period about 15 years that it was partly for that reason that he was unwilling to work out any table for the expectation of life, which he considered would be vitiated by short enumeration at that age. A possible explanation is, in the case of females, to be found in the practice in several parts of India of secluding girls at the age of puberty; for at any rate certain castes consider it necessary to shut up and conceal pubescent girls independently of any shame at their being unmarried. Thus Dāsaris, Dhangars and Killekyatas seclude girls at puberty for 3 to 8 days, and Jains from 9 to 15 days. This seclusion of girls when they reach the age of puberty is probably part of a widely spread custom which may be observed also in Africa and in Oceania. At the same time it is more than doubtful if there is any general shortage of enumeration as suggested by the actuary, and it is clear from the returns that the ages of males are similarly misstated at that period; this the actuary, in 1921, attributed to the desire to appear either definitely as a boy or definitely as a man, and it is possible that the practice of early marriage results in some exaggeration of the ages of those just married and a corresponding understatement of the ages of those who are not. In the case of males later in life there is apparently a tendency for widowers and bachelors who are becoming elderly to understate their ages, particularly if they are wishful to remarry. On the other hand the Indian age returns do not appear to suffer from any understatement in the ages of adult women, though recently married girls, and particularly those who are mothers, tend to overstate their age, or rather to have their age overstated for them, no doubt since a matron's position gives an impression of age which is not necessarily a true one, particularly in a country in which women are married when exceptionally young. In the case of the old it is a natural tendency on the part of both sexes to exaggerate, and women in particular, being very ignorant of the periods which mark the passage of time, are inclined to give the most wild statements as to their age; in fact as a magistrate in court the writer has heard a woman of about 35 to 40 years, who gave her age as 100 years and caused a titter at the bar, hurriedly restate it as 200 years. The enumerators, it is true, were instructed to correct ridiculous returns of age, but it may be doubted whether they were in all cases competent to do so. The fact that the average life in India is shorter than in the West possibly encourages exaggeration in the eyes of those who do pass their allotted three score years and ten, and this tendency is in some places likely to be encouraged by the practice of performing a ceremony to celebrate the attainment of sixty years of life. Obviously a guess is least inaccurate in the case of the young, where the margin for variation is least, and most inaccurate for the aged, where an error of even twenty years may be difficult to detect.

Another reason for the misstatement of the correct age is a superstitious belief that it is unwise to state one's age correctly, as this is liable to reduce one's length of years. The *Niti Shashtra* apparently lays down that a man's age is one of the nine things which he must carefully conceal; such beliefs are probably dying out, but they probably die extremely hard and they are not peculiar to India. Another point which affects all ages returned at the census is the practice common, if not general, in India of reckoning age from the time of conception and not from that of birth, while yet another element of inaccuracy is to be found in curious methods of reckoning periods of time; thus a common method in the Assam hills is to reckon by harvests. A child born in September would have his age stated in November as one year and in the following November as two years old, a form of reckoning which is also applied to events so that an event which took place just over a year previously would be said to have been taken place two years ago on the ground that two harvests had intervened. The error arising from a practice of this kind would be insignificant when applied to mature years, were it not for the fact that later on the computation is made not by harvests but by the harvesting of a particular plot; a man will remember that within his knowledge such and such plots have been harvested so many times and that the normal cycle of cultivation is, say, seven years (reference is of course not to permanently cultivated but periodically cultivated *jhum* lands); this will give a fair approximation to his real age, provided the cycle of cultivation remains at seven years. There is no certainty, however, that it may not have been 20 years and been gradually reduced with the result that it very much distorts the return of age given.

It is possible that deliberate misstatements of age could be reduced if the persons enumerated could be made to appreciate the fact that their names are eliminated from the returns at the first stage of compilation and that their individual ages are merged into groups. Such confidence, however, is at present wanting, nor was the legislative protection given to the privacy of returns enough to prevent attempts being made to use census schedules as evidence of age in courts of law, and as long as there is that possibility the necessary confidence is certain to be absent.

Ignorance is, however, the principal reason for the inaccuracy of the age returns, and the Census Superintendent of Central India may here be quoted :—

"The Hindus have the custom of casting horoscopes but they are never produced before the enumerator. A horoscope may not often show the true age. It is easily recast to suit one's needs especially of a matrimonial nature and at times it is re-edited when lowering of age is required while seeking Government service .... The vast majority are both indifferent and ignorant towards the question. Ignorance is natural in a population which is illiterate and which never keeps any document. Indifference arises from the outlook on life. The average man or woman in India matures early and is short-lived. Life presses heavily on them and fatalism overpowers them. Childhood, adolescence, middle life and old age, are well-marked stages in life and the Hindu social system has laid down conduct of life and has prescribed rules for the observance of customs and practices. It matters not if the precise age is not known. Apart from any question of reticence, the villager will stare at what he deems an irrelevant enquiry when you ask him to state his age; will hesitate; will sometimes ask 'Is it my age?' and when pressed will return some absurd answer especially if he is over 45 or 50. So the age recorded in the Census is the one guessed either by the enumerated or the enumerator. If our enumerator is somewhat conscientious he would ask a person when he took to the plough or how old he was when the great famine of 1899 broke out. He may in such cases approach to a nearer approximation. By far the heaviest burden that falls on the enumerator is to guess the age of practically everyone in his block. In the tribal areas, it is a matter of great difficulty to make the tribes return any age at all for many of them are not used to counting. A local event such as a Raja's marriage or installation was usually a serviceable guide to the enumerator in fixing the age according to his judgment."

The Madras Census Superintendent writes of—

"The peculiarly practical and realist outlook on life of the average Indian, who yet is often thought to be impractical and visionary. After all, years are a mere convenience for reckoning; to exalt them into an absolute standard as is done in western countries, is to give them an undue importance. Capacity is what matters. Thus to the Indian our application of age-limits to govern retirement and general insistence on birth certificates seem probably to show a defective and—to use a popular word in India—bureaucratic attitude towards life."

Preferential Digits.

70. Again, the age returns of past censuses have made it quite clear that adult Indians have a very marked preference for certain particular digits. This was effectively demonstrated by the Actuary to the Government of India in his Report on the 1921 census, the preference taking the following order :—0, 5, 2, 8, 4, 6 and then the odd numbers 3, 7, 1, 9. With reference to this the Actuary wrote as follows :—

"The method of grouping ages previously adopted, namely, the method by which the numbers living at ages which are multiples of 5 were always treated as the youngest in each group, and with ages stated as age last birthday, produced less accurate results than would be obtained by any other method for which the smallest semblance of justification could be advanced".

As an illustration of the effect on the age returns of this preference for certain digits the accompanying histogram has been compiled on the actual age returns in 1931 of 100,000 of each sex from Madras Presidency. A glance is enough to show that such returns cannot possibly represent the real age distribution of the population.

Formation of age groups.

71. In view of this criticism on the Indian Census practice of throwing all ages returned into quinary groups beginning with the digits 0 or 5, it was decided not only to have age returned as 'age at the nearest birthday' instead of as the number of years completed, but to recast the system of obtaining the quinary groups in the way recommended by the Actuary. The method which he recommended, and which has been followed at this census, was to group the ages from 4 upwards into alternate groups of three and seven. Thus the years 4, 5 and 6 form the first ternary group which is followed by a septenary group of the years 7-13. In this way the favourite digit '0' forms the centre of one group, the next favourite digit '5', the centre of the other. The actual limits of age corresponding to these two groups, assuming that the returns are perfectly correct, would be $3\frac{1}{2}$ to $6\frac{1}{2}$ years in the first case and $6\frac{1}{2}$ to $13\frac{1}{2}$ years in the second case. The alternate ternary and septenary groups thus obtained were formed into quinary groups by a process of combining their halves, so that the group 10-15 years was obtained by combining half the group 7-13 with half the group 14-16, while the group 15-20 was formed from the remaining half of those aged 14-16 plus half of those aged 17-23. The single year groups below the ages of five years were formed by splitting up group 4-6 into six parts, two of which went to compose the group 5-10, three of which remained to represent the group 4-5, and one of which went to supplement half the number of those whose age to the nearest birthday was returned as three years to make the group 3-4. The group 0-1 was composed of those whose age was returned as *nil* plus half those whose nearest birthday was given as one year. The result has been to give a series of age groups undoubtedly very much more accurate in their representation of the actual ages of the general population than could have been obtained by following the old method. It should be made clear, of course, that this method of quinary grouping is not a substitute for the return of ages by annual integers, which can be examined and smoothed by any one interested in so doing. The method of sorting followed at this as at previous censuses necessitates, for purposes of speed and economy, a direct sort into groups instead of a sort by single years and return accordingly. The alternative therefore to a sort into alternate ternary and septenary groups, subsequently to be smoothed into the usual quinary groups, was not a sort into single years but a sort direct into quinary groups beginning with 5 and ending with 0, or *vice versa,* with all the inaccuracies involved by the preference for particular digits referred to above. For certain purposes the unsmoothed ternary and septenary groups have been retained as will appear in the general body of the tables and as will be indicated later in this report. It will be clear of course that there is this additional difference between the two sets of groups. The ternary and septenary groups are in terms of age to the nearest birthday, so that theoretically the groups are divided not at the year of completed age but at the semester before and after. Thus group 7-13 should include all persons who have completed six years and six months and who have not actually completed thirteen years and six months, whereas the quinquennial groups represent a division by years actually completed, so that group 10-15 should include all who have actually reached their 10th birthday and have failed actually to reach their fifteenth, though it be but by hours.

The Actuary recommended a further adjustment to rectify the continuous decrement caused by death in the numbers living in the successive age periods of the population, since the method of distributing equal halves of the ternary and septenary groups into quinary groups involved a small error from this course. To rectify this error he recommended a transfer, from each group to the next younger, of the number in the older group multiplied by the mean of the rates of mortality applicable to the youngest and oldest ages respectively in the group. These transfers, based on the rates of mortality for All-India Males deduced by the Actuary from the 1921 Census returns, involve the following transfers :—

0·84	per cent.	of group	5-10	to group	0-5
1·24	,,	,,	10-15	,,	5-10
1·55	,,	,,	20-25	,,	15-20
2·38	,,	,,	30-35	,,	25-30
3·66	,,	,,	40-45	,,	35-40
5·09	,,	,,	50-55	,,	45-50
6·87	,,	,,	60-65	,,	55-60
7·43	,,	,,	70 and over	,,	65-70

HISTOGRAM OF AGE-RETURNS OF 100,000 MALES AND 100,000 FEMALES FROM MADRAS SHOWING HOW CRUDE AGE RETURNS ARE INACCURATELY WEIGHTED BY THE PREFERENCE SHOWN FOR CERTAIN DIGITS

1931

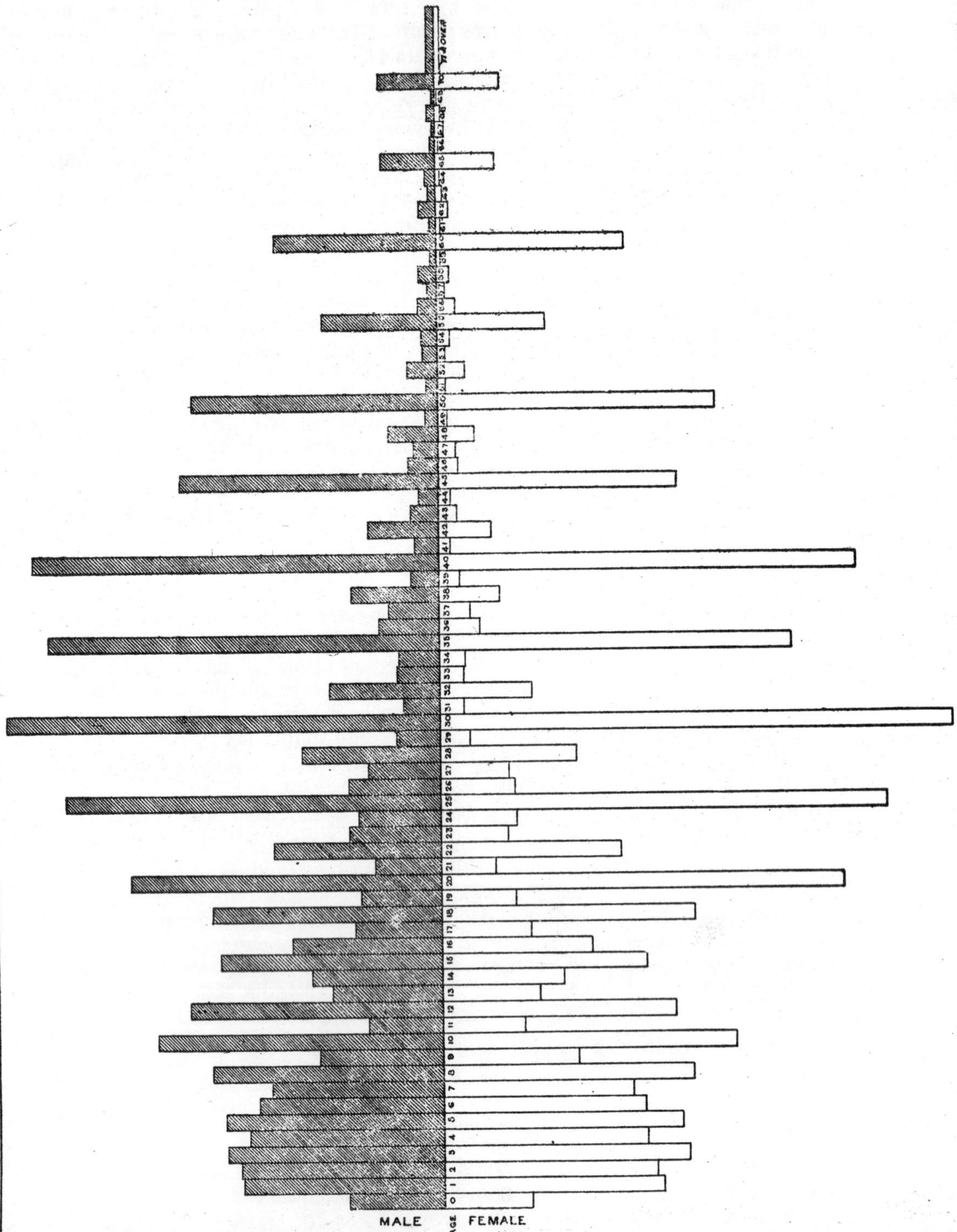

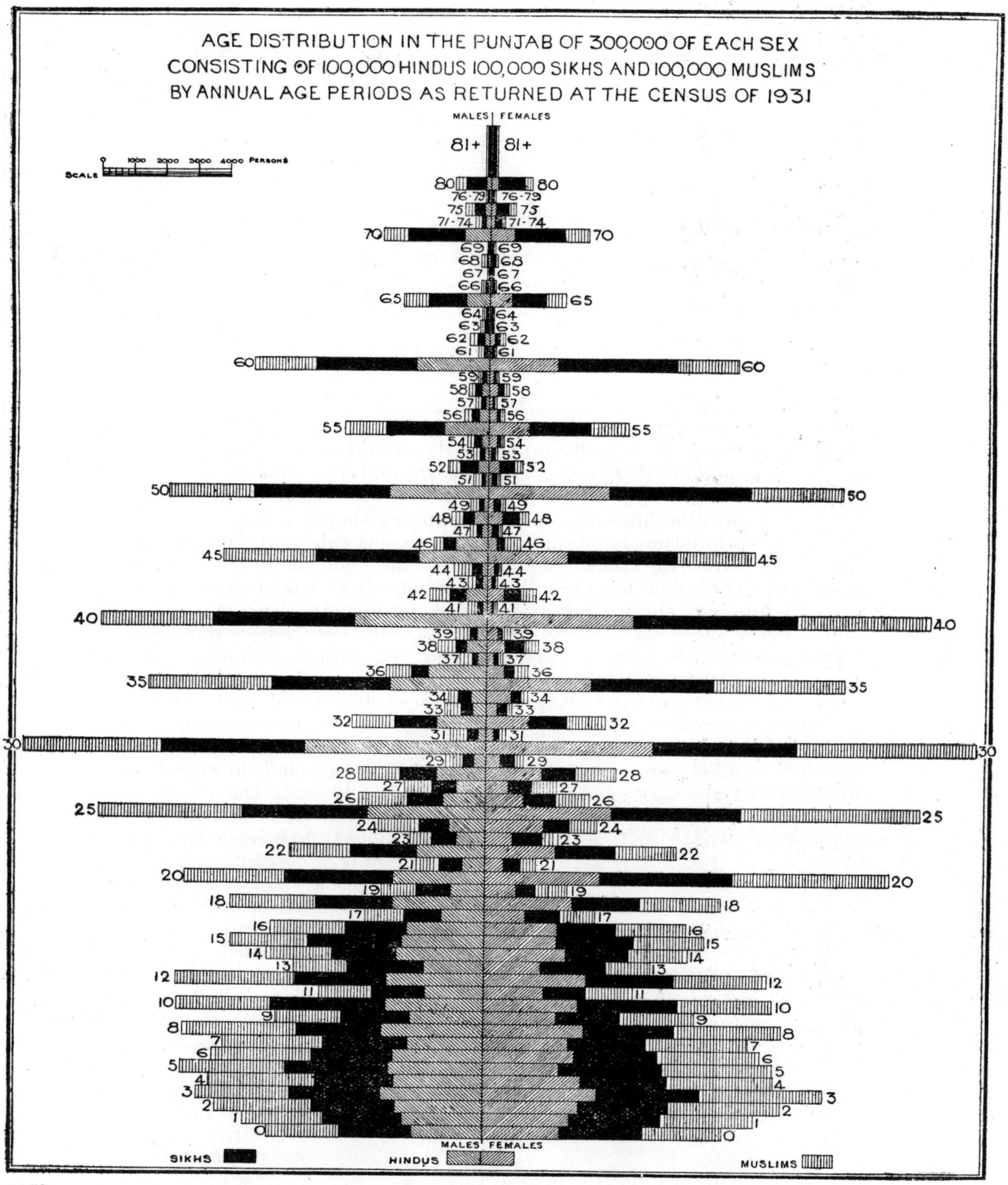
AGE DISTRIBUTION IN THE PUNJAB OF 300,000 OF EACH SEX
CONSISTING OF 100,000 HINDUS 100,000 SIKHS AND 100,000 MUSLIMS
BY ANNUAL AGE PERIODS AS RETURNED AT THE CENSUS OF 1931
MALES
FEMALES
SCALE
0 1000 2000 3000 4000 PERSONS
SIKHS
HINDUS
MUSLIMS

These adjustments were not made in any of the provincial returns and have not been made in the age returns as shown in Table VII in Part II of this Report. They have, however, been worked out for All Religions for all India and the results will be found in Subsidiary Table I to this chapter. The other subsidiary tables in which all India figures of age by religion are involved have also been based on the unadjusted quinary groups, and the same procedure has been followed in the case of the tables in which civil condition is involved. In any case the adjustment to be made for the continuous decrement in successive age periods is so small that for all practical purposes it can be ignored, and in point of fact Mr. Vaidyanathan who examines the 1931 age returns in the annexure to this chapter prefers a different adjustment to that of Mr. Meikle.

Periodic Variation.

72. Clearly the smoother quinquennial age groups of 1931 are not strictly comparable to those of previous censuses which are unevenly weighted by preferential digits. This bias however does not affect the decennial group in which all the series of digits appear, and the comparison with previous censuses has therefore been made by decennial periods. The table below shows the age distribution of 10,000 males and females of the Indian population by 10-yearly age groups for the 5 decades 1891—1931 adjusted for mortality like Subsidiary Table I.

Age group.	1931.		1921.		1911.		1901.		1891.	
	Males.	Females.	Males.	Females.	Males.	Females.	Males.	Females.	Males.	Females.
0—10 ..	2,802	2,889	2,673	2,810	2,710	2,816	2,648	2,721	2,837	2,923
10—20 ..	2,086	2,062	2,087	1,896	2,013	1,823	2,130	1,917	1,974	1,758
20—30 ..	1,768	1,856	1,640	1,766	1,718	1,839	1,666	1,787	1,678	1,801
30—40 ..	1,431	1,351	1,461	1,398	1,451	1,391	1,457	1,408	1,455	1,401
40—50 ..	968	891	1,013	967	1,014	969	1,019	991	1,004	949
50—60 ..	561	545	619	606	609	607	614	621	590	596
60—70 ..	269	281	347	377	340	380	466	555	462	573
70 and over	115	125	160	180	145	175				
Mean age ..	23·2	22·8	24·8	24·7	24·7	24·7	24·7	25·1	24·4	24·9

The decennium 1881-91, which was like that of 1921-31 free from any marked catastrophes, showed what may be taken as a normal increase of 9·6%. This percentage has been exceeded by the increase during the past decade, but only by 1·0%. The intervening three decades were much below normal by these standards, but it is possible that in India a decade free from any disturbing catastrophe in the way of famine, pestilence or epidemic is rather the exception than the rule. The accompanying diagrams compare the age groups by sex in 1931 and 1921 and also the quinquennial age groups in Northern Ireland in 1926. The following changes in the age constitution of India are to be noticed : (*i*) The increase in children under five years old ; this reduces the mean age, though the consequent reduction does not indicate any curtailment of longevity. This increase is directly attributable to the prosperity of the decade since 1921 : (*ii*) the low numbers in group 5-10 ; this presumably results from the after effects of the influenza epidemic at the end of the last decade, though in point of fact the first half of the decade under review was more prosperous than the last half : (*iii*) the increase in females in age groups 10-30 ; this should theoretically lead to an increased number of births in the next decade, just as the decrease in the 5-10 years group should involve a corresponding reduction of births in the decade after that : (*iv*) the decrease in the oldest group, where those aged 70 and over have decreased by nearly a million ; this is probably again traceable to the after effects of the influenza epidemic, which is to be very clearly traced

Age.		*1921.*	1931.
0-5	..	*39,656,410*	53,465,289
5-10	..	*46,747,388*	45,506,909

Age.		Females.	
		1921.	1931.
10-15	..	*16,570,526*	19,061,522
15-20	..	*12,496,066*	15,897,514
20-25	..	*13,502,280*	16,695,096
25-30	..	*13,573,002*	14,724,565

also in the following table in the figures of those aged 40 to 60 in 1921 :—

Age groups 1901 to 1931 (1891 = 100,000).

1901.		1911.		1921.		1931.	
Age group.	Population.	Age group.	Population.	Age group.	Population.	Age group.	Population.
				0-10 ..	100,000	10-20 ..	84,000
		0-10 ..	100,000	10-20 ..	72,800	20-30 ..	73,200
0-10 ..	100,000	10-20 ..	76,300	20-30 ..	68,200	30-40 ..	61,800
10-20 ..	72,000	20-30 ..	67,300	30-40 ..	54,650	40-50 ..	39,550
20-30 ..	94,500	30-40 ..	83,000	40-50 ..	58,300	50-60 ..	36,350
30-40 ..	84,400	40-50 ..	62,250	50-60 ..	38,750	60 and over	28,600
40-50 ..	72,000	50-60 ..	46,400	60 and over	40,900		
50-60 ..	64,700	60 and over	58,000				
60 and over	88,050						

The table above is designed to illustrate the decrement from census to census of any particular ten years age group. Thus group 0–10 in 1891 becomes group 10–20 in 1901, 20–30 in 1911, 30–40 in 1921 and 40–50 in 1931. The table is therefore composed to illustrate the decennial decrease in an unit of 100,000 persons starting whenever possible from 1891. The 1931 figure for age group 0–10, based on the 1921 figure for 0–10=100,000, would be 114,000, indicating the great increase in the number of children found at this census. The age groups 10-20 of 1921 and 20-30 of 1931 represent of course an impossibility as the apparent increase, where there should be a decrease on account of mortality, cannot be accounted for except by misstatements of age in 1921 or in 1931.

Age distribution.

73. According to Sundbärg a normal population has about one half of its total between the ages of 15 and 50, and the proportion of those above that age group to those below it indicates whether the population is increasing, stationary or decreasing. The youngest of the three population groups must be double the eldest if the population is to continue to grow. Just short of that point it may be stationary, but if the elder continue to exceed the younger the population must be regressive. In the marginal tables, the populations of the different provinces and of different religions are shown arranged in order of progressiveness as determined from the 1931 census returns and it will be seen that all of them are clearly progressive according to Sundbärg's classification, except that of the Parsis which must be regarded as stationary, though it is possible, as pointed out below that Sundbärg's categories need readjustment before they can be satisfactorily applied to Indian conditions. The proportions of children to adults are also shown in subsidiary table IV at the end of this chapter with the figures of several censuses compared. In 1921 the Census Commissioner pointed out that the apparent rise in the ratio of children to adults was not an indication of increased fertility during the decade 1911-21, but was due to a depletion of the adult categories by the influenza epidemic. In the 1931 figures the effects of this depletion are still to be seen in the fall of the older age categories with regard to the reproductive ages. On the other hand the proportion of children has still further increased and this time it is clearly due to increased propagation during the years of prosperity. If the total population aged 15 to 50 be taken as

Province or State.	Percentage of population aged		
	0—15 years.	15—50 years.	50 years and over.
Ajmer-Merwara ..	38·8	52·0	9·2
Andaman and Nicobar Islands.	28·7	63·6	7·7
Assam	42·2	49·8	8·0
Baluchistan	24·9	70·9	4·2
Bengal	40·8	51·1	8·1
Bihar and Orissa ..	40·2	50·2	9·6
Bombay (*excluding Aden*)	39·7	51·2	9·1
Aden	26·2	66·3	7·5
Burma	37·4	51·3	11·3
Central Provinces and Berar.	40·1	50·0	9·9
Coorg	35·0	57·2	7·8
Delhi	36·3	55·9	7·8
Madras	38·9	50·5	10·6
N. W. F. Province ..	41·0	50·4	8·6
Punjab	41·2	48·1	10·7
United Provinces ..	38·9	51·3	9·8
Baroda State ..	39·1	50·4	10·5
Central India Agency ..	40·1	51·5	8·4
Gwalior State ..	39·4	52·0	8·6
Hyderabad State ..	39·9	50·0	10·1
Jammu and Kashmir State.	40·6	50·3	9·1
Cochin State	41·7	48·2	10·1
Travancore State ..	42·6	47·7	9·7
Mysore State	40·1	49·9	10·0
Punjab States Agency ..	39·9	49·3	10·8
Rajputana Agency ..	40·7	49·5	9·8
Sikkim State	40·9	47·6	11·5
Western India States Agency.	42·0	47·9	10·1
India ..	**39·9**	**50·5**	**9·6**

Community.	Percentage of population aged		
	0—15 years.	15—50 years.	50 and over.
Tribal	43·9	47·8	8·3
Muslim	42·2	49·3	8·5
Christian ..	41·7	49·2	9·1
Jew	37·7	53·6	8·7
Hindu	39·2	50·9	9·9
Sikh	39·5	48·2	12·3
Jain	36·7	51·7	11·6
Parsi	27·2	56·7	16·1

AGE DISTRIBUTION OF 10,000 OF EACH SEX IN INDIA 1931 AND IN NORTHERN IRELAND 1926

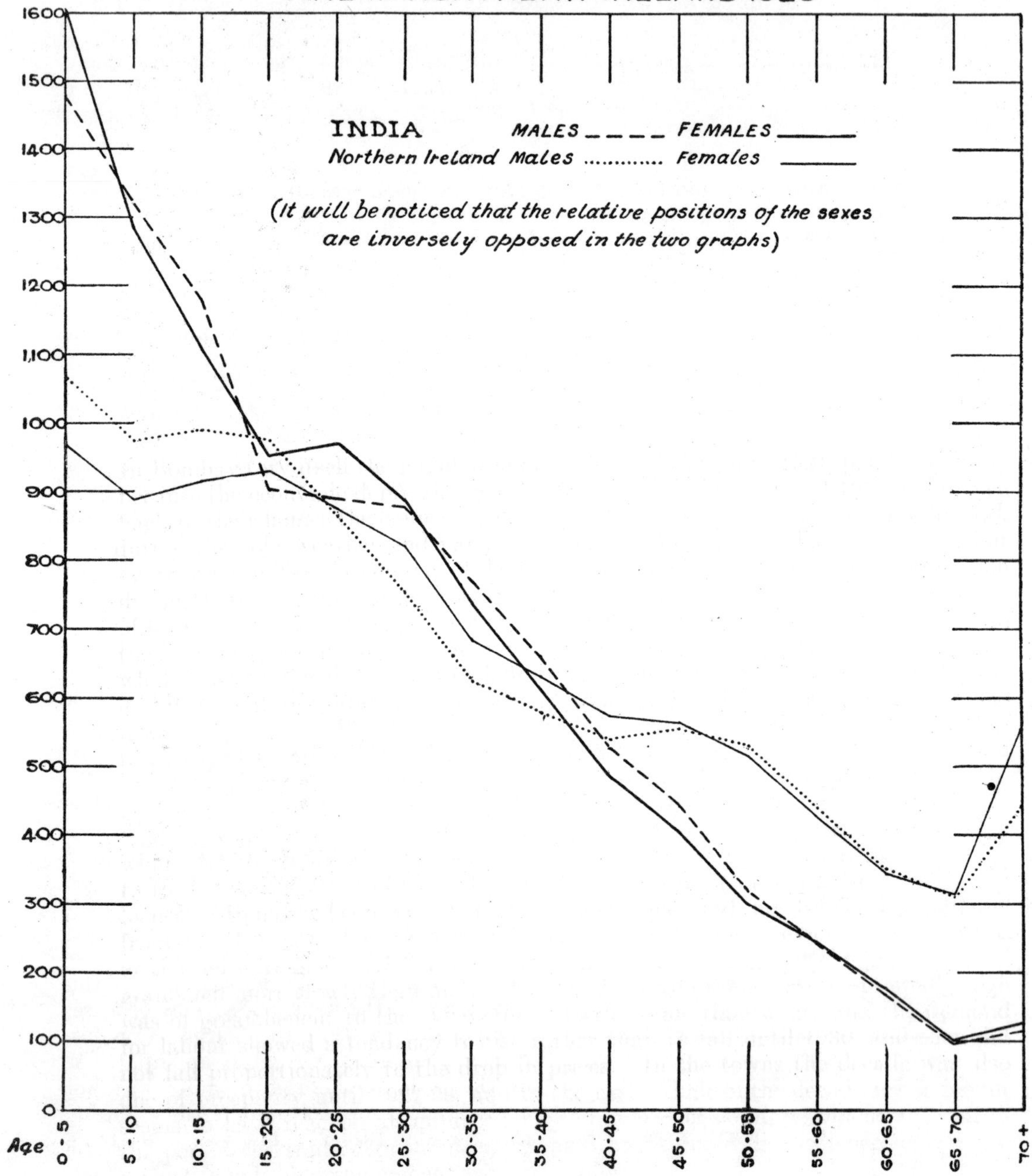

AGE DISTRIBUTION BY QUINQUENNIAL GROUPS OF 10,000 OF EACH SEX IN 1931 & 1921

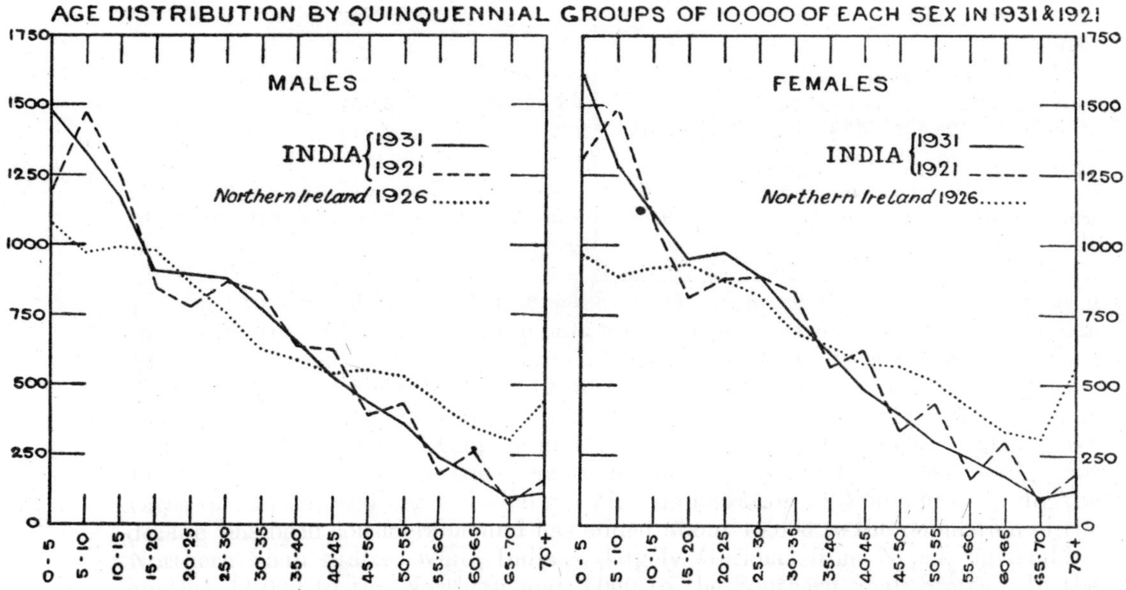

AGE DISTRIBUTION BY DECENNIAL GROUPS OF 10,000 OF EACH SEX AT THREE CONSECUTIVE DECADES

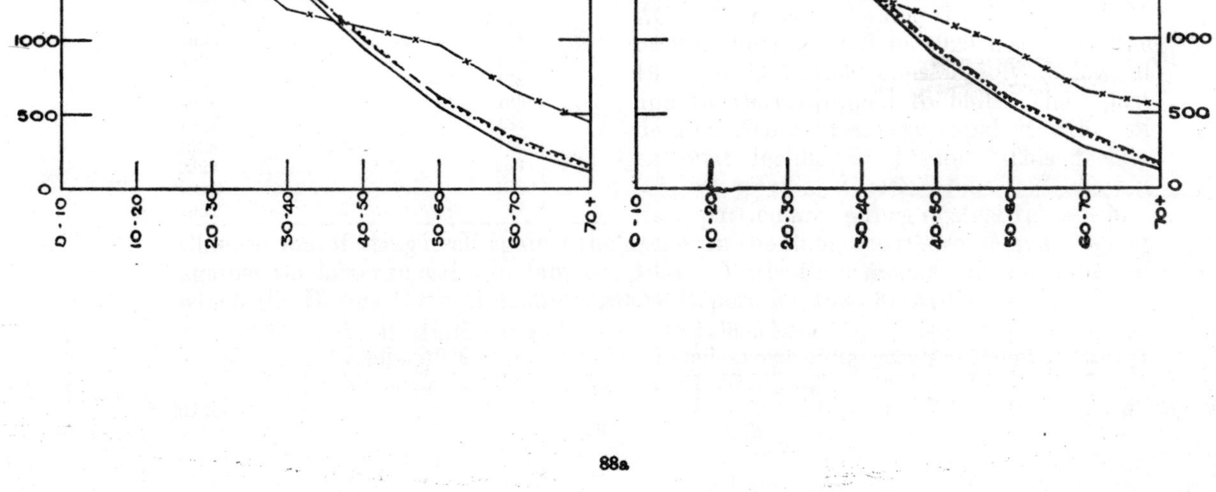

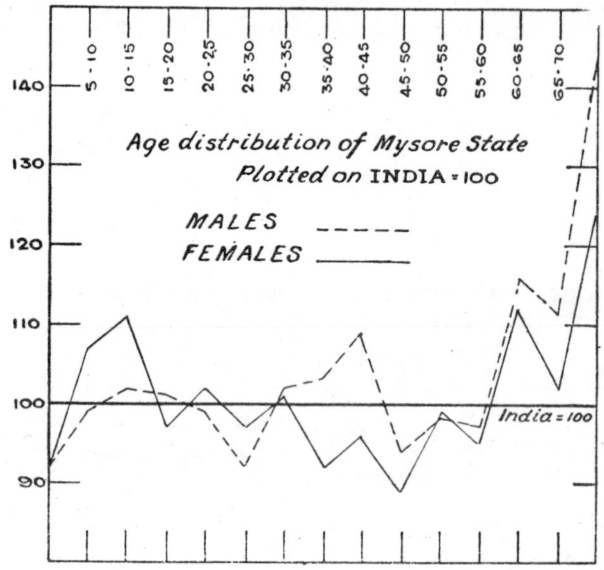
Age distribution of Mysore State
Plotted on INDIA = 100
MALES
FEMALES
India = 100

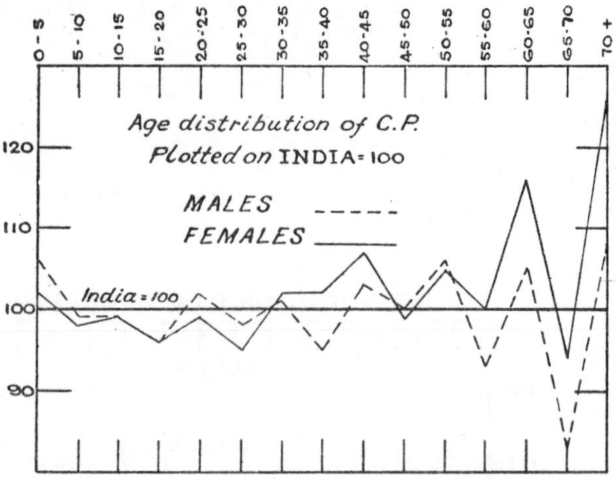
Age distribution of C.P.
Plotted on INDIA = 100
MALES
FEMALES
India = 100

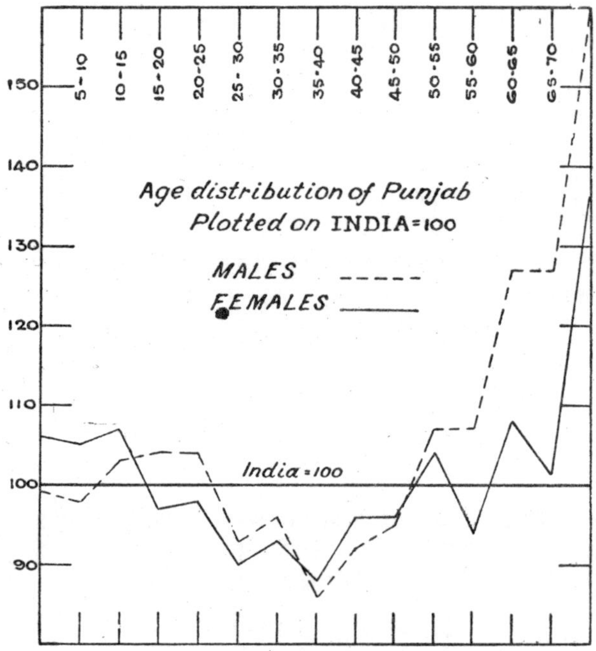
Age distribution of Punjab
Plotted on INDIA = 100
MALES
FEMALES
India = 100

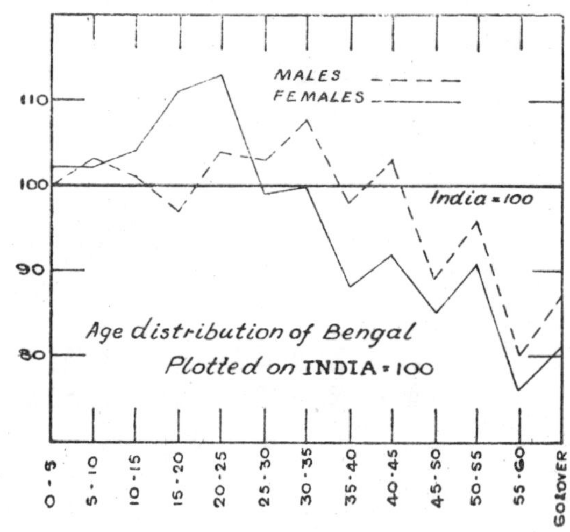
MALES
FEMALES
India = 100
Age distribution of Bengal
Plotted on INDIA = 100

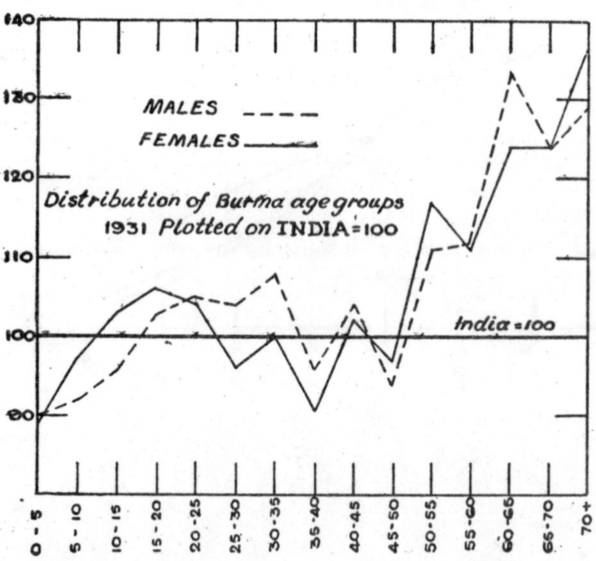
MALES
FEMALES
Distribution of Burma age groups
1931 Plotted on INDIA = 100
India = 100

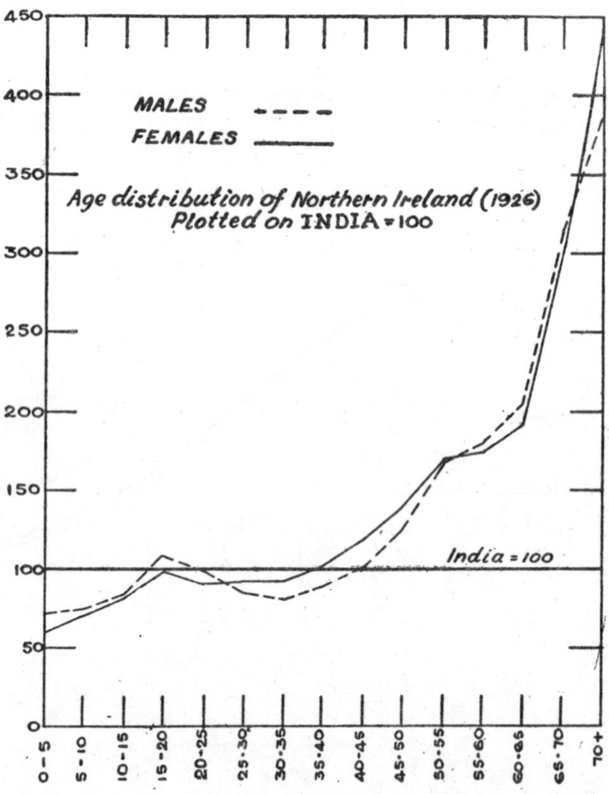
MALES
FEMALES
Age distribution of Northern Ireland (1926)
Plotted on INDIA = 100
India = 100

100, those aged 50 and over were 23 in 1921 and have fallen to 19 in 1931, whereas those aged 0 to 15 have risen from 78·8 to 79·1. In 1891 after a similar decade of prosperity and increase the corresponding figures were likewise 79 for those aged 0 to 15, and 22 for those aged 50 and over, whereas after the following decade, which had suffered much from famine, the corresponding figure for those over 50 was still 22 but for those from 0—15 only 76. The diagrams accompanying this chapter show the distribution of 10,000 of each sex by age groups giving for comparative purposes the corresponding distribution by age groups in Northern Ireland. As an indication of comparative fertility the proportion borne by children 0—10 to married females of 15—40 may be examined and the marginal table gives figures for some communities. Similarly the proportion of persons aged sixty and over to those aged 15 to 40 is an indication of comparative longevity. Comparison suggests that fertility and longevity, though not quite in inverse ratio, approach such a position. In the case of Anglo-Indians the only age groups available necessitate the use of slightly different ages. The results in their case may be compared with the others as approximately equivalent. In the case of castes quinquennial age groups are not available and 0—6 is used for 0—10, 17—43 for 15—40. It may be observed that the castes which head the list in the marginal table all practise adult marriage. The low point at which the mean age falls rather suggests that for India the three age-groups of Sundbärg might need modification, and that 15 and 50 years are a little too old at which to start the second and third age groups respectively. This was in fact pointed out by Sir Edward Gait in 1911, and he took as his standard for comparison the numbers aged 0—10, 15—40 and 60 and over, thus omitting the population from 10 to 15 and from 40 to 60. It would perhaps be more satisfactory to take the total population into account dividing it into 0—13½, 13½ to 45 and 45 and over, a method which would give in 1931 the following result :—

Community.	No. aged 0—10.	No. of married women aged 15—40.	No. of children aged 0—10 to each married woman aged 15—40.
Tribal ..	2,443,237	1,247,270	1·96
Christian ..	1,760,983	908,570	1·94
Sikh	1,194,247	621,095	1·92
Muslim ..	22,972,076	12,870,165	1·78
Jain	319,953	195,063	1·64
Hindu ..	66,177,624	40,378,332	1·64
Parsi	19,404	12,142	1·60

Community.	Sex.	No. aged 60 and over.	No. aged 15—40.	Percentage of those aged 60 and over on those aged 15—40.
1	2	3	4	5
Tribal ..	M.	123,846	1,455,660	8·5
	F.	*139,208*	*1,529,419*	*9·1*
Muslim ..	M.	1,547,638	16,179,065	9·6
	F.	*1,277,130*	*15,011,484*	*8·5*
Hindu ..	M.	4,782,296	50,089,524	9·5
	F.	*5,044,122*	*48,354,902*	*10·4*
Jain ..	M.	28,276	266,275	10·6
	F.	*30,340*	*246,619*	*12·3*
Sikh ..	M.	147,828	963,229	15·3
	F.	*106,023*	*719,448*	*14·7*
Parsi ..	M.	3,957	24,150	16·4
	F.	*3,730*	*23,348*	*16·0*

Anglo-Indians.

	No. aged 60 and over.	No. aged 17—39.	Percentage of persons aged 60 and over on persons aged 19 to 39.
M.	3,164	27,419	11·5
F.	*3,553*	*25,023*	*13·7*

Caste or Tribe.	No. of children aged 0—6.	No. of married women aged 17—43.	No. of children 0—6 to each married woman 17—43.
Karen ..	160,577	107,455	1·49
Bhil	169,254	117,247	1·44
Nayar ..	310,456	230,371	1·35
Brahui ..	924	695	1·33
Santal ..	530,232	400,942	1·32
Baidhya ..	21,645	16,543	1·31
Gujar.. ..	410,035	322,711	1·27
Momin ..	499,214	394,353	1·27
Bhangi ..	142,360	117,010	1·22
Chamar ..	2,446,885	2,054,425	1·19
Kayastha ..	437,847	375,279	1·17
Teli	1,341,910	1,153,892	1·16
Kahar ..	402,294	346,204	1·16
Rajput ..	1,661,211	1,453,941	1·14
Dhobi ..	296,094	262,154	1·13
Brahman ..	2,320,692	2,095,937	1·11
Kunbi ..	1,065,981	977,863	1·09

0—13½, 128,465,421 persons, 13½ to 43½, 167,523,422, and 43½ and over, 53,770,475 ; stated in percentages the corresponding figures are 37, 48 and 15.

Mean Age.

74. The mean age in England and Wales in 1921 was 30·6 and that in Northern Ireland in 1926 was the same, whereas that of India is only 23·02 and it would seem that the expectation of life at 24 years is under 25 years except in

Madras. This conclusion is arrived at from the actuarial report on the 1901 census, which also indicates that the expectation of life in India 30 years ago was greatest between 4 and 9 years and at no age attained 40 years, though it came nearest to doing so in Madras. In the Public Health Commissioner's Report for 1927 the expectation of life in India at the age of five was quoted as 35 years. Returning to the 1901 actuarial report it appears that Burma was better off in this respect as the expectation of life at from 3 to 6 years of age exceeded 42 years for males and at from 3 to 5 years exceeded 43 for females. The infant mortality rate obtained from the same tables is only 23 per cent. in Burma as against almost 30 per cent. in most of India. The mean ages by sex for the different provinces and states and for religions are :—

	All Religions.		Hindu.		Jain.		Tribal.		Christian.		Muslim.	
Province or State.	Males.	Females.	Males.	Females.	Males.	Females.	Males.	Females.	Males.	Females.	Males.	Females
1	2	3	4	5	6	7	8	9	10	11	12	13
India ..	23·2	22·8	23·5	23·3	24·6	24·5	21·8	21·5	22·5	22·0	22·4	21·5
Ajmer-Merwara ..	23·8	23·5	23·7	23·6	25·8	26·1	22·1	22·9	23·1	21·8	23·9	22·8
Andaman and Nicobar Islands.	27·8	21·6	*	*	*	*	*	*	*	*	*	*
Assam ..	22·7	21·6	23·9	22·2	*	*	23·2	22·5	*	*	22·0	20·1
Baluchistan ..	25·2	20·0	*	*	*	*	*	*	*	*	*	*
Bengal	23·3	21·7	*	*	*	*	22·6	20·9	*	*	*	*
Bihar and Orissa	23·0	23·6	23·4	24·0	*	*	21·4	21·7	21·1	21·3	22·6	23·0
Bombay	23·4	22·8	*	*	24·9	23·7	*	*	*	*	*	*
Burma	24·3	23·6	*	*	*	*	*	*	*	*	*	
Central Provinces and Berar.	23·7	23·8	24·2	24·3	25·0	25·0	23·1	23·2	22·0	21·7	24·2	23·3
Coorg	25·0	23·2	*	*	*	*	*	*	*	*	*	*
Delhi	24·4	22·2	24·4	22·4	*	*	*	*	25·0	23·2	24·4	21·8
Madras	24·4	24·3	24·5	24·4	27·3	27·3	23·4	23·4	23·9	23·4	23·1	23·0
North-West Frontier Province.	22·6†	21·8†	24·0	21·9	*	*	*	*	*	*	23·2	22·5
Punjab (*including Agency*).	24·3	23·1	24·7	23·4	*	*	*	*	22·9	21·5	23·8	22·7
United Provinces of Agra and Oudh (British Territory).	24·5	24·5	24·1‡	24·3‡	*	*	*	*	*	*	23·8	23·3
Baroda State ..	23·7	23·6	23·7	23·6	25·2	25·8	22·6	20·8	*	*	24·0	23·9
Central India Agency.	23·3	23·2	23·3	23·3	26·1	25·7	21·4	20·9	*	*	24·3	23·4
Gwalior State ..	23·4	23·2	24·4	24·2	26·0	23·7	*	*	26·1	24·7	24·2	23·2
Hyderabad State	23·5	22·6	*	*	*	*	*	*	*	*	23·6	22·9
Jammu and Kashmir State.	23·6	23·1	26·9	25·2	*	*	*	*	*	*	23·5	22·5
Cochin State ..	23·7	24·1	23·9	24·6	24·0	21·5	*	*	23·3	23·3	23·0	22·5
Travancore State ..	23·0	22·8	23·3	23·3	*	*	*	*	22·6	22·2	22·2	21·6
Mysore State ..	25·1	24·4	24·7	23·8	25·5	24·6	22·7	21·7	24·5	23·7	23·9	21·9
Rajputana Agency	23·5	23·4	23·6	23·5	24·8	25·8	20·4	20·3	23·4	21·4	23·5	22·7
Sikkim State ..	23·0	22·8	*	*	*	*	*	*	*	*	*	*
Western India States Agency.	22·6	22·8	*	*	*	*	*	*	*	*	*	*

NOTE.—The figures against the respective Provinces include attached States, except in the case of Madras which excludes Cochin and Travancore.

* Figure unavailable or unimportant.

† Calculated on enumerated population only.

‡ Brahmanic Hindus only.

Expectation of life.

75. According to the 1901 investigation the expectation of life in India is slightly greater at birth for females than for males but thereafter is appreciably less until the age of 20 years, when females may again expect a longer life than males of the same age, and thereafter their expectation of life is slightly better throughout. The inference is that the female infant has greater vitality at birth, but is more likely to succumb first on account of the greater tendency in India to neglect girls in favour of boys and secondly on account of the risks of early marriage. The actuarial examination in 1911 however gave, with less probability perhaps, a better expectation of life for females at all ages up to 80 when the expectations

were equalised, the male expectation going very slightly ahead at 84 years. At the same time the 1911 examination gave a slightly decreased expectation of life for both sexes and all ages as compared with that of 1901, while the 1901 expectations repeated there were not quite so high as those of 1891. No rates at all were worked out from the census returns of 1921, as the actuary considered that their interest would be purely academic, and that the returns were not reasonably dependable. It would therefore be unwise to attach too much importance to the life tables of previous decades. The constant figure for the mean age at this census as compared with previous ones and in conjunction with the consistency of the decennial age groups suggests that the expectation of life has not much altered since 1891, though until the report of the actuary on the 1931 age returns is available it is not possible to say for certain*. Such a report is under preparation at the time of writing and will be found in the annexure which follows this chapter. As regards Indian mortality rates generally, it is to be inferred from two articles published in the *Journal of the Institute of Actuaries* in July 1929 that the mortality rate rises to maximum at about 55, though in other respects following a similar course to that of the United Kingdom. It also appears that of Indians who insure their lives Hindu mortality is slightly higher than that of other groups, Parsis experiencing ·66 of Hindu mortality, European ·75, Anglo-Indian ·79 and Muslims ·92, though this last figure must be accepted with reserve, as owing to their objection to insurance on religious grounds very few Muslims insure their lives at all. The age distribution of the population in 1931 as compared with 1921 will be found presented for India as a whole and for main communities in Subsidiary Tables I and II at the end of this chapter. A recurrent feature of the Indian age returns is the dip in the curve (*v. inf.* para. 81) at the age group of 15—20. This feature, which is much the same in both sexes, is usually ascribed to more or less intentional misstatement of the ages of both sexes in their ' teens '. It is just possible that this dip in the 1931 curve is the result in part of the depletion, by the influenza epidemic of the end of the last decade, of females of the reproductive ages. It is however pointed out by the Census Superintendent for Central India that there is a general tendency to lower the age of boys for whom matrimonial arrangements are being made; allusion to the prevailing misstatement of the age of girls has already been made, while in regard to boys the Superintendent of Census Operations for Madras may again be quoted :—

> " The Indian outlook on age is, as remarked, much more functional and the advent of so pronounced a vital phenomenon as puberty exercises probably a considerable influence on age returns. If it has arrived the tendency will be to attribute definitely mature years ; if it has not the tendency may be to diminish the actual tale of years due. Much of this is of course conjectural but the actual age return curves dealt with already do show peculiar aggregations at ages between 10 and 15 and after 20 ".

The difference in the age groups of those who live in towns may be inferred by referring to paras. 43 and 48 in chapter II above.

Vital Statistics.

76. The vital statistics of India, are well known to be defective. They are compiled from records maintained locally by means which vary in different provinces, but generally they are kept up by the reports of village officials in rural areas and by municipalities in urban. In the latter case their accuracy will naturally depend on the amount of interest taken in the matter by the urban authorities. This is not great, and even the rural returns are probably more accurate on the whole. In them however, the reporting of the occurrence of births and deaths is often a troublesome duty which the village headman or chaukidar is apt to neglect. Obviously in the case of births he is likely to wait and see whether a child will live and so save himself in many cases the necessity of making a second report for its death, while he no doubt hesitates to report deaths which would give any excuse for the unwelcome visits of unduly suspicious police officers. Taken on the whole the defect in vital statistics is probably to be estimated at about 20 per cent., though it is much higher at its maximum. For example in Mysore State the deficiency is put at 50 per cent. or even more. The returns from which birth and mortality rates are deduced, and the figures given in the subsidiary tables to this

* The expectation of life as deduced by the Actuary from the 1931 returns shows an expectation at birth of 26·56 years for females and 26·91 for males ; at the ages of 4 and 5 years, respectively, when the expectation is at its best, it is 36·75 for females and 38·96 for males. Attention is drawn to the superior expectation enjoyed by males. The figures are for India as a whole.

chapter and to chapter 1, can therefore be only accepted subject to reservation. They are however probably reliable enough as indications of the general trend of birth and death rates, even though the gross figures themselves are understated in both directions, and in Madras Province the returns are accurate enough to have made it possible for the department of Public Health to prognosticate the result of the 1931 Census with an error (on the excess side) of not more than 2 per cent. Bengal and the United Provinces, in that order, are believed to be the next most accurate in respect of their returns, although the Census Superintendent of the latter province estimates the percentage of error in the record of births as 15 per cent. and in that of deaths as 22 per cent. In Assam the Census Superintendent considers that "at least one third of vital occurrences go unreported", and that with reference only to the areas in which vital statistics are theoretically maintained.

Infantile and Puerperal mortality.

77. The question of population and age necessarily involves some reference to the question of infant mortality—that is to the number of infants, per mille born, who die during the first year of life. The infant mortality rate has long been notoriously high in India as compared with most countries in the west of Europe, but is not nearly so high as that, for instance, of Chile, and from 1910-1925 was comparable with that of Hungary, while it was considerably lower than that of the Straits Settlements. The rate of infant mortality in India during the decade under review shows an appreciable reduction on the rate of the previous decade even if allowance be made for the heavy mortality of the influenza years. The marginal table shows the infant mortality rates for the two decades in so far as the figures are available, as 1930 is latest year for which India figures have been obtained by the Public Health Commissioner. The diagram at the end of this chapter, derived from his Report for 1930, gives an indication of the respective conditions of different provinces in the matter of infantile mortality, a curious feature being the high rate consistently prevailing in Coorg, which, as a rural province comparatively free from *purdah*, practising post-puberty marriage and situated at a high altitude, might be presumed to have a low infant death rate; the graphs illustrating the infant mortality of India and of some of the Provinces were also prepared by Colonel Russell and are reproduced here with his permission. It is in towns that the highest infantile mortality is found and the. marginal table shows the rates from 1925 to 1929 for Presidency Towns and certain provincial capitals. The causes of infantile mortality as analysed by the Executive Health Officer for Bombay from time to time show that by far the greater number are due to infantile debility and malformation including premature birth, respiratory diseases coming next, then convulsions, and then diarrhœa and enteritis. A special enquiry was made in Bombay in 1930 as to the infant mortality rates among working and non-working mothers, the results of which are conveniently summarized in Mr. Sorley's report on the cities of Bombay:—

British India—Infant mortality rate per 1,000 births.

Year.	Infant mortality rates per 1,000 live births.	Year.	Infant mortality rates per 1,000 live births.
1911 ..	204·98	1921 ..	197·9
1912 ..	207·65	1922 ..	175·09
1913 ..	194·61	1923 ..	175·56
1914 ..	211·83	1924 ..	188·66
1915 ..	201·90	1925 ..	174·40
1916 ..	202·34	1926 ..	189·04
1917 ..	205·18	1927 ..	166·93
1918 ..	266·96	1928 ..	172·94
1919 ..	224·40	1929 ..	178·39
1920 ..	194·93	1930 ..	180·83

City.	Infantile mortality rates per 1,000 live-births during 1925.	1926.	1927.	1928.	1929.	1930.
Bombay ..	357	255	316	314	301	298
Calcutta ..	326	372	340	276	259	268
Madras ..	279	282	240	289	259	246
Rangoon ..	352	320	294	341	321	278
Lucknow ..	260	287	256	301	269	329
Lahore ..	222	241	201	204	214	187
Nagpur ..	258	302	254	299	291	270
Delhi ..	183	238	201	210	259	199

"The enquiry covered 2,053 cases. Of these 39·2 per cent. were working mothers and 60·8 per cent. non-working mothers; 91·48 per cent. were Hindus, 3·80 Muslims and 4·72 Indian Christian; and 75 per cent. of the workers were textile workers. The average number of live births per working mother in all areas was 2·85 and per non-working mother was 2·75. In Naigaum a sanitary area, the figures were 2·91 and 2·78 respectively. As regards still births in proportion to live births the figures were, for all areas, working mothers 34 per cent. and for non-working mothers 33 per cent.; and for Naigaum the figures were 31 per cent. and 27 per cent. respectively. It will be obvious that the working class mothers have more children and more still births than non-working mothers, and that the Naigaum figures are better than the general figures. The statistics are curious. The greater prolificness of working class mothers seems to be due to their better economic condition which leads to their having more and better food than the non-working mothers. But the unfavourable figures for still births amongst working mothers seem to suggest that industrial labour, while not interfering with the conception of children has had effect on child bearing itself. It is by no means unlikely that working mothers work too late before and too soon after child-birth and so are liable to certain influences which do not affect non-working mothers. The table below shows the infant mortality by age groups :—

Age at death.	Rate of infant mortality per 1,000 live-births.		
	Working mothers.	Non-working mothers.	All mothers.
Under 1 day	8	8	8
1 day and under 7 days	26	38	33
7 days and under 1 month	26	23	24
1 month and under 3 months	21	22	21
3 months and under 6 months	22	27	25
6 months to 1 year	99	85	91
Total under 1 year ..	202	203	202

The rate of mortality among infants under six months is greater in the case of non-working mothers than for working mothers, the actual figures being 118 as against 103 ".

In Calcutta the three principal causes of infant mortality are returned as congenital debility, premature birth and *tetanus neonatorum*, syphilis being largely responsible for the second of these. The infantile mortality in Baroda State is said to be chiefly caused by " child marriage, faulty feeding, contamination of the milk supply, ignorant management of children, frequency of motherhood and insanitary conditions ". In Calcutta a high rate of infantile mortality among Muslims is reported to be a constant feature of the vital statistics and this is to be ascribed in the main to the strict purdah observed even among the poorest Muslims living in *bastis*, where all health visitors report that they meet with most opposition to healthy innovations. The above read again with the Bombay figures suggests that immature maternity, purdah and primitive obstetrics are probably still principally responsible for the high rate of mortality among Indian infants and an otherwise somewhat severe critic of the 1911 census report admitted early marriage as a prime cause of the low ratio of females to males and predicted a continued fall of that ratio at the next census and until this cause should be removed. This point of view is supported by what is known of maternity mortality. Obviously the causes of death in child-birth are likely to bear an immediate relation to those of death in the first year of life, and an investigation made in Madras into causes of maternal mortality in 7,324 cases in four cities led to the following conclusions (among others) :—

In 6% of confinements the mother was under the age of 15.

In 3% of confinements instrumental delivery or other surgical interference was required.

The maternal mortality is at its maximum in the earliest ages, being highest in the first confinement, and the earlier the age of the mother the greater the risk of her death.

More than 60% of puerperal deaths were due to sepsis or septicaemia.

Economic conditions had no bearing on maternal mortality ; they seemed almost to have an inverse relationship to neo-natal mortality.

The incidence of neo-natal mortality was greatest in the case of first births, and when the mother was under 20 years of age.

Only about one third of confinements received skilled medical aid.

In a written statement made to the Age of Consent Committee the Assistant Director of Public Health observed that proportionate to the high maternal and child mortality " there is a vast number of invalids or physical wrecks among the survivals ", and even in Travancore State, more advanced in this respect, perhaps, than any part of India except the adjoining state of Cochin, the Census Commissioner of the State is able to pronounce that—

" The highest female mortality, which exceeds that of males by 60 to 61 per 1,000 occurs in the age-period 15—30, and must certainly be attributed to the early marriage of girls and the consequent premature maternity. Death of young mothers at child-birth is not an uncommon occurrence, but more common than this, however, is the death of women in the later period of maturity, say, between the years of 20 and 30, brought on by the physical exhaustion, the nervous break-down and other ailments, which are the aftermath of premature child-bearing."

INFANTILE MORTALITY PER MILLE OF LIVE BIRTHS IN BRITISH INDIA AND PROVINCES FROM 1892-1930

With acknowledgments to Lt. Col. A. J. H. Russell C.B.E. I.M.S. Public Health Commissioner with the Govt. of India in whose report for 1930 the originals will be found.

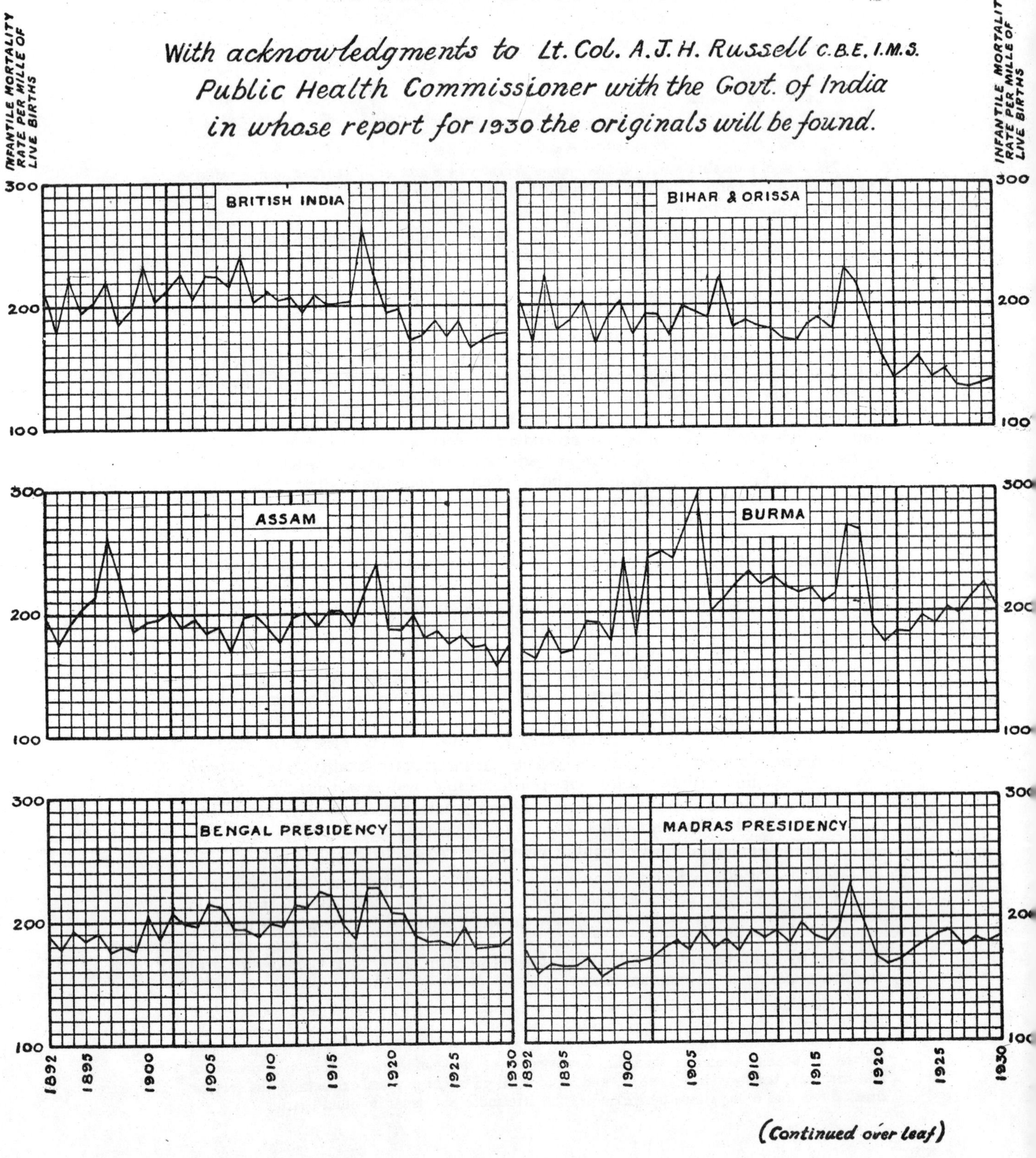

(Continued over leaf)

INFANTILE MORTALITY PER MILLE OF LIVE BIRTHS IN BRITISH INDIA AND PROVINCES FROM 1892 - 1930

(Continued)

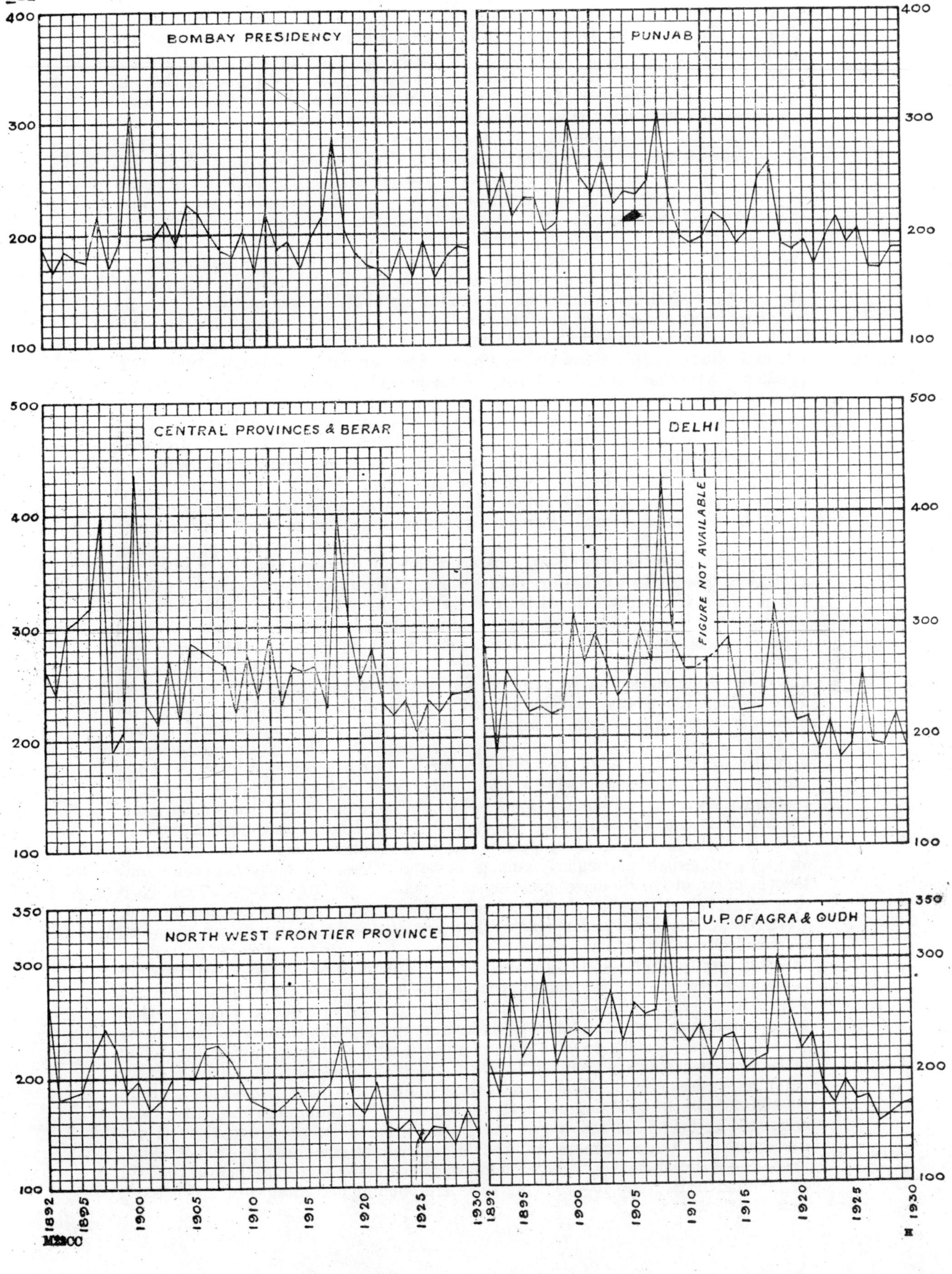

The Age of Consent Committee pointed out that the law as to the age of consent was " practically unknown throughout the country. A knowledge of it was confined to judges, lawyers and a few educated men " (Report p. 18, §. 38). The committee also pointed out that early marriage is normally followed by early consummation and in consequence by early maternity. " Consummation soon after puberty ", they say (*Report* pp. 97, 98 § 226, 228) " is almost universal among classes which practise early marriage............... Smriti texts are invoked to prove the need of consummation soon after puberty—preferably within 16 days of the first menses ". Again (page 67, § 159) " it is admitted on all hands that the practice of early marriage is widely prevalent throughout Bengal.........It is also established that .... pre-puberty consummations are common and that violations of the Law of Consent occur in many cases ". One witness states (*Evidence*, IV, page 510) that " cases are not uncommon in which girls bring forth six or seven children before they attain their eighteenth year ". Yet the consequences of early maternity are clear enough. The Age of Consent Committee compares the evil with that of *sati* in the following terms (page 102 § 232) :—" *Satis* were few and far between...........In the case of early maternity the evil is widespread...... ....so extensive as to affect the whole framework of society. After going through the ordeal, if a woman survives to the age of 30 she is in many cases an old woman, almost a shadow of her former self..........In the case of *sati* the utter hideousness of the incident shocked the conscience ; in this case the familiarity of the evil blinds us to its ghastly results ". The committee concludes (page 152, §§ 339 and 341) that there is " a large element of truth in the theory that frequency of birth has a very direct bearing on maternal and infantile mortality " ; that " according to the medical evidence the effect of frequency of births at short intervals is far more disastrous when maternity starts at an early age ", and that whatever methods may be needed or applied, " early consummation leading to early maternity ought in any event to be prohibited ". If anyone doubt the evil effects of early maternity stated in such moderate language by the committee in their report he need only examine the volumes of evidence, much of which, in particular the medical evidence, it is quite impossible to read with anything approaching equanimity. And the evils of early maternity are complicated and amplified by the conditions under which child-birth takes place. These have been described among others by Dr. H. Suhrawardy, M.D., F.R.C.S.I., in his treatise on " Child Welfare ". They are well known and it is not proposed to transcribe their description here, but it does seem necessary to refer to the evidence given before the Age of Consent Committee as indicating that infant mortality is higher among Hindus than among the other communities on account of early marriage and premature births (*Evidence*, volume I, page 439), and that in a very large number of cases the first born child dies, some witnesses even declaring that they had never known one to survive (*ibid*, I, 414, II, 490). It is worth notice in this connection that an investigation at Johnstown, Pa., U. S. A. showed that still births for mothers under 20 years of age numbered 11·1% as compared to 4% for mothers aged 20—24. The results of early maternity with the consequent rapid fall in the numbers of married women after the age of 25 is to be seen in the age curves of both Hindus and Muslims, though possibly in the latter case an important factor in the decrease may be the greater strictness of purdah, particularly among the poorer class. In both these communities the curve of female marriage reaches its peak in the group 20 to 25 and then drops sharply to the age group 35—40, after which the steepness is less pronounced. In the case of males the peak is reached 10 years later and the fall between 35 and 40 is much less marked, while in the case of Burmese the marriage curves of both sexes follow generally similar and less violent lines. This may be expressed otherwise in percentages thus :—Of the communities in which the greatest number of married women are found between the ages of 20 to 25 the total number of females in that age group is found to have fallen in the age group 35—40 in the case of Muslims to 52·4%, and of Hindus to 63·5% as compared with a corresponding fall among males from the same age group to 70·8 % and 72·7% respectively. On the other hand in the case of Sikhs, while the maximum of married women also occurs in group 20—25, 59% of the total number in that group are still found in the group 35—40 as compared to 58·6% of males. If the Burmese be taken the comparison is not quite even, as the maximum number of married women falls five years later, in the 25—30 group, and of the total number of females in that group there are 60·7% to be found in the group 40—45, while the corresponding percentage of males is 63·7.

The total numbers in any age group may of course be determined by factors such as disease or migration, but as between different sexes and different communities the comparisons between successive age-groups have some validity. In 1927 the maternal mortality rate for Madras, as disclosed by a special enquiry set on foot by Colonel A. J. H. Russell, was approximately 20 per 1,000 live births, though the figure in the Public Health Commissioner's Report shows only 5·3, and this rate of 20 per mille may be contrasted with the rate of 2·6 in the Netherlands or 6·5 per mille in the U. S. A. The question of infantile and maternity mortality and of the measures taken to reduce them will be found dealt with in the Annual Reports of the Public Health Commissioner with the Government of India for 1927, 1928, 1929 and in particular for 1930, and it is clear not only that there are a number of voluntary societies at work on the question of infantile mortality—such societies as the Seva Sadan Society of Poona or the Indian Red Cross Society in its Health Welfare activities, or the Bombay Presidency Infant Welfare Society, to name three only of many, but that the rate of infantile mortality has been effectively reduced since the census of 1921 in spite of a greatly increased population. At the same time the warning of the Age of Consent Committee as to the inadequacy of such institutions quoted in a later chapter applies also in this connection. Sir John Megaw estimates that "100 out of every 1,000 girl wives are doomed to die in child-birth before they have ceased to have babies, and about 200,000 mothers die in giving birth to children every year in India". What is really wanted is fewer babies but better ones, and it is possible that efforts should be concentrated less on infant welfare directly than on the reduction of immature maternity, on a general improvement in the standard of living and culture, and on the removal of the causes generally rather than on the treatment of the symptoms*.

INFANTILE MORTALITY PER MILLE OF BIRTHS IN 1930

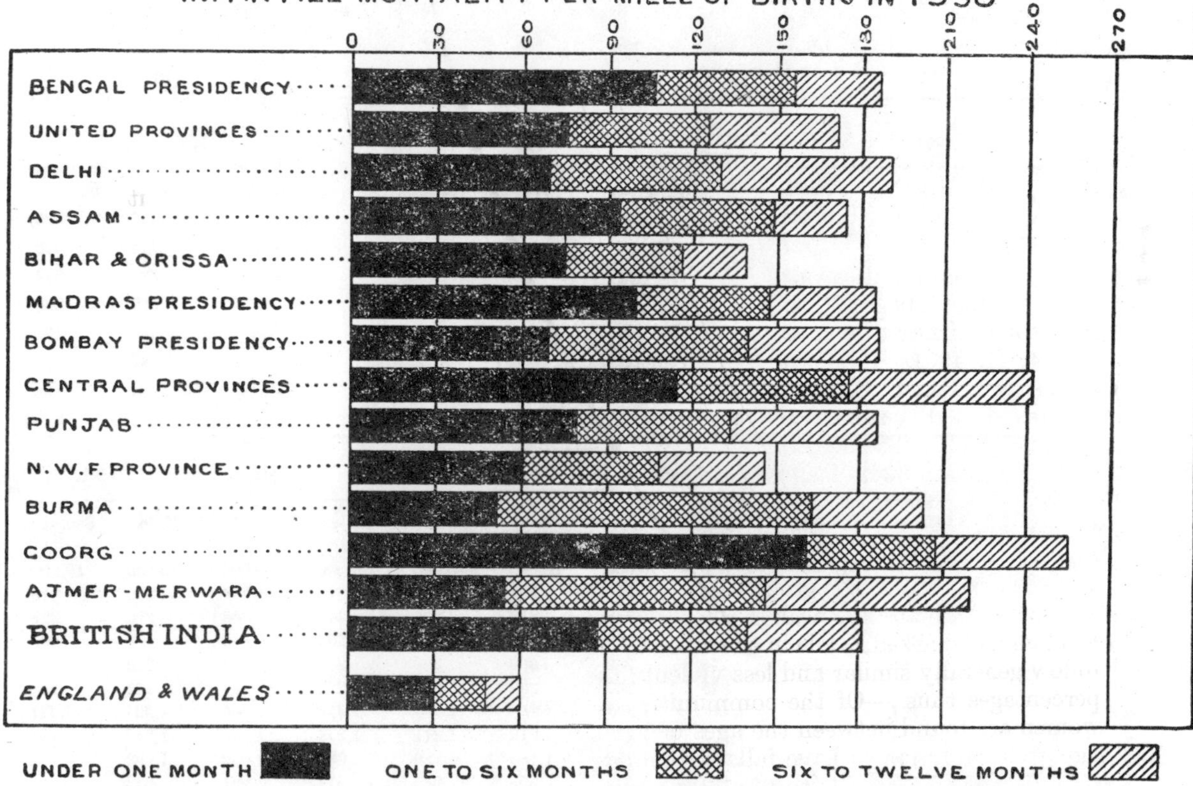

*It may be added that nothing in the vital statistics or the infant mortality rates as ascertained by the Public Health Department can be found to support the statement, which seems, if correctly reported by the *Daily Herald* and the *Times of India*, to be a grave and quite unjustifiable exaggeration, made at Geneva in 1930 by Mrs. Tarini Sinha that 446 infants of every 1,000 born in India died from the effects of opium given them by their mothers. If the most ample allowance be made for incomplete returns the gross infantile mortality rate for India can hardly be computed at much more than half the figure propounded by Mrs. Sinha for deaths from the effects of opium alone, a cause which does not even figure specifically in the Bombay Health Officer's list.

SUBSIDIARY TABLE I.

Age distribution of 10,000 of each sex in India.

Age.	1931. Males.	1931. Females.	1921. Males.	1921. Females.	1911. Males.	1911. Females.	1901. Males.	1901. Females.	1891. Males.	1891. Females.
1	2	3	4	5	6	7	8	9	10	11
India including Burma.										
Total	10,000	10,000	10,000	10,000	10,000	10,000	10,000	10,000	10,000	10,000
0—1	299	322	286	300	320	336	266	276	326	347
1—2	275	305	138	150	161	176	163	175	173	188
2—3	298	334	230	257	271	298	274	297	287	319
3—4	305	330	271	311	294	329	276	303	318	354
4—5	301	314	277	298	281	294	275	288	305	319
Total 0—5	*1,478*	*1,605*	*1,202*	*1,316*	*1,327*	*1,433*	*1,254*	*1,339*	*1,409*	*1,527*
5—10	1,324	1,284	1,471	1,494	1,383	1,383	1,394	1,382	1,428	1,396
10—15	1,182	1,110	1,245	1,081	1,165	997	1,264	1,082	1,139	946
15—20	904	952	842	815	848	826	866	835	835	811
20—25	891	969	775	881	822	930	787	892	802	897
25—30	877	887	865	885	896	909	879	895	876	904
30—35	770	738	825	833	829	835	848	851	842	846
35—40	661	613	636	565	622	556	609	557	613	555
40—45	527	486	621	621	634	631	649	652	638	626
45—50	441	405	392	346	380	338	370	339	366	323
50—55	318	300	434	438	432	443	437	452	411	426
55—60	243	245	185	168	177	164	177	169	179	170
60—65	171	179	266	298	257	305				
65—70	98	102	81	79	83	75	466	555	462	573
70 and over	115	125	160	180	145	175				
Mean age	23·2	22·8	24·8	24·7	24·7	24·7	24·7	25·1	24·4	24·9

India Proper.

Age group.	1931. Males.	1931. Females.	Age group.	1931. Males.	1931. Females.	Age group.	1931. Males.	1931. Females.
Total	10,000	10,000	5—10	1,325	1,282	40—45	547	505
0—1	299	321	10—15	1,200	1,124	45—50	424	389
1—2	273	303	15—20	888	935	50—55	334	314
2—3	296	334	20—25	904	984	55—60	229	230
3—4	305	330	25—30	856	869	60—65	182	191
4—5	300	313	30—35	787	756	65—70	87	90
Total 0—5	1,473	1,601	35—40	640	596	70 and over	124	134
						Mean age	22·3	22·8

Burma.

Age.	1931. Males.	1931. Females.	1921. Males.	1921. Females.	1911. Males.	1911. Females.	1901. Males.	1901. Females.	1891. Males.	1891. Females.
1	2	3	4	5	6	7	8	9	10	11
Total	10,000	10,000	10,000	10,000	10,000	10,000	10,000	10,000	10,000	10,000
0—1	257	283	234	256	218	241	228	252	280	310
1—2	267	293	210	228	217	236	248	266	210	226
2—3	271	293	232	256	266	289	293	315	270	286
3—4	269	287	270	289	302	323	309	326	312	327
4—5	260	278	248	269	269	291	272	287	253	268
Total 0—5	*1,324*	*1,434*	*1,194*	*1,298*	*1,272*	*1,380*	*1,350*	*1,446*	*1,325*	*1,417*
5—10	1,214	1,245	1,205	1,273	1,276	1,341	1,232	1,282	1,247	1,293
10—15	1,130	1,138	1,152	1,132	1,163	1,126	1,088	1,042	1,192	1,148
15—20	927	1,004	977	1,071	893	967	874	961	912	1,022
20—25	938	1,004	910	948	857	884	888	929	913	910
25—30	910	852	866	819	860	810	909	857	881	806
30—35	835	737	813	710	846	737	877	766	799	684
35—40	637	556	639	538	677	578	648	547	635	539
40—45	550	498	603	561	594	557	567	523	553	514
45—50	413	391	435	393	399	365	396	361	389	358
50—55	353	351	410	413	370	384	381	393	366	393
55—60	271	271	234	239	223	231	231	236	222	232
60—65	228	222	262	259	263	272				
65—70	122	126	122	119	124	122	559	657	566	684
70 and over	148	171	178	227	183	246				
Mean age	24·30	23·6	25·70	25·14	25·32	24·98	25·28	25·06	25·00	24·91

SUBSIDIARY TABLE II.

Age distribution of 10,000 of each sex in each main Religion.

Age and Religion.	1931.		1921.		1911.		1901.		1891.		1881.	
	Males.	Females.	Males.	Females.	Males.	Females.	Males.	Females.	Males.	Females.	Males.	Females.
Hindu	10,000	10,000	10,000	10,000	10,000	10,000	10,000	10,000	10,000	10,000	10,000	10,000
0—5	1,441	1,556	1,165	1,270	1,293	1,388	1,206	1,286	1,367	1,484	1,277	1,375
5—10	1,299	1,252	1,442	1,461	1,336	1,332	1,361	1,346	1,400	1,372	1,400	1,354
10—15	1,189	1,103	1,237	1,073	1,151	984	1,268	1,082	1,134	938	1,220	1,011
15—20	889	917	835	779	851	805	871	814	831	782	821	769
20—40	3,211	3,237	3,139	3,200	3,216	3,276	3,157	3,229	3,169	3,234	3,216	3,282
40—60	1,580	1,502	1,679	1,637	1,673	1,642	1,682	1,676	1,635	1,596	1,601	1,612
60 and over	391	433	503	580	480	573	455	567	464	594	465	597
Mean Age ..	23·5	23·3	25·1	25·2	24·9	25·2	24·9	25·5	24·6	25·2	24·6	25·4
Muslim	10,000	10,000	10,000	10,000	10,000	10,000	10,000	10,000	10,000	10,000	10,000	10,000
0—5	1,544	1,717	1,282	1,442	1,397	1,550	1,380	1,495	1,545	1,680	1,415	1,524
5—10	1,400	1,364	1,584	1,628	1,526	1,548	1,509	1,510	1,515	1,469	1,528	1,460
10—15	1,233	1,178	1,268	1,077	1,208	1,015	1,261	1,068	1,131	925	1,197	976
15—20	885	991	837	881	833	872	840	869	847	888	777	800
20—40	3,150	3,151	3,029	3,109	3,047	3,123	3,010	3,097	3,040	3,136	3,023	3,132
40—60	1,402	1,247	1,493	1,378	1,493	1,395	1,506	1,439	1,471	1,396	1,545	1,518
60 and over	386	352	507	485	496	497	494	522	451	506	515	590
Mean Age ..	22·4	21·5	24·1	23·3	23·9	23·3	24·1	24·0	23·7	23·8	24·3	24·6
Christian ..	10,000	10,000	10,000	10,000	10,000	10,000	10,000	10,000	10,000	10,000	10,000	10,000
0—5	1,576	1,657	1,289	1,391	1,356	1,491	1,290	1,449	1,347	1,551	1,266	1,457
5—10	1,333	1,342	1,382	1,463	1,314	1,411	1,384	1,479	1,308	1,421	1,298	1,450
10—15	1,221	1,217	1,261	1,246	1,199	1,178	1,283	1,244	1,122	1,111	1,127	1,138
15—20	942	992	917	928	882	945	865	905	869	922	828	884
20—40	3,107	3,079	3,193	3,114	3,357	3,132	3,299	3,099	3,485	3,147	3,722	3,208
40—60	1,428	1,323	1,501	1,406	1,466	1,398	1,483	1,394	1,468	1,389	1,383	1,394
60 and over	393	390	457	452	426	445	396	430	401	459	376	460
Mean Age ..	22·5	22·0	24·2	23·4	24·0	23·3	24·0	23·4	24·2	23·6	24·2	23·[illegible]
Tribal	10,000	10,000	10,000	10,000	10,000	10,000	10,000	10,000	10,000	10,000	10,000	10,000
0—5	1,758	1,840	1,362	1,457	1,640	1,724	1,370	1,449	1,544	1,687	Not available.	
5—10	1,449	1,373	1,696	1,660	1,583	1,521	1,565	1,515	1,718	1,642		
10—15	1,217	1,144	1,280	1,129	1,099	960	1,323	1,151	1,249	1,054		
15—20	808	913	770	799	753	802	872	898	744	763		
20—40	3,034	3,087	2,935	3,117	3,085	3,234	3,080	3,196	2,890	3,068		
40—60	1,407	1,279	1,549	1,385	1,455	1,312	1,453	1,383	1,450	1,313		
60 and over	327	364	408	453	385	447	337	408	405	473		
Mean Age ..	21·8	21·5	23·4	23·2	22·9	22·8	23·2	23·3	22·8	23·0		

SUBSIDIARY TABLE III.

Age distribution of 1,000 of each sex in certain Castes.

Castes.	Males—Number per mille aged—						Females—Number per mille aged—					
	0—6	7—13	14—16	17—23	24—43	44 & over.	0—6	7—13	14—16	17—23	24—43	44 & over.
1	2	3	4	5	6	7	8	9	10	11	12	13
1. Baniya ..	170	158	70	133	291	178	191	160	67	133	276	173
2. Bhangi ..	205	177	75	119	286	138	222	160	69	129	288	132
3. Bhil ..	223	192	71	117	260	137	253	181	78	128	244	116
4. Brahman ..	164	156	69	123	300	188	178	151	64	125	292	190
5. Chamar ..	206	180	73	110	290	141	218	162	66	117	296	141
6. Chetti ..	183	161	65	130	294	167	199	154	67	135	270	175
7. Darzi ..	180	164	72	124	270	190	204	168	77	128	261	162
8. Dom ..	176	160	74	126	312	152	188	151	73	137	305	146
9. Gond ..	205	169	70	105	293	158	203	154	65	122	291	165
10. Gujar ..	188	178	75	112	284	163	217	168	69	119	278	149
11. Iluvan ..	221	182	69	117	264	147	216	172	69	130	264	149
12. Jat	185	173	70	119	276	177	215	171	63	119	268	164
13. Kachhi ..	192	160	76	117	309	146	219	146	72	124	298	141
14. Kahar ..	188	166	75	114	286	171	202	159	69	121	284	165
15. Kallan ..	182	181	63	109	302	163	171	165	52	123	321	168
16. Kayastha ..	168	161	71	130	294	176	188	163	66	134	280	169
17. Khatri ..	177	158	67	130	293	175	206	172	64	120	273	165
18. Kumhar ..	197	174	74	115	279	161	214	163	68	121	275	159
19. Kunbi ..	172	166	81	116	285	180	184	169	70	121	279	177
20. Mahar ..	189	172	85	120	273	161	196	159	82	129	269	165
21. Maratha ..	171	150	92	109	300	178	186	154	102	117	278	163
22. Megh ..	153	162	104	118	280	183	176	160	105	137	264	158
23. Momin (Julaha, etc.)	199	172	70	119	274	166	215	174	70	125	272	144
24. Naibrahman ..	185	171	77	123	284	160	206	162	68	123	284	157
25. Namasudra ..	178	175	66	127	288	166	200	163	72	145	276	144
26. Nayar (Nair)	206	167	67	119	272	169	195	155	63	128	273	186
27. Od	196	181	80	110	275	158	188	184	84	123	271	150
28. Pathan ..	188	175	69	118	286	164	213	164	63	118	288	154
29. Prabhu ..	169	171	80	137	320	123	204	179	92	156	245	124
30. Rajput ..	171	164	71	121	294	179	190	154	61	121	296	178
31. Santal ..	214	191	64	107	291	133	230	169	66	128	276	131
32. Shan ..	180	158	56	116	318	172	184	157	63	142	291	163
33. Tanti ..	192	181	61	100	310	156	189	157	55	116	321	162
34. Teli ..	196	177	68	112	287	160	205	169	61	126	285	154
35. Viswabrahman, etc.	183	167	72	119	285	174	200	166	67	127	276	164
36. Yadava ..	186	175	71	108	298	162	197	163	65	115	296	164

SUBSIDIARY TABLE IV.

Proportion of children under 10 and of persons over 60 to those aged 15—40; also of married females aged 15—40 per 100 females.

Province, State or Agency.	Proportion of children, both sexes per 100. Persons aged 15—40.			Married females aged 15—40.			Proportion of persons over 60 per 100 aged 15—40. 1931.		1921.		1911.		Number of married females aged 15—40 per 100 females of all ages.		
	1931.	1921.	1911.	1931.	1921.	1911.	Males.	Females.	Males.	Females.	Males.	Females.	1931.	1921.	1911.
INDIA ..	**69**	**69**	**68**	**170**	**174**	**167**	**10**	**10**	**13**	**14**	**12**	**14**	**34**	**32**	**34**
Provinces ..	**68**	**68**	**69**	**169**	**172**	**169**	**10**	**10**	**13**	**14**	**12**	**14**	**34**	**33**	**33**
1. Ajmer-Merwara ..	66	62	58	160	164	144	7	9	10	13	8	11	36	34	39
2. Andaman and Nicobar Islands.	42	20	29	176	148	179	4	8	5	11	12	13	38	35	33
3. Assam	74	75	78	189	195	197	8	7	10	9	10	10	34	32	33
4. Baluchistan ..	28	*	*	150	*	*	2	4	*	*	*	*	43	*	*
5. Bengal	68	68	73	169	172	181	8	8	10	10	11	12	36	34	34
6. Bihar and Orissa ..	70	70	73	162	165	168	9	11	12	15	12	16	35	33	33
7. Bombay (including Aden).	66	67	64	165	174	159	8	9	11	13	10	12	36	33	35
8. Burma	62	60	65	205	201	211	12	12	13	15	14	16	26	25	26
9. Central Provinces and Berar.	69	78	73	156	180	160	10	11	15	18	12	15	36	32	36
10. Coorg	49	52	45	159	171	150	6	7	7	10	5	8	33	31	32
11. Delhi	53	54	†	153	150	†	6	7	9	10	†	†	39	38	†
12. Madras	67	65	68	163	160	165	11	11	15	15	15	15	33	32	32
13. North-West Frontier Province (*Districts and Administered Territories*).	72	77	82	195	206	212	10	8	16	15	16	13	33	32	32
14. Punjab	74	77	70	197	199	183	13	12	18	17	15	15	33	32	34
15. United Provinces of Agra and Oudh.	67	66	62	161	161	150	9	10	13	15	12	14	36	34	35
States and Agencies	**71**	**72**	**67**	**174**	**182**	**162**	**10**	**10**	**13**	**14**	**11**	**13**	**34**	**32**	**34**
16. Assam States ..	78	78	88	218	217	232	11	12	15	16	14	15	28	26	27
17. Baluchistan States ..	33	*	*	170	*	*	1	2	*	*	*	*	41	*	*
18. Baroda State ..	68	69	60	157	167	145	10	11	11	13	8	10	36	33	38
19. Bengal States ..	70	72	74	191	197	200	8	6	10	8	11	10	33	32	33
20. Bihar and Orissa States.	76	76	79	178	189	189	6	8	7	10	8	11	34	31	33
21. Bombay States ..	76	80	68	183	195	160	10	10	12	15	10	12	33	31	36
22. Central India Agency	67	71	64	162	176	158	7	8	10	13	8	11	36	33	36
23. Central Provinces States.	81	87	84	181	203	188	8	10	11	14	9	12	35	32	35
24. Gwalior State ..	64	69	‡	164	180	‡	7	9	11	13	‡	‡	35	32	‡
25. Hyderabad State ..	71	69	68	173	175	157	11	11	16	17	14	15	34	31	35
26. Jammu and Kashmir State.	68	77	77	162	183	183	11	9	18	15	17	14	38	35	34
27. Madras States Agency	76	65	66	196	177	170	11	11	11	11	11	12	30	30	33
Cochin State ..	*75*	*67*	*66*	*195*	*178*	*170*	*11*	*11*	*10*	*12*	*9*	*11*	*30*	*30*	*32*
Travancore State ..	*78*	*65*	*65*	*200*	*180*	*171*	*11*	*11*	*10*	*11*	*10*	*11*	*31*	*30*	*32*
Other Madras States	*59*	*	*	*148*	*	*	*11*	*11*	*	*	*	*	*32*	*	*
28. Mysore State ..	68	66	64	174	174	163	12	11	16	16	15	16	33	31	31
29. North-West Frontier Province (*Agencies and Tribal Areas*).	3	*	*	205	*	*	..	6	*	*	*	*	37	*	*
30. Punjab States ..	59	72	63	144	184	163	15	12	18	16	14	14	36	33	35
31. Punjab States Agency	70			179			13	11					35		
32. Rajputana Agency ..	72	74	63	175	189	151	9	10	12	14	10	12	34	31	37
33. Sikkim State ..	73	67	72	197	180	186	13	14	16	17	15	17	30	29	31
34. United Provinces States	67	62	66	158	145	152	9	10	12	14	12	14	36	35	36
35. Western India States Agency.	76	§	§	177	§	§	10	12	§	§	§	§	34	§	§

* Figures not available. † Included against Punjab. ‡ Included against Central India Agency.
§ Included against Bombay for past censuses.

SUBSIDIARY TABLE V.

Proportion of children under 10 and of persons over 60 to those aged 15—40 in certain religions; also of married females aged 15—40 per 100 females.

Religion.	Proportion of children, both sexes per 100.		Proportion of persons over 60 per 100 aged 15—40.		Number of married females aged 15—40 per 100 females of all ages.
	Persons aged 15—40.	Married females aged 15—40.	Males.	Females.	
India.					
All Religions	69	170	10	10	34
India Proper.					
All Religions	69	169	10	10	35
Hindu	67	164	10	10	35
Muslim	74	178	10	9	36
Sikh	71	192	15	15	33
Tribal	82	196	9	9	33
Burma.					
All Religions	62	205	12	12	26
Burmese	65	206	14	13	25

SUBSIDIARY TABLE VI.

Variation in population at certain age periods.

Province, State or Agency.	Period.	Variation per cent. in population (Increase +). (Decrease —).					
		All Ages.	0—10	10—15	15—40	40—60	60 and over.
1	2	3	4	5	6	7	8
India	**1881—1891**	**+11·2**	**+16·1**	**+4·3**	**+10·8**	**+9·7**	**+8·0**
	1891—1901	**+1·8**	**—5·1**	**+14·5**	**+2·3**	**+5·2**	**+0·3**
	1901—1911	**+6·6**	**+9·7**	**—1·7**	**+7·3**	**+5·1**	**+8·6**
	1911—1921	**+0·9**	**+0·1**	**+8·5**	**—1·0**	**+1·1**	**+3·1**
	1921—1931	**+10·9**	**+14·5**	**+10·6**	**+15·1**	**+3·1**	**—14·9**
Ajmer-Merwara	1881—1891	+17·7	+20·1	+55·5	+5·5	+23·2	+36·2
	1891—1901	—12·1	—44·5	+8·4	+5·1	—4·3	—34·5
	1901—1911	+5·1	+53·5	—39·6	+0·8	—1·7	+20·5
	1911—1921	—1·2	—4·4	+57·5	—10·9	+1·3	+7·2
	1921—1931	+13·1	+23·3	+7·1	+15·8	+3·6	—14·7
Andaman and Nicobar Islands ..	1901—1911	+52·4	+249·4	+204·9	+42·9	+22·5	+38·7
	1911—1921	+5·5	—14·2	+35·4	+27·3	—20·3	—32·0
	1921—1931	+6·9	+97·9	+32·7	—5·6	—11·1	—21·6
Assam	1881—1891	+15·5	+14·1	+25·5	+16·4	+11·8	+9·8
	1891—1901	+7·4	+4·2	+7·1	+12·2	+7·0	—9·7
	1901—1911	+15·2	+19·8	+9·8	+12·6	+16·4	+18·8
	1911—1921	+13·2	+8·5	+28·4	+12·5	+15·4	+11·2
	1921—1931	+15·7	+17·7	+16·7	+18·8	+7·8	—4·6
Bengal	1881—1891	+7·5	+9·6	+11·5	+7·9	+3·2	—1·6
	1891—1901	+7·7	+6·8	+15·1	+9·4	+6·7	+1·2
	1901—1911	+8·0	+9·3	+5·8	+10·1	+3·6	+0·9
	1911—1921	+2·8	—1·2	+8·3	+5·3	+2·5	—5·9
	1921—1931	+7·3	+8·7	+10·6	+9·0	+3·5	—14·6
Bihar and Orissa	1901—1911	+8·1	+11·5	+4·6	+8·3	+4·8	+6·1
	1911—1921	—1·2	—5·5	+4·9	—0·8	+2·8	—5·5
	1921—1931	+11·5	+14·8	+8·2	+14·6	+7·9	—12·2
Bombay	1881—1891	+15·8	+22·3	—3·5	+14·3	+19·2	+28·7
	1891—1901	—3·5	—12·3	+21·2	—3·0	—1·2	—12·6
	1901—1911	+6·3	+8·4	—10·5	+8·7	+7·5	+12·8
	1911—1921	—1·5	—0·1	+9·8	—5·4	—2·8	+3·5
	1921—1931	+13·4	+16·1	+13·8	+18·4	+4·5	—14·5
Burma	1881—1891	+24·6	+19·6	+22·9	+28·6	+23·1	+30·1
	1891—1901	+21·3	+22·3	+13·2	+23·8	+22·1	+14·7
	1901—1911	+16·2	+15·3	+24·7	+14·2	+17·4	+15·5
	1911—1921	+9·4	+3·2	+9·1	+11·8	+15·3	+5·6
	1921—1931	+11·2	+16·8	+10·4	+12·7	+4·8	—3·1

Province, State or Agency.	Period.	Variation per cent. in population (Increase +). (Decrease —). All Ages.	0—10	10—15	15—40	40—60	60 and over.
1	2	3	4	5	6	7	8
Central Provinces and Berar ..	1881—1891	+10·7	+11·5	+18·3	+6·6	+12·3	+11·8
	1891—1901	—7·9	—21·8	+4·1	+0·1	—4·0	—30·5
	1901—1911	+17·9	+33·5	—11·3	+15·0	+15·0	+42·2
	1911—1921	—0·3	—2·1	+27·4	—8·1	+3·0	+10·3
	1921—1931	+12·6	+10·8	+8·5	+23·4	+4·9	—17·5
Coorg	1881—1891	—2·9	+10·6	—18·6	—8·3	+8·1	+8·2
	1891—1901	+4·4	—3·9	+33·8	+1·8	+7·1	+9·4
	1901—1911	—3·1	—7·4	—13·6	—1·1	+3·6	+12·1
	1911—1921	—6·4	+1·8	—5·8	—11·1	—6·4	+8·3
	1921—1931	—0·3	—3·4	+4·5	+2·7	—3·5	—19·8
Delhi	1921—1931	+30·3	+34·9	+47·2	+36·1	+7·8	—8·2
Madras	1881—1891	+18·5	+29·2	—3·0	+16·1	+21·5	+23·9
	1891—1901	+7·8	+4·3	+31·3	+3·3	+11·6	+6·3
	1901—1911	+8·4	+3·9	+2·7	+11·8	+10·2	+14·7
	1911—1921	+2·2	—0·8	+5·5	+3·5	+0·8	+4·6
	1921—1931	+10·3	+16·7	+7·4	+14·3	+2·3	—15·6
North-West Frontier Province ..	1881—1891	+17	+33	+2	+26	—8	—43
	1891—1901	+10	—3	+38	+3	+33	+106
	1901—1911	+7	+9	+6	+3	+11	+16
	1911—1921	+3·8	—2·1	+1·9	+7·9	+3·7	+12·3
	1921—1931	+7·7	+8·3	+18·8	+14·6	—4·3	—31·0
Punjab	1901—1911	—2·4	+0·3	—6·2	—1·9	—3·2	—4·6
	1911—1921	+5·5	+10·5	+10·3	—0·6	+4·0	+18·2
	1921—1931	+13·5	+14·9	+17·1	+20·6	+3·4	—14·2
United Provinces of Agra and Oudh ..	1881—1891	+6·3	+9·9	—0·3	+5·5	+6·1	+9·5
	1891—1901	+1·6	—3·2	+12·2	+1·6	+4·3	—4·2
	1901—1911	—0·9	—1·1	—4·1	+0·7	—1·6	—3·0
	1911—1921	—3·1	—0·3	—3·7	—5·5	—2·1	—0·3
	1921—1931	+6·7	+12·5	+7·1	+11·2	—3·8	—21·6
Baroda State	1881—1891	+10·5	+14·6	—0·8	+10·9	+9·1	+16·7
	1891—1901	—19·2	—35·6	+1·1	—12·4	—14·7	—40·6
	1901—1911	+4·1	+22·0	—28·4	+2·2	+4·9	+20·9
	1911—1921	+4·6	+6·1	+42·5	—7·1	+8·7	+23·0
	1921—1931	+14·9	+17·1	+13·1	+18·0	+8·4	+4·5
Central India Agency	1921—1931	+10·6	+10·8	+10·5	+18·2	+1·3	—22·9
Cochin State	1891—1901	+12·3	+11·8	+18·4	+11·6	+11·1	+9·1
	1901—1911	+13·1	+12·8	+7·9	+14·4	+13·7	+15·8
	1911—1921	+6·6	+5·8	+11·6	+2·6	+11·6	+11·5
	1921—1931	+23·1	+33·1	+18·9	+19·2	+20·5	+17·9
Gwalior State	1901—1911	+5·9	+30·8	—12·9	—1·3	+5·0	+14·2
	1911—1921	+3·0	+7·5	+30·0	—6·1	+1·3	+18·9
	1921—1931	+10·3	+9·6	+16·9	+17·6	—1·1	—24·1
Hyderabad State	1881—1891	+19·2	+26·9	+2·7	+17·0	+19·9	+30·2
	1891—1901	—3·4	—14·2	+18·7	—2·8	+3·4	—12·2
	1901—1911	+20·0	+28·8	+3·1	+18·0	+18·9	+36·6
	1911—1921	—6·8	—8·5	+6·9	—10·2	—6·6	+0·1
	1921—1931	+15·8	+26·5	+5·8	+23·0	+2·4	—18·8
Jammu and Kashmir State ..	1891—1901	+15·0	+8·0	+48·1	+13·2	+14·1	+14·1
	1901—1911	+6·8	+8·2	+1·6	+8·6	+2·6	+9·5
	1911—1921	+5·0	+5·1	+7·7	+4·9	+1·2	+9·1
	1921—1931	+11·9	+8·2	+15·0	+22·7	+3·2	—24·0
Mysore State	1881—1891	+18·1	+42·1	—22·3	+10·9	+28·6	+49·6
	1891—1901	+12·1	+9·0	+59·5	—0·7	+20·8	+21·3
	1901—1911	+4·8	—4·4	+3·9	+12·7	+0·4	+15·2
	1911—1921	+3·0	+8·0	—0·2	+3·8	—5·3	+7·2
	1921—1931	+9·7	+15·6	+13·4	+13·3	—0·5	—19·0
Rajputana Agency	1901—1911	+6·9	+32·5	—24·5	+4·4	+3·2	+8·5
	1911—1921	—6·5	—1·2	+26·6	—16·6	—8·8	+1·2
	1921—1931	+14·0	+16·6	+15·1	+19·2	+5·0	—13·0
Travancore State	1891—1901	+15·4	+21·5	+21·4	+14·3	+9·3	+0·4
	1901—1911	+16·2	+19·1	+19·4	+13·6	+14·6	+19·8
	1911—1921	+16·9	+16·1	+22·5	+16·2	+15·6	+16·7
	1921—1931	+27·2	+44·4	+20·9	+20·7	+21·4	+21·3
Western India States Agency ..	1901—1911	+7·3	+25·1	—32·4	+1·9	+22·4	+53·0
	1911—1921	+0·5	+7·7	+47·6	—13·8	+2·0	+11·1
	1921—1931	+12·9	+12·1	+13·5	+18·6	+5·2	—1·4

NOTE.—Column 3 shows variation in population enumerated by age, not in total population.

SUBSIDIARY TABLE VII.

Reported birth rate by sex and province.

Number of births per 1,000 of total population at each year.

Province, State or Agency.	1921.		1922.		1923.		1924.		1925.		1926.		1927.		1928.		1929.		1930.	
	Males.	Females.	Males.	Females.	Males.	Females.	Males.	Females.	Males.	Females.	Males.	Females.	Males.	Females.	Males.	Females.	Males.	Females.	Males.	Females.
1	2	3	4	5	6	7	8	9	10	11	12	13	14	15	16	17	18	19	20	21
Ajmer-Merwara	16·6	14·5	16·1	14·2	17·3	15·3	18·1	15·2	17·8	15·4	17·0	14·4	16·5	13·9	18·1	15·2	18·8	15·6	18·4	15·2
Assam	29·4	29·8	28·0	28·8	28·4	29·2	30·7	31·3	28·7	29·4	30·4	31·2	29·9	30·5	30·9	31·5	32·4	33·1	30·8	31·9
Bengal	28·1	27·9	27·5	27·1	29·7	29·5	28·9	28·8	29·0	28·6	26·6	26·4	26·7	26·4	28·3	28·0	27·8	27·6	25·1	25·0
Bihar and Orissa	36	33	37	34	39	36	37	34	37	34	39	36	39	36	40	37	37	35	37	35
Bombay	32	33	32	32	35	35	35	36	34	35	36	37	36	38	38	38	38	39	37	38
Burma	15·3	14·5	15·0	14·3	14·8	14·0	13·7	12·8	12·5	11·8	13·3	12·8	12·0	11·4	12·3	11·7	12·4	11·8	13·4	12·7
Central Provinces and Berar ..	19·5	18·4	18·3	17·5	23·4	22·3	22·6	21·6	22·5	21·4	23·6	22·5	23·4	22·2	23·9	22·6	22·6	21·4	24·5	23·2
Coorg	14·0	13·4	13·8	12·3	13·3	12·3	10·9	10·3	9·7	9·2	11·8	11·0	10·1	9·1	9·2	8·8	11·5	10·7	12·3	11·3
Delhi	21·7	19·9	21·4	19·9	21·6	19·4	21·2	19·2	20·2	18·5	18·9	18·1	18·7	16·9	21·7	19·6	20·6	19·3	20·7	19·2
Madras	13·8	13·2	15·2	14·6	16·6	15·9	17·4	16·7	16·5	15·9	17·5	16·9	17·5	16·9	17·8	17·1	17·9	17·2	18·7	17·7
North-West Frontier Province	26·5	25·3	23·2	21·9	27·0	25·6	26·7	24·7	26·5	24·6	29·9	27·5	29·0	26·8	32·3	29·6	30·5	28·2	25·4	23·5
Punjab	22	20	20	18	22	20	20	18	20	18	21	18	21	18	22	20	21	19	20	18
United Provinces of Agra and Oudh.	18·1	16·3	17·1	15·3	19·1	17·0	18·2	16·4	17·1	15·2	17·8	15·8	18·9	16·9	19·5	17·4	17·3	15·4	18·6	16·6
Baroda State	23·1	21·9	25·8	24·4	26·7	25·7	28·2	26·7	26·0	24·9	26·7	24·8	25·3	24·4	24·6	23·5	26·2	25·2	28·4	26·7
Cochin State	16·4	14·7	15·4	13·8	14·0	12·8	13·3	12·3	12·8	11·7	15·0	13·8	15·3	14·1	15·3	14·5	17·2	15·9	17·3	15·6
Gwalior State	5·8	4·7	5·8	4·7	5·9	5·1	*	*	7·1	6·2	11·8	10·9	11·7	10·7	13·7	13·2	15·1	14·3	12·9	13·8
Mysore State	8·7	8·2	9·4	8·9	9·5	9·0	9·5	8·9	8·9	8·6	10·7	10·2	9·7	9·2	9·6	9·1	10·2	9·6	10·3	9·7
Travancore State	18·5	18·2	17·2	17·1	16·5	16·2	16·8	16·7	14·1	13·5	17·1	15·9	18·9	18·1	19·7	18·6	20·8	19·7	22·5	21·7

* Figures not available.

N.B.—The methods of calculating the rates for this table and Table VIII followed by different provinces are not consistent. Ajmer-Merwara, Assam, Bihar and Orissa, Bombay, Central Provinces and Berar, Coorg, North-West Frontier Province, Gwalior, Cochin and Mysore have calculated the rates on the 1921 population; Bengal, Burma, Delhi, Punjab, United Provinces of Agra and Oudh, Baroda and Travancore have allowed for annual increases in population. Madras gives figures on both bases, the latter being adopted here. In the case of the United Provinces the births are calculated per 1,000 of population and not per 1,000 of the appropriate sex.

SUBSIDIARY TABLE VIII.

Reported death rate by sex and province.

Number of deaths per 1,000 of total population at each year.

Province, State or Agency.	1921.		1922.		1923.		1924.		1925.		1926.		1927.		1928.		1929.		1930.	
	Males.	Females.	Males.	Females.	Males.	Females.	Males.	Females.	Males.	Females.	Males.	Females.	Males.	Females.	Males.	Females.	Males.	Females.	Males.	Females.
1	2	3	4	5	6	7	8	9	10	11	12	13	14	15	16	17	18	19	20	21
Ajmer-Merwara	27·7	29·1	21·4	23·1	25·4	25·8	24·5	25·5	22·9	24·2	30·4	33·2	25·0	27·5	25·5	26·3	29·5	30·7	27·3	28·6
Assam	26·9	25·9	27·0	26·6	24·0	22·9	27·6	26·9	23·1	21·8	23·2	22·8	23·4	23·4	22·2	22·0	21·0	20·8	21·4	21·3
Bengal	30·6	29·7	25·8	24·3	25·8	24·5	26·3	24·3	24·8	23·6	24·2	23·6	24·5	24·6	24·2	24·5	22·0	22·6	21·0	21·2
Bihar and Orissa	35	31	26	22	26	24	31	27	25	22	27	24	26	24	27	24	28	26	31	28
Bombay	26	26	24	23	26	26	27	28	23	24	28	29	25	26	27	28	30	32	29	30
Burma	22·2	20·7	22·8	21·1	21·1	19·7	21·5	20·2	18·5	17·4	20·3	19·2	19·0	17·5	20·3	19·0	20·7	19·6	19·1	18·6
Central Provinces and Berar ..	46·0	42·0	31·0	27·6	32·1	28·9	34·4	30·7	29·0	25·6	36·0	32·7	32·8	29·8	35·4	32·0	36·0	32·2	39·6	35·9
Coorg	28·0	29·3	32·9	36·6	27·7	30·9	39·0	43·5	30·9	30·7	34·2	34·1	30·9	31·9	30·5	32·1	22·6	25·1	24·2	26·5
Delhi	28·8	36·5	21·9	29·1	32·3	43·4	27·8	37·5	24·4	31·7	33·5	45·8	24·2	30·0	21·9	29·3	27·5	35·0	23·0	30·4
Madras	10·2	10·0	10·6	10·2	10·9	10·8	12·1	11·7	11·9	11·6	12·3	12·0	11·6	11·3	12·5	12·1	11·9	11·5	11·8	11·5
North-West Frontier Province	30·3	29·8	20·8	20·6	22·5	23·0	27·9	31·6	19·0	18·8	20·6	21·0	21·4	20·6	18·3	18·6	22·1	23·2	21·2	20·5
Punjab	30	31	21	22	29	32	39	44	27	30	33.	36	25	26	22	23	25	27	26	27
United Provinces of Agra and Oudh.	40·0	39·1	25·8	24·5	23·9	22·9	28·4	27·7	25·0	23·8	25·1	24·1	22·5	21·4	23·4	23·1	23·3	22·8	26·0	25·3
Baroda State	15·7	14·4	19·9	18·2	22·1	20·3	20·8	19·4	18·5	17·2	22·8	21·8	17·8	17·4	20·1	18·2	21·4	19·7	23·5	22·3
Cochin State	10·9	9·5	10·2	8·6	11·0	9·4	8·6	7·6	8·8	8·1	8·9	7·8	10·7	9·3	9·9	8·2	9·3	8·3	11·3	10·1
Gwalior State	5·5	4·9	4·7	4·3	5·6	4·9	*	*	6·2	5·2	9·8	7·6	9·8	9·9	10·8	9·3	11·1	9·8	14·8	12·7
Mysore State	7·6	7·0	7·7	7·2	8·5	8·0	11·0	10·3	9·2	8·5	7·7	7·3	7·4	6·9	8·3	7·7	7·4	7·1	7·9	7·6
Travancore State	12·9	11·2	11·9	10·3	11·5	10·0	11·6	10·0	9·2	8·0	8·4	7·6	9·4	9·0	9·2	8·4	10·9	10·1	10·0	9·6

*Figures not available.

APPENDIX TO CHAPTER IV.

(*W. H. Shoobert*).

A Nagpur centenarian.

The following extract is taken from the Census Report on the Central Provinces and Berar and relates to an aged wrestler of the name of Siddi Wastad, son of a Negro father and an Arab mother, and now for many years a resident of Nagpur.

" Probably the oldest man in the Province is Siddi Wastad, a retainer of the family of Sirdar Venkatrao Gujar of Nagpur City..............In Nagpur he is generally supposed to have passed his 150th year.... ....He was one of the famous wrestlers at the court of His Highness the Maharaja Khanderao Gaikwar, father of the present Ruler of Baroda, and must have been almost past his prime as an athlete in about 1850 A. D. He claims to remember the war in Mysore and the death of Tippu Sultan as incidents of his youth. He also saw the last Moghul Emperor and his predecessor. The old man, of course, remembers the Indian Mutiny of 1857 very well and recalls that when he first went to Lahore from Baroda he travelled by road, because there was no railway.

He visited Nagpur twice when he was residing at Baroda and was eventually employed as a professional wrestler and instructor in physical training for Krishnarao Abasaheb, the father of Sirdar Venkatrao Gujar. This was about the year 1855 and as Siddi Wastad was reputed to have a son of sixty years in Baroda at the time, it would seem probable that the date of his own birth was soon after 1775 A. D. When he came to Nagpur to live with the Gujar family there was no railway line but land had been acquired for constructing a rail road and earth-work was in progress. His arrival in the City was just before the destruction of the Mahal by fire. Even allowing for considerable exaggeration, his age would be about 130.

Sirdar Venkatrao's father....was, when Siddi Wastad was first employed as his trainer, about 16 or 17 years of age......The old athlete has now been living in Sirdar Venkatrao Gujar's house for over 75 years and his influence in the family has been very great indeed. It has been the custom in the past for every famous wrestler visiting Nagpur to make a point of paying his respects to Siddi Wastad before giving any exhibition. His own final public contest was with a sepoy in the old military cantonment at Amraoti. He defeated this man and became unpopular among the troops as a result.

Until the year of the influenza epidemic of 1918 this remarkable man remained in perfect health. He was himself attacked by the scourge and in the ten years following is reported to have had attacks of paralysis and cholera. Since then he has gradually lost his teeth and his hair has turned white. Until 1918 it was not his habit to lie down or to go to bed. A short nap in a chair at night was quite enough for him, and he offered his prayers five times a day. His diet up to that time was about 6 lbs. of flour for one meal, apart from vegetables, rice, mutton and four seers of milk each day. His meal used to take him full three hours when his teeth were sound and he now eats, apparently heartily, on his hardened gums. When ill, he has never taken doctor's drugs but he prepares his own medicines and medicated oils and treats himself.

How greatly he is held in awe by the family of his employer and friend is indicated by the fact that he will not allow the room in which he resides to be swept by anybody. Once during his absence Sirdar Venkatrao himself ventured to attempt to clean the room, but he found three large scorpions underneath the prayer rug ' with the result............that he was severely admonished for this venture ! '

REPORT ON THE ESTIMATED AGE-DISTRIBUTION OF THE INDIAN POPULATION AS RECORDED AT THE CENSUS OF 1931 AND THE RATES OF MORTALITY DEDUCED FROM A COMPARISON OF THE CENSUS RETURNS FOR 1921 AND 1931.

I had the honour to be invited by the Government of India to make an investigation into the estimated age distribution of the Indian population as indicated by the Census figures of 1931 and to prepare Life Tables as deduced by a comparison of the Census records of 1931 with one or more of the preceding Census enumerations ; and now beg to submit the results of my investigation.

This is the sixth of a series of investigations into the Mortality of the Indian population conducted in connection with each decennial Census from 1881 onwards. The first three were made by the late Sir George Hardy, the fourth by the late Mr. T. G. Ackland and the fifth in connection with the 1921 Census by Mr. H. G. W. Meikle, the then Actuary to the Government of India.

PROVINCES DEALT WITH IN THIS REPORT.

The larger Feudatory Indian States that conduct separately their own Census operations were not included in any of the previous investigations. The areas dealt with in these investigations were mainly British Provinces and the smaller Feudatory States under the direct political control of the Provincial administration. I decided, however, to conduct the present investigation on the Census Statistics available for the whole Indian Empire including all the Feudatory States whether small or large. The Indian Subcontinent, covering an area of more than 1,800,000 square miles and containing a population of almost 353 millions, was divided for the purpose of my enquiry into the following ten large geographical units :

(1) Sind, Baluchistan and North-West Frontier Province.

(2) Punjab, Delhi and Kashmir.

(3) Rajputana, Ajmer-Merwara, Gwalior and Central India Agency.

(4) The United Provinces.

(5) Central Provinces, Berar and Hyderabad State.

(6) Bihar and Orissa.

(7) Bengal and Assam.

(8) Bombay Presidency (excluding Sind), Baroda State and the Western India States.

(9) The Madras Presidency, Coorg, Mysore, Travancore and Cochin States.

(10) Burma (Burmans only excluding foreign born).

Each British Province includes the small State or States, if any, in direct political relationship with it.

Though Sind is politically a part of Bombay, in view of its great distance from Bombay and the greater affinity of the population of Sind to its immediate neighbours, it was decided to amalgamate it with Baluchistan and North-West Frontier Province.

The data supplied to me for the purpose of my investigation included :—

(1) The Census Returns of 1931 showing in each Province and for each sex the numbers living at the ages of 0, 1, 2, 3 and in alternate ternary and septenary groups 4-6, 7-13, 14-16, 17-23, etc., with one large group at the end of 74 and over.

(2) Specimen Schedules, in connection with the 1921 Census, showing out of a selected number, usually about 100,000 of each sex in each Province, the numbers recorded as living at each individual age last birth-day throughout life.

(3) Birth-place Returns showing—

(a) the number of emigrants born in each Province or State and enumerated elsewhere, and (*b*) the number of immigrants enumerated in each Province or State and born elsewhere.

(4) The Provincial and All-India Census Reports on the 1921 Census.

(5) The Actuarial Reports based on the 1921 and the preceding Censuses.

No returns at individual ages, except those at the very early ages from 0 to 3, and no specimen schedules showing the distribution of the population at each age, except in the case of the Punjab and Madras out of a sample of 100,000 in each sex, were available in connection with the 1931 Census. This has proved to me a very great handicap* and I could not apply to the 1931 Census certain lines of investigation I made with the aid of the specimen schedules available in the Actuarial Reports of the earlier Censuses, especially in connection with the enquiry whether the very large errors in the Age Returns in India show a tendency to diminish or increase. Nor are their uses confined to the study of errors in age as there are bound to be other lines of Statistical Research in which individual Age Returns of the population will be of great help. By the time the Government of India requisitioned my services in connection with the Actuarial Analysis of the 1931 Census, I learnt to my disappointment that only ternary and septenary groups above referred to were available. I do not think it should entail any great expense if Tables are given for each Province showing the distribution of the population according to individual ages in each sex. The population statistics of England and Wales are available for each age. If, however, for one reason or other, this is considered impracticable for the next few decades in the Census history of India I cannot too strongly recommend that specimens showing distribution of the population at each age should be collected in each Province and in each State that conducts its own Census operations. The characteristics of the specimen are summarised in statistical language in the words " Representative Random Sample ". A sample of 100,000 may be a representative one for a small area but may not be so for a large one. The magnitude of the sample should, therefore, depend on the area dealt with. Where again a large area is concerned, the sample should be taken from two or more localities widely separated from one another: otherwise the sample will neither represent the entire area nor be a random one.

SECTION I.

Characteristics of the Decennium 1921-1931.

1. The method to be adopted in the Actuarial Analysis of the Census material of India is very largely influenced by the economic and hygienic conditions prevailing in the decade preceding the Census. A population of which 90 per cent. or more is rural, subsisting mainly on the produce of the soil and cattle, leading a practically insular life in the village of its occupation, with its needs necessarily brought down to the barest minimum, should be extremely sensitive to the caprice of nature. If the rainfall is seasonal and sufficient a good harvest is reaped and the population, remunerated in most cases in kind, moves in harmony with the season. With bountiful harvest, a feeling of optimism permeates the entire atmosphere and conditions are conducive to health and abundant supply of babies. On the other hand, a lean harvest, engendered by the failure of the monsoon, leads to undernourishment and to contamination of any available scanty water supply which makes epidemics of the nature of Cholera, particularly connected with the bowels, break out. The death rate soars very high claiming a very large toll from the very young and the very old and underfeeding due to scarcity usually gives the people, under such circumstances, very little stamina to withstand the attack. The fall in the birth rate, combined with the very high mortality affecting childhood, leaves a deep chasm in the age curve noticeable in the Age Returns of several subsequent decennial Censuses just as a permanent scar from a deep wound.

2. If the next few years after a famine happen to be good or even normal monsoon years, the surviving population consisting mainly of those that have weathered the storm is known to have more than made up for the children lost

* It is usual to have 100,000 individuals of each sex sorted by individual ages for each province. This was not done in 1931 as the Actuary to the Government of India advised that it would not be necessary if Mr. Meikle's method of grouping were adopted.—J. H. H.

during the famine years. By the side of the deep chasm in the age curve above referred to, there would usually appear a big hump and as it very rarely happens that any Province in India is uninterruptedly immune from these seasonal disturbances for a decennial period, the age curve is generally full of undulations at successive short ranges which are either accentuated or masked by the preference for particular digits and the systematic errors in the ages returned by the population. To bring out the true or nearly true age curve from such irregular data, the Actuarial microscope has to be used rather very minutely and the method adopted is made to suit the nature of the statistics presented to the Actuary which in its turn is primarily influenced by the conditions obtaining in the decennium under consideration.

3. In illustration of the point made out in the last two paragraphs, the following Table showing the number of children under 5 per 10,000 of the total population in India in each of the Census enumerations may be found of interest. Corresponding figures for some representative countries in Europe and the United States of America are given which bring out in relief the very large fluctuations in the Indian birth rate due to the effect of famines and the rapidly recuperative nature of the population during normal or sumptuous years.

TABLE I.

Number of children under 5 per 10,000 of population.

Country.	1880-81.	1890-91.	1900-01.	1910-11.	1920-21.	1930-31.
England and Wales ..	1,356	1,225	1,143	1,068	877	..
Germany	1,365	1,300	1,308	1,206	634	..
Sweden	1,232	1,218	1,147	1,121	955	..
Belgium	1,237	1,159	1,171	1,024	694	..
France	923	872	862	886	618	..
Switzerland	Not available.		1,140	1,076	848	..
United States ..	1,379	1,222	1,210	1,156	1,095	..
India	1,369	1,468	1,297	1,379	1,258	1,529

4. The deficiency in the number of young children in the 1881 enumeration is to be traced to the famine of 1876-78 which affected the Provinces of Madras and Bombay. It will be noticed that, in spite of the large reduction of the young shown in the returns of two very large Provinces, the total for India was appreciably in excess of several European countries and was only slightly in defect of the number for the United States of America. The 1891 Census followed a period of general prosperity which is evidenced in the very large proportion of children in the age distribution of the population. The widespread nature of the famine of 1899-1901 is reflected in the very small number of children under 5 returned at the 1901 Census which low record has been beaten only by the 1921 enumeration. The conditions obtaining in the decennium preceding the 1911 Census, though generally free from scarcity and consequent famine, were less favourable than those of the period 1881-1891 as reflected in the number of children under 5 which, though appreciably in excess of the other countries brought in the comparison, is very much in defect of the high level reached in 1891.

5. The particularly low figure for 1921, lower than any previous famine record, bears eloquent testimony to the fact that the young ages were subject to a two-fold depletion due to the selective incidence of the Influenza mortality of 1918-1919. The first wave was particularly fatal to children, while the second and the more virulent one, by claiming a very large toll from the adult ages and proving particularly fatal to women in pregnancy, had struck a heavy blow at the very source of child supply.

6. As against the large fluctuations in the number of children in India with the normality or otherwise of the conditions obtaining during the decade preceding the Census can be set the steady trend towards fall of the number of children in the Western countries due purely to sociological reasons.

7. Where the decade preceding the Census was subject to dire visitations such as famine and pestilence, the method adopted by the renowned Actuaries, who wrote the Reports in connection with the earlier Censuses, was to estimate average rates

of mortality by combining the data of the Census on hand with those of a few earlier Censuses thereby eliminating, as far as this could be done, the effects of the disturbances above referred to.

8. Thus with respect to his 1881 Report, the late Sir George Hardy obtained average rates of mortality, firstly because the earlier Census enumeration was known to be extremely defective and secondly because of the famine of 1876-1878 which affected the two Provinces of Bombay and Madras. Since, however, the decennium ending with the 1891 Census was practically free from famine or epidemic that usually follows in the trail of a famine, he limited his investigation to a comparison of the 1881 and 1891 Census figures. The 1901 Census closely followed on the heels of the severe famine of 1899-1901, which affected extensive tracts in India, and also an epidemic of Plague. Sir George, therefore, deduced average rates of mortality by combining the Census figures of 1881, 1891 and 1901 by giving double weight to the 1891 Return. The decennium preceding the 1911 Census was, in spite of disturbances of moderate intensity in certain localities, taking the country as a whole, generally free from any calamitous visitation, and the late Mr. T. G. Ackland deduced rates of mortality relating to the decennium by combining the 1891 and the 1901 Census figures only. The conditions attending the 1921 Census were, however, exceptional. The population had not by then fully emerged from the devastating effects caused by the great Influenza epidemic which was estimated to have claimed as its victim nearly 7 per cent. of the total population of India. Mr. H. G. W. Meikle, the Actuary to the Government of India, who wrote the Report with the 1921 Census, with the view to deduce average rates of mortality, combined all the previous enumerations from 1881 onwards with the 1921 figures.

9. Though the decennium under consideration opened and closed in gloom, it has been on the whole a prosperous one. In the opening years of the decennium the effects of the Influenza epidemic that prevailed at the close of the last decade and the bad monsoon of 1920 were still evident. This position rapidly altered and a series of good monsoons followed interrupted only by floods notably in Bengal, Gujarat, Sind and South India. Famines were practically local and not very serious and the advancement in Medical Research minimised to a great extent deaths from Tropical diseases such as Cholera, Plague and Kala-azar. These favourable conditions are naturally reflected in the very large increase (10·6 per cent.) in the population which the decennium has witnessed. The closing years of the decennium, however, brought the position practically back to that of the opening ones, with this difference that towards the close there was considerably larger number of mouths to feed than at the commencement on practically identical economic conditions. Trade was depressed to an unprecedented level and the prices of agricultural products fell so low as to be entirely unremunerative to the cultivator. The consequent distress to a population of which nearly four-fifths live directly by agriculture could be easily imagined. Whether the prosperity of the few middle years of the decennium has been of such magnitude as to justify the very large increase of 10·6 per cent. of the population or in absolute figures 33,895,298, an increase which, in the words of Dr. Hutton, the Census Commissioner for India, is "a figure approaching equality with that of the total population of France or Italy and appreciably greater than that of such important European Powers as Poland and Spain" is a subject on which I shall have something to say in another section of this Report. Here I am mainly concerned with the fact that in the decade under consideration the population did contribute a very large—almost abnormally large—increase, apparently both by saving in deaths and by abundant supply of babies and on this account I felt justified in making use of the 1921 and 1931 Census figures only thereby confining my attention solely to the conditions obtaining in the decennium.

SECTION II.

On the peculiar nature of the Methods to be adopted in constructing Mortality Tables from Indian Census Returns.

1. In the preceding section of this Report attention was directed to the characteristics of the decennium under consideration being the main factor influencing the decision of the Actuary as to whether the mortality Table to be constructed should be an average one embodying the experience of more than one decennium or

should be confined only to that of the decennium preceding the Census. In this section I shall consider the peculiar novelty and difficulty of the problem of mortality Table construction as applied to this country caused by the fact that the records of vital occurrences are entirely undependable, which makes it necessary to discard the usual methods of construction of mortality Tables and adopt special ones as I explain below.

2. Where a reasonable amount of reliance can be placed on the ages and numbers returned at the Census enumeration and the records of deaths during the intercensal period, the method almost invariably employed to obtain the rate of mortality at each age of a given population is to compare the living at the various ages as recorded in the Census Returns with the registered deaths at the corresponding ages. The task of the Actuary becomes, under such conditions, comparatively easy for the analysed material will practically tell its own tale and smoothing or graduation will be required only with the view, on the one hand to arrive, very nearly, at that ideal flow of the rates of mortality from age to age that would have been obtained had the volume of statistics analysed not been limited in extent and to eliminate any small irregularities due to minor mis-statements of the age on the other. But the records of vital occurrences in India are yet deplorably undependable as will be evident from the following Table :—

TABLE II.

Comparison between enumerated and deduced population.

Province (British Territory only).	Variation 1921-1930 according to Vital Statistics (Excess of Births over Deaths+, Deficiency —). Total.	Variation 1921-1931 according to Census (Excess +, Deficiency—). Total.	Difference. Excess or defect of column 3 over column 2.
1	2	3	4
Assam	+450,854	+1,163,123	+712,269
Bengal	+1,463,484	+3,411,695	+1,948,211
Bihar and Orissa	+3,254,095	+3,682,158	+428,063
*Bombay	+1,728,161	+2,587,404	+859,243
Burma	+715,458	+1,454,954	+739,496
C. P. and Berar	+1,423,608	+1,594,963	+171,355
Delhi	+53,132	+147,794	+94,662
Madras	+4,398,902	+4,421,122	+22,220
N. W. F. Province	+94,759	+173,736	+78,977
Punjab	+2,428,382	+2,895,374	+466,992
United Provinces	+3,927,768	+3,033,694	—894,074
Total ..	+19,938,603	+24,566,017	+4,627,414

* Excludes Aden.

3. The natural assumption to be made, in drawing conclusions from the above Table, is that the censused figures are very nearly correct and all irregularities are traceable to records of Vital Statistics. As between the records of births and deaths, larger inaccuracies are naturally traceable to the former than to the latter. A study of the figures in the Table will show that Delhi, Assam and Bengal are almost in the vanguard of Provinces that maintain inaccurate vital records as the increases in the population of the decade in these Provinces traced through vital records are nearly 64, 61 and 57 per cent. respectively in defect of the increases revealed by the Census enumeration. Burma and the North-West Frontier Province closely follow with the respective deficiencies of 51 and 45 per cent. Bombay shows a deficiency of 35 per cent. The United Provinces show a large excess of 29 per cent. As this is an emigrating Province, the only explanation is that in this Province the records of deaths are more inaccurate than the

records of births. Madras alone, of all the Provinces, is remarkably accurate as the deficiency is only one-half per cent. It outpaces the second best Province—the Central Provinces and Berar—by a considerable distance as the deficiency in this Province is as much as 11 per cent. It might be possible to approach the censused population with very great accuracy through records of vital occurrences, even if the latter be inaccurately maintained and therefore subject to very large errors, provided such errors are of the same or nearly the same absolute magnitude. For, in arriving at the population on any date with the aid of the records of births and deaths, the numbers relating to births and deaths occcur with opposite signs and therefore the errors in these two records are of a compensatory nature. One is therefore forced either to assume that the records of vital occurrences in Madras are maintained up to a great degree of accuracy, or that both the records of births and deaths are teeming with inaccuracies and these inaccuracies happen by chance to be very nearly equal, so as to reproduce the censused population within an error of one-half per cent. As observed above, the records of births in all Provinces except the United Provinces are relatively more inaccurate than the records of deaths. With the Province of Madras, however, as between assuming that both the records of births and deaths are inaccurate or both of them are very accurate, I am inclined to the latter view which is also borne out by the relatively greater accuracy shown by that Province in the statement of ages as will be seen in the section on "Errors in Age". It may, therefore, be of interest to construct mortality Tables for the Province of Madras according to the usual method of mortality Table construction when the records of births and deaths are dependable and compare the results so obtained with those deduced by making use of Census enumerations only. As, however, I have not been supplied with the full statement of deaths in Madras occurring in the decennium according to each age, this investigation could not be taken up before the time my Report was expected to be ready.

4. With the records of vital occurrences teeming with inaccuracies in each Province, as shown by the above Table, the Actuary has no course open but to make as best an estimate as he could of the rates of mortality prevailing amongst the population by making use of the Census enumerations only, without any reference to the records of births and deaths.

5. For the convenience of the reader who will not take anything on trust, I have tried to set out in the next few articles the *rationalé* of the method to be adopted when mortality Tables are constructed by making use of Census Returns only. As a hint, however, to such of the readers as would let anything in the nature of Mathematics alone, I have placed an asterisk to these articles which can safely be passed over. But they are requested to assume that for the construction of the mortality Table the Actuary requires a series of smooth numbers representing the mean population living from age to age in the period under consideration and also another set of smooth numbers denoting the rate at which the population has increased or decreased at each age in the same period.

Construction of Mortality Tables from Census Returns only.

*6. In countries where a reasonable degree of reliance can be placed on vital occurrences the only correct method of constructing a mortality Table is to make use of Census Returns along with the records of deaths. At the infantile ages, however, where the Census figures are subject to irregularities of a two-fold nature due to both overstatement of age and non-enumeration of infants, use has to be made of the records of births also in the quinquennium preceding the date of the Census to correct the Census figures relating to these early ages. If we are dealing with an ideal population where only as many die in a year as are born in the year, where there are no migration disturbances (called by Actuaries a Stationary Population) and where the adult population has come to such a high level of literacy as to give correct particulars at a Census, we shall arrive at the same results when constructing a mortality Table from Censuses alone as when we make use of both Census Returns and records of vital occurrences. If $P_x^{(1)}$ persons are recorded as having attained age x on their birthday preceding the Census date, their average age taking one with another can be assumed to be $x+\frac{1}{2}$. If at the Census taken 10 years later there are returned $P_{x+10}^{(10)}$ persons of age $x+10$ last birthday, the latter will be the survivors from amongst the group of $P^{(1)}_x$ persons of age x last birthday recorded at the preceding Census and will be of average age $x+\frac{1}{2}+10$. Provided that the chief desiderata of a stationary population as to the constancy of birth and death rates as also immunity from migration disturbances are actually realized, the ratio $P^{(10)}_{x+10}/P^{(1)}_x$ may be taken as very nearly equivalent to ${}_{10}p_{x+\frac{1}{2}}$ which is the probability of surviving 10 years at exact age $x+\frac{1}{2}$. It will, however, be necessary to find the probability of surviving one year, instead of 10 years for the construction of the mortality Table, which can be obtained as follows :—

*7. Under the ideal conditions of a stationary population which we have assumed, it can be easily seen that the numbers returned at the latter Census at any age x will be identical with the numbers returned at the Census 10 years earlier at the same age. This equality will hold whatever may be the interval between the two Censuses. If two Censuses are taken with an interval of only one year separating them we shall obtain the equation† ${}_1p_{x+\frac{1}{2}}= P^{(2)}_{x+1}/P^{(1)}_x$ where ${}_1p_{x+\frac{1}{2}}$ is the probability of surviving one year at age $x+\frac{1}{2}$ and $P^{(2)}_{x+1}$ represents the population returned as of age $x+1$ last birthday at the latter of the two Censuses. Since the numbers returned at the same age in any two Censuses are identical we have $P^{(2)}_{x+1}/P^{(1)}_{x+1}=P^{(1)}_{x+1}/P^{(1)}_x$ so that ${}_1p_{x+\frac{1}{2}}=P^{(1)}_{x+1}/P^{(1)}_x$. It will be evident from an inspection of the above equations that given a stationary population the numbers returned at each age at one Census enumeration would easily supply the numerical values of the probabilities required for the construction of the mortality Table. But no community conforms to the rigorous conditions imposed for being called a stationary one and we shall have to modify our formula yielding numerical values of the probabilities of surviving at each age when the ideal requirements are relaxed one by one and we pass on from an imaginary stationary community to one actually met with subject to varying birth and death rates combined with disturbances due to emigration and immigration.

Varying Birth Rate with Constant Death Rate and no Migration Disturbance.

*8. Let us assume that the number of births has been increasing uniformly from year to year for a considerable number of years in geometrical progression while the death rate has been constant at each age and there has been no migration. On our assumptions, the number of births per annum increased from, say, l_0 in that period of one year just preceding the first Census date to $r^{10} l_0$ in that period of one year just preceding the next decennial Census date. Let us denote the number of children of age less than 1 (age 0 last birthday) returned at the earlier of the two Censuses we are considering by L_0. These are the survivors out of the l_0 births in the year preceding that Census. The population returned at age 1 last birthday will number $\frac{1}{r}L_1$, for, these are the survivors from amongst the $\frac{1}{r}\,l_0$ births in that period of one year which commenced exactly two years before the Census date on the basis of a geometrical increase in the number of births. We shall therefore have the total population at each age last birthday returned at the first Census given as follows :—

$L_0,\ \frac{1}{r}L_1,\ \frac{1}{r^2}L_2\ \ldots\ \frac{1}{r^{10}}L_{10}\ldots\frac{1}{r^{20}}L_{20}\ldots\frac{1}{r^{100}}L_{100}$, etc. On the same assumption, the population returned at the next Census at each age last birthday will be as follows :—

$$r^{10}L_0,\ r^9L_1,\ r^8L_2\ldots L_{10},\ \frac{1}{r}L_{11},\ldots\ \frac{1}{r^{10}}L_{20}\ldots\frac{1}{r^{90}}L_{100},\ \text{etc.}$$

The L's in the two series with the appropriate suffixes denote the population in each age that would have been returned had the number of births not varied from year to year, that is, on the assumption that all the conditions of a stationary population had been satisfied.

*9. The mean population at any age, meaning thereby the population that would have been returned had a Census been taken at a date exactly at the middle

† Students of Actuarial Science will note that the prefix 1 in ${}_1p_{x+\frac{1}{2}}$ is usually omitted.

point of the two decennial Censuses, is given by $\frac{1}{2}L_x\left(\frac{1}{r^x}+\frac{1}{r^{x-10}}\right)$, $\sqrt{\frac{L_x}{r^x}\cdot\frac{L_x}{r^{x-10}}}$ or $\frac{2L_x}{r^x+r^{x-10}}$, according as we take the Arithmetic, Geometric or Harmonic Mean. Let us denote the expressions by L^A_x, L^G_x and L^H_x respectively. It can easily be verified that $\frac{L^A_{x+1}}{L^A_x}=\frac{L^G_{x+1}}{L^G_x}=\frac{L^H_{x+1}}{L^H_x}=\frac{1}{r}\cdot\frac{L_{x+1}}{L_x}=\frac{1}{r}\ {}_1p_{x+\frac{1}{2}}$ That this result should be true whatever may be the mean population we are taking could have been foreseen inasmuchas it is true for the populations enumerated at each of the two Censuses we are considering. I could not take it for granted since it may not be evident to one and all of the readers. I have, however, assumed in the case under consideration the death rate to be the same as in the case first considered but only the birth rate to vary. The probability, therefore, of surviving one year at age $x+\frac{1}{2}$ is even now ${}_1p_{x+\frac{1}{2}}\left(=\frac{L_{x+1}}{L_x}\right)$ being identical with its value when all the conditions of a stationary population are satisfied. The natural conclusion to be drawn is that, whereas when a population has attained an absolutely stationary condition the number at any age of one Census enumeration, or, what is the same thing, of the intercensal (mean) population between two Censuses, divided by the number at the age next below yields the probability of surviving one year at the half age midway between the two ages, when one of the conditions, namely, constancy of births from year to year, is relaxed, the ratio above described no longer gives the required probability of survivorship, but we shall have to take into account the rate of increase of the population and multiply by this rate the ratio of the mean numbers at consecutive ages to obtain the probabilities of survivorship at each half age from which the mortality Table can be easily constructed.

*10. Since the population at age x of one Census becomes by survival that at age $x+10$ at the next decennial Census and both of them are the survivors to ages x and $x+10$ in the two Censuses respectively out of births occurring in the same year, we can, by dividing the number returned at any age $x+10$ at a Census by the number returned at age x at the preceding decennial Census, obtain the value of ${}_{10}p_{x+\frac{1}{2}}$ (the probability of surviving 10 years at age $x+\frac{1}{2}$) and thereby eliminate any necessity for bringing into account the rate of increase in the population. From the values of ${}_{10}p_{x+\frac{1}{2}}$ those of ${}_1p_{x+\frac{1}{2}}$ can be obtained by a suitable method of interpolation. Before, however, this method could be adopted, one has to be absolutely certain that the only cause contributing towards a return of varying numbers at the same age from one Census to another is variation in birth rate, of which the magnitude is exactly ascertainable, and the rate of mortality has been practically invariable and the population has also been immune from disturbances due to migration. Such conditions are ideal and are not true to populations that are usually met with. It might be observed in passing that with only varying birth rate, if Census-taking be an annual function, we shall obtain the value of ${}_1p_{x+\frac{1}{2}}$ at each central age by taking the ratio $P^{(2)}_{x+1}/P^{(1)}_x$ where $P^{(1)}$ represents the population at the earlier Census and $P^{(2)}$ at the Census taken one year later, and thereby avoid the necessity for ascertaining the rate at which the population has been varying due to variation in birth rate.

*11. With the view to make it easy for the general reader I have assumed the variation in the population to be brought about by the number of births increasing in a geometrical progression of constant common ratio r. The arguments will still hold if the variation be not at the uniform rate from year to year but at varying rates r_1, r_2, r_3, etc., and some of these r's may be greater and others less than unity so that the number of births may be increasing in some and decreasing in other years.

Varying Death Rate and Constant Birth Rate and no Migration Disturbance.

*12. I have so far considered the construction of a mortality Table from Census Returns alone firstly when the population satisfied all the conditions necessary for its being called a stationary one and secondly when only one of the conditions, *viz.*, constancy of the number of births from year to year, was relaxed. We can now assume the births to remain constant from year to year while the death rate varies. When the birth rate alone varies, either uniformly at a constant rate r or at rates changing from year to year, the force or forces that bring about variation in the population returned at the same age in the several Census enumerations all act at one particular point of age, namely, at birth. When, however, variation in population is a result of continuously varying death rate only, the other conditions of a stationary population holding, these forces act at all age points and the variation at any age between two Census enumerations represents the cumulative effect of these forces from birth up to the age in question. In spite of this apparent complication, since on our assumption the variation in the Census material is introduced by an irregular flow only in rates of death from year to year and from age to age and the assignment of a numerical value of this factor (rate of death) being the object of our enquiry, we shall yet be able to obtain the average value of ${}_{10}p_{x+\frac{1}{2}}$ by the ratio $P^{(10)}_{x+10}/P^{(1)}_x$ as evidently the population numbering $P^{(10)}_{x+10}$ at the later Census at age $x + 10$ are the survivors out of $P^{(1)}_x$ at age x at the earlier Census when the latter were subject to irregular incidence of mortality during the intercensal period. The quantity $1—P^{(10)}_{x+10}/P^{(1)}_x$ would give the average value of the probability of death within 10 years at age $x + \frac{1}{2}$ prevailing in the intercensal period and the probabilities of death or survival for one year at each half age will have to be obtained by interpolation though the resulting values might be very rough and require graduation due to the irregular incidence of mortality. The results of two annual Censuses will have to be made use of if interpolation is to be avoided as in the case when only the birth rate varied.

*13. If P^M_x be the mean population at age x between two decennial Censuses, whether it is the Arithmetic, Geometric or Harmonic mean or mean computed in any other manner, the ratio P^M_{x+1}/P^M_x does not yield the value of ${}_1p_{x+\frac{1}{2}}$ as it does when the population has been absolutely stationary. The cause is not far to seek if it is remembered that on our assumption P^M_{x+1} and P^M_x which represent survivors to the middle date of the intercensal period out of births in different, though consecutive, years have been depleted differently by varying incidences of mortality from birth up to age x in each case and the ratio P^M_{x+1}/P^M_x instead of depending upon the mortality rate from age $x+\frac{1}{2}$ to $x+\frac{1}{2}+1$ is coloured by the varying incidences of mortality above referred to at all ages below age x. To make the ratio P^M_{x+1}/P^M_x yield the value ${}_1p_{x+\frac{1}{2}}$ we must multiply it by a quantity r' which represents the ratio of the cumulative effect of mortality from birth to age x for the mean population P^M_x to the corresponding effect of mortality for the mean population P^M_{x+1}. The problem in this case is analogous to that when only the number of births varied, for, it will be remembered in that case to obtain the value of ${}_1p_{x+\frac{1}{2}}$ it was necessary to multiply the ratio P^M_{x+1}/P^M_x by r where r is the ratio of the number of births in that year of which P^M_x are the survivors to the births in the year of which P^M_{x+1} are the survivors.

*14. Where, however, it is not possible to ascertain and make allowance for the varying incidences of mortality in the two quantities P^M_x and P^M_{x+1} above referred to, due to the death registers not having been accurately maintained, the only method to be adopted is to ascertain for each age an average rate of increase or decrease in the population for the intercensal period and starting from the mean population between the two Censuses as base obtain the population that would have been returned six months anterior and six months posterior to the middle date of the intercensal period from which the values of ${}_1p_{x+\frac{1}{2}}$ can be easily deduced.

Varying Birth and Death Rates.

*15. It can now be seen that when both the birth and death rates vary the equation $P^{(10)}_{x+10}/P^{(1)}_x = {}_{10}p_{x+\frac{1}{2}}$ will yet hold. For $P^{(10)}_{x+10}$ and $P^{(1)}_x$ being persons at ages $x + 10$ and x in the latter and earlier Censuses respectively are the survivors out of the births occurring in the same year and in taking the ratio of the one to the other the disturbing effect in the constant flow of population from birth to age $x + \frac{1}{2}$ due to variation in the birth rate (the r of the geometric increase or decrease) is eliminated. Again the same fact, namely, that the populations $P^{(10)}_{x+10}$ and $P^{(1)}_x$ relate to births in the same year, is responsible for eliminating in the ratio $P^{(10)}_{x+10}/P^{(1)}_x$ the rates of mortality from birth to age $x+\frac{1}{2}$ and making it depend solely on the rates of mortality for the period of 10 years after age $x+\frac{1}{2}$. From the values of ${}_{10}p_{x+\frac{1}{2}}$ those of ${}_{1}p_{x+\frac{1}{2}}$ and then of ${}_{1}p_{x}$ can be obtained by interpolation.

*16. The question might naturally be asked at this stage as to why this apparently easy method of arriving at the values of ${}_{10}p_{x+\frac{1}{2}}$ at each half age should not be adopted. The answer is not far to seek if it is remembered that all along we have assumed that the individuals composing the community have come to realize the importance of giving correct particulars both as to numbers and ages at the Census enumeration and do give them. But the necessity for employing the rather out of the way method of constructing the mortality Table by comparing two or more Census enumerations only, without any reference to the record of vital occurrences in the intercensal period, arose out of the fact that the latter were quite unreliable. It will, therefore, be entirely unjustifiable to assume that the ages returned at the Censuses are correct when the birth and death records are entirely undependable. What usually happens with every step taken forward in the scale of literary evolution of a community is that the accuracy of the ages recorded in the death registers precede that of Census Returns. Apart from the fact that Law, under pain of penalties, compels the registration of births and deaths, the usual inducement for overstatement or understatement at particular periods of life which exist with respect to living persons at a Census enumeration is very nearly absent when giving the ages of the dead. That is why it is often said that the only correct method of constructing a mortality Table is to compare the living with the dead with further help from the register of births at infantile ages.

*17. It will hardly need any demonstration to show that, when the Census material is subject to variations due to the combined effect of irregular birth and death rates, the ratio P^{M}_{x+1}/P^{M}_{x} obtained from the mean of the two Census enumerations will not yield the value of ${}_{1}p_{x+\frac{1}{2}}$. It will be remembered that the ratio did not yield the value of this quantity even when only one of the two disturbing influences was present. To make the above ratio yield the value of ${}_{1}p_{x+\frac{1}{2}}$ we shall have to isolate the disturbance caused to the uniform flow of population from year to year by irregular variation in births from the disturbance caused by irregular variation in deaths and multiply the above ratio by suitable factors which, in addition to being a complicated process, assumes accurate knowledge of vital occurrences, records of which are extremely defective with respect to the population we are dealing with.

Migration.

*18. The correction for disturbances caused to the censused population due to immigration and emigration is easy to allow for if statistics of the immigrant and emigrant population have been maintained according to age.

*19. If I_x and E_x be the number of immigrants and emigrants respectively at age x during the intercensal period and if out of the excess of immigrants over emigrants there have occurred D_x deaths in the period, we shall have to take for the population at age $x+10$ at the latter of the two Censuses $P^{(10)}_{x+10}$—(I-E-D) instead of $P^{(10)}_{x+10}$ in each of the ratios given above yielding probabilities of surviving 10 years.

*20. The disturbance due to migration except in the cases of a few Indian Provinces is not very material. Further, Migration Statistics are not available according to age. The Actuary has, therefore, to make as good an estimate as possible of the age distribution of the migrant population. The deaths amongst the net immigrant population though comparatively of small significance will have to be allowed for by him in each age group by using his best judgment.

*21. I think a few words at summarising the results arrived at so far will, in view of the help it may give at clarifying the point under consideration, not be considered redundant. For the sake of simplicity I shall assume either that disturbances due to migration do not exist at all or if they do, appropriate corrections have been made to the censused population to eliminate as far as possible errors due to them. If correct ages are returned at the Census we shall obtain the following results :—

I. On the supposition that the population has been absolutely stationary for a long period so that the number of births in a year is equal to the number of deaths we shall have $\frac{P^{(10)}_{x+1}}{P^{(1)}_x}=\frac{P^{(2)}_{x+1}}{P^{(1)}_x}=\frac{P^{(1)}_{x+1}}{P^{(1)}_x}=\frac{P^{M}_{x+1}}{P^{M}_x}={}_1p_{x+\frac{1}{2}}$.

II. If the variation in the populations returned from Census to Census be due solely to variation in birth rate the ratio $\frac{P^{M}_{x+1}}{P^{M}_x}$ will have to be multiplied by a factor r as explained above which will have the effect of eliminating irregularity due to varying flow of birth rate from year to year and make the product $r\frac{P^{M}_{x+1}}{P^{M}_x}$ yield the value of ${}_1p_{x+\frac{1}{2}}$ which we require for the construction of the mortality Table.

III. Similarly when the population has been subject to varying death rate only, we shall have to multiply $\frac{P^{M}_{x+1}}{P^{M}_x}$ by a quantity r^1 (explained above) to make the product equal to ${}_1p_{x+\frac{1}{2}}$.

IV. When the population has been subject to irregular variation in both births and deaths we shall have to multiply by two different factors r and r^1 the ratio $\frac{P^{M}_{x+1}}{P^{M}_x}$ to make the product equal to ${}_1p_{x+\frac{1}{2}}$. The factor r eliminates variation due to the irregular flow of births and is obtained by an analysis of the records of births maintained for a long period in the past and the factor r^1 eliminates variation due to irregular incidence of rates of death from birth to age x and is obtained by an analysis of the records of deaths. In all the four cases $P^{(10)}_{x+10}/P^{(1)}_x={}_{10}p_{x+\frac{1}{2}}$ from which the values of ${}_1p_{x+\frac{1}{2}}$ can be obtained by interpolation.

*22. These methods are available if, and only if, both the desiderata given below hold:

(1) that the ages returned at the Census are absolutely correct, and

(2) that accurate records of births and deaths, the latter according to correct ages, have been maintained in the past.

*23. Since the ages returned at the Indian Censuses (including the latest one) have been manifestly full of errors both of a major and minor nature, added to which is the proverbial inaccuracy of the records of Vital Statistics maintained by the Provinces, we shall have to adopt special methods and construct mortality Tables by using Census enumerations alone. The fact that the Census enumerations are full of errors rules out the method of decennial interpolation from the equality $P^{(10)}_{x+10}/P^{(1)}_x={}_{10}p_{x+\frac{1}{2}}$. The fact that the records of Vital Statistics are not maintained accurately makes it impossible to find out the factors r and r^1 (mentioned above) representing correcting factors for the irregular incidences of births and deaths.

*24. The question will naturally be asked as to what is the method to be adopted which will minimise the effect of the errors in the Census material and provide mortality rates on which reasonable reliance can be placed. The answer is naturally suggested by the equation $P^{(10)}_{x+10}/P^{(1)}_x={}_{10}p_{x+\frac{1}{2}}$ when Census operations are undertaken once in 10 years or by the equation $P^{(2)}_{x+1}/P^{(1)}_x={}_1p_{x+\frac{1}{2}}$ when Censuses are taken annually. Taking the former of the two equalities it will be seen that if the numbers at each age returned at the two Censuses could be successfully graduated so as to remove errors we shall obtain the value of ${}_{10}p_{x+\frac{1}{2}}$ at each age. The disadvantage of this method is due to the fact that methods of graduation are not entirely successful in removing major deliberate errors. Since the values of ${}_{10}p_{x+\frac{1}{2}}$ are to be obtained from two sets of numbers $P^{(10)}$ and $P^{(1)}$ independently graduated and having residual errors in themselves, the errors in the computed values of ${}_{10}p_{x+\frac{1}{2}}$ will be accentuated or masked according as the residual errors in $P^{(10)}$ and $P^{(1)}$ are in opposite or in the same direction with the natural result that small errors in the graduated values of $P^{(1}$ and $P^{(1)}$ may be magnified in the computed values of ${}_{10}p_{x+\frac{1}{2}}$. With such errors magnified in them these values will not give as accurate a measure as desirable of the manner in which the number $P^{(1)}_x$ at the first

Census diminished to P^{10}_{x+10} at the next decennial Census due to the operation of mortality.

*25. The only other method that would to a large extent minimise this error is suggested by the equality $(r\, r^1)\, P^M_{x+1}/P^M_x = {}_1p_{x+\frac{1}{2}}$. According to this method we graduate the mean population of the intercensal period and by comparing the two Census enumerations in suitable age groups obtain and graduate the rates of natural increase of the population which will provide smooth values of r_x the rate of natural increase or decrease of the population at each age x in the decennium due to the combined operation of varying incidences in the birth and death rates. By multiplying the graduated mean population at each age x, P^M_x, by $r_x^{-\frac{1}{20}}$ and $r_x^{\frac{1}{20}}$ respectively we obtain the respective number of people that would have been returned at each age had two Censuses been taken, one on a date six months anterior and the other six months posterior to the middle day of the decennial period. By this device, from the figures of two Censuses taken with an interval of 10 years between them, we obtain the figures of two Censuses with only one year separating them. The values of ${}_1p_{x+\frac{1}{2}}$ at each half age are then obtained from the equality $r_{x+1}^{\frac{1}{20}}\, P^M_{x+1}/r_x^{-\frac{1}{20}}\, P^M_x = {}_1p_{x+\frac{1}{2}}$. This is the method that has been adopted in the construction of the mortality Tables for all the Provinces.

26. No apology, I hope, is needed for this lengthy description of the peculiar methods to be adopted in constructing mortality Tables from Indian Census Returns without which, I am sure, those for whose benefit Census publications are usually meant will find it difficult to appreciate why for instance the mean population should be calculated or, as a matter for that, what has the rate of increase in the population to do with the rate of death. The average man of letters is afraid of anything in the nature of statistics on the ground that "it is all dull stuff". It might take several years before the average reader realizes that statistics are nothing but numerical expression of facts a knowledge of which is essential to enable one to be prepared for difficulties which might occcur. They are more inclined to swear at statistics whereas they should swear by them. It will therefore be necessary, in the language of my esteemed friend, Mr. S. V. Mukherjea, Census Commissioner for Baroda, "to humanise the document". Talking of the general apathy of the public towards Census publications, Mr. Mukherjea in his characteristic style writes: "My experience has been that a Census Report, although intended for the general benefit of students and officers, is rarely read. Officers and publicists like to get a complimentary copy—for it is the thing to do so—look at its opening pages and then relegate it to their shelves, resorting to it most occasionally as an inducement to sleep when all other "drowsy syrup" of the doctors failed. What destiny is reserved for these humble pages, their author will be the last person to know".

27. If this is the language in which Mr. Mukherjea deplores the lack of interest of the public to a Census Report, my lot has been cast with a drier subject and the lengthy description given above is an humble attempt to "humanise my document".

SECTION III.

Errors in age.

1. The huge magnitude and the very wide range of the errors in the ages returned at the Indian Censuses constitute another important contributing factor towards making the task of the investigating Actuary particularly difficult. So much has been said in the past by successive Census Commissioners and Census Superintendents of each Province and State of the errors that abound in the ages returned at the Indian Census that any lengthy description by me of the psychological factors that lie at the root of these errors would be to emphasise the obvious. A large part of the Actuarial Report in connection with the 1921 Census is devoted to a consideration of the question of errors in age.

2. Before I consider the actual nature and extent of the errors in age one special characteristic of vital importance more or less peculiar to Indian Census has to be mentioned, namely, that people have no clear notions as to the distinction between age last birthday and age next birthday and always mix up the two. This was proved beyond doubt by my predecessor by reference to the 1891 and the 1901 Censuses of the Punjab. Curiously enough, in the former of the two Censuses,

the people of that Province were asked to state their age next birthday whereas in other Provinces the age asked for was the age last birthday. In the subsequent Census, however, the age asked for in the Punjab as well as in the rest of India was age last birthday. In the former of the two Censuses, to bring the Punjab figures in conformity with the figures for the rest of India, conversion was effected from age next birthday to age last birthday by scheduling the number returned at each age opposite the next younger age.

3. A part of the full Table appearing on page 7 of Mr. Meikle's Report on the "Age Distribution and Rates of Mortality" relating to the two Censuses of the Punjab is given below.

TABLE III.

Numbers recorded at each age in 1891 and 1901 out of 100,000 persons in the Punjab.

Age.	1891.		1901.	
	Males.	Females.	Males.	Females.
27—28	1,491	1,500	801	656
28—29	348	400	1,665	1,661
29—30	5,511	6,180	373	374
30—31	219	148	5,257	6,039
31—32	1,830	1,567	200	148
32—33	465	281	1,971	1,748

It will be seen that the large number 5,511 appearing in column 1 was the total population out of 100,000 males returned at age 30 next birthday and is, therefore, scheduled opposite to age 29 last birthday. This number 29 is really a very unpopular one as is evident from the small number 373 returned at that age last birthday at the 1901 Census. Successive Censuses have revealed that numbers, relatively large as compared to the adjoining ages, have been returned at ages ending with 2 and 8.* This is evident from the comparatively large numbers entered opposite age periods 27-28 and 31-32 in the 1891 Census as these were returned for ages 28 and 32 next birthday respectively. In the subsequent Census, however, numbers more or less equally large were returned for ages 28 and 32 last birthday respectively. A study of the full Table to which reference has been made will show that this characteristic is repeated round about all ages which end in 0 or 5. It is, therefore, evident that people fixed their attention only on the number indicating the age to be returned and were not influenced in the least by the age asked for being either the age last birthday or next birthday. Mr. Meikle states that it may, therefore, be assumed that the ages returned are the nearest birthday. What, however, appears to me to be the reasonable conclusion to draw is that the numbers returned at each age would have been the same whether ages next birthday or last birthday or nearest birthday had been asked for. A confusion similar to the one between age last birthday and age next birthday in India affected also the returns as to duration of marriage asked for in the 1911 Census of the United Kingdom as was pointed out by Sir Alfred Watson in the discussion on a Paper submitted by Dr. Stevenson on the "Fertility of the various Social Classes" to the Royal Statistical Society in April 1920.

4. The change made in the 1931 Census of recording age nearest birthday instead of last birthday appears to be one in the right direction on the primary ground that the greater care and thought necessary in giving an age to the nearest birthday taking into account the number of completed months after the last integral age, are more conducive to correct ages being returned when age nearest birthday is asked for than when age last birthday or next birthday is asked for. This appears to have been the main idea at the back of the mind of the Census Joint Committee in the United Kingdom when at the Census of 1921, for the first time, ages were required to be given in years and months though the change was made not with the intention of tabulating ages in years and months.

5. Taking up now the actual errors in the statement of ages at the Census it is said that an investigation into these errors is a study in idiosyncrasy. It would, however, give some consolation if it could be proved that each succeeding Census

* Whether the two digits are really centres of attraction or repulsion is a matter that requires detailed examination and is dealt with lower in this section.

showed that idiosyncrasy was slowly yielding place to sanity. It was, however, impossible for me to make any investigation in this direction with the 1931 Census Returns as by the time Government announced their intention to have the Actuarial Report in connection with this Census written by me the only available statistics were the ternary and septenary groups into which the individual Age Returns were straightaway sorted. Whether the ternary and septenary groupings could be modified so as to secure a more accurate balance of errors in each group is a subject which I shall take up under the head of "Grouping" in this section, but I cannot help observing here at the risk of repeating it that it will be undesirable to make the Census Analysis forego the demographic and psychological study which the distribution at each age out of a representative and random sample of 100,000 persons of each sex in each Province provides.

6. The principal sources of error in Census Statistics are of two kinds, namely, (*a*) Minor Errors of short range, unbiassed in character, and (*b*) Major Errors of a biassed nature and wide range that produce considerable distortion of the age curve.

7. *Minor Errors.*—The minor errors are attributable mainly to ignorance. Many people, in a country predominantly illiterate, are so indifferent as regards their age that, when questioned by the enumerator, they return round numbers which are primarily the nearest decennial ages and secondarily the nearest quinquennial ages. These errors are cyclical in character affecting ages which are multiples of 10 and 5 and recur, therefore, in cycles of ten-year age periods.

8. It has been held, by an examination of the relatively large numbers returned at ages ending in 2 and 8 as compared with the respective adjoining ages, that these digits are minor centres of attraction, meaning thereby that the numbers returned at these ages are more than the correct numbers at them. It is true that the preference for age 12 is so marked as to throw in the shade the general preference for a multiple of 5 in the age period 10-20 and 8 is very often preferred to age 5 in the period 0-10. A reference to the row "Deviation" in Tables IX, X and XI will show that, beyond the partiality above indicated, preferences for ages ending in 2 and 8 are not so very pronounced in the other sections of the decennial age periods. As a matter of fact, in most provinces, except Bengal, 8 is a centre of repulsion* to a certain extent. All the other digits are repulsed in the order 6, 4, 7, 3, 9 and 1 as is evident from the results of the three Census Returns analysed in Tables IX, X and XI above referred to. The method of construction of these Tables, the conclusions to be drawn from a study of them regarding the magnitude of the attraction or repulsion for ages ending in the several digits from 0 to 9 and the order in which the various digits have been preferred are taken up in greater detail in a few paragraphs of this section occurring later. These minor mis-statements of age are removed by a good method of graduation and disappear if the population is grouped in suitable decennial age periods.

9. *Major Errors.*—The major errors, that affect population statistics producing serious distortion of the age curve and of the rates of mortality deduced therefrom, consist primarily of the transfer of persons from one age period to another and secondarily of substantial omissions in the Census Records especially in ages of infancy and childhood.

10. If accurate records of deaths and migration are maintained according to each age it might be possible to identify the magnitude and locate the position of these major errors to a certain degree of accuracy, by comparing the number returned at any age, say, x at one Census with that returned at age $x+10$ at the next decennial Census by making suitable allowance for deaths and disturbances due to migration to which the first number had been subject in the intercensal period. It is hardly necessary to add that such an investigation is nextto impossible with the present condition of death and migration records in India. These wilful mis-statements are generally due tovanity especially in the case of old persons who generally give themselves the advantage of a few more years. There might also be financial reasons for overstatement at the old ages if the laws of the country provide for an old age pension. In a certain number of cases these mis-statements are also due to resentment against the personal nature of the questions

* A digit is a centre of repulsion when the number returned as of that digit is less than the correct number at it.

and suspicion of their motives. Whatever may be the causes for these deliberate mis-statements they are ultimately traceable to ignorance; not ignorance of age itself to which the minor errors are due but to ignorance of the fact that the Census Analysis does not deal with individuals but only with groups and the individuals are merged unidentifiably in the groups dealt with.

11. At the appropriate place in this section comparisons will be effected between the extent and magnitude of the errors in age in India and those of some other countries where the level of education is decidedly higher than in India. The errors in the ages returned at the Censuses in India do not show any tendency to diminish and will not do so, so long as illiteracy permeates the population to the extent it is now doing. We cannot expect better results till education spreads and as a natural result the ignorance of the people in matters relating to the Census is substantially minimised. Talking of this ignorance Mr. G. H. Knibbs in a Paper read before the Royal Statistical Society in 1920 said :—

> "It would be easy to publish primers showing the purpose of a Census or of the greater branches of Statistics. Such primers could readily be prepared so as to be supplied to primary and other schools—in such a form as to serve the purpose of a systematic and most useful instruction in Statistical Method—instruction which would be of business value. In this way a popular recognition of the utility of Statistics could readily be created and the work of securing accurate data greatly facilitated."

12. One would entirely agree with Mr. Knibbs' view that education relating to statistical enquiries of all kinds, which, to make them serve their high purpose, should be presented in an interesting form devoid of all dull series of numerical Tables, should form a compulsory part of the education, in his boyhood, of the future citizen. This will to a large extent mend the no more than a *dilettante* interest shown even by a person of more than average education in matters relating to the Census.

On the Nature and Extent of the Errors in Age in Census Returns.

13. In his Actuarial Report in connection with the 1911 Census the late Mr. T. G. Ackland illustrated the preference for particular digits of age by the following Table :—

TABLE IV.

Showing in each of the six Provinces undermentioned the numbers out of a total of 1,000 returned in respect of each digit of age ; also the mean values for the six Provinces and the order in which the several digits were recorded.

	DIGIT OF AGE RECORDED IN CENSUS									
	0	1	2	3	4	5	6	7	8	9
Numbers (per 1,000) recorded in respect of each digit of age										
Bengal	253	43	121	56	64	187	76	57	106	37
	(1)	(9)	(3)	(8)	(6)	(2)	(5)	(7)	(4)	(10)
Bombay	292	43	110	56	60	215	66	47	78	33
	(1)	(9)	(3)	(7)	(6)	(2)	(5)	(8)	(4)	(10)
Burma	187	76	106	98	78	142	85	80	84	64
	(1)	(9)	(3)	(4)	(8)	(2)	(5)	(7)	(6)	(10)
Madras	264	48	113	64	73	171	89	48	90	40
	(1)	(9)	(3)	(7)	(6)	(2)	(5)	(8)	(4)	(10)
Punjab	279	44	110	55	67	198	78	49	84	36
	(1)	(9)	(3)	(7)	(6)	(2)	(5)	(8)	(4)	(10)
United Provinces	294	47	113	45	65	186	83	43	91	33
	(1)	(7)	(3)	(8)	(6)	(2)	(5)	(9)	(4)	(10)
Totals ..	1,569	301	673	374	407	1,099	477	324	533	243
Mean values	262	50	112	62	68	183	79	54	89	41
Order of Record	(1)	(9)	(3)	(7)	(6)	(2)	(5)	(8)	(4)	(10)

14. This Table was intended to show not only the magnitude of concentration at ages ending in certain favourite digits but also the order in which the digits were preferred. Mr. Ackland drew his conclusions on the assumption that had correct ages been returned the number with respect to each digit shown in the Table would have been 100 being a tenth of the total population which was reduced to 1000 for the purpose of this enquiry. In his Actuarial Report with the 1921 Census, Mr. Meikle did not publish any figures based on a similar analysis of the

1921 Census material but evidently indicated his acquiescence with the arguments and conclusions of Mr. Ackland by quoting the order of preference for each particular digit as deduced by the latter for the whole of India.

15. There is however some fallacy in this method. The count evidently commences at age 0 and a cycle is complete at age 9. At age 10 another cycle commences which is completed at age 19 and so on. Each age, therefore, ending with the digit, say, 9 is nine years lower down the scale than age 0 of the same cycle and has therefore been depleted by deaths occurring in these nine years of lifetime. Had there been no preference for particular digits of age, that is, if people had returned their correct ages, even then the total number returned at ages having 9 in the unit's place would have been considerably smaller than the number returned at ages ending in 0. There would have been a progressive and smooth diminution as we go downwards from age 0 to age 9. The method of analysis adopted at the 1911 Report does not make allowance for this progressive diminution due to mortality and therefore loads the scales against ages at the lower half of the cycle in favour of those at the upper half.

16. In illustration of the case in point, I have taken Mr. Ackland's graduation of the specimen schedule of 100,000 males of the Province of Bombay. The graduated numbers are smooth and do not exhibit any preference for any particular digit of age but only diminish smoothly from age to age due to the operation of mortality. The results are set out in the following Table :—

TABLE V.

Distribution of 100,000 Males of the Province of Bombay according to the digit of age in the unit's place.

1911 Census.

	Unit figure in age last birthday.									
	0	1	2	3	4	5	6	7	8	9
A. ..	12,225	11,400	10,845	10,382	9,987	9,638	9,318	9,017	8,732	8,456
B. ..	1·45	1·35	1·28	1·23	1·18	1·14	1·10	1·07	1·03	1·00

17. In the row A the graduated numbers are given while row B shows the ratio which the number at each digit bears to that at digit 9. The latter figures indicate that, without showing any preference for ages ending in particular digits, the total population returned at ages ending in 0 should be 45%, those at ages ending in 1, 35%, at 2, 28%, etc., in excess of those returned at ages ending in 9. Hence, before conclusions are drawn, allowance should be made for this natural excess at all other digits as compared with the number at digit 9.

18. A method that eliminates this fallacy is to obtain for each digit the ratio of the sum of the ungraduated to that of the graduated numbers at that digit and compare these ratios. It is not claimed that the graduated numbers represent absolute truth. A good method of graduation would produce figures which deviate, if at all, from the true figures within the limits of errors due to random sampling. It can, therefore, be claimed that, where the original statistics are manifestly full of errors, the graduated figures represent as near an approach to the true figures as possible; the greater the reliability of the original statistics the closer will be the graduated to the true figures.

19. The three Tables IX, X and XI appearing on pages 128-130 show for the six main Provinces of India in each of the three Censuses (1911, 1901 and 1891) the numbers returned in respect of each digit of age out of a total male population of 1,000 in each Province, the corresponding graduated numbers and the ratios of the ungraduated to the graduated total for each digit. The deviations (excess+, deficiency—) of the ungraduated from the graduated numbers are given in the next row and the row following shows the order in which the different digits have been preferred while returning ages obtained by a comparison of the ratio of the ungraduated to the graduated numbers. The last row gives the rank allotted to each digit by the method adopted at the 1911 Analysis by a comparison of the size of the ungraduated numbers only without making any allowance for their progressive diminution due to the operation of mortality as explained above. I could not carry this enquiry down to the 1931 Census as with that Census, with which my work is intimately connected, no returns at individual ages either of the

whole population or of samples, as I have several times said in this Report, are available, while with respect to the 1921 Census, though the numbers at individual ages of specimens are available, the graduated numbers are available only in groups.

20. It should be observed at the outset, at the risk of repeating it, that digits should be allotted their rank in the order of record only by a comparison of the ratio of the ungraduated to the graduated numbers and not by a comparison of the magnitude of the absolute numbers representing deviation. In illustration of this point, we can take the digits 1 and 9 for the United Provinces at the 1911 Census. The ratio for the former digit is ·4196 and for the latter ·3837 which shows that out of every 10,000 males whose ages had 1 in the unit's place only 4196 returned correct ages and the remaining 5804 other ages. As for the digit 9 the ratio shows that only 3837 out of 10,000 whose ages ended with 9 returned correct ages. It is now evident that, as between the two digits, ages ending with digit 9 were repelled by the U. P. males in 1911 more than ages ending with digit 1. If we had drawn our conclusions from the relative magnitude of the deviation for each digit we would have inferred that 9 was more popular than 1 in that Province. The deviations have their own use in giving a numerical measure of the magnitude of the error at each digit out of each sample of 1,000 of the population having the same age distribution as the total population. For instance, in such a sample of 1,000 persons in the United Provinces in 1911, as many as 112 persons would have been found at ages ending in the digit 1 of which only 47 returned correct ages and the remaining 65 returned incorrect ages. The ratio of 65 to 112 is smaller than the ratio of 53 to 86 showing that the unpopularity of 1 in U. P. at the 1911 Census was less than that of 9 though the absolute figures of deviations for these digits are 65 and 53 respectively. The "total deviation irrespective of sign" gives the total number of males out of each representative sample of 1,000 persons that returned incorrect ages.

21. It will be seen, from a scrutiny of the figures in Tables IX, X and XI, that ages ending with the digits 0, 5 and 2 proved centres of attraction. Confining first our attention to the figures relating to All-India in Table IX, it will be seen that as many as 141 per mille of the total population whose ages did not end with the digit 0 returned ages ending with that digit at the 1911 Census. This is the average figure for the whole of India and varies from a maximum of 175 in the United Provinces to a minimum of 68 in Burma. The magnitude of the plumpings at ages 0 in the other Censuses can be obtained similarly from the figures for these Censuses appearing in Tables X and XI. The next popular digit is 5 though in the age period 10-19 age 12 has a greater degree of concentration than age 15. Next in rank in the order of preference comes the digit 2, followed by 8. From an examination of the All-India ratios for these two digits in all the three Censuses, it will be seen that the numbers returned at these ages are very nearly accurate. The former is the centre of a small attraction though it has been consistently repelled by Burma, and by Madras in two out of the three Censuses analysed. The latter is, if anything, a small centre of repulsion. In the 1891 and 1901 Censuses 1 per mille and 5 per mille respectively of the total population who were of an age ending with digit 8 repelled their true ages and returned other ages. At the 1911 Census, however, 1 per mille of the total population whose age did not end with the digit 8 returned an age ending with that digit. Bengal alone, of all the Provinces, appears to have consistently shown a great partiality for these two digits. I feel it essential to emphasise the fact that the errors at ages ending in digits 2 and 8 are not very material, except at the single age 12 and the single age 8, as it appears to me that it has been assumed in the past that at ages ending in these two digits there has been a substantial overstatement of numbers.

22. The other digits are definite centres of repulsion as in every one of them the actual numbers returned are less, in some considerably less, than the expected or graduated numbers. The same fact is confirmed by the ratios applicable to these digits either for the Provinces or for the whole of India as these ratios are in every case substantially less than unity, which, by the way, would have been the value of the ratio for any digit had correct numbers been returned at that digit.

23. What might, however, prove of interest is the fact that the unpopularity of digits 6, 7, 8 and 9 appearing in the lower half of the cycle has been accentuated and that of digits 1, 3 and 4 in the upper half masked by the method of comparison

adopted at the 1911 Report which omitted to make allowance for the influence of mortality above referred to. For a similar reason the popularity of ages ending in 0 has been further magnified and that of ages ending in 5 not fully brought out by the inherent fault in the old method which compared the several digits as regards their popularity by the absolute magnitude of the crude figures returned at the Census. To take an example, it would appear, by paying attention only to the numbers returned at the Census, that in the Province of Bengal at the 1911 Census as many as 153 per mille of the total population who were not of ages ending with 0 returned such ages whereas the correct number as given by "Deviation" should be only 129. The ungraduated figure for digit 5 would indicate that the cluster round ages ending in 5 was only 87 per mille whereas the correct number is larger being 91. This method of basing conclusions from the magnitude of the crude figures only returned at the Census without allowing for the fall in numbers due to mortality from age to age did perhaps the greatest injustice to digit 5 as against digit 0 at the 1901 Census in the two Provinces of Bombay and Madras. I am not aware if it had been realised that in these two Provinces at the 1901 Census the cluster round ages ending in 5 was proportionately larger than that round ages ending in digit 0. The ratios (which alone give the correct method of assessing the popularity of different digits) relating to these digits show that in the Province of Bombay at the 1901 Census the numbers returned at ages ending in 5 were 208 per cent. of the correct number whereas for digit 0 they were only 192 per cent. The corresponding percentages for Madras were 142 and 141. Since the absolute magnitude of the numbers returned at 0 is considerably larger than that at 5 it is very likely that the fact, that at the 1901 Census in the Provinces of Bombay and Madras, ages ending in digit 5 were more popular than ages ending in digit 0, thereby reversing the usual order of preference of these two digits, was overlooked.

24. The method of comparing ungraduated Census figures has also reversed the relative positions of digits 1 and 9 and the latter has come in for a measure of unpopularity rather undeserved. It will be seen from a reference to Table IV that digit 9 has been given the last rank in the order of record for all the Provinces and naturally for the whole of India and digit 1 the next higher rank in almost all Provinces and for the whole of India, while in the United Provinces this digit was given as high a rank as the 7th. It will, however, appear from a comparison of the sizes of the ratios that at the 1911 Census in all the Provinces and in the whole of India 9 was more popular than 1 except in the United Provinces where the order was reversed. A reference to all the three Tables IX, X and XI will show that except in two instances (1901 Burma, and 1911 U. P.) digit 9 always secured the 9th rank and 1 the last, *viz.*, 10th rank, thereby proving clearly the greater popularity of ages ending in digit 9 as compared with ages ending in digit 1. The other incorrect ranks allotted by the old method are all indicated in Table IX.

25. Exigencies of space and time forbid my making any further elaboration on this subject relating to the order in which ages ending in the different digits were preferred at the three Censuses that have been analysed for this study. It is, however, necessary to state in closing this topic that the other odd numbers excluding 5 were preferred in the order 3, 7, 9 and 1 and not in the order 3, 7, 1 and 9, as made out in the older Reports. As between digits 3 and 7 it is not quite decisive which of the two is the more popular. Each is repelled practically to the same extent as is evident by the extreme closeness of the ratios relating to these two digits in all the three Censuses for the whole of India.

26. As regards how far these errors show a tendency to diminish, I fear, I am not in a position to make any statement that would show a satisfactory state of things. Information in this respect is given by the numbers called "total deviation irrespective of sign" in Tables IX, X and XI. For the whole of India about 522 per mille of the male population returned incorrect ages at the 1891 Census which happily dwindled down to 376 at the 1901 Census but at the 1911 Census the number rose again to 466. If we examine particular digits the same tendency is revealed. For instance, the concentration at age 0 at the 1891 Census was 166 per mille which diminished to 108 at the 1901 Census and again rose to 141 in 1911. It will be found that in the case of all Provinces except Burma there has been a set-back in this respect from the 1901 to the 1911 Census. It is not possible to say how far Burma has been consistent

in the tendency for improvement it has shown, as this Province, for reasons ex plained by Sir George Hardy, was not included in the 1891 Actuarial Analysis. Madras which showed a very large deviation of 562 at the 1891 Census was remarkably accurate at the 1901 Census, for, at that Census only 180 per mille of the total male population gave incorrect ages. At the 1901 Census the accuracy shown by Madras was substantially superior to that of all the other Provinces including Burma. But it has since taken fast strides in the retrograde direction as will be evident from the large number, 450 per mille, that returned incorrect ages at the 1911 Census. This figure, though significantly smaller than the figures of the other Provinces excluding Burma, is almost double that of Burma and shows Madras as exactly two and a half times worse off in this respect as judged by the standard set up by Madras itself at the 1901 Census. It is not, I hope, necessary to make further comments as the figures of 'ratios', 'deviation' and 'total deviation irrespective of sign' tell their own tale. The general conclusion to be drawn from a scrutiny of these figures is that the tendency towards improvement shown by all the Provinces from 1891 to 1901 practically vanished in 1911, Burma alone being an exception. What has happened since 1911 I am not in a position to pronounce any opinion upon backed by Statistical Analysis, as, for reasons I have already explained more than once, it has not been possible for me to make any investigations in this direction with the 1921 and 1931 Census materials.

27. It has often been held, not without justification, that the magnitude of these errors is directly correlated with the percentage of illiteracy in a country. It might, therefore, be instructive to compare in this respect India with some representative countries of the world. An easy method of comparison is obtained by using the "Index of Concentration" devised by the United States Census Bureau. By this method the number of persons between 23 and 62 years whose ages are returned as multiples of 5 is compared with one-fifth of the total number between the two ages. The method is based on the justifiable assumption that had there been no concentration on multiples of 5 these two figures would be "about equal". The limits 23 and 62 were selected as they covered the period in which the concentration under investigation was most marked. The method suffers, to a certain extent, from the same disadvantage as attaches to that adopted at the 1911 Actuarial Analysis in proving the order of preference for particular digits of age. Since, however, numbers ending in 5 and 0 are symmetrically placed in each cycle that commences with 3 and ends with 2, any bias in favour of 5 introduced by the method is neutralized by the bias contrariwise against 0. Again, since the small error yet attaching to the method affects more or less equally all the countries, comparison of one country with another is not vitiated by this method. The following Table effects such a comparison in which the total for multiples of 5 is expressed as a percentage of the total for all ages from 23 to 62 and is taken from the 1921 Report for the Province of Bombay by Mr. Sedgwick. It should, however, be stated that 100 would mean no concentration at all and 500, the maximum value of the index, would mean that all ages returned between 23 and 62 were multiples of 5.

TABLE VI.

Region.	*Index of concentration.*
Bombay—Males. Selected area 1	325
Bombay—Males. Selected area 2	314
Bulgaria	245
Russia	182
Hungary	133
United States	120
Canada	110
France	106
Germany	102
Sweden	101
England and Wales	100
Belgium	100

28. Another method of indicating the tendencies of people to concentrate at ages ending in certain digits and avoid others is to find the ratio of the total number returned at ages ending in particular digits to the corresponding graduated total which was also explained earlier in this section. The following Table, compiled by Mr. G. H. Knibbs, gives for males and females of Australia the ratio described above for the three Censuses taken in 1891, 1901 and 1911.

TABLE VII.

Ratio of number recorded to adjusted number. Censuses—1891, 1901 and 1911—Australia.

Year of Census.		Unit figure in age last birth-day.									
		0	1	2	3	4	5	6	7	8	9
						MALES.					
1891	..	1·1388	·9167	1·0088	·9545	·9969	1·0366	1·0207	·9513	1·0055	·9532
1901	..	1·1044	·9369	1·0072	·9677	·9809	1·0343	1·0134	·9636	1·0144	·9667
1911	..	1·0485	·9956	·9944	·9787	·9990	1·0085	1·0097	·9691	1·0191	·9695
						FEMALES.					
1891	..	1·1251	·9288	·9978	·9848	·9943	1·0077	1·0117	·9640	1·0125	·9558
1901	..	1·0926	·9270	1·0039	·9861	·9979	1·0106	1·0128	·9708	1·0165	·9738
1911	..	1·0367	·9895	·9935	·9895	1·0056	1·0050	1·0066	·9770	1·0148	·9760

A Table similar to the above, with respect to the male population only of the whole of India for the same three Censuses, is given below :—

TABLE VIII.

Ratio of number recorded to adjusted number. Censuses—1891, 1901, and 1911—All-India—Males.

Year of Census.		Unit figure in age last birthday.									
		0	1	2	3	4	5	6	7	8	9
1891	..	2·3719	·3596	1·0556	·5481	·6800	1·9175	·8065	·5444	·9773	·4471
1901	..	1·8925	·5575	1·0556	·6923	·7600	1·7708	·8298	·7143	·9432	·5882
1911	..	2·1652	·4425	1·0370	·5962	·6800	1·8865	·8404	·6000	1·0114	·4824

29. It need hardly be stated that unity for any digit would mean that ages ending in that digit have been correctly returned. A cursory scrutiny of the above Tables will make it evident how very slight the bunchings are in Australia at ages ending in 0 and 5 as compared with the pronounced cluster round these ages in India. The same characteristic might also be noted at ages which are centres of repulsion. The chief reason why these Tables are given here is to show that, whereas in Australia there is a pronounced tendency for the ratios relating to each digit to approach unity, that is, for the errors in age, already very small, to show a definite tendency towards diminution, no such tendency is exhibited by the figures relating to India. I have only to repeat what I have already observed that though 1901 Census figures showed some improvement on those of 1891, the figures relating to the 1911 Census indicated a definite move in the retrograde direction as is also evident from Table VIII.

Grouping.

30. Germane to the subject of errors in age is that of the groupings to be adopted to minimise the effect of the accidental errors that affect Age Returns. This is, however, a topic on which opinion is divided and whether one partciular method or another is to be preferred will depend on the certainty with which it will be possible to say how far the statistics collected are afflicted with errors of overstatement or understatement and whether the range of these errors is short or long. The central idea underlying all methods of grouping is that groups should be formed as far as possible containing the popular age along with the adjoining ages from which the former has drawn numbers so that, though returns at individual ages may be incorrect, the total of the group may be considered reasonably correct and the group totals are used as the basic data for any subsequent investigations. The most satisfactory grouping is that which makes the deviations between the total in each group and the ideal total in that group that would have been evident had correct

ages been returned a minimum. We are then faced with the problem of giving due weight to the rival claims of two considerations each acting contrary to the other. With the view to minimise the errors left over in them it is desirable to form large groups; on the other hand, large groups may have the effect of obscuring peculiar conditions prevailing in the decennium affecting only short range or ranges in the age curve.

31. Had the plumpings been confined only to ages ending in 0, groups 5-14, 15-24, etc., would deal effectively with such errors on the assumption that the concentration at ages ending in 0 is only drawn from the adjoining four or five ages on either side. The records of deaths of England and Wales were presented in this form for many years. Since, however, ages ending in 5 are also secondary centres of disturbance, the decennial groups above referred to will have to be abandoned in favour of quinquennial groups. Had there been concentrations of equal intensity at ages 0 and 5, groups 3-7, 8-12, etc., wherein the digit of concentration occupies the central position in each group would have been satisfactory. Indian Census Returns have, however, indicated concentration of greater intensity at all decennial ages than at quinquennial ones. This is the main point of criticism against this method added to which is the fact that ages ending in 2 which are also favoured to a certain extent occur at the end of alternate groups. In what follows this will be referred to as the 3-7 group. Had the concentrations at the two favourite digits been due to systematic over-statements of ages only, groups 1-5, 6-10, etc., would have eliminated them. Similarly groups 0-4, 5-9, etc., would have satisfactorily dealt with understatements. Except, however, at particular short periods of life there is no reason why systematic over-statement or under-statement alone should affect the Age Returns. The former method (0-4 group) had been adopted in the past as the standard one for grouping and presenting Census figures. This was condemned by my predecessor, Mr. Meikle, as the least accurate of all the methods of grouping and I find myself in entire agreement with his condemnation of the method as I shall show lower down in the course of this enquiry. I should also make special mention here of the great service rendered by Mr. Meikle to the cause of Indian Census by focussing attention on this important subject of grouping. The recommendations made by him, though in my opinion could be improved upon, were decidedly in the nature of improvements on the old methods. There are two more groupings, namely, 2-6, 7-11, etc., and 4-8, 9-13, etc. Five different methods of grouping have altogether been mentioned respectively designated as 0-4, 1-5, 2-6, 3-7 and 4-8 groups. We can also call 0-4 grouping as the 1st place method designating the method of grouping by the position of the most popular age of the group relative to it. For a similar reason 4-8 group will be called 2nd place method and 3-7, 2-6 and 1-5 will respectively be called 3rd, 4th and 5th place methods. Each of these methods of grouping could be associated with either age last birthday, next birthday or nearest birthday thereby giving rise to 15 different methods. In India, however, since people do not make any distinction in returning ages between age last birthday, next birthday or nearest birthday, there are only five different methods to be taken into account.

32. For adoption in connection with the 1931 Census Mr. Meikle recommended a method of grouping in alternate ternary and septenary groups 4-6, 7-13, etc., to be used in conjunction with the age nearest birthday. This method of grouping, according to my analysis, is a decided improvement on the old 0-4 method. There is, however, an inherent defect in the method in so far as it exaggerates bunchings in ages which are multiples of 10 and does not give full weight to those at ages which are multiples of 5. Ages of the former type occupy the central place amongst seven ages while those of the latter type occupy the central place amongst three ages only. It will, therefore, be evident that this method of grouping is based on the assumption that the concentration at ages ending in 0 is very nearly three times that at ages ending in 5. By reference to the ratios in Tables IX, X and XI it will be seen this is by no means the case. It was also pointed out earlier in this section that in two instances (Bombay and Madras, 1901) the actual proportion of concentration at ages ending in 5 was in excess of that at ages ending in 0.

33. It will, therefore, be desirable to slightly diminish the number of ages grouped along with an age ending in 0 and increase correspondingly the number grouped along with an age ending in 5. Since there is markedly greater concentration about ages ending in 0 than about 5, the number of ages in the former group should be larger than at the latter very nearly in proportion to the relative concentrations. I have, therefore, considered the claim for recognition of the following quaternary

and senary groupings in conjunction with age last birthday at the date of Census. A quaternary group is formed about an age ending in 5 which is placed centrally with an age and a half on either side of it. A senary group is formed about an age ending in 0 placed centrally with 2½ ages on either side of it. The earliest quaternary group comprises all persons whose ages are 3, 4, 5 and 6 last birthday. The next higher quaternary group is composed of persons of ages 13, 14, 15 and 16 last birthday and so on. The earliest senary group is formed of persons of ages from 7 to 12 last birthday, the next higher from 17 to 22 and so on. It would appear that these groups could easily be formed if the age asked for at the Census is last birthday. It will, however, be desirable not to sacrifice the greater accuracy secured, if any, in the ages returned by asking for the nearest age. If as at the 1931 Census groups are to be formed from the nearest age, the suggested quaternary and senary method of grouping will only necessitate dividing into two equal halves the numbers returned at all ages ending in 3 and 7. One half of the number at an age ending in 3 will be taken with the upper senary group and the other half with the lower quaternary group. Similarly half of the number returned at an age ending in 7 will be taken with the upper quaternary group and the other half with the lower senary group.

34. We have now to consider the relative accuracy of seven different methods of grouping which are described as follows :—

(1) 0-4 group called also 1st place method.

(2) 4-8 group called also 2nd place method.

(3) 3-7 group called also 3rd place method.

(4) 2-6 group called also 4th place method.

(5) 1-5 group called also 5th place method.

(6) The Ternary and Septenary method.

(7) The Quaternary and Senary method.

TABLE IX.

1911 Males.

Provinces.		Unit figure in age last birthday.									
		0	1	2	3	4	5	6	7	8	9
Bengal.	Ungraduated	253	43	121	56	64	187	76	57	106	37
	Graduated	124	115	109	104	100	96	93	89	86	84
	Ratio	2·0403	·3739	1·1101	·5385	·6400	1·9479	·9172	·6405	1·2326	·4440
	Deviation	+129	—72	+ 12	—48	—36	+91	—17	—32	+20	—47
	Order of record	(1)	(10)	(4)	(8)	(7)	(2)	(5)	(6)	(3)	(9)
	Ackland's order of record	(1)	(9)	(3)	(8)	(6)	(2)	(5)	(7)	(4)	(10)
	Total deviation irrespective of sign 504										
Bombay.	Ungraduated	292	43	110	56	60	215	66	47	78	33
	Graduated	122	114	109	104	100	96	93	90	87	85
	Ratio	2·3934	·3772	1·0092	·5385	·6000	2·2396	·7097	·5222	·8966	·3882
	Deviation	+170	—71	+1	—48	—40	+119	—27	—43	—9	—52
	Order of record .. .	(1)	(10)	(3)	(7)	(6)	(2)	(5)	(8)	(4)	(9)
	Ackland's order of record	(1)	(9)	(3)	(7)	(6)	(2)	(5)	(8)	(4)	(10)
	Total deviation irrespective of sign 580										
Burma.	Ungraduated	187	76	106	98	78	142	85	80	84	64
	Graduated	119	113	108	104	100	97	94	91	88	86
	Ratio	1·5714	·6725	·9815	·9423	·7800	1·4639	·9043	·8791	·9545	·7442
	Deviation	+68	—37	—2	—6	—22	+45	—9	—11	—4	—22
	Order of record .. .	(1)	(10)	(3)	(5)	(8)	(2)	(6)	(7)	(4)	(9)
	Ackland's order of record	(1)	(9)	(3)	(4)	(8)	(2)	(5)	(7)	(6)	(10)
	Total deviation irrespective of sign 226										

Provinces.		Unit figure in age last birthday. 0	1	2	3	4	5	6	7	8	9
Madras.	Ungraduated	264	48	113	64	73	171	89	48	90	40
	Graduated	120	112	108	104	100	97	94	91	88	86
	Ratio	2·2000	·4285	1·0463	·6154	·7300	1·7629	·9468	·5275	1·0227	4651
	Deviation	+144	—64	+5	—40	—27	+74	—5	—43	+2	—46
	Order of record	(1)	(10)	(3)	(7)	(6)	(2)	(5)	(8)	(4)	(9)
	Ackland's order of record	(1)	(9)	(3)	(7)	(6)	(2)	(5)	(8)	(4)	(10)
	Total deviation irrespective of sign 450										
Punjab.	Ungraduated	279	44	110	55	67	198	78	49	84	36
	Graduated	120	113	108	104	100	97	94	91	88	85
	Ratio	2·3250	·3894	1·0185	·5288	·6700	2·0412	·8298	5385	·9545	·4275
	Deviation	+159	—69	+2	—49	—33	+101	—16	—42	—4	—49
	Order of record	(1)	(10)	(3)	(8)	(6)	(2)	(5)	(7)	(4)	(9)
	Ackland's order of record..	(1)	(9)	(3)	(7)	(6)	(2)	(5)	(8)	(4)	(10)
	Total deviation irrespective of sign 524										
United Provinces.	Ungraduated	294	47	113	45	65	186	83	43	91	33
	Graduated	119	112	108	104	100	97	94	91	89	86
	Ratio	2·4706	·4196	1·0463	·4327	·6500	1·9175	·8830	·4725	1·0225	·3837
	Deviation	+175	—65	+5	—59	—35	+89	—11	—48	+2	—53
	Order of record	(1)	(9)	(3)	(8)	(6)	(2)	(5)	(7)	(4)	(10)
	Ackland's order of record	(1)	(7)	(3)	(8)	(6)	(2)	(5)	(9)	(4)	(10)
	Total deviation irrespective of sign 542										
All-India.	Ungraduated	262	50	112	62	68	183	79	54	89	10
	Graduated	121	113	108	104	100	97	94	90	88	85
	Ratio	2·1652	·4425	1·0370	·5962	·6800	1·8865	·8404	·6000	1·0114	4824
	Average deviation ..	+141	—63	+4	—42	—32	+86	—14	—36	+1	—45
	Order of record	(1)	(10)	(3)	(8)	(6)	(2)	(5)	(7)	(4)	(9)
	Ackland's order of record	(1)	(9)	(3)	(7)	(6)	(2)	(5)	(8)	(4)	(1)
	Total deviation irrespective of sign 466										

TABLE X.

1901 Males.

Provinces.		0	1	2	3	4	5	6	7	8	9
Bengal.	Ungraduated	234	47	135	57	74	169	82	60	98	44
	Graduated	123	114	109	104	100	96	93	90	87	84
	Ratio	1·9024	·4123	1·2385	·5481	·7400	1·7604	·8817	·6667	1·1264	·5238
	Deviation	+111	—67	+26	—47	—26	+73	—11	—30	+11	—40
	Order of record	(1)	(10)	(3)	(8)	(6)	(2)	(5)	(7)	(4)	(9)
	Total deviation irrespective of sign 442										
Bombay.	Ungraduated	235	57	119	63	68	200	68	59	81	50
	Graduated	122	114	108	104	100	96	93	90	88	85
	Ratio	1·9262	·5000	1·1018	·6058	·6800	2·0833	·7312	·6556	·9205	·5882
	Deviation	+113	—57	+11	—41	—32	+104	—25	—31	—7	—35
	Order of record	(2)	(10)	(3)	(8)	(6)	(1)	(5)	(7)	(4)	(9)
	Total deviation irrespective of sign 456										
Burma.	Ungraduated	199	74	96	99	78	155	81	86	77	55
	Graduated	119	113	108	104	100	97	94	91	88	86
	Ratio	1·6723	·6549	·8889	·9519	·7800	1·5979	·8617	·9451	·8750	·6395
	Deviation	+80	—39	—12	—5	—22	+58	—13	—5	—11	—31
	Order of record	(1)	(9)	(5)	(3)	(8)	(2)	(7)	(4)	(6)	(10)
	Total deviation irrespective of sign 276										
Madras.	Ungraduated	169	104	100	93	90	138	81	77	76	72
	Graduated	120	113	108	104	100	97	94	91	88	85
	Ratio	1·4083	·9204	·9259	·8942	·9000	1·4227	·8617	·8462	·8636	·8471
	Deviation	+49	—9	—8	—11	—10	+41	—13	—14	—12	—13
	Order of record	(2)	(4)	(3)	(6)	(5)	(1)	(8)	(10)	(7)	(9)
	Total deviation irrespective of sign 180										

Provinces.		Unit figure in age last birthday. 0	1	2	3	4	5	6	7	8	9
Punjab.	Ungraduated	274	40	119	57	67	198	74	49	86	36
	Graduated	122	114	108	104	100	96	93	90	88	85
	Ratio	2·2459	·3509	1·1018	·5481	·6700	2·0625	·7957	·5444	·9773	·4235
	Deviation	+152	—74	+11	—47	—33	+102	—19	—41	—2	—49
	Order of record	(1)	(10)	(3)	(7)	(6)	(2)	(5)	(8)	(4)	(9)
	Total deviation irrespective of sign 530										
United Provinces.	Ungraduated	262	58	113	65	78	162	80	56	81	45
	Graduated	119	112	107	104	100	97	94	92	89	86
	Ratio	2·2016	·5179	1·0561	·6250	·7800	1·6701	·8511	·6087	·9101	·5233
	Deviation	+143	—54	+6	—39	—22	+65	—14	—36	—8	—41
	Order of record	(1)	(10)	(3)	(8)	(6)	(2)	(5)	(7)	(4)	(9)
	Total deviation irrespective of sign 428										
All-India.	Ungraduated	229	63	114	72	76	170	78	65	83	50
	Graduated	121	113	108	104	100	96	94	91	88	85
	Ratio	1·8925	·5575	1·0556	·6923	·7600	1·7708	·8298	·7143	·9432	·5882
	Average deviation ..	+108	—50	+6	—32	—24	+74	—16	—26	—5	—35
	Order of record	(1)	(10)	(3)	(8)	(6)	(2)	(5)	(7)	(4)	(9)
	Total deviation irrespective of sign 376										

TABLE XI.

1891 Males.

Province		0	1	2	3	4	5	6	7	8	9
Bengal.	Ungraduated	249	49	122	61	70	170	79	61	94	45
	Graduated	122	114	108	104	100	97	93	90	87	85
	Ratio	2·0410	·4298	1·1296	·5865	·7000	1·7526	·8495	·6778	1·0804	·5294
	Deviation	+127	—65	+14	—43	—30	+73	—14	—29	+7	—40
	Order of record	(1)	(10)	(3)	(8)	(6)	(2)	(5)	(7)	(4)	(9)
	Total deviation irrespective of sign. 442										
Bombay.	Ungraduated	288	37	116	51	66	213	67	44	78	40
	Graduated	122	114	108	104	100	97	93	90	87	85
	Ratio	2·3606	·3246	1·0741	·4904	·6600	2·1959	·7204	·4889	·8966	·4706
	Deviation	+166	—77	+8	—53	—34	+116	—26	—46	—9	—45
	Order of record	(1)	(10)	(3)	(7)	(6)	(2)	(5)	(8)	(4)	(9)
	Total deviation irrespective of sign 580										
Burma	.. ..	*	..	..	..	..	..	..	..	..	..
Madras.	Ungraduated	310	33	102	59	68	185	77	44	92	30
	Graduated . ..	121	113	108	104	100	97	93	91	88	85
	Ratio	2·5620	·2920	·9444	·5673	·6800	1·9072	·8280	·4835	1·0456	·3529
	Deviation	+189	—80	—6	—45	—32	+88	—16	—47	+4	—55
	Order of record	(1)	(10)	(4)	(7)	(6)	(2)	(5)	(8)	(3)	(9)
	Total deviation irrespective of sign 562										
Punjab	.. ..	†	..	..	..	..	..	..	..	..	..
United Provinces.	Ungraduated	301	45	114	56	67	177	78	47	80	35
	Graduated	120	113	108	104	100	97	94	91	88	85
	Ratio	2·5083	·3982	1·0555	·5384	·6700	1·8247	·8298	·5165	·9091	·4118
	Deviation	+181	—68	+6	—48	—33	+80	—16	—44	—8	—50
	Order of record	(1)	(10)	(3)	(8)	(6)	(2)	(5)	(7)	(4)	(9)
	Total deviation irrespective of sign 534										
All-India.	Ungraduated	287	41	114	57	68	186	75	49	86	38
	Graduated	121	114	108	104	100	97	93	90	88	85
	Ratio	2·3719	·3596	1·0556	·5481	·6800	1·9175	·8065	·5444	·9773	·4471
	Average deviation ..	+166	—73	+6	—47	—32	+89	—18	—42	—1	—48
	Order of record	(1)	(10)	(3)	(8)	(6)	(2)	(5)	(7)	(4)	(9)
	Total deviation irrespective of sign 522										

* For reasons explained by him Sir George Hardy did not make any investigation with the Burma figures.

† It was not possible to include the Punjab in the 1891 Analysis as the ages next birthday were tabulated for that Province at that Census.

35. It will be desirable here to say a few words about the two criteria by which the suitability of any method of grouping is generally tested. The first criterion is what is called "goodness of fit". According to this criterion that method of grouping is the best which yields values at individual ages which deviate the least in the aggregate from the originally observed values. The second criterion relates to "smoothness" and helps to single out that method of grouping as the best which makes the values progress smoothly from one group to another.

36. Each of the first five methods of grouping was the subject of more than one severe test in the past with the view to find out which of them gave the most satisfactory result. In that gigantic work in connection with the preparation of Life Tables for the United States of America for 1890, 1901, 1910 and 1901-1910, Mr. James W. Glover, Professor of Insurance in the University of Michigan, conducted elaborate investigations with the statistics relating to the male population in the State of New York estimated as of July 1910 and the deaths of the three-year period 1909-1911.

37. In testing "goodness of fit" his first method was to obtain the rates of mortality for all ages from 15 to 85 by a method of osculatory interpolation when the population and the deaths were combined according to each of the five quinquennial age groups. These rates were compared with the rates of mortality obtained from the average of these five sets of graduated populations and statistics of deaths. The smallness of the deviations and the frequency with which these deviations changed sign were made the criterion by which to judge which method of grouping gave the most satisfactory result. By his second method he obtained the deviations of the expected from the actual deaths for each of the five methods of grouping. His third criterion was to consider that method of grouping the best which made the weighted squared deviations of the graduated values from the observed values a minimum. Each of the three methods detailed above can only be of theoretical interest to us in India so long as the records of Vital Statistics are in the present state of unreliability.

38. Instead of comparing the rates of mortality as deduced by every one of the methods of quinquennial grouping with the average for all groupings or with the observed rates of mortality as Professor Glover did because the data supplied to him comprised *inter alia* dependable statistics of deaths, I had, in the absence of this desideratum, no other option but to compare the actual numbers in each group for each method with the corresponding expected (or what is the same thing graduated) number. Whatever may be the actual groups in which the original statistics are collected they have to be finally transformed to the 0-4 groups (1st place method). This is more or less essential as the Age Statistics of most other countries and of India itself have all been published in this form and if any other method of grouping be adopted for the final presentation of population figures, comparisons with other countries and with past Censuses of India itself, which are always of very great value in Census study, would be practically impossible. The three Tables XV, XVI and XVII appearing at the end of this section show for the All-India Males in each of the three Censuses, 1891, 1901 and 1911, the deviations between the actual numbers returned at the Censuses and the graduated numbers in 5-9, 10-14, etc., groups for all the methods of grouping. It will be seen that, according to all the other methods except the first, the original statistics are not collected in 0-4 groups (*i.e.*, according to the 1st place method). All the other six methods were transformed from their respective groups to the 0-4, etc., groups which, as observed above, is desirable with the view to effect useful comparisons with other Census Statistics.

39. A word of explanation as to how this transformation from the original grouping to the 0-4 grouping should be effected may be necessary. Taking for instance the 2nd place method, the group, say, 4-8 should part with a fifth of the total ungraduated number in that group to the previous group and obtain a fifth of the total ungraduated number from the following, namely, 9-13 group. The result can very nearly be taken to be the 5-9 group and so on for transforming other groups. Similarly the 3rd place method of grouping should cede the population relating to ages ending in 3 and 4 to the preceding group and obtain the population relating to ages ending in 8 and 9 from the succeeding group. Each group should therefore cede two-fifths of its number to the preceding group and

obtain two-fifths of the number in the succeeding group. The adjustments to be made to the 4th and 5th place methods of grouping to transform them to the 1st place method should now be evident.

40. The assumption is made in this process of transforming one group into another that the numbers in all the ages in a quinquennial group are equal and no allowance is made for the progressive diminution of the population from age to age in that group. I have, however, satisfied myself that except at the ages of infancy and childhood and at the extreme old ages (say, above 70) the resulting error is of small magnitude. At the early ages, however, statistics of population should be tabulated according to single age periods and at the very old ages the statistics are usually combined into a single group, say, 70 and over. It will, therefore, be evident that at those age periods where the grouping device is adopted to minimise the effects of minor mis-statements of age the error introduced by the above assumption is of no great moment. The ternary-septenary and the quaternary-senary methods of grouping are transformed easily into 0-4, etc., groups by the dichotomous process explained by Mr. Meikle with respect to the former method of grouping which he advocated. By this method groups are formed by taking the sum of one-half of any two consecutive groups and the resulting new groups are of the 0-4, 5-9, etc., type.

41. The smallness of the number called "total deviation without sign" is the basis by which to judge each of the seven methods for the first criterion, namely, "goodness of fit".* This number shows the sum of the deviations (whether in excess or in defect) of the recorded numbers from the graduated numbers when the former in each of the six methods of grouping (except of course the first which is in the required form) are finally transformed into 0-4, 5-9, etc., groups by processes of which full explanation was given above. The algebraic sum of the deviations does not provide the criterion by which to judge the methods, as two deviations, one very large and positive and another negative and equal or very nearly equal, would produce a small algebraic sum of the deviations in spite of the large error of the observed number in each case from the ideal number. Judged by the criterion of the smallness of the "total deviation without sign" it will be evident that the 4th place method (2-6, 7-11, etc., groups) is foremost in rank of all the seven methods considered. The sum of the deviations irrespective of sign is the smallest for this method in each of the three Censuses considered. Second in rank as regards accuracy is the "Quaternary and Senary" method explained in detail earlier in this section though the "Ternary and Septenary" method shows itself as slightly superior at the 1891 Census, but this is more than compensated for by the very large differences in the other two Censuses in favour of the former method. It will be of interest to note that the 1st place method (0-4, etc., groups) shows the largest deviation of all the seven methods in all the three Censuses. This is the method of grouping of the population that had been adopted in the past and Mr. Meikle was quite justified in condemning this method as the least accurate of all the methods of grouping population statistics in India.

42. I felt it might be of interest to ascertain which of the seven methods gave the least deviation between graduated and ungraduated numbers in their original groups themselves before the transformation into 0-4, etc., groups was effected. The results are set out in the following Table:—

TABLE XII.

All-India—Males.

Year of Census.	Total deviation without sign.						
	1st place method. '0—4.'	2nd place method. '4—8.'	3rd place method. '3—7.'	4th place method. '2—6.'	5th place method. '1—5.'	Ternary and Septenary method.	Quaternary and Senary method.
1891	49,062	51,348	67,473	43,373	50,470	39,227	46,083
1901	66,580	61,227	81,085	51,174	55,564	59,563	52,122
1911	58,531	57,874	73,915	47,487	62,561	52,148	52,798

43. It will be seen from an examination of the figures of deviations in the above Table that '2-6' method shows the least deviation between ungraduated and graduated numbers before the original groups in which the population statistics are

* This test is usually adopted to judge the closeness of fit of the graduated numbers to the observed ones. Here, however, it has to be used contrariwise.

summed are altered to produce the '0-4' groups. In one instance (1891) when the errors in age were very large in magnitude, the Ternary and Septenary method shows a deviation smaller than the '2-6' method. But this is more than compensated for by the large difference between the deviations of the two methods in favour of the '2-6' method at the other two Censuses. The deviations appearing in the above Table do not provide a very important criterion by which to judge the methods as ultimately all the six methods (except the first) are altered to the groupings of the first one.

44. As for the second criterion, namely, "smoothness" by which to judge the methods of grouping, it is satisfactory to be able to say that I have been able to adopt the same method of analysis as was adopted by Professor Glover with the population statistics relating to the United States of America above referred to. The smoothness of a series of values grouped in five ages is tested by the regularity of progression of the ratio $\frac{G_x}{G_{x-5}+G_{x+5}}$ where G_x is the total for ages from x to $x+4$ inclusive. Such ratios were formed from '0-4' groups for each of the seven methods of grouping considered. As when testing the methods for "goodness of fit", the groupings in such of them, six in number, as were not originally in the '0-4' groups were transformed to these groups. Where the earliest age in a quinquennial group in the numerator of the above ratio is a multiple of 10 the ratio is called ${}_0M_x$ and where the earliest age is a multiple of 5 it is called ${}_5M_x$. For instance, the ratio $\frac{G_{20}}{G_{15}+G_{25}}$ is called ${}_0M_{20}$ and the ratio $\frac{G_{25}}{G_{20}+G_{30}}$ is called ${}_5M_{25}$. The three Tables XVIII, XIX and XX give the values of ${}_0M_x$ and ${}_5M_x$ for each of the seven methods of grouping in each of the three Censuses 1891, 1901 and 1911. The average values of ${}_0M_x$ and ${}_5M_x$ and the difference between the average values of these quantities are given below each method of grouping. To make it easy to understand that the method which gives smooth progression of the grouped values is that for which the difference between the average value of ${}_0M_x$ and ${}_5M_x$ is a minimum, the values of ${}_0M_x$ and ${}_5M_x$ for the graduated population in each Census are also given. The graduated numbers of the population progress smoothly from age to age and therefore the quinquennial groups formed from them should also progress smoothly. That they do so is demonstrated by the extremely small magnitude of the difference between the average value of ${}_0M_x$ and ${}_5M_x$ for the graduated population in each of the three Censuses considered. The seven methods of grouping population statistics under consideration are arranged in each Table according to the smoothness of progression of the grouped values judged by the criterion of the smallness of the difference between the average value of ${}_0M_x$ and ${}_5M_x$.

45. The first rank of the '2-6' method amongst all the seven methods considered will be evident. The "Quaternary and Senary" method secures the second rank and the "Ternary and Septenary" method the third. It is not by a narrow margin that the '2-6' method secures the first rank. Even at the 1911 Census where the "Quaternary and Senary" method which is always second in rank makes the closest approach to the '2-6' method, the difference between the average ${}_0M_x$ and ${}_5M_x$ according to the former is more than 50 per cent. larger than the corresponding difference of the latter. What may be of interest is that the '0-4' method (the method of grouping population statistics adopted so far) in addition to occupying uniformly the last rank in all the three Censuses shows at each Census a figure of difference several times larger than that of the '2-6' method and in the 1901 Census it was very nearly 20 times as large. The method, therefore, so far adopted in grouping population statistics has been the least accurate of all the methods considered from every point of view.

46. As a result of his analysis, Prof. Glover rejected the '0-4' and '1-5' methods as unsuitable and was not able to pronounce as decisive an opinion in favour of one of the other three methods, '2-6', '3-7' and '4-8', as it has been possible to do with the analysis on Indian Age Returns for the main reason that the mis-statements of age in the American Census Returns are not so pronounced as in the case of the Indian Returns. He ultimately decided in favour of the '4-8' method and his arguments for so doing may be quoted in his own words. "However, the decision as to groups '2-6', '3-7' and '4-8' still remains a problem. As between these three groups it will be observed that groups '2-6' and '3-7'

contain both the ages ending in the digits 0 and 8 in the same quinquennial age group while the adjacent five-year groups contain the ages ending in the digit 5. This tends to exaggerate unduly alternate quinquennial age groups in these sets. With the group '4-8', however, the ages ending in the digits 5 and 8 are in the same quinquennial group and the ages ending in the digit 0 are in the adjacent five-year groups. Since the exaggeration for ages which are multiples of 10 is undoubtedly greater than for ages which end in the digit 5, the group '4-8' would seem to furnish a better balanced grouping than the group '2-6' or '3-7'."

47. It will be evident from Prof. Glover's arguments that the chief reason why he decided in favour of the '4-8' grouping is the fact that in U. S. A. Age Returns ages ending in digit 8 formed definite centres of attraction next in popularity after the two digits 0 and 5. To secure, therefore, a better balance of the errors between two consecutive quinquennial groups he decided to keep the most favoured digit 0 in one group and the next two favoured digits 5 and 8 together in the adjacent quinquennial group. The late Mr. George King who analysed the population of England and Wales with the 1911 Census also pronounced in favour of the '4-8' method as his analysis also revealed that ages ending in digit 8 were nearly as favoured as ages ending in 5 which is shown by the following Table :—

TABLE XIII.

England and Wales, Males—1911. Ages 10—89.

Digit of age.	0	1	2	3	4	5	6	7	8	9
Ratio of recorded to graduated number on basis of 100,000 graduated at each age ..	1·0887	·9230	1·0094	·9687	·9941	1·0031	1·0016	·9661	1·0320	·9991
Ratio to digit 9 as shown by Mr. King ..	1·090	·924	1·010	·970	·995	1·004	1·003	·967	1·033	1·000

48. The results of three Australian Censuses appearing in Table VII also indicate concentration at ages ending in 8 of an intensity next only to ages 0 and 5.

49. Apart from the fact that the results of the analysis to which the three Censuses have been subjected have indicated the decided superiority of the '2-6' method of grouping over all the other methods taken in the comparison, we could have, on precisely the same arguments as induced Messrs. Glover and King to decide in favour of the '4-8' method, pronounced in favour of the '2-6' method. Their chief argument was that the second and third favoured digits, 5 and 8, should appear in one quinquennial group to balance the pronounced concentration at digit 0 which is the first favourite. Tables IX, X and XI appearing in this section have clearly indicated that in India digit 2 is the third favourite after 0 and 5 and **not** digit 8.

50. We should, therefore, include digits 2 and 5 in the same quinquennial group. The '2-6' and the '1-5' methods are the only two that satisfy this condition but the latter having an age of pronounced concentration at the end of a group can be *prima facie* rejected as unsuitable, leaving the choice only on the '2-6' method.

51. We are now in a position to see why the '2-6' method gives results, judged by any criterion, markedly superior to all the other methods. Any two consecutive groups of this method are formed from the two sets of digits, 2, 3, 4, 5, 6 and 7, 8, 9, 0, 1. It was shown earlier in this section that as between the two digits 3 and 7 it was not quite decisive which was repelled the more. These two digits appearing one along with digit 5 in one group and the other along with digit 0 in the other introduce, in so far as they are concerned, balancing errors in two adjacent groups. The marked concentration at digit 0 as compared with digit 5 should then be neutralized by combining with the former digits relatively unpopular as compared with those combining with the latter. The '2-6' method of grouping is able to effect this as digits 1 and 9 which are the least liked of the ten digits are grouped along with 0 as against 4 and 6 grouped with 5. The combination of 2 with the 5 group and that of 8 with the 0 group serve as the final correcting factor in this respect.

Recommendations for adoption at the 1941 Census.

52. (*a*) *Grouping.*—They say that figures speak more emphatically and convincingly than words and if that is so, it can be claimed that the unique position of the '2-6' method of grouping amongst all the seven methods considered, in minimising the effects of mis-statements of age in population statistics, has been established beyond any pale of doubt. I, therefore, very strongly recommend its being adopted at the 1941 Census.

53. (*b*) *Age.*—The method of grouping recommended is particularly easy to adopt if age last birthday is asked for at the Census. The change made in the 1931 Census of asking people to return their age on nearest birthday, though theoretically expected to diminish significantly the errors in the ages returned, does not appear to have had the desired effect. This is evident from the distribution according to each age at the 1931 Census of a sample of 100,000 persons of each sex of the Presidency of Madras and the Punjab which alone were forwarded to me as the available statistics showing the distribution of any sample at individual ages. Amongst the larger Indian States the Census Commissioner for Baroda has given age distribution of the population at individual ages. These samples indicate the same degree of concentration, as in the earlier Censuses, at the usual favourite digits. Had the change made in this respect at the 1931 Census any effect at all, the concentration at ages ending in 0 should have been more or less equally divided between ages ending in 0 and 1, for, if a person returns his or her completed age as a favourite figure, say, 30, it is as likely that the person has passed more than six months since completing age 30 as less than six months. If, therefore, all those persons, who usually give ages clustering round numbers ending in digits 0 and 5 when age last birthday is asked for, were to give a moment's thought to the change in the age to be returned because what is asked for is no longer age last birthday but nearest birthday, very nearly one half of them would have returned nearest ages ending in 0 and the other half those ending in 1. This would have had the effect of very nearly levelling up the concentration at digits ending in 0 by dividing it more or less equally between ages ending in 0 and 1. For a similar reason the concentration at ages ending in 5 should have been more or less equally divided between ages ending in 5 and 6. The statistics to which reference has been made do not exhibit any such tendency as the following Table for Madras clearly indicates thereby confirming the statement made at an earlier part of this section that people were not in the least influenced by the age asked for being last birthday, nearest birthday or next birthday.

TABLE XIV.

Madras—Males.

Numbers returned at each digit of age out of a total population of 1000.

Date of Census.	Digit of age. 0	1	2	3	4	5	6	7	8	9
1891	310	33	102	59	68	185	77	44	92	30
1901	169	104	100	93	90	138	81	77	76	72
1911	264	48	113	64	73	171	89	48	90	40
1931	253	53	108	64	62	208	68	52	95	37

The large deficiencies noticed in ages ending in 1 and 6 do not show any tendency to close up as a result of the change made in the 1931 Census in recording the age. On the other hand, the deficiency at 6 has been the largest at 1931 of all the four Censuses.

54. It has been observed in other countries that the form of the age enquiry has an appreciable influence on the accuracy of the Age Returns. Dr. A. A. Young, in his Report on ages at the 12th U. S. A. Census, applied a test to the data of several countries some of which obtained ages in years, others in years and months and a third set actually called for the date of birth. He concluded, as a result of his test, that the statistics were most dependable when the date of birth was called for.

55. To call for the date of birth will be an impossibility for several decades in the Census history of India. At the same time, while returning ages to the enumerator, people's minds should be set about thinking for a while instead of

returning any age at random. I should, therefore, recommend ages being called for in completed number of years and months. The enumerator should write in his form the number of completed years and months. While grouping, however, according to the '2-6' plan recommended, the months should be ignored. We shall thereby get the age last birthday which is best suited to the method of grouping recommended without in any way sacrificing the accuracy, if any, that might accrue to the Age Statistics by calling for something more than mere age last birthday. In those cases where the number of months passed since the last birthday cannot be obtained it is immaterial as the grouping is according to the completed number of years (that is, age last birthday) only. I do not make myself bold to say that the suggested method of asking for age last birthday and the number of months completed since last birthday will have any metamorphic effect at the 1941 Census. It might, however, have some effect of slowly curing the Age Returns of its ills as decades pass on, as otherwise, with the existing system of calling only for ages whether last birthday, next birthday or nearest birthday, the malady shows no signs of coming under control. If, however, it is considered too early in the Census history of India to burden the schedule with ages and months (though the latter are to be ignored in the grouping) the age last birthday with the suggested '2-6' method of grouping could be depended upon to give the best results of all the other methods of grouping.

56. In adopting the '2-6' method of grouping, returns for ages 0, 1, 2, etc., up to 6 last birthday should be scheduled separately and groups should be formed of ages 7-11, 12-16, 17-21, etc., to 67-71 with a last group of 72 and over. Table XXI gives a practical example of how the population supposed to have been straightaway sorted in the above groups are further transformed into 5-9, 10-14, etc.,......65-69, 70 and over groups, with the returns at ages 0, 1, 2, 3 and 4 stated individually.

TABLE XV.

1891—All-India—Males.

Deviations.

Age group.	1st place method. '0—4'.	2nd place method. '4—8'.	3rd place method. '3—7'.	4th place method. '2—6'.	5th place method. '1—5'.	Ternary and Septenary method.	Quaternary and Senary method.
5—9	+6,254	+7,956	+8,348	+5,086	+7,253	+3,312	+5,479
10—14	—382	—1,488	—296	+465	—2,810	+1,276	—664
15—19	—8,901	—6,209	—7,626	—4,635	—2,269	—7,907	—7,437
20—24	—5,448	—5,508	—1,508	—1,466	—584	—1,952	—1,968
25—29	+1,393	+2,773	+1,822	+2,757	+3,888	+1,924	+2,118
30—34	+4,947	+3,013	+3,106	+1,718	—1,079	+2,387	+2,005
35—39	—488	+548	+838	+3,023	+4,719	+1,013	+1,217
40—44	+5,658	+3,690	+2,492	+110	—1,761	+1,268	+1,119
45—49	—2,029	—1,013	—626	+832	+1,704	—325	—234
50—54	+4,519	+2,507	+1,088	—992	—3,207	+81	—33
55—59	—2,678	—1,822	—1,027	+199	+1,164	—634	—586
60—64	+4,024	+2,643	+1,404	—106	—1,481	+660	+609
65—69	—1,327	—1,158	—1,021	—757	—605	—1,049	—1,004
70—74	+936	+535	+195	—207	—597	+15	—23
75—79	—78	+5	+76	+238	+288	+97	+106
	+27,731	+23,670	+19,369	+14,428	+19,016	+12,033	+12,653
	—21,331	—17,198	—12,104	—8,163	—14,393	—11,867	—11,949
Total deviation without sign.	49,062	40,868	31,473	22,591	33,409	23,900	24,602

TABLE XVI.

1901—Males—All-India.

Deviations.

Age group.	1st place method. '0—4'.	2nd place method. '4—8'.	3rd place method. '3—7'.	4th place method. '2—6'.	5th place method. '1—5'.	Ternary and Septenary method.	Quaternary and Senary method.
5—9	+11,543	+12,417	+12,513	+9,585	+12,265	+8,821	+10,485
10—14	+8,718	+6,151	+6,106	+6,960	+5,199	+8,125	+5,655
15—19	—10,595	—6,689	—7,219	—4,387	—4,034	—10,341	—9,024
20—24	—9,752	—9,111	—5,524	—5,142	—4,517	—5,418	—5,661
25—29	—407	+892	—60	+162	+1,700	—464	—71
30—34	+3,361	+1,537	+2,264	+1,490	—866	+2,084	+1,398
35—39	—1,771	—618	—459	+1,437	+2,215	—1,259	—809
40—44	+3,539	+1,709	+827	—747	—1,366	+198	—158
45—49	—1,535	—446	+1,124	+1,245	+1,905	—223	+21
50—54	+5,201	+3,118	+2,447	—214	—2,665	+916	+699
55—59	—2,029	—1,089	—2,157	+860	+1,866	—391	—223
60—64	+4,750	+3,021	+1,553	—112	—579	+843	+684
65—69	—1,500	—1,216	—1,102	—841	—893	—1,331	—1,236
70—74	+1,545	+877	+407	+17	—370	+317	+199
75—79	+334	+444	+525	+636	+660	+342	+414
	+38,991	+30,166	+27,766	+22,392	+25,810	+21,646	+19,555
	—27,589	—19,169	—16,521	—11,443	—15,290	—19,427	—17,182
Total deviation without sign.	66,580	49,335	44,287	33,835	41,100	41,073	36,737

TABLE XVII.

1911—All-India—Males.

Deviations.

Age group.	1st place method. '0—4'.	2nd place method. '4—8'.	3rd place method. '3—7'.	4th place method. '2—6'.	5th place method. '1—5'.	Ternary and Septenary method.	Quaternary and Senary method.
5—9	+6,619	+8,489	+8,760	+4,883	+8,501	+4,167	+6,351
10—14	+3,268	+1,038	+2,053	+2,651	—892	+3,574	+1,270
15—19	—10,130	—6,428	—7,928	—3,925	—643	—9,303	—8,310
20—24	—6,483	—6,279	—880	—774	—465	—1,235	—1,431
25—29	+2,540	+4,519	+2,714	+3,563	+5,285	+2,283	+2,693
30—34	+5,275	+3,031	+4,182	+2,792	—744	+3,558	+2,949
35—39	+388	+1,219	+1,298	+3,798	+5,648	+1,114	+1,432
40—44	+6,794	+4,399	+3,047	+513	—1,582	+1,827	+1,551
45—49	—1,253	—237	+101	+1,796	+2,772	+278	+436
50—54	+6,261	+3,590	+1,883	—687	—3,596	+684	+487
55—59	—3,338	—2,109	—1,384	—198	+842	—1,140	—1,053
60—64	+4,530	+2,802	+1,501	—89	—1,352	+719	+651
65—69	—861	—940	—1,103	—2,704	—1,085	—1,529	—1,396
70—74	+262	—219	—586	—1,069	—1,706	—714	—832
75—79	—529	—418	—262	—10	+184	—231	—211
	+35,937	+29,087	+25,539	+19,996	+23,232	+18,204	+17,820
	—22,594	—16,630	—12,143	—9,456	—12,065	—14,152	—13,233
Total deviation without sign.	58,531	45,717	37,682	29,452	35,297	32,356	31,053

TABLE XVIII.

1891 Census—All-India—Males.

Values of $_0M_x$ and $_5M_x$.

Transformed Age Groups.	Age group in which Population is originally summed.															
	Graduated.		'2—6'.		Quaternary and Senary method.		Ternary & Septenary method.		'3—7'.		'1—5'.		'4—8'.		'0—4'.	
	$_0M_x$.	$_5M_x$.	$_0M_x$.	$_5M_x$.	$_0M_x$.	$_5M_x$.	$_0M_x$.	$_5M_x$.	$_0M_x$.	$_5M_x$.	$_0M_x$.	$_5M_x$.	$_0M_x$.	$_5M_x$.	$_0M_x$.	$_5M_x$.
(1)	(2)		(3)		(4)		(5)		(6)		(7)		(8)		(9)	
10—14	·495	..	·498	..	·498	..	·536	..	·488	..	·441	..	·470	..	·505	..
15—19	..	·501	..	·451	..	·425	..	·409	..	·419	..	·494	..	·466	..	·424
20—24	·501	..	·494	..	·511	..	·516	..	·521	..	·483	..	·448	..	·476	..
25—29	..	·500	..	·540	..	·532	..	·526	..	·515	..	·573	..	·563	..	·525
30—34	·500	..	·482	..	·506	..	·515	..	·529	..	·420	..	·522	..	·576	..
35—39	..	·499	..	·540	..	·493	..	·484	..	·464	..	·630	..	·450	..	·404
40—44	·498	..	·458	..	·513	..	·520	..	·556	..	·394	..	·594	..	·676	..
45—49	..	·495	..	·534	..	·473	..	·467	..	·430	..	·642	..	·392	..	·333
50—54	·492	..	·436	..	·507	..	·514	..	·570	..	·331	..	·661	..	·815	..
55—59	..	·488	..	·528	..	·444	..	·438	..	·384	..	·725	..	·310	..	·241
60—64	·483	..	·495	..	·598	..	·607	..	·692	..	·358	..	·871	..	1·110	..
65—69	..	·470	..	·398	..	·333	..	·325	..	·299	..	·526	..	·248	..	·204
70—74	·441	..	·446	..	·529	..	·545	..	·588	..	·346	..	·704	..	·860	..
Total	3·410	2·953	3·309	2·991	3·662	2·700	3·753	2·649	3·944	2·511	2·773	3·590	4·270	2·429	5·018	2·131
Average	·487	·492	·473	·499	·523	·450	·536	·442	·563	·419	·396	·598	·610	·405	·717	·355
Difference between $_0M_x$. and $_5M_x$.	·005		·026		·073		·094		·144		·202		·205		·362	

TABLE XIX.

1901 Census—All-India—Males.

Values of $_0M_x$ and $_5M_x$.

Transformed Age Groups.	Age group in which Population is originally summed.															
	Graduated.		'2—6'.		Quaternary and Senary method.		Ternary and Septenary method.		'1—5'.		'3—7'.		'4—8'.		'0—4'.	
	$_0M_x$.	$_5M_x$.	$_0M_x$.	$_5M_x$.	$_0M_x$.	$_5M_x$.	$_0M_x$.	$_5M_x$.	$_0M_x$.	$_5M_x$.	$_0M_x$.	$_5M_x$.	$_0M_x$.	$_5M_x$.	$_0M_x$.	$_5M_x$.
(1)	(2)		(3)		(4)		(5)		(6)		(7)		(8)		(9)	
10—14	·495	..	·526	..	·531	..	·561	..	·503	..	·520	..	·518	..	·555	..
15—19	..	·500	..	·458	..	·427	..	·407	..	·465	..	·439	..	·457	..	·418
20—24	·500	..	·472	..	·490	..	·500	..	·470	..	·482	..	·441	..	·458	..
25—29	..	·500	..	·521	..	·522	..	·513	..	·547	..	·517	..	·551	..	·530
30—34	·500	..	·508	..	·521	..	·535	..	·468	..	·529	..	·516	..	·553	..
35—39	..	·499	..	·513	..	·480	..	·468	..	·546	..	·473	..	·470	..	·435
40—44	·498	..	·466	..	·502	..	·513	..	·446	..	·506	..	·535	..	·586	..
45—49	..	·496	..	·530	..	·491	..	·481	..	·579	..	·486	..	·444	..	·397
50—54	·493	..	·463	..	·513	..	·524	..	·390	..	·569	..	·594	..	·684	..
55—59	..	·491	..	·524	..	·462	..	·452	..	·641	..	·371	..	·379	..	·320
60—64	·488	..	·482	..	·556	..	·571	..	·399	..	·655	..	·698	..	·837	..
65—69	..	·479	..	·425	..	·373	..	·361	..	·482	..	·357	..	·314	..	·265
70—74	·454	..	·467	..	·525	..	·551	..	·424	..	·534	..	605	..	·722	..
Total	3·428	2·965	3·384	2·971	3·638	2·755	3·755	2·682	3·100	3·260	3·795	2·643	3·907	2·615	4·395	2·365
Average	·490	·494	·483	·495	·520	·459	·536	·447	·443	·543	·542	·441	·558	·436	·628	·394
Difference between $_0M_x$. and $_5M_x$.	·004		·012		·061		·089		·100		·101		·122		·214	

TABLE XX.

1911 Census—All-India—Males.

Values of $_0M_x$ and $_5M_x$.

Transformed Age Groups.	Age group in which Population is originally summed.															
	Graduated.		'2—6'.		Quaternary and Senary method.		Ternary and Septenary method.		'3—7'.		'4—8'.		'1—5'.		'0—4'.	
	$_0M_x$.	$_5M_x$.	$_0M_x$.	$_5M_x$.	$_0M_x$.	$_5M_x$.	$_0M_x$.	$_5M_x$.	$_0M_x$.	$_5M_x$.	$_0M_x$.	$_5M_x$.	$_0M_x$.	$_5M_x$.	$_0M_x$.	$_5M_x$.
(1)	(2)		(3)		(4)		(5)		(6)		(7)		(8)		(9)	
10—14	·497	..	·513	..	·513	..	·543	..	·509	..	·497	..	·464	..	·534	..
15—19	..	·501	..	·363	..	·435	..	·418	..	·433	..	·469	..	·501	..	·431
20—24	·501	..	·495	..	·514	..	·522	..	·517	..	·452	..	·477	..	·475	..
25—29	..	·500	..	·525	..	·519	..	·511	..	·510	..	·564	..	·560	..	·532
30—34	·499	..	·490	..	·509	..	·520	..	·523	..	·501	..	·435	..	·542	..
35—39	..	·498	..	·527	..	·488	..	·478	..	·470	..	·468	..	·594	..	·433
40—44	·497	..	·463	..	·507	..	·515	..	·534	..	·560	..	·414	..	·616	..
45—49	..	·495	..	·533	..	·484	..	·476	..	·452	..	·422	..	·614	..	·372
50—54	493	..	·457	..	·513	..	·521	..	·559	..	·620	..	·368	..	·737	..
55—59	..	·491	..	·497	..	·439	..	·433	..	·400	..	·348	..	·620	..	·280
60—64	·489	..	·558	..	·583	..	·593	..	·627	..	·714	..	·432	..	·856	..
65—69	..	·480	..	·326	..	·392	..	·379	..	·384	..	·357	..	·511	..	·321
70—74	·462	..	·490	..	·451	..	·476	..	·468	..	·514	..	·310	..	·576	..
Total	3·438	2·965	3·466	2·771	3·590	2·757	3·690	2·695	3·737	2·649	3·858	2·628	2·900	3·400	4·336	2·369
Average	·491	·494	·495	·462	·513	·460	·527	·449	·534	·442	·551	·438	·414	·567	·619	·395
Difference between $_0M_x$ and $_5M_x$.	·003		·033		·053		·078		·092		·113		·153		·224	

TABLE XXI.

Age group.	Original population as sorted straight according to groups stated in (1).	·4×5 year groups of Col. (2).	—Δ of Col. (3).	(4) + (2) = adjusted population in '5—9' etc., groups.	Age group.
(1)	(2)	(3)	(4)	(5)	(6)
0	1,179	..	..	..	..
1	2,513	..	..	..	..
2	2,519	..	..	1,179	0
3	2,700	..	..	2,513	1
4	2,425	..	..	2,519	2
5	2,718	..	..	2,700	3
6	2,295	..	..	2,425	4
7—11	10,951	4,380	— 4,380	11,584	5—9
12—16	10,935	4,374	+ 6	10,941	10—14
17—21	9,641	3,856	+ 518	10,159	15—19
22—26	10,133	4,053	— 197	9,936	20—24
27—31	9,065	3,626	+ 427	9,492	25—29
32—36	8,086	3,234	+ 392	8,478	30—34
37—41	7,471	2,988	+ 246	7,717	35—39
42—46	5,119	2,048	+ 940	6,059	40—44
47—51	4,332	1,733	+ 315	4,647	45—49
52—56	2,442	977	+ 756	3,198	50—54
57—61	2,566	1,026	— 49	2,517	55—59
62—66	1,200	480	+ 546	1,746	60—64
67—71	899	360	+ 120	1,019	65—69
72 and over	811	0	+ 360	1,171	70 and over
	100,000	..	..	100,000	..

SECTION IV.

1. In this section I shall attempt a brief description of the methods adopted in the construction of mortality Tables for the various Provincial groups detailed in the opening pages of this Report with some discussion on topics relevant thereto.

2. It was explained in an earlier section of this Report, that, in view of the conditions prevailing in the decennium 1921-1931, the Table of mortality of each area was to embody the experience of this decennium only. The statistics of population used therefore were only those relating to the 1921 and 1931 Censuses without any reference to earlier enumerations. The population of each area at the 1931 Census is available for nearest age on Census day—this having been the age asked for according to instructions to enumerators—for ages 0, 1, 2 and 3 stated separately and in alternate ternary and septenary groups 4-6, 7-13, 14-16, 17-23, etc., to 67-73 with one large group at the end of 74 and over. The passage from ternary and septenary groups to the ordinary quinquennial age groups 0-4, 5-9, etc., is effected very easily by taking half the sum of two consecutive age groups. For instance, the age group 5-9 is obtained by taking the sum of one half of the ternary group 4-6 and one half of the septenary group 7-13. It should also be noted that the resulting quinary group 5-9, on the assumption that the ages returned were the ages nearest birthday, would include all persons whose ages were 5, 6, 7, 8, and 9 last birthday. In this way the statistics of the population returned at the 1931 Census were arranged in quinquennial age periods 0-4, 5-9, etc., to 65-69 with one large group at the end of 70 and over, according to age last birthday in conformity with the method of grouping adopted at the previous enumerations in India to facilitate comparison. The numbers in each age group were reduced by a constant ratio so as to produce a total of 100,000 for all ages.

Correction for Mortality.

3. The method described above of redistributing the original ternary and septenary age groups into quinary groups introduces an error—though not very material—due to the fact that in the process of redistribution the assumption has been made that the numbers relating to each age in each septenary and ternary group are equal to one another and no allowance has been made for the progressive diminution of these numbers as age increases in each group due to the operation of mortality.

4. To allow for this error Mr. Meikle recommended certain percentages being transferred from groups like 10-14, 20-24, 30-34, etc., to the respective earlier groups, 5-9, 15-19, 25-29, etc. I have, however, to state with regret that I have not been able to satisfy myself as to how quinquennial groups with the earliest age a multiple of 10 like 20-24, 30-34, etc., alone have to part with certain percentages to the respective earlier groups. Taking, for instance, the transformed quinary group 30-34 one can easily see that this age group is made up of the lower half of the septenary group 27-33 and the upper half of the ternary group 34-36. In so far as it is made up of the lower half of the septenary group 27-33 it owes a certain number to the upper half of the same septenary group which is amalgamated with the quinary group 25-29. Again in so far as this age group 30-34 is made up of the upper half of the ternary group 34-36 it took rather less than its correct quota from that group when it was bisected and the upper half taken with the 30-34 group and the lower half with the 35-39 group. I think therefore any age group like 30-34 owes a certain number to the previous age group 25-29 and has to get another number from the succeeding age group 35-39. This is the case with respect to all transformed quinary groups. It is true that age groups like 30-34, 40-44 and so on with the earliest number in the group a multiple of 10 owe to the respective preceding quinary groups more than what they have to get from the succeeding ones with the result that on final adjustment they have to meet with a net diminution. But if we deal with the net diminution only and transfer this net amount entirely to the upper age group we shall be, what in common parlance is called, "robbing Peter to pay Paul" and our final adjustments will not be quite correct in transferring numbers from one age group to another to that degree of approximation which it is desirable to have if mortality correction is to be given effect to.

5. I have, on the same assumption as made by Mr. Meikle which is accurate enough for our present purpose, calculated this mortality correction to be applied

to each group. I shall represent by the symbol s_{30} the total number in the septenary group of which 30 is the middle age and so on for other septenary groups. Similarly t_{25} represents the total in the ternary group of which 25 is the middle age and so on for other ternary groups. The total number s_{30} in the septenary group 27-33, for instance, can be assumed approximately to be distributed at each of the seven ages in that group as follows :—

$\frac{s_{30}}{7}(1+3\,q_{30})$ as of nearest age 27,

$\frac{s_{30}}{7}(1+2\,q_{30})$ as of nearest age 28,

$\frac{s_{30}}{7}(1+\,q_{30})$ as of nearest age 29,

$\frac{s_{30}}{7}$ as of nearest age 30,

$\frac{s_{30}}{7}(1-q_{30})$ as of nearest age 31,

$\frac{s_{30}}{7}(1-2\,q_{30})$ as of nearest age 32,

$\frac{s_{30}}{7}(1-3\,q_{30})$ as of nearest age 33.

The upper half of the above distribution relating to the age group from exact age $26\frac{1}{2}$ to exact age 30 should contain (the q's denoting rates of mortality throughout) $\frac{s_{30}}{7}(1+3q_{30})+\frac{s_{30}}{7}(1+2q_{30})+\frac{s_{30}}{7}(1+q_{30})+\frac{1}{2}\frac{s_{30}}{7}$ which is equal to $\frac{1}{2}\,s_{30}+\frac{6}{7}\,s_{30}\,q_{30}$.

Instead, therefore, of taking $\frac{1}{2}\,s_{30}+\frac{6}{7}\,s_{30}q_{30}$ as relating to the upper half of the septenary group 27-33 and $\frac{1}{2}\,s_{30}-\frac{6}{7}\,s_{30}q_{30}$ to the lower half, the method of bisection takes $\frac{1}{2}\,s_{30}$ to both the halves. It will therefore be evident that age group 30-34 has to cede $\frac{6}{7}\,s_{30}q_{30}$ to the group 25-29. Considering similarly the ternary group 34-36 it can easily be seen by a similar analysis that the group 30-34 has to get $\frac{1}{3}\,t_{35}q_{35}$ from the group 35-39. The whole scheme of correction is given in the following Table :—

Quinquennial age group.	Should give to the preceding quinquennial group.	Should get from the succeeding quinquennial group.
0—4	..	$\frac{1}{3}\,q_5\,t_5$
5—9	$\frac{1}{3}\,q_5\,t_5$	$\frac{6}{7}\,q_{10}\,s_{10}$
10—14	$\frac{6}{7}\,q_{10}\,s_{10}$	$\frac{1}{3}\,q_{15}\,t_{15}$
15—19	$\frac{1}{3}\,q_{15}\,t_{15}$	$\frac{6}{7}\,q_{20}\,s_{20}$
20—24	$\frac{6}{7}\,q_{20}\,s_{20}$	$\frac{1}{3}\,q_{25}\,t_{25}$
25—29	$\frac{1}{3}\,q_{25}\,t_{25}$	$\frac{6}{7}\,q_{30}\,s_{30}$
30—34	$\frac{6}{7}\,q_{30}\,s_{30}$	$\frac{1}{3}\,q_{35}\,t_{35}$
35—39	$\frac{1}{3}\,q_{35}\,t_{35}$	$\frac{6}{7}\,q_{40}\,s_{40}$
40—44	$\frac{6}{7}\,q_{40}\,s_{40}$	$\frac{1}{3}\,q_{45}\,t_{45}$
45—49	$\frac{1}{3}\,q_{45}\,t_{45}$	$\frac{6}{7}\,q_{50}\,s_{50}$
50—54	$\frac{6}{7}\,q_{50}\,s_{50}$	$\frac{1}{3}\,q_{55}\,t_{55}$
55—59	$\frac{1}{3}\,q_{55}\,t_{55}$	$\frac{6}{7}\,q_{60}\,s_{60}$
60—64	$\frac{6}{7}\,q_{60}\,s_{60}$	$\frac{1}{3}\,q_{65}\,t_{65}$
65—69	$\frac{1}{3}\,q_{65}\,t_{65}$	$\frac{6}{7}\,q_{70}\,s_{70}$
70 and over	$\frac{6}{7}\,q_{70}\,s_{70}$	..

To give effect to the mortality correction in each Provincial group I adopted the rates of mortality from the 1911 Actuarial Report relating to the Province. Where any Provincial group is dealt with for the first time the rates of mortality relating to the whole of India were taken.

6. The population of each area according to the 1921 Census is available in the usual 0-4, 5-9, etc., groups according to age last birthday. With the view, however, to bring the population statistics of 1921 in conformity with those of 1931, ternary and septenary groups were formed from the sample of 100,000 for each sex available in respect of each area. These samples are available for each Census unit. To obtain samples applicable to each of the ten large geographical groups for which separate mortality Tables were to be constructed, the distribution according to each age in each Census unit was weighted according to the population in that unit and a new sample applicable to the geographical area dealt with was formed.

7. For instance, the Madras group is composed of the following Census units :—

(a) The British Province of Madras (including the small States of Pudukkottah, Banganapalli and Sandur).
(b) Mysore State.
(c) Travancore State.
(d) Cochin State.
(e) Coorg.

The sample age distribution out of a total of 100,000 for each sex in each of the above areas was weighted at each age according to the population (taken to the nearest million) in that area and the sum of the products thus obtained was divided by the sum of the weights. In this manner was formed the sample distribution at each age out of a total population of 100,000 in each sex for each of the ten large areas into which the whole of India (including Burma) was divided for the purpose of this analysis. I have also made suitable adjustments to transform each ternary and septenary age group of the 1921 population in each area from age last birthday to age nearest birthday. From the ternary and septenary age groups, quinary groups 0-4, 5-9, etc., for ages last birthday were formed in the same manner as with the 1931 Return.

Migration.

8. Allowance was made at this stage for the disturbance caused by migration in the case of those Provincial groups where it was of such magnitude as to affect the rate of increase of the population or its age distribution. Taking India as a whole, for its size and the magnitude of its population, immigration and emigration, as observed by the Census Commissioner, Dr. Hutton, are practically unimportant. The direct effect of dividing India into ten large sections including British Provinces and the adjoining States has been to neutralize the large movement of population between contiguous political divisions where these are grouped together. The grouping has rendered ineffective, for instance, making any allowance for the presence of the large number of Bengalis in Assam and Madrasis in Mysore, Travancore and Cochin States and *vice versa.* In the Provincial groups of Madras and the United Provinces and in the group Bengal and Assam, migration, in spite of the neutralizing force above referred to, was too significant to be ignored. In the case of the first two groups the balance of migration was adverse in each of the two Censuses taken in 1921 and 1931. The total number of net emigrants per 100,000 of the total population at the respective Censuses in the case of each of these two Provincial groups was added to the quinquennial groups above referred to representing age distribution per 100,000 of total population in each sex. The age distribution of the migrant population was taken to be the same as was estimated by Sir George Hardy in 1891 by reference to the three Provinces, Coorg, Berar and Lower Burma where the immigrant population was relatively very large. Sir George has given full explanation of the methods followed by him in his 1891 Report. In the case of the Provincial group, Bengal and Assam, the balance of migration was in favour. The disturbance caused in the case of Burma by the presence in that Province of a large immigrant male population was eliminated by confining my investigation to Buddhists only who form almost entirely the indigenous population of that Province engaged almost exclusively in agricultural pursuits and of a non-migratory temperament. In this respect my investigation has fallen in line with all the earlier ones and

it is desirable that it should do so from another point of view. The Burman Buddhists have been observed in the past, as has also been confirmed by my investigation, to experience mortality markedly superior to that of Hindus or Muhammadans. To have combined the Buddhists of Burma with those following other religions would have introduced an element of heterogeneity in the investigation very much undesirable. The assumed age distribution of the emigrant population in the case of Madras and the United Provinces and of the immigrant population of Bengal and Assam enabled the correction due to migration disturbances being easily applied in each age group to the population of these Provincial groups in 1921 and 1931 respectively. The corrected population in each Census was again proportioned for in each quinary group relative to a total of 100,000 and the arithmetic mean of the two corrected populations was obtained in each age group.

Graduation.

9. It is now necessary to graduate or adjust the figures in each quinary group of the mean population, obtained by processes described above, with the view to remove or at best reduce to a minimum the effect of major and minor errors (referred to in detail in the last section) inherent to population statistics particularly in India. With this end in view it was decided to adopt a mathematical formula which, while producing a smooth progression of numbers from one quinquennial group to another, provided also a law by which the number at each age could be easily obtained.

10. The method of graduation adopted was with reference to a standard Table recommended by the late Mr. Alfred Henry in the discussion on a Paper submitted to the Institute of Actuaries by Mr. Ackland in connection with his 1911 Report to the Government of India. Mr. Meikle also adopted this method though that of Mr. Ackland was curve fitting and Sir George Hardy made use of a formula of graduation based on a modification of Makeham's Law. The choice of the Table to be used as the standard was a matter that required some investigation. The standard chosen has to be perfectly smooth and should preferably have been graduated by a mathematical formula. A first attempt was made by using the English Life Table No. 9. A suitable addition was made to the age in the ungraduated Indian population statistics to allow for the higher mortality prevailing in India as compared to England. Several trial graduations were made and the number of years added to the age in each quinary group of the Indian population before effecting comparison with the English population in corresponding age groups was varied from trial to trial. It was ultimately found that a rating up of between 10 and 11 years to the Indian age gave a smooth progression of the population from age to age, which, combined with the graduated rates of increase to be described later, gave satisfactory rates of mortality from only about age 35 onwards. It would therefore have been necessary to modify the Proclaimed Clans experience, more than half a century old by now, not only to supply the rates of mortality at the ages of infancy and childhood up to age 12, at which that experience stopped, but also to fill up the large gap between ages 12 and 35 by a smooth junction at both ends. This would have been entirely unsatisfactory. Mr. Meikle rejected, quite rightly, the Proclaimed Clans experience as entirely unsuitable for his purpose. They are still more so now. Mr. Ackland had made suitable adjustments to the Proclaimed Clans experience, on the basis of the rates of mortality derived by him at the older ages, to make it yield rates which would approximately reflect the mortality at the ages of infancy and childhood. One advantage, therefore, in adopting the Indian Life Table for 1911, which was also graduated by a mathematical formula and therefore satisfied the condition of being perfectly smooth, was to have on hand a Table in which the experience relating to the very young ages has been brought up to comparatively recent times. Another advantage, which is in my view rather substantial, is the fact that comparisons could be made and the requisite ratios—the subject of graduation—could be formed without making any addition to the age of the ungraduated population. I have found that in comparing with English Life Table the addition to the age which was necessary to produce a good fit at ages, say, from 30 to 65 or 70 was too large at the very young and the very old ages. I therefore adopted the Male Life Table prepared for the whole of India by Mr. Ackland as the standard Table for the graduation of the male experience in each of the ten areas dealt with by me.

11. The mean in each age group, relative to a total of 100,000 of the population for each area corrected for migration in certain cases as explained above, was summed from the bottom upwards to produce the population aged 0 and upwards, 5 and upwards, etc. These were denoted by the respective symbols T_0, T_5, T_{10}, etc., to T_{70}. Corresponding sums for the standard Table adopted were denoted by the symbols T_0', T_5' T_{10}', etc., to T'_{70}. The ratio $\frac{T}{T'}$ was made the subject of graduation. A cubical parabola given by the equation $y=1+ax+bx^2+cx^3$ was fitted to the observed ratios of $\frac{T}{T'}$ in each case. It is not necessary to go fully into the technical details of this process of graduation. I desire, however, to state that I have found the process of fitting a curve by the method of "Least Squares" particularly suitable not only for its easy application but also for the facility this method afforded for discarding the ratio at any age if due to gross mis-statement in age it was found to be entirely undependable. The graduated ratio multiplied by the population according to the standard at any age yielded the graduated mean population at that age.

Rates of increase.

"*A Nation ought to devote its best energies to the self-imposed task of carrying out in its manifold details the following general programme* :—

(*i*) *of steadily raising the natural level of successive generations, Morally, Physically and Intellectually by every reasonable means,*

(*ii*) *of keeping its Numbers within approximate limits,*

(*iii*) *of developing the Health and Vigour of the people. In short, to make every individual efficient both through Nature and by Nurture.*"

FRANCIS GALTON.

12. To deduce, from the graduated mean population obtained by processes explained in the last few paragraphs of this section, the fundamental column of the mortality Table showing the number of survivors at each age out of a fixed number of births, say, 100,000, it is necessary to determine the average rate of increase of the population in each of the various Provincial groups during the period taken into account which in the present case is the decennium 1921-1931. The following Tables taken mainly from Mr. Marten's Report for 1921 show the average rate of increase, both real and actual (the latter based on Census figures only), in each decennial period since the first general Census of India in 1872.

TABLE XXII.

Census of	Population.	Variation per cent. since previous Census.
1872	206,162,360	..
1881	253,896,330	+23·2
1891	287,314,671	+13·2
1901	294,361,056	+2·5
1911	315,156,396	+7·1
1921	318,942,480	+1·2
1931	352,837,778	+10·6

TABLE XXIII.

Period.	Increase due to Inclusion of new areas.	Increase due to Improvement of method.	Real increase of population.	Total.	Rate per cent. of real increase.
(1)	(2)	(3)	(4)	(5)	(6)
	Millions.	Millions.	Millions.	Millions.	
1872-1881	33·0	12·0	3·0	48·0	1·5
1881-1891	5·7	3·5	24·3	33·5	9·6
1891-1901	2·7	·2	4·1	7·0	1·4
1901-1911	1·8	..	18·7	20·5	6·4
1911-1921	·1	..	3·7	3·8	1·2
1921-1931	..	..	..	..	10·6

13. The rates of increase shown in Table XXII are not of any practical interest as they have been coloured substantially by artificial increases due to inclusion of new areas and to progressive increase in the accuracy of the enumeration from Census to Census.

14. It will be seen that the real rate of increase has been the largest in the decennium 1921-1931 of all the periods. It may not be out of place at this stage to make some observations as to the desirability or otherwise of the very large rate of increase in the population which the decennium has witnessed, applied particularly to this country where the standard of living is proverbially low. Otherwise, the poignant words of Francis Galton, inscribed in bold characters on the walls of the Biometric Laboratory of University College, London, by Galton's worthy and famous disciple Prof. Karl Pearson and quoted at the beginning of this topic, would be irrelevant.

15. The rate of increase of the population has always remained a matter of absorbing interest during the one hundred and thirty-five years since Malthus in his *Essay on Principle of Population* expressed real alarm at the rapid rate at which population was increasing and presented a very vivid and horrid picture of the results of indiscriminate multiplication. He enunciated a law which in mathematical language can be stated thus: If the population of a confined area increases in geometrical progression, while the food production increases only in an arithmetical progression, the former must inevitably overtake and surpass the latter and within a short period there will be several people without any food. A few sentences may be quoted from Malthus' Essay in illustration of his graphic description :—

> "The population of the island (Great Britain) is computed to be about 7 millions and we will suppose the present produce equal to the support of such a number. In the first 25 years the population would be 14 millions and the food being also doubled, the means of subsistence would be equal to the increase. In the next 25 years the population would be 28 millions and the means of subsistence only equal to the support of 21 millions. In the next period the population would be 56 millions and the means of subsistence just sufficient for half that number. And at the conclusion of the first century the population would be 112 millions and the means of subsistence just only equal to the support of 35 millions which would leave a population of 77 millions totally unprovided for."

16. Malthus has been the subject of a certain amount of criticism on the score of having depicted too horrid and too gruesome a picture. He might have indulged in a little bit of exaggeration of which he should have been quite conscious. It should, however, be remembered that he was practically the pioneer amongst the great thinkers of the world who directed their attention to this great problem relating to population and its increase. Just as in the realm of Literature a Tragedy is considered to inculcate a moral better than a Comedy, so also, in this case, Malthus having felt himself to be in the role of a teacher of the moral regarding population and its uncontrolled growth had to depict a shocking picture to impress on the imagination of the public the consequences if the moral was disobeyed. He has also been criticised for making the starving millions breed and multiply in each period. The surplus population would not be straightaway wiped out but the immediate effect of population overtaking the means of subsistence would be a fall in the standard of living for the majority in the area which would give an impetus to indiscriminate multiplication making the standard of living fall still lower thereby completing what is called the vicious circle, of which India provides a good example. That birth rate is very highly and inversely correlated with status in the social scale, that is, with the standard of living, is illustrated by the following Table relating to England and Wales appearing in Mr. Carr-Saunders' book on Population.

TABLE XXIV.

The number of births in the year 1911 per 1,000 married men under 55 years of age in England and Wales grouped according to the occupation of the father.

Occupation of the father.	Number of births.
(1) Upper and middle classes	119
(2) Intermediate	132
(3) Skilled workmen	153
(4) Intermediate	158
(5) Unskilled workmen	213

17. Let us now examine the truth of the Malthusian proposition enunciated at the end of paragraph 15.

Let r be the common ratio of the geometrical progression in which population is increasing.

If P_0 be the population in the area under consideration at the commencement of an epoch and P_t the population at time t measured from the beginning of the epoch we shall have $\frac{dP_t}{dt}=P_t r$, giving $\frac{1}{P_t}\frac{dP_t}{dt}=r$ or $\frac{d \log P_t}{dt}=r$ leading to $\log P_t = rt +$ constant, or $P_t = P_0 e^{rt}$ since when $t=0$, $P_t=P_0$. Therefore the population at any time t measured in years is $P_0 e^{rt}$.

If the means of subsistence increase in an arithmetical progression at a rate K times the rate at which the population is increasing so that the common difference of the arithmetical progression of increase of foodstuffs and other necessaries of life is Kr, we shall, on the supposition that the available amount of the necessaries of life at the commencement of the epoch was just sufficient to support the population then existing in the area, *viz.*, P_0, obtain for the number of people which the resources of the area then available can support at the end of time t the quantity $P_0(1+Krt)$. If on Malthus' assumption the population, increasing in geometrical progression, were to overtake the means of subsistence increasing in an arithmetical progression, though at a rate several times larger than the rate at which the population is increasing, we should have a value of t satisfying the equality

$$P_0 e^{rt} = P_0(1+Krt)$$

$$\text{or } 1+ rt + \frac{r^2t^2}{2} + \frac{r^3t^3}{2\cdot 3} + \ldots\ldots\ldots\ldots = 1 + Krt \text{————} (A).$$

The values of t given by the equation (A) give the period at the end of which population would overtake means of subsistence and there would subsequently result a shortage of food. One value of t is 0 corresponding to the commencement of the epoch, when the assumption was made that population had just sufficient for subsistence. Another value of t, if one exists, would give the critical number of years at the end of which the food problem in the community would come to tell. Practical values of r are never greater than ·03. Only undeveloped countries like Canada and New Zealand show anything near this rate. Even for Australia the value of r is about ·02. For all practical values of r and practical values of K (the number of times food supply exceeds the needs of population) it is possible to find value of t by a process of successive approximation so well known to students of Actuarial Science. The values of t, the number of years at the end of which the population would overtake the food supply for practical values of r and K, have been called "Malthusian equivalent intervals". These values have been calculated by Mr. G. H. Knibbs and are exhibited in the following Table.

TABLE XXV.

Malthusian equivalent intervals corresponding to various rates of increase.

Number of times food supply exceeds needs of population.	Number of years (t) before population overtakes food-supply, the former increasing in a geometrical progression of ratio r and the latter in an arithmetical progression of common difference Kr.			
K	$r=0\cdot01$	$r=0\cdot015$	$r=0\cdot02$	$r=0\cdot03$
2	126	84	63	42
4	234	156	117	78
8	332	221	166	111
16	423	282	211	141

18. The annual rate of increase of population in India which the decennium under consideration has engendered is very nearly 1%. The above Table shows that if population continues to increase at this rate and if the food supply were to increase at double this rate, *i.e.*, at 2% (on the supposition that the present food supply in India is just sufficient for supporting the present population, which is far from being the case), food shortage would come to tell at the end of 126 years.

If food supply increases at 4% while population increases only at 1% the critical period will be reached at the end of 234 years. For 8 and 16 per cent. increases in food supply, population and food supply will attain equality at the end of 332 and 423 years respectively. These are small as compared with historical and geological periods. Thus the truth of the Malthusian proposition is established beyond doubt.

19. The adage " Population begets Population " naturally points at a geometrical progression as the law governing the rate of increase of population. If, however, we proceed on this assumption, we are faced with incongruous results. Mr. Knibbs, several times referred to by me, has computed the average rate of increase of the population of the world weighted according to the population of each country during the quinquennium 1906-1911 to be 1·159 per cent. per annum. The largest annual rate of increase of 2·98% was shown by Canada. Ireland was the only one of all the countries that indicated an annual rate of decrease of ·006%. Amongst countries that showed an increase, France exhibited the lowest rate per annum being ·016%. Referring to the average rate of increase of the population of the world of 1·159% per annum, Mr. Knibbs has some very interesting observations to make which I am quoting *in extenso* :—

" Either this rate of increase must be enormously greater than has existed in the past history of the world or enormous numbers of human beings must have been blotted out by catastrophes of various kinds from time to time. For, putting the present population (of the world) at 1,649,000,000 at the average rate of increase, this number would be produced from a single pair of human beings in about 1,782 years, that is to say, since A. D. 132 or since Salvius Julianus revised under Hardian the Edicts of the Praetors. Even the rate given by the world-populations 1804 and 1914, *viz.*, (0·0086) gives only 2,397 years, carrying us back to only B. C. 483, or since the days of Darius I of Persia.

" The profound significance of this fact, accentuated also by the extraordinary increase in the length of life (expectation of life at age 0) which has revealed itself of recent years, is obvious when the correlative food requirements are taken into account. The resources of Nature will have to be exploited in the future more successfully than in the past to maintain this rate of increase (0·01159) which doubles the population every 60·15 years and would give for 10,000 years the colossal number 22,184 with 46 noughts (10^{46}) after it.

" This number is so colossal that it is difficult to appreciate its magnitude. Assuming the earth to be a globe of 3,960 miles radius, of a density 5·527 compared with water, that water weighs about 62½ lbs: per cubic foot, and that a human being weighs on the average, say, 100 lbs. (7 st. 2 lbs.) the actual mass of the earth would be equivalent only to say, $132{,}265 \times 10^{18}$ persons ; that is, it would require $16{,}771 \times 10^{23}$ times as much " matter " as there is in the earth. Or, to consider it as a question of surface, allowing 1½ square feet per person, the earth's entire surface area would provide standing room for only $36{,}625 \times 10^{11}$ persons. That is, the population would be $60{,}570 \times 10^{30}$ times as great as there would be standing room if the whole earth's surface were available. It is evident from this that the rate of increase of human beings must have been more approximate to the rate for France at the present time if the earth has been peopled for 10,000 years : the French rate, 0·0016, would require 12,842 years to give the present population from a single pair. This rate, however, would give a population of only 17·55 millions in 10,000 years.

" The foregoing analysis of the effect of the rate of increase, with which we are familiar, established the fact that the rate must have passed through great changes, and could not have been maintained for any long period, either at its present average, or that characteristic of the last century. It is not improbable that the rate of the last quinquennium will not be long maintained ; and it is certain that however great human genius or effort may be, in enlarging the world's food supplies, that rate cannot possibly be maintained for many centuries. The contention of Malthus is thus placed beyond question, from a different point of view. "

20. From the above vivid description, it will be evident that the power of population just as the power of compound interest over a period measured in centuries is just as to shock the imagination. While solving problems in compound interest, how many of us did not regret the fact that a great-great-grandparent of ours of a couple of centuries back did not invest a few rupees at a small rate of interest, compounding annually, so as to amount to several lakhs for our present use. With increasing experience, however, we realize that in the realm of practical finance this is an absurdity. Similarly it is absurd to try to forecast the population in a given area, say, a thousand years hence, on the basis that the present rate of increase will continue to progress in a geometrical ratio. Correcting factors will

be at work to keep down the rate of growth. Malthus indulged purposely in some exaggeration when he omitted to make mention of the correcting factors.

21. If geometrical progression is to be ruled out, the question might naturally be asked as to what the law underlying population growth is. Quetelet's brilliant analogy between the growth of population and the motion of a body through a resisting medium suggests a rational solution. In the case of such a body when the velocity is small, the force to impede the velocity is also small. As the velocity increases, the resistance also increases till the body cannot move in the medium at a velocity greater than a particular one, called the limiting velocity, whatever may be the magnitude of the force acting on the body making it move forward. Similarly, when the resources of a country and the amount of space available are large as compared to the population, very little impediment will be felt to the growth of population and it may actually increase at a rate approximating to the geometric progression. As density increases, and as the ratio of the undeveloped resources of the area to the population diminishes, the rate of growth will be arrested and will slowly diminish, attaining the value 0 when the population in the area will attain a stationary or constant value beyond which it cannot increase.

22. To evolve a mathematical formula for the law of population growth on the above analogy was, however, left first to Verhulst and then, quite independently of him, to Pearl and Reed. It is not necessary to give in detail here the mathematical processes by which the equation to the curve of population growth is obtained. The reader is referred to either " Studies in Human Biology " by R. Pearl or to the Presidential address delivered by Mr. G. Udny Yule before the Royal Statistical Society and appearing in Volume 88 of the Journal of that body.

23. The rate per unit of time at which the population in a given area increases at any moment depends upon the absolute magnitude of the population in the area at that moment subject to a retarding influence or, in mathematical language, a reducing factor depending on the difference between the maximum population which the area can support and the population at that moment. This leads to a differential equation for the law of population growth of the form $\frac{dy}{dt}=\frac{y}{\alpha}(1-\frac{y}{L})$ which when solved leads to the equation,

$$y = \frac{L}{1+e^{\frac{\beta-\alpha}{t}}} \qquad \text{——————} \quad \text{(B)}$$

where y is the population at any time t and L is the limiting value of the population which is approached when t becomes infinitely great. The form of the curve given by equation (B) representing a rational law of population growth is given by the accompanying diagram.

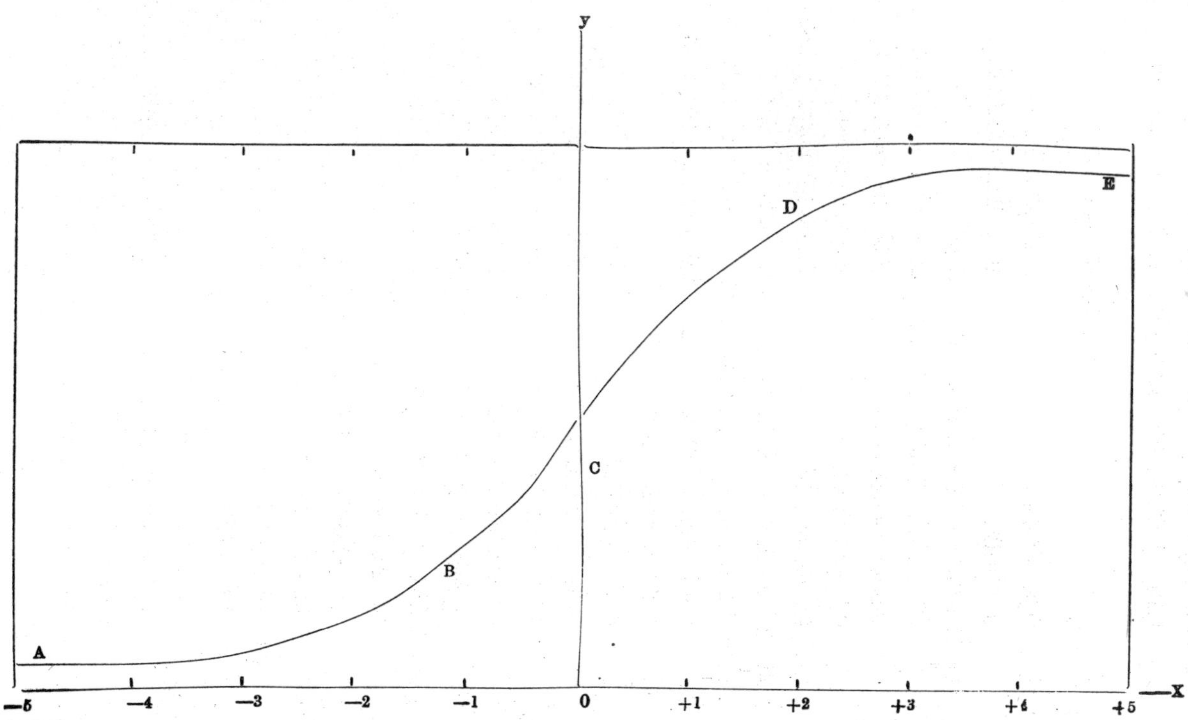

Time is measured along the X axis and the population along the Y axis. The part ABC of the curve of population growth is convex to the X axis (the axis of time) showing that in this section the increase of population in any year is larger than in the preceding year. Up to the point C corresponding to time β, the density of population in the area is not very large and the impediment to growth of population is not very intense. When the population already existing in the area is small compared with the limiting population L, we can prove that the rate of increase in the population is very nearly in a geometrical progression. For, in the differential equation to the curve, namely, $\frac{1}{y}\frac{dy}{dt}=\frac{1}{\alpha}(1-\frac{y}{L})$ by making y very small as compared with L we obtain the simplified equation $\frac{1}{y}\frac{dy}{dt}=\frac{1}{\alpha}$ or $y=Ae^{t/\alpha}$ which is the same as a logarithmic curve, or the curve of a geometrical progression.

24. At the point C, the density of population in the area is one-half the limiting density and this is a point of inflexion at which the curve changes from convexity to concavity. Over the section CDE of the curve the increase of population in any year is smaller than in the preceding one and goes on diminishing from year to year till the increase vanishes and the population attains a limiting value based on the area available for occupation and the capacity of the area to provide means of subsistence. That this curve for the law of population growth very nearly fits in with the observed facts with respect to several countries has been proved by Messrs. Yule and Pearl in the Papers by these authors referred to above.

25. It appears, from the above analysis, it is reasonable to assume that in those countries such as for instance Canada, Australia, etc., where the available resources are not fully mobilized and the density is small as compared with the area fit for human habitation, population would continue to increase very nearly in conformity with the law "Population begets Population", that is, in a geometrical progression. That this rate of increase will in course of time be compelled to slow down by such methods as modern civilization would tolerate and vanish when the population would attain its limiting value appears to be the only rational assumption.

26. In those countries, where the level of education is high, this final or limiting value of the population will be reached by a voluntary and deliberate limitation of the birth-rate which will bring as a natural reward a fall in the death-rate thereby minimising misery. That most of the countries in Europe did substantially restrict the size of their families is proved with all the force of statistical analysis. The fall in the French birth-rate is proverbial. In England the fall practically synchronised with the famous Bradlaugh Case (1877) which served to attract with an extraordinary force public interest to a pamphlet giving information on birth-control written by Dr. Knowlton of which Bradlaugh and Mrs. Besant were the publishers. The Germans were rather late in taking interest in the subject. But when once they did they were systematic and thorough and flooded their country with literature on the subject. The fall in the German birth-rate in the years just before the Great War was phenomenal.

27. In other countries, of which India is a good example, where due to lack of imagination which education inculcates and the consequent *laissez faire* attitude of the people towards matters of vital importance, actions are not intelligently directed towards safeguarding the happiness of the future, but by adopting a policy of drift pinning faith on the proverb "with every mouth God sends a pair of hands" the limiting population will be reached by a high birth-rate bringing in its trail a high death-rate and the inevitable physical and mental suffering which a high death-rate would naturally entail. The following Table comparing England and Wales and India over a quinquennium shows that in England and Wales where the birth-rate is low, due to a larger fall in death rate, the survival rate is really larger than in India where the effect of a larger birth-rate is neutralized by a heavy death rate.

TABLE XXVI.

Year.	England and Wales.			British India.		
	Birth-rate.	Death-rate.	Survival rate.	Birth-rate.	Death-rate.	Survival rate.
1910	25	13	12	40	33	7
1911	24	14·5	9·5	39	32	7
1912	24	13	11	39	30	9
1913	24	14	10	39	29	10
1914	24	14	10	40	30	10

28. The statistics relating to most other countries of Western Europe go to confirm what was observed with respect to England and Wales, that the fall in the birth-rate synchronised with a larger fall in the death-rate as the following Table taken from the journal of the Royal Statistical Society, Volume 83, page 33, clearly indicates.

TABLE XXVII.

Decreases in the death-rate and the birth-rate between 1871-80 and 1901-10 in certain States of Western Europe : points per 1,000 of the population.

Country or State.	Fall in.	
	Death-rate.	Birth-rate.
1. Hamburg	11·5	12·2
2. Wurtemburg	11·3	10·3
3. Saxony	10·8	10·8
4. Bavaria	9·2	5·9
5. Netherlands	9·2	5·7
6. Baden	8·3	5·8
7. Prussia	8·2	5·5
8. Austria	8·2	4·3
9. Hesse	8·0	5·9
10. Alsace-Lorraine	7·9	5·4
11. Belgium	6·4	6·2
12. England and Wales	6·0	8·2
13. Denmark	5·2	2·8
14. Scotland	5·0	6·5
15. Finland	4·0	5·8
16. Sweden	3·4	4·7
17. Norway	2·8	3·6
18. Italy	2·6	2·3
19. Switzerland	2·3	3·8

29. Those countries that restrict their birth-rate help Nature in her task of keeping the numbers within the bounds of the capacity of the area, while others that allow the birth-rate to soar high will have to pay large penalties in the shape of heavy death rates, for Nature is a relentless task-mistress and will always have her own way.

30. One can judge whether or not a country is suffering from the effects of over-population by the standard of living obtaining in the country as economists

hold that low standard of living is a sure index of over-population. When the number of mouths is considerably larger than the capacity of the soil to provide food for them, the standard of living should naturally fall. Let me quote from what Carr-Saunders says in this connection with particular reference to India and China.

"Infanticide was employed in India and China until recently; it has now been abandoned and no other method of keeping the size of the families small has taken its place. An examination of the social conditions suggests that the people are not living as well as they might; famines are not uncommon and are never far off. The symptoms point to over-population, of which the cause would seem to be the failure to replace the custom of infanticide by some other method of regulation."

31. No greater proof is required of the fact that what primarily ails India is over-population than the low, miserably low, standard of living of the masses. This would indicate that the actual position of the Indian population in the Logistic curve of population growth given in page 147 is in the section CDE of the curve, possibly very near E round about which point, if Nature's Law is to be obeyed, any further increase in the population should be practically nil. In other words, there should be, very nearly, only as many babies born as there is wastage due to deaths. To subject the soil to increased pressure due to the addition of nearly 34 millions in a decade when the standard of living is proverbially low is a situation that should cause real alarm in the minds of well-wishers of India. Without an addition in real wealth of, at least, the same extent, of which there has been no very large indication, the existing low standard of living is sure to be depressed further, leading, as has already been indicated, to further over-population and consequent increase in the loss of the spirit of enterprise. For, successive generations of life on less than bare margin of subsistence and the natural indolence and despondency which such a state engenders have probably made the majority of Indians abstain from making any strenuous effort to raise their standard of living, which could be achieved in the first instance by limiting the size of the families. Being itself both the cause and effect of over-population the low standard of living of the average Indian completes what is called the "vicious circle".

32. That the primary cause of the abnormally heavy mortality experienced by the masses in India is traceable to very low economic status is illustrated by the difference between the rates of mortality and the expectations of life relating to males between the experience of the Oriental Government Security Life Assurance Company embracing the period of two decades 1905-1925 and those of the male population of India ascertained after the 1931 Census as clearly shown by fhe following Table :—

TABLE XXVIII.

Age.	Oriental—Males Ultimate 1905-1925.		All India Males 1931.	
	Mortality per cent.	Mean after life-time.	Mortality per-cent.	Mean after life-time.
20	·725	37·16	1·27	29·57
25	·817	33·53	1·53	26·50
30	·887	29·89	1·93	23·60
35	1·001	26·22	2·41	20·99
40	1·263	22·58	2·94	18·60
45	1·743	19·11	3·49	16·40
50	2·513	15·95	4·10	14·31
55	3·663	13·18	4·81	12·27
60	5·097	10·86	5·79	10·25
65	6·685	8·88	7·27	8·26
70	8·643	7·15	9·76	6·35
75	11·254	5·60	14·27	4·61
80	15·145	4·25	21·80	3·13
85	20·351	3·12	36·08	1·95
90	26·890	2·14	57·70	1·12
95	54·300	·48	..	..

33. It need hardly be stated that the economic status of the policy-holders of the Oriental must necessarily be much higher than that of the general population in India. The rates of mortality of the latter are more than 100 per cent. heavier up to the middle age of life than those of the former. The low economic status of the masses in India is firstly the direct cause of heavier mortality through under-nourishment and secondly it helps to maintain mortality at a very high level by depressing the standard of living which brings about a very large increase both in birth and death rates.

34. The remedy, in short, lies in Birth Control among families of poor economic status. In the Census Report for Mysore State, just to hand, one is pleased to find the following sentence: "By an order issued a year ago Government instituted in the Maternity Hospital at Bangalore a Birth-Control clinic for advice and supply of contraception appliances to married women who, for reasons of health or household economy, wish to restrict conception." India's primary need is the opening of several centres of the type of the Bangalore Birth-Control Clinic covering its entire area. If this is done, the second in rank amongst the three self-imposed tasks which, according to Galton, a nation ought to devote its best energies to will be directly achieved and, as a by-product, the other two will naturally follow.

---

35. The populations returned at the two Censuses, after having been corrected for migration in the cases of certain Provincial groups, as explained above, were compared in decennial age groups 0-9, 10-19, etc., and rates of increase of the population applicable to each of these groups were obtained. The logarithms of the rates of increase ($\log r_x$) were made the subject of graduation. The graduating curve was in this case also a cubical parabola and the process of fitting the curve was, as in the case of the graduation of the population, the method of "Least Squares".

36. In this manner were obtained the graduated values of r_x (the rate of increase at age x) in each Provincial group. The graduated population L_x at age x multiplied into $r_x^{\frac{1}{20}}$ (that is, $r_x^{\frac{1}{20}} L_x$) gave the population that would have been returned had a Census been taken six months posterior to middle date of the decennium. Similarly $r_x^{-\frac{1}{20}} L_x$ gave the population on a date six months anterior to the middle date of the decennium. The values of $p_{x+\frac{1}{2}}$ (the probability of surviving one year at age $x+\frac{1}{2}$) were obtained from the ratio $\frac{r_{x+1}^{\frac{1}{20}} L_{x+1}}{r_x^{-\frac{1}{20}} L_x}$ from which the values of p_x and q_x were obtained. The methods adopted for obtaining the rates of mortality q_x relating to females were identical with those adopted in the case of the males, except that to allow for the mortality correction above referred to and for the standard Table made use of in the graduation corresponding female Tables of the 1911 Census were adopted.

37. The method detailed above yielded the rates of mortality from age 1 onwards to the end of life in each Provincial group. The important problem of allotting a value to the rate of mortality at age 0 (q_0) remained. Sir George Hardy graduated the Proclaimed Clans figures available for infantile ages up to 12 for the years from 1876 to 1891 by a formula of the type

$$l_x = A + Hx + Bc^x + \frac{m}{n\ x+1} \text{ ——— } (1).$$

Students of Actuarial Science will easily see that according to Makeham's modification of Gompertz's law for the Force of Mortality the following equality holds:—

$$\log l_x = A + Hx + Bc^x \text{ ——— } (2).$$

Sir George, evidently, made two modifications to the Makeham formula. Firstly he dealt with l_x instead of $\log l_x$. This appears to have been adopted mainly for the facility the l_x form gave to obtain the values of L_x (the population at each age) at the young ages by integration and not from the more easy and approximate formula $L_x = \frac{l_x + l_{x+1}}{2}$ applicable to adult ages which due to the rapid fluctuation of mortality rates at the ages of infancy and childhood is inapplicable at these ages. The principle of "uniform seniority" which is obeyed by the formula when $\log l_x$ is equated to the right-hand side of equation (2) will naturally be sacrificed when l_x is equated to the same quantity. This is immaterial while constructing mortality Tables not mainly intended for financial operations and even if they are, the sacrifice of the conveniences derived from this principle at the very young ages is not of any consequence. The second modification made by Sir George was the addition of the term $\frac{m}{nx+1}$ to provide for the higher mortality and the consequent faster decrement of the numbers surviving to each age at the infantile ages and ages of childhood as compared with the adult ages. This term has its maximum value at age 0 and diminishes rapidly as age increases.

38. The rate of mortality at age 0 (q_0) of Burma males was first obtained as follow :—From the graduated values of q_1, q_2, q_3, q_4, etc., the fundamental column of the mortality Table showing the numbers surviving to each age up to 4 (l_2, l_3, l_4,) out of a fixed number commencing age 1 (l_1) were calculated. The values of the constants appearing in equation (1) were obtained from these values of l. The resulting equation took the following form :—

$$l_x = 97191\cdot335 - 1762\cdot505x + 30178\cdot684\ (\cdot45)^x + \frac{13488\cdot550}{29\cdot8125x+1} \text{———(3).}$$

39. Having found the value of l_0 from equation (3) the constants in this equation were proportionately reduced so as to make $l_0 = 100{,}000$, the usual convenient radix of a mortality Table. The modified equation is given below.

$$l_x = 68999\cdot235 - 1251\cdot259x + 21424\cdot812\ (\cdot45)^x + \frac{9575\cdot953}{29\cdot8125x+1} \text{———(4).}$$

The resulting value of the function l_x at the young ages provided the value of q_0 for Burma and the values of this quantity for the other Provincial groups were obtained graphically using the values for Burma for the first five ages as base.

40. For constructing the mortality Table for each sex relating to the whole of India, an average age distribution applicable to each of the two Censuses 1921 and 1931 out of a total of 100,000 in each sex was obtained by weighting the numbers in each age group in each area by the total population in that area taken to the nearest million. Having thus obtained the age distribution in each Census, applicable to the whole of India out of a total of 100,000 in the usual quinary age groups 0-4, 5-9, etc., the construction of the mortality Table followed identically on the lines of the method adopted for each Provincial group.

41. The mortality Tables for each sex and for each Provincial group including those for All-India, constructed by methods detailed above, are given in pages 173—194 and called A, B, C, etc., to V.

Explanation of the Columns of the Mortality Table.

42. It is usual to say a few words at this stage explaining the fundamental columns of the mortality Table. The column, headed "Living at age x", usually denoted by the symbol l_x, represents the number of persons alive at the beginning of each age interval out of 100,000 persons born alive. The words "born alive" are used with the view to call attention to the fact that still-births are excluded and the column refers only to survivors of living births. It should also be particularly noted that the meaning of the heading "Living at age x" is living at the beginning of the age interval x to $x+1$, that is, at the precise moment of completing the integral number of years of age x. It may also be added that the 100,000 persons under observation from birth are not assumed as having been born at the same moment. The main point to be stressed is that the flow of lives from age to age in this column is based on the assumption that every one of the 100,000 births is kept under observation from the moment of birth and a regular record is maintained as to how many are alive at exact age one year, how many at exact age two years, and so on to the end of life. The total number counted as alive at exact age one year is entered opposite to age 1 in this column and so on for other ages. This is the fundamental column of the mortality Table and shows the decrement of life from age to age throughout the whole range of life. Taking, for example, Table A, relating to All-India Males, we see that out of 100,000 chil-

dren born alive only 52,439 attain age 18, the age of majority in India. The original number is reduced to one half at about age $21\frac{1}{2}$. The proverbial "three-score and ten years" is attained only by 7,036 out of every 100,000 born.

43. The next column 3 headed "Dying between ages x and $x+1$" shows the number dying after attaining the age shown in column 1 but before attaining the next higher age out of 100,000 persons born alive. It is merely the decrement of the numbers in column 2 and is obtained by taking the difference between successive numbers in that column. The number of deaths, very high for the age interval 0 to 1, diminishes rapidly till about age 10, 11 or 12 (there being minor variation from Province to Province) which is the most favourable period in life. From this point onwards the number of deaths increases till it attains a maximum more or less in the neighbourhood of age 40 for males and then slowly tails off to zero. In countries where the rates of mortality till about middle age are not so heavy as in India this maximum appears much later in life, that is, after age 70. Since this column indicates the number of deaths occurring in each age interval amongst a diminishing number of persons alive at the beginning of that age interval, it cannot give an adequate idea of the rate of mortality at each age. This is however given by the next column.

44. The next column headed "Mortality per cent." shows the number dying in each age interval among 100 alive at the beginning of the interval. Just as in the case of the preceding column relating to the number dying between the ages x and $x+1$ the mortality per cent. which is very large for age 0 rapidly diminishes to age 11 or 12. From this point onwards it increases slowly at first and more rapidly from and after age 50 and towards the end of the Table the rate of increase is extremely rapid.

45. Column 5 with the heading "Living between ages x and $x+1$" has to be particularly distinguished from column 2 headed "Living at age x". It might be of interest here to mention that the Life Table or mortality Table under explanation shows the number of persons surviving to each year of age and the number of persons dying between two consecutive integral ages in a *stationary population* undisturbed by migration and where only as many are born as die during the year in all the age periods. In other words, in the construction of the mortality Table, disturbances due to migration and irregular flow of births and deaths from year to year over the period considered are eliminated and rates of mortality obtained as applicable to the population when freed from these disturbing influences. This column shows the number of persons that would have been enumerated at each age last birthday in a stationary population supported by 100,000 births had a Census been taken at any moment during the year. In other words, the total number opposite to age 25, say, is the population between ages 25 and 26 at all fractional ages between these two integral ones.

46. The number in column 6 recorded opposite to any age shows the total population that would have been returned as of that age and all older ages to the end of the Table at a Census taken at any time. It is obtained by adding the population in the preceding column from the current age to the end of the Table. The number in this column opposite to age 0 represents the total population maintained by 100,000 births per annum in a community subject to the rates of mortality given in column 4. This column is of particular interest in so far as it enables two countries or two communities subject to different rates of mortality to be compared as regards their age distribution. Due to the heavy rates of mortality to which Indian population is subject, we find on reference, for instance, to the All-India Male Table A that about half the population is under age 24 and the other half aged 24 and above and only about a quarter of the population lives aged 40 and above, whereas, in countries subject to lighter rates of mortality these proportions occur at ages substantially later. For instance, in the United States of America (1910 experience) half the population is over 31 years of age and about one-fourth over age 50. The corresponding ages for England and Wales (1911 experience) are 33 and 51. The numbers appearing in this column can also be interpreted in another way. The number appearing, for instance, opposite to age 25 not only represents, as explained above, the total population aged 25 and upwards but also the total number of years of future life-time that would be lived by those alive at the beginning of age 25 given in column 2, namely, 47,787.

47. The next and the last column headed " Mean after life-time at age x " is also commonly known as the " expectation of life ". Being, as is more or less explained by the heading itself, the mean or average future life-time lived by all persons attaining a particular age x, the number in this column opposite to any age, on the basis of the explanation given towards the end of the last paragraph, is obtained by dividing the number in column 6 by the number in column 2 appearing opposite to the same age. This expression " expectation of life " is associated in public minds with not a little confusion due to the unfortunate choice of the word " expectation " which has however come to stay. It is much better to call it " mean after life-time " or " average after life-time ". People usually consider the expectation of life at any age to represent the number of years any individual of that age may " reasonably expect " still to live. This is, however, not the case. Given a large number of individuals, say, aged 30 not chosen by any selective process, we shall find persons in all states of health. The expectation of life at age 30 means only the average life-time lived by all persons of that age in the future, some living very long and others having only a short span of life. In the process of averaging we take the excess from those who live long and distribute it among those who die early, so as to place all on an equality. As applied, therefore, to any particular individual, the expectation of life has no significance whatsoever. If he is in a very bad state of health his future life-time may be far shorter and if he be in sound health it may be far longer than the expectation of life. The chief importance of this function lies in the fact that it affords a ready means of comparing two mortality Tables for the cumulative effect of mortality at all ages above any particular age.

Comparisons.

48. It will be essential before concluding the Report to compare the results arrived at by my investigations with the earlier ones. Before, however, this is done, it is necessary to stress that a few important points should be borne in mind. The essential difference between my investigation and those of my predecessors is traceable to the fact that, whereas I included in each area the British Province and the adjoining Feudatory Indian States, their investigations were confined to British Provinces only. A certain amount, therefore, of the difference between the rates of mortality as deduced by me and by my predecessors with respect to each Provincial group can, naturally, be traced to the variations in the areas dealt with. In the absence of mortality Tables constructed separately relating to the larger Indian States, it will not be possible to say how far their inclusion has tended either to increase or diminish the aggregate mortality of the respective British Province with which each of them has been grouped. It was, however, felt that the vitality of the Indian Empire should be appraised in suitable geographical groups without omitting any area and on the Census Commissioner expressing his opinion in favour of this procedure, I agreed very gladly to conduct my investigations on these lines as I was also very strongly in favour of adopting this course.

49. Another point to bear in mind, when comparing the mortality of the same Province in two different Censuses, is the fact that the rates of mortality may appear as having improved, whereas they may have deteriorated, due to improved efficiency in methods of Census enumeration showing artificially a very large increase. In illustration of this point I have only to refer to Tables XXIX and XXX showing the rates of mortality and Tables XXXI and XXXII showing expectations, of life for males and females respectively in the Provincial group, Central Provinces and Hyderabad. By referring to either of these Tables, it will be evident that the mortality in this area is considerably superior in 1931 as compared with what it was in 1881. The Hyderabad State has returned at the 1931 Census a total population which is nearly 15¾% in excess of the population returned at the 1921 Census, whereas the rate of increase for the whole of India is only about 10½ per cent. The very large increase in the population, shown by the Hyderabad State at the 1931 Census, has been attributed by the Census Commissioner to increased efficiency of the Census staff and there can be no other convincing explanation. Since the rates of mortality depend on the rates of increase, the very large increase in population shown by the Hyderabad State should have lightened significantly the mortality rates relating to the Central Provinces, Berar and Hyderabad group. A substantial part, therefore, of the improvement in vitality shown by the Central Provinces between 1881 and 1931 might be traced to this cause.

50. There is yet a third point to be borne in mind consequent upon the deduced rates of mortality being to a certain extent sensitive to the methods of graduation adopted both with respect to the population and the rates of increase. With respect to the latter, whether a constant rate of increase at all ages or a variable one from age to age has been adopted (after graduation) also affects the results to a certain extent. Where, however, the collected statistics are subject only to minor errors due to the paucity of the data, different methods of graduation will have very little effect upon the deduced rates of mortality. With respect to the Indian Census Returns, where the errors are of very large magnitude, smoothing formulas of very great power have to be adopted with the result, above mentioned, that the calculated rates of mortality depend to a significant extent upon the smoothing formula or the formula of graduation. This is particularly so at the ages of infancy and childhood where, even in countries which place a substantial reliance on the statistics at the other ages, help has to be derived from the records of births and deaths to correct irregularities relating to them. We are without any guide whatsoever in India with respect to the flow of vital occurrences at the very young ages. The only small material on hand is nearly half a century old and therefore quite obsolete for our present purpose. It also refers only to a limited area which, as compared to the size of the Indian Subcontinent, is entirely unrepresentative of parts distant from itself. All these factors have to be borne in mind before comparisons are effected between either the results of one Province from one Census to another or of one Province with another in the same Census. If, therefore, in effecting comparison on the above lines the differences traced are only very small, it will be unsafe to attach any large significance to them.

51. The task of comparing the results brought out by me with those of my predecessors appears a huge one as I have constructed as many as twenty-two Tables for both the sexes after dividing India and Burma into ten large geographical areas. The mortality Tables corresponding to three of these areas, namely, Bihar and Orissa ; Rajputana, Ajmere-Merwara and the Central India States and Agency group ; Sind, Baluchistan and N. W. F. Province, have been constructed by me for the first time. With respect to these areas, therefore, in the absence of mortality Tables relating to the earlier Censuses, it will not be possible to say in what direction variation in mortality lay. As regards the other Provinces, I propose to draw conclusions relating to the trend of mortality on broad and general lines only.

52. The obvious way of comparing two Tables of mortality either with respect to the same locality at different epochs or of two different localities or communities at the same epoch is to compare the rates of mortality, that is, the numbers appearing in the column headed "Mortality per cent." in the Life Tables A to V. Though this method provides an effective way of comparing the trend of mortality at individual ages without the comparison being vitiated by variations at all other ages between the Tables compared, it suffers from the disadvantage of being too laborious as every age has to be compared individually. Where, therefore, it is considered desirable to eliminate minor fluctuations at individual ages, Tables could be compared in large groups of quinquennial or decennial age periods by computing what is called the probability of dying over 5 or 10 year age periods. Tables XXIX and XXX give for each sex the rates of mortality at all quinquennial age points, 0, 5, 10, etc., in each Province from the 1881 to 1931 Censuses wherever these are available. Though a general tendency may be discerned in the case of some Provinces for the rates of mortality at the adult and older ages to diminish, this is, however, subject to such large fluctuations as to make any statement to this effect devoid of its emphasis. Burma, however, shows itself to have slightly deteriorated even at these ages. A substantial improvement in the rates of mortality at the very young ages is, however, apparent in each Province. It would have been unsafe to place too much reliance on the lighter mortality, exhibited at the young ages as a result of the present analysis, due to the great unreliability of the data relating to these ages but for the fact that the available statistics of deaths pertaining to these ages have gone to confirm this inference. These statistics of deaths are, of course, not dependable but they are no more so now than formerly and, on the supposition that the amount of error has remained constant, there is room for drawing the conclusion that the mortality at the very young ages, notably in the first year after birth, has improved to a certain extent. It would,

therefore, appear that the several Baby-Week Exhibitions and other propaganda relating to the proper bringing-up of children carried on frequently during the last decade have come to bear some fruit. The Nation, therefore, should feel grateful to the organisers of these exhibitions.

53. Another point of great importance which must cause concern to workers in the cause of public welfare, especially in connection with minimising the perils attendant on maternity revealed not only by the 1931 Actuarial Analysis but also by the earlier ones, is the heavier mortality of females as compared with males practically from about age 12 to about age 45. In the other sections of the Table, female mortality is lighter than that of males. It will be of interest in this connection to refer to the rates of mortality of both the sexes with respect to England and Wales given in Tables XXIX and XXX. It will be observed that in England female mortality is, in the major part of the Table, substantially lighter than male mortality and between ages 10 and 15 where female mortality rises relatively to male mortality it only approaches the latter without exceeding it. A reference to the Life-Tables relating to other countries notably the United States of America also indicates that female mortality is throughout lighter than male mortality. The heavier mortality of females as compared with that of males from about the age of adolescence to the age when capacity for child-bearing may be expected to cease appears to be a feature of the mortality experience of Indian females. A considerable part of the heavy mortality of girls in their teens can naturally be traced to immature maternity if correct statistics are maintained according to age and cause of death. That noble piece of Legislation called by the name "Sarda Act" has not been sufficiently long on the Statute Book for its effects to make themselves evident in the decennium considered. The salutary restriction imposed by this Act against the marriage of immature boys and girls combined with increasing knowledge on matters relating to maternity and to pre-natal and post-natal ailments, will, it is hoped, make considerable part of the excess mortality of females at the reproductive ages diminish.

54. Another method of comparing mortality Tables that has been very largely adopted in the past is to compare what has been called "the mean after life-time" which is also commonly known as "the expectation of life" the method of calculation of which from the fundamental column, showing the number of survivors from age to age, of a mortality Table was explained in an earlier paragraph. The chief advantage of this quantity lies in the fact that by its use one is able to compare mortality Tables for the cumulative effect of mortality over its entire length from any given age. For instance, comparing two mortality Tables by their expectations of life, say, at age 25, one would be able to judge which of the two Tables shows in the aggregate lighter mortality from age 25 up to the end of the mortality Table. This method of comparison by expectation of life has, therefore, the advantage of not giving prominence to minor fluctuations in mortality rates at particular ages. Where, however, it is desired to compare mortality Tables over short ranges, the function called temporary expectation of life can be made use of. Tables XXXI and XXXII give the expectations of life for all the Provincial groups from 1881 to 1931 for males and females separately. By comparing the expectation of life at age 0 for two Provinces or for two different Censuses of the same Province, one is able to compare the mortality rates to which the populations of the two Provinces are subject in the former case and the variation in the mortality of the Province from one Census to another in the latter. It need hardly be mentioned that the larger the expectation of life the lighter is the mortality. It will be seen that the expectation of life at age 0 shows a substantial improvement at the 1931 Census over the other four Censuses brought in the comparison excluding that of 1921 with respect to which no expectation of life was calculated. Since the rates of mortality relating to the very young ages in India are not entirely dependable, one would rather be inclined to draw conclusions by eliminating these ages, that is, by comparing the expectation of life at age 5 or preferably age 10.

55. I shall make a few observations relating to the trend of mortality in each Province by comparing the expectations of life at age 10. These observations will be mostly confined to the male Tables. It will however be easy for any one to draw his own conclusions from the experience of female lives from a study of Table XXXII on more or less identical lines. The mortality in the Province of

Bengal does not show any decided tendency to improve substantially. Though the expectation of life at age 10 in 1931 is somewhat larger than in 1901 and in 1911, it is to a certain extent smaller than in 1891 and substantially so as compared with 1881. Bihar and Orissa, which have been dealt with separately in one group for the first time after the 1931 Census, exhibit expectations of life up to age 50 markedly superior to those of the adjoining Province of Bengal. Bombay and Madras have substantially improved as compared with 1881 but it will be remembered that they had to bear the brunt of the 1876-78 famine which accounted for the very heavy mortality and the consequent low expectations of life of these two Provinces in 1881. The expectations of life at age 10 in these two Provinces in 1931 are smaller than in 1891, the decade 1881-1891 having been one of comparative prosperity for them. Bombay shows substantial improvement in 1931 as compared with 1901 and 1911. As regards the main cause of the low expectation of life shown by Bombay in 1901 it should be observed that this Province along with Central Provinces was affected by the 1899-1901 famine though Madras was unaffected by it. The expectation of life at age 10 for the province of Madras has been keeping more or less steady from 1911 onwards. Burma has always been noted for its lighter mortality as compared with other Indian Provinces in the past which reputation it yet maintains though the expectation of life of this Province does not indicate any decided tendency to increase but is keeping more or less steady. The first Life-Table with respect to the Central Provinces was constructed after the 1881 Census and the second one after the 1931 Census. The latter, however, includes the experience of the very large population contained in H. E. H. The Nizam's Dominions. It will be seen that the Central Provinces show substantial improvement in mortality in 1931 as compared with 1881. As has already been observed, a large portion of this improvement should naturally be traced to the improved machinery of Census-taking set up by the Hyderabad State at the 1931 Census. The Punjab group, comprising the British Provinces of the Punjab and the adjoining smaller Indian States together with Kashmir, the biggest in area of all the Indian States, shows in 1931 an improvement in mortality which is decidedly substantial. In 1911, however, this Province showed the heaviest mortality of all the Indian Provinces except perhaps the United Provinces. The improvement noticed in 1931 has been such as to bring the position practically back to the 1891 level when the experience of the Province as to mortality was the lightest of all the decennial investigations. It is highly probable that a part of the improvement has been due to combining the Punjab with Kashmir noted for its highly salubrious and temperate climate. It is, however, not possible to make any definite statement to this effect before proving by Actuarial analysis that the people in Kashmir are subject to lighter mortality than those in the Punjab as other factors may be at work, for instance, low economic status, neutralising the effect of the salubrious climate. Rajputana and Ajmere-Merwara as also Sind, Baluchistan and North-West Frontier Province are two Provincial groups with respect to which mortality Tables have been constructed for the first time at the 1931 Census. The former group has indicated the heaviest mortality for males of all Provincial groups dealt with. The United Provinces show some improvement in mortality in 1931 though it is not very substantial as indicated by the small increase averaging about a year as compared with 1891 in the expectation of life up to about age 40. The improvement in mortality for the male population of the whole of India in 1931 is indicated by the value of the expectation of life at age 10 which is very nearly one year in excess of the highest value of this function which was reached in 1891. Generally speaking, it can be said that the influence of the hygienic and economic factors that prevailed in the decennium 1921-1931 was such as to bring the condition of the Indian population as to its mortality experience nearly back to the 1891 position.

56. Amongst all the Provincial groups analysed, Burma shows the lightest mortality. As a matter of fact, it has been keeping up the first rank in this respect in all the three Censuses analysed with respect to this Province. Madras which used to keep always the second rank appears to have lost a little bit of ground, as the Punjab, judged by the value of the expectation of life at age 10, has superseded it in 1931. Whether the grouping of the British Province of Madras with the adjoining Indian States has proved a disadvantage to it and the grouping of the Punjab with Kashmir has proved an advantage to the Punjab group is a matter

which requires further detailed analysis. It is, however, somewhat significant that the two Provinces, Burma and Madras, which have been indicating substantially lighter mortality than that of the other Indian Provinces, have been the least inaccurate in returning ages. Bihar and Orissa for which a Life Table has been constructed for the first time in connection with the 1931 Census indicate mortality at all ages up to 50 substantially lighter than the adjoining Provincial group, Bengal and Assam, which exhibits the worst vitality of all the Provinces except perhaps Rajputana and Ajmere-Merwara group. The difference between the vitalities of these two Provincial groups is not, however, very substantial.

57. The comparative statements detailed above have been made with special reference to the expectations of life relating to male lives of the various Provincial groups and for All-India appearing in Table XXXI. The corresponding expectations of life relating to females are given in Table XXXII. Here again Burma females show the lightest mortality. As between Madras and the Punjab females, the former show lighter mortality at all young ages up to 30 and after this age the position is reversed. The heaviest mortality amongst females is shown by the Sind, Baluchistan and North-West Frontier Province group. This is very probably due to the strict ' purdah ' observed by the females in this group of which the population is predominantly Muhammadan. Vitality, only superior to that of the Provincial group just considered but inferior to the rest of India, is shown by Bengal and Assam, and Rajputana and Ajmere-Merwara groups. The former shows heavier mortality than the latter upto about age 40 after which the position is reversed. Taking female mortality as a whole it can be stated that the deterioration which set in from 1901 onwards has not yet taken a definite turn towards improvement. Whereas in the case of males the position in 1931 with respect to vitality was such as to bring it back very nearly up to the high level reached in 1891, the female vitality, however, does not indicate any recovery of the lost ground.

58. So far I have compared either the same Province at different Censuses or one Province with another at the same Census. It will, however, be interesting to compare Indian mortality with that of the other countries of the world. It has often been said that the Indian population exhibits the worst vitality of all the countries of the world which have analysed their mortality experience but, except perhaps for Tables comparing India with England, no statistics have been published so far to indicate the force of the statement that India exhibits the heaviest mortality of all civilised countries. Believing in the truism that figures speak more forcibly than words, I have taken advantage of the publication in Prof. Glover's admirable volume, "United States Life-Tables 1890—1910" of the mortality Tables relating to no less than thirteen representative countries of the world including India. These are exhibited in the six Tables from XXXIII to XXXVIII three of which relate to males and the other three to females. Prof. Glover has given in his volume extensive figures for all the functions of the mortality Tables and for each age to which none, interested in studying the comparative mortality of the countries of the world, can help referring. I have, however, chosen only three of these mortality functions and have also further condensed my Tables by giving values only at quinquennial ages. Tables XXXIII and XXXIV give for males and females respectively the number of persons that die in a year out of 1,000 observed at each quinquennial age. The very heavy rate of mortality experienced by the Indian population as compared with all the other twelve countries will be evident. It will also be observed that the ratio of the mortality in India to the mortality of the other countries is very large at the younger ages and at some age points the mortality in India is more than nearly seven times as heavy as that of countries which exhibit light mortality. As age advances there is a tendency for the ratio to diminish; yet the Indian mortality keeps substantially heavier than that of the other countries. Tables XXXV and XXXVI, showing for the two sexes how rapidly the numbers surviving to each quinquennial age out of 100,000 children born diminish, might be considered as affording a better basis for comparative study by some people. It will be seen that, in India, before age 5 is reached nearly 45,000 young lives out of 100,000 children born are lost, whereas even the country that exhibits the lowest survivorship amongst the other twelve brought into the comparison shows a wastage of only about 27,000 and Norway noted for its very light mortality loses only something less than 12,000 in the first 5 ages. Survivors to age 10 are only about half the number of children born in India and the very large number surviving

to this age in other countries will be evident from a study of the Tables. The two Tables afford a ready means of making such comparisons at all quinquennial ages and the appallingly heavy toll claimed by death in India will be evident even from a cursory scrutiny of them. Tables XXXVII and XXXVIII give the values of the expectations of life for all the countries and the small values, as compared with other countries, of this function relating to India as a sure indication of the very heavy mortality experienced by it will be evident.

59. In bringing this Report to a close, I have to draw the special attention of the authorities in charge of the registration of the vital occurrences in India to the extreme desirability, nay necessity, of focussing particular attention on a limited area in each Province with the view to obtain complete statistics of births and deaths in the locality, the latter either according to individual ages or quinquennial age periods grouped in the same manner as recommended by me for the 1941 Census enumeration. As many as six Actuarial analyses undertaken in connection with Indian Censuses have been performed by methods more or less in the nature of makeshifts and it will be extremely desirable to make the seventh and subsequent ones, at least, follow the normal and, therefore, comparatively more easy method of mortality Table construction. I know it will be practically impossible to expect the records of vital statistics with respect to the entire area in each Province in India to come up to the requisite degree of accuracy within a decade. That is why I am recommending a representative small area in each Province being subject to special scrutiny so that it may provide, by the time of the next Census, dependable records of vital occurrences. The relatively great accuracy of the records of vital statistics in the Presidency of Madras have been commented upon earlier in this Report. If this accuracy is maintained and further improved upon, we shall have by 1941 sufficient material on hand with respect to one very large Province supplying a long felt want.

60. Just when this Report is nearing completion, practically at the very moment I am writing these lines, I have received from the Census Commissioner a Table showing the deaths in the Presidency of Madras that occurred during the ten calendar years, 1921 to 1930, both inclusive. It will, therefore, not be possible for me to make any investigations making use of the statistics of deaths, in such time as to enable the results to be incorporated in this Report. This will, however, be done in a Paper I propose to submit to the Institute of Actuaries, London. The infantile deaths, *i.e.*, deaths below age one, are divided in this Table into four useful categories as follows: "under one week", "over one week (and under one month)", "over one month but not exceeding six months" and "over six months but not exceeding twelve months". With respect to higher ages, however, up to age 20. one finds the orthodox quinquennial groupings '1—4', '5—9', '10—14' and '15—19'. From age 20 onwards the groupings are decennial with one large group at the end of 60 and over. The groups could preferably be modified to be in conformity with those to be adopted in collecting population statistics at the 1941 Census. It will be essential, if the Life Tables to be constructed after the 1941 Census are to include the Indian States in the same way as the Life Tables constructed now do, that the Indian States should also make efforts to supply reliable statistics of vital occurrences in the inter-censal period between now and the date of the next Census. If this is not done and if reliable records of births and deaths are only available for British Provinces there will be no other alternative but to revert to the old method of constructing Life Tables only with reference to the British Provinces in India.

61. The situation takes a different aspect altogether when we come to consider the ages of infancy and childhood. Here without exaggeration we are simply groping in the dark and it has only been repeated too often by my predecessors and myself that the Proclaimed Clans experience of nearly half a century ago is entirely useless as giving any basis to deduce mortality rates at the very young ages applicable to the present generation of children. If the recommendations made in the previous paragraph are given effect to from now there would be sufficient statistics on hand by about the next Census date which would provide reliable basis to the investigating Actuary to deduce mortality rates not only at the ages of infancy and childhood but also at the older ages. If, however, it is found not possible just yet to give immediate effect to them in their entirety, steps should be taken to maintain accurate records of births and deaths up to

age 15 at least in representative small areas in each Province. This will provide the Actuary at the next Census with sufficient material to deduce reliable rate of mortality at the very young ages. Recommendations to this effect were made by Sir George Hardy after the 1901 Census, repeated by Mr. Ackland after 1911 Census and emphasised by Mr. Meikle after the 1921 Census, but, one has to state with regret, to no purpose. Mr. Ackland said in this connection "The record and investigation of these statistics (Proclaimed Clans statistics) apparently ceased in 1904 and, as explained earlier in the present Report and in Mr. Hardy's 1901 Report, the data furnished between 1891 and 1904 were so limited as to age as to be practically useless for the purposes desired. It is clear that results based on statistics referring to the period 1876-1890, could not properly be employed in any future investigation of Census Returns; and it is therefore most desirable, and indeed essential, if complete Life-Tables are to be deduced in future, that some effort should be made to secure trustworthy data as to the births in the several Provinces, and the deaths at the ages of infancy and childhood". Ackland's words expressed in the above terms twenty years ago, will hold even more emphatically by the time the next Census falls to be taken. It is, therefore, earnestly hoped that the Government of each Province will take the necessary steps to give effect to the recommendations in this respect at least.

Acknowledgments.

62. It is now my pleasant duty to acknowledge help from various persons which I received not only in the preparation of this Report but also in making the very elaborate calculations which the construction of the twenty-two Life Tables had involved, of which only those that have had any experience in conducting statistical investigations in all their various details would have an adequate idea. I had naturally to be in constant correspondence with Dr. Hutton, the Census Commissioner for India, and his replies to my various enquiries were prompt, full and marked by an extreme measure of courtesy which is gratefully acknowledged. I found his intimate knowledge of the conditions obtaining in the different parts of India and of Indian sociology of particular help in forming my Provincial groups. I have to express my indebtedness to my friend and colleague in the Oriental Life Office, Mr. Douglas Forrest, F.F.A., who read the Report in manuscript and gave suggestions of a useful character. As regards the help I received to complete the laborious work in connection with the preparation of the Life Tables I have been particularly fortunate, for, what I received was not help of a purely clerical nature, but help from young men aspiring for Actuarial honours and therefore imbued with the desire to learn the work. It was a pleasure to see these young men from day to day ever ready to take up with a cheerful countenance the large quantity of laborious work they were called upon to do. To one and all of them I express my gratitude and do hope that the training they received will stand them in good stead, when in the fullness of time some of them at least may be called upon to undertake investigations of a similar nature. My sincere thanks are also due to Mr. Minocher J. S. Khras, F.S.S., a friend and colleague of mine whose very long association with the Royal Statistical Society extending over a period of more than a quarter of a century was particularly helpful in placing at my disposal the vast store of Statistical knowledge carefully preserved in the pages of the Journals of that body to which and to the pages of the Journals of the Institute of Actuaries—that storehouse of knowledge on Actuarial matters—I had constantly to refer to derive inspiration when the work was in progress.

L. S. VAIDYANATHAN,

M.A., F.I.A.

ORIENTAL BUILDINGS,

Bombay, 29th March 1933.

TABLE XXIX.

Comparative Rates of Mortality ($100q_x$) at quinquennial ages, as deduced from the results of the 1881, 1891, 1901, 1911, 1921 and 1931 Censuses respectively in the several Provinces specified and over the combined area, with corresponding values for England.

MALE LIVES.

Age.	Bengal. 1881.	Bengal. 1891.	Bengal. 1901.	Bengal. 1911.	Bengal. 1921. Hindus	Bengal. 1921. Mahomedans.	Bengal. 1931.	Bihar and Orissa. 1931.	Bombay. 1881.	Bombay. 1891.	Bombay. 1901.	Bombay. 1911.	Bombay. 1921. Hindus.	Bombay. 1921. Mahomedans.	Bombay. 1931.
0	28·27	28·82	29·89	29·86	..	..	24·96	23·75	28·44	26·35	29·79	29·69	..	..	23·85
5	2·29	2·86	3·03	2·97	2·00	2·65	2·22	1·51	2·43	2·58	2·81	2·60	2·95	2·53	1·78
10	1·04	1·22	1·49	1·42	·90	1·17	1·04	·45	1·13	1·10	1·26	1·03	1·28	·95	·60
15	1·51	1·22	1·47	1·51	1·04	1·48	1·11	·74	1·62	1·04	1·15	·95	1·30	·91	·92
20	1·76	1·56	1·75	1·82	1·40	1·69	1·38	1·11	1·93	1·18	1·30	1·53	1·43	·96	1·27
25	1·86	1·92	2·07	2·06	1·81	1·97	1·81	1·36	2·13	1·38	1·55	2·12	1·81	1·32	1·56
30	1·99	2·32	2·42	2·34	2·36	2·38	2·41	1·66	2·35	1·64	1·90	2·63	2·29	1·95	1·88
35	2·17	2·72	2·77	2·74	3·04	2·93	3·02	2·15	2·60	1·98	2·40	3·09	2·84	2·61	2·27
40	2·46	3·16	3·12	3·24	3·80	3·57	3·65	2·81	2·88	2·44	3·05	3·56	3·50	3·32	2·76
45	2·89	3·68	3·48	3·77	4·48	4·15	4·25	3·52	3·29	3·05	3·85	4·06	4·20	4·00	3·31
50	3·47	4·30	3·97	4·38	5·19	4·78	4·81	4·32	3·97	3·85	4·80	4·67	5·03	4·82	4·04
55	4·38	5·06	4·74	5·14	5·86	5·40	5·43	5·30	5·07	4·90	5·90	5·44	5·95	5·66	5·03
60	5·88	6·21	5·97	6·30	6·58	6·11	6·17	6·60	6·71	6·30	7·26	6·46	7·11	6·73	6·32
65	8·25	7·92	8·08	8·31	7·52	7·10	7·35	8·51	9·35	8·26	9·29	7·89	8·68	8·24	8·17
70	11·96	10·48	11·52	11·80	..	..	9·42	11·32	13·42	11·11	12·52	10·01	..	..	11·00
75	17·53	14·30	17·01	17·86	..	..	14·07	15·04	19·56	15·21	17·74	13·46	..	..	15·71
80	25·32	19·99	25·27	28·32	..	..	23·43	22·56	28·33	21·35	25·73	19·74	..	..	23·58
85	36·65	28·49	36·59	44·82	..	..	38·43	35·63	41·54	30·50	37·50	31·16	..	..	37·62
90	60·00	41·20	51·22	65·73	..	..	58·57	54·38	100·00	43·89	54·00	48·72	..	..	62·13

Age.	Burma. 1901.	Burma. 1911.	Burma. 1921.	Burma. 1931.	Central Provinces and Hyderabad. 1881.	Central Provinces and Hyderabad. 1931.	Madras. 1881.	Madras. 1891.	Madras. 1901.	Madras. 1911.	Madras. 1921.	Madras. 1931.
0	23·83	22·34	..	22·30	28·44	24·90	28·75	26·35	26·81	27·39	..	23·55
5	1·93	1·74	1·99	1·59	2·43	1·53	2·71	2·58	2·34	2·55	2·43	1·64
10	·83	·75	·89	·54	1·13	·56	1·25	1·10	1·03	1·14	1·22	·66
15	·91	·77	·90	·87	1·62	·92	1·73	1·04	1·01	1·08	1·17	·91
20	1·20	1·15	·95	1·14	1·95	1·30	2·06	1·18	1·21	1·15	1·23	1·18
25	1·47	1·55	1·08	1·30	2·15	1·56	2·22	1·38	1·41	1·31	1·39	1·37
30	1·73	1·82	1·35	1·52	2·39	1·85	2·37	1·61	1·66	1·64	1·72	1·73
35	1·96	1·91	1·77	2·02	2·69	2·31	2·55	1·90	2·06	2·12	2·19	2·28
40	2·19	2·04	2·29	2·49	3·03	2·89	2·79	2·24	2·66	2·71	2·79	2·81
45	2·43	2·32	2·76	2·78	3·47	3·35	3·11	2·64	3·40	3·19	3·33	3·33
50	2·73	2·73	3·29	3·12	4·13	3·73	3·61	3·13	4·20	3·72	3·97	3·90
55	3·18	3·25	3·87	3·68	5·27	4·12	4·46	3·83	5·01	4·33	4·66	4·50
60	3·98	4·51	4·59	4·62	6·99	4·73	5·84	4·93	5·93	5·06	5·49	5·43
65	5·38	6·57	5·69	6·36	9·73	6·34	8·01	6·59	7·44	6·10	6·67	6·87
70	7·75	9·36	..	9·09	13·96	10·11	11·44	9·06	10·16	7·78	..	9·37
75	11·76	13·56	..	14·07	20·32	16·92	16·79	12·78	14·66	10·70	..	13·96
80	18·00	19·74	..	21·74	29·43	26·85	24·91	18·32	21·40	16·38	..	21·88
85	27·18	28·58	..	31·90	44·90	39·91	35·48	26·62	31·07	27·22	..	35·53
90	39·71	40·49	..	44·64	100·00	56·09	60·00	38·99	44·40	45·74	..	55·48

TABLE XXIX—(*contd.*)

Comparative Rates of Mortality ($100q_x$) at quinquennial ages, as deduced from the results of the 1881, 1891, 1901, 1911, 1921 and 1931 Censuses respectively, in the several Provinces specified and over the combined area, with corresponding values for England.

MALE LIVES.

Age.	Punjab.						Rajputana and Ajmer-Merwara.	Sind & N. W. F. Provinces.	United Provinces.							All India.						England.	
	1881.	1891.	1901.	1911.	1921.	1931.	1931.	1931.	1881.	1891.	1901.	1911.	1921. Hindus.	1921. Mahomedans.	1931.	1881.	1891.	1901.	1911.	1921.	1931.	1911.	1921.
0	28·27	26·35	29·79	29·79	..	23·98	27·39	26·01	28·44	26·35	26·81	29·79	..	..	27·86	28·41	27·26	28·54	29·00	..	24·87	12·04	9·00
5	2·29	2·58	2·81	2·81	2·50	2·07	2·47	1·89	2·43	2·58	2·33	2·81	2·64	2·18	2·37	2·41	2·68	2·67	2·75	2·52	1·93	·49	·42
10	1·04	1·10	1·26	1·22	1·36	·77	1·30	·90	1·14	1·10	1·03	1·26	1·27	1·06	1·05	1·11	1·14	1·24	1·25	1·22	·79	·19	·18
15	1·41	1·02	1·24	1·77	1·38	·91	1·22	1·09	1·56	1·15	·95	1·27	1·36	1·32	1·11	1·56	1·13	1·17	1·32	1·26	·98	·23	·22
20	1·65	1·12	1·52	2·04	1·48	1·25	1·29	1·35	1·87	1·49	1·13	1·93	1·68	1·63	1·34	1·85	1·39	1·43	1·69	1·42	1·27	·35	·35
25	1·85	1·36	1·86	2·30	1·67	1·53	1·67	1·61	[illegible]·11	1·88	1·46	2·52	2·03	1·91	1·56	2·00	1·69	1·69	2·03	1·68	1·53	·40	·40
30	2·05	1·67	2·16	2·62	2·01	1·78	2·33	2·11	2·33	2·28	1·91	2·94	2·37	2·29	1·91	2·18	2·04	2·02	2·37	2·10	1·93	·48	·43
35	2·26	2·04	2·46	3·04	2·49	2·07	2·92	2·82	2·56	2·72	2·50	3·30	2·87	2·72	2·40	2·38	2·43	2·49	2·77	2·67	2·41	·62	·55
40	2·51	2·49	2·76	3·61	3·07	2·42	3·51	3·52	2·85	3·19	3·23	3·65	3·60	3·24	2·99	2·66	2·85	3·01	3·24	3·33	2·94	·81	·69
45	2·85	3·02	3·06	4·18	3·58	2·82	4·10	4·17	3·31	3·72	4·06	4·06	4·27	3·78	3·61	3·05	3·37	3·64	3·72	4·00	3·49	1·09	·88
50	3·34	3·62	3·43	4·62	4·07	3·32	4·71	4·76	4·04	4·36	4·90	4·62	5·08	4·41	4·30	3·66	3·98	4·30	4·28	4·72	4·10	1·48	1·18
55	4·10	4·36	3·99	5·14	4·61	4·06	5·51	5·36	5·22	5·21	5·77	5·41	6·00	5·12	5·16	4·61	4·78	5·09	4·98	5·46	4·81	2·11	1·76
60	5·35	5·22	4·99	5·80	5·28	5·24	6·65	6·06	7·01	6·41	6·98	6·52	7·20	6·12	6·34	6·12	5·93	6·25	6·00	6·31	5·79	3·04	2·56
65	7·30	6·47	6·70	6·68	6·30	7·17	8·43	7·37	9·86	8·21	9·05	8·05	8·83	7·68	8·05	8·50	7·64	8·14	7·57	7·43	7·27	4·38	3·98
70	10·32	8·42	9·62	8·76	..	10·34	11·22	11·05	14·22	10·89	12·28	10·27	..	..	10·77	12·18	10·16	11·36	10·17	..	9·76	6·47	6·00
75	14·95	11·30	14·35	14·15	..	15·63	16·05	17·62	20·71	14·92	17·26	13·52	..	..	15·37	17·68	13·93	16·12	14·71	..	14·27	9·75	9·38
80	21·47	15·62	21·59	22·04	..	24·30	24·15	26·50	30·05	20·96	24·69	19·54	..	..	23·18	25·28	19·58	23·55	22·55	..	21·80	14·30	14·00
85	31·47	22·07	32·12	36·23	..	37·10	37·37	38·24	42·00	30·01	35·14	33·04	..	..	37·30	36·17	28·03	33·88	36·35	..	36·08	19·91	19·97
90	9050·00	31·77	46·72	58·39	..	54·05	57·58	52·70	100·00	43·50	50·90	58·64	..	..	60·10	62·50	40·62	47·86	57·20	..	57·70	27·40	26·75

TABLE XXX.

Comparative Rates of Mortality ($100q_x$) at quinquennial ages, as deduced from the results of the 1881, 1891, 1901, 1911, 1921 and 1931 Censuses respectively, in the several Provinces specified and over the combined area, with corresponding values for England.

FEMALE LIVES.

Age.	Bengal 1881.	Bengal 1891.	Bengal 1901.	Bengal 1911.	Bengal 1921. Hindus.	Bengal 1921. Mahomedans.	Bengal 1931.	Bihar and Orissa. 1931.	Bombay. 1881.	Bombay. 1891.	Bombay. 1901.	Bombay. 1911.	Bombay. 1921. Hindus.	Bombay. 1921. Mahomedans.	Bombay. 1931.	Burma 1901.	Burma 1911.	Burma 1921.	Burma 1931.	C. P. and Hyderabad. 1881.	C. P. and Hyderabad. 1931.	Madras. 1881.	Madras. 1891.	Madras. 1901.	Madras. 1911.	Madras. 1921.	Madras. 1931.
0	24·12	25·36	26·05	29·76	..	..	23·36	23·23	20·29	23·19	25·85	29·58	..	..	23·45	19·06	22·07	..	20·30	24·29	22·76	24·60	23·19	23·60	25·70	..	21·46
5	2·08	2·80	3·15	2·90	2·81	3·43	1·93	1·42	2·22	2·53	2·85	2·48	3·38	3·35	2·06	1·89	1·42	2·00	1·23	2·22	1·24	2·50	2·53	2·45	2·34	2·04	1·12
10	1·06	1·39	1·71	1·44	1·55	1·93	1·07	·60	1·16	1·25	1·39	·96	1·88	1·84	1·08	·85	·53	1·08	·52	1·16	·63	1·27	1·25	1·21	1·34	1·25	·50
15	1·70	1·67	1·84	1·59	1·61	2·09	1·42	1·15	1·81	1·45	1·61	·94	1·45	1·30	1·30	1·17	·66	1·09	·99	1·81	1·20	1·92	1·44	1·32	1·24	1·27	·94
20	2·05	2·01	2·11	1·92	1·78	2·31	2·01	1·84	2·22	1·59	1·62	1·56	1·69	1·60	1·71	1·66	1·12	1·16	1·59	2·24	1·83	2·35	1·59	1·44	1·25	1·40	1·49
25	2·13	2·25	2·50	2·11	1·94	2·49	2·52	2·26	2·40	1·68	1·72	2·18	2·04	2·00	2·02	1·97	1·58	1·57	1·96	2·42	2·24	2·47	1·68	1·58	1·37	1·59	1·85
30	2·19	2·50	2·74	2·36	2·29	2·83	3·00	2·51	2·55	1·80	1·93	2·68	2·45	2·42	2·28	2·11	1·93	1·82	2·18	2·59	2·53	2·57	1·77	1·73	1·64	1·92	2·17
35	2·26	2·75	2·75	2·70	2·74	3·26	3·45	2·72	2·69	2·00	2·39	3·09	3·00	2·99	2·56	2·10	2·02	1·94	2·35	2·78	2·77	2·65	1·93	2·05	2·05	2·32	2·51
40	2·40	3·01	2·72	3·16	3·31	3·79	3·88	3·02	2·82	2·31	2·99	3·48	3·60	3·59	2·92	1·96	2·09	2·06	2·56	2·97	3·02	2·75	2·11	2·57	2·60	2·85	2·94
45	2·61	3·28	2·89	3·65	3·85	4·30	4·25	3·53	3·04	2·69	3·63	3·93	4·17	4·11	3·31	1·94	2·31	2·44	2·78	3·21	3·23	2·85	2·29	3·23	3·01	3·25	3·38
50	2·96	3·65	3·28	4·20	4·42	4·81	4·60	4·23	3·46	3·27	4·29	4·50	4·77	4·73	3·82	2·20	2·66	2·95	3·07	3·62	3·47	3·10	2·55	3·88	3·48	3·71	3·88
55	3·65	4·18	3·98	4·92	5·02	5·32	4·94	5·14	4·35	4·11	5·24	5·23	5·33	4·97	4·48	2·59	3·12	3·51	3·50	4·55	3·84	3·74	3·04	4·48	4·03	4·25	4·47
60	5·11	5·27	5·12	6·09	5·76	5·97	5·46	6·32	5·95	5·45	6·40	6·21	6·33	5·78	5·47	3·25	4·36	4·28	4·27	6·21	4·45	5·07	4·08	5·16	4·75	4·97	5·30
65	7·48	7·00	7·18	8·11	6·87	6·98	6·49	8·03	8·56	7·42	8·36	7·66	6·83	6·56	7·02	4·44	6·41	5·45	5·72	8·96	5·70	7·24	5·75	6·52	5·81	6·12	6·68
70	11·21	9·58	10·66	11·63	..	..	8·57	10·58	12·65	10·29	11·79	9·80	..	..	9·54	6·87	9·20	..	8·40	13·19	8·05	10·66	8·24	9·26	7·53	..	8·99
75	16·84	13·44	16·13	17·71	..	..	12·65	14·77	18·76	14·41	17·07	13·29	..	..	13·88	10·89	13·41	..	12·98	19·54	12·43	16·11	11·96	13·78	10·47	..	13·24
80	24·74	19·19	24·29	28·21	..	..	20·93	20·98	27·54	20·60	24·88	19·60	..	..	21·54	17·18	19·62	..	20·22	28·79	22·59	24·33	17·57	20·47	16·19	..	21·02
85	36·00	27·78	35·71	44·74	..	..	34·95	30·65	43·85	29·80	35·80	31·08	..	..	35·02	26·45	28·49	..	30·05	43·66	38·80	35·02	25·92	29·39	27·08	..	32·84
90	57·14	40·60	50·34	65·69	..	..	57·14	47·03	100·00	43·28	49·90	48·67	..	..	58·14	39·11	40·43	..	42·49	100·00	55·01	60·00	38·38	40·29	45·64	..	48·78

TABLE XXX—(*contd.*)

Comparative Rates of Mortality ($100q_x$) *at quinquennial ages, as deduced from the results of the 1881, 1891, 1901, 1911, 1921 and 1931 Censuses respectively, in the several Provinces specified and over the combined area, with corresponding values for England.*

FEMALE LIVES.

Age.	Punjab.				Rajputana and Ajmer Merwara.	Sind & N.-W. F. Provinces.	United Provinces.							All India.						England.	
	1881.	1891.	1921.	1931.	1931.	1931.	1881.	1891.	1901.	1911.	1921. Hindus.	1921. Mahomedans.	1931.	1881.	1891.	1901.	1911.	1921.	1931.	1911.	1921.
0	24·12	23·19	..	23·65	24·26	25·66	24·29	23·19	27·28	29·75	..	..	25·38	24·26	23·99	25·88	28·46	..	23·23	9·77	6·94
5	2·08	2·53	3·17	2·02	1·81	1·65	2·22	2·53	2·92	2·79	2·49	2·57	2·14	2·20	2·63	2·91	2·62	2·78	1·65	·48	·42
10	1·06	1·25	1·80	1·04	·82	1·24	1·16	1·27	1·35	1·28	1·25	1·40	·98	1·14	1·31	1·49	1·29	1·55	·81	·20	·18
15	1·60	1·43	1·90	1·29	1·13	1·50	1·75	1·60	1·18	1·29	1·55	1·56	1·23	1·75	1·56	1·48	1·34	1·57	1·15	·24	·23
20	1·94	1·53	2·05	1·75	1·66	1·88	2·16	1·94	1·37	1·89	1·81	1·81	1·76	2·14	1·81	1·72	1·70	1·73	1·76	·29	·31
25	2·12	1·67	2·19	2·13	2·09	2·30	2·38	2·21	1·76	2·41	2·03	2·02	2·20	2·27	2·01	2·00	2·00	1·92	2·16	·34	·35
30	2·25	1·83	2·53	2·44	2·51	3·00	2·53	2·46	2·07	2·80	2·38	2·36	2·56	2·37	2·21	2·24	2·31	2·24	2·51	·41	·39
35	2·35	2·07	2·89	2·70	2·94	3·88	2·65	2·75	2·44	3·11	2·84	2·76	2·86	2·47	2·46	2·46	2·66	2·72	2·93	·52	·45
40	2·45	2·36	3·40	2·91	3·43	4·59	2·79	3·04	2·87	3·49	3·38	3·27	3·17	2·59	2·71	2·77	3·08	3·26	3·45	·66	·53
45	2·59	2·66	3·88	3·01	3·95	5·22	3·05	3·32	3·39	3·94	3·91	3·82	3·45	2·79	2·99	3·21	3·53	3·81	3·90	·85	·67
50	2·83	3·04	4·36	3·32	4·53	5·74	3·53	3·71	4·05	4·50	4·68	4·44	3·78	3·15	3·37	3·76	4·06	4·40	4·31	1·14	·92
55	3·37	3·57	4·88	3·84	5·27	6·19	4·51	4·33	4·87	5·27	5·51	5·17	4·21	3·89	3·97	4·49	4·74	5·01	4·75	1·61	1·32
60	4·58	4·35	5·53	4·67	6·26	6·95	6·23	5·47	6·12	6·34	6·56	6·14	4·96	5·35	5·05	5·59	5·78	5·77	5·43	2·31	1·90
65	6·53	5·61	6·58	6·00	7·75	8·38	9·08	7·29	8·15	7·86	8·12	7·70	6·31	7·73	6·77	7·50	7·44	6·99	6·66	3·34	2·99
70	9·56	7·57	..	82·47	10·33	11·67	13·47	10·00	11·40	10·02	..	..	8·75	11·42	9·32	10·67	10·12	..	8·88	5·26	4·65
75	14·30	10·50	..	12·38	14·63	18·85	19·98	14·07	16·44	13·36	..	..	13·90	17·02	13·13	15·79	14·60	..	13·01	8·08	7·59
80	21·00	14·87	..	19·48	22·35	32·03	29·43	20·16	23·94	19·41	..	..	22·24	24·93	18·83	23·24	22·49	..	20·66	12·42	11·77
85	31·13	21·37	..	32·75	35·85	53·13	41·67	29·30	34·49	32·95	..	..	33·77	36·84	27·36	33·26	36·28	..	34·76	17·34	17·47
90	48·84	31·16	..	51·82	56·14	..	100·00	42·93	48·22	58·60	..	..	48·50	63·63	40·06	45·23	59·07	..	56·67	23·83	23·85

M22CC

TABLE XXXI.

Comparative Expectations of Life at decennial ages, as deduced from the results of the 1881, 1891, 1901, 1911 and 1931 Censuses respectively, in the several Provinces specified and over the combined area, with corresponding values for England.

MALE LIVES.

Age.	Bengal.					Bihar and Orissa.	Bombay.					Burma.			C. P. and Hyderabad.	
	1881	1891.	1901.	1911.	1931.	1931.	1881.	1891.	1901.	1911.	1931.	1901.	1911.	1931.	1881.	1931.
0	24·50	22·78	21·57	21·47	24·91	28·88	23·04	26·12	22·77	22·52	27·84	30·29	31·48	30·61	22·83	28·10
10	35·04	33·85	32·95	32·54	33·68	37·59	32·87	37·20	34·62	33·33	36·72	39·39	39·88	39·55	32·46	37·29
20	29·56	27·77	27·50	27·10	27·08	29·97	27·38	30·87	28·39	26·43	29·61	33·28	32·82	32·49	26·92	30·22
30	24·62	22·51	22·64	22·15	21·39	23·55	22·71	24·67	22·27	21·32	23·70	27·68	27·30	26·28	22·20	24·42
40	19·43	17·98	18·28	17·56	17·11	17·93	18·01	18·54	16·90	17·23	18·43	22·58	22·04	20·90	17·55	19·42
50	14·25	13·83	13·93	13·39	13·62	13·36	13·17	13·88	12·48	13·51	13·73	17·45	16·51	16·04	12·85	15·18
60	9·42	9·89	9·52	9·27	10·16	9·39	8·66	9·56	8·73	9·94	9·55	12·18	11·00	11·04	8·43	10·57
70	5·49	6·35	5·61	5·40	6·38	5·96	5·01	6·05	5·38	6·55	5·89	7·37	6·66	6·52	4·85	5·77
80	2·86	3·59	2·86	2·49	2·92	3·08	2·51	3·39	2·81	3·48	2·95	3·84	3·61	3·28	2·42	2·67
90	1·00	1·69	1·07	·95	1·00	1·20	·50	1·65	1·07	1·41	1·00	1·75	1·77	1·62	·50	1·22

Age.	Madras.					Punjab.					Rajputana & Ajmer-Merwara.	Sind & North-West Frontier Provinces.	United Provinces.				
	1881	1891.	1901.	1911.	1931.	1881.	1891.	1901.	1911.	1931	1931.	1931.	1881.	1891.	1901.	1911.	1931.
0	22·35	26·92	26·21	25·92	28·71	24·80	26·58	23·18	21·23	28·05	23·60	25·43	23·10	24·45	25·30	21·21	24·56
10	32·92	38·70	36·93	37·78	37·61	35·57	38·07	35·45	31·38	38·07	33·60	34·47	32·97	34·10	35·26	31·44	35·45
20	27·86	32·55	30·43	31·60	30·60	29·92	31·76	29·59	26·12	31·22	27·41	27·79	27·38	27·75	28·43	25·27	29·06
30	23·59	26·57	24·24	25·35	24·36	24·96	25·60	24·54	21·60	25·45	21·45	21·77	22·63	22·35	22·01	20·89	23·11
40	19·06	21·06	18·60	20·06	19·17	20·05	20·22	19·99	17·55	20·13	16·95	17·10	17·46	17·74	16·76	17·18	17·96
50	14·28	15·91	14·05	15·74	14·79	15·07	15·56	15·43	14·15	15·09	13·10	13·43	12·91	13·56	12·64	13·47	13·61
60	9·60	11·06	10·10	11·70	10·56	10·25	11·41	10·70	10·63	10·22	9·35	9·74	8·36	9·63	8·92	9·84	9·64
70	5·66	6·94	6·27	7·68	6·45	6·19	7·60	6·39	6·53	5·98	5·80	5·57	4·78	6·15	5·50	6·50	5·98
80	2·92	3·85	3·35	3·98	3·13	3·32	4·48	3·28	3·11	2·91	2·92	2·73	2·41	3·43	2·96	3·42	2·98
90	1·00	1·82	1·56	1·50	1·13	1·20	2·26	1·38	1·13	1·19	1·00	1·07	·50	1·60	1·23	1·11	·71

Age.	All India.					England.		
	1881.	1891.	1901.	1911.	1931.	1901.	1911.	1921.
0 ..	23·67	24·59	23·63	22·59	26·91	44·07	46·04	55·62
10 ..	34·00	35·46	34·73	33·36	36·38	49·65	52·35	44·64
20 ..	28·55	29·24	28·59	27·46	29·57	41·04	43·67	45·78
30 ..	23·80	23·66	22·90	22·45	23·60	33·06	35·29	37·40
40 ..	18·90	18·75	17·91	18·01	18·60	25·65	27·27	29·19
50 ..	13·93	14·28	13·59	13·97	14·31	18·89	19·85	21·36
60 ..	9·25	10·12	9·53	10·00	10·25	12·90	13·83	14·36
70 ..	5·44	6·48	5·80	6·19	6·35	8·02	8·25	8·75
80 ..	2·87	3·65	3·07	3·06	3·13	4·40	4·64	4·93
90 ..	1·00	1·69	1·23	1·15	1·12	2·32	2·37	2·82

TABLE XXXII.

Comparative Expectations of Life at decennial ages, as deduced from the results of the 1881, 1891, 1901, 1911 and 1931 Censuses respectively, in the several Provinces specified and over the combined area, with corresponding values for England.

FEMALE LIVES.

Age.	Bengal.					Bihar & Orissa.	Bombay.					Burma.			Central Provinces and Hyderabad.	
	1881.	1891.	1901.	1911.	1931.	1931.	1881.	1891.	1901.	1911.	1931.	1901.	1911.	1931.	1881.	1931.
0	26·51	23·73	22·51	21·58	24·80	26·90	24·89	27·07	24·05	22·86	26·37	32·21	32·61	31·00	24·65	28·21
10	34·48	32·76	32·03	32·44	31·31	33·78	32·26	36·15	33·69	33·50	34·41	38·92	40·22	37·23	31·84	34·79
20	29·47	27·76	27·55	27·20	25·27	27·07	27·20	30·92	28·52	26·54	28·48	32·98	32·67	30·40	26·72	28·33
30	25·34	23·52	23·86	22·45	20·98	22·54	23·27	25·69	22·98	21·57	23·66	28·96	27·21	25·76	22·69	24·08
40	20·60	19·43	19·99	17·91	17·61	18·11	19·00	20·31	17·78	17·60	19·15	24·62	22·24	21·33	18·50	20·24
50	15·33	15·16	15·14	13·67	14·51	13·72	14·10	15·07	13·37	13·81	14·79	19·00	16·75	16·64	13·75	16·19
60	9·97	10·65	10·18	9·40	10·95	9·75	9·15	10·24	9·30	10·13	10·48	13·16	11·15	11·63	8·90	11·60
70	5·69	6·68	5·87	5·43	6·85	6·21	5·19	6·33	5·58	6·62	6·46	7·77	6·72	6·89	5·03	6·88
80	2·90	3·70	2·95	2·48	3·22	3·40	2·55	3·47	2·92	3·49	3·17	3·96	3·63	3·49	2·46	2·95
90	1·07	1·59	1·31	·95	1·10	1·53	·50	1·59	1·20	1·42	1·11	1·83	1·77	1·68	·50	1·25

Age.	Madras.					Punjab.			Rajputana and Ajmer-Merwara.	Sind and North-West Frontier Provinces.	United Provinces.				
	1881.	1891.	1901.	1911.	1931.	1881.	1891.	1931.	1931.	1931.	1881.	1891.	1901.	1911.	1931.
0	24·18	27·99	27·13	27·65	30·04	26·85	27·62	26·57	25·96	23·28	24·94	25·25	23·93	21·50	25·09
10	32·39	37·78	36·27	37·62	36·17	35·05	37·13	34·80	33·45	29·87	32·35	32·97	34·90	31·94	33·97
20	27·77	32·78	30·65	32·02	29·05	29·88	31·97	28·88	26·78	23·81	27·18	27·71	28·89	25·88	27·75
30	24·24	27·90	25·06	26·01	23·83	25·77	26·87	24·44	21·74	18·65	23·13	23·31	23·33	21·42	23·24
40	20·20	22·78	19·56	20·73	19·22	21·35	21·89	20·49	17·47	15·07	18·73	19·15	18·38	17·51	19·32
50	15·37	17·41	15·03	16·28	14·99	16·28	17·08	16·14	13·62	12·25	13·75	14·85	13·82	13·69	15·37
60	10·17	11·89	10·86	12·00	10·81	10·90	12·33	11·48	9·87	9·05	8·81	10·36	9·52	9·99	11·00
70	5·88	7·28	6·60	7·79	6·69	6·43	8·01	7·03	6·19	5·24	4·94	6·45	5·74	6·56	6·5
80	2·96	3·97	3·51	4·00	3·29	3·37	4·63	3·43	3·09	2·16	2·38	3·54	3·02	3·43	3·1
90	·93	1·85	1·77	1·50	1·34	1·30	2·30	1·31	1·15	..	·50	1·65	1·50	1·06	1·41

Age.	All India.					England.		
	1881.	1891.	1901.	1911.	1931.	1901.	1911.	1921.
0	25·58	25·54	23·96	23·31	26·56	47·70	50·02	59·58
10	33·42	34·40	33·86	33·74	33·61	51·98	55·02	57·53
20	28·44	29·28	28·64	27·96	27·08	43·45	46·36	48·73
30	24·48	24·69	23·82	22·99	22·30	35·43	37·84	40·26
40	20·03	20·20	19·12	18·49	18·23	27·81	29·65	31·86
50	14·96	15·59	14·50	14·28	14·65	20·63	21·87	23·69
60	9·79	10·87	10·02	10·11	10·81	14·08	14·81	16·22
70	5·63	6·80	5·98	6·22	6·74	8·74	9·13	9·95
80	2·88	3·76	3·12	3·06	3·25	4·84	5·10	5·56
90	·91	1·75	1·64	1·10	1·18	2·68	2·55	3·13

TABLE XXXIII.

Foreign Countries—Males—Annual rate of Mortality per thousand.

Taken from the published Life Tables of various countries, based on their official population and Death Statistics and exhibited here in tabular form so that a comparison may be made at each age.

Age.	Australia. 1901–1910.	Denmark. 1906–1910.	England. 1901–1910.	France. 1898–1903.	Germany. 1901–1910.	Holland. 1900–1909.	India. 1901–1910.	Italy. 1901–1910.	Japan. 1898–1903.	Norway. 1901–1910.	Sweden. 1901–1910.	Switzerland. 1901–1910.	United States. 1901–1910.
(1)	(2)	(3)	(4)	(5)	(6)	(7)	(8)	(9)	(10)	(11)	(12)	(13)	(14)
Males.													
0	95·10	120·67	144·34	163·26	202·34	140·46	289·98	167·71	156·86	81·45	92·55	138·40	127·38
5	2·81	2·85	5·42	6·35	5·28	4·96	27·50	7·68	7·87	4·38	5·02	4·13	5·24
10	1·79	1·81	1·82	3·03	2·44	2·26	12·50	2·26	3·31	2·98	3·22	2·25	2·61
15	2·55	2·48	2·61	3·75	2·77	2·60	13·20	4·12	4·75	4·08	3·22	2·70	3·19
20	3·70	3·86	3·78	6·99	5·04	5·07	16·90	6·19	8·30	9·07	6·41	5·16	5·46
25	4·48	4·04	4·54	7·52	5·13	4·92	20·30	6·85	8·38	8·78	6·28	5·56	6·22
30	5·19	4·47	5·66	7·86	5·56	4·75	23·50	6·67	7·87	7·57	6·04	6·20	7·31
35	6·33	5·28	7·32	9·42	6·97	5·37	27·80	7·06	8·69	7·35	6·37	7·54	9·14
40	8·16	6·89	9·31	11·04	9·22	6·79	32·30	8·48	10·40	7·78	7·57	9·83	10·40
45	10·83	9·38	12·23	13·63	12·44	8·98	37·20	10·31	13·28	8·92	9·25	13·08	13·10
50	13·95	11·87	16·57	17·01	16·93	11·77	42·80	13·45	17·75	11·11	11·24	17·88	15·28
55	18·16	17·07	23·08	21·53	23·57	16·86	49·90	17·73	24·48	14·16	15·26	24·85	21·38
60	25·84	23·89	32·62	30·84	32·60	24·29	59·80	26·62	35·06	19·14	20·66	35·43	29·90
65	38·59	34·03	45·57	44·30	47·06	37·20	75·50	39·83	51·21	28·80	30·04	50·42	42·92
70	61·62	53·63	67·08	68·32	69·36	57·43	101·70	64·49	74·45	42·76	46·40	73·93	59·90
75	96·10	80·79	100·62	108·70	106·40	89·21	148·00	102·62	107·50	66·91	74·60	108·89	90·15
80	137·95	131·97	141·63	167·80	157·87	137·00	228·70	169·78	155·80	106·34	120·81	166·92	133·66
85	197·01	191·64	203·15	230·50	231·60	204·00	366·30	251·60	225·80	164·09	192·27	232·16	195·04
90	277·36	290·48	295·66	276·80	320·02	290·00	545·50	358·74	327·20	235·78	286·99	317·20	261·48
95	381·11	..	369·66	341·50	413·99	600·00	..	517·41	474·00	329·32	398·02	425·31	339·81
100	525·36	..	449·69	460·00	496·68	..	..	..	686·90	458·00	495·00	675·97	436·52

TABLE XXXIV.

Foreign Countries—Females—Annual rate of Mortality per thousand.

Taken from the published Life Tables of various countries based on their official population and Death Statistics and exhibited here in tabular form so that a comparison may be made at each age.

Age.	Australia. 1901–1910.	Denmark. 1906–1910.	England. 1901–1910.	France. 1898–1903.	Germany. 1901–1910.	Holland. 1900–1909.	India. 1901–1910.	Italy. 1901–1910.	Japan. 1898–1903.	Norway. 1901–1910.	Sweden. 1901–1910.	Switzerland. 1901–1910.	United States. 1901–1910.
(1)	(2)	(3)	(4)	(5)	(6)	(7)	(8)	(9)	(10)	(11)	(12)	(13)	(14)
Females.													
0	97·53	97·71	117·43	136·49	170·48	117·69	284·60	152·11	140·92	66·79	75·98	112·58	105·51
5	2·58	2·57	5·53	6·49	5·31	4·63	26·20	8·50	8·10	4·28	5·16	4·06	5·00
10	1·59	2·08	1·99	3·28	2·56	2·28	12·90	2·90	3·77	3·19	3·25	2·26	2·36
15	2·19	2·91	2·58	4·47	3·02	3·21	13·40	4·89	6·38	4·58	4·19	3·81	3·09
20	3·29	3·78	3·25	6·27	4·22	3·84	17·00	6·48	9·64	6·13	5·26	5·40	4·90
25	4·30	4·44	3·86	7·35	5·37	4·48	20·00	7·33	9·92	6·66	5·96	6·18	5·91
30	5·19	4·87	4·84	7·59	5·97	5·17	23·10	7·58	9·98	6·93	6·12	6·63	6·87
35	6·17	5·50	6·17	8·20	6·86	5·97	26·60	7·89	10·67	7·43	6·50	7·22	7·77
40	7·18	6·23	7·66	8·79	7·71	7·10	30·80	8·54	11·38	7·73	7·00	8·22	8·54
45	8·07	7·34	9·70	10·03	8·54	7·64	35·30	8·80	11·49	8·06	7·68	9·07	10·27
50	9·56	8·97	12·67	12·44	11·26	10·09	40·60	10·66	13·80	9·46	9·11	12·34	12·78
55	12·77	11·87	17·98	16·32	16·19	13·37	47·40	14·44	18·52	11·94	11·96	17·53	18·08
60	19·20	17·44	25·39	24·36	24·73	20·75	57·80	23·26	26·50	16·11	16·60	27·01	25·53
65	29·98	28·20	35·34	36·64	39·60	32·36	74·40	37·54	39·87	24·12	24·92	43·27	37·33
70	47·77	46·18	56·43	58·50	62·06	51·74	101·20	64·07	60·72	37·13	40·32	67·14	54·72
75	77·79	72·06	86·43	94·54	98·31	81·62	146·00	103·74	92·00	60·72	67·02	104·03	81·13
80	113·33	119·06	124·29	146·70	146·50	127·80	224·90	168·42	137·20	96·29	109·48	154·71	122·14
85	164·59	170·35	182·03	206·70	217·39	188·30	362·80	247·27	204·50	150·31	173·55	220·16	178·61
90	242·21	257·06	257·81	240·60	295·66	270·00	590·70	356·92	304·80	218·48	252·73	309·20	246·87
95	341·45	..	330·96	275·70	368·57	560·00	..	521·98	454·40	311·60	360·75	402·96	324·90
100	500·73	..	405·44	329·00	420·77	1000·00	..	..	677·30	396·00	440·00	590·07	393·81

TABLE XXXV.

Foreign Countries—Males—Number of survivors out of 100,000 born alive.

Taken from the published Life Tables of various countries based on their official population and Death Statistics and exhibited here in tabular form so that a comparison may be made at each age.

Age.	Australia. 1901-1910.	Denmark. 1906-1910.	England. 1901-1910.	France. 1898-1903.	Germany. 1901-1910.	Holland. 1900-1909.	India. 1901-1910.	Italy. 1901-1910.	Japan. 1898-1903.	Norway. 1901-1910.	Sweden. 1901-1910.	Switzerland. 1901-1910.	United States. 1901-1910.
(1) *Males.*	(2)	(3)	(4)	(5)	(6)	(7)	(8)	(9)	(10)	(11)	(12)	(13)	(14)
0	100,000	100,000	100,000	100,000	100,000	100,000	100,000	100,000	100,000	100,000	100,000	100,000	100,000
5	87,585	85,229	79,398	77,692	74,211	80,243	55,308	72,816	76,887	88,366	86,491	82,469	82,195
10	86,622	84,240	78,083	75,944	72,827	78,850	50,212	71,325	74,891	86,769	84,762	81,201	80,605
15	85,789	83,461	77,297	74,818	72,007	78,010	47,213	70,264	73,602	85,475	83,533	80,335	79,544
20	84,493	82,205	76,113	72,948	70,647	76,612	43,833	68,579	71,310	82,817	81,638	78,797	77,957
25	82,802	80,523	74,546	70,230	68,881	74,684	39,973	66,303	68,304	79,068	79,037	76,718	75,679
30	80,844	78,862	72,741	67,653	67,092	72,907	35,831	64,108	65,596	75,866	76,619	74,506	73,222
35	78,607	76,988	70,472	64,839	65,104	71,155	31,533	61,962	62,976	73,104	74,331	72,060	70,342
40	75,887	74,773	67,668	61,641	62,598	69,090	27,136	59,669	60,101	70,408	71,897	69,100	66,996
45	72,479	71,879	64,230	58,033	59,405	66,532	22,803	56,962	56,743	67,579	69,050	65,364	63,304
50	68,221	68,284	59,903	53,818	55,340	63,265	18,658	53,799	52,629	64,356	65,702	60,692	58,963
55	63,107	63,730	54,435	49,004	50,186	59,107	14,787	49,838	47,523	60,507	61,601	54,703	54,075
60	56,782	57,639	47,564	43,199	43,807	53,551	11,229	44,902	41,160	55,862	56,548	47,298	47,701
65	48,670	50,114	39,278	35,998	36,079	46,287	8,002	38,198	33,384	49,827	50,040	38,402	39,996
70	38,275	40,684	29,898	27,465	27,136	36,866	5,134	29,835	24,519	41,911	41,680	28,306	31,050
75	25,962	29,370	19,754	17,815	17,586	25,800	2,736	19,762	15,570	32,206	31,227	18,014	21,547
80	14,330	17,333	10,608	8,774	8,987	14,681	1,032	10,079	7,964	21,083	19,350	8,928	12,295
85	5,995	7,373	4,349	3,037	3,212	6,085	202	3,245	2,918	10,610	8,732	3,068	5,214
90	1,652	1,968	1,117	728	683	1,636	11	580	631	3,656	2,380	645	1,492
95	244	..	149	122	74	111	..	38	57	747	332	75	266
100	15	..	13	11	4	..	..	..	1	72	20	2	25

TABLE XXXVI.

Foreign Countries—Females—Number of survivors out of 100,000 born alive.

Taken from the published Life Tables of various countries based on their official population and Death Statistics and exhibited here in tabular form so that a comparison may be made at each age.

Age.	Australia. 1901-1910.	Denmark. 1906-1910.	England. 1901-1910.	France. 1898-1903.	Germany. 1901-1910.	Holland. 1900-1909.	India. 1901-1910.	Italy. 1901-1910.	Japan. 1898-1903.	Norway. 1901-1910.	Sweden. 1901-1910.	Switzerland. 1901-1910.	United States 1901-1910.
(1) *Females.*	(2)	(3)	(4)	(5)	(6)	(7)	(8)	(9)	(10)	(11)	(12)	(13)	(14)
0	100,000	100,000	100,000	100,000	100,000	100,000	100,000	100,000	100,000	100,000	100,000	100,000	100,000
5	89,285	87,558	82,178	80,496	77,334	82,690	56,608	73,935	78,339	89,922	88,285	85,054	84,668
10	88,395	86,566	80,756	78,616	75,845	81,314	51,450	72,136	76,245	88,308	86,509	83,760	83,143
15	87,619	85,596	79,898	77,248	74,887	80,341	48,304	70,830	74,568	86,726	85,049	82,686	82,129
20	86,459	84,180	78,756	75,246	73,564	78,937	44,828	68,891	71,652	84,459	83,053	80,778	30,581
25	84,875	82,500	77,391	72,732	71,849	77,326	40,901	66,545	68,186	81,788	80,771	78,489	78,437
30	82,909	80,598	75,779	70,068	69,848	75,501	36,745	64,103	64,874	79,064	78,382	76,025	76,009
35	80,618	78,565	73,769	67,377	67,679	73,433	32,471	61,679	61,632	76,279	76,007	73,456	73,295
40	78,001	76,341	71,308	64,583	65,283	71,109	28,139	59,215	58,308	73,449	73,496	70,706	70,383
45	75,103	73,818	68,359	61,661	62,717	68,556	23,839	56,673	55,065	70,607	70,878	67,766	67,235
50	71,945	70,990	64,742	58,385	59,812	65,733	19,714	54,097	51,794	67,660	68,005	64,362	63,539
55	68,199	67,428	60,179	54,452	55,984	62,092	15,813	50,894	47,898	64,224	64,639	59,931	59,053
60	63,247	62,958	54,157	49,441	50,780	57,299	12,165	46,638	42,998	60,032	60,387	53,897	53,104
65	56,256	56,545	46,716	42,694	43,540	50,471	8,747	40,310	36,668	54,552	54,733	45,607	45,654
70	46,793	47,405	37,646	34,053	34,078	41,243	5,637	31,742	28,745	47,135	46,943	34,922	36,512
75	34,479	35,651	26,418	23,454	23.006	29,770	3,022	20,997	19,745	37,350	36,453	22,944	26,163
80	21,356	22,300	15,545	12,789	12,348	17,659	1,159	10,667	11,106	25,413	23,715	11,903	15,831
85	10,527	10,437	7,094	5,037	4,752	7,818	231	3,499	4,585	13,698	11,564	4,396	7,265
90	3,566	3,309	2,158	1,452	1,131	2,317	12	642	1,148	5,195	3,654	1,023	2,307
95	687	—	393	334	157	245	..	42	122	1,181	653	129	450
100	56	—	43	59	13	...	..	..	3	144	55	5	51

TABLE XXXVII.

Foreign Countries—Males—Complete expectation of life in years.

Taken from the published Life Tables of various countries based on their official population and Death Statistics and exhibited here in tabular form so that a comparison may be made at each age.

Age.	Australia. 1901—1910.	Denmark. 1906—1910.	England. 1901—1910.	France. 1898—1903.	Germany. 1901—1910.	Holland. 1900—1909.	India. 1901—1910.	Italy. 1901—1910.	Japan. 1898—1903.	Norway. 1901—1910.	Sweden. 1901—1910.	Switzerland. 1901—1910.	United States. 1901—1910.
(1)	(2)	(3)	(4)	(5)	(6)	(7)	(8)	(9)	(10)	(11)	(12)	(13)	(14)
Males.													
0	55·20	54·9	48·53	45·74	44·82	51·0	22·59	44·24	43·97	54·84	54·53	49·25	49·32
5	57·91	59·4	55·90	53·57	55·15	58·3	35·01	55·32	51·90	56·92	57·90	54·52	54·82
10	53·53	55·1	51·81	49·75	51·16	54·3	33·36	51·44	48·23	52·92	54·03	50·34	50·86
15	49·03	50·5	47·31	45·45	46·71	49·8	30·32	47·17	44·02	48·69	49·79	45·86	46·50
20	44·74	46·3	43·01	41·53	42·56	45·7	27·46	43·27	40·35	45·16	45·88	41·70	42·39
25	40·60	42·2	38·86	39·03	38·59	41·8	24·86	39·66	37·02	42·18	42·31	37·76	38·59
30	36·52	38·0	34·76	34·35	34·55	37·8	22·44	35·94	33·44	38·86	38·57	33·80	34·80
35	32·49	33·9	30·79	30·71	30·53	33·6	20·16	32·09	29·73	35·24	34·68	29·87	31·12
40	28·56	29·7	26·96	27·15	26·64	29·5	18·02	28·23	26·03	31·49	30·77	26·03	27·55
45	24·78	25·9	23·27	23·64	22·94	25·6	15·97	24·45	22·42	27·70	26·93	22·37	24·01
50	21·16	22·1	19·76	20·26	19·43	21·8	13·97	20·73	18·97	23·96	23·17	18·90	20·59
55	17·67	18·5	16·48	16·95	16·16	18·1	11·99	17·18	15·73	20·32	19·54	15·68	17·21
60	14·35	15·2	13·49	13·81	13·14	14·7	10·00	13·78	12·76	16·79	16·06	12·73	14·17
65	11·31	12·1	10·80	10·96	10·40	11·6	8·04	10·74	10·14	13·51	12·81	10·09	11·40
70	8·67	9·3	8·39	8·42	7·99	8·9	6·17	8·02	7·89	10·57	9·85	7·78	8·96
75	6·58	6·9	6·41	6·34	5·97	6·7	4·47	5·82	6·00	7·98	7·29	5·81	6·79
80	4·96	5·1	4·86	4·87	4·38	4·9	3·04	4·06	4·44	5·86	5·22	4·27	5·07
85	3·65	3·7	3·53	3·91	3·18	3·5	1·94	2·90	3·19	4·26	3·66	3·18	3·79
90	2·64	2·6	2·56	3·29	2·35	2·2	1·23	2·01	2·22	3·11	2·60	2·38	2·90
95	1·88	..	2·07	2·66	1·80	1·0	..	1·29	1·48	2·24	1·89	1·63	2·21
100	1·18	..	1·53	1·93	1·50	..	..	..	·50	1·50	1·45	1·00	1·66

TABLE XXXVIII.

Foreign Countries—Females—Complete expectation of life in years.

Taken from the published Life Tables of various countries based on their official population and Death Statistics and exhibited here in tabular form so that a comparison may be made at each age.

Age.	Australia. 1901—1910.	Denmark. 1906—1910.	England. 1901—1910.	France. 1898—1903.	Germany. 1901—1910.	Holland. 1900—1909.	India. 1901—1910.	Italy. 1901—1910.	Japan. 1898—1903.	Norway. 1901—1910.	Sweden. 1901—1910.	Switzerland. 1901—1919.	United States. 1901—1910.
(1)	(2)	(3)	(4)	(5)	(6)	(7)	(8)	(9)	(10)	(11)	(12)	(13)	(14)
Females.													
0	58·84	57·9	52·38	49·13	48·33	53·4	23·31	44·83	44·85	57·72	56·98	52·15	52·54
5	60·80	61·1	58·53	55·75	57·27	59·4	35·40	55·20	51·97	59·06	59·40	56·15	56·89
10	56·39	56·7	54·53	52·03	53·35	55·4	33·74	51·53	48·34	55·09	55·58	51·98	52·89
15	51·86	52·4	50·08	47·90	49·00	51·0	30·78	47·43	44·36	51·05	51·48	47·62	48·51
20	47·52	48·2	45·77	44·02	44·84	46·9	27·96	43·69	41·06	47·35	47·66	43·69	44·39
25	43·36	44·1	41·54	40·51	40·84	42·8	25·40	40·14	38·02	43·81	43·93	39·89	40·53
30	39·33	40·1	37·36	36·93	36·94	38·8	22·99	36·58	34·84	40·24	40·20	36·10	36·75
35	35·37	36·1	33·31	33·29	33·04	34·8	20·69	32·92	31·54	36·61	36·38	32·27	33·01
40	31·47	32·0	29·37	29·60	29·16	30·8	18·49	29·18	28·19	32·93	32·53	28·43	29·28
45	27·59	28·1	25·53	25·86	25·25	26·9	16·38	25·38	24·71	29·15	28·64	24·55	25·53
50	23·69	24·1	21·81	22·14	21·35	22·9	14·28	21·47	21·11	25·31	24·74	20·71	21·86
55	19·85	20·2	18·27	18·52	17·64	19·1	12·20	17·65	17·61	21·53	20·90	17·05	18·32
60	16·20	16·5	15·01	15·08	14·17	15·5	10·11	14·02	14·32	17·85	17·19	13·67	15·09
65	12·88	13·0	11·99	11·97	11·09	12·3	8·10	10·81	11·35	14·38	13·69	10·67	12·13
70	9·96	10·0	9·25	9·21	8·45	9·4	6·22	8·02	8·77	11·23	10·53	8·15	9·52
75	7·59	7·5	7·10	7·00	6·30	7·0	4·52	5·83	6·61	8·49	7·81	6·09	7·29
80	5·73	5·5	5·36	5·38	4·65	5·2	3·06	4·11	4·85	6·29	5·64	4·51	5·43
85	4·19	4·0	3·94	4·39	3·40	3·7	1·93	2·94	3·45	4·57	4·02	3·34	4·05
90	2·99	2·9	2·94	3·84	2·59	2·4	1·10	2·01	2·36	3·31	2·91	2·45	3·05
95	2·10	..	2·32	3·33	2·10	1·1	..	1·31	1·55	2·43	2·10	1·76	2·37
100	1·24	..	1·80	2·59	1·87	..	..	..	·83	1·81	1·70	1·10	1·90

TABLE—A.

LIFE TABLE—ALL INDIA.

Males.

Age.	Living at age x.	Dying between ages x and $x+1$.	Mortality per cent.	Living between ages x and $x+1$.	Living above age x.	Mean after life-time at age x.
(1)	(2)	(3)	(4)	(5)	(6)	(7)
0	100,000	24,874	24·87	85,443	2,690,881	26·91
1	75,126	6,896	9·18	71,352	2,605,438	34·68
2	68.230	3,850	5·64	66,174	2,534,086	37·14
3	64,380	2,524	3·92	63,037	2,467,912	38·33
4	61,856	1,695	2·74	60,954	2,404,875	38·88
5	60,161	1,159	1·93	59,551	2,343,921	38·96
6	59,002	853	1·45	58,576	2,284,370	38·72
7	58,149	669	1·15	57,814	2,225,794	38·28
8	57,480	539	·94	57,211	2,167,980	37·72
9	56,941	474	·83	56,704	2,110,769	37·07
10	56,467	447	·79	56,243	2,054,065	36·38
11	56,020	452	·81	55,794	1,997,822	35·66
12	55,568	465	·84	55,336	1,942,028	34·95
13	55,103	484	·88	54,861	1,886,692	34·24
14	54,619	507	·93	54,365	1,831,831	33·54
15	54,112	532	·98	53,846	1,777,466	32·85
16	53,580	558	1·04	53,301	1,723,620	32·17
17	53,022	583	1·10	52,731	1,670,319	31·50
18	52,439	607	1·16	52,135	1,617,588	30·85
19	51,832	629	1·21	51,518	1,565,453	30·20
20	51,203	649	1·27	50,878	1,513,935	29·57
21	50,554	668	1·32	50,220	1,463,057	28·94
22	49,886	684	1·37	49,544	1,412,837	28·32
23	49,202	700	1·42	48,852	1,363,293	27·71
24	48,502	715	1·47	48,145	1,314,441	27·10
25	47,787	730	1·53	47,422	1,266,296	26·50
26	47,057	747	1·59	46,683	1,218,874	25·90
27	46,310	767	1·66	45,927	1,172,191	25·31
28	45,543	792	1·74	45,147	1,126,264	24·73
29	44,751	820	1·83	44,341	1,081,117	24·16
30	43,931	850	1·93	43,506	1,036,776	23·60
31	43,081	875	2·03	42,643	993,270	23·06
32	42,206	897	2·13	41,758	950,627	22·52
33	41,309	915	2·22	40,851	908,869	22·00
34	40,394	933	2·31	39,928	868,018	21·49
35	39,461	950	2·41	38,986	828,090	20·99
36	38,511	965	2·51	38,028	789,104	20·49
37	37,546	980	2·61	37,056	751,076	20·00
38	36,566	995	2·72	36,069	714,020	19·53
39	35,571	1,008	2·83	35,067	677,951	19·06
40	34,563	1,017	2·94	34,054	642,884	18·60
41	33,546	1,023	3·05	33,035	608,830	18·15
42	32,523	1,026	3·15	32,010	575,795	17·70
43	31,497	1,029	3·27	30,982	543,785	17·26
44	30,468	1,029	3·38	29,954	512,803	16·83
45	29,439	1,027	3·49	28,925	482,849	16·40
46	28,412	1,025	3·61	27,900	453,924	15·98
47	27,387	1,020	3·72	26,877	426,024	15·56
48	26,367	1,013	3·84	25,860	399,147	15·14
49	25,354	1,006	3·97	24,851	373,287	14·72
50	24,348	998	4·10	23,849	348,436	14·31
51	23,350	988	4·23	22,856	324,587	13·90
52	22,362	975	4·36	21,875	301,731	13·49
53	21,387	962	4·50	20,906	279,856	13·09
54	20,425	949	4·65	19,950	258,950	12·68
55	19,476	936	4·81	19,008	239,000	12·27
56	18,540	923	4·98	18,079	219,992	11·87
57	17,617	909	5·16	17,162	201,913	11·46
58	16,708	895	5·36	16,261	184,751	11·06
59	15,813	880	5·57	15,373	168,490	10·66
60	14,933	864	5·79	14,501	153,117	10·25
61	14,069	848	6·03	13,645	138,616	9·85
62	13,221	832	6·29	12,805	124,971	9·45
63	12,389	816	6·59	11,981	112,166	9·05
64	11,573	800	6·91	11,173	100,185	8·66
65	10,773	783	7·27	10,381	89,012	8·26
66	9,990	766	7·67	9,607	78,631	7·87
67	9,224	748	8·11	8,850	69,024	7·48
68	8,476	730	8·61	8,111	60,174	7·10
69	7,746	710	9·17	7,391	52,063	6·72
70	7,036	687	9·76	6,693	44,672	6·35
71	6,349	665	10·47	6,016	37,979	5·98
72	5,684	640	11·26	5,364	31,963	5·62
73	5,044	613	12·08	4,738	26,599	5·27
74	4,431	583	13·16	4,139	21,861	4·93
75	3,848	549	14·27	3,574	17,722	4·61
76	3,299	512	15·52	3,043	14,148	4·29
77	2,787	470	16·86	2,552	11,105	3·98
78	2,317	425	18·34	2,104	8,553	3·69
79	1,892	378	19·98	1,703	6,449	3·41
80	1,514	330	21·80	1,349	4,746	3·13
81	1,184	283	23·90	1,043	3,397	2·87
82	901	238	26·42	782	2,354	2·61
83	663	195	29·41	565	1,572	2·37
84	468	152	32·48	392	1,007	2·15
85	316	114	36·08	259	615	1·95
86	202	80	39·44	162	356	1·76
87	122	53	43·29	96	194	1·59
88	69	33	47·61	52	98	1·42
89	36	19	52·41	27	46	1·28
90	17	10	57·70	12	19	1·12
91	7	4	63·46	5	7	1·00
92	3	2	69·70	2	2	·67
93	1	1	76·42	...	..	..

TABLE—B.

LIFE TABLE—ALL INDIA.

Females.

Age.	Living at age x.	Dying between ages x and $x+1$.	Mortality per cent.	Living between ages x and $x+1$.	Living above age x.	Mean after life-time at age x.
(1)	(2)	(3)	(4)	(5)	(6)	(7)
0	100,000	23,234	23·23	86,437	2,656,400	26·56
1	76,766	6,639	8·65	73,114	2,569,963	33·48
2	70,127	3,551	5·06	68,222	2,496,849	35·60
3	66,576	2,262	3·40	65,368	2,428,627	36·48
4	64,314	1,497	2·33	63,519	2,363,259	36·75
5	62,817	1,038	1·65	62,271	2,299,740	36·61
6	61,779	773	1·25	61,393	2,237,469	36·22
7	61,006	616	1·01	60,698	2,176,076	35·67
8	60,390	531	·88	60,125	2,115,378	35·03
9	59,859	490	·82	59,614	2,055,253	3[illegible]·33
10	59,369	481	·81	59,128	1,995,639	33·61
11	58,888	494	·84	58,641	1,936,511	32·88
12	58,394	511	·88	58,139	1,877,870	32·16
13	57,883	540	·93	57,613	1,819,731	31·44
14	57,343	586	1·02	57,050	1,762,118	30·73
15	56,757	655	1·15	56,429	1,705,068	30·04
16	56,102	731	1·30	55,737	1,648,639	29·39
17	55,371	795	1·44	54,973	1,592,902	28·77
18	54,576	849	1·56	54,152	1,537,929	28·18
19	53,727	894	1·66	53,280	1,483,777	27·62
20	52,833	931	1·76	52,367	1,430,497	27·08
21	51,902	961	1·85	51,422	1,378,130	26·55
22	50,941	985	1·93	50,448	1,326,708	26·04
23	49,956	1,004	2·01	49,454	1,276,260	25·55
24	48,952	1,020	2·08	48,442	1,226,806	25·06
25	47,932	1,033	2·16	47,416	1,178,364	24·58
26	46,899	1,044	2·23	46,377	1,130,948	24·11
27	45,855	1,053	2·30	45,328	10,84,571	23·65
28	44,802	1,060	2·37	44,272	1,039,243	23·20
29	43,742	1,067	2·44	43,209	994,971	22·75
30	42,675	1,073	2·51	42,138	951,762	22·30
31	41,602	1,078	2·59	41,063	909,624	21·86
32	40,524	1,082	2·67	39,983	868,561	21·43
33	39,442	1,086	2·75	38,899	828,578	21·01
34	38,356	1,090	2·84	37,811	789,679	20·59
35	37,266	1,093	2·93	36,720	751,868	20·18
36	36,173	1,096	3·03	35,625	715,148	19·77
37	35,077	1,098	3·13	34,528	679,523	19·37
38	33,979	1,101	3·24	33,429	644,995	18·98
39	32,878	1,100	3·35	32,328	611,566	18·60
40	31,778	1,096	3·45	31,230	579,238	18·23
41	30,682	1,087	3·54	30,138	548,008	17·86
42	29,595	1,076	3·64	29,057	517,870	17·50
43	28,519	1,063	3·73	27,987	488,813	17·14
44	27,456	1,047	3·81	26,933	460,826	16·78
45	26,409	1,029	3·90	25.894	433,893	16·43
46	25,380	1,010	3·98	24,875	407,999	16·08
47	24,370	990	4·06	23,875	383,124	15·72
48	23,380	969	4·14	22,896	359,249	15·37
49	22,411	947	4·23	21,937	336,353	15·01
50	21,464	925	4·31	21,002	314,416	14·65
51	20,539	903	4·40	20,087	293,414	14·29
52	19,636	880	4·48	19,196	273,327	13·92
53	18,756	857	4·57	18,328	254,131	13·55
54	17,899	834	4·66	17,482	235,803	13·17
55	17,065	811	4·75	16,659	218,321	12·79
56	16,254	790	4·86	15,859	201,662	12·41
57	15,464	769	4·97	15,080	185,803	12·02
58	14,695	751	5·11	14,319	170,723	11·62
59	13,944	734	5·26	13,577	156,404	11·22
60	13,210	718	5·43	12,851	142,827	10·81
61	12,492	703	5·63	12,141	129,976	10·40
62	11,789	689	5·84	11,444	117,835	10·00
63	11,100	676	6·09	10,762	106,391	9·58
64	10,424	663	6·36	10,093	95,629	9·17
65	9,761	650	6·66	9,436	85,536	8·76
66	9,111	639	7·01	8,791	76,100	8·35
67	8,472	627	7·40	8,159	67,309	7·94
68	7,845	615	7·84	7,537	59,150	7·54
69	7,230	603	8·33	6,929	51,613	7·14
70	6,627	589	8·88	6,332	44,684	6·74
71	6,038	574	9·51	5,751	38,352	6·35
72	5,464	559	10·23	5,185	32,601	5·97
73	4,905	542	11·04	4,634	27,416	5·59
74	4,363	522	11·96	4,102	22,782	5·22
75	3,841	500	13·01	3,591	18,680	4·86
76	3,341	474	14·18	3,104	15,089	4·52
77	2,867	445	15·53	2,644	11,985	4·18
78	2,422	414	17·10	2,215	9,341	3·86
79	2,008	377	18·78	1,820	7,126	3·55
80	1,631	337	20·66	1,462	5,306	3·25
81	1,294	296	22·85	1,146	3,844	2·97
82	998	253	25·36	872	2,698	2·70
83	745	210	28·18	640	1,826	2·45
84	535	168	31·31	451	1,186	2·22
85	367	128	34·76	303	735	2·00
86	239	92	38·51	193	432	1·81
87	147	63	42·58	115	239	1·63
88	84	39	46·97	65	124	1·48
89	45	23	51·66	33	59	1·31
90	22	12	56·67	16	26	1·18
91	10	6	61·99	7	10	1·00
92	4	3	67·63	3	3	·75
93	1	1	73·57	..	..	..

TABLE—C.

LIFE TABLE—BENGAL, ASSAM AND SIKKIM.

Males.

Age.	Living at age x.	Dying between ages x and $x+1$.	Mortality per cent.	Living between ages x and $x+1$.	Living above age x.	Mean after life-time at age x.
(1)	(2)	(3)	(4)	5)	(6)	(7)
0	100,000	24,956	24·96	85,397	2,491,271	24·91
1	75,044	6,954	9·27	71,248	2,405,874	32·06
2	68,090	3,960	5·82	65,978	2,334,626	34·29
3	64,130	2,635	4·11	62,732	2,268,648	35·38
4	61,495	1,826	2·97	60,532	2,205,916	35·87
5	59,669	1,323	2·22	58.976	2,145,384	35·95
6	58,346	1,008	1·73	57,842	2,086,408	35·76
7	57,338	812	1·42	56,932	2,028,566	35·38
8	56,526	690	1·22	56,181	1,971,634	34·88
9	55,836	616	1·10	55,528	1,915,453	34·30
10	55,220	572	1·04	54,934	1,859,925	33·68
11	54,648	550	1·01	54,373	1,804,991	33·03
12	54,098	546	1·01	53,825	1,750,618	32·36
13	53,552	552	1·03	53,276	1,696,793	31·68
14	53,000	564	1·06	52,718	1,643,517	31·01
15	52.436	580	1·11	52,146	1,590,799	30·34
16	51,856	599	1·15	51,557	1,538,653	29·67
17	51,257	620	1·21	50,947	1,487,096	29·01
18	50,637	640	1·26	50,317	1,436,149	28·36
19	49,997	660	1·32	49.667	1,385,832	27·72
20	49,337	681	1·38	48,996	1,336,165	27·08
21	48,656	703	1·45	48,305	1,287,169	26·45
22	47,953	728	1·52	47,589	1,238,864	25·83
23	47,225	757	1·60	46,846	1,191,275	25·23
24	46,468	791	1·70	46,073	1,144,429	24·63
25	45,677	829	1·81	45.262	1,098,356	24·05
26	44,848	867	1·93	44,415	1,053,094	23·48
27	43,981	903	2·05	43,529	1,008,679	22·93
28	43,078	936	2·17	42,610	965,150	22·40
29	42,142	966	2·29	41,659	922,540	21·89
30	41,176	992	2·41	40,680	880,881	21·39
31	40,184	1,017	2·53	39,676	840,201	20·91
32	39,167	1,039	2·65	38,647	800,525	20·44
33	38,128	1,057	2·77	37,600	761,878	19·98
34	37,071	1,073	2·89	36,534	724,278	19·54
35	35,998	1,087	3·02	35,455	687,744	19·11
36	34,911	1,097	3·14	34,362	652,289	18·68
37	33,814	1,106	3·27	33,261	617,927	18·27
38	32,708	1,111	3·40	32.153	584,666	17·88
39	31,597	1,114	3·52	31,040	552,513	17·49
40	30,483	1,113	3·65	29,926	521,473	17·11
41	29,370	1,108	3·77	28,816	491,547	16·74
42	28,262	1,100	3·89	27,712	462,731	16·37
43	27,162	1,090	4·01	26,617	435,019	16·02
44	26,072	1,076	4·13	25,534	408,402	15·66
45	24,996	1,061	4·25	24,466	382,868	15·32
46	23,935	1,044	4·36	23,413	358,402	14·97
47	22,891	1,022	4·46	22,380	334,989	14·63
48	21,869	1,000	4·57	21,369	312,609	14·29
49	20,869	978	4·69	20,380	291,240	13·96
50	19,891	956	4·81	19,413	270,860	13·62
51	18,935	934	4·93	18,468	251,447	13·28
52	18,001	910	5·06	17,546	232,979	12·94
53	17,091	886	5·18	16,648	215,433	12·61
54	16,205	860	5·31	15,775	198,785	12·27
55	15,345	833	5·43	14,928	183,010	11·93
56	14,512	806	5·55	14,109	168,082	11·58
57	13,706	780	5·69	13,316	153,973	11·23
58	12,926	754	5·83	12,549	140,657	10·88
59	12,172	729	5·99	11,808	128,108	10·52
60	11,443	706	6·17	11,090	116,300	10·16
61	10,737	684	6·37	10,395	105,210	9·80
62	10,053	662	6·59	9,722	94,815	9·43
63	9.391	640	6·82	9.071	85,093	9·09
64	8,751	618	7·06	8,442	76,022	8·66
65	8,133	598	7·35	7,834	67,580	8·31
66	7,535	578	7·67	7,246	59,746	7·93
67	6,957	558	8·02	6,678	52,500	7·55
68	6,399	538	8·41	6,130	45,822	7·16
69	5,861	520	8·87	5,601	39,692	6·77
70	5,341	503	9·42	5.089	34,091	6·38
71	4,838	486	10·05	4,595	29,002	5·99
72	4.352	469	10·78	4,118	24,407	5·61
73	3,883	453	11·67	3,656	20,289	5·23
74	3,430	437	12·74	3,212	16,633	4·85
75	2,993	421	14·07	2,782	13,421	4·48
76	2,572	401	15·59	2,372	10,639	4·14
77	2,171	374	17·23	1,984	8,267	3·81
78	1,797	342	19·03	1,626	6.283	3·50
79	1,455	307	21·10	1,301	4,657	3·20
80	1,148	269	23·43	1,014	3,356	2·92
81	879	229	26·05	764	2,342	2·66
82	650	188	28·92	556	1,578	2· 3
83	462	148	32·03	388	1,022	2·21
84	314	110	35·03	259	634	2·02
85	204	78	38·43	165	375	1·84
86	126	53	42·03	100	210	1·67
87	73	33	45·85	56	110	1·51
88	40	20	49·88	30	54	1·35
89	20	11	54·12	15	24	1·20
90	9	5	58·57	6	9	·00
91	4	3	63·24	3	3	·75
92	1	1	68·12	..	..	..

M 22CC

N

TABLE—D.

LIFE TABLE—BENGAL, ASSAM AND SIKKIM.

Females.

Age.	Living at age x.	Dying between ages x and $x+1$.	Mortality per cent.	Living between ages x and $x+1$.	Living above age x.	Mean after life-time at age x.
(1)	(2)	(3)	(4)	(5)	(6)	(7)
0	100,000	23,356	23·36	86,324	2,479,720	24·80
1	76,644	6,438	8·40	73,126	2,393,396	31·23
2	70,206	3,636	5·18	68,265	2,320,270	33·05
3	66,570	2,405	3·61	65,292	2,252,005	33·83
4	64,165	1,655	2·58	63,293	2,186,713	34·08
5	62,510	1,209	1·93	61,880	2,123,420	33·97
6	61,301	950	1·55	60,826	2,061,540	33·63
7	60,351	783	1·30	59,960	2,000,714	33·15
8	59,568	696	1·17	59,220	1,940,754	32·58
9	58,872	649	1·11	58,547	1,881,531	31·96
10	58,223	624	1·07	57,911	1,822,987	31·31
11	57,599	628	1·09	57,285	1,765,076	30·64
12	56,971	652	1·14	56,645	1,707,791	29·98
13	56,319	688	1·22	55,975	1,651,146	29·32
14	55,631	733	1·32	55,265	1,595,171	28·67
15	54,898	782	1·42	64,507	1,539,906	28·05
16	54,116	833	1·54	53,699	1,485,399	27·45
17	53,283	884	1·66	52,841	1,431,700	26·87
18	52,399	932	1·78	51,933	1,378,859	26·31
19	51,467	975	1·90	50,980	1,326,926	25·78
20	50,492	1,013	2·01	49,985	1,275,946	25·27
21	49,479	1,045	2·11	48,957	1,225,961	24·87
22	48,434	1,073	2·21	47,897	1,177,004	24·30
23	47,361	1,098	2·32	46,812	1,129,107	23·84
24	46,263	1,120	2·42	45,703	1,082,295	23·39
25	45,143	1,138	2·52	44,574	1,036,592	22·96
26	44,005	1,152	2·62	43,429	992,018	22·54
27	42,853	1,164	2·72	42,271	948,589	22·14
28	41,689	1,172	2·81	41,103	906,318	21·74
29	40,517	1,178	2·91	39,928	865,215	21·35
30	39,339	1,180	3·00	38,749	825,287	20·98
31	38,159	1,180	3·09	37,569	786,538	20·61
32	36,979	1,177	3·18	36,391	748,969	20·25
33	35,802	1,171	3·27	35,216	712,578	19·90
34	34,631	1,163	3·36	34,050	677,362	19·56
35	33,468	1,153	3·45	32,891	643,312	19·22
36	32,315	1,141	3·53	31,745	610,421	18·89
37	31,174	1,128	3·62	30,610	578,676	18·56
38	30,046	1,114	3·71	29,489	548,066	18·24
39	28,932	1,098	3·80	28,383	518,577	17·92
40	27,834	1,080	3·88	27,294	490,194	17·61
41	26,754	1,060	3·96	26,224	462,900	17·30
42	25,694	1,038	4·04	25,175	436,676	17·00
43	24,656	1,014	4·11	24,149	411,501	16·69
44	23,642	989	4·18	23,147	387,352	16·38
45	22,653	963	4·25	22,172	364,205	16·08
46	21,690	937	4·32	21,221	342,033	15·77
47	20,753	911	4·39	20,298	320,812	15·46
48	19,842	885	4·46	19,399	300,514	15·15
49	18,957	859	4·53	18,528	281,115	14·83
50	18,098	833	4·60	17,681	262,587	14·51
51	17,265	806	4·67	16,862	244,906	14·19
52	16,459	779	4·73	16,070	228,044	13·86
53	15,680	752	4·80	15,304	211,974	13·52
54	14,928	727	4·87	14,564	196,670	13·17
55	14,201	702	4·94	13,850	182,106	12·82
56	13,499	678	5·02	13,160	168,256	12·40
57	12,821	655	5·11	12,494	155,096	12·10
58	12,166	634	5·21	11,849	142,602	11·72
59	11,532	614	5·32	11,225	130,753	11·34
60	10,918	596	5·46	10,620	119,528	10·95
61	10,322	580	5·62	10,032	108,908	10·55
62	9,742	564	5·79	9,460	98,876	10·15
63	9,178	550	6·00	8,903	89,416	9·74
64	8,628	537	6·22	8,359	80,513	9·33
65	8,091	525	6·49	7,829	72,154	8·92
66	7,566	514	6·79	7,309	64,325	8·50
67	7,052	504	7·15	6,800	57,016	8·09
68	6,548	496	7·57	6,300	50,216	7·67
69	6,052	487	8·05	5,808	43,916	7·26
70	5,565	477	8·57	5,327	38,108	6·85
71	5,088	467	9·18	4,854	32,781	6·44
72	4,621	456	9·87	4,393	27,927	6·04
73	4,165	445	10·68	3,943	23,534	5·65
74	3,720	432	11·61	3,504	19,591	5·27
75	3,288	416	12·65	3,080	16,087	4·89
76	2,872	399	13·88	2,672	13,007	4·53
77	2,473	378	15·29	2,284	10,335	4·18
78	2,095	354	16·90	1,918	8,051	3·84
79	1,741	327	18·78	1,578	6,133	3·52
80	1,414	296	20·93	1,266	4,555	3·22
81	1,118	261	23·35	987	3,289	2·94
82	857	222	25·90	746	2,302	2·69
83	635	182	28·66	544	1,556	2·45
84	453	144	31·79	381	1,012	2·23
85	309	108	34·95	255	631	2·04
86	201	76	37·81	163	376	1·87
87	125	50	40·00	100	213	1·70
88	75	33	44·00	59	113	1·51
89	42	21	50·00	31	54	1·29
90	21	12	57·14	15	23	1·10
91	9	6	66·67	6	8	·89
92	3	2	79·84	2	2	·67
93	1	1	97·90	..	..	..

TABLE—E.

LIFE TABLE—BIHAR AND ORISSA.

Males.

Age.	Living at age x.	Dying between ages x and $x+1$.	Mortality per cent.	Living between ages x and $x+1$.	Living above age x.	Mean after life-time at age x.
(1)	(2)	(3)	(4)	(5)	(6)	(7)
0	100,000	23,745	23·75	86,144	2,888,060	28·88
1	76,255	6,830	8·96	72,504	2,801,916	36·74
2	69,425	3,681	5·30	67,446	2,729,412	39·31
3	65,744	2,294	3·49	64,513	2,661,966	40·49
4	63,450	1,453	2·29	62,672	2,597,453	40·94
5	61,997	935	1·51	61,498	2,534,781	40·89
6	61,062	619	1·01	60,753	2,473,283	40·50
7	60,443	434	·72	60,226	2,412,530	39·91
8	60,009	331	·55	59,843	2,352,304	39·20
9	59,678	282	·47	59,537	2,292,461	38·41
10	59,396	266	·45	59,263	2,232,924	37·59
11	59,130	275	·46	58,993	2,173,661	36·76
12	58,855	303	·51	58,703	2,114,668	35·93
13	58,552	341	·58	58,382	2,055,965	35·11
14	58,211	384	·66	58,019	1,997,583	34·32
15	57,827	429	·74	57,612	1,939,564	33·54
16	57,398	473	·82	57,162	1,881,952	32·79
17	56,925	516	·91	56,667	1,824,790	32·06
18	56,409	554	·98	56,132	1,768,123	31·34
19	55,855	585	1·05	55,562	1,711,991	30·65
20	55,270	611	1·11	54,965	1,656,429	29·97
21	54,659	634	1·16	54,342	1,601,464	29·30
22	54,025	655	1·21	53,697	1,547,122	28·64
23	53,370	674	1·26	53,033	1,493,425	27·98
24	52,696	692	1·31	52,350	1,440,392	27·33
25	52,004	709	1·36	51,650	1,388,042	26·69
26	51,295	726	1·42	50,932	1,336,392	26·05
27	50,569	744	1·47	50,197	1,285,460	25·42
28	49,825	763	1·53	49,443	1,235,263	24·79
29	49,062	783	1·60	48,671	1,185,820	24·17
30	48,279	803	1·66	47,877	1,137,149	23·55
31	47,476	827	1·74	47,063	1,089,272	22·94
32	46,649	854	1·83	46,222	1,042,209	22·34
33	45,795	882	1·93	45,354	995,987	21·75
34	44,913	913	2·03	44,456	950,633	21·17
35	44,000	945	2·15	43,528	906,177	20·59
36	43,055	978	2·27	42,566	862,649	20·04
37	42,077	1,012	2·41	41,571	820,083	19·49
38	41,065	1,045	2·54	40,542	778,512	18·96
39	40,020	1,072	2·68	39,484	737,970	18·44
40	38,948	1,095	2·81	38,401	698,486	17·93
41	37,853	1,115	2·95	37,295	660,085	17·44
42	36,738	1,134	3·09	36,172	622,790	16·95
43	35,604	1,151	3·23	35,029	586,618	16·48
44	34,453	1,165	3·38	33,870	551,589	16·01
45	33,288	1,172	3·52	32,702	517,719	15·55
46	32,116	1,179	3·67	31,527	485,017	15·10
47	30,937	1,182	3·82	30,346	453,490	14·66
48	29,755	1,184	3·98	29,163	423,144	14·22
49	28,571	1,185	4·15	27,978	393,981	13·79
50	27,386	1,184	4·32	26,794	366,003	13·36
51	26,202	1,179	4·50	25,613	339,209	12·95
52	25,023	1,172	4·68	24,437	313,596	12·53
53	23,851	1,164	4·88	23,269	289,159	12·12
54	22,687	1,153	5·08	22,110	265,890	11·72
55	21,534	1,140	5·30	20,964	243,780	11·32
56	20,394	1,126	5·52	19,831	228,816	11·22
57	19,268	1,110	5·76	18,713	202,985	10·53
58	18,158	1,093	6·02	17,612	184,272	10·15
59	17,065	1,075	6·30	16,527	166,660	9·77
60	15,990	1,056	6·60	15,462	150,133	9·39
61	14,934	1,035	6·93	14,417	134,671	9·02
62	13,899	1,011	7·28	13,393	120,254	8·65
63	12,888	986	7·65	12,395	106,861	8·29
64	11,902	959	8·06	11,423	94,466	7·94
65	10,943	931	8·51	10,477	83,043	7·59
66	10,012	901	9·00	9,562	72,566	7·25
67	9,111	868	9·52	8,677	63,004	6·92
68	8,243	831	10·08	7,827	54,327	6·59
69	7,412	792	10·68	7,016	46,500	6·27
70	6,620	749	11·32	6,246	39,484	5·96
71	5,871	704	11·99	5,519	33,238	5·66
72	5,167	656	12·70	4,839	27,719	5·36
73	4,511	606	13·44	4,208	22,880	5·07
74	3,905	555	14·22	3,627	18,672	4·78
75	3,350	504	15·04	3,098	15,045	4·49
76	2,846	458	16·08	2,617	11,947	4·20
77	2,388	414	17·35	2,181	9,330	3·91
78	1,974	372	18·85	1,788	7,149	3·62
79	1,602	330	20·57	1,437	5,361	3·35
80	1,272	287	22·56	1,129	3,924	3·08
81	985	243	24·67	863	2,795	2·84
82	742	200	26·95	642	1,932	2·60
83	542	161	29·71	462	1,290	2·38
84	381	124	32·55	319	828	2·17
85	257	92	35·63	211	509	1·98
86	165	64	38·93	133	298	1·81
87	101	43	42·45	79	165	1·63
88	58	27	46·20	45	86	1·48
89	31	16	50·18	23	41	1·32
90	15	8	54·38	11	18	1·20
91	7	4	58·81	5		1·00
92	3	2	63·46	2		·67
83	1	1	68·34	..		

TABLE—F.

LIFE TABLE—BIHAR AND ORISSA.

Females.

Age.	Living at age x.	Dying between ages x and $x+1$.	Mortality per cent.	Living between ages x and $x+1$.	Living above age x.	Mean after life-time at age x.
(1)	(2)	(3)	(4)	(5)	(6)	(7)
0	100,000	23,225	23·23	86,481	2,689,787	26·90
1	76,775	6,879	8·96	72,983	2,603,306	33·91
2	69,896	3,594	5·14	67,959	2,530,323	36·20
3	66,302	2,197	3·31	65,121	2,462,364	37·14
4	64,105	1,373	2·14	63,370	2,397,243	37·40
5	62,732	889	1·42	62,259	2,333,873	37·20
6	61,843	612	·99	61,537	2,271,614	36·73
7	61,231	457	·75	61,003	2,210,077	36·09
8	60,774	379	·62	60,584	2,149,074	35·36
9	60,395	354	·59	60,218	2,088,490	34·58
10	60,041	361	·60	59,861	2,028,272	33·78
11	59,680	392	·66	59,484	1,968,411	32·98
12	59,288	445	·75	59,065	1,908,927	32·20
13	58,843	511	·87	58,588	1,849,862	31·44
14	58,332	585	1·00	58,039	1,791,274	30·71
15	57,747	662	1·15	57,416	1,733,235	30·01
16	57,085	739	1·29	56,716	1,675,819	29·36
17	56,346	812	1·44	55,940	1,619,103	28·74
18	55,534	880	1·58	55,094	1,563,163	28·15
19	54,654	939	1·72	54,184	1,508,069	27·59
20	53,715	988	1·84	53,221	1,453,885	27·07
21	52,727	1,024	1·94	52,215	1,400,664	26·56
22	51,703	1,052	2·04	51,177	1,348,449	26·08
23	50,651	1,074	2·12	50,114	1,297,272	25·61
24	49,577	1,089	2·20	49,033	1,247,158	25·16
25	48,488	1,098	2·26	47,939	1,198,126	24·71
26	47,390	1,101	2·32	46,839	1,150,186	24·27
27	46,289	1,100	2·38	45,739	1,103,347	23·84
28	45,189	1,097	2·43	44,641	1,057,608	23·40
29	44,092	1,090	2·47	43,547	1,012,967	22·97
30	43,002	1,081	2·51	42,461	969,420	22·54
31	41,921	1,071	2·56	41,386	926,959	22·11
32	40,850	1,060	2·59	40,320	885,573	21·68
33	39,790	1,048	2·63	39,266	845,253	21·24
34	38,742	1,036	2·67	38,224	805,987	20·80
35	37,706	1,024	2·72	37,194	767,763	20·36
36	36,682	1,012	2·76	36,176	730,569	19·92
37	35,670	1,002	2·81	35,169	694,393	19·47
38	34,668	995	2·87	34,170	659,224	19·02
39	33,673	989	2·94	33,179	625,054	18·56
40	32,684	986	3·02	32,191	591,875	18·11
41	31,698	984	3·10	31,206	559,684	17·66
42	30,714	982	3·20	30,223	528,478	17·21
43	29,732	980	3·30	29,242	498,255	16·76
44	28,752	979	3·40	28,262	469,013	16·31
45	27,773	979	3·53	27,284	440,751	15·87
46	26,794	978	3·65	26,305	413,467	15·43
47	25,816	976	3·78	25,328	387,162	15·00
48	24,840	974	3·92	24,353	361,834	14·57
49	23,866	971	4·07	23,380	337,481	14·14
50	22,895	968	4·23	22,411	314,101	13·72
51	21,927	964	4·40	21,445	291,690	13·30
52	20,963	958	4·57	20,484	270,245	12·89
53	20,005	951	4·75	19,530	249,761	12·48
54	19,054	942	4·94	18,583	230,231	12 08
55	18,112	931	5·14	17,646	211,648	11·68
56	17,181	918	5·34	16,722	194,002	11·29
57	16,263	905	5·56	15,811	177,280	10·90
58	15,358	890	5·80	14,913	161,469	10·51
59	14,468	875	6·04	14,030	146,556	10·13
60	13,593	859	6·32	13,164	132,526	9·75
61	12,734	843	6·62	12,312	119,362	9·37
62	11,891	824	6·93	11,479	107,050	9·00
63	11,067	805	7·27	10,665	95,571	8·64
64	10,262	784	7·64	9,870	84,906	8·27
65	9,478	761	8·03	9,097	75,036	7·92
66	8,717	738	8·47	8,348	65,939	7·56
67	7,979	712	8·92	7,623	57,591	7·22
68	7,267	685	9·43	6,925	49,968	6·88
69	6,582	657	9·99	6,253	43,043	6·54
70	5,925	627	10·58	5,612	36,790	6·21
71	5,298	597	11·28	4,999	31,178	5·88
72	4,701	566	12·03	4,418	26,179	5·57
73	4,135	532	12·86	3,869	21,761	5·26
74	3,603	496	13·78	3,355	17,892	4·97
75	3,107	459	14·77	2,878	14,537	4·68
76	2,648	420	15·85	2,438	11,659	4·40
77	2,228	379	17·00	2,038	9,221	4·14
78	1,849	337	18·24	1,681	7,183	3·88
79	1,512	296	19·55	1,364	5,502	3·64
80	1,216	255	20·98	1,088	4,138	3·40
81	961	217	22·53	853	3,050	3·17
82	744	180	24·25	654	2,197	2·95
83	564	148	26·16	490	1,543	2·74
84	416	118	28·28	357	1,053	2·53
85	298	91	30·65	252	696	2·34
86	207	69	33·28	173	444	2·14
87	138	50	36·21	113	271	1·96
88	88	35	39·46	70	158	1·80
89	53	23	43·06	42	88	1·66
90	30	14	47·03	23	46	1·53
91	16	8	51·41	12	23	1·44
92	8	4	56·22	6	11	1·38
93	4	2	61·49	3	5	1·25
94	[illegible]	1	67·24	1	2	1·00
95	1	1	73·50		..	

TABLE—G.

LIFE TABLE—BOMBAY.

Males.

Age.	Living at age x.	Dying between ages x and $x+1$.	Mortality per cent.	Living between ages x and $x+1$.	Living above age x.	Mean after life-time at age x.
(1)	(2)	(3)	(4)	(5)	(6)	(7)
0	100,000	23,850	23·85	86,086	2,783,652	27·84
1	76,150	6,919	9·09	72,368	2,697,566	35·42
2	69,231	3,869	5·59	67,159	2,625,198	37·92
3	65,362	2,470	3·78	64,037	2,558,039	39·14
4	62,892	1,586	2·52	62,052	2,494,002	39·66
5	61,306	1,094	1·78	60,724	2,431,950	39·67
6	60,212	745	1·24	59,840	2,371,226	39·38
7	59,467	538	0·90	59,198	2,311,386	38·87
8	58,929	423	0·72	58,717	2,252,188	38·22
9	58,506	365	0·62	58,324	2,193,471	37·49
10	58,141	350	0·60	57,966	2,135,147	36·72
11	57,791	362	0·63	57,610	2,077,181	35·94
12	57,429	386	0·67	57,236	2,019,571	35·17
13	57,043	425	0·75	56,830	1,962,335	34·40
14	56,618	474	0·84	56,381	1,905,505	33·66
15	56,144	516	0·92	55,886	1,849,124	32·94
16	55,628	554	1·00	55,351	1,793,238	32·24
17	55,074	591	1·07	54,779	1,737,887	31·56
18	54,483	621	1·14	54,172	1,683,108	30·89
19	53,862	650	1·21	53,537	1,628,936	30·24
20	53,212	677	1·27	52,874	1,575,399	29·61
21	52,535	700	1·33	52,185	1,522,525	28·98
22	51,835	719	1·39	51,475	1,470,340	28·37
23	51,116	739	1·45	50,747	1,418,865	27·76
24	50,377	758	1·50	49,998	1,368,118	27·16
25	49,619	776	1·56	49,231	1,318,120	26·56
26	48,843	793	1·62	48,446	1,268,889	25·98
27	48,050	810	1·69	47,645	1,220,443	25·40
28	47,240	826	1·75	46,827	1,172,798	24·83
29	46,414	842	1·81	45,993	1,125,971	24·26
30	45,572	858	1·88	45,143	1,079,978	23·70
31	44,714	874	1·95	44,277	1,034,835	23·14
32	43,840	890	2·03	43,395	990,558	22·59
33	42,950	905	2·11	42,498	947,163	22·05
34	42,045	920	2·19	41,585	904,665	21·52
35	41,125	935	2·27	40,657	863,080	20·99
36	40,190	949	2·36	39,716	822,423	20·46
37	39,241	963	2·45	38,759	782,707	19·95
38	38,278	976	2·55	37,790	743,948	19·44
39	37,302	989	2·65	36,808	706,158	18·93
40	36,313	1,001	2·76	35,812	669,350	18·43
41	35,312	1,011	2·86	34,807	633,538	17·94
42	34,301	1,019	2·97	33,791	598,731	17·46
43	33,282	1,025	3·08	32,770	564,940	16·97
44	32,257	1,029	3·19	31,742	532,170	16·50
45	31,228	1,033	3·31	30,712	500,428	16·02
46	30,195	1,037	3·43	29,676	469,716	15·56
47	29,158	1,041	3·57	28,638	440,040	15·09
48	28,117	1,045	3·72	27,594	411,402	14·63
49	27,072	1,048	3·87	26,548	383,808	14·18
50	26,024	1,051	4·04	25,499	357,260	13·73
51	24,973	1,052	4·21	24,447	331,761	13·28
52	23,921	1,053	4·40	23,394	307,314	12·85
53	22,868	1,053	4·61	22,342	283,920	12·42
54	21,815	1,049	4·81	21,290	261,578	11·99
55	20,766	1,043	5·03	20,245	240,288	11·57
56	19,723	1,036	5·25	19,205	220,043	11·16
57	18,687	1,026	5·49	18,174	200,838	10·75
58	17,661	1,015	5·75	17,153	182,664	10·34
59	16,646	1,003	6·03	16,145	165,511	9·94
60	15,643	989	6·32	15,148	149,366	9·55
61	14,654	973	6·64	14,168	134,218	9·16
62	13,681	955	6·98	13,203	120,050	8·77
63	12,726	935	7·35	12,259	106,847	8·40
64	11,791	913	7·74	11,334	94,588	8·02
65	10,878	889	8·17	10,434	83,254	7·65
66	9,989	863	8·64	9,557	72,820	7·29
67	9,126	835	9·15	8,709	63,263	6·93
68	8,291	805	9·70	7,888	54,554	6·58
69	7,486	772	10·31	7,100	46,666	6·23
70	6,714	739	11·00	6,345	39,566	5·89
71	5,975	703	11·77	5,623	33,221	5·56
72	5,272	665	12·61	4,940	27,598	5·23
73	4,607	624	13·55	4,295	22,658	4·92
74	3,983	581	14·58	3,692	18,363	4·61
75	3,402	534	15·71	3,135	14,671	4·31
76	2,868	486	16·96	2,625	11,536	4·02
77	2,382	437	18·36	2,164	8,911	3·74
78	1,945	387	19·92	1,751	6,747	3·47
79	1,558	337	21·65	1,390	4,996	3·21
80	1,221	288	23·58	1,077	3,606	2·95
81	933	240	25·77	813	2,529	2·71
82	693	196	28·22	595	1,716	2·48
83	497	154	31·00	420	1,121	2·26
84	343	117	34·12	284	701	2·04
85	226	85	37·62	184	417	1·85
86	141	59	41·54	111	233	1·65
87	82	38	45·92	63	122	1·49
88	44	22	50·79	33	59	1·34
89	22	12	56·18	16	26	1·18
90	10	6	62·13	7	10	1·00
91	4	3	68·67	3	3	·75
92	1	1	75·85	·	··	··

TABLE—H.

LIFE TABLE—BOMBAY.

Females.

Age.	Living at age x.	Dying between ages x and $x + 1$.	Mortality per cent.	Living between ages x and $x + 1$.	Living above age x.	Mean after life-time at age x.
(1)	(2)	(3)	(4)	(5)	(6)	(7)
0	100,000	23,450	23·45	86,270	2,637,235	26·37
1	76,550	6,482	8·47	73,013	2,550,965	33·32
2	70,068	3,708	5·29	68,092	2,477,952	35·36
3	66,360	2,482	3·74	65,045	2,409,860	36·31
4	63,878	1,735	2·72	62,965	2,344,815	36·71
5	62,143	1,279	2·06	61,476	2,281,850	36·72
6	60,864	1,001	1·64	60,364	2,220,374	36·48
7	59,863	826	1·38	59,450	2,160,010	36·08
8	59,037	719	1·22	58,677	2,100,560	35·58
9	58,318	658	1·13	57,989	2,041,883	35·01
10	57,660	625	1·08	57,348	1,983,894	34·41
11	57,035	615	1·08	56,727	1,926,546	33·78
12	56,420	624	1·11	56,108	1,869,819	33·14
13	55,796	645	1·16	55,474	1,813,711	32·51
14	55,151	675	1·22	54,813	1,758,237	31·88
15	54,476	710	1·30	54,121	1,703,424	31·27
16	53,766	746	1·39	53,393	1,649,303	30·68
17	53,020	782	1·48	52,629	1,595,910	30·10
18	52,238	815	1·56	51,831	1,543,281	29·54
19	51,423	844	1·64	51,001	1,491,450	29·00
20	50,579	867	1·71	50,145	1,440,449	28·48
21	49,712	885	1·78	49,270	1,390,304	27·97
22	48,827	898	1·84	48,378	1,341,034	27·47
23	47,929	911	1·90	47,473	1,292,656	26·97
24	47,018	921	1·96	46,558	1,245,183	26·48
25	46,097	929	2·02	45,632	1,198,625	26·00
26	45,168	935	2·07	44,701	1,152,993	25·53
27	44,233	939	2·12	43,763	1,108,292	25·06
28	43,294	941	2·17	42,824	1,064,529	24·59
29	42,353	943	2·23	41,881	1,021,705	24·12
30	41,410	944	2·28	40,938	979,824	23·66
31	40,466	944	2·33	39,994	938,886	23·20
32	39,522	944	2·39	39,050	898,892	22·74
33	38,578	943	2·44	38,107	859,842	22·29
34	37,635	942	2·50	37,164	821,735	21·83
35	36,693	941	2·56	36,222	784,571	21·38
36	35,752	940	2·63	35,282	748,349	20·93
37	34,812	939	2·70	34,343	713,067	20·48
38	33,873	937	2·77	33,464	678,724	20·04
39	32,936	936	2·84	32,468	645,320	19·59
40	32,000	934	2·92	31,533	612,852	19·15
41	31,066	929	2·99	30,602	581,319	18·71
42	30,137	924	3·07	29,675	550,717	18·27
43	29,213	920	3·15	28,753	521,042	17·84
44	28,293	913	3·23	27,836	492,289	17·40
45	27,380	907	3·31	26,927	464,453	16·96
46	26,473	900	3·40	26,023	437,526	16·53
47	25,573	893	3·49	25,126	411,503	16·09
48	24,680	886	3·59	24,237	386,377	15·66
49	23,794	880	3·70	23,354	362,140	15·22
50	22,914	875	3·82	22,477	338,786	14·79
51	22,039	869	3·94	21,604	316,309	14·35
52	21,170	860	4·06	20,740	294,705	13·92
53	20,310	852	4·20	19,884	273,965	13·49
54	19,458	844	4·34	19,036	254,081	13·06
55	18,614	835	4·48	18,197	235,045	12·63
56	17,779	826	4·65	17,366	216,848	12·20
57	16,953	817	4·82	16,544	199,482	11·77
58	16,136	810	5·02	15,731	182,938	11·34
59	15,326	802	5·23	14,925	167,207	10·91
60	14,524	794	5·47	14,127	152,282	10·48
61	13,730	787	5·73	13,337	138,155	10·06
62	12,943	778	6·01	12,554	124,818	9·64
63	12,165	769	6·32	11,780	112,264	9·23
64	11,396	759	6·66	11,017	100,484	8·82
65	10,637	747	7·02	10,263	89,467	8·41
66	9,890	735	7·43	9,523	79,204	8·01
67	9,155	722	7·89	8,794	69,681	7·61
68	8,433	707	8·38	8,079	60,887	7·22
69	7,726	690	8·93	7,381	52,808	6·84
70	7,036	671	9·54	6,701	45,427	6·46
71	6,365	650	10·21	6,040	38,726	6·08
72	5,715	629	11·01	5,400	32,686	5·72
73	5,086	604	11·88	4,784	27,286	5·36
74	4,482	574	12·80	4,195	22,502	5·02
75	3,908	542	13·88	3,637	18,307	4·68
76	3,366	507	15·07	3,113	14,670	4·36
77	2,859	470	16·43	2,624	11,557	4·04
78	2,389	430	18·00	2,174	8,933	3·74
79	1,959	385	19·68	1,766	6,759	3·45
80	1,574	339	21·54	1,405	4,993	3·17
81	1,235	293	23·71	1,088	3,588	2·91
82	942	247	26·18	819	2,500	2·65
83	695	200	28·82	595	1,681	2·42
84	495	157	31·79	416	1,086	2·19
85	338	118	35·02	279	670	1·98
86	220	86	39·03	177	391	1·78
87	134	58	43·06	105	214	1·60
88	76	36	47·58	58	109	1·43
89	40	21	52·61	30	51	1·28
90	19	1	58·14	13	21	1 11
91	8	5	64·18	6	8	1·00
92	3	2	70·72	2	2	·87
93	1	1	77·77	..	..	..

TABLE—I.

LIFE TABLE—BURMA.

Males.

Age.	Living at age x.	Dying between ages x and $x+1$.	Mortality per cent.	Living between ages x and $x+1$.	Living above age x.	Mean after life-time at age x.
(1)	(2)	(3)	(4)	(5).	(6)	(7)
0	100,000	22,300	22·30	87,026	3,060,866	30·61
1	77,700	6,707	8·63	74,025	2,973,840	38·57
2	70,993	3,690	5·20	69,015	2,899,815	40·85
3	67,303	2,351	3·49	66,046	2,830,800	42·06
4	64,952	1,523	2·35	64,140	2,674,754	42·57
5	63,429	1,008	1·59	62,893	2,700,614	42·58
6	62,421	688	1·10	62,056	2,637,721	42·26
7	61,733	497	·81	61,149	2,575,665	41·72
8	61,236	391	·64	61,040	2,514,516	41·06
9	60,845	338	·56	60,676	2,453,476	40·32
10	60,507	324	·54	60,345	2,392,800	39·55
11	60,183	352	·58	60,007	2,332,455	38·76
12	59,831	387	·65	59,638	2,272,448	37·98
13	59,444	427	·72	59,230	2,212,810	37·23
14	59,017	472	·80	58,781	2,153,580	36·49
15	58,545	512	·87	58,289	2,094,799	35·78
16	58,033	547	·94	57,759	2,036,510	35·09
17	57,486	577	1·00	57,198	1,978,751	34·42
18	56,909	602	1·06	56,608	1,921,553	33·77
19	56,307	622	1·10	55,996	1,864,945	33·12
20	55,685	637	1·14	55,367	1,808,949	32·49
21	55,048	650	1·18	54,723	1,753,582	31·86
22	54,398	660	1·21	54,068	1,698,859	31·23
23	53,738	668	1·24	53,404	1,644,791	30·61
24	53,070	673	1·27	52,734	1,591,387	29·99
25	52,397	679	1·30	52,057	1,538,653	29·37
26	51,718	687	1·33	51,375	1,486,596	28·74
27	51,031	697	1·37	50,682	1,435,221	28·12
28	50,334	710	1·41	49,979	1,384,539	27·51
29	49,624	725	1·46	49,261	1,334,560	26·89
30	48,899	745	1·52	48,527	1,285,299	26·28
31	48,154	770	1·60	47,769	1,236,772	25·68
32	47,384	802	1·69	46,983	1,189,003	25·09
33	46,582	839	1·80	46,162	1,142,020	24·52
34	45,743	875	1·91	45,306	1,095,858	23·96
35	44,868	908	2·02	44,414	1,050,552	23·41
36	43,960	938	2·13	43,491	1,006,138	22·89
37	43,022	963	2·24	42,540	962,647	22·38
38	42,059	981	2·33	41,569	920,107	21·88
39	41,078	993	2·42	40,582	878,538	21·39
40	40,085	1,000	2·49	39,585	837,956	20·90
41	39,085	995	2·55	38,587	798,371	20·43
42	38,090	990	2·60	37,595	759,784	19·95
43	37,100	985	2·66	36,608	722,189	19·47
44	36,115	980	2·71	35,625	685,581	18·98
45	35,135	975	2·78	34,647	649,956	18·50
46	34,160	970	2·84	33,675	615,309	18·01
47	33,190	964	2·90	32,708	581,634	17·52
48	32,226	957	2·97	31,748	548,926	17·03
49	31,269	951	3·04	30,793	517,178	16·54
50	30,318	947	3·12	29,845	486,385	16·04
51	29,371	944	3·21	28,899	456,540	15·54
52	28,427	942	3·31	27,956	427,641	15·04
53	27,485	941	3·42	27,014	399,685	14·54
54	26,544	940	3·54	26,074	372,671	14·04
55	25,604	941	3·68	25,134	346,597	13·54
56	24,663	943	3·82	24,191	321,463	13·03
57	23,720	946	3·99	23,247	297,272	12·53
58	22,774	951	4·18	22,299	274,025	12·03
59	21,823	957	4·39	21,345	251,726	11·53
60	20,866	965	4·62	20,383	230,381	11·04
61	19,901	974	4·89	19,414	209,998	10·55
62	18,927	984	5·20	18,435	190,584	10·07
63	17,943	994	5·54	17,446	172,149	9·59
64	16,949	1,005	5·93	16,447	154,703	9·13
65	15,944	1,014	6·36	15,437	138,256	8·67
66	14,930	1,009	6·76	14,425	122,819	8·23
67	13,921	1,004	7·21	13,419	108,394	7·79
68	12,917	1,001	7·75	12,417	94,975	7·35
69	11,916	998	8·38	11,417	82,558	6·93
70	10,918	992	9·09	10,422	71,141	6·52
71	9,926	982	9·89	9,435	60,719	6·12
72	8,944	964	10·78	8,462	51,284	5·73
73	7,980	939	11·77	7,510	42,822	5·37
74	7,041	906	12·87	6,588	35,312	5·02
75	6,135	863	14·07	5,704	28,724	4·68
76	5,272	811	15·38	4,866	23,020	4·37
77	4,461	749	16·79	4,087	18,154	4·07
78	3,712	679	18·30	3,372	14,067	3·79
79	3,033	607	20·02	2,730	10,695	3·53
80	2,426	528	21·74	2,162	7,965	3·28
81	1,898	447	23·57	1,674	5,803	3·06
82	1,451	370	25·50	1,266	4,129	2·85
83	1,081	298	27·53	932	2,863	2·65
84	783	232	29·66	667	1,931	2·47
85	551	176	31·90	463	1,264	2·29
86	375	129	34·34	311	801	2·14
87	246	90	36·69	201	490	1·99
88	156	61	39·23	125	289	1·85
89	95	40	41·89	75	164	1·73
90	55	25	44·64	43	89	1·62
91	30	14	47·50	23	46	1·53
92	16	8	50·46	12	23	1·44
93	8	4	53·53	6	11	1·38
94	4	2	56·70	3	5	1·25
95	2	1	59·97	2	2	1·00
96	1	1	63[illegible]			

M22CC

TABLE—J.

LIFE TABLE—BURMA.

Females.

Age.	Living at age x.	Dying between ages x and $x+1$.	Mortality per cent.	Living between ages x and $x+1$.	Living above age x.	Mean after life-time at age x.
(1)	(2)	(3)	(4)	(5)	(6)	(7)
0	100,000	20,300	20·30	88,207	3,099,990	31·00
1	79,700	6,187	7·76	76,295	3,011,783	37·79
2	73,513	3,275	4·45	71,750	2,935,488	38·98
3	70,238	2,017	2·87	69,154	2,863,738	40·77
4	68,221	1,265	1·86	67,543	2,794,584	40·96
5	66,956	822	1·23	66,519	2,727,041	40·73
6	66,134	567	·86	65,848	2,660,522	40·23
7	65,567	424	·65	65,355	2,594,674	39·57
8	65,143	352	·54	64,967	2,529,319	38·83
9	64,791	329	·51	64,626	2,464,352	38·04
10	64,462	335	·52	64,295	2,399,726	37·23
11	64,127	365	·57	63,945	2,335,431	36·42
12	63,762	414	·65	63,550	2,271,486	35·62
13	63,348	476	·75	63,110	2,207,936	34·85
14	62,872	546	·87	62,599	2,144,826	34·11
15	62,326	619	·99	62,017	2,082,227	33·41
16	61,707	692	1·12	61,361	2,020,210	32·74
17	61,015	762	1·25	60,634	1,958,849	32·10
18	60,253	827	1·37	59,840	1,898,215	31·50
19	59,426	884	1·49	58,984	1,838,375	30·94
20	58,542	933	1·59	58,076	1,779,391	30·40
21	57,609	970	1·68	57,124	1,721,315	29·88
22	56,639	999	1·76	56,140	1,664,191	29·38
23	55,640	1,022	1·84	55,129	1,608,051	28·90
24	54,618	1,039	1·90	54,099	1,552,922	28·43
25	53,579	1,051	1·96	53,053	1,498,823	27·97
26	52,528	1,057	2·01	51,999	1,445,770	27·52
27	51,471	1,060	2·06	50,941	1,393,771	27·08
28	50,411	1,060	2·10	49,881	1,342,830	26·64
29	49,351	1,057	2·14	48,823	1,292,949	26·20
30	48,294	1,052	2·18	47,768	1,244,126	25·76
31	47,242	1,046	2·21	46,719	1,196,358	25·32
32	46,196	1,038	2·25	45,677	1,149,639	24·89
33	45,158	1,030	2·28	44,643	1,103,962	24·45
34	44,128	1,022	2·32	43,617	1,059,319	24·01
35	43,106	1,014	2·35	42.599	1,015,702	23·56
36	42,092	1,006	2·39	41,589	973,103	23·12
37	41,086	999	2·43	40,587	931,514	22·67
38	40,087	991	2·47	39,592	890,927	22·23
39	39,096	984	2·51	38,604	851,335	21·78
40	38,112	977	2·56	37,624	812,731	21·33
41	37,135	967	2·60	36,646	775,107	20·87
42	36,168	958	2·65	35,684	738,461	20·42
43	35,210	949	2·69	34,736	702,777	19·96
44	34,261	938	2·74	33,792	668,041	19·50
45	33,323	927	2·78	32,860	634,249	19·03
46	32,396	917	2·83	31,938	601,389	18·56
47	31,479	906	2·87	31,026	569,451	18·09
48	30,573	897	2·93	30,125	538,425	17·61
49	29,676	889	3·00	29,232	508,300	17·13
50	28,787	883	3·07	28,346	479,068	16·64
51	27,904	877	3·14	27,466	450,722	16·15
52	27,027	871	3·22	26,591	423,256	15·66
53	26,156	865	3·31	25,723	396,665	15·17
54	25,291	859	3·40	24,862	370,942	14·67
55	24,432	855	3·50	24,005	346,080	14·17
56	23,577	852	3·61	23,151	322,075	13·66
57	22,725	850	3·74	22,300	298,924	13·15
58	21,875	852	3·89	21,449	276,624	12·65
59	21,023	855	4·07	20,596	255,175	12·14
60	20,168	861	4·27	19,738	34,579	11·63
61	19,307	868	4·49	18,873	214,841	11·13
62	18,439	874	4·74	18,002	195,968	10·63
63	17,565	883	5·03	17,124	177,966	10·13
64	16,682	893	5·35	16,235	160,842	9·64
65	15,789	904	5·72	15,337	144,607	9·16
66	14,885	914	6·14	14,428	129,270	8·69
67	13,971	922	6·60	13,510	114,842	8·22
68	13,049	929	7·12	12,585	101,332	7·77
69	12,120	935	7·71	11,653	88,747	7·32
70	11,185	939	8·40	10,715	77,094	6·89
71	10,246	933	9·11	9,779	66,379	6·48
72	9,313	923	9·90	8,852	56,600	6·08
73	8,390	907	10·82	7,937	47,748	5·69
74	7,483	887	11·85	7,039	39,811	5·32
75	6,596	857	12·98	6,168	32,772	4·97
76	5,739	816	14·23	5,331	26,604	4·64
77	4,923	766	15·57	4,540	21,273	4·32
78	4,157	707	17·02	3,804	16,733	4·03
79	3,450	641	18·57	3,130	12,929	3 75
80	2,809	568	20·22	2,525	9,799	3·49
81	2,241	493	21·98	1,995	7,274	3·25
82	1,748	417	23·84	1,540	5,279	3·02
83	1,331	344	25·81	1,159	3,739	2·81
84	987	275	27·88	850	2,580	2·61
85	712	214	30·05	605	1,730	2·43
86	498	161	32·33	417	1,125	2·26
87	337	117	34·72	279	708	2·10
88	220	82	37·20	179	429	1·95
89	138	55	39·80	111	250	1·81
90	83	35	42·49	66	139	1·68
91	48	22	45·29	37	73	1·52
92	26	13	48·19	20	36	1·39
93	13	7	51·20	9	16	1·23
94	6	3	54·20	5	7	1·17
95	3	2	57·42	2	2	·67
96		1	60·74	..		..

TABLE—K.

LIFE TABLE—CENTRAL PROVINCES, BERAR AND HYDERABAD.

Males.

Age.	Living at age x.	Dying between ages x and $x+1$.	Mortality per cent.	Living between ages x and $x+1$.	Living above age x.	Mean after life-time at age x.
(1)	(2)	(3)	(4)	(5).	(6)	(7)
0	100.000	24,895	24·90	85,440	2,809,528	28·10
1	75,105	6,915	9·21	71,302	2,724,088	36·27
2	68,190	3,682	5·40	66,209	2,652,786	38·90
3	64,508	2,280	3·53	63,284	2,586,577	40·10
4	62,228	1,437	2·31	61,459	2,523,293	40·55
5	60,791	928	1·53	60,296	2,461,834	40·50
6	59,863	626	1·05	59,550	2,401,538	40·12
7	59,237	455	·77	59,010	2,341,988	39·54
8	58,782	367	·62	58,598	2,282,978	38·84
9	58,415	330	·56	58,250	2,224,380	38·08
10	58,085	325	·56	57,923	2,166,130	37·29
11	57,760	343	·59	57,588	2,108,207	36·50
12	57,417	378	·66	57,228	2,050,619	35·71
13	57,039	422	·74	56,828	1,993,391	34·95
14	56,617	469	·83	56,383	1,936,563	34·20
15	56,148	515	·92	55,890	1,880,180	33·49
16	55,633	560	1·01	55,353	1,824,290	32·79
17	55,073	603	1·09	54,772	1,768,937	32·12
18	54,470	639	1·17	54,150	1,714,165	31·47
19	53,831	669	1·24	53,497	1,660,015	30·84
20	53,162	693	1·30	52,815	1,606,518	30·22
21	52,469	714	1·36	52,112	1,553,703	29·61
22	51,755	730	1·41	51,390	1,501,591	29·01
23	51,025	745	1·46	50,653	1,450,201	28·42
24	50,280	759	1·51	49,900	1,399,548	27·84
25	49,521	773	1·56	49,135	1,349,648	27·25
26	48,748	787	1·61	48,354	1,300,513	26·68
27	47,961	799	1·67	47,562	1,252,159	26·11
28	47,162	812	1·72	46,756	1,204,597	25·54
29	46,350	825	1·78	45,937	1,157,841	24·98
30	45,525	842	1·85	45,104	1,111,904	24·42
31	44,683	859	1·92	44,254	1,066,800	23·87
32	43,824	880	2·01	43,384	1,022,546	23·33
33	42,944	902	2·10	42,493	979,162	22·80
34	42,042	925	2·20	41,579	936,669	22·28
35	41,117	951	2·31	40,642	895,090	21·77
36	40,166	977	2·43	39,677	854,448	21·27
37	39,189	999	2·55	38,690	814,771	20·79
38	38,190	1,019	2·67	37,680	776,081	20·32
39	37,171	1,034	2·78	36,654	738,401	19·86
40	36,137	1,044	2·89	35,615	701,747	19·42
41	35,093	1,050	2·99	34,568	666,132	18·98
42	34,043	1,052	3·09	33,517	631,564	18·55
43	32,991	1,050	3·18	32,466	598,047	18·13
44	31,941	1,044	3·27	31,419	565,581	17·71
45	30,897	1,036	3·35	30,379	534,162	17·29
46	29,861	1,025	3·43	29,349	503,783	16·87
47	28,836	1,011	3·51	28,330	474,434	16·45
48	27,825	996	3·58	27,327	446,104	16·03
49	26,829	981	3·66	26,339	418,777	15·61
50	25,848	965	3·73	25,365	392,438	15·18
51	24,883	948	3·81	24,409	367,073	14·75
52	23,935	930	3·89	23,470	342,664	14·32
53	23,005	91	3·96	22,550	319,194	13·87
54	22,094	892	4·04	21,648	296,644	13·43
55	21,202	874	4·12	20,765	274,996	12·97
56	20,328	857	4·22	19,899	254,231	12·51
57	19,471	841	4·32	19,051	234,332	12·03
58	18,630	826	4·43	18,217	215,281	11·56
59	17,804	813	4·57	17,397	197,064	11·07
60	16,991	804	4·73	16,589	179,667	10·57
61	16,187	799	4·94	15,788	163,078	10·07
62	15,388	799	5·19	14,988	147,290	9·57
63	14,589	802	5·50	14,188	132,302	9·07
64	13,787	810	5·88	13,382	118,114	8·57
65	12,977	822	6·34	12,566	104,732	8·07
66	12,155	836	6·88	11,737	92,166	7·58
67	11,319	851	7·52	10,894	80,429	7·11
68	10,468	865	8·26	10,035	69,535	6·64
69	9,603	876	9·13	9,165	59,500	6·20
70	8,727	883	10·11	8,286	50,335	5·77
71	7,844	880	11·22	7,404	42,049	5·36
72	6,964	868	12·46	6,530	34,645	4·97
73	6,096	843	13·82	5,674	28,115	4·61
74	5,253	804	15·31	4,851	22,441	4·27
75	4,449	753	16·92	4,073	17,590	3·95
76	3,696	690	18·66	3,351	13,517	3·66
77	3,006	617	20·52	2,697	10,166	3·38
78	2,389	538	22·50	2,120	7,469	3·13
79	1,851	456	24·62	1,623	5,349	2·89
80	1,395	375	26·85	1,208	3,726	2·67
81	1,020	298	29·21	871	2,518	2·47
82	722	229	31·70	607	1,647	2·28
83	493	169	34·31	409	1,040	2·11
84	324	120	37·05	264	631	1·95
85	204	81	39·91	163	367	1·80
86	123	53	42·90	97	204	1·66
87	70	32	46·01	54	107	1·53
88	38	19	49·24	28	53	1·39
89	19	10	52·61	14	25	1·32
90	9	5	56·09	7	11	1·22
91	4	2	59·70	3	4	1·00
92	2	1	63·44	1	1	·50
93	1	1	67·30	..	..	..

TABLE—L.

LIFE TABLE—CENTRAL PROVINCES, BERAR AND HYDERABAD.

Females.

Age.	Living at age x.	Dying between ages x and $x+1$.	Mortality per cent.	Living between ages x and $x+1$.	Living above age x.	Mean after life-time at age x.
(1)	(2)	(3)	(4)	(5)	(6)	(7)
0	100,000	22,758	22·76	86,702	2,820,506	28·21
1	77,242	6,398	8·28	73,722	2,733,804	35·39
2	70,844	3,378	4·77	69,019	2,660,082	37·55
3	67,466	2,029	3·01	66,372	2,591,063	38·41
4	65,437	1,243	1·90	64,770	2,524,691	38·58
5	64,194	794	1·24	63,772	2,459,921	38·32
6	63,400	549	·87	63,125	2,396,149	37·79
7	62,851	421	·67	62,641	2,333,024	37·12
8	62,430	368	·59	62,246	2,270,383	36·37
9	62,062	363	·58	61,880	2,208,137	35·58
10	61,699	386	·63	61,506	2,146,257	34·79
11	61,313	430	·70	61,098	2,084,751	34·00
12	60,883	490	·81	60,638	2,023,653	33·24
13	60,393	561	·93	60,113	1,963,015	32·50
14	59,832	636	1·06	59,514	1,902,902	31·80
15	59,196	711	1·20	58,840	1,843,388	31·14
16	58,485	784	1·34	58,093	1,784,548	30·51
17	57,701	853	1·48	57,275	1,726,455	29·92
18	56,848	914	1·61	56,391	1,669,180	29·36
19	55,934	966	1·73	55,451	1,612,789	28·83
20	54,968	1,007	1·83	54,464	1,557,338	28·33
21	53,961	1,040	1·93	53,441	1,502,874	27·85
22	52,921	1,065	2·01	52,389	1,449,433	27·39
23	51,856	1,086	2·09	51,313	1,397,044	26·94
24	50,770	1,102	2·17	50,219	1,345,731	26·51
25	49,668	1,113	2·24	49,111	1,295,512	26·08
26	48,555	1,120	2·31	47,995	1,246,401	25·67
27	47,435	1,123	2·37	46,874	1,198,406	25·26
28	46,312	1,123	2·43	45,750	1,151,532	24·86
29	45,189	1,120	2·48	44,629	1,105,782	24·47
30	44,069	1,116	2·53	43,511	1,061,153	24·08
31	42,953	1,109	2·58	42,399	1,017,642	23·69
32	41,844	1,100	2·63	41,294	975,243	23·31
33	40,744	1,090	2·68	40,199	933,949	22·92
34	39,654	1,080	2·72	39,114	893,750	22·54
35	38,574	1,069	2·77	38,039	854,636	22·16
36	37,505	1,058	2·82	36,976	816,597	21·77
37	37,447	1,046	2·87	35,924	779,621	21·39
38	35,401	1,034	2·92	34,884	743,697	21·01
39	34,367	1,021	2·97	33,857	708,813	20·62
40	33,346	1,008	3·02	32,842	674,956	20·24
41	32,338	994	3·07	31,841	642,114	19·86
42	31,344	979	3·12	30,854	610,273	19·47
43	30,365	962	3·17	29,884	579,419	19·08
44	29,403	942	3·20	28,932	549,535	18·69
45	28,461	920	3·23	28,001	520,603	18·29
46	27,541	900	3·27	27,091	492,602	17·89
47	26,641	880	3·30	26,201	465,511	17·47
48	25,761	862	3·35	25,330	439,310	17·05
49	24,899	847	3·40	24,476	413,980	16·63
50	24,052	834	3·47	23,635	389,504	16·19
51	23,218	821	3·54	22,807	365,869	15·76
52	22,397	808	3·61	21,993	343,062	15·32
53	21,589	795	3·68	21,192	321,069	14·87
54	20,794	782	3·76	20,403	299,877	14·42
55	20,012	769	3·84	19,627	279,474	13·97
56	19,243	756	3·93	18,865	259,847	13·50
57	18,487	744	4·02	18,115	240,982	13·04
58	17,743	735	4·14	17,376	222,867	12·56
59	17,008	728	4·28	16,644	205,491	12·08
60	16,280	724	4·45	15,918	188,847	11·60
61	15,556	722	4·64	15,195	172,929	11·12
62	14,834	722	4·87	14,473	157,734	10·63
63	14,112	721	5·11	13,751	143,261	10·15
64	13,391	721	5·38	13,031	129,510	9·67
65	12,670	722	5·70	12,309	116,479	9·19
66	11,948	724	6·06	11,586	104,170	8·72
67	11,224	727	6·48	10,860	92,584	8·25
68	10,497	729	6·94	10,133	81,724	7·79
69	9,768	730	7·47	9,403	71,591	7·33
70	9,038	728	8·05	8,674	62,188	6·88
71	8,310	724	8·71	7,948	53,514	6·44
72	7,586	717	9·45	7,227	45,566	6·01
73	6,869	707	10·29	6,516	38,339	5·58
74	6,162	695	11·28	5,814	31,823	5·16
75	5,467	679	12·43	5,128	26,009	4·76
76	4,788	660	13·78	4,458	20,881	4·36
77	4,128	636	15·41	3,810	16,423	3·98
78	3,492	607	17·38	3,188	12,613	3·61
79	2,885	570	19·77	2,600	9,425	3·27
80	2,315	523	22·59	2,054	6,825	2·95
81	1,792	463	25·83	1,560	4,77	2·66
82	1,329	386	29·08	1,136	3,211	2·42
83	943	305	32·32	791	2,075	2·20
84	638	227	35·56	524	1,284	2·01
85	411	159	38·80	332	760	1·85
86	252	106	42·04	199	428	1·70
87	146	66	45·29	113	229	1·57
88	80	39	48·53	60	116	1·45
89	41	21	51·77	31	56	1·37
90	20	11	55·01	14	25	1·25
91	9	5	58·26	7	11	1·22
92	4	2	61·50	3	4	1·00
93	2	1	64·74	1	1	·50
94	1	1	67·98	..	..	..

TABLE—M.

LIFE TABLE—MADRAS.

Males.

Age.	Living at age *x*.	Dying between ages *x* and *x* + 1.	Mortality per cent.	Living between ages *x* and *x* + 1.	Living above age *x*.	Mean after life-time at age *x*.
(1)	(2)	(3)	(4)	(5)	(6)	(7)
0	100,000	23,550	23·55	88,225	2,870,764	28·71
1	76,450	6,839	8·95	73,031	2,782,539	36·40
2	69,611	3,738	5·37	67,742	2,709,508	38·92
3	65,873	2,361	3·58	64,692	2,641,766	40·10
4	63,512	1,528	2·41	62,748	2,577,074	40·58
5	61,984	1,019	1·64	61,475	2,514,326	40·56
6	60,965	714	1·17	60,608	2,452,851	40·23
7	60,251	582	0·97	59,960	2,392,243	39·71
8	59,669	446	0·75	59,446	2,332,283	39·09
9	59,223	359	0·61	59,043	2,272,837	38·38
10	58,864	388	0·66	58.670	2,213,794	37·61
11	58,476	396	0·68	58,278	2,155,124	36·86
12	58,080	418	0·72	57,871	2,096,846	36·10
13	57,662	449	0·78	57,438	2,038,975	35·36
14	57,213	485	0·85	56,970	1,981,537	34·63
15	56 728	518	0·91	56,469	1,924,567	33·93
16	56,210	549	0·98	55,936	1,868,098	33·23
17	55,661	580	1·04	55,371	1,812,162	32·56
18	55,081	603	1·10	54,779	1,756,791	31·90
19	54,478	621	1·14	54,168	1,702,012	31·24
20	53,857	634	1·18	53,540	1,647,844	30·60
21	53,223	646	1·21	52,900	1,594,304	29·96
22	52,577	657	1·25	52,248	1,541,404	29·32
23	51,920	666	1·28	51,587	1,489,156	28·68
24	51,254	679	1·32	50,915	1,437,569	28·05
25	50,575	694	1·37	50,228	1,386,654	27·42
26	49,881	709	1·42	49,526	1,336,426	26·79
27	49,172	729	1·48	48,808	1,286,900	26·17
28	48,443	753	1·56	48,066	1,238,092	25·56
29	47,690	782	1·64	47,299	1,190,026	24·95
30	46,908	813	1·73	46,502	1,142,727	24·36
31	46,095	847	1·84	45,671	1,096,225	23·78
32	45,248	881	1·95	44,808	1,050,554	23·22
33	44,367	910	2·05	43,912	1,005,746	22·67
34	43,457	938	2·16	42,988	961,834	22·13
35	42,519	968	2·28	42,035	918,846	21·61
36	41,551	989	2·38	41,056	876,811	21·10
37	40,562	1,006	2·48	40,059	835,755	20·60
38	39,556	1,024	2·59	39,044	795,696	20·12
39	38,532	1,040	2·70	38,012	756,652	19·64
40	37,492	1,052	2·81	36,966	718,640	19·17
41	36,440	1,063	2·92	35,909	681,674	18·71
41	35,377	1,067	3·02	34,843	645,765	18·25
43	34,310	1,071	3·12	33,775	610,922	17·81
44	33,239	1,072	3·23	32,703	577,147	17·36
45	32,167	1,072	3·33	31,631	544,444	16·93
46	31,095	1,070	3·44	30,560	512,813	16·49
47	30,025	1,067	3·55	29,491	482,253	16·06
48	28,958	1,063	3·67	28,427	452,762	15·64
49	27,895	1,057	3·79	27,366	424,335	15·21
50	26,838	1,048	3·90	26,314	396,969	14·79
51	25,790	1,037	4·02	25,272	370,655	14·37
52	24,753	1,024	4·14	24,241	345,383	13·95
53	23,729	1,007	4·24	23,225	321,142	13·53
54	22,722	991	4·36	22,227	297,917	13·11
55	21,731	977	4·50	21,242	275,690	12·69
56	20,754	967	4·66	20,271	254,448	12·26
57	19,787	955	4·83	19,309	234,177	11·84
58	18,832	944	5·01	18,360	214,868	11·41
59	17,888	932	5·21	17,422	196,508	10·99
60	16,956	921	5·43	16,496	179,086	10·56
61	16,035	909	5·67	15,580	162,590	10·14
62	15,126	896	5·92	14,678	147,010	9·72
63	14,230	885	6·22	13,788	132,332	9·30
64	13,345	872	6·53	12,909	118,544	8·88
65	12,473	857	6·87	12,044	105,635	8·47
66	11,616	843	7·26	11,195	93,591	8·06
67	10,773	829	7·70	10,358	82,396	7·65
68	9,944	812	8·17	9,538	72,038	7·24
69	9,132	797	8·73	8,734	62,500	6·84
70	8,335	781	9·37	7,944	53,766	6·45
71	7,554	763	10·10	7,173	45,822	6·07
72	6,791	741	10·91	6,420	38,649	5·69
73	6,050	719	11·88	5,691	32,229	5·33
74	5,331	688	12·91	4,987	26,538	4·98
75	4,643	648	13·96	4,319	21,551	4·63
76	3,995	611	15·30	3,689	17,232	4·31
77	3,384	562	16·62	3,103	13,543	4·00
78	2,822	513	18·17	2,566	10,440	3·70
79	2,309	459	19·90	2,079	7,874	3·41
80	1,850	405	21·88	1,648	5,795	3·13
81	1,445	348	24·10	1,271	4,147	2·87
82	1,097	292	26·58	951	2,876	2·62
83	805	236	29·32	687	1,925	2·39
84	569	184	32·30	477	1,238	2·18
85	385	137	35·53	316	761	1·98
86	248	97	39·02	200	445	1·79
87	151	65	42·76	118	245	1·63
88	86	40	46·75	66	127	1·48
89	46	23	50·99	35	61	1·33
90	23	13	55·48	16	26	1·13
91	10	6	60·22	7	10	1·00
92	4	3	65·22	3	3	·75
93	1	1	70·46	..	..	..

TABLE—N.

LIFE TABLE—MADRAS.

Females.

Age.	Living at age x.	Dying between ages x and $x+1$.	Mortality per cent.	Living between ages x and $x+1$.	Living above age x.	Mean after life-time at age x.
(1)	(2)	(3)	(4)	(5)	(6)	(7)
0	100,000	21,456	21·46	89,272	3,003,486	30·04
1	78,544	6,198	7·89	75,445	2,914,214	37·10
2	72,346	3,186	4·40	70,753	2,838,769	39·24
3	69,160	1,893	2·74	68,214	2,768,016	40·02
4	67,267	1,143	1·70	66,695	2,699,802	40·14
5	66,124	743	1·12	65,753	2,633,107	39·82
6	65,381	514	·79	65,124	2,567,354	39·27
7	64,867	385	·59	64,674	2,502,230	38·57
8	64,482	323	·50	64,321	2,437,556	37·80
9	64,159	317	·50	64,000	2,373,235	36·99
10	63,842	323	·50	63,681	2,309,235	36·17
11	63,519	345	·54	63,346	2,245,554	35·35
12	63,174	381	·60	62,984	2,182,208	34·54
13	62,793	444	·71	62,571	2,119,224	33·75
14	62,349	510	·82	62,094	2,056,653	32·99
15	61,839	579	·94	61,549	1,994,559	32·25
16	61,260	649	1·06	60,936	1,933,010	31·55
17	60,611	714	1·18	60,254	1,872,074	30·89
18	59,897	772	1·29	59,511	1,811,820	30·25
19	59,125	822	1·39	58,714	1,752,309	29·64
20	58,303	871	1·49	57,867	1,693,595	29·05
21	57,432	903	1·57	56,981	1,635,728	28·48
22	56,529	929	1·64	56,064	1,578,747	27·87
23	55,600	952	1·71	55,124	1,522,683	27·39
24	54,648	974	1·78	54,161	1,467,559	26·85
25	53,674	990	1·85	53,179	1,413,398	26·33
26	52,684	1,005	1·91	52,182	1,360,219	25·82
27	51,679	1,022	1·98	51,168	1,308,037	25·31
28	50,657	1,034	2·04	50,140	1,256,869	24·81
29	49,623	1,045	2·11	49,100	1,206,729	24·32
30	48,578	1,054	2·17	48,051	1,157,629	23·83
31	47,524	1,062	2·24	46,993	1,109,578	23·35
32	46,462	1,070	2·30	45,927	1,062,585	22·87
33	45,392	1,076	2·37	44,854	1,016,658	22·40
34	44,316	1,081	2·44	43,776	971,804	21·93
35	43,235	1,086	2·51	42,692	928,028	21·47
36	42,149	1,092	2·59	41,603	885,336	21·01
37	41,057	1,097	2·67	40,508	843,733	20·55
38	39,960	1,102	2·76	39,409	803,225	20·10
39	38,858	1,106	2·85	38,305	763,816	19·66
40	37,752	1,108	2·94	37,198	725,511	19·22
41	36,644	1,109	3·04	36,090	688,313	18·78
42	35,535	1,109	3·12	34,980	652,223	18·35
43	34,426	1,102	3·20	33,875	617,243	17·93
44	33,324	1,095	3·29	32,777	583,368	17·51
45	32,229	1,088	3·38	31,685	550,591	17·08
46	31,141	1,080	3·47	30,601	518,906	16·66
47	30,061	1,072	3·57	29,525	488,305	16·24
48	28,989	1,063	3·67	28,457	458,780	15·83
49	27,926	1,054	3·77	27,399	430,323	15·41
50	26,872	1,043	3·88	26,351	402,924	14·99
51	25,829	1,032	4·00	25,313	376,573	14·58
52	24,797	1,018	4·11	24,288	351,260	14·17
53	23,779	1,003	4·22	23,277	326,972	13·75
54	22,776	988	4·34	22,282	303,695	13·33
55	21,788	973	4·47	21,302	281,413	12·92
56	20,815	959	4·61	20,335	260,111	12·50
57	19,856	945	4·76	19,384	239,776	12·08
58	18,911	931	4·92	18,445	220,392	11·65
59	17,980	918	5·11	17,521	201,947	11·23
60	17,062	905	5·30	16,610	184,426	10·81
61	16,157	893	5·53	15,710	167,816	10·39
62	15,264	881	5·77	14,824	152,106	9·97
63	14,383	869	6·04	13,948	137,282	9·54
64	13,514	857	6·34	13,086	123,334	9·13
65	12,657	845	6·68	12,234	110,248	8·71
66	11,812	833	7·05	11,396	98,014	8·30
67	10,979	819	7·46	10,569	86,618	7·89
68	10,160	804	7·91	9,757	76,049	7·49
67	9,354	788	8·42	8,960	66,292	7·09
70	8,566	770	8·99	8,181	57,332	6·69
71	7,796	751	9·63	7,421	49,151	6·30
72	7,045	730	10·36	6,680	41,730	5·92
73	6,315	707	11·20	5,961	35,050	5·55
74	5,608	682	12·16	5,267	29,089	5·19
75	4,926	652	13·24	4,600	23,822	4·84
76	4,274	618	14·46	3,965	19,222	4·50
77	3,656	578	15·81	3,367	15,257	4·17
78	3,078	533	17·32	2,812	11,890	3·86
79	2,545	485	19·06	2,302	9,078	3·57
80	2,060	433	21·02	1,844	6,776	3·29
81	1,627	377	23·17	1,438	4,932	3·03
82	1,250	318	25·44	1,091	3,494	2·80
83	932	258	27·68	803	2,403	2·58
84	674	202	29·97	573	1,606	2·38
85	472	155	32·84	395	1,033	2·19
86	317	113	35·65	260	638	2·01
87	204	78	38·24	165	378	1·85
88	126	52	41·27	100	213	1·57
89	74	34	45·95	58	113	1·53
90	41	20	48·78	30	55	1·34
91	20	11	55·00	15	25	1·25
92	9	5	56·53	6	10	1·11
93	4	2	60·51	3	4	1·00
94	2	1	64·67	1	1	·50
95	1	1	68·99	..	..	..

TABLE—O.

LIFE TABLE—PUNJAB

Males.

Age.	Living at age x.	Dying between ages x and $x+1$.	Mortality per cent.	Living between ages x and $x+1$.	Living above age x.	Mean after life-time at age x.
(1)	(2)	(3)	(4)	(5)	(6)	(7)
0	100,000	23,975	23·98	86,009	2,804,650	28·05
1	76,025	6,950	9·14	72,233	2,718,641	35·76
2	69,075	3,964	5·74	66,960	2,646,408	38·31
3	65,111	2,620	4·02	63,719	2,579,448	39·62
4	62,491	1,784	2·86	61,547	2,515,729	40·26
5	60,707	1,255	2·07	60,046	2,454,182	40·43
6	59,452	913	1·54	58,995	2,394,136	40·27
7	58,539	697	1·19	58,191	2,335,141	39·89
8	57,842	563	·97	57,560	2,276,950	39·36
9	57,279	482	·84	57,038	2,219,390	38·75
10	56,797	437	·77	56,579	2,162,352	38·07
11	56,360	418	·74	56,151	2,105,773	37·36
12	55,942	422	·75	55,731	2,049,622	36·64
13	55,520	441	·79	55,299	1,993,891	35·91
14	55,079	467	·85	54,846	1,938,592	35·20
15	54,612	498	·91	54,363	1,883,746	34·49
16	54,114	530	·98	53,849	1,829,383	33·81
17	53,584	563	1·05	53,302	1,775,534	33·14
18	53,021	594	1·12	52,724	1,722,232	32·48
19	52,427	622	1·19	52,116	1,669,508	31·84
20	51,805	647	1·25	51,482	1,617,392	31·22
21	51,158	669	1·31	50,823	1,565,910	30·61
22	50,489	689	1·36	50,145	1,515,087	30·01
23	49,800	707	1·42	49,446	1,464,942	29·42
24	49,093	723	1·47	48,732	1,415,496	28·83
25	48,370	738	1·53	48,001	1,366,764	28·26
26	47,632	751	1·58	47,257	1,318,763	27·69
27	46,881	762	1·63	46,500	1,271,506	27·12
28	46,119	773	1·68	45,733	1,225,006	26·56
29	45,346	783	1·73	44,954	1,179,273	26·01
30	44,563	793	1·78	44,167	1,134,319	25·45
31	43,770	802	1·83	43,369	1,090,152	24·91
32	42,968	811	1·89	42,562	1,046,783	24·36
33	42,157	820	1·95	41,747	1,004,221	23·82
34	41,337	829	2·01	40,923	962,474	23·28
35	40,508	838	2·07	40,089	921,551	22·75
36	39,670	846	2·13	39,247	881,462	22·22
37	38,824	854	2·20	38,397	842,215	21·69
38	37,970	862	2·27	37,539	803,818	21·17
39	37,108	870	2·34	36,673	766,279	20·65
40	36,238	878	2·42	35,799	729,606	20·13
41	35,360	885	2·50	34,918	693,807	19·62
42	34,475	891	2·58	34,029	658,889	19·11
43	33,584	895	2·67	33,137	624,860	18·61
44	32,689	897	2·74	32,241	591,723	18·10
45	31,792	898	2·82	31,343	559,482	17·60
46	30,894	899	2·91	30,445	528,139	17·10
47	29,995	901	3·00	29,544	497,694	16·59
48	29,094	903	3·11	28,643	468,150	16·09
49	28,191	905	3·21	27,739	439,507	15·59
50	27,286	907	3·32	26,833	411,768	15·09
51	26,379	910	3·45	25,924	384,935	14·59
52	25,469	913	3·58	25,013	359,011	14·10
53	24,556	916	3·73	24,098	333,998	13·60
54	23,640	919	3·89	23,180	309,900	13·11
55	22,721	922	4·06	22,260	286,720	12·62
56	21,799	926	4·25	21,336	264,460	12·13
57	20,873	930	4·46	20,408	243,124	11·65
58	19,943	935	4·69	19,476	222,716	11·17
59	19,008	942	4·96	18,537	203,240	10·69
60	18,066	947	5·24	17,593	184,703	10·22
61	17,119	951	5·56	16,644	167,110	9·76
62	16,168	953	5·89	15,691	150,466	9·31
63	15,215	955	6·28	14,738	134,775	8·86
64	14,260	956	6·70	13,782	120,037	8·42
65	13,304	954	7·17	12,827	106,255	7·99
66	12,350	950	7·69	11,875	93,428	7·57
67	11,400	942	8·26	10,929	81,553	7·15
68	10,458	929	8·88	9,994	70,624	6·75
69	9,529	912	9·57	9,073	60,630	6·36
70	8,617	891	10·34	8,172	51,557	5·98
71	7,726	864	11·18	7,294	43,385	5·62
72	6,862	832	12·13	6,446	36,091	5·26
73	6,030	794	13·17	5,633	29,645	4·92
74	5,236	751	14·34	4,860	24,012	4·59
75	4,485	701	15·63	4,135	19,152	4·27
76	3,784	645	17·05	3,461	15,017	3·97
77	3,139	585	18·62	2,847	11,556	3·68
78	2,554	520	20·35	2,294	8,709	3·41
79	2,034	452	22·24	1,808	6,415	3·15
80	1,582	384	24·30	1,390	4,607	2·91
81	1,198	318	26·53	1,039	3,217	2·69
82	880	255	28·92	753	2,178	2·48
83	625	197	31·48	527	1,425	2·28
84	428	146	34·21	355	898	2·10
85	282	105	37·10	229	543	1·93
86	177	71	40·16	142	314	1·77
87	106	46	43·38	83	172	1·62
88	60	28	46·77	46	89	1·48
89	32	16	50·33	24	43	1·34
90	16	9	54·05	12	19	1·19
91	7	4	57·94	5	7	1·06
92	3	2	62·00	2	2	·67
93	1	1	66·22	..	..	..

TABLE—P-

LIFE TABLE—PUNJAB.

Females.

Age.	Living at age x.	Dying between ages x and $x+1$.	Mortality per cent.	Living between ages x and $x+1$.	Living above age x.	Mean after life-time at age x.
(1)	(2)	(3)	(4)	(5)	(6)	(7)
0	100,000	23,653	23·65	86,146	2,657,223	26·57
1	76,347	6,501	8·51	72,798	2,571,077	33·68
2	69,846	3,703	5·30	67,871	2,498,279	35·77
3	66,143	2,464	3·72	64,836	2,430,408	36·74
4	63,679	1,713	2·69	62,777	2,365,572	37·15
5	61,966	1,254	2·02	61,311	2,302,795	37·16
6	60,712	973	1·60	60,226	2,241,484	36·92
7	59,739	798	1·34	59,340	2,181,258	36·51
8	58,941	692	1·17	58,595	2,121,918	36·00
9	58,249	631	1·08	57,933	2,063,323	35·42
10	57,618	600	1·04	57,318	2,005,390	34·80
11	57,018	592	1·04	56,722	1,948,072	34·17
12	56,426	604	1·07	56,124	1,891,350	33·52
13	55,822	625	1·13	55,510	1,835,226	32·88
14	55,197	660	1·20	54,867	1,779,716	32·24
15	54,537	703	1·29	54,185	1,724,849	31·63
16	53,834	748	1·39	53,460	1,670,664	31·03
17	53,086	788	1·48	52,692	1,617,204	30·46
18	52,298	824	1·58	51,886	1,564,512	29·92
19	51,474	857	1·66	51,046	1,512,626	29·39
20	50,617	888	1·75	50,173	1 461,580	28·88
21	49,729	912	1·83	49,273	1,411,407	28·38
22	48,817	932	1·91	48,351	1,362,134	27·90
23	47,885	950	1·98	47,410	1,313,783	27·44
24	46,935	965	2·06	46,452	1,266,373	26·98
25	45,970	978	2·13	45,481	1,219,921	26·54
26	44,992	986	2·19	44,499	1,174,440	26·10
27	44,006	993	2·26	43,510	1,129,941	25·68
28	43,013	997	2·32	42,514	1,086,431	25·26
29	42,016	999	2·38	41,517	1,043,917	24·85
30	41,017	999	2·44	40,517	1,002,400	24·44
31	40,018	997	2·49	39,520	961,883	24·04
32	39,021	993	2·54	38,524	922,363	23·64
33	38,028	987	2·60	37,535	883,839	23·24
34	37,041	980	2·65	36,551	846,304	22·85
35	36,061	972	2·70	35,575	809,753	22·46
36	35,089	962	2·74	34,608	774,178	22·06
37	34,127	952	2·79	33,651	739,570	21·67
38	33,175	940	2·83	32,705	705,919	21·28
39	32,235	927	2·87	31,771	673,214	20·88
40	31,308	912	2·91	30,852	641,443	20·49
41	30,396	894	2·94	29,949	610,591	20·09
42	29,502	875	2·96	29,065	580,642	19·68
43	28,627	855	2·99	28,199	551,577	19·27
44	27,772	833	3·00	27,356	523,378	18 85
45	26,939	811	3·01	26,533	496,022	18·41
46	26,128	796	3·05	25,730	469,489	17·97
47	25,332	786	3·10	24,939	443,759	17·52
48	24,546	777	3·17	24,158	418,820	17·06
49	23,769	770	3·24	23,384	394,662	16·60
50	22,999	763	3·32	22,617	371,278	16·14
51	22,236	757	3·40	21,858	348,661	15·68
52	21,479	752	3·50	21,103	326,803	15·22
53	20,727	747	3·60	20,353	305,700	14·75
54	19,980	742	3·71	19,609	285,347	14·28
55	19,238	739	3·84	18,869	265,738	13·81
56	18,499	736	3·98	18,131	246,869	13·34
57	17,763	733	4·13	17,396	228,738	12·88
58	17,030	731	4·29	16,665	211,342	12·41
59	16,299	729	4·47	15,934	194,677	11·94
60	15,570	727	4·67	15,207	178,743	11·48
61	14,843	726	4·89	14,480	163,536	11·02
62	14,117	724	5·13	13,755	149,056	10·56
63	13,393	722	5·39	13,032	135,301	10·10
64	12,671	720	5·68	12,311	122,269	9·65
65	11,951	717	6·00	11,592	109,958	9·20
66	11,234	713	6·35	10,878	98,366	8·76
67	10,521	709	6·74	10,166	87,488	8·32
68	9,812	704	7·17	9,460	77,322	7·88
69	9,108	699	7·67	8,758	67,862	7·45
70	8,409	693	8·24	8,063	59,104	7·03
71	7,716	685	8·88	7,373	51,041	6·61
72	7,031	676	9·61	6,695	43,668	6·21
73	6,355	665	10·46	6,023	36,975	5·82
74	5,690	648	11·39	5,366	30,952	5·44
75	5,042	624	12·38	4,730	25,586	5·07
76	4,418	595	13·46	4,120	20,856	4·72
77	3,823	563	14·72	3,542	16,736	4·38
78	3,260	527	16·18	2,996	13,194	4·05
79	2,733	485	17·74	2,491	10,198	3·73
80	2,248	438	19·48	2,029	7,707	3·43
81	1,810	390	21·52	1,615	5,678	3·14
82	1,420	339	23·87	1,250	4,063	2·86
83	1,081	287	26·53	938	2,813	2·60
84	794	234	29·49	677	1,875	2·36
85	560	183	32·75	468	1,198	2·14
86	377	137	36·32	309	730	1·94
87	240	96	40·20	192	421	1·75
88	144	63	44·07	112	229	1·59
89	81	39	47·95	62	117	1·44
90	42	22	51·82	31	55	1·31
91	20	11	55·70	14	24	1·20
92	9	5	59·57	7	10	1·11
93	4	3	63·45	3	3	·75
94	1	1	67·32	..	..	..

TABLE—Q.

LIFE TABLE—RAJPUTANA.

Males.

Age.	Living at age x.	Dying between ages x and $x+1$.	Mortality per cent.	Living between ages x and $x+1$.	Living above age x.	Mean after life-time at age x.
(1)	(2)	(3)	(4)	(5)	(6)	(7)
0	100,000	27,385	27·39	83,869	2,360,428	23·60
1	72,615	6,894	9·49	68,854	2,276,559	31·35
2	65,721	3,956	6·02	63,615	2,207,705	33·59
3	61,765	2,676	4·33	60,350	2,144,090	34·71
4	59,089	1,897	3·21	58,093	2,083,740	35·26
5	57,192	1,415	2·47	56,455	2,025,647	35·42
6	55,777	1,114	2·00	55,220	1,969,192	35·30
7	54,663	925	1·69	54,201	1,913,972	35·01
8	53,738	806	1·50	53,335	1,859,771	34·61
9	52,932	729	1·38	52,567	1,806,436	34·13
10	52,203	678	1·30	51,864	1,753,869	33·60
11	51,525	644	1·25	51,203	1,702,005	33·03
12	50,881	624	1·23	50,569	1,650,802	32·44
13	50,257	611	1·22	49,952	1,600,233	31·84
14	49,646	603	1·21	49,344	1,550,281	31·23
15	49,043	597	1·22	48,745	1,500,937	30·60
16	48,446	592	1·22	48,150	1,452,192	29·98
17	47,854	591	1·23	47,558	1,404,042	29·34
18	47,263	591	1·25	46,968	1,356,484	28·70
19	46,672	591	1·27	46,376	1,309,516	28·06
20	46,081	595	1·29	45,784	1,263,140	27·41
21	45,486	603	1·33	45,184	1,217,356	26·76
22	44,883	619	1·38	44,574	1,172,172	26·12
23	44,264	642	1·45	43,943	1,127,598	25·47
24	43,622	671	1·54	43,286	1,083,655	24·84
25	42,951	718	1·67	42,592	1,040,369	24·22
26	42,233	765	1·81	41,851	997,777	23·63
27	41,468	804	1·94	41,066	955,926	23·05
28	40,664	841	2·07	40,243	914,860	22·50
29	39,823	878	2·20	39,384	874,617	21·96
30	38,945	906	2·33	38,492	835,233	21·45
31	38,039	930	2·44	37,574	796,741	20·95
32	37,109	954	2·57	36,632	759,167	20·46
33	36,155	971	2·69	35,670	722,535	19·98
34	35,184	987	2·81	34,690	686,865	19·52
35	34,197	999	2·92	33,698	652,175	19·07
36	33,198	1,010	3·04	32,693	618,477	18·63
37	32,188	1,016	3·16	31,680	585,784	18·20
38	31,172	1,021	3·28	30,661	554,104	17·78
39	30,151	1,023	3·39	29,640	523,443	17·36
40	29,128	1,022	3·51	28,617	493,803	16·95
41	28,106	1,019	3·63	27,596	465,186	16·55
42	27,087	1,014	3·74	26,580	437,590	16·15
43	26,073	1,008	3·87	25,569	411,010	15·76
44	25,065	997	3·98	24,567	385,441	15·38
45	24,068	986	4·10	23,575	360,874	14·99
46	23,082	972	4·21	22,596	337,299	14·61
47	22,110	957	4·33	21,631	314,703	14·23
48	21,153	941	4·45	20,683	293,072	13·85
49	20,212	925	4·58	19,749	272,389	13·48
50	19,287	909	4·71	18,833	252,640	13·10
51	18,378	892	4·85	17,932	233,807	12·72
52	17,486	875	5·00	17,048	215,875	12·35
53	16,611	858	5·17	16,182	198,827	11·97
54	15,753	840	5·33	15,333	182,645	11·59
55	14,913	822	5·51	14,502	167,312	11·22
56	14,091	804	5·71	13,689	152,810	10·84
57	13,287	786	5·92	12,894	139,121	10·47
58	12,501	768	6·14	12,117	126,227	10·10
59	11,733	749	6·38	11,359	114,110	9·73
60	10,984	730	6·65	10,619	102,751	9·35
61	10,254	711	6·93	9,898	92,132	8·98
62	9,543	692	7·25	9,197	82,234	8·62
63	8,851	673	7·60	8,515	73,037	8·25
64	8,178	654	8·00	7,851	64,522	7·89
65	7,524	634	8·43	7,207	56,671	7·53
66	6,890	611	8·87	6,584	49,464	7·18
67	6,279	587	9·35	5,986	42,880	6·83
68	5,692	564	9·91	5,410	36,894	6·48
69	5,128	540	10·53	4,858	31,484	6·14
70	4,588	515	11·22	4,330	26,626	5·80
71	4,073	488	11·98	3,829	22,296	5·47
72	3,585	461	12·86	3,355	18,467	5·15
73	3,124	432	13·82	2,908	15,112	4·84
74	2,692	400	14·87	2,492	12,204	4·53
75	2,292	368	16·05	2,108	9,712	4·24
76	1,924	334	17·35	1,757	7,604	3·95
77	1,590	299	18·80	1,440	5,847	3·68
78	1,291	263	20·40	1,160	4,407	3·41
79	1,028	228	22·18	914	3,247	3·16
80	800	193	24·15	703	2,333	2·92
81	607	160	26·33	527	1,630	2·69
82	447	128	28·72	383	1,103	2·47
83	319	100	31·35	269	720	2·26
84	219	75	34·23	182	451	2·06
85	144	54	37·37	117	269	1·87
86	90	37	40·80	71	152	1·69
87	53	24	44·51	41	81	1·53
88	29	14	48·54	22	40	1·38
89	15	8	52·89	11	18	1·20
90	7	4	57·58	5	7	1·00
91	3	2	62·63	2	3	·67
92	1	1	68·04	..	..	..

TABLE—R.

LIFE TABLE—RAJPUTANA.

Females.

Age.	Living at age x.	Dying between ages x and $x+1$.	Mortality per cent.	Living between ages x and $x+1$.	Living above age x.	Mean after life-time at age x.
(1)	(2)	(3)	(4)	(5)	(6)	(7)
0	100,000	24,256	24·26	85,761	2,595,598	25·96
1	75,744	6,424	8·48	72,230	2,509,837	33·14
2	69,320	3,593	5·18	67,399	2,437,607	35·16
3	65,727	2,341	3·56	64,481	2,370,208	36·06
4	63,386	1,580	2·49	62,550	2,305,727	36·38
5	61,806	1,116	1·81	61,220	2,243,177	36·29
6	60,690	834	1·37	60,273	2,181,957	35·95
7	59,856	660	1·10	59,526	2,121,684	35·45
8	59,196	557	0·94	58,918	2,062,158	34·84
9	58,639	501	0·86	58,388	2,003,240	34·16
10	58,138	477	0·82	57,900	1,944,852	33·45
11	57,661	477	0·83	57,422	1,886,952	32·72
12	57,184	497	0·87	56,936	1,829,530	31·99
13	56,687	532	0·94	56,421	1,772,594	31·27
14	56,155	576	1·03	55,867	1,716,173	30·56
15	55,579	625	1·13	55,266	1,660,306	29·87
16	54,954	678	1·23	54,615	1,605,040	29·21
17	54,276	729	1·34	53,912	1,550,425	28·57
18	53,547	777	1·45	53,158	1,496,513	27·95
19	52,770	822	1·56	52,359	1,443,355	27·35
20	51,948	861	1·66	51,518	1,390,996	26·78
21	51,087	893	1·75	50,640	1,339,478	26·22
22	50,194	921	1·84	49,734	1,288,838	25·68
23	49,273	948	1·92	48,799	1,239,104	25·15
24	48,325	971	2·01	47,839	1,190,305	24·63
25	47,354	992	2·09	46,858	1,142,466	24·13
26	46,362	1,009	2·18	45,858	1,095,608	23·63
27	45,353	1,024	2·26	44,841	1,049,750	23·15
28	44,329	1,038	2·34	43,810	1,004,909	22·67
29	43,291	1,049	2·42	42,766	961,099	22·20
30	42,242	1,059	2·51	41,713	918,333	21·74
31	41,183	1,066	2·59	40,650	876,620	21·29
32	40,117	1,072	2·67	39,581	835,970	20·84
33	39,045	1,077	2·76	38,506	796,389	20·40
34	37,968	1,081	2·85	37,428	757,883	19·96
35	36,887	1,084	2·94	36,345	720,455	19·53
36	35,803	1,086	3·03	35,260	684,110	19·11
37	34,717	1,087	3·13	34,173	648,850	18·69
38	33,630	1,086	3·23	33,087	614,677	18·28
39	32,544	1,083	3·33	32,003	581,590	17·87
40	31,461	1,079	3·43	30,921	549,587	17·47
41	30,382	1,072	3·53	29,846	518,666	17·07
42	29,310	1,065	3·63	28,778	488,820	16·68
43	28,245	1,056	3·74	27,717	460,042	16·29
44	27,189	1,046	3·85	26,666	432,325	15·90
45	26,143	1,034	3·95	25,626	405,659	15·52
46	25,109	1,020	4·06	24,599	380,033	15·14
47	24,089	1,005	4·17	23,586	355,434	14·76
48	23,084	990	4·29	22,589	331,848	14·38
49	22,094	974	4·41	21,607	309,259	14·00
50	21,120	957	4·53	20,642	287,652	13·62
51	20,163	940	4·66	19,693	267,010	13·24
52	19,223	923	4·80	18,761	247,317	12·87
53	18,300	906	4·95	17,847	228,556	12·49
54	17,394	888	5·11	16,950	210,709	12·11
55	16,506	870	5·27	16,071	193,759	11·74
56	15,636	851	5·44	15,211	177,688	11·36
57	14,785	832	5·63	14,369	162,477	10·99
58	13,953	813	5·83	13,546	148,108	10·61
59	13,140	793	6·03	12,744	134,562	10·24
60	12,347	773	6·26	11,960	121,818	9·87
61	11,574	753	6·51	11,198	109,858	9·49
62	10,821	733	6·77	10,454	98,660	9·12
63	10,088	713	7·07	9,732	88,206	8·74
64	9,375	693	7·39	9,028	78,474	8·37
65	8,682	673	7·75	8,346	69,446	8·00
66	8,009	653	8·15	7,682	61,100	7·63
67	7,356	633	8·61	7,040	53,418	7·26
68	6,723	613	9·12	6,416	46,378	6·90
69	6,110	592	9·69	5,814	39,962	6·54
70	5,518	570	10·33	5,233	34,148	6·19
71	4,948	546	11·03	4,675	28,915	5·84
72	4,402	519	11·79	4,143	24,240	5·51
73	3,883	490	12·62	3,638	20,097	5·18
74	3,393	460	13·56	3,163	16,459	4·85
75	2,933	429	14·63	2,718	13,296	4·53
76	2,504	396	15·81	2,306	10,578	4·22
77	2,108	362	17·17	1,927	8,272	3·92
78	1,746	327	18·73	1,583	6,345	3·63
79	1,419	291	20·48	1,273	4,762	3·36
80	1,128	252	22·35	1,002	3,489	3·09
81	876	215	24·53	769	2,487	2·84
82	661	178	26·99	572	1,718	2·60
83	483	143	29·64	411	1,146	2·37
84	340	111	32·61	285	735	2·16
85	229	82	35·85	188	450	1·97
86	147	58	39·36	118	262	1·78
87	89	38	43·15	70	144	1·62
88	51	24	47·21	39	74	1·45
89	27	14	51·54	20	35	1·30
90	13	7	56·14	9	15	1·15
91	6	4	61·02	4	6	1·00
92	2	1	66·16	2	2	1·00
93	1	1	71·59	..	..	..

TABLE—S.

LIFE TABLE—N. W. F. P., SIND AND BALUCHISTAN.

Males.

Age.	Living at age x.	Dying between ages x and $x+1$.	Mortality per cent.	Living between ages x and $x+1$.	Living above age x.	Mean after life-time at age x.
(1)	(2)	(3)	(4)	(5)	(6)	(7)
0	100,000	26,013	26·01	86,994	2,542,761	25·43
1	73,987	6,912	9·34	70,531	2,455,767	33·19
2	67,075	3,805	5·67	65,172	2,385,236	35·56
3	63,270	2,426	3·83	62,057	2,320,064	36·67
4	60,844	1,608	2·64	60,040	2,258,007	37·11
5	59,236	1,117	1·89	58,678	2,197,967	37·11
6	58,119	826	1·42	57,706	2 139,289	36·81
7	57,293	678	1·18	56,954	2,081,583	36·33
8	56,615	598	1·06	56,316	2,024,629	35·76
9	56,017	533	·95	55,750	1,968,313	35·14
10	55,484	498	·90	55,235	1,912,563	34·47
11	54,986	488	·89	54,742	1,857,328	33·78
12	54,498	502	·92	54,247	1,802,586	33·08
13	53,996	521	·96	53,736	1,748,339	32·38
14	53,475	551	1·03	53,199	1,694,603	31·69
15	52,924	578	1·09	52,635	1,641,404	31·01
16	52,346	602	1·15	52,045	1,588,769	30·35
17	51,744	624	1·21	51,432	1,536,724	29·70
18	51,120	643	1·26	50,799	1,485,292	29·06
19	50,477	659	1·33	50,147	1,434,493	28·42
20	49,818	672	1·35	49,482	1,384,346	27·79
21	49,146	684	1·39	48,804	1,334,864	27·16
22	48,462	697	1·43	48,114	1,286,060	26·54
23	47,765	711	1·49	47,409	1,237,946	25·92
24	47,054	726	1·54	46,691	1,190,537	25·30
25	46,328	746	1·61	45,955	1,143,846	24·69
26	45,582	767	1·68	45,199	1,097,891	24·09
27	44,815	792	1·77	44,419	1,052,692	23·49
28	44,023	824	1·87	43,611	1,008,273	22·90
29	43,199	854	1·99	42,772	964,662	22·33
30	42,345	894	2·11	41,898	921,890	21·77
31	41,451	934	2·25	40,984	879,992	21·23
32	40,517	971	2·40	40,031	839,008	20·71
33	39,546	1,004	2·54	39,044	798,977	20·20
34	38,542	1,033	2·68	38,026	759,933	19·72
35	37,509	1,058	2·82	36,980	721,907	19·25
36	36,451	1,078	2·96	35,912	684,927	18·79
37	35,373	1,097	3·10	34,824	649,015	18·35
38	34,276	1,113	3·25	33,720	614,191	17·92
39	33,163	1,123	3·39	32,601	580,471	17·50
40	32,040	1,129	3·52	31,476	547,870	17·10
41	30,911	1,131	3·66	30,345	516,394	16·71
42	29,780	1,129	3·79	29,216	486,049	16·32
43	28,651	1,123	3·92	28,089	456,833	15·94
44	27,528	1,114	4·05	26,971	428,744	15·57
45	26,414	1,102	4·17	25,863	401,773	15·21
46	25,312	1,086	4·29	24,769	375,910	14·85
47	24,226	1,068	4·41	23,692	351,141	14·49
48	23,158	1,048	4·53	22,634	327,449	14·14
49	22,110	1,027	4·65	21,597	304,815	13·79
50	21,083	1,004	4·76	20,581	283,218	13·43
51	20,079	980	4·88	19,589	262,637	13·08
52	19,099	955	5·00	18,621	243,048	12·73
53	18,144	929	5·12	17,680	224,427	12·37
54	17,215	902	5·24	16,764	206,747	12·01
55	16,313	874	5·36	15,876	189,983	11·65
56	15,439	846	5·48	15,016	174,107	11·28
57	14,593	818	5·61	14,182	159,091	10·90
58	13,771	791	5·74	13,375	144,909	10·52
59	12,980	765	5·89	12,598	131,534	10·13
60	12,215	740	6·06	11,845	118,936	9·74
61	11,475	717	6·25	11,118	107,091	9·33
62	10,762	694	6·49	10,415	95,973	8·92
63	10,068	672	6·68	9,732	85,558	8·50
64	9,396	655	6·98	9,069	75,826	8·07
65	8,741	644	7·37	8,419	66,757	7·64
66	8,097	639	7·89	7,777	58,338	7·20
67	7,458	635	8·51	7,141	50,561	6·78
68	6,823	631	9·25	6,507	43,420	6·36
69	6,192	625	10·09	5,880	36,913	5·96
70	5,567	615	11·05	5,259	31,033	5·57
71	4,952	601	12·14	4,652	25,774	5·20
72	4,351	579	13·30	4,061	21,122	4·85
73	3,772	552	14·63	3,496	17,061	4·52
74	3,220	518	16·09	2,961	13,565	4·21
75	2,702	476	17·62	2,464	10,604	3·92
76	2,226	426	19·14	2,013	8,140	3·66
77	1,800	374	20·78	1,613	6,127	3·40
78	1,426	322	22·58	1,265	4,514	3·17
79	1,104	270	24·46	969	3,249	2·94
80	834	221	26·50	724	2,280	2·73
81	613	175	28·55	525	1,556	2·54
82	438	136	30·96	370	1,031	2·35
83	302	100	33·21	252	661	2·19
84	202	72	35·67	166	409	2·03
85	130	50	38·24	105	243	1·87
86	80	33	40·92	64	138	1·72
87	47	21	43·70	36	74	1·57
88	26	12	46·59	20	38	1·46
89	14	7	49·59	11	18	1·29
90	7	4	52·70	5	7	1·07
91	3	2	55·91	2	2	·82
92	1	1	59·13	..	..	..

TABLE—T.

LIFE TABLE—N. W. F. P., SIND AND BALUCHISTAN.

Females.

Age.	Living at age x.	Dying between ages x and $x + 1$.	Mortality per cent.	Living between ages x and $x + 1$.	Living above age x.	Mean after life-time at age x.
(1)	(2)	(3)	(4)	(5)	(6)	(7)
0	100,000	25,663	25·66	84,891	2,328,185	23·28
1	74,337	6,469	8·70	70,808	2,243,294	30·18
2	67,868	3,558	5·24	66,429	2,172,486	32·01
3	64,310	2,086	3·24	63,217	2,106,057	32·75
4	62,224	1,514	2·43	61,467	2,042,840	32·83
5	60,710	999	1·65	60,211	1,981,373	32·64
6	59,711	878	1·47	59,272	1,921,162	32·17
7	58,833	810	1·38	58,428	1,861,890	31·65
8	58,023	760	1·31	57,643	1,803,462	31·08
9	57,263	723	1·26	56,901	1,745,819	30·49
10	56,540	700	1·24	56,190	1,688,918	29·87
11	55,840	690	1·24	55,495	1,632,728	29·24
12	55,150	705	1·28	54,798	1,577,233	28·60
13	54,445	730	1·34	54,080	1,522,435	27·96
14	53,715	760	1·42	53,335	1,468,355	27·34
15	52,955	790	1·50	52,560	1,415,020	26·72
16	52,165	818	1·57	51,756	1,362,460	26·12
17	51,347	846	1·65	50,924	1,310,704	25·53
18	50,501	871	1·72	50,065	1,259,780	24·95
19	49,630	894	1·80	49,183	1,209,715	24·37
20	48,736	916	1·88	48,278	1,160,532	23·81
21	47,820	936	1·96	47,352	1,112,254	23·26
22	46,884	955	2·04	46,407	1,064,902	22·71
23	45,929	974	2·12	45,442	1,018,495	22·18
24	44,955	992	2·21	44,459	973,053	21·65
25	43,963	1,010	2·30	43,458	928,594	21·12
26	42,953	1,029	2·40	42,438	885,136	20·61
27	41,924	1,049	2·50	41,400	842,698	20·10
28	40,875	1,074	2·63	40,338	801,298	19·60
29	39,801	1,109	2·77	39,246	760,960	19·12
30	38,692	1,161	3·00	38,112	721,714	18·65
31	37,531	1,215	3·24	36,923	683,602	18·21
32	36,316	1,250	3·44	35,691	646,679	17·81
33	35,066	1,263	3·60	34,435	610,988	17·42
34	33,803	1,267	3·75	33,169	576,553	17·06
35	32,536	1,263	3·88	31,905	543,384	16·70
36	31,273	1,257	4·02	30,644	511,479	16·36
37	30,016	1,249	4·16	29,392	480,835	16·02
38	28,767	1,238	4·30	28,148	451,443	15·69
39	27,529	1,225	4·45	26,916	423,295	15 38
40	26,304	1,207	4·59	25,701	396,379	15·07
41	25,097	1,185	4·72	24,504	370,678	14·77
42	23,912	1,160	4·85	23,332	346,174	14·48
43	22,752	1,133	4·98	22,186	322,842	14·19
44	21,619	1,103	5·10	21,067	300,656	13·91
45	20,516	1,071	5·22	19,986	279,589	13·63
46	19,455	1,038	5·34	18,931	259,603	13·34
47	18,407	1,004	5·45	17,905	240,672	13·08
48	17,403	968	5·56	16,919	222,767	12·80
49	16,435	930	5·66	15,970	205,848	12·52
50	15,505	890	5·74	15,060	189,878	12·25
51	14,615	851	5·82	14,189	174,818	11·96
52	13,764	813	5·91	13,358	160,629	11·67
53	12,951	776	5·99	12,563	147,271	11·37
54	12,175	741	6·09	11,804	134,708	11·06
55	11,434	708	6·19	11,080	122,904	10·75
56	10,726	677	6·31	10,388	111,824	10·43
57	10,049	647	6·44	9,725	101,436	10·09
58	9,402	619	6·58	9,093	91,711	9·75
59	8,783	593	6·75	8,486	82,618	9·41
60	8,190	569	6·95	7,906	74,132	9·05
61	7,621	547	7·18	7,347	66,226	8·69
62	7,074	524	7·41	6,812	58,879	8·32
63	6,550	503	7·68	6,299	52,067	7·95
64	6,047	484	8·00	5,805	45,768	7·57
65	5,563	466	8·38	5,330	39,963	7·18
66	5,097	449	8·81	4,872	34,633	6·79
67	4,648	435	9·36	4,431	29,761	6·40
68	4,213	421	9·99	4,002	25,330	6·01
69	3,792	408	10·76	3,588	21,328	5·62
70	3,384	395	11·67	3,187	17,740	5·24
71	2,989	381	12·75	2,798	14,553	4·87
72	2,608	364	13·96	2,426	11,755	4·51
73	2,244	345	15·37	2,072	9,329	4·16
74	1,899	323	17·01	1,737	7,257	3·82
75	1,576	297	18·85	1,428	5,520	3·50
76	1,279	267	20·88	1,145	4,092	3·20
77	1,012	236	23·32	894	2,947	2·91
78	776	201	25·59	676	2,053	2·65
79	575	166	28·87	492	1,377	2·39
80	409	131	32·03	343	885	2·16
81	278	99	35·61	229	542	1·95
82	179	71	39·66	143	313	1·75
83	108	47	43·52	85	170	1·57
84	61	29	47·54	46	85	1·39
85	32	17	53·13	24	39	1·22
86	15	9	60·34	10	15	1·00
87	6	4	70·12	4	5	·83
88	2	2	75·87	1	1	·50

TABLE—U.

LIFE TABLE—UNITED PROVINCES.

Males.

Age.	Living at age x.	Dying between ages x and $x+1$.	Mortality per cent.	Living between ages x and $x+1$.	Living above age x.	Mean after life-time at age x.
(1)	(2)	(3)	(4)	(5)	(6)	(7)
0	100,000	27,856	27·86	83,576	2,455,930	24·56
1	72,144	6,910	9·58	68,378	2,372,354	32·88
2	65,234	3,985	6.11	63,112	2,303,976	35·32
3	61,249	2,674	4·37	59,832	2,240,864	36·59
4	58,575	1,860	3·18	57,694	2,181,032	37·23
5	56,715	1,345	2·37	56,010	2,123,438	37·44
6	55,370	1,017	1·84	54,862	2,067 428	37·34
7	54,353	808	1·49	53,949	2,012,566	37·03
8	53,545	677	1·26	53 206	1,958,617	36·58
9	52,868	596	1·13	52,570	1,905,411	36·04
10	52,272	547	1·05	51,999	1,852,841	35·45
11	51,725	522	1·01	51,464	1,800,842	34·82
12	51,203	517	1·01	50,944	1,749,378	34·17
13	50,686	522	1·03	50,425	1,698,434	33·51
14	50,164	534	1·06	49,897	1,648,009	32·85
15	49,630	550	1·11	49,355	1,598,112	32·20
16	49,080	568	1·16	48,796	1,548,757	31·56
17	48,512	587	1·21	48,219	1,499,961	30·92
18	47,925	605	1·26	47,622	1,451,742	30·29
19	47,320	618	1·31	47,011	1,404,120	29·67
20	46,702	627	1·34	46,389	1,357,109	29·06
21	46,075	637	1·38	45,756	1,310,720	28·45
22	45,438	646	1·42	45,115	1,264,964	27·84
23	44,792	656	1·46	44,464	1,219,849	27·23
24	44,136	666	1·51	43,803	1,175,385	26·63
25	43,470	678	1·56	43,131	1,131,582	26·03
26	42,792	691	1·61	42,447	1,088,451	25·44
27	42,101	707	1·68	41,747	1,046,004	24·85
28	41,394	722	1·74	41,033	1,004,257	24·26
29	40,672	740	1·82	40.302	963,224	23·68
30	39,932	763	1·91	39,551	922,922	23·11
31	39,169	782	2·00	38,778	883,371	22·55
32	38,387	805	2·10	37,984	844,593	22·00
33	37,582	825	2·20	37,170	806,609	21·46
34	36,757	845	2·30	36,334	769,439	20·93
35	35,912	864	2·40	35,480	733,105	20·41
36	35,048	881	2·51	34,608	697,625	19·90
37	34,167	898	2·63	33,718	663,017	19·41
38	33,269	914	2:75	32,812	629,299	18·92
39	32,355	927	2·87	31,891	596,487	18·44
40	31,428	939	2·99	30,959	564,596	17·96
41	30,489	948	3·11	30,015	533,637	17·50
42	29,541	954	3·23	29,064	503,622	17·05
43	28,587	959	3·35	28,107	474,558	16·60
44	27,628	961	3·48	27,148	446,451	16·16
45	26,667	962	3·61	26,186	419,303	15·72
46	25,705	961	3·74	25,224	393,117	15·29
47	24,744	957	3·87	24,266	367,893	14 87
48	23,787	953	4·01	23,310	343,627	14·45
49	22,834	948	4·15	22,360	320,317	14·03
50	21,886	942	4·30	21,415	297,957	13·61
51	20,944	934	4·46	20,477	276,542	13·20
52	20,010	925	4·62	19,548	256,065	12·80
53	19,085	915	4·79	18,627	236,517	12·39
54	18,170	903	4·97	17,719	217,890	11·99
55	17,267	891	5·16	16,821	200,171	11·59
56	16,376	879	5·37	15,937	183,350	11·20
57	15,497	864	5·58	15.065	167,413	10·80
58	14,633	849	5·80	14,208	152,348	10·41
59	13,784	835	6·06	13,367	138,140	10·02
60	12,949	820	6·34	12,539	124,773	9·64
61	12,129	804	6·63	11,727	112,234	9·25
62	11,325	786	6·94	10,932	100,507	8·87
63	10,539	767	7·28	10,155	89,575	8·50
64	9,772	747	7·65	9,399	79,420	8·13
65	9,025	727	8·05	8,661	70,021	7·76
66	8,298	705	8·50	7,946	61,360	7·39
67	7,593	681	8·97	7,252	53,414	7·03
68	6,912	657	9·51	6,584	46,162	6·68
69	6,255	633	10·12	5,938	39,578	6·33
70	5,622	606	10·77	5,319	33,640	5·98
71	5,016	577	11·51	4,728	28,321	5·65
72	4,439	547	12·33	4,165	23,593	5·31
73	3,892	516	13·25	3,634	19,428	4·99
74	3,376	482	14·27	3,135	15,794	4·68
75	2,894	445	15·37	2,672	12,659	4·37
76	2,449	407	16·61	2,245	9,987	4·08
77	2,042	367	18·00	1,859	7,742	3·79
78	1,675	327	19·55	1,511	5,883	3·51
79	1,348	287	21·26	1,205	4,372	3·24
80	1,061	246	23·18	938	3,167	2·98
81	815	207	25·36	711	2,229	2·73
82	608	169	27·84	524	1,518	2·50
83	439	134	30·48	372	994	2·26
84	305	102	33·58	254	622	2·04
85	203	76	37·30	165	368	1·81
86	127	53	41·80	100	203	1·60
87	74	35	47·23	57	103	1·39
88	39	21	53·59	28	46	1·18
89	18	11	60·88	12	18	1·00
90	7	5	69·10	4	5	·71
91	2	2	78·25	1	1	·50

TABLE—V.

LIFE TABLE—UNITED PROVINCES.

Females.

Age.	Living at age x.	Dying between ages x and $x + 1$.	Mortality per cent.	Living between ages x and $x + 1$.	Living above age x.	Mean after life-time at age x.
(1)	(2)	(3)	(4)	(5)	(6)	(7)
0	100,000	25,389	25·39	85,113	2,509,376	25·09
1	74,611	6,855	9·19	70,864	2,424,263	32·49
2	67,756	3,864	5·70	65,694	2,353,399	34·73
3	63,892	2,560	4·01	62,533	2,287,705	35·81
4	61,332	1,764	2·88	60,401	2,225,172	36·28
5	59,568	1,272	2·14	58,902	2,164,771	36·34
6	58,296	967	1·66	57,813	2,105,869	36·12
7	57,329	773	1·35	56,942	2,048,056	35·72
8	56,556	652	1·15	56,230	1,991,114	35·21
9	55,904	582	1·04	55,613	1,934,884	34·61
10	55,322	544	·98	55,050	1,879,271	33·97
11	54,778	533	·97	54,512	1,824,221	33·30
12	54,245	543	1·00	53,973	1,769,709	32·62
13	53,702	568	1·06	53,418	1,715,736	31·95
14	53,134	604	1·14	52,832	1,662,318	31·29
15	52,530	647	1·23	52,207	1,609,486	30·64
16	51,883	693	1·33	51,536	1,557,279	30·02
17	51,190	740	1·45	50,820	1,505,743	29·41
18	50,450	782	1·55	50,059	1,454,923	28·84
19	49,668	823	1·66	49,257	1,404,864	28·29
20	48,845	861	1·76	48,414	1,355,607	27·75
21	47,984	891	1·85	47,539	1,307,193	27·24
22	47,093	916	1·95	46,635	1,259,654	26·75
23	46,177	939	2·03	45,707	1,213,019	26·27
24	45,238	959	2·12	44,758	1,167,312	25·80
25	44,279	975	2·20	43,792	1,122,554	25·35
26	43,304	987	2·28	42,811	1,078,762	24·91
27	42,317	996	2·35	41,819	1,035,951	24·48
28	41,321	1,002	2·43	40,820	994,132	24·06
29	40,319	1,005	2·49	39,816	953,312	23·64
30	39,314	1,005	2·56	38,812	913,496	23·24
31	38,309	1,004	2·62	37,807	874,684	22·83
32	37,305	1,000	2·68	36,805	836,877	22·43
33	36,305	995	2·74	35,808	800,072	22·04
34	35,310	989	2·80	34,816	764,264	21·64
35	34,321	982	2·86	33,830	729,448	21·25
36	33,339	974	2·92	32,852	695,618	20·86
37	32,365	966	2·98	31,882	662,766	20·48
38	31,399	956	3·05	30,921	630,884	20·09
39	30,443	946	3·11	29,970	599,963	19·71
40	29,497	935	3·17	29,030	569,993	19·32
41	28,562	922	3·23	28,101	541,096	18·94
42	27,640	908	3·28	27,186	512,862	18·56
43	26,732	894	3·34	26,285	485,676	18·17
44	25,838	878	3·40	25,399	459,391	17·78
45	24,960	862	3·45	24,529	433,992	17·39
46	24,098	846	3·51	23,675	409,463	16·99
47	23,252	831	3·57	22,837	385,788	16·59
48	22,421	816	3·64	22,013	362,951	16·19
49	21,605	801	3·71	21,205	340,938	15·78
50	20,804	786	3·78	20,411	319,733	15·37
51	20,018	768	3·84	19,634	299,322	14·95
52	19,250	754	3·93	18,873	279,688	14·53
53	18,496	742	4·01	18,125	260,815	14·10
54	17,754	730	4·11	17,389	242,690	13·67
55	17,024	717	4·21	16,666	225,301	13·23
56	16,307	705	4·31	15,955	208,635	12·79
57	15,602	694	4·45	15,255	192,680	12·35
58	14,908	686	4·60	14,565	177,425	11·90
59	14,222	678	4·77	13,883	162,860	11·45
60	13,544	672	4·96	13,208	148,977	11·00
61	12,872	667	5·18	12,538	135,769	10·55
62	12,205	661	5·42	11,875	123,231	10·10
63	11,544	656	5·68	11,216	111,356	9·65
64	10,888	651	5·98	10,563	100,140	9·20
65	10,237	646	6·31	9,914	89,577	8·75
66	9,591	642	6·69	9,270	79,663	8·31
67	8,949	635	7·10	8,632	70,393	7·87
68	8,314	629	7·56	8,000	61,761	7·43
69	7,685	623	8·11	7,373	53,761	7·00
70	7,062	618	8·75	6,753	46,388	6·57
71	6,444	614	9·53	6,137	39,635	6·15
72	5,830	608	10·43	5,526	33,498	5·75
73	5,222	599	11·46	4,923	27,972	5·36
74	4,623	583	12·61	4,331	23,049	4·99
75	4,040	562	13·90	3,759	18,718	4·63
76	3,478	533	15·31	3,212	14,959	4·30
77	2,945	496	16·85	2,697	11,747	3·99
78	2,449	454	18·52	2,222	9,050	3·70
79	1,995	405	20·32	1,793	6,828	3·42
80	1,590	354	22·24	1,413	5,035	3·17
81	1,236	300	24·29	1,086	2,622	2·93
82	936	248	26·47	812	2,536	2·71
83	688	198	28·78	589	1,724	2·51
84	490	153	31·21	413	1,135	2·32
85	337	114	33·77	280	722	2·14
86	223	81	36·46	183	442	1·98
87	142	56	39·28	114	259	1·82
88	86	36	42·22	68	145	1·69
89	50	23	45·30	39	77	1·54
90	27	13	48·50	20	38	1·41
91	14	7	51·83	11	18	1·29
92	7	4	55·28	5	7	1·06
93	3	2	58·86	2	2	·66
94	1	1	62·58	..	..	..

CHAPTER V.

Sex.

Section i.—Interpretation of the Returns.

78. The figures of the population of India by sexes show a further continuation of the steady fall in the proportion of females to males that has been going on since 1901. Various reasons have frequently been repeated to explain this shortage of females which is so characteristic of the population of India as compared to **Sex Ratio.**

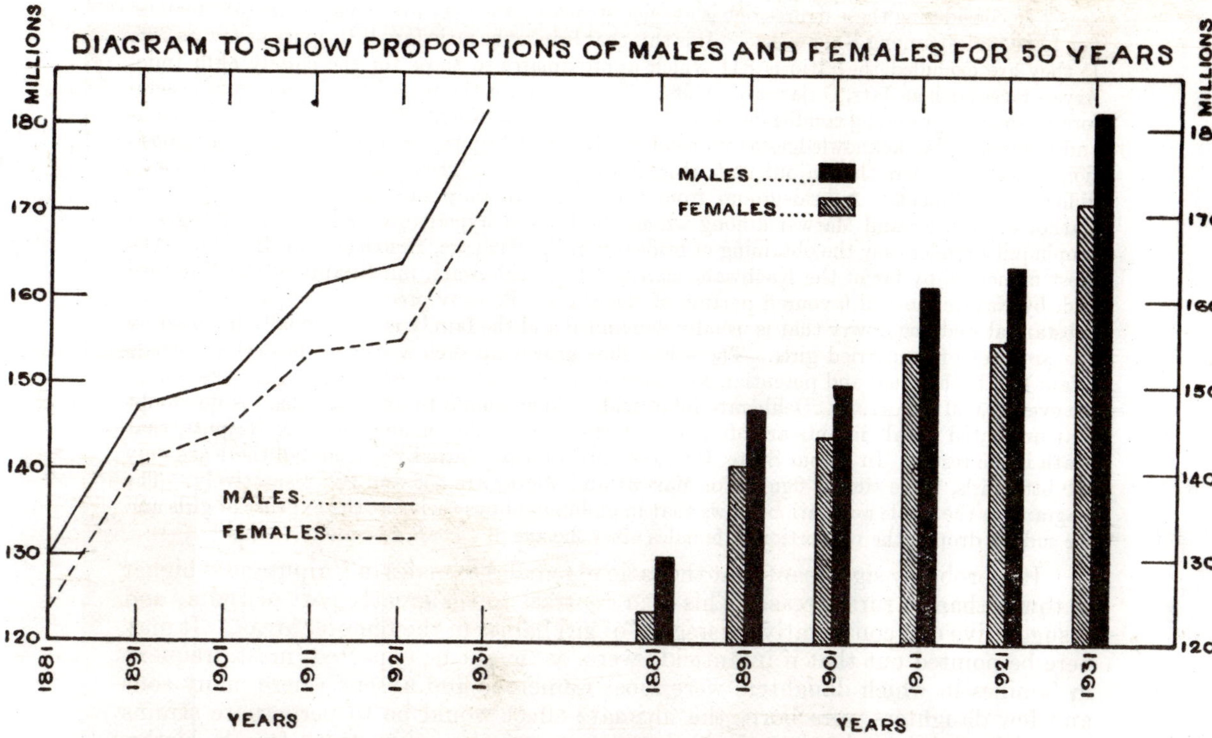

that of most European countries. The female infant is definitely better equipped by nature for survival than the male, but in India the advantage she has at birth is probably neutralised in infancy by comparative neglect and in adolescence by the strain of bearing children too early and too often. Sons are everywhere desired not only among Hindus, where a son is necessary to his father's salvation, but almost equally so among other communities as well; daughters in many parts of India mean great pecuniary expense in providing for their marriage, which moreover, among the majority perhaps of Hindus, must be arranged by the time they reach puberty. So strong indeed is the prejudice against the birth of daughters that abortion is reported to be sometimes practised if the child in the womb is foretold to be a girl. In every province in India the available vital statistics indicate that fewer females are born than males. It is admitted that the vital statistics are incomplete and that there is a definite tendency to omit to report the birth of females in a greater degree than that of the similar omission with regard to males; at the same time the inequality which can be attributed to this source is not enough to balance the excess of male births reported; nor is there any evidence to justify an assumption of widespread female infanticide, though that practice no doubt lingers in isolated or remote areas, since as lately as 1930 the Jammu and Kashmir State Government had to take special measures to suppress it in certain Rajput villages, while the extraordinarily low female ratio of the Shekhawat branch of the Kachwaha clan of Rajputs in Jaipur State, 530 females per 1,000 males, is indubitably suggestive of deliberate interference with the natural ratio, when considered with the Rajput tradition. The next worst Rajput ratios are those of the Bhadauria and Tonwar Rajputs in Gwalior State which are 634 and 622 females per 1,000 males respectively and these are also so low as to appear extremely suspicious of the same thing, being very much lower than the ratio (754) for the Hindu Rajputs of Jammu and Kashmir. Comparative neglect of female children is however admittedly common and taking the population as a whole the superior vitality of the female is unable to become operative at all until she reaches the age of 20 years. Further, among Hindus and Jains the effect of the consequent limitation in the number of females as compared to males is accentuated by a ban on widow re-marriage.

In regard to the female ratio of the Kachwaha Rajputs, it is necessary to quote the Census Superintendent of Rajputana :—

" In considering these figures one is at once struck by the very low female ratio (584 females per 1,000 males) among Kachwahas. It is this that brings the ratio for all Rajputs as low as 796. If they are excluded the ratio is 841 which approximates to those for the closely akin Indo-Aryan races such as Jats, Gujars and Ahirs. The reason for the paucity of females must therefore be sought for among conditions that are peculiar to the Kachwahas. This large, important and numerous clan acknowledges as its head the Ruler of Jaipur, a State the geographical position of which renders the Rajput matrimonial adage of "*Pachcham ka beta aur Purab ki beti*" difficult of fulfilment. A bridegroom from the West can only suitably be sought from the Rathor of Bikaner and Marwar among whom the laws of hypergamy and the advantages of propinquity render easy the obtaining of brides from the Parihars, Sesodias and Bhattis. The most numerous by far of the Kachwaha clan are the Shekhawats, inhabitants of the Northern and, by Nature most ill-favoured portion of the State. Poverty precludes the payment of the substantial wedding dowry that is usually demanded and the family is traditionally haunted by the prospect of unmarried girls. There has thus grown up such a studied neglect of female infant life, both actual and potential, as results in a recorded ratio of 530 female Shekhawats for every 1,000 males......Deliberate infanticide seldom comes to light but there is no doubt that unwanted female infants are often so neglected, especially in some clans of Rajputs, that death is the result. In Jaipur State, for 1,000 little Rajput boys aged from 0-6 there are only 659 little girls, while similar figures for Marwar and Mewar are 856 and 982 respectively. The diagram for the whole population shows that in childhood boys thrive at the expense of girls and the sudden drop in the proportion of females after the age of 4 bears testimony to this "

It is probably significant that the ratio of females to males in Rajputana is higher in towns than in rural areas. This is in contrast to the greater part of India, and is suggestive of a conservative disregard of girl babies in the remoter areas. It may here be pointed out that if infanticide were, as might be expected, most frequent in families in which daughters were most numerous and absent where many sons and few daughters were born, the ultimate effect would be to perpetuate strains in which males predominated at the expense of those favouring female births, a point of some importance in connection with the considerations in the following paragraph.

Masculinity and Decline.

79. A good deal of recent work on sex ratios has tended to the view that an increase in masculinity is an indication of declining population. Clearly that is not the case in India as a whole. On the other hand it may have some correlation to the low rate of increase among Hindus and Jains as compared to that in other religious bodies, as it is among Hindus and Jains that the disharmony resulting from the low proportion of women is likely to be most acutely felt on account of the non-remarriage of widows. It is not unlikely moreover that the caste system itself definitely tends towards a preponderance of masculinity. Westermarck takes the view that a mixture of race leads to an increase in the proportion of females and he cites (*History of Human Marriage*, pages 476 to 482, 3rd edn.) a number of observations from various parts of the world to support this view, and quotes incidentally Dr. Nagel's experiments in the self-fertilization of plants as producing an excess of male flowers, several cases of inbreeding herds of cattle in which bull calves greatly exceed heifers, and two independent experiments in horse-breeding indicating that fillies predominate among foals in proportion as the sire and dam differ in colour. Heape, arguing from the breeding of dogs, likewise concludes that inbreeding increases masculinity (quoted by Pitt-Rivers, *Clash of Culture*). The obvious inference is that marriage within the caste will ultimately, at any rate, increase the proportion of male to female children, and it is worth noticing that the belief that endogamy has this result does not merely arise from modern enquiries into the subject, since the Talmud is quoted as stating that mixed marriages produce only girls. It cannot, however, be taken as definitely proved that femininity increases with hybridization, as some investigations point in the opposite direction, and it may be noted in passing that among the Andamanese, who are certainly declining faster than any race in India, women exceed men among the pure-bred aborigines, whereas males exceed females among the half-breeds. The same is the case with the Cochin Jews, where the White Jews, who are strictly endogamous and pure bred and who seem to be approaching extinction, number more females than males, whereas the hybridized Black Jews, who show some increase since 1921, have more males than females. The population concerned is, however, so small in the cases of the Andamanese and the White Jews that it is not safe to draw any conclusion, but Anglo-Indian males exceed Anglo-Indian females, whose ratio per 1,000 males is 942, and the disproportion is maintained throughout the reproductive period. Pitt-Rivers, while admitting that miscegenation has lowered the excessive masculinity of the pure Maori, attributes this to the greater adaptability of the mixed stock to vitally changed conditions and not to the effect of an admixture of blood directly, and, if he is right in this, it is possible that the failure of hybridization to increase the sex ratio in the case of Anglo-Indians is symptomatic of a decreased adaptability to an unchanged environment, but on the other hand the Anglo-Indian is anything but decreasing in numbers, his increase during the past decade has been 22·4% and during the past 50 years 122·9%. The apparent connection therefore between inbreeding and masculinity may be due to some other factor hitherto not appreciated. At the same time the fact remains that there is a good deal of evidence to support the theory that inbred or pure-blooded societies produce an excess of males, and Miss King's experiments with rats (quoted by Pitt-Rivers, *op. cit.*) afforded evidence that the normal sex ratio could be changed by breeding from litters which contained an excess of males. Mr. Sedgwick, in the Bombay Census Report for 1921, pointed out that the Indian caste system with its exogamous *gotra* and endogamous caste " is a perfect method of preserving what is called in Genetics the 'pure line'. The endogamy prevents external hybridisation, while the (internal) exogamy prevents the possibility of a fresh pure line arising within the old one by the isolation of any character not common to the whole line. With the preservation of the pure line the perpetuation of all characters common to it necessarily follows." Whether this proposition be entirely acceptable or not, it may be conceded that if once a caste, whether as a result of inbreeding or of some totally different factor, has acquired the natural condition of having an excess of males, this condition is likely to be perpetuated as long as inbreeding is maintained. Caste therefore would appear to be of definite assistance to the Hindu in his superlative anxiety for male children; moreover, since the higher the caste the stricter, in the past at any rate, the ban on external exogamy, this tendency would show more patently in the higher caste and explain why the proportion of females to males increases in inverse ratio to social status. In any case it would be interesting to have reliable statistics of the sexes of the offspring of intercaste marriages.

Sex Ratio and community.

80. It is not, however, only Hindu society which suffers in India from a shortage of females, though in the case of Muslims, as also of Christians and of the Black Jews above referred to, the original stock from which the community has been recruited must have been very largely Hindu originally and may therefore be still influenced by the proclivities encouraged by previous inbreeding. Local conditions may also have some bearing on the case, as the proportion of females to males is much higher in the damp climate of the south and east than in the drier Deccan and north-west, though here again it is not safe to infer, as was inferred in 1921 by Marten, that climate is responsible for the ratio, since in that case the ratio of females to males should be still higher in the Nicobars than in Madras. In the Nicobars, however, the indigenous ratio is 927 females to every 1,000 males, while in the Andamans, where the basis of the local-born population is drawn from all over India and Burma and where the climate approximates to that of Madras and Burma, the ratio is far less, 356 female births being recorded for every 1,000 males among non-Andamanese. The Andamans figures rather suggest that race is more likely to be the responsible factor than climate. One other factor has to be mentioned and that is the great reduction of recent years in mortality from famine. The India Census Report of 1911 (pages 220—222) adduces some evidence to suggest that famine leads to a higher mortality among males, and may therefore function as a corrective to an excessive male ratio, so that a reduction of mortality from famine would automatically reduce the ratio of females to males.

It is generally recognised that the ratio of females to males increases inversely with social standing among Hindus. This is well illustrated by the figures for Bombay where the whole Hindu population has been divided up according to education and social status into advanced, intermediate, backward and depressed classes. For the advanced castes the ratio of women to men is 878 per 1,000, for the intermediate castes it is 935 per 1,000, for the aboriginal tribes 956 and for other backward 953 while for the depressed classes it rises to 982 per 1,000 males. On the other hand the ratio for Muslims taken as a whole in the same province is only 809 females to per 1,000 males, and even if the States of Western India, where Muslim females actually exceed males in number, be reckoned in with Bombay it only raises the ratio for Muslim women to 829 per 1,000 males. These figures are possibly not quite representative as they stand, since many of the Muslims in Bombay are immigrants, while climatic or racial factors may enter in since Sind is preponderatingly Muslim as compared to the rest of the Bombay Presidency, and as has already been stated, the preponderance of males is greater in the dry areas in the north-west of India, whatever the reason may be. The figures are, however, generally indicative of the fact that the preponderance of males over females is certainly no less among Muslims generally than among Hindus. It is probable that some proportion of the excess number of males both among Muslims and Brahmans or other high class Hindus is to be accounted for by the *purdah* system, not so much because there is any deliberate concealment of females, as because it makes the household generally more difficult of access to the enumerator, who might be tempted to put down the names of the members of the household personally known to him and to omit those unknown, among whom the women of the household would naturally preponderate, to avoid having to make himself a nuisance to the inmates. There is, however, no reason to believe that the short enumeration of women due to this cause accounts for more than a very small part of the excess of males disclosed by the census. The Census Superintendent for Bombay has argued with some plausibility for the view that in the north-west of India, particularly among Muslims, the census returns have consistently understated the number of females between 0 and 15

FEMALES PER 1000 MALES

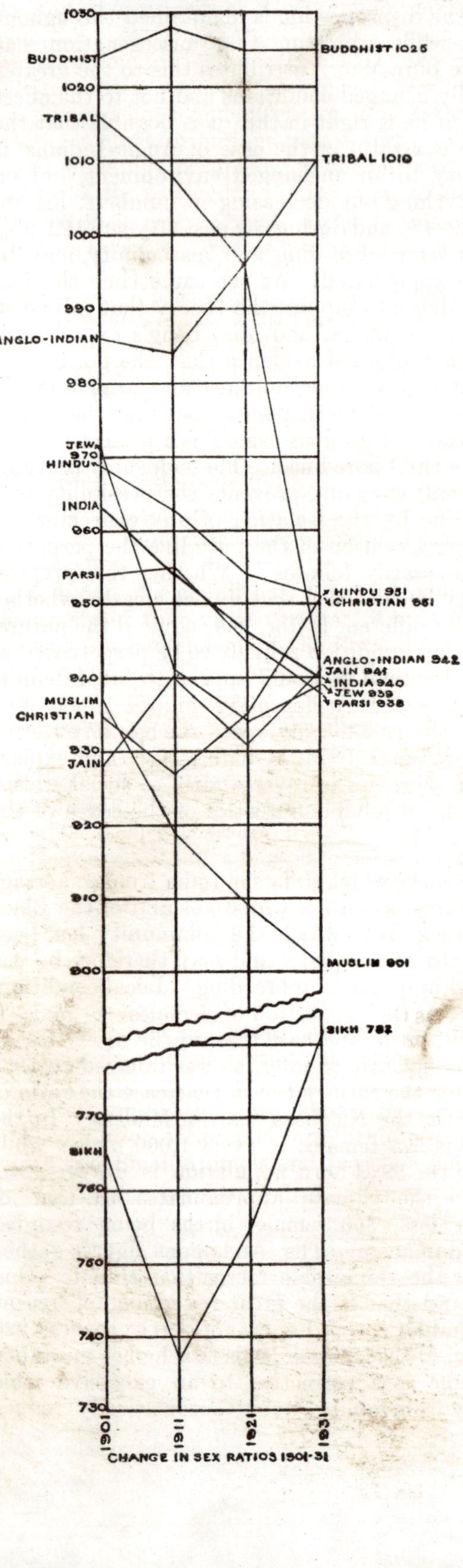

CHANGE IN SEX RATIOS 1901-31

on account of indifference to their existence or of deliberate concealment; his arguments are attractive, but fail to account for the fact that the ratio of females aged 0-1 is much higher than the total ratio, whereas it is just at that period that it might be expected to be least, not only on account of the greater number of males born but because concealment would presumably be just as active a factor at that age as during the next 10 years or so while indifference might be expected to be possibly even more active, nor does it account for the existence of a progressive decline in the ratio from census to census. The all-India ratio (Burma included) is 901 females per 1,000 males for Muslims and 951 females per 1,000 males for Hindus. Here again, however, it has to be remembered that Muslims predominate in the north-west where the ratio of females to males is lower in all communities than in the south and east. If the Punjab alone be taken the Muslims have the higher ratio 841 females per 1,000 males, Hindus having 826 and Sikhs only 799 females per 1,000 males. The only provinces in which there is actually an excess of women over men are Madras and Bihar and Orissa, though the Central Provinces can be added if Berar be excluded. In the Central Provinces and Berar taken together males have exceeded females for the first time since 1891, though in the natural population alone females still exceed males. In Burma again if Burmese alone be taken there is an excess of women over men, and the excess of males, as in the Federated Malay States, is due entirely to the immigration of foreign males. Conversely the excess of females in Bihar and Orissa, in the Central Provinces, other than Berar, and in Madras is partly accounted for by the emigration of males. The excess in Bihar and Orissa is mainly in Chota Nagpur and Orissa, including the States. If the natural as distinct from the actual populations of these provinces be taken, there is a ratio of 1,004 females per 1,000 males in the Central Provinces, 984 females per 1,000 males in Bihar and Orissa and 1,010 females per 1,000 males in Madras. Where females are in excess the excess is still most marked in the lower castes and does not always extend to the higher. Thus in Bihar and Orissa there are 964 Brahman females to every 1,000 Brahman males, but in the Hari caste there are 1,009 females to every 1,000 males. Similarly in the Central Provinces there are 863 Brahman females to 1,000 males, but 965 Sonar, 1,017 Kalar and 1,117 Ghasia females to 1,000 males of their respective castes. The aboriginal tribes which have retained their tribal religions show for India as a whole, an excess of females per 1,000, males, their ratio being 1,009. For British Territory there is a decidedly higher ratio of 1,018 females to every 1,000 males, which is mainly due to the high ratio of females (1,025 per 1,000 males) among the non-Hinduised tribes of Chota Nagpur and the Santal Parganas, since elsewhere except in Burma (1,021) and in Madras (1,006 females per 1,000 males) the tribal population shows a slight excess of males, the ratio being on the average 994 females per 1,000 males. It seems likely that this high ratio of females among the aborigines of Chota Nagpur and of the Agency Tracts of Madras is partly due to the recruiting of males for labour on the Assam tea gardens and the figures for emigration to Assam confirm the supposition, as the Census Superintendent for that province remarks on the very poor recruitment of women coolies during the decade. The ratio is higher in the Bihar and Orissa States (1,038) and in Chota Nagpur

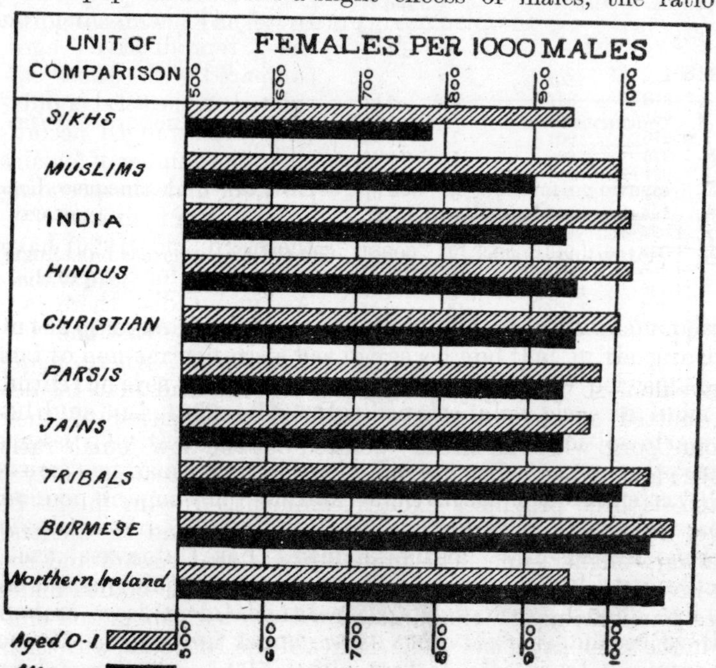

(1,040) than in the Santal Parganas though for Indian States generally there are only 993 tribal females per 1,000 males. Generally speaking however, except in the Nicobars the numbers of the sexes are fairly well balanced in non-Hinduised tribes, being much more nearly equal than in either Hindus or Muslims in India as a whole. The general conclusion as to the sex ratios of the population as a whole of India proper is therefore that in the aboriginal tribes the numbers of the two sexes are approximately equal, whereas in the rest of the community males exceed females. The all-India ratio of the latter per 1,000 of the former is lowest among Sikhs (782 for India as a whole), next lowest among Muslims (901), and is 951 among Hindus; but this higher ratio is only maintained as compared to Muslims if the whole population be taken together, since the bulk of the Muslim population is located in the area where the females ratio for the whole community is lowest. Taken by separate areas the ratio of females to males among Muslims is equal to or higher than the ratio among Hindus; thus in Madras there are approximately 1,026 females per 1,000 males in both communities and in the Punjab the Muslim ratio of females per 1,000 males is, as we have seen already, higher than the Hindu ratio. Within the Hindu community the ratio increases in inverse proportion to social position and education. The table in the margin and diagram above show the female ratio in the first year of life as compared to that at all ages censused, indicating the comparative wastage of female life from whatever causes.

Females per 1,000 males. (of population returned by age.) In	Aged 0-1.	All ages.	Variation % between columns 2 and 3.
Sikhs	947	784	—17·2
Muslims	999	904	—9·5
India	*1,013*	*941*	*—7·1*
Hindus	1,017	953	—6·3
Christians	1,002	952	—5·0
Parsis	981	940	—4·2
Jains	972	941	—3·2
Tribals	1,045	1,009	—3·4
Burmese	1,076	1,046	—2·8
Northern Ireland	*951*	*1,066*	*+12·0*

Reproductive period.

81. From the point of view, however, of the immediate increase or decrease of population the sex ratio of the total community is of less importance than the sex ratio of the breeding part of it, since on account of age or immaturity a considerable proportion of the population is neutral as regards reproduction. If we examine the relative proportions of females aged 15 to 45 and of males aged 20 to 50, which may be taken to represent roughly the breeding age period of the population of India, it becomes immediately apparent that the proportion of female to male is generally higher than it is when the ratio is based on the total population. The marginal figures show the provincial ratios in British India, calculated first on the reproductive ages, compared with those calculated on the total population, and arranged according to the number of females per 1,000 males in ascending order. The figures of Northern Ireland (1926) have been added for comparison. As in India there are areas, or at least one, Co. Fermanagh, where males exceed females, and have done so for fifty years. Delhi and the Andaman Islands have been purposely omitted on account of the artificial composition of their populations. Apart from Coorg, where as already pointed out the low female ratio seems quite out of place and which calls for some special explanation not yet forthcoming, the position of three provinces excites comment. Assam might be expected to figure lower down in the list, the Nicobars lower still, and the Central Provinces on the contrary higher up. The probability is that Assam and the Central Provinces are inversely affected by migration, that is by able-bodied males of the reproductive ages immigrating to the first as tea garden labour and emigrating from the other in the same capacity. The figures of the Nicobars, with their very small population, have been to some extent biassed by the presence of

Serial No.	Province.	Females per 1,000 males reproductive age periods.	Females per 1,000 males total population.	Serial number according to column 4.	Difference per 1,000 males between columns 3 and 4.
1	2	3	4	5	6
1	Coorg	805	803	1	2
2	Punjab	918	831	2	+87
3	N. W. F. P.	961	843	3	+118
4	Bombay	970	901	7	+69
5	Ajmer-Merwara	976	892	5	+84
6	Nicobar Islands	991	881	4	+110
7	Assam	991	900	6	+91
8	United Provinces	995	902	8	+93
9	Bengal	1,037	924	9	+113
10	Burma	1,039	958	10	+81
11	Central Provinces	1,106	998	11	+108
12	Bihar and Orissa	1,130	1,005	12	+125
13	Madras	1,177	1,025	13	+152
	Northern Ireland	*1,231*	*1,066*		*+165*

foreign traders and the crews of Chinese pearling boats, etc., whose comparatively small numbers are nevertheless enough to impair the balance of the sex returns. If these be excluded the number of Nicobarese females per 1,000 Nicobarese males is 927 ; and if the reproductive ages only be considered, it becomes 991. Taking India as a whole therefore, the sex ratio is very far from being as unfavourable to a progressive population as the total sex figures suggest at first sight. At the same time it must not be forgotten that the point at which the number of females is adequate to the number of males is limited to the ages from 15 to 30, and the probability is that their deficiency from the ages of 30 to 60 is due to exhaustion by breeding as soon as the reproductive period is reached. The Age of Consent Committee reports as follows :—

> " Inquiries into a large number of cases show that when the marriage of young people is consummated at an early age, say, when the boy is not more than 16 years or the girl is 12 or 13, a fairly large percentage of wives die of phthisis or some other disease of the respiratory organs or from some ovarian complication within 10 years of the consummation of marriage "

The earlier deficiency is also responsible, since were the excess of females in age group 0-5 maintained till group 15 to 20 the parity between the sexes would be maintained for a greater period after that point. Actually more males are born but there are more females in age group 0-5, after which the sudden drop in the ratio may be taken to indicate the effect of discriminative neglect in favour of male children during the earlier years. The Census Superintendent for Bombay comes, among others, to the following definite conclusion :—

> " The death-rate amongst females is higher than amongst males in the 5 to 10 years age group ; this is due to the neglect of female children. There is no reliable evidence showing whether the tendency to neglect female children is more powerful in certain communities and castes than in others, but *prima facie* it is probable that neglect of female children varies to some extent with economic circumstances. A study of the specific death-rates shows that after the age of 5 only in the 40 and over age groups is the female death-rate lower than the male. 65·8 per cent. of the female population is aged between 5 and 40 so that the heavy death-rate affects the larger proportion of the female population."

There are more females again at 20 to 25 and for the third time more females at

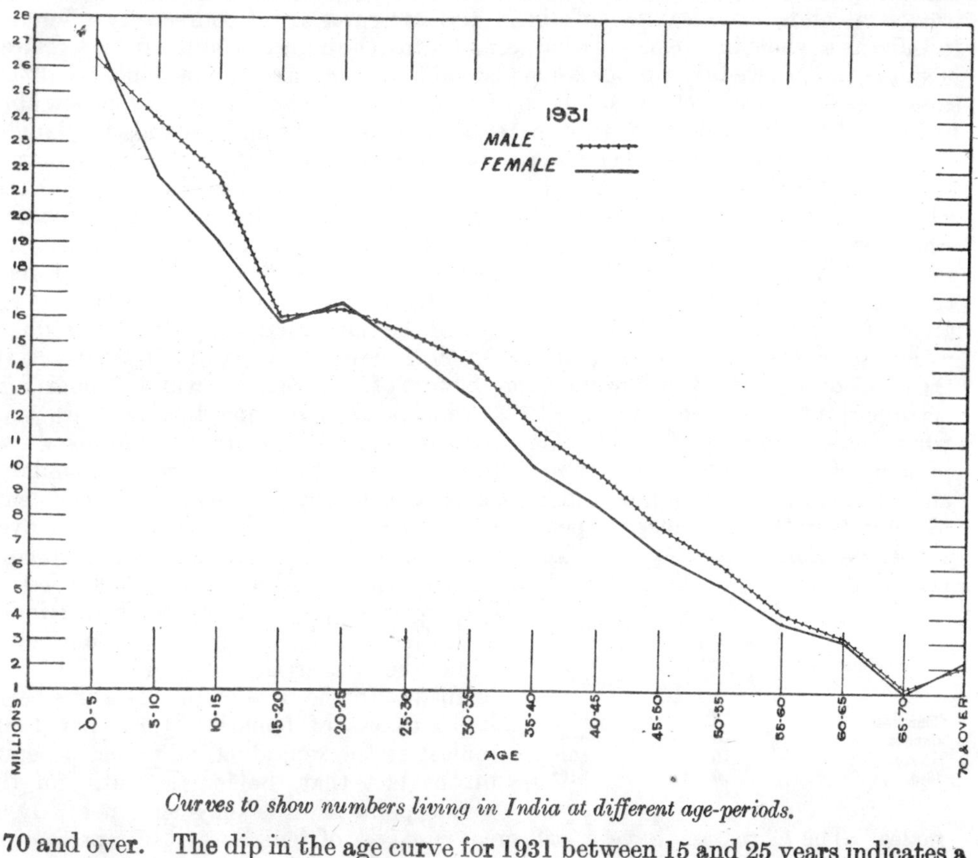

Curves to show numbers living in India at different age-periods.

70 and over. The dip in the age curve for 1931 between 15 and 25 years indicates a recurrent feature of Indian age-returns, already referred to in the last chapter.

Writing with reference to the curves of male and female vital statistics in the United Provinces the Census Superintendent shows very lucidly the effects there of immature maternity on the ratio of the sexes :—

Age.			Number of female deaths per 1,000 male deaths, in the United Provinces of Agra and Oudh.	
			1931.	1921.
0-1	..	..	838	877
1-5	..	..	916	981
5-10	..	..	871	910
10-15	..	..	847	865
15-20	..	..	*1,000*	*981*
20-30	..	..	*1,070*	*1,044*
30-40	..	..	912	935
40-50	..	..	758	816
50-60	..	..	784	834
60 and over		..	877	936

" Nothing could demonstrate more plainly the dangers to which the women of this province are exposed owing to the conditions under which they bear children ; and the fact that the curve rises between 20 and 30 illustrates the fact that those dangers are not limited to the birth of the first-born, but continue as the result of subsequently bearing too many and too frequent children, or as the result of disorders and diseases arising from child-birth.

In the margin I give the sex-ratio at the various age periods for 1921 and 1931. They are most striking. Here we see at once that whereas the sex-ratio in deaths has fallen since 1921 at all other ages, it has risen at the reproductive ages of 15-30. This bears out what I have said elsewhere, *viz* :—that in the absence of selective epidemic diseases the effect of the usual very high mortality of females at the reproductive ages becomes more noticeable, and so the sex-ratio in deaths rises."

In Cochin State on the other hand these conditions have been remedied :—

" Further a steady rise in the age of marriage consequent on the rapid progress of female education in the State and the gradual displacement of primitive methods of midwifery by modern and scientific methods have considerably reduced the dangers which almost all women have to face, and lowered the death-rate among young mothers to an appreciable extent. The gradual rise in the sex ratio is but the natural outcome of these improved conditions."

It is necessary now to examine the figures by certain religions in the same manner. Communities in which the women outnumber the men, figures of which present no abnormal features, need not perhaps occupy our attention further. Thus indigenous Burmese races show no marriages under 5 years and very few indeed under 10 years, and their total figures of married persons show a slight excess of females which is in no way remarkable. Indian figures are of course very different. In India as a whole in all except tribal communities the males outnumber the females, in spite of which we find a progressive instead of a regressive population, and at the same time the contradictory condition in many places that parents of sons are able to demand considerable sums from parents anxious to obtain husbands for daughters. The latter custom is of course partly due to the rule that a girl must be married before puberty, a point to which reference must be made in the next chapter, while the progressive nature of the population has already been indicated when pointing out that the inequality between the sexes was less at the reproductive ages than when taken as a whole. It is from this point of view that communities must be examined individually. Taking the Hindus it appears that there are 54,473,448 females of the reproductive ages to 51,450,266 males, an excess of three million or 1,059 females to every 1,000 males. In the case of the Hindus however the factor of the ban on widow remarriage is important, for there are 8,313,773 widows at the reproductive ages and when these are excluded the female excess is reduced to a deficiency of over five million, of over 10 per cent. that is, leaving only 897 per 1,000 males. Similarly among Jains the exclusion of widows leaves a deficiency of nearly 20 per cent. of females in the reproductive period. Sikhs have an actual deficiency of over 15 per cent. of females at the reproductive period in any case, and though a considerable number of their potentially reproductive males remain unmarried in consequence, they are, compared to Hindus and Jains, a late marrying community, while the remarriage of widows is not banned. In the case of the Muslims there is an excess of females (1,026 per 1,000 males) at the reproductive period, in spite of the fact that the female ratio for the whole population is only 901 per 1,000 males. The Christians have a still greater excess of females at the reproductive

Community.		Increase per cent. 1921—1931	Females 15—45 per 1,000 males 20—50.
Christian	..	32	1,080
Muslim	..	13	1,026
Hindu	..	10	897*
Jain ..	..	6	810*

* After exclusion of widows.

ages, having 1,080 females per 1,000 males of that period. It seems likely that these proportions have some definite bearing on the rates of increase in the different communities. It offers an explanation of the particularly small rate of increase of Jains, and a reason why Hindus have increased at a slower rate than Muslims. The comparative rate of Hindu increase would be lower still were it not for the large additions received from tribal communities, a source of recruitment which will not be available indefinitely. The exceptionally high Christian rate of increase is of course similarly affected by the inclusion of converts, but the sex-ratio is probably contributive. In the case of the Sikhs, which is very obviously an instance to the contrary, it is impossible to ascertain what proportion of the abnormal increase is due to accretions from Hinduism. Considerable numbers of Hindus, particularly of the Arora caste, are reported to have turned Sikh in the Punjab, and there is some evidence of a considerable propaganda about the time of the census to induce depressed castes in the Punjab to return themselves as Sikhs. Sahejdhari Sikhs who returned themselves as Hindu in 1921 may have returned themselves as Sikh in 1931, and it is more than probable that this was the case in the Punjab, where they can register as voters in Sikh constituencies by making a declaration that they are Sikhs. In some provinces, *e.g.*, Sind, there have been extraordinary fluctuations in the numbers returned as Sikhs probably on account of a varying classification of Sahejdharis. The Sind variations are mentioned below (Chapter XI, para. 165) and must cause the exceptional increase of 1931 to be regarded with much reserve. The percentages of variation in Sind, where there were 127,000 Sikhs returned in 1881, were —99 in 1891 and —100 in 1901. In 1911, 12,000 were returned and the variations for 1921 and 1931 were —42 per cent. and +164 per cent. In any case it is likely that the practice of late marriage by the community in general would tend to a higher birth rate, or rather a higher survival rate, since it seems clear that premature maternity is likely not only to deplete the number of married women in the later age groups of the reproductive period but to reduce the number of healthy children born to them. If this be so the same consideration would apply to the analogous case of the Anglo-Indians already mentioned above. Another striking case which at first sight appears to conflict with the hypothesis proposed is that of the Tribal Religions which suffer a decrease of 15 per cent. in spite of the very favourable sex ratio of 1,143 females to 1,000 males in the reproductive period. It will be seen from the figures given in Chapter XI that this decrease can be entirely attributed to transfers from Tribal Religions to Hinduism and to Christianity, but chiefly to the former. In this connection a reference may be made to the diagram of the sex ratios at the last four censuses at paragraph 80 above. It will be noticed that the Christian and Sikh communities, which have both shown very remarkable increase in population at this census, have had a rising female ratio for the past two decades, and it is possible that the rising female ratio of the Anglo-Indians from 1911 to 1921 is also intimately associated with their 1931 increase, in which case the falling ratio of 1921-31 should indicate a much reduced rate of increase after 1941 if not before. No other community has shown any increase in the female ratio since 1911, except the slight increases during the past decade among Jains, Jews and Tribes. The steadily falling Muslim ratio is of some importance and must inevitably lead to the cessation of the high increase in that community. It is possibly to be imputed to the observance of the purdah system by the poorer classes and the consequent prevalence of consumption and early mortality among women. It also suggests a possible lowering of the age of marriage and maternity.

Community.	Variation per cent. 1921—1931.	Females 15—45 per 1,000 males 20—50.
Sikh	+34	848
Tribal	—15	1,143

Sex Ratio by Caste.

82. An examination of the sex ratio by caste might be expected to show an immediate correlation to the ratio of prevalence of infant marriage to which allusion is made in the next chapter, whereas at first sight these ratios appear in almost inverse relationship. It must however be borne in mind first that the ratio of the prevalence of infant marriage has been calculated on the number of married aged 0—6 only, excluding all figures of marriage for girls beyond that age group and secondly that the mere ceremony of marriage cannot of itself affect the ratio. The practices which govern the female ratio in India, apart from possible climatic or racial factors, the nature, degree and very existence of which are doubtful, are those relating to the care of female children and to too early and too frequent maternity,

neither of which have any necessary connection with the frequency of the marriage ceremony when the bride is under six and a half years old—an age at which even the most precocious can hardly bear children. The marginal table therefore must be regarded as merely suggestive of the possible prevalence of the neglect of female children and/or of too early and too frequent maternity as likely to be contributive to a low ratio of females to males in the total caste population. It may here be pointed out that the figures for Rajputs (India) include from some provinces both Sikh and Muslim Rajputs, and that in Jammu and Kashmir State, where it has recently (1930) been found necessary to take special measures to prevent infanticide among Hindu Rajputs, the sex ratio among Hindu Rajputs is 754 females per 1,000 males, that among Muslim Rajputs being 918. The Census Superintendent of the United Provinces points out that there still appears to exist a differential treatment of girl babies between different castes and continues :—

Caste or Tribe.	Females per 1,000 males.
Rajput (*Rajputana*)	798
Jat	805
Gujar	832
Brahman (*Bengal*)	847
Rajput (*India*)	868
Sayyid	884
Kayastha	888
Momin	898
Brahman (*India*)	902
Gadaria	929
Kunbi	937
Komati	938
Yadava	948
Dom	952
Chamar	967
Teli	979
Mahar	1,001
Maratha	1,004
Sawara	1,019
Gond	1,045
Nayar (*India*)	1,049
Tanti	1,058
Nayar (*Cochin*)	1,154

"It is only by preserving the girl babies that a sufficiency of females will remain at all ages. The dangers of child-birth (dependent in large measure on the customs of the caste in respect of the age of the consummation of marriage) largely control the ratio of the sexes in the total population of every caste."

A reference may be made in this connection to the marginal table and diagram above (paragraph 80) in which the difference between the female ratio in the first year of life and the female ratio for the population as a whole is clearly indicated.

Only two purely Muslim groups have been tabulated and of these the figure for Sayyids is so low as to make it doubtful if it represents a complete enumeration of the females of the group. This doubt arises from an examination of the returns under the head 'Pathan' which, though available from eight provinces and states, afford the very low ratio of 864 females per 1,000 males and suggest that either some of the Pathans enumerated were temporary visitors whose females reside outside the scope of census enumeration (*e.g.*, in the N.-W. F. P. Tribal Areas) or that females of the Pathan group have been returned as Muslims merely without specification of tribe. It is possible that something of this sort may have affected the returns of Sayyids also since the Muslim groups, except perhaps in the case of the Momins, are not by any means so clearly defined as are Hindu castes or primitive tribes. In the case of the latter again it must not be forgotten that under one head are sometimes included not only tribesmen living a detached and tribal life in their own hills but also Hinduised tribesmen whose life and customs are hardly if at all distinguishable from those of other castes occupying the same areas. Thus 'Sawara' includes not only the hillmen of the Ganjam Agency whose life and religion is purely tribal, but the Saharias of Gwalior who are completely Hinduised. This difference is perhaps reflected in their sex ratios, for the Gwalior Saharias have only 977 females per 1,000 males whereas the Madras branch of the tribe have 1,024 and the C. P. branch 1,043. It has already been pointed out that the highest female ratio is generally to be found either among primitive tribes or low castes, among both of whom marital cohabitation does not usually take place till approximate maturity is reached. The sex ratio is also similarly high among the *marumakkathayam* communities of the Malabar coast where female children are no less cared for than male and where, owing to the prevalence of adult marriage very early maternity is unusual.

Section ii.—Fertility.

Fertility statistics.

83. Figures of the size and composition of families, and statistics bearing on the rate of propagation in India are so inadequate that it was decided to attempt to obtain some figures of fertility at this census in spite of the many difficulties. The figures obtained will be found in Appendix I to Part ii (*Tables*) of this volume. Financial considerations were one obstacle and others were the difficulty of getting ordinary enumerators, and the still greater difficulty of getting suitable persons to carry out the rather delicate enquiries needed for this purpose. In Baroda State the enquiries made were particularly careful and thorough, and the Census Commissioner for that State, Mr. S. V. Mukerjea, has dealt admirably with the whole subject in his report. In Travancore also 105,000 returns were collected, of which only 2·7 per cent. had to be rejected, and they have been carefully discussed in detail by Dr. Pillai. In the United Provinces the Local Government decided that no such enquiries could be made, but in most other provinces and states some attempt was made to obtain figures of fertility. Various agencies were used, generally educational or medical, and wherever possible the figures were collected through women. The total number of families for which returns of some kind were obtained was about 900,000 drawn from all grades of society and (except the United Provinces) from every part of India, so that the resulting figures may be taken as a well-mixed sample, though admittedly inadequate numerically. As the information obtained was very variable in degree and quality it was necessary to reject for one table or another those returns which were inadequate in some respect, and in consequence the numbers dealt with in each table fall very far short of the total number of returns received, amounting in some cases to less than half. In the tables volume gross figures have been compiled for India, with sub-totals by all communities for which more than one provincial figure exists. Thus in the case of Hindus a sub-total of 'Other Interior Castes' has been compiled, and a further sub-total of Yadavas; on the other hand no separate sub-total of Bafinda appears, as a separate figure for this caste is available for one state only, and as it can be found in the provincial figures there was no object in repeating the total for India. The figures that follow in this chapter are those compiled for India only, and for provincial or state sub-totals it will be necessary to refer to the Tables volume.

Sex of first-born.

84. The first statement shows the proportion of male and female children returned as the first born of the families examined. Whether Jastrzebski's theory that the sex of subsequent births is influenced in the direction of masculinity or femininity by the sex of the first child be valid or not, it is likely that males will predominate among the first-born, as it seems to be a universal phenomenon that although fewer survive infancy more males are actually born than females, and this majority can hardly fail to be reflected in the proportions of male to female first-born. In any case the enquiry in Burma showed that in 61 per cent. of the families in which a girl was born first female children predominated, and in 75 per cent. of those in which the first-born was a boy, male children predominated, but the figures dealt with were not large. In Baroda, however, the figures of 29,000 families yielded precisely the same percentages. The corresponding percentages in Travancore were 52 and 61. The marginal table shows that there is a general, if not very exact, correspondence between the ratio of the sexes of first births and the ratios throughout India of the natural population of provinces, though the comparative symmetry of the figures is marred in particular those of by Delhi, the Punjab, the Andaman Islands, Mysore and the Central Provinces. At any rate it is clearly in the north-west that the female ratio is lowest among the first-born as among the total population, and in the south that it is, correspondingly, the highest. This rather suggests that the lower ratio of females to males in the north-west is due in part to an actual insufficiency of female births, though if the sex ratio of first births be maintained throughout subsequent births the Punjab and Delhi should show a higher survival rate than they do, as also Mysore.

Province or State.	Number of females first born per 1,000 males first born.	Number of females per 1,000 males in natural population.
Baluchistan	566	832
Jammu and Kashmir ..	590	869
Baroda	699	923
Gwalior	726	908
Bengal	730	942
Central India	732	940
Delhi	759	793
Punjab	786	823
Central Provinces ..	795	1,004
Bombay	808	923
Western India States ..	829	965
Travancore	862	987
Andaman Islands ..	875	893
Assam	879	945
Madras	882	1,010
Cochin	924	1,023
Mysore	967	965

STATEMENT I.

Sex of First-Born.

Number of females first-born.	Number of males first-born.	Number of females first-born per 1,000 males first-born.	Number of slips examined.
238,462	305,963	779	575,495

Fertility and Age at Marriage.

85. The second statement shows the proportion of sterile to fertile marriages according to the duration of marriage, and the age of the wife at the time of marriage. No account is taken of still-born children and such are not counted as births at all in any of these tables. The general percentage of sterility in marriages that have lasted 15 years and over is 6 per cent. This percentage falls in the case of wives married under 12 years to 2 per cent. but the numbers available are few and the percentage unreliable for that reason. There is less reason to doubt the result in the case of wives married at 13 to 14 years of age when the percentage of sterility is only 4, rising to 7 in the case of wives married above the age of 14 years. These results have, however, to be read with those obtained from the next table which shows the average size of the family correlated to the age of the wife at marriage. Here we find that while the average number of children born from wives married at all ages is 4·2 and the survival rate 2·9, both the number born and the survival rate seem to increase with the age of the wife at marriage and are at the highest for wives married at 30 years and over, 5·1 and 3·6 respectively, while for wives married at 20 to 30 years they are 4·3 and 3·1. The general inference is that although an increase in the age of marriage for girls slightly increases the risk of the marriage proving sterile, possibly on account of greater exposure to sterilizing diseases, it also increases the number of children born alive when the marriage is, as it will be in at least ·92 per cent. of cases, fertile, and it likewise increases the probability of survival to the children.

STATEMENT II.

Proportion of fertile and sterile marriages.

Age of wife at marriage.	Duration of Marriage. 0–4 years.		5–9 years.		10–14 years.		15 years and longer	
	Fertile.	Sterile.	Fertile.	Sterile.	Fertile.	Sterile.	Fertile.	Sterile
All Ages ..	164,491	71,502	213,807	41,930	214,696	27,433	444,161	26,513
0–12 ..	1,588	1,592	5,933	1,188	11,792	645	26,767	604
13–14 ..	63,803	28,590	93,718	16,982	91,871	10,106	203,135	9,509
15–19 ..	81,610	34,427	92,905	19,473	87,890	13,509	165,421	12,917
20–29 ..	15,751	6,085	19,350	3,711	20,710	2,727	43,098	3,020
30 and over .	1,739	808	1,901	576	2,433	446	5,740	463

STATEMENT III.

Average size of family correlated with age of wife at marriage.

Wife married at	Number of families.	Number of children born alive.	Average observed.	Number of children surviving.	Average observed.
All Ages	568,628	2,368,172	4·2	1,661,448	2·9
0–12 years	40,729	154,120	3·8	112,127	2·8
13–14 years	191,783	809,891	4·2	552,345	2·9
15–19 years	249,874	1,022,209	4·1	726,118	2·9
20–29 years	75,758	328,181	4·3	232,804	3·1
30 years and over	10,484	53,771	5·1	38,054	3·6

Size of Family by Occupation.

86. In the fourth statement, which shows the size of family by the occupation of the husband, the average number of children born per family, which in this case is calculated on a smaller number of families, works out at the slightly higher figure of 4·3, and the survival rate obtained, 3·0, is similarly slightly higher. This is stated in the form of the numbers surviving per 1,000 born, 697 per 1,000 for all the families examined. The families are classified by occupation on the lines of the Occupation Table (X), but the result of this has been that the numbers in some occupational orders, on which averages have been calculated, are really too small for any safe conclusion. The general average size of family is exceedingly constant about the number 4. In five instances it rises to 5·0 or over, the maximum being 5·6, but in three of these cases the numbers dealt with are very low. In the other two, where the numbers are higher, the rate may perhaps, be accepted. These two are the orders of Religion and of Persons living on their Income. In the latter the survival rate is also high, as might be expected, 712 per 1,000, though not as high as in the case of Law, Medicine and Instruction, where the survival rate is 760 per 1,000 while the average family is only 3·7. Apparently physicians, if unable to heal themselves, can yet heal their children. At any rate this is the highest survival rate found in any occupation, the next highest being those of the families of men employed in textile industries and in the Army, 731 and 729 respectively, with average families of 3·7 and 3·6. Public administration comes next with an average family of 3·9 and a survival rate of 721 per 1,000. The lowest survival rates, all those below 600 in fact, are calculated on figures too small to be worth considering, but it is possibly significant that the survival rate in Industry as a whole is only 687 children per 1,000 born, though the general level is in the neighbourhood of 700, and Class C (Public Administration and Liberal Arts) as a whole has the rate of 716, but with smaller families.

STATEMENT IV.

Size of families by occupation of husband.

N. B.—Totals in this table include figures which could not be distributed to sub-totals owing to the method adopted in compilation.

Occupation.	Number of families examined.	Number of children born.	Average per family.	Number of children surviving.	Proportion of total surviving to 1,000 born.
Total of all classes	**408,161**	**1,740,399**	**4·3**	**1,213,457**	**697**
A.—Production of Raw Materials	**223,391**	**978,750**	**4·4**	**683,540**	**698**
Exploitation of animals and vegetation ..	223,077	976,746	4·4	682,233	698
Pasture and Agriculture	*213,025*	*911,655*	*4·3*	*631,841*	*693*
Cultivation	*203,948*	*866,547*	*4·2*	*602,655*	*695*
Cultivating owners	*23,381*	*102,932*	*4·4*	*68,584*	*666*
Agricultural Labourers	*13,421*	*57,691*	*4·3*	*40,507*	*702*
Forestry	*139*	*529*	*3·8*	*355*	*671*
Stock-Raising	*5,038*	*20,487*	*4·1*	*13,847*	*676*
B.—Preparation and supply of Material Substances.	**92,323**	**387,301**	**4·2**	**266,963**	**689**
Industry	48,203	201,825	4·2	138,608	687
Textiles	*5,670*	*20,835*	*3·7*	*15,237*	*731*
Hides, skins and hard materials from the animal kingdom.	*57*	*255*	*4·5*	*154*	*604*
Wood	*1,521*	*6,220*	*4·1*	*4,192*	*674*
Sawyers, carpenters, turners and joiners ..	*24,705*	*106,492*	*4·3*	*71,716*	*673*
Metals	*688*	*2,628*	*3·8*	*1,756*	*668*
Blacksmiths, other workers in iron, makers of implements, workers in brass, copper and bell metal.	*959*	*3,674*	*3·8*	*2,582*	*703*
Ceramics	*181*	*678*	*3·7*	*458*	*676*
Chemical products properly so-called and analogous.	*215*	*823*	*3·8*	*586*	*712*
Food Industries	*983*	*4,269*	*4·3*	*3,043*	*713*
Industries of dress and the toilet	*8,147*	*31,678*	*3·9*	*22,118*	*698*
Building Industries	*1,117*	*4,506*	*3·8*	*3,053*	*673*

Occupation.	Number of families examined.	Number of children born.	Average per family.	Number of children surviving.	Proportion of total surviving to 1,000 born.
Construction of means of transport ..	*77*	*383*	*5·0*	*229*	*598*
Production and transmission of physical force.	*35*	*137*	*3·9*	*76*	*555*
Miscellaneous and undefined Industries ..	*4,310*	*18,475*	*4·3*	*12,573*	*681*
Scavenging	*3,547*	*15,428*	*4·3*	*10,485*	*680*
Transport	4,077	14,893	3·7	10,245	688
Transport by water	*297*	*1,544*	*5·2*	*1,002*	*649*
Transport by road	*1,499*	*5,660*	*3·8*	*3,784*	*669*
Transport by rail	*451*	*1,577*	*3·5*	*1,122*	*711*
Trade	*40,943*	*170,583*	*4·3*	*118,110*	*692*
C.—Public Administration and Liberal Arts ..	**34,453**	**139,219**	**4·0**	**99,701**	**716**
Public Force	2,671	10,464	3·9	7,108	679
Army	*1,543*	*5,486*	*3·6*	*3,999*	*729*
Police	*743*	*2,754*	*3·7*	*1,734*	*630*
Public Administration	19,232	74,688	3·9	53,842	721
Professions and Liberal Arts	12,550	54,067	4·3	38,751	719
Religion	*2,407*	*12,629*	*5·2*	*7,970*	*631*
Law, Medicine and Instruction	*7,360*	*27,412*	*3·7*	*20,824*	*760*
D.—Miscellaneous	**57,994**	**235,129**	**4·1**	**163,253**	**694**
Persons living on their income.	3,407	17,054	5·0	12,146	712
Domestic Service	6,401	24,068	3·8	16,526	687
Insufficiently described occupations ..	30,125	123,062	4·1	85,128	692
Labourers and workmen otherwise unspecified	*29,142*	*118,134*	*4·1*	*81,979*	*694*
Unproductive..	14,585	58,668	4·0	41,692	711
Inmates of jails, asylums and almshouses, beggars and vagrants	*2,204*	*9,551*	*4·3*	*6,774*	*709*
Other unclassified non-productive Industries	*58*	*326*	*5·6*	*204*	*626*
Unemployed and occupations unspecified	15,517	60,061	3·9	41,797	696

Size of family and duration of marriage by community.

87. The fifth statement correlates the duration of marriage with the community of the married and the number of quick births, and dealing with considerably larger numbers the average number of children born falls to 3·9, the lowest general figure yielded by any of these tables, but this of course is determined by the fact that large numbers of the marriages examined are incomplete. In marriages of ten to nineteen years duration the average number of children born is four and in marriages of 33 years duration and over it is 5·8 rising in the case of a few Kurmi marriages to 9, and in that of one Jewish family to 10. In Buddhist families on the other hand, where marriage is late, the average number born falls in cases of duration over 33 years and is at its highest in marriages of 20 to 31 years duration with an average per family of 6·1, only equalled in that duration term by Christians and Kurmis with the same number. The latter however rise to 7·0 in the later duration term in which the Buddhist average falls. Some conclusions can also be drawn from this table as to the frequency of births, the general inference being that two children are born alive during the first few years of marriage and that after ten years of married life have been accomplished the rate is approximately 1 child per decade up to 32 years of marriage.

In the sixth statement, which correlates the size of family to its community, the number of families examined is again rather fewer, and the total survival rate for 1,000 children born alive appears as 700 instead of the 697 yielded by Table IV, 700 being approximately the figure obtained likewise from Table III. The average per family, 4·3 in Table IV, is 4·2 by Tables III and VI, though it rises to 6·3 for Kayasthas and falls to 2·5 for Bhils. In the latter case the low birth-rate is compensated for by a high survival rate, 741, but the nomadic castes who have an average family of only 3·3 do not reach the general standard survival rate of 700, having one of 651 only, no doubt indicating the effects of their habits of life. The lowest survival rates are shown by Kurmis and Chamars, both under 600 and both having the majority of their wives married under 15 years of age, whereas the Sikh with the majority married over that age has a survival rate of 714, and the same combination of a high survival rate with a late age of wives at marriage appears in Parsis, Christians and above all in Buddhists, but the number dealt with in the first and third of these three communities is regrettably small, while Muslims, also with a majority of marriages with the wife aged 15 or over, have a survival rate of one below the general standard.

M22CC

Statement V.

Duration of Marriage correlated with Caste or Religion of Family.

Community of Husband.	Total.			Duration of Marriage with Present Wife. Under 10 years.			10 years.			10—19 years.			20—31 years.			32 years.			33 years and over.		
	Number of slips examined.	Number of children born alive.	Average per family.	Number of families.	Number of children born alive.	Average per family.	Number of families.	Number of children born alive.	Average per family.	Number of families.	Number of children born alive.	Average per family.	Number of families.	Number of children born alive.	Average per family.	Number of families.	Number of children born alive.	Averge per family.	Number of families.	Number of children born alive.	Average per family.
1	2	3	4	5	6	7	8	9	10	11	12	13	14	15	16	17	18	19	20	21	22
India																					
Total	**899,783**	**3,477,211**	**3·9**	**218,240**	**373,197**	**1·7**	47,931	148,153	3·1	268,487	1,073,908	4·0	**259,738**	**1,266,330**	**4·9**	**20,583**	**121,909**	**5·9**	**84,804**	**493,714**	**5·8**
Hindus	509,257	2,002,396	3·9	125,179	207,513	1·7	26,042	75,362	2·9	158,172	616,987	3·9	137,332	737,251	5·4	13,924	83,536	5·8	48,608	281,747	5·8
Brahman ..	32,461	112,495	3·5	8,916	12,948	1·5	1,371	3,761	2·7	9,962	28,496	3·0	8,007	42,727	5·3	909	5,478	6·0	3,296	19,085	5·8
Other Interior Castes	83,309	316,527	3·8	21,778	30,074	1·4	3,847	10,247	2·7	24,638	95,079	3·9	24,415	129,798	5·3	1,684	9,953	5·9	6,947	41,376	6·0
Kayastha ..	706	2,722	3·9	167	237	1·4	27	67	2·5	121	506	4·2	121	644	5·3	55	213	3·9	215	1,055	4·9
Kurmi ..	316	1,409	4·5	90	177	2·0	20	62	3·1	111	539	4·9	76	462	6·1	2	17	8·5	17	152	9·0
Rajput ..	4,698	16,076	3·4	1,133	1,634	1·4	328	772	2·4	1,488	4,939	3·3	1,274	6,202	4·9	85	415	4·9	390	2,114	5·4
Viswakarma	1,847	6,461	3·5	473	710	1·5	140	382	2·7	605	2,171	3·9	470	2,521	5·4	28	147	5·3	131	530	4·0
Yadava ..	938	2,675	2·9	262	281	1·1	71	170	2·4	284	868	3·1	247	918	3·7	3	18	6·0	71	420	6·0
Nomadic Castes ..	197	653	3·3	71	104	1·5	14	30	2·1	41	158	3·9	51	256	5·0	6	21	3·5	14	84	6·0
Exterior Castes ..	36,761	44,678	3·9	9,823	7,117	1·7	2,255	7,055	3·1	11,281	46,277	4·1	10,206	54,671	5·4	537	3,166	5·9	2,659	16,392	6·2
Chamar ..	3,155	10,713	3·4	848	1,389	1·6	198	630	3·2	1,073	3,544	3·3	840	4,022	4·8	36	179	5·0	160	949	5·9
Sikhs	25,740	105,185	4·1	6,419	12,220	1·9	1,471	4,271	2·9	7,313	29,606	4·1	6,856	37,897	5·5	445	2,598	5·8	3,236	18,593	5·7
Jains	4,632	19,288	4·2	1,193	1,898	1·6	258	800	3·1	1,322	5,545	4·2	1,177	6,879	5·8	155	994	6·4	527	3,172	6·0
Buddhists	2,167	9,964	4·6	492	1,800	3·6	11	44	4·0	463	2,430	5·2	593	3,640	6·1	309	1,200	3·9	299	850	2·8
Parsis	1,127	4,823	4·3	170	299	1·8	40	120	3·0	288	1,248	4·3	303	1,559	5·1	50	230	4·6	276	1,367	5·4
Jews	7	41	5·9	2	6	3·0	1	10	10·0	2	11	5·5	1	4	4·0	..	..	..	1	10	10·0
Muslims	264,542	940,469	3·6	60,840	109,206	1·8	15,926	54,029	3·4	74,686	310,007	4·2	87,392	324,170	3·7	3,560	19,890	5·6	22,138	123,167	5·6
Christians	37,506	169,798	4·5	9,341	12,809	1·4	1,280	3,733	2·9	8,729	37,598	4·3	12,359	75,255	6·1	842	5,689	6·9	4,955	34,714	7·0
Tribal	28,155	116,407	4·1	6,612	11,548	1·8	1,228	3,579	2·9	8,950	35,122	3·9	7,619	43,441	5·7	884	5,190	5·9	2,862	7,527	6·1
Bhil	574	1,655	2·9	231	261	1·1	54	152	2·8	154	547	3·6	91	418	4·6	4	33	8·2	40	244	6·1
Other or Unspecified ..	26,650	108,840	4·1	7,992	98	2·0	1,674	6,205	3·7	8,652	35,354	4·1	6,106	36,234	5·9	414	2,582	6·3	1,902	12,567	6·6

STATEMENT VI.

Size of families by caste or religion of family.

Community.	Number of slips examined.	Total number of children born alive.	Average per family.	Number of children surviving.	Proportion of total surviving to 1,000 born.	Number of families with wife married at 0—12	13—14	15—19	20—30	30 & over
1	2	3	4	5	6	7	8	9	10	11
Total	**528,864**	**2,242,711**	**4.2**	**1,569,983**	**700**	**41,950**	**172,286**	**229,408**	**72,471**	**10,321**
Hindus	302,403	1,291,923	4·3	899,948	697	18,334	117,807	130,495	29,647	4,310
Brahman	7,875	40,599	5·2	26,255	647	541	4,149	2,423	413	91
Other Interior Castes ..	21,624	106,732	4·9	74,182	695	1,010	5,252	9,552	3,834	415
Kayastha	280	1,759	6·3	1,166	663	14	116	120	22	8
Kurmi	316	1,409	4·5	805	571	7	199	92	16	2
Rajput	1,168	5,637	4·8	3,896	691	157	215	571	170	55
Viswakarma ..	174	879	5·1	558	635	4	65	76	22	7
Yadava	257	1,011	3·9	674	667	80	61	85	28	3
Nomadic Castes ..	199	662	3·3	431	651	72	27	74	22	4
Exterior Castes ..	35,349	149,302	4·2	104,217	698	870	13,100	16,838	4,112	429
Chamar	859	4,847	5·6	2,860	590	63	440	243	87	26
Sikhs	23,391	96,550	4·1	68,982	714	3,872	4,713	10,633	3,655	518
Jains	1,739	7,240	4·2	5,044	697	38	867	765	65	4
Buddhists	617	2,357	3·8	1,916	813	..	32	221	281	83
Parsis	713	3,252	4·6	2,299	707	1	231	245	219	17
Jews	69	264	3·8	189	716	9	24	30	6	..
Muslims	141,526	577,778	4·1	403,704	699	12,543	29,871	61,420	32,408	4,756
Christians	22,396	111,546	5·0	85,699	768	1,475	6,178	11,563	2,887	293
Tribal	9,640	48,415	5·0	30,918	639	689	3,340	3,629	1,778	182
Bhil	396	1,006	2·5	745	741	77	83	191	40	5
Other or Unspecified	26,370	103,386	3·9	71,284	689	4,989	9,223	10,407	1,525	158

NOTE.—The total of columns 7-11 falls short of the figure in column 2 by 2,428 owing to the absence of details by age of wife at marriage for 2,406 families from Bengal and for 22 from the Andaman Islands.

General Conclusions.

88. It may be added in conclusion that the numbers examined in these fertility tables hardly admitof safe conclusions except on the broader lines. It is not unlikely that the results obtained for India as a whole bear a reasonable approximation to the general average for the whole country, deduced as they are from returns from half a million families or more of all kinds and conditions. On the other hand no broad generalization from the individual figures of a single caste can be regarded as of very much authority. There is also some doubt as to how far the returns given by the persons questioned represent really accurate statements of fact. At the same time the general conclusion may fairly be drawn that the average married woman in India has four children born alive and that 2·9 in every four, 70 % that is, survive. It is interesting to note that the Census Superintendent of Bombay arrives at a similar conclusion from a calculation based on the number of persons of varying ages per 1,000 houses. It may also be concluded that raising the age of marriage for women will not reduce the number of children but will increase the proportion of those that survive.

It may be added that although in all provinces ' baleful prophecies were rife ' to the effect that the enquiry into fertility would arouse resentment and opposition and would have serious consequences, the prophets proved both false and foolish, for the enquiry did none of these things. A few people took umbrage at them, but those that did were not obliged to answer, and the collection of information was much easier and more efficient than in the attempts made in 1921. The employment of intelligent women for this purpose has many advantages.

SUBSIDIARY TABLE I.

General proportions per mille of the sexes by Provinces and States.

Province, State or Agency.	Actual Population.	Natural Population.
1	2	3
India	**940**	**940**
Provinces	**940**	**943**
Ajmer-Merwara	892	861
Andaman and Nicobar Islands	495	893
Assam (*including States*)	909	945
Baluchistan (*Districts and Administered Territories*)	717	815
Bengal	924	942
Bihar and Orissa	1,005	979
Bombay (*including Aden*)	901	924
Burma	958	1,025
Central Provinces and Berar	998	1,004
Coorg	803	922
Delhi	722	793
Madras	1,025	1,009
North-West Frontier Province (*Districts and Administered Territories*).	843	851
Punjab	831	824
United Provinces of Agra and Oudh	902	890
States and Agencies	**941**	**938**
Baluchistan States	855	850
Baroda State	942	923
Bengal States	886	939
Bihar and Orissa States	1,033	1,029
Bombay States	952	921
Central India Agency	948	940
Central Provinces States	1,010	999
Gwalior State	887	908
Hyderabad State	959	974
Jammu and Kashmir State	881	869
Cochin State	1,043	1,023
Travancore State	987	987
Other Madras States	1,079	1,062
Mysore State	955	965
North-West Frontier Province (*Agencies and Tribal Areas*)	864	888
Punjab States (*including Agency*)	832	816
Rajputana Agency	908	900
Sikkim State	967	986
United Provinces States	951	933
Western India States Agency	974	965

NOTE.—The estimated populations referred to on the fly-leaf of Table I in Part II of this Report have been included for purposes of calculating Actual and Natural population ; it being assumed for purposes of the latter figures that the entire population so estimated was indigenous.

SUBSIDIARY TABLE II.

Number of females per 1,000 males at different age-periods by main religions at each of the last three censuses.

Age.	All Religions.			Hindu.			Muslim.			Tribal.		
	1931.	1921.	1911.	1931.	1921.	1911.	1931.	1921.	1911.	1931.	1921.	1911.
1	2	3	4	5	6	7	8	9	10	11	12	13
0—1	1,012	991	1,001	1,017	993	1,004	999	983	991	1,045	1,009	1,020
1—2	1,044	1,027	1,041	1,051	1,030	1,046	1,030	1,021	1,029	1,078	1,055	1,067
2—3	1,058	1,058	1,050	1,068	1,066	1,053	1,040	1,045	1,046	1,090	1,098	1,080
3—4	1,018	1,085	1,065	1,024	1,098	1,074	1,003	1,066	1,051	1,057	1,101	1,098
4—5	980	1,017	1,001	989	1,019	1,002	955	1,007	993	1,013	1,059	1,035
Total 0—5	1,022	1,035	1,030	1,029	1,041	1,034	1,005	1,023	1,020	1,056	1,067	1,060
5—10	910	960	954	919	967	959	880	936	933	957	976	969
10—15	880	821	817	884	828	823	864	773	773	948	879	880
15—20	989	916	930	983	890	911	1,012	957	962	1,139	1,034	1,074
20—25	1,023	1,075	1,079	1,026	1,074	1,076	1,024	1,089	1,089	1,145	1,237	1,277
25—30	955	968	968	973	971	970	906	948	952	1,026	1,077	1,078
Total 0—30	961	956	960	967	957	960	945	943	947	1,033	1,021	1,036
30—40	891	905	910	912	922	933	824	842	854	957	967	937
40—50	866	902	912	886	922	928	798	836	854	891	873	879
50—60	910	926	950	940	947	973	815	848	867	967	923	965
60 and over..	994	1,040	1,092	1,055	1,101	1,151	825	871	921	1,124	1,106	1,173
Total 30 and over ..	899	927	944	926	951	967	815	846	866	957	949	952
Total All Ages	940	946	954	953	954	963	904	909	919	1,009	996	1,008

NOTE.—The figures in this statement relate to India proper, *i.e.*, exclude details for Burma, where the sort for age was by Race in stead of by Religion.

SUBSIDIARY TABLE III.

Number of females per 1,000 males at different age-periods by Religion.

Age.	All Religions.	Hindu.	Muslim.	Christian.	Tribal.
1	2	3	4	5	6
Total All ages	941	953	904	952	1,009
0—1	1,013	1,017	999	1,002	1,045
1—2	1,044	1,051	1,030	1,006	1,078
2—3	1,058	1,068	1,040	1,005	1,090
3—4	1,018	1,024	1,003	1,003	1,057
4—5	982	989	955	988	1,013
Total 0—5	1,023	1,029	1,005	1,001	1,056
5—10	912	919	880	959	957
10—15	884	884	864	949	948
15—20	991	983	1,012	1,003	1,139
20—25	1,023	1,026	1,024	1,001	1,145
25—30	952	973	906	945	1,026
Total 0—30	962	967	945	977	1,033
30—40	889	912	824	903	957
40—50	866	886	798	871	891
50—60	912	940	815	902	967
60 and over	994	1,055	825	947	1,124

NOTE.—The figures below All Religions relate to India as a whole but those for the respective religions refer to India proper, *i.e.*, exclude details for Burma where the sort for age was by Race instead of by Religion.

SUBSIDIARY TABLE IV.

Number of females per 1,000 males for certain selected Castes and Tribes.

Caste.	All Ages.	0—6	7—13	14—16	17—23	24—43	44 and over.
1	2	3	4	5	6	7	8
Baniya	881	994	892	837	881	834	860
Bhangi	909	985	824	837	986	914	867
Bhil	981	1,108	927	1,080	1,071	921	834
Brahman	902	980	875	828	917	878	911
Chamar	967	1,023	870	882	1,031	985	965
Chetti	1,011	1,098	970	1,048	1,045	928	1,057
Darzi	950	1,078	973	1,016	978	918	810
Dom	952	1,018	896	943	1,036	932	915
Gond	1,045	1,038	954	971	1,212	1,037	1,088
Gujar	832	961	782	763	887	815	764
Iluvan	1,026	1,003	970	1,023	1,142	1,030	1,036
Jat	805	936	794	730	808	782	744
Kachhi	879	1,005	800	831	934	846	853
Kahar	933	1,004	896	852	990	923	904
Kallan	1,083	1,017	988	890	1,218	1,151	1,119
Kayastha	888	996	896	823	914	845	855
Khatri	813	948	886	773	749	758	767
Kumhar	913	993	856	841	953	902	900
Kunbi	937	1,003	951	805	977	917	923
Mahar	1,001	1,041	920	965	1,082	987	1,024
Maratha	1,004	1,097	1,029	1,108	1,073	932	920
Megh	993	1,145	980	1,002	1,154	934	858
Momin (Julaha)	898	968	909	901	952	889	779
Naibrahman	903	1,007	852	799	900	902	892
Namasudra	961	1,080	893	1,053	1,105	920	830
Nayar (Nair)	1,049	989	980	991	1,122	1,056	1,153
Od	965	926	982	1,010	1,073	954	917
Pathan	864	979	811	789	863	870	812
Prabhu	883	1,063	923	1,023	1,006	677	884
Rajput	868	964	813	748	874	873	861
Santal	998	1,076	883	1,017	1,196	947	983
Shan	989	1,013	985	1,092	1,205	906	940
Tanti	1,058	1,046	918	961	1,227	1.095	1,092
Teli	979	1,022	933	883	1,104	971	943
Viswabrahman	905	989	901	841	959	879	853
Yadava	948	1,005	882	863	1,009	943	960

SUBSIDIARY TABLE V.

Number of deaths per 1,000 of the population for each sex at different ages as reported for British Districts in India.

Age.	1921.		1922.		1923.		1924.		1925.		1926.		1927.		1928.		1929.		1930.	
	Males.	Females.	Males.	Females.	Males.	Females.	Males.	Females.	Males.	Females.	Males.	Females.	Males.	Females.	Males.	Females.	Males.	Females.	Males.	Females.
1	2	3	4	5	6	7	8	9	10	11	12	13	14	15	16	17	18	19	20	21
0—1	205·16	190·14	183·21	166·38	182·56	167·99	196·72	179·94	181·21	167·02	196·61	179·57	174·01	159·30	180·93	164·32	185·46	169·49	189·12	171·88
1—5	54·11	49·61	41·22	36·74	43·63	39·75	52·67	47·44	45·42	40·79	52·13	46·80	48·82	43·83	48·16	43·48	51·83	46·94	57·11	51·25
5—10	15·25	13·81	10·56	9·62	10·88	10·29	12·93	12·13	10·27	9·56	10·83	10·16	10·12	9·35	10·04	9·56	10·11	9·56	10·74	9·96
10—15	10·84	10·34	7·99	8·01	8·54	8·83	10·46	10·98	8·10	8·28	8·44	8·97	7·55	7·90	7·53	8·20	7·15	7·75	7·21	7·54
15—20	13·60	15·36	10·46	12·23	10·80	12·91	13·30	15·58	10·77	12·88	11·33	14·05	10·50	13·19	10·40	13·74	9·96	13·16	10·25	13·13
20—30	16·16	17·15	12·23	13·20	12·23	13·52	14·37	15·68	12·23	13·25	12·55	14·24	11·98	13·68	12·03	14·50	11·56	14·03	11·65	14·05
30—40	19·44	19·02	15·04	14·56	14·66	14·51	16·99	16·89	14·59	14·09	14·94	15·03	14·46	14·47	14·63	15·00	14·20	14·67	14·25	14·79
40—50	26·28	22·02	20·44	16·81	19·85	16·76	22·65	19·50	20·27	16·53	20·38	17·25	19·52	16·26	19·81	16·71	19·85	16·74	20·18	17·19
50—60	41·13	35·87	32·18	27·25	31·28	27·06	35·38	31·14	31·64	27·15	32·57	28·23	30·56	26·31	31·08	27·04	31·96	27·84	32·48	28·53
60 and over ..	84·49	76·59	66·91	59·77	66·19	60·04	73·89	67·20	68·18	61·51	71·23	65·36	67·54	61·23	68·66	62·57	72·32	66·52	74·04	68·43

CHAPTER VI.

Civil Condition.

89. The instructions issued to enumerators were to record for each individual whether he or she were unmarried, married or widowed. Divorced persons who had not remarried were to be entered in the third category. The instructions as regards the second category were that a woman who had never been married should be shown in the first category even though she were a prostitute or concubine, but that persons recognised by custom as married were to be entered as such even though they had not been through any proper ceremony, while persons living together whose religious or social tenets allowed cohabitation without preliminary formalities were likewise to be entered as married. The intention was to widen as far as possible the definition of marriage as used in 1921, since it is in no way the concern of the census whether a couple are legally married to one another or to other persons or not at all, if they are living together in such a manner as to beget children and form a family. Prostitutes who may be married to a god are rightly excluded, as far as the conditions of enumeration permit, from the census return of married, since though they may have children occasionally no family unit is constituted. **Instructions for enumeration.**

90. The general statistics of Civil Condition will be found in Table VII of part ii, and the figures of selected castes in Table VIII. Proportional figures are embodied in the subsidiary tables at the end of this chapter. It is evident at the first glance that the returns of Civil Condition are in very marked contrast to the figures of previous decades. The marginal figures show the number of males and females per mille of those aged 0—15 returned as married during the past 50 years. It will be seen that from 1881 to 1921 there has been a steady decrease of those married under the age of 15 years. This decrease has become an increase in 1931, for the number of married males under 15 has risen by 51% and the number of married females under 15 by 26% since 1921, an increase which is undoubtedly due to the enormous number of infant marriages which took place in the six months' interval between the passing of the Sarda Act and its coming into operation, some account of which has been given below. On the other hand Hindu widows under the age of 15 have fallen from 8 per mille in 1921 to 5·5 per mille, but while this may be taken as indicating a real decrease it is to be feared that the figures for the married cannot be taken at their face value. It is an obvious and striking fact that, although in all previous census figures the number of married women exceeds the number of married men, as must necessarily be the case in a country where there are a considerable number of polygynous marriages, on this occasion the figures are entirely reversed, presenting the impossible position of at least 601,244 married men with non-existent wives, and that at the maximum allowance of one each for those that have them. Polygyny is not widely practiced in India among either Muslims or Hindus, but it has been found at all previous census operations ; the first half of the decade was prosperous and the economic check upon it unlikely to have operated before the end of the decade, and there is no reason to suppose that customs have changed to the extent of obliterating the very low ratio of eight co-wives to every thousand wives in a population of some three hundred million odd.* It is not to be supposed on the other hand that a practice has suddenly **The statistics.**

Number of married per 1,000 of those aged 0—15 years.

Sex.		1881	1891	1901	1911	1921	1931
Males	..	63	59	59	54	51	77
Females	..	187	170	162	156	144	181

Persons returned as "married" in 1931.

Locality and Religions.		Females.	Males.
India (with Burma)			
All Religions	..	83,607,223	84,208,467
India proper—			
Hindu	..	58,353,082	58,663,574
Jain	..	266,941	267,510
Sikh	..	898,020	895,659
Buddhist	..	93,284	95,668
Muslim	..	18,241,410	18,300,813
Christian	..	1,213,375	1,219,421
Tribal	..	1,728,085	1,691,634
Others	..	127,655	130,254
Burma—			
All Races	..	2,680,877	2,934,902
Indigenes	..	2,527,527	2,516,134
Indians (Hindu and Muslim).		116,535	343,758
Indians (other)	..	7,533	16,015
All others	..	29,282	58,995

*An examination of the composition of families in a very limited area in Mysore disclosed 17 per cent. of co-wives to wives in Muslim and 3 per cent. in Hindu families, both a great deal higher rates than 8 per mille.

arisen of marrying males to a goddess ; nor can the excess of married males in 1931 be imputed to a sudden increase of polyandrous marriages. It is true that there are in the Himalayas a certain number of tribes or castes practising polyandry. Most of them are Buddhists, and finding, as we do, that married males exceed married females in that community, if Burmese Buddhists be excluded, and that this is a recurrent feature of Indian census returns, we may accept that excess as correct. An excess of Christian married males over married females is also a normal feature of Indian census returns, and may be imputed primarily to the numbers of married British soldiers, officials, etc., whose wives are in Europe. This excess of Christian married males is noticeably less than usual—6,046 as compared to 16,887 in 1921 and 19,656 in 1911. The excess is absent in the case of Tribal Religions and of Sikhs in both of which communities prepuberty marriage is very rarely if ever practised and in which the married women exceed the married men ; the unnatural excess can therefore be ascribed to Hindus, Jains and Muslims, at any rate in the main. It is not difficult to divine the cause. In all these communities early marriage is practised, and the Sarda Act came into force a year before the census. Although that Act has in practice been virtually a dead letter, it is certain that a considerable number of persons who have married off their children in contravention of the Act will have hesitated to state specifically that a child aged so and so (and Age may be asked by the enumerator before Civil Condition) is married, knowing that such a statement will lay him open to the possibility of prosecution. Moreover in at least one case a Brahman association had bound its members not to divulge marriages made in contravention of the new law. The fact that the number of such concealments has been so much greater in the case of females than of males as to reverse the proportions of the married is the natural consequence of the fact that the bride is normally younger than the bridegroom and the impulse to conceal the age is therefore more frequent. It may be here added that more than one attempt was made to use the census schedules as evidence for prosecution under the Sarda Act, so that the fear of those who returned their married daughters under 14 as unmarried was not entirely ill-founded. It was ultimately ruled that the schedule had to be produced, an indication of faulty legislative provision for the protection of the census enquiry, but fortunately by that time the records had been compiled and the original schedules destroyed in accordance with the customary procedure.

Correction of error.

91. It is necessary therefore to arrive at some computation of the error involved. The proportion of married males and females, as returned in 1931, are 1,007 males to every 1,000 females, or 993 married females to every 1,000 married males. Now an examination of the sex proportions of the last fifty years shows that the number of married females per 1,000 married males varies from 1,005 to 1,011, and the number of married males per 1,000 married females from 989 to 993. The average works out at 1,008 married females, or 992 married males, per 1,000 married of the opposite sex. The existence of concealment of the marriage of females makes it more than probable that there has been concealment of the marriage of males also, but for the purposes of this computation it is necessary to assume that the number of males returned as married is correct ; clearly it is a minimum. Now to maintain the average marriage ratio of the past fifty years 85,000,000 married females are required, and for the lowest ratio found, that of 1891, at least 84,653,970 married females are required, whereas the actual number returned is 83,607,223. We are therefore brought to the unwelcome conclusion that at the very least 1,046,747 married females have been returned as unmarried, and that all these are under the age of 14 years, since otherwise there would be no purpose in concealing their married condition. In all probability the number is not less than one and a quarter million. Taking the lowest figure the ratio of females aged 0—15 who are married becomes 196 per 1,000 instead of the ratio of 181 indicated by the returns, an increase of 52 in every 1,000 married females aged 0—15, that is of at least 36 per cent. on the ratio of 1921, or considerably more than the 13 per cent. shown by the unqualified figures, and a reversion beyond the position of 1891. An attempt will be made below to distribute this concealment of married females as between different communities, but it is not possible to locate or to distribute it with any certainty as between different provinces. It is unlikely that much concealment has taken place in Indian States which have had no legislation comparable to the Sarda Act, and it may be taken as certain that Cochin and Travancore States have contributed little or nothing to it, since infant marriage is not practised on the Malabar Coast. On the other hand it is inferred by the Census Superintendent for Rajputana from the statistics provided by that Agency that "recent legislation, although inapplicable to the States, has apparently had the effect of hastening on the marriages of immature persons of both sexes." It is possible however that this lowering of the age of marriage may be partially due, as pointed out elsewhere, to the automatic and inevitable action of the existing sex ratio aggravated by the ban on widow remarriage. In some cases a denial of marriage at the census may have been the result of failure by the bridegroom's party to provide the dowry promised, as cases of this kind are reported to have led to attempted repudiation of the marriage, when the census took place, in Tippera district in Bengal. An actual excess of 864,125 married males is to be found in Burma and in Bengal together. In Burma however they are all immigrants whose wives are likely to be found mostly in Madras or in the United Provinces, and the Burmans themselves do not in any case practise infant marriage, while Bengal usually has an excess of married males, mostly immigrants to Calcutta, equal to less than two thirds of their excess at this census. It has already been shown that this excess of 600,000 odd does not by any means represent the actual shortage of married females in the returns.

Group bias.

92. In considering the statistics there is another point which has to be borne in mind as regards the age groups. The method recommended by the actuary who examined the 1921 returns has been described in Chaper IV, and has greatly improved the value of the returns of age. This improvement however cannot equally be postulated of the age groups by civil condition. Under the old system of sorting directly into quinquennial groups there was a very heavy accumulation of returns at the ages ending in the digits 5 or 0, but the consequent error was the same for both Age by itself or Age as a factor in Civil Condition. The method adopted at this census has improved the returns of age without effecting an equivalent improvement in the age groups when read with civil condition, as the number of individuals of any civil condition is not identical with the total returns of any given age. Thus of those returned as aged 14-16 there will be a greater number married at the latter age than at the former, and by dividing the group into equal halves of which one contributes to the group 10—15 and the other to the group 15 to 20, the numbers of married shown in the lower age group will be increased beyond their correct proportion and conversely the number of unmarried in the higher group will also be proportionately inflated. The error caused will only be seriously operative up to the point at which the vast majority become all of the same married condition, and again at the point at which many become widowed; and it would appear from the returns that its effect has been to counterbalance the tendency to over-estimate the age of young married females which has been indicated in all previous census returns. An excellent example of the actual effect of the working of the method of smoothing on the ages of the married and widowed will be found in the following table which is taken from the Report on Bihar and Orissa :—

Age.	Married.						Widowed.					
	Actual number.			Number per mille.			Actual number.			Number per mille.		
	Persons.	Males.	Females.	P.	M.	F.	Persons.	Males.	Females.	P.	M.	F.
	Unsmoothed.											
4—6	**360,693**	131,019	229,674	**88**	63	112	**12,132**	3,795	8,337	**3**	2	4
7—13	**2,105,252**	839,474	1,265,778	**288**	217	368	**56,322**	19,546	36,776	**8**	5	11
14—16	**1,472,192**	583,066	889,126	**593**	448	753	**43,328**	15,984	27,344	**17**	12	23
17—23	**3,742,710**	1,478,972	2,263,738	**796**	667	919	**148,560**	48,242	100,318	**32**	21	40
	Smoothed.											
4—5	**120,231**	43,673	76,558	**87**	64	112	**4,044**	1,265	2,779	**3**	2	4
5—10	**1,232,973**	485,247	747,726	**216**	163	273	**34,227**	11,670	22,557	**6**	4	8
10—15	**1,788,722**	711,270	1,077,452	**366**	275	467	**49,825**	17,765	32,060	**10**	7	14
15—20	**2,697,451**	1,031,019	1,576,432	**726**	586	860	**95,944**	32,113	63,831	**27**	18	35
20—25	**3,103,157**	1,319,723	1,783,434	**826**	734	910	**151,277**	48,810	102,467	**40**	27	52

The exact working of the age group bias is, however, better illustrated still by figures for Gwalior State whence returns by annual ages were available up to 16 years. The following statement shows these returns as compiled from the schedule ; the operation of preferences for certain digits is obvious :—

Actual returns of Age by Civil Condition for Gwalior State, excluding Nimach Cantonment.

		Males.			Females.		
Age.	Total.	Unmarried.	Married.	Widowed.	Unmarried.	Married.	Widowed
0	62,851	32,069	110	19	30,382	222	49
1	96,846	48,174	235	31	47,852	463	91
2	96,630	47,406	445	37	47,788	890	64
3	102,798	49,371	556	47	51,566	1,111	147
	94,436	47,285	842	125	44,404	1,479	301
5	106,718	54,187	784	109	49,317	2,005	316
6	94,943	48,010	939	164	43,105	2,324	401
7	91,828	44,920	1,134	133	41,902	3,492	247
8	105,305	54,283	1,987	125	43,182	5,462	266
9	64,821	31,132	1,676	114	25,729	5,937	233
10	116,624	59,072	5,715	343	35,945	14,812	737
11	50,256	23,276	2,804	142	14,657	8,945	432
12	124,198	60,973	10,504	523	22,621	28,758	819
13	46,485	20,489	5,384	287	6,628	13,254	443
14	62,423	25,676	8,563	446	6,469	20,505	764
15	97,901	34,653	17,772	874	6,246	37,082	1,274
16	100,518	29,160	23,460	1,140	4,775	40,301	1,682

The next statement shows the same figures as grouped by sorters into the alternate ternary and septenary groups (from 4 years upwards) as they would have been if sorted direct into groups as was done elsewhere :—

		Males.			Females.		
Age.	Total.	Unmarried.	Married.	Widowed.	Unmarried.	Married.	Widowed.
0	62,851	32,069	110	19	30,382	222	49
1	96,846	48,174	235	31	47,852	463	91
2	96,630	47,406	445	37	47,788	890	64
3	102,798	49,371	556	47	51,566	1,111	147
4—6	296,097	149,482	2,565	398	136,826	5,808	1,018
7—13	647,527	342,155	29,204	1,667	190,664	80,660	3,177
14—16	260,842	89,489	49,795	2,460	17,490	97,888	3,720

The third of these statements shows the final appearance of these figures in the adjusted groups, in which the figures for marriage and widowhood in the group

5-10 are clearly inflated at the expense of the higher group 10-15, though the figures of the lowest group are little affected.

Age.	Total.	Males. Unmarried.	Males. Married.	Males. Widowed.	Females. Unmarried.	Females. Married.	Females. Widowed.
0—1	*123,822*	*56,238*	*313*	*43*	*66,376*	*748*	*104*
1—2	*97,940*	*48,338*	*406*	*48*	*47,988*	*1,051*	*109*
2—3	*·98,697*	*48,503*	*576*	*64*	*48,188*	*1,212*	*154*
3—4	*100,751*	*49,599*	*706*	*91*	*48,588*	*1,524*	*243*
4—5	*98,699*	*49,827*	*855*	*133*	*45,609*	*1,936*	*339*
0—5	519,909	252,505	2,856	379	256,749	6,471	949
5—10	373,115	195,991	15,030	901	118,137	41,298	1,758
10—15	316,980	142,740	32,413	1,681	67,814	69,593	2,739

For comparison with the above the figures are given below grouped as they would have been had the 1921 method of return to last (instead of nearest) birthday been followed and the figures sorted direct into quinquennial groups by the method followed at that census :—

Age.	Total.	Males. Unmarried.	Males. Married.	Males. Widowed.	Females. Unmarried.	Females. Married.	Females. Widowed.
0—1	*111,276*	*56,156*	*228*	*35*	*54,308*	*454*	*95*
1—2	*96,737*	*47,790*	*340*	*34*	*47,820*	*676*	*77*
2—3	*99,715*	*48,389*	*500*	*42*	*49,677*	*1,001*	*106*
3—4	*98,617*	*48,328*	*699*	*86*	*47,985*	*1,295*	*224*
4—5	*100,577*	*50,736*	*813*	*117*	*46,861*	*1,742*	*308*
0—5	506,922	251,399	2,580	314	246,651	5,168	810
5—10	468,568	234,974	8,986	762	196,549	25,623	1,674
10—15	390,623	177,277	38,998	2,006	71,470	97,409	3,463

The figures are next shown in the form of a distribution of 1000 of each civil condition between the ages of 0 and 15 first according to figures reached by the 1931 method and then comparatively by figures provided by the 1921 method :—

Age.	Unmarried. 1931 method.	Unmarried. 1921 method.	Married. 1931 method.	Married. 1921 method.	Widowed. 1931 method.	Widowed. 1921 method.
			(*a*) *Males.*			
0—1	*95*	*85*	*6*	*4*	*15*	*11*
1—2	*82*	*72*	*8*	*7*	*16*	*11*
2—3	*82*	*73*	*11*	*10*	*21*	*14*
3—4	*84*	*73*	*14*	*14*	*31*	*28*
4—5	*84*	*76*	*18*	*16*	*44*	*38*
0—5	427	379	57	51	127	102
5—10	332	354	299	178	303	247
10—15	241	267	644	771	570	651
			(*b*) *Females.*			
0—1	*150*	*106*	*7*	*4*	*19*	*16*
1—2	*108*	*93*	*9*	*5*	*20*	*13*
2—3	*109*	*96*	*10*	*8*	*28*	*18*
3—4	*110*	*93*	*13*	*10*	*45*	*38*
4—5	*103*	*91*	*16*	*13*	*62*	*52*
0—5	580	479	55	40	174	137
5—10	267	382	352	200	323	281
10—15	153	139	593	760	503	582

Finally the following table, taken from the Gwalior Report, shows the comparative distribution by civil condition of 1000 of each sex at the three main age groups first as arrived at by the 1931 method, and then as reached by the 1921 procedure :—

Civil Condition.	0—5 Males.	0—5 Females.	5—10 Males.	5—10 Females.	10—15 Males.	10—15 Females.
Unmarried	988	974	930	784	822	529
Married ..	11	22	66	207	169	453
Widowed ..	1	4	4	9	9	18
Unmarried	989	976	960	878	812	415
Married ..	10	21	37	114	179	565
Widowed ..	1	3	3	8	9	20

It is quite obvious that in the tables as they stand in part *ii* of this volume the high figures of marriage at the group 5—10 will be misleading. On the other hand it must unfortunately be pointed out that the necessity of allowing for an adjustment of not less than one million girls returned as unmarried though actually married has to be balanced against the bias indicated above, to say nothing of the tendency to exaggerate the ages of young married girls. When allowing for the adjustment of misstated civil condition, the age-bias, inflating group 5—10 as regards the married, may be regarded as operating to adjust the difficulty of distributing to different groups the numbers of those inaccurately returned as unmarried in 1931. It will of course be quite clear that this corrective was not intentional, and would have been avoided had the bias given to the returns of Civil Condition been detected in time. This could easily have been done by sorting for civil condition before sorting for age, but when the Census Superintendent of Bengal, the first of us to detect the bias, pointed it out, sorting had everywhere been completed. Ages as stated to enumerators in India are always so inaccurate, and the old method of grouping under which the age returns were influenced by preferential digits was so unsatisfactory, that it cannot be held that the inaccuracy of the grouping by Civil Condition is necessarily any greater at this census than in previous decades, but it probably is, and in any case it is unfortunate that the greater accuracy which might have been obtained by reversing the order of sorting must be deferred to the next census, and even if the method used has acted as a corrective in one respect it would have been more satisfactory to have been able to ascertain that error precisely and to apply the necessary corrective afterwards. Meanwhile it is necessary to bear in mind this flaw in grouping when considering the increase in infant marriage disclosed in the returns which form another point in striking contrast to those of recent decades. Were the returns of married females complete it would be clear that some allowance would have to be made for the tendency towards weighting the lower ages at the expense of the higher. As however it must be taken as quite certain that some million married girls under 14 years of age have been returned as unmarried, and in all probability a still larger number of girls and a considerable number of boys, the returns as they stand may be taken as an indication correct enough of the proportion of married at the more infantile ages, and to correct the weighting caused by the method of grouping the correction necessary in the figures of the married may be made to fall entirely at the highest age groups possible. For the purposes therefore of the marginal table a transfer of 1,046,747 females has been made from the category of unmarried to that of married and shown entirely under the highest age group under 15 years. The weighting of the lower age groups will be more apparent in the case of the widowed. Not only will the tendency for the returns of widowed to be more numerous at the higher age groups be greater, and

Married persons per 1,000 of the population aged

Census of	0 to 1. M.	0 to 1. F.	1 to 2. M.	1 to 2. F.	2 to 3. M.	2 to 3. F.	3 to 4. M.	3 to 4. F.	4 to 5. M.	4 to 5. F.	5 to 10. M.	5 to 10. F.	10 to 15. M.	10 to 15. F.
1881	(0—10, *males 24 and females 75*)												151	500
1891 . ..	(0—5, *males 5 and females 13*)										36	123	154	494
1901	2	3	3	6	5	9	8	16	13	27	36	102	134	423
1911	2	3	4	7	6	11	9	17	14	30	37	105	129	430
1921	1	2	3	5	4	8	7	13	12	23	32	88	116	382
1931	7	8	8	12	12	20	22	42	31	66	79	193	149	381

the inequitable distribution to lower age groups therefore greater, but the inclination to concealment or to exaggerate age will perhaps have been less, in which case the bias involved by the method of sorting will be less balanced by its operation as a corrective. Except in the case of Hindus and Jains the numbers are not of any very great significance as elsewhere the ban on remarriage does not exist. In the case of Hindus and Jains the number of widows at each age group in 1931 should lose a certain proportion to the group above, and the actual state of widowhood as presented by the 1931 census figures is actually a little better than it appears to be from the record, indicating a very remarkable decrease in the number of child widows during the last ten years. It is to be feared that unless the practice of the remarriage of child widows is greatly extended during the coming decade, the reduction found at this census will be found in 1941 to have been converted again to a grave increase as a result of the great increase that took place during the early months of 1930 in child marriages hurriedly undertaken to forestall the Sarda Act. Indeed the year that elapsed between the rush of anticipatory marriages and the taking of the census left time enough for many infants married in haste to become widows for life, and the marked rise in the number of widows under ten years as compared with 1921, in spite of a decline in the proportion of widows on the whole, is probably significant of sorrows to come, particularly as, if widows under five years alone be examined, the 1921 figures are found to have more than doubled. It is likely that there was no marked lowering of the age of marriage until 1930, although as pointed out elsewhere an excess of males will tend in that direction ; it is evident, however, if only from the increase of married aged 0-3 where the possible influence of sorting methods is inoperative, that there has been a decided temporary fall in the age of marriage ; this fall is probably attributable almost entirely to anticipation of the Marriage Restraint Act.

Census of	Hindu and Jain females returned as widowed per 1,000 aged						
	0-1	1-2	2-3	3-4	4-5	5-10	10-15
1881	*(0—10—2·9 per 1,000)*						21·1
1891	*(0—5—0·7 per 1,000)*					4·1	16·1
1901	0·3	0·6	0·7	1·3	2·9	5·7	20·6
1911	0·3	0·4	0·5	1·2	2·5	5·5	17·3
1921	0·2	0·3	0·5	0·9	2·2	5·5	20·5
1931	0·3	0·4	0·7	1·9	3·2	5·7	11·3

Marriage Ratios of Communities.

93. It was stated above that some attempt would be made to distribute by religion the 1,046,747 or so married girls under 14 who must have been returned as unmarried. It is assumed that in view of the extraordinary rush to get children married before the operation of the Sarda Act, and of the large number of married who have undoubtedly been returned as unmarried, it is justifiable to calculate for individual communities on the mean ratio of married females found, although for the total ratio for all communities the lowest recorded proportion of married females to males has been taken. Now the mean of the highest and lowest recorded Muslim ratios of married women to married men found from 1881 onwards is 1,018 married women to 1,000 married men. To make up this ratio 366,598 more married women are required than have actually been returned. Similarly the mean Hindu ratio of married women to married men found from 1881 onwards is 1,006. To make the number of married women up to this ratio another 627,890 Hindu women should have been returned as married. The ratio between these figures for Hindus and Muslims corresponds nearly enough to the ratio between the actual excess numbers of married males returned by each community from India and Burma together when Burmese Muslims are excluded. Similarly 999 Jain and 4,716 Sikh females need to be transferred from unmarried to married to raise their ratios respectively to the mean of the highest and lowest possible figures since 1881. This accounts for all but 46,544 of the minimum numbers required, and this must be left to be accounted for by the other communities or by still higher ratios, for it is not impossible but that the actual ratios of married females to married males are even higher than those assumed. If the additional numbers of married females

Number of males returned as married in excess of total of married females of the same community.	
Hindu	468,051
Muslims	134,067
Jain	569

under 14 years actually arrived at be now transferred from the unmarried females aged 0—15 to the married of that age, the rates per 1,000 come to 213 and 210 for Hindus and Muslims respectively instead of 199 and 186. Jains are raised from 125 to 130, and Sikhs from 80 to 86 married females per 1,000 aged 0—15. The table in the margin shows the number of females per 1,000 aged 0—15 who were returned as married for six decades in five religious communities.

Community.	Married females aged 0-15 per 1,000 females of that age.						
	1881.	1891.	1901.	1911.	1921.	1931.	1931 *as adjusted.*
Hindu	208	193	186	184	170	199	213
Muslim	153	141	131	123	111	186	210
Jain	189	172	164	130	117	125	130
Sikh	120	143	101	88	72	80	86
Christian	33	37	38	39	32	43	..

Clearly this vitiation by false returns of the numbers of unmarried females must be taken into account in any consideration of civil condition. Thus while the proportions of the unmarried, married and widowed returned at the census are :—

Males .. unmarried 47·9%, married 46·7%, widowed 5·4%,

Females .. unmarried 35·2%, married 49·3%, widowed 15·5%,

these figures if applied to the actual numbers, merely result in the absurdity of married males whose wives are unmarried. It is therefore necessary to correct them to the extent already indicated together with certain component parts, and the resulting percentages are given in the marginal table. Figures of Northern Ireland (1926) are added for the sake of comparison. In the diagram that follows no attempt has been made to distribute the married returned as unmarried which probably remain after the adjustment of the Hindu, Jain, Sikh and Muslim ratios as above. The Christians, who are likely to have a good many of them, show a higher ratio of married females to married males than ever before, and the other communities show no such marked change in proportions as would enable any definite transfer from the unmarried to the married category.

Unit.	Sex.	Unmarried.	Married.	Widowed.
INDIA ..	males ..	47·9	46·7	5·4
	females ..	*34·6*	*49·9*	*15·5*
Burma ..	males ..	56·1	39·2	4·7
	females ..	*52·1*	*37·4*	*10·5*
India (*ex-* Burma).	males ..	47·6	47·0	5·4
	females ..	*33·8*	*50·5*	*15·7*
Hindus ..	males ..	46·3	48·0	5·7
	females ..	*32·4*	*50·7*	*16·9*
Jains ..	males ..	50·3	41·5	8·2
	females ..	*33·7*	*44·2*	*22·1*
Sikhs ..	males ..	55·0	37·0	8·0
	females ..	*41·1*	*47·5*	*11·4*
Muslims ..	males ..	50·0	45·6	4·4
	females ..	*35·8*	*51·3*	*12·9*
Others ..	males ..	53·6	42·6	3·8
	females ..	*45·2*	*43·9*	*10.9*
Northern Ireland.	males ..	64·4	31·5	4·1
	females ..	*61·1*	*30·5*	*8·4*

Marriage Ratios by Age. **94.** Similarly when examining the ages of the married it is necessary to take into account the false returns of unmarried so far as possible. These false returns must be assumed to refer in any case to females married under the age of 14 years so that the adjustment is simple enough when considering the proportionate ages of the married, provided the ages below 15 years are not considered separately. The marginal table therefore shows for each sex the percentage of married persons who are under the age of 15 years. It is at once noticeable that the ratio of females married under 15 is higher among Muslims than among Hindus, nor is this merely the result of the adjustment, carried out above, of the million odd married females returned as unmarried ; on the bare figures as returned at the census the Muslim ratio of married females under 15 years to the total of married females is higher than the Hindu ratio. In 1921 the Hindu ratio was 4% higher than the Muslim. In England and Wales in 1921

Province, etc.	Number per 1,000 of total married who are under 15 years.	
	Males.	Females.
India	65·7	157·3
Burma	1·8	6·7
India Proper	68·0	161·8
Hindu	*73·1*	*164·1*
Jain	*32·5*	*108·3*
Muslim	*59·4*	*174·3*
Tribal	*49·6*	*93·3*
Sikh	*26·9*	*74·6*
Christian	*15·4*	*43·3*

and in Northern Ireland in 1926 no females under 15 years were returned as married.

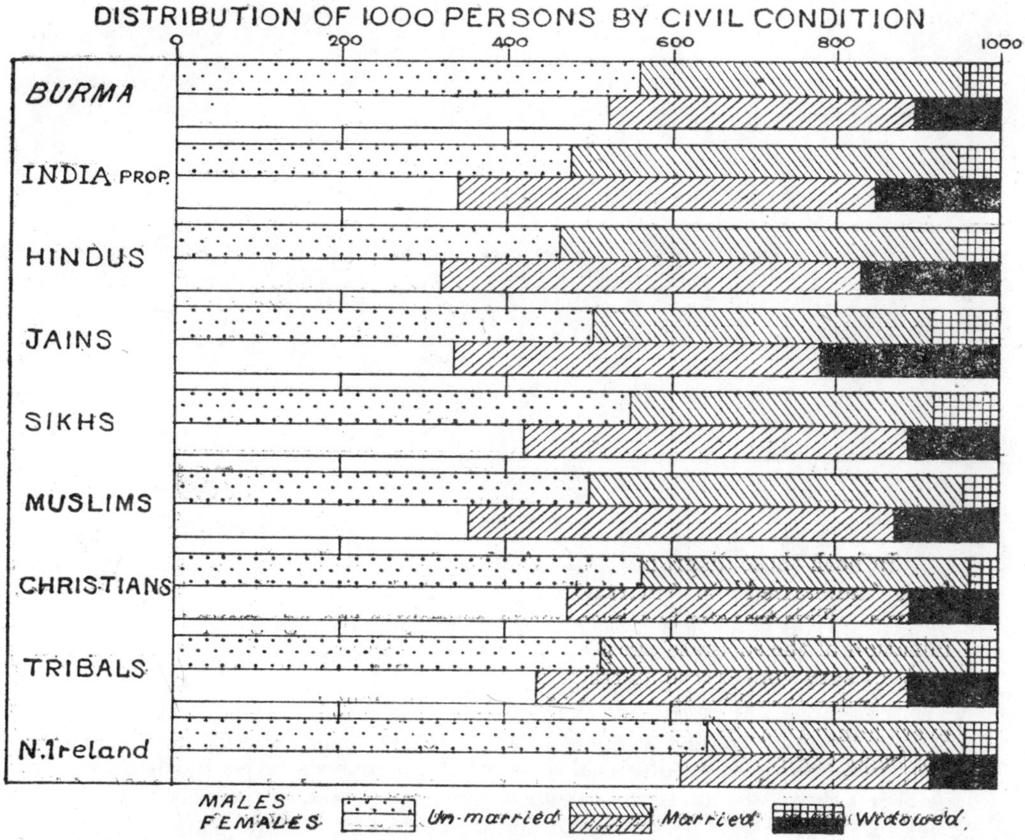

Some examination of civil condition by actual age groups seems called for, and the accompanying diagrams show in one case an age group pyramid, based on the actual numbers returned at each age period, which also displays the marital condition of each group, and in the other a representation of the ratio of marital condition per 1,000 of each sex at each age period.

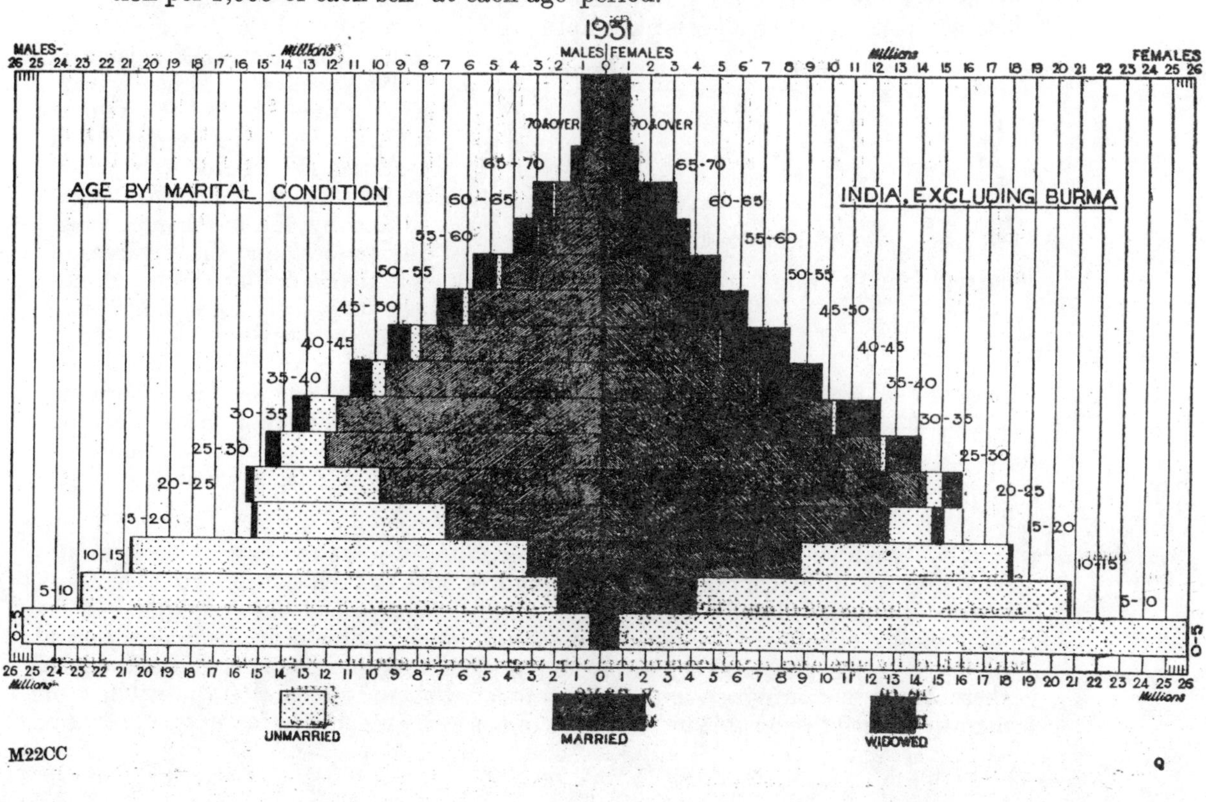

DISTRIBUTION BY CIVIL CONDITION OF 1000 OF EACH SEX IN DIFFERENT AGE GROUPS

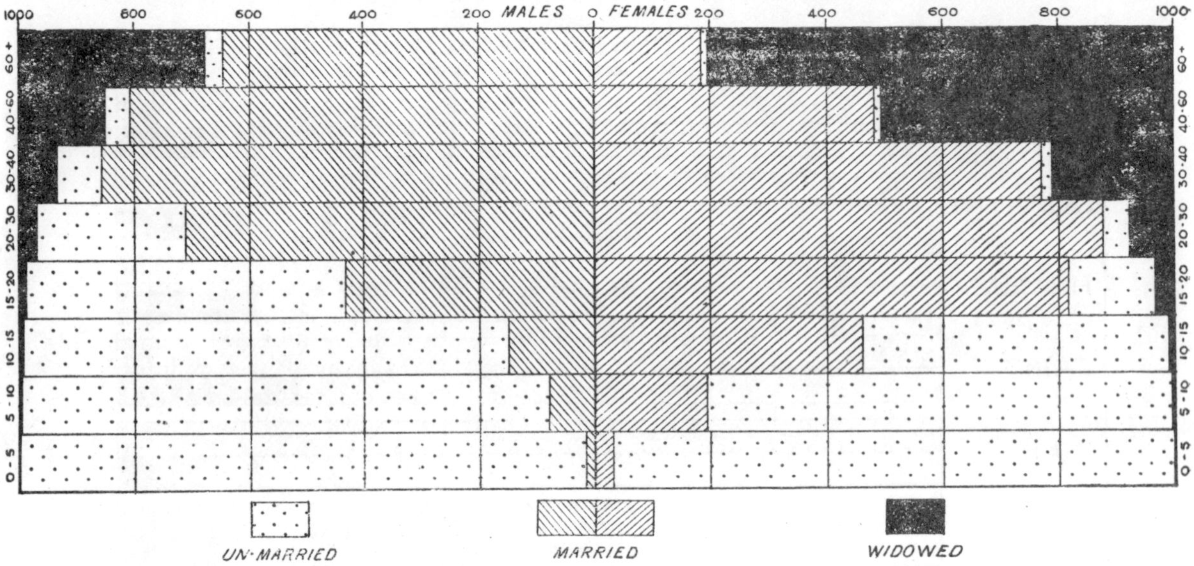

In both these diagrams a transfer has been made of over a million females from 'unmarried' to 'married' to correct the impossible ratio of the actual returns. This transfer has been made entirely in the age group 10—15. An examination of the separate age groups for females shows that little more than one per cent. of survivors escape marriage (as compared for instance to about 26% in Northern Ireland) and by the age of 15 years nearly 40% have been married and one in every hundred is already a widow. By the age of 20 almost 85% have been married, 3% being widowed, as compared to only 45% of males married by that age. In the next ten years the maximum extent of marriage is reached, nearly 98% of females having been married by the age of 30 and more than a tenth part of them already widowed, while of males 86% have been married. By 50 years more than half the female population of that age are already widows, though only 15% of the males of that age are widowed, and of females over 70 years more than 85% are widows, although less than 40% of males over 70 are widowers. In Northern Ireland 48% of women aged 65 and over or 62% of those aged 75 and over are widows, and of males over 65 over 29% are widowers. The tremendous increase in the married of both sexes at very early ages is most noticeable. From 10 to 15 the increase on the actual figures returned is comparatively reasonable, but the marginal table shows the figures without the correction required to bring the figures of married females up to the ratio necessitated by the number of married males, and the figures of married females from 0 to 15 appear as returned, more than a million short. Similarly it is at the very early ages that there has been a phenomenal increase in widowhood, though there is an actual decrease in widows of 10 to 15 years, indicating both the definite improvement that had preceded the passing of the Sarda Act and the rush of hasty infant marriages which it precipitated.

Age.	Males.		Females.	
	1921.	1931.	*1921.*	1931.
0-1 ..	*6,921*	36,882	*9,066*	44,082
1-2 ..	*6,687*	41,228	*11,595*	63,954
2-3 ..	*16,484*	63,375	*32,197*	114,099
3-4 ..	*28,915*	118,844	*60,755*	232,813
4-5 ..	*51,677*	168,897	*104,850*	346,904
5-10 ..	*757,405*	1,883,773	*2,016,687*	4,200,534
10-15 ..	*2,344,066*	3,217,626	*6,330,207*	7,269,208

Age.	Widows.	
	1921.	1931.
0-1	*759*	1,515
1-2	*612*	1,785
2-3	*1,600*	3,485
3-4	*3,475*	9,076
4-5	*8,693*	15,019
5-10	*102,293*	105,482
10-15	*279,124*	185,339

Civil condition by Caste.

95. When we come to examine civil condition by caste it is possible to locate some portion of the concealed marriage figures, and the relation between the false returns of unmarried and the practice of infant marriage is at once apparent. It is only possible of course to be reasonably certain of concealment in the case of castes tabulated by age and civil condition for very considerable portions of India, since where one or two provinces only have tabulated there is generally a possibility of migration being responsible for an excess of one sex, except in a few cases of certain castes of limited range. Thus of the 627,890 missing married Hindu females only about 267,000 to 268,000 can be located by the excess of married males in certain castes. Bengal Brahmans lead the way with 55,500 married males in excess of females, Brahmans elsewhere making up the total to 85,000. Kayasthas have an excess of 40,600, Rajputs of 34,000, Yadavas of 26,000, Komatis of 13,000, Kunbis of 17,000 and the 'Viswabrahman' group of artizan castes 14,000 between them. Khatris have 9,000, Namasudras 7,700, Kumhars 5,000, Gadarias 2,800 and Baidyas 1,600. Of the tribes Santals have 4,500 and Bhils 2,600. Few Muslim groups have been tabulated, but, of the few that have been, both Sayyids and Momins show an excess of 7,000 husbands, accounting for 14,000 of the 366,589 needed.

In the marginal table a number of castes are shown in the order of prevalence of infant marriage. This list must be taken as a sample only, and the incidence of infant marriage has been calculated on the number of females returned as married aged 0 to 6 years. No attempt has been made to adjust the ratios for the concealed marriages as the ages of these are not known, and it is clear that several of the castes mentioned above, *e.g.* Brahmans, Kayasthas, Rajputs, Komatis, Yadavas, would stand higher in the list than they do had they not concealed their marriages carried out in contravention of the Sarda Act between April 1930 and February 1931, while the Kunbi or Kurmi group would probably take the unenviable place at the head of the list which would seem to be theirs by prescriptive tradition. In any case their high ratio of infant marriage supports the speculation made in paragraph 97 of this Chapter (*cf.* also Chapter XII page 457). In the provincial volumes the castes in Table VIII should be arranged in order of the prevalence of infant marriage, but as this order is likely to vary from province to province even for the same castes, and as very few castes indeed have been tabulated for the whole of India in Table VIII, the marginal list can only claim to give an indication of the relative position of various important castes with regard to the age of marriage. A reference to Table VIII (part II of this volume) will show that the general caste figures were largely influenced by the numbers located in the United Provinces, where a low age of marriage seems more universal than in other provinces. In the case of the Pathans shown in the list the U. P. figures alone have been given, and the ratio should not be regarded as at all typical of Pathans elsewhere. Only two other Muslim groups are given, that of weavers shown collectively as Momin, and Sayyids; the rest are Hindu, Jain or Tribal. For it will be noticed that even tribes like Oraons and Santals appear in the list, but there is every reason to suppose that infant marriage in their case is an acquired habit, as it is not common to the Austroasiatic tribes, though it is probably more natural to Kunbis than it is to Rajputs.

Caste.	Females aged 0-6 married or widowed per 1,000 of total females in the caste.
Tanti	25·1
Kunbi	20·5
Bhar	15·9
Maratha	15·7
Yadava	12·6
Dom	12·1
Mahar	11·9
Komati	10·6
Chamar	10·3
Shaha	9·1
Teli	9·1
Momin	9·0
Darzi	8·9
Dhobi	8·6
Gadaria	8·2
Nai	8·2
Pathan (U. P.)	8·0
Sawara	7·6
Lingayat	7·3
Kumhar	7·1
Namasudra	7·1
Megh	6·7
Gond	6·6
Od	6·5
Kahar	5·5
Kayastha	5·1
Oraon	4·6
Santal	4·2
Brahman	3·6
Sayyid	3·6
Kachhi	3·5
Rajput	3·4

Interpretation of "Married".

96. It is hardly necessary to point out that marriage as found and returned by an Indian census is not to be understood in the sense of marriage as returned in an European census, in which effective cohabitation of man and wife is a normal assumption. The practice of child marriage involves as a necessary corollary some postponement of effective marriage, and in the case of Muslims and of the majority of Hindus prepuberty consummation is not practised, though the prevailing Hindu custom certainly involves consummation at a very early date thereafter. On the other hand it is not accurate to state, though the statement is frequently met, that the Hindu child marriage is merely an "irrevocable betrothal". Apart from the fact that this expression is a contradiction in terms, for betrothal implies the possibility of breaking a troth which has only a moral obligation as its sanction, there exists no necessity in the case of the Hindu marriage for any further ceremony to cement the union, which also remains valid and final in the case of the bridegroom's death, whereas completion by a subsequent ceremony would be essential to a mere betrothal. It is true that a further ceremony is frequently performed either when the wife is taken to her husband's house or as a preliminary to consummation, but such ceremonies are neither universal nor essential. The Age of Consent Committee's report has made this quite clear ; thus, in section 159, "the practice of *gaona*, according to which the girl-wife is not sent to the husband's family till some time after marriage, and generally after puberty, does not prevail in Bengal, with the result that soon after marriage, at any age, the girl lives with her husband and consummation invariably follows on attainment of puberty ". Again (section 54) "the custom of *gaona*......obtains in the Punjab to a fair extent ......but is fast disappearing, and in any case the period which elapses between marriage and *gaona* is becoming shorter and shorter." Again in Assam (section 145) "*garbhadhan* is still mostly practised. It takes place soon after puberty and precedes consummation. Amongst some educated people it is falling into disuse ". In the case of widowers remarrying "the ceremony is almost invariably ignored ", section 41. Again, writing of India generally, section 227, "There is a growing tendency everywhere to drop this practice (*gaona, garbhadhan dwiragaman, doli, rukhsati*, etc.)...... It......is falling into disuse more and more......and none of the ceremonies are any protection to unions before 16." Finally in section 383 the Committee conclude that "the practice of *gaona, garbhadhana* or similar consummation ceremonies does not obtain throughout India and wherever it existed once it is fast dying out ". Were the practice of *gaona* or *garbhadhana* the most important part of the marriage ceremony it is possible that a return of married might be made to coincide with one of effective marriage, but as these ceremonies are neither essential to marriage nor its invariable concomitant it is obviously quite impossible to make their completion the test of a marriage for census purposes, and marriage in these statistics can only be interpreted subject to the reservation that it is not ordinarily effective before puberty, and under the age of 15 years can probably be ignored, as far as the purely statistical consideration of the propagation of the species is concerned.

Infant Marriage.

97. To say that in one aspect marriages before the age of 15 can be ignored is not of course to suggest that child marriage is of no demographical importance. Its bearing on the population question has already been considered in the two preceding chapters. The map below shows roughly the prevalence of the custom of child marriage, for though it cannot attempt to take into account the number of married children returned at the census as unmarried, it must be recognised that infant marriage on the scale that preceded the Sarda Act at this census was of an abnormal nature and is hardly consistent with the steady improvement in the age of marriage that has taken place during the past 50 years. It is perhaps worth observing that this distribution suggests a correlation with the brachycephalic non-Armenoid Alpine element in the population of India, and it may be observed that according to Vámbéry (quoted by Westermarck, *History of Human Marriage*, 1901, page 214) "all peoples of the Turkish stock are in the habit of betrothing babies ". The racial connection between Tajik and Indian brachycephalic stock is indicated in Chapter XII, and a probable connection with Russia also pointed out. It may therefore be observed here that at the end of the last century (1867-75) Russia was the only country in Europe where marriage approached the universality of marriage in India, 68·31% of persons being married, and the only country where the marriage age was anything like so young, 57·27% of married women being under the age of 20, Hungary being the next with 35·16%. Various views have been held as to the origin of the custom of child marriage. It seems never to have extended to the Malabar coast and is not nearly so prevalent in the extreme south, along the east coast, or in the north-west as in the west, in Bengal and in the Deccan. Clearly it is very ancient and the suggestion that attributes it to the Muslim invasions is not even momentarily entertainable. Megasthenes presumably refers to the practice when he records that the girls of the Pandaian kingdom bear children at the age of seven, adding that they are old at 40. Risley regards the custom as due primarily to hypergamy which, by limiting the choice of bridegrooms, impels parents to marry off their girls at the earliest age possible. Whether hypergamy has or has not contributed to the establishment of the custom, it might equally well have been due, as it almost certainly is in one tribe in Assam, to a paucity of women and the necessity of making sure of a wife before someone else snapped her up, and not to a paucity of bridegrooms in a country where males exceed females. Gait regards infant marriage as the result of the impact of ' Aryan ' and ' Dravidian ', and as a device to guard against pre-marital communism, and this again is likely to have been a contributing factor (*cf. infra* Chapter XII, page 457). More weight however than was given by him seems due to the late Sir J. Campbell's opinion quoted on page 271 of the 1911 Census Report. Campbell's opinion was that early marriage was due to a belief in the danger of dying with unfulfilled wishes combined with the great wish of a Hindu to marry and have children. As stated this is probably the wrong way round. The wish to marry and have children is the cause of the fear of dying unmarried. It will be pointed out later (Chapter XI, page 379) that the penalty for failure to marry is extinction in a future existence. This belief appears in the tradition of primitive tribes from Assam to Fiji, where " not a single unmarried Fijian ghost is known to have reached the mansions of the blest ", and is still so lively in some parts of India that the corpse of a person dying unmarried is married before cremation. In China this feeling is so strong that the very souls of the unmarried dead are married and given in marriage *post mortem*, and that the idea is not absent in Europe may be inferred from the belief once current in England that maids who died unwed ' lead apes in hell '. It would be rash to say that this superstition was the cause of early marriage, but it seems more than probable that the underlying idea which imputes blame to failure to marry and propagate is the same as that which enjoins fertilization at the earliest opportunity.

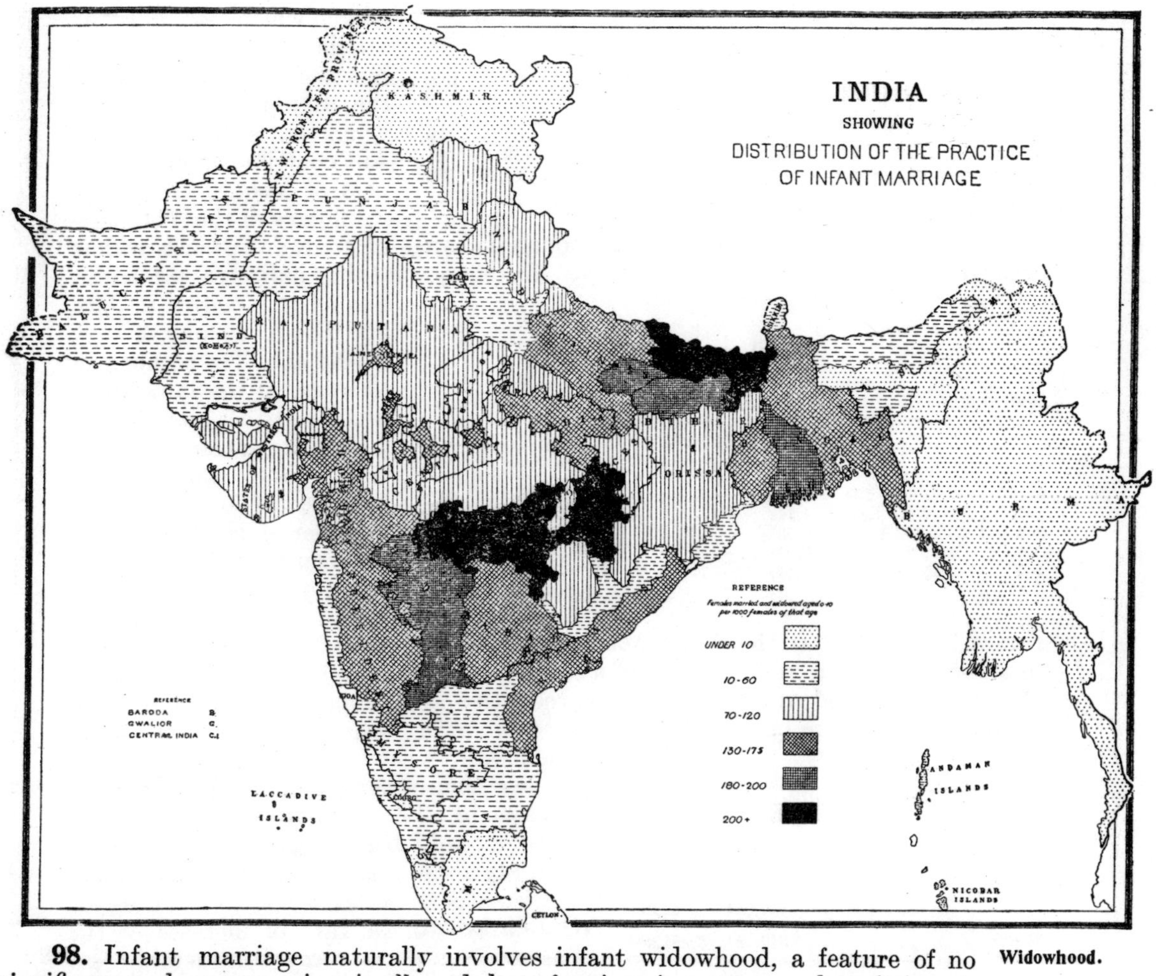

98. Infant marriage naturally involves infant widowhood, a feature of no significance where remarriage is allowed, but of serious importance where it is not. It has already been pointed out that there is an excess of males in India generally and that this is likely to tend, when associated with child marriage, towards an increasing disparity between the ages of husband and wife if it does not actually tend towards prepuberty marriage of the latter. Widows who can be remarried do not **Widowhood.**

complicate the position, but the existence of numbers of youthful widows who cannot must accentuate this tendency. In the case of older widows it is obvious that their numbers will affect the population question little once the reproductive ages are over, while in the case of widowers their loss to reproduction is governed only by their inability or disinclination to find wives, and at the reproductive ages their numbers at any given time are probably mainly those of males in the intermediate and temporary stage between bereavement and remarriage. In any case there is an excess of males and in consequence a solitary life is compulsory for a certain number and it makes little difference whether they are bachelors or widowers. The consideration of widowhood may therefore be confined to a consideration of its existence as a permanent bar to remarriage. It has already been pointed out that the general ratio of widowed females has decreased as compared with 1921. At that census there were 175 widows in every 1,000 females, a figure which had fallen in 1931 to 155. It is however only Jains and Hindus who place an effective ban on widow remarriage, and in both these communities the total ratio of widows has fallen ; Jain widows in 1931 were 253 per 1,000 females, but in 1931 only 221. Similarly the 1921 figure of 191 widows in every 1,000 Hindu females has fallen to 169 ; in both these as in all other communities the decrease must be largely attributed to the absence of famine and pestilence during the past decade. Famine at any rate seems definitely selective of males. On the other hand, as already pointed out, there has already been a very remarkable increase in child widows, particularly under the age of 5 years, which can only be attributed to the rush of marriages anticipatory to the Sarda Act, a rush which it is to be feared will contribute large numbers of young widows to the figures of the 1941 census unless there is before then a very pronounced change of attitude towards widow remarriage in Hindu society generally. The marginal table indicates the variation at this census in Jain and Hindu widows of very tender age. The numbers in the case of the Jains are so small as to deprive them of significance ; those of Hindus, though small enough in regard to the total number of Hindu widows, who numbered just under twenty million in 1931, are of some importance in regard to the effect of the Sarda Act in causing an unprecedented orgy of infant marriages involving in the course of a single year a most unfortunate increase in the number of child widows. If the reproductive ages alone be considered, that is years 15-40, there has been a decrease in Jain widows since 1921, while Hindu widows show an increase of less than 3%, less than a third that is of the rate of increase in the population as a whole. It has already been suggested (Chapter V, para. 81) above that the ratio of reproductive females to males seems to be in direct relationship to the rate of increase of the community, so that any considerable increase during the present decade in the number of widows who cannot remarry is likely to reduce the proportion borne by the Hindu and Jain communities to the population as a whole, if not in 1941 then certainly in 1951, so that from one point of view at least reform in the direction of widow remarriage of much more intensity than has been waged hitherto would

Community.	Widows, per 10,000 of all ages, under the age of— 5 years.		10 years.		15 years.	
	1921.	1931.	*1921.*	1931.	*1921.*	1931.
Hindu ..	*6*	12	*48*	55	*163*	129
Jain ..	*8*	11	*40*	33	*119*	81
All Religions	*6*	12	*44*	52	*148*	123

Widows aged.	Hindu. 1921.	1931.	Variation per cent.	Jain. 1921.	1931.	Variation per cent.
0–1 ..	597	1,081	+81	15	20	+33
1–2 ..	494	1,342	+172	4	8	+100
2–3 ..	1,257	2,695	+114	23	16	—30
3–4 ..	2,837	7,078	+150	26	21	—19
4–5 ..	6,707	11,471	+71	51	78	+53

Widows aged 15-40 years.	1921.	1931.
Jain	47,041	41,672
Hindu	5,817,781	5,981,096

seem to be indicated in their own interests, as well as in those of the Sarda Act widows, on the part of Hindus in general. It has already been suggested that the caste system leads to the production of an excess of males ; that the excess exists is in any case incontrovertible. It seems also an unavoidable conclusion that an excess of males must tend to lower the age of marriage for females since the number of mature females will not be enough to go round. The ban on widow remarriage must accentuate the evils of this vicious circle as well as contributing very largely to excessive disparity in the ages of married couples where a widower remarries, a disparity which is apt to begin in unhappiness and conclude in sterility, for marriages of this kind are undoubtedly less fertile than those between persons of more equal ages. It is not without significance that the Census Commissioner of Baroda State records that there is a

> " Growing consciousness of the fact that remarriage is becoming a social necessity in Gujarat. The 1911 Report mentioned a number of petitions from..........places in which the Government of the State was actually requested to make remarriage of widows compulsory : the disgruntled bachelors recounted their woes in these petitions owing to the fewness of virgin brides in their castes. The local Arya Samaj in recent years has attempted to popularise the idea of remarriage of widows amongst higher castes. A permissive Act for the remarriage of widows has been in existence for many years and yet very few persons amongst the higher castes have so far taken advantage of it. Census Committees report very little change in the general attitude of the higher castes. The Porwads in South Gujarat however are understood to have given a general permit to the widows to remarry ".

Similarly the Census Superintendent in Rajputana points out that for every 256 potential bridegrooms in Rajputana there exist at present only 162 potential brides, and if the latter are not married till they are 15 years old many males will reach 20 years unmarried. He writes :—

> " From 15-30, ages at which males contemplate or achieve marriage, there are 46 unmarried males per 1,000 persons, while there are only 4 unmarried females at similar ages. It therefore follows that these 46 males must arrange marriages with girls who are aged from 5-10 and from 10-15 of whom there are 82. Observing these proportionate figures the approximate number of girls that have reached the age of 14 is 11 while boys of 18, 19 and 20 may be assessed as 30. It looks therefore as if the discrepancy of 4 years fixed by the Sarda Act of 14 for females and 18 for males is for the present insufficient in practice and that if the provisions of the Act are rigidly complied with, the age of marriage for males will automatically rise to 21-23 for some years to come for want of sufficient girls who have reached the age of at least 14 ".

In short the course indicated by the census figures for Hindus is to raise the age of maternity and the ban on widow remarriage ; for Muslims to relieve the rigours of purdah when combined with penury and to raise likewise the age of maternity at any rate in those parts of India where Muslims practise infant marriage. It is not suggested that Hindus and Muslims are alone concerned in these matters, but it is they who constitute the vast bulk of the population of India proper, and it is their progeny that will determine the quality of future generations.

The Child Marriage Restraint Act, 1930.

99. As a matter of fact the last three or four years of the decade under review have been particularly marked by social movements and legislation bearing on the marital condition of the people and therefore destined ultimately to affect that side of social life with the census returns for which this chapter is concerned. Dewan Bahadur Harbilas Sarda's bill to prohibit, in the case of Hindus only, the marriage of girls under the age of 12 and boys under the age of 15 was first debated in the Legislative Assembly on September 15th, 1927, and was then referred to a select committee by which it was converted to a penal measure applicable to all communities. The Act, as passed in its final form as the Child Marriage Restraint Act on 28th September 1929, provided penalties for the solemnization of marriages of male children under 18 and of female children under 14 years of age, but did not invalidate marriages made in contravention of its provisions. It was to take effect from April 1st, 1930, and it was this interval between the date when the Act was passed and the date on which it came into force which was very largely responsible for the enormous increase in the numbers of those married below the age of ten years. This period was naturally an opportunity for a campaign against the Act by those who regarded it as objectionable. The opposition of a conservative section of orthodox Hindus was natural, and the objection was of course based on religious grounds, though all Brahmans, *e.g.*, the Nambudris, do not practise prepuberty marriage and those who do not have not thereby lost their status. Generally speaking, the Act met with wide approval among educated Hindus interested in social reform, and advantage was taken of the great Kumbh Mela at Allahabad in February just before the Act was to become operative to undertake propaganda on its behalf, though some of the orthodox resented the distribution of vernacular translations of the Act and the Sanatan Dharma Sabha organised a demonstration. In Poona a Yajurvediya Brahman *sabha* adopted resolutions making it obligatory on members of their community to refrain from divulging marriages made in contravention of the new law. Rather an unlooked for opposition to the Act came from a section of the Muslim community based apparently on the arguments that any act controlling the age of marriage must *ipso facto* be an encroachment on the authority of the Shariat, and that the Quran itself, at any rate by implication, provided for child marriages in certain cases. The possibility of prepuberty marriage certainly seems to be implied in the Book ' Divorce ' where three months are prescribed as the term within which a divorce shall not become absolute in the case of wives " who have not yet had their courses ". On the other hand it has been stated that consummation before puberty is forbidden by the Shariat, and in any case a female married as a minor is entitled to repudiate the marriage on attaining majority, and the position of the Muslim objectors to the Act seemed to be that no restriction was required in their case and that any legislation made a precedent for inter ference with their religious law. Other Muslims hold marriage to be a civil contract, and all agree that prepuberty consummation is not practised, but it seems clear that in the North-West Frontier Province, as in east Bengal and in Assam, prepuberty betrothal has the sanctity of marriage in the eyes of custom, while the actual returns of Muslim marriages at this census have suggested to at least one census superintendent that " it is also probable that through close association with their Hindu neighbours they [that is Muslims] are gradually assimilating more and more the social customs of the major community." As it was, a Muslim conference was held under the auspices of the " Committee for the Protection of Religion " and passed a resolution calling for a campaign of civil disobedience against the Act and urging Muslims to celebrate marriages in contravention of it, as if they were desirous to prove the Act unnecessary by creating new conditions in which it would be needed. Similar propaganda led to Muslim processions and a hartal in Peshawar but failed to bring about a large number of marriages before April 1st as its promoters had intended, and a somewhat artificial nature is suggested for the Muslim propaganda by the fact that in Baroda State an Infant Marriage Prevention Act had operated since 1904, without any opposition for almost a generation, although at any rate one Hindu community there had obtained exemption from the Act's provisions.

Meanwhile there took place all over India a rush to marry off minor children before the Act became effective. Gujarat and Bengal seem to have been particularly active in this respect, but other parts of India were not far behind. *Liberty* (13th March, 1930), with substantial accuracy in spite of somewhat hyperbolical wording, thus described the state of affairs in March 1930 :—

> " A matrimonial wave is just passing over the country. Bride in embryo is being mated to groom in the cradle. The Sarda Act is coming into force and the pig-tailed pundits have sanctioned—rather sanctified juvenile unions to stave off perdition. Poor girl just learning to suck the feeding bottle is being carried over to the wedding bower. Urchins are being snatched from the arms of their playmates to don the garb of a groom. As an emergency measure the elastic pundits have issued an edict whereby they have certified the month of *Chaitra* to be the proper season for matrimonial alliances .... our pundits have extended the limit this year .... We are sure before the 1st of April come in there will hardly be left a single unmarried man or woman in India ".

Two thousand child marriage contracts had been reported from Gujarat as early as the previous November, and demands for dowries were said to have become exorbitant and the businesses of money-lenders brisk. Among the Kadva Kunbis of Gujarat, however, the spate of marriage was partly attributed to the custom by which marriages are celebrated only " when the goddess speaks ", an occasion which is determined in the temple of Umia Mata at Unjha by lots drawn by Brahman priests and astrologers after worship with the two headmen of that place in the Mehsana district of the Baroda State. Consequently marriage opportunities for this section of the community occur only at intervals and possibly as rarely as once in twelve years. One such occasion occurred just before the census of 1911. The total population of Kadva Kunbis was 269,348 according to the census of 1921 and in 1931 there were 219,161 in Baroda alone. The rush of marriages in Gujarat went on in December, and 1,000 were reported to have taken place in Surat on December 12th alone, while all the towns in that district were festive with marriage processions, music and illuminations, the great majority of which marriages undoubtedly took place in anticipation of the operation of the restricting Act. Similar scenes were enacted in Bengal in the following February and March particularly in the districts of Hughli, Bankura, Dinajpur, Nadia, Dacca and Chittagong. In Bakarganj " the monthly average of minor marriages registered during 1921 to 1929 was 305. In the four months from January to April (1930), the numbers registered were respectively 419, 1,320, 8,782 and 4,452 ", and these figures refer of course to Muslim marriages only. In Bankura child marriages were reported to be taking place at the rate of 1000 a day on propitious days in February ; in Dinajpur some 10,000 marriages were reputed to have taken place, mostly in order to anticipate the Act, between the middle of January and the middle of March ; in the Chuadanga subdivision of Nadia some 4,000 marriages were reported to have involved difficulties in the engagement of musicians, palanquin-bearers, and even of motor-cars and 'buses, and to have sent up the prices of fish, curds and sweetmeats to exorbitant figures, as was the case also in Chittagong. One account from Bengal states that money-lenders and others who stood to profit by the celebration of marriages circulated a rumour that the Act prohibited any marriage's taking place for the space of 14 years. A similar rush of marriages was reported from Allahabad at the end of the auspicious season for marriages in March, as also from Manbhum in Bihar. In the Tamil districts of southern India hundreds of child marriages were likewise reported in March, and it was reported from Madura that on March 12th and 15th, days found propitious by the astrologers, 200 vakils of that town " married off their children, practically all of whom were within the ages of 6 to 10". In Bombay there was a similar rush of marriages in March ; these were mostly Hindus, but in Goalpara in Assam both Hindus and Muslims celebrated a rush of marriages to an extent sufficient to run up the price of many commodities, while towards the end of March the Marriage Registration offices in the Munshiganj sub-division of Dacca in Bengal were registering 100 marriages a day among Muslims. In Sind likewise Muslims as well as Hindus hurried on marriages to forestall the Act. In Larkana town alone 300 pairs of infants were reported to have had their marriages arranged for March, while in the Larkana and Upper Sind Frontier districts the number of marriages taking place was so great that difficulty was experienced in getting the services not only of musicians, it was said, but even of priests. In many cases, of course, the children married in all this haste were the merest infants. Apart from vague descriptions of the children married as " mere babes " (Gujarat) or as " aged only a few months " (Dhanbad) many specific cases were reported of marriages in which the bridegroom and bride were respectively, to give some of the actual instances, 25 and two and a half years (Bankura), seven years and three years old (Calcutta), two years old and twenty one days (Serajganj), three years old and ten days old (Brahmanbaria), four years and three years (Sind), while in another Sind case a Muslim gentleman of position was reported to have married a yet unweaned son to a girl of 4 years, and on March 25th in another province the six-year old son of an influential Muslim nobleman was married to the four year old daughter of a very prominent judge.

Not unnaturally this rush of hasty marriages involved unforeseen consequences. Criminal cases followed marriages hurried though without the consent of parents or others in which the caste of an emergency bridegroom had been misrepresented, a deluded Kayastha in Bengal, for instance, marrying his daughter to a Napit. Other such marriages had to be stopped by injunctions, and in one case in Nasik the court interfered to prevent the marriage of a Brahman girl of 10 to a deformed cripple nearly four times her age. Her father's excuse was that the Act would shortly be in force, it was against the Shastras to keep his daughter unmarried till she was 14, and in the short time available no more suitable husband could be found. In this case a properly indignant neighbour had moved the court, but it is to be feared that many other such cases are likely to have occurred in which there was no interference. But that some sections of the public are alive to such abuses is indicated not only by this case but by another earlier in the year, also in Bombay, in which the Youth League interfered to obtain an injunction against the second marriage of a boy of 12 who was sickly and whose first wife was alive. In this case however the marriage was carried through outside British territory, after which the boy died leaving two child widows. Of a different sort were the consequences of the pre-Sarda Act marriages in Assam, where the expenses incurred on these marriages by Muslim immigrants from Maimansingh were followed by very low prices for jute and paddy and thus materially contributed to agricultural distress and to the consequent necessity for the distribution of loans. Similarly in Bengal anxiety to forestall the Act is reputed to have led to reckless borrowing on a large scale, with "fantastic rates of interest" which are reported to have mounted as high as 78% in Bogra District. In Broach district in Bombay the President of the District Congress Committee publicly complained that the people were too engrossed in marrying to care for political meetings.

In fact marriages did not stop when the Act came into force, but were celebrated, particularly by Muslims, by way of protest and challenge. On April 4th a congregation of some 12,000 Muslims, for instance, were assembled at the Jama Masjid in Delhi to witness the marriage of a boy of 13 to a girl of 9, and the District Magistrate was then petitioned to prosecute all concerned. Similar marriages were celebrated by Muslims in Multan, and orthodox Hindus as well as Muslims continued to protest against the Act and to advocate defiance. On the other hand supporters of the Act were active in protest against any rumour of its amendment and a representation to the same effect was made to H. E. the Viceroy by an influential body of Muslim ladies, while the support given by the leading Indian Christians to the Act brought out an aspect of the situation unfamiliar to many, in that it indicated the retention of purely secular marriage among the rural Christian community on account of the fact that early marriage could not be celebrated under the Christian Marriage Act. This retention of secular marriage after conversion is familiar enough in the case of many hill tribes on account of the difficulty of obtaining divorce in the case of marriages under the Christian Marriage Act, but in their case the question of age does not lead to any difficulty as they mostly practise adult marriage. In spite of educated support, however, the agitation against the Act resulted in Mr. Surpat Singh's motion in July 1930 to amend the Act so as to permit of the marriage of persons below the specified ages on the production by such person's guardians of the certificate of a Civil Court of its satisfaction that the marriage should be permitted for family reasons or on conscientious grounds. Other amending bills have since been introduced either to repeal the Act altogether or to exempt from its operation communities in which post-puberty marriage is forbidden by their religious usages or customs, but none of them have got further than that stage. Meanwhile corresponding legislation has been passed in a number of Indian States including Kashmir and Baroda. Mysore, which had an Infant Marriage Prevention Regulation, forbidding the marriage of girls under eight years, as early as 1894, introduced a bill in 1931 making punishable marriages below the ages prescribed in the Sarda Act but providing for the reduction of the age for special reasons to 12 in the case of girls, under the orders of the District Magistrate and on condition that consummation should not take place till after the age of 14. At the time of writing this bill has not yet become law, but a law has been enacted in Jammu and Kashmir, and the pre-existing law in Baroda was at once brought into conformity with that in British India. In the Idar State the Act proposed by the State Council likewise prescribes the ages of 18 and 14 and contains the additional proviso that a man over 45 years of age shall not marry a woman of less than half his age. On the other hand the Kadva Kunbis, whose custom of observing periodic marriage occasions has already been mentioned, are to be permitted to continue to celebrate under-age marriages provided consummation is postponed. The Baroda Government on the contrary, which had an Infant Marriage Prevention Act in 1904, and which had since 1922 exempted the Kadva Kunbis from its application, withdrew that privilege in the 1930 amendment, and at the same time stiffened the Act by invalidating all marriages below the ages of 8 and 6 in the cases of boys and girls respectively, and made the parties responsible for all marriages under 16 or 14, as the case might be, punishable by imprisonment as well as by fine. As a matter of fact the Kadva Kunbis cannot be regarded as suffering very severe hardship under any child marriage restraint act, as they can fulfil their obligation to the goddess by marrying the child to a bunch of flowers which is afterwards thrown away, when the child can be remarried by the *natra* form used for the widowed. Apart from this particular group of Kunbis, the Kunbi, Kurmi or Kurmikshattriya group generally have been somewhat conspicuous for the practice of infant marriage ; this is probably an ancient characteristic, but may possibly be now-a-days a factor in their campaign of social scansion.

The instructions of the Government of India were that the provisions of the Child Marriage Restraint Act should on coming into operation be administered with due care and discretion, and the cry was raised that the Act was intended to be a dead letter. It is of course obvious from the nature of the Act that nothing will come of it if no one bothers to prosecute, a duty which has been deliberately left to the private citizen ; the Census Superintendent for Bihar and Orissa quotes a number of correspondents who agree that the Act is ineffective in that province, and the Census Superintendent of Assam describes it as quite inoperative in that province, and this perhaps is the general view of the functioning of the Act in most parts of India, for the Act depends for its success on the vigorous working of public opinion. The first conviction under the Act was reported from Lahore in July 1930, and up to February 1931, when the census took place, there had been thirty-three prosecutions, at least three of which related to Muslims and one to Christians. Since then not less than a score of convictions and more injunctions have served to show that the Act *can* operate successfully *where there are public associations or private individuals prepared to deposit security and take up cases* in which the law is being transgressed. Thus the Gujarat Social Reform Association has taken action in a number of cases including two in which men of 40 or 50 were to marry girls of 6. At the same time, the warning of the Age of Consent Committee (Report, Section 291, page 133) applies here with some force. It points out that the number of such institutions " is so small and the places where they exist so few, that it will be a travesty of facts to suggest that these associations would serve the purpose of reporting even grave cases of breaches of the law. The rural areas may be altogether wiped out of the map if all hope is concentrated on the manner in which these associations will function ". In one case dealt with by the courts in Noakhali in Bengal two brothers aged 50 and 45 were punished for marrying, in defiance of the Act, their two cousins age 4 and 2. They were Muslims and the intention was to obtain final control of the property and persons of the two children whose guardians they were, a motive which would apparently put the marriage in any case into the category of those banned in the rather obscure verse at the beginning of that book of the Quran called ' The Women '. They were fined Rs. 150 each, not an excessively severe penalty, in view of the fact that they had presumably effected their object. In a case in Madras a village munsiff who transgressed the Act was dismissed by the Collector but re-instated with a warning by higher authority. It is, however, still easy enough in many places to evade the Act entirely by celebrating a marriage outside British territory, and a specific instance may be quoted of parties in Ajmer who went to Kishengarh State to celebrate a marriage illegal in British India. This however seems to indicate that the law is something more than a mere dead letter, and that the unfortunate increase in the existing numbers of infants and children married and widowed at a tender age, which has been occasioned by the advantage taken by the orthodox to marry while an open season yet remained, may ultimately be compensated for by the numbers which will benefit from the future working of the Act. There is also hope that once the practice of prepuberty marriage ceases (if it does) there will be an automatic improvement in the position of the unfortunate father of daughters who must under present conditions almost ruin himself financially in order to avoid the stigma of their growing up unmarried. In the Baroda State Council a bill has been moved to make it a punishable offence for a bridegroom or his guardians to ask for any remuneration as the price of his willingness to accept a girl as a bride, and the proposed penalty is a fine of Rs. 500 or six months simple imprisonment or both. It is doubtful if it would be possible to enforce such a law, any more than the Sarda Act can be enforced if the public do not prosecute, but it " professes the most noble sentiments ".

One point has to be borne in mind with regard to the marriage of girls and that is that an excess of males, particularly when it is almost compulsory for men to have a son, since " there is no heaven for a sonless man ", is bound to lower the age of marriage for females. When there are not enough to go round it becomes a necessity to secure a girl while she is still young enough not to have been snapped up by some one else, and if as we have suggested elsewhere (*vide supra* para. 79) an excess of males is biologically inherent in the present caste system, a relaxation of that system will be necessary to increase the proportion of females to males and to remove the growing shortage of the former, which must, if it continue to increase, tend irresistibly in the end towards making the early marriage of girls almost compulsory.

Widow Remarriage and Divorce.

100. Restriction in infant marriage is not the only direction towards which reforming movements have been directed. Permission for Hindu widows to remarry is a natural corollary of the abandonment of the practice of *sati*, but though *sati* has gone the social ban on the remarriage of the widow remains, and in every thousand Hindu women there are still 169 widowed twenty-two of whom are under thirty years of age and over a quarter of those under 20. The widower however incurs no stigma in remarrying unless there be great disparity of age and then only among the more progressively-minded. Among the latter there is a definite and pronounced prejudice against the remarriage of middle-aged men to young girls, and the Idar State, as just pointed out, has gone so far as to prohibit the marriage of a man over 45 years old to any woman less than half his age. A similar movement is at work in the Jain community, and the Jain Swetambar Conference at Junnar in 1930 passed a resolution limiting the marriageable age of males to 45 years. The point of view which would prohibit a man's marrying when past 45 involves perhaps a tacit assumption that his marriage with a widow or a spinster of mature years is out of the question, an assumption natural enough in the present condition of Hindu and Jain society where marriageable girls of mature years are not to be found and widows may not be remarried ; it would appear an unnatural point of view were the prejudice against post-puberty marriage and widow remarriage less strigently operative, though some schools of Hindu thought would probably uphold the attitude in any case. In Hyderabad State a bill to legalise the remarriage of Hindu widows on the lines of the existing law in British India, where marriages of Hindu widows were made legal by Act XV of 1856, was opposed by orthodox Hindus, but received general support from public opinion, and in one community of Reddis, who normally prohibit widow remarriage, the remarriage of a girl who had been widowed at 7 years old met with general approval and the orthodox, who succeeded in preventing a similar union by dissuading the bride, were themselves outcasted for their interference. Generally speaking, however, remarriage of Hindu widows among the higher castes is still uncommon enough to attract attention in Indian papers to its infrequent occurrences.

If remarriage is not easy for the Hindu widow, divorce is much more difficult. The husband who wishes to marry another wife can do so, but the tie between husband and any wife once married is indissoluble in Hindu law. The Madras courts have recognised divorce when allowed by caste custom, but even this practice has not been generally applied. The only case in which it seems to be definitely certain that a Hindu marriage can be nullified is in the case of one affected by the Native Christians' Marriage Act of 1866 in which one party to the marriage embraces Christianity and is in consequence deserted by the other. In 1929 however a bill to permit the Hindu community to resort to divorce in certain circumstances was introduced in the Legislative Council of the Baroda State and received the Gaekwar's assent in 1931.

On the Malabar coast, owing to the prevalence of the *marumakkathayam* system, the position of women generally has been better than in any other part of civilized India. The Nambudri Brahmans, however, follow the *makkathayam* system and the great majority of Nambudri women are condemned by ancient custom to remain unmarried, as only the eldest son in a Nambudri family marries a wife of his own caste. The others marry Nayar women with whom they live in the form of union known as *sambandham*, easily dissoluble by either party. Legislation is now in progress to enable the younger brothers of a Nambudri family to contract marriages within their own caste and also to give legal recognition and binding effect to *sambandham* marriages (as was done in Cochin State by the Nayar Regulation of 1920), whether hypergamous or endogamous, while securing to the wife the right of divorce and, with her children, the right of maintenance by the husband, together with the right to inherit a moiety of undisposed self-acquired property left by the husband. By the customary law all responsibility for the maintenance of the children lay with the woman's family, and any property acquired by the husband reverted to his family at his death. Obviously modern conditions call for some relaxation of this customary law, for the *marumakkathayam* system, perhaps the best in the world when taken by itself, has possibly in the past been exploited by the Nambudris to their own profit. But it would be as great an error to replace the *marumakkathayam* system by the ordinary *makkathayam* one as to suppose that the former is either primitive, barbarous or in any way less respectable than the latter, although it is less widely distributed. On the contrary it seems likely that the *marumakkathayam* was the ancient and civilised system, which was replaced in most countries of southern Europe and southern Asia by the *makkathayam* under the stress of conquest by a ruder people from the steppes of southern Russia.

Inter-Caste Marriage.

101. It is not possible to leave the subject of divorce without a reference to the Indian Christian Marriage Act. The Roman Catholic Church while objecting strongly to the Indian Divorce Act as making it possible for Catholics to obtain dissolution of marriage, which is contrary to Canon Law, simultaneously objects to the fact that the laws governing Christian marriage make no provision for what is known as 'the Pauline privilege', that is for the right of the Church to dissolve a marriage contracted before conversion, a practice that would require the strictest control on the part of the state to prevent abuses, as conversion has been known to be utilized by individuals with the mere object of shaking off unwanted partners without incurring the liability to maintain them. On the other hand the Act is criticised from the opposite side for making it possible for courts to hold, as they have done, with reference to section 4 of the Act, that any marriage in which one or both the parties are Christians must be solemnized in one of the ways provided by section 5, from which it is held that no marriage can be contracted by a Christian except under the provisions of the Act, and that to perform or abet the performance of the marriage of a Christian convert according to the rites of another faith is punishable under the Act.

The difficulty of marrying into another religion without a change of creed is not one confined to Indian Christians, and until 1923 there was no law under which Hindus could contract a valid inter-caste marriage except under the Special Marriage Act of 1872, which involved a declaration that the party to the ceremony was neither a Muslim nor a Hindu. In 1910 a bill was brought to legalise marriages between persons of different castes and different religions, but it failed, and the same fate befell another bill in 1919, to legalise inter-caste marriages. In 1923 the bill referred to above was framed to legalise marriages between persons of different religions, as well as different castes, but the opposition it met with resulted in the exclusion of all communities other than Hindus, Sikhs, Jains and Buddhists. Recourse to this law, however, involves to a Hindu the loss of his personal law, and he not only loses his joint family membership, his right to manage Hindu trust property and his right of adoption, but his succession to property is governed by the Indian Succession Act. Nevertheless the Arya Marriage Validity bill brought in 1930, to provide for valid Hindu inter-caste marriages, has not become law, while Sir H. S. Gour's Special Marriage (amendment) Bill, brought forward in 1931, to provide for civil marriage between members of different communities without involving a declaration abjuring their religion, met with uncompromising opposition in the Assembly and was unhesitatingly rejected.

Devadasis.

102. In the same autumn of 1927 that the Sarda Bill was first debated in the Assembly, the Council of State discussed the motion of a Madras member for the prevention of the dedication of girls as *devadasis* in Hindu temples on the ground that such dedication inevitably entailed a life of prostitution for the girl so dedicated. The motion was opposed by the Law Member on the ground that the alleged consequences of such dedication were not inevitable and that, in so far as they might be, the case was covered by Act XVIII of 1924, which amended Sections 372 and 375 of the Indian Penal Code so as to extend their scope to cover cases of girls dedicated to Hindu temples. The motion was withdrawn on Government's undertaking that if a bill were introduced it should be circulated for opinion. In November of the same year the Madras Legislative Council passed unanimously a resolution recommending Government to undertake preventive legislation, and on that principle the Council legislated for the enfranchisement of inamholding Devadasis, that is of dedicated women holding land in virtue of temple service. Dr. Muthulaksmi Reddi brought a bill in the Madras Council in 1930, to prohibit the performance of the dedicatory ceremony in any Hindu temple and to enable dedicated women to contract a legal marriage, and in the same year Mr. Jayakar gave notice of his intention to introduce in the Legislative Assembly a similar bill to be of general application, but the bill was not introduced. Early in 1930, the Chief of Sawantwadi raised the minimum age of dedication to 18 in that State, and in July of the same year the Maharani of Travancore abolished dedication in the temples maintained by the Government of her State. The Mysore Government had prohibited the dedication of girls in State-controlled temples as early as 1910. The question of Devadasis is introduced here because it clearly has a bearing on the census returns of marital condition. It is probable that the great majority of such women return themselves as married, regarding themselves as married to the god, and it has also to be borne in mind that a life of immorality is not necessarily the consequence of dedication. In several castes in Madras, particularly in Bellary and the neighbourhood, it is the practice, if a male heir be wanting, to dedicate a daughter in the temple. Thenceforward she becomes by established custom the heir to her parents' property and can perform their funeral rites as if she were a son. She takes to herself a mate of her own selection of any equal or higher caste, but continues to live in her father's house, and her children take his name and belong to his family and not to their father's. If she has a son he inherits the property and continues the family, while if she have a daughter only the daughter will in her turn become a *basavi* and renew the attempt. No social stigma attaches to her, but rather the contrary, for her presence at weddings is auspicious, probably because she cannot become a widow. Clearly no immorality is inherent in this custom, which is merely a method of temporarily reverting to the *marumakkathayam* system when the family lacks a male heir and the *makkathayam* system proves irksome or inadequate.

As has been already suggested, it is probable that a matrilineal system formerly obtained throughout Dravidian-speaking India, as it did in southern Europe, Asia Minor, Egypt and Mesopotamia.* The western Asiatic affinities of the *devadasi* custom of the Tamilnad, for it is perhaps only there that the custom is still general, are clear enough. Apart from the familiar account of Herodotus of the offering made by women of their chastity in the temple of Mylitta at Babylon, a reference to which custom is made also in the 43rd verse of the Epistle of Jeremy in the Book of the apocryphal Prophet Baruch, Lucian mentions the same custom at Byblus in Phoenicia; there the goddess of a temple, connected at a very early date with Egypt, was a fish from the waist downwards and had by her temple a pool of sacred fish with a stone *chattri* in its midst, and a woman had the alternative of shaving her head and offering her hair (*cf.* pp. 398, 411 *infra*) instead of her chastity. Lucian as a matter of fact puts it the other way "the women who do not chuse to be shaved are obliged in lieu of it to expose their persons, and submit to the embraces of strangers in the public market-place for hire, during the space of one whole day; the money arising from it is consecrated to the service of the goddess and expended on a sacrifice to her" (Lucian, *On the Syrian Goddess*, tr. Franklin). Hair was offered by Argive maidens to Athene before marriage, and those of Megara offered clippings of their hair at the tomb of Iphinoe; in Delos both youths and maidens offered their hair before marriage at a tomb of corn-maidens in the sanctuary of Artemis; hair was polled and offered to the goddess of health at Titane near Corinth whose image was "swathed in strips of Babylonish raiment", and it is still shorn and offered to the Holy Virgin at Tenos as a thanksgiving for recovery from sickness; at Troezen every maiden before marriage dedicated a lock of her hair, in this case to a male deity, in the temple of Hippolytus. In all these cases, with the possible exception of that of the goddess of health, the association seems to be between hair and fertility of the soil and of the body, and is probably the same association in India that makes the Abbé Dubois note on the commonness of the offering of hair in temples by men and women in fulfilment of a vow. (*People of India*, III, iii). This practice obtains now even at the *darga* of the Mirgan Sahib at Nagore in Tanjore district, where there is a tank, such as those commonly found

* For a map showing the ancient sites here mentioned see the last page of ch. XII.

at Hindu temples, to which Hindu women come to bathe who have vowed their hair to the Muslim Saint. The element of a vow seems also to have entered into the practice of sacred prostitution at Comana in Pontus, where Strabo records that people assembled on account of vows made to sacrifice to the goddess, describing the place as "full of women trafficking in their persons, the most of them sacred",* that is to the moon goddess. Similar customs were observed at the Phoenician colony of Sicca on the north African coast; at Heliopolis in Syria likewise women prostituted themselves from religious motives, and in Armenia, at the temple of Anaitis, Strabo tells us that "they dedicate male and female slaves, a fact in no way remarkable, but further the most illustrious of the people dedicate their virgin daughters, who according to custom prostitute themselves for a long period in the service of the goddess and are afterwards given in marriage". Similarly it appears that in some Indian temples it is usual for a *devadasi* to serve for a period in the temple and thereafter be kept as a concubine outside. Consecrated hetaerae were associated with the worship of Aphrodite at Corinth, and an inscription from Tralles in Lydia is referred to by Frazer which shows that the custom obtained in Asia Minor as late as the second century A. D. "It records", he says, "of a certain woman, Aurelia Aemilia by name, not only that she herself served the god in the capacity of a harlot at his express command, but that her mother and female ancestors had done the same before her". Strabo records a practice of dedicating girls in the temple of Ammon in Egypt not dissimilar to that in Armenia except that in the case of Ammon the deity was male and the dedicated girls, when given to a human husband after serving their term as the wives of the god, were mourned as dead. This practice of marriage to the god appears again, but at an earlier date, in Mesopotamia. Marduk and the Sun-god Shamash both had female votaries who were married to them and who had human children and the word used for these dedicated women was the same as the Hebrew word for a temple harlot. It is hardly necessary to point out that the *devadasi* is likewise married to the god, but may have children by men. Dedications of virility were also made in the temple of the Syrian goddess, whose priests were eunuchs who had dedicated themselves by castration, and it is possible that an Indian survival of the same cult is to be seen in the dedication of natural eunuchs or otherwise deformed males to the goddess Huligamma, and in the cult of the goddess Chatushringi, whose temple on a hill near Poona is served by men (said to be natural eunuchs) who dress in women's clothes and spend their lives begging and worshipping the goddess, at whose temple they collect in large numbers to celebrate the Dasehra. In the Deccan, besides the girls dedicated to the god Khandoba as *murli*, boys (*vāghyā*) are also dedicated and are brought up as temple servants and mendicants. This god Khandoba is worshipped at the Dasehra in association with Ekavira, who is definitely a fertility goddess worshipped during the Dasehra in Maratha house-holds in little Gardens of Adonis. In any case the general parallel between the practice in southern India and that in Syria and Asia Minor is too close to be fortuitous, and offers another link between Dravidian India and the eastern Mediterranean (*cf.* Chapters X, XI, XII). It is true that the Asian deity was more often a goddess and that in India a god is served, but there is much other evidence to indicate that in India as in Greece and Italy† and as also in Asia Minor, the mother goddess and a matrilineal system preceded a change to the patrilineal system of nordic or proto-nordic invaders. It is, of course, impossible to dissociate the custom by which all worshippers propitiate the deity once in their lives by an offering of their chastity from that of dedicating some individuals to do it for a period of their lives. Indeed the custom alluded to above of dedicating a daughter as a *basavi* for the sake of reviving the otherwise inoperative *marumakkathayam* inheritance rather suggests that the practice of dedication in one form or another, real or symbolic, may have at one time been the universal concomitant of the matrilineal system in India as in Asia Minor or in Cyprus. It is possible that the *talikettu* ceremony on the Malabar coast points in the same direction; the Brahman explanation of it as a purificatory sacrament (Iyer, *Cochin Tribes and Castes,*

---

* *Καί ἄλλοι δε κατ' εὐχὴν ἀεί τινες ἐπιδημοῦσι, θυσίας τε ἐπιτελοῦντες τῃθεῷ .... πλῆθος γυναικῶν ἐργαζομένων ἀπὸ του σώματος, ὧν αἱ πλείους εἰσιν ἱεραί*—Strabo, XII, 559.

† *Vide* Frazer, *The Magic Art and the Evolution of Kings*, II, ch. xviii. The institution of kingship on a matrilineal system seems to have accompanied the worship of the mother goddess.

II page 29), read with Hamilton's account of the Zamorin's nuptials (*New Account of the East Indies*, page 310), is not antagonistic. At any rate the custom of dedication prevailed as far west as Cyprus, where there was a custom, Herodotus mentions it, similar to that of Babylon, and on the African coast to Sicca Veneria and probably to Carthage herself. The Cyprian shrines were connected in form in respect of their horn and pillar cult with Crete and Mycenæ, while the cones which were the emblem of the goddess at Byblus and other places in Asia Minor have been found in the most ancient sanctuary of Cyprus and as far west as Malta. There can be no doubt but that the custom of consecrated prostitution originates in a commerce regarded as essentially necessary to ensure that life should be propagated and that the earth should fructify, and in a further reference below (Chapter XI, page 416) the significance of the participation of a stranger is suggested. According to Bernier the virgin married to Vishnu at Puri consulted the god as to the abundance of the coming harvest, an association which is most significant. Marco Polo in giving an account of the custom of prostitution to strangers in the province of Kamul tells us how it was indignantly prohibited by the Emperor of China. The order was obeyed for three years and then rescinded, as it was found that the land became barren in consequence and the earth no longer brought forth her fruit in due season.

SUBSIDIARY TABLE I.

Distribution by Civil Condition of 1,000 of each sex, religion and main age period at each of the last five censuses.

Age.	Unmarried.					Married.					Widowed.				
	1931.	1921.	1911.	1901.	1891.	1931.	1921.	1911.	1901.	1891.	1931.	1921.	1911.	1901.	1891.
1	2	3	4	5	6	7	8	9	10	11	12	13	14	15	16
						ALL RELIGIONS.									
Males ..	479	498	490	492	487	467	438	456	454	465	54	64	54	54	48
0—5 ..	983	994	993	993	994	16	6	7	7	6	1	..	..	..	..
5—10 ..	919	966	962	962	962	79	32	37	36	36	2	2	1	2	2
10—15 ..	847	879	866	860	841	149	116	129	134	154	4	5	5	6	5
15—20 ..	553	687	665	650	621	434	298	322	334	368	13	15	13	16	11
20—30 ..	255	292	276	275	255	713	663	687	686	715	32	45	37	39	30
30—40 ..	74	83	79	87	75	859	835	857	847	868	67	82	64	66	57
40—60 ..	40	44	44	49	38	807	797	819	816	837	153	159	137	135	125
60 and over..	32	37	38	39	28	646	641	660	669	687	322	322	302	292	285
Females ..	352	358	344	344	339	493	467	483	476	485	155	175	173	180	176
0—5 ..	969	988	985	986	986	30	11	14	13	13	1	1	1	1	1
5—10 ..	802	907	891	893	874	193	88	105	102	123	5	5	4	5	3
10—15 ..	609	601	555	559	491	381	382	430	423	495	10	17	15	18	14
15—20 ..	148	188	163	179	132	818	771	800	777	833	34	41	37	44	35
20—30 ..	44	38	34	40	26	878	870	884	868	893	78	92	82	92	81
30—40 ..	17	17	16	21	13	771	769	784	765	779	212	214	200	214	208
40—60 ..	11	13	12	13	10	482	493	487	484	477	507	494	501	503	513
60 and over..	10	12	12	12	8	188	174	158	163	143	802	814	830	825	849
						HINDU.									
Males ..	462	479	470	475	472	480	452	472	466	478	58	69	58	59	50
0—5 ..	981	993	990	992	993	18	7	10	8	7	1	..	..	..	..
5—10 ..	905	956	950	952	953	93	42	48	46	45	2	2	2	2	2
10—15 ..	823	849	835	833	811	172	144	159	160	183	5	7	6	7	6
15—20 ..	523	644	626	613	587	462	339	359	369	401	15	17	15	18	12
20—30 ..	237	276	259	260	245	729	677	703	698	725	34	47	38	42	30
30—40 ..	70	81	77	87	77	859	831	856	843	865	71	88	67	70	58
40—60 ..	39	45	45	51	40	797	785	811	805	831	164	170	144	144	129
60 and over..	30	37	37	40	29	637	630	649	654	675	333	333	314	306	296
Females ..	330	332	317	321	319	501	477	495	485	495	169	191	188	194	186
0—5 ..	968	985	981	983	983	31	14	18	16	16	1	1	1	1	1
5—10 ..	779	883	863	872	850	215	111	132	122	146	6	6	5	6	4
10—15 ..	572	543	495	511	442	417	437	488	468	542	11	20	17	21	16
15—20 ..	112	138	122	141	100	850	814	836	810	862	38	48	42	49	38
20—30 ..	29	26	23	32	19	884	871	887	867	895	87	103	90	101	86
30—40 ..	12	14	13	20	12	759	755	773	751	772	229	231	214	229	216
40—60 ..	8	10	9	11	9	461	471	468	467	468	531	519	523	522	523
60 and over..	6	10	8	8	6	170	156	142	150	133	824	834	850	842	861

SUBSIDIARY TABLE I—*contd.*

Distribution by Civil Condition of 1,000 of each sex, religion and main age period at each of the last five censuses—*contd.*

Age.	Unmarried.					Married.					Widowed.				
	1931.	1921.	1911.	1901.	1891.	1931.	1921.	1911.	1901.	1891.	1931.	1921.	1911.	1901.	1891.
1	2	3	4	5	6	7	8	9	10	11	12	13	14	15	16
						MUSLIM.									
Males ..	500	531	527	526	519	456	418	427	432	440	44	51	46	42	41
0—5 ..	985	997	998	997	997	15	3	2	3	3	..	..	..	..	..
5—10 ..	932	985	984	982	983	67	14	15	17	16	1	1	1	1	1
10—15 ..	872	931	922	914	904	125	66	75	83	93	3	3	3	3	3
15—20 ..	567	749	727	714	674	421	241	263	276	316	12	10	10	10	10
20—30 ..	257	305	295	290	257	712	656	671	679	714	31	39	34	31	29
30—40 ..	64	73	72	77	62	877	858	869	870	886	59	69	59	53	52
40—60 ..	28	34	34	38	28	845	836	848	856	862	127	130	118	106	110
60 and over	22	28	28	29	20	686	681	697	717	731	292	291	275	254	249
Females ..	368	390	379	376	365	503	465	473	471	475	129	145	148	153	160
0—5 ..	964	993	995	992	992	35	6	5	7	7	1	1	..	1	1
5—10 ..	798	947	932	927	914	198	50	65	70	83	4	3	3	3	3
10—15 ..	598	644	596	597	514	394	344	393	391	474	8	12	11	12	12
15—20 ..	129	153	137	161	104	845	815	834	808	867	26	32	29	31	29
20—30 ..	35	30	27	33	20	904	901	909	898	911	61	69	64	69	69
30—40 ..	14	14	14	17	11	797	799	806	801	786	189	187	180	182	203
40—60 ..	10	11	10	12	9	495	513	505	505	462	495	476	485	483	529
60 and over	8	11	10	10	8	202	194	170	175	142	790	795	820	815	850
						CHRISTIAN.									
Males ..	565	565	563	574	570	399	393	401	391	399	36	42	36	35	31
0—5 ..	996	998	998	998	997	4	2	2	2	2	..	..	..	..	1
5—10 ..	986	993	993	994	994	13	7	6	5	5	1	..	1	1	1
10—15 ..	968	973	970	972	979	31	26	29	26	20	1	1	1	2	1
15—20 ..	761	862	829	841	840	233	133	166	155	157	6	5	5	4	3
20—30 ..	393	428	445	465	490	589	548	539	518	500	18	24	16	17	10
30—40 ..	86	92	99	105	104	871	856	862	853	865	43	52	39	42	31
40—60 ..	33	40	38	39	40	861	848	862	861	870	106	112	100	100	90
60 and over	24	33	27	26	26	697	686	704	707	712	279	281	269	267	262
Females ..	474	474	460	465	456	417	413	422	409	420	109	113	118	126	124
0—5 ..	995	997	996	997	997	5	3	4	3	3	..	..	..	..	..
5—10 ..	970	984	984	984	987	29	15	15	15	12	1	1	1	1	1
10—15 ..	888	912	884	885	882	110	85	113	108	116	2	3	3	7	2
15—20 ..	391	477	418	428	398	594	510	570	554	591	15	13	12	18	11
20—30 ..	125	109	99	92	89	828	841	854	855	866	47	50	47	53	45
30—40 ..	39	49	42	38	40	816	815	821	809	817	145	136	137	153	143
40—60 .	27	41	29	26	31	582	590	571	546	545	391	369	400	428	424
60 and over	23	43	23	22	25	250	243	205	174	180	727	714	772	804	795

SUBSIDIARY TABLE I—*concld.*

Distribution by Civil Condition of 1,000 of each sex, religion and main age period at each of the last five censuses—*concld.*

Age.	Unmarried.					Married.					Widowed.				
	1931.	1921.	1911.	1901.	1891.	1931.	1921.	1911.	1901.	1891.	1931.	1921.	1911.	1901.	1891.
1	2	3	4	5	6	7	8	9	10	11	12	13	14	15	16
						TRIBAL.									
Males ..	516	541	539	537	552	446	411	427	413	414	38	48	34	50	34
0—5 ..	984	996	996	995	996	16	4	4	5	4	..	..	..	..	..
5—10 ..	953	986	990	980	990	46	13	10	19	9	1	1	..	1	1
10—15 ..	894	937	944	917	934	104	60	55	78	64	2	3	1	5	2
15—20 ..	567	753	743	719	710	420	236	249	261	281	13	11	8	20	9
20—30 ..	225	299	279	294	276	744	656	691	653	697	31	45	30	53	27
30—40 ..	59	72	66	71	61	887	851	888	852	891	54	77	46	77	48
40—60 ..	28	34	28	31	21	860	847	883	837	889	112	119	89	132	90
60 and over	23	26	25	24	13	737	727	754	741	772	240	247	221	235	215
Females ..	438	459	450	442	467	452	418	436	419	422	110	123	114	139	111
0—5 ..	980	995	995	992	995	19	5	4	7	5	1	..	1	1	..
5—10 ..	910	972	976	968	976	87	26	22	29	22	3	2	2	3	2
10—15 ..	761	820	816	805	805	232	172	179	183	189	7	8	5	12	6
15—20 ..	263	424	376	389	367	711	548	602	567	611	26	28	22	44	22
20—30 ..	83	99	77	91	77	862	836	873	818	872	55	65	50	91	51
30—40 ..	28	35	28	30	24	826	813	848	784	853	146	152	124	186	123
40—60 ..	19	23	18	21	16	577	588	588	544	621	404	389	394	435	363
60 and over	19	20	17	18	12	268	255	226	245	241	713	725	757	737	747
						BURMA.									
Males ..	561	559	569	565	558	392	389	389	393	394	47	52	42	42	48
0—5 ..	1,000	1,000	1,000	1,000	1,000	..	..	..	..	..	..	..	..	..	..
5—10 ..	999	1,000	1,000	1,000	1,000	1	..	..	..	..	..	..	..	..	..
10—15 ..	994	999	999	995	999	6	1	1	5	1	..	..	..	..	..
15—20 ..	807	927	919	922	932	184	69	78	75	63	9	4	3	3	5
20—40 ..	309	302	298	298	268	652	651	665	666	686	39	47	37	36	46
40—60 ..	85	72	89	88	49	797	809	817	814	843	118	119	94	98	108
60 and over	78	63	89	83	41	633	645	656	652	679	289	292	255	265	280
Females ..	521	509	519	510	506	374	377	376	381	378	105	114	105	109	116
0—5 ..	1,000	1,000	1,000	1,000	1,000	..	..	..	..	..	..	..	..	..	..
5—10 ..	999	1,000	1,000	1,000	1,000	1	..	..	..	..	..	..	..	..	..
10—15 ..	977	996	993	987	995	21	4	7	13	5	2	..	..	..	..
15—20 ..	608	733	726	720	732	366	248	259	265	246	26	19	15	15	22
20—40 ..	213	165	160	160	130	710	750	763	764	780	77	85	77	76	90
40—60 ..	70	52	70	68	35	633	661	665	653	686	297	287	265	279	279
60 and over	64	52	91	83	48	302	287	289	282	392	634	661	620	635	560

NOTE.—Owing to the sort for Civil Condition's having been confined to Race in Burma, the 1931 figures under the various religions refer only to India proper except in the case of the figures for All Religions which are inclusive of Burma.

M22CC

SUBSIDIARY TABLE II.

Distribution by Civil Condition of 1,000 of each sex at certain ages as returned by each Province, State or Agency.

ALL RELIGIONS.

Males.

	All Ages.			0—5			5—10			10—15			15—40			40 and over		
	Unmarried.	Married.	Widowed.	Unmarried.	Married.	Widowed.	Unmarried.	Married.	Widowed.	Unmarried.	Married.	Widowed.	Unmarried.	Married.	Widowed.	Unmarried.	Married.	Widowed.
INDIA	**479**	**467**	**54**	**983**	**16**	**1**	**919**	**79**	**2**	**847**	**149**	**4**	**257**	**703**	**40**	**38**	**774**	**188**
Ajmer-Merwara	450	482	68	974	25	1	890	106	4	797	196	7	236	716	48	52	717	231
Assam	536	420	44	999	1	..	982	17	1	953	45	2	313	645	42	21	829	150
Bengal	469	498	33	981	19	..	931	68	1	867	131	2	217	757	26	14	864	122
Bihar and Orissa	420	529	51	968	31	1	833	163	4	718	275	7	169	789	42	23	805	172
Bombay (*including Aden*).	474	473	53	983	16	1	932	66	2	864	132	4	246	716	38	30	778	192
Burma	561	392	47	994	6	..	807	184	9	309	652	39	85	797	118	78	633	289
Central Provinces and Berar.	413	540	47	973	26	1	854	143	3	730	266	4	145	817	38	27	886	87
Coorg	554	393	53	999	1	..	996	4	..	993	7	..	457	501	42	33	791	176
Delhi	459	465	76	999	1	..	951	47	2	864	131	5	275	663	62	55	687	258
Madras	527	433	40	997	3	..	982	18	..	958	41	1	335	640	25	25	829	146
North-West Frontier Province.	574	379	47	1,000	..	..	995	5	..	975	23	2	398	562	40	49	778	173
Punjab (*including Agency*).	541	383	76	998	2	..	973	26	1	926	72	2	353	593	54	73	662	265
United Provinces of Agra and Oudh.	438	483	79	976	23	1	861	136	3	746	247	7	214	723	63	58	682	260
Baroda State	454	479	67	996	4	..	916	79	5	810	182	8	217	739	44	40	730	230
Central India Agency	444	495	61	981	18	1	895	102	3	780	214	6	193	756	51	40	747	213
Cochin State	587	379	34	1,000	..	..	1,000	..	..	997	3	..	407	570	23	21	847	132
Gwalior State	468	456	76	988	11	1	930	66	4	822	169	9	230	706	64	256	676	68
Hyderabad State	424	526	50	953	45	2	858	138	4	745	248	7	189	775	36	37	796	167
Jammu and Kashmir State.	534	412	54	1,000	..	..	982	18	..	948	51	1	309	643	48	40	748	212
Mysore State	556	393	51	1,000	..	..	999	1	..	995	5	..	394	576	30	21	787	192
Rajputana Agency	491	438	71	990	10	..	938	60	2	852	144	4	255	696	49	60	684	256
Travancore State	584	387	29	1,000	..	..	999	1	..	991	9	..	397	585	18	29	857	114
Western India States Agency.	470	469	61	959	40	1	888	110	2	809	187	4	227	730	43	30	744	226

Females.

	All Ages			0—5			5—10			10—15			15—40			40 and over.		
	Unmarried.	Married.	Widowed.	Unmarried.	Married.	Widowed.	Unmarried.	Married.	Widowed.	Unmarried.	Married.	Widowed.	Unmarried.	Married.	Widowed.	Unmarried.	Married.	Widowed.
INDIA	**352**	**493**	**155**	**969**	**30**	**1**	**802**	**193**	**5**	**609**	**381**	**10**	**59**	**829**	**112**	**11**	**415**	**574**
Ajmer-Merwara	317	527	156	951	48	1	761	235	4	538	455	7	25	884	91	4	395	601
Assam	415	444	141	993	7	..	900	98	2	715	277	8	69	812	119	8	392	600
Bengal	310	514	176	952	47	1	702	291	7	450	534	16	21	824	155	4	320	676
Bihar and Orissa	312	527	161	948	50	2	719	273	8	519	467	14	37	847	116	6	429	565
Bombay (*including Aden*).	339	506	155	967	32	1	776	219	5	569	421	10	45	847	108	11	397	592
Burma	521	374	105	977	21	2	608	366	26	213	710	77	70	633	297	64	302	634
Central Provinces and Berar.	305	549	146	950	49	1	693	301	6	469	521	10	22	817	161	6	439	555
Coorg	444	396	160	998	2	..	990	9	1	942	55	3	150	725	125	9	361	630
Delhi	376	517	107	997	3	..	892	107	1	671	326	3	54	881	65	8	485	507
Madras	377	445	178	988	12	..	906	92	2	769	224	7	76	792	132	9	373	618
North-West Frontier Province.	458	433	109	1,000	..	..	982	18	..	876	121	3	119	805	76	28	502	470
Punjab (*including Agency*).	419	464	117	995	5	..	917	82	1	762	235	3	87	846	67	12	502	486
United Provinces of Agra and Oudh.	317	532	151	970	29	1	756	239	5	516	475	9	31	875	94	7	435	558
Baroda State	329	524	147	989	10	1	798	197	5	580	412	8	36	881	83	2	451	547
Central India Agency	331	513	156	970	29	1	771	223	6	529	460	11	39	849	112	12	392	596
Cochin State	467	387	146	1,000	..	..	993	7	..	930	67	3	170	728	102	12	440	548
Gwalior State	328	502	170	974	22	4	784	206	10	529	453	18	34	838	128	13	364	623
Hyderabad State	311	533	156	925	71	4	659	328	13	414	565	21	46	836	118	22	425	553
Jammu and Kashmir State.	404	489	107	1,000	..	..	957	42	1	777	217	6	44	920	36	6	495	499
Mysore State	404	418	177	1,000	..	..	951	48	1	804	192	4	60	796	144	10	341	649
Rajputana Agency	348	496	156	981	18	1	824	173	3	592	401	7	30	867	103	4	411	585
Travancore State	475	406	119	1,000	..	..	992	8	..	920	78	2	151	774	75	13	495	492
Western India States Agency.	357	496	147	948	51	1	824	173	3	647	348	5	41	866	93	3	436	561

M22CC

SUBSIDIARY TABLE II—*contd.*

Distribution by Civil Condition of 1,000 of each sex at certain ages as returned by each Province, State or Agency—*contd.*

HINDU.*

Males.

	All Ages.			0—5.			5—10.			10—15.			15—40.			40 and over.		
	Unmarried.	Married.	Widowed.	Unmarried.	Married.	Widowed.	Unmarried.	Married.	Widowed.	Unmarried.	Married.	Widowed.	Unmarried.	Married.	Widowed.	Unmarried.	Married.	Widowed.
INDIA ..	**463**	**480**	**57**	**981**	**18**	**1**	**905**	**93**	**2**	**823**	**172**	**5**	**240**	**717**	**43**	**37**	**765**	**198**
Ajmer-Merwara ..	434	500	66	972	27	1	875	120	5	772	220	8	204	750	46	44	725	231
Assam	535	410	55	1,000	..	..	990	9	1	971	27	2	340	611	49	26	794	180
Bengal	469	486	45	984	16	..	955	44	1	909	90	1	262	707	31	21	816	163
Bihar and Orissa ..	412	535	53	968	31	1	826	170	4	708	285	7	167	790	43	23	799	178
Bombay (*including Aden*).	460	488	52	982	17	1	925	73	2	849	147	4	214	750	36	24	784	192
Central Provinces and Berar.	397	553	50	971	28	1	835	162	3	700	295	5	128	833	39	22	816	162
Coorg	557	387	56	999	1	..	996	4	..	993	7	..	451	504	45	33	781	186
Delhi	440	475	85	999	1	..	942	57	1	840	155	5	244	689	67	59	647	294
Madras	521	438	41	997	3	..	980	20	..	955	44	1	330	645	25	25	826	149
North-West Frontier Province.	506	440	54	1,000	..	..	990	9	1	968	30	2	373	585	42	77	716	207
Punjab (*including Agency*).	514	401	85	997	3	..	961	38	1	895	102	3	324	616	60	88	625	287
United Provinces of Agra and Oudh.	435	485	80	976	24	..	857	140	3	738	255	7	211	725	64	62	675	263
Baroda State ..	447	486	67	996	4	..	909	86	5	795	197	8	203	752	45	40	730	230
Central India Agency	438	500	62	980	19	1	889	108	3	766	227	7	187	761	52	41	742	217
Cochin State ..	583	381	36	1,000	..	..	1,000	..	..	997	3	..	408	565	27	22	846	132
Gwalior State ..	468	457	75	988	11	1	928	68	4	818	173	9	227	708	65	69	674	257
Hyderabad State ..	414	532	54	952	46	2	848	147	5	725	267	8	181	780	39	39	784	177
Jammu and Kashmir State.	527	397	76	1,000	..	..	969	30	1	939	59	2	382	567	51	88	673	239
Mysore State ..	554	394	52	1,000	..	..	999	1	..	994	6	..	390	579	31	21	782	197
Rajputana Agency ..	488	441	71	991	9	..	936	62	2	846	150	4	250	701	49	62	679	259
Travancore State ..	590	381	29	1,000	..	..	999	1	..	994	6	..	424	556	20	37	853	110
Western India States Agency.	455	483	62	955	44	1	871	127	2	782	214	4	206	750	44	26	746	228

Females.

	All Ages.			0—5.			5—10.			10—15.			15—40.			40 and over.		
	Unmarried.	Married.	Widowed.	Unmarried.	Married.	Widowed.	Unmarried.	Married.	Widowed.	Unmarried.	Married.	Widowed.	Unmarried.	Married.	Widowed.	Unmarried.	Married.	Widowed.
INDIA ..	**330**	**501**	**169**	**968**	**31**	**1**	**779**	**215**	**6**	**572**	**417**	**11**	**41**	**835**	**124**	**7**	**396**	**597**
Ajmer-Merwara ..	306	537	157	945	54	1	733	263	4	505	488	7	19	890	91	2	391	607
Assam	413	431	156	999	1	..	932	66	2	764	228	8	67	799	134	6	376	618
Bengal	293	481	226	972	26	2	731	260	9	473	505	22	22	768	210	4	290	706
Bihar and Orissa ..	302	531	167	949	49	2	710	281	9	504	481	15	31	849	120	4	423	573
Bombay (*including Aden*).	326	513	161	963	36	1	745	250	5	528	461	11	35	851	114	10	386	604
Central Provinces and Berar.	290	560	150	943	55	2	655	339	6	424	566	10	20	890	90	5	437	558
Coorg	450	391	159	998	2	..	990	9	1	948	50	2	155	720	125	9	360	631
Delhi	355	530	115	997	3	..	871	128	1	624	373	3	39	888	73	5	461	534
Madras	370	448	182	986	14	..	896	101	3	756	237	7	72	793	135	8	369	623
North-West Frontier Province.	435	436	129	1,000	..	..	963	35	2	817	179	4	80	825	95	19	405	576
Punjab (*including Agency*).	379	479	142	994	6	..	879	119	2	682	313	5	53	855	92	8	435	557
United Provinces of Agra and Oudh.	311	533	156	971	28	1	751	244	5	504	487	9	26	875	99	6	427	567
Baroda State ..	321	533	146	988	11	1	781	215	4	551	441	8	28	890	82	2	453	545
Central India Agency	323	518	159	967	31	2	754	240	6	506	481	13	37	847	116	12	388	600
Cochin State ..	450	387	163	1,000	..	..	991	9	..	920	76	4	161	721	118	9	415	576
Gwalior State ..	325	504	171	974	23	3	778	212	10	521	461	18	31	839	130	12	362	626
Hyderabad State ..	295	539	166	916	79	5	614	370	16	369	606	25	40	832	128	21	409	570
Jammu and Kashmir State.	355	461	184	1,000	..	..	927	69	4	708	280	12	39	847	128	2	364	634
Mysore State ..	400	419	181	1,000	..	..	948	51	1	799	197	4	57	795	148	9	337	654
Rajputana Agency ..	341	500	159	981	18	1	813	184	3	572	420	8	26	869	105	3	407	590
Travancore State ..	467	399	134	1,000	..	..	993	7	..	925	73	2	155	759	86	13	461	526
Western India States Agency.	348	511	141	939	60	1	794	203	3	606	388	6	34	879	87	3	446	551

SUBSIDIARY TABLE II—*concld.*

Distribution by Civil Condition of 1,000 of each sex at certain ages as returned by each Province, State or Agency—*concld.*

MUSLIMS.*

Males.

	All Ages.			0—5			5—10			10—15			15—40			40 and over.		
	Unmarried.	Married.	Widowed.	Unmarried.	Married.	Widowed.	Unmarried.	Married.	Widowed.	Unmarried.	Married.	Widowed.	Unmarried.	Married.	Widowed.	Unmarried.	Married.	Widowed.
INDIA ..	**499**	**457**	**44**	**985**	**15**	..	**932**	**67**	**1**	**872**	**125**	**3**	**259**	**705**	**36**	**27**	**811**	**162**
Ajmer-Merwara ..	495	437	68	977	22	1	933	65	2	869	126	5	306	635	59	61	725	214
Assam ..	526	449	25	998	2	..	963	36	1	913	85	2	248	725	27	9	903	88
Bengal	468	510	22	978	22	..	913	86	1	835	163	2	175	804	21	7	911	82
Bihar and Orissa ..	412	547	41	956	43	1	807	189	4	683	311	6	138	827	35	12	848	140
Bombay (*including Aden*).	521	422	57	989	11	..	959	40	1	917	80	3	340	612	48	46	754	200
Central Provinces and Berar.	492	458	50	985	14	1	960	39	1	923	75	2	273	689	38	22	813	165
Coorg	528	442	30	1,000	..	..	997	3	..	995	5	..	487	488	25	26	887	87
Delhi	488	449	63	998	2	..	970	29	1	911	86	3	316	630	54	44	755	201
Madras	583	389	28	999	1	..	996	4	..	990	10	..	394	585	21	21	871	108
North-West Frontier Province.	579	374	47	1,000	..	..	995	5	..	975	23	2	392	568	40	47	783	170
Punjab (*including Agency*).	554	378	68	998	2	..	980	19	1	944	54	2	362	588	50	52	702	246
United Provinces of Agra and Oudh.	451	476	73	976	23	1	880	117	3	792	203	5	219	721	60	32	727	241
Baroda State ..	497	439	64	997	3	..	962	36	2	913	84	3	294	662	44	38	744	218
Central India Agency	467	471	62	989	10	1	932	66	2	871	125	4	254	694	52	25	775	200
Cochin State ..	598	377	25	1,000	..	..	999	1	..	996	4	..	416	563	21	13	889	98
Gwalior State ..	471	458	71	986	12	2	950	46	4	877	115	8	250	684	59	40	736	224
Hyderabad State ..	468	493	39	975	24	1	879	118	3	829	168	3	283	690	27	40	828	132
Jammu and Kashmir State.	530	416	54	1,000	..	..	985	15	..	949	50	1	289	664	47	22	775	203
Mysore State ..	584	385	32	1,000	..	..	999	1	..	996	4	..	429	551	20	16	856	128
Rajputana Agency ..	496	436	68	988	11	1	939	59	2	877	119	4	270	679	51	31	729	240
Travancore State ..	612	367	21	1,000	..	..	998	2	..	994	6	..	436	548	16	13	808	89
Western India States Agency.	532	413	55	969	30	1	958	41	1	928	70	2	311	649	40	39	759	202

Females.

	All Ages.			0—5			5—10			10—15			15—40			40 and over.		
	Unmarried.	Married.	Widowed.	Unmarried.	Married.	Widowed.	Unmarried.	Married.	Widowed.	Unmarried.	Married.	Widowed.	Unmarried.	Married.	Widowed.	Unmarried.	Married.	Widowed.
INDIA ..	**368**	**533**	**129**	**964**	**35**	**1**	**798**	**198**	**4**	**598**	**394**	**8**	**51**	**857**	**92**	**9**	**430**	**561**
Ajmer-Merwara ..	355	512	133	968	31	1	838	158	4	615	379	6	31	894	75	5	435	560
Assam ..	382	491	127	982	18	..	809	188	3	548	442	10	16	908	76	4	326	670
Bengal	318	542	140	937	62	1	674	320	6	421	567	12	16	871	113	3	343	654
Bihar and Orissa ..	296	555	149	920	78	2	658	335	7	443	545	12	23	867	110	5	435	560
Bombay (*including Aden*).	384	483	133	983	16	1	900	98	2	732	263	5	65	848	87	11	441	548
Central Provinces and Berar.	386	472	142	982	17	1	894	103	3	698	296	6	47	866	87	9	399	592
Coorg	379	455	166	997	3	..	977	23	..	861	129	10	79	793	128	4	347	649
Delhi	411	497	92	998	2	..	927	72	1	749	248	3	64	886	50	7	523	470
Madras	426	415	159	999	1	..	970	29	1	845	150	5	94	783	123	9	372	619
North-West Frontier Province.	430	432	108	1,000	..	..	983	16	1	881	116	3	121	803	76	28	508	464
Punjab (*including Agency*).	443	452	105	996	4	..	934	65	1	803	194	3	106	837	57	16	527	457
United Provinces of Agra and Oudh.	349	528	123	964	35	1	778	218	4	573	421	6	55	878	67	14	481	505
Baroda State ..	368	475	157	987	5	8	903	86	11	760	236	4	67	847	86	4	426	570
Central India Agency	363	491	146	981	18	1	863	133	4	659	334	7	46	868	86	12	395	592
Cochin State ..	470	398	132	1,000	..	..	991	9	..	913	83	4	130	761	109	5	430	565
Gwalior State ..	363	491	146	969	25	6	841	150	9	622	364	14	62	842	96	24	411	565
Hyderabad State ..	360	496	144	955	42	3	848	151	7	634	354	12	66	835	99	22	439	539
Jammu and Kashmir State.	415	497	88	1,000	..	..	963	36	1	792	205	3	58	895	47	5	538	457
Mysore State ..	456	417	127	1,000	..	..	981	18	1	852	146	2	69	841	90	6	397	597
Rajputana Agency ..	381	493	126	979	20	1	861	136	3	674	320	6	51	872	77	6	467	527
Travancore State ..	485	402	113	1,000	..	..	993	7	..	920	77	3	127	790	83	7	482	511
Western India States Agency.	401	449	150	988	11	1	944	55	1	811	186	3	72	838	90	4	427	569

NOTE.—The above proportions for Provinces are calculated inclusively of the population of the Indian States attached to them, except in the case of Madras where Cochin and Travancore are excluded.

* Excludes figures for Burma as the sort for Civil Condition in that province was by Race instead of by Religion.

SUBSIDIARY TABLE III.

Distribution by main age periods and Civil Condition of 10,000 of each Sex and Religion.

Religion and age.	Males.			Females.		
	Unmarried.	Married.	Widowed.	Unmarried.	Married.	Widowed.
All Religions	4,791	4,673	536	3,521	4,931	1,548
0—5	9,833	162	5	9,692	297	11
5—10	9,189	792	19	8,017	1,935	48
10—15	8,472	1,492	36	6,089	3,814	97
15—20	5,527	4,337	136	1,485	8,180	335
20—40	1,739	7,782	479	328	8,327	1,345
40—60	397	8,067	1,536	113	4,816	5,071
60 and over ..	319	6,464	3,217	100	1,877	8,023
Hindus	4,625	4,802	573	3,298	5,012	1,690
0—5	9,812	182	6	9,676	311	13
5—10	9,053	924	23	7,792	2,150	58
10—15	8,233	1,723	44	5,719	4,168	113
15—20	5,230	4,623	147	1,116	8,505	379
20—40	1,615	7,882	503	213	8,307	1,480
40—60	385	7,974	1,641	75	4,613	5,312
60 and over ..	301	6,368	3,331	60	1,700	8,240
Muslims	4,994	4,564	442	3,676	5,033	1,291
0—5	9,844	152	4	9,640	350	10
5—10	9,322	666	12	7,984	1,978	38
10—15	8,722	1,253	25	5,985	3,937	78
15—20	5,674	4,207	119	1,292	8,453	255
20—40	1,722	7,845	433	267	8,612	1,121
40—60	283	8,449	1,268	98	4,946	4,956
60 and over ..	220	6,860	2,920	81	2,024	7,895
Christians	5,651	3,992	357	4,740	4,171	1,089
0—5	9,963	35	2	9,951	46	3
5—10	9,860	135	5	9,697	293	10
10—15	9,679	312	9	8,881	1,097	22
15—20	7,611	2,332	57	3,915	5,934	151
20—40	2,606	7,107	287	899	8,230	871
40—60	335	8,606	1,059	271	5,816	3,913
60 and over ..	235	6,973	2,792	228	2,498	7,274
Sikhs	5,503	3,696	801	4,137	4,726	1,137
0—5	9,985	14	1	9,969	29	2
5—10	9,805	187	8	9,378	613	9
10—15	9,353	627	20	7,914	2,064	22
15—20	6,546	3,324	130	2,393	7,501	106
20—40	3,026	6,381	593	360	8,998	642
40—60	1,258	6,589	2,153	101	6,400	3,499
60 and over ..	874	4,847	4,279	72	2,683	7,245
Tribals	5,158	4,466	376	4,378	4,520	1,102
0—5	9,836	160	4	9,796	196	8
5—10	9,528	462	10	9,098	873	29
10—15	8,940	1,037	23	7,611	2,323	66
15—20	5,665	4,200	135	2,629	7,111	260
20—40	1,499	8,089	412	599	8,464	937
40—60	284	8,597	1,119	190	5,773	4,037
60 and over ..	231	7,368	2,401	187	2,678	7,135

NOTE.—The figures for All Religions relate to India General but the details for the respective religions refer exclusively to India Proper, *i.e.*, excluding Burma where the sort for Civil Condition was by Race and not Religion.

SUBSIDIARY TABLE IV.

Proportion of Sexes by Civil Condition in the main Provinces.

Province and Religion.	Number of females per 1,000 males.		
	All ages.		
	Unmarried.	Married.	Widowed.
1	2	3	4
INDIA*	**691**	**993**	**2,717**
Hindu	679	995	2,810
Sikh	589	1,003	1,112
Muslim	665	997	2,637
Christian	799	995	2,903
Tribal	857	1,022	2,954
Assam	**705**	**961**	**2,883**
Hindu	689	936	2,535
Muslim	654	988	4,599
Tribal	889	1,010	2,463
Bengal	**610**	**953**	**4,996**
Hindu	568	899	4,518
Muslim	636	994	5,900
Buddhist	789	1,010	2,886
Bihar and Orissa	**748**	**1,004**	**3,200**
Hindu	735	999	3,155
Muslim	731	1,032	3,746
Tribal	889	1,024	3,095
Bombay (*including Aden*)	**650**	**970**	**2,671**
Hindu	664	984	2,902
Muslim	596	924	1,862
Jain	575	885	2,383
Burma	**890**	**913**	**2,142**
Burmese	967	1,005	2,386
Central Provinces and Berar	**741**	**1,015**	**3,073**
Hindu	730	1,014	3,081
Muslim	706	933	2,704
Tribal	826	1,058	3,207
Madras	**735**	**1,051**	**4,563**
Hindu	729	1,049	4,531
Muslim	750	1,096	5,827
Christian	826	1,035	3,902
Punjab	**644**	**1,005**	**1,285**
Hindu	615	998	1,401
Muslim	672	1,004	1,280
Sikh	592	1,026	1,111
United Provinces	**654**	**995**	**1,734**
Hindu	646	995	1,771
Muslim	696	997	1,521
Christian	658	1,006	1,380

*The figures against this entry refer to India General, *i.e.*, including Burma, though the details against the respective religions relate to India Proper only.

NOTE.—The Provincial figures are inclusive of the States attached to them, except Madras which excludes Cochin and Travancore.

SUBSIDIARY TABLE V.

Proportion who are married and widowed at certain ages.

Province, State or Agency.	Number per 1,000 aged 0—10 who are married.										Number per 1,000 aged 15—40 who are widowed.									
	Males.					Females.					Males.					Females.				
	1931.	1921.	1911.	1901.	1891.	1931.	1921.	1911.	1901.	1891.	1931.	1921.	1911.	1901.	1891.	1931.	1921.	1911.	1901.	1891
										HINDU.										
INDIA	**53**	**26**	**29**	**28**	**28**	**113**	**66**	**74**	**70**	**70**	**43**	**56**	**44**	**47**	**36**	**124**	**138**	**124**	**137**	**123**
Ajmer-Merwara	70	29	18	25	30	143	74	45	67	73	46	82	63	80	34	91	126	99	135	71
Assam	4	2	2	3	2	29	11	14	18	16	49	58	54	54	40	134	155	158	181	168
Bengal	30	6	7	6	5	130	49	64	75	89	31	36	31	31	33	210	232	224	240	257
Bihar and Orissa	99	59	77	80	67	155	100	132	138	122	43	57	49	41	41	120	138	125	120	114
Bombay†	44	30	35	25	31	133	98	109	83	113	36	59	40	63	33	114	136	117	148	96
Burma	9	1	3	3	..	11	1	8	3	..	24	34	25	26	23	48	49	43	56	61
Central Provinces and Berar	89	34	29	28	27	179	99	99	84	95	39	59	39	61	38	89	104	78	125	80
Coorg	3	3	1	4	4	5	5	2	3	7	45	39	32	46	32	126	132	132	149	134
Madras	11	7	6	5	6	54	28	31	27	36	25	27	21	24	18	135	131	120	131	128
North-West Frontier Province	4	2	2			15	5	5			42	45	54			95	98	108		
Delhi	*27	12	12	9	17	*56	30	32	29	48	*67	94	72	50	59	*73	78	106	88	127
Punjab (*including Agency*)	*20	13				*56	36				*60	77				*92	98			
United Provinces	78	33	30	32	25	121	60	59	61	53	64	79	64	51	48	99	111	104	102	92
Baroda State	42	34	80	66	85	102	72	144	108	173	44	78	66	107	37	82	105	112	182	80
Central India Agency	62	38	47	49	..	124	88	77	86	..	52	76	54	82	..	116	131	119	160	..
Gwalior State	38	36				108	78				65	94				130	150			
Cochin State	..	..	..	..	1	4	1	1	1	12	27	34	29	26	12	118	124	122	110	55
Hyderabad State	89	32	25	26	21	189	134	127	107	126	38	54	26	42	27	124	147	101	133	105
Jammu and Kashmir State	15	7	6	7	..	30	54	54	46	..	51	54	52	41	..	127	143	150	144	..
Mysore State	..	1	..	..	1	25	4	4	10	26	31	40	22	30	26	148	160	133	142	154
Rajputana Agency	35	14	11	21	..	91	48	35	57	..	49	86	50	83	..	105	141	108	152	..
Travancore State	..	..	1	1	1	3	1	2	2	3	20	28	36	41	10	86	91	104	99	44
Western India States Agency†	84	..	..	..	..	125	..	..	..	..	44	..	..	..	..	87	..	..	..	..
										MUSLIM.										
INDIA.	**40**	**9**	**9**	**10**	**9**	**107**	**30**	**35**	**39**	**43**	**36**	**43**	**38**	**34**	**33**	**91**	**99**	**94**	**98**	**103**
Ajmer-Merwara	42	15	12	19	15	86	45	29	30	41	59	70	57	56	34	75	88	77	80	64
Assam	18	2	1	3	1	90	10	9	12	13	27	31	31	29	22	104	113	109	131	115
Bengal	53	7	7	8	7	176	36	47	57	61	21	26	22	23	22	113	120	113	120	126
Bihar and Orissa	116	34	41	40	37	197	71	86	89	90	35	45	42	36	35	110	122	123	130	125
Bombay	25	10	10	11	10	53	26	25	26	28	47	65	43	48	36	87	98	85	101	77
Burma	3	..	1	1	..	5	..	..	1	..	25	37	31	34	28	72	74	63	69	80
Central Provinces and Berar	25	13	12	18	9	55	28	27	39	27	38	48	40	49	35	87	98	94	128	96
Coorg	2	4	2	6	4	13	4	5	3	5	25	21	22	22	15	127	141	140	153	119
Madras	2	2	2	2	3	14	6	7	7	11	21	26	23	22	13	123	119	119	119	104
North-West Frontier Province	2	..	1			7	1	3			40	41	35			75	68	58		
Delhi	15	5	5	3	6	33	20	14	10	19	54	60	57	38	47	50	51	65	59	89
Punjab (*including Agency*)	10	5				31	13				50	59				57	62			
United Provinces	67	17	18	22	15	115	40	42	43	38	60	70	62	46	45	67	77	73	73	69
Baroda State	18	16	26	87	40	41	33	51	113	68	44	60	57	103	36	86	99	106	172	89
Central India Agency	37	21	32	25	..	69	47	50	51	..	52	64	57	77	..	86	100	104	138	..
Gwalior State	28	27				80	50				59	75				96	108			
Cochin State	..	..	..	..	..	4	1	..	1	3	21	23	21	23	10	109	102	97	92	64
Hyderabad State	76	23	10	20	12	90	39	27	42	40	27	42	21	32	21	99	125	84	106	98
Jammu and Kashmir State	7	8	5	7	..	16	21	19	20	..	48	44	36	31	..	46	50	51	52	..
Mysore State	..	..	..	1	2	9	1	2	5	9	20	25	18	26	18	90	101	96	100	106
Rajputana Agency	34	19	10	18	..	71	40	30	28	..	51	80	47	61	..	77	95	78	113	..
Travancore State	1	2	..	1	3	3	1	2	2	4	16	23	30	30	12	83	76	85	72	43
Western India States Agency	35	†	†	†	†	32	†	†	†	†	40	†	†	†	†	90	†	†	†	†

NOTES.—(1) The proportions for Provinces include those for Indian States attached to them, except in the case of Madras, where they exclude Cochin and Travancore.

†(2) Separate figures for the Western India States Agency, which has been treated as an independent unit on this occasion, are not available for previous censuses and the figures against Bombay, previous to 1931, must therefore be read as including this unit.

* Excluding Addharmis.

SUBSIDIARY TABLE VI.

Distribution by Civil Condition of 1,000 of each sex at certain ages for selected castes.

Distribution of 1,000 males of each age by Civil Condition.

Caste.	All Ages.			0—6			7—13			14—16			17—23.			24—43.			44 and over.		
	Un-married.	Married.	Wi-dowed.	Un-married.	Married.	Wi-dowed.	Un-married.	Married.	Wi-dowed.	Un-married.	Married.	Wi-dowed.	Un-married.	Married.	Wi-dowed.	Un-married.	Married.	Wi-dowed.	Un-married.	Married.	Wi-dowed.
1	2	3	4	5	6	7	8	9	10	11	12	13	14	15	16	17	18	19	20	21	22
Baniya	494	411	95	992	7	1	948	50	2	751	239	10	413	564	23	174	725	101	98	559	343
Bhangi	457	470	73	982	17	1	865	130	5	577	400	23	279	672	49	75	834	91	34	689	277
Bhil	504	463	33	993	7	..	948	51	1	710	285	5	296	688	16	41	914	45	33	828	139
Brahman	486	435	79	986	13	1	931	67	2	759	230	11	494	484	22	167	754	79	82	641	277
Chamar	415	523	62	964	35	1	769	225	6	471	509	20	224	742	34	52	874	74	27	731	242
Chetti	560	406	34	1,000	..	..	999	1	..	975	25	..	776	217	7	161	800	39	17	841	142
Darzi	450	466	84	987	12	1	911	85	4	682	291	27	328	628	44	89	826	85	47	672	281
Dom	392	542	66	964	35	1	811	182	7	530	439	31	242	716	42	53	874	73	48	730	222
Gond	446	509	45	977	22	1	880	118	2	652	338	10	298	679	23	54	893	53	27	809	164
Gujar	509	414	77	994	5	1	927	71	2	737	254	9	458	516	26	143	767	90	59	647	294
Iluvan	599	374	27	1,000	..	..	999	1	..	988	11	1	768	222	10	132	838	30	22	855	123
Jat	539	382	79	996	4	..	953	46	1	798	196	6	530	451	19	204	713	83	82	619	299
Kachhi	441	472	87	987	12	1	894	102	4	591	391	18	279	685	36	83	812	105	38	635	327
Kahar	446	469	85	983	16	1	874	121	5	644	339	17	329	631	40	80	820	100	45	665	290
Kallan	549	408	43	999	1	..	996	4	..	981	19	..	762	228	10	131	821	48	15	816	169
Kayastha	509	432	59	983	16	1	939	58	3	811	176	13	624	353	23	156	785	59	46	742	212
Khatri	559	373	68	999	1	..	983	16	1	923	72	5	672	314	14	212	719	69	91	649	260
Kumhar	442	484	74	976	23	1	831	164	5	567	418	15	308	661	31	82	834	84	34	690	276
Kunbi	367	548	85	926	70	4	687	302	11	440	536	24	217	743	40	85	821	94	44	683	273
Mahar	429	511	60	968	29	3	824	167	9	548	402	50	292	650	58	62	875	63	34	784	182
Maratha	434	496	70	978	18	4	855	137	8	652	326	22	415	560	25	82	840	78	51	721	228
Megh	474	443	83	970	22	8	918	69	13	757	202	41	437	501	62	124	789	87	62	697	241
Momin (Julaha, etc.)	449	473	78	974	24	2	853	142	5	615	367	18	317	650	33	81	823	96	32	697	271
Naibrahman	451	469	80	975	24	1	857	139	4	631	355	14	337	629	34	97	808	95	43	666	291
Namasudra	472	472	56	979	19	2	921	70	9	781	199	20	458	526	16	87	855	58	15	784	201
Nayar (Nair)	612	353	35	1,000	..	..	999	1	..	990	10	..	864	129	7	230	729	41	42	820	138
Od	499	439	62	965	33	2	903	89	8	756	220	24	508	453	39	94	832	74	25	763	212
Pathan	528	410	62	987	12	1	935	62	3	817	171	12	591	381	28	158	767	75	45	735	220
Prabhu	580	385	35	997	3	..	971	28	1	870	126	4	845	149	6	179	794	27	24	775	201
Rajput	508	418	74	988	11	1	931	66	3	766	223	11	504	474	22	187	737	76	86	647	267
Santal	498	464	38	983	17	..	924	75	1	723	265	12	397	576	27	69	882	49	22	834	144
Shan	534	381	85	1,000	..	..	1,000	..	..	981	16	3	703	242	55	164	719	117	41	717	242
Tanti	353	593	54	927	71	2	610	377	13	404	564	32	251	710	39	41	896	63	15	818	167
Teli	457	491	52	975	24	1	836	161	3	645	346	9	426	552	22	79	862	59	22	782	196
Viswabrahman, etc.	470	453	77	983	16	1	900	96	4	689	295	16	420	552	28	112	798	90	45	690	265
Yadava	412	511	77	959	39	2	762	230	8	523	451	26	311	649	40	84	827	89	30	708	262

SUBSIDIARY TABLE VI—*concld.*

Distribution by Civil Condition of 1,000 of each sex at certain ages for selected castes—*concld.*

Distribution of 1,000 females of each age by Civil Condition.

Caste.	All Ages.			0—6			7—13			14—16			17—23			24—43			44 and over.		
	Un-married.	Married.	Wi-dowed.	Un-married.	Married.	Wi-dowed.	Un-married.	Married.	Wi-dowed.	Un-married.	Married.	Wi-dowed.	Un-married.	Married.	Wi-dowed.	Un-married.	Married.	Wi-dowed.	Un-married.	Married.	Wi-dowed.
1	23	24	25	26	27	28	29	30	31	32	33	34	35	36	37	38	39	40	41	42	43
Baniya	349	458	193	982	17	1	849	148	3	263	717	20	34	916	50	9	747	244	6	317	677
Bhangi	355	529	116	974	25	1	715	280	5	179	804	17	42	930	28	15	861	124	10	422	568
Bhil	448	464	88	992	8	..	862	136	2	359	631	10	69	913	18	14	884	102	8	481	511
Brahman	315	469	216	980	19	1	769	223	8	228	736	36	40	884	76	11	731	258	7	321	672
Chamar	320	551	129	953	46	1	587	405	8	131	847	22	34	936	30	11	853	136	7	410	583
Chetti	422	422	156	1,000	..	..	978	21	1	656	332	12	155	812	33	22	819	159	6	378	616
Darzi	350	506	144	956	42	2	697	296	7	291	690	19	62	894	44	19	816	165	16	414	570
Dom	284	558	158	936	63	1	538	451	11	177	786	37	43	902	55	15	797	188	26	370	604
Gond	353	510	137	968	31	1	765	230	5	329	652	19	75	897	28	22	852	126	9	415	576
Guj	377	503	120	987	12	1	781	216	3	286	701	13	58	915	27	14	861	125	6	453	541
Iluvan	487	381	132	1,000	..	..	995	5	..	818	175	7	253	708	39	35	816	149	13	405	582
Jat	407	477	116	992	8	..	860	138	2	479	572	9	106	876	18	20	877	103	9	467	524
Kachhi	338	516	146	984	14	2	707	286	7	127	847	26	34	928	38	13	825	162	13	350	637
Kahar	340	519	141	973	25	2	722	271	7	227	749	24	56	911	33	14	838	148	10	432	558
Kallan	403	416	181	999	1	..	986	14	..	784	212	4	192	776	32	15	785	200	5	328	667
Kayastha	351	451	198	973	25	2	853	141	6	285	678	37	44	876	80	11	735	254	6	329	665
Khatri	429	424	147	998	2	..	957	42	1	579	414	7	117	855	28	23	818	159	11	387	602
Kumhar	343	525	132	967	32	1	669	325	6	215	764	21	55	912	33	14	851	135	7	435	558
Kunbi	260	580	160	889	108	3	467	519	14	118	848	34	40	914	46	11	816	173	7	423	570
Mahar	322	528	150	939	57	4	622	362	16	258	680	62	73	869	58	20	821	159	17	428	555
Maratha	318	532	150	916	79	5	611	379	10	355	622	23	70	878	52	23	811	166	16	412	572
Megh	380	468	152	962	29	9	754	219	27	376	548	76	156	764	80	74	733	193	62	459	479
Momin (Julaha, etc.)	359	521	120	958	41	1	694	300	6	238	737	25	69	900	31	21	855	124	13	435	552
Naibrahman	340	523	137	960	38	2	693	301	6	227	750	23	64	898	38	18	841	141	13	420	567
Namasudra	297	484	219	964	34	2	569	420	11	65	889	46	16	867	117	11	661	328	7	254	739
Nayar (Nair)	444	370	186	1,000	..	.	989	10	1	735	250	15	260	683	57	48	744	208	13	337	650
Od	384	460	156	965	33	2	838	150	12	396	568	36	67	868	65	17	791	192	12	386	602
Pathan	416	460	124	983	16	1	875	123	2	489	495	16	147	823	30	38	838	124	23	434	543
Prabhu	505	375	120	981	14	5	970	25	5	803	185	12	298	675	27	34	791	175	21	409	570
Rajput	345	474	181	982	17	1	806	188	6	322	650	28	68	881	51	17	782	201	9	356	635
Santal	417	461	122	982	17	1	854	140	6	371	599	30	117	829	54	20	833	147	8	445	547
Shan	456	391	153	1,000	..	.	1,000	..	..	789	180	31	294	610	96	67	782	151	24	400	576
Tanti	245	585	170	868	127	5	428	550	22	137	829	34	28	928	44	8	810	182	2	375	623
Teli	348	507	145	956	43	1	707	287	6	297	688	15	70	899	31	15	824	161	8	389	603
Viswabrahman, etc.	356	494	150	972	27	1	757	237	6	292	683	25	71	882	47	17	815	168	11	411	578
Yadava	**306**	**535**	**159**	**936**	**61**	**3**	**600**	**386**	**14**	**202**	**760**	**38**	**52**	**895**	**53**	**12**	**814**	**174**	**9**	**405**	**586**

APPENDIX TO CHAPTER VI.

(A. C. TURNER).

Some notes on marriage in the United Provinces.

A general tendency is noticeable among the more educated Hindus to omit the less important ceremonies in connexion with marriage, and to spend less on the celebration of marriages and other social events. This is largely economic. For instance, the *thauna* (third and final visit of husband to bring his bride from her house to his) and *ala chala* (after which the wife is free to go backwards and forwards between her parents' house and her husband's without ceremony) are often omitted by Hindus; and those Muslims who formerly practised them now pay less observance to *manjha* or *kona baithana* (the segregation of the bride from her parents and elders just prior to the wedding), *chauthi* (the first visit of the wife to her parents' home after the *rukhsati* and her subsequent return with her husband), and *chala*. The commonest form of marriage among ordinary castes is *paupujia* or *dola*. This differs from the *charhawa* marriage of the higher castes only in that the bride and her people come to the bridegroom's house for the *biyah* rites to be performed instead of those rites taking place at the bride's home. The bridegroom goes to fetch her at the *gauna*.

A variation of the *paupujia* custom occurs in the case of certain Vaishya sub-castes. After the marriage has been arranged and the date fixed the bride's parents go to the town or village where the bridegroom's family lives, take a house on rent and all the ceremonies are performed in this rented house instead of at the bride's home. This variation is known as *utha biyah.* Rajbhat Umars, a sub-class of the Umar Vaishyas, practise yet another variation. When the marriage has been settled the bridegroom's father with some of his relatives visit the bride's home for 2 or 3 days. Then they depart with the bride to their home and all the pre-marriage ceremonies which are normally carried out at her home are performed at the bridegroom's. The bride's people come 2 or 3 days before the marriage and stay at the bridegroom's house and then the marriage takes place on the appointed day. This practice is, however, falling into disfavour.

Ghar Damadi, Gharjawai, or Gharjamai.

In paragraph 231 on page 220 of the 1911 Report Mr. Blunt refers to Beena marriage. Here the suitor goes to live with the girl's family and works there, in a capacity which is part servant, part debtor, for a certain period before he marries her. Mr. Blunt gave two views as to its origin which were not mutually exclusive and added "At the present day, whatever the original object of the custom, it is used as a means of getting a wife without paying a dowry in cash or kind. It is restricted to poor people who work out the dowry in labour. Nominally at all events, connubial intercourse is forbidden, the son-in-law *in futuro* gets maintenance, but has no claim on the father-in-law's property. The custom is found among the Bhuiyar, Bind, Chero, Ghasiya, Kharwar, Majhwar, Gond and Parahiya castes: its usual name is *ghar-jawai gharjaiyan*, or *ghardamada*. The normal period appears to be three years." This practice, which has in it the elements of marriage by purchase, still continues among not only the above castes but also among Kuchbandia Kanjars and Kalabaz Nats. There is no fixed period of service. Among Brijbasi Gual Nats of Sahaswan tahsil in district Budaun, a bridegroom married in this way cannot leave his father-in-law's house even after serving the agreed period and marrying the girl but must stay and serve after marriage so long as his wife's parents are alive. If he wishes to leave earlier he must pay the parents a bride-price which is then fixed by the tribal *panchayat*.

But this practice in a somewhat modified form is now to be found among most Hindu castes and even among Muslims. Formerly a man who lived in his father-in-law's house or in his sister's husband's house was very much looked down upon, so much so that there was a more forcible Hindi proverb than that quoted by Mr. Blunt at the foot of page 220, which ran—

"*Kutta pale so kutta, sas ghar jamai aur bahin ghar bhai.*"

(he who tames a dog is a dog, a man living in his mother-in-law's house and a man living where his sister is married are the other two dogs).

There has, however, been a perceptible change in the social outlook and although such arrangements are still not regarded with much favour the three 'dogs' are not treated with quite such contempt as in the past. Almost everywhere some cases are met with of a son-in-law going to live with his wife's parents, under the following circumstances :—

(*i*) when the girl's father is well-to-do and has no sons ;

(*ii*) when the girl's family is very poor and wants the help or a strong man ; and

(*iii*) when the son-in-law is a poor man and cannot pay a dower.

In such cases the man usually settles permanently with his 'in-laws'. If the girl's family is well-to-do and the bridegroom is in fair circumstances the bride's father often has to pay large sum to the latter to induce him to accept the stigma attaching to a *ghar-jawai*; otherwise there is no payment, the suitor being treated as the debtor. In this form the practice is not at all uncommon being found chiefly among the lower Hindu castes and poor members of the higher castes, reported from districts as far apart as Bahraich, Ballia, Hamirpur, Budaun, etc. As regards actual numbers Rae Bareli district reports the following 2,490 instances—

Chamar	433
Ahir	373
Pasi	371
Lodh	174
Kurmi	155
Murao	135
Brahman	125
Koeri	87
Rajput	85
Gadaria	80
Muslim	62
Others	410

Etawah district reports some 2,000 instances of *ghar-jawai* and of a man living at his brother-in-law's house. These together included roughly Rajputs 800, Brahmans 400, Ahirs 300 and Chamars 100.

Bara Banki district reports the following 100 instances :—

Kurmi	18
Brahman	16
Pasi	16
Ahir	11
Chamar	8
Rajput	6
Others	25

Other districts reported fewer members. From Gonda comes the following—One father with an only daughter entertained a succession of *ghar-jawais*. The first actually married her and died. Another man was brought to take his place. He proved unsuitable and was turned out after 18 months, before marriage. The same fate overtook the next suitor. When yet another hopeful took up residence the *panchayat* thought matters had gone far enough and intervened. It cost the father a fine of Rs. 46 and a goodly feast for the *panches*.

Ghar baithna. Somewhat allied to the custom of *ghar-jawai* is the practice of *ghar baithna*. Here the woman is usually a widow and mistress of her own house and property with no male collaterals or other relations of her husband. As a result the man who marries her usually belongs to a religion or caste that permits widow re-marriage. The husband proceeds to live in his wife's house. Gonda district reports this as quite common. From Rae Bareli district the following figures were collected—

Ahir	414
Pasi	369
Chamar	353
Lodh	232
Murao	135
Koeri	131
Gadaria	107
Kurmi	89
Teli	72
Brahman	60
Muslim	60
Nai	47
Kachhi	46
Bharbunja	41
Vaishya	37
Lohar	35
Kumhar	31
Goriya	28
Tamboli	27
Rajput	26
Kahar	22
Others	190
Total	2,552

This practice is viewed with dislike and among the higher castes the *garh baitha* is despised and outcasted. It is therefore most common among the lower castes: Brahmans, Rajputs and Vaishyas would only contract such an alliance if they were very poor men and the widow's possessions attractive.

Marriage by capture. Marriage by capture is non-existent, thought as Mr. Blunt mentioned there are traces of its past existence in some of the marriage rites. Quite different in nature is the curious custom observed by Goriyas of the Gorakhpur district (who appear to be the outcome of fusion between a sub-caste of Mallahs and a sub-caste of Kahars). Before the rite of *sendhurdan* (marking the parting of the bride's hair with red lead) is performed the bridegroom leaves the wedding party in assumed umbrage and goes and sits on a roof erected specially for the purpose. The bride then goes to him and entreats him to marry her saying " My lord, come and marry me. You need do no work as I will work and earn money for you". The bridegroom and bride then descend from the roof and the marriage proceeds. The origin of this peculiar rite is unknown....

Marriage by exchange .... In this province the practice is found in two forms. The first is *adala badala, santa*, or *golawat*, in which form the son of one man marries the daughter of the other, and the second man's son marries the first man's daughter. This form is found chiefly among the ordinary castes such as Kuchband Kanjars, Gual Nats, Dharkars, Tarkihars, Chhipis, Khatiks, Gadarias, Barhais, Lohars, Kurmis and Kahars. In some parts Sonars adopt it, and it is quite common among Mathuria Chaube Brahmans. Jains sometimes arrange such marriages. This form, however, is not popular and is often looked down upon.

The more popular form is known as *tigadda*, or *tiptha* which is a triangular arrangement thus:—

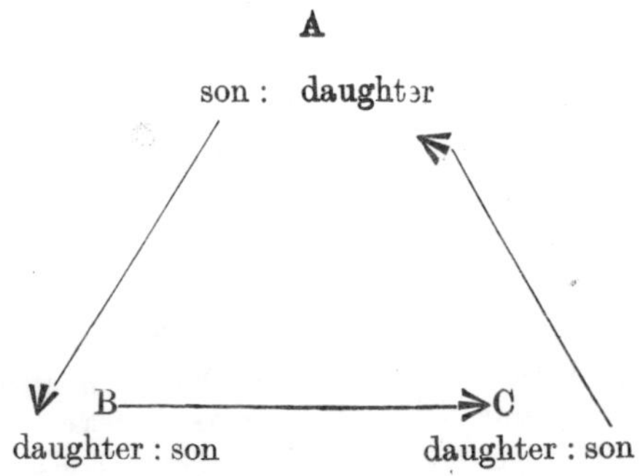

This arrangement is common everywhere among the ordinary castes an. often among the higher, including Vaishyas. In the east of the province where Muslims are largely descendants of converts from Hinduism who have retained many Hindu customs, they too practise the custom.

Polyandry. Polyandry is still practised among all classes and castes in Jaunsar-Bawar (district Dehra Dun). A few of the more educated have taken to monogamy themselves but at the same time have no objection to giving a daughter in marriage to all the brothers of one family. The reason given by these folk is economic. Separate marriages of brothers may lead to division of the family property which when broken up would not suffice to maintain individual members of the family with their own separate establishments. That polyandry does not continue in Jaunsar-Bawar entirely on account of the dearth of females is shown by the fact that many girls from there are married into the Punjab............................

Divorce. *Chhut* (divorce) is practised in Jaunsar-Bawar. A husband can at any time divorce his wife either verbally or in writing provided the next man who takes her to wife pays double the *jeodhan*. Divorces without serious reasons are, however, growing less common......................... In Chakrata tahsil of Dehra Dun (Jaunsar-Bawar) the bridegroom has to pay a small sum to the bride's father as *jeodhan* (as ceremonial gift) which is intended to cover the expenses of the marriage. ....

Adoption. Under the Hindu law, a son may be adopted but not a daughter. Among Jogila Nats, Khalkhor Nats (reported from Budaun) and Kuchband Kanjars, however, the custom of adopting a daughter also exists.

CHAPTER VII.

Infirmities.

103. As in the previous census the enumerators were instructed to record the fact for each individual who was found to be insane, deaf and dumb, blind of both eyes or suffering from corrosive leprosy. They were also warned against recording as blind those who suffered from loss of the sight in one eye only, or as lepers persons who suffered from leucoderma. In Bengal blind of both eyes was defined as " unable to count the fingers of a hand held up at one yard's distance ". These instructions were counsels of perfection and it is not claimed that the figures published in Table IX are as reliable as those published in the other tables in the same volume. The return of infirmities at the Indian census has probably never been satisfactory. Notwithstanding instructions to the contrary, it seems likely that many feeble minded and dotards are entered as insane and that many who are partially blind are returned as totally blind. It is probable of course, that the excess numbers so obtained do not even balance the omissions in the return of the infirmities at all where these infirmities none the less exist. In the case of leprosy,* however, it is practically certain that the census figures in India fail entirely to represent the true state of affairs. Dr. Muir and others, who have investigated the prevalence of leprosy by means of local surveys, have concluded that the census figures represent one tenth of the actual. The attempt to record physical disabilities through the medium of the census was abandoned in England and Wales ten years ago as a failure, and earlier still in the United States of America. It was nevertheless decided not to abandon the attempt to return this disease at the census, as the figures which the census is able to provide afford some basis for an estimate of true numbers in the light of the difference between the figures obtained from local surveys and the census returns for the same areas. At the same time the tabulation of infirmity by caste was abandoned in the interests of economy.

Instructions to enumerators.

104. One obvious criticism on the return of infirmities is that while the first three mentioned are defects which may be observed by an enumerator, the fourth is a disease which can only be detected by expert eyes and should not be made the subject of a purely lay return. Those cases which are obvious to the lay eye are burnt out cases no longer infectious. The infectious cases are those at an earlier stage of development, and it is by a comparison of the number of these early cases with the number of those in which the disease has run its course that the increase or decrease of prevalence can be ascertained. Enumerators cannot be expected to add medical diagnosis to their limited ability to record fact. Apart from this, it is quite obvious that there will be much wilful concealment of such a disease as leprosy, and since the number of females returned as lepers is 40,019 against 107,892 males, it may perhaps be inferred that concealment among females is greater, as indeed might be expected in view of customs such as that of purdah. On the other hand it seems to be generally held that leprosy attacks a greater proportion of males than of females, so that it is impossible to say in what degree the lower figures for females are due to the natural incidence of the disease and in what degree to the circumstances of enumeration, and the concealment inevitable from it. Similarly insanity is likely to be concealed particularly in the case of females, while there is certain to be a tendency to conceal cases of deaf-mute children. Moreover, the use of such a term as insanity is frequently a matter of personal temperament and of the very variable value that different individuals attach to identical words. In fact a young lady in Lucknow Cantonment, filling in the schedule for her husband, who was out at his work but had doubtless had the misfortune to offend her, described him as insane, deaf-mute, blind and leprous—an extreme case, no doubt, but illuminating. One may fancy an enumerator enquiring as he fills in his schedule as to the sanity of some individual whose behaviour struck him as unusual. The first villager might answer " Oh, he does be a bit queer, but not what you'd call mad ", whereas the next might perfectly well say of the same individual " Mad, is it ? Indeed, a March hare 'd be sane to him ". What is the enumerator to put down, and what will be the value of his record statistically or demographically ? The

Defects of the Returns.

*A return of elephantiasis would probably present less difficulty to the census staff and in Travancore State such a return was added, though even of this infirmity it was found that concealment was general there. In the Nicobar Islands it was proposed to substitute this return for that of leprosy, which is either absent or undetected, whereas elephantiasis is a common scourge, but the proposal was not in the end carried out.

term 'blind' is liable to a not dissimilar diversity of interpretation, and although the instructions are that only those blind in both eyes shall be recorded as such, this is definitively effective only to the extent of excluding from the record persons with one unquestionably sound eye. It is true of course that the bias of one enumerator is apt to be corrected by the bias of another in the opposite direction, and possible that exaggeration and meiosis so balance one another in the returns that a fairly correct conclusion is reached, but none the less it is impossible to doctor the returns of infirmity like the admittedly inaccurate returns of age, so as to produce out of amalgamated inaccuracies results which are a sufficiently accurate representation of the facts. Moreover, some of the inexplicable fluctuations from census to census, and inconsistencies that appear between provinces, make the accuracy of the figures even of blindness open to impeachment, though the returns of blindness have generally been regarded as comparatively accurate, and it is perhaps significant that the Blind Relief Association found by a count that the totally blind in Bijapur District in 1920 numbered 260 per 100,000 as against 70 returned at the census of 1911. On the other hand it cannot be denied that the ratios of the infirm to the rest of the population at successive ages do show a consistency from census to census which is incompatible with any kind of error but a constant one, indicating that however inaccurate our figures may be numerically they have some real comparative value from census to census. The census figures of infirmity are therefore presented subject to the proviso that although they do indicate tendencies on general lines their value is only comparative, as they cannot be taken to represent actual numbers. Their treatment is therefore primarily confined to this comparative aspect whether in time or in place, and in view of the nature of the material is perhaps justifiably brief.

Reference to statistics.

105. The main statistics will be found in Imperial Table IX, and the subsidiary tables at the end of this chapter give proportionate and comparative figures. The marginal statement shows the total number of persons suffering from each of the four infirmities recorded for the last fifty years. The decrease from 1881 to 1891 was regarded by the Census Commissioner for that year as due to increasing accuracy of enumeration. In 1901 the still further decrease was again attributed in part to the same cause and in part to severe famine mortality, the incidence of which is likely to be most heavy on those unfitted by infirmity to survive excessive privation. It is to be feared that except in the case of blindness after 1881 the theory of increasing accuracy as an explanation of decreasing infirmity was after all a delusion, for the figures of insanity have increased beyond that of 1881, and in 1911, the figures of deaf-mutes passed those of 1881, while the figures of leprosy are believed from the results of scientific surveys of limited areas to represent about one-tenth of the actual number of sufferers from that disease. The marginal table gives the numbers, per 100,000, of those afflicted with the four diseases according to the census figures, affording a better means of comparison than the crude figures. In 1921 the effect of the influenza epidemic was regarded in Bihar and Orissa as responsible for exceptional mortality among the afflicted. In the Central Provinces on the other hand the unexpected rise in their numbers and still more in their ratio was put down to the incidence of influenza's being adversely

Infirmity.	Number afflicted.					
	1931.	1921.	1911.	1901.	1891.	1881.
Insanity	120,304	88,305	81,006	66,205	74,279	81,132
Deaf-muteness	230,895	189,644	199,891	153,168	196,861	197,215
Blindness	601,370	479,637	443,653	354,104	458,868	526,748
Leprosy	147,911	102,513	109,094	97,340	126,244	131,968
Total	1,095,678*	860,099	833,644	670,817	856,252	937,063

* Excludes multiple infirmities.

Infirmity.	No. afflicted per 100,000 of population.					
	1931.	1921.	1911.	1901.	1891.	1881.
Insanity	34	28	26	23	27	35
Deaf-muteness	66	60	64	52	75	86
Blindness	172	152	142	121	167	229
Leprosy	42	32	35	33	46	57
Total	314*	272	267	229	315	407

* Excludes multiple infirmities.

selective of healthy adults, and our confidence in even the comparative reliability of the figures is still further shaken. The total number of persons, 1,095,678, returned as afflicted in 1931 included 120,304 insane, 230,895 deaf-mute, 601,370 blind and 147,911 lepers. The marginal table shows their distribution by provinces, their provincial increase since 1921, and the ratio of this increase to that of the increase of population. The general increase in ratio as well as in numbers may be attributed provisionally to increased accuracy of enumeration. As however even a considerable increase in that direction must be far removed from real accuracy, the explanation is offered as likely but without any enthusiastic conviction of reality. The Census Superintendent of Bihar and Orissa regards the increase in the numbers of afflicted persons as due to the favourable economic condition of the decade causing "Charity to

Province, State or Agency.	Infirm per 100,000 of population 1931.	Variation, increase+ decrease— since 1921.	Ratio of increase+ decrease— infirm per 100,000 of increase of population.
INDIA.	313	+238,141	+690
1. Ajmer-Merwara	501	+1,255	+1,930
2. Andamans and Nicobars	88	—39	—1,641
3. Assam	297	+5,918	+471
4. Baluchistan	316	—556	—806
5. Bengal	226	+14,753	+423
6. Bihar and Orissa	263	+43,904	+1,004
7. Bombay (including Aden).	346	+27,152	+762
8. Burma	466	+10,940	+740
9. Central Provinces and Berar.	434	+11,618	+578
10. Coorg	152	+112	+21,918
11. Delhi	141	+4	+3
12. Madras	285	+51,475	+1,170
13. N.-W. F. P.	206	—937	—539
14. Punjab	350	+2,873	+85
15. United Provinces	396	+46,015	+1,482
16. Baroda	456	+2,245	+709
17. Central India	272	+3,866	+613
18. Cochin	287	+873	+386
19. Gwalior	244	+170	+52
20. Hyderabad	154	—7,085	—361
21. Jammu and Kashmir.	405	+2,850	+737
22. Mysore	198	+3,018	+522
23. Rajputana	337	+13,976	+1,003
24. Sikkim	184	+9	+32
25. Travancore	214	+3,732	+342
26. Western India States	535	*	*

* As separate figures are not available for 1921 this unit has been combined with the Bombay Presidency for purposes of calculating variation.

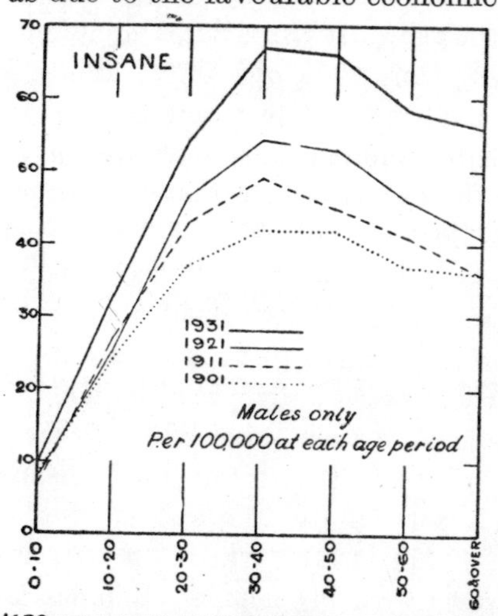

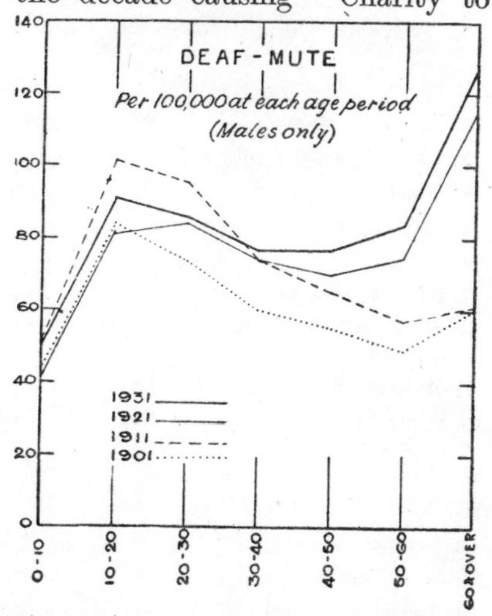

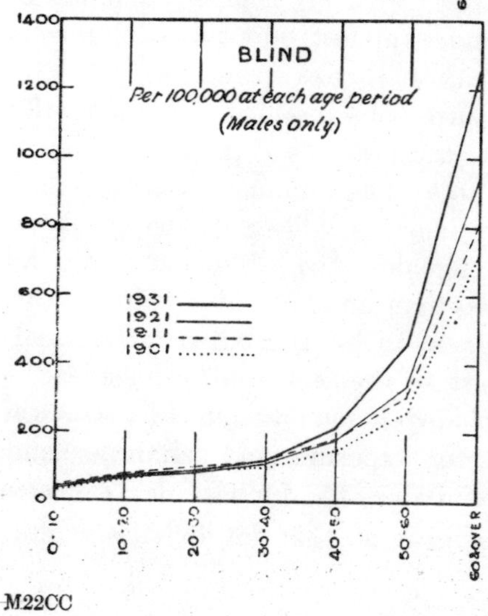

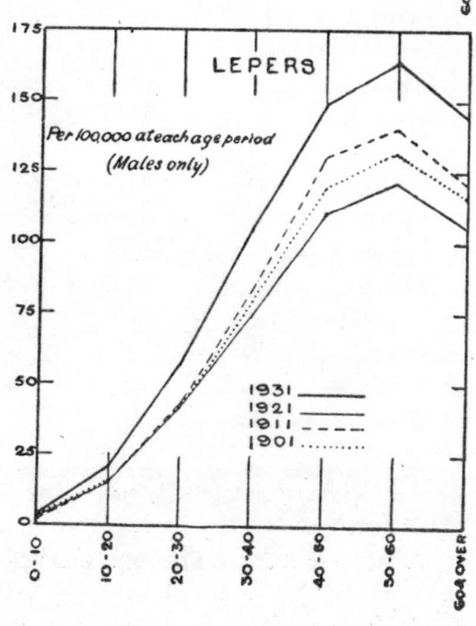

unloose her purse-strings" and increasing the likelihood of the survival of the unfit, an opinion with which the Census Superintendent of the United Provinces agrees; nor can the probability of this as a factor in the increase be denied. In illustrating the ages of the incidence of infirmity by diagram the curves by sexes have been drawn on the actual figures in preference to the figures of the ratio of the infirm to the population. At previous censuses these curves have been drawn for each sex on the number of infirm per 100,000 of population, but as the infirm are likely to have a very different death rate to the healthy, and as the relation of their numbers to the population figure is in any case dubious, curves drawn on the ratios would seem to be more likely to be misleading in case of inaccurate figures than a curve of which the inaccuracy is the visible inaccuracy of defective figures and not the less obvious distortion of a ratio based on them. A reference to the diagrams of Chapters IV and V will give the necessary comparison between the age curves of the infirm and those of the population as a whole. For the sake of comparison, and to illustrate the undoubted consistency between the infirmity returns of successive decades, ratio curves based on the figures of males only (as being more accurate than the figures for females) are shown above for four decennia.

Insanity. **106**. The marginal table shows the number of insane per 100,000 of the population in India and the various provinces and the variation correlated to the increase in population since 1921 on the same basis. The vague and unsatisfactory nature of the return of insanity is admirably illustrated in the different views of Census Superintendents themselves; thus while one says "idiocy is usually a congenital defect and one would have expected a much higher proportion of insane in the earlier age periods" another condemns his returns for showing just such an increase on the ground that "complete insanity manifests itself at adolescence" and "returns to be accurate must exclude the congenitally weak-minded". In Assam one district showed an extraordinary rise in the number of insane in 1921 from 52 to 255 and a similar drop to 62 in 1931, while an adjoining district with a smaller population living under almost identical conditions shows in 1931 a rise from 242 to 430. The return of insanity is naturally lowest in the lowest age groups. Lunacy is likely to be undetermined among young children; idiocy is unlikely to be admitted. Among females the incidence at all ages is less than among males. Part of this difference is to be attributed to concealment, part to the fact that women lead a more secluded if monotonous life, are less subject to exposure and anxiety, and are less liable to indulge in excesses of various kinds. The age curves (which in the case of that for females should

Province, State or Agency.	No. of insane per 100,000 of population, 1931.	Variation per 100,000 of increase since 1921.
1. India	34	+93
2. Ajmer-Merwara	39	+191
3. Andamans and Nicobars	24	—1,136
4. Assam	59	+106
Baluchistan	48	+1
6. Bengal	44	+81
7. Bihar and Orissa	21	+118
8. Bombay (including Aden).	48	+92
9. Burma	88	+90
10. Central Provinces and Berar.	28	+72
11. Coorg	19	+3,131
12. Delhi	14	+8
13. Madras	33	+156
14. N.-W. F. P.	31	+53
15. Punjab	29	+37
16. United Provinces	23	+136
17. Baroda	56	+120
18. Central India	23	+115
19. Cochin	53	+113
20. Gwalior	13	—1
21. Hyderabad	15	—16
22. Jammu and Kashmir.	39	+36
23. Mysore	27	+158
24. Rajputana	23	+98
25. Sikkim	5	—21
26. Travancore	41	+73
27. Western India States	45	*

* For purposes of calculating variation this unit has been combined with Bombay of which it formed part in 1921.

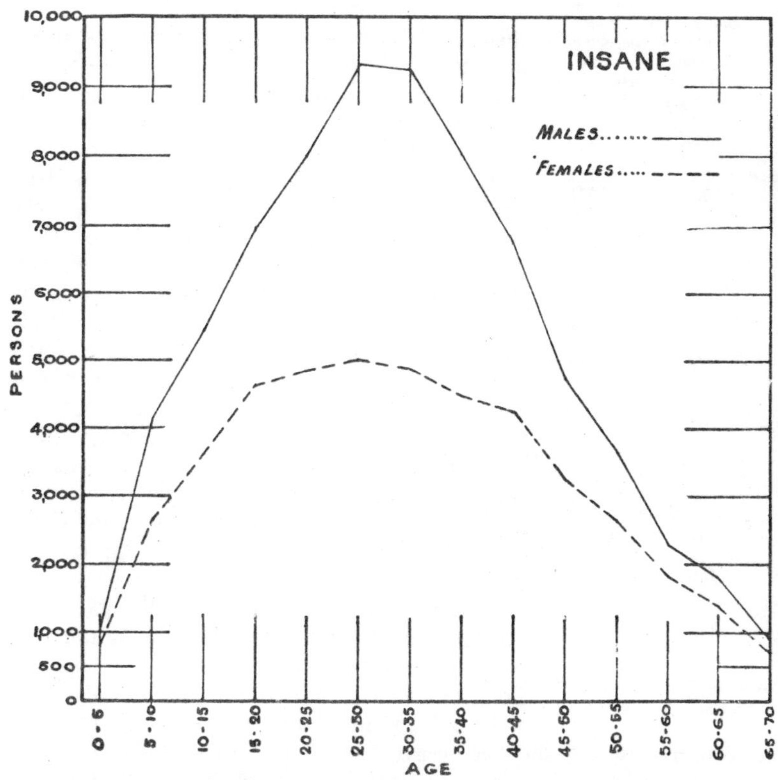

be transposed to a greater height to allow for concealment) show this clearly, as that for females reaches a point much nearer its maximum at 15 to 20 years than that for males, and is without the 25-35 peak. This relatively earlier rise in the figures among females is to be attributed to the strain of premature and excessive maternity, while the later rise in the male figures corresponds to the entry into life with family and working cares. From the age of maturity—about 35 years, the males die off more quickly than the unaffected, while for women the curve is far less steep and the fall is not marked until after the climacteric. Generally speaking insanity is an affliction of the adult period, unlike deafmuteness, which is one of the young, or blindness, which is severest in old age. To judge by the Reports of the Public Health Commissioner on mental hospitals the principal causes of insanity in India are mental strain, critical periods of life (*e.g.*, puberty), *cannabis indica*, presumably in the form of ganja or some other preparation, privation, and diseases consequent on malnutrition, epilepsy and syphilis. The total number of patients in mental hospitals in 1930 was 11,147. In 1921 it was 9,919. If any interest is felt in the extravagant and unpleasant methods of treating insanity in Indian folk-medicine a reference may be made to pages 415-417 of Mr. O'Malley's Report on Bengal, Bihar and Orissa for 1911.

Deaf-muteness.

107. The figures of this defect if rightly returned should show a curve decreasing with each age group, since the disease is congenital. Before 1921 the instructions contained the words 'deaf-mute from birth', omitted in 1921 and 1931. The results in 1921 were unsatisfactory as the omission led to an increased number of returns of aged deaf-mutes, presumably cases of deafness in senility, and though this was not the case in all units, *e.g.*, in Cochin State, the error caused by the inclusion of aged persons, probably deaf only, was so marked that it would have been better to have reverted to the 1911 practice of including the words " from birth ", though this on the other hand may lead to the omission of a certain number whose condition is not realised to have been congenital and the Census Superintendent of the United Provinces considers that the omission of the words " from birth " has led to increased accuracy of the return of infirmities as a whole, since it has frequently happened that enumerators apply the words " from birth " to all infirmities instead of to deaf-muteness only. Deaf-muteness in India, as elsewhere, is frequently associated with cretinism and goitre and may therefore be attributed in part to the absence of iodine salts in the soil and consequently in the drinking water. Naturally the absence is most likely to occur in rainy and hilly country where the salts have been washed out of the surface soil at sites inhabited or cultivated for a long period of time. Thus in Baroda the Census Commissioner for that State points out the heavy incidence of deaf-muteness on the upper reaches of certain streams and in the proximity of the Rann of Cutch. In addition therefore to the marginal table of the distribution and variation of this defect by provinces a map has been added indicating

Province, State or Agency.	No. of deaf mute per 100,000 of population 1931.	Variation per 100,000 of increase since 1921.
1. India	66	+120
2. Ajmer-Merwara	73	+418
3. Andamans and Nicobars	27	+252
4. Assam	75	+113
5. Baluchistan	67	—145
6. Bengal	70	+110
7. Bihar and Orissa	63	+147
8. Bombay (including Aden).	78	+230
9. Burma	116	+344
10. Central Provinces and Berar.	78	—56
11. Coorg	62	+15,851
12. Delhi	23	—5
13. Madras	71	+274
14. N.-W. F. P.	66	—173
15. Punjab	69	—95
16. United Provinces	52	+77
17. Baroda	52	+211
18. Central India	29	+23
19. Cochin	40	—7
20. Gwalior	37	—33
21. Hyderabad	26	+17
22. Jammu and Kashmir.	159	+329
23. Mysore	60	+59
24. Rajputana	28	+39
25. Sikkim	149	+71
26. Travancore	57	+66
27. Western India States	91	*

* For purposes of calculating variation this unit has been combined with Bombay of which it formed part in 1921.

its distribution according to the census returns but based on district instead of provincial figures, as this gives a better correlation with geographical features. The returns however are not very reliable and the present census shows an entirely inexplicable drop in the Naga and Garo Hills in Assam, the former of which had in 1921 seven times the total of the rest of that province. Similar fluctuations are recorded in Cochin and in Madras, where the Census Superintendent suggests an apparent cycle of 20 years, and also an association with insanity. This however is admittedly not borne out by the Madras returns and the Census Superintendent for Central India, on the look-out for the same association finds his figures on the whole against it. The Madras Superintendent adds that there is nothing in that province to support any association of deaf-muteness with goitre but the association undoubtedly exists in Assam and Burma. In Madras it may be observed that a high incidence of this deficiency seems to coincide to some extent with a high incidence of scarcity or famine; in all provinces the returns by sex show a greater number of males afflicted than females. There seems to be no biological reason for this, so one is inclined to look for the reason to two possible causes—firstly concealment, secondly a greater loss of deaf-mute girl children as a result of more or less deliberate neglect. Girl children are often enough not wanted anyhow, and the deaf-mutes among them must be so much the more superfluous, once their affliction is realised. The Hyderabad Census Commissioner states that the preponderence of males is a "phenomenon .... common to most forms of congenital malformation", but quotes no authority for this hard saying, though as more males than females are born the statement is likely to be true at least to that extent, and in Northern Ireland male deaf-mutes exceeded female by 30 per cent. in 1926, and in England and Wales in 1921, 55 per cent. of the inmates of homes for the deaf and dumb were males. In the case of deaf-mutes in India it cannot be denied that the close correspondence in outline of the male and

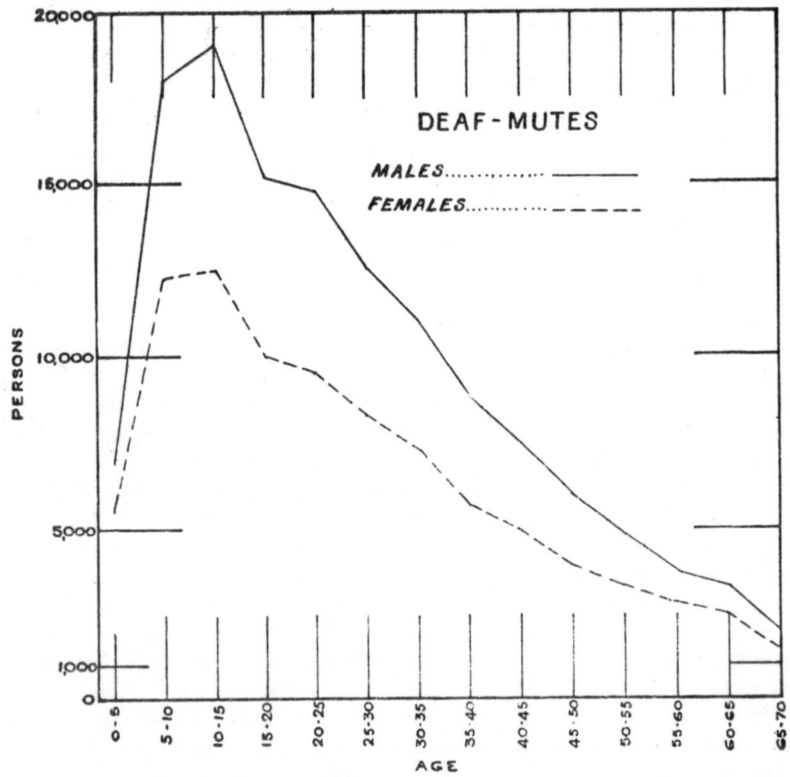

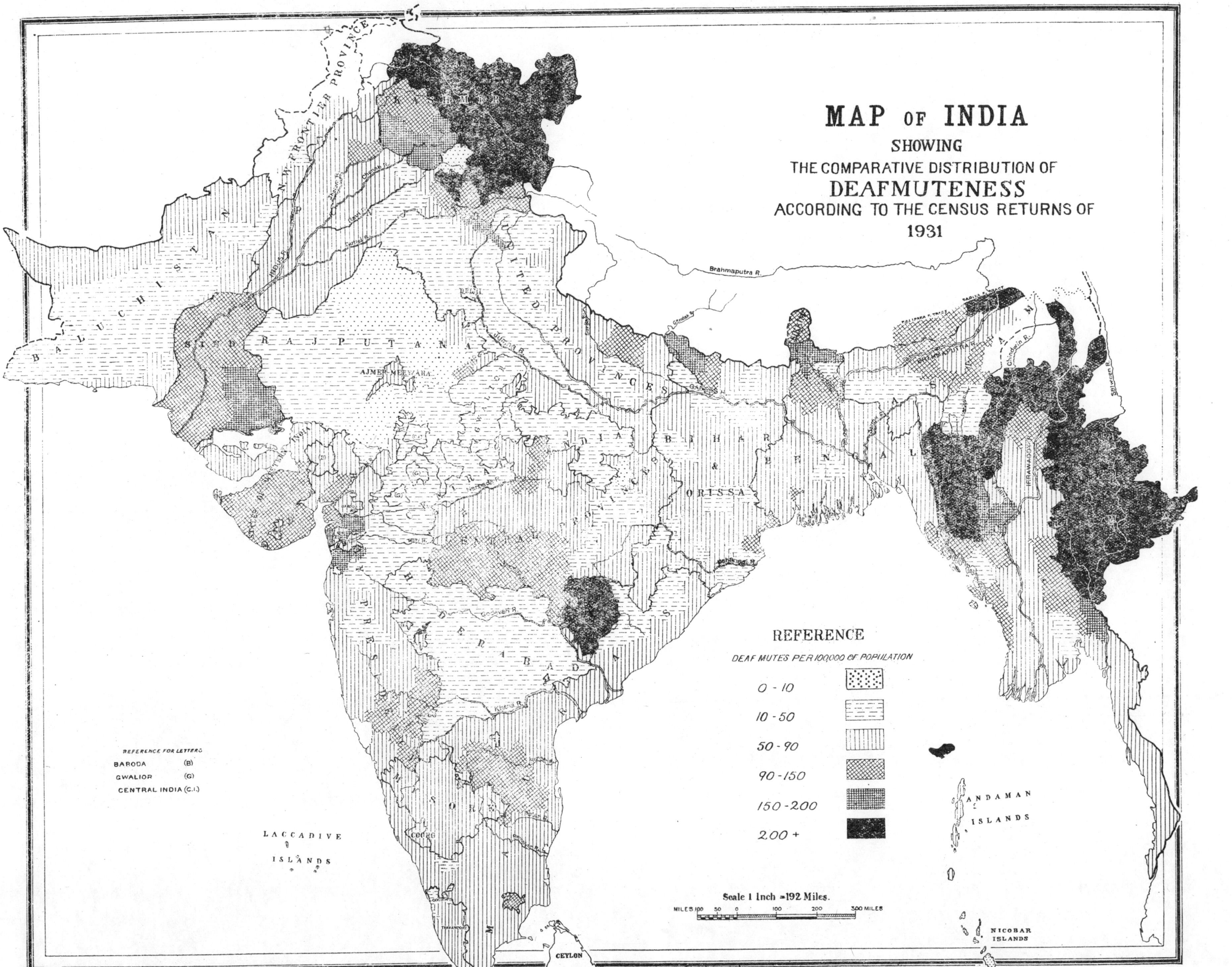

MAP OF INDIA
SHOWING
THE COMPARATIVE DISTRIBUTION OF
DEAFMUTENESS
ACCORDING TO THE CENSUS RETURNS OF
1931
REFERENCE
DEAF MUTES PER 100,000 OF POPULATION
0 - 10
10 - 50
50 - 90
90 - 150
150 - 200
200 +
REFERENCE FOR LETTERS
BARODA (B)
GWALIOR (G)
CENTRAL INDIA (C.I.)
Scale 1 Inch = 192 Miles.
MILES 100 50 0 100 200 300 MILES
N.W. FRONTIER PROVINCE
BALUCHISTAN
SIND
RAJPUTANA
AJMER-MERWARA
UNITED PROVINCES
CENTRAL INDIA
BIHAR & ORISSA
BENGAL
CENTRAL PROVINCES
HYDERABAD
MYSORE
COORG
MADRAS
ORISSA
Brahmaputra R.
Ganges R.
Indus R.
Godavari R.
Kistna R.
Narbada R.
Chindwin R.
Irrawaddy R.
Salween R.
LACCADIVE ISLANDS
ANDAMAN ISLANDS
NICOBAR ISLANDS
CEYLON

female curves suggests that they are governed by the same factors. Concealment would account for this, but if it were the only or principal factor one might expect perhaps to see less correspondence in the female to the male curve from 10 to 20 years and a greater correspondence from 0 to 10 years. It will be noticed that the steep rise from 0-5 to 5-10 and the slight rise from that group to the next correspond to the ages at which deaf-muteness becomes first indubitable to the child's parents and then cannot be concealed from neighbours, the girl's curve being here less steep, as one might expect ; from the point at which the infirmity is patent there is a steady fall, corresponding to the natural decrease in deaf-mutes, who are usually short-lived, except for a depression at the 15-20 group corresponding to the age of marriage which may indicate a slight inflation of the previous and subsequent groups at the expense of the 15-20 group. There is no clear rise in old age though the increased figure for the group 70 and over must represent a certain inclusion of dotards. As in the case of the other infirmities, this group has not been plotted on the curve, since it covers an indefinite number of age groups and is liable to be misleading. A geometrically decreasing ratio from the 60-65 group would not bring extinction before 135 years, but the inaccuracy of return indicated is less than that of 1921, and whereas the group for 70 and over in all other infirmities shows an increase on the 1921 figure, corresponding no doubt to the increased population, that for deaf-muteness shows a decrease in 1931. The geographical distribution of deaf-muteness shows that the return is not so inaccurate as to obscure the connection between this infirmity and locality, and localities showing a high frequency in 1921 continue to do so in 1931. In particular the distribution of this infirmity shows an association with steep and rapidly drained valleys at comparatively high elevations, and with tarai country which is rapidly drained. Its incidence is lower on plateaux and on alluvial plains, but seems to increase again here and there in deltaic land and also in areas particularly subject to famine, perhaps a not unnatural association for a deficiency disease. Bengal has several institutions for the deaf and dumb which turn out articulating, literate and self-supporting individuals. Madras and Bombay have similar institutions and figures of these institutions and those for teaching the blind, and the numbers of pupils are given in chapter IX, but the total number of pupils compared to those afflicted is insignificant entirely.

Blindness.

108. The figures of blindness have generally been held by census officers in India to be much the most accurate of the infirmity returns on the ground that there is no particular motive for concealment as this affliction excites neither contempt nor disgust ; even so the returns are in some cases open to doubt and in any case concealment is likely in the case of girls of marriageable age. In Ajmer-Merwara and in Madras the incidence in 1921 was heavier on males than on females. This has been reversed in 1931. In Assam the heavier ratio of blindness in the hills has been in the past put down to the insanitary houses of primitive tribes, but it is found to have increased most in 1931 precisely in those districts where education and sanitation have made the most progress. Figures of blindness are on the whole heavier in the drier, dustier and sandier parts of India, but the Census Superintendent in Central India questions the close association between blindness and environment and points out that in western countries 25 per cent. of blindness is caused by congenital anomalies, *opthalmia neonatorum* is responsible for another 25 per cent. and syphilis, injuries and atrophy of the optic nerve for another 10 per cent. each. Even so in Rajputana we find that Jaisalmer, which is nearly all sand, has a low ratio of blindness while " the highest is returned from two such geographical

Census figures of blindness, 1931.

Province, State or Agency.	Number of blind per 100,000 of population, 1931.	Variation per 100,000 of increase since 1921.
1. India	172	+353
2. Ajmer-Merwara	386	+1,313
3. Andamans & Nicobars	31	+168
4. Assam	107	+175
5. Baluchistan	195	—577
6. Bengal	73	+91
7. Bihar and Orissa	126	+508
8. Bombay (including Aden).	178	+370
9. Burma	189	+217
10. Central Provinces and Berar.	262	+310
11. Coorg	61	+1,370
12. Delhi	103	—2
13. Madras	111	+344
14. N.-W. F. P.	102	—298
15. Punjab	245	+136
16. United Provinces	291	+1,214
17. Baroda	329	+391
18. Central India	206	+479
19. Cochin	132	+150
20. Gwalior	182	+83
21. Hyderabad	87	—337
22. Jammu and Kashmir.	156	+272
23. Mysore	100	+236
24. Rajputana	282	+855
25. Sikkim	24	—4
26. Travancore	63	+139
27. Western India States	395	*

*For purposes of calculating variation this unit has been combined with Bombay of which it formed part in 1921.

extremes as Bharatpur and Sirohi.........Blindness is not marked by a high ratio in the hot and dry states in the west of the agency where it might be expected to prevail ". This the Census Superintendent suggests may be due to faulty enumeration. Again in Bihar and Orissa, though south Bihar conforms to the environmental criterion, north Bihar, just as dusty, returns little more blindness than Orissa and Chota Nagpur, which are comparatively green and wooded, while the extraordinary fluctuations of the number of the blind, 107 per 100,000 in 1911, 82 in 1921 and 126 in 1931 make the returns suspect. On the other hand in Hyderabad State blindness is much more prevalent in Marathwara with a greater intensity of heat, glare and dust-laden winds than in the Telingana. "Black cotton soil" says the Census Commissioner of that state " is highly prejudicial to the eyesight ". Cochin State shows a similar fluctuation to that of Bihar and Orissa, but a generally increased ratio, while Travancore shows, as in 1921, a higher ratio of blindness among males than among females, but greater increase among the latter. The Census Commissioner for that state adds " The evil of defective eyesight is evidently increasing among young adults, especially students in the higher forms of English schools and in colleges. The Government of Travancore have realised the seriousness of this evil and arranged for the periodical medical inspection of the students ". This consideration has possibly

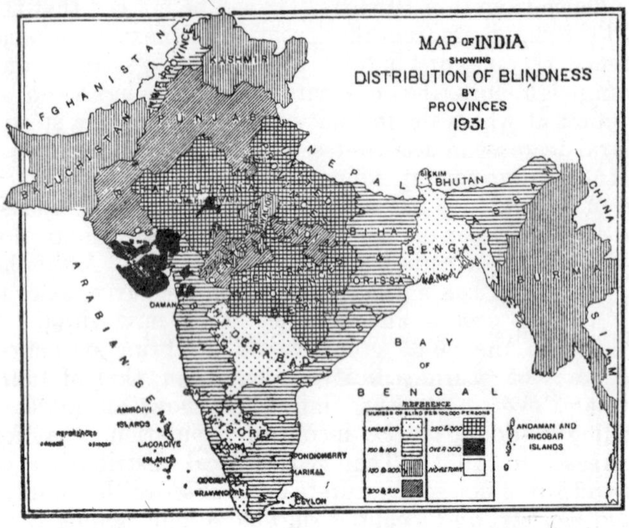

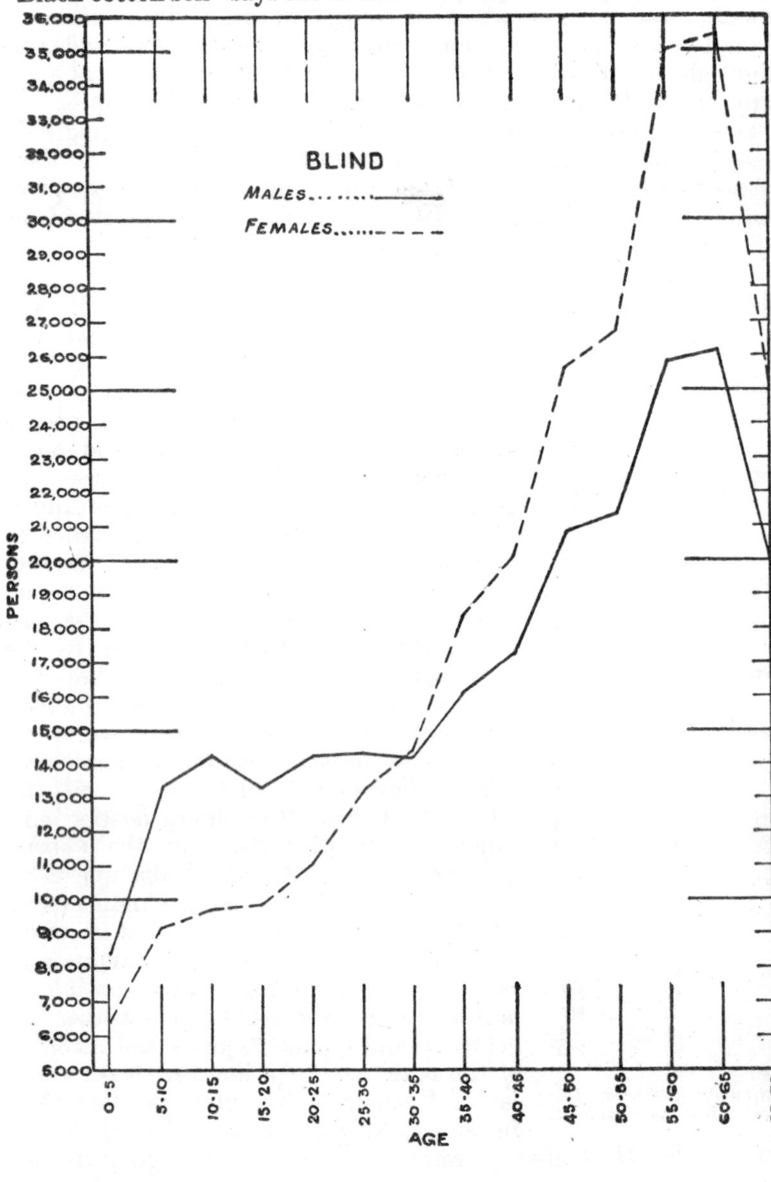

something to do with the curve by age groups, which shows juvenile blindness as rather a male than a female phenomenon, even though concealment may account for the depression of the female curve at 15-20, the marriageable age; the steadier increase for females, which is characteristic of Indian returns of blindness in general, is usually put down to their task of cooking over smoky fires. Apart from the greater incidence of juvenile blindness in males the two curves show, like the curves of deaf-muteness, a striking similarity of outline which suggests the possibility of a greater accuracy of the census figures than we have claimed for them in this chapter. Cataract and glaucoma are causes of much blindness which only appear with increasing age, but glaucoma heads the Public Health Commissioner's list (1929) of the main causes of blindness in India, *opthalmia neonatorum*, small-pox, conjunctivitis, and trachoma following in that order, after which are put 'neglect of simple diseases of the eyes in childhood' and 'dust and glare especially in the dry zone'. To these are added 'eye-strain under bad lighting conditions' and the medicaments of quacks. In this connection the Census Superintendent of Madras notes that—

"The general knowledge that cataract can be treated surgically has an unfortunate illustration in the prevalence of the operation known as 'couching'. This is a practice of vaids and hakims of merely pushing into deeper parts of the eye, the cloud or 'flower' which constitutes the cataract. There it may, and frequently does, cause much injury even though it can no longer be seen. European surgical practice is to remove the cloud altogether. Careful investigations made at the Ophthalmic Hospital, Madras, showed that out of 836 persons whose cataract had been couched only 176 had retained useful sight. The success return from proper surgical practice, on the other hand, is 90 per cent. and even of the remaining 10 per cent. most derive benefit from the operation. Here again propaganda is the only remedy and this point is dealt with among others in the literature issued by medical officers in Madras".

A Blind Relief Association, now known as the All-India Blind Relief Association, was founded in Bombay in 1919, and is now affiliated to the International Association for the Prevention of Blindness. It aims in particular at conveying relief and prevention into rural areas in different parts of India where treatment is generally inaccessible. Much of the blindness in India is curable and more is preventible. One serious difficulty is the economic one. Cultivators suffering from eye complaints cannot afford to leave the work on their fields for a prolonged stay in hospital either for themselves or to look after their children there. Consequently proper treatment is only obtained, if at all, too late to be of value, while affections of the eyes are often made worse by the improper treatment of local quacks. No apology is needed for quoting again and at length the Census Superintendent of Madras :—

"The chief tragedy of blindness is that so much of it in India (probably more than half) is preventable and that the majority of incurably or partially blind become so when infants or young children. We are apt to dwell too much on cataract and the more spectacular manifestations of blindness and forget the large share which parental folly and neglect, improper food and housing play in producing the 50,000 blind recorded in this presidency. Blindness from cataract despite the large number of cases is of less real importance in the life of the community, is generally associated with advanced years and is curable. Even if no cure is effected the victim has had during the useful stages of his life the power of sight. Opthalmia neonatorum, syphilis, small-pox, keratomalacia, on the other hand, as causes of blindness all mark their victims before adult years are reached and the loss and burden they bring on the community are difficult to assess. In the first two the fault of the parents is complete. It is their disease which appears as blindness in their child and if all parents established their own soundness before begetting children blindness of this sort would vanish. Ophthalmia neonatorum is in any case preventable after birth by a simple precaution which every woman ought to know but which many, including 'dais', unfortunately do not. Indeed it has frequently been discovered that a fully qualified doctor or midwife had been present at the birth of a child subsequently produced for treatment of this affliction. Blindness from small-pox is simply neglected vaccination and parental responsibility runs high. It is higher still when we consider the blindness caused by violent irritants put into the eyes to rouse the child or cure some simple ailment. Chewed red pepper, tobacco juice, red-hot coals, strong solution of alum all seem preposterous to Western ears, but all are frequently put into the eyes of Indian children with generally the tragic result of blindness. The application of irritants is probably at least as great a cause of blindness in India as ophthalmia neonatorum. Misfortune comes to all, but there is something peculiarly tragic, about misfortune occasioned by another's folly.

Keratomalacia and trachoma come in a different category and the latter is a disease of adults as well as children. Its precise cause is not yet known but it is usually associated with bad housing and ventilation. In the opinion of Colonel Wright trachoma is not in India nearly so serious a cause of blindness as in other parts of the world. This may reflect the fact that the Indian house is often much more a receptacle than a dwelling in the European sense and much of the occupants' day is actually spent in the open air.

Keratomalacia is in the opinion of Colonel Wright the greatest single cause of preventable blindness in India. This is not generally recognized. In Madras blindness is a more common sequel to it than to ophthalmia neonatorum. It is really a multiple-deficiency complex in which ophthalmic features, however noteworthy, are but localized signs. Its chief primary aetiological factor is apparently lack of fat-soluble vitamin A in the diet, and its prevention lies in proper feeding of children. It is thus linked by cause to the wide range of ailments that begin in malnutrition and it is a significant pendant to McCarrison's views on the merits of India's various diets that whereas keratomalacia is common in the rice-eating south and the Ganges valley it is practically unknown in the wheat and milk consuming Punjab. A large proportion of the poorer population of this presidency is in what McCarrison would call the twilight zone of nutrition where a small change in dietary may precipitate a deficiency disease. Colonel Wright brought to notice in 1925 a sudden precipitation of keratomalacia in adults who had acquired liver disease.

The mode of operation against these preventable causes of blindness is more obvious in some cases than in others but in all propaganda plays a large part. This has been realized and for some years past much has been done by oral and pictorial exhortation to make more widely known what the public should do to reduce or remove preventable blindness. Keratomalacia presents a difficult problem and is not separable from the very much wider economic problem represented by the low standard of living and unsatisfactory dietary prevailing in so large a part of the population. Its prevention is in fact primarily an economic question. The same apparently applies to trachoma. The above causes of blindness which operate so heavily in the first five years of life have a profound influence on the actual total number of blind persons and if they were reduced to proper proportions the blindness diagram would undergo a marked alteration."

Leprosy.

109. Were it not for their inaccuracy the figures of leprosy would be the most important of the returns of infirmity made at the census. It is, however, an unsuitable subject for diagnosis by enumerators and it is also one in which concealment is likely to be particularly obstinate. This is reflected in all probability in the great excess returned of male over female lepers, for though it is stated by some authorities that the male is more exposed to this disease, and though it is clear that this is true in the sense that he is the more likely to contract it away from home, it seems equally probable that the male, who so contracts it, is on the whole a more likely source of contagion to the women of the household he lives in than the exterior source from which he obtained it was for him. The difference in the incidence of this disease on the two sexes is therefore to be regarded as most suspicious in itself, and the more so in that concealment in the case of women is so easy under the purdah system as to be almost certain in probably the majority of cases of female lepers. The same factor must be taken into account in regard to the expert surveys of leprosy, for here too the tendency must be for more females than males to escape observation. As regards the sex incidence in Bihar and Orissa the Census Superintendent writes "doubtless ...... men are more liable to develop this disease than women are, but the extent to which this is true bears no relation to the disproportion exhibited by the census figures, which can only be due to systematic concealment." Other Census Superintendents

Census figures of leprosy, 1931.

Province, State or Agency.	No. of lepers per 100,000 of population.	Variation per 100,000 of increase since 1921.
1. India	42	+132
2. Ajmer-Merwara	3	+8
3. Andamans and Nicobars	7	—926
4. Assam	59	+76
5. Baluchiatan	6	—80
6. Bengal	42	+154
7. Bihar and Orissa	54	+241
8. Bombay (including Aden)	41	+34
9. Burma	76	+92
10. Central Provinces and Berar.	70	+223
11. Coorg	10	+1,761
12. Delhi	1	—1
13. Madras	71	+399
14. N.-W. F. P.	10	+22
15. Punjab	10	+1
16. United Provinces	30	+69
17. Baroda	24	+7
18. Central India	16	+21
19. Cochin	62	+123
20. Gwalior	12	+2
21. Hyderabad	26	—24
22. Jammu and Kashmir.	62	+140
23. Mysore	11	+72
24. Rajputana	5	+10
25. Sikkim	6	—14
26. Travancore	55	+67
27. Western India States	4	*

*For purposes of calculating variation this unit has been combined with Bombay of which it formed part in 1921.

take the same view. It is perhaps significant in regard to the true sex incidence of leprosy that in Hyderabad State among the few Christian lepers found there were almost as many women as men. The census figures are mainly important as an indication of distribution. On the day after the 1921 census Dr. Muir asked 30 lepers, who knew that they were lepers, if they had been returned as such and found that only two had been so returned. The census figures have also been used to estimate the actual number of lepers by computing a figure for the whole of India on the basis of the ratio found to exist in limited areas between the census figures and the numbers obtained by expert survey. This method is also liable to be highly erroneous on account of the very great variations shown in the ratio of census to expert survey returns for different areas. The figures resulting from survey are always higher than the census figures* but the difference seems generally to vary from about 10 times the census figure downwards over large units. In very small units the excess is sometimes much greater, and a municipality in Malda district (Bengal), that of English Bazar, had a census figure of 3 and a survey figure of 67. On the other hand the Census Superintendent for Bombay regards the inaccuracy of return as varying according to the incidence of the disease. He writes—

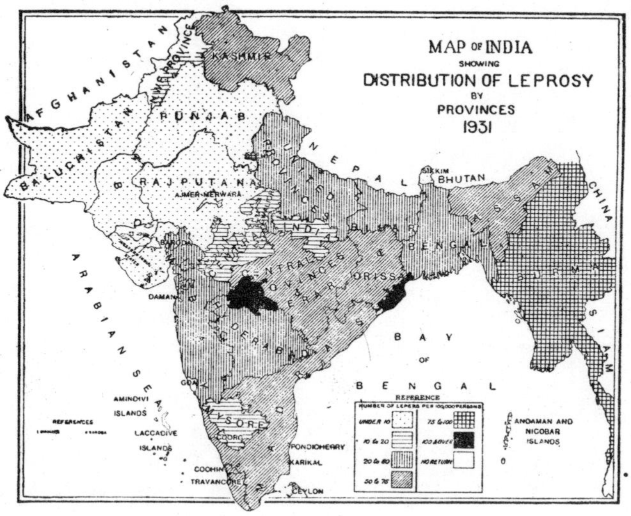

> "The leprosy returns in the Bombay Presidency vary in accuracy probably from within two-thirds to one-tenth of the truth, the accuracy depending more than anything on the incidence of the disease in particular areas. Where the disease is widely prevalent it is not properly reported. Where it is only occasionally found there is no doubt the Census statistics are nearer the truth. In the Ahmednagar district the medical authorities believe that the Census statistics of leprosy are about two-thirds correct. In Bombay City the statistics are believed not to be more than one-tenth correct".

The 10 to 1 ratio is possibly the commoner; in one thana of Bengal a survey figure of 274 was returned against a census figure of 30, though three or four times the census figure seems more usual in that province, and in a taluk of Hyderabad State 538 against 53, but Dr. Lowe estimates the total number of lepers in the Nizam's Dominions as 60,000 against a census figure of 3,738. The Census Commissioner of that State describes the 1891 leprosy return of 10,508 as a "glaring error in enumeration", though it would seem to have been much nearer the numerical truth than the subsequent ones. His aspersions are perhaps justified by the unusual sex incidence—males 2,598, females 7,910, such an antithesis to all other Indian returns as to suggest an error in compilation or printing. Surveys over larger units show a smaller excess than 10 to 1, but it seems not unlikely that the larger the unit the less close the survey. In Ajmer-Merwara the census return is 18 lepers only, but 30 persons were actually treated for leprosy in 1930. In Assam the leprosy survey found 11,720 lepers in five districts which returned only 3,843 at the census—less than one-third, and the Census Superintendent estimates that there are at the very least 20,000 lepers in Assam. His census figure is 5,420. In Bihar and Orissa the census returns for 450 odd villages occupying 328 square miles in Puri district, 72 per cent. of which were found to be infected, gave 179 lepers per 100,000 against 1,344 found by the survey—eight times as many, and in Muzaffarpur district 374 cases were returned against

* A solitary instance to the contrary. is reported from Ganjam where a leprosy survey yielded less than a fourth of the census return. Not unnaturally the survey figure is suspect.

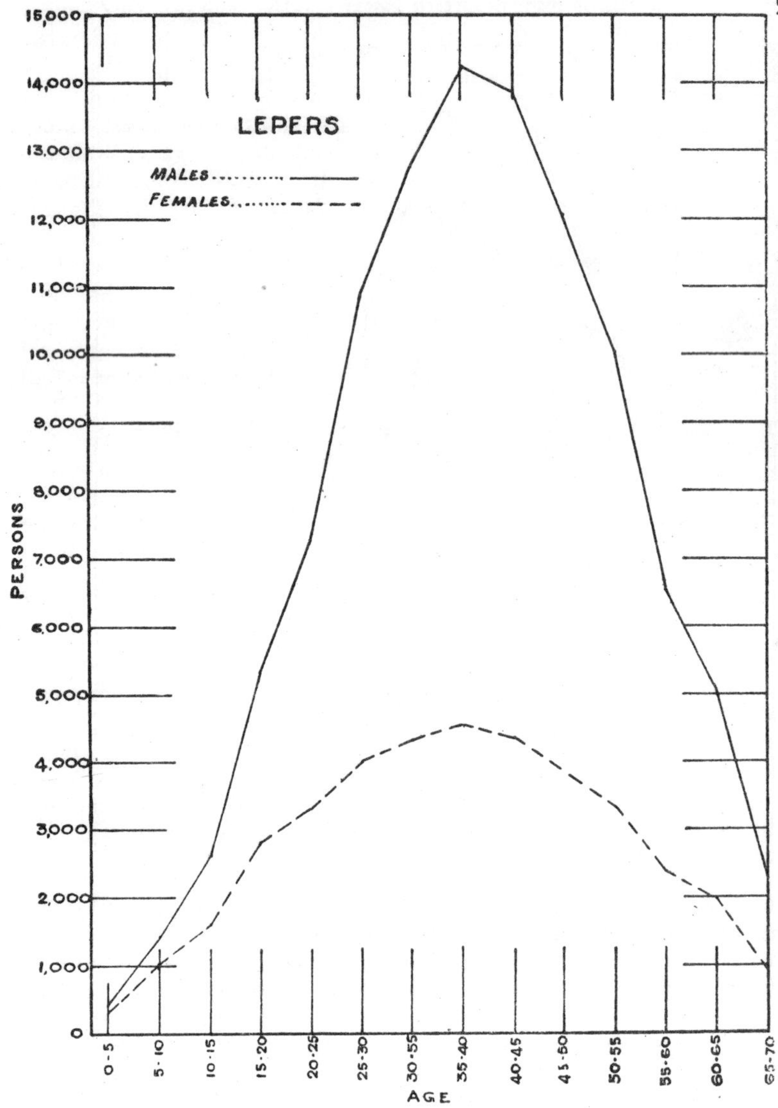

2,455 found by the doctors, 75 per cent. of 652 villages being found infected. In one district in Madras the survey party returned the ratio as 852 per 100,000, the census figure being 131. Leprosy shortens life, and the age curves of leprosy show steady increases after maturity until the period of old age is approached when they fall rapidly. The peak is later than that in the curve for insasanity and corresponds in both sexes. Otherwise the leprosy and insanity curves are not dissimilar, particularly in the marked difference between the sexes in the numbers of their afflicted.

As regards circumstances contributing to the prevalence of leprosy the Pub ic Health Commissioner (1929) states that a high leprosy rate is associated with a poor soil where vegetables and fodder do not thrive and where the cereal crops are apt to fail; with the inadequate consumption of vegetables and milk, and with the consumption of food of bad quality such as spoiled rice and rotten fish. It is of interest to compare conclusions formed by Dr. Mayer in Nigeria. Apart from certain factors of purely local significance, he mentions poor food conditions (smoke-dried fish is excessively popular), over-crowding of houses and prolonged periods of drought and frequent famines as having increased susceptibility to the disease on account of resultant starvation and dirtiness of clothing. He mentions as predisposing diseases scabies, intimately connected with leprosy, malaria, yaws, syphilis, ankylostomiasis, dracontiasis and one or two others "because of their tendency to cause long periods of poor health, which is well known to favour infection, the development of a latent infection and to increase the severity of established leprosy. .... Malaria, yaws and syphilis may be considered as the most common predisposing causes of leprosy in Nigeria ". One or other of all the diseases here mentioned as well as, it may be added, *kala-azar* may be found alongside leprosy in this country, and pyorrhœa is regarded by some as another serious contributor. Ignorance of the danger of contamination is an important factor in the spread of the disease, and the attitude of the Indian village is very different from that of the Nigerian Yoruba tribe which cures lepers dead with a drastic remedy of cold steel. This ignorance or indifference to the disease is well illustrated by the Census Superintendent for Madras :—

"The survey parties found that a number of male patients attributed their infection to contact with leprous paramours or concubines. Apparently young women rejected on account of leprosy as unfit for marriage are allowed to have other connections. The part played by such activities in the spread of the disease needs no stressing. In South Arcot one man with highly infectious leprosy was found undergoing the preliminary ceremonies of marriage. With the aid of the villagers the marriage was postponed for six months, an encouraging instance of communal action for the public weal. One village in Salem district has a number of male lepers to whom infection was conveyed through the ministerations of a leper barber........ In another village an actively infectious leprosy case was found sharing a hooka with the other men of the village ; this illustrates well the part played by ignorance in the spread of the disease. Leprosy is easily conveyed if the skin is already abraded."

Oldrieve notes the following cases, among others, of observed lepers from one small district :—A scullion at a railway refreshment room ; another in a missionary's house ; a preparer of oil for curries ; another such ; a ghi-seller's wife ; a woman milk-seller ; another milk-woman ; a vegetable seller ; a sweetmeat maker ; a baker ; a cigarette-maker ; and his wife ; a stitcher of leaves for wrapping food ; a sub-assistant surgeon working in a hospital ! The Census Superintendent of Madras remarks that leprosy like tuberculosis is a 'disease of semi-civilization' :—

"It is in the contact zones that these diseases have their widest range. Where a primitive mode of life is in contact with a more advanced, where simple habits have been modified but adaptation is not complete, leprosy finds a wide field. Coolies and factory hands provide the bulk of the specimens. In these cases a new mode of life is in most obvious impingement upon a simpler predecessor."

Similarly it is observed in Nigeria that tribes which have recently taken to clothing as a result of contact between Muslims in the north and Europeans in the south are at a stage in which they are more liable to acquire leprosy. The reason given is that they wear clothing but do not wash it, having forsaken the healthy nakedness of their forefathers to adopt foreign fashions of clothing without the necessary corollary of soap and water and changes of raiment. That the spread of leprosy can be unexpectedly rapid is shown by the records of a case in East Prussia where from a single importation 50 lepers were found to have been infected in the course of 30 years. It may be added that in many, possibly in all parts of India a leper's body is not burned but buried or cast into water. It is perhaps improbable that infection is ever thus conveyed but it seems a pity that cremation is not employed.

Apart from the leprosy centre at the School of Tropical Medicine the two most important bodies engaged in the anti-leprosy campaign in India are the British Empire Leprosy Relief Association (Indian Council) and the Mission to Lepers. The marginal statement shows the number of lepers treated in medical institutions in British India in 1929. In Hyderabad State the Leprosy Hospital has been over-crowded since 1926 and at least 1,000 patients were refused admission in consequence. In 1930 alone 260 patients were refused admission. Anti-leprosy campaigns have been in progress throughout India during at any rate the latter half of the decade. Thus in the Chhattisgarh Division of the Central Provinces "Propaganda-Treatment-Survey Units" moved from thana to thana and made surveys, gave lectures with the help of lanterns, and opened 32 treatment centres. Bihar and Orissa has six asylums, 2 colonies and 28 clinics for the treatment of out-patients. Of 6,393 persons examined in Puri in 1929, 288 were found to be lepers, a rate of 4,500 per 100,000. Tangi Thana and other places yielded rates of 1,133, 1,236 and 923 per 100,000. Puri is a malarial district and also attracts lepers since devotions at the shrine of Jagannath were held to be a cure, so that the growth of an endemic area there has been doubly favoured. Assam initiated a survey in 1925 which continued till lack of funds brought it to a close in 1928 during which time 5 districts had been surveyed and 11,720 lepers diagnosed at a cost of Rs. 1,00,154. In addition to the existing three small leper asylums two small colonies were opened at Tura and Dhubri. There are at present 81 clinics and it is proposed to make every

Lepers treated in institutions, 1929.

Province	Number	Province	Number
Assam ..	991	Delhi ..	116
Baluchistan ..	11	Madras ..	17,552
Bengal ..	3,923	N. W. F. P.	15
Bihar and Orissa	9,451	Punjab ..	209
Bombay ..	3,223	United Provinces.	5,279
Burma ..	3,083		
Central Provinces. ..	2,720		

kala-azar dispensary and out-centre a leprosy clinic as well which should raise the number to 237. Lepers treated in 1930 numbered 1,898. In the Punjab there are four leprosy Hospitals managed by the Mission to Lepers in the East assisted by a Government grant; special surgeons have been trained in diagnosis and treatment, surveys are in progress, and propaganda is carried on by means of the distribution of pamphlets and of lantern lectures. In Madras there has been a rough survey which detected 48,000 cases and the expert estimate puts the real total at 100,000. Out of 1,097 schoolboys examined at Villupuram in South Arcot 3·67% were found to be infected, and in East Godavari 5% of factory hands. An organised campaign has been undertaken by dividing the province into six areas with an expert medical officer in charge of each whose efforts are directed to the opening of clinics and to the dissemination of propaganda knowledge as well as to the treatment of active cases. There is no compulsory segregation or detention but the object is to treat the infectious rather than to offer asylums to burnt out cases which, though no longer infectious, form the majority of lepers recognizable as such by laymen.

Elephantiasis.

110. The only other infirmity made a subject of census returns was elephantiasis, which was recorded in Travancore State. This disease is said to be easy to recognize, but the Census Commissioner of the State reports that concealment is undoubtedly practised, as in Trivandrum itself 3,268 persons out of 31,021 who were tested for the disease gave positive results to microscopic examination for filarial disease. Of the 3,268 who proved to have filaria in their blood 533 actually suffered from elephantiasis of the hand or foot. But only 180 persons in the town out of 96,016 were returned as suffering from elephantiasis at the census. The total population afflicted in Travancore according to the returns is 14,709, that is 288 per 100,000 the proportion of females being returned as 746 per 1,000 males, the difference being more likely to be due to concealment than to spiteful discrimination in favour of her own sex by the mosquito that carries the parasite.

Other diseases.

111. With other diseases the census is only indirectly concerned on account of their effect on population figures, and of their predisposing influence, where it exists, to infirmities recorded. The accompanying diagram taken from the Public Health Commissioner's Report for 1929 shows the mean of mortality for the years 1920-29 as distributed between fevers, respiratory diseases, cholera, dysentery and diarrhœa, plague, small-pox and others. Considerably more than half the total deaths from all causes are due to fevers. Anti-malarial work is carried on in all provinces. Kala-azar, which has depopulated whole valleys in Assam and for which the mortality rate was over 90% has been defeated during the decade by the discovery of its treatment

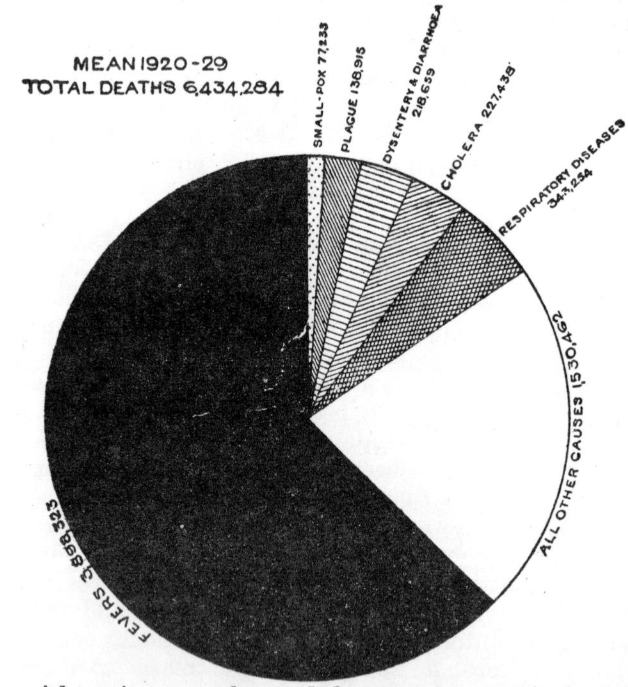

with antimony salts, and there are now 90% of recoveries. Of respiratory diseases tuberculosis is a serious problem in India particularly in thickly populated areas and it is probably more prevalent than figures indicate. It has been pointed out that Indian students in Europe very frequently contract tuberculosis. King George's Thanksgiving Fund, with a capital of over 9½ lakhs raised by public subscription, aims at the prevention of tuberculosis by educational measures, and at a survey of the prevalence of the disease. Mortality from tuberculosis has been reduced by over 50% in western countries and could undoubtedly be similarly reduced in India. 200 000 cases were treated in hospitals in 1929. Cholera was less than usual during the decade and is regarded as decreasing, but slowly. Pilgrimages are important distributors, and the great Kumbh mela of 1930 at Allahabad proved to be followed, as anticipated, by a year of high epidemicity. Plague has similarly been greatly reduced during the decade. Mortality from plague in the Punjab was higher in 1924 than in any year since 1907, when it was considerably more than twice the 1924 figure, and it was also above normal in 1926. The United Provinces figure for 1923-26 exceeded those of 1915 and 1916, but has not reached the mortality of any other year in the previous decade, and the other provinces have all shown a generally corresponding improvement. 1921, 1922, 1927, 1928 and 1929 were all years of exceptionally low plague mortality and the figure for 1930 has been lower than for any year since plague came to India through Bombay. Probably the rats of India are developing immunity, as the extent to which they appear to be immune is greatest where plague has been worst. On the other hand Assam and in a lesser degree Bengal and Burma are free from plague though their rat population is reported to be highly susceptible. This freedom has not been satisfactorily explained. Karachi, India's chief port for the export of grain has been free from plague since 1926. Mortality from small-pox was slightly less for 1921-1929 than for the corresponding 9 years of the previous decade, but India remains the greatest centre of small-pox in the world. Some 600,000 cases of venereal disease are treated annually in hospitals but no other statistics of these diseases are available. Beri-beri is endemic round the western stores of the Bay of Bengal, the centre of the focus of infection lying round about Masulipatam towards the north of the Coromandel Coast. The disease is seasonal, prevailing during the later part of the monsoon, and is commonest in communities living on raw-milled and polished rice, and as might be expected outbreaks occur in small communities living under special conditions, such as felling camps in forests, or military police outposts—obviously among persons living on milled rice supplied as rations. In 22,000 cases treated in 1929 there were 300 deaths. Of other diseases ankylostomiasis (hookworm), dracontiasis (guineaworm) and yaws are of some importance. Hookworm disease, in spite of a fairly widespread incidence of the parasite, is virtually non-existent in the greater part of India. Thus the North-West Frontier Province, Kashmir, Sind, the Punjab and Rajputana are for all practical purposes entirely free, and though in the eastern parts of the two last there is a fairly high incidence of very light infections, "infections severe enough to be of pathogenic significance are practically unknown". Similarly the Deccan and western India generally, as well as Mysore, are free for practical purposes, as also Central India and the greater part of the Central Provinces. In the eastern provinces and in Madras, where infection is appreciably more prevalent, the infection is in most places so slight as to be negligible except in certain localities. The seriously infected areas may be regarded as confined to the intermediate zone in the plains of Burma (between the delta and the dry zone, that is), the Brahmaputra and Surma valleys in Assam, the Duars and Darjiling district in Bengal, in Madras the west coast and the east coast from Tanjore to Nellore, and the State of Travancore. Cases treated in hospitals in 1929 were by far the heaviest in Madras (104,542) where 266,000 treatments were issued to the general population and an intensive educational propaganda by motion pictures, lantern lectures, pamphlets, etc., was instituted; 58,000 egg-counts were carried out and the infection average for the Presidency was found to be 73%. Control has proved to be a matter of the control of soil pollution. In Travancore a survey was conducted in 1930. Out of 27,791 examinations made 25,714 positive cases were found with an average egg-count of 1,400 per c.c.; 87 to 93% of positive cases were found among persons tested in various parts of the State. The incidence of the disease was found to be highest among Government servants, and during the course of a six month's campaign 71,285 persons were treated. It is not generally understood how great the economic effect of this disease, not merely in respect of poor outturn and lethargic work, but in the creation of large numbers who are in fact parasitic on their less infected fellows. Hookworm produces habitual criminals and village pests of the petty pilfering order and probably innumerable beggars, and the writer when in charge of one of the smallest jails in India (one of the few still controlled by the district magistrate) found by deliberate experiment that habitual pilferers and village parasites could by being tested for hookworm and by treatment in jail be made into useful members of their communities. Guineaworm is reported to be prevalent to a varying extent in several districts in Madras. Yaws is very prevalent in the Chin Hills and the Upper Chindwin district and in some other parts of Burma including Mergui, in the Assam hills, in the Nicobar Islands, in Bastar State, in the Chanda and Chhattisgarh uplands of the Central Provinces and in the Agency tracts and on the Malabar coast of Madras. The distribution of yaws, which is common in Africa and in Melanesia appears to be more or less racial, and is possibly connected in India with Melanesian race elements. As in Nigeria, and like hookworm and guineaworm, it probably predisposes to leprosy. It is likely that in the past, and even in the present, cases of yaws have been frequently diagnosed as syphilis. Fortunately it is susceptible to the same treatment. For detailed information as to the prevalence of and mortality from various diseases in India reference should be made to the Annual Reports of the Public Health Commissioner with the Government of India. Figures of death from certain diseases will be found in Subsidiary Table XI to Chapter I (p. 39).

SUBSIDIARY TABLE I.

Distribution of 10,000 of each sex of the Infirm by Age.

Age.	Insane. Males. 1931.	1921.	1911.	1901.	1891.	Insane. Females. 1931.	1921.	1911.	1901.	1891.	Deaf-Mutes. Males. 1931.	1921.	1911.	1901.	1891.	Deaf-Mutes. Females. 1931.	1921.	1911.	1901.	1891.
1	2	3	4	5	6	7	8	9	10	11	12	13	14	15	16	17	18	19	20	21
Total	**10,000**	**10,000**	**10,000**	**10,000**	**10,000**	**10,000**	**10,000**	**10,000**	**10,000**	**10,000**	**10,000**	**10,000**	**10,000**	**10,000**	**10,000**	**10,000**	**10,000**	**10,000**	**10,000**	**10,000**
0—5	145	121	102	150	170	180	142	139	196	183	502	313	403	410	453	596	387	469	486	532
5—10	559	539	547	582	588	577	553	568	633	567	1,317	1,284	1,458	1,484	1,420	1,314	1,313	1,446	1,548	1,439
10—15	739	761	833	921	820	783	803	876	954	820	1,382	1,373	1,529	1,621	1,310	1,340	1,332	1,454	1,525	1,152
15—20	946	810	940	928	945	999	904	1,028	1,013	967	1,101	1,042	1,217	1,270	1,078	1,071	1,004	1,223	1,211	1,029
20—25	1,088	1,024	1,118	1,027	1,054	1,049	993	1,095	1,012	1,011	1,072	972	1,142	999	969	1,027	961	1,143	976	953
25—30	1,263	1,273	1,270	1,217	1,232	1,087	1,053	1,013	968	990	917	987	1,049	982	899	889	883	975	888	862
30—35	1,257	1,342	1,316	1,232	1,263	1,053	1,131	1,126	1,103	1,103	805	886	877	858	824	776	847	861	870	803
35—40	1,087	1,049	976	989	953	989	867	790	798	863	641	648	570	545	605	609	573	529	501	548
40—45	918	987	960	962	986	910	1,025	996	1,001	971	550	620	576	580	623	536	664	611	590	630
45—50	644	618	574	572	560	712	634	571	537	592	432	398	309	317	379	426	383	302	313	366
50—55	495	581	558	576	563	576	733	706	665	719	353	429	333	347	456	361	479	369	397	485
55—60	313	272	239	246	278	399	305	297	274	317	272	228	136	139	246	300	229	140	149	250
60 and over	546	623	567	598	588	686	857	795	846	897	656	819	401	448	738	755	945	478	546	951

Age.	Blind. Males. 1931.	1921.	1911.	1901.	1891.	Blind. Females. 1931.	1921.	1911.	1901.	1891.	Lepers. Males. 1931.	1921.	1911.	1901.	1891.	Lepers. Females. 1931.	1921.	1911.	1901.	1891.
1	22	23	24	25	26	27	28	29	30	31	32	33	34	35	36	37	38	39	40	41
Total	**10,000**	**10,000**	**10,000**	**10,000**	**10,000**	**10,000**	**10,000**	**10,000**	**10,000**	**10,000**	**10,000**	**10,000**	**10,000**	**10,000**	**10,000**	**10,000**	**10,000**	**10,000**	**10,000**	**10,000**
0—5	297	265	317	303	411	203	201	226	211	278	40	58	30	46	45	91	101	67	100	92
5—10	474	549	557	585	648	290	357	360	385	415	137	119	70	108	89	259	203	150	206	196
10—15	506	581	599	692	648	307	342	366	448	411	242	257	209	271	240	400	448	408	456	421
15—20	471	464	541	575	588	313	301	376	410	409	495	422	381	418	406	705	629	647	662	625
20—25	501	480	604	601	607	350	361	457	458	449	675	612	587	581	586	829	767	835	781	735
25—30	505	546	646	665	632	418	433	510	520	517	1,008	897	886	911	877	992	960	946	926	926
30—35	502	600	687	696	662	457	547	646	641	620	1,183	1,174	1,176	1,220	1,202	1,081	1,159	1,186	1,146	1,188
35—40	569	531	546	541	560	581	507	507	506	535	1,319	1,195	1,206	1,159	1,209	1,147	999	980	930	998
40—45	610	693	775	754	698	636	756	831	822	753	1,286	1,426	1,561	1,514	1,522	1,094	1,299	1,268	1,291	1,296
45—50	734	571	538	519	564	812	597	549	522	584	1,120	1,023	1,050	980	998	973	844	803	752	776
50—55	753	904	915	866	749	846	1,038	1,075	1,027	888	930	1,129	1,189	1,187	1,163	837	983	1,079	1,081	991
55—60	910	535	442	453	623	1,108	629	487	487	697	609	520	491	483	493	601	447	449	420	457
60 and over	3,168	3,281	2,833	2,750	2,160	3,679	3,931	3,610	3,563	3,444	956	1,168	1,164	1,122	1,170	991	1,161	1,182	1,249	1,299

NOTE.—In this table, those infirm whose age was not specified, have been left out of account.

SUBSIDIARY

Number of persons afflicted per 100,000 of the population

Province, State or Agency.	Insane. Males. 1931.	1921.	1911.	1901.	1891.	Insane. Females. 1931.	1921.	1911.	1901.	1891.	Deaf-Mutes. Males. 1931.	1921.	1911.	1901.	1891.	Deaf-Mutes. Females. 1931.	1921.	1911.
1	2	3	4	5	6	7	8	9	10	11	12	13	14	15	16	17	18	19
INDIA ..	**41**	**33**	**31**	**28**	**33**	**27**	**22**	**20**	**17**	**21**	**76**	**70**	**74**	**62**	**86**	**55**	**49**	**53**
Provinces ..	**43**	**35**	**33**	**30**	**34**	**29**	**23**	**21**	**19**	**22**	**81**	**74**	**80**	**67**	**94**	**58**	**51**	**56**
1. Ajmer-Merwara ..	49	22	25	24	22	27	15	12	4	9	88	32	23	29	39	56	23	9
2. Assam	65	57	51	47	62	52	45	37	35	48	82	78	87	87	95	68	60	66
3. Baluchistan ..	60	62	57	..	..	33	40	28	..	..	81	107	103	..	..	49	56	50
4. Bengal	49	47	50	50	58	38	35	36	35	44	81	79	81	72	102	58	55	58
5. Bihar and Orissa ..	28	14	16	17	20	15	7	8	9	10	77	66	90	95	139	49	40	55
6. Bombay (including Aden).	59	52	37	24	38	36	31	20	13	23	93	63	73	43	72	61	46	49
7. Burma	98	93	85	61	98	77	82	74	45	83	122	96	77	33	55	109	84	65
8. Central Provinces and Berar.	35	28	19	18	20	21	17	11	9	12	92	104	54	54	51	63	72	39
9. Coorg	14	10	11	16	26	25	8	10	20	25	61	13	42	59	80	63	11	59
10. Delhi	16	18	..	..	..	11	12	..	..	..	28	32	..	..	..	16	32	..
11. Madras	39	24	24	23	25	27	17	17	15	18	81	58	87	74	87	62	44	68
12. North-West Frontier Province.	41	47	54	37	41	18	25	25	1	24	82	97	113	100	109	47	69	75
13. Punjab (including Agency).	36	35	31*	43*	36*	21	20	20*	26*	21*	79	106	95*	91*	115*	56	72	70*
14. United Provinces of Agra and Oudh.	29	21	23	19	16	17	11	12	10	8	61	60	67	46	88	41	39	45
States and Agencies ..	**32**	**24**	**22**	**14**	**26**	**21**	**16**	**14**	**9**	**16**	**57**	**50**	**45**	**33**	**52**	**42**	**36**	**33**
15. Baroda State ..	65	54	30	15	43	47	39	21	9	27	55	34	29	41	45	48	22	13
16. Central India Agency	28	16	10 (16 and 17 together)	5 (16 and 17 together)	..	18	11	6 (16 and 17 together)	2 (16 and 17 together)	..	32	35	27 (16 and 17 together)	19 (16 and 17 together)	..	25	23	19 (16 and 17 together)
17. Gwalior State ..	16	18				10	10				40	52				34	35	
18. Cochin State ..	61	44	34	27	32	45	34	30	23	27	48	57	39	77	66	33	47	33
19. Hyderabad State ..	18	23	23	4	18	12	17	15	2	10	30	31	37	7	46	22	23	29
20. Jammu and Kashmir State.	49	51	48	60	..	28	27	30	37	.	180	153	107	136	..	135	122	87
21. Mysore State ..	31	17	26	21	25	23	12	20	16	19	67	70	86	62	78	53	50	68
22. Rajputana Agency ..	29	16	18	12	32	16	8	9	8	19	32	32	36	22	..	23	20	21
23. Sikkim State ..	5	22	13	46	..	4	5	7	32	..	159	200	297	355	..	139	152	233
24. Travancore State ..	45	37	20	20	19	36	27	16	14	11	69	63	34	31	34	44	45	24
25. Western† India States Agency.	59	..	..	..	..	3	..	..	..	..	101	..	..	..	..	80	..	..

* Includes Delhi.

† Separate figures for previous Censuses are not available for this unit, but the ratios in the 1921 to 1891 columns against Bombay are inclusive

TABLE II.

at each of the last five censuses.

		Blind.										Lepers.										
		Males.					Females.					Males.					Females.					
1901.	1891.	1931.	1921.	1911.	1901.	1891.	1931.	1921.	1911.	1901.	1891.	1931.	1921.	1911.	1901.	1891.	1931.	1921.	1911.	1901.	1891.	
20	21	22	23	24	25	26	27	28	29	30	31	32	33	34	35	36	37	38	39	40	41	
42	**57**	**157**	**145**	**138**	**121**	**164**	**185**	**160**	**145**	**120**	**171**	**59**	**46**	**51**	**48**	**68**	**23**	**18**	**18**	**17**	**23**	
45	**61**	**158**	**144**	**140**	**133**	**164**	**183**	**158**	**145**	**133**	**168**	**67**	**48**	**55**	**54**	**73**	**26**	**19**	**20**	**19**	**25**	
16	24	327	248	248	120	181	452	283	301	125	209	4	3	3	8	7	2	2	2	3	3	1
62	75	101	97	94	97	107	114	96	87	91	105	83	80	90	125	182	32	30	32	39	60	2
..	..	201	252	235	..	..	187	276	260	..	..	8	18	14	..	..	3	7	5	..	..	3
49	68	76	78	78	80	84	70	66	63	67	75	59	48	56	69	104	23	18	19	23	36	4
56	78	121	82	111	112	122	131	82	104	104	123	79	48	71	76	82	29	17	23	24	26	5
29	49	167	167	136	84	149	192	207	153	87	156	55	48	52	38	69	26	23	23	15	24	6
22	47	170	168	131	105	172	209	205	150	117	229	102	98	79	56	117	49	49	37	25	52	7
40	37	210	204	173	155	166	313	307	239	201	192	88	61	58	78	91	51	39	33	38	39	8
56	64	64	47	47	45	49	58	69	45	63	51	12	3	6	6	13	8	7	..	4	14	9
..	..	93	135	..	..	..	118	136	..	..	..	2	3	..	..	..	..	1	..	..	..	10
55	65	105	87	83	91	101	116	86	79	88	104	107	56	62	54	53	35	19	20	17	18	11
75	69	103	132	161	128	198	100	133	151	132	245	12	11	17	18	16	8	7	8	10	7	12
66*	77*	239	259	249*	298*	343*	252	259	261*	314*	361*	13	15	17*	26*	37*	6	6	8*	11*	13*	13
28	52	259	217	208	168	229	328	256	234	178	241	47	44	48	36	58	11	11	11	11	13	14
23	**37**	**151**	**144**	**128**	**55**	**165**	**194**	**171**	**143**	**50**	**193**	**35**	**31**	**29**	**17**	**31**	**16**	**14**	**11**	**8**	**12**	
28	30	246	249	129	75	161	417	395	204	95	235	31	35	31	18	2	15	16	12	10	15	15
13	..	166	152	109	41	..	248	203	128	35	..	22	21	19	6	..	10	10	9	4	–	16
		130	162				241	227				15	18				9	8				17
60	43	129	127	133	113	133	136	128	125	107	105	94	70	73	57	66	31	25	28	25	31	18
4	30	88	150	122	15	100	85	157	121	9	84	36	47	41	4	39	16	20	15	2	13	19
92	..	149	142	154	115	..	165	144	152	97	..	71	60	59	72	..	38	30	26	36	..	20
48	62	106	93	104	79	108	94	80	94	67	105	16	8	18	17	22	6	3	8	8	11	21
15	–	234	173	185	78	272	334	230	242	79	372	6	6	9	6	21	3	2	3	3	7	22
385	..	25	27	36	71	..	22	40	21	57	..	9	14	16	55	..	4	12	40	25	–	23
23	24	71	49	42	42	46	55	35	29	29	33	79	73	49	68	53	30	29	16	28	22	24
..	..	309	..	..	..	..	484	..	..	..	..	5	..	..	..	..	2	..	..	..	–	25

of the W. I. S. Agency.

M2200

SUBSIDIARY TABLE III.

Number afflicted per 100,000 persons of each Age-period and number of females afflicted per 1,000 males.

Age-period.	Number afflicted per 100,000.								Number of Females afflicted per 1,000 males.			
	Insane.		Deaf-mutes.		Blind.		Lepers.		Insane.	Deaf-mutes.	Blind.	Lepers.
	Males.	Females.	Males.	Females.	Males.	Females.	Males.	Females.				
1	2	3	4	5	6	7	8	9	10	11	12	13
All ages	41	27	76	55	157	186	60	24	626	678	1,113	371
0—5	4	3	26	21	32	24	2	1	778	805	760	849
5—10	17	12	76	56	56	42	6	5	647	676	682	703
10—15	25	19	88	65	67	51	12	8	663	657	676	613
15—20	43	29	94	63	83	62	33	18	662	659	738	528
20—25	49	29	90	57	87	66	45	20	604	649	778	456
25—30	60	34	81	56	93	90	70	27	539	657	920	365
30—35	65	38	78	56	100	113	83	34	524	653	1,014	339
35—40	69	45	76	56	140	182	123	46	570	645	1,137	323
40—45	69	49	77	58	176	235	141	51	620	661	1,161	316
45—50	62	50	78	60	273	389	158	59	692	668	1,232	322
50—55	61	50	80	63	355	499	166	63	730	693	1,251	334
56—60	56	47	90	71	621	890	158	61	799	748	1,356	367
60 and over	56	45	126	99	1,257	1,636	144	56	788	780	1,293	384

CHAPTER VIII.

Occupation.

Section i—Classification and distribution.

112. Occupation is quite the most troublesome and complicated return called for on the census schedule. Four columns were devoted to this return in which the enumerator was to describe the enumerated as an earner or a dependant, and to enter in the case of an earner his principal occupation, his most important subsidiary occupation if he had any, and the industry in which he was employed. A complete compilation of figures of subsidiary occupations has been attempted at this census for the first time, and Table X gives complete details by sex for each group instead of for orders only. A dependant was not regarded as having any principal occupation but was to be recorded in the column for subsidiary occupation as following any occupation which contributed to the family maintenance. Such a dependant was distinguished as a 'working dependant' from the non-working dependants following no occupation, and in this chapter the term 'earner' is used of a wage receiver or subsistence obtainer in either principal or subsidiary occupation, and the term 'worker' is used of all such persons together with those following an occupation as working dependants, *i.e.* not themselves receiving the wage or controlling the means of subsistence gained. The term 'actual worker' is used with reference to all workers in principal and dependant occupations excluding the numbers of individuals duplicated by their appearing also as earners by means of subsidiary occupations, but in this chapter the subject is approached rather from the aspect of the total number of different means of subsistence engaging the whole working population than from the aspect of the maximum number of the actual workers occupied. **Instructions to Enumerator.**

The definition of industry was employment on wages in company with any other person by a third person. This definition of course covers many non-industrial forms of employment but it was intended to eliminate these in the process of selection for compilation and to tabulate only those industries known to be of importance in any given locality. Unfortunately the imperative need for drastic economy led to the abandonment of any sort for or tabulation of industry, this particular item in the census programme being one of those selected for curtailment as the reports from most provinces suggested that the returns of industry were not entirely satisfactory owing to misunderstandings on the part of enumerators as to exactly what was wanted. They did however often prove very useful in enabling occupations to be classified.

Misunderstandings such as those affecting the return of industry are familiar in the Indian census schedule and were the cause of one of the changes in the form of the schedule made at this census. In 1911 and 1921 enumerators were instructed to return in the case of dependants the "occupation on which dependent", an instruction which always gave rise to much misunderstanding and consequently unsatisfactory results. The abandonment of this instruction means that there can be no final distribution of the dependence of the total population on the various occupations derived from the individual returns, but there is no reason to suppose that an estimate of this distribution cannot be obtained from an examination of the returns of earners and working dependants, which will be as satisfactory for practical purposes as the one obtained from the incompletely comprehended and unsatisfactory returns of occupation on which dependent obtained on previous occasions, for a change was also involved in the instructions that a dependant might be regarded as having an occupation. The former division was into workers and dependants, and the instruction was that all persons contributing to the family maintenance should be regarded as workers, so that the 'earners' *plus* 'working dependants' of 1931 are in effect equivalent to the 'workers' of 1921 with the advantage that it is, or should be, possible to distinguish between those who are actually in receipt of earnings and those who are merely helpers; thus in Cochin, for instance, the proportion of 'earners' *plus* 'working dependants' to the total population in 1931 is almost identical with the proportion that 'workers' were to it in 1921. On the other hand there was in some cases a tendency to try and interpret 'earner' in the sense attached to the word 'worker' in 1921, thus obscuring the distinction between earner and working dependant, while the figures of working dependants and others have probably been biassed here and there by a snobbish feeling that it is not so respectable for women to be working as to be non-working dependants, particularly where the observance of purdah is a mark of social superiority.

Reference to figures.

113. The figures of occupation will be found in Table X of part II, and the proportional figures in the subsidiary tables at the end of this chapter are preceded by a copy of the complete scheme of classification. In interpreting the returns the method here followed is first to attempt some examination of the distribution of occupation on broad lines, that is by classes and sub-classes involving divisions on very general lines only, and then to attempt some examination of the statistics in greater detail with reference to orders, and where necessary to individual groups, as classified in the scheme appended to this chapter. The final section consists of a brief note on occupation and caste with reference to Table XI in part II.

Workers and Dependants.

114. Instead of the proportion of non-working dependants to workers having been reduced by the new distinction between earners and working dependants, as was anticipated, the proportion of non-working dependants has increased. In 1921 out of every hundred persons 46 were workers to 54 dependants. In 1931 there were 44 workers to 56 dependents. That this is due in part, to a predilection for returning total instead of working dependence is possibly indicated by the figures for sexes engaged in agriculture, in which the number of males returned as workers has increased during the decade by nearly two million, while the number of females has so far decreased, that is by nearly five million, as to reduce the total number of agricultural workers to less than the total of 1921. The quite exceptional increase in females under head domestic service shows at once however where the bulk of these workers appears. It is certainly regarded as much more socially respectable for a wife to be engaged at home on household duties than to labour in the fields, and there is a generally increasing tendency, as castes aspire to a higher social standing, to keep their women at home. On the other hand the proportion of children to adults, and therefore of dependants to workers is unquestionably higher than it was in 1921, while it is not unlikely that part of the increase in dependence as compared with work is due to the increasing difficulty of getting employment and earning an independent livelihood, keeping youths, in the middle classes at any rate, dependent on their families whereas 10 years ago they would have been earning.

Earners and Workers.

115. The proportion of earners to working dependants is about nine to two, that is of the total working population 81·4 per cent. is in direct receipt of wages or of other means of subsistence whereas the other 18·6 per cent. are helpers of the wage-earners. This statement however is to be accepted only with considerable reserve, as the practice of previous decades in which the division was merely into workers and dependants, all who contributed indirectly in the earning of wages being shown in the former category, undoubtedly influenced in practice the distinction drawn at this census between receivers of earnings and their helpers, a distinction difficult enough in any case where the nature of the occupation is such that the earnings are obtained in the form of natural products which are consumed by the producer without ever being exchanged for coin. Occupations of this sort, including as they do both agriculture and stock-rearing, at any rate to a considerable degree, probably form the great majority in India, and the instructions given were that in such cases the owner or householder should be regarded as the earner and the working members of this family as working dependants. The figures returned however indicate that the interpretation of earner has frequently been wider than was intended by the instructions given, at any rate in class A, sub-class 1. It would appear also from the returns that the instruction that the actual occupation followed should be returned by working dependants, and not the occupation of the principal earner where the two differed, has been often misunderstood. Thus it is difficult to see how the male and female working dependants returned under group 157, *Police,* can represent persons whose occupation is the preservation of the public peace or the arrest of offenders, since generally speaking police officers are appointed under special warrants and it is an offence to impersonate them. On the other hand the numbers in this case are few, and in out of the way parts of India the most unexpected conditions are apt to prevail, and it is not inconceivable that police are to be found whose office is hereditary or an *ex-officio* accompaniment of some other post and is automatically filled by the relatives of the usual functionary when he is indisposed or engaged in other pursuits, while the term 'police' would include for census purposes persons whose services were essentially in that department though not themselves involving the alleged unhappiness of constabulary duties. The females whose principal occupation is found in this group include of course wardresses in prisons as well as policewomen. Similarly the 21 female working dependants on the Air Force are easily explicable as the wives and families of caretakers, bhistis, etc., who help the earner or deputize in his absence. Nevertheless the difficulty of obtaining correct returns of occupation as required by the census code is illustrated by the return from the remote Himalayan principality of Poonch of 40,000 odd females whose principal or subsidiary occupation was stated as 'mechanic, unspecified.' The not unnatural enquiry suggested by these remarkable figures, coming from, with the possible exception of the Amindivi Islands, about the most unlikely area within the scope of operations to produce quantities of female mechanics, resulted in their reclassification under domestic service.

116. It has already been pointed out that the returns of this census do not provide any direct figure for the distribution of the total population according to its dependence on various occupations. Such a distribution would seem to have little but academic value, but if it be considered necessary it can be inferred from an examination of the distribution of dependants at previous censuses. The marginal table shows the percentage of workers to dependants in each class and sub-class in 1911 and in 1921. The figures for 1901 are not comparable except in a few cases and in these also the percentages are given. Now if the total percentage of actual workers to non-working dependants be taken for 1931, it is found to be **44** per cent. workers to 56 per cent. dependants. Now the

Class or Sub-class in Occupation Table.	Ratio of workers to non-working dependants. According to the returns of 1911.	1921.	Assumed for 1931.
I*	47 : 53	46 : 54	44 : 56
II	58 : 42	64 : 36	62 : 38
III	50 : 50	47 : 53	45 : 55
IV†	48 : 52	45 : 55	43 : 57
V	45 : 55	44 : 56	42 : 58
VI	45 : 55	48 : 52	46 : 54
VII	37 : 63	38 : 62	36 : 64
VIII‡	42 : 58	41 : 59	39 : 61
D	57 : 43	54 : 46	44 : 56
Totals§	47 : 53	46 : 54	44 : 56

* 46 : 54 in 1901. ‡ 41 : 59 in 1901.

† 44 : 56 in 1901. § 47 : 53 in 1901.

Incidence of Dependency.

difference between this ratio and that of 1921 may be applied to all sub-classes except those in class D, where owing to the nature of the returns a large number of persons, mostly female, who were formerly classified in sub-class I, now appear in sub-class X as domestic instead of agricultural workers. This will affect the percentage of workers to dependants inferred from the 1911 and 1921 returns, and sub-class D must be calculated on a different basis. The ratio for the whole population is obviously determined by that for the agricultural portion of it and the inclusion of some 7,000,000 additional agriculturalists in class D is likely to bring that class into line with class A. In the fourth column therefore of the marginal table above will be found the ratio of dependants to workers for different sub-classes which is assumed for the purpose of the distribution of total dependence in 1931. In the table below are shown the results of the application of those ratios to the occupation returns of 1931, offered for what they are worth :—

Class or sub-class.	Occupation.	No. of workers (in lakhs).	Percentage of total workers.	No. of non-working dependants (in lakhs).	Total maintained (in lakhs).	Percentage of total population.
A, B and C.						
I	Exploitation of Animals and Vegetation.	1,033	67·1	1,315	2,348	67·0
II	Exploitation of Minerals ..	3	·2	2	5	·1
III	Industry	154	10·0	188	342	9·7
IV	Transport	23	1·5	30	53	1·5
V	Trade	79	5·1	109	188	5·4
VI	Public Force	8	·6	9	17	·5
VII	Public Administration ..	10	·7	18	28	·8
VIII	Professions and Liberal Arts.	23	1·5	36	59	1·7
D	Miscellaneous (Persons living on their income, Domestic Service, Insufficiently described and Unproductive Occupations).	205	13·3	261	466	13·3

It will be observed that the proportion of the total population maintained by the various sub-classes corresponds very closely to the proportion of workers in each of those classes, which is precisely what might be expected on *a priori* grounds, and from the figures in paragraph 86 above, which indicate that there is no very great variation according to occupation in the number of children born and that what variation there is is equalised by a survival rate which varies inversely to the number of births.

Occupational Classification.

117. Occupations were classified as in 1911 and in 1921 according to the Bertillon system, which was fully described by Sir Edward Gait in his report on the former census. The scheme has come in for a great deal of criticism at the hands of Census Superintendents and others, but none of the critics have succeeded in propounding any satisfactory alternative, and while criticisms are usually directed to the complexity and alleged excessive detail in the grouping, suggestions for improvement offered by departments of Government usually take the form of requiring much more detailed grouping than that already provided. This latter attitude results from losing sight of the fact that (to quote Sir Edward Gait) "the whole scheme, as adapted for India, is based on the axiom that a census does not supply data which are suitable for minute classification ". If this axiom be not strictly observed it becomes impossible to keep down the number of detailed heads, and classification in the compilation offices would be made unconscionably slow and difficult, while the already existing degree of inaccuracy would probably be greatly enhanced. As it is the problem of sorting the occupation of each individual into his proper category is too intricate to be carried out with entire satisfaction and as it is in ability to classify correctly that Indian sorting offices are particularly deficient, it is likely that the degree of error in classification is already greater in the occupation table than that in any other. Indeed problems frequently arise in classification which offer very considerable difficulty. It is simple enough when confronted with a return of "*Bande Mataram*" as a means of subsistence to allocate the individual to group 195, *Other unclassified non-productive industries*, probably the most fit place for him whatever he had returned, but " Professional identifying witness " is more difficult. Should he go into the same category, or should it be group 168, *Lawyers' clerks, petition writers, etc.*? The latter would probably wish to relegate him to group 157, but there is much virtue in an ' etcetera '. " Charity-receiver on burial ground " suggests mendicancy at first sight, but probably represents a Mahabrahman and would be rightly classified in group 166, . *Servants in religious edifices, burial grounds, etc.*, together with " Pourer of water on gods ", but one is a little puzzled as to whether " Driving away epidemics by charms " should go with " Averters of hailstorms " into group 181, *Astrologers, fortune tellers, horoscope-casters, wizards, witches and mediums*, or into group 170, *Persons (unregistered) practising the healing art*, with the leech, familiar in India with his little horns and cupping tools, who returned his occupation as " Sucking bad blood ". " Ear wax remover " should probably go into the same category, but the alternative of order 12, Industries of dress and the toilet, where the barbers are found, inevitably occurs to one, as it does in the case of " Setting gold nails in teeth ", which might also be group 171, *Dentists*, or 98, *Makers of jewellery and ornaments*. " Breaking the horns of dead bullocks " is probably group 53, but one would like to know more of the eschatology of the said horns, and " Searcher of conch shells ", particularly in the Central Provinces whence returned, is completely defeating. Indeed it is most suggestive as a basis of archæological as well as industrial enquiry and it can hardly be classified in group 19, *collectors of forest produce*, though it might conceivably be a Naga from Assam looking for the cheapest market to buy in. " Cradle-swinger " not only adds a touch of domesticity, but indicates the extreme differentiation of function which so often characterizes the life of a household in India.

Difficulties of classification being what they are, it was natural to attempt at the outset to simplify the occupational scheme by a widening of categories and a reduction of groups; as a result however of the insatiable desire of departments for more detailed figures the attempt ended in an increase of groups from 191 to 195, as the amalgamations which it was possible to induce them to accept were more than counterbalanced by the additional details which opportunity instigated them to require. On the whole, however, the occupational grouping was probably more satisfactory than in 1921 from the census point of view, and as far as their comparative value goes there has been little if any loss, as there has been no rearrangement at all of classes, sub-classes or orders except for the reduction of one order in sub-class II, Exploitation of Minerals, where the three orders of 1921, Mines, Quarries, and Salt, embracing six groups between them, have become two orders only, *Metallic minerals* and *Non-metallic minerals*, a much more logical division but embracing now thirteen groups instead of six.

A few minor transfers have been made among groups, where the existing classification seemed unsuitable or inaccurate. Thus group 101 of 1921 including persons employed in places of entertainment, which then appeared under order 18, ' Other miscellaneous and undefined industries,' now appears as group 183, order 49, sub-class VIII ' Professions and Liberal Arts '. The title of the order, *Letters, Arts and Sciences*, hardly seems appropriate, but this order contains perforce a number of other groups not covered by its definition which contribute to the education or entertainment of the public. Similarly witches and wizards have moved from group 189 of 1921, which they then shared unreasonably with beggars and vagrants, to group 181 of the same order of Letters, Arts and Sciences to be kennelled in their proper pack with astrologers, fortune-tellers and mediums. Literary they are not, but scientific they think they are, and artful they must be.

Similarly a certain number of occupations wrongly classified in 1921 have been allocated to different groups at this census. Saddle-cloth makers and embroiderers have been reclassified as workers in textiles instead of in leather, while sellers of the finished article have been included under trade in textiles instead of trade in means of transport. Sellers of grasshoppers were classified in 1921 under " trade of other sorts ", they have been reclassified this time under " trade in foodstuffs ". Changes of this kind, and few at that, are not likely to have affected the comparative values of the returns. A complete scheme of the occupational classification in 1931 will be found at the end of this chapter, and it will be convenient to reprint here the note of 1911 in which Sir Edward Gait explains the principles then and since followed in classifying occupation.

" (1) Where a person both makes and sells, he is classed under the industrial head; the commercial one is reserved for persons engaged in trade pure and simple. On the same principle when a person extracts some substance, such as saltpetre, from the ground, and also refines it, he is shown under the mining and not under the industrial head.

(2) Industrial and trading occupations are divided into two main categories :—

(*a*) those where the occupation is classified according to the material of which the articles are made, and

(*b*) those where it is classified according to the use which they serve. As a general rule, the first category is reserved for the manufacture or sale of articles the use of which is not finally determined, but it also includes that of specified articles for which there is no separate head, and also the occupations, so common in India, which are characterized by the material used rather than the particular articles made. The ordinary village *mochi*, for instance, makes not only shoes, but also waterbags and all other articles of leather, which he tans himself.

(3) As a general rule, when a man's personal occupation is one which involves special training, *e.g.*, that of a doctor, engineer, surveyor, etc., he is classed under the head reserved for that occupation, irrespective of the agency by which he is employed. A ship's doctor, for instance, is shown as a doctor and not as a ship's officer. An exception is made in cases where the work in which an individual is employed involves further specialization, *e.g.*, that of a marine or sanitary engineer. Only those Government servants are shown in sub-class VII who are engaged in the general administration. Officers of the medical, irrigation, opium, post office and other similar services are classed under the special heads provided for these occupations.

As a further means of facilitating the classification of the entries recorded in the schedules and of maintaining uniformity of procedure an elaborate alphabetical index of occupation was prepared and circulated to all Provincial Superintendents for the guidance of their staff."

Distribution of Occupations.

118. The proportional distribution of occupations, according to classes, sub-classes and orders will be found in some detail in the subsidiary tables at the end of this volume, the actual figures of the returns appearing by classes, sub-classes, orders and groups in Table X of part II, but for convenience of reference the latter statistics have been reduced to a distribution of 10,000 livelihoods according to classes and sub-classes and are given in the following table :—

Class and sub-class.	Means of subsistence.	Total.	Principal occupation.		Dependent occupation.		Subsidiary occupation.	
			Males.	Females.	Males.	Females.	Males.	Females.
A, B, C & D.	**All occupations** ..	**10,000**	**5,772**	**1,649**	**454**	**1,241**	**673**	**211**
A	Production of Raw Materials.	6,584	4,081	1,103	344	610	375	71
I	*Exploitation of Animals and Vegetation.*	*6,560*	*4,066*	*1,099*	*343*	*610*	*372*	*70*
II	*Exploitation of Minerals*	*24*	*15*	*4*	*1*	..	*3*	*1*
B	Preparation and Supply of Material Substances.	1,756	1,054	305	54	104	202	37
III	*Industry*	*1,038*	*610*	*193*	*30*	*76*	*108*	*21*
IV	*Transport*	*165*	*118*	*10*	*7*	*4*	*24*	*2*
V	*Trade*	*553*	*326*	*102*	*17*	*24*	*70*	*14*
C	Public Administration and Liberal Arts.	286	210	18	14	4	38	2
VI	*Public Force* ..	*56*	*49*	..	*1*	..	*6*	..
VII	*Public Administration* ..	*69*	*55*	*2*	*2*	*1*	*9*	..
VIII	*Professions and Liberal Arts.*	*161*	*106*	*16*	*11*	*3*	*23*	*2*
D	Miscellaneous ..	1,374	427	223	42	523	58	101
IX	*Persons living on their income.*	*16*	*9*	*2*	*1*	..	*4*	..
X	*Domestic Service* ..	*751*	*107*	*53*	*17*	*469*	*14*	*91*
XI	*Insufficiently described occupations.*	*503*	*260*	*142*	*12*	*46*	*34*	*9*
XII	*Unproductive* ..	*104*	*51*	*26*	*12*	*8*	*6*	*1*

It will of course be observed that the 10,000 occupations above do not represent 10,000 individuals, 884 of these occupations are subsidiary to others, so that the whole 10,000 occupations afford a means of subsistence to 9,116 workers only. Of these 9,116, earners number 7,421, of whom 884, that is nearly one-eighth, have secondary occupations in addition to their principal occupations. The remaining 1,691 are dependants assisting earners either directly in the occupation by which they earn, or indirectly, *e.g.* by working on the land of a husband or father whose occupation is returned as cultivating owner, or, to give another instance, by weaving, for the occupation of dependants has been shown according to the occupation itself and not according to the occupation of the earner on which dependent. It is hardly necessary to draw attention to the great preponderance of agriculture, whether as the principal or subsidiary occupation and for dependants no less than for earners, and of the females returned as having domestic service as a dependent occupation it is practically certain that a large proportion also help in the fields. Those returned as being of insufficiently described occupations probably belong for the most part to Class B, consisting as they do of persons who have returned their occupation by some such vague term as contractor, shop-keeper, clerk, labourer, without giving the information necessary to classify them in any definite category. It is likely therefore that those engaged in the preparation and supply of material substances number some 2,000 in every 10,000 instead of only 1,756.

PROPORTIONATE DISTRIBUTION OF OCCUPATIONS

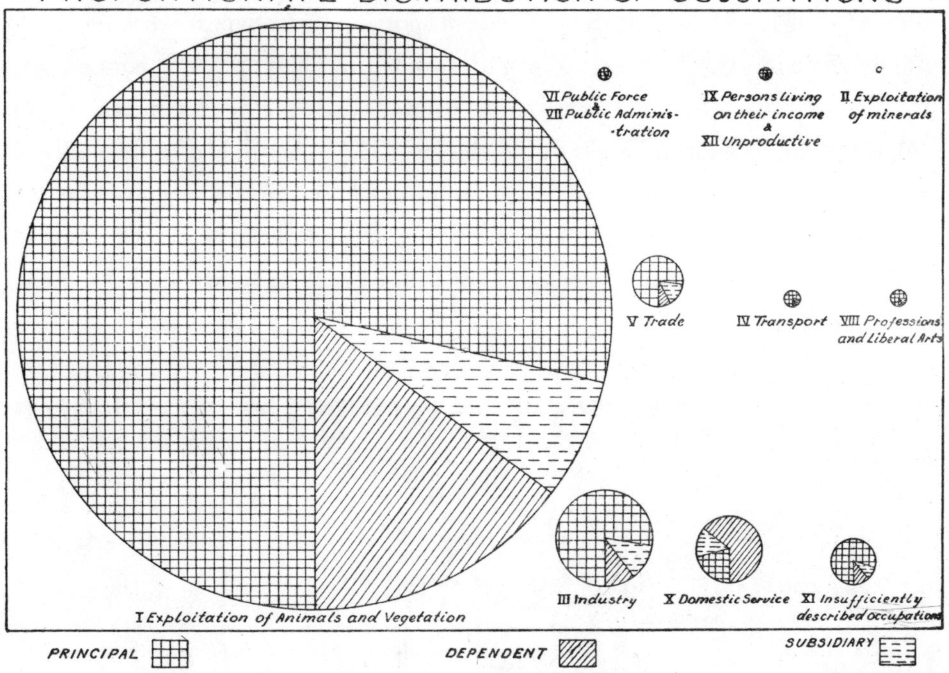

The comparative occupational constitution of the larger geographical units is shown in the following table and illustrated graphically in the diagram below, subsidiary occupations being included in both cases :—

Class or sub-class and description of occupation.	Distribution of 1,000 occupations in									
	Assam.	Bengal.	Bihar and Orissa.	Bombay.	Burma.	Central Provinces.	Madras.	Punjab.	United Provinces.	Hyderabad State.
A. and B.										
I. Exploitation of animals and vegetation.	814	680	747	676	678	800	462	634	745	568
II. Exploitation of Minerals.	4	2	8	1	6	2	1	1	..	4
III. Industry ..	83	88	83	113	118	83	88	170	117	107
IV. Transport ..	17	20	9	20	41	12	13	21	9	45
V. Trade ..	38	68	44	51	93	44	42	60	51	119
C. Public Administration, Professions & Liberal Arts.	18	28	17	39	44	20	22	41	20	38
D. Others	26	114	92	100	20	39	372	73	58	119

Some of the apparent vagaries of these figures call for a word of comment. The very high figure against D in Madras is caused by the large numbers of insufficiently described occupations, probably to be redistributed between I, III and V. The high proportion of industrial occupations in the Punjab is a recurrent feature and was noticed at any rate in 1911. In Burma the high proportion of trade is largely induced by the extent to which women engage in trade both as a principal and as a subsidiary occupation ; the unexpected industrial figure is again occasioned by the participation of women as dependent workers and probably by the extent to which village industries are practised as subsidiary to agriculture or other occupations and the high figure of transport reflects the comparatively sparse population scattered in many cases on long lines of communication by river or by road. Similarly in Hyderabad State the high proportion of transport workers is possibly due to the comparative absence, at any rate till recently, of easy communications by road or rail. It should perhaps be pointed out that in Assam tea appears in sub-class I as agricultural and not in sub-class III. The table of course only shows the comparative distribution within each province, but in the diagram that follows, the base of each distribution column is proportionate to the total population of each province, subsidiary occupations again being included in the distribution of occupations.

COMPARATIVE DISTRIBUTION OF OCCUPATIONS IN THE LARGER PROVINCES

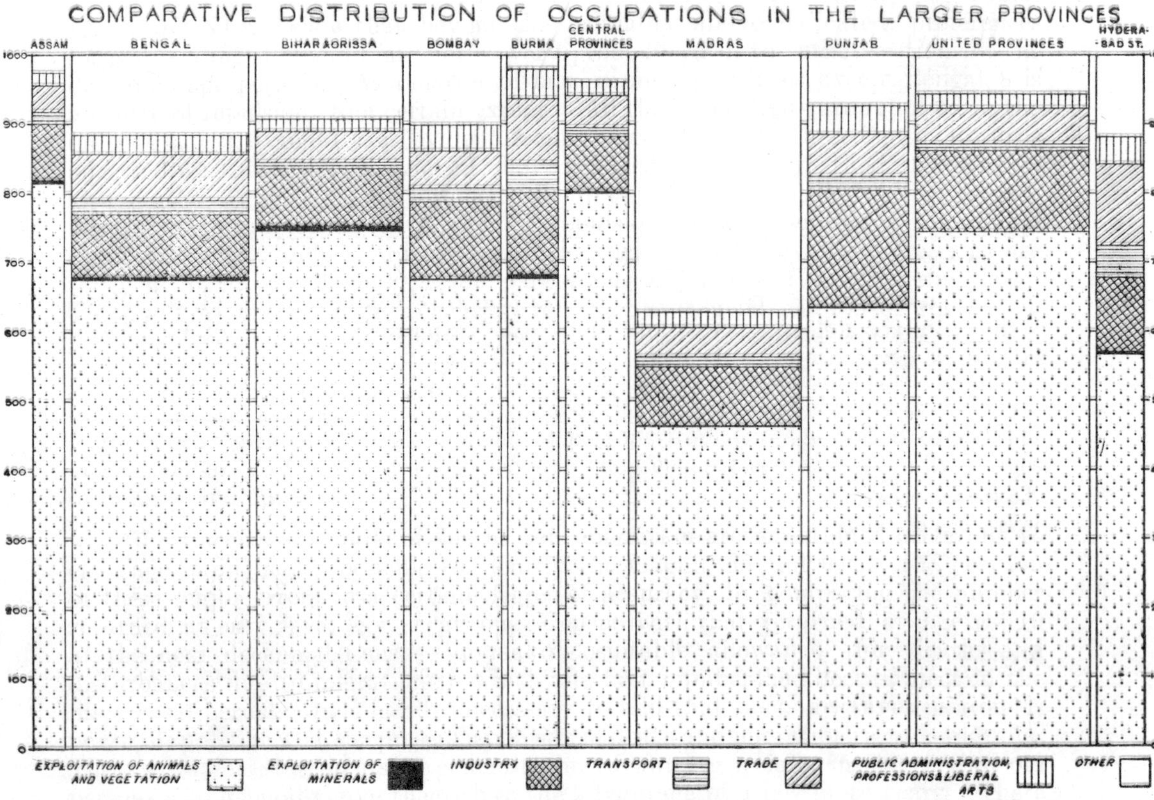

Changes in Distribution. **119.** In order to compare the distribution of occupations in 1931 with that disclosed by the census of 1921 it is necessary to exclude from the 1931 figures the numbers of subsidiary occupations and to calculate the 1921 figures on workers

only. The marginal table gives the comparative results. It should be made clear at the outset that the decrease in class A, caused undoubtedly by the decrease in sub-class I, for II has hardly changed, is apparent rather than real. The decrease on paper is one of 507, per 10,000, and this is more than balanced by the increase of 535 in class X. The change is due to the number of females, 572 per 10,000 workers, who have returned their occupation as domestic service. In 1921 these would have appeared as workers (mainly if not entirely agricultural) in the occupations in which they assisted the male members of their families. Similarly the decrease in class B of 94 per 10,000 divided between Industry,—78, and Trade,—35, but balanced in part by the increase under Transport, is largely met by the increase of 99 in class XI.

Class or sub-class.	Means of subsistence.	Distribution of 10,000 workers in	
		1921.	1931.
A.	Production of Raw Material	7,241	6,734
I	*Exploitation of Animals and Vegetation.*	*7,217*	*6,711*
II	*Exploitation of Minerals* ..	*24*	*23*
B.	Preparation and Supply of Material Substances.	1,759	1,665
III	*Industry*	*1,075*	*997*
IV	*Transport*	*134*	*153*
V	*Trade*	*550*	*515*
C.	Public Administration and Liberal Arts.	283	269
VI	*Public Force*	*71*	*55*
VII	*Public Administration* ..	*69*	*64*
VIII	*Professions and Liberal Arts.*	*143*	*150*
D.	Miscellaneous	717	1,332
IX	*Persons living on their income.*	*13*	*14*
X	*Domestic Service*	*173*	*708*
XI	*Insufficiently described occupations.*	*406*	*505*
XII	*Unproductive*	*125*	*105*

The insufficiently described occupations in that class are, at any rate in the great majority of cases, general terms connected with industry and trade such as 'shopkeeper', 'trade', 'contractor' or 'coolie' which cannot be allotted to any particular category. It is possible that the greater prevalence of unemployment in 1931 as compared to 1921 has contributed to diverting returns from definite to indefinite categories. The census schedule contained no provision for any distinction between a man employed in his normal calling and one having a calling but temporarily unoccupied, and in the case of many callings in industry and trade the distinctive function of the individual will largely depend on what he is doing at the time when the census takes place, since the particular direction of his energies will normally vary from time to time according to the demand for labour or goods or the nature of openings that present themselves. Thus a labour contractor might be returned at one census under transport by road, at another transport by rail and at a third under transport by water according to the purpose for which he supplied the labour. If without a contract, he would be a contractor and nothing more, and therefore relegated to class XI. The same obviously applies to much labour and in point of fact to a considerable volume of industrial and trading occupations in India where industry in general is less specialised and functions less differentiated than in highly industrialized countries of the west. The other changes since 1921 call for little comment. The increase in sub-class IV, Transport, is natural and expected. Communications have everywhere increased, roads are better, and motor traffic has become ubiquitous during the decade. Indeed if there is any cause for doubt it is whether the increase has not really been greater than that indicated by the figures. The increase in sub-class VIII, Professions and Liberal Arts, is the natural accompaniment of the gradual spread of literacy. The decreases in sub-classes VI and VII—Public Force and Public Administration, indicate either that there has been no increase in those occupations which is commensurate with the increase in population, or an absolute decrease which is very slight except in the case of the Army. There has also been a decrease in sub-class XII which comprises inmates of asylums, gaols and institutions, beggars, vagrants, prostitutes and similar classes. It will be observed from the more detailed examination of the figures in § *ii* of this chapter that there is a general tendency towards increase in what may be described as modernized occupations, though the degree of that increase is perhaps less than one would be inclined to expect to find.

Subsidiary Occupations.

120. For subsidiary occupations no complete means of comparison with 1921 is available. In 1911 however figures were given of the numbers of actual workers who were partly agricultural but whose principal occupation was not agriculture. These totalled 53 per 1,000 for India while those who returned agriculture as a subsidiary occupation in 1931 numbered 44 per 1,000, almost certainly an understatement, and it is probably not without significance that there are just 9 females per mille of all occupations who have returned domestic service as their subsidiary occupation ; it is likely that they help in agriculture as well. The tendency when in doubt is to return agriculture as the principal occupation on account of its respectable status, in preference to returning it as subsidiary, and in any case the returns of subsidiary occupations of all kinds are probably below the real figure. The distribution of 1,000 subsidiary occupations is shown in the marginal table, and the diagram below shows a comparison between the distribution of occupations followed as principal and as subsidiary as well as the occupations of dependent workers. It will be noticed that the distribution by subsidiary occupation corresponds generally to that by principal occupation after allowing for the preference already pointed out for returning an agricultural profession as principal in case of any conflict between that and some non-agricultural calling. In class D the subsidiary occupations are weighted by the returns of domestic service as subsidiary, this representing the contribution of women to the general family maintenance by their household services often performed in addition to help in the fields, and in Assam and Burma in addition to spinning, weaving and dyeing silk or cotton and other cottage industries such as the rearing of silkworms. The importance of subsidiary occupations was brought out by the enquiries of the Banking Enquiry Committee which in the United Provinces at any rate attributed to their subsidiary occupations the comparative freedom of a considerable proportion of the peasantry from heavy indebtedness.

Class and sub-class.	Distribution of 1,000 workers each in	
	Principal occupations.	Subsidiary occupations.
A.	698	505
I	*696*	*500*
II	*2*	*5*
B.	183	270
III	*108*	*146*
IV	*17*	*29*
V	*58*	*95*
C.	31	45
VI	*7*	*7*
VII	*8*	*10*
VIII	*16*	*28*
D.	88	180
IX	*2*	*4*
X	*22*	*119*
XI	*54*	*49*
XII	*10*	*8*
Total ..	1,000	1,000

Dependent Occupations.

121. The occupations of dependants, as might be expected are a little differently distributed. The marginal table shows the comparative distribution of 1,000 of each of principal and dependent occupations. The main difference here is in the comparatively small proportion of dependants who are occupied in class C (a difference which naturally follows from the nature of the occupations falling into that class) and in the high figures of class D. These figures are determined by those of sub-class X, which contains the large numbers of female dependants who have returned domestic service as their occupation. In very many cases it is combined with assistance given in other occupations as already indicated. Otherwise the distribution is again generally on similar lines to that in principal and subsidiary occupations, indicating that the census figures as a whole give a reasonably accurate conception of the general distribution of functions in the community.

Class and sub-class.	Distribution of 1,000 each of	
	Earners (principal occupation).	Working Dependants.
A.	698	563
I	*696*	*562*
II	*2*	*1*
B.	183	93
III	*108*	*63*
IV	*17*	*6*
V	*58*	*24*
C.	31	11
VI	*7*	*1*
VII	*8*	*2*
VIII	*16*	*8*
D.	88	333
IX	*2*	..
X	*22*	*287*
XI	*54*	*34*
XII	*10*	*12*
Total ..	1,000	1,000

It is, however, very clear that the proportion of working to non-working dependants is very much higher in agriculture (sub-class I) than in any other means of subsistence. Excluding sub-class X, in which the females who have returned domestic service as a dependent or subsidiary occupation really belong to some other sub-class, working dependants are to earners as 19 to 100 in agriculture, etc., as 14 to 100 in insufficiently described occupations, as 13 to 100 in Industry, and as 9 to 100 in Trade.

COMPARATIVE DISTRIBUTION OF OCCUPATIONS DEPENDENT, PRINCIPAL & SUBSIDIARY

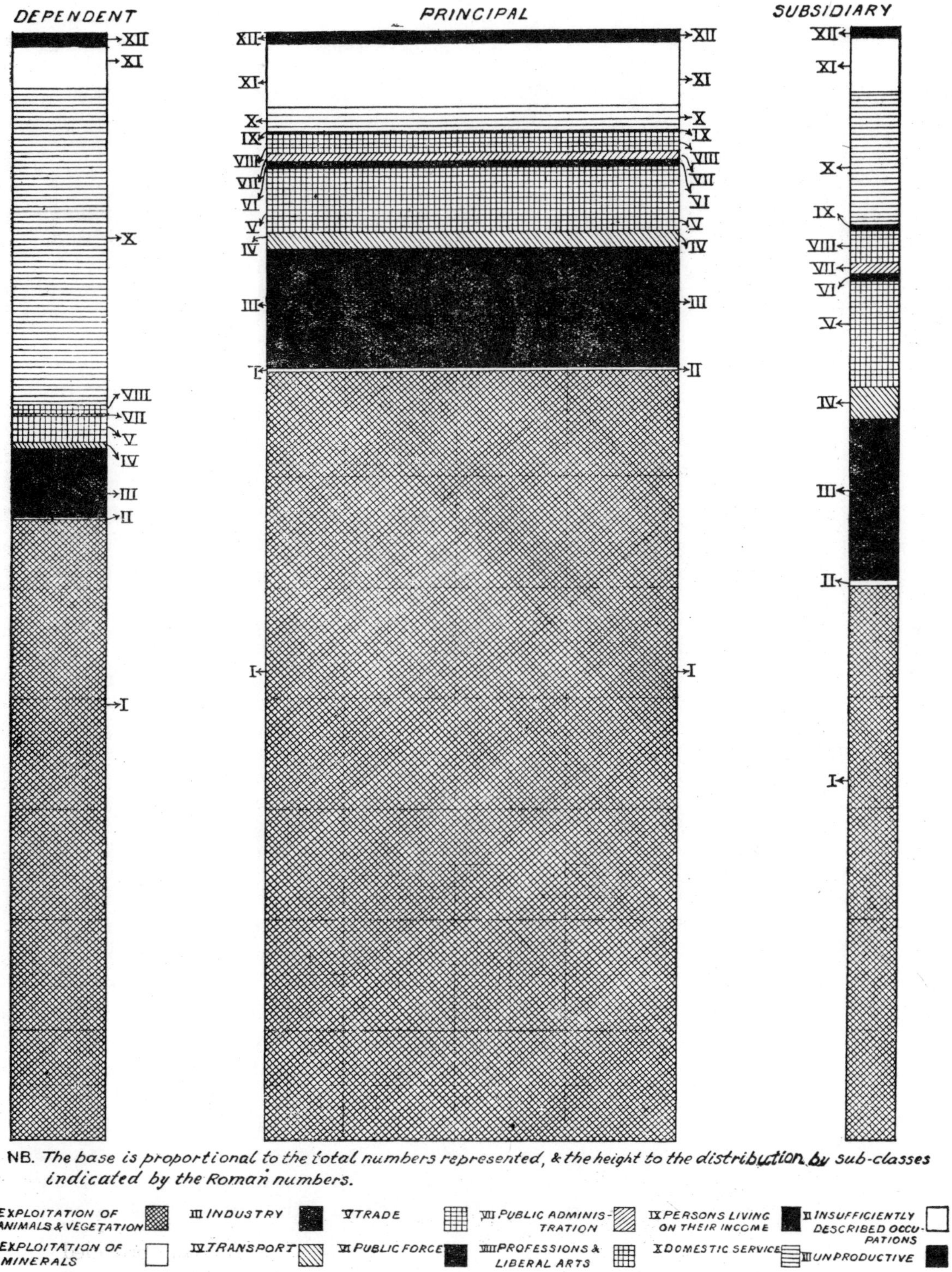

NB. *The base is proportional to the total numbers represented, & the height to the distribution by sub-classes indicated by the Roman numbers.*

Occupation by Sex.

122. The distribution of occupation by sex is indicated in the marginal table which shows the proportion by sex for one thousand in each sub-class. Dependent and subsidiary workers are included, though the proportion of females to males is naturally much higher among working dependants than it is among earners either in principal or subsidiary occupations. Thus in subsidiary occupations alone there are in every 1,000 earners only 239 females to 761 males, while if 'domestic service' be excluded, the figure of females per 1,000 workers falls to 154. Among earners in principal occupations again the number of females per 1,000 earners is 222. Among working dependants on the other hand females number 733 to 267 males, while if principal and dependent occupations be taken together, excluding subsidiary occupations, which only represent the duplication of occupations by individuals already counted, the proportion of actual female workers to male is 317 to 683 in every 1,000. The proportion of actual female workers has likewise fallen heavily in all sub-classes with the exception of course of X, which shows a great increase, the fall being particularly marked in in sub-classes I, II, XI and XII and only rather less so in III, V and IX. The figures are given for 1931 in the margin. The proportion of actual female workers to male in the whole population has increased since last census from 455 per mille of actual male workers to 465, undoubtedly on account of the inclusion of domestic service as a possible return of occupation for working dependants. If this sub-class X, be excluded, together with XI, Insufficiently described, and XII Unproductive occupations, the highest proportion of actual female workers is in Industry, but this proportion is determined by the figures in a very few groups. In order 9, Ceramics, group 63, *Potters and makers of earthenware*, shows 309 actual female workers per mille to 691 males; in order 12, Industries of dress, etc., group 85, *Washing and cleaning*, has a higher ratio with 417 females to 583 males; but it is in order 11, Food industries, that the female ratio goes highest (522). Here in group 74, *Makers of sugar, molasses and gur* there are 527 actual female workers to 473 male, in group 72, *grain-parchers*, there are 626 to 374, and in group 71, *Rice-pounders and huskers, and flour grinders* there are 815 females to every 185 actual male workers. The next sub-class in order of the female ratio is agriculture, where the female element is principally provided in the form of labour in the fields—group 7

Number and descripton of sub-class.	Number per 1,000 workers in principal, dependent and subsidiary occupations, of Males.	Females.
I.—Exploitation of animals and vegetation	729	271
II.—Exploitation of Minerals ..	758	242
III.—Industry ..	720	280
IV.—Transport ..	901	99
V.—Trade ..	747	253
VI.—Public Force ..	992	8
VII.—Public Administration.. ..	970	30
VIII.—Professions and Liberal Arts ..	872	128
IX.—Persons living on their incomes ..	820	180
X.—Domestic Service	184	816
XI.—Insufficiently described occupations	608	392
XII.—Unproductive	658	342

AGRICULTURAL & PASTORAL OCCUPATIONS

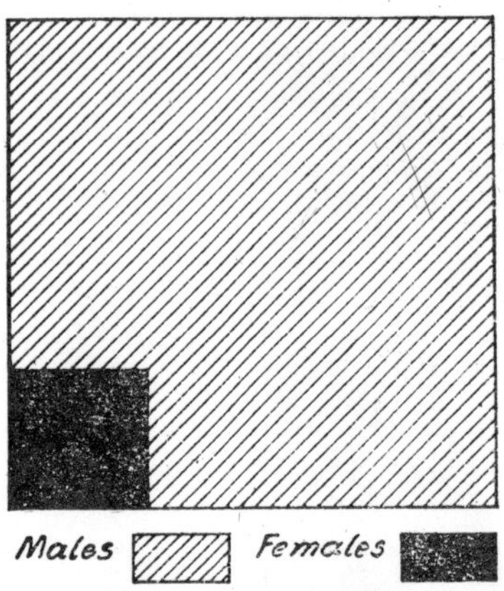

Sub-class.	Number of females in every 1,000 actual workers.
All	317
I	279
II	250
III	297
IV	103
V	269
VII	33
VIII	140
IX	218
X	808
XI	409
XII	351

has 457 actual female workers to 543 male, and in that of labour in special cultivation, for group 15, *Tea*, shows 456 female to 544 actual male workers. Group 19, *Collectors of forest produce*, has a majority of female workers but the absolute numbers are very small in any case. The next highest ratio is found in sub-class V, Trade. Here order 32 (other trade in foodstuffs) shows a high proportion of female workers in group 131, *Dairy produce, eggs and poultry*, 514 females to 486 males, and order 37, Trade in fuel, shows 557 female to 443 male workers as *Dealers in charcoal, cowdung and firewood*. Finally in sub-class VIII, Professions and Liberal Arts, order 47, Medicine, shows a ratio of 707 actual female workers to 293 male in group 172, *Midwives, compounders, nurses, etc.*, in which the female element is obviously likely to be high, though the figures of this group are not enough to affect perceptibly the ratio for the sub-class as a whole, in which it is lower than in any other sub-classes except Public Force, Public Administration and Transport.

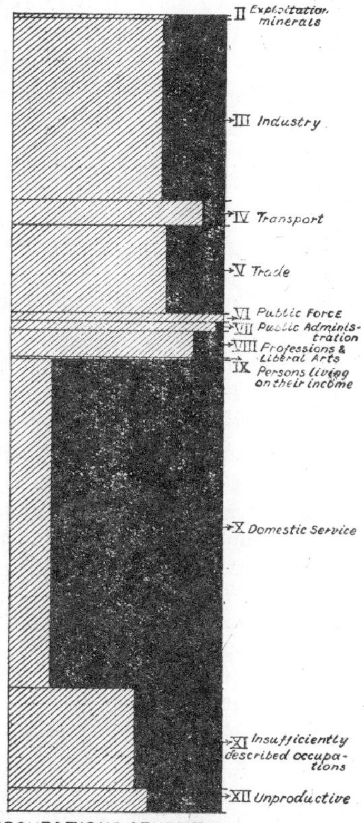

OCCUPATIONS OTHER THAN AGRICULTURE ETC.

Males ▨ Females ■

123. It has already been explained that at this census special returns from establishments employing organized labour were not called for, and that owing to the necessity for retrenchment at the compilation stage one of the sorts abandoned was that for the return of industry made on the general schedule, as most Census Superintendents regarded the returns in this column as not very satisfactory. In any case the number of workers employed in organized labour is extraordinarily low for a population the size of India's and the daily average number of hands employed by establishments in British India to which the Factories Act applies is only 1,553,169. The total India figure for persons occupied in plantations, mines, industry and transport in 1921 was 24,239,555 of whom only 2,685,909 were employed in mines, plantations or organised industrial establishments having 10 or more employees. **Organized Industry.** The total figure under the three same heads in 1931 amounts to 26,187,689, and if labour in similar establishments is in the same proportion it will now number 2,901,776. Figures of the daily average of persons employed indicate that it has increased during the last decade at the rate of about 30 per cent., in which case it will now number 3,500,000. Probably 5,000,000 may be fairly taken as the figure of organized labour in India in 1931, as the figure of 3½ million represents only the daily attendance in registered factories. It has been claimed that Indian factory labour is very largely of the casual description; that it is not skilled and it is not recruited even from the hereditary trades to which it might be expected to look for its supply; that while the hereditary weaver is maintaining a precarious existence weaving *khaddar* at greater cost than is required for machine-made fabric, the mills producing the latter seek their labour in the casual labour market, recruiting very largely from agriculturists who come and work in the mills for a time and then go back to their villages; and that the same applies to most forms of factory labour in India. It is true that industrial labour is continually changing—a fact obvious enough at the census when the final enumeration was checked against the preliminary one, but the bulk of it is probably semi-skilled, and in any case factory conditions bear little relation to hereditary handicraft. The conditions under which it lives are frequently incredibly squalid and overcrowded (*vide*, for instance, paragraphs 43 and 51 above) and there is little wonder that countrymen will not bring their wives and families to live in industrial centres if they can help it. Housing conditions may be bad in villages but there is at any rate plenty of space outside the village. The general result is that factory labour is largely recruited from younger sons for whom there is no land or need at home, village servants for whom there is no work and whom the village is unwilling to maintain, cultivators in debt who

need cash to pay off a mortgage, ne'er-do-weels who have attracted too much attention to themselves at home, and women frequently of equivocal status. The conditions under which this labour force lives result in a very heavy incidence of disease and mortality; it has already been pointed out (paragraph 109 above) that coolies and factory hands provide the majority of leprosy cases. This kind of labour when unprotected is easily sweated. The growth, for instance, of the tobacco industry is pointed out below, and the number of persons employed in this industry has increased from less than 48,000 in 1921 to nearly 148,000 in 1931. They work mainly in *biri* factories which employ no mechanical power and are therefore outside the operation of the Factories Act. Much child labour is employed and the Whitley Commission remarked that "workers as young as five years of age may be found in some of these places working without adequate meal intervals or weekly rest days, and often for 10 or 12 hours daily, for sums as low as 2 annas in the case of those of tenderest years". The factories themselves are often merely slum buildings occupied for the purpose. The Census Superintendent of Madras writes of the *biri* making industry as follows :—

"There is great variety in size in the manufacturing units; it depends chiefly on the premises available. Where a godown or shed is used the employees may run up to 150 or 200; where a house is used 50 would be a maximum and 30 an average. There is a good deal of employment of children and long hours. Parents take a small advance from the employer of their children and so are little disposed to protest unduly or to withdraw them. The lighting and sanitary arrangements of the establishments are far from good, or are almost nil. Payment is by outturn, generally about 12 annas a thousand. The ordinary workman's performance would be about 100 an hour. Children are usually paid by the week, payment varying with capacity and age. The Factory Act does not apply to these places because no power is used. If section 2 were extended to them, it could be defeated by keeping the numbers below ten. A tendency towards smaller units seems already apparent. North Arcot is one of the strongholds of beedi making, with 74 factories and 1,200 workers, half of whom were children. These factories are essentially fluctuating in nature. They can be set up, closed and transferred with equal ease. It is certain that a good deal of this form of employment has not entered the census returns."

A non-official bill has been introduced to deal with the *biri* industry in Madras, but the evil is very far from being confined to that province and the Census Superintendent of the Central Provinces and Berar draws attention to the conditions of this industry in Bhandara and Jubbulpore. Similar conditions will probably be found to exist in other industries which do not employ mechanical power, and India may be fortunate in the present backwardness of her industrial development if it enables her to avoid allowing it to grow further on these lines. There are, it is true, a few notable exceptions to the general conditions of the housing and treatment of labour, and Jamshedpur has already been mentioned (paragraph 51); Messrs. Binny at Madras and the Empress Mills at Nagpur might be added, but the industrial concerns which pay much attention to the accommodation of their employees outside the factory itself are the exception and very far from being the rule, though inside the factories themselves conditions are generally satisfactory in the case of establishments within the scope of the Factories Act.

Section ii—Statistics of Orders and Groups.

Exploitation of animals and Vegetation.

124. Order I, **Pasture and Agriculture,** occupies 71 per cent. of the actual workers of India, or, if those be excluded who follow it only as subsidiary to some other occupation, 67 per cent. The great majority of these are occupied in agriculture proper, and are shown in sub-order (*a*) **Cultivation** as distinct from (*b*) Cultivation of Special Crops, Fruit, etc., (*c*) Forestry, (*d*) Stock-raising and (*e*) the Raising of Small Animals and Insects. The marginal table shows the proportional figures of the sub-orders of Order I. Sub-order (*a*) was in 1921 divided into Rent-receivers, Cultivators, Agents, etc., Farm servants and Field labourers. No attempt was made to distinguish the two latter categories this time, but that of cultivators was divided into cultivating owners, cultivating tenants and cultivators of jhum and shifting areas, and the category of

Distribution of 1,000 occupations in Order I.
Pasture and Agriculture.

Sub-order.	No. per mille of total.
(*a*) Cultivation	943
(*b*) Cultivation of Special Crops, Fruit, etc.	17
(*c*) Forestry	4
(*e*) Stock-raising	35
(*d*) Raising of Insects, etc. ..	1

agents was divided up into agents of owners, agents of Government, rent collectors, clerks, etc. The first group, that of landlords, is in effect the same as in 1921, for though it was desired to distinguish real agricultural non-cultivating proprietors from those whose interest in the land was indirect, it proved quite impossible in practice and it was ultimately necessary to define landlords as rent-receivers and include all non-cultivators receiving income in money or kind from the labours of others on the land. Rights in land in India are complicated and involved to a degree incredible to persons familiar only with the simpler tenures of western Europe, and between the man who cultivates it and the man who nominally owns it there are often a number of intermediate holders of some interest or other in the produce of the land. Holders of such intermediate rights have technical names which vary from one locality to another and any attempt to classify and sort for them would involve technicalities much too numerous and intricate for a census staff to deal with, apart from the fact that the actual rights involved are frequently the subject of highly controversial dispute among the parties concerned. Group I therefore of *Non-cultivating Proprietors taking Rent in Money or Kind*, includes all persons returned under the convenient label of 'rent receiver', a simple definition easily understood, and numbers 4 per cent. of the total of occupations described as 'cultivation', of which percentage less than a quarter are subsidiary to some other calling. The great bulk of cultivators appear in groups 5, 6 and 7 as *Cultivating Owners*, *Tenant Cultivators* or *Agricultural Labourers*, fairly evenly divided as regards total numbers, owners being the fewest of the three and labourers including large numbers of working dependants who assist either owners or tenants in the cultivation of their holdings. A difficulty of definition was also raised by the term 'cultivating owners'. Freehold tenures, as understood in Britain, are conspicuous by their absence in India generally, and the variety of tenancies and sub-tenancies particularly in Bengal, is legion. A census definition of ownership was found unexpectedly difficult to frame in any simple manner which would be consistent in most provinces, and ultimately ownership was defined as the possession of rights of occupancy, a term which covered all cultivators holding on a lease from Government as well as many others with a conditional or preferential right to their holdings subject to periodic reassessment of rents. Such owners formed 27 per cent. of the total engaged in cultivation and 18 per cent. of the total of actual workers in all occupations, these percentages including those for whom such ownership was only a subsidiary means of subsistence. The only previous figures which attempted to make any sort of distinction between owners and tenants were those of 1891. They are not strictly comparable, as the figures given include all non-working dependants, but in so far as they afford any comparison they indicate an increased proportion in 1931 of cultivating owners to cultivating tenants. The figures are given below:

1891.			1931.		
Census description.	Population supported.	Ratio.	Census description.	Number of workers.	Ratio.
Land occupants, cultivating.	45,354,183	533	Cultivating owners	28,397,214	784
Tenants and sharers, cultivating.	85,164,663	1,000	Tenant cultivators	36,238,654	1,000

On the other hand the Census Superintendent in Burma reports that alienation of land to non-agriculturists has increased and that in the principal districts of Lower Burma the area held by Chettiars increased by 140 per cent. between July 1st, 1930 and June 30th, 1932. That this has also taken place in India generally is perhaps suggested by the apparent increase in the proportion of agricultural labourers to owners and tenant cultivators. These two categories appeared in 1921 under the common designation " ordinary cultivators ", and for every 1,000 ordinary cultivators there were 290 agricultural labourers who then appeared in two groups as " farm servants " and " field labourers ". In 1931 it must be remembered that the working dependants of owner and tenant cultivators have appeared as dependent workers in the category of agricultural labour, and the proportion therefore of agricultural labourers to cultivators is inflated by these figures, yielding 515 labourers for 1,000 cultivators if all actual workers are taken and 519 if subsidiary occupation be also included. If however we rely on principal occupation alone, into which the figures of working dependants do not enter at all in 1931, we find that to every 1,000 cultivators there are 466 agricultural labourers, a very much higher ratio than in 1921. Probably the fairest comparison would be to take the 1931 figures of cultivating owners and tenant cultivators both principal and dependent and to compare them with the number of those only who returned agricultural labour as their principal occupation, in which case the resulting ratio is 407 agricultural labourers to every 1,000 cultivators. In any case the change in ratio is somewhat remarkable, even when adopting the lowest ratio which can be compared with that of 1921. Possibly the explanation is that a large increase has taken place in the agricultural population without a corresponding increase in actual holders of land whether as tenants or owners though it is likely that a concentration of land in the hands of non-cultivating owners is also taking place.

	1921. Workers.		1931.	
	Farm servants *plus* Field labourers.	Ordinary Cultivators.	Principal occupation. Agricultural labourers.	Actual Workers. Cultivating owners *plus* Tenant cultivators.
Total figures ..	21,676,107	74,664,886	24,925,357	61,180,004
Ratio ..	291	1,000	407	1,000

The marginal table shows the distribution per 1,000 of occupations defined as cultivation and the number of each per 1,000 of actual workers in all occupations. Cultivators of *jhum*, *taungya* and shifting areas are mostly members of hill and forest tribes whose land is irrigable if at all only with excessive difficulty and who are therefore compelled to clear fresh areas for cultivation, as the growth of weeds in cleared areas makes cultivation impossible after a couple of years. After a period of fallow, which varies according to the land available, the plot is again cleared and cultivated. The method is wasteful and leads to denudation of the hillsides but is not only the sole method commonly known to those that practise it, and their only means of subsistence, but frequently the only method of cultivation possible on hilly and ill-watered slopes. Cultivators of shifting areas have been classified separately from cultivating owners as not only are the methods practised and the results obtained very different, but the right of possession in individual plots has not everywhere been recognised by the state, though among the tribesmen themselves the land thus intermittently cultivated is frequently regarded as a permanent and heritable possession, the subject of sales, mortgages, wills and marriage settlements.

	Distribution of 1,000 occupations in Order I (*a*) *Cultivation*.				Number per 1,000 of total actual workers.
Group number.	Total.	Principal.	Dependent.	Subsidiary.	
1. Rent-receivers	40	29	3	8	27
5. Cultivating owners.	275	228	33	14	184
6. Cultivating tenants.	350	288	42	20	235
7. Agricultural labourers.	324	241	63	20	218
8. Cultivators of shifting areas.	8	7	1	..	5
2, 3 and 4, Agents, clerks, etc.	3	1	..	1	2

If a comparison be made between the area of land under crops and the number of agriculturalists actually engaged in cultivation the result found for British India is that for each agriculturalist there is 2·9 acres of cropped land of which 0·65 of an acre is irrigated. The corresponding figures for 1921 are 2·7 and 0·61. If however we take only the figures of owner and tenant cultivators, excluding, rent-receivers, agents and agricultural labourers, we find that each cultivator has four and a half acres to cultivate, and of irrigated land, excluding in this case the *jhumiyas* (cultivators of shifting areas), each cultivator has just over an acre. The apparent increase in cultivated area per cultivator over 1921 in this case is nearly an acre, but the 1921 figures of ordinary cultivators probably include a number of dependants who have appeared in 1931 under 'domestic service', and the real extent of the increase in land under cultivation per cultivator is probably not more than one-fifth of an acre if indeed there is any such increase at all. Similarly the apparent decrease of agriculturalists since 1921 suggested by the figures in the margin is not to be taken at its face value, on account of the transfer of returns to 'domestic service' and to the unspecified category, and even the apparent decrease indicated in the margin is transformed to an increase of three millions when the states are included. This is not without significance, as it is in the states that there has been the greatest rate of increase in population since 1921, and in the states as a whole that there is the least pressure of population on space, though the available land is generally poorer than in British India. It seems likely therefore that the increase of agriculturalists is resulting in the extension of cultivation to areas which yield a low economic return.

British India.

Census.	Cultivated acreage.	Cultivators.	Agriculturalists.
1921 ..	212,259,506	59,205,285	79,654,841
1931 ..	228,160,853	50,015,428	78,545,253

The cultivation of special crops occupies a mere fraction of the population concerned in pasture and agriculture, under 2%, the greater part of which is engaged in the production of tea. The persons whose principal, dependent or subsidiary occupation contributes to tea-production number over a million, and over 45% of them women. If the miscellaneous group of market-gardeners, flower and fruit growers be omitted, the special crop occupying the next highest number is coconut, on which 203,000 odd are employed, though here there must be a very considerable output grown by ordinary cultivators who do not even appear at all as growers of special crops. Similarly in the case of *pan*, though normally this is a specialized crop, considerable quantities are grown, at any rate in the hills, by cultivators who combine the care of *pan*-vines grown in the forest with their other avocations.

Distribution of 1,000 occupied in the growing of special crops.

Cinchona	1
Coconut	106
Coffee	29
Pan-vine	56
Rubber	10
Tea	561
Miscellaneous	237

Forestry, Order 1 (*c*), employs still fewer than special cultivation—4 per mille only of the total in order 1 and more than half of them woodcutters and charcoal-burners. Forest officers, rangers and guards amount to less than an eighth of this 4 per mille and the rest are collectors of forest produce, among whom collectors of lac have fallen since 1921 by more than 50%. The value of lac has fallen since the war-time boom, but it is possible that this decrease is more than balanced by the coming into existence of 34,000 lac cultivators—Order 1(*e*), **Raising of Small Animals and Insects,** who do not figure at all in the 1921 Occupation Table and whose numbers are not apparently relevant to those of the corresponding sub-order at that census, as keepers of bees and birds show an increase and of silkworms only a numerically small decrease, which becomes an increase if subsidiary occupations are included.

The remaining Sub-Order, 1(*d*), **Stock raising** is, after cultivation, that which provides most occupations, but only 36 per mille of the whole order of pasture and agriculture. Cattle and buffalo graziers account for over a million, shepherds, goat-herds, pig-breeders, etc., for nearly three million, and breeders of horses and other transport animals for less than 45,000.

Order 2, **'Fishing and Hunting'** employs even fewer than Sub-order 1(*b*) of special cultivation. Here again fishing is an occupation often combined with agriculture. Moreover, it is one which in Hindu society is looked on askance, and this probably tends to reduce the number of returns very considerably. As a principal occupation the numbers occupied in fishing and pearling run into six figures only in Bengal and Madras.

Exploitation of Minerals.

125. Reference has already been made to the changes in the arrangement of the groups in class II, in which the three orders of 1921, Mines, Quarries and Salt, have given place to two only, **Metallic** and **Non-metallic minerals,** while the six groups, under the former three orders have become thirteen. The figures under each group are unexpectedly low, the largest being those under coal which occupies 205,000 persons, and none of the other groups reach a quarter of this figure. There has been a positive decrease of actual workers since 1921 amounting to over 1,000, a decrease of 26,000 female workers being balanced by an increase of 25,000 male workers, probably in part at any rate as a result of legislation restricting the employment of women underground. After coal the extraction of building materials, including stone, clays and material for cement, occupies the next highest number, then the manufacture of salt and saline substances and then the extraction of petroleum. The relative figures are given in marginal table.

Distribution of 1,000 workers in the extraction of minerals.

Metallic minerals—	
Gold	30
Iron	30
Lead, silver and zinc	23
Manganese	35
Tin and wolfram	12
Others	4
Non-metallic minerals—	
Coal	507
Petroleum	69
Building materials	125
Mica	31
Precious stones	19
Salt, etc.	108
Others	7
Total	1,000

Industry.

126. Industry occupies 10% of India's workers as compared to 11% in 1921. The figures throughout the thirteen orders in this sub-class have a general correspondence to those of 1921 and are remarkable more for their consistency than for any change during the decade. Even in **Textiles** (Order 5), in which some marked increase might have been expected, the increase according to the returns is only 2% in actual workers, while for those whose employment is subsidiary no 1921 figures are available for comparison. Here again the slight decrease in the number of female workers, which is of course more than balanced by an increase in male, may possibly be accounted for by returns in sub-classes X or XI, but this decrease is one of less than 5,000 and therefore of no very great significance. The one industrial order in which a marked increase has taken place is No. 16, **Production and Transmission of Physical Force,** that is in heat, light, electricity, motive power, etc. This Order in 1921 occupied 11,514 actual workers, whereas the number has now risen to 23,650 in addition to which 1,257 have a subsidiary occupation under this head. If a more detailed examination be made, the same feature of a general constancy in the industrial returns is obvious, most groups showing a small increase though here and there a change is noticeable. Thus there has been an increase in silk spinners and weavers (group 47 in 1931, groups 34 and 35 in 1921) from 80,700 to 114,500 and 9,000 more have returned it as a subsidiary occupation. On the other hand group 50, *Lace, Crêpe, Embroideries etc., and insufficiently described Textile Industries,* has

Distribution of 1,000 workers in sub-class III, Industry.

Order.	Persons.
5. Textiles	258
6. Hides, skins, etc.	21
7. Wood	113
8. Metals	48
9. Ceramics	68
10. Chemical products, etc.	42
11. Food Industries	95
12. Industries of dress, etc.	223
13. Furniture	1
14. Building	40
15. Construction of means of Transport.	2
16. Production and Transmission of Heat, Power, etc.	1
17. Miscellaneous and Undefined.	88
Total	1,000

shrunk from 174,000 in 1921 to 32,000 in 1931, even when those employed in it as a subsidiary occupation only have been included. Similarly in Order 8, **Metals,** group 57, *Smelting, Forging and Rolling of Iron and Other Metals,* shows a noticeable decrease, while there is a pronounced increase in group 62, *Workers in Mints, Die-sinkers, etc.* In Order 9 (**Ceramics**) again *Brick and Tile Makers,* have decreased while *Other Workers in Ceramics* have increased, a difference possibly due merely to classification. Such an explanation however does not apply to the changes in order 10, **Chemical Products, etc.,** where there has been an increase of over 130% in group 66, *Manufacture of Matches, Fire-works and Other Explosives,* and of over 120% in group 67, *Manufacture of Aerated and Mineral Waters and Ice.* In Order 11, **Food Industries** the very marked decline in the numbers of group 76, *Toddy drawers,* and the decline, somewhat less marked, in group 77, *Brewers and Distillers,* was only to be expected and possibly represents an unwillingness to admit to an unpopular occupation as well as a real reduction in the numbers following these callings. On the other hand there has been a very considerable increase indeed in manufacturers of tobacco, an indication of the very rapid extension of the *biri*-making industry to which attention has already been drawn above (paragraph 123), and in regard to which the Census Superintendent for Madras writes as follows :—

	Number of actual workers in 1921.	Number of actual workers in 1931.
Toddy drawers	254,377	186,915
Brewers and Distillers.	6,893	5,953
Tobacco manufacturers.	47,857*	147,197†

*Includes manufacturers of ganja and opium.

†Includes 10,785 for whom the occupation is subsidiary to some other.

> " A general growth in the smoking habit has been noticeable to ordinary observation during the decade. The application of a tariff and the setting up of tobacco manufacture in or adjoining the presidency (Bangalore is a notable centre) led to considerable encouragement of cigarette smoking. At the end of the decade came the boycott of imported cigarettes and the *Beedi* came into its own. This is in essence a small quantity of powdered tobacco rolled in a special kind of leaf (usually imported from Bombay). Much *beedi* making is done as house industry, notably by Muslim women. It is among Muslims that *beedi* smoking seems to be most common, a fact borne out by the prominence of tobacco dealers in Malabar and North Arcot. *Beedis* are actually exported from Madras to Burma and the Malay States."

The 1921 figures given in the margin above include manufacturers of opium and *ganja* whose figure is not separable in the 1921 classification. These two have been returned separately this time and number only 604 taken together. Order 13, **Furniture Industries,** shows a considerable rise, from 10,000 to 17,000, in group 88, *Cabinet-makers, Carriage-painters, etc.,* while order 14, **Building Industries,** amalgamated this time into one group, shows a marked decline, 812,000 to 693,000, even when those following them as a subsidiary occupation are added. In Order 15, **Construction of Means of Transport,** the numbers in group 91, *Persons engaged in making, assembling or repairing motor vehicles or cycles,* shows a very natural increase from less than 5,000 to more than 13,000, exclusive of another 800 for whom it is a subsidiary occupation. *Carriage-makers and Wheelwrights* (group 92) however show no decrease but on the contrary quite a normal rise in numbers. *Ship and Boat Builders* (group 93), with whom aeroplane builders, if there are any, are classified, do nevertheless show an unmistakable decrease, and at least one Census Superintendent has pointed out that there has been a definite decline in the use of water transport. Reference has already been made to Order 16, and the final order in this sub-class, No. 17, **Miscellaneous and undefined industries** shows an increase in groups 96, *Makers of Musical Instruments,* and 97, *Makers of Clocks and Surgical or Scientific Instruments* but a decrease in group 98, *Makers of Jewellery and Ornaments.* Group No. 100, *Scavenging* also shows a decrease.

127. An increase in the proportion of workers employed in transport has already been indicated (paragraph 119). The distribution of 1,000 workers in transport is **Transport.**

shown in the marginal table. The sub-class is classified in five orders of which 20, **Transport by Road,** occupies more than double the numbers of any other. It is this order which shows the principal change in this sub-class since 1921, and the change is primarily due to the development in road communications and motor traffic that has taken place during the decade. Workers employed in group No. 106, *Labour on Roads and Bridges* have increased from 285,000 to 424,000 in addition to which there are 74,500 occupied in it as a subsidiary occupation. Group No. 107, *Owners, Managers and Employees connected with Mechanically Driven Vehicles*, has increased from 20,000 to 84,000, and there are another 5,000 who find a subsidiary occupation in it. At the same time, though group 109, *Palki-bearers and owners, etc.*, shows a decrease from 66,000 to 57,500, which is less than might be expected (and there are 23,000 others for whom it is a subsidiary occupation), there is no decrease in group 108, *Owners, etc., of vehicles other than mechanical.* On the contrary they have increased from 364,500 to 405,000, and another 201,000 find in it a subsidiary occupation, a growth which confirms the increase in group 92 (paragraph 126). *Owners and drivers of pack-animals* too (group 110) show just a slight increase without taking into account those for whom this occupation is subsidiary. Turning to Order 21, **Transport by Rail,** it is clear at once that the increase of the numbers occupied in road transport has not been at the expense of the numbers of those occupied in rail traffic, and the decrease in the latter in respect to the former is not absolute, but merely a relatively lower rate of increase, since railway employees of all kinds have increased, and group 113 *Labour employed on Railways* has risen from 179,000 to 286,000, in addition to which there are 30,000 for whom it provides a subsidiary occupation. The same applies to Order 19, **Transport by Water,** under which group 104, *Labour employed on Harbours, Docks, Rivers and Canals*, has increased from 29,000 to 55,000, exclusive of 4,000 for whom it is subsidiary to some other occupation, though on the other hand ship and boatbuilders have decreased and there is some reason for supposing that transport by water has decreased. Apparently the decrease is in the use of water for internal transport, and the increase in harbours for external transport by sea, *e.g.*, at Vizagapatam and in Cochin. Order 22, **Post Office, Telegraph and Telephone Services** likewise occupies an increased number of persons, and the only order in this sub-class which shows an absolute decrease is perhaps unexpectedly No. 18, **Transport by Air,** which shows a decrease from 335 to 306 leaving out of account 24 persons who found in it a subsidiary occupation in 1931. The numbers are of course insignificant in any case. As regards the increase of labour on transport generally it should perhaps be pointed out that part of this increase may merely be due to the fact that the census fell earlier this time than in 1921 and therefore nearer the height of the working season. How far this affected the numbers it is impossible to say, but it is not likely to have accounted for more than a fraction of the increase.

Distribution of 1,000 Transport workers.

Order.	1931.	*1921.*
Transport by Road.	580	*513*
Transport by Rail	244	*270*
Transport by Water.	144	*178*
Post, Telegraphs, etc.	32	*39*

Trade.

128. The figures for Trade generally show a slight absolute decrease as compared with 1921, apart from the relative decrease shown by the table in paragraph 119 above, for the number of workers occupied declined from just over to just under eight million, taking no account, of course, of the million and a half who returned trade of some kind as a subsidiary occupation in 1931. It is tempting to put down this decline to the economic depression generally, which was possibly making itself felt in individual trades before the effect was perceptible to the community as a whole. Such a reason can perhaps be safely relied on to explain the fall in the number of workers occupied in group 115, *Bank managers, Money-lenders, etc., and their employees* (from 345,000 in 1921 to 329,500 in 1931, when there were also 153,000 who found in it a subsidiary occupation), and in group 116, *Brokers, Commission Agents, Commercial travellers, etc.*, which declined from 91,000 to 64,000. Seventeen orders are included in sub-class V, Trade, and the marginal table below shows their comparative strength in 1931. Trade in foodstuffs, otherwise than in hotels, eating houses, cookshops, etc., accounts for nearly half of the whole subclass, and if the numbers occupied in the different orders be scrutinized generally it will be seen that the decrease is by no means equally distributed. Orders No. 26, **Trade in skin leather and furs**, 27, **Trade in Wood**, 28, **Trade in Metals**, 29, **Trade in Pottery, Brick and Tiles**, 30, **Trade in Chemical Products**, 31, **Hotels, Cafés, Restaurants, etc.**, and 38, **Trade in Articles of Luxury and in those pertaining to Letters and the Arts and Sciences**, all show an increase, if in most cases only a slight one. On the other hand Orders 23, **Banks, etc.**, 24, **Brokerage**, 25, **Trade in Textiles**, 32, **Other trade in Foodstuffs**, 33, **Trade in Clothing and Toilet Articles** 34, **Trade in Furniture**, 35, **Trade in Building Materials**, 36, **Trade in Means of Transport** and 37, **Trade in Fuel**, all show an absolute decline on the number of workers occupied, though here again it is in many cases slight. Of the increases the most noticeable is that in group 127, *Owners and managers of hotels, cookshops, etc., and their employees*, a rise of 53 per cent. from 99,000 to 152,000, indicating probably a greater mobility of the population and a definite change in manners. The other increases are none of them particularly significant unless it be that in Order 38, which is mainly occasioned by an increase in group 148, *Publishers, Booksellers, Stationers, Dealers in Music, etc.*, indicative of the gradual spread of literacy. Among the decreases the heaviest is that in Order 32, where workers occupied in trade in foodstuffs apart from eating houses have fallen from 4,258,000 to 3,837,000. In spite of an increase in makers of furniture, group 88 (paragraph 126 above), workers in Order 34 have declined in number from 72,000 to 61,000, possibly a change in classification only, and workers in Order 35 from 39,000 to 22,000. In Order 36 there has naturally been a rise in group 142, *Dealers and hirers in mechanical transport*, from 3,000 to 8,200, although group 143, *Dealers and hirers in other carriages, carts, boats, etc.* (compare groups 92 and 108) shows a rise of not far from double, from 19,000 to 35,600. As already pointed out however this order as a whole has fallen, the fall being determined by the decrease in group 144, *Dealers and hirers in elephants, camels, horses, asses, mules, etc.*, the decrease in which has so far overbalanced the increase in 142 and 143 as to cause a decrease in the three combined from 135,000 to 111,000. In Order 39, **Trade of other sorts**, the rise of over 209,000 is almost entirely accounted for by the rise in group 150, *General store keepers and shopkeepers otherwise unspecified.*

Distribution of 1,000 workers in subclass V, Trade.

Order No.	Persons.
23. Banks, etc.	52
24. Brokerage, etc. ..	8
25. Textiles	56
26. Hides, etc.	11
27. Wood	21
28. Metals	3
29. Pottery, Bricks, etc. ..	6
30. Chemical Products ..	8
31. Hotels, etc.	59
32. Other Foodstuffs ..	485
33. Clothing and Toilet ..	13
34. Furniture	7
35. Building Materials ..	3
36. Means of Transport ..	15
37. Fuel	40
38. Luxury, letters, etc. ..	26
39. Miscellaneous	187

Public Force and Administration.

129. Turning to sub-class VI, Public Force, the decrease shown in paragraph 119 above is not only relative but absolute, since the total number employed under this head, exclusive of those (99,900) who find a subsidiary occupation therein (mostly as village watchmen) for whom no comparative figures are available, has fallen from 1,040,000 to 841,000. The decrease in the **Army**, both Imperial and State Forces has been one of 28 per cent., the figures having fallen from 440,000 to 317,000. The **Navy** and **Air Force** have increased, but the numbers are insignificant, amounting only to about 3,000 in all. *Police* (group 157) have increased by 7 per cent. only, less than the rate of increase of the total population, while *village watchmen* (group 158) have decreased by 95,700, a figure which suggests that this occupation has been returned at this census as subsidiary by about that number who returned it in 1921 as their principal occupation. In sub-class VII, again taking no account of those who found in 1931 only a subsidiary livelihood in **Public Administration**, there has been an absolute decrease of 10,000, as well as a relative decrease, at any rate in the figures returned, though as the decrease in actual workers has been primarily determined by a decrease of 52,000 in group

Distribution of 1,000 persons occupied in Public Force and Administration.

Navy and Air Force ..	2
Army	158
Police	155
Village watchmen	135
Service of the state ..	185
Service of Indian and Foreign States.	133
Municipal service	72
Village officials and servants	160

162, *Village officials and servants other than watchmen*, an occupation returned in 1931 as subsidiary by 112,000 persons, it is not unlikely that the decrease has been caused by the return of the occupation as subsidiary instead of principal. Of the other three groups in this order group 160, *Service of Indian and Foreign States*, shows a decrease of 17,000, while group 159, *Service of the State*, shows an increase of over 8,000. The returns under these two heads are often confused, and it is impossible to be certain either that the decrease in group 160 or the increase in group 159 does not really refer to the other group in each case, but taken together the decrease in the service of the state amounts to nearly 9,000. On the other hand there has been an unequivocal rise amounting to just under 51,000 in group 161, *Municipal Service*, which now affords an occupation to 145,000 persons, as against 94,000 in 1921; to say nothing of some 6,000 who find a subsidiary occupation in the same group. This increase is clearly due to the extension of local self-government.

Professions and Liberal Arts.

130. The total returns under sub-class VIII show an increase over 1921 of about 229,000, as well as 414,000 who find a subsidiary occupation in this sub-class which is divided into five orders. Of these Orders No. 45, **Religion** shows a decrease although but a slight one of 14,600 persons, while 220,600 return a subsidiary occupation in this order. The majority of persons returning occupations in this order are in group 163, *Priests, ministers, etc.*, No. 164, *Monks, Nuns and Religious Mendicants*, coming next (there is one of these to every 664 workers in India), then No. 166, *Temple Servants, etc.*, and finally group 165, *Other Religious Workers*. Order No. 49, **Letters, Arts and Sciences** also shows a decrease (—19,000). This is a heterogeneous order including, as it does actors, dancers, entertainers of all sorts, musicians, artists, scientists, witches, astrologers, economists, journalists and public scribes. In this order a very noticeable decrease, half as much again that in the order as a whole, is found under group 177, *Architects, Surveyors, Engineers and their employees (not being State servants)*. The decrease here of over 26,000 persons is difficult to account for, but may conceivably be correlated with the decrease in building industries already pointed out. They cannot all have been employed on building New Delhi in 1921 and have gone out of business since, nor can they have returned their employment as subsidiary, as that total in this group amounts to 1,430 only. Probably the 1921 returns included those who were State servants, but here again there is no corresponding increase except under group 161, municipal servants, where part of this decrease may perhaps be sought. Group 182, *Musicians, Actors, Dancers, etc.*, shows a decrease in females only. The other orders in this sub-class show an increase. The most pronounced is that in order 47, **Medicine,** which shows an increase of 63,000, *i.e.* of 25 per cent., the number following occupations in this order (apart from those for whom they are subsidiary 50,900) being now 318,600 against 255,500 in 1921. Much of the increase is represented by females. The distribution of 1,000 workers in this order is shown in the marginal table. There has also been an increase in order 48, **Instruction,** of 49 per cent., group 174, *Professors and Teachers of all kinds* having risen from 310,000 to 462,800, apart from 51,000 who find a subsidiary occupation in this category. Group 175, *Clerks and servants connected with education*, has risen almost proportionally. Order 46, **Law,** has also increased by 36 per cent. from 98,000 to 133,000 in addition to which there are 10,000 who find a subsidiary occupation here. Including the latter this gives a whole attorney of some kind to every 1,100 workers.

Distribution of 1,000 occupations in sub-class VIII.

Religion	458
Law	53
Medicine	135
Instruction	204
Letters, Arts, and Sciences ..	150

Distribution of 1,000 workers in Medicine.

Registered practitioners (including oculists).	241
Unregistered persons practising the healing art.	381
Dentists ..	11
Midwives, vaccinators, compounders, nurses, etc.	355
Veterinary surgeons ..	12

Private Income and Domestic Service.

131. In class D, Miscellaneous, there are six orders. In the first of these, No. 50, **Persons living on their income,** an order which includes pensioners, scholarships holders, etc., the number has risen since 1921 in proportion to the general population, the proportion to the total of workers having risen from 13 to 14 per 10,000, excluding 65,000 in 1931 who had some definite occupation as well. It may however be noted that the number of females returned in this order has fallen in absolute figures, though if to the 1931 total be added the total who returned living on their income as subsidiary to some other occupation, the 1921 total of females in this order (50,809) is almost equalled by the 50,535 obtained in 1931. This suggests that some of those who returned a private income as their means of subsistence in 1921 have this time returned some other occupation, perhaps domestic service, as their principal means of subsistence in 1931. It has already been pointed out that this order 51, **Domestic Service** has been unnaturally swollen in 1931 by returns of females at the expense of other orders, in particular probably of agriculture, but no doubt also of others, including possibly not only those just referred to but also dancing girls and prostitutes, both of which categories show a noticeable decrease in 1931. Even the number of male domestic servants shows a remarkable increase since 1921, from 1,710,000 to 2,095,000, an increase of 22 per cent. or, if working dependants be excluded in 1931, of 6 per cent. The apparent increase however in female domestic servants is by 971 per cent. from 822,000 to 8,804,000. Clearly this can only be explained by the resort to a return of domestic service as a substitute for a return of some other kind, and the 1931 figure that is really comparable with the 1921 return of female domestic servants is that of the 887,000 who have returned it as their principal occupation, this occupation being returned as dependent by the remaining 7,917,000, in addition to which 1,533,400 females have returned domestic service as a subsidiary occupation. The only other point to be noticed in this order is the increase in group 186, *Private motor-drivers and cleaners* from 18,800 to 68,000, a rise consistent with that in groups 107 and 142 already noticed.

Insufficiently Described and Unproductive Occupations.

132. In order 52, which contains four groups of **Insufficiently described occupations**, only one point calls for comment here and that is the disappearance of some 70,000 women from group 188, *Manufacturers, Businessmen and Contractors otherwise unspecified,* since 1921. Here again they have probably gone to Order 51, which has formed a convenient receptacle for all sorts of women whose occupation is not easy to define in precise terms. That the general increase in order 52 is in part due to prevailing unemployment has already been suggested in paragraph 119 above. There remains sub-class XII euphemistically described as 'Unproductive'. In this sub-class Order 53, **Inmates of Jails, Asylums and Almshouses,** shows a regrettable increase of 37 per cent., that is from 128,393 in 1921 to 176,128 in 1931. Of the latter figure approximately 140,000 are prisoners undergoing rigorous imprisonment, but as the provinces and states in some cases misunderstood the instructions and amalgamated the figures of convicts sentenced to simple imprisonment with those sentenced to rigorous the figure can only be accepted with caution. In addition to the above there appear in the returns 238 mysterious persons who find a subsidiary occupation in being an inmate of some almshouse, jail, or perhaps more plausibly (for there is no 'Cat and Mouse' act in force in India) asylum. On the other hand in Order 54, **Beggars, Vagrants, Prostitutes,** group 193, *Beggars and Vagrants* shows a fall of 20 per cent. from 1,593,000 to 1,397,000, which latter figure includes the 115,000 odd who returned beggary as a subsidiary means of subsistence, while in group 194, *Procurers and Prostitutes,* there has been a fall in the returns of 23 per cent., from 94,000 to 72,500, the latter figure including those for whom this occupation affords only a subsidiary livelihood. How far this is a real decline and how far it is due to an increasing distaste for returning a disreputable occupation it is impossible to say, but perhaps the two alternatives are in either case symptomatic of the same tendency, and the existence of the one involves the other, at any rate sooner or later. The last group 195, *Other unclassified non-productive industries* shows a slight decrease in the number of males returned, unless subsidiary occupations are included, but an in explicably high increase of females entirely in the form of working dependants. The group includes among others a certain number of persons who returned their occupation as 'Congress worker', but this can hardly account for those working dependants whose principals are apparently returned under some other occupation.

Section iii.—Occupation by Caste and Race.

Occupation and Caste.

133. Table XI contains some figures of certain castes by occupations, showing the numbers dealt with, the numbers following the traditional caste occupations, and

the numbers following other occupations, the latter classified on broad lines by sub-classes. This table was an optional table and was not compiled by all provinces, and where compiled was not exhaustive, so that the figures compiled for the India table offer only samples, the method having been to compile it as far as possible for all castes for which figures were available and which were well distributed by provincial tables, omitting those castes tabulated for Table XI in only one or two provinces. This table was omitted entirely in 1921 but it is of some importance as indicating the extent of the tendency of castes to abandon hereditary callings and take up others. In certain directions of course this tendency has long existed. Agriculture for instance is a respectable calling and it is one which at any rate can be conveniently combined with many caste occupations, and the tendency to substitute agriculture for other pursuits must be of very long-standing and many castes whose names imply some other occupation are now mainly agricultural. Possibly many have always been so, for the typical Indian village system, in which various occupational castes pursue their callings in a single village for the benefit of the whole village community, seems to be of comparatively late growth and is possibly the result of deliberate administrative arrangements. Indeed the Bengal Report for 1901 points out how in Orissa where a new village is formed the presence of the necessary occupational castes required to make the village self-contained and self-supporting is obtained by free grants of land known as *chākrān jagir*. On the other hand the Jatakas suggest a distribution of occupation by village, mentioning a village of wheelwrights, a village of potters, etc. Such a distribution appears more primitive in type and would have contributed in no small degree to the original stabilization of functional castes. Functional societies of this kind are likely to have been extremely favourable to the perpetuation of inherited aptitude and to the secretion of processes and technique. Such a distribution of function by village is still found in Burma and in a very active form in the hill districts between Burma and Assam, particularly in the unadministered areas.

Apart from agriculture the abandonment of caste functions is operative in particular directions to the exclusion of others. There is no tendency for instance for other castes to encroach on the dhobi's monopoly of washing, though all castes aim at entering the learned professions and in particular government service, and there is a similar tendency to give up caste callings for trade. The tendency to leave caste callings for learned professions is one which is making itself severely felt by those castes, Brahmans and Kayasthas in particular, who have in the past held a virtual monopoly of them. They are being submitted to severe competition in the special callings to which they have been accustomed to work for their livelihood, and the pinch is accentuated by the policy approved by Government of communal representation in Government service, a policy not confined to administrative posts but extended to clerical ones, and detrimental to those castes whose hereditary function is clerical, and who have neither aptitude nor inclination for industry or trade, as well as to the performance of the functions themselves.

A general examination of the castes tabulated by occupation enables the position to be roughly summarized as follows :—In the majority of cases about half the males tabulated retain their traditional occupation and varying numbers up to, but rarely exceeding, a quarter, have other subsidiary occupations. About a quarter or less of the half that have abandoned their hereditary occupations as their principal means of subsistence retain them as subsidiary. One or two exceptions are worth stating. Of the Chamars hardly more than one in thirteen return their traditional occupation as the principal means of subsistence and only one in 40 as the subsidiary means. The Bhats again form a similar exception and not unnaturally, as the demand for genealogists is probably less than that for tanners and their occupation as heralds is one of the past entirely. In the case of Jhinwars again the greater decrease of the numbers following their traditional occupation is the natural corollary of the decline in the number of palki owners and bearers already noticed in regard to the figures of group 109 in Order 20 (Transport by Road), while the extremely limited extent to which the mali pursues his hereditary calling of gardener is perhaps dictated by the limited numbers of persons who can afford to employ gardeners. On the other hand the agricultural communities of Jat and Kurmi have not gone nearly so far as to abandon their hereditary occupation to the extent of 50 per cent. Turning to the callings adopted, agriculture is easily the most popular, though industry, trade and transport claim fair numbers and many appear as 'insufficiently described'. The Chamar is mostly agricultural, as also the Bhat and the Mali, while the Nai is drawn to professions and liberal arts and to domestic service.

Occupation and Race.

134. The second part of Table XI deals with the occupations of Europeans and Anglo-Indians. Omitting all dependants and taking males only of workers, 66 per cent. of Europeans are employed in Public Force — that is in the Army, Navy, Air Force or Police. The next highest proportions are occupied in Transport, 7·5 per cent., Industry, 4·5 per cent., Professions and Liberal Arts 4 per cent., Public Administration 4 per cent., Trade 4 per cent., and Agriculture 3 per cent. Of European females 61 per cent. are occupied in Professions and Liberal Arts. Anglo-Indian males find their most frequent occupation in Transport 34 per cent., Industry coming next with 11 per cent., then Public Administration with 10 per cent. In the case of females 38 per cent. are occupied in Professions and Liberal Arts. The marginal table shows the occupational distribution of 1,000 each of European and Anglo-Indian males. The large proportion of Europeans in sub-class VI is due of course to the presence in India of British troops.

Distribution by principal occupation of 1,000 European and Anglo-Indian males.

Sub-class.	Europeans.	Anglo-Indians.
I.—Agriculture etc.	34	32
II.—Minerals ..	16	18
III.—Industry ..	45	107
IV.—Transport ..	75	336
V.—Trade ..	39	94
VI.—Public Force	662	56
VII.—Public Administration.	44	103
VIII.—Professions and Arts.	45	84
IX.—Private Income.	12	50
X.—Domestic service.	5	31
XI.—Insufficiently described.	23	85
XII.—Unproductive	..	4

Scheme of occupations for the Census of 1931 :—

Class.	Sub-class.	Order.	Group.
A.—*PRODUCTION OF RAW MATERIALS.*	I—EXPLOITATION OF ANIMALS AND VEGETATION.	1. *Pasture and Agriculture*— (*a*) Cultivation ..	1. Non-cultivating proprietors taking rent in money or kind.
			2. Estate agents and managers of owners.
			3. Estate agents and managers of Government.
			4. Rent collectors, clerks, etc.
			5. Cultivating owners.
			6. Tenant cultivators.
			7. Agricultural labourers.
			8. Cultivators of *jhum, taungya* and shifting areas.
		(*b*) Cultivation of special crops, fruit, etc., (Planters, managers, clerks and labourers).	9. Cinchona.
			10. Coconut.
			11. Coffee.
			12. Ganja.
			13. Pan-vine.
			14. Rubber.
			15. Tea.
			16. Market gardeners, flower and fruit growers.
		(*c*) Forestry .	17. Forest officers, rangers, guards, etc.
			18. Woodcutters and charcoal burners.
			19. Collectors of forest produce.
			20. Collectors of lac.

Class.	Sub-class.	Order.	Group.
A.—*PRODUCTION OF RAW MATERIALS*—contd.	I.—EXPLOITATION OF ANIMALS AND VEGETATION—*contd.*	(*d*) Stock raising ..	21. Cattle and buffalo breeders and keepers.
			22. Breeders of transport animals.
			23. Herdsmen, shepherds and breeders of other animals.
		(*e*) Raising of small animals and insects.	24. Birds, bees, etc.
			25. Silkworms.
			26. Lac cultivation.
		2. *Fishing and Hunting.*	27. Fishing and pearling.
			28. Hunting.
	II.—EXPLOITATION OF MINERALS.	3. *Metallic Minerals.*	29. Gold.
			30. Iron.
			31. Lead, silver and zinc.
			32. Manganese.
			33. Tin and wolfram.
			34. Other metallic minerals.
		4. *Non-Metallic Minerals.*	35. Coal.
			36. Petroleum.
			37. Building materials (including stone, materials for cement-manufacture and clays).
			38. Mica.
			39. Precious and semi-precious stones.
			40. Salt, saltpetre and other saline substances.
			41. Other non-metallic minerals.
B.—*PREPARATION AND SUPPLY OF MATERIAL SUBSTANCES.*	III.—INDUSTRY ..	5. *Textiles*	42. Cotton ginning, cleaning and pressing.
			43. Cotton spinning, sizing and weaving.
			44. Jute pressing, spinning and weaving.
			45. Rope, twine string and other fibres.
			46. Wool carding, spinning and weaving.
			47. Silk spinning and weaving.
			48. Hair (horse-hair), etc.
			49. Dyeing, bleaching, printing, preparation and sponging of textiles.
			50. Lace, crêpe, embroideries, fringes, etc., and insufficiently described textile industries.
		6. *Hides, skins and hard materials from the animal kingdom.*	51. Working in leather.
			52. Furriers and persons occupied with feathers, and bristles ; brush-makers.
			53. Bone, ivory, horn, shell, etc. workers (except buttons).

Class.	Sub-class.	Order.	Group.
B.—*PREPARATION AND SUPPLY OF MATERIAL SUBSTANCES—contd.*	III.—INDUSTRY—*contd.*	7. *Wood*	54. Sawyers.
			55. Carpenters, turners and joiners, etc.
			56. Basket makers and other industries of woody materials, including leaves, and thatchers and builders working with bamboo, reeds or similar materials.
		8. *Metals*	57. Smelting, forging and rolling of iron and other metals.
			58. Makers of arms, guns, etc.
			59. Blacksmiths, other workers in iron, makers of implements.
			60. Workers in brass, copper and bell metal.
			61. Workers in other metals (except precious metals).
			62. Workers in mints, die-sinkers, etc.
		9. *Ceramics* ..	63. Potters and makers of earthenware.
			64. Brick and tile makers.
			65. Other workers in ceramics.
		10. *Chemical products properly so-called and analogous.*	66. Manufacture of matches, fireworks, and other explosives.
			67. Manufacture of aerated and mineral waters and ice.
			68. Manufacture and refining of vegetable oils.
			69. Manufacture and refining of mineral oils.
			70. Others.
		11. *Food Industries* ..	71. Rice pounders and huskers, and flour grinders.
			72. Grain parchers, etc.
			73. Butchers.
			74. Makers of sugar, molasses and gur.
			75. Sweetmeat and condiment makers.
			76. Toddy drawers.
			77. Brewers and distillers.
			78. Manufacturers of tobacco.
			79. Manufacturers of opium.
			80. Manufacturers of ganja.
			81. Others.
		12. *Industries of dress and the toilet.*	82. Boot, shoe, sandal and clog makers.
			83. Tailors, milliners, dress-makers and darners.
			84. Embroiderers, hat-makers and makers of other articles of wear.
			85. Washing and cleaning.
			86. Barbers, hairdressers and wigmakers.
			87. Other industries connected with the toilet.

Class.	Sub-class.	Order.	Group.
B.—*PREPARATION AND SUPPLY OF MATERIAL SUBSTANCES*—contd.	III.—INDUSTRY—*concld.*	13. *Furniture Industries.*	88. Cabinet-makers, carriage painters, etc.
			89. Upholsterers, tent-makers, etc.
		14. *Building Industries.*	90. Lime burners, cement workers; Excavators and well sinkers; Stone cutters and dressers; Bricklayers and masons; builders (other than buildings made of bamboo or similar materials); Painters, decorators of houses, tilers, plumbers, etc.
		15. *Construction of means of transport.*	91. Persons engaged in making, assembling or repairing, motor vehicles or cycles.
			92. Carriage, cart, palki, etc., makers and wheelwrights.
			93. Ship, boat, aeroplane builders.
		16. *Production and transmission of physical forces.*	94. Heat, light, electricity, motive power, etc.; gas works and electric light and power.
		17. *Miscellaneous and undefined Industries.*	95. Printers, engravers, bookbinders, etc.
			96. Makers of musical instruments.
			97. Makers of clocks and surgical or scientific instruments, etc.
			98. Makers of jewellery and ornaments.
			99. Other miscellaneous and undefined industries (toy-making, taxidermy, etc.)
			100. Scavenging.
	IV—TRANSPORT ..	18. *Transport by air* ..	101. Persons concerned with aerodromes and aeroplanes.
		19. *Transport by water*	102. Ship-owners, boat-owners and their employees, officers, mariners, etc. Ship-brokers, boatmen and towmen.
			103. Persons (other than labourers) employed in harbours, docks, rivers and canals, including pilots.
			104. Labourers, employed on harbours, docks, rivers and canals.
		20. *Transport by road*	105. Persons (other than labourers) employed on the construction and maintenance of roads and bridges.
			106. Labourers employed on roads and bridges.
			107. Owners, managers and employees (excluding personal servants) connected with mechanically driven vehicles (including trams).

Class.	Sub-class.	Order.	Group.
B.—*PREPARATION AND SUPPLY OF MATERIAL SUBSTANCES*—contd.	IV.—TRANSPORT—*contd.*	20. *Transport by road*—contd.	108. Owners, managers and employees (excluding personal servants) connected with other vehicles.
			109. Palki, etc., bearers and owners.
			110. Pack elephant, camel, mule, ass and bullock, owners and drivers.
			111. Porters and messengers.
		21. *Transport by rail*	112. Railway employees of all kinds other than coolies.
			113. Labourers employed on railway construction and maintenance and coolies and porters employed on railway premises.
		22. *Post Office, Telegraph and Telephone services.*	114. Post Office, Telegraph and Telephone services.
	V.—TRADE ..	23. *Banks, Establishments of credit, exchange and insurance.*	115. Bank managers, money-lenders, exchange and insurance agents, money changers and brokers and their employees.
		24. *Brokerage, commission and export.*	116. Brokers, commission agents, commercial travellers, warehouse owners and employees.
		25. *Trade in textiles*	117. Trade in piece-goods, wool, cotton, silk, hair and other textiles.
		26. *Trade in skins, leather and furs.*	118. Trade in skins, leather, furs, feathers, horn, etc., and the articles made from these.
		27. *Trade in wood* ..	119. Trade in wood (not fire-wood).
			120. Trade in barks.
			121. Trade in bamboos and canes.
			122. Trade in thatches and other forest produce.
		28. *Trade in metals*	123. Trade in metals, machinery, knives, tools, etc.
		29. *Trade in pottery, bricks and tiles.*	124. Trade in pottery, bricks and tiles.
		30. *Trade in chemical products.*	125. Drugs, dyes, paints, petroleum, explosives, etc.
		31. *Hotels, cafés, restaurants, etc.*	126. Vendors of wine, liquors, aerated waters and ice.
			127. Owners and managers of hotels, cook-shops, sarais, etc. (and employees).
			128. Hawkers of drink and food stuffs.
		32. *Other trade in food stuffs.*	129. Grain and pulse dealers.
			130. Dealers in sweetmeats, sugar and spices.

Class.	Sub-class.	Order.	Group.
B.—*PREPARATION AND SUPPLY OF MATERIAL SUBSTANCES*—concld.	V.—TRADE—*contd.*	32. *Other trade in food stuffs*—contd.	131. Dealers in dairy products, eggs and poultry.
			132. Dealers in animals for food.
			133. Dealers in fodder for animals.
			134. Dealers in other food stuffs.
			135. Dealers in tobacco.
			136. Dealers in opium.
			137. Dealers in ganja.
		33. *Trade in clothing and toilet articles.*	138. Trade in ready-made clothing and other articles of dress and the toilet (hats, umbrellas, socks, ready-made shoes, perfumes, etc.).
		34. *Trade in furniture*	139. Trade in furniture, carpets, curtains and bedding.
			140. Hardware, cooking utensils, porcelain, crockery, glassware, bottles, articles for gardening, etc.
		35. *Trade in building materials.*	141. Trade in building materials (other than bricks, tiles and woody materials).
		36. *Trade in means of transport.*	142. Dealers and hirers, in mechanical transport, motors, cycles, etc.
			143. Dealers and hirers in other carriages, carts, boats, etc.
			144. Dealers and hirers of elephants, camels, horses, cattle, asses, mules, etc.
		37. *Trade in fuel* ..	145. Dealers in firewood, charcoal, coal, cowdung, etc.
		38. *Trade in articles of luxury and those pertaining to letters and the arts and sciences.*	146. Dealers in precious stones, jewellery (real and imitation), clocks, optical instruments, etc.
			147. Dealers in common bangles, bead necklaces, fans, small articles, toys, hunting and fishing tackle, flowers, etc.
			148. Publishers, booksellers, stationers, dealers in music, pictures, musical instruments and curiosities.
		39. *Trade of other sorts*	149. Dealers in rags, stable refuse, etc.
			150. General store-keepers and shopkeepers otherwise unspecified.
			151. Itinerant traders, pedlars, and hawkers (of other than food, etc.)
			152. Other trades (including farmers of pounds, tolls and markets)

Class.	Sub-class.	Order.	Group.
C.—*PUBLIC ADMINISTRATION AND LIBERAL ARTS.*	VI.—PUBLIC FORCE	40. *Army* ..	153. Army (Imperial).
			154. Army (Indian States).
		41. *Navy*	155. Navy.
		42. *Air Force* ..	156. Air Force.
		43. *Police* ..	157. Police.
			158. Village watchmen.
	VII.—PUBLIC ADMINISTRATION.	44. *Public Administration.*	159. Service of the State.
			160. Service of Indian and Foreign States.
			161. Municipal and other local (not village) service.
			162. Village officials and servants other than watchmen.
	VIII.—PROFESSIONS AND LIBERAL ARTS.	45. *Religion* ..	163. Priests, ministers, etc.
			164. Monks, nuns, religious mendicants.
			165. Other religious workers.
			166. Servants in religious edifices, burial and burning grounds, pilgrim conductors, circumcisers, etc.
		46. *Law*	167. Lawyers of all kinds, including qazis, law agents and mukhtiars.
			168. Lawyers' clerks, petition-writers, etc.
		47. *Medicine* ..	169. Registered medical practitioners including oculists.
			170. Other persons practising the healing arts without being registered.
			171. Dentists.
			172. Midwives, vaccinators, compounders, nurses, masseurs, etc.
			173. Veterinary surgeons.
		48. *Instruction* ..	174. Professors and teachers of all kinds.
			175. Clerks and servants connected with education.
		49. *Letters, arts and sciences* (other than 44).	176. Public scribes, stenographers, etc.
			177. Architects, surveyors, engineers, and their employees (not being state servants).
			178. Authors, editors, journalists and photographers.
			179. Artists, sculptors and image-makers.
			180. Scientists (astronomers, botanists, etc.).
			181. Astrologers, fortune-tellers, horoscope-casters, wizards, witches and mediums.

Class.	Sub-class.	Order.	Group.
C.—*PUBLIC ADMINISTRATION AND LIBERAL ARTS*—contd.	VIII.—PROFESSIONS AND LIBERAL ARTS —*contd.*	49. *Letters, arts and sciences* (other than 44)—contd.	182. Musicians (composers and performers other than military), actors, dancers, etc.
			183. Managers and employees of places of public entertainment, race-courses, societies, clubs.
			184. Conjurors, acrobats, reciters, exhibitors of curiosities and wild animals, etc.
D.—*MISCELLANEOUS.*	IX.—PERSONS LIVING ON THEIR INCOME.	50. *Persons living principally on their income.*	185. Proprietors (other than of agricultural land), fund and scholarship holders and pensioners.
	X.—DOMESTIC SERVICE.	51. *Domestic service..*	186. Private motor-drivers and cleaners.
			187. Other domestic service.
	XI.—INSUFFICIENTLY DESCRIBED OCCUPATIONS.	52. *General terms which do not indicate a definite occupation.*	188. Manufacturers, business men and contractors otherwise unspecified.
			189. Cashiers, accountants, book-keepers, clerks and other employees in unspecified offices and warehouses and shops.
			190. Mechanics otherwise unspecified.
			191. Labourers and workmen otherwise unspecified.
	XII.—UNPRODUCTIVE.	53. *Inmates of jails, asylums and alms houses.*	192. Inmates of jails, asylums and alms houses.
		54. *Beggars, vagrants, prostitutes.*	193. Beggars and vagrants.
			194. Procurers and prostitutes.
		55. *Other unclassified non-productive industries.*	195. Other unclassified non-productive industries.

SUBSIDIARY TABLE I.

General distribution of workers at each occupation per 10,000 of total population.

Class, Sub-class and Order.	Number per 10,000 of total population. Earners (principal occupation) and working dependants.	Earners as subsidiary occupation.
Non-working dependants=5609		
All occupations	**4,391**	**425**
A. PRODUCTION OF RAW MATERIALS ..	*2,957*	*215*
I.—EXPLOITATION OF ANIMALS AND VEGETATION	**2,947**	**213**
1. Pasture and agriculture	2,923	208
(a) **Cultivation**	**2,766**	**185**
(b) **Special crops**	**47**	7
(c) **Forestry**	**9**	**3**
(d) **Stock-raising**	**100**	**12**
(e) **Raising of small animals and insects**	**1**	**1**
2. Fishing and hunting	24	5
II.—EXPLOITATION OF MINERALS	**10**	**2**
3. Metallic minerals	1	..
4. Non-metallic minerals	9	2
B. PREPARATION AND SUPPLY OF MATERIAL SUBSTANCES.	*731*	*115*
III.—INDUSTRY	**438**	**62**
5. Textiles	117	12
6. Hides, skins and hard materials from the animal kingdom.	9	1
7. Wood..	47	10
8. Metals	20	4
9. Ceramics	29	5
10. Chemical products properly so called and analogous ..	17	4
11. Food Industries	42	5
12. Industries of dress and the toilet	96	15
13. Furniture industries	1	..
14. Building industries	18	2
15. Construction of means of transport	1	..
16. Production and transmission of Physical force ..	1	..
17. Miscellaneous and undefined industries	40	4
IV.—TRANSPORT	**67**	**12**
18. Transport by air	..	..
19. Transport by water	10	1
20. Transport by road	36	10
21. Transport by rail	18	1
22. Post Office, telegraph and telephone services ..	3	..
V.—TRADE	**226**	**41**
23. Banks, establishments of credit, exchange and insurance.	9	4
24. Brokerage, commission and export	2	..
25. Trade in textiles	13	2
26. Trade in skins, leather and furs	3	1

SUBSIDIARY TABLE I—*concld.*

General distribution of workers at each occupation per 10,000 of total population.

Class, Sub-class and Order.	Number per 10,000 of total population. Earners (principal occupation) and working dependants.	Earners as subsidiary occupation.
V.—TRADE—*concld.*		
27. Trade in wood ..	4	2
28. Trade in metals	1	..
29. Trade in pottery, bricks and tiles ..	1	..
30. Trade in chemical products	2	..
31. Hotels, cafes, restaurants, etc.	14	2
32. Other trade in foodstuffs	110	20
33. Trade in clothing and toilet articles	3	..
34. Trade in furniture	2	..
35. Trade in building materials	1	..
36. Trade in means of transport	3	1
37. Trade in fuel ..	8	2
38. Trade in articles of luxury and those pertaining to letters and the arts and sciences.	6	1
39. Trade of other sorts	44	6
C. PUBLIC ADMINISTRATION AND LIBERAL ARTS.	*118*	*19*
VI.—PUBLIC FORCE	**24**	**3**
40. Army	9	..
41. Navy	..	..
42. Air force	..	..
43. Police	15	3
VII.—PUBLIC ADMINISTRATION	**28**	**4**
44. Public administration	28	4
VIII.—PROFESSIONS AND LIBERAL ARTS	**66**	**12**
45. Religion	29	6
46. Law ..	4	..
47. Medicine	9	2
48. Instruction	14	2
49. Letters, Arts and sciences (other than 44)	10	2
D. MISCELLANEOUS	*585*	*76*
IX.—PERSONS LIVING ON THEIR INCOME	**6**	**2**
50. Persons living principally on their income	6	2
X.—DOMESTIC SERVICE	**311**	**51**
51. Domestic service	311	51
XI.—INSUFFICIENTLY DESCRIBED OCCUPATIONS	**222**	**20**
52. General terms which do not indicate a definite occupation.	222	20
XII.—UNPRODUCTIVE	**46**	3
53. Inmates of jails, asylums and alms houses	5	..
54. Beggars, vagrants and prostitutes	38	3
55. Other unclassified non-productive industries	3	..

SUBSIDIARY TABLE II(a).

Earners (principal occupation) and working dependants.

Province, State or Agency.	Total 1,000. Non-working dependants.	Total 1,000. Working dependants.	Total 1,000. Earners principal occupation.	Sub-class I Exploitation of animals and vegetation.	Sub-class II Exploitation of minerals.	Sub-class III Industry.	Sub-class IV Transport.	Sub-class V Trade.	Sub-class VI Public Force.	Sub-class VII Public Administration.	Sub-class VIII Professions and Liberal Arts.	Sub-class IX Persons living on their income.	Sub-class X Domestic Service.	Sub-class XI Insufficiently described occupations.	Sub-class XII Unproductive.
				Number per mille of the total population occupied as Earners (principal occupation) and as Working Dependants in											
1	2	3	4	5	6	7	8	9	10	11	12	13	14	15	16
INDIA	**561**	**82**	**357**	**295**	**1**	**44**	**7**	**22**	**2**	**3**	**6**	**1**	**31**	**22**	**5**
Provinces	**571**	**69**	**360**	**288**	**1**	**43**	**6**	**21**	**2**	**2**	**6**	**1**	**32**	**23**	**4**
1. Ajmer-Merwara	476	154	370	327	1	67	26	35	7	5	15	1	11	21	8
2. Andaman and Nicobar Islands.	289	227	484	384	..	37	33	23	26	25	6	1	27	140	9
3. Assam	550	113	337	377	2	34	6	13	1	1	5	..	4	4	3
4. Baluchistan (*Districts and Administered Territories*).	605	30	365	224	1	33	32	20	52	5	7	1	14	2	4
5. Bengal	712	13	275	197	1	25	6	19	1	1	6	..	16	12	4
6. Bihar and Orissa	587	13	400	320	3	27	3	15	1	1	4	..	5	32	2
7. Bombay (*including Aden*) ..	611	52	337	256	..	46	9	21	3	6	7	1	8	23	9
Aden	*507*	*27*	*466*	*21*	*1*	*75*	*118*	*69*	*24*	*5*	*10*	*2*	*68*	*93*	*7*
8. Burma	576	69	355	295	3	45	15	38	2	3	14	..	3	4	2
9. Central Provinces and Berar	467	96	437	429	2	42	6	22	3	3	5	..	6	11	4
10. Coorg	316	166	518	372	..	24	10	18	1	2	6	..	170	80	1
11. Delhi	578	43	379	105	1	116	34	56	12	11	12	3	38	29	5
12. Madras	446	171	383	269	..	49	6	22	1	3	7	1	137	56	3
13. North-West Frontier Province (*Districts and Administered Territories*).	646	40	314	218	..	45	8	25	16	4	9	1	5	18	5
14. Punjab	647	59	294	214	..	66	8	22	4	3	8	1	10	9	8
15. United Provinces of Agra and Oudh.	514	68	418	369	..	54	4	23	2	2	6	..	10	12	4
States and Agencies ..	**525**	**125**	**350**	**317**	**1**	**47**	**8**	**27**	**4**	**5**	**8**	**1**	**30**	**21**	**6**
16. Assam States	514	169	317	390	1	50	5	17	2	2	6	..	4	8	1
17. Baluchistan States ..	664	20	316	275	..	25	8	11	4	3	3	1	3	..	3
18. Baroda State	504	103	393	350	1	53	7	28	6	5	12	2	3	27	2
19. Bengal States	709	23	268	238	..	13	5	13	1	1	4	..	6	4	6
20. Bihar and Orissa States ..	555	48	397	353	3	42	4	17	2	1	3	..	6	11	3
21. Bombay States	595	105	300	313	..	31	2	14	1	5	4	1	6	23	5
22. Central India Agency ..	490	44	466	387	1	43	4	20	5	6	5	1	8	23	7
23. Central Provinces States ..	499	188	313	438	..	32	4	11	2	1	2	..	5	3	3
24. Gwalior State	507	57	436	358	1	46	2	21	5	5	6	..	8	34	7
25. Hyderabad State	529	137	334	268	2	50	21	55	4	6	9	1	33	12	10
26. Jammu and Kashmir State	472	306	222	224	..	23	3	8	2	4	4	1	157	98	4
27. Madras States Agency ..	509	175	316	199	1	71	8	31	1	4	11	1	139	24	1
Cochin State	*491*	*122*	*387*	*213*	..	*89*	*12*	*35*	*1*	*4*	*14*	*2*	*117*	*21*	*1*
Travancore State ..	*528*	*182*	*290*	*185*	*1*	*69*	*7*	*31*	*1*	*3*	*11*	..	*140*	*23*	*1*
Other Madras States ..	*358*	*230*	*412*	*322*	*2*	*41*	*5*	*28*	*1*	*5*	*8*	*1*	*184*	*42*	*3*
28. Mysore State	545	97	358	347	2	36	4	20	3	5	5	1	7	22	3
29. North-West Frontier Province (*Agencies and Tribal Areas*).	107	1	892	50	..	44	24	23	707	21	2	..	2	19	1
30. Punjab States	390	306	304	541	..	33	3	12	2	2	4	1	5	3	4
31. Punjab States Agency ..	575	100	325	311	..	47	6	20	5	4	7	1	7	9	8
32. Rajputana Agency ..	472	153	375	379	1	61	5	26	5	6	14	..	8	16	7
33. Sikkim State	333	17	650	636	..	4	5	8	..	1	1	..	11	1	..
34. United Provinces States ..	494	116	390	421	..	34	2	19	2	3	5	..	8	9	3
35. Western India States Agency	612	125	263	231	2	52	10	29	4	8	10	1	6	28	7

SUBSIDIARY TABLE II(b).

Earners (subsidiary occupation).

Province, State or Agency.	Number per mille of total population of earners having a subsidiary occupation in Sub-class I.	Sub-class II.	Sub-class III.	Sub-class IV.	Sub-class V.	Sub-class VI.	Sub-class VII.	Sub-class VIII.	Sub-class IX.	Sub-class X.	Sub-class XI.	Sub-class XII.
1	2	3	4	5	6	7	8	9	10	11	12	13
INDIA	**21**	..	**6**	**1**	**4**	..	..	**1**	..	**5**	**2**	..
Provinces	**20**	..	**6**	**1**	**4**	..	..	**1**	..	**5**	**2**	..
1. Ajmer-Merwara	24	..	6	1	5	..	1	2	1	..	2	1
2. Andaman and Nicobar Islands ..	4	..	9	1	2	1	..	..	..	..	1	..
3. Assam	39	..	7	3	6	..	..	2	..	..	1	..
4. Baluchistan (*Districts and Administered Territories*).	76	..	3	4	16	..	1	1	2	..	..	1
5. Bengal	14	..	2	1	3	..	..	1	..	1	1	..
6. Bihar and Orissa	18	1	9	1	5	..	..	2	..	1	4	..
7. Bombay (*including Aden*)	13	..	2	1	1	..	1	..	..	..	1	..
Aden	*4*	..	*1*	..	*1*	..	..	..	..	..	..	..
8. Burma	13	..	8	4	4	..	1	1	..	..	..	..
9. Central Provinces and Berar	20	..	6	1	5	..	..	1	..	..	1	..
10. Coorg	11	..	7	5	5	..	2	2	..	49	..	..
11. Delhi	9	..	2	1	1	1	1	..	1	..	1	..
12. Madras	13	..	5	2	4	..	1	1	..	27	3	..
13. North-West Frontier Province (*Districts and Administered Territories*).	12	..	2	1	1	2	1	1	1	1	1	..
14. Punjab	16	..	4	1	2	..	1	1	1	..	..	..
15. United Provinces of Agra and Oudh ..	37	..	11	1	5	..	..	1	..	1	3	1
States and Agencies	**27**	..	**7**	**1**	**5**	..	**1**	**1**	..	**4**	**2**	**1**
16. Assam States	42	..	8	3	8	..	..	1	..	..	5	..
17. Baluchistan States	50	..	2	5	2	..	..	1	..	..	..	..
18. Baroda State	13	..	4	1	3	1	1	1	..	..	3	..
19. Bengal States	13	..	1	..	2	1	..	1	..	..	..	..
20. Bihar and Orissa States	30	1	11	1	6	1	1	2	..	..	3	..
21. Bombay States	13	..	4	1	2	..	1	1	1	1	2	..
22. Central India Agency	23	..	7	1	5	..	1	1	..	1	2	1
23. Central Provinces States	11	..	5	1	2	..	..	1	..	..	..	..
24. Gwalior State	30	..	7	1	5	1	..	1	..	1	6	1
25. Hyderabad State	37	..	8	3	9	..	1	1	..	4	2	1
26. Jammu and Kashmir State	46	..	5	1	2	1	1	1	..	1	1	..
27. Madras States Agency	46	..	7	1	5	..	..	2	..	30	3	..
Cochin State	*29*	..	*9*	*2*	*7*	..	..	*2*	*1*	*30*	*2*	..
Travancore State	*52*	..	*7*	*1*	*4*	..	..	*1*	..	*29*	*2*	..
Other Madras States	*30*	..	*9*	*6*	*7*	..	*2*	*3*	..	*38*	*7*	..
28. Mysore State	13	..	9	2	5	1	3	2	..	..	2	..
29. North-West Frontier Province (*Agencies and Tribal Areas*).	24	..	7	..	15	22	3	..	..	4	7	..
30. Punjab States	14	..	10	1	3	1	3	3	1	1	1	..
31. Punjab States Agency	26	..	6	1	2	..	1	1	1	1		..
32. Rajputana Agency	24	..	6	1	4	..	1	1	..	..	1	1
33. Sikkim State	25	..	3	2	1	..	1	2	..	6	..	..
34. United Provinces States	19	..	7	..	3	..	..	2	..	1	2	..
35. Western India States Agency ..	4	..	1	..	1	..	..	..	..	..	1	

SUBSIDIARY TABLE III.
Occupations of Females.

Group No.	Occupation.	Number of actual workers (Earners *plus* Working Dependants). Males.	Females.	Number of females per 1,000 males.
1	2	3	4	5
	All Occupations	**105,086,333**	**48,829,717**	**465**
	A. PRODUCTION OF RAW MATERIALS	*74,700,585*	*28,939,854*	*387*
	I.—EXPLOITATION OF ANIMALS AND VEGETATION.	**74,441,002**	**28,853,437**	**388**
	1. Pasture and agriculture	**73,763,185**	**28,690,962**	**389**
	(a) Cultivation	**69,619,876**	**27,353,496**	**393**
1	Non-cultivating proprietors taking rent in money or kind.	2,419,817	837,574	346
2	Estate agents and managers of owners	56,151	7,689	137
3	Estate agents and managers of government	8,070	1,868	231
5	Cultivating owners	22,469,143	4,536,957	202
6	Tenant cultivators	26,896,149	7,277,755	271
7	Agricultural labourers	17,110,466	14,369,753	840
8	Cultivators of jhum, taungya and shifting areas.	510,996	317,503	621
	(b) Cultivation of special crops, fruit, etc. (Planters, managers, clerks and labourers).	**1,003,931**	**654,287**	**652**
9	Cinchona	1,222	957	783
10	Coconut	98,933	40,496	409
11	Coffee	34,228	17,815	520
15	Tea	555,451	464,881	837
16	Market gardners, flower and fruit growers	233,564	114,155	489
	(c) Forestry	**213,043**	**97,449**	**457**
18	Wood cutters and charcoal burners	132,621	40,532	306
20	Collectors of lac	1,564	1,027	657
	(d) Stock raising	**2,915,259**	**579,642**	**199**
21	Cattle and buffalo breeders and keepers	822,079	152,730	186
23	Herdsmen, shepherds and breeders of other animals.	2,056,669	425,813	207
	(e) Raising of small animals and insects	**11,076**	**6,088**	**550**
24	Birds, bees, etc.	4,546	1,446	318
25	Silk worms	2,869	2,793	974
26	Lac cultivation	3,661	1,849	505
	2. Fishing and hunting	**677,817**	**162,475**	**240**
27	Fishing and pearling	638,941	151,809	238
28	Hunting	38,876	10,666	274
	II.—EXPLOITATION OF MINERALS	**259,583**	**86,417**	**333**
	3. Metallic minerals	**37,728**	**10,651**	**282**
30	Iron	4,932	4,092	830
32	Manganese	7,695	4,838	629
	4. Non-metallic minerals	**221,855**	**75,766**	**342**
35	Coal	124,874	49,957	400
37	Building materials (including stone, materials for cement manufacture and clays).	35,350	10,262	290
38	Mica	4,923	2,946	598
39	Precious and semi-precious stones	5,260	1,316	250
40	Salt, saltpetre and other saline substances	22,257	10,488	471

SUBSIDIARY TABLE III—*contd.*

Occupations of Females—*contd.*

Group No.	Occupation.	Number of actual workers (Earners *plus* Working Dependants). Males.	Females.	Number of females per 1,000 males.
1	2	3	4	5
	B. PREPARATION AND SUPPLY OF MATERIAL SUBSTANCES.	*18,682,341*	*6,924,615*	*371*
	III.—INDUSTRY	**10,797,527**	**4,554,426**	**422**
	5. Textiles	**2,531,411**	**1,570,725**	**620**
42	Cotton ginning, cleaning and pressing ..	195,966	61,239	312
43	Cotton spinning, sizing and weaving ..	1,761,267	1,122,306	637
44	Jute pressing, spinning and weaving ..	235,804	36,649	155
45	Rope, twine, string and other fibres ..	121,996	207,838	1,704
46	Wool carding, spinning and weaving ..	63,934	45,413	710
47	Silk spinning and weaving	57,023	57,498	1,008
48	Hair (horse-hair), etc.	747	773	1,035
49	Dyeing, bleaching, printing, preparation and sponging of textiles.	77,781	25,989	334
50	Lace, crêpe, embroideries, fringes, etc., and insufficiently described textile industries.	16,893	13,020	771
	6. Hides, skins and hard material from the animal kingdom.	**265,904**	**46,170**	**174**
51	Working in leather	256,515	44,429	173
52	Furriers and persons occupied with feathers, and bristles, brush makers.	1,072	239	223
53	Bone, ivory, horn, shell, etc., workers (except buttons).	8,317	1,502	181
	7. Wood	**1,289,419**	**342,304**	**265**
54	Sawyers	86,080	2,503	29
55	Carpenters, turners and joiners	881,586	23,379	27
56	Basket makers and other industries of woody materials including leaves, and thatchers and builders working with bamboo, reeds or similar materials.	321,753	316,422	983
	8. Metals	**659,635**	**53,435**	**81**
57	Smelting, forging and rolling of iron and other metals.	28,715	3,782	132
	9. Ceramics	**727,559**	**297,271**	**409**
63	Potters and makers of earthenware ..	600,628	268,595	447
65	Other workers in ceramics	27,261	8,822	324
	10. Chemical products properly so called and analogous.	400,785	202,519	505
66	Manufacture of matches fireworks and other explosives.	13,185	4,166	316
68	Manufacture and refining of vegetable oil ..	355,488	192,541	542
70	Others	13,561	4,043	298
	11. Food industries	**706,281**	**770,714**	**1,091**
71	Rice pounders and huskers and flour grinders	102,676	453,788	4,420
72	Grain parchers, etc.	104,730	175,291	1,674
74	Makers of sugar molasses and gur ..	19,437	21,612	1,112
75	Sweetmeat and condiment makers ..	87,427	26,552	304
77	Brewers and distillers	4,220	1,733	411
78	Manufacturers of tobacco	78,694	57,718	733
79	Manufacturers of opium	191	49	257
80	Manufacturers of ganja	246	64	260

SUBSIDIARY TABLE III—*contd.*

Occupations of Females—*contd.*

Group No.	Occupation.	Number of actual workers (Earners *plus* Working Dependants). Males.	Females.	Number of females per 1,000 males.
1	2	3	4	5
	B. PREPARATION AND SUPPLY OF MATERIAL SUBSTANCES—contd.			
	III.—INDUSTRY—*concld.*			
	12. Industries of dress and the toilet ..	**2,565,594**	**815,230**	**318**
83	Tailors, milliners, dress makers and darners..	493,116	155,248	315
84	Embroiderers, hat makers and makers of other articles of wear.	15,884	9,589	604
85	Washing and cleaning	637,859	456,469	716
87	Other industries connected with the toilet ..	15,410	9,841	639
	13. Furniture industries	**16,980**	**4,029**	**237**
88	Cabinet-makers, carriage painters, etc. ..	14,394	2,438	169
89	Upholsterers, tent makers, etc.	2,586	1,591	615
90	**14. Building industries**	**528,344**	**90,183**	**171**
	15. Construction of means of transport ..	**28,599**	**566**	**20**
92	Carriage, cart, palki makers and wheel-wrights.	7,115	209	29
94	**16. Production and transmission of physical force.**	**21,403**	**2,247**	**105**
	17. Miscellaneous and undefined industries	**1,055,613**	**359,033**	**340**
99	Other miscellaneous and undefined industries (toy making, taxidermy, etc.).	34,852	13,198	379
100	Scavenging	387,695	314,326	811
	IV.—Transport	**2,099,198**	**242,208**	**115**
101	**18. Transport by air**	**295**	**11**	**37**
	19. Transport by water	**348,695**	**13,279**	**38**
104	Labourers employed on harbours, docks, rivers and canals.	46,775	8,575	183
	20. Transport by Road	**1,083,080**	**176,347**	**163**
106	Labourers employed on roads and bridges ..	285,633	138,339	484
	21. Transport by rail	**584,376**	**51,755**	**89**
113	Labourers employed on railway construction and maintenance and coolies and porters employed on railway premises.	238,947	46,878	196
114	**22. Post Office, telegraph and telephone services.**	**82,752**	**816**	**10**
	V.—TRADE	**5,785,616**	**2,127,981**	**368**
115.	**23. Banks establishments of credit exchange and insurance.**	**292,739**	**36,743**	**126**
116	**24. Brokerage, commission and export** ..	**62,444**	**1,504**	**24**
117	**25. Trade in textiles**	**411,315**	**47,587**	**116**
118	**26. Trade in skins, leather and furs** ..	**81,204**	**7,594**	**94**
	27. Trade in wood	**94,058**	**45,196**	**481**
121	Trade in bamboos and canes	20,296	11,689	576
122	Trade in thatches and other forest produce	7,120	9,746	1,369
123	**28. Trade in metals**	**24,103**	**3,101**	**129**
124	**29. Trade in pottery bricks and tiles** ..	**26,112**	**20,376**	**780**
125	**30. Trade in chemical products**	**46,517**	**16,147**	**347**
	31. Hotels, cafes, restaurants, etc.	**335,638**	**154,179**	**459**
126	Vendors of wine, liquors, ærated waters and ice.	166,261	89,234	537
128	Hawkers of drink and food stuffs	42,943	39,596	922

SUBSIDIARY TABLE III—*concld.*

Occupations of Females—*concld.*

Group No.	Occupation.	Number of actual workers (Earners *plus* Working Dependants). Males.	Females	Number of females per 1,000 males.
1	2	3	4	5
	B. PREPARATION AND SUPPLY OF MATERIAL SUBSTANCES—concld.			
	V.—TRADE—*concld.*			
	32. Other trade in food stuffs	**2,515,266**	**1,321,654**	**525**
130	Dealers in sweetmeats, sugar and spices ..	245,701	112,414	458
131	Dealers in dairy products, eggs and poultry	229,908	243,587	1,059
133	Dealers in fooder for animals	56,162	85,771	1,527
134	Dealers in other food stuffs	1,184,910	633,192	534
138	**33. Trade in clothing and toilet articles** ..	**98,517**	**13,611**	**138**
	34. Trade in furniture	**47,486**	**13,588**	**286**
139	Trade in furniture, carpets, curtains and bedding.	12,270	3,826	312
141	**35. Trade in building materials**	**16,639**	**5,764**	**346**
	36. Trade in means of transport	**105,437**	**5,083**	**48**
145	**37. Trade in fuel**	**129,476**	**163,080**	**1,260**
	38. Trade in articles of luxury and those pertaining to letters and the arts and sciences.	**164,743**	**55,854**	**339**
147	Dealers in common bangles, bead necklaces, fans, small articles, toys, hunting and fishingtackle, flowers, etc.	83,539	50,644	606
	39. Trade of other sorts	**1,333,922**	**216,920**	**163**
149	Dealers in rags, stable refuse, etc. ..	18,974	4,487	236
	C. PUBLIC ADMINISTRATION AND LIBERAL ARTS.	*3,783,454*	*363,445*	*96*
	VI.—PUBLIC FORCE	**834,453**	**7,021**	**8**
	40. Army	**314,810**	**1,728**	**5**
155	**41. Navy**	**1,390**	**8**	**6**
156	**42. Air force**	**1,838**	**25**	**14**
	43. Police	**516,415**	**5,260**	**10**
	VII.—(44)—PUBLIC ADMINISTRATION ..	**962,741**	**32,543**	**34**
	VIII.—PROFESSIONS AND LIBERAL ARTS.	**1,986,260**	**323,881**	**163**
	45. Religion	**907,163**	**119,731**	**132**
	46. Law	**132,591**	**498**	**4**
	47. Medicine	**222,536**	**96,045**	**432**
172	Midwives, vaccinators, compounders, nurses, masseurs, etc.	35,555	85,909	2,416
	48. Instruction	**443,239**	**58,413**	**132**
	49. Letters, arts and sciences (other than 44)	**280,731**	**49,194**	**175**
182	Musicians (composers and performers other than military) actors, dancers, etc.	179,183	38,740	216
	D. MISCELLANEOUS	*7,917,432*	*12,601,208*	*1,592*
185	**IX.—(50).—PERSONS LIVING PRINCIPALLY ON THEIR INCOME.**	**168,829**	**47,045**	**279**
	X.—(51).—DOMESTIC SERVICE	**2,094,487**	**8,803,790**	**4,203**
187	Other domestic service	2,031,302	8,798,706	4,332
	XI.—(52).—INSUFFICIENTLY DESCRIBED OCCUPATIONS.	**4,599,238**	**3,179,404**	**691**
191	Labourers and workmen otherwise unspecified.	3,752,546	3,122,718	832
	XII.—UNPRODUCTIVE	**1,054,878**	**570,969**	**541**
192	**53. Inmates of jails, asylums and alms houses.**	**167,493**	**8,635**	**52**
	54. Beggars, vagrants, prostitutes ..	**864,440**	**486,539**	**563**
194	Procurers and prostitutes	5,811	63,229	10,881
195	**55. Other unclassified non-productive industries.**	**22,945**	**75,795**	**3,303**
	Earners whose occupations are not returned	2,521	595	236

SUBSIDIARY TABLE IV.

Selected Occupations.

Occupation.	Actual Workers. 1931.	1921.	1911.	Percentage of Variation 1921-31.
Total Workers	***153,916,050**	**146,413,562**	**148,885,003**	**+5.1**
A. PRODUCTION OF RAW MATERIALS.	*103,640,439*	*106,035,722*	*106,508,881*	*—2·3*
I.—EXPLOITATION OF ANIMALS AND VEGETATION	**103,294,439**	**105,688,373**	**106,200,432**	**—2·3**
1. Pasture and Agriculture	102,454,147	104,943,712	105,335,379	—2·4
2. Fishing and hunting	840,292	744,661	865,053	+12·8
II.—EXPLOITATION OF MINERALS	**346,000**	**347,349**	**308,449**	**—0·4**
3. Metallic minerals	48,379	47,895	50,281	+1·0
4. Non-metallic minerals	297,621	299,454	258,168	—0·6
B.—PREPARATION AND SUPPLY OF MATERIAL SUBSTANCES.	*25,606,956*	*25,734,692*	*28,002,567*	*—0·5*
III.—INDUSTRY	**15,351,953**	**15,714,907**	**17,506,279**	**—2·3**
5. Textiles	4,102,136	4,030,674	4,449,449	+1·8
6. Hides, skins and hard materials from the animal kingdom.	312,074	310,113	294,794	+0·6
7. Wood	1,631,723	1,581,006	1,730,920	+3·2
8. Metals	713,070	725,227	737,307	1·7
9. Ceramics	1,024,830	1,085,335	1,159,168	—5·6
10. Chemical products properly so called and analogous.	603,304	577,204	630,079	+4·5
11. Food Industries	1,476,995	1,653,464	2,134,045	—10·7
12. Industries of dress and the toilet	3,380,824	3,403,842	3,747,755	—0·7
13. Furniture Industries	21,009	12,066	18,163	+74·1
14. Building Industries	618,527	811,945	962,115	—23·8
15. Construction of means of transport	29,165	22,894	24,938	+27·4
16. Production and transmission of physical force.	23,650	11,514	7,257	+105·4
17. Miscellaneous and undefined industries	1,414,646	1,489,623	1,610,289	—5·0
IV.—TRANSPORT	**2,341,406**	**1,970,400**	**2,394,882**	**+18·8**
18. Transport by air	306	335	..	—8·7
19. Transport by water	361,974	349,721	481,605	+3·5
20. Transport by road	1,259,427	1,010,734	1,362,504	+24·6
21. Transport by rail	636,131	532,136	474,184	+19·5
22. Post office, telegraph and telephone services.	83,568	77,474	76,589	+7·9
V.—TRADE	**7,913,597**	**8,049,385**	**8,101,406**	**—1·7**
23. Banks, establishments of credit, exchange and insurance.	329,482	345,135	421,464	—4·5
24. Brokerage, commission and export	63,948	90,812	89,149	—29·6
25. Trade in textiles	458,902	493,393	513,030	—7·0
26. Trade in skins, leather and furs	88,798	88,302	114,557	+0·6
27. Trade in wood	139,254	105,220	109,398	+32·3
28. Trade in metals	27,204	24,925	22,523	+9·1
29. Trade in pottery, bricks and tiles	46,488	33,571	54,159	+38·5
30. Trade in chemical products	62,664	50,244	76,500	+24·7
31. Hotels, cafes, restaurants, etc.	489,817	349,044	351,889	+40·3

*Includes 3,116 earners whose occupations were not returned.

SUBSIDIARY TABLE IV—*concld.*

Selected Occupations—*concld.*

Occupation.	Actual Workers. 1931.	1921.	1911.	Percentage of Variation 1921-31.
B. PREPARATION AND SUPPLY OF MATERIAL SUBSTANCES—concld.				
V.—TRADE—*concld.*				
32. Other trade in food stuffs ..	3,836,920	4,257,723	4,477,113	—9·9
33. Trade in clothing and toilet articles ..	112,128	116,764	122,863	—4·0
34. Trade in furniture	61,074	72,366	72,448	—15·6
35. Trade in building materials ..	22,403	38,668	39,741	—42·1
36. Trade in means of transport ..	110,520	134,618	97,810	—17·9
37. Trade in fuel	292,556	308,157	335,000	—5·1
38. Trade in articles of luxury and those pertaining to letters arts and sciences.	220,597	198,631	234,716	+11·1
39. Trade of other sorts	1,550,842	1,341,812	969,046	+15·6
C. PUBLIC ADMINISTRATION AND LIBERAL ARTS.	*4,146,899*	*4,125,676*	*4,302,535*	*+0·5*
VI.—PUBLIC FORCE	**841,474**	**1,039,538**	**1,069,424**	**—19·1**
40. Army	316,538	440,351	384,074	—28·1
41. Navy	1,398	250	2,229	+459·2
42. Air force	1,863	856	..	+117·6
43. Police	521,675	598,081	683,121	—12·8
VII.—PUBLIC ADMINISTRATION	**995,284**	**1,005,346**	**970,521**	**—1·0**
44. Public Administration	995,284	1,005,346	970,521	—1·0
VIII.—PROFESSIONS AND LIBERAL ARTS	**2,310,141**	**2,080,792**	**2,262,590**	**+11·0**
45. Religion	1,026,894	1,041,459	1,195,129	—1·4
46. Law	133,089	98,067	82,461	+35·7
47. Medicine	318,581	255,526	270,302	+24·7
48. Instruction	501,652	336,543	271,668	+49·1
49. Letters, arts and sciences (other than 44).	329,925	349,197	443,030	—5·5
D. MISCELLANEOUS ..	*20,518,640*	*10,517,472*	*10,071,020*	*+95·1*
IX.—PERSONS LIVING ON THEIR INCOME	**215,874**	**184,259**	**206,070**	**+17·2**
50. Persons living principally on their income.	215,874	184,259	206,070	+17·2
X.—DOMESTIC SERVICE ..	**10,898,277**	**2,531,866**	**2,725,856**	**+330·4**
51. Domestic service	10,898,277	2,531,866	2,725,856	+330·4
XI.—INSUFFICIENTLY DESCRIBED OCCUPATIONS.	**7,778,642**	**5,946,713**	**5,067,700**	**+30·8**
52. General terms which do not indicate a definite occupation.	7,778,642	5,946,713	5,067,700	+30·8
XII.—UNPRODUCTIVE	**1,625,847**	**1,854,634**	**2,071,394**	**—12·3**
53. Inmates of jails, asylums and alms houses.	176,128	128,393	124,563	—37·2
54. Beggars, vagrants, prostitutes ..	1,350,979	1,686,737	1,946,831	—19·9
55. Other unclassified non-productive industries.	98,740	39,504	..	+149·9

SUBSIDIARY TABLE V.

Occupations in selected cities.

Cities.	Number per 10,000 of actual workers by each class and sub-class of occupation.																Number per cent. of			
	A. Production of raw materials.	I—Exploitation of animals and vegetation.	II—Exploitation of minerals.	B. Preparation and supply of material substances.	III—Industry.	IV—Transport.	V.—Trade.	C. Public administration and liberal arts.	VI—Public force.	VII—Public administration.	VIII—Professions and liberal arts.	D. Miscellaneous.	IX—Persons living on their income.	X—Domestic service.	XI—Insufficiently described occupations.	XII—Unproductive.	All occupations.	Actual workers.	Non-working dependants.	Number of female workers per 100 males.
1	2	3	4	5	6	7	8	9	10	11	12	13	14	15	16	17	18	19	20	21
Amritsar	831	830	1	6,299	3,120	554	2,625	796	157	193	446	2,074	49	791	1,020	214	10,000	37	63	3
Bombay*	211	192	19	5,547	3,116	896	1,535	1,083	160	570	353	3,104	33	712	2,227	132	10,000	49	51	11
Calcutta (including Howrah) ..	267	262	5	4,430	1,932	911	1,587	873	106	302	465	4,430	178	1,518	2,502	232	10,000	49	51	8
Cawnpore	569	569	..	5,893	3,395	511	1,987	829	324	161	344	2,709	195	988	1,394	132	10,000	43	57	10
Delhi (excluding New Delhi and Cantonment).	489	464	25	6,635	3,498	1,122	2,015	790	197	206	387	2,086	101	1,157	733	95	10,000	40	60	7
Hyderabad (Deccan).. ..	1,089	1,081	8	3,506	977	1,125	1,404	2,260	704	871	685	3,145	404	1,453	844	444	10,000	62	38	39
Karachi	507	471	36	4,820	1,887	1,217	1,716	1,764	659	418	687	2,909	86	400	2,084	339	10,000	32	68	12
Lahore	966	961	5	5,542	2,266	1,723	1,553	1,754	465	798	491	1,738	110	758	566	304	10,000	42	58	4
Madras	421	419	2	3,428	1,649	690	1,089	787	115	257	415	5,364	170	3,434	1,606	154	10,000	50	50	61
Poona	875	875	..	3,710	2,115	434	1,161	2,457	981	871	605	2,958	232	808	1,211	707	10,000	31	69	20
Rangoon	193	190	3	7,417	3,117	1,914	2,386	1,173	128	441	604	1,217	73	708	304	132	10,000	56	44	10

*The discrepancy between the sum of the figures in columns 2—17 and the figure in column 18 is due to the exclusion from the former columns 3,116 persons (*i. e.* 55 : 10,000) occupation details for whom are not available.

SUBSIDIARY TABLE VI.

(i) Number of persons employed on the 26th February 1931 in the Railway Department.

Province, State or Agency.	Persons Directly Employed.										Persons Indirectly Employed.								Grand Total.	
	Officers.		Subordinates drawing more than Rs. 75 per mensem.		Subordinates drawing from rs. 20 to 75 per mensem.		Subordinates drawing under Rs. 20 per mensem.		Total		Contractors.		Contractors' regular employees.		Coolies.		Total.			
	Europeans and Anglo-Indians.	Indians.	Europeans and Anglo-Indians.	Indians.	Europeans and Anglo-Indians.	Indians.	Europeans and Anglo-Indians.	Indians.	Europeans and Anglo-Indians.	Indians.	Europeans and Anglo-Indians.	Indians.	Europeans and Anglo-Indians.	Indians.	Europeans and Anglo-Indians.	Indians.	Europeans and Anglo-Indians.	Indians.	Europeans and Anglo-Indians.	Indians.
Total (a)	**426**	**207**	**2,378**	**11,338**	**1,615**	**74,941**	**129**	**109,002**	**4,548**	**195,488**	**1**	**662**	..	**2,271**	..	**27,996**	**1**	**30,929**	**4,549**	**226,417**
Ajmer-Merwara	31	8	412	1,435	98	7,963	1	4,045	542	13,451	..	18	..	107	..	533	..	658	542	14,109
Assam	33	6	58	404	38	3,132	3	9,229	132	12,771	..	149	..	281	..	7,713	..	8,143	132	20,914
Bombay	292	122	1,518	7,930	1,246	53,817	64	71,725	3,120	133,594	1	151	..	1,007	..	10,046	1	11,204	3,121	144,798
Burma	15	18	1	139	5	90	1	1,685	22	1,932	..	207	..	35	..	4,798	..	5,040	22	6,972
N.-W. F. Province	1	2	19	138	..	2,399	..	1,288	20	3,827	..	9	..	54	..	220	..	283	20	4,110
Cochin State	..	1	4	36	..	202	..	407	4	646	..	3	..	..	..	..	..	3	4	649
Mysore State	12	21	104	169	207	1,763	60	4,412	383	6,365	..	48	..	313	..	772	..	1,133	383	7,498
Rajputana Agency	42	29	262	1,087	21	5,575	..	16,211	325	22,902	..	77	..	474	..	3,914	..	4,465	325	27,467
	Officers.		Subordinates on scales of pay rising to Rs. 250 per mensem or over.		Subordinates on scales of pay Rising from Rs. 30 to Rs. 249 per mensem.		Subordinates on scales under Rs. 30 per mensem.		Total.											
Total (b)	**997**	**569**	**4,220**	**2,233**	**7,732**	**167,132**	**503**	**388,637**	**13,452**	**558,571**	**Not available.**								**13,452**	**558,571**
Bengal	355	199	1,354	802	2,281	58,549	60	94,310	4,050	153,850	Not available								4,050	153,860
Bihar and Orissa	106	36	650	166	782	15,355	10	59,777	1,548	75,334	Not available								1,548	75,334
Central Provinces	49	17	322	113	499	7,417	5	33,453	875	41,000	Not available								875	41,000
Delhi	11	10	20	30	15	851	3	1,191	49	2,082	Not available								49	2,082
Madras	164	89	426	193	2,307	22,967	348	51,834	3,245	75,083	Not available								3,245	75,083
Punjab	178	154	683	655	708	37,362	52	66,275	1,621	104,446	Not available								1,621	104,446
United Provinces..	121	47	687	209	1,053	20,922	22	66,393	1,883	87,571	Not available								1,883	87,571
Baroda State	1	12	7	19	7	1,775	1	4,817	16	6,623	Not available								16	6,623
Central India	12	5	70	44	76	1,812	2	10,263	160	12,124	Nor available								160	12,124
Jammu and Kashmir	..	..	..	..	..	..	..	80	..	100	Not available								..	100
Travancore State..	..	..	1	2	4	20,102	..	244	5	348	Not available								5	348

NOTE.—The Railways in the majority of the Provinces and States were not able to supply conveniently the information for this table in the form prescribed, and therefore figures according to the form followed by them were accepted and are reproduced under the head (b) above.

SUBSIDIARY TABLE VI—*contd.*

(ii) Number of persons employed on the 26th February 1931 in the Irrigation Department.

Province, State or Agency.	Total persons employed.		Persons directly employed. Total.		Officers.		Upper Subordinates.		Lower Subordinates.		Clerks.		Peons and other servants.		Coolies.		Persons indirectly employed. Total.		Contractors.		Contractors' regular employees.		Coolies.	
	Europeans and Anglo-Indians.	Indians.	Europeans and Anglo-Indians.	Indians.	Europeans and Anglo-Indians.	Indians.	Europeans and Anglo-Indians.	Indians.	Europeans and Anglo-Indians.	Indians.	Europeans and Anglo-Indians.	Indians.	Europeans and Anglo-Indians.	Indians.	Europeans and Anglo-Indians.	Indians.	Europeans and Anglo-Indians.	Indians.	Europeans and Anglo-Indians.	Indians.	Europeans and Anglo-Indians.	Indians.	Europeans and Anglo-Indians.	Indians.
1	2	3	4	5	6	7	8	9	10	11	12	13	14	15	16	17	18	19	20	21	22	23	24	25
Total	**419**	**262,109**	**366**	**89,460**	**263**	**841**	**25**	**1,428**	**8**	**2,528**	**21**	**6,703**	**31**	**34,707**	**18**	**43,253**	**53**	**172,649**	**45**	**7,709**	**8**	**28,166**	..	**136,774**
Bengal	45	4,074	16	2,238	16	37	..	2	..	130	..	346	..	1,707	..	16	29	1,836	29	408	..	561	..	867
Bihar and Orissa ..	4	6,349	4	2,289	3	21	..	75	..	82	1	335	..	1,285	..	491	..	4,060	..	268	..	124	..	3,668
Bombay	83	76,271	79	26,700	48	158	15	166	1	561	1	1,609	2	4,908	12	19,298	4	49,571	1	714	3	21,251	..	27,606
Burma	22	6,972	22	1,932	15	18	1	139	5	90	1	177	..	328	..	1,180	..	5,040	..	207	..	35	..	4,798
Central Provinces* ..	13	16,302	13	7,988	12	29	1	107	..	197	..	239	..	757	..	6,659	..	8,314	..	158	..	262	..	7,894
Delhi	..	379	..	60	..	2	..	..	..	2	..	3	..	19	..	34	..	319	..	9	..	5	..	305
Madras	53	35,137	52	11,945	17	107	4	249	..	239	1	561	24	3,850	6	6,939	1	23,192	..	651	1	331	..	22,210
N.-W. F. Province ..	8	2,783	8	1,655	8	14	..	27	..	14	..	69	..	1,007	..	524	..	1,128	..	82	..	60	..	986
Punjab	108	68,461	107	23,167	86	245	2	548	..	299	16	1,171	3	14,613	..	6,291	1	45,294	1	2,041	..	3,494	..	39,759
United Provinces ..	74	32,170	62	9,035	58	126	1	4	..	414	1	1,606	2	5,472	..	1,413	12	23,135	8	2,049	4	1,470	..	19,616
Baroda State]	..	43	..	43	..	..	..	..	..	..	..	11	..	26	..	6	..	..	..	..	..	..	..	..
Central India Agency ..	..	336	..	141	..	2	..	..	..	6	..	11	..	91	..	31	..	195	..	20	..	8	..	167
Cochin State	..	96	..	96	..	..	..	..	..	1	..	1	..	94	..	..	..	..	..	..	..	..	..	..
Gwalior State	..	815	..	460	..	11	..	30	..	46	..	226	..	147	..	..	..	355	..	160	..	..	..	195
Mysore State	9	11,082	3	1,270	..	65	1	65	2	437	..	278	..	224	..	201	6	9,812	6	902	..	539	..	8,371
Travancore State ..	..	839	..	441	..	6	..	16	..	10	..	60	..	179	..	170	..	398	..	40	..	26	..	332

* Includes persons employed in the Government and Quasi Government Irrigation works not under the Public Works Department.

SUBSIDIARY TABLE VI—*contd.*

(iii) Number of persons employed on the 26th February 1931 in the Post Office and Telegraph Department.

Province, State or Agency.	Supervising Officers (including Probationary Superintendents and Inspectors of Post Offices and Assistant and Deputy Superintendent of Telegraphs and all officers of higher rank than these.				Post Masters, including Deputy, Assistant, Sub and Branch Post Masters.				Signalling establishment, including warrant officers, non-commissioned officers, military telegraphists and their employees.				Miscellaneous agents, schoolmasters, stationmasters, etc.				Clerks of all kinds.				Postmen.				Skilled labour establishment including foremen, instrument makers, carpenters, blacksmiths, mechanics, sub-inspectors, linemen and line-riders and other employees.			
	Post Office.		Telegraph Department.		Post Office.		Telegraph Department.		Post Office.		Telegraph Department.		Post Office.		Telegraph Department.		Post Office.		Telegraph Department.		Post Office.		Telegraph Department.		Post Office.		Telegraph Department.	
	Europeans and Anglo-Indians.	Indians.	Europeans and Anglo-Indians.	Indians.	Europeans and Anglo-Indians.	Indians.	Europeans and Anglo-Indians.	Indians.	Europeans and Anglo-Indians.	Indians.	Europeans and Anglo-Indians.	Indians.	Europeans and Anglo-Indians.	Indians.	Europeans and Anglo-Indians.	Indians.	Europeans and Anglo-Indians.	Indians.	Europeans and Anglo-Indians.	Indians.	Europeans and Anglo-Indians.	Indians.	Europeans and Anglo-Indians.	Indians.	Europeans and Anglo-Indians.	Indians.	Europeans and Anglo-Indians.	Indians.
1	2	3	4	5	6	7	8	9	10	11	12	13	14	15	16	17	18	19	20	21	22	23	24	25	26	27	28	29
Total	**68**	**699**	**329**	**201**	**107**	**8,141**	**26**	**3**	..	**40**	**1,860**	**1,525**	**15**	**14,747**	**2**	**65**	**234**	**18,147**	**94**	**2,112**	..	**32,754**	**2**	..	..	**134**	**69**	**6,185**
Ajmer-Merwara	..	2	3	1	1	20	3	3	..	..	21	21	..	27	..	..	1	62	..	11	..	83	..	..	..	..	..	13
Andamans and Nicobars ..	..	..	1	..	..	..	..	..	..	..	5	..	..	..	..	..	..	..	..	..	..	..	..	..	..	..	..	3
Assam	3	25	5	1	..	509	..	..	..	..	21	30	..	732	..	..	6	654	..	23	..	1,383	..	..	..	..	..	171
Bengal	8	141	58	45	9	1,222	..	..	..	..	219	342	..	..	..	..	21	3,467	26	424	..	5,668	..	..	..	9	14	1,566
Bihar and Orissa	2	42	19	10	1	659	..	..	..	..	26	49	..	1,107	..	..	..	965	..	41	..	2,127	..	..	..	2	4	320
Bombay (*excluding Aden*) ..	10	98	36	41	3	946	..	..	..	..	431	373	..	2,646	..	..	19	3,263	18	518	..	4,799	..	..	..	15	..	871
Burma	6	20	48	13	5	451	23	..	..	..	182	69	3	181	..	..	34	973	12	232	..	1,435	..	..	..	..	1	496
Central Provinces and Berar ..	2	24	20	7	3	278	..	..	..	..	72	29	..	738	..	..	14	594	7	58	..	1,118	..	..	..	..	..	236
Madras	8	84	34	34	36	1,754	..	..	..	..	283	218	5	2,970	..	..	79	2,586	21	250	..	4,941	..	..	..	100	..	580
* North-West Frontier Province ..	..	11	4	4	2	168	..	..	..	..	29	13	..	298	..	..	..	303	..	80	..	481	..	..	..	..	..	178
* Punjab and Delhi	11	91	71	34	13	760	..	..	..	37	234	219	3	2,938	..	..	22	2,100	3	263	..	3,197	..	..	..	5	20	934
United Provinces	12	104	18	3	17	276	..	..	..	..	276	131	1	1,968	..	..	10	2,259	5	144	..	4,631	..	..	..	..	30	551
Baroda State	..	6	1	..	..	65	..	..	..	1	..	..	..	241	..	..	..	123	..	..	..	365	2	..	..	..	..	16
Central India Agency	..	5	9	1	1	124	..	..	..	1	12	11	..	210	2	23	..	70	..	..	..	298	..	..	..	3	..	75
‡ Cochin State	..	1	..	..	1	9	..	..	..	..	..	..	1	37	..	..	..	19	..	..	..	38	..	..	..	..	..	..
† Gwalior State	..	20	..	7	..	174	..	..	..	..	..	9	..	61	..	42	..	117	..	18	..	382	..	..	..	..	..	36
* Jammu and Kashmir State ..	1	4	1	..	..	58	..	..	..	1	4	2	..	87	..	..	..	72	..	1	..	488	..	..	..	..	..	59
Mysore State	3	8	1	..	12	387	..	..	..	..	34	3	..	160	..	..	24	231	2	47	..	614	..	..	..	..	..	..
Rajputana Agency	2	10	..	..	1	240	..	..	..	..	1	5	..	283	..	..	..	233	..	..	..	593	..	..	..	..	..	69
‡ Travancore State	..	3	..	..	2	41	..	..	..	..	10	1	2	63	..	..	4	56	..	2	..	113	..	..	..	..	..	1

* The figures for Telegraph Department also include those for the Engineering Department.

† The figures for Telegraph Department also include those for the Telephone Department.

‡ Excludes persons working in the Anchal Department.

SUBSIDIARY TABLE VI—*concld.*

(iii) Number of persons employed on the 26th February 1931 in the Post Office and Telegraph Department—*concld.*

Province, State or Agency.	Unskilled labour establishment including line coolies, cable guards, battery men, telegraph messengers, peons and other employees. Post Office.		Telegraph Department.		Road establishment consisting of overseers, runners, clerks and booking agents, boatmen, syces, coachmen, bearers and others.‖ Post Office.		Telegraph Department.		Railway Mail service. Supervising officers (including) Superintendents and Inspectors of Sorting).		Clerks of all‖ kinds.		Sorters.		Mail Guards, Mail Agents, Van peons, Porters, etc.		Messengers.		Other servants.		Combined offices. Signallers.		Messengers and other servants.		Total.	
	Europeans and Anglo-Indians.	Indians.	Europeans and Anglo-Indians.	Indians.	Europeans and Anglo-Indians.	Indians.	Europeans and Anglo-Indians.	Indians.	Europeans and Anglo-Indians.	Indians.	Europeans and Anglo-Indians.	Indians.	Europeans and Anglo-Indians.	Indians.	Europeans and Anglo-Indians.	Indians.	Europeans and Anglo-Indians.	Indians.	Europeans and Anglo-Indians.	Indians.	Europeans and Anglo-Indians.	Indians.	Europeans and Anglo-Indians.	Indians.	Europeans and Anglo-Indians.	Indians.
	30	31	32	33	34	35	36	37	38	39	40	41	42	43	44	45	46	47	48	49	50	51	52	53	54	55
Total	2	9,041	..	3,572	..	18,674	..	21	5	110	..	198	4	4,905	..	3,392	—	16	..	1	15	3,038	..	3,756	2,832	131,477
Ajmer-Merwara	..	33	..	16	..	23	..	..	..	3	..	18	..	70	..	46	..	..	..	1	..	3	..	9	29	465
Andamans and Nicobars ..	..	..	..	8	..	..	..	..	..	..	..	..	..	..	..	..	..	..	..	..	..	..	..	..	6	11
Assam	..	306	..	80	..	1,558	..	..	..	4	..	1	..	85	..	97	..	..	..	..	..	57	..	312	35	6,028
Bengal	2	1,700	..	1,003	..	2,995	..	17	1	12	..	21	..	692	..	463	..	..	..	..	1	383	..	543	359	20,713
Bihar and Orissa	..	737	..	44	..	1,775	..	..	..	14	..	11	..	406	..	263	..	..	..	..	..	174	..	379	52	9,125
Bombay	..	1,845	..	710	..	1,210	..	3	3	20	..	52	..	692	..	543	..	..	..	..	..	186	..	595	520	19,426
Burma	..	564	..	340	..	134	..	..	..	5	..	4	2	139	..	146	..	..	..	..	13	188	..	215	329	5,605
Central Provinces and Berar	..	275	..	67	..	1,087	..	..	..	6	..	4	..	193	..	151	..	..	..	..	..	38	..	166	118	5,069
Madras	..	1,617	..	399	..	2,688	..	..	1	14	..	53	2	773	..	560	..	..	..	..	..	1,106	..	568	469	21,295
*North-West Frontier Province	..	185	..	89	..	168	..	..	..	..	..	4	..	23	..	29	..	..	..	..	..	44	..	72¶	35	2,150
*Punjab and Delhi	..	1,127	..	441	..	1,537	..	..	..	24	..	15	..	832	..	501	..	..	..	..	..	232	..	328	377	15,615
United Provinces	..	..	..	267	..	3,986	..	..	§	§	..	..	..	729	..	394	..	..	..	..	..	490	..	286	369	16,229
Baroda State	..	57	..	..	..	54	..	..	..	3	..	1	..	85	..	43	..	..	..	..	..	7	..	60	3	1,127
Central India Agency ..	..	91	..	27	..	244	..	..	..	3	..	6	..	107	..	72	..	..	..	..	..	95	..	74	24	1,540
‡Cochin State	..	17	..	..	..	27	..	..	..	..	..	..	..	..	..	..	..	..	..	..	..	..	..	..	2	148
†Gwalior State	..	39	..	19	..	39	..	1	..	..	..	1	..	3	..	5	..	..	..	..	..	..	..	..	..	973
*Jammu and Kashmir State	..	47	..	17	..	530	..	..	..	..	..	..	..	..	..	1	..	..	..	..	..	2	..	12	6	1,381
Mysore State	..	192	..	24	..	234	..	..	..	..	..	..	..	..	..	..	..	16	..	..	‖	‖	..	..	76	1,916
Rajputana Agency ..	..	173	..	5	..	330	..	..	..	2	..	7	..	76	..	78	..	..	..	..	..	20	..	114	4	2,238
‡Travancore State	..	36	..	16	..	55	..	..	..	..	..	..	..	..	..	..	..	..	..	..	1	13	..	23	19	423

§Included among supervising officers under columns 2 and 3. ‖Included against item 3. ¶Includes 38 belonging to the Telegraph Department.

NOTE.—The figures in columns 38—53 refer expressly to Post Office personnel. For *, ‡ an † see footnote on page 318.

SUBSIDIARY TABLE VII.

Statistics of Factories in British India subject to the Indian Factories Act in 1930.

Industry.	Enumerated Factories.	Average daily number of persons employed.
Total	8,148	1,528,302
Textiles	*2,789*	*884,221*
Cotton (spinning, weaving, ginning, bailing and other factories).	2,392	492,284
Dyeing and bleaching	38	5,188
Indigo	16	859
Jute mills	212	369,387
Lac	18	1,995
Rope Works	15	3,831
Silk Mills	7	1,712
Woollen Mills	12	4,247
Miscellaneous	79	4,718
Hides, Skins, etc.	*58*	*9,758*
Bone and Manure	21	3,736
Leather and Shoes	11	2,626
Tanneries	21	3,345
Miscellaneous	5	51
Wood	*235*	*19,740*
Carpentry and Cabinet-making.	36	3,686
Saw Mills	199	16,054
Metals	199	80,327
Foundries	73	3,250
Iron and steel smelting and steel rolling mills.	5	30,484
Kerosene tinning and packing.	28	10,170
Lead smelting and lead rolling mills.	6	4,489
Mints	2	1,436
Metal Stamping	28	3,198
Ordnance	25	21,664

Industry.	Enumerated Factories.	Average daily number of persons employed.
Steel trunk, lock and cutlery.	3	808
Miscellaneous	29	4,828
Ceramics	*105*	*15,760*
Bricks and tiles	76	9,611
Cement, lime and Potteries	29	6,149
Chemical products, etc.	*436*	*52,819*
Chemicals	12	3,653
Ice and aerated waters	80	3,160
Matches	41	17,137
Oil Mills	249	11,919
Paints	8	1,409
Petroleum refineries	12	12,034
Soaps	9	891
Turpentine and rosin	2	229
Miscellaneous	23	2,387
Food Industries	*3,044*	*179,731*
Bakeries, biscuit and confectionery.	22	1,398
Breweries and distilleries	32	2,140
Coffee	15	4,265
Dairy produce	3	237
Flour Mills	73	5,482
Food canning and bottling	2	22
Forage Presses	10	389
Rice Mills	1,615	78,271
Sugar	48	15,203
Tea	959	60,161
Tobacco	18	6,040
Miscellaneous	247	6,123

Industry.	Enumerated Factories.	Average daily number of persons employed.
Industries of dress and toilet	*44*	*3,912*
Clothing	3	1,470
Hosiery	41	2,442
Building Industries	*10*	*693*
Stone dressing	10	693
Construction and means of Transport.	*287*	*166,251*
Coach-building and motor-car repairing.	95	6,462
Railway workshops	153	130,700
Ship-building and engineering.	30	26,289
Tramway works	9	2,800
Production and Transmission of physical force.	*464*	*62,925*
Electrical Engineering	41	5,140
Electrical generating and transforming stations.	39	5,363
Gas works	18	1,826
General Engineering	303	43,542
Telegraphs	2	1,300
Water pumping stations	26	2,520
Miscellaneous	35	3,234
Miscellaneous and undefined Industries.	*477*	*52,165*
Glass	19	2,390
Paper Mills	7	5,597
Paper pulp	2	1361
Printing, bookbinding, etc.	381	37,545
Miscellaneous	68	5,272

NOTE.—The above figures have been extracted from the Government of India's Report for the year 1930 on the factories subject to the Indian Factories Act. Details of the persons employed by age or sex are not available separately for each branch of industry but of the average number employed in all factories (*i.e.*, 1,528,302) 1,235,425 were men, 254,905 women, 39,968 boys and 6,875 girls. Factories engaged in two or more classes of work are shown only under the principal class in this table.

Appendix to Chapter VIII.

A Note on the Ages of Male Earners and Dependants.

(By B. L. Cole.)

Statement showing the occupational distribution per mille of Population in certain Provinces and States, etc.

Province, etc.	Earners.		Working Dependants.		Non-Working Dependants.	
	Males.	Females.	Males.	Females.	Males.	Females.
Travancore ..	219	71	32	151	252	275
Madras	273	110	20	152	201	244
Gwalior	343	93	20	37	167	340
Baroda	291	101	18	85	206	299
Ajmer-Merwara ..	313	56	29	125	186	291
Rajputana	308	67	35	118	181	291

At first sight these figures suggest that there existed wide differences of opinion concerning the definitions of the three terms. 'Earner', 'Working Dependant' and 'Non-Working Dependant'. Before definitely ascribing the differences in the ratios to this reason, it is as well to remember that they are influenced not only by economic conditions due to environment and locality, but also by the proportions of the sexes and the age constitution of the population when set down in figures for 1,000 *persons*. For the purpose of this enquiry it will suffice to examine the figures for males only and to start by assuming that all males aged under 10 years and over 60 are non-working dependants. This assumption as regards those aged over 60 is perhaps somewhat arbitrary but it provides a basis for certain deductions as will be seen hereafter.

Starting from the South, we get from Imperial Table VII the age constitution of males among 1,000 *persons* in Travancore and Madras to be as shown in the following statements. Following the assumption referred to above, all males aged under 10 and over 60 provides the majority of non-working dependants supplemented where necessary by the requisite number of those aged 10—15. The remainder of those so aged are then placed in the categories of Working Dependants and Earners to the extent required leaving all those aged 15 to 20 in the category of Earners wherever possible.

Travancore. Density 668.

Earners—

0—10 —153 }
10—15 — 62 } {15 } =230+22 =252 Non-Working Dependants.
15—20 — 47 {15, 32} = 32 Working Dependants.
20—60 —221 {219 =219 Earners.
{2 }
60 & over. —20 } = 22
—— ——
503 503

Now there are in this State 503 males in every 1,000 persons in the population, and it is unlikely that nearly one-third of those aged from 15 to 20 are non-working dependants. In this densely populated and prosperous State it is far more probable that the older males give up leading an active life before they are aged 60 and that the majority of the male working dependants are lads aged from 10—15, that all aged from 15—20 are earners* leaving 49 out of 221 aged from 20—60 to retire from active life and free to join the ranks of the non-working dependants.

The figures for the Madras Presidency present somewhat similar features, but here the male ratio in 1,000 persons is 494, *i.e.*, 9 less than in Travancore.

Madras Density 328.

0—10—136 }
} =178+23=201 Non-Working Dependants.
10—15— 59 {42, 17}
} = 20= 20 Working Dependants.
15—20— 43 {3, 40}
20—60—233 } =273=273 Earners.
60 & over. —23
—— ——
494 494

* This is, I think, most unlikely.—J. H. H.

It is unlikely that as many as 42 out of 59 of those aged 10—15 are non-working dependants. The probability is that all the 20 Working Dependants are furnished by this group and that of the remaining 39 only a few of the younger ones are non-workers and that quite 25 are earners. Pursuing this assumption, we therefore find that the 273 Earners consist of 25 who are aged 10—15, 43 aged 15—20 and 205 aged 20—60. This leaves the 28 older males of this latter age group free to join the non-working category. The constitution would then be something like this :—

```
0—10     —136  ⎫
               ⎬ =150+28+23=201  N. W. D.
           ⎧ 14⎭
10—15 — 59 ⎨ 20            = 20  W. D.
           ⎩ 25⎫
15—20 — 43     ⎬ =273      =273  Earners.
           ⎧205⎭
20—60 —233 ⎩         28
60 & over. —23
          ----             ----
           494              494
```

These figures for the South of India lead one to the conclusions that a man's working life is over before the age of 60 is reached owing to a sufficiency of younger men to take up the responsibilities of earners.

For conditions in the central areas of the Continent, the figures for Gwalior and Baroda States may be examined. Bearing in mind that the male ratios in 1,000 persons are 530 and 515 respectively, one is struck by the large figure of 343 earners in Gwalior.

Gwalior. Density 134.

```
0—10     —141  ⎫
               ⎬ =151+16=167  N. W. D.
           ⎧ 10⎭
10—15 — 66 ⎨ 20         = 20  W. D.
           ⎩ 36⎫
15—20 — 53     ⎬ =343   =343  Earners.
20—60 —254     ⎭
60 & over. — 16
          ----          ----
           530           530
```

No other distribution appears probable. It is not likely that many more than 36 boys out of the 66 aged from 10—15 are Earners and if there are fewer, it entails putting some of the 16 old men of over 60 into this category.

Baroda. Density 299.

```
0—10     —141  ⎫
               ⎬ =184+22=206 N. W. D.
           ⎧ 43⎭
10—15 — 62 ⎨ 18          = 18 W. D.
           ⎩  1⎫
15—20 — 50     ⎬ =291    =291 Earners.
20—60 —240     ⎭
60 & over. —22
          ----          ----
           515           515
```

The striking feature of this distribution is that only 1 boy out of the 62 aged from 10—15 is an earner and that 43 of them are non-workers. The progressive educational policy of this State is well known and may be a contributing factor. The proportion of 43 represents an actual population of 105,049. Of those aged from 10—15, 62,330 can at least read, so that the remaining 42,719 must be wholly illiterate and are therefore not likely to be sitting idle. The inference therefore, is that, as in the South, men probably cease working before they reach the age of 60.

Let us now examine the figures for another typical tract of country—the sparsely populated Rajputana Agency and the small province of Ajmer-Merwara.

Rajputana. Density 87.

```
0—10     —147  ⎫
               ⎬ =162+19=181 N. W. D.
           ⎧ 15⎭
10—15 — 66 ⎨ 35          = 35 W. D.
           ⎩ 16⎫
15—20 — 50     ⎬ =308    =308 Earners.
20—60 —242     ⎭
60 & over. —19
          ----          ----
           524           524
```

The distribution here seems to be reasonably normal and calls for no special comment.

Ajmer-Merwara. Density 207.

0—10 —140 } =170+16=186 N. W. D.
10—15 — 61 { 30 }
{ 29 = 29 W. D.
{ 2 }
15—20 — 53 } =313 =313 Earners.
20—60 —258 }
60 & over —16
528 528

The distribution of the boys aged from 10 to 15 is so different to that shown in the adjoining Agency of Rajputana as to call for remark. Out of a total population of 560,292 persons no fewer than 119,524 or 21 per cent. are found in Ajmer City.

Ajmer City.

0—10 —128 }
10—15 — 58 } =202+16=218 N. W. D.
15—20 — 59 { 16 }
{ 5 = 5 W. D.
{ 38 } =329 =329 Earners.
20—60 —291 }
60 & over —16
552 552

A disproportionate number of males and a small proportion of working dependants cannot but have a disturbing effect on the figures for the Province as a whole. The proportion of 16 non-workers aged from 15—20 represents in actual figures 2,912 males and there are certainly not this number attending schools and colleges and therefore non-working dependants. A truer picture would therefore be obtained by assuming that a man's active life ceases before the age of 60, that the working dependants are aged from 10—15 and quite 50 out of 59 aged 15—20 are earners.

CHAPTER IX.

Literacy.

Reference to statistics.

135. For the purposes of census literacy was defined as the ability to write a letter and to read the answer to it, and the figures are therefore strictly comparable with those from 1901 onwards. They exclude those who can read but not write, of whom there is a considerable number, mostly Muslims able to read the Quran in Arabic. Particulars of this latter class have been recorded in Baroda State where they form 50 per mille of the population over 5 years old (males 32 females 18), but in the rest of India the population has been divided into literate and illiterate, alleged literates under the age of 5 being reckoned illiterate. The vernacular script of literacy was not generally recorded, and a reference to this point with such details as are available will be found in the following chapter on Language. Literacy in English was, as hitherto, recorded in a separate column. The general figures of literacy will be found in Table XIII of part ii of this volume, Table XIV containing figures by literacy for selected castes, while the main aspects of literacy will be found more conveniently exhibited by proportional figures at the end of this chapter.

Increase since 1921.

136. The actual number of literates has increased since 1921 by 5,515,205 persons, that is by 24·4 per cent. as compared to the increase in the total population of 10·6 per cent., and of 10·9 per cent. in the population enumerated by literacy. The literates in 1921 numbered 22,623,651, that is 7·1 per cent. of the total population; the actual increase of literates has been 16·3 per cent. of the actual increase of population, so that there has been an increase of literacy relative to the total population in 1931 as compared to 1921; but seeing that the total increase of population since then has been 33,895,298, although literacy has increased appreciably faster than the population, the percentage correspondingly literate now is still not more than 8·0. The marginal table shows the percentage of increase in each province taking its number of literates in 1921 as 100, and including in the provincial figures the figures of the states in political relations with each. The second table shows in the same way the states which formed separate census units. Excluding the Andamans and Nicobars, where the decrease is due to the abandonment of the penal settlement, the only unit showing a decrease is Aden. The provinces in order of extent of literacy in 1921 were Burma, Bengal, Madras, Bombay, Assam, Bihar and Orissa, North West Frontier Province, Central Provinces, Punjab and the United Provinces. To some extent therefore, but by no means consistently, most progress has been made where there was most room for it. Bihar and Orissa proves an exception, while Burma and to a less extent Assam have increased more rapidly than some provinces with more room for expansion. The order of literacy in the States and Agencies in 1921 was Travancore, Cochin, Baroda, Mysore, Sikkim, Gwalior, Rajputana, Central India, Hyderabad, Jammu and Kashmir, so that the same principle of an increase in literacy being most usual where there is most need of it is still at work, though Cochin and to a less extent Baroda are exceptional in a direction the reverse of Bihar and Orissa's. If the increases in states are noticeably higher on the whole than in British India, this is merely another instance of the same thing, as the states as a whole were behind British India in literacy in 1921, though Travancore, Cochin and Baroda were ahead of all units but Burma. In considering the proportion of literacy to the population, however, it is usual to exclude at least that part of the population aged 0—5 years, and also that part of the population (3,078,460) not enumerated

Increase % in Provinces (No. of literates 1921=100).

Province	Increase %
Delhi	+70·6
Punjab	+46·9
Assam	+41·0
Central Provinces and Berar	+38·1
United Provinces	+34·4
Burma	+27·2
INDIA	+24·4
Coorg	+22·7
Bombay	+20·9
North-West Frontier Province	+19·3
Madras	+19·1
Ajmer-Merwara	+19·1
Bengal	+ 9·7
Baluchistan	+ 9·1
Bihar and Orissa	+ 8·9
Andaman and Nicobar Islands	—13·4
Aden	—18·1

Increase % in States and Agencies (No. of literates 1921 = 100).

State/Agency	Increase %
Cochin	+87·0
Jammu and Kashmir	+71·5
Hyderabad	+63·1
Baroda	+59·6
Central India	+55·3
Mysore	+34·2
Gwalior	+28·1
Travancore	+25·8
Rajputana	+22·4
Western India States	+20·7
Sikkim	+ 1·0

GROWTH OF LITERACY PER MILLE OF TOTAL POPULATION 1881-1931

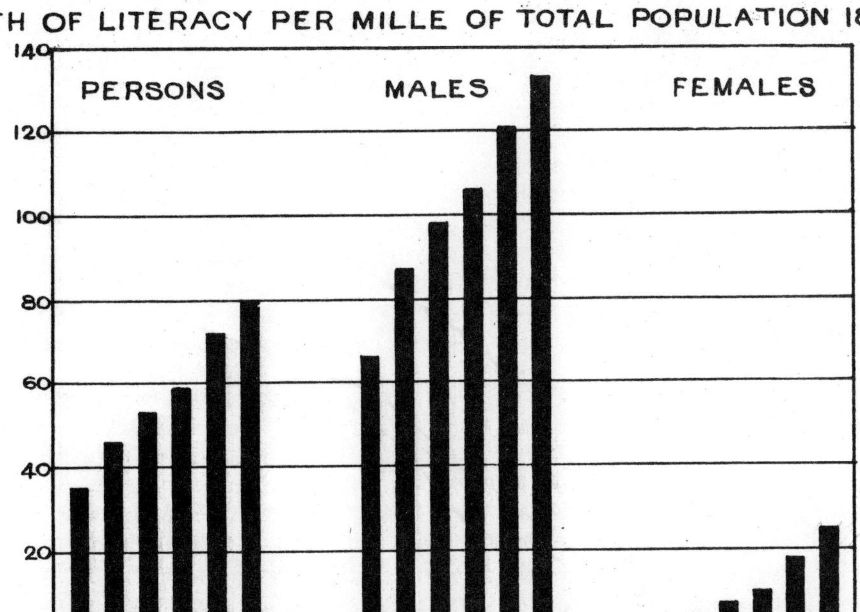

LITERACY IN ENGLISH PER 10,000, 1891 To 1931

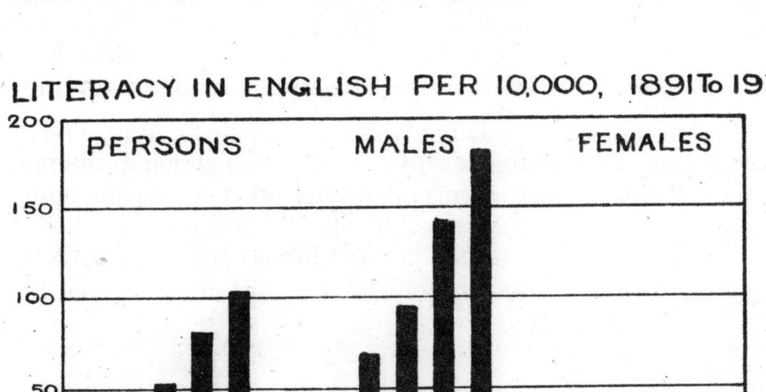

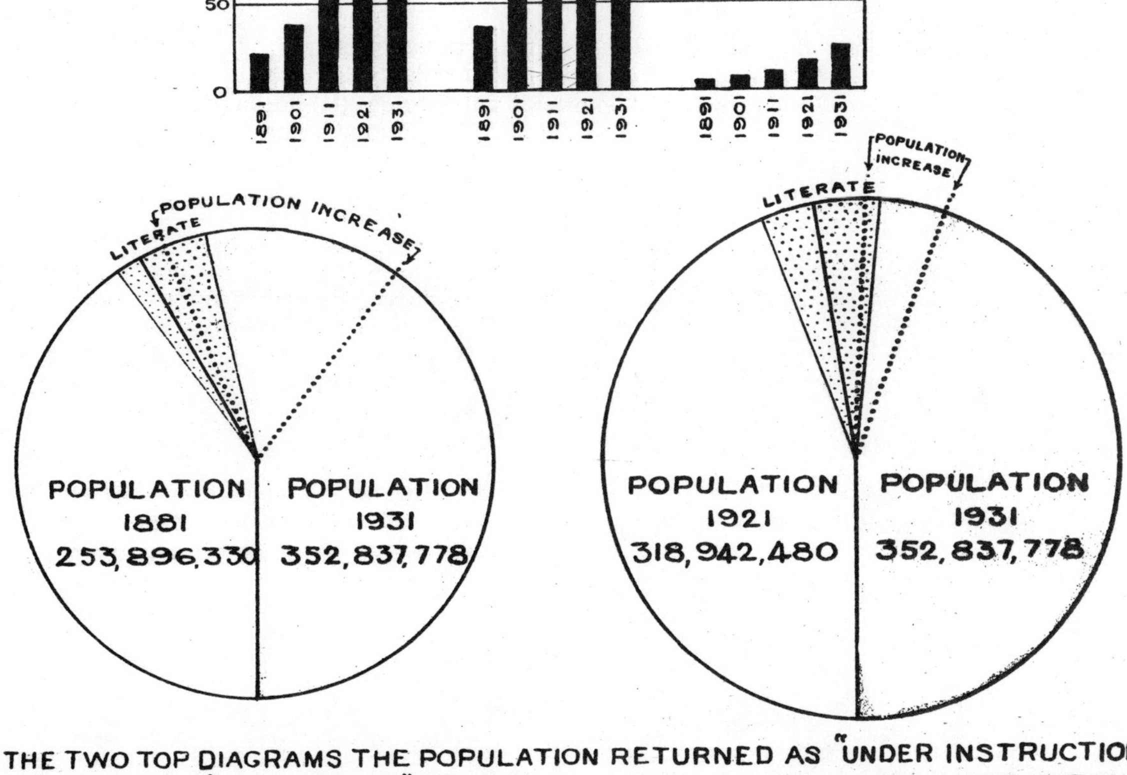

IN THE TWO TOP DIAGRAMS THE POPULATION RETURNED AS "UNDER INSTRUCTION" "LEARNING" OR "UNSPECIFIED" HAS BEEN OMITTED. IN THE LEFT HAND BOTTOM DIAGRAM THOSE RETURNED IN 1881 AS "UNDER INSTRUCTION" HAVE BEEN INCLUDED AS LITERATE.

by literacy. The total population figure to be considered therefore with reference to the figure of literacy is 296,294,029 (males 153,770,850, females 142,523,179) and subsequent calculations will be based on that figure. The figures above represent the actual variation of literates since 1921 in each of the units named, but the real variation of literacy can only be accurately estimated by the variation of the ratio of literates to the population as a whole. A small increase in literates, such as that of 1 per cent. in Sikkim may, and in that case does, represent an actual decrease of literacy, which has failed to keep pace with a growth in population. The marginal table therefore shows the numbers literate per mille of the total population aged 5 and over, and of the corresponding male and female population separately, in 1931 as compared to 1921. Subsidiary Table V shows the growth per mille since 1901. Before that the classification of literacy was into illiterate, learning and literate, and in the diagram showing the growth of literacy since 1881 those shown as "under instruction" in 1881 and as "learning" in 1891 have been excluded from the total taken as literate, the loss of those who were under instruction but would in 1901 and after have been returned as 'literate' is perhaps balanced at any rate in 1881 by the exclusion of the very large number whose literacy or illiteracy was unspecified in the return and most of whom were probably illiterate; since 1901 the return has been 'literate' or 'illiterate' simply. The diagram is also based on the figures per mille of the total population, not on that aged 5 and over only. For the purpose of demonstrating growth the standard taken is immaterial and age groups are lacking in the literacy table of 1881.

Literates per mille aged 5 and over.

	1921.	1931.
Persons	*82*	95
Males	*139*	156
Females	*21*	29

Distribution of Literacy.

137. The literacy of different provinces is given by ratio per mille in Subsidiary Table II at the end of this chapter, and its progress is illustrated in Subsidiary Table V. It is also illustrated graphically in the accompanying diagram

NUMBER OF LITERATE PER MILLE AGED 5 YEARS AND OVER

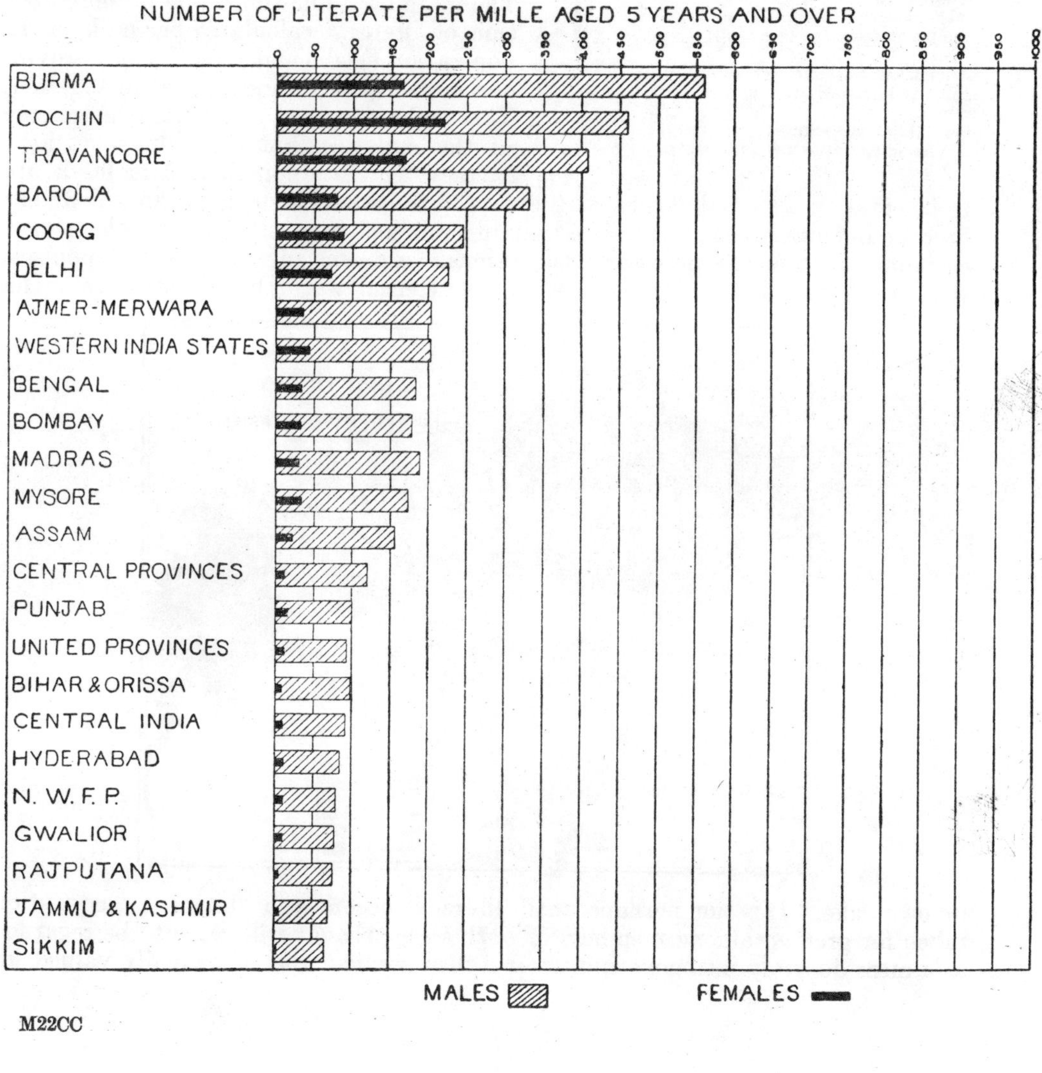

based on the figures of provinces (British territory) and of major states. A warning must here be given against certain figures in the Subsidiary Tables. The exceptionally high figures for Baluchistan and the North-West Frontier Province Agencies and Tribal Areas are entirely misleading, as they are calculated on a very small proportion of the population consisting principally of troops and persons living in cantonments or frontier posts and having no reference at all to the real inhabitants of the area to which they refer. In the marginal table, the North-West Frontier Province agencies are omitted and the Baluchistan figures, British territory and States together, are calculated roughly on the whole population aged 5 and over instead of only on those enumerated by literacy; as however there are no figures for the whole population of Baluchistan by age, the figure for those aged five and over is only an estimate, and Baluchistan is given credit in the accompanying map for a somewhat higher rate. In comparing these figures with those of 1921 some difficulty is experienced in that the 1921 India Report gives no separate figures for provincial states, whereas on this occasion the figures for British India have been separated from those of the states in political relation with various provinces. The marginal table shows the present position of literacy calculated per mille of the population aged 5 and over for all provinces and states, taking the sexes together. This probably gives the truest impression of the real distribution of literacy, as a literacy which is confined to males is apt to be of rather a special nature, and, except in those castes or classes in which male literacy and learning is a natural heritage or a religious necessity, is apt to be a mere economic implement—necessary to business, a means of livelihood, a political weapon, or useful for intercourse with the external world, but of little value for

Province, State, etc.	Literate per mille aged 5 and over.
Burma	368
Cochin	337
Travancore	289
Baroda	209
Aden	182
Coorg	176
Andamans and Nicobars	170
Delhi	163
Ajmer-Merwara	125
Western India States	125
Madras States*	121
Bengal	111
Bombay†	108
Madras	108
Mysore	106
Assam	93
Bombay States	71
Central Provinces	66
Punjab	63
Assam States	61
Bengal States	61
United Provinces	55
Baluchistan	54
Bihar and Orissa	53
Central India	52
Hyderabad	50
North-West Frontier Province ..	49
United Provinces States	49
Gwalior	47
Rajputana	43
Punjab States	42
Punjab States Agency	42
Jammu and Kashmir	40
Bihar and Orissa States	39
Sikkim	35
Central Provinces States	23

**Excluding Cochin and Travancore.*
†*Including Aden.*

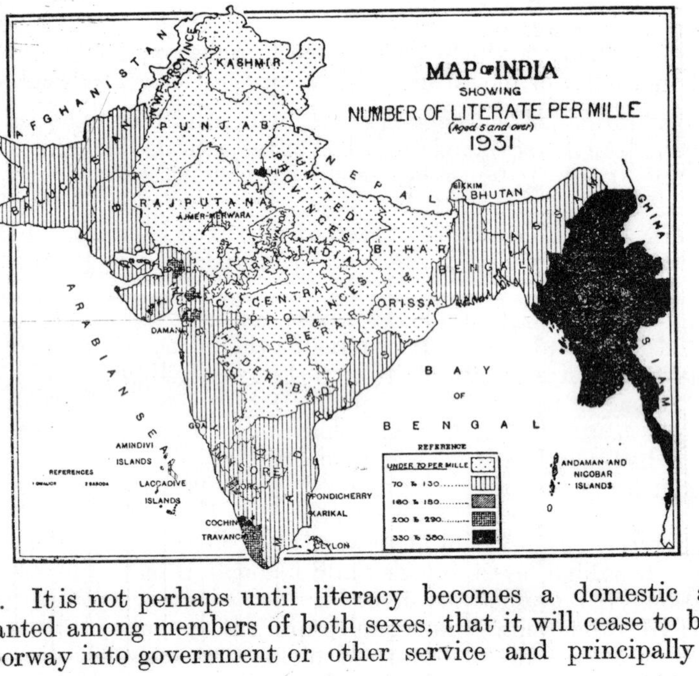

its own sake. It is not perhaps until literacy becomes a domestic acquisition taken for granted among members of both sexes, that it will cease to be regarded as a mere doorway into government or other service and principally valued for its potentiality to that entry. The Census Superintendent of Cochin State ascribes a definite falling off in the number both of institutions and of pupils in the lower secondary and in the primary classes less to the general economic depression than to a growing realisation that literacy is losing its economic value as a qualification for a career. He points out that graduates of Madras University join the Police Department on a salary of Rs. 10 to Rs. 12 per month and are held fortunate in getting employment at all. On the other hand there is no falling off in the higher secondary classes but a continued increase, which he ascribes to such pupils having gone too far to withdraw. The falling off in primary education he rightly regards as a bad sign, and he argues the necessity of completely recasting the educational system. However that may be, the distribution of male literacy shows some divergence from that of general literacy, as may be seen in the accompanying diagram in which provinces and states are arranged in order of general literacy but in which male and female literacy are taken separately for graphic representation.

In the relative position of provinces and states in order of literacy there is little change during the decade. Cochin State, in spite of a very rapid growth in population, has been able to do more than keep pace with that growth, in spite of having started with a very high ratio. Burma easily maintains her lead, for there literacy even if not of a very high order, is a habit, traditional in both sexes and all classes, both boys and girls being taught in the monasteries of which almost every Burman village has at least one. No need perhaps for compulsory education here. In India however it had been introduced by 1930 in 133 urban areas and in 3,137 rural areas of which 2,303 are in the Punjab, though apparently with no very marked success.

138. It is a commonplace that literacy is much more prevalent in towns than in the country, as both the need for it and the opportunities of acquiring it are greater. Thus an examination of the 34 cities tabulated in Table XIII shows that of the total population the proportion literate per 1,000 is 348 males and 149 females as compared to 133 and 25 respectively in India as a whole. A reference may also be made in this respect to the table in paragraph 41 of chapter II. There is naturally a still greater contrast in literacy in English, the figures for the same 34 cities being 1,473 males literate in English per 10,000 of the total population and 434 females, as compared to 181 and 23 respectively for the whole of India. **Literacy in Cities.**

139. The distribution of literacy among females has already been indicated when dealing with the distribution of literacy generally, and a reference to the diagram above will show that the extent of literacy among women is not necessarily determined by its extent among men, but is generally correlative though much less in extent. It will also show the comparative absence of female literacy throughout India proper except in Kerala. In the Bihar and Orissa States, to take an extreme case, there is only one literate female to every fifteen literate males, and in Sikkim less than one to every twenty-two ; even in Burma there are 3·5 literate males to every literate female. In Kerala and Baroda alone is the situation other than in the rest of India, for Cochin State has more than one literate female to every two literate males and Travancore only a little less, while Malabar has nearly one to every three, Coorg a little less than one to every three, Baroda a little fewer and Mysore one to every five. Cochin now leads India in female literacy with Travancore a fair second and Burma a very close third. Comparative progress is illustrated in Subsidiary Table V at **Female Literacy.**

Total number of literate females in

	1921.	1931.
India	*2,782,213*	4,169,105
Assam	*46,002*	81,133
Bengal	*407,831*	664,507
Bihar and Orissa ..	*109,735*	139,083
Bombay and Western India States.	*300,952*	372,154
Burma	*625,706*	1,010,298
Central Provinces ..	*52,304*	79,949
Madras	*456,895*	616,247
North-West Frontier Province.	*8,987*	11,412
Punjab and Punjab States Agency.	*78,339*	163,200
United Provinces ..	*134,004*	218,299
Baroda	*41,300*	79,667
Central India	*15,514*	25,572
Cochin	*49,320*	113,789
Gwalior	*9,689*	15,195
Hyderabad	*43,340*	68,039
Kashmir	*4,007*	9,078
Mysore	*57,023*	90,086
Rajputana	*18,851*	25,258
Sikkim	*118*	150
Travancore	296,067	351,611

the end of this chapter, and the marginal table gives the crude numbers for the larger provinces and states for 1921 and 1931, the figures of provinces being in this case inclusive of the states in political relation with them. It shows an increase of almost 50 per cent. against an increase of 11·4 per cent. in the female population enumerated by literacy, but the figures of female literacy are still absurdly low. Besides the difficulty, still felt very strongly in most provinces, of getting good women teachers, one of the most serious obstacles to the spread of female education is the early age of marriage, which causes girls to be taken from school before they have reached even the standard of the primary school leaving certificate. The report on Education in India in 1929-30 gives a table, reproduced in the margin, showing that of 1·3 million girls in class I only 26 per cent. went on to class II, of 311 thousand in class II only, 63 per cent. went on to class III, and of 183 thousand in class III only 58 per cent. went on to class IV. The total wastage involved is about 90 per cent. Here we are found in a vicious circle, since the early age of marriages prevents the growth of female literacy, while the absence of female literacy seems largely responsible for the absence of any general change in the early age of marriage. Burma and the Malabar Coast are the two exceptions and in Cochin State an increasing tendency is reported for women to seek careers of their own in preference to marriage at all. For the extent of female literacy in different communities and in different castes, a reference may be made to the marginal tables given in paragraphs 140 and 141 below.

Class.	1928-29.	1929-30.	Wastage.
I	1,317,575	..	..
II	311,281	340,221	977,354
III ..	183,143	197,231	113,960
IV ..	93,234	105,665	77,478

Literacy by community.

140. The accompanying diagram shows the number per mille literate in each sex in the different main religions and in Burma. Owing to the tabulation's having

LITERACY PER MILLE AGED 5 AND OVER IN MAIN COMMUNITIES.

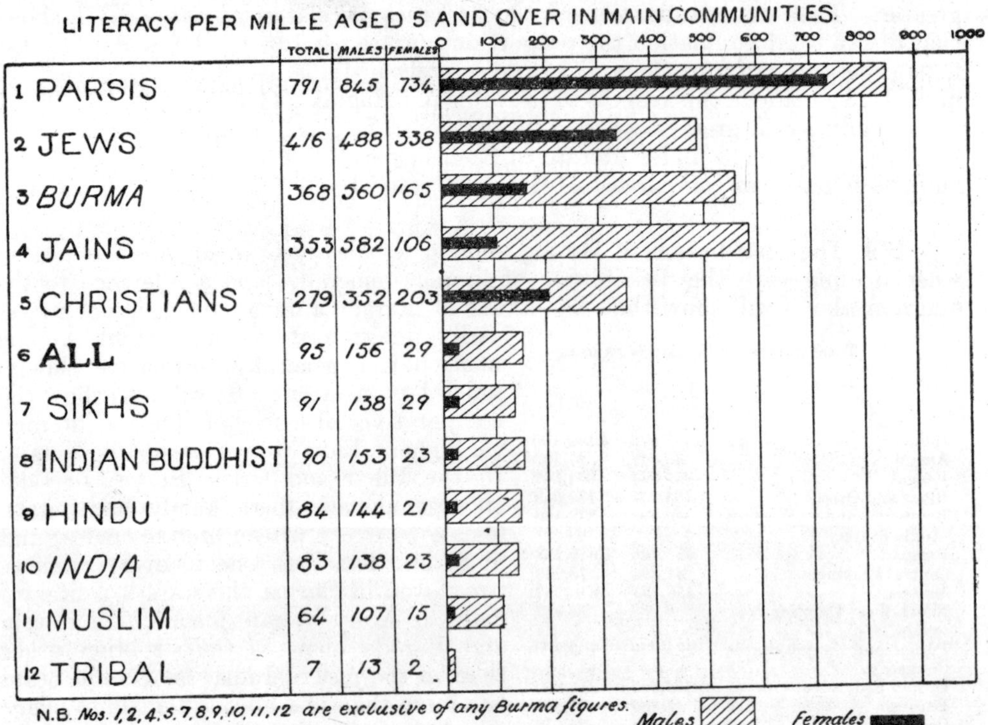

N.B. Nos. 1, 2, 4, 5, 7, 8, 9, 10, 11, 12 are exclusive of any Burma figures.

been based on racial instead of religious groups in Burma the figures of literacy by religion are to this extent discrepant with those of last census as the latter included Hindus, Muslims, etc., in Burma, whereas the present ones are confined to India proper and the figures for Burma are not distinguished by religion except in the case of Hindus and Muslims. This being so it has been thought better here as elsewhere to show Burma as a single unit in the subsidiary tables in this chapter;

it is predominantly composed, of course, of Burmese Buddhists, and though figures for Indian Hindus, Indian Muslims and other Indians will be found in Table XIII, the general standard of literacy in Burma is determined by that of the Buddhist Burmese. Taking the figures as a whole, the greatest progress has been made by Sikhs, Jains, Muslims, and Hindus in that order, while Tribal, Parsis and Christians have all declined in their proportion of literacy since 1921. The unexpected decline among Parsis is confined to males and it is just possible that it can be ascribed to the economic depression. The decline among both Christians and Tribal is to be put down if not wholly at any rate in part, to the exclusion of Burma figures, though it is also possible that the figures of Christians have suffered by the inclusion of illiterate converts and those of Tribal by the return of literate tribesmen as Hindus. The marginal table shows the variations in the descending order of total increase, but it will be noticed that this order is not always retained if the sexes are taken separately. Thus both Parsis and Tribal show a slight increase in feminine literacy in spite of the fall of literacy on their whole population. Again Jains although only second in the rate of growth of general literacy come first in growth in literacy among females, but are behind both Hindus and Muslims in growth among males. The growth in Sikh literacy is noticeable, as they showed hardly any increase at all in the preceding decade and the Census Superintendent of the Punjab in 1921 wrote of their educational stagnation. This time they easily lead in rate of increase except among women, where they are second to the Jains. It is hardly necessary to point out that the high standard of literacy among Parsis, Jews and Jains is partly due to the fact that they are mainly composed of trading classes for whom literacy is essential, and that where literacy is so general as it is among the Parsis, for instance, the rate of growth per mille is not strictly comparable to the rate of growth in a comparatively illiterate community. At the same time it is noteworthy that in Burma where the prevalence of literacy is much greater than in any Indian communities except Parsis and Jains the rate of increase should be as high as 51 per mille for the total population and 50 and 53 for males and females respectively.

Variation in literacy per mille, 1921—1931.

Community.	Total.	Males.	Females.
Sikh	+23	+31	+13
Jain	+12	+7	+19
Muslim	+11	+14	+6
Hindu	+9	+14	+5
Tribal	—2	—3	+1
Parsi	—3	—9	+3
Christian	—6	—3	—7

In considering literacy among the different communities it will perhaps be useful to examine briefly their respective position with regard to literacy of 20 years and over, since such figures might affect any franchise based on literacy. The marginal table gives the figures of literates per mille aged 20 and over by communities for adults only of both sexes as compared to the figure when the whole population over 5 years is considered. If females alone be considered the difference between the comparative figures is more marked and the order they appear in is in one case different, as Christians have a higher proportion of literate females than Jains have. Literacy figures by religion and sex for the various provinces will be found in Subsidiary Table III at the end of this chapter. The following table shows the number literate in British territory in each province in each main community per mille (1) of adults of

Community.	Literates per mille: aged 5 and over.	aged 20 and over.
Parsi	791	851
Jewish	416	482
Jain	353	389
Christian	279	305
Sikh	91	107
Hindu	84	96
Muslim	64	77
Minor and Unspecified ..	19	23
Tribal	7	8
Burma	*368*	*427*

Community.	Literate females per mille: aged 5 and over.	aged 20 and over.
Parsi	734	780
Jewish	338	368
Christian	203	200
Jain	106	90
Sikh	29	29
Hindu	21	19
Muslim	15	14
Minor and Unspecified ..	5	5
Tribal	2	1
Burma	*165*	*171*

the community concerned, (2) of all adults in the province :—

Province, etc.	Hindu. Literates per mille aged 20 and over.		Muslim. Literates per mille aged 20 and over.		Christian. Literates per mille aged 20 and over.		Tribal. Literates per mille aged 20 and over.	
	Of own community.	Of all communities.	Of own community.	Of all communities.	Of own community.	Of all communities.	Of own community.	Of all communities.
India (*excluding Burma*)	96	69	77	17	305	5	8	·2
Ajmer-Merwara ..	113	87	143	24	887	11	3	.01
Assam*	127	74	83	23	232	6	21	2
Bengal	180	83	85	44	496	2	11	·1
Bihar and Orissa ..	64	53		*Separate details not available*			8	·4
Bombay (*excluding Aden*).	118	90	86	18	420	6	5	.03
Central Provinces and Berar.	71	61	180	8	595	2	7	·6
Coorg	195	172	173	16	387	9	0	0
Delhi	170	107	177	56	581	17	0	0
Madras	120	106	154	10	229	8	3	.002
North-West Frontier Province.	335	21	28	25	834	6	0	0
Punjab	123	34	39	22	123	2	0	0
United Provinces Agra and Oudh.	59	50	68	10	317	1	0	0

N.B.—The use of 0 implies the absence of any of that community in the province.
* Assam includes the States, elsewhere excluded, except for India as a whole.

It will be seen that under each community the left-hand column read downwards shows the relative literacy of that community in the different provinces, while the right hand columns read across show the proportions per 1,000 adults in each province who are literate in each of the four communities. Tribal figures are shown in this table as, numerically at any rate, they are the fourth most important community in India excluding Burma, while in literacy they are exceptionally backward. In certain provinces however there are other communities of much local importance. Thus in Bombay **Parsis**, aged 20 and over have 853 literates per 1,000 of their own community and 4 per 1,000 of the adults in the province. In the same province **Jains** have 391 literate of every 1,000 adults and very nearly 4 literate of every 1,000 adults in the province. Of every 1,000 literates in Bombay Province 30 are Jains and 32 are Parsis. In the Punjab **Sikhs** have 110 literate of every 1,000 adult, 15 literate in every 1,000 adults of the province, and 1·0 literate in every 1,000 adults in India proper; of literate adults in the Punjab 200 in every 1,000 are Sikhs. Literacy in Burma has been tabulated by race, qualified in the case of Indians by the differentiation of Hindus and Muslims. The marginal table shows the figures corresponding to those in the table above for India. The difference in literacy between Burma and India is very marked.

Literacy per mille aged 20 and over in Burma.	of own race.	of all races.
Burmans	530	307
Other Indigenous ..	257	79
Indo-Burmans ..	346	4
Indian Hindus ..	314	15
Indian Muslims ..	349	10
Other Indians ..	514	2
Chinese	414	6
Others	961	3

Literacy by Caste.

141. The two dozen castes and tribes shown in the marginal table arranged in order of total literacy per mille indicate the extreme variation of literacy among different social or racial groups. It is not possible to give more than a sample here, and even the much larger number appearing in Table XIV, where castes are shown by literacy and by province, is merely a brief selection by way of illustrating the great divergence between the literacy of different castes in India and between the same castes in different provinces. The proportionate figures for the same castes are given with reference to locality in subsidiary table V at the end of this chapter where comparative figures for 1921 are available. Those with a high social status are not by any means always so high in order of literacy, though of necessity the trading classes are always

Caste or Tribe.	Literate per mille. Males.	Females.
Baidhya	782	486
Nayar	603	276
Kayastha	607	191
Khatri	451	126
Brahman	437	96
Lushei	260	31
Viswabrahman.. ..	197	21
Rajput	153	13
Kurmi	126	12
Teli	114	6
Mali	80	4
Momin	59	8
Parayan	56	6
Jat	53	6
Mahar	44	4
Oraon	35	11
Yadava	39	2
Kumhar	35	4
Bhangi	19	2
Baloch	19	1
Dom	16	2
Gond	16	1
Bhil	11	1
Chamar	10	1

high in male literacy, while the figures of feminine literacy do not necessarily correspond at all to those of masculine, except that they are naturally always less than the latter in the same group; only among the Baidhyas of Bengal and Assam do they reach 50 per cent. of the male figure. The primitive tribes generally are very low in the list except in Assam, where the Lushei show how literate an isolated hill tribe may become when given the opportunity. The high literacy of the Malabar Coast is exemplified in this list by the Nayars, but the high literacy of that coast, and of Travancore and Cochin States, in particular, has influenced the figures of some other castes including even those of the Paraiyans. As regards literacy among exterior castes the proportion per mille literate in each province and the total per mille literate in British provinces and in the States is shown in the marginal table; in India as a whole the exterior castes of Hinduism are a little better equipped than the primitive tribes, but not very much. The details of the castes contributing to the marginal figures are different in different provinces and are detailed in the appendix on the Exterior Castes at the end of this volume. The primitive tribes are very many of them greatly handicapped in the acquisition of literacy by the fact that they are so often given their primary education in a language which is not their own. This is not the case in Assam, where the local vernacular is usually used in primary schools in hill districts, a policy the results of which are reflected in the literacy of the Lusheis and Khasis; if the Nagas are backward it is to be put down largely to the incredibly polyglot nature of their habitat where there are as many vernaculars in a small area as will be found in the rest of India outside Assam and Burma. Generally however the policy seems to be to use the vernacular of the adjacent plains for the primary instruction of hill tribes, and the backwardness of the Santals, for instance, in literacy is attributed by Mr. P. O. Bodding, the best authority on that tribe, to that policy. As regards the difficulties in the way of acquisition of literacy by the depressed classes reference may be made to Appendix I to this volume, on the Exterior Castes.

Literacy among the Exterior Castes.

Province.	Literate per mille.	Province.	Literate per mille.
Baluchistan	69	*Total Provinces* ..	*16*
Bengal	50	Central Provinces ..	15
North-West Frontier Province.	36	Coorg	15
		Madras	15
Assam	31	Delhi	14
Total States ..	*31*	Punjab	8
Bombay	28	Bihar and Orissa ..	6
Ajmer-Merwara ..	22	United Provinces ..	5
India	*19*		

Literacy by Age.

142. In any comparison between literacy in 1931 and in 1921 there is one factor that has to be borne in mind which has already been examined in Chapter VI, and that is the method of sorting by age. The number of literates at any given year will not necessarily be proportional to the total number of that year living, and when the years are grouped the upper limit of any group will contain a higher proportion of literates than the lower until majority is reached. The method of sorting therefore will exclude from the group 5 to 10 a certain number who have appeared in that group in 1921. Some of these will be correctly excluded owing to the preference for the digit 5 which then depleted in some degree the 4 year group in favour of the higher age, but probably more than the correct number will be excluded. This matters little enough as far as real literacy is concerned, as literacy at the age of 5 is only nominal, but the comparative values will suffer a little, the actual position as compared to 1921 being really a little better than the bare figures indicate. The comparable value of the other figures of literacy by age will similarly be slightly impaired in regard to 1921, but the total figure of literacy of course only loses by the small number unduly excluded from the group 5—10 to the group 0—5, and this number can probably be ignored for practical purposes. Subject to this caution we may proceed to compare the figures of literacy at different ages. The marginal table contains the figures per mille for the different age groups in 1921 and 1931. Except for males aged 10-15 there has in all groups been a marked increase particu-

Literacy per mille.

Aged.	*1921.*		1931.	
	Males.	*Females.*	Males.	Females.
5—10	*29*	*10*	59	20
10—15	*110*	*28*	109	34
15-20	*174*	*36*	195	44
20 and over	*171*	*20*	185	28

larly in the proportion of literate females. In the lowest age group the numbers literate have doubled, and the loss in the 10—15 group is only 1 per mille in males, females gaining by 6 per mille. In 1921 also it was this group which showed the lowest ratio of increase over 1911. After group 5—10, group 15—20 shows the next highest increase. It is this group which is usually regarded as most indicative of the growth of literacy, and the lower ratio of the subsequent group is in accordance with normal expectations. Obviously however this need not be necessarily or permanently the case, since once literacy becomes general the reduction in literacy aged 20 and over will depend on the relative proportion of literate to illiterate deaths and on the extent to which literacy is lost. Generally speaking it seems likely that the average literate leads a life less exposed to casual dangers than the average illiterate does, while there is less tendency to lose literacy if its use is involved in the calling pursued. It is perhaps natural therefore that among Parsis, the most longlived community in India, and also one which is mostly engaged in trade and unlikely to suffer from loss of literacy, the ratio of literacy should be even higher above the age of 20 than it is from 15 to 20, and the same considerations may explain the same phenomenon among male Jews. It is also to be seen however among Burmese and among Indian Buddhists (*vide* Subsidiary Table I at the end of this chapter), and the explanations suggested in the India Report 1911 do not seem to account for this satisfactorily. Possibly the case of Burma is met by the fact that literacy is general enough among males to prevent any excess in the ratio literate from 15 to 20, but this explanation cannot be applied to Indian Buddhists.

Literacy in English.

143. Literacy in English has increased, that is in ratio to the numbers of the community, among all communities except Christians, where it has failed to keep pace with the growth in numbers. Sikhs have shown the most rapid increase, having very nearly doubled their ratio during the decade, the next highest proportional increase being among Muslims. Subsidiary Table I shows the distribution of literacy in English among communities, Subsidiary Table IV shows it by age, sex and province, and gives comparative figures for 1921 and 1911. The proportional figures are too small to show conveniently per 1,000, so figures of literacy in English are given per 10,000 of the population aged 5 and over. The Parsis have 5,041, Jews 2,636, Christians 919, Jains 306, Sikhs 151, Indian Buddhists 119, Hindus 113, Muslims 92 and Tribal 4 persons literate in English in every 10,000 of their population. As regards the provinces the figures are again deceptive unless read with caution. The figures for Baluchistan are fictitious for the reasons given in paragraph 137 above ; Delhi and Ajmer-Merwara show high figures on account of the very high proportion of urban population. As pointed out in paragraph 138 above, literacy in English is particularly high in cities on account of the greater opportunities for its acquisition and its greater economic value in use. The high figures of the Andamans and Nicobars are also more or less artificial. Cochin State really leads in literacy in English with 307 so literate per 10,000 of her population aged 5 and over. Coorg follows with 238, Bengal being third with 211. The next is Travancore State with 158. The figures of literacy in English by caste are interesting, as these figures show some divergence from those for vernacular literacy, and the marginal table may be compared with that given in paragraph 141 above.

Caste.	Literate in English per 10,000 of population.	
	Males.	Females.
Baidhya	5,279	1,373
Kayastha	2,418	293
Khatri	1,320	109
Brahman	1,073	86
Nayar	693	137
Lùshei	160	9
Rajput	135	5
Viswabrahman.. ..	86	4
Jat	70	3
Kunbi	69	2
Mali	53	2
Oraon	46	9
Teli	48	0·5
Momin	43	6
Parayan	25	3
Yadava	23	1
Mahar	15	0·8
Kumhar	16	0·5
Baloch	17	0·4
Dom	9	0·9
Bhangi	6	2
Gond	4	0·4
Chamar	3	0·3
Bhil	1	..

Literacy for Franchise.

144. It was suggested when the advent of the Franchise Committee was at hand in 1931 that figures should be obtained at the census of all persons who had reached the leaving standard of primary schools, since such statistics would be useful if any decision were made to base the franchise on some such qualification. It was however found impossible to devise any uniform definition of the necessary standard which could be applied to all provinces. Apart from this it is obvious that the possession of a school leaving certificate, or another of a similar description, applied as a test of literacy would leave unqualified a large number of persons who are literate but possess no such certificate. Some will have left school before such certificates were given at all ; others will have neglected to sit for the examination ; others again will have acquired literacy by private tuition, at a private institution, or in the course of business. It is very doubtful therefore if such a test could conveniently be made use of in determining the qualification for franchise. Many provinces and states however did undertake an enquiry of this kind and the results are referred to in the provincial reports..

It is perhaps worth while in this connection to reproduce here an interesting paragraph from the Central Provinces Report. The Census Superintendent writes :

" It seems proper, at a time when Franchise problems are claiming much attention, to place on record some figures to show to what extent the various tribes, castes and communities of the province are represented in the local Legislative Council. The subjoined table gives those figures :—

Name of caste.	Number of elected members in				Number of nominated members in			
	First Council.	Second Council.	Third Council.	Council of 1931.	First Council.	Second Council.	Third Council.	Council of 1931.
Maratha Brahmin ..	10	19	11	3	1	..	1	3
Other Brahmins ..	11	10	6	7	..	1	..	..
Prabhu	2	1	3	..	..	1	..	2
Rajput	1	2	2	..	..	..	..	1
Bania	6	5	9	2	..	..	..	..
Kayastha	2	2	1	2	1	..	..	..
Maratha and Kunbi	7	6	9	2	..	..	..	6
Madrasi non-Brahmin	..	1	1	1	..	..	..	..
Vidur	..	..	2	..	..	..	..	..
Kalar	1	..	2	2	..	..	..	..
Gond	..	..	..	..	..	..	1	..
Mahar	..	..	..	..	2	2	3	..
Chamar	1	..	..	..	..	..	1	..
Jaiswara	..	..	..	1	..	..	..	..
Barber	..	..	..	3	..	..	..	..
Gwala	..	..	..	1	..	..	..	..
Other Hindus ..	3	..	1	4	1	1	..	2
Christian	2	1	1	1	2	2	2	..
Parsee	1	..	..	3	..	..	..	..
Muslim	6	7	7	4	1	1	..	3

The figures tell their own story. The note below recorded after the third Council explains the tendencies, further rapid development of which is evident from the statistics of 1931. The growth of the strength of the non-Brahmin party is obvious. The inadequate representation of the aboriginal tribes is most striking.

The strongest elements purely from the point of view of caste are the Brahmins, Banias and Marathas and Kunbis. Of these, the Maratha Brahmins and the Marathas and Kunbis each represent communities closely bound by caste, customs and geographical distribution, whilst " Other Brahmins " and " Banias " comprise a number of widely differing castes, in origin mostly foreign to the province, and possessing no such common characteristic as would constitute either of them distinct political entities. It will be noticed that Brahmins were most strongly represented in the second Council when the Swarajists decided to participate in the elections for the first time. The solidity of the Maratha Brahmin element will be realised when it is stated that they then held 14 out of the 24 non-Muhammadan seats in the Berar and Nagpur divisions. This number is now reduced to 8. The total number of Brahmins shows a heavy fall from 29 in the second Council to 17 in the present Council, justifying the inference that a political consciousness is being evoked in other communities. Even now, however, the higher castes account for over two-thirds of the members elected from general constituencies, and the only challenge, slight though it is, to their predominance, comes from the Maratha Kunbis who have succeeded in increasing their numbers in the Council and reproduce a powerful element in the electorate. Only one member of the depressed classes has been elected, and that in the first Council when owing to the boycott there was little competition. The number of members nominated from the depressed classes has been raised from two to four in the third Council, and is made up of three Mahars and one Chamar."

Mr. Shoobert has drawn attention to the inadequate representation of the aboriginal tribes. It should be explained that these tribes number over four million in the Central Provinces and attached states, and form between a fifth and a quarter of the total population, 1,969,214 being adherents of tribal religions while the remainder were returned as Hindus or Christians, but mainly as Hindus.

Comparison with returns of the Education Department.

145. Some comparison is necessary between the figures of literacy returned at the census and the figures compiled by the Education Department showing the number* of schools, colleges and other educational institutions, the pupils under instruction, and their proportion in different provinces and communities in British India. The departmental figures are taken from *Education in India, 1930-31.* The first marginal table therefore shows the number of pupils in 1931 distributed between the different communities and their ratio per mille on the figures of the same communities as obtained by the census returns. These ratios may be compared with the ratio of literacy in the same communities given above in paragraph 140. For calculating the ratio of Buddhists, Burmese have been taken as equivalent to 'Buddhists' in Burma. The exact ratio is uncertain as there are many literate Shans and other Buddhists in Burma who are not included under the term Burmese, and probably many illiterate also. In any case the number of the Department's pupils in Burma bears little relation to vernacular literacy in that province.

Community.	No. of pupils 1931 (Education Department's).	No. per mille of community (1931 census).
Parsis	19,790	205
Europeans and Anglo-Indians.	50,084	185
Indian Christians	418,934	120
Sikhs	195,814	61
Buddhists	653,071	52
Muslims	3,357,593	50
Hindus	7,821,007	44
Others	171,915	25
Total	12,688,308	46

The second table below shows the number of institutions and the number of pupils in them in 1921 and in 1931 and the percentage of variation :—

Institutions.	Number in 1921.	Number in 1931.	Increase per cent.	Number of pupils 1921.	Number of pupils 1931.	Increase per cent.
Universities	13	16		..	8,189	
Arts Colleges	*154*	244	58	*46,737*	66,837	43
Professional Colleges	*66*	73	11	*12,903*	17,002	32
Secondary Schools	*8,816*	13,581	54	*1,237,656*	2,286,411	85
Primary Schools	*158,792*	204,384	29	*6,299,836*	9,362,748	49
Special Schools	*3,946*	8,891	125	*126,758*	315,650	149
Unrecognised Institutions	*33,229*	34,879	5	*592,975*	632,249	7
Total	*205,016*	262,068	28	*8,316,865*	12,689,086	53

It is to be noticed that 74 per cent. of the pupils are in primary schools, a decline of 2 per cent. in the proportion of primary pupils during the decade, so that the already unduly low proportion of primary to secondary education appeared to be falling instead of rising. This aspect of the relation between the two is indicated by the comparative rates of growth (*vide* Subsidiary Table VII at the end of this chapter). While since 1901 the number of primary schools has increased by 110 per cent., those of secondary schools have increased by 151 per cent. and those of colleges by 71 per cent. ; again since 1921 the growth in the number of primary schools has been 28 per cent. only, whereas secondary schools and colleges have increased by 51 per cent. and 44 per cent. respectively. This point is further emphasised by the statement of expenditure. About half the money spent on education is contributed by Government, and of the whole amount, after the exclusion of Direction, Inspection, Buildings, Universities, Boards, Special Schools, and Miscellaneous, we find that Rs. 6,82,07,867 are spent on primary education as compared to Rs. 9,45,23,607 on secondary. Admittedly primary education cannot be extended without spending money on secondary education, but the sums spent on the latter and the number of pupils under secondary instruction appear disproportionately high in view of the large illiterate population. It has been estimated that about two-thirds of the villages in India have no schools, and for the 500,000 census villages in British territory the Education Department figures show little over 200,000 recognised schools, while the addition of all unrecognised rural schools fails to bring the total to 230,000. The average cost per pupil in all recognised institutions worked out at just over Rs. 23 for 1930, but a separate analysis of the cost of primary and secondary pupils respectively gave Rs. 8-5-5 and Rs. 179-4-3 as the cost of each primary and each secondary male pupil for that year, and Rs. 10-3-6 and Rs. 467-3-5 respectively as the corresponding costs of each female pupil (*vide Education in India, 1929-1930*). The high cost of girl pupils is no doubt due in a great degree to their comparative paucity, and is to that extent unavoidable, but the figures do suggest that the amount spent on secondary education is disproportionate to that spent on primary. The reason is simple enough. As a result of the caste system there is an insistent demand for education on the part of those castes who have been accustomed to look to literacy to provide them with a livelihood, and their tendency under competition is to demand higher education. On the other hand there is no widespread demand among other castes for education at all, and this is illustrated by the tremendous wastage in primary schools. This amounts to two-thirds of the total in the case of boys and a great deal more than that in the case of girls, who are apt to leave school when they are married.

This wastage again explains the inordinate excess of pupils shown by the Education Department as under instruction over the numbers returned as literate aged 5—20 by the census, which might have been expected to show some relation to the number of pupils. The comparative figures are shown in the third marginal table, which shows also for comparison the number returned at the census as literate, 20 years and over. These figures may be regarded perhaps as those of effective literacy, which really only begins at about 20 years, and if they appear unduly low when compared to the figures of pupils under instruction, this must be put down to the wastage already mentioned which involves a discard of at least two-thirds of the primary pupils, that is of a half of the total number of pupils. Burma is of course exceptional as most of her literacy is obtained in village monasteries and not through the Education Department. The high figure of Delhi is no doubt due in part to its being mainly an urban area and in part to the concentration there of ministerial officers of Government and their families.

Province.	No. of pupils, 1931, per 1,000 of population aged 5 and over.	Numbers returned as literate at census per 1,000 of population aged 5 and over.	
		Aged 5—20.	Aged 20 and over.
Ajmer-Merwara	40	38	87
Assam*	44	29	62
Baluchistan†	12	14	40
Bengal	63	34	77
Bihar and Orissa	32	15	38
Bombay	67	33	75
Burma	43	106	262
Central Provinces	33	21	45
Coorg	69	53	123
Delhi	73	46	117
Madras	72	32	76
North-West Frontier Province	40	14	35
Punjab	63	20	43
United Provinces	35	17	38

* The figures on which the Assam ratios are calculated include those of Assam States.

† The figures, in which States are again included, are calculated on an estimated figure for the population aged 5 and over, as returns by age and literacy apply only to a small portion of the population.

The Education Department consider that four years at school is required to give permanent literacy, and that the number of literates turned out in any year can therefore be gauged by the number of pupils reading in Class IV in that year. The marginal figures give their numbers annually for the past decade, making a total of 7,660,419. Of these persons it is considered that at least 20% and possibly as much as 25% would be found unfit for promotion, that is to say they have not been rendered permanently literate, so that almost that portion of them may be regarded as having already relapsed into illiteracy by 1931, resulting in a minimum estimate of

Year.	No. of class IV pupils in British India.
1922	635,604
1923	646,962
1924	672,412
1925	668,345
1926	710,895
1927	767,921
1928	803,155
1929	857,409
1930	899,619
1931	998,097
Total	7,660,419

5,750,000 persons rendered literate in British India during the decade. Now the actual increase in the number of literates in British India since 1921 is 4,073,030 a figure which is fairly comparable with the Education Department's estimate when allowance has been made both for the decrease to be replaced among previous literates on account of their normal mortality during the decade and for casualties among the new literates themselves.

	Total number of literates in India in	
	1921.	1931.
India ..	22,623,651	28,131,315
Provinces ..	18,654,541	22,727,571
States ..	3,969,110	5,403,744

The next marginal table, for comparison with the number of pupils per mille of population shown in the third, shows the number of pupils of the Exterior Castes and the ratio of literacy returned by members of these castes at the census. It should be explained that the departmental figures of depressed class pupils have been taken and the ratio per mille at school calculated on the census figures of the Exterior Castes for the various provinces shown. It is possible that the actual castes treated as depressed or exterior do not entirely correspond, and although the difference is likely to be small, except perhaps in Bengal, where the figures include all "educationally backward" classes, the ratios must be treated with caution on this account. It should be added that the census figures for literacy in exterior castes are not quite complete as literacy figures were not available for about 8 per cent. of those treated as exterior. The ratio however has been calculated on the remaining 92 per cent., so that the small deficiency affects only the third column of the table.

Province.	Depressed class pupils (Education Department).	Exterior castes literate at census.	Number per mille of exterior castes: at school.	literate.
Bengal	433,686	230,206	54	50
Bihar and Orissa ..	24,187	32,150	4	6
Bombay	62,903	49,012	36	28
Central Provinces ..	43,008	43,886	15	15
Madras	352,162	107,817	48	15
Punjab	36,279	10,384	30	8
United Provinces ..	125,383	42,858	11	5

The final table in this paragraph shows the number of schools for defectives and the number of pupils attending them according to the Education Department's returns, together with the ratio of those under instruction to the total number of blind and deafmute aged 0—20 as returned at the census from each province possessing schools of this nature. In addition to the schools shown in the statement there is a mission school for the blind at Rajpur,

Province.	Number of schools.			Number of pupils.			Number aged 0—20 at census.			Percentage under instruction.		
	For deaf-mute.	For the blind.	Total.	Deaf-mute.	Blind.	Total.	Deaf-mute.	Blind.	Total.	Deaf-mute.	Blind.	Total.
Bengal . ..	5	1	6	237	80	317	17,429	6,332	23,761	1·4	1·3	1·3
Bihar and Orissa ..	0	2	2	0	79	79	11,068	9,712	20,780	0	·8	·04
Bombay ..	4	3	7	169	125	294	6,491	5,749	12,240	2·6	2·2	2·4
Burma	1	2	3	24	48	72	5,778	2,753	8,531	·4	1·7	·8
Central Provinces ..	1	1	2	20	18	38	3,884	5,156	9,040	·5	·3	·4
Madras	3	4	6*	115	198	370	15,869	7,130	22,999	·7	2·8	1·6
Punjab	..	1	2	..	26	62	7,215	6,986	14,201	..	·4	·4
United Provinces ..	..	1	1	0	12	12	10,424	19,399	29,823	0	·006	·004

* One institution is combined.

Dehra Dun, for which statistics are not available. The totals in the fourth and seventh columns include certain figures for institutions or for pupils whose precise classification as blind or deafmute is unknown. The percentage in the last three columns suggest that the instruction provided by these schools for the defective is virtually irrelevant.

Educated Unemployed.

146. In response to requests from several quarters it was decided to attempt at the 1931 census to obtain figures of the educated unemployed generally believed to be exceedingly high. The general schedule was already inconveniently crowded, and as the return was intended to touch only those who were fully literate a separate schedule was prepared to be filled in by the enumerated himself and not by the enumerator. The instructions on the form employed stated that the information was required in the interest of the public, of the State and of the unemployed themselves, and it might have been anticipated that a general response would have been

made to this effort to obtain information. The attempt was however a failure, as though many forms were issued very few were filled in and returned to the enumerators, and although some provinces and states obtained figures which they considered were worth incorporating in their statistical tables, the results for India as a whole were so unsatisfactory that the figures must have been misleading if credited, and it was decided to omit them from part II of the India volume. Such as they are, they are included in this chapter, but the degree of their probable understatement may be inferred by a comparison of the figures with those obtainable from the Education Department. The latter showed that there were, in 1930, 25,716 candidates who passed for matriculation, 13,633 who passed the Intermediate Arts or Science examination, 9,300 who passed examinations for their B. A. or B. Sc., and 1,426 who passed examinations for their M. A. or M. Sc., a total of over 50,000 of whom over 10,000 were graduates, and the number of graduates turned out annually in India from 1921 onwards has not been less than 7,000 and has at least twice been over 10,000, making over 55,000 graduates alone between 1921 and 1930, apart from those who have failed to graduate; in comparison with this the 15,000 odd returned as unemployed, most of whom were only matriculates, can hardly be regarded as affording a satisfactory explanation of the outcry there is about the lack of employment for the educated or the vast number of applications that are received for any vacancy for which some educational qualification is necessary.

Educated Unemployed (*i*) By Class.

Serial No.	Class.	Total un-employed.	Aged 20—24. Un-employed for less than one year.	Aged 20—24. Un-employed for one year or more.	Aged 25—29. Un-employed for less than one year.	Aged 25—29. Un-employed for one year or more.	Aged 30—34. Un-employed for less than one year.	Aged 30—34. Un-employed for one year or more.	Aged 35—39. Un-employed for less than one year.	Aged 35—39. Un-employed for one year or more.
1.	Brahmans	4,245	668	1,938	168	903	47	341	14	166
2.	Depressed Hindus ..	303	21	117	12	90	11	39	3	10
3.	Other Hindus ..	6,860	1,001	3,082	278	1,597	77	585	23	217
4.	Muslims	2,580	318	1,081	107	683	30	265	14	82
5.	Anglo-Indians ..	80	13	28	7	9	4	9	2	8
6.	Burmans	37	12	11	2	4		2	3	3
7.	All Other Classes* ..	1,204	195	540	79	258	7	90	9	26
	Total Unemployed ..	15,309	2,228	6,797	653	3,544	176	1,331	68	512

* Includes 51 Indians (class unspecified) in Burma.

Total English-knowing Unemployed under 20 years	2,666
Ditto ditto over 40 years	488
Total number of Educated Unemployed whose fathers were Soldiers	82
Ditto ditto ditto Cultivators	6,428
Ditto ditto ditto Artizans	340
Ditto ditto ditto Menials or servants	983
Total number of Educated Unemployed passed Matric. or S. L. C. who though not totally unemployed failed to obtain employment with which they were satisfied	3,123

Educated Unemployed (*ii*) By Degree.

Degrees.	Total Un-employed.	Aged 20—24.	Aged 25—29.	Aged 30—34.	Aged 35—39.
1	2	3	4	5	6
1. British Degrees..	30	4	9	11	6
2. Continental Degrees	3	..	2	..	1
3. American Degrees	8	2	1	..	5
4. Other Foreign Degrees	5	..	1	1	3
5. Indian Degrees—					
Medical	154	20	68	53	13
Legal	149	14	59	52	24
Agricultural	21	15	4	2	..
Commerce	111	55	42	8	6
M. A.	113	31	44	28	10
M. Sc.	41	10	18	9	4
B. A.	1,370	708	474	133	55
B. Sc.	169	76	72	19	2
B. Eng. or L. C. E.	42	13	20	7	2
B. T. or L. T.	35	10	22	3	..
Intermediate	284	145	80	37	22
School L. C. or Matric	11,317	7,150	2,902	951	314
Non-qualified	1,457*	772	379	193	113
Total Unemployed ..	15,309	9,025	4,197	1,507	580

* From Bombay, the United Provinces, Baroda and the Western India States.

The reasons given for the failure of the return were various. In Burma the educated but unemployed are largely Indians and mostly to be found in Rangoon. The reason given for their failure to make the return was that they feared use would be made of it to repatriate to India those who were without employment. In Bengal the reason alleged was a fear on the part of the unemployed *bhadralok* that all that was wanted was a list of them for the police as political suspects, while another rumour accused the Government of trying to win over the unemployed from the congress party by false hopes of employment. In Madras the attitude of the recipient of the unemployment schedule was described as "You will not give me employment, why should I fill up your schedule?" and it seems likely that this feeling, together with a dislike of admitting failure to have found employment and general apathy towards the census is to be taken as the most common cause of the schedule's failure. This failure is not only indicative of the uselessness of expecting to obtain a voluntary return of information failure to comply with which involves no penalty, but a warning against attempts to collect special information on separate schedules returned by the individual as distinct from information collected by an enumerator who retains the schedule himself throughout the proceedings.

In connection with educated unemployment and in explanation of what he aptly labels the *cacoethes matriculandi* the Census Superintendent for Assam quotes the following passage from a note written by Mr. Cunningham (many years Director of Public Instruction in Assam) for the Calcutta University Commission in 1917, and it is still true to-day :—

> "There is a constant conflict in educational policy between the Government and people—the one desiring to improve the standard of education, the other crying on behalf of the hungry who are not fed, for the relaxation of standards and the wider spread of education, good or bad....... The privileged classes do not take to commerce or industry, the unprivileged follow the lead of the privileged. It has been said that in these parts the social order is a despotism of caste tempered by matriculation. It is only by matriculating and taking the part in the after-life which has been reserved for those who have matriculated that the lower castes can raise themselves to consideration. It is only so that they can raise a representation strong enough to fight for their social and political interests; and it is only by education that the privileged classes can qualify themselves to oppose effectively the conservatism of Government. On both hands this literary education is what every man desires. And if new ways are opened which lead to profit, the best amongst the lower classes will still press forward, undiverted, to the university unless the new employment is socially esteemed, and certificated by the fact that the *bhadralog* compete for it."

The Census Superintendent himself sums up the position as follows :—

> "Matriculation has in fact assumed much the same importance in the social sphere as a public school education has done in England. The ambition to 'make a gentleman' of their son is not confined to the parents of the lower classes of any one country and in Assam this takes the form of matriculation and a job which does not involve manual labour. The respectability of a community in Assam, can, in fact, be generally measured by the number of persons belonging to that community who are in Government service."

SUBSIDIARY TABLE I.

Literacy by Age, Sex and Religion.

Religion.	Number per mille who are literate.											Number per mille aged 5 and over who are illiterate.			Number per 10,000 aged 5 and over who are literate in English.		
	All ages 5 and over.			5—10.		10—15.		15—20.		20 and over.							
	Persons.	Males.	Females.	Males.	Females.	Males.	Females.	Males.	Females.	Males.	Females.	Persons.	Males.	Females.	Persons.	Males.	Females.
1	2	3	4	5	6	7	8	9	10	11	12	13	14	15	16	17	18
All Religions (India)	95	156	29	59	20	109	34	195	44	185	28	905	844	971	123	212	28
All Religions (Burma).	368	560	165	227	103	385	161	618	210	662	171	632	440	835	128	202	50
All Religions (India proper).	83	138	23	52	16	98	28	176	36	165	21	917	862	977	123	212	27
Hindu ..	84	144	21	55	15	104	26	184	34	168	19	916	856	979	113	204	16
Sikh	91	138	29	39	16	88	30	179	50	159	29	909	862	971	151	251	21
Jain	353	582	106	250	88	433	144	682	174	670	90	647	418	894	306	571	20
Buddhist ..	90	153	23	37	13	69	18	149	29	203	26	910	847	977	119	207	26
Zoroastrian ..	791	845	734	463	430	661	632	871	824	925	780	209	155	266	5,041	6,396	3,592
Muslim ..	64	107	15	38	11	71	18	134	23	131	14	936	893	985	92	164	11
Christian ..	279	352	203	159	128	278	220	454	296	402	200	721	648	797	919	1,174	649
Jew	416	488	338	230	212	311	300	498	397	583	368	584	512	662	2,636	3,492	1,710
Tribal	7	13	2	5	1	9	2	18	2	15	1	993	987	998	4	7	..
Others	19	30	5	10	3	21	4	43	8	36	5	981	970	995	28	47	6

Details against individual religions refer to India proper excluding Burma.

SUBSIDIARY TABLE II.

Literacy by Age, Sex and Locality.

Province, State or Agency.	Number per mille who are literate.										
	All ages 5 and over.			5—10.		10—15.		15—20.		20 and over.	
	Persons.	Males.	Females.	Males.	Females.	Males.	Females.	Males.	Females.	Males.	Females.
1	2	3	4	5	6	7	8	9	10	11	12
INDIA	95	156	29	59	20	109	34	195	44	185	28
Provinces	99	163	29	61	20	112	33	203	43	194	29
1. Ajmer-Merwara	125	203	35	83	26	140	41	232	48	240	33
2. Andamans and Nicobars ..	170	223	46	30	18	128	53	187	69	253	47
3. Assam	93	156	22	65	19	116	30	193	33	183	19
4. Baluchistan (Districts and administered Territories).	336	397	156	188	111	301	171	453	162	412	162
5. Bengal	111	182	33	74	24	128	37	220	42	217	32
6. Bihar and Orissa	53	98	8	37	6	66	9	122	12	119	8
7. Bombay Presidency (including Aden).	108	176	31	67	21	127	37	232	49	204	30
Aden	182	258	46	40	24	155	49	229	59	302	47
8. Burma	368	560	165	227	103	385	161	618	210	662	171
9. Central Provinces and Berar	66	120	12	49	10	90	15	164	19	138	10
10. Coorg	176	246	87	108	56	178	94	274	137	279	82
11. Delhi	163	226	72	79	44	145	71	254	90	264	75
12. Madras	108	188	30	64	20	121	36	236	51	227	28
13. North-West Frontier Province (Districts and Administered territories).	49	80	12	22	8	44	13	114	20	98	12
14. Punjab	63	100	17	30	9	69	18	141	29	118	17
15. United Provinces of Agra and Oudh.	55	94	11	37	7	71	13	120	18	108	11
States and Agencies ..	82	130	29	50	21	100	37	171	48	151	25
16. Assam States	61	98	25	30	13	65	27	129	42	119	24
17. Baluchistan States ..	182	228	52	75	36	148	63	195	53	253	55
18. Baroda State	209	331	79	157	75	301	132	470	147	354	55
19. Bengal States ..	61	104	11	30	7	59	13	138	16	127	10
20. Bihar and Orissa States ..	39	73	5	28	4	49	6	86	7	91	5
21. Bombay States	71	123	15	48	11	92	19	172	27	144	14
22. Central India Agency ..	52	92	9	35	7	61	10	112	14	111	9
23. Central Provinces States ..	23	42	3	10	2	24	3	62	5	52	3
24. Cochin State	337	460	220	264	191	439	303	575	321	498	187
25. Gwalior State	47	78	11	31	7	54	10	90	14	94	11
26. Hyderabad State	50	85	12	39	9	71	13	137	20	90	11
27. Jammu and Kashmir State ..	40	70	6	18	5	38	8	89	10	87	6
28. Madras States (excluding Cochin and Travancore).	121	230	21	35	9	170	30	245	39	290	19
29. Mysore State	106	174	33	41	17	153	46	205	55	208	30
30. North-West Frontier Province (Agencies and Tribal Areas).	374	383	72	144	37	224	65	368	103	392	79
31. Punjab States	42	74	6	17	3	39	5	85	9	90	6
32. Punjab States Agency ..	42	70	7	14	3	32	7	81	11	90	7
33. Rajputana Agency ..	43	76	6	23	3	43	5	86	8	96	6
34. Sikkim State	35	66	3	7	1	16	2	59	3	96	4
35. Travancore State ..	289	408	168	166	113	314	200	530	274	475	153
36. United Provinces States ..	49	90	4	36	3	66	5	104	6	106	4
37. Western India States Agency	125	204	43	98	31	166	53	252	66	236	39

SUBSIDIARY TABLE III.

Literacy by Religion, Sex and Locality.

Province, State, or Agency.	Number per mille who are literate.									
	Hindu.		Jain.		Muslims.		Christian.		Tribal.	
	Males.	Females.	Males.	Females.	Males.	Females.	Males.	Females.	Males.	Females.
1	2	3	4	5	6	7	8	9	10	11
India	**144**	**21**	**582**	**106**	**107**	**15**	**352**	**203**	**13**	**2**
Ajmer-Merwara	164	23	799	82	196	28	848	773	5	..
Andaman and Nicobar Islands	261	64	..	..	194	42	472	299	1	..
Assam (inclusive of States)	186	25	716	54	115	16	277	144	31	4
Baluchistan	516	146	778	111	44	3	786	644	..	
Bengal	263	50	644	203	116	17	487	389	14	4
Bihar and Orissa	102	7	601*	164*	100*	11*	158*	82*	13	1
Bombay including Aden	178	26	540	108	121	16	455	286	10	..
Burma†	338	109	..	..	372	60	..	..	..	..
Central Provinces and Berar	118	9	625*	100*	265	35	626	502	12	1
Coorg	246	88	600	324	203	31	432	215	..	..
Delhi	208	60	588	154	213	55	542	436	..	..
Madras	182	26	612	98	229	21	278	147	6	..
North-West Frontier Province (Districts and Administered Territories).	416	101	..	..	42	3	786	544	..	..
Punjab	166	26	502	87	58	8	121	74	..	..
United Provinces of Agra and Oudh	91	9	590	128	97	16	327	241	..	..
Baluchistan States	400	8	..	..	10	..	750	500	..	..
Baroda State	315	72	849	298	420	79	506	263	37	4
Bengal States	119	13	766	85	74	6	218	44	..	..
Bihar and Orissa States	78	5	..	..	..	..	..	..	5	..
Bombay States	114	13	383	68	138	16	301	150	5	..
Central Indian Agency	83	7	637	100	198	8	679	530	2	..
Central Provinces States	50	3	..	..	272	32	65	26	3	..
Cochin State	428	169	716	177	276	49	580	388	..	..
Gwalior State	69	9	398	64	156	28	645	687	..	..
Hyderabad State	70	8	319	66	205	35	221	115	10	2
Jammu and Kashmir State	187	19	802	386	34	2	294	305	16	..
Madras States (excluding Cochin and Travancore).	221	21	579	125	336	15	280	23	..	..
Mysore State	161	24	442	77	284	101	488	341	22	1
North-West Frontier Province (Agencies and Tribal areas).	430	91	..	..	177	36	947	171	..	..
Punjab States	74	5	658	67	56	5	622	636	..	..
Punjab States Agency	98	8	443	38	34	4	212	178	..	..
Rajputana Agency	62	4	607	32	71	7	649	563	..	..
Sikkim State	73	4	1,000	..	813	..	617	322	55	..
Travancore State	399	142	611	..	253	30	460	251	38	2
United Provinces States	100	4	388	105	55	5	38	20	..	..
Western India States Agency	168	35	670	196	253	23	766	706	37	27

* Includes States.

† Otherwise compiled by Races :—

	Other Indians.	Burmese.	Other Indigenous Races.	Indo-Burman Races.	Chinese.	Others.
Males	536	717	350	402	454	914
Females	323	210	80	180	171	885

SUBSIDIARY TABLE IV.

Literacy in English by Age, Sex and Locality.

Literate in English per 10,000.

Province, State or Agency.	1931. 5—10 Males.	1931. 5—10 Females.	1931. 10—15 Males.	1931. 10—15 Females.	1931. 15—20 Males.	1931. 15—20 Females.	1931. 20 and over. Males.	1931. 20 and over. Females.	1931. All ages 5 and over. Males.	1931. All ages 5 and over. Females.	1921. All ages 5 and over. Males.	1921. All ages 5 and over. Females.	1911. All ages 5 and over. Males.	1911. All ages 5 and over. Females.
INDIA	**52**	**15**	**129**	**13**	**336**	**47**	**250**	**27**	**212**	**28**	**160**	**18**	**109**	**12**
Provinces	57	16	136	31	351	47	265	28	224	29	176	19	121	13
Ajmer-Merwara	112	41	260	71	643	96	530	73	447	71	364	56	269	36
Andaman and Nicobar Islands	76	46	385	114	889	130	534	135	513	118	315	111	329	170
Assam	38	8	117	18	346	25	272	14	220	15	189	11	111	5
Baluchistan	474	347	928	502	1,378	409	1,438	749	1,338	608	184	25	119	21
Bengal	145	32	306	58	642	68	495	46	427	48	339	23	228	15
Bihar and Orissa	21	4	52	7	143	11	113	7	92	7	78	5	47	3
Bombay	45	22	125	49	424	92	361	60	286	56	230	37	168	25
Burma	66	35	133	62	284	81	233	45	202	50	155	38	104	24
Central Provinces and Berar	23	8	61	14	179	21	133	12	111	13	84	9	64	6
Coorg	104	66	266	135	574	218	457	96	405	112	301	65	188	35
Delhi	162	89	405	148	1,111	224	1,088	205	895	183	566	102	..	..
Madras	61	19	154	39	428	65	302	33	257	35	193	23	140	15
North-West Frontier Province	30	10	83	14	382	21	333	23	255	20	169	15	98	9
Punjab *including Agency*	30	8	105	17	344	32	219	20	188	19	117	12	92	12
United Provinces of Agra and Oudh	27	8	66	13	174	19	128	14	109	13	73	10	55	8
States and Agencies	27	9	95	25	264	45	176	21	151	22	97	16	62	9
Baroda States	33	8	169	23	578	42	313	15	281	18	153	10	104	5
Central India Agency	16	5	43	11	151	16	113	10	92	10	68	6	41	3
Cochin State	104	54	383	183	1,118	406	663	137	582	163	353	76	233	36
Gwalior State	17	3	42	5	102	9	99	7	79	6	56	2	..	..
Hyderabad State	31	10	78	16	171	21	118	12	105	13	55	10	39	6
Jammu and Kashmir State	24	3	66	6	209	10	130	6	113	6	68	3	42	1
Mysore State	20	13	187	57	460	87	321	48	271	48	202	33	133	25
Rajputana Agency	16	2	35	3	87	5	66	4	56	4	34	3	24	2
Sikkim State	8	..	19	2	73	4	75	3	56	3	70	3	41	1
Travancore State	52	27	167	76	538	162	371	66	308	72	247	58	152	23
Western India States Agency	29	2	120	7	384	15	243	8	205	7	*	*	*	*

*Included against Bombay.

SUBSIDIARY TABLE V.
Literacy by Caste.

Caste.	Number per 1,000 who are literate.				Number per 10,000 literate in English.			
	1931		1921		1931		1921	
	Males.	Females.	Males.	Females.	Males.	Females.	Males.	Females.
1	2	3	4	5	6	7	8	9
ASSAM.								
Ahom	246	14	167	9	451	7	355	6
Jugi	266	26	156	11	112	2	88	2
Kachari (Tribal)	62	3	17	..	54	..	10	..
BALUCHISTAN.								
Baluch (Biloch)	8	..	8	..	4	..	2	..
Brahui	12	..	9	..	5	..	2	..
Pathan	21	1	13	..	23	1	8	..
BENGAL.								
Baidya	777	476	714	431	5,295	1,402	4,458	613
Brahman	645	216	654	169	2,888	332	2,504	103
Kayastha	571	209	559	154	2,740	354	2,285	123
Barui	284	56	356	38	721	58	716	13
Kamar	250	37	322	24	450	42	413	9
Jogi (Jugi)	240	33	290	14	396	32	288	7
Napit..	198	25	245	16	333	28	308	7
Baishnab	284	37	259	18	417	35	224	7
Kaibartta (Chasi)	324	39	218	11	472	19	241	3
Goala..	165	24	181	12	293	19	227	5
Dhoba	137	19	142	8	150	12	148	3
Namasudra	145	15	142	6	224	9	134	2
Kaibartta (Jalia)	120	22	110	6	133	22	102	3
Jolaha	133	40	81	4	209	65	39	1
Bagdi	34	4	40	2	20	3	30	..
Hari	36	5	36	1	18	4	14	..
Bauri	14	5	11	1	9	..	7	..
Santal	14	4	8	..	7	..	2	..
BIHAR AND ORISSA.								
Kayastha	605	118	591	84	1,813	153	1,592	51
Brahman	356	28	304	19	371	16	260	8
Babhan	233	25	222	20	143	3	120	3
Rajput	217	13	208	9	156	3	182	2
Khandait	197	9	160	7	82	1	56	..
Teli	114	4	93	2	36	1	23	..
Kurmi	93	4	76	2	39	..	20	..
Chasa	95	3	75	2	18	..	14	..
Jolaha	67	8	50	7	40	1	42	4
Gaura	50	2	35	1	13	..	7	1
Goala..	37	2	26	1	17	..	14	..
Dhobi	29	2	20	1	5	..	6	1
Ho	17	1	14	1	13	..	17	1
Pan (Hindu)	23	..	15	..	1	..	2	..
Santal (Hindu)..	12	1	13	..	4	..	4	..
Oraon (Tribal)	14	7	12	1	12	..	4	1
Dosadh	12	1	8	1	4	..	2	..
Munda (Tribal)	11	2	10	1	6	..	3	1
Santal (Tribal)	8	1	7	1	2	..	4	..
Chamar	10	1	8	..	2	..	1	..

SUBSIDIARY TABLE V—*contd.*

Caste.	Number per 1,000 who are literate				Number per 10,000 literate in English.			
	1931		1921		1931		1921	
	Males.	Females.	Males.	Females.	Males.	Females.	Males.	Females.
1	2	3	4	5	6	7	8	9
BOMBAY.								
Brahman	788	231	652	144	2,507	221	1,612	72
Lohana	470	74	343	77	790	25	443	61
Lingayat	293	20	231	15	136	1	69	1
Maratha	223	28	58	3	148	2	20	1
Agri	98	3	41	3	14	1	9	..
Mahar, Dhed	63	5	23	1	28	1	13	1
Bharwad	25	2	10	1	3	..	2	..
Bhil	10	..	4	..	1	..	..	..
BURMA.								
Arakanese	678	163	552	79	230	37	105	15
Mon Group	457	124	402	101	85	18	30	7
Karen Group	341	144	222	78	101	52	86	41
Taungthu	275	31	158	17	22	6	15	1
Kuki Chin Group	30	..	102	8	13	..	9	4
Palaung-Wa Group	115	2	87	1	3	..	3	..
Kachin	46	13	21	3	10	1	5	..
CENTRAL PROVINCES AND BERAR.								
Baniya	598	74	430	41	462	11	199	6
Brahman	581	122	386	63	1,345	10?	812	40
Rajput	209	15	137	11	165	6	156	9
Kalar..	180	10	127	6	70	11	59	3
Kurmi	124	4	82	3	27	..	19	..
Kunbi	144	5	78	2	51	2	24	1
Mali	92	3	66	3	36	..	28	..
Lodhi	86	3	61	3	12	..	22	..
Teli	103	3	59	4	22	..	18	1
Lohar	147	4	55	6	24	1	24	7
Dhobi	62	3	39	4	13	..	15	..
Ahir	33	2	31	4	12	..	26	3
Mehra	56	3	27	1	22	..	6	..
Dhimar	33	2	23	3	10	2	9	..
Gond	17	1	10	1	3	..	2	..
Chamar	16	1	8	1	3	..	3	..
MADRAS. (Including Cochin and Travancore.)								
Brahman	800	286	608	152	3,271	183	1,895	83
Nayar	604	276	491	215	694	137	433	49
Komati	615	68	521	54	354	13	288	9
Chetti	447	97	387	25	348	15	235	5
Vaniyan	152	8	298	21	78	..	109	6
Kammalan	462	95	277	26	73	8	69	3
Labbai	438	27	300	15	240	6	92	4
Kaikolan	186	10	261	18	172	6	79	2
Kshatriya	764	625	244	38	3,329	723	263	17
Kallan	235	8	163	5	98	3	38	1
Telaga	149	25	119	17	220	8	182	6
Mappilla	265	45	117	8	96	4	19	..

Caste.	Number per 1,000 who are literate.				Number per 10,000 literate in English.			
	1931		1921		1931		1921	
	Males.	Females.	Males.	Females.	Males.	Females.	Males.	Females.
1	2	3	4	5	6	7	8	9
MADRAS.								
(Including Cochin and Travancore)—*contd.*								
Idaiyan	472	264	112	9	1,288	135	90	4
Pallan	56	1	46	2	10	..	7	..
Paraiyan	56	6	37	3	25	3	16	1
Golla	45	3	29	3	40	1	26	1
Mala	16	1	16	1	7	..	7	
Madiga	9	1	9	1	4	..	5	
Cheruman	13	3	8	1	..	..	1	..
NORTH-WEST FRONTIER PROVINCE.								
Awan	67	10	28	2	167	29	43	..
Pathan	48	6	23	1	120	14	30	..
PUNJAB.								
Khatri	438	114	377	61	1,277	85	1,006	39
Baniya (Agarwal)	490	34	386	20	468	17	324	10
Arora..	364	64	294	30	435	29	255	10
Brahman	268	34	214	19	453	20	342	8
Saiyid	216	33	172	26	483	26	341	11
Sheikh	198	43	141	24	545	43	351	11
Pathan	140	26	100	13	356	21	226	7
Kashmiri	140	32	64	11	409	33	167	7
Rajput	89	11	58	6	169	9	85	6
Tarkhan	70	9	38	5	95	3	30	1
Jat	55	7	32	3	76	3	36	1
Kanet	49	1	36	1	29	..	24	..
Awan..	60	6	36	1	96	3	43	..
Arain	56	8	28	3	112	9	52	1
Nai	48	4	28	2	50	1	24	1
Mirasi	41	3	28	1	28	1	17	1
Lohar	51	5	26	2	55	3	36	1
Ahir	30	2	22	1	49	1	27	1
Jhinwar (Jhiwar)	42	4	22	2	39	2	22	..
Julaha	32	3	20	1	28	1	10	..
Biloch	24	2	16	1	23	1	12	..
Teli	24	2	13	1	24	1	9	..
Mochi	20	2	10	1	16	..	4	..
Kumhar	21	2	9	1	21	1	7	..
Chamar	14	1	9	..	7	..	2	..
Machhi	17	2	7	1	19	1	5	..
Chuhra	13	3	4	..	14	4	4	..
UNITED PROVINCES OF AGRA AND OUDH.								
Kayastha	702	191	523	90	1,964	215	1,122	50
Saiyid	380	87	210	38	895	36	227	13
Brahman	293	25	191	13	244	19	122	8
Rajput	183	14	114	12	118	4	57	5
Jat	81	8	51	2	71	4	38	1
Julaha	54	5	30	3	24	1	9	..
Barhai	44	4	27	2	19	2	15	7
Kurmi	54	1	30	1	17	..	10	..

SUBSIDIARY TABLE V—*concld.*

Caste.	Number per 1,000 who are literate.				Number per 10,000 literate in English.			
	1931		1921		1931		1921	
	Males.	Females.	Males.	Females.	Males.	Females.	Males.	Females.
1	2	3	4	5	6	7	8	9
UNITED PROVINCES OF AGRA AND OUDH—*cond.*								
Teli	43	2	22	1	10	..	5	..
Lohar	46	2	20	1	22	..	6	..
Gujar..	31	2	19	1	13	..	4	..
Nai	39	2	17	2	16	..	6	1
Lodha	24	1	13	1	4	..	2	1
Ahir	20	1	12	..	8	..	4	..
Dom	10	..	12	..	2	..	3	..
Kahar	18	1	17	1	8	1	6	..
Mallah	22	..	10	..	5	..	2	..
Gadariya	11	1	6	..	5	2	14	..
Kumhar	11	1	6	..	6	1	4	..
Bhangi	10	1	5	..	6	2	3	..
Dhobi	7	1	3	..	2	2	2	..
Bhar	8	..	4	..	1	..	2	..
Pasi	4	..	3	..	2	..	1	..
Chamar	6	..	2	..	2	..	1	..
BARODA.								
Brahman	780	284	600	158	1,838	89	909	32
Kunbi	478	97	267	38	256	4	97	1
CENTRAL INDIA.								
Baniya	501	34	323	15	317	10	110	1
Brahman	265	27	123	5	317	19	38	2
Rajput	166	21	75	13	109	5	38	3
Gujar..	50	1	25	2	10	..	3	..
Bhil	5	..	7	..	..	..	..	..
Gond	6	..	6	..	..	..	1	..
GWALIOR.								
Baniya	263	61	352	27	234	12	165	4
Brahman	197	48	182	27	338	17	233	10
Rajput	126	10	77	16	55	2	48	1
HYDERABAD.								
Brahman	701	79	437	63	708	67	338	36
Komati	258	17	270	10	78	14	36	2
Lingayat	88	8	76	3	60	4	26	1
Kapu	64	8	47	2	50	7	12	..
Telaga	42	4	26	3	76	3	36	1
Maratha	30	4	23	2	24	2	9	..
Madiga	10	1	2	1	7	1	1	..
MYSORE.								
Brahman	783	344	707	203	3,386	345	2,399	112
Sheikh	302	102	206	50	350	34	187	7
Lingayat	301	22	203	11	140	5	63	1
Vakkaliga	122	5	75	3	53	3	25	1
Kuruba	68	3	40	1	34	..	13	..
Beda	58	4	36	3	21	1	8	..
RAJPUTANA.								
Baniya (Mahajan)	592	23	442	17	189	5	103	1
Brahman	237	14	169	10	274	4	81	3
Rajput	70	11	52	9	95	2	32	2
Jat	12	1	10	..	15	..	3	..
Gujar..	8	..	7	..	3	..	2	..
Mina	10	..	6	..	1	..	..	..
Meo	5	..	5	..	..	..	1	..
Kumhar	11	..	5	1	8	..	2	..

SUBSIDIARY TABLE VI.

Progress of literacy since 1901.

Number literate per mille

Province, State or Agency.	All ages 10 and over. Males.				All ages 10 and over. Females.				15—20. Males.				15—20. Females.				20 and over. Males.				20 and over. Females.			
	1931.	1921.	1911.	1901.	1931.	1921.	1911.	1901.	1931.	1921.	1911.	1901.	1931.	1921.	1911.	1901.	1931.	1921.	1911.	1901.	1931.	1921.	1911.	1901.
1	2	3	4	5	6	7	8	9	10	11	12	13	14	15	16	17	18	19	20	21	22	23	24	25
INDIA	174	161	140	129	31	23	13	9	195	174	144	132	44	36	21	14	185	171	150	139	28	20	12	8
Provinces	178	167	147	134	30	22	14	9	199	179	151	138	42	35	22	14	190	178	157	145	27	19	12	8
Ajmer-Merwara	223	210	163	142	37	28	17	10	232	211	160	119	48	44	37	13	240	227	171	157	33	26	14	9
Andaman and Nicobar Islands	240	246	224	311	51	38	36	109	187	153	176	512	69	32	37	169	253	260	228	304	47	39	36	90
Assam	169	144	117	89	23	15	8	6	189	164	126	92	33	23	12	8	179	150	121	94	20	13	7	5
Baluchistan	409	76	56	..	162	6	4	..	450	301	287	..	160	217	164	..	410	346	376	..	161	166	152	..
Bengal	201	210	187	138	34	23	15	7	219	214	189	175	41	28	19	13	215	225	199	175	32	21	13	9
Bihar and Orissa	108	114	104		8	7	5		118	111	103		11	10	7		116	126	114		7	7	4	
Bombay	186	181	158	148	30	30	17	11	222	217	171	168	46	53	28	19	195	184	163	153	27	24	15	9
Burma	614	576	496	498	175	123	79	57	618	569	479	485	210	156	109	77	662	620	544	537	171	118	75	53
Central Provinces and Berar	122	103	87	79	11	10	4	3	152	142	109	91	17	18	8	4	127	104	87	83	9	9	3	2
Coorg	264	238	194	159	92	64	36	20	274	226	167	162	137	121	57	37	279	256	214	173	82	52	31	16
Delhi	246	201	*	*	77	44	*	*	254	190	*	*	90	55	*	*	264	217	*	*	75	42	*	*
Madras	211	199	183	160	32	26	17	12	236	204	184	166	51	44	29	22	227	214	198	175	28	22	14	10
North-West Frontier Province	104	95	81	88	13	12	8	7	131	114	82	76	20	20	12	9	113	102	91	101	12	11	8	7
Punjab	112	90	84	86	18	11	8	4	140	96	78	82	29	17	12	6	118	94	95	95	16	9	7	4
United Provinces of Agra and Oudh	104	85	78	75	12	8	6	3	120	92	83	77	17	12	9	4	108	89	82	81	11	7	6	3
States and Agencies	154	127	107	100	35	29	12	8	181	144	106	104	55	47	20	12	160	132	115	108	30	24	10	7
Baroda State	361	277	229	199	80	52	25	9	470	354	258	206	147	105	40	13	354	265	216	208	55	34	15	7
Central India Agency	103	76	64	68	10	7	3	4	112	78	61	76	14	11	5	8	111	81	69	72	9	6	3	3
Cochin State	497	365	329	302	225	127	79	59	575	359	303	282	321	174	104	77	498	397	367	343	187	113	73	56
Gwalior State	87	77	†	†	12	8	†	†	90	78	†	†	14	11	†	†	94	83	†	†	11	7	†	†
Hyderabad State	93	65	67	70	12	9	5	4	137	86	69	77	20	14	7	6	90	67	72	75	11	8	4	4
Jammu and Kashmir State	79	54	53	52	7	3	2	1	89	53	42	45	10	4	2	1	87	61	62	60	6	3	2	1
Mysore State	198	163	142	..	36	24	15	..	205	174	137	144	55	43	24	18	208	169	152	129	30	19	13	8
*Punjab States Agency	79	*	*	*	7	*	*	*	81	*	*	*	11	*	*	*	90	*	*	*	7	*	*	*
Rajputana Agency	86	81	79	75	6	5	3	2	86	80	70	76	8	7	4	3	96	90	88	83	6	5	3	2
Sikkim State	77	101	108	125	4	4	4	3	59	70	73	85	3	5	3	3	96	127	132	155	4	4	4	3
Travancore State	454	425	329	283	178	178	64	39	530	437	318	264	274	226	97	58	475	440	369	320	153	160	56	35
Western India States Agency	225	§	§	§	45	§	§	§	252	§	§	§	66	§	§	§	236	§	§	§	39	§	§	§

NOTE.—The figures for provinces are inclusive of the States attached to them, except in the case of Madras, where they exclude Cochin and Travancore for which separate details have been given.

* Included against Punjab. † Included against Central India. § Included against Bombay.

SUBSIDIARY TABLE VII.

Number of Institutions and pupils according to the returns of the Education Department since 1901.

Class of Institution.	Number of Institutions.				Scholars.			
	1931.	1921.	1911.	1901.	1931.	1921.	1911.	1901.
1	2	3	4	5	6	7	8	9
Universities and Colleges	333	233	193	186	92,028	59,595	31,447	20,447
Secondary Schools	13,581	8,816	6,442	5,416	2,286,411	1,239,524	890,061	582,551
Primary Schools	204,384	158,792	118,413	97,116	9,362,748	6,310,451	4,575,465	3,150,678
Special Schools	8,891	3,946	5,783	956	315,650	132,706	164,544	33,950
Unrecognized Institutions	34,879	33,929	39,491	43,292	632,249	639,125	630,438	617,818
Total ..	262,068	206,016	179,322	146,966	12,689,086	8,381,401	6,281,955	4,405,988

CHAPTER X.

Language.

Section i.—The Returns.

Extension of the language return.

147. For the return of language in the 1931 census two columns were provided—one for the speakers of mother-tongue, and the other for any language or languages habitually spoken, in addition to the mother-tongue, in daily or domestic life. Infants and deaf and dumb persons were to be credited with the same language as their mothers. The distribution and classification of Indian languages has been so exhaustively dealt with in the Linguistic Survey of India, the very important introductory volume to which appeared as recently as 1927, that little remains for a census to do with regard to the main languages of the country beyond recording their corresponding increase and decrease, since the area of any given tongue is hardly ever stable. In one respect, however, existing information was lacking and that was the extent of the overlap of different languages in the numberless areas in which two or more co-exist. It is not suggested that this overlap is a permanent feature, and that areas speaking two languages at present will necessarily continue to do so in perpetuity, but in view of the not unreasonable desire of many Indians for a redistribution of provinces on a linguistic basis, as well as of the possibility of extensions of franchise to very considerable populations speaking some tribal language as their mother-tongue, to say nothing of the desirability of starting all primary education in the real language of the child to be taught, the record of this overlap has more than a purely academic interest. Moreover, apart from linguistics, the extent of the survival of tribal languages is a better index than that of the survival of tribal religion to the social cohesion of the tribe, since the test of language is easier and more definite than that of religion where the borderland of Hinduism is often vague and obscure. As a matter of fact the material collected of the distribution of mother-tongue and subsidiary languages in *Orissa irredenta* and the coasts thereof was requisitioned by the Orissa Boundary Committee before it had been extracted from the schedules, and it was only by working himself and his staff to the verge of collapse that the Superindendent of Census Operations in Madras was able to provide adequate data in time for the Committee to use it.

Subsidiary language and Orissa boundaries.

148. In the case of Orissa unfortunately the very facts which the census schedule was designed to elicit operated towards impairing its value. This was on account of the stupid and unintelligent propaganda which was deliberately directed to misrepresent as Oriya what was not Oriya, or as non-Oriya what was. The result of this propaganda was the sort of foolishness which made both enumerated and enumerator 'plump' for one language. If a man spoke Oriya as an alternative language with, say, Bengali as his mother-tongue he would return his mother-tongue as Bengali and perversely return Bengali again in the subsidiary column for fear of giving support to the Oriya case. *Vice versa* Oriya speakers equally at home in Telugu would conceal the fact by returning Oriya in both columns. Of the various agitators the Oriyas were easily the worst. So high did feeling run in the Orissa boundaries of Madras that special officers had to be appointed to superintend enumeration and abstraction. Nevertheless the return of subsidiary language, incomplete as it was, made it possible to indicate clearly enough the debatable areas where two languages were spoken and must have been of very considerable value to the Boundary Committee. The general percentage increase in Oriya-speakers since 1921 is in close relation to the average increase in population, and the consistency of the language returns in Ganjam as compared with those of previous censuses, excepting always that of 1901, indicates their general accuracy. The marginal table gives the figures from 1881 onwards taking in 1931 the total speakers of Oriya by mother-tongue only. If those speaking Oriya as a subsidiary language be added, it makes a total number of persons having a command of the Oriya language of 1,184,909—that is of no more than 57·7 per cent. of the

Census of		Total population of Ganjam Plains.	Number returned as speaking Oriya.	Percentage of Oriya-speakers.
1881	..	1,503,301	748,904	50
1891	..	1,590,208	797,132	53
1901	..	1,689,754	1,274,975	75
1911	..	1,870,826	958,661	51
1921	..	1,835,562	931,790	51
1931	..	2,053,381	1,079,337	53

population of the Ganjam plains, to which the figures relate, as compared to the 52·6 per cent. whose mother-tongue it is, but it is probable that there has been some understatement both of Oriya and of Telugu in the return of subsidiary language, as Oriya-Telugu bilingualism is extensive. The inaccuracy of the 1901 figure was recognised at the time, and actually during the course of compilation a reference was made to the Census Superintendent as to the return of Reddika, a Telugu caste, as Oriya speakers. The compilation was however continued in accordance with the return in the schedule. The Madras Government had a special enquiry made in 1904 as to the language returns of 1901 and reported that the inaccuracy of the census figures in that year was due to the desire of Telugus to participate in the special advantages given to encourage the education of Oriyas; to the belief that it was easier for Oriyas to obtain Government service than for Telugus; and to the fact that there were more Oriya enumerators than Telugu, that they would ask their questions in Oriya, and would probably put down as Oriya speaking all who answered in that language. Ganjam is predominantly bilingual and the return of subsidiary language was first introduced in 1931. So deep does bilingualism go in parts of Ganjam that from very infancy many grow up speaking both Oriya and Telugu and are so much at home in both that they cannot tell which to return as their mother-tongue. Some officers unfamiliar with this phenomenon found difficulty in appreciating the fact that small children can be bilingual, and rejected returns of a subsidiary language under the age at which they considered it possible for a child to have learned a second one thoroughly, but in point of fact it is perfectly possible for a child to be bilingual from his first learning to speak, and the phenomenon is familiar in some parts of India where marriages between persons of different linguistic groups are common. The late Khan of Kalat spoke Brahui to his mother and Balochi to his father from infancy, and children lisping in two radically different tongues are common enough in the hills of Assam.

Bilingualism

149. Elsewhere than in and about Orissa the subsidiary language return was fortunately not coloured by immediate politics, though not always free from political bias, as in the case of Bhopal State, where Urdu was returned "in deliberate disregard of the actual facts" in order to give effect to a sentiment that Hindus as well as Muslims living in that State ought to have the peculiarly Muslim variety of Hindustani as their mother-tongue instead of Rajasthani and even instead of Gondi. A similar sentiment caused Muslims in many parts of India to return Urdu (Hindustani) as their mother-tongue and the local vernacular as their subsidiary language though the precise opposite was the real fact; and the same sort of feeling was at work in the case of some Gonds who, considering Gondi of inferior social reputation, returned Halbi, a Marathi dialect, as their mother-tongue, giving Gondi, if at all, as subsidiary. In fact Mr. Grigson, when Administrator in Bastar State in 1930, stated that it was common for Gonds to affirm in court that they knew no language but Halbi, when as a matter of fact their wives and mothers coming to give evidence would be found to understand no tongue but Gondi, on which husbands and sons would admit that they did speak Gondi in their homes. The first stage in the disappearance of any language is the use of another as well in ordinary daily intercourse, and in cases of this kind it is probable that the provision for the return of a second language has extended the area of record of many of the hill and jungle languages now in the process of becoming submerged, a process likely to be much accelerated by the ubiquitous increase of easy communications. It has proved impossible to plot this overlap with precise reference to the numbers involved on a scale small enough to reproduce as an all-India map for this volume. The linguistic map therefore which accompanies this report deals only with the distribution of mother-tongues, and for detailed information as to subsidiary languages the student is referred to the various provincial reports in all of which, except in that for the United Provinces, where Hindustani alone is spoken, will be found a map showing the distribution by population figures not only of mother-tongue but of the actual numbers speaking various subsidiary languages in each district and in some cases in even smaller units. In the provincial volumes (Table XV, ii) will be found the details of subsidiary languages by the smallest territorial units for which it was practicable to give them where such languages were not evenly distributed over a district or larger area. A summary of this information will be found in Table

XV (ii), in part ii of this volume and in the corresponding subsidiary table at the end of this chapter.

Changes in classification.

150 A few alterations of minor importance have been made in the classification of languages as compared with that of 1921. India thus appears with 225 instead of 222 languages although the Tibeto-Burman Sub-family is credited with only 128 instead of 134 languages. This reduction of six, increased to seven by the omission of unspecified Pahari, is more than balanced by an addition of one to the Eranian branch—Persian, a dialect of which is the mother-tongue of a number of villages in Baluchistan, having here been added to the vernaculars of India; of one to the Dardic branch, that is of Bashgali in the Kafir group which did not appear at all in 1921; of one to the southern group of the Indo-Aryan branch, Konkani being treated as a separate language and not (as in 1921) as a dialect of Marathi; and of seven to the unclassed languages, Burushaski appearing for the first time, Andamanese being shown as two languages instead of one (since the language of the Jarawas, Sentinelese and Onges differs much from that of the Great Andaman coast tribes), and the unclassed Gipsy tongues appearing as six instead of one, though there has been no change in nomenclature or classification except that they are not pooled as in 1921. In the case however of the Tibeto-Burman languages there are changes in grouping and nomenclature which need to be stated. In the Bodo group the speakers of the language shown in 1921 as "Tipara or Mrung" have been returned partly under the same head and partly under the term *Tsakchip* in the Old Kuki sub-group of the Kuki-Chin group. In the Naga group Khoirao and Marāmi have been merged in Memi (="Sopvoma or Mao" of 1921), and Chang, the cis-frontier speakers of which are very few, in the new term *Other Eastern Naga languages*, which includes also Phom and some trans-frontier languages spoken by casual individuals found inside the frontier at census time. Mikir has been put in a group by itself, as besides having affinities to the Kachha Naga and Kabui languages it has strong affinities to the Bodo tongues and some to the Kuki ones. Maring has also been omitted from the Naga-Kuki sub-group and shown in the Old Kuki sub-group of the Kuki-Chin group, with which it seems to have at least as much affinity as with the Naga. In the Kuki-Chin group there have been changes of nomenclature and amalgamation resulting in the disappearance from the list of Purum, Hiroi-Lamgāng, Chote, Vaiphei, Kamhow, Laiyo, Kwingly, Yokwa, Kaungtso, Kwelshin, Hualngo, Kyaw and Taungtha, and in the addition of Pankhu, Chinbok, Chinme, Rongtu and Tsakchip as well as of Maring transferred from the Naga group. Sokte now includes Kamhow, Thado includes Jangsen, Lai includes Kaungtso, Kwangli, Kwelshin, Tlangtlang, Laiyo and Yokwa, and Tashon includes Hualngo. The Mān and Karen languages probably have affinity with the Mon-Khmer, with which indeed they were actually classified in 1911, but they are also reported to have Tai characteristics and the combination may be due to contact or to the amalgamation of tribes. They have been associated this time for convenience with the Tibeto-Chinese family, as Przyluski treats them as affiliated to the Tai. Information on these and on the other groups of Burma languages is still very scanty as the Linguistic Survey of Burma has never been carried out. Among the foreign languages (C. *Languages of Europe*) is included a number of persons who returned their mother-tongue as "Swiss". This however is not a new international language, but appears to be a relic of war-time mentality and an euphemism accordingly for 'German', to which category they have been added in the detailed table. From somewhat similar motives, perhaps, Flemish seems to have been returned as "Belgian".

Some slight alterations in the classification adopted in provincial and state reports have been made in the India tables. The speakers of Palaung (842) and Pale (114) returned from the Chittagong Hill Tracts, Tripura State and elsewhere in Bengal cannot apparently be correct, as all the Palaungs are located in the Shān States to the east of Burma. I have therefore no doubt whatever that Palaung should have been classified as Palaing, the name of a Kuki-Chin clan in the area from which the returns are made. Pale is more doubtful. It may be the name of another clan—there is certainly one called Palow—or it may be a return of Pali made by Buddhist priests in the spirit that provokes many returns of Sanskrit by learned Hindus or of Arabic by Muslims; in any case it is most unlikely to be the Pale of the Palaung-Wa country.

Language groups.	No. of languages spoken.	No. of speakers as mother-tongue and subsidiary 1931 (bilinguals shown twice).	No. of speakers 1921.	No. of speakers mother-tongue only, 1931	Difference between columns 4 and 5 (increase in 1931+ decrease in 1931—).	Difference between columns 4 and 3 (increase + decrease —).
1	2	3	4	5	6	7
A.—Language of India and Burma.	**225**	**366,430,537**	**315,525,177**	**349,887,527**	**+94,362,350**	**+50,905,360**
(i) *Austric Languages—*						
1. Indonesian languages ..	2	6,542	5,561	6,542	+981	+981
2. Mon-Khmer languages ..	10	734,204	549,917	726,578	+176,661	+184,287
3. Munda languages ..	7	4,710,685	3,973,873	4,609,588	+635,715	+736,812
(ii) *Tibeto-Chinese Languages—*						
1. Tibeto-Burman languages	128	14,167,611	11,959,011	12,982,840	+1,023,829	+2,208,600
2. Tai-Chinese languages ..	11	1,150,220	926,335	1,027,656	+101,321	+223,885
3. Man and Karen languages*	17	1,351,291	1,114,617	1,342,278	+227,661	+236,674
(iii) *Dravidian Languages—*						
1. Dravida languages ..	7	47,032,874	37,285,594	41,454,593	+4,168,999	+9,747,280
2. Intermediate languages ..	5	3,661,277	3,056,598	3,609,418	+552,820	+604,679
3. Andhra language ..	1	28,195,824	23,601,492	26,373,727	+2,772,235	+4,594,332
4. N. W. language.. ..	1	231,581	184,368	207,049	+22,681	+47,213
(iv) *Indo-European Languages—*						
1. Eranian languages ..	3	2,457,134	1,981,675	2,270,466	+288,791	+475,459
2. Dardic languages ..	5	1,543,031	1,304,319	1,522,936	+218,617	+238,712
3. Indo-Aryan languages ..	19	261,105,909	229,560,555	253,699,403	+24,138,848	+31,545,354
(v) *Unclassed Languages—*						
1. Andamanese	2	466	580	466	—114	—114
2. Burushaski	1	26,076	..	26,076	+26,076	+26,076
3. Gipsy dialects† ..	6	25,999	15,018	25,999	+10,981	+10,981
4. Languages not returned and unspecified.	..	29,813‡	5,664	1,912	—3,752	+24,149
B. Languages of other Asiatic countries and Africa.	**17**	**305,386**	**211,894**	**302,324**	**+90,430**	**+93,492**
C. Languages of Europe ..	**20**	**452,099**	**319,112**	**339,706**	**+20,594**	**+132,987**

* The correct classification of these two langauges is doubtful. Przyluski treats them as Tai (Meillet and Cohen, *Langues du Monde* 380), but it is probable they have Austric affinities.

† These dialects are drawn from various Indian languages and contain such diverse elements that they cannot fairly be allotted to one family rather than another.

‡ Includes Hill and aboriginal subsidiary languages (27,841).

Survival of Tribal Languages.

151. The table above shows in a very general way the linguistic position and the importance therein of the subsidiary language return, but it is really only by reference to the various provincial reports that individual areas can be dealt with. There are far too many languages and dialects in India to treat individually without prolonging this chapter to an inordinate length. The question however of tribal languages and of their survival or displacement is of such interest, at any rate in several provinces, that no justification is required for quoting here at length from the provincial reports to which reference must be made for details. The Census Superintendent for the United Provinces draws attention to the disappearance of gipsy languages :—

"These gypsy languages........are dying out in this province. These wandering tribes are taking to a more settled manner of living, cultivation and the like, and with this change comes the need to use the language of their neighbours. As a result the majority of the present members of these tribes have never learnt these dialects, but speak from their youth some form or other of Hindustani......even those who returned a gypsy language as mother-tongue in every case returned Hindustani as subsidiary language."

And the Census Superintendent of Mysore State reports precisely the same phenomenon. Of tribal languages in Central India the Census Superintendent of the Central India Agency writes as follows :—

"Despite the presence of a large Tribal population in Central India, the question of the non-Aryan dialects giving place to the advancing tide of Aryan culture and civilization does not present itself for the very obvious reason that the process of displacement has already taken place, perhaps a long time ago. The Kol, Baiga and other Munda tribes in Rewa, the Sonr in Bundelkhand, the Saharia in northern Malwa and Gwalior, have in the present day no languages of their own. They speak the Indo-Aryan vernacular of the locality in which they reside. Whether the Bhil had a language of his own we do not know. Probably the basis of his language was Munda but his present language is throughly overlaid with an Aryan superstructure..............The Gondi (so-called) of Rewa is practically a broken Bagheli. If that be so, the Aryan language has already supplanted the language of the Gonds. The small number of Korkus who live in the villages in the Narbada valley have practically abandoned their language and speak Malvi."

For the tribes in Baroda the Census Commissioner for that State points out that where the members of a tribe have no economic independence, Hinduization involves the loss of the tribal language. Thus Gujarati is rapidly supplanting, if it has not supplanted, the Bhili dialects of the Dublas and Talavias, who are agricultural labourers dependent on Gujarati-speaking masters. But on the other hand where there is economic independence with a consequent social consciousness the tribal language survives Hinduization and value is attached to its retention, as for instance by the Chodhras. This helps to explain the obvious vitality of tribal languages in eastern India in spite of the rapid Hinduization of the past decade. This vitality is on the whole pronounced in the Central Provinces, in Bihar and Orissa, in Bengal and in Assam, though there are one or two exceptions in each of these provinces. At the same time bilingualism is on the increase and there can be little doubt of the ultimate fate of these tribal languages. The Census Superintendent for the Central Provinces writes :—

"In border areas poly-linguism is in fact frequently encountered. A well-known, but humble, Gond shikari in south Chanda can speak and understand Hindi, Telugu, Gondi and Marathi, and such cases are by no means exceptional.........., wherever a tribal language is spoken, the great majority of the adult men using it, and a large proportion of the adult women, are bi-lingual. So faithfully indeed is this fact accepted that in Seoni district it was found that among the Gonds infants in arms were being recorded as bi-lingual."

Nevertheless of the tribal languages themselves he finds that :—

"Kherwari was the only non-Aryan language for which numbers substantially below those of 1911 were returned. In fact the apparent fall in 1921 of those speaking almost all tribal languages must evidently be attributed to the influenza epidemic, for it can be proved from the figures of the 1931 Census that, although the danger of their displacement is obvious, the actual state of affairs has not really been changing for many years past............. In the first place, except for Korku, the Munda languages have either disappeared or are, it seems, in process of disappearance in this province. Of 84,971 Sawara or Saonrs enumerated not a single one returned the tribal language. There is no doubt that the Sawaras of Chhattisgarh and the territories outside the Central Provinces adjoining it are the same as the isolated tribe known as Saonrs in Saugor and Damoh............some ethnologists have insisted that Korwas and Korkus are branches of the same tribe. If this is accepted the concentration of the Saonrs in the forests of the Vindhyan foothills, far from the Sawaras of Chhattisgarh, and the Korkus in the Mahadeo hills and the Melghat, far from the Korwas of the Chhota Nagpur plateau irresistibly suggests the withdrawal of those who spoke Munda languages in the first instance into the remote and isolated tracts of the province before the approach of Dravidian and Aryan languages. The Munda elements which remained in the local language in the open tracts merged into mixed jargons. Even in the hills Sawara also disappeared. Of the others Korku, which is still spoken among themselves by the greater number of the members of the tribe, Korwa, Kharia and Gadaba alone survive. Gadaba the mother-tongue of a handful of people in Bastar State numbering not more than 400 was returned by slightly more than that number of people at the Census. Sir George Grierson's remarks regarding Nihali, classed as a dialect of Korku, are relevant in connection with this discussion. Mentioning that there are many instances of tribes which even in historic times have abandoned one language and taken to another he wrote :—

"A striking example is afforded by the tribe of Nahals in the Central Provinces. These people appear to have originally spoken a Munda language akin to Korku. It came under Dravidian influence and has become a mixed form of speech, half Munda and half Dravidian. This in its turn has fallen under the spell of Aryan tongues, and is now in fair way to becoming an Aryan language. If we were to judge by language a hundred years ago we should have called the tribe Munda."

Korku itself was returned as their mother-tongue by 161,975 members of the tribe out of a total population of 176,616, the corresponding figures having been 112,194, and 140,440 in 1921. It is to be observed that of these 54,716 males and 50,974 females speak the language of the tract in which they reside as subsidiary to their mother-tongue. On the other hand the number of persons returning mother-tongue Hindi or Marathi and subsidiary language Korku was negligible.

Apart from the few tribes which still speak Munda or Dravidian languages there are a number speaking either Aryan dialects, distinguished by the names of the tribes themselves or else the language of the tract in which they are found. Whether the original language of these tribes was Munda or Dravidian it is generally impossible to trace. For instance Bhili is now classed as a language of the Aryan sub-family ; while the Kamars, Bhatras, and Halbas all speak dialects of Aryan languages. On the other hand the Baigas, a typical forest people numbering 37,086 in the province, have now really no language of their own. Baigani returned by 3,641 persons almost all in Balaghat, is merely a broken dialect of Chhattisgarhi. Others who have lost their original language, whatever it was, are Bhuinhars, Binjhwars, Kolis, Rautias, Kawars and Pandos. Binjhwari, returned by 2,339 speakers in Raipur and Surguja is recognized as a sub-dialect of Chhattisgarhi. Bhuihari, spoken by 28 persons in Korea, and Pando, by 502 in Udaipur, have been identified by Rai Bahadur Hiralal to be broken dialects of Chhattisgarhi.

It is interesting to notice that among these tribes which have assimilated Aryan language are some, if not all, of those regarded as the true aboriginals or autochthonoi of the Eastern Central Provinces—for instance the Binjhwars, the Kamars and the Baigas. The Gonds, Halbas and others have been classed as semi-aboriginals, probably outsiders who have been domiciled in the province since before historic times. Binjhwars, Baigas and Kamars have all been described by Russell as " Dravidian tribes ". It cannot be said what was the original form of their language but the claim that they are true aboriginals of the province appears to be just as strong as that for the Korkus who according to Russell, being an offshoot of the great Kol or Munda tribe, came much further west than their kinsmen and settled in the Mahadeo hills. According to their own traditions, however they claim to be born of the soil and to have been especially created by Mahadeo as a population for his hills at the request of Rawan, the demon King of Ceylon ".

In Bihar and Orissa even the Austroasiatic languages, which have almost disappeared further west, are flourishing, and the Census Superintendent there reports that—

" Since 1921 there has been an increase of about 577,000 or 17·7 per cent., in the number of persons speaking. . . .tribal languages. They have in fact more than kept pace with the general increase in population, with the result that the proportion of the total population accounted for by them has risen from 859 to 907 per 10,000. Two principal reasons may be advanced to explain this . . . . The first is that the aboriginal peoples themselves have multiplied more quickly than most other communities—partly because their natural rate of growth is superior, and partly because many emigrants have returned during the last decade from the industrial centres of Bengal and the tea gardens of Assam. The second reason is that the procedure adopted at the present census of recording " mother-tongue " and " subsidiary language " separately, instead of the single language " ordinarily spoken ", has undoubtedly led to a more complete return of tribal languages as the mother-tongue of persons who are bi-lingual. To this latter cause must clearly be attributed the fact that in the district of Champaran 5,511 persons are shown as speaking Oraon at the present census, out of whom, 5,508 speak Hindustani as a subsidiary language. In 1921, although there were nearly 10,000 Oraons in that district, not a single one was returned as speaking his tribal tongue. Similarly, in Balasore the number of Santali speakers has gone up abruptly from 9,655 to 15,120, and more than 10,000 of the latter are now shown as speaking a second language (Oriya) . . . . .very few of the tribal languages are falling into disuse. The only ones in which the proportion of speakers is appreciably lower than it was ten years ago are Bhumij, Juang, Kharia, Mahili and Turi. In the case of Mahili the decrease probably has not much significance, for this dialect (like Karmali) is little more than a variant of Santali, and it is probable that Santali was entered fairly often as the mother-tongue of persons speaking Mahili. The decline in Bhumij is most noticeable in the districts of Manbhum and Singhbhum, where the " Hinduization " of this tribe is proceeding apace ; in Mayurbhanj state, although Hinduism is now returned as the religion of the great majority, the tribal feeling persists, with the result that the tribal language too is still vigorous in that area. Speakers of Juang have increased in number since 1921 from 10,531 to 14,583. . . . . To all intents and purposes this language is as full of vitality as ever it was. Nor is the loss sustained by the Kharia language material, though the proportion of speakers has fallen off slightly both in Ranchi and in the Orissa states, the two localities where this particular tribe is numerous. Turi, however, is definitely on he wane. In 1911 it was spoken by 2,701 persons, in 1921 by 1,808, and now it is spoken by only 1,215. . . . . But in these days there is little to distinguish Turis from an ordinary low Hindu caste, and the loss of their old tribal language is not a matter for surprise.

The particularly marked increase in the proportion of persons speaking Kora is due primarily to vagaries of classification. . . . . .Still more abrupt is the increase from 383 to 6,270 in the number of persons speaking Gondi. This represents a swing back to (and beyond) the position in 1911, when there were 4,212 speakers of this language. The fact is that in this province nearly every Gond has acquired the knowledge of a secondary language, and at the last census the tendency to return this secondary language in preference to the tribal dialect was apparently carried to a much further length with the Gonds than with most of the other aboriginal races.

Taking together. . . . . . . .18 tribes. . . . . . . .the proportion of their members speaking tribal languages is 820 per mille, as compared with 802 per mille in 1921. . . . . .In areas where primitive races are most numerous a pleader, a zamindar or a village mahajan may find it absolutely necessary as a matter of business to acquaint himself with their manner of speech. Thus, in the Sadr sub-division of Singhbhum the supremacy of Ho as the *lingua franca* of the countryside is unchallenged. In Ranchi a considerable number of the Aryan inhabitants speak Mundari and (to a less extent) Oraon. Curiously enough, Santali in the Santal Parganas seems to be treated much more cavalierly, and as a subsidiary language it is spoken just as widely in Manbhum. This can hardly be in accordance with the actual facts, and it is probable that, both in the Santal Parganas and in other parts of the plateau, the returns fail to do justice to the extent to which the use of tribal languages is current among non-aboriginals. Some foolish notion of prestige may have restrained people from admitting that they were in the habit of speaking these dialects...........

Tribal language.			No. of speakers.	No. per mille using some subsidiary language.
TOTAL		..	3,837,768	419
Asuri	..	..	2,769	842
Bhumij	..	..	117,356	746
Birhor	..	..	731	557
Birjia	..	..	628	998
Ho	..	..	526,443	226
Juang	..	..	14,583	901
Karmali	..	..	10,047	122
Kharia	..	..	113,680	871
Kora	..	..	9,739	465
Korwa	..	..	12,434	950
Mahili	..	..	13,704	254
Mundari	..	..	521,891	486
Santali	..	..	1,628,957	283
Turi	..	..	1,215	913
Gondi	..	..	6,270	769
Kondhi	..	..	133,682	448
Oraon	..	..	656,188	723
Malto	..	..	67,451	122

The marginal statement shows for each tribal lanaguage the proportion of persons who speak some subsidiary language....................

It will be noticed that among the smaller tribes, such as the Asurs (including Birjias), the Juangs and the Korwas, the acquisition of a second language has proved to be almost universally necessary. This is only natural, for with such limited numbers they obviously could not maintain themselves in water-tight compartments. It is interesting to find that bi-lingualism is so comparatively rare among the Santals and Hos; also that as between the Oraons and Mundas who for the most part are found in close association, the former tribe is in this matter the more sophisticated of the two. In all, 1,607,250 speakers of these tribal languages are bi-lingual, and this means that three out of every four persons in the province who use a secondary language in every day life belong to one or other of these tribes. One would naturally expect bi-lingualism to be a good deal more common among males than among females, but the returns do not bear out this expectation. So far as the aboriginal races are concerned, the ratio is 82 males to 79 females. It is not improbable that the returns are inaccurate in this respect, and that women were sometimes shown as speaking a second language simply because their husbands did so."

In Bengal the Austroasiatic languages are out of their environment and find survival more difficult, while of Dravidian languages Kurukh indeed has increased a little but Malto has decreased. On the other hand the Tibeto-Burmese languages seem hardy enough on the whole, though some have declined. Of these languages the Census Superintendent of Bengal writes :—

"The total number speaking languages of the Bara group is 246 thousand compared with 226 thousand in 1921......... Tipura spoken by nearly 192,000 persons .... makes the largest contribution towards this group and those speaking it have increased from 158,734 in 1921 .... Those speaking Garo, Koch and Kachari have all declined in numbers.. .... Rabha was not returned as a language in spite of there being over 3,000 members of the tribe returned by the tribal name .... The total numbers speaking the Kuki-Chin group of languages is rather less than 43 thousand compared with nearly 30 thousand in 1921 .... It is the persons speaking Tibeto-Himalayan languages who are most extensively bi-lingual in Bengal. In Darjeeling amongst those speaking Bhotia tongues five times as many speak some subsidiary language as the number of those without any subsidiary language at all; and even in Sikkim rather more of those whose mother-tongue is a Bhotia language are bilingual than not .... Similarly for every three persons in Sikkim speaking Rong as mother tongue with no subsidiary language there are four who speak also some subsidiary language. In the whole of Bengal amongst persons speaking Tibeto-Himalayan languages there are only 11 speaking no subsidiary language to every 89 who are bilingual, and in Sikkim the corresponding proportions are almost one to two. Those speaking Austro-Asiatic languages appear to have the next greatest facility or necessity for acquiring subsidiary languages. Throughout the whole of Bengal in every 100 persons speaking these languages there are 33 who are bilingual to every 67 who are not................ Those speaking Kherwari adopt by preference Bengali as their subsidiary tongue whereas those speaking Kharia more generally use Hindustani."

Similarly in Assam the Census Superintendent is emphatic as to the vitality of tribal languages :—

"We can .... say definitely that the indigenous hill languages are as vigorous as ever and show no signs of erosion. As regards the tribal languages spoken in the plains ...... Kachari (including Dimasa) and Rabha, both of which showed a decrease in 1921, have a considerable increase in the number of their speakers at this census. ....To show the vigour of Kachari I need only mention that out of the 57,000 persons in Darrang who have returned their caste as Kachari 51,000 speak the Kachari language and in Kamrup out of 107,000 Kacharis 93,000 still claim Kachari as their mother-tongue. The question of Rabha is difficult because owing to conversion to Hinduism the actual number of people who returned their tribe or caste as Rabha has been steadily decreasing since 1911. In that year there were 79,000 Rabhas : in 1921 only 70,000 and at this census 69,000, yet the number of speakers of Rabha is practically the same now (27,000) as in 1911 (28,000), and considerably more than in 1921 (22,000).

As for Lalung..................the speakers of this language have declined at every census since 1901 but that I doubt whether the census figures represent the real number of speakers. On the whole I think we are justified in concluding that the tribal languages in the plains are holding their own in a wonderful manner. Even the small Deori community—about 4,000 strong—appear to be in no danger of forgetting Chutiya, their mother-tongue. Mr. McSwiney remarked in 1911 that the Chutiya language was practically defunct though it continued to retain a small spark of life. That spark is still burning and shows no sign of being extinguished.

It will be of intense interest to observe whether the Assamese language itself—against the inroads of which the tribal languages of the plains have, for hundreds of years, put up such a stout fight—will, in its turn, be able in the future, to defend itself against a new and a very powerful invader in the shape of Bengali which, with the coming of the Eastern Bengal settlers, has established itself firmly in all the districts of lower and central Assam."

Of bilingualism in Assam the Census Superintendent concludes that—

"The statistics of bi-lingualism are smaller than might have been expected and.......... the only people in Assam who are bilingual to any extent are the speakers of Tibeto-Burmese languages in Goalpara, Kamrup, Darrang, Sibsagar and Nowgong and ...... except in Goalpara, (where two-thirds of the Tibeto-Burmese speakers have Assamese and one-third Bengali as their subsidiary language) the only subsidiary language which they can speak fluently is Assamese."

This, of course, excludes the consideration of Tibeto-Burmese languages *inter se*, as the Census Superintendent, in view of their unconscionable number and variety, has necessarily treated them as a whole for statistical purposes. These languages are however so variable and multiform that each differs totally from its neighbour as a spoken vernacular, and there are cases in the Naga Hills where the mother-tongues of opposite sides of the village street are so different that, although one is always known to both sides, the one in lesser use may be incomprehensible across the road, and it is common to hear two people colloguing while answering each in his own tongue the questions of his *vis-a-vis* asked in the other's. The Census Superintendent for Assam has thus fallen into the very certain error of stating that the Assam hill tribes are not good linguists. It is true that few know Assamese. Little opportunity have they to learn, and less to learn Bengali or Hindustani, but there are small villages where the children grow up fluent in five languages each of which would puzzle a Dutchman to learn a little of in two years, and in the State of Manipur the majority of male tribesmen are bilingual in their own tongues and Manipuri, while a combined knowledge of some Kuki language, some Naga language and the Manipuri language must be extremely frequent. The incredible rapidity with which a Naga or Kuki interpreter acquires an additional language with the most limited opportunity for doing so has to be experienced to be appreciated, and there are some villages which in addition to real languages compose jargons and counter-jargons of their own in order to be able to chatter incomprehensibly in the presence of others, particularly when discussing a proposition of purchase, sale or barter.

Difficulties in classifying Indo-Aryan Languages.

152. The fact that no linguistic map was prepared for the United Provinces as mentioned above is involved in a difficulty not of subsidiary languages but of mother-tongues, a difficulty which was very far from being confined to the United Provinces. This difficulty was that, familiar from former census reports, of distinguishing in the census record between the various dialects of Hindustani classified by Sir George Grierson as different languages. Generally speaking one dialect fades into another by indistinct and gradual changes so that it is very difficult to draw a hard and fast line and say for instance 'here the Eastern group ends and the Mediate begins ; here ends Mediate Hindi and beyond is Western'. It was anticipated that this difficulty would be found to operate in the case of all the languages of the Indo-Aryan branch of the Indo-European family, but as a matter of fact this did not prove to be the case with all of them. Rajasthani and Bhili, for instance, gave little difficulty, but the distinction between Eastern and Western Hindi in the Central Provinces and Central India, and between Lahnda and Panjabi in the Punjab was more than the census enumerators could grasp. As for the enumerated, each of course very properly considers his Hindi to be the true Hindi and is not prepared to qualify it by an adjective of locality implying that it is merely a dialect. Too much precision must not therefore be expected of figures representing the use of Eastern and Western Hindi and of Lahnda and Panjabi, as it was necessary in the course of compilation to assign large numbers of speakers of Hindi, and similarly of Panjabi, more or less arbitrarily to one or the other group according to locality, since the returns were inevitably unqualified. In the United Provinces no attempt was made to distinguish Eastern from Western Hindi and for the purpose of the linguistic maps the line has been taken arbitrarily as the boundary (more or less) of Agra and Oudh provinces, which is probably as nearly correct as any other convenient boundary that could be chosen.

Script. **153.** The United Provinces again proved a stumbling block to a return of script. Some idea of the respective numbers who use each of the various vernacular scripts is unquestionably a desideratum. That such a return is possible has been shown by the Punjab, in which a return was made of the script of literacy and numbers are available of those who use the Urdu, Nagari, and Gurmukhi scripts respectively; similarly by the Central Provinces and Berar, where figures are now available for literacy in Hindi, (or Marathi) and Urdu respectively; by the Central India Agency for which the returns cover the same three scripts and Gujarati; by Hyderabad, and by Jammu and Kashmir State. But in the United Provinces an ancient controversy about the use of the terms Hindi and Urdu for the spoken language apparently gave rise to the fear that a similar controversy would arise as a result of asking for the script of literacy. As there can be no argument as to whether a given script is Urdu or Hindi it is difficult to comprehend the relevancy of this fear and it might have been surmised that the Local Government would have found the return of script useful. In the case of the spoken language admittedlythe use of the terms Urdu and Hindi do give rise to embittered controversy between two schools which are generally speaking conterminous with Hinduism and Islam in religion. In point of practice it is impossible to define any boundary between Urdu and Hindi as spoken, since the difference consists merely in a preference for a Persian or for a Sanskrit vocabulary, and as an illiterate man uses only the language of common speech it is generally the bias of the enumerator which would determine the category of his return. As far as spoken language goes therefore it was decided, as in 1921, to use the term Hindustani only in the return for the United Provinces, and with the omission of the script of literacy the use of the term Urdu disappeared. This disappearance caused some searching of heart among Muslims who did not realise that the reason for omitting the term Urdu was that no general record of the script was being made at the census. For H. E. H. the Nizam's Dominions a return of literacy in Urdu has been added to that of English.

Prov. or State.	Persons literate in				
	Gurmukhi.	Hindi.	Marathi.	Urdu.	Roman.
Baluchistan ..	3,490	7,111	1,083	18,422	3,844
C. P. and Berar ..	..	380,950*	..	44,247	..
Delhi ..	1,821	26,008	..	47,358	175
Punjab	198,484	216,296	..	908,521	6,587
Central India Agency	..	255,981	15,616	29,453	..
Hyderabad ..	..	..	..	192,039	..
Jammu and Kashmir	..	776	..	3,178	..

*Includes Marathi.

Figures not available from other provinces.

The need for a common script for India is probably even greater than that for a common tongue. English is tending to supply in a minor degree the place of the latter, but even Hindustani, the most widely used Indian language appears in totally different characters. Historical sentiment and local patriotism alike militate against the abandonment of any of the numerous scripts in use in India, but it seems probable that sooner or later some common script will have to be adopted, and the Roman script now adopted by Turkey would probably be the most satisfactory compromise in spite of its alien origin and its paucity of symbols. Hindustani in the Roman script is already in use in the Army and proves eminently satisfactory, and owing to the discharge of soldiers accustomed to use it, it must be spreading slowly in all areas in which the Indian Army recruits. The inclusion in the census schedule of a return of script would have provided figures for its diffusion and a basis for subsequent comparisons, but unfortunately the already over-crowded schedule could not be made to carry more, and the only returns of it available are those for the Punjab, where 6,587 persons were recorded as literate in that script, for Baluchistan with 3,844, and Delhi with 175. Meanwhile the paradox continues of the most anti-British elements in India having to debate their politics in English, while in an article advocating the substitution of Hindi for English as a common language for India an Indian newspaper (itself published in English) adopted as a slogan the words "Linguistic Inqilab Zindabad", translatable perhaps "Up the *Zabāni* Rebels!", and to complete the picture the existing superfluity of vernacular scripts has been inflicted with an addition during the decade under review. In Burma a Chin reformer named Pao Chin Hao (*vide infra*, appendix to this chapter) has invented a new religion together with a script inspired by the deity, whose literal designs seem derived from the Burmese and Roman alphabets. This script, intended to fill the absence of any indigenous Chin system of writing, has unfortunately got so far in its short period of existence as to be used in a spelling book and in a printed translation into the Kamhao-Sokte language of the Sermon on the Mount, though both these appear to be produced from photozincographic blocks and not from founded type. A specimen passage from the Sermon on the Mount will be found with a transliteration in the chapter on Language in the Burma Census Report and the first two pages of the spelling book appear below with a transliteration.

Section ii.—Linguistic Pre-history.

154. In 1867 it was pointed out by Mr. E. Thomas in a letter to the Asiatic Society of Bengal that the Aryan invaders of southern Europe and south-west Asia had invented no alphabet of their own in the course of their wanderings, but were in every case indebted to the country in which they settled for the provision of characters for the reduction of their speech to writing. His inference was that in the case of India the Sanskrit alphabet had its ultimate source in some method of writing known to the pre-Aryan inhabitants. This suggestion was immediately attacked and scouted as incompatible with the then unquestioned view that the Indo-Europeans found India a completely uncivilized country inhabited by barbarous tribes, and while a probably Semitic origin for the earliest form of the Devanagari script was generally admitted, it was regarded as a post-Aryan importation. It has taken sixtyfive years to find evidence that the Brahmi alphabet is after all derived from the symbols used on their seals by the pre-Aryans of the Indus Valley*, and that the theory that the symbols of the Brahmi script were imported from Phœnicia during the first millenium B. C., or locally invented after the Indo-European invasion, is not only now unnecessary but improbable. For although Professor Konow and some others are not yet entirely satisfied, Professor Langdon seems to have effectively demonstrated the connection between the Brahmi script and the signs of the Mohenjodaro seals, while Dr. Pran Nath seems to have arrived independently at the same conclusion, and Mr. Thomas seems to be justified at last in the analogy he drew between the sources of the Indo-European alphabets in Greece and in India respectively. What Langdon says is that if his two main hypotheses are true, *i.e.*, the identity of the Indus with the Sumerian signs and the derivation of the Brahmi characters from the Indus signs 'then it must follow that the Aryan Sanskritists gave values derived from their own language to these characters. In other words they knew the ideographic meanings, translated them into Sanskrit, and derived the syllabic values from the Sanskrit words". This alone is enough to explode the theory, if any retain it, that the existing civilization of India postdates the Indo-European invasion, for had the people of the Indus valley been exterminated or expelled their symbols could not have furnished the basis for the literature of their conquerors, and though it is possible that the Indus valley itself had, as Sir John Marshall holds, been vacated before the Rigvedic Aryans came in, it is quite obvious that there must have been a fusion of culture either there or elsewhere, and it was probably, in fact it must have been, in the Ganges basin. **The Brahmi alphabet.**

155. This raises the question, which cannot be answered at any rate until the Mohenjodaro script is completely deciphered, as to what language was spoken in Upper India before the Indo-Europeans. The most natural hypothesis would be that the language was a Dravidian one, since that is the most widely spread family in **Austroasiatic**

* Mr. Kanakasabhai states (*The Tamils 1,800 Years Ago*, page 45) that "it was from the Nagas that the Aryas first learnt the art of writing; and hence Sanskrit characters are to this day known as Deva-Nagari", but he quotes no authority or reference for what is perhaps a mere surmise based on a verbal similarity.

India after the Indo-European, against which it has successfully held its own in the south. The general tendency among languages appears to be for the easier and the socially more useful to supplant the more difficult or less useful, though the latter may at the same time by a similar process be replacing other less efficient or less estimated tongues. Thus the Goidelic language, probably at one time the prevailing language of Wales, was pushed to the western coast by the later Brythonic, and the latter has followed it in turn and is now in some parts of Wales the slowly disappearing tongue of descendants of those whose natural speech was at one time Goidelic (which only survives in certain forms of enumeration, place-names and a few words of Irish or the so-called fairy speech), and in some cases probably an even earlier and pre-Goidel language. Similarly it seems probable that many tribes in India who now speak a Dravidian language formerly spoke a Munda one. At any rate the fact that the Oraon, for instance, speaks a Dravidian language is no evidence at all that he is not racially nearly allied to the Munda with whom his culture would appear to connect him, though culture again like language, is not a criterion of race.* Similarly the Malers or Sauria Paharias of the Rajmahal hills still speak a Dravidian language, though their relatives the Mal Paharias have adopted an Indo-European one. Both tribes have apparently been pushed back from their more fertile lands by Santals who have come up from the isolation of the Chota Nagpur Plateau with what is probably a still more ancient language than Dravidian, and one which is actually likely to have been the original language of both Mal and Sauria Paharias. The position in India has been much complicated by its history, for it seems that probably Munda languages once occupied the greater part of Upper India, but were pushed back to the hills and forests by the early civilization of the Indus and Ganges valleys speaking probably Dravidian languages. In the alternative the language of the earliest civilization may itself have been a Munda language and been superseded by the Dravidian of later arrivals. The Austroasiatic languages are the most widely distributed in the world as far as geographical distances go, being found from the Punjab in the North to New Zealand in the south and from Madagascar in the west to Easter Island in the east. Von Baer's zoological law that the most widely distributed in space are also the most widely distributed in time can probably be applied with equal force to all languages which have preceded modern methods of rapid distribution, and if so indicates unquestionably that the Austroasiatic is an older group of tongues than the Dravidian, and the obvious inference is that they preceded Dravidian in India. The Dravidian speakers however were thrust out of their domain by Indo-European languages before they had more than partially penetrated the hill fastnesses, and while some of the Munda speakers have retained their languages to this day others were apparently Indo-Europeanised in tongue without passing through a genuinely Dravidian stage, though having assimilated a number of borrowed words, while others, whose Munda language seems to have survived both the Dravidian and Indo-European occupations of the Ganges valley, have been Dravidianised after the latter event by a northerly movement of tribes from the Dravidianised south. There is however, a serious void in our knowledge in that no intensive work appears to have been done on the tribal dialects of southern India, so that it is impossible to say whether the Munda languages ever penetrated to the extreme south of India or not. The Linguistic Survey unfortunately did not include southern India in its scope, and there is therefore a crying need for an intensive study of the dialects spoken by such tribes as the Kadar, Kurumans, Paliyans, Paniyans and Ṭhanda-Pulayans with the object of discovering whether or no any Munda survivals are to be found. If Munda languages extended to southern India, they must inevitably have left some traces in the speech of the pre-Dravidian inhabitants. If they did not we need to know what was the pre-Dravidian language there. Some tribes or castes, *e.g.*, the Kakkalans of Travancore, are reported to have languages peculiar to themselves.

Another obscure and debatable point in regard to the distribution of the Munda languages is the direction from which they reached India. Their connection with

---

* Dr. Guha regards Oraon skulls as showing some physical differences from those of Mundas, but admits, I think, a very close relationship. At any rate the co-efficients of racial likeness given by him for Oraon and Munda show a difference of only 1·79.

the rest of the Austroasiatic family has suggested diffusion from the east westwards, in which case they must have penetrated north-west up the Ganges Valley and along the foot of the Himalayas and up into the hills by such routes as the Kangra Valley, surviving now only in the inner ranges between Ladakh and Sikkim. South-westwards on the other hand they survive in the west of the Central Provinces and must have extended to the Vindhyas and possibly to the west coast, as Bhili at any rate contains some Munda remnants and the very name of the Kolis suggests Munda affinities. Southwards the Sawaras of the Vizagapatam and Ganjam hills and the Gadabas of the adjoining tracts in the Central Provinces have definitely Munda tongues, though the western branches of this tribe, which extends at least to the borders of Rajputana, have lost their distinctive speech, and several of the Gond groups have culture elements which suggest Austroasiatic affinities, the Maria Gonds, for instance, the Koyas, the Bhatras and the Parjas of Bastar and Jeypore, where the so-called Bonda Parjas call themselves Bonda simply (as if Munda with a cold in the head), shave the heads of their women like Konyak Nagas of the Chagyik group and dress them in masses of bead ornaments and narrow petticoats open on one hip exactly like some of the Konyak Naga tribes among whom Mon-Khmer linguistic survivals can be traced. It may be noted in passing that this narrow petticoat is very suggestive of the garment worn by the clay figurines of the (?) Mother Goddess found in quantities in Harappa and Mohenjodaro as also in Crete. The Ods or Waddars, who seem to have Munda affinities, go further south on their wanderings, but their homeland is Orissa, and it seems possible that the Badagas of the Nilgiris may have cultural affinities with some Munda tribes. Nevertheless the most southerly point to which the Munda languages have yet been traced is north of the Godavari river. The southerly distribution of the Munda languages however does not necessarily affect the question of the direction from which they reached India, and it seems just as likely that they came from the north-west and spread down the Ganges Valley to the east as that they came up the valley in the opposite direction. Moreover, if Munda's affinity with the languages of south-east Asia and the Pacific be unquestioned it is also possible that it had affinities with the agglutinative Sumerian language westwards of it, and it would possibly be the safest hypothesis that various branches of the Austroasiatic languages originally radiated in a more or less southerly direction from a common centre in central or south-east Asia, even though it seems certain that the Indus Valley civilization affords a link between Upper India and Sumer.*

An important position in the distribution of the Austroasiatic languages in India is held by the Nicobar Islands. Nicobarese according to the Linguistic Survey, occupies a position intermediate between Munda and Mon-Khmer. Meillet and Cohen (*Les Langues du Monde*) classify Nicobarese with the Mon-Khmer family, but remark that it forms an exception to the rest of that group, in retaining the use of suffixes to form derivatives, a character which it has in common with Munda, "Il est difficile de décider", they continue, "si la nikobarais a innové sous des influences occidentales ou s'il a conservé un trait ancien, aboli depuis longtemps dans les langues parlées à l'est". The very isolation of the Nicobars, and their complete absence of contact for many hundreds of years with any language of the Munda group is in itself a solution to the doubt expressed, and the inference is that the Munda languages generally retain a more ancient characteristic lost by the Mon-Khmer branch, a consideration which inclines one to the view that their distribution has at any rate not been from east to west. On the other hand some account must be taken of the theory, favoured apparently by Prof. Sylvain Lévi and by Prof. Craighill Handy, for instance, of Oceanic intrusions into India. In a paper on Polynesian origins (*Bernice P. Bishop Museum, Occnl. Papers, IX, 8*) Professor Handy attributes to an intrusion from Polynesia to the Asiatic mainland some of the cultural phenomena to be found in Indo-China, Burma, Assam and the west coast of India, mentioning specifically the outrigger canoe on the west coasts of India and Ceylon. This fits in with the known colonization of Madagascar from Indonesia, onto the route of which Ceylon would fall, and the clear traditions of immigrants such as the Iruvar (Izhavas), who form a fifth of the population of Travancore and Cochin, and

* Prof. Hodson points out to me that Hevesy (*Es gibt keine Austric Sprache*) has put forward the theory of a connection between the Munda and the Ugro-Finnish languages.

are almost equally numerous in British Malabar, having come from the direction of Ceylon within the historic period. It is posssible that the coconut palm, the planting of which in Orissa is still regarded as ceremonially dangerous except for Brahmans, has also been an introduction from Indonesia; in the case of the Malabar coast its Malayalam name, *thengai*, ' fruit of the south ', suggests its having been brought by way of Ceylon. It is also clear that the traditions of the Mon-Khmer speaking Khasi point very definitely to migration from the east westwards as do some other traditions in Assam associated with cultures suggestive of Oceania. The words used, for instance, by the Naga tribes for a communal tabu (*penna*, *pini*) can be traced through the Malayan *puni* to New Zealand with a cognate meaning throughout. A recent article published by the Kern Institute suggests an Indonesian origin for the bronze " kettle drums " of the Karens of Burma which are found elsewhere in south-east Asia and were still being made at the end of the last century by the Shans of Nwedaung near Loikaw in the Karenni. Another cultural point of some importance is the " shouldered celt ". Handy claims this as an old Polynesian form, which is incontestable, and its distribution includes parts of the Indian Archipelago, Indo-China. Burma and parts of India. The natural inference is that its distribution has, like that of the Bachelors' House, which is much too widely spread among the primitive tribes of India to be attributed to Oceanic intrusions, started from India and spread to Polynesia, and this may indeed be the true interpretation of facts, but there are certain features of its Indian distribution which appear to point in the other

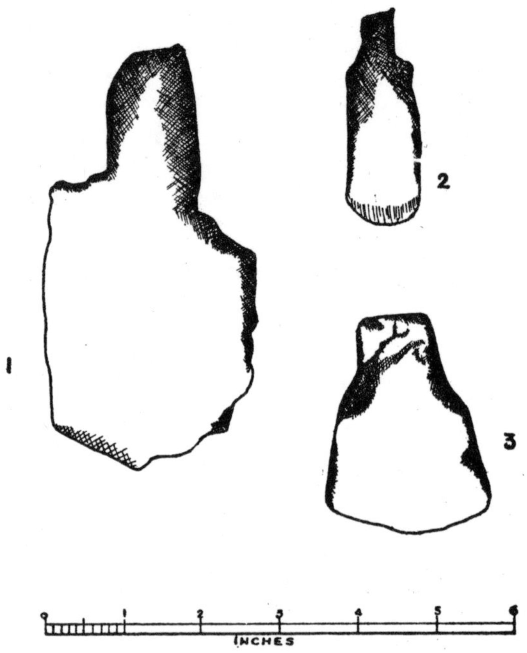

ROUGHLY SHOULDERED CELTS
1. FROM RAJGIR, BIHAR
2. FROM MADRAS (*Locality unspecified; Agency tracts?*)
3. FROM ASSAM (*?Naga Hills*)

direction. Square-shouldered adzes abound in the Irrawadi valley; specimens are found very rarely in the Santal Parganas and the Madras Agency tracts, and somewhat more frequently apparently in Chota Nagpur. They do not seem to occur elsewhere in India and are quite distinct from the usual type of Indian celt, which prevails in the Santal Parganas and in central and south India generally, and which may be correlated to the copper and bronze types of Mohenjodaro which are all unshouldered. In the Chota Nagpur area, however, shouldered copper celts are obtained, generally, it seems, from

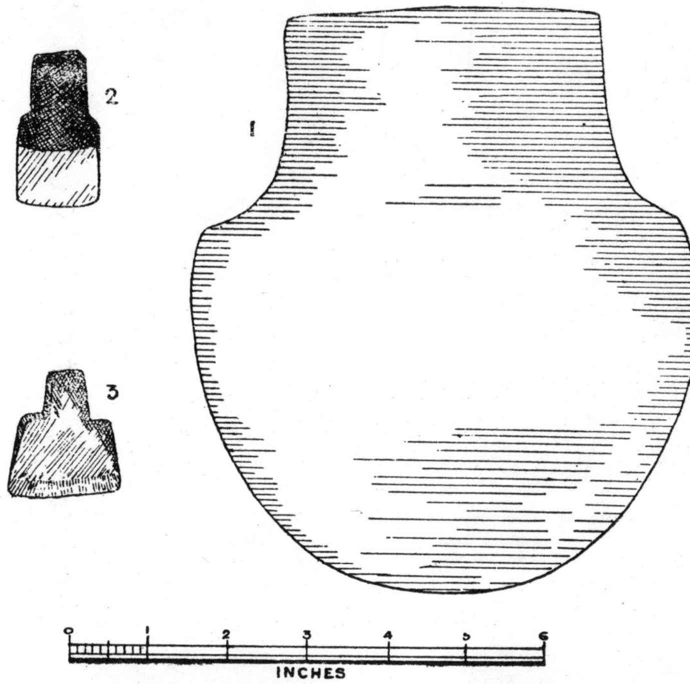

1. SHOULDERED COPPER IMPLEMENT, MANBHUM
2 & 3. HIGHLY FINISHED SHOULDERED CELTS, BURMA
(*From Specimens in the Indian Museum*)

pre-historic burials, and these must be associated with the shouldered stone ones, as must the shouldered iron hoes still used by the Khasis

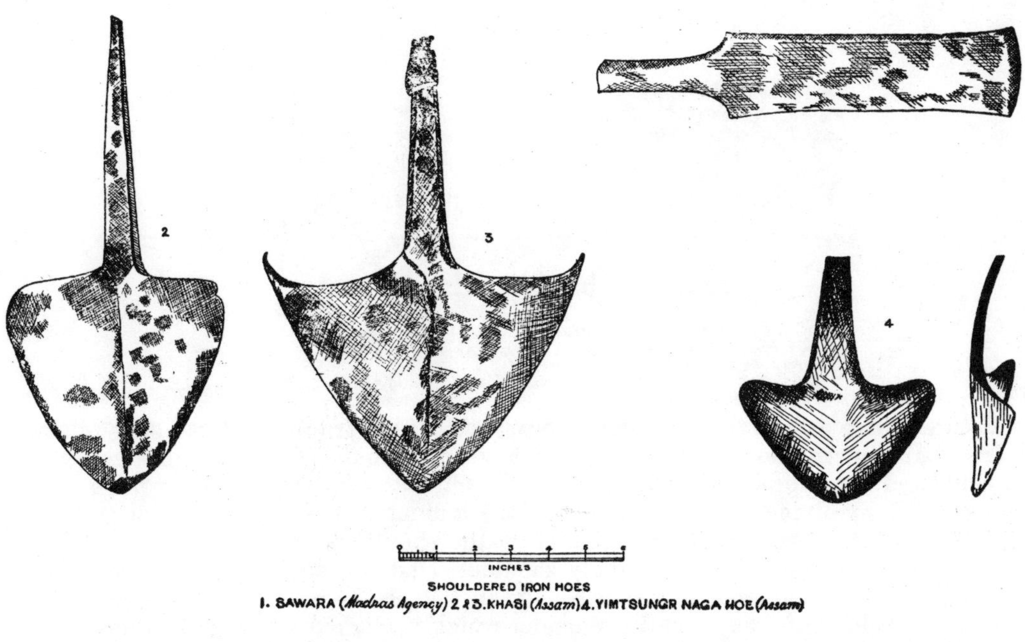

SHOULDERED IRON HOES
1. SAWARA (*Madras Agency*) 2 & 3. KHASI (*Assam*) 4. YIMTSUNGR NAGA HOE (*Assam*)

and by some Nagas in Assam, as by Sawaras and other Munda tribes in India proper. These hoes are as pronounced in type and as distinctive from the hoes in general use as the corresponding shouldered celts are among neolithic adzes. The distribution of the shouldered adze and hoe in stone and metal is not coextensive with that of the Munda language and is not reported from the Nicobars, and the

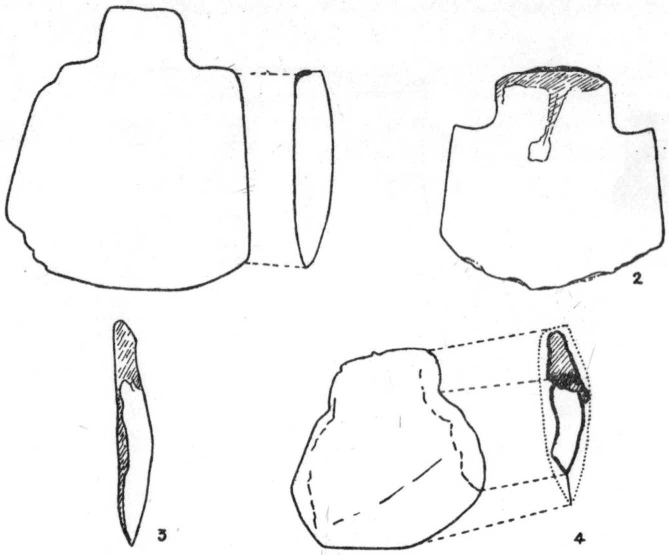

1. SHOULDERED CELT FROM BAPUGWEMA NAGA HILLS ASSAM ⅓ NAT. SIZE
2, 3 & 4. SHOULDERED CELTS FROM WAICHONG (2) KOBAK
(3) BOLASAN (4) IN THE NORTH CACHAR HILLS ASSAM. ½ NAT. SIZE

inference is that it is either an intrusion from Oceania or a development which started in eastern India and thence spread to the islands. One rather curious

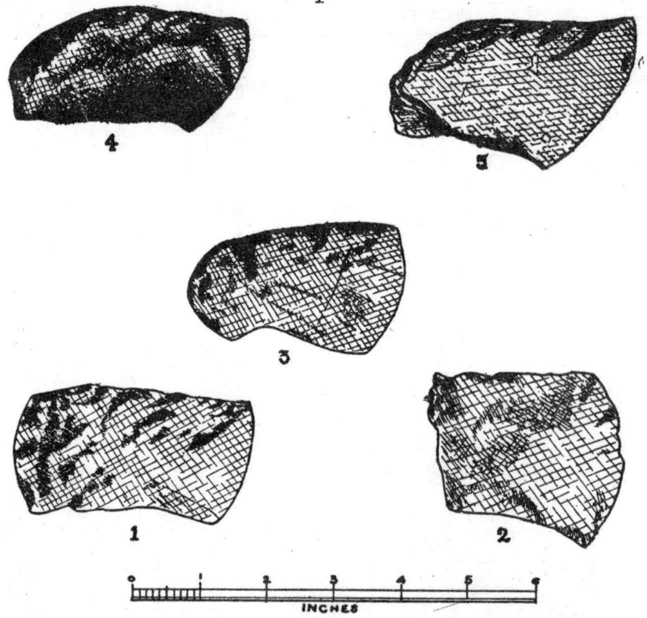

1 & 2 CELTS FROM INDIAN MUSEUM LABELLED "INDIA" LOCALITY UNSPECIFIED BUT PROBABLY FROM SANTAL PARGANAS, WHERE SIMILAR ARTEFACTS HAVE BEEN FOUND BY BODDING.
3, 4 & 5. CELTS FROM PAHANG (*Malay peninsula*) AFTER EVANS JOURNAL F. M. S. MUS. XII. PL. IV

feature in this case is the sporadic appearance of the true shouldered adze of the Irrawadi type in India, accompanied by a very common prevalence of a roughly shouldered type probably almost equally effective for practical purposes but obviously involving far less labour in the making. The true Irrawadi type of adze is not only very exactly squared at the shoulders but is worked flat and polished throughout. The roughly shouldered adze common in the Naga Hills and the Santal Parganas is polished only on the plano-convex cutting edge, the tang end being left rough, and a shoulder roughly worked sometimes on one side of the adze only. In the N. Cachar Hills, in an area occupied by a number of prehistoric groups of enormous monolithic urns of phallic shape, which contained the ashes of the dead and are probably forerunners of the Khasi stone cists and clan burials, a number of stone axes and adzes have been found. The axes are triangular, flat and polished, but the adzes, or possibly hoes, have in many cases the appearance of having been worked in imitation of metal blades with a curved back like the existing Khasi or Yimtsung Naga hoes.* A similar inference is

* Specimens may be seen in the Pitt Rivers Museum at Oxford

suggested by the shape of the curved stone axes found in the Santal Parganas and described by Bodding, which have a close parallel in some curved axe heads from Pahang in Malaya (see Journ. F. M. S. Mus. vol. xv, pl. iv), though here again the eastern type is much more pertect than the western. This suggests the possibility that the shouldered stone adze may be a derivation from the metal type and not its original, which would involve a distribution eastwards from the centre in which the copper originals are found and which corresponds closely with that of the non-Aryan kingdoms of the Saudyumnas, plausibly identified with the Munda and Mon-Khmer by Pargiter, and occcupying a country still occupied by Sawara and Munda tribes. This hypothesis would also account for the apparently quite unnecessary labour expended on the fabrication of the square-shouldered Irrawadi celt which is difficult to understand if it were not the natural result of an attempt to copy a metal original as exactly as the available material permitted. If this hypothesis be rejected we must regard the shouldered copper celt as subsequent to the shouldered stone adze. Either or both might have given rise to the existing iron hoe, since there seems to have been no copper age in Assam or Burma. But if the copper celt be later it supports the hypothesis that the shouldered adze is intrusive from Indonesia, whereas if the copper form be the original type the stone form must have reached Oceania from the west, and not India or Indonesia from the south-east. In the latter case it has to be considered whether the roughly shouldered adzes of the Naga Hills and Santal Parganas are degenerate forms of the flat square-shouldered and highly polished Irrawadi adze or their undeveloped prototype, and the development of so unnecessarily laborious a type as the square-shouldered adze from an equally efficient if less polished implement seems unlikely. If on the other hand the prototype be Oceanian it cannot be Indian and in that case we must regard the square-shouldered adze as having degenerated in its original material in one place while leading perhaps simultaneously to improved copper and iron types in others, not perhaps an impossibility. It would appear however on the face of it that the shouldered adze is a type much more likely to originate in metal than in stone.*

Shouldered adzes have involved a digression from the matter of language, but it is difficult to consider the question of the Munda languages entirely apart

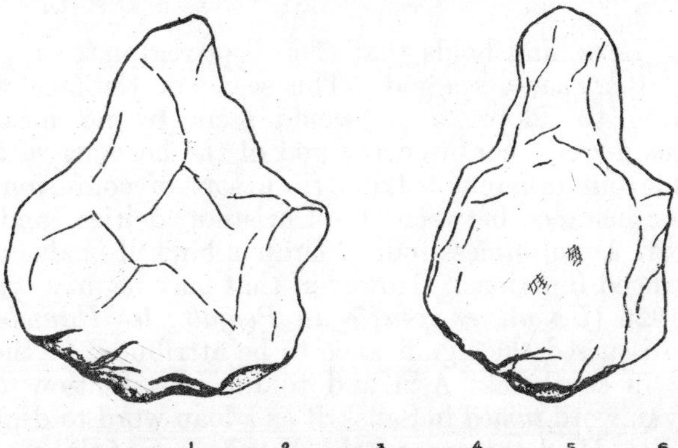

SHOULDERED HOES FROM AL-UBAID (*after Hall & Woolley*)

* The following bibliography of shouldered adzes is given here as the articles are many of them obscure and unknown to the general reader. Those marked with an asterisk are illustrated. *Proceedings of the Asiatic Society of Bengal, 1875,** and No. 1 of 1876. *Journal of the Asiatic Society of Bengal,* No. 3 *of* 1879 (Cockburn),* LXIII, iii, I of 1894 (Cockburn)* ; LXV, iii, No. I of 1896 (Peal)* ; LXX, iii, No. 1 of 1901 (Bodding)* ; LXXIII, iii, No. 2 of 1904 (Bodding) ; XXI, No. 3 of 1926 (Hutton)* ; XXV, No. 1 of 1929 (Mills and Hutton)*. *Man,* XVII-74 (July 1917, Balfour)* ; XXIV, 15, (February 1924, Hutton)*. See also Gurdon, *The Khasis* (1914), page 12 *et seq.* and Hutton, *The Sema Nagas* pages 254—258.

In the matter of canoes and their association with a westward drift from Polynesia the following may be referred to :—Hornell, *Origins, etc., of Indian Boat Designs, Memoirs of the Asiatic Society of Bengal,* VII, No. 3, pages 139-256 (1920)* ; Mills, *The Ao Nagas,* pages 76 and 79, notes (1926)* and Hutton, correspondence in *Folklore* XXXIX, No. 1, pages 94-95 (1928), and *M. A. S. B.* XI No. 1, pages 32, 39, 60, 63, 68* ; Peal, *Visit to the Naga Hills, J. A. S. B.* 1872*. It is to be noted that the dug-out "canoe" drum occurs in China, *vide* Colquhoun, *Across Chryse,* II, page 308, and its arrival in the Assam Hills from the direction of Indonesia is open to grave doubt.

from any cultural features which form part of the same complex. Although shouldered hoes of chert are clearly depicted (Hall and Woolley, *al-Ubaid*, plate XIII) as found in Sumer, while Mackay has found pottery hoes at Kish distinctly suggestive of the shouldered type, and Sir Flinders Petrie illustrates one polished stone "axe" of similar pattern from predynastic Egypt (*Prehistoric Egypt*, pl. XXVII), this particular feature does not seem to appear in India west of Chota Nagpur, but the vestiges of Munda occupation are to be found as already indicated all over northern India. Prof. Przyluski in a series of articles in the *Memoires* and in the *Bulletin* of the *Société dé Linguistique* has pointed out a number of Austroasiatic loans in vocabularies of Indo-European languages spoken in India. Indeed in a paper in the Royal Asiatic Society's Journal in 1931 he derives the name of *Varuna* as well as the Hittite *Aruna* from a Sumerian root and an Austroasiatic

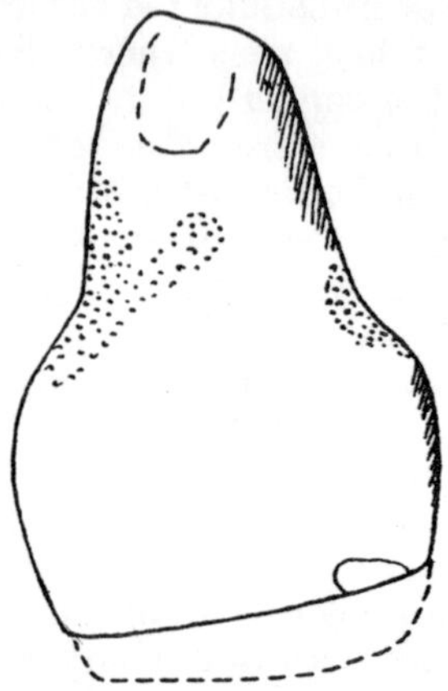

STONE IMPLEMENT:— PREDYNASTIC EGYPT
(after Sir Flinders Petrie)

god of the sea, *Baru*, and holds that there is no reason to suppose that Varuna was ever anything other than a sea god. This seems on the face of it an unnecessarily extreme position to adopt, as it would seem by no means unlikely that the Indo-Europeans merely confused the god of the heavens with an indigenous god of similar name but different attributes, a sort of confusion that has frequently taken place for instance between pre-Christian deities and Christian saints in Europe (*e.g.*, St. Anne), unless indeed Uranus himself is also to be identified as a *Baru* with changed functions. However that may be, in a paper in the *Journal Asiatique* in 1926 (*Un ancien peuple du Penjab : les Udumbara*) Przyluski has penetratingly discussed the significance to be attributed to the gourd-origin myth so widespread in south-east Asia and to the distribution of names associated with a pre-Aryan word *tumba* in Sanskrit as a loan word to designate the colocynth *Lagenia vulgaris*. He demonstrates the distribution of this word in Indonesia and its association with the similar fruit of the *Ficus glomerata*, called in Sanskrit *udumbara*, with certain names of musical instruments made of gourds, and so with one of the functions of the widespread caste of degraded musicians known as Dōm, Domna, Dombar, etc., who may be regarded as representing early inhabitants of northern India. If we accept, as we must, the force of his argument we may see a survival of the Munda-speaking Austroasiatic population of northern India not only in the Doms, and no doubt in the very similar Korava group, but in the Kurumbas of southern India, to whose former predominance the tract in Malabar still known as Kurumbranad yet testifies and who are still associated like the ancient Kodumbara with the keeping of sheep and the production of woollen cloth, and with the Gadaba (no Telugu ear would tolerate "Gadamba"* and the *m* would drop out as easily as it has from Kuruba), who still speak a Munda language and seem to be associated with the kindred Bhatra tribe

* That this was the original form is perhaps confirmed by the existence in Vizagapatam district of the variants Gutob and Gutumuo for Gadaba.

in the Orissa hinterland as Przyluski's Udumbara with his Bhadra. By an

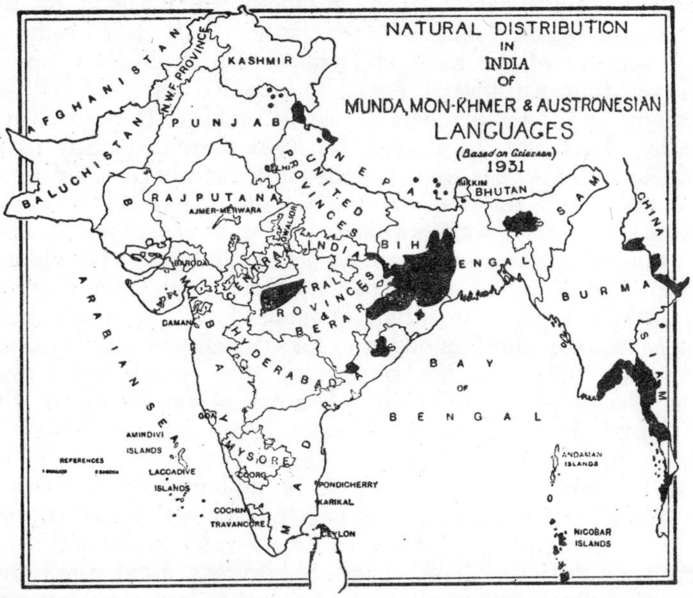

ingenious equation of these tribes with the Padaei of Herodotus, Przyluski associates these Munda-speakers with the Melanesians through the practice of eating their aged relatives like the Bataks of Sumatra, and this practice has been attributed to the Birhors of Chota Nagpur who speak a Mundari tongue (*cf. infra*, page 404). It remains to be pointed out that the Kuruba as also the Kuruman are still associated with megalithic and dolmenic burials like so many of the tribes who have retained their Austroasiatic speech, while the stories of aged-relative-eating have a distribution corresponding roughly with that of Munda languages

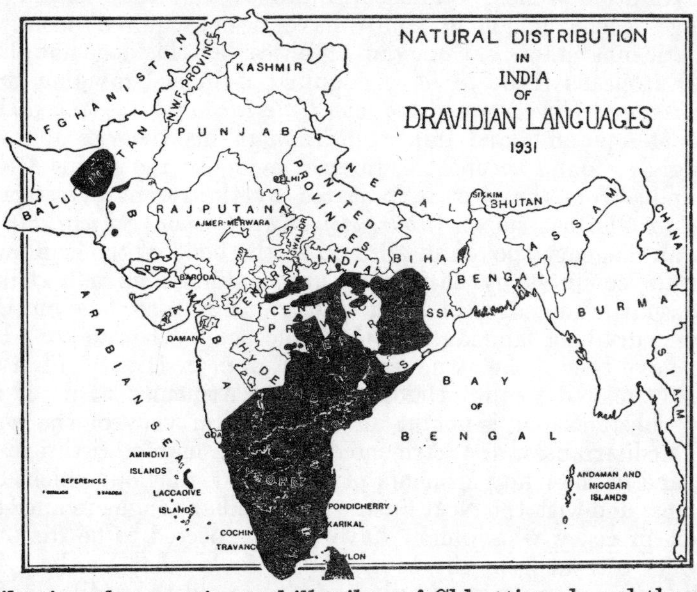

to-day, attributing the practice to hill tribes of Chhattisgarh and the Amarkantak tableland, to the Birhors of Chota Nagpur, to hill tribes in Assam, to some Kachins in north-west of Burma and to the Wa in the east of it. "The fruit is ripe", they say according to the Shans, "let us eat it", as they shake down their aged parents from the branches they have made them ascend.

156. One conclusion of Przyluski's however, it does not seem possible to accept. He seems to regard the Austroasiatic speakers in northern India generally as having pushed out the Dravidian speakers from the whole of the fertile valleys of northern India leaving a mere island of Dravidian speakers in Baluchistan. It seems to us far more probable, in view of what has already been stated as to the wider distribution and greater antiquity of Austroasiatic languages, and maps of the distribution of Dravidian and Munda languages support **Dravidian.**

this view, that the Munda preceded the Dravidian in the Peninsula generally, and was pushed to the south-east by the Dravidian which was in its turn superseded by the Indo-European tongues. Przyluski has laid some emphasis on Herodotus' account of the races of India, and identifies the warlike race of the north with the Indo-Europeans, the Ethiopianlike race of the far south with the Dravidians, and the intermediate races, of which Herodotus describes two, as Austroasiatic. Herodotus says, however, that there are many nations of Indians speaking different languages, and that the most easterly part is desert. Apparently Herodotus' knowledge did not extend eastwards beyond the Thar desert and must have been confined southwards to the west coast perhaps no further than Bombay. It is also not clear in what sense the term "Dravidian" is used by Przyluski as he appears to refer to the Dravidian languages but to the pre-Dravidian physical type. Dravidian languages have left much clearer survivals in north-west India than the Munda ones, for though the latter have, as effectively demonstrated by Przyluski, left strong traces in vocabulary, the former have affected the actual speech of the Indo-Europeans, providing it with cerebrals to the extent of requiring distinctive letters of the alphabet, while Dravidian loan words have been indicated in much greater number than have Munda ones so far, and the story of the Deluge, which is undoubtedly of Mesopotamian origin and absent from the Rigveda, retains, as pointed out by Caldwell, words of Dravidian origin for two of its most important features—water (*nira*) and fish (*mina*), while, as pointed out by Professor N. K. Dutt, Satyavrata Manu, the Indian counterpart of Noah, is described in the Puranas as "the lord of Dravida". Professor Rapson (*Cambridge History of India, I, 41*) regards Dravidian languages as having been "actually flourishing in the western regions of Northern India at the period when languages of the Indo-European type were introduced." It seems therefore necessary to regard the Dravidian speakers as having been the latest pre-Indo-European occupants of Upper India, as having reached India from the north-west where their language remains among the Brahui, who actually regard the Mohenjo-daro ruins as the work of their ancestors,* and as having brought with them the ancient civilization of Mesopotamia, Asia Minor and the eastern Mediterranean. The Deluge legend might of course have been acquired locally in India from Austroasiatic inhabitants of Sumerian affinities, but this does not alter the fact that the Indo-Europeans seem to have acquired it in a Dravidian dress. Schoener (*Alt-dravidisches: Eine Namenkundliche Untersuchung*) has traced Dravidian place-names in Mesopotamia and Iran, and although his theories do not seem to have been generally found acceptable, further evidence that this Dravidian tongue reached India from the west is indicated by the recent investigations (1930) of G. W. Brown who has shown (*Jour. American Oriental Society*, 50, 273. *sqq.*) that the Khărian language spoken in Mitanni at the bend of the Euphrates both before and after its conquest by the Indo-European invaders has striking similarities to the Dravidian languages of India today, as it also has on the other hand with some surviving languages of the Caucasus. Kharian (or Hurrian) is also stated to have been "the true non-Indo-European Hittite of Asia Minor" and to be nearly related to the Haldian of early Armenia. This, if it prove to be definitely substantiated, is not at all surprising in view of the wide distribution of both Mediterranean and Armenoid physical characteristics in the population of India, and of the many elements in the Hindu religion which connect it with Mesopotamia and with the Near East. A Dravidian tongue in ancient Mesopotamia is in fact precisely what might have been expected to be discovered now that we know for certain from the Indus Valley finds what has long been suspected, that India was not an isolated welter of australoid tribes till the Indo-Europeans entered it in the 2nd millenium B. C., but had a civilisation, comparable to and in communication with the ancient kingdoms of Mesopotamia, far older and in most ways more highly developed than that of the Indo-European invaders who established themselves in India precisely as they did in Babylon, as barbarian rulers of more cultured peoples.

Indo-European. **157.** With the advent in India of the Indo-European we come at any rate within the range of historical tradition and the distribution and

---

* Personal information from Mr. E. J. H. Mackay while he was engaged in excavating that site. Colonel Sewell, however, regards the tradition as spurious and suggested by the excavators themselves.—J. H. H.

inter-relation of the Indo-European languages has been so exhaustively treated

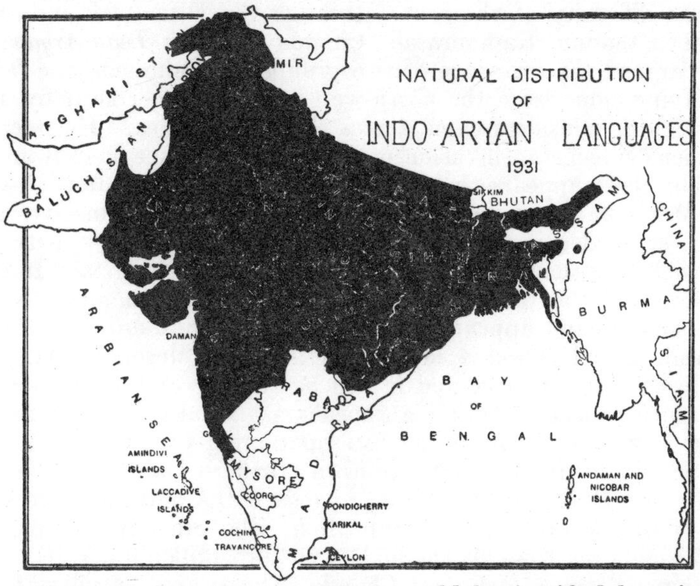

by Sir George Grierson that the most that would be justified here is to sum up very briefly his conclusions. He tells us that Sanskrit is the purified literary language arising from the dialects of the Rigveda; that the languages of the "Outer Branches", that is Lahnda or Western Panjabi, Sindhi, Marathi, Oriya, Bihari, Bengali and Assamese, are derived from a different dialect of the original Indo-European tongue than are the languages of the "Inner Branch", Western Hindi, Panjabi, Gujarati, Bhili, Khandeshi, Rajasthani and the Pahari dialects. Eastern Hindi is intermediate between the two, while of the Inner Branch languages Gujarati at any rate retains traces of the Outer language which it has superseded. From the same colloquial source as Sanskrit arose the Midland language of the Inner Branch always regarded as not only the true type of the Indo-Aryan tongue

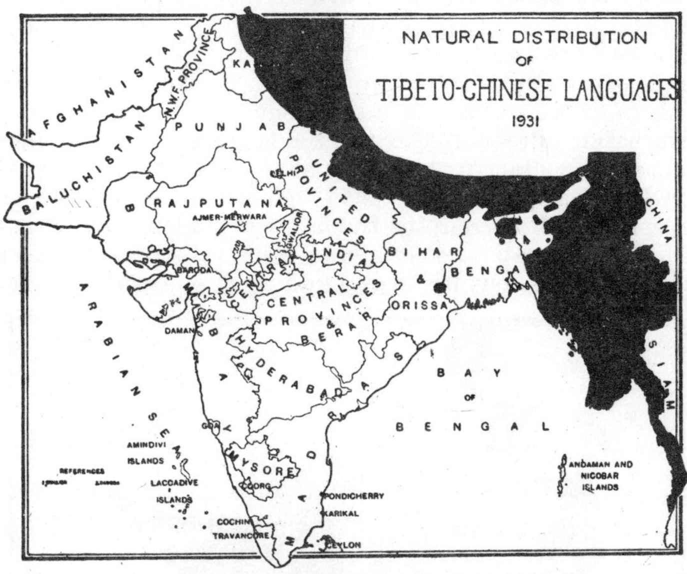

but as the tongue of the true and pure Indo-Aryan people. This difference between the Inner and Outer languages is regarded as a confirmation of Hoernle's theory of the first and second wave of Indo-European immigration, the second wave being supposed to have entered India through Chitral to the east of the first already established in the Punjab. A further confirmation of this view is said to have been found in the racial differences between the inhabitants of the Punjab and those of the United Provinces.

No definite proof of the truth of this theory has, however, been found, and it does not seem essential to an interpretation of the facts as accepted, though it is not of course in conflict with them. It appears on the face of it unlikely on account of the difficulty of the route through the Himalayas indicated by the theory. Rai Bahadur Ramaprasad Chanda in his *Indo-Aryan Races* has convincingly argued the existence of two groups of Brahmans, one fair which he regards as having come from the north-west, and the other swarthy from south-west Asia which he considers came across the Arabian Sea. He infers from this and from other evidence an invasion of Indo-European speakers from the east of Babylonia, but there appears to be no evidence whatever that the earlier nordic invaders of Mesopotamia, who seem to have established themselves as rulers of the Hittites, succeeded in effectively imposing their language on their subjects, though it is believed that the Kanesian dialect, in which certain Indo-European features occur, was the official tongue of the Hittite Empire. Similarly the above-mentioned Kharri appear to have been a non-nordic race with nordic chieftains, and their location is in the north-west of Mesopotamia. If therefore Chanda's theory is to be accepted it will be simpler and safer to regard these Mesopotamian invaders as Dravidian speakers. In any case their culture and religion must have been that of the Mesopotamian basin, and the movement of peoples and culture from Mesopotamia to northern India must be put at such an early date that it is hardly possible to regard the movement as having had any impulse from the proto-nordic steppe folk, who only appear to have begun to invade Mesopotamia towards the end of the 3rd millenium B. C. Modified to this extent there is much to support Chanda's theory, which will not then differ in effect from that already advanced of a previous invasion of Dravidian speakers.

There is moreover another interpretation possible of the distribution of the Inner and the Outer Bands of Indo-Aryan languages. The Outer Band is that of languages which have retained certain features characteristic of the Pisacha or Dardic group, a group of languages still spoken in the Pamirs and in the north-western hills of India. The Inner Band has none of these features. It may be added that it is the Inner Band which has developed a script, on which the Outer is dependent. It will be pointed out in a subsequent chapter that there is very good reason for supposing that between the end of the Mohenjodaro civilisation in the Indus valley and the entry of the Rigvedic Aryans the Indus valley was subjected to an invasion of Alpines from the Pamirs. It is not improbable that these Alpines had acquired an Indo-European language, and they may even have had proto-nordic leaders. The oldest language in the Pamirs, and it is one which is stated by Grierson to exist as a substratum to all the Dardic tongues, is the so far unclassed language the present form of which is known as Burushaski. Probably this was the language of the Alpine inhabitants before they came into contact with the common ancestors of the Avesta Iranians and the Rigvedic Aryans. But these had left their northern steppes and were wandering in the neighbourhood of the Iranian plateau long before they descended on the plains of the Punjab, and may have been responsible not only for the disturbance of the Alpines, but for their adoption of a variety of their language.

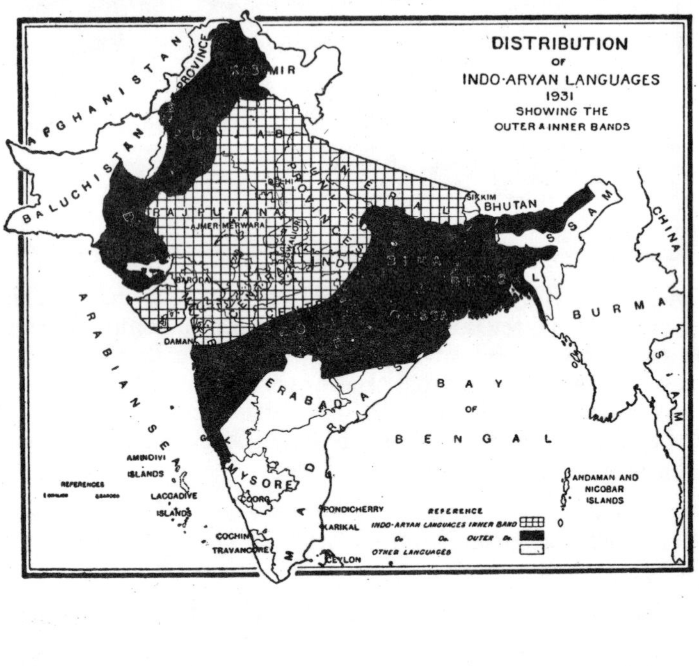

It is also possible that they had infected the Alpine culture and religion with some affinity to their own by supplying it with rulers and war-lords as they did to the Alpine peasants in Central Europe. The Pisacha language introduced in northern India would naturally be pushed out by the later Rigvedic Aryans, though their continued occupation of the whole of the west bank of the Indus and both banks of its upper waters would be quite enough to account for the assimilation to the Outer Band language of the narrow strip of land between Peshawar and Sialkot, which, if this theory be correct, should belong to the Inner group, much as the extension of the Inner Band to the Gujarat coast has interrupted the former continuity of the Outer Band from Baluchistan to Kanara, if indeed Gujarati should not still be classified with the Outer Band, which is at least a debatable proposition. Indeed some such strip of country lost to the Inner Branch must somewhere remain whatever be the hypothesis adopted, and Grierson (*Linguistic Survey*, I.i, 108) gives other reasons for a southward movement of Eranians or Pamiris subsequent to the Indo-Aryan invasion.

In any case Hoernle's theory of the second invasion from the north seems less likely than Professor Rapson's view of the occupation of the Punjab as occurring in the course of migration while that of the Ganges valley belongs to a later epoch of colonization. It must be recognised that if Sanskrit owes its script to the previous civilization of northern India there must have been amalgamation and an interchange of cultural ideas between the colonists and the pre-existing population, whether or not they already worshipped Vedic deities. The culture of Mesopotamia, when invaded by the Kassites and other northern warrior tribes, was vastly more developed in many respects than that of the invaders and there is no reason to imagine that the same was not the case in India. Hence it was that it was in the area of colonization and amalgamation that the Indo-European languages developed both writing and literature to the greatest heights. It was in the Attic language of Athens, where the invading northerner fused with the darkhaired Ionian, that literature and philosophy flourished, not at Dorian Sparta, where the population remained more martial perhaps, but less cultured, as the Punjab compared to the Madhyadesa. The most important and lasting gift of the Aryans to India was probably their language, a vehicle of communication and expression belonging to a family of languages which has proved its superiority in all parts of the world by superseding any other languages with which any of its members have come into effective competition.

SUBSIDIARY TABLE I.

Distribution of the population of each sex by language.

Language.	Total number of speakers (000's omitted). 1931. Males.	1931. Females.	1921. Males.	1921. Females.	Number per 10,000 of total population 1931. Males.	1931. Females.	Where chiefly spoken.
1	2	3	4	5	6	7	8
Vernaculars of India ..	**180,215**	**169,673**	**162,125**	**153,400**	**9,978**	**9,986**	
Austric Family	**2,676**	**2,667**	**2,260**	**2,269**	**148**	**157**	
Austro-nesian Sub-Family (Malay Group).	*3*	*3*	*3*	*3*	..	..	..
Malay	2	2	2	2	..	..	Burma.
Salon	1	1	1	1	..	..	Do.
Austro-asiatic Sub-Family ..	*2,673*	*2,664*	*2,257*	*2,267*	*148*	*157*	
Mon Group (Talaing) ..	*154*	*151*	*97*	*92*	*9*	*9*	Burma.
Palaung-Wa Group ..	*88*	*88*	*74*	*74*	*5*	*5*	
Wa	11	11	7	7	1	1	Burma.
Palaung	70	70	59	59	4	4	Do.
Khasi Group (Khasi) ..	*114*	*120*	*98*	*107*	*6*	*7*	Assam.
Nicobar Group (Nicobarese)	*5*	*5*	*5*	*4*	..	..	Andamans and Nicobars.
Munda Branch	*2,310*	*2,299*	*1,984*	*1,990*	*128*	*135*	
Kherwari	2,018*	2,014*	1,748	1,755	112	119	Assam, Bengal, Bihar and Orissa and Central Provinces.
Korku	85	85	61	60	5	5	Central Provinces and Berar.
Kharia	79	73	68	69	4	4	Bihar and Orissa and Central Provinces.
Sawara	98	97	84	83	5	6	Madras.
Gadaba	22	22	17	16	1	1	Do.
Tibeto-Chinese Family ..	**6,909**	**7,101**	**6,364**	**6,521**	**383**	**418**	
Tibetan Group	*127*	*125*	*117*	*115*	*7*	*7*	
Bhotia	*127*	*125*	*117*	*115*	*7*	*7*	
Bhotia of Baltistan ..	68	69	74	74	4	4	Jammu and Kashmir State.
Bhotia of Ladakh ..	21	21	17	17	1	1	Ditto.
Pronominalized Himalayan Group.	*56*	*58*	*53*	*54*	*3*	*3*	
Kanauri	12	14	10	12	1	1	Punjab.
Kiranti	44	44	42†	41†	2	3	Bengal and Sikkim.
Non-Pronominalized Himalayan Group.	*52*	*50*	*53*	*48*	*3*	*3*	
Murmi	22	21	20	19	1	1	Bengal and Sikkim.
Magari	9	9	11	9	..	1	Bengal, Assam and Sikkim.
Rong or Lepcha ..	13	12	10	10	1	1	Bengal and Sikkim.
North Assam Branch ..	*9*	*9*	*8*	*7*	*1*	*1*	
Abor	7	7	7	7	..	..	Assam.
Bara or Bodo Group ..	*466*	*445*	*363*	*353*	*25*	*26*	
Bodo‡	148	143	138	133	8	8	Assam.
Garo	117	113	110	106	6	7	Do.
Tipura (Mrung) ..	104	94	82	81	6	6	Assam and Bengal.
Mikir Language (Mikir) ..	*64*	*62*	*56*	*53*	*4*	*4*	Assam.
Naga Group	*173*	*176*	*147*	*148*	*10*	*10*	
Angami	22	21	22	21	1	1	Assam.
Sema	19	19	17	18	1	1	Do.
Ao	15	18	14	16	1	1	Do.
Tangkhul	14	15	11	13	1	1	Do.
Naga (unclassed) ..	4	4	12	11	..	..	Do.
Kuki-Chin Group	*476*	*497*	*392*	*404*	*26*	*29*	
Manipuri	192§	200§	171	172	11	12	Assam.
Thado	28	29	16	17	2	2	Do.
Lushei	28	32	36	41	2	2	Do.
Chin (other unspecified) ..	60	61	55	56	3	4	Burma.
Kuki (other unspecified) ..	5	5	12†	13	..	..	Assam and Bengal.

*Include Santali, Mundari, Ho, etc.
†Limbu, Khambu and Rai Combined.
‡1931 figures are only for Bara Bodo or Plains Kachari.
§Include Kathé also.

SUBSIDIARY TABLE I—*contd.*

Distribution of the population of each sex by language—*contd.*

Language.	Total number of speakers (000's omitted). 1931. Males.	1931. Females.	1921. Males.	1921. Females.	Number per 10,000 of total population 1931. Males.	1931. Females.	Where chiefly spoken.
1	2	3	4	5	6	7	8
Kachin Group (Kachin) ..	*76*	*81*	*73*	*78*	*4*	*5*	Burma.
Burma Group	*4,881*	*5,079*	*4,575*	*4,738*	*270*	*299*	
Burmese	4,332	4,522	4,135	4,288	240	266	Burma.
Arakanese	156	152	153	151	9	9	Burma and Bengal.
Intha	28	29	27	28	2	2	Burma.
Lolo-Muhso Group ..	*48*	*45*	*39*	*36*	*3*	*3*	
Akha	21	19	18	16	1	1	Burma.
Tai Group	*517*	*511*	*464*	*462*	*29*	*30*	
Khun..	16	16	16	17	1	1	Burma.
Shan	475	470	422	421	26	28	Do.
Karen Family	**669**	**672**	**558**	**556**	**37**	**40**	
Dravidian Family	**35,848**	**35,797**	**32,078**	**32,050**	**1,985**	**2,107**	
Dravida Group	*20,644*	*20,810*	*18,589*	*18,697*	*1,143*	*1,225*	
Tamil	10,073	10,339	9,284	9,496	558	608	Madras and Mysore State.
Malayalam	4,533	4,605	3,736	3,762	251	271	Madras, Cochin and Travancore.
Kanarese	5,690	5,516	5,253	5,121	315	325	Bombay, Madras, Hyderabad and Mysore.
Kodagu or Coorgi ..	23	22	22	18	1	1	Coorg.
Tulu	324	328	293	299	18	19	Madras.
Intermediate Group ..	*1,797*	*1,812*	*1,512*	*1.544*	*100*	*107*	
Kurukh or Oraon ..	521	517	430	436	29	30	Bihar and Orissa.
Malto..	35	36	33	33	2	2	Bihar and Orissa.
Gondi	926	939	798	819	51	55	C. P. and Berar and Central India Agency.
Kandhi or Kui	288	298	239	244	16	18	Madras and Bihar and Orissa.
Kolami	16	13	12	12	1	1	Central Provinces and Berar.
Andhra Language Group (Telugu).	*13,291*	*13,083*	*11,874*	*11,727*	*736*	*770*	Madras, Hyderabad and Mysore.
North Western Language (Brahui).	115	92	103	81	6	5	Baluchistan.
Indo-European Family ..	**134,083**	**123,410**	**120,851**	**111,995**	**7,423**	**7,263**	
Eastern Group (Eranian Branch)	*1,242*	*1,029*	*1,091*	*890*	*69*	*61*	
Balochi	344	284	272	213	19	17	Baluchistan and Bombay.
Pashto	895	742	819	677	50	44	N.-W. F. Province and Baluchistan.
Dard Group	*820*	*690*	*705*	*599*	*45*	*41*	
Shina	36	32	14	14	2	2	Jammu and Kashmir State.
Kashmiri	783	656	687	581	43	39	Ditto.
North-Western Group ..	*6,803*	*5,769*	*4,893*	*4,131*	*377*	*340*	
Lahnda or Western Panjabi	4,603	3,963	3,050	2,602	255	233	Punjab and N.-W. F. Province.
Sindhi	2,200	1,807	1,843	1,528	122	106	Bombay.
Southern Group	*10,817*	*10,544*	*9,509*	*9,289*	*599*	*621*	..
Marathi	10,573	10,317	9,296	9,095	585	607	Bombay, C. P. and Berar and Hyderabad.
Eastern Group	*48,059*	*46,580*	*31,090*	*30,082*	*2,661*	*2,739*	
Oriya	5,485	5,709	4,952	5,192	304	336	Bihar and Orissa and Madras.
Bihari	14,015	13,912	4	4	776	819	Rajputana, C. I. Agency and Bihar and Orissa.
Bengali	27,517	25,952	25,239	24,055	1,523	1,527	Bengal and Assam.
Assamese	1,042	967	895	932	58	56	Assam.
Mediate Group (Eastern Hindi)	*4,210*	*2,657*	*704*	*695*	*233*	*215*	C. I. Agency, C. P. and Berar.

SUBSIDIARY TABLE I—*concld.*

Distribution of the Population of each sex by language—*concld.*

Language.	Total number of speakers (000's omitted). 1931. Males.	1931. Females.	1921. Males.	1921. Females.	Number per 10,000 of total population 1931. Males.	1931. Females.	Where chiefly spoken.
1	2	3	4	5	6	7	8
Central Group	*60,652*	*53,905*	*71,833*	*65,416*	*3,358*	*3,173*	
Western Hindi ..	37,743	33,804	50,210	46,504	2,090	1,990	U. P., Punjab, C. P. and Berar, C. I. Agency, Rajputana, Hyderabad State and Gwalior.
Rajasthani	7,271	6,627	6,656	6,025	403	390	Rajputana, C. I. Agency and Gwalior State.
Gujarati	5,610	5,240	4,967	4,585	311	308	Bombay, Baroda State and Western India States Agency.
Punjabi	8,799	7,040	8,961	7,272	487	414	Punjab and Jammu and Kashmir State.
Bhili	1,110	1,079	932	924	61	64	Bombay, C. I. Agency and Rajputana.
Pahari Group	*1,472*	*1,280*	*1,025*	*893*	*82*	*75*	
Central Pahari ..	6	1	4	..	..	..	United Provinces.
Eastern Pahari (Khas-Kura or Naipali).	251	162	167	113	14	10	Bengal, Assam and Sikkim State.
Western Pahari ..	1,211	1,115	854	780	67	66	Punjab and Jammu and Kashmir State.
Unclassed Languages ..	**29**	**25**	**8**	**7**	**2**	**1**	
Gipsy Languages ..	13	13	8	7	1	1	Bombay, Punjab, Jammu and Kashmir State and Rajputana.
Vernaculars of other Asiatic Countries and Africa.	**198**	**105**	**143**	**69**	**11**	**6**	
Indo-European Family ..	**25**	**14**	**15**	**10**	**1**	**1**	
Persian Group	*23*	*12*	*14*	*9*	*1*	*1*	
Persian	23	12	14	9	1	1	Bombay, Baluchistan and N.-W. F. Province.
Tibeto-Chinese Family ..	**124**	**62**	**89**	**39**	**7**	**4**	
Chinese Group	*124*	*62*	*89*	*39*	*7*	*4*	
Semitic Family	**37**	**23**	**30**	**14**	**2**	**1**	
Arabic	34	20	29	13	2	1	Bombay and Hyderabad.
Hamitic Family (Ethiopic Group, Somali).	3	2	4	2	..	..	Bombay.
Mongolian family	*8*	*4*	*1*	..		..	
Japanese Group (Japanese)	*3*	*1*	*1*	..	..	..	Bombay and Burma.
European Languages ..	**208**	**131**	**198**	**121**	**12**	**8**	
Indo-European Family ..	**208**	**131**	**194**	**119**	**12**	**8**	
Romance Group	*9*	*6*	*2*	*2*	*1*	..	
Portuguese	6	4	2	1	..	..	Bombay and Madras.
Teutonic Group	*198*	*125*	*191*	*117*	*11*	*7*	
English	196	123	191	117	11	7	

NOTE.—Owing to the omission of the minor languages and dialects the details in the above table do not work up in every case to the totals of Groups, which in turn do not work up to those for Families, the difference being due to the conversion of absolute figures into thousands

SUBSIDIARY TABLE II.

Distribution by Mother Tongue of the population of each Province, State or Agency.

Province and Language.	Number of speakers per 10,000 of population.
India.	
Western Hindi	2,041
Bengali	1,525
Bihari	797
Telugu	752
Marathi	596
Tamil	582
Panjabi	452
Rajasthani	397
Kanarese	320
Gujarati	310
Oriya	319
Burmese	253
Malayalam	261
Lahnda or Western Panjabi	244
Kherwari	115
Sindhi	114
Bhili	63
Assamese	57
Western Pahari	66
Gondi	53
Pashto	47
Eastern Hindi	224
Kashmiri	41
Other Languages	371
Ajmer-Merwara.	
Rajasthani	7,633
Western Hindi	2,193
Other Languages	174
Andamans and Nicobars.	
Nicobarese	3,355
Other Langauges	6,645
Assam.	
Bengali	4,289
Assamese	2,157
Eastern Hindi	638
Manipuri	398
Bodo (Plains Kachari)	305
Kherwari	318
Khasi	253
Garo	208
Oriya	219
Mikir	137
Eastern Pahari	147
Other Languages	931
Baluchistan.	
Balochi	3,073
Pashto	2,385
Brahui	1,468
Sindhi	1,750
Lahnda or Western Panjabi	591
Panjabi	225
Western Hindi	197
Other Languages	311
Bengal.	
Bengali	9,226
Eastern Hindi	320
Western Hindi	50
Kherwari	172
Oriya	31
Kurukh or Oraon	37
Tipura or Mrung	38
Eastern Pahari	26
Other Languages	100
Bihar and Orissa.	
Bihari	6,596
Oriya	2,017
Kherwari	672
Bengali	458
Kurukh or Oraon	155
Kharia	27
Malto	16
Other Languages	59
Bombay.	
Marathi	4,223
Gujarati	1,854
Sindhi	1,278
Kanarese	1,215
Western Hindi	595
Bhili	220
Rajasthani	115
Balochi	113
Khandesi	84
Telugu	62
Other Languages	241

SUBSIDIARY TABLE II—*contd.*

Distribution by Mother Tongue of the population of each Province, State or Agency—*contd.*

Province and Language.	Number of speakers per 10,000 of population.
Burma.	
Burmese	6,036
Shangale	624
Sgaw	341
Pwo	323
Shan (unsepcified)	2
Bengali	257
Yanbye	223
Arakanese	152
Taungthu	152
Talaing	208
Western Hindi	132
Telugu	110
Tamil	126
Kachin	105
Tavoyan	109
Palaung and Pale	95
Other Languages	1,005
Central Provinces and Berar.	
Western Hindi	3,116
Marathi	3,122
Gondi	714
Oriya	214
Rajasthani	193
Kurku	90
Kurukh or Oraon	79
Other Languages	2,472
Coorg.	
Kanarese	3,990
Kodagu or Coorgi	2,730
Malayalam	1,527
Tulu	874
Other Languages	879
Delhi.	
Western Hindi	9,225
Rajasthani	106
Panjabi	370
Other Languages	299
Madras.	
Tamil	4,013
Telugu	3,768
Malayalam	790
Oriya	391
Kanarese	366
Western Hindi	265
Marathi	28
Other Languages	379
North-West Frontier Province.	
Pashto	5,221
Lahnda or Western Panjabi	4,195
Panjabi	351
Rajasthani	3
Western Hindi	96
English	47
Other Languages	87
Punjab.	
Panjabi	5,095
Lahnda or Western Panjabi	2,590
Western Hindi	1,400
Western Pahari	593
Rajasthani	215
Other Languages	107
United Provinces.	
Western Hindi	9,968
Other Languages	32
Baroda State.	
Gujarati	8,676
Bhili	738
Western Hindi	320
Other Languages	266
Central India Agency.	
Rajasthani	2,483
Western Hindi	3,627
Eastern Hindi	2,247
Bhili	881
Gondi	534
Gujarati	95
Marathi	82
Other Languages	51

SUBSIDIARY TABLE II—*concld.*

Distribution by Mother Tongue of the population of each Province, State or Agency—*concld.*

Province and Language.	Number of speakers per 10,000 of population.	Province and Language.	Number of speakers per 10,000 of population.
Cochin State.		*Rajputana Agency.*	
Malayalam	9,030	Rajasthani	7,667
Tamil	549	Western Hindi	1,533
Marathi	43	Bhili	641
Telugu	101	Other Languages	159
Other Languages	277		
Gwalior State.			
Western Hindi	6,327	*Sikkim State.*	
Rajasthani	3,216		
Bhili	214	Eastern Pahari	3,539
Marathi	61		
Gujarati	81	Kiranti	2,608
Other Languages	101	Bhotia of Sikkim	994
Hyderabad State.			
Telugu	4,830	Rong or Lepcha	1,203
Marathi	2,623	Murmi	636
Kanarese	1,122	Other Languages	1,020
Western Hindi	1,090		
Rajasthani	188		
Gondi	53	*Travancore State.*	
Other Languages	94		
Jammu and Kashmir State.		Malayalam	8,361
Kashmiri	3,876	Tamil	1,547
Punjabi	2,414	Marathi	14
Western Pahari	1,737		
Rajasthani	878	Other Languages	78
Bhotia of Baltistan or Balti	378		
Lahnda or Western Panjabi	264	*Western India States Agency.*	
Other Languages	453		
Mysore State.		Gujarati	8,711
Kanarese	6,983	Sindhi	1,045
Telugu	1,572	Western Hindi	168
Western Hindi	584	Rajasthani	58
Tamil	478		
Other Languages	383	Other Languages	18

NOTE.—The figures for Provinces are inclusive of the states attached to them except in the case of Madras where they exclude Cochin and Travancore.

SUBSIDIARY TABLE III.

Number of persons speaking tribal languages compared with the strength of tribe.

Tribe and Language.	Strength of tribe as given in Table XVII.	Tribal mother-tongue only.	Number of persons speaking a subsidiary language in addition to tribal mother-tongue.	Province, State or Agency dealt with.
1	2	3	4	5
1. Arakanese	208,251	221,945	*	Burma.
2. Badaga	43,075	42,526	*	Madras.
3. Balochi	1,006,459	625,708	235,791	Baluchistan, Bombay and Punjab.
4. Bhili	1,973,435	2,185,876	209,328	Bombay, Baroda, Central India, C. P. and Berar, Gwalior, Hyderabad and Rajputana.
5. Brahui	224,415	207,040	48,585	Baluchistan and Bombay.
6. Chutiya	*	4,315	*	Assam.
7. Gadaba	47,026	43,667	31,886	Madras.
8. Garo	231,701	230,672	*	Assam and Bengal.
9. Gond	1,875,870	1,720,790	867,574	Bengal, Bihar and Orissa, C. P. and Berar, C. I. Agency and Hyderabad.
10. Kachari,† Mech and Dimasa	3,45,248	306,056	*	Assam and Bengal.
11. Kandhi or Kui	662,946	578,928	194,239	Bihar and Orissa and Madras.
12. Karen Group	1,367,673	1,341,066	782,832	Burma.
13. Kharia	159,303	137,659	108,266	Bengal, Bihar and Orissa and C. P.
14. Khasi	232,530‡	233,872	1,879	Assam.
15. Kherwari	1,174,976	894,732	298,777	Bengal, C. P. and Bihar and Orissa.
16. Koch	81,299	9,529	*	Assam and Bengal.
17. Kodagu or Coorgi ..	54,502	44,585	44,585	Coorg.
18. Korku	176,616	161,975	105,690	Central Provinces and Berar.
19. Kurukh or Oraon ..	865,272	984,486	620,889	Bengal and Bihar and Orissa.
20. Lalung	43,448	9,017	*	Assam.
21. Malto	59,891	70,755	9,732	Bengal and Bihar and Orissa.
22. Meithei or Manipuri ..	330,545	391,891	*	Assam, Bengal and Burma.
23. Mikir	129,797	126,457	*	Assam.
24. Murmi	42,241	42,642	37,348	Bengal and Sikkim.
25. Naga	272,527	349,111	*	Burma and Assam.
26. Newar	16,451	9,455	8,554	Bengal and Sikkim.
27. Palaung	138,746	138,656	*	Burma.
28. Rabha	69,154	27,006	*	Assam.
29. Rong or Lepcha ..	25,780	25,149	16,805	Bengal and Sikkim.
30. Salon	1,930	1,908	*	Burma.
31. Sawara	211,781	185,562	71,448	Madras.
32. Shina	14,139	68,199	413	Jammu and Kashmir.
33. Tai Group	1,037,406	1,021,909	247,781	Burma.
34. Tipara	203,069	191,725	*	Assam.
35. Toda	597	597	*	Madras.
36. Wa	10,465	22,142	*	Burma.

* Information not available. † Including Plains-Kachari.

‡ Excludes certain others included under Naipali Castes.

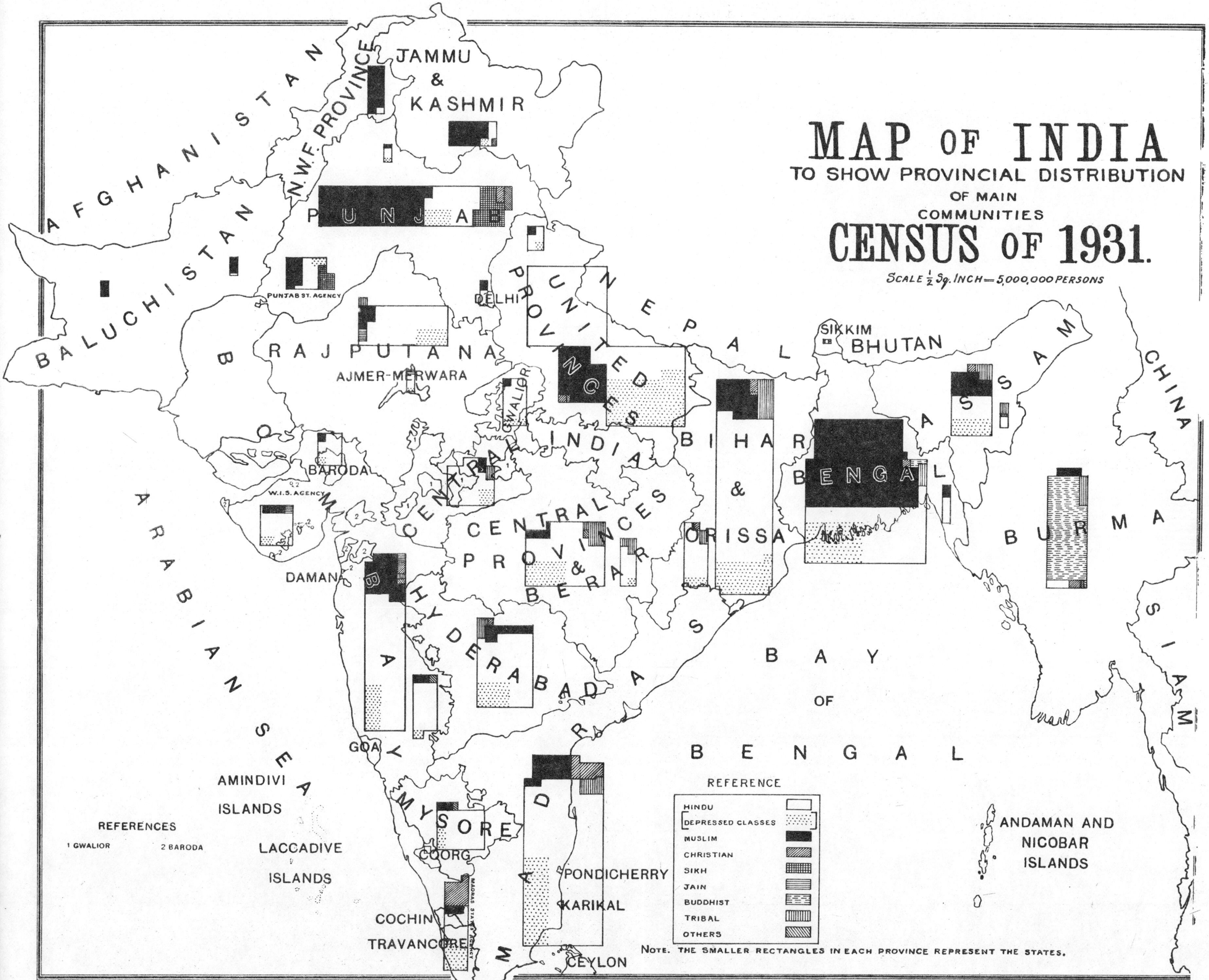

REG. No. 2905. E. 32.

HELIO. S. I. O. CALCUTTA

Pages 1 and 2 of 'Spelling Book in Kamhow-Sokte' by Pau-Chin-Hau and Than-Chin-Kham.

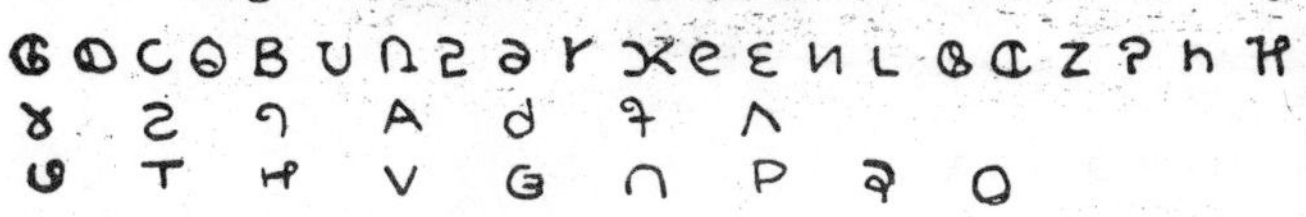

pa ka la ma da ya va nga ha ga xa hsa ba tga ta hta na hpa ra fa **cha**
à ài i aw u ua ia
ab ag ad am an al au ang ai

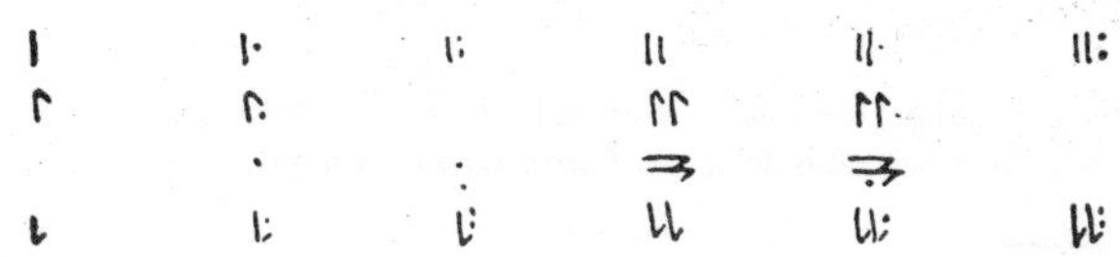

These are tonal signs

pà	pai	pi	paw	pu	pua	pia
kà	kai	ki	kaw	ku	kua	kia
là	lai	li	law	lu	lua	lia
mà	mai	mi	maw	mu	mua	mia
dà	dai	di	daw	du	dua	dia
yà	yai	yi	yaw	yu	yua	yia
và	vai	vi	vaw	vu	vua	via
ngà	ngai	ngi	ngaw	ngu	ngua	ngia
hà	hai	hi	haw	hu	hua	hia
gà	gai	gi	gaw	gu	gua	gia
xà	xai	xi	xaw	xu	xua	xia
hsà	hsai	hsi	hsaw	hsu	hsua	hsia
bà	bai	bi	baw	bu	bua	bia
tgà	tgai	tgi	tgaw	tgu	tgua	tgia
tà	tai	ti	taw	tu	tua	tia
htà	htai	hti	htaw	htu	htua	htia
nà	nai	ni	naw	nu	nua	nia
hpà	hpai	hpi	hpaw	hpu	hpua	hpia
rà	rai	ri	raw	ru	rua	ria
fà	fai	fi	faw	fu	fua	fia
chà	chai	chi	chaw	chu	chua	chia

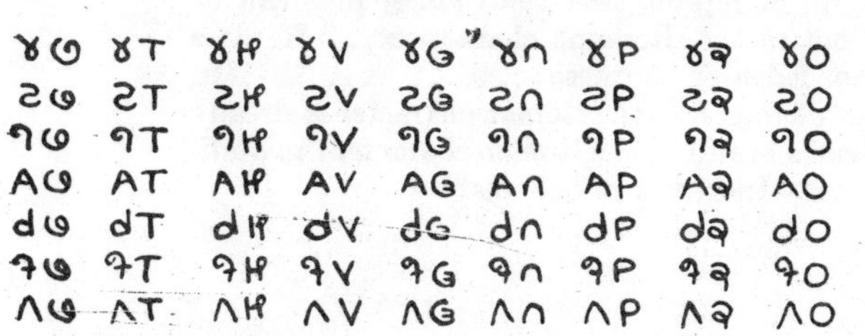

ab	ag	ad	am	an	al	aau	ang	aia
aib	aig	aid	aim	ain	ail	aiau	aing	aiia
ib	ig	id	im	in	il	iau	ing	iia
awb	awg	awd	awm	awn	awl	awau	awng	awia
ub	ug	ud	um	un	ul	uau	ung	uia
uab	uag	uad	uam	uan	ual	uaau	uang	uaia
iab	iag	iad	iam	ian	ial	iaau	iang	iaia

pab	pag	pad	pam	pan	pal	paau	pang	paia
paib	paig	paid	paim	pain	pail	paiau	paing	paiia
pib	pig	pid	pim	pin	pil	piau	ping	piia
pawb	pawg	pawd	pawm	pawn	pawl	pawau	pawng	pawia
pub	pug	pud	pum	pun	pul	puau	pung	puia
puab	puag	puad	puam	puan	pual	puaau	puang	puaia
piab	piag	piad	piam	pian	pial	piaau	piang	piaia

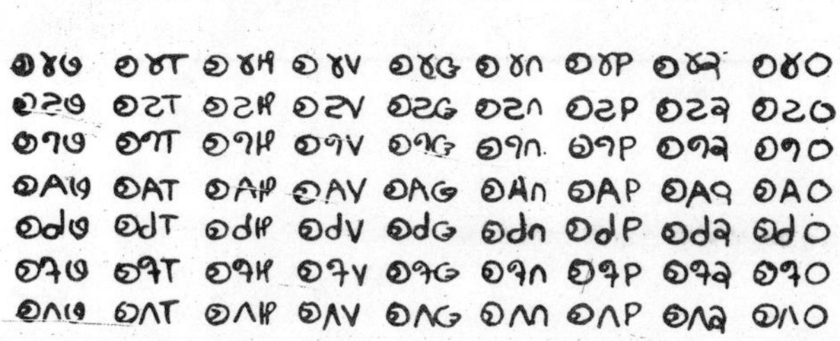

kab	kag	kad	kam	kan	kal	kaau	kang	kaia
kaib	kaig	kaid	kaim	kain	kail	kaiau	kaing	kaiia
kib	kig	kid	kim	kin	kil	kiau	king	kiia
kawb	kawg	kawd	kawm	kawn	kawl	kawau	kawng	kawia
kub	kug	kud	kum	kun	kul	kuau	kung	kuia
kuab	kuag	kuad	kuam	kuan	kual	kuaau	kuang	kuaia
kiab	kiag	kiad	kiam	kian	kial	kiaau	kiang	kiaia

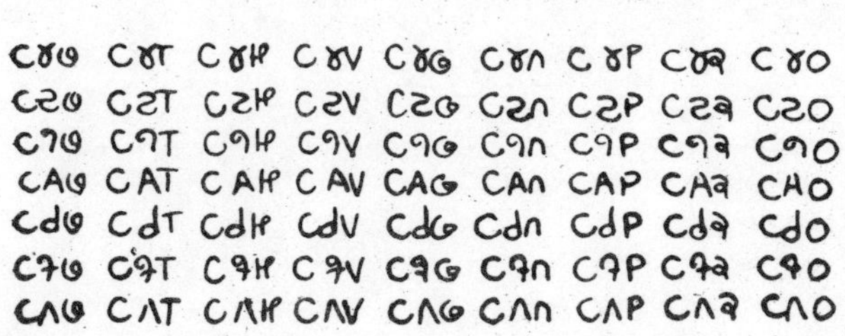

lab	lag	lad	lam	lan	lal	laau	lang	laia
laib	laig	laid	laim	lain	lail	laiau	laing	laiia
lib	lig	lid	lim	lin	lil	liau	ling	liia
lawb	lawg	lawd	lawm	lawn	lawl	lawau	lawng	lawia
lub	lug	lud	lum	lun	lul	luau	lung	luia
luab	luag	luad	luam	luan	lual	luaau	luang	luaia
liab	liag	liad	liam	lian	lial	liaau	liang	liaia

APPENDIX TO CHAPTER X.

Extracts from correspondence between the Census Commissioner for India and Mr. J. J. Bennison, Census Superintendent of Burma in regard to a new written character in Burma and Assam.

(*i*) FROM CENSUS COMMISSIONER FOR INDIA TO CENSUS SUPERINTENDENT FOR BURMA, DATED THE 24TH MARCH 1932.

" I think I am right in saying that the character that has been revealed to Pao Chin Hao involves an alphabet of an unconscionable length, since he has a different character, I think, for every possible monosyllable. At any rate, that is the line on which his revelation ran according to the information I had from Manipur. One official sent me sheets of Pao Chin Hao's characters and said they were too many to record completely."

(*ii*) FROM CENSUS SUPERINTENDENT FOR BURMA, TO CENSUS COMMISSIONER FOR INDIA, DATED THE 9TH MAY 1932.

" I understand from the Rev. W. Sherratt, (Agent of the British and Foreign Bible Society in Burma) that the original alphabet as revealed to Pow Chin How did contain a very large number of characters. Mr. Sherratt visited the Chin Hills in March 1931 and pointed out to him that the large number of characters was a very great drawback. Pow Chin How and a few of his followers then got together and reduced the number considerably. Three or four of them then came down and saw Mr. Sherratt about May 1931 and eventually ' The Sermon on the Mount ' was printed. A copy is enclosed herewith. Mrs. Sherratt wrote out the words in Indian ink and this was photographed and zinc plates made. There are only 21 consonants in the alphabet but in addition to the usual vowels there are a few ' final syllables ', similar to those in Burmese. There are also a few tones. Pow Chin How's eldest son (Shian Ko Chin) and another of his followers (Than Chin Kham) came down in March this year to see Mr. Sherratt and I saw them once. Than Chin Kham is a vernacular school-teacher in Tonzan village near Tiddim and he knows Burmese. I understand he has played a large part in producing the new alphabet. He is translating St. Matthew into the new characters. He uses the Burmese version of St. Matthew and also a Chin version (in the Roman character) which was done by Mr. Cope, the American Baptist Missionary in the Chin Hills. He maintains that the Chin sounds can be properly represented in these new characters but not in the Roman characters.....He does not know any English but he has a fairly good knowledge of Burmese ....Mr. Cope apparently thinks there is no need for another character as the Roman character is already well-known in the Chin Hills and the school text-books are all in the Roman character: in addition to being an A. B. M.* padre he is also an Honorary Inspector of Schools."

---

* American Baptist Mission.

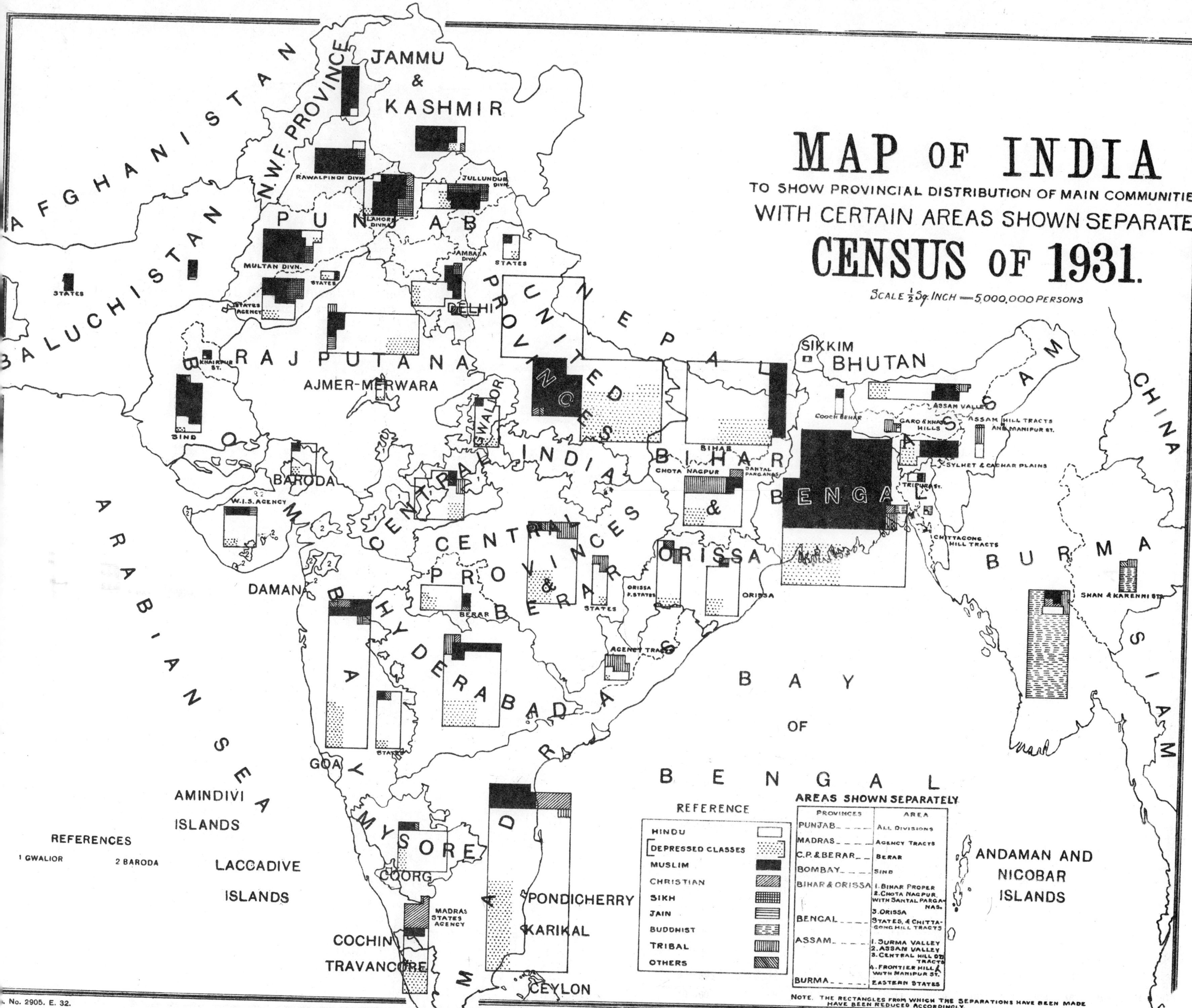

No. 2905. E. 32.

HELIO. S. I. O. CALC.

CHAPTER XI.

Religion.

Section i.—Religion and the Census.

158. Although on the face of it religion would appear to be a concern purely for the individual, and in spite of the recent pronouncement of an eminent Frenchman to the effect that the deity is an academic subject (" *la question de Dieu manque d'actualité* "), yet strongly held religious convictions inevitably react on political situations and cannot be divorced from those aspects of social life of which the State and therefore the census must take cognizance. This is particularly the case in India, which is still the most religious country in the world, and must be regarded as the justification for the importance attached to religion in the census of India as compared, for example, with that of United States of America, where culture is comparatively independent of religion. In India the two are so inseparably bound up that religion, always a conservative force, appears as a positive obstacle to cultural unity. **'Religion'.**

It has been argued that the census statistics of religion tend to perpetuate communal divisions; the census cannot, however, hide its head in the sand like the proverbial ostrich, but must record as accurately as possible facts as they exist, and there is no question of the existence of communal differences which are reflected at present in political constituencies. It is not in its devotional aspect that the census is concerned with religion, but in its social, and it cannot be denied but society in India is still largely organised on a basis of caste and religion, and social conduct is much influenced by practices which may not be in themselves religious but which are subject to religious sanctions. The age of marriage, the practice of remarriage, the observance of purdah, the occupations of women, the inheritance of property and the maintenance of widows, even diet, to name a few obvious cases, vary according to the caste and the religious community of the individual. The time will no doubt come when occupation will serve the purpose at present served by religion and caste in presenting demographic data, but that time is not yet, and at the present moment their barriers have not so far decayed that their social importance can be ignored for public purposes, though progress in this direction may well prove much faster than one anticipates. The social importance of religious differences is reflected in the controversial disputes about religious terminology for census purposes. The census terms are :—Hindu, Jain, Buddhist, Sikh, Zoroastrian, Jew, Muslim, Christian, Tribal and Others. This is the most practical division available but is admittedly not satisfactory since difficulty arises in the case of many of these terms, particularly so in that of the term *Hindu* which is not entirely exclusive of some of the other terms used. Many Hindus for instance claim that Sikhs, Jains and Buddhists are also Hindu inasmuch as their faiths had their origin in the Hindu religion. On the other hand this claim is stoutly repudiated by the great majority of Sikhs and it was therefore necessary to treat the terms Hindu and Sikh as mutually exclusive. In the case of Jains many, but by no means all, regard themselves as Hindu and orders were issued that any Jain who wished to record the fact that he was also Hindu could do so and the tables would show in a footnote the number of Jains who consider themselves Hindus. In the United Provinces the Census Superintendent reports that the present tendency among Jains is towards segregation from rather than amalgamation with Hindus and that intermarriage with Hindu families is becoming more unpopular, though there is less objection to taking Hindu wives than to giving brides to Hindu males. It was claimed by the Hindu Mahasabha that a few Buddhists adopted the same position as Jains who regard themselves as Hindus, but from Buddhists as well as Jains protests were received against the possibility of their being classified as Hindus. In order to get round the ambiguity it was also ordered that Buddhists might likewise describe themselves as Hindu, and the totals of Buddhists who so regard themselves will be found in footnotes in Table XVI. In all 12,326 out of a total for India of 1,252,631 Jains, and 70 Buddhists out of 12,786,831 described themselves as being Hindus, and of these 526 Jains and 25 Buddhists actually appear as Hindus in the statistical tables.

159. Some other schismatics have similarly an ambiguous position. In 1881 Kabirpanthi and Satnami were shown as religions separate from Hinduism. Since that year they have been incorporated with Hindus and on this occasion they **Ambiguous Sects.**

have been similarly treated except in Bombay where a few Kabirpanthis and Dadupanthis who did not return themselves as Hindu have been shown under "Others". It would be natural to suppose that the remaining religions might at any rate be regarded as quite distinct, yet while the border line between tribal religions and some aspects of Hinduism is not at all easy to draw, it is often just as hard to define it between Hinduism and Islam, and even between Hinduism and Christianity, in the case of a number of intermediate sects which offer points of identity with both.

Except for a body in Tinnevelly that claims to be both Jew and Christian, the Jews remain a much more clearly defined body, and in their case Hindu influence would seem to go no further than inducing the Beni-Israel to add a Hindu or a Hinduised second name to the Hebraic one, but the Indian Christians of South India go further. Caste is admittedly observed by Catholics*, while some Protestants who profess not to admit it do admit a ban on commensality. The Catholics appear to use caste marks in some cases, and there was a *cause célèbre* in the Madras courts in which an overzealous imported priest, who had destroyed as unchristian the wall which ran the length of the aisle to separate the caste from the outcaste Christians, was prosecuted by his flock in consequence. The Catholics, besides observing caste even to conventional privileges in dress and ornaments, use the *tali* instead of a ring in marriage and permit the retention of other customs, such as a tabu " for reasons of hygiene " on contacts with persons polluted by childbirth.

On the other hand certain features of the Lingayat belief seem to have been borrowed from Christianity, as a doctrine of immaculate conception and the practice of burying the dead. A forest tribe in North Kanara, now Hindu, has family names of Christian origin. In the case of Islam however the border line is much less definite. Even saints of Christianity, Islam and Judaism are themselves subject to some confusion. In the Near East Elijah, al-Khidr (The Green One) and St. George are confused or identified generally, while boys born on St. Demetrius' Day are called Kasim. Confusion of this kind is probably to be found among Indian outcastes such as Lalbegis, who have drawn on both Hindu and Muslim sources for their religious tenets, but it goes still further with the Chet-Rami sect of the Punjab, who worship the Christian Trinity plus a Hindu-Muslim trinity consisting of Allah the Creator, Parameshwar the Preserver, and Khuda the Destroyer. There is thus a very real difficulty sometimes in deciding whether a particular body is Muslim or Hindu, and since the census actually took place there have been some searchings of heart as to the Sathpantis, or Pirpantis, of Gujarat, Kachh and Khandesh. These people are Mathia Kunbis by caste, and an offshoot of the Leva Kunbis, and seem to have been returned at the census as Hindus ; they are said to follow the Atharva Veda, which is perhaps more magical than religious, and they worship at the tombs of Muslim saints at Pirana and elsewhere, from which they get the alternative name for their sect, and they observe as their sacred book a collection of the precepts of Imam Shah, the Pir of Pirana ; they observe the Ramazan, repeat the *kalima* and bury their dead with both Muslim and Hindu prayers. On the other hand they keep the *holi* and *diwali* and their marriages are conducted by Brahmans, so that they appear, on the whole, to be Hindus socially but rather Muslims by religion. This position is emphasized by the fact that while a religious authority, the Shankaracharya of the Sankeshwar and Karavir Maths, pronounces them to be without the pale of Hinduism, the Hindu Mahasabha, a frankly communal organisation, proclaims that they are within it. Another Hindu organisation has urged these Mathias to abandon the worship of Muslim saints, but in truth mere worship at the burial places of holy men is hardly a test of religion at all, since there are many shrines holy to more than one faith, and the holy ones of one religion often survive the superimposition of another and adapt themselves to the change as Badar Makan, the shrine of a Muslim pir in Chittagong, becomes Buddha Makan to an Arakan Buddhist. So in Paphos the Cypriot peasant worships even the Virgin Herself as Panhagia Aphroditessa. The truth is that the shrines of the dead are places impregnated with the fertilising soul-matter† of the departed great ones and the cult of them goes back to a totally pre-Hindu phase, which is still represented in the tribal religions, and appears in

---

* At the time of going to press a Catholic youth is reported to have started a fast to the death outside the residence of the Bishop of Trichinopoly to secure the removal of the iron railings which separate the caste from the outcaste Catholics in that bishoprick.

† See below page 409 for details of the Karen belief in which this idea is crystallized.

other practices of some Muslims, the implications of which have been forgotten though the practices rema n, as in the use of tombstones of phallic design, which may be seen even in the Khyber Pass, for instance, while the Muslims of Malaya use stone ones of different but likewise significant designs for the different sexes. A case not unlike that of the Mathia Kunbis is to be seen in that of the Nayitas of Malwa who " share in equal degree the Muslim and Hindu religious beliefs ", worshipping Ganesh as well as Allah, using Hindu names and dress and observing Hindu festivals. It may also be found in the Kuvachandas of Sind and again in the Hussaini Brahmans, who like the Mathias are more or less converted to Islam in faith but retain Brahmanical practices and claim to eat only with the Sayyids among Muslims. The Malkanas of the United Provinces are another somewhat similar group of Rajput, Jat and Bania origin observing both Hindu and Muslim ceremonies. Many became definitely Hindu as a result of the *shuddhi* movement and others returned themselves as Muslim at the census, but the bulk apparently continue to halt between two opinions, and in 1926 when the *shuddhi* and *tanzim* movements were at their height these Malkanas started taking money for conversion and it is said that many made considerable sums by conversion and reconversion to and from Hinduism, Islam and Christianity for which communal zealots were then at any rate able to find money. Bengal affords a number of instances of border line sects such as that of the Bhagwania or Satyadharma community, recruited from both Hindus and Muslims, though even within the sect there is no intermarriage, while the Nagarchis of Bakarganj, the Kirtanias of Pabna and Maimansingh and the Chitrakars or Patuas of West Bengal are in the nature of castes rather than sects, whose religion and customs have both Hindu and Muslim features as in the case of the Mathia Kunbis. A fresh movement aimed at the reconciliation of Hinduism and Islam was started during the decade under review by a man who claimed to be an incarnation of Channabasaveswara, but his teachings, though they gained some adherents, aroused much antagonism among the Virasaivas of Mysore State, where the movement started, and led to its suppression.

Another aspect of the confused border line between Islam and Hinduism is to be seen in the customs of the outcastes of the Punjab, where Chuhras for instance take Muslim names and even utilise the services of mullahs where they serve Muslim villages or wards, though in the eastern Punjab generally they follow Hindu customs and use Hindu names. Yet there is no such marked difference between one Chuhra and the other that a valid distinction between these two religions can be drawn in his case. At this census it has been left to each individual to return his religion as he thought fit and some Chuhras have returned Islam others Hinduism. Many again have described themselves as belonging to *Ad-dharm*, ' the original religion ', probably without any clear idea of what that faith may be, but desiring merely to emphasize the distinction between themselves and caste Hindus without committing themselves to Islam or Christianity. Chuhras in the Punjab who returned their religion as " Chuhra " simply (and there were many) have been included with Hindus, following the precedent of the previous census, though it is a moot question whether they should not have been shown as Tribal, and it seems not impossible that they are by origin a degraded branch of the aboriginal tribe known in Gujarat as Chodhra.

Generally speaking, there would seem to be no insuperable reason why the Muslim and the Hindu should not dwell together in harmony, and there are Hindu temples in Madura and Tanjore which have hereditary Muslim trustees. At any rate the obstacle is probably less the divergence of religious belief than their reliance on different historical pasts. In the early glories of Hinduism and Buddhism, under rulers like Chandragupta and Asoka, Islam has no concern, and the great historic characters of the Muslims in India were mostly earth-seizing monarchs whose victories were over Hindus and whose culture was of external origin.

Interpretation of ' Hindu '.

160. Part of the difficulty of defining the term Hindu arises from the fact that it is as much a social as a religious term and really denotes membership of a system of organized society with great latitude of religious beliefs and practices, so that it is possible for a man to be a Hindu socially and to have a religious belief shared with others who do not regard themselves as members of the same society, a possibility illustrated by a tribal Korwa of the Central Provinces who said to his Census Superintendent " if we had plough cattle we should be Hindus ". Conversely there is no compelling necessity that all others of his society should share his beliefs, and the Census Superintendent of Mysore State, himself a Brahman, thus defines a Hindu :—

"What makes a man Hindu is the fact that he is an Indian by birth ; that he shares religious belief of a kind familiar to the majority of the people ; that he is a member of the social order accepted by that majority ; and that he worships one or other of the deities in the pantheon commonly accepted by that same majority."

This is a feature particularly associated with Hinduism but it is not exclusively confined to that religion, as at least one case arose of a Muslim who wished to be included with the social community of Islam but who returned his religion as Agnosticism. He appears to have been unique and his difficulty was evaded by showing him as a Muslim for all tables except that of religion, a position which recalls that of Maurice Barrès who said of himself "I am an atheist, but of course I am a Catholic", but the number of Hindus whose attitude to their community and their beliefs might be expressed in a somewhat similar paradox must be very large, and the cross division of religion and society is clearly going to create a difficult position for census operations in the future unless a return of "community" be substituted for that of religion and caste. Thus the Sahejdhari Sikhs who worship the ninth Guru but not the tenth, and who cut their hair instead of allowing it to grow, form a sect half-way between the Hindu and Sikh religions and for census purposes had to declare themselves to belong to one or to the other with the result that some are included in the Hindu and others in the Sikh total, but no substitute for "Hindu" as a religious term can be found, nor is it possible to disentangle its religious from its social significance. This is inherent in the history of Hindu society which has been formed by the accretion of a number of races within a polity indirectly hierarchical. It is probably significant that many an ignorant Hindu, if asked his religion, will not give "Hindu" as an answer but will give the name of his caste or of the particular sect to which he belongs. As far as Sikhs go, the criteria that separate them from Hindus are not very marked on the social side, whatever they may be doctrinally. The daughter of a Sikh ruler can marry a cadet of the house of Nepal, and Hindus can enter the Golden Temple of Amritsar which is normally barred to Muslims and Christians. Indeed there are apparently cases in which a father may bring up one son as a Hindu and another as a Sikh. The Sikhs in general, however, emphatically protest that they are not Hindus, in spite of the Hindu Mahasabha which says that they are, and this is particularly so in the case of the Akali Sikhs, who are mainstay of the Sikhs in the army, while the Sahejdhari Sikhs vote in Sikh constituencies in the Punjab on making a solemn affirmation that they are Sikhs.

Buddhists were claimed as Hindus by the Hindu Mahasabha with less justice than Sikhs, since Buddhism arose as a definite reaction against Hinduism, and considerations of politics have probably been allowed to bias the critical faculty in putting forward this claim, since it may be doubted whether even the Hindu Mahasabha would claim all Japanese Buddhists as Hindus. The common element in the two religions, and this is of course apparent, even to the parallel between the Indian *holi* and the chaster Burmese Water Carnival, is often derived from a more primitive religion, but to claim Buddhists as Hindus by religion appears to the disinterested just about as reasonable as it would be to claim Christians as Jews.

When they do not split away like the Sikhs, there seems to be a tendency for reforming elements in Hinduism to crystallize eventually into a closed caste. This has been the case with the Lingayats, who started as a reforming sect of Hindus founded by Basava in the twelfth century, with the Kabirpanthis and with others, the Vaisnava sect in Bengal for instance, and probably would have been the case with the Sikhs had they remained within the pale. In the case of the Brahmo and Arya Samajists, however, neither are closed but on the contrary recruit steadily from among Brahmanic Hindus ; nevertheless there appeared some tendency on the part of one section of the Arya Samaj to disclaim Hinduism at this census, though the schism between Aryas and orthodox Hindus is perhaps less marked on the whole than when the Arya movement started, which is perhaps due to a weakening of the strictly orthodox position. Of this 'weakening', if the term be permissible, the Census Superintendent of Cochin State writes, a little pessimistically perhaps, as follows :—

"Broadly speaking, a two-fold movement is discernible in this connection. Among those placed in the lower grades of Hindu society it is a movement for the purification and elevation of their religious rites and practices ; while those born in the higher grades reveal a growing indifference in all matters connected with religion......... To the generality of English-educated persons—be it remembered in this connection that the caste Hindus have progressed much more than all others in English education—religion is now a matter of utter indifference or unconcern and its rites and practices a mass of superstition to be derided and condemned by all right-thinking people........... Apart from this, the attitude of a great majority of the English-educated young men of caste Hindu communities towards their religion is now one of veiled hostility because, in these days of communal demand for equal representation of all creeds and classes in the public service, they find that the unlucky accident of their birth within the Hindu fold is an almost impassable barrier against their entry in government or quasi-government service, the only career for which they are fit by training and temperament alike."

161. The Jains, as already pointed out, were claimed as Hindus with more reason, since some Jains do actually consider themselves to be Hindus, though their customs of succession and adoption are not the same as those in Hindu law. It seems probable indeed that this sect represents the continuity of an anti-Brahmanistic teaching which may trace its derivation to a pre-Vedic age and to opposition at the outset to the rise of Brahmanic Hinduism. It is not likely that Mahavira was regarded as the 23rd *tirthankara* gratuitously, in spite of his having been the first historical one of the series and the apparent founder of the religion. Moreover, this view of the Jain position would explain how it is that although the teaching of Mahavira was emphatically antivedic, the rules of Jain and of Brahmanic asceticism are almost identical, if the suggestion be accepted, that is, which is generally advanced here, that Brahmanic Hinduism was not an entirely new religion imported from outside by Indo-European invaders into a country peopled by darkskinned savages, but an indigenous growth produced by the impact of these invaders, having a religion akin to that of classical Greece and Rome, upon a pre-existing more civilized people with a religion drawn from Mesopotamia, Asia Minor or the eastern Mediterranean. It may be noted incidentally that such a hypothesis would do something towards reconciling the difficulty in that whereas the Jains describe the Tirthankara Parswa who preceded Mahavira as the son of a king Aswasena of Benares, no king of that name is known to Brahmanical literature except a king of the " Nagas ". Professor Tucci's opinion that Jainism embodies a revival of very ancient rituals and forms " probably even pre-Aryan ", goes to support the same view, and it cannot be denied that the nudity cult of the Digambar Jains is of great antiquity, much older than the familiar accounts of Megasthenes of the 3rd century B.C. This nudity cult still causes local sensations from time to time and some Jain *munis* were in April 1931 charged with indecency in the Court of the City Magistrate at Surat. The case was withdrawn on an understanding given by the Jains that such " sky-clad " ascetics should only move about in public surrounded by a discreet bodyguard. In May however in Dholpur State the appearance of sky-clad Jains in the village of Rajakhera, where the populace was less tolerant, gave rise to a serious riot. The Jain like the Hindu community is not unmoved by the spirit of reform, and opinion has run very high on the question of the initiation of minors as religious ascetics (*muni*), leading in Ahmadabad to blows between the two factions in July 1930 and to action by the Magistrate who had to take security against breaches of the peace in January 1931. **Jainisim.**

162. Some indications of a tendency to change and reform have appeared in the other important religious communities, even the Parsis having apparently experienced dissensions between the Shenshais and the Kadmis, and between the supporters and opponents of Bahaism, while as an instance of the change effected by modern means of transport it is interesting to note that the holy fire for a Parsi temple at Allahabad was brought from Bombay in a specially consecrated motor lorry in which the sacred fire was fed with sandalwood by a priest. In Islam an attack by the Ahl-i-Hadis sect on the Hanafi sect resulted in a criminal prosecution, and the Dawudi Borah sect was divided by a *fatwa* which excommunicated those members of the society who might forbear to wear beards. The insignificance however of dissensions of this kind serves merely to emphasize the general unity of the community as a whole, and the Christian communities of India, who, Roman Catholics apart, show sects as multifarious as those of Hinduism, have made a notable movement towards unity in the attempt, partially if not completely successful, to unite the Wesleyan, Congregational and Presbyterian communities into a United Church, or rather into two united churches, those of Southern and Northern India respectively. It was hoped that the figures of Christian sects would be available to show the extent and effect of this unifying movement from which certain sections of those three bodies withheld themselves, but unfortunately the necessity **Reforming movements.**

for economy at the abstraction stage prohibited the necessary sort being made Similarly separate figures are not available for the Anglican Communion, the form under which were returned members of the Church of England and of the newly established independent branch of that community in India. The disestablishment of the Anglican Church in India, which will in future be independent of the State, as well as of the ecclesiastical control of the Church of England, and will receive no aid from Government as in the past, is too recent for its consequences to be foreseen, but it is possible that it will seek to unite with the other united Protestant communities, while it is also not unlikely that its sympathies politically will be definitely nationalist. Among Catholics exception was taken to the separate return of Catholics of the Chaldaean and of the Latin rite. As it was impossible to include the Catholics of the Chaldaean rite among Roman Catholics generally and also to show them as Syrian Christians, and as from their history and traditions the Syrians as a whole form a striking and important community in Southern India, where they have been established as long as Christianity has in most parts of Europe, and have quite as much right to be regarded as an indigenous religious body as have Muslims and Parsis, the Catholics of Chaldaean rites were shown as a separate unit, other Syrians being taken together like the Protestants. These other Syrians include Nestorians, whose numbers have been much depleted by secessions to the Jacobites and to Rome; Jacobites, who form the next largest Syrian body to Romans of the Chaldaean rite; Reformed or Mar Thoma Syrians, and a small schismatic body known as Yuyomayam. The Jacobite community has been rent since 1910 by a schism resulting from the excommunication by the Patriarch of Antioch of the Jacobite metropolitan Mar Dionysius, who refused to recognise the decree or to surrender his temporalities or to submit to the findings of the secular court, which in turn adjudicated on the case. About the time the census was taken the Patriarch came to India and the good offices of Lord Irwin were obtained and the decree of excommunication was revoked and a synod was called to arrange for a reconciliation of the divisions which the schism had caused. The Catholics of Chaldaean rites have had Indian bishops from their own community since 1896, but during the decade preceding this census the first Indian bishop of Latin rites was also appointed (1923). There is also now an Indian bishop of the American Episcopal Methodist Church. The part played by the Indian Christians in the nationalist movement is not without importance, and it is during the past decade that their attitude has tended to change from that of a separatist minority towards co-operation with the moderate nationalists, a change expressed by the formation of a Christian Nationalist Party in Bombay.

Pilgrimages.

163. One difficulty which was little felt at this census as compared with some previous ones was the temporary displacement of population by great pilgrimages. Religious pilgrimages play a greater feature in Indian life than in the life of any other nation, though they have always been popular on the shores of the Mediterranean. Even the very ancient pilgrimages to St. James of Compostella however and the modern ones to the grotto of Lourdes are probably insignificant compared to such assemblies as the Kumbh *mela* at Allahabad, which occurred fortunately in 1930 and not in 1931. This pilgrimage habit, for in India it is nothing less, appears to be maintained by regular and hereditary canvassers attached to different shrines who go round the country inducing villagers to leave everything and embark, sometimes with their families as well, on visits to distant shrines and tours of holy places which may even take years to accomplish. The shrines undoubtedly benefit, but it is impossible not to speculate as to whether the moral or physical benefit of the pilgrim is proportionate to the loss in time, in labour and in expense, though the justice of such a materialistic reflection is perhaps questionable when made by one who has not himself experienced the religious emotion inspired in the pilgrims. Canvassing, however, is not always needed to start a pilgrimage. In February 1930 the gas generated by night-soil in a trenching-ground near Delhi issued from the earth in flame, and the spot promptly became the scene of a local pilgrimage to the goddess-favoured site, large numbers of people of the more ignorant classes coming and removing mephitic earth from the empyreumatic spot hallowed, as some said, by the goddess of small-pox. The goddess in this case proved obligingly susceptible of chemical analysis, which showed that her ambrosial composition was 70 per cent. methane, 20 per cent. carbon-dioxide and 10 per cent. inert gases.

Propaganda.

164. If, however, the census was untroubled by pilgrimages or great fairs it had other troubles to meet from religious sentiment to which allusion has already been made. There was the energetic propaganda by the Hindu Mahasabha which practically amounted to an advocacy of returning as Hindu every person whose religion could not be found to have been originated outside India, that is practically every one but Muslims, Christians, Parsis and Jews, regardless of whether the followers of other Indian religions wished to be returned as Hindu or not, and equally regardless of the facts of the case. They also proposed to include as Hindus all persons of doubtful position half-way between Hinduism and Islam, without insisting on the *shuddhi* ceremony. In the fear apparently that the depressed classes would not be returned as Hindus attempts were also made to minimise their numbers, though it is only fair to say that the depressed classes organizations were not behind hand in claiming as " depressed " a number of castes almost certainly not in that category. Non-Hindu hill tribes such as the Khasi of Assam were claimed as Hindus, though one Assam paper naively distinguished between '*kutcha*' and '*pucca*' Hindus, while a proposal was actually mooted by certain members of the Central Legislature that wherever the majority of the members of a hill tribe had been Hinduised, the complete tribe should be shown as Hindu. It was not suggested that where a minority were Hindu the whole tribe should be returned as Tribal, though this may of course have been implied. The Census Superintendent for Bombay regards the figure of Tribal Religions for that province (155,038) as " grossly understated " and thus accounts for their deficiency :

" Whenever an individual disclaims membership of any recognised religion, the tendency is to enter Hindu without further enquiry, more particularly if the individual in question is undoubtedly a member of a tribe, long established in the locality. The process of thought is something as follows :—This land is called Hindustan and is the country of the Hindus, and all who live in it must be Hindus unless they definitely claim another recognised religion. This attitude pervades all grades of Hindu Society and I have been questioned on this basis, as to the propriety of the instructions issued, by many Hindus, including Government officers, who possessed the qualification of B.A. and who held the rank of Mamlatdar. Though they submitted to the orders given, there is little doubt that these orders were not passed on in their entirety and with the clarity necessary to impress them upon all Enumerators........ It is certain that the very vast bulk of the Bhils, Katkaris and Thakurs in this Presidency are not Hindus. It cannot also be denied that Bhils and Thakurs, living in isolated groups in Hindu villages are gradually yielding to the influence of association and conforming to the rites of Hindu worship as practised locally but in the absence of adequate data it is impossible to compute the number of persons who have abandoned their primitive beliefs and adopted Hinduism in their place. My personal view is that the process of assimilation is very slow, much slower than is commonly believed to be the case, even in areas where individual members of the Aboriginal Tribes have descended into the plains and are brought into contact with all the influence of village life."

What took place in Assam is typical and it is simplest to quote the Census Superintendent himself :

" Just before the census I received several petitions from Kacharis in Kamrup stating that they had been returned as Hindus in the census schedules and that they objected to the action of the enumerators recording their religion as Hindu. The Census Officer in forwarding the petitions noted as follows and I think his note sums up exactly what went on in most districts of the Assam Valley :— ' It is true to some extent that due to propaganda by the Hindu Sabha some of the Kacharis have willingly allowed themselves to be recorded as Hindu by religion ; in some cases some of the enumerators have persuaded them to have themselves recorded as such ; and in some cases some of the enumerators have recorded them as such of their own accord, they being ignorant of what was recorded of them '."

The Census Superintendent continues:

" The propaganda work of the Hindu Mission was certainly a great success in Assam from their point of view and had an enormous influence on the tribal peoples hovering in the borderland between Hinduism and Animism .... some Lalungs came to see me in Nowgong in January 1930 and asked my advice as to how they should return their religion. I questioned them about their religion, ascertained that it was purely a tribal one and advised them to tell the truth. A meeting of Lalungs was subsequently held and a resolution was passed that the Lalung community should return their religion as Lalung. In spite, however, of this resolution the vast majority of Lalungs returned themselves as Hindus, in many cases, I have no doubt, voluntarily. But there can be no doubt that many enumerators under the influence of the propaganda entered Hindu against the names of tribal persons who found it difficult to state precisely what their religion was and if there was any doubt Hinduism got the benefit of it .... In Darrang.............the Deputy Commissioner reports that......... he had good reason to suspect a Charge Superintendent—a Government officer—of using his influence to get Animist Kacharis returned as Hindus."

In another passage the Census Superintendent remarks that attempts were made to return as Hindus even the Naga and Kuki tribes of the North Cachar Hills, and he quotes as follows from the Deputy Commissioner of Darrang District :—

" The Hindu enumerator (and they are nearly all Hindus) tends to record all animistic and aboriginal tribes, such as Kacharis, Mikirs, Mundas and Santhals, as Hindus. Even if the enumerator fails, the supervisor or checking officer tends to keep him up to the scratch. An instance was brought to my notice at Halem where the enumerator had written Miri, but the checking officer changed it to 'Hindu Miri'. There is no remedy though I have done what I can ; the enumerator, if questioned, says that they say they are Hindus. In the great majority of cases I do not imagine they do say so. Those I have asked say (in the great majority of cases) that they are, *e.g.*, of the 'Miri' religion. The net result must be that the religion statistics collected at this census will be very inaccurate in areas where there are animistic or aboriginal tribes."

Agitation among the Gonds and Oraons resulted in a large number, who were returned as Tribal in 1921, particularly of the former, returning themselves or being returned as Hindus, though their Hinduism in parts of the areas concerned is highly problematical. In the case of the Gonds in Berar alone these rather dubious Hindus numbered over 100,000, and in the Central Provinces and Berar together they amounted to more than three lakhs. In India as a whole the tribesmen who changed from Tribal religions to Hinduism numbered a million and a half.* In Gwalior State over 14,000 Bhils in the remoter forests and hills, whose tribal name was returned as their religion, were classified notwithstanding as " Hinduized Tribal " and included in the total of Hindus, involving a total transfer from " Tribal " in 1921 to " Hindu " in 1931 of some 162,000 Bhils. In Cochin State some 5,000 hill or forest tribesmen were classified as 'Hindu' though very doubtfully conforming to such a description, and a similar procedure has probably been followed elsewhere. On the other hand again counter-agitation in the Punjab against being returned as Hindu led 400,000 of the depressed castes to return themselves as *Ad-Dharmi*, i.e., " of the original faith ", as distinct from the terms used by their congeners of other provinces in northern India—*Adi-Hindu*, an expression which allowed of their inclusion in the total of Hindus, correctly of course, since in spite of their disabilities they are Hindu by religion, and if not, would not agitate for admission to Hindu temples†. Feeling on the subject of the return of religion ran highest in the Punjab, where many attempts were made to weight the census. False statements were circulated probably to arouse enthusiasm, such as a *canard* that all the sweepers of Simla had been returned as Muslims, which was published as a fact before even the preliminary enumeration of Simla had begun. A good deal of heat was similarly engendered on the question of the Udasi Sadhus. Members of this sect at one time regarded themselves generally as Sikhs, but since then they have reverted to the original fold and are now Hindus. Unfortunately an obsolete direction was reproduced in the Punjab Census Code from 1921 directing the inclusion of Udasis as Sikhs in the absence of information to the contrary. This was at once withdrawn when the circumstances were made clear. A great deal of misunderstanding was also aroused by the provision in the Code that Aryas and Brahmos should not be entered in the schedule as Hindu. This provision is an old one and is merely intended to facilitate the sorting of the Brahmo and Arya slips, but it was assumed by uninstructed persons who obtained access to the Code that the provision was intended to exclude Brahmos and Aryas from the Hindu total, which was not of course the case.

In Bengal even compilation was subject to propaganda and in one sorting office it was discovered that payment had been made for copying slips for fictitious Hindus while 74 Muslims were converted to Hinduism during the slip copying process. The insignificance of the numbers involved and the fact that the chicanery was detected and corrected is rather a testimony to the general accuracy of compilation than otherwise.

---

* Some figures of the turnover are as follows :—

Cochin State	5,000
Gwalior	162,000
Rajputana	252,000
Central Provinces	145,000
Assam Valley	350,000
Total	914,000

† In the social map these *Ad-dharmis* have been shown in pale blue amalgamating them with the other depressed castes.

Other communities showed no particular reluctance to act on lines similar to those of the Mahasabha, and in the Punjab in particular attempts made by Hindus, Sikhs and Muslims alike to bully the depressed castes into returning themselves as the canvassers desired probably left little to choose between them ; reports from the Punjab indicate that if any discrimination can be made the Sikhs were the most and the Muslims the least active of the three in this respect. Ultimately the depressed classes were so harassed that they made a big demonstration in Lahore, insisting on being returned under their own religious designation of *Ad-dharmi.* As they denied that they were Hindus it was necessary to show them separately.

Section ii.—The figures.

165. The figures for Religion will be found in Table XVI in part ii of this volume and comparative and proportional figures in the subsidiary tables at the end of this chapter ; for convenience an abstraction is given below :— **Hindus.**

Religion.	Actual Number in 1931 (000's omitted).	Proportion per 10,000 of population in						Variation per cent (Increase+) (Decrease—)					
		1931.	1921.	1911.	1901.	1891.	1881.	1921-1931.	1911-1921.	1901-1911.	1891-1901.	1881-1891.	1881-1931.
Hindu	239,195	6,824	6,856	6,939	7,037	7,232	7,432	+10·4	—0·4	+5·0	+0·3	+10·1	**+26·8**
Jain	1,252	36	37	40	45	49	48	+6·2	—5·6	—6·4	—5·8	+15·9	**+2·5**
Buddhist	12,787	365	366	342	322	248	135	+10·5	+7·9	+13·1	+32·9	+108·6	**+274·1**
Sikh	4,336	124	103	96	75	67	73	+33·9	+7·4	+37·3	+15·1	+2·9	**+133·9**
Zoroastrian ..	110	3	3	3	3	3	3	+7·8	+1·7	+6·3	+4·7	+5·3	**+28·5**
Muslim	77,678	2,216	2,174	2,126	2,122	1,996	1,974	+13·0	+5·1	+6·7	+8·9	+14·3	**+55·0**
Christian	6,297	179	150	124	99	79	73	+32·5	+22·6	+32·6	+28·0	+22·6	**+238·1**
Jew	24	1	1	1	1	1	1	+10·9	+3·8	+15·1	+6·0	+43·1	**+101·0**
Tribal	8,280	236	309	328	292	323	259	—15·3	—5·1	+19·9	—7·5	+41·2	**+28·8**
Minor religions and religions not returned.	571	16	1	1	4	2	2	+3072·6	—51·5	—71·4	+203·7	—28·7	**+179·3**

The Hindu population has increased during the decade by 10·4% to a total of 239,195,140. The composition of this total will appear from the accompanying table, in which the figures for "Other Hindus" contain the sum of those who returned their religion as Adi-Hindu, Adi-Dravida and Adi-Karnataka, together with certain sects such as that of the Dev Samaj for which separate figures are shown in some provinces. The depressed castes who returned themselves as Ad-Dharmi in the Punjab (except for 7,287 who returned themselves as "Hindu Ad-Dharmi" and are included accordingly as 'Other Hindus') have been included under the head "Others", and not as Hindus since they objected to being so included, and though their religion does not seem to differ from that of Adi-Hindus in any way, and it would seem proper to have included them in the Hindu total, the only position which is possible to the census is to accept the individual's own statement of his religion provided it can be classified under one of the standard heads, and the return of Ad-Dharm has therefore been included with "Others". The numbers were 399,307. Had this group been added to the Hindu total, the percentage of increase would have been raised by an additional 0·2. The difference which would have been made in the Punjab by the inclusion of Ad-Dharmis as Hindus would have been to transform the decrease of —3·81%, which the Hindus of that province suffered, into an increase of 2·3%. Even so the figure is low as compared to the 16·5% increase of Muslims and 34% of Sikhs in that province ; these figures relate to British Districts, but the figures for the states and for the Punjab States Agency are not dissimilar.

The increase under the head of Brahmanic Hindus is not entirely the result of the normal propagation of the species. Apart from conversion or rather perhaps reconversion (*shuddhi*) of a certain number of Muslims and Christians, the numbers have been increased by large adhesions to Hinduism of hill and forest tribesmen. Reference has already been made to Gonds, Oraons and Bhils. The organ of the Hindu Mission claims 62,844 converts from Muslims, Christians and Tribal Religions for the year 1927-28 alone, and having stated that the Mission commenced work in 1926 "in order to stem the tide of conversion to Christianity" goes on to say "In 1930 a large number of our workers carried an intensive propaganda for several months before the census operation. We........were convinced of a substantial increase of Hindu population in these provinces (Assam, Bengal and Bihar) in consequence of the absorption of Animists". The conviction was well founded, as Tribal religions in Assam show a decrease of 280,000, as compared to an increase in Christians of 117,000, and a reference to the Assam Census Report will show how large the turnover from 'Tribal' to 'Hindu' in the return of religion for some of the plains tribes in that province. The table (see below paragraph 173, *Tribal*) hardly shows complete figures for the change, as it can only give the numbers of those tribes which returned their tribe in column 8 of the schedule, and there were certainly many Christians who did not do so and probably appreciable numbers of Hindus. On the other hand against the increase from these sources must be set off some decrease due to defection from orthodox Hinduism to the Arya or Brahmo Samaj, though the total figure of Hindus is not thereby affected, to the exclusion of the Ad-Dharmis already explained, and perhaps in some small degree to the conversion of the depressed castes and others to Islam or Christianity. It should be pointed out that the term Brahmanic as used at this and past censuses includes not only Sanatanists and orthodox Hindus of recognised Hindu sects but also many, such as Lingayats, Kabirpanthis or the Jugi caste of Assam, who do not recognise Brahmanic authority.

Similarly the increase of Aryas is to be attributed to the adhesion of "Brahmanic" Hindus drawn very largely but by no means entirely from the lower ranks of Hindu society, which find in the Arya Samaj an opportunity of rising socially without abandoning Hinduism, since the Arya Samaj does not attach that importance to caste which is characteristic of orthodox Brahmanism. This reason was given for the increase of Aryas in Kashmir from 1,000 in 1911 to 23,000 in 1921, their present figures being 94,000. The Arya Samaj has been the most active of the Hindu proselytising bodies, and the All-India Shuddhi Conference, meeting under its auspices at the Kumbh Mela of 1930 at Allahabad, propounded (if correctly reported) the amazing proposition that "it is an undisputed fact that the founders of all the religions of the world were either Hindus or their descendants who drifted away from the present body", and it appealed for the reconversion of their followers in the interests of the future progress of mankind.

The Brahmo Samaj is a more eclectic body with a better claim to provide a catholic religion in that it does not insist on the infallibility of the Vedas, but inculcates the worship of one God, Creator and Preserver, who punishes sin remedially and is to be served in prayer and moral conduct, a belief in the immortality of the soul, and the view that no prophet, and no scriptures of any religion are finally and exclusively authoritative. It is probable that the very broadness of this creed militates against its appeal to any but the most intellectual classes, and though there are a number of Brahmo missions the increase by conversion is very much less numerically than that effected by the Arya Samaj. Its position in Hinduism both religiously and socially offers a near parallel to that of the Unitarians in Christianity in Britain.

Sikhs.

166. The increase of 33·9% under this head cannot be regarded as an entirely natural increase of population. Allowance must be made for a considerable amount of conversion from Hinduism not only in the Mazhbi section of the community, which is recruited from rather a different class than the rest, but in Sikhs proper by adhesion from Hindi-speaking castes, such as Jats and Aroras, even in the eastern part of the Punjab. This conversion seems to have been partly due to the impression that there was something to be gained by belonging to a community comparatively speaking little represented in Government services, and cases are actually reported in which some sons are brought up as Hindus and others as Sikhs so as to better the opportunities of the family as a whole in the search for posts under Government. How far the figures given represent a complete return of Sikhs it is not easy to say, as it is not known whether the Sahejdhari Sikhs generally returned themselves as Sikhs or Hindus. The orders given to enumerators were that a return of "Sikh, Hindu" would not be accepted, and that the person enumerated must decide in which body he would be returned. The probability is that the bulk of the Sahejdhari Sikhs returned themselves as Hindus in Baluchistan and in the N.-W. F. P. but it is doubtful if such is the case in the Punjab where the Sahejdhari is recognised as a Sikh for electoral purposes if he desires to be so regarded. The figures of Sikhs in Sind show a remarkable fluctuation from census to census, largely on account of the varying classification of the Sahejdhari. Thus in 1881, 127,000 Sikhs were censused in Sind, in 1891 under a thousand, in 1901

Census year.	Actual number of Sikhs.	Increase per cent. since 1881.
1881	1,853,426	..
1891	1,907,833	2·9
1901	2,195,339	18·4
1911	3,014,466	62·6
1921	3,238,803	74·7
1931	4,335,771	133·9

none, in 1911 about 11,000, in 1921 about 7,000 and in 1931 18,500. The decennial increase in the number of Sikhs is shown in the marginal table above. Their fertility is probably higher than that of Hindus on account of later marriage and the free remarriage of widows. The great bulk of the Sikhs shown as such in the census reports belong to the Keshadhari or Akali division which outnumbered those Sahejdhari who returned themselves as Sikhs in 1921 by about 1,200%. A noticeable feature in connection with the Sikhs is their appreciable increase in centres distant from the Punjab, to which they migrate largely for the sake of employment as mechanics. The phenomenal increase of over 30% in the Punjab itself, must be largely ascribed to the inclusion by conversion of Hindu castes.

Jains.

167. The Jain community is gradually decreasing in number proportionately to the population of the country as a whole. This is probably due in part to the practice of child marriage and the prohibition of widow remarriage, and partly also to the small size of the community which, attracting as it does no adherents from outside, cannot increase at the same rate as much larger ones. Dr. Guha suggests with some force that the Jains have a lowered fertility and an increased infant mortality rate on account of their division into small endogamous groups, some of which in Ahmadabad do not exceed 500 souls. The percentage of increase among Jains at this census was 6·2 and the Jain community now stands at 0·36% of the population of India instead of the 0·37% of last census and the 0·49% of 1891. 11,800 out of 1,252,105 Jains returned themselves as also Hindu, while the category 'Hindu, Others' includes 526 in the Punjab who returned themselves as also Jain.

Buddhists.

168. Contrariwise to the Jains the population of Buddhists to the rest of the population has steadily gone up with the increasing population of Burma, where 96·6% of the Buddhists recorded at this census are found. The great bulk of these are Burmans; Shans, Karens and Talaings making up about one-fifth to a quarter between them. In India the bulk of the Buddhists are found in Sikkim and the adjoining hills. There are a few in Assam, the descendants either of ancient immigrants from Burma *via* the Hukong valley or of isolated parties left behind by the army of invasion in the early 19th century. A few Sinhalese Buddhists are reported from Cochin State but most of the Buddhists there are educated Malayali Iruvas who have abandoned Hinduism on account of their social disabilities in that community. A colony of Buddhists in Chittagong, however, claims to represent the ancient Buddhist population of Maghada, and to be distinct from the Buddhists of the adjoining Hill Tracts, whose origin is Talaing or Arakanese, and from the Maghs of Chittagong whose religion has also been brought from Burma. Of Indian Buddhists 45 returned themselves as also Hindu, while 25 Buddhists in the Punjab who returned themselves as Hindu first and Buddhist afterwards are included under the head of 'Other Hindus'.

Distribution of Buddhists.

Province or State.	1931.	1921.
1. Burma	12,348,037	11,201,943
2. Bengal	316,031	265,604
3. Kashmir	38,724	37,685
4. Sikkim	35,412	26,788
5. Assam	14,955	13,162
6. Bengal States ..	14,532	10,155
7. Rest of India ..	19,115	15,931

Zoroastrians.

169. In spite of pressing invitations to return to Persia, which the Parsis have shown little inclination to accept, the Parsis have increased by 7·8% during the decade. Of the total number of 109,752, 99,010 are found in Bombay province, in Baroda, and the states of Western India. It was pointed out at last census that the birth rate was very low among Parsis, though the survival rate was exceptionally high. Both phenomena are due primarily to the high economic and cultural condition of the community, prosperity with education being the only really efficient check on the birth-rate yet discovered. So severely did this check operate by 1921, that in that year the birth-rate was lower even than in France. Like the Jains the Parsis are declining in numbers proportionately to the population as a whole, and it is possible that in their case also fertility may be lowered by too much inbreeding.

Population of Parsis.

Province or State.	Total number of Parsis.	Percentage of total Parsis.	Percentage of provincial population.
Bombay Presidency ..	89,544	81·6	·41
Baroda	7,127	6·5	·29
Bombay States ..	1,468	1·3	·03
Western India States Agency.	871	0·8	·02
Rest of India ..	10,742	9·8	.003

Jews.

170. As in the case of the Parsis, the Jews (Beni-Israel they are called in Bombay) are practically a closed body and receive no addition by conversion. Their increase from 21,778 to 24,141 (10·9%) shows that unlike the Parsis they are not losing in numbers proportionately to the rest of the population of India. The bulk of them are found in Bombay Presidency and in Cochin, being divided in both cases into "Black" and "White" Jews, though there appears to be no tradition of any connection between the Bombay and Cochin colonies, which are of very great antiquity.

Jews.

Province or State.	Total No. of Jews.	Percentage of total Jews.	Percentage of local population.
Bombay Presidency ..	17,739	73·5	·08
Cochin	1,451	6·0	·12
Rest of India ..	4,951	20·5	·002

Muslims.

171. Probably owing to the practices of polygyny, of widow remarriage and on the whole, of later consummation of marriage than is the prevailing practice among most Hindus, the Muslims are at present increasing at a greater rate. Some of the increase may be attributed to the *tanzim* movement for conversion to Islam, which naturally sprang up in reply to *shuddhi*, but it is believed that the increase attributable to this cause is not appreciable. The movement was primarily directed to the reconversion of the *shuddhi* converts and met with some success in the Agra and Mathura districts. Possibly the more rapid rate of increase may account to some extent for the lower level of intellectual attainment on the part of the Muslim population, but this would appear to be contradicted by the much more rapid increase of Sikhs. It is however to be borne in mind that comparison in the rates of increase between groups of very different size are apt to be fallacious and it is not to be expected that taking India as a whole the Hindus who form such a large majority should increase on the same scale as smaller units, limited as in the case of the Sikhs for instance, almost to a single area. Figures of the principal Muslim sects are not available as some local Governments decided to ignore these divisions, and others took cognizance of Sunni and Shia only, ignoring smaller bodies such as the Ahmadiya, Ahl-i-Hadis and Dawudi. It is noticeable that in most provinces the rate of increase of Muslims is decidedly higher than that of Hindus, though this is most markedly so in the Punjab. On the other hand in Bengal, where in the previous decade the Muslim population showed an increase of 5·2% against a Hindu decrease of 0·7, the Hindus at this census show an increase much nearer to that of the Muslims in rate, though still behind. Hindus have increased by 6·7% as against the Muslims 9·1%. If adults only be regarded, the comparative figures of Muslims to Hindus are lower, the higher fertility ratio rather naturally being accompanied by a higher rate of immature mortality. In the Punjab, on the other hand the respective ratios of Muslims, Hindus and Sikhs are very much the same whether the total population be considered or the adult population only.

Muslims, 1881—1931.

Province, etc.	Variation % 1921-1931.	Variation % 1881—1931.
India	+13·0	+55·0
British provinces ..	+12·7	+48·5
Ajmer-Merwara ..	—4·6	+68·0
Assam	+25·1	+109·3
Baluchistan ..	+10·4	..
Bengal	+9·1	} +46·3
Bihar and Orissa ..	+15·6	
Bombay	+16·7	+47·5
Burma	+16·8	+246·3
C. P. & Berar	+21·2	+47·4
Coorg	+5·8	+9·9
Madras	+16·4	+71·0
Delhi	+46·0	}
Punjab	+16·5	+49·8
N.-W. F. Province ..	+8·0	
United Provinces ..	+10·8	+21.3
States and Agencies ..	+14·7	+113·4

Comparative figures of Hindus and Muslims in Bengal.

British districts.	All ages.	Percentage of total.	Adults only (aged 20 and over).	Percentage of total.
Total population of Bengal.	50,114,002	100	24,873,309	100
Muslims ..	27,497,624	55	12,855,470	52
Hindus ..	21,570,407	43	11,503,668	46

Christians

172. The increase under the head of Christian is of course largely due to conversion which causes a steady transfer to Christianity from the depressed classes and still more, except in Madras, from the hill and forest tribes. If the natural increase be 12%, then over 20% out of the total increase of 32·5% must be due to conversion. Figures for the different denominations of Protestants and of Syrians other than Catholics are not available except for certain areas, and in any case those of Protestant sects would have been much confused by the cross divisions of

Presbyterians and others who have for certain purposes combined as a United Church, but some of whom returned their unitary designation only while others returned only their sectarian one. Of the Christians returned from the whole of India about 2·7% are Europeans, 2·2% are Anglo-Indians and the remainder, at any rate for all practical purposes, are Indians. Unitarians, who were returned in 1921 under 'Indefinite Beliefs' have been included as Protestants on this occasion. Their position among Christian sects is somewhat analogous to that of the Brahmos in Hinduism, appealing likewise to a limited intellectual group of the upper and middle classes, though there is in Assam an Unitarian mission which claims a number of converts in the Khasi Hills.

Tribal Religions.

173. The figures of Tribal religions show a decrease of 15·3% since 1921, this figure being primarily due to losses by conversion to Hinduism or Christianity. In the case of the latter, typical figures are afforded by the Assam Hill Tribes in districts in which conversion to Hinduism has been inoperative. Thus in the Naga Hills and in the hill areas of the Manipur State the variation in Christians has been +162% and +157% respectively compared to +2% and + 17% on the part of tribal religions. As an instance of loss by conversion to Hinduism the most outstanding cases are those of Assam again and of the Central Provinces. In Assam the census superintendent attributes 350,000, that is half the increase of Hindus in the Assam valley, to accretions from Tribal religions. In the Central Provinces the turnover from Tribal to Hinduism and Christianity, but mainly to Hinduism, in various parts of the province is shown in the marginal table, and these, of course are only the actual figures by which adherents of tribal religion have decreased as compared with 1921, making no allowance for the actual increase of population which might have been anticipated in tribal religions. In Rajputana the Tribal religions have lost at least 250,000 to Hinduism. So again in Gwalior State the figures under Tribal Religion in 1921 were 161,629, and this time are shown as *nil*, a mere 14,291, who are specifically stated to have returned the name of their tribe as that of their religion, being returned in spite of that as Hinduized Tribes. Clearly it is most unlikely that the change has been as complete as all this, when Bhils who are not Hindu are found living even in mixed villages in Rajputana, and there has probably been arbitrary classification of Tribal religion as Hindu. The figures given in the margin cannot be regarded as complete since many missionaries objected to their converts recording their tribe in column 8 of the Schedule and instructed them to return "Indian Christian" thus depriving the census of real figures of the tribe. The numbers of Tribal religion have also suffered depletion owing to the decay, which attacks so many primitive tribes when brought into contact with civilisation. Thus the Andamanese have declined from 1882 in 1901 to 460 in 1931, a loss of 75·6% in 30 years, at which rate they will be virtually extinct by the end of the century. This aspect of tribal figures may be examined in Table XVIII and with reference to appendix II to this volume.

Jubbulpore	41,000
Nagpur	42,000
Bhandara	36,000
Raipur	41,000
Drug	63,000
Berar	112,000

Tribe.	1931. Total.	Hindu.	Muslim.	Christian.	1921. Total.	Hindu.
Bhil	2,013,177	1,569,365	8,332	133	1,795,808	968,199
Birhor	2,350	1,723	..	1	..	..
Gadaba ..	47,154	281	..	3	..	..
Garo	231,701	44,013	..	29,490	161,915	3,422
Gond	3,069,069	1,627,491	4	35	2,902,592	1,026,707
Ho	523,184	129,680	..	2,078	440,174	49,530
Kachari.. ..	345,248	259,283	..	8,808	207,266	71,192
Korku	194,433	107,018	..	16	140,440	46,553
Korwa	40,101	20,854	..	71	..	..
Lushei	117,569	1,742	..	61,654	61,090	195
Miri	85,038	79,848	..	38	68,725	45,424
Munda	658,450	226,883	..	136,763	593,839	236,833
Oraon	1,021,355	413,889	..	200,509	765,680	202,400
Santals	2,508,789	1,020,001	..	24,033	2,265,282	739,976

Others.

174. The head 'others' includes the comparatively insignificant number of persons who return themselves as deists, agnostics, free thinkers, rationalists, theosophists, Christian Scientists, etc., those eccentrics who made such returns of religion as "*Ahimsa*", "Truth", "Reason" and "Freedom for India" (one of them described himself as "spiritually universal", but manifestly could not be distributed to all the various heads), and those who returned themselves as having no religion or who merely failed from indifference, or from inability to express themselves, to make any return of religion at all. It includes Confucians, a term used indiscriminately by census officers in India for any Chinese and usually rendered by enumerators and compilers, perhaps not inaptly, " Confusionist ", and also a number of Chinese ancestor-worshippers returned as Animists (*i.e.*, *Nat* worshippers) from Burma. It also includes 418,789 Ad-Dharmis who objected to being described as Hindus, an objection which they continued to reiterate during the compilation stage of the census. The followers, some thousands in number, of a prophet, or a rogue, named Pao Chin Hao, who has recently arisen in the Chin Hills in Burma and started a new religion, which includes an inspired script and one or two most engaging features, such as the institution of religious police whose business it is to arrest diseases, were included among ' Animists ' in the Burma returns and their numbers are not accurately known ; a brief notice of this creed will be found in the appendix volume.

Comparative numbers.

175. The following table shows the relative proportions of the various religious communities in 1931 as compared to 1921 throughout India. Their comparative proportions since 1891 will be found in subsidiary Table I to this chapter. It brings out very clearly the extent to which the Hindu community is indebted to accretion from tribal religions for its growth at this census. With the exception of Baluchistan, where the Hindus are generally speaking immigrants and their number easily influenced by the composition of military units in Quetta, no province has shown any proportionate increase of Hindus to the general population except where there have been tribal religions to draw from. Muslims on the other hand have increased their ratio to the total population in all provinces except Ajmer-Merwara where the 1921 Muslim figure was artificially swollen by the Urs pilgrims.

Distribution by Religion of 10,000 persons in India, in the provinces and in the States, 1921 and 1931.

Province, etc.	Year.	Hindu.	Muslim.	Buddhist.	Tribal.	Christian.	Sikh.	Jain.	Other.
India	*1921*	*6,856*	*2,174*	*366*	*309*	*150*	*103*	*37*	*5*
	1931	6,824	2,216	365	236	179	124	36	20
Provinces	*1921*	*6,606*	*2,407*	*465*	*280*	*123*	*96*	*18*	*5*
	1931	6,548	2,469	468	213	142	118	17	25
Ajmer-Merwara	*1921*	*7,356*	*2,055*	..	*96*	*112*	*4*	*372*	*5*
	1931	7,755	1,734	..	27	124	6	348	6
Andamans and Nicobars ..	*1921*	*3,278*	*1,515*	*979*	*3,387*	*586*	*144*	*0*	*111*
	1931	2,586	2,280	988	3,379	496	220	0	51
Assam	*1921*	*5,434*	*2,896*	*17*	*1,479*	*168*	*1*	*5*	..
	1931	5,720	3,196	17	825	235	3	3	1
Baluchistan	*1921*	*920*	*8,731*	*4*	*0*	*159*	*182*	..	*4*
	1931	894	8,744	1	1	174	181	1	4
Bengal	*1921*	*4,327*	*5,399*	*57*	*181*	*31*	..	*3*	*2*
	1931	4,304	5,487	63	105	36	2	2	1
Bihar and Orissa	*1921*	*8,284*	*1,085*	..	*553*	*76*	*1*	*1*	..
	1931	8,231	1,132	..	544	91	1	1	0
Bombay	*1921*	*7,658*	*1,974*	*1*	*64*	*137*	*4*	*111*	*51*
	1931	7,605	2,039	1	59	145	10	92	49
Burma	*1921*	*368*	*380*	*8,506*	*534*	*195*	*4*	*1*	*12*
	1931	390	399	8,430	444	226	7	1	103
C. P. and Berar	*1921*	*8,354*	*405*	..	*1,160*	*30*	*1*	*49*	*1*
	1931	8,601	440	..	872	33	3	50	1
Coorg	*1921*	*7,733*	*795*	*1*	*1,265*	*194*	*0*	*12*	..
	1931	8,939	844	..	0	210	0	5	2
Delhi	*1921*	*6,669*	*2,904*	..	*0*	*273*	*57*	*96*	*1*
	1931	6,285	3,253	1	0	267	101	84	9
Madras	*1921*	*8,864*	*671*	..	*137*	*322*	..	*6*	..
	1931	8,831	707	..	75	380	..	7	..
N.-W. F. P...	*1921*	*666*	*9,162*	..	*0*	*47*	*125*	..	..
	1931	590	9,184	..	0	51	175	0	..
Punjab	*1921*	*3,181*	*5,533*	*1*	*0*	*159*	*1,109*	*17*	..
	1931	2,684	5,655	2	0	176	1,299	15	169
United Provinces	*1921*	*8,509*	*1,428*	..	*0*	*44*	*3*	*15*	*1*
	1931	8,450	1,484	..	0	42	10	14	..
States	*1921*	*7,748*	*1,343*	*12*	*415*	*250*	*126*	*104*	*2*
	1931	7,771	1,347	12	316	307	141	101	5

N. B.—A blank indicates that the number per 10,000 is fractional ; 0 indicates that none at all were returned.

In the case of Assam the Khasi States are included in the 1921 figures. Otherwise all states are excluded from provinces.

Section iii.—General.

Hinduism in its relation to Primitive Religion in India.

176. The question of religion in India cannot, of course, be entirely disentangled from that of race, and the views expressed here must be read with those in the subsequent chapter, but it may be convenient to state here briefly the general

DISTRIBUTION BETWEEN COMMUNITIES OF 10,000 PERSONS IN PROVINCES AND STATES SHOWING 1931 AS COMPARED TO 1921

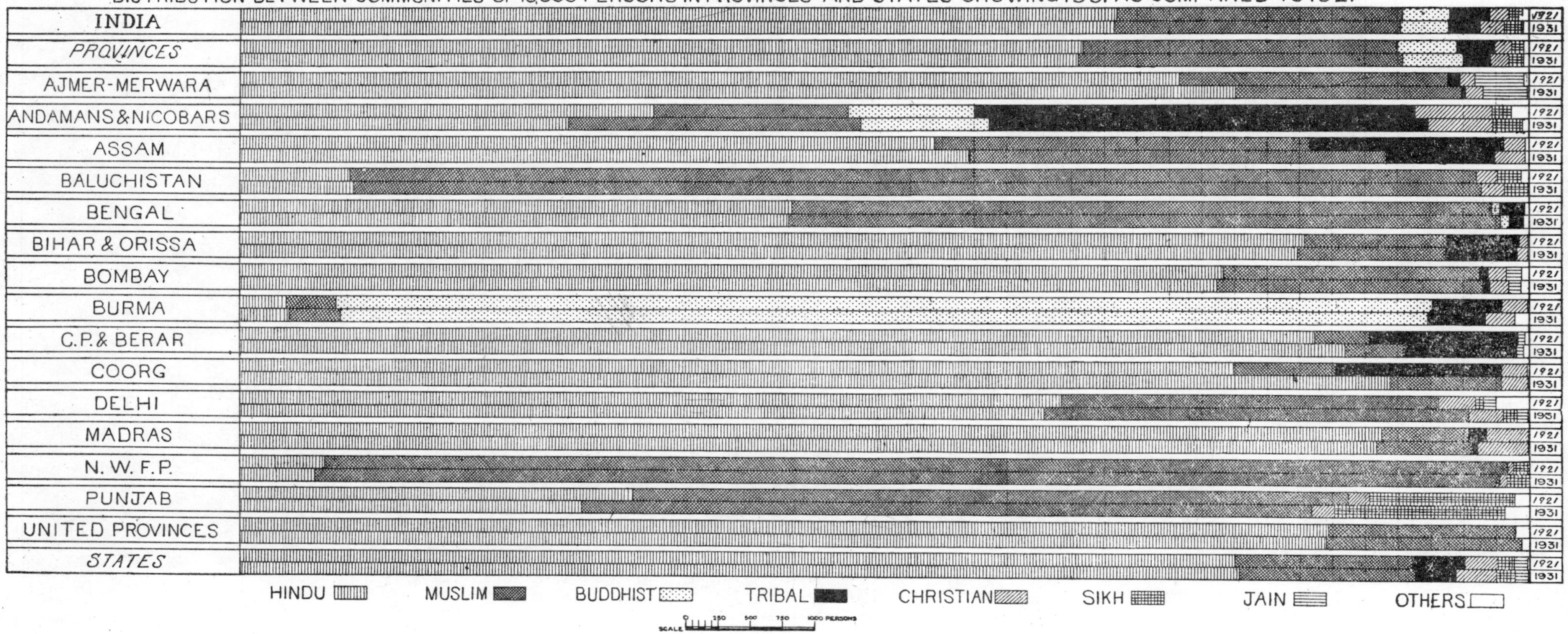

hypothesis reached. That is that a number of successive racial intrusions into and occupations of India have contributed to the elements now found in the Hindu religion, which took its final form as the result of the impact of the social ascendency of the Indo-European invaders of the 2nd millenium B. C. on pre-existing religious institutions. The first occupants of India were probably Negritos, and elements of their belief, perhaps including the reverence for the pipal tree and possibly a primitive phallic fertility cult, may have been perpetuated by the proto-australoids who were the next comers and probably contributed the totemic theory, or at least the basis thereof. The next elements were probably of Mediterranean origin contributing a phallic and a megalithic culture and the life essence theory, but the relative positions of the Dravidian-speaking Mediterranean+Armenoid, the proto-australoid and the Munda and Mon-Khmer or Austroasiatic races is difficult to determine and there is little material from which to draw a conclusion, and many would identify the proto-australoid and Munda racial elements. If the Munda speaking elements be distinct from the proto-australoid, it would be conveniently orderly to suppose that the Mundas came after them with a life-essence theory and the Mediterraneans still later to develop it into reincarnation, and bringing in the worship of the Great Mother, but it is conceivable that the Mediterraneans brought both the theory and its development and the Munda came later as a barbarian invader, though no doubt, already in possession of the soul-matter philosophy, since at any rate the hill tribes of Assam, Burma and Indo-China appear to contain an element of Caucasian stock which penetrated to the S. E. of Asia before the southern migration of Mongolians of the Pareoean branch, and the soul-matter theory must have arisen very early in the history of the human race. Both Munda and Mediterranean must have been followed by religious elements from Asia Minor, brought *via* Mesopotamia by traders and settlers from the west, which superseded the fertility and soul-matter cult by one of personified deities, sacrificial propitiation and a formalised worship, again with phallic elements and such institutions as that of the *deva-dasi* (*vide supra* para. 102), together with astronomical lore and cults of the heavenly bodies and priestly institutions which formed the basis of modern Hinduism, the final form of which was determined by the successful conflict of this proto-Hinduism on the religious side with the imported religion of the " Aryan " invaders, to whom, however, it had to concede much socially, resulting in the socio-religious position of the priestly order so familiar in India.

The generally accepted view of the Hindu religion or society regards it as originating in Aryan invaders of about B. C. 1500 who came in with a higher civilization and a fairer skin to find the great peninsula inhabited by dark skinned barbarians on whom they imposed the religion of the Vedas. It is more than doubtful if this view can any longer be accepted, and the doubts cast on it appear to be confirmed by recent discoveries including that of a figure of Shiva among the remains at Mohenjodaro, while Sir John Marshall has clearly shown that the pre-Aryan religion of the Indus valley involved a cult of the bull, and of the snake—typical Mediterranean cults, to be found in Crete—and also of phallic symbols, including " ring " and baetylic stones, which are probably all part of the soul-fertility cult which is associated throughout India with menhirs, dolmens and a megalithic culture generally ; indeed Heine-Geldern connects the megalithic Mycenean theatre with India and so with the Far East and the Pacific Islands. It has been pointed out with some aptness that in modern Hinduism only those elements of Vedic rites have survived which are essentially social, such as the marriage ceremonies ; the argument being that though society was, or aimed at being, Aryan, its religion is older than that of the so called Aryan invasion. The god of the Rigveda Indo-Europeans is Indra, the thunder god, who fills in later developments an entirely minor role, apparently being absorbed into the Hindu pantheon just as the minor gods of primitive tribes have been, retaining, however, his personal identity by virtue of a social prestige or privilege which other tribal gods have lost in the process of assimilation. The historical Hindu religion first appears not in the Punjab, which must be regarded as the area most completely occupied by the Indo-European invaders, but to the east of that in the Brahmarshidesha where stable fusion between these Indo-European invaders and the previous inhabitants probably took place. When alien cultures and religions fuse to form a new culture or religion, it will not be found that this fusion takes place where the intrusive culture is strong enough to predominate. It will rather appear away from the centre where the intrusion is strongest, in some area where the previous culture was strong enough to resist complete suppression and make its influence felt on the new one. Thus it is that the efflorescence of Hellenic culture took place not in Sparta, where was the purest blood of the northern invaders, but in Athens where the grasshopper-wearing inhabitants regarded themselves as autochthones and where there was probably effective fusion between the fair-haired northerner and the dark-haired Pelasgian. Similarly there is some reason to believe that Rome grew from a fusion between the ancient Etruscans and later invaders, whether the latter came from the east or from the north. In the same way it is suggested that Hindu religion and society finally took form and flourished as a result of the impact of the invading Indo-European on the indigenous religion that he found in India. It is quite clear that the previous inhabitants of India lived in cities and had a high civilization, probably of western Asiatic origin, and it is significant that Hinduism is remarkable for the similarity of many of its tenets and practices to those of Asia Minor and Mesopotamia. The indigenous religion of any country inevitably starts with an advantage over that of an invading people, since it is the priest of the country who knows how to approach the gods of the soil and propitiate them, and for that reason there is always a tendency for a local religion to establish its ascendency over an intrusive one. This appears to have been the case in India where the important position of Shiva, Vishnu and Kali, as compared to the unimportant one which Indra now holds, signalizes the triumph of the older gods. The religious history of pre-Vedic India was probably similar and parallel to that of the eastern Mediterranean and of Asia Minor. Prof. Tucci points out that though the moon does not appear to have been an independent divinity, ancient lunar cults have been assimilated by Devi in the forms of Durga, Kali and Tripura-sundari. The cult of snakes, the worship of a mother goddess were probably brought in by earlier invaders of Mediterranean or of Armenoid race, speaking no doubt a Dravidian language, whose religion must also be associated with fertility cults, phallic symbolism, the Devadasi cult and probably human sacrifice. Recent discoveries in Crete have revealed a remarkable snake cult associated with the symbol of the double axe. With Mesopotamia too we must perhaps associate a moon god and sun goddess whose sex was changed with a change from matrilineal to patrilineal descent perhaps under the influence of the Rigvedic invaders. It is worth pointing out that the deification and worship of kings, very typical of the Hindu attitude to kingship, is stated by Langdon (*J. R. A. S.*, 1931, page 367) to be characteristic of Sumerian religion in contrast to Semitic. It would also appear not characteristic of the religion of the Rigveda, but on the contrary to be connected with the beliefs in the external soul and in life-essence discussed below, inasmuch as the king contains or represents the life-principle of the community he rules. Like the cult of the snake, the transmigration of souls too appears to be a doctrine in no way typical of northern religions in which the dead live on underground, and Fustel de Coulanges has pointed out that it is not a feature of any northern religion though it has survived and been incorporated in them from the more ancient religions of Greece and Italy. Ancestor worship again is very strong in India and this too would appear foreign to northern European religion, and indeed it is almost impossible that nomads should be ancestor worshippers, and the Aryan invasion, so-called, was probably an invasion of steppe-dwelling tribes, pastoral in habit and still nomadic. Cremation they may have brought in and if so, they gave it a social cachet which is still leading to its gradual adoption by tribes which have previously practised burial or exposure, but it seems much more likely that the Rigvedic Aryans buried their dead and adopted cremation from the inhabitants whom they conquered. The 8th book of the Rigveda contains the following words addressed to the dead " I place this barrier (of stones) for the living........that no other may go beyond it. May they live a hundred numerous autumns, keeping death at a distance by this hill........Enter the mother earth........Earth, let his breath rise upward (easily) ; oppress him not ....Even as a mother covers her son with the end of her cloth, so do ye, earth, cover him........may these homes........for all time be his asylum. I heap up earth above thee, etc., " (Rajendralala Mitra, *Indo-Aryans*, II, 123). This passage seems very clearly to indicate burial in a tumulus, and the word translated ' barrier ' is stated in a note to be *paridhi* which may mean part of a circle of stones. It is true that the 10th hymn of the Rigveda clearly refers to cremation, but the author above quoted rightly regards it as the later passage, and suggests that ritual exigencies involved the dislocation of the verses and their fusion for ceremonial purposes in the Yajurveda and the Sutras, the reference to inhumation being then interpreted as indicating the burial of the ashes. It appears, however, quite clear that the hymn quoted above can only refer to the inhumation of the body, and that this practice as well as that of cremation was in use at the time of the Rigveda, while cremation is not mentioned until the 10th hymn, admittedly a much later composition than the earlier ones ; cremation also seems definitely to have been the practice in the Indus valley of the Mohenjodaro period, and therefore the more likely one of the two to have been adopted as an alternative by the Rigvedic Aryans at their period of fusion with the preexisting population. The Aryan sanctity of fire seems likely to have been incompatible with cremation, and it will be remembered that Herodotus taxes Cambyses with impiety for having had the body of Amasis burned "for the Persians regard fire as a god and therefore to burn the dead is on no account allowed......for they say that it is not right to offer to a god the corpse of a man." It may be noticed both that Wilson (*Infanticide in Western India,* 74) remarks of the Rajputs of Kachh and Kathiawar that they encouraged their concubines to commit *sati* in preference to their wives and actually gives as the reason that *sati* was a custom of low castes and therefore derogatory to Rajputs, and also that Rajputs in Gujarat who forbid widow remarriage are called *Vānkā,* 'crooked', and those who allow it *Pādhrā,* 'straight' (*Bombay Gazetteer,* IX, *i,* page 123-n).

With Asia Minor or Mesopotamia again we must associate astronomy and the worship of the heavenly bodies, which form an important part of Hindu culture, and in particular the cult of the moon god. Sun worship appears to be less important in the Rigveda than at a later date when the Bhavishya Purana is largely devoted to a cult of the sun. It is however possible that it was the influence of Rigvedic invaders which changed the sex of the sun from female to male and gave rise to the sun-descended nobility as distinct from the moon-descended. In Rigveda X Soma the moon is represented as male and as marrying Sūryā the daughter of the Sun. The name of the latter suggests that the Sun himself, Sūryă, was originally the female that married the Moon and that there has been a change of sex associated in so many parts of the world with variations of the Phaethon legend. Similarly again the existing holy places of the Hindus are outside Brahmavarta where one might have expected to find them, if it were really the fact that the religion actually arose in that area, while to find them elsewhere is consistent with a view that they are places regarded with devotion by the religions which preceded the invasion. This view is sometimes emphasised by the existence of Hindu shrines where priests and custodians are not Brahmans but some pseudo-Brahman or Sudra caste, *e.g.* the Malis who are the officiating priests of some Orissa temples and probably the Panda Brahmans of the same region. It is doubtless significant that sacrifice of cattle was "detested by the public" though enjoined by the earlier vedas, the inference from which is that the reverence paid to cattle predates the Rigvedic invasion, and Buddhism and Jainism, the latter of which contains extremely ancient ceremonial survivals, may represent a reaction towards the pre-Vedic religion to which the majority of the inhabitants of northern India were attached and which was modified but not destroyed by contact with the invaders. The first prohibition of cow-killing seems to be found in the comparatively late Atharva Veda and to be applied specially if not exclusively to Brahmans, while elsewhere we learn that the cow, although a fit offering for Mitra and Varuna, should not be sacrificed because such sacrifice is opposed to public feeling, a clear indication of the contrast between the religions of the socially superior Aryan invaders and the cattle-cherishing inhabitants who formed the bulk of the population. In Southern India, the Census Superintendent for Madras points out, "the cow is as much revered in those areas of the presidency with the lightest tincture of Brahmanism as in those more affected", which "may be taken to indicate that reverence for the cow in India is older than the Vedic religion." In any case the sanctity of the cow is foreign to the Rigveda and appears far more suggestive of the religions of Asia Minor, Egypt and Crete than of the Indo-European invaders who came from the steppes of the north-west to conquer northern India in the strength of their horses and of their iron. Indra moreover appears as the author of sacrifice and in the Yajur Veda it seems still to be Indra and Varuna who are the principal recipients of sacrificed cattle. It does not seem possible to accept Sir John Marshall's antithesis between the worship of the bull and the worship of the cow. Both are surely different aspects of the same reverence for cattle which characterises the pre-equine civilisations of the

Mediterranean basin, and in India are pre-" Aryan " in origin. The Vedas after all enjoined *gaumedha*, and the Black Yajur Veda lays down an elaborate list of deities to whom bulls, oxen and cows can be appropriately sacrificed. Vishnu, Shiva and Kali the great gods of Hinduism are not Rigvedic deities at all. Sakti is probably a cult derived from the Great Mother goddess of Asia Minor, and the cult of Shiva is inevitably associated with it, the two being bound up with the phallic religion of southern Asia and of the eastern Mediterranean. It is probably significant that the word *linga* is definitely of non-Aryan origin, as Przyluski has demonstrated, while the word *puja* is also believed to be a non-Sanskritic loan word. With the worship of Shiva, too, is to be associated the snake cult of which there are so many survivals in southern India and which appears to have been at an early date in definite opposition to Brahmanistic Hinduism, the conflict between the two being indicated, for instance, by Krishna's exploits against serpents, by the destruction of serpents at the burning of the forests of Khandava and the slaughter of serpents in the Mahabharata. Vishnu, apparently a post-Rigvedic god, is perhaps the fruit of the reaction of what we may call proto-Hinduism to the Rigvedic invaders, as also the present ascendency of male over female conceptions of the deity, and Przyluski in one of his most recent essays (*Archiv Orientálni, IV*, 2, August 1932) ascribes a Dravidian origin to the name ' Vishnu '. At the same time Vishnu would seem to have some associations with religious beliefs which must be regarded as represented chiefly in beliefs yet surviving among primitive tribes. Indra apparently is himself declared in the Mahabharata to be guilty of brahmanicide in killing Vrtra and Namuci who were Danavas, though the Rigveda praises him for the same deed. Pargiter adduces considerable evidence to show that the true Brahman families were of pre-Rigvedic origin and that the Aryan kings of Madhyadesha were their own priests and in the earliest times had no Brahmans. Strabo remarks that it is recorded that " The Indians worshipped Zeus Ombrios, the river Ganges and the indigenous gods " (τοὺς ἐγχωρίους δαίμονας—XV, 718) and as Zeus Ombrios is clearly Indra, the thunder god, the suggestion that the other gods worshipped are of indigenous origin is probably very near to the truth and the traditional view that the Hindu religion is a growth entirely subsequent to the Rigveda, or rather to the Rigvedic invasions, is no longer tenable. Rai Bahadur Ramaprasad Chanda in a paper on the " Non-vedic elements in Brahmanism " has made a number of points which indicate the continued existence of the pre-Rigvedic religions alongside of or in opposition to the orthodox Hinduism of the Brahmarshidesha. Quoting Kumārila and Medhātithi he points out that the Smartas include non-Vedic elements ; thus of the four orders named in the *Dharmasutra* of Gautama (Student, Householder, Ascetic and Hermit) only that of householder (*grihastha*) is prescribed in the Vedas that the Upanishads were not originally recognised as part of the Vedic canon at all and had their origin outside Vedic Hinduism ; that the Yatis destroyed by Indra are probably the forerunners of the Yatis of the Upanishads and the Smritis and that the latter order were organised on a pre-Vedic model ; that the Pancharatra and Pasupata systems were condemned by Kumārila as non-Vedic and that the Vaishnavite and Saivite sects are derived respectively from those two systems ; that contact with Pasupatas, Saivas, Jainas, etc., involved purification ; that by the time of the Mahabharata, however, Pancharatra and Pasupata are placed on a footing of recognised and orthodox religious authority. His general conclusion is that the cults of Vishnu, Shiva and Sakti " originated among a people of different ethnic origins from the midlandic Aryans ". The point to be emphasised here is not so much Chanda's precise conclusions as the evidence he adduces of the survival of pre-Vedic religion alongside and inside the later forms of Hinduism, and of their gradual absorption and acceptance as a recognised part of it, which has perhaps since developed into the position of their forming the most important part of it.

If the view be accepted that the Hindu religion has its origin in pre-Vedic times and that in its later form it is the result of the reaction by the religion of the country to the intrusive beliefs of the northern invaders, many features of Hinduism will become at once more comprehensible, while the very striking difference between the religion of the Rigveda and that of the Dharmashastras will seem natural. It will, however, be still necessary to look westward for the source of Hindu religion, though its spread in India was possibly in the nature of a peaceful infiltration along the trade routes from Asia Minor of beliefs and practices which associated themselves with those already followed by the indigenous inhabitants. This will explain Hinduism's amalgamation with and absorption of local cults and its excessive multiformity, and is moreover in entire accordance with the manner in which it still spreads at the present day, absorbing tribal religions in virtue of its social prestige and by identification of local gods with its own , by an experimental resort to Hindu priests, and by the social promotion of pagan chiefs who, are provided with suitable mythological pedigrees. Onto the early Hindu beliefs spread in this manner the religion of the Rigveda has been imposed, and absorbed. Features survive curiously in out of the way parts beyond the pale of Hinduism itself. Thus the horse sacrifice has become a fertility rite among the non-Hindu Garos of the Assam hills and appears likewise in the wilds of Sumatra, though it has failed to establish itself in orthodox Hinduism. Similarly, though the sacrifice of cattle is anathema to the true Hindu, the *Taittiriya Brahmana* recommended a whole series of animal slaughterings, including both bulls and cows, to be performed at the *Panchasaradiya Sava* and at the *Asvamedha*, a series extremely suggestive of the scales laid down for successive feasts for the acquirement of social merit at such ceremonies as the *Terhengi* of the Angami Nagas, while the *Grihya Sutra* enjoins the *Sulagava*, "spitted cow" ceremony (corresponding roughly to the Angami *Sekrengi*, as the *Panchasaradiya* does to the *Terhengi*) at which the beast was killed, as to-day by Sema Nagas, with a pointed stake, and its death accompanied by the erection of a wooden post with a round top mortised on to it and by the distribution of the animal's flesh.

Viewed in this light it is not difficult to understand the claim of certain politicians that the term Hinduism should cover all religions having their origin in India, even though we hold that the original impulse came from the Mediterranean or Asia Minor, since Jainism, Buddhism and Sikhism are all offshoots of the same root. The claim is less logical when applied to tribal religions which have not yet reached the stage of accepting Brahmans as priests or of attaching any sanctity to the cow or of worshipping in Hindu temples in their own villages. An occasional visit to Hindu temples away from home is not quite a safe test since many such shrines undoubtedly occupy sites dedicated originally to more ancient indigenous deities and subsequently Hinduised, and in any case it is typical of primitive religions to propitiate the gods of any locality they may visit. Admittedly however the line is hard to draw between Hinduism and tribal religions. The inclusion of the latter within the Hindu fold is easy and wherever hill or forest tribes live in permanent daily contact with Hindus their religion rapidly assimilates itself to that of their neighbours though the old method of thinking is unchanged. Thus it is that religious or quasi-religious beliefs and practices among Hindus appear very frequently to be based on the principles of magic, *mana* or other ideas common in primitive religion. The very word *brahma* itself seems to have probably connoted originally supernatural power or influence of the nature of *mana*—a view apparently supported by the Atharva Veda, and these beliefs and practices survive and operate with all their primitive qualities alongside the loftiest heights of asceticism and philosophy. If it appears that the latter aspect of the Hindu religion is lost sight of in these pages, it is because their purpose is rather to articulate the fragments of the more primitive and material philosophy that preceded it, than to emphasise what is already of long-standing and undisputed recognition.

We may therefore expect to find very ancient and primitive beliefs continuing under the guise of Hinduism. The sanctity of the fig tree for instance is possibly to be associated with the beliefs of the Negrito inhabitants who appear to have formed the earliest population of India. It is probably on account of its milk-like sap that the *ficus* is associated with fertility cults in Africa, Italy and New Guinea as well as in Assam and in southern India, and it is generally also connected with the spirits of the dead. This cult appears to be shared by the Andamanese who are an approximately pure Negrito race and perhaps the only race still surviving in the world comparatively unmixed in blood. At any rate they and their beliefs have probably been isolated for some five thousand years at least. Similarly, though the probability is that this element of Hinduism is due to some pre-Aryan immigrant cult from the direction of Asia Minor, the possibility that some tribal and totemic taboo has acted as a contributory factor in the religious sanctity attaching to cattle cannot be entirely overlooked. Thus the flesh of cattle is tabooed by certain clans among primitive tribes of Assam and Indonesia who do not appear to have come even remotely under the influence of Hinduism, while on the other hand the cow is regarded as completely tabooed by the Shins of Chilas, who are described by Leitner as a Hindu tribe with nowadays a veneer of Islam, the highest caste in Dardistan and really Brahmans themselves though expelled from India or from Kashmir by Brahmans. Not only do they taboo the flesh of the cow but also its milk and only touch a calf at the end of a prong.

Pargiter's view of the original conception of *brahma* as akin to that of *mana* has already been mentioned and this view seems naturally to associate itself with the views on soul-matter, or life itself as a transferable and material substance, which are so familiar in Indonesia and further India but which are actually common enough in India itself. It is on this theory of the indestructibility and transferability of life-matter that the underlying principle of head-hunting is based in Assam; in other parts of the same cultural area it is manifest in human sacrifice or in cannibalism, the latter perhaps being its most primitive manifestation and the former its most developed. That the principle is still strong in India may be inferred from a number of recent instances several of which are given later. In the form of head-hunting this theory involves that which regards the head as the particular seat of the soul, and this belief is apparent in India proper in the sanctity which attaches to the head or to the hair, as also in many cases where the (soul-impregnated ?) hair does duty for the individual, as in the case of the Naga who dies far from home and a portion of whose hair is brought back by his companions to be attached to the head of the wooden effigy which is then the subject of the usual funeral ceremonies, and as also in the case of the head-hunter who so often substitutes the hair of his dead or even of his living, and unwitting, victim for the head he cannot carry off.* The Ujli Minas when unsuccessful in dacoity will only shave at home and after propitiating their goddess. Probably they fear that they may be suffering from a loss of life-essence as Samson did when his hair was cut. Conversely a Korku woman of the Central Provinces tries to obtain as a cure for barrenness a hair from the mother of a large family which she buries under her bathing stone. The same theory may perhaps be the origin of the familiar caste mark placed in front of the forehead just between eyebrows. The Angami Naga tribe regards this particular place as the special seat of the soul, conceived of as a diminutive human shape, which it is necessary to guard from the infectious influence of strangers by means of disinfectants. This is done by attaching to that particular spot on the forehead a small fragment of the leaf of the wormwood—an effective disinfectant of spiritual influences, like other aromatic plants. It seems likely that it is in a practice of this sort and as a protection against danger to the soul that the use of the caste mark may have first originated.

Fertility cults have already been mentioned. These like head-hunting and human sacrifice are intimately associated with agriculture and the line is hard to draw at the point at which a purely magical fertility rite begins to develop into ceremonial of a genuinely religious nature. At any rate a point is easily reached by the former which is correlated to the latter, and the tribal cult ceases to be purely tribal and is identified with some definitely religious festival so that the magical, ceremonial and devotional aspects become merged. Magical fertility rites, originally regarded as necessary to ensure the processes of nature, are thus conserved and crystallized and continue to be accepted as a natural feature in the ceremony when the reason of their being there is forgotten. So too features of such rites which in the beginning are natural and inevitable, since they are regarded as essentially necessary to make the rite effective, and for this reason are performed without any sense of impropriety or obscenity, become, when they cease to be essential to the ceremony, effectively indecent but are not recognised as such as long as the traditional form of the ceremony continues to be unquestioned. In this form ceremonies and practices survive long after the conditions of society in which they originated have changed. Thus rites essentially priapic survived at Isernia near Naples at any rate into the 19th century actually under the aegis of the Church, and it is only on contact with and under criticism from some external source that familiar and therefore unquestioned practices are seen in a new and critical light. That this process is now taking place in Hindu society is sufficiently obvious. The Cochin Government has prohibited the singing of

---

* *Cf.* also *supra* para. 102.

obscene songs, etc., at the *Holi* festival, and advanced Hindu opinion would probably welcome a similar prohibition in many parts of British India, where already the festival seems to be generally celebrated with less excess than used to be the case. The Government of Mysore has abolished the institution of Devadasis, and here again an influential element in Hindu society is loud in its approval.

It is perhaps symptomatic of the tendency to reform and to even more drastic change in Hinduism that it should prove possible, as apparently it has in Bombay, to constitute an " Anti-Priestcraft Association ", the professed purpose of which is " to combat all religious and social beliefs and customs and institutions which cannot stand the test of reason ", and members of which are reported to entertain a frankly bolshevist attitude towards all religions and to advocate the destruction of all temples, churches and mosques. On the other hand little effective has been accomplished in the way of removing untouchability in its real sense. It is often said that the conditions of modern life have broken down the idea that contact with certain castes involves pollution, and this is true just to that extent to which the use of conveniences such as trams, 'buses and trains necessitates a relaxation of the rule that certain castes pollute by touch and still more that they can pollute by mere proximity. Further there is a tendency obviously consequent on the necessity of relaxation referred to above to relax the rule of pollution by touch in the case of members of untouchable castes who do not pursue untouchable avocations. This does not necessarily involve any real abandonment of the attitude of caste Hindus to what the Census Superintendent of Assam conveniently describes as the " Exterior Castes ". The water they touch is still undrinkable, food they touch becomes impure and they are not admitted to places of worship or to restaurants nor will the ordinary barbers serve them. Indeed the most that seems to have been yet accomplished* is the occasional staging of inter-caste meals, gestures which appear so far to have had little practical effect on the general attitude of the caste to the outcaste Hindu. But it must not be forgotten that the attempts of the depressed classes to obtain the right of entry to temples is perhaps sometimes as much inspired by social motives as by religious ones, and produces an antagonistic reaction which might be absent if religion alone were involved.

The tribal religions, as has been indicated already, represent, as it were, surplus material not yet built into the temple of Hinduism. How similar this surplus is to the material already used will appear in many ways and may be noticed, to start with, in the cults of the dead. The Hindu rites of the *shradh* provide for the creation of a new body to house the soul of the deceased and, though theoretically renewed every year to maintain it, they are usually as a matter of fact gradually abandoned with the lapse of time. In the tribal religions this cult of the dead is seen in a precisely parallel form but at a very much more matter of fact and materialistic stage of the development of the idea. Thus in Mysore the Hasalar tribe redeem the soul with a pig from the magician who has caused the death and domicile it in a pot where it is supplied with food and water. The Nicobarese and some Naga tribes fashion wooden figures on which the skull of the deceased is placed in order that the soul may leave it and enter the wooden figure. It is for a time kept supplied with all worldly necessities. A similar practice must formerly have obtained among the Garos of Assam, but it has disappeared and in the wooden figures now used the pegs that held the skull in place have become unrecognizable, surviving apparently as a sort of a pair of ornamental horns, though an obsolete grave figure in the Indian Museum in Calcutta has a pair of horns much more nearly approximating to the trans-frontier Konyak Naga type. Further west and south the Sawara of the Ganjam Agency tracts uses a similar but more conventionalised wooden figure to accommodate the soul of his cremated dead during the interval between death and cremation and the time for the erection of a stone or stones for the souls of the dead during the year past, which is done annually about the time of the sowing of the crop. Still further west the Kunbi of the Central Provinces make an image of their dead in brass which is kept until the

* This was written before Mr. Gandhi's fast, which has certainly given more impetus to the movement against untouchability, while the younger generation, students and schoolboys in particular, has for some time been manifestly more tolerant than their elders, particularly in Bengal and Assam.

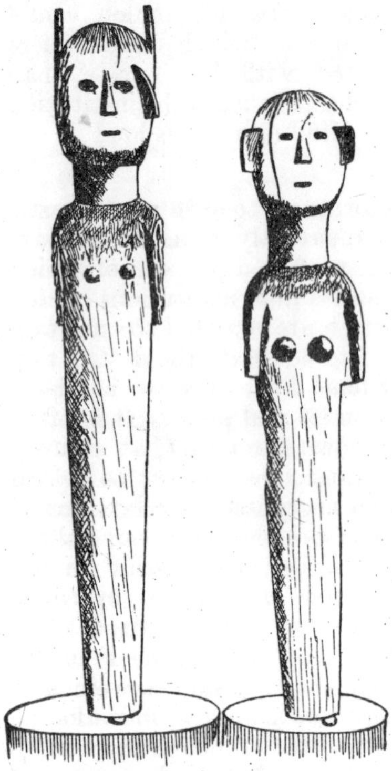

OBSOLETE TYPE OF GARO GRAVE FIGURE (KIMA)
From specimens now in the Indian Museum, Calcutta

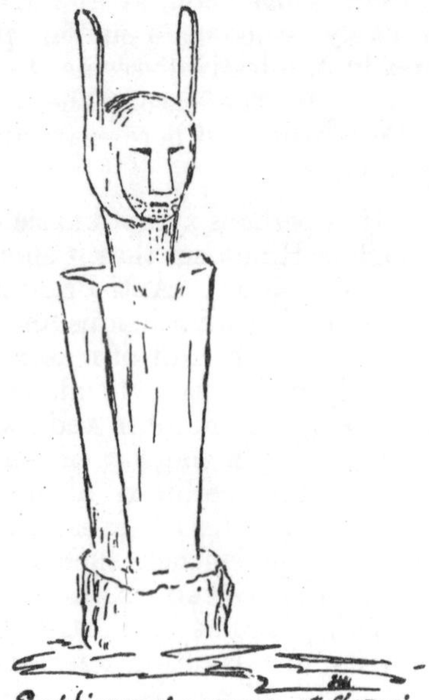

Soul-figure of a woman at Chongvi with horns for keeping her skull in place (Konyak Naga tribe).

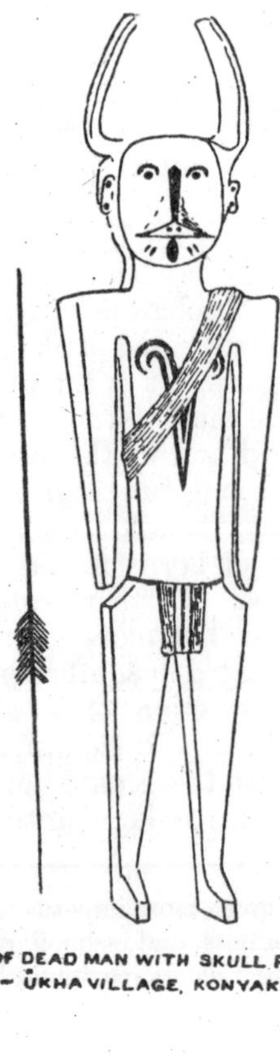

STATUE OF DEAD MAN WITH SKULL RECEPTACLE ON HEAD – ŪKHA VILLAGE, KONYAK NAGA.

Statue of Nicobarese with skull of deceased as head.
The wooden body serves as a cupboard for his bones.
Teressa Is. 1930.

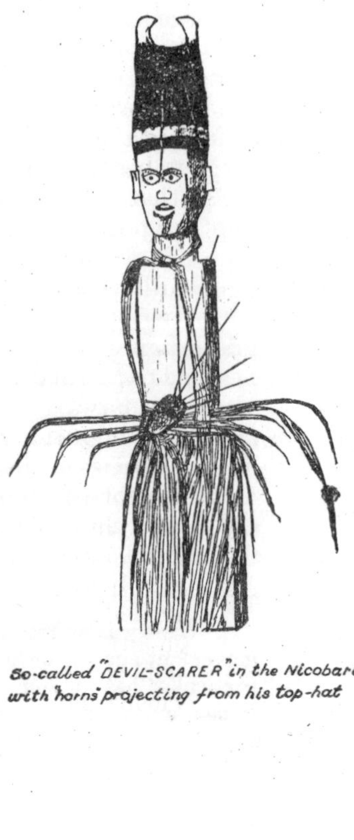

So-called "DEVIL-SCARER" in the Nicobars with "horns" projecting from his top-hat

superfluity of such images necessitates their deposit in the water of some sacred river. In the north the statues of the dead made by the head-hunting Kafirs of

Kafir memorial effigies, A & B male, C female, set up one year after death.
Sketched by the late General R.G. Woodthorpe at Apsai, Bashkol R. Kafiristan, 29th September, 1885.
(By the courtesy of Mr Henry Balfour)

the western Himalayas had probably the same purpose, while in western India may be seen the chattries of deceased Hindu Maratha rulers in which the recumbent bull and a lingam face the waxen images of the dead prince and his wife, which latter are piously supplied with food and other requisites and are entertained with music and have their clothes changed regularly once a week. In the very south of India the Malayarayans of Travancore make a metal effigy of the dead, which is kept in a miniature stone cist covered with a capstone (like the tattoed skull of a Konyak Naga in the north-east) and erected on high ground. The image is brought out annually and feasted and worshipped with tulsi leaves on its head.

Allusion* has already been made to the theory of soul-matter as a fertilizer of the crops and a producer of life generally, a theory which appears to pervade the magico-religious thought and practice throughout Indonesia and south-west Asia and survives in strength in further India. The Sawara custom above is probably a mere manifestation of the same idea, since the collective disposal of the village's dead at the time of sowing is clearly associated in some Naga tribes with their aspect as crop fertilizers, while the Oraons of Chota Nagpur again temporarily inter their dead, if the paddy has sprouted, to be cremated the following year before it sprouts. The connection between the souls of the dead and the fertilization of the ground is reflected again in their very frequent association with water. It is hardly necessary to call to mind the value set by Hindus upon the immersion of their dead in the Ganges, but there are a number of parallel beliefs in more or less primitive tribes which do not seem to owe their existence to Hindu influence but rather to share their origin with the ingredients of that religious system. Thus the Meithei practice of disposing of the frontal bone of the deceased in the Ganges appears, at first sight, to be the result of their Hinduization, and no doubt their choice of the Ganges is such a result, but their neighbours the Kacharis, when yet unhinduized, used to consign their frontal bone to the Kopili river after the harvest, while the Rengma Naga makes a pool for water at the grave of any notable man that the rain, and rice, may be plentiful, and at least one other Naga tribe pours water on a grave to cause rain, while the Palaungs of eastern Burma fetch a bier pole from a grave and put it in a stream for the same purpose. The Santal again have the practice, at any rate under certain circumstances, of consigning a piece of bone from the head and another from the breast of the dead to the waters of the Damodar river. The Panwar mourner, besides throwing into the Narbada the

* See above on page 398, and for an instance of such a specific theory page 409, below.

bones of the dead, throws in with them some of his own hair also, thus perhaps vicariously accompanying the soul. The Kunbi practice of consigning to the Ganges the brass images of his ancestors has already been mentioned and the Bishnoi Brahmans of Sind were described by Tod as burying their dead at their thresholds and raising over them small altars on which they place an image of Shiva (? a lingam) and a jar of water (*Rajasthan, VIII, ii*). Though nothing is said of any fertilizing effect these various practices would seem not unconnected. It is even possible that there may be some similar association with the dead or their avenging spirits in the ordeal by water described by Warren Hastings as practised by Hindus in the Ganges, the accused man submerging himself and holding to the foot of a Brahman, a form of ordeal parallels to which are practised by a number of primitive tribes from Western India to Vizagapatam and from the Central Provinces *via* Assam and Burma to Indo-China. Even in the Rigveda itself there seems to be some notion of the souls of the dead as departing to the waters or vegetation, in spite of the more definite and prevailing idea of a house of the dead, and in the later Vedic rite of *garbhadhana* to promote conception the husband infused grass in water and then poured the water down his wife's nostril, which looks as though it were intended that soul-matter from the grass should enter the woman to cause her to conceive.

The idea of soul-matter as a fertilizing agent is probably also responsible for distinctive treatment of the bodies of those who die by "bad" deaths and are therefore probably either unfertile or unsuitable or likely to lead to the reproduction of bad results. It is thus that we find everywhere special treatment accorded to the bodies of women who die in child-birth, while other forms of death are treated differently, *i.e.*, as bad or otherwise, by different tribes. In the case of persons killed by wild beasts the idea is perhaps the soul-stuff of the dead is absorbed by the wild animal, and this is illustrated by the widespread belief that the soul of the dead rides on the tiger, as told for instance by the Annamites of Cambodia and the Baigas of Central India. The idea that the soul of a person killed enters the killer is found elsewhere, *e.g.*, in Australia.

The same doctrine of soul-matter is probably the principle which underlies head-hunting, human sacrifice and cannibalism. The first of these has been recognised in India only in Kafiristan and in Assam, though it is reported of the Bhils that they were at one time accustomed to bring back the heads of their enemies and hang them up in trees (*Rajputana Census Report*, 1931), while the Kondhs circulated a head, hair and fingers as a signal for a rising in 1882, and of four heads taken in that rising one at any rate was "affixed as a trophy" to a tamarind tree near Billat village; again a Brahui clan explain their name of Sarparra as meaning 'decapitator' and have been identified with Strabo's "Saraparae, that is Decapitators" who lived near the Guranii and the Medes and were "savage intractable mountainy men" who "slash round the legs* and cut off the heads of strangers." The theory however on which it is based, that the soul-matter is specially located in the head, may be detected elsewhere. Thus the Andamanese attach special importance to the jaw† and to the skull in mourning, and at any rate one case is recorded of their carrying off the cranium of a victim killed in warfare. The Newars of Nepal apparently show traces of the separate treatment of the head in burial, a feature frequently associated with head-hunting in Assam, Indonesia and Oceania, Melanesia in particular, and undoubtedly based on the same idea. Head-hunting as a

---

* The generally preferred reading, *περισκυθιστάς* for *περισκελιστάς* is translated "scalp in the Scythian manner" but this is hardly compatible with decapitation, either would seem to be *ἅπαξ λεγόμενον* and the former reading is much more likely the emendation of a scholiast who knew his Herodotus, but was as unacquainted with what is a common feature of head-hunting practice as with the unusual word coined by Strabo to describe it; Casaubon indeed explains the name of the tribe as a facetious metaphor from Persian trousers (*σαράβαρα* = 'jodhpurs') 'diminishing at the knee.' A Naga headhunter who does not actually remove and suspend from the village head-tree the foot and leg of his victim will frequently slash the legs in order to entitle him to wear the embroidered gaiters of a warrior who has taken his enemy's legs, while some tribes on the north bank of the Brahmaputra are reported to cut off the hands and feet of their enemies (though they do not decapitate) probably to hamper possible attempts of the ghost to pursue and harm them.

† *N. B.*—Special importance often attaches to the lower jaw among head-hunters both in Asia and Africa and sometimes to the tongue which is regarded as the seat of life.

necessary preliminary to marriage, as it is in most if not all genuine head-hunting tribes, is to be explained by the idea that unless a man has taken heads he has no surplus soul-matter about him to beget offspring.* Probably the same notion is to be seen in the Chang Naga practice of naming a child after a village raided by his father. Thus the present chief of Yongemdi is named Longkhong and his brother Ongli after the Ao villages Lungkhung and Ungr which were successfully raided by their father with considerable slaughter about the time that they came respectively into this world. The same notion is clearly present in the cases that come to light from time to time in India of murder as a remedy for barrenness in women. Thus in October 1929 the High Court of the Punjab had to deal with a case in which a girl, desperately anxious to bear her husband a son, killed a child, cut off its hands and feet and bathed herself standing upon them. It cannot be doubted but that the idea was that the life of the dead child should become the life of a fresh child in her womb. Again early in 1930 a case occurred in Gujarat of the murder by means of sulphuric acid of a 12 months old boy by a girl of 20 who had no child, and it was part of the prosecution case that it was a comparatively common practice on the part of barren women to attempt to quicken themselves by burning marks on children in the street, a practice no doubt ultimately derived from one which involved the taking of the child's life, and which may be compared with that of branding children offered to the Syrian Goddess referred to below (page 411). And if head-hunting is rare in India, human sacrifice, on the other hand, has been widespread and has clearly been ultimately based on the same conception of the necessity or at any rate the desirability of releasing soul-matter to fertilize the earth. No doubt it was later interpreted as the placation or propitiation of an earth deity, but this must be regarded as a sophisticated justification of a practice the true meaning of which had become obscure or been forgotten. The Kondhs are described as having performed their Meriah sacrifices to the earth mother, but the details of the ceremony and the practice of distributing fragments of the sacrificial meat in their fields and granaries show a very patent connection with the disposal of enemy flesh by head-hunting Nagas and the underlying idea is undoubtedly the same. In one form of the sacrifice the victim was squeezed to death in a cleft in a green tree, and in another the tears caused by his sufferings brought rain in proportion to their profusion. Similarly the Wa of Burma definitely associate their head-hunting with the sowing of the crop, while the successful Kafir head-hunter was greeted, on his return from the foray with his trophy, by a shower of grain. In Kulu the transplanting of the rice is accompanied by the sacrifice of a rough dough image of a man to the house god. So again the Dasehra festival, now associated by all Hindus with the killing of Ravana by Rama, coincides throughout most of India with the sowing of the winter crops, in particular with that of millet, a more ancient staple in south Asia than rice, as well as with that of wheat. It is this festival that is associated in western India with the worship of weapons of war (and it is still regarded there as a proper day on which to go forth and loot) while it is then that human sacrifices used to be performed in eastern India, and it is still on this festival that the *gupta puja*, the hidden rite, to ensure the prosperity of the person, house or family, would be resorted to if ever. The association of human sacrifice with the prosperity of the individual and with the success of the state in war seems clear enough, and its association with crops may be inferred with equal safety. It was probably some such association of soul-substance with fertility and perhaps with some notion of a higher fertility value attaching to Europeans that led Oraons to remove portions of the body of a recently buried European not very long ago. The evidence at the trial made it clear that special value attached to European bones for magical purposes (see *Indian Antiquary*, Dec. 1929). The location of the soul in the head and the confusion of the soul with the shadow are illustrated in the Himalayan cure for fever in which the patient stands in the sun and a bone filled with grain is buried in the spot where the head of the shadow falls (Crooke, *Religion and Folklore of N. India*, 1926, page 222). The same idea of soul-matter as a fertiliser is probably at the bottom of human sacrifice as a cure for illness, as in the case of a Santal of Dhanbad who in 1931 garlanded and then beheaded his infant son in order to effect a cure of his own maladies.

---

* Conversely I have known a Brahman gardener in the Simla Hills refrain from setting grafts himself since to do so would prejudice his chance of begetting children, clearly on account of the loss of life-matter; instead he called in an old man past the breeding age to do it for him.

True cannibalism is only traditional in India but vestiges of ceremonial cannibalism survive in many places or have done until recently. Thus Portman records the practice of Andamanese homicides, who drank of the blood and ate of the raw fat of the victim and of the flesh of his breast, the latter apparently cooked. In the north-west the Kafirs used to eat a piece of the heart and drink some of the blood of their enemies they killed. In the north-east the Lushei of Assam used to taste the liver and lick from the spear-head the blood of the first victim slain in war. The nearly related Thado eats his first meal after taking life with hands deliberately imbued with his enemy's blood and still uncleansed therefrom, a custom practised as late as 1919, and the same custom obtains in a decayed form among the independent Semas of the Assam frontier, where a returning head-taker must eat at least a morsel of food before entering his village ; the insistence is on the meal now, but it is eaten with still ensanguined fingers as he may not cleanse himself until after he has taken this meal. The intention in all these cases is certainly to transfer to the slayer the soul-matter or life-matter of the slain, just as the soul-matter of so many kings has been transferred to their successors by their murder. Similar in principle is the practice of anointing at his succession the intrusive Rajput ruler with the blood of the indigenous Bhil who regards the right to give it as a precious privilege, even though the giver is believed always to die within the year, his soul-matter exhausted no doubt in providing for the fertility and prosperity of the State. It was no doubt a similar idea to that of the Kafir and the Thado which inspired the action of Nana Pharari, a notorious dacoit of Nasik in Bombay Presidency who stabbed a personal enemy in July 1930, pulled out his knife from the victim and applied its gory blade to his forehead and to his tongue. The action of applying the blood to the forehead offers a very close parallel to that of the Angami Naga who never drinks liquor without applying on the tips of his finger a drop to his forehead for the benefit of the material soul resident within. The drinking of human blood and the tasting of human flesh is common in Indonesia and Oceania and it is likely that it has at one time been more prevalent in India than it is now. It was reported of the Wa of Burma by Sir George Scott that probably human flesh was eaten on special occasions, possibly at the harvest festival. The Wa are also credited by the Shans with eating their dead relatives like the Battak of Sumatra, and this, a practice probably arising rather from a belief in reincarnation than directly from that in life or soul-matter, has also been reported of some tribes in India. Thus Herodotus mentions the Callatians as an Indian tribe known by Darius to practise this, and he attributes the same custom to the Padaei, for whom an identification has been suggested with the Birhor of Chota Nagpur whom Dalton states to have admitted its former pratice by their tribes. The same custom has been likewise attributed to the Lobas of north-east Assam (called Mishu Ting Ba by the Tibetans) in particular, to the hill tribes of Chhattisgarh and of the Amarkantak tableland, as to the hill tribes of Assam, in general, and to some of the transfrontier Kachins of north-west Burma, though in these cases there is no well authenticated evidence. A possible survival of the same practice is to be found in the Kharia custom in the Central Provinces of catching, and eating communally, a fish on the third day after a person's death, the fish being a common vehicle of the soul as is noted elsewhere in this chapter. All this points to some pre-existence of this practice and to a clear cultural link between the more primitive tribes of India and those of the Indian archipelago.

Perhaps the crudest form in which the doctrine of soul substance appears is the vulgar but widely credited superstition which attributes to the European the practice of catching fat black boys and hanging them by the heels over a slow fire to distil from a puncture in the skull the seven drops of vital essence which imparts to sahibs in general their energy in field sports and their activity of mind and body. Curiously enough this life essence, this *momiyai*, seems to have started as bitumen simply and to have been used as a quite legitimate medicine, then to have become a spurious substitute in the form of resin, the supposed virtues of which were later attributed by confusion to the embalmed bodies from which this resin was most readily obtained. From the dead body a fourth transfer has taken place and superstition now imputes the virtue of the medicine to its distillation from the living body in the form of its life-essence. This belief caused several harmless strangers to be beaten in Saharanpur recently on the suspicion that they were manufacturers of this elixir. Enthoven mentions that it gave some trouble in the outbreak of plague in 1896 in Bombay, and the belief is clearly still active. Possibly it has some bearing on the reluctance felt in India to remain in a hospital. Here again it is by Hindus, or persons classified as such, that this superstition is generally held, and the Kabuli trader who brings *momiyai* for sale from Afghanistan is probably under no delusion as to its composition or virtue. The theory is also to be seen in the Aghoripanth philosophy (Russell, *Tribes and Castes of the C. P.*, Vol. II) and in occasional cases of cannibalism that come to light in the criminal courts. Thus in September 1931 two men, one apparently a Rarhi Brahman ascetic and the other a Mahabrahman were accused in Bankura of having dug up the newly buried corpse of a child, of having taken it to their *asram* and of having there cooked and eaten part of it ; the Rarhi Brahman admitted having eaten a little of the heart " as he believed it was a part of his religion to do so". It is perhaps partly due to the influence of the primitive belief in this life-giving soul-matter that so much importance is attached in India to the reproduction of the species to pass it on reduplicated to the next generation, so that the penalty of failure to marry is among the more primitive tribes extinction at the hands of a demon who bars the pathway of the dead, while among a number of Hindu castes, as also among the Todas of southern India, the corpse of a person dying unmarried is married before cremation as a necessary qualification to future happiness. The doctrine of soul-substance as a fertiliser is naturally not less applicable to animals than to human beings, and it is therefore not surprising to find the Malas of southern India and Ahirs at the Gaidaur festival causing their cattle—the young in particular—to trample a pig to death, after which according to the ancient custom, the corpse of the pig is eaten by the Ahirs who thus share in the transfer of the porcine life-substance to their cattle. In the case of the Koravas, who have a similar practice, an instance of the substitution of a human being for the more usual pig is actually on record (Thurston, *Castes and Tribes of South India*, III, 463 sq.), the unfortunate having been buried to his neck before the cattle were driven over him.

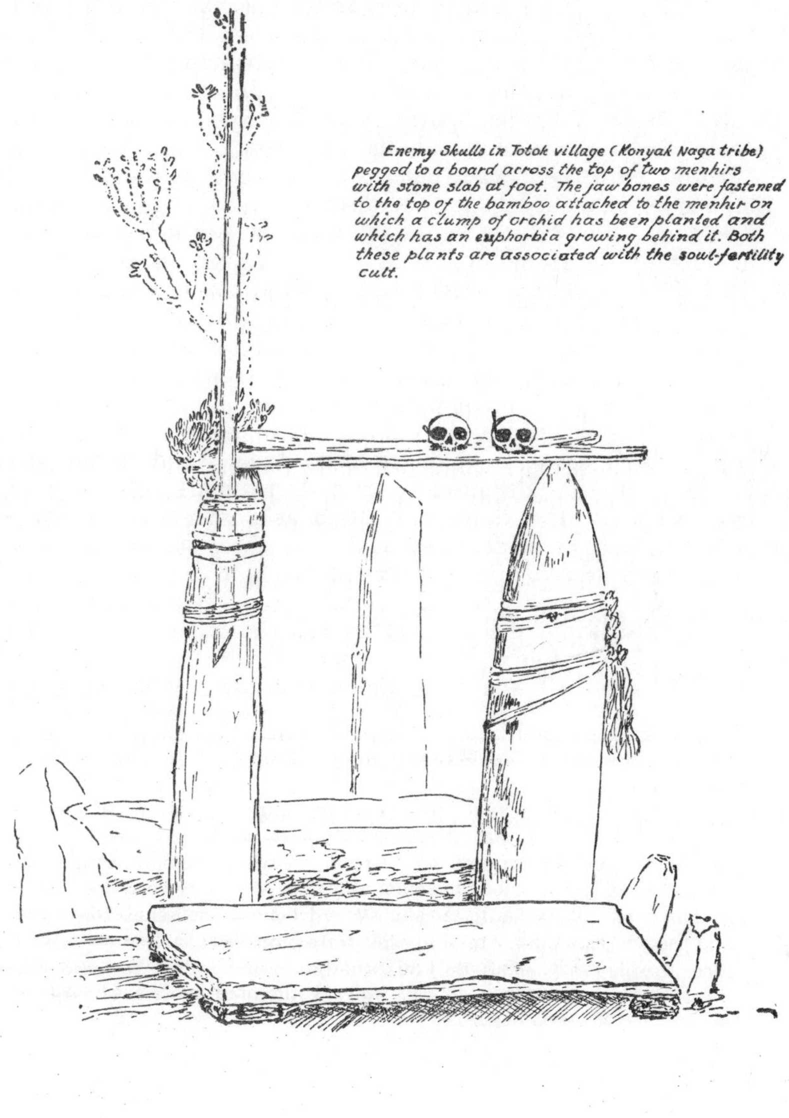

Involved again in the belief in soul-matter probably is the practice of erecting megalithic monuments and wooden images of the dead. The two practices are not completely separable as both appear primarily to be intended to afford a temporary dwelling for the soul pending its operation as a fertilizer of the crop. The megalithic monument appears very often as merely a permanent substitute for the impermanent wooden statue which can be given greater resemblance to the human body. Thus the wooden statues of the dead put up by the Angami Nagas of Assam are in some villages destroyed after the harvest and the others have a small stone erected behind them to do duty when they have perished. In other villages again a man's youngest son succeeding to his father's house must put up a monolith for his deceased parents, an act corresponding to that of some other villages in which the monoliths are erected during their lifetime by specially prosperous persons to enhance the prosperity of the community as a whole. The significance of the latter monolith is quite definitely phallic and ancient specimens still exist whose form puts this beyond dispute, both as a solid menhir and as hollow monoliths which contained the ashes of the dead, and there is no doubt but the association is here again with the soul-matter as a fertility agent, and an echo of the doctrine is perhaps to be found in the Vijayanagara legend of the head of the hero Ramanatha which when returned to Kummata became united with the *lingam* of Shiva. It may be noted that Kampila, the defender of Kummata appears, or at least his troops do, under the guise of head-hunters (*Journal of the Mythic Society*, January 1930), while dolmens have actually been used as Saivite temples; in the Naga Hills the cult of head-hunting is, like that of the dead, associated with menhirs and dolmens and other symbols of fertility like the milky *ficus* or *euphorbia* trees. The remains of this megalithic culture in India are widespread though in most places completely decadent, and they generally show sporadically very similar traits. Thus the disposal of the dead of the community during the sowing season has already been mentioned and in further India it is, or used to be, associated with a certain amount of mummification of the dead to make them keep, some tribes, *e.g.*, the Ao Nagas smoke-drying the body, others *e.g.*, the Khasis, embalming it in honey. The use of a soul-figure is merely a different method of obtaining the same end, and by the Konyak Naga of Assam a wooden figure is provided to house the soul until the head can be separated and disposed of in a phallic stone cist. The Sawara of the Ganjam Agency in Madras burn their dead, but a wooden figure is provided to house the soul till the erection of monoliths for the dead which takes places annually about the time of sowing. Soul-figures, probably of similar purpose in the first instance, are made in earth by the Handi Jogi of Mysore. The Nicobarese, like some Nagas, place the skull of the dead on a wooden body, and at this census such a figure was to be seen on the island of Teressa, the skull doing duty as a head incongruously surmounted by an old top hat, the treasured headgear of the dead man. It is impossible not to see the same idea underlying the waxen figures of deceased Hindu princes already referred to accompanied as they are by a stone lingam. It seems therefore not unlikely that the carved stones erected to the memory of Rajput dead of both sexes have a similar origin, and table stones may occasionally be seen in Rajputana erected to mark the site of a *Sati*, recalling the fact that the dolmen is used as a memorial of the dead by the Munda of Chota Nagpur, while by some Assam tribes the upright monolith and recumbent dolmen are used to correspond respectively to the male and to the female sexes. A reference to Volume IX of the Bombay Gazetteer definitely confirms the supposition that the Rajput memorial stone has the same origin as the Naga or Khasi menhir. Unhewn stones (*khatra*) or carved stones are raised, we learn, by most classes of Hindus in Gujarat for deceased persons, sometimes for all, but more particularly for those that have died a violent death* or been remarkable

* The Census Superintendent of Madras may be conveniently quoted here on similar practices in South India :—

> "*Pudams* or shrines exist to which no priests or temples are attached and the prevailing worship is in fact a kind of goblin propitiation, the goblins being usually the spirits of persons who died a violent death. Animal sacrifice and frequent admixture of human blood are commonplaces in their ceremonies. One such shrine in Tinnevelly district is to the spirit of a European killed in the Travancore wars and the offerings made are of articles considered peculiarly acceptable to one of his race, bread, fowls, cheroots and brandy......In effect the real religion of the presidency, in the south, at any rate, is directed rather towards shrines and saints than towards deities."

for their holiness*. These stones are sometimes placed in a shrine, sometimes under a pipal tree. Until the shrine is set up the spirit of the deceased is dangerous. We may perhaps infer that the reason why such stones are set up, particularly for persons whose spirits are likely to be dangerous, is in order to appease them by providing an abiding place for them and so conforming to an ancient custom otherwise liable to be foregone. The carved stones take the ordinary form of a Rajputana or Kathiawar memorial stone or may be replaced by " a bust of black marble, brick or wood " but it is significant that they are worshipped by the newly married, or by a bridegroom on the way to fetch the bride, recalling the ceremony performed by childless Konyak Nagas on their phallic stone skull cists, and the practice of barren women to strip themselves at dawn and embrace naked the stone slab carved with the image of Hanuman†. At certain temples in southern India barren women are or were seated astride a particular stone to get offspring, success depending upon the experience of an orgasm while in this position. In the Punjab hills again, Chamba for instance, monoliths, or wooden substitutes, are put up for the dead with feasting on a great scale, and for the sake of acquiring merit. A rough effigy of the deceased is usually carved on the stone and the wooden substitute sometimes has a hole and a spout for water, when it is set up in the stream beside which it would otherwise be placed. Sometimes a circular stone is placed on the top of the monolith (recalling the former Khasi practice) and in the case of ruling families (*e.g.* of Mandi and Suket, where the practice is confined to royalty) the wife and concubine of the deceased are also represented on the stones as they are by Assam hill tribes. The Malayarayans of Travancore make a metal effigy of the

Memorial stones in Chamba State placed in a water course.

dead and put it into a miniature cist of stone verticals and a capstone which is erected on high ground and worshipped annually. Even the method of transporting

*" The spirit of Muhammad even is said to inform one granite pillar in Tinnevelly where daily " puja " is done by Hindu votaries. Vows are made to it by Hindus who flock to seek cure of disease, rain and other boons. Ganja and cheroots are the form the offerings take, these being considered peculiarly attractive to Muhammadans " (M. W. M. Yeatts, *Madras Census Report*, 1931).

† One may compare with these practices that of embracing a certain pillar in the church of the Virgin at Orcival in Auvergne or sitting in the chair of St. Fiacre in the church of the village of that name, the stone seat of which, like the pillar at Orcival, had the power of rendering barren women fertile. It was necessary, however, that there should be no garment between the stone and the sitter's body. Similarly in the chapel of St. Antoine de Paule at Saragossa there was a tombstone on which barren women lay in order to become fruitful. (Dulaure, *Des Divinités Génératrices*, page 251).

megaliths seems to have left traces in western India. The Nagas, like the people of Nias in the Indian archipelago, transport megaliths on wooden sledges made from the forked trunk of a tree which are dragged by very large numbers of men pulling on cane or creeper ropes. In the case of the Naga at any rate an essential implication of the ceremony is the infection of the village with the prosperity of the celebrant, and when the ceremony is performed with wooden instead of stone emblems these emblems are formally dragged all round the village with this express purpose. Very suggestive of a degenerate form of this ceremony is the village festival (*ghasbavji*) in Rajputana at which the "god", consisting of a large waterworn boulder, is dragged round the village on a sled made out of a forked tree trunk. Probably of similar origin also is the general veneration paid to stones throughout India, particularly of course to those of queer or unusual shape. Crooke (in *The Religion and Folklore of Northern India*) gives a very large number of examples which it is unnecessary to recapitulate, but it may be recorded here that a suit was argued in the Calcutta High Court on the 25th of April 1929 about a stone about 5 feet square, apparently of black slate or marble from Jaipur, which changed hands for Rs. 10,000 (£750) as being "very efficacious in the matter of getting a son". The suit arose because the stone failed to function, and it was stated in evidence that numbers of even quite well-educated Hindus believed in the efficacy of stones of this kind when used with the correct rites, and that so much as a lakh might be paid for such a stone. It was also mentioned that sitting on a stone is an essential feature in many Jain rites.

It may here be urged that the reverence and superstition paid to stones in general, is not, as Crooke suggests, a vague supersitition which develops into the use of memorial stones but on the contrary is the degenerated remnant of the life-essence fertility cult. The use of a stone or mere pebble as a *pretyasila* "stone of the disembodied spirit" by Hindus in western India seems a definite instance of this process of decay. The stone is picked up by the chief mourner at the place where the corpse was put down and is anointed with oil (recalling the baetyls of Naga fertility cults), a crow is induced to eat corn scattered about it and the pebble is then thrown into running water or kept among the household deities. Similarly the Komati caste of Mysore invokes the soul of the deceased to enter a pebble temporarily, while the ashes of the deceased are cast into a sacred river or some other water. It seems therefore much more likely that a veneration of stones on account of the indwelling soul has been transferred to peculiar stones in general on account of similar possibilities, than that a vague reverence of stones should exist without reason and be elaborated into a coherent creed which really turns on a belief in the power of soul-matter to promote the fertility of nature. An extension of the same idea would seem to appear in the practice of requiring spirit or soul-matter of the dead to impart permanence or, to use our own metaphor, "life" to buildings. This practice is referred to as that of foundation "sacrifices", but the idea of sacrifice, if present at all, is clearly later than the practice itself, which is essentially of the same origin in India, where at least a belief in the necessity survives, and in Oceania, where in Fiji and in the Marquesas, for instance, human sacrifices were required to invest a building or a canoe with the necessary *mana*. This belief is still so prevalent in India as to be the cause of a good deal of disturbance from time to time. In 1922 the Deputy Commissioner of Dibrugarh had to issue a notice reassuring people against *mur katas* (= "headcutters") coming to kill or behead male children for some unkown purpose and to threaten with prosecution anyone assisting to spread the rumour. In 1923 on the 27th May a riot took place on Cinnamara tea estate on account of a scare about the kidnapping of children for the foundation of a new bridge. In June 1924 a rumour in Calcutta that the Port Commissioners were seeking for children to bury in the foundation of the new Kidderpore dockyard led to Punjabi taxidrivers being killed in the belief that they were agents decoying children for this purpose, and in the same month strangers in Patna were maltreated in connection with a similar scare about a bridge in Bihar. In 1926 in north Lakhimpur there was a rumour that *arkas* (*i.e.*, head-takers ?) were trying to obtain children's heads for the construction of a railway bridge. In the same year the district engineeer constructing the recent bridge on the Sibsagar Road-Khowang Railway had trouble from a kidnapping scare, which was so much intensified when a retaining wall burst that schoolboys asked leave in order to stay at home for fear of being kidnapped on their way to school. Several petitions were filed in the

S. D. O.'s office, also against suspected kidnappers, while villagers insisted on visiting and counting tea-garden coolies during the night in order to assure themselves that they were not concealing victims in their lines, and a number of assaults took place, one serious. In July of the same year there was a scare in Cachar that a human sacrifice was required for the oil-borings to promote the flow of oil in the Burmah Oil Company's wells. A strange coolie was roughly handled on the 12th of that month in Cachar and a stranger from Sylhet was beaten and confined on the same suspicion on the 10th. In January 1929 a rumour in Bombay that children were being kidnapped for the construction of a bridge in Baroda led to an attack on Pathans, and on a Greek engineer, to the death of a Hindu carpenter and ultimately during two days time to the killing of 17 Pathans while two other Muslims and three Hindus were killed in the consequent affrays, very many other persons being injured. In the subsequent riots 149 people were killed and the damage to property came to at least 5 lakhs of rupees. In May 1929, in Bihar again this time, a man was beaten to death in the belief that he was seeking to kidnap a child as a "foundation sacrifice" for a bridge at Jamshedpur, while the floods in the Surma valley of the same year led to a scare that children were being kidnapped for the reconstruction of certain embankments in the Manipur State. In certain tribes of the Naga Hills in Assam a live chicken is still placed in the hole dug for the main house post and the post stepped on to it, while it is asserted that certain transfrontier tribes use a human being thus, as formerly in Fiji, "to hold up the post". The same idea is to be seen in a practice attributed by Mr. S. N. Roy, (in *Man in India*, IX, page 272) to Bengali boat-builders who have had to dispute their dues with a customer; a few drops of the ship-wright's blood are plugged into a cavity in the planking, when the boat acquires a malevolent vitality, drowns its crew and continues an independent existence as an aquatic phantom. A sword used in sacrifice acquires a similar vitality from the blood of the victims it decapitates, and like boats it is furnished with eyes painted in vermilion.

It has been already indicated that the soul is often conceived in the tribal religions of India as having the form of a manikin and being located in the head, and though this conception is apparently at conflict with the theory of soul-matter or a material life-substance it is held concurrently with it without any consciousness of inconsistency. There is nothing remarkable in this, but the question arises whether these two conceptions are of different origin or may have come into being from the same source, and it is here submitted that the conception of the soul as a manikin is merely the effect, on a rather vague conception as to the nature of life, of that tendency towards anthropomorphism which is inevitable when man is to conceive of a material with some of his own attributes and no known shape and which is apparent in the conception of the deity in the great majority of religions. The Karen of Burma have a doctrine of a material substance which is the cause of life, or rather which is actually life itself, a sort of ectoplasm of life, which leaves the dying body to enter the herbs of the field or the seeds of the earth, and which then passes through grass into cattle and through grain, or indirectly through the meat of grazing animals, into man and passes through the seminal fluid to generate fresh life, precisely as if it consisted of carbohydrates*. This doctrine may perhaps be regarded as having arisen very early in the history of mankind as a natural result of speculation as to the cause of the change that takes place at death and as to the nature of that which has left the body. Speculation of some kind would be inevitable, if only as a result of the natural curiosity required by any animal, human or otherwise, to adapt itself to environment in the struggle to survive. Abstract ideas come late in the development of a language and presumably therefore late in the development of thought, and hence the necessity, before any philosophic idea of life can be framed, of regarding it as a material substance and of thinking of that substance as taking some form. The idea then of a manikin living behind the forehead whose movements are registered on an infant's fontanelle is a not unnatural symptom of the development, or degeneration, of the life-substance theory and may perhaps be traced in that doctrine of the Vedanta school of Hindu philosophy which regards the soul as encased in a series of sheaths the interior of which accompany the soul on its migration while the exterior constitutes the material body; and the location

* It seems certain that the strange provision in the Brahmanical code which makes the Telis an untouchable caste (but not the Tili, who only sells not presses oil) is due to their practice of destroying the seed in the pursuit of their occupation without provision for its transfer to another living organism, a suggestion confirmed, I think, by Manu, *iv.* 85.

of the soul in the head is illustrated by the Hindu belief that it escapes through the "crevice of Brahma", through which ascetics can project their soul (and so die) at will, while for less holy persons it is necessary to fracture the skull with a conch shell to let out the soul. The *salagrama* held to the aperture perhaps served the same purpose as the *pretyasila* mentioned above. One is also reminded of the story in the Aitareya Brahmana (*vide* Rajendralala Mitra, *Indo-Aryans*, II, 76) of how the gods killed a man for their sacrifice, but the part in him fit for an offering went out, leaving him deformed, and entered a horse, and so on through an ox (which turned to a gayal when the fit part left it), a sheep and a goat and entered the earth, where the gods surrounded it so that no escape was possible, when it turned into rice. Father Schmidt considers that in India "the materialistic Sankhyan philosophy most certainly arose from matrilineal animism," and he suggests that the spiritual philosophies of classical Greece may have had at least in part a similar source. Having got as far as materializing our life principle, its conception as similar in feature to that of the body is inescapable, and the way is clear for the doctrine of reincarnation. The doctrine reached is logically irreconcilable with the theory with which we started but experience shows that the two can be held simultaneously, at any rate by primitive man, without any consciousness of inconsistency. There are probably, however, steps by the way which contribute to this belief—the idea of the soul coming back as an insect is one, and one to which the conception of the soul as able to leave the body and flit about at night, derived in part no doubt if not entirely from the phenomena of dreams, has contributed. As instances the Lhota Nagas of Assam and the Kunbis of Bombay and the Kamis of Bengal may all be quoted as watching for an insect after a person's death, or the Ahirs, Kamars and Gonds who go to a river and bring back an insect or a fish as containing the soul and sometimes, in the case of the Gonds at least, eat it to ensure its rebirth. Another contributory observation to the insect notion is perhaps the mysterious way in which large numbers of insects appear from nowhere in particular, as if caused by superfluity as it were of life-substance, an idea which would have been comprehensible enough to the ancient world, which regarded for instance insect life as spontaneously engendered in dung dropped under a waxing moon, etc. (*vide* Pliny, *Nat. Hist.*, Bk. II), or which regarded the Nile floods as pouring soul into the sods so as to fashion live creatures from the very soil (*Nilus . . . . . glaebis etiam infundat animas, ex ipsaque humo vitalia effingat*—Pomponius Mela, I, 52), bringing us back again to that fertility cult which associates soul with water. Similarly Diodorus Siculus (I, *i*) says "moisture generates creatures from heat, as from a seminal principle" and a little further on "they say that about Thebes in Egypt, after the overflowing of the river Nile, the earth thereby being covered with mud and slime, many places putrefy through the heat of the sun, and thence are bred multitudes of mice. It is certain, therefore, that out of the earth . . . . animals are generated". These ideas of life in dung and water seem to have been combined in the practice which so disgusted the Abbé Dubois at the temple of Nanjanagud in Mysore some 150 years ago. Barren women and their husbands were described by him as drinking out of the temple sewer from hands soiled by setting aside a portion of the ordure to be examined a few days later whether insects or vermin were engendered in it, which was regarded as "a favourable prognostic for the woman". The same belief probably accounts for the practice of throwing dung at a bridal pair, a practice common for instance in the Assam Hills. Whatever be its origin, however, a vague belief in reincarnation is common to most of the tribal religions in India and is generally associated more or less with some degree of ancestor worship, a tendency to which is everywhere apparent. This reincarnation belief is to be seen very clearly in the ancient Brahmanic theory that after the birth of a son the sexual relationship of husband and wife should cease, since the son is the father's self and the father's wife has become his mother also. It is stated of the Kochhar sub-caste of the Khatri, a trading caste of the Punjab, that a father's funeral rites are performed in the fifth month of his wife's first pregnancy, which points to the same idea. The Bishnoi of Hissar bury an infant at the threshold that its soul may re-enter the mother and be born again. Among the Bhuiyas every child is regarded as a reincarnation of some deceased relative, while the Mikirs, it may be noticed, believe in reincarnation except for the souls of those who have been killed by tigers. Among the Lushei the reincarnated soul sometimes appears as a hornet, sometimes as dew and in the latter form the belief is hardly distinguishable from the Karen theory of life substance. So again it is a common practice with the tribes mentioned that while a dead grandfather's name or that of another ancestor must be given to a child, the name of a living ancestor shall not be given as either he or the new born child will die. The practice was perhaps similar in ancient Indian society as in old lists of kings it is common to find a grandson named after the grandfather. This practice seems, however, to have changed as the name of any ancestor living or dead is reported now to be avoided by Hindus.

The association of reincarnation with the soul fertility cult is perhaps confirmed to some extent by Malcolm's record of the practice of jumping off certain high rocks in Central India in order to be reborn in a royal house. Forsyth (*Highlands of Central India*) also records the account of an eyewitness, Captain Douglas, Political Assistant in Nimar, of a scene at Omkar, a shrine of Shiva on Mandhatta island in the Narbada, at which a young man leaped off a rock 90 ft. high to his death in 1822, and mentions a later case of an old woman who hesitated and was pushed over. In the case of this rock apparently if the jumper survived, he was killed by a "priestess" with a dagger, but in the case of another of these rocks if a man survived the fall he was made Raja and the association between the soul and the fertility of the land impinges on that between the fertility of the land and the king as the living receptacle or embodiment of the life-spirit, and one which must not be allowed to grow old. One is reminded, however, by this habit of jumping off a cliff to royal incarnation of a number of similar practices associated in each case with the fertility of the soil.* Thus rope-sliding (*beduart*) in the Himalayas would appear to be a definite survival of a similar form of voluntary or involuntary human sacrifice. The slider, an acrobat or dancer (*beda*) by caste, is worshipped as Mahadeo, bathed in milk, dressed in new clothes, and carried round the village fields before the ceremony, which is resorted to when harvests have been bad. That this is a survival of human sacrifice is clearly indicated by the fact that both the rope used and the hair of the slider are distributed as fertility charms while the slider himself becomes infertile, for his fields go barren and the seed he sows fails to burgeon. He is in fact spiritually dead† and his life-matter has been distributed to his neighbours. We are recalled to the Kondh *meriah* whose parent was consoled by his neighbours in words which Macpherson has recorded—"Your child has died that all the world may live". It is worth remarking that the hereditary caste of rope-sliders is the Nat caste and that the women of that caste are associated in many parts of India with dancing and prostitution. Both are probably closely connected with fertility rites and it may be that the professions of tight-rope walker, acrobat, dancer and prostitute take their origin in services performed primarily for the benefit of the crops. In former days it is said that the slider who fell off the rope was cut to pieces at the bottom, and the rite as a whole suggests a chastened form of human sacrifice in which it was essential that the victim should fall from a great height. It recalls insistently the ceremony described as practiced at the temple of the Syrian Goddess where from a very lofty porch between two gigantic phalli the animal or sometimes apparently human victims were hurled to the ground and where worshippers let their children down in a sack aft er branding them (*cf. supra* p. 403) as devoted to the deity. In the northeast corner of India the Angami Naga still hurls from the roof of a house his sacrificial victim, a puppy dog invested with the symbolic attributes of a man, while a calf released below is literally torn to pieces by the crowd. Meanwhile ashes representing clouds and cotton seeds representing hail are thrown by the priest from the roof, clearly showing that not only is a distribution of the victims' life-essence involved but a fall of fertilizing water probably intended to be magically ensured by a fall of the victim from above.

One phenomenon of primitive religion which cannot be ignored when writing of India is totemism, traces of which are shown by primitive tribes in all parts of India and by not a few castes that have reached or retained a high social position. From the Bhils in the west to the Wa of eastern Burma; from the

* Tod (*Annals*, XI, ch. iv) says "love of off-spring" is the motive, but he does not explain and one is almost inclined to suspect him of facetiousness.

† Like the Maithil Brahman mentioned by Wilson (*Indian Caste*, II, 194), who was outcasted by his family because he recovered after his funeral ceremonies had actually been performed in expectation of his decease, and like the Bhil referred to above (p. 1) who dies within a year of the use of his blood to anoint his lord as king.

Kanets of the Simla hills to members of Telugu castes of southern India, clear traces of totemism are found to survive, and it is needless here to go into details already sufficiently well-known and recorded. It may be enough to recall "the longtailed Ranas of Saurasthra", Jethwa Rajputs who claim descent from Hanuman, and the ruler of the Malabar coast whose death involves abstention from fishing lest the soul-inhabited fish be captured, to show that totemistic ideas are not entirely confined to primitive tribes and to castes low in the social scale. Various theories have been put forward to account for totemism of which the most satisfactory is Sir James Frazer's "conceptional" theory. His position, put briefly, is that a period must have existed in human history when the function of the male in producing offspring was as yet unrecognised; consequently the female on consciousness of conception sought for a cause to explain the phenomenon and attributed it to some animal or plant. Clearly we need not, indeed cannot, suppose that the existing beliefs of the Australian tribes, on which Sir James bases his diagnosis, represent the belief in totem birth in its original form, and assuming that his theory is correct we may probably imagine conception as first attributed to something eaten, touched or even merely seen by the conceiving woman. Granting the coexistence of the soul-matter theory of life and death and the inclusion in that theory of plants or fruit, it would be easy to speculate as to the source of the new life within the womb from soul-matter taken in food. In any case ignorance of paternity can hardly have lasted for a very long period in most branches of the human race, and in the well-known instance of the Trobriand Islands Moubray (*Matriarchy in the Malay Peninsula*, p. 53) has plausibly argued that the Trobrianders' emphatic denial of the father's share in procreation is the result of a decay of society starting from the point of development at which matriliny was about to swing over patriliny. Be that as it may, it is obvious that once the idea of totemism be started it would be kept alive and fed by ideas and sentiments not adequate in themselves perhaps to start the theory. The psychological considerations sometimes urged as causes of totemism cannot be regarded as the actual causes since ideas must have some ultimate reference to observed experience, but they will contribute to the retention of an idea which would not otherwise survive.

Frazer himself has pointed out the theory of the external soul as apparently responsible for some forms which, if not actually totemism, resemble it so closely as makes no matter; and while it has been recently argued by an American anthropologist that totemism arises from food restrictions, others have traced it to theories of the transmigration of soul. Bullock (*Man*, *XXXI*, 185) regards totemism as developing subsequently to exogamy and as being merely the machinery by which exogamy is implemented. This conclusion is based on a study of the institutions of the Mashona, where, he says, "the connection between totemism and exogamy is undoubted". This, however, does not prove that such a connection always existed, since no society is in a static condition and an accidental coincidence may easily develop into a coalescence. Durkheim with greater plausibility (*L'année sociologique*, vol. i) regards totemism as the cause of a taboo on incest and consequently as the cause of exogamy. It is simplest, perhaps, to accept Frazer's view of the origin of totemism and to regard the other explanations as having contributed to extend or support the belief after a period at which the observation of the fact of paternity would otherwise have put a natural end to it. If it so happened that exogamy originated at an early totemic period of the human race, it is natural to find it surviving where totemism survives either in some semblance of its earliest form as a conception theory or in a developed form into which other beliefs have entered. Such a view of totemism also agrees with the extreme variety of its manifestations, ranging from the sacramental consumption of the totem or its use for magical augmentation of the food supply, to the merest peg for exogamy to hang upon, and it is in the latter form that it is commonest in India where it has generally decayed into a mere totemistic clan name. There are, however, traces of taboos and beliefs essential to it at an earlier stage. Some tribes with what appear to be totemistic clan names no longer regard them as such. Thus the Thevoma clan of the Angami, Nagas and the Awomi of the Sema would appear in both cases to bear names translatable as "Pigmen", but no such meaning is ascribed by the Angamis, who explain the name as a human patronymic, while the corresponding Sema clan gives an adventitious explanation of an ancestor who was bitten by a pig; on the other hand the Ao Naga neighbours of these tribes have a dog clan which still claims canine characteristics, *e.g.*, speed of foot and doglike features*; moreover they taboo the dog as food or rather used to taboo it until recently they found it desirable to break the taboo in order to benefit by the medicinal virtues of dog-flesh. Another Ao clan again, the Wozakumr—Hornbill people, claim descent from a woman who conceived as a result of a feather dropping in her lap from a hornbill flying overhead, and it is taboo for them to kill a hornbill or even to see a dead one. It may likewise be noted that the Hindu Chasa of Orissa regard the injuring of their clan totem as punished by leprosy, a fate which the Brahman regards as caused by killing a cow.

Into this conception theory of totemism the belief in life-matter seems hardly to enter unless it be perhaps to the extent that the supply of totem soul is limited and is continually passing through death and rebirth from one member of the clan to another. This appears to be the case in Australia but it is not reported of any tribe in India. On the other hand the external soul, which seems to be a development of the life-matter belief, does appear as connected with totemism in India much as it is in parts of Africa. As a possible source of the connection between totemism and the external soul the phenomena of birth may be suggested. The afterbirth is well known to be intimately associated with the idea of the external soul and is regarded in some cases as actually containing it. Thus among the Baganda it is buried under a plantain tree and a woman may conceive if pollinated, as it were, by the dropping on her of a plantain flower. In the case of the chief, however, the placenta is carefully preserved and brought to him to handle and return to safe keeping on state occasions. Here we are reminded of the placenta standard on the palette of Narmer. No doubt as the abode of the king's vital essence the proximity of such a standard in time of danger would be useful and if the standard be the abode of the external soul we have the explanation both of the association of totems with standards and the apparent paradox of taking into danger a very highly prized emblem the capture of which is regarded by the enemy as of great significance.† One may recall the Fairy Banner of the McLeods which not only brings victory but causes a cow to drop her calf or a pregnant woman to give birth on the sight of it. It may be inferred that its quickening property is due to its being the seat of external soul-matter.‡ If the placenta be thus regarded as the location of the external soul, a possible origin of totemism at once suggests itself in the possibility of the placenta being devoured by some scavenging animal or bird or being associated with the tree on which it is placed for security or with some plant which springs up on the spot where it is buried. It is necessary of course to postulate a subsequent transfer of the totem from the individual to the exogamous clan descended from him or her, but such an origin would perhaps account for a purely social form of totemism in which there was no sacramental element and no magical food production. It would also account for a soul-transmigration form of totemism.

It is worth while in this connection to draw attention to the case of the plantain tree as deriving Baganda soul-matter from a placenta at its root in Africa

* In the Nicobars where descent is claimed from a dog and a woman the dress of men is said to be intended to simulate a doggy appearance, consisting of a fillet round the head with two ends sticking up from the knot on the forehead to resemble dog's ears, while the private parts are concealed in a blue bag with a long red point to it, and the waist-band is arranged to fall down behind in a tail.

† The earliest Roman standards are said to have consisted of a bundle of hay on a pole. Can it have been held that such a bundle of hay would be, like a growth of mistletoe, a convenient hiding place for external soul matter, just as the Kayan leaves the leafy tops of trees unpruned in order to afford a refuge for the spirits of vegetation when clearing the fields? It might be that the same idea was present in the bandaged pole which on an Egyptian temple represented the god, the hieroglyphic for which resembles a flag though it is described as a hatchet and stated to be in effect a bandaged pole with a loose flap projecting.

‡ Strasser (*The Mongolian Horde*, p. 104) relates that the Tashal Lama of Urga in Mongolia "pressed his standards to the slit throats of his victims, saturating them in their spurting life blood." One is tempted to see in this an attempt to imbue the standards with soul-matter which would no doubt contribute towards their victorious progress.

and as being used as the equivalent of a human being in Assam and Oceania.* Thus a "plantain tree" is in many parts of the Naga hills an euphemism for a slave for decapitation. The same equation appears in Micronesia, Fiji, Polynesia, Madagascar and nearer home among the Palaungs of Burma, with whom the tree is also an emblem of fertility, while it is frequently a plantain tree which is used in India in the mock marriages sometimes performed for elder children to enable their juniors to be married before them. A close parallel to the Baganda theory of conception from a plantain flower is to be found in India in the Muslim belief that a woman may conceive if the flowers of a rose tree or jasmine which is growing from the tomb of a dead saint should fall upon her. One may also call attention to the existence in the case of the Ho of a clan whose peculiar totem is the hole of a mouse or rat, a totem immediately explicable on the placenta theory when one is informed that the tribe is descended from a person whose placenta at his birth was buried in a rat hole. The same placenta theory perhaps also appears in the Kora story reported by Risley from Bengal to account for the fruit of a certain tree's being taboo to the tribe since their ancestor once accidentally ate a human placenta which had been exposed in a tree of that particular variety.

Another origin of totems has been suggested as likely to be found in food restrictions. We should be inclined rather to put it the other way round and regard it as perhaps to be found in peculiarities of diet. The discovery and search for forms of vegetable food must have held a very important place in early domestic economy. Under any conditions in which food was scarce and its collection uncertain and laborious, as is probably frequently if not normally the case in a pre-agricultural stage of existence, there must have been a tendency to conceal as long as possible the source of some hitherto unknown supply of food lest that supply be exhausted by other gatherers. Experiment in strange vegetables is dangerous, particularly in the tropics. It is therefore suggested that to the discovery and communication to the kindred and concealment from other clans of new forms of vegetable food must be ascribed the importance of certain wild vegetables in clan ceremonial among the Naga tribes of Assam. The test of whether a clan in one tribe is to be identified or not with a clan in another tribe speaking a totally different language often depends on the vegetable used in certain ceremonies. If the identical plant is used the clans would be regarded as related and clansmen of one tribe going on a trading expedition into the territory of another will feel secure in a house of a related clan, whereas otherwise they would lie down, if at all, in fear of being awoken from their slumber by the sharp *dao* of decapitation. It is true that the wild vegetables used in these clan ceremonies are not always regular articles of food, but it is the writer's impression that they are always edible. Here surely is another possible source of ideas leading to the adoption of a vegetable totem by a given clan.

It is not argued that all totems are accounted for directly by any of the ideas suggested above. Pigs' tripe, for instance, will not quite fit, though we might perhaps suppose a fragment to have got left in a pot in which an afterbirth was hung up; buffalo dung is harder still, unless dung be regarded (*vide supra* p. 410) as a source of spontaneous life. It is, however, likely from every point of view that totemism in general has received accretions from a number of sources, and that while it may have originally started with the conception theory in ignorance of the fact of paternity, it has been encouraged and perpetuated by the ideas of life-matter, a separable soul, transmigration and probably other connected ideas, and that a number of these have contributed to totemism as still found in India.

Magic, when limited to purely imitative or sympathetic magic, is rather within the domain of science than religion. There is nothing religious at all about the effort of an Ao Naga to influence the rice by planting a root or two in earth put in the hollow top of a bamboo, and so raised above the rest of the field which is thus induced to grow high; in the rather inconsiderate Kuki plan of putting a bug into the bundle of the departing guest in order that the rest of the vermin may leave the house likewise, or in the custom of giving a Prabhu bride a grind-

* *Cf.* also *Census of Nigeria, 1931.* VI, 7—"It is said that some of the Yoruba eat the placenta............In the Cameroons it is usually buried under a plantain tree and the fruit is henceforth taken by the native doctor and later by the child".

stone to hold which she gives to her husband saying "take the baby". When however the efficacy of such magic depends not on the practice but on the practitioner, we may suspect that the idea of soul-matter is present and that it is, often at any rate, the superfluity of this material that enables the magician to make his magic successful. Here again one may perhaps see the reaction of the simple belief that like produces like to an independent belief in the existence of soul-matter. However, that may be, a belief in magic both white and black pervades all the more ignorant classes in India and is frequently responsible for serious crime, nor is it always eliminated by culture and education, as witness the comparatively educated persons frequently victimised by rogues who profess to be able to double currency notes miraculously. Thus, to give a single instance, in May 1931, a well-to-do merchant of Indore imprudently handed over Rs. 2,800 to one Pandit Sri Krishna who claimed to have a marvellous process of doubling notes. Ignorant villagers are much more easily imposed on, as in the case of a village near Multan in the Punjab which about the same time parted with Rs. 15,000 in cash and ornaments to a Muslim Fakir who first called down a few rupees from heaven to inspire confidence in his piety and miraculous powers, and then professed to be able to turn silver ornaments into gold or one rupee into three. A belief in magic again, for it can hardly be described as anything else, even if it involve the theory of the impregnation of matter with soul-essence, appears in the practice, reported on good authority in Rangoon, of a director of an international trading corporation who, when ill, has sewn into the seat of his pyjama trousers by his Catholic wife a pious fragment of the holy St. Theresa's petticoat. What the effect on a male Naga would be of wearing a piece of any woman's petticoat, however saintly, we hesitate to set down in print, but presumably Herr Direktor experiences benefit.

Often a belief in witchcraft leads to the murder of the reputed witch. In 1928 in Bihar for instance nine cases of murder were ascribed to witchcraft, and in 1931 in the Yarpur mahalla of Patna a small Lohar girl was murdered in retaliation for the supposed enchantments of her mother, while an "aboriginal" woman suspected of being a witch was killed in Ghatsila district. In Fyzabad in 1927, a man was killed on the advice of a medicine man as being the cause of another's prolonged dysentery, and in Budaun a chamar who was suspected of having bewitched an idiot of good family was pegged out and periodically belaboured while the bewitched one was watched for improvement in his condition. Ultimately, as there was none, the chamar succumbed. In July 1920 a mob in the Nizam's Dominions killed a woman who was believed to have brought cholera on the village, a belief arising from the hysterical statement of a possessed woman into whom had entered the spirit of the goddess who was being worshipped at the time by the village. In November 1930 in Gonda in the United Provinces a wizard was murdered by his own pupil in the belief that he, the wizard, had caused an evil spirit to destroy his pupil's wife and would cause it also to destroy him himself, and as the pupil was one of ten years' standing this instance testifies to the wizard's belief in his own system.

On the other hand the witches themselves likewise commit murders for their own ends and to that extent anyhow justify their persecution. A boy was sacrificed in Bhagalpur in 1928, for the purpose of exorcising evil spirits from a possessed woman, while on the eve of the Dasehra festival of 1930 two sorcerers of Sambalpur, described by the High Court as "men of standing", sacrificed a boy for some nefarious purpose of their own. This case however may possibly have been one rather of a homicide of the kind alluded to above as occasioned by the belief in the need for soul-matter. The use of human sacrifice in order to exorcise spirits is probably unusual, as it is commoner to treat the body of the possessed by more direct methods. Indeed a Hindu girl was beaten to death in Lahore in November 1929, in the attempt to cure her of possession, and this apparently at a shrine frequented by persons in order to experience possession by the deity. In view however of the extent of illiteracy and of the population concerned, the amount of violent crime actually due to a belief in witchcraft appears to be unexpectedly small, though naturally apt to increase with the appearance of calamities or epidemics, which are ascribable to the malevolence of witches, and in Chota Nagpur there are professional witch-doctors called *sokha* whose business it is to indicate the witch responsible for calamity or epidemic that has occurred.

Personal magic, however, is not the only form in which magic appears. Tribal magic, in which the community combines, usually at some festival, in rites or dances intended to secure fertility or prosperity, is a normal feature of tribal religion. Such festivals or rites are usually associated with the agricultural year and may involve sexual licence which is probably intended to have a magical effect on the fertility of the crop and of the community itself, and no better instance of such a festival can be quoted than the *holi*, which has survived as a Hindu festival throughout India.* It is tempting, if possibly fanciful, to trace the origin of the widespread belief in the magic effect of coition on the fertility of the soil, of animals and of people in general to a period in human history when the relation between cause and effect in the begetting of children was not yet fully comprehended, but when the two were already seen to have some association, so that what was really the cause of the conception of one particular child was regarded as merely the cause of parturition in general.† Such a stage in the process of deduction from observed facts, if its existence be credible, would account for the common practice of assisting the fertility of the crops by the act of sexual coition. A reference has already been made (*v. supra* ch. VI. para. 102) to the probable connection between fertility cults and the practice of sacred prostitution. An explanation may here be offered of the peculiar part played by strangers in this cult. Both in the sacred prostitution of Babylon and Byblus it is clear that the dedicated woman gave herself to strangers; similarly it was commerce with strangers which was so necessary to the fertility of the fields of Kamul and so contributive to the prosperity of the people of Caindu. Yule mentions the custom as reported of the Hazaras and of other peoples, including even the Nayars (*Travels of Marco Polo*, I, 212, II, 56). It seems not unlikely that the underlying motive is the acquisition from the stranger of additional life-matter not already inherent in the soil or its inhabitants. The soul-matter of any given place may be regarded as limited in extent and the transfer from one individual to another merely redistributes but does not increase, whereas the reception of soul-material from a stranger is additional to that already in circulation and will naturally therefore increase fertility. This hypothesis likewise offers a possible explanation of the custom mentioned by Gait of the Todas (*Census of India*, 1911, I, p. 260), who are reported to call in a person from another village to deflower a girl about to attain puberty, who otherwise finds it difficult to marry, and perhaps also of the *talikettu* ceremony in south India generally. A possible association of the distribution in India of the brachycephalic Eurasiatic type with the practice of infant marriage has already been suggested (*supra*, ch. VI, para. 102). The fact that approval of commerce with strangers, which is perhaps associated always with the fertility of the soil, is reported of the Uighars, Hazaras, Chukchis, Koryaks (*vide* Yule, *Travels of Marco Polo*, I, p. 212 n., II, 56 n.), and (by a Xth century Arab traveller) of some Turks, makes it possible that this custom also has Alpine associations. Dancing likewise has probably a magical origin, and it certainly has a magical aspect as when it involves leaping up in the air to encourage the growth of paddy, and Russell has acutely suggested that acrobatic displays have originated in the same idea. Similarly animal dancing, such as that for instance of the Gonds, Bhatras and Parjas of the Central Provinces, probably originates in an attempt to increase or perhaps merely to concentrate by magic the wild animals on which the community partly depends for its food supply. When, however, the spring hunting is considered, it is apparent that the soul-matter cult is again prominent. The *Aheria* of the Rajput in western India, the hunting festival of the Halvakki Vakkals in Kanara, the *Jur Sital* of Bihar,

---

* Unless it be the marriage festival annually celebrated in June by the lord of a feudal manor in Normandy who after participating in the bridal festivities of his serfs picked out the couples who appeared to him to be the most amorous, and caused them to consummate their marriages in the boughs of trees or in the waters of the local river. Dulaure speaks of this practice as one of tyrannical jesting, but the interpretation here assumed is perhaps more likely. Fertility rites survived in Europe in spite of the Church;—" *le femmes prostituées......qui suivaient la Cour......étaient tenues, tant que le moi de mai durait, de faire le lit du roi des ribauds* " (Dulaure), and sometimes even under its auspices as at Isernia.

† I have heard a Sema chief of great tribal authority and experience, Inato of Lumitsami, affirm that it was ridiculous to suppose that pregnancy would result from coition on one occasion only, which indicates that even now the relation between cause and effect in this particular is not completely grasped in that tribe.

the spring hunt of the Chota Nagpur tribes, and of the Bhatras, Gonds and Gadabas of the Central Provinces and Madras, the *Sekrengi* hunt of the Angami Nagas and the corresponding festivals of other Assam tribes are all designed to secure prosperity through the coming year, and inasmuch as all manner of living things are destroyed they are probably intended (the *Sekrengi* certainly is) to collect a supply of life-essence and are to be regarded in much the same light as the spring man-hunt of the Wa of Burma.

It would be impossible here to go into all the aspects of the tribal religion in India but enough has perhaps been said to show that the beliefs held are not mere vague imaginings of superstitious and untaught minds, "amorphous" as they were described in the Census report of 1911, but the *débris* of a real religious system, a definite philosophy, to the one time widespread prevalence of which the manifold survivals in Hinduism testify, linking together geographically the austroasiatic and australoid cultures of the forest-clad hills where the isolated remains of the original religion still hold out in an unassimilated form. It is probably this philosophy of life-essence which accounts for the fact that in so many parts of the world, *e.g.* in India and southern and eastern Europe, Greece and Italy in particular, the real religion of the people is hagiolatry. It is less the orthodox gods of the religion who are worshipped than shrines and holy places, generally tombs particularly associated with some deceased saint or hero likely to have been rich in soul-matter, the benefit of which may be obtained at the grave, originally no doubt in the form of a material emanation. Be that as it may, showing traces in Europe on the one hand and stretching down into Australasia on the other, this creed must have been in its time a great religion, not so great perhaps in altruism, but great in extent and in constituting a very definite rung in that poor ladder up which the race still tries to climb in its effort to ascertain the unknowable, to scale the ramparts of infinity.

SUBSIDIARY

Proportional strength of the main religions in each Pro

Number per 10,000

Province, State or Agency.	Hindu.*					
	1931	1921	1911	1901	1891	1881
INDIA	**6,824**	**6,841**	**6,931**	**7,034**	**7,231**	**7,432**
Provinces	**6,548**	**6,589**	**6,688**	**6,835**	**7,014**	**7,197**
Ajmer-Merwara	7,755	7,326	7,750	7,977	8,054	8,162
Andaman and Nicobar Islands	2,586	3,254	3,578	3,758	..	..
Assam	5,720	5 433	5,418	5,578	5,472	6,273
Baluchistan	894	869	622	643	..	..
Bengal	4,304	4,327	4,480	4,660	4,727	4,855
Bihar and Orissa	8,231	8,282	8,223	8,333	8,290	8,430
Bombay	7,605	7,657	7,585	7,651	7,756	7,480
Burma†	390	*368*	*514* 322	*436* 272	*306* 228	*236* ..
Central Provinces and Berar	8,601	8,353	8,261	8,320	8,244	8,266
Coorg	8,939	7,733	7,939	8,849	9,063	9,113
Delhi	6,285	6,417	3,297	3,873	4,077	4,130
Punjab	2,684	3,084				
Madras	8,831	8,864	8,889	8,914	8,981	9,141
North-West Frontier Province	590	666	546	629	638	708
United Provinces	8,450	8,464	8,504	8,532	8,609	8,627
States and Agencies	**7,771**	**7,742**	**7,788**	**7,769**	**7,957**	**8,277**
Assam States	4,362	5,994	5,816	5,996	..	5,921
Baluchistan States	302	334	282	342	..	..
Baroda State	8,809	8,193	8,349	7,922	8,850	8,480
Bengal States	6,593	6,752	6,900	6,985	6,955	6,262
Bihar and Orissa States	9,017	8,684	8,589	8,624	8,627	8,245
Bombay States†	8,775	8,676	8,401	8,278	8,414	7,962
Central India Agency	8,823	8,688	8,830	8,081	7,468	8,422
Gwalior State	9,286	8,807				
Central Provinces States	7,202	7,308	6,195	6,802	7,386	8,621
Cochin State	6,477	6,599	6,706	6,826	6,938	7,152
Hyderabad State	8,435	8,545	8,693	8,860	8,941	9,033
Jammu and Kashmir State	2,019	2,016	2,183	2,371	2,720	..
Madras States Agency	6,400	6,642	6,903	7,111	7,456	7,467
Mysore State	9,174	9,168	9,199	9,206	9,248	9,308
North-West Frontier Province (Agencies and Tribal Area)	2,939	4,563	1,984	..	..	..
Punjab States	8,769	5,001	4,953	5,582	5,849	5,495
Punjab States Agency	4,220					
Rajputana	8,533	8,296	8,311	8,327	8,351	8,750
Sikkim State	4,287	6,673	6,674	6,491	..	..
United Provinces States	7,883	7,819	7,008	6,962	6,934	6,764
Travancore State	6,152	6,365	6,657	6,895	7,318	7,312
Western India States Agency‡	8,119	8,077	7,914	..	..	..

* The 1881-1921 figures for "Others" are inclusive of those for Aryas and Brahmo.
† Figures for 1881-1901 for all the religions are inclusive of those for Western
‡ Figures for 1881-1901 are included in the

NOTE.—The *Italic* figures against Burma relate to Lower Burma only. The figures for Tribal Religions are
The proportions in the case of Agencies and Tribal Areas of the North-West

TABLE I.

vince, State or Agency at each of the last six censuses.

of the population.

Sikh.						Jain.						Buddhist.					
1931	1921	1911	1901	1891	1881	1931	1921	1911	1901	1891	1881	1931	1921	1911	1901	1891	1881
124	**103**	**96**	**75**	**67**	**73**	**36**	**37**	**40**	**45**	**49**	**48**	**365**	**366**	**342**	**322**	**248**	**135**
118	**96**	**89**	**68**	**64**	**63**	**17**	**18**	**19**	**21**	**22**	**23**	**468**	**465**	**436**	**406**	**321**	**172**
6	4	18	6	4	4	348	372	405	418	497	528	..	..	..	..	..	..
220	144	172	150	..	..	..	..	..	25	..	..	988	979	604	755	..	..
3	1	1	1	..	..	3	5	3	3	2	..	17	17	16	15	14	14
181	182	128	85	..	..	1	..	..	..	..	..	1	4	..	..	..	..
2	..	1	..	..	..	2	3	1	1	1	..	63	57	53	50	48	43
1	1	1	..	..	..	1	1	1	1	1	..	..	..	..	..	..	..
10	4	6	1	1	77	92	111	108	123	127	132	1	1	..	..	..	..
7	*4*	*4*	*3*	*1*	..	1	*1*	*1*	..	..	..	8,430	*8,506*	*8,351*	*8,533*	*8,680*	*8,702*
		6	6	5	..			1	..	..	..			8,571	8,755	9,053	..
3	1	2	2	..	1	50	49	50	56	52	55	..	..	..	..	..	..
..	..	..	..	..	..	5	12	6	6	7	6	..	1	..	..	..	..
101	57	1,048	746	737	658	84	96	20	21	21	21	1	..	2	2	3	2
1,299	1,109					15	17					2	1				
..	..	..	..	..	..	7	6	7	7	8	8	..	..	..	..	..	..
175	125	138	125	103	50	..	..	..	..	..	..	..	..	..	..	..	..
10	3	3	3	2	1	14	15	16	18	18	18	..	..	..	..	..	..
141	**126**	**122**	**99**	**76**	**109**	**101**	**104**	**114**	**136**	**140**	**140**	**12**	**12**	**11**	**10**	**5**	..
4	1	..	..	..	..	3	3	3	..	..	..	1	9	..	5	..	..
2	3	74	..	..	..	..	..	..	..	..	..	..	..	..	..	..	..
2	..	1	..	..	..	198	203	214	247	208	214	..	..	..	..	..	..
.	..	..	..	..	..	5	6	7	5	3	2	149	113	73	81	66	..
..	..	..	..	..	..	1	1	..	..	..	..	3	3	4	2	4	2
2	2	3	1	..	..	195	200	203	446	391	406	..	..	..	..	..	..
2	1	1	2	2	2	76	74	94	131	87	54	..	..	..	..	..	..
2	2					128	122					..	..				
1	1	1	1	..	..	8	7	5	5	3	1	..	..	..	..	..	..
..	..	..	..	..	..	2	1	1	..	..	..	1	..	..	..	..	
4	2	3	4	4	4	15	15	16	18	24	8	..	..	..	..	..	..
139	119	100	89	45	..	2	2	1	1	2	..	106	113	116	121	116	..
..	..	..	..	..	..	1	..	..	..	..	..	..	..	..	1	..	..
..	..	1	..	..	..	45	35	30	25	27	26	2	2	1	..	..	..
1,168	892	823	..	..	..	..	..	..	..	..	..	..	21	..	..	..	..
248	1,841	1,875	1,325	1,127	1,541	9	16	17	16	14	18	30	6	8	6	1	..
2,228						17						2					
37	9	9	2	1	..	268	284	316	349	338	375	..	..	..	..	..	.
..	..	..	1	..	..	..	1	..	..	..	.	3,225	3,278	3,289	3,481	..	..
1	..	..	..	..	..	2	2	4	2	3	.	..	..	..	..	1	..
..	..	..	..	..	..	..	..	..	..	..	..	..	..	..	1	..	..
..	..	..	..	..	..	509	535	564	..	..	..	..	..	..	..	..	..

while 1931 figures for All Hindus are shown in column 2.
India States Agency.
figures for the Bombay States.
in many cases (*e.g.* Coorg, Madras, Hyderabad) included in those for Hindus in 1881.
Frontier Province relate to trans-frontier posts only.

Proportional strength of the main religions in each Pro

Province State or Agency.	Muslim.					
	1931	1921	1911	1901	1891	1881
INDIA	**2,216**	**2,174**	**2,126**	**2,122**	**1,996**	**1,974**
Provinces	**2,469**	**2,407**	**2,351**	**2,324**	**2,240**	**2,260**
Ajmer-Merwara	1,734	2,055	1,616	1,510	1,369	1,255
Andaman and Nicobar Islands	2,280	1,515	1,731	1,707	..	..
Assam	3,196	2,896	2,810	2,689	2,710	2,698
Baluchistan	8,744	8,731	9,106	9,150	..	..
Bengal	5,487	5,399	5,274	5,158	5,108	5,009
Bihar and Orissa	1,132	1,085	1,063	1,061	1,076	1,089
Bombay	2,039	1,974	2,046	2,026	1,871	1,836
Burma	399	*380*	{ *547*	*509*	*452*	*452* }
			{ 347	323	333	.. }
Central Provinces and Berar	440	405	406	421	385	386
Coorg	844	795	751	756	732	703
Delhi	{ 3,253	2,904 }	5,485	5,325	5,136	5,173
Punjab	{ 5,655	5,533 }				
Madras	707	671	662	643	631	623
North-West Frontier Province	9,184	9,162	9,286	9,221	9,230	9,212
United Provinces	1,484	1,428	1,411	1,411	1,353	1,343
States and Agencies	**1,347**	**1,343**	**1,331**	**1,376**	**1,176**	**946**
Assam States	393	455	419	365	..	221
Baluchistan States	9,696	9,663	9,643	9,658	..	..
Baroda State	748	763	791	845	781	801
Bengal States	3,210	3,070	3,009	2,885	2,902	2,886
Bihar and Orissa States	42	40	42	39	40	48
Bombay States‡	929	913	977	1,217	1,060	1,085
Central India	{ 568	553 }	46	606	546	551
Gwalior State	{ 580	555 }				
Central Provinces States	94	89	95	96	87	85
Cochin State	729	702	695	671	642	556
Hyderabad State	1,063	1,041	1,032	1,037	987	940
Jammu and Kashmir State	7,728	7,675	7,594	7,416	7,051	..
Madras States	692	667	654	634	609	573
Mysore State	608	570	542	523	512	479
North-West Frontier Province (Agencies and Tribal Areas)	4,970	3,917	7,095	..	..	..
Punjab States	{ 933 }	3,100	3,133	3,068	3,006	2,945
Punjab States Agency	{ 3,480 }					
Rajputana	953	915	936	952	811	853
Sikkim State	10	3	5	4	..	..
United Provinces States	2,090	2,149	2,961	3,026	3,061	3,236
Travancore State	693	675	661	646	621	612
Western India States§	1,364	1,377	1,412	..	..	..

* The 1921-1881 figures for "Others" are inclusive of those for Aryas and Brahmos
† This is due to the inclusion of 120,091 persons who were shown under head
‡ Figures for 1901-1881 for all the religions are inclusive of those for Western
§ Figures for 1901-1881 are included in the

NOTE.—The *Italic* figures against Burma relate to Lower Burma only. The figures for Tribal Religions are in many cases
The proportions in the case of Agencies and Tribal Areas of the North-

TABLE I.

vince, State or Agency at each of the last six censuses.

Number per 10,000 of the population.

Christian.						Tribal.						Others.*					
1931	1921	1911	1901	1891	1881	1931	1921	1911	1901	1891	1881	1931	1921	1911	1901	1891	1881
179	150	124	99	79	73	236	309	328	292	323	259	20	20	13	11	7	6
142	123	102	82	68	58	213	280	301	250	264	221	25	22	14	14	7	6
124	112	108	78	50	48	27	96	79	..	..	..	6	35	24	11	26	3
496	586	214	197	..	..	3,379	3,387	3,670	3,326	..	..	51	135	31	82	..	..
235	168	99	61	31	15	825	1,479	1,652	1,652	1,771	1,000	1	1	1	1	..	..
174	159	121	116	..	..	1	..	..	..	..	..	4	55	23	6	..	..
36	31	29	25	21	20	105	181	161	105	93	70	1	2	1	1	2	3
91	76	67	51	34	18	544	553	644	554	598	454	..	2	1	..	1	9
145	137	119	112	86	84	59	64	87	38	113	342	49	52	49	49	46	49
226	195	*281* 173	*237* 141	*240* 159	*225* ..	444	534	*300* 579	*281* 381	*320* 221	*384* ..	103	*12*	*2* 1	*1* 122†	*1* 1	*1* ..
33	30	25	23	11	11	872	1,160	1,254	1,176	1,307	1,281	1	2	2	2	1	..
210	194	203	204	196	177	..	1,265	1,099	183	..	..	2	..	2	2	2	1
267 176	273 159	99	33	26	16	.. ..	.. ..	..	..	..	..	9 169	253 97	49	..	..	..
380	322	288	268	243	227	75	137	154	168	133	..	..	..	..	..	4	1
51	47	30	25	29	30	..	..	..	..	..	..	..	..	..	..	..	..
42	44	38	22	13	11	..	..	..	..	..	..	..	46	28	14	5	..
307	250	200	162	120	128	316	415	425	445	520	394	5	8	9	3	6	6
746	105	4	2	..	..	4,491	3,433	3,758	3,632	..	3,858	..	..	..	..	..	..
..	..	1	..	..	..	..	..	..	..	..	..	..	..	..	..	..	..
30	35	35	39	3	3	184	767	568	903	124	465	29	39	42	44	34	37
29	22	3	4	6	2	14	36	7	39	14	848	..	1	1	1	54	..
161	117	97	9	6	3	775	1,154	1,267	1,326	1,314	1,702	1	1	1	..	9	..
36	34	29	16	10	10	58	169	381	36	121	532	5	6	6	6	4	5
16 3	15 5	10	10	6	8	514 ..	666 507	517	1,168	1,890	962	1 1	3 2	2	2	1	1
208	176	183	4	2	..	2,487	2,419	3,521	3,092	2,522	1,293	..	..	..	..	..	..
2,779	2,682	2,539	2,441	2,404	2,272	..	4	46	48	..	..	12	12	13	14	16	21
105	50	41	21	18	14	377	345	214	59	25	..	1	2	1	1	1	1
8	5	3	1	1	..	..	..	..	..	..	..	..	70	3	1	65	..
2,900	2,664	2,399	2,174	1,931	1,956	4	24	41	77	..	..	3	3	3	3	4	4
134	119	103	90	77	70	36	105	124	156	136	117	1	1	..	..	..	..
923	607	98	..	..	..	..	..	..	..	..	..	..	..	..	..	..	..
5 10	9	4	2	1	1	.. ..	..	..	..	..	..	6 43	27	10	1	2	..
5	5	4	3	2	1	204	488	422	366	496	..	..	3	2	1	1	21
25	45	32	23	..	..	2,453	..	..	..	..	..	..	..	..	..	..	..
24	22	21	6	1	..	..	..	..	..	..	..	..	8	6	4	..	..
3,149	2,928	2,636	2,362	2,060	2,076	6	31	46	95	..	..	..	1	..	1	1	..
4	3	4	..	..	..	2	5	4	..	..	..	2	3	102	..	..	..

while 1931 figures for All Hindus are shown in column 2.
"Minor Religions and Religions not returned".
India States Agency.
figures for the Bombay States.
(*e.g.* Coorg, Madras, Hyderabad) included in those for Hindus in 1881.
West Frontier Province relate to trans-frontier posts only.

M22CC'

Distribution of Urban

Province, State or Agency.	Total Population	Hindu.		Sikh.		Jain.		Buddhist.		
		Urban.	Rural.	Urban.	Rural.	Urban.	Rural.	Urban.	Rural.	Urban.
1	2	3	4	5	6	7	8	9	10	11
INDIA	**350,529,557**	**25,124,727**	**214,070,413**	**344,678**	**3,991,093**	**433,773**	**818,332**	**912,911**	**11,873,895**	**98,085**
Provinces	**271,431,549**	**18,887,622**	**158,840,366**	**282,974**	**2,938,023**	**169,491**	**284,078**	**909,800**	**11,783,289**	**87,758**
Ajmer-Merwara	560,292	112,911	321,598	335	6	6,490	13,007	4	..	300
Andaman and Nicobar Islands ..	29,463	..	7,618	..	649	..	..	..	2,912	..
Assam	8,622,251	153,673	4,778,087	432	2,065	880	1,756	278	14,677	6
Baluchistan (*Districts and Administered Territories*).	463,508	33,387	8,045	7,002	1,366	32	..	68	..	167
Bengal	50,114,002	2,541,062	19,029,345	6,627	693	5,643	3,524	15,609	300,422	1,350
Bihar and Orissa	37,677,576	1,235,093	29,776,381	3,982	1,671	1,852	1.882	140	779	226
Bombay (*including Aden*)	21,854,866	3,368,464	13,252,757	9,191	11,702	64,528	135,487	1,862	34°	81,189
Burma	14,647,497	309,043	261,910	6,195	4,712	599	122	890,684	11,457,353	403
Central Provinces and Berar ..	15,507,723	1,314,016	12,024,207	2,265	1,976	24,968	52,927	44	22	1,953
Coorg	163,327	6,440	139,567	..	..	50	33	..	3	27
Delhi	636,246	244,745	155,118	6,324	113	4,581	764	76	..	126
Madras	46,740,107	5,119,713	36,157,657	515	22	7,134	24,072	813	546	485
North-West Frontier Province (*Districts and Administered Territories*).	2,425,076	93,127	49,850	25,377	17,133	..	..	2	..	60
Punjab	23,580,852	1,126,247	5,202,341	205,681	2,858,463	21,620	13,664	39	5,684	511
United Provinces of Agra and Oudh	48,408,763	3,229,701	37,675,885	9,048	37,452	31,114	36,840	181	549	955
States and Agencies	**79,098,008**	**6,237,105**	**55,230,047**	**61,704**	**1,053,070**	**264,282**	**534,254**	**3,111**	**90,606**	**10,327**
Assam States	625,606	86,885	186,005	193	39	141	26	31	59	2
Baluchistan States	405,109	1,097	11,152	27	30	..	..	..	..	..
Baroda State	2,443,007	411,443	1,740,628	500	21	20,393	28,015	2	41	5,789
Bengal States	973,336	22,702	618,960	14	..	357	145	2	14,530	..
Bihar and Orissa States	4,652,007	44,106	4,150,772	41	175	1	317	..	1,376	..
Bombay States	4,468,396	483,358	3,437,730	40	674	19,908	67,445	4	..	387
Central India Agency	6,632,790	469,334	5,382,870	991	435	18,234	32,034	13	..	921
Central Provinces States	2,483,214	65,025	1,723,376	50	229	971	989	3	..	15
Gwalior State	3,523,070	285,905	2,985,671	269	412	16,986	28,093	..	..	223
Hyderabad State	14,436,148	1,048,901	11,127,826	3,441	1,737	6,141	15,402	38	14	1,520
Jammu and Kashmir State ..	3,646,243	99,148	637,074	4,664	45,998	594	3	1,707	37,017	4
Madras States Agency	6,754,484	536,773	3,786,377	5	7	281	1	37	123	15
Cochin State	*1,205,016*	*113,051*	*667,433*	..	..	*209*	*1*	*34*	*62*	*3*
Travancore State	*5,095,973*	*354,581*	*2,780,307*	*5*	*7*	*41*	..	*3*	*61*	*12*
Other Madras States	*453,495*	*69,141*	*338,637*	..	..	*31*	..	..	..	..
Mysore State	6,557,302	800,606	5,215,274	49	51	7,461	22,152	1,237	2	323
North West Frontier Province *Agencies and Tribal Areas*).	46,451	..	13,651	..	5,425	..	..	..	1	..
Punjab States	437,787	7,718	376,165	475	10,379	207	201	..	1,308	..
Punjab States Agency .. .	4,472,218	191,680	1,695,569	49,434	947,192	3,636	3,812	2	720	17
Rajputana Agency	11,225,712	1,074,055	8,504,750	1,431	40,174	92,565	208,183	1	..	289
Sikkim State	109,808	..	47,074	..	..	..	2	..	35,412	..
United Provinces States	1,206,070	44,732	905,992	40	70	124	90	..	1	..
Western India States Agency ..	3,999,250	563,637	,683,131	40	22	76,282	127,344	34	2	322

TABLE II.

and Rural Population.

Zoroastrian.	Muslim.		Christian.		Jew.		Tribal.		Others.	
Rural.	Urban.	Rural.	Urban.	Rural.	Urban.	Rural.	Urban.	Rural.	Urban.	Rural.
12	13	14	15	16	17	18	19	20	21	22
11,667	**10,567,672**	**67,109,873**	**1,276,462**	**5,020,301**	**21,225**	**2,916**	**91,771**	**8,188,576**	**38,388**	**532,799**
8,791	**8,175,856**	**53,844,587**	**952,915**	**2,913,745**	**19,564**	**1,642**	**59,913**	**5,719,796**	**36,841**	**514,498**
1	53,905	43,228	6,202	745	49	..	1	1,508	2	..
1	..	6,719	..	1,461	..	..	—	9,955	..	148
1	53,067	2,702,847	3,385	199,201	..	18	1,678	709,754	22	424
..	43,416	361,893	7,904	140	15	..	28	38	6	1
170	1,029,374	26,468,250	76,440	103,859	1,851	16	4,847	523,190	1,527	203
15	374,490	3,890,300	29,698	312,196	5	19	8,343	2,040,466	8	30
8,355	1,141,638	3,315,259	189,327	127,715	16,180	1,559	5,100	124,035	149	27
16	191,283	393,556	71,688	259,418	1,206	12	32,349	618,039	16,587	132,322
139	308,641	374,213	29,346	21,238	147	6	7,090	1,344,525	—	—
..	2,459	11,318	851	2,574	—	..	—	—	..	5
..	180,018	26,942	11,122	5,867	11	..	—	—	439	—
22	837,740	2,468,197	370,317	1,403,959	23	..	477	348,286	39	90
..	256,189	1,971,114	11,411	802	11	..	—	..	..	..
35	1,629,660	11,702,800	65,636	349,152	10	2	—	—	18,060	381,247
36	2,073,976	5,107,951	79,588	125,418	56	10	—	—	2	1
2,876	**2,391,816**	**8,265,286**	**323,547**	**2,106,556**	**1,661**	**1,274**	**31.858**	**2,468,780**	**1,547**	**18,301**
..	2,577	22,023	4,921	41,739	..	..	7,739	273,219	7	—
..	9,437	383,347	14	1	2	—	—	2	—	—
1,338	81,173	101,457	2,699	4,563	47	8	957	43,933	..	—
..	4,471	308,005	59	2,709	..	—	5	1,377	—	—
23	1,268	18,248	254	74,578	..	..	45	360,555	..	248
1,081	99,025	315,906	4,602	11,404	77	852	62	25,841	..	..
55	178,828	197,809	6,823	3,653	38	..	2,488	338,264	..	..
2	5,977	17,277	1,399	50,302	..	..	1,625	615,974	..	..
16	91,179	113,118	747	451	..	..	..	..	..	..
264	514,281	1,020,385	26,261	125,121	27	..	16,371	528,418	..	..
1	234,915	2,582,721	1,277	986	..	..	5	129	..	..
1	94,521	372,875	204,517	1,754,294	1,355	394	5	2,902	..	1
..	*18,440*	*69,462*	*76,538*	*261,332*	*1,065*	*386*	—	—	..	..
1	*67,497*	*285,777*	*129,354*	*1,475,121*	*290*	*8*	*5*	*2,902*	..	*1*
..	*8,584*	*17,636*	*1,625*	*17,841*	..	..	..	..	..	..
8	170,349	228,279	64,219	23,319	39	..	653	23,175	106	..
2	..	23,086	..	4,286	..	..	—	—	..	..
1	6,125	34,720	9	197	..	..	..	—	..	282
5	192,150	1,364,441	1,100	3,259	1	..	..	—	1,431	17,769
30	383,045	686,280	3,307	2,471	38	..	1,574	227,518	—	1
..	..	104	..	276	..	..	—	26,940	—	—
..	81,107	171,024	135	2,755	..	..	—	—	—	..
49	241,388	304,181	1,204	192	37	20	329	533	3	..

SUBSIDIARY TABLE III.

Distribution of Christians—Number and Variation.

Province, State or Agency.	Actual number of Christians in 1931	1921	1911	1901	1891	1881	Variation per cent. (Increase + Decrease —). 1921-31	1911-21	1901-11	1891-1901	1881-91	1881-1931
INDIA	**6,296,763**	**4,754,064**	**3,876,203**	**2,923,241**	**2,284,380**	**1,862,634**	**+ 32·5**	**+ 22·6**	**+ 32·6**	**+ 28·0**	**+ 22·6**	**+238·1**
Provinces	**4,089,849**	**3,158,364**	**2,601,761**	**1,935,358**	**1,516,356**	**1,175,738**	**+ 29·5**	**+ 21·4**	**+ 34·4**	**+ 27·6**	**+ 29·0**	**+247·9**
Ajmer-Merwara	6,947	5,631	5,432	3,712	2,683	2,225	+ 25·6	+ 1·8	+ 46·3	+ 38·4	+ 20·6	+212·2
Andaman and Nicobar Islands.	1,461	1,586	566	486	483	..	— 7·9	+180·2	+ 16·5	+ 0·6	..	..
Assam	249,246	132,106	66,562	35,969	16,844	7,093	+ 88·7	+ 98·5	+ 85·1	+113·5	+137·2	+3,414·0
Baluchistan	8,059	6,693	5,085	4,026	3,008	..	+ 20·4	+ 31·6	+ 26·3	+ 33·8	..	..
Bengal	183,067	149,069	129,746	106,596	82,339	72,289	+ 22·8	+ 14·8	+ 21·7	+ 29·5	+ 13·9	+153·2
Bihar and Orissa	416,726	303,358	268,265	172,340	110,360	55,943	+ 37·4	+ 13·1	+ 55·7	+ 56·2	+ 97·3	+644·9
Bombay	333,048	277,989	244,392	220,087*	170,009*	145,154*	+ 19·8	+ 13·7	+ 11·0	+ 29·5	+ 17·1	+129·4
Burma	331,106	257,106	210,081	147,525	120,922	84,219†	+ 28·8	+ 22·3	+ 42·4	+ 22·2	..	+293·1
Central Provinces and Berar.	102,285	77,718	73,401	27,252	14,451	13,174	+ 31·6	+ 5·9	+169·3	+ 88·6	+ 9·3	+676·4
Coorg	3,425	3,182	3,553	3,683	3,392	3,152	+ 7·6	— 10·4	— 3·5	+ 8·6	+ 7·6	+ 8·7
Delhi	16,989	13,320	199,751	66,591	48,472	28,054	+ 27·5	+73·3	+200·0	+ 37·4	+ 72·8	+1,455·4
Punjab	419,353	332,939					+ 26·0					
Madras	1,793,742	1,380,672	1,208,515	1,038,863	879,438	711,117	+ 29·9	+ 14·2	+ 16·3	+ 18·1	+ 23·7	+152·[illegible]
North-West Frontier Province.	16,499	13,916	6,718	5,273	5,437	5,645	+ 18·6	+107·1	+ 27·4	— 3·0	— 3·7	+192·3
United Provinces	207,896	203,179	179,694	102,955	58,518	47,673	+ 2·3	+ 13·1	+ 74·5	+ 75·9	+ 22·7	+336·1
States and Agencies	**2,206,914**	**1,595,700**	**1,274,442**	**987,883**	**768,024**	**686,896**	**+ 38·3**	**+ 25·2**	**+29·0**	**+ 28·6**	**+ 11·8**	**+ 221·3**
Baroda	7,262	7,421	7,203	7,691	646	771	— 2·1	+ 3·0	— 6·3	+ 1,090·6	— 16·2	+841·9
Central India	10,476	9,062	9,358	8,113	5,992	7,065	+15·6	+14·4	+ 15·3	+ 35·4	— 15·2	+65·2
Gwalior	1,198	1,649					—27·3					
Cochin	334,870	262,595	233,092	198,239	173,831	136,361	+27·5	+ 12·7	+ 17·6	+ 14·0	+ 27·5	+145·6
Hyderabad	151,382	62,656	54,296	22,996	20,429	13,614	+141·6	+ 15·4	+136·1	+ 12·6	+ 50·1	+1,012·0
Jammu and Kashmir	2,263	1,634	975	422	218	..	+ 38·5	+ 67·6	+131·0	+ 93·6	..	..
Mysore	87,538	71,395	59,844	50,059	38,135	29,249	+ 22·6	+ 19·3	+ 19·5	+ 31·3	+ 30·4	+199·3
Rajputana	5,778	4,911	4,256	2,841	1,862	1,294	+ 17·7	+ 15·4	+ 49·8	+ 52·6	+ 43·9	+346·5
Sikkim	276	370	285	135	..	..	— 25·4	+ 29·8	+111·1	..	..	..
Travancore	1,604,475	1,172,934	903,868	697,387	526,911	498,542	+ 36·8	+ 29·8	+ 29·6	+ 32·4	+ 5·7	+221·8
Western India States	1,396	1,073	1,265	‡	‡	‡	+ 30·1	— 15·2	..	..	..	..

* Includes figures for Western India States. † Refers to Lower Burma only. ‡ Included in Bombay.

CHAPTER XII.

Caste, Tribe and Race.

Enumeration of Caste and Race.

177. Column eight in the general schedule provided for an entry of 'caste tribe or race'. The term 'caste' needs no definition in India; 'tribe' was provided to cover the many communities still organised on that basis in whose case the tribe has not become a caste; it was likewise determinate enough, and no attempt was made to define the term 'race', which is generally used so loosely as almost to defy definition. Nor is it intended to do anything so rash as to attempt to define it here, while in the census schedule its very looseness enabled it to cover returns which, though not strictly referable all to the same category, were quite adequate for the purpose intended, which was primarily to obtain a return of Indians to whom the terms 'caste' and 'tribe' are inapplicable and a means of identifying Anglo-Indians whose birthplace might be an inadequate means of identification. If an interpretation of the term 'race' as used in this chapter is demanded by the reader he must rest content with Sir Flinders Petrie's definition of it as "a group of human beings, whose type has become unified by their rate of assimilation's exceeding the rate of change produced by foreign elements". It would have been inexpedient to prescribe this definition as a guide for enumerators. Generally speaking foreigners were asked to give their nationality though this is not necessarily identical with their race, and the term 'British', if used with reference to nationality, might be correctly held to cover a Cypriot or a Maltese, or even a South American Indian with a birth place in the U. S. A., a quasi-Spanish name. and an infelicitous domicile in what was once the Kingdom of Ireland.

European British Subjects.

178. In the Provincial Census Reports foreigners generally will be found returned in Table VI by the continent of their origin divided under the three heads of British Dominions (including, for convenience, mandated territories) Non-British countries, and Unspecified, while in the India tables they are shown in greater detail. The total number of foreigners censused in India in 1931, including European British subjects and Armenians, only amounted to 168,134 (117,336 males and 50,798 females) or ·05 per cent. of the total population. The European British subjects totalled 155,555 of whom 110,137 were males and 45,418 females. Of these again 7,205 males and 3,422 females were found in Burma, and while in Burma the figures show a total increase of 1,434 males and 1,365 females since 1921, the figures for India proper show a further fall since 1921 and are now little more than 80 per cent. of those recorded in 1911, while males taken alone are fewer than in 1901.

European British Subjects according to Census Returns.

	1931.		1921.		1911.		1901.	
	Males.	Females.	Males.	Females.	Males.	Females.	Males.	Females.
India	110,137	45,418	119,149	46,336	134,950	50,484	112,687	42,004
Ajmer-Merwara ..	1,172	352	1,080	320	1,369	333	644	273
Andamans and Nicobars	180	34	171	38	193	50	222	47
Assam	2,168	959	1,806	863	1,556	616	1,484	484
Baluchistan	3,795	1,219	3,967	787	3,360	809	2,961	491
Bengal	13,116	7,788	12,449	7,567	14,659	7,668	15,767	8,271
Bihar and Orissa ..	3,443	2,232	3,563	2,182	3,489	2,157	..	..
Bombay (*including Aden*)	16,679	7,452	23,161	7,880	21,157	7,826	19,872	7,182
Burma	7,205	3,422	5,771	2,057	8,904	2,924	6,481	2,125
Central Provinces and Berar.	3,815	1,309	4,338	1,289	5,323	1,710	3,408	1,587
Coorg	69	53	38	56	109	65	126	86
Delhi	2,879	1,330	3,401	916	622	246	Incld. in Punjab.	
Madras	6,423	4,253	5,253	4,697	8,143	4,965	7,852	4,705
N.-W. F. P.	10,116	1,427	9,397	1,056	4,898	800	4,053	587
Punjab	14,597	4,926	15,860	5,686	23,457	7,407	19,791	5,781
United Provinces ..	16,868	5,193	17,805	6,638	24,461	8,350	20,363	7,237
Baroda State ..	78	33	49	31	72	51	44	36
Central India Agency	1,788	572	2,705	614	3,414	554	3,133	580
Cochin State ..	38	34	19	4	Incld. in Madras		31	14
Gwalior State ..	54	47	489	60	Included in C. I. figures		32	29
Hyderabad State ..	1,760	93	2,960	543	4,251	979	2,760	387
Jammu and Kashmir State.	69	82	123	140	124	102	101	88
Mysore State ..	2,929	1,978	4,132	2,504	4,697	2,426	2,748	1,439
Rajputana Agency ..	463	393	462	342	682	445	504	381
Sikkim State ..	4	3	1	6	10	1	..	..
Travancore State ..	299	157	149	60	Incld. in Madras		310	194
W. I. S. Agency ..	130	79	Included against Bombay.					

The figures above show comparisons since 1901. These figures must be taken with some qualification as they certainly represent more than the actual numbers on account of the tendency of Anglo-Indians who are not handicapped by excessive pigmentation to return themselves as Europeans. The total returned as European British subjects in India including Burma was 155,555, but the total number of those who were returned as born in Great Britain and Ireland was 100,150. To these may be added British subjects born in Gibraltar and Malta giving a total of 100,586. The difference between this total and that of the persons who returned themselves as European British subjects, *i.e.*, 54,969, gives some indication of the number of Anglo-Indians who returned themselves as Europeans. In this connection it is necessary to examine the proportion of India-born to Europe-born in the successive age groups. In the lowest age group only 31·6 per cent. of those returned as E. B. subjects were born in Great Britain or Ireland. In group 14 to 16 this percentage rises to 39·7 per cent.; in group 17—23 to 74 per cent., or in the two taken together, *i.e.*, 14—23, to 70·2 per cent.; in group 24—33, where the percentage of Europe-born is highest, to 77·4 per cent. After that it falls to about 63 per cent. between the ages 34—53, and to 54·4 in the group 54 and over. As no separate figures are available for European British subjects born outside Great Britain and Ireland it is necessary to make some arbitrary adjustment of figures to arrive at an estimate of the number of Anglo-Indians returned as European British subjects more accurate than the mere indication given by the difference in the figures. If something over 5 per cent. be allowed for the Indian, colonial and foreign-born of pure non-domiciled European parentage in the lower age-groups and about half that in the highest, and if an additional 5 per cent. be allowed in the lowest group for children of European British subjects who are taken to Europe at an early age and do not return, we arrive at the figure of 58 per cent. as born in India in the lowest age-group, 25 per cent. in the next group 14—23, and 18 per cent. in group 24—33, rising to 32 in the next two groups and to 43 per cent. in the last group. The figures thus arrived at for persons born and domiciled in India but returned as European British subjects are 12,841 aged 0—13, 8,286 aged 14—23, 8,987 aged 24—33, 8,019 aged 34—43, 4,656 aged 44—53 and 3,969 aged 54 and over, making a total of approximately 47,000. The relative proportions are illustrated in the accompanying diagrams, and the figures thus adjusted of the Europe-born and India-born clearly indicate that the latter represents a comparatively normal age series, whereas the former is obviously abnormal and is entirely governed by migration. Probably it is primarily controlled by the ages of British troops, the total number of which in India amounted at the time of the census to 70,034 (there were 72,151 in 1921), but in any case it completely dominates the combined curve after the age of 4 years, as may be seen by comparing the curves of annual ages for Europe-born males and females. The numbers of those born and remaining in India however, excluding as they must do the great majority of Europeans, seem to be much too high to represent only the unmixed domiciled Europeans, and it seems certain that a high proportion of this population is really Anglo-Indian. If, after making an allowance as above indicated for those European, British subjects of non-Indian domicile who may have been born outside Great Britain and Ireland, some 35 per cent. of the remaining India-born in each age group be regarded as enough, as they probably are, to represent the total of domiciled European British Subjects, we may take 30,000 as the number of Anglo-Indians who should be deducted from the total of European British subjects and added to that of those returned as Anglo-Indians. It has to be borne in mind that cases of marriage between male European British subjects and female Anglo-Indians are probably more frequent than the reverse, and in such cases it is more than likely that the whole family will be returned as European British subjects whereas in fact that description may really apply to one member only. Be that as it may, by this calculation the figure of Europeans in India would be reduced to 125,555—say 125,500, while that of Anglo-Indians is correspondingly raised from 138,395 to 168,400. In the tables, of course, the numbers are given as returned at the census (part *ii*, Table XIX). The figures for European British subjects, whether in the form returned or thus adjusted, are to be compared with 185,434 persons returned as European British subjects in 1911, the Delhi Durbar year, when the figures were higher than ever before or since, of whom 122,919 were returned as born in the United Kingdom. It is possible of course that to make the adjusted figure for 1931 comparable a similar

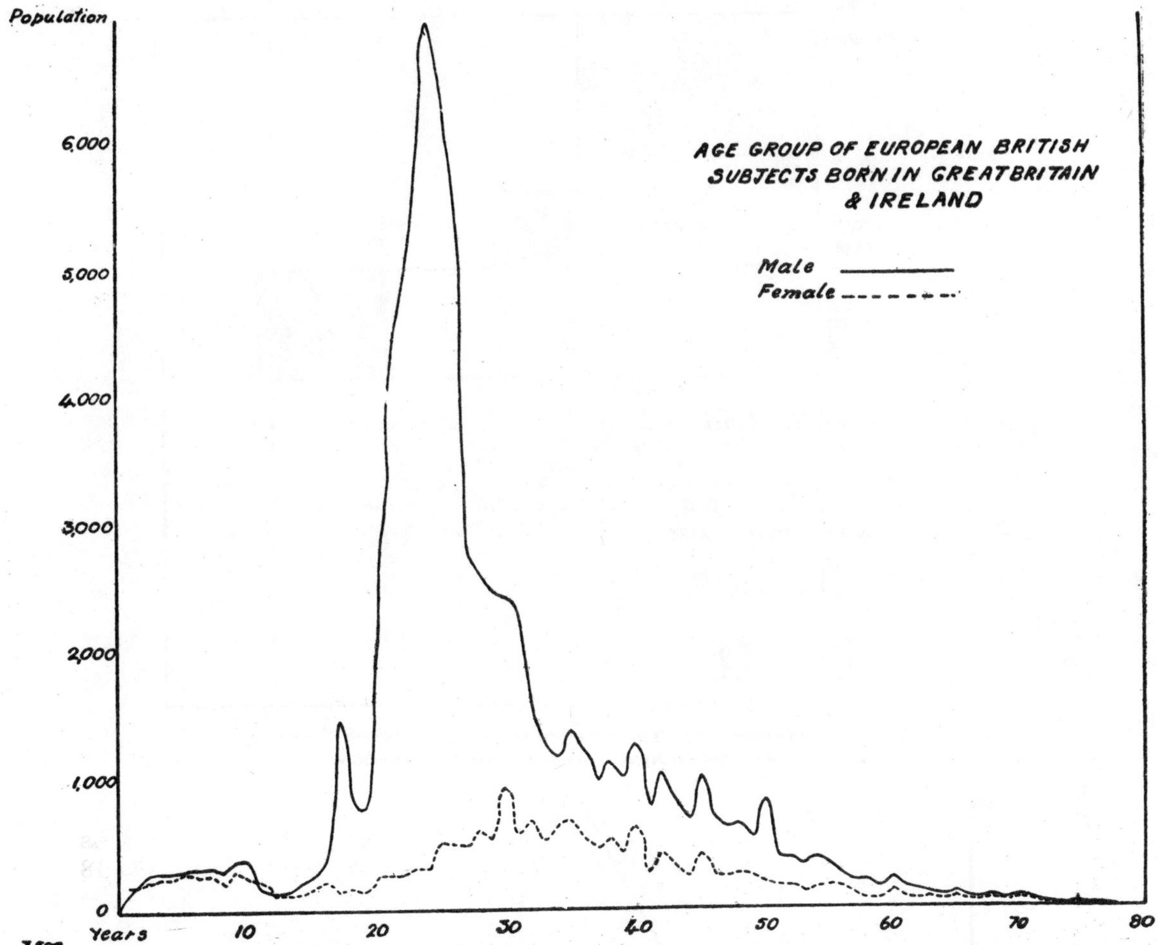
Population
6,000
5,000
4,000
3,000
2,000
1,000
0
Years
10
20
30
40
50
60
70
80
AGE GROUP OF EUROPEAN BRITISH SUBJECTS BORN IN GREATBRITAIN & IRELAND
Male
Female

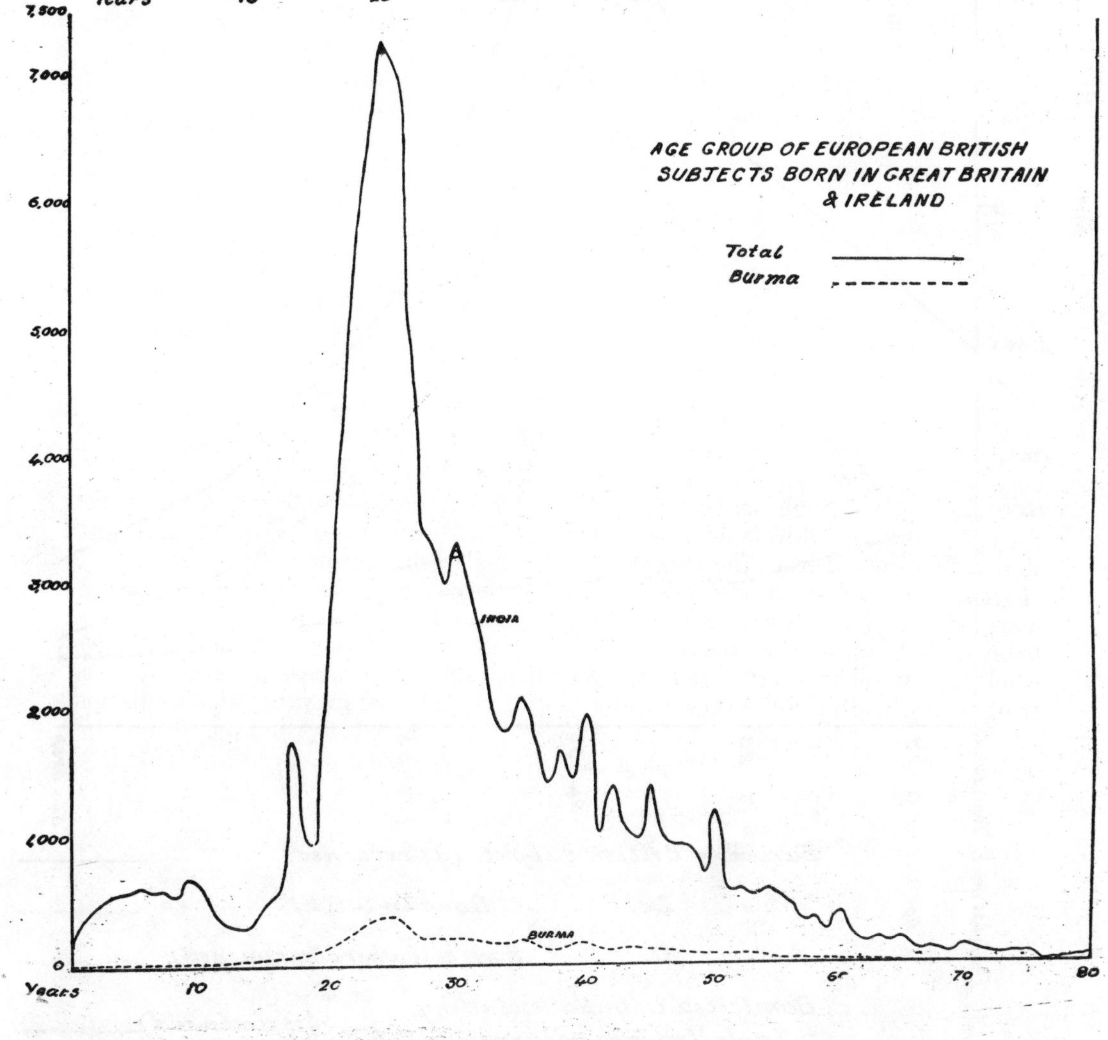
7,500
7,000
6,000
5,000
4,000
3,000
2,000
1,000
0
Years
10
20
30
40
50
60
70
80
AGE GROUP OF EUROPEAN BRITISH SUBJECTS BORN IN GREAT BRITAIN & IRELAND
Total
Burma
INDIA
BURMA

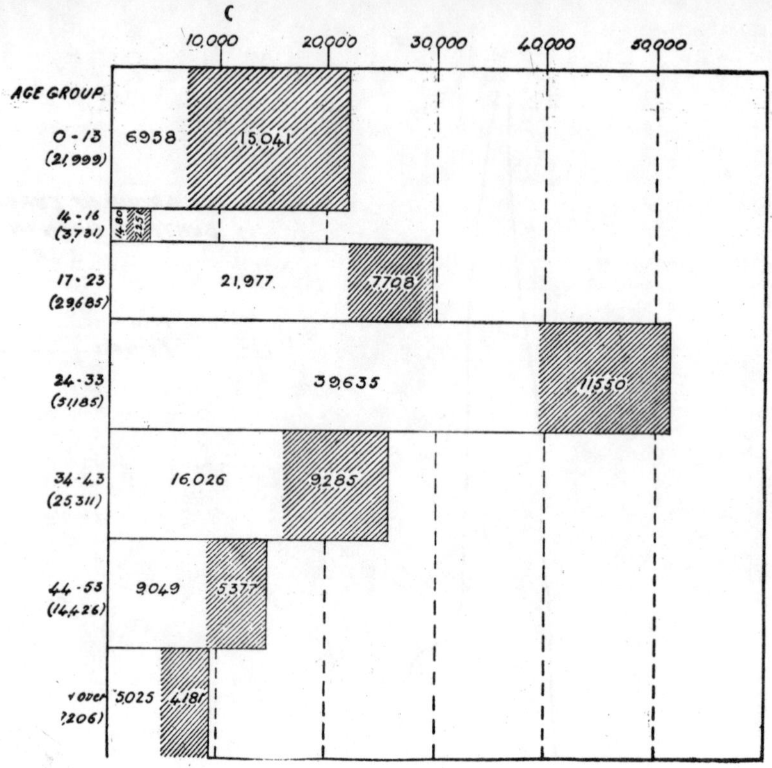

Age Groups of persons returned as European British Subjects.
The unshaded portions represent those born in Europe.

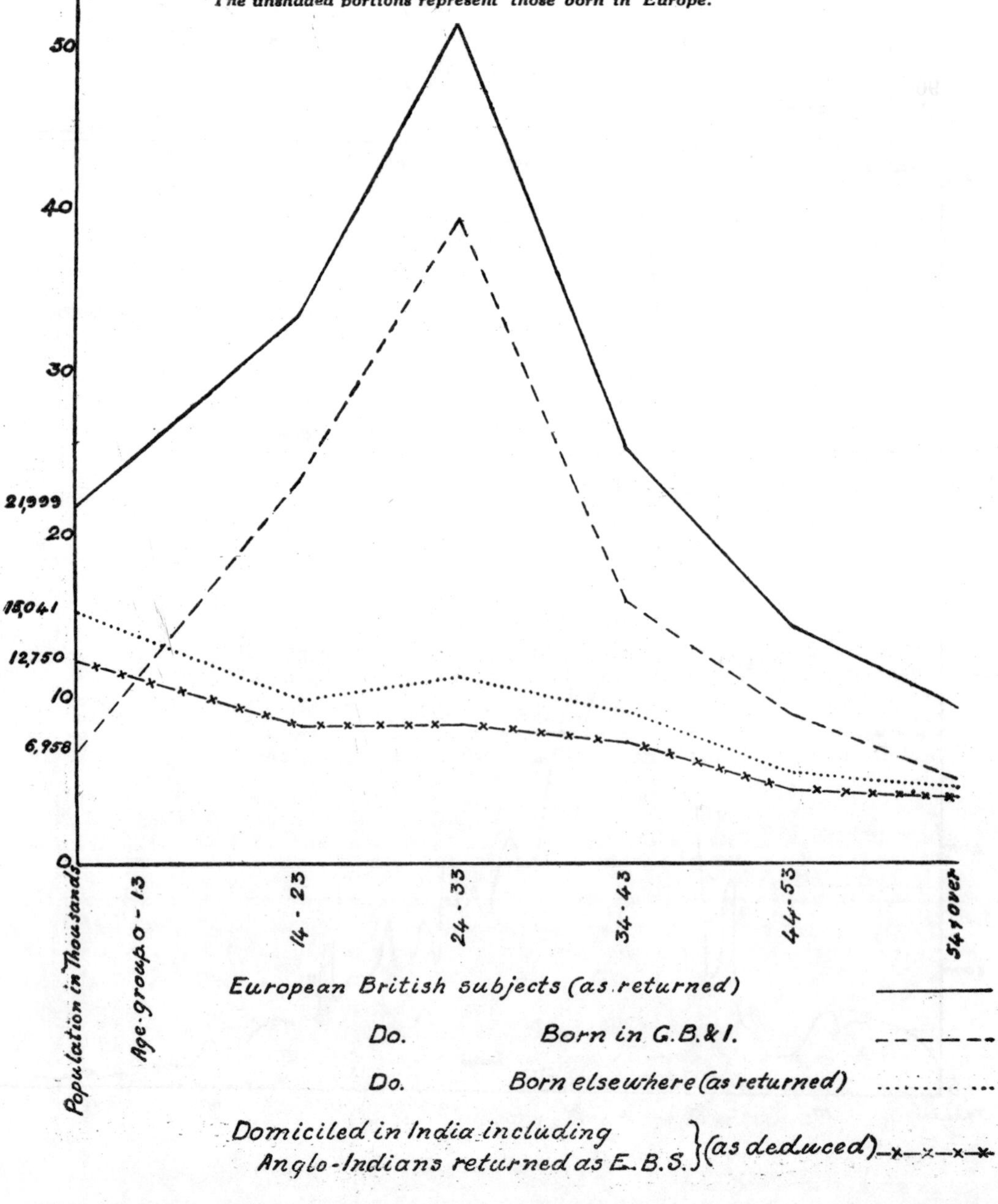

adjustment is needed for this 185,434 also. If worked out on the same proportior it would reduce the number of European British subjects in 1911 to less than the number who returned a birth-place in the United Kingdom by some 3,000, which is impossible, and would add 19,000 odd to the Anglo-Indian total of that census (155,560 : 100,590 : : 185,400 : 119,900), and reduce the total of genuine European British subjects to 166,100. In any case the decrease of the latter in 1931 is marked and unequivocal.

Whereas in the Indian Empire the number of European British subjects is decreasing, in Burma taken by herself, on the contrary, the number of European British subjects censused in 1931 has definitely increased since 1921, though the figure at that census—7,828, showed a marked decrease on the number recorded in 1911, which was 11,828. Nor has this total been regained in 1931, for the Burma figure at this census is 10,627 for European British subjects and 19,200 for Anglo-Indians. In Burma again if a similar adjustment be made for the return of Anglo-Indians as Europeans, the adjusted figures become 7,900 for European British subjects in Burma in 1931 and 21,900 for Anglo-Indians. Some of the European British subjects were probably tourists, as the tourist season was not entirely over by the end of February. Precise figures are not available, but as far as can be ascertained the number is not likely to be more than about 1,000 for India and Burma together. The actual total number of all foreign tourists that passed through Burma between October and March was only 5,287.

One noticeable feature of the 1931 figures for European British subjects is to be found in the increase of females relative to males. While the numbers (unadjusted) of males have decreased by 9,000 since 1921, those of females have decreased by 900 only. In Burma they have not only increased relatively to males but absolutely by 1,365 over the 1921 figure. This increase of females is partly perhaps to be accounted for by an increasing number of Europeans in India, particularly since the war, who marry comparatively young, partly perhaps by more wives and daughters brought out to India since war conditions ceased, and in some small degree perhaps by the number of Indians who go abroad for their education and return with European wives.

Other Foreigners.

179. The total number of Europeans other than British subjects censused in the Indian Empire was 14,353 in 1911 (Armenians included) 10,546 in 1921 just after the war, and 12,579 in 1931. Of these nearly half did not specify the country of their birth, merely returning it as Europe, and of those who did specify the birth-place some 1,500 came from France, 1,000 from Germany, 900 from Italy, 500 each from Belgium and Turkey, and 300 from Switzerland, no other Continental nation contributing as many as 300 persons. Details will be found in part ii of this Volume, Table VI.

Anglo-Indians.

180. Turning to Anglo-Indians we find that in contrast to Europeans the number returned at the census shows an increase of 22·4 per cent. over that in 1921 and of 122·9 per cent. on the total returned in 1881. In 1921 an Anglo-Indian was described for census purposes as a person of mixed European and Indian descent, but for the 1931 census a slightly different definition was suggested, for use where a definition was asked for, describing an Anglo-Indian for census purposes as a person whose father, grand-father or other progenitor in the male line was an European, since it was assumed that others would probably prefer to be returned as Indians. It is possible however that this consideration was inoperative in the case of the progeny of an European or Anglo-Indian woman by an Indian Christian, and the definition adopted may have been at least to that extent unsatisfactory. The actual number returned in 1931 was 138,395 (71,247 males and 67,148 females), of which 61,363 males and 57,832 females were found in India proper and 19,200 (9,884 males and 9,316 females) in Burma, but if to these totals we add the number by which it was calculated that the total of European British subjects had to be reduced, we get a total of 168,400 as the probable real number of Anglo-Indians in the Indian Empire, of whom 22,000 are in Burma. Here again however some allowance must be made in India proper for the return of Indian Christians as Anglo-Indians. It is probable that a number of the descendants of Portuguese dependants, whose practice it was to take their masters' names and who are found in certain districts in Bombay and Bengal where they are known respectively as "East Indians" and "Feringhis," returned themselves at this census, as in previous decades, as Anglo-Indians. The figures show that outside Bombay and Calcutta the number of such returns is very small, but it is difficult to estimate their number in the Presidency towns. It may fairly be taken, perhaps, as 3,400, so that the total number of Anglo-Indians may be put at 165,000. Attention has already been drawn to their remarkable fecundity.

Tribe.

181. Indians returned by tribe instead of by caste form rather a heterogeneous category including Muslim tribes of Pathans, Baluchis, Brahuis or Mappillas; comparatively primitive tribes like the Toda or the Nicobarese who still worship their own tribal deities; others who have become partly Hinduised like most of the Bhils and Gonds where the tribal name is on the way to become a caste name; others largely Christianised like the Oraon or the Lushei, and others again wholly Hindu like the Manipuri, but retaining their distinctive language and culture. In the case of the primitive tribes who are partly Christianised, comparison with the figures of previous decades has been made very difficult by the irritating practice of some missionaries to induce their converts to abandon their tribal name and return themselves nondescriptly as "Indian Christians", as though they had some cause to be ashamed of their forefathers. As the question of the welfare of primitive tribes in contact with changing conditions and progressive culture is of some importance, at any rate to the tribesmen themselves, the comparative figures of such tribes have as far as possible been collected in Table XVIII for successive decades.

The Return of Caste.

182. As on the occasion of each successive census since 1901, a certain amount of criticism has been directed at the census for taking any note at all of the fact of caste. It has been alleged that the mere act of labelling persons as belonging to a caste tends to perpetuate the system, and on this excuse a campaign against any record of caste was attempted in 1931 by those who objected to any such returns being made. It is, however, difficult to see why the record of a fact that actually exists should tend to stabilize that existence. It is just as easy to argue and with at least as much truth, that it is impossible to get rid of any institution by ignoring its existence like the proverbial ostrich, and indeed facts themselves demonstrate that in spite of the recognition of caste in previous decades the institution is of itself undergoing considerable modification. Indeed the treatment of caste at the 1931 census may claim to make a definite, if minute, contribution to Indian unity. Thus in the tables for literacy and civil condition by selected castes the arrangement which has hitherto been on a purely provincial basis, has been changed to show collectively corresponding units from different parts of India, while the same principle has been attempted in the tabulation of castes. How far the agitation, which was strongest in the Punjab, for the return of no caste was really due to a *bona-fide* desire to see caste abolished, and how far it may have been due to entirely other considerations of a political nature, we cannot pretend to say. It does seem clear, however, that in some degree political considerations did contribute to an agitation which probably started with a quite disinterested impulse. It is possible also that the desire of certain sects of Hinduism to extend their numbers and influence may have contributed from a sectarian as distinct from the political standpoint. No total of Hindus who returned themselves as of no caste in India at the last census is available, but 20,993 Hindus appeared in the Punjab census tables as "caste unspecified", about half of them coming from Bahawalpur State. In 1931, a definite return of nil was accepted for caste as distinct from the individuals who on account of ignorance or accident failed to state any caste at all. These returns of 'caste nil' totalled 1,883,464 for India, 98 % of which came from Bengal. In addition to it there were 60,715 Hindus for whom no return of caste was obtained. No return of caste was insisted on from Arya or Brahmo Hindus or from Sikhs, Jains, Buddhists, Muslims or Christians unwilling to make one, but where volunteered it was recorded, and has in the case of some Muslim groups been tabulated where such groups present functional or social features obviously derived from the caste system. It is not suggested that caste rules are observed by Muslims as they are by Hindus but, though there is no ban on commensality, inter-group marriage is apt to be restricted in the case of Muslim groups derived from Hindu castes, and is perhaps hardly as free as it is among the corresponding groups of Sikhs. Indian Christians who did not return their caste, and the majority do not do so, generally appeared on the schedule in this column under the designation 'Indian Christian'. Caste, however, as pointed out elsewhere is by no means ignored after conversion. Only last June (1932) a writer in *The Guardian* (Madras) quoted the case of a Christian pastor in Madras, who, after presiding at a church committee meeting, went for a meal to the catechist's house. As he was an Adi-Dravida he could only be allowed to eat by himself in the veranda and "had to remove his leaf-plate himself". The same writer laid stress upon the part played by caste in church politics and the greater tolerance with which the institution is regarded by the Roman Church. It is of course the desire to escape from the stigma of an outcaste name that leads Indian Christians generally to return no caste, though curiously enough some Christians in the Central Provinces returned their caste as *Satnami*, in itself a religious sect probably schismatic from Hinduism but now little more than an euphemism for 'Chamar'.

It has already been suggested that facts themselves show that caste is undergoing a change. There are, however, influences at work which sometimes cut both ways. The introduction of railways, 'buses and quick communications has often been credited with a tendency to break down caste and there can be no doubt that this is true with regard to some aspects of caste, *e.g.*, distance pollution. On the other hand rapid communications seem to have acted to a certain extent as a strengthening bond, since they render possible the practice of continuing to marry within the group in spite of a change of residence to a distant place. There is no doubt whatever that in the past the migration of small groups to the areas in which they have been out of touch with their religion or caste fellows, and perhaps in mediaeval times subject to different sets of caste rules promulgated by rulers with different policies or views, has led to the splitting of castes into a number of endogamous groups which might have retained their original uniformity but for distance and failure of contact. The railway and the omnibus operate against such fission.

There is, however, apparently a tendency towards the consolidation of groups at present separated by caste rules. The best instance of such a tendency to consolidate a number of castes into one group is to be found in the grazier castes which aim at combining under the term "Yadava" Ahirs, Goalas, Gopis, Idaiyans and perhaps some other castes of milkmen, a movement already effective in 1921. This movement is generally speaking, however, poorly co-ordinated as yet and within a given group of castes the tendency some times shows itself in contradictory directions, but we may quote as typical of the movement for consolidation the desire of the artisan castes in many parts of India to appear under a common name; thus carpenters, smiths, goldsmiths and some others of similar occupations desired in various parts of India to be returned by a common denomination such as *Vishwakarma* or *Jangida*, usually desiring to add a descriptive noun implying that they belonged to one of the two highest *varnas* of Hinduism, either Brahman or Rajput. Of the two, Brahman was usually desired at this census though in some cases a caste which had applied in one province to be called Brahman asked in another to be called Rajput and there are several instances at this census of castes claiming to be Brahman who claimed to be Rajput ten years ago. Of course this movement for consolidation with a new designation implying a high social origin is partially to be ascribed to a very proper desire to rise in the social estimation of other people. It is also attributable in some cases to a desire for the backing of a large community in order to count for more in political life. There is little evidence as yet that intermarriage is being practised within these consolidating groups, but it is a development the possibility of which may not be overlooked, and the Census Superintendent of the Central Provinces quotes "specific instances ...... of marriage between members of different sub-castes of Brahmans, and between members of different sub-castes of Kalars, whose union would formerly have been condemned". Another point that has been raised at this census is a difficulty of stating a caste in the case of intercaste marriages, which, few enough in pro-

Some new ranks claimed by old castes.

Old name.	*1921 claims.*	*1931 claims.*
Kamar	Kshattriya	Brahman.
Sonar	Kshattriya Rajput	Brahman. Vaisya.
Sutradar	Vaisya	Brahman.
Nai	Thakur	Brahman.
Napit	Baidya	Brahman.
Rawani (Kahar).	Vaisya	Kshattriya.
Muchi	Baidya Rishi	..
Chamar	..	Gahlot Rajput.

portion to the population, appear to be increasing in number and rather tend towards the feeling, already in existence as a result of other causes, that the splitting of Hindu society into a number of castes is dangerous to the body as a whole and that divisions corresponding to the four *varnas* of the Vedas are sufficient in themselves. There is, however, a very marked repugnance in all the castes who have anything to say about the matter to being designated *sudras*, though the term seems to have been quite respectable up to a comparatively recent date. On the whole it is fair to conclude that there is a tendency for the limitations of caste to be loosened and for rigid caste distinctions to be broken down, and if that be the case there seems to be little support for the argument that a return of caste at the census operates in the other direction. On the other hand in the present state of society it was not possible to dispense with that return since in a very considerable number of cases it is essential to a knowledge of the position in his environment of the individuals concerned. It is possible that in another ten years it may be feasible to substitute some other criterion and it would certainly be desirable, if it were so feasible, to adopt for census purposes some much larger grouping than that of castes. The use of *varna*, however, is quite impossible since practically every Hindu who claims to be a Hindu at all would claim to be either Brahman or Kshattriya. Even castes of Chamars in the United Provinces have dropped their characteristic nomenclature and at this census returned themselves as Sun-or Moon-descended Rajputs. This, of course, does not imply any correspondingly respectful treatment of them by their neighbours. It is obviously impossible for the Census authorities to do anything other than accept the nomenclature of the individuals making the return, since to discriminate and to allot to different groups would involve entering into discusssion on the basis of largely hypothetical data. Experience at this census has shown very clearly the difficulty of getting a correct return of caste and likewise the difficulty of interpreting it for census purposes. The Superintendent of Census Operations for Madras in this connection writes as follows :—

> "Sorting for caste is really worthless unless nomenclature is sufficiently fixed to render the resulting totals close and reliable approximations. Had caste terminology the stability of religious returns caste sorting might be worth while. With the fluidity of present appellations it is certainly not .... 227,000 Ambattans have become 10,000 ......Navithan, Nai, Nai Brahman, Navutiyan, Pariyari claim about 140,000—all terms unrecorded or untabulated in 1921 ...... Individual fancy apparently has some part in caste nomenclature. For example, an extremely dark individual pursuing the occupation of waterman on the Coorg border described his caste as Suryavamsa, the family of the sun."

Many of the claims made and appellations used recall irresistibly the ruse of that hero of W. S. Gilbert's who "christened himself 'Darwinian Man'", and the difficulty of classifying by occupation is instanced by the fact that cultivation in northern India is a most respectable occupation whereas in certain parts of southern India it is largely associated with the "exterior" castes and is consequently less respectable. Similarly the term 'merchant' would cover all sorts of different social classes and units from the Gujarati *bania* to the gipsy Banjara. Moreover, though it is conceded that the position of individuals belonging to exterior castes (that is to castes hitherto described as "depressed") has been much ameliorated as far as public life is concerned, and that untouchability has in that respect been very appreciably reduced, all available information goes to show that in private intercourse, as in religious observances, the castes whose water cannot be accepted are held at as great a distance as before. In so far as their position has been improved it seems to be less the result of a change of heart towards them than of a concession by caste to caste for its own convenience and not by caste to outcaste for the benefit of the latter. The present position of the exterior castes is examined in an appendix to this volume.

The Tabulation of Caste.

183. For several reasons therefore the usual treatment of caste at this census has been modified. In the first place provincial Superintendents were informed that it was not necessary generally to tabulate figures of castes for which the Local Government did not regard such tabulation as important, while as the standard of population of castes for tabulation four per mille, instead of two per mille as in 1921, was suggested as a minimum. An exception was made in the case of exterior castes, and primitive tribes, with regard to which the instructions were that all should be tabulated, and in the case of a dozen or so selected castes of wide distribution which might serve as specimens so to speak of society for all India purposes in Tables VIII, XI and XIV. In tabulating castes for Table XVII the method of 1901, retained in 1911 and 1921, has been abandoned in favour of the 1891 method in which they appear grouped roughly by traditional occupation, references being given in different groups to individual castes to enable examples to be found in the three tables of Civil Condition, Occupation and Literacy above mentioned. In reverting to the 1891 method of tabulating caste for Table XVII, the occupation scheme used has been as far as possible assimilated to the Bertillon scheme, which has long been the basis of the Occupational Table (X). Admittedly this method of tabulating caste is far from being entirely satisfactory, since it can only recognise traditional occupation, which is not always a non-contentious question, and cannot simultaneously recognise more than one of several traditional occupations for the same caste, as, for instance, basket-making, scavenging and music for Doms. It does, however, admit of associating together many castes which are nearly related in function and origin instead of divorcing them entirely on account of an alphabetical chasm between the initial letters of their appellations. It also avoids any semblance of arrangement by order of social precedence. All subsequent census officers in India must have cursed the day when it occurred to Sir Herbert Risley, no doubt in order to test his admirable theory of the relative nasal index, to attempt to draw up a list of castes according to their rank in society. He failed, but the results of his attempt are almost as troublesome as if he had succeeded, for every census gives rise to a pestiferous deluge of representations, accompanied by highly problematical histories, asking for recognition of some alleged fact or hypothesis of which the census as a department is not legally competent to judge and of which its recognition, if accorded, would be socially valueless. Moreover, as often as not direct action is requested against the corresponding hypotheses of other castes. For the caste that desires to improve its social position seems to regard the natural attempts of others to go up with it as an infringement of its own prerogative ; its standing is in fact to be attained by standing upon others rather than with them. For these reasons an abandonment of the return of caste would be viewed with relief by census officers. This question is one which it will only be possible to determine when the time comes, but if the exterior castes were to agree to return their religion or their community as "Adi-Hindu" or by some similar adventitious label, it might be possible even to omit the return of caste, while in any case it would afford a collective term which might make it possible to ignore individual castes for the purpose of tabulation and a tentative experiment in this direction has been made in presenting Table XVII.

The Origin of Caste.

184. How far an abandonment of the return of caste would be a really popular move is rather a different question. Caste is still of vital consideration in the structure of Indian society and of intense importance as well as interest to the majority of Hindus. It impinges in innumerable ways on questions not only of race and religion but also of economics, since it still goes far to determine the occupation, society and conjugal life of every individual born into its sphere. Some consideration of its origin cannot therefore be avoided and a number of different explanations have been offered for the existence of what is, as it is found to-day, a system unique in the world, since there is no other country or nation which possesses anything approaching the elaborate caste system of India, nor is there any other country known to have ever possessed one of the same kind. It has been described on the one hand as leading to "a degree of social disunity to which no parallel can be found in human history*", though on the other it has probably played a very important historical role as a great contributor to political and cultural stability, and there is much that is true in the Abbé Dubois' eulogium of the caste system. Roughly speaking, there may be said to be five important theories of the origin of caste, apart from the minor variations and combinations of these five ; there is first the traditional view of the origin of caste typified in the Code of Manu ; there is the occupational explanation, of which Nesfield was the best known exponent ; the tribal and religious explanation of Ibbetson ; the family or gentile explanation offered by Senart, and the racial and hypergamous explanation of Risley. None of these explanations are at all satisfactory by themselves, though all contain a definite appreciation of what should perhaps be rather described as features than causes of the caste system. The

* Nesfield—*Brief View of the Caste System of the N.-W. Provinces and Oudh,* page 116.

nearest approach to a satisfactory explanation is probably to be found in two articles by Stanley Rice which appeared in the *Asiatic Review* in 1929. Even Mr. Rice, however, hardly seems to appreciate the full implications of the view he adopts*, while credit must also be given to Oldenberg for having seen as early as 1907, that tabus on commensality were pre-Aryan in origin.

Before attempting to suggest the true causes which have led to the growth of caste in India, it will perhaps be necessary to examine briefly the various views mentioned above. The first of these is the traditional view of which the Code of Manu may be taken as the prime exponent. Caste, according to this view, is based on four *varnas* or " colours " sprung from different parts of the Creator's body and subject to certain prohibitions as to marriage, food and occupation, breach of which has led to loss of position, while the enormous number of existing castes between which inter-marriage and commensality is banned, is accounted for by unions, licit or illicit, between one and another of these castes ; hypergamous marriages having given rise to clean castes, and marriages, which we may perhaps describe as hypogamous, between a male of a lower position and a female of higher, stigmatised as *pratiloma* that is ' against the grain ', having given rise to the out-castes who, though Hindu or at least quasi-Hindu by religion, are outside the pale of decent Hindu society. This traditional view is based on a Rigvedic hymn which, if it cannot be said to be spurious, is at least much later in composition than the bulk of the Rigveda. The view is generally discarded by all critics as an artificial systematisation composed centuries after the origin which it professes to explain, and has been clearly shown by Senart to be an attempt to interpret in terms of an Indo-European social system parallel to that of Rome an existing order, which, at any rate at the time of application, the terms cannot be made to fit.

The second view derives caste entirely from occupation. The principal exponent of this view was Nesfield who regarded the present division of Indian society into castes, which are largely occupational, as indicating the origin of the whole system. His position is supported by Dahlmann who likewise sees in a village community practising a particular trade or craft the origin of a caste through the formation of a guild which in course of time has become exclusive both in the matter of commensality and that of marriage. One of the arguments on which this view of the origin of caste is based is drawn from a supposition that the lowest castes in this scale are those which practise a craft in which no metal is used, the higher castes being those which involve the use of metal, the inference being that the non-metal using castes became closed guilds as a result of the arrival of subsequent peoples using metal, and these in their turn became closed guilds which did not intermarry with the former non-metal-using villagers. This theory will hardly stand critical examination. It is true that basket-making is an occupation of one of the lowest castes ; at the same time the black-smiths' caste is very far from being more highly esteemed, though it must be considerably later in point of time, than that of the coppersmith or the goldsmith. Moreover, this scheme does not explain at all the varying positions of agriculturalists who are of low castes in certain parts of southern India but generally of respectable if not of high caste in northern India. It should be, however, mentioned in this connection that it does appear to be a custom in southern India or in parts of southern India to provide a craftsman, that is, a man of the carpenter's or blacksmith's or goldsmith's profession with a grave made of stone slabs in a cist form in place of the simple unlined grave which is given to a cultivator, and this does suggest either a difference in status or in custom between the aborigines and immigrants who brought in tools and crafts, or in the alternative some difference in eschatology between the cultivator and the craftsman. The parallel, however, which is drawn between caste and the guild system of the later Roman Empire, although at first it appears quite close, breaks down on examination. The later Roman Empire attempted to compel every person to follow the profession into which he was born, but this was purely economic in origin

* This applies also to Dr. Bonnerjea's hypothesis published in the *Indian Antiquary* in 1931. While criticising Rice for regarding caste as predating the Aryan invasion he regards the system as introduced by the Indo-Europeans, but nevertheless ascribes the institution to primitive superstition and to a belief in magic. Dr. Guha advanced a similar view in a thesis before Havard University in 1924. I agree in ascribing caste to a belief in magic, though I cannot accept the rest of Dr. Bonnerjea's hypothesis which appears to me to be contradictory. It may be added that the theory of caste here put forward was arrived at before I had seen either Rice's or Bonnerjea's articles and was independent of their conclusions.

and did not involve any ban on commensality between one profession and another, and what might appear to be a ban on intermarriage in that a man was compelled under certain conditions to adopt the profession of his wife's father, was really only an attempt to recruit persons for certain unpopular professions a shortage in which was inconvenient to the State. It is inconceivable that any such purely artificial system as a caste distinction based solely on function could possibly give rise to the vivid and lasting prejudices that accompany caste distinctions in India.

The third explanation of the caste system has been sought in a tribal origin. Ibbetson attributed the development of caste to a combination of tribal origins, functional guilds and 'a Levitical religion', and he laid the greater stress in this on the tribe. It is quite clear that tribes are just as much responsible for the origin of certain castes as it is that certain castes are or have been in the past restricted to particular functions. At the same time Ibbetson's explanation of the origin of caste is really only a summary of certain observable features of caste. These features, that is, tribes, guilds and religious monopolies, have certainly contributed to the growth of the caste system, having no doubt done much to consolidate and perpetuate it, but they can in no sense be regarded as causes. They are features which are not unique and are common to many countries, whereas caste is something that is found nowhere else. Given caste, a tribe, a guild or a priestly order may very easily become a caste, but if the essentials of caste are not there to start with it is difficult to see how any of these groups with the possible exception of the priestly order, would be likely to develop into one.

The fourth attempt to explain caste that we have mentioned is Senart's ascription of its origin to the *gens* and to family worship. Here again we are unable to agree with the explanation put forward. The *gens* would appear to be essentially other than caste and to correspond to *gotra*, which so far from being synonymous with caste, definitely runs counter to it. A caste in India seldom if ever claims a common ancestor, though the *gotra* like the *gens* insists on common ancestry. Moreover the mere existence of a number of gotras within a caste, but not confined to it, seems to preclude Senart's supposition that the exclusiveness of caste originated in family worship.

The fifth explanation of caste is Risley's derivation from colour and hypergamy. This derivation appears to fail to explain satisfactorily the taboo on food and marriage. In order to base caste on hypergamy, Risley has found it necessary to postulate a fictitious point at which the result of intermarriage provides enough women to enable a society to close its ranks and become a caste, although there still exist outside it more women of the same community from which it has been drawing its wives and with whom it has been in more or less intimate relations. Apart from this consideration the nearest parallel to caste which can be found goes somewhat perhaps to support Risley's theory; that is, the position of the negroes in the southern states of the U. S. A. Westermarck (*History of Human Marriage*, 1901, pages 365-7) supports this view; but although separate carriages, separate restaurants and even separate towns are provided for negroes, no pollution takes place as a result of having negro servants and there is no hard and fast line which is really analogous to a caste division between, say quadroons and octoroons, nor have the many social factors, which have tended in India to produce similar results in regard to foreigners, such as the Moghals or the English, really succeeded in making Muslims or Anglo-Indians into a caste in the Hindu sense, and where Muslims form a real caste it is always one which has been converted from pre-Muslim inhabitants and retained its pre-Islamic organisation. Colonel Sewell points out an additional respect in which the parallel breaks down in that in the Indian case the superior population consisted of invaders presumably anxious to preserve their racial identity and their social superiority, whereas in the American case the negro was in the first instance imported for the purpose of providing labour. In any case, if we reject Risley's derivation of caste from race, we must nonetheless admit the part that *varna* has played in crystallising and perpetuating that institution, which could hardly have come down to posterity in its present form without having been subjected to the reagent of racial prejudice and discrimination.

Of recent Indian writers on caste, one, Prof. N. K. Dutt*, while criticising Risley adopts in effect his theory of origin, though attaching much more value to

* *Origin and growth of Caste in India* (Calcutta, 1931).

the code of Manu, and Mr. Hayavadana Rao*, and Dr. Ghurye† likewise regard caste as having arisen largely as a result of racial difference. The latter emphasises the factor of priestly manipulation by Brahmans attempting to maintain the purity of race of the Aryan invaders. Like the others the latter theory cannot be regarded as adequate in itself, and though it may represent an important contribution to the ultimate establishment of a hard and fast system, it does not appear probable on the face of it that priestly dominance could have effected so much, unless the essential factors of the system were already present and predisposed to be used for such a purpose ; and in this connection it seems necessary to draw attention to an important paper‡ by A. M. T. Jackson (J. A. S. B. III, No. 7 of July 1907) who points out effectively the contributions of political divisions and of the royal prerogative in early India to the formation of sub-castes. The latter author, however, explicitly disclaims any attempt to indicate the origin of the system, and it is with its ultimate origin rather than the process of its development that we are here concerned.

Seeing that light is required on the origin of caste it would seem not unreasonable, as in the case of religion, to examine first those cultures that survive in India least altered from antiquity in case they can illumine origins elsewhere obscured by changes and developments due to growing civilization and to external contacts. Caste, as it now is, is an institution which has grown and developed through many centuries, but since it is so firmly rooted in India, and since it is found nowhere else, it would appear almost certain, on the face of it, that its first beginnings are to be sought in India and not outside, and we have fortunately in the more inaccessible corners of this vast country still a few tribes whose primitive conditions of life have changed so little in a thousand years as to be witnesses of value. Pliny the Elder, writing in the first century A. D., mentions *Abariman*, the untamed hills of the eastern Himalayas, whose inhabitants are still spoken of by the Assamese in the precise term used by Pliny—*abari manu*, and Ptolemy, writing in the second, locates "the Nanga-logae, that is the realm of the naked" precisely where the *Naga log* are found today, some tribes of them still unclothed, still untouched by contact with the people of the plains, tribes who have never seen a white man nor a horse nor know what is gun-powder, and whose language is still unspoken by any one outside their own community save some of their immediate neighbours. Hinduism, Buddhism and Islam have never penetrated here, and caste as it exists in the plains is unknown and undreamed of, but nevertheless institutions are found which seem to throw a definite light on caste and religion as they have developed in another environment.§ Thus in the unadministered area to the east of the Naga Hills, where each village is an independent political unit, there is very often to be seen a distribution by villages of certain occupations. Thus some villages make pots but do not weave cloth ; others weave, and others again are occupied principally with blacksmiths' work, the one village bartering its products with its neighbours, when not prevented by mutual hostilities, in spite of differences of language, customs and sometimes perhaps of race between one village and another. Here we have clearly the occupational aspect of caste origins on which so much emphasis has been laid by Nesfield and Ibbetson, and indeed the remnants of such a condition seem to have survived in northern India until the Buddhistic age, as the Jatakas indicate that certain trades were localised in separate villages, some containing potters, others smiths and so forth, but it is not the only aspect. It frequently happens that upheavals in village politics end in battle, vendetta and sudden death, and that as a consequence part of a village community, usually an exogamous clan or sept, is compelled to migrate to some other village. It might be anticipated that a group of weaving families would be welcomed in a pot-making village which only obtained cloth by barter, and *vice versa*, and up to a point this is indeed the case ; numbers are strength and such immigrants are generally welcomed and allowed to settle and cultivate,—but not to ply their ancestral craft when that differs from the occupation of their hosts. That is tabu, and should the strangers insist on it they must again go elsewhere to some village in which it is permitted. Instances of this have occurred within the writer's personal knowledge, and the underlying feeling seems to be that the practice of the tabued craft will affect the crops and the fruits of the earth generally, perhaps, because it is an offence to the

* *Indian Caste System* (Bangalore 1931).

† *Caste and Race in India* (London, 1932).

‡ Pointed out to me by Dr. B. S. Guha to whom my acknowledgments are due.

§ *Cf.*, T. C. Hodson *Naga Tribes of Manipur*, p. 83, and *Genna in Assam*, J.R.A.I., 1906, p. 92.

ancestral spirits who are generally regarded as the source of fructification; or it may be that the particular form of *mana* or *aren* which enables the manufacture of the article made by the strangers is liable to neutralise the corresponding magic on which the traditional village industry depends. Here however there is generally speaking no tabu on commensality or on intermarriage, and for the sources of these aspects of caste we must look elsewhere.

For a possible source of the commensal tabu, however, we need not look far from that of the occupational one. The same Naga communities which we have been considering afford abundant instances of tabus on certain foods, of a vivid belief in *mana* or, as the Ao Naga calls it, *aren*, and of the magical effects of food on the consumer. It has already been pointed out (*v. sup.*, page 414) that certain foods are peculiar to certain exogamous clans, and are in many cases associated with clan ceremonial, and it may be offered as one hypothesis that the presence of strange craftsmen practising their craft is condoned or rather rendered less dangerous by the prohibition of intimate relations with them, reducing thus the inconvenient strictness of one tabu by erecting another which at the start may be less irksome. That this is in accordance with the spirit of the primitive society under consideration is demonstrated by the readiness with which in some tribes the proximity of Christian converts is tolerated, even though they cultivate on tabued days, provided they live outside the village fence and therefore form a more or less separate community, though here again commensality is not barred, except indeed in so far as the Christians refuse to eat such flesh as they are taught to regard as "meats offered to idols". Another hypothesis, and there is no reason to suppose the suggested explanations to be mutually exclusive, is the theory that the food of strangers is itself dangerous. Senart's citation of the tabu on strangers at the family meal would doubtless lead back to this and Rice's view of the tabu on commensality as derived from a belief in totemism agrees in effect with the hypothesis here put forward, since both depend for their force on the belief in *mana* and in the resulting tabu on food or other contacts which may be infected with the dangerous soul-matter of strangers; this soul-matter is particularly perilous if such strangers have new and, what is the same thing, mysterious arts and therefore magical powers. Thus when the writer was touring in previously unvisited Naga territory in 1923-24 he found villages which not only objected to accepting presents or purchase money of any kind from the strangers or to parting with any possession to them for fear of the influence to which they might thus become subject by proxy as it were, but they actually destroyed mats or other property lent to build shelters when the visitors who had used them had gone, and threw away their tainted coins in the jungle. The differentiation between cooked and uncooked food as a vehicle of pollution so familiar to any observer of caste in India is clearly traceable to this view of the infection, by the act of cooking, of the food cooked with the *mana* of the cooker. Similarly among the Maori, to quote Eldon Best, "the most soul-destroying thing according to native ideas" is *tamaoa*, deprivation of *tapu* by means of cooked food. A tabu on intermarriage could easily be traced to a similar source if not to the same one (among the Mafulu of New Guinea no girl who is not a near relative of a bachelor may even see him eat), and once accepted would be tremendously strengthened and indefinitely perpetuated by the practice of hypergamy and by the comparative racial exclusiveness as regards marriage of the Indo-European invaders of the 2nd millenium B. C.

The sentiments and beliefs, therefore, on which caste is based presumably go back to the totemistic proto-australoid and to the austroasiatic inhabitants of pre-Dravidian India and we may conceive of their becoming effective on contact with Dravidian-speaking strangers bringing new crafts from the west. Hence would arise local tabus against certain crafts and persons, tabus tending to become tribal and to erect rigid divisions between communities. Even in early vedic literature different words appear for identical occupations. With culturally superior strangers hypergamy must almost certainly arise, and if there came a foreign priesthood with the ancient sciences of south-west Asia, the belief in their magical powers would make them the most heavily tabued of all. The sea has receded in the Persian Gulf, and Larsa and Lagash, Ur* and Eridu were no great

* Indeed it is stated that "a bead of amazonite from the Nilghary Hills of India was dug up from a prediluvian layer at Ur", (O. G. S. Crawford in *Antiquity, VI 259*), but Mr. Mackay states that "there must have been other sources of green felspar as it was largely used in Egypt from pre-dynastic times downwards".

cry from Makranistan and the delta of the Indus, and it is hard to conceive that India was unknown to them before the barbarian invader swept down from the north; all the requisites for the growth of caste seem to have been present long before that date, and the fact that caste is still far stronger in southern than in northern India, and there is weakest in the Punjab, is of the greatest significance. It must have remained for the Indo-European invader, with that pride of race which has ever and everywhere characterised him, to have the effect of crystallizing, on the basis of a fixed social scale, the pre-existing tabus arising from magical ideas, ultimately resulting in an attempt to describe in terms of an intrusive Indo-Aryan society a social system really based on the tabus of pre-existing conditions. Hence the formalist fictions of the Code of Manu by which all castes are derived from four varnas and arranged in a scheme of which the practice of hypergamy is the key-stone. Obviously the fixation of the extensive and rigid restrictions typical of caste in its later form would take time to establish, and it is natural therefore to find allusions in the later vedas to the absence of any absolute ban on the taking of food cooked by sudras, and Apastamba's statement (II, 2, 3; a reference for which I am indebted to Rai Bahadur Ramaprasad Chanda) clearly suggests that for nonceremonial purposes it was not necessary to be so particular. It is therefore argued not that caste in its present form is not a post-Aryan development, but that the essential ingredients which made the growth of caste possible were of pre-Aryan origin and without them the development of caste would not and could not have taken place.

In this connection there is a bye issue worth consideration; that is the position in Manu's code of the *pratiloma* castes. The explanation of the degraded position they there hold is generally regarded as a more or less fictitious exposition of the hypergamous ideal, but even from the most diehardly hypergamous point of view it is a little difficult to see why the fruit of an hypogamous union should stand lower in the social scale than castes whose ancestors contained no drop at all of the blood of the patrician invader. Granting that for the sake of schematic balance and of the Aristotelian principle of *perversio optimi pessimum* the offspring of a Brahman woman by a Sudra should rank below that of a Kshattriya by a Sudra, it might still have been expected that either would be regarded as superior to a mere Sudra of unmixed blood. It is therefore suggested that Manu's rules of precedence are derived in this respect from social conditions in which the union of a woman of the invading race with one of the indigenous race was necessarily anomalous. Now if the invaders were, like the Indo-Europeans elsewhere, a patrilineal society and if the indigenous race was matrilineal as the original Mediterraneans seem to have been and as the Dravidian-speakers of Malabar still are, the fruit of a male invader and a female indigene would have a recognised position in either society under either the *makkathayam* or the *marumakkathayam* principle, and whether the marriage were patrilocal or matrilocal, but the issue of a female invader by an indigenous male would have no place in either. Since he could not claim kinship through his mother with her exogamous patrilineal class, nor through his father with his matrilocal matrilineal family, and having no claim on family property under either system, his position would tend to become degraded, which would account for the low status given in Manu's code promulgated at a date when the precise causes of the low position were no longer clear and called for some sort of formalist explanation. A reflection of this amalgamation of the two cultures is possibly to be seen in the employment by Hindus of the daughter's or sister's son or husband in certain rites as an alternative to the employment of a Brahman (v. *Punjab Tribes and Castes*, I, 392). It is hardly necessary to point out that such circumstances, under which patrilineal invaders took wives from matrilineal indigenes, would also operate very strongly towards the erection of a purdah system. The woman under the matrilineal system has a freedom not dissimilar to that of the man under the patrilineal. The woman taken from a matrilineal society and having ties of language, kinship, acquaintance and custom with that society, but expected to live according to strange and probably repugnant domestic and marital rules, could only be effectively restrained to that end by cutting off her freedom of movement in and association with the society to which she belonged. It may appear at first sight that the case of a Nambudri Brahman married to a Nayar wife is a contrary instance, since she does not observe purdah at all, but the fact that in this case the children follow the matrilineal system supports the argument that purdah was necessary to the combination of a patrilineal system with the practice of taking wives from a matrilineal society. That purdah should exist so strongly in the case of the Nambudri wives of the elder sons must be explained by the necessity for maintaining a barrier against the encroachment of a matrilineal environment and by the probability that the Nambudri already practised purdah when they first arrived in Malabar. That the purdah system was alien to the Rigvedic Aryans when they invaded India, the Rigveda itself is a witness, while there is nothing whatever to associate it with the Mediterranean stock which seems to have followed the matrilineal system in which purdah has no natural place at all. It is perhaps significant in this connection that purdah is weaker in the south of India than in the north, and in Madras at any rate gets weaker from north to south, where, conversely, caste gets stronger. It is conceivable that the same circumstances gave rise to the practice of the pre-puberty marriage of girls as to that of purdah, and, infant marriage again is least prevalent in the extreme south.

The view that caste corresponds to race has here been rejected, as it is clear that the two do not coincide. The Brahman of the United Provinces has a long head (c. i. 73·1), he of Bengal a round one (c. i. 79·0); the cephalic index of the Chamar of the U. P. is 72·8, and that of the Bihar Chamar 76, and the same differences, which correspond, as explained later, to different migrations into India, are to be found likewise in other castes. At the same time that is not to say that there is no correlation of any kind between caste and race. Though curiously enough the relative position of the corresponding U. P. and Bihar castes in each pair named above is reversed according to that test, Risley's theory of the nasal index has a definite basis on facts. It cannot be denied that there is usually a clear relation between social status and the nasal index and that the latter varies according to the admixture of aboriginal, that is of proto-australoid, blood, though in regard to later immigrant strains caste cannot be similarly correlated to race on any systematic basis. Further in any consideration of caste and race it is impossible to overlook the effect of the famines which have frequently visited India in the past. Famine so severe as to reduce people even to eating their own kind is vouched for by more than one account,* and there can be little doubt but that from time to time such famines must have led to loss of caste on a considerable scale, and though where many have lost it together the result may have been merely the formation of sub-castes, small groups must have often been driven to associating with some caste lower in status rather than live an isolated existence. In effect therefore there must be racial elements common to all castes though in very varying degrees, and racial elements have again been imported into caste by the formation of castes from tribes. This process must have been common enough in the past, and indeed may still be seen working. Jats, Gujars, Kolis or Kaibarttas may be cited as examples in which the process is complete, while it is still in duration in the cases of Panikas, Gonds and Oraons, for instance, and it must frequently have happened that the chiefs of a tribe have ultimately been accepted as Rajputs while the rank and file have failed to achieve so high a status. It is similarly a commonplace that castes frequently owe their origin to religious sects which, after recruiting adherents from many sources, close their ranks to external marriage.

It has been pointed out that the social estimation accorded to any given caste in northern India depreciates from west to east. That is to say that under the hypergamous system it is much more common to take brides from the east and to give them to the west than the reverse. This at first sight would perhaps appear to be occasioned by the much greater shortage of women in proportion to men that is found in the north-west than in the east, but it seems far from impossible but that the practice has also been occasioned by the fact that the patrilineal races which have invaded India have come from the north-west and have hypergamously cavilled at giving their daughters to cousins whose blood was less pure, though showing less compunction in taking wives from such a stock. Just so is it commoner to find Europeans with Anglo-Indian wives than the reverse, and it is perhaps an implication of the same question that east coast Brahmans are, taken as a whole, regarded as less orthodox than those of the west coast.

185. The Census Report of 1901 laid the foundations on which has since been based all work that has been done on the racial composition of India, but the results of such work in the thirty years that have passed since that report was published have so far changed the whole complexion of the problem that a restatement of the **Race.**

* For instance see pages 4 to 8 of Findlay Shirras' *Poverty and Kindred Economic Problems in India*, and *Travels of Peter Mundy, II*, pages 39—52 and 275, 276, Appendix A, and introduction pages lxiii—lxix.

position is now required. Risley's work remains, but his data have been supplemented and his conclusions must be revised. Roughly speaking he recognised three main racial types in India, the Dravidian, the Indo-Aryan, and the Turko-Iranian, the latter of which was confined to the North-West Frontier and the two former of which were modified by two subsidiary elements—the Scythian and the Mongolian, respectively introducing the brachycephalic elements found in western and eastern India. Risley's deductions were coloured by an erroneous belief in the ethnic isolation of India, and an analysis of India's racial ingredients is unfortunately a far more complicated matter than was then realised. Indeed, a later writer on the subject has likened India to a net collecting in its great peninsula the flotsam and jetsam of all Asia. In any case it is necessary to clear the deck by throwing overboard some of Risley's deductions. The Dravidian, as conceived of by him, has been the first to go, and has been replaced by at least three races where he recognised only one, so that the term Dravidian has acquired in consequence an ambiguity with reference to race which makes it essential to confine its use entirely to linguistics, and (except in quotations from other writers) it is only in a linguistic sense that it will be found in this volume. The element which Risley regarded as "Scythian" must be re-classified and re-examined. It is very doubtful if any "Scythian" invaders of India were ever numerous enough to make much impression on pre-existing racial types, and secondly what we know of Scythians suggests that they were probably at least as much dolicho as brachycephalic. In the east again it is impossible to accept the view that the brachycephaly of the Brahmans of Bengal is due to a Mongolian element. If that were so the degree of brachycephaly should increase inversely with social status, whereas the contrary is the case except where genuinely Mongolian peoples are concerned like the Maghs of Arakan; also the Brahman, most brachycephalic of Bengalis, lacks the epicanthic fold. Since 1901 important work has been done on history, such as the first volume of the *Cambridge History of India*, Pargiter's *Ancient Indian Historical Tradition*, Slater's *Dravidian Elements in Indian Culture*, or Chanda's *Indo-Aryan Races*, to name but four of many; on language, including the completion of the *Linguistic Survey of India* by Sir G. Grierson and Professor Sten Konow, the work done by P. Schmidt and more recently by Przyluski and others in Paris, by Morgenstierne on the Dardic languages and by Langdon on the Mohenjodaro signs; on archæology, such as the discovery and exploration of the Indus valley cities by the Archæological Survey, and the work done by Sir Aurel Stein in Baluchistan and the Makran, and on physical anthropology like the work of Haddon, Thurston, Dudley Buxton (*Peoples of Asia*) or Colonel Seymour Sewell's *Racial Ethnology of India* (VIIth Congress of the Far Eastern Association of Trop. Medicine, 1927) and his and Dr. Guha's *Excavations in Baluchistan* and their Chapter XXX of Sir John Marshall's *Mohenjodaro*, and Sir Arthur Keith's important appendix to Thomas' *Arabia Felix*. All this and much other such work has of necessity provided an entirely different conception of the early history of the racial composition of the Indian sub-continent. Mention has been made here of the merest fraction of the number of works that have definitely added to our knowledge of relevant facts since Sir Herbert Risley's great report.

The material available for the determination of the racial elements and affinities of the Indian peoples may be divided for practical purposes into physical, linguisitic and cultural features, to which a very brief attention is all that can be given here. The physical features are dealt with at length by Dr. Guha in the volume of appendices, easily the most important contribution to the physical anthropology of India since Risley's survey; the linguistic have already been referred to in Chapter X, and the cultural in Chapters VI and XI and elsewhere in this volume. It is merely necessary to indicate here the prehistoric cranial material available for a study of race in India. Of such material the important finds are few; Adichanallur and a few other places in southern India, Sialkot, Bayana near Agra, Nal in Baluchistan, and Mohenjodaro comprise the whole field of pre-historic craniology in India.* The important literature may be recapitulated as briefly—Lapicque, *Note Sommaire*, etc., *Bull. Mus. d'Histoire Naturelle*, pages 283-285 (1905) [quoted by Sewell and Guha], Thurston, *Castes and Tribes of S. India*, volume I, pages xxvi-xxviii (1909), Keith, *Journ. Anthropological Society of Bombay*, XI No. 6, pages 663-72 (1917) [quoted by Sewell and Guha], Elliot Smith, footnote on page 81 of Slater's *Dravidian Elements* (1924), and Sewell and Guha *Report on the Bones excavated at Nal* (Mem. Archæol. Survey of India No. 35, Appendix V) and Chapter XXX 'Human Remains' in Marshall's *Mohenjodaro and the Indus Civilization*. The general conclusion is that

* For a map of ancient sites, etc., see the last page of this Chapter.

the Mohenjodaro skulls of the type described as Proto-Australoid are related to skulls of the "massive" type reported on by Buxton from Kish, to the skulls found at Adichanallur in southern India and to those of the modern Veddahs. One of the

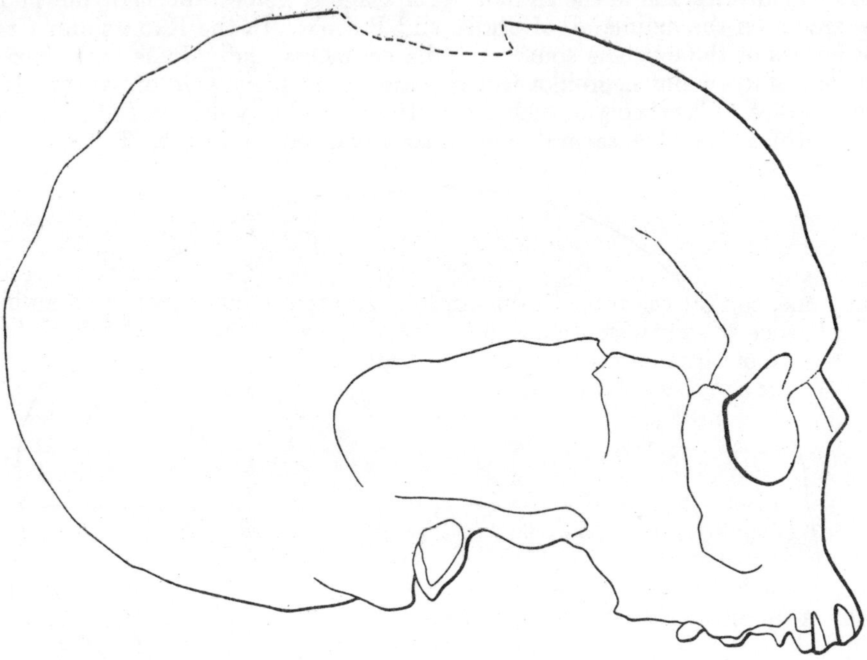

Skull from Adichanallur.

Adichanallur skulls was described by Elliot Smith as "indistinguishable from the early Egyptian type" that is, presumably, the Badarian, and the other as "well within the range of variation of that type". In his *Evolution of Man* he refers to these two skulls in somewhat different words: "One of them is clearly and unmistakeably Proto-Australian in type and the second one conforms more nearly to the racial type known as Mediterranean." The Mohenjodaro skulls of the type described as Mediterranean are related to the Sialkot and the Nal skulls and to the dolichocephalic skulls of Kish, Ur and Anau as well as to the Bayana skull. Mohenjodaro has also yielded one brachycephalic skull of Alpine type in immature condition and one typically Mongolian skull. The physical material for most of India's population seems to have been present in the Indus valley at an early date.

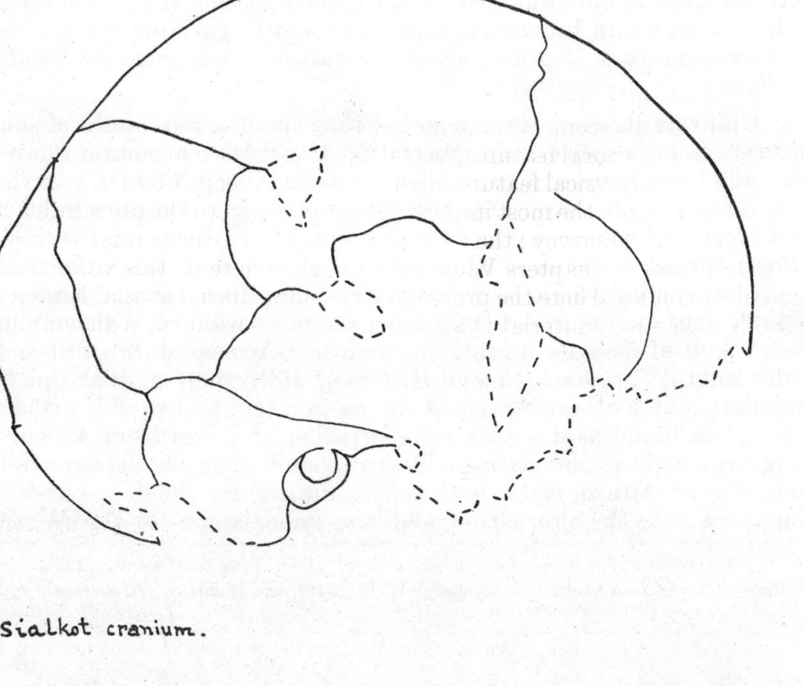

The Sialkot cranium.

The earliest inhabitants of the Indian Peninsula were probably negroid in type, and the Negrito, rapidly disappearing though he is, still survives in the Andaman Islands. His kinship to less isolated and therefore more hybridized tribes in the Malay Peninsula and in the Indian Archipelago is well established, but he has left few traces on the mainland of India and Burma. In the Kadars and Uralis of the forests of the extreme south of India occasional individuals with frizzly hair and low stature and negrolike features are very suggestive of survivals of the Negrito race. The theory of such a negrito survival in southern India, particularly among the Kadar, has several times been advanced, *e.g.*, by K. T. Preuss, Keane

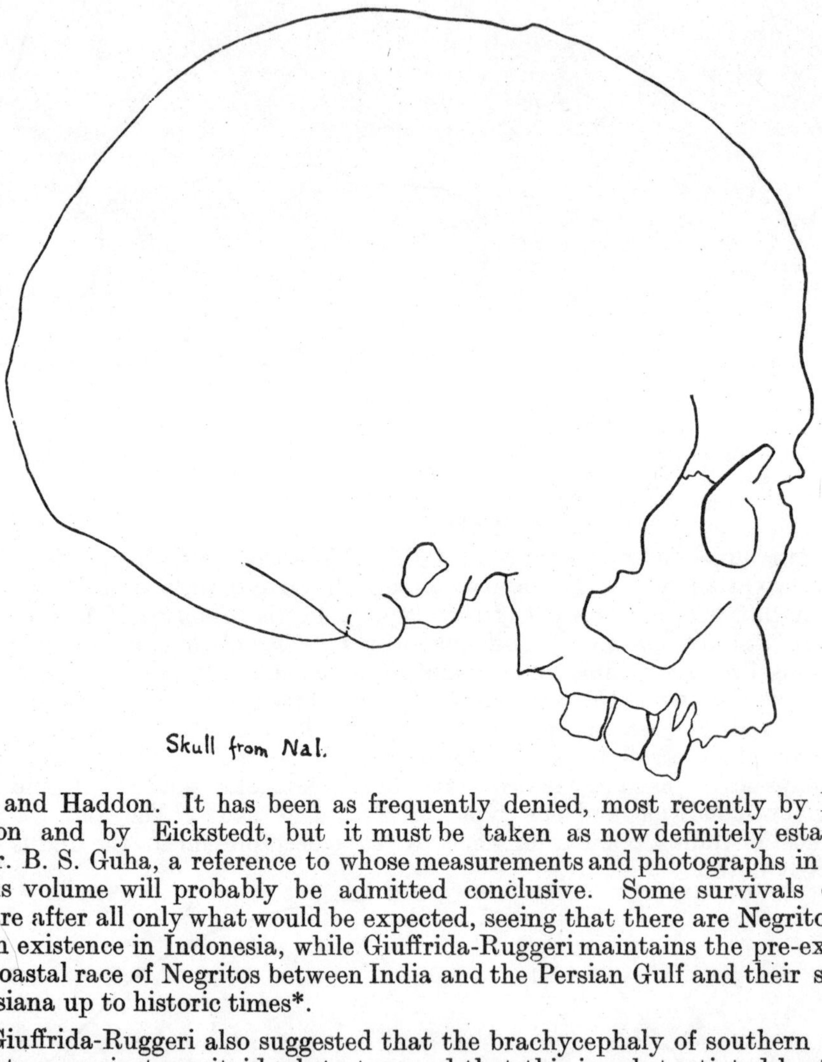

Skull from Nal.

Sergi and Haddon. It has been as frequently denied, most recently by Dudley Buxton and by Eickstedt, but it must be taken as now definitely established by Dr. B. S. Guha, a reference to whose measurements and photographs in part iii of this volume will probably be admitted conclusive. Some survivals of this sort are after all only what would be expected, seeing that there are Negrito tribes still in existence in Indonesia, while Giuffrida-Ruggeri maintains the pre-existence of a coastal race of Negritos between India and the Persian Gulf and their survival in Susiana up to historic times*.

Giuffrida-Ruggeri also suggested that the brachycephaly of southern Arabia is due to an ancient negritoid substratum and that this is substantiated by the low stature of southern Arabs and their occasional curly hair. Sir Arthur Keith does not, however, put forward the suggestion of Negrito affinities in his analysis of the head forms of southern Arabia in Appendix I to Bertram Thomas' *Arabia Felix* (1932), though he confirms Seligman's conclusion that the southern Arab is brachycephalic, coming to the conclusion that despite a certain Armenoid admixture " there exists in South Arabia a brachycephaly which is relatively unique ; a wide short skull of medium height, but with non-Armenoid dimensions (*i.e.*, postauricular length) ". Dixon (*Racial History of Man*) suggests that this brachycephalic population of southern Arabia is Alpine in origin and would explain the negroid characters found as due to the importation of slaves from Africa. If Giuffrida-Ruggeri is right in postulating a Negrito strain along the Persian Gulf, it is conceivable that an African origin is thereby indicated for the distribution of Negritos in Indonesia. In the alternative, and the pre-existence of the Negrito in Elam or

* *First Outlines of a Systematic Anthropology of Asia*, page 50 (Calcutta, 1921). He quotes Hüsing *Volkerschichten in Iran* (Anthrop. Gesellsch., Wien, 1916), and Dienlafoy, *La necropole de Suse.*

Arabia can hardly be said to have been established, we can only postulate a very early distribution from Central Asia. The former origin would perhaps be more in accordance with Keith's view (*Human Races Old and New*) of three main types having arisen in Europe, Asia and Africa respectively, whereas the latter would be necessary to Hooton's view, which is ably supported by Sewell (*Origin of Man and the Population of India*), that dolichocephaly has its origin in Africa and brachycephaly in Asia. In the latter event we must perhaps conclude that the negroid characters of Negrito tribes are modifications as a result of an environment similar to that which has acted upon the Negro of Africa. In either case it is generally admitted that the Negrito represents the oldest surviving type of man and it is possible even that he preceded Neanderthal man, by whom, according to Griffith-Taylor, he was displaced and dispersed. In any case the Negrito seems to have been the first inhabitant of south-eastern Asia. As already indicated traces of his stock are still to be seen in some of the forest tribes of the higher hills of the extreme south of India, and similar traces appear to exist in the inaccessible areas between Assam and Burma, where a dwarfish stature is combined with frizzly hair such as appears to result from recent admixtures of the pure or virtually pure Negrito stock of the Andamans with blood from the mainland of India or Burma. There are also legends among the Kuki and Kachari tribes of Assam of former contact with and of the extermination of a dwarf race armed with bows and spears living in dense forest and of an implacable hostility such as that still displayed by the Jarawas of Great Andaman Island to all their neighbours. What, if anything, in the way of culture the Negrito has bequeathed to his supplanter is a matter for speculation, but since he has existed in the Andamans in a condition of hostile isolation for many centuries it is just possible that the bow is his invention. It is also to be noted that he possesses a cult of the *ficus* tree which is or has been associated in southern Europe, Africa* and Oceania with fertility and with the souls of the dead, as it still is in India, and that he also possesses his own version of the legend of the Path of the Dead to Paradise guarded by an avenging demon, which is so wide-spread in Indonesia and its neighbourhood. If he did not evolve these conceptions for himself and bequeath them to others, the fact that he possesses them at any rate points to their distribution at a very early period of human prehistory.

If the Negrito was the earliest inhabitant of southern Asia he must have been early displaced or supplanted by the Proto-australoid. This dolichocephalic type appears to have had its origin in the west. The view that the Australian is connected with Neanderthal man, though repeatedly rejected by weighty authorities, seems to die hard, since Hrdlicka apparently regards the Neanderthal as having contributed to existing human types, while Sewell (*Origin of Man, etc.*) appears to revert to that theory of Australian origins, and in his account of the Mohenjodaro skulls he definitely associates the Indian Proto-australoid type with the Australian aboriginal on the one hand and with the Rhodesian skull on the other. In this view he seems to have since been justified by the discovery near Mt. Carmel in 1932 of *palaeanthropus palestinus*, whom Keith describes as bridging "the gap between European Neanderthalians and more primitive forms of modern man." It is however also claimed that *homo soloensis* recently discovered in Java is the direct ancestor of the Australian aborigines. Nevertheless Colonel Sewell has himself pointed out to this writer the possibility of the derivation of the Proto-australoid type in India from a leptorrhine western type through a series of climatic modifications. What he writes is "a comparison of the Mohenjodaro skulls with those from Kish, Al-Ubaid, Aditanallur and the skulls of the Veddahs indicates that we have a transition-series commencing in the Kish skulls with a nose that is long and narrow, passing through the Al-Ubaid skulls where the nose is slightly shorter and broader, then through the Aditanallur and Mohenjodaro skulls in which these changes are more marked to the maximum alteration found in the Veddahs...... Similarly the series presents corresponding relations in the height of the orbit and the degree of prognathism, as well as in the bizygomatic breadth". He has added in conversation that the series could be prolonged unbroken from Kish westwards to terminate in an Anglo-Saxon skull, but would probably admit the possibility of modification by hybridization as a possible alternative to modifiation by climate.

* *E.g.*, among the Akikuyu ; also in ancient Egypt where the *ficus sycomorus* was tenanted by Hathor, a goddess of bovine and Asiatic associations, who fed the souls of the dead with water (or milk ?) from the tree. Pictorial representations, says Mr. Mackay, are very common in tombs of the XVIII and XIX dynasties at Thebes.

Meanwhile Elliot Smith has emphasised the ikeness of the Adichanallur skulls to one type of predynastic Egyptian, and similarly pottery found in megalithic tombs in the Deccan has been stated by Balfour to have a close resemblance to that of predynastic Egypt, while lapis lazuli said to be from Afghanistan is found in early predynastic Egyptian graves, though according to Mr. Mackay it is more likely to have been from Persia, which was a prolific source of this stone and probably provided the quantities found at Sumer, whereas there has been comparatively little found at Mohenjodaro. Peake and Fleure regard this Badarian culture as likely to have introduced the microlithic flint implements of the 'Final Capsian' culture, and they state that the Hamitic dialects of north Africa are believed to represent the language of the Final Capsians and appear to have no relation to Dravidian ; the safest hypothesis at present therefore appears to be that the Proto-australoid type in India is derived from a very early migration from the west and that its special features have been finally determined and permanently characterized in India itself. It is represented in its purest form in the Veddahs, Malavedans, Irulas, Sholagas and similar tribes in the hunting stage in Ceylon and southern India (where it often shows a strain of Mediterranean admixture and sometimes occasional traces of a negroid blend, as the kindred Sakai in Malaya), and perhaps in as pure a form as any in the nearly related Paliyans of the Palni hills, whose sole implement is the digging stick. But, apart from its extension into Indonesia to the east and possibly to south Arabia on the west, as a contributory element in the population of India it is to be found from Kashmir to Cape Comorin and from Kalat to the Karenni, particularly of course in the lower castes and much stronger in the south than in the north. It is this type which is primarily responsible for the platyrrhine and dark-skinned elements in India which decrease generally in accordance with the increase in the social position of the subject examined, but which are present to some extent in all castes, though but rarely in the highest castes of northern India. We have already seen that this type was present in Mohenjodaro, though it is not clear from Sir John Marshall's book that any of the skeletons that have been preserved from that site are of equal antiquity to that of their surroundings and the inferences to be drawn from the accounts given indicate that the human skeletal material is probably of comparatively late date and in any case does not afford a reliable clue to the character of its original inhabitants. What the contribution of the Proto-australoid race to Indian culture has been is not very clear, they probably introduced pottery, and they may have had the beginnings of a neolithic culture, since some of the Badarian celts in Egypt have their side ground to a flatsurface. Badarian pottery is perhaps the oldest known, and Peake and Fleure suggest that the first pottery was made from leathern models in the neighbourhood of the sources of the Tigris and Euphrates or north Syria, while Frankfort considers that the earliest Susa pottery had such an origin. The presence of the boomerang, as also of the blowgun in south India and in a rudimentary or degenerate form in Assam, may possibly be credited to them, and in the domain of religion probably totemism.

Like the Proto-australoid and unlike the Negrito the Melanesian division of the Oceanic Negroes is dolichocephalic, and the frizzly hair which is so typical of the Melanesian possibly indicates a hybrid origin, and it seems likely that the Melanesian represents a stabilised type derived from mixed Negrito and Proto-australoid elements. However that may be, Melanesian elements are apparent in India and Burma, though limited in distribution and doubtful in origin, as there seems to have been at any rate some slight migration from east to west which may have brought back with it certain cultural elements which had their source of distribution from India thus running their foil, so to speak, and greatly complicating analysis. As a physical type the Melanesian occurs very markedly in the hilly tracts that divide Assam from Burma, and in the Nicobars, in both of which areas it has a mongoloid admixture. It seems to occur also but without the same strong mongoloid element on the Malabar coast, though here it is easy to be misled by directly African elements, indications of which are plentiful enough. Culturally the Melanesian stock in Assam, Burma and in the Nicobars is associated with disposal of the dead by exposure and the separation of the skull, communal houses, head-hunting and a canoe cult. Its connection with the Indian Archipelago is marked by a series of striking cultural parallels between Assam and New Guinea, but as it exists nowhere in India as a separate isolated type with a culture of its own, and as the Indonesian cultures, and therefore presumably those of New Guinea, seem to be generally derived from the mainland, it is impossible to isolate the Melanesian for examination not only from the Austroasiatic and Indonesian groups referred to below, but also from Malay intrusions which are present in Burma, in Assam and probably elsewhere.

The term Austroasiatic is a linguistic rather than a racial term and as such has been referred to above in Chapter X, where the questions involved in that of the Munda languages have been briefly discussed. Linguistic as it is however the term Austroasiatic has certain quite definite cultural association in India, Burma and Indonesia, the most prominent of which have already been mentioned, but to which might tentatively be added the practice of terraced cultivation, which north of the Godavari in India is found roughly corresponding to the distribution of Austric languages, though by no means universally. Thus the Sawara (*Sora*) of the Madras Agency Tracts have terraced fields which will almost compare with those of the Angami Nagas, while their cousins the Santals (*Hor*) apparently have not. It is however a practice that might easily be lost in the course of migration, and the Sawara (" Saharia ") of Central India has himself apparently lost it thus, or in the alternative has failed to acquire it. It has been suggested that the least unsatisfactory theory of the distribution of these languages is that they have migrated eastwards down the Ganges valley to the Bay of Bengal. The suggestion that they are connected with the agglutinative Sumerian language has more than once been put forward (*e.g.*, by Rivet in 1929) and apparently with some degree of plausibility, and in that case it seems likely that we must look still further west for their origin. Handy in his suggested map of Polynesian origins traces two courses of pre-historic migration from west to east, one round the coasts of India the other north of the Himalayas.* It seems reasonable to postulate an alternative route across India and the Bay of Bengal for Elamites and dwellers in Mesopotamia of the Mediterranean race to have reached the Indian Archipelago. For overlaid as it is with Pareoean elements and confused with submerged negroid races, the basic type of the nesiot race is generally regarded as Mediterranean in origin and as having derived even its pre-historic cultures from the mainland of Asia. It seems just possible that the leptorrhine features and fair skins so often to be seen among the Namasudras of Bengal which are so much at variance with their low social position may be due to settlements left behind in the course of this migration.†

The possibility of repercussions from the Indonesian area westwards on India has already been mentioned in Chapter X. It seems definitely clear that there has been a movement north-westwards from the coast of Burma to the hills of Assam, and it is not impossible that similar movements have taken place from the east coast of India, as already suggested in an earlier chapter. It may be noted for instance that the Oraons according to a tradition quoted by Gait came from the Carnatic‡. It is true that they speak a Dravidian language but their culture is closely allied to that of the Mundas and it is wellknown how easily languages are changed. There are no recorded traces of any Austroasiatic language south of the Godavari, but no systematic examination of tribal dialects has been made there. There is much about Mysore, including a form of the shouldered iron hoe and terraced cultivation that is strongly suggestive of Indonesian culture, and the Paniyans of the Wynad, Coorg, and the Malabar ghats use a typically Indonesian method of making fire ; a typical Indonesian snare of the " scissors " type (*Man*. XXII, 103) was found by the writer in the hills of Travancore in 1931, and in the Cochin State museum in

* Terrien de Lacouperie argued for a migration towards the end of the third millenium B. C. from near the Caspian Sea across Asia to China where he supposes the migrants to have introduced the beginnings of culture and the germs of the Chinese script, and Peake (*Bronze Age and the Celtic world*, page 74 has suggested a resuscitation of that hypothesis, which might provide a vehicle for Rivet's connection of the Ainu language with the Sumerian and for a culture similar to that associated with Austroasiatic languages to each China though the date of this migration seems too late for that of the Austroasiatic speakers across India. Yunnan has clearly much in common with Indonesia, including elaborate terraced cultivation, but the general trend of migration and culture in south-east Asia seems to have been from north to south rather than from the islands to the mainland. Moderately longheaded skulls dated c. 3000 B. C. have been found at Anau (Peake and Fleure, *Priests and Kings*, page 189).

† It is possible to see in the Hindu tradition of the struggle with a buffalo-headed deity a struggle between the Aryan invader and a matrilineal buffalo-keeping race. The Mahishyas of Bengal might connect with those of Java, if *k'bo-Kewat, Kaibartta* [vide *Dt. Census of Midnapur* 1891, Hunter *Statist. Acct. of Bengal* (Raja of Mayanachoura) and J. R. A. S. 1877 VIII-X, page 16, part 9]. Is it possible to see in the title *Mahishi* given by the vedas to the chief queen a survival of the same culture ?

‡ The term Carnatic is usually applied to the lowlands between the Eastern Ghats and the Coromandel Coast. The temptation to derive *Oraon* from *Orang* must be shunned as they call themselves Kurukh.

Trichur he saw a single specimen of a crescent-shaped mother-of-pearl breast

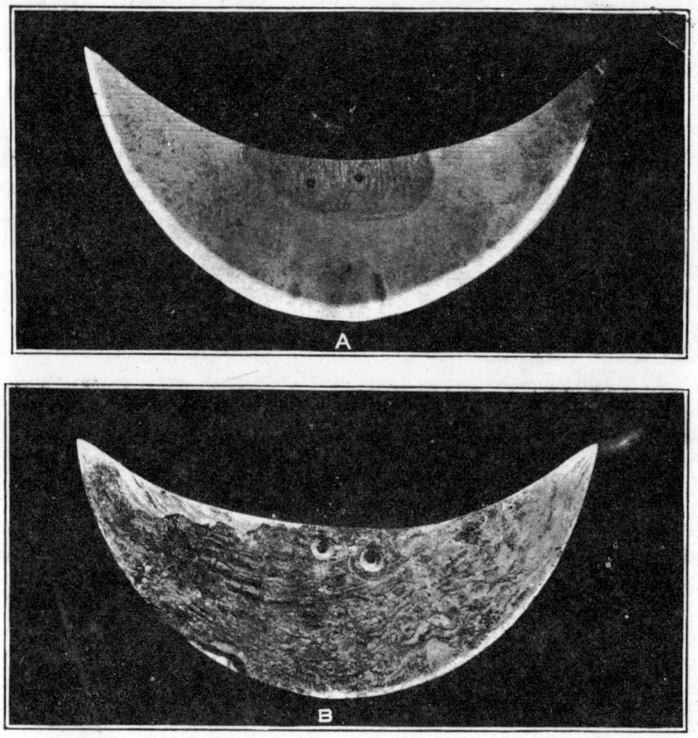

PEARL - SHELL CRESCENT (A *front*, B *back*) FORMERLY WORN BY NAYADI TRIBE, MALABAR COAST

From the only known specimen now in the Cochin state museum at Trichur

ornament extremely suggestive of Oceania, which was an obsolete ornament formerly used by the Nayadis, a wandering jungle tribe of Malabar. But it is possible that these stray parallels are to be connected with the Malabar Coast, which Indonesian voyagers have unquestionably reached at one time or another. It also seems possible that the vague suggestion of the mongoloid, which is so often given by the appearance of the hillmen of Chota Nagpur, of Bastar State in the Central Provinces and of the Madras Agency Tracts, may be due to a strain of Pareoean blood which has come in by sea from the east. One is insistently reminded in these areas of the Assam hill tribes, and both Haddon and Buxton have drawn attention to this strain, which struck the present writer quite independently and contrary to his expectations; and the admitted proto-australoid element in these tribes is no obstacle to this, since it must have extended at some period throughout what is now the archipelago to the Australian Continent, apart from the probability of its absorption on the mainland. Haddon says (*Races of Man*, page 108) " there is something in the facial appearance of many Kolarians which enables an observer to pick out a typical inhabitant of Chota Nagpur from a crowd of southern Dravidians and among some (Munda, etc.) there is often a reminiscence of Mongoloid traits ", and the truth of this is incontestable. A noticeable feature in the legends of the hill tribes of Assam is the story of a tremendous cataclysm in which the world was overwhelmed by fire followed by darkness and a formidable rise of waters. This tradition seems to be shared by the Mundas, and the Santals have a story of a rain of fire though apparently without a flood, while the Andamanese, the Nicobarese and most of the peoples of the Indian Archipelago have a somewhat similar story of a flood, though the preliminary rain of fire does not seem to appear in the accounts recorded, although a reminiscence of it perhaps appears in the Ongtong Java myth (*vide* Frazer, *Myths of the Origin of Fire*, page 53), and both in this and in one of the Sumatra myths there is a reference to the depression or submergence of the land below sea level, while the volcanic cataclysm is possibly to be seen in the Madagascar myth of the contest between Fire and Water. In the case of the eastern Assam hill tribes, however, the stories of the cataclysm occur repeatedly and all agree in indicating that the survivors of the rain of fire were driven by great floods up into the hills,

INDONESIA RESTORED AT THE 100 FATHOM LINE (after Peake & Fleure)

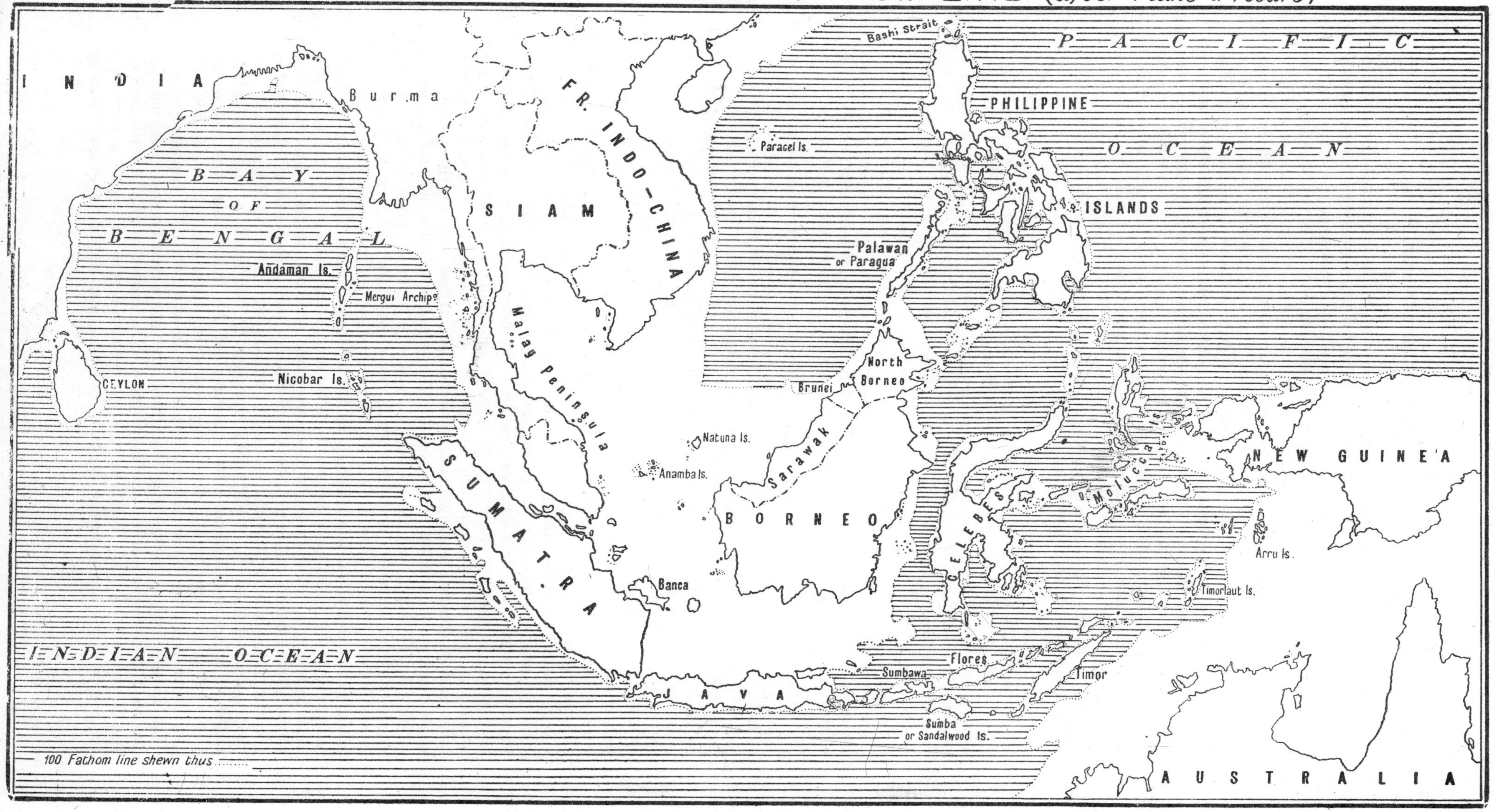

and it is tempting to suppose that they relate to some volcanic upheaval, which overtook what is now the Indian Archipelago and was followed by a subsidence of land below sea level. Peake and Fleure (*Priests and Kings*, page 184) have made a map of the area reconstucting land at the 100 fathom line. The result of this is to extend the land area of south-east Asia to include Sumatra, Java, Borneo and Bali, leaving only narrow channels of sea between this reconstructed area and the Philippines, the Celebes, Lombok, Flores and Timor, and providing the easiest of short passages from island to island from Borneo and Bali to New Guinea and Australia. Not only does this reconstruction explain the connection between the Proto-australoids of India, and Indonesia, and the Australians proper, but if it is a correct reconstruction, and to account for the peopling of Australia in pre-historic times it is perhaps a necessary one, it is then clear that its disappearance must have involved either some great cataclysm or a series of smaller ones accounting not only for traditions such as those of the Assam hills but also for a dispersal of part of the population westwards having Austroasian languages and probably strains of Melanesian and of Pareoean or even Malayan blood.

The above speculation has been offered with some diffidence as likely to be condemned as fantastic, and indeed it is tendered in profound ignorance of geology. At the same time it may be permitted to a layman to observe that during the last decade the researches of acknowledged geologists have been somewhat seismic themselves, and the eruptions of Wegener and Kroeber have shaken several previously accepted hypotheses. Molengraaff and Weber have pointed out that the distribution of fresh-water fish in the Islands suggests that they had the elevation indicated in the not very distant past. In any case it may here be added that the theory put forward of an Indonesian cataclysm is anything but essential to an hypothesis of intrusions on the mainland of India and Burma of nesiot speech and culture. Even less is it required to explain the presence of mongoloid elements.

If the map of the area occupied by Tibeto-Chinese languages in para. 157 be again referred to it will be seen that although it may be said to fringe upon the area of Indo-European languages, there is a very considerable overlap in places. In all this overlapping area the Indo-European languages are definitely intrusive and the mongoloid element in the population is strong enough to retain its own languages. It is further possible that the extension of mongoloid physical elements has gone a good deal further than the present range of their languages would suggest. One of the Mohenjodaro skulls has been identified as definitely Mongolian, and from the lowest stratum of the excavations have been recovered terracotta figurines with unmistakable Mongolian features, having the typical sloping narrow eyes of caricatures of that type. Some wear a big round fan-shaped head-dress very suggestive of head-dresses still to be seen in the Himalayas. On the other side of India the physical type of the Muslim cultivator in Eastern Bengal is strongly suggestive of a mixed Mongolian and Proto-australoid strain. Buxton, as we have seen, suggests that the Pareoean element extends to southern India. Burma, of course, is almost completely mongoloid and though the existence of other strains is undoubted they are no longer easy to isolate. There are proto-australoid elements probably in some of the hill tribes, and on the Assam side a Melanesian strain is to be expected. The survival of Mon-Khmer languages in the Mon, Palaung and Wa tribes suggests the probable presence of a nesiot strain of blood likewise, and the strain may be taken as certainly present in the Mawken (Selung) tribe ; the Burmese type generally is brachycephalic and platyrrhine, and these features appear to be predominant throughout Burma, and to have imposed themselves on the remnants of the Mons of Pegu, originally alien to them, in which case the Burman seems to have assimilated that race physically as he has culturally, the Mon having before that already assimilated the dolichocephalic leptorrhine element introduced from Telingana by the Talaings, an element still occasionally traceable in Mon families, unless it be that this is only another instance of the survival of the Indonesian type frequently met with at any rate in the hills to the west of the Chindwin. It is possible that the Karen has also some nesiot element, as in culture and appearance the Hill Karen seems to merge into Wa tribes, and the Karen language has so far not been definitely classified and may prove to be nearer to the Austric than to the Chinese-Tai groups. The bulk of evidence with regard to the Karens points to their having come from the direction of China, but McMahon quotes Cross as recording a tradition that the Karens once lived to the east of a great body of water, "the largest in the world", which "runs backward to its source", and as interpreting this as the Bay of Bengal, but in that case it seems highly improbable that this *Kaw* or *Kho* would not have been explicitly pointed out as such, since the Karens are still in contact with the shores of that Bay. The Changs of the Naga Hills have a similar story of a great river far to the south that runs downwards till it meets a rock and thence with great force flows upwards, so that navigators are carried away. Handy has pointed out (*Polynesian Origins*) that from the Bashi Strait between Luzon and Formosa there rushes out "a current so strong that any sailing vessel sucked into it is flung out toward Micronesia". The Chinese called it "a monster that swallows unwary vessels", and Handy goes on to quote a Cantonese book of the XIIth century which says "To the east of Java is the great Eastern Ocean-Sea where (the surface of) the water begins to go downward; there is the kingdom of women. Still further east is the place where the Wei-lu drains it, the world from which men do not return". This he regards as a reference to the Bashi Strait, which is however, as he points out, north-east of Java. It is tempting to see in that current the river of Karen and Chang tradition, and it may be added that the Changs have other stories very suggestive of Mon-Khmer affinities, identical as they are with legends of the Khasis and Syntengs. Subsequent waves of Mongolian immigration have passed over Burma since, obliterating the traces of former movements and assimilating their stock, and both these processes have been intensified by the policy of massacre and deportation which makes the mediæval history of Burma so profoundly depressing to read. The race-movement of Mongolians southwards still continues among the Kachin tribes, while the Kuki-Chin tribes have barely settled down after reaching the Bay of Bengal and starting to work northwards again on the Assam side of the dividing ranges. The bulk of Burma in any case is primarily mongoloid, and any non-Mongolian streams of migration that may have reached India through Burma have absorbed a vast quantity of Mongolian blood. In Assam even the Khasis and Syntengs, though they have managed to retain their Austric language, differ little in physique from their Tibeto-Burman speaking neighbours. Elsewhere in India south of the Himalayas even Mongolian languages have not survived, and there is little trace of their influence except in the mongoloid cast of physical features that crops up unexpectedly with fair frequency in northern India, particularly along the foot of the hills. Their contribution to Indian culture west of Assam has probably been negligible.

From the east of India it is now necessary to turn to the west, and we have there to account for the presence of a non-Armenoid Alpine population of a brachycephalic leptorrhine type which appears indeed in Bengal in the east but is much more marked in the west of India, extending as it does from Baluchistan to Coorg, whence perhaps it has penetrated the extreme south-east of the peninsula. Risley explains this type as Turko-Iranian in the north, and as Scytho-Dravidian in the south, but there appears to be no justification, for his distinction, since there seems to be no change in type toward the south which is not explicable by assuming, and with every probability, a proto-australoid admixture increasing inversely to the degree of latitude. If "Scythian" has any precise meaning it must refer to the Saka, who appear to have been a dolichocephalic people probably nearly allied to the Indo-Aryans and unable to introduce the brachycephalic element even if they entered India in sufficient numbers, which is highly improbable. The Turki and Tungus invaders on the other hand were of Mongolian affinities and the type of brachycephaly which we are considering does not appear to belong to that family. In any case Crooke, Haddon, Giuffrida-Ruggeri and Buxton agree in rejecting Risley's diagnosis of the western brachycephaly and Chanda has offered a basis for a much more satisfactory hypothesis. He postulates a Tokharian-speaking branch of *homo alpinus* occupying the Pamirs which also invaded India only to find the middle of the Gangetic plain occupied by Vedic Aryans and therefore pushed round them to give rise to Grierson's "outer band" of Indo-European languages. The theory of an invasion of Alpines from the Pamirs as the explanation of west Indian brachycephaly may be unreservedly accepted. Indeed there is no other explanation which meets the facts. It is accepted by Haddon that "it is evident that there has been a mixture with a strong brachycephalic stock, which must have belonged to the Eurasiatic group since there is no trace whatever of 'Mongolian' characters", though "there is no evidence to suggest when this immigration took place". Sir Aurel Stein's discovery of this type of Alpine in the region of Lob-Nor dating from the first centuries A. D. supports the hypothesis. It is not however possible to accept Chanda's hypothesis as regards date. It appears on the face of it that a much simpler and more satisfactory view would be to regard the brachycephalic stock as preceding the Rigvedic Aryans. We may suppose them to have entered the Indus valley during or after the Mohenjodaro period and to have extended down the west coast of India as far as Coorg forming the physical basis of several of the brachycephalic or mesaticephalic castes of western India—Prabhus, Marathas, Kunbis, Billavas, etc., and introducing the brachycephalic element into the Brahui. The brachycephals who remained in northern India will have at a later date been pushed outwards by the Vedic Aryans carrying the roundheaded element eastwards to Bengal down the Ganges Valley, where the Bengali element in the delta seems very definitely intrusive, forming a wedge between Orissa and Assam the inhabitants of which offer many similarities of custom, caste, religion and dialect in contrast to intervening Bengal. In support of the hypothesis that the Eurasiatic Alpine stock antedates the Rigvedic invasion Giuffrida-Ruggeri, who otherwise accepts Chanda's view, may conveniently be quoted. "Evidently", he says, "*the introduction of the brachycephals must go back to a pre-historic epoch*". The italics are his. Dixon (*Racial History of Man*, p. 265) suggests "the second or even the third millenium B. C." for the intrusion of this type into India, and supports the supposition that it preceded the Indo-Aryans. In another passage he suggests a movement of Alpines from the Iranian plateau as a result of the expansion of the Indo-European Kassites (who were raiding the Babylonian frontier before the end of the 3rd millenium B. C.), though he does not himself associate this movement with the Alpine extension in India. If we assume that these Alpines spoke an Indo-European language, of which there is no direct evidence, their distribution will fit in well enough with Grierson's theory of the "outer band" of Indo-Aryan languages, but it is an assumption which is not necessary to the hypothesis advanced or necessarily relevant to the question of race, though as Chanda has pointed out, Grierson finds traces of Pisacha dialects, of Pamiri origin, as far south as the Konkan, which supports such an assumption. The Chitrali (Khowar) are brachycephalic and speak an Indo-Aryan (Dardic) language. The Hunza-Nagar seem to be of mixed type* and speak Burushaski, an unclassed language unrelated so far as at present suggested to any recognised group. Khowari has a Burushaski element which Morgenstierne regards as due to contact. Grierson however says (*L. S.* VIII, ii, 6) "over the whole of Dardistan there is an underlayer of Burushaski words. These words are found far from the present habitat of Burushaski." We may infer that the Burushaski language is the original indigenous one and that the Pisacha languages are immigrant, possibly acquired by the brachycephalic Alpines through contact with speakers of an Aryan tongue before the pressure of the latter compelled them to migrate southwards, though the Khowari with a Sanskritic tongue appear to be more brachycephalic than their neighbours the Hunza-Nagars with a Burushaski one. The traditions of the pre-Rigvedic wanderings of the Aryans which are recorded in the Avesta, make it probable that the Aryans had come into contact with the Iranian Alpines long before they reached the Punjab (*v. infra* p. 458, 461). From north-western India their stream pushed on down through Gujarat, where the Pisacha tongue has since been overlaid by the midland Aryan (*vide* Grierson) and down the west coast, where it survives in Marathi and Konkani. In Kanara the language turns to a Dravidian one, but the brachycephalic element must have left the coast line for it is to be traced on the Mysore plateau (it is very strong in Coorg) whence it has passed to the Tamilnad, missing the Malabar Coast. It may probably be supposed to have remained in occupation of the more cultivable areas in north-western India till the Rigvedic invasion, and the association of type and frequently of caste between Gujarat and Bengal may possibly be put down to the

* Risley's measurements were brachycephalic, Leitner's mesaticephalic and Dixon's, the only series of any length, give a mean cephalic index of 77·45±26. The information as to Dixon's measurements was given me by Dr. Guha who tells me that he has received in Mss. from Professor Dixon the series of 92 heads measured.

dispersal west, south and east caused by the Rigvedic irruption. Associations have been recently traced between the Nagar Brahmans of Gujarat and the Kayasthas of Bengal; similarly there are Bagdes, Vagris and Bagris in Kolhapur, Gujarat and Bengal. Where they have not been disturbed they are peaceable and law-abiding cultivators and fishermen but the branch that got unsettled in the centre has never recovered and has ever since been criminally and nomadically inclined. This of course is hypothesis not history, but the closely connected caste of Bauri (Bawaria, Baori, etc.), can be definitely associated across India from Rajputana and Delhi, where it is restless and criminal, to the U. P., where it is less so, to Bihar and Bengal where it is a decent and peaceable caste closely associated with the Bagdi. Crooke says of it in the U. P. that it seems "to fall into two branches—those........in the Upper Duab who still retain some of their original customs and manners" (*i.e.*, the criminal manners familiar further west) "and those to the east who......have abandoned their original predatory life". We suggest that the peaceable life was the original one and that invasion on invasion, for the western Bauria must have suffered many, has been responsible for their anti-social proclivities.

To return to the Alpine immigration one consideration arises of an entirely different nature. Recent researches into the racial distribution of blood groups have shown that the predominance of group B in India is in strong contrast to western Europe, where group B is markedly absent. This group however increases in south-east Europe, a percentage of 18 being found in Silesia, 20 in Warsaw and, by Hoche and Moritsch, even in Vienna. In Russia the percentage of B group bloods rises rapidly, generally exceeding 20 %, reaching 29 in Perm and 32 in Krimtshack, the maximum recorded, and attention may be drawn in passing to the psychological affinity between Russia and India which has often been pointed out (also *v. supra* Ch. VI, para. 97). Further south the percentage is 20 in Transylvania, 23 in Macedonia. In the far east the percentage is higher than in Russia, China rising to 35 %, Malays to 29 % and Filipinos to 30 % and in one series even to 44 %. On the other hand the Japanese show percentages of B group ranging consistently from 19 to 23. In Africa percentages of B group go up as high as 29·2 but the highest percentages all seem to congregate on the mainland of Asia and the adjoining islands of Indonesia. The percentages in India itself run from 37·2 to 41·2, a marked contrast to the percentages noted in England which vary from 7·2 to 10·7 rising to 17·4 in Liverpool where there is probably an appreciable mixture of blood from the crews of foreign vessels*. Lattes' opinion is that it is definitely established that the distribution of blood groups in a given population is related to its ethno-anthropological constitution. Group A decreases going east and south from western Europe and B increases inversely, while O is characteristic of long isolated and marginal communities such as Australian aborigines, Eskimos and Laplanders. If the AB group be also taken into account and the total value of B be taken, the results, according to Lattes, show the value of B to be from 12 to 16 in western Europe, 20 to 28 in the Balkans, 28 to 43 in Russians, 44 in Gipsies and Chinese, 47 in Manchurians and 49 in Indians ("Hindus"). In Koreans the percentage is 39; in Indo-Chinese it falls to 36 and in Malays to 21. In Australian aborigines it is 4·5. Malone and Lahiri in the Indian Journal of Medical Research for April 1929 published some tests taken mostly on Indian troops and also on miscellaneous castes of the U. P. and on a number of so called "Dravidians" whose castes they do not distinguish and who were apparently low castes and primitive tribes of upper India, to whom the term 'Dravidian' is of very doubtful application indeed. The military castes they classified in groups according to Risley, and these groups it is better to ignore. The *p. q. r.* values have therefore been here worked out for the individual castes on Bernstein's formula, and the race-index on Hirszfeld's. The results place the Baloch with the highest index (1·00), then the Pathan (·95), Rajputs and Khatris (·88 each), "Dravidians" (·81), Jats (·74), Hindus of the U. P. (·72) and Hazaras (·67) last as might be expected, since their home is nearest the Pamirs. Taking B group

* These figures are all taken from Lattes' *Individuality of the Blood*, translated by Bertie, 1932. It may be noted that in that work the term "Indian" is always used with reference to American Indians, the term "Hindu", perhaps without its religious connotation, being used of Indians proper.

alone only the Baloch (24·3 per cent.) falls below 33 per cent., while the Hazara has 39 per cent. of B. These figures confirm Lattes' conclusions as regards India in general but suggest that a proper investigation of blood groups by caste would yield most valuable results. Clearly there is some factor at work common to Indians and to Manchus and in a lesser degree to eastern Europe and Africa. It can hardly be environment, as India and Manchuria have nothing in common, and it has been proved that blood groups are hereditary. The factor can hardly be Mongolian as it is not associated with the necessary physique in India or in eastern Europe. It is not Armenoid, as the Armenians have a low percentage of group B, and a similar factor in western Europe bars the Mediterranean and Nordic races. By a process of exhaustion the hypothesis is reached that this distribution of blood group B must be sought in the brachycephalic Eurasiatic race that seems to have spread from a centre in or near the Pamirs. The Ainu have been regarded by Haddon as an outlier of the Alpine race, and their likeness to the Russian peasant has frequently been remarked*; their blood groups show 32·7 to 38·5 per cent. of B; and Haddon in any case thus describes the range of *homo alpinus*:—" Galcha, Tajik, Wakhi, etc., of Persia, the Pamirs and neighbouring areas, and extending in a north-easterly direction to Manchuria ". Add to that the southward extension to the Deccan suggested by Chanda and the distribution of B blood group fits well enough. One more item testifies to the soundness of this view. The Gipsies of Europe show blood groups with 44 per cent. of B, a figure approaching the Indian percentage; and the Romany tongue of the Gipsies of Europe, in common that is with Konkani Marathi, " still retains many forms which can best be explained by a Dardic origin " (Grierson, *Linguistic Survey*, I, 109). The accuracy of the theory can be tested. If it be correct the Telugus and Malayalis should show a lower percentage of B value than the Tamil and a still lower percentage than the Kodagu, the Maratha or the Gujarati.

Caste or Tribe.	No. of persons.	Per cent. of groups				Index A : B (Hirszfeld).	p.	q.	r.	p+q+r.
		O.	A.	B.	AB.		(Bernstein).			
Baloch	74	47·2	24·3	24·3	4·2	1·00	15·5	15·5	68·7	99·7
Pathan ..	150	29·3	31·3	33·3	6·1	·95	20·9	22·2	54·1	97·2
Khatri ..	99	33·3	25·3	30·3	11·1	·88	20·3	23·5	57·7	101·5
Rajput ..	118	28·8	28·0	33·0	10·2	·88	24·4	24·7	53·6	102·7
" Dravidian " ..	589	24·3	27·5	36·8	11·4	·81	21·9	28·1	49·2	99·2
Jat ..	277	33·2	24·5	35·5	6·8	·74	17·2	24·1	57·6	98·9
U. P. Hindu ..	2,357	30·2	24·5	37·2	8·1	·72	17·9	26·1	54·9	98·9
Hazara ..	100	32·0	25·0	39·0	4·0	·67	15·8	24·6	56·5	96·9
Indians—										
(Malone and Lahiri). ..	3,764	32·3	26·3	33·7	7·7	·82	19·2	23·6	56·5	99·3
(Hirszfeld) ..	1,000	31·3	19·0	41·2	8·5	·56	14·9	29·1	55·9	99·9
(Bais and Verhoef).	348	37·9	23·0	31·6	7·5	·78	16·6	22·0	61·5	100·1

The Eurasiatic Alpine type, however, is not alone responsible for non-Mongolian brachycephaly in India. The Armenoid type of head, characterised by a very steep and high but flattened occiput and described as " hypsibrachycephalic" occurs frequently enough in India to be noticeable to a watchful eye. This type is probably a specialised off-shoot from the standard Alpine stock and appears to have arisen in the highlands of south-west Asia in the neighbourhood of which isolated communities such as the Druses and the Maronites still retain the old type with marked purity. While typical of Armenia and Anatolia, it is, generally speaking, still to be found sporadically all over S. E. Europe, Asia Minor and Mesopotamia, mingled in varying proportions with the dolichocephalic Mediterranean type. It probably constituted the most important element in the population of Sumer. In a type modified by hybridization, it is common enough in India, but does not seem to be confined to any particular caste though perhaps more often noticeable among Brahmans and Banias than among others, and is most common in Dravidian-speaking India and in the upland valleys of the east Punjab and the United Provinces. This race appears to have been at any rate partly responsible for the highly developed civilization of ancient Mesopotamia and Asia Minor and in both areas it has everywhere mingled with the Mediterranean race which it found in occupation. As we have little means of knowing the proportionate contribution by these two races to the early culture of western Asia, and thence to India, it will be safer to consider the two together as a blend

* Allusion has already been made (on the last page) to the psychological affinity between India and Russia; those acquainted with India only might refer to an article on Russian mentality in *The Fortnightly Review* for November 1932, by Mr. Harold Jenks.

to which the Mediterranean has contributed the most physically, while the Armenoid may have contributed more culturally. He is claimed as the principal contributor to the culture of Sumer and of Babylon, but the evidence does not seem to justify so exclusive a claim. On the other hand it seems to have been a blend of the Armenoid with the Mediterranean which produced the "prospector" type associated in western Europe with the early metallic industries and perhaps with megalithic monuments which seem in the Near East to be the result of "the interplay of Cycladic and Mesopotamian cultures". It seems likely that this type reached India either in association with the Mediterranean or in their footsteps, the latter being the more likely. Although at least one has been discovered at Harappa, no Armenoid skulls appear to have yet been discovered at Mohenjodaro, but the skulls found and preserved from this site are probably all of latish date, and do not necessarily represent the early inhabitants, while some of the stone statues are strongly suggestive of the Armenoid type of head. Thurston figures a typically Armenoid skull at p. xlvi of vol. I of *Castes and Tribes of Southern India* as a Hindu skull and speaks of its character as very familiar among all sorts and conditions in southern India, and the type is well represented in his photograph of a Banajiga.

The Mediterranean race appears to be the one that has contributed most to the physical composition of the peoples of India, and perhaps also to its culture. The centre from which it dispersed appears to have been the eastern Mediterranean, but that it reached India at a very early date is to be inferred from the crania found at Nal in Baluchistan, at Sialkot and at Bayana, which link the inhabitants of northern India to the dolichocephalic skulls of similar type found at Kish and at Anau. On the evidence of the Indian skulls Sewell and Guha conclude that "it would seem probable that the Mediterranean stock had become established in northern India at a period that clearly antedates the civilisation at Nal and along the Indus valley, and the differences that have been shown to exist between the human remains at Anau, Kish and Nal indicate that a sufficient length of time had elapsed for certain local variations to have become evolved and established" (*Excavation in Baluchistan*, p. 80). We may therefore infer that northern India was occupied by Mediterraneans before the Armenoid stock began to mingle with them, and it is possible that they were connected with the Indonesian race, now submerged, which seems to have left patches of speakers of Austroasiatic languages along both sides of the Ganges valley in the course of its migrations. Civilisation, however, appears to have its origins in the 'Fertile Crescent' which skirts the hills north of Mesopotamia from Syria to the Persian Gulf. This area was also occupied at a very early date by people of the same Mediterranean type, whose area of characterisation was on the shores of that sea and whose range in early neolithic times seems to have extended as far as the Indian Archipelago along the southern fringe of the mountains that stretch from Asia Minor to the Himalayas. They appear to have occupied the earliest sites at Susa and at a later date to have been also among the early occupants of Anau north of those mountains and near the Caspian Sea. Sir Aurel Stein's most recent discoveries in the Zhob valley have yielded stone implements of neolithic type, copper weapons and ornaments and painted pottery closely resembling that from culture strata ascribed to pre-Sumerian times in Mesopotamian sites, under conditions indicating prolonged occupation by a homogeneous culture of the sites excavated. Very close similarity is also found with remains from sites in southern Seistan, and there is marked resemblance to material from Mohenjodaro and Harappa. It seems likely, however, that the 'Fertile Crescent' contained from a very early period an admixture of racial types, and it was perhaps as a result of this that civilisation arose there, since "Rivers has shown that the establishment of contacts between peoples with different training and equipment produces new ideas and liberates initiative"* and the Sumerians whose civilisation, at any rate in this area if not in the world, is the oldest yet discovered, seem to have been of mixed race and to have included types of both the hypsibrachycephalic Armenoid and the dolichocephalic Mediterranean.†

* Peak and Fleure, *Peasants and Potters*, page 132.

† Peake and Fleure (*Peasants and Potters*, page 132) suggest also the probability of the presence of some of the dolichocephalic "Northern steppe-folk" (of Aryan affinities) and of Alpines from the Pamir.

A combination of Armenoid and Mediterranean is found in India, particularly among the Tamils, and that inter-communications took place between the Mohenjodaro civilisation and the ancient civilisation of Mesopotamia has been demonstrated by the discovery of objects of common type in both areas, and Sir John Marshall concludes that there was a "lively intercourse between the Indus valley and Elamite and Mesopotamian sites at the end of the fourth millenium B. C." The Mohenjodaro civilisation occupied according to Marshall the period between 3250 and 2750 B. C. and its connection with Mesopotamia is dated back to its very beginnings. It is assumed by Marshall that it developed in India but failing evidence to that effect it seems a much safer hypothesis that the main features came in from Mesopotamia, to the early civilisations of which it obviously bears a close affinity. Some points of this affinity have already been indicated (*e.g.*, para. 102 *supra*), and the fish-cults so numerous in India, but particularly in the east and south and on the Malabar Coast, are another case in point, but the question with which we are primarily concerned here is that of the race or races which imported or developed this civilisation. The worshippers of Indo-Aryan gods do not appear to have begun to encroach on the civilisation of the 'Fertile Crescent' till towards the end of the third millenium when a period of race movement began, possibly occasioned by climatic changes to the north. The Indo-European languages were, as we have already seen, preceded in India by both Austric and Dravidian languages and have been influenced by both, but while there is nothing to indicate that the speakers of the Austric languages had any advanced culture we find the Dravidian speakers of to-day not only having a culture of very great antiquity, but also one very strongly suggestive of Mesopotamian affinities, while its early megalithic cults surviving all over southern India and sporadically in northern and further India can hardly be considered without reference to the megalithic cultures of the Mediterranean. It is probable that there were direct contacts between southern India and Mesopotamia by sea, but the existence of the Brahui in Baluchistan makes the existence of land contacts equally likely. The Sumerian civilisation at the head of the Persian Gulf seems to have been largely dependent on the cultivation of the date; the Sumerians located their Garden of Eden in Dilmun, then also a date-bearing land, where is now Bushire on the coastal route to Makran, and the date is still the staple crop in the valleys of the Makran coast on the natural route between the ancient parts of Sumeria and the Indus delta, whether the medium of travel be land or sea. Maritime communications were certainly developing during the third millenium B. C. but early voyages must have been primarily coasting voyages. On the other hand a migration by a land route from Mesopotamia was probably at one time a matter of much less difficulty than it was found by Alexander's army, since at one time the whole of that now inhospitable area was undoubtedly fertile country, and apart from the Nal find already mentioned, Sir Aurel Stein's tour in Gedrosia in 1928 has disclosed scores of sites of ancient habitation yielding pottery, which links them with the earliest Susa zone, copper objects* and hundreds of terracotta figurines of the mother goddess (as at Mohenjodaro) and of the humped bull which is the *vahana* of Shiva. Everywhere in southern Baluchistan there are remains of enormous dams and *bands* proving that at one time the land was elaborately irrigated and pointing perhaps to the period at which its natural waters began to fail on account of climatic changes involving the undertaking of conservancy on a larger scale, and we are probably justified in picturing Baluchistan, a land of hills and valleys indeed but now barren and sandswept, as five thousand years ago a good land of fountains and depths, drinking water of the rain of heaven.

In either case the presence in Baluchistan of the Brahui, speaking a Dravidian language, living among remnants of a lost civilization, in a country rendered, inhospitable by a change of climate, professing a skin-deep allegiance to Islam but in practice worshipping at pre-Islamic shrines and phallic stones (*vide* Bray, *Census of Baluchistan, 1911*, p. 63), and using circles of stones to dance in, and

* Mr. H. Hargreaves found at Nal a copper tool containing a very high percentage of nickel. The nickel found in Mohenjodaro copper is definitely less, and it was stated at the Oriental Congress in Oxford in 1928 that the only copper ore containing so high a percentage of nickel was from Oman. The analysis of this copper adze was as follows :—*Cu.* 93·05%, *Ni.* 4·90, *Pb.* 2·14, *As.* traces, *S.*, *Fe.* *nil.* If the connection with Oman is proved, it increases the probability of migration by sea, as it presumably involves a maritime connection with the Arabian shore of the gulf.

exorcising devils by the dancing of medicine-men like the people of the Malabar Coast, points very suggestively to speakers of Dravidian languages as the ancient inhabitants of Mohenjodaro and perhaps the givers of culture to India, while the fact that they claim Aleppo as their place of origin and bury their dead to face westwards, indicates their ancient connection with Mediterranean. Bloch (*Bulletin de la Societé de Linguistique de Paris,* XXV; I owe the reference to Dr. Guha) has pointed out a connection between Malto, Kurukh, Kanarese and Brahui as distinct from the Gondi, Tamil and Telugu groups, and has indicated both the influence of the former group on Kashmiri and Syrian Gypsy, and also the very early connection between the Dravidian and Indo-Aryan languages; he regards the Dravidian languages of the Deccan as having definitely come southwards from northern India. Evidence is also forthcoming to indicate that Dravidian languages were at one time spoken in Gujarat, while Bloch's tentative suggestion that Brahui might be immigrant from the south-east not only seems unlikely on *a priori* grounds but is rebutted by Morgenstierne in his *Report on a Linguistic Mission to N. W. India* (Oslo, 1932). Rapson remarks that the reason why the Brahui has not been accepted as representing the Dravidian is that the racial character of the Brahui is Iranian and he adds that their tribal system is the antithesis of the caste system, and uses this argument to explain the change of racial character that he believes to have taken place. Haddon, however, says of the Dehwar and the Brahui that "in all essentials they belong to the dolicho-mesocephalic series" and must be regarded as a mixed type, while Bray reports that the Brahui skull is deliberately rounded in infancy, though babes are alleged to be born long-headed. Guha's opinion is that they were originally dolichocephalic but are now mesocephalic verging on brachycephalic as a result of a heavy admixture of Balochi blood, while artificial deformation possibly contributes to their roundness of head, a roundness which he agrees is accompanied by a long face.* As for their tribal system, it is true that strangers have been incorporated in considerable numbers, but there exists, in spite of their undoubtedly mixed racial type to-day, a very strong preference among the Brahui for endogamy (decidedly suggestive of the caste system, this) and by one authority the Mamashahi and the Nichari clans and the Dehwars are specifically reported to be definitely endogamous, and these are the oldest and aboriginal groups. Sir Denis Bray's report of 1911, shows that the traces of a former matrilineal system are clear enough, and the story recorded by Lieut. Carloss of his visit to the cave dwellings of Gondrani in 1838 (J. A. S. B., March 1839), when he was shown the palace of Badul Jamaul, the princess married by the stranger "a son of the King of Egypt" who became king of the matrilineal and matrilocal kingdom, is exceedingly suggestive of Mediterranean affinities, while the Shrine of Bibi Nāni near Hinglaj, also in Las Bela, is a place of pilgrimage "celebrated from the Euphrates to the Ganges" and the resort alike of Muslim and Hindu pilgrims. Sir Thomas Holdich says of it "the object of their veneration is probably the same goddess who was known to the Chaldeans under the same old-world name (Nana) a thousand years before the time of Abraham. Nothing testifies so strongly to the unchangeable nature of the geographical link formed by Makran between East and West than (*sic*) does this remarkable *ziarat* hidden away in the deep folds of the Malan mountains."† It has already been pointed out (para. 156) that the Dravidian language is now being found to have Mesopotamian and Caucasian affinities, and failing evidence to the contrary it is not unreasonable to conclude that the civilisation of the Indus valley was associated with speakers of Dravidian languages of Mediterranean race with an Armenoid admixture and a developed culture derived from the Near East. Indeed the Brahui themselves regard the Mohenjodaro ruins as the work of their own ancestors,‡ though it seems probable that this may be a *quasi*-tradition acquired from the suggestions of the excavators themselves. Moreover though this culture seems to have disappeared in the Indus valley it seems to have handed on to the later Indo-European invaders the pictographs

* Total facial length 117·77; facial index 89·34; nasal index 71·46; cephalic index 79·1.

† Quoted at page 36 of the *Las Bela Gazetteer* in the actual words here given. Nana or Nanai was the mother of Attis and identified with Ishtar, Astarte, Artemis, Anaitis or Aphrodite. Alone of her pilgrims devotees and unmarried girls pay no tax to the State. Naina Devi of the Kulu Valley, where her image is a black stone 3 ft. high, and of places in Sirmur and Bilaspur States, and probably elsewhere in the lower Himalayas, is likely to be the same goddess.

‡ Personal information from Mr. Mackay, the archæologist who was exploring the site.

from which their Brahmi script was derived, and unquestionably a number of elements in their language. How then and where did this take place? The cults and customs of Asia Minor are still strong in India, as also the Dravidian tongue, but it is clear that the fusion between the earlier civilisation and the Rigvedic Aryans did not take place in southern India to which the latter penetrated only in historic times. It did not apparently take place in the Indus valley and it must therefore have occurred in the Ganges basin where the middle kingdom has always been regarded as the true focus of Hindustan and the standard for the rest of Sanskrit India both of language and religion.

This is not only what might be expected on *a priori* grounds but it fits in convincingly both with known facts and with probable hypotheses. Sir John Marshall has pointed out that the latest date for the survival of the Mohenjodaro civilisation is early in the third millenium, and he has taken the jar burials at Harappa as indicative of the arrival of a fresh people with different customs. The practice of fragmented burial in jars appears to have very strong Iranian associations* and the Indus valley is right in the path of the Pisacha migration from the Iranian plateau and the Pamirs to the west coast of India. Here, it seems is the explanation of the break in continuity between the Indus valley civilisation and the arrival of the Rigvedic Aryans. We do not know at what date the Dravidian speakers pushed southwards to occupy the peninsula, but it seems likely that they must have taken a western route and have penetrated south India before the Alpines came in from the Pamirs. Some of the features of south Indian culture suggest not merely Asia Minor, *e.g.*, the fire walking ceremonies such as are common in south India and formed a feature of the worship of Artemis in Cappadocia, but Crete, where there was a cult of snakes†, which indeed were vehicles of the soul throughout Greece, and worship of the mother goddess, and where the vogue of slender waists for males is very suggestive of mediaeval Indian sculpture, while the popular sport among the Kallar and Maravar‡ of jumping onto enraged bulls with sharpened horns to pluck off a cloth put there for the purpose and prove themselves men in the eyes of their women folk is most reminiscent not only of the bull-baiting of Provence, where a rosette must be snatched from the points of the horns of an infuriated bull, but also of the bull-jumping scenes on Cretan vases, though in southern India the practice does not extend to somersaults nor to the fairer sex. Terracotta figurines of the mother goddess have been excavated in Crete not dissimilar to those from Mohenjodaro, and to others excavated in 1926-27 in Bihar at Buxar from a site 52 feet below the present surface and 13 feet below the Maurya stratum, indicating the extension of the Indus valley culture to the Ganges Valley and the Madhyadesa. The cult of the bull is common to the early cultures of Crete, of Egypt, of the Near East, of the Indus valley and of Hindu India. Dr. Guha points out that the brachycephalic admixture extends to the Tamilnad but not to the Andhradesa, a conclusion which is substantiated not only by the appearance of the people but also by their character, the Tamil being far the more pragmatical and more sensible of hard facts and economic values, whereas the Telugu has precisely that volatile, artistic and sensitive temperament that one is accustomed to associate with the Mediterranean stock. The Telugu, perhaps the purest Mediterranean stock in India, has in historic times been pushing up north-eastwards along the Coromandel Coast, and apparently the thrust of Alpines south-east across the Mysore plateau has failed to follow back north-eastwards just as it failed to penetrate the high ranges and heavy jungle of the Western Ghats which isolated the Malabar Coast from the brachycephalic influence.

If the hypothesis that the civilized inhabitants of the Indus valley were Dravidian-speakers be rejected, the only available alternative seems to be that they spoke some language of the Munda family. This is not impossible, and if the language of ancient Sumer was agglutinative as is Dravidian, so also are the Munda languages. The hypothesis however that the early civilization of India was Dravidian rather than Munda seems much easier to adopt, though it is still possible that it

---

* See for instance Sir J. J. Modi on *Gaurtappas*, Journ. Anthropological Society of Bombay, XIV, No. 3.

† The cult of snakes is also strong in the lower Himalayas, like Armenoid features, it is likewise found there in the significant company of Naina Devi, megalithic monuments, and marriage customs not unsuggestive of Babylon, and fertility rites which are spoken of by the *Punjab Castes and Tribes* as "Paphian" but which are not described. Devi in the hills is often spoken of as Devi Mai or Devi Mata—The Mother Goddess.

‡ In the case of the Kallar it is to be noticed that they include a boomerang among their wedding gifts, practise circumcision, and bury their dead and perform their Karuppan worship with the face to the north, probably indicating migration into India by land. The rite of circumcision is paid for the boy's father's sister, mother of his potential wife.

may have been first Munda-speaking and later Dravidian; any how it may be noted that the Munda themselves speak of Asuras as metal-using foreigners, while the Sanskrit-speakers in their turn used the term *asura* for a race found by them in India. If both these alternatives be rejected we are forced to suppose that the language spoken by the Indus valley civilization has totally disappeared, a supposition which seems, to say the least of it, highly improbable in view of the undoubted survivals in the field of religion, and it may here be pointed out that Przyluski (*Archiv Orientalni* IV, 2, August 1932, *vide Indian Antiquary*, January 1933) suggests a non-Indo-European origin for the name of the god Vishnu and a Dravidian origin for the god himself.

The early culture of the Mediterraneans and Armenoids in India may perhaps be most conveniently described as pre-Vedic Hinduism. Although this culture disappeared from the Indus valley, it must have survived across the Jamna with sufficient vigour to react to the Rigvedic Aryans whom it probably supplied with a script, and whose religious beliefs it ultimately submerged in its own philosophy. Slater* has aptly pointed out that Krishna himself was of Naga descent and the traditional blue colour in which Hindu art depicts him possibly represents the brunette colouring of the Mediterranean as distinguished on the one hand from the blond Aryans and on the other from the dusky aboriginals. Slater again points out that Sukra the chief priest of the Asuras is stated by the Mahabharata to have become "the spiritual guide of both the Daityas and the Devas", thus recording the success of the prevedic priestly class in imposing their spiritual authority on the Aryans also, and this same Sukra, or another one, according to the Vishnu Purana said *mantras* for the success of the Asuras and restored to life the Danavas slain by Indra. His father was the rishi Bhrigu whose sons were Brahmans and priests of the Daityas. Clearly there were Brahmans before the Rigvedic Aryans, and we must look for the origin of that caste in the priests of the presumably Dravidian-speaking civilisation who must have been acquainted with the mathematical and astronomical knowledge of contemporary Babylonia. At the same time it does not seem possible that the prevedic Hindu culture can have remained unaffected by the Iranian immigration from the Pamirs, which probably displaced it in the Indus valley during the 3rd millenium B. C. It seems that while the greater number migrated towards southern India by a western route, enough must have penetrated the Ganges valley to affect the physical features of a portion at any rate of the population. It is significant that the degree of brachycephaly in the Bengali castes decreases from Brahman downwards if we except the mongoloid groups like the Maghs.† We have also seen that enough of the prevedic civilisation remained to have a very definite and lasting influence on the religion and culture of the Rigvedic Aryans. The Alpine peoples have generally evinced a disposition for peaceful penetration rather than warlike domination and we may conclude that the irruption of the Pamiri invaders was less violent than that of their successors in the second millenium, and their settlements must have been rural rather than urban, in contrast to the Mediterranean-Armenoid culture. In fact the bulk of the descendants of the Alpine invaders are probably to be found in the great cultivating castes of Kunbis, Kurmis and Kapus representing the Tajiks of Iran (*vide* Keane, *Man Past and Present*, 1920, page 542), and it is worth notice that one of the Tajik tribes is spoken of as "Purmuli or Fermuli"; mutate *pf* for *kw* and then *k*, a philological process familiar enough, and the result is something very near 'Kurmi'. The prevedic Mediterraneans probably had a matrilineal system which would have facilitated the amalgamation of the Alpines, but it generally happens that people with such a system tend to substitute a patrilineal one where the two come into contact, and it is likely that the change from a matrilineal to a patrilineal system started to take place in upper India as a result of the Pamiri immigration, while it is not unlikely that the same process tended to substitute the worship of male for female deities. The process of Hinduising the female village deities of southern India by providing them with orthodox male husbands from the official Hindu pantheon is still perhaps in process. In Madura the fisheyed goddess Minakshi is annually so married with great pomp and *éclat*, but in the villages the goddess is still the real deity and protectress of the people rather than the recognised Hindu gods. So also in Bengal the *Dharma-puja-paddhati* records that Adyā, the mother of the gods, was married to Shiva with "traditional ceremonies not enjoined

---

* *Dravidian Element in Indian Culture*, pages 55 sqq.

† This conclusion is based on Risley, Dr. Guha's figures not being ready at the time of writing.

in the Shastras but somehow or other accepted as inviolable by them and known as stri-āchāra (lit. female custom)" performed by women before the Brahmans officiated (Sarkar, *Folk Element in Hindu Culture*, 231), and the same author maintains elsewhere that goddesses have been accorded (in folk-custom presumably) a higher position than the gods. According to the Mahabharata a matrilineal system survived in mediaeval India in the kingdom of Mahishmati about the Narbadā river, where the women had liberty to choose a plurality of husbands, and among the Arattas, somewhere apparently in the Punjab, "whose heirs are their sisters' children not their own". With the exception of the Nambudris, who follow the Rigveda, Brahmans in southern India, many of whom at any rate follow the Samaveda Yajurveda or Atharvaveda, are accustomed to marry the daughter of their mother's brother. This, which Dr. Chanda has pointed out to me as "opposed to the letter and spirit of the Brahmanic code" is clearly a survival of a matrilineal system; orthodoxy would appear to enjoin the patrilineal prohibition of such marriages. The Pandyan dynasty seems to have been originally matrilineal as Tamil poems are said to allude to its founder as a woman, and the tradition recorded by Megasthenes is that it was founded by a daughter of Heracles, while Pliny describes the Indian people "*gens Pandœ, sola Indorum regnata foeminis*". The worship of goddesses in whose honour annual fairs are held, is more important in the Himalayas of the Punjab and United Provinces than that of the orthodox gods, and such goddesses, though now regarded as incarnations of Devi, are frequently associated with the worship of snakes, while it seems likely that the Nanagotri Brahmans of Tehri-Garhwal represent families which originally traced their descent through the female line (*nana*=mother's brother). It is possible that the Pisacha variety of the Indo-European tongue was introduced at the same time as the Eurasiatic Alpine stock from the Pamirs, and either passed on to the Rigvedic Aryans the peculiarities it retained from the Dravidian it replaced, or never completely displaced its predecessor as the prevailing vernacular. An alternative hypothesis might be that the Pamiri stock did not cross the Jamna but migrated eastwards down its right bank thus leaving more or less intact the prevedic Hindus east of the Jamna and north of the Ganges until the narrowing of the valley towards the trijunction of the Son, the Ganges and the Gogra urged it across. However that may be, it is clear that the penetration of the Alpine element was much more limited in the east than in the west and that in the former at any rate it did not obliterate the pre-existing culture.

This prevedic Hindu culture, modified somewhat in all probability by contact with the Alpine, must have still been vigorous enough in the Madhyadesa to react to the stimulus of the Rigvedic Aryans, when these invaders, near cousins of the Kassites who about the same time overthrew the rulers of Babylon and established themselves as lords of Mitanni, occupied the Punjab about the middle of the 2nd millenium B. C. Their previous traditions as gleaned from the Avesta are conveniently summarised by Peake and Fleure (*Merchant Venturers in Bronze*, page 130). Driven from their northern home on account of its becoming ice-bound and uninhabitable they moved south to Sughda (Sogdiana) and Mura (Merv, Bokhara). Locusts and hostile tribes drove them to Bakhdi (Balkh) whence they moved to Nisaya. There they divided one part going to Haroyu (Herat) and the other probably to Kabul and thence to the Punjab at a date not later than 1400 B. C. and probably a century or so earlier. Their occupation of the country between the Indus and the Jamna, where the Rigveda seems to have been composed, but not written, must have taken the form of migratory movement and was probably effected without much difficulty. The description of their enemies as "noseless" suggests conflict with tribes of proto-australoid affinities, and there seems every probability that tribes such as the Bhils and the Chodhras would have continued to occupy hill and forest areas in spite of the Mediterranean and Alpine migrations. If the prevedic civilisation in the Indus valley had really declined, this may have enabled such tribes to re-occupy parts of the open country. The mention however, *e.g.*, in the *civ*th hymn of the first book of the Rigveda, of the cities, castles and great wealth of an enemy whose womenfolk bathed themselves in milk, suggests that the ancient civilisation was far from being extinct, and it is not impossible but that many aborigines were employed as servants and as auxiliary troops or as allies against the invader, a practice which was common enough in mediaeval India. The development of a written literature clearly took place at the second stage of their invasion described by Rapson as a colonising stage in contrast to that of mass migration. It is just at such a stage that amalgamation with the pre-existing inhabitants is most likely, and the influence of the latter can clearly be traced in the change in vedic religion which appears even in the tenth book of the Rigveda, and in the Yajurveda, as well as in the Atharvaveda, for this last consists, principally at any rate, of magic while the pantheistic philosophy later developed in the Upanishads is already apparent in the tenth book of the Rigveda. Pargiter points out that though the name of the compiler of the Rigveda was well known to the later epic and pauranic tradition, the very mention of Vyasa is ignored or suppressed in Vedic literature. It is possible to infer from this that the immediate post-Rigvedic brahmans may have been the inheritors of the prevedic tradition which was adverse to the Rigveda and supported the indigenous deities by preference. It is possible that the contest between Vasistha and Viswamitra, as a result of which the Kshattriya became a Brahman, may symbolise the amalgamation of the two cultures, and Viswamitra's formal renunciation of Kshattriya ways the final ascendancy of the pre-Aryan religion. In any case it is more than probable that the post-Rigvedic literature, in which the 10th book of the Rigveda must be included, would contain importations from pre-Rigvedic indigenous tradition, while the cerebral letters acquired by the Indo-Aryan from the indigenous languages "play an increasingly important part in the development of Indo-Aryan in its subsequent phases", just as the use of rice and the areca nut, equally of pre-Aryan origin, have affected the subsequent developments on the cultural side. The development of the art of writing from the prevedic pictographs must have gone on simultaneously and was, as suggested by Macdonell, no doubt first used for purely secular purposes and was not at first regarded as proper for application to religious hymns and formulae. This would fit in well with its derivation from the signs on the Mohenjodaro seals which seem to have been primarily used for commerce, as cotton fabric bearing a seal impressed with an Indus valley stamp has been recovered from a prehistoric site in Iraq. It seems unlikely in the extreme that the language, religion and culture of the invaders could have been influenced by the pre-existing civilisation without an admixture of race taking place, and the fact that later tradition and literature definitely describes some of the rishis and their descendants as non-Aryan, indicates, that this admixture extended to the priesthood* as it probably did to all other classes. Thus the legends of the origin of the Baidhyas of Bengal, a caste not only of acknowledged respectability, and the repository of traditional medical knowledge, but also one which provided a ruling dynasty in the XIth century A. D., have been justly interpreted as indicating a matrilineal origin (*v.* Risley, *Census of India*, 1901, I, Ethnographic Appendices page 185), while another version definitely describes their descent as *pratiloma* in spite of its being ascribed to the Twin Brethren of Vedic mythology. It is tempting to see in the two strains the origin of the two great Rajput houses of the Sun and of the Moon, the latter typical of Mesopotamian cults while the former is more suggestive of the Rigveda. The Agnikula branch was probably added at a later date to include the conquering families of Hun or Saka origin. On the other hand the Brahman in the Rigveda seems to have been second in social importance to the Rajanya and it seems not impossible that traditions of the conflict between the Brahmans and the Kshattriyas and the extermination of the latter by Parasurama, represent a revolt against the Aryan aristocracy led by a priestly class of mixed origin, which would naturally have the support of the people in general. In the United Provinces the population from Brahman downward is predominantly dolichocephalic, but as the Mediterraneans were no less dolichocephalic than the (?) proto-Nordic Aryans, the Armenoid admixture being probably slight, their fusion with the Aryans would not be traceable in the cephalic index, though it would tend to a substitution of dark hair and eyes for the fairer colouring of the Aryans. The element of brachycephaly introduced by the Alpines would be again modified in the direction of dolichocephaly by the new comers, and it is thus that we find in all the castes of Bihar a higher degree of brachycephaly than in the United Provinces where the Rigvedic Aryan element is the stronger. On the other hand the platyrrhine element, indicating the proto-australoid strain is fairly constant in both races and appears with little respective variation in the two provinces, for instance, in the cultivating Brahmans or the Kurmis, though the cephalic indices differ considerably. Thus in Risley's arrangement by nasal indices (*People of India*, Appendix III, summary of measurements, *Aryo-Dravidian* type) the castes of the U. P. and of Bihar appear almost alternately, but if the series be re-arranged by cephalic indices the Bihar castes fall into a separate

* Some of the rishis actually appear to have had a sort of totemistic origin ascribed to them "Achela Muni was born of an elephant, and Kesha Pingala of an owl, and Agastya Muni from the *agasti* flower, and Kausika Muni from the *kusha* grass, and Kapila from a monkey, etc." (Quoted by Wilson, *Indian Caste*, I, page 297, from the *Vajra Shuchi*, a Buddhist *sutra*).

group of 74 and over. Risley's apophthegm that the nasal index indicates the social precedence of any caste was true enough, but he failed to distinguish between the proto-australoids, the true aborigines of India if it be correct that their characterisation was in India itself, and the Mediterranean, likewise dolichocephalic but leptorrhine not platyrrhine, who seems to have introduced civilisation and the art of working in metal. Even to-day in the Deccan an artizan who dies too poor to be burned is buried in a stone-lined grave of dolmen pattern while a cultivator is put into a plain earth grave. Risley's classification also failed to diagnose accurately the origin of brachycephaly in western India, and its extension across, India to Bengal interrupted as it is by the dolichocephalic elements which both preceded and followed it. As pointed out by Childe, the great gift of the Aryans to India was neither their religion nor their physique but a vastly superior language with its corresponding opportunities for mental and cultural development.

It is not suggested that the above views are the final word on race in India, but it is submitted that the hypotheses put forward do offer a scheme into which the fact at present known will fit without distortion, and it will perhaps be convenient at this point briefly to recapitulate. The earliest occupants of India were probably of the Negrito race, but they have left little trace on the mainland of the peninsula. The Protoaustraloids who followed them and whose origin must be sought in Palestine, where up to the present the earliest ancestors of their race have been found*, may claim to be the true aborigines on the ground that their racial type was ultimately fixed in India. They were followed by an early branch probably of the Mediterranean race, speaking an agglutinative tongue from which the present Austroasiatic languages are derived, which migrated down the Ganges valley mingling no doubt with the Protoaustraloids and in the van at any rate penetrating to the farthest south-east of the Asiatic continent. This early branch of the Mediterranean race may have carried with it the beginnings of culture with a rudimentary knowledge of agriculture. They may also have taken the practice of erecting rude stone monuments and perhaps of primitive navigation. This migration was followed by a later immigration of civilised Mediterraneans from the Persian Gulf, but ultimately from eastern Europe, who brought with them the knowledge of metals but not of iron and were followed by later waves of immigrants and a generally advanced culture, which maintained a connection with the cities of Mesopotamia and evolved or developed the prehistoric civilisation of the Indus valley and in all probability a similar civilisation in the Ganges valley. All these immigrants were of the dolichocephalic type, but mixed with this last race, possibly even with the first comers but in any case as later settlers, was a brachycephalic element coming ultimately from the Anatolian plateau in the form of the Armenoid branch of the Alpine race. The civilisation which arose in India under the auspices of these races had developed by the end of the 4th millenium B. C. a high standard of comfort, art and sanitation in city life, and a religion which bears many resemblances to the earlier religions of the eastern Mediterranean. The language in use was probably Dravidian, and there was a pictographic script analogous to those in use in prehistoric Mesopotamia. This civilisation was flooded in the west during the third millenium B. C. by an immigration from the Iranian plateau and the Pamirs of a brachycephalic race speaking perhaps an Indo-European language of the Pisacha or Dardic family, the main course of which migration went down the west of India and across the Mysore plateau to the south, missing the Malabar coast which has thus preserved much of the ancient civilisation of Dravidian-speaking India. Another branch of these immigrants fewer in number penetrated the Ganges valley but was not strong enough to obliterate the Armenoid-Mediterranean civilisation, though it probably modified it a good deal. Meanwhile in the extreme east of India other movements were going on, as there was a widespread race movement of the southern Mongoloids southwards to the Bay of Bengal and into Indonesia, which had some reflex influence on India from the east. Finally about 1500 B. C. came the Indo-Aryan migration into the Punjab, which first occupied the area between the Indus and the Jamna and later sent colonies across the Jamna into Hindustan. These imposed themselves upon the surviving civilisation there, which so reacted to this powerful stimulant as to produce from the combined material the philosophy, religon, art and letters that were the glory of ancient India, though it yet remains for the descendants of those early races to accomplish the vision of the Bhavishya Purana and unite the peoples of India in the fulness of time to be of one caste, a united nation.

* Unless the recently found remains of "Solo man" in Java prove to be earlier.

SUGGESTED ROUTES OF EARLIER (*POST-AUSTRALOID*) MIGRATIONS INTO INDIA

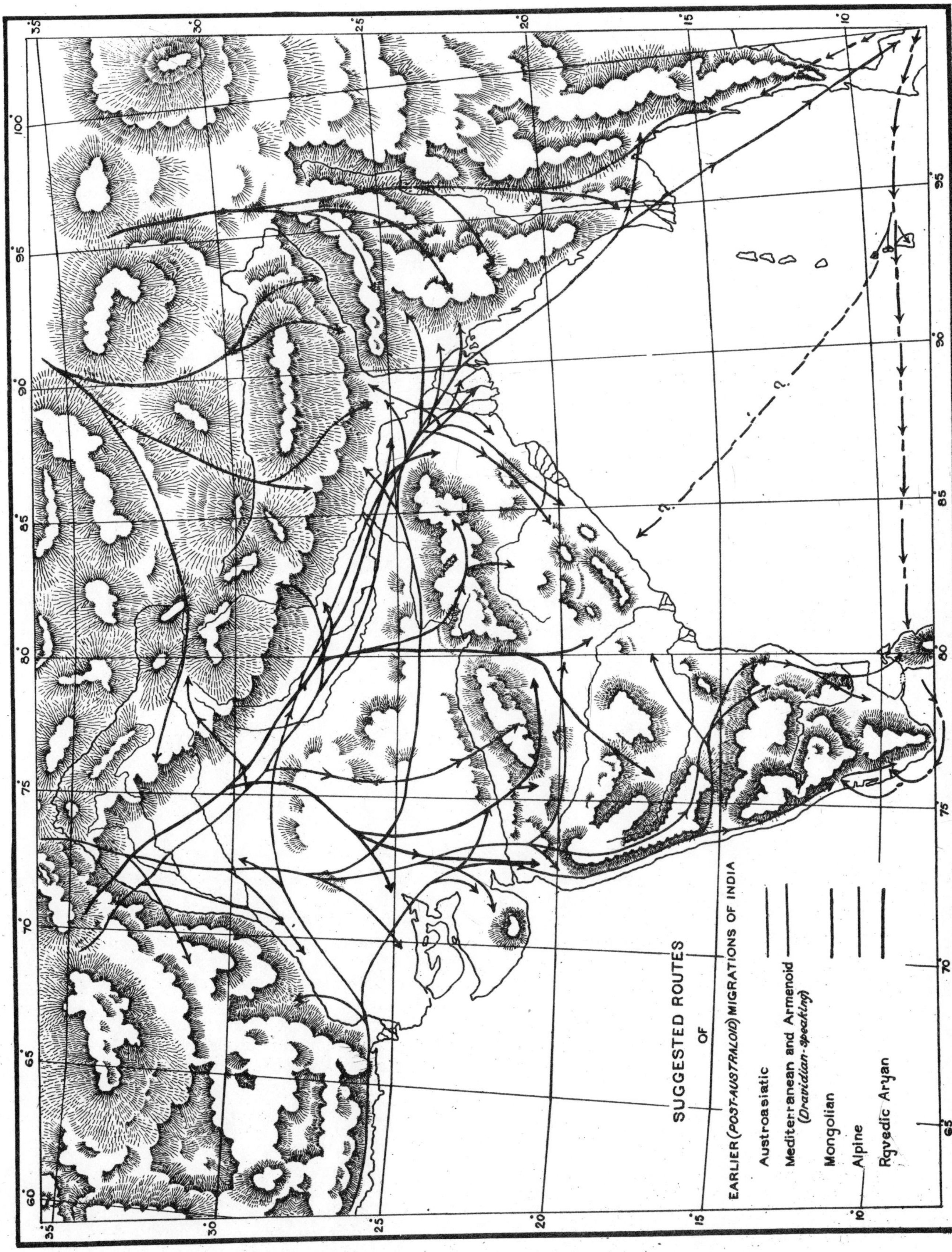

MAP OF ANCIENT SITES TO ILLUSTRATE CHAPTERS VII, X, XI & XII

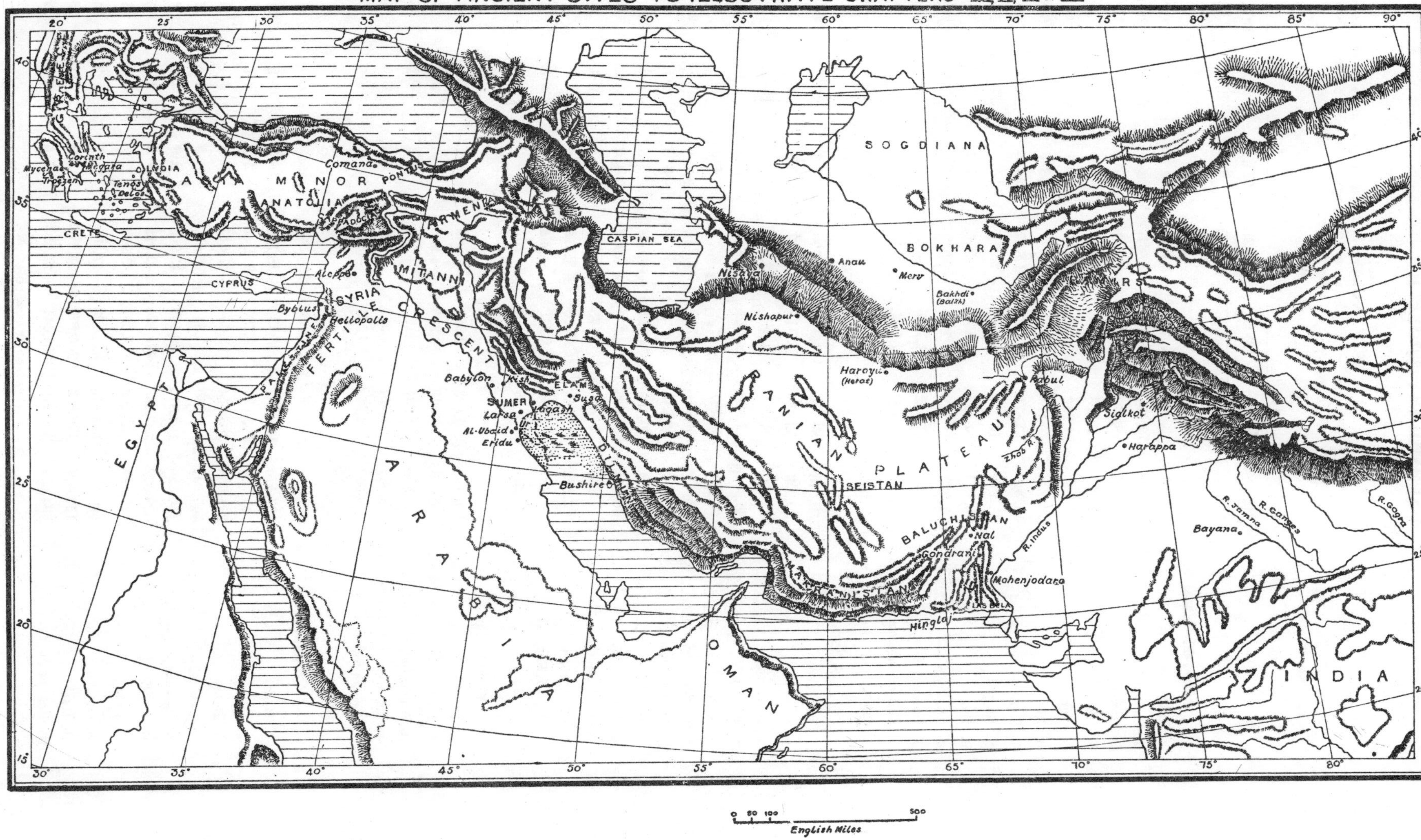

SUBSIDIARY TABLE I.

Race, Tribe or Caste.	Population in			Net variation Increase (+) Decrease (—).	Number per mille of the total population of Province, State or Agency.		
	1931.	1921.	1911.	1911-31.	1931.	1921.	1911.
1	2	3	4	5	6	7	8
Ajmer-Merwara.							
1. Brahman	27,670	23,643	24,220	+3,450	49·4	47·7	48·3
2. Chamar	15,915	12,278	13,351	+2,564	28·4	24·8	26·6
3. Daroga	10,182	8,579	8,952	+1,230	18·2	17·3	17·9
4. Dhobi	2,827	2,413	2,882	—55	5·0	4·9	5·7
5. Gujar	35,063	31,912	35,059	+4	62·6	64·4	69·9
6. Jat	29,992	25,896	30,497	—505	53·5	52·3	60·8
7. Kumhar	16,005	13,871	14,120	+1,885	28·6	28·0	28·2
8. Rajput	17,273	13,772	14,302	+2,971	30·8	27·8	28·5
9. Teli	4,773	4,126	4,406	+367	8·5	8·3	8·8
10. Anglo-Indians ..	1,232	746	710	+522	2·2	1·5	1·4
11. Europeans	1,676	1,442	1,755	—79	3·0	2·9	3·5
British Subjects ..	*1,524*	*1,400*	*1,702*	*—178*	*2·7*	*2·8*	*3·4*
Others	*152*	*42*	*53*	*+99*	*0·3*	*0·1*	*0·1*
Assam.							
1. Brahman	159,116	159,696	131,317	+27,799	17·2	20·0	18·6
2. Dhobi	30,919	33,466	33,946	—3,027	3·3	4·2	4·8
3. Kayastha	135,590	121,711	81,967	+53,623	14·7	15·2	11·6
4. Kurmi	26,331	27,980	24,520	+1,811	2·8	3·5	3·5
5. Mali	45,631	46,597	*	..	4·9	5·8	*
6. Namasudra	170,519	166,564	172,753	—2,234	18·4	20·8	24·5
7. Napit (Nai)	33,434	32,793	*	..	3·6	4·1	*
8. Rabha	69,154	70,491	79,022	—9,868	7·5	8·8	11·2
9. Teli and Tili	40,664	39,555	38,757	+1,907	4·4	5·0	5·5
10. Anglo-Indians ..	650	491	475	+175	0·1	0·1	0·1
11. Europeans	3,362	2,768	2,250	+1,112	0·4	0·3	0·3
British Subjects ..	*3,127*	*2,669*	*2,172*	*+955*	*0·3*	*0·3*	*0·3*
Others	*235*	*99*	*78*	*+157*	*0·0*	*0·0*	*0·0*
Baluchistan.							
1. Dehwar	5,317	5,433	7,326	—2,009	6·1	6·8	8·8
2. Lori	5,653	6,890	10,936	—5,283	6·5	8·6	13·1
3. Anglo-Indians ..	379	234	123	+256	0·4	0·3	0·1
4. Europeans	5,034	4,757	4,210	+824	5·8	5·9	5·0
British Subjects ..	*5,014*	*4,754*	*4,169*	*+845*	*5·8*	*5·9*	*5·0*
Others	*20*	*3*	*41*	*—21*	*0·0*	*0·0*	*0·0*
Bengal.							
1. Bagdi	987,570	895,397	1,015,738	—28,168	19·3	18·8	21·9
2. Baidya	110,739	102,931	88,796	+21,943	2·2	2·2	1·9
3. Bauri	331,268	303,054	313,654	+17,614	6·5	6·4	6·7
4. Brahman	1,447,691	1,309,539	1,253,841	+193,850	28·3	27·6	27·1
5. Chamar	150,458	152,372	136,553	+13,905	2·9	3·2	2·9
6. Dhobi	229,672	227,468	231,890	—2,218	4·5	4·8	5·0
7. Dom	140,067	150,263	173,991	—33,924	2·7	3·2	3·8
8. Goala	599,283	583,970	646,473	—47,190	11·7	12·3	14·0
9. Hari	132,401	148,847	265,679	—133,278	2·6	3·1	5·7
10. Jogi or Jugi	384,634	365,910	361,141	+23,493	7·5	7·7	7·8

* Figures not available.

SUBSIDIARY TABLE I—*contd.*

Race, Tribe or Caste.	Population in			Net variation Increase (+) Decrease (—).	Number per mille of the total population of Province, State or Agency.		
	1931.	1921.	1911.	1911-31.	1931.	1921.	1911.
1	2	3	4	5	6	7	8
Bengal—*concld.*							
11. Mumin (Jolaha) ..	270,292	255,164	282,705	—12,413	5·3	5·4	6·1
12. Kaibartta (Chasi & Jalia)	2,733,338	2,594,733	2,487,403	+245,935	53·5	54·5	53·7
13. Kayastha	1,558,475	1,297,736	1,113,684	+444,791	30·5	27·3	24·0
14. Kumhar ..	289,810	284,653	294,545	—4,735	5·7	6·0	6·4
15. Kurmi ..	194,652	181,447	176,779	+17,873	3·8	3·8	3·8
16. Namasudra	2,094,957	2,006,259	1,909,794	+185,163	41·0	42·1	41·2
17. Nai (Napit)	451,068	444,188	458,035	—6,967	8·8	9·3	9·9
18. Pod (Poundra) ..	667,731	588,394	536,568	+131,163	13·1	12·4	11·6
19. Rajbansi (Kshattriya)	1,806,390	1,727,111	1,808,790	—2,400	35·4	36·3	39·1
20. Rajput (Chattri) ..	156,978	125,513	130,221	+26,757	3·1	2·6	2·8
21. Tanti (Tatwa) ..	330,518	319,613	322,983	+7,535	6·5	6·7	7·0
22. Teli and Tili	503,189	491,832	419,122	+84,067	9·8	10·3	9·0
23. Anglo-Indians ..	27,573	22,250	19,833	+7,740	0·5	0·5	0·4
24. Europeans	23,030	22,730	25,451	—2,421	0·5	0·5	0·5
British Subjects ..	*20,904*	*20,016*	*22,327*	*—1,423*	*0·4*	*0·4*	*0·5*
Others	*2,126*	*2,714*	*3,124*	*—998*	*0·0*	*0·1*	*0·1*
Bihar and Orissa.							
1. Babhan (Bhumihar Brahman).	895,602	979,369	1,129,735	—234,133	21·1	25·8	29·4
2. Baniya	220,071	178,231	140,575	+79,496	5·2	4·7	3·7
3. Bauri	315,038	269,687	292,503	+22,535	7·4	7·1	7·6
4. Brahman	2,101,287	1,879,226	1,755,424	+345,863	49·6	49·5	45·7
5. Chamar	1,296,001	1,147,230	1,114,467	+181,534	30·6	30·2	29·0
6. Dhobi (Dhoba) ..	414,221	432,688	427,079	—12,858	9·8	11·4	11·1
7. Dom	269,346	218,733	241,903	+27,443	6·4	5·7	6·3
8. Dosadh	1,290,936	1,167,686	1,189,274	+101,662	30·5	30·8	30·9
9. Goala (Ahir)	3,455,141	3,192,242	3,250,415	+204,726	81·6	84·1	84·6
10. Hajjam	456,779	417,778	455,758	+1,021	10·8	11·0	11·9
11. Hari	115,613	103,602	119,468	—3,855	2·7	2·7	31·1
12. Jolaha	983,843	841,377	826,391	+157,452	23·2	22·2	21·5
13. Kayastha	383,435	344,022	347,613	+35,822	9·1	9·1	9·0
14. Khandait	1,010,146	822,016	769,353	+240,793	23·9	21·7	20·0
15. Kumhar	599,038	528,720	513,327	+85,711	14·2	13·9	13·4
16. Kurmi	1,452,724	1,315,417	1,312,832	+139,892	34·3	34·7	34·2
17. Pasi	172,061	150,136	150,142	+21,919	4·1	4·0	3·9
18. Rajput (Chhatri) ..	1,412,440	1,256,906	1,239,826	+172,614	33·4	33·1	32·?
19. Rajwar	133,952	109,323	131,971	+1,981	3·2	2·9	3·4
20. Tanti (Tatwa) ..	689,791	602,412	613,277	+76,514	16·3	15·9	16·0
21. Teli	1,210,496	1,076,705	1,071,906	+138,590	28·6	28·4	27·9
22. Anglo-Indians ..	6,638	4,134	3,405	+3,233	0·2	0·1	0·1
23. Europeans	6,389	6,346	6,316	+73	0·2	0·2	0·2
British Subjects ..	*5,675*	*5,745*	*5,646*	*+29*	*0·1*	*0·2*	*0·1*
Others	*714*	*601*	*670*	*+44*	*0·0*	*0·0*	*0·0*
Bombay (*including W. I. S. Agency*).							
1. Ahir	185,931	174,248	183,919	+2,012	6·1	6·5	6·8
2. Banjari (Banjara) ..	143,371	109,025	143,586	—215	4·7	4·1	5·3
3. Berad (Bedar) ..	206,883	186,434	184,871	+22,012	6·8	7·0	6·8

SUBSIDIARY TABLE I—*contd.*

Race, Tribe or Caste.	Population in 1931.	Population in 1921	Population in 1911.	Net variation Increase (+) Decrease (—). 1911-31.	Number per mille of the total population of Province, State or Agency. 1931.	1921.	1911.
1	2	3	4	5	6	7	8
Bombay—(*including W. I. S. Agency*)—contd.							
4. Bhangi (Halalkhor) ..	123,375	121,747	140,714	—12,339	4·2	4·5	5·2
5. Bohra	137,957	132,299	126,011	+11,946	4·5	4·9	4·7
6. Brahman	1,128,941	1,030,119	1,067,681	+61,260	37·1	38·5	39·4
7. Chambhar	337,982	282,400	302,536	+35,446	11·1	10·6	11·2
8. Dhobi	84,348	79,752	79,707	+4,641	2·8	3·0	2·9
9. Kunbi (including Maratha).	6,434,861	5,832,488	5,768,726	+666,135	211·7	218·0	213·0
10. Kumbhar	297,700	265,816	254,542	+43,158	9·8	9·9	9·4
11. Mahar (Holiya and Dhed)	1,438,550	1,337,463	1,470,992	—32,442	47·3	50·0	54·3
12. Mang (Madig) ..	309,938	259,427	274,037	+35,901	10·2	9·7	10·1
13. Rajput	579,153	472,718	457,723	+121,430	19·1	17·7	16·9
14. Teli	187,054	167,146	168,848	+18,206	6·2	6·2	6·2
15. Vaddar (Od)	110,503	99,810	102,842	+7,661	3·6	3·7	3·8
16. Vaghri	89,067	86,114	82,016	+7,051	2·9	3·2	3·0
17. Anglo-Indians ..	16,646	10,543	9,175	+7,471	0·5	0·4	0·3
18. Europeans	26,533	33,863	32,727	—6,194	0·9	1·3	1·2
British Subjects ..	*24,338*	*31,041*	*28,983*	*—4,645*	*0·8*	*1·2*	*1·1*
Others	*2,195*	*2,822*	*3,744*	*—1,549*	*0·1*	*0·1*	*0·1*
Burma.							
1. Arakanese	259,866*	300,628	344,123	—84,257	17·7	22·8	28·4
2. Burmese	8,596,031	7,824,191	7,479,433	+1,116,598	586·1	592·2	617·4
3. Other Burman† ..	315,222	286,011	145,834	+169,388	21·5	21·6	12·0
4. Zerbadi	122,705	94,270	59,729	+62,976	8·4	7·1	4·9
5. Anglo-Indians ..	19,200	16,688	11,106	+8,094	1·3	1·3	0·9
6. Europeans	11,651	8,665	13,443	—1,792	0·8	0·7	1·1
British Subjects ..	*10,627*	*7,828*	*11,828*	*—1,201*	*0·7*	*0·6*	*1·0*
Others	*1,024*	*837*	*1,615*	*—591*	*0·1*	*0·1*	*0·1*
Central Provinces and Berar.							
1. Ahir	818,105	602,747	738,192	+79,913	45·5	37·7	46·0
2. Banjara	155,353	122,973	169,505	—14,152	8·6	7·7	10·6
3. Basor	54,987	44,046	52,947	+2,040	3·1	2·8	3·3
4. Brahman	517,765	457,377	445,744	+72,021	28·8	28·6	27·8
5. Dhobi	187,594	165,624	165,427	+22,167	10·4	10·4	10·3
6. Kayastha	38,829	34,330	33,584	+5,245	2·2	2·1	2·1
7. Kewat	197,035	174,542	169,395	+27,640	11·0	10·9	10·6
8. Kori	34,994	38,208	39,628	—4,634	1·9	2·4	2·5
9. Kumhar	131,311	121,408	118,520	+12,791	7·3	7·6	7·4
10. Kunbi	1,281,184	1,253,306	1,356,734	—75,550	71·2	78·4	84·6
11. Kurmi	317,399	301,747	302,588	+14,811	17·6	18·9	18·9
12. Lodhi (Lodha) ..	318,577	295,612	313,900	+4,677	17·7	18·5	19·6
13. Mang	101,226	84,239	83,660	+17,566	5·6	5·3	5·2
14. Maratha	287,189	206,144	93,901	+193,288	16·0	12·9	5·9
15. Mehra	1,307,962	1,170,737	1,165,177	+142,785	72·7	73·3	72·7
16. Nai	133,256	160,127	148,750	—15,494	7·4	10·0	9·3
17. Rajput	506,087	455,906	441,231	+64,856	28·1	28·5	27·5
18. Teli	1,022,881	890,240	869,370	+153,511	56·9	55·7	54·2

*Includes 51,615 Arakan Muslims.

†Here refers only to Danu, Intha, Tavoyan Yabein, Hpon, Taungyo and Yaw.

SUBSIDIARY TABLE I—*contd.*

Race, Tribe or Caste.	Population in			Net variation Increase (+) Decrease (—).	Number per mille of the total population of Province, State or Agency.		
	1931.	1921.	1911.	1911-31.	1931.	1921.	1911.
1	2	3	4	5	6	7	8
Central Provinces and Berar—*concld.*							
19. Anglo-Indians ..	5,065	3,574	3,488	+1,577	0·3	0·2	0·2
20. Europeans	5,650	5,892	7,333	—1,683	0·3	0·4	0·5
British Subjects ..	*5,124*	*5,627*	*7,033*	*—1,909*	*0·3*	*0·4*	*0·4*
Others	*526*	*265*	*300*	*+226*	*0·0*	*0·0*	*0·0*
Coorg.							
1. Brahman	2,723	6,187	2,521	+202	16·7	37·8	14·4
2. Kodaga	41,026	44,476	39,228	+1,798	251·2	271·5	224·2
3. Kuruba	6,867	7,335	7,394	—527	42·0	44·8	42·3
4. Vakkaliga	7,948	7,751	10,576	—2,628	48·7	47·3	60·4
5. Anglo-Indians ..	84	47	138	—54	0·5	0·3	0·8
6. Europeans	138	156	207	—69	0·8	1·0	1·2
British Subjects ..	*122*	*94*	*174*	*—52*	*0·7*	*0·6*	*1·0*
Others	*16*	*62*	*33*	*—17*	*0·1*	*0·4*	*0·2*
Madras (*including Cochin and Travancore*).							
1. Ambattan (Barbers) ..	362,592	255,532	234,876	+127,716	6·7	5·3	5·1
2. Brahman	1,473,836	1,564,111	1,401,566	+72,270	27·6	32·7	30·3
3. Chakkaliyan	613,942	550,245	529,060	+84,882	11·5	11·5	11·4
4. Maravan	437,411	459,786	373,138	+64,273	8·2	9·6	8·1
5. Pallan	857,329	878,689	877,354	—20,025	16·0	18·4	19·0
6. Telaga	699,089	604,123	498,762	+200,327	13·1	12·6	10·8
7. Vaniyan	250,449	220,117	211,037	+39,412	4·7	4·6	4·6
8. Vannan	215,356	252,595	288,447	—73,091	4·0	5·3	6·2
9. Anglo-Indians ..	31,201	29,495	30,219	+982	0·6	0·6	0·7
10. Europeans	13,076	11,291	15,382	—2,306	0·2	0·2	0·3
British Subjects ..	*11,204*	*10,182*	*13,108*	*—1,904*	*0·2*	*0·2*	*0·3*
Others	*1,872*	*1,109*	*2,274*	*—402*	*0·0*	*0·0*	*0·0*
North West Frontier Province.							
1. Arora	61,402	69,046	69,215	—7,813	13·1	13·6	18·1
2. Brahman	17,200	21,884	13,208	+3,992	3·7	4·3	3·5
3. Dhobi	11,870	18,644	14,877	—3,007	2·5	3·7	3·9
4. Khatri	35,046	44,792	35,720	—674	7·5	8·8	9·4
5. Kumhar	23,202	24,054	22,664	+538	5·0	4·7	5·9
6. Nai	27,242	27,335	24,777	+2,465	5·8	5·4	6·5
7. Teli	7,179	11,446	6,932	+247	1·5	2·3	1·8
8. Anglo-Indians ..	161	200	100	+61	0·0	0·0	0·0
9. Europeans	11,576	10,473	5,741	+5,835	2·5	2·1	1·5
British Subjects ..	*11,543*	*10,453*	*5,698*	*+5,845*	*2·5*	*2·1*	*1·5*
Others	*33*	*20*	*43*	*—10*	*0·0*	*0·0*	*0·0*
Punjab (*including Delhi*).							
1. Ahir	234,984	213,889	208,594	+26,390	8·1	8·4	8·6
2. Arain	1,334,629	1,093,116	977,601	+357,028	45·8	42·7	40·4
3. Arora	775,734	716,415	673,665	+102,069	26·6	28·0	27·8
4. Brahman	1,108,908	1,035,568	1,017,743	+91,165	38·1	40·5	42·0
5. Chamar	1,148,271	1,185,243	1,139,941	+8,330	39·4	46·3	47·1
6. Chhimba	96,269	125,570	129,338	—33,069	3·3	4·9	5·3

SUBSIDIARY TABLE I—*contd.*

Race, Tribe or Caste.	Population in			Net variation Increase (+) Decrease (—).	Number per mille of the total population of Province, State or Agency.		
	1931.	1921.	1911.	1911-31.	1931.	1921.	1911.
1	2	3	4	5	6	7	8
Punjab (*including Delhi*)—concld.							
7. Chuhra	1,114,797	1,125,201	1,235,103	—120,306	38·3	44·0	51·0
8. Dhobi	179,751	170,839	156,046	+23,705	6·2	6·7	6·4
9. Ghirath	124,340	137,153	171,129	—46,789	4·3	5·4	7·1
10. Kumhar	629,754	582,962	550,450	+79,304	21·6	22·8	22·7
11. Mali	91,534	101,850	193,579	—102,045	3·1	4·0	8·0
12. Nai	385,903	366,230	350,456	+35,447	13·2	14·3	14·5
13. Pathan	376,405	284,393	292,689	+83,716	12·9	11·1	12·1
14. Saini	165,190	129,523	112,719	+52,471	5·7	5·1	4·7
15. Sayad	312,480	260,980	247,388	+65,092	10·7	10·2	10·2
16. Sheikh	532,703	336,845	338,873	+193,830	18·3	13·2	14·0
17. Anglo-Indians ..	4,635	4,916	3,479	+1,156	0·2	0·2	0·1
18. Europeans	24,405	26,325	32,278	—7,873	0·8	1·0	1·3
British Subjects ..	*23,732*	*25,863*	*31,732*	*—8,000*	*0·8*	*1·0*	*1·3*
Others	*673*	*462*	*546*	*+127*	*0·0*	*0·0*	*0·0*
United Provinces of Agra and Oudh.							
1. Ahar	427,170	419,992	269,604	+157,566	8·6	9·0	5·6
2. Ahir	3,896,788	3,691,294	3,903,745	—6,957	78·5	79·4	81·3
3. Brahman	4,555,965	4,513,264	4,701,179	—145,214	91·8	97·0	97·9
4. Chamar	6,312,203	5,842,900	6,083,401	+228,802	127·2	125·6	126·7
5. Dhobi	776,159	709,262	725,719	+440	15·6	15·2	15·1
6. Julaha	1,005,203	882,023	991,263	+13,940	20·3	19·0	20·7
7. Kahar	1,154,961	1,083,938	1,112,421	+42,540	23·3	23·3	23·2
8. Kayastha	478,657	452,911	485,073	—6,416	9·6	9·7	10·1
9. Kewat	550,162	482,963	445,121	+105,041	11·1	10·4	9·3
10. Khatik	215,531	177,264	182,495	+33,036	4·3	3·8	3·8
11. Kori	923,410	798,817	860,434	+62,976	18·6	17·2	17·9
12. Kumhar	782,639	699,528	726,361	+56,278	15·8	15·0	15·1
13. Kurmi	1,756,214	1,748,217	1,890,371	—134,157	35·4	37·6	39·4
14. Lodha	1,099,225	1,043,842	1,114,408	—15,183	22·2	22·4	23·2
15. Nai	906,457	857,370	912,828	—6,371	18·3	18·4	19·0
16. Pasi	1,460,326	1,338,446	1,311,415	+148,911	29·4	28·8	27·3
17. Rajput	3,756,936	3,468,884	3,657,557	+99,379	75·7	74·6	76·2
18. Teli	1,005,558	937,729	968,132	+37,426	20·3	20·2	20·2
19. Anglo-Indians ..	11,272	9,267	8,094	+3,178	0·2	0·2	0·2
20. Europeans	23,501	25,161	33,411	—9,910	0·5	0·5	0·7
British Subjects ..	*22,061*	*24,443*	*32,811*	*—10,750*	*0·4*	*0·5*	*0·7*
Others ..	*1,440*	*718*	*600*	*+840*	*0·0*	*0·0*	*0·0*
Baroda State.							
1. Bhangi	31,026	27,549	26,406	+4,620	12·7	13·0	13·0
2. Brahman	123,714	113,825	113,412	+10,302	50·6	53·5	55·8
3. Chamar	42,884	35,147	32,210	+10,674	17·6	16·5	15·8
4. Dhed	107,988	99,627	99,806	+8,182	44·2	46·8	49·1
5. Ghanchi	21,726	16,408	16,481	+5,245	8·9	7·7	8·1
6. Hajjam	29,164	26,355	26,266	+2,898	11·9	12·4	12·9
7. Kanbi	502,888	434,469	402,657	+100,231	205·8	204·3	198·1
8. Kumhar . ..	51,893	43,769	43,733	+8,160	21·2	20·6	21·5

SUBSIDIARY TABLE I—*contd.*

Race, Tribe or Caste.	Population in 1931.	Population in 1921.	Population in 1911.	Net variation Increase (+) Decrease (—). 1911-31.	Number per mille of the total population of Province, State or Agency. 1931.	1921.	1911.
1	2	3	4	5	6	7	8
Baroda State—*concld.*							
9. Maratha	12,165	13,326	14,785	—2,620	5·0	6·3	7·3
10. Vaghri	35,805	30,659	28,129	+7,676	14·7	14·4	13·8
11. Anglo-Indians ..	63	44	82	—19	0·0	0·0	0·0
12. Europeans	135	103	159	—24	0·1	0·0	0·1
British Subjects ..	*111*	*80*	*123*	*—12*	*0·0*	*0·0*	*0·1*
Others	*24*	*23*	*36*	*—12*	*0·0*	*0·0*	*0·0*
Central India Agency (including Gwalior State).							
1. Ahir	364,464	351,322	325,719	+38,745	35·9	38·2	34·8
2. Baniya	212,234	291,026	83,247	+128,987	20·9	31·6	8·9
3. Bansphor (Basor) ..	56,451	55,641	52,465	+3,986	5·6	6·1	5·6
4. Brahman	869,503	715,509	986,206	—116,703	85·6	77·8	105·3
5. Chamar	929,847	823,486	859,438	+70,409	91·6	89·6	91·7
6. Dhobi	95,385	82,692	82,405	+12,980	9·4	9·0	8·8
7. Kayastha	71,018	61,525	71,392	—374	7·0	6·7	7·6
8. Kunbi	42,182	78,863	*	..	4·2	8·6	*
9. Kurmi	252,948	211,190	215,359	+37,589	24·9	23·0	23·0
10. Kumhar	161,507	137,753	145,274	+16,233	15·9	15·0	15·5
11. Lodhi	227,327	222,658	228,235	—908	22·4	24·2	24·4
12. Nai	150,322	138,564	156,395	—6,073	14·8	15·1	16·7
13. Rajput	782,018	643,521	755,819	+26,199	77·0	70·0	80·7
14. Teli	196,690	173,564	186,820	+9,870	19·4	18·9	19·9
15. Anglo-Indians ..	867	732	565	+302	0·1	0·1	0·1
16. Europeans	2,588	4,142	4,582	—1,994	0·3	0·5	0·5
British Subjects ..	*2,461*	*3,868*	*3,968*	*—1,507*	*0·2*	*0·4*	*0·4*
Others	*127*	*274*	*614*	*—487*	*0·0*	*0·0*	*0·1*
Hyderabad State.							
1. Balija	39,300	33,364	*	..	2·7	2·7	*
2. Bedar (Bendar) ..	237,774	237,741	208,096	+29,678	16·5	19·1	15·6
3. Brahman	376,468	247,126	261,241	+115,227	26·1	19·8	19·5
4. Chambhar (Madiga, Mang, Mochi).	1,281,092	1,112,577	1,222,993	+58,099	88·7	89·2	91·4
5. Kumhar (Kummara) ..	154,148	117,157	151,986	+2,162	10·7	9·4	11·4
6. Kurma	173,318	156,189	144,688	+28,630	12·0	12·5	10·8
7. Mahar (Mala, Dher) ..	1,076,539	922,023	1,137,589	—61,050	74·6	73·9	85·1
8. Telaga (Munnur, Mutrasi)	966,190	883,206	947,746	+18,444	66·9	70·8	70·9
9. Waddar	138,082	107,668	131,799	+6,283	9·6	8·6	9·9
10. Wanjari (Banjara, Lambada).	371,402	263,844	435,322	—63,920	25·7	21·2	32·5
11. Anglo-Indians ..	3,370	2,237	3,004	+366	0·2	0·2	0·2
12. Europeans	2,627	3,690	5,384	—2,757	0·2	0·3	0·4
British Subjects ..	*1,853*	*3,503*	*5,230*	*—3,377*	*0·1*	*0·3*	*0·4*
Others	*774*	*187*	*154*	*+620*	*0·0*	*0·0*	*0·0*
Jammu and Kashmir State							
1. Arain	22,922	26,370	20,621	+2,301	6·3	7·9	6·5
2. Bafinda	33,872	28,162	26,830	+7,042	9·3	8·5	8·5
3. Brahman	253,529	190,187	241,362	+12,167	69·5	57·3	76·4
4. Chamar (Chamiar) ..	41,220	39,091	39,099	+2,121	11·3	11·8	12·4

* Figures not available.

SUBSIDIARY TABLE I—*concld.*

Race, Tribe or Caste.	Population in 1931.	Population in 1921.	Population in 1911.	Net variation Increase (+) Decrease (—). 1911-31.	Number per mille of the total population of Province, State or Agency. 1931.	1921.	1911.
1	2	3	4	5	6	7	8
Jammu and Kashmir State—*concld.*							
5. Dom (Dum)	34,341	30,617	52,099	—17,758	9·4	9·2	16·5
6. Khatri	23,206	22,682	18,517	+4,689	6·4	6·8	5·9
7. Rajput	256,020	222,275	211,328	+44,692	70·2	66·9	66·9
8. Anglo-Indians ..	123	48	17	+106	0·0	0·0	0·0
9. Europeans	198	270	251	—53	0·0	0·1	0·1
British Subjects ..	*151*	*263*	*226*	*—75*	*0·0*	*0·1*	*0·1*
Others	*47*	*7*	*25*	*+22*	*0·0*	*0·0*	*0·0*
Mysore State.							
1. Banajiga	152,250	134,815	132,955	+19,295	23·2	22·5	22·9
2. Beda	301,463	271,134	268,454	+33,009	46·0	45·3	46·2
3. Brahman	245,163	215,574	194,576	+50,587	37·4	36·1	33·5
4. Ganiga	44,960	41,973	40,469	+4,491	6·9	7·0	7·0
5. Kumbara	48,657	44,289	41,810	+6,847	7·4	7·4	7·2
6. Banjara (Lambani) ..	64,368	53,300	51,168	+13,200	9·8	8·9	8·8
7. Maratha	60,528	53,034	45,898	+14,630	9·2	8·9	7·9
8. Nayinda	46,216	42,360	39,414	+6,802	7·0	7·1	6·8
9. Vakkaliga	1,312,264	1,294,801	1,336,182	—23,918	200·1	216·6	230·1
10. Vodda	164,876	152,188	142,482	+22,394	25·1	25·5	24·5
11. Anglo-Indians ..	8,309	6,778	5,827	+2,482	1·3	1·1	1·0
12. Europeans	5,411	6,901	7,463	—2,052	0·8	1·2	1·3
British Subjects ..	*4,907*	*6,636*	*7,123*	*—2,216*	*0·7*	*1·1*	*1·2*
Others	*504*	*265*	*340*	*+164*	*0·1*	*0·0*	*0·6*
Rajputana Agency.							
1. Ahir	182,165	163,311	169,129	+13,036	16·2	16·6	16·1
2. Bishnoi	69,873	52,843	52,879	+16,994	6·2	5·4	5·0
3. Brahman	854,634	772,156	959,752	—105,118	76·1	78·5	91·2
4. Chamar	767,263	696,904	734,110	+33,153	68·3	70·9	69·8
5. Charan	35,548	31,436	37,574	—2,026	3·2	3·2	3·6
6. Daroga	177,104	100,833	118,914	+58,190	15·8	10·3	11·3
7. Dhobi	43,832	40,739	45,801	—1,969	3·9	4·1	4·4
8. Kumhar	357,751	299,055	309,234	+48,517	31·9	30·4	29·4
9. Kunbi	57,815	48,522	48,202	+9,613	5·2	4·9	4·6
10. Lodha	57,560	53,329	54,726	+2,834	5·1	5·4	5·2
11. Rajput	633,830	612,587	687,292	—53,462	56·5	62·3	65·3
12. Teli	80,015	79,216	78,560	+1,455	7·1	8·1	7·5
13. Anglo-Indians ..	828	641	529	+299	0·1	0·1	0·1
14. Europeans	932	840	1,179	—247	0·1	0·1	0·1
British Subjects ..	*856*	*804*	*1,127*	*—271*	*0·1*	*0·1*	*0·1*
Others	*76*	*36*	*52*	*+24*	*0·0*	*0·0*	*0·0*
Sikkim State.							
1. Bhotia	15,192	11,580	12,414	+2,778	138·4	141·7	141·2
2. Khas	11,044	6,616	6,210	+4,834	100·6	81·0	70·6
3. Murmi	7,017	6,180	7,436	—419	63·9	75·6	84·6
4. Newar	3,811	2,516	2,937	+874	34·7	30·8	33·4
5. Anglo-Indians ..	2	..	4	—2	0·0	..	0·0
6. Europeans	8	7	14	—6	0·1	0·1	0·2
British Subjects ..	*7*	*7*	*11*	*—4*	*0·1*	*0·1*	*0·1*
Others	*1*	..	*3*	*—2*	*0·0*	..	*0·0*

SUBSIDIARY TABLE II.

Statistics of Europeans and Anglo-Indians.

Province, State or Agency.	Number of persons born in Europe, America and Australia. 1931.	1921.	Table XIX. Europeans and Allied Races in 1931. British Subjects.	Others.	Total.	Total Europeans and Allied Races in 1921.	Anglo-Indians. 1931.	1921.
1	2	3	4	5	6	7	8	9
INDIA ...	**123,438**	**125,869**	**155,555**	**12,579**	**168,134**	**176,031**	**138,395**	**113,090**
Provinces	**113,793**	**113,455**	**144,474**	**10,824**	**155,298**	**159,623**	**121,898**	**96,607**
1. Ajmer-Merwara ..	1,281	1,118	1,524	152	1,676	1,442	1,232	746
2. Andaman and Nicobar Islands ..	151	144	214	..	214	209	97	25
3. Assam	2,659	1,889	3,127	235	3,362	2,768	650	491
4. Baluchistan ..	4,127	4,189	5,014	20	5,034	4,757	379	234
5. Bengal	14,092	14,107	20,904	2,126	23,030	22,730	27,573	22,250
6. Bihar and Orissa ..	3,668	3,687	5,675	714	6,389	6,346	6,638	4,134
7. Bombay* ..	17,568	22,409†	24,131	2,164	26,295	33,863†	16,218	10,543†
8. Burma	7,729	7,298	10,627	1,024	11,651	8,665	19,200	16,688
9. Central Provinces and Berar ..	4,502	4,598	5,124	526	5,650	5,892	5,065	3,574
10. Coorg	77	90	122	16	138	156	84	47
11. Delhi	3,196	2,948	4,209	97	4,306	4,370	1,010	417
12. Madras	8,088	6,399	10,676	1,701	12,377	10,836	28,694	23,492
13. North-West Frontier Province ..	10,625	9,727	11,543	33	11,576	10,473	161	200
14. Punjab (including Agency) ..	17,406	16,669	19,523	576	20,099	21,955	3,625	4,499
15. United Provinces of Agra and Oudh	18,624	18,183	22,061	1,440	23,501	25,161	11,272	9,267
States and Agencies	**9,645**	**12,414**	**11,081**	**1,755**	**12,836**	**16,408**	**16,497**	**16,483**
16. Baroda State ..	104	85	111	24	135	103	63	44
17. Central India Agency	2,057	2,903	2,360	117	2,477	3,513	736	472
18. Cochin State ..	73	50	72	40	112	66	1,717	2,182
19. Gwalior State ..	75	584	101	10	111	629	131	260
20. Hyderabad State ..	2,661	3,680	1,853	774	2,627	3,690	3,370	2,237
21. Jammu and Kashmir State	212	167	151	47	198	270	123	48
22. Mysore State ..	3,238	4,162	4,907	504	5,411	6,901	8,309	6,778
23. Rajputana Agency	469	401	856	76	932	840	828	641
24. Sikkim State ..	7	11	7	1	8	7	2	..
25. Travancore State	536	371	456	131	587	389	790	3,821
26. Western India States Agency ..	213	..	207	31	238	..	428	..

*Including Aden. †Includes figures for Western India States Agency.

SUBSIDIARY TABLE III.

Age.	Persons born in Great Britain and Northern* Ireland.		
	Persons.	Males.	Females.
1	2	3	4
Total	**100,150**	**79,442**	**20,708**
0—13	6,958	3,697	3,261
14—16	1,480	832	648
17—23	21,977	20,376	1,601
24—33	39,635	33,857	5,778
34—43	16,026	10,985	5,041
44—53	9,049	6,391	2,658
54 and over	5,007	3,286	1,721
Age Unspecified	18	18	..

*Also includes 1,101 persons (922 Males and 179 Females) who returned their birth place as Ireland without qualification.

APPENDIX I.

Exterior Castes.

N.B.—*No attempt has been made here to deal with events that have taken place since 1931.*

This term for the Hindu castes hitherto known as " depressed " was originally suggested by the Census Superintendent for Assam and has been adopted in this report as the most satisfactory alternative to the unfortunate and depressing label " depressed class ". It has been criticised as being the same term as ' outcaste ' only of five instead of two syllables, and it must be admitted that ' exterior ' is but old ' out ' writ large. At the same time it is here submitted that outcaste, with an *e*, has not unnaturally attracted to its connotation the implications of the quite differently derived outcast, with no *e*. Outcaste correctly interpreted seems to mean no more than one who is outside the caste system and is therefore not admitted to Hindu society, but since in practice the exterior castes also contained those who had been cast out from the Hindu social body for some breach of caste rules ' outcaste ' and ' outcast ' were in some cases synonymous and the derogatory implications of obliquity attaching to the latter term have unjustly coloured the former, a taint which is not conveyed by the substitution of the word ' exterior ', which may connote exclusion but not extrusion.

The instructions of the Government of India for the taking of this census concluded with the following enjoinder :—

> " The Government of India also desire that attention should be paid to the collection of information conducive to a better knowledge of the backward and depressed classes and of the problem involved in their present and future welfare."

In that connection the following instructions were issued to the various Superintendents of Census Operations in India :—

> " For this purpose it will be necessary to have a list of castes to be included in depressed classes and all provinces are asked to frame a list applicable to the province. There are very great difficulties in framing a list of this kind and there are insuperable difficulties in framing a list of depressed classes which will be applicable to India as a whole."

A subsequent instruction ran as follows :—

> " I have explained depressed castes as castes, contact with whom entails purification on the part of high caste Hindus. It is not intended that the term should have any reference to occupation as such but to those castes which by reason of their traditional position in Hindu society are denied access to temples, for instance, or have to use separate wells or are not allowed to sit inside a school house but have to remain outside or which suffer similar social disabilities. These disabilities vary in different parts of India being much more severe in the south of India than elsewhere. At the same time the castes which belong to this class are generally known and can in most parts of India be listed for a definite area, though perhaps the lists for India as a whole will not coincide."

The question of the preparation of lists for each province was discussed at a meeting of the Superintendents of Census Operations in January 1931 before the census took place. It was agreed that each province should make a list of castes who suffered disability on account of their low social position and on account of being debarred from temples, schools or wells. No specific definition of depressed castes was framed and no more precise instructions were issued to the Superintendents of Census Operations, because it was realised that conditions varied so much from province to province and from district to district, even, within some provinces, that it would be unwise to tie down the Superintendents of Census Operations with too meticulous instructions. The general method of proceeding prescribed was that of local enquiry into what castes were held to be depressed and why and the framing of a list accordingly. It was decided that Muslims and Christians should be excluded from the term " depressed class " and that, generally speaking, hill and forest tribes, who had not become Hindu but whose religion was returned as Tribal, should also be excluded and in the numbers of the exterior castes given below these principles have been followed. A note on the depressed and backward classes in Assam submitted to the Franchise Committee by the Superintendent of Census Operations for that province affords a very clear example of the way in which these principles were intended to be applied and have been applied by Superintendents of Census Operations, and an extract from it is given towards the end of this appendix.

Both for social and political reasons it is obviously necessary to know the number of these classes not only in India as a whole but also in different provinces. The matter is of importance not only with reference to their representation in the body politic, but also with reference to any social work that is to be done towards raising them from their present backward position to one more nearly comparable with that of more advanced social groups.

The Census Commissioner in 1921 (Census of India, Volume I, part I, paragraph 193) gave what he describes as *minimum* numbers of the Depressed Classes in various provinces, making a total of 52,680,000. This figure he states, must be taken as a low estimate, since it does not include all those who should have been included, and he says, "We may confidently place the numbers of these Depressed Classes all of whom are considered impure, at something between 55 and 60 millions in India proper". Of the 52½ million for which the Census Commissioner gave actual figures, less than 43½ million were to be found in British India. This figure agrees fairly well with the 42 million odd given as the figure of Depressed Classes by the Franchise Committee of 1919. It is also not greatly at variance with the 44½ million estimated by the Nair Central Committee of 1929 as the figure of Depressed Classes in British India, but it varies very considerably from the Hartog Committee's figure of approximately 30 million. Clearly it is time that some more definite figures were obtained than the estimates hitherto employed. There are however a considerable number of difficulties in arriving at a determined figure.

The definition to be used in arriving at the figure of Depressed Classes is a very difficult matter. The following possible tests are to be considered :—

(1) Whether the caste or class in question can be served by clean Brahmans or not.

(2) Whether the caste or class in question can be served by the barbers, water-carriers, tailors, etc., who serve the caste Hindus.

(3) Whether the caste in question pollutes a high caste Hindu by contact or by proximity.

(4) Whether the caste or class in question is one from whose hands a caste Hindu can take water.

(5) Whether the caste or class in question is debarred from using public conveniences, such as, roads, ferries, wells or schools.

(6) Whether the caste or class in question is debarred from the use of Hindu temples.

(7) Whether in ordinary social intercourse a well educated member of the caste or class in question will be treated as an equal by high caste men of the same educational qualifications.

(8) Whether the caste or class in question is merely depressed on account of its own ignorance, illiteracy or poverty and but for that would be subject to no social disability.

(9) Whether it is depressed on account of the occupation followed and whether but for that occupation it would be subject to no social disability.

Now it is obvious that several of these tests themselves involve an unknown factor—What is a clean Brahman ? What is the line between a high caste and a low caste Hindu, since both adjectives may and ordinarily would have a merely comparative sense ? What constitutes pollution or what constitutes the right to use a temple, since here again there are grades from those who must remain entirely outside and not approach a temple at all to those who are admitted to the inner sanctuary ? In deciding what is an Exterior Caste, none of these tests can be taken alone. From the point of view of the State the important test is the right to use public conveniences—roads, wells and schools, and if this be taken as the primary test, religious disabilities and the social difficulties indirectly involved by them may be regarded as contributory only. Some importance must be attached to them, since obviously if the general public regards the persons of certain groups as so distasteful that concerted action is resorted to in order to keep them away, persons of those groups do suffer under a serious disability. It is not enough to say that a road is a public road, and that if A considers himself polluted by the presence of B at a distance of 30 yards and no compulsion rests on B to remove himself from the road to let A pass, the disability is A's and not B's, since A must leave the road or be polluted. That is all very well if B and his friends are in such a position as to be able to impose on A the position of being one to leave the road. If, however, it is possible for A and his friends by boycotting B and his friends for certain purposes to bring pressure on B to disregard his legal rights and to conform to A's religious prejudices and leave the road whenever A is seen at a distance, clearly B has in practice no freedom of action in the matter of the road whether his religious scruples are involved or not. This question of the use of roads has been taken as an illustration, but in point of fact the restriction of the use of roads is one which seems to be generally disappearing and has possibly disappeared to such an extent that the question may be ignored as far as British India is concerned. The use of wells, however, is another matter and the disability of the exterior castes varies from not being allowed to approach the village well at all to the position common in Bengal in which persons of certain castes may not draw water themselves but must await someone of a clean caste who draws water for them at the well. The question of schools is another very real problem for the exterior castes, since in many parts of India if they sit inside the school they would be made to suffer in some other way by the higher castes using the school, and whereas the acquisition of reading and writing at least may be taken for granted in the case of the children of any Brahman, and of other castes as well, it is an exception in the case of the exterior castes, the presence of whose children is disliked in the school by their social superiors and whose children, if they read at all, must sit outside in the sun and dust. It is often argued that untouchability is merely dependent on the occupation, so that an untouchable person or caste abandoning an unclean occupation becomes touchable. This may be true in a literal sense, but it is not true morally, since members of exterior castes who may have abandoned their traditional calling for two or three generations are still liable to be treated as outside the pale of decent society, and their presence is apt to be regarded as an offence by members of interior castes, while they would not be ordinarily admitted to social functions on a footing of equality.

For purposes therefore of deciding what persons are to be included in the numbers of the exterior castes it has been necessary for each province to deal with the problem in its own way and to produce its own list. It is not possible to say generally that such and such a caste is exterior to Hindu society and to apply that dictum to the whole of India. It may be possible to do so in the case of certain castes, such as those of Dom and Bhangi, but it certainly is not the case that a caste which is depressed in one part of India is depressed everywhere. Consequently each provincial superintendent has had to draw up his own list, taking into account the various factors enumerated above, and to reckon as depressed only those castes or classes who definitely suffer from serious social and political handicap on account of their degraded position in the Hindu social scheme. So much is this the position that, in the Central Provinces for instance, the castes to be treated as depressed for purposes of figures in this Report have varied from district to district and no list is possible at all which is applicable to the whole of the province for all the castes concerned. Many castes and tribes who would be included by some, at any rate, of the tests mentioned above have been excluded from the list on the ground that they suffer no tangible disability as a result of their inferiority in the Hindu system. Many primitive tribes for instance are in an ambiguous position by reason of their not really being Hindus at all. Such tribes when they come within the Hindu system often become automatically depressed, largely on account of the fact that they have no prejudices against occupations and food which are taboo to interior Hindus. On the other hand, the socially superior individuals of these identical tribes are very frequently able to get themselves incorporated into the Hindu system as Rajputs or Kshattriyas, though their fellow tribesmen may remain exterior. In some cases, however, a complete tribe has succeeded in establishing its claim to a more or less equivocal twice-born status. In these circumstances, therefore, non-Hinduised hill and forest tribes have been excluded from the total of the Exterior Castes, as until they reach the stage of incorporation in regular Hindu society, they do not really suffer by their potential position in that scheme. Similarly criminal tribes have not been included unless their condition be such that even if they ceased to be criminal by habit or profession and lived as peaceable and law-abiding citizens, they would still be depressed on account of their social position as distinct from their occupational stigma. Again there are numbers of castes who, though they are regarded by interior Hindus as ceremonially polluting and such as from whose hands water cannot be taken, have in many cases such strong caste organisations and include so many individuals of substance and education that they have built up for themselves a strong position which obviates the need of any special measures for their social, political or religious protection. It is these considerations which have caused the Census Superintendent of Cochin State to exclude the Iruvans from the number of those depressed, while the Shahas, Telis and Mahishyas of Bengal and Assam would themselves protest at any such inclusion.

The note on the Depressed and Backward Classes in Assam by the Census Superintendent for that province, which forms an appendix to the Assam Census Report, affords an excellent example of the facts and considerations taken into account in determining what constitutes a depressed caste. In the case of Assam the numbers of the exterior castes are so high in comparison to the total number of interior Hindus or rather the number of interior Hindus is so comparatively small in a province in which the numbers of backward classes and hill tribes is high, that the disabilities attaching to depression are slight compared to those in most provinces, but the factors to be taken into account are the same everywhere. The non-Hindus and the hill and forest tribes included by the Assam Census Superintendent as Backward Classes have been excluded from the figures given in the table below which amount for all India to just a little over fifty million.

These figures are given province by province in this place; tables in a somewhat different form will be found towards the end of this appendix. The total number of exterior castes in British India appears in Table XVII as 39,137,405, the difference being due to the fact that in two provinces the figures in Provincial Table II on which that table is based differ slightly from the figures obtained from the caste table for individual castes.

Caste.	Population.
Aheri	87
Bagri	584
Balai	19,871
Bambhi	5,764
Bansphor	13
Bargi	75
Bhangi	6,976
Chamar	15,914
Dabgar	57
Dhanak	1,680
Garoda	48
Ghancha	90
Kalbelia	393
Kanjar	625
Khangar	2
Kuchband	69
Mahar	31
Meghwal	10
Nat	518
Pasi	49
Raigar	22,601
Rawal	113
Sansi	406
Sargara	762
Satia	71
Thori	2
Tirgar	5
Total	76,816

1. *Ajmer-Merwara.*—These figures (*76,816*) differ by 81 from the total found in Provincial Table II for the province where the total of Depressed Classes appears as 76,735. This smaller figure is due to the omission from the Provincial Table of the numbers of 80 Bagris and one Sansi, (total 81) whose religion was dubiously returned as "tribal".

Caste	Population
Bhangi	29
Chamar	204
Kori	47
Pasi	232
Total	512

2. *Andaman Islands.*—No return was made by the Census Superintendent and these figures (*512*) have been extracted by me from his tables as representing castes unequivocally depressed.

Caste	Population
Province—	
Bhangi	2,364
Namasudra	170,519
Jaliya Kaibartta	149,074
Tea garden coolie castes	1,233,512
Others	1,839
Surma Valley—	
Bhuinmali	38,635
Dhobi	22,521
Dugla	9,523
Jhalo and Malo	10,826
Jugi	83,922
Mahara	5,424
Muchi	7,312
Patni	51,408
Sutradhar	12,575
Brahmaputra Valley—	
Brittial Bania	14,348
Hira	16,628
Total	1,830,430

3. *Assam.*—Here it will be noticed that the list (total 1,830,430) varies in different parts of the province. Jugis, for instance, are found in both valleys, but are treated as exterior in the Surma valley and not in the Brahmaputra valley. 'Others' in the figures applicable to the whole province do not include any castes not in the list, but merely castes listed for one valley or the other but enumerated elsewhere, of which a separate tally is not now available. Of the total *1,421* are found in the Assam States, the remainder *1,829,009* being in British territory.

Caste	Population
Chuhras	4,533
Kori	477
Pasi	228
Nat	227
Chamar (including Jaiswara)	227
Khatik	19
Shudar	7
Ramdasi	3
Ghasia	1
Total	5,722

4. *Baluchistan.*—Of this total of 5,722, only *20* are found in Baluchistan States, remainder (*5,702*) being in British territory. In addition to the castes in the above list the following castes appear in the Baluchistan list, figures of which have not been accepted by me, as the exterior position of several of them is at least open to dispute, and it appeared to me that the local net had been cast too wide and I therefore rejected for the India list the following castes which appeared to me to be doubtfully exterior:—

Caste	Population
Dhobi	749
Mochi	388
Nai	125
Kurmi	109
Kabirpanthi	56
Kumhar	71
Gadaria	46
Julaha	31
Kohli	28
Teli	21
Total	1,624

Caste.	Population.
Bhuinmali	72,804
Dom	140,067
Halalkhor	876
Hari	132,393
Kaora	107,908
Kichak	2
Lalbegi	4,965
Mehtor	23,278
Bagdi	987,570
Bahelia	4,449
Bauri	331,238
Bhuiya	49,370
Bind	19,518
Binjhia	317
Chamar	150,458
Dhenuar	44
Dhobi	229,672
Doai	1,960
Dosadh	36,420
Ghasi	5,312
Kadar	1,078
Kan	66
Kanwar	133
Kotal	7,651
Lohar	50,167
Mal	111,167
Mallah	26,252
Muchi	414,219
Musahar	11,714
Naiya	40
Namasudra	2,094,957
Palaiya	43,160
Pan	1,855
Pasi	18,925
Patni	40,766
Pod	667,731
Pundari	31,255
Rajwar	21,337
Sunri	76,920
Tiyar	96,413
Turi	16,199
Baiti	8,888
Bediya	7,243
Beldar	3,139
Berua	367
Bhatiya	322
Damai	6,039
Gonrhi	5,149
Jalia Kaibartta	352,072
Jhalo, Malo	198,099
Kalwar	13,531
Kandra	4,724
Kapali	165,583
Kapuria	170
Karenga	9,855
Khatik	1,157
Konai	41,058
Mahar	1,986
Nagar	16,164
Nat	7,348
Raju	56,778
Shagirdapesha	333
Total	6,930,631

5. *Bengal.*— Of this total of 6,930,631, *30,822* are found in the Bengal States, leaving *6,899,809* in British districts. Here again a number of names have been added by the Local Government, some of which are also regarded as Exterior by the Census Superintendent. Most of these are primitive tribes whose names I have rejected for that reason. These tribes are marked with an asterisk, and it must, of course, be borne in mind that many of them are actually in the process of being transformed into exterior castes of Hinduism, if they have not already become so. Of the others not so marked some are admittedly doubtful and their inclusion as exterior castes might be justified; others on the contrary appear to me to be such that their inclusion would be entirely unjustified, *e.g.*, Khandait, while Suklis have definitely protested against their inclusion, and the attitude of the Rajbansis has been equivocal. It is understood that the Local Government are also including Kurmis in their list of Depressed Classes, but I do not myself regard this as even a doubtful case. They will not be found in this list. The additional names in the Local Government's list are—

*Agaria	230
*Asur	..
*Bhumij	84,447
*Birhor	..
*Garo	37,909
*Hadi	14,334
*Hajang	19,69?
*Ho	23
*Kandh	1,525
Kastha	2,601
*Kaur	1,781
*Khaira	38,287
Khandait	35,080
*Kochh	81,299
*Koda (Kora)	46,789
Koiri	16,021
*Korwa	..
Lodha	11,001
*Mahli	16,262
*Malpaharia	11,782
*Mech	4,875
*Munda	63,107
*Nageshia	2,088
Nuniya	28,100
*Oraon	136,427
*Rabha	2,076
Rajbangshi	1,806,390
*Santal	433,502
Sukli	3,860
Tipara	195,855

Caste.	Population.
Bauri	314,979
Bhogta	66,054
Bhuiya	621,062
Bhumij	266,464
Chamar	1,296,001
Chaupal	2,737
Dhobi	414,221
Dom	269,340
Dosadh	1,290,936
Ghasi	75,579
Ghusuria	1,846
Godra	1,553
Gokha	48,622
Halalkhor	20,742
Hari	115,613
Irika	332
Kandra	155,113
Kanjar	2,566
Kela	9,493
Kurariar	631
Lalbegi	105
Mahuria	2,389
Mangan	184
Mochi	22,863
Musahar	720,051
Nat	9,628
Pan	411,770
Pasi	172,061
Siyal	9,281
Turi	54,041
Total	6,376,257

6. *Bihar and Orissa.*—This total (6,376,257) excludes the figures of Rajwar (133,935) which have been included by the Census Superintendent who gives the total number of his depressed classes as 6,510,192. The figure that appears however in his provincial table II is 6,409,337 of which 649,266 appear in the states, the remainder, that is 5,760,071, being in British territory, a figure little higher than that reached by me after excluding Rajwars, and differing from his report total on account of some omissions in the provincial table. The case of the Rajwars in Bihar seems to me to be open to doubt and they do not appear in the United Provinces' list. In my opinion the Franchise Committee was not justified in excluding from the depressed castes Bauri, Bhogta, Bhuiya, Bhumij, Ghasi, Pan and Turi. With the possible exception of Bhumij and Bhuiya these seven cannot be regarded as retaining much, if any, tribal cohesion, and they are outwardly Hinduised. Of the total 6,376,257 in my list not more than *631,864* are found in the Bihar and Orissa States, leaving not less than *5,744,393* in British districts.

Caste.	Population.
Agar	6,680
Bhambi	8,729
Bhangi, etc.	79,403
Chambhar	291,811
Dhor	18,277
Khalpa	11,485
Kolcha (Kolgha)	1,114
Koli-Dhor	15,923
Kotwalia	1,418
Mahar	1,264,104
Mang	309,938
Mang-Garudi	4,334
Meghwal	69,797
Timali	68
Turi	1,053
Vitholia	526
Wansfoda	664
Others	13,674
Total	2,098,998

7. *Bombay.*—Of this total of 2,098,998, *348,574* are found in the Bombay States, the remaining *1,750,424* being in British territory.

Caste.	Population.
*Audhelia	749
Basor	53,204
*Balahi	33,776
*Bedar	490
*Bahna	6
Chamar	528,039
*Chadar	21,071
*Chauhan	2,026
Dom	4,660
*Dhobi	73,966
*Dhimar	46,071
*Dohor	6,616
*Dewar	1,786
*Dahayat	833
*Dhanuk	3
Ganda	108,843
*Ghasia	45,409
*Holiya	3,439
*Jangam	12
*Kori	30,477
*Katia	24,510
*Kumhar	23,863
*Khatik	11,327
*Khangar	7,650
*Kaikari	2,157
Mahar, Mehra	1,255,703
Mang	101,142
Mehtar, Bhangi	30,950
Mochi	6,179
*Madgi	10,070
Carried over	2,435,027

8. *Central Provinces and Berar.*—Of this total of 3,071,078, not more than *252,732* appear in the states, not less than the remaining *2,818,346* being in British territory. It will be noticed that an asterisk appears against a large number of castes in the marginal list, and only those castes have been treated as exterior throughout the province against which no asterisk appears. Wherever a caste is asterisked the implication is that in some parts of the province it is treated as Exterior and in other parts it is treated as Interior. Details of this distribution may be obtained from the provincial tables if required. The numbers shown against each caste refer, of course, to the numbers actually treated as exterior and not to the number of the castes found in the province. The Census Superintendent gives the figure of 3,180,075 as the total of the depressed classes in the Central Provinces and Berar, both in Chapter XII of his report and in Provincial Table II and in Appendix II to his

Caste.	Population.
Brought forward ..	2,435,027
*Mala	1,048
*Nagarchi	5,970
*Ojha	1,718
*Pardhi	41
*Pardhan	71,906
*Panka	204,304
*Rajjhar	1,217
Satnami	349,847
Total ..	3,071,078

8. *Central Provinces and Berar*—contd.

report. In the latter place the total given for British Districts is misprinted as 2,927,936 instead of 2,927,343. As these figures include those returning tribal religions, I have taken as the total of the depressed castes the sum of those returned as Hindu by religion, the figures of which appear here.

Caste.	Population.
Adi-Dravida	52
Adiya	5
Balagai	130
Holeya	320
Kalloda	2
Korama	128
Kudiya	549
Lippara	4
Madiga	217
Maleya	123
Medara	41
Muchi	20
Mundala	87
Nale Kanavaru	9
Pale	3,192
Panchama	19,571
Pannikar	5
Paraiyan	340
Samagara	5
Surava	3
Total ..	24,803

9. *Coorg.*—Of the total (*24,803*) of these castes Kudiya appears also as a primitive tribe and there is therefore an overlap of 549 between exterior castes and primitive tribes in Coorg, or of 1,089 if the Marratha (540) be included in the former category ; for the purposes of these figures it has been omitted.

Caste.	Population.
Bawaria	32
Chamar	42,952
Chuhra	17,901
Dagi and Koli	6,928
Dhanak	1,321
Khatik	3,522
Sansi	227
Total ..	72,883

10. *Delhi.*—This total (*72,883*) agrees with that given in Provincial Table II.

Caste.	Population.
Adi-Andhra	664,844
Adi-Dravida	1,619,227
Adi-Karnataka	644
Ajila	659
†Aranadan	60
Arunthuthiyar	17,396
Baira	1,879
Bakuda	806
Bandi	553
Bariki	3,695
Battada	558
Bavuri	42,810
Bellara	87
Byagari	8,459
Chachati	5,130
Chakkiliyan	606,775
Chalavadi	3,422
Chamar	140
Chandala	2,113
Cheruman	214,878
Dandasi	44,248
Devendrakulathan	4,019
†Dombo	79,643
Ghasi	6,081
Godagali	969
Godari	419
Godda	146
Gosangi	244
Haddi	17,433
Hasla	368
Holeya	49,567
Jaggali	3,020
Jambuvulu	6,701
†Kadan	491
Kalladi	5,737
Kanakkan	22,046
†Karimpalan	2,807
†Kattunayakan	1,581
Kodalo	28,410
Koosa	818
Koraga	4,042
†Kudiya	3,497
Carried over ..	3,476,422

11. *Madras.*—This total (7,299,400) is taken from the Madras Caste Table for 1931, *65,296* being found in the Madras States other than Cochin and Travancore, *i.e.*, in Pudukkottai, Banganapalle and Sandur ; the remaining *7,234,104* are found in British territory. The total differs from that given in Madras Provincial Table II by a figure of 34,053. This represents the numbers of the Marathi or Marratha tribe, a caste or tribe found in South Kanara (its name has nothing to do with 'Maratha' as ordinarily understood) and described by the Census Superintendent and the district officer as a primitive tribe, but listed by the Madras Government as a depressed caste. In southern India, *i.e.*, in India south of the Godavari, little difference is to be distinguished as a rule in the treatment of primitive tribes and of exterior castes ; both alike are regarded as untouchables or pollute at a distance, though the same does not apply to all the tribes in the Agency tract which is to the north of the Godavari. This Marratha tribe however should probably be excluded from the list of depressed castes proper, and I have therefore excluded it in this list, following the caste table and not Provincial Table II, the numbers of which include this tribe. Several other tribes appear in the Madras table both as primitive tribes and as depressed castes. They have been included by the Madras Census Superintendent both in his Caste Table and in Provincial Table II, and their names will be found in the above list marked with a dagger. The total numbers of these tribes involve an overlap between the

Caste.	Population.
Brought forward ..	3,476,422
†Kudubi	12,011
Kudumban	827
Kuravan	2,110
†Kurichchan	7,112
†Kuruman	10,447
Madari	6,617
Madiga	612,411
Maila	1,431
Mala	837,718
Mala Dasu	2,399
†Malasar	5,101
Matangi	623
†Mavillan	1,341
Moger	773
Muchi	1,842
Mundala	6,250
Nalakeyava	1,489
Nayadi	520
Pagadai	771
Paidi	39,437
Painda	92
Paky	2,017
Pallan	825,224
Pambada	335
Pamidi	424
Panchama	75,574
Paniyan	32,410
Panniandi	54
†Pano	70,527
Paraiyan	1,117,197
Paravan	826
Pulayan	23,378
Puthirai Vannan	74
Raneyar	1,480
Relli	24,239
Samagara	2,018
Samban	557
Sapari	462
Semman	1,198
Thoti	1,639
Tiruvalluvar	207
Valluvan	59,202
Valmiki	4,289
Vettuvan	28,325
Total	7,299,400

11. *Madras.*—contd.

primitive tribes and exterior castes of 194,618 or of 228,671 if the Marratha (34,053) be included. The Marrathas have however been excluded from my figures, though treated as 'Depressed' by the Government of Madras.

Caste.	Population.
Chuhra	5,783
Chamar	227
Total	6,010

12. *North-West Frontier Province.*—This figure (6,010) exceeds the figure *5,468* appearing in the North-West Frontier Provincial Table II by *542*. The explanation is that this figure 542 refers to exterior castes enumerated in trans-frontier posts which were therefore outside the scope of Provincial Table II, and the correct figure is the one given here.

Caste.	Population.
1. Bawaria	16,120
2. Chamar	941,312
3. Chuhra	454,772
4. Dagi and Koli	181,472
5. Dumna	37,205
6. Megh	22,363
7. Sansi	31,165
8. Sarera	7,083
9. Others (Ad-Dharmi)	75,313
Total	1,766,805

13. *Punjab.*—The total figure here arrived at (1,766,805) differs by 82,576 from the figure which is given by the Census Superintendent for the Punjab in his Provincial Table II; this latter figure is 1,684,229, but it does not include all the depressed castes, as Bawaria, Dumna, Megh and Sarera are omitted in Provincial Table II. In Appendix I to Chapter XI the Census Superintendent gives his total figure of depressed castes as 1,798,623, which exceeds the total accepted by me for the India figures by 31,818. Of the castes given in my list above *94,347* are found in the Punjab States, *392,999* are found in the Punjab States Agency, and the remainder, *1,279,459*, are in the British districts. These figures include all those who returned their religion as Ad-Dharmi the total number of whom is 399,307 in British districts and 19,482 in the States and the Agency together. I have taken for India the figures of the eight castes in the above list and such others who returned themselves as Ad-Dharmi. The Census Superintendent for the Punjab, however, names sixteen castes as "Depressed and Backward". Excluding the 8 castes etc., given by me the other castes named by him include :—

Bagaria	2,282
Dhobi	12,543
Ghosi	1,904
Julaha	53,488
Kahar	62,422
Mahtam	15,482
Od	19,583
Ramdasia	12,235
Total	179,939*

The last two of these castes are regarded by him as quite definitely depressed.

* Total Punjab—includes the States approximately 4,800 and the Agency approximately 32,500.

Caste.	Population
Agariya Bhuiya Bhuiyar Chero Ghasiya Khairaha Kharwar (excluding Banbasi) Majhwar (Manjhi) Panka Parahiya Patari	68,044
Kol	76,845
Korwa	467
Banmanu Bayar Dhangar Musahar	78,770
Saun	2,275
Silpkar	313,737
Balahar Bansphor Dharkar Basor Dom Domar	109,906
Aheriya	23,084
Bahelia	45,458
Bandi Kabaria	513
Khatik Chik	209,668
Pasi (includes Yarmali)	1,459,940
Balai	136
Bhar (excluding Rajbhar)	461,624
Bhil	28
Dhari Kingharia Pawaria	7,599
Dusadh	73,522
Beriya Bangali Bhantu	12,105
Karwal or Karaul	108
Habura	1,915
Kanjar (including Sapera and Saparia).	23,311
Sansia	886
Badi Bajania Bajgi Gual Kalabaz	34
Nat	37,038
Badhik	1,367
Barwar	4,314
Bawariya (Bauria)	15,956
Sahariya	14,113
Sanaurhiya	31
Gidhiya	191
Bhangi	482,718
Chamar	6,292,338
Dabgar Gharmi	657
Dhobi	665,905
Kori	922,357
Mochi	5,752
Arakh	85,907
Kaparia	803
Khairwa	81
Kotwar	64
Tharu	31,578
Total	11,531,145

14. *United Provinces.*—Of this total figure of 11,531,145, *208,864* are found in the States and the remaining *11,322,281* in British districts. In addition to the above the Census Superintendent for the United Provinces includes the following castes (1,288,804) in his list. There is some doubt about the correct classification of the castes in this second list and I have excluded them from my figures :—

Beldar	44,206
Kharot	356
Kumhar	772,945
Luniya	471,297
Total	1,288,804

The castes accepted by me include a number of quasi-aboriginal tribes. In the case of the United Provinces I consider them correctly classified as exterior castes, as with the possible exception of some 200 Korwas they are reported to be completely detribalized and their social position is indistinguishable from that of other depressed castes included.

States.—The total figure for depressed castes in States and Agencies appears in Table XVII as *11,112,942*. This figure includes the figures already mentioned of depressed castes found in the states in political relation with the various provinces. The States and Agencies forming census units are dealt with separately below :—

Caste.	Population.
Bhangi	31,018
Bansphor	478
Chamar (including Khalpa)	42,802
Garoda	7,796
Holar	54
Mahar	572
Mang	37
Nadia	622
Shenva	9,643
Thori	56
Turi	1,711
Vankar including Dhed	107,988
Others (Arya)	266
Total	203,043

15. *Baroda.*—The marginal list of depressed castes, total *203,043*, agrees with the figures given by the Baroda Census Superintendent as depressed in his Appendix IX to his Chapter XII.

Caste.	Population.
Balai	191,194
Basor	43,399
Bhambi	6,560
Bhangi	28,429
Chamar	513,897
Dharkar	4,850
Dher	51
Dom	51
Domar	442
Jhamral	1,519
Mahar	4,885
Mang	1,252
Meghwal	1,373
Total	797,902

16. *Central India Agency.*—The total given above, *797,902*, exceeds the total appearing in the Agency Provincial Table II by 58, the reason being that it includes 58 Chamars whose religion was returned as 'Tribal' and who, therefore, appeared in a different column in the Provincial Table. Except in this case and in that of Ajmer-Merwara, in both of which the correctness of the return seems open to considerable doubt, individuals returning a tribal religion have been rigidly excluded from my figures.

Caste.	Population.
Bagri	23,209
Balai	97,828
Barar	1,384
Bargunda	1,931
Basor	13,052
Beria	5,807
Bhangi	27,405
Chamar	415,950
Kanjar	402
Khatik	15,800
Koli	75,351
Total	678,119

17. *Gwalior.*—No return of depressed castes was made in State Table II, and the figures here are taken from Chapter XII of the Gwalior Report

Caste.	Population.
Dher (including Mala, Mahar)	1,076,539
Madiga (including Mang)	1,281,092
Others	115,599
Total	2,473,230

18. *Hyderabad.*—The total in this State is *2,473,230*. 'Others' in this list include a number of minor exterior castes, *e.g.* Bhangi, for which separate totals are not given in the State Tables.

Caste.	Population.
Barwala	5,682
Basith	6,213
Batwal	5,645
Chamar	41,189
Chuhra	1,607
Dhiyar	3,165
Dom	34,329
Gardi	173
Jolaha	40
Megh	70,030
Ratal	488
Saryara	2,354
Watal	13
Total	170,928

19. *Jammu and Kashmir.*—The castes in the above list (total *170,928*) are those reported as exterior by the Census Commissioner for the State, and the numbers are those that appear against the castes named in the State Caste Table. They agree with the numbers of depressed classes given in the State Table II.

Caste.	Population.
Eravalan	541
Irulan	240
Kadan	267
Kanakkan	13,192
Kavera	790
Kootan	228
Malayan	3,185
Nayadi	152
Pulayan	82,043
Sambavan (including Paraiyan)	11,914
Ullatan	778
Valluvan	212
Vettuvan	11,797
Total	125,339

20. *Cochin.*—Here the numbers given (*125,339*) are those of the castes described as exterior by the Census Superintendent for the State. His State Table II gives the total of depressed classes as 126,652 exceeding the total given here by 1,313. This total refers to the Vadukan caste, and its classification as depressed is erroneous ; it was included in the provincial table accidentally and I have therefore omitted it.

Caste.	Population.
Adi-Dravida	966
Alavan	734
Ampattan	305
Arayan	23,380
Bavuri	164
Bharathar	275
Chackaravar	3,536
Chakkiliyan	6,188
Chavalakkaran	1,730
Chayakkaran	2,168
Ilavan	869,863
Ilavathi	6,955
Kaikolan	455
Kakkalan	1,666
Kaniyan	15,652
Kathikkaran	161
Kavathi	2,293
Keralamuthali	1,423
Kuravan	87,071
Marakkan	353
Maravan	14,399
Medara	363
Mukkuvan	596
Nadar	233,982
Nayadi	144
Nulayan	3,129
Pallan	29,880
Panan	3,812
Panikkan	397
Paravan	13,602
Paraiyan	70,684
Pulayan	207,337
Pulluvan	527
Thantan	41,214
Thantapulayan	795
Thontaman	684
Valan	21,172
Vannan	13,433
Varnavar	166
Velakkithalanayar	30,603
Velan	16,253
Veluthadanayar	14,878
Vetan	9,496
Vettakkaran	498
Yadavan	8,457
Minor and Unspecified	7,896
Total	1,769,735

21. *Travancore.*—The Census Commissioner for Travancore State gives a list of castes regarded as depressed in that State, the number of which is extracted from his Caste Table and added up amounts to *1,769,735* but the number that appears in his State Table II is 1,787,380. I have therefore accepted for India figure the smaller total obtained from his caste table. The larger total in State Table II includes the hill tribes, probably with justice.

22. *Mysore.*—The real exterior castes of Mysore State are the Holeyas and Madigas, numbering between them *1,000,326*, who have been jointly returned at at this census as *Adikarnatakas*.

Caste.	Population.
Holeya, Madiga	1,000,326
Total	1,000,326

In addition the Mysore Government treats as depressed the following four castes :—

Banjara	50,709
Koracha	10,238
Korama	13,607
Vodda	164,876

which accounts for the total appearing in the Mysore State Table II of 1,239,856. It seems clear that at any rate the Banjara and Vodda are not strictly exterior castes and the case of the other two, apparently two names for the same caste, is doubtful; they are more criminal than depressed. For the purposes of Indian figures therefore the total of 1,000,326 is taken for Mysore.

Caste.	Population.
Aheri	1 204
Bagri	10,397
Balai	218,857
Bambhi	162,863
Bansphor	926
Bargi	1,593
Bazigar	372
Bhangi	92,747
Bidakia	63
Chamar	766,643
Dabgar	652
Dhanak	30,733
Dhed	19,907
Garoda	8,699
Ghancha	4,772
Kalbelia	3,740
Kanjar	3,553
Khangar	2,925
Koria	11,303
Kuchband	326

23. *Rajputana.*—The total of these castes (*1,565,409*), reported as depressed by the Census Superintendent and compiled from figures extracted from his Caste Table, agrees with his total in Provincial Table II.

Caste.	Population.
Brought forward ..	1,342,275
Mahar	5,362
Meghwal	23,273
Nat	6,416
Pasi	43
Raigar	130,103
Rawal	677
Sansi	6,719
Sarbhangi	23
Sargara	31,300
Satia	1,113
Thori	17,397
Tirgar	708
Total ..	1,565,409

23. *Rajputana*—contd.

Caste.	Population.
Lalbegi	23
Mehtar	3
Muchi	19
Sunri	2
Bhuiya	3
Damai	1,866
Dhobi	6
Kalwar	96
Lohar	11
Total ..	2,029

24. *Sikkim.*—The figures (*2,029*) are extracted from the Bengal and Sikkim Caste Table and represent the castes returned as depressed by the Census Superintendent. No State Table is published.

Caste.	Population.
Ager	428
Bhambi	1
Bhangi (including Halalkhor) ..	33,422
Chamar	47,728
Garoda	5,594
Koli Dhor	10,435
Kotwalia	51
Mahar	174,446
Meghwal	43,909
Turi	2,206
Total ..	318,220

25. *Western India States Agency.*—The figures (*318,220*) agree with those in Provincial Table II and include all castes returned by the Census Superintendent as depressed.

Grand Total		
	India ..	.. *50,195,770*
	Provinces	.. *41,091,490*
	States ..	.. *9,104,280*

N.B.—The total here given for provinces includes that of the states attached to them. For separate figures see Table B below. The totals do not precisely correspond to those given in Table XVII of Part II, as the latter figures are taken from the Provincial Table II in the cases of Bihar and Orissa and of the Central Provinces and Berar, in both of which the details do not tally precisely with those given for the whole province.

These then being the numbers of the depressed classes in India some estimate is necessary of their position at the present time, and it has already been pointed out that their disabilities can be roughly divided into two categories. Firstly, that under which they are barred from public utilities, such as, the use of roads and tanks, and secondly, their religious disabilities which debar them from the use of temples, burning grounds, *mats* and some other institutions. In addition to the above, but arising out of the second of these, there are the disabilities involved in relation with private individuals, such as the services of barbers and the admission to tea-shops, hotels or theatres owned by private individuals. A resolution of the Anti-Untouchability Conference of 1929 in Madras regretted " to note that in Restaurants, Coffee Hotels, Hair Dressing Saloons, Water Pandals, etc., notices are hung prominently excluding the untouchables ", and the Census Superintendent for the Central Provinces writes " The fact that a sweeper may sit beside a high-class Hindu in a railway carriage or a motor-lorry without any question of his right to do so has not yet made it any more easy in the interior for a touring officer to persuade cartmen of some castes to carry his sweeper from camp to camp. In fact in certain districts it is always essential to employ at least one cartman of humble caste for this purpose ".

Theoretically perhaps the admission to Hindu temples would be enough, once it is conceded, to remove all the other disabilities, for the temple is not merely a religious institution but is also in many ways a social one, for the term must be taken to include such buildings as *namgarhs* which, as temples do in some parts of India, serve as a village hall or a town hall for the public generally. A temple also contains a school, so that the absence of the right of entering the temple may debar an individual from the possibility of attending the school. In some Hindu temples, such as the Parbati Temple in Poona, the Kalarama Temple at Nasik, the Hajo Temple in Assam, it has been in the past the practice to admit non-Hindus, such as Christians and Muslims to a point to which the untouchable Hindus were never admitted at all. It is however not quite certain how far under present conditions the actual right of admission to a temple would, if conceded, remove the social disabilities of the depressed castes since it might have the effect of merely driving the higher castes to shun the temples to which the untouchables were admitted. In any case the right varies much in different places. An Iruva or a Thiyya in Malabar must stay 325 feet from the curtain wall of the temple of Guruvayur, for instance, and this wall is 350 feet square with the temple in the centre. Yet the Iruva have not been treated, in Cochin State at any rate, as a depressed caste at all, since though deprived there likewise of temple entry they are otherwise well-to-do and not ill educated.

As regards the civil rather than the religious disabilities to which the depressed classes are at present subjected, the first one mentioned above is the right to use the public roads; up to how recently the use of public roads has been debarred in certain cases may be gathered from the fact that the untouchables of Travancore made an organised attempt in 1924 to obtain the use of roads which skirted the temple at Vaikom. These roads were public roads, maintained by the State for the use of everybody, but on account of their proximity to the temple building, the untouchables were not allowed to use certain sections which skirted the temple too closely. Ultimately, as a result of satyagraha, the temple compound was enlarged and the ban on the roads was removed, the roads having been realigned so that their users were no longer within the polluting distance of the temple. In 1926 and again in 1930, a similar case occurred in Travancore in connection with Sachindram Temple which is one of the richest in the State. Here again the depressed classes wanted the right to use a road maintained by public funds and belonging to the State. In the matter of the use of roads generally, however, the depressed castes are no longer in the position in which some of them were when the Mangalore District Gazetteer was written, when the Ande Koragas had to carry a spittoon round their necks as being so highly polluting that they could not be allowed to expectorate on the public road, though it has recently been reported that a caste has been found in the Tamilnad, the very sight of which is polluting, so that its unfortunate members are compelled to follow nocturnal habits, leaving their dens after dark and scuttling home at the false dawn like the badger, hyaena or aard-vark. *The Hindu* of December 24th, 1932, writes of them as follows :—" In this (Tinnevelly) district there is a class of unseeables called Purada Vannans. They are not allowed to come out during day time because their sight is considered to be pollution." Some of these people, who wash the clothes of other exterior castes, working between midnight and daybreak, were with difficulty persuaded to leave their houses to interview Mr. A. V. Thakkar, who described them as coming only after repeated persuasion and then with " their whole bodies shaking and trembling ".

The case of wells has already been alluded to, and is a far more widespread and real grievance than any which may still survive in regard to the use of roads. Generally speaking, if the exterior castes have succeeded in asserting their right to use public wells, the higher castes have given them up. Here again the difficulty about the use of wells will be found to be most prevalent in the drier parts of India where water is scarce. In Assam this difficulty is not worth mentioning and in Bengal where it exists, it is usually got over by water being drawn for the exterior castes by some interior caste Hindu. This arrangement is obviously open to certain drawbacks but it is not so serious as the custom in many parts of upper India and southern India which prohibits the exterior castes from having water at all from the well which is used by interior Hindus. The same applies to the use of dharamshalas and of public burning ghats and the burial grounds in regard to all of which the position of the exterior castes is much the same as it is in regard to the use of wells.

With regard to schools, the Director of Public Instruction for Bombay reporting for the year 1928-29, remarks that admission to schools was not refused to the children of the depressed classes in the schools under the control of any local body except the District Local Board at Ratnagiri, some schools of the District Local Board of the Nasik District and in the Ahmadabad and Surat districts. In the latter districts the students generally used to sit in temples, dharamshalas or private houses and the pupils of the depressed classes were objected to, but the objection was withdrawn on being warned that such schools would loose any grants that they enjoyed from the Government. How far this withdrawal of objection was effective is doubtful, since at any rate in one case the depressed classes at Surat had to withdraw their children from the school as a result of the indirect pressure exerted on them by higher castes. Similarly in some cases the depressed caste pupils find it better to sit outside the school, as if they sit inside they are boycotted and compelled to leave the school. Thus at Kaira in April 1931 some Dheds took their seats with other Hindu boys in the municipal school. Kaira had been one of the centres of Mr. Gandhi's activities and no objection was raised on that day, but when the parents of the interior caste boys heard of it they threatened a boycott of the school and of the teacher if the Dhed boys were allowed to sit with theirs, or even to occupy the same class room, with the result that the next day the Dheds were refused admission to the school premises. On the other hand in Sind and in the central and southern divisions of Bombay it was reported that there were no primary schools managed by the local authorities which refused admission to the depressed castes' children. Similarly in Assam no inconvenience appears to have been experienced by the exterior castes in the matter of school attendance. On the other hand in many parts of India the inconvenience is greater than it is in Bombay. Very few of the exterior castes attend schools nominally accessible to them in

Negapatam, Kumbakonam, Tinnevelly, Cocanada, Bezwada and Narsapur and other towns in southern India, though in Madras, Madura, Sivaganga and some other towns a number of exterior castes' children attend schools which are not especially reserved for them and which are not boycotted by the higher castes. In most parts of southern India it is necessary to have special schools for the exterior castes, since it is not yet possible to induce the higher castes to learn in their company. In July 1931, when it was decided to admit exterior castes into all the aided schools, a number of schools had to close and from some other schools the higher caste children were withdrawn. Similarly in Baroda State the abolition of separate schools in November 1931, is reported to have given great resentment to the caste Hindus who in some cases withdrew their children from schools and in others destroyed the crops of the exterior castes or poured kerosene oil into the wells used by them. In Bengal the Rural Primary Education Bill passed in 1930, appears to have been opposed by members representing the caste Hindus, and it is alleged that this opposition was aimed at depriving the non-caste Hindus and also the poorer Muslims from the benefits of literacy. In Cochin State on the other hand much has been done to open all educational institutions to the exterior castes though this has involved in some cases the removal of the school to another site, while cases have occurred of some ill-treatment of the castes now admitted to the schools. Generally speaking, however, during the last decade the exterior castes at school in Cochin have increased in number from some 1,500 to some 14,000 and out of 700 recognised schools only 3 are still reserved to the higher castes, and a Protector of the backward and depressed classes has recently been appointed. Cochin, however, is probably in many ways exceptional.

In regard to the matter of the right to enter Hindu temples, the exterior castes were advised by Mr. Gandhi not to attempt to gain entry by his own method of satyagraha as God resided in their breasts. A temple, however, as has been pointed out, is more than a purely religious institution and the right of temple entry is by some regarded as the key position with regard to the removal of untouchability. The claim to enter temples is not opposed only by high-caste Hindus ; even *Justice*, the organ of the anti-Brahman Party, writes as follows :—

> " For many centuries these peoples, most of whom until recently were Animists, were content to worship at their own shrines, and to try to force themselves into Hindu temples is not..........to make themselves popular. Nor can we think that any grave wrong is done by their continued exclusion ...... they would be better occupied in improving their own condition than in a violent attempt to assert rights which no one had heard of till a few years ago."

There is on the other hand a definite movement among many more advanced Hindus to remove the ban on the temple entry, a movement which has since the census been given much impetus by Mr. Gandhi's fast and the negotiations following it for the admission of untouchables to Hindu temples generally, and it may be mentioned as an instance of this that 8 temples of a Telugu community in Bombay were reported to have been opened to untouchables in February 1930. On the other hand recent cases of attempts to obtain entry by depressed castes have led to violence. Some 2,000 untouchables collected outside the Kala Ram temple at Nasik on March 3rd, 1930, and a meeting which attempted to bring about a settlement was stoned by the orthodox. Ultimately some 150,000 Mahars and Chamars were reported to have collected at Nasik and the temple had to be closed for about a month to keep them from entering it. The admission of caste Hindus by a private passage ended in violence in which the orthodox were the aggressors, and which was extended to Mahar villages in the neighbourhood where the depressed castes were violently attacked by caste Hindus, their wells polluted and in some cases their houses burned. A similar attempt to force an entrance a year later had similar results, and in December 1931 the same sort of situation arose on an attempt of the depressed castes to bathe in the Ramakund, the sacred pool at Nasik, and again in April over the dragging of the *rath*. Similarly at Singanallur in south India the question of entry to a temple led to a free fight in 1930, and at some other places also. In Nagpur a temple was voluntarily opened to untouchables and in the Dacca Division in Bengal a *satyagraha* of 9 months duration ended in the temple doors being forced open by a band of high caste women who sympathised with the *satyagrahis*. This was in May, but it was reported in October that the temple was deserted by high caste Hindus. One wonders therefore how far the higher castes are likely to make use of a pan-Hindu temple recently endowed at Ratnagiri with a view to providing a common place of worship for all castes.

The prohibition against exterior castes entering the Hindu temples naturally raises the question whether they can really be called Hindu at all. Generally speaking, the answer must be that they are definitely Hindus ; they worship the same deities and, though refused entry to the temples, boxes are placed outside, at the limits to which they can approach, to receive their offerings. The degree of Hinduism does, however, vary considerably ; thus the Mahars and Chamars in general are very decidedly Hindu, whereas the Chuhra of the Punjab is very doubtfully so, taking a Hindu tone when living by a Hindu village, a Muslim tone in a Muslim village and that of a Sikh in a Sikh village ; perhaps the Chuhra should really be described as tribal by religion, and the possibly connected Chodhra of the Bombay Presidency is definitely regarded as a forest tribe rather than a caste. In any case, in the Punjab the question has been partly solved at this census by the Chuhra returning himself as an *Ad-Dharmi*, that is to say a follower of the original religion. For him it means the customs immemorially observed by his caste or tribe, but of course the term might mean very different things to different peoples. In the Punjab its use as distinct from Hindu (in other provinces the exterior castes have frequently returned themselves as *Adi-Hindu*, *Adi-Dravida*, etc., with a similar implication to that of *Ad-Dharmi*) is probably a political expedient in order to obtain more effective representation on the provincial legislative body, and in spite of the occasional use of the word 'Hindu' with reference to caste Hindus and excluding the exterior castes it must be held that these castes generally are Hindu by religion even if they are not Hindu socially, hence the expression "exterior caste" is suitably applied to castes who follow the Hindu religion but are not admitted to Hindu society.

This social bar tends to foster conversion to the Sikh faith, to Islam, or to Christianity, though even after conversion the social stigma does not vanish at once. This is hardly to be expected. The Mazhbi Sikhs are looked down upon by the Sikhs who are not Mazhbi. The Southern Indian Christians distinguish between the castes of their converts in their seating accommodation in churches, and the dislike of the exterior castes does not immediately disappear when they turn Muslim. At the same time once they are converted it does not take them very long before they can rise in the social scale, and in the case of Indian Christians in southern India a period of about three generations often, perhaps usually, sees them accepted as the equal of previous converts of most castes.

There are other points in which the exterior castes suffer socially. Thus exception is taken to their wearing the ornaments usually worn by higher castes, and in some cases they are not allowed to wear gold ornaments at all. Cases are on record in which Chamars for instance have been beaten for dressing like Rajputs, and the mounting of an exterior caste bridegroom upon a horse for his bridal procession has led to a boycott of the caste in question by the higher caste neighbours. In December 1930 the Kallar in Ramnad propounded eight prohibitions, the disregard of which led to the use of violence by the Kallar against the exterior castes whose huts were fired, whose granaries and property were destroyed and whose livestock was looted. These eight prohibitions were as follows :—

"(*i*) that the Adi-Dravidas shall not wear ornament of gold and silver ;

(*ii*) that the males should not be allowed to wear their clothes below their knees or above the hips ;

(*iii*) that their males should not wear coats or shirts or baniyans ;

(*iv*) no Adi-Dravida shall be allowed to have his hair cropped ;

(*v*) that the Adi-Dravidas should not use other than earthenware vessels in their homes ;

(*vi*) their women shall not be allowed to cover the upper portion of their bodies by clothes or ravukais or thavanies ;

(*vii*) their women shall not be allowed to use flowers or saffron paste ; and

(*viii*) the men shall not use umbrellas for protection against sun and rain nor should they wear sandals ".

In June 1931, the eight prohibitions not having been satisfactorily observed by the exterior castes in question, the Kallar met together and framed eleven prohibitions, which went still further than the original eight, and an attempt to enforce these led to more violence. These eleven prohibitions were :—

"1. The Adi-Dravidas and Devendrakula Vellalars should not wear clothes below their knees.

2. The men and women of the above said depressed classes should not wear gold jewels.

3. Their women should carry water only in mud pots and not in copper or brass vessels. They should use straw only to carry the water pots and no cloths should be used for that purpose.

4. Their children should not read and get themselves literate or educated.

5. The children should be asked only to tend the cattle of the Mirasdars.

6. Their men and women should work as slaves of the Mirasdars in their respective Pannais.

7. They should not cultivate the land either on *waram* or lease from the Mirasdars.

8. They must sell away their own lands to Mirasdars of the village at very cheap rates, and if they don't do so, no water will be allowed to them to irrigate their lands. Even if something is grown by the help of rain-water, the crops should be robbed away, when they are ripe for harvest.

9. They must work as coolies from 7 A.M. to 6 P.M. under the Mirasdars and their wages shall be for men Re. 0-4-0 per day and for women Re. 0-2-0 per day.

10. The above said communities should not use Indian Music (Melam, etc.), in their marriages and other celebrations.

11. They must stop their habit of going on a horse in procession before tying the Thali thread in Marriage, and they must use their house doors as a palanquin for the marriage processions and no vehicle should be used by them, for any purpose."

It is not suggested that the eight or eleven injunctions of the Kallar would be taken very seriously by any one but themselves, but they are quoted here to indicate the attitude often adopted towards the exterior castes. Similarly in Bengal the use by a Namasudra bridegroom of a palanquin in a marriage procession led to a disturbance, and other instances could probably be quoted from other parts of India.

Economically the exterior castes in eastern India are generally speaking self-supporting and by no means desperately poor. In western India their position often is that of scavenger or village menial for whose service there is a certain amount of necessity which is recompensed by a traditional provision of certain village lands or by other methods of payment in kind. The trouble frequently is that the number of these menials has become superfluous and they none the less expect to be fed by the village for unwanted services, and if they do not get so fed they steal the grain, no doubt regarding it as theirs by right. In southern India again the exterior castes are generally derived from various classes of cultivating serfs who until recently were tied to the soil. In northern India their economic position varies a good deal, since leather-workers for instance in industrial towns find a ready livelihood, whereas the exterior castes in the agricultural areas, where they can only obtain the worst land and the worst wells, are very often extremely poverty-stricken.

The origin of the position of the exterior castes is partly racial, partly religious and partly a matter of social custom. There can be little doubt that the idea of untouchability originates in taboo. Reminiscences of such a taboo are still to be seen in Burma where gravedigging is a profession involving a social stigma of a kind which will not permit of association with persons of other professions. A comparison of this custom with the position of those who dig graves for the hill tribes in the surrounding areas leaves little doubt but that the repulsion originates in the fear of some death infection, and the underlying idea is not that the person himself is polluted by unclean work but that his mere association with death may infect others with whom the grave-digger comes into contact with the probability of dying. The treatment of washermen all over India as a depressed caste is almost certainly traceable to a similar taboo, the objection perhaps arising from an association with the menstrual clothes of women and consequently an infection which, in the first instance, is magical though it later comes to be regarded merely as a matter of personal cleanliness. The untouchability which has originated in taboo has undoubtedly been accentuated by differences of race and the racial antipathies which seem common to every branch of the human family and have reinforced the magical taboo. An instance of this sort of thing may again be found in Burma, which, as there is no caste in the Indian sense, is useful as providing examples of the process of caste formation. Here pagoda slaves, the status of whom is hereditary, are looked down upon by other classes. In general pagoda slaves have been recruited from non-Burmese races. Large numbers of Arakanese, Talaings, Manipuris and Siamese have been settled in various parts of Burma by various conquering monarchs as slaves of different pagodas. This racial element is probably to be traced again in the prohibition of the wearing of ornaments by certain castes. Thus in the Naga Hills in Assam in the Ao tribe one of the sub-tribal groups, which is apparently of different origin to the rest of the tribe, is not allowed to wear ivory on both arms. Similar restrictions are found in the Laccadive Islands. The same element probably appears in the practice of hypergamy, and the first step which any section of an exterior caste takes in order to raise its social standing is to deny to other sections the right to marry its daughters though continuing for the time being to take wives from among them. Thus have the Haliya Kaibarttas severed themselves from the Jaliya Kaibarttas and established themselves as a separate caste, no longer depressed, and even so a section of the Namasudras is now attempting to segregate itself. Indeed as between different sections of the exterior castes prejudice is just strong as between the interior castes and the exterior castes generally. The Mahars in Bombay have objected to sharing their counsels and conferences with Chamars, and Mahars and Chamars have unanimously spurned the Bhangi. Similarly in Madras Pallars have objected to being classed with Chaklis whom they regard as no less inferior to them than the Paraiyans though all alike are untouchables to a good caste Hindu. Religion of ourse with its apparatus of holy vessels, sacred animals and sacrosanct priests has also contributed to the creation of the idea of untouchability, and society in general by its natural dislike of certain unclean occupations and by its very proper antipathy to criminal professions has done much to depress and stereotype the position of the exterior castes.

In 1916 and again in 1920, the Government of India called for a report as to the moral and material condition of the depressed classes and for proposals for their amelioration from all local governments. The records of the consequent reports will be found under *Proceedings of the Government of India in the Home Department*, Nos. 130—131 of July 1916, 329—341 of August 1920.

During the past decade a good deal has been done particularly in Madras to benefit the exterior castes in various ways. Not only has the Madras Government appointed a Commissioner of Labour entrusted with the task of encouraging the education of the depressed classes and of looking after their economic interests, but many private societies have also been at work. Besides a number of Christian Missions, the Depressed Classes Union, the Poor School Society, the Social Service League, the Andhra Deena Seva Sangam, and the Depressed Classes Mission of Mangalore are some of the institutions working for this object. The Arcot Mission has started an agricultural school and Local Boards have also been spending money towards the same end. In addition to this much has been done by the Self-Respect movement and the Depressed Classes Conference. The actual steps taken by the Government of Madras have been, besides the appointment of a Commissioner of Labour, the insistence on the right of admission of exterior caste pupils into all publicly managed schools, the refusal of grants-in-aid to privately managed schools which do not admit exterior caste pupils, the removal of publicly managed schools from places inaccessible to exterior castes, the opening of special schools and hostels for the exterior castes, the remission of their fees, and the provision of scholarships and of special facilities for the training of exterior caste teachers. On the economic side the Government of Madras has taken steps towards the provision of house sites for the relief of congestion and for purposes of freeing the exterior castes from oppression by their landlords, the organisation and running of co-operative societies, the provision of drinking water by constructing new wells and repairing old, the provision of burial grounds and sanitary requirements for the exterior castes, the assignment of land for cultivation both by reservation for and free assignment to exterior castes of lands not classed as valuable, that is, lands not affected by irrigation projects, and by reservation for exterior castes of lands classed as valuable and assignment to them on payment of market value in easy instalments. As a result of these measures some progress has been made. In 1920, there were 150,000 pupils of exterior castes in schools, in 1930, there were 230,000. Over 100,000 of these were in Christian Mission schools and many of the remainder in schools maintained by the societies mentioned above. Most of these schools are only primary schools, there being only about 2,700 pupils in educational institutions above the primary stage of whom about 50 only were in colleges. Out of 230,000 reading in schools in 1930 about 7,500 were girls. Of the 230,000 only 16,000, however, were reading in ordinary schools not reserved for exterior castes while over 70,000 pupils who did not belong to the exterior castes were reading in schools specially maintained for those castes. As compared with the rest of the population, while about 6 per cent. of the population of Madras was going to school when this census took place, only about 4 per cent. of the exterior castes were at school, and of that total less than 1 per cent. was beyond the primary stage. Economically very considerable sums have been spent by the Madras Government during the past ten years in financing and organising co-operative societies for the acquisition of land for house sites and for the granting of agricultural loans and for purposes of flood relief, rural credit and collective bargaining. In 1920, there were over 14,600 members of exterior castes in about 100 co-operative societies; as a result of the work done during the decade there are now about 2,000 such societies consisting mainly of exterior castes and during recent years new societies have been registered at the rate of over 100 a year. Over 55,000 house sites have been provided and some 300,000 acres of land have been assigned to exterior caste cultivators. But at the time of this census there were still six districts in Madras untouched by the activities of the Commissioner of Labour. In Bombay apart from the work done by private institutions among which the Servants of India Society is very prominent, little has yet been done. A Committee was appointed by the Government of Bombay to enquire into the condition of the depressed castes and aboriginal tribes in the Presidency in November 1928. As a result of the recommendations of that Committee an officer was appointed in 1931, charged with the duty of watching over the progress of and of upholding the rights of the backward classes. In addition to that a Resolution of the Government of Bombay directed the recruitment of members of the depressed classes in the police. It is perhaps significant that the Committee found it necessary to include in their recommendations an addition to the Government Servants' Conduct Rules framed with a view to enforcing polite treatment of the depressed classes by the officials of Government. In regard to the education of these classes in British India generally some information has already been given in Chapter IX. Many of the Indian States have also recognised the necessity for special measures for the uplift of exterior castes, in particular, Baroda, Cochin and Travancore; while in Gwalior and Jaipur action has been taken more particularly in regard to the criminal tribes of which there are considerable numbers in those States. In Jaipur areas of land have been allotted to the criminal tribes and special schools have been opened for the education of their children, and the same has been done in Gwalior.

The occasion of this census, coming as it did at a time when political reforms appeared imminent, complicated the already plentiful difficulties in the way of getting an exact return of number of exterior castes. A number of conflicting forces were at work, as, apart from the natural desire of individuals of exterior castes to raise their own social status by making themselves out to be something other than they were recognised to be by their neighbours, a definite movement was set afoot by the Hindu Mahasabha for the return of all Hindus as Hindu simply with no qualifications of caste or sect. In 1928 the Hindu Mahasabha itself passed a resolution declaring that the so called untouchables had equal rights with other Hindus to study in schools, and to use wells and roads and temples, and the same resolution called on priests, barbers and washermen to afford their services to untouchables. At this census, however, political considerations probably overweighed all else and many efforts were made to induce untouchables to record themselves as 'Hindus' and nothing else. The exterior castes themselves were, however, generally alive to the fact that their interests required their numbers to be definitely known; at the same time they were not unconscious of the fact that it might be advantageous to them to represent as many castes as possible as being depressed in order to swell their numbers in importance. Consequently, while in the Punjab the All-India Shradhanand Depressed Classes Mission was calling on the exterior castes to return themselves as Arya Hindus instead of, for instance, Achuts or Dalits, the exterior castes' own leaders were calling on their followers to return themselves as *Ad-Dharmi* by religion and not Hindu at all; and in other provinces the associations of the exterior castes were representing as 'depressed' castes which very doubtfully fall into that category and many of which have been excluded on scrutiny. Generally speaking, however, it is believed that the figures for the exterior classes obtained at this census have been accurate on the whole and the methods adopted in different provinces to determine what constitutes an exterior caste have already been referred to, while extracts from some of the Provincial Reports will be found below.

Little information exists as to the actual numbers of these exterior castes who are entitled to a vote under the present constitution of the provinces. Except in the case of Madras, nomination has been resorted to to secure the representation of depressed classes. Four members have been so nominated in the Central Provinces, two each in Bombay and in Bihar and Orissa, one each in Bengal and in the United Provinces and none in the Punjab or in Assam. In Madras ten members were nominated to represent nine specified communities recorded as depressed, while individuals of the exterior castes were not debarred of course from voting in a general constituency if they happened to be qualified as electors. It has been estimated that there are in Madras rather less than 57,000 exterior caste electors in a total of more than 1¼ million "non-Mahomedan" voters, that is to say, about 4½ per cent., though the exterior castes form some 16 per cent. of the total non-Muslim population. In Bombay a rough estimate has been made that there are 15,600 exterior caste voters out of a total of 759,000 voters in all the general constituencies, that is, about 2 per cent. of the exterior castes have votes, whereas they comprise over 8 per cent. of the population of the Presidency.

The following Tables A and B will give some indication of the numerical constitution of the depressed castes and of their distribution and comparative literacy. It should be made clear that figures for literacy are available in part only, and the percentage shown as literate is the percentage calculated on that total only for which figures of literacy are available.

TABLE A.

Name of Caste, etc.	Total number treated as exterior.	Locality in which treated as exterior.	Remarks.
Adiya	5	Coorg.	
Ager	7,108	Bombay, Western India States Agency.	
Aheri (Aheria)	24,375	Ajmer-Merwara, United Provinces and Rajputana.	
Ajila	659	Madras.	
Alavan	734	Travancore.	
Ambattan	305	Travancore]	Barber castes elsewhere not treated as exterior.
Arakh	85,907	United Provinces.	
Aranadan	60	Madras.	
Arayan	23,380	Travancore.	
Arunthuthiyar			Included with Chakkiliyan.
Audhelia	749	Chattisgarh (C. P.).	
Bagri (Bagdi, Badhik) ..	1,023,127	Ajmer-Merwara, Bengal, U. P., Gwalior, Rajputana.	
Bahelia	49,907	Bengal, United Provinces.	
Bahna	6	Amraoti (Berar).	
Baira	1,879	S. Kanara (Madras).	
Baiti	8,888	Bengal.	
Bajania, etc.	34	United Provinces	Total recorded 7,876 elsewhere not treated as exterior.
Bakuda	806	S. Kanara (Madras).	
Balai (Balahi)	561,662	Ajmer-Merwara, Central Provinces and Berar (parts) United Provinces, Central India, Gwalior, Rajputana.	

Name of Caste, etc.	Total number treated as exterior.	Locality in which treated as exterior.	Remarks.
Balagai	130	Coorg.	
Bandi (Kabaria)	1,066	United Provinces, S. Kanara (Madras).	
Barar	1,384	Gwalior.	
Bargi	1,668	Ajmer-Merwara, Rajputana.	
Bargunda	1,931	Gwalior.	
Bariki	3,695	Ganjam and Vizagapatam (Madras).	
Barwala (Barwar)	9,996	U. P., Jammu and Kashmir.	
Basith	6,213	Jammu and Kashmir State.	
Battada	558	S. Kanara (Madras).	
Batawal	5,645	Jammu and Kashmir State.	
Bauri (Bavari, Bawaria)	721,299	Bengal, Bihar and Orissa, Delhi, Madras, Punjab, United Provinces, Travancore.	
Bazigar	372	Rajputana	Total recorded 2,734. Not elsewhere treated as exterior.
Bedar	490	Central Provinces and Berar (part)	Total recorded 991,536. Not elsewhere treated as exterior.
Beldar	3,139	Bengal	Total Beldar, Bind, Nuniya, Od and Waddar recorded as 561,926 for India. Only reported exterior in Bengal and Punjab but latter figures not included here. Treated also as depressed by Mysore State.
Bellara	87	S. Kanara (Madras).	
B riya (Bediya)	25,155	Bengal, Gwalior, United Provinces.	
Berua	367	Bengal.	
Bhambi (Bambhi)	183,917	Ajmer-Merwara, Bombay, Central India, Rajputana, Western India States Agency.	
Bhangi (Lalbegi, Mehtar, Halalkhor).	865,453	Ajmer-Merwara, Andamans and Nicobars, Assam, Bengal, Bihar and Orissa, Bombay, Central Provinces and Berar, United Provinces, Baroda, Central India, Gwalior, Rajputana, Sikkim, Western India States Agency.	
Bhar	461,324	United Provinces	See Rajwar.
Bharathar	275	Travancore.	
Bhatiya	322	Bengal.	
Bhil	28	United Provinces.	
Bhogta	66,054	Bihar and Orissa.	
Bhuinmali	111,439	Assam, Bengal.	
Bhuiya, etc.	738,479	Bengal, Bihar and Orissa, Sikkim, United Provinces.	Includes Agaria, Chero, etc., in U. P.
Bhumij	266,464	Bihar and Orissa.	
Bidakia	63	Rajputana.	
Bind	19,518	Bengal.	
Binjhia	317	Bengal.	
Byagari	8,459	Bellary (Madras).	
Chachati	5,130	Vizagapatam (Madras).	
Chadar	21,071	Central Provinces.	
Chakkaravar	3,536	Travancore.	
Chakkiliyan	630,359	Madras and Travancore.	
Chalavadi	3,422	Bellary (Madras).	
Chamar (Chambhar, Khalpa, Samagara, Satnami).	11,751,187	Ajmer-Merwara, Andamans and Nicobars, Baluchistan, Bengal, Bihar and Orissa, Bombay, Central Provinces and Berar, Coorg, Delhi, Madras, North-West Frontier Province, Punjab, United Provinces, Baroda, Central India Agency, Gwalior, Jammu and Kashmir, Rajputana, Western India States.	India total 12,195,516 returned from the Provinces here mentioned.
Chauhan	2,026	Drug (Central Provinces).	
Chaupal	2,737	Bihar and Orissa.	
Chavalakkaran	1,730	Travancore.	
Chayakkaran	2,168	Travancore.	
Chuhra	484,596	Baluchistan, Delhi, N.-W. F. P., Punjab, Jammu and Kashmir.	
Dabgar	1,366	Ajmer-Merwara, United Provinces, Rajputana.	See Muchi.

Name of Caste, etc.	Total number treated as exterior.	Locality in which treated as exterior.	Remarks.
Dahayat	833	Damoh (Central Provinces).	
Damai	7,905	Bengal and Sikkim.	
Dandasi	44,248	Ganjam (Madras).	
Devendrakulathan ..	4,019	Tamilnad (Madras).	
Dewar	1,786	Chhattisgarh (Central Provinces).	
Dhanak	33,737	Ajmer-Merwara, Saugor (Central Provinces), Delhi, Rajputana.	India total (with Kandra, *q.v.*) 758,671.
Dhenuar	44	Bengal.	
Dhimar	46,071	Central Provinces and Berar (parts). ..	Not elsewhere treated as exterior.
Dhiyar	3,165	Jammu and Kashmir.	
Dhobi	1,406,291	Assam, Bengal, Bihar and Orissa, Central Provinces and Berar, United Provinces, Sikkim.	India total including Vannan (*q. v.*), Parit and Veluttedan 3,161,428.
Dhor (Dohor)	24,983	Bombay, Central Provinces and Berar.	
Doai	1,960	Bengal.	
Dom (Domar, Dombo, Dumna, Bansphor, Basor, Dharkar, Patni, Wansfoda).	884,403	Ajmer-Merwara, Assam, Baroda, Bengal, Bihar and Orissa, Bombay, Central Provinces and Berar, Madras, Punjab, United Provinces, Central India, Jammu and Kashmir, Rajputana, Gwalior.	*N.B.*—Hyderabad figures probably included under "Others".
Dugla	9,523	Assam.	
Dusadh	1,400,878	Bengal, Bihar and Orissa, United Provinces.	
Eravalan	541	Cochin.	
Ganda	108,843	Central Provinces	*See* Pan.
Gardi	173	Jammu and Kashmir.	
Garoda	22,137	Ajmer-Merwara, Baroda, Rajputana, Western India States Agency.	
Ghancha	4,862	Ajmer-Merwara, Rajputana.	
Ghasia	132,382	Baluchistan, Bengal, Bihar and Orissa, Central Provinces, Ganjam and Vizagapatam (Madras).	
Ghokha	48,622	Bihar and Orissa.	
Ghusuria	1,846	Bihar and Orissa.	
Gidhiya	191	United Provinces.	
Godagali	969	Ganjam and Vizagapatam (Madras).	
Godari	419	Do.	
Godda	146	S. Kanara (Madras).	
Godra	1,553	Bihar and Orissa.	
Gonrhi	5,149	Bengal.	
Gosangi	244	Chingleput (Madras).	
Habura	1,915	United Provinces.	
Haddi (Relli)	41,672	Ganjam and Vizagapatam (Madras) ..	No doubt the same caste originally.
Hari (Brittial)	262,354	Assam, Bengal, Bihar and Orissa ..	
Hasala	368	S. Kanara (Madras).	
Hira	16,628	Assam.	
Ilavathi..	6,955	Travancore.	
Iravan	869,863	Travancore.	
Irika	332	Bihar and Orissa.	
Irulan	240	Cochin.	
Jaggali	3,020	Ganjam and Vizagapatam (Madras).	
Jaliya Kaibartta ..	501,146	Assam, Bengal.	
Jambuvulu	6,701	Godavari (Madras).	
Jangam	12	Bhandara (Central Provinces).	
Jhalo Malo	208,925	Surma Valley (Assam), Bengal.	
Jhamral	1,519	Central India.	
Jolaha	40	Jammu and Kashmir.	
Jugi	83,922	Surma Valley (Assam).	
Kadan	758	Madras, Cochin	Strictly speaking a jungle tribe, but treated as untouchable.
Kadar	1,078	Bengal.	
Kaikari	2,157	Central Provinces and Berar.	

Name of Caste, etc.	Total number treated as exterior.	Locality in which treated as exterior.	Remarks.
Kaikolan	455	Travancore.	
Kakkalan	1,666	Travancore.	
Kalbelia	4,133	Ajmer-Merwara, Rajputana.	
Kalladi, Kalloda	5,739	Malabar (Madras), Coorg.	
Kalwar	13,627	Bengal, Sikkim.	
Kan	66	Bengal.	
Kanakkan	35,238	Malabar (Madras), Cochin.	
Kandra	159,837	Bengal, Bihar and Orissa.	*See* Dhanak.
Kaniyan	15,652	Travancore.	
Kanjar	30,457	Ajmer-Merwara, Bihar and Orissa, United Provinces, Gwalior, Rajputana.	
Kaora	107,908	Bengal.	
Kapali	165,583	Bengal.	
Kaparia	973	Bengal, United Provinces.	
Karenga	9,855	Bengal.	
Karimpalan	2,807	Malabar (Madras).	
Karwal	108	United Provinces.	
Kathikkaran	161	Travancore.	
Katia	24,510	Central Provinces.	
Kattunayakan	1,581	Malabar (Madras).	
Kavathi	2,293	Travancore.	
Kavera	790	Cochin.	
Kela	9,493	Bihar and Orissa.	
Keralamuthali	1,423	Travancore.	
Khairwa	81	United Provinces.	
Khangar	10,577	Ajmer-Merwara, Central Provinces and Berar (part), Rajputana.	
Khatik	241,493	Baluchistan, Bengal, Central Provinces and Berar (part), Delhi, United Provinces, Gwalior.	India total recorded, 412,620.
Kichak	2	Bengal.	
Kingharia (incl. Dharhi, Pawaria).	7,599	United Provinces.	
Kodalo	28,410	Ganjam (Madras).	
Kol	76,845	United Provinces	Treated as an exterior caste in United Provinces only, elsewhere as a forest tribe.
Kolcha	1,114	Bombay.	
Koli and Dagi	263,751	Delhi, Punjab, Gwalior.	
Koli Dhor	26,358	Bombay, Western India States Agency.	
Konai	41,058	Bengal.	
Konwar	133	Bengal.	
Koosa	818	S. Kanara (Madras).	
Kootan	228	Cochin.	
Koraga	4,042	Bellary, S. Kanara (Madras).	
Korama (Kuruman) ..	10,575	Coorg, Malabar (Madras).	
Kori (Koria)	964,661	Andamans and Nicobars, Baluchistan, Central Provinces and Berar (part), United Provinces, Rajputana.	
Korwa	467	United Provinces	Elsewhere treated as a primitive tribe.
Kotal	7,651	Bengal.	
Kotwar	64	United Provinces.	
Kotwalia	1,469	Bombay, Western India States.	
Kuchband	395	Ajmer-Merwara, Rajputana.	
Kudiya	4,046	Coorg, S. Kanara (Madras).	
Kudubi	12,011	Madras.	
Kudumban	827	Tamilnad (Madras).	
Kumhar	23,863	Central Provinces and Berar (part).	
Kurariar	631	Bihar and Orissa.	
Kuravan	89,181	Travancore, Malabar (Madras).	
Kurichchan	7,112	Malabar (Madras).	
Lippara	4	Coorg.	

Name of Caste, etc.	Total number treated as exterior.	Locality in which treated as exterior.	Remarks.
Lohar	50,178	Bengal, Sikkim.	Probably refers to the Gurkhali Lohar generally treated as exterior.
Mahar, (Cheruman, Dher, Holeya*, Holar, Mal, Mala Mehra, Pulayan, Vankar).	5,447,947	Ajmer-Merwara, Assam, Bengal, Bombay Coorg, Central Provinces and Berar, Madras, United Provinces, Baroda, Central India, Rajputana, Hyderabad, Cochin, Travancore, Western India States Agency.	* With Adikarnataka in Mysore.
Mahuria	2,389	Bihar and Orissa.	
Maila	1,431	S. Kanara (Madras).	
Mala Dasu	2,399	Andhradesh (Madras).	
Malasar	5,101	Madras.	
Malayan	3,185	Cochin.	
Maleya	123	Coorg.	
Mallah	26,252	Bengal.	
Mang (Madiga, Matangi, Megh, Meghwal, Madgi).	2,547,537	Ajmer-Merwara, Coorg, Bombay, Central Provinces and Berar, Madras, Punjab, Baroda, Central India, Hyderabad Jammu and Kashmir, Rajputana, Western India States Agency.	Madiga is included with Adikarnataka in Mysore.
Mang Garudi	4,334	Bombay.	
Mangan	184	Bihar and Orissa.	
Maravan	14,399	Travancora.	
Marakkan	353	Travancore.	
Mavillan	1,341	Malabar (Madras).	
Medara (Madari)	7,021	Coorg, Madras, Travancore.	
Moger	773	S. Kanara (Madras).	
Muchi (Mochi, Mucchi) ..	458,206	Assam, Bengal, Bihar and Orissa Central Provinces, and Berar, Coorg, Ganjam (Madras), United Provinces, Sikkim.	India total (including Dabgar and Jingar) 1,026,405 but not everywhere treated as exterior.
Mukkuvan	596	Travancore.	
Mundala	6,337	Coorg, S. Kanara (Madras).	
Musahar	810,535	Bengal, Bihar and Orissa, United Provinces.	
Nadar	233,982	Travancore.	
Nadia	622	Baroda.	
Nagar	16,164	Bengal.	
Nagarchi	5,970	Central Provinces and Berar.	
Naiya	40	Bengal.	
Nale Kanavaru	9	Coorg.	
Nalekeyeva	1,489	S. Kanara (Madras).	
Namasudra (Chandala) ..	2,267,589	Assam, Bengal, Vizagapatam (Madras).	
Nat	61,175	Ajmer-Merwara, Baluchistan, Bengal, Bihar and Orissa, United Provinces, Rajputana.	
Nayadi	816	Malabar (Madras), Cochin, Travancore.	
Nulayan	3,129	Travancore.	
Ojha	1,718	Central Provinces (parts).	
Pagadai	771	Tamilnad (Madras).	
Paidi	39,437	Ganjam, Vizagapatam (Madras).	
Painda	92	Ganjam (Madras).	
Paky	2,017	N. Circars (Madras).	
Palaiya	43,160	Bengal.	
Pale	3,192	Coorg.	
Pallan	855,104	Madras, Travancore.	
Pambada	335	S. Kanara (Madras).	
Pamidi	424	Ganjam (Madras).	
Pan (Panka, Pano, Panik)	688,456	Bengal, Bihar and Orissa, Central Provinces (part), Madras.	Total recorded (with Ganda, *q. v.*, and Baraik) 1,241,322.
Panan	3,812	Travancore.	
Panchama	95,145	Coorg, Madras.	
Panikkan	402	Coorg, Travancore.	
Paniyan	32,410	Malabar (Madras).	
Panniandi	54	Tamilnad (Madras).	
Paraiyan (Sambavam) ..	1,200,135	Coorg, Madras, Cochin, Travancore.	
Paravan	14,428	Madras, Travancore.	
Pardhan	71,906	Central Provinces and Berar.	
Pardhi	41	Narsinghpur (Central Provinces).	
Pasi	1,651,478	Ajmer-Merwara, Andamans and Nicobars, Baluchistan, Bengal, Bihar and Orissa, United Provinces, Rajputana.	
Pod	667,731	Bengal.	
Pulluvan	527	Travancore.	

Name of Caste, etc.	Total number treated as exterior.	Locality in which treated as exterior.	Remarks.
Pundari	31,255	Bengal.	
Puthirai Vannan ..	74	Tamilnad (Madras).	
Rajgar	152,704	Ajmer-Merwara, Rajputana.	
Raju	56,778	Bengal.	
Rajwar (Rajjhar) ..	22,554	Bengal, Central Provinces (part) ..	Treated as exterior also by Census Superintendent of Bihar and Orissa. Total recorded for India (with Bhar, *q. v.*) 630,708.
Raneyar	1,480	Madras.	
Ratal	488	Jammu and Kashmir.	
Rawal	790	Ajmer-Merwara, Rajputana.	
Relli	..	.. ..	Included in Haddi.
Sansi	39,403	Ajmer-Merwara, Delhi, Punjab, United Provinces, Rajputana.	
Sahariya	14,113	United Provinces.	
Sanaurhiya	31	United Provinces.	
Sarbhangi	23	Rajputana.	
Sargara	32,062	Ajmer-Merwara, Rajputana.	
Saryara (Sarera)	9,437	Punjab, Jammu and Kashmir.	
Satia	1,184	Ajmer-Merwara, Rajputana.	
Saun	2,275	United Provinces.	
Silpkar	313,737	United Provinces.	
Siyal	9,281	Bihar and Orissa.	
Shagirdapesha ..	333	Bengal.	
Shenva	9,643	Baroda.	
Sunri	76,922	Bengal, Sikkim.	
Surava	3	Coorg.	
Sutradhar	12,575	Assam	A boat building caste; distinct from "Viswabrahmans".
Samban..	557	Tamilnad (Madras).	
Sapari	462	Vizagapatam (Madras).	
Semman	1,198	Tamilnad (Madras).	
Tirgar	713	Ajmer-Merwara, Rajputana.	
Tiruvalluvar	207	Madras.	
Thantan	41,214	Travancore.	
Thantapulayan	795	Travancore.	
Tharu	31,578	United Provinces.	Treated as a primitive tribe in Bihar and Orissa. Not treated as depressed in Bengal.
Thontaman	684	Travancore.	
Thoti	1,639	Chingleput (Madras).	
Thori	17,455	Ajmer-Merwara, Rajputana, Baroda.	
Timali	68	Bombay.	
Tiyar	96,413	Bengal.	
Turi	70,240	Bihar and Orissa, Bengal	A depressed tribal unit.
Turi	4,970	Baroda, Western India States Agency, Bombay.	
Ullatan	778	Cochin.	
Valan	21,172	Travancore.	
Valluvan	59,414	Madras, Cochin.	
Vannan	13,433	Travancore.	
Varnavar	166	Do.	
Velakkithalanayar ..	30,603	Do.	
Velan	16,253	Do.	
Veluthadanayar	14,878	Do.	
Vetan	9,496	Do.	
Vettakkaran	498	Do.	
Vettuvan	40,122	Madras, Cochin.	
Vitholia..	526	Bombay.	
Watal	13	Jammu and Kashmir.	
Yadavan	8,457	Travancore.	
Adi-Andhra	664,844	Madras.	
Adi-Dravida	2,620,571	Coorg, Madras, Mysore, Travancore.	
Adi-Karnataka	644	Madras.	
Tea Garden Coolie castes ..	1,233,512	Assam.	
Others (Sudra, Valmiki, Ramdasia, unnamed, minor and unspecified).	218,846	Assam, Baluchistan, Bombay, Madras, Baroda, Hyderabad, Travancore, Punjab	
Total ..	50,195,770		

TABLE B.

Province or State.	Total Population.	Total Hindu.	Total Exterior castes.	Percentage of Exterior castes on— Hindu Population.	Total Population.	Percentage of Exterior castes who are literate.
INDIA	**350,529,557**	**239,195,140**	**50,195,770**	21	14	1·9
Provinces	**271,431,549**	**177,727,988**	**39,064,009**	22	14	1·6
1. Ajmer Merwara	560,292	434,509	76,816	18	14	2·2
2. Andamans and Nicobars ..	29,463	7,618	512	7	2	?
3. Assam	8,622,251	4,931,760	1,829,009	37	21	3·1
4. Baluchistan (*Districts and Administered Territories*).	463,508	41,432	5,702	14	1	6·9
5. Bengal	50,114,002	21,570,407	6,899,809	32	14	5·0
6. Bihar and Orissa	37,677,576	31,011,474	5,744,393	19	15	0·6
7. Bombay	21,854,866	16,621,221	1,750,424	11	8	2·8
8. Burma	14,647,497	570,953	No return of caste.			
9. Central Provinces and Berar ..	15,507,723	13,338,223	2,818,346	21	18	1·5
10. Coorg	163,327	146,007	24,803	17	15	1·5
11. Delhi	636,246	399,863	72,883	18	11	1·4
12. Madras	46,740,107	41,277,370	7,234,104	18	15	1·5
13. North-West Frontier Province ..	2,425,076	142,977	5,468	4	..	3·6
14. Punjab	23,580,852	6,328,588	1,279,459	20	5	0·8
15. United Provinces of Agra and Oudh	48,408,763	40,905,586	11,322,281	28	23	0·5
States and Agencies	**79,098,088**	**61,467,152**	**11,131,761**	18	14	3·1
16. Assam States	625,606	272,890	1,421	1	..	12·9
17. Baluchistan States	405,109	12,249	20	..	..	2·5
18. Baroda State	2,443,007	2,152,071	203,043	9	8	10·3
19. Bengal States	973,336	641,662	30,822	5	3	?
20. Bihar and Orissa States	4,652,007	4,194,878	631,864	15	14	1·0
21. Bombay States	4,468,396	3,921,088	348,574	9	8	2·8
22. Central India Agency	6,632,790	5,852,204	797,902	14	12	0·3
23. Central Provinces States.. ..	2,483,214	1,788,401	252,732	14	10	0·5
24. Gwalior State	3,523,070	3,271,576	678,119	21	19	?
25. Hyderabad State	14,436,148	12,176,727	2,473,230	20	17	0·6
26. Jammu and Kashmir State ..	3,646,243	736,222	170,928	23	5	0·5
27. Madras States Agency	6,754,484	4,323,150	1,960,370	45	29	13·8
Cochin State	*1,205,016*	*780,484*	*125,339*	*16*	*10*	*4·8*
Travancore State	*5,095,973*	*3,134,888*	*1,769,735*	*56*	*35*	*14·9*
Other Madras States	*453,495*	*407,778*	*65,296*	*16*	*14*	*3·5*
28. Mysore State	6,557,302	6,015,880	1,000,326	17	15	1·4
29. North-West Frontier Province (*Agencies and Tribal Areas*).	46,451	13,651	542	4	1	?
30. Punjab States	437,787	383,883	94,347	25	22 }	0·3
31. Punjab States Agency	4,472,218	1,887,249	392,999	21	9 }	
32. Rajputana Agency	11,225,712	9,578,805	1,565,409	16	14	0·4
33. Sikkim State	109,808	47,074	2,029	4	2	?
34. United Provinces States.. ..	1,206,070	950,724	208,864	22	17	0·2
35. Western India States Agency ..	3,999,250	3,245,768	318,220	10	8	1·9

The following extracts are taken from the Provincial and State Reports on the subject of the depressed classes.

The treatment of the subject by the Census Superintendent of Assam has already been mentioned as typical of the method adopted in all provinces at this census. He writes as follows :—

Assam.—Under the orders of the Census Commissioner for India a list of depressed and backward classes has to be prepared for every province in India. The invidious task of preparing such a list for Assam has, therefore, been laid upon me and I am compelled, however reluctantly, to assume the functions of a modern Ballal Sen.................... "Depressed" as used in India in connection with caste has come to be associated particularly with persons belonging to certain castes in Madras who are unapproachable, whose touch necessitates immediate purification and who are not allowed to read in the schools along with other boys.

There is, I am glad to say, no such degree of dep ession in Assam ; an un-approachable caste is unknown here and boys of all castes are freely admitted into all schools and colleges. Nor are there any difficulties worth mentioning as regards the drawing of water by all castes from public 'tanks' and wells.

Hence I would be loath to apply to any caste in this province an adjective which has come to connote an extreme state of degradation. The expression "depressed castes" does however occur frequently in this note in the extracts quoted from the opinions of various officers. This is merely because these opinions were received before I had decided that I would not use the term in Assam.

The unusual expression "Hindu Exterior Castes" has been invented by me in accordance with the permission given by the Census Commissioner for India to Provincial Superintendents to use any expression which they considered more suitable to local conditions than the hackneyed term "depressed".

To return to our three divisions :—

(1) "*Hindu Exterior Castes*".—This, as I have confessed, is an expression to which I plead guilty. I am by no means proud of it and it is open to many criticisms. I have however asked many Indian gentlemen to give me a better one but they have not succeeded. The expression, as it stands, connotes castes which are Hindu castes but which are outside something and that is really what I mean to imply.

What are they outside ? The answer is that they are outside the social pale of Hindu Society ; that they are "below the salt" ; that they are on the other side of a barrier which prevents them from moving upwards.

But before going further I must define what I mean by "Hindu Exterior Castes".

By this expression I mean castes recognized definitely as Hindu castes whose water is not acceptable and who, *in addition*, are so deficient as castes in education, wealth and influence or, for some reason connected with their traditional occupations, are so looked down upon that there seems little hope of their being allowed by Hindu Society to acquire any further social privileges within—at any rate—the next decade.

By the use of the word "exterior caste" I certainly do not intend to imply that such a caste can never raise itself to a higher level. On the contrary I intend to imply that this can happen, as it actually has happened in the past, and that an exterior caste may in the course of time possibly become what I may call an "interior" one.

It is impossible to lay down any simple test to distinguish members of the Hindu exterior castes in Assam from others. The main test to distinguish "clean" castes from "unclean" castes is whether the water of the caste is accepted by members of the upper castes. A caste whose water is acceptable is known in the Surma Valley as "*jalchal*" and a caste whose water is not accepted may be conveniently defined as "*jal-achal*". In Assam the words "*pani chale*" and "*pani na chale*" are in vogue. But we cannot apply this simple test alone in order to find out which castes are exterior and which are not. It is true that all exterior castes are *jal-achal* but it is not true that all *jal-achal* castes are exterior. For example in the Sylhet district the Shahas are technically a *jal-achal* caste but they are a very wealthy and influential community who are treated with considerable respect in society and by a peculiar social convention are permitted to purchase their brides from the higher castes.

The Shahas are in fact a good example of a caste which though technically unclean have by their own efforts raised themselves to a position in which the upper classes simply cannot afford to ignore them.

I have not therefore classed the Shahas as an "Exterior Caste". One of my friendly critics, Babu K. C. Dutta, Extra Assistant Commissioner, has taken up this point.

> "You do not class" he writes "the Shahas as an exterior caste simply because of their education and the wealth and influence they command. Yet they are not *jal-chal*, they are not allowed entrance into the *Thakurghar* of the cleaner castes and the disability is not likely to be relaxed in the next decade. I do not concede for a moment that the disabilities that bar the Shahas are any more pronounced in the case of the less influential and uncultured castes. These exterior castes are suffering from want of education, wealth, culture, in fact, all that contributes to social influence. As soon as they have achieved these, their position will be akin to that of the Shahas—neither clean nor depressed."

The Shahas are, of course, exterior to the extent that they fall on the other side of the great line which divides Hindu Society—the *jal-chal* line—but though this line is still of great importance other things must be taken into consideration.

If, for example, the Patnis and Namasudras could shake off the tradition which associates them with occupations regarded as low (most of them are now cultivators but tradition associates them with fishing and boat-plying) and could acquire, as a caste, a reputation for wealth and culture they would, I admit, be in much the same position as the Shahas are to-day.

This process will, however, take many generations and in the meantime they are, in my opinion, clearly suffering from greater disabilities than the Shahas, the disabilities being the very absence of those factors which have made the Shahas a respected caste.

Thus while the *jal-chal* line is a useful line of division between the upper and the lower castes it is not of much use as a test for determining the "Exterior Castes". Nor does the test of temple entry afford us much assistance.

Generally speaking in the Surma Valley all castes which are "*jal-achal*" are not allowed into the actual *Thakurghar* of temples in which the higher castes worship and are not allowed to assist in the ceremonies by bringing tulsi and flowers with which to decorate the idol. *Jal-achal* castes are however allowed "darshan" and are permitted to come into the compound of the temple. In the Assam Valley where the "*Namghar*" generally takes the place of the temple the same principle holds good but a distinction is made between different classes of *jal-achal* castes. Nadiyals and Banias for example are not allowed at all into the *Namghars* of higher castes whereas Katonis and Suts are allowed in some districts to enter the part not regarded as particularly holy, *i.e.*, they are not allowed to enter the *Monikhut*.

The whole matter being, therefore, so indeterminate how, it may be asked, can I possibly venture to say, with any degree of certainty, what castes are exterior. The only possible method was to find out by local enquiry in each district the general social position of all castes which might be thought to come under the definition of "exterior castes". This is the method I adopted..

Caste in the Assam Valley is not, as elsewhere, chiefly a functional division; it is really a racial division and functional castes are very few.

Probably for that reason Hinduism in that valley is tolerant towards the tribal communities which have not yet been completely absorbed into its organism. It must, in fact, be extremely difficult for an Assamese Hindu to despise at heart a man whose Hinduism is open to considerable doubt but who considers that he is just as good a man as any Koch or Kalita. In fact people like the Deoris consider that they are much better and don't care who knows it. Nobody can be depressed who hits you with a big stick if you attempt to show your contempt for him.

As a result the only castes in the Assam Valley which can be called exterior are castes which are either traditionally associated with some degrading occupation (such as selling fish) or whose traditional origin is associated with a bar sinister. About some castes in this valley there is however, no possible doubt. Let us deal with these first.

There is, I consider, no doubt that in the Assam Valley the caste which at this census has adopted the name of Bania and which at previous censuses was styled Brittial-Bania is an exterior caste. Some of the leading men of this community have in fact informed me that their position in society is hopeless and have asked to be classed as a depressed caste.

That this caste is an exterior caste is also the unanimous opinion of all responsible officers whom I have consulted.

Nor is there any doubt about the large class which has now adopted the caste name of Kaibartta—and which was previously known as Nadiyal; nor about the Charals of Lower Assam who now call themselves Namasudras with their offshoot the Hiras. The general opinion about all these castes is unanimous.

Thus the Census Officer, Dhubri, reports :—

> "Namasudras or Nadiyals or Jaluas or Charals or Kaibarttas or Doms are considered untouchable by caste Hindus who neither admit them into their places of worship nor take water touched by them"

and the Census Officer, Jorhat :—

> "Among the indigenous Assamese castes the following are depressed :—
>
> (1) Kaibarttas or Nadiyals or Doms.
>
> (2) Brittial-Banias.
>
> (3) Hiras or Charals (found in Lower Assam only)".

From Darrang comes further evidence :—

> " That Doms, Nadiyals, Namasudras, Charals, Hiras and Brittial-Banias are depressed, is admitted by the members of the community themselves who were consulted," writes the Census Officer.

In fact in every district of the Assam Valley the opinion is unanimous that the Brittial-Banias and the Kaibarttas (which name may be taken to include Charals, Nadiyals, Hiras and all the other names which from time to time have been applied to various branches of this family) are the most exterior castes in the whole of the Assam Valley.

These castes are socially " outside the pale " and though the Brittial-Banias have worked hard to improve their position and have a considerable number of educated men amongst them they appear to be as far off as ever from any sort of social recognition.

Ancient custom and practice have ordained that members of these castes are to be treated as practically untouchable. It is true that the former necessity of taking a bath if touched by a member of one of these castes has fallen into disuse but a Brahman officer of about 30 years of age has informed me that when he was a small boy he had to take a bath if, by accident, he was touched by one of the hated Doms.

Above these castes came others whose position seemed to me for a long time to be extremely doubtful. They are the Naths or Jugis (known in Upper Assam as Katonis) and the Suts who are also commonly called Borias.

A careful study of the position of these castes has however convinced me that I would be wrong to class them as exterior............The truth about the Naths and the Suts appears to be that they are exterior castes who have made considerable efforts to raise themselves socially and that their efforts are beginning to bear fruit. There is a bar against them but they are beginning to break through it : they are really " superior exterior castes " who are moving upwards. There is, in fact, hope for them. As one Assamese officer has briefly expressed it :—

> " All Assamese low castes have a chance of rising in the social scale except the Doms and Haris whose case is hopeless."

The Suts and Naths do not themselves desire to be classed as depressed or exterior and in fact strongly object to it...............

> " The Education Department in 1915 provided three general dining halls and four separate rooms and the understanding has always been tha the upper caste boys are to dine in the general dining halls and the depressed or backward class boys are to use the above four rooms.............. For the last two years, there has been a very strong movement for admitting these remaining ' backward ' caste boys into the general dining hall—there is an overwhelming majority in their favour, only a small minority of about five or six still being in the opposition."

Professor Sen Gupta has subsequently informed me that the movement referred to in the last paragraph of his note resulted in August 1931 in the abolition of the remaining restriction and that—as a tentative measure—permission was given to the students who had formerly dined in the four rooms set apart to dine in the general dining hall. The Professor thinks it probable that the concession will continue.

This last piece of information, I confess, surprised me. If the concession is allowed to continue it will reflect great credit on the liberal spirit of Professor Sen Gupta's mess and may, in time, have a far-reaching effect on social custom in the Assam Valley. It does not, however, change my opinion that the Kaibarttas and Banias are definitely " exterior castes ".

On the whole I feel fairly confident that my classification of exterior castes in the Assam Valley is correct......................

I only wish I felt as confident about the exterior castes in the Surma Valley.

Conditions in that Valley are very different from those in the Assam Valley. Sylhet is linguistically and ethnologically connected with Bengal and the inclusion of this large district in Assam was originally merely a measure of administrative convenience.

Sylhet and Cachar (which is largely populated by people of Sylhetti origin) are therefore essentially Bengali in their culture. Hence there are many more functional castes than in the Assam Valley where, as I have already explained, caste is largely racial. Moreover, the presence of a large upper caste zamindar class in Sylhet—the arbitrators of social usage—has not tended to encourage any relaxation in the treatment of the lower orders of society........... Take for example the case of a M. A. of the Sylhet Mali caste occupying a good Government post. Many responsible Hindu officers have informed me definitely that if such a person came alone to see them in their paternal homes a chair would not be offered to the guest. A *jol-chauki* (small wooden stool) *might* be offered. Even Muslims treat these low castes in the same way. A Muslim Sub-divisional Officer tells me that if a Dhubi friend of his occupying a good position in Government service were to come to his house to see him " I would not offer him a chair. I would simply say " sit down " and the Dhubi would not take a chair."

Surely if the upper caste Hindus wished to help the lower castes the least they might do is to treat the educated men among the lower castes with the same courtesy as they would extend to an educated Muslim.

The following opinion of a responsible Hindu Government officer is of interest: " Some low caste men by their *submissive attitude* win the hearts of the upper caste men and get partial admission into society. Others claim as of right and get refused. A lot depends on the man himself. If he claims too much he gets badly snubbed. In places where orthodoxy is strong he will not, in any case, get fair treatment. In the towns treatment is more liberal than in the villages. In the villages orthodoxy still prevails. If a Patni is the tenant of a Zemindar he will never get fair social treatment however highly educated he is. Orthodoxy is strongest amongst the Zemindars. But if the low caste man is an executive officer such as a Sub-Deputy Collector or an Extra Assistant Commissioner he would be given better treatment than a non-executive officer, *e.g.*, than a Deputy Inspector of Schools". The above remarks refer, of course, only to private social intercourse. On all social and public occasions the educated Mali or Patni is simply nowhere. He has (if he goes to the ceremony) to sit along with his other caste-men outside the house on the mat provided for their caste, while the higher castes sit inside the house.

Add the following facts :—

(1) Members of castes like Mali, Patni, Muchi, etc., are not allowed to enter into the temples set up by the higher castes ;

(2) The upper castes will not take water or food touched by them ; and one begins to realize the dreadful sense of mingled inferiority and hatred which an educated member of one of these exterior castes must feel in most cases towards the higher castes.

The exterior castes themselves are, however, guilty of similar treatment to each other and an exterior caste which considers itself to be on a higher social level than another exterior caste adopts exactly the same attitude as the higher castes do towards the exterior castes. A case which recently happened in Sunamganj illustrates this point. The local ferryman there (a Patni by caste) was prosecuted for refusing to row a Muchi across the river. His defence was that, according to social custom, a Patni could not row for a Muchi and that it has always been the practice, if a Muchi wanted to cross the river, for the paddle to be given to him so that he could row himself across.

After careful consideration and analysis of the evidence I have collected, I have come to the conclusion that the following are the main castes in the Surma Valley which should be classed as exterior. They are arranged in alphabetical order :—

1. Dhupi or Dhobi.
2. Dugla or Dholi.
3. Jhalo and Malo.
4. Yogi (Jugi) (Nath).
5. Kaibartta (Jalliya).
6. Mahara.
7. Mali (Bhuinmali).
8. Namasudra.
9. Patni.
10. Sutradhar.

There is general consensus of evidence that these castes are exterior throughout the Surma Valley though the position of some of them seems to be much more hopeful in Cachar than it is in Sylhet. I have no doubt that this is due largely to the absence of a Zemindari class in Cachar which is a temporarily-settled district............I have been told by several officers that the Maharas are a *jal-chal* caste and that people of this caste were made 'clean' by some ancient Raja of Sylhet—the idea being that the Maharas used to carry the Raja's palanquin and, as Raja wanted to smoke in it, he had to have as palanquin-bearers people who could attend to his smoking requirements. On the other hand some officers completely deny this story and say that the Maharas are not a *jal-chal* caste....the Maharas are principally to be found in South Sylhet. The Sub-divisional Officer (a Muslim) reported as follows :—

" I have made close and careful enquiries and there is a general consensus of opinion that the Maharas are not *jal-chal* and are a depressed class. The story that Raja Subid Narayan made them *jal-chal* for smoking requirements only, seems to be true. If the Maharas are at all *jal-chal*, they are *jalchal* only in the sense that a man of higher caste can smoke a *huka* filled with water by a Mahara. There is not a single graduate among the Maharas in this subdivision and not even a single matriculate can be found. The Deputy Inspector of Schools reports that the only educated Maharas he has met in the whole subdivision are three persons working as Vernacular teachers in Primary and Middle English Schools. So the Maharas are depressed both socially and educationally................

One gentleman from Karimganj—himself a Nath—has, indeed, no hesitation in including his community among the exterior castes. He writes as follows :—

"So far as my knowledge goes, amongst the Hindus inhabiting this sub-division the Patnis, Jogis (Naths), Namasudras, Malis, Dhubis and Duglas are to be properly included in the list of depressed classes. The reasons of depression regarding each of these communities are almost the same, namely :—

(1) The members of these communities are not allowed by the so called high caste Hindus, to enter the temple ; even their shadow defiles the image in the temple.

(2) The high class Hindus never take any food and water touched or shadowed by these people.

(3) Brahmins of caste Hindus never agree to officiate as priests in ceremonies performed by these people even if they request them.

(4) Some of these communities are not allowed to have the same barber who works amongst the high class Hindus to work for them.

In conclusion I beg to say that these are but few amongst the many disadvantages from which these people suffer."

Previous census reports show that for the last forty years the Naths have been endeavouring to raise their social position by giving up widow re-marriage and refusing food prepared by other castes. In spite, however, of these efforts the Nath community of the Surma Valley is still very much looked down upon and I must, I consider, class them as an "exterior caste".

This classification may seem peculiar inasmuch as I have not classed the Naths (Katonis) of the Assam Valley as exterior. How far the Assam Naths are connected with the Sylhet Naths is a matter into which I intend to enquire further but I doubt whether there is any very close connection. In any case a sufficient explanation of this difference in treatment would appear to be that Hinduism in Sylhet is not so tolerant as it is in the Assam Valley. Even in the Murarichand College caste restrictions seem to be much more closely observed than in the Cotton College. I have received a note on the system of messing in that college and it appears that even the Sahas are not allowed to take their meals in the general dining hall reserved for the upper caste students. In fact the *jal-chal* line is strictly observed there—at least nominally—and the students who do not belong to the upper castes have their meals served to them "either in their own rooms or in those set apart in the main block or in two out-houses provided for the purpose".

Of the Chuhras the Census Superintendent of Baluchistan writes :—

Baluchistan.—"The Chuhras censused in Baluchistan have returned themselves as belonging to the religious groups named below :—

Column 4 of Schedule, *i.e.*, Religion.	Column 8 of Schedule *i.e.*, Caste or Tribe.
Hindu Balmiki	Chuhra.
Hindu Lal Begi	Chuhra.
Musalman Lal Begi	Chuhra.
Musalman Balashai	Chuhra.
Sikh Mazhabi	Chuhra.
Chuhra	Chuhra.

Although these persons without exception are not allowed to drink from wells belonging to real Hindus, Muslims or Sikhs and are not permitted to enter their places of worship, I include them in the figures for the various religions to which they claim to belong giving separately the numbers (Males and Females) of these untouchables in a footnote in each case."

Madras.—The following extracts are taken from the Census Report for Madras where the Census Superintendent gives as the total number of depressed classes 7,300,000 in round figures, or 15½ per cent. of the population of that province. He goes on :—

"For reasons already given this figure cannot be taken as an absolute tale of those to whom the peculiar disabilities summed up in the broad term 'depressed' attach. There are many Christian converts on whom disabilities press no whit lighter than in the untouchable communities they owned before. These are not included, for personal and local and sectarian variations enter too largely for census allocation to be possible. There are other bodies the difficulties of whose life are hardly less than those of any Adi-Dravida but to whom the technical stigma of untouchability does not apply. Such do not figure in the census list. The census total therefore can fairly be termed only an approximation. It is however a good approximation and, as an indication of the general dimensions of untouchability and through it of the depressed classes problem, is absolutely reliable. Whether its approximation is above or below would depend on the point from which approached. If this viewed primarily the existence of heavy social disabilities, the figure 7,300,000 is a minimum, if it considers strict personal polluting power it is a maximum. The general dimensions of seven millions are beyond contest.

The 7,300,000 figures and the discussions above refer of course only to persons enumerated within the province on census night...... A third of the emigrants belong to the depressed classes and consequently, were the natural population to be considered, eight millions would have to be taken as the round figure for them instead of seven. . . . .

Only one of the communities represented shows an increase at all over the decade and for the Chakkiliyans the caste record seems full and as accurate as any census figures of caste can be expected to be. Apparently the Chakkiliyan is still content with the old name of his community and is practically free from that seeking after new names which has afflicted the depressed as a whole. His fellow leather worker of the north has not escap. the contagion for Madigas have diminished apparently 16 per cent. More pronounced declin. however is apparent in their hereditary enemies, the Malas, who have shed a million, while in the south the Paraiyans have dropped 1½ millions and the Totis have practically disappeared......the figures returned for the Adi family......sufficiently account for the above phenomena. The Andhra section (the name seems to have taken on most in East Godavari), now two-thirds million strong, had no returns in 1921 while that year could yield only 50,000 Adi-Dravidas as against 1931 's 1,619,000, thirty-two times greater. The drift from the old names is nearly as marked on the West Coast. Holeyas were 92,000 in 1921, 50,000 ten years later. They were 155,000 in 1891 and have declined steadily. The few hundred Adi-Karnatakas do not come near bridging the gap and are in any case a Bellary and Coimbatore, not a Kanara production.

It may be that the emergence of 23,000 Pulayans, a community not recorded from Malabar in 1921, accounts for some of the missing Holeyas. The words are identical, with merely the characteristic substitution of a Kanarese 'h' for a Tamil or other 'p' and it is difficult to see how Pulayans could have vanished in 1921 when they are a well-known feature of the region. On the other hand 98 per cent. of the Holeyas of 1921 returned languages other than Malayalam, which goes against the Pulayan theory. The presence of 16,000 Adi-Dravidas in South Kanara clearly accounts for part of the 40,000 and it is interesting that his term should be preferred to Adi-Karnataka. The preference is understandable when it is remembered that the Holeyas are essentially a Tulu, not a Kanarese, community and that while Adi-Dravida does mean something it is extremely doubtful whether Adi-Karnataka or for that matter, Adi-Andhra, has any even theoretical justification at all.

Even the Oriya depressed are not immune from the general decline, for Bavuris and Haddis show a marked decline in numbers. Ghasis, Chachatis, Kodalos, Medaris and Barikis now appear in the records however in numbers considerably greater than the diminution in Bavuris and Haddis and their emergence is the explanation of the others' decline. Other depressed classes of the Oriya region all show an increase, Dandasi, Relli, Paidi, Pano, Dombo, etc., and the quest for euphemisms has not seriously begun in this area, an indication, as already remarked, of the much less acuteness which attends the whole depressed class question there. Conditions in fact reflect those of north India rather than south. The Dandasi community has of recent years made considerable efforts at reform of its own customs and practices, with success ; it has not thought it necessary to discard its rather attractive and sonorous caste title but has wisely devoted its attention to contents rather than label.

There is something infinitely pathetic in the vain idea that a change of name can reverse the stigma of centuries ; yet this community would apparently retort to Juliet that all lies in a name. It is a mistake to encourage terms which obscure real social units. That so ugly and clumsy a term as Adi-Andhra should come to obliterate real and lively distinctions as Mala and Madiga is hardly to the good. Communities of such numerical importance and pronounced individuality should be encouraged to retain and develop a pride in their cognomens..........

It cannot be said that the social disabilities under which these communities labour are in sight of extinction despite the growth of tolerance and the inevitable effect of the development of communications and of urban life. Distinguished individual effort........ is by no means rare but it remains individual. Communities cannot yet be said even to have altered appreciably in outlook. I came across in a Telugu delta district a subordinate officer of the Labour Department occupying the dak bungalow, an unusual thing for such officers, who ordinarily put up with some casteman in the village. His castemen however shied off him, because of his employment, which brought him into constant association with the depressed classes. This man was of no notably exalted caste but a Telaga. It is probable that resentment at special consideration shown to the depressed classes in land assignment and other directions is reflected also in such an attitude, the resentment that the rising of the under-dog never fails to arouse in those who have kept him down, a feature not peculiar to India. It remains however an indication of the true position in the rural areas where the depressed classes are most represented . . . .

A peculiar refinement of the untouchability theory was distance pollution. This set out certain castes as polluting not merely on contact but by mere approach. The Nayadis were the backmarkers in this handicapping system and were practically denied ordinary use of public ways. When the system was in full force Nayadi progress must have borne a strong resemblance to that of a malefactor for whom a warrant is out and whose one object is to avoid close contact with his fellow men. A lifetime so spent can hardly produce elevation of thought or desire and a community whose chief aspiration is to avoid notice cannot contribute much to national life. This remarkable development of the superiority theory was practically confined to the West Coast and of late years has greatly weakened even there, probably more because of development of communications and increase of population than from any conscious realisation that there is in such a system something hardly compatible with claims to culture and advancement. It is probably becoming evident that a person of such rare texture that a presence sixty feet away pollutes him had better seek out some desert island or develop a less fragile purity. The train began the breakdown of this preposterous system ; the bus may complete it.

Contact pollution on the other hand existed and exists all over the presidency.

An instance of the modification and at the same time of the persistence of discrimination is afforded by the river and canal ferries of the Telugu delta districts. According to petitions quoted in a Government Order of 1919 a member of the depressed classes might have to wait for hours before being taken over as he and a Brahman would never be taken together and the Brahman always had priority. In the bigger boats plying on the two rivers and larger canals there is now no such preference ; any person waiting is admitted on board. Depressed classes however have to keep to a different end of the boat from Brahmans. In the cross-river ferries the disappearance is not so complete and an influential Brahman would be taken over in preference to a crowd of depressed classes of prior arrival. In other cases either the Brahman or the depressed class person would hold back to avoid travelling with the other. The extent to which prejudice and preference have scope varies from village to village and with the importance of the Brahman or enlightenment of the depressed. It has been noticed that Christians of depressed class origin make no bones about getting into the boat whether a Brahman is waiting or not. The ferryman occasionally too has prejudices.

On the small canal ferries Brahman precedence is still the general rule, but where the traffic is considerable and the balakats big, as at Nidadavole before the bridge was built, conditions resembled those on the river boats.

The same petition complained that in certain municipalities depressed classes were denied the use of water taps reserved for higher castes, despite circumstances of proximity and convenience. Such restriction if it ever existed as an official practice no longer does.

Despite their lowly status, these communities play a large and important part in the life of the presidency. It is they who furnish the backbone of agricultural labour in the chief ricegrowing districts. In one form or another they have been the victims of an agrestic serfdom wherever they have been. This generally took (and still takes) the form of compulsory advances from their employers which could never be repaid in full and thus tied the borrower to the soil. This was most noticeable in Tanjore but a parallel system of advances produced the same effect in South Kanara. It must be laid to the credit of Ceylon and other estates that they have done more to raise the self-respect of the South Indian depressed classes worker than any other single circumstance. It is possibly for the same reason that emigration is opposed in certain quarters. The Madras Government appointed an officer as Commissioner of Labour and among his particular functions are the attending to the needs of depressed classes. The decade has seen much expenditure on provision of wells for them, of schools, and a most important feature, the buying of house sites for them mainly in the delta areas. A notable example of a breakaway from caste traditions is in the Nambudri who was schoolmaster in a depressed classes school in Malabar. The Nayadi colony of Olavakkot formed to house members of possibly the most contemned community in Malabar has been able to develop its activities more than it anticipated. Recently however some difficulties have arisen through a boycott by other castes of a school which received some Nayadi pupils."

APPENDIX II.

Primitive Tribes.

The purpose of this appendix is not to give an account of Primitive Tribes but to estimate their numbers and distribution, to indicate briefly certain important considerations which bear on their welfare and administration, and to point out where more detailed information is available.

Numbers. Since 1891 no serious attempt seems to have been made to arrive at the figure of Hill and Forest tribes. The figure given in Table XVII in 1891 was 15,806,914 but it was clearly incomplete, excluding as it did the Musahars (622,034 at that census) and others such as the Dublas and Talavias of Bombay and Baroda (172,052 in 1891). The Census Commissioner in 1921 roughly estimated the strength of hill and forest tribes at 16 million (page 226, Section 194 Census Report, 1921), but his estimate was based apparently on the figures of major tribes of which a number are recorded in Section 87 of his Chapter IV (page 112). He does not mention tribes so important numerically as Bhumij (240,229 in 1921), Kol (328,425 in 1921), Bharia (630,862 in 1921), or Karen (1,220,356 in 1921), and as the percentage of the population laid down as qualifying a caste or tribe to be separately tabulated must have ruled out of tabulation entirely a very large number of small units, he probably failed to realise the very large figure which is composed of broken and scattered tribes small and insignificant individually. At this census special injunctions were given that all primitive tribes were to be tabulated whatever their numbers and irrespective of the percentage proviso for the individual tabulation of castes. It is therefore now possible to give accurate numbers of any identifiable tribal unit, though it is less easy to indicate the extent to which such a unit remains primitive in its habits.

The basic figure indicating the total number of primitive tribes is to be obtained from Table XVII by adding together the total figures of groups I, II and III. This figure amounts to 26,735,339, but some adjustments are necessary. These adjustments cannot be carried out with precision, as so many tribes, particularly in the Bhil, Koli, and Gond groups, fade off into castes wherever they live in the plains or open country as ordinary Hindu villagers, but if certain complete groups be deducted and others allowed to remain, since it is impossible to deal with broken units, and if no attempt made to include a certain number of nomadic tribes whose condition is doubtful and, if properly described as primitive, it is perhaps the result of degeneration rather than failure to rise, tribes such as Banjara, for instance, or Kaikadi, Yerukalas Pardhis or Sansis (*vide* Table XVII group XI, 14), or the Koracha, Korama and Kuruba of Mysore where 12,333 persons have been returned as of tribal religion (apart from their 250,000 fellow tribesmen returned as Hindu), none of whom have been included in the figures here given of primitive tribes, then a reasonably accurate figure can be reached as representing the total population which can properly be described by the term 'primitive tribes'; there will still be inevitably a slight overlap with the figures of the exterior castes given in Appendix I, *e.g.* in the case of Turi in Bihar and Orissa.

Although this test has by no means been rigidly adhered to, the tribes given in Table XVII relate primarily to primitive tribes enumerated in more than one province; many other primitive tribes will be found in Table XVIII, but while some appear in both, others are likely to be found in neither table and reference for their details has to be made to provincial or state volumes. It is consequently necessary here to add to the basic figure the following :—

Primitive Tribes of Travancore State not included in Table XVII.

Tribe.	Population.
Kanikkaran	6,659
Malankuravan	66
Malapantaram	187
Malapulayan	254
Malayarayan	3,182
Mannan	1,276
Muthuvan	1,301
Thantapulayan	795
Ullatan	5,121
Vettuvan*	1,322
Vishavan	166
Total	20,329

*Included in Table XVII as a caste under group VI, 2.

1. *To group III.*—
   Travancore Tribes .. 20,329
   (Plains Uralis have been omitted, Mala-Uralis only (916) having been reckoned here as 'Primitive'; they appear in Table XVII, as also Paliyans (483).
   Kaniyan in Madras 1,470

2. *To group 3.*—Andh in Hyderabad State 6,100
   Andh in Central Provinces and Berar 58,549
3. *To group 6.*—Bagata in Madras .. 34,379
4. *To group 7.*—Tipara in Bengal .. 203,069
   Tipara in Assam 4,000
5. *To group 8.*—Khyang in Bengal 1,002
6. *To group 11.*—The following tribes in Assam :—

Abor	14,042
Aka	38
Dafla	1,600
Deori Chutiya	4,000†
Lalung	43,448
Mikir	129,797
Miri	85,038
Mishmi	2,234

†Vide *Assam Census Report*, 1931, page 222. Precise figures have not been tabulated.

7. *To group 11.*—The following tribes in Bengal—

Bhotia	14,783
Chakma	135,508
Dhimal	376
Khambu	32,601
Murmi	35,224
Lepcha	12,720
Toto	334
Yakka	873
and in Sikkim—	
Bhotia	15,192
Khambu	18,565
Murmi	7,017
Yakka	142
To group 11.—In Assam—Alien Tribes on tea-gardens	53,121*
In Burma—Lolo-Muhso	93,214

These additions add up to 1,028,765 making with the first mentioned figure a total of 27,764,104.

From this total certain deductions clearly have to be made—

1. *From group 2* Minas and Meos (1,110,479) and Mers and Merats (139,528) should be excluded. They cannot now be regarded in general as primitive, though the Mina may in some cases retain some primitive characteristics.

2. *From groups 2 and 3* the difference between the number returned by Baroda as Primitive and Forest Tribes and the numbers for that State included in these groups. This difference is 230,897, the figure by which the latter exceeds the former.

3. *From group 3,* 182,235 Kolis enumerated in the Punjab, and 6,934 Kolis in Delhi, a caste in these cases rather than a tribe.

4. *From group 8* Meitheis both in Assam (324,432) and Burma (6,113) must be deducted. They cannot be treated as primitive.

5. *From group 10* Ahoms (249,434) and Shans (900,204) must be deducted for the same reason.

This makes a total for deduction of 3,150,256 giving a remainder of 24,613,848 as the total population of primitive tribes in India 1931. It is unlikely that this total is understated and its tendency is obviously to decrease rather than increase with the lapse of time.

Religion. Of this total number of 24,613,848 only 8,280,347 have been returned as adhering to their tribal religions. The remainders are mainly Hindu, but in certain tribes there are large numbers of Christians, some Buddhists, and a few, like the Tadvis of Khandesh, are Muslims. Table XVIII will show for many tribes not only the respective proportions in 1931 but the change from census to census wherever figures are available.

Distribution. The main figures of distribution can again be obtained from Table XVII where figures for provinces and states are shown in brackets against each group of tribes. Those indicated above are to be added and subtracted respectively and the resulting figures are stated by provinces below :—

Ajmer-Merwara	18,904
Andamans and Nicobars	10,405
Assam	1,678,419
Bengal	1,927,299
Bihar and Orissa	6,681,228
Bombay	2,841,080
Burma	2,206,356
Central Provinces	4,065,277
Coorg	1,089
Madras	1,262,369
United Provinces	400,184
Provinces	*21,092,610*
States	*3,521,238*
Baroda	313,273
Central India	1,342,081
Cochin	1,048
Gwalior	281,033
Hyderabad	222,806
Rajputana	802,178
Sikkim	41,257
Travancore	21,728
Western India States	495,834
Total ..	24,613,848

* *N. B.*—These figures refer chiefly to tribes from Chota Nagpur and the Madras Agency tracts but exclude any who have returned their religion as Hindu. The latter, that is of course the vast majority, appear in Appendix I as exterior castes.

As a check on these figures we may compare them with those arrived at by Provincial Census Superintendents. Thus the figure here for Bihar and Orissa is 6,681,228 and the figure for primitive tribes arrived at by Mr. Lacey for that province is 5,643,431 in addition to which he records 1,437,667 as the figure of tribes or castes on the border line. Of the total 7,000,000, roughly 2,000,000 have been treated as exterior castes indicating that the overlap in the figure of primitive tribes and of exterior castes in the appendices is not very great at any rate in Bihar and Orissa, which contributes nearly a quarter of the whole. Again the figures for primitive tribes available from the Central Provinces is 4,111,972 (vide *Census Report for Central Provinces and Berar*, 1931, page 359) a figure which embodies Halba (120,754), and Ojha (5,106) not included in these figures. From Madras again the number obtained from the tables is 1,428,938, but this includes 166,569 who are described both as depressed castes and as primitive tribes. They have been omitted here and are covered by the figures in Appendix I.

Groups returned from Madras both as primitive tribes and as depressed castes and excluded from the figures given here for Primitive Tribes.

Dombo	79,643
Karimpalan	2,807
Katturayakan	1,581
Kudubi	12,011
Pano	70,527
Total	166,569

Administrative Problem.

The total figure of primitive tribes in India may then be taken as 25,000,000 in round numbers, of which about 20,000,000 are in British India of whom again 2,500,000 are found in Burma, for there are in Burma a number of hill tribes who were only partially enumerated at the census. It has already been indicated that their position in surroundings of a more developed culture presents certain problems of administration. As long as a primitive tribe remains in isolation conducting its own affairs according to its own laws and customs it presents no problem except that required to prevent raiding or other forms of aggression on more civilised or less warlike neighbours. For this purpose a military occupation of territory may be necessary and a loose system of political control or administration of some sort which need not involve more than a minimum of interference with tribal customs and the expense of which, if greater, as it normally will be, than any revenue yielded by such an area, is in the nature of insurance. Where communications are meagre or non-existent contact with the outer world will be so slow that the effect of its impact will not be rapid enough for observation and no change will take place in the primitive community except the gradual adaptation and alteration resulting from the intercourse on the fringes of the area inhabited. Changes of this kind involving a very slow change of environment and outlook are familiar enough in India and have been going on for centuries if not millennia. No serious problem arises until this process of slow adaptation is interfered with by a development of communication and a sudden increase of contacts.

Even excise laws, although in many ways to the benefit of primitive tribes, may operate as a hardship, and would be found excessively severe if the very proper restrictions on distilling were extended to *pachwai* and *tari* made for household consumption and forming a very important part of the diet of tribes that cannot grow sugar and are too poor to buy it. For three months in the hot weather the Marias of Chanda live almost exclusively on a very mildly alcoholic beverage, much as the Angami Naga does to a less degree in Assam. Any one well acquainted with either tribe will vividly realise the hardship that might be wrought by bigoted prohibitionists anxious to disallow to others that freedom which they do not value for themselves, and total prohibition is a policy shared by Hindus and Muslims. The prohibition of distilling itself may be a hardship, as for the Gond who must offer to his god liquor distilled by the family of worshippers, but this is probably one of those that must be borne in the interests of the community, like the game laws that prevent a Kachha Naga or a Kuki from offering game at the graves of the dead during the close season, or the troublesome restrictions on homicide which prevent a Wa from fertilizing his crop with the life-essence of a stranger, or the Kondh from doing the same with the *meriah* he has reared for that purpose.

The rapid opening up of communications, involving contact at many points and often the practical settlement of tribal country, entirely alters the aspect of any gradual changes that may have been taking place. Generally speaking it substitutes conflict for contact. Not necessarily, that is, a conflict of arms but of culture and of material interest. Attempts to develop minerals, forests or land for intensive cultivation can only be made at the expense of the tribe whose isolation is thus invaded. The customs which regulate the ownership, usufruct or transfer of land among primitive tribes are generally at variance with those observed by more sophisticated communities, and in the conflict between the two the tribal custom is normally superseded by a code which is neither valued nor understood by the tribe and in the application of which the tribe is deprived of its property, generally in the name of law, either by alienation to foreigners or by transforming the trusteeship of a tribal chief into absolute ownership of a kind quite foreign to the customs of the tribe. This has befallen both the Mundas, for instance and the hill tribes of Chittagong, to mention two instances only, while even in Rajputana a somewhat similar process has been at work. Here an authority thoroughly conversant with the people and conditions in that Agency states that during the last 25 years there has been a very marked change in the position of landlords from the chiefs downwards :—

"What..........has happened in Rajputana in the last century is a complete departure from the ancient relationship of peasant and chief, wherein the chief has become securely established in 'rights' that were not his a hundred years ago, and the peasant has been deprived both of rights and responsibilities. It would not have been difficult to establish universal franchise a century ago ; as a matter of fact it was exercised (and is still exercised in inaccessible places) without being labelled. To day it would be so difficult as almost to seem an impossible task to make the peasant withdraw his watchful gaze from his landlord's activities, just within the borders of the law, long enough to exercise an intelligent vote, let alone a responsible one...... In the century the operation of British law and its influence has set up the ruling chiefs in a security, authority and prestige that never appertained to their position in earlier times, and..............the peasant has been deprived of just so much as has accrued to the other..........Progressively, and at an accelerated pace since Lord Minto's commencement of the policy of non-interference, the common people have been deprived both of authority and responsibility. The British idea of law and application of it has made this process easy and apparently natural."

A similar application of alien law also usually disturbs the tribal customs of debt. Tribal customs of debt are frequently, perhaps normally, stated in terms of extravagant usury. Such terms however represent less the real customs observed in practice than the ideal which the lender considers ought to be the return, and in point of fact they are qualified by very important considerations. In the first place there is commonly no law of limitation, and the borrower may not expect to repay before the next generation while the lender is very often so placed that there is a moral compulsion to lend under certain circumstances even if no return is expected in his lifetime. Thus it is often the custom for a chief to lend paddy to the most indigent and unprofitable of his villagers in times of scarcity though he knows repayment to be extremely unlikely. In any case when repayment does take place there is normally a settlement by accommodation between both parties which bears little relation to the payment due on a strict interpretation of the law of usury as formally stated by the tribe. It is only natural that tribesmen whose views of debt are dictated by this sort of vague custom are perfectly ready to subscribe without demur to the most flagrantly usurious agreements exacted by foreign moneylenders who intend to invoke a foreign code to compel repayment on the letter of the agreement and at the time when it suits them to do so instead of at such time as the debtor finds himself in a position to pay. Similarly the criminal law of a civilized community is often entirely at variance with what is felt to be just and proper by tribal custom. Afforestation again is a frequent grievance, and in forests which were common property under a tribal regime it becomes a punishable offence to exercise what the tribe regards as an inalienable right. Thus under the Assam Forest Regulations tribal land used for *jhuming* is held to be Unclassed State Forest, and as such at the absolute disposal of Government. It can be taken and its possessors ousted without any sort of compensation. But this land has by the great majority of hill tribes been regarded for many generations as their most valuable real property. Further under a recent regulation it has been held that a man quarrying stone, for his own use, on his own jhum land is liable to pay Rs. 10 per month or Rs. 100 a year as a permit fee on the ground that the land from which he takes the stone is Unclassed State Forest, although it may have been the subject of bequest, mortgage, or transfer by sale and purchase for twenty generations, and its boundaries a matter of common knowledge in the village. Indeed a recent case occurred in which a young and inexperienced officer announced, on the strength of this Unclassed State Forest doctrine that he would recognize no individual rights in jhum land, and even fined a man for letting land bought by his own grandfather to another man on lease. Such an action would in some tribes have been almost enough to cause a rebellion by itself ; but it was in no way inconsistent with the theory that the tribal land is unclassed State forest. In the Madras Agency Tracts again the same attitude has been taken towards *jhum*, there called *podu*, and has been carried to the extent of the prohibition of cultivation, twice bringing the Sawara tribe to the verge of open rebellion. *Dahia* (or *bewar*), as it is there called, is similarly forbidden in the Central Provinces, compelling the forest tribes to cultivate only under the land settlement system which is in many cases unsuited to them. Primitive systems of agriculture are frequently extremely wasteful of forest land and may in hill country prove damaging to adjoining plains on account of denudation, the too rapid escape of rain and consequent inundation below. At the same time wasteful cultivation of this kind is very often the only known means of subsistence. It cannot be abandoned in a day for other methods with which the cultivator, whose knowledge is traditional, is unfamiliar. Again the exploitation of minerals not only involves the taking up of tribal land but generally the introduction of an alien population, usually of an extremely mixed character and not infrequently exceptionally dissolute. This impinges on tribal life in a number of disconcerting ways. Even the invasion of missionaries is liable to produce as much evil as good, if not more, for their conduct and objects are generally in extreme conflict with tribal religion and with tabus of all kinds, and their point of view, readily comprehensible to an alien administration which understands the tribal position very vaguely if at all, and backed as it so often is by influentially vocal societies at a distance, is much more likely to obtain the support of authority than tabus which are on the face of them unreasonable to all except those to whom they are the most vitally important things in life. A similar misunderstanding of the tribal point of view is apt to arise in the case of many customs, and it may be enough to mention that of marriage by a form of capture common to both Bhils and Gonds, and, although quite familiar to the tribesmen themselves, often capable of being treated by British courts as cases of abduction. It is true that the law would normally require a complaint to move it to action, but it is obvious that a knowledge of the possibility of moving it is likely to encourage complaints from persons who would otherwise have acquiesced contentedly in tribal custom, and to result in a quite unjust punishment of the party complained against for following a law really known to and admitted by the complainant. A Bhil was convicted and sentenced by a British court just about the time of the 1931 census for just such a breach of the penal code in entire accordance with Bhil custom. Apart from laws in themselves their manner of application may be extremely severe on people whose methods of dealing with antisocial actions or persons is entirely different. No apology is required for quoting at length from Rai Bahadur Sarat Chandra Roy, himself a practising lawyer in Bihar and Orissa courts :

"The British system of administration of justice......has unintentionally produced certain deplorable effects on the moral character of the aborigines. This complicated system of law and legal procedure, which is..........suited to advanced districts and people, was naturally not comprehended by the simple aborigines and was not suited to their level of culture. Although the judges and magistrates were inspired with a desire to do justice, very few of them were, or still are, conversant with the languages, customs and mentality of the people. And thus this complicated system of administration of justice has tendered to impair the natural truthfulness and honesty of the people in many cases. By repeated painful experience the people have found that under the complicated and cumbrous Procedure Codes and a too technical Law of Evidence which are now in force and which are beyond their comprehension, their native straight-forwardness and veracity is no match for the chicanery and falsehood and the many subtle tricks employed against them by many of their adversaries. And "law-touts" and other petty-fogging "advisers" are not wanting to induce them to adopt the ways of their adversaries. Such advice unhappily they now not unoften follow, though rather clumsily. But, as is inevitable, the expensive system of litigation through one court after another—Courts of Original Jurisdiction, Courts of First Appeal and Courts of Second Appeal,—is ruinous for the poor aboriginal, who, in most cases, cannot fight up to the last, and even those who can, only find themselves in the end utterly ruined through the expenses and trouble of securing ultimate victory. In this way the complicated British-Indian system of administration of justice has more often than not helped in ruining the aboriginals economically and in degrading them morally.

The British system of law and administration has further tended to impair the social solidarity of the tribes and has weakened the authority of the social heads or Panches and the respect they formerly commanded. Until recently, when Government orders validating tribal customary law regarding succession and inheritance were promulgated, the Courts often disregarded the custom against inheritance by daughters and applied to them a Succession Act quite inconsistent with the fundamental social structures and ideas of kinship of the tribes. Until recently when rules against alienation of ancestral lands were promulgated by Government, the ancient tribal custom against such alienation was utterly disregarded, and through such alienation, alien Hindus and Mahomedans were admitted to the villages resulting in the further disintegration of the old village community. The recent restrictions against alienation have come so late, and the people have been now so long accustomed to such transfers, that a large section of the people now feel these restrictions irksome and no longer needed, and subterfuges are often resorted to in order to evade them." *Effects on the Aborigines of Chota Nagpur of their Contact with Western Civilisation—Journ. Bihar and Orissa Research Soc. 1931.*

It is easy to see how a combination of anti-tribal forces is likely to create a condition of excessive discomfort in tribal life, the most serious aspect of which is the complete breakdown of the communal organization. A tribe living in comparative isolation will usually be found to have developed an adaptation to its environment which within certain limits approaches perfection, an adaptation which may have taken many millennia to accomplish, and the breakdown of which may be the ruin of the tribe, for it is likely to proceed at a far greater rate than either the gradual change in physical environment or than the still slower process of adaptation to that change.

In the past the administration of tribal areas as non-regulation districts has in very many cases done much to make the position easier for the tribes affected. However uncomprehending and uncomprehended the administration may have been it was in a position to temper the conflict of interest, and to that position have been due precautions such as the Chota Nagpur Tenancy Act, or such as exemption from the provisions of the Indian Succession Act or of the Stamp Act, or restrictions on the appearance of pleaders in courts hearing tribal cases. Even where such exemptions have been made they have often been too half-hearted and too easily nullified. Of some 30 primitive tribes in the Central Provinces only 9 are specifically exempted from the operation of the Indian Succession Act, while in Assam a hillman who subscribes as he must do when in Government service, to the General Provident Fund cannot nominate as his heir his brother or his brother's son according to his own venerated custom but if he has no issue must nominate his wife. This is reasonable no doubt to a Britisher, but is completely at variance with sentiment and custom in the Assam hills, and generally with good and sufficient reason. Similarly the Post Office Savings Bank recognizes Hindu and Muslim law but not tribal custom. It seems more than likely that the incorporation of tribal areas into regulation areas, when such areas are governed by more or less democratic forms of government on the constitution of which the tribes will be placed in an insignificant minority, will bring their interests into direct conflict with the interests of their neighbours under conditions in which the administration of the tribal area will have very little power to modify the severity with which it will react on the tribes. Tribes occupying such an area realize little or nothing of the method in which laws are administered outside it ; if they do they have no means of making themselves heard.

The consequence is that a few alien settlers who are able to do so and are wishful to live under the ordinary codes, which give tremendous advantages to traders and others dealing with simple and unlettered men, are likely to succeed (it has under existing conditions often been done) in getting a method of administration extended to a tribal area the disadvantages of which to the tribesmen are completely unappreciated by them until they find themselves irrevocably within its grip. In the process of accommodation, it is only too likely that a previously nonhinduised hill tribe may become a mere depressed caste as has happened to the Turis, Koras and Kharias, to mention only three instances from the same part of India,* while the cultivator is deprived of his rights in tribal land and degraded to that of a landless labourer, a process pointed out in the case of Gonds and kindred tribes by the Census Superintendent for the Central Provinces in Appendix III of his report.

In the alternative they may retain a sort of emasculated tribal life, deprived of the customs and festivals that gave it meaning and cohesion, and fall into that psychical apathy and physical decline which has decimated so many tribal communities in the Pacific and elsewhere; and this decline is accelerated in another way by the opening up of communications. Many new diseases are imported against which no immunity has been evolved, since they did not form part of the environment to which the tribe is adapted, and the result is a staggering mortality from which there may be no recovery. The rapidly approaching extinction of the tribes of Great Andaman has largely been due to diseases imported into the penal settlement and communicated to the Andamanese by convicts. The use of distilled liquor, of opium and even of mercury (as a drug) is performing a similar disservice for other tribes and is likewise the result of the improved communications which corrupt good manners. The Durbar of a State known to the writer vetoed the advent of rail communications on the ground that railways were an evil: they only brought in dirt, disease, crime and strangers, and the state was better without,—a judgement in which we may find very much indeed to commend.

Meanwhile the difficulties under which primitive tribes are placed with regard to education have already been pointed out (*vide* paragraph 141 in Chapter IX), and in Bihar and Orissa a memorandum of the Government itself, submitted to the Statutory Commission, states that in the matter of education the aboriginals of that province " as a whole are, relatively to the general population, in a worse position than they were in 1921. They have got a little less than their general share of the big advance made in primary education and decidedly less of the advance in high and middle education ". Education in itself is a doubtful blessing in so far as it is apt to unfit them for their environment, but it is probably a necessary weapon of defence for them in the circumstances in which they are placed, perhaps the only one of any permanent value, though the real solution of the problem would appear to be to create self-governing tribal areas with free power of self-determination in regard to surrounding or adjacent provincial units.

It remains to add a list of all papers in the 1931 census series which deal with primitive tribes from one aspect or another. Some of them are collected in part III of this volume but others can only be found by reference to the provincial volumes concerned.

References.

List of passages in Provincial and State Census Reports (1931) bearing on the customs, conditions or welfare of primitive tribes. Items marked with an asterisk appear in Part III of this volume; items marked † are also reproduced but in part only, or in a different form.

Census volume and province, etc.	Chapter or passage to which reference is made.	Subject.	Author.
II. Andaman and Nicobar Islands.	A. Andaman Islands, † Chapter V.	*The Aborigines*	M. C. C. Bonington.
	B. Nicobar Islands,† Chapters V-VII.	*Ethnology, etc., of Nicobarese*	Do.
	Appendix A*	*The Shompen*	Do.
	Appendix B*	*Religion of Kar Nikobar* ..	G. Stevenson.
III. Assam	Chapter XII, Appendix I(2)	*Backward Tribes*	C. S. Mullan.
	Appendix A*	*Effect on Primitive Tribes of contacts with civilization.*	J. P. Mills.
	Appendix B*	*Notes on certain Hill Tribes* ..	J. P. Mills and others.
V. Bengal	Appendix II*	*Notes on the Peoples of the Chittagong Hill Tracts.*	J. P. Mills and others.
VII. Bihar and Orissa ..	Appendix V*	*The Kurmis of Chota Nagpur*	W. G. Lacey.
	Appendix VI†	*The Santals*	W. G. Lacey and P. O. Bodding.
VIII. Bombay ..	Appendix B	*Notes on the aboriginals and Hill tribes found in the Presidency.*	*H. T. Sorley.*

*These instances might be increased indefinitely Practically all the primitive tribes south of the Godavari river have become mere depressed castes.

Census volume and province, etc.	Chapter or passage to which reference is made.	Subject.	Author.
XI. Burma	Chapter VI, Section 63† ..	*Lahu and Kaw marriage customs.*	J. H. Talford.
	Appendix C*	*Notes on the Indigenous Races of Burma.*	J. H. Green.
	Appendix E†	*Naga Tribes and their customs.*	T. P. Dewar.
XII. Central Provinces and Berar.	Chapter XII, Section 13 ..	*Primitive Tribes*	W.H. Shoobert and others.
	Appendix III*	*Aboriginal Tribes of the Central Provinces.*	Do.
XIV. Madras	Chapter XII†, pp. 360-392	*Primitive Tribes*	M. W. M. Yeatts and others.
XVIII. United Provinces	Chapter XII, appendix D..	*Monographs on certain Castes and Tribes.*	A. C. Turner.
XIX. Baroda	Chapter XII, Section 407	*Forest and Primitive Tribes* ..	
	Appendix IX (Caste glossary).	s. v. *Primitive and Forest Tribes.*	S. V. Mukherjea.
XX. Central India ..	Appendix I†	*Ethnographic account of the Bhils of Central India.*	C. S. Venkatachar.
	Appendix II*	*Migration of Castes and Tribes into Central India and their distribution.*	Do.
XXI. Cochin	Appendix I†	*The Forest Tribes of Cochin*	K. Govinda Menon.
XXIII. Hyderabad ..	†	*The Chenchus*	G. A. Khan.
XXV. Mysore ..	Appendix X	*Some facts regarding four primitive tribes.*	M. Venkatesa Iyangar.
XXVIII. Travancore ..	Appendix I†	*The Primitive Tribes* ..	N. Kunjan Pillai and L. A. Krishna Iyer.

INDEX.

N. B.—Figures in clarendon type indicate paragraphs.

Figures in ordinary type indicate pages.

A

A—*contd.*

B

B—*contd.*

C

C—*contd.*

D

E

E—*contd.*

F

G

H

H—*contd.*

I

J

K

M22CC

K—*contd.*

L

M

M—*contd.*

N

O

P

S—*concld.*

T

T—*contd.*

U

V

M22CC—2,510—26-7-33—GIPS

CENSUS OF INDIA
1931

CENSUS OF INDIA 1931

WITH COMPLETE SURVEY OF TRIBAL LIFE AND SYSTEM

(IN THREE VOLUMES)
(VOLUME II)

J.H. HUTTON

With An Introduction by

K.S. SINGH
Anthropological Survey of India, Delh

GYAN
GYAN PUBLISHING HOUSE
NEW DELHI - 110002

Census of india 1931

ISBN : 81-212-0171-3 (Set)

Reprinted in 2010 in India by
Gyan Publishing House
23, Main Ansari Road, Darya Ganj, N.D. 110002
Phones: 23282060, 23261060 Fax : 91-11-23285914
E-Mail : books@gyanbooks.com, gyanbook@vsnl.com,
Website : gyanbooks.com

Printed at : Gian Ridhi Offset Printers, Delhi

CENSUS OF INDIA, 1931.

VOLUME I—PART II.

M8CC

Preface.

The arrangement of this volume differs a little from that of the corresponding volume in 1921. In that volume figures for cities were given separately at the end. This time each table that has been compiled separately for cities follows the general table to which it relates. The figures of the cities table are, of course, also included under the relevant head in the general table. The fly-leaf of each table indicates the table in 1921 to which the 1931 table corresponds in every case in which the numerical order differs ; some rearrangement has been made in the tables in order that they may be as relevant as possible to the treatment of their contents in the Report Volume. Table XII, as will be seen from the Table of Contents, does not appear in this volume ; the results obtained were so unsatisfactory that it has not been printed as an Imperial Table, the figures have however been compiled and will be found given in Chapter IX of the Report. An appendix (*iv*) has been added to show the area and population of provinces when redistributed with Orissa and Sind as separate units instead of as part of the provinces in which they were incorporated at the date of the census.

It should be noted that all the figures in the main Tables are determined by the actual distribution of population as it happened to be found on the night on which the census was taken, irrespective of its prevailing distribution or of abnormalities caused by seasonal, temporary or fortuitous movements. Tables not so qualified by date or geography at the moment of census have been placed in appendices.

TABLE I.

Area, Houses, and Population.

1. The figures in this table relate to the whole of the Indian Empire except certain tracts beyond the administrative frontier in Assam and Burma. They do not relate to those parts of the peninsula which are outside the Indian Empire.

2. The Settlement of Aden including Perim Island is included, but not the Aden Protectorate.

3. Details of some of the principal States included in the Agencies and Provincial States groups will be found on page 4 where also is shown the population of the areas under British Administration in certain Indian States.

4. The figures in this table are based on a detailed enumeration on the standard schedule except in the following cases :—

	Persons.
1. Andaman and Nicobar Islands—	
Andamanese (Part)	370
Nicobarese (Shompen)	200
2. Baluchistan—	
Tribal Areas	757,768
3. Bombay Presidency—	
Ahmadabad City (Part)	75,735
4. Burma—	
East Manglun (Northern Shan States)	19,649
5. North-West Frontier Province—	
Agencies and Tribal Areas	2,212,837

In the case of the Baluchistan Tribal Areas a simplified form of schedule was employed. In the other areas in the above list the population was estimated after a careful inquiry. For the manner in which the estimates were made, reference should be made to the corresponding reports.

5. The 33 units which appear in the 1921 table have now become 35 in consequence of the following changes :—

1. The Western India States Agency has been separated from Bombay.
2. The Punjab States Agency has been separated from the Punjab.

The Madras States Agency has similarly been separated from Madras, but this has not involved any change in this table, as it appeared separately in 1921. The census of the Madras States has, however, been carried out by the Superintendent of Census Operations for Madras Province, except in the case of Travancore and Cochin, which as before have acted independently, their reports being included in the India series.

6. In the Province of Assam the Khasi States, previously included for census purposes in British Assam, have now been shown separately under the head 'Assam States' which formerly had reference to Manipur State only. Separate figures for these States do not appear in Table XX, but with the exception of these and other very small States figures will be found in that table not only for the districts of each province but for the States which are not shown separately in the general tables.

7. The topographical surveys carried out during the decade in various parts of India have resulted in a revision of area figures which accounts for some discrepancies between areas given here and in 1921 and for an increase of 1,045 sq. miles in the computation of the area censused in that year. Other changes are accounted for by inter-provincial transfers. The remaining areas are at present under revision but the figures are not yet available. An area of 908 square miles incorporated into British India from the previously unadministered tracts on the Assam frontier, and an area estimated at 1,400 sq. miles similarly incorporated into the Chin Hills District in Burma have been included for the first time, while 6 square miles formerly in the United Provinces have been ceded to Nepal, making a total addition of 2,302 square miles to the area of India on its external boundaries. Para. 2 of the fly leaf to Table II gives the corresponding population figures of these areas.

Table I—Area, Houses

Province, State or Agency.	Area in square miles.	Towns.	Villages.	Occupied Houses. Total.	In towns.	In villages.
1	2	3	4	5	6	7
INDIA	**1,808,679**	**2,575**	**696,831**	**71,062,228**	**7,935,989**	**63,126,239**
Provinces	**1,096,171**	**1,698**	**499,359**	**54,533,192**	**5,908,418**	**48,624,774**
1. Ajmer-Merwara	2,711	5	747	122,213	37,778	84,435
2. Andaman and Nicobar Islands	3,143	..	239	5,710	..	5,710
Andaman Islands	*2,508*	..	*90*	*4,267*	..	*4,267*
Nicobar Islands	*635*	..	*149*	*1,443*	..	*1,443*
3. Assam	55,014	28	32,879	1,771,295	43,646	1,727,649
4. Baluchistan .. .. .. (*Districts and Administered Territories*).	54,228	12	1,425	90,116	15,559	74,557
5. Bengal	77,521	139	86,618	9,743,944	789,218	8,954,726
6. Bihar and Orissa	83,054	78	83,402	7,222,758	341,940	6,880,818
Bihar	*42,335*	*53*	*47,165*	*4,795,811*	*232,801*	*4,563,010*
Orissa	*13,706*	*9*	*15,523*	*1,134,679*	*40,805*	*1,093,874*
Chota Nagpur	*27,013*	*16*	*20,714*	*1,292,268*	*68,334*	*1,223,934*
7. Bombay	123,679	217	26,634	4,323,165	858,166	3,464,999
Bombay Presidency	*77,221*	*184*	*21,484*	*3,571,958*	*703,566*	*2,868,392*
Sind	*46,378*	*30*	*5,150*	*745,079*	*148,472*	*596,607*
Aden	*80*	*3*	..	*6,128*	*6,128*	..
8. Burma	233,492	92	32,387	3,140,423	314,668	2,825,755
9. Central Provinces and Berar	99,920	112	39,756	3,168,788	353,787	2,815,001
Central Provinces	*82,153*	*70*	*33,825*	*2,439,990*	*244,336*	*2,195,654*
Berar	*17,767*	*42*	*5,931*	*728,798*	*109,451*	*619,347*
10. Coorg	1,593	2	378	33,906	1,942	31,964
11. Delhi	573	6	307	138,875	98,483	40,392
12. Madras	142,277	340	51,487	9,248,879	1,136,393	8,112,486
13. North-West Frontier Province .. .. (*Districts and Administered Territories*).	13,518	27	2,830	486,876	73,790	413,086
14. Punjab	99,200	199	34,630	4,894,035	607,281	4,286,754
15. United Provinces of Agra and Oudh ..	106,248	441	105,640	10,142,209	1,235,767	8,906,442
Agra	*82,094*	*367*	*81,311*	*7,393,844*	*1,033,806*	*6,360,038*
Oudh	*24,154*	*74*	*24,329*	*2,748,365*	*201,961*	*2,546,404*
States and Agencies	**712,508**	**877**	**197,472**	**16,529,036**	**2,027,571**	**14,501,465**
16. Assam States	12,320	2	2,847	127,439	20,843	106,596
Manipur	*8,620*	*1*	*1,372*	*89,151*	*17,463*	*71,688*
Khasi States	*3,700*	*1**	*1,475*	*38,288*	*3,380*	*34,908*
17. Baluchistan States	80,410	5	2,076	76,528	2,386	74,142
18. Baroda State	8,164	50	2,920	562,798	136,254	426,544
19. Bengal States	5,434	5	4,582	189,131	5,538	183,593
20. Bihar and Orissa States	28,648	7	19,378	952,141	10,772	941,369
21. Bombay States	27,994	81	8,838	893,084	125,174	767,910
22. Central India Agency	51,597	56	23,252	1,433,711	169,626	1,264,085
23. Central Provinces States	31,175	10	8,960	423,234	15,981	407,253
24. Gwalior State	26,367	43	10,852	767,830	97,655	670,175
25. Hyderabad State	82,698	135	21,697	3,312,222	395,482	2,916,740
26. Jammu and Kashmir State	84,516	39	8,903	671,638	60,942	610,696
27. Madras States Agency	10,698	69	4,711	1,230,403	141,752	1,088,651
Cochin State	*1,480*	*12*	*272*	*207,563*	*32,506*	*175,057*
Travancore State	*7,625*	*46*	*3,936*	*929,930*	*93,196*	*836,734*
Other Madras States	*1,593*	*11*	*503*	*92,910*	*16,050*	*76,860*
28. Mysore State	29,326	108	16,483	1,311,445	205,567	1,105,878
29. North-West Frontier Province .. .. (*Agencies and Tribal Areas*).	22,838	..	..	..	..	..
30. Punjab States	5,820	4	2,610	95,112	3,368	91,744
31. Punjab States Agency	31,241	43	13,451	954,505	103,650	850,855
32. Rajputana Agency	129,059	145	33,688	2,392,110	308,271	2,083,839
33. Sikkim State	2,818	..	367	27,101	..	27,101
34. United Provinces States	5,943	9	5,361	252,368	25,121	227,247
35. Western India States Agency	35,442	66	6,496	856,236	199,189	657,047

*The Shillong Municipality lies partly in British and partly in non-British territory

and Population.

Population.								
Persons.			Males.			Females.		
Total. 8	Urban. 9	Rural. 10	Total. 11	Urban. 12	Rural. 13	Total. 14	Urban. 15	Rural. 16
352,837,778	38,985,427	313,852,351	181,828,923	21,485,055	160,343,868	171,008,855	17,500,372	153,508,483
271,526,9×8	29,658,469	241,868,464	139,931,556	16,603,709	123,327,847	131,595,377	13,054,760	118,540,617
560,292	180,199	380,093	296,081	98,874	197,207	264,211	81,325	182,886
29 463	..	29,463	19,702	..	19,702	9,761	..	9,761
19,223	..	19,223	14,258	..	14,258	4,965	..	4,965
10,240	..	10,240	5,444	..	5,444	4,796	..	4,796
8,622,251	213,421	8,408,830	4,537,206	135,320	4,401,886	4,085,045	78,101	4,006,944
463,508	92,025	371,483	270,004	65,913	204,091	193,504	26,112	167,392
50,114,002	3,684,330	46,429,672	26,041,698	2,301,537	23,740,161	24,072,304	1,382,793	22,689,511
37,677,576	1,653,837	36,023,739	18,794,138	908,690	17,885,448	18,883,438	745,147	18,138,291
25,727,500	1,152,117	24,575,383	12,896,660	633,488	12,263,172	12,830,840	518,629	12,312,211
5,306,142	191,429	5,114,713	2,549,251	102,777	2,446,474	2,756,891	88,652	2,668,239
6,643,934	310,291	6,333,643	3,348,227	172,425	3,175,802	3,295,707	137,866	3,157,841
21,930,601	4,953,363	16,977,238	11,535,903	2,794,419	8,741,484	10,394,698	2,158,944	8,235,754
17,992,053	4,202,578	13,789,475	9,322,604	2,355,773	6,966,831	8,669,449	1,846,805	6,822,644
3,887,070	699,307	3,187,763	2,180,954	406,301	1,774,653	1,706,116	293,006	1,413,110
51,478	51,478	..	32,345	32,345	..	19,133	19,133	..
14,667,146	1,520,037	13,147,109	7,490,601	903,980	6,586,621	7,176,545	616,057	6,560,488
15,50·,723	1,688,470	13,819,253	7,761,818	895,282	6,866,536	7,745,905	793,188	6,952,717
12,065,885	1,160,357	10,905,528	6,002,239	614,165	5,388,074	6,063,646	546,192	5,517,454
3,441,838	528,113	2,913,725	1,759,579	281,117	1,478,462	1,682,259	246,996	1,435,263
163,327	9,827	153,500	90,575	5,848	84,727	72,752	3,979	68,773
636,246	447,442	188,804	369,497	267,979	101,518	266,749	179,463	87,286
46,740,107	6,337,256	40,402,851	23,082,999	3,179,721	19,903,278	23,657,108	3,157,535	20,499,573
2,425,076	386,177	2,038,899	1,315,818	235,126	1,080,692	1,109,258	151,051	958,207
23,580,852	3,067,464	20,513,388	12,880,510	1,805,872	11,074,638	10,700,342	1,261,592	9,438,750
48,408,763	5,424,621	42,984,142	25,445,006	3,005,148	22,439,858	22,963,757	2,419,473	20,544,284
35,613,784	4,499,908	31,113,876	18,805,132	2,489,610	16,315,522	16,808,652	2,010,298	14,798,354
12,794,979	924,713	11,870,266	6,639,874	515,538	6,124,336	6,155,105	409,175	5,745,930
81,310,845	9,326,958	71,983,887	41,897,367	4,881,346	37,016,021	39,413,478	4,445,612	34,967,866
625,606	102,496	523,110	306,927	49,136	257,791	318,679	53,360	265,319
445,6?6	85,804	359,802	215,815	40,157	175,658	229,791	45,647	184,144
180,000	16,692	163,308	91,112	8,979	82,133	88,888	7,713	81,175
405,109	10,577	394,532	218,410	5,648	212,762	186,699	4,929	181,770
2,443,007	523,003	1,920,004	1,257,817	272,552	985,265	1,185,190	250,451	934,739
973,336	27,610	945,726	516,162	16,672	499,490	457,174	10,938	446,236
4,652,007	45,715	4,606,292	2,288,422	23,105	2,265,317	2,363,585	22,610	2,340,975
4,468,396	607,463	3,860,933	2,288,623	314,672	1,973,951	2,179,773	292,791	1,886,982
6,632,790	677,670	5,955,120	3,405,438	363,490	3,041,948	3,227,352	314,180	2,913,172
2,483,214	75,065	2,408,149	1,235,385	37,361	1,198,024	1,247,829	37,704	1,210,125
3,523,?70	395,309	3,127,761	1,867,031	214,586	1,652,445	1,656,039	180,723	1,475,316
14,436,148	1,616,981	12,819,167	7,370,010	836,874	6,533,136	7,066,138	780,107	6,286,031
3,646,243	342,314	3,303,929	1,938,338	192,199	1,746,139	1,707,905	150,115	1,557,790
6,754,484	837,509	5,916,975	3,373,032	424,851	2,948,181	3,381,452	412,658	2,968,794
1,205,016	206,340	998,676	589,813	104,231	485,582	615,203	102,109	513,094
5,095,973	551,788	4,544,185	2,565,073	282,180	2,282,893	2,530,900	269,608	2,261,292
453,495	79,381	374,114	218,146	38,440	179,706	235,349	40,941	194,408
6,557,302	,045,042	5,512,260	3,353,963	546,822	2,807,141	3,203,339	498,220	2,705,119
2,259,288	..	2,259,288	1,212,347	..	1,212,347	1,046,941	..	1,046,941
437,787	14,534	423,253	229,290	7,907	221,383	208,497	6,627	201,870
4,472,218	439,451	4,032,767	2,451,394	251,470	2,199,924	2,020,824	187,981	1,832,843
11,225,712	1,556,305	9,669,407	5,885,028	813,605	5,071,423	5,340,684	742,700	4,597,984
109,808	..	109,808	55,825	..	55,825	53,983	..	53,983
1,206,070	126,138	1,079,932	618,171	67,432	550,739	587,899	58,706	529,193
3,999,250	883,776	3,115,474	2,025,754	442,964	1,582,790	1,973,496	440,812	1,532,684

ınd has been ıntegrally included against Khasi States.

Details for Principal States in Agencies and Provincial Groups.

Name of State and Province.	Area in square miles.	Towns and villages.	Occupied houses.	Population. Persons.	Males.	Females.
Assam States—						
Manipur	8,620	1,373	89,151	445,606	215,815	229,791
Baluchistan States—						
Kalat..	73,278	1,801	65,007	342,101	184,915	157,186
Bengal States—						
Cooch Behar	1,318	1,204	116,813	590,886	313,230	277,656
Tripura	4,116	3,383	72,318	382,450	202,932	179,518
Bihar and Orissa States—						
Mayurbhanj	4,243	3,709	169,674	889,603	442,378	447,225
Bombay States—						
Kolhapur	3,217	1,054	182,464	957,137	490,336	466,801
Mahi Kantha Agency	3,124	1,866	114,860	518,164	263,398	254,766
Rewa Kantha Agency	4,968	2,992	169,412	888,086	459,133	428,953
Southern Mahratta States ..	3,036	612	142,697	691,111	351,520	339,591
Burma States—						
Federated Shan States	56,335	17,173	311,673	1,506,337	773,120	733,217
Central India Agency—						
Bhopal	6,902	3,005	168,489	729,955	377,961	351,994
Dhar	1,784	721	51,650	243,430	123,775	119,655
Indore	9,518	3,661	298,696	1,318,237	689,655	628,582
Orchha	2,080	802	74,237	314,661	163,272	151,389
Rewa	13,000	6,466	315,005	1,587,445	795,381	792,064
Central Provinces States—						
Bastar	13,062	2,443	91,143	524,721	263,248	261,473
Surguja	6,055	1,654	72,488	501,939	254,923	247,016
Madras States Agency—						
Pudukkottai	1,179	435	81,565	400,694	191,134	209,560
Punjab States Agency—						
Bahawalpur	15,003	2,376	211,462	984,612	545,103	439,509
Patiala	5,942	3,539	343,998	1,625,520	900,597	724,923
Rajputana Agency—						
Alwar	3,158	1,765	154,310	749,751	396,261	353,490
Bharatpur	1,978	1,323	104,246	486,954	263,325	223,629
Bikaner	23,317	2,757	185,418	936,218	501,153	435,065
Bundi	2,220	813	48,335	216,722	113,101	103,621
Dholpur	1,221	528	54,905	254,986	140,497	114,489
Jaipur	15,579	5,912	566,662	2,631,775	1,387,067	1,244,708
Kotah	5,684	2,529	153,688	685,804	355,056	330,748
Marwar	35,016	4,151	449,459	2,125,982	1,109,912	1,016,070
Mewar	12,694	8,085	334,790	1,566,910	807,184	759,726
Tonk	2,553	1,281	71,488	317,360	164,401	152,959
United Provinces States—						
Benares	870	1,368	73,760	391,272	194,236	197,036
Rampur	893	1,084	104,137	465,225	250,618	214,607
Tehri-Garhwal	4,180	2,918	74,471	349,573	173,317	176,256
Western India States Agency—						
Cutch	8,250	954	122,805	514,307	248,845	265,462
Gondal	1,024	175	44,061	205,846	103,758	102,088
Bhavanagar	2,961	655	109,261	500,274	257,156	243,118
Junagadh	3,284	835	11,513	545,152	278,866	266,286
Palanpur	1,769	549	60,471	264,179	136,445	127,734
Nawanagar	3,791	690	81,119	409,192	205,767	203,425

Areas under British Administration in certain Indian States (exclusive of Administered Territories such as Berar and parts of Merwara, and of Railway* lands over which jurisdiction has been ceded).

Tract.	Area in square miles.	Population. Persons.	Males.	Females.
1. *Assam—*				
British Reserve in Manipur	0·7	3,625	2,212	1,413
The Shillong (Rifle Range) Cantonment	0·1	..	..	..
2. *Bombay Presidency—*				
Sadar Bazar in the Mahi Kantha Agency	1·0	1,978	1,061	917
Kolhapur Civil Station	0·3	226	130	96
3. *Baroda State*—Baroda Cantonment	1·0	3,221	2,021	1,200
4. *Central India Agency—*				
Mhow Cantonment	5·8	31,177	17,496	13,681
Nowgong Cantonment	6·6	5,794	3,166	2,628
Indore Residency	1·4	15,197	8,874	6,323
Baghelkund Agency Headquarters	0·1	210	143	67
Bundelkhand Agency Headquarters	1·0	665	430	235
Other Areas	0·05	118	74	44
5. *Gwalior State—*				
Nimach Cantonment	4·1	9,542	5,063	4,479
Gwalior Residency Headquarters	1·0	181	120	61
6. *Hyderabad State—*				
Residency Bazars	0·1	14,472	8,116	6,356
Secunderabad including Bolarum Cantonment	19·0	120,801	64,738	56,063
Aurangabad Cantonment	3·5	7,582	4,490	3,092
7. *Mysore State*—Civil and Military Station of Bangalore ..	14·0	134,113	69,409	64,704
8. *Punjab*—Kasumpti Municipality	0·1	108	74	34
9. *Rajputana Agency*—Abu District	6·0	4,532	2,753	1,779
10. *Western India States Agency—*				
Rajkot Civil Station	2·0	11,627	6,404	5,223
Wadhwan Civil Station	1·0	13,344	7,185	6,159

* Details of Railway lands in States over which jurisdiction has been ceded will be found in notification No. 555-1, dated the 30th September 1930, of the Foreign and Political Department.

TABLE II.

Variation in Population during fifty years.

1. The population enumerated at previous censuses has been corrected as far as possible in order to allow for subsequent inter-provincial transfers. The adjustments in the 1921 population consequent on such transfers are detailed below. In the case of the totals of the Provinces and States not detailed in this statement no adjustment is needed.

Province or State.	Population as given in Imperial Table II of 1921.	Adjusted 1921 Population.	Increase or decrease in population.	Details of Transfers.
Bengal	47,592,462	47,599,233	+ 6,771	Thirteen inhabited *Mauzas* transferred from Bihar and Orissa to Bengal with an aggregate population of 6,948 persons. An interchange between these provinces of two villages of unequal populations resulted in a decrease to Bengal of 177 persons. *An uninhabited area of 1 square mile was also transferred from United Provinces to Bihar and Orissa on account of diluvion.
*Bihar and Orissa ..	37,961,858	37,955,087	—6,771	
United Provinces ..	46,510,668	46,509,950	—718	Fractions of a square mile were transferred from the United Provinces by diluvion and alluvion by the Jumna to the Punjab—Gurgaon and Karnal being effected in that Province, Muzaffarnagar and Bulandshar in the former. These areas taken together, at the time of the transfer were populated by 454 persons, which represents the only such alteration to the Punjab in the decade. A further 264 persons were transferred to Delhi Province from Meerut (U. P.) as a result of a change in the boundary between these two provinces.
Punjab	25,101,060	25,101,514	+454	
Delhi	488,188	488,452	+264	
Rajputana Agency ..	9,844,384	9,831,755	—12,629	Nandwai Pargana of Indore transferred to the C. I. Agency with a population of 3,682 persons, together with the Pargana of Gangapur transferred to Gwalior State with a population of 9,401. Nimrol (Gwalior), with a population of 454 persons, has been included in the census of the Rajputana Agency. Certain villages have been transferred to Indore and Dhar from Gwalior State in exchange for certain portions of Sundarsi, together with Pathari Estate. The population involved in this exchange was 6,658 persons—4,252 persons being added to Central India and 2,406 to Gwalior State.
Central India Agency	5,997,023	6,002,551	+5,528	
Gwalior State ..	3,186,075	3,193,176	+7,101	

2. Tracts enumerated for the first time at this census are noted below ; the figures in brackets relate to population :—

The 'Malandri' tract in Swat Territory (1,020) together with certain desert areas on the tribal borders of the North-West Frontier Province (estimated in 1921). An area in the Chin Hills district (18,327) in Burma. The Melomi-Primi area (4,620) in the Sadr Sub-division, and certain villages (2,200) in the Mokokchung Sub-division of the Naga Hills ; the area known as the 'Zongling' area (1,696) to the south of the Lushai Hills, and certain Abor and Naga villages (7,195) in the Sadiya Frontier Tract, all in Assam.

Total .. 35,058

Corresponding details for previous decades will be found on the fly-leaf of Imperial Table II of the 1921 India Report—Part II, or may be ascertained from the provincial reports. The figures below represent the total populations of areas included for the first time at each successive census :—

1931.	1921.	1911.	1901.	1891.	1881.
35,058	86,633	1,793,365	2,672,077	5,713,902	33,139,081

3. The cause of the discrepancy in the sex details of the 1881 population of the North-West Frontier Province referred to in the first paragraph of the fly-leaves to the corresponding India tables of the two previous censuses, has been traced, and reconciled in the present table.

4. A reduction of 6 sq. miles in the U. P., with a population of 130 persons (M. 78, F. 52) in 1921, has been excluded in 1931, the area in question having been ceded to Nepal.

5. Additional details for certain States which are not shown separately in the body of the table are given on page 10 of this volume.

Table II.—Variation in

	Province, State or Agency.	Persons. 1931.	1921.	1911.	1901.	1891.	1881.
	1	2	3	4	5	6	7
	INDIA	**352,837,778**	**318,942,480**	**315,156,396**	**294,361,056**	**287,314,671**	**253,896,330**
	Provinces	**271,526,933**	**246,856,191**	**243,797,647**	**231,142,489**	**220,765,285**	**198,448,631**
1	1. Ajmer-Merwara	560,292	495,271	501,395	476,912	542,358	460,722
2	2. Andaman and Nicobar Islands ..	29,463	27,086	26,459	24,649	15,609	14,628
	3. Assam	8,622,251	7,459,128	6,578,768	5,725,871	5,363,777	4,811,572
3	4. Baluchistan (*Districts and Administered Territories*). ..	463,508	420,648	414,412	382,106	..	..
4	5. Bengal	50,114,002	46,702,307	45,489,697	42,147,895	39,095,855	36,322,302
	6. Bihar and Orissa	37,677,576	33,995,418	34,482,452	33,236,045	32,869,962	30,982,615
5	*Bihar*	*25,727,500*	*23,373,517*	*23,745,337*	*23,353,474*	*23,574,943*	*22,412,662*
6	*Orissa*	*5,306,142*	*4,968,873*	*5,131,753*	*4,982,142*	*4,666,227*	*4,343,964*
	Chota Nagpur	*6,643,934*	*5,653,028*	*5,605,362*	*4,900,429*	*4,628,792*	*4,225,989*
	7. Bombay	21,930,601	19,348,219	19,696,266	18,574,289	18,904,606	16,514,923
7	*Bombay Presidency*	*17,992,053*	*16,012,342*	*16,136,666*	*15,319,405*	*15,985,427*	*14,063,006*
	Sind	*3,887,070*	*3,279,377*	*3,513,435*	*3,210,910*	*2,875,100*	*2,417,057*
	Aden	*51,478*	*56,500*	*46,165*	*43,974*	*44,079*	*34,860*
	8. Burma	14,667,146	13,212,192	12,115,217	10,490,624	7,722,053	3,736,771
8	9. Central Provinces and Berar ..	15,507,723	13,912,760	13,916,158	11,971,328	13,048,845	11,943,251
9	*Central Provinces*	*12,065,885*	*10,837,444*	*10,858,996*	*9,217,312*	*10,151,354*	*9,270,578*
	Berar	*3,441,838*	*3,075,316*	*3,057,162*	*2,754,016*	*2,897,491*	*2,672,673*
10	10. Coorg	163,327	163,838	174,976	180,607	173,055	178,302
11	11. Delhi	636,246	488,452	413,851	405,819	373,136	350,848
12	12. Madras	46,740,107	42,318,985	41,405,404	38,229,654	35,644,428	30,841,154
13	13. North-West Frontier Province (*Districts and Administered Territories*). ..	2,425,076	2,251,340	2,196,933	2,041,534	1,857,519	1,575,943
14	14. Punjab	23,580,852	20,685,478	19,579,047	19,942,715	18,652,614	16,939,312
15	15. United Provinces of Agra and Oudh ..	48,408,763	45,375,069	46,806,612	47,312,441	46,501,468	43,776,288
	Agra	*35,613,784*	*33,208,427*	*34,248,608*	*34,479,273*	*33,850,544*	*32,388,456*
	Oudh	*12,794,979*	*12,166,642*	*12,558,004*	*12,833,168*	*12,650,924*	*11,387,832*
16	**States and Agencies** ..	**81,310,845**	**72,086,289**	**71,358,749**	**63,218,567**	**66,549,386**	**55,447,699**
	16. Assam States	625,606	531,118	481,753	401,074	114,103*	317,819*
17	17. Baluchistan States	405,109	378,977	420,291	428,640	..	..
18	18. Baroda State	2,443,007	2,126,522	2,032,798	1,952,692	2,415,396	2,182,158
19	19. Bengal States	973,336	896,926	822,565	740,299	716,310	698,261
20	20. Bihar and Orissa States	4,652,007	3,959,669	3,945,209	3,314,474	3,028,018	2,410,611
21	21. Bombay States	4,468,396	3,867,819	3,863,473	3,609,431	4,099,470	3,485,047
22	22. Central India Agency ..	6,632,790	6,002,551	6,133,764	5,435,038	10,154,521†	9,094,057†
23	23. Central Provinces States ..	2,483,214	2,066,900	2,117,152	1,631,264	1,712,689	1,387,406
24	24. Gwalior State	3,523,070	3,193,176	3,235,303	3,073,651	..	..
25	25. Hyderabad State	14,436,148	12,471,770	13,374,676	11,141,142	11,537,040	9,845,594
26	26. Jammu and Kashmir State ..	3,646,243	3,320,518	3,158,126	2,905,578	2,543,952	..
27	27. Madras States Agency ..	6,754,484	5,460,312	4,811,841	4,188,086	3,700,622	3,344,849
	Cochin State	*1,205,016*	*979,080*	*918,110*	*812,025*	*722,906*	*600,278*
	Travancore State	*5,095,973*	*4,006,062*	*3,428,975*	*2,952,157*	*2,557,736*	*2,401,158*
	Other Madras States	*453,495*	*475,170*	*464,756*	*423,904*	*419,980*	*343,413*
28	28. Mysore State	6,557,302	5,978,892	5,806,193	5,539,399	4,943,604	4,186,188
29	29. North-West Frontier Province (*Agencies and Tribal Areas*). ..	2,259,288	2,825,136	1,622,094	83,962	..	..
30	30. Punjab States	437,787	408,019	412,173	411,764	392,525	360,423
31	31. Punjab States Agency	4,472,218	4,008,017	3,800,621	4,012,634	3,870,755	3,501,260
32	32. Rajputana Agency	11,225,712	9,831,755	10,518,345	9,842,482	12,153,631	10,102,105
33	33. Sikkim State	109,808	81,721	87,920	59,014	30,458	..
34	34. United Provinces States	1,206,070	1,134,881	1,189,874	1,163,454	1,179,947	1,099,460
35	35. Western India States Agency ..	3,999,250	3,541,610	3,524,578	3,284,489	3,956,345	3,432,461

* Figures for Khasi States only.
† Includes Gwalior State.

Population during fifty years.

Variation { Increase (+), Decrease (—).					Net Variation in period 1881-1931. Increase (+), Decrease (—).	
1921 to 1931.	1911 to 1921.	1901 to 1911.	1891 to 1901.	1881 to 1891.		
8	9	10	11	12	13	
+33,895,298	**+3,786,084**	**+20,795,340**	**+7,046,385**	**+33,418,341**	**+98,941,448**	
+24,670,742	**+3,058,544**	**+12,655,158**	**+10,377,204**	**+22,316,654**	**+73,078,302**	
+65,021	—6,124	+24,483	—65,446	+81,636	+99,570	1
+2,377	+627	+1,810	+9,040	+981	+14,835	2
+1,163,123	+880,360	+852,897	+362,094	+552,205	+3,810,679	3
+42,860	+6,236	+32,306	..	..		4
+3,411,695	+1,212,610	+3,341,802	+3,052,040	+2,773,553	+13,791,700	5
+3,682,158	—487,034	+1,246,407	+366,083	+1,887,347	+6,694,961	6
+2,353,983	—371,820	+391,863	—221,469	+1,162,281	+3,314,838	
+337,269	—162,880	+149,611	+315,915	+322,263	+962,178	
+990,906	+47,666	+704,933	+271,637	+402,803	+2,417,945	
+2,582,382	—348,047	+1,121,977	—330,317	+2,389,683	+5,415,678	7
+1,979,711	—124,324	+817,261	—666,022	+1,922,421	+3,929,047	
+607,693	—234,058	+302,525	+335,810	+458,043	+1,470,013	
—5,022	+10,335	+2,191	—105	+9,219	+16,618	
+1,454,954	+1,096,975	+1,624,593	+2,768,571	+3,985,282	+10,930,375	8
+1,594,963	—3,398	+1,944,830	—1,077,517	+1,105,594	+3,564,472	9
+1,228,441	—21,552	+1,641,684	—934,042	+880,776	+2,795,307	
+366,522	+18,154	+303,146	—143,475	+224,818	+769,165	
—511	—11,138	—5,631	+7,552	—5,247	—14,975	10
+147,794	+74,601	+8,032	+32,683	—22,288	+285,398	11
+4,421,122	913,581	+3,175,750	+2,585,226	+4,803,274	+15,898,953	12
+173,736	+54,407	+155,399	+184,015	+281,576	+849,133	13
+2,895,374	+1,106,431	—363,668	+1,290,101	+1,713,302	+6,641,540	14
+3,033,694	—1,431,543	—505,829	+810,973	+2,725,180	+4,632,475	15
+2,405,357	—1,040,181	—230,665	+628,729	+1,462,088	+3,225,328	
+628,337	—391,362	—275,164	+182,244	+1,263,092	+1,407,147	
+9,224,556	**+727,540**	**+8,140,182**	**—3,330,819**	**+11,101,687**	**+25,863,146**	
+94,488	+49,365	+80,679		..	+307,787	16
+26,132	—41,314	—8,349	..	..	..	17
+316,485	+93,724	+80,106	—462,704	+233,238	+260,849	18
+76,410	+74,361	+82,266	+23,989	+18,049	+275,075	19
+692,338	+14,400	+630,735	+286,456	+617,407	+2,241,396	20
+600,577	+4,346	+254,042	—490,039	+614,423	+983,349	21
+630,239	—131,213	+698,726	—4,719,483	+1,060,464	—2,461,267	22
+416,314	—50,252	+485,888	—81,425	+325,283	+1,095,808	23
+329,894	—42,127	+161,652	..	..	..	24
+1,964,378	—902,906	+2,233,534	—395,898	+1,691,446	+4,590,554	25
+325,725	+162,392	+252,548	+361,626	..	..	26
+1,294,172	+648,471	+623,755	+487,464	+355,773	+3,409,635	27
+225,936	+60,970	+106,085	+89,119	+122,628	+604,738	
+1,089,911	+577,087	+476,818	+394,421	+156,578	+2,694,815	
—21,675	+10,414	+40,852	+3,924	+76,567	+110,082	
+578,410	+172,699	+266,794	+595,795	+757,416	+2,371,114	28
—565,848	+1,203,042	+1,538,132	..	..	..	29
+29,768	—4,154	+409	+19,239	+32,102	+77,364	30
+464,201	+207,396	—212,013	+141,879	+369,495	+970,958	31
+1,393,957	—686,590	+675,863	—2,311,149	+2,051,526	+1,123,607	32
+28,087	—6,199	+28,906	+28,556	..	..	33
+71,189	—54,993	+26,420	—16,493	+80,487	+106,610	34
+457,640	+17,032	+240,089	—671,856	+523,884	+566,789	35

Table II.—Variation

Province, State or Agency.	Males. 1931.	1921.	1911.	1901.	1891.	1881.
1	14	15	16	17	18	19
INDIA	**181,828,923**	**163,995,554**	**161,338,935**	**149,951,824**	**146,769,629**	**129,949,300**
Provinces	**139,931,556**	**126,798,887**	**124,641,244**	**117,426,782**	**112,335,393**	**101,119,128**
1. Ajmer-Merwara	296,081	269,566	266,198	251,026	288,325	248,844
2. Andaman and Nicobar Islands ..	19,702	20,793	19,570	18,695	13,375	12,640
3. Assam	4,537,206	3,887,880	3,401,309	2,948,331	2,765,702	2,471,182
4. Baluchistan (*Districts and Administered Territories*).	270,004	255,014	239,181	219,523	..	..
5. Bengal	26,041,698	24,154,563	23,368,445	21,491,387	19,800,792	18,206,758
6. Bihar and Orissa	18,794,138	16,760,525	16,856,289	16,199,376	16,071,266	15,274,742
Bihar	*12,896,660*	*11,580,305*	*11,602,792*	*11,360,502*	*11,502,398*	*11,036,849*
Orissa	*2,549,251*	*2,350,793*	*2,476,284*	*2,429,608*	*2,291,095*	*2,144,324*
Chota Nagpur	*3,348,227*	*2,829,427*	*2,777,213*	*2,409,266*	*2,277,773*	*2,093,569*
7. Bombay	11,535,903	10,176,969	10,258,017	9,591,005	9,795,898	8,533,932
Bombay Presidency	*9,322,604*	*8,301,310*	*8,287,403*	*7,798,685*	*8,194,561*	*7,192,596*
Sind	*2,180,954*	*1,837,265*	*1,939,324*	*1,761,790*	*1,570,423*	*1,318,601*
Aden	*32,345*	*38,394*	*31,290*	*30,530*	*30,914*	*22,735*
8. Burma	7,490,601	6,756,969	6,183,494	5,342,033	3,937,936	1,991,005
9. Central Provinces and Berar .. .	7,761,818	6,951,399	6,930,315	5,926,293	6,573,493	6,056,252
Central Provinces	*6,002,239*	*5,385,525*	*5,379,701*	*4,531,993*	*5,081,667*	*4,675,760*
Berar	*1,759,579*	*1,565,874*	*1,550,614*	*1,394,300*	*1,491,826*	*1,380,492*
10. Coorg	90,575	89,501	97,279	100,258	95,907	100,439
11. Delhi	369,497	281,777	230,865	217,921	200,514	185,002
12. Madras	23,082,999	20,870,749	20,382,955	18,851,329	17,626,390	15,264,417
13. North-West Frontier Province .. (*Districts and Administered Territories*).	1,315,818	1,229,316	1,182,102	1,105,709	1,007,653	866,343
14. Punjab	12,880,510	11,306,507	10,770,985	10,734,532	10,056,695	9,167,186
15. United Provinces of Agra and Oudh ..	25,445,006	23,787,359	24,454,240	24,429,364	24,101,447	22,740,386
Agra	*18,805,132*	*17,488,690*	*17,969,540*	*17,861,158*	*17,610,646*	*16,888,682*
Oudh	*6,639,874*	*6,298,669*	*6,484,700*	*6,568,206*	*6,490,801*	*5,851,704*
States and Agencies ..	**41,897,367**	**37,196,667**	**36,697,691**	**32,525,042**	**34,434,236**	**28,830,172**
16. Assam States	306,927	261,348	237,337	195,686	54,546	155,546
17. Baluchistan States	218,410	205,986	227,238	225,997	..	..
18. Baroda State	1,257,817	1,100,564	1,055,935	1,008,634	1,252,983	1,138,139
19. Bengal States	516,162	477,143	438,368	393,877	374,053	363,136
20. Bihar and Orissa States	2,288,422	1,946,186	1,955,125	1,653,592	1,525,643	1,224,568
21. Bombay States	2,288,623	1,974,121	1,961,282	1,830,166	2,087,547	1,779,221
22. Central India Agency	3,405,438	3,071,770	3,107,903	2,754,101	5,312,925	4,794,220
23. Central Provinces States	1,235,385	1,029,398	1,053,707	812,034	862,567	700,951
24. Gwalior State	1,867,031	1,695,355	1,699,808	1,612,623		..
25. Hyderabad State	7,370,010	6,345,071	6,797,118	5,673,629	5,873,129	5,002,137
26. Jammu and Kashmir State	1,938,338	1,757,122	1,674,367	1,542,057	1,353,229	
27. Madras States Agency	3,373,032	2,744,921	2,411,758	2,098,048	1,853,976	1,662,540
Cochin State	*589,813*	*482,959*	*457,342*	*405,200*	*361,904*	*301,815*
Travancore State	*2,565,073*	*2,032,553*	*1,731,363*	*1,490,165*	*[illegible],290,415*	*1,197,134*
Other Madras States	*218,146*	*229,409*	*223,053*	*202,683*	*[illegible]01,657*	*163,591*
28. Mysore State	3,353,963	3,047,117	2,934,621	2,797,024	2,483,451	2,085,842
29. North-West Frontier Province .. (*Agencies and Tribal Areas*).	1,212,347	1,517,791	864,876	53,608	..	..
30. Punjab States	229,290	215,633	216,853	217,794	209,124	194,597
31. Punjab States Agency	2,451,394	2,210,150	2,106,055	2,192,015	2,114,967	1,917,706
32. Rajputana Agency	5,885,028	5,178,428	5,509,023	5,165,931	6,427,145	5,461,527
33. Sikkim State	55,825	41,492	45,059	30,795	15,742	..
34. United Provinces States	618,171	581,230	609,309	592,190	602,548	569,438
35. Western India States Agency ..	2,025,754	1,795,841	1,791,949	1,675 241	2,030,681	[illegible]

in Population during fifty years—*concld.*

Females.						
1931.	1921.	1911.	1901.	1891.	1881.	
20	21	22	23	24	25	
171,008,855	**154,946,926**	**153,817,461**	**144,409,232**	**140,545,042**	**123,947,080**	
131,595,377	**120,057,304**	**119,156,403**	**118,715,707**	**108,429,892**	**97,329,508**	
264,211	225,705	235,197	225,886	254,033	211,878	1
9,761	6,293	6,889	5,954	2,234	1,988	2
4,085,045	3,571,248	3,177,459	2,777,540	2,598,075	2,340,390	3
193,504	165,634	175,231	162,583	..	..	4
24,072,304	22,547,744	22,121,252	20,656,508	19,295,063	18,115,544	5
18,883,438	17,234,893	17,626,163	17,036,669	16,798,696	15,707,873	6
12,830,840	*11,793,212*	*12,142,545*	*11,992,972*	*12,072,545*	*11,375,813*	
2,756,891	*2,618,080*	*2,655,469*	*2,552,534*	*2,375,132*	*2,199,640*	
3,295,707	*2,823,601*	*2,828,149*	*2,491,163*	*2,351,019*	*2,132,420*	
10,394,698	9,171,250	9,438,249	8,983,284	9,108,708	7,980,991	7
8,669,449	*7,711,032*	*7,849,263*	*7,520,720*	*7,790,866*	*6,870,410*	
1,706,116	*1,442,112*	*1,574,111*	*1,449,120*	*1,304,677*	*1,098,456*	
19,133	*18,106*	*14,875*	*13,444*	*13,165*	*12,125*	
7,176,545	6,455,223	5,931,723	5,148,591	3,784,117	1,745,766	8
7,745,905	6,961,361	6,985,843	6,045,035	6,475,352	5,886,999	9
6,063,646	*5,451,919*	*5,479,295*	*4,685,319*	*5,069,687*	*4,594,818*	
1,682,259	*1,509,442*	*1,506,548*	*1,359,716*	*1,405,665*	*1,292,181*	
72,752	74,337	77,697	80,349	77,148	77,863	10
266,749	206,675	182,986	187,898	172,622	165,846	11
23,657,108	21,448,236	21,022,449	19,378,325	18,018,038	15,576,737	12
1,109,258	1,022,024	1,014,831	935,825	849,866	709,600	13
10,700,342	9,378,971	8,808,062	9,208,183	8,595,919	7,772,126	14
22,963,757	21,587,710	22,352,372	22,883,077	22,400,021	21,035,902	15
16,808,652	*15,719,737*	*16,279,068*	*16,618,115*	*16,239,898*	*15,499,774*	
6,155,105	*5,867,973*	*6,073,304*	*6,264,962*	*6,160,123*	*5,536,128*	
39,413,478	**34,889,622**	**34,661,058**	**30,693,525**	**32,115,150**	**26,617,527**	
318,679	269,770	244,416	205,388	59,557	162,273	16
186,699	172,991	193,053	202,643	..	..	17
1,185,190	1,025,958	976,863	944,058	1,162,413	1,044,019	18
457,174	419,783	384,197	346,422	342,257	335,125	19
2,363,585	2,013,483	1,990,084	1,660,882	1,502,375	1,186,043	20
2,179,773	1,893,698	1,902,191	1,779,265	2,011,923	1,705,826	21
3,227,352	2,930,781	3,025,861	2,680,937	4,841,596	4,299,837	22
1,247,829	1,037,502	1,063,445	819,230	850,122	686,455	23
1,656,039	1,497,821	1,535,495	1,461,028	..	..	24
7,066,138	6,126,699	6,577,558	5,467,513	5,663,911	4,843,457	25
1,707,905	1,563,396	1,483,759	1,363,521	1,190,723	..	26
3,381,452	2,715,391	2,400,083	2,090,038	1,846,646	1,682,309	27
615.203	*496,121*	*460,768*	*406,825*	*361,002*	*298,463*	
2,530,900	*1,973,509*	*1,697,612*	*1,461,992*	*1,267,321*	*1,204,024*	
235,349	*245,761*	*241,703*	*221,221*	*218,323*	*179,822*	
3,203,339	2,931,775	2,871,572	2,742,375	2,460,153	2,100,346	28
1,046,941	1,307,345	757,218	30,354	..	..	29
208,497	192,386	195,320	193,970	183,401	165,826	30
2,020,824	1,797,867	1,694,566	1,820,619	1,755,788	1,582,554	31
5,340,684	4,653,327	5,009,322	4,676,551	5,726,486	4,640,578	32
53,983	40.229	42,861	28,219	14,716	..	33
587,899	553,651	580,565	571,264	577,399	530,022	34
1,973,496	1,745,769	1,732,629	1,609,248	1,925,684	1,651,857	35

Details of Variation in the Population of the Principal States.

Name of State and Province.	Persons. 1931.	1921.	1911.	1901.	1891.	1881.	Variation Increase (+), Decrease (—). 1921-1931.	1911-1921.	1901-1911.	1891-1901.	1881-1891.	Net Variation in period 1881-1931 Increase(+), Decrease(—).
1	2	3	4	5	6	7	8	9	10	11	12	13
Assam States—												
Manipur ..	445,606	384,016	346,222	284,465	..	221,070	+61,590	+37,794	+61,757	..	..	+224,536
Baluchistan States—												
Kalat ..	342,101	328,281	359,086	372,531	..	..	+13,820	—30,805	—13,445	..	..	..
Bengal States—												
Cooch Behar ..	590,886	592,489	592,952	566,974	578,868	602,624	—1,603	—463	+25,978	—11,894	—23,756	—11,738
Tripura ..	382,450	304,437	229,613	173,325	137,442	95,637	+78,013	+74,824	+56,288	+35,883	+41,805	+286,813
Bihar and Orissa States—												
Mayurbhanj	889,603	754,314	729,218	610,383	532,238	385,737	+135,289	+25,096	+118,835	+78,145	+146,501	+503,866
Bombay States—												
Kolhapur ..	957,137	833,726	833,441	910,011	913,131	800,189	+123,411	+285	—76,570	—3,120	+112,942	+156,948
Mahi Kantha Agency.	518,164	450,478	412,631	361,545	581,568	517,485	+67,686	+37,847	+51,086	—220,023	+64,083	+679
Rewa Kantha Agency.	888,086	753,058	665,099	479,065	733,506	549,892	+135,028	+87,959	+186,034	—254,441	+183,614	+338,194
Southern Maratha States.	691,111	608,362	618,139	626,084	639,270	523,753	+82,749	—9,777	—7,945	—13,186	+115,517	+167,358
Burma States—												
Federated Shan States.	1,506,337	1,433,542	1,348,740	1,136,359	17,378*	..	+72,795	+84,802	+212,381	..	..	..
Central India Agency—												
Bhopal ..	729,955	692,448	738,124	679,053	963,610	965,290	+37,507	—45,676	+59,071	—284,557	—1,680	—235,335
Dhar ..	243,430	229,771	191,788	171,434	..	..	+13,659	+37,983	+20,354	..	..	..
Indore ..	1,318,237	1,150,840	1,051,893	904,283	1,141,108	1,089,154	+167,397	+98,947	+147,610	—236,825	+51,954	+229,083
Orchha ..	314,661	284,948	330,032	321,678	333,020	311,514	+29,713	—45,084	+8,354	—11,342	+21,506	+3,147
Rewa ..	1,587,445	1,401,524	1,515,237	1,327,184	1,508,180	1,305,124	+185,921	—113,713	+188,053	—180,996	+203,056	+282,321
Central Provinces States—												
Bastar ..	524,721	464,407	433,310	306,501	310,884	196,248	+60,314	+31,097	+126,809	—4,383	+114,636	+328,473
Surguja ..	501,939	377,679	428,703	351,011	324,552	270,311	+124,260	—51,024	+77,692	+26,459	+54,241	+231,628
Madras States Agency—												
Pudukkottai ..	400,694	426,813	411,886	380,440	373,096	302,127	—26,119	+14,927	+31,446	+7,344	+70,969	+98,567
Punjab States Agency—												
Bahawalpur	984,612	781,191	780,641	720,877	650,042	573,494	+203,421	+550	+59,764	+70,835	+76,548	+411,118
Patiala ..	1,625,520	1,499,739	1,407,659	1,596,692	1,583,521	1,467,433	+125,781	+92,080	—189,033	+13,171	+116,088	+158,087
Rajputana Agency—												
Alwar ..	749,751	701,154	791,688	828,487	767,786	682,926	+48,597	—90,534	—36,799	+60,701	+84,860	+66,825
Bharatpur ..	486,954	496,437	558,785	626,665	640,303	645,540	—9,483	—62,348	—67,880	—13,638	—5,237	—158,586
Bikaner ..	936,218	659,685	700,983	584,755	832,065	509,077	+276,533	—41,298	+116,228	—247,310	+322,988	+427,141
Bundi ..	216,722	187,068	218,730	171,227	295,675	254,701	+29,654	—31,662	+47,503	—124,448	+40,974	—37,979
Dholpur ..	254,986	230,188	263,593	271,496	279,890	249,657	+24,798	—33,405	—7,903	—8,394	+30,233	+5,329
Jaipur ..	2,631,775	2,338,802	2,636,647	2,658,666	2,823,966	2,527,142	+292,973	—297,845	—22,019	—165,300	+296,824	+104,633
Kotah ..	685,804	630,060	639,089	544,879	718,771	707,402	+55,744	—9,029	+94,210	—173,892	+11,369	—21,598
Marwar ..	2,125,982	1,841,642	2,057,553	1,935,565	2,528,178	1,757,618	+284,340	—215,911	+121,988	—592,613	+770,560	+368,364
Mewar ..	1,566,910	1,366,980	1,281,284	1,018,805	1,710,579	1,443,144	+199,930	+85,696	+262,479	—691,774	+267,435	+123,766
Tonk ..	317,360	287,898	303,181	273,267	380,069	338,029	+29,462	—15,283	+29,914	—106,802	+42,040	—20,669
United Provinces States—												
Benares ..	391,272	362,860	357,838	361,357	387,456	357,710	+28,412	+5,022	—3,519	—26,099	+29,746	+33,562
Rampur ..	465,225	453,607	531,217	533,212	551,249	541,914	+11,618	—77,610	—1,995	—18,037	+9,335	—76,689
Tehri-Garhwal	349,573	318,414	300,819	268,885	241,242	199,836	+31,159	+17,595	+31,934	+27,643	+41,406	+149,737
Western India States Agency—												
Cutch ..	514,307	484,547	513,429	488,022	558,415	512,084	+29,760	—28,882	+25,407	—70,393	+46,331	+2,223
Gondal ..	205,846	167,071	161,916	162,859	161,036	135,604	+38,775	+5,155	—943	+1,823	+25,432	+70,242
Bhavanagar ..	500,274	426,404	441,367	412,664	467,282	400,323	+73,870	—14,963	+28,703	—54,618	+66,959	+99,951
Junagadh ..	545,152	465,493	434,222	395,428	484,190	387,499	+79,659	+31,271	+38,794	—88,762	+96,691	+157,653
Palanpur ..	264,179	236,694	226,250	222,627	274,864	234,402	+27,485	+10,444	+3,623	—52,237	+40,462	+29,777
Nawanagar ..	409,192	345,353	349,400	336,779	379,611	316,147	+63,839	—4,047	+12,621	—42,832	+63,464	+93,045

Name of State and Province.	Males. 1931.	1921.	1911.	1901.	1891.	1881.	Females. 1931.	1921.	1911.	1901.	1891.	1881.
1	14	15	16	17	18	19	20	21	22	23	24	25
Assam States—												
Manipur ..	215,815	188,119	170,666	139,632	...	109,557	229,791	195,897	175,556	144,833	...	111,513
Baluchistan States—												
Kalat ..	184,915	179,003	194,598	196,279	...	...	157,186	149,278	164,488	176,252	...	...
Bengal States—												
Cooch Behar ..	313,230	315,628	316,548	301,382	302,457	311,678	277,656	276,861	276,404	265,592	276,411	290,946
Tripura ..	202,932	161,515	121,820	92,495	71,596	51,458	179,518	142,922	107,793	80,830	65,846	44,179
Bihar and Orissa States—												
Mayurbhanj	442,378	374,319	362,570	303,266	265,880	194,827	447,225	379,995	366,648	307,117	266,358	190,910
Bombay States—												
Kolhapur ..	490,336	428,543	424,435	460,874	467,572	410,647	466,801	405,183	409,006	449,137	445,559	389,542
Mahi Kantha Agency.	263,398	226,974	208,922	182,368	296,646	266,566	254,766	223,504	203,709	179,177	284,922	250,919
Rewa Kantha Agency.	459,133	386,756	340,376	245,205	376,146	283,445	428,953	366,302	324,723	233,860	357,360	266,447
Southern Maratha States.	351,520	309,952	312,500	315,148	320,531	260,136	339,591	298,410	305,639	310,936	318,739	263,617
Burma States—												
Federated Shan States.	773,120	726,291	675,022	565,551	*10,833	...	733,217	707,251	673,718	570,808	*6,545	...
Central India Agency—												
Bhopal ..	377,961	358,135	374,716	340,144	497,969	504,309	351,994	334,313	363,408	338,909	465,641	460,981
Dhar ..	123,775	115,675	96,041	85,975	...	...	119,655	114,096	95,747	85,459	...	...
Indore ..	689,655	600,330	543,108	468,279	...	...	628,582	550,510	508,785	436,004	...	...
Orchha ..	163,272	147,466	168,633	165,747	172,989	162,611	151,389	137,482	161,399	155,931	160,031	148,903
Rewa ..	795,381	698,322	752,554	659,488	758,416	654,182	792,064	703,202	762,683	667,696	749,764	650,942
Central Provinces States—												
Bastar ..	263,248	234,824	218,015	155,683	159,656	103,046	261,473	229,583	215,295	150,818	151,228	93,202
Surguja ..	254,923	192,547	217,749	177,961	165,294	137,389	247,016	185,132	210,954	173,050	159,258	132,922
Madras States Agency—												
Pudukkottai ..	191,134	205,033	196,566	180,794	177,912	142,810	209,560	221,780	215,320	199,646	195,184	159,317
Punjab States Agency—												
Bahawalpur	545,103	430,090	430,254	395,684	355,153	314,395	439,509	351,101	350,387	325,193	294,889	259,099
Patiala ..	900,597	837,479	792,540	877,197	871,467	806,984	724,923	662,260	615,119	719,495	712,054	660,449
Rajputana Agency—												
Alwar ..	396,261	371,975	413,659	431,035	403,898	360,384	353,490	329,179	378,029	397,452	363,888	322,542
Bharatpur ..	263,325	272,345	302,254	335,156	347,830	350,475	223,629	224,092	256,531	291,509	292,473	295,065
Bikaner ..	501,153	347,690	371,489	306,462	440,114	293,684	435,065	311,995	329,494	278,293	391,951	215,393
Bundi ..	113,101	97,635	113,211	88,731	156,033	133,103	103,621	89,433	105,519	82,496	139,642	121,598
Dholpur ..	140,497	127,078	144,455	147,880	157,123	138,342	114,489	103,110	119,138	123,616	122,767	111,315
Jaipur ..	1,387,067	1,242,742	1,385,750	1,405,458	1,505,765	1,365,194	1,244,708	1,096,060	1,250,897	1,253,208	1,318,201	1,161,948
Kotah ..	355,056	327,015	330,324	280,912	375,210	371,255	330,748	303,045	308,765	263,967	343,561	336,147
Marwar ..	1,109,912	971,115	1,075,269	1,015,531	1,329,478	973,065	1,016,070	870,527	982,284	920,034	1,198,700	784,553
Mewar ..	807,184	705,396	664,287	532,046	894,577	772,685	759,726	661,584	616,997	486,759	816,002	670,459
Tonk ..	164,401	149,168	156,390	140,928	200,097	176,869	152,959	138,730	146,791	132,339	179,972	161,160
United Provinces States—												
Benares ..	194,236	181,718	177,869	177,776	193,078	184,739	197,036	181,142	179,969	183,581	194,378	172,971
Rampur ..	250,618	243,014	282,978	280,987	291,092	282,359	214,607	210,593	248,239	252,225	260,157	259,555
Tehri-Garhwal	173,317	156,498	148,462	133,427	118,378	102,340	176,256	161,916	152,357	135,458	122,864	97,496
Western India States Agency—												
Cutch ..	248,845	235,363	252,453	244,643	278,441	260,251	265,462	249,184	260,976	243,379	279,974	251,833
Gondal ..	103,758	82,995	80,252	81,397	81,497	70,105	102,088	84,076	81,664	81,462	79,539	65,499
Bhavanagar ..	257,156	220,303	227,700	212,427	242,479	207,858	243,118	206,101	213,667	200,237	224,803	192,465
Junagadh ..	278,866	237,264	220,863	201,724	249,947	202,204	266,286	228,229	213,359	193,704	234,243	185,295
Palanpur ..	136,445	122,383	116,644	115,280	142,005	122,051	127,734	114,311	109,606	107,347	132,859	112,351
Nawanagar ..	205,767	174,275	176,312	171,120	194,496	163,462	203,425	171,078	173,088	165,659	185,115	152,685

* Figures for Mong Mit State only.

TABLE III.

Towns and Villages Classified by Population.

The total population dealt with in this table falls short of that shown in Table I owing to the omission of 2,278,937 persons, as no statistics were available of the number of villages situated in the Agencies and Tribal Areas of the North-West Frontier Province (2,259,288 persons), while in Burma no classification was possible of the 19,649 persons referred to in paragraph 4, sub-clause 4, on page 1 of this volume. The omission of the former population accounts for the discrepancy between the number of units dealt with here and in Table I.

2. In this table, as in Tables I, IV and V, all Municipalities, Civil Lines and Cantonments have been treated as separate towns.

3. In the districts in which a revenue and cadastral survey has been carried out the *mauza* or survey village has been taken as the census village, except in the case of Burma where the figures represent village tracts which may include a village or group of villages and adjacent lands ; elsewhere the census village, the residential village or independent group of houses bearing a separate name, small outlying hamlets being ordinarily treated as part of the residential villages to which they relate.

4. Travellers enumerated in encampments, boats and trains, will be found detailed separately in this table, while in Tables IV and V this moving population has been included in the population of the town within which they were actually enumerated.

Table III.—Towns and Villages

Province, State or Agency.	Total Number of inhabited towns and villages.	Population.	Under 500.	
			Number.	Population.
1	2	3	4	5
INDIA	**699,406**	**350,558,841**	**509,786**	**97,514,496**
Provinces	**501,057**	**271,507,284**	**351,920**	**69,650,013**
1. Ajmer-Merwara	752	560,292	509	114,117
2. Andaman and Nicobar Islands ..	239	29,463	224	14,886
3. Assam	32,907*	8,622,251	28,662	4,769,228
4. Baluchistan .. .. .. (*Districts and Administered Territories*).	1,437	463,508	1,229	161,483
5. Bengal	86,757	50,114,002	59,246	12,554,148
6. Bihar and Orissa	83,480	37,677,576	62,080	12,451,997
Bihar	*47,218*	*25,727,500*	*32,338*	*6,829,628*
Orissa	*15,532*	*5,306,142*	*12,424*	*2,332,235*
Chota Nagpur	*20,730*	*6,643,934*	*17,318*	*3,290,134*
7. Bombay	26,851	21,930,601	15,125	3,679,016
Bombay Presidency	*21,668*	*17,992,053*	*12,284*	*2,988,008*
Sind	*5,180*	*3,887,070*	*2,841*	*691,008*
Aden	*3*	*51,478*	..	..
8. Burma	32,479	14,647,497	23,621	2,911,383
9. Central Provinces and Berar ..	39,868	15,507,723	31,832	6,475,758
Central Provinces	*33,895*	*12,065,885*	*27,808*	*5,550,034*
Berar	*5,973*	*3,441,838*	*4,024*	*925,724*
10. Coorg	380	163,327	269	66,946
11. Delhi	313	636,246	183	49,054
12. Madras	51,827	46,740,107	28,306	4,996,332
13. North-West Frontier Province .. (*Districts and Administered Territories*).	2,857	2,425,076	1,601	367,033
14. Punjab	34,829	23,580,852	20,952	4,928,206
15. United Provinces of Agra and Oudh	106,081	48,408,763	78,081	16,110,426
Agra	*81,678*	*35,613,784*	*62,127*	*12,265,823*
Oudh	*24,403*	*12,794,979*	*15,954*	*3,844,603*
States and Agencies	**198,349**	**79,051,557**	**157,866**	**27,864,483**
16. Assam States	2,849*	625,606	2,625	325,218
17. Baluchistan States	2,081	405,109	1,916	246,626
18. Baroda State	2,970	2,443,007	1,580	400,578
19. Bengal States	4,587	973,336	4,094	454,427
20. Bihar and Orissa States	19,385	4,652,007	17,324	2,937,100
21. Bombay States	8,919	4,468,396	6,480	1,243,214
22. Central India Agency	23,308	6,632,790	20,486	3,509,026
23. Central Provinces States	8,970	2,483,214	7,756	1,484,975
24. Gwalior State	10,895	3,523,070	9,331	1,703,192
25. Hyderabad State	21,832	14,436,148	12,601	2,851,391
26. Jammu and Kashmir State ..	8,942	3,646,243	6,914	1,383,302
27. Madras States Agency	4,780	6,754,484	1,676	363,588
Cochin State	*284*	*1,205,016*	*8*	*1,673*
Travancore State	*3,982*	*5,095,973*	*1,446*	*309,369*
Other Madras States	*514*	*453,495*	*222*	*52,546*
28. Mysore State	16,591	6,557,302	13,282	2,721,707
29. Punjab States	2,614	437,787	2,433	207,706
30. Punjab States Agency	13,494	4,472,218	10,968	1,409,780
31. Rajputana Agency	33,833	11,225,712	28,688	4,771,209
32. Sikkim State	[illegible]67	109,808	327	73,537
33. United Provinces States	5,370	1,206,070	4,922	708,376
34. Western India States Agency ..	6,562	3,999,250	4,463	1,069,531

*The Shillong Municipality lies partly in British and partly in non-British Territory and

classified by Population.

500—1,000.		1,000—2,000.		2,000—5,000.		
Number.	Population.	Number.	Population.	Number.	Population.	
6	7	8	9	10	11	
113,541	**79,189,377**	**53,908**	**73,707,758**	**18,836**	**53,556,566**	
87,632	**61,370,395**	**43,442**	**59,479,012**	**15,452**	**43,915,597**	
149	103,618	59	79,238	31	86,487	1
12	8,049	2	2,209	1	3,988	2
3,303	2,239,458	787	1,059,545	137	360,108	3
137	93,844	49	65,142	16	49,775	4
15,653	10,964,216	7,985	11,025,002	3,440	9,745,344	5
13,440	9,299,848	5,900	8,038,714	1,824	5,146,626	6
8,552	*5,974,951*	*4,527*	*6,230,659*	*1,605*	*4,565,743*	
2,272	*1,554,731*	*727*	*961,677*	*97*	*247,458*	
2,616	*1,770,166*	*646*	*846,378*	*122*	*333,425*	
6,865	4,855,080	3,433	4,675,644	1,145	3,293,790	7
5,459	*3,847,891*	*2,696*	*3,670,028*	*979*	*2,846,327*	
1,406	*1,007,189*	*736*	*1,003,652*	*166*	*447,463*	
..	..	*1*	*1,964*	..	..	
4,617	3,348,813	3,333	4,534,194	808	2,200,954	8
5,865	4,001,849	1,669	2,222,136	385	1,067,849	9
4,576	*3,086,373*	*1,182*	*1,557,637*	*262*	*709,375*	
1,289	*915,476*	*487*	*664,499*	*123*	*358,474*	
89	59,541	20	26,218	1	3,832	10
73	52,396	43	59,694	8	22,651	11
9,656	6,982,882	8,466	11,881,934	4,582	13,366,902	12
637	452,816	379	524,546	203	597,263	13
8,240	5,842,674	4,142	5,647,569	1,239	3,529,082	14
18,896	13,065,311	7,175	9,637,227	1,632	4,440,946	15
13,075	*9,011,008*	*5,001*	*6,740,395*	*1,241*	*3,390,305*	
5,821	*4,054,303*	*2,174*	*2,896,832*	*391*	*1,050,641*	
25,909	**17,818,982**	**10,466**	**14,228,746**	**3,384**	**9,640,969**	
167	112,094	49	64,691	5	12,990	16
117	75,682	37	50,964	11	31,837	17
777	547,123	419	569,393	157	442,677	18
322	220,019	141	187,448	24	58,264	19
1,659	1,100,753	350	443,761	46	128,004	20
1,443	1,007,613	692	950,515	249	716,385	21
2,093	1,388,275	545	715,987	143	397,950	22
1,033	682,695	158	204,465	16	45,857	23
1,083	742,206	371	500,370	87	239,640	24
5,439	3,819,128	2,808	3,843,747	884	2,440,955	25
1,377	955,878	520	701,349	118	309,288	26
1,029	754,169	1,136	1,610,740	762	2,285,327	27
14	*10,942*	*54*	*81,926*	*143*	*462,740*	
867	*637,111*	*978*	*1,391,515*	*585*	*1,728,478*	
148	*106,116*	*104*	*137,299*	*34*	*94,109*	
2,406	1,611,984	702	931,888	157	440,571	28
92	66,159	69	100,931	19	57,867	29
1,572	1,095,398	718	961,555	198	562,736	30
3,511	2,415,979	1,180	1,606,227	348	1,008,165	31
30	19,530	10	16,741	..	..	32
347	231,093	77	102,792	18	48,384	33
1,412	973,204	484	665,182	142	414,072	34

has been integrally included against Assam States as in Table I.

Table III.—Towns and Villages

Province, State or Agency.	5,000—10,000.		10,000—20,000.	
	Number.	Population.	Number.	Population.
1	12	13	14	15
INDIA	**2,330**	**15,412,217**	**632**	**8,537,719**
Provinces	**1,843**	**12,147,276**	**471**	**6,409,946**
1. Ajmer-Merwara	1	7,179	..	..
2. Andaman and Nicobar Islands ..	..	..	..	..
3. Assam	12	82,637	4	55,882
4. Baluchistan .. .. .. (*District and Administered Territories*).	4	30,422	..	..
5. Bengal	321	2,070,803	73	1,001,309
6. Bihar and Orissa	183	1,223,507	33	455,723
Bihar	*161*	*1,068,833*	*22*	*306,531*
Orissa	*5*	*32,568*	*5*	*74,436*
Chota Nagpur	*17*	*122,106*	*6*	*74,756*
7. Bombay	191	1,256,613	54	761,236
Bombay Presidency	*171*	*1,111,532*	*47*	*661,697*
Sind	*20*	*145,081*	*6*	*87,372*
Aden	..	..	*1*	*12,167*
8. Burma	69	466,578	17	221,284
9. Central Provinces and Berar ..	66	458,317	33	461,778
Central Provinces	*35*	*239,127*	*19*	*270,982*
Berar	*31*	*219,190*	*14*	*190,796*
10. Coorg	1	5,995	..	..
11. Delhi	3	22,382	1	16,347
12. Madras	614	4,018,784	134	1,821,192
13. North-West Frontier Province .. (*Districts and Administered Territories*).	27	180,778	4	50,730
14. Punjab	171	1,145,512	50	633,121
15. United Provinces of Agra and Oudh	180	1,177,769	68	931,344
Agra	*139*	*910,246*	*53*	*712,921*
Oudh	*41*	*267,523*	*15*	*218,423*
States and Agencies	**487**	**3,264,941**	**161**	**2,127,773**
16. Assam States	1	5,079	1*	16,692
17. Baluchistan States	..	..	..	..
18. Baroda State	23	152,993	9	125,723
19. Bengal States	5	41,089	1	11,837
20. Bihar and Orissa States	6	42,389	..	..
21. Bombay States	41	272,833	10	118,825
22. Central India Agency	24	158,332	11	153,689
23. Central Provinces States	4	25,484	3	38,917
24. Gwalior State	13	92,964	7	80,900
25. Hyderabad State	65	430,431	26	343,042
26. Jammu and Kashmir State ..	9	55,779	2	21,439
27. Madras States Agency	136	899,730	30	373,608
Cochin State	*48*	*328,755*	*14*	*186,608*
Travancore State	*84*	*547,034*	*15*	*176,341*
Other Madras States	*4*	*23,941*	*1*	*10,659*
28. Mysore State	31	205,686	7	92,596
29. Punjab States	1	5,124	..	..
30. Punjab States Agency	22	145,173	10	133,801
31. Rajputana Agency	70	489,940	26	359,836
32. Sikkim State	..	..	..	..
33. United Provinces States	4	28,027	1	12,493
34. Western India States Agency ..	32	213,888	17	244,375

classified by Population—*concld.*

20,000—50,000.		50,000—100,000.		100,000—and over.		Encampments, Boat and Railway Population unclassed.	
Number 16	Population. 17	Number. 18	Population. 19	Number. 20	Population. 21	22	
269	**7,940,572**	**66**	**4,566,885**	**38**	**9,640,132**	**493,119**	
216	**6,379,364**	**52**	**3,535,737**	**29**	**8,213,675**	**406,269**	
2	49,588	..	..	1	118,579	1,486	1
..	..	..	..	..	..	331	2
2	42,505	..	..	..	..	12,888	3
2	60,272	..	..	..	..	2,570	4
33	939,109	3	194,498	3	1,552,983	66,590	5
12	399,249	7	484,909	1	159,690	17,313	6
8	*293,608*	*4*	*285,391*	*1*	*159,690*	*12,466*	
1	*37,568*	*1*	*65,263*	..	..	*206*	
3	*68,073*	*2*	*134,255*	..	..	*4,641*	
28	923,392	5	416,721	5	2,061,906	7,203	7
26	*859,204*	*2*	*188,918*	*4*	*1,814,115*	*4,333*	
1	*26,841*	*3*	*227,803*	*1*	*247,791*	*2,870*	
1	*37,347*	..	..	..	..	..	
11	295,216	1	63,454	2	515,311	90,310	8
16	495,228	..	..	2	319,482	5,326	9
11	*327,743*	..	..	*2*	*319,482*	*5,132*	
5	*167,485*	..	..	..	..	*194*	
..	..	..	..	..	..	795	10
..	..	1	55,959	1	346,687	11,076	11
47	1,369,972	18	1,158,599	4	1,070,438	73,072	12
5	147,098	1	87,440	..	..	17,372	13
26	688,488	6	379,140	3	773,311	13,749	14
32	969,247	10	695,017	7	1,295,288	86,188	15
27	*844,904*	*9*	*635,190*	*6*	*1,044,349*	*58,643*	
5	*124,343*	*1*	*59,827*	*1*	*250,939*	*27,545*	
53	**1,561,208**	**14**	**1,031,148**	**9**	**1,426,457**	**86,850**	
..	..	1	85,804	..	..	3,038	16
..	..	..	..	..	..	..	17
4	94,881	..	..	1	109,639	..	18
..	..	..	..	..	..	252	19
..	..	..	..	..	..	..	20
3	88,160	1	69,860	..	..	991	21
4	114,109	1	60,901	1	126,282	8,239	22
..	..	..	..	..	..	821	23
1	21,999	2	132,459	..	..	9,340	24
6	178,441	1	62,119	2	466,894	..	25
1	38,474	..	..	1	166,592	14,142	26
10	343,610	1	95,674	..	..	28,038	27
3	*119,887*	..	..	..	..	*12,485*	
6	*194,947*	*1*	*95,674*	..	..	*15,504*	
1	*28,776*	..	..	..	..	*49*	
2	43,632	1	85,058	3	412,871	11,309	28
..	..	..	..	..	..	..	29
5	108,374	1	55,129	..	..	272	30
7	243,726	2	180,601	1	144,179	5,850	31
..	..	..	..	..	..	..	32
..	..	1	74,216	..	..	689	33
10	285,802	2	129,327	..	..	3,869	34

TABLE IV.

Towns Classified by Population with variation since 1881.

For purpose of this table a town was defined as any self-governing urban unit, irrespective of size, including every municipality, every cantonment, all civil lines not included within municipal limits, and also every other continuous collection of houses ordinarily inhabited by not less than 5,000 persons and having an urban character though not necessarily self-governing. Cantonments have been shown separately from the cities or towns to which they are adjacent, and not amalgamated with them as in 1921.

2. The towns are grouped in six classes. The first class consists of towns with a population of 100,000 and over; the second of towns the populations of which number from 50,000 to 100,000; the third 20,000 to 50,000; the fourth 10,000 to 20,000; the fifth 5,000 to 10,000, and the sixth under 5,000. In the first three classes the towns, other than the three Presidency towns which come first and are placed in order of magnitude, are arranged alphabetically in each class; in the last three only the number of towns and their aggregate population are given.

3. This table covers six censuses and gives the net variation for the period 1881-1931 as well as for each intervening decade. The separate detailing of certain cantonments and civil lines, for which complete figures for past censuses are not available, has in certain cases caused deflections in the variation figures against the respective municipalities under which they were formerly included, and therefore for comparative purposes their figures, which if not shown separately in this table will be found in Provincial Reports, should be included with those for the municipalities bearing the same names. As no uniformity appears to have been observed in the compilation of this table at previous censuses, adjustments (details of which are given in Provincial Reports) of previous figures have been found necessary in certain cases to provincial tables and consequently to the general table given here. The totals of each class therefore represent the total number of persons living in towns of that class in the year of record, and, except for 1931, are not the sum of the figures below them, affected as they have been by subsequent transfers from one class to another. The same remarks apply to the figures shown against India.

4. The following figures show the population of certain hill stations according to a census taken during the season of 1931 in the Punjab and of 1930 in the United Provinces.

Province.	Town.	Persons.	Males.	Females.
Punjab	Simla Municipality	51,706	37,157	14,549
United Provinces.	Naini Tal Municipality	17,375	12,167	5,208
	Naini Tal Cantonment	1,535	1,118	417
	Ranikhet Cantonment	9,489	7,246	2,243
	Almora Cantonment	942	498	444
	Mussoorie Municipality	17,115	12,362	4,753
	Landour Cantonment	2,878	2,071	807
	Chakrata Cantonment	5,935	4,918	1,017
	Lansdowne Cantonment	5,900	4,383	1,517

5. Additional figures for cantonments will be found in the second statement appended to this table.

6. The 1921 class totals have been adjusted to make an allowance for the population of the three towns of Aden for which Table IV was not prepared in that year.

M8CC

Table IV.—Towns classified by

Name of Town.	Province, District, State or Agency, etc.	Population. 1931.	1921.	1911.	1901.	1891.	1881.	Variation: 1921 to 1931.
1	2	3	4	5	6	7	8	9
INDIA	**2,575 Towns**	**38,985,427**	**32,475,276**	**29,748,228**	**29,244,221**	**27,251,176**	**23,773,376**	**+6,510,151**
Class I (100,000 and over).	**38 Towns**	**9,674,032**	**8,211,704**	**7,075,782**	**6,605,837**	**6,173,123**	**5,304,172**	**+1,462,328**
Calcutta (Corpn.)	Bengal	1,193,651	1,074,508	1,038,896	945,814	766,194	695,843	+ 119,143
Bombay (Corpn.)	Bombay	1,161,383	1,175,914	979,445	776,006	821,764	773,196	— 14,531
Madras (Corpn.)	Madras	645,586	526,911	518,660	509,346	452,518	405,848	+ 118,675
Agra (M.)	United Provinces (Agra)	205,487	163,750	163,935	188,022	168,662	160,203	+ 41,737
Ahmadabad (M.)	Bombay (Ahmadabad)	310,000	270,775	214,000	181,774	144,451	124,767	+ 39,225
Ajmer (M.)	Ajmer-Merwara	119,524	113,512	86,222	73,839	68,843	48,735	+ 6,012
Allahabad (M.)	United Provinces (Allahabad).	173,895	145,605	159,701	172,032	175,246	160,118	+ 28,290
Amritsar (M.)	Punjab (Amritsar)	263,210	157,031	151,339	161,039	135,401	150,665	+ 106,179
Bangalore (M.)	Mysore (Bangalore)	172,357	118,556	88,651	69,447	80,285	62,317	+ 53,801
Bangalore Civil and Military Station (M.).	Mysore (Bangalore)	134,113	118,940	100,834	89,599	100,081	93,540	+ 15,173
Bareilly (M.)	United Provinces (Bareilly)	134,179	119,175	117,521	133,167	122,837	115,138	+ 15,004
Baroda (M.)	Baroda	109,639	91,778	95,867	100,628	112,471	101,818	+ 17,861
Benares (M.)	United Provinces (Benares)	201,037	195,373	199,868	213,079	223,375	218,573	+ 5,664
Cawnpore (M.)	United Provinces (Cawnpore)	219,189	195,085	157,040	202,797	194,048	155,369	+ 24,104
Dacca (M.)	Bengal (Dacca)	138,518	119,450	108,551	89,733	81,585	78,369	+ 19,068
Delhi (M.)	Delhi	347,539	248,259	229,144	206,534	189,648	170,245	+ 99,280
Howrah (M.)	Bengal (Howrah)	224,873	195,301	179,006	157,594	116,606	90,813	+ 29,572
Hyderabad (M.)	Hyderabad	346,093	309,036	387,133	352,028	415,039*a*	367,417*a*	+ 37,057
Indore (M.)	Central India (Indore)	127,327	93,091	44,947	86,686	82,984	75,401	+ 34,236
Jaipur (M.)	Rajputana (Jaipur)	144,179	120,207	137,098	160,167	158,787	142,578	+ 23,972
Jubbulpore (M.)	C. P. and Berar (Jubbulpore).	104,317	86,796	79,009	77,376	73,356	76,023	+ 17,521
Karachi (M.)	Bombay (Karachi)	247,791	201,691	140,511	108,644	98,195	68,332	+ 46,100
Lahore (M.)	Punjab (Lahore)	400,075	257,295	210,271	186,884	159,597	130,960	+ 142,780
Lucknow (M.)	United Provinces (Lucknow)	251,097	217,167	232,332	256,239	264,953	253,729	+ 33,930
Madura (M.)	Madras (Madura)	182,018	138,894	134,130	105,984	87,428	73,807	+ 43,124
Mandalay (M.)	Burma (Mandalay)	134,950	134,839	124,914	167,721	170,071	..	+ 111
Moradabad (M.)	United Provinces (Moradabad).	110,562	82,671	81,118	75,082	72,876	69,309	+ 27,891
Multan (M.)	Punjab (Multan)	108,351	74,270	85,747	74,627	64,265	57,471	+ 34,081
Mysore (M.)	Mysore	107,142	83,951	71,306	68,111	74,048	60,292	+ 23,191
Nagpur (M.)	C. P. and Berar (Nagpur)	215,165	145,193	101,415	127,734	117,014	98,299	+ 69,972
Patna (M.)	B. and O. (Patna)	159,690	119,976	136,153	134,785	165,192	170,654	+ 39,714
Poona (M.)	Bombay (Poona)	198,078	163,713	127,174	121,075	126,296	99,622	+ 34,365
Rangoon (M.)	Burma (Rangoon)	398,967	335,491	284,935	221,160	165,768	124,524	+ 63,476
Salem (M.)	Madras (Salem)	102,179	52,244	59,153	70,621	67,710	50,667	+ 49,935
Secunderabad (including Bolarum) (C.)	Hyderabad	120,801	95,151	113,490	96,438	†	†	+ 25,650
Sholapur (M.)	Bombay (Sholapur)	144,654	119,581	61,345	75,288	61,915	59,890	+ 25,073
Srinagar (M.)	Jammu and Kashmir (Kashmir South).	173,573	139,520	124,240	122,618	118,960	..	+ 34,053
Trichinopoly (M.)	Madras (Trichinopoly)	142,843	120,422	123,512	104,721	90,609	84,449	+ 22,421
Class II (50,000 to 100,000).	**65 Towns**	**4,572,113**	**3,517,749**	**3,010,281**	**3,414,188**	**3,255,175**	**2,880,899**	**+ 1,054,364**
Bandar (Masulipatam). (M).	Madras (Kistna)	56,928	43,940	42,123	39,507	38,809	35,056	+ 12,988
Bezwada (M.)	Madras (Kistna)	60,427	44,159	32,867	24,224	20,741	9,336	+ 16,268
Bhagalpur (M.)	B. and O. (Bhagalpur)	83,847	68,878	74,349	75,760	69,106	68,238	+ 14,969
Bhatpara (M.)	Bengal (Twenty-four Parganas).	84,975	65,609	50,414	21,540	14,135	10,239	+ 19,366
Bhavanagar (M.)	Western India States Agency (Bhavanagar).	75,594	59,392	60,694	56,442	57,653	47,792	+ 16,202
Bhopal (M.)	Central India (Bhopal)	61,037	45,094	56,204	77,023	70,338	55,402	+ 15,943
Bikaner (M.)	Rajputana (Bikaner)	85,927	69,410	55,826	53,075	50,513	33,154	+ 16,517
Calicut (M.)	Madras (Malabar)	99,273	82,334	78,417	76,981	66,078	57,085	+ 16,939
Chittagong (M.)	Bengal (Chittagong)	53,156	36,030	28,766	22,140	24,069	20,969	+ 17,126
Cocanada (M.)	Madras (Godavari)	65,952	53,348	54,110	48,096	40,553	28,856	+ 12,604
Coimbatore (M.)	Madras (Coimbatore)	95,198	65,788	47,007	53,080	46,383	38,967	+ 29,410
Conjeeveram (M.)	Madras (Chingleput)	65,258	61,376	53,864	46,164	42,548	37,275	+ 3,882
Cuddalore (M.)	Madras (South Arcot)	59,057	50,527	56,574	52,216	47,355	43,545	+ 8,530
Cuttack (M.)	B. and O. (Cuttack)	65,263	51,007	52,528	51,364	47,186	42,656	+ 14,256
Darbhanga (M.)	B. and O. (Darbhanga)	60,676	53,700	62,628	66,244	73,561	65,955	+ 6,976
Ellore (M.)	Madras (Kistna)	57,342	45,862	37,819	33,521	29,382	25,092	+ 11,480
Farrukhabad-cum-Fategarh (M.).	United Provinces (Farrukhabad).	56,503	48,331	56,573	67,338	78,032	79,761	+ 8,172
Fyzabad-cum-Ajodhya (M.)	United Provinces (Fyzabad).	59,992	51,342	47,519	71,179	74,806	67,652	+ 8,650
Gaya (M.)	B. and O. (Gaya)	88,005	67,562	49,921	71,288	80,383	76,415	+ 20,443
Gorakhpur (M.)	United Provinces (Gorakhpur).	59,369	50,498	48,358	64,148	63,620	59,908	+ 8,871
Gujranwala (M.)	Punjab (Gujranwala)	58,716	37,887	29,472	29,224	26,785	22,884	+ 20,829
Guntur (M.)	Madras (Guntur)	65,179	48,184	40,529	30,833	23,359	19,646	+ 16,995
Hubli (M.)	Bombay (Dharwar)	89,982	69,206	61,440	60,214	52,595	36,677	+ 20,776
Hyderabad (M)	Bombay (Sind)	96,021	73,951	69,140	64,790	54,569	45,195	+ 22,070
Imphal*	Assam (Manipur)	85,804	80,003	74,650	72,234	..	..	+ 5,801
Jamnagar (M)	W. I. Sts. Agency. (Nawanagar).	55,056	42,495	44,887	53,844	48,530	39,668	+ 12,561
Jamshedpur*	B. and O. (Singbhum)	83,738	57,360	5,672	..	..	..	+ 26,378
Jhansi (M.)	United Provinces (Jhansi)	64,591	54,385	58,236	55,724	53,779	32,987	+ 10,206
Jodhpur (M.)	Rajputana (Marwar)	94,736	73,480	79,756	79,109	80,405	63,329	+ 21,256
Jullundur (M.)	Punjab (Jullundar)	74,295	59,085	55,354	54,455	50,375	42,651	+ 15,210
Kharakpur*	Bengal (Midnapore)	58,134	25,280	18,957	..	..	..	+ 32,854
Koil-Aligarh (M.)	United Provinces (Aligarh).	83,878	36,963	66,344	72,084	62,925	63,906	+ 16,915
Kolar Gold Fields (M.)	Mysore (Kolar)	85,103	87,682	83,743	70,874	24,111	..	— 2,579
Kolhapur (M.)	Bombay (Kolhapur)	69,860	53,243	45,849	54,373	45,815	38,599	+ 16,617
Kumbakonam (M.)	Madras (Tanjore)	62,317	60,700	64,647	59,673	54,307	50,098	+ 1,617
Lashkar (M.)	Gwalior (Gird)	78,680	80,387	46,952	89,154	104,083	88,066	— 1,707
Ludhiana (M.)	Punjab (Ludhiana)	66,098	50,312	43,152	48,211	46,024	..	+ 15,786
Mangalore (M.)	Madras (South Kanara)	66,756	53,877	48,412	44,108	40,922	32,099	+ 12,879
Meerut (M.)	United Provinces (Meerut)	91,181	77,7[illegible]	76,755	118,539	119,805	99,911	+ 1[illegible]

a Includes Secunderabad. † Included in Hyderabad (Serial No. 18)

population with variation since 1881.

Increase (+), Decrease (—).				Variation in period 1881 to 1931. Increase (+) Decrease (—).	Males.			Females.			
1911 to 1921.	1901 to 1911.	1891 to 1901.	1881 to 1891.		1931.	1921.	1911.	1931.	1921.	1911.	
10	11	12	13	14	15	16	17	18	19	20	
+2,727,048	**+504,007**	**+1,993,045**	**+3,477,800**	**+15,212,051**	**21,485,055**	**17,845,248**	**16,108,304**	**17,500,372**	**14,630,028**	**13,639,924**	
+ 1,135,922	**+ 469,945**	**+ 432,714**	**+ 868,951**	**+ 4,369,860**	**5,687,045**	**4,886,083**	**4,135,392**	**3,986,987**	**3,325,621**	**2,940,390**	
+ 35,612	+ 93,082	+ 179,620	+ 70,351	+ 497,808	812,287	721,724	693,946	381,364	352,784	344,950	1
+ 196,469	+ 203,439	— 45,758	+ 48,568	+ 388,187	747,381	771,332	640,288	414,002	404,582	339,157	2
+ 8,251	+ 9,314	+ 56,828	+ 46,670	+ 239,738	340,068	276,107	266,465	305,518	250,804	252,195	3
— 185	— 24,087	+ 19,360	+ 8,459	+ 45,284	113,320	90,823	88,943	92,167	72,927	74,992	4
+ 56,775	+ 32,226	+ 37,323	+ 19,684	+ 185,233	166,935	153,274	115,502	143,065	117,501	98,498	5
+ 27,290	+ 12,383	+ 4,996	+ 20,108	+ 70,789	66,014	67,597	47,354	53,510	45,915	38,868	6
— 14,096	— 12,331	— 3,214	+ 15,128	+ 13,777	97,909	81,701	87,806	75,986	63,904	71,895	7
+ 5,692	— 9,700	+ 25,638	— 15,264	+ 112,545	157,823	92,437	87,828	105,387	64,594	63,511	8
+ 29,905	+ 19,204	— 10,838	+ 17,968	+ 110,040	91,680	63,911	45,997	80,677	54,645	42,654	9
+ 18,106	+ 11,235	— 10,482	+ 6,541	+ 40,573	69,409	61,576	51,752	64,704	57,364	49,082	10
+ 1,654	— 15,646	+ 10,330	+ 7,699	+ 19,041	72,830	64,068	62,127	61,349	55,107	55,394	11
— 4,089	— 4,761	— 11,843	+ 10,653	+ 7,821	60,723	49,739	51,342	48,916	42,039	44,525	12
— 4,495	— 13,211	— 10,296	+ 4,802	— 17,536	111,587	104,204	103,126	89,450	91,169	96,742	13
+ 38,045	— 45,757	+ 8,749	+ 38,679	+ 63,820	129,276	116,411	89,806	89,913	78,674	67,234	14
+ 10,899	+ 18,818	+ 8,148	+ 3,216	+ 60,149	79,365	67,333	63,091	59,153	52,117	45,460	15
+ 19,115	+ 22,610	+ 16,886	+ 19,403	+ 177,294	203,869	143,679	130,775	143,670	104,580	98,369	16
+ 16,295	+ 21,412	+ 40,988	+ 25,793	+ 134,060	145,120	128,472	114,566	79,753	66,829	64,440	17
— 78,097	+ 35,105	— 63,011	+ 47,622	— 21,324	182,885.	157,860	197,699	163,208	151,176	189,434	18
+ 48,144	— 41,739	+ 3,702	+ 7,583	+ 51,926	73,450	52,738	24,792	53,877	40,353	20,155	19
— 16,891	— 23,069	+ 1,380	+ 16,209	+ 1,601	77,933	64,382	70,846	66,246	55,825	66,252	20
+ 7,787	+ 1,633	+ 4,020	— 2,667	+ 28,294	56,613	46,883	41,783	47,704	39,913	37,226	21
+ 61,180	+ 31,867	+ 10,449	+ 29,863	+ 179,459	145,052	121,565	82,026	102,739	80,126	58,485	22
+ 47,024	+ 23,387	+ 27,287	+ 28,637	+ 269,115	253,846	161,055	129,513	146,229	96,240	80,758	23
— 15,165	— 23,907	— 8,714	+ 11,224	— 2,632	143,876	119,873	127,275	107,221	97,294	105,057	24
+ 4,764	+ 28,146	+ 18,556	+ 13,621	+ 108,211	91,676	70,289	67,091	90,342	68,605	67,639	25
+ 9,925	— 42,807	— 2,350	..	..	69,849	69,102	61,816	65,101	65,737	63,098	26
+ 1,553	+ 6,036	+ 2,206	+ 3,567	+ 41,253	61,346	44,685	43,353	49,216	37,986	37,765	27
— 11,477	+ 11,120	+ 10,362	+ 6,794	+ 50,880	60,800	40,975	46,987	47,551	33,295	38,760	28
+ 12,645	+ 3,195	— 5,937	+ 13,756	+ 46,850	56,772	43,783	36,112	50,370	40,168	35,194	29
+ 43,778	— 26,319	+ 10,720	+ 18,715	+ 116,866	116,403	77,906	53,696	98,762	67,287	47,719	30
— 16,177	+ 1,368	— 30,407	— 5,462	— 10,964	92,238	65,777	70,841	67,452	54,199	65,312	31
+ 36,539	+ 6,099	— 5,221	+ 26,674	+ 98,456	107,542	87,242	67,394	90,536	76,471	59,780	32
+ 50,556	+ 63,775	+ 55,392	+ 41,244	+ 274,443	270,017	232,149	201,819	128,950	103,342	83,116	33
— 6,909	— 11,468	+ 2,911	+ 17,043	+ 51,512	51,786	26,418	29,232	50,393	25,826	29,921	34
— 18,339	+ 17,052	..	..	..	64,738	50,935	60,755	56,063	44,216	52,735	35
+ 58,236	— 13,943	+ 13,373	+ 2,025	+ 84,764	76,837	63,115	31,891	67,817	56,466	29,454	36
+ 15,280	+ 1,622	+ 3,658	..	..	94,793	75,152	66,994	78,780	64,368	57,246	37
— 3,090	+ 18,791	+ 14,112	+ 6,160	+ 58,394	72,997	60,574	61,560	69,846	59,848	61 952	38
+ 507,468	**— 403,907**	**+ 159,013**	**+ 374,276**	**+ 1,691,214**	**2,497,626**	**1,926,963**	**1,634,234**	**2,074,487**	**1,590,786**	**1,376,047**	
+ 1,817	+ 2,616	+ 698	+ 3,753	+ 21,872	29,269	21,878	20,536	27,659	22,062	21,587	1
+ 11,292	+ 8,643	+ 3,483	+ 11,405	+ 51,091	31,675	23,107	17,026	28,752	21,052	15,841	2
— 5,471	— 1,411	+ 6,654	+ 868	+ 15,609	46,868	37,218	39,947	36,979	31,660	34,402	3
+ 15,195	+ 28,874	+ 7,405	+ 3,896	+ 74,736	60,134	45,723	34,739	24,841	19,886	15,675	4
— 1,302	+ 4,252	— 1,211	+ 9,861	+ 27,802	39,894	30,785	31,869	35,700	28,607	28,825	5
— 11,110	— 20,819	+ 6,685	+ 14,936	+ 5,635	32,718	24,033	29,043	28,319	21,061	27,161	6
+ 13,584	+ 2,751	+ 2,562	+ 17,359	+ 52,773	45,832	36,712	28,275	40,095	32,698	27,551	7
+ 3,917	+ 1,436	+ 10,903	+ 8,993	+ 42,188	51,030	42,527	40,680	48,243	39,807	37,737	8
+ 7,264	+ 6,626	— 1,929	+ 3,100	+ 32,187	35,049	24,117	18,779	18,107	11,913	9,987	9
— 762	+ 6,014	+ 7,543	+ 11,697	+ 37,096	33,692	26,346	26,629	32,260	27,002	27,481	10
+ 18,781	— 6,073	+ 6,697	+ 7,416	+ 56,231	49,880	33,417	23,399	45,318	32,371	23,608	11
+ 7,512	+ 7,700	+ 3,616	+ 5,273	+ 27,983	32,367	30,714	26,451	32,891	30,662	27,413	12
— 6,047	+ 4,358	+ 4,861	+ 3,810	+ 15,512	29,892	25,079	28,012	29,165	25,448	28,562	13
— 1,521	+ 1,164	+ 4,178	+ 4,530	+ 22,607	36,357	27,315	28,504	28,906	23,692	24,024	14
— 8,928	— 3,616	— 7,317	+ 7,606	— 5,279	32,274	27,024	31,274	28,402	26,676	31,354	15
+ 8,043	+ 4,298	+ 4,139	+ 4,290	+ 32,250	28,216	22,630	18,302	29,126	23,232	19,517	16
— 8,242	— 10,765	— 10,694	— 1,729	— 23,258	30,865	26,311	30,342	25,638	22,020	26,231	17
+ 3,823	— 23,660	— 3,627	+ 7,154	— 7,660	34,933	29,173	25,921	25,059	22,169	21,598	18
+ 17,641	— 21,367	— 9,095	+ 3,968	+ 11,590	50,625	37,336	26,310	37,380	30,226	23,611	19
+ 2,140	— 15,790	+ 528	+ 3,712	— 539	33,041	27,237	25,662	26,328	23,261	22,696	20
+ 8,415	+ 248	+ 2,439	+ 3,901	+ 35,832	34,216	21,728	16,271	24,500	16,159	13,201	21
+ 7,655	+ 9,696	+ 7,474	+ 3,713	+ 45,533	33,228	24,337	20,826	31,951	23,847	19,703	22
+ 7,766	+ 1,226	+ 7,619	+ 15,918	+ 53,305	47,495	36,392	31,577	42,487	32,814	29,863	23
+ 4,811	+ 4,350	+ 10,221	+ 9,374	+ 50,826	53,339	40,518	37,204	42,682	33,433	31,936	24
+ 5,353	+ 2,416	..	..	..	40,157	38,268	36,393	45,647	41,735	38,257	25
— 2,392	— 8,957	+ 5,314	+ 8,862	+ 15,388	27,824	21,307	22,025	27,232	21,188	22,862	26
+ 51,688	..	..	..	..	51,137	35,385	3,380	32,601	21,975	2,292	27
— 3,851	+ 2,512	+ 1,945	+ 20,792	+ 31,604	33,908	28,731	30,143	30,683	25,654	28,093	28
— 6,276	+ 647	— 1,296	+ 17,076	+ 31,407	52,165	39,747	41,838	42,571	33,733	37,918	29
+ 3,731	+ 899	+ 4,080	+ 7,724	+ 31,644	41,321	33,062	30,539	32,974	26,023	24,815	30
+ 6,323	..	..	..	..	33,443	15,154	11,739	24,691	10,126	7,218	31
+ 619	— 5,740	+ 9,159	— 981	+ 19,972	48,264	38,034	37,297	35,614	28,929	29,047	32
+ 3,939	+ 12,869	+ 46,763	..	..	45,051	47,487	46,521	40,052	40,195	37,222	33
+ 7,394	— 8,524	+ 8,558	+ 7,216	+ 31,261	38,033	28,237	24,158	31,827	25,006	21,691	34
— 3,947	+ 4,974	+ 5,366	+ 4,209	+ 12,219	30,738	29,626	31,327	31,579	31,074	33,320	35
+ 33,435	— 42,202	— 14,929	+ 16,017	— 9,386	42,538	44,595	24,245	36,142	35,792	22,707	36
+ 7,160	— 5,059	+ 2,187	..	..	38,218	29,061	24,765	27,880	21,251	18,387	37
+ 5,465	+ 4,304	+ 3,186	+ 8,823	+ 34,657	34.672	28.204	25.129	32,[illegible]34	25,673	23.283	38
956	— [illegible]		[illegible]	[illegible]							

Table IV.—Towns classified by

	Name of Town.	Province, District, State or Agency, etc.	Population. 1931.	1921.	1911.	1901.	1891.	1881.	Variation: 1921 to 1931.
	1	2	3	4	5	6	7	8	9
	Class II (50,000 to 100,000)—*concld.*								
40	Mirzapur-cum-Bindhyachal (M.)	United Provinces (Mirzapur)	61,184	54,994	32,332	66,071	69,602	70,621	+ 6,190
41	Monghyr (M.)	B. and O. (Monghyr)	52,863	46,825	46,913	35,880	57,077	55,372	+ 6,038
42	Moulmein (M.)	Burma (Amherst)	65,506	61,301	57,582	58,446	55,785	53,107	+ 4,205
43	Muttra (M.)	United Provinces (Muttra)	60,590	42,615	54,332	60,042	61,195	57,724	+ 17,975
44	New-Delhi (M.)	Delhi	64,855	31,456	..	..	..	..	+ 33,399
45	Palamcottah (M.)	Madras (Tinnevelly)	51,990	46,643	44,909	39,545	18,686	17,964	+ 5,347
46	Patiala (M.)	Punjab St. Agency (Patiala)	55,129	47,531	46,974	53,545	55,856	53,629	+ 7,598
47	Peshawar (M.)	N. W. F. Province (Peshawar).	87,440	79,427	74,062	73,343	63,079	59,292	+ 8,013
48	Rajahmundry (M.)	Madras (Godavari)	63,526	53,791	48,417	36,408	28,397	24,555	+ 9,735
49	Rampur (M.)	United Provinces (Rampur)	74,216	73,156	74,316	78,758	76,733	74,250	+ 1,060
50	Ranchi (M.)	B. and O. (Ranchi)	50,517	39,628	32,994	25,970	20,306	18,443	+ 10,889
51	Rawalpindi (M.)	Punjab (Rawalpindi)	75,767	55,251	46,642	47,077	35,925	26,785	+ 20,516
52	Saharanpur (M.)	United Provinces (Saharanpur).	78,655	62,261	62,850	66,254	63,194	59,194	+ 16,394
53	Shahjahanpur (M.)	United Provinces (Shahjahanpur).	79,316	72,616	71,778	76,458	78,522	77,404	+ 6,700
54	Shikarpur (M.)	Bombay (Sukkur)	62,505	55,503	53,944	49,491	42,004	42,496	+ 7,002
55	Sialkot (M.)	Punjab (Sialkot)	85,093	55,911	48,595	44,789	39,612	33,850	+ 29,182
56	Sukkur (M.)	Bombay (Sukkur)	69,277	42,759	35,294	31,316	29,302	27,389	+ 26,518
57	Surat (M.)	Bombay (Surat)	98,936	117,434	114,868	119,306	109,229	109,844	— 18,498
58	Tanjore (M.)	Madras (Tanjore)	66,889	59,913	60,341	57,870	54,390	54,745	+ 6,976
59	Tinnevelly (M.)	Madras (Tinnevelly)	57,078	53,783	44,805	40,469	24,768	23,221	+ 3,295
60	Trivandrum (M.)	Madras (Travancore)	96,016	72,784	63,561	57,882	27,887	41,173	+ 23,232
61	Tuticorin (M.)	Madras (Tinnevelly)	60,395	44,522	40,185	28,048	25,107	16,281	+ 15,873
62	Ujjain (M.)	Gwalior (Ujjain)	53,779	43,908	39,295	39,892	34,691	32,932	+ 9,871
63	Vellore (M.)	Madras (North Arcot)	57,265	50,210	49,746	43,537	44,925	37,491	+ 7,055
64	Vizagapatam (M.)	Madras (Vizagapatam)	57,303	44,711	43,413	40,892	34,487	30,291	+ 12,592
65	Warangal (M.)	Hyderabad (Warangal)	62,119	5,422	5,542	4,741	3,433	..	+ 56,697
	Class III (20,000 to 50,000.)	**268 Towns**	**8,091,288**	**5,968,794**	**5,545,820**	**4,940,251**	**4,492,113**	**3,907,329**	**+ 2,122,494**
1	Aden	Bombay	37,347	43,119	36,876	35,790	34,968	34,711	— 5,772
2	Adoni (M.)	Madras (Bellary)	35,635	30,232	31,645	30,416	26,243	22,441	+ 5,403
3	Agra Cantonment	United Provinces (Agra)	24,277	21.782	21,514	..	..	..	+ 2,495
4	Ahmadnagar (M.)	Bombay (Amadnagar)	41,890	33,139	33,878	35,784	36,083	32,903	+ 8,751
5	Akola (M.)	C. P. and Berar (Akola)	47,632	37,864	25,826	29,289	21,470	16,614	+ 9,768
6	Akyab (M.)	Burma (Akyab)	38,094	36,569	37,893	35,680	37,938	33,989	+ 1,525
7	Alleppey (M.)	Madras (Travancore)	43,838	32,074	25,665	24,918	22,768	25,754	+ 11,764
8	Alwar (M.)	Rajputana (Alwar)	47,900	44,760	41,305	56,771	51,427	49,867	+ 3,140
9	Amalner (M.)	Bombay (Khandesh East)	23,491	17,072	13,232	10,294	7,978	7,627	+ 6,419
10	Ambala (M.)	Punjab (Ambala)	35,193	27,287	24,493	26,744	26,856	26,159	+ 7,906
11	Ambala Cantonment	Punjab (Ambala)	49,368	47,745	54,223	50,438	51,016	40,686	+ 1,623
12	Ambur (P. B.)	Madras (North Arcot)	24,217	19,220	18,264	15,903	10,586	10,390	+ 4,997
13	Amraoti (M.)	C. P. and Berar (Amraoti)	46,832	40,694	34,270	34,216	28,946	23,550	+ 6,138
14	Amreli (M.)	Baroda (Amreli)	20,186	17,793	17,443	17,997	15,653	13,642	+ 2,393
15	Amroha (M.)	United Provinces (Moradabad).	44,948	40,448	42,410	41,071	36,103	37,040	+ 4,500
16	Anakapalle (M.)	Madras (Vizagapatam)	23,376	20,360	20,625	18,539	17,010	13,341	+ 3,016
17	Arrah (M.)	B. and O. (Shahabad)	48,922	40,769	38,549	46,170	46,905	42,998	+ 8,153
18	Aruppukkottai (P. B.)	Madras (Ramnad)	33,848	31,579	26,681	23,633	12,673	10,831	+ 2,269
19	Asansol (M.)	Bengal (Burdwan)	31,286	26,499	21,919	14,906	..	..	+ 4,787
20	Aurangabad (M.)	Hyderabad (Aurangabad)	29,288	28,540	22,949	36,837	33,887	30,219	+ 748
21	Bahawalpur*	Punjab (Bahawalpur)	20,943	18,494	18,414	18,546	18,716	13,635	+ 2,449
22	Bahraich (M.)	United Provinces (Bahraich).	33,783	27,371	26,907	27,304	24,046	21,998	+ 6,412
23	Bally (M.)	Bengal (Howrah)	30,347	23,209	22,394	18,662	16,700	14,815	+ 7,138
24	Banda (M.)	United Provinces (Banda)	22,415	20,029	21,061	22,565	23,071	28,974	+ 2,386
25	Bandra (M.)	Bombay (Bombay Suburban).	43,290	29,271	24,286	22,075	18,317	14,987	+ 14,019
26	Bankura (M.)	Bengal (Bankura)	31,703	25,412	23,453	20,737	18,743	18,747	+ 6,291
27	Bannu (M.)	N. W. F. Province (Bannu)	24,768	16,361	11,751	10,070	6,550	5,260	+ 8,407
28	Baranagar (M.)	Bengal (Twenty-four Parganas).	37,050	32,084	25,895	25,432	22,556	19,729	+ 4,966
29	Barisal (M.)	Bengal (Bakarganj)	35,716	26,744	22,473	18,978	15,482	13,186	+ 8,972
30	Barsi (M.)	Bombay (Sholapur)	27,610	22,074	18,097	24,242	20,569	16,126	+ 5,536
31	Basirhat (M.)	Bengal (Twenty-four Parganas).	21,287	19,267	18,331	17,001	15,109	14,843	+ 2,020
32	Bassein (M.)	Burma (Bassein)	45,662	42,563	37,081	31,864	30,177	28,147	+ 3,099
33	Basti (T. A.)	United Provinces (Basti)	22,526	17,691	11,447	14,761	13,630	5,536	+ 4,835
34	Batala (M.)	Punjab (Gurdaspur)	33,204	26,122	23,430	27,365	27,223	24,281	+ 7,082
35	Beawar (M.)	Ajmer-Merwara	28,342	22,362	22,800	21,928	20,978	15,829	+ 5,980
36	Belgaum (M.)	Bombay (Belgaum)	41,204	38,306	31,451	26,237	28,423	23,115	+ 2,898
37	Bellary (M.)	Madras (Bellary)	47,573	39,842	34,956	58,247	59,467	53,460	+ 7,731
38	Berhampore (M.)	Bengal (Murshidabad)	27,403	26,670	26,143	24,397	23,515	23,605	+ 733
39	Berhampur (M.)	Madras (Ganjam)	37,750	32,731	31,456	25,729	25,653	23,599	+ 5,019
40	Bettiah (M.)	B. and O. (Champaran)	27,941	24,291	25,793	24,696	22,780	21,263	+ 3,650
41	Bhadreswar (M.)	Bengal (Hooghly)	22,992	22,081	24,353	15,150	9,639	9,241	+ 911
42	Bharatpur (M.)	Rajputana (Bharatpur)	30,173	33,495	33,918	43,601	67,555	66,163	— 3,322
43	Bhatinda*	Punjab (Patiala)	22,771	20,154	15,037	13,185	8,536	5,084	+ 2,617
44	Bhiwani (M.)	Punjab (Hissar)	35,866	33,270	31,100	35,917	35,487	33,762	+ 2,596
45	Bhuj (M.)	W. I. Sts. Agcy. (Cutch)	21,859	19,281	21,579	26,362	25,421	22,308	+ 2,578
46	Bhusaval (M.)	Bombay (Khandesh East)	27,989	25,557	18,312	16,363	13,169	9,613	+ 2,432
47	Bihar (M.)	B. and O. (Patna)	46,994	36,720	35,151	45,063	47,723	48,968	+ 10,274
48	Bijapur (M.)	Bombay (Bijapur)	39,747	32,485	27,615	23,811	16,759	11,424	+ 7,262
49	Bijnor (M.)	United Provinces (Bijnor)	23,520	18,095	17,439	17,583	16,236	15,147	+ 5,425
50	Bilaspur (M.)	C. P. and Berar (Bilaspur)	31,374	24,295	19,850	18,937	11,122	7,775	+ 7,079
51	Bobbili (P. B.)	Madras (Vizagapatam)	20,544	18,179	18,261	17,387	14,468	14,943	+ 2,365
52	Bodinayakkanur (M.)	Madras (Madura)	27,036	20,341	20,183	22,209	17,570	14,759	+ 6,695
53	Brahmanbaria (M.)	Bengal (Tippera)	26,662	23,414	22,295	19,915	18,006	17,438	+ 3,248
54	Broach (M.)	Bombay (Broach)	34,276	42,648	43,403	42,896	40,168	37,281	— 8,372
55	Budaun (M.)	United Provinces (Budaun)	45,455	39,118	38,230	39,031	35,372	33,680	+ 6,337
56	Budge-Budge (M.)	Bengal (Twenty-four Parganas)	24,183	25,723	17,982	13,051	..	..	— 1,540

population with variation since 1881—*continued.*

Increase (+), Decrease (—).				Variation in period 1881 to 1931. Increase (+), Decrease (—).	Males.			Females.			
1911 to 1921.	1901 to 1911.	1891 to 1901.	1881 to 1891.		1931.	1921.	1911.	1931.	1921.	1911.	
10	11	12	13	14	15	16	17	18	19	20	
+ 22,662	— 33,739	— 3,531	— 1,019	— 9,437	32,538	28,674	16,361	28,646	26,320	15,471	40
— 88	+ 11,033	— 21,197	+ 1,705	— 2,509	27,843	24,364	24,053	25,020	22,461	22,860	41
+ 3,719	— 864	+ 2,661	+ 2,678	+ 12,399	38,399	38,076	35,130	27,107	23,225	22,452	42
— 11,717	— 5,710	— 1,153	+ 3,471	+ 2,866	33,148	23,290	29,624	27,442	19,325	24,708	43
..	..	..	..	..	41,307	20,126	..	23,548	11,330	..	44
+ 1,734	+ 5,364	+ 20,859	+ 722	+ 34,026	24,384	22,246	21,231	27,606	24,397	23,678	45
+ 557	— 6,571	— 2,311	+ 2,227	+ 1,500	33,139	28,476	28,663	21,990	19,055	18,311	46
+ 5,365	+ 719	+ 10,264	+ 3,787	+ 28,148	50,151	45,384	40,993	37,289	34,043	33,069	47
+ 5,374	+ 12,009	+ 8,011	+ 3,842	+ 38,971	32,078	26,758	23,761	31,448	27,033	24,656	48
— 1,160	— 4,442	+ 2,025	+ 2,483	— 34	39,603	39,082	38,833	34,613	34,074	35,483	49
+ 6,634	+ 7,024	+ 5,664	+ 1,863	+ 32,074	26,918	20,623	16,978	23,599	19,005	16,016	50
+ 8,609	— 435	+ 11,152	+ 9,140	+ 48,982	46,086	35,493	28,948	29,681	19,758	17,694	51
— 589	— 3,404	+ 3,060	+ 4,000	+ 19,461	45,282	36,040	35,416	33,373	26,221	27,434	52
+ 838	— 4,680	— 2,064	+ 1,118	+ 1,912	42,690	38,125	36,789	36,626	34,491	34,989	53
+ 1,559	+ 4,453	+ 7,487	— 492	+ 20,009	33,744	30,212	28,532	28,761	25,291	25,412	54
+ 7,316	+ 3,806	+ 5,177	+ 5,762	+ 51,243	49,071	30,771	26,651	36,022	25,140	21,944	55
+ 7,465	+ 3,978	+ 2,014	+ 1,913	+ 41,888	43,282	25,708	21,069	25,995	17,051	14,225	56
+ 2,566	— 4,438	+ 10,077	— 615	— 10,908	52,958	61,711	59,634	45,978	55,723	55,234	57
— 428	+ 2,471	+ 3,480	— 355	+ 12,144	33,590	29,353	28,777	33,299	30,560	31,564	58
+ 8,978	+ 4,336	+ 15,701	+ 1,547	+ 33,857	27,600	26,563	21,246	29,478	27,220	23,559	59
+ 9,223	+ 5,679	+ 29,995	— 13,286	+ 54,843	49,392	37,344	32,292	46,624	35,440	31,269	60
+ 4,337	+ 12,137	+ 2,941	+ 8,826	+ 44,114	30,497	22,781	20,320	29,898	21,741	19,865	61
+ 4,613	— 597	+ 5,201	+ 1,759	+ 20,847	30,055	24,350	20,864	23,724	19,558	18,431	62
+ 464	+ 6,209	— 1,388	+ 7,434	+ 19,774	28,626	24,899	23,831	28,639	25,311	25,915	63
+ 1,298	+ 2,521	+ 6,405	+ 4,196	+ 27,012	29,449	22,153	21,465	27,854	22,558	21,948	64
— 120	+ 801	+ 1,308	..	..	33,326	2,731	2,754	28,793	2,691	2,788	65
+ 422,974	**+ 605,569**	**+ 448,138**	**+ 584,784**	**+ 4,183,959**	**4,444,867**	**3,275,835**	**2,976,399**	**3,646,421**	**2,692,959**	**2,569,421**	
+ 6,243	+ 1,086	+ 822	+ 257	+ 2,636	24,207	30,288	25,845	13,140	12,831	11,031	1
— 1,413	+ 1,229	+ 4,173	+ 3,802	+ 13,194	17,963	15,561	16,080	17,672	4,671	15,565	2
+ 268	..		..	..	14,416	13,228	12,392	9,861	8,554	9,122	3
— 739	— 1,906	— 299	+ 3,180	+ 8,987	21,494	16,854	17,465	20,396	16,285	16,413	4
+ 12,038	— 3,463	+ 7,819	+ 4,856	+ 31,018	26,401	20,718	14,006	21,231	17,146	11,820	5
— 1,324	+ 2,213	— 2,258	+ 3,949	+ 4,105	28,724	27,693	29,509	9,370	8,876	8,384	6
+ 6,409	+ 747	+ 2,150	— 2,986	+ 18,084	23,677	16,885	13,370	20,161	15,189	12,295	7
+ 3,455	— 15,466	+ 5,344	+ 1,560	— 1,967	25,584	23,433	22,254	22,316	21,327	19,051	8
+ 3,840	+ 2,938	+ 2,316	+ 351	+ 15,864	12,500	8,839	6,951	10,991	8,233	6,281	9
+ 2,794	— 2,251	— 112	+ 697	+ 9,034	20,045	15,298	13,589	15,148	11,989	10,904	10
— 6,478	+ 3,785	— 578	+ 10,330	+ 8,682	29,991	29,691	34,446	19,377	18,054	19,777	11
+ 956	+ 2,361	+ 5,317	+ 196	+ 13,827	11,900	9,308	8,544	12,317	9,912	9,720	12
+ 6,424	+ 54	+ 5,270	+ 5,396	+ 23,282	25,746	21,802	18,147	21,086	18,892	16,123	13
+ 350	— 554	+ 2,344	+ 2,011	+ 6,544	10,129	8,929	8,893	10,057	8,864	8,550	14
— 1,962	+ 1,339	+ 4,968	— 937	+ 7,908	22,525	19,985	20,550	22,423	20,463	21,860	15
— 265	+ 2,086	+ 1,529	+ 3,669	+ 10,035	11,448	10,088	10,165	11,928	10,272	10,460	16
+ 2,220	— 7,621	— 735	+ 3,907	+ 5,924	26,635	21,564	19,955	22,287	19,205	18,594	17
+ 4,898	+ 3,048	+ 10,960	+ 1,842	+ 23,017	16,574	15,465	12,988	17,274	16,114	13,693	18
+ 4,580	+ 7,013	..	..	..	18,710	15,464	12,486	12,576	11,035	9,433	19
+ 5,591	- 13,888	+ 2,950	+ 3,668	— 931	15,132	14,529	11,293	14,156	14,011	11,656	20
+ 80	— 132	— 170	+ 5,081	+ 7,308	11,809	10,520	10,493	9,134	7,974	7,921	21
+ 464	— 397	+ 3,258	+ 2,048	+ 11,785	18,617	14,716	14,227	15,166	12,655	12,680	2
+ 815	+ 3,732	+ 1,962	+ 1,885	+ 15,532	20,944	15,264	14,217	9,403	7,945	8,177	2
— 1,032	— 1,504	— 506	— 5,903	— 6,559	12,288	10,315	10,543	10,127	9,714	10,518	2
+ 4,985	+ 2,211	+ 3,758	+ 3,330	+ 28,303	24,668	16,491	13,250	18,622	12,780	11,036	2
+ 1,959	+ 2,716	+ 1,994	— 4	+ 12,956	17,280	13,523	12,156	14,423	11,889	11,297	26
+ 4,610	+ 1,681	+ 3,520	+ 1,290	+ 19,508	14,619	9,657	6,908	10,149	6,704	4,843	27
+ 6,189	+ 463	+ 2,876	+ 2,827	+ 17,321	23,116	19,989	14,982	13,934	12,095	10,913	28
+ 4,271	+ 3,495	+ 3,496	+ 2,296	+ 22,530	23,588	17,584	15,488	12,128	9,160	6,985	29
+ 3,977	— 6,145	+ 3,673	+ 4,443	+ 11,484	14,393	11,267	9,256	13,217	10,807	8,841	30
+ 936	+ 1,330	+ 1,892	+ 266	+ 6,444	11,106	10,162	9,517	10,181	9,105	8,814	31
+ 5,482	+ 5,217	+ 1,687	+ 2,030	+ 17,515	29,148	28,406	24,246	16,514	14,157	12,835	32
+ 6,244	— 3,314	+ 1,131	+ 8,094	+ 16,990	13,416	10,237	6,543	9,110	7,454	4,904	33
— 308	— 935	+ 142	+ 2,942	+ 8,923	18,102	13,929	14,180	15,102	12,193	12,250	34
— 438	+ 872	+ 950	+ 5,149	+ 12,513	15,307	12,016	12,328	13,035	10,346	10,472	35
+ 6,855	+ 5,214	— 2,186	+ 5,308	+ 18,089	21,453	19,973	16,232	19,751	18,333	15,219	36
+ 4,886	— 23,291	— 1,220	+ 6,007	— 5,887	25,405	21,113	18,474	22,168	18,729	16,482	37
+ 527	+ 1,746	+ 882	— 90	+ 3,798	15,166	14,719	14,302	12,237	11,951	11,841	38
+ 1,275	+ 5,727	+ 76	+ 2,054	+ 14,151	18,490	16,001	15,331	19,260	16,730	16,125	39
— 1,502	+ 1,097	+ 1,916	+ 1,517	+ 6,678	14,659	12,577	13,096	13,282	11,714	12,697	40
— 2,272	+ 9,203	+ 5,511	+ 398	+ 13,751	14,938	14,487	15,862	8,054	7,594	8,491	41
— 423	— 9,683	— 23,954	+ 1,392	— 35,990	16,736	19,268	18,803	13,437	14,227	15,115	42
+ 5,117	+ 1,852	+ 4,649	+ 3,452	+ 17,687	13,575	12,484	9,232	9,196	7,670	5,805	43
+ 2,170	— 4,817	+ 430	+ 1,725	+ 2,104	19,135	17,746	16,249	16,731	15,524	14,851	44
— 2,298	— 4,783	+ 941	+ 3,113	— 449	10,805	9,308	10,556	11,054	9,973	11,023	45
+ 7,245	+ 1,949	+ 3,194	+ 3,556	+ 18,376	15,422	14,422	10,056	12,567	11,135	8,256	46
+ 1,569	— 9,912	— 2,660	— 1,245	— 1,974	24,532	18,259	16,995	22,462	18,461	18,156	47
+ 4,870	+ 3,804	+ 7,052	+ 5,335	+ 28,323	20,823	16,951	14,345	18,924	15,534	33,270	48
+ 656	— 144	+ 1,347	+ 1,089	+ 8,373	12,930	9,809	9,209	10,590	8,286	8,230	49
+ 4,445	+ 913	+ 7,815	+ 3,347	+ 23,599	16,366	12,454	9,983	15,008	11,841	9,867	50
— 82	+ 874	+ 2,919	— 475	+ 5,601	10,125	8,892	8,849	10,419	9,287	9,412	51
+ 158	— 2,026	+ 4,639	+ 2,811	+ 12,277	13,240	9,767	9,671	13,796	10,574	10,512	52
+ 1,119	+ 2,380	+ 1,909	+ 568	+ 9,224	13,973	12,367	11,671	12,689	11,047	10,624	53
— 755	+ 507	+ 2,728	2,887	— 3,005	18,872	22,668	22,630	15,404	19,980	20,773	54
+ 888	— 801	+ 3,659	+ 1,692	+ 11,775	24,129	20,453	20,048	21,326	18,665	18,182	55
+ 7,741	+ 4,931	..	..	..	15,514	17,883	11,529	8,669	7,840	6,453	56

Table IV.—Towns classified by

	Name of Town.	Province, District, State or Agency, etc.	Population. 1931.	1921.	1911.	1901.	1891.	1881.	Variation: 1921 to 1931.
	1	2	3	4	5	6	7	8	9
	Class III (20,000 to 50,000—contd.								
57	Bulandshahr (M.)	United Provinces (Bulandshahr).	24,898	19,509	19,383	18,959	16,931	17,863	+ 5,389
58	Burdwan (M.)	Bengal (Burdwan)	39,618	34,616	35,921	35,022	34,477	34,080	+ 5,002
59	Burhanpur (M.)	C. P. and Berar (Nimar)	44,066	35,916	22,777	33,341	32,252	30,017	+ 8,150
60	Cambay (M.)	Bombay (Cambay)	31,877	27,251	28,098	31,780	31,390	36,007	+ 4,626
61	Cannanore (M.)	Madras (Malabar)	34,236	27,705	28,957	27,811	27,418	26,386	+ 6,531
62	Cawnpore (Cantt.)	United Provinces (Cawnpore)	24,566	21,351	21,517	..	..	..	+ 3,215
63	Champdani (M.)	Bengal (Hooghly)	25,365	24,652	..	..	..	..	+ 713
64	Chanda (M.)	C. P. and Berar (Chanda)	28,138	22,981	19,866	17,803	16,175	16,137	+ 5,157
65	Chandausi (M.)	United Provinces (Moradabad).	26,768	25,164	22,255	25,711	28,111	27,521	+ 1,604
66	Chapra (M.)	B. and O. (Saran)	47,448	42,415	42,373	45,901	57,352	51,670	+ 5,033
67	Changanachery (M.)	Madras (Travancore)	24,201	18,955	17,242	14,264	..	..	+ 5,246
68	Chidambaram (M.)	Madras (South Arcot)	25,084	22,501	21,327	19,909	18,640	19,837	+ 2,583
69	Chiniot (M.)	Punjab (Jhang)	25,841	17,513	14,085	15,685	13,476	10,731	+ 8,328
70	Chittoor (M.)	Madras (Chittoor)	22,018	17,941	15,108	10,893	9,965	5,809	+ 4,077
71	Churu (M.)	Rajputana (Bikaner)	21,965	16,932	16,038	15,657	14,014	10,666	+ 5,033
72	Cochin (M.)	Madras (Malabar)	22,818	20,637	20,023	19,274	17,601	15,698	+ 2,181
73	Comilla (M.)	Bengal (Tippera)	31,365	25,914	22,692	19,169	14,680	13,372	+ 5,451
74	Cuddapah (M.)	Madras, (Cuddapah)	22,602	19,517	17,807	16,432	17,379	18,982	+ 3,085
75	Damoh (M.)	C. P. and Berar (Damoh)	20,728	15,296	17,042	13,355	11,753	8,665	+ 5,432
76	Davanagere (M.)	Mysore (Chitaldrug)	23,155	16,971	10,074	10,402	8,061	6,362	+ 6,184
77	Dehra Dun (M.)	United Provinces (Dehra Dun).	40,409	33,500	30,301	28,095	25,684	18,959	+ 6,909
78	Deoband (M.)	United Provinces (Saharanpur).	22,126	17,891	18,614	20,167	19,250	22,116	+ 4,235
79	Dera-Ghazi Khan (M.)	Punjab (Dera-Ghazi Khan)	23,468	20,731	18,466	23,731	27,886	22,309	+ 2,737
80	Dera-Ismail Khan (M.)	N. W. F. Province (Dera-Ismail Khan).	38,956	33,885	29,401	28,287	23,246	18,988	+ 5,071
81	Devakȯttai (P. B.)	Madras (Ramnad)	20,393	16,143	13,329	9,503	9,929	8,451	+ 4,250
82	Dharwar (M.)	Bombay (Dharwar)	41,671	34,750	30,289	31,279	32,841	26,520	+ 6,921
83	Dhoraj (M.)	W. I. Sts. Agcy. (Gondal)	29,302	25,666	24,116	24,815	20,406	16,121	+ 3,636
84	Dhulia (M.)	Bombay (Khandesh West)	39,939	30,605	30,800	24,726	21,880	18,449	+ 9,334
85	Dinapore (M.)	B. and O. (Patna)	24,221	21,667	21,066	22,858	44,419	37,893	+ 2,554
86	Dindigul (M.)	Madras (Madura)	43,617	30,922	25,052	25,182	20,203	14,182	+ 12,695
87	Dohad (M.)	Bombay (Panch Mahals)	22,093	16,076	9,303	13,990	12,935	12,394	+ 6,017
88	Ellichpore (M.)	C. P. and Berar (Amraoti)	28,592	23,899	13,909	26,082	26,637	26,728	+ 4,693
89	Ernakulam (M.)	Madras (Cochin)	36,638	23,192	21,195	21,901	17,870	15,467	+ 13,446
90	Erode (M.)	Madras (Coimbatore)	33,672	22,911	16,701	15,529	12,330	9,864	+ 10,761
91	Etawah (M.)	United Provinces (Etawah)	46,948	41,558	45,350	42,570	38,793	34,721	+ 5,390
92	Firozabad (M.)	United Provinces (Agra)	23,154	20,183	13,571	16,849	15,278	16,023	+ 2,971
93	Ferozepore (M.)	Punjab (Ferozepore)	34,337	29,695	24,678	23,475	25,337	20,870	+ 4,642
94	Ferozepore (Cantt).	Punjab (Ferozepore)	30,297	24,656	26,158	25,866	25,100	18,700	+ 5,641
95	Gadag-Bettigiri (M.)	Bombay (Dharwar)	45,852	41,208	30,429	30,652	23,899	17,001	+ 4,644
96	Gauhati (M.)	Assam (Kamrup)	21,797	16,480	12,481	11,661	8,283	11,695	+ 5,317
97	Ghazipur (M.)	United Provinces (Ghazipur)	27,498	24,708	22,165	39,429	44,970	43,232	+ 2,790
98	Giridih (M.)	B. and O. (Hazaribagh)	21,122	18,874	10,668	9,433	..	..	+ 2,248
99	Godhra (M.)	Bombay (Panch Mahals)	35,110	26,979	22,144	20,915	14,691	13,342	+ 8,131
100	Gondal (M).	W. I. Sts. Agcy. (Gondal)	24,573	17,418	15,141	19,592	15,343	13,523	+ 7,155
101	Gudiyattam (M.)	Madras (North Arcot)	24,688	22,803	23,390	21,335	18,747	10,641	+ 1,885
102	Gujrat (M.)	Punjab (Gujrat)	25,604	21,274	18,692	19,048	17,671	18,162	+ 4,330
103	Gulbarga (M.)	Hyderabad (Gulbarga)	41,083	35,820	32,437	29,228	28,200	22,834	+ 5,263
104	Gwalior (M.)	Gwalior (Gird)	21,999	13,037	14,694	16,807	..	..	+ 8,962
105	Hapur (M.)	United Provinces (Meerut)	25,116	20,388	19,142	17,796	14,977	13,212	+ 4,728
106	Hardwar (M.)	United Provinces (Saharanpur).	33,287	30,764	28,682	25,597	29,125	28,106	+ 2,523
107	Hathras (M.)	United Provinces (Aligarh)	39,784	38,763	37,854	42,578	39,181	34,932	+ 1,021
108	Hazaribagh (M.)	B. and O. (Hazaribagh)	20,977	17,060	17,009	15,799	16,672	15,306	+ 3,917
109	Henzada (M.)	Burma (Henzada)	28,542	23,651	25,052	24,756	19,762	16,724	+ 4,891
110	Hinganghat (M.)	C. P. and Berar (Wardha)	22,601	17,200	14,943	12,662	10,964	9,000	+ 5,401
111	Hissar (M.)	Punjab (Hissar)	25,179	21,415	17,162	17,647	16,854	14,167	+ 3,764
112	Hooghly Chinsura (M.)	Bengal (Hooghly)	32,634	29,938	28,916	29,383	33,060	31,177	+ 2,696
113	Hoshiarpur (M.).	Punjab (Hoshiarpur)	25,925	20,413	16,980	17,037	21,099	20,638	+ 5,512
114	Hospet (M.)	Madras (Bellary)	21,673	18,337	16,937	18,482	12,878	10,219	+ 3,336
115	Insein (M.)	Burma (Insein)	20,487	14,308	13,992	..	..	..	+ 6,179
116	Jagraon (M.)	Punjab (Ludhiana)	27,108	17,731	15,039	18,760	18,116	16,873	+ 9,377
117	Jalgaon (M.)	Bombay (Khandesh East)	34,375	23,710	17,867	16,259	14,672	9,918	+ 10,665
118	Jalna (M.)	Hyderabad (Aurangabad)	22,408	16,912	18,993	20,270	19,128	16,199	+ 5,496
119	Jamalpur (M.)	B. & O. (Monghyr)	30,346	24,827	20,526	13,929	18,089	13,213	+ 5,519
120	Jamalpur (M.)	Bengal (Mymensingh)	23,077	23,113	21,109	17,965	15,388	14,727	— 36
121	Jammu (M).	Jammu and Kashmir (Jammu).	38,613	31,506	31,726	36,130	34,542	..	+ 7,107
122	Jaora (M.)	Central India (Jaora)	20,998	17,151	18,054	23,854	21,844	19,902	+ 3,847
123	Jaunpur (M.)	United Provinces (Jaunpur)	37,675	32,569	30,473	42,771	42,819	42,845	+ 5,106
124	Jetpur*	W. I. Sts. Agcy. (W. Kathiawar).	22,973	18,694	16,513	15,919	13,646	11,813	+ 4,279
125	Jhang-Maghiana (M.)	Punjab (Jhang)	36,035	30,139	25,914	24,382	23,290	21,629	+ 5,896
126	Jubbulpore (Cantt).	C. P. & Berar (Jubbulpore)	20,065	21,997	21,642	13,157	11,326	..	— 1,932
127	Junagadh*	W. I. Sts. Agcy. (Junagadh)	39,890	33,221	35,413	34,251	31,640	24,679	+ 6,669
128	Kadaiyanallur (P. B.)	Madras (Tinnevelly)	23,819	19,693	17,077	13,939	8,200	7,467	+ 4,126
129	Kalyan (M.)	Bombay (Thana)	26,291	17,829	12,600	10,749	12,608	12,910	+ 8,462
130	Kamarhati (M.)	Bengal (Twenty-four Parganas).	30,334	23,018	18,015	13,216	11,722	10,253	+ 7,316
131	Kamptee (M.)	C. P. and Berar (Nagpur)	20,787	17,531	14,869	38,888	43,159	50,987	+ 3,256
132	Kanauj (M.)	United Provinces (Farrukhabad).	20,360	18,258	18,105	18,552	17,648	16,646	+ 2,102
133	Kapurthala (M.)	Punjab (Kapurthala).	20,210	16,242	16,367	18,519	16,747	15,237	+ 3,968
134	Karaikoudi (M.)	Madras (Ramnad)	21,672	15,350	14,648	11,801	6,579	5,541	+ 6,322
135	Karnal (M).	Punjab (Karnal)	25,371	21,841	21,018	22,703	21,530	22,528	+ 3,530
136	Kasganj (M.)	United Provinces (Etah)	23,100	20,988	16,429	19,686	16,050	16,535	+ 2,112
137	Kasur (M.)	Punjab (Lahore)	46,815	31,018	24,783	22,022	20,290	17,336	+ 15,797
138	Khamgaon (M.)	C. P. and Berar (Buldhana)	23,462	19,962	10,123	18,341	15,598	12,390	+ 3,500
139	Khandwa (M.)	C. P. and Berar (Nimar)	34,622	26,802	21,604	19,401	15,589	15,142	+ 7,820
140	Khurja (M.)	United Provinces (Bulands	31,279	25,719	27,387	[illegible]	[illegible]		

population with variation since 1881—*continued.*

Increase (+), Decrease (—). 1911 to 1921.	1901 to 1911.	1891 to 1901.	1881 to 1891.	Variation in period 1881 to 1931. Increase (+), Decrease (—).	Males. 1931.	1921.	1911.	Females. 1931.	1921.	1911.
10	11	12	13	14	15	16	17	18	19	20
+ 126	+ 424	+ 2,028	— 932	+ 7,035	14,248	11,056	10,679	10,650	8,453	8,704
— 1,305	+ 899	+ 545	+ 397	+ 5,538	23,485	19,583	20,527	16,133	15,033	15,394
+ 13,139	— 10,564	+ 1,089	+ 2,235	+ 14,049	23,056	18,886	11,624	21,010	17,030	11,153
— 847	— 3,682	+ 390	— 4,617	— 4,130	16,296	13,547	13,858	15,581	13,704	14,240
— 1,252	+ 1,146	+ 393	+ 1,032	+ 7,850	16,934	13,159	14,241	17,302	14,546	14,716
— 166	..	..	..	..	14,596	13,353	13,510	9,970	7,998	8,007
..	..	..	..	..	17,497	17,193	..	7,868	7,459	..
+ 3,115	+ 2,063	+ 1,628	+ 38	+ 12,001	14,394	11,539	10,077	13,744	11,442	9,789
+ 2,909	— 3,456	— 2,400	+ 590	— 753	14,898	14,058	12,367	11,870	11,106	9,888
+ 42	— 3,528	— 11,451	+ 5,682	— 4,222	25,934	22,492	21,601	21,514	19,923	20,772
+ 1,713	+ 2,978	..	..	..	12,615	9,814	8,826	11,586	9,141	8,416
+ 1,174	+ 1,418	+ 1,269	— 1,197	+ 5,247	12,449	11,214	10,279	12,635	11,287	11,048
+ 3,428	— 1,600	+ 2,209	+ 2,745	+ 15,110	14,027	9,008	7,073	11,814	8,505	7,012
+ 2,833	+ 4,215	+ 928	+ 4,156	+ 16,209	10,892	8,942	7,398	11,126	8,999	7,710
+ 894	+ 381	+ 1,643	+ 3,348	+ 11,299	11,107	8,462	7,793	10,858	8,470	8,245
+ 614	+ 749	+ 1,673	+ 1,903	+ 7,120	11,950	11,222	10,764	10,868	9,415	9,259
+ 3,222	+ 3,523	+ 4,489	+ 1,308	+ 17,993	18,530	15,533	13,706	12,835	10,381	8,986
+ 1,710	+ 1,375	— 947	— 1,603	+ 3,620	11,522	9,866	8,675	11,080	9,651	9,132
— 1,746	+ 3,687	+ 1,602	+ 3,088	+ 12,063	10,726	7,993	8,732	10,002	7,303	8,310
+ 6,897	— 328	+ 2,341	+ 1,699	+ 16,793	12,069	8,978	5,257	11,086	7,993	4,817
+ 3,199	+ 2,206	+ 2,411	+ 6,725	+ 21,450	24,862	20,669	18,111	15,547	12,831	12,190
— 723	— 1,553	+ 917	— 2,866	+ 10	12,407	9,953	10,065	9,719	7,938	8,549
+ 2,265	— 5,265	— 4,155	+ 5,577	+ 1,159	12,759	11,386	10,428	10,709	9,345	8,038
+ 4,484	+ 1,114	+ 5,041	+ 4,258	+ 19,968	22,141	19,446	16,829	16,815	14,439	12,572
+ 2,814	+ 3,826	— 426	+ 1,478	+ 11,942	9,684	7,520	6,176	10,709	8,623	7,153
+ 4,461	— 990	— 1,562	+ 6,321	+ 15,151	21,957	18,258	15,528	19,714	16,492	14,761
+ 1,550	— 699	+ 4,409	+ 4,285	+ 13,181	13,813	11,654	10,950	15,489	14,012	13,166
— 195	+ 6,074	+ 2,846	+ 3,431	+ 21,490	20,917	15,946	16,231	19,022	14,659	14,569
+ 601	— 1,792	— 21,561	+ 6,526	— 13,672	12,347	10,981	10,133	11,874	10,686	10,933
+ 5,870	— 130	+ 4,979	+ 6,021	+ 29,435	22,351	15,809	12,720	21,266	15,113	12,332
+ 6,773	— 4,687	+ 1,055	+ 541	+ 9,699	11,911	8,189	4,729	10,182	7,887	4,574
+ 9,990	— 12,173	— 555	— 91	+ 1,864	14,822	12,183	7,027	13,770	11,716	6,882
+ 1,997	— 706	+ 4,031	+ 2,403	+ 21,171	19,363	12,638	11,944	17,275	10,554	9,251
+ 6,210	+ 1,172	+ 3,199	+ 2,466	+ 23,808	17,765	11,481	8,402	15,907	11,430	8,299
— 3,792	+ 2,780	+ 3,777	+ 4,072	+ 12,227	25,461	22,469	24,249	21,487	19,089	21,101
+ 6,612	— 3,278	+ 1,571	— 745	+ 7,131	13,053	11,240	7,184	10,101	8,943	6,387
+ 5,017	+ 1,203	— 1,862	+ 4,467	+ 13,467	19,679	17,022	13,930	14,658	12,673	10,748
— 1,502	+ 292	+ 766	+ 6,400	+ 11,597	19,205	15,662	17,529	11,092	8,994	8,629
+ 10,779	— 223	+ 6,753	+ 6,898	+ 28,851	24,139	21,708	15,570	21,713	19,500	14,859
+ 3,999	+ 820	+ 3,378	— 3,412	+ 10,102	14,506	10,786	8,138	7,291	5,694	4,343
+ 2,543	— 17,264	— 5,541	+ 1,738	— 15,734	15,011	13,277	12,005	12,487	11,431	10,160
+ 8,206	+ 1,235	..	..	..	11,122	9,885	5,713	10,000	8,989	4,955
+ 4,835	+ 1,229	+ 6,224	+ 1,349	+ 21,768	18,827	14,243	11,599	16,283	12,736	10,545
+ 2,277	— 4,451	+ 4,249	+ 1,820	+ 11,050	12,603	8,670	7,668	11,970	8,748	7,473
— 587	+ 2,055	+ 2,588	+ 8,106	+ 14,047	12,272	11,201	11,386	12,416	11,602	12,004
+ 2,582	— 356	+ 1,377	— 491	+ 7,442	13,956	11,384	9,657	11,648	9,890	9,035
+ 3,383	+ 3,209	+ 1,028	+ 5,366	+ 18,249	21,567	18,720	16,849	19,516	17,100	15,588
— 1,657	— 2,113	..	..	..	12,306	6,675	7,458	9,693	6,362	7,236
+ 1,246	+ 1,346	+ 2,819	+ 1,765	+ 11,904	14,266	11,523	10,758	10,850	8,865	8,384
+ 2,082	+ 3,085	— 3,528	+ 1,019	+ 5,181	19,374	18,338	16,624	13,913	12,426	12,058
+ 909	— 4,724	+ 3,397	+ 4,249	+ 4,852	22,688	22,114	21,360	17,096	16,649	16,494
+ 51	+ 1,210	— 873	+ 1,366	+ 5,671	10,903	8,561	8,564	10,074	8,499	8,445
— 1,401	+ 296	+ 4,994	+ 3,038	+ 11,818	15,765	12,974	14,009	12,777	10,677	11,043
+ 2,257	+ 2,281	+ 1,698	+ 1,964	+ 13,601	11,812	8,887	7,690	10,789	8,313	7,253
+ 4,253	— 485	+ 793	+ 2,687	+ 11,012	15,065	12,326	9,710	10,114	9,089	7,452
+ 1,022	— 467	— 3,677	+ 1,883	+ 1,457	18,799	16,723	15,817	13,835	13,215	13,099
+ 3,433	— 57	— 4,062	+ 461	+ 5,287	14,689	11,536	9,576	11,236	8,877	7,404
+ 1,400	— 1,545	+ 5,604	+ 2,659	+ 11,454	10,858	9,132	8,408	10,815	9,205	8,529
+ 316	..	..	..	..	13,420	9,520	10,046	7,067	4,788	3,946
+ 2,692	— 3,721	+ 644	+ 1,243	+ 10,235	17,151	9,771	8,128	9,957	7,960	6,911
+ 5,843	+ 1,608	+ 1,587	+ 4,754	+ 24,457	18,771	12,687	9,490	15,604	11,023	8,377
— 2,081	— 1,277	+ 1,142	+ 2,929	+ 6,209	11,764	8,660	9,711	10,644	8 252	9,282
+ 4,301	+ 6,597	— 4,160	+ 4,876	+ 17,133	16,378	13,343	10,881	13,968	11,484	9,645
+ 2,004	+ 3,144	+ 2,577	+ 661	+ 8,350	12,629	12,566	11,728	10,448	10,547	9,381
— 220	— 4,404	+ 1,588	..	..	23,361	19,121	19,362	15,252	12,385	12,364
— 903	— 5,800	+ 2,010	+ 1,942	+ 1,096	10,946	8,656	9,146	10,052	8,495	8,908
+ 2,096	— 12,298	— 48	— 26	— 5,170	20,353	17,376	15,888	17,322	15,193	14,585
+ 2,181	+ 594	+ 2,273	+ 1,833	+ 11,160	11,102	8,967	7,674	11,871	9,727	8,839
+ 4,225	+ 1,532	+ 1,092	+ 1,661	+ 14,406	19,275	15,714	13,212	16,760	14,425	12,702
+ 355	+ 8,485	+ 1,831	..	..	12,645	14,871	14,252	7,420	7,126	7,390
— 2,192	+ 1,162	+ 2,611	+ 6,961	+ 15,211	21,212	17,255	18,565	18,678	15,966	16,848
+ 2,616	+ 3,138	+ 5,739	+ 733	+ 16,352	11,886	9,769	8,330	11,933	9,924	8,747
+ 5,229	+ 1,851	— 1,859	— 302	+ 13,381	15,143	9,979	6,973	11,148	7,850	5,627
+ 5,003	+ 4,799	+ 1,494	+ 1,469	+ 20,081	20,087	14,965	11,243	10,247	8,053	6,772
+ 2,662	— 24,019	— 4,271	— 7,828	— 30,200	10,806	8,601	7,617	9,981	8,930	7,252
+ 153	— 447	+ 904	+ 1,002	+ 3,714	10,721	9,695	9,337	9,639	8,563	8,768
— 125	— 2,152	+ 1,772	+ 1,510	+ 4,973	11,772	9,340	9,485	8,438	6,902	6,882
+ 702	+ 2,847	+ 5,222	+ 1,038	+ 16,131	10,935	7,223	6,768	10,737	8,127	7,880
+ 823	— 1,685	+ 1,173	— 998	+ 2,843	14,314	12,054	11,233	11,057	9,787	9,785
+ 4,559	— 3,257	+ 3,636	— 485	+ 6,565	12,729	11,281	9,237	10,371	9,707	7,192
+ 6,235	+ 2,761	+ 1,732	+ 2,954	+ 29,479	28,067	17,125	13,769	18,748	13,893	11,014
+ 9,839	— 8,218	+ 2,743	+ 3,208	+ 11,072	13,113	10,664	5,545	10,349	9,298	4,578
+ 5,198	+ 2,203	+ 3,812	+ 447	+ 19,480	19,060	14,423	11,511	15,562	12,379	10,093
— 1,668	— 1,890	+ 2,928	— 841	+ 4,089	17,135	13,963	14,549	14,144	11,756	12,838

Table IV.—Towns classified by

Name of Town.	Province, District, State or Agency, etc.	Population. 1931.	1921.	1911.	1901.	1891.	1881.	Variation. 1921 to 1931.
1	2	3	4	5	6	7	8	9
Kohat (M.)	N. W. F. Province (Kohat)	25,100	18,547	16,697	18,092	14,347	13,490	+ 6,553
Kotah (M.)	Rajputana (Kotah)	37,876	31,707	32,753	33,657	38,620	40,270	+ 6,169
Kottayam (M.)	Madras (Travancore)	25,236	18,833	15,141	17,552	7,090	11,293	+ 6,403
Krishnagar (M.)	Bengal (Nadia)	24,284	22,309	23,475	24,547	25,500	27,477	+ 1,975
Kurla (M.)	Bombay (Bombay Suburban).	30,311	26,059	15,081	14,831	11,469	9,715	+ 4,252
Kurnool (M.)	Madras (Kurnool)	35,314	27,908	26,040	25,376	24,376	20,329	+ 7,406
Lahore (Cantt.)	Punjab (Lahore)	29,672	24,486	18,416	16,080	17,257	18,409	+ 5,186
Larkana (M.)	Bombay (Larkana)	26,841	17,723	16,097	14,543	12,019	13,188	+ 9,118
Latur (M.)	Hyderabad (Osmanabad)	30,760	16,233	7,574	10,479	9,063	8,648	+ 14,527
Lucknow (Cantt.)	United Provinces (Lucknow)	23,562	23,399	19,782	..	..	..	+ 163
Lyallpur (M.)	Punjab (Lyallpur)	42,922	28,136	19,578	9,171	..	..	+ 14,786
Madaripur (M.)	Bengal (Faridpur)	26,894	25,297	19,073	17,463	13,772	12,298	+ 1,597
Malegaon (M.)	Bombay (Nasik)	32,462	23,711	19,542	19,054	19,261	14,402	+ 8,751
Maler Kotla (M.)	Punjab (Maler Kotla)	22,396	24,564	23,880	21,122	21,754	20,621	— 2,168
Malwan (M.)	Bombay (Ratnagiri)	29,817	22,215	22,080	19,626	17,053	15,565	+ 7,602
Mandvi (M.)	W. I. Sts. Agcy. (Cutch)	25,342	22,638	24,235	24,683	38,155	35,980	+ 2,704
Mannargudi (M.)	Madras (Tanjore)	22,764	21,636	21,398	20,449	20,395	19,409	+ 1,128
Mardan (M.)	N. W. F. P. (Peshawar)	23,848	7,433	6,134	..	..	..	+ 16,415
Mattancheri (M.)	Madras (Cochin)	39,645	24,664	23,508	20,061	17,254	14,634	+ 14,981
Mau (N. A.)	United Provinces (Azamgarh).	21,354	17,998	16,751	17,696	15,547	14,945	+ 3,356
Mayavaram (M.)	Madras (Tanjore)	31,887	28,617	27,121	24,276	23,765	23,044	+ 3,270
Meerut (Cantt.)	United Provinces (Meerut)	45,528	44,898	39,876	..	..	..	+ 630
Mergui (M.)	Burma (Mergui)	20,405	17,297	14,889	11,987	10,137	8,633	+ 3,108
Mhow (Cantt.)	Central India (Indore)	31,177	31,737	29,820	36,039	31,773	27,227	— 560
Midnapur (M.)	Bengal (Midnapore)	32,021	28,965	32,740	33,140	32,264	33,560	+ 3,056
Miraj (M.)	Bombay (Miraj Senior)	26,465	21,424	21,168	18,425	26,060	20,616	+ 5,041
Montgomery (M.)	Punjab (Montgomery)	26,164	14,601	8,129	6,602	5,159	3,178	+ 11,563
Murwara (M.)	C. P. and Berar (Jubbulpore)	21,959	19,682	15,812	14,137	9,460	8,612	+ 2,277
Muzaffarnagar (M)	United Provinces (Muzaffarnagar)	35,347	23,937	23,811	23,444	18,166	15,080	+ 11,410
Muzaffarpur (M.)	B. & O. (Muzaffarpur)	42,812	32,755	43,668	45,617	49,192	42,460	+ 10,057
Myingyan (M.)	Burma (Myingyan)	25,457	18,931	16,379	16,205	19,790	..	+ 6,526
Mymensingh (M.)	Bengal (Mymensingh)	30,480	25,287	19,853	14,668	11,555	10,561	+ 5,193
Nadiad (M.)	Bombay (Kaira)	34,584	31,939	27,145	31,435	29,048	28,304	+ 2,645
Nagercoil (M.)	Madras (Travancore)	42,945	34,406	29,883	25,782	11,187	16,534	+ 8,539
Nagina (M.)	United Provinces (Bijnor)	25,427	18,736	19,625	21,412	22,150	20,503	+ 6,691
Naihati (M.)	Bengal (24-Parganas)	30,908	23,286	18,219	13,831	9,077	6,576	+ 7,622
Najibabad (M.)	United Provinces (Bijnor)	28,473	18,504	18,460	19,568	19,410	17,750	+ 9,969
Nander (M.)	Hyderabad (Nander)	26,992	21,470	17,625	14,184	13,105	14,091	+ 5,522
Nandyal (M.)	Madras (Kurnool)	22,608	18,124	16,230	15,137	10,737	8,907	+ 4,484
Narayanganj (M.)	Bengal (Dacca)	34,189	30,602	27,876	24,472	17,715	12,508	+ 3,587
Narnaul*	Punjab (Patiala)	21,905	20,410	21,350	19,489	21,159	20,052	+ 1,495
Nasik (M.)	Bombay (Nasik)	48,703	42,756	33,463	21,490	24,429	24,101	+ 5,947
Nasirabad (Cantt.)	Ajmer-Merwara	21,397	19,651	20,241	22,494	21,710	21,320	+ 1,746
Navsari (M.)	Baroda (Navsari)	24,397	19,437	17,982	21,451	16,276	14,920	+ 4,960
Nellore (M.)	Madras (Nellore)	45,895	35,863	33,246	32,040	29,336	27,505	+ 10,032
Negapatam (M.)	Madras (Tanjore)	48,527	54,016	60,168	57,190	59,221	53,855	— 5,489
Ootacamund (M.)	Madras (Nilgiris)	24,616	19,467	18,829	18,596	15,053	12,335	+ 5,149
Pabna (M.)	Bengal (Pabna)	21,904	19,343	19,274	18,424	16,486	15,267	+ 2,561
Pakokku (M.)	Burma (Pakokku)	23,115	19,507	20,010	19,456	19,972	..	+ 3,608
Palanpur*	W. I. Sts. Agcy. (Palanpur)	20,347	17,843	17,221	17,799	21,092	17,547	+ 2,504
Palghat (M.)	Madras (Malabar)	49,064	45,487	44,319	44,177	39,481	36,339	+ 3,577
Pandharpur (M.)	Bombay (Sholapur)	29,460	25,210	28,550	32,405	19,954	16,910	+ 4,250
Panipat (M.)	Punjab (Karnal)	32,915	27,343	26,342	26,914	27,547	25,022	+ 5,572
Parlakimedi (M.)	Madras (Ganjam)	20,072	18,719	18,370	17,336	16,390	10,812	+ 1,353
Patan (M.)	Baroda (Kadi)	29,830	27,017	28,339	31,402	32,646	32,712	+ 2,813
Pegu (M.)	Burma (Pegu)	21,712	18,769	17,104	14,132	10,762	5,891	+ 2,943
Periyakulam (M.)	Madras (Madura)	23,004	16,478	18,715	17,960	16,363	16,446	+ 6,526
Pilibhit (M.)	United Provnces (Pilibhit)	36,892	32,344	31,554	33,490	33,799	29,721	+ 4,548
Pollachi (M.)	Madras (Coimbatore)	22,112	11,875	10,909	8,958	5,805	5,082	+ 10,237
Poona (Cantt.)	Bombay (Poona)	35,807	32,726	32,226	32,777	35,094	10,129	+ 3,081
Poonamallee (P. B.)	Madras (Chingleput)	20,340	17,549	16,342	15,323	14,948	14,638	+ 2,791
Porbandar*	W. I. Sts. Agcy. (Porbandar)	33,383	28,699	24,821	24,620	18,805	14,569	+ 4,684
Proddatur (M.)	Madras (Cuddapah)	20,124	15,906	15,756	14,370	6,841	6,510	+ 4,218
Prome (M.)	Burma (Prome)	28,295	26,067	26,911	27,375	30,022	28,813	+ 2,228
Pudukkottai (M.)	Madras (Pudukkottai)	28,776	26,101	26,850	20,347	16,885	15,384	+ 2,675
Puliyangudi (P. B.)	Madras (Tinnevelly)	21,173	18,437	15,463	15,729	13,818	12,104	+ 2,736
Puri (M.)	B. and O. (Puri)	37,568	38,694	39,686	49,334	28,794	22,095	— 1,126
Purulia (M.)	B. and O. (Manbhum)	25,974	22,161	20,886	17,291	12,128	9,305	+ 3,813
Peshawar (Cantt.)	N. W. F. Province (Peshawar).	34,426	25,025	23,873	21,804	21,112	20,690	+ 9,401
Quetta (M.)	Baluchistan (Quetta-Pishin)	34,881	27,220	17,021	13,517	11,302	..	+ 7,661
Quetta (Cantt.)	Baluchistan (Quetta-Pishin)	25,391	21,781	16,901	11,067	7,500	..	+ 3,610
Quilon (M.)	Madras (Travancore)	33,739	25,135	18,839	15,691	15,375	13,588	+ 8,604
Raichur (M.)	Hyderabad (Raichur)	27,910	26,374	25,034	22,165	23,174	15,387	+ 1,536
Raipur (M.)	C. P. and Berar (Raipur)	45,390	38,341	35,335	32,114	23,759	24,948	+ 7,049
Rajapalaiyam (P. B.)	Madras (Ramnad)	38,693	33,184	28,412	25,360	13,301	12,021	+ 5,509
Rajkot (M.)	W. I. Sts. Agcy. (Rajkot).	47,485	36,057	26,412	27,159	21,564	15,139	+ 11,428
Rajshahi (M.)	Bengal (Rajshahi)	27,064	24,598	23,406	21,589	21,407	19,228	+ 2,466
Rangpur (M.)	Bengal (Rangpur)	20,749	19,076	16,429	15,960	14,216	13,320	+ 1,673
Ratlam*	Central India (Ratlam)	37,675	30,133	27,957	36,321	29,822	31,066	+ 7,542
Ratnagiri (M.)	Bombay (Ratnagiri)	23,906	18,540	15,858	16,094	14,303	12,616	+ 5,366
Rawalpindi (Cantt.)	Punjab (Rawalpindi)	43,517	45,891	39,841	40,611	37,870	26,190	— 2,374
Rewa*	Central India (Rewa)	25,206	20,977	26,247	24,608	23,626	22,016	+ 4,229
Rewari (M.)	Punjab (Gurgaon)	26,269	23,129	24,780	27,295	27,934	23,972	+ 3,140
Rishra Konnagar (M.)	Bengal (Hooghly)	26,868	23,259	..	..	..	..	+ 3,609
Rohtak (M.)	Punjab (Rohtak)	34,112	24,701	19,862	19,766	16,191	15,160	+ 9,411
Saidapet (M.)	Madras (Chingleput)	33,037	27,404	15,635	14,254	5,702	10,290	+ 5,633
Sambhal (M.)	United Provinces (Moradabad).	44,300	41,585	45,276	42,838	40,153	37,963	+ 2,715
Sangli (M.)	Bombay (Sangli)	29,818	21,112	16,141	16,829	14,798	13,272	+ 8,706
Santipur (M.)	Bengal (Nadia)	24,992	24,792	26,703	26,898	30,437	29,687	+ 200
Sargodha (M.)	Punjab (Shahpur)	26,761	17,728	8,849	..	..	..	+ 9,033

population with variation since 1881—*continued.*

Increase (+), Decrease (—). 1911 to 1921.	1901 to 1911.	1891 to 1901.	1881 to 1891.	Variation in period 1881 to 1931. Increase (+), Decrease (—).	Males. 1931.	1921.	1911.	Females. 1931.	1921.	1911.	
10	11	12	13	14	15	16	17	18	19	20	
+ 1,850	— 1,395	+ 3,745	+ 857	+ 11,610	14,236	10,856	9,295	10,864	7,691	7,402	141
— 1,046	— 904	— 4,963	— 1,650	— 2,394	20,259	16,790	16,949	17,617	14,917	15,804	142
+ 3,692	— 2,411	+ 10,462	— 4,203	+ 13,943	13,280	9,855	7,863	11,956	8,978	7,278	143
— 1,166	— 1,072	— 953	— 1,977	— 3,193	12,807	11,377	11,767	11,477	10,932	11,708	144
+ 10,978	+ 250	+ 3,362	+ 1,754	+ 20,596	17,914	15,217	8,598	12,397	10,842	6,483	145
+1,868	+ 664	+ 1,000	+ 4,047	+ 14,985	17,949	13,844	12,766	17,365	14,064	13,274	146
+ 6,070	+ 2,336	— 1,177	— 1,152	+ 11,263	20,741	18,295	13,736	8,931	6,191	4,680	147
+ 1,626	+ 1,554	+ 2,524	— 1,169	+ 13,653	15,641	10,273	8,836	11,200	7,450	7,261	148
+ 8,659	— 2,905	+ 1,416	+ 415	+ 22,112	16,609	8,767	3,843	14,151	7,466	3,731	149
+ 3,617	..	..	..	..	15,582	15,740	13,283	7,980	7,659	6,499	150
+ 8,558	+ 10,407	..	..	..	27,489	18,875	13,353	15,433	9,261	6,225	151
+ 6,224	+ 1,610	+ 3,691	+ 1,474	+ 14,596	15,204	14,309	10,549	11,690	10,988	8,524	152
+ 4,169	+ 488	— 207	+ 4,859	+ 18,060	16,705	12,156	10,083	15,757	11,555	9,459	153
+ 684	+ 2,758	— 632	+ 1,133	+ 1,775	12,230	14,466	13,538	10,166	10,098	10,342	154
+ 135	+ 2,454	+ 2,573	+ 1,488	+ 14,252	14,494	10,315	10,327	15,323	11,900	11,753	155
— 1,597	— 448	— 13,472	+ 2,175	— 10,638	12,103	10,122	11,238	13,239	12,516	12,997	156
+ 238	+ 949	+ 54	+ 986	+ 3,355	11,339	10,808	10,556	11,425	10,828	10,842	157
+ 1,299	..	..	..	..	13,631	4,435	3,835	10,217	2,998	2,299	158
+ 1,156	+ 3,447	+ 2,807	+ 2,620	+ 25,011	20,925	12,933	12,625	18,720	11,731	10 883	159
+ 1,247	— 945	+ 2,149	+ 602	+ 6,409	11,149	9,214	8,320	10,205	8,784	8,431	160
+ 1,496	+ 2,845	+ 511	+ 721	+ 8,843	15,572	14,007	13,264	16,315	14,610	13,857	161
+ 5,022	..	..	..	..	27,961	28,864	24,269	17,567	16,034	15,607	162
+ 2,408	+ 2,902	+ 1,850	+ 1,504	+ 11,772	10,969	9,540	8,100	9,436	7,757	6,789	163
+ 1,917	— 6,219	+ 4,266	+ 4,546	+ 3,950	17,496	19,218	17,723	13,681	12,519	12,097	164
— 3,775	— 400	+ 876	— 1,296	— 1,539	17,807	15,724	17,577	14,214	13,241	15,163	165
+ 256	+ 2,743	— 7,635	+ 5,444	+ 5,849	13,750	10,941	10,747	12,715	10,483	10,421	166
+ 6,472	+ 1,527	+ 1,443	+ 1,981	+ 22,986	17,392	10,011	5,773	8,772	4,590	2,356	167
+ 3,870	+ 1,675	+ 4,677	+ 848	+ 13,347	11,572	10,359	8,173	10,387	9,323	7,639	168
+ 126	+ 367	+ 5,278	+ 3,086	+ 20,267	21,131	13,706	13,973	14,216	10,231	9,838	169
— 10,913	— 1,949	— 3,575	+ 6,732	+ 352	24,841	18,201	23,836	17,971	14,554	19,832	170
+ 2,552	+ 174	— 3,585	..	..	13,769	10,374	8,765	11,688	8,557	7,614	171
+ 5,434	+ 5,185	+ 3,113	+ 994	+ 19,919	19,733	16,597	13,462	10,747	8,690	6,391	172
+ 4,794	— 4,290	+ 2,387	+ 744	+ 6,280	18,528	17,435	14,364	16,056	14,504	12,781	173
+ 4,523	+ 4,101	+ 14,595	— 5,347	+ 26,411	20,873	16,994	14,553	22,072	17,412	15,330	174
— 889	— 1,787	— 738	+ 1,647	+ 4,924	14,476	9,846	10,072	10,951	8,890	9,553	175
+ 5,067	+ 4,388	+ 4,754	+ 2,501	+ 24,332	20,123	15,464	11,685	10,785	7,822	6,534	176
+ 44	— 1,108	+ 158	+ 1,660	+ 10,723	16,023	9,612	9,699	12,450	8,892	8,761	177
+ 3,845	+ 3,441	+ 1,079	— 986	+ 12,901	14,332	11,435	9,281	12,660	10,035	8,344	178
+ 1,894	+ 1,093	+ 4,400	+ 1,830	+ 13,701	11,646	9,194	8,165	10,962	8,930	8,065	179
+ 2,726	+ 3,404	+ 6,757	+ 5,207	+ 21,681	21,526	19,442	18,738	12,663	11,160	9,138	180
— 940	+ 1,861	— 1,670	+ 1,107	+ 1,853	11,270	10,536	10,985	10,635	9,874	10,365	181
+ 9,293	+ 11,973	— 2,939	+ 328	+ 24,602	25,333	21,974	16,897	23,370	20,782	16,566	182
— 590	— 2,253	+ 784	+ 390	+ 77	11,861	11,311	11,298	9,536	8,340	8,943	183
+ 1,455	— 3,469	+ 5,175	+ 1,356	+ 9,477	12,013	9,478	8,690	12,384	9,959	9,292	184
+ 2,617	+ 1,206	+ 2,704	+ 1,831	+ 18,390	22,810	17,769	16,180	23,085	18,094	17,066	185
— 6,152	+ 2,978	— 2,031	+ 5,366	— 5,328	23,143	26,321	29,995	25,384	27,695	30,173	186
+ 638	+ 233	+ 3,543	+ 2,718	+ 12,281	13,164	10,217	9,955	11,452	9,250	8,874	187
+ 69	+ 850	+ 1,938	+ 1,219	+ 6,637	11,970	10,352	10,056	9,934	8,991	9,218	188
— 503	+554	— 516	..	..	11,881	9,665	9,658	11,234	9,842	10,352	189
+ 622	— 578	— 3,293	+ 3,545	+ 2,800	10,509	9,141	8,562	9,838	8,702	8,659	190
+ 1,168	+ 142	+ 4,696	+ 3,142	+ 12,725	24,234	22,619	21,776	24,830	22,868	22,543	191
— 3,340	— 3,855	+ 12,451	+ 3,044	+ 12,550	15,095	12,631	14,591	14,365	12,579	13,959	192
+ 1,001	— 572	— 633	+ 2,525	+ 7,893	18,010	14,666	13,554	14,905	12,677	12,788	193
+ 349	+ 1,034	+ 946	+ 5,578	+ 9,260	9,604	8,818	8,638	10,468	9,901	9,732	194
— 1,322	— 3,063	— 1,244	— 66	— 2,882	14,884	13,487	13,904	14,946	13,530	14,435	195
+ 1,665	+ 2,972	+ 3,370	+ 4,871	+ 15,821	11,920	10,728	10,232	9,792	8,041	6,872	196
— 2,237	+ 755	+ 1,597	— 83	+ 6,558	11,109	7,844	8,817	11,895	8,634	9,898	197
+ 790	— 1,936	— 309	+ 4,078	+ 7,171	19,569	17,004	16,817	17,323	15,340	14,737	198
+ 966	+ 1,951	+ 3,153	+ 723	+ 17,030	11,720	6,241	5,393	0,392	5,634	5,516	199
+ 500	— 551	— 2,317	+ 24,965	+ 25,678	20,657	18,990	18,200	15,150	13,736	14,026	200
+ 1,207	+ 1,019	+ 375	+ 310	+ 5,702	10,409	8,783	8,093	9,931	8,766	8,249	201
+ 3,878	+ 201	+ 5,815	+ 4,236	+ 18,814	17,088	14,434	12,672	16,295	14,265	12,149	202
+ 150	+ 1,386	+ 7,529	+ 331	+ 13,614	10,280	8,105	7,988	9,844	7,801	7,768	203
— 844	— 464	— 2,647	+ 1,209	— 518	15,332	14,340	14,385	12,963	11,727	12,526	204
— 749	+ 6,503	+ 3,462	+ 1,501	+ 13,392	14,326	12,932	13,108	14,450	13,169	13,742	205
+ 2,974	—266	+ 1,911	+ 1,714	+ 9,069	10,417	9,168	7,639	10,756	9,269	7,824	206
— 992	— 9,648	+ 20,540	+ 6,699	+ 15,473	20,703	21,805	22,905	16,865	16,889	16,781	207
+ 1,275	+ 3,595	+ 5,163	+ 2,823	+ 16,669	14,388	12,169	11,377	11,586	9,992	9,509	208
+ 1,152	+ 2,069	+ 692	+ 422	+ 13,736	25,702	19,508	18,687	8,724	5,517	5,186	209
+ 10,199	+ 3,504	+ 2,215	..		22,838	19,024	11,456	12,043	8,106	5,565	210
+ 4,880	+ 5,834	+ 3,567	..	..	19,589	18,385	13,813	5,802	3,396	3,088	211
+ 6,296	+ 3,148	+ 316	+ 1,787	+ 20,151	17,381	13,065	9,649	16,358	12,070	9,190	212
+ 1,340	+ 2,869	— 1,009	+ 7,787	+ 12,523	14,026	13,323	12,681	13,884	13,051	12,353	213
+ 3,006	+ 3,221	+ 8,355	— 1,189	+ 20,442	24,060	19,910	18,038	21,330	18,431	17,297	214
+ 4,772	+ 3,052	+ 12,059	+ 1,280	+ 26,672	19,812	16,628	14,108	18,881	16,556	14,304	215
+ 9,645	— 747	+ 5,595	+ 6,425	+ 32,346	24,249	18,369	13,267	23,236	17,688	13,145	216
+ 1,192	+ 1,817	+ 182	+ 2,179	+ 7,836	15,178	13,831	13,057	11,886	10,767	10,349	217
+ 2,647	+ 469	+ 1,744	+ 896	+ 7,429	12,808	12,059	10,509	7,941	7,017	5,920	218
+ 2,176	— 8,364	+ 6,499	— 1,244	+ 6,609	20,175	16,079	14,340	17,500	14,054	13,617	219
+ 2,682	— 236	+ 1,791	+ 1,687	+ 11,290	11,863	9,189	7,964	12,043	9,351	7,894	220
+ 6,050	— 770	+ 2,741	+ 11,680	+ 17,327	29,885	34,687	28,503	13,632	11,204	11,338	221
— 5,270	+ 1,639	+ 982	+ 1,610	+ 3,190	13,767	11,220	14,248	11,439	9,757	11,999	222
— 1,651	— 2,515	— 639	+ 3,962	+ 2,297	14,383	12,586	12,885	11,886	10,543	11,895	223
..	..	..	..	..	17,528	15,030	..	9,340	8,229	..	224
+ 4,839	+ 96	+ 3,575	+ 1,031	+ 18,952	19,907	14,199	10,622	14,205	10,502	9,240	225
+ 11,769	+ 1,381	+ 8,552	— 4,588	+ 22,747	17,129	13,947	7,958	15,908	13,457	7,677	226
— 3,691	+ 2,438	+ 2,685	+ 2,190	+ 6,337	23,190	21,462	23,234	21,110	20,123	22,042	227
+ 4,971	— 688	+ 2,031	+ 1,526	+ 16,546	15,901	11,325	8,622	13,917	9,787	7,519	228
— 1,911	— 195	— 3,539	+ 750	— 4,695	12,016	11,342	12,186	12,976	13,450	14,517	229
+ 8,879	..	..	..	..	16,498	11,602	6,180	10,263	6,128	2,660	230

Table IV.—Towns classified by

	Name of Town.	Province, District, State or Agency, etc.	Population. 1931.	1921.	1911.	1901.	1891.	1881.	Variation: 1921 to 1931.
	1	2	3	4	5	6	7	8	9
231	Sasaram (M.) .	. B. and O. (Shahabad) .	25,175	22,308	23,097	23,644	22,713	21,818	+ 2,867
232	Satara (M.) .	. Bombay (Satara) .	26,379	22,454	19,145	26,022	29,601	29,028	+ 3,925
233	Saugor (M.) .	. C. P. and Berar (Saugor) .	38,517	28,571	34,876	31,412	32,736	44,416	+ 9,946
234	Sembiyam (P. B.)	. Madras (Chingleput) .	33,127	24,235	21,325	17,567	14,276	11,901	+ 8,892
235	Sirajganj (M.) .	. Bengal (Pabna) .	32,467	25,518	24,777	23,114	23,267	21,037	+ 6,949
236	Serampore (M.) .	. Bengal (Hooghly) . .	39,056	33,197	49,594	44,451	35,952	25,559	+ 5,859
237	Shahabad (M.) .	. United Provinces (Hardoi).	21,101	18,696	19,545	20,036	20,153	18,510	+ 2,405
238	Shillong (M.) .	. Assam (Khasi and Jaintia Hills).	21,300	15,469	11,128	7,430	5,910	4,288	+ 5,831
239	Shimoga (M.) .	. Mysore (Shimoga) . .	20,661	15,090	13,118	6,240	11,340	12,040	+ 5,571
240	Sidhpur (M.) .	Baroda (Kadi) .	20,468	16,187	15,447	14,743	16,224	13,688	+ 4,281
241	Sikar* . .	. Rajputana (Jaipur) .	26,297	21,080	22,317	21,523	19,897	17,739	+ 5,217
242	Sitapur (M.) .	. United Provinces (Sitapur)	24,720	21,584	21,578	22,557	21,380	18,544	+ 3,136
243	South-Suburban (M.)	Bengal (Twenty-four Parganas).	39,499	33,345	31,533	26,374	30,967	26,378	+ 6,154
244	Srirangam (M.)	. Madras (Trichinopoly, .	24,663	23,153	24,799	23,039	21,632	19,773	+ 1,510
245	Srivilliputtur (M.)	. Madras (Ramnad) .	32,385	31,195	29,066	26,382	21,448	18,256	+ 1,190
246	Sylhet (M.) .	. Assam (Sylhet) . .	21,435	16,912	14,457	13,893	14,027	14,407	+ 4,523
247	Tanda (M.) .	. United Provinces (Fyzabad)	21,177	18,058	19,378	19,853	19,724	19,954	+ 3,119
248	Tavoy (M.) .	. Burma (Tavoy) . .	29,018	27,480	25,074	22,371	15,099	13,372	+ 1,538
249	Tellicherry (M.) .	. Madras (Malabar) . .	30,349	27,576	29,258	27,883	27,196	26,410	+ 2,773
250	Tenali (M.) .	. Madras (Guntur) . .	34,580	23,230	18,195	10,204	6,074	4,747	+ 11,350
251	Tenkasi (P. B.) .	. Madras (Tinnevelly) .	27,338	22,071	19,940	18,128	12,861	11,987	+ 5,267
252	Thana (M.) .	. Bombay (Thana) .	21,816	22,639	15,591	16,011	17,455	14,456	— 823
253	Tiruvarur (M.) .	. Madras (Tanjore) . .	20,371	24,124	16,408	15,436	12,934	9,181	— 3,753
254	Tiruvannamalai (M.	. Madras (North Arcot) .	27,769	21,912	21,244	17,069	12,155	9,592	+ 5,857
255	Titagarh (M.) .	. Bengal (Twenty-four Parganas).	49,584	52,451	45,171	16,065	.	..	— 2,867
256	Tallygunge (M.) .	. Bengal (Twenty-four Parganas).	24,476	21,637	18,433	12,821	15,054	12,824	+ 2,839
257	Tonk* . .	. Rajputana (Tonk) . .	35,798	30,374	33,864	38,759	45,944	40,726	+ 5,424
258	Toungoo (M.) .	. Burma (Toungoo) .	23,223	19,332	18,546	16,146	19,232	17,199	+ 3,891
259	Trichur (M.) .	. Madras (Cochin) . .	45,658	27,897	23,574	15,585	12,945	10,822	+ 17,761
260	Udaipur* . .	. Rajputana (Mewar) . .	44,035	34,789	33,229	45,976	46,693	38,214	+ 9,246
261	Vaniyambadi (M.)	. Madras (North Arcot) .	22,940	20,090	20,406	12,005	15,838	15,426	+ 2,850
262	Vengurla (M.) .	. Bombay (Ratnagiri) .	20,158	19,126	17,294	19,018	10,134	8,947	+ 1,032
263	Veraval* . .	. W. I. Sts. Agcy. (Junagadh)	21,114	19,365	15,563	16,775	15,339	12,111	+ 1,749
264	Villupuram (M.) .	. Madras (South Arcot) .	20,127	17,423	16,157	11,263	7,950	8,241	+ 2,704
265	Virudunagar (M.)	. Madras (Ramnad) .	33,081	21,821	21,355	16,837	14,075	9,506	+ 11,260
266	Vizianagram (M.)	. Madras (Vizagapatam) .	44,696	39,299	37,550	37,270	30,881	22,577	+ 5,397
267	Wazirabad (M.)	. Punjab (Gujranwala) .	20,707	18,645	17,146	18,069	15,786	16,462	+ 2,062
268	Yeotmal (M.) .	. C. P. and Berar (Yeotmal)	20 967	17,238	13,525	10,545	6,464	4,445	+ 3,729
	Class IV (10,000—20,000)	**543 Towns . . .**	**7,449,402**	**6,220,889**	**6,163,954**	**6,457,339**	**5,487,983**	**4,764,257**	**+ 1,228,513**
	Class V (5,000—10,000)	**987 Towns . . .**	**6,992,832**	**6,223,011**	**5,944,503**	**5,945,905**	**6,164,900**	**5,334,663**	**+ 769,821**
	Class VI (Under 5,000)	**674 Towns . . .**	**2,205,760**	**2,333,129**	**2,007,888**	**1,880,701**	**1,677,882**	**1,582,056**	**— 127,369**

* The abbreviations used in the table are as follows:—Corporation (Corpn.), Municipality (M.), Cantonment (Cantt.), Notified Area (N. A.), Panchayat

population with variation since 1881—*concluded.*

Increase (+), Decrease (—). 1911 to 1921	1901 to 1911.	1891 to 1901.	1881 to 1891.	Variation in period 1881 to 1931. Increase (+), Decrease (—).	Males. 1931.	1921.	1911.	Females. 1931.	1921.	1911.
10	11	12	13	14	15	16	17	18	19	20
— 789	— 547	+ 931	+ 895	+ 3,357	12,473	10,674	10,483	12,702	11,634	12,614
+ 3,309	— 6,877	— 3,579	+ 573	— 2,649	13,772	11,547	9,775	12,607	10,907	9,370
— 6,305	+ 3,464	— 1,324	— 11,680	— 5,899	19,735	14,965	17,820	18,782	13,606	17,056
+ 2,910	+ 3,758	+ 3,291	+ 2,375	+ 21,226	17,252	12,438	11,000	15,875	11,797	10,325
+ 741	+ 1,663	— 153	+ 2,230	+ 11,430	17,981	13,756	13,236	14,486	11,762	11,541
— 16,397	+ 5,143	+ 8,499	+ 10,393	+ 13,497	23,985	20,210	30,363	15,071	12,987	19,231
— 849	— 491	— 117	+ 1,643	+ 2,591	11,115	9,713	10,171	9,986	8,983	9,374
+ 4,341	+ 3,698	+ 1,520	+ 1,622	+ 17,012	12,087	8,667	6,101	9,213	6,802	5,027
+ 1,972	+ 6,878	— 5,100	— 700	+ 8,621	11,056	7,995	6,617	9,605	7,095	6,501
+ 740	+ 704	— 1,481	+ 2,536	+ 6,780	10,218	8,110	7,585	10,250	8,077	7,862
— 1,237	+ 794	+ 1,626	+ 2,158	+ 8,558	13,363	10,737	11,504	12,934	10,343	10,813
+ 6	— 979	+ 1,177	+ 2,836	+ 6,176	14,159	12,561	12,359	10,561	9,023	9,219
+ 1,812	+ 5,159	— 4,593	+ 4,589	+ 13,121	22,183	19.083	17,683	17,316	14,262	13,850
— 1,646	+ 1,760	+ 1,407	+ 1,859	+ 4,890	11,917	11,139	11.683	12,746	12,014	13,116
+ 2,129	+ 2,684	+ 4,934	+ 3,192	+ 14,129	15,903	15,437	14.331	16,482	15,758	14,735
+ 2,455	+ 564	— 134	— 380	+ 7,028	13,100	10,032	8,314	8,335	6,880	6,143
— 1,320	— 475	+ 129	— 230	+ 1,223	10,991	9,336	9,635	10,186	8 722	9,743
+ 2,406	+ 2,703	+ 7,272	+ 1,727	+ 15,646	14,601	13,818	12,573	14,417	13,662	12,501
— 1,682	+ 1,375	+ 687	+ 786	+ 3,939	14,211	13,090	14,275	16,138	14,486	14,983
+ 5,035	+ 7,991	+ 4,130	+ 1,327	+ 29,833	17,951	12,065	9,320	16,629	11,165	8,875
+ 2,131	+ 1,812	+ 5,267	+ 874	+ 15,351	13,196	10,718	9,495	14,142	11,353	10,445
+ 7,048	— 420	— 1,444	+ 2,999	+ 7,360	12,297	12,497	8,640	9,519	10,142	6,951
+ 7,716	+ 972	+ 2,502	+ 3,753	+ 11,190	10,024	12,309	7,938	10,347	11,815	8,470
+ 668	+ 4,175	+ 4,914	+ 2,563	+ 18,177	13,930	10,847	10,621	13,839	11,065	10,623
+ 7,280	+ 29,106	..	..	..	34,252	36,533	31,225	15,332	15,918	13,946
+ 3,204	+ 5,612	— 2,233	+ 2,230	+ 11,652	14,800	13,326	11,183	9,676	8,311	7,250
— 3,490	— 4,895	— 7,185	+ 5,218	— 4,928	18,201	15,097	16,837	17,597	15,277	17,027
+ 786	+ 2,400	— 3,086	+ 2,033	+ 6,024	13,215	11,150	11,106	10,008	8,182	7,440
+ 4,323	+ 7,989	+ 2,640	+ 2,123	+ 34,836	22,840	13,783	12,089	22,818	14,114	11,485
+ 1,560	— 12,747	— 717	+ 8,479	+ 5,821	23,775	18,315	17,460	20,260	16,474	15,769
— 316	+ 8,401	— 3,833	+ 412	+ 7,514	10,834	9,283	9,205	12,106	10,807	11,201
+ 1,832	— 1,724	+ 8,884	+ 1,187	+ 11,211	9,773	9,157	8,436	10,385	9,969	8,858
+ 3,802	— 1,212	+ 1,436	+ 3,228	+ 9,003	10,517	10,146	7,831	10,597	9,219	7,732
+ 1,266	+ 4,894	+ 3,313	— 291	+ 11,886	10,447	9,046	8,290	9,680	8,377	7,867
+ 466	+ 4,518	+ 2,762	+ 4,569	+ 23,575	16,430	10,799	10,710	16,651	11,022	10,645
+ 1,749	+ 280	+ 6,389	+ 8,304	+ 22,119	22,165	19,381	17,897	22,531	19,918	19,653
+ 1,499	— 923	+ 2,283	— 676	+ 4,245	11,778	10,478	9,456	8,929	8,167	7,690
+ 3,713	+ 2,980	+ 4,081	+ 2,019	+ 16,522	11,434	9,298	7,249	9,533	7,940	6,276
+ 56,935	— 293,385	+ 969,356	+ 723,726	+ 2,685,145	3,967,072	3,271,228	3,221,431	3,482,330	2,949,661	2,942,523
+ 278,508	— 1,402	— 218,995	+ 830,237	+ 1,658,169	3,691,457	3,241,891	3,077,287	3,301,375	2,981,120	2,867,216
+ 325,241	+ 127,187	+ 202,819	+ 95,826	+ 623,704	1,196,988	1,243,248	1,063,561	1,008,772	1,089,881	944,327

Board (P. B.) and Town Area (T. A.) an asterisk denotes a town treated as such for census purposes though neither a Municipality nor a Cantonment.

Statement showing the net variation during the decade 1921-1931, in places treated as towns at both censuses.

Province, State or Agency.	Places treated as towns in 1921 but now omitted. Number.	Places treated as towns in 1921 but now omitted. Aggregate population in 1921.	Places now treated as towns which were not so treated in 1921. Number.	Places now treated as towns which were not so treated in 1921. Aggregate population in 1931.	Net variation in decade 1921-31, due to differences in the list of towns.	Variation in aggregate population of places which were treated as towns at both censuses.
1	2	3	4	5	6	7
INDIA	75	289,300	257	1,328,398	+1,039,098	+ 5,476,075
Ajmer-Merwara	..	..	..	..	..	+ 15,502
Assam	..	..	..	..	..	+ 57,769
Baluchistan	..	..	3	4,255	+ 4,255	+ 19,284
Bengal	3	9,667	11	70,865	+ 61,198	+ 439,438
Bihar and Orissa	1	4,271	4	24,824	+ 20,553	+ 268,929
Bombay	8	36,311	30	108,851	+ 72,540	+ 564,388
Burma	2	9,411	12	71,289	+ 61,878	+ 166,632
Central Provinces and Berar	10	51,584	8	45,481	— 6,103	+ 328,208
Coorg	..	..	..	..	..	+ 986
Delhi	..	..	1	8,262	+ 8,262	+ 134,760
Madras	7	34,435	40	285,671	+ 251,236	+ 860,595
North-West Frontier Province	2	10,611	1	5,780	— 4,831	+ 55,159
Punjab Punjab States Agency	4	11,223	37	189,778	+ 178,555	+ 746,216
United Provinces of Agra and Oudh	28	92,489	12	71,950	— 20,539	+ 650,911
Baroda State	..	..	2	6,516	+ 6,516	+ 75,664
Central India Agency	..	..	6	28,727	+ 28,727	+ 98,089
Cochin State	..	..	3	17,519	+ 17,519	+ 61,680
Gwalior State	3	9,903	15	60,469	+ 50,566	+ 36,360
Hyderabad State	..	..	48	222,169	+ 222,169	+ 207,515
Jammu and Kashmir State	3	9,637	4	5,357	— 4,280	+ 54,901
Mysore State	3	5,930	6	19,342	+ 13,412	+ 169,002
Rajputana Agency	..	..	3	18,811	+ 18,811	+ 219,852
Travancore State	..	..	8	45,574	+ 45,574	+ 101,560
Western India States Agency	1	3,828	3	16,908	+ 13,080	+ 142,675

NOTE 1.—The figures in this statement include the States attached to each Province, but those for Madras exclude Cochin and Travancore.

2.—Unless they have come into existence since last census, Cantonments and Civil Lines, which have been classified separately this census, have not been taken into account in this statement, since their population was treated as urban in 1921 and the only change is in their presentation as separate units.

Statement showing the Civil and Military Population of British Cantonments.

Cantonment	Province, State or Agency.	Population. Persons.	Males.	Females.	Civil Population.	Military Population.
1	2	3	4	5	6	7
Abbottabad	N.-W. F. Province	8,527	6,663	1,864	4,128	4,399
Agra	United Provinces	24,277	14,416	9,861	21,996	2,281
Ahmadabad	Bombay Presidency	3,789	2,421	1,368	2,492	1,297
Ahmadnagar	Do.	15,639	9,133	6,506	11,141	4,498
Allahabad	United Provinces	10,019	6,253	3,766	8,336	1,683
Almora	Do.	973	557	416	685	288
Ambala	Punjab	49,368	29,991	19,377	42,299	7,069
Amritsar	Do.	1,630	1,162	468	966	664
Attock	Do.	1,826	1,332	494	396	1,430
Aurangabad	Hyderabad	7,582	4,490	3,092	..	7,582
Bakloh	Punjab	3,239	2,114	1,125	1,002	2,237
Balun (Dalhousie)	Do.	852	591	261	695	157
Bangalore (Civil and Military Station)	Mysore	134,113	69,409	64,704	124,950	9,163
Bannu	N.-W. F. Province	5,559	4,658	901	2,523	3,036
Bareilly	United Provinces	9,852	6,559	3,293	7,119	2,733
Baroda	Baroda State	3,221	2,021	1,200	2,585	636
Barrackpore	Bengal	10,982	7,002	3,980	8,921	2,061
Belgaum	Bombay Presidency	11,430	7,032	4,398	8,220	3,210
Benares	United Provinces	4,278	2,964	1,314	2,974	1,304
Campbellpur	Punjab	3,697	2,187	1,510	1,871	1,826
Cawnpore	United Provinces	24,566	14,596	9.970	23,278	1,288
Chakrata	Do.	1,374	1,125	249	1,256	118
Chaman	Baluchistan	2,354	1,923	431	431	1,923
Cherat	N.-W. F. Province	843	708	135	627	216
Dagshai	Punjab	1,469	923	546	1,448	21
Dehra-Dun	United Provinces	9,721	7,392	2,329	5,517	4,204
Delhi (New) Cantt.	Delhi	8,798	6,093	2,705	4,322	4,476
Delhi Fort	Do.	1,641	1,314	327	..	1,641
Deolali	Bombay Presidency	7,805	4,439	3,366	6,114	1,691
Dera-Ismail Khan	N.-W. F. Province	1,375	910	465	1,039	336
Dharamsala	Punjab	2,383	1,527	856	326	2,057
Dinapur	Bihar and Orissa	10,217	5,909	4,308	9,072	1,145
Farrukhabad-*cum*-Fatehgarh	United Provinces	3,851	2,483	1,368	3,057	794
Drigh-Road near Karachi	Bombay	22	17	5	Not available.	
Ferozepore	Punjab	30,297	19,205	11,092	20,232	10,065
Fort Sandeman	Baluchistan	2,637	2,597	40	301	2,336
Fort William (*and Maidan*)	Bengal	3,083	2,661	422	350	2,733
Fyzabad	United Provinces	5,726	4,299	1,427	3,962	1,764
Hyderabad	Bombay (Sind)	5,678	3,461	2,217	4,530	1,148
Jalapahar	Bengal	718	421	297	563	155
Jhansi	United Provinces	12,121	8,166	3,955	8,545	3,576
Jhelum	Punjab	6,233	5,312	921	2,449	3,784
Jubbulpore	Central Provinces	20,065	12,645	7,420	12,271	7,794
Jullundur	Punjab	14,735	9,798	4,937	9,990	4,745
Jutogh	Do.	470	332	138	429	41
Kamptee	Central Provinces	5,554	3,704	1,850	3,699	1,855
Karachi*	Bombay (Sind)	15,774	11,068	4,706	6,240	9,534
Kasauli	Punjab	2,852	1,968	884	2,452	400
Kirkee	Bombay Presidency	16,302	9,940	6,362	9,976	6,326
Kohat	N.-W. F. Province	9,250	7,538	1,712	4,747	4,503
Kolhapur	Bombay States	2,632	1,433	1,199	297	2,335
Lahore	Punjab	29,672	20,741	8,931	19,634	10,038
Landaur	United Provinces	1,150	880	270	1,149	1
Lansdowne	Do.	4,399	3,322	1,077	3,038	1,361
Lebong	Bengal	564	352	212	437	127
Loralai	Baluchistan	2,626	2,157	469	1,267	1,359

* Includes Manora (2,018 Persons—1,255 males and 763 females).

The Civil and Military Population of British Cantonments—*concluded.*

Cantonment.	Province, State or Agency.	Population. Persons.	Males.	Females.	Civil Population.	Military Population.
1	2	3	4	5	6	7
Lucknow	United Provinces	23,562	15,582	7,980	16,125	7,437
Madras Ft. St. George	Madras	1,644	1,155	489	..	1,644
Mandalay	Burma	12,982	7,818	5,164	10,567	2,415
Mardan	N.-W. F. Province	2,431	1,705	726	1,716	715
Maymyo	Burma	4,749	3,761	988	..	4,749
Meerut	United Provinces	45,528	27,961	17,567	41,481	4,047
Mhow	Cnetral India Agency	31,177	17,496	13,681	26,806	4,371
Mingaladon	Burma	3,910	2,930	980	812	3,098
Multan	Punjab	11,106	7,319	3,787	7,933	3,173
Murree	Do.	450	388	62	425	25
Muttra	United Provinces	3,439	2,354	1,085	2,321	1,118
Muzaffarpur	Bihar and Orissa.	237	209	28	108	129
Naini Tal	United Provinces	932	640	292	869	63
Nasirabad	Ajmer-Merwara	21,397	11,861	9,536	19,347	2,050
Nimach	Gwalior State	9,542	5,063	4,479	8,719	823
Nowgong	Central India Agency	6,459	3,596	2,863	5,902	557
Nowshera	N.-W. F. Province	16,137	11,913	4,224	12,124	4,013
Pachmarhi	Central Provinces	4,699	2,564	2,135	4,562	137
Peshawar	N.-W. F. Province	34,426	25,702	8,724	28,904	5,522
Pishin	Baluchistan	810	766	44	138	672
Poona	Bombay Presidency	35,807	20,657	15,150	28,257	7,550
Quetta	Baluchistan	25,391	19,589	5,802	13,651	11,740
Rangoon	Burma	1,448	1,046	402	736	712
Ranikhet	United Provinces	3,772	2,558	1,214	3,742	30
Rawalpindi	Punjab	43,517	29,885	13,632	34,474	9,043
Risalpur	N. W. F. Province	8,016	5,685	2,331	5,959	2,057
Roorkee	United Provinces	3,532	2,601	931	2,255	1,277
Sabathu	Punjab	1,327	748	579	1,315	12
Santa-Cruz	Bombay Presidency	2,461	1,442	1,019	2,030	431
Saugor	Central Provinces	10,345	5,571	4,774	9,040	1,305
Secunderabad (*including Bolarum*)	Hyderabad	120,801	64,738	56,063	107,093	13,708
Shahjahanpur*	United Provinces	4,448	2,556	1,892	4,448	..
Shillong	Assam	5,236	3,547	1,689	3,447	1,789
Sialkot	Punjab	15,851	10,795	5,056	8,861	6,990
Sitapur	United Provinces	3,100	1,965	1,135	2,899	201
St. Thomas-*cum*-Pallavaram	Madras	9,293	5,129	4,164	7,954	1,339
Wellington	Do.	7,289	4,245	3,044	5,976	1,313

* No troops were at Shahjahanpur at the time of final enumeration.

TABLE V.

Towns arranged Territorially with Population by Religion.

This Table shows the territorial distribution of the urban population by religion.

2. The definition of a town given on the fly-leaf to Table IV applies to this Table: the number of categories into which towns are arranged being also identical. The towns in each Province or State are arranged according to population in the first three classes, while those in the last three are not shown in detail, the total number of towns being given with the aggregate population. The name of the district where indentical with the town is sometimes omitted.

3. This table was not prepared for Aden, and there is therefore a difference of three in the number of towns shown here and in Tables I and IV; consequently the figure of the total urban population in this table falls short of that in I and IV by 51,478 persons. A further discrepancy in the population figures is caused by the omission of the estimated population of Ahmadabad, referred to on the fly-leaf of Table I.

4. Details are given below for persons included under the head 'Others'.

Province, State or Agency.	Religion.	Persons.	Males.	Females.
Ajmer-Merwara	Unspecified	2	2	..
Assam	No Religion	7	5	2
	Indefinite Beliefs	15	7	8
Baluchistan	Indefinite Beliefs	6	3	3
Bengal	Confucian	1,374	1,131	243
	Indefinite Beliefs	75	65	10
	Religion not returned	78	59	19
Bihar and Orissa	Agnostic	6	5	1
	Khumbhipatia	2	1	1
Bombay	Confucian	10	10	..
	Indefinite Beliefs	110	91	19
	Religion not returned	29	16	13
Burma	Confucian	16,232	11,025	5,207
	Shintoist	317	241	76
	Indefinite Beliefs	38	16	22
Delhi	Ad-Dharmis	439	246	193
Madras	Indefinite Beliefs	36	23	13
	No Religion	3	2	1
Punjab	Ad-Dharmis	18,060	10,379	7,681
United Provinces	Indefinite Beliefs	2	2	..
Assam States	No Religion	7	5	2
Mysore State	Confucian	11	9	2
	No Religion	95	42	53
Punjab States Agency	Ad-Dharmis	1,431	830	601
Western India States Agency	Indefinite Beliefs	3	3	..

The term 'Indefinite beliefs' includes 'Atheist', 'Agnostic' and similar returns, which are specified on the fly-leaf of Table XVI.

Table V.—Towns Arranged Territorially

	District or State.	Town, Municipality, Suburb, Cantonment, etc.		Population. Persons.	Males.	Females.	Hindus. Persons.	Males.	Females.
	1	2		3	4	5	6	7	8
	INDIA ..	**2,572 Towns**		**38,858,214**	**21,422,036**	**17,436,178**	**25,123,142**	**13,794,200**	**11,328,942**
	Provinces	**1,695 Towns**		**29,531,256**	**16,540,690**	**12,990,566**	**18,886,037**	**10,531,993**	**8,354,044**
	Ajmer-Merwara ..	**5-Towns**		**180,199**	**98,874**	**81,325**	**112,911**	**61,420**	**51,491**
1	**Class I**	**Ajmer**	.. M	**119,524**	**66,014**	**53,510**	**71,314**	**39,121**	**32,193**
	Class III	**2-Towns**	..	**49,739**	**27,168**	**22,571**	**33,223**	**17,909**	**15,314**
2	Ajmer-Merwara ..	Beawar	.. M	28,342	15,307	13,035	20,105	10,851	9,254
3	Ajmer-Merwara ..	Nasirabad	.. C	21,397	11,861	9,536	13,118	7,058	6,060
	Classes IV to VI ..	**2-Towns**		**10,936**	**5,692**	**5,244**	**8,374**	**4,390**	**3,984**
	Assam	**28-Towns**		**213,421**	**135,320**	**78,101**	**153,673**	**97,979**	**55,694**
	Class III	**2-Towns**		**43,232**	**27,606**	**15,626**	**28,057**	**18,643**	**9,414**
1	Kamrup	Gauhati	.. M	21,797	14,506	7,291	16,812	11,356	5,456
2	Sylhet	Sylhet ..	.. M	21,435	13,100	8,335	11,245	7,287	3,958
	Classes IV to VI ..	**26-Towns**		**170,189**	**107,714**	**62,475**	**125,616**	**79,336**	**46,280**
	Baluchistan ..	**12-Towns**		**92,025**	**65,913**	**26,112**	**33,387**	**24,193**	**9,194**
	Class III	**2-Towns**		**60,272**	**42,427**	**17,845**	**22,144**	**15,757**	**6,387**
1	Quetta-Pishin ..	Quetta ..	.. M	34,881	22,838	12,043	11,956	8,038	3,918
2	Quetta-Pishin ..	Quetta ..	.. C	25,391	19,589	5,802	10,188	7,719	2,469
	Classes IV to VI ..	**10-Towns**		**31,753**	**23,486**	**8,267**	**11,243**	**8,436**	**2,807**
	Bengal	**139-Towns**		**3,684,330**	**,301,537**	**,382,793**	**2,541,062**	**1,575,267**	**965,795**
	Class I	**3-Towns**		**1,557,042**	**,036,772**	**520,270**	**1,074,648**	**705,043**	**369,605**
1	Calcutta	Calcutta	Corpn.	1,193,651	812,287	381,364	821,011	546,730	274,281
2	Howrah .. .	Howrah	.. M	224,873	145,120	79,753	173,613	111,511	62,102
3	Dacca	Dacca ..	.. M	138,518	79,365	59,153	80,024	46,802	33,222
	Class II	**3-Towns**		**196,265**	**128,626**	**67,639**	**123,674**	**80,786**	**42,888**
4	Twenty-four Parganas	Bhatpara	.. M	84,975	60,134	24,841	56,279	39,101	17,178
5	Midnapore	Kharakpur*	..	58,134	33,443	24,691	43,418	24,793	18,625
6	Chittagong ..	Chittagong	.. M	53,156	35,049	18,107	23,977	16,892	7,085
	Class III	**32-Towns**		**956,457**	**575,263**	**381,194**	**662,824**	**397,320**	**265,504**
7	Twenty-four Parganas	Tittagarh	.. M	49,584	34,252	15,332	36,297	24,620	11,677
8	Burdwan	Burdwan	.. M	39,618	23,485	16,133	30,135	18,067	12,068
9	Twenty-four Parganas	South Suburban	.. M	39,499	22,183	17,316	32,462	18,106	14,356
10	Hooghly	Serampore	.. M	39,056	23,985	15,071	33,693	20,325	13,368
11	Twenty-four Parganas	Baranagar	.. M	37,050	23,116	13,934	29,419	17,906	11,513
12	Bakarganj ..	Barisal	.. M	35,716	23,588	12,128	21,721	13,896	7,825
13	Dacca	Narayanganj	.. M	34,189	21,526	12,663	17,328	11,318	6,010
14	Hooghly	Hooghly Chinsura	M	32,634	18,799	13,835	28,501	16,093	12,408
15	Pabna	Sirajganj	.. M	32,467	17,981	14,486	13,009	7,537	5,472
16	Midnapore	Midnapore	.. M	32,021	17,807	14,214	25,248	14,003	11,245
17	Bankura	Bankura	.. M	31,703	17,280	14,423	29,570	16,000	13,570
18	Tippera	Comilla	.. M	31,365	18,530	12,835	14,625	9,253	5,372
19	Burdwan	Asansol	.. M	31,286	18,710	12,576	20,323	12,272	8,051
20	Twenty-four Parganas	Naihati	.. M	30,908	20,123	10,785	24,897	15,879	9,018
21	Mymensingh ..	Mymensingh	.. M	30,480	19,733	10,747	20,566	13,433	7,133
22	Howrah	Bally	.. M	30,347	20,944	9,403	22,548	14,902	7,646
23	Twenty-four Parganas	Kamarhati	.. M	30,334	20,087	10,247	21,539	13,773	7,766
24	Murshidabad ..	Berhampore	.. M	27,403	15,166	12,237	22,843	12,637	10,206
25	Rajshahi	Rajshahi	.. M	27,064	15,178	11,886	15,476	8,635	6,841
26	Faridpur	Madaripur	.. M	26,894	15,204	11,690	16,141	8,989	7,152
27	Hooghly	Rishra Konnagar	.. M	26,868	17,528	9,340	20,286	12,717	7,569
28	Tippera	Brahmanbaria	.. M	26,662	13,973	12,689	15,352	8,101	7,251
29	Hooghly	Champdani	.. M	25,365	17,497	7,868	18,749	12,481	6,268
30	Nadia	Santipur	.. M	24,992	12,016	12,976	16,857	8,100	8,757
31	Twenty-four Parganas	Tollygunge	.. M	24,476	14,800	9,676	17,231	10,642	6,589
32	Nadia	Krishnagar	.. M	24,284	12,807	11,477	16,878	8,950	7,928
33	Twenty-four Parganas	Budge Budge	.. M	24,183	15,514	8,669	17,447	11,261	6,186
34	Mymensingh ..	Jamalpur	.. M	23,077	12,629	10,448	7,437	4,438	2,999
35	Hooghly	Bhadreswar	.. M	22,992	14,938	8,054	16,979	10,616	6,363
36	Pabna	Pabna ..	.. M	21,904	11,970	9,934	11,620	6,573	5,047
37	Twenty-four Parganas	Basirhat	.. M	21,287	11,106	10,181	13,511	7,073	6,438
38	Rangpur	Rangpur	.. M	20,749	12,808	7,941	14,136	8,724	5,412
	Classes IV to VI ..	**101-Towns** ..	..	**974,566**	**560,876**	**413,690**	**679,916**	**392,118**	**287,798**
	Bihar and Orissa ..	**78-Towns** ..		**1,653,837**	**908,690**	**745,147**	**1,235,093**	**684,891**	**550,202**
1	**Class I**	**Patna** ..	.. M	**159,690**	**92,238**	**67,452**	**119,644**	**69,285**	**50,359**
	Class II	**7-Towns** ..	..	**484,909**	**272,022**	**212,887**	**349,017**	**198,008**	**151,009**
2	Gaya	Gaya ..	.. M	88,005	50,625	37,380	66,462	38,502	27,960
3	Bhagalpur	Bhagalpur	.. M	83,847	46,868	36,979	58,348	33,299	25,049
4	Singhbhum ..	Jamshedpur*	..	83,738	51,137	32,601	60,494	36,395	24,099
5	Cuttack	Cuttack	.. M	65,263	36,357	28,906	52,853	30,217	22,636
6	Darbhanga ..	Darbhanga	.. M	60,676	32,274	28,402	42,217	22,769	19,448
7	Monghyr	Monghyr	.. M	52,863	27,843	25,020	40,926	21,691	19,235
8	Ranchi	Ranchi ..	.. M	50,517	26,918	23,599	27,717	15,135	12,582
	Class III	**12-Towns**		**399,500**	**214,915**	**184,585**	**293,769**	**160,328**	**133,441**
9	Shahabad	Arrah ..	.. M	48,922	26,635	22,287	35,793	19,866	15,927
10	Saran	Chapra ..	.. M	47,448	25,934	21,514	35,873	19,888	15,985
11	Patna	Bihar ..	.. M	46,994	24,532	22,462	27,240	14,189	13,051
12	Muzaffarpur ..	Muzaffarpur	.. M	42,812	24,841	17,971	30,648	18,340	12,308
13	Puri	Puri ..	.. M	37,568	20,703	16,865	36,891	20,239	16,652
14	Monghyr	Jamalpur	.. M	30,346	16,378	13,968	24,256	13,077	11,179
15	Champaran	Bettiah	.. M	27,941	14,659	13,282	16,723	9,198	7,525
16	Manbhum	Purulia .	.. M	25,974	14,388	11,586	22,128	12,337	9,791
17	Shahabad	Sasaram	.. M	25,175	12,473	12,702	14,797	7,524	7,273
18	Patna	Dinapur	.. M	24,221	12,347	11,874	19,570	9,988	9,582
19	Hazaribagh ..	Giridih	.. M	21,122	11,122	10,000	15,202	8,000	7,202
20	Hazaribagh ..	Hazaribagh	.. M	20,977	10,903	10,074	14,648	7,682	6,966
	Classes IV to VI ..	**58-Towns**		**609,738**	**329,515**	**280,223**	**472,663**	**257,270**	**215,393**

with Population by Religion.

Sikhs.			Jains.			Buddhists.			Muslims.			
Persons. 9	Males. 10	Females. 11	Persons. 12	Males. 13	Females. 14	Persons. 15	Males. 16	Females. 17	Persons. 18	Males. 19	Females. 20	
344,668	**218,401**	**126,267**	**433,572**	**229,165**	**204,407**	**912.808**	**460,504**	**452,304**	**10,524,834**	**5,897,206**	**4,627,628**	
282,964	**179,658**	**103,306**	**169,290**	**96,598**	**72,692**	**909,697**	**458,907**	**450,790**	**8,133,018**	**4,639,814**	**3,493,204**	
335	**227**	**108**	**6,490**	**3,527**	**2,963**	**4**	**4**	..	**53,905**	**29,881**	**24,024**	
270	**181**	**89**	**2,942**	**1,580**	**1,362**	**4**	**4**	..	**40,548**	**22,746**	**17,802**	1
51	**37**	**14**	**3,004**	**1,641**	**1,863**	..	..	..	**11,393**	**6,169**	**5,224**	
15	13	2	2,706	1,481	1,225	..	..	..	5,069	2,707	2,362	2
36	24	12	298	160	138	..	..	..	6,324	3,462	2,862	3
14	**9**	**5**	**544**	**306**	**238**	..	..	..	**1,964**	**966**	**998**	
432	**307**	**125**	**880**	**642**	**238**	**278**	**218**	**60**	**53,067**	**33,186**	**19,881**	
86	**64**	**22**	**93**	**76**	**17**	**12**	**11**	**1**	**14,128**	**8,341**	**5,787**	
64	47	17	59	52	7	10	10	..	4,146	2,663	1,483	1
22	17	5	34	24	10	2	1	1	9,982	5,678	4,304	2
346	**243**	**103**	**787**	**566**	**221**	**266**	**207**	**59**	**33,939**	**24,845**	**14,094**	
7,002	**5,172**	**1,830**	**82**	**20**	**12**	**68**	**53**	**15**	**43,416**	**30,820**	**12,596**	
4,786	**3,399**	**1,387**	**32**	**20**	**12**	**40**	**25**	**15**	**26,081**	**18,184**	**7,897**	
3,310	2,180	1,130	25	13	12	29	16	13	18,101	11,799	6,302	1
1,476	1,219	257	7	7	..	11	9	2	7,980	6,385	1,595	2
2,216	**1,773**	**443**	..	..	..	**28**	**28**	..	**17,335**	**12,636**	**4,399**	
6,627	**4,927**	**1,700**	**5,643**	**4,089**	**1,554**	**15,609**	**9,097**	**6,512**	**1,029,374**	**659,729**	**369,645**	
4,863	**3,734**	**1,129**	**3,211**	**2,400**	**811**	**3,077**	**2,465**	**612**	**416,864**	**293,067**	**123,797**	
4,683	3,587	1,096	3,149	2,356	793	3,002	2,408	594	310,814	229,003	81,811	1
164	133	31	57	42	15	49	41	8	48,286	31,863	16,423	2
16	14	2	5	2	3	26	16	10	57,764	32,201	25,563	3
1,207	**749**	**458**	**32**	**17**	**15**	**747**	**571**	**176**	**64,401**	**42,938**	**21,463**	
10	6	4	..	..	..	46	37	9	27,645	20,299	7,346	4
1,159	706	453	32	17	15	3	3	..	9,558	5,714	3,844	5
38	37	1	..	..	..	698	531	167	27,198	16,925	10,273	6
315	**248**	**67**	**899**	**701**	**198**	**319**	**227**	**92**	**279,820**	**169,879**	**109,941**	
7	7	..	2	..	2	11	11	..	12,987	9,396	3,591	7
34	23	11	41	25	16	..	..	..	8,621	4,941	3,680	8
8	8	..	..	..	..	1	1	..	6,021	3,428	2,593	9
..	..	..	5	3	2	..	..	..	5,079	3,480	1,599	10
7	7	..	11	8	3	..	..	..	7,215	4,994	2,221	11
..	..	..	..	..	..	1	1	..	12,459	8,886	3,573	12
..	..	..	..	..	..	..	..	..	16,704	10,111	6,593	13
..	..	..	..	..	..	..	..	..	4,010	2,628	1,382	14
3	3	..	128	115	13	..	..	..	19,284	10,296	8,988	15
..	..	..	..	..	..	..	..	..	6,253	3,544	2,709	16
..	..	..	..	..	..	..	..	..	1,629	1,005	624	17
..	..	..	..	..	..	27	12	15	16,595	9,207	7,388	18
23	11	12	26	22	4	29	22	7	8,462	4,974	3,488	19
..	..	..	..	..	..	2	2	..	5,801	4,108	1,693	20
2	2	..	55	38	17	2	1	1	9,342	6,161	3,481	21
49	49	..	17	13	4	13	11	2	7,259	5,706	1,553	22
7	7	..	195	133	62	..	..	..	8,478	6,089	2,389	23
..	..	..	13	11	2	..	..	..	4,394	2,460	1,934	24
..	..	..	92	63	29	2	2	..	11,362	6,423	4,939	25
..	..	..	..	..	..	..	..	..	10,698	6,185	4,513	26
..	..	..	1	1	..	6	5	1	6,506	4,756	1,750	27
..	..	..	..	..	..	..	..	..	11,228	5,852	5,376	28
..	..	..	11	6	5	37	32	5	6,515	4,944	1,571	29
..	..	..	..	..	..	..	..	..	8,133	3,915	4,218	30
..	..	..	9	7	2	156	98	58	6,457	3,652	2,805	31
..	..	..	..	..	..	..	..	..	6,119	3,282	2,837	32
165	124	41	8	8	..	32	29	3	6,122	3,832	2,290	33
..	..	..	4	4	..	..	..	..	15,629	8,183	7,446	34
..	..	..	..	..	..	..	..	..	5,905	4,247	1,658	35
..	..	..	2	1	1	..	..	..	10,225	5,369	4,856	36
..	..	..	..	..	..	..	..	..	7,769	4,028	3,741	37
10	7	3	279	243	36	..	..	..	6,259	3,797	2,462	38
242	**196**	**46**	**1,501**	**971**	**530**	**11,466**	**5,834**	**5,632**	**268,289**	**153,845**	**114,444**	
3,982	**2,592**	**1,390**	**1,852**	**1,040**	**812**	**140**	**99**	**41**	**374,490**	**199,879**	**174,611**	
149	**94**	**55**	**33**	**26**	**7**	**15**	**14**	**1**	**38,238**	**22,241**	**15,997**	1
3,186	**2,130**	**1,056**	**728**	**414**	**314**	**102**	**72**	**30**	**111,120**	**60,516**	**50,604**	
44	30	14	375	190	185	1	1	..	20,596	11,626	8,970	2
..	..	..	69	37	32	..	..	..	24,555	12,946	11,609	3
3,130	2,091	1,039	175	126	49	95	65	30	13,797	9,126	4,671	4
4	4	..	31	16	15	2	2	..	9,956	5,145	4,811	5
..	..	..	..	..	..	..	..	..	18,308	9,432	8,876	6
..	..	..	1	1	..	..	..	..	11,812	6,102	5,710	7
8	5	3	77	44	33	4	4	..	12,096	6,139	5,957	8
298	**159**	**139**	**772**	**383**	**389**	**17**	**10**	**7**	**98,643**	**51,014**	**47,629**	
..	..	..	492	232	260	10	4	6	12,432	6,439	5,993	9
..	..	..	6	6	..	..	..	..	11,505	6,006	5,499	10
..	..	..	14	7	7	..	..	..	19,736	10,336	9,400	11
1	1	..	..	..	..	1	1	..	11,801	6,345	5,456	12
2	2	..	..	..	..	..	..	..	475	344	131	13
..	..	..	..	..	..	4	3	1	4,888	2,606	2,282	14
9	7	2	..	..	..	..	..	..	9,495	4,690	4,805	15
..	..	..	..	..	..	..	..	..	2,964	1,596	1,368	16
268	135	133	..	..	..	..	..	..	10,084	4,806	5,278	17
..	..	..	..	..	..	..	..	..	4,634	2,349	2,285	18
..	..	..	47	27	20	..	..	..	5,654	2,987	2,667	19
18	14	4	213	111	102	2	2	..	4,975	2,510	2,465	20
349	**209**	**140**	**319**	**217**	**102**	**6**	**3**	**3**	**126,489**	**66,108**	**60,381**	

Table V.—Towns Arranged Territorially

No.	District or State. 1	Town, Municipality, Suburb, Cantonment, etc. 2		Christians. Persons. 21	Christians. Males. 22	Christians. Females. 23	Zoroastrians. Persons. 24	Zoroastrians. Males. 25	Zoroastrians. Females. 26
	INDIA	**2,572 Towns**		**1,274,217**	**683,721**	**590,496**	**97,740**	**50,478**	**47,262**
	Provinces	**1,695 Towns**		**950,670**	**517,739**	**432,931**	**87,413**	**45,807**	**41,606**
	Ajmer-Merwara	**5-Towns**		**6,202**	**3,642**	**2,560**	**300**	**141**	**159**
1	**Class I**	**Ajmer**	M	**4,161**	**2,242**	**1,919**	**240**	**111**	**129**
	Class III	**2-Towns**		**2,001**	**1,379**	**622**	**60**	**30**	**30**
2	Ajmer-Merwara	Beawar	M	420	242	178	20	10	10
3	Ajmer-Merwara	Nasirabad	C	1,581	1,137	444	40	20	20
	Classes IV to VI	**2-Towns**		**40**	**21**	**19**	..	..	..
	Assam	**28 Towns**		**3,385**	**1,923**	**1,462**	**6**	**5**	**1**
	Class III	**2-Towns**		**748**	**406**	**342**	..	..	..
1	Kamrup	Gauhati	M	609	321	288	..	..	..
2	Sylhet	Sylhet	M	139	85	54	..	..	..
	Classes IV to VI	**26-Towns**		**2,637**	**1,517**	**1,120**	**6**	**5**	**1**
	Baluchistan	**12-Towns**		**7,904**	**5,526**	**2,378**	**167**	**90**	**77**
	Class III	**2-Towns**		**7,012**	**4,948**	**2,064**	**160**	**83**	**77**
1	Quetta-Pishin	Quetta	M	1,319	716	603	137	72	65
2	Quetta-Pishin	Quetta	C	5,693	4,232	1,461	23	11	12
	Classes IV to VI	**10-Towns**		**892**	**578**	**314**	**7**	**7**	..
	Bengal	**139-Towns**		**76,440**	**42,212**	**34,228**	**1,350**	**783**	**567**
	Class I	**3-Towns**		**49,300**	**26,796**	**22,504**	**1,283**	**756**	**527**
1	Calcutta	Calcutta	Corpn.	46,101	25,058	21,043	1,199	692	507
2	Howrah	Howrah	M	2,516	1,408	1,108	84	64	20
3	Dacca	Dacca	M	683	330	353	..	..	..
	Class II	**3-Towns**		**5,516**	**3,101**	**2,415**	**3**	**3**	..
4	Twenty-four Parganas	Bhatpara	M	444	301	143	..	..	..
5	Midnapore	Kharakpur*		3,850	2,147	1,703	1	1	..
6	Chittagong	Chittagong	M	1,222	653	569	2	2	..
	Class III	**32-Towns**		**10,619**	**5,760**	**4,859**	**15**	**8**	**7**
7	Twenty-four Parganas	Tittagarh	M	214	167	47	6	2	4
8	Burdwan	Burdwan	M	185	85	100	..	..	..
9	Twenty-four Parganas	South Suburban	M	648	368	280	..	..	..
10	Hooghly	Serampore	M	257	159	98	..	..	..
11	Twenty-four Parganas	Baranagar	M	366	184	182	..	..	..
12	Bakarganj	Barisal	M	1,535	805	730	..	..	..
13	Dacca	Narayanganj	M	157	97	60	..	..	..
14	Hooghly	Hooghly Chinsura	M	122	77	45	1	1	..
15	Pabna	Sirajganj	M	43	30	13	..	..	..
16	Midnapore	Midnapore	M	512	257	255	..	..	..
17	Bankura	Bankura	M	444	232	212	..	..	..
18	Tippera	Comilla	M	118	58	60	..	..	..
19	Burdwan	Asansol	M	2,398	1,387	1,011	7	4	3
20	Twenty-four Parganas	Naihati	M	208	134	74	..	..	..
21	Mymensingh	Mymensingh	M	206	91	115	..	..	..
22	Howrah	Bally	M	431	244	187	1	1	..
23	Twenty-four Parganas	Kamarhati	M	74	51	23	..	..	..
24	Murshidabad	Berhampore	M	153	58	95	..	..	..
25	Rajshahi	Rajshahi	M	115	48	67	..	..	..
26	Faridpur	Faridpur	M	55	30	25	..	..	..
27	Hooghly	Rishra Konnagar	M	69	49	20	..	..	..
28	Tippera	Brahmanbaria	M	82	20	62	..	..	..
29	Hooghly	Champdani	M	53	34	19	..	..	..
30	Nadia	Santipur	M	2	1	1	..	..	..
31	Twenty-four Parganas	Tollygunge	M	267	133	134	..	..	..
32	Nadia	Krishnagar	M	1,287	575	712	..	..	..
33	Twenty-four Parganas	Budge Budge	M	408	260	148	..	..	..
34	Mymensingh	Jamalpur	M	7	4	3	..	..	..
35	Hooghly	Bhadreswar	M	74	53	21	..	..	..
36	Pabna	Pabna	M	57	27	30	..	..	..
37	Twenty-four Parganas	Basirhat	M	7	5	2	..	..	..
38	Rangpur	Rangpur	M	65	37	28	..	..	..
	Classes IV to VI	**101-Towns**		**11,005**	**6,555**	**4,450**	**49**	**16**	**33**
	Bihar and Orissa	**78-Towns**		**29,698**	**15,390**	**14,308**	**226**	**138**	**88**
1	**Class I**	**Patna**	M	**1,570**	**548**	**1,022**	**25**	**14**	**11**
	Class II	**7-Towns**		**15,266**	**7,939**	**7,327**	**177**	**111**	**66**
2	Gaya	Gaya	M	508	262	246	7	2	5
3	Bhagalpur	Bhagalpur	M	769	493	276	..	..	..
4	Singhbhum	Jamshedpur*		3,748	2,091	1,657	166	107	59
5	Cuttack	Cuttack	M	2,400	960	1,440	4	2	2
6	Darbhanga	Darbhanga	M	151	73	78	..	..	..
7	Monghyr	Monghyr	M	124	49	75	..	..	..
8	Ranchi	Ranchi	M	7,566	4,011	3,555	..	..	..
	Class III	**12-Towns**		**5,692**	**2,862**	**2,830**	**11**	**6**	**5**
9	Shahabad	Arrah	M	195	94	101	..	..	..
10	Saran	Chapra	M	64	34	30	..	..	..
11	Patna	Bihar	M	4	..	4	..	..	..
12	Muzaffarpur	Muzaffarpur	M	348	145	203	6	2	4
13	Puri	Puri	M	200	118	82	..	..	..
14	Monghyr	Jamalpur	M	1,194	689	505	4	3	1
15	Champaran	Bettiah	M	1,713	763	950	1	1	..
16	Manbhum	Purulia	M	879	452	427	..	..	..
17	Shahabad	Sasaram	M	26	8	18	..	..	..
18	Patna	Dinapur	M	17	10	7	..	..	..
19	Hazaribagh	Giridih	M	192	94	98	..	..	..
20	Hazaribagh	Hazaribagh	M	860	455	405	..	..	..
	Classes IV to VI	**58-Towns**		**7,170**	**4,041**	**3,129**	**13**	**7**	**6**

with Population by Religion—*continued.*

Jews.			Tribals.			Others.			
Persons. 27	Males. 28	Females. 29	Persons. 30	Males. 31	Females. 32	Persons. 33	Males. 34	Females. 35	
17,074	**8,873**	**8,201**	**91,771**	**55,270**	**36,501**	**38,388**	**24,218**	**14,1[illegible]0**	
15,413	8,064	7,349	59,913	38,781	21,132	36,841	23,329	13,512	
49	29	20	1	1	..	2	2	..	
42	26	16	1	1	..	2	2	..	1
7	3	4	..	..	..	..	..	.	
7	3	4	..	..	..	..	..	..	
..	..	..	..	..	..	..	..	..	2
..	..	..	..	..	..	..	..	..	3
..	..	..	1,678	1,048	630	22	12	10	
..	..	..	103	62	41	5	3	2	
..	..	..	97	57	40	..	..	..	1
..		..	6	5	1	5	3	2	2
..	..	..	1,575	986	589	17	9	8	
15	12	3	28	24	4	6	3	3	
12	9	3	..	..	..	5	2	3	
4	4	..	..	..	..	..	..	..	1
8	5	3	..	..	..	5	2	3	2
3	3	..	28	24	4	1	1	..	
1,851	949	902	4,847	3,229	1,618	1,527	1,255	272	
1,829	931	898	529	384	145	1,438	1,196	242	
1,829	931	898	426	327	99	1,437	1,195	242	1
..	..	..	103	57	46	1	1	..	2
..	..	..	..	..	..	..	..	..	3
3	3	–	671	458	213	11	..	11	
..	..	..	551	390	161	..	..	..	4
3	3	..	110	59	51	..	..	..	5
..	..	..	10	9	1	11	..	11	6
7	6		1,594	1,081	518	45	33	12	
..	..	..	16	16	..	44	33	11	7
..	..	..	602	344	258	..	..	..	8
1	1	..	358	271	87	..	..	..	9
..	..	..	22	18	4	..	..	..	10
..	..	..	32	17	15	..	..	..	11
..	..	..	..	..	..	..	..	..	12
..	..	..	..	..	..	..	..	..	13
..	..	..	..	..	..	..	..	..	14
..	..	..	..	..	..	..	..	..	15
..	..	..	8	3	5	..	..	..	16
..	..	..	60	43	17	..	..	..	17
..	..	..	..	..	..	..	..	..	18
1	1	..	17	17	..	..	..	..	19
..	..	..	..	..	..	..	..	..	20
..	..	..	7	7	..	..	..	..	21
..	..	..	29	18	11	..	..	..	22
4	4	..	37	30	7	..	..	..	23
..	..	..	..	..	..	..	..	..	24
1	..	1	16	7	9	..	..	..	25
..	..	..	..	..	..	..	..	..	26
..	..	..	..	..	..	..	..	..	27
..	..	..	..	..	..	..	..	..	28
..	..	..	..	..	..	..	..	..	29
..	..	..	..	..	..	..	..	..	30
..	..	..	356	268	88	..	..	..	31
..	..	..	..	..	..	..	..	..	32
..	..	..	..	..	..	1	..	1	33
..	..	..	..	..	..	..	..	..	34
..	..	..	34	22	12	..	..	..	35
..	..	..	..	..	..	..	..	..	36
..	..	..	..	..	..	..	..	..	37
..	..	..	..	..	..	..	..	..	38
12	9	3	2,053	1,306	747	33	26	7	
5	4	1	8,343	4,651	3,692	8	6	2	
..	..	..	15	15	..	1	1	..	1
3	2	1	5,307	2,828	2,479	3	2	1	
..	..	..	12	12	..	..	..	..	2
..	..	..	106	93	13	..	..	..	3
..	..	..	2,133	1,136	997	..	..	..	4
3	2	1	10	9	1	..	..	..	5
..	..	..	..	..	..	..	..	..	6
..	..	..	..	..	..	..	..	..	7
..	..	..	3,046	1,578	1,468	3	2	1	8
2	2	–	295	150	145	1	1	..	
..	..	..	..	..	..	..	..	..	9
..	..	..	..	..	..	..	..	..	10
..	..	..	..	..	..	..	..	..	11
..	..	..	6	6	..	1	1	..	12
..	..	..	..	..	..	..	..	..	13
..	..	..	..	..	..	..	..	..	14
..	..	..	..	..	..	..	..	..	15
..	..	..	3	3	..	..	..	..	16
..	..	..	..	..	..	..	..	..	17
..	..	..	..	..	..	..	..	..	18
2	2	..	25	12	13	..	..	..	19
..	..	..	261	129	132	..	..	..	20
..	..	..	2,726	1,658	1,068	3	2	1	

Table V.—Towns Arranged Territorially

No.	District or State.	Town, Municipality, Suburb, Cantonment, etc.		Population.			Hindus.		
				Persons.	Males.	Females.	Persons.	Males.	Females.
	1	2		3	4	5	6	7	8
	Bombay	**214-Towns**		**4,826,150**	**2,731,400**	**2,094,750**	**3,366,879**	**1,889,451**	**1,477,428**
	Class I	**5-Towns**		**1,986,171**	**1,213,073**	**773,098**	**1,348,677**	**819,828**	**528,849**
1	Bombay	Bombay	Corpn.	1,161,383	747,381	414,002	789,861	505,588	284,273
2	Karachi	Karachi..	.. M	247,791	145,052	102,739	115,465	69,606	45,859
3	Ahmadabad ..	Ahmadabad	.. M	234,265	136,261	98,004	161,703	93,496	68,207
4	Poona	Poona ..	.. M	198,078	107,542	90,536	170,214	91,837	78,377
5	Sholapur	Sholapur	.. M	144,654	76,837	67,817	111,434	59,301	52,133
	Class II	**5-Towns**		**416,721**	**230,818**	**185,903**	**272,290**	**148,006**	**124,284**
6	Surat	Surat ..	.. M	98,936	52,958	45,978	67,005	36,461	30,544
7	Hyderabad ..	Hyderabad	.. M	96,021	53,339	42,682	67,664	36,426	31,238
8	Dharwar	Hubli ..	.. M	89,982	47,495	42,487	59,104	31,244	27,860
9	Sukkur	Sukkur ..	.. M	69,277	43,282	25,995	38,897	23,042	15,855
10	Sukkur	Shikarpur	.. M	62,505	33,744	28,761	39,620	20,833	18,787
	Class III	**27-Towns**		**885,072**	**473,362**	**411,710**	**627,750**	**334,981**	**292,769**
11	Nasik	Nasik ..	.. M	48,703	25,333	23,370	40,741	21,125	19,616
12	Dharwar	Gadag (Bettigiri)	M	45,852	24,139	21,713	34,739	18,189	16,550
13	Bombay Suburban	Bandra ..	.. M	43,290	24,668	18,622	21,759	13,065	8,694
14	Ahmadnagar ..	Ahmadnagar	.. M	41,890	21,494	20,396	30,789	15,910	14,879
15	Dharwar	Dharwar	.. M	41,671	21,957	19,714	30,970	16,382	14,588
16	Belgaum	Belgaum	.. M	41,204	21,453	19,751	30,472	15,956	14,516
17	West-Khandesh ..	Dhulia ..	.. M	39,939	20,917	19,022	29,817	15,631	14,186
18	Bijapur	Bijapur	.. M	39,747	20,823	18,924	27,163	14,318	12,845
19	Poona	Poona Cantt.	.. C	35,807	20,657	15,150	17,852	10,110	7,742
20	Panch Mahals ..	Godhra ..	.. M	35,110	18,827	16,283	15,231	8,482	6,749
21	Kaira	Nadiad ..	.. M	34,584	18,528	16,056	27,533	14,801	12,732
22	East Khandesh ..	Jalgaon	.. M	34,375	18,771	15,604	27,817	15,066	12,751
23	Broach	Broach	.. M	34,276	18,872	15,404	20,950	11,752	9,198
24	Nasik	Malegaon	.. M	32,462	16,705	15,757	12,766	6,437	6,329
25	Bombay Suburban ..	Kurla ..	.. M	30,311	17,914	12,397	19,895	11,741	8,154
26	Ratnagiri	Malwan	.. M	29,817	14,494	15,323	28,023	13,540	14,483
27	Sholapur	Pandharpur	.. M	29,460	15,095	14,365	27,024	13,837	13,187
28	East-Khandesh ..	Bhusaval	.. M	27,989	15,422	12,567	20,106	10,922	9,184
29	Sholapur	Barsi ..	.. M	27,610	14,393	13,217	23,525	12,295	11,230
30	Larkana	Larkana	.. M	26,841	15,641	11,200	15,709	8,753	6,956
31	Satara	Satara ..	.. M	26,379	13,772	12,607	22,437	11,764	10,673
32	Thana	Kalyan ..	.. M	26,291	15,143	11,148	20,230	11,578	8,652
33	Ratnagiri	Ratnagiri	.. M	23,906	11,863	12,043	18,167	9,191	8,976
34	East-Khandesh ..	Amalner	.. M	23,491	12,500	10,991	17,937	9,560	8,377
35	Panch Mahals ..	Dohad ..	.. M	22,093	11,911	10,182	10,229	5,812	4,417
36	Thana	Thana ..	.. M	21,816	12,297	9,519	17,931	10,053	7,878
37	Ratnagiri	Vengurla	.. M	20,158	9,773	10,385	17,938	8,711	9,227
	Classes IV to VI ..	**177-Towns**		**1,538,186**	**814,147**	**724,039**	**1,118,162**	**586,636**	**531,526**
	Burma	**92-Towns**		**1,520,037**	**903,980**	**616,057**	**309,043**	**240,031**	**69,012**
	Class I	**2-Towns**		**533,917**	**339,866**	**194,051**	**151,321**	**119,683**	**31,638**
1	Rangoon	Rangoon	.. M	398,967	270,017	128,950	140,301	112,304	27,997
2	Mandalay ..	Mandalay	.. M	134,950	69,849	65,101	11,020	7,379	3,641
3	**Class II Moulmein** ..	**Moulmein**	. M	**65,506**	**38,399**	**27,107**	**15,960**	**11,797**	**4,163**
	Class III	**11-Towns**		**304,010**	**178,744**	**125,266**	**50,900**	**40,553**	**10,347**
4	Bassein	Bassein	.. M	45,662	29,148	16,514	10,748	9,160	1,588
5	Akyab	Akyab ..	.. M	38,094	28,724	9,370	10,996	10,267	729
6	Tavoy	Tavoy ..	.. M	29,018	14,601	14,417	1,235	977	258
7	Henzada	Henzada	.. M	28,542	15,765	12,777	3,588	2,765	823
8	Prome	Prome ..	.. M	28,295	15,332	12,963	4,065	2,808	1,257
9	Myingyan ..	Myingyan	.. M	25,457	13,769	11,688	1,539	1,199	340
10	Toungoo	Toungoo	.. M	23,223	13,215	10,008	3,967	2,845	1,122
11	Pakokku	Pakokku	.. M	23,115	11,881	11,234	473	386	87
12	Pegu	Pegu ..	.. M	21,712	11,920	9,792	4,275	2,947	1,328
13	Insein	Insein ..	.. M	20,487	13,420	7,067	7,380	5,267	2,113
14	Mergui	Mergui ..	.. M	20,405	10,969	9,436	2,634	1,932	702
	Classes IV to VI ..	**78-Towns**		**616,604**	**346,971**	**269,633**	**90,862**	**67,998**	**22,864**
	Central Provinces and Berar	**112-Towns**		**1,688,470**	**895,282**	**793,188**	**1,314,016**	**694,862**	**619,154**
	Class I	**2-Towns**		**319,482**	**173,016**	**146,466**	**249,941**	**135,316**	**114,625**
1	Nagpur	Nagpur	.. M	215,165	116,403	98,762	176,237	95,077	81,160
2	Jubbulpore ..	Jubbulpore	.. M	104,317	56,613	47,704	73,704	40,239	33,465
	Class III	**16-Towns**		**495,732**	**265,748**	**229,984**	**370,929**	**198,028**	**172,901**
3	Akola	Akola ..	.. M	47,632	26,401	21,231	35,202	19,612	15,590
4	Amraoti	Amraoti	.. M	46,832	25,746	21,086	36,529	20,087	16,442
5	Raipur	Raipur	.. M	45,390	24,060	21,330	36,491	19,412	17,079
6	Nimar	Burhanpur	.. M	44,066	23,056	21,010	26,001	13,511	12,490
7	Saugor	Saugor ..	.. M	38,517	19,735	18,782	29,034	14,804	14,230
8	Nimar	Khandwa	.. M	34,622	19,060	15,562	23,595	13,147	10,448
9	Bilaspur	Bilaspur	.. M	31,374	16,366	15,008	25,372	13,232	12,140
10	Amraoti	Ellichpur	.. M	28,592	14,822	13,770	19,792	10,317	9,475
11	Chanda	Chanda	.. M	28,138	14,394	13,744	25,203	12,889	12,314
12	Buldhana	Khamgaon	.. M	23,462	13,113	10,349	17,916	10,012	7,904
13	Wardha	Hinghanghat	.. M	22,601	11,812	10,789	19,213	10,010	9,203
14	Jubbulpore ..	Murwara	.. M	21,959	11,572	10,387	17,799	9,422	8,377
15	Yeotmal	Yeotmal	.. M	20,967	11,434	9,533	17,858	9,691	8,167
16	Nagpur	Kamptee	.. M	20,787	10,806	9,981	13,673	7,045	6,628
17	Damoh	Damoh	.. M	20,728	10,726	10,002	15,416	7,952	7,464
18	Jubbulpore ..	Jubbulpore	.. C	20,065	12,645	7,420	11,835	6,885	4,950
	Classes IV to VI ..	**94-Towns**		**873,256**	**456,518**	**416,738**	**693,146**	**361,518**	**331,628**
	Coorg—Class V ..	**2-Towns**		**9,827**	**5,848**	**3,979**	**6,440**	**3,805**	**2,635**
	Delhi	**6-Towns**		**447,442**	**267,979**	**179,463**	**244,745**	**148,039**	**96,706**
1	**Class I**	**Delhi City**	M	**347,539**	**203,869**	**143,670**	**178,298**	**105,552**	**72,746**
2	**Class II**	**New Delhi**	M	**64,855**	**41,307**	**23,548**	**46,715**	**29,686**	**17,029**
	Classes IV to VI ..	**4-Towns**		**35,048**	**22,803**	**12,245**	**19,732**	**12,801**	**6,931**

with Population by Religion—*continued.*

Sikhs.			Jains.			Buddhists.			Muslims.			
Persons. 9	Males. 10	Females. 11	Persons. 12	Males. 13	Females. 14	Persons. 15	Males. 16	Females. 17	Persons. 18	Males. 19	Females. 20	
9,181	6,378	2,803	64,327	37,920	26,407	1,759	1,437	322	1,098,800	635,727	463,073	
3,059	2,136	923	21,563	14,199	7,364	1,699	1,396	303	438,264	274,857	163,407	
985	752	233	12,424	8,998	8,426	1,630	1,359	271	209,246	143,918	65,328	1
1,916	1,266	650	620	360	260	53	28	25	118,412	67,349	51,063	2
71	56	15	4,796	2,588	2,208	..	..	..	62,883	37,453	25,430	3
83	58	25	2,130	1,367	763	16	9	7	19,041	10,951	8,090	4
4	4	..	1,593	886	707	..	..	..	28,682	15,186	13,496	5
3,175	2,149	1,026	3,622	1,985	1,637	13	9	4	125,775	72,686	53,089	
12	10	2	2,786	1,485	1,301	..	..	..	23,393	12,298	11,095	6
851	538	313	23	13	10	..	..	..	27,116	16,167	10,949	7
..	..	..	813	487	326	13	9	4	24,970	13,037	11,933	8
2,094	1,452	642	..	..	..	..	..	..	27,642	18,427	9,215	9
218	149	69	..	..	..	..	..	..	22,654	12,757	9,897	10
385	256	129	12,320	7,090	5,230	34	24	10	192,634	104,080	88,554	
3	3	..	351	215	136	..	..	..	6,478	3,426	3,052	11
..	..	..	414	284	130	..	..	..	9,399	4,970	4,429	12
53	33	20	223	163	60	..	..	..	7,051	4,309	2,742	13
18	12	6	1,620	831	789	2	2	..	6,415	3,383	3,032	14
..	..	..	390	237	153	..	..	..	9,464	4,887	4,577	15
..	..	..	1,794	916	878	..	..	..	8,331	4,355	3,976	16
11	6	5	808	442	366	5	1	4	8,594	4,475	4,119	17
..	..	..	448	306	142	..	..	..	11,850	6,064	5,786	18
43	35	8	861	583	278	5	4	1	6,881	4,179	2,702	19
..	..	..	880	449	431	..	..	..	18,532	9,636	8,896	20
..	..	..	206	105	101	..	..	..	5,751	2,996	2,755	21
..	..	..	378	222	156	8	8	..	5,999	3,379	2,620	22
..	..	..	468	251	217	..	..	..	10,991	6,002	4,989	23
..	..	..	255	149	106	..	..	..	19,406	10,100	9,306	24
48	37	11	193	161	32	10	5	5	7,824	4,713	3,111	25
..	..	..	53	24	29	..	..	..	556	351	205	26
..	..	..	490	259	231	..	..	..	1,817	947	870	27
16	10	6	400	216	184	1	1	..	5,545	3,232	2,313	28
..	..	..	559	294	265	..	..	..	3,464	1,772	1,692	29
170	104	66	..	..	..	..	..	..	10,945	6,777	4,168	30
6	5	1	155	87	68	..	..	..	3,366	1,737	1,629	31
17	11	6	218	183	35	..	..	..	4,609	2,674	1,935	32
..	..	..	60	46	14	3	3	..	5,469	2,514	2,955	33
..	..	..	549	339	210	..	..	..	4,757	2,484	2,273	34
..	..	..	361	186	175	..	..	..	7,078	3,500	3,578	35
..	..	..	177	136	41	..	..	..	1,674	1,032	642	36
..	..	..	9	6	3	..	..	..	388	186	202	37
2,562	1,837	725	26,822	14,646	12,176	13	8	5	342,127	184,104	158,023	
6,195	4,451	1,744	599	386	213	890,684	447,289	443,395	191,283	137,145	54,138	
1,490	1,152	338	453	304	149	238,620	120,807	117,813	85,853	64,523	21,330	
1,343	1,053	290	443	296	147	135,383	69,896	65,487	70,526	55,924	14,602	1
147	99	48	10	8	2	103,237	50,911	52,326	15,327	8,599	6,728	2
66	43	23	90	61	29	30,877	15,547	15,330	12,306	7,614	4,692	3
355	240	115	18	1	17	198,186	100,492	97,694	35,288	25,949	9,339	
12	12	..	1	1	..	24,620	13,067	11,553	6,412	4,738	1,674	4
5	4	1	..	..	..	13,516	6,984	6,532	12,771	10,906	1,865	5
10	8	2	..	..	..	24,552	11,603	12,949	1,827	1,096	731	6
17	8	9	..	..	..	21,805	10,966	10,839	1,453	1,047	406	7
37	32	5	12	..	12	20,413	9,947	10,466	2,541	1,759	782	8
31	21	10	..	..	..	22,360	11,549	10,811	952	634	318	9
121	81	40	..	..	..	12,754	6,657	6,097	2,495	1,282	1,213	10
33	18	15	..	..	..	21,621	10,799	10,822	689	488	201	11
..	..	..	..	..	..	14,888	7,266	7,622	1,572	1,093	479	12
83	52	31	5	..	5	8,694	5,489	3,205	1,628	1,203	425	13
6	4	2	..	..	..	12,963	6,165	6,798	2,948	1,703	1,245	14
4,284	3,016	1,268	38	20	18	423,001	210,443	212,558	57,836	39,059	18,777	
2,265	1,584	681	24,968	13,137	11,831	44	30	14	308,641	164,941	143,700	
450	278	172	3,535	1,862	1,673	28	20	8	52,689	28,953	23,736	
444	274	170	1,833	955	878	3	2	1	28,042	15,628	12,414	1
6	4	2	1,702	907	795	25	18	7	24,647	13,325	11,322	2
1,067	774	293	7,268	3,915	3,353	14	9	5	105,924	57,137	48,787	
41	20	21	590	330	260	2	2	..	11,208	6,118	5,090	3
6	4	2	639	340	299	..	..	..	9,582	5,272	4,310	4
108	68	40	496	274	222	..	..	..	7,227	3,798	3,429	5
..	..	..	262	145	117	..	..	..	17,675	9,328	8,347	6
5	4	1	1,752	962	790	..	..	..	7,321	3,790	3,531	7
21	16	5	588	323	265	1	1	..	9,572	5,166	4,406	8
80	56	24	13	6	7	11	6	5	4,213	2,265	1,948	9
..	..	..	162	85	77	..	..	..	8,606	4,406	4,200	10
6	3	3	197	114	83	..	..	..	2,157	1,100	1,057	11
67	40	27	302	163	139	..	..	..	4,976	2,847	2,129	12
..	..	..	394	207	187	..	..	..	2,729	1,466	1,263	13
24	14	10	483	273	210	..	..	..	3,135	1,742	1,393	14
3	3	..	198	101	97	..	..	..	2,430	1,376	1,044	15
15	12	3	46	20	26	..	..	..	6,959	3,678	3,281	16
9	5	4	985	489	496	..	..	..	3,759	1,923	1,836	17
682	529	153	161	83	78	..	..	..	4,375	2,862	1,513	18
748	532	216	14,165	7,360	6,805	2	1	1	150,028	78,851	71,177	
...	..	..	50	22	28	..	..	..	2,459	1,545	914	
6,824	4,191	2,133	4,581	2,568	2,013	76	59	17	180,018	106,540	73,478	
3,169	2,107	1,062	4,238	2,362	1,876	10	9	1	158,287	91,836	66,451	1
2,142	1,339	803	238	134	104	63	48	15	12,111	8,176	3,935	2
1,013	745	268	105	72	33	3	2	1	9,620	6,528	3.092	

Table V.—Towns Arranged Territorially

	District or State.	Town, Municipality, Suburb, Cantonment, etc.		Christians.			Zoroastrians.		
	1	2		Persons. 21	Males. 22	Females. 23	Persons. 24	Males. 25	Females. 26
	Bombay	**214-Towns**		**187,082**	**109,134**	**77,948**	**80,844**	**42,150**	**38,694**
	Class I	**5-Towns**		**99,633**	**61,759**	**37,874**	**62,584**	**33,195**	**29,389**
1	Bombay	Bombay	Corpn.	80,728	51,466	29,262	57,765	30,595	27,170
2	Karachi	Karachi	M	7,852	4,599	3,253	2,408	1,271	1,137
3	Ahmadabad	Ahmadabad	M	3,277	1,832	1,445	1,321	725	596
4	Poona	Poona	M	5,153	2,575	2,578	786	440	346
5	Sholapur	Sholapur	M	2,623	1,287	1,336	304	164	140
	Class II	**5-Towns**		**6,599**	**3,523**	**3,076**	**5,222**	**2,447**	**2,775**
6	Surat	Surat	M	790	399	391	4,938	2,298	2,640
7	Hyderabad	Hyderabad	M	352	186	166	11	8	3
8	Dharwar	Hubli	M	4,925	2,641	2,284	157	77	80
9	Sukkur	Sukkur	M	525	293	232	111	63	48
10	Sukkur	Shikarpur	M	7	4	3	5	1	4
	Class III	**27-Towns**		**39,195**	**20,498**	**18,697**	**7,582**	**3,688**	**3,894**
11	Nasik	Nasik	M	904	371	533	222	191	31
12	Dharwar	Gadag (Bettigiri)	M	1,290	691	599	10	5	5
13	Bombay Suburban	Bandra	M	11,986	6,073	5,913	2,060	947	1,113
14	Ahmadnagar	Ahmadnagar	M	2,930	1,293	1,637	50	29	21
15	Dharwar	Dharwar	M	806	428	378	30	15	15
16	Belgaum	Belgaum	M	593	221	372	14	5	9
17	West-Khandesh	Dhulia	M	432	216	216	52	32	20
18	Bijapur	Bijapur	M	237	111	126	47	24	23
19	Poona	Poona Cantt.	C	7,600	4,529	3,071	2,394	1,134	1,260
20	Panch Mahals	Godhra	M	293	164	129	156	86	70
21	Kaira	Nadiad	M	1,076	614	462	13	9	4
22	East Khandesh	Jalgaon	M	129	72	57	39	22	17
23	Broach	Broach	M	394	212	182	1,457	644	813
24	Nasik	Malegaon	M	17	9	8	5	3	2
25	Bombay Suburban	Kurla	M	2,016	1,083	933	177	94	83
26	Ratnagiri	Malwan	M	1,185	579	606	..	..	..
27	Sholapur	Pandharpur	M	129	52	77	..	..	..
28	East-Khandesh	Bhusaval	M	1,671	918	753	214	107	107
29	Sholapur	Barsi	M	51	27	24	11	5	6
30	Larkana	Larkana	M	7	3	4	3	1	2
31	Satara	Satara	M	342	146	196	59	25	34
32	Thana	Kalyan	M	993	577	416	185	99	86
33	Ratnagiri	Ratnagiri	M	205	107	98	2	2	..
34	East-Khandesh	Amalner	M	88	25	63	44	31	13
35	Panch Mahals	Dohad	M	586	338	248	46	29	17
36	Thana	Thana	M	1,413	770	643	291	148	143
37	Ratnagiri	Vengurla	M	1,822	869	953	1	1	..
	Classes IV to VI	**177-Towns**		**41,655**	**23,354**	**18,301**	**5,456**	**2,820**	**2,636**
	Burma	**92-Towns**		**71,688**	**39,433**	**32,255**	**403**	**250**	**153**
	Class I	**2-Towns**		**34,132**	**18,600**	**15,532**	**361**	**221**	**140**
1	Rangoon	Rangoon	M	30,408	16,759	13,649	355	219	136
2	Mandalay	Mandalay	M	3,724	1,841	1,883	6	2	4
3	**Class II** Moulmein	**Moulmein**	M	**3,470**	**1,669**	**1,801**	**7**	**5**	**2**
	Class III	**11-Towns**		**12,573**	**6,891**	**5,682**	**10**	**9**	**1**
4	Bassein	Bassein	M	2,805	1,417	1,388	..	..	..
5	Akyab	Akyab	M	344	224	120	..	..	..
6	Tavoy	Tavoy	M	659	373	286	5	5	..
7	Henzada	Henzada	M	1,164	613	551	2	1	1
8	Prome	Prome	M	377	194	183	..	..	..
9	Myingyan	Myingyan	M	358	209	149	..	..	..
10	Toungoo	Toungoo	M	3,343	1,990	1,353	1	1	..
11	Pakokku	Pakokku	M	154	88	66	..	..	..
12	Pegu	Pegu	M	360	177	183	..	..	..
13	Insein	Insein	M	2,532	1,280	1,252	..	..	..
14	Mergui	Mergui	M	477	326	151	2	2	..
	Classes IV to VI	**78-Towns**		**21,513**	**12,273**	**9,240**	**25**	**15**	**10**
	Central Provinces and Berar	**112-Towns**		**29,346**	**15,945**	**13,401**	**1,953**	**1,022**	**931**
	Class I	**2-Towns**		**10,165**	**5,207**	**4,958**	**1,162**	**617**	**545**
1	Nagpur	Nagpur	M	6,449	3,359	3,090	963	516	447
2	Jubbulpore	Jubbulpore	M	3,716	1,848	1,868	199	101	98
	Class III	**16-Towns**		**9,352**	**5,276**	**4,076**	**327**	**165**	**162**
3	Akola	Akola	M	521	286	235	45	23	22
4	Amraoti	Amraoti	M	69	38	31	6	5	1
5	Raipur	Raipur	M	959	440	519	27	11	16
6	Nimar	Burhanpur	M	47	21	26	74	45	29
7	Saugor	Saugor	M	397	171	226	8	4	4
8	Nimar	Khandwa	M	746	365	381	88	37	51
9	Bilaspur	Bilaspur	M	1,645	773	872	7	3	4
10	Amraoti	Ellichpur	M	19	9	10	5	2	3
11	Chanda	Chanda	M	401	210	191	13	6	7
12	Buldhana	Khamgaon	M	178	39	139	23	12	11
13	Wardha	Hinghanghat	M	31	15	16	1	1	..
14	Jubbulpore	Murwara	M	509	118	391	9	3	6
15	Yeotmal	Yeotmal	M	276	158	118	10	7	3
16	Nagpur	Kamptee	M	91	48	43	3	3	..
17	Damoh	Damoh	M	455	301	154	8	3	5
18	Jubbulpore	Jubbulpore	C	3,008	2,284	724	..	..	..
	Classes IV to VI	**94-Towns**		**9,829**	**5,462**	**4,367**	**464**	**240**	**224**
	Coorg—Class V	**2-Towns**		**851**	**464**	**387**	**27**	**12**	**15**
	Delhi	**6-Towns**		**11,122**	**6,247**	**4,875**	**126**	**81**	**45**
1	**Class I**	**Delhi City**	M	**3,008**	**1,695**	**1,313**	**83**	**57**	**26**
2	**Class II**	**New Delhi**	M	**3,541**	**1,898**	**1,643**	**41**	**23**	**18**
	Classes IV to VI	**4 Towns**		**4,573**	**2,654**	**1,919**	**2**	**1**	**1**

with Population by Religion—*continued*.

Jews. Persons. 27	Jews. Males. 28	Jews. Females. 29	Tribals. Persons. 30	Tribals. Males. 31	Tribals. Females. 32	Others. Persons. 33	Others. Males. 34	Others. Females. 35	
12,029	**6,297**	**5,732**	**5,100**	**2,789**	**2,311**	**149**	**117**	**32**	
10,375	**5,471**	**4,904**	**186**	**127**	**59**	**131**	**105**	**26**	
8,621	4,604	4,017	2	2	..	121	99	22	1
925	480	445	135	91	44	5	2	3	2
211	108	103	3	3	..	..	..	..	3
605	271	334	45	30	15	5	4	1	4
13	8	5	1	1	..	..	..	..	5
25	**13**	**12**	..	—	—	—	—	..	
12	7	5	..	..	..	..	..	..	6
4	1	3	..	..	..	..	..	..	7
..	..	..	..	..	..	..	..	..	8
8	5	3	..	..	..	..	..	..	9
1	..	1	..	..	..	..	..	..	10
910	**447**	**463**	**4,249**	**2,288**	**1,961**	**13**	**10**	**3**	
4	2	2	..	..	..	..	..	..	11
..	..	..	..	..	..	..	..	..	12
152	73	79	..	..	..	6	5	1	13
12	6	6	54	28	26	..	..	..	14
11	8	3	..	..	..	..	..	..	15
..	..	..	..	..	..	..	..	..	16
..	..	..	220	114	106	..	..	..	17
2	..	2	..	..	..	..	..	..	18
171	83	88	..	..	..	..	..	..	19
..	..	..	18	10	8	..	..	..	20
..	..	..	5	3	2	..	..	..	21
5	2	3	..	..	..	..	..	..	22
..	..	..	16	11	5	..	..	..	23
1	1	..	12	6	6	..	..	..	24
148	80	68	..	..	..	..	..	..	25
..	..	..	..	..	..	..	..	..	26
..	..	..	..	..	..	..	..	..	27
29	11	18	..	..	..	7	5	2	28
..	..	..	..	..	..	..	..	..	29
7	3	4	..	..	..	..	..	..	30
14	8	6	..	..	..	..	..	..	31
24	12	12	15	9	6	..	..	..	32
..	..	..	..	..	..	..	..	..	33
..	..	..	116	61	55	..	..	..	34
..	..	..	3,793	2,046	1,747	..	..	..	35
330	158	172	..	..	..	..	..	..	36
..	..	..	..	..	..	..	..	..	37
719	**366**	**353**	**665**	**374**	**291**	5	2	3	
1,206	**619**	**587**	**32,349**	**23,094**	**9,255**	**16,587**	**11,282**	**5,305**	
1,109	**563**	**546**	**6,784**	**4,713**	**2,071**	**13,794**	**9,300**	**4,494**	
1,069	544	525	5,500	3,820	1,680	13,639	9,202	4,437	1
40	19	21	1,284	893	391	155	98	57	2
3	2	1	2,605	1,574	1,031	122	87	35	3
30	**24**	**6**	**6,004**	**4,124**	**1,880**	**646**	**461**	**185**	
10	10	..	1,052	741	311	2	2		4
3	2	1	70	62	8	384	270	114	5
..	..	..	691	513	178	42	30	12	6
..	..	..	478	343	135	37	23	14	7
..	..	..	736	503	233	114	89	25	8
..	..	..	212	152	60	4	4	..	9
1	..	1	528	360	168	14	..	14	10
..	..	..	124	87	37	21	15	6	11
1	1	..	613	433	180	3	3	..	12
10	6	4	146	114	32	7	7	..	13
5	5	..	1,354	816	538	18	18	..	14
64	**30**	**34**	**16,956**	**12,683**	**4,273**	**2,025**	**1,434**	**591**	
147	**83**	**64**	**7,090**	**3,678**	**3,412**	..	..	..	
98	**59**	**39**	**1,414**	**704**	**710**	..	..	..	
31	20	11	1,163	572	591	..	..	..	1
67	39	28	251	132	119	..	..	..	2
36	**17**	**19**	**815**	**427**	**388**	..	..	..	
8	3	5	15	7	8	..	..	..	3
..	..	..	1	..	1	..	..	..	4
9	6	3	73	51	22	..	..	..	5
..	..	..	7	6	1	..	..	..	6
..	..	..	..	..	..	..	..	..	7
..	..	..	11	5	6	..	..	..	8
7	2	5	26	23	3	..	..	..	9
..	..	..	8	3	5	..	..	..	10
..	..	..	161	72	89	..	..	..	11
..	..	..	..	..	..	..	..	..	12
4	2	2	229	111	118	..	..	..	13
..	..	..	..	..	..	..	..	..	14
6	3	3	186	95	91	..	..	..	15
..	..	..	..	..	..	..	..	..	16
2	1	1	94	52	42	..	..	..	17
..	..	..	4	2	2	..	..	..	18
13	7	6	4,861	2,547	2,314	..	..	..	
..	..	..	..	..	..	..	..	..	
11	8	3	..	..	..	**439**	**246**	**193**	
7	5	2	..	..	..	**439**	**246**	**198**	1
4	3	1	..	..	..	..	..	—	2
..	..	..	..	..	..	..	—	—	

Table V.—Towns Arranged Territorially

	District or State.	Town, Municipality, Suburb, Cantonment, etc.		Population.			Hindus.		
				Persons.	Males.	Females.	Persons.	Males.	Females.
	1	2		3	4	5	6	7	8
	Madras ..	.. **340-Towns**		**6,337,256**	**3,179,721**	**3,157,535**	**5,119,713**	**2,570,683**	**2,549,030**
	Class I ..	.. **4-Towns**		**1,072,626**	**556,527**	**516,099**	**872,404**	**452,009**	**420,395**
1	Madras ..	.. Madras ..	Corpn.	645,586	340,068	305,518	519,633	273,355	246,278
2	Madura ..	.. Madura ..	M	182,018	91,676	90,342	158,734	80,025	78,709
3	Trichinopoly	.. Trichinopoly ..	M	142,843	72,997	69,846	102,783	52,485	50,298
4	Salem ..	.. Salem ..	M	102,179	51,786	50,393	91,254	46,144	45,110
	Class II ..	.. **18-Towns**		**1,168,133**	**590,883**	**577,250**	**935,161**	**473,667**	**461,494**
5	Malabar ..	.. Calicut ..	M	99,273	51,030	48,243	57,965	30,002	27,963
6	Coimbatore	.. Coimbatore ..	M	95,198	49,880	45,318	80,147	41,950	38,197
7	Tanjore ..	.. Tanjore ..	M	66,889	33,590	33,299	56,478	28,486	27,992
8	South Canara	.. Mangalore ..	M	66,756	34,672	32,084	40,839	21,616	19,223
9	Godavari East	.. Coconada ..	M	65,952	33,692	32,260	60,874	31,057	29,817
10	Chingleput ..	.. Conjeeveram ..	M	65,258	32,367	32,891	61,992	30,635	31,357
11	Guntur ..	.. Guntur ..	M	65,179	33,228	31,951	45,657	23,398	22,259
12	Godavari East	.. Rajahmundry ..	M	63,526	32,078	31,448	58,746	29,736	29,010
13	Tanjore ..	.. Kumbakonam ..	M	62,317	30,738	31,579	57,255	28,206	29,049
14	Kistna ..	.. Bezwada ..	M	60,427	31,675	28,752	47,788	24,981	22,807
15	Tinnevelly ..	.. Tuticorin ..	M	60,395	30,497	29,898	43,258	21,953	21,305
16	South Canara	.. Cuddalore ..	M	59,057	29,892	29,165	53,636	27,005	26,631
17	Godavari East	.. Ellore ..	M	57,342	28,216	29,126	49,695	24,342	25,353
18	Vizagapatam	.. Vizagapatam ..	M	57,303	29,449	27,854	51,299	26,208	25,091
19	North Arcot	.. Vellore ..	M	57,265	28,626	28,639	42,363	21,126	21,237
20	Tinnevelly ..	.. Tinnevelly ..	M	57,078	27,600	29,478	49,024	23,741	25,283
21	Kistna ..	.. Bandar (Masulipatam)	M	56,928	29,269	27,659	48,163	24,782	23,381
22	Tinnevelly ..	.. Palamcottah ..	M	51,990	24,384	27,606	29,982	14,443	15,539
	Class III ..	.. **48-Towns**		**1,396,927**	**699,240**	**697,687**	**1,089,751**	**544,953**	**544,798**
23	Malabar	.. Palghat ..	M	49,064	24,234	24,830	39,521	19,339	20,182
24	Tanjore	.. Negapatam ..	M	48,527	23,143	25,384	34,340	16,896	17,444
25	Bellary ..	.. Bellary ..	M	47,573	25,405	22,168	28,760	15,073	13,687
26	Nellore ..	.. Nellore ..	M	45,895	22,810	23,085	33,187	16,531	16,656
27	Vizagapatam	.. Vizianagram ..	M	44,696	22,165	22,531	41,860	20,740	21,120
28	Madura ..	.. Dindigul ..	M	43,617	22,351	21,266	31,264	16,037	15,227
29	Ramnad ..	.. Rajapalaiyam ..	P.B.	38,693	19,812	18,881	37,115	19,070	18,045
30	Ganjam ..	.. Berhampur	M	37,750	18,490	19,260	35,810	17,508	18,302
31	Bellary ..	.. Adoni	M	35,635	17,963	17,672	21,963	10,988	10,975
32	Kurnool ..	.. Kurnool ..	M	35,314	17,949	17,365	17,760	8,895	8,805
33	Guntur ..	.. Tenali ..	M	34,580	17,951	16,629	27,901	14,365	13,536
34	Malabar ..	.. Cannanore ..	M	34,236	16,934	17,302	16,597	8,517	8,080
35	Ramnad ..	.. Aruppukkottai ..	P.B.	33,848	16,574	17,274	31,829	15,608	16,221
36	Coimbatore	.. Erode ..	M	33,672	17,765	15,907	28,764	15,094	13,670
37	Chingleput ..	.. Sembiyam ..	P.B.	33,127	17,252	15,875	28,437	14,754	13,683
38	Ramnad ..	.. Virudunagar ..	M	33,081	16,430	16,651	30,078	14,946	15,132
39	Chingleput ..	.. Saidpet ..	M	33,037	17,129	15,908	30,501	15,799	14,702
40	Ramnad ..	.. Srivilliputtur ..	M	32,385	15,903	16,482	30,530	15,120	15,410
41	Tanjore ..	.. Mayavaram ..	M	31,887	15,572	16,315	29,704	14,538	15,166
42	Malabar ..	.. Tellicherry ..	M	30,349	14,211	16,138	16,743	7,998	8,745
43	North Arcot	.. Tiruvannamalai ..	M	27,769	13,930	13,839	22,798	11,270	11,528
44	Tinnevelly ..	.. Tenkasi ..	P.B.	27,338	13,196	14,142	20,863	10,050	10,813
45	Madura ..	.. Bodinayakkanur ..	M	27,036	13,240	13,796	24,618	12,048	12,570
46	South Arcot	.. Chidambaram ..	M	25,084	12,449	12,635	23,205	11,511	11,694
47	North Arcot	.. Gudiyattam ..	M	24,688	12,272	12,416	20,217	9,958	10,259
48	Trichinopoly	.. Srirangum ..	M	24,663	11,917	12,746	24,452	11,810	12,642
49	Nilgiris ..	.. Ootacamand ..	M	24,616	13,164	11,452	14,119	7,949	6,170
50	North Arcot	.. Ambur ..	P.B.	24,217	11,900	12,317	13,768	6,887	6,881
51	Tinnevelly	.. Kodaiyanallur ..	P.B.	23,819	11,886	11,933	16,425	8,149	8,276
52	Vizagapatam	.. Anakapalle ..	M	23,376	11,448	11,928	23,034	11,274	11,760
53	Madura ..	.. Periyakulam ..	M	23,004	11,109	11,895	19,065	9,160	9,905
54	North Arcot	.. Vaniyambadi ..	M	22,940	10,834	12,106	10,209	4,946	5,263
55	Malabar ..	.. Cochin ..	M	22,818	11,950	10,868	5,147	2,826	2,321
56	Tanjore ..	.. Mannargudi ..	M	22,764	11,339	11,425	21,131	10,447	10,684
57	Kurnool ..	.. Nandyal ..	M	22,608	11,646	10,962	12,520	6,350	6,170
58	Cuddapah ..	.. Cuddapah ..	M	22,602	11,522	11,080	10,778	5,519	5,259
59	Coimbatore ..	.. Pollachi ..	M	22,112	11,720	10,392	19,651	10,359	9,292
60	Chittoor ..	.. Chittoor ..	M	22,018	10,892	11,126	18,628	9,320	9,308
61	Bellary ..	.. Hospet ..	M	21,673	10,858	10,815	16,853	8,367	8,486
62	Ramnad ..	.. Karaikudi ..	M	21,672	10,935	10,737	20,301	10,160	10,141
63	Tinnevelly ..	.. Puliyangudi ..	P.B.	21,173	10,417	10,756	17,842	8,720	9,122
64	Vizagapatam	.. Bobbili ..	P.B.	20,544	10,125	10,419	19,896	9,830	10,066
65	Ramnad ..	.. Devakottai ..	P.B.	20,393	9,684	10,709	18,893	8,925	9,968
66	Tanjore ..	.. Tiruvarur ..	M	20,371	10,024	10,347	17,220	8,540	8,680
67	Chingleput ..	.. Poonamalle ..	P.B.	20,340	10,409	9,931	17,005	8,666	8,339
68	South Arcot	.. Villupuram ..	M	20,127	10,447	9,680	15,587	8,065	7,522
69	Cuddapah ..	.. Proddatur ..	M	20,124	10,280	9,844	13,272	6,657	6,615
70	Ganjam ..	.. Parlakimedi ..	M	20,072	9,604	10,468	19,650	9,374	10,276
	Classes IV to VI	.. **270-Towns**		**2,699,570**	**1,833,071**	**1,366,499**	**2,222,397**	**1,100,054**	**1,122,343**
	North-West Frontier Province.	**27-Towns**		**386,177**	**235,126**	**151,051**	**93,127**	**56,311**	**36,816**
1	**Class II** ..	.. **Peshawar** ..	**M**	**87,440**	**50,151**	**37,289**	**11,594**	**6,781**	**4,813**
	Class III ..	.. **5-Towns**		**147,098**	**90,329**	**56,769**	**46,046**	**26,647**	**19,399**
2	**Dera Ismail Khan**	.. **Dera Ismail Khan**	**M**	**38,956**	**22,141**	**16,815**	**16,421**	**8,703**	**7,718**
3	**Peshawar** ..	.. **Peshawar** ..	**C**	**34,426**	**25,702**	**8,724**	**10,379**	**7,189**	**3,190**
4	**Kohat** ..	.. **Kohat** ..	**M**	**25,100**	**14,236**	**10,864**	**3,249**	**1,898**	**1,351**
5	**Bannu** ..	.. **Bannu** ..	**M**	**24,768**	**14,619**	**10,149**	**13,277**	**7,230**	**6,047**
6	**Peshawar** ..	.. **Mardan** ..	**M**	**23,848**	**13,631**	**10,217**	**2,720**	**1,627**	**1,093**
	Classes IV to VI	.. **21-Towns**		**151,639**	**94,646**	**56,993**	**35,487**	**22,883**	**12,604**

with Population by Religion—*continued.*

Sikhs.			Jains.			Buddhists.			Muslims.			
Persons. 9	Males. 10	Females. 11	Persons. 12	Males. 13	Females. 14	Persons. 15	Males. 16	Females. 17	Persons. 18	Males. 19	Females. 20	
515	**438**	**77**	**7,134**	**4,835**	**2,299**	**813**	**479**	**334**	**837,740**	**418,899**	**418,841**	
266	**232**	**34**	**2,334**	**1,617**	**717**	**356**	**204**	**152**	**111,353**	**59,904**	**51,449**	
29	27	2	2,279	1,574	705	343	198	145	69,959	38,281	31,678	1
1	1	..	3	3	..	5	3	2	13,186	6,801	6,385	2
234	202	32	49	37	12	..	..	..	19,456	10,256	9,200	3
2	2	..	3	3	..	8	3	5	8,752	4,566	4,186	4
9	**7**	**2**	**1,223**	**837**	**386**	**86**	**55**	**31**	**144,268**	**73,693**	**70,575**	
..	..	..	104	53	51	18	12	6	34,843	17,761	17,082	5
3	3	..	67	56	11	14	10	4	7,038	3,864	3,174	6
4	2	2	156	84	72	..	..	..	4,033	2,038	1,995	7
..	..	..	72	54	18	..	..	..	7,315	4,216	3,099	8
..	..	..	62	47	15	1	1	..	3,236	1,699	1,537	9
..	..	..	134	73	61	6	4	2	2,840	1,529	1,311	10
..	..	..	63	57	6	6	3	3	13,909	7,205	6,704	11
..	..	..	94	80	14	..	..	..	2,763	1,424	1,339	12
..	..	..	94	56	38	14	6	8	3,029	1,513	1,516	13
..	..	..	207	173	34	6	2	4	7,390	4,002	3,388	14
..	..	..	..	..	..	3	3	..	3,087	1,674	1,413	15
..	..	..	73	48	25	..	..	..	3,120	1,678	1,442	16
..	..	..	14	9	5	..	..	..	5,899	3,047	2,852	17
2	2	..	4	2	2	11	10	1	2,955	1,689	1,266	18
..	..	..	69	39	30	7	4	3	12,704	6,418	6,286	19
..	..	..	..	..	..	..	..	..	6,735	3,223	3,512	20
..	..	..	10	6	4	..	..	..	6,512	3,342	3,170	21
..	..	..	..	..	..	..	..	..	16,860	7,371	9,489	22
29	**14**	**15**	**1,375**	**961**	**414**	**167**	**119**	**48**	**231,714**	**116,816**	**114,898**	
..	..	..	11	6	5	..	..	..	8,223	4,209	4,014	23
24	9	15	4	1	3	..	..	..	10,953	4,633	6,320	24
..	..	..	226	171	55	12	10	2	16,041	9,009	7,032	25
..	..	..	8	7	1	..	..	..	9,059	4,627	4,432	26
..	..	..	..	..	..	..	..	..	2,182	1,132	1,050	27
..	..	..	12	7	5	..	..	..	5,129	2,690	2,439	28
..	..	..	..	..	..	..	..	..	1,175	540	635	29
..	..	..	..	..	..	24	15	9	1,274	666	608	30
..	..	..	105	72	33	1	1	..	13,358	6,793	6,565	31
..	..	..	75	68	7	..	..	..	16,376	8,415	7,961	32
..	..	..	159	138	21	6	3	3	3,996	2,124	1,872	33
3	3	..	..	..	..	..	..	..	14,049	6,689	7,360	34
..	..	..	..	..	..	..	..	..	1,206	559	647	35
..	..	..	6	2	4	1	1	..	3,466	1,935	1,531	36
..	..	..	117	73	44	51	30	21	1,679	912	767	37
..	..	..	..	..	..	..	..	..	1,512	659	853	38
..	..	..	88	54	34	..	..	..	1,341	722	619	39
..	..	..	..	..	..	..	..	..	523	263	260	40
..	..	..	3	2	1	..	..	..	676	345	331	41
..	..	..	..	..	..	..	..	..	11,836	5,367	6,469	42
..	..	..	54	29	25	1	1	..	4,001	2,074	1,927	43
..	..	..	..	..	..	..	..	..	6,133	3,005	3,128	44
..	..	..	10	5	5	..	..	..	1,759	891	868	45
..	..	..	28	15	13	..	..	..	1,732	860	872	46
..	..	..	11	8	3	1	1	..	4,284	2,226	2,058	47
..	..	..	..	..	..	..	..	..	60	36	24	48
..	..	..	62	53	9	5	4	1	2,778	1,547	1,231	49
..	..	..	17	11	6	15	7	8	9,914	4,730	5,184	50
..	..	..	..	..	..	..	..	..	7,349	3,711	3,638	51
..	..	..	3	3	..	..	..	..	285	149	136	52
..	..	..	..	..	..	..	..	..	2,511	1,222	1,289	53
..	..	..	..	..	..	..	..	..	12,534	5,787	6,747	54
..	..	..	..	..	..	46	43	3	5,558	3,105	2,453	55
..	..	—	118	59	59	..	..	..	938	493	445	56
..	..	..	14	13	1	..	..	..	8,076	4,203	3,873	57
..	..	..	50	44	6	..	..	..	11,118	5,585	5,533	58
..	..	..	..	..	..	1	1	..	1,854	1,055	799	59
..	..	..	2	2	..	..	..	..	2,572	1,292	1,280	60
..	..	..	53	36	17	..	..	..	4,641	2,388	2,253	61
..	..	..	..	..	..	3	2	1	1,062	601	461	62
..	..	..	..	..	..	..	..	..	2,396	1,227	1,169	63
..	..	..	..	..	..	..	..	..	352	199	153	64
2	2	..	1	1	..	..	..	..	1,294	648	646	65
..	..	..	33	12	21	..	..	..	2,926	1,377	1,549	66
..	..	..	68	45	23	..	..	..	2,615	1,362	1,253	67
..	..	..	37	24	13	..	..	..	2,455	1,330	1,125	68
..	..	..	..	..	..	..	..	..	6,159	3,273	2,886	69
..	..	..	..	..	..	..	..	..	304	151	153	70
211	**185**	**26**	**2,202**	**1,420**	**782**	**204**	**101**	**103**	**350,405**	**168,486**	**181,919**	
25,377	**16,407**	**8,970**	—	—	—	**2**	**2**	..	**256,189**	**153,891**	**102,298**	
5,150	**2,992**	**2,158**	..	..	..	..	..	..	**69,893**	**39,915**	**29,978**	1
10,885	**6,730**	**4,155**	—	—	—	**2**	**2**	—	**85,599**	**53,744**	**31,855**	
638	376	262	..	..	..	..	—	—	21,709	12,959	8,750	2
3,480	2,535	945	..	..	..	2	2	—	16,476	13,034	3,442	3
1,110	645	465	..	..	..	..	..	—	20,655	11,647	9,008	4
3,136	1,713	1,423	..	..	..	..	..	..	8,171	5,574	2,597	5
2,521	1,461	1,060	..	..	..	..	..	..	18,588	10,530	8,058	6
9,342	**6,685**	**2,657**	—	—	—	—	..	..	**100,697**	**60,232**	**40,465**	

Table V.—Towns Arranged Territorially

	District or State. 1	Town, Municipality, Suburb, Cantonment, etc. 2		Christians. Persons. 21	Males. 22	Females. 23	Zoroastrians. Persons. 24	Males. 25	Females. 26
	Madras	**340-Towns**		**370,317**	**183,829**	**186,488**	**485**	**252**	**233**
	Class I	**4-Towns**		**85,641**	**42,411**	**43,230**	**236**	**127**	**109**
1	Madras	Madras	Corpn.	53,086	26,491	26,595	229	122	107
2	Madura	Madura	M	10,081	4,840	5,241	..	..	..
3	Trichinopoly	Trichinopoly	M	20,318	10,014	10,304	3	3	..
4	Salem	Salem	M	2,156	1,066	1,090	4	2	2
	Class II	**18-Towns**		**87,154**	**42,506**	**44,648**	**106**	**61**	**45**
5	Malabar	Calicut	M	6,325	3,192	3,133	18	10	8
6	Coimbatore	Coimbatore	M	7,919	3,990	3,929	10	7	3
7	Tanjore	Tanjore	M	6,213	2,977	3,236	5	3	2
8	South Canara	Mangalore	M	18,510	8,775	9,735	20	11	9
9	Godavari East	Cocanada	M	1,768	881	887	10	6	4
10	Chingleput	Conjeeveram	M	286	126	160	..	..	..
11	Guntur	Guntur	M	5,510	2,555	2,955	20	10	10
12	Godavari East	Rajahmundry	M	1,923	838	1,085	..	..	..
13	Tanjore	Kumbakonam	M	1,925	957	968	..	..	..
14	Kistna	Bezwada	M	4,935	2,467	2,468	8	6	2
15	Tinnevelly	Tuticorin	M	14,041	6,861	7,180	5	5	..
16	South Canara	Cuddalore	M	2,228	1,161	1,067	..	..	..
17	Godavari East	Ellore	M	1,734	818	916	..	..	..
18	Vizagapatam	Vizagapatam	M	3,011	1,527	1,484	10	3	7
19	North Arcot	Vellore	M	2,122	1,039	1,083	..	..	..
20	Tinnevelly	Tinnevelly	M	1,313	633	680	..	..	..
21	Kistna	Bandar (Masulipatam)	M	2,243	1,139	1,104	..	..	..
22	Tinnevelly	Palamcottah	M	5,148	2,570	2,578	..	..	..
	Class III	**48-Towns**		**73,690**	**36,266**	**37,424**	**101**	**35**	**66**
23	Malabar	Palghat	M	1,309	680	629	..	..	..
24	Tanjore	Negapatam	M	3,206	1,604	1,602	..	..	..
25	Bellary	Bellary	M	2,528	1,140	1,388	6	2	4
26	Nellore	Nellore	M	3,641	1,645	1,996	..	..	..
27	Vizagapatam	Vizianagram	M	654	293	361	..	..	..
28	Madura	Dindigul	M	7,212	3,617	3,595	..	..	..
29	Ramnad	Rajapalaiyam	P.B.	403	202	201	..	..	..
30	Ganjam	Berhampur	M	638	297	341	..	..	..
31	Bellary	Adoni	M	208	109	99	..	..	..
32	Kurnool	Kurnool	M	1,163	571	592	..	..	..
33	Guntur	Tenali	M	2,518	1,321	1,197	..	..	..
34	Malabar	Cannanore	M	3,568	1,713	1,855	16	9	7
35	Ramnad	Aruppukkottai	P.B.	813	407	406	..	..	..
36	Coimbatore	Erode	M	1,433	732	701	..	..	..
37	Chingleput	Sembiyam	P.B.	2,837	1,480	1,357	6	3	3
38	Ramnad	Virudunagar	M	1,491	825	666	..	..	..
39	Chingleput	Saidpet	M	1,099	550	549	8	4	4
40	Ramnad	Srivilliputtur	M	1,332	520	812	..	..	..
41	Tanjore	Mayavaram	M	1,504	687	817	..	..	..
42	Malabar	Tellicherry	M	1,769	846	923	..	..	..
43	North Arcot	Tiruvannamalai	M	915	556	359	..	..	..
44	Tinnevelly	Tenkasi	P.B.	342	141	201	..	..	..
45	Madura	Bodinayakkanur	M	649	296	353	..	..	..
46	South Arcot	Chidambaram	M	119	63	56	..	..	..
47	North Arcot	Gudiyattam	M	175	79	96	..	..	..
48	Trichinopoly	Srirangum	M	151	71	80	..	..	..
49	Nilgiris	Ootacamand	M	7,553	3,572	3,981	60	14	46
50	North Arcot	Ambur	P.B.	503	265	238	..	..	..
51	Tinnevelly	Kodaiyanallur	P.B.	45	26	19	..	..	..
52	Vizagapatam	Anakapalle	M	54	22	32	..	..	..
53	Madura	Periyakulam	M	1,427	726	701	1	1	..
54	North Arcot	Vaniyambadi	M	197	101	96	..	..	..
55	Malabar	Cochin	M	12,062	5,973	6,089	..	..	..
56	Tanjore	Mannargudi	M	577	340	237	..	..	..
57	Kurnool	Nandyal	M	1,998	1,080	918	..	..	..
58	Cuddapah	Cuddapah	M	656	374	282	..	..	..
59	Coimbatore	Pollachi	M	606	305	301	..	..	..
60	Chittoor	Chittoor	M	816	278	538	..	..	..
61	Bellary	Hospet	M	126	67	59	..	..	..
62	Ramnad	Karaikudi	M	306	172	134	..	..	..
63	Tinnevelly	Puliyangudi	P.B.	935	470	465	..	..	..
64	Vizagapatam	Bobbili	P.B.	290	90	200	..	..	..
65	Ramnad	Devakottai	P.B.	203	108	95	..	..	..
66	Tanjore	Tiruvarur	M	192	95	97	..	..	..
67	Chingleput	Poonamallee	P.B.	652	336	316	..	..	..
68	South Arcot	Villupuram	M	2,048	1,028	1,020	..	..	..
69	Cuddapah	Proddatur	M	689	348	341	4	2	2
70	Ganjam	Parlakimedi	M	78	45	33	..	..	..
	Classes IV to VI	**270-Towns**		**123,832**	**62,646**	**61,186**	**42**	**29**	**13**
	North-West Frontier Province.	**27-Towns**		**11,411**	**8,474**	**2,937**	**60**	**30**	**30**
1	**Class II**	**Peshawar**	M	**792**	**452**	**340**	..	..	..
	Class III	**5-Towns**		**4,539**	**3,192**	**1,347**	**27**	**14**	**13**
2	Dera Ismail Khan	Dera Ismail Khan	M	188	103	85	..	..	..
3	Peshawar	Peshawar	C	4,062	2,928	1,134	27	14	13
4	Kohat	Kohat	M	86	46	40	..	..	..
5	Bannu	Bannu	M	184	102	82	..	..	..
6	Peshawar	Mardan	M	19	13	6	..	..	..
	Classes IV to VI	**21-Towns**		**6,080**	**4,830**	**1,250**	**33**	**16**	**17**

with Population by Religion—*continued.*

Jews.			Tribals.			Others.			
Persons.	Males.	Females.	Persons.	Males.	Females.	Persons.	Males.	Females.	
27	28	29	30	31	32	33	34	35	
28	**14**	**9**	**477**	**267**	**210**	**39**	**25**	**14**	
10	**4**	**6**	..	..	..	**26**	**19**	**7**	
2	1	1	..	..	..	26	19	7	1
8	3	5	..	..	..	..	..	..	2
..	..	..	..	..	..	..	..	..	3
..	..	..	..	..	..	..	..	..	4
2	**2**	..	**118**	**52**	**66**	**6**	**3**	**3**	
..	..	..	..	..	..	..	..	..	5
..	..	..	..	..	..	..	..	..	6
..	..	..	..	..	..	..	..	..	7
..	..	..	..	..	..	..	..	..	8
1	1	..	..	..	..	..	..	..	9
..	..	..	..	..	..	..	..	..	10
..	..	..	14	..	14	..	..	..	11
..	..	..	..	..	..	..	..	..	12
..	..	..	..	..	..	..	..	..	13
..	..	..	93	44	49	..	..	..	14
1	1	..	..	..	..	..	..	..	15
..	..	..	..	..	..	..	..	..	16
..	..	..	..	..	..	..	..	..	17
..	..	..	11	8	3	..	..	..	18
..	..	..	..	..	..	..	..	..	19
..	..	..	..	..	..	6	3	3	20
..	..	..	..	..	..	..	..	..	21
..	..	..	..	..	..	..	..	..	22
10	**7**	**3**	**86**	**67**	**19**	**4**	**2**	**2**	
..	..	..	..	..	..	..	..	..	23
..	..	..	..	..	..	..	..	..	24
..	..	..	..	..	..	..	..	..	25
..	..	..	..	..	..	..	..	..	26
..	..	..	..	..	..	..	..	..	27
..	..	..	..	..	..	..	..	..	28
..	..	..	..	..	..	..	..	..	29
..	..	..	4	4	..	..	..	..	30
..	..	..	..	..	..	..	..	..	31
..	..	..	..	..	..	..	..	..	32
..	..	..	..	..	..	..	..	..	33
3	3	..	..	..	..	..	..	..	34
..	..	..	..	..	..	..	..	..	35
2	1	1	..	..	..	..	..	..	36
..	..	..	..	..	..	..	..	..	37
..	..	..	..	..	..	..	..	..	38
..	..	..	..	..	..	..	..	..	39
..	..	..	..	..	..	..	..	..	40
..	..	..	..	..	..	..	..	..	41
..	..	..	..	..	..	1	..	1	42
..	..	..	..	..	..	..	..	..	43
..	..	..	..	..	..	..	..	..	44
..	..	..	..	..	..	..	..	..	45
..	..	..	..	..	..	..	..	..	46
..	..	..	..	..	..	..	..	..	47
..	..	..	..	..	..	..	..	..	48
..	..	..	36	23	13	3	2	1	49
..	..	..	..	..	..	..	..	..	50
..	..	..	..	..	..	..	..	..	51
..	..	..	..	..	..	..	..	..	52
..	..	..	..	..	..	..	..	..	53
..	..	..	..	..	..	..	..	..	54
5	3	2	..	..	..	..	..	..	55
..	..	..	..	..	..	..	..	..	56
..	..	..	..	..	..	..	..	..	57
..	..	..	..	..	..	..	..	..	58
..	..	..	..	..	..	..	..	..	59
..	..	..	..	..	..	..	..	..	60
..	..	..	..	..	..	..	..	..	61
..	..	..	..	..	..	..	..	..	62
..	..	..	..	..	..	..	..	..	63
..	..	..	6	6	..	..	..	..	64
..	..	..	..	..	..	..	..	..	65
..	..	..	..	..	..	..	..	..	66
..	..	..	..	..	..	..	..	..	67
..	..	..	..	..	..	..	..	..	68
..	..	..	..	..	..	..	..	..	69
..	..	..	40	34	6	..	..	..	70
1	**1**	—	**273**	**148**	**125**	**3**	**1**	**2**	
11	**11**	..	..	..	..	..	..	..	
11	11	..	..	..	..	..	..	..	1
..	..	..	..	..	..	..	..	..	
..	..	..	..	..	..	..	..	..	2
..	..	..	..	..	..	..	..	..	3
..	..	..	..	..	..	..	..	..	4
..	..	..	..	..	..	..	..	..	5
..	..	..	..	..	..	..	..	..	6
..	..	..	..	..	..	..	..	..	

Table V.—Towns Arranged Territorially

	District or State.	Town, Municipality, Suburb, Cantonment, etc.		Population.			Hindus.		
				Persons.	Males.	Females.	Persons.	Males.	Females.
	1	2		3	4	5	6	7	8
	Punjab	**199-Towns**		**3,067,464**	**1,805,872**	**1,261,592**	**1,126,247**	**667,944**	**458,303**
	Class I	**3-Towns**		**771,636**	**472,469**	**299,167**	**261,104**	**162,968**	**98,136**
1	Lahore	Lahore	M	400,075	253,846	146,229	127,016	83,592	43,424
2	Amritsar	Amritsar	M	263,210	157,823	105,387	96,975	58,890	38,085
3	Multan	Multan	M	108,351	60,800	47,551	37,113	20,486	16,627
	Class II	**5-Towns**		**359,969**	**208,912**	**151,057**	**95,050**	**55,596**	**39,454**
4	Sialkot	Sialkot	M	85,093	49,071	36,022	13,275	7,744	5,531
5	Rawalpindi	Rawalpindi	M	75,767	46,086	29,681	24,806	14,549	10,257
6	Jullundur	Jullundur	M	74,295	41,321	32,974	20,756	11,888	8,868
7	Ludhiana	Ludhiana	M	66,098	38,218	27,880	19,255	11,384	7,871
8	Gujranwala	Gujranwala	M	58,716	34,216	24,500	16,958	10,031	6,927
	Class III	**24-Towns**		**762,650**	**451,543**	**311,107**	**309,117**	**182,515**	**126,602**
9	Ambala	Ambala	C	49,368	29,991	19,377	27,369	16,203	11,166
10	Lahore	Kasur	M	46,815	28,067	18,748	8,245	5,003	3,242
11	Rawalpindi	Rawalpindi	C	43,517	29,885	13,632	15,355	10,120	5,235
12	Lyallpur	Lyallpur	M	42,922	27,489	15,433	19,992	12,880	7,112
13	Jhang	Jhang Maghiana	M	36,035	19,275	16,760	16,724	8,594	8,130
14	Hissar	Bhiwani	M	35,866	19,135	16,731	27,906	14,836	13,070
15	Ambala	Ambala	M	35,193	20,045	15,148	11,716	7,057	4,659
16	Ferozepore	Ferozepore	M	34,337	19,679	14,658	13,667	7,913	5,754
17	Rohtak	Rohtak	M	34,112	19,907	14,205	16,238	10,003	6,235
18	Gurdaspur	Batala	M	33,204	18,102	15,102	9,149	5,052	4,097
19	Karnal	Panipat	M	32,915	18,010	14,905	8,003	4,616	3,387
20	Ferozepore	Ferozepore	C	30,297	19,205	11,092	13,269	8,206	5,063
21	Lahore	Lahore	C	29,672	20,741	8,931	12,109	8,075	4,034
22	Ludhiana	Jagraon	M	27,108	17,151	9,957	6,851	4,163	2,688
23	Shahpur	Sargodha	M	26,761	16,498	10,263	11,674	7,021	4,653
24	Gurgaon	Rewari	M	26,269	14,383	11,886	13,201	7,362	5,839
25	Montgomery	Montgomery	M	26,164	17,392	8,772	11,014	7,142	3,872
26	Hoshiarpur	Hoshiarpur	M	25,925	14,689	11,236	11,097	6,562	4,535
27	Jhang	Chiniot	M	25,841	14,027	11,814	8,711	4,903	3,808
28	Gujrat	Gujrat	M	25,604	13,956	11,648	5,772	3,225	2,547
29	Karnal	Karnal	M	25,371	14,314	11,057	13,251	7,519	5,732
30	Hissar	Hissar	M	25,179	15,065	10,114	13,846	8,501	5,345
31	Dera Gazi Khan	Dera Ghazi Khan	M	23,468	12,759	10,709	9,284	4,845	4,439
32	Gujranwala	Wazirabad	M	20,707	11,778	8,929	4,674	2,714	1,960
	Classes IV to VI	**167-Towns**		**1,173,209**	**672,948**	**500,261**	**460,976**	**266,865**	**194,111**
	United Provinces	**441-Towns**		**5,424,621**	**3,005,148**	**2,419,473**	**3,229,701**	**1,817,117**	**1,412,584**
	Class I	**7-Towns**		**1,295,446**	**730,144**	**565,302**	**777,874**	**445,320**	**332,554**
1	Lucknow	Lucknow	M	251,097	143,876	107,221	142,461	83,425	59,036
2	Cawnpore	Cawnpore	M	219,189	129,276	89,913	150,374	89,117	61,257
3	Agra	Agra	M	205,487	113,320	92,167	127,088	70,951	56,137
4	Benares	Benares	M	201,037	111,587	89,450	137,754	77,265	60,489
5	Allahabad	Allahabad	M	173,895	97,909	75,986	114,150	64,782	49,368
6	Bareilly	Bareilly	M	134,179	72,830	61,349	62,824	34,990	27,834
7	Moradabad	Moradabad	M	110,562	61,346	49,216	43,223	24,790	18,433
	Class II	**10-Towns**		**695,259**	**386,781**	**308,478**	**419,142**	**235,304**	**183,838**
8	Meerut	Meerut	M	91,181	52,112	39,069	44,388	25,741	18,647
9	Aligarh	Koil Aligarh	M	83,878	48,264	35,614	45,859	26,373	19,486
10	Shahjahanpur	Shahjahanpur	M	79,316	42,690	36,626	35,580	19,910	15,670
11	Saharanpur	Saharanpur	M	78,655	45,282	33,373	29,039	17,537	11,502
12	Jhansi	Jhansi	M	64,591	33,908	30,683	47,525	24,885	22,640
13	Mirzapur	Mirzapur-*cum*-Bindhyachal.	M	61,184	32,538	28,646	48,510	25,686	22,824
14	Muttra	Muttra	M	60,590	33,148	27,442	46,170	25,301	20,869
15	Fyzabad	Fyzabad-*cum*-Ajodhya.	M	59,992	34,933	25,059	44,619	26,498	18,121
16	Gorakhpur	Gorakhpur	M	59,369	33,041	26,328	37,658	21,454	16,204
17	Farrukhabad	Farrukhabad-*cum*-Fatehgarh.	M	56,503	30,865	25,638	39,794	21,919	17,875
	Class III	**33-Towns**		**991,773**	**555,469**	**436,304**	**536,824**	**306,660**	**230,164**
18	Etawah	Etawah	M	46,948	25,461	21,487	31,331	17,164	14,167
19	Meerut	Meerut	C	45,528	27,961	17,567	24,545	14,717	9,828
20	Budaun	Budaun	M	45,455	24,129	21,326	18,516	10,215	8,301
21	Moradabad	Amroha	M	44,948	22,525	22,423	11,362	6,062	5,300
22	Moradabad	Sambhal	M	44,300	23,190	21,110	13,307	7,063	6,244
23	Dehra Dun	Dehra Dun	M	40,409	24,862	15,547	25,418	15,856	9,562
24	Aligarh	Hathras	M	39,784	22,688	17,096	33,394	19,047	14,347
25	Jaunpur	Jaunpur	M	37,675	20,353	17,322	22,655	12,427	10,228
26	Pilibhit	Pilibhit	M	36,892	19,569	17,323	19,398	10,652	8,746
27	Muzaffarnagar	Muzaffarnagar	M	35,347	21,131	14,216	20,952	12,834	8,118
28	Bahraich	Bahraich	M	33,783	18,617	15,166	15,301	8,848	6,453
29	Saharanpur	Hardwar	M	33,287	19,374	13,913	24,025	14,382	9,643
30	Bulandshahr	Khurja	M	31,279	17,135	14,144	16,164	9,233	6,931
31	Bijnor	Najibabad	M	28,473	16,023	12,450	11,958	6,852	5,106
32	Ghazipur	Ghazipur	M	27,498	15,011	12,487	18,325	10,268	8,057
33	Moradabad	Chandausi	M	26,768	14,898	11,870	19,191	10,809	8,382
34	Bijnor	Nagina	M	25,427	14,476	10,951	6,188	3,384	2,804
35	Meerut	Hapur	M	25,116	14,266	10,850	14,444	8,158	6,286
36	Bulandshahr	Bulandshahr	M	24,898	14,248	10,650	13,790	8,080	5,710
37	Sitapur	Sitapur	M	24,720	14,159	10,561	15,323	9,210	6,113
38	Cawnpore	Cawnpore	C	24,566	14,596	9,970	15,134	8,779	6,355
39	Agra	Agra	C	24,277	14,416	9,861	14,980	8,665	6,315
40	Lucknow	Lucknow	C	23,562	15,582	7,980	12,889	7,915	4,974
41	Bijnor	Bijnor	M	23,520	12,930	10,590	9,995	5,755	4,240
42	Agra	Firozabad	M	23,154	13,053	10,101	12,959	7,436	5,523
33	Etah	Kasganj	M	23,100	12,729	10,371	14,726	8,177	6,549

with Population by Religion—*continued.*

Sikhs.			Jains.			Buddhists.			Muslims.			
Persons. 9	Males. 10	Females. 11	Persons. 12	Males. 13	Females. 14	Persons. 15	Males. 16	Females. 17	Persons. 18	Males. 19	Females. 20	
205,681	**126,992**	**78,689**	**21,620**	**11,584**	**10,036**	**39**	**30**	**9**	**1,629,660**	**948,892**	**680,768**	
55,093	**33,694**	**21,399**	**1,700**	**919**	**781**	**10**	**7**	**3**	**437,180**	**265,849**	**171,331**	
21,010	13,802	7,208	725	404	321	10	7	3	238,033	148,708	89,325	1
31,855	18,627	13,228	604	329	275	..	..	..	132,016	79,118	52,898	2
2,228	1,265	963	371	186	185	..	..	..	67,131	38,023	29,108	3
26,516	**16,090**	**10,426**	**4,710**	**2,542**	**2,168**	**7**	**6**	**1**	**224,669**	**129,857**	**94,812**	
3,203	1,997	1,206	1,532	841	691	..	..	..	64,713	37,217	27,496	4
12,388	7,327	5,061	974	533	441	3	2	1	36,663	23,120	13,543	5
2,167	1,480	687	892	458	434	..	..	..	47,798	26,017	21,781	6
2,879	1,846	1,033	334	167	167	4	4	..	42,254	24,238	18,016	7
5,879	3,440	2,439	978	543	435	..	..	..	33,241	19,265	13,976	8
39,545	**26,090**	**13,455**	**6,983**	**3,777**	**3,206**	**20**	**15**	**5**	**381,742**	**222,408**	**159,334**	
1,981	1,482	499	509	282	227	5	3	2	16,565	9,968	6,597	9
1,529	1,052	477	144	72	72	..	..	..	36,658	21,825	14,833	10
3,144	2,072	1,072	51	30	21	6	4	2	18,974	13,612	5,362	11
5,181	3,243	1,938	65	47	18	..	..	..	15,534	10,115	5,419	12
1,243	684	559	..	..	..	..	..	..	18,042	9,984	8,058	13
8	6	2	274	140	134	..	..	..	7,567	4,102	3,465	14
1,898	1,139	759	760	412	348	..	..	..	20,816	11,436	9,380	15
3,034	1,830	1,204	108	54	54	..	..	..	17,128	9,660	7,468	16
240	130	110	1,325	729	596	..	..	..	16,180	8,975	7,205	17
1,327	740	587	..	..	..	2	2	..	22,323	12,060	10,263	18
71	46	25	860	458	402	..	..	..	23,930	12,861	11,069	19
1,405	1,069	336	403	209	194	1	1	..	11,336	7,100	4,236	20
2,467	1,724	743	66	38	28	4	4	..	11,282	7,778	3,504	21
3,785	2,880	905	228	125	103	..	..	..	14,175	8,690	5,485	22
5,201	3,333	1,868	1	1	..	..	..	..	9,146	5,786	3,360	23
13	7	6	632	324	308	..	..	..	12,224	6,588	5,636	24
3,356	2,342	1,014	13	11	2	2	1	1	11,168	7,570	3,598	25
1,097	679	418	472	271	201	..	..	..	12,609	6,801	5,808	26
208	139	69	..	..	..	..	..	..	16,913	8,977	7,936	27
587	374	213	..	..	..	..	..	..	18,938	10,197	8,741	28
137	85	52	182	93	89	..	..	..	11,729	6,578	5,151	29
336	279	57	749	403	346	..	..	..	10,128	5,836	4,292	30
91	56	35	125	71	54	..	..	..	13,953	7,777	6,176	31
1,206	699	507	16	7	9	..	..	..	14,424	8,132	6,292	32
84,527	**51,118**	**33,409**	**8,227**	**4,346**	**3,881**	**2**	**2**	..	**586,069**	**330,778**	**255,291**	
9,048	**5,992**	**3,056**	**31,114**	**16,828**	**14,286**	**181**	**110**	**71**	**2,073,976**	**1,118,739**	**955,237**	
2,622	**1,581**	**1,041**	**3,332**	**1,868**	**1,464**	**73**	**45**	**28**	**488,751**	**269,758**	**218,993**	
793	521	272	239	140	99	7	1	6	101,673	56,682	44,991	1
130	86	44	265	165	100	3	2	1	65,460	38,397	27,063	2
1,308	719	589	2,053	1,141	912	3	3	..	72,049	39,143	32,906	3
113	75	38	131	71	60	10	8	2	61,866	33,636	28,230	4
103	68	35	302	163	139	42	27	15	54,189	30,217	23,972	5
90	56	34	25	11	14	7	3	4	69,804	37,035	32,769	6
85	56	29	317	177	140	1	1	..	63,710	34,648	29,062	7
2,092	**1,177**	**915**	**4,104**	**2,264**	**1,840**	**1**	**1**	..	**263,567**	**144,911**	**118,656**	
89	73	16	987	568	419	..	..	..	44,735	25,348	19,387	8
580	322	258	639	349	290	1	1	..	35,938	20,851	15,087	9
26	15	11	..	..	..	..	..	..	43,312	22,627	20,685	10
241	157	84	1,852	1,003	849	..	..	..	46,347	25,910	20,437	11
56	36	20	231	139	92	..	..	..	15,620	8,222	7,398	12
20	17	3	45	27	18	..	..	..	12,276	6,648	5,628	13
980	500	480	232	119	113	..	..	..	12,678	6,961	5,717	14
60	31	29	15	9	6	..	..	..	15,082	8,269	6,813	15
17	11	6	..	..	..	..	..	..	21,522	11,470	10,052	16
23	15	8	103	50	53	..	..	..	16,057	8,605	7,452	17
2,573	**1,893**	**680**	**6,069**	**3,325**	**2,744**	**3**	**3**	..	**425,739**	**230,071**	**195,668**	
8	4	4	914	522	392	..	..	..	14,621	7,735	6,886	18
809	686	123	663	365	298	1	1	..	15,855	9,567	6,288	19
17	9	8	..	..	..	..	..	..	26,447	13,629	12,818	20
..	..	..	83	41	42	1	1	..	32,972	16,122	16.850	21
1	1	..	35	20	15	..	..	..	30,776	16,008	14,768	22
512	311	201	374	204	170	..	..	..	12,054	7,483	4,571	23
15	10	5	96	61	35	..	..	..	5,530	3,175	2,355	24
9	7	2	..	..	..	..	..	..	14,970	7,903	7,067	25
5	5	..	2	2	..	..	..	..	17,042	8,685	8,357	26
33	19	14	1,098	621	477	..	..	..	13,142	7,596	5,546	27
42	29	13	91	56	35	..	..	..	18,284	9,647	8,637	28
144	104	40	77	34	43	..	..	..	8,975	4,810	4,165	29
211	103	108	123	59	64	..	..	..	14,262	7,475	6,787	30
1	1	..	225	117	108	..	..	..	16,057	8,925	7,132	31
35	17	18	..	..	..	..	..	..	8,922	4,608	4,314	32
10	8	2	45	29	16	..	..	..	7,309	3,937	3,372	33
..	..	..	38	19	19	..	..	..	19,029	10,987	8,042	34
7	7	..	167	91	76	..	..	..	10,302	5,914	4,388	35
74	57	17	78	41	37	..	..	..	10,773	5,977	4,796	36
23	16	7	34	15	19	..	..	..	9,134	4,818	4,316	37
24	14	10	8	3	5	..	..	..	7,230	4,250	2,980	38
172	125	47	16	12	4	1	1	..	6,316	3,657	2,659	39
379	333	46	32	17	15	..	..	..	6,450	4,083	2,367	40
10	5	5	136	51	85	..	..	..	13,152	7,042	6,110	41
..	..	..	739	412	327	..	..	..	9,326	5,190	4,136	42
..	..	..	85	57	28	..	..	..	8,005	4,363	3,642	43

Table V.—Towns Arranged Territorially

District or State. 1	Town, Municipality, Suburb, Cantonment, etc. 2		Christians. Persons. 21	Christians. Males. 22	Christians. Females. 23	Zoroastrians. Persons. 24	Zoroastrians. Males. 25	Zoroastrians. Females. 26
Punjab ..	.. **199-Towns**		**65,636**	**39,731**	**25,905**	**511**	**315**	**196**
Class I ..	.. **3-Towns**		**15,212**	**8,258**	**6,954**	**200**	**113**	**87**
1 Lahore ..	.. Lahore ..	M	13,153	7,257	5,896	128	76	52
2 Amritsar ..	.. Amritsar ..	M	1,555	734	821	41	24	17
3 Multan ..	.. Multan ..	M	504	267	237	31	13	18
Class II ..	.. **5-Towns**		**6,138**	**3,222**	**2,916**	**1**	**1**	..
4 Sialkot ..	.. Sialkot ..	M	2,344	1,267	1,077	..	..	..
5 Rawalpindi ..	.. Rawalpindi ..	M	933	555	378	..	..	..
6 Jullundur ..	.. Jullundur ..	M	190	97	93	..	..	..
7 Ludhiana ..	.. Ludhiana ..	M	1,011	366	645	1	1	..
8 Gujranwala	.. Gujranwala ..	M	1,660	937	723	..	..	..
Class III ..	.. **24-Towns**		**20,867**	**14,065**	**6,802**	**180**	**80**	**50**
9 Ambala ..	.. Ambala ..	C	2,936	2,050	886	2	2	..
10 Lahore ..	.. Kasur ..	M	227	105	122	6	4	2
11 Rawalpindi..	.. Rawalpindi ..	C	5,917	4,007	1,910	65	37	28
12 Lyallpur ..	.. Lyallpur ..	M	1,988	1,102	886	7	7	..
13 Jhang ..	.. Jhang Maghiana	M	26	13	13	..	..	..
14 Hissar ..	.. Bhiwani ..	M	111	51	60	..	..	..
15 Ambala ..	.. Ambala ..	M	3	1	2	..	..	..
16 Ferozepore	.. Ferozepore ..	M	344	183	161	..	..	..
17 Rohtak ..	.. Rohtak ..	M	129	70	59	..	..	..
18 Gurdaspur ..	.. Batala ..	M	306	174	132	..	..	..
19 Karnal ..	.. Panipat ..	M	51	29	22	..	..	..
20 Ferozepore	.. Ferozepore ..	C	2,598	1,857	741	24	16	8
21 Lahore ..	.. Lahore ..	C	3,722	3,111	611	22	11	11
22 Ludhiana ..	.. Jagraon ..	M	69	52	17	..	..	—
23 Shahpur ..	.. Sargodha ..	M	704	341	363	..	..	..
24 Gurgaon ..	.. Rewari ..	M	199	102	97	..	..	..
25 Montogomery	.. Montgomery ..	M	581	309	272	3	2	1
26 Hoshiarpur	.. Hoshiarpur ..	M	58	30	28	..	..	..
27 Jhang ..	.. Chiniot ..	M	..	..	..	..	..	..
28 Gujrat ..	.. Gujrat ..	M	307	160	147	..	..	..
29 Karnal ..	.. Karnal ..	M	72	39	33	..	..	..
30 Hissar ..	.. Hissar ..	M	119	45	74	1	1	..
31 Dera Gazi Khan	.. Dera Ghazi Khan	M	15	10	5	..	..	..
32 Gujranwala	.. Wazirabad ..	M	385	224	161	..	..	..
Classes IV to VI	.. **167-Towns**		**23,419**	**14,186**	**9,233**	**130**	**121**	**59**
United Provinces	.. **441-Towns**		**79,588**	**45,789**	**33,799**	**955**	**538**	**417**
Class I ..	.. **7-Towns**		**22,307**	**11,300**	**11,007**	**472**	**263**	**209**
1 Lucknow ..	.. Lucknow ..	M	5,807	3,040	2,767	116	67	49
2 Cawnpore ..	.. Cawnpore ..	M	2,825	1,440	1,385	124	66	58
3 Agra ..	.. Agra ..	M	2,903	1,317	1,586	82	45	37
4 Benares ..	.. Benares ..	M	1,155	526	629	8	6	2
5 Allahabad ..	.. Allahabad ..	M	4,992	2,584	2,408	113	64	49
6 Bareilly ..	.. Bareilly ..	M	1,410	725	685	19	10	9
7 Moradabad	.. Moradabad ..	M	3,215	1,668	1,547	10	5	5
Class II ..	.. **10-Towns**		**6,174**	**3,027**	**3,147**	**161**	**86**	**75**
8 Meerut ..	.. Meerut ..	M	982	382	600	..	..	..
9 Aligarh ..	.. Koil Aligarh ..	M	854	363	491	6	4	2
10 Shahjahanpur	.. Shahjahanpur ..	M	397	137	260	1	1	..
11 Saharanpur	.. Saharanpur ..	M	1,147	659	488	22	12	10
12 Jhansi ..	.. Jhansi ..	M	1,043	564	479	116	62	54
13 Mirzapur ..	.. Mirzapur-*cum*-Bindhyachal.	M	330	158	172	..	..	..
14 Muttra ..	.. Muttra ..	M	527	265	262	2	1	1
15 Fyzabad ..	.. Fyzabad-*cum*-Ajodhya.	M	213	125	88	2	..	2
16 Gorakhpur ..	.. Gorakhpur ..	M	156	99	57	11	5	6
17 Farrukhabad	.. Farrukhabad-*cum*-Fatehgarh.	M	525	275	250	1	1	..
Class III ..	.. **33-Towns**		**20,401**	**13,414**	**6,987**	**152**	**96**	**56**
18 Etawah ..	.. Etawah ..	M	70	33	37	4	3	1
19 Meerut ..	.. Meerut ..	C	3,651	2,623	1,028	3	2	1
20 Budaun ..	.. Budaun ..	M	475	276	199	..	..	..
21 Moradabad	.. Amroha ..	M	530	299	231	..	..	..
22 Moradabad	.. Sambhal ..	M	181	98	83	..	..	..
23 Dehra Dun	.. Dehra Dun ..	M	2,018	986	1,032	28	19	9
24 Aligarh ..	.. Hathras ..	M	712	372	340	37	23	14
25 Jaunpur ..	.. Jaunpur ..	M	41	16	25	..	..	..
26 Pilibhit ..	.. Pilibhit ..	M	445	225	220	..	..	..
27 Muzaffarnagar	.. Muzaffarnagar ..	M	122	61	61	..	..	..
28 Bahraich ..	.. Bahraich ..	M	65	37	28	..	..	..
29 Saharanpur	.. Hardwar ..	M	66	44	22	..	..	..
30 Bulandshahr	.. Khurja ..	M	518	264	254	1	1	..
31 Bijnor ..	.. Najibabad ..	M	232	128	104	..	..	..
32 Ghazipur ..	.. Ghazipur ..	M	216	118	98	..	..	..
33 Moradabad	.. Chandausi ..	M	211	113	98	2	2	..
34 Bijnor ..	.. Nagina ..	M	172	86	86	..	..	..
35 Meerut ..	.. Hapur ..	M	196	96	100	..	..	..
36 Bulandshahr	.. Bulandshahr ..	M	183	93	90	..	..	..
37 Sitapur ..	.. Sitapur ..	M	206	100	106	..	..	..
38 Cawnpore ..	.. Cawnpore ..	C	2,140	1,528	612	25	19	6
39 Agra ..	.. Agra ..	C	2,748	1,934	814	43	21	22
40 Lucknow ..	.. Lucknow ..	C	3,808	3,231	577	4	3	1
41 Bijnor ..	.. Bijnor ..	M	227	77	150	..	—	..
42 Agra ..	.. Firozabad ..	M	127	12	115	3	3	..
43 Etah ..	.. Kasganj ..	M	282	132	150	2	..	2

with Population by Religion—*continued.*

Jews.			Tribals.			Others.			
Persons. 27	Males. 28	Females. 29	Persons. 30	Males. 31	Females. 32	Persons. 33	Males. 34	Females. 35	
10	**5**	**5**	..	..	..	**18,060**	**10,379**	**7,681**	
..	..	..	..	..	..	**1,137**	**661**	**476**	
..	..	..	..	..	..	..	..	..	1
..	..	..	..	..	..	164	101	63	2
..	..	..	..	..	..	973	560	413	3
..	..	..	..	..	..	**2,878**	**1,598**	**1,280**	
..	..	..	..	..	..	26	5	21	4
..	..	..	..	..	..	..	..	..	5
..	..	..	..	..	..	2,492	1,381	1,111	6
..	..	..	..	..	..	360	212	148	7
..	..	..	..	..	..	..	..	..	8
6	**4**	**2**	..	..	..	**4,240**	**2,589**	**1,651**	
1	1	..	..	..	..	..	..	..	9
..	..	..	..	..	..	6	6	..	10
5	3	2	..	..	..	..	..	..	11
..	..	..	..	..	..	155	95	60	12
..	..	..	..	..	..	..	..	..	13
..	..	..	..	..	..	..	..	..	14
..	..	..	..	..	..	..	..	..	15
..	..	..	..	..	..	56	39	17	16
..	..	..	..	..	..	..	..	..	17
..	..	..	..	..	..	97	74	23	18
..	..	..	..	..	..	..	..	..	19
..	..	..	..	..	..	1,261	747	514	20
..	..	..	..	..	..	..	..	..	21
..	..	..	..	..	..	2,000	1,241	759	22
..	..	..	..	..	..	35	16	19	23
..	..	..	..	..	..	..	..	..	24
..	..	..	..	..	..	27	15	12	25
..	..	..	..	..	..	592	346	246	26
..	..	..	..	..	..	9	8	1	27
..	..	..	..	..	..	..	..	..	28
..	..	..	..	..	..	..	..	..	29
..	..	..	..	..	..	..	..	..	30
..	..	..	..	..	..	..	..	..	31
..	..	..	..	..	..	2	2	..	32
4	**1**	**3**	..	..	..	**9,805**	**5,531**	**4,274**	
56	**33**	**23**	..	..	..	**2**	**2**	..	
15	**9**	**6**	..	..	..	..	..	..	
1	..	1	..	..	..	..	..	..	1
8	3	5	..	..	..	..	..	..	2
1	1	..	..	..	..	..	..	..	3
..	..	..	..	..	..	..	..	..	4
4	4	..	..	..	..	..	..	..	5
..	..	..	..	..	..	..	..	..	6
1	1	..	..	..	..	..	..	..	7
17	**10**	**7**	..	..	..	**1**	**1**	..	
..	..	..	..	..	..	..	..	..	8
1	1	..	..	..	..	..	..	..	9
..	..	..	..	..	..	..	..	..	10
7	4	3	..	..	..	..	..	..	11
..	..	..	..	..	..	..	..	..	12
3	2	1	..	..	..	..	..	..	13
..	..	..	..	..	..	1	1	..	14
1	1	..	..	..	..	..	..	..	15
5	2	3	..	..	..	..	..	..	16
..	.	..	..	..	..	..	..	..	17
11	**6**	**5**	..	..	..	**1**	**1**	..	
..	..	..	..	..	..	..	..	..	18
1	..	1	..	..	..	..	..	..	19
..	..	..	..	..	..	..	..	..	20
..	..	..	..	..	..	..	..	..	21
..	..	..	..	..	..	..	..	..	22
5	3	2	..	..	..	..	..	..	23
..	..	..	..	..	..	..	..	..	24
..	..	..	..	..	..	..	..	..	25
..	..	..	..	..	..	..	..	..	26
..	..	..	..	..	..	..	..	..	27
..	..	..	..	..	..	..	..	..	28
..	..	..	..	..	..	..	..	..	29
..	..	..	..	..	..	..	..	..	30
..	..	..	..	..	..	..	..	..	31
..	..	..	..	..	..	..	..	..	32
..	..	..	..	..	..	..	..	..	33
..	..	..	..	..	..	..	..	..	34
..	..	..	..	..	..	.	..	..	35
..	..	..	..	..	..	.	..	..	36
..	..	..	..	..	..	..	..	..	37
5	3	2	..	..	..	..	..	..	38
..	..	..	..	..	..	1	1	..	39
..	..	..	..	..	..	..	..	..	40
..	..	..	..	..	..	..	..	..	41
..	..	..	..	..	..	..	..	..	42
..	..	..	..	..	..	..	..	..	33

Table V.—Towns Arranged Territorially

District or State. 1	Town, Municipality, Suburb, Cantonment, etc. 2		Population. Persons. 3	Males. 4	Females. 5	Hindus. Persons. 6	Males. 7	Females. 8
United Provinces—*concld.*								
Class III—*concld.*								
44 Basti	Basti ..	T. A.	22,526	13,416	9,110	17,213	10,344	6,869
45 Banda	Banda ..	.. M	22,415	12,288	10,127	16,195	9,011	7,184
46 Saharanpur ..	Deoband ..	.. M	22,126	12,407	9,719	7,446	4,180	3,266
47 Azamgarh	Mau ..	.. N.A.	21,354	11,149	10,205	8,983	4,827	4,156
48 Fyzabad	Tanda ..	.. M	21,177	10,991	10,186	8,615	4,456	4,159
49 Hardoi	Shahabad ..	.. M	21,101	11,115	9,986	10,821	5,784	5,037
50 Farrukhabad ..	Kanauj ..	.. M	20,360	10,721	9,639	11,281	6,070	5,211
Classes IV to VI ..	**391 Towns**		**2,442,143**	**1,332,754**	**1,109,389**	**1,495,861**	**829,833**	**666,028**
States and Agencies ..	**877 Towns**		**9,326,958**	**4,881,346**	**4,445,612**	**6,237,105**	**3,262,207**	**2,974,898**
Assam States ..	**2 Towns**		**102,496**	**49,136**	**53,360**	**86,885**	**41,510**	**45,375**
1 **Class II** Manipur State—	Imphal* ..	..	**85,804**	**40,157**	**45,647**	**81,612**	**38,060**	**43,552**
Classes IV—VI ..	**1 Town**		**16,692†**	**8,979**	**7,713**	**5,273**	**3,450**	**1,823**
Baluchistan States—								
Classes IV to VI ..	**5 Towns**		**10,577**	**5,648**	**4,929**	**1,097**	**657**	**440**
Baroda State ..	**50 Towns**		**523,003**	**272,552**	**250,451**	**411,443**	**215,391**	**196,052**
1 **Class I**	Baroda City	.. M	**109,639**	**60,723**	**48,916**	**87,752**	**48,395**	**39,357**
Class III	**4 Towns**		**94,881**	**47,244**	**47,637**	**66,498**	**34,780**	**33,718**
2 Kadi	Patan ..	.. M	29,830	14,884	14,946	22,567	11,323	11,244
3 Navsari	Navsari ..	.. M	24,397	12,013	12,384	16,886	8,626	8,260
4 Kadi	Sidhpur ..	.. M	20,468	10,218	10,250	13,909	7,084	6,825
5 Amreli	Amreli ..	.. M	20,186	10,129	10,057	15,136	7,747	7,389
Classes IV to VI ..	**45 Towns**		**318,483**	**164,585**	**153,898**	**255,193**	**132,216**	**122,977**
Bengal States—								
Classes IV to VI ..	**5 Towns** ..	..	**27,610**	**16,672**	**10,938**	**22,702**	**13,603**	**9,099**
Bihar and Orissa States—								
Class V	**7 Towns**		**45,715**	**23,105**	**22,610**	**44,106**	**22,270**	**21,836**
Bombay States ..	**81 Towns**		**607,463**	**314,672**	**292,791**	**483,358**	**249,784**	**233,574**
1 **Class II**—Kolhapur State—	Kolhapur ..	.. M	**69,860**	**38,033**	**31,827**	**60,331**	**32,856**	**27,525**
Class III	**3 Towns**		**88,160**	**45,947**	**42,213**	**65,337**	**34,021**	**31,316**
2 Cambay State ..	Cambay ..	.. M	31,877	16,296	15,581	22,303	11,444	10,859
3 Sangli State ..	Sangli ..	.. M	29,818	15,901	13,917	23,965	12,707	11,258
4 Miraj State ..	Miraj ..	.. M	26,465	13,750	12,715	19,069	9,870	9,199
Classes IV to VI ..	**77 Towns**		**449,443**	**230,692**	**218,751**	**357,640**	**182,907**	**174,733**
Central India Agency	**56 Towns**		**677,670**	**363,490**	**314,180**	**469,334**	**252,850**	**216,484**
1 **Class I**—Indore State—	Indore ..	.. M	**127,327**	**73,450**	**53,877**	**96,437**	**55,793**	**40,644**
2 **Class II**—Bhopal State—	Bhopal ..	.. M	**61,037**	**32,718**	**28,319**	**21,791**	**11,676**	**10,115**
Class III	**4 Towns**		**115,056**	**62,384**	**52,672**	**70,303**	**38,351**	**31,952**
3 Ratlam State ..	Ratlam* ..	..	37,675	20,175	17,500	23,124	12,547	10,577
4 Indore State ..	Mhow ..	.. C	31,177	17,496	13,681	18,261	9,960	8,301
5 Rewa State ..	Rewa* ..	..	25,206	13,767	11,439	20,014	11,143	8,871
6 Jaora State ..	Jaora* ..	..	20,998	10,946	10,052	8,904	4,701	4,203
Classes IV to VI ..	**50 Towns**		**374,250**	**194,938**	**179,312**	**280,803**	**147,030**	**133,773**
Central Provinces States—								
Classes IV to VI ..	**10 Towns**		**75,065**	**37,361**	**37,704**	**65,025**	**32,161**	**32,864**
Gwalior State ..	**43 Towns**		**395,309**	**214,586**	**180,723**	**285,905**	**155,937**	**129,968**
Class II	**2 Towns**		**132,459**	**72,593**	**59,866**	**95,493**	**52,488**	**43,005**
1 Gird	Lashkar	.. M	78,680	42,538	36,142	58,900	31,796	27,104
2 Ujjain	Ujjain ..	.. M	53,779	30,055	23,724	36,593	20,692	15,901
3 **Class III**—Gird ..	Gwalior ..	.. M	**21,999**	**12,306**	**9,693**	**16,778**	**9,481**	**7,297**
Classes IV to VI ..	**40 Towns**		**240,851**	**129,687**	**111,164**	**173,634**	**93,968**	**79,666**
Hyderabad State ..	**185 Towns**		**1,616,981**	**836,874**	**780,107**	**1,048,901**	**538,739**	**510,162**
Class I ..	**2 Towns**		**466,894**	**247,623**	**219,271**	**252,577**	**132,150**	**120,427**
1 Hyderabad ..	Hyderabad City ..	M	346,093	182,885	163,208	167,349	87,887	79,462
2 Hyderabad ..	Secunderabad (including Bolarum).	C	120,801	64,738	56,063	85,228	44,263	40,965
3 **Class II**—Warangal—	Warangal City ..	M	**62,119**	**33,326**	**28,793**	**46,535**	**24,738**	**21,797**
Class III	**6 Towns**		**178,441**	**93,430**	**85,011**	**108,205**	**56,634**	**51,571**
4 Gulbarga	Gulbarga City ..	M	41,083	21,567	19,516	20,937	11,180	9,757
5 Osmanabad ..	Latur ..	.. M	30,760	16,609	14,151	21,220	11,634	9,586
6 Aurangabad ..	Aurangabad City	M	29,288	15,132	14,156	14,973	7,655	7,318
7 Raichur	Raichur ..	.. M	27,910	14,026	13,884	20,345	10,023	10,322
8 Nander	Nander ..	.. M	26,992	14,332	12,660	16,999	8,995	8,004
9 Aurangabad ..	Jalna ..	.. M	22,408	11,764	10,644	13,731	7,147	6,584
Classes IV to VI ..	**126 Towns**		**909,527**	**462,495**	**447,032**	**641,584**	**335,217**	[illegible]

† Relates to the portion of the Shillong Municipality lying in the Khasi States.

with Population by Religion—*continued.*

Sikhs.			Jains.			Buddhists.			Muslims.			
Persons. 9	Males. 10	Females. 11	Persons. 12	Males. 13	Females. 14	Persons. 15	Males. 16	Females. 17	Persons. 18	Males. 19	Females. 20	
6	6	..	10	5	5	..	..	..	5,243	3,035	2,208	44
9	6	3	291	156	135	..	..	..	5,841	3,065	2,776	45
..	..	..	403	211	192	..	..	..	13,985	7,855	6,130	46
4	..	4	..	..	..	..	..	..	12,354	6,315	6,039	47
7	4	3	21	11	10	..	..	..	12,528	6,516	6,012	48
5	5	..	..	..	..	..	..	..	10,150	5,245	4,905	49
1	1	..	185	93	92	..	..	..	8,703	4,454	4,249	50
1,761	**1,341**	**420**	**17,609**	**9,371**	**8,238**	**104**	**61**	**43**	**895,919**	**473,999**	**421,920**	
61,704	**38,743**	**22,961**	**264,282**	**132,567**	**131,715**	**3,111**	**1,597**	**1,514**	**2,391,816**	**1,257,392**	**1,134,424**	
193	**151**	**42**	**141**	**97**	**44**	**31**	**26**	**5**	**2,577**	**1,373**	**1,204**	
30	**21**	**9**	**139**	**95**	**44**	**5**	**5**	..	**1,720**	**838**	**882**	1
163	**130**	**33**	**2**	**2**	..	**26**	**21**	**5**	**857**	**535**	**322**	
27	**22**	**5**	..	..	..	..	..	..	**9,437**	**4,956**	**4,481**	
500	**435**	**65**	**20,393**	**10,306**	**10,087**	**2**	**1**	**1**	**81,173**	**41,964**	**39,209**	
50	**44**	**6**	**2,639**	**1,436**	**1,203**	..	..	..	**17,975**	**10,196**	**7,779**	1
2	**2**	..	**4,764**	**2,308**	**2,456**	..	..	..	**17,729**	**8,680**	**9,049**	
..	..	..	3,318	1,591	1,727	..	..	..	3,937	1,967	1,970	2
..	..	..	425	230	195	..	..	..	3,229	1,698	1,531	3
2	2	..	273	131	142	..	..	..	6,271	2,993	3,278	4
..	..	..	748	356	392	..	..	..	4,292	2,022	2,270	5
448	**389**	**59**	**12,990**	**6,562**	**6,428**	**2**	**1**	**1**	**45,469**	**23,088**	**22,381**	
14	**4**	**10**	**357**	**273**	**84**	**2**	**1**	**1**	**4,471**	**2,756**	**1,715**	
41	**29**	**12**	**1**	**1**	..	..	..	..	**1,268**	**634**	**634**	
	29	**11**	**19,908**	**10,601**	**9,307**	**4**	**2**	**2**	**99,025**	**51,668**	**47,357**	
..	..	..	**2,314**	**1,338**	**976**	..	..	..	**6,423**	**3,508**	**2,915**	1
..	..	..	**5,208**	**2,750**	**2,458**	**4**	**2**	**2**	**16,239**	**8,419**	**7,820**	
..	..	..	2,869	1,399	1,470	4	2	2	6,564	3,372	3,192	2
..	..	..	1,788	1,047	741	..	..	..	3,633	1,907	1,726	3
..	..	..	551	304	247	..	..	..	6,042	3,140	2,902	4
40	**29**	**11**	**12,386**	**6,513**	**5,873**	..	..	..	**76,363**	**39,741**	**36,622**	
991	**622**	**369**	**18,234**	**9,716**	**8,518**	**13**	**13**	..	**178,828**	**94,420**	**84,408**	
468	**295**	**173**	**4,385**	**2,552**	**1,833**	..	..	..	**25,574**	**14,528**	**11,046**	1
197	**97**	**100**	**834**	**425**	**409**	..	..	..	**37,618**	**20,164**	**17,454**	2
110	**68**	**42**	**4,954**	**2,509**	**2,445**	**3**	**3**	..	**34,592**	**18,319**	**16,273**	
27	19	8	3,545	1,788	1,757	..	..	..	9,716	5,172	4,544	3
49	29	20	172	85	87	3	3	..	9,018	5,027	3,991	4
30	18	12	82	38	44	..	..	..	5,038	2,546	2,492	5
4	2	2	1,155	598	557	..	..	..	10,820	5,574	5,246	6
216	**162**	**54**	**8,061**	**4,230**	**3,831**	**10**	**10**	..	**81,044**	**41,409**	**39,635**	
50	**40**	**10**	**971**	**542**	**429**	**3**	**1**	**2**	**5,977**	**2,995**	**2,982**	
269	**167**	**102**	**16,986**	**9,308**	**7,678**	..	..	..	**91,179**	**48,735**	**42,444**	
136	**90**	**46**	**3,004**	**1,687**	**1,317**	..	..	..	**33,458**	**18,141**	**15,317**	
96	60	36	1,098	607	491	..	..	..	18,312	9,941	8,371	1
40	30	10	1,906	1,080	826	..	..	..	15,146	8,200	6,946	2
..	..	..	**192**	**107**	**85**	..	..	..	**5,024**	**2,716**	**2,308**	3
133	**77**	**56**	**13,790**	**7,514**	**6,276**	..	..	..	**52,697**	**27,878**	**24,819**	
3,441	**2,226**	**1,215**	**6,141**	**3,263**	**2,878**	**38**	**20**	**18**	**514,281**	**269,005**	**245,276**	
1,002	**690**	**312**	**312**	**194**	**118**	**38**	**20**	**18**	**192,343**	**103,095**	**89,248**	
761	493	268	114	66	48	36	19	17	170,191	90,590	79,601	1
241	197	44	198	128	70	2	1	1	22,152	12,505	9,647	2
114	**72**	**42**	..	..	..	..	..	..	**14,460**	**8,003**	**6,457**	3
1,511	**930**	**581**	**1,532**	**842**	**690**	..	..	..	**65,120**	**34,003**	**31,117**	
4	4	..	181	88	93	..	..	..	19,792	10,228	9,564	4
26	26	..	474	267	207	..	..	..	8,993	4,649	4,344	5
157	87	70	328	196	132	..	..	..	13,492	7,023	6,469	6
212	194	18	61	35	26	..	..	..	6,856	3,565	3,291	7
1,104	615	489	110	52	58	..	..	..	8,540	4,546	3,994	8
8	4	4	378	204	174	..	..	..	7,447	3,992	3,455	9
814	**534**	**280**	**4,297**	**2,227**	**2,070**	..	..	..	**242,358**	**123,904**	**118,454**	

Table V.—Towns Arranged Territorially

	District or State.	Town, Municipality, Suburb, Cantonment, etc.		Christians.			Zoroastrians.		
				Persons.	Males.	Females.	Persons.	Males.	Females.
	1	2		21	22	23	24	25	26
	United Provinces—*concld.*								
	Class III—*concld.*								
44	Basti ..	.. Basti	T. A.	54	26	28	..	..	..
45	Banda ..	.. Banda	.. M	79	50	29	..	..	..
46	Saharanpur	.. Deoband	.. M	292	161	131	..	..	..
47	Azamgarh	.. Mau	N.A.	13	7	6	..	..	..
48	Fyzabad	.. Tanda	.. M	6	4	2	..	..	..
49	Hardoi ..	.. Shahabad	.. M	125	81	44	..	..	..
50	Farrukhabad	.. Kanauj	.. M	190	103	87	..	..	..
	Classes IV to VI ..	**391 Towns**	—	**30,706**	**18,048**	**12,658**	**170**	**93**	**77**
	States and Agencies ..	**877 Towns**	—	**323,547**	**165,982**	**157,565**	**10,327**	**4,671**	**5,656**
	Assam States ..	**2 Towns** ..	...	**4,921**	**2,376**	**2,545**	**2**	**1**	**1**
1	**Class II**—Manipur State— Imphal* ..		..	**127**	**73**	**54**	..	..	..
	Classes IV to VI ..	**1 Town** ..	—	**4,794**	**2,303**	**2,491**	**2**	**1**	**1**
	Baluchistan States—								
	Classes IV to VI	**5 Towns** ..	..	**14**	**11**	**3**	..	..	..
	Baroda State ..	**59 Towns**	..	**2,699**	**1,616**	**1,083**	**5,789**	**2,328**	**3,461**
1	**Class I**	Baroda City	.. M	**748**	**425**	**323**	**447**	**216**	**231**
	Class III	**4 Towns** ..	—	**59**	**28**	**31**	**3,800**	**1,432**	**2,368**
2	Kadi	Patan	.. M	6	2	4	2	1	1
3	Navsari	Navsari	.. M	45	22	23	3,783	1,423	2,360
4	Kadi	Sidhpur	.. M	8	4	4	5	4	1
5	Amreli	Amreli	.. M	..	..	..	10	4	6
	Classes IV to VI ..	**45 Towns** ..	..	1,892	1,163	729	1,542	680	862
	Bengal States—								
	Classes IV to VI ..	**5 Towns** ..	..	**59**	**34**	**25**	..	..	..
	Bihar and Orissa States—								
	Class V ..	**7 Towns** ..	..	**254**	**146**	**108**	..	..	..
	Bombay States ..	**81 Towns** ..	..	**4,602**	**2,298**	**2,304**	**387**	**204**	**183**
1	**Class II**—Kolhapur State—Kolhapur		.. M	**738**	**328**	**410**	**4**	**3**	**1**
	Class III ..	**3 Towns**	..	**1,253**	**683**	**570**	**103**	**58**	**45**
2	Cambay State ..	Cambay	.. M	68	42	26	68	36	32
3	Sangli State ..	Sangli	.. M	416	226	190	1	1	..
4	Miraj State ..	Miraj	.. M	769	415	354	34	21	13
	Classes IV to VI ..	**77 Towns** ..	..	**2,611**	**1,287**	**1,324**	**280**	**143**	**137**
	Central India Agency	**56 Towns** ..	..	**6,823**	**4,009**	**2,814**	**921**	**470**	**451**
1	**Class I**—Indore State— Indore ..		.. M	**302**	**187**	**115**	**100**	**55**	**45**
2	**Class II**—Bhopal State— Bhopal ..		.. M	**387**	**201**	**186**	**37**	**19**	**18**
	Class III	**4 Towns** ..	..	**4,347**	**2,734**	**1,613**	**517**	**253**	**264**
3	Ratlam State ..	Ratlam*	..	1,009	498	511	96	58	38
4	Indore State ..	Mhow ..	.. C	3,249	2,195	1,054	412	190	222
5	Rewa State ..	Rewa* ..	..	38	20	18	4	2	2
6	Jaora State ..	Jaora* ..	..	51	21	30	5	3	2
	Classes IV to VI ..	**50 Towns**	..	1,787	887	900	267	143	124
	Central Provinces States—								
	Classes IV to VI ..	**10 Towns**	..	**1,399**	**649**	**750**	**15**	**10**	**5**
	Gwalior State ..	**43 Towns**	..	**747**	**349**	**398**	**223**	**90**	**133**
	Class II	**2 Towns**	..	**275**	**152**	**123**	**93**	**35**	**58**
1	Gird	Lashkar	.. M	190	102	88	84	32	52
2	Ujjain	Ujjain ..	.. M	85	50	35	9	3	6
3	**Class III**—Gird ..	Gwalior..	.. M	**5**	**2**	**3**	..	..	..
	Classes IV to VI ..	**40 Towns**	..	**467**	**195**	**272**	**130**	**55**	**75**
	Hyderabad State ..	**135 Towns**	..	**26,261**	**14,407**	**11,854**	**1,520**	**793**	**727**
	Class I ..	**2 Towns**	.. M	**16,123**	**9,217**	**6,906**	**1,092**	**548**	**544**
1	Hyderabad ..	Hyderabad City	.. M	4,560	2,284	2,276	415	210	205
2	Hyderabad ..	Secunderabad (including Bolarum).	C	11,563	6,933	4,630	677	338	339
3	**Class II**—Warangal ..	Warangal City	.. M	**748**	**357**	**391**	**7**	**7**	..
	Class III	**6 Towns**		**1,136**	**556**	**580**	**190**	**104**	**86**
4	Gulbarga	Gulbarga City	.. M	145	50	95	16	9	7
5	Osmanabad ..	Latur ..	.. M	..	..		2	2	..
6	Aurangabad ..	Aurangabad City	M	12	7	5	159	88	71
7	Raichur	Raichur..	.. M	130	61	69		..	..
8	Nander	Nander ..	.. M	194	108	86	3	1	2
9	Aurangabad ..	Jalna ..	.. M	655	330	325	10	4	6
	Classes IV to VI ..	**126 Towns**	..	8,254	4,277	3,977	231	134	97

with Population by Religion—*continued.*

Jews. Persons. 27	Jews. Males. 28	Jews. Females. 29	Tribals. Persons. 30	Tribals. Males. 31	Tribals. Females. 32	Others. Persons. 33	Others. Males. 34	Others. Females. 35	
..	..	..	..	..	..	..	..	..	44
..	..	..	..	..	..	..	..	..	45
..	..	..	..	..	..	..	..	..	46
..	..	..	..	..	..	..	..	..	47
..	..	..	..	..	..	..	..	..	48
..	..	..	..	..	..	..	..	..	49
..	..	..	..	..	..	..	..	..	50
13	8	5	..	..	..	..	..	..	
1,661	809	852	31,858	16,489	15,369	1,547	889	658	
..	..	..	7,739	3,597	4,142	7	5	2	
..	..	..	2,171	1,065	1,106	..	..	..	1
..	..	..	5,568	2,532	3,036	7	5	2	
2	2	..	..	..	..	..	..	..	
47	20	27	957	491	466	..	..	..	
28	11	17	..	..	..	..	..	..	1
1	..	1	28	14	14	..	..	..	
..	..	..	..	..	..	..	..	..	2
1	..	1	28	14	14	..	..	..	3
..	..	..	..	..	..	..	..	..	4
..	..	..	..	..	..	..	..	..	5
18	9	9	929	477	452	..	..	..	
..	..	..	5	1	4	..	..	..	
..	..	..	45	25	20	..	..	..	
77	35	42	62	51	11	..	..	..	
..	..	..	..	..	..	..	..	..	1
1	1	..	15	13	2	..	..	..	
1	1	..	..	..	..	..	..	..	2
..	..	..	15	13	2	..	..	..	3
..	..	..	..	..	..	..	..	..	4
76	34	42	47	38	9	..	..	..	
38	18	20	2,488	1,372	1,116	..	..	..	
17	9	8	44	31	13	..	..	..	1
2	1	1	171	135	36	..	..	..	2
7	3	4	223	144	79	..	..	..	
..	..	..	158	93	65	..	..	..	3
7	3	4	6	4	2	..	..	..	4
..	..	..	..	..	..	..	..	..	5
..	..	..	59	47	12	..	..	..	6
12	5	7	2,050	1,062	988	..	..	..	
..	..	..	1,625	963	662	..	..	..	
..	..	..	..	..	..	..	..	..	
..	..	..	..	..	..	..	..	..	
..	..	..	..	..	..	..	..	..	
..	..	..	..	..	..	..	..	..	1
..	..	..	..	..	..	..	..	..	2
..	..	..	..	..	..	..	..	..	3
27	11	16	16,371	8,410	7,961	..	..	..	
27	11	16	8,380	1,698	1,682	..	..	..	
27	11	16	2,640	1,325	1,315	..	..	..	
..	..	..	740	373	367	..	..	..	1
						..	..	..	2
..	..	..	55	149	106	..	..	..	3
..	..	..	747	361	386	..	..	..	
..	..	..	8	8	..	..	..	..	
..	..	..	45	31	14	..	..	..	4
..	..	..	167	76	91	..	..	..	5
..	..	..	306	148	158	..	..	..	6
..	..	..	42	15	27	..	..	..	7
..	..	..	179	83	96	..	..	..	8
..	..	..	11,989	6,202	5,787	..	..	..	9

Table V.—Towns arranged Territorially

	District or State.	Town, Municipality, Suburb, Cantonment, etc.		Population. Persons.	Population. Males.	Population. Females.	Hindus. Persons.	Hindus. Males.	Hindus. Females.
	1	2		3	4	5	6	7	8
	Jammu and Kashmir State.	**39 Towns**		**342,314**	**192,199**	**150,115**	**99,148**	**57,013**	**42,135**
1	**Class I**	Srinagar	M	**173,573**	**94,793**	**78,780**	**33,670**	**18,447**	**15,223**
2	**Class III**	Jammu	M	**38,613**	**23,361**	**15,252**	**24,102**	**14,354**	**9,748**
	Classes IV to VI	**37 Towns**		**130,128**	**74,045**	**56,083**	**41,376**	**24,212**	**17,164**
	Madras States Agency	**69 Towns**		**837,509**	**424,851**	**412,658**	**536,773**	**270,948**	**265,825**
1	**Class II—Travancore**	Trivandrum	M	**96,016**	**49,392**	**46,624**	**75,354**	**38,618**	**36,736**
	Class III	**9 Towns**		**320,676**	**165,280**	**155,396**	**174,921**	**90,265**	**84,656**
2	Cochin	Trichur	M	45,658	22,840	22,818	22,352	11,400	10,952
3	Travancore	Alleppey	M	43,838	23,677	20,161	18,986	10,254	8,732
4	Travancore	Nagercoil	M	42,945	20,873	22,072	32,211	15,873	16,338
5	Cochin	Mattancheri	M	39,645	20,925	18,720	16,110	8,607	7,503
6	Cochin	Ernakulam	M	36,638	19,363	17,275	18,170	9,853	8,317
7	Travancore	Quilon	M	33,739	17,381	16,358	18,017	9,291	8,726
8	Madras States	Pudukkottai	M	28,776	14,326	14,450	25,867	12,841	13,026
9	Travancore	Kottayam	M	25,236	13,280	11,956	11,626	6,128	5,498
10	Travancore	Changanachery	M	24,201	12,615	11,586	11,582	6,018	5,564
	Classes IV to VI	**59 Towns**		**420,817**	**210,179**	**210,638**	**286,498**	**142,065**	**144,433**
	Mysore State	**108 Towns**		**1,045,042**	**546,822**	**498,220**	**800,606**	**417,321**	**383,285**
	Class I	**3 Towns**		**413,612**	**217,861**	**195,751**	**303,322**	**159,916**	**143,406**
1	Bangalore	Bangalore city	M	172,357	91,680	80,677	144,529	76,645	67,884
2	Bangalore	Bangalore Civil and Military Station.	M	134, 113	69,409	64,704	74,004	38,537	35,467
3	Mysore	Mysore City	M	107,142	56,772	50,370	84,789	44,734	40,055
4	**Class II—Kolar**	Kolar Gold Fields	M	**85,103**	**45,051**	**40,052**	**62,313**	**32,695**	**29,818**
	Class III	**2 Towns**		**43,816**	**23,125**	**20,691**	**33,003**	**17,348**	**15,655**
5	Chitaldrug	Devangere	M	23,155	12,069	11,086	18,119	9,397	8,722
6	Shimoga	Shimoga	M	20,661	11,056	9,605	14,884	7,951	6,933
	Classes IV to VI—	**102 Towns**		**502,511**	**260,785**	**241,726**	**401,968**	**207,362**	**194,606**
	Punjab States.								
	Classes IV to VI—	**4 Towns**		**14,534**	**7,907**	**6,627**	**7,718**	**4,227**	**3,491**
	Punjab States Agency	**43 Towns**		**439,451**	**251,470**	**187,981**	**191,680**	**110,687**	**80,993**
1	**Class II—Patiala**	Patiala	M	**55,129**	**33,139**	**21,990**	**22,764**	**13,416**	**9,348**
	Class III	**5 Towns**		**108,225**	**60,656**	**47,569**	**41,659**	**23,514**	**18,145**
2	Patiala	Bhatinda*		22,771	13,575	9,196	11,026	6,553	4,473
3	Maler Kotla	Maler Kotla	M	22,396	12,230	10,166	4,601	2,637	1,964
4	Patiala	Narnaul*		21,905	11,270	10,635	12,605	6,662	5,943
5	Bahawalpur	Bahawalpur*		20,943	11,809	9,134	7,166	4,030	3,136
6	Kapurthala	Kapurthala	M	20,210	11,772	8,438	6,261	3,632	2,629
	Classes IV to VI—	**37 Towns**		**276,097**	**157,675**	**118,422**	**127,257**	**73,757**	**53,500**
	Rajputana Agency	**145 Towns**		**1,556,305**	**813,605**	**742,700**	**1,074,055**	**566,726**	**507,329**
1	**Class I—Jaipur**	Jaipur	M	**144,179**	**77,933**	**66,246**	**92,364**	**50,076**	**42,288**
	Class II	**2 Towns**		**180,663**	**97,997**	**82,666**	**127,896**	**70,347**	**57,549**
2	Marwar	Jodhpur	M	94,736	52,165	42,571	66,199	36,899	29,300
3	Bikaner	Bikaner	M	85,927	45,832	40,095	61,697	33,448	28,249
	Class III	**7 Towns**		**244,044**	**129,025**	**115,019**	**148,889**	**79,487**	**69,402**
4	Alwar	Alwar	M	47,900	25,584	22,316	32,568	17,392	15,176
5	Mewar	Udaipur	M	44,035	23,775	20,260	26,973	14,614	12,359
6	Kotah	Kotah	M	37,876	20,259	17,617	25,614	13,995	11,619
7	Tonk	Tonk*		35,798	18,201	17,597	15,657	7,974	7,683
8	Bharatpur	Bharatpur	M	30,173	16,736	13,437	20,216	11,214	9,002
9	Jaipur	Sikar*		26,297	13,363	12,934	14,217	7,384	6,833
10	Bikaner	Churu	M	21,965	11,107	10,858	13,644	6,914	6,730
	Classes IV to VI	**135 Towns**		**987,419**	**508,650**	**478,769**	**704,906**	**366,816**	**338,090**
	United Provinces States	**9 Towns**		**126,138**	**67,432**	**58,706**	**44,732**	**24,222**	**20,510**
1	**Class II—Rampur**	Rampur	M	**74,216**	**39,603**	**34,613**	**14,903**	**8,048**	**6,855**
	Classes IV to VI	**8 Towns**		**51,922**	**27,829**	**24,093**	**29,829**	**16,174**	**13,655**

with Population by Religion—*continued.*

Sikhs. Persons. 9	Sikhs. Males. 10	Sikhs. Females. 11	Jains. Persons. 12	Jains. Males. 13	Jains. Females. 14	Buddhists. Persons. 15	Buddhists. Males. 16	Buddhists. Females. 17	Muslims. Persons. 18	Muslims. Males. 19	Muslims. Females. 20	
4,664	**2,851**	**1,813**	**594**	**317**	**277**	**1,707**	**850**	**857**	**234,915**	**130,497**	**104,418**	
870	**634**	**236**	**3**	**3**	—	**5**	**5**	—	**138,764**	**75,583**	**63,181**	1
1,296	**757**	**539**	**563**	**297**	**266**	**9**	**4**	**5**	**12,036**	**7,621**	**4,415**	2
2,498	**1,460**	**1,038**	**28**	**17**	**11**	**1,693**	**841**	**852**	**84,115**	**47,293**	**36,822**	
5	**2**	**3**	**281**	**159**	**122**	**37**	**24**	**13**	**94,521**	**48,908**	**45,613**	
5	**2**	**3**	—	—	—	—	—	—	**6,910**	**3,699**	**3,211**	1
—	—	—	**249**	**138**	**111**	**37**	**24**	**13**	**42,261**	**22,251**	**20,010**	
..	..	..	..	..	..	14	10	4	1,783	939	844	2
..	..	..	40	21	19	2	2	..	13,224	7,104	6,120	3
..	..	..	..	..	..	..	..	..	3,855	1,777	2,078	4
..	..	..	205	114	91	..	..	..	9,054	4,827	4,227	5
..	..	..	4	3	1	20	11	9	2,406	1,381	1,025	6
..	..	..	..	..	..	1	1	..	6,299	3,278	3,021	7
..	..	..	..	..	..	..	..	..	2,033	1,030	1,003	8
..	..	..	..	..	..	..	..	..	1,222	702	520	9
..	..	..	..	..	..	..	—	..	2,385	1,213	1,172	10
	—	—	**32**	**21**	**11**	..	—	..	**45,350**	**22,958**	**22,392**	
49	**40**	**9**	**7,461**	**4,443**	**3,018**	**1,237**	**639**	**598**	**170,349**	**91,744**	**78,605**	
49	**40**	**9**	**2,516**	**1,580**	**936**	**314**	**168**	**146**	**66,228**	**36,034**	**30,194**	
..	..	..	1,153	724	429	35	18	17	19,831	10,975	8,856	1
32	29	3	814	484	330	260	143	117	28,625	15,398	13,227	2
17	11	6	549	372	177	19	7	12	17,772	9,661	8,111	[illegible]
..	—	—	**447**	**262**	**185**	**920**	**469**	**451**	**6,771**	**4,045**	**2,726**	4
..	..	..	**404**	**266**	**138**	..	—	..	**8,777**	**4,649**	**4,128**	
..	..	..	271	174	97	..	..	..	4,182	2,190	1,992	5
..	..	..	133	92	41	..	..	.	4,595	2,459	2,136	6
..	..	..	**4,094**	**2,335**	**1,759**	**3**	**2**	**1**	**88,573**	**47,016**	**41,557**	
475	**278**	**197**	**207**	**107**	**100**	..	..	..	**6,125**	**3,289**	**2,836**	
49,434	**30,844**	**18,590**	**3,636**	**1,956**	**1,680**	**2**	**2**	..	**192,150**	**106,498**	**85,652**	
10,462	**7,087**	**3,375**	**183**	**92**	**91**	..	..	..	**21,591**	**12,465**	**9,126**	1
5,797	**3,793**	**2,004**	**1,561**	**842**	**719**	..	..	..	**58,708**	**32,193**	**26,515**	
3,598	2,255	1,343	60	35	25	..	..	..	7,743	4,523	3,220	2
202	137	65	1,236	670	566	..	..	..	16,326	8,765	7,561	3
52	39	13	238	122	116	..	..	..	9,002	4,440	4,562	4
29	26	3	..	..	..	..	..	..	13,735	7,745	5,990	5
1,916	1,336	580	27	15	12	..	..	..	11,902	6,720	5,182	6
33,175	**19,964**	**13,211**	**1,892**	**1,022**	**870**	**2**	**2**	..	**111,851**	**61,840**	**50,011**	
1,431	**957**	**474**	**92,565**	**44,176**	**48,389**	**1**	**1**	..	**383,045**	**198,701**	**184,344**	
147	**94**	**53**	**7,242**	**3,828**	**3,414**	..	..	..	**44,072**	**23,780**	**20,292**	1
273	**188**	**85**	**11,730**	**5,524**	**6,206**	..	..	..	**40,097**	**21,543**	**18,554**	
12	5	7	4,773	2,465	2,308	..	..	..	23,239	12,495	10,744	2
261	183	78	6,957	3,059	3,898	..	..	..	16,858	9,048	7,810	3
154	**92**	**62**	**10,649**	**5,492**	**5,157**	..	..	..	**82,722**	**42,899**	**39,823**	
36	20	16	961	500	461	..	..	..	14,278	7,637	6,641	4
8	5	3	5,076	2,706	2,370	..	..	..	10,988	5,772	5,216	5
63	36	27	1,034	537	497	..	..	..	11,018	5,599	5,419	6
4	2	2	762	406	356	..	..	..	19,329	9,789	9,540	7
40	27	13	435	233	202	..	..	..	9,117	5,055	4,062	8
..	..	..	748	349	399	..	..	..	11,321	5,624	5,697	9
3	2	1	1,633	761	872	..	..	..	6,671	3,423	3,248	10
857	**583**	**274**	**62,944**	**29,332**	**33,612**	**1**	**1**	..	**216,154**	**110,479**	**105,675**	
40	**16**	**24**	**124**	**66**	**58**	..	..	..	**81,107**	**43,058**	**38,049**	
—	..	—	**106**	**56**	**50**	..	..	..	**59,190**	**31,495**	**27,695**	1
40	**16**	**24**	**18**	**10**	**8**	..	.	..	**21.917**	**11,563**	**10,354**	

Table V.—Towns arranged Territorially

	District or State.	Town, Municipality, Suburb, Cantonment, etc.		Christians.			Zoroastrians.		
	1	2		Persons. 21	Males. 22	Females. 23	Persons. 24	Males. 25	Females. 26
	Jammu and Kashmir State.	39 Towns	—	1,277	668	609	4	3	1
1	Class I — —	Srinagar	— M	257	118	139	4	3	1
2	Class III — —	Jammu —	— M	602	328	274	—	—	—
	Classes IV to VI —	37 Towns	—	418	222	196	—	—	..
	Madras States Agency	69 Towns	—	204,517	104,124	100,393	15	11	4
1	Class II—Travancore —	Trivandrum	— M	13,746	7,072	6,674	—	—	—
	Class III — —	9 Towns —	—	102,129	52,078	50,051	15	11	4
2	Cochin	Trichur	.. M	21,509	10,491	11,018	..	..	..
3	Travancore ..	Alleppey	.. M	11,574	6,286	5,288	12	10	2
4	Travancore ..	Nagercoil	.. M	6,879	3,223	3,656	..	..	..
5	Cochin	Mattancheri	.. M	13,856	7,199	6,657	..	..	..
6	Cochin	Ernakulam	.. M	15,391	7,779	7,612	3	1	2
7	Travancore ..	Quilon ..	.. M	9,422	4,811	4,611	..	..	..
8	Madras States ..	Pudukkottai	.. M	876	455	421	..	..	..
9	Travancore ..	Kottayam	.. M	12,388	6,450	5,938	..	..	..
10	Travancore ..	Changanachery	.. M	10,234	5,384	4,850	..	..	..
	Classes IV to VI ..	59 Towns	—	88,642	44,974	43,668	—	—	..
	Mysore State ..	108 Towns	—	64,219	32,064	32,155	323	163	160
	Class I	3 Towns	..	40,723	19,899	20,824	308	154	154
1	Bangalore	Bangalore city	.. M	6,754	3,291	3,463	28	11	17
2	Bangalore	Bangalore Civil and Military Station.	M	30,022	14,652	15,370	244	120	124
3	Mysore	Mysore City	.. M	3,947	1,956	1,991	36	23	13
4	Class II—Kolar —	Kolar Gold Fields.	M	14,651	7,579	7,072	—	—	—
	Class III	2 Towns	..	1,158	611	547	8	5	3
5	Chitaldrug	Devangere	.. M	131	67	64	8	5	3
6	Shimoga	Shimoga	.. M	1,027	544	483	..	—	—
	Classes IV to VI— —	102 Towns	.. M	7,687	3,975	3,712	7	4	3
	Punjab States.								
	Classes IV to VI— ..	4 Towns	..	9	6	3	..	—	—
	Punjab States Agency	43 Towns	..	1,100	639	461	17	14	3
1	Class II—Patiala —	Patiala	— M	127	78	49	2	1	1
	Class III — —	5 Towns	—	315	193	122	1	1	—
2	Patiala — —	Bhatinda*	.. ..	229	135	94	—	—	—
3	Maler Kotla ..	Maler Kotla	.. M	31	21	10	..	—	—
4	Patiala	Narnaul	.. M	8	7	1	..	..	—
5	Bahawalpur ..	Bahawalpur*	.. ..	12	7	5	1	1	—
6	Kapurthala ..	Kapurthala	.. M	35	23	12	..	..	—
	Classes IV to VI— ..	37 Towns	—	658	368	290	14	12	2
	Rajputana Agency .	145 Towns	—	3,307	1,794	1,513	289	156	133
1	Class I—Jaipur —	Jaipur	— M	329	143	186	17	8	9
	Class II — ..	2 Towns	..	580	337	243	58	29	29
2	Marwar	Jodhpur	.. M	441	251	190	43	21	22
3	Bikaner	Bikaner	.. M	139	86	53	15	8	7
	Class III — ..	7 Towns	—	681	388	293	5	3	2
4	Alwar . ..	Alwar ..	.. M	57	35	22	—	—	—
5	Mewar	Udaipur*	.. ..	94	53	41	—	—	—
6	Kotah	Kotah ..	.. M	108	58	50	..	—	—
7	Tonk	Tonk* ..	.. ..	37	25	12	..	—	—
8	Bharatpur	Bharatpur	.. M	363	206	157	2	1	1
9	Jaipur	Sikar* ..	.. ..	8	4	4	3	2	1
10	Bikaner	Churu ..	.. M	14	7	7	..	..	—
	Classes IV to VI ..	135 Towns	..	1,717	926	791	209	116	93
	United Provinces States	9 Towns	—	135	70	65	—	—	—
1	Class II—Rampur	Rampur	— M	17	4	13	—	—	—
	Classes IV to VI ..	8 Towns	..	118	66	52	—	—	—

with Population by Religion—*continued.*

Jews.			Tribals.			Others.			
Persons. 27	Males. 28	Females. 29	Persons. 30	Males. 31	Females. 32	Persons. 33	Males. 34	Females. 35	
..	..	..	5	..	5	..	..	..	
..	..	..	..	..	..	..	..	..	1
..	..	..	5	..	5	..	..	..	2
..	..	..	..	..	..	..	..	..	
1,355	672	683	5	3	2	..	..	..	
..	..	..	1	1	..	..	..	..	1
1,064	513	551	..	..	..	..	..	..	
..	..	..	..	..	..	..	..	..	2
..	..	..	..	..	..	..	..	..	3
..	..	..	..	..	..	..	..	..	4
420	178	242	..	..	..	..	..	..	5
644	335	309	..	..	..	..	..	..	6
..	..	..	..	..	..	..	..	..	7
..	..	..	..	..	..	..	..	..	8
..	..	..	..	..	..	..	..	..	9
..	..	..	..	..	..	..	..	..	10
291	159	132	4	2	2	..	..	..	
39	13	26	653	344	309	106	51	55	
39	13	26	7	6	1	106	51	55	
12	5	7	..	..	..	15	11	4	1
21	6	15	.	..	..	91	40	51	2
6	2	4	7	6	1	..	..	..	3
..	..	..	1	1	..	..	..	..	4
..	..	..	466	246	220	..	..	..	
..	..	..	444	236	208	..	..	..	5
..	..	..	22	10	12	..	..	..	6
..	..	..	179	91	88	..	..	..	
..	..	..	..	..	.	..	..	..	
1	..	1	..	..	..	1,431	830	601	
..	..	..	..	..	..	..	..	..	1
..	..	..	..	..	..	184	120	64	
..	..	..	..	..	..	115	74	41	2
..	..	..	..	..	..	..	..	..	3
..	..	..	..	..	..	..	..	..	4
..	..	..	..	..	..	..	..	..	5
..	..	..	..	..	..	69	46	23	6
1	..	1	..	..	..	1,247	710	537	
38	18	20	1,574	1,076	498	..	..	..	
..	..	..	8	4		..	..	..	1
..	..	..	29	29	..	..	..	..	
..	..	..	29	29	..	..	..	..	2
..	..	..	..	..	..	..	..	..	3
..	..	..	944	664	280	..	..	..	
..	..	..	..	..	..	..	..	..	4
..	..	..	896	625	271	..	..	..	5
..	..	..	39	34	5	..	..	..	6
..	..	..	9	5	4	..	..	..	7
..	..	..	..	..	..	..	..	..	8
..	..	..	..	..	..	..	..	..	9
..	..	..	..	..	..	..	..	..	10
38	18	20	593	379	214	..	..	..	
..	..	..	..	..	..	..	..	..	
..	..	..	..	..	..	..	..	..	1
..	..	..	..	..	..	..	..	..	

Table V.—Towns arranged Territorially

	District or State.	Town, Municipality, Suburb, Cantonment, etc.		Population.			Hindus.		
				Persons.	Males.	Females.	Persons.	Males.	Females.
	1	2		3	4	5	6	7	8
	Western India States Agency.	**66 Towns** ..	..	**883,776**	**442,964**	**440,812**	**563,637**	**288,161**	**275,476**
	Class II ..	.. **2 Towns** ..	..	**130,650**	**67,718**	**62,932**	**89,101**	**46,672**	**42,429**
1	Bhavnagar	.. Bhavnagar ..	M	75,594	39,894	35,700	56,000	29,646	26,354
2	Nawanagar	.. Jamnagar ..	M	55,056	27,824	27,232	33,101	17,026	16,075
	Class III ..	.. **10 Towns** ..		**286,268**	**144,001**	**142,267**	**172,794**	**89,257**	**83,537**
3	Rajkot ..	.. Rajkot ..	M	47,485	24,249	23,236	36,052	18,602	17,450
4	Junagadh ..	.. Junagadh* ..		39,890	21,212	18,678	22,088	11,871	10,217
5	Porbandar ..	.. Porbandar*	..	33,383	17,088	16,295	25,756	13,441	12,315
6	Gondal ..	.. Dhoraji ..	M	29,302	13,813	15,489	12,746	6,583	6,163
7	Cutch ..	.. Mandvi ..	M	25,342	12,103	13,239	12,827	6,202	6,625
8	Gondal ..	.. Gondal ..	M	24,573	12,603	11,970	17,334	9,084	8,250
9	W. K. Agency	.. Jetpur* ..		22,973	11,102	11,871	11,598	5,975	5,623
10	Cutch ..	.. Bhuj ..	M	21,859	10,805	11,054	12,486	6,285	6,201
11	Junagadh ..	.. Veraval* ..		21,114	10,517	10,597	10,578	5,336	5,242
12	Palanpur ..	.. Palanpur* ..		20,347	10,509	9,838	11,329	5,878	5,451
	Classes IV to VI ..	**54 Towns**	..	**466,858**	**231,245**	**235,613**	**301,742**	**152,232**	**149,510**

	District or State.	Town, Municipality, Suburb, Cantonment, etc.		Christians.			Zoroastrians.		
				Persons.	Males.	Females.	Persons	Males.	Females.
	1	2		21	22	23	24	25	26
	Western India States Agency.	**66 Tonws**	..	**1,204**	**722**	**482**	**822**	**428**	**394**
	Class II ..	.. **2 Towns**	..	**338**	**203**	**135**	**393**	**198**	**195**
1	Bhavnagar ..	.. Bhavnagar	.. M	254	145	109	282	149	133
2	Nawanagar	.. Jamnagar	.. M	84	58	26	111	49	62
	Class III ..	.. **10 Towns**	..	**332**	**225**	**107**	**139**	**73**	**66**
3	Rajkot ..	.. Rajkot	.. M	13	3	10	5	3	2
4	Junagadh ..	.. Junagadh*	..	96	60	36	11	6	5
5	Porbandar ..	.. Porbandar*	..	128	94	34	58	28	30
6	Gondal ..	.. Dhoraji	.. M	..	..	..	1	1	..
7	Cutch ..	.. Mandvi	.. M	16	12	4	13	7	6
8	Gondal ..	.. Gondal	.. M	20	13	7	6	3	3
9	W. K. Agency	.. Jetpur*	..	4	3	1	..	..	..
10	Cutch ..	.. Bhuj	.. M	34	27	7	31	17	14
11	Junagadh ..	.. Veraval*	..	8	5	3	5	3	2
12	Palanpur ..	.. Palanpur*	..	13	8	5	9	5	4
	Classes IV to VI	.. **54 Towns**	..	**534**	**294**	**240**	**290**	**157**	**133**

The abbreviations used in the table are as follows :—Corporation (Corpn.) ; Municipality (M.) ; Cantonment (C.) ; Notified Area (N. A.) ; Town Area (T. A.) and Panchayat Board (P. B.).

An asterisk denotes a town treated as such for Census purposes though neither a Municipality nor a Cantonment.

with Population by Religion—*concluded.*

Sikhs.			Jains.			Buddhists.			Muslims.			
Persons. 9	Males. 10	Females. 11	Persons. 12	Males. 13	Females. 14	Persons. 15	Males. 16	Females. 17	Persons. 18	Males. 19	Females. 20	
40	**30**	**10**	**76,282**	**37,236**	**39,046**	**34**	**17**	**17**	**241,388**	**116,191**	**125,197**	
..	..	..	**11,699**	**5,938**	**5,761**	..	..	..	**29,117**	**14,705**	**14,412**	
..	..	..	6,744	3,498	3,246	..	..	..	12,312	6,454	5,858	1
..	..	..	4,955	2,440	2,515	..	..	..	16,805	8,251	8,554	2
33	**25**	**8**	**19,539**	**9,436**	**10,103**	..	..	..	**93,336**	**44,938**	**48,398**	
..	..	..	4,582	2,220	2,362	..	..	..	6,751	3,380	3,371	3
7	7	..	1,408	739	669	..	..	..	16,280	8,529	7,751	4
3	2	1	1,108	520	588	..	..	..	6,329	3,003	3,326	5
..	..	..	1,447	706	741	..	..	..	15,108	6,523	8,585	6
3	2	1	2,292	1,073	1,219	..	..	..	10,191	4,807	5,384	7
..	..	..	2,096	1,018	1,078	..	..	..	5,117	2,485	2,632	8
..	..	..	1,792	899	893	..	..	..	9,578	4,224	5,354	9
20	14	6	1,196	551	645	..	..	..	8,092	3,911	4,181	10
..	..	..	1,105	488	617	..	..	..	9,418	4,685	4,733	11
..	..	..	2,513	1,222	1,291	..	..	..	6,472	3,391	3,081	12
7	**5**	**2**	**45,044**	**21,862**	**23,182**	**34**	**17**	**17**	**118,935**	**56,548**	**62,387**	

Jews.			Tribals.			Others.			
Persons. 27	Males. 28	Females. 29	Persons. 30	Males. 31	Females. 32	Persons. 33	Males. 34	Females. 35	
37	**20**	**17**	**329**	**156**	**173**	3	3	..	
..	..	..	..	..	..	2	2	..	
..	..	..	..	..	..	2	2	..	1
..	..	..	..	..	..	..	..	..	2
1	..	1	**94**	**47**	**47**	..	..	..	
..	..	..	82	41	41	..	..	..	3
..	..	..	..	..	..	..	..	..	4
1	..	1	..	..	..	..	..	..	5
..	..	..	..	..	..	..	..	..	6
..	..	..	..	..	..	..	..	..	7
..	..	..	..	..	..	..	..	..	8
..	..	..	1	1	..	..	..	..	9
..	..	..	..	..	..	..	..	..	10
..	..	..	..	..	..	..	..	..	11
..	..	..	11	5	6	..	..	..	12
36	20	16	**235**	**109**	**126**	1	1	..	

TABLE VI.

Birthplace.

The population dealt with in this table falls short of that shown in Table I by the estimated population referred to in items 3—5 of paragraph 4 on the fly-leaf to that table.

2. The discrepancy between the respective populations of the Assam British Districts and Assam States given here and in Table I, is due to the inclusion of the Khasi States in the British District of the Khasi and Jaintia Hills in Parts I and III of this table. The statistics below the entry Assam State, *i.e.*, columns 50—52 in Part I, and column 22 in Part III, only relate therefore to Manipur State, though the figures in both these parts against Serial Nos. 17 and 16 respectively, column 1 appertain to both Manipur and the Khasi States in all columns except 11—13 and 50—52.

3. The total population of cities in this table includes the population of adjoining Cantonments, Civil Lines, Notified Areas, etc., and in consequence the figures do not tally numerically with the population figures shown against the corresponding cities in Class I of Table IV from which such subsidiary figures have been excluded. The same remarks apply to all subsequent tables of this volume in which city details appear.

4. The present table corresponds to Table XI of the 1921 Census, Parts I, II and III of which have been amalgamated on this occasion into one form, which constitutes Part I of this table, Part II contains the corresponding table for cities, the population of which is of course included in the figures given in Part I, and Part III gives figures of Internal Migration as in Part IV of the 1921 table. Of Part III, column 1 gives the provinces and states for which the balance of migration is to be considered ; column 2 the number of immigrants born elsewhere in India and found on enumeration in the unit under consideration ; column 3 the number of persons born in the province or state under consideration (column 1) but enumerated elsewhere in India at the census ; column 4 gives the net balance of migration with reference to the unit under consideration ; the remaining columns show the details contributing to the totals in columns 2 and 3, and the + or − signs prefixed to the figures indicate with reference to the province under consideration (column 1) its loss or gain with reference to the province named at the top of the column in which they appear. Thus in column 10, under Bihar and Orissa, appears against Assam, in column 1, the figure +441,618, indicating that Assam, the province under consideration, has gained that number of immigrants from Bihar and Orissa ; conversely, in col. 7 under Assam, and against Bihar and Orissa in col. 1, appears the figure − 441,618, indicating that Bihar and Orissa has lost that number of emigrants to Assam, since this population was born in that province but enumerated in Assam. These figures represent the net balance only. A reference to Part I will show that 443,412 persons born in Bihar and Orissa were enumerated in Assam and that 1,794 persons born in Assam were enumerated in Bihar and Orissa ; 441,618 is the difference and represents the excess of emigrants to Assam, over immigrants from Assam, in Bihar and Orissa ; in Assam, *vice versa*. As Part III refers to internal migration only, figures of emigrants and immigrants to and from the French and Portuguese Settlements, as well as other foreign countries, are excluded from the statistics. For figures of immigration to and emigration from India as a whole, reference must be made to Chapter III of the Report volume. The statement at the end of Part III gives available details according to birthplace of the persons included against the entry A (*e*) (*i.e.*, French and Portuguese Settlements) in column 1 of Part I of this table.

Table VI—Part I—

Province or State

	Birthplace	India.			Ajmer-Merwara.			Andaman and Nicobar Islands.		
		Persons.	Males.	Females.	Persons.	Males.	Females.	Persons.	Males.	Females.
	1	2	3	4	5	6	7	8	9	10
	Total Population ..	**350,529,557**	**180,620,612**	**169,908,945**	**560,292**	**296,081**	**264,211**	**29,463**	**19,702**	**9,761**
	A. Born in India ..	349,797,353	180,127,460	169,669,893	558,786	294,855	263,931	28,973	19,241	9,732
	(a) Provinces	271,319,335	139,671,560	131,647,775	477,535	259,078	218,457	27,986	18,435	9,551
1	Ajmer-Merwara ..	514,757	276,605	238,152	453,848	245,110	208,738	24	24	..
2	Andaman and Nicobar Islands.	15,270	8,067	7,203	..	..	..	14,718	7,754	6,964
3	Assam	7,464,517	3,848,998	3,615,519	21	16	5	152	134	18
4	Baluchistan .. .. (*Districts and Administered Territories*).	412,061	227,038	185,023	58	54	4	20	20	..
5	Bengal..	49,374,373	25,422,812	23,951,561	430	267	163	967	814	153
6	Bihar and Orissa ..	39,034,944	19,727,324	19,307,620	100	60	40	620	565	55
7	Bombay	21,303,830	11,077,440	10,226,390	2,067	1,181	886	504	446	58
	Aden	*25,617*	*12,510*	*13,107*	..	..	..	..	..	..
8	Burma..	13,895,731	6,860,691	7,035,040	33	19	14	2,971	2,453	518
9	Central Provinces and Berar.	15,431,500	7,698,517	7,732,983	457	241	216	433	373	60
10	Coorg	127,840	66,513	61,327	1	..	1	7	7	..
11	Delhi	442,485	246,770	195,715	1,169	665	504	8	6	2
12	Madras	47,628,570	23,679,259	23,949,311	323	197	126	2,747	1,896	851
13	North-West Frontier Province. (*Districts and Administered Territories.*)	2,369,354	1,280,173	1,089,181	289	237	52	398	335	63
14	Punjab	23,844,603	13,072,274	10,772,329	3,124	2,188	936	1,983	1,598	385
15	United Provinces of Agra and Oudh.	49,414,925	26,151,515	23,263,410	15,615	8,843	6,772	2,434	2,010	424
16	Provinces Unspecified ..	44,575	27,564	17,011	..	..	..	..	..	..
	(b) States and Agencies	78,358,782	40,384,751	37,974,031	80,892	35,539	45,353	284	233	51
17	Assam States	447,613	218,430	229,183	..	..	..	..	..	..
18	Baluchistan States ..	409,266	221,277	187,989	..	..	..	..	..	..
19	Baroda State	2,323,604	1,208,009	1,115,595	71	39	32	19	17	2
20	Bengal States	813,691	419,729	393,962	1	1	..	..	..	..
21	Bihar and Orissa States ..	4,542,932	2,239,315	2,303,617	5	5	..	..	..	..
22	Bombay States	4,361,165	2,270,244	2,090,921	90	62	28	10	9	1
23	Central India Agency ..	6,514,560	3,357,331	3,157,229	2,439	1,177	1,262	54	39	15
24	Central Provinces States ..	2,325,924	1,163,773	1,162,151	..	..	..	..	..	..
25	Gwalior State	3,538,341	1,854,589	1,683,752	4	4	..	34	32	2
26	Hyderabad State ..	14,520,955	7,354,733	7,166,222	450	274	176	7	6	1
27	Jammu and Kashmir State	3,676,502	1,966,995	1,709,507	34	23	11	14	11	3
28	Madras States Agency ..	6,607,260	3,305,033	3,302,227	13	11	2	27	17	10
	Cochin State ..	*1,163,389*	*573,997*	*589,392*	..	.	..	*15*	*9*	*6*
	Travancore State ..	*5,010,803*	*2,520,971*	*2,489,832*	..	..	..	*12*	*8*	*4*
	Other Madras States	*433,068*	*210,065*	*223,003*	*13**	*11*	*2*	..	..	..
29	Mysore State	6,337,948	3,224,682	3,113,266	95	59	36	29	22	7
30	North-West Frontier Province. (*Agencies and Tribal Areas*).	33,688	22,058	11,630	..	..	..	..	..	..
31	Punjab States (*including Agency*).	4,674,919	2,573,696	2,101,223	830	523	307	..	..	..
32	Rajputana Agency ..	11,741,584	6,180,490	5,561,094	76,374	33,079	43,295	67	58	9
33	Sikkim State	101,603	51,154	50,449	..	..	..	..	..	..
34	United Provinces States..	1,197,754	619,770	577,984	164	91	73	..	..	..
35	Western India States Agency.	4,183,261	2,128,873	2,054,388	322	191	131	23	22	1
36	States Unspecified ..	6,212	4,570	1,642	..	..	..	..	..	..
	(c) French and Portuguese Settlements.	82,271	48,485	33,786	338	228	110	..	..	..
	(d) India Unspecified ..	36,965	22,664	14,301	21	10	11	703	573	130

* Includes Cochin and Travancore.

Birthplace.

enumerated.

Assam (including Khasi States). Persons. 11	Males. 12	Females. 13	Baluchistan (Districts and Administered Territories). Persons. 14	Males. 15	Females. 16	Bengal. Persons. 17	Males. 18	Females. 19	
8,802,251	**4,628,318**	**4,173,933**	**463,508**	**270,004**	**193,504**	**50,114,002**	**26,041,698**	**24,072,304**	
8,708,963	4,565,580	4,143,383	440,144	253,776	186,368	49,987,753	25,962,578	24,025,175	
8,622,092	4,514,057	4,108,035	427,397	244,631	182,766	49,901,732	25,907,959	23,993,773	(a)
77	57	20	100	63	37	507	367	140	1
4	3	1	2	2	..	16	12	4	2
7,391,113	3,807,337	3,583,776	10	4	6	26,638	15,728	10,910	3
245	212	33	368,574	200,396	168,178	111	79	32	4
572,570	325,852	246,718	578	352	226	48,292,950	24,764,179	23,528,771	5
443,412	256,246	187,166	44	35	9	1,114,260	791,197	323,063	6
6,395	3,795	2,600	4,450	3,218	1,232	7,518	5,106	2,412	7
..	..	..	..	..	..		..	..	
6,285	3,153	3,132	60	36	24	3,777	2,375	1,402	8
70,187	37,644	32,543	203	120	83	44,093	25,940	18,153	9
1	..	1	2	1	1	3	3	..	10
106	83	23	742	529	213	2,158	1,783	375	11
57,442	31,019	26,423	185	118	67	40,269	22,050	18,219	12
592	561	31	6,066	4,687	1,379	1,915	1,549	366	13
5,878	4,604	1,274	34,610	25,522	9,088	23,611	18,285	5,326	14
67,785	43,491	24,294	11,771	9,548	2,223	343,906	259,306	84,600	15
..	..	..	..	..	..	..	..	..	16
86,674	**51,374**	**35,300**	**12,512**	**8,982**	**3,530**	**84,463**	**53,565**	**30,898**	(b)
6,182	4,652	1,530	7	2	5	686	527	159	17
..	..	..	7,436	4,830	2,606	79	72	7	18
232	107	125	10	6	4	263	196	67	19
2,443	1,182	1,261	..	..	..	28,699	15,722	12,977	20
28,189	14,015	14,174	..	..	..	10,670	6,325	4,345	21
152	105	47	429	373	56	127	108	19	22
14,884	8,256	6,628	56	35	21	932	468	464	23
11,853	6,788	5,065	..	..	..	33	19	14	24
262	183	79	71	53	18	1,581	1,281	300	25
389	223	166	148	104	44	847	632	215	26
23	16	7	2,054	1,766	288	209	147	62	27
23	7	16	5	4	1	83	50	33	28
1	*1*	..	*2*	*1*	*1*	*23*	*14*	*9*	
1	*1*	..	*3*	*3*	..	*8*	*8*	..	
21	*5*	*16*	..	..	..	*52*	*28*	*24*	
85	54	31	107	64	43	322	199	123	29
	..	..	34	19	15	2	2	..	30
175	127	48	987	811	176	1,343	775	568	31
21,537	15,495	6,042	907	710	197	32,011	23,673	8,338	32
61	44	17	45	36	9	6,320	3,223	3,097	33
184	120	64	31	24	7	256	146	110	34
..	..	..	185	145	40	..	..	..	35
	..	..	..	..	..	..	..	..	36
22	**15**	**7**	**128**	**103**	**25**	**1,291**	**913**	**378**	(c)
175	**134**	**41**	**107**	**60**	**47**	**267**	**141**	**126**	(d)

Table VI.—Part I—

Province or State

Birthplace.	Bihar and Orissa.			Bombay (*including Aden*).			Burma.	
	Persons.	Males.	Females.	Persons.	Males.	Females.	Persons.	Males.
1	20	21	22	23	24	25	26	27
Total Population ..	**37,677,576**	**18,794,138**	**18,883,438**	**21,854,866**	**11,505,229**	**10,349,637**	**14,647,497**	**7,480,676**
A. Born in India	**37,634,635**	**18,777,380**	**18,857,255**	**21,794,214**	**11,459,827**	**10,334,387**	**14,489,055**	**7,364,954**
(a) Provinces	**37,525,075**	**18,736,277**	**18,788,798**	**20,865,539**	**10,980,985**	**9,884,554**	**14,467,144**	**7,348,025**
1 Ajmer-Merwara ..	121	86	35	20,308	12,839	7,469	24	11
2 Andaman and Nicobar Islands.	4	3	1	80	65	15	82	43
3 Assam	1,794	.,327	467	475	370	105	1,113	825
4 Baluchistan (*Districts and Administered Territories*).	7	2	5	35,223	20,996	14,227	110	98
5 Bengal..	149,396	75,664	73,732	5,885	4,428	1,457	158,055	139,366
6 Bihar and Orissa	37,138,759	18,535,431	18,603,328	1,171	799	372	18,344	16,295
7 Bombay	6,140	4,086	2,054	20,446,436	10,693,491	9,752,945	8,436	6,442
Aden	..	..	..	*25,479*	*12,442*	*13,037*	*6*	*4*
8 Burma..	253	92	161	820	466	354	13,871,534	6,846,931
9 Central Provinces and Berar.	63,223	32,425	30,798	54,389	32,233	22,156	775	683
10 Coorg	6	6	..	144	120	24	2	..
11 Delhi	309	207	102	5,277	3,847	1,430	503	437
12 Madras	26,006	12,470	13,536	58,814	36,906	21,908	297,543	241,412
13 North-West Frontier Province (*Districts and Administered Territories*).	782	730	52	11,464	9,334	2,130	907	723
14 Punjab	13,286	9,526	3,760	89,684	61,369	28,315	23,550	19,245
15 United Provinces of Agra and Oudh.	124,989	64,222	60,767	135,369	103,722	31,647	86,166	75,514
16 Provinces Unspecified ..	..	..	..	..	..	..	..	..
(b) States and Agencies ..	108,089	40,525	67,564	852,980	429,256	423,724	20,990	16,175
17 Assam States	6	2	4	..	..	..	3,362	2,034
18 Baluchistan States ..	5	5	..	..	..	..	5	5
19 Baroda State	47	28	19	111,949	48,529	63,420	342	266
20 Bengal States	19	11	8	..	..	..	43	31
21 Bihar and Orissa States ..	79,915	24,674	55,241	..	..	..	388	334
22 Bombay States	350	284	66	257,174	124,674	132,500	293	266
23 Central India Agency ..	1,902	1,182	720	12,396	6,582	5,814	153	107
24 Central Provinces States ..	5,128	1,392	3,736	..	..	..	258	227
25 Gwalior State	173	93	80	2,081	1,354	727	90	74
26 Hyderabad State ..	431	243	188	161,676	73,546	88,130	939	690
27 Jammu and Kashmir State	78	55	23	1,255	932	323	127	121
28 Madras States Agency ..	38	29	9	3,643	1,159	2,484	1,145	991
Cochin State	..	..	..	*3,025*	*695*	*2,330*	*239*	*191*
Travancore State ..	..	..	..	*618*	*464*	*154*	*816*	*723*
Other Madras States ..	*38**	*29*	*9*	..	..	..	*90*	*77*
29 Mysore State	372	244	128	17,085	8,869	8,216	1,409	915
30 North-West Frontier Province. (*Agencies and Tribal Areas*).	475	437	38	..	..	..	..	..
31 Punjab States (*including Agency*).	89	63	26	..	..	..	1,360	1,132
32 Rajputana Agency ..	18,987	11,733	7,254	96,537	61,861	34,676	1,909	1,355
33 Sikkim State	26	15	11	724	283	441	17	16
34 United Provinces States..	4	2	2	..	..	..	261	152
35 Western India States Agency.	44	33	11	188,460	101,467	86,993	8,889	7,459
36 States Unspecified ..	..	..	..	..	..	..	..	..
(c) French and Portuguese Settlements.	285	169	116	54,073	34,607	19,466	893	735
(d) India Unspecified ..	1,186	409	777	21,622	14,979	6,643	28	19

Birthplace—*continued.*

where enumerated.

	Central Provinces and Berar.			Coorg.			Delhi.			
Females. 28	Persons. 29	Males. 30	Females. 31	Persons. 32	Males. 33	Females. 34	Persons. 35	Males. 36	Females. 37	
7,166,821	**15,507,723**	**7,761,818**	**7,745,905**	**163,327**	**90,575**	**72,752**	**636,246**	**369,497**	**266,749**	
7,124,101	15,501,577	7,757,015	7,744,562	163,228	90,522	72,706	632,221	366,449	265,772	
7,119,119	15,119,846	7,575,791	7,544,055	150,121	83,211	66,910	585,334	337,905	247,429	(a)
13	3,380	2,122	1,258	..	..	..	777	419	358	1
39	92	69	23	..	..	..	..	..	..	2
288	432	244	188	..	..	..	83	55	28	3
12	709	599	110	..	..	..	189	128	61	4
18,689	5,558	2,905	2,653	..	..	..	6,168	3,681	2,487	5
2,049	24,457	11,599	12,858	..	..	..	710	517	193	6
1,994	98,422	51,190	47,232	..	..	..	2,275	1,402	873	7
2	..	..	..	..	..	..	*4*	*2*	*2*	
7,024,603	147	84	63	7	6	1	84	52	32	8
92	14,851,267	7,422,029	7,429,238	..	..	..	862	535	327	9
2	251	35	216	124,609	64,926	59,683	..	..	..	10
66	755	526	229	..	..	..	373,058	215,184	157,874	11
56,131	9,509	5,298	4,211	25,333	18,142	7,191	1,441	836	605	12
184	1,109	967	142	..	..	..	1,758	1,362	396	13
4,305	13,630	10,336	3,294	..	..	..	83,412	42,662	40,750	14
10,652	110,128	67,788	42,340	..	..	..	114,517	71,072	43,445	15
..	..	..	..	172	137	35	..	..	..	16
4,815	381,122	180,888	200,234	13,091	7,302	5,789	46,745	28,476	18,26	(b)
1,328	6	3	3	..	..	..	..	..	..	17
..	..	..	..	..	..	..	..	..	..	18
76	501	274	227	..	..	..	65	41	24	19
12	175	165	10	..	..	..	..	..	..	20
54	1,031	464	567	..	..	..	5	..	5	21
27	5,853	3,799	2,054	..	..	..	..	..	..	22
46	158,905	75,225	83,680	..	..	..	310	171	139	23
31	64,984	26,337	38,647	..	..	..	..	..	..	24
16	8,736	3,880	4,856	..	..	..	1,651	978	673	25
249	90,743	39,570	51,173	21	11	10	278	169	109	26
6	270	247	23	..	..	—	470	386	84	27
154	167	111	56	96	68	28	26	19	7	28
48	..	..	—	*71*	*50*	*21*	*17*	*12*	*5*	
93	..	..	..	*24*	*18*	*6*	*4*	*4*	—	
13	*167**	*111*	*56*	*1*	—	*1*	*5*	*3*	*2*	
494	691	364	327	12,971	7,220	5,751	142	86	56	29
..	9	8	1	..	..	—	—	—	—	30
228	579	394	185	—	—	—	5,200	3,333	1,867	31
554	48,184	29,864	18,320	—	—	—	36,951	22,245	14,706	32
1	12	12	—	—	—	—	—	—	—	33
109	276	171	105	—	—	—	1,647	1,048	599	34
1,430	—	—	—	—	—	—	—	—	—	35
..	—	—	—	3	3	—	—	—	—	36
158	525	296	229	9	8	1	73	48	25	(c)
9	84	40	44	7	1	6	69	20	49	(d)

* Includes Cochin and Travancore.

Table VI.—Part I—

Birthplace.	Province or State						
	Madras.			North-West Frontier Province (*Districts and Administered Territories*).			
	Persons.	Males.	Females.	Persons.	Males.	Females.	Persons.
1	38	39	40	41	42	43	44
Total Population	**46,740,107**	**23,082,999**	**23,657,108**	**2,425,076**	**1,315,818**	**1,109,258**	**23,580,852**
A. Born in India ..	46,720,898	23,071,578	23,649,320	2,385,528	1,289,930	1,095,598	23,541,725
(a) Provinces	46,502,190	22,965,932	23,536,258	2,348,293	1,264,779	1,083,514	22,996,429
1 Ajmer-Merwara ..	..	..	..	68	52	16	753
2 Andaman and Nicobar Islands.	..	..	..	2	..	2	104
3 Assam	..	..	..	36	21	15	306
4 Baluchistan .. .. (*Districts and Administered Territories*).	..	..	..	426	209	217	3,898
5 Bengal..	..	..	..	704	513	191	4,320
6 Bihar and Orissa ..	..	..	..	129	88	41	1,150
7 Bombay	..	..	..	655	455	200	6,419
Aden	..	..	..	..	..	..	*16*
8 Burma..	3,158	1,509	1,649	76	39	37	1,852
9 Central Provinces and Berar.	..	..	..	248	209	39	1,904
10 Coorg	..	..	..	..	..	..	..
11 Delhi . ..	..	..	..	515	372	143	33,065
12 Madras	46,454,913	22,937,135	23,517,778	461	312	149	1,447
13 North-West Frontier Province (*Districts and Administered Territories*).	..	..	..	2,269,885	1,208,857	1,061,028	50,046
14 Punjab	..	..	..	66,890	47,361	19,529	22,685,326
15 United Provinces of Agra and Oudh.	..	..	..	8,198	6,291	1,907	205,839
16 Provinces Unspecified ..	44,119	27,288	16,831	..	..	..	..
(b) States and Agencies ..	202,194	97,958	104,236	36,597	24,626	11,971	544,454
17 Assam States	..	..	..	..	..	..	7
18 Baluchistan States ..	..	..	..	..	..	..	..
19 Baroda State	..	..	..	8	5	3	127
20 Bengal States	..	..	..	..	..	..	..
21 Bihar and Orissa States ..	..	..	..	7	2	5	6
22 Bombay States	..	..	..	29	19	10	84
23 Central India Agency ..	..	..	..	280	275	5	228
24 Central Provinces States ..	..	..	..	27	..	27	129
25 Gwalior State	..	..	..	74	73	1	1,182
26 Hyderabad State ..	58,108	27,223	30,885	171	102	69	707
27 Jammu and Kashmir State	..	..	..	5,849	5,030	819	75,028
28 Madras States Agency ..	51,724	26,257	25,467	..	..	..	44
Cochin State ..	*14,743*	*8,330*	*6,413*	..	..	..	..
Travancore State ..	*16,604*	*10,113*	*6,491*	..	..	..	*1*
Other Madras States ..	*20,377*	*7,814*	*12,563*	..	..	..	*43*
29 Mysore State	86,203	39,936	46,267	83	40	43	260
30 North-West Frontier Province. (*Agencies and Tribal Areas*).	..	..	..	27,852	17,258	10,594	..
31 Punjab States (*including Agency*).	..	..	..	1,121	902	219	335,800
32 Rajputana Agency ..	..	..	..	1,096	920	176	130,154
33 Sikkim State	..	..	..	..	..	..	..
34 United Provinces States..	..	..	..	..	..	..	698
35 Western India States Agency	..	..	..	..	..	..	..
36 States Unspecified ..	6,159	4,542	1,617	..	..	..	..
(c) French and Portuguese Settlements.	15,964	7,433	8,531	34	30	4	11
(d) India Unspecified ..	550	255	295	604	495	109	831

Birthplace—*continued.*

where enumerated.

Punjab.		United Provinces of Agra and Oudh.			Assam State (*Manipur*).			
Males. 45	Females. 46	Persons. 47	Males. 48	Females. 49	Persons. 50	Males. 51	Females. 52	
12,880,510	**10,700,342**	**48,408,763**	**25,445,006**	**22,963,757**	**445,606**	**215,815**	**229,791**	
12,851,277	10,690,448	48,343,613	25,400,107	22,943,506	444,178	214,805	229,373	
12,625,792	10,370,637	48,016,702	25,279,376	22,737,326	7,371	4,150	3,221	(a)
386	367	3,392	1,802	1,590	..	..	..	1
69	35	140	29	111	..	..	..	2
141	165	1,094	623	471	5,246	2,961	2,285	3
2,454	1,444	449	350	99	..	..	.	4
2,286	2,034	30,519	16,540	13,979	186	113	73	5
482	668	66,515	18,695	47,820	185	102	83	6
3,789	2,630	8,144	4,846	3,298	5	2	3	7
	9	..	..	..	..	..	..	
1,039	813	1,387	759	628	1,502	786	716	8
768	1,136	14,759	6,809	7,950	5	4	1	9
..	..	89	85	4	..	..	..	10
11,873	21,192	14,946	5,808	9,138	1	1	..	11
941	506	3,081	1,868	1,213	6	4	2	12
31,331	18,715	3,534	3,206	328	1	1	..	13
12,465,889	10,219,437	92,021	48,597	43,424	77	57	20	14
104,344	101,495	47,776,632	25,169,359	22,607,273	157	119	38	15
..	..	..	..	..	..	..	.	16
225,079	319,375	325,898	120,219	205,679	436,807	210,655	226,152	(b)
2	5	6	2	4	436,553	210,462	226,091	17
..	..	3	..	3	..	..	..	18
74	53	324	143	181	..	..	..	19
..	..	2	2	..	..	..	..	20
3	3	18	5	13	..	..	..	21
49	35	245	84	161	..	..	..	22
114	114	109,039	36,916	72,123	3	2	1	23
59	70	421	245	176	..	..	..	24
541	641	47,285	16,393	30,892	..	..	..	25
332	375	1,858	886	972	..	..	..	26
42,797	32,231	1,383	1,031	352	1	1	..	27
12	32	60	32	28	..	..	..	28
..	..	..	..	..	..	..	..	
..	*1*	*60*	*32*	*28*	..	..	..	
12	*31*	..	..	..	..	..	..	
190	70	525	185	340	..	..	..	29
..	..	2	..	2	..	..	..	30
122,508	213,292	4,317	3,087	1,230	4	4	..	31
58,100	72,054	81,674	33,845	47,829	243	184	59	32
..	..	2	..	2	3	2	1	33
298	400	78,692	27,345	51,347	..	..	..	34
..	..	42	18	24	..	..	..	35
..	..	..	..	..	..	..	..	36
5	6	91	79	12	..	..	..	(c)
401	430	922	433	489	..	..	..	(d)

Table VI.—Part I—

Province or State

	Birthplace.	Baluchistan States.			Baroda State.			Bengal States.		
		Persons.	Males.	Females.	Persons.	Males.	Females.	Persons.	Males.	Females.
	1	53	54	55	56	57	58	59	60	61
	Total Population.	**405,109**	**218,410**	**186,699**	**2,443,007**	**1,257,817**	**1,185,190**	**973,336**	**516,162**	**457,174**
	A. Born in India ..	**404,962**	**218,325**	**186,637**	**2,441,505**	**1,256,928**	**1,184,577**	**972,247**	**515,414**	**456,833**
	(a) Provinces	**3,314**	**2,057**	**1,257**	**191,190**	**80,912**	**110,278**	**186,180**	**110,299**	**75,881**
1	Ajmer-Merwara ..	17	10	7	529	340	189	9	..	9
2	Andaman and Nicobar Islands.	..	..	..	1	..	1	1	1	..
3	Assam	..	..	..	11	8	3	35,374	18,844	16,530
4	Baluchistan .. .. (*Districts and Administered Territories.*)	1,025	636	389	..	..	..	2	1	1
5	Bengal..	..	..	..	393	293	100	129,677	77,439	52,238
6	Bihar and Orissa ..	..	..	..	110	88	22	12,842	9,241	3,601
7	Bombay	355	284	71	179,435	72,041	107,394	88	61	27
	Aden	..	..	..	*19*	*7*	*12*	..	..	..
8	Burma..	..	..	..	265	138	127	14	6	8
9	Central Provinces and Berar.	..	..	..	647	379	268	1,609	876	733
10	Coorg	..	..	..	..	..	..	..	..	..
11	Delhi	10	7	3	350	268	82	1	..	1
12	Madras	1	1	..	555	330	225	2,168	1,410	758
13	North-West Frontier Province. (*District and Administered Territories.*)	82	55	27	338	302	36	47	47	..
14	Punjab	1,719	968	751	1,556	1,278	278	123	65	58
15	United Provinces of Agra and Oudh.	105	96	9	7,000	5,447	1,553	4,225	2,308	1,917
16	Provinces Unspecified ..	..	..	..	..	..	..	..	..	..
	(b) States and Agencies	**401,647**	**216,267**	**185,380**	**2,249,339**	**1,175,595**	..	**786,066**	**405,115**	**380,951**
17	Assam States	..	..	..	..	..	..	718	687	31
18	Baluchistan States ..	401,529	216,178	185,351	200	181	19	..	..	..
19	Baroda State	12	5	7	2,118,428	1,125,312	993,116	87	67	20
20	Bengal States	..	..	..	..	..	..	782,304	402,614	379,690
21	Bihar and Orissa States ..	..	..	..	3	3	..	1,078	479	599
22	Bombay States	30	23	7	41,224	12,911	28,313	64	41	23
23	Central India Agency ..	..	..	..	974	513	461	790	503	287
24	Central Provinces States ..	..	..	..	4	3	1	109	2	107
25	Gwalior State	..	..	..	491	302	189	..	..	..
26	Hyderabad State ..	2	1	1	337	204	133	2	2	..
27	Jammu and Kashmir State	27	27	..	30	29	1	..	..	..
28	Madras States Agency ..	1	1	..	23	16	7	..	..	..
	Cochin State ..	*1*	*1*	..	*14*	*8*	*6*	..	..	..
	Travancore State ..	..	..	..	*9*	*8*	*1*	..	..	..
	Other Madras States	..	..	..		..	..	..	..	..
29	Mysore State	..	..	..	72	41	31	..	..	..
30	North-West Frontier Province. (*Agencies and Tribal Areas.*)	1	1	..	3	3	..	.	..	..
31	Punjab States .. .. (*including Agency*).	29	21	8	136	121	15	7	7	..
32	Rajputana Agency ..	7	3	4	8,973	5,651	3,322	895	701	194
33	Sikkim State	..	..	..	..	.	..	..	..	..
34	United Provinces States..	..	..	..	12	10	2	12	12	..
35	Western India States Agency	9	7	2	78,429	30,295	48,134	..	..	..
36	States Unspecified ..	..	..	..	..	..	..	..	..	..
	(c) French and Portuguese Settlements	**1**	**1**	..	**824**	**341**	**483**	**1**	..	**1**

Birthplace—*continued.*

where enumerated.

Bihar and Orissa States. Persons.	Males.	Females.	Bombay States. Persons.	Males.	Females.	Central India Agency. Persons.	Males.	Females.	
62	63	64	65	66	67	68	69	70	
4,652,007	**2,288,422**	**2,363,585**	**4,468,396**	**2,288,623**	**2,179,773**	**6,632,790**	**3,405,438**	**3,227,352**	
4,651,674	2,288,165	2,363,509	4,467,488	2,287,933	2,179,555	6,630,126	3,403,333	3,226,793	
224,628	93,023	131,605	334,291	129,722	204,569	293,982	122,501	171,481	(a)
2	1	1	169	124	45	4,326	2,543	1,783	1
..	..	..	1	1	..	4	3	1	2
230	139	91	..	..	..	32	18	14	3
4	4	..	227	193	34	162	117	45	4
8,108	3,650	4,458	120	69	51	844	509	335	5
183,309	72,930	110,379	333	139	194	953	460	493	6
736	553	183	328,008	125,675	202,333	37,783	19,518	18,265	7
..	..	..	..	..	..	..	..	..	
45	24	21	9	5	4	50	24	26	8
18,350	9,110	9,240	1,067	630	437	98,166	38,610	59,556	9
..	..	..	..	..	..	1	..	1	10
50	44	6	40	35	5	1,113	762	351	11
10,451	4,359	6,092	1,385	758	627	715	380	335	12
42	30	2	222	182	40	524	447	77	13
1,765	1,164	601	1,232	934	298	4,630	3,512	1,118	14
1,536	1,015	521	1,478	977	501	144,679	55,598	89,081	15
..	..	..	..	..	..	..	..	..	16
4,427,046	2,195,142	2,231,904	4,127,489	2,156,061	1,971,428	6,335,648	3,280,495	3,055,153	(b)
..	..	..	..	..	..	..	..	..	17
..	..	..	..	..	..	..	..	..	18
16	9	7	53,528	19,382	34,146	1,620	817	803	19
1	1	..	..	..	..	..	..	..	20
4,417,763	2,191,177	2,226,586	..	..	..	32	15	17	21
90	69	21	4,041,183	2,121,889	1,919,294	4,673	1,729	2,944	22
173	88	85	1,502	568	934	6,032,024	3,152,773	2,879,251	23
2,616	938	1,678	..	..	..	1,901	863	1,038	24
11	8	3	122	72	50	184,922	67,369	117,553	25
37	29	8	8,409	3,326	5,083	1,321	751	570	26
14	10	4	30	24	6	160	128	32	27
4,291	1,644	2,647	10	2	8	21	19	2	28
..	..	..	*10*	*2*	*8*	..	..	..	
..	..	..	..	..	..	..	..	..	
*4,291**	*1,644*	*2,647*	..	..	..	*21**	*19*	*2*	
31	17	14	522	246	276	265	155	110	29
..	..	..	..	..	..	9	8	1	30
190	123	67	..	..	..	722	449	273	31
1,769	996	773	11,935	5,218	6,717	105,405	53,772	51,633	32
..	..	..	..	..	..	..	..	..	
10	9	1	..	..	..	454	308	146	34
34	24	10	10,248	5,334	4,914	2,119	1,339	780	35
..	..	..	..	..	..	..	..	..	36
..	..	..	5,019	1,862	3,157	360	222	138	(c)
..	..	..	689	288	401	136	115	21	(d)

* Includes Cochin and Travancore.

Table VI.—Part I.–

Birthplace.	Province or State						
	Central Provinces States.			Cochin State.			Gwalior
	Persons.	Males.	Females.	Persons.	Males.	Females.	Persons.
1	71	72	73	74	75	76	77
Total Population.	**2,483,214**	**1,235,385**	**1,247,829**	**1,205,016**	**589,813**	**615,203**	**3,523,070**
A. Born in India ..	2,482,850	1,235,237	1,247,613	1,204,813	589,707	615,106	3,522,870
(a) Provinces	218,461	94,683	123,778	55,048	23,392	31,656	69,604
1 Ajmer-Merwara ..	49	35	14	..	..	..	2,316
2 Andaman and Nicobar Islands.	4	4	..	..	..	..	..
3 Assam	149	66	83	3	..	3	2
4 Baluchistan .. .. (*Districts and Administered Territories.*)	.	..	..	8	4	4	7
5 Bengal..	1,213	659	554	33	17	16	260
6 Bihar and Orissa ..	22,625	10,323	12,302		..	..	102
7 Bombay	445	265	180	291	180	111	4,050
Aden	..	..	..		..	..	..
8 Burma..	9	6	3	31	15	16	4
9 Central Provinces and Berar.	180,768	75,853	104,915	11	8	3	9,013
10 Coorg	3		3	2	1	1	..
11 Delhi .. .	40	21	19	1	1	..	662
12 Madras	3,369	1,713	1,656	54,614	23,122	31,492	85
13 North-West Frontier Province. (*Districts and Administered Territories.*)	49	33	16	2	2	..	144
14 Punjab	1,391	916	475	19	15	4	2,576
15 United Provinces of Agra and Oudh.	8,347	4,789	3,558	33	27	6	50,383
16 Provinces Unspecified ..	..	..	..	..	..	..	..
(b) States and Agencies ..	2,264,377	1,140,548	1,123,829	1,149,634	566,221	583,413	3,451,506
17 Assam States	..	..	..	..	..	..	..
18 Baluchistan States ..	..	..	..	..	..	..	..
19 Baroda State	8	5	3	3	1	2	492
20 Bengal States	..	..	..	..	..	..	..
21 Bihar and Orissa States ..	3,806	1,808	1,998	..	..	..	..
22 Bombay States	293	172	121	..	..	..	165
23 Central India Agency ..	17,897	9,555	8,342	1	..	1	131,333
24 Central Provinces States ..	2,238,344	1,126,827	1,111,517	2	2	..	..
25 Gwalior State	70	49	21	..	..	..	3,241,520
26 Hyderabad State ..	322	168	154	13	11	2	232
27 Jammu and Kashmir State	3	2	1	1	1	..	39
28 Madras States Agency ..	..	..	..	1,148,775	565,716	583,059	..
Cochin State ..	..	..	..	*1,117,599*	*553,453*	*564,146*	..
Travancore State ..	..	..	..	*31,167*	*12,257*	*18,910*	..
Other Madras States ..	..	..	..	*9*	*6*	*3*	..
29 Mysore State	20	14	6	127	62	65	31
30 North-West Frontier Province. (*Agencies and Tribal Areas*).	..	..	..	..	..	..	..
31 Punjab States .. .. (*including Agency*).	175	90	85	..	..	..	320
32 Rajputana Agency ..	3,437	1,858	1,579	12	4	8	76,480
33 Sikkim State	..	..	..	..	..	..	..
34 United Provinces States..	2	..	2	..	..	..	539
35 Western India States Agency	..	..	..	700	424	276	355
36 States Unspecified ..	..	..	..	..	..	..	..
(c) French and Portuguese Settlements.	3	2	1	66	52	14	17
(d) India Unspecified ..	9	4	5	65	42	23	1,743

Birthplace—*continued.*

where enumerated.

State.		Hyderabad State.			Jammu and Kashmir State.			
Males.	Females.	Persons.	Males.	Females.	Persons.	Males.	Females.	
78	79	80	81	82	83	84	85	
1,867,031	**1,656,039**	**14,436,148**	**7,370,010**	**7,066,138**	**3,646,243**	**1,938,338**	**1,707,905**	
1,866,888	1,655,982	14,431,167	7,366,000	7,065,167	3,643,236	1,936,284	1,706,952	
31,956	37,648	229,123	154,629	74,494	60,119	27,596	32,523	(a)
1,241	1,075	1,525	602	923	6	4	2	1
..	..	..	..	..	..	..	..	2
1	1	5	2	3	7	2	5	3
1	1	21	17	4	93	54	39	4
151	109	313	167	146	111	67	44	5
66	36	564	354	210	23	15	8	6
2,247	1,803	67,734	36,637	31,097	180	109	71	7
..	..	..	..	..	..	..	..	
4	..	105	36	69	29	14	15	8
4,194	4,819	14,289	6,702	7,587	45	32	13	9
..	..	6	3	3	..	..	..	10
416	246	949	641	308	83	57	26	11
52	33	132,952	102,545	30,407	33	25	8	12
102	42	184	145	39	6,384	3,759	2,625	13
1,724	852	3,190	2,220	970	52,366	22,934	29,432	14
21,752	28,631	7,286	4,558	2,728	759	524	235	15
..	..	..	..	..	..	..	..	16
1,834,251	1,617,255	14,200,862	7,210,775	6,990,087	3,582,973	1,908,601	1,674,372	(b)
..	..	..	..	..	..	..	..	17
..	..	..	..	..	..	..	..	18
230	262	37	26	11	22	15	7	19
..	..	..	..	.	..	..	..	20
..	..	..	..	.	..	..	..	21
137	28	324	192	132	19	12	7	22
52,053	79,280	558	293	265	11	8	3	23
..	..	..	..	..	..	..	..	24
1,745,984	1,495,536	717	528	189	22	19	3	25
157	75	14,188,353	7,203,129	6,985,224	19	14	5	26
30	9	42	26	16	3,582,047	1,908,041	1,674,006	27
..	..	61	38	23	..	..	..	28
..	..	*31*	*22*	*9*	..	..	..	
..	..	*28*	*16*	*12*	..	..	..	
..	..	*2*	..	*2*	..	..	..	
18	13	2,869	1,728	1,141	2	2	..	29
..	..	..	..	..	88	49	39	30
188	132	541	422	119	668	388	280	31
34,872	41,608	6,608	4,040	2,568	64	50	14	32
..	..	..	..	..	2	1	1	33
308	231	752	353	399	9	2	7	34
274	81	..	..	..	..	..	..	35
..	..	..	..	..	..	..	..	36
12	5	157	98	59	17	17	..	(c)
669	1,074	1,025	498	527	127	70	57	(d

Table VI.—Part I—

Province or State

	Birthplace.	Madras States (*excluding Cochin and Travancore*). Persons.	Males.	Females.	Mysore State. Persons.	Males.	Females.	North-West (*Agencies*) Persons.
	1	86	87	88	89	90	91	92
	Total Population.	**453,495**	**218,146**	**235,349**	**6,557,302**	**3,353,963**	**3,203,339**	**46,451**
	A. Born in India ..	452,401	217,573	234,828	6,553,410	3,351,314	3,202,096	38,701
	(a) Provinces	43,645	16,802	26,843	331,360	181,896	149,464	29,315
1	Ajmer-Merwara ..	..	..	..	183	140	43	20
2	Andaman and Nicobar Island.	..	..	..	10	6	4	..
3	Assam	..	..	..	11	5	6	12
4	Baluchistan .. .. (*Districts and Administered Territories*).	..	..	..	95	68	27	18
5	Bengal..	..	..	..	617	311	306	91
6	Bihar and Orissa ..	..	..	..	58	43	15	28
7	Bombay Presidency ..	..	..	..	30,606	16,395	14,211	68
	Aden	..	..	..	..	..	..	..
8	Burma..	23	18	5	382	163	219	..
9	Central Provinces and Berar.	..	..	..	693	371	322	32
10	Coorg	..	..	..	2,703	1,320	1,383	..
11	Delhi	..	..	..	132	86	46	116
12	Madras	43,338	16,645	26,693	294,024	161,615	132,409	315
13	North-West Frontier Province. (*Districts and Administered Territories.*)	..	..	..	93	60	33	9,413
14	Punjab	..	..	..	1,193	922	271	16,228
15	United Provinces of Agra and Oudh.	..	..	..	560	391	169	2,979
16	Provinces Unspecified ..	284	139	145	..	..	..	..
	(b) States and Agencies ..	408,708	200,746	207,962	6,221,275	3,168,980	3,052,295	9,202
17	Assam States	..	..	..	1	1	..	32
18	Baluchistan States ..	..	..	..	..	..	..	..
19	Baroda State	..	..	..	51	30	21	..
20	Bengal States	..	..	..	..	..	..	..
21	Bihar and Orissa States ..	..	..	..	..	..	..	..
22	Bombay States	..	..	..	461	240	221	..
23	Central India Agency ..	..	..	..	110	79	31	..
24	Central Provinces States ..	..	..	..	..	..	..	31
25	Gwalior State	..	..	..	26	12	14	82
26	Hyderabad State ..	368	220	148	4,224	2,384	1,840	11
27	Jammu and Kashmir State	..	..	..	73	47	26	2,414
28	Madras States Agency ..	408,008	200,374	207,634	1,058	732	326	..
	Cochin State ..	*77*	*60*	*17*	*543*	*400*	*143*	..
	Travancore State ..	*152*	*91*	*61*	*422*	*283*	*139*	..
	Other Madras States	*407,779*	*200,223*	*207,556*	*93*	*49*	*44*	..
29	Mysore State	282	127	155	6,212,710	3,163,517	3,049,193	65
30	North-West Frontier Province. (*Agencies and Tribal Areas*).	..	..	..	..	..	..	5,211
31	Punjab States (*including Agency*). ..	..	..	..	3	2	1	907
32	Rajputana Agency ..	..	..	..	2,348	1,793	555	449
33	Sikkim State	..	..	..	..	..	..	..
34	United Provinces States..	..	..	..	..	..	..	..
35	Western India States Agency.	..	..	..	210	143	67	..
36	States Unspecified ..	50	25	25	..	..	..	..
	(c) French and Portuguese Settlements.	48	25	23	585	304	281	33
	(d) India unspecified ..	..	..	..	190	134	56	151

Birth place—*continued.*

where enumerated.

Frontier Province. *and Tribal Areas.)* Males.	Females.	Punjab States *(including Punjab States Agency).* Persons.	Males.	Females.	Rajputana Agency. Persons.	Males.	Females.	
93	94	95	96	97	98	99	100	
44,635	**1,816**	**4,910,005**	**2,680,684**	**2,229,321**	**11,225,712**	**5,885,028**	**5,340,684**	
37,028	1,673	4,905,889	2,677,624	2,228,265	11,224,686	5,884,346	5,340,340	
28,589	726	539,055	222,605	316,450	219,935	97,118	122,817	(a)
20	..	178	61	117	21,522	7,875	13,647	1
..	..	1	..	1	..	..	..	2
12	..	8	5	3	83	41	42	3
17	1	165	122	43	44	39	5	4
91	..	298	159	139	1,003	553	450	5
23	..	125	76	49	436	267	169	6
66	2	2,084	1,205	879	9,970	4,671	5,299	7
..	..	*1*	..	*1*	..	..	..	
..	..	195	128	67	70	18	52	8
32	..	384	226	158	2,914	1,108	1,806	9
..	..	..	..	..	2	2	..	10
116	..	4,054	1,743	2,311	1,962	1,053	909	11
315	..	111	67	44	258	150	108	12
9,021	392	2,727	1,820	907	277	217	60	13
15,919	309	503,442	203,283	300,159	113,855	57,502	56,353	14
2,957	22	25,283	13,710	11,573	67,539	23,622	43,917	15
..	..	..	..			..	..	16
8,257	**945**	**4,366,801**	**2,454,997**	**1,911,804**	**11,003,705**	**5,786,848**	**5,216,857**	(b)
32	..	1	..	1	41	23	18	17
..	..	2	2	..	7	4	3	18
..	..	16	9	7	745	397	348	19
..	..	..	..	..	4	..	4	20
	..	..	..	..	16	6	10	21
..	..	24	24	..	4,362	1,642	2,720	22
..	..	103	71	32	26,335	9,629	16,706	23
31	..	2	2	..	81	37	44	24
82	..	378	195	183	46,601	14,940	31,661	25
11	..	90	41	49	200	123	77	26
,410	4	4,663	3,545	1,118	104	70	34	27
..	..	..	..	..	4	2	2	28
..	..	..	..	..	*2*	*1*	*1*	
..	..	..	..	..	*1*	*1*	..	
..	..	..	..	..	*1*	..	*1*	
65	..	33	10	23	72	37	35	29
4,271	940	..	..	..	2	2	..	30
907	..	4,292,137	2,425,906	1,866,231	26,527	10,845	15,682	31
448	1	69,060	25,025	44,035	10,894,773	5,747,387	5,147,386	32
..	..	..		..	..	.	..	33
..	..	292	167	125	234	159	75	34
..	..	..	..	..	3,597	1,545	2,052	35
..	..	..	..	..	..	..	..	36
33	..	**22**	**18**	**4**	**163**	**122**	**41**	(c)
[illegible]	[illegible]	11	4	7	883	258		

Table VI.—Part I—

Birthplace.	Province or State					
	Sikkim State.			Travancore State.		
	Persons.	Males.	Females.	Persons.	Males.	Females.
	101	102	103	104	105	106
Total Population.	**109,808**	**55,825**	**53,983**	**5,095,973**	**2,565,073**	**2,530,900**
A. Born in India ..	**96,821**	**49,031**	**47,790**	**5,094,722**	**2,564,308**	**2,530,414**
(a) Provinces	**2,315**	**1,427**	**888**	**105,231**	**55,641**	**49,590**
1 Ajmer-Merwara ..	..	..	..	1	1	..
2 Andaman and Nicobar Islands.	..	..	..	2	2	..
3 Assam	6	2	4	..	..	..
4 Baluchistan .. .. (*Districts and Administered Territories.*)	..	..	..	..	..	..
5 Bengal	1,707	900	807	222	195	27
6 Bihar and Orissa ..	305	288	17	1	..	1
7 Bombay	..	..	..	517	356	161
Aden	..	..	..	..	..	..
8 Burma..	..	..	..	30	14	16
9 Central Provinces and Berar.	..	..	..	14	12	2
10 Coorg	..	..	..	8	4	4
11 Delhi	1	..	1	..	..	..
12 Madras	..	..	..	104,277	54,920	49,357
13 North-West Frontier Province. (*Districts and Administered Territories*).	..		..	7	2	5
14 Punjab	164	135	29	93	82	11
15 United Provinces of Agra and Oudh.	132	102	30	59	53	6
16 Provinces Unspecified ..	..	..	..	..	..	..
(b) States and Agencies ..	**94,506**	**47,604**	**46,902**	**4,988,372**	**2,507,898**	**2,480,474**
17 Assam States	5	1	4	..	..	..
18 Baluchistan States ..	..	..	..	..	..	..
19 Baroda State	..	..	..	9	7	2
20 Bengal States	..	..	..	..	..	..
21 Bihar and Orissa States ..	..	..	..	..	..	..
22 Bombay States	..	..	..	..	..	..
23 Central India Agency ..	..	..	..	..	..	..
24 Central Provinces States ..	..	..	..	..	..	..
25 Gwalior State	..	..	..	1	1	..
26 Hyderabad State ..	..	..	..	25	16	9
27 Jammu and Kashmir State	..	..	..	..	..	..
28 Madras States Agency ..	..	..	..	4,987,899	2,507,711	2,480,188
Cochin State ..	..	..	..	*26,964*	*10,738*	*16,226*
Travancore State ..	..	..	..	*4,960,870*	*2,496,939*	*2,463,931*
Other Madras States ..	..	..	..	*65*	*34*	*31*
29 Mysore State	..	..	..	380	134	246
30 North-West Frontier Province. (*Agencies and Tribal Areas.*)	..	..	..	..	..	
31 Punjab States .. (*including Agency*).	..	..	..	..	..	..
32 Rajputana Agency ..	110	81	29	39	21	18
33 Sikkim State	94,391	47,522	46,869	..	..	..
34 United Provinces States..	..	..	..	..	..	..
35 Western India States Agency.	..	..	..	19	8	11
36 States Unspecified ..	..	..	..	..	..	..
(c) French and Portuguese Settlements.	..	..	..	226	165	61
	..					

Birthplace—*continued.*

where enumerated.

United Provinces States.			Western India States Agency.			
Persons.	Males.	Females.	Persons.	Males.	Females.	
107	108	109	110	111	112	
1,206,070	**618,171**	**587,899**	**3,999,250**	**2,025,754**	**1,973,496**	
1,205,923	618,086	587,837	3,996,371	2,024,062	1,972,309	
91,544	28,300	63,244	50,209	22,029	28,180	(a)
7	1	6	519	269	250	1
..	..	..	2	1	1	2
69	65	4	2	2	..	3
3	2	1	168	161	7	4
429	297	132	648	325	323	5
3,200	847	2,353	79	53	26	6
76	49	27	43,538	17,679	25,859	7
..	..	..	*92*	*48*	*44*	
1	1	..	523	278	245	8
36	17	19	657	344	313	9
..	..	..	..	..	..	10
182	109	73	127	90	37	11
18	10	8	381	238	143	12
26	23	3	47	46	1	13
818	563	255	1,161	899	262	14
86,679	26,316	60,363	2,357	1,644	713	15
..	..	..	..	..	..	16
1,114,378	589,785	524,593	3,941,456	1,999,713	1,941,743	(b)
..	..	..	..	..	..	17
..	..	..	..	..	..	18
2	2	..	34,570	11,970	22,600	19
..	..	..	..	..	..	20
..	..	..	..	..	..	21
1	..	1	3,416	1,331	2,085	22
203	50	153	965	599	366	23
1	1	..	..	..	..	24
18	8	10	136	81	55	25
18	10	8	199	125	74	26
38	22	16	22	20	2	27
..	..	..	15	11	4	28
..	..	..	*12*	*9*	*3*	
..	..	..	*3*	2	1	
..	..	..	..	..	..	
..	..	..	88	62	26	29
..	..	..	..	..	..	30
752	568	184	..	..	..	31
120	79	41	12,469	5,369	7,100	32
..	..	..	..	..	..	33
1,113,225	589,045	524,180	..	..	..	34
..	..	..	3,889,576	1,980,145	1,909,431	35
..	..	..	..	..		36
..	..	..	992	542	450	(c)
1	1	..	3,714	1,778	1,936	(d)

Table VI.—Part I—

Birthplace.	India.			Ajmer-Merwara.			Andaman and Islands	
	Persons.	Males.	Females.	Persons.	Males.	Females.	Persons.	Males.
1	2	3	4	5	6	7	8	9
B. Born in other Asiatic countries	**595,078**	**391,776**	**203,302**	**172**	**130**	**42**	**328**	**317**
Within British Dominions ..	**13,178**	**7,521**	**5,657**	**10**	**8**	**2**	**11**	**11**
37 British North Borneo ..	53	46	7	..	..	..	..	..
38 Ceylon	8,366	4,851	3,515	8	6	2	8	8
39 Cyprus	33	27	6	..	..	..	..	..
40 Hongkong	214	171	43	..	..	..	1	1
41 Labuan	25	19	6	..	..	..	..	..
42 Maldives	81	60	21	..	..	..	..	..
43 Palestine	211	100	111	..	..	..	..	..
44 Sarawak	4	3	1	..	..	..	..	..
45 Malaya	4,191	2,244	1,947	2	2	..	2	2
Outside British Dominions ..	**577,403**	**380,945**	**196,458**	**161**	**122**	**39**	**317**	**306**
46 Afghanistan	81,053	56,474	24,579	65	62	3	..	..
47 Arabia	23,613	18,182	5,431	20	10	10	..	..
48 Armenia	89	56	33	1	1	..	..	..
49 Bali	4	3	1	..	..	..	..	..
50 Bhutan	5,236	3,766	1,470	..	..	..	..	..
51 Bokhara	62	59	3	7	7	..	..	..
52 Celebes	1	1	..	..	..	..	..	..
53 China	120,745	88,903	31,842	6	5	1	179	168
54 Chinese Turkistan ..	58	57	1	..	..	..	..	..
55 French Indo-China ..	174	139	35	1	1	..	..	..
56 Iraq	386	231	155	2	2	..	..	..
57 Japan	2,334	1,812	522	..	..	..	135	135
58 Java	110	82	28	..	..	..	..	..
59 Mongolia	2	1	1	..	..	..	..	..
60 Nepal	327,028	200,817	126,211	49	27	22	3	3
61 Persia	2,821	1,772	1,049	8	5	3	..	..
62 Philippines	62	49	13	..	..	..	..	..
63 Russia in Asia	19	9	10	..	..	..	..	..
64 Russian Turkistan	61	31	30	2	2	..	..	..
65 Siam	9,663	5,959	3,704	..	..	..	..	..
66 Sumatra	27	18	9	..	..	..	..	..
67 Syria	86	78	8	..	..	..	..	..
68 Tibet	3,556	2,286	1,270	..	..	..	..	..
69 Turkey in Asia	213	160	53	..	..	..	..	..
70 **Asia Unspecified**	**4,497**	**3,310**	**1,187**	**1**	..	**1**	..	..
C. Born in Europe	**118,089**	**90,833**	**27,256**	**1,266**	**1,053**	**213**	**148**	**136**
Within British Dominions ..	**106,049**	**83,043**	**23,006**	**1,207**	**1,023**	**184**	**145**	**133**
71 United Kingdom	104,293	82,027	22,266	1,201	1,019	182	145	133
72 *England and Wales* ..	*84,513*	*66,588*	*17,925*	*1,105*	*959*	*146*	*131*	*121*
73 *Scotland*	*12,697*	*10,168*	*2,529*	*56*	*30*	*26*	*3*	*3*
74 *Northern Ireland*	*1,836*	*1,293*	*543*	..	..	..	..	..
75 *Channel Islands and Isle of Man.*	*655*	*330*	*325*	..	..	..	..	..
76 *United Kingdom Unspecified*	*1,375*	*1,100*	*275*	..	..	..	*5*	*4*
77 *Ireland Unspecified* ..	*3,217*	*2,548*	*669*	*40*	*30*	*10*	*6*	*5*
78 Irish Free State	1,320	680	640	..	..	..	..	..
79 Gibraltar	114	75	39	6	4	2	..	..
80 Malta	322	261	61	..	..	..	..	..
Outside British Dominions ..	**6,670**	**4,198**	**2,472**	**59**	**30**	**29**	**3**	**3**
81 Austria	87	54	33	..	..	..	..	..
82 Belgium	493	324	169	..	..	..	..	..
83 Bulgaria	10	5	5	..	..	..	..	..
84 Czechoslovakia	17	11	6	..	..	..	..	..
85 Denmark	154	74	80	1	..	1	..	..
86 Finland	11	1	10	..	..	..	..	..
87 France	1,498	774	724	40	18	22	..	..
88 Germany	1,048	632	416	3	2	1	1	1
89 Greece	118	88	30	..	..	..	..	..
90 Holland	289	230	59	..	..	..	..	..
91 Hungary	8	5	3	2	2	..	..	..
92 Iceland	11	2	9	..	..	..	..	..
93 **Italy**	902	622	280	1	1	..	..	..

Province or State

Birthplace—*continued.*

where enumerated.										
Nicobar.	Assam (*including Khasi States*).			Baluchistan. (*Districts and Administered Territories.*)			Bengal.			
Females. 10	Persons. 11	Males. 12	Females. 13	Persons. 14	Males. 15	Females. 16	Persons. 17	Males. 18	Females. 19	
11	90,561	60,748	29,813	19,199	12,875	6,324	112,049	69,572	42,477	B.
..	27	14	13	20	10	10	209	153	56	
..	..	..	..	..	..	..	2	2	..	37
..	12	8	4	12	3	9	104	71	33	38
..	..	..	..	..	..	..	1	1	..	39
..	1	1	..	3	3	..	41	29	12	40
..	..	..	..	..	..	..	..	..	..	41
..	..	..	..	..	..	..	..	..	..	42
..	..	..	..	..	..	..	..	..	..	43
..	..	..	..	..	..	..	..	..	..	44
..	14	5	9	5	4	1	61	50	11	45
11	90,533	60,733	29,800	19,179	12,865	6,814	111,826	69,405	42,421	
..	1,346	1,316	30	14,916	9,538	5,378	3,755	3,651	104	46
..	18	17	1	7	6	1	196	150	46	47
..	..	..	..	..	..	..	78	48	30	48
..	..	..	..	..	..	..	..	..	..	49
..	1,571	1,180	391	1	1	..	3,533	2,508	1,025	50
..	..	..	..	1	1	..	..	..	..	51
..	..	..	..	..	..	..	..	..	..	52
11	640	580	60	34	24	10	3,507	2,939	568	53
..	..	..	..	1	1	..	1	1	..	54
..	..	..	..	..	..	..	..	..	..	55
..	..	..	..	6	3	3	18	8	10	56
..	..	..	..	1	..	1	538	416	122	57
..	1	1	..	..	..	..	45	43	2	58
..	..	..	..	..	..	..	..	..	..	59
..	86,897	57,599	29,298	3,868	3,120	748	97,631	58,201	39,430	60
..	38	19	19	310	140	170	902	557	345	61
..	..	..	..	..	..	..	9	8	1	62
..	..	..	..	..	..	..	11	4	7	63
..	..	..	..	..	..	..	..	..	..	64
..	..	..	..	..	..	..	8	6	2	65
..	..	..	..	..	..	..	1	1	..	66
..	..	..	..	..	..	..	..	..	..	67
..	20	20	..	25	24	1	1,538	830	708	68
..	2	1	1	9	7	2	55	34	21	69
..	1	1	..	..	..	..	14	14	..	70
12	2,514	1,857	657	4,080	3,297	783	13,550	9,190	4,360	C.
12	2,327	1,715	612	4,058	3,285	773	12,220	8,235	3,985	
12	2,327	1,715	612	3,915	3,194	721	12,200	8,223	3,977	71
10	*1,423*	*1,010*	*413*	*2,923*	*2,309*	*614*	*8,948*	*5,910*	*3,038*	72
..	*760*	*605*	*155*	*913*	*833*	*80*	*2,554*	*1,895*	*659*	73
..	..	..	..	*79*	*52*	*27*	*11*	*8*	*3*	74
..	..	..	..	..	..	..	..	..	..	75
1	..	..	..	..	..	..	*36*	*6*	*30*	76
1	*144*	*100*	*44*	..	..	..	*651*	*404*	*247*	77
..	..	..	..	124	82	42	..	..	..	78
..	..	..	..	1	..	1	3	3	..	79
..	..	..	..	13	9	9	17	9	8	80
..	176	134	[illegible]	22	12	10	1,316	948	368	
..	1	1	..	..	..	..	30	23	7	81
..	..	..	..	..	..	..	124	95	29	82
..	..	..	..	..	..	..	4	..	4	83
..	..	..	..	..	..	..	4	2	2	84
..	4	2	2	2	1	1	25	23	2	85
..	..	..	..	..	..	..	..	..	..	86
..	35	19	16	7	3	4	203	93	110	87
..	6	3	3	4	1	3	164	115	49	88
..	..	..	..	..	..	..	43	38	5	89
..	7	5	2	..	..	..	129	121	8	90
..	..	..	..	..	..	..	2	1	1	91
..	..	..	..	..	..	..	10	1	9	92
..	95	84	11	2	1	1	277	226	51	93

Table VI.—Part I—

	Birthplace.	Province or State							
		Bihar and Orissa.			Bombay (*including Aden*).			Burma.	
	1	Persons. 20	Males. 21	Females. 22	Persons. 23	Males. 24	Females. 25	Persons. 26	Males. 27
B.	**Born in other Asiatic countries**	**37,994**	**13,316**	**24,678**	**38,460**	**29,790**	**8,670**	**150,514**	**109,755**
	Within British Dominions ..	**22**	**12**	**10**	**522**	**432**	**90**	**1,358**	**997**
37	British North Borneo ..	..	..	..	31	31	..	8	7
38	Ceylon	18	9	9	353	281	72	748	596
39	Cyprus	..	..	..	11	9	2	1	1
40	Hongkong	1	1	..	69	67	2	2	..
41	Labuan	..	..	..	9	9	..	..	..
42	Maldives	..	..	..	16	15	1	15	15
43	Palestine	1	1	..	5	4	1	4	3
44	Sarawak	..	..	..	..	..	..	..	..
45	Malaya	2	1	1	28	16	12	580	375
	Outside British Dominions ..	**37,969**	**13,301**	**24,668**	**33,965**	**26,412**	**7,553**	**149,151**	**108,757**
46	Afghanistan	1,362	1,329	33	10,416	8,027	2,389	132	129
47	Arabia	40	21	19	20,426	15,827	4,599	58	48
48	Armenia	..	..	..	..	..	..	5	3
49	Bali	..	..	..	..	..	..	..	..
50	Bhutan	32	24	8	..	..	..	2	2
51	Bokhara	..	..	..	..	..	..	..	..
52	Celebes	..	..	..	..	..	..	1	1
53	China	29	20	9	670	598	72	114,270	83,684
54	Chinese Turkistan ..	..	..	..	..	..	..	..	..
55	French Indo-China ..	..	..	..	..	..	..	168	136
56	Iraq	2	1	1	63	37	26	197	98
57	Japan	2	1	1	859	656	203	570	411
58	Java	2	1	1	21	14	7	14	10
59	Mongolia	2	1	1	..	..	..	..	..
60	Nepal	36,410	11,846	24,564	1,138	935	203	23,889	18,139
61	Persia	80	53	27	231	185	46	181	122
62	Philippines	..	..	..	..	..	..	37	35
63	Russia in Asia	..	..	..	..	..	..	..	..
64	Russian Turkistan	2	2	..	..	..	..	..	..
65	Siam	..	..	..	..	..	..	9,619	5,933
66	Sumatra	..	..	..	1	1	..	4	3
67	Syria	..	..	..	83	75	3	..	..
68	Tibet	4	2	2	57	57	..	3	3
69	Turkey in Asia	2	..	2	..	..	..	1	..
70	**Asia Unspecified**	3	3	..	3,973	2,946	1,027	5	1
	C. Born in Europe	**3,338**	**2,270**	**1,068**	**16,282**	**12,080**	**4,202**	**7,098**	**5,464**
	Within British Dominions ..	**3,029**	**2,120**	**909**	**11,328**	**8,345**	**2,983**	**6,440**	**4,975**
71	United Kingdom	2,960	2,083	877	11,008	8,067	2,941	6,187	4,831
72	*England and Wales* ..	*2,549*	*1,832*	*717*	*8,349*	*6,115*	*2,234*	*4,968*	*3,848*
73	*Scotland*	*310*	*191*	*119*	*1,105*	*834*	*271*	*1,156*	*936*
74	*Northern Ireland*	*101*	*60*	*41*	..	..	..	*62*	*46*
75	*Channel Islands and Isle of Man.*	..	..	..	*645*	*322*	*323*	*1*	*1*
76	*United Kingdom Unspecified*	..	..	..	..	..	..	..	..
77	*Ireland Unspecified* ..	..	..	..	*909*	*796*	*113*	..	..
78	Irish Free State	62	31	31	..	..	..	239	138
79	Gibraltar	1	1	..	85	57	28	..	..
80	Malta	6	5	1	235	221	14	14	6
	Outside British Dominions ..	**304**	**145**	**159**	**1,407**	**1,039**	**368**	**658**	**489**
81	Austria	8	2	6	16	11	5	4	2
82	Belgium	87	58	29	58	57	1	8	2
83	Bulgaria	..	..	..	5	4	1	..	..
84	Czechoslovakia	..	..	..	7	4	3	3	3
85	Denmark	24	5	19	8	1	7	13	11
86	Finland	..	..	..	..	..	..	..	..
87	France	19	6	13	230	150	80	135	80
88	Germany	61	15	46	352	255	97	97	89
89	Greece	8	3	5	..	..	..	29	23
90	Holland	10	10	..	29	22	7	51	45
91	Hungary	..	..	..	..	..	..	..	
92	Iceland	..	..	..	..	..	..	..	
93	Italy	9	4	5	23	22	1	127	75

Birthplace—*continued.*

where enumerated.

	Central Provinces and Berar.			Coorg.			Delhi.			
Females. 28	Persons. 29	Males. 30	Females. 31	Persons. 32	Males. 33	Females. 34	Persons. 35	Males. 36	Females. 37	
40,759	**1,608**	**1,303**	**305**	**13**	**9**	**4**	**789**	**603**	**186**	**B.**
361	**154**	**87**	**67**	**9**	**6**	**3**	**13**	**8**	**5**	
1	..	..	..	..	..	..	..	..	..	37
152	48	34	14	9	6	3	11	7	4	38
..	..	..	..	..	..	..	..	..	..	39
2	38	20	18	..	..	..	..	..	..	40
..	..	..	..	..	..	..	..	..	..	41
..	30	18	12	..	..	..	..	..	..	42
1	37	14	23	..	..	..	..	..	..	43
..	..	..	..	..	..	..	..	..	..	44
205	1	1	..	..	..	..	2	1	1	45
40,394	**1,337**	**1,116**	**221**	**3**	**3**	..	**707**	**535**	**172**	
3	810	750	60	2	2	..	184	154	30	46
10	16	15	1	..	..	..	16	12	4	47
2	..	..	..	..	..	..	..	..	..	48
..	..	..	..	..	..	..	..	..	..	49
..	..	..	..	..	..	..	1	1	..	50
..	..	..	..	..	..	..	..	..	..	51
..	..	..	..	..	..	..	..	..	..	52
30,586	31	26	5	1	1	..	29	21	8	53
..	..	..	..	..	..	..	..	..	..	54
32	..	..	..	..	..	..	..	..	..	55
99	2	2	..	..	..	..	2	2	..	56
159	12	7	5	..	..	..	2	2	..	57
4	..	..	..	..	..	..	..	..	..	58
..	..	..	..	..	..	..	..	..	..	59
5,750	427	289	138	..	..	..	427	315	112	60
59	33	23	10	..	..	..	18	7	11	61
2	..	..	..	..	..	..	..	..	..	62
..	2	..	2	..	..	..	..	..	..	63
..	..	..	..	..	..	..	..	..	..	64
3,686	2	2	..	..	..	..	..	..	..	65
1	..	..	..	..	..	..	..	..	..	66
..	..	..	..	..	..	..	..	..	..	67
..	..	..	..	..	..	..	26	19	7	68
1	2	2	..	..	..	..	2	2	..	69
4	**117**	**100**	**17**	**1**	..	**1**	**69**	**60**	**9**	70
1,634	**4,152**	**3,314**	**838**	**72**	**39**	**33**	**3,136**	**2,404**	**732**	**C.**
1,465	**3,986**	**3,227**	**759**	**66**	**37**	**29**	**3,107**	**2,385**	**722**	
1,356	3,983	3,226	757	64	36	28	3,063	2,357	706	71
1,120	*2,450*	*1,986*	*464*	*47*	*27*	*20*	*2,866*	*2,219*	*647*	72
220	*111*	*70*	*41*	*17*	*9*	*8*	*154*	*106*	*48*	73
16	..	..	..	..	..	..	*43*	*32*	*11*	74
..	..	..	..	..	..	..	..	..	..	75
..	*1,248*	*1,033*	*215*	..	..	..	..	..	..	76
..	*174*	*137*	*37*	..	..	..	..	..	..	77
101	..	..	..	2	1	1	44	28	16	78
..	..	..	..	..	..	..	..	..	..	79
8	3	1	2	..	..	..	..	..	..	80
169	**90**	**37**	**53**	**6**	**2**	**4**	**22**	**14**	**8**	
2	..	..	..	..	..	..	..	..	..	81
6	2	..	2	..	..	..	..	..	..	82
..	..	..	..	..	..	..	..	..	..	83
..	1	1	..	..	..	..	..	..	..	84
2	2	..	2	..	..	..	..	..	..	85
..	..	..	..	..	..	..	..	..	..	86
55	23	10	13	6	2	4	..	..	..	87
8	14	6	8	..	..	..	3	1	2	88
6	4	4	..	..	..	..	..	..	..	89
6	5	4	1	..	..	..	..	..	..	90
..	1	..	1	..	..	..	..	..	..	91
..	..	..	..	..	..	..	..	..	..	92
52	4	1	3	..	..	..	14	9	5	

Table VI.—Part I—

Province or State

	Birthplace.	Madras.			North-West Frontier Province. (*Districts and Administered Territories.*)			
	1	Persons. 38	Males. 39	Females. 40	Persons. 41	Males. 42	Females. 43	Persons. 44
B.	**Born in other Asiatic countries**	**9,274**	**5,145**	**4,129**	**32,601**	**20,043**	**12,558**	**21,261**
	Within British Dominions ..	**8,370**	**4,460**	**3,910**	**21**	**17**	**4**	**184**
37	British North Borneo ..	12	6	6	..	..	..	..
38	Ceylon	5,197	2,824	2,373	4	..	4	51
39	Cyprus	20	16	4	..	..	..	..
40	Hongkong	29	27	2	15	15	..	11
41	Labuan	16	10	6	..	..	..	..
42	Maldives	20	12	8	..	..	..	..
43	Palestine	144	68	76	2	2	..	..
44	Sarawak	4	3	1	..	..	..	..
45	Malaya	2,928	1,494	1,434	..	..	..	122
	Outside British Dominions ..	**822**	**648**	**174**	**32,573**	**20,026**	**12,547**	**21,073**
46	Afghanistan	305	222	83	27,855	16,221	11,634	13,385
47	Arabia	47	40	7	26	20	6	369
48	Armenia	..	..	..	..	..	..	..
49	Bali	..	..	..	..	..	..	..
50	Bhutan	..	..	..	..	..	..	20
51	Bokhara	..	..	..	53	50	3	..
52	Celebes	..	..	..	..	..	..	..
53	China	95	68	27	21	13	8	830
54	Chinese Turkistan ..	..	..	..	..	..	..	..
55	French Indo-China ..	2	2	..	..	..	..	1
56	Iraq	30	29	1	..	..	..	36
57	Japan	90	85	5	2	1	1	17
58	Java	1	1	..	..	..	..	14
59	Mongolia	..	..	..	..	..	..	..
60	Nepal	216	181	35	4,540	3,686	854	5,216
61	Persia	26	14	12	19	9	10	432
62	Phillppines	..	..	..	..	..	..	1
63	Russia in Asia	..	..	..	..	..	..	2
64	Russian Turkistan	..	..	..	54	25	29	3
65	Siam	8	4	4	..	..	..	4
66	Sumatra	..	..	..	..	..	..	14
67	Syria	..	..	..	..	..	..	1
68	Tibet	..	..	..	..	..	..	620
69	Turkey in Asia	2	2	..	3	1	2	108
70	**Asia Unspecified ..**	**82**	**37**	**45**	**7**	..	**7**	**4**
	C. Born in Europe ..	**7,517**	**5,044**	**2,473**	**6,841**	**5,772**	**1,069**	**16,832**
	Within British Dominions ..	**6,302**	**4,400**	**1,902**	**6,628**	**5,697**	**931**	**15,450**
71	United Kingdom	5,701	4,168	1,533	6,628	5,697	931	15,407
72	*England and Wales* ..	*4,975*	*3,707*	*1,268*	*6,119*	*5,294*	*825*	*14,317*
73	*Scotland*	*583*	*394*	*189*	*271*	*222*	*49*	*541*
74	*Northern Ireland*	*143*	*67*	*76*	..	..	..	*549*
75	*Channel Islands and Isle of Man.*	..	..	..	..	..	..	..
76	*United Kingdom Unspecified*	..	..	..	..	..	..	..
77	*Ireland Unspecified* ..	..	..	..	*238*	*181*	*57*	..
78	Irish Free State	590	228	362	..	..	..	35
79	Gibraltar	5	4	1	..	..	..	4
80	Malta	6	..	6	..	..	..	4
	Outside British Dominions ..	**1,115**	**606**	**509**	**71**	**21**	**50**	**175**
81	Austria	11	3	8	..	..	..	1
82	Belgium	43	12	31	3	2	1	45
83	Bulgaria	1	1	..	..	..	..	..
84	Czechoslovakia ..	..	..	..	..	..	..	..
85	Denmark	39	17	22	7	..	7	1
86	Finland	8	..	8	..	..	..	..
87	France	464	264	200	13	5	8	30
88	Germany	118	67	51	22	4	18	36
89	Greece	4	4	..	1	..	1	1
90	Holland	44	17	27	1	..	1	2
91	Hungary	3	2	1	..	..	..	..
92	Iceland	..	..	..	..	..	..	..
93	Italy	159	79	80	3	3	..	2

Birthplace—*continued.*

where enumerated.

Punjab.		United Provinces of Agra and Oudh.			Assam State (*Manipur*).			
Males. 45	Females. 46	Persons. 47	Males. 48	Females. 49	Persons. 50	Males. 51	Females. 52	
15,710	**5,551**	**45,883**	**29,355**	**16,528**	**1,411**	**1,002**	**409**	**B**
98	**86**	**106**	**48**	**58**	**1**	**1**	..	
..	..	..	..	..	..	..	..	37
38	13	74	36	38	..	..	..	38
..	..	..	..	..	..	..	..	39
5	6	..	..	..	..	..	..	40
..	..	..	..	..	..	..	..	41
..	..	..	..	..	..	..	..	42
..	..	14	5	9	..	..	..	43
..	..	..	..	.	..	..	..	44
55	67	18	7	11	1	1	..	45
15,611	**5,462**	**45,773**	**29,305**	**16,468**	**1,410**	**1,001**	**409**	
9,907	3,478	1,375	1,281	94	..	..	..	46
288	81	153	81	72	..	..	..	47
..	..	..	..	..	..	..	..	48
..	..	..	..	..	..	..	..	49
10	10	30	15	15	..	..	..	50
..	..	..	..	..	..	..	..	51
..	..	..	..	..	..	..	..	52
480	350	112	71	41	..	..	..	53
..	..	..	..	..	..	..	..	54
..	1	..	..	..	..	..	..	55
30	6	..	..	..	..	..	..	56
16	1	29	17	12	1	..	1	57
7	7	11	4	7	..	..	..	58
..	..	..	..	..	..	..	..	59
3,919	1,297	43,387	27,373	16,014	1,409	1,001	408	60
294	138	88	71	17	..	..	..	61
1	..	4	1	3	..	..	..	62
1	1	3	3	..	..	..	..	63
2	1	..	..	..	..	..	..	64
2	2	11	6	5	..	..	..	65
11	3	5	1	4	..	..	..	66
1	..	2	2	..	..	..	..	67
551	69	553	371	182	..	..	..	68
91	17	10	8	2	..	..	..	69
1	3	4	2	2	..	..	..	70
13,022	**3,810**	**17,934**	**14,928**	**3,006**	**14**	**7**	**7**	**C**
12,370	**3,080**	**17,575**	**14,772**	**2,803**	**14**	**7**	**7**	
12,341	3,066	17,436	14,672	2,764	14	7	7	71
11,637	*2,680*	*13,027*	*10,794*	*2,233*	*12*	*6*	*6*	72
334	*207*	*2,795*	*2,528*	*267*	*2*	*1*	*1*	73
370	*179*	*815*	*639*	*176*	..	..	..	74
..	..	*8*	*7*	*1*	..	..	..	75
..	..	*32*	*21*	*11*	..	..	..	76
..	..	*759*	*683*	*76*	..	..	..	77
27	8	120	88	32	..	..	..	78
..	4	7	5	2	..	..	..	79
2	2	12	7	5	..	..	..	80
105	**70**	**352**	**151**	**201**	..	..	..	
1	..	5	3	2	..	..	..	81
24	21	9	3	6	..	..	..	82
..	..	..	..	..	..	..	..	83
..	..	..	..	..	..	..	..	84
1	..	3	1	2	..	..	..	85
..	..	..	..	..	..	..	..	86
10	20	67	34	33	..	..	..	87
19	17	92	25	67	..	..	..	88
1	..	6	..	6	..	..	..	89
..	2	10	5	5	..	..	..	90
..	..	..	..	..	..	..	..	91
..	..	..	..	..	..	..	..	92
2	..	63	39	24	..	..	..	93

Table VI.—Part I—

Birthplace.	Province or State						
	Baluchistan States.			Baroda State.			
	Persons.	Males.	Females.	Persons.	Males.	Females.	Persons.
1	53	54	55	56	57	58	59
B. Born in other Asiatic countries	145	84	61	460	381	79	1,082
Within British Dominions ..	—	—	—	6	5	1	..
37 British North Borneo ..	..	..	..	..	..	..	..
38 Ceylon	..	..	..	6	5	1	..
39 Cyprus	..	..	..	..	..	..	..
40 Hongkong	..	..	..	..	..	..	..
41 Labuan	..	..	..	..	..	..	..
42 Maldives	..	..	..	..	..	..	..
43 Palestine	..	..	..	..	..	..	..
44 Sarawak	..	..	..	..	..	..	..
45 Malaya	..	..	..	..	..	..	..
Outside British Dominions ..	145	84	61	454	376	78	1,082
46 Afghanistan	37	34	3	122	111	11	82
47 Arabia	..	..	..	28	20	8	2
48 Armenia	..	..	..	..	..	..	..
49 Bali	..	..	..	..	..	..	..
50 Bhutan	..	..	..	..	..	..	4
51 Bokhara	..	..	..	..	..	..	..
52 Celebes	..	..	..	..	..	..	..
53 China	..	..	..	3	1	2	..
54 Chinese Turkistan ..	..	..	..	..	..	..	..
55 French Indo-China ..	..	..	..	..	..	..	..
56 Iraq	..	..	..	..	..	..	1
57 Japan	..	..	..	44	40	4	..
58 Java	1	1	..	..	..	..	..
59 Mongolia	..	..	..	..	..	..	..
60 Nepal	..	..	..	239	190	49	989
61 Persia	107	49	58	6	5	1	..
62 Philippines	..	..	..	..	..	..	..
63 Russia in Asia	..	..	..	1	1	..	..
64 Russian Turkistan	..	..	..	..	..	..	..
65 Siam	..	..	..	6	3	3	4
66 Sumatra	..	..	..	..	..	..	..
67 Syria	..	..	..	..	..	..	..
68 Tibet	..	..	..	..	..	..	..
69 Turkey in Asia	..	..	..	5	5	..	..
70 **Asia Unspecified**	..	..	..	..	..	..	..
C. Born in Europe	2	1	1	88	64	24	7
Within British Dominions ..	2	1	1	75	58	17	3
71 United Kingdom	2	1	1	72	55	17	3
72 *England and Wales*	*1*	*1*	..	*49*	*34*	*15*	..
73 *Scotland*	..	..	..	*23*	*21*	*2*	*2*
74 *Northern Ireland*	*1*	..	*1*	..	..	..	..
75 *Channel Islands and Isle of Man.*	..	..	..	..	..	..	..
76 *United Kingdom Unspecified*	..	..	..	..	..	..	..
77 *Ireland Unspecified* ..	..	..	..	..	..	..	*1*
78 Irish Free State	..	..	..	3	3	..	..
79 Gibraltar	..	..	..	..	..	..	..
80 Malta	..	..	..	..	..	..	..
Outside British Dominions ..	..	..	..	13	6	7	4
81 Austria	..	..	..	..	..	..	..
82 Belgium	..	..	..	..	..	..	..
83 Bulgaria	..	..	..	..	..	..	..
84 Czechoslovakia ..	..	..	..	..	..	..	..
85 Denmark	..	..	..	..	..	..	..
86 Finland	..	..	..	..	..	..	..
87 France	..	..	..	11	5	6	..
88 Germany	..	..	..	..	..	..	..
89 Greece	..	..	..	..	..	..	..
90 Holland	..	..	..	..	..	..	..
91 Hungary	..	..	..	..	..	..	..
92 Iceland	..	..	..	..	..	..	..
93 Italy	..	..	..	1	1	..	..

Birthplace—*continued.*

where enumerated.

	Bengal States.		Bihar and Orissa States.			Bombay States.		
	Males.	Females.	Persons.	Males.	Females.	Persons.	Males.	Females.
	60	61	62	63	64	65	66	67
B	**744**	**338**	**248**	**199**	**49**	**689**	**609**	**80**
	..	..	**2**	**2**	..	**8**	**8**	..
37	..	..	..	..	..	..	..	..
38	..	..	2	2	..	7	7	..
39	..	..	..	..	..	..	..	..
40	..	..	..	..	..	..	..	..
41	..	..	..	..	..	..	..	..
42	..	..	..	..	..	..	..	..
43	..	..	..	..	..	..	..	..
44	..	..	..	..	..	..	..	..
45	..	..	..	..	..	1	1	..
	744	**338**	**246**	**197**	**49**	**646**	**585**	**61**
46	79	3	61	56	5	346	303	43
47	1	1	1	1	..	39	38	1
48	..	..	..	..	..	..	..	..
49	..	..	..	..	..	..	..	..
50	4	..	4	2	2	..	..	..
51	..	..	..	..	..	..	..	..
52	..	..	..	..	..	..	..	..
53	..	..	1	..	1	48	48	..
54	..	..	..	..	..	..	..	..
55	..	..	..	..	..	..	..	..
56	1	..	..	..	..	..	..	..
57	..	..	..	..	..	10	10	..
58	..	..	..	..	..	..	..	..
59	..	..	..	..	..	..	..	..
60	657	332	176	135	41	185	170	15
61	..	..	3	3	..	18	16	2
62	..	..	..	..	..	..	..	..
63	..	..	..	..	..	..	..	..
64	..	..	..	..	..	..	..	..
65	2	2	..	..	..	..	..	..
66	..	..	..	..	..	..	..	..
67	..	..	..	..	..	..	..	..
68	..	..	..	..	..	..	..	..
69	..	..	..	..	..	..	..	..
70	..	..	..	..	..	35	16	19
C	**4**	**3**	**75**	**50**	**25**	**63**	**30**	**33**
	2	**1**	**48**	**29**	**19**	**53**	**24**	**29**
71	2	1	47	29	18	53	24	29
72	..	..	*40*	*24*	*16*	*47*	*21*	*26*
73	*2*	..	*5*	*4*	*1*	*5*	*2*	*3*
74	..	..	*2*	*1*	*1*	..	..	..
75	..	..	..	..	..	..	..	..
76	..	..	..	..	..	..	..	..
77	..	*1*	..	..	..	*1*	*1*	..
78	..	..	1	..	1	..	..	..
79	..	..	..	..	..	..	..	..
80	..	..	..	..	..	..	..	..
	2	**2**	**27**	**21**	**6**	**6**	**4**	**2**
81	..	..	..	..	..	..	..	..
82	..	..	23	19	4	..	..	..
83	..	..	..	..	..	..	..	..
84	..	..	..	..	..	..	..	..
85	..	..	..	..	..	..	..	..
86	..	..	..	..	..	..	..	..
87	..	..	..	..	..	2	2	..
88	..	..	3	1	2	3	2	1
89	..	..	..	..	..	..	..	..
90	..	..	..	..	..	..	..	..
91	..	..	..	..	..	..	..	..
92	..	..	..	..	..	..	..	..
93	..	..	..	..	..	..	..	..

Table VI.—Part I—

Province or State

Birthplace.	Central India Agency.			Central Provinces States.			
	Persons.	Males.	Females.	Persons.	Males.	Females.	Persons.
1	68	69	70	71	72	73	74
B. Born in other Asiatic countries	**585**	**459**	**126**	**297**	**103**	**194**	**124**
Within British Dominions	**20**	**10**	**10**	**4**	**2**	**2**	**110**
37 British North Borneo ..	..	..	..	..	..	..	..
38 Ceylon	19	10	9	4	2	2	62
39 Cyprus	..	..	..	..	..	..	..
40 Hongkong	..	..	..	..	..	..	..
41 Labuan	..	..	..	..	..	..	..
42 Maldives	..	..	..	..	..	..	..
43 Palestine	..	..	..	..	..	..	..
44 Sarawak ..	..	..	..	..	..	..	..
45 Malaya	1	..	1	..	..	..	48
Outside British Dominions ..	**560**	**447**	**113**	**293**	**101**	**192**	**14**
46 Afghanistan	216	170	37	24	23	1	3
47 Arabia	28	20	8	..	..	..	2
48 Armenia	..	..	..	..	..	..	..
49 Bali	..	..	..	..	..	..	..
50 Bhutan	..	..	..	..	..	..	..
51 Bokhara	..	..	..	..	..	..	..
52 Celebes	..	..	..	..	..	..	..
53 China	36	29	7	..	..	..	2
54 Chinese Turkistan ..	..	..	..	..	..	..	..
55 French Indo-China ..	..	..	..	..	..	..	..
56 Iraq	3		..	..	..	..	..
57 Japan	..	..	..	6	4	2	1
58 Java	..	..	..	..	..	..	..
59 Mongolia	..	..	..	.	..	..	..
60 Nepal	266	210	56	56	71	185	2
61 Persia	10	5	5	7	3	4	2
62 Philippines	..	..	..	..	..	..	..
63 Russia in Asia	..	..	..	..	..	..	..
64 Russian Turkistan ..	..	..	..	..	..	..	..
65 Siam	1	1	..	..	..	..	..
66 Sumatra	..	..	..	..	..	..	2
67 Syria	..	..	..	..	..	..	..
68 Tibet	..	..	..	..	..	..	..
69 Turkey in Asia	..	..	..	..	..	..	..
70 Asia Unspecified	5	2	3	..	..	..	
C. Born in Europe	**1,960**	**1,593**	**367**	54	39	15	68
Within British Dominions ..	**1,898**	**1,577**	**321**	38	27	11	38
71 United Kingdom	1,895	1,577	318	38	27	11	38
72 *England and Wales* ..	*1,785*	*1,509*	*276*	*1*		*1*	*23*
73 *Scotland*	*54*	*38*	*16*	..	..	..	*13*
74 *Northern Ireland*	*4*	*3*	*1*	..	..	..	*2*
75 *Channel Islands and Isle of Man.*	..	..	..	..	..	..	..
76 *United Kingdom Unspecified*	..	..	..	*37*	*27*	*10*	..
77 *Ireland Unspecified* ..	*52*	*27*	*25*	..	..	..	..
78 Irish Free State	..	..	..	..	..	..	..
79 Gibraltar	..	..	..	..	..	..	..
80 Malta	3	..	3	..	..	..	..
Outside British Dominions ..	**54**	**14**	**40**	**14**	**11**	3	30
81 Austria	..	..	..	..	..	..	—
82 Belgium	..	..	..	9	9	..	3
83 Bulgaria	..	..	..	..	..	..	..
84 Czechoslovakia	..	..	..	.	..	..	..
85 Denmark	..	..	..	..	..	..	..
86 Finland		..	..	..	..	..	..
87 France	40	8	32	5	2	3	..
88 Germany	8	3	5	..	..	..	2
89 Greece	..	..	..	..	..	..	2
90 Holland	1	1	..	..	..	..	..
91 Hungary	..	..	..	..	..	..	..
92 Iceland	..	..	..	..	..	..	..
93 Italy	..	..	..	..	..	..	9

Birthplace—*continued.*

where enumerated.

Cochin State. Males. 75	Cochin State. Females. 76	Gwalior State. Persons. 77	Gwalior State. Males. 78	Gwalior State. Females. 79	Hyderabad State. Persons. 80	Hyderabad State. Males. 81	Hyderabad State. Females. 82	
65	**59**	**124**	**99**	**25**	**2,258**	**1,659**	599	B
55	**55**	**3**	**2**	**1**	**15**	**14**	**1**	
..	..	..	..	..	..	..	..	37
31	31	2	1	1	11	10	1	38
..	..	..	..	..	..	..	..	39
..	..	..	..	..	..	..	..	40
..	..	..	..	..	..	..	..	41
..	..	..	..	..	..	..	..	42
..	..	..	..	..	2	2	..	43
..	..	..	..	..	..	..	..	44
24	24	1	1	..	2	2	..	45
10	**4**	**119**	**96**	**23**	**2,235**	**1,637**	598	
3	..	52	43	9	181	154	27	46
1	1	4	3	1	1,831	1,355	476	47
..	..	..	..	..	5	4	1	48
..	..	..	..	..	4	3	1	49
..	..	..	..	..	..	..	..	50
..	..	..	..	..	..	..	..	51
..	..	..	..	..	..	..	..	52
1	1	..	..	..	13	5	8	53
..	..	..	..	..	..	..	..	54
..	..	..	..	..	..	..	..	55
..	..	..	..	..	1	1	..	56
1	..	..	..	..	12	8	4	57
..	..	..	..	..	..	..	..	58
..	..	..	..	..	..	..	..	59
1	1	56	44	12	14	8	6	60
2	..	3	3	..	172	97	75	61
..	..	..	..	..	..	..	..	62
..	..	..	..	..	..	..	..	63
..	..	..	..	..	..	..	..	64
..	..	..	..	..	..	..	..	65
1	1	..	..	..	..	..	..	66
..	..	..	..	..	..	..	..	67
..	..	1	1	..	..	..	..	68
..	..	3	2	1	2	2	..	69
..	..	2	1	1	8	8	..	70
37	**31**	**56**	**37**	**19**	**2,548**	**2,234**	**314**	C
22	**16**	**48**	**34**	**14**	**2,088**	**1,944**	**144**	
22	16	43	31	12	2,086	1,942	144	71
13	*10*	*36*	*27*	*9*	*2,052*	*1,921*	*131*	72
8	*5*	*7*	*4*	*3*	*30*	*17*	*13*	73
1	*1*	..	..	..	..	..	..	74
..	..	..	..	..	..	..	..	75
..	..	..	..	..	..	..	..	76
..	..	..	..	..	*4*	*4*	..	77
..	..	5	3	2	..	..	..	78
..	..	..	..	..	1	1	..	79
..	..	..	..	..	1	1	..	80
15	**15**	**8**	**3**	**5**	**237**	**131**	106	
..	..	..	..	..	4	3	1	81
..	3	3	1	2	2	1	1	82
..	..	..	..	..	..	..	..	83
..	..	..	..	..	..	..	..	84
..	..	1	..	1	7	5	2	85
..	..	..	..	..	..	..	..	86
..	..	..	..	..	30	13	17	87
..	2	1	..	1	3	2	1	88
2	..	..	..	..	10	4	6	89
..	..	..	..	..	..	..	..	90
..	..	..	..	..	..	..	..	91
..	..	..	..	..	..	..	..	92
..	9	1	1	..	42	23	19	93

Table VI.—Part I—

	Birthplace	Province or State — Jammu and Kashmir State. Persons.	Males.	Females.	Madras States. (*excluding Cochin and Travancore*). Persons.	Males.	Females.
	1	83	84	85	86	87	88
	B. Born in other Asiatic countries	**2,786**	**1,961**	**825**	**1,077**	**561**	**516**
	Within British Dominions ..	**6**	**5**	**1**	**1,074**	**560**	**514**
37	British North Borneo ..	..	..	..	..	..	..
38	Ceylon	5	4	1	910	489	421
39	Cyprus	..	..	..	..	..	..
40	Hongkong	..	..	..	..	..	..
41	Labuan	..	..	..	..	..	..
42	Maldives	..	..	..	..	..	..
43	Palestine	..	..	..	..	..	..
44	Sarawak	..	..	..	..	..	..
45	Malaya	1	1	..	164	71	93
	Outside British Dominions ..	**2,768**	**1,944**	**824**	**2**	**1**	**1**
46	Afghanistan	1,607	1,026	581	1	1	..
47	Arabia	5	4	1	..	..	..
48	Armenia	..	..	..	..	..	..
49	Bali	..	..	..	..	..	..
50	Bhotan	..	..	..	..	..	..
51	Bokhara	1	1	..	..	..	..
52	Celebes	..	..	..	..	..	..
53	China	5	1	4	..	..	..
54	Chinese Turkistan ..	56	55	1	..	..	..
55	French Indo-China ..	..	..	..	..	..	..
56	Iraq	5	2	3	..	..	..
57	Japan	..	..	..	..	..	..
58	Java	..	..	..	..	..	..
59	Mongolia	..	..	..	..	..	..
60	Nepal	974	765	209	1	..	1
61	Persia	21	13	8	..	..	..
62	Philippines	..	..	..	..	..	..
63	Russia in Asia	..	..	..	..	..	..
64	Russian Turkistan	..	..	..	..	..	..
65	Siam	..	..	..	..	..	..
66	Sumatra	..	..	..	..	..	..
67	Syria	..	..	..	..	..	..
68	Tibet	93	76	17	..	..	..
69	Turkey in Asia	1	1	..	..	..	..
70	**Asia Unspecified**	12	12	..	1	..	1
	C. Born in Europe	**183**	**84**	**99**	**8**	**5**	**3**
	Within British Dominions ..	**147**	**64**	**83**	**6**	**4**	**2**
71	United Kingdom	146	64	82	4	2	2
72	*England and Wales* ..	*108*	*47*	*61*	*4*	*2*	*2*
73	*Scotland*	*22*	*9*	*13*	..	..	..
74	*Northern Ireland*	..	..	..	..	..	..
75	*Channel Island and Isle of Man.*	..	..	..	..	..	..
76	*United Kingdom Unspecified*	*3*	*2*	*6*	..	..	..
77	*Ireland Unspecified* ..	*8*	*6*	*2*	..	..	..
78	Irish Free State	..	..	..	2	2	..
79	Gibraltar	..	..	..	..	..	..
80	Malta	1	..	1	..	..	..
	Outside British Dominions ..	**29**	**13**	**16**	**2**	**1**	**1**
81	Austria	1	..	1	..	..	..
82	Belgium	..	..	..	..	..	..
83	Bulgaria	..	..	..	..	..	..
84	Czechoslovakia	1	1	..	..	..	..
85	Denmark	3	2	1	2	1	1
86	Finland	..	..	..	..	..	..
87	France	2	1	1	..	..	..
88	Germany	4	2	2	..	..	..
89	Greece	1	1	..	..	..	..
90	Holland	..	..	..	..	..	..
91	Hungary	..	..	..	..	..	..
92	Iceland	..	..	..	..	..	..
93	Italy	7	2	5	..	..	..

Birthplace—*continued.*

where enumerated.

Mysore State. Persons. 89	Mysore State. Males. 90	Mysore State. Females. 91	North-West Frontier Province (*Agencies and Tribal Areas.*) Persons. 92	Males. 93	Females. 94	Punjab States (*including Punjab States Agency*). Persons. 95	Males. 96	Females. 97	
468	**278**	**190**	**4,011**	**3,876**	**135**	**3,655**	**2,812**	**843**	**B**
235	**118**	**117**	**3**	**3**	..	**21**	**18**	**3**	
..	..	..	..	..	..	..	..	..	37
200	102	98	1	1	..	2	1	1	38
..	..	..	..	..	..	..	..	..	39
..	..	..	1	1	..	2	1	1	40
..	..	..	..	..	..	..	..	..	41
..	..	..	..	..	..	..	..	..	42
1	1	..	..	..	..	..	..	..	43
..	..	..	..	..	..	..	..	..	44
34	15	19	1	1	..	17	16	1	45
215	**146**	**69**	**3,986**	**3,851**	**135**	**3,592**	**2,785**	**807**	
78	70	8	469	337	132	1,469	1,113	356	46
40	16	24	..	..	..	3	1	2	47
..	..	..	..	..	..	..	..	..	48
..	..	..	..	..	..	..	..	..	49
..	..	..	..	..	..	..	..	..	50
..	..	..	..	..	..	..	..	..	51
..	..	..	..	..	..	..	..	..	52
25	21	4	2	2	..	133	79	54	53
..	..	..	..	..	..	..	..	..	54
2	..	2	..	..	..	..	..	..	55
5	4	1	..	..	..	13	8	5	56
3	2	1	..	..	..	..	..	..	57
..	..	..	..	..	..	..	..	..	58
..	..	..	..	..	..	..	..	..	59
25	18	7	3,511	3,511	..	1,706	1,445	261	60
28	11	17	4	1	3	9	7	2	61
8	3	5	..	..	..	..	..	..	62
..	..	..	..	..	..	..	..	..	63
..	..	..	..	..	..	..	..	..	64
..	..	..	..	..	..	..	..	..	65
..	..	..	..	..	..	..	..	..	66
..	..	..	..	..	..	..	..	..	67
..	..	..	..	..	..	258	131	127	68
1	1	..	..	..	..	1	1	..	69
18	**14**	**4**	**22**	**22**	..	**42**	**9**	**33**	70
3,162	**2,241**	**921**	**3,717**	**3,713**	**4**	**157**	**88**	**69**	**C**
2,905	**2,110**	**795**	**3,708**	**3,704**	**4**	**139**	**80**	**59**	
2,810	2,061	749	3,708	3,704	4	139	80	59	71
2,550	*1,914*	*636*	*2,762*	*2,759*	*3*	*113*	*68*	*45*	72
141	*75*	*66*	*863*	*863*	..	*9*	*5*	*4*	73
..	..	..	..	..	..	*14*	*6*	*8*	74
1	..	*1*	..	..	..	..	..	..	75
6	*6*	..	..	..	..	*3*	*1*	*2*	76
112	*66*	*46*	*83*	*8'*	*1*	..	..	..	77
93	49	44	..	..	..	..	..	..	78
..	..	..	..	..	..	..	..	..	79
2	..	2	..	..	..	..	..	..	80
253	**128**	**125**	**7**	**7**	..	**18**	**8**	**10**	
5	4	1	..	..	..	..	..	..	81
37	25	12	..	..	..	..	..	..	82
..	..	..	..	..	..	..	..	..	83
..	..	..	..	..	..	..	..	..	84
6	2	4	..	..	..	..	..	..	85
..	..	..	..	..	..	..	..	..	86
106	32	74	2	2	..	4	..	4	87
30	8	22	1	1	..	2	2	..	88
..	..	..	4	4	..	..	..	..	89
..	..	..	..	..	..	..	..	..	90
..	..	..	..	..	..	..	..	..	91
..	..	..	..	..	..	..	..	..	92
49	44	5	..	..	..	3	..	3	93

Table VI.—Part I—

	Birthplace.	Province or State					
		Rajputana Agency.			Sikkim State.		
		Persons.	Males.	Females.	Persons.	Males.	Females.
	1	98	99	100	101	102	103
	B. Born in other Asiatic countries	**524**	**391**	**133**	**12,980**	**6,792**	**6,188**
	Within British Dominions ..	**3**	**2**	**1**	..	..	..
37	British North Borneo ..	..	..	..	..	..	..
38	Ceylon	3	2	1	..	..	..
39	Cyprus	..	..	..	..	..	..
40	Hongkong	..	..	..	..	..	..
41	Labuan	..	..	..	..	..	..
42	Maldives	..	..	..	..	..	..
43	Palestine	..	..	..	..	..	..
44	Sarawak	..	..	..	..	..	..
45	Malaya	..	..	..	..	..	..
	Outside British Dominions ..	**521**	**389**	**132**	**12,980**	**6,792**	**6,188**
46	Afghanistan	260	233	27	1	1	..
47	Arabia	15	11	4	..	..	..
48	Armenia	..	..	..	..	..	..
49	Bali	..	..	..	..	..	..
50	Bhutan	1	1	..	37	18	19
51	Bokhara	..	..	..	..	..	..
52	Celebes	..	..	..	..	..	..
53	China	2	1	1	15	11	4
54	Chinese Turkistan .	..	..	..	..	..	..
55	French Indo-China ..	..	..	..	..	..	..
56	Iraq	..	..	..	..	..	..
57	Japan	..	..	..	..	..	..
58	Java	..	..	..	..	..	..
59	Mongolia	..	..	..	..	..	..
60	Nepal	230	139	91	12,571	6,563	6,008
61	Persia	6	3	3	..	..	..
62	Philippines	3	1	2	..	..	..
63	Russia in Asia	..	..	..	..	..	..
64	Russian Turkistan	..	..	..	..	..	..
65	Siam	..	..	..	..	..	..
66	Sumatra	..	..	..	..	..	..
67	Syria	..	..	..	..	..	..
68	Tibet	..	..	..	356	199	157
69	Turkey in Asia	4	..	4	..	..	..
70	**Asia Unspecified**	..	..	..	..	..	..
	C. Born in Europe	**440**	**276**	**164**	**5**	**2**	**3**
	Within British Dominions ..	**406**	**257**	**149**	**3**	**2**	**1**
71	United Kingdom	405	257	148	3	2	1
72	*England and Wales* ..	*298*	*186*	*112*	*2*	*1*	*1*
73	*Scotland*	*78*	*48*	*30*	..	..	..
74	*Northern Ireland*	..	..	..	..	..	..
75	*Channel Islands and Isle of Man*	..	..	..	..	..	..
76	*United Kingdom Unspecified*	..	..	..	..	..	..
77	*Ireland Unspecified* ..	*29*	*23*	*6*	*1*	*1*	..
78	Irish Free State	..	..	..	..	..	..
79	Gibraltar	1	..	1	..	..	..
80	Malta	..	..	..	..	..	..
	Outside British Dominions ..	**34**	**19**	**15**	**2**	..	**2**
81	Austria	..	..	..	..	..	..
82	Belgium	1	..	1	..	..	..
83	Bulgaria	..	..	..	..	..	..
84	Czechoslovakia	..	..	..	..	..	..
85	Denmark	5	1	4	..	..	..
86	Finland	..	..	..	1	..	1
87	France	10	5	5	1	..	1
88	Germany	5	5	..	..	..	..
89	Greece	..	..	..	..	..	..
90	Holland	..	..	..	..	..	..
91	Hungary	..	..	..	..	..	..
92	Iceland	..	..	..	..	..	..
93	Italy	4	2	2	..	..	..

Birthplace—*continued.*

where enumerated.									
Travancore State.			United Provinces States.			Western India States Agency.			
Persons.	Males.	Females.	Persons.	Males.	Females.	Persons.	Males.	Females.	
104	105	106	107	108	109	110	111	112	
676	**411**	**265**	**126**	**76**	**50**	**646**	**543**	**103**	**B**
600	**338**	**262**	..	..	..	**31**	**17**	**14**	
..	..	..	..	..	..	..	..	..	37
453	248	205	..	..	..	22	9	13	38
..	..	..	..	..	..	..	..	..	39
..	..	..	..	..	..	..	..	..	40
..	..	..	..	..	..	..	..	..	41
..	..	..	..	..	..	..	..	..	42
1	..	1	..	..	..	..	..	..	43
..	..	..	..	..	..	..	..	..	44
146	90	56	..	..	..	9	8	1	45
76	**73**	**3**	**126**	**76**	**50**	**544**	**465**	**79**	
24	23	1	11	11	..	101	85	16	46
2	2	..	4	3	1	217	171	46	47
..	..	..	..	..	..	..	..	..	48
..	..	..	..	..	..	..	..	..	49
..	..	..	..	..	..	..	..	..	50
..	..	..	..	..	..	..	..	..	51
..	..	..	..	..	..	..	..	..	52
2	2	..	1	1	..	3	3	..	53
..	..	..	..	..	..	..	..	..	54
..	..	..	..	..	..	..	..	..	55
..	..	..	..	..	..	..	..	..	56
..	..	..	..	..	..	..	..	..	57
..	..	..	..	..	..	..	..	..	58
..	..	..	..	..	..	..	..	..	59
1	1	..	107	58	49	212	197	15	60
47	45	2	1	1	..	11	9	2	61
..	..	..	..	..	..	..	..	..	62
..	..	..	..	..	..	..	..	..	63
..	..	..	..	..	..	..	..	..	64
..	..	..	..	..	..	..	..	..	65
..	..	..	..	..	..	..	..	..	66
..	..	..	..	..	..	..	..	..	67
..	..	..	2	2	..	..	..	..	68
..	..	..	..	..	..	..	..	..	69
..	..	..	..	..	..	71	61	10	70
498	**312**	**186**	**20**	**9**	**11**	**204**	**137**	**67**	**C**
377	**263**	**114**	**17**	**6**	**11**	**168**	**109**	**59**	
377	263	114	17	6	11	168	109	59	71
290	*200*	*90*	*17*	*6*	*11*	*126*	*81*	*45*	72
77	*55*	*22*	..	..	..	*37*	*26*	*11*	73
10	*8*	*2*	..	..	..	..	..	..	74
..	..	..	..	..	..	..	..	..	75
..	..	..	..	..	..	..	..	..	76
..	..	..	..	..	..	*5*	*2*	*3*	77
..	..	..	..	..	..	..	..	..	78
..	..	..	..	..	..	..	..	..	79
..	..	..	..	..	..	..	..	..	80
118	**49**	**69**	**3**	**3**	..	**35**	**27**	**8**	
..	..	..	1	1	..	..	..	..	81
36	16	20	..	..	..	..	..	..	82
..	..	..	..	..	..	..	..	..	83
1	..	1	..	..	..	..	..	..	84
1	1	..	..	..	..	..	..	..	85
2	1	1	..	..	..	..	..	..	86
4	1	3	1	1	..	8	8	..	87
13	3	10	..	..	..	..	..	..	88
..	..	9	..	..	..	5	4	1	89
..	..	..	..	..	..	..	..	..	90
..	..	..	..	..	..	..	..	..	91
1	1	..	..	..	..	..	..	..	92
7	3	4	..	..	..	..	..	..	93

Table VI.—Part I—

Province or State

	Birthplace.	India.			Ajmer-Mewara.			Andaman and	
		Persons.	Males.	Females.	Persons.	Males.	Females.	Persons.	Males.
	1	2	3	4	5	6	7	8	9
	C. Born in Europe—*concluded.*								
94	Latvia	1	1	..	..	..	..	..	..
95	Norway	245	183	62	..	..	..	..	..
96	Poland	19	11	8	..	..	..	..	..
97	Portugal	231	173	58	6	5	1	..	..
98	Rumania	9	4	5	..	..	..	..	..
99	Russian Union	142	63	79	2	..	2	..	..
100	Spain	175	130	45	3	2	1	..	..
101	Sweden	288	163	125	..	..	..	2	2
102	Switzerland	326	175	151	1	..	1	..	..
103	Turkey in Europe	544	430	114	..	.	..	..	..
104	Yugoslavia	44	43	1	..	.	..	..	..
105	**Europe Unspecified**	**5,370**	**3,592**	**1,778**	..	..	..	..	..
	D. Born in Africa	**11,408**	**6,248**	**5,160**	**40**	**29**	**11**	**3**	..
	Within British Dominions	**2,625**	**1,290**	**1,335**	**8**	**8**	—	..	..
106	British East Africa (Kenya)	184	84	100	..	..	..	..	..
107	Cape Colony	92	55	37	2	2	..	..	..
108	Mauritius	145	97	48	..	..	..	..	..
109	Natal	1,292	634	658	..	..	..	..	..
110	Sierra Leone	8	2	6	..	..	..	..	..
111	Somaliland	533	230	303	..	..	..	..	..
112	St. Helena	5	4	1	1	1	..	..	..
113	Sudan	11	6	5	..	..	..	..	..
114	Tanganyika	1	1	..	..	..	..	..	..
115	Transvaal	174	84	90	..	..	..	..	..
116	Uganda	55	24	31	..	..	..	..	..
117	Zanzibar	125	69	56	..	..	..	..	..
	Outside British Dominions	**2,710**	**1,719**	**991**	..	..	..	..	..
118	Abyssinia	27	8	19	..	..	..	..	..
119	Congo	1	..	1	..	..	..	..	..
120	Egypt	158	92	66	..	..	..	..	..
121	Madagascar	4	3	1	..	..	..	..	..
122	Mozambique	2,520	1,616	904	..	..	..	..	..
123	**Africa Unspecified**	**6,073**	**3,239**	**2,834**	**37**	**26**	**11**	**3**	..
	E. Born in America	**4,455**	**2,305**	**2,150**	**10**	**4**	**6**	**3**	**2**
	Within British Dominions	**1,104**	**628**	**476**	..	..	..	..	..
124	Bermudas	17	9	8	..	..	..	..	..
125	British Guiana	49	24	25	..	..	..	..	..
126	British West Indies	332	177	155	..	..	..	..	..
127	Canada	628	372	256	..	..	..	..	..
128	Jamaica	67	37	30	..	..	..	..	..
129	Newfoundland	11	9	2	..	..	..	..	..
	Outside British Dominions	**1,536**	**821**	**715**	..	..	..	**3**	2
130	Argentine Republic	38	21	17	..	..	..	..	..
131	Brazil	23	12	11	..	..	..	..	..
132	Chile	2	2	..	..	..	..	..	..
133	Greenland	1	1	..	..	..	..	..	..
134	Mexico	16	7	9	..	..	..	..	..
135	Panama	1	1	..	..	..	..	..	..
136	Peru	4	2	2	..	..	..	..	..
137	United States	1,451	775	676	..	..	..	3	2
138	America Unspecified	1,815	856	959	10	4	6	..	..
	F. Born in Australasia	1,516	796	720	10	4	6	8	6
139	Australia	569	259	310	3	2	1	..	
140	Fiji Islands	387	205	182	5	1	4	8	6
141	New Zealand	160	82	78	2	1	1	..	..
142	Tasmania	165	132	33	..	..	..	..	..
143	**Australasia Unspecified**	235	118	117	..	..	..	..	..
	G. Born at Sea	16	7	9	..	..	—	—	—
	H. Birthplace not returned	1,642	1,187	455	8	6	2	—	—

Birthplace—*continued.*

where enumerated.

Nicobar.	Assam (*including Khasi States*).			Baluchistan. (*Districts and Administered Territories.*)			Bengal.			
Females.	Persons.	Males.	Females.	Persons.	Males.	Females.	Persons.	Males.	Females.	
10	11	12	13	14	15	16	17	18	19	
..	..	..	..	..	..	..	..	..	..	94
..	1	..	1	..	..	..	67	66	1	95
..	2	2	..	..	..	..	3	3	..	96
..	3	2	1	2	2	..	30	26	4	97
..	..	..	..	..	..	..	1	..	1	98
..	2	2	..	1	..	1	64	21	43	99
..	6	6	..	3	3	..	44	32	12	100
..	13	7	6	..	..	..	44	37	7	101
..	1	1	..	1	1	..	39	19	20	102
..	..	..	..	..	..	..	5	3	2	103
..	..	..	..	..	..	..	4	3	1	104
..	11	8	3	..	..	..	14	7	7	105
3	76	57	19	29	18	11	112	72	40	D
..	21	15	6	5	3	2	16	12	4	
..	..	..	..	1	1	..	1	..	1	106
..	..	..	..	..	..	..	1	1	..	107
..	..	..	..	1	..	1	3	3	..	108
..	6	3	3	..	..	..	4	2	2	109
..	..	..	..	..	..	..	..	..	..	110
..	..	..	..	..	..	..	..	..	..	111
..	..	..	..	..	..	..	..	..	..	112
..	..	..	..	..	..	..	7	6	1	113
..	..	..	..	..	..	..	..	..	..	114
..	15	12	3	3	2	1	..	..	..	115
..	..	..	..	..	..	..	..	..	..	116
..	..	..	..	..	..	..	..	..	..	117
..	3	2	1	18	9	9	11	8	3	
..	..	..	..	..	..	..	..	..	..	118
..	..	..	..	..	..	..	..	..	..	119
..	3	2	1	18	9	9	11	8	3	120
..	..	..	..	..	..	..	..	..	..	121
..	..	..	..	..	..	..	..	..	.	122
3	52	40	12	6	6	..	85	52	33	123
1	107	63	44	41	26	15	393	218	175	E
..	3	3	..	27	18	9	324	168	156	
..	..	..	..	2	2	..	..	..	..	124
..	2	2	..	1		1	..	..	..	125
..	..	..	..	1	1	..	280	146	134	126
..	..	..	..	21	14	7	44	22	22	127
..	1	1	..	2	1	1	..	..	..	128
..	..	..	..	..	..	..	..	..	..	129
1	73	40	33	7	4	3	69	50	19	
..	..	..	..	1	1	..	..	..	..	130
..	..	..	..	..	..	..	..	..	..	131
..	..	..	..	1	1	..	..	..	..	132
..	..	..	..	..	..	..	..	..	..	133
..	..	..	..	1	..	1	..	..	..	134
..	..	..	..	..	..	..	..	..	..	135
..	..	..	..	..	..	..	..	..	..	136
1	73	40	33	4	2	2	69	50	19	137
..	31	20	11	7	4	3	..	..	..	138
2	28	12	16	15	12	3	143	66	77	F
..	16	6	10	2	2	..	116	48	68	139
2	7	4	3	..	..	..	1	..	1	140
..	5	2	3	2	2	..	26	18	8	141
..	..	..	..	..	..	..	..	..	..	142
..	..	..	..	11	8	3	..	..	..	143
..	2	1	1	..	..	..	2	2	..	G
..	..	..	..	..	..	..	..	..	..	H

Table VI.—Part I—

Province or State

Birthplace.	Bihar and Orissa. Persons.	Males.	Females.	Bombay (*including Aden*). Persons.	Males.	Females.	Burma. Persons.	Males.
1	20	21	22	23	24	25	26	27
C. Born in Europe—*concluded.*								
94 Latvia	..	..	..	..	..	..	..	..
95 Norway	24	13	11	63	33	30	34	33
96 Poland	9	3	6	..	..	..	3	1
97 Portugal	13	10	3	50	38	12	43	40
98 Rumania	2	1	1	..	..	..	2	1
99 Russian Union	5	2	3	5	3	2	22	16
100 Spain	11	11	..	15	8	7	7	..
101 Sweden	2	1	1	72	37	35	15	14
102 Switzerland	12	1	11	92	67	25	22	14
103 Turkey in Europe	..	..	..	382	327	55	3	..
104 Yugoslavia	..	..	..	..	..	..	40	40
105 **Europe Unspecified**	5	5	..	3,547	2,696	851	..	..
D. Born in Africa	41	26	15	4,680	2,740	1,940	173	102
Within British Dominions	7	2	5	675	324	351	10	7
106 British East Africa (Kenya)	2	..	2	2	1	1	..	..
107 Cape Colony	1	1	..	46	25	21	..	..
108 Mauritius	2	1	1	37	37	..	6	6
109 Natal	2	..	2	8	7	1	1	1
110 Sierra Leone	..	..	..	8	2	6	..	..
111 Somaliland	..	..	..	530	227	303	..	..
112 St. Helena	..	..	..	..	..	..	..	..
113 Sudan	..	..	..	..	..	..	..	..
114 Tanganyika	..	..	..	..	..	..	..	..
115 Transvaal	..	..	..	23	15	8	..	..
116 Uganda	..	..	..	5	1	4	..	..
117 Zanzibar	..	..	..	16	9	7	3	..
Outside British Dominions	2	2	..	2,524	1,619	905	17	11
118 Abyssinia	..	..	..	..	..	..	..	..
119 Congo	..	..	..	..	..	..	..	..
120 Egypt	1	1	..	6	5	1	17	11
121 Madagascar	..	..	..	..	..	..	..	..
122 Mozambique	1	1	..	2,518	1,614	904	..	..
123 **Africa Unspecified**	32	22	10	1,481	797	684	146	84
E. Born in America	226	116	110	932	592	340	489	297
Within British Dominions	9	3	6	279	208	71	39	26
124 Bermudas	..	..	..	14	6	8	..	..
125 British Guiana	..	..	..	19	9	10	..	..
126 British West Indies	..	..	..	25	15	10	..	..
127 Canada	9	3	6	211	173	38	39	26
128 Jamaica	..	..	..	6	3	3	..	..
129 Newfoundland	..	..	..	4	2	2	..	..
Outside British Dominions	203	109	94	256	169	87	338	200
130 Argentine Republic	..	..	..	31	15	16	..	..
131 Brazil	..	..	..	23	12	11	..	..
132 Chile	1	1	..	..	..	..	..	..
133 Greenland	..	..	..	..	..	..	..	..
134 Mexico	1	..	1	11	6	5	..	..
135 Panama	..	..	..	..	..	..	..	..
136 Peru	..	..	..	4	2	2	..	..
137 United States	201	108	93	187	134	53	338	200
138 **America Unspecified**	14	4	10	397	215	182	112	71
F. Born in Australasia	26	8	18	298	200	98	168	104
139 Australia	17	5	12	40	13	27	130	74
140 Fiji Islands	..	..	..	10	10	..	4	..
141 New Zealand	3	1	2	24	18	6	10	8
142 Tasmania	1	..	1	155	127	28	2	..
143 **Australasia Unspecified**	5	2	3	69	32	37	22	22
G. Born at Sea	1	1	..	..	..	..	..	..
H. Birthplace not returned	1,815	1,021	294	..	..	..	..	..

Birthplace—*continued.*

where enumerated.

	Central Provinces and Berar.			Coorg.			Delhi.			
Females.	Persons.	Males.	Females.	Persons.	Males.	Females.	Persons.	Males.	Females.	
28	29	30	31	32	33	34	35	36	37	
..	..	..	..	..	..	..	..	..	..	94
1	2	1	1	..	..	..	..	..	..	95
2	..	..	..	..	..	..	..	..	..	96
3	1	1	..	..	..	..	..	..	..	97
1	..	..	..	..	..	..	..	..	..	98
6	..	..	..	..	..	..	..	..	..	99
7	..	..	..	..	..	..	..	..	..	100
1	24	6	18	..	..	..	..	..	..	101
8	7	3	4	..	..	..	4	4	..	102
3	..	..	..	..	..	..	1	..	1	103
..	..	..	..	..	..	..	..	..	..	104
..	76	50	26	..	..	..	7	5	2	05
71	87	56	31	7	3	4	28	18	10	D
3	18	8	10	..	..	..	..	..	..	
..	8	4	4	..	..	..	..	..	..	106
..	..	..	..	..	..	..	..	..	..	107
..	..	..	..	..	..	..	..	..	..	108
..	3	2	1	..	..	..	..	..	..	109
..	..	..	..	..	..	..	..	..	..	110
..	..	..	..	..	..	..	..	..	..	111
..	3	2	1	..	..	..	..	..	..	112
..	4	..	4	..	..	..	..	..	..	113
..	..	..	..	..	..	..	..	..	..	114
..	..	..	..	..	..	..	..	..	..	115
..	..	..	..	..	..	..	..	..	..	116
3	..	..	..	..	..	..	..	..	..	117
6	1	..	1	..	..	..	1	1	—	
..	..	..	..	..	..	..	..	..	..	118
..	..	..	..	..	..	..	..	..	..	119
6	1	..	1	..	..	..	1	1	..	120
..	..	..	..	..	..	..	..	..	..	121
..	..	..	..	..	..	..	..	..	..	122
62	68	48	20	7	3	4	27	17	10	123
192	266	113	153	5	2	3	55	17	38	E
13	12	9	3	4	1	3	5	1	4	
..	..	..	..	..	..	..	..	..	..	124
..	..	..	..	..	..	..	..	..	..	125
..	..	..	..	..	..	..	..	..	..	126
13	10	7	3	4	1	3	5	1	4	127
..	..	..	..	..	..	..	..	..	..	128
..	2	2	..	..	..	..	..	..	..	129
138	101	34	67	1	1	—	..	..	..	
..	..	..	..	..	..	..	..	..	..	130
..	..	..	..	..	..	..	..	..	..	131
..	..	..	..	..	..	..	..	..	..	132
..	..	..	..	..	..	..	..	..	..	133
..	..	..	..	..	..	..	..	..	..	134
..	..	..	..	..	..	..	..	..	..	135
..	..	..	..	..	..	..	..	..	..	136
138	101	34	67	1	1	—	..	..	..	137
41	153	70	83	—	—	—	50	16	34	188
64	21	13	8	2	—	2	17	6	11	F
56	12	7	5	..	..	..	..	..	..	139
4	2	1	1	..	..	..	..	..	..	140
2	2	..	2	—	..	..	5	2	3	141
2	3	3	—		..	..	..	..	..	142
..	2	2	..	2	..	2	12	4	8	143
..	1	1	..	—	—	—	—	—	..	G
—	11	3	8	—	..	—	—	—	..	H

Table VI.—Part I—

Province or State

Birthplace.	Madras.			North-West Frontier Province (*Districts and Administered Territories.*)			
	Persons.	Males.	Females.	Persons.	Males.	Females.	Persons.
1	38	39	40	41	42	43	44
C. Born in Europe—*concluded.*							
94 Latvia	..	..	..	..	..	..	1
95 Norway	35	31	4	3	2	1	..
96 Poland	2	2	..	..	..	..	..
97 Portugal	31	22	9	1	1	..	3
98 Rumania	1	1	..	..	..	..	2
99 Russian Union	7	3	4	8	3	5	4
100 Spain	19	18	1	..	..	..	4
101 Sweden	64	32	32	..	..	..	3
102 Switzerland	61	30	31	7	..	7	3
103 Turkey in Europe	1	1	..	2	1	1	37
104 Yugoslavia	..	..	..	..	..	..	..
105 **Europe Unspecified** ..	100	38	62	142	54	88	1,207
D. Born in Africa ..	1,771	945	826	45	32	13	631
Within British Dominions ..	1,161	590	571	..	..	..	..
106 British East Africa (Kenya)	6	2	4	..	..	..	..
107 Cape Colony	7	4	3	..	..	..	..
108 Mauritius	52	29	23	..	..	..	..
109 Natal	1,095	554	541	..	..	..	..
110 Sierra Leone	..	..	..	..	..	..	..
111 Somaliland	..	..	..	..	..	..	..
112 St. Helena	..	..	..	..	..	..	..
113 Sudan	..	..	..	..	..	..	..
114 Tanganyika	..	..	..	..	..	..	..
115 Transvaal	..	..	..	..	..	..	..
116 Uganda	..	..	..	..	..	..	..
117 Zanzibar	1	1	..	..	..	..	..
Outside British Dominions ..	8	4	4	15	8	7	36
118 Abyssinia	..	..	..	..	..	..	..
119 Congo	1	..	1	..	..	..	..
120 Egypt	7	4	3	15	8	7	36
121 Madagascar	..	..	..	..	..	..	..
122 Mozambique	..	..	..	..	..	..	..
123 **Africa Unspecified** ..	602	351	251	30	24	6	593
E. Born in America ..	496	236	260	29	19	10	298
Within British Dominions ..	77	35	42	11	8	3	23
124 Bermudas	..	..	..	..	..	..	..
125 British Guiana	4	1	3	..	..	..	1
126 British West Indies ..	1	..	1	..	..	..	..
127 Canada	66	31	35	7	4	3	22
128 Jamaica	6	3	3	..	..	..	..
129 Newfoundland	..	..	..	4	4	..	..
Outside British Dominions ..	224	102	122	6	4	2	9
130 Argentine Republic ..	..	..	..	2	2	..	..
131 Brazil	..	..	..	..	..	..	..
132 Chile	..	..	..	..	..	..	..
133 Greenland	..	..	..	..	..	..	..
134 Mexico	2	..	2	..	..	..	..
135 Panama	..	..	..	..	..	..	..
136 Peru	..	..	..	..	..	..	..
137 United States	222	102	120	4	2	2	9
138 **America Unspecified** ..	195	99	96	12	7	5	266
F. Born in Australasia ..	149	50	99	32	22	10	105
139 Australia	47	14	33	7	2	5	67
140 Fiji Islands	24	7	17	..	..	..	21
141 New Zealand	18	5	13	10	10	..	15
142 Tasmania	1	1	..	..	..	..	..
143 [illegible]				15	10	5	2

Birthplace—*continued.*

where enumerated.

Punjab.		United Provinces of Agra and Oudh.			Assam State (*Manipur*).			
Males.	Females.	Persons.	Males.	Females.	Persons.	Males.	Females.	
45	46	47	48	49	50	51	52	
1	..	..	..	..	..	..	..	94
..	..	8	..	8	..	..	..	95
..	..	..	..	..	..	..	..	96
3	..	11	2	9	..	..	..	97
1	1	1	..	1	..	..	..	98
1	3	6	3	3	..	..	..	99
3	1	20	12	8	..	..	..	100
..	3	42	22	20	..	..	..	101
3	..	6	2	4	..	..	..	102
35	2	3	..	3	..	..	..	103
..	..	..	..	..	..	..	..	104
547	660	7	5	2	—	—	—	105
350	281	343	175	168	—	—	—	D
..	—	129	60	69	—	—	—	
..	..	12	2	10	—	..	—	106
..	..	18	12	6	..	..	..	107
..	..	21	11	10	..	..	..	108
..	..	73	31	42	..	..	..	109
..	..	..	..		..	..	..	110
..	..	..	..	..	..	..	..	111
..	—	1	1	—	—	..	—	112
..	..	..	..	..	..	..	..	113
..	..	..	..	..	..	..	..	114
..	..	..	..	..	..	..	..	115
..	..	..	..	..	..	..	..	116
..	..	4	3	1	—	..	.	117
25	13	36	17	19	—	—	..	
..	..	..	..	..	..	..	..	118
..	..	..	..	..	..	..	..	119
25	13	36	17	19	—	..	..	120
..	..	..	—	..	—	..	..	121
..	..	..	..	..	..	..	..	122
325	268	178	98	80	—	—	—	123
112	186	624	251	373	3	1	2	E
7	16	128	70	58	—	..	..	
..	..	1	1	..	..	..	..	124
..	1	22	12	10	..	..	—	125
..	..	7	6	1	..	..	..	126
7	15	51	23	28	—	..	..	127
..	..	46	27	19	..	..	..	128
..	..	1	1	..	..	..	—	129
..	9	118	37	81	3	1	2	
..	..	1	1	..	..	..	..	130
..	..	..	..	..	..	..	..	131
..	..	..	—	..	..	..	..	132
..	..	1	1	..	..	..	..	133
..	..	1	1	..	..	..	..	134
..	..	..	..	..	..	—	..	135
..	..	..	..	..	..	..	..	136
..	9	115	34	81	3	1	2	137
105	161	378	144	234	—	..	..	138
39	66	353	189	164	—	—	—	F
27	40	33	15	18	..	..	..	139
8	13	299	167	132	..	..	..	140
4	11	11	4	7	..	..	..	141
..	—	1	1	..	..	..	..	142
..	2	9	2	7	..	..	..	143
..	—	4	..	4	—	—	..	G
..		9	1	8	—	—	—	H

Table VI.—Part I—

Province of State

Birthplace.	Baluchistan States.			Baroda State.			
	Persons.	Males.	Females.	Persons.	Males.	Females.	Persons.
1	53	54	55	56	57	58	59
C.—Born in Europe—*concluded.*							
94 Latvia	..	..	..	..	..	..	..
95 Norway	..	..	..	..	..	..	..
96 Poland	..	..	..	..	..	..	..
97 Portugal	..	..	..	..	..	..	..
98 Rumania	..	..	..	..	..	..	..
99 Russian Union	..	..	..	1	..	1	..
100 Spain	..	..	..	..	..	..	..
101 Sweden	..	..	..	..	..	..	..
102 Switzerland	..	..	..	..	..	..	4
103 Turkey in Europe	..	..	..	..	..	..	..
104 Yugoslavia	..	..	..	..	..	..	..
105 **Europe Unspecified**	—	—	—	—	..	—	—
D. Born in Africa	..	..	..	**938**	**439**	**499**	..
Within British Dominions	—	..	..	**371**	**159**	**212**	..
106 British East Africa (Kenya)	..	..	..	101	47	54	..
107 Cape Colony	..	..	..	12	5	7	..
108 Mauritius	..	..	..	17	9	8	..
109 Natal	..	..	..	85	26	59	..
110 Sierra Leone	..	..	..	..	..	..	..
111 Somaliland	..	..	..	..	..	..	..
112 St. Helena	..	..	..	..	..	..	..
113 Sudan	..	..	..	..	..	..	..
114 Tanganyika	..	..	..	..	..	..	..
115 Transvaal	..	..	..	133	55	78	..
116 Uganda	..	..	..	..	..	..	..
117 Zanzibar	..	..	..	23	17	6	..
Outside British Dominions	—	—	—	**27**	8	19	—
118 Abyssinia	..	..	..	27	8	19	..
119 Congo	..	..	..	..	..	..	..
120 Egypt	..	..	..	..	..	..	..
121 Madagascar	..	..	..	..	..	..	..
122 Mozambique	..	..	..	..	..	..	..
123 **Africa Unspecified**	—	..	—	**540**	**272**	**268**	—
E. Born in America	—	..	..	**15**	**4**	**11**	—
Within British Dominions	..	..	—	..	..	—	—
124 Bermudas	..	..	..	..	..	—	—
125 British Guiana	..	..	..	..	..	..	..
126 British West Indies	..	..	..	..	..	..	..
127 Canada	..	..	..	..	..	..	..
128 Jamaica	..	..	..	..	..	..	..
129 Newfoundland	..	..	..	..	..	..	..
Outside British Dominions	—	—	—	**15**	**4**	**11**	..
130 Argentine Republic	..	..	..	..	..	..	..
131 Brazil	..	..	..	..	..	..	..
132 Chile	..	..	..	..	..	..	..
133 Greenland	..	..	..	..	..	..	..
134 Mexico	..	..	..	..	..	..	..
135 Panama	..	..	..	..	..	..	..
136 Peru	..	..	..	..	..	..	..
137 United States	..	..	..	15	4	11	..
138 **America Unspecified**	—	—	—	..	..	..	—
F. Born in Australasia	—	—	—	**1**	1	—	—
139 Australia	..	..	..	..	..	..	..
140 Fiji Islands	..	..	..	..	..	..	..
141 New Zealand	..	..	..	1	1	..	..
142 Tasmania	..	..	..	..	..	..	..
143 **Australasia Unspecified**	—	..	—	—	—	—	—
G. Born at Sea	—	—	—	—	—	—	—
H. Birthplace not returned	—	—	—	—	—	—	—

Birthplace—*continued.*

where enumerated.

Bengal States.		Bihar and Orissa States.			Bombay States.			
Males.	Females.	Persons.	Males.	Females.	Persons.	Males.	Females.	
60	61	62	63	64	65	66	67	
..	..	..	..	..	..	..	..	94
..	..	..	..	..	..	..	..	95
..	..	..	..	..	..	..	..	96
..	..	..	..	..	..	..	..	97
..	..	..	..	..	..	..	..	98
..	..	1	1	..	..	..	..	99
..	..	..	..	..	..	..	..	100
2	2	..	..	..	..	..	..	101
..	..	..	..	..	..	..	..	102
..	..	..	..	..	1	..	1	103
..	..	..	..	..	..	..	..	104
..	..	..	—	—	4	2	2	105
..	..	2	1	1	84	23	61	D
..	..	..	..	..	..	..	..	
..	..	..	..	..	..	..	..	106
..	..	..	..	..	..	..	..	107
..	..	..	..	..	..	..	..	108
..	..	..	..	..	..	..	..	109
..	..	..	..	..	..	..	..	110
..	..	..	..	..	..	..	..	111
..	..	..	..	..	..	..	..	112
..	..	..	..	..	..	..	..	113
..	..	..	..	..	..	..	..	114
..	..	..	..	..	..	..	..	115
..	..	..	..	..	..	..	..	116
..	..	..	..	..	..	..	..	117
..	—	—	—	—	1	1	—	
..	..	..	..	..	..	..	..	118
..	..	..	..	..	..	..	..	119
..	..	..	..	..	..	..	..	120
..	..	..	..	..	..	..	..	121
..	..	..	..	..	1	1	..	122
—	—	2	1	1	83	22	61	123
—	—	4	3	1	67	25	42	E
..	—	—	—	..	17	5	12	
..	..	..	..	..	—	—	..	124
..	..	..	..	..	..	—	..	125
..	..	..	..	..	12	4	8	126
..	..	..	..	..	—	—	..	127
..	..	..	..	..	5	1	4	128
..	..	..	..	..	..	—	..	129
..	..	4	3	1	3	2	1	
..	..	..	..	..	3	2	1	130
..	..	..	..	..	..	—	..	131
..	..	..	..	..	—	—	—	132
..	..	..	..	..	..	—	..	133
..	..	..	—	..	—	..	—	134
..	..	..	..	..	..	..	..	135
..	..	..	..	..	—	—	..	136
..	..	4	3	1	..	—	—	137
..	..	—	—	—	47	18	29	138
..	..	4	4	—	5	3	2	F
—	—	4	4	..	4	3	1	139
..	..	..	..	..	..	—	..	140
..	..	..	..	..	1	—	1	141
..	..	..	..	..	..	—	..	142
..	..	..	..	..	..	..	..	143
..	..	..	..	..	..	—	..	G
		..	..	..	..	..		

Table VI.—Part I—

Province or State

Birthplace.	Central India Agency.			Central Provinces States.			
	Persons.	Males.	Females.	Persons.	Males.	Females.	Persons.
1	68	69	70	71	72	73	74
C. **Born in Europe**—*concluded.*							
94 Latvia	..	..	..	..	..	..	..
95 Norway	2	..	2	..	..	..	..
96 Poland	..	..	..	..	..	..	..
97 Portugal	..	..	..	..	..	..	..
98 Rumania	..	..	..	..	..	..	..
99 Russian Union	..	..	..	..	..	..	..
100 Spain	2	2	..	..	..	..	11
101 Sweden	..	..	..	..	..	..	..
102 Switzerland	1	..	1	..	..	..	1
103 Turkey in Europe	..	..	..	..	..	..	2
104 Yugoslavia	..	..	..	..	..	..	..
105 **Europe Unspecified**	8	2	6	2	1	1	..
D. Born in Africa	22	15	7	..	..	..	5
Within British Dominions	9	9	..	..	..	..	5
106 British East Africa (Kenya)	..	..	..	..	..	..	4
107 Cape Colony	..	..	..	..	..	..	..
108 Mauritius	1	1	..	..	..	..	..
109 Natal	..	..	..	..	..	..	1
110 Sierra Leone	..	..	..	..	..	..	..
111 Somaliland	2	2	..	..	..	..	..
112 St. Helena	..	..	..	..	..	..	..
113 Sudan	..	..	..	..	..	..	..
114 Tanganyika	..	..	..	..	..	..	..
115 Transvaal	..	..	..	..	..	..	..
116 Uganda	..	..	..	..	..	..	..
117 Zanzibar	6	6	..	..	..	..	..
Outside British Dominions	..	..	..	..	..	..	..
118 Abyssinia	..	..	..	..	..	..	..
119 Congo	..	..	..	..	..	..	..
120 Egypt	..	..	..	..	..	..	..
121 Madagascar	..	..	..	..	..	..	..
122 Mozambique	..	..	..	..	..	..	..
123 **Africa Unspecified**	13	6	7	..	..	..	..
E. Born in America	88	32	56	13	6	7	3
Within British Dominions	70	25	45	..	..	..	..
124 Bermudas	..	..	..	..	..	..	..
125 British Guiana	..	..	..	..	..	..	..
126 British West Indies	5	5	..	..	..	..	..
127 Canada	65	20	45	..	..	..	..
128 Jamaica	..	..	..	..	..	..	..
129 Newfoundland	..	..	..	..	..	..	..
Outside British Dominions	..	..	..	8	4	4	3
130 Argentine Republic	..	..	..	..	..	..	..
131 Brazil	..	..	..	..	..	..	..
132 Chile	..	..	..	..	..	..	..
133 Greenland	..	..	..	..	..	..	..
134 Mexico	..	..	..	..	..	..	..
135 Panama	..	..	..	..	..	..	..
136 Peru	..	..	..	..	..	..	..
137 United States	..	..	..	8	4	4	3
138 **America Unspecified**	18	7	11	5	2	3	..
F. Born in Australasia	9	6	8	..	..	..	2
139 Australia	8	5	3	..	..	..	..
140 Fiji Islands	..	..	..	..	..	..	..
141 New Zealand	1	1	..	..	..	..	2
142 Tasmania	..	..	..	..	..	..	..
143 **Australasia Unspecified**	..	..	..	..	..	..	..
G. Born at Sea	..	..	..	..	..	..	1
H. Birthplace not returned		..	..	..	..		..

Birthplace—*continued.*

or State where enumerated.

Cochin State.		Gwalior State.			Hyderabad State.			
Males.	Females.	Persons.	Males.	Females.	Persons.	Males.	Females.	
75	76	77	78	79	80	81	82	
..	..	..	..	..	..	..	..	94
..	..	..	..	..	..	..	..	95
..	..	..	..	..	..	..	..	96
..	..	..	..	..	25	13	12	97
..	..	..	..	..	..	..	..	98
..	..	1	1	..	..	..	..	99
10	1	1	..	1	6	5	1	100
..	..	..	..	..	..	..	..	101
1	..	..	..	..	1	1	..	102
2	..	..	..	..	107	61	46	103
..	..	..	..	..	..	..	..	104
..	..	..	..	..	223	159	64	105
3	2	..	..	..	4	3	1	D.
3	2	..	..	..	4	3	1	
2	2	..	..	..	4	3	1	106
..	..	..	..	..	..	..	..	107
..	..	..	..	..	..	..	..	108
1*	..	..	..	..	..	..	..	109
..	..	..	..	..	..	..	..	110
..	..	..	..	..	..	..	..	111
..	..	..	..	..	..	..	..	112
..	..	..	..	..	..	..	..	113
..	..	..	..	..	..	..	..	114
..	..	..	..	..	..	..	..	115
..	..	..	..	..	..	..	..	116
..	..	..	..	..	..	..	..	117
..	..	..	..	..	..	..	..	
..	..	..	..	..	..	..	..	118
..	..	..	..	..	..	..	..	119
..	..	..	..	..	..	..	..	120
..	..	..	..	..	..	..	..	121
..	..	..	..	..	..	..	..	122
..	..	..	..	..	..	..	..	123
1	2	19	7	12	92	70	22	E.
..	..	16	7	9	22	19	3	
..	..	..	..	..	..	..	..	124
..	..	..	..	..	..	..	..	125
..	..	..	..	..	..	..	..	126
..	..	16	7	9	22	19	3	127
..	..	..	..	..	..	..	..	128
..	..	..	..	..	..	..	..	129
1	2	..	..	..	46	30	16	
..	..	..	..	..	..	..	..	130
..	..	..	..	..	..	..	..	131
..	..	..	..	..	..	..	..	132
..	..	..	..	..	..	..	..	133
..	..	..	..	..	..	..	..	134
..	..	..	..	..	..	..	..	135
..	..	..	..	..	..	..	..	136
1	2	..	..	..	46	30	16	137
..	..	3	..	3	24	21	3	138
..	2	..	..	..	21	12	9	F
..	..	..	..	..	17	12	5	139
..	..	..	..	..	..	..	..	140
..	2	..	..	..	4	..	4	141
..	..	..	..	..	..	..	..	142
..	..	..	..	..	..	..	..	143
..	1	1	..	1	..	..	..	G.
..	..	..	..	..	58	32	26	H.

Table VI.—Part I—

Province or State

	Birthplace.	Jammu and Kashmir State.			Madras States. (*Excluding Cochin and Travancore.*)			
		Persons.	Males.	Females.	Persons.	Males.	Females.	Persons.
	1	83	84	85	86	87	88	89
	C. Born in Europe—*concluded.*							
94	Latvia	..	..	..	..	..	..	..
95	Norway	..	..	..	..	..	..	..
96	Poland	..	..	..	..	..	..	..
97	Portugal	1	..	1	..	..	..	..
98	Rumania	..	..	..	..	..	..	..
99	Russian Union	3	2	1	..	..	..	4
100	Spain	2	..	2	..	..	..	4
101	Sweden	..	..	..	..	..	..	1
102	Switzerland	4	2	2	..	..	..	11
103	Turkey in Europe	..	..	..	..	..	..	..
104	Yugoslavia	..	..	..	..	..	..	..
105	**Europe Unspecified**	7	7	—	—	..	—	4
	D. Born in Africa	9	2	7	8	6	2	167
	Within British Dominions	2	1	1	..	..	..	31
106	British East Africa (Kenya)	1	..	1	..	..	..	2
107	Cape Colony	1	1	..	..	..	..	..
108	Mauritius	..	..	..	..	..	..	..
109	Natal	..	..	..	..	..	..	14
110	Sierra Leone	..	..	..	..	..	..	..
111	Somaliland	..	..	..	..	..	..	..
112	St. Helena	..	..	..	..	..	..	..
113	Sudan	..	..	..	..	..	..	..
114	Tanganyika	..	..	..	..	..	..	..
115	Transvaal	..	..	..	..	..	..	..
116	Uganda	..	..	..	..	..	..	..
117	Zanzibar	..	..	..	..	..	..	15
	Outside British Dominions	..	..	..	..	—	..	1
118	Abyssinia	..	..	..	..	..	..	..
119	Congo	..	..	..	..	..	..	..
120	Egypt	..	..	..	..	..	..	1
121	Madagascar	..	..	..	..	..	..	..
122	Mozambique	..	..	..	..	..	..	..
123	**Africa Unspecified**	7	1	6	8	6	2	135
	E. Born in America	12	4	8	1	1	..	63
	Within British Dominions	10	3	7	1	1	..	5
124	Bermudas	..	..	..	..	..	..	..
125	British Guiana	..	..	..	..	..	..	..
126	British West Indies	..	..	..	..	..	..	1
127	Canada	10	3	7	..	..	..	4
128	Jamaica	..	..	..	1	1	..	..
129	Newfoundland	..	..	..	..	..	..	..
	Outside British Dominions	2	1	1	—	..	..	32
130	Argentine Republic	..	..	..	..	..	..	..
131	Brazil	..	..	..	..	..	..	..
132	Chile	..	..	..	..	..	..	..
133	Greenland	..	..	..	..	..	..	..
134	Mexico	..	..	..	..	..	..	..
135	Panama	..	..	..	..	..	..	..
136	Peru	..	..	..	..	..	..	..
137	United States	2	1	1	..	..	..	32
138	**America Unspecified**	..	—	—	—	..	—	26
	F. Born in Australasia	17	3	14	—	—	—	30
139	Australia	12	3	9	..	—	..	9
140	Fiji Islands	..	..	..	..	..	..	1
141	New Zealand	3	..	3	..	..	..	4
142	Tasmania	2	..	2	..	..	..	..
143	**Australasia Unspecified**	..	..	..	..	..	..	16
	G. Born at Sea	—	—	—	—	..	—	2
	H. Birthplace not returned	..	—	—	..	..	..	—

Birthplace—*continued.*

where enumerated.

Mysore State.		North-West Frontier Province (*Agencies and Tribal Areas.*)			Punjab States. (*Including Punjab States Agency.*)			
Males.	Females.	Persons.	Males.	Females.	Persons.	Males.	Females.	
90	91	92	93	94	95	96	97	
..	..	..	..	..	..	..	..	94
..	..	..	..	..	1	..	1	95
..	..	..	..	..	..	..	..	96
..	..	..	..	..	5	3		97
..	..	..	..	..	..	..	..	98
..	4	..	..	..	3	3	..	99
1	3	..	..	..	..	..	..	100
1	..	..	..	..	..	..	..	101
11	..	..	..	..	..	..	..	102
..	..	..	..	..	..	..	..	103
..	..	..	..	..	..	..	..	104
3	1	2	2	..	..	..	..	105
86	81	1	1	..	26	16	10	D.
14	17	..	..	..	—	—	—	
2	..	..	..	..	..	..	..	106
..	..	..	..	..	..	..	..	107
..	..	..	..	..	..	..	..	108
7	7	..	..	..	..	..	..	109
..	..	..	..	..	..	..	..	110
..	..	..	..	..	..	..	..	111
..	..	..	..	..	..	..	..	112
..	..	..	..	..	..	..	..	113
..	..	..	..	..	..	..	..	114
..	..	..	..	..	..	..	..	115
..	..	..	..	..	..	..	..	116
5	10	..	..	..	..	..	..	117
1	—	—	—	—	—	—	—	
..	..	..	..	..	..	..	..	118
..	..	..	..	..	..	..	..	119
1	..	..	..	..	..	..	..	120
..	..	..	..	..	..	..	..	121
..	..	..	..	..	..	..	..	122
71	64	1	1	..	26	16	10	123
26	37	15	15	..	21	14	7	E.
1	4	4	4	..	2	1	1	
..	..	..	..	..	..	..	..	124
..	..	..	..	..	..	..	..	125
..	1	..	..	..	..	..	..	126
1	3	4	4	..	2	1	1	127
..	..	..	..	..	..	..	..	128
..	..	..	..	..	..	..	..	129
16	16	4	4	..	—	—	—	
..	..	..	..	..	..	..	..	130
..	..	..	..	..	..	..	..	131
..	..	..	..	..	..	..	..	132
..	..	..	..	..	..	..	..	133
..	..	..	..	..	..	..	..	134
..	..	..	..	..	..	..	..	135
..	..	..	..	..	..	..	..	136
16	16	4	4	..	..	..	..	137
9	17	7	7	..	19	13	6	138
17	13	6	2	4	16	6	10	F.
6	3	2	2	..	16	6	10	139
1	..	..	..	..	..	..	..	140
1	3	4	..	4	..	..	..	141
..	..	..	..	..	..		..	142
9	7	..	..	..	..	..	..	143
..	1	—	—	—	..	..	..	G
..	—	..	—	—	241	124	117	H

Table VI.—Part I—

Province

	Birthplace.	Rajputana Agency. Persons.	Rajputana Agency. Males.	Rajputana Agency. Females.	Sikkim State. Persons.	Sikkim State. Males.	Sikkim State. Females.	Persons.
		98	99	100	101	102	103	104
	C. Born in Europe—*concluded.*							
94	Latvia	..	..	..	..	..	..	..
95	Norway	..	..	..	..	..	..	2
96	Poland	..	..	..	..	..	..	..
97	Portugal	2	1	1	..	..	..	3
98	Rumania	..	..	..	..	..	..	..
99	Russian Union	3	2	1	..	..	..	..
100	Spain	—	—	—	..	..	..	17
101	Sweden	1	1	..	..	..	..	1
102	Switzerland	3	2	1	..	..	..	30
103	Turkey in Europe	..	..	..	..	..	..	..
104	Yugoslavia	..	..	..	..	..	..	..
105	**Europe Unspecified** ..	..	..	..	..	..	..	3
	D. Born in Africa ..	28	8	20	—	—	—	29
	Within British Dominions ..	6	1	5	—	—	—	—
106	British East Africa (Kenya)	6	1	5	..	..	..	..
107	Cape Colony	..	..	..	..	..	..	..
108	Mauritius	..	..	..	..	..	..	..
109	Natal	..	..	..	..	..	..	..
110	Sierra Leone	..	..	..	..	..	..	..
111	Somaliland	..	..	..	..	..	..	..
112	St. Helena	..	..	..	..	..	..	..
113	Sudan	..	..	..	..	..	..	
114	Tanganyika	..	..	..	..	..	..	..
115	Transvaal	..	..	..	..	..	..	..
116	Uganda	..	..	..	..	..	..	..
117	Zanzibar	..	..	..	..	..	..	..
	Outside British Dominions	—	—	—	—	—	..	..
118	Abyssinia	..	..	..	..	..	..	
119	Congo	..	..	..	..	..	..	..
120	Egypt	..	..	..	..	..	..	
121	Madagascar	..	..	..	..	..	..	..
122	Mozambique	..	..	..	..	..	..	..
123	**Africa Uspecified** ..	22	7	15	..	..	..	29
	E. Born in America ..	23	5	18	1	..	1	32
	Within British Dominions ..	7	1	6	1	—	1	2
124	Bermudas	..	..	..	..	..	..	..
125	British Guiana	..	..	..	..	..	..	..
126	British West Indies ..	..	..	..	..	..	..	..
127	Canada	7	1	6	1	..	1	2
128	Jamaica	..	..	..	..	..	..	..
129	Newfoundland	..	..	..	..	..	..	..
	Outside British Dominions ..	6	2	4	—	—	—	1
130	Argentine Republic ..	..	..	..	..	..	..	..
131	Brazil	..	..	..	..	..	..	..
132	Chile	..	..	..	..	..	..	..
133	Greenland	..	..	..	..	..	..	..
134	Mexico	..	..	..	..	..	..	..
135	Panama	..	..	..	..	..	..	1
136	Peru	..	..	..	..	..	..	..
137	United States	6	2	4	..	..	..	..
138	**America Unspecified** ..	10	2	8	—	..	..	29
	F. Born in Australasia ..	11	2	9	1	—	1	16
139	Australia	6	2	4	..	..	..	..
140	Fiji Islands	5	..	5	..	..	..	—
141	New Zealand	..	..	..	1	..	1	6
142	Tasmania	..	..	..	..	..	..	..
143	**Australasia Unspecified** ..	..	..	..	—	—	—	10
	G. Born at Sea	—	—	—	..	..	—	—
	H. Birthplace not returned ..	—	—	—	—	..	—	—

Birthplace—*concluded.*

or State where enumerated.

Travancore State.		United Provinces States.			Western India States Agency.			
Males.	Females.	Persons.	Males.	Females.	Persons.	Males.	Females.	
105	106	107	108	109	110	111	112	
..	..	..	..	..	..	..	..	94
1	1	..	..	..	3	3	..	95
..	..	..	..	..	..	..	..	96
3	..	1	1	..	..	..	..	97
..	..	..	..	..	..	..	..	98
..	..	..	..	..	..	..	..	99
17	..	..	..	..	..	..	..	100
1	..	..	..	..	..	..	..	101
1	29	..	..	..	19	12	7	102
..	..	..	..	..	..	..	..	103
..	..	..	..	..	..	..		104
..	3	..	..	..	1	1	..	105
16	13	..	..	..	2,019	1,006	1,013	D.
—	—	..	—	—	152	76	76	
..	..	..	..	..	34	19	15	106
..	..	..	..	..	4	4	..	107
..	..	..	..	..	5	..	5	108
..	..	..	..	..	..	..	..	109
..	..	..	..	..	..	..	..	110
..	..	..	..	..	1	1	..	111
..	..	..	..	..	..	..	..	112
..	..	..	..	..	..	..	..	113
..	..	..	..	..	1	1	..	114
..	..	..	..	..	..	..	..	115
..	..	..	..	..	50	23	27	116
..	..	..	..	..	57	28	29	117
..	..	..	..	..	7	3	4	
..	..	..	..	..	..	..	..	118
..	..	..	..	..	..	..	..	119
..	..	..	..	..	3	..	3	120
..	..	..	..	..	4	3	1	121
..	..	..	..	..	..	..	..	122
16	13	..	..	..	1,860	927	933	123
19	13	1	..	1	8	4	4	E.
..	2	—	—	—	6	4	2	
..	..	..	..	..	..	..	..	124
..	..	..	..	..	..	..	..	125
..	..	..	..	..	..	..	..	126
..	2	..	..	..	6	4	2	127
..	..	..	..	..	..	..	..	128
..	..	..	..	..	..	..	..	129
1	..	1	..	1	—	..	..	
..	..	..	..	..	..	..	..	130
..	..	..	..	..	..	..	..	131
..	..	..	..	..	..	..	..	132
..	..	..	..	..	..	..	..	133
..	..	..	..	..	..	..	..	134
1	..	..	..	..	..	..	..	135
..	..	..	..	..	..	..	..	136
..	..	1	..	1	..	..	..	137
18	11	..	..	..	2	—	2	138
7	9	..	..	..	2	2	—	F.
..	..	..	..	..	1	1	..	139
..	..	..	..	..	..	..	..	140
4	2	..	..	..	..	..	..	141
..	..	..	..	..	..	..	..	142
3	7	..	..	..	1	1	..	143
..	..	..	—	—	—	..	..	G.
..	..	..	..	—	—	—	—	H.

Table VI.—Part II—

Birthplace.	Calcutta (*excluding Howrah*). Persons.	Males.	Females.	Bombay. Persons.	Males.	Females.	Persons.
1	2	3	4	5	6	7	8
Total Population	**1,196,734**	**814,948**	**381,786**	**1,161,383**	**747,381**	**414,002**	**647,230**
A. Born in India	**1,179,836**	**802,560**	**377,276**	**1,146,118**	**735,679**	**410,439**	**643,596**
(a) Provinces	**1,156,280**	**784,957**	**371,323**	**969,172**	**619,927**	**349,245**	**626,082**
1 Ajmer-Merwara	197	115	82	3,588	3,036	552	..
2 Andamans and Nicobars	3	3	..	77	64	13	..
3 Assam	4,616	3,918	698	221	207	14	..
4 Baluchistan (*Districts and Administered Territories*).	..	..	..	1,266	848	418	..
5 Bengal	795,903	487,933	307,970	2,476	1,902	574	..
6 Bihar and Orissa	223,698	191,531	32,167	544	362	182	..
7 Bombay	4,467	2,955	1,125	836,138	513,996	322,142	..
8 Burma	1,461	1,512	336	258	183	75	1,041
9 Central Provinces and Berar	3,000	2,187	813	4,814	3,470	1,344	..
10 Coorg	2	2	..	124	104	20	..
11 Delhi	1,558	1,307	251	3,320	2,496	824	..
12 Madras	5,287	3,348	1,939	21,415	14,876	6,539	618,524
13 N.-W. F. Province (*Districts and Administered Territories*).	611	439	172	3,091	2,697	394	..
14 Punjab	12,445	9,879	2,566	8,517	6,863	1,654	..
15 United Provinces of Agra and Oudh.	103,032	80,215	22,817	83,323	68,823	14,500	..
16 Provinces unspecified	..	..	..	..	..	..	6,467
(b) States and Agencies.	**22,671**	**16,859**	**5,812**	**135,737**	**87,566**	**48,171**	**13,984**
17 Assam States	203	170	33	..	..	..	..
18 Baluchistan States	79	72	7	..	..	..	..
19 Baroda State	233	171	62	6,027	3,900	2,127	..
20 Bengal States	3,505	2,487	1,018	..	..	..	..
21 Bihar and Orissa States	1,053	917	136	..	..	..	..
22 Bombay States	88	81	7	20,631	14,002	6,629	..
23 Central India Agency	186	60	126	3,330	2,063	1,267	..
24 Central Provinces States	26	12	14	..	..	..	..
25 Gwalior State	908	718	190	606	402	204	..
26 Hyderabad State	380	283	97	15,914	11,031	4,883	2,623
27 Jammu and Kashmir State	93	69	24	376	311	65	..
28 Madras States Agency	48	30	18	3,486	1,064	2,422	3,096
Cochin State	*23*	*14*	*9*	*2,946*	*642*	*2,304*	*1,010*
Travancore State	*8*	*8*	..	*540*	*422*	*118*	*1,850*
Other Madras States	*17*	*8*	*9*	..	..	..	*236*
29 Mysore State	171	108	63	2,937	2,036	901	6,063
30 N.-W. F. Province (*Agencies and Tribal Areas*).	..	..	..	..	..	..	..
31 Punjab States and Agency	258	194	64	..	..	..	..
32 Rajputana Agency	14,881	11,180	3,701	8,389	6,834	1,555	..
33 Sikkim State	313	171	142	724	283	441	..
34 United Provinces States	246	136	110	..	..	..	..
35 Western India States Agency	..	..	..	73,317	45,640	27,677	..
36 States unspecified*	..	..	..	..	..	..	2,202
(c) French and Portuguese Settlements.	**861**	**723**	**138**	**38,702**	**25,915**	**12,787**	**3,537**
(d) India Unspecified	**24**	**21**	**3**	**2,507**	**2,271**	**236**	**43**
B. Born in Other Asiatic Countries.	**7,548**	**6,068**	**1,480**	**7,832**	**6,465**	**1,367**	**797**
C. Born in Europe	**8,971**	**6,108**	**2,863**	**6,665**	**4,736**	**1,929**	**2,331**
D. Born in Africa	**64**	**43**	**21**	**373**	**205**	**168**	**393**
E. Born in America	**226**	**126**	**100**	**210**	**142**	**68**	**80**
F. Born in Australasia	**89**	**43**	**46**	**185**	**154**	**31**	**33**
G. Born at Sea	..	..	..	..	..	..	..
H. Birthplace not returned	..	..	..	..	..	..	..

Birthplace—Cities.

Madras.		Hyderabad. (Deccan.)			Delhi (*including New Delhi*).			
Males.	Females.	Persons.	Males.	Females.	Persons.	Males.	Females	
9	10	11	12	13	14	15	16	
341,223	306,007	466,894	247,623	219,271	439,180	263,178	176,002	
338,794	304,802	463,580	244,759	218,821	435,797	260,740	175,057	A
328,371	297,661	48,538	31,122	17,416	391,324	233,496	157,828	(a)
..	..	600	211	389	749	404	345	1
..	..	..	..	..	..	..	..	2
..	..	5	2	3	81	53	28	3
..	..	5	5	..	183	123	60	4
..	..	220	100	120	6,135	3,664	2,471	5
..	..	264	225	39	710	517	193	6
..	..	12,170	6,063	6,107	2,237	1,378	859	7
497	544	92	25	67	81	50	31	8
..	..	3,032	1,155	1,877	767	447	320	9
..	..	6	3	3	..	..	..	10
..	..	463	298	165	226,962	126,741	100,221	11
323,560	294,964	22,692	17,232	5,460	1,432	829	603	12
..	..	112	97	15	1,718	1,338	380	13
..	..	2,882	2,210	672	54,557	35,368	19,189	14
..	..	5,995	3,496	2,499	95,712	62,584	33,128	15
4,314	2,153	..	..	..	..	..	..	16
8,575	5,409	414,905	213,550	201,355	44,333	27,176	17,157	(b)
..	..	..	..	..	..	..	..	17
..	..	..	..	..	..	..	..	18
..	..	22	16	6	65	41	24	19
..	..	..	..	..	..	..	..	20
..	..	..	..	..	5	..	5	21
..	..	148	59	89	..	..	..	22
..	..	56	31	25	295	157	138	23
.	..	..	..	..	..	..	..	24
..	..	342	292	50	1,628	961	667	25
1,741	882	408,636	209,706	198,930	256	155	101	26
..	..	35	21	14	440	358	82	27
2,019	1,077	43	26	17	26	19	7	28
657	*353*	*25*	*18*	*7*	*17*	*12*	*5*	
1,227	*623*	*18*	[illegible]	*10*	*4*	*4*	..	
135	*101*	..	..	..	*5*	*3*	*2*	
3,103	2,960	1,779	1,125	654	137	82	55	29
..	..	..	..	..	..	..	..	30
..	..	493	386	107	4,769	3,128	1,641	31
..	..	2,669	1,576	1,093	35,076	21,238	13,838	32
..	..	..	..	..	..	..	..	33
..	..	682	312	370	1,636	1,037	599	34
..	..	..	..	..	..	..	..	35
1,712	490	..	..	..	..	..	..	36
1,823	1,714	137	87	50	72	48	24	(c)
25	18	..	..	..	68	20	48	(d)
484	313	881	765	116	727	560	167	B
1,651	680	2,270	1,990	280	2,562	1,839	723	C
226	167	4	3	1	21	16	5	D
55	25	80	62	18	56	17	39	E
13	20	21	12	9	17	6	11	F
..	..	..	...	..	..	...	..	G
..	..	58	32	26	..	..	..	H

Table VI.—Part II—

Birthplace.	Lahore.			Rangoon.			
	Persons.	Males.	Females.	Persons.	Males.	Females.	Persons.
1	17	18	19	20	21	22	23
Total Population ..	429,747	274,587	155,160	400,415	271,063	129,352	274,659
A. Born in India	423,708	270,199	153,509	378,136	254,601	123,535	270,395
(a) Provinces ..	404,475	255,626	148,849	370,529	248,860	121,669	268,521
1 Ajmer-Merwara	154	103	51	..	..	..	166
2 Andamans and Nicobars ..	20	17	3	..	..	..	..
3 Assam	49	37	12	295	271	24	26
4 Baluchistan (*Districts and Administered Territories*).	385	278	107	..	..	..	25
5 Bengal	1,255	856	399	29,426	27,166	2,260	2,148
6 Bihar and Orissa	110	90	20	4,013	3,843	170	727
7 Bombay	1,554	1,028	526	2,876	2,016	860	616
8 Burma	121	81	40	196,429	99,424	97,005	35
9 Central Provinces and Berar	195	145	50	..	..	..	223
10 Coorg	..	..	..	..	..	..	..
11 Delhi	2,416	1,527	889	..	..	..	379
12 Madras	455	307	148	107,390	88,635	18,755	278
13 N.-W. F. Province .. (*Districts and Administered Territories*).	7,060	4,969	2,091	..	..	..	273
14 Punjab	361,895	225,105	136,790	3,032	2,481	551	4,816
15 United Provinces of Agra and Oudh.	28,806	21,083	7,723	26,409	24,511	1,898	258,806
16 Provinces unspecified ..	..	..	..	659	513	146	..
(b) States and Agencies.	19,097	14,452	4,645	6,876	5,146	1,730	1,874
17 Assam States	..	..	..	4	2	2	1
18 Baluchistan States ..	..	..	..	..	..	..	..
19 Baroda State	37	27	10	..	..	..	23
20 Bengal States	..	..	..	4	1	3	..
21 Bihar and Orissa States ..	1	1	..	..	..	..	..
22 Bombay States	42	27	15	..	..	..	.
23 Central India Agency ..	23	23	..	..	..	..	128
24 Central Provinces States ..	41	18	23	..	..	..	28
25 Gwalior State	143	92	51	..	..	..	134
26 Hyderabad State	136	90	46	..	..	..	120
27 Jammu and Kashmir State ..	8,469	7,165	1,304	..	..	..	80
28 Madras States Agency ..	13	8	5	468	405	63	8
Cochin State ..	..	..	..	..	..	..	..
Travancore State ..	..	..	..	..	..	..	*8*
Other Madras States ..	*13*	*8*	*5*	*468*	*405*	*63*	..
29 Mysore State	128	118	10	..	..	..	26
30 N.-W. F. Province .. (*Agencies and Tribal Areas*).	..	..	..	..	..	..	..
31 Punjab States and Agency ..	4,151	2,882	1,269	..	..	..	164
32 Rajputana Agency ..	5,603	3,875	1,728	..	..	..	904
33 Sikkim State	..	..	..	..	..	..	..
34 United Provinces States ..	310	126	184	..	..	..	258
35 Western India States Agency	..	..	..	3,706	2,850	856	..
36 States unspecified ..	..	..	..	2,694	1,888	806	..
(c) French and Portuguese Settlements.	11	5	6	716	585	131	..
(d) India unspecified ..	125	116	9	15	10	5	..
B. Born in Other Asiatic Countries.	1,040	778	262	19,013	14,037	4,976	624
C. Born in Europe ..	4,792	3,482	1,310	2,872	2,179	693	3,550
D. Born in Africa	128	86	42	126	71	55	32
E. Born in America ..	63	33	30	151	92	59	58
F. Born in Australasia ..	16	9	7	117	83	34	..
G. Born at Sea	..	..	..	..	..	..	..
H. Birthplace not returned	..	..	..	..	..	..	..

Birthplace—Cities—*continued.*

Lucknow.		Amritsar.			Karachi.			
Males.	Females.	Persons.	Males.	Females.	Persons.	Males.	Females.	
24	25	26	27	28	29	30	31	
159,458	115,201	264,840	158,985	105,855	263,565	156,120	107,445	
155,858	114,537	264,222	158,414	105,808	262,409	155,501	106,908	A
154,437	114,084	256,011	152,558	103,453	259,484	153,532	105,952	(a)
85	81	2	..	2	16	9	7	1
..	..	3	3	..	..	..	..	2
9	17	6	3	3	..	..	..	3
20	5	23	11	12	352	193	159	4
1,276	872	98	63	35	1,190	813	377	5
520	207	3	2	1	..	..	..	6
410	206	309	230	79	*209,215	119,469	89,746	7
28	7	10	8	2	..	..	..	8
131	92	66	15	51	11,455	9,817	1,638	9
..	..	..	..	..	..	..	..	10
230	149	..		..	11	11	..	11
154	124	19	13	6	1,582	1,141	441	12
210	63	954	467	487	2,045	1,519	526	13
3,552	1,267	249,635	148,512	101,123	22,218	13,702	8,516	14
147,812	110,994	4,883	3,231	1,652	11,400	6,858	4,542	15
..	..	..	..	..	..	..	..	16
1,421	453	8,211	5,856	2,355	2,730	1,789	941	(b)
1	..	..	..	..	..	..	..	17
..	..	..	..	..	..	..	..	18
23	..	1	..	1	6	6	..	19
..	..	..	..	..	..	..	..	20
..	..	..	..	..	..	..	..	21
..	..	..	..	..	1,817	1,310	507	22
71	57	..	..	..	..	..	..	23
20	8	..	..	..	..	..	..	24
85	49	4	1	3	..	..	..	25
67	53	11	8	3	2	2	..	26
64	16	..	..	..	1	1	..	27
3	5	..	..	..	..	..	..	28
..	..	..	..	..	..	..	..	
3	5	..	..	..	..	..	..	
..	..	..	..	..	..	..	..	
22	4	2	2	..	7	4	3	29
..	..	..	..	..	..	..	..	30
142	22	7,121	5,073	2,048	..	..	..	31
753	151	1,072	772	300	10	6	4	32
..	..	..	..	..	..	..	..	33
170	88	..	..	..	..	..	..	34
..	..	..	..	..	887	460	427	35
..	..	..	..	..	..	..	..	36
..	..	..	..	..	195	180	15	(c)
..	..	..	..	..	..	..	..	(d)
427	197	450	412	38	98	45	53	B
3,129	421	161	155	6	823	443	380	C
21	11	6	4	2	10	9	1	D
23	35	..	..	..	225	122	103	E
..	..	1	..	1	..	..	..	F
..	..	..	..	..	..	..	..	G
..	..	..	..	..	..	..	..	H

* Includes British Districts and States unspecified (2,030 males, 5,042 females).

Table VI.—Part II—

	Birthplace.	* Poona. Persons.	Males.	Females.	Cawnpore. Persons.	Males.	Females.	Persons.
	1	32	33	34	35	36	37	38
	Total Population ..	256,003	141,291	114,712	243,755	143,872	99,883	229,764
	A. Born in India	252,206	138,278	113,928	241,862	142,410	99,452	227,980
	(a) Provinces ..	239,738	130,608	109,130	239,668	141,103	98,565	216,360
1	Ajmer-Merwara	1,046	835	211	32	18	14	476
2	Andamans and Nicobars ..	..	..	..	..	..	..	..
3	Assam	54	..	54	18	13	5	18
4	Baluchistan (*Districts and Administered Territories*).	169	128	41	4	..	4	18
5	Bengal	147	96	51	1,159	658	501	1,051
6	Bihar and Orissa	..	..	..	286	209	77	61
7	Bombay	†227,352	221,778	105,574	440	239	201	741
8	Burma	14	10	4	14	10	4	81
9	Central Provinces and Berar	1,291	746	545	419	177	242	845
10	Coorg	..	..	..	..	..	..	2
11	Delhi	201	179	22	396	252	144	1,657
12	Madras	4,229	2,471	1,758	151	105	46	278
13	N.-W. F. Province .. .. (*Districts and Administered Territories*).	60	56	4	7	5	2	46
14	Punjab	3,763	3,160	603	1,477	983	494	4,659
15	United Provinces of Agra and Oudh.	1,412	1,149	263	235,265	138,434	96,831	206,427
16	Provinces unspecified		..	..	..	..	..	..
	(b) States and Agencies.	8,850	5,264	3,586	2,016	1,224	792	11,558
17	Assam States	..	..	..	..	..	..	4
18	Baluchistan States ..	..	..	..	..	..	..	..
19	Baroda State	443	205	238	4	2	2	10
20	Bengal States	..	..	..	..	..	..	..
21	Bihar and Orissa States ..	..	..	..	..	..	..	..
22	Bombay States	..	..	..	..	..	..	2
23	Central India Agency ..	139	63	76	431	258	173	323
24	Central Provinces States ..	..	..	..	56	16	40	44
25	Gwalior State	122	84	38	484	316	168	890
26	Hyderabad State	5,882	3,395	2,487	45	26	19	45
27	Jammu and Kashmir State ..	41	1	40	22	15	7	16
28	Madras States Agency ..	..	..	..	..	..	..	8
	Cochin State ..	..	..	..	..	..	..	..
	Travancore State ..	..	..	..	..	..	..	8
	Other Madras States ..	..	..	..	..	..	..	..
29	Mysore State	555	330	225	28	28	..	28
30	N.-W. F. Province .. (*Agencies and Tribal Areas*).	..	..	..	..	..	..	..
31	Punjab States and Agency ..	..	..	..	88	53	35	50
32	Rajputana Agency ..	1,594	1,185	409	753	444	309	9,883
33	Sikkim State	..	..	..		..	..	..
34	United Provines States ..	..	..	..	105	66	39	253
35	Western India States Agency	74	1	73	..	..	..	2
36	States unspecified ..	..	..	..	..	..	..	..
	(c) French and Portuguese Settlements.	901	639	262	15	15	..	8
	(d) India Unspecified ..	2,717	1,767	950	163	68	95	54
	B. Born in Other Asiatic Countries.	690	506	184	284	192	92	168
	C. Born in Europe ..	2,962	2,425	537	1,568	1,250	318	1,563
	D. Born in Africa	87	55	32	16	13	3	10
	E. Born in America ..	..	..	..	20	7	13	26
	F. Born in Australasia ..	58	27	31	5	..	5	8
	G. Born at Sea	..	..	..	..	..	..	..
	H. Birthplace not returned	..	..	..	..	..	..	9

* Here relates to Poona Taluka, and therefore includes 5,816 persons (3,152 males and 2,664 females) enumerated in the immediate neighbourhood of Poona City.

Birthplace—Cities—*continued.*

Agra.		Howrah.			Nagpur.			
Males.	Females.	Persons.	Males.	Females.	Persons.	Males.	Females.	
39	40	41	42	43	44	45	46	
127,736	**102,028**	**224,873**	**145,120**	**79,753**	**215,165**	**116,403**	**98,762**	
126,270	**101,710**	**223,428**	**143,998**	**79,430**	**214,808**	**116,188**	**98,620**	A
119,692	**96,668**	**221,667**	**142,747**	**78,920**	**208,886**	**112,677**	**96,209**	(a)
273	203	11	7	4	188	123	65	1
..	..	..	..	.	10	..	10	2
8	10	97	70	27	10	8	2	3
16	2	2	2	..	27	21	6	4
665	386	144,828	83,648	61,180	1,174	620	554	5
27	34	33,181	26,393	6,788	59	36	23	6
433	308	226	169	57	5,616	3,479	2,137	7
46	35	47	27	20	22	14	8	8
490	355	794	459	335	191,246	101,481	89,765	9
2	..	..	..	..	..	..	..	10
888	769	53	33	20	246	205	41	11
160	118	2,661	1,372	1,289	2,167	1,332	835	12
25	21	26	19	7	61	58	3	13
3,078	1,581	797	603	194	1,321	1,000	321	14
113,581	92,846	38,944	29,945	8,999	6,739	4,300	2,439	15
..	..		..	..	..	..	..	16
6,556	**5,002**	**1,742**	**1,244**	**498**	**5,598**	**3,320**	**2,278**	(b)
..	4	5	2	3	..	..	..	17
..	..	..	..	..	..	..	..	18
4	6	..	..	..	96	53	43	19
..	..	36	27	9	4	3	1	20
..	..	181	135	46	23	4	19	21
..	2	..	..	..	298	167	131	22
154	169	5	4	1	2,529	1,624	905	23
36	8	..	..	..	640	372	268	24
462	428	145	114	31	87	55	32	25
24	21	22	15	7	667	345	322	26
13	3	7	3	4	1	1	..	27
8	..	..	..	..	22	9	13	28
..	..	..	..	..	..	..	..	
8	..	..	..	..	..	..	..	
..	..	..	..	..	**22*	*9*	*13*	
10	18	..	..	..	131	101	30	29
..	..	..	..	..	..	..	..	30
32	18	..	..	..	41	27	14	31
5,664	4,219	1,335	939	396	1,059	559	500	32
..	..	6	5	1	..	..	..	33
149	104	..	..	..	..		..	34
..	2	..	..	..	..	...	..	35
..	..	..	..	..	..	..	..	36
3	**5**	**1**	**1**	..	**324**	**191**	**133**	(c)
19	**35**	**18**	**6**	**12**	..	..	...	(d)
107	**61**	**1,080**	**876**	**204**	**85**	**63**	**22**	B
1,337	**226**	**343**	**232**	**111**	**237**	**134**	**103**	C
7	**3**	**7**	**5**	**2**	**17**	**12**	**5**	D
11	**15**	**11**	**6**	**5**	**18**	**6**	**12**	E
3	5	4	3	1	..	..	..	F
..		..	..	..	..	...	..	G
1	8	..	..	..	..	...	...	H

* Includes Cochin and Travancore.

Table VI.—Part II—

Birthplace.	Benares.			Allahabad.			
	Persons.	Males.	Females.	Persons.	Males.	Females.	Persons
1	47	48	49	50	51	52	53
Total Population ..	**205,315**	**114,551**	**90,764**	**183,914**	**104,162**	**79,752**	**182,018**
A. Born in India	**204,313**	**113,935**	**90,378**	**182,382**	**103,053**	**79,329**	**181,765**
(a) Provinces ..	**202,945**	**113,168**	**89,777**	**180,693**	**102,029**	**78,664**	**180,469**
1 Ajmer-Merwara	153	89	64	69	41	28	..
2 Andamans and Nicobars ..	1	1	..	1	..	1	..
3 Assam	125	68	57	44	23	21	..
4 Baluchistan (*Districts and Administered Territories.*)	..	..	..	21	10	11	..
5 Bengal	8,310	4,689	3,621	2,953	1,569	1,384	..
6 Bihar and Orissa	2,191	1,549	642	1,350	793	557	..
7 Bombay	553	339	214	582	334	248	..
8 Burma	14	10	4	46	18	28	..
9 Central Provinces and Berar	374	306	68	770	403	367	49
10 Coorg	..	..	..	79	77	2	..
11 Delhi	69	47	22	139	82	57	..
12 Madras	552	302	250	349	188	161	180,058
13 N.-W. F. Province (*Districts and Administered Territories*).	10	10	..	38	27	11	..
14 Punjab	789	542	247	1,300	850	450	..
15 United Provinces of Agra and Oudh.	189,804	105,216	84,588	172,952	97,614	75,338	..
16 Provinces unspecified ..	..	..	..	..	..	..	362
(b) States and Agencies.	**1,368**	**767**	**601**	**1,685**	**1,021**	**664**	**1,233**
17 Assam States	..	..		..	..	..	..
18 Baluchistan States ..	..	..	..	..	..	..	..
19 Baroda State	6	6	..	4	..	4	..
20 Bengal States	..	..	..	1	1	..	..
21 Bihar and Orissa States ..	..	..	..	..	..	..	..
22 Bombay States	1	1	..	14	10	4	..
23 Central India Agency ..	105	75	30	833	489	344	..
24 Central Provinces States ..	..	..	..	6	6	..	..
25 Gwalior State	142	89	53	120	65	55	..
26 Hyderabad State	96	69	27	123	72	51	63
27 Jammu and Kashmir State.	38	24	14	35	22	13	..
28 Madras States Agency ..	..	..	..	..	..	..	995
Cochin State	..	..	..	..	..	..	*115*
Travancore State ..	..	..	..	..	..	..	*712*
Other Madras States ..	..	..	..	..	..	..	*168*
29 Mysore State	253	29	224	31	8	23	167
30 N.-W. F. Province (*Agencies and Tribal Areas*).	..	..	..	..	..	..	..
31 Punjab States and Agency ..	..	..	..	38	33	5	..
32 Rajputana Agency ..	511	355	156	388	254	134	..
33 Sikkim State	..	..	..	..	..	..	..
34 United Provinces States ..	216	119	97	92	61	31	..
35 Western India States Agency	..	..	..	..	..	..	..
36 States unspecified ..	..	..	..	..	..	..	8
(c) French and Portuguese Settlements.	..	..	..	4	3	1	63
(d) India Unspecified ..	..	..	..	..	..	..	..
B. Born in Other Asiatic Countries.	800	454	346	315	201	114	149
C. Born in Europe ..	185	152	33	1,157	882	275	74
D Born in Africa	5	1	4	10	8	2	6
E. Born in America ..	9	7	2	40	13	27	21
F. Born in Australasia ..	3	2	1	10	5	5	3
G. Born at Sea	..	..	..	..	..	..	..
H. Birthplace not returned	..	..	..	..	..	..	..

Birthplace—Cities—*continued.*

Madura.		Srinagar.			Bangalore. (*excluding Civil and Military Station*).			
Males.	Females.	Persons.	Males.	Females.	Persons.	Males.	Females.	
54	55	56	57	58	59	60	61	
91,676	**90,342**	**173,573**	**94,793**	**78,780**	**172,357**	**91,680**	**80,677**	
91,544	**90,221**	**173,230**	**94,601**	**78,629**	**172,071**	**91,535**	**80,536**	A
90,801	**89,668**	**1,045**	**687**	**358**	**35,726**	**19,441**	**16,285**	(*a*)
..	..	1	1	..	19	12	7	1
..	..	..	..	..	..	..	..	2
..	..	4	1	3	..	..	..	3
..	..	6	4	2	23	18	5	4
..	..	32	13	19	65	38	27	5
..	..	7	4	3	4	3	1	6
..	..	9	7	2	1,629	1,003	626	7
27	22	3	1	2	31	12	19	8
..	..	..	..	..	87	56	31	9
..	..	..	..	..	175	96	79	10
..	..	12	10	2	26	17	9	11
90,550	89,508	10	9	1	33,496	18,065	15,431	12
..	..	66	41	25	6	5	1	13
..	..	824	559	265	92	69	23	14
..	..	71	37	34	73	47	26	15
224	138	..	..	..	..	..	..	16
712	521	**172,120**	**93,872**	**78,248**	**136,225**	**72,022**	**64,203**	(b)
..	..	..	..	..	..	..	..	1
..	..	..	..	..	..	..	..	18
..	..	1	1	..	13	9	4	19
..	..	..	..	..	..	..	..	20
..	..	..	..	..	..	..	..	21
..	..	3	2	1	39	15	24	22
..	..	4	2	2	..	..	..	23
..	..	..	..	..	..	..	..	24
..	..	3	2	1	..	..	..	25
27	36	..	..	..	389	227	162	26
..	..	172,095	93,861	78,234	19	14	5	27
602	393	..	..	..	219	139	80	28
76	*39*	..	..	..	*71*	*41*	*30*	
460	*252*	..	..	..	*88*	*67*	*21*	
66	*102*	..	..	..	*60*	*31*	*29*	
80	87	..	..	..	135,120	71,278	63,842	29
..	..	..	..	..	..	..	..	30
..	..	7	1	6	..	..	..	31
..	..	5	2	3	365	309	56	32
..	..	2	1	1	..	..	..	33
..	..	..	..	..	..	..	..	34
..	..	..	..	..	61	31	30	35
3	5	..	..	..	..	..	..	36
31	32	14	14	..	90	52	38	(c)
..	..	51	28	23	30	20	10	(d)
76	73	232	146	86	76	55	21	B
45	29	103	43	60	184	77	107	C
4	2	1	1	..	13	8	5	D
7	14	3	1	2	10	4	6	E
..	3	4	1	3	3	1	2	F
..	..	..	..	..	..	..	..	G
..	..	..	..	..	..	..	..	H

Table VI.—Part II—

Birthplace.	Patna. Persons.	Patna. Males.	Patna. Females.	Mandalay. Persons.	Mandalay. Males.	Mandalay. Females.	Persons.
1	62	63	64	65	66	67	68
Total Population	**159,690**	**92,238**	**67,452**	**147,932**	**77,667**	**70,265**	**144,179**
A. Born in India	**159,209**	**91,924**	**67,285**	**146,059**	**76,250**	**69,809**	**144,119**
(a) Provinces	**158,582**	**91,599**	**66,983**	**145,529**	**75,820**	**69,709**	**4,072**
1 Ajmer-Merwara	3	2	1	—	—	—	444
2 Andamans and Nicobars	..	..	—	—	—	—	—
3 Assam	94	59	35	18	14	4	—
4 Baluchistan (*Districts and Administered Territories*).	3	1	2	..	..	..	—
5 Bengal	4,411	2,531	1,880	2,487	2,028	459	222
6 Bihar and Orissa	150,230	86,572	63,658	191	179	12	—
7 Bombay	97	47	50	517	396	121	227
8 Burma	12	4	8	133,123	65,643	67,480	—
9 Central Provinces and Berar	54	21	33	..	..	..	33
10 Coorg	..	..	..	..	..	..	..
11 Delhi	39	28	11	..	..	..	296
12 Madras	70	34	36	3,727	2,916	811	..
13 N.-W. F. Province (*Districts and Administered Territories*).	13	9	4	..	..	..	..
14 Punjab	403	269	134	1,699	1,340	359	857
15 United Provinces of Agra and Oudh.	3,153	[illegible],022	1,131	3,600	3,153	447	1,904
16 Provinces unspecified	..	..	..	167	151	16	90
(b) States and Agencies.	**617**	**315**	**302**	**521**	**422**	**99**	**140,034**
17 Assam States	..	..	..	..	..	..	..
18 Baluchistan States	..	..	..	..	—	..	..
19 Baroda State	1	..	1	—	..	..	—
20 Bengal States	..	..	..	—	—	—	—
21 Bihar and Orissa States	10	8	2	—	..	—	—
22 Bombay States	..	..	..	—	..	..	—
23 Central India Agency	116	30	86	—	..	—	77
24 Central Provinces States	..	..	..	..	..	—	—
25 Gwalior State	..	..	..	—	..	—	65
26 Hyderabad State	53	16	37	..	—	—	—
27 Jammu and Kashmir State	7	7	..	..	—	—	—
28 Madras States Agency	3	3	..		2	3	—
Cochin State	..	..	..	..	—	—	—
Travancore State	..	..	..	—	—	—	—
Other Madras States	**3	*3*	..		*2*	*3*	—
29 Mysore State	15	8	7	..	..	—	—
30 N.-W. F. Province (*Agencies and Tribal Areas*).	..	..	..	..	..	..	—
31 Punjab States and Agency	2	..	2	..	..	—	—
32 Rajputana Agency	410	243	167	..	..	—	139,825
33 Sikkim State	..	..	..	..	..	—	—
34 United Provinces States	..	..	..	..	—	—	—
35 Western India States Agency	..	..	..	—	—	—	—
36 States unspecified	..	..	—	516	420	96	67
(c) French and Portuguese Settlements.	5	5	..	9	8	1	8
(d) India Unspecified	5	5	—	—	—	—	5
B. Born in Other Asiatic Countries.	306	233	73	1,487	1,129	358	21
C. Born in Europe	167	78	89	363	279	84	33
D. Born in Africa	4	1	3	5	1	4	1
E. Born in America	1	1	—	12	5	7	—
F. Born in Australasia	3	1	2	6	3	3	—
G. Born at Sea	—	—	—	—	—	—	—
H. Birthplace not returned	—	—	—	—	—	—	—

* Includes Cochin and Travancore.

Birthplace—Cities—*continued.*

Jaipur.		Bareilly.			Trichinopoly.			
Males.	Females.	Persons.	Males.	Females.	Persons.	Males.	Females.	
69	70	71	72	73	74	75	76	
77,933	66,246	144,031	79,389	64,642	142,843	72,997	69,846	
77,900	66,219	142,918	78,447	64,471	142,406	72,740	69,666	
2,355	1,717	140,888	77,022	63,866	189,312	71,153	68,159	(a)
193	251	35	13	22	..	..	..	1
..	—	..	..	..	..	..	..	2
—	—	8	5	3	..	..	..	3
—	—	4	4	..	..	..	..	4
115	107	343	229	114	..	..	..	5
—	—	29	17	12	—	..	..	6
126	101	150	101	49	..	..	..	7
..	—	11	4	7	114	59	55	8
19	13	51	21	30	..	..	..	9
—	—	..	..	..	..	..	..	10
157	139	135	81	54	..	..	..	11
..	—	56	39	17	138,182	70,222	67,960	12
..	—	107	97	10	..	..	..	13
554	303	1,435	1,117	318	..	..	..	14
1,135	769	138,524	75,294	63,230	..	..	..	15
56	34	—	..	..	1,016	872	144	16
75,533	64,501	1,948	1,391	557	2,837	1,475	1,362	(b)
..	..	—	..	..	..	..	..	17
—	—	—	—	—	..	..	..	18
..	—	4	2	2	..	..	..	19
—	—	—	—	—	..	..	..	20
..	—	—	—	—	..	—	..	21
—	—	—	—	..	..	..	..	22
38	39	55	16	39	..	..	..	23
..	—	9	9	..	..	..	..	24
39	26	40	17	23	..	..	..	25
—	—	14	6	8	112	62	50	26
—	—	91	84	7	..	..	..	27
—	—	1	1	—	2,179	1,144	1,035	28
—	—	—	—	—	*163*	*117*	*46*	
—	—	*1*	*1*	—	*303*	*201*	*102*	
—	—	—	—	—	*1,713*	*826*	*887*	
—	—	6	4	2	479	220	259	29
..	—	—	..	..	—	—	..	30
—	—	26	22	4	—	—	..	31
75,422	64,403	310	241	69	—	—	..	32
—	—	—	..	..	—	—	..	33
—	—	1,392	989	403	—	—	..	34
—	—	—	..	..	..	—	..	35
34	33	—	..	..	67	49	18	36
8	—	..	..	..	256	112	144	(c)
4	1	82	34	48	1	—	1	(d)
17	4	61	52	9	266	155	111	B
15	23	1,029	879	150	152	97	55	C
1	—	9	5	4	13	4	9	D
—	—	12	5	7	5	1	4	E
—	—	2	1	1	1	—	1	F
—	—	—	—	—	—	—	..	G
—	—	—	—	—	—	—	—	H

Table VI.—Part II—

Birthplace.	Dacca. Persons.	Dacca. Males.	Dacca. Females.	Meerut. Persons.	Meerut. Males.	Meerut. Females.	Persons.
1	77	78	79	80	81	82	83
Total Population ..	**138,518**	**79,365**	**59,153**	**136,709**	**80,073**	**56,636**	**134,113**
A. Born in India	**138,049**	**78,988**	**59,061**	**134,399**	**78,180**	**56,219**	**131,390**
(a) Provinces ..	**137,717**	**78,822**	**58,895**	**132,077**	**77,096**	**54,981**	**29,231**
1 Ajmer-Merwara	5	..	5	214	127	87	16
2 Andaman and Nicobar Islands	..	..	..	1	1	..	5
3 Assam	1,376	1,014	362	5	5	..	9
4 Baluchistan (*Districts and Administered Territories*).	7	..	7	38	25	13	30
5 Bengal	127,819	72,525	55,294	790	422	368	436
6 Bihar and Orissa	6,008	3,658	2,350	35	24	11	30
7 Bombay	78	58	20	240	130	110	1,468
8 Burma	53	23	30	25	11	14	275
9 Central Provinces and Berar	168	98	70	106	56	50	458
10 Coorg	..	..	..	..	..	..	230
11 Delhi	..	..	..	1,000	590	410	55
12 Madras	28	22	6	99	59	40	25,275
13 N.-W. F. Province .. (*Districts and Administered Territories*).	13	9	4	2,302	2,226	76	62
14 Punjab	125	101	24	5,713	3,911	1,802	536
15 United Provinces of Agra and Oudh.	2,037	1,314	723	121,509	69,509	52,000	346
16 Provinces unspecified ..	..	..	..	..	..	..	..
(b) States and Agencies	**332**	**166**	**166**	**2,155**	**945**	**1,210**	**101,882**
17 Assam States	..	..	..	..	..	..	..
18 Baluchistan States ..	..	..	..	..	..	..	..
19 Baroda State	..	..	..	1	1	..	15
20 Bengal States	256	102	154	..	..	..	..
21 Bihar and Orissa States ..	..	..	..	..	..	..	..
22 Bombay States	..	—	—	—	..	..	38
23 Central India Agency ..	..	..	..	72	42	30	23
24 Central Provinces States ..	..	..	..	..	—	—	..
25 Gwalior State	..	..	..	139	43	96	8
26 Hyderabad State	41	38	3	645	180	465	1,428
27 Jammu and Kashmir State ..	4	..	4	35	15	20	48
28 Madras States Agency ..	..	..	..	..	—	..	218
Cochin State ..	..	..	..	..	..	..	*67*
Travancore State ..	..	..	..	..	..	..	*144*
Other Madras States ..	..	..	..	..	..	..	*7*
29 Mysore State	1	1	..	12	4	8	99,449
30 N.-W. F. Province (*Agencies and Tribal Areas*).	..	..	..	..	..	..	..
31 Punjab States and Agency ..	..	..	..	135	104	31	—
32 Rajputana Agency ..	21	17	4	473	224	249	609
33 Sikkim State	9	8	1	..	..	—	—
34 United Provinces States ..	—	..	..	643	332	311	—
35 Western India States Agency	—	..	..	..	—	..	46
36 States unspecified ..	—	..	..	..	—	—	—
(c) French and Portuguese Settlements.	—	..	..	12	12	..	240
(d) India Unspecified —	—	..	..	155	127	28	37
B. Born in Other Asiatic Countries.	387	330	57	62	35	27	214
C. Born in Europe —	76	44	32	2,223	1,850	373	2,330
D. Born in Africa .. —	—	..	..	7	1	6	132
E. Born in America —	4	3	1	12	5	7	31
F. Born in Australasia —	2	..	2	5	2	3	15
G. Born at Sea — —	—	..	..	1	..	1	1
H. Birthplace not returned	..	—	—	—	—	—	—

Birthplace—Cities—*concluded.*

Bangalore (*Civil and Military Station*).		Indore.			Jubbulpore.			
Males.	Females.	Persons.	Males.	Females.	Persons.	Males.	Females.	
84	85	86	87	88	89	90	91	
69,409	**64,704**	**127,327**	**73,450**	**53,877**	**124,382**	**69,258**	**55,124**	
67,485	**63,905**	**127,258**	**73,403**	**53,855**	**122,030**	**67,335**	**54,695**	A.
15,954	**13,277**	**26,063**	**16,510**	**9,553**	**107,519**	**59,257**	**48,262**	(a)
11	5	661	384	277	36	12	24	1
3	2	..	..	..	10	5	5	2
4	5	4	2	2	43	18	25	3
20	10	17	15	2	32	15	17	4
199	237	91	48	43	611	329	282	5
23	7	54	38	16	201	100	101	6
778	690	7,385	4,260	3,125	1,923	1,165	758	7
111	164	5	4	1	37	18	19	8
217	241	4,193	2,373	1,820	87,731	46,471	41,260	9
133	97	..	..	..	..	..	..	10
37	18	329	212	117	..	.	..	11
13,781	11,494	122	69	53	1,207	671	536	12
40	22	60	52	8	342	308	34	13
360	176	1,230	872	358	3,267	2,647	620	14
237	109	11,912	8,181	3,731	12,079	7,498	4,581	15
..	..	..	..	..	..	..		16
51,387	**50,495**	**101,142**	**56,857**	**44,285**	**14,465**	**8,078**	**6,387**	(b)
..	..	..	..	..	..	..	..	17
..	..	..	..	..	..	..	..	18
12	3	341	189	152	..	..	..	19
..	..	..	..	..	..	..	..	20
..	..	..	..	..	..	..	..	21
15	23	124	73	51	14	7	7	22
12	11	73,037	40,075	32,962	13,221	7,308	5,913	23
..	..	2	2	..	53	26	27	24
1	7	10,252	5,740	4,512	214	136	78	25
732	696	461	270	191	320	199	121	26
28	20	10	6	4	62	54	8	27
125	93	..	..	..	..	..	..	28
44	*23*	..	..	..	..	..	..	
76	*68*	..	..	..	..	..	..	
5	*2*	..	..	..	..	..	..	
50,056	49,393	65	38	27	45	23	22	29
..	..	..	..	..	..	..	..	30
..	..	..	..	..	23	6	17	31
376	233	16,020	9,928	6,092	509	319	190	32
..	..	..	..	..	..	..	..	33
..	..	28	19	9	4	..	4	34
30	16	802	517	285	..	..	..	35
..	..	..	..	..	..	..	..	36
107	**133**	**53**	**36**	**17**	**46**	..	**46**	(c)
37	..	..	..	..	..	..	..	(d)
110	**104**	**46**	**33**	**13**	**101**	**82**	**19**	B.
1,724	**606**	**20**	**11**	**9**	**2,208**	**1,818**	**390**	C.
66	**66**	**1**	**1**	..	**8**	**7**	**1**	D.
15	**16**	**2**	**2**	..	**33**	**15**	**18**	E.
8	**7**	..	..	..	**2**	**1**	**1**	F.
1	..	..	..	..	..	..	..	G.
..	..	..	..	..	..	..	..	H.

Table VI.—Part III—

Province, State or Agency.	Immigrants born elsewhere in India.	Emigrants born in Province or State.	Excess of Immigrants (+) or Emigrants (—).	NET INTERCHANGE OF POPULATION. Ajmer-Merwara.	Andamans and Nicobars.	Assam.	Baluchistan (*Districts and Administered Territories*).	Bengal.	Bihar and Orissa.
1	2	3	4	5	6	7	8	9	10
Provinces ..	**8,316,778**	**8,811,591**	**—494,813**	**+5,844**	**—12,742**	**—1,198,825**	**—17,376**	**—673,632**	**+1,284,596**
1 Ajmer-Merwara ..	104,579	60,909	+43,670	..	—24	—56	—42	—77	—21
2 Andaman and Nicobar Islands.	13,552	552	+13,000	+24	..	+148	+18	+951	+616
3 Assam	1,317,653	73,404	+1,244,249	+56	—148	..	+235	+545,932	+441,618
4 Baluchistan ..	71,335	43,487	+27,848	+42	—18	—235	..	+467	+35
5 Bengal	1,693,245	1,081,423	+611,822	+77	—951	—545,932	—467		+964,864
6 Bihar and Orissa ..	494,405	1,896,185	—1,401,780	+21	—616	—441,618	—35	—964,864	..
7 Bombay	1,272,083	857,394	+414,689	+18,241	—424	—5,920	+30,773	—1,633	—4,969
8 Burma	616,600	24,197	+592,403	—9	—2,889	—5,172	+50	+154,278	+18,091
9 Central Provinces and Berar.	649,701	580,233	+69,468	+2,923	—341	—69,755	+506	—38,535	—38,766
10 Coorg	38,603	3,231	+35,372	—1	—7	—1	—2	—3	—4
11 Delhi	259,021	69,427	+189,594	—392	—8	—23	—553	+4,010	+401
12 Madras	249,471	1,173,657	—924,186	—323	—2,747	—57,442	—185	—40,269	—26,006
13 North-West Frontier Province.	115,005	99,469	+15,536	—221	—396	—556	—5,640	—1,211	—653
14 Punjab	855,557	1,159,277	—303,720	—2,371	—1,879	—5,572	—30,712	—19,291	—12,136
15 United Provinces ..	565,968	1,638 293	—1,072,325	—12,223	—2,294	—66,691	—11,322	—313,387	—58,474
16 Provinces unspecified	..	50,453	..	..	..	..	..	..	
States and Agencies ..	**4,379,398**	**3,884,585**	**+494,813**	**—49,514**	**—258**	**—45,424**	**—10,472**	**+61,810**	**+117,184**
17 Assam States ..	7,625	11,060	—3,435	..	..	—936	—7	—500	+179
18 Baluchistan States ..	3,432	7,737	—4,305	+17	..	..	—6,411	—79	—5
19 Baroda State ..	322,101	205,176	+116,925	+458	—18	—221	—10	+130	+69
20 Bengal States ..	189,942	31,387	+158,555	+8	+1	+32,931	+2	+100,978	+12,823
21 Bihar and Orissa States	233,911	125,169	+108,742	—3	..	—27,959	+2	—2,562	+103,394
22 Bombay States ..	420,597	319,982	+100,615	+79	—9	—152	—202	—7	—17
23 Central India Agency	597,606	482,536	+115,070	+1,887	—50	—14,852	+106	—88	—949
24 Central Provinces States	244,494	87,580	+156,914	+49	+4	—11,704	..	+1,180	+17,497
25 Cochin State ..	87,083	45,790	+41,293	..	—15	+2	+6	+10	..
26 Gwalior State ..	279,590	296,821	—17,231	+2,312	—34	—260	—64	—1,321	—71
27 Hyderabad State ..	241,632	332,602	—90,970	+1,075	—7	—384	—127	—534	+133
28 Jammu and Kashmir State.	61,045	94,455	—33,410	—28	—14	—16	—1,961	—98	—69
29 Madras States* ..	44,574	25,289	+19,285	—13	..	—21	..	—52	—38
30 Mysore State ..	339,925	125,238	+214,687	+88	—19	—74	—12	+295	—314
31 N.-W. F. Province (*Agencies and Tribal Areas*).	33,306	28,477	+4,829	+20	..	+12	—16	+89	—452
32 Punjab States and Agency	613,719	382,782	+230,937	—652	+1	—167	—822	—1,045	+36
33 Rajputana Agency ..	328,867	846,811	—517,944	—54,852	—67	—21,454	—863	—31,008	—18,551
34 Sikkim State ..	2,430	7,212	—4,782	..	..	—55	—45	—4,613	+279
35 Travancore State ..	132,733	49,933	+82,800	+1	—10	—1	—3	+214	+1
36 United Provinces States	92,697	84,529	+8,168	—157	..	—115	—28	+173	+3,196
37 Western India States Agency.	102,089	293,685	—191,596	+197	—21	+2	—17	+648	+43
38 States unspecified ..	..	334	..	..	..	..	..	..	..

Birthplace—Internal Migration.

BETWEEN PROVINCES AND STATES.

Bombay (*including Aden*).	Burma.	Central Provinces and Berar.	Coorg.	Delhi.	Madras.	N.-W. F. P. (*Districts and Administered Territories*).	Punjab.	United Provinces of Agra and Oudh.	Total Provinces.	Total States and Agencies.	
11	12	13	14	15	16	17	18	19	20	21	
—267,678	**—574,700**	**—17,046**	**—24,836**	**—152,723**	**+521,443**	**+452**	**+140,576**	**+986,647**	..	**—494,813**	
—18,241	+9	—2,923	+1	+392	+323	+221	+2,371	+12,223	**—5,844**	**+49,514**	1
+424	+2,889	+341	+7	+8	+2,747	+396	+1,879	+2,294	**+12,742**	**+258**	2
+5,920	+5,172	+69,755	+1	+23	+57,442	+556	+5,572	+66,691	**+1,198,825**	**+45,424**	3
—30,773	—50	—506	+2	+553	+185	+5,640	+30,712	+11,322	**+17,376**	**+10,472**	4
+1,633	—154,278	+38,535	+3	—4,010	+40,269	+1,211	+19,291	+313,387	**+673,632**	**—61,810**	5
+4,969	—18,091	+38,766	+4	—401	+26,006	+653	+12,136	+58,474	**—1,284,596**	**—117,184**	6
	—7,616	—44,033	+144	+3,002	+58,814	+10,809	+83,265	+127,225	**+269,678**	**+147,011**	7
+7,616	..	+628	—5	+419	+294,385	+831	+21,698	+84,779	**+574,700**	**+17,703**	8
+44,033	—628	..	+251	—107	+9,509	+861	+11,726	+95,369	**+17,046**	**+52,422**	9
—144	+5	—251	..	..	+25,333	..	..	—89	**+24,836**	**+10,361**	10
—3,002	—419	+107	..	..	+1,441	+1,243	+50,347	+99,571	**+152,723**	**+36,871**	11
—58,814	—294,385	—9,509	—25,333	—1,441	..	—461	—1,447	—3,081	**—521,443**	**—453,021**	12
—10,809	—831	—861	..	—1,243	+461	..	+16,844	+4,664	**—452**	**+15,988**	13
—83,265	—21,698	—11,726	..	—50,347	+1,447	—16,844	..	+113,818	**—140,576**	**—163,144**	14
—127,225	—84,779	—95,369	+89	—99,571	+3,081	—4,664	—113,818	..	**—986,647**	**—85,678**	15
..	..	..	..	..	..	..	..	..	..	.	16
—147,011	**—17,703**	**—52,422**	**—10,361**	**—36,871**	**+453,021**	**—15,988**	**+163,144**	**+85,678**	**+494,813**	..	
+5	—1,860	—1	..	+1	+6	+1	+70	+151	**—2,891**	**—544**	17
+355	—5	..	..	+10	+1	+82	+1,719	+102	**—4,214**	**—91**	18
+67,486	—77	+146	..	+285	+555	+330	+1,429	+6,676	**+77,238**	**+39,687**	19
+88	—29	+1,434	..	+1	+2,168	+47	+123	+4,223	**+154,798**	**+3,757**	20
+736	—343	+17,319	+2	+45	+10,451	+35	+1,759	+1,518	**+104,394**	**+4,348**	21
+70,834	—284	—4,786	..	+40	+1,385	+193	+1,148	+1,233	**+69,455**	**+31,160**	22
+25,387	—103	—60,739	+1	+803	+715	+244	+4,402	+35,640	**—7,596**	**+122,666**	23
+445	—249	+115,784	+3	+40	+3,369	+22	+1,262	+7,926	**+135,628**	**+21,286**	24
—2,734	—208	+11	—69	—16	+39,871	+2	+19	+33	**+36,912**	**+4,381**	25
+1,969	—86	+277	..	—989	+85	+70	+1,394	+3,098	**+6,380**	**—23,611**	26
—93,942	—834	—76,454	—15	+671	+74,844	+13	+2,483	+5,428	**—87,650**	**—3,320**	27
—1,075	—98	—225	..	—387	+33	+535	—22,662	—624	**—26,689**	**—6,721**	28
..	—67	—167	—1	—5	+22,961	..	—43	..	**+22,554**	**—3,603**	29
+13,521	—1,027	+2	—10,268	—10	+207,821	+10	+933	+35	**+210,981**	**+3,706**	30
+68	..	+23	..	+116	+315	—18,439	+16,228	+2,977	**+941**	**+3,888**	31
+2,084	—1,165	—195	..	—1,146	+111	+1,606	+167,642	+20,966	**+187,254**	**+43,683**	32
—86,567	—1,839	—45,270	+2	—34,989	+258	—819	—16,299	—14,135	**—326,453**	**—19,191**	33
—724	—17	—12	..	+1	..	..	+164	+130	**—4,892**	**+110**	34
—101	—786	+14	—16	—4	+87,673	+7	+92	—1	**+87,080**	**—4,280**	35
+76	—260	—240	..	—1,465	+18	+26	+120	+7,987	**+9,331**	**—1,163**	36
—144,922	—8,366	+657	..	+127	+381	+47	+1,161	+2,315	**—147,748**	**—43,848**	37
..	..	..	..	..	..	..	..	..	..	..	38

figures for which are given separately.

Table VI.—Part III—

Province, State or Agency.	NET INTERCHANGE OF POPULATION								
	Assam State (Manipur).	Baluchistan States.	Baroda State.	Bengal States.	Bihar and Orissa States.	Bombay States.	Central India Agency.	Central Provinces States.	Cochin State.
1	22	23	24	25	26	27	28	29	30
Provinces.	+2,891	+4,214	—77,238	—154,798	—104,394	—69,455	+7,596	—135,628	—36,912
1. Ajmer-Merwara ..	..	—17	—458	—8	+3	—79	—1,887	—49	..
2. Andaman and Nicobar Islands.	..	..	+18	—1	..	+9	+50	—4	+15
3. Assam	+936	..	+221	—32,931	+27,959	+152	+14,852	+11,704	—2
4. Baluchistan ..	+7	+6.411	+10	—2	—2	+202	—106	..	—6
5. Bengal	+500	+79	—130	—100,978	+2,562	+7	+88	—1,180	—10
6. Bihar and Orissa ..	—179	+5	—69	—12,823	—103,394	+17	+949	—17,497	..
7. Bombay ..	—5	—355	—67,486	—88	—736	—70,834	—25,387	—445	+2,734
8. Burma	+1,860	+5	+77	+29	+343	+284	+103	+249	+208
9. Central Provinces and Berar ..	+1	..	—146	—1,434	—17,319	+4,786	+60,739	–115,784	—11
10. Coorg	..	..	..	..	—2	..	—1	—3	+69
11. Delhi	—1	—10	—285	—1	—45	—40	—803	—40	+16
12. Madras	—6	—1	—555	—2,168	—10,451	—1,385	—715	—3,369	—39,871
13. North-West Frontier Province	—1	—82	—330	—47	—35	—193	—244	—22	—2
14. Punjab	—70	—1,719	—1,429	—123	—1,759	—1,148	—4,402	—1,262	—19
15. United Provinces ..	—151	—102	—6,676	—4,223	—1,518	—1,233	—35,640	—7,926	—33
16. Provinces Unspecified	..	..	..	..	..	..	..	..	..
States and Agencies.	+544	+91	—39,687	—3,757	—4,348	—31,160	—122,666	—21,286	—4,381
17. Assam States ..	..	..	..	—718	..	..	+3	..	..
18. Baluchistan States ..	..	..	—188	..	..	+30	..	..	+1
19. Baroda State ..	..	+188	..	—87	—19	—12,304	—646	—4	+11
20. Bengal States ..	+718	..	+87	..	+1,077	+64	+790	+109	..
21. Bihar & Orissa States	..	..	+19	—1,077	..	+90	+141	—1,190	..
22. Bombay States ..	..	—30	+12,304	—64	—90	..	—3,171	—293	+10
23. Central India Agency	—3	..	+646	—790	—141	+3,171	..	—15,996	—1
24. Central Provinces States	..	..	+4	—109	+1,190	+293	+15,996	..	—2
25. Cochin State ..	..	—1	—11	..	..	—10	+1	+2	..
26. Gwalior State ..	..	..	+1	..	—11	+43	—53,589	—70	..
27. Hyderabad State ..	..	—2	—300	—2	—37	—8,085	—763	—322	+18
28. Jammu and Kashmir State.	—1	—27	—8	..	..	—11	—149	—3	—1
29. Madras States*	..	..	..	..	—4,291	..	—21	..	+68
30. Mysore State ..	+1	..	—21	..	—31	—61	—155	—20	+416
31. N.-W. F. Province (*Agencies and Tribal Areas*)	+32	—1	—3	..	..	..	—9	+31	..
32. Punjab States and Agency.	—3	—27	—120	—7	—190	+24	—619	—173	..
33. Rajputana Agency ..	—202	..	—8,228	—891	—1,753	—7,573	—79,070	—3,356	—10
34. Sikkim State ..	+2	..	..	..	..	..	..	..	..
35. Travancore State	..	..	..	..	..	..	..	..	—4,203
36. United Provinces States	..	..	—10	—12	—10	+1	—251	—1	..
37. Western India States Agency.	..	—9	—43,859	..	—42	—6,832	—1,154	..	—688
38. States unspecified ..	..	..	..	..	..	..	..	..	..

*Excludes Cochin and Travancore

Birthplace—Internal Migration—*concluded.*

BETWEEN PROVINCES AND STATES.

Gwalior State.	Hyderabad State.	Jammu and Kashmir State.	Madras States*.	Mysore State.	N.-W. F. P. (*Agencies and Tribal Areas.*)	Punjab States and Agency.	Rajputana Agency.	Sikkim State.	Travancore State.	United Provinces States.	Western India States Agency.	
31	32	33	34	35	36	37	38	39	40	41	42	
—6,380	+87,650	+26,689	—22,554	—210,981	—941	—187,254	+326,453	+4,892	—87,080	—9,331	+147,748	
—2,312	—1,075	+28	+13	—88	—20	+652	+54,852	..	—1	+157	—197	1
+34	+7	+14	..	+19	..	—1	+67	..	+10	..	+21	2
+260	+384	+16	+21	+74	—12	+167	+21,454	+55	+1	+115	—2	3
+ 64	+127	+1,961	..	+12	+16	+822	+863	+45	+3	+28	+17	4
+1,321	+534	+98	+52	—295	—89	+1,045	+31,008	+4,613	—214	—173	—648	5
+71	—133	+69	+38	+314	+452	—36	+18,551	—279	—1	—3,196	—43	6
—1,969	+93,942	+1,075	..	—13,521	—68	—2,084	+86,567	+724	+101	—76	+144,922	7
+86	+834	+98	+67	+1,027	..	+1,165	+1,839	+17	+786	+260	+8,366	8
—277	+76,454	+225	+167	—2	—23	+195	+45,270	+12	—14	+240	—657	9
..	+15	..	+1	+10,268	..	..	—2	..	+16	..	..	10
+989	—671	+387	+5	+10	—116	+1,146	+34,989	—1	+4	+1,465	—127	11
—85	—74,844	—33	—22,961	—207,821	—315	—111	—258	..	—87,673	—18	—381	12
—70	—13	—535	..	—10	+18,439	—1,606	+819	..	—7	—26	—47	13
—1,394	—2,483	+22,662	+43	—933	—16,228	—167,642	+16,299	—164	—92	—120	—1,161	14
—3,098	—5,428	+624	..	—35	—2,977	—20,966	+14,135	—130	+1	—7,987	—2,315	15
..	..	..	..	..	..	..	..	..	..	..	..	16
+28,611	+3,320	+6,721	+3,603	—3,706	—3,888	—43,583	+191,491	—110	+4,280	+1,163	+43,848	
..	..	+1	..	—1	—32	+3	+202	—2	..	..	..	17
..	+2	+27	..	..	+1	+27	..	..	..	..	+9	18
—1	+300	+8	..	+21	+3	+120	+8,228	..	..	+10	+43,859	19
..	+2	..	..	..	..	+7	+891	..	..	+12	..	20
+11	+37	..	+4,291	+31	..	+190	+1,753	..	..	+10	+42	21
—43	+8,085	+11	..	+61	..	—24	+7,573	..	..	—1	+6,832	22
+53,589	+763	+149	+21	+155	+9	+619	+79,070	..	..	+251	+1,154	23
+70	+322	+3	..	+20	—31	+173	+3,356	..	..	+1	..	24
..	—18	+1	—68	—416	..	..	+10	..	+4,203	..	+698	25
..	—485	+17	..	+5	—82	—58	+29,879	..	—1	+521	+219	26
+485	..	+23	—366	—1,355	—11	+451	+6,408	..	+3	+734	—199	27
—17	—23	..	..	—71	—2,326	—3,995	—40	+2	..	—29	—22	28
..	+366	..	..	+189	..	..	—1	..	+87	..	..	29
—5	+1,355	+71	—189	..	—65	—30	+2,276	..	+42	..	+122	30
+82	+11	+2,326	..	+65	..	+907	+447	..	..	..	..	31
+58	—451	+3,995	..	+30	—907	..	+42,533	..	..	—460	..	32
—29,879	—6,408	+40	+1	—2,276	—447	—42,533	..	—110	—38	+114	—8,872	33
..	..	—2	..	..	..	..	+110	..	..	..	..	34
+1	—3	..	—87	—42	..	..	+38	..	..	..	+16	35
—521	—734	+29	..	..	..	+460	—114	..	..	..	..	36
—219	+199	+22	..	—122	..	..	+8,872	..	—16	..	..	37
..	..	..	..	..	..	..	..	..	..	..	..	38

figures for which are given separately.

Statement showing available details of the Persons Born in the French and Portuguese Settlements in India.

Province, State or Agency.	Sex.	French Settlements.				Portuguese Settlements.			French and Portuguese Settlements Unspecified.
		Pondicherry.	Chandarnagore.	Elsewhere.	Unspecified.	Goa.	Elsewhere.	Unspecified	
India	**Males**	**146**	**91**	**50**	**12**	**1,896**	**237**	**734**	**45,319**
	Females	**97**	**197**	**20**	**26**	**704**	**416**	**131**	**32,195**
Ajmer-Merwara	Males	..	..	..	..	..	..	..	228
	Females	..	..	..	..	..	..	..	110
Assam	Males	..	2	..	..	13	..	..	..
	Females	..	..	..	..	7	..	..	..
Baluchistan	Males	..	..	..	..	104	..	..	..
	Females	..	..	..	..	25	..	..	..
Bengal	Males	7	84	..	5	98	..	719	..
	Females	3	191	..	21	37	..	127	..
Bihar and Orissa	Males	..	..	..	..	..	..	..	169
	Females	..	..	..	..	..	..	..	116
Bombay	Males	..	..	..	..	..	..	..	36,469
	Females	..	..	..	..	..	..	..	22,623
Burma	Males	53	..	7	..	675	..	..	..
	Females	47	..	1	..	110	..	..	..
Central Provinces & Berar	Males	7	1	..	..	271	..	..	19
	Females	5	..	..	..	206	..	..	19
Coorg	Males	..	..	..	..	..	..	..	8
	Females	..	..	..	..	..	..	..	1
Delhi	Males	6	..	..	..	42	..	..	..
	Females	4	..	..	..	21	..	..	..
Madras	Males	..	..	..	..	..	..	..	7,458
	Females	..	..	..	..	..	..	..	8,554
North-West Frontier Province	Males	..	..	..	..	63	..	..	..
	Females	..	..	..	..	4	..	..	..
Punjab	Males	..	..	..	..	23	..	..	..
	Females	..	..	..	1	9	..	..	..
United Provinces of Agra and Oudh	Males	..	3	..	..	76	..	..	..
	Females	..	6	..	..	6	..	..	..
Baroda	Males	..	..	..	1	103	237	..	..
	Females	..	..	..	1	66	416	..	..
Central India	Males	2	..	..	..	220	..	..	..
	Females	..	..	..	..	138	..	..	..
Cochin	Males	2	..	15	..	35	..	..	..
	Females	2	..	6	..	6	..	..	..
Gwalior	Males	..	1	..	..	11	..	..	..
	Females	..	..	..	..	5	..	..	..
Hyderabad	Males	14	..	2	6	61	..	15	..
	Females	2	..	..	3	50	..	4	..
Jammu and Kashmir	Males	..	..	..	..	17	..	..	..
	Females	..	..	..	..	..	..	..	..
Mysore	Males	..	..	..	..	..	..	..	304
	Females	..	..	..	..	..	..	..	281
Rajputana	Males	..	..	..	..	..	..	..	122
	Females	..	..	..	..	..	..	..	41
Travancore	Males	55	..	26	..	[illegible]4	..	..	..
	Females	34	..	13	..	14	..	..	..
Western India States	Males	..	..	..	..	..	..	..	542
	Females	..	..	..	..	..	..	..	450

TABLE VII.

Age, Sex and Civil Condition by Religion.

1. This table is divided into three parts. Part I gives a general summary of the total population by Civil Condition and Age for All Religions, the total population by Civil Condition and Age by All Religions for India proper, and by individual religions, from which the Andamans and Nicobars, where no sort by Civil Condition and Religion was made, are excluded, (Part I-A) ; also the total population by Civil Condition and Age for racial groups in Burma, where civil condition was sorted for by race instead of by religion (Part I-B.)

2. Part II shows the distribution (excluding Burma), by individual provinces and states, of the total population by All Religions by Civil Condition and Age, and also of the population of numerically important religious communities. Part III gives similar information for cities, but with age statistics in less detail.

3. The population dealt with in this table excludes the estimated populations referred to in paragraph 4, clauses 2—5 on the fly leaf to Table I of this volume together with such persons as were not recorded by age, the numbers of the latter are as follows :—

	Persons.	Males.	Females.
Andaman and Nicobar Islands	1,520	817	703
Bombay British Districts	1,643	1,341	302
Aden	22	20	2
Bombay States	8,452	4,172	4,280
Western India States Agency	834	461	373
Total ..	12,471	6,811	5,660

4. Figures for Aryas and Brahmos in Part I-A exclude details for the following provinces in which the information was not extracted :—

Ajmer-Merwara, the Andaman and Nicobar Islands, Bombay, the North-West Frontier Province, Rajputana, and the Western India States Agency.

5. Divorced persons have been included as " Widowed "; persons recognised by custom as married have been shown as such, whether or not a formal ceremony has taken place.

Table VII.—Age, Sex and Civil Condition. Part I.—General Table.

Age and Religion.	Population.			Unmarried.		Married.		Widowed.	
	Persons.	Males.	Females.	Males.	Females.	Males.	Females.	Males.	Females.
1	2	3	4	5	6	7	8	9	10
All Religions ..	**349,759,318**	**180,205,584**	**169,553,734**	**86,338,001**	**59,698,043**	**84,208,467**	**83,607,223**	**9,659,116**	**26,248,468**
0—1 ..	10,768,547	5,349,103	5,419,444	5,311,425	5,373,847	36,882	44,082	796	1,515
1—2 ..	10,045,853	4,914,082	5,131,771	4,871,935	5,066,032	41,228	63,954	919	1,785
2—3 ..	10,946,797	5,320,176	5,626,621	5,255,189	5,509,037	63,375	114,099	1,612	3,485
3—4 ..	11,028,301	5,464,709	5,563,592	5,342,266	5,321,703	118,844	232,813	3,599	9,076
4—5 ..	10,675,791	5,386,664	5,289,127	5,211,894	4,927,204	168,897	346,904	5,873	15,019
Total 0—5 ..	*53,465,289*	*26,434,734*	*27,030,555*	*25,992,709*	*26,197,823*	*429,226*	*801,852*	*12,799*	*30,880*
5—10 ..	45,506,909	23,796,001	21,710,908	21,867,197	17,404,892	1,883,773	4,200,534	45,031	105,482
10—15 ..	40,634,216	21,572,694	19,061,522	18,276,462	11,606,975	3,217,626	7,269,208	78,606	185,339
15—20 ..	31,937,792	16,040,278	15,897,514	8,865,682	2,360,984	6,956,249	13,003,768	218,347	532,762
20—25 ..	33,009,771	16,314,675	16,695,096	5,894,600	1,029,773	10,039,581	14,788,688	380,494	876,635
25—30 ..	30,190,648	15,466,083	14,724,565	2,200,319	354,878	12,613,545	12,789,487	652,219	1,580,200
30—35 ..	27,027,522	14,217,036	12,810,486	1,281,031	248,934	12,164,396	10,561,969	771,609	1,999,583
35—40 ..	21,633,271	11,548,383	10,084,888	633,945	145,708	9,963,516	7,091,132	950,922	2,848,048
40—45 ..	18,411,820	9,852,087	8,559,733	458,075	112,010	8,372,439	5,366,353	1,021,573	3,081,370
45—50 ..	14,221,408	7,632,488	6,588,920	289,682	71,913	6,191,098	3,118,118	1,151,708	3,398,889
50—55 ..	11,381,206	6,025,595	5,355,611	214,720	55,218	4,734,833	2,190,823	1,076,042	3,109,570
55—60 ..	8,083,945	4,155,676	3,928,269	135,237	37,695	3,020,651	1,091,985	999,788	2,798,589
60—65 ..	6,569,452	3,307,296	3,262,156	104,380	30,886	2,310,703	744,403	892,213	2,486,867
65—70 ..	3,146,284	1,597,385	1,548,899	50,420	15,854	1,020,203	276,297	526,762	1,256,748
70 and over	4,539,785	2,245,173	2,294,612	73,542	24,500	1,290,628	312,606	881,003	1,957,506

Part I-A.—India Proper.

Age and Religion.	Persons.	Males.	Females.	Unmarried Males.	Unmarried Females.	Married Males.	Married Females.	Widowed Males.	Widowed Females.
All Religions ..	**335,111,821**	**172,724,908**	**162,386,913**	**82,143,233**	**55,963,907**	**81,273,565**	**80,926,346**	**9,308,110**	**25,496,660**
0—1 ..	10,373,279	5,156,701	5,216,578	5,119,023	5,170,981	36,882	44,082	796	1,515
1—2 ..	9,635,717	4,714,266	4,921,451	4,672,120	4,855,713	41,227	63,953	919	1,785
2—3 ..	10,533,831	5,117,401	5,416,430	5,052,419	5,298,849	63,370	114,096	1,612	3,485
3—4 ..	10,621,728	5,263,769	5,357,959	5,141,340	5,116,081	118,830	232,802	3,599	9,076
4—5 ..	10,282,481	5,192,477	5,090,004	5,017,737	4,728,105	168,870	346,881	5,870	15,018
Total 0—5 ..	*51,447,036*	*25,444,614*	*26,002,422*	*25,002,639*	*25,169,729*	*429,179*	*801,814*	*12,796*	*30,879*
5—10 ..	43,705,947	22,887,591	20,818,356	20,959,352	16,513,160	1,883,218	4,199,747	45,021	105,449
10—15 ..	38,973,209	20,727,071	18,246,138	17,435,804	10,810,142	3,212,831	7,251,998	78,436	183,998
15—20 ..	30,525,177	15,346,901	15,178,276	8,306,296	1,923,657	6,828,659	12,740,225	211,946	514,394
20—25 ..	31,588,372	15,612,691	15,975,681	5,473,949	751,893	9,771,654	14,376,829	367,088	846,959
25—30 ..	28,899,533	14,785,289	14,114,244	2,025,434	256,410	12,132,950	12,320,544	626,905	1,537,290
30—35 ..	25,874,159	13,592,046	12,282,113	1,166,156	180,691	11,682,031	10,147,282	743,859	1,954,140
35—40 ..	20,757,596	11,071,559	9,686,037	577,492	110,185	9,574,097	6,784,657	919,970	2,791,195
40—45 ..	17,643,301	9,440,870	8,202,431	416,708	83,274	8,034,823	5,101,720	989,339	3,017,437
45—50 ..	13,632,877	7,323,908	6,308,969	264,652	52,700	5,942,111	2,937,922	1,117,145	3,318,347
50—55 ..	10,865,422	5,761,254	5,104,168	194,323	39,256	4,525,691	2,041,115	1,041,240	3,023,797
55—60 ..	7,687,438	3,953,322	3,734,116	120,981	25,556	2,870,507	1,001,310	961,834	2,707,250
60—65 ..	6,240,043	3,137,175	3,102,868	92,538	20,725	2,189,632	679,815	855,005	2,402,328
65—70 ..	2,964,839	1,505,957	1,458,882	43,115	10,127	963,446	251,275	499,396	1,197,480
70 and over	4,306,872	2,134,660	2,172,212	63,794	16,402	1,232,736	290,093	838,130	1,865,717
Hindus ..	**238,598,653**	**122,172,534**	**116,426,119**	**56,505,005**	**38,391,969**	**58,663,574**	**58,353,082**	**7,003,955**	**19,681,068**
0—1 ..	7,149,361	3,544,656	3,604,705	3,518,960	3,574,855	25,082	28,769	614	1,081
1—2 ..	6,780,232	3,306,618	3,473,614	3,274,960	3,429,816	30,937	42,456	721	1,342
2—3 ..	7,306,585	3,533,783	3,772,802	3,486,142	3,694,238	46,345	75,869	1,296	2,695
3—4 ..	7,371,669	3,642,128	3,729,541	3,549,427	3,558,645	89,747	163,818	2,954	7,078
4—5 ..	7,119,826	3,579,011	3,540,815	3,446,043	3,276,062	128,287	253,282	4,681	11,471
Total 0—5 ..	*35,727,673*	*17,606,196*	*18,121,477*	*17,275,532*	*17,533,616*	*320,398*	*564,194*	*10,266*	*23,667*
5—10 ..	30,449,951	15,870,748	14,579,203	14,367,881	11,360,534	1,465,896	3,134,749	36,971	83,920
10—15 ..	27,358,875	14,522,361	12,836,514	11,956,146	7,340,929	2,502,281	5,350,136	63,934	145 449
15—20 ..	21,536,107	10,863,103	10,673,004	5,680,899	1,191,126	5,022,574	9,077,711	159,630	404,167
20—25 ..	22,338,876	11,023,717	11,315,159	3,711,863	453,316	7,043,873	10,193,335	267,981	668,508
25—30 ..	20,706,617	10,496,272	10,210,345	1,385,227	161,380	8,655,390	8,836,580	455,655	1,212,385
30—35 ..	18,664,309	9,691,247	8,973,062	818,648	117,109	8,324,798	7,326,326	547,801	1,529,627
35—40 ..	15,198,517	8,015,185	7,183,332	420,944	72,543	6,892,987	4,944,380	701,254	2,166,409
40—45 ..	13,004,413	6,885,867	6,118,546	309,353	54,489	5,813,070	3,731,380	763,444	2,332,677
45—50 ..	10,054,448	5,337,978	4,716,470	197,916	34,442	4,275,442	2,135,446	864,620	2,546,582
50—55 ..	8,036,369	4,207,195	3,829,174	146,233	25,503	3,254,719	1,481,740	806,243	2,321,931
55—60 ..	5,696,080	2,870,369	2,825,711	90,221	16,683	2,046,724	719,792	733,424	2,089,236
60—65 ..	4,624,219	2,268,628	2,355,591	68,453	13,468	1,554,296	484,538	645,879	1,857,585
65—70 ..	2,166,699	1,065,762	1,100,937	31,414	6,573	668,390	176,491	365,958	917,873
70 and over	3,035,500	1,447,906	1,587,594	44,275	10,258	822,736	196,284	580,895	1,381,052
Aryas ..	***955,512***	***529,333***	***426,179***	***263,388***	***168,249***	***223,652***	***204,260***	***42,293***	***53,670***
0—1 ..	*33,212*	*16,876*	*16,336*	*16,857*	*16,325*	*19*	*11*	..	..
1—2 ..	*26,420*	*13,400*	*13,020*	*13,390*	*13,002*	*9*	*17*	*1*	*1*
2—3 ..	*28,676*	*14,630*	*14,046*	*14,604*	*14,018*	*24*	*27*	*2*	*1*
3—4 ..	*28,685*	*14,723*	*13,962*	*14,614*	*13,868*	*102*	*90*	*7*	*4*
4—5 ..	*26,878*	*14,161*	*12,717*	*13,938*	*12,547*	*209*	*154*	*14*	*16*
Total 0—5 ..	143,871	73,790	70,081	73,403	69,760	363	299	24	22
5—10 ..	*115,902*	*62,915*	*52,987*	*60,102*	*47,723*	*2,678*	*5,138*	*135*	*126*
10—15 ..	*111,791*	*62,466*	*49,325*	*54,992*	*34,911*	*7,161*	*14,144*	*313*	*270*
15—20 ..	*98,214*	*55,187*	*43,027*	*32,331*	*8,921*	*21,794*	*33,177*	*1,062*	*929*
20—25 ..	*97,234*	*53,304*	*43,930*	*20,660*	*3,934*	*30,775*	*38,276*	*1,869*	*1,720*
25—30 ..	*84,007*	*46,720*	*37,287*	*7,937*	*1,203*	*35,674*	*33,071*	*3,109*	*3,013*
30—35 ..	*74,140*	*42,823*	*31,317*	*5,279*	*665*	*33,862*	*26,918*	*3,682*	*3,734*
35—40 ..	*55,402*	*32,142*	*23,260*	*2,644*	*332*	*25,263*	*17,703*	*4,235*	*5,225*
40—45 ..	*46,742*	*20,891*	*19,851*	*2,008*	*252*	*20,448*	*13,642*	*4,435*	*5,957*
45—50 ..	*38,273*	*21,970*	*16,303*	*1,364*	*186*	*15,659*	*8,944*	*4,947*	*7,173*
50—55 ..	*30,463*	*17,483*	*12,980*	*1,037*	*134*	*11,750*	*6,233*	*4,696*	*6,613*
55—60 ..	*21,820*	*12,514*	*9,306*	*639*	*85*	*7,581*	*3,189*	*4,294*	*6,032*
60—65 ..	*17,279*	*9,778*	*7,501*	*476*	*58*	*5,555*	*2,062*	*3,747*	*5,381*
65—70 ..	*8,832*	*5,069*	*3,763*	*237*	*32*	*2,488*	[illegible]	[illegible]	
		[illegible]	*5,261*	*279*					

Table VII.—Age, Sex and Civil Condition. Part I-A.—India Proper—*contd.*

Age and Religion.	Population.			Unmarried.		Married.		Widowed.	
	Persons.	Males.	Females.	Males.	Females.	Males.	Females.	Males.	Females.
1	2	3	4	5	6	7	8	9	10
Brahmos ..	***4,446***	***2,471***	***1,975***	***1,330***	***1,014***	***1,038***	***777***	***103***	***184***
0—1 ..	*121*	*59*	*62*	*59*	*61*	..	*1*	..	..
1—2 ..	*75*	*36*	*39*	*36*	*39*	..	..	..	..
2—3 ..	*88*	*37*	*51*	*37*	*51*	..	..	..	..
3—4 ..	*66*	*27*	*39*	*27*	*39*	..	..	..	..
4—5 ..	*101*	*53*	*48*	*52*	*48*	*1*	..	..	..
Total 0—5 ..	451	212	239	211	238	1	1	..	..
5—10 ..	*439*	*236*	*203*	*228*	*192*	*8*	*10*	..	*1*
10—15 ..	*595*	*343*	*252*	*327*	*227*	*16*	*25*	..	..
15—20 ..	*580*	*336*	*244*	*274*	*177*	*59*	*64*	*3*	*3*
20—25 ..	*525*	*281*	*244*	*162*	*106*	*115*	*129*	*4*	*9*
25—30 ..	*462*	*255*	*207*	*65*	*26*	*181*	*162*	*9*	*19*
30—35 ..	*327*	*190*	*137*	*21*	*17*	*158*	*101*	*11*	*19*
35—40 ..	*283*	*159*	*124*	*17*	*15*	*134*	*89*	*8*	*20*
40—45 ..	*247*	*156*	*91*	*11*	*6*	*130*	*70*	*15*	*15*
45—50 ..	*199*	*137*	*62*	*9*	*3*	*118*	*45*	*10*	*14*
50—55 ..	*112*	*65*	*47*	*3*	*2*	*52*	*30*	*10*	*15*
55—60 ..	*95*	*45*	*50*	*1*	*2*	*36*	*27*	*8*	*21*
60—65 ..	*44*	*17*	*27*	..	*2*	*13*	*10*	*4*	*15*
65—70 ..	*46*	*20*	*26*	..	*1*	*11*	*9*	*9*	*16*
70 and over ..	*41*	*19*	*22*	*1*	..	*6*	*5*	*12*	*17*
Sikhs	**4,323,730**	**2,423,738**	**1,899,992**	**1,333,869**	**785,924**	**895,659**	**898,020**	**194,210**	**216,048**
0—1 ..	159,173	81,732	77,441	81,703	77,409	26	26	3	6
1—2 ..	116,019	59,439	56,580	59,410	56,501	24	72	5	7
2—3 ..	125,159	64,671	60,488	64,617	60,329	50	153	4	6
3—4 ..	125,216	65,486	59,730	65,344	59,478	134	245	8	7
4—5 ..	120,605	63,859	56,746	63,597	56,314	235	399	27	33
Total *0—5* ..	*646,172*	*335,187*	*310,985*	*334,671*	*310,031*	*469*	*895*	*47*	*59*
5—10 ..	548,075	300,445	247,630	294,593	232,235	5,629	15,166	223	229
10—15 ..	513,305	287,855	225,450	269,241	178,411	18,037	46,533	577	506
15—20 ..	408,447	233,074	175,373	152,560	41,965	77,481	131,542	3,033	1,866
20—25 ..	401,556	227,874	173,682	108,367	13,029	114,047	157,355	5,460	3,298
25—30 ..	334,782	191,303	143,479	51,971	2,930	129,629	134,016	9,703	6,533
30—35 ..	298,873	174,480	124,393	37,557	2,200	124,494	112,853	12,429	9,340
35—40 ..	239,019	136,498	102,521	23,028	1,415	97,771	85,329	15,699	15,777
40—45 ..	213,081	119,817	93,264	17,811	1,139	84,294	72,458	17,712	19,667
45—50 ..	189,720	108,761	80,959	13,583	846	72,973	52,557	22,205	27,556
50—55 ..	156,211	90,272	65,939	10,385	595	58,028	38,683	21,859	26,661
55—60 ..	120,638	70,344	50,294	7,180	363	41,154	22,183	22,010	27,748
60—65 ..	100,974	58,733	42,241	5,680	319	32,554	15,633	20,499	26,289
65—70 ..	60,305	36,110	24,195	3,090	198	17,690	6,437	15,330	17,560
70 and over ..	92,572	52,985	39,587	4,152	248	21,409	6,380	27,424	32,959
Jains ..	**1,251,340**	**644,611**	**606,729**	**324,198**	**205,543**	**267,510**	**266,941**	**52,903**	**134,245**
0—1 ..	38,131	19,333	18,798	19,163	18,645	157	133	13	20
1—2 ..	33,524	16,690	16,834	16,559	16,640	126	186	5	8
2—3 ..	33,656	16,448	17,208	16,301	16,885	144	307	3	16
3—4 ..	32,391	15,995	16,396	15,791	15,885	193	490	11	21
4—5 ..	33,537	16,536	17,001	16,062	16,041	438	882	36	78
Total *0—5* ..	*171,239*	*85,002*	*86,237*	*83,876*	*84,096*	*1,058*	*1,998*	*68*	*143*
5—10 ..	148,714	76,876	71,838	74,266	64,181	2,510	7,359	100	298
10—15 ..	139,315	73,407	65,908	68,093	46,595	5,122	18,670	192	643
15—20 ..	117,648	61,277	56,371	37,992	6,811	22,539	47,086	746	2,474
20—25 ..	119,455	61,151	58,304	25,565	1,683	34,270	52,179	1,316	4,442
25—30 ..	101,194	52,216	48,978	10,416	621	39,347	39,907	2,453	8,450
30—35 ..	93,136	49,201	43,935	7,422	414	38,416	32,686	3,363	10,835
35—40 ..	81.461	42.430	39,031	4,880	355	32,469	23,205	5,081	15,471
40—45 ..	73,029	38,131	34,898	3,930	249	28,140	18,032	6,061	16,617
45—50 ..	61,459	32,334	29,125	2,879	175	21,860	10,982	7,595	17,968
50—55 ..	50,098	26,205	23,893	2,108	104	16,831	7,541	7,266	16,248
55—60 ..	35,976	18,105	17,871	1,234	70	10,537	3,649	6,334	14,152
60—65 ..	28,799	13,925	14,874	820	67	7,761	2,357	5,344	12,450
65—70 ..	13,531	6,794	6,737	354	52	3,388	759	3,052	5,926
70 and over ..	16,286	7,557	8,729	363	70	3,262	531	3,932	8,128
Buddhists ..	**435,857**	**224,232**	**211,625**	**120,037**	**96,572**	**95,668**	**93,284**	**8,527**	**21,769**
0—1 ..	13,797	6,932	6,865	6,857	6,785	73	76	2	4
1—2 ..	12,277	6,156	6,121	6,101	6,042	54	77	1	2
2—3 ..	14,244	7,048	7,196	6,980	7,104	67	90	1	2
3—4 ..	14,254	7,120	7,134	7,036	7,045	79	78	5	11
4—5 ..	13,519	6,880	6,639	6,777	6,536	96	86	7	17
Total *0—5* ..	*68,091*	*34,136*	*33,955*	*33,751*	*33,512*	*369*	*407*	*16*	*36*
5—10 ..	57,284	29,835	27,449	29,279	26,389	543	992	13	68
10—15 ..	50,581	26,217	24,364	25,324	21,220	873	3,015	20	129
15—20 ..	40,455	19,821	20,634	14,207	7,968	5,436	12,102	178	564
20—25 ..	40,468	19,819	20,649	9,791	3,982	9,691	15,864	337	803
25—30 ..	37,232	19,151	18,081	3,375	1,392	15,127	15,457	649	1,232
30—35 ..	33,001	17,518	15,483	1,878	906	14,933	13,133	707	1,444
35—40 ..	24,667	13,339	11,328	698	313	11,919	9,240	722	1,775
40—45 ..	21,341	11,478	9,863	533	265	10,210	7,647	735	1,951
45—50 ..	17,197	9,198	7,999	372	174	7,946	5,316	880	2,509
50—55 ..	14,756	7,829	6,927	265	139	6,721	4,318	843	2 470
55—60 ..	10,734	5,627	5,107	178	89	4,588	2,478	861	2,540
60—65 ..	8,798	4,594	4,204	144	82	3,626	1,776	824	2,346
65—70 ..	4,509	2,317	2,192	92	56	1,636	735	589	1,401
70 and over ..	6,743	3,353	3,390	150	85	2,050	804	1,153	2,501

Table VII.—Age, Sex and Civil Condition. Part I-A.—India Proper—*contd.*

Age and Religion.	Population.			Unmarried.		Married.		Widowed.	
	Persons.	Males.	Females.	Males.	Females.	Males.	Females.	Males.	Females.
1	2	3	4	5	6	7	8	9	10
Parsis ..	**109,329**	**56,366**	**52,963**	**31,388**	**25,816**	**22,801**	**20,581**	**2,177**	**6,566**
0—1 ..	1,767	892	875	892	873	..	2	..	..
1—2 ..	1,639	832	807	830	806	2	1	..	..
2—3 ..	1,864	929	935	923	933	6	2	..	..
3—4 ..	1,909	978	931	972	924	6	7	..	..
4—5 ..	2,156	1,092	1,064	1,077	1,057	15	7	..	..
Total 0—5 ..	*9,335*	*4,723*	*4,612*	*4,694*	*4,593*	*29*	*19*	..	..
5—10 ..	10,069	5,208	4,861	5,144	4,806	62	53	2	2
10—15 ..	10,339	5,349	4,990	5,239	4,872	109	115	1	3
15—20 ..	10,009	5,066	4,943	4,696	4,005	361	910	9	28
20—25 ..	9,944	4,999	4,945	4,260	3,189	722	1,709	17	47
25—30 ..	9,621	4,809	4,812	2,708	1,508	2,046	3,178	55	126
30—35 ..	9,433	4,768	4,665	1,921	1,098	2,777	3,368	70	199
35—40 ..	8,491	4,508	3,983	946	578	3,428	2,977	134	428
40—45 ..	7,815	4,185	3,630	692	440	3,345	2,628	148	562
45—50 ..	6,633	3,542	3,091	390	300	2,909	1,913	243	878
50—55 ..	5,762	3,067	2,695	304	204	2,503	1,552	260	939
55—60 ..	4,191	2,185	2,006	178	104	1,696	937	311	965
60—65 ..	3,455	1,773	1,682	128	66	1,355	685	290	931
65—70 ..	1,935	1,024	911	57	29	725	288	242	594
70 and over ..	2,297	1,160	1,137	31	24	734	249	395	864
Muslims ..	**76,344,231**	**40,099,103**	**36,245,128**	**20,023,832**	**13,324,218**	**18,300,813**	**18,241,410**	**1,774,458**	**4,679,500**
0—1 ..	2,525,858	1,263,275	1,262,583	1,253,077	1,248,653	10,059	13,570	139	360
1—2 ..	2,234,561	1,100,863	1,133,698	1,092,150	1,113,925	8,574	19,387	139	386
2—3 ..	2,555,761	1,252,574	1,303,187	1,237,632	1,267,317	14,690	35,176	252	694
3—4 ..	2,580,391	1,288,081	1,292,310	1,262,020	1,226,739	25,495	63,766	566	1,805
4—5 ..	2,519,424	1,288,490	1,230,934	1,251,981	1,141,954	35,533	85,920	976	3,060
Total 0—5 ..	*12,415,995*	*6,193,283*	*6,222,712*	*6,096,860*	*5,998,588*	*94,351*	*217,819*	*2,072*	*6,305*
5—10 ..	10,556,081	5,613,744	4,942,337	5,232,951	3,945,885	373,839	977,464	6,954	18,988
10—15 ..	9,216,115	4,945,085	4,271,030	4,313,316	2,556,028	619,585	1,681,518	12,184	33,484
15—20 ..	7,137,399	3,546,893	3,590,506	2,012,387	463,830	1,492,384	3,035,044	42,122	91,632
20—25 ..	7,397,146	3,655,045	3,742,101	1,344,878	180,174	2,229,579	3,414,188	80,588	147,739
25—30 ..	6,534,098	3,428,054	3,106,044	475,328	60,138	2,814,235	2,778,316	138,491	267,590
30—35 ..	5,735,133	3,121,457	2,613,676	248,923	40,460	2,715,642	2,222,243	156,892	350,973
35—40 ..	4,386,773	2,427,616	1,959,157	106,279	24,528	2,150,812	1,420,374	170,525	514,255
40—45 ..	3,632,028	2,013,376	1,618,652	69,967	18,549	1,769,483	1,038,311	173,926	561,792
45—50 ..	2,789,617	1,557,767	1,231,850	41,446	11,570	1,325,109	593,637	191,212	626,643
50—55 ..	2,186,815	1,208,595	978,220	29,163	8,680	1,003,214	404,558	176,218	564,982
55—60 ..	1,532,263	840,550	691,713	18,240	5,433	650,882	199,392	171,428	486,888
60—65 ..	1,240,038	672,241	567,797	14,538	4,442	500,567	138,504	157,136	424,851
65—70 ..	606,765	338,877	267,888	6,787	2,067	233,023	52,420	99,067	213,401
70 and over ..	977,965	536,520	441,445	12,769	3,846	328,108	67,622	195,643	369,977
Christians ..	**5,963,999**	**3,054,580**	**2,909,419**	**1,726,007**	**1,379,145**	**1,219,421**	**1,213,375**	**109,152**	**316,899**
0—1 ..	208,484	104,134	104,350	103,978	104,168	145	168	11	14
1—2 ..	192,055	95,738	96,317	95,582	96,117	147	194	9	6
2—3 ..	194,790	97,167	97,623	96,935	97,302	221	307	11	14
3—4 ..	187,454	93,565	93,889	93,142	93,308	410	557	13	24
4—5 ..	180,673	90,859	89,814	90,068	88,725	755	1,020	36	69
Total 0—5 ..	*963,456*	*481,463*	*481,993*	*479,705*	*479,620*	*1,678*	*2,246*	*80*	*127*
5—10 ..	797,527	407,149	390,378	401,475	378,559	5,484	11,439	190	380
10—15 ..	726,950	372,967	353,983	361,001	314,385	11,621	38,810	345	788
15—20 ..	576,366	287,778	288,588	219,019	112,972	67,105	171,250	1,654	4,366
20—25 ..	572,804	286,315	286,489	157,698	52,392	125,287	225,998	3,330	8,099
25—30 ..	494,223	254,066	240,157	54,526	13,719	193,052	209,943	6,488	16,495
30—35 ..	435,889	226,435	209,454	25,735	9,095	192,853	178,773	7,847	21,586
35—40 ..	342,139	182,315	159,824	9,413	5,363	163,344	122,606	9,558	31,855
40—45 ..	292,093	156,440	135,653	6,607	4,198	139,774	96,122	10,059	35,333
45—50 ..	220,072	117,296	102,776	3,653	2,714	101,678	59,939	11,965	40,123
50—55 ..	181,524	95,853	85,671	2,666	2,090	81,291	44,761	11,896	38,820
55—60 ..	127,593	66,627	60,966	1,686	1,447	52,670	23,141	12,271	36,378
60—65 ..	102,866	53,483	49,383	1,236	1,092	40,693	15,467	11,554	32,824
65—70 ..	53,961	27,725	26,236	679	628	19,192	6,272	7,854	19,336
70 and over ..	76,536	38,668	37,868	908	871	23,699	6,608	14,061	30,389
Jews ..	**22,923**	**11,825**	**11,098**	**6,719**	**5,642**	**4,801**	**4,323**	**305**	**1,133**
0—1 ..	585	295	290	294	289	1	1	..	..
1—2 ..	579	270	309	270	308	..	1	..	..
2—3 ..	608	306	302	305	302	1	..	..	..
3—4 ..	579	292	287	291	286	1	1	..	..
4—5 ..	701	339	362	333	357	6	5	..	..
Total 0—5 ..	*3,052*	*1,502*	*1,550*	*1,493*	*1,542*	*9*	*8*	..	..
5—10 ..	2,881	1,431	1,450	1,407	1,419	23	30	1	1
10—15 ..	2,711	1,373	1,338	1,318	1,266	55	71	..	1
15—20 ..	2,403	1,227	1,176	1,055	714	167	450	5	12
20—25 ..	2,244	1,142	1,102	788	389	348	694	6	19
25—30 ..	2,051	1,021	1,030	304	143	691	837	26	50
30—35 ..	1,819	967	852	169	83	774	696	24	73
35—40 ..	1,477	779	698	72	25	686	554	21	119
40—45 ..	1,348	754	594	49	21	673	441	32	132
45—50 ..	937	538	399	36	16	461	235	41	148
50—55 ..	748	402	346	14	9	349	157	39	180
55—60 ..	455	249	206	4	4	214	66	31	136
60—65 ..	412	231	181	6	8	192	40	33	133
65—70 ..	173	95	78	3	1	70	22	22	55
70 and over ..	212	114	98	1	2	80	22	24	74

Table VII.—Age, Sex and Civil Condition. Part I-A.—India Proper—*concld.*

Age and Religion.	Population.			Unmarried.		Married.		Widowed.	
	Persons.	Males.	Females.	Males.	Females.	Males.	Females.	Males.	Females.
1	2	3	4	5	6	7	8	9	10
Tribal ..	**7,611,803**	**3,788,282**	**3,823,521**	**1,954,037**	**1,674,093**	**1,691,634**	**1,728,085**	**142,611**	**421,343**
0—1	258,619	126,464	132,155	125,112	130,791	1,338	1,334	14	30
1—2	252,209	121,345	130,864	119,945	129,258	1,361	1,572	39	34
2—3	287,020	137,319	149,701	135,437	147,470	1,838	2,174	44	57
3—4	293,345	142,639	150,706	139,884	146,873	2,714	3,704	41	129
4—5	278,194	138,179	140,015	134,674	134,720	3,404	5,012	101	283
Total 0—5	*1,369,387*	*665,946*	*703,441*	*655,052*	*689,112*	*10,655*	*13,796*	*239*	*533*
5—10	1,073,850	548,731	525,119	522,835	477,776	25,376	45,836	520	1,507
10—15	898,473	461,194	437,279	412,311	332,798	47,826	101,593	1,057	2,888
15—20	655,179	306,242	348,937	173,503	91,713	128,614	248,146	4,125	9,078
20—25	665,210	310,108	355,102	103,890	42,690	198,978	298,735	7,240	12,677
25—30	643,616	317,608	326,008	37,600	14,139	268,049	288,018	11,959	23,851
30—35	570,744	287,289	283,455	21,064	9,071	253,232	245,127	12,993	29,257
35—40	450,330	234,413	215,917	9,797	4,872	209,487	167,244	15,129	43,801
40—45	377,236	198,744	178,492	6,748	3,752	176,648	127,583	15,348	47,157
45—50	275,689	146,549	129,140	3,784	2,365	126,512	73,003	16,253	53,772
50—55	219,848	114,256	105,592	2,794	1,868	96,738	54,210	14,724	49,514
55—60	149,187	73,356	75,831	1,800	1,324	58,268	27,524	13,288	46,983
60—65	121,400	58,251	63,149	1,308	1,140	45,295	19,263	11,648	42,746
65—70	51,580	24,079	27,501	543	495	17,547	7,172	5,989	19,834
70 and over	90,074	41,516	48,558	1,008	978	28,409	10,835	12,099	36,745
Others ..	422,013	230,752	191,261	109,614	71,062	102,652	102,751	18,486	17,448
0—1	16,691	8,601	8,090	8,600	8,087	1	3	..	..
1—2	11,986	6,009	5,977	6,007	5,970	2	7	..	..
2—3	13,348	6,759	6,589	6,750	6,570	8	18	1	1
3—4	13,772	7,093	6,679	7,041	6,542	51	136	1	1
4—5	13,231	6,902	6,329	6,795	6,054	101	268	6	7
Total 0—5	*69,028*	*35,364*	*33,664*	*35,193*	*33,223*	*163*	*432*	*8*	*9*
5—10	59,106	32,100	27,006	28,207	20,310	3,846	6,642	47	54
10—15	54,550	30,147	24,403	22,729	12,886	7,293	11,412	125	105
15—20	39,246	21,273	17,973	9,155	2,387	11,693	15,396	425	190
20—25	37,980	20,698	17,282	5,891	999	14,049	15,991	758	292
25—30	32,414	17,967	14,447	3,059	430	13,653	13,480	1,255	537
30—35	28,272	15,913	12,359	2,180	248	12,246	11,354	1,487	757
35—40	22,097	12,425	9,672	1,054	185	9,750	8,235	1,621	1,252
40—45	18,876	10,507	8,369	741	164	8,073	6,710	1,693	1,495
45—50	15,827	8,969	6,858	467	93	6,506	4,657	1,996	2,108
50—55	12,379	6,901	5,478	302	49	4,818	3,437	1,781	1,992
55—60	9,863	5,584	4,279	223	29	3,545	2,084	1,816	2,166
60—65	8,749	5,086	3,663	201	28	3,130	1,517	1,755	2,118
65—70	5,228	3,093	2,135	89	17	1,729	666	1,275	1,452
70 and over	8,398	4,725	3,673	123	14	2,158	738	2,444	2,921

Table VII.—Age, Sex and Civil Condition—*contd.*

Part I-B.—Burma.

Age and Religion.	Population.			Unmarried.		Married.		Widowed.	
	Persons.	Males.	Females.	Males.	Females.	Males.	Females.	Males.	Females.
1	2	3	4	5	6	7	8	9	10
All Races ..	**14,647,497**	**7,480,676**	**7,166,821**	**4,194,768**	**3,734,136**	**2,934,902**	**2,680,877**	**351,006**	**751,808**
0—1	395,268	192,402	202,866	192,402	202,866	..	..	..	..
1—2	410,136	199,816	210,320	199,815	210,319	1	1	..	..
2—3	412,966	202,775	210,191	202,770	210,188	5	3	..	..
3—4	406,573	200,940	205,633	200,926	205,622	14	11	..	..
4—5	393,310	194,187	199,123	194,157	199,099	27	23	3	1
Total 0—5	*2,018,253*	*990,120*	*1,028,133*	*990,070*	*1,028,094*	*47*	*38*	*3*	*1*
5—10	1,800,962	908, 410	892,552	907,845	891,732	555	787	10	33
10—15	1,661,007	845,623	815,384	840,658	796,833	4,795	17,210	170	1,341
15—20	1,412,615	693,377	719,238	559,386	437,327	127,590	263,543	6,401	18,368
20—25	1,421,399	701,984	719,415	420,651	277,880	267,927	411,859	13,406	29,676
25—30	1,291,115	680,794	610,321	174,885	98,468	480,595	468,943	25,314	42,910
30—35	1,153,363	624,990	528,373	114,875	68,243	482,365	414,687	27,750	45,443
35—40	875,675	476,824	398,851	56,453	35,523	389,419	306,475	30,952	56,853
40—45	768,519	411,217	357,302	41,367	28,736	337,616	264,633	32,234	63,933
45—50	588,531	308,580	279,951	25,030	19,213	248,987	180,196	34,563	80,542
50—55	515,784	264,341	251,443	20,397	15,962	209,142	149,708	34,802	85,773
55—60	396,507	202,354	194,153	14,256	12,139	150,144	90,675	37,954	91,339
60—65	329,409	170,121	159,288	11,842	10,161	121,071	64,588	37,208	84,539
65—70	181,445	91,428	90,017	7,305	5,727	56,757	25,022	27,366	59,268
70 and over	232,913	110,513	122,400	9,748	8,098	57,892	22,513	42,873	91,789

Table VII.—Age, Sex and Civil Condition. Part I-B.—Burma—*contd.*

Age and Religion.	Population.			Unmarried.		Married.		Widowed.	
	Persons.	Males.	Females.	Males.	Females.	Males.	Females.	Males.	Females.
1	2	3	4	5	6	7	8	9	10
Burmese	**8,596,031**	**4,202,079**	**4,393,952**	**2,399,439**	**4,320,404**	**1,612,566**	**1,619,978**	**190,074**	**453,570**
0—1	231,008	111,294	119,714	111,294	119,714	..	..	..	..
1—2	241,634	116,725	124,909	116,725	124,909	..	..	..	..
2—3	241,058	117,430	123,628	117,430	123,628	..	..	..	..
3—4	237,801	116,618	121,183	116,618	121,183	..	..	..	..
4—5	230,567	113,025	117,542	113,025	117,542	..	..	..	..
Total 0—5	*1,182,068*	*575,092*	*606,976*	*575,092*	*606,976*	..	..	..	..
5—10	1,083,371	541,455	541,916	541,442	541,890	13	24	..	2
10—15	1,003,788	503,384	500,404	502,099	493,689	1,239	6,329	46	386
15—20	825,525	386,671	438,854	314,693	280,384	69,253	149,406	2,725	9,064
20—25	809,925	374,036	435,889	222,928	181,897	145,371	238,246	5,737	15,746
25—30	716,084	347,858	368,226	80,487	67,568	256,269	276,004	11,102	24,654
30—35	643,678	321,009	322,669	54,445	48,081	254,022	247,849	12,542	26,739
35—40	496,499	250,061	246,438	29,140	25,311	205,907	187,422	15,005	33,705
40—45	445,297	221,602	223,695	22,280	20,821	182,972	164,642	16,350	38,232
45—50	352,069	173,700	178,369	14,504	14,295	140,496	115,911	18,700	48,163
50—55	315,382	153,745	161,637	12,294	11,854	122,068	97,536	19,383	52,247
55—60	248,713	122,649	126,064	9,316	9,268	91,046	60,514	22,287	56,282
60—65	206,658	103,361	103,297	7,983	7,740	73,172	43,197	22,206	52,360
65—70	117,705	57,519	60,186	5,409	4,432	35,129	17,409	16,981	38,345
70 and over	149,269	69,937	79,332	7,318	6,198	35,609	15,489	27,010	57,645
Other Indigenous Races.	**4,623,991**	**2,307,725**	**2,316,266**	**1,309,968**	**1,170,943**	**873,251**	**876,016**	**124,506**	**260,307**
0—1	133,911	66,013	67,898	66,013	67,898	..	..	..	..
1—2	136,208	66,909	69,299	66,909	69,299	..	..	..	..
2—3	138,413	68,431	69,982	68,431	69,982	..	..	..	..
3—4	136,173	67,746	68,427	67,746	68,427	..	..	..	..
4—5	131,526	65,163	66,363	65,163	66,363	..	..	..	..
Total 0—5	*676,231*	*334,262*	*341,969*	*334,262*	*341,969*	..	..	..	..
5—10	580,410	293,005	287,405	292,984	287,338	19	64	2	3
10—15	529,345	268,674	260,671	267,631	253,701	961	6,240	82	730
15—20	442,823	209,458	233,365	173,501	138,218	32,993	87,040	2,964	8,107
20—25	435,825	202,528	233,297	125,526	85,040	70,930	136,022	6,072	12,235
25—30	398,347	197,924	200,423	48,164	26,606	138,905	157,883	10,855	15,934
30—35	356,200	184,152	172,048	28,906	17,186	143,985	138,733	11,261	16,129
35—40	272,023	142,902	129,121	12,221	8,490	119,278	100,924	11,403	19,707
40—45	239,494	124,765	114,729	9,041	6,591	104,274	86,223	11,450	21,915
45—50	183,041	94,797	88,244	5,324	4,084	77,588	56,501	11,885	27,659
50—55	159,704	81,092	78,612	4,377	3,452	64,797	46,287	11,918	28,873
55—60	122,437	61,851	60,586	2,835	2,436	46,493	27,307	12,523	30,843
60—65	102,208	52,233	49,975	2,259	2,065	37,911	19,497	12,063	28,413
65—70	53,995	27,086	26,909	1,208	1,107	17,205	6,947	8,673	18,855
70 and over	71,908	32,996	38,912	1,729	1,660	17,912	6,348	13,355	30,904
Chinese	**193,594**	**127,049**	**66,545**	**69,471**	**36,333**	**51,897**	**24,557**	**5,681**	**5,655**
0—1	4,293	2,283	2,010	2,283	2,010	..	..	..	..
1—2	4,339	2,267	2,072	2,267	2,072	..	..	..	..
2—3	4,683	2,472	2,211	2,472	2,211	..	..	..	..
3—4	4,730	2,534	2,196	2,534	2,196	..	..	..	..
4—5	4,585	2,457	2,128	2,457	2,128	..	..	..	..
Total 0—5	*22,630*	*12,013*	*10,617*	*12,013*	*10,617*	..	..	..	..
5—10	20,379	11,106	9,273	11,096	9,246	10	26	..	1
10—15	18,904	10,639	8,265	10,545	8,123	92	139	2	3
15—20	18,245	11,902	6,343	10,095	4,014	1,733	2,257	74	72
20—25	19,840	13,748	6,092	9,772	2,269	3,808	3,696	168	127
25—30	20,074	14,485	5,589	6,126	709	7,916	4,620	443	260
30—35	18,331	13,333	4,998	4,198	466	8,620	4,225	515	307
35—40	15,014	11,057	3,957	2,097	276	8,278	3,294	682	387
40—45	13,056	9,670	3,386	1,557	225	7,380	2,689	733	472
45—50	8,916	6,553	2,363	770	136	5,061	1,438	722	789
50—55	7,135	5,126	2,009	540	108	3,914	1,085	672	816
55—60	4,376	3,050	1,326	292	62	2,207	496	551	768
60—65	3,495	2,413	1,082	218	43	1,695	350	500	689
65—70	1,509	982	527	82	23	618	125	282	379
70 and over	1,690	972	718	70	16	565	117	337	585
Indian Hindus	**565,609**	**425,389**	**140,220**	**189,866**	**63,278**	**219,534**	**66,975**	**16,189**	**9,967**
0—1	8,982	4,399	4,583	4,399	4,583	..	..	..	..
1—2	9,793	4,864	4,929	4,863	4,928	1	1	..	..
2—3	10,553	5,257	5,296	5,252	5,293	5	3	..	..
3—4	9,995	5,062	4,933	5,048	4,924	14	9	..	..
4—5	9,074	4,721	4,353	4,694	4,333	24	19	3	1
Total 0—5	*48,397*	*24,303*	*24,094*	*24,256*	*24,061*	*44*	*32*	*3*	*1*
5—10	40,154	22,646	17,508	22,253	17,063	385	436	8	9
10—15	38,668	24,136	14,532	22,889	12,594	1,221	1,896	26	42
15—20	57,078	42,856	14,222	28,889	3,823	13,627	10,131	340	268
20—25	77,917	60,921	16,996	31,923	2,295	28,242	14,293	756	408
25—30	84,278	69,223	15,055	22,738	1,129	44,945	13,297	1,540	629
30—35	73,245	61,254	11,991	15,989	802	43,378	10,446	1,887	743
35—40	49,963	42,246	7,717	8,212	456	31,807	6,171	2,227	1,090
40—45	37,193	31,246	5,947	5,390	343	23,732	4,419	2,124	1,185
45—50	21,226	17,413	3,813	2,709	220	12,856	2,325	1,848	1,268
50—55	15,184	12,164	3,020	1,995	165	8,636	1,652	1,533	1,203
55—60	8,710	6,700	2,010	1,067	110	4,354	861	1,279	1,039
60—65	6,983	5,399	1,584	758	95	3,458	589	1,183	900
65—70	3,023	2,303	720	282	50	1,416	203	605	467
70 and over	3,590	2,579	1,011	316	72	1,433	224	830	715

Table VII.—Age, Sex and Civil Condition. Part I-B.—Burma—*concld.*

Age and Religion.	Population			Unmarried.		Married.		Widowed.	
	Persons.	Males.	Females.	Males.	Females.	Males.	Females.	Males.	Females.
1	2	3	4	5	6	7	8	9	10
Indian Muslims ..	**396,594**	**271,514**	**125,080**	**137,841**	**64,340**	**124,224**	**49,560**	**9,449**	**11.180**
0—1 ..	9,040	4,458	4,582	4,458	4,582	..	..	..	..
1—2 ..	9,771	4,890	4,881	4,890	4,881	..	..	..	..
2—3 ..	9,837	4,989	4,848	4,989	4,848	..	..	..	..
3—4 ..	9,502	4,750	4,752	4,750	4,751	..	1	..	..
4—5 ..	9,281	4,595	4,686	4,592	4,683	3	3	..	.
Total 0—5 ..	*47,431*	*23,682*	*23,749*	*23,679*	*23,745*	*3*	*4*	..	..
5—10 ..	40,941	22,185	18,756	22,068	18,527	117	212	..	17
10—15 ..	38,086	22,281	15,805	21,081	12,788	1,186	1,878	14	139
15—20 ..	41,993	28,718	13,275	20,812	3,954	7,704	8,801	202	520
20—25 ..	49,928	36,033	13,895	20,866	2,022	14,693	11,222	474	651
25—30 ..	47,472	36,862	10,610	12,358	760	23,552	9,107	952	743
30—35 ..	40,312	32,328	7,984	8,215	507	23,044	6,705	1,069	772
35—40 ..	26,230	20,930	5,300	3,371	300	16,446	3,985	1,113	1,015
40—45 ..	20,144	15,841	4,303	2,092	236	12,705	3,007	1,044	1,060
45—50 ..	13,911	10,539	3,372	1,156	139	8,524	1,888	859	1,345
50—55 ..	10,739	7,811	2,928	793	115	6,229	1,471	789	1,342
55—60 ..	7,014	5,104	1,910	506	88	3,794	627	804	1,195
60—65 ..	5,850	4,315	1,535	426	71	3,100	396	789	1,068
65—70 ..	2,970	2,301	669	210	36	1,580	127	511	506
70 and over ..	3,573	2,584	989	208	52	1,547	130	829	807
Other Indians ..	**55,622**	**37,008**	**18,614**	**19,527**	**9,693**	**16,015**	**7,533**	**1,466**	**1,388**
0—1 ..	1,319	647	672	647	672	..	..	..	..
1—2 ..	1,269	602	667	602	667	..	..	..	..
2—3 ..	1,322	641	681	641	681	..	..	..	..
3—4 ..	1,300	652	648	652	647	..	1	..	..
4—5 ..	1,205	607	598	607	597	..	1	..	..
Total 0—5 ..	*6,415*	*3,149*	*3,266*	*3,149*	*3,264*	..	*2*	..	..
5—10 ..	5,404	2,906	2,498	2,901	2,492	5	6	..	..
10—15 ..	5,026	2,865	2,161	2,828	2,033	37	125	..	3
15—20 ..	5,565	3,594	1,971	2,932	824	639	1,114	23	33
20—25 ..	6,724	4,538	2,186	3,020	488	1,473	1,646	45	52
25—30 ..	6,632	4,864	1,768	1,868	214	2,886	1,473	110	81
30—35 ..	5,807	4,347	1,460	1,219	156	2,995	1,199	133	105
35—40 ..	4,251	3,244	1,007	602	78	2,483	775	159	154
40—45 ..	3,467	2,707	760	419	55	2,102	538	186	167
45—50 ..	2,190	1,705	485	212	25	1,308	270	185	190
50—55 ..	1,596	1,219	377	158	20	899	186	162	171
55—60 ..	997	741	256	96	15	491	105	154	136
60—65 ..	763	575	188	66	14	382	57	127	117
65—70 ..	369	267	102	33	8	156	19	78	75
70 and over ..	416	287	129	24	7	159	18	104	104
Indo-Burman Races ..	**182,166**	**90,307**	**91,859**	**56,730**	**51,481**	**30,317**	**31,533**	**3,260**	**8,845**
0—1 ..	5,951	2,909	3,042	2,909	3,042	..	..	..	..
1—2 ..	6,393	3,186	3,207	3,186	3,207	..	..	..	..
2—3 ..	6,329	3,159	3,170	3,159	3,170	..	..	..	..
3—4 ..	6,321	3,199	3,122	3,199	3,122	..	..	..	..
4—5 ..	6,357	3,252	3,105	3,252	3,105	..	..	..	..
Total 0—5 ..	*31,351*	*15,705*	*15,646*	*15,705*	*15,646*	..	..	..	..
5—10 ..	26,9[illegible]	13,405	13,524	13,399	13,506	6	17	..	1
10—15 ..	23,975	12,037	11,938	11,980	11,303	57	597	..	38
15—20 ..	18,119	8,370	9,749	6,747	4,913	1,551	4,537	72	299
20—25 ..	17,569	7,946	9,623	4,633	2,959	3,165	6,221	148	443
25—30 ..	14,566	7,256	7,310	1,730	1,063	5,232	5,670	294	577
30—35 ..	12,579	6,599	5,980	1,064	727	5,216	4,645	319	608
35—40 ..	9,051	4,766	4,285	464	401	3,986	3,170	316	714
40—45 ..	7,569	3,940	3,629	350	305	3,286	2,516	304	808
45—50 ..	5,565	2,835	2,730	217	195	2,310	1,520	308	1,015
50—55 ..	4,739	2,350	2,389	136	156	1,916	1,231	298	1,002
55—60 ..	3,556	1,828	1,728	94	112	1,414	655	320	961
60—65 ..	2,912	1,502	1,410	90	90	1,104	432	308	888
65—70 ..	1,563	783	780	54	46	525	164	204	570
70 and over ..	2,123	985	1,138	67	59	549	158	369	921
Others	**33,890**	**19,605**	**14,285**	**12,126**	**8,664**	**7,098**	**4,725**	**381**	**896**
0—1 ..	764	399	365	399	365	..	..	..	..
1—2 ..	729	373	356	373	356	..	..	..	..
2—3 ..	771	396	375	396	375	..	..	..	..
3—4 ..	751	379	372	379	372	..	..	..	..
4—5 ..	715	367	348	367	348	..	..	..	..
Total 0—5 ..	*3,730*	*1,914*	*1,816*	*1,914*	*1,816*	..	..	..	..
5—10 ..	3,374	1,702	1,672	1,702	1,670	..	2	..	..
10—15 ..	3,215	1,607	1,608	1,605	1,602	2	6	..	..
15—20 ..	3,267	1,808	1,459	1,717	1,197	90	257	1	5
20—25 ..	3,671	2,234	1,437	1,983	910	245	513	6	14
25—30 ..	3,662	2,322	1,340	1,414	419	890	889	18	32
30—35 ..	3,211	1,968	1,243	839	318	1,105	885	24	40
35—40 ..	2,644	1,618	1,026	337	211	1,234	734	47	81
40—45 ..	2,299	1,446	853	238	160	1,165	599	43	94
45—50 ..	1,613	1,038	575	138	119	844	343	56	113
50—55 ..	1,305	834	471	104	92	683	260	47	119
55—60 ..	704	431	273	50	48	345	110	36	115
60—65 ..	540	323	217	42	43	249	70	32	104
65—70 ..	311	187	124	27	25	128	28	32	71
70 and over ..	344	173	171	16	34	118	29	39	108

Table VII.—Age, Sex and Civil Condition. Part II. Provinces and States.

Age and Religion.	Population.			Unmarried.		Married.		Widowed.	
	Persons.	Males.	Females.	Males.	Females.	Males.	Females.	Males.	Females.
1	2	3	4	5	6	7	8	9	10
Aden.									
All Religions ..	***51,456**	**32,325**	**19,131**	**16,859**	**8,186**	**14,786**	**8,113**	**677**	**2,832**
0—1 ..	542	291	251	291	251	..	..	..	..
1—2 ..	898	464	434	464	434	..	..	..	..
2—3 ..	895	458	437	458	437	..	..	..	..
3—4 ..	936	475	461	475	460	..	1	..	..
4—5 ..	901	448	453	448	453	..	..	..	..
Total 0—5 ..	*4,172*	*2,136*	*2,036*	*2,136*	*2,035*	..	*1*	..	..
5—10 ..	4,848	2,593	2,255	2,583	2,245	8	9	2*	1
10—15 ..	4,456	2,875	1,581	2,796	1,489	79	86	..	6
15—20 ..	4,876	3,007	1,869	2,582	1,011	421	805	4	53
20—25 ..	6,464	4,162	2,302	2,742	515	1,385	1,654	35	133
25—30 ..	6,869	4,591	2,278	1,903	348	2,591	1,738	97	192
30—35 ..	5,781	3,902	1,879	974	207	2,854	1,405	74	267
35—40 ..	4,440	3,101	1,339	516	98	2,492	985	93	256
40—45 ..	3,526	2,328	1,198	299	96	1,938	703	91	399
45—50 ..	2,154	1,419	735	141	46	1,205	337	73	352
50—55 ..	1,824	1,088	736	94	43	911	234	83	459
55—60 ..	664	394	270	23	15	342	58	29	197
60—65 ..	813	451	362	46	29	356	63	49	270
65—70 ..	199	94	105	6	4	80	12	8	89
70 and over	370	184	186	18	5	127	23	39	158
Ajmer-Merwara.									
All Religions ..	**560,292**	**296,081**	**264,211**	**133,452**	**83,798**	**142,706**	**139,410**	**19,923**	**41,003**
0—1 ..	18,658	9,274	9,384	9,104	9,216	166	163	4	5
1—2 ..	16,777	8,315	8,462	8,174	8,243	134	212	7	7
2—3 ..	17.360	8,487	8,873	8,316	8,500	162	366	9	7
3—4 ..	16,647	8,252	8,395	7,985	7,788	256	595	11	12
4—5 ..	15,613	7,948	7,665	7,601	6,921	334	727	13	17
Total 0—5 ..	*85,055*	*42,276*	*45,779*	*41,180*	*40,668*	*1,052*	*2,063*	*41*	*48*
5—10 ..	68,572	36,408	32,164	32,414	24,482	3,851	7,568	143	114
10—15 ..	63,558	34,404	29,154	27,428	15,683	6,734	13,279	242	192
15—20 ..	55,704	29,565	26,139	13,795	1,959	15,215	23,651	555	529
20—25 ..	57,363	30,621	26,742	9,039	453	20,719	25,435	863	854
25—30 ..	45,877	24,646	21,231	3,179	158	20,243	19,397	1,224	1,676
30—35 ..	39,217	20,968	18,249	1,968	119	17,593	15,812	1,407	2,318
35—40 ..	35,609	18,946	16,663	1,417	80	15,510	12,021	2,019	4,562
40—45 ..	31,919	17,219	14,700	1,251	63	13,652	9,333	2,316	5,304
45—50 ..	25,689	14,360	11,329	690	42	10,820	4,969	2,850	6,318
50—55 ..	20,055	11,188	8,867	502	30	8,071	3,177	2,615	5,660
55—60 ..	12,605	6,488	6,117	246	18	4,148	1,271	2,094	4,828
60—65 ..	10,121	4,854	5,267	179	19	2,977	878	1,698	4,370
65—70 ..	3,914	1,848	2,066	66	9	1,019	257	763	1,800
70 and over ..	5,034	2,290	2,744	98	15	1,102	299	1,090	2,430
Andaman and Nicobar Islands.									
All Religions ..	**†27,943**	**18,885**	**9,058**	**8,527**	**3,923**	**9,032**	**4,494**	**1,326**	**641**
0—1 ..	813	387	426	387	426	..	..	..	..
1—2 ..	636	306	330	306	330	..	..	..	..
2—3 ..	796	397	399	397	399	..	..	..	..
3—4 ..	748	392	356	392	356	..	..	..	..
4—5 ..	615	330	285	330	285	..	..	..	..
Total 0—5 ..	*3,608*	*1,812*	*1,796*	*1,812*	*1,796*	..	..	..	..
5—10 ..	2,409	1,324	1,085	1,314	1,066	10	17	..	2
10—15 ..	1,995	1,116	879	1,086	752	29	125	1	2
15—20 ..	1,918	1,147	771	823	166	305	588	19	17
20—25 ..	2,689	1,823	866	958	50	810	781	55	35
25—30 ..	3,685	2,822	863	920	10	1,731	812	171	41
30—35 ..	3,550	2,771	779	659	7	1,866	723	246	49
35—40 ..	2,625	2,051	574	381	8	1,444	513	226	53
40—45 ..	2,041	1,571	470	277	8	1,113	408	181	54
45—50 ..	1,278	976	302	126	5	715	237	135	60
50—55 ..	912	679	233	89	15	479	158	111	60
55—60 ..	458	326	132	37	10	229	64	60	58
60—65 ..	333	230	103	24	13	163	35	43	55
65—70 ..	153	81	72	7	11	56	13	18	48
70 and over	289	156	133	14	6	82	20	60	107
Baluchistan.									
All Religions ..	**‡110,849**	**80,197**	**30,652**	**37,351**	**13,037**	**39,362**	**15,658**	**3,484**	**1,907**
0—1 ..	2,566	1,285	1,281	1,285	1,281	..	..	..	..
1—2 ..	2,160	1,115	1,045	1,115	1,045	..	..	..	..
2—3 ..	2,380	1,212	1,168	1,212	1,168	..	..	..	..
3—4 ..	2,235	1,125	1,110	1,125	1,110	..	..	..	..
4—5 ..	2,015	1,056	959	1,056	959	..	..	..	..
Total 0—5 ..	*11,356*	*5,793*	*5,563*	*5,793*	*5,563*	..	..	..	..
5—10 ..	8,484	4,682	3,802	4,620	3,667	62	135	..	..
10—15 ..	7,764	4,539	3,225	4,328	2,635	206	585	5	5
15—20 ..	14,260	10,686	3,574	7,180	617	3,383	2,920	123	37
20—25 ..	19,215	15,008	4,207	8,246	270	6,464	3,875	298	62
25—30 ..	16,649	13,388	3,261	3,981	111	8,888	3,043	519	107
30—35 ..	13,027	10,612	2,415	1,958	76	8,093	2,211	561	128
35—40 ..	7,300	5,837	1,463	584	45	4,764	1,196	489	222
40—45 ..	5,079	3,985	1,094	322	31	3,242	805	421	258
45—50 ..	3,025	2,330	695	138	25	1,847	387	345	283
50—55 ..	1,984	1,480	504	82	22	1,156	246	242	236
55—60 ..	1,020	733	287	48	10	534	99	151	178
60—65 ..	779	535	244	35	5	370	75	130	164
65—70 ..	333	218	115	12	3	140	33	66	79
70 and over	574	371	203	24	7	213	48	134	148

*Excludes 22 persons (20 males and 2 females) of unspecified age.

† Excludes 1,520 persons (817 males and 703 females) who were not recorded by age.

‡ These figures, which relate to the British Districts and States in Baluchistan, exclude 757, 768 persons (408, 217 males and 349,551 females) who were not recorded by age.

Table VII.—Age, Sex and Civil Condition.—Part II. Provinces and States—*contd*

*Assam.

Age and Religion.	Population.			Unmarried.		Married.		Widowed.	
	Persons.	Males.	Females.	Males.	Females.	Males.	Females.	Males.	Females.
1	2	3	4	5	6	7	8	9	10
All Religions	**9,247,857**	**4,844,133**	**4,403,724**	**2,595,453**	**1,828,682**	**2,033,641**	**1,955,002**	**215,039**	**620,040**
0—1	314,649	156,908	157,741	156,903	151,721	5	20	..	..
1—2	308,555	151,624	156,931	151,588	156,813	35	118	1	..
2—3	335,279	163,583	171,696	163,480	171,141	101	548	2	7
3—4	326,217	160,867	165,350	160,580	163,463	285	1,846	2	41
4—5	311,477	156,087	155,390	155,591	152,435	477	2,844	19	111
Total 0—5	*1,596,177*	*789,069*	*807,108*	*788,142*	*801,573*	*903*	*5,376*	*24*	*159*
5—10	1,249,517	653,574	595,943	641,759	536,231	11,448	58,376	367	1,336
10—15	1,056,778	555,922	500,856	529,917	357,913	25,173	138,842	832	4,101
15—20	850,665	403,581	447,084	286,565	79,515	111,997	349,164	5,019	18,405
20—25	882,894	424,067	458,827	208,043	33,278	205,796	397,462	10,228	28,087
25—30	813,548	432,696	380,852	74,024	7,869	338,515	327,883	20,157	45,100
30—35	723,338	401,463	321,875	36,945	4,812	341,715	262,396	22,803	54,667
35—40	546,655	313,761	232,894	11,790	2,266	277,064	157,618	24,907	73,010
40—45	452,794	261,391	191,403	7,566	1,709	229,571	114,061	24,254	75,633
45—50	331,454	191,563	139,891	3,917	1,023	163,496	59,027	24,150	79,841
50—55	266,829	152,379	114,450	2,779	818	127,454	42,099	22,146	71,533
55—60	172,008	96,305	75,703	1,441	534	76,482	18,296	18,382	56,873
60—65	136,285	74,680	61,605	1,096	421	58,058	13,141	15,526	48,043
65—70	61,590	34,162	27,428	520	229	25,204	4,749	8,438	22,450
70 and over	107,325	59,520	47,805	949	491	40,765	6,512	17,806	40,802
Hindus	**5,204,650**	**2,751,657**	**2,452,993**	**1,472,047**	**1,013,865**	**1,128,396**	**1,055,799**	**151,214**	**383,329**
0—1	175,447	87,778	87,669	87,778	87,667	..	2	..	..
1—2	167,869	82,881	84,988	82,875	84,983	6	5	..	..
2—3	179,512	87,878	91,634	87,857	91,588	20	43	1	3
3—4	175,093	86,605	88,488	86,540	88,265	64	208	1	15
4—5	167,870	84,445	83,425	84,324	83,037	115	349	6	39
Total 0—5	*865,791*	*429,587*	*436,204*	*429,374*	*435,540*	*205*	*607*	*8*	*57*
5—10	674,444	351,440	323,004	348,143	300,916	3,085	21,456	212	632
10—15	568,907	299,155	269,752	290,596	206,059	8,067	61,546	492	2,147
15—20	464,386	226,088	238,298	171,743	44,485	51,429	182,572	2,916	11,241
20—25	489,355	240,727	248,628	131,881	16,718	102,726	214,189	6,120	17,721
25—30	472,191	253,323	218,868	51,381	3,906	188,721	185,782	13,221	29,180
30—35	427,254	238,018	189,236	26,711	2,499	195,709	151,658	15,598	35,079
35—40	326,193	188,637	137,556	8,771	1,200	161,811	90,918	18,055	45,438
40—45	272,647	158,479	114,168	5,625	903	135,020	66,574	17,834	46,691
45—50	201,612	117,401	84,211	2,929	547	96,288	34,347	18,184	49,317
50—55	164,962	95,111	69,851	2,095	435	76,194	24,656	16,822	44,760
55—60	104,552	58,819	45,733	1,051	251	44,167	9,898	13,601	35,584
60—65	81,382	44,776	36,606	786	180	32,671	6,761	11,319	29,665
65—70	34,616	19,112	15,504	364	77	13,017	2,178	5,731	13,249
70 and over	56,358	30,984	25,374	597	149	19,286	2,657	11,101	22,568
Muslims	**2,780,514**	**1,461,762**	**1,318,752**	**769,446**	**503,409**	**655,983**	**648,233**	**36,333**	**167,110**
0—1	93,117	46,240	46,877	46,238	46,861	2	16	..	..
1—2	95,731	46,661	49,070	46,636	48,970	25	100	..	..
2—3	106,991	51,833	55,158	51,763	54,679	70	475	..	4
3—4	104,285	51,141	53,144	50,947	51,547	193	1,572	1	25
4—5	99,509	49,742	49,767	49,437	47,338	297	2,377	8	52
Total 0—5	*499,633*	*245,617*	*254,016*	*245,021*	*249,395*	*587*	*4,540*	*9*	*81*
5—10	405,758	216,128	189,630	208,089	153,443	7,910	35,563	129	624
10—15	345,938	184,848	161,090	168,824	88,287	15,767	71,149	257	1,654
15—20	272,957	125,589	147,368	75,566	7,799	48,772	134,822	1,251	4,747
20—25	281,774	132,357	149,417	49,573	2,312	80,300	140,473	2,484	6,632
25—30	236,051	126,918	109,133	13,570	761	109,333	97,549	4,015	10,823
30—35	201,969	114,812	87,157	5,443	543	105,204	72,287	4,165	14,327
35—40	146,765	86,121	60,644	1,396	300	80,924	39,549	3,801	20,795
40—45	117,368	69,631	47,737	843	208	65,257	25,693	3,531	21,836
45—50	86,015	50,935	35,080	431	111	47,103	12,135	3,401	22,834
50—55	65,675	38,445	27,230	264	90	35,214	7,627	2,967	19,513
55—60	42,827	24,783	18,044	147	63	21,925	3,088	2,711	14,893
60—65	33,998	19,236	14,762	118	42	16,727	2,161	2,391	12,559
65—70	15,688	9,398	6,290	56	22	7,828	698	1,514	5,570
70 and over	28,098	16,944	11,154	105	33	13,132	899	3,707	10,222
Tribal	**992,390**	**493,755**	**498,635**	**272,475**	**242,352**	**198,717**	**200,703**	**22,563**	**55,580**
0—1	36,953	18,324	18,629	18,322	18,627	2	2	..	..
1—2	36,331	17,847	18,484	17,845	18,472	2	12	..	..
2—3	39,303	19,214	20,089	19,206	20,061	8	28	..	..
3—4	37,634	18,547	19,087	18,522	19,031	25	55	..	1
4—5	35,296	17,535	17,761	17,479	17,658	52	88	4	15
Total 0—5	*185,517*	*91,467*	*94,050*	*91,374*	*93,849*	*89*	*185*	*4*	*16*
5—10	132,624	67,434	65,190	67,050	64,002	364	1,120	20	68
10—15	109,025	55,153	53,872	54,031	48,431	1,060	5,186	62	255
15—20	86,077	39,102	46,975	28,855	19,912	9,551	25,099	696	1,964
20—25	85,350	38,576	46,774	19,148	10,325	18,128	33,406	1,300	3,043
25—30	81,559	39,955	41,604	6,217	2,422	31,445	35,053	2,293	4,129
30—35	73,296	37,283	36,013	3,186	1,313	31,689	30,484	2,408	4,216
35—40	58,560	30,754	27,806	968	547	27,302	21,907	2,484	5,352
40—45	50,069	26,463	23,606	623	430	23,475	17,597	2,365	5,579
45—50	35,146	18,512	16,634	303	275	16,088	10,257	2,121	6,102
50—55	29,199	15,061	14,138	236	218	12,879	8,124	1,946	5,796
55—60	20,098	10,404	9,694	139	154	8,557	4,474	1,708	5,066
60—65	17,209	8,865	8,344	111	144	7,228	3,603	1,526	4,597
65—70	9,366	4,774	4,592	57	91	3,694	1,614	1,023	2,887
70 and over	19,295	9,952	9,343	177	239	7,168	2,594	2,607	6,510

* Includes Assam States.

Table VII.—Age, Sex and Civil Condition. Part II.—Provinces and States—*contd.*

Age and Religion.	Population.			Unmarried.		Married.		Widowed.	
	Persons.	Males.	Females.	Males.	Females.	Males.	Females.	Males.	Females.
1	2	3	4	5	6	7	8	9	10
				Bihar and Orissa.					
All Religions	**37,677,576**	**18,794,138**	**18,883,438**	**7,698,809**	**5,664,954**	**10,089,629**	**10,120,350**	**1,005,700**	**3,098,134**
0—1	927,550	459,557	467,993	455,360	463,034	4,123	4,809	74	150
1—2	1,013,551	488,849	524,702	482,273	515,509	6,429	8,953	147	240
2—3	1,185,564	561,812	623,752	549,144	602,677	12,382	20,463	286	612
3—4	1,256,641	611,471	645,170	580,824	591,213	29,861	52,158	786	1,799
4—5	1,219,289	612,016	607,273	567,484	528,818	43,270	75,716	1,262	2,739
Total 0—5	*5,602,595*	*2,733,705*	*2,868,890*	*2,635,085*	*2,701,251*	*96,065*	*162,099*	*2,555*	*5,540*
5—10	5,073,200	2,642,921	2,430,279	2,157,262	1,690,174	474,090	718,244	11,569	21,861
10—15	4,346,269	2,302,350	2,043,919	1,599,408	998,693	685,493	1,014,695	17,449	30,531
15—20	3,184,908	1,563,970	1,620,938	583,579	148,447	949,959	1,414,236	30,432	58,255
20—25	3,335,591	1,600,627	1,734,964	364,091	57,095	1,190,860	1,584,178	45,676	93,691
25—30	3,304,941	1,617,586	1,687,355	140,166	22,839	1,404,543	1,480,026	72,877	184,490
30—35	3,038,521	1,506,842	1,531,679	87,488	16,672	1,335,936	1,273,321	83,418	241,686
35—40	2,412,959	1,207,217	1,205,742	44,913	9,718	1,064,570	853,530	97,734	342,494
40—45	2,078,609	1,046,319	1,032,290	32,413	7,092	907,211	654,826	106,695	370,372
45—50	1,598,020	818,724	779,296	19,563	3,944	680,804	379,565	118,357	395,787
50—55	1,269,517	643,356	626,161	14,294	3,108	520,081	267,767	108,981	355,286
55—60	900,134	426,396	473,738	8,018	2,097	320,660	139,374	97,718	332,267
60—65	718,011	325,230	392,781	5,714	1,731	235,577	94,169	83,939	296,881
65—70	324,786	144,860	179,926	2,503	755	95,921	36,119	46,436	143,052
70 and over	489,515	214,035	275,480	4,312	1,338	127,859	48,201	81,864	225,941
Hindus	**31,011,474**	**15,493,257**	**15,518,217**	**6,197,854**	**4,472,644**	**8,419,514**	**8,398,716**	**875,880**	**2,646,857**
0—1	748,403	371,101	377,302	368,020	373,572	3,018	3,614	63	116
1—2	822,032	396,421	425,611	391,419	418,678	4,875	6,741	127	192
2—3	956,714	452,937	503,777	442,929	487,445	9,763	15,820	245	512
3—4	1,009,620	491,208	518,412	466,113	474,827	24,435	42,043	660	1,542
4—5	976,972	491,081	485,891	454,383	421,829	35,665	61,733	1,033	2,329
Total 0—5	*4,513,741*	*2,202,748*	*2,310,993*	*2,122,864*	*2,176,351*	*77,756*	*129,951*	*2,128*	*4,691*
5—10	4,099,789	2,139,192	1,960,597	1,726,047	1,339,296	402,878	602,217	10,267	19,084
10—15	3,532,362	1,876,406	1,655,956	1,278,241	779,090	582,688	850,403	15,477	26,463
15—20	2,619,681	1,294,711	1,324,970	470,901	101,248	797,502	1,173,948	26,308	49,774
20—25	2,756,552	1,330,477	1,426,075	297,749	34,968	993,506	1,310,925	39,222	80,182
25—30	2,738,626	1,344,855	1,393,771	115,693	14,058	1,166,459	1,222,365	62,703	157,348
30—35	2,526,375	1,255,523	1,270,852	73,160	10,534	1,110,030	1,054,394	72,333	205,924
35—40	2,016,444	1,008,760	1,007,684	38,734	5,860	884,764	709,507	85,262	292,317
40—45	1,745,278	878,126	867,152	28,281	4,037	756,333	546,424	93,512	316,691
45—50	1,346,065	689,291	656,774	16,876	2,242	568,478	315,859	103,937	338,673
50—55	1,069,616	541,900	527,716	12,196	1,723	433,857	221,573	95,847	304,420
55—60	760,098	359,662	400,436	6,849	1,098	267,257	115,116	85,556	284,222
60—65	605,842	273,636	332,206	4,822	931	195,531	77,380	73,283	253,895
65—70	274,133	121,688	152,445	2,051	440	79,325	29,771	40,312	122,234
70 and over	406,872	176,282	230,590	3,390	768	103,150	38,883	69,742	190,939
Tribal	**2,043,809**	**1,011,522**	**1,037,287**	**530,575**	**469,058**	**442,797**	**455,347**	**38,150**	**112,882**
0—1	66,728	32,527	34,201	32,003	33,619	524	576	..	6
1—2	62,330	29,837	32,493	29,275	31,857	558	633	4	3
2—3	75,338	35,980	39,358	35,222	38,442	754	908	4	8
3—4	80,922	39,495	41,427	38,382	39,939	1,103	1,445	10	43
4—5	76,828	38,189	38,639	36,854	36,802	1,308	1,751	27	86
Total 0—5	*362,146*	*176,028*	*186,118*	*171,736*	*180,659*	*4,247*	*5,313*	*45*	*146*
5—10	303,082	155,073	148,009	145,376	132,113	9,536	15,312	161	584
10—15	254,468	130,784	123,684	113,405	93,492	17,004	29,118	375	1,074
15—20	177,446	83,539	93,907	43,882	28,601	38,390	62,695	1,267	2,611
20—25	173,074	81,236	91,838	26,493	14,849	52,733	73,320	2,010	3,669
25—30	170,394	84,066	86,328	11,526	6,242	69,307	73,207	3,233	6,879
30—35	153,029	76,334	76,695	7,309	4,410	65,607	63,759	3,418	8,526
35—40	116,403	59,132	57,271	3,592	2,430	51,566	43,073	3,974	11,768
40—45	96,615	49,179	47,436	2,507	1,928	42,618	33,362	4,054	12,146
45—50	72,710	36,864	35,846	1,600	1,300	30,865	20,722	4,399	13,824
50—55	60,865	30,336	30,529	1,261	1,045	24,952	16,360	4,123	13,124
55—60	40,968	19,200	21,768	722	751	14,808	8,348	3,670	12,669
60—65	32,163	14,618	17,545	535	596	11,034	5,620	3,049	11,329
65—70	12,801	5,432	7,369	221	229	3,761	1,899	1,450	5,241
70 and over	22,645	9,701	12,944	410	413	6,369	3,239	2,922	9,292
				Bombay. *(Excluding Aden.)*					
All Religions	**21,801,745***	**11,471,543**	**10,330,202**	**5,408,573**	**3,476,218**	**5,459,366**	**5,244,934**	**603,604**	**1,609,050**
0—1	647,732	323,471	324,261	320,853	321,312	2,518	2,805	100	144
1—2	618,120	303,544	314,576	300,193	310,087	3,241	4,331	110	158
2—3	658,016	320,883	337,133	316,344	329,899	4,382	7,008	157	226
3—4	664,102	331,733	332,369	325,292	317,706	6,229	14,308	212	355
4—5	660,609	337,624	322,985	328,921	300,723	8,250	21,514	453	748
Total 0—5	*3,248,579*	*1,617,255*	*1,631,324*	*1,591,603*	*1,579,727*	*24,620*	*49,966*	*1,032*	*1,631*
5—10	2,819,745	1,486,771	1,332,974	1,386,561	1,032,682	97,497	293,957	2,713	6,335
10—15	2,476,229	1,331,194	1,145,035	1,151,085	649,370	175,627	484,478	4,482	11,187
15—20	1,951,538	1,002,201	949,337	552,962	104,412	437,296	816,003	11,943	28,922
20—25	2,099,396	1,064,436	1,034,960	379,626	46,794	663,571	939,438	21,239	48,728
25—30	1,962,285	1,044,706	917,579	151,590	20,062	854,463	808,119	38,653	89,398
30—35	1,799,045	992,194	806,851	88,769	14,848	853,635	670,349	49,790	121,654
35—40	1,419,172	789,476	629,696	41,054	8,987	685,295	441,402	63,127	179,307
40—45	1,168,371	642,151	526,220	26,424	6,803	548,455	322,265	67,272	197,152
45—50	885,406	480,256	405,150	14,621	4,093	391,017	182,343	74,618	218,714
50—55	689,259	368,944	320,315	10,014	3,028	289,083	119,336	69,847	197,951
55—60	486,384	251,432	234,952	5,573	2,020	181,746	55,968	64,113	176,964
60—65	390,183	195,529	194,654	4,215	1,590	134,837	36,674	56,477	156,390
65—70	172,578	87,923	84,655	1,705	691	55,931	11,961	30,287	72,003
70 and over	233,575	117,075	116,500	2,771	1,111	66,293	12,675	48,001	102,714

*Excludes 1,643 persons (1,341 males and 302 females) who were not recorded by age.

Table VII.—Age, Sex and Civil Condition. Part II.—Provinces and States—*contd.*

Bombay (*Excluding Aden*)—*concld.*

Age and Religion.		Population.			Unmarried.		Married.		Widowed.	
		Persons.	Males.	Females.	Males.	Females.	Males.	Females.	Males.	Females.
1		2	3	4	5	6	7	8	9	10
Hindus	..	**16,616,819**	**8,606,594**	**8,010,225**	**3,917,600**	**2,570,448**	**4,244,551**	**4,136,614**	**444,443**	**1,303,163**
0—1	..	506,426	251,691	254,735	249,435	252,244	2,175	2,364	81	127
1—2	..	484,251	237,081	247,170	234,158	243,341	2,828	3,690	95	139
2—3	..	504,613	244,865	259,748	240,920	253,510	3,809	6,033	136	205
3—4	..	501,727	249,027	252,700	243,699	239,830	5,151	12,564	177	306
4—5	..	495,257	251,100	244,157	244,269	224,687	6,475	18,877	356	593
Total 0—5	..	*2,492,274*	*1,233,764*	*1,258,510*	*1,212,481*	*1,213,612*	*20,438*	*43,528*	*845*	*1,370*
5—10	..	2,156,820	1,123,360	1,033,460	1,038,144	762,916	83,006	264,890	2,210	5,654
10—15	..	1,909,166	1,010,748	898,418	856,773	465,584	150,340	422,952	3,635	9,882
15—20	..	1,492,973	751,488	741,485	381,201	60,660	361,349	656,719	8,938	24,106
20—25	..	1,584,559	786,233	798,326	241,014	26,205	530,430	732,309	14,789	39,812
25—30	..	1,460,853	763,753	697,100	79,817	12,167	658,117	612,168	25,819	72,765
30—35	..	1,350,090	731,947	618,143	45,943	9,709	652,198	508,687	33,806	99,747
35—40	..	1,072,411	585,718	486,693	22,651	6,120	518,444	334,333	44,623	146,240
40—45	..	887,472	478,719	408,753	15,284	4,677	414,594	244,097	48,841	159,979
45—50	..	680,871	362,271	318,600	8,889	2,853	297,463	138,898	55,919	176,849
50—55	..	535,210	281,752	253,458	6,247	2,098	221,915	90,739	53,590	160,621
55—60	..	379,101	192,816	186,285	3,550	1,417	140,000	42,165	49,266	142,703
60—65	..	303,294	149,059	154,235	2,651	1,150	103,131	27,204	43,277	125,881
65—70	..	136,025	68,213	67,812	1,140	494	43,558	8,969	23,515	58,349
70 and over		175,700	86,753	88,947	1,815	786	49,568	8,956	35,370	79,205
Muslims	..	**4,414,048**	**2,447,438**	**1,966,610**	**1,272,407**	**753,869**	**1,033,523**	**953,013**	**141,508**	**259,728**
0—1	..	120,771	61,581	59,190	61,282	58,809	289	375	10	6
1—2	..	114,159	56,719	57,440	56,369	56,907	342	519	8	14
2—3	..	132,377	65,681	66,696	65,187	65,895	479	787	15	14
3—4	..	141,981	72,525	69,456	71,555	67,965	942	1,451	28	40
4—5	..	144,450	75,912	68,538	74,335	66,260	1,502	2,154	75	124
Total 0—5	..	*653,738*	*332,418*	*321,320*	*328,728*	*315,836*	*3,554*	*5,286*	*136*	*198*
5—10	..	570,644	315,716	254,928	302,789	229,646	12,537	24,750	390	532
10—15	..	480,678	275,043	205,635	252,420	151,004	21,924	53,545	699	1,086
15—20	..	383,406	210,242	173,164	142,559	30,653	65,012	138,321	2,671	4,190
20—25	..	436,417	235,060	201,357	114,311	13,032	114,860	180,474	5,889	7,851
25—30	..	430,321	240,462	189,859	59,888	5,112	168,742	170,269	11,832	14,478
30—35	..	383,334	222,321	161,013	35,713	3,209	171,949	139,006	14,659	18,798
35—40	..	294,684	173,636	121,048	15,451	1,777	141,449	91,127	16,736	28,144
40—45	..	236,863	138,128	98,735	9,067	1,305	112,549	65,791	16,512	31,639
45—50	..	171,849	99,516	72,333	4,529	711	78,482	36,180	16,505	35,442
50—55	..	128,318	72,933	55,385	2,930	546	55,867	23,562	14,136	31,277
55—60	..	89,786	49,326	40,460	1,558	379	34,917	11,279	12,851	28,802
60—65	..	73,252	39,455	33,797	1,231	278	26,776	7,838	11,448	25,681
65—70	..	30,428	16,536	13,892	412	121	10,328	2,417	5,796	11,354
70 and over		50,330	26,646	23,684	821	260	14,577	3,168	11,248	20,256
Jains	..	**199,808**	**109,633**	**90,175**	**51,810**	**29,529**	**50,078**	**42,470**	**7,745**	**18,176**
0—1	..	5,507	2,706	2,801	2,686	2,769	18	31	2	1
1—2	..	5,003	2,462	2,541	2,429	2,489	31	50	2	2
2—3	..	5,079	2,471	2,608	2,439	2,535	29	72	3	1
3—4	..	4,902	2,446	2,456	2,410	2,354	34	99	2	3
4—5	..	5,299	2,692	2,607	2,597	2,421	87	174	8	12
Total 0—5	..	*25,790*	*12,777*	*13,013*	*12,561*	*12,568*	*199*	*426*	*17*	*19*
5—10	..	23,601	12,316	11,285	11,825	9,255	467	1,960	24	70
10—15	..	22,438	12,122	10,316	11,132	6,434	950	3,763	40	119
15—20	..	19,401	10,849	8,552	6,890	787	3,835	7,428	124	337
20—25	..	19,949	11,027	8,922	4,729	197	6,090	8,172	208	553
25—30	..	17,601	10,029	7,572	1,707	92	7,925	6,463	397	1,017
30—35	..	16,694	9,938	6,756	1,148	59	8,238	5,310	552	1,387
35—40	..	13,484	7,950	5,534	603	39	6,574	3,439	773	2,056
40—45	..	11,385	6,599	4,786	428	15	5,318	2,536	853	2,235
45—50	..	8,847	5,047	3,800	295	32	3,729	1,356	1,023	2,412
50—55	..	7,044	3,955	3,089	207	24	2,729	840	1,019	2,225
55—60	..	5,212	2,822	2,390	123	10	1,760	398	939	1,982
60—65	..	4,101	2,121	1,980	82	7	1,259	226	780	1,747
65—70	..	1,899	986	913	46	3	524	80	416	830
70 and over	..	2,362	1,095	1,267	34	7	481	73	580	1,187
Tribal	..	**129,135**	**64,721**	**64,414**	**36,393**	**31,821**	**26,343**	**27,306**	**1,985**	**5,287**
0—1	..	4,346	2,113	2,233	2,112	2,222	1	11	..	..
1—2	..	4,555	2,225	2,330	2,216	2,316	9	14	..	..
2—3	..	4,985	2,399	2,586	2,385	2,567	14	19	..	..
3—4	..	4,956	2,407	2,549	2,392	2,528	15	20	..	1
4—5	..	4,733	2,375	2,358	2,349	2,327	26	28	..	3
Total 0—5	..	*23,575*	*11,519*	*12,056*	*11,454*	*11,960*	*65*	*92*	..	*4*
5—10	..	20,111	10,201	9,910	10,019	9,606	175	295	7	9
10—15	..	17,566	9,038	8,528	8,569	7,535	457	986	12	7
15—20	..	11,350	5,649	5,701	3,513	1,904	2,085	3,757	51	40
20—25	..	10,819	5,458	5,361	1,886	557	3,467	4,734	105	70
25—30	..	9,530	4,906	4,624	486	83	4,250	4,407	170	134
30—35	..	8,624	4,377	4,247	218	55	3,971	3,971	188	221
35—40	..	7,062	3,572	3,490	101	38	3,257	2,986	214	466
40—45	..	6,185	3,143	3,042	64	29	2,851	2,447	228	568
45—50	..	4,847	2,471	2,376	35	15	2,189	1,558	247	803
50—55	..	3,606	1,773	1,833	20	11	1,555	1,070	198	752
55—60	..	2,452	1,129	1,323	11	11	914	508	204	804
60—65	..	1,921	849	1,072	7	9	655	310	187	753
65—70	..	655	292	363	2	5	216	89	74	269
70 and over	..	832	344	488	8	5	236	96	100	387

Table VII.—Age, Sex and Civil Condition. Part II.—Provinces and States—*contd.*

Bengal.

Age and Religion.		Population.			Unmarried.		Married.		Widowed.	
		Persons.	Males.	Females.	Males.	Females.	Males.	Females.	Males.	Females.
1		2	3	4	5	6	7	8	9	10
All Religions	...	**50,114,002**	**26,041,698**	**24,072,304**	**12,202,178**	**7,438,555**	**12,999,949**	**12,389,849**	**839,571**	**4,243,900**
0—1	..	1,663,618	830,020	833,598	818,202	818,125	11,707	15,079	111	394
1—2	..	1,310,060	636,763	673,297	628,821	654,849	7,870	18,022	72	426
2—3	..	1,622,284	782,861	839,423	769,818	807,217	12,923	31,337	120	869
3—4	..	1,625,417	803,204	822,213	783,441	767,318	19,440	52,834	323	2,061
4—5	..	1,564,340	794,427	769,913	770,937	698,565	23,056	68,422	434	2,926
Total 0—5	..	*7,785,719*	*3,847,275*	*3,938,444*	*3,771,219*	*3,746,074*	*74,996*	*185,694*	*1,060*	*6,676*
5—10	..	6,726,769	3,563,257	3,163,512	3,313,405	2,216,247	246,487	924,547	3,365	22,718
10—15	..	5,903,139	3,117,274	2,785,865	2,698,453	1,247,786	413,568	1,494,770	5,253	43,309
15—20	..	4,825,066	2,281,751	2,543,315	1,188,892	120,234	1,076,384	2,289,449	16,475	133,632
20—25	..	5,054,079	2,419,485	2,634,594	786,613	51,237	1,600,759	2,377,020	32,113	206,337
25—30	..	4,469,830	2,349,919	2,119,911	231,163	20,776	2,055,505	1,758,026	63,251	341,109
30—35	..	3,953,458	2,167,718	1,785,740	110,827	14,141	1,982,169	1,361,802	74,722	409,797
35—40	..	2,989,960	1,688,120	1,301,840	38,509	7,415	1,561,518	782,284	88,093	512,141
40—45	..	2,501,878	1,418,136	1,083,742	25,969	5,251	1,299,152	551,463	93,015	527,028
45—50	..	1,828,826	1,018,748	810,078	13,516	3,319	906,741	282,477	98,491	524,282
50—55	..	1,453,298	794,102	659,196	9,458	2,630	692,671	188,657	91,973	467,909
55—60	..	959,392	507,403	451,989	4,938	1,269	422,932	86,364	79,533	364,356
60—65	..	744,796	385,108	359,688	3,611	876	312,751	58,039	68,746	300,773
65—70	..	362,432	190,122	172,310	1,865	482	146,186	22,499	42,071	149,329
70 and over	..	555,360	293,280	262,080	3,740	818	208,130	26,758	81,410	234,504
Muslims..	...	**27,497,624**	**14,200,142**	**13,297,482**	**6,638,311**	**4,225,060**	**7,247,952**	**7,210,671**	**313,879**	**1,861,751**
0—1	..	956,331	477,436	478,895	470,080	467,909	7,317	10,777	39	209
1—2	..	781,638	378,897	402,741	373,895	388,010	4,963	14,502	39	229
2—3	..	968,081	466,685	501,396	457,943	475,495	8,680	25,480	62	421
3—4	..	967,815	477,314	490,501	463,803	448,010	13,337	41,403	174	1,088
4—5	..	929,761	469,175	460,586	453,164	406,339	15,762	52,582	249	1,665
Total 0—5	..	*4,603,626*	*2,269,507*	*2,334,119*	*2,218,885*	*2,185,763*	*50,059*	*144,744*	*563*	*3,612*
5—10	..	3,953,395	2,089,461	1,863,934	1,906,359	1,256,428	180,928	596,517	2,174	10,989
10—15	..	3,421,242	1,796,341	1,624,901	1,498,240	684,560	294,777	921,829	3,324	18,512
15—20	..	2,663,891	1,220,182	1,443,709	549,204	54,229	661,777	1,344,469	9,201	45,011
20—25	..	2,751,028	1,282,572	1,468,456	329,238	20,737	936,370	1,379,912	16,964	67,807
25—30	..	2,361,584	1,232,054	1,129,530	79,045	8,591	1,123,899	996,219	29,110	124,720
30—35	..	2,068,577	1,132,321	936,256	32,354	6,008	1,068,246	764,940	31,721	165,308
35—40	..	1,532,495	863,292	669,203	9,608	3,154	821,724	433,584	31,960	232,465
40—45	..	1,254,097	711,010	543,087	6,169	2,266	673,476	295,729	31,365	245,092
45—50	..	912,646	513,536	399,110	3,292	1,253	478,971	146,117	31,273	251,740
50—55	..	710,967	394,307	316,660	2,287	783	363,457	94,104	28,563	221,773
55—60	..	465,465	254,801	210,664	1,158	448	227,321	41,334	26,322	168,882
60—65	..	360,639	194,061	166,578	850	331	169,800	28,062	23,411	138,185
65—70	..	170,058	95,037	75,021	479	162	79,544	10,464	15,014	64,395
70 and over	..	267,914	151,660	116,254	1,143	347	117,603	12,647	32,914	103,260
Hindus ..	..	**21,570,407**	**11,299,914**	**10,270,493**	**5,284,923**	**2,992,718**	**5,507,584**	**4,952,357**	**507,407**	**2,325,418**
0—1	..	671,871	335,071	336,800	330,833	332,601	4,169	4,021	69	178
1—2	..	499,418	243,588	255,830	240,828	252,324	2,730	3,314	30	192
2—3	..	618,326	298,778	319,548	294,717	313,548	4,006	5,558	55	442
3—4	..	621,030	308,047	312,983	302,142	301,015	5,770	11,036	135	932
4—5	..	599,994	307,911	292,083	300,827	275,496	6,905	15,378	179	1,209
Total 0—5	..	*3,010,639*	*1,493,395*	*1,517,244*	*1,469,347*	*1,474,984*	*23,580*	*39,307*	*468*	*2,953*
5—10	..	2,631,341	1,400,316	1,231,025	1,336,145	896,426	63,027	323,151	1,144	11,448
10—15	..	2,359,554	1,257,707	1,101,847	1,141,177	516,597	114,678	561,003	1,852	24,247
15—20	..	2,065,205	1,015,875	1,049,330	609,635	52,362	399,391	910,211	6,849	86,757
20—25	..	2,205,030	1,089,914	1,115,116	436,949	23,937	638,656	955,284	14,309	135,895
25—30	..	2,015,726	1,069,514	946,212	144,825	10,202	892,163	723,414	32,526	212,596
30—35	..	1,802,027	990,334	811,693	74,344	6,981	874,830	564,508	41,160	240,204
35—40	..	1,395,362	789,641	605,721	27,445	3,701	707,935	327,850	54,261	274,170
40—45	..	1,195,232	677,095	518,137	18,793	2,530	598,477	239,775	59,825	275,832
45—50	..	887,950	483,445	394,505	9,629	1,739	408,601	127,048	65,215	265,718
50—55	..	711,282	382,365	328,917	6,752	1,591	314,075	87,491	61,538	239,835
55—60	..	473,502	241,422	232,080	3,548	661	186,325	41,606	51,549	189,813
60—65	..	368,157	182,428	185,729	2,594	415	135,988	27,674	43,846	157,640
65—70	..	184,541	91,061	93,480	1,282	249	63,617	11,099	26,162	82,132
70 and over	..	274,859	135,402	139,457	2,458	343	86,241	12,936	46,703	126,178
Christians	...	***180,380**	**95,920**	**84,460**	**52,139**	**39,852**	**41,167**	**36,084**	**2,614**	**8,524**
0—1	..	6,146	3,088	3,058	3,035	2,969	52	87	1	2
1—2	..	4,528	2,264	2,264	2,217	2,212	46	51	1	1
2—3	..	5,175	2,605	2,570	2,546	2,494	59	73	..	3
3—4	..	5,122	2,510	2,612	2,429	2,529	79	74	2	9
4—5	..	4,889	2,465	2,424	2,372	2,357	92	59	1	8
Total 0—5	..	*25,860*	*12,932*	*12,928*	*12,599*	*12,561*	*328*	*344*	*5*	*23*
5—10	..	21,873	11,435	10,438	10,970	9,940	457	483	8	15
10—15	..	20,727	10,725	10,002	10,167	8,519	549	1,446	9	37
15—20	..	17,958	8,810	9,148	6,832	3,713	1,941	5,262	37	173
20—25	..	18,103	9,045	9,058	5,321	2,168	3,642	6,610	82	280
25—30	..	17,091	9,398	7,693	2,603	968	6,599	6,206	196	519
30—35	..	15,324	8,679	6,645	1,691	654	6,744	5,343	244	648
35—40	..	11,544	6,616	4,928	652	330	5,669	3,645	295	953
40—45	..	9,906	5,819	4,087	461	273	5,044	2,773	314	1,041
45—50	..	6,970	4,140	2,830	303	214	3,527	1,565	310	1,051
50—55	..	5,537	3,227	2,310	226	178	2,716	1,152	285	980
55—60	..	3,383	1,910	1,473	117	113	1,555	531	238	829
60—65	..	2,640	1,449	1,191	91	92	1,154	374	204	725
65—70	..	1,343	702	641	49	47	517	152	136	442
70 and over	..	2,121	1,033	1,088	57	82	725	198	251	808

*Includes 81 persons (71 males and 10 females) of Indefinite Beliefs.

Table VII.—Age, Sex and Civil Condition. Part II.—Provinces and States—*contd.*

Central Provinces and Berar.

Age and Religion.		Population.			Unmarried.		Married.		Widowed.	
		Persons.	Males.	Females.	Males.	Females.	Males.	Females.	Males.	Females.
1		2	3	4	5	6	7	8	9	10
All Religions	..	**15,507,723**	**7,761,818**	**7,745,905**	**3,147,619**	**2,286,142**	**4,234,679**	**4,300,476**	**379,520**	**1,159,287**
0—1	..	542,591	268,663	273,928	264,615	269,706	3,966	4,087	82	135
1—2	..	460,410	219,350	241,060	215,480	235,843	3,718	5,045	152	172
2—3	..	479,990	230,048	249,942	224,932	240,305	4,912	9,353	204	284
3—4	..	487,487	242,789	244,698	234,166	224,591	8,325	19,594	298	513
4—5	..	453,671	227,312	226,359	215,989	198,551	10,893	27,059	430	749
Total 0—5	..	*2,424,149*	*1,188,162*	*1,235,987*	*1,155,182*	*1,168,996*	*31,814*	*65,138*	*1,166*	*1,853*
5—10	..	1,958,964	998,119	960,845	847,816	647,725	147,521	307,413	2,782	6,007
10—15	..	1,755,245	903,256	851,989	654,024	382,300	245,155	460,887	4,077	8,802
15—20	..	1,398,959	683,585	715,374	237,761	46,142	435,783	652,151	10,041	17,081
20—25	..	1,463,205	711,239	751,966	131,652	17,245	562,831	707,380	16,756	27,341
25—30	..	1,312,706	665,251	647,455	43,906	6,709	595,485	590,037	25,860	50,709
30—35	..	1,173,218	597,394	575,824	26,516	4,768	540,891	500,298	29,987	70,758
35—40	..	959,637	483,043	476,594	15,607	3,411	430,663	357,125	36,773	116,058
40—45	..	831,859	425,268	406,591	11,974	2,926	372,918	271,410	40,376	132,255
45—50	..	665,543	348,923	316,620	7,864	1,893	295,031	158,577	46,028	156,150
50—55	..	515,108	266,033	249,075	5,500	1,223	218,991	106,553	41,542	141,299
55—60	..	376,265	182,305	193,960	3,408	874	140,920	54,756	37,977	138,330
60—65	..	307,425	143,811	163,614	2,912	750	107,378	37,686	33,521	125,178
65—70	..	141,828	65,674	76,154	1,498	380	45,724	14,410	18,452	61,364
70 and over	..	223,612	99,755	123,857	1,999	800	63,574	16,955	34,182	106,102
Hindus ..	..	**13,338,223**	**6,671,326**	**6,666,897**	**2,623,304**	**1,881,844**	**3,716,576**	**3,772,609**	**331,446**	**1,012,444**
0—1	..	470,219	232,776	237,443	229,124	233,674	3,583	3,660	69	109
1—2	..	393,395	186,871	206,524	183,384	201,732	3,350	4,640	137	152
2—3	..	409,387	196,405	212,982	191,774	203,891	4,442	8,835	189	256
3—4	..	416,769	208,440	208,329	200,421	189,020	7,731	18,825	288	484
4—5	..	385,505	193,463	192,042	182,889	165,363	10,183	26,003	391	676
Total 0—5	..	*2,075,275*	*1,017,955*	*1,057,320*	*987,592*	*993,680*	*29,289*	*61,963*	*1,074*	*1,677*
5—10	..	1,681,203	856,644	824,559	713,402	527,320	140,615	291,562	2,627	5,677
10—15	..	1,510,768	777,552	733,216	542,311	300,440	231,449	424,583	3,792	8,193
15—20	..	1,201,358	587,223	614,135	184,474	30,096	393,807	568,807	8,942	15,232
20—25	..	1,256,583	610,183	646,400	99,150	11,574	496,344	610,588	14,689	24,238
25—30	..	1,125,859	570,287	555,572	33,485	5,125	514,383	505,854	22,419	44,593
30—35	..	1,010,642	514,256	496,386	21,281	3,702	466,876	430,407	26,099	62,277
35—40	..	826,208	415,126	411,082	12,528	2,733	370,519	307,070	32,079	101,279
40—45	..	716,889	365,519	351,370	9,732	2,398	320,502	233,650	35,285	115,322
45—50	..	574,995	300,587	274,408	6,462	1,553	253,990	137,297	40,135	135,558
50—55	..	445,749	229,533	216,216	4,519	967	188,667	92,370	33,247	122,879
55—60	..	326,970	157,895	169,075	2,813	692	121,964	47,829	33,118	120,554
60—65	..	267,153	124,618	142,535	2,489	596	93,014	32,924	29,115	109,015
65—70	..	124,284	57,365	66,919	1,328	301	39,975	12,828	16,062	53,790
70 and over	..	194,287	86,583	107,704	1,738	667	55,182	14,877	29,663	92,160
Muslims ..	..	**682,854**	**358,900**	**323,954**	**178,140**	**125,603**	**163,536**	**152,460**	**17,224**	**45,891**
0—1	..	21,942	10,999	10,943	10,881	10,811	112	121	6	11
1—2	..	20,679	10,242	10,437	10,129	10,298	109	133	4	6
2—3	..	21,693	10,497	11,196	10,357	11,051	138	142	2	3
3—4	..	21,624	10,554	11,070	10,386	10,859	164	204	4	7
4—5	..	21,129	10,537	10,592	10,314	10,281	208	282	15	29
Total 0—5	..	*107,067*	*52,829*	*54,238*	*52,067*	*53,300*	*731*	*882*	*31*	*56*
5—10	..	90,157	46,468	43,689	44,731	39,160	1,689	4,412	48	117
10—15	..	79,458	41,711	37,747	38,616	26,453	3,015	11,097	80	197
15—20	..	64,620	33,613	31,007	20,832	3,792	12,387	26,555	394	660
20—25	..	68,233	35,663	32,570	13,822	1,330	21,037	30,122	804	1,118
25—30	..	57,016	30,950	26,066	3,785	469	25,825	23,595	1,340	2,002
30—35	..	49,493	27,372	22,121	1,866	335	24,042	19,037	1,464	2,749
35—40	..	40,232	21,647	18,585	832	226	19,162	13,642	1,653	4,717
40—45	..	34,044	18,438	15,606	557	167	16,133	10,053	1,748	5,386
45—50	..	26,932	14,975	11,957	400	99	12,671	5,586	1,904	6,272
50—55	..	20,667	11,484	9,183	288	77	9,507	3,591	1,689	5,515
55—60	..	15,366	8,329	7,037	122	54	6,533	1,685	1,674	5,298
60—65	..	12,987	6,808	6,179	101	52	5,144	1,256	1,563	4,871
65—70	..	6,023	3,230	2,793	43	31	2,248	406	939	2,356
70 and over	..	10,559	5,383	5,176	78	58	3,412	541	1,893	4,577
Tribal ..	..	**1,351,615**	**660,755**	**690,860**	**308,923**	**253,156**	**324,713**	**347,049**	**27,119**	**90,655**
0—1	..	45,938	22,522	23,416	22,254	23,107	261	296	7	13
1—2	..	42,685	20,438	22,247	20,182	21,973	246	261	10	13
2—3	..	45,123	21,337	23,786	21,017	23,414	309	347	11	25
3—4	..	45,423	22,010	23,413	21,597	22,868	407	523	6	22
4—5	..	43,338	21,480	21,858	20,992	21,125	467	694	21	39
Total 0—5	..	*222,507*	*107,787*	*114,720*	*106,042*	*112,487*	*1,690*	*2,121*	*55*	*112*
5—10	..	171,381	86,730	84,651	81,749	74,277	4,884	10,182	97	192
10—15	..	149,696	76,082	73,614	65,896	50,038	10,003	23,215	183	361
15—20	..	119,035	55,405	63,630	27,693	10,401	27,061	52,239	651	990
20—25	..	123,905	57,490	66,415	14,766	3,391	41,568	61,387	1,156	1,637
25—30	..	118,037	57,542	60,495	4,936	878	50,732	56,115	1,874	3,502
30—35	..	102,937	50,330	52,607	2,508	557	45,684	47,117	2,138	4,933
35—40	..	84,857	41,855	43,002	1,715	329	37,454	33,801	2,686	8,872
40—45	..	73,517	37,291	36,226	1,296	262	33,087	25,715	2,908	10,249
45—50	..	57,895	30,161	27,734	824	171	25,901	14,608	3,436	12,955
50—55	..	44,302	22,600	21,702	560	121	19,021	9,892	3,019	11,689
55—60	..	30,953	14,598	16,355	400	91	11,393	4,852	2,805	11,412
60—65	..	24,985	11,283	13,702	279	74	8,476	3,244	2,528	10,384
65—70	..	10,389	4,515	5,874	104	29	3,161	1,099	1,250	4,746
70 and over	..	17,219	7,086	10,133	155	50	4,598	1,462	2,333	8,621

Table VII.—Age, Sex and Civil Condition. Part II.—Provinces and States—*contd.*

Age and Religion. 1	Population. Persons. 2	Population. Males. 3	Population. Females. 4	Unmarried. Males. 5	Unmarried. Females. 6	Married. Males. 7	Married. Females. 8	Widowed. Males. 9	Widowed. Females. 10
Coorg.									
All Religions	**163,327**	**90,575**	**72,752**	**50,212**	**32,323**	**35,582**	**28,835**	**4,781**	**11,594**
0—1	4,313	2,127	2,186	2,126	2,182	1	4	..	..
1—2	4,378	2,184	2,194	2,183	2,190	1	4	..	..
2—3	3,931	1,911	2,020	1,908	2,015	3	5	..	..
3—4	3,498	1,721	1,777	1,719	1,774	2	3	..	..
4—5	3,402	1,725	1,677	1,721	1,670	4	5	..	2
Total 0—5	*19,522*	*9,668*	*9,854*	*9,657*	*9,831*	*11*	*21*	...	*2*
5—10	18,616	9,527	9,089	9,491	8,995	36	86	..	8
10—15	18,954	9,993	8,961	9,925	8,442	66	493	2	26
15—20	16,639	9,129	7,510	8,232	3,241	859	4,064	38	205
20—25	17,991	9,879	8,112	7,133	1,392	2,612	6,276	134	444
25—30	16,867	9,740	7,127	3,185	167	6,111	6,055	444	905
30—35	15,216	9,175	6,041	1,557	93	7,001	4,803	617	1,145
35—40	11,435	7,164	4,271	489	51	5,991	2,786	684	1,434
40—45	9,021	5,607	3,414	259	45	4,733	1,921	615	1,448
45—50	6,281	3,771	2,510	117	25	3,119	1,042	535	1,443
50—55	4,801	2,784	2,017	77	15	2,239	673	468	1,329
55—60	3,063	1,634	1,429	36	9	1,215	306	383	1,114
60—65	2,346	1,213	1,133	22	8	857	186	334	939
65—70	1,130	585	545	16	3	360	61	209	481
70 and over	1,445	706	739	16	6	372	62	318	671
Delhi.									
All Religions	**636,246**	**369,497**	**266,749**	**169,583**	**100,393**	**171,844**	**137,975**	**28,070**	**28,381**
0—1	20,084	10,141	9,943	10,141	9,943	..	..	..	..
1—2	16,033	8,065	7,968	8,063	7,967	2	1	..	..
2—3	18,164	9,123	9,041	9,122	9,040	1	1	..	..
3—4	17,492	8,872	8,620	8,855	8,586	17	34	..	..
4—5	15,933	8,277	7,656	8,236	7,582	38	74	3	..
Total 0—5	*87,706*	*44,478*	*43,228*	*44,417*	*43,118*	*58*	*110*	*3*	..
5—10	72,429	39,366	33,063	37,448	29,486	1,860	3,552	58	25
10—15	71,057	39,683	31,374	34,304	21,055	5,199	10,212	180	107
15—20	68,674	39,707	28,967	21,489	4,106	17,333	24,441	885	420
20—25	72,724	42,860	29,864	15,897	1,378	25,343	27,729	1,620	757
25—30	63,186	38,697	24,489	6,540	419	29,523	22,577	2,634	1,493
30—35	54,723	34,491	20,232	3,928	299	27,609	18,014	2,954	1,919
35—40	40,505	25,623	14,882	2,017	189	20,513	11,638	3,093	3,055
40—45	32,340	20,372	11,968	1,402	137	15,921	8,420	3,049	3,411
45—50	23,655	14,862	8,793	795	79	10,865	4,762	3,202	3,952
50—55	17,813	10,928	6,885	541	63	7,516	3,182	2,871	3,640
55—60	11,689	6,853	4,836	335	35	4,113	1,580	2,405	3,221
60—65	9,632	5,658	3,974	237	19	3,263	1,080	2,158	2,875
65—70	4,410	2,673	1,737	98	6	1,338	353	1,237	1,378
70 and over	5,703	3,246	2,457	135	4	1,390	325	1,721	2,128
North-West Frontier Province. (*Districts and Administered Territories.*)									
All Religions	**2,425,076**	**1,315,818**	**1,109,258**	**761,820**	**508,291**	**491,044**	**749,733**	**62,954**	**121,234**
0—1	74,859	38,257	36,602	38,257	36,602	..	..	..	..
1—2	67,391	33,606	33,785	33,606	33,785	..	..	..	..
2—3	80,958	40,153	40,805	40,153	40,805	..	..	..	..
3—4	82,517	41,690	40,827	41,690	40,827	..	..	..	..
4—5	80,994	41,966	39,028	41,966	39,028	..	..	..	..
Total 0—5	*386,719*	*195,672*	*191,047*	*195,672*	*191,047*	..	..	..	..
5—10	334,706	183,669	151,037	182,738	148,290	857	2,661	74	86
10—15	288,425	163,622	124,803	159,554	109,329	3,817	15,122	251	352
15—20	215,504	117,251	98,253	90,806	30,168	25,096	66,241	1,349	1,844
20—25	226,255	119,063	107,192	67,884	13,223	48,470	89,929	2,709	4,040
25—30	221,499	117,355	104,144	30,241	5,303	81,823	91,318	5,291	7,523
30—35	194,565	106,608	87,957	16,885	3,637	83,608	75,544	6,115	8,776
35—40	139,663	76,883	62,780	6,471	2,243	64,136	47,572	6,276	12,965
40—45	115,205	63,005	52,200	4,351	1,758	52,516	36,424	6,138	14,018
45—50	89,533	50,251	39,282	2,695	1,146	41,005	21,826	6,551	16,310
50—55	70,951	39,420	31,531	1,699	860	31,756	15,734	5,965	14,937
55—60	49,524	28,423	21,101	995	461	21,464	7,563	5,964	13,077
60—65	40,328	23,185	17,143	769	344	17,056	5,245	5,360	11,554
65—70	18,011	10,729	7,282	336	143	7,206	1,879	3,187	5,260
70 and over	34,188	20,682	13,506	724	339	12,234	2,675	7,724	10,492
Muslims	**2,227,303**	**1,196,120**	**1,031,183**	**696,336**	**474,152**	**443,251**	**445,275**	**56,533**	**111,756**
0—1	68,647	35,093	33,554	35,093	33,554	..	..	..	..
1—2	62,369	31,063	31,306	31,063	31,306	..	..	..	..
2—3	75,267	37,293	37,974	37,293	37,974	..	..	..	..
3—4	76,896	38,856	38,040	38,856	38,040	..	..	..	..
4—5	75,557	39,174	36,383	39,174	36,383	..	..	..	..
Total 0—5	*358,737*	*181,479*	*177,257*	*181,479*	*177,257*	..	..	..	..
5—10	312,253	171,728	140,525	170,908	138,164	759	2,293	61	68
10—15	268,655	152,709	115,946	148,971	102,138	3,502	13,493	236	315
15—20	193,848	103,440	90,408	80,804	28,666	21,445	60,054	1,191	1,688
20—25	201,114	102,470	98,644	58,238	12,604	41,857	82,304	2,375	3,736
25—30	200,065	102,868	97,197	25,741	5,013	72,486	85,250	4,641	6,934
30—35	176,766	94,562	82,204	14,469	3,420	74,721	70,775	5,372	8,009
35—40	128,117	69,570	58,547	5,587	2,108	58,398	44,590	5,585	11,849
40—45	106,074	57,333	48,741	3,783	1,657	48,079	34,286	5,471	12,798
45—50	82,753	46,001	36,752	2,365	1,085	37,807	20,646	5,829	15,021
50—55	65,834	36,257	29,577	1,482	818	29,463	14,955	5,312	13,804
55—60	46,187	26,426	19,761	876	435	20,127	7,219	5,423	12,107
60—65	37,760	21,671	16,089	687	328	16,080	5,016	4,904	10,745
65—70	16,803	9,995	6,808	288	136	6,795	1,801	2,912	4,871
70 and over	32,338	19,611	12,727	658	323	11,732	2,593	7,221	9,811

Table VII.—Age, Sex and Civil Condition. Part II.—Provinces and States—*contd.*

Madras.

Age and Religion.	Population.			Unmarried.		Married.		Widowed.	
	Persons.	Males.	Females.	Males.	Females.	Males.	Females.	Males.	Females.
1	2	3	4	5	6	7	8	9	10
All Religions ..	**46,740,107**	**23,082,999**	**23,657,108**	**12,149,098**	**8,923,018**	**10,010,551**	**10,520,571**	**928,350**	**4,213,519**
0—1 ..	1,306,829	642,155	664,674	641,565	663,523	559	1,104	31	47
1—2 ..	1,313,939	644,748	669,191	643,881	666,262	849	2,860	18	69
2—3 ..	1,411,023	688,315	722,708	686,838	716,210	1,441	6,357	36	141
3—4 ..	1,411,826	693,480	718,346	690,616	704,494	2,807	13,514	57	338
4—5 ..	1,335,983	664,290	671,693	660,029	651,964	4,108	19,058	153	671
Total 0—5 ..	*6,779,600*	*3,332,988*	*3,446,612*	*3,322,029*	*3,402,453*	*9,764*	*42,893*	*295*	*1,266*
5—10 ..	6,010,063	3,031,434	2,978,629	2,974,489	2,695,289	55,686	276,003	1,259	7,337
10—15 ..	5,422,941	2,777,955	2,644,986	2,662,102	2,029,802	113,857	597,526	1,996	17,658
15—20 ..	4,177,902	2,008,379	2,169,523	1,497,757	469,228	500,241	1,619,537	10,381	80,758
20—25 ..	4,358,627	1,997,358	2,361,269	1,016,863	184,826	956,868	2,028,779	23,627	147,664
25—30 ..	3,997,702	1,880,280	2,117,422	327,539	48,407	1,503,211	1,791,502	49,530	277,513
30—35 ..	3,600,237	1,767,391	1,832,396	164,238	32,446	1,542,897	1,460,684	60,756	339,266
35—40 ..	2,989,255	1,535,940	1,453,315	65,867	19,215	1,387,996	968,332	82,077	465,768
40—45 ..	2,552,084	1,321,076	1,231,008	44,232	14,261	1,186,749	726,428	90,095	490,319
45—50 ..	1,929,214	985,975	943,239	24,244	8,412	857,195	415,231	104,536	519,596
50—55 ..	1,583,167	798,127	785,040	17,471	6,417	676,616	293,652	104,040	484,971
55—60 ..	1,180,829	589,283	591,546	11,600	4,495	466,616	140,043	111,067	447,008
60—65 ..	980,355	481,199	499,156	9,060	3,566	367,500	93,563	104,639	402,027
65—70 ..	491,391	243,322	248,069	4,497	1,764	171,464	32,147	67,361	214,158
70 and over ..	686,690	331,792	354,898	6,210	2,437	213,891	34,251	111,691	318,210
Hindus ..	***41,277,410**	**20,380,283**	**20,897,127**	**10,611,745**	**7,725,774**	**8,929,045**	**9,366,540**	**839,493**	**3,804,813**
0—1 ..	1,145,982	562,565	583,417	562,015	582,319	522	1,052	28	46
1—2 ..	1,144,372	561,209	583,663	560,394	580,838	798	2,758	17	67
2—3 ..	1,235,228	601,693	633,535	600,314	627,187	1,345	6,212	34	136
3—4 ..	1,239,384	607,664	631,720	604,947	618,084	2,660	13,301	57	335
4—5 ..	1,169,853	580,640	589,213	576,668	569,974	3,830	18,609	142	630
Total 0—5 ..	*5,935,319*	*2,913,771*	*3,021,548*	*2,904,338*	*2,978,402*	*9,155*	*41,932*	*278*	*1,214*
5—10 ..	5,271,868	2,656,440	2,615,428	2,601,520	2,341,953	53,712	266,536	1,208	6,939
10—15 ..	4,754,569	2,437,571	2,316,998	2,326,179	1,746,754	109,495	553,995	1,897	16,249
15—20 ..	3,664,287	1,766,949	1,897,338	1,300,247	388,438	457,509	1,436,421	9,193	72,479
20—25 ..	3,841,833	1,763,497	2,078,336	881,467	152,378	861,063	1,793,482	20,967	132,476
25—30 ..	3,542,652	1,667,538	1,875,114	287,369	40,407	1,335,803	1,584,056	44,366	250,651
30—35 ..	3,193,089	1,568,686	1,624,403	146,023	27,164	1,367,932	1,290,470	54,731	306,769
35—40 ..	2,661,163	1,366,478	1,294,685	59,144	16,017	1,232,653	858,128	74,681	420,540
40—45 ..	2,276,449	1,176,972	1,099,477	39,765	11,877	1,054,782	645,193	82,425	442,407
45—50 ..	1,725,217	879,799	845,418	21,845	6,971	762,051	369,285	95,903	469,162
50—55 ..	1,417,514	712,775	704,739	15,783	5,382	601,580	261,405	95,412	437,952
55—60 ..	1,060,174	527,351	532,823	10,416	3,665	415,376	124,610	101,559	404,548
60—65 ..	880,869	430,785	450,084	8,161	2,938	327,180	83,208	95,444	363,938
65—70 ..	440,241	217,147	223,094	3,983	1,412	152,172	28,084	60,992	193,598
70 and over ..	612,166	294,524	317,642	5,505	2,016	188,582	29,735	100,437	285,891
Muslims ..	**†3,305,938**	**1,631,716**	**1,674,222**	**951,686**	**713,341**	**634,435**	**695,107**	**45,595**	**265,774**
0—1 ..	98,707	49,201	49,506	49,190	49,483	10	22	1	1
1—2 ..	106,278	52,761	53,517	52,742	53,481	19	36	..	..
2—3 ..	108,606	53,782	54,824	53,746	54,773	35	51	1	..
3—4 ..	104,957	52,535	52,422	52,503	52,343	32	78	..	1
4—5 ..	100,895	51,133	49,762	51,040	49,542	89	197	4	23
Total 0—5 ..	*519,443*	*259,412*	*260,031*	*259,221*	*259,622*	*185*	*384*	*6*	*25*
5—10 ..	451,417	230,328	221,089	229,443	214,422	864	6,417	21	250
10—15 ..	412,029	210,018	202,011	207,810	170,510	2,164	30,460	44	1,041
15—20 ..	315,493	147,883	167,610	123,134	43,551	24,013	117,934	736	6,125
20—25 ..	313,693	141,138	172,555	84,930	15,206	54,468	146,219	1,740	11,130
25—30 ..	269,345	124,859	144,486	25,598	3,699	96,127	122,664	3,134	18,123
30—35 ..	240,872	117,390	123,482	11,214	2,311	102,696	99,783	3,450	21,388
35—40 ..	194,049	99,234	94,815	3,869	1,339	91,379	64,119	3,986	29,357
40—45 ..	162,529	84,199	78,330	2,472	952	77,651	46,371	4,076	31,007
45—50 ..	121,371	62,807	58,564	1,321	523	57,041	25,701	4,445	32,340
50—55	97,554	50,067	47,487	897	337	44,807	17,373	4,363	29,777
55—60 ..	72,121	36,734	35,387	608	318	31,110	8,053	5,016	27,016
60—65 ..	59,647	29,743	29,904	481	266	24,368	5,401	4,894	24,237
65—70 ..	30,723	15,641	15,082	275	132	11,968	2,018	3,398	12,932
70 and over ..	45,652	22,263	3,389	383	153	15,594	2,210	6,286	21,026
Christians ..	**‡1,774,299**	**878,513**	**895,786**	**483,757**	**403,544**	**353,636**	**371,246**	**31,070**	**120,996**
0—1 ..	52,150	25,514	26,606	25,528	26,593	15	13	1	..
1—2 ..	52,244	25,666	26,578	25,652	26,548	14	28	..	2
2—3 ..	54,791	26,822	27,969	26,795	27,929	26	38	1	2
3—4 ..	54,302	26,838	27,464	26,773	27,393	65	71	..	
4—5 ..	51,977	26,018	25,959	25,888	25,784	127	165	3	10
Total 0—5 ..	*265,464*	*130,888*	*134,576*	*130,636*	*134,247*	*247*	*315*	*5*	*14*
5—10 ..	236,353	118,962	117,391	118,251	115,151	690	2,134	21	106
10—15 ..	214,586	108,719	105,867	107,380	95,462	1,307	10,128	32	277
15—20 ..	165,443	78,511	86,932	64,049	31,997	14,169	53,215	293	1,720
20—25 ..	168,308	76,997	91,311	43,935	14,917	32,461	73,048	601	3,346
25—30 ..	148,934	70,021	78,913	12,178	3,662	56,411	67,968	1,432	7,283
30—35 ..	132,884	64,960	67,924	5,632	2,581	57,409	55,961	1,919	9,382
35—40 ..	107,245	55,558	51,687	2,240	1,611	50,767	36,855	2,551	13,221
40—45 ..	91,218	47,681	43,537	1,600	1,248	43,354	28,150	2,727	14,139
45—50 ..	68,425	35,429	32,996	876	818	31,171	16,878	3,382	15,300
50—55 ..	56,927	29,202	27,725	656	631	25,020	12,448	3,526	14,646
55—60 ..	41,353	21,463	19,890	488	461	17,155	6,271	3,820	13,158
60—65 ..	34,016	17,690	16,326	354	328	13,633	4,216	3,703	11,782
65—70 ..	18,104	9,358	8,746	208	198	6,482	1,764	2,668	6,784
70 and over ..	25,039	13,074	11,965	274	232	8,410	1,895	4,390	9,838

* Includes 40 persons (26 males and 14 females) of Indefinite Beliefs.
† Includes one female of Indefinite Belief.
‡ Includes 23 persons (20 males and 3 females) of Indefinite Beliefs.

Table VII.—Age, Sex and Civil Condition. Part II.—Provinces and States—*contd.*

Punjab.

Age and Religion.		Population.			Unmarried.		Married.		Widowed.	
		Persons.	Males.	Females.	Males.	Females.	Males.	Females.	Males.	Females.
1		2	3	4	5	6	7	8	9	10
All Religions	..	**23,580,852**	**12,880,510**	**10,700,342**	**7,019,221**	**4,560,404**	**4,897,276**	**4,910,530**	**964,013**	**1,229,408**
0—1	..	877,522	443,644	433,878	443,551	433,738	82	126	11	14
1—2	..	661,227	333,732	327,495	333,579	327,165	133	312	20	18
2—3	..	737,801	374,302	363,499	373,815	362,625	448	851	39	23
3—4	..	745,547	382,577	362,970	381,351	360,432	1,171	2,473	55	65
4—5	..	718,452	374,923	343,529	372,989	339,400	1,797	3,933	137	196
Total 0—5	..	*3,740,549*	*1,909,178*	*1,831,371*	*1,905,285*	*1,823,360*	*3,631*	*7,695*	*262*	*316*
5—10	..	3,143,832	1,691,328	1,452,504	1,648,441	1,337,511	41,369	113,374	1,518	1,619
10—15	..	2,851,094	1,571,550	1,279,544	1,460,509	988,094	107,179	287,522	3,862	3,928
15—20	..	2,190,257	1,203,432	986,825	798,242	237,812	387,440	733,693	17,750	15,320
20—25	..	2,193,921	1,187,358	1,006,563	556,327	92,455	596,884	886,645	34,147	27,463
25—30	..	1,900,592	1,045,976	854,616	239,955	26,287	744,555	776,012	61,466	52,317
30—35	..	1,683,077	949,494	733,583	150,146	17,258	725,241	645,748	74,107	70,577
35—40	..	1,298,931	727,958	570,973	78,510	11,216	564,137	453,027	85,311	106,730
40—45	..	1,118,461	621,532	496,929	56,636	8,352	473,104	362,691	91,792	125,886
45—50	..	946,870	535,234	411,636	39,209	5,850	387,982	245,353	108,043	160,433
50—55	..	763,217	432,178	331,039	29,176	4,484	300,658	175,989	102,344	150,566
55—60	..	573,809	329,030	244,779	20,031	2,599	207,024	95,813	101,975	146,367
60—65	..	480,814	276,771	204,043	16,054	2,086	165,423	67,126	95,294	134,831
65—70	..	270,890	159,781	111,109	8,329	1,131	85,141	27,482	66,311	82,496
70 and over	..	424,538	239,710	184,828	12,371	1,909	107,508	32,360	119,831	150,559
Muslims..	..	**13,332,460**	**7,241,612**	**6,090,848**	**4,018,185**	**2,712,924**	**2,730,337**	**2,743,041**	**493,090**	**634,883**
0—1	..	501,246	252,222	249,024	252,177	248,951	39	67	6	6
1—2	..	383,606	193,471	190,135	193,373	189,949	84	179	14	7
2—3	..	432,902	219,831	213,071	219,511	212,511	295	549	25	11
3—4	..	439,692	225,786	213,906	224,990	212,407	761	1,463	35	36
4—5	..	427,042	222,569	204,473	221,398	202,205	1,103	2,172	68	96
Total 0—5	..	*2,184,488*	*1,113,879*	*1,070,609*	*1,111,449*	*1,066,023*	*2,282*	*4,430*	*148*	*156*
5—10	..	1,822,654	978,898	843,756	959,886	788,698	18,223	54,281	789	777
10—15	..	1,610,827	887,055	723,772	838,825	583,887	46,286	137,946	1,944	1,939
15—20	..	1,210,478	659,280	551,198	460,345	153,957	189,759	389,508	9,176	7,733
20—25	..	1,232,029	658,675	573,354	325,101	65,940	315,094	493,726	18,480	13,688
25—30	..	1,081,888	589,823	492,065	134,759	18,143	421,618	448,405	33,446	25,517
30—35	..	951,639	532,608	419,031	78,236	11,212	415,488	373,686	38,884	34,133
35—40	..	721,262	402,337	318,925	36,899	7,598	322,967	259,530	42,471	51,797
40—45	..	615,716	339,952	275,764	24,606	5,516	270,233	207,643	45,113	62,605
45—50	..	519,759	292,116	227,643	15,172	3,823	223,720	140,909	53,224	82,911
50—55	..	416,727	234,125	182,602	11,136	3,032	172,638	101,017	50,351	78,553
55—60	..	311,964	177,861	134,103	7,612	1,729	119,197	55,279	51,052	77,095
60—65	..	262,064	150,882	111,182	6,016	1,358	96,694	39,016	48,172	70,808
65—70	..	147,259	86,714	60,545	2,926	700	49,932	16,189	33,856	43,656
70 and over	..	243,706	137,407	106,299	5,217	1,308	66,206	21,476	65,984	83,515
Hindus ..	..	**6,328,588**	**3,465,534**	**2,863,054**	**1,804,266**	**1,108,251**	**1,363,236**	**1,348,446**	**298,032**	**406,357**
0—1	..	227,208	114,908	112,300	114,886	112,263	20	36	2	1
1—2	..	169,832	85,275	84,557	85,245	84,495	27	58	3	4
2—3	..	187,998	94,330	93,668	94,221	93,513	98	149	11	6
3—4	..	187,896	95,344	92,552	95,064	91,832	267	699	13	21
4—5	..	177,341	92,103	85,238	91,640	83,940	428	1,237	35	6.
Total 0—5	..	*950,275*	*481,960*	*468,315*	*481,056*	*466,043*	*840*	*2,179*	*64*	*93*
5—10	..	806,808	430,878	375,930	414,939	332,778	15,405	42,524	534	628
10—15	..	765,555	419,127	346,428	376,709	240,164	41,019	104,737	1,399	1,527
15—20	..	617,594	340,821	276,773	206,123	43,628	128,896	227,219	5,802	5,926
20—25	..	606,045	330,042	276,003	137,776	12,266	181,725	252,968	10,541	10,769
25—30	..	518,347	287,693	230,654	60,475	4,255	208,324	205,497	18,894	20,902
30—35	..	464,142	264,180	199,962	41,199	3,183	199,385	168,690	23,596	28,089
35—40	..	366,024	206,850	159,174	23,818	1,763	154,295	116,209	28,737	41,202
40—45	..	314,313	177,209	137,104	18,568	1,315	127,537	89,471	31,104	46,318
45—50	..	260,564	148,777	111,787	13,887	938	99,269	56,642	35,621	54,207
50—55	..	210,184	120,437	89,747	10,261	699	76,681	39,464	33,495	49,584
55—60	..	155,948	89,803	66,145	6,931	427	51,002	19,876	31,870	45,842
60—65	..	129,093	73,748	55,345	5,660	332	39,064	13,496	29,024	41,517
65—70	..	69,185	40,797	28,388	3,028	179	18,873	5,023	18,896	23,186
70 and over	..	94,511	53,212	41,299	3,836	281	20,921	4,451	28,455	36,567
Sikhs	..	**3,064,144**	**1,703,584**	**1,360,560**	**945,221**	**570,352**	**620,358**	**636,467**	**138,005**	**153,741**
0—1	..	114,701	59,058	55,643	59,036	55,619	19	18	3	6
1—2	..	82,515	42,301	40,214	42,280	40,141	18	66	3	7
2—3	..	88,954	46,017	42,937	45,980	42,802	36	130	1	5
3—4	..	89,781	47,050	42,731	46,959	42,559	88	166	3	6
4—5	..	86,988	46,221	40,767	46,052	40,514	149	228	20	25
Total 0—5	..	*462,939*	*240,647*	*222,292*	*240,307*	*221,635*	*310*	*608*	*30*	*49*
5—10	..	395,365	217,179	178,186	213,356	168,738	3,697	9,306	126	142
10—15	..	366,576	205,771	160,805	193,472	129,881	11,934	30,595	365	329
15—20	..	280,813	158,524	122,289	104,994	30,846	51,451	90,168	2,079	1,275
20—25	..	274,269	152,960	121,309	73,326	10,094	75,880	108,886	3,754	2,329
25—30	..	231,831	129,638	102,193	35,465	2,521	87,456	94,973	6,717	4,699
30—35	..	209,484	119,960	89,524	25,835	1,959	85,435	80,825	8,690	6,740
35—40	..	167,840	94,185	73,655	15,722	1,277	67,559	61,332	10,904	11,046
40—45	..	150,914	83,490	67,424	11,994	1,040	59,150	52,650	12,346	13,734
45—50	..	135,350	76,714	58,636	9,239	776	52,044	38,868	15,431	18,992
50—55	..	111,831	63,915	47,916	7,139	545	41,618	28,970	15,158	18,401
55—60	..	87,235	50,677	36,558	5,056	327	30,042	16,942	15,579	19,289
60—65	..	73,523	42,715	30,808	4,011	295	23,948	12,007	14,756	18,506
65—70	..	45,141	26,836	18,305	2,227	185	13,346	5,154	11,263	12,966
70 and over	..	71,033	40,373	30,660	3,078	233	16,488	5,183	20,807	25,244

Table VII.—Age, Sex and Civil Condition. Part II.—Provinces and States—*contd.*

United Provinces.

Age and Religion.	Population.			Unmarried.		Married.		Widowed.	
	Persons.	Males.	Females.	Males.	Females.	Males.	Females.	Males.	Females.
1	2	3	4	5	6	7	8	9	10
All Religions ..	**48,408,763**	**25,445,006**	**22,963,757**	**11,146,564**	**7,275,588**	**12,291,464**	**12,222,231**	**2,006,978**	**3,465,938**
0—1 ..	1,497,178	747,733	749,445	741,821	742,857	5,823	6,394	89	194
1—2 ..	1,415,426	693,979	721,447	685,717	711,898	8,158	9,337	104	212
2—3 ..	1,471,988	714,554	757,434	702,980	742,347	11,345	14,688	229	399
3—4 ..	1,514,915	754,949	759,966	730,005	726,825	24,300	31,855	644	1,286
4—5 ..	1,433,364	742,313	691,051	704,847	644,080	36,489	44,927	977	2,044
Total 0—5 ..	*7,332,871*	*3,653,528*	*3,679,343*	*3,565,370*	*3,568,007*	*86,115*	*107,201*	*2,043*	*4,135*
5—10 ..	6,044,830	3,246,268	2,798,562	2,795,292	2,117,304	440,804	667,457	10,172	13,801
10—15 ..	5,461,379	3,008,463	2,452,916	2,244,911	1,265,167	743,436	1,166,150	20,116	21,599
15—20 ..	4,317,976	2,303,535	2,014,441	975,604	162,523	1,272,245	1,802,641	55,686	49,277
20—25 ..	4,467,869	2,320,857	2,147,012	628,122	61,389	1,601,387	2,001,116	91,348	84,507
25—30 ..	4,267,712	2,223,782	2,043,930	307,542	30,079	1,770,929	1,843,645	145,311	170,206
30—35 ..	3,839,897	2,023,231	1,816,666	210,704	23,641	1,644,469	1,565,582	168,058	227,443
35—40 ..	3,129,710	1,659,950	1,469,760	128,437	14,770	1,325,655	1,093,607	205,858	361,383
40—45 ..	2,679,415	1,429,483	1,249,932	97,974	11,328	1,109,981	827,609	221,528	410,995
45—50 ..	2,118,743	1,140,023	978,720	65,870	6,810	822,850	477,898	251,303	494,012
50—55 ..	1,672,085	885,001	787,084	48,725	4,833	605,925	329,958	230,351	452,293
55—60 ..	1,149,260	593,080	556,180	30,547	3,389	362,130	157,106	200,403	395,685
60—65 ..	919,913	465,411	454,502	23,249	2,810	269,914	103,888	172,248	347,804
65—70 ..	427,061	214,515	212,546	10,157	1,221	110,894	37,562	93,464	173,763
70 and over ..	580,042	277,879	302,163	14,060	2,317	124,730	40,811	139,089	259,035
Hindus	**40,905,586**	**21,488,425**	**19,417,161**	**9,351,263**	**6,030,392**	**10,417,307**	**10,354,783**	**1,719,855**	**3,031,986**
0—1 ..	1,262,937	631,656	631,281	626,450	625,568	5,136	5,547	70	166
1—2 ..	1,187,839	581,486	606,353	574,277	598,220	7,121	7,946	88	187
2—3 ..	1,238,267	600,582	637,685	590,646	625,003	9,747	12,348	189	334
3—4 ..	1,274,505	635,442	639,063	614,198	612,322	20,725	25,663	519	1,078
4—5 ..	1,192,689	614,835	577,854	584,331	540,550	29,738	35,578	766	1,726
Total 0—5 ..	*6,156,237*	*3,064,001*	*3,092,236*	*2,989,902*	*3,001,663*	*72,467*	*87,082*	*1,632*	*3,491*
5—10 ..	5,065,415	2,722,556	2,342,859	2,333,939	1,761,668	379,803	569,100	8,814	12,091
10—15 ..	4,598,142	2,542,701	2,055,441	1,875,721	1,035,735	649,331	1,000,504	17,649	19,202
15—20 ..	3,628,131	1,940,138	1,687,993	803,541	117,673	1,089,118	1,526,625	47,479	43,695
20—25 ..	3,755,714	1,952,340	1,803,374	516,289	42,047	1,359,251	1,686,351	76,800	74,976
25—30 ..	3,628,900	1,887,667	1,741,233	264,326	20,853	1,499,796	1,567,980	123,545	152,400
30—35 ..	3,284,708	1,729,527	1,555,181	186,945	16,643	1,398,160	1,335,063	144,422	203,475
35—40 ..	2,675,194	1,417,087	1,258,107	116,186	11,046	1,122,068	926,165	178,833	320,896
40—45 ..	2,292,684	1,222,331	1,070,353	89,283	8,160	940,166	698,813	192,882	363,380
45—50 ..	1,803,753	967,752	836,001	60,290	4,753	689,379	399,913	218,083	431,335
50—55 ..	1,425,063	751,792	673,271	44,549	3,328	507,684	276,248	199,559	393,695
55—60 ..	975,298	498,333	476,965	27,847	2,429	299,037	131,167	171,449	343,369
60—65 ..	779,317	389,409	389,908	21,000	1,980	222,087	86,394	146,322	301,534
65—70 ..	358,724	177,015	181,709	9,089	822	89,352	30,858	78,574	150,029
70 and over ..	478,306	225,776	252,530	12,356	1,592	99,608	32,520	113,812	218,418
Muslims	**7,181,927**	**3,780,453**	**3,401,474**	**1,700,956**	**1,184,878**	**1,804,838**	**1,799,991**	**274,659**	**416,605**
0—1 ..	224,056	110,860	113,196	110,159	112,327	682	841	19	28
1—2 ..	218,334	107,751	110,583	106,709	109,173	1,026	1,385	16	25
2—3 ..	224,270	109,196	115,074	107,571	112,676	1,585	2,333	40	65
3—4 ..	230,987	114,732	116,255	111,082	109,921	3,528	6,128	122	206
4—5 ..	231,714	122,850	108,864	115,976	99,326	6,670	9,227	204	311
Total 0—5 ..	*1,129,361*	*565,389*	*563,972*	*551,497*	*543,423*	*13,491*	*19,914*	*401*	*635*
5—10 ..	941,075	503,226	437,849	441,939	339,575	59,965	96,617	1,322	1,657
10—15 ..	828,100	446,690	381,410	352,529	217,669	91,783	161,417	2,378	2,324
15—20 ..	657,155	344,912	312,243	160,543	40,877	176,506	266,027	7,863	5,339
20—25 ..	676,538	347,674	328,864	101,064	16,883	232,703	302,879	13,907	9,102
25—30 ..	608,445	318,774	289,671	37,586	8,157	260,361	264,622	20,827	16,892
30—35 ..	530,442	280,149	250,293	20,987	6,243	236,490	221,218	22,672	22,832
35—40 ..	435,554	232,440	203,114	11,135	3,290	195,464	160,997	25,841	38,827
40—45 ..	370,614	198,165	172,449	7,854	2,859	162,929	123,831	27,382	45,759
45—50 ..	302,242	165,232	137,010	5,030	1,895	128,471	74,855	31,731	60,260
50—55 ..	236,760	127,597	109,163	3,716	1,389	94,503	51,504	29,378	56,270
55—60 ..	166,877	90,906	75,971	2,410	862	60,858	24,862	27,638	50,247
60—65 ..	135,033	73,051	61,982	2,054	744	46,216	16,783	24,781	44,455
65—70 ..	65,629	36,029	29,600	984	352	20,816	6,435	14,229	22,813
70 and over ..	98,102	50,219	47,883	1,628	660	24,282	8,030	24,309	39,193
Christians ..	**205,009***	**111,650**	**93,359**	**61,499**	**40,414**	**43,627**	**43,935**	**6,524**	**9,010**
0—1 ..	6,487	3,283	3,204	3,279	3,202	4	2	..	..
1—2 ..	5,994	3,044	2,950	3,038	2,947	6	3	..	..
2—3 ..	6,172	3,102	3,070	3,095	3,065	7	5	..	..
3—4 ..	6,192	3,139	3,053	3,119	3,015	20	37	..	1
4—5 ..	5,889	3,025	2,864	2,983	2,788	41	73	1	3
Total 0—5 ..	*30,734*	*15,593*	*15,141*	*15,514*	*15,017*	*78*	*120*	*1*	*4*
5—10 ..	24,842	13,167	11,675	12,396	10,363	753	1,287	18	25
10—15 ..	22,574	12,153	10,421	10,353	7,511	1,739	2,869	61	41
15—20 ..	21,424	12,138	9,286	7,846	2,848	4,048	6,316	244	122
20—25 ..	23,815	14,080	9,735	8,104	1,928	5,532	7,599	444	208
25—30 ..	19,810	11,309	8,501	4,194	892	6,544	7,237	571	372
30—35 ..	15,588	8,356	7,232	1,732	651	6,094	6,106	530	475
35—40 ..	11,887	6,401	5,486	490	400	5,292	4,250	619	836
40—45 ..	10,007	5,468	4,539	345	285	4,495	3,282	628	972
45—50 ..	7,577	4,123	3,454	175	141	3,224	1,990	724	1,323
50—55 ..	5,974	3,207	2,767	136	107	2,394	1,393	677	1,267
55—60 ..	3,964	2,115	1,849	90	89	1,401	658	624	1,102
60—65 ..	3,119	1,613	1,506	64	77	992	455	557	974
65—70 ..	1,489	787	702	26	43	449	178	312	481
70 and over ..	2,205	1,140	1,065	34	62	592	195	514	808

*Includes 3 males of Indefinite Beliefs.

Table VII.—Age, Sex and Civil Condition. Part II.—Provinces and States—*contd.*

Age and Religion.	Population.			Unmarried.		Married.		Widowed.	
	Persons.	Males.	Females.	Males.	Females.	Males.	Females.	Males.	Females.
1	2	3	4	5	6	7	8	9	10
Baroda State.									
All Religions ..	**2,443,007**	**1,257,817**	**1,185,190**	**571,233**	**389,766**	**602,056**	**620,694**	**84,528**	**174,730**
0—1 ..	87,439	44,279	43,160	44,279	43,160	..	..	..	..
1—2 ..	72,703	36,492	36,211	36,492	36,211	..	..	..	..
2—3 ..	68,471	33,837	34,634	33,837	34,634	..	..	..	..
3—4 ..	68,370	34,448	33,922	34,172	33,121	244	736	32	65
4—5 ..	66,093	34,463	31,630	34,024	30,368	398	1,149	41	113
Total 0—5 ..	*363,076*	*183,519*	*179,557*	*182,804*	*177,494*	*642*	*1,885*	*73*	*178*
5—10 ..	304,213	160,033	144,180	146,567	115,027	12,714	28,460	752	693
10—15 ..	288,872	152,007	136,865	123,082	79,375	27,746	56,430	1,179	1,060
15—20 ..	241,691	122,832	118,859	54,448	12,902	66,360	103,619	2,024	2,338
20—25 ..	232,906	117,074	115,832	32,252	3,313	82,028	108,998	2,794	3,521
25—30 ..	182,911	92,954	89,957	10,104	573	78,651	82,816	4,199	6,568
30—35 ..	169,920	87,756	82,164	6,830	343	75,491	72,010	5,435	9,811
35—40 ..	153,009	78,244	74,765	4,496	212	66,143	56,961	7,605	17,592
40—45 ..	136,989	70,518	66,471	3,501	175	58,127	45,778	8,890	20,518
45—50 ..	113,419	60,101	53,318	2,465	115	46,540	27,892	11,096	25,311
50—55 ..	90,212	47,988	42,224	1,874	86	35,577	18,649	10,537	23,489
55—60 ..	62,400	32,515	29,885	1,131	54	21,910	8,552	9,474	21,279
60—65 ..	51,093	25,850	25,243	848	40	16,466	5,647	8,536	19,556
65—70 ..	23,185	12,083	11,102	380	26	6,810	1,662	4,893	9,414
70 and over ..	29,111	14,343	14,768	451	31	6,851	1,335	7,041	13,402
Bihar and Orissa States.									
All Religions ..	**4,652,007**	**2,288,422**	**2,363,585**	**1,165,640**	**963,217**	**1,056,023**	**1,066,907**	**66,759**	**333,461**
0—1 ..	158,890	78,335	80,555	78,335	80,555	..	..	..	..
1—2 ..	146,349	71,142	75,207	71,142	75,207	..	..	..	..
2—3 ..	168,006	80,798	87,208	80,778	87,153	20	53	..	2
3—4 ..	166,277	80,927	85,350	80,709	84,859	218	471	..	20
4—5 ..	153,541	76,375	77,166	75,969	76,284	403	842	3	40
Total 0—5 ..	*793,063*	*387,577*	*405,486*	*386,933*	*404,058*	*641*	*1,366*	*3*	*62*
5—10 ..	639,001	324,669	314,332	313,411	284,154	11,157	29,482	101	696
10—15 ..	547,101	283,004	264,097	256,911	199,811	25,777	62,757	316	1,529
15—20 ..	407,132	194,563	212,569	111,822	44,797	81,060	162,196	1,681	5,576
20—25 ..	421,946	196,790	225,156	64,793	17,124	128,863	199,256	3,134	8,776
25—30 ..	408,527	200,578	207,949	16,744	4,907	178,486	185,606	5,348	17,436
30—35 ..	369,613	184,622	184,991	7,589	3,186	171,199	157,847	5,834	23,958
35—40 ..	288,618	145,825	142,793	2,696	1,660	136,051	100,416	7,078	40,717
40—45 ..	237 409	119 242	118,167	1,856	1,255	110,088	73,992	7,298	42,920
45—50 ..	173,586	86,595	86,991	1,040	740	77,419	39,496	8,136	46,755
50—55 ..	138,087	67,353	70,734	752	573	59,077	27,926	7,524	42,235
55—60 ..	87,943	39,247	48,696	399	328	32,268	12,212	6,580	36,156
60—65 ..	69,645	30,020	39,625	295	256	24,040	7,572	5,685	31,797
65—70 ..	26,899	10,939	15,960	115	113	8,098	2,865	2,726	12,982
70 and over ..	43,437	17,398	26,039	284	255	11,799	3,918	5,315	21,866
Hindus ..	**4,194,878**	**2,063,008**	**2,131,870**	**1,040,260**	**849,348**	**962,094**	**974,370**	**60,654**	**308,152**
0—1 ..	142,060	70,055	72,005	70,055	72,005	..	..	..	..
1—2 ..	131,078	63,681	67,397	63,681	67,397	..	..	..	..
2—3 ..	149,977	72,042	77,935	72,025	77,880	17	53	..	2
3—4 ..	147,950	71,985	75,965	71,791	75,501	194	444	..	20
4—5 ..	136,588	67,985	68,603	67,627	67,783	356	783	2	37
Total 0—5 ..	*707,653*	*345,748*	*361,905*	*345,179*	*360,566*	*567*	*1,280*	*2*	*59*
5—10 ..	571,638	290,538	281,100	280,036	252,122	10,410	28,319	92	659
10—15 ..	490,788	254,366	236,422	229,935	175,729	24,142	59,259	289	1,434
15—20 ..	367,686	176,296	191,390	100,043	37,099	74,729	149,156	1,524	5,135
20—25 ..	382,582	178,472	204,110	57,750	13,563	117,882	182,463	2,840	8,084
25—30 ..	369,517	181,509	188,008	14,401	3,703	162,284	168,273	4,824	16,032
30—35 ..	334,290	166,977	167,313	6,447	2,496	155,277	142,724	5,253	22,093
35—40 ..	261,612	131,635	129,977	2,331	1,320	122,934	91,067	6,370	37,590
40—45 ..	215,788	107,962	107,826	1,616	994	99,721	67,118	6,625	39,714
45—50 ..	158,762	78,932	79,830	917	580	70,583	35,833	7,432	43,417
50—55 ..	126,358	61,488	64,870	659	456	53,955	25,204	6,874	39,210
55—60 ..	80,471	35,934	44,537	352	253	29,594	10,926	5,988	33,358
60—65 ..	63,538	27,371	36,167	259	188	21,938	6,725	5,174	29,254
65—70 ..	24,641	9,968	14,673	94	86	7,360	2,566	2,514	12,021
70 and over ..	39,554	15,812	23,742	241	193	10,718	3,457	4,853	20,092
Tribal ..	**360,600**	**176,918**	**183,682**	**98,597**	**90,054**	**73,453**	**73,364**	**4,868**	**20,264**
0—1 ..	13,278	6,534	6,744	6,534	6,744	..	..	..	..
1—2 ..	12,191	5,934	6,257	5,934	6,257	..	..	..	..
2 - 3 ..	14,387	6,923	7,464	6,920	7,464	3	..	..	..
3—4 ..	14,659	7,095	7,564	7,080	7,545	15	19	..	..
4—5 ..	13,591	6,714	6,877	6,684	6,834	29	41	1	2
Total 0—5 ..	*68,106*	*33,200*	*34,906*	*33,152*	*34,844*	*47*	*60*	*1*	*2*
5—10 ..	53,055	26,808	26,247	26,215	25,320	586	897	7	30
10—15 ..	43,761	22,205	21,556	20,839	18,662	1,342	2,814	24	80
15—20 ..	30,585	14,076	16,509	9,100	5,954	4,841	10,188	135	367
20—25 ..	30,709	14,166	16,543	5,597	2,781	8,320	13,200	249	562
25—30 ..	31,060	14,985	16,075	1,959	902	12,594	14,038	432	1,135
30 —35 ..	28,385	14,019	14,366	953	603	12,593	12,244	473	1,519
35—40 ..	21,801	11,448	10,353	302	299	10,568	7,494	578	2,560
40—45 ..	17,321	9,055	8,266	195	230	8,305	5,425	555	2,611
45—50 ..	11,593	5,973	5,620	97	139	5,322	2,793	554	2,688
50—55 ..	9,153	4,549	4,604	74	103	3,971	2,072	504	2,429
55—60 ..	5,721	2,506	3,215	37	69	2,018	950	451	2,196
60—65 ..	4,695	2,016	2,679	31	63	1,590	627	395	1,989
65—70 ..	1,716	729	987	12	26	552	224	165	737
70 and over ..	2,939	1,183	1,756	34	59	804	338	345	1,359

Table VII.— Age, Sex and Civil Condition. Part II.—Provinces and States—*contd.*

Age and Religion.	Population.			Unmarried.		Married.		Widowed.	
	Persons.	Males.	Females.	Males.	Females.	Males.	Females.	Males.	Females.
1	2	3	4	5	6	7	8	9	10
Bengal States.									
All Religions ..	**973,336**	**516,162**	**457,174**	**261,185**	**162,925**	**228,386**	**210,633**	**26,591**	**83,616**
0—1 ..	34,043	16,972	17,071	16,642	16,750	330	318	..	3
1—2 ..	25,319	12,297	13,022	12,172	12,861	122	159	3	2
2—3 ..	32,272	15,555	16,717	15,393	16,439	158	268	4	10
3—4 ..	33,060	16,196	16,864	15,990	16,354	196	480	10	30
4—5 ..	32,143	16,008	16,135	15,770	15,441	231	652	7	42
Total 0—5 ..	*156,837*	*77,028*	*79,809*	*75,967*	*77,845*	*1,037*	*1,877*	*24*	*87*
5—10 ..	133,701	70,045	63,656	67,937	50,387	2,050	12,753	58	516
10—15 ..	114,576	60,265	54,311	56,230	29,276	3,912	23,870	123	1,165
15—20 ..	92,712	43,630	49,082	27,550	2,987	15,554	41,947	526	4,148
20—25 ..	97,158	46,645	50,513	19,758	1,084	25,850	43,487	1,037	5,942
25—30 ..	87,322	47,594	39,728	7,390	594	37,948	30,862	2,256	8,272
30—35 ..	78,022	44,796	33,226	3,741	502	38,216	23,388	2,839	9,336
35—40 ..	57,867	34,598	23,269	1,106	84	30,139	12,829	3,353	10,356
40—45 ..	47,347	28,671	18,676	741	55	24,593	8,748	3,337	9,873
45—50 ..	34,771	20,674	14,097	295	34	17,179	4,634	3,200	9,429
50—55 ..	26,877	15,579	11,298	201	25	12,654	3,138	2,724	8,135
55—60 ..	16,986	9,810	7,176	114	21	7,470	1,342	2,226	5,813
60—65 ..	13,593	7,763	5,830	79	13	5,743	945	1,941	4,872
65—70 ..	6,015	3,462	2,553	25	5	2,399	360	1,038	2,188
70 and over ..	9,552	5,602	3,950	51	13	3,642	453	1,909	3,484
Bombay States.									
All Religions ..	***4,459,944**	**2,284,451**	**2,175,493**	**1,110,426**	**764,387**	**1,049,926**	**1,076,974**	**124,099**	**334,132**
0—1 ..	134,666	67,351	67,315	66,781	66,537	552	766	18	12
1—2 ..	134,132	65,276	68,856	64,443	67,449	801	1,382	32	25
2—3 ..	141,120	67,766	73,354	66,638	71,203	1,089	2,099	39	52
3—4 ..	143,779	70,277	73,502	68,595	69,644	1,632	3,742	50	116
4—5 ..	149,185	73,638	75,547	71,216	69,004	2,309	6,292	113	251
Total 0—5 ..	*702,882*	*344,308*	*358,574*	*337,673*	*343,837*	*6,383*	*14,281*	*252*	*456*
5—10 ..	624,925	326,142	298,783	303,754	233,275	21,725	63,781	663	1,727
10—15 ..	549,465	293,940	255,525	253,164	147,110	39,687	105,443	1,089	2,972
15—20 ..	389,923	200,085	189,838	106,734	19,337	90,737	164,113	2,614	6,388
20—25 ..	396,647	196,407	200,240	62,300	7,494	129,724	182,481	4,383	10,265
25—30 ..	356,394	177,913	178,481	19,472	3,628	151,213	156,840	7,228	18,013
30—35 ..	324,986	166,574	158,412	10,897	2,749	146,536	131,168	9,141	24,495
35—40 ..	272,361	142,143	130,218	5,747	1,958	124,385	92,290	12,011	35,970
40—45 ..	231,993	121,402	110,591	3,823	1,499	104,443	69,850	13,136	39,242
45—50 ..	185,229	98,225	87,004	2,380	1,108	80,348	41,914	15,497	43,982
50—55 ..	146,478	77,623	68,855	1,707	868	60,985	27,812	14,931	40,175
55—60 ..	106,023	54,270	51,753	1,056	554	39,108	12,921	14,106	38,278
60—65 ..	86,487	42,510	43,977	846	469	29,249	8,910	12,415	34,598
65—70 ..	38,383	19,311	19,072	373	194	12,042	2,656	6,896	16,222
70 and over ..	47,768	23,598	24,170	500	307	13,361	2,514	9,737	21,349
Hindus ..	**3,920,786**	**1,998,198**	**1,922,588**	**961,432**	**668,106**	**929,894**	**957,437**	**106,872**	**297,045**
0—1 ..	118,883	59,439	59,444	58,923	58,729	498	704	18	11
1—2 ..	118,697	57,734	60,963	56,965	59,669	739	1,270	30	24
2—3 ..	124,054	59,490	64,564	58,470	62,608	982	1,908	38	48
3—4 ..	126,042	61,456	64,586	59,926	61,059	1,485	3,420	45	107
4—5 ..	130,124	64,285	65,839	62,097	59,843	2,083	5,768	105	228
Total 0—5 ..	*617,800*	*302,404*	*315,396*	*296,381*	*301,908*	*5,787*	*13,070*	*236*	*418*
5—10 ..	552,415	287,165	265,250	266,435	204,128	20,121	59,526	609	1,596
10—15 ..	487,324	259,310	228,014	221,651	128,559	36,659	96,722	1,000	2,733
15—20 ..	342,012	174,623	167,389	90,258	15,861	82,092	145,780	2,273	5,748
20—25 ..	345,723	170,136	175,587	50,733	6,149	115,693	160,255	3,710	9,183
25—30 ..	309,440	153,468	155,972	14,570	3,008	132,871	136,908	6,027	16,056
30—35 ..	283,823	144,448	139,375	8,186	2,308	128,561	115,211	7,701	21,856
35—40 ..	239,121	123,859	115,262	4,517	1,706	109,079	81,548	10,263	32,008
40—45 ..	204,476	106,269	98,207	3,040	1,365	91,947	62,014	11,282	34,828
45—50 ..	164,182	86,460	77,722	1,970	1,020	71,030	37,567	13,460	39,135
50—55 ..	129,875	68,391	61,484	1,409	791	53,903	24,923	13,079	35,770
55—60 ..	93,558	47,612	45,946	869	477	34,459	11,490	12,284	33,979
60—65 ..	76,298	37,198	39,100	707	411	25,706	7,915	10,785	30,774
65—70 ..	33,674	16,808	16,866	312	174	10,517	2,333	5,979	14,359
70 and over ..	41,065	20,047	21,018	394	241	11,469	2,175	8,184	18,602
Muslims ..	**414,921**	**221,578**	**193,343**	**117,086**	**75,500**	**91,439**	**91,248**	**13,053**	**26,595**
0—1 ..	11,982	6,022	5,960	5,979	5,911	43	48	..	1
1—2 ..	11,861	5,835	6,026	5,781	5,966	52	59	2	1
2—3 ..	13,262	6,503	6,759	6,408	6,661	94	96	1	2
3—4 ..	14,065	7,060	7,005	6,921	6,843	135	155	4	7
4—5 ..	14,612	7,457	7,155	7,267	6,904	184	237	6	14
Total 0—5 ..	*65,782*	*32,877*	*32,905*	*32,356*	*32,285*	*508*	*595*	*13*	*25*
5—10 ..	56,871	30,682	26,189	29,317	23,171	1,319	2,937	46	81
10—15 ..	48,137	26,904	21,233	24,417	14,785	2,415	6,287	72	161
15—20 ..	36,602	19,545	17,057	12,746	2,626	6,538	13,972	261	459
20—25 ..	39,674	20,502	19,172	9,228	1,111	10,730	17,276	544	785
25—30 ..	37,084	19,373	17,711	4,175	547	14,210	15,758	988	1,406
30—35 ..	32,078	17,318	14,760	2,294	391	13,861	12,511	1,163	1,858
35—40 ..	25,304	14,076	11,228	1,012	186	11,680	8,194	1,384	2,848
40—45 ..	20,731	11,487	9,244	620	114	9,435	5,949	1,432	3,181
45—50 ..	15,472	8,714	6,758	310	68	6,906	3,224	1,498	3,466
50—55 ..	12,085	6,759	5,326	228	62	5,207	2,154	1,324	3,110
55—60 ..	9,097	4,875	4,222	143	63	3,410	1,076	1,322	3,083
60—65 ..	7,539	3,952	3,587	107	48	2,641	771	1,204	2,768
65—70 ..	3,376	1,804	1,572	46	11	1,119	246	639	1,315
70 and over ..	5,089	2,710	2,379	87	32	1,460	298	1,163	2,049

*Excludes 8,452 persons (4,172 males and 4,280 females) of unspecified age.

Table VII.—Age, Sex and Civil Condition. Part II.—Provinces and States—*contd.*

Central India Agency.

Age and Religion.	Population.			Unmarried.		Married.		Widowed.	
	Persons.	Males.	Females.	Males.	Females.	Males.	Females.	Males.	Females.
1	2	3	4	5	6	7	8	9	10
All Religions	**6,632,790**	**3,405,438**	**3,227,352**	**1,513,564**	**1,069,354**	**1,684,155**	**1,655,107**	**207,719**	**502,891**
0—1	183,146	90,987	92,159	89,967	90,980	990	1,135	30	44
1—2	195,576	94,228	101,348	93,241	99,775	952	1,519	35	54
2—3	209,970	99,374	110,596	97,841	108,145	1,481	2,364	52	87
3—4	211,657	103,011	108,646	100,564	104,354	2,362	4,108	85	184
4—5	199,351	100,399	98,952	97,240	92,989	3,011	5,612	148	351
Total 0—5	*999,700*	*487,999*	*511,701*	*478,853*	*496,243*	*8,796*	*14,738*	*350*	*720*
5—10	862,419	450,538	411,881	403,236	317,543	45,943	91,907	1,359	2,431
10—15	794,585	423,984	370,601	330,467	195,941	90,851	170,352	2,666	4,308
15—20	626,772	321,416	305,356	134,839	26,143	180,047	269,281	6,530	9,932
20—25	639,912	323,690	316,222	79,217	11,151	234,428	289,636	10,045	15,435
25—30	589,052	303,524	285,528	31,383	6,836	256,791	250,065	15,350	28,627
30—35	511,882	265,638	246,244	19,649	5,542	228,324	203,895	17,665	36,807
35—40	421,053	217,128	203,925	11,782	3,146	181,983	139,210	23,363	61,569
40—45	357,289	186,204	171,085	8,986	2,430	152,188	102,868	25,030	65,787
45—50	270,890	144,606	126,284	5,728	1,796	111,778	53,857	27,100	70,631
50—55	209,652	110,319	99,333	4,011	1,215	82,741	35,827	23,567	62,291
55—60	137,216	68,578	68,638	2,188	487	47,195	15,898	19,195	52,253
60—65	113,388	54,928	58,460	1,642	392	36,479	10,778	16,807	47,290
65—70	39,810	19,324	20,486	625	200	11,628	3,076	7,071	17,210
70 and over	59,170	27,562	31,608	958	289	14,983	3,719	11,621	27,600
Hindus	**5,852,204**	**3,002,203**	**2,850,001**	**1,316,560**	**919,955**	**1,499,589**	**1,476,446**	**186,054**	**453,600**
0—1	160,812	80,252	80,560	79,362	79,467	865	1,055	25	38
1—2	170,367	82,249	88,118	81,333	86,636	884	1,430	32	52
2—3	183,158	86,798	96,360	85,367	94,077	1,383	2,200	48	83
3—4	185,155	90,239	94,916	87,923	90,835	2,232	3,905	84	176
4—5	174,131	87,863	86,268	84,927	80,655	2,805	5,300	131	313
Total 0—5	*873,623*	*427,401*	*446,222*	*418,912*	*431,670*	*8,169*	*13,890*	*320*	*662*
5—10	756,762	396,033	360,729	351,871	272,045	42,876	86,415	1,286	2,269
10—15	700,590	374,221	326,369	286,884	165,253	84,839	157,073	2,498	4,043
15—20	555,142	284,705	270,437	114,850	21,147	163,943	240,118	5,912	9,172
20—25	565,474	285,893	279,581	66,879	9,464	210,019	255,881	8,995	14,236
25—30	522,922	268,955	253,967	27,060	6,298	228,242	221,291	13,653	26,378
30—35	454,962	235,474	219,488	17,386	5,168	202,327	180,519	15,761	33,801
35—40	372,601	191,485	181,116	10,625	2,831	159,883	122,358	20,977	55,927
40—45	316,458	164,267	152,191	8,153	2,183	133,566	90,515	22,548	59,493
45—50	240,086	127,606	112,480	5,228	1,630	97,991	47,381	24,387	63,469
50—55	185,803	97,206	88,597	3,722	1,092	72,314	31,527	21,170	55,978
55—60	121,013	60,067	60,946	2,008	413	40,900	13,961	17,159	46,572
60—65	99,845	48,018	51,827	1,506	330	31,557	9,475	14,955	42,022
65—70	35,116	16,881	18,235	584	172	10,053	2,756	6,244	15,307
70 and over	51,807	23,991	27,816	892	259	12,910	3,286	10,189	24,271
Muslims	**376,637**	**98,346**	**178,291**	**92,565**	**64,758**	**93,394**	**87,443**	**12,387**	**26,090**
0—1	10,181	4,923	5,258	4,888	5,212	32	41	3	5
1—2	11,109	5,387	5,722	5,351	5,669	33	52	3	1
2—3	11,460	5,451	6,009	5,403	5,902	44	106	4	1
3—4	11,361	5,499	5,862	5,436	5,729	62	128	1	5
4—5	10,883	5,462	5,421	5,349	5,219	101	180	12	22
Total 0—5	*54,994*	*26,722*	*28,272*	*26,427*	*27,731*	*272*	*507*	*23*	*34*
5—10	48,134	25,186	22,948	23,486	19,804	1,653	3,050	47	94
10—15	43,703	23,339	20,364	20,331	13,412	2,915	6,802	93	150
15—20	35,206	18,390	16,816	10,398	2,045	7,652	14,383	340	388
20—25	37,478	19,490	17,988	6,974	746	11,885	16,641	631	601
25—30	32,665	17,451	15,214	2,246	258	14,212	13,856	993	1,100
30—35	28,357	15,526	12,831	1,117	196	13,299	11,155	1,110	1,480
35—40	24,144	13,079	11,065	595	162	11,166	8,084	1,318	2,819
40—45	20,378	11,121	9,257	420	127	9,350	5,937	1,351	3,193
45—50	15,898	8,851	7,047	222	95	7,124	3,122	1,505	3,830
50—55	12,537	6,948	5,589	122	68	5,486	2,078	1,340	3,443
55—60	8,549	4,617	3,932	90	44	3,403	865	1,124	3,023
60—65	7,235	3,813	3,422	83	37	2,676	585	1,054	2,800
65—70	2,861	1,575	1,286	26	17	1,020	164	529	1,105
70 and over	4,498	2,238	2,260	28	16	1,281	214	929	2,030
Tribal	**340,752**	**170,828**	**169,924**	**87,292**	**74,437**	**76,884**	**78,138**	**6,652**	**17,349**
0—1	10,434	4,923	5,511	4,891	5,474	32	37	..	..
1—2	12,443	5,778	6,665	5,753	6,631	25	33	..	1
2—3	13,690	6,315	7,375	6,270	7,320	45	54	..	1
3—4	13,557	6,491	7,066	6,430	6,995	61	69	..	2
4—5	12,710	6,267	6,443	6,181	6,326	82	106	4	11
Total 0—5	*62,834*	*29,774*	*33,060*	*29,525*	*32,746*	*245*	*299*	4	*15*
5—10	50,511	25,755	24,756	24,463	22,620	1,268	2,087	24	49
10—15	43,742	22,964	20,778	20,071	15,111	2,822	5,580	71	87
15—20	30,169	14,811	15,358	7,349	2,567	7,231	12,539	231	252
20—25	30,258	14,516	15,742	3,460	744	10,698	14,609	358	389
25—30	27,785	13,893	13,892	1,148	202	12,182	12,907	563	783
30—35	23,561	11,838	11,723	621	124	10,610	10,520	607	1,079
35—40	20,046	10,249	9,797	264	106	9,186	7,536	799	2,155
40—45	16,687	8,740	7,947	171	81	7,753	5,498	816	2,368
45—50	11,852	6,445	5,407	98	46	5,511	2,837	836	2,524
50—55	8,887	4,817	4,070	51	36	4,068	1,879	698	2,155
55—60	5,952	3,002	2,950	29	22	2,377	902	596	2,026
60—65	5,012	2,448	2,564	19	16	1,882	624	547	1,924
65—70	1,278	577	701	4	7	402	127	171	567
70 and over	2,178	999	1,179	19	9	649	194	331	976

Tabla VII.—Age, Sex and Civil Condition. Part II.—Provinces and States—*contd.*

Central Provinces States.

Age and Religion.	Population.			Unmarried.		Married.		Widowed.	
	Persons.	Males.	Females.	Males.	Females.	Males.	Females.	Males.	Females.
1	2	3	4	5	6	7	8	9	10
All Religions	**2,483,214**	**1,235,385**	**1,247,829**	**559,016**	**460,584**	**630,564**	**639,416**	**45,805**	**147,829**
0—1	91,703	45,264	46,439	44,601	45,810	627	604	36	25
1—2	84,502	40,771	43,731	40,228	43,088	533	626	10	17
2—3	89,680	44,646	45,034	43,907	43,933	718	1,080	21	21
3—4	89,039	46,317	42,722	45,018	40,719	1,271	1,938	28	65
4—5	96,017	43,239	52,778	41,513	50,168	1,683	2,494	43	116
Total 0—5	*450,941*	*220,237*	*230,704*	*215,267*	*223,718*	*4,832*	*6,742*	*138*	*244*
5—10	344,941	177,276	167,665	156,147	134,521	20,868	32,580	261	564
10—15	284,259	148,637	135,622	113,982	80,949	34,096	53,698	559	975
15—20	200,754	95,536	105,218	35,792	11,536	58,073	91,034	1,671	2,648
20—25	217,576	102,747	114,829	20,084	4,818	79,888	105,853	2,775	4,158
25—30	215,155	106,641	108,514	7,158	1,990	95,483	99,046	4,000	7,478
30—35	197,707	99,373	98,334	4,588	1,306	90,317	87,003	4,468	10,025
35—40	150,195	78,000	72,195	2,383	623	70,683	57,167	4,934	14,405
40—45	124,058	64,752	59,306	1,684	436	58,021	43,045	5,047	15,825
45—50	90,670	47,944	42,726	737	226	42,220	24,445	4,987	18,055
50—55	69,939	35,843	34,096	518	149	30,987	17,059	4,338	16,888
55—60	48,976	21,795	27,181	250	118	17,792	9,151	3,753	17,912
60—65	41,301	17,727	23,574	231	98	14,025	6,582	3,471	16,894
65—70	17,354	7,092	10,262	68	29	5,284	2,668	1,740	7,565
70 and over	29,388	11,785	17,603	127	67	7,995	3,343	3,663	14,193
Hindus	**1,788,401**	**886,123**	**902,278**	**375,275**	**306,838**	**476,619**	**481,328**	**34,229**	**114,112**
0—1	65,004	31,970	33,034	31,529	32,531	407	481	34	22
1—2	58,867	28,257	30,610	27,894	30,112	355	481	8	17
2—3	60,419	30,457	29,962	29,901	29,089	538	854	18	19
3—4	59,373	31,757	27,616	30,753	25,970	982	1,597	22	49
4—5	69,070	29,738	39,332	28,418	37,183	1,290	2,068	30	81
Total 0—5	*312,733*	*152,179*	*160,554*	*148,495*	*154,885*	*3,572*	*5,481*	*112*	*188*
5—10	243,829	125,474	118,355	107,102	89,844	18,168	28,093	204	418
10—15	203,897	107,110	96,787	77,293	51,963	29,371	44,081	446	743
15—20	145,469	69,643	75,826	21,858	5,507	46,420	68,345	1,365	1,974
20—25	157,435	74,548	82,887	11,218	2,054	61,120	77,819	2,210	3,014
25—30	154,629	76,805	77,824	3,837	966	69,950	71,535	3,018	5,323
30—35	142,168	71,269	70,899	2,321	650	65,679	62,957	3,269	7,292
35—40	109,337	55,969	53,368	1,127	341	51,274	42,314	3,568	10,713
40—45	91,658	46,957	44,701	806	242	42,474	32,482	3,677	11,977
45—50	68,857	35,822	33,035	482	130	31,656	18,771	3,684	14,134
50—55	53,482	26,975	26,507	334	88	23,415	13,100	3,226	13,319
55—60	37,397	16,226	21,171	161	66	13,252	6,926	2,813	14,179
60—66	31,594	13,213	18,381	131	53	10,474	4,929	2,608	13,399
65—70	13,600	5,336	8,264	43	13	3,960	2,077	1,333	6,174
70 and over	22,316	8,597	13,719	67	36	5,834	2,418	2,696	11,265
Muslims	**23,254**	**11,733**	**11,521**	**5,070**	**3,754**	**6,229**	**5,910**	**434**	**1,857**
0—1	752	356	396	353	395	3	..	..	1
1—2	611	283	328	281	328	2	..	..	..
2—3	673	306	367	303	356	3	11	..	..
3—4	690	332	358	326	339	6	18	..	1
4—5	683	340	343	325	323	15	18	..	2
Total 0—5	*3,409*	*1,617*	*1,792*	*1,588*	*1,741*	*29*	*47*	..	*4*
5—10	2,809	1,470	1,339	1,320	1,115	145	217	5	7
10—15	2,446	1,298	1,148	1,068	716	222	416	8	16
15—20	2,073	1,007	1,066	497	109	493	928	17	29
20—25	2,406	1,210	1,196	345	34	834	1,110	31	52
25—30	2,139	1,130	1,009	132	14	962	906	36	89
30—35	2,111	1,103	1,008	86	11	969	855	48	142
35—40	1,488	752	736	16	6	694	542	42	188
40—45	1,290	669	621	10	1	609	390	50	230
45—50	940	498	442	3	3	452	208	43	231
50—55	766	383	383	..	1	339	142	44	240
55—60	497	224	273	1	1	194	70	29	202
60—65	438	185	253	..	1	150	52	35	200
65—70	171	76	95	1	..	58	16	17	79
70 and over	271	111	160	3	1	79	11	29	148
Tribal	**617,599**	**310,156**	**307,443**	**163,018**	**136,831**	**136,788**	**141,098**	**10,350**	**29,514**
0—1	23,357	11,628	11,729	11,409	11,604	217	123	2	2
1—2	22,871	11,158	11,713	10,980	11,568	176	145	2	..
2—3	26,224	12,722	13,502	12,542	13,285	177	215	3	2
3—4	26,617	13,062	13,555	12,776	13,217	280	323	6	15
4—5	24,150	12,087	12,063	11,702	11,623	372	407	13	33
Total 0—5	*123,219*	*60,657*	*62,562*	*59,409*	*61,297*	*1,222*	*1,213*	*26*	*52*
5—10	90,125	46,069	44,056	43,484	39,686	2,533	4,232	52	138
10—15	71,240	36,652	34,578	32,160	25,566	4,399	8,803	103	209
15—20	48,738	22,673	26,065	12,087	5,387	10,318	20,070	268	608
20—25	53,363	24,895	28,467	7,924	2,562	16,474	24,868	498	1,037
25—30	54,190	26,579	27,611	3,081	975	22,612	24,671	886	1,965
30—35	49,641	25,057	24,584	2,130	622	21,842	21,499	1,085	2,463
35—40	36,529	19,778	16,751	1,216	265	17,314	13,197	1,248	3,289
40—45	28,792	15,910	12,882	853	186	13,819	9,311	1,238	3,385
45—50	19,162	10,754	8,408	239	92	9,355	4,936	1,160	3,380
50—55	14,257	7,746	6,511	174	59	6,614	3,423	958	3,029
55—60	10,070	4,872	5,198	84	49	3,970	1,968	818	3,181
60—65	8,522	4,006	4,516	97	42	3,141	1,492	768	2,982
65—70	3,339	1,574	1,765	23	16	1,192	549	359	1,200
70 and over	6,412	2,923	3,489	57	27	1,983	866	883	2,596

Table VII.—Age, Sex and Civil Condition. Part II.—Provinces and States—*contd.*

Gwalior State.

Age and Religion.	Population.			Unmarried.		Married.		Widowed.	
	Persons.	Males.	Females.	Males.	Females.	Males.	Females.	Males.	Females.
1	2	3	4	5	6	7	8	9	10
All Religions	**3,523,070**	**1,867,031**	**1,656,039**	**874,082**	**542,564**	**851,956**	**831,717**	**140,993**	**281,758**
0—1	111,641	56,593	55,048	56,323	54,484	233	465	37	99
1—2	97,046	48,321	48,725	47,937	47,965	349	682	35	78
2—3	99,993	49,075	50,918	48,529	49,807	505	1,006	41	105
3—4	101,288	50,660	50,628	49,788	48,792	757	1,568	115	268
4—5	99,046	50,974	48,072	49,961	45,755	871	1,966	142	351
Total 0—5	*509,014*	*255,623*	*253,391*	*252,538*	*246,803*	*2,715*	*5,687*	*370*	*901*
5—10	448,541	239,108	209,433	222,230	164,106	15,872	43,254	1,006	2,073
10—15	431,207	233,911	197,296	192,292	104,420	39,553	89,430	2,066	3,446
15—20	352,983	186,671	166,312	85,022	12,784	96,912	146,628	4,737	6,900
20—25	353,248	185,484	167,764	51,785	5,133	126,554	152,241	7,145	10,390
25—30	303,758	162,907	140,851	22,268	2,406	130,222	121,087	10,417	17,358
30—35	267,031	145,826	121,205	15,147	1,797	118,055	97,619	12,624	21,789
35—40	222,880	121,433	101,447	9,962	1,215	94,772	67,070	16,699	33,162
40—45	188,838	102,652	86,186	7,846	1,012	76,935	48,314	17,871	36,860
45—50	143,771	78,451	65,320	5,313	702	55,039	25,779	18,099	38,839
50—55	109,023	58,716	50,307	3,810	532	39,408	16,765	15,498	33,010
55—60	75,312	38,595	36,717	2,147	489	23,932	7,844	12,516	28,384
60—65	61,307	30,206	31,101	1,635	515	18,139	5,483	10,432	25,103
65—70	23,221	11,489	11,732	772	282	5,983	1,958	4,734	9,492
70 and over	32,936	15,959	16,977	1,315	368	7,865	2,558	6,779	14,051
Hindus	**3,271,576**	**1,732,247**	**1,539,329**	**810,312**	**500,889**	**791,200**	**775,189**	**130,735**	**263,251**
0—1	103,855	52,717	51,138	52,463	50,642	220	424	34	72
1—2	90,135	44,877	45,258	44,519	44,573	329	627	29	58
2—3	92,899	45,589	47,310	45,086	46,295	467	925	36	90
3—4	94,053	47,066	46,987	46,277	45,290	679	1,448	110	249
4—5	92,089	47,437	44,652	46,504	42,496	801	1,837	132	319
Total 0—5	*473,031*	*237,686*	*235,345*	*234,849*	*229,296*	*2,496*	*5,261*	*341*	*788*
5—10	417,747	222,857	194,890	206,795	151,768	15,119	41,170	943	1,952
10—15	402,041	218,279	183,762	178,546	95,952	37,794	84,565	1,939	3,245
15—20	328,566	173,755	154,811	77,977	11,381	91,313	136,950	4,465	6,480
20—25	327,655	171,923	155,732	47,118	4,495	118,106	141,451	6,699	9,786
25—30	281,952	150,979	130,973	20,427	2,057	120,862	112,558	9,690	16,358
30—35	248,114	135,230	112,884	13,989	1,516	109,522	90,894	11,719	20,474
35—40	206,954	112,600	94,354	9,264	1,020	87,784	62,204	15,552	31,130
40—45	175,277	95,076	80,201	7,336	860	71,079	44,709	16,661	34,632
45—50	133,139	72,368	60,771	4,996	600	50,535	23,804	16,837	36,367
50—55	100,632	53,939	46,693	3,566	451	36,002	15,440	14,371	30,802
55—60	69,219	35,248	33,971	1,973	428	21,766	7,155	11,509	26,388
60—65	56,309	27,545	28,764	1,514	473	16,471	5,014	9,560	23,277
65—70	21,146	10,371	10,775	726	258	5,340	1,766	4,305	8,751
70 and over	29,794	14,391	15,403	1,236	334	7,011	2,248	6,144	12,821
Muslims	**204,297**	**109,412**	**94,885**	**51,546**	**34,450**	**50,133**	**46,586**	**7,733**	**13,849**
0—1	6,407	3,178	3,229	3,165	3,171	11	35	2	23
1—2	5,740	2,849	2,891	2,829	2,828	15	47	5	16
2—3	5,914	2,906	3,008	2,870	2,930	31	66	5	12
3—4	6,002	2,985	3,017	2,916	2,899	67	104	2	14
4—5	5,776	2,943	2,833	2,878	2,691	57	115	8	27
Total 0—5	*29,839*	*14,861*	*14,978*	*14,658*	*14,519*	*181*	*367*	*22*	*92*
5—10	25,459	13,430	12,029	12,757	10,121	620	1,804	53	104
10—15	23,920	12,769	11,151	11,199	6,939	1,466	4,056	104	156
15—20	20,078	10,613	9,465	5,725	1,217	4,663	7,944	225	304
20—25	21,047	11,209	9,838	3,789	541	7,042	8,867	378	430
25—30	17,688	9,735	7,953	1,362	288	7,777	6,976	596	689
30—35	15,138	8,498	6,640	782	236	7,005	5,507	711	897
35—40	12,736	7,052	5,684	429	176	5,732	4,024	891	1,484
40—45	10,744	6,005	4,739	293	124	4,817	2,968	895	1,647
45—50	8,326	4,770	3,556	165	77	3,723	1,600	882	1,879
50—55	6,483	3,685	2,798	138	67	2,766	1,064	781	1,667
55—60	4,691	2,585	2,106	108	53	1,742	558	735	1,495
60—65	3,936	2,083	1,853	71	38	1,364	402	648	1,413
65—70	1,595	839	756	29	23	509	165	301	568
70 and over	2,617	1,278	1,339	41	31	726	284	511	1,024
Jains	**45,079**	**24,238**	**20,841**	**11,629**	**6,695**	**10,148**	**9,578**	**2,461**	**4,568**
0—1	1,319	672	647	669	637	2	6	1	4
1—2	1,118	571	547	565	535	5	8	1	4
2—3	1,120	550	570	543	552	7	15	..	3
3—4	1,154	573	581	559	560	11	16	3	5
4—5	1,116	564	552	550	533	12	14	2	5
Total 0—5	*5,827*	*2,930*	*2,897*	*2,886*	*2,817*	*37*	*59*	*7*	*21*
5—10	5,099	2,695	2,404	2,554	2,111	131	277	10	16
10—15	5,022	2,746	2,276	2,434	1,429	291	802	21	45
15—20	4,147	2,225	1,922	1,256	126	923	1,682	46	114
20—25	4,353	2,253	2,100	819	64	1,368	1,864	66	172
25—30	3,944	2,094	1,850	448	42	1,520	1,500	126	308
30—35	3,593	1,990	1,603	355	30	1,447	1,163	188	410
35—40	3,043	1,693	1,350	260	14	1,184	796	249	540
40—45	2,692	1,489	1,203	210	22	972	607	307	574
45—50	2,216	1,258	958	146	22	740	356	372	580
50—55	1,817	1,039	778	97	8	604	242	338	528
55—60	1,337	723	614	62	5	393	120	268	489
60—65	1,020	552	468	48	2	285	61	219	405
65—70	467	272	195	17	1	129	26	126	168
70 and over	502	279	223	37	2	124	23	118	198

Table VII.—Age, Sex and Civil Condition. Part II.—Provinces and States—*contd.*

Hyderabad State.

Age and Religion		Population			Unmarried.		Married.		Widowed.	
		Persons.	Males.	Females.	Males.	Females.	Males.	Females.	Males.	Females.
1		2	3	4	5	6	7	8	9	10
All Religions	..	**14,436,148**	**7,370,010**	**7,066,138**	**3,124,066**	**2,199,822**	**3,878,362**	**3,763,422**	**367,582**	**1,102,894**
0—1	..	437,224	206,994	230,230	203,708	226,116	3,207	3,976	79	138
1—2	..	488,250	234,050	254,200	229,064	247,588	4,891	6,382	95	230
2—3	..	490,396	233,577	256,819	226,193	246,161	7,111	10,169	273	489
3—4	..	475,857	232,359	243,498	218,253	221,453	13,361	20,478	745	1,567
4—5	..	536,492	251,849	284,643	227,694	232,086	23,004	49,615	1,151	2,942
Total *0—5*	..	*2,428,219*	*1,158 829*	*1,269,390*	*1,104,912*	*1,173,404*	*51,574*	*90,620*	*2,343*	*5,366*
5—10	..	1,758,013	914,853	843,160	784,278	555,270	126,537	276,844	4,038	11,046
10—15	..	1,575,481	827,213	748,268	616,285	309,878	205,207	422,442	5,721	15,948
15—20	..	1,294,390	638,789	655,601	273,315	55,253	355,928	572,499	9,546	27,849
20—25	..	1,360,945	673,215	687,730	168,628	31,988	489,033	613,872	15,554	41,870
25—30	..	1,259,758	635,407	624,351	65,374	19,617	548,201	535,468	21,832	69,266
30—35	..	1,060,369	553,799	506,570	36,700	14,853	491,849	407,625	25,250	84,092
35—40	..	889,841	474,600	415,241	19,744	11,121	420,299	285,400	34,557	118,720
40—45	..	755,754	406,456	349,298	15,401	8,689	353,829	213,945	37,226	126,664
45—50	..	593,770	324,795	268,975	11,329	6,288	270,308	126,913	43,158	135,774
50—55	..	473,350	256,884	216,466	9,751	4,437	206,644	89,961	40,489	122,068
55—60	..	351,869	185,613	166,256	7,338	3,072	138,432	49,024	39,843	114,160
60—65	..	288,606	147,839	140,767	4,020	2,597	107,791	36,788	35,128	101,382
65—70	..	150,688	76,921	73,767	2,565	1,457	52,043	18,870	22,313	53,440
70 and over	..	195,095	94,797	100,298	3,526	1,898	60,687	23,151	30,584	75,249
Hindus ..	—	**12,176,727**	**6,203,053**	**5,973,674**	**2,571,180**	**1,792,752**	**3,308,661**	**3,221,299**	**323,212**	**959,623**
0—1	..	368,577	174,185	194,392	171,620	190,801	2,509	3,477	56	114
1—2	..	410,385	196,021	214,364	191,881	208,668	4,093	5,502	47	194
2—3	..	411,054	194,625	216,429	188,620	207,049	5,809	8,954	196	426
3—4	..	398,539	194,165	204,374	182,097	184,748	11,400	18,166	668	1,460
4—5	..	451,869	210,367	241,502	189,628	193,521	19,705	45,328	1,034	2,653
Total *0—5*	..	*2,040,424*	*969,363*	*1,071,061*	*923,846*	*984,787*	*43,516*	*81,427*	*2,001*	*4,847*
5—10	..	1,477,030	767,967	709,063	653,524	444,262	110,767	254,599	3,676	10,202
10—15	..	1,328,885	697,366	631,519	508,993	237,563	183,093	379,325	5,280	14,631
15—20	..	1,085,375	532,860	552,515	213,722	39,442	310,503	487,904	8,635	25,169
20—25	..	1,143,191	565,722	577,469	129,101	24,904	422,788	515,418	13,833	37,147
25—30	..	1,065,041	537,603	527,438	50,286	16,257	468,203	449,886	19,114	61,295
30—35	..	898,972	468,492	430,480	29,397	12,300	417,075	344,199	22,020	73,981
35—40	..	753,644	401,710	351,934	16,078	9,428	355,128	238,673	30,504	103,833
40—45	..	640,567	343,860	296,707	12,610	7,319	298,192	178,893	33,058	110,495
45—50	..	505,255	274,290	230,965	9,482	5,389	226,580	107,759	38,228	117,817
50—55	..	402,618	217,522	185,096	8,594	3,774	173,274	76,105	35,654	105,217
55—60	..	298,586	156,938	141,648	6,337	2,614	115,537	40,815	35,064	98,219
60—65	..	246,191	126,026	120,165	4,178	2,005	91,066	31,079	30,782	87,081
65—70	..	127,851	65,043	62,808	2,259	1,200	43,552	16,212	19,232	45,396
70 and over	..	163,097	78,291	84,806	2,773	1,508	49,387	19,005	26,131	64,293
Muslims —	—	**1,534,666**	**791,435**	**743,231**	**370,211**	**267,799**	**390,149**	**368,284**	**31,075**	**107,148**
0—1	..	45,459	21,480	23,979	20,988	23,630	474	332	18	17
1—2	..	50,171	24,662	25,509	24,121	24,981	515	507	26	21
2—3	..	50,129	24,784	25,345	23,858	24,539	875	765	51	41
3—4	..	48,351	24,169	24,182	22,828	22,846	1,281	1,257	60	79
4—5	..	54,888	26,940	27,948	24,576	25,254	2,281	2,486	83	208
Total *0—5*	..	*248,998*	*122,035*	*126,963*	*116,371*	*121,250*	*5,426*	*5,347*	*238*	*366*
5—10	..	182,954	95,048	87,906	83,629	73,288	11,175	14,012	244	606
10—15	..	164,680	86,439	78,241	71,590	49,633	14,564	27,658	285	950
15—20	..	147,168	75,384	71,784	43,803	11,219	30,973	58,545	608	2,020
20—25	..	151,417	74,626	76,791	29,447	4,591	44,063	68,502	1,116	3,698
25—30	..	133,044	66,238	66,806	10,874	2,064	53,496	58,635	1,868	6,107
30—35	..	111,137	58,837	52,300	5,262	1,691	51,260	42,829	2,315	7,780
35—40	..	94,788	50,292	44,496	2,782	1,011	44,610	32,180	2,900	11,305
40—45	..	80,217	43,190	37,027	2,130	862	38,099	23,991	2,961	12,174
45—50	..	62,900	35,737	27,163	1,398	597	30,931	13,131	3,408	13,435
50—55	..	50,251	27,953	22,298	856	454	23,739	9,233	3,358	12,611
55—60	..	38,412	20,593	17,819	671	336	16,565	5,594	3,357	11,889
60—65	..	29,954	15,059	14,895	565	414	11,371	3,940	3,123	10,541
65—70	..	15,936	8,281	7,655	195	153	5,919	1,671	2,167	5,831
70 and over	..	22,810	11,723	11,087	638	236	7,958	3,016	3,127	7,835
Tribal ...	—	**544,789**	**280,584**	**264,205**	**139,769**	**109,005**	**132,130**	**130,101**	**8,685**	**25,099**
0—1	..	18,049	8,712	9,337	8,521	9,183	188	147	3	7
1—2	..	21,915	10,430	11,485	10,166	11,129	243	341	21	15
2—3	..	23,263	11,156	12,107	10,763	11,708	369	383	24	16
3—4	..	23,335	11,208	12,127	10,635	11,190	561	917	12	20
4—5	..	23,113	11,571	11,542	10,801	10,025	748	1,465	22	52
Total *0—5*	..	*109,675*	*53,077*	*56,598*	*50,886*	*53,235*	*2,109*	*3,253*	*82*	*110*
5—10	..	77,228	40,809	36,419	37,269	30,140	3,441	6,116	99	163
10—15	..	62,465	32,760	29,705	27,304	17,948	5,355	11,502	101	255
15—20	..	45,095	21,798	23,297	11,386	3,163	10,206	19,673	206	461
20—25	..	48,266	23,280	24,986	6,854	1,651	15,994	22,638	432	697
25—30	..	45,719	23,029	22,690	2,736	916	19,722	20,523	571	1,251
30—35	..	36,995	19,460	17,535	1,394	573	17,517	15,371	549	1,591
35—40	..	30,174	16,761	13,413	579	427	15,477	10,548	705	2,438
40—45	..	25,282	14,167	11,115	395	280	12,999	8,116	773	2,719
45—50	..	18,144	10,641	7,503	268	145	9,398	4,245	975	3,113
50—55	..	14,568	8,191	6,377	179	141	7,037	3,329	975	2,907
55—60	..	10,619	5,757	4,862	235	83	4,562	1,919	960	2,860
60—65	..	9,106	4,914	4,192	127	130	3,974	1,328	813	2,734
65—70	..	4,862	2,552	2,310	77	53	1,856	684	619	1,573
70 and over	..	6,591	3,388	3,203	80	120	2,483	856	825	2,227

Table VII.—Age, Sex and Civil Condition. Part II.—Provinces and States—*contd.*

Jammu and Kashmir State.

Age and Religion.	Population.			Unmarried.		Married.		Widowed.	
	Persons.	Males.	Females.	Males.	Females.	Males.	Females.	Males.	Females.
1	2	3	4	5	6	7	8	9	10
All Religions	**3,646,243**	**1,938,338**	**1,707,905**	**1,025,160**	**690,139**	**799,073**	**834,460**	**114,105**	**183,306**
0—1	115,930	58,323	57,607	58,323	57,607	..	..	..	..
1—2	118,293	59,284	59,009	59,284	59,009	..	..	..	..
2—3	117,790	59,099	58,791	59,099	58,790	..	1	..	..
3—4	115,806	58,525	57,281	58,523	57,267	2	14	..	..
4—5	111,623	56,700	54,923	56,617	54,829	82	84	1	10
Total 0—5	*579,542*	*291,931*	*287,611*	291,846	287,502	*84*	*99*	*1*	*10*
5—10	469,120	253,182	215,938	248,562	206,597	4,512	9,055	108	286
10—15	429,988	234,021	195,967	221,797	152,339	11,877	42,605	347	1,023
15—20	350,597	178,694	171,903	120,218	30,842	56,165	137,426	2,311	3,635
20—25	364,687	182,675	182,012	80,253	7,269	97,466	169,172	4,956	5,571
25—30	323,912	167,877	156,035	27,278	1,996	131,202	145,270	9,397	8,769
30—35	287,468	156,681	130,787	14,456	1,354	131,227	118,272	10,998	11,161
35—40	215,654	120,001	95,653	6,560	707	102,282	78,031	11,159	16,915
40—45	164,794	91,981	72,813	4,562	453	77,013	53,839	10,406	18,521
45—50	127,624	72,028	55,596	3,054	313	57,823	32,485	11,151	22,798
50—55	101,362	57,413	43,949	2,263	236	44,767	22,578	10,383	21,135
55—60	76,943	43,698	33,245	1,549	172	30,984	11,248	11,165	21,825
60—65	64,878	36,427	28,451	1,231	133	24,897	8,203	10,299	20,115
65—70	31,348	18,084	13,264	552	78	11,059	2,762	6,473	10,424
70 and over	58,326	33,645	24,681	979	148	17,715	3,415	14,951	21,118
Muslims	**2,817,636**	**1,497,252**	**1,320,384**	**793,219**	**548,544**	**622,590**	**656,226**	**81,443**	**115,614**
0—1	89,960	45,223	44,737	45,223	44,737	..	..	..	..
1—2	94,926	47,580	47,346	47,580	47,346	..	..	..	..
2—3	94,485	47,347	47,138	47,347	47,137	..	1	..	..
3—4	92,246	46,736	45,510	46,734	45,497	2	13	..	..
4—5	88,368	45,392	42,976	45,348	42,928	44	48	..	..
Total 0—5	*469,985*	*232,278*	*227,707*	*232,232*	*227,645*	*46*	*62*	..	..
5—10	372,408	201,588	170,820	198,460	164,520	3,067	6,162	61	138
10—15	339,907	185,953	153,954	176,496	121,885	9,217	31,505	240	564
15—20	273,180	139,253	133,927	91,814	25,163	45,643	106,658	1,796	2,106
20—25	285,425	142,345	143,080	58,995	5,807	79,376	134,091	3,974	3,182
25—30	252,669	130,021	122,648	17,999	1,280	104,652	116,543	7,370	4,825
30—35	222,964	120,825	102,139	8,414	848	103,983	94,984	8,428	6,307
35—40	165,195	92,033	73,162	3,345	502	80,523	62,377	8,165	10,283
40—45	121,925	68,316	53,609	2,168	284	58,852	41,961	7,296	11,364
45—50	91,735	51,810	39,925	1,233	176	43,040	24,985	7,537	14,764
50—55	71,868	40,588	31,280	786	128	32,926	17,401	6,876	13,751
55—60	53,474	30,492	22,982	436	96	22,487	8,561	7,569	14,325
60—65	45,286	25,471	19,815	345	77	18,086	6,296	7,040	13,442
65—70	20,912	12,180	8,732	157	39	7,728	2,030	4,295	6,663
70 and over	40,703	24,099	16,604	339	94	12,964	2,610	10,796	13,900
Hindus	**736,222**	**393,699**	**342,523**	**207,560**	**121,645**	**156,253**	**157,962**	**29,886**	**62,916**
0—1	22,901	11,521	11,380	11,521	11,380	..	..	..	..
1—2	20,648	10,342	10,306	10,342	10,306	..	..	..	..
2—3	20,614	10,393	10,221	10,393	10,221	..	..	..	..
3—4	20,742	10,390	10,352	10,390	10,352	..	..	..	..
4—5	20,558	9,972	10,586	9,937	10,543	34	34	1	9
Total 0—5	*105,463*	*52,618*	*52,845*	*52,583*	*52,802*	*34*	*34*	*1*	*9*
5—10	85,225	45,535	39,690	44,096	36,789	1,395	2,759	44	142
10—15	79,796	42,696	37,100	40,083	26,263	2,510	10,402	103	435
15—20	69,295	35,540	33,755	25,897	4,202	9,184	28,111	459	1,442
20—25	70,993	36,397	34,596	19,683	679	15,836	31,643	878	2,274
25—30	63,701	34,074	29,627	8,700	378	23,514	25,513	1,860	3,736
30—35	57,714	32,257	25,457	5,659	283	24,216	20,591	2,382	4,583
35—40	45,021	25,090	19,931	2,978	68	19,327	13,624	2,785	6,239
40—45	38,271	21,223	17,048	2,188	50	16,144	10,254	2,891	6,744
45—50	31,897	18,070	13,827	1,645	36	13,079	6,307	3,346	7,484
50—55	26,102	15,019	11,083	1,336	22	10,431	4,186	3,252	6,875
55—60	20,824	11,812	9,012	1,011	27	7,496	2,049	3,305	6,936
60—65	17,257	9,712	7,545	796	16	5,956	1,408	2,960	6,121
65—70	9,057	5,170	3,887	342	8	2,905	499	1,923	3,380
70 and over	15,606	8,486	7,120	563	22	4,226	582	3,697	6,516
Sikhs	**50,662**	**26,457**	**24,205**	**14,729**	**10,470**	**10,324**	**11,285**	**1,404**	**2,450**
0—1	2,002	1,033	969	1,033	969	..	..	..	..
1—2	1,837	916	921	916	921	..	..	..	..
2—3	1,828	913	915	913	915	..	..	..	..
3—4	1,802	920	882	920	881	..	1	..	..
4—5	1,770	869	901	865	898	4	2	..	1
Total 0—5	*9,239*	*4,651*	*4,588*	*4,647*	*4,584*	*4*	*3*	..	*1*
5—10	7,087	3,856	3,231	3,808	3,098	46	127	2	6
10—15	6,224	3,359	2,865	3,237	2,219	119	629	3	17
15—20	4,730	2,236	2,494	1,528	426	682	2,022	26	46
20—25	4,692	2,156	2,536	911	67	1,189	2,415	56	54
25—30	4,139	2,068	2,071	247	20	1,715	1,936	106	115
30—35	3,697	2,011	1,686	136	14	1,751	1,507	124	165
35—40	2,688	1,477	1,211	68	10	1,286	961	123	240
40—45	2,139	1,197	942	46	5	1,021	689	130	248
45—50	1,713	971	742	29	14	800	426	142	302
50—55	1,300	745	555	20	11	599	279	126	265
55—60	979	566	413	18	1	405	129	143	283
60—65	815	472	343	15	..	316	85	141	258
65—70	449	265	184	8	1	161	38	96	145
70 and over	771	427	344	11	..	230	39	186	305

Table VII.—Age, Sex and Civil Condition. Part II.—Provinces and States—*contd.*

Mysore State.

Age and Religion.	Population.			Unmarried.		Married.		Widowed.	
	Persons.	Males.	Females.	Males.	Females.	Males.	Females.	Males.	Females.
1	2	3	4	5	6	7	8	9	10
All religions ..	**6,557,302**	**3,353,963**	**3,203,339**	**1,866,180**	**1,295,533**	**1,318,017**	**1,339,597**	**169,766**	**568,209**
0—1 ..	176,771	86,822	89,949	86,822	89,949	..	..	..	..
1—2 ..	181,494	88,935	92,559	88,935	92,559	..	..	..	..
2—3 ..	191,638	93,117	98,521	93,117	98,521	..	..	..	..
3—4 ..	190,352	93,004	97,348	92,999	97,333	5	14	..	1
4—5 ..	189,705	93,976	95,729	93,970	95,704	6	25	..	..
Total 0—5 ..	*929,960*	*455,854*	*474,106*	*455,843*	*474,066*	*11*	*39*	..	*1*
5—10 ..	882,466	440,978	441,488	440,602	419,942	359	21,224	17	322
10—15 ..	814,673	420,275	394,398	417,939	317,240	2,270	75,699	66	1,459
15—20 ..	602,622	305,621	297,001	260,784	53,349	43,851	233,262	986	10,390
20—25 ..	612,368	295,141	317,227	180,474	15,055	111,695	281,163	2,972	21,009
25—30 ..	549,596	272,035	277,561	59,277	4,561	204,546	232,002	8,212	40,998
30—35 ..	501,043	262,459	238,584	26,985	3,337	223,715	183,795	11,759	51,452
35—40 ..	409,297	228,090	181,207	9,823	2,243	201,770	113,990	16,497	64,974
40—45 ..	341,640	192,177	149,463	5,740	1,712	168,307	81,770	18,130	65,981
45—50 ..	255,608	139,621	115,987	3,012	1,142	116,840	47,636	19,769	67,209
50—55 ..	199,137	104,432	94,705	2,043	880	84,009	33,056	18,380	60,769
55—60 ..	153,599	78,970	74,629	1,325	675	58,157	16,714	19,488	57,240
60—65 ..	130,456	66,415	64,041	1,019	572	46,825	11,257	18,571	52,212
65—70 ..	69,937	36,518	33,419	525	305	23,645	4,024	12,348	29,090
70 and over ..	104,900	55,377	49,523	789	454	32,017	3,966	22,571	45,103
Hindus ..	**6,015,880**	**3,066,332**	**2,949,548**	**1,698,330**	**1,179,037**	**1,207,961**	**1,235,571**	**160,041**	**534,940**
0—1 ..	161,716	79,268	82,448	79,268	82,448	..	..	..	..
1—2 ..	165,354	80,860	84,494	80,860	84,494	..	..	..	..
2—3 ..	174,573	84,718	89,855	84,718	89,855	..	..	..	..
3—4 ..	173,434	84,725	88,709	84,721	88,694	4	14	..	1
4—5 ..	172,471	85,538	86,933	85,532	86,908	6	25	..	..
Total 0—5 ..	*847,548*	*415,109*	*432,439*	*415,099*	*432,399*	*10*	*39*	..	*1*
5—10 ..	807,003	402,406	404,597	402,069	383,786	320	20,506	17	305
10—15 ..	746,570	384,525	362,045	382,342	289,420	2,119	71,246	64	1,379
15—20 ..	550,128	278,191	271,937	236,609	46,886	40,693	215,209	889	9,842
20—25 ..	559,172	267,787	291,385	162,030	12,795	103,002	258,619	2,755	19,971
25—30 ..	504,708	248,382	256,326	53,418	3,943	187,250	213,331	7,714	39,052
30—35 ..	461,437	240,377	221,060	24,489	2,913	204,839	169,183	11,049	48,964
35—40 ..	378,017	209,842	168,175	9,027	1,950	185,222	104,854	15,593	61,371
40—45 ..	315,642	176,916	138,726	5,308	1,497	154,409	75,135	17,199	62,094
45—50 ..	235,930	128,158	107,772	2,746	995	106,721	43,850	18,691	62,927
50—55 ..	183,965	95,842	88,123	1,880	757	76,556	30,489	17,406	56,877
55—60 ..	142,341	72,674	69,667	1,195	578	53,061	15,401	18,418	53,688
60—65 ..	121,211	61,292	59,919	938	501	42,813	10,374	17,541	49,044
65—70 ..	64,976	33,687	31,289	466	251	21,634	3,710	11,587	27,328
70 and over ..	97,232	51,144	46,088	714	366	29,312	3,625	21,118	42,097
Muslims ..	**398,628**	**213,381**	**185,247**	**124,513**	**84,477**	**82,067**	**77,290**	**6,801**	**23,480**
0—1 ..	10,996	5,539	5,457	5,539	5,457	..	..	..	..
1—2 ..	12,047	5,981	6,066	5,981	6,066	..	..	..	..
2—3 ..	12,772	6,225	6,547	6,225	6,547	..	..	..	..
3—4 ..	12,805	6,213	6,592	6,213	6,592	..	..	..	..
4—5 ..	13,301	6,478	6,823	6,478	6,823	..	..	..	..
Total 0—5 ..	*61,921*	*30,436*	*31,485*	*30,436*	*31,485*	..	..	..	..
5—10 ..	57,145	29,284	27,861	29,256	27,337	28	510	..	14
10—15 ..	50,954	26,955	23,999	26,848	20,439	105	3,500	2	60
15—20 ..	38,074	20,184	17,890	17,840	3,792	2,278	13,735	66	363
20—25 ..	38,610	20,020	18,590	13,349	914	6,516	16,977	155	699
25—30 ..	32,593	17,228	15,365	4,014	171	12,850	13,869	364	1,325
30—35 ..	28,846	16,207	12,639	1,649	109	14,041	10,795	517	1,735
35—40 ..	22,829	13,505	9,324	504	69	12,372	6,737	629	2,518
40—45 ..	18,826	11,270	7,556	257	41	10,370	4,790	643	2,725
45—50 ..	14,195	8,445	5,750	149	31	7,576	2,663	720	3,056
50—55 ..	10,913	6,309	4,604	84	22	5,556	1,790	669	2,792
55—60 ..	8,022	4,560	3,462	48	27	3,789	871	723	2,564
60—65 ..	6,570	3,688	2,882	24	12	2,959	593	705	2,277
65—70 ..	3,473	2,034	1,439	23	13	1,478	217	533	1,209
70 and over ..	5,657	3,256	2,401	32	15	2,149	243	1,075	2,143
Christians ..	**87,538**	**45,164**	**42,374**	**27,048**	**21,273**	**16,671**	**15,692**	**1,445**	**5,409**
0—1 ..	2,499	1,256	1,243	1,256	1,243	..	..	..	..
1—2 ..	2,557	1,322	1,235	1,322	1,235	..	..	..	..
2—3 ..	2,634	1,353	1,281	1,353	1,281	..	..	..	..
3—4 ..	2,442	1,247	1,195	1,247	1,195	..	..	..	..
4—5 ..	2,317	1,161	1,156	1,161	1,156	..	..	..	..
Total 0—5 ..	*12,449*	*6,339*	*6,110*	*6,339*	*6,110*	..	..	..	..
5—10 ..	10,904	5,520	5,384	5,516	5,354	4	30	..	..
10—15 ..	10,345	5,180	5,165	5,161	4,798	19	362	..	5
15—20 ..	9,134	4,490	4,644	4,070	2,224	410	2,334	10	86
20—25 ..	9,269	4,666	4,603	3,504	1,241	1,137	3,185	25	177
25—30 ..	7,573	3,994	3,579	1,314	408	2,616	2,863	64	308
30—35 ..	6,578	3,562	3,016	587	301	2,885	2,328	90	387
35—40 ..	5,140	2,812	2,328	176	220	2,520	1,519	116	589
40—45 ..	4,412	2,379	2,033	104	171	2,151	1,198	124	664
45—50 ..	3,348	1,799	1,549	68	112	1,566	724	165	713
50—55 ..	2,668	1,425	1,243	51	98	1,221	505	153	640
55—60 ..	1,975	1,062	913	56	67	827	298	179	548
60—65 ..	1,625	866	759	44	59	650	204	172	496
65—70 ..	899	475	424	28	39	321	71	126	314
70 and over ..	1,219	595	624	30	71	344	71	221	482

Table VII.—Age, Sex and Civil Condition. Part II.—Provinces and States—*contd.*

Age and Religion.	Population.			Unmarried.		Married.		Widowed.	
	Persons.	Males.	Females.	Males.	Females.	Males.	Females.	Males.	Females.
1	2	3	4	5	6	7	8	9	10
***Madras States.**									
All Religions ..	**453,495**	**218,146**	**235,349**	**119,230**	**92,979**	**88,772**	**96,815**	**10,144**	**45,555**
0—1 ..	6,451	3,178	3,273	3,178	3,273	..	..	..	..
1—2 ..	10,810	5,248	5,562	5,248	5,562	..	..	..	..
2—3 ..	10,203	5,031	5,172	5,031	5,171	..	1	..	..
3—4 ..	13,006	6,366	6,640	6,365	6,639	1	1	..	..
4—5 ..	11,479	5,679	5,800	5,678	5,794	1	6	..	..
Total 0—5 ..	*51,949*	*25,502*	*26,447*	*25,500*	*26,489*	*2*	*8*	..	..
5—10 ..	59,246	29,285	29,961	29,257	29,680	27	270	1	11
10—15 ..	51,296	26,255	25,041	26,028	23,511	224	1,497	3	33
15—20 ..	39,925	19,886	20,039	18,204	10,105	1,653	9,644	29	290
20—25 ..	38,871	17,695	21,176	10,987	2,072	6,586	17,948	122	1,156
25—30 ..	41,762	18,942	22,820	5,594	580	12,819	19,894	529	2,346
30—35 ..	37,322	16,890	20,432	1,990	228	14,098	16,329	802	3,875
35—40 ..	32,192	15,859	16,333	777	138	14,070	11,413	1,012	4,782
40—45 ..	27,994	13,191	14,803	404	74	11,693	8,219	1,094	6,510
45—50 ..	21,096	10,231	10,865	170	55	8,924	5,036	1,137	5,774
50—55 ..	18,359	8,236	10,123	148	46	6,851	3,439	1,237	6,638
55—60 ..	11,985	5,947	6,038	75	16	4,738	1,609	1,134	4,413
60—65 ..	10,714	4,991	5,723	46	19	3,688	939	1,257	4,765
65—70 ..	4,673	2,320	2,353	17	4	1,628	310	675	2,039
70 and over ..	6,111	2,916	3,195	33	12	1,771	260	1,112	2,923
Cochin State.									
All Religions ..	**1,205,016**	**589,813**	**615,203**	**346,342**	**287,327**	**223,439**	**238,324**	**20,032**	**89,552**
0—1 ..	40,043	20,083	19,960	20,083	19,960	..	..	..	..
1—2 ..	44,940	22,477	22,463	22,477	22,463	..	..	..	..
2—3 ..	41,802	20,933	20,869	20,933	20,869	..	..	..	..
3—4 ..	37,072	18,629	18,443	18,629	18,443	..	..	..	..
4—5 ..	34,240	17,304	16,936	17,304	16,934	..	1	..	1
Total 0—5 ..	*198,097*	*99,426*	*98,671*	*99,426*	*98,669*	..	*1*	..	*1*
5—10 ..	156,302	79,218	77,084	79,195	76,551	22	512	1	21
10—15 ..	148,115	74,869	73,246	74,607	68,155	249	4,885	13	206
15—20 ..	117,905	55,964	61,941	47,350	27,168	8,307	32,864	307	1,909
20—25 ..	108,729	49,736	58,993	36,630	11,275	18,413	44,577	693	3,141
25—30 ..	91,521	42,145	49,376	7,686	2,121	33,282	41,994	1,177	5,261
30—35 ..	84,494	40,050	44,444	3,705	1,301	35,092	36,701	1,253	6,442
35—40 ..	69,792	34,736	35,056	1,325	687	31,849	25,627	1,562	8,742
40—45 ..	61,286	30,793	30,493	896	545	28,186	20,388	1,711	9,560
45—50 ..	47,363	23,748	23,615	549	316	21,170	12,631	2,029	10,668
50—55 ..	40,625	20,478	20,147	429	229	17,800	9,274	2,249	10,644
55—60 ..	29,219	14,448	14,771	225	131	11,797	4,461	2,426	10,179
60—65 ..	23,256	11,174	12,082	160	95	8,768	2,825	2,246	9,162
65—70 ..	12,410	5,871	6,539	79	35	4,191	951	1,601	5,553
70 and over ..	15,902	7,157	8,745	80	49	4,313	633	2,764	8,063
Hindus ..	**780,484**	**377,933**	**402,551**	**220,430**	**181,190**	**143,845**	**155,846**	**13,658**	**65,515**
0—1 ..	25,406	12,645	12,761	12,645	12,761	..	..	..	..
1—2 ..	28,741	14,282	14,459	14,282	14,459	..	..	..	..
2—3 ..	26,741	13,308	13,433	13,308	13,433	..	..	..	..
3—4	23,467	11,777	11,690	11,777	11,690	..	..	..	..
4—5 ..	21,606	10,925	10,681	10,925	10,679	..	1	..	1
Total 0—5 ..	*125,961*	*62,937*	*63,024*	*62,937*	*63,022*	..	*1*	..	*1*
5—10 ..	98,770	50,177	48,593	50,168	48,169	8	409	1	15
10—15 ..	93,838	47,514	46,324	47,351	42,612	154	3,543	9	169
15—20 ..	75,492	35,365	40,127	30,107	16,895	5,000	21,648	258	1,584
20—25 ..	70,234	31,535	38,699	19,572	7,149	11,379	29,015	584	2,535
25—30 ..	60,100	27,257	32,843	5,149	1,371	21,175	27,397	933	4,075
30—35 ..	55,628	25,972	29,656	2,571	819	22,457	23,977	944	4,860
35—40 ..	46,388	22,703	23,685	923	395	20,681	16,845	1,099	6,445
40—45 ..	40,818	20,183	20,635	625	300	18,384	13,340	1,174	6,995
45—50 ..	31,703	15,619	16,084	378	157	13,891	8,146	1,350	7,781
50—55 ..	27,250	13,458	13,792	289	120	11,689	5,950	1,480	7,722
55—60 ..	19,648	9,452	10,196	151	74	7,699	2,817	1,602	7,305
60—65 ..	15,768	7,344	8,424	111	56	5,746	1,794	1,487	6,574
65—70 ..	8,359	3,842	4,517	51	24	2,755	587	1,036	3,906
70 and over ..	10,527	4,575	5,952	47	27	2,827	377	1,701	5,548
Christians ..	**334,870**	**166,195**	**168,675**	**98,603**	**85,470**	**62,384**	**64,982**	**5,208**	**18,223**
0—1 ..	11,763	5,950	5,813	5,950	5,813	..	..	..	..
1—2 ..	12,881	6,509	6,372	6,509	6,372	..	..	..	..
2—3 ..	11,881	5,999	5,882	5,999	5,882	..	..	..	..
3—4 ..	10,752	5,392	5,360	5,392	5,360	..	..	..	..
4—5 ..	9,918	4,991	4,927	4,991	4,927	..	..	..	..
Total 0—5 ..	*57,195*	*28,841*	*28,354*	*28,841*	*28,354*	..	..	..	..
5—10 ..	45,410	22,819	22,591	22,813	22,536	6	52	..	3
10—15 ..	42,833	21,490	21,393	21,414	20,491	72	888	4	14
15—20 ..	33,305	16,139	17,166	13,411	8,560	2,706	8,462	22	144
20—25 ..	29,958	14,176	15,782	8,480	3,555	5,639	11,908	57	319
25—30 ..	24,278	11,454	12,824	1,830	671	9,473	11,387	151	766
30—35 ..	22,349	10,798	11,551	832	436	9,755	10,024	211	1,091
35—40 ..	18,243	9,271	8,972	327	269	8,587	7,018	357	1,685
40—45 ..	16,107	8,232	7,875	228	227	7,576	5,725	428	1,923
45—50 ..	12,513	6,397	6,116	147	148	5,687	3,763	563	2,205
50—55 ..	10,831	5,619	5,212	116	104	4,852	2,855	651	2,253
55—60 ..	7,798	4,046	3,752	62	53	3,279	1,438	705	2,261
60—65 ..	6,139	3,122	3,017	45	36	2,426	910	651	2,071
65—70 ..	3,370	1,635	1,715	26	10	1,141	323	488	1,382
70 and over ..	4,491	2,136	2,355	31	20	1,185	229	920	2,106

* Excludes Cochin and Travancore, separate details for which have been given.

Table VII.—Age, Sex and Civil Condition, Part II.— Provinces and States—*contd.*

Age and Religion.		Population.			Unmarried.		Married.		Widowed.	
		Persons.	Males.	Females.	Males.	Females.	Males.	Females.	Males.	Females.
1		2	3	4	5	6	7	8	9	10

Travancore State.

Age and Religion.		Persons.	Males.	Females.	Unmarried Males.	Unmarried Females.	Married Males.	Married Females.	Widowed Males.	Widowed Females.
Religions ..	..	**5,095,973**	**2,565,073**	**2,530,900**	**1,498,635**	**1,202,104**	**993,386**	**1,027,297**	**73,052**	**301,499**
0—1	..	211,940	106,460	105,480	106,460	105,480	..	..	..	..
1—2	..	184,135	91,998	92,137	91,998	92,137	..	..	..	..
2—3	..	172,712	86,936	85,776	86,936	85,776	..	..	..	..
3—4	..	158,571	79,741	78,830	79,741	78,830	..	..	..	..
4—5	..	149,884	75,716	74,168	75,716	74,168	..	..	..	..
Total 0—5	..	*877,242*	*440,851*	*436,391*	*440,851*	*436,391*	..	..	..	..
5—10	..	673,095	341,345	331,750	340,936	329,195	388	2,484	21	71
10—15	..	617,939	313,728	304,211	310,930	279,988	2,722	23,714	76	509
15—20	..	487,912	238,499	249,413	193,904	96,735	43,472	147,589	1,123	5,089
20—25	..	461,356	221,670	239,686	131,831	38,861	87,491	192,115	2,348	8,710
25—30	..	389,368	193,529	195,839	38,823	7,700	150,401	172,989	4,305	15,150
30—35	..	358,098	181,818	176,280	19,944	4,822	157,103	152,438	4,771	19,020
35—40	..	288,368	150,647	137,721	7,275	2,546	137,860	108,358	5,512	26,817
40—45	..	251,634	131,767	119,867	5,033	1,944	120,665	87,210	6,069	30,713
45—50	..	194,623	100,884	93,739	3,193	1,235	90,088	55,286	7,603	37,218
50—55	..	165,984	86,050	79,934	2,491	970	75,479	41,265	8,080	37,699
55—60	..	118,704	60,335	58,369	1,270	627	50,437	21,059	8,628	36,683
60—65	..	95,449	48,006	47,443	924	473	38,702	13,651	8,380	33,319
65—70	..	50,932	25,241	25,691	523	259	18,709	4,857	6,009	20,575
70 and over	..	65,269	30,703	34,566	707	358	19,869	4,282	10,127	29,926
Hindus ..	..	**3,134,888**	**1,567,925**	**1,566,963**	**925,474**	**732,135**	**596,843**	**625,107**	**45,601**	**209,721**
0—1	..	128,936	64,604	64,332	64,604	64,332	..	..	..	..
1—2	..	111,382	55,486	55,896	55,486	55,896	..	..	..	..
2—3	..	104,837	52,471	52,366	52,471	52,366	..	..	..	..
3—4	..	96,342	48,436	47,906	48,436	47,906	..	..	..	..
4—5	..	90,245	45,494	44,751	45,494	44,751	..	..	..	..
Total 0—5		*531,742*	*266,491*	*265,251*	*266,491*	*265,251*	..	..	..	..
5—10	..	402,939	204,082	198,857	203,909	197,452	160	1,362	13	43
10—15	..	370,245	187,834	182,411	186,680	168,676	1,102	13,372	52	363
15—20	..	296,862	143,821	153,041	122,237	61,122	20,784	88,138	800	3,781
20—25	..	283,702	135,005	148,697	86,981	25,490	46,364	116,790	1,660	6,417
25—30	..	243,333	119,983	123,350	27,743	5,187	89,297	107,159	2,943	1,004
30—35	..	224,827	113,330	111,497	14,723	3,330	95,407	94,575	3,200	3,592
35—40	..	182,132	94,455	87,677	5,665	1,756	85,255	67,061	3,535	18,860
40—45	..	159,183	82,647	76,536	3,937	1,326	74,904	53,804	3,806	21,406
45—50	..	123,598	63,360	60,238	2,536	839	56,150	33,555	4,674	25,844
50—55	..	105,779	54,198	51,581	2,002	634	47,248	24,693	4,948	26,254
55—60	..	76,429	38,233	38,196	993	379	31,941	12,267	5,299	25,550
60—65	..	61,544	30,413	31,131	712	303	24,537	7,707	5,164	23,121
65—70	..	32,257	15,599	16,658	368	166	11,597	2,503	3,634	13,989
70 and over	..	40,316	18,474	21,842	497	224	12,097	2,121	5,880	19,497

North-West Frontier Province.
(*Agencies and Tribal Areas.*)

Age and Religion.		Persons.	Males.	Females.	Unmarried Males.	Unmarried Females.	Married Males.	Married Females.	Widowed Males.	Widowed Females.
All Religions	..	**46,451**	**44,635**	**1,816**	**19,415**	**881**	**23,827**	**802**	**1,393**	**133**
0—1	..	174	90	84	90	84	..	..	..	..
1—2	..	133	59	74	59	74	..	..	..	..
2—3	..	145	73	72	73	72	..	..	..	..
3—4	..	151	79	72	79	72	..	..	..	..
4—5	..	147	76	71	76	71	..	..	..	..
Total 0—5	..	*750*	*377*	*373*	*377*	*373*	..	..	..	..
5—10	..	641	368	273	363	269	5	4	..	..
10—15	..	778	562	216	522	186	39	29	1	1
15—20	..	8,791	8,607	184	5,721	30	2,777	150	109	4
20—25	..	12,983	12,763	220	7,481	11	5,065	202	217	7
25—30	..	10,035	9,872	163	3,160	2	6,366	155	346	6
30—35	..	7,008	6,892	116	1,299	3	5,286	108	307	5
35—40	..	2,677	2,598	79	290	4	2,164	62	144	13
40—45	..	1,451	1,393	58	134	..	1,159	41	100	17
45—50	..	600	558	42	32	1	460	24	66	17
50—55	..	360	332	28	21	..	268	12	43	16
55—60	..	154	132	22	7	..	106	5	19	17
60—65	..	112	88	24	2	1	70	6	16	17
65—70	..	43	36	7	1	..	25	2	10	5
70 and over		68	57	11	5	1	37	2	15	8

Punjab States.

Age and Religion.		Persons.	Males.	Females.	Unmarried Males.	Unmarried Females.	Married Males.	Married Females.	Widowed Males.	Widowed Females.
All Religions	..	**437,787**	**229,290**	**208,497**	**103,208**	**71,253**	**107,046**	**107,869**	**19,036**	**29,375**
0—1	..	13,392	6,630	6,762	6,630	6,760	..	2	..	..
1—2	..	9,988	4,937	5,051	4,937	5,051	..	..	..	..
2—3	..	11,123	5,383	5,740	5,382	5,738	1	2	..	..
3—4	..	11,482	5,613	5,869	5,598	5,835	15	34	..	..
4—5	..	11,287	5,618	5,669	5,577	5,582	37	85	4	2
Total 0—5	..	*57,272*	*28,181*	*29,091*	*28,124*	*28,966*	*53*	*123*	*4*	*2*
5—10	..	50,210	25,975	24,235	24,816	20,950	1,120	3,235	39	50
10—15	..	47,466	25,198	22,268	22,108	14,551	2,986	7,556	104	161
15—20	..	39,635	20,436	19,199	11,226	3,203	8,739	15,530	471	466
20—25	..	39,332	19,831	19,501	7,166	1,533	11,888	17,267	777	701
25—30	..	37,367	19,083	18,284	3,188	597	14,606	16,467	1,289	1,220
30—35	..	35,474	18,569	16,905	2,222	428	14,804	14,848	1,543	1,629
35—40	..	28,853	15,490	13,363	1,280	279	12,432	10,558	1,778	2,526
40—45	..	24,727	13,426	11,301	958	220	10,645	8,198	1,823	2,883
45—50	..	21,343	11,858	9,485	678	161	9,101	5,562	2,079	3,762
50—55	..	18,115	10,099	8,016	520	137	7,555	4,191	2,024	3,688
55—60	..	13,460	7,516	5,944	340	83	5,095	2,066	2,081	3,795
60—65	..	11,038	6,156	4,882	274	58	3,984	1,429	1,898	3,395
65—70	..	5,497	3,142	2.355	132	33	1,820	423	1,190	1,899
70 and over	..	7,998	1,330	3,668	176	54	2,218	416	1,936	3,198

Table VII.—Age, Sex and Civil Condition. Part II.—Provinces and States—*contd.*

Punjab States Agency.

Age and Religion.	Population.			Unmarried.		Married.		Widowed.	
	Persons.	Males.	Females.	Males.	Females.	Males.	Females.	Males.	Females.
1	2	3	4	5	6	7	8	9	10
All Religions ..	**4,472,218**	**2,451,394**	**2,020,824**	**1,297,878**	**791,109**	**960,224**	**976,378**	**193,292**	**253,337**
0—1 ..	159,820	80,496	79,324	80,442	79,304	54	20	..	..
1—2 ..	122,235	61,544	60,691	61,432	60,627	111	63	1	1
2—3 ..	136,470	68,787	67,683	68,584	67,481	200	201	3	1
3—4 ..	135,100	69,018	66,082	68,622	65,452	387	615	9	15
4—5 ..	128,714	67,024	61,690	66,419	60,634	581	1,013	24	43
Total 0—5 ..	*682,339*	*346,869*	*335,470*	*345,499*	*333,498*	*1,333*	*1,912*	*37*	*60*
5—10 ..	571,280	307,758	263,522	297,560	236,495	9,858	26,630	340	397
10—15 ..	529,591	291,950	237,641	265,685	170,277	25,457	66,466	808	898
15—20 ..	427,034	233,003	194,031	143,541	33,183	85,852	157,463	3,610	3,385
20—25 ..	429,205	231,340	197,865	100,668	9,901	124,044	182,204	6,628	5,760
25—30 ..	366,086	201,714	164,372	47,141	2,729	143,171	151,140	11,402	10,503
30—35 ..	319,786	180,836	138,950	31,086	1,767	135,796	123,080	13,954	14,103
35—40 ..	255,013	143,905	111,108	18,565	935	107,958	87,308	17,382	22,865
40—45 ..	220,205	124,012	96,193	14,403	734	90,796	69,024	18,813	26,435
45—50 ..	186,745	107,900	78,845	10,776	526	74,231	44,529	22,893	33,790
50—55 ..	150,884	87,701	63,183	8,231	392	57,657	31,480	21,813	31,311
55—60 ..	114,271	66,583	47,688	5,424	262	39,591	16,170	21,568	31,256
60—65 ..	95,704	55,357	40,347	4,311	186	31,431	11,247	19,615	28,914
65—70 ..	48,930	29,354	19,576	2,127	77	14,553	3,761	12,674	15,738
70 and over ..	75,145	43,112	32,033	2,861	147	18,496	3,964	21,755	27,922
Hindus ..	**1,887,249**	**1,020,180**	**867,069**	**517,314**	**312,186**	**418,821**	**429,234**	**84,045**	**125,699**
0—1 ..	64,455	32,119	32,336	32,072	32,326	47	10	..	..
1—2 ..	49,286	24,556	24,730	24,458	24,691	98	38	..	1
2—3 ..	55,635	27,680	27,955	27,519	27,843	161	112	..	..
3—4 ..	55,417	27,883	27,534	27,594	27,128	287	397	2	9
4—5 ..	52,742	27,147	25,595	26,734	24,906	401	661	12	28
Total 0—5 ..	*277,535*	*139,385*	*138,150*	*138,377*	*136,894*	*994*	*1,218*	*14*	*38*
5—10 ..	235,874	125,146	110,728	119,139	95,297	5,842	15,204	165	227
10—15 ..	221,824	120,469	101,355	106,320	65,824	13,735	35,032	414	499
15—20 ..	182,974	98,464	84,510	56,512	9,798	40,231	72,791	1,721	1,921
20—25 ..	180,169	95,344	84,825	37,918	2,278	54,448	79,280	2,978	3,267
25—30 ..	153,676	83,074	70,602	17,512	705	60,553	63,872	5,009	6,025
30—35 ..	137,397	76,218	61,179	12,431	506	57,648	52,618	6,139	8,055
35—40 ..	110,259	61,162	49,097	7,705	256	45,710	36,656	7,747	12,185
40—45 ..	95,295	53,171	42,124	6,058	191	38,651	28,455	8,462	13,478
45—50 ..	80,948	46,307	34,641	4,698	134	31,500	18,039	10,109	16,468
50—55 ..	66,077	38,131	27,946	3,741	106	24,819	12,773	9,571	15,067
55—60 ..	50,210	29,085	21,125	2,561	74	17,094	6,310	9,430	14,741
60—65 ..	42,314	24,203	18,111	2,054	55	13,572	4,362	8,577	13,694
65—70 ..	21,111	12,463	8,648	986	22	6,199	1,315	5,278	7,311
70 and over ..	31,586	17,558	14,028	1,302	46	7,825	1,309	8,431	12,673
Muslims ..	**1,556,591**	**852,700**	**703,891**	**463,489**	**300,602**	**328,714**	**329,255**	**60,497**	**74,034**
0—1 ..	57,907	29,270	28,637	29,266	28,629	4	8	..	..
1—2 ..	45,938	23,166	22,772	23,157	22,748	9	24	..	..
2—3 ..	51,430	25,945	25,485	25,913	25,414	32	71	..	..
3—4 ..	50,932	26,182	24,750	26,096	24,587	82	158	4	5
4—5 ..	49,035	25,706	23,329	25,556	23,079	141	237	9	13
Total 0—5 ..	*255,242*	*130,269*	*124,973*	*129,988*	*124,457*	*268*	*498*	*13*	*18*
5—10 ..	208,758	113,764	94,994	111,224	88,558	2,438	6,320	102	116
10—15 ..	184,358	102,750	81,608	96,024	63,497	6,500	17,834	226	277
15—20 ..	141,694	76,037	65,657	49,742	13,882	25,166	50,760	1,129	1,015
20—25 ..	150,358	79,652	70,706	36,603	5,244	40,740	63,713	2,309	1,749
25—30 ..	133,558	73,000	60,558	16,970	1,765	51,988	55,749	4,042	3,044
30—35 ..	113,159	63,812	49,347	9,248	1,111	49,770	44,284	4,794	3,952
35—40 ..	87,077	49,311	37,766	4,460	597	39,247	30,406	5,604	6,763
40—45 ..	73,454	41,482	31,972	3,108	472	32,605	23,555	5,769	7,945
45—50 ..	59,577	34,872	24,705	2,095	350	25,948	14,439	6,829	9,916
50—55 ..	46,549	27,201	19,348	1,509	259	19,391	10,058	6,301	9,031
55—60 ..	34,860	20,444	14,416	900	163	13,139	5,169	6,405	9,084
60—65 ..	29,263	17,186	12,077	715	113	10,553	3,618	5,918	8,346
65—70 ..	14,244	8,588	5,656	338	47	4,554	1,294	3,696	4,315
70 and over ..	24,440	14,332	10,108	565	87	6,407	1,558	7,360	8,463
Sikhs ..	**996,626**	**561,238**	**435,388**	**308,498**	**172,243**	**205,406**	**210,947**	**47,334**	**52,198**
0—1 ..	36,157	18,435	17,722	18,432	17,720	3	2	..	..
1—2 ..	26,070	13,344	12,726	13,339	12,725	4	1	1	..
2—3 ..	28,360	14,624	13,736	14,614	13,718	7	17	3	1
3—4 ..	27,805	14,459	13,346	14,439	13,285	17	60	3	1
4—5 ..	26,067	13,717	12,350	13,679	12,236	35	112	3	2
Total 0—5 ..	*144,459*	*74,579*	*69,880*	*74,503*	*69,684*	*66*	*192*	*10*	*4*
5—10 ..	122,618	66,697	55,921	65,131	50,865	1,497	5,009	69	47
10—15 ..	119,507	66,614	52,893	61,509	39,591	4,943	13,190	162	112
15—20 ..	99,260	56,856	42,404	36,474	9,224	19,649	32,758	733	422
20—25 ..	95,705	54,776	40,929	25,636	2,286	27,847	37,936	1,293	707
25—30 ..	76,363	44,285	32,078	12,432	223	29,599	30,483	2,254	1,372
30—35 ..	66,947	39,505	27,442	9,233	124	27,365	25,308	2,907	2,010
35—40 ..	55,836	32,383	23,453	6,283	65	22,198	19,598	3,902	3,790
40—45 ..	49,955	28,524	21,431	5,167	61	18,912	16,496	4,445	4,874
45—50 ..	44,954	25,992	18,962	3,939	38	16,278	11,697	5,775	7,227
50—55 ..	37,277	21,810	15,467	2,957	23	13,073	8,399	5,780	7,045
55—60 ..	28,474	16,637	11,837	1,935	21	9,112	4,568	5,590	7,248
60—65 ..	23,522	13,620	9,902	1,528	18	7,097	3,178	4,995	6,706
65—70 ..	13,183	8,071	5,112	789	8	3,679	1,104	3,603	4,000
70 and over ..	18,566	10,889	7,677	982	12	4,091	1,031	5,816	6,634

Table VII.—Age, Sex and Civil Condition. Part II.—Provinces and States—*contd.*

Age and Religion.	Population.			Unmarried.		Married.		Widowed.	
	Persons.	Males.	Females.	Males.	Females.	Males.	Females.	Males.	Females.
1	2	3	4	5	6	7	8	9	10
Rajputana Agency.									
All Religions ..	**11,225,712**	**5,885,028**	**5,340,684**	**2,888,862**	**1,857,155**	**2,579,453**	**2,648,241**	**416,713**	**835,288**
0—1 ..	346,766	172,374	174,392	171,708	173,475	621	844	45	73
1—2 ..	343,154	169,005	174,149	168,193	172,895	794	1,219	18	35
2—3 ..	359,065	175,296	183,769	174,073	181,566	1,194	2,119	29	84
3—4 ..	349,990	174,235	175,755	172,032	171,079	2,144	4,510	59	166
4—5 ..	336,364	172,187	164,177	168,642	157,105	3,351	6,702	194	370
Total 0—5 ..	*1,735,339*	*863,097*	*872,242*	*854,648*	*856,120*	*8,104*	*15,394*	*345*	*728*
5—10 ..	1,472,995	783,824	689,171	735,178	567,911	47,248	119,096	1,398	2,164
10—15 ..	1,364,988	745,362	619,626	635,214	366,662	107,061	248,308	3,087	4,656
15—20 ..	1,064,302	563,456	500,846	287,343	42,833	267,361	444,616	8,752	13,397
20—25 ..	1,049,804	544,510	505,294	170,269	12,123	360,223	471,659	14,018	21,512
25—30 ..	881,282	460,573	420,709	64,893	3,552	373,215	376,750	22,465	40,407
30—35 ..	768,253	403,402	364,851	42,366	2,511	333,343	309,981	27,693	52,359
35—40 ..	691,034	362,456	328,578	29,239	1,786	291,025	234,933	42,192	91,859
40—45 ..	606,013	321,423	284,590	23,485	1,299	249,988	181,967	47,950	101,324
45—50 ..	494,616	269,231	225,385	16,531	773	193,794	105,374	58,906	119,238
50—55 ..	395,814	214,115	181,699	12,204	555	147,487	72,802	54,424	108,342
55—60 ..	272,038	139,756	132,282	7,156	375	85,688	32,669	46,912	99,238
60—65 ..	226,578	112,872	113,706	5,519	334	66,373	22,231	40,980	91,141
65—70 ..	89,277	45,521	43,756	2,093	114	23,374	6,376	20,054	37,266
70 and over ..	113,379	55,430	57,949	2,724	207	25,169	6,085	27,537	51,657
Hindus ..	**9,578,805**	**5,029,620**	**4,549,185**	**2,452,204**	**1,551,397**	**2,218,088**	**2,275,171**	**359,328**	**722,617**
0—1 ..	292,761	145,462	147,299	144,953	146,609	491	652	18	38
1—2 ..	291,270	143,288	147,982	142,592	146,912	683	1,053	13	17
2—3 ..	305,304	149,074	156,230	148,024	154,349	1,024	1,818	26	63
3—4 ..	297,246	148,191	149,055	146,300	144,984	1,836	3,930	55	141
4—5 ..	285,308	146,279	139,029	143,339	132,964	2,779	5,765	161	300
Total 0—1 ..	*1,471,889*	*732,294*	*739,595*	*725,208*	*725,818*	*6,813*	*13,218*	*273*	*559*
5—10 ..	1,251,331	667,306	584,025	624,593	474,847	41,528	107,341	1,185	1,837
10—15 ..	1,165,093	638,395	526,698	539,911	301,242	95,786	221,444	2,698	4,012
15—20 ..	909,809	483,441	426,368	241,968	31,581	234,007	383,274	7,466	11,513
20—25 ..	894,041	464,883	429,158	141,524	8,788	311,570	401,982	11,789	18,388
25—30 ..	752,208	394,121	358,087	54,810	2,799	320,254	320,541	19,057	34,747
30—35 ..	655,590	344,637	310,953	36,325	1,968	284,687	263,874	23,625	45,111
35—40 ..	593,383	311,519	281,864	25,761	1,445	249,299	200,655	36,459	79,764
40—45 ..	521,082	276,660	244,422	20,818	1,061	214,157	155,388	41,685	87,973
45—50 ..	424,930	231,515	193,415	14,691	614	165,431	89,527	51,393	103,274
50—55 ..	339,565	183,797	155,768	10,864	428	125,558	61,626	47,375	93,714
55—60 ..	233,029	119,437	113,592	6,407	295	72,496	27,385	40,534	85,912
60—65 ..	194,619	96,613	98,006	4,976	257	56,292	18,664	35,345	79,085
65—70 ..	76,210	38,547	37,663	1,903	91	19,476	5,284	17,168	32,288
70 and over ..	96,026	46,455	49,571	2,445	163	20,734	4,968	23,276	44,440
Muslims ..	**1,069,325**	**565,962**	**503,363**	**280,897**	**191,983**	**246,759**	**247,948**	**38,306**	**63,432**
0—1 ..	35,003	17,473	17,530	17,367	17,374	88	134	18	22
1—2 ..	33,725	16,862	16,863	16,777	16,729	82	117	3	17
2—3 ..	34,536	16,932	17,604	16,795	17,358	134	227	3	19
3—4 ..	33,967	16,825	17,142	16,580	16,646	241	474	4	22
4—5 ..	32,777	16,735	16,042	16,310	15,264	406	733	19	45
Total 0—5 ..	*170,008*	*84,827*	*85,181*	*83,829*	*83,371*	*951*	*1,685*	*47*	*125*
5—10 ..	142,809	75,807	67,002	71,141	57,647	4,494	9,129	172	226
10—15 ..	129,681	70,234	59,447	61,589	40,060	8,358	18,998	287	389
15—20 ..	101,322	53,427	47,895	30,152	7,123	22,361	39,761	914	1,011
20—25 ..	102,819	53,423	49,396	19,180	2,176	32,618	45,607	1,625	1,613
25—30 ..	86,261	45,159	41,102	6,360	492	36,326	37,749	2,473	2,861
30—35 ..	74,645	39,927	34,718	3,469	337	33,613	30,739	2,845	3,642
35—40 ..	62,984	33,955	29,029	1,735	235	28,460	22,429	3,760	6,365
40—45 ..	53,502	29,186	24,316	1,237	167	23,991	17,111	3,958	7,038
45—50 ..	43,256	24,301	18,955	776	116	18,843	10,037	4,682	8,802
50—55 ..	35,117	19,643	15,474	580	95	14,652	7,119	4,411	8,260
55—60 ..	25,007	13,500	11,507	326	59	9,001	3,519	4,173	7,929
60—65 ..	20,835	11,056	9,779	260	59	7,011	2,434	3,785	7,286
65—70 ..	8,870	4,949	3,921	94	17	2,830	794	2,025	3,110
70 and over ..	12,209	6,568	5,641	169	29	3,250	837	3,149	4,775
Jains ..	**300,748**	**146,004**	**154,744**	**75,521**	**49,631**	**56,889**	**66,843**	**13,594**	**38,270**
0—1 ..	9,464	4,818	4,646	4,775	4,582	35	52	8	12
1—2 ..	8,563	4,269	4,294	4,243	4,254	24	39	2	1
2—3 ..	8,365	4,111	4,254	4,087	4,205	24	47	..	2
3—4 ..	7,810	3,877	3,933	3,837	3,863	40	67	..	3
4—5 ..	7,824	3,944	3,880	3,818	3,720	116	140	10	20
Total 0—5 ..	*42,026*	*21,019*	*21,007*	*20,760*	*20,624*	*239*	*345*	*20*	*38*
5—10 ..	35,634	18,234	17,400	17,618	15,971	593	1,359	23	70
10—15 ..	32,455	16,684	15,771	15,496	11,404	1,142	4,177	46	190
15—20 ..	27,053	13,036	14,017	7,496	1,096	5,346	12,169	194	752
20—25 ..	28,427	13,341	15,086	5,127	234	7,882	13,508	332	1,344
25—30 ..	23,220	10,912	12,308	2,331	83	8,030	9,798	551	2,427
30—35 ..	21,254	10,059	11,195	1,757	71	7,505	8,048	797	3,076
35—40 ..	20,124	9,400	10,724	1,369	51	6,638	5,997	1,393	4,676
40—45 ..	18,817	8,925	9,892	1,212	36	6,012	4,761	1,701	5,095
45—50 ..	16,381	7,954	8,427	916	21	4,892	2,952	2,146	5,454
50—55 ..	13,266	6,442	6,824	656	12	3,759	2,038	2,027	4,774
55—60 ..	8,910	4,141	4,769	365	6	2,147	883	1,629	3,880
60—65 ..	7,034	3,108	3,926	241	6	1,533	553	1,334	3,367
65—70 ..	2,944	1,344	1,600	86	4	597	152	662	1,444
70 and over ..	3,203	1,405	1,798	91	12	575	103	739	1,683

Table VII.—Age, Sex and Civil Condition. Part II.—Provinces and States—*concld.*

Age and Religion.	Population.			Unmarried.		Married.		Widowed.	
	Persons.	Males.	Females.	Males.	Females.	Males.	Females.	Males.	Females.
1	2	3	4	5	6	7	8	9	10
Sikkim State.									
All Religions	**109,808**	**55,825**	**53,983**	**28,814**	**25,389**	**25,354**	**24,080**	**1,657**	**4,514**
0—1	3,526	1,740	1,786	1,739	1,780	1	6	..	..
1—2	3,348	1,652	1,696	1,649	1,692	3	4	..	..
2—3	3,587	1,795	1,792	1,790	1,787	5	4	..	1
3—4	3,444	1,724	1,720	1,716	1,712	7	7	1	1
4—5	3,252	1,618	1,634	1,610	1,623	7	10	1	1
Total 0—5	*17,157*	*8,529*	*8,628*	*8,504*	*8,594*	*23*	*31*	*2*	*3*
5—10	14,457	7,336	7,121	7,175	6,835	158	278	3	8
10—15	13,296	6,919	6,377	6,311	5,609	598	749	10	19
15—20	10,727	5,463	5,264	3,251	2,244	2,164	2,936	48	84
20—25	10,402	5,257	5,145	2,162	1,301	3,018	3,719	77	125
25—30	8,872	4,521	4,351	707	403	3,686	3,729	125	219
30—35	7,539	3,801	3,738	330	175	3,349	3,306	122	257
35—40	5,529	2,806	2,723	123	65	2,565	2,321	118	337
40—45	4,877	2,486	2,391	74	49	2,269	1,985	143	357
45—50	4,291	2,283	2,008	62	37	2,056	1,556	165	415
50—55	3,825	2,057	1,768	44	27	1,868	1,323	145	418
55—60	3,012	1,548	1,464	26	21	1,343	860	179	583
60—65	2,602	1,292	1,310	27	15	1,095	700	170	595
65—70	1,243	611	632	7	5	496	266	108	361
70 and over	1,979	916	1,063	11	9	663	321	242	738
United Provinces States.									
All Religions	**1,206,070**	**618,171**	**587,899**	**272,635**	**188,650**	**303,499**	**311,844**	**42,037**	**87,405**
0—1	34,657	17,247	17,410	17,075	17,257	167	146	5	7
1—2	36,313	17,561	18,752	17,375	18,533	182	216	4	3
2—3	38,022	18,130	19,892	17,852	19,502	273	379	5	11
3—4	38,223	18,747	19,476	18,260	18,737	473	707	14	32
4—5	35,977	18,114	17,863	17,477	16,631	615	1,182	22	50
Total 0—5	*183,192*	*89,799*	*93,393*	*88,039*	*90,660*	*1,710*	*2,630*	*50*	*103*
5—10	151,173	78,371	72,802	68,586	53,823	9,552	18,608	233	371
10—15	133,477	71,946	61,531	54,792	32,379	16,672	28,570	482	582
15—20	110,523	55,662	54,861	25,293	6,104	28,929	47,446	1,440	1,311
20—25	113,607	57,197	56,410	17,116	2,963	37,737	51,178	2,344	2,269
25—30	107,020	53,906	53,114	7,370	809	43,260	48,104	3,276	4,201
30—35	89,537	47,293	42,244	4,126	593	39,542	36,280	3,625	5,371
35—40	76,423	38,960	37,463	2,250	441	32,439	28,275	4,271	8,747
40—45	69,564	34,427	35,137	1,726	344	28,347	24,950	4,354	9,843
45—50	48,732	28,431	20,301	1,127	155	22,404	7,957	4,900	12,189
50—55	43,069	22,911	20,158	842	130	17,510	8,474	4,559	11,554
55—60	30,212	15,268	14,944	500	88	10,675	4,541	4,093	10,315
60—65	24,115	11,937	12,178	389	70	7,981	2,779	3,567	9,329
65—70	11,014	5,279	5,735	185	28	3,182	1,040	1,912	4,667
70 and over	14,412	6,784	7,628	294	63	3,559	1,012	2,931	6,553
Hindus	**950,724**	**482,153**	**468,571**	**207,165**	**144,593**	**242,683**	**252,516**	**32,305**	**71,462**
0—1	27,346	13,608	13,738	13,447	13,585	157	146	4	7
1—2	27,976	13,490	14,486	13,321	14,299	165	184	4	3
2—3	29,720	14,137	15,583	13,894	15,279	239	298	4	6
3—4	30,013	14,692	15,321	14,266	14,688	416	610	10	23
4—5	28,039	14,078	13,961	13,511	12,841	548	1,082	19	38
Total 0—5	*143,094*	*70,005*	*73,089*	*68,439*	*70,692*	*1,525*	*2,320*	*41*	*77*
5—10	119,195	61,336	57,859	52,495	40,940	8,641	16,609	200	310
10—15	105,144	56,391	48,753	41,241	24,115	14,749	24,146	401	492
15—20	86,646	43,079	43,567	18,187	4,579	23,809	37,903	1,083	1,085
20—25	87,645	43,586	44,059	12,264	2,394	29,626	39,772	1,696	1,893
25—30	84,031	41,311	42,720	5,449	555	33,501	38,657	2,361	3,508
30—35	70,748	36,922	33,826	3,171	406	31,038	28,926	2,713	4,494
35—40	60,907	30,549	30,358	1,803	298	25,458	22,878	3,288	7,182
40—45	56,381	27,192	29,189	1,384	227	22,428	20,865	3,380	8,097
45—50	38,088	22,580	15,508	934	107	17,855	5,675	3,791	9,726
50—55	34,302	18,172	16,130	706	92	13,953	6,881	3,513	9,157
55—60	24,350	12,015	12,335	411	64	8,409	3,836	3,195	8,435
60—65	19,517	9,410	10,107	312	51	6,281	2,350	2,817	7,706
65—70	9,188	4,302	4,886	145	21	2,608	890	1,549	3,975
70 and over	11,488	5,303	6,185	224	52	2,802	808	2,277	5,325
Western India States Agency.									
All Religions	**3,998,416***	**2,025,293**	**1,973,123**	**952,343**	**705,207**	**949,133**	**977,608**	**123,817**	**290,308**
0—1	125,553	62,570	62,983	61,376	61,743	1,150	1,209	44	31
1—2	127,436	62,345	65,091	60,371	62,547	1,919	2,506	55	38
2—3	124,837	60,094	64,743	57,516	61,316	2,515	3,373	63	54
3—4	122,979	60,296	62,683	57,171	58,443	3,062	4,164	63	76
4—5	121,283	60,778	60,505	57,119	55,501	3,564	4,872	95	132
Total 0—5	*622,088*	*306,083*	*316,005*	*293,553*	*299,550*	*12,210*	*16,124*	*320*	*331*
5—10	552,224	286,046	266,178	253,929	219,235	31,517	46,191	600	752
10—15	506,773	268,829	237,944	217;628	153,975	50,229	82,726	972	1,243
15—20	384,001	197,162	186,839	93,670	22,541	100,761	160,398	2,731	3,900
20—25	368,407	183,981	184,426	52,859	5,824	126,901	172,104	4,221	6,498
25—30	285,887	142,139	143,748	14,590	1,265	121,282	130,070	6,267	12,413
30—35	261,687	130,217	131,470	8,944	870	113,112	112,897	8,161	17,703
35—40	239,084	118,970	120,114	5,507	623	101,480	88,802	11,983	30,689
40—45	206,837	104,454	102,383	4,106	489	87,275	68,822	13,073	33,072
45—50	168,439	88,329	80,110	2,675	265	69,697	40,885	15,957	38,960
50—55	133,450	69,438	64,012	1,962	180	52,760	28,669	14,716	35,163
55—60	100,012	48,613	51,399	1,185	148	33,234	14,303	14,194	36,948
60—65	87,587	41,752	45,835	917	122	27,406	9,995	13,429	35,718
65—70	33,274	16,772	16,502	336	51	9,813	2,851	6,623	13,600
70 and over	48,666	22,508	26,158	482	69	11,456	2,771	10,570	23,318

* Excludes 834 persons (461 males and 373 females) of unspecified age.

Table VII.—Age, Sex and Civil Condition. Part III.—Cities.

Age and Religion.	Population.			Unmarried.		Married.		Widowed.	
	Persons.	Males.	Females.	Males.	Females.	Males.	Females.	Males.	Females.
1	2	3	4	5	6	7	8	9	10
Part III.—Cities.									
Calcutta.									
All Religions ..	**1,196,734**	**814,948**	**381,786**	**283,099**	**126,392**	**509,722**	**186,149**	**22,127**	**69,245**
0—1 ..	22,186	11,956	10,230	11,850	10,151	104	76	2	3
1—2 ..	17,500	9,070	8,430	8,958	8,342	110	85	2	3
2—3 ..	21,077	10,770	10,307	10,617	10,169	152	130	1	8
3—4 ..	20,772	10,724	10,048	10,492	9,808	227	215	5	25
4—5 ..	19,892	10,478	9,414	10,192	9,088	280	283	6	43
Total 0—5	*101,427*	*52,998*	*48,429*	*52,109*	*47,558*	*873*	*789*	*16*	*82*
5—10	95,388	53,498	41,890	49,442	37,223	4,008	4,492	48	175
10—15	98,301	58,547	39,754	49,832	27,369	8,625	12,049	90	336
15—20	128,230	88,480	39,750	50,522	6,253	37,479	31,578	479	1,919
20—30	312,661	230,679	81,982	63,990	4,990	163,574	67,261	3,115	9,731
30—40	234,395	176,501	57,894	12,038	1,718	159,308	41,136	5,155	15,040
40—50 ..	128,908	93,194	35,714	3,288	723	84,655	18,724	5,251	16,267
50—60 ..	60,658	40,029	20,629	1,041	334	34,845	7,069	4,143	13,226
60 and over ..	36,766	21,022	15,744	837	224	16,355	3,051	3,830	12,469
Bombay.									
All Religions ..	**1,161,383**	**747,381**	**414,002**	**286,869**	**145,115**	**446,185**	**222,775**	**14,327**	**46,112**
0—1 ..	16,226	8,033	8,193	8,025	8,182	8	11	..	..
1—2 ..	19,322	9,848	9,474	9,824	9,458	24	15	..	1
2—3 ..	23,203	11,891	11,312	11,847	11,280	44	30	..	2
3—4 ..	22,546	11,786	10,760	11,736	10,708	50	48	..	4
4—5 ..	22,041	11,948	10,093	11,812	9,966	131	122	5	5
Total 0—5 ..	*103,338*	*53,506*	*49,832*	*53,244*	*49,594*	*257*	*226*	*5*	*12*
5—10 ..	93,921	53,713	40,208	52,705	38,840	992	1,320	16	48
10—15 ..	86,031	50,852	35,179	48,410	30,233	2,414	4,844	28	102
15—20 ..	115,323	67,890	47,433	45,060	12,040	22,640	34,737	190	656
20—30 ..	332,120	216,827	115,293	64,043	10,121	151,202	100,987	1,582	4,185
30—40 ..	264,426	195,820	68,606	18,088	2,719	174,269	56,115	3,463	9,772
40—50 ..	107,602	75,708	31,894	3,948	1,022	67,918	17,291	3,842	13,581
50—60 ..	40,490	23,553	16,937	986	390	19,643	5,320	2,924	11,227
60 and over ..	17,836	9,256	8,580	368	156	6,850	1,895	2,038	6,529
Age Unspecified	296	256	40	17	..	..	40	239	..
Madras.									
All Religions ..	**647,230**	**341,223**	**306,007**	**173,974**	**112,272**	**156,229**	**146,303**	**11,020**	**47,432**
0—1 ..	13,469	6,702	6,767	6,702	6,766		1	..	
1—2 ..	14,779	7,397	7,382	7,397	7,381	..	1	..	..
2—3 ..	16,008	8,006	8,002	8,005	7,997	1	3	..	2
3—4 ..	15,678	7,853	7,825	7,850	7,822	3	3	..	
4—5 ..	14,934	7,558	7,376	7,542	7,340	16	30	..	6
Total 0—5 ..	*74,868*	*37,516*	*37,352*	*37,496*	*37,306*	*20*	*38*	..	*8*
5—10 ..	69,561	35,600	33,961	35,476	32,939	121	993	3	29
10—15 ..	66,083	33,863	32,220	33,552	26,914	306	5,196	5	110
15—20 ..	67,539	33,738	33,801	28,090	8,261	5,564	24,694	84	846
20—30 ..	140,257	71,868	68,389	32,226	4,958	38,758	58,834	884	4,597
30—40 ..	105,818	59,529	46,289	5,247	1,047	52,272	35,511	2,010	9,731
40—50 ..	65,980	37,844	28,136	1,249	485	34,018	14,827	2,577	12,824
50—60 ..	35,520	19,408	16,112	448	243	16,384	4,879	2,576	10,990
60 and over ..	21,604	11,857	9,747	190	119	8,786	1,331	2,881	8,297
Agra.									
All Religions ..	**229,764**	**127,736**	**102,028**	**59,440**	**39,192**	**58,563**	**50,657**	**9,733**	**12,179**
0—1 ..	6,821	3,392	3,429	3,392	3,429	..	..	..	..
1—2 ..	7,151	3,558	3,593	3,558	3,593		..	..	
2—3 ..	6,921	3,409	3,512	3,406	3,508	3	..	..	4
3—4 ..	6,782	3,447	3,335	3,437	3,319	10	11	..	5
4—5 ..	6,297	3,316	2,981	3,305	2,959	11	20	..	2
Total 0—5 ..	*83,972*	*17,122*	*16,850*	*17,098*	*16,808*	*24*	*31*	..	*1*
5—10 ..	27,113	15,103	12,010	14,477	10,590	603	1,400	23	20
10—15 ..	25,387	14,054	11,333	12,390	7,839	1,605	3,381	59	113
15—20 ..	23,940	12,890	11,050	6,462	2,116	6,072	8,666	356	268
20—30 ..	47,286	26,794	20,492	6,735	775	18,594	18,786	1,465	931
30—40 ..	31,958	18,795	13,163	1,327	359	15,506	10,784	1,962	2,020
40—50 ..	20,141	11,731	8,410	495	326	9,124	5,014	2,112	3,070
50—60 ..	11,604	6,585	5,019	291	206	4,351	1,877	1,943	2,936
60 and over ..	8,363	4,662	3,701	165	173	2,684	718	1,813	2,810
Ajmer.									
All Religions ..	**119,524**	**66,014**	**53,510**	**29,153**	**18,086**	**32,359**	**27,493**	**4,502**	**7,931**
0—1 ..	3,780	1,847	1,933	1,818	1,911	27	21	2	1
1—5 ..	12,672	6,295	6,377	6,154	6,172	131	191	10	4
Total 0—5	*16,452*	*8,142*	*8,310*	*7,972*	*8,083*	*158*	*212*	*12*	*15*
5—10 ..	13,218	7,097	6,121	6,622	5,161	454	938	21	22
10—15	12,731	6,940	5,791	5,976	3,644	924	2,100	40	47
15—20	12,966	7,059	5,907	3,758	676	3,150	5,084	151	147
20—30	25,110	14,235	10,875	3,564	303	9,992	9,910	679	662
30—40	17,513	10,420	7,093	744	112	8,719	5,554	957	1,427
40—50 ..	11,334	6,736	4,598	295	54	5,416	2,437	1,025	2,107
50—60 ..	6,245	3,490	2,755	136	29	2,479	823	875	1,903
60 and over ..	3,955	1,895	2,060	86	24	1,067	435	742	1,601

Table VII.—Age, Sex and Civil Condition. Part III.—Cities—*contd.*

Allahabad.

Age and Religion. 1		Population. Persons. 2	Males. 3	Females. 4	Unmarried. Males. 5	Females. 6	Married. Males. 7	Females. 8	Widowed. Males. 9	Females. 10
All Religions	..	**183,914**	**104,162**	**79,752**	**42,192**	**26,837**	**54,987**	**42,131**	**6,983**	**10,784**
0—1	..	4,359	2,210	2,149	2,172	2,095	37	53	1	1
1—2	..	4,830	2,426	2,404	2,364	2,352	62	51	..	1
2—3	..	5,084	2,543	2,541	2,447	2,473	92	68	4	..
3—4	..	5,043	2,547	2,496	2,431	2,388	113	104	3	4
4—5	..	4,686	2,419	2,267	2,302	2,138	114	120	3	9
Total *0—5*	..	*24,002*	*12,145*	*11,857*	*11,716*	*11,446*	*418*	*396*	*11*	*15*
5—10	..	20,479	10,984	9,495	9,906	7,945	1,057	1,514	21	36
10—15	..	18,860	10,427	8,433	8,598	5,416	1,792	2,970	37	47
15—20	..	18,222	10,588	7,634	5,376	1,022	5,015	6,464	197	148
20—30	..	36,543	21,324	15,219	5,041	595	15,389	13,921	894	703
30—40	..	28,344	16,866	11,478	972	211	14,574	9,611	1,320	1,656
40—50	..	19,656	11,777	7,879	334	102	9,793	4,866	1,650	2,911
50—60	..	10,936	6,282	4,654	170	50	4,616	1,830	1,496	2,774
60 and over	..	6,872	3,769	3,103	79	50	2,333	559	1,357	2,494

Amritsar.

Age and Religion. 1		Persons. 2	Males. 3	Females. 4	Males. 5	Females. 6	Males. 7	Females. 8	Males. 9	Females. 10
All Religions	..	**264,840**	**158,985**	**105,855**	**86,492**	**47,072**	**62,712**	**47,385**	**9,781**	**11,398**
0—1	..	7,567	3,819	3,748	3,819	3,748	..	..	..	..
1—2	..	6,314	3,169	3,145	3,169	3,145	..	..	..	..
2—3	..	7,318	3,660	3,658	3,660	3,658	..	..	..	..
3—4	..	7,050	3,590	3,460	3,587	3,460	3	..	..	..
4—5	..	6,590	3,416	3,174	3,408	3,170	8	3	..	1
Total *0—5*	..	*34,839*	*17,654*	*17,185*	*17,643*	*17,181*	*11*	*3*	..	*1*
5—10	..	30,983	16,916	14,067	16,748	13,761	145	292	23	14
10—15	..	29,729	17,122	12,607	16,599	10,749	482	1,832	41	26
15—20	..	27,850	17,546	10,304	12,700	2,690	4,623	7,453	223	161
20—30	..	54,683	35,266	19,417	14,500	1,574	19,329	17,085	1,437	758
30—40	..	38,716	24,761	13,955	5,255	566	17,299	11,732	2,207	1,657
40—50	..	24,238	15,211	9,027	1,605	293	11,483	5,849	2,123	2,885
50—60	..	13,335	8,143	5,192	853	139	5,520	2,239	1,770	2,814
60 and over	..	10,467	6,366	4,101	589	119	3,820	900	1,957	3,082

Bangalore City.

Age and Religion. 1		Persons. 2	Males. 3	Females. 4	Males. 5	Females. 6	Males. 7	Females. 8	Males. 9	Females. 10
All Religions	..	**172,357**	**91,680**	**80,677**	**49,698**	**31,321**	**38,573**	**37,204**	**3,409**	**12,152**
0—1	..	4,662	2,312	2,350	2,312	2,350	..	..	..	..
1—2	..	4,830	2,388	2,442	2,388	2,442	..	..	..	..
2—3	..	5,155	2,539	2,616	2,539	2,616	..	..	..	..
3—4	..	5,004	2,456	2,548	2,456	2,548	..	..	..	..
4—5	..	4,619	2,287	2,332	2,287	2,331	..	1	..	..
Total *0—5*	..	*24,270*	*11,982*	*12,288*	*11,982*	*12,287*	..	*1*	..	..
5—10	..	20,870	10,564	10,306	10,546	9,798	18	503	..	5
10—15	..	19,553	10,185	9,368	10,122	7,101	62	2,237	1	30
15—20	..	18,870	10,165	8,705	8,327	1,206	1,810	7,264	28	235
20—30	..	34,442	18,390	16,052	7,577	589	10,539	14,253	274	1,210
30—40	..	23,648	13,483	10,165	822	163	12,096	7,704	565	2,298
40—50	..	15,215	8,619	6,596	180	93	7,721	3,447	718	3,056
50—60	..	8,621	4,673	3,948	79	47	3,878	1,298	716	2,603
60 and over	..	6,868	3,619	3,249	63	37	2,449	497	1,107	2,715

Bangalore.

(*Civil and Military Station.*)

Age and Religion. 1		Persons. 2	Males. 3	Females. 4	Males. 5	Females. 6	Males. 7	Females. 8	Males. 9	Females. 10
All Religions	..	**134,113**	**69,409**	**64,704**	**40,003**	**29,062**	**26,855**	**26,347**	**2,551**	**9,295**
0—1	..	3,548	1,765	1,783	1,765	1,783	..	..	..	..
1—2	..	3,908	1,945	1,963	1,945	1,963	..	..	..	..
2—3	..	4,048	2,013	2,035	2,013	2,035	..	..	..	..
3—4	..	3,870	1,919	1,951	1,919	1,951	..	..	..	..
4—5	..	3,641	1,831	1,810	1,831	1,810	..	..	..	..
Total *0—5*	..	*19,015*	*9,473*	*9,542*	*9,473*	*9,542*	..	..	..	..
5—10	..	16,938	8,658	8,280	8,648	8,108	10	167	..	5
10—15	..	15,595	7,875	7,720	7,830	6,650	44	1,054	1	16
15—20	..	13,742	6,839	6,903	5,877	2,235	942	4,526	20	142
20—30	..	25,695	13,271	12,424	6,663	1,537	6,450	10,052	158	835
30—40	..	17,801	9,748	8,053	1,019	453	8,353	5,982	376	1,618
40—50	..	11,805	6,342	5,463	246	230	5,612	2,905	484	2,328
50—60	..	7,194	3,804	3,390	127	141	3,123	1,161	554	2,088
60 and over	..	6,328	3,399	2,929	120	166	2,321	500	958	2,263

Bareilly.

Age and Religion. 1		Persons. 2	Males. 3	Females. 4	Males. 5	Females. 6	Males. 7	Females. 8	Males. 9	Females. 10
All Religions	..	**144,031**	**79,389**	**64,642**	**39,673**	**25,949**	**34,346**	**30,291**	**5,370**	**8,402**
0—1	..	3,995	2,002	1,993	2,001	1,993	1	..	..	..
1—2	..	4,226	2,111	2,115	2,107	2,111	4	4	..	..
2—3	..	4,341	2,122	2,219	2,115	2,211	7	7	..	1
3—4	..	4,387	2,175	2,212	2,170	2,198	5	12	..	2
4—5	..	4,145	2,123	2,022	2,116	2,004	7	17	..	1
Total *0—5*	..	*21,094*	*10,533*	*10,561*	*10,509*	*10,517*	*24*	*40*	..	*4*
5—10	..	17,353	9,247	8,106	9,104	7,734	137	355	6	17
10—15	..	15,546	8,541	7,005	8,128	5,579	393	1,395	20	31
15—20	..	14,266	7,997	6,269	5,263	1,188	2,583	4,951	151	130
20—30	..	28,177	15,946	12,231	5,115	507	10,039	11,124	792	600
30—40	..	19,552	11,373	8,179	948	205	9,431	6,880	994	1,094
40—50	..	13,549	7,761	5,788	348	150	6,296	3,643	1,117	1,995
50—60	..	8,291	4,638	3,653	153	42	3,399	1,368	1,086	2,243
60 and over	..	6,203	3,353	2,850	105	27	2,044	535	1,204	2,288

Table VII.—Age, Sex and Civil Condition. Part III.—Cities—*contd.*

Age and Religion.	Population.			Unmarried.		Married.		Widowed.	
	Persons.	Males.	Females.	Males.	Females.	Males.	Females.	Males.	Females.
1	2	3	4	5	6	7	8	9	10
Baroda.									
All Religions ..	**112,860**	**62,744**	**50,116**	**28,242**	**15,338**	**29,844**	**25,005**	**4,658**	**9,773**
0—1 ..	3,484	1,746	1,738	1,746	1,738	..	..	..	..
1—2 ..	2,914	1,476	1,438	1,476	1,438	..	..	..	..
2—3 ..	2,635	1,350	1,285	1,350	1,285	..	..	..	..
3—4 ..	2,584	1,343	1,241	1,318	1,201	23	36	2	4
4—5 ..	2,369	1,262	1,107	1,234	1,057	28	49	..	1
Total 0—5 ..	*13,986*	*7,177*	*6,809*	*7,124*	*6,719*	*51*	*85*	*2*	*5*
5—10 ..	11,326	6,132	5,194	5,638	4,390	483	788	11	16
10—15 ..	11,368	6,240	5,128	5,243	3,255	979	1,838	18	35
15—20 ..	12,757	7,219	5,538	4,190	648	2,927	4,730	102	160
20—30 ..	23,745	13,821	9,924	4,473	240	8,779	8,928	569	756
30—40 ..	16,682	9,797	6,885	960	44	7,898	5,183	939	1,658
40—50 ..	11,584	6,544	5,040	363	30	5,048	2,429	1,133	2,581
50—60 ..	6,893	3,656	3,237	175	8	2,471	803	1,010	2,426
60 and over ..	4,519	2,158	2,361	76	4	1,208	221	874	2,136
Benares.									
All Religions ..	**205,315**	**114,551**	**90,764**	**43,983**	**26,851**	**61,899**	**48,044**	**8,669**	**15,869**
0—1 ..	3,929	2,038	1,891	2,001	1,845	35	44	2	2
1—2 ..	4,816	2,386	2,430	2,350	2,365	35	58	1	7
2—3 ..	5,309	2,600	2,709	2,530	2,631	67	70	3	8
3—4 ..	5,385	2,723	2,662	2,621	2,561	98	94	4	7
4—5 ..	5,087	2,639	2,448	2,533	2,326	102	111	4	11
Total 0—5 ..	*24,526*	*12,386*	*12,140*	*12,035*	*11,728*	*337*	*377*	*14*	*35*
5—10 ..	22,196	11,977	10,219	11,065	8,373	880	1,801	32	45
10—15 ..	20,965	11,682	9,283	9,695	5,331	1,924	3,880	63	72
15—20 ..	19,681	11,409	8,272	4,979	662	6,190	7,414	240	196
20—30 ..	39,169	22,715	16,454	4,224	417	17,341	15,069	1,150	968
30—40 ..	30,019	17,414	12,605	1,067	166	14,822	10,269	1,525	2,170
40—50 ..	22,644	13,186	9,458	449	89	10,842	5,676	1,895	3,693
50—60 ..	14,002	7,642	6,360	220	49	5,718	2,410	1,704	3,901
60 and over ..	12,113	6,140	5,973	249	36	3,845	1,148	2,046	4,789
Cawnpore.									
All Religions ..	**243,755**	**143,872**	**99,883**	**54,065**	**31,276**	**77,842**	**56,907**	**11,965**	**11,700**
0—1 ..	4,576	2,301	2,275	2,301	2,275	..	..	..	..
1—2 ..	5,704	2,805	2,899	2,804	2,899	1	..	..	..
2—3 ..	5,642	2,791	2,851	2,785	2,837	6	14	..	..
3—4 ..	5,737	2,956	2,781	2,923	2,734	31	43	2	4
4—5 ..	5,477	2,880	2,597	2,827	2,531	50	59	3	7
Total 0—5 ..	*27,136*	*13,733*	*13,403*	*13,640*	*13,276*	*88*	*116*	*5*	*11*
5—10 ..	23,906	13,407	10,499	12,721	9,436	637	1,032	49	31
10—15 ..	22,112	12,834	9,278	11,253	6,379	1,478	2,857	103	42
15—20 ..	23,034	13,219	9,815	6,751	1,141	6,058	8,525	410	149
20—30 ..	56,534	33,413	23,121	7,240	702	24,096	21,666	2,077	753
30—40 ..	45,239	28,854	16,385	1,661	215	24,185	14,350	3,008	1,820
40—50 ..	26,077	16,823	9,254	506	79	13,552	5,952	2,765	3,223
50—60 ..	12,250	7,431	4,819	172	29	5,327	1,734	1,932	3,056
60 and over ..	7,467	4,158	3,309	121	19	2,421	675	1,616	2,615
Dacca.									
All Religions ..	**138,518**	**79,365**	**59,153**	**38,799**	**21,929**	**38,667**	**27,458**	**1,899**	**9,766**
0—1 ..	3,862	1,912	1,950	1,827	1,851	85	95	..	4
1—2 ..	3,142	1,529	1,613	1,488	1,578	40	34	1	1
2—3 ..	3,890	1,876	2,014	1,826	1,946	49	66	1	2
3—4 ..	3,861	1,903	1,958	1,853	1,878	48	73	2	7
4—5 ..	3,639	1,852	1,787	1,804	1,724	46	52	2	11
Total 0—5 ..	*18,394*	*9,072*	*9,322*	*8,798*	*8,977*	*268*	*320*	*6*	*25*
5—10 ..	16,207	8,917	7,290	8,569	6,327	342	928	6	35
10—15 ..	15,174	8,471	6,703	7,878	4,346	576	2,290	17	67
15—20 ..	15,074	8,739	6,335	5,985	1,099	2,717	4,920	37	316
20—30 ..	28,587	17,579	11,008	6,421	690	10,918	9,153	240	1,165
30—40 ..	19,251	11,688	7,563	778	157	10,556	5,478	354	1,928
40—50 ..	12,821	7,667	5,154	219	176	7,049	2,793	399	2,185
50—60 ..	7,412	4,308	3,104	94	140	3,822	1,120	392	1,845
60 and ove ..	5,598	2,924	2,674	57	17	2,419	456	448	2,201
***Delhi.**									
All Religions ..	**365,527**	**215,778**	**149,749**	**98,416**	**57,060**	**102,128**	**76,960**	**15,234**	**15,729**
0—1 ..	10,322	5,237	5,085	5,237	5,085	..	..	..	..
1—2 ..	8,556	4,304	4,252	4,302	4,251	2	1	..	..
2—3 ..	9,960	4,982	4,978	4,981	4,978	1	..	..	..
3—4 ..	9,785	4,958	4,827	4,953	4,824	5	3	..	..
4—5 ..	9,099	4,738	4,361	4,722	4,352	13	9	3	..
Total 0—5 ..	*47,722*	*24,219*	*23,503*	*24,195*	*23,490*	*21*	*13*	*3*	..
5—10 ..	40,105	21,941	18,164	21,281	17,004	636	1,152	24	8
10—15 ..	38,916	21,963	16,953	19,826	12,435	2,065	4,458	72	60
15—20 ..	39,433	23,187	16,246	13,516	2,664	9,170	13,361	501	221
20—30 ..	80,463	49,155	31,308	14,057	1,038	32,513	29,132	2,585	1,138
30—40 ..	56,917	36,571	20,346	3,561	251	29,462	17,473	3,548	2,622
40—50 ..	34,083	21,903	12,180	1,278	115	17,173	7,799	3,452	4,266
50—60 ..	17,013	10,470	6,543	446	45	7,356	2,616	2,668	3,882
60 and over ..	10,875	6,369	4,506	256	18	3,732	956	2,381	3,532

*Excludes New Delhi and Cantonment.

Table VII.—Age, Sex and Civil Condition. Part III—Cities—*contd.*

Age and Religion. 1	Population. Persons. 2	Population. Males. 3	Population. Females. 4	Unmarried. Males. 5	Unmarried. Females. 6	Married. Males. 7	Married. Females. 8	Widowed. Males. 9	Widowed. Females. 10
Howrah.									
All Religions	224,873	145,120	79,753	49,451	25,634	91,482	40,871	4,187	13,248
0—1	4,703	2,409	2,294	2,311	2,270	97	22	1	2
1—2	3,688	1,944	1,744	1,901	1,720	43	23	..	1
2—3	4,447	2,346	2,101	2,287	2,072	59	27	..	2
3—4	4,299	2,269	2,030	2,197	1,977	69	49	3	4
4—5	4,062	2,165	1,897	2,094	1,824	71	67	..	6
Total 0—5	*21,199*	*11,133*	*10,066*	*10,790*	*9,863*	*339*	*188*	*4*	*15*
5—10	18,963	10,665	8,298	9,876	7,016	783	1,248	6	34
10—15	19,643	11,028	8,615	9,440	5,470	1,568	3,068	20	77
15—20	23,654	14,699	8,955	7,920	1,576	6,664	6,975	115	404
20—30	55,917	38,460	17,457	9,169	1,043	28,652	14,665	639	1,749
30—40	43,050	31,321	11,729	1,683	363	28,644	8,750	994	2,616
40—50	24,263	17,010	7,253	406	174	15,611	3,891	993	3,188
50—60	11,537	7,205	4,332	109	106	6,330	1,387	766	2,839
60 and over	6,647	3,599	3,048	58	23	2,891	699	650	2,326
Hyderabad.									
All Religions	466,894	247,623	219,271	108,207	70,374	118,210	97,117	21,206	51,780
0—1	8,614	4,191	4,423	4,171	4,406	20	17	..	..
1—5	44,656	18,759	25,897	18,542	25,648	206	228	11	21
Total 0—5	*53,270*	*22,950*	*30,320*	*22,713*	*30,054*	*226*	*245*	*11*	*21*
5—10	42,105	20,289	21,816	19,126	19,491	1,147	2,209	16	116
10—15	40,686	23,831	16,855	22,080	12,258	1,722	4,398	29	199
15—20	53,654	29,773	23,881	18,473	3,693	10,840	18,317	460	1,871
20—30	98,180	51,518	46,662	21,048	3,199	28,870	37,132	1,600	6,331
30—40	69,018	37,853	31,165	3,076	734	31,002	20,506	3,775	9,925
40—50	52,895	29,793	23,102	988	467	23,247	10,416	5,558	12,219
50—60	35,012	21,072	13,940	406	323	15,171	2,685	5,495	10,932
60 and over	22,074	10,544	11,530	297	155	5,985	1,209	4,262	10,166
Indore.									
All Religions	127,327	73,450	53,877	31,606	16,551	36,265	28,162	5,579	9,164
0—1	2,920	1,443	1,477	1,429	1,460	13	15	1	2
1—2	3,134	1,547	1,587	1,533	1,569	13	15	1	3
2—3	3,087	1,467	1,620	1,454	1,599	12	18	1	3
3—4	2,923	1,429	1,494	1,417	1,471	11	19	1	4
4—5	2,684	1,405	1,279	1,388	1,257	14	17	3	5
Total 0—5	*14,748*	*7,291*	*7,457*	*7,221*	*7,356*	*63*	*84*	*7*	*17*
5—10	12,572	6,859	5,713	6,588	4,920	254	771	17	22
10—15	12,918	7,256	5,662	6,500	3,349	724	2,272	32	41
15—20	14,612	8,450	6,162	4,853	458	3,439	5,548	158	156
20—30	29,132	17,575	11,557	4,810	272	11,893	10,566	872	719
30—40	19,381	12,195	7,186	1,020	113	9,946	5,444	1,229	1,629
40—50	12,439	7,450	4,989	362	44	5,773	2,402	1,315	2,543
50—60	7,038	4,019	3,019	160	22	2,827	791	1,032	2,206
60 and over	4,487	2,355	2,132	92	17	1,346	284	917	1,831
Jaipur.									
All Religions	144,179	77,933	66,246	30,387	17,608	40,658	35,918	6,888	12,720
0—1	3,821	1,929	1,892	1,922	1,887	6	3	1	2
1—5	13,432	6,769	6,663	6,688	6,454	77	200	4	9
Total 0—5	*17,253*	*8,698*	*8,555*	*8,610*	*8,341*	*83*	*203*	*5*	*11*
5—10	14,663	7,889	6,774	7,255	5,125	615	1,617	19	32
10—15	14,256	7,711	6,545	6,291	3,278	1,379	3,205	41	62
15—20	14,136	7,543	6,593	3,200	440	4,167	5,974	176	179
20—30	28,120	15,426	12,694	3,019	216	11,637	11,487	770	991
30—40	21,619	12,016	9,603	956	99	9,852	7,336	1,208	2,168
40—50	16,380	9,075	7,305	558	51	6,899	4,015	1,618	3,239
50—60	10,590	5,735	4,855	314	32	3,859	1,544	1,562	3,279
60 and over	7,162	3,840	3,322	184	26	2,167	537	1,489	2,759
Jubbulpore.									
All Religions	124,382	69,258	55,124	31,622	19,230	34,142	27,940	3,494	7,954
0—1	3,972	1,958	2,014	1,940	2,000	17	13	1	1
1—2	3,524	1,708	1,816	1,674	1,789	33	25	1	2
2—3	3,579	1,704	1,875	1,671	1,842	32	30	1	3
3—4	3,420	1,683	1,737	1,651	1,703	32	33		1
4—5	3,171	1,606	1,565	1,567	1,527	37	35	2	3
Total 0—5	*17,666*	*8,659*	*9,007*	*8,503*	*8,861*	*151*	*136*	*5*	*10*
5—10	13,574	7,284	6,290	6,924	5,540	354	738	6	12
10—15	12,578	6,943	5,635	6,156	3,646	762	1,958	25	31
15—20	12,986	7,239	5,747	4,117	622	3,000	4,985	122	140
20—30	28,104	16,360	11,744	4,675	366	11,108	10,655	577	723
30—40	19,026	11,429	7,597	859	94	9,762	6,023	808	1,480
40—50	11,289	6,593	4,696	284	48	5,500	2,458	809	2,190
50—60	5,758	3,127	2,631	60	31	2,424	734	643	1,866
60 and over	3,401	1,624	1,777	44	22	1,081	253	499	1,502

Table VII.—Age, Sex and Civil Condition. Part III—Cities—*contd.*

Age and Religion.	Population.			Unmarried.		Married.		Widowed.	
	Persons.	Males.	Females.	Males.	Females.	Males.	Females.	Males.	Females.
1	2	3	4	5	6	7	8	9	10
Karachi.									
All Religions ..	**247,791**	**145,052**	**102,739**	**70,432**	**43,046**	**68,105**	**47,187**	**6,515**	**12,506**
0—1 ..	6,718	3,369	3,349	3,368	3,349	..	..	1	..
1—2 ..	6,604	3,236	3,368	3,234	3,366	..	1	2	1
2—3 ..	7,335	3,565	3,770	3,558	3,767	6	3	1	..
3—4 ..	7,058	3,467	3,591	3,452	3,576	14	11	1	4
4—5 ..	6,630	3,360	3,270	3,338	3,251	21	15	1	4
Total 0—5 ..	*34,345*	*16,997*	*17,348*	*16,950*	*17,309*	*41*	*30*	*6*	*9*
5—10 ..	28,171	15,139	13,032	14,855	12,376	271	640	13	16
10—15 ..	24,918	13,913	11,005	13,203	8,916	682	2,045	28	44
15—20 ..	24,961	14,412	10,549	9,453	2,397	4,555	7,934	404	218
20—30 ..	55,909	34,458	21,451	11,618	1,499	21,668	18,874	1,172	1,078
30—40 ..	40,671	26,883	13,788	3,149	328	22,248	11,127	1,486	2,333
40—50 ..	21,969	13,875	8,094	814	130	11,674	4,542	1,387	3,422
50—60 ..	10,495	6,084	4,411	250	56	4,774	1,416	1,060	2,939
60 and over ..	6,352	3,291	3,061	140	35	2,192	579	959	2,447
Lahore.									
All Religions ..	**429,747**	**274,587**	**155,160**	**145,490**	**66,828**	**114,444**	**73,905**	**14,653**	**14,427**
0—1 ..	12,531	6,661	5,870	6,656	5,870	3	..	2	..
1—2 ..	10,006	5,491	4,515	5,487	4,514	1	1	3	..
2—3 ..	11,487	6,190	5,297	6,174	5,290	10	7	6	..
3—4 ..	10,838	5,665	5,173	5,653	5,159	11	13	1	1
4—5 ..	9,875	5,183	4,692	5,172	4,664	9	23	2	5
Total *0—5* ..	*54,737*	*29,190*	*25,547*	*29,142*	*25,497*	*34*	*44*	*14*	*6*
5—10 ..	43,583	23,707	19,876	23,465	17,965	231	1,896	11	15
10—15 ..	42,660	24,618	18,042	23,745	14,209	837	3,802	36	31
15—20 ..	52,093	34,748	17,345	25,493	5,106	8,860	12,037	395	202
20—30 ..	104,633	72,388	32,245	31,604	2,789	38,229	28,435	2,555	1,021
30—40 ..	66,883	47,551	19,332	8,742	707	35,189	16,450	3,620	2,175
40—50 ..	35,913	24,059	11,854	2,190	328	18,626	7,635	3,243	3,891
50—60 ..	17,115	10,940	6,175	639	134	8,013	2,545	2,288	3,496
60 and over ..	12,130	7,386	4,744	470	93	4,425	1,061	2,491	3,590
Lucknow.									
All Religions ..	**274,659**	**159,458**	**115,201**	**67,350**	**40,329**	**80,120**	**59,089**	**11,988**	**15,783**
0—1 ..	5,182	2,656	2,526	2,653	2,526	3	..	..	..
1—2 ..	5,787	2,916	2,871	2,913	2,871	3	..	..	..
2—3 ..	6,122	3,045	3,077	3,041	3,072	4	5	..	.
3—4 ..	6,367	3,220	3,147	3,203	3,125	17	21	..	1
4—5 ..	6,138	3,173	2,965	3,143	2,929	29	34	1	2
Total *0—5* ..	*29,596*	*15,010*	*14,586*	*14,953*	*14,523*	*56*	*60*	*1*	*3*
5—10 ..	27,967	15,054	12,913	14,550	11,998	490	903	14	12
10—15 ..	26,183	14,695	11,488	13,428	8,897	1,222	2,552	45	39
15—20 ..	27,195	16,294	10,901	9,860	2,583	6,082	8,082	352	236
20—30 ..	60,238	36,456	23,782	11,200	1,751	23,536	20,905	1,720	1,126
30—40 ..	46,404	28,516	17,888	2,218	312	23,733	15,161	2,565	2,415
40—50 ..	30,060	18,215	11,845	691	165	14,742	7,494	2,782	4,186
50—60 ..	16,054	9,119	6,935	258	59	6,587	2,813	2,274	4,063
60 and over ..	10,962	6,099	4,863	192	41	3,672	1,119	2,235	3,703
Madura.									
All Religions ..	**182,018**	**91,676**	**90,342**	**46,968**	**32,615**	**42,098**	**41,960**	**2,610**	**15,767**
0—1 ..	3,971	1,911	2,060	1,911	2,060	..	..	..	...
1—2 ..	4,880	2,383	2,497	2,383	2,497	..	..	..	...
2—3 ..	5,367	2,639	2,728	2,639	2,728	..	..	..	..
3—4 ..	4,853	2,399	2,454	2,399	2,454	..	..	..	..
4—5 ..	4,279	2,128	2,151	2,127	2,151	1	..	...	...
Total 0—5 ..	*23,350*	*11,460*	*11,890*	*11,459*	*11,890*	*1*	..	...	...
5—10 ..	20,618	10,402	10,216	10,379	9,883	23	329	...	4
10—15 ..	19,524	10,036	9,488	9,950	7,845	84	1,623	2	20
15—20 ..	18,026	9,124	8,902	7,351	1,789	1,744	6,894	29	219
20—30 ..	35,922	17,469	18,453	6,694	851	10,551	16,094	224	1,508
30—40 ..	28,367	14,693	13,674	790	203	13,440	10,262	463	3,209
40—50 ..	18,574	9,770	8,804	207	103	9,025	4,604	538	4,097
50—60 ..	10,870	5,443	5,427	85	41	4,741	1,674	617	3,712
60 and over ..	6,767	3,279	3,488	53	10	2,489	480	737	2,998
Moradabad.									
All Religions ..	**110,562**	**61,346**	**49,216**	**29,996**	**22,557**	**26,719**	**21,039**	**4,631**	**5,620**
0—1 ..	3,547	1,798	1,749	1,798	1,749	...	..	..	..
1—2 ..	3,502	1,753	1,749	1,753	1,749		..	..	..
2—3 ..	3,596	1,733	1,863	1,733	1,863	..	..	..	..
3—4 ..	3,478	1,722	1,756	1,524	1,554	197	197	1	5
4—5 ..	3,225	1,683	1,542	1,288	1,139	393	395	2	8
Total 0—5 ..	*17,348*	*8,689*	*8,659*	*8,096*	*8,054*	*590*	*592*	*3*	*13*
5—10 ..	13,224	7,001	6,223	5,310	4,580	1,678	1,619	13	24
10—15 ..	12,183	6,495	5,688	4,741	3,754	1,729	1,917	25	17
15—20 ..	11,661	6,389	5,272	3,496	1,748	2,747	3,430	146	94
20—30 ..	21,969	12,550	9,419	4,327	2,113	7,518	6,870	705	436
30—40 ..	14,266	8,577	5,689	1,855	1,212	5,858	3,739	864	738
40—50 ..	9,688	5,765	3,923	1,135	678	3,648	1,919	982	1,326
50—60 ..	5,953	3,460	2,493	631	316	1,895	669	934	1,508
60 and over ..	4,270	2,420	1,850	405	102	1,056	284	959	1,464

Table VII.—Age, Sex and Civil Condition. Part III—Cities—*contd.*

Age and Religion.		Population.			Unmarried.		Married.		Widowed.	
		Persons.	Males.	Females.	Males.	Females.	Males.	Females.	Males.	Females
1		2	3	4	5	6	7	8	9	10
Multan.										
All Religions	..	**119,457**	**68,119**	**51,338**	**36,449**	**24,903**	**27,229**	**19,870**	**4,441**	**6,565**
0—1	..	3,630	1,797	1,833	1,797	1,832	..	1	..	..
1—2	..	2,594	1,278	1,316	1,278	1,315	..	1	..	..
2—3	..	3,207	1,589	1,618	1,588	1,610	..	7	1	1
3—4	..	3,151	1,592	1,559	1,590	1,549	2	9	..	1
4—5	..	2,927	1,514	1,413	1,508	1,405	5	6	1	2
Total 0—5	..	*15,509*	*7,770*	*7,739*	*7,761*	*7,711*	*7*	*24*	*2*	*4*
5—10	..	13,820	7,554	6,266	7,457	6,105	96	155	1	6
10—15	..	13,200	7,436	5,764	7,227	4,935	203	818	6	11
15—20	..	12,748	7,340	5,408	5,563	2,327.	1,695	3,002	82	79
20—30	..	25,304	14,977	10,327	6,328	3,384	8,039	6,434	610	509
30—40	..	17,125	10,397	6,728	1,357	263	6,168	5,455	872	1,010
40—50	..	10,990	6,482	4,508	456	97	4,982	2,693	1,044	1,718
50—60	..	6,125	3,598	2,527	184	42	2,545	976	869	1,509
60 and over	..	4,636	2,565	2,071	116	39	1,494	313	955	1,719
Mysore.										
All Religions	..	**107,142**	**56,772**	**50,370**	**31,014**	**19,326**	**23,346**	**22,661**	**2,412**	**8,383**
0—1	..	2,470	1,248	1,222	1,248	1,222	..	..	..	..
1—2		2,576	1,290	1,286	1,290	1,286	..	..	..	..
2—3	..	2,957	1,444	1,513	1,444	1,513	..	..	..	..
3—4	..	2,938	1,443	1,495	1,443	1,495	..	..	..	..
4—5	..	2,818	1,396	1,422	1,396	1,422	..	..	..	..
Total 0—5	..	*13,759*	*6,821*	*6,938*	*6,821*	*6,938*	..	—	—	—
5—10	..	13,695	7,091	6,604	7,083	6,274	8	324	..	6
10—15	..	13,024	6,947	6,077	6,910	4,703	37	1,352	..	22
15—20	..	11,036	5,975	5,061	4,996	834	959	4,051	20	176
20—30	..	20,153	10,539	9,614	4,541	392	5,812	8,421	186	801
30—40	..	14,865	8,089	6,776	458	86	7,246	5,092	385	1,598
40—50	..	10,042	5,619	4,423	120	49	4,979	2,290	520	2,084
50—60	..	5,898	3,209	2,689	49	29	2,613	823	547	1,837
60 and over		4,670	2,482	2,188	36	21	1,692	308	754	1,859
Nagpur.										
All Religions	..	**215,165**	**116,403**	**98,762**	**49,149**	**32,119**	**62,601**	**52,440**	**4,653**	**14,203**
0—1	..	5,501	2,783	2,718	2,743	2,668	29	38	11	12
1—2	..	5,724	2,884	2,840	2,807	2,756	58	62	19	22
2—3	..	5,877	2,907	2,970	2,800	2,865	88	84	19	21
3—4	..	5,685	2,822	2,863	2,713	2,738	91	104	18	21
4—5	..	5,419	2,744	2,675	2,641	2,519	84	131	19	25
Total 0—5	..	*28,206*	*14,140*	*14,066*	*13,704*	*13,546*	*350*	*419*	*86*	*101*
5—10	..	24,545	12,792	11,753	11,780	9,468	934	2,180	78	105
10—15	..	23,167	12,345	10,822	10,373	6,576	1,889	4,131	83	115
15—20	..	22,531	11,971	10,560	6,093	1,349	5,750	9,001	128	210
20—30	..	44,590	24,377	20,213	5,495	714	18,306	18,531	576	968
30—40	..	31,927	18,619	13,308	1,072	193	16,684	10,846	863	2,269
40—50	..	20,353	11,746	8,607	365	124	10,368	4,820	1,013	3,663
50—60	..	11,405	6,243	5,162	155	77	5,228	1,700	860	3,385
60 and over		8,441	4,170	4,271	112	72	3,092	812	966	3,387
Patna.										
All Religions	..	**159,690**	**92,238**	**67,452**	**34,338**	**20,598**	**51,847**	**35,159**	**6,053**	**11,695**
0—1	..	2,953	1,427	1,526	1,419	1,474	7	52	1	—
1—2	..	3,393	1,677	1,716	1,659	1,663	18	53	—	—
2—3	..	4,054	1,990	2,064	1,940	2,040	50	22	—	2
3—4	..	4,009	2,040	1,969	1,924	1,925	114	42	2	2
4—5	..	3,850	2,042	1,808	1,885	1,751	153	54	4	3
Total 0—5	..	*18,259*	*9,176*	*9,083*	*8,827*	*8,853*	*342*	*223*	*7*	*7*
5—10	..	17,434	9,617	7,817	8,529	6,465	1,069	1,335	19	17
10—15	..	17,326	10,031	7,295	7,690	4,314	2,306	2,934	35	47
15—20	..	16,931	10,457	6,474	4,495	664	5,782	5,636	180	174
20—30	..	32,325	19,971	12,354	3,816	233	15,318	11,309	837	812
30—40	..	23,586	13,964	9,622	605	28	12,283	7,553	1,076	2,041
40—50	..	16,733	9,734	6,999	214	19	8,218	3,800	1,302	3,180
50—60	..	9,406	5,436	3,970	110	9	4,110	1,511	1,216	2,450
60 and over	..	7,690	3,852	3,838	52	13	2,419	858	1,381	2,967
Poona.										
All Religions	..	**162,901**	**86,784**	**76,117**	**43,979**	**30,558**	**39,229**	**31,539**	**3,576**	**14,020**
0—1	..	4,385	2,264	2,121	2,262	2,116	2	5	..	—
1—2	..	4,342	2,202	2,140	2,199	2,126	3	10	..	2
2—3	..	4,286	2,079	2,207	2,075	2,193	4	13	..	1
3—4	..	4,059	1,958	2,101	1,951	2,077	6	23	1	1
4—5	..	3,894	1,929	1,965	1,915	1,925	12	36	2	4
Total 0—5	..	*20,966*	*10,432*	*10,534*	*10,402*	*10,439*	*27*	*87*	*3*	*8*
5—10	..	18,129	9,594	8,535	9,183	7,657	405	850	6	28
10—15	..	17,544	9,519	8,025	8,801	5,898	708	2,072	10	55
15—20	..	18,015	9,682	8,333	6,968	2,509	2,664	5,563	50	261
20—30	..	35,114	19,055	16,059	7,051	3,142	11,596	11,477	408	1,440
30—40	..	25,538	14,531	11,007	1,128	787	12,655	6,980	748	3,240
40—50	..	14,797	7,695	7,102	296	76	6,563	3,041	836	3,985
50—60	..	7,874	3,938	3,936	107	28	3,054	1,048	777	2,860
60 and over	..	4,924	2,338	2,586	43	22	1,557	421	738	2,143

Table VII.—Age, Sex and Civil Condition. Part III—Cities—*concld.*

Age and Religion. 1	Population. Persons. 2	Population. Males. 3	Population. Females. 4	Unmarried. Males. 5	Unmarried. Females. 6	Married. Males. 7	Married. Females. 8	Widowed. Males. 9	Widowed. Females. 10
Rangoon.									
All Religions	**400,415**	**271,063**	**129,352**	**115,243**	**62,992**	**149,396**	**53,750**	**6,424**	**12,610**
0—1	6,042	2,919	3,123	2,919	3,123	..	..	..	..
1—2	5,916	2,911	3,005	2,910	3,005	1	..	..	..
2—3	6,430	3,196	3,234	3,195	3,234	1	..	..	..
3—4	6,263	3,146	3,117	3,142	3,116	4	1	..	..
4—5	5,960	3,019	2,941	3,014	2,938	5	3	..	..
Total 0—5	*30,611*	*15,191*	*15,420*	*15,180*	*15,416*	*11*	*4*	..	..
5—10	30,036	15,928	14,108	15,813	14,029	115	78	..	1
10—15	31,037	17,352	13,685	16,807	13,014	542	658	3	13
15—20	43,775	29,555	14,220	21,208	7,523	8,272	6,541	75	156
20—30	110,224	81,601	28,623	32,758	7,466	48,148	20,227	695	930
30—40	82,043	62,392	19,651	9,430	2,919	51,589	14,796	1,373	1,936
40—50	42,779	30,933	11,846	2,648	1,459	26,666	7,435	1,619	2,952
50—60	19,012	12,266	6,746	929	715	10,043	2,902	1,294	3,129
60 and over	10,898	5,845	5,053	470	451	4,010	1,109	1,365	3,493
Salem.									
All Religions	**102,179**	**51,786**	**50,393**	**27,269**	**19,827**	**22,885**	**22,912**	**1,632**	**7,654**
0—1	2,869	1,408	1,461	1,408	1,461	..	..	..	..
1—2	3,181	1,570	1,611	1,568	1,611	2	..	..	..
2—3	3,553	1,751	1,802	1,749	1,802	2	..	..	..
3—4	3,334	1,655	1,679	1,654	1,678	1	1	..	..
4—5	2,992	1,515	1,477	1,513	1,475	2	2	..	..
Total 0—5	*15,929*	*7,899*	*8,030*	*7,892*	*8,027*	*7*	*3*	..	..
5—10	13,376	6,829	6,547	6,799	6,203	30	340	..	4
10—15	11,977	6,113	5,864	6,022	4,474	91	1,370	..	20
15—20	10,098	4,963	5,135	3,433	696	1,507	4,301	23	138
20—30	18,879	9,243	9,636	2,661	327	6,429	8,555	153	754
30—40	13,898	7,427	6,471	326	56	6,841	4,952	260	1,463
40—50	8,950	4,777	4,173	86	23	4,362	2,238	329	1,912
50—60	5,183	2,601	2,582	24	13	2,217	829	360	1,740
60 and over	3,889	1,934	1,955	26	8	1,401	324	507	1,623
Sholapur.									
All Religions	**135,574**	**72,079**	**63,495**	**32,273**	**20,292**	**36,587**	**33,014**	**3,219**	**10,189**
0—1	4,344	2,149	2,195	2,122	2,173	27	22	..	..
1—2	4,104	2,033	2,071	2,009	2,045	24	26	..	..
2—3	3,843	1,901	1,942	1,870	1,909	31	33	..	..
3—4	3,585	1,798	1,787	1,762	1,722	35	63	1	2
4—5	3,532	1,807	1,725	1,766	1,628	41	94	..	3
Total 0—5	*19,408*	*9,688*	*9,720*	*9,529*	*9,477*	*158*	*238*	*1*	*5*
5—10	15,776	8,249	7,527	7,796	5,989	439	1,514	14	24
10—15	14,965	7,836	7,129	6,884	3,855	928	3,219	24	55
15—20	14,660	7,464	7,196	3,907	480	3,476	6,502	81	214
20—30	28,663	15,487	13,176	3,499	300	11,567	11,896	421	980
30—40	19,627	11,468	8,159	447	104	10,364	6,085	657	1,970
40—50	11,572	6,420	5,152	130	52	5,598	2,437	692	2,663
50—60	6,374	3,255	3,119	46	22	2,589	777	620	2,320
60 and over	4,529	2,212	2,317	35	13	1,468	346	709	1,958
Srinagar.									
All Religions	**173,573**	**94,793**	**78,780**	**51,630**	**31,635**	**37,529**	**38,039**	**5,634**	**9,106**
0—1	3,578	1,842	1,736	1,842	1,736	..	..	..	..
1—2	4,393	2,200	2,193	2,200	2,193	..	..	..	..
2—3	4,940	2,481	2,459	2,481	2,459	..	..	..	..
3—4	5,098	2,580	2,518	2,580	2,518	..	..	..	..
4—5	4,869	2,466	2,403	2,466	2,403	..	..	..	..
Total 0—5	*22,878*	*11,569*	*11,309*	*11,569*	*11,309*	..	..	..	..
5—10	22,147	11,502	10,645	11,485	10,523	17	115	..	7
10—15	20,688	11,021	9,667	10,811	8,026	200	1,608	10	33
15—20	18,656	10,114	8,542	7,519	1,339	2,492	6,992	103	211
20—30	35,289	19,177	16,112	7,605	324	10,866	15,052	706	736
30—40	25,055	14,690	10,365	1,706	77	11,801	8,875	1,183	1,413
40—50	15,683	9,063	6,620	615	20	7,161	4,013	1,287	2,587
50—60	8,380	4,866	3,514	231	9	3,436	1,136	1,199	2,369
60 and over	4,797	2,791	2,006	89	8	1,556	248	1,146	1,750
Trichinopoly.									
All Religions	**142,843**	**72,997**	**69,846**	**39,688**	**26,672**	**30,719**	**29,769**	**2,590**	**13,405**
0—1	3,131	1,531	1,600	1,531	1,600	..	..	..	..
1—2	3,394	1,623	1,771	1,623	1,771	..	..	..	..
2—3	3,664	1,768	1,896	1,768	1,896	..	..	..	..
3—4	3,491	1,726	1,765	1,726	1,764	..	1	..	..
4—5	3,219	1,630	1,589	1,630	1,585	..	4	..	..
Total 0—5	*16,899*	*8,278*	*8,621*	*8,278*	*8,616*	..	*5*	..	..
5—10	16,241	8,136	8,105	8,111	7,894	25	209	..	2
10—15	15,879	7,978	7,901	7,904	6,767	71	1,116	3	18
15—20	15,745	8,289	7,456	6,894	1,947	1,367	5,286	28	223
20—30	29,031	15,185	13,846	7,015	1,001	7,971	11,514	199	1,331
30—40	20,652	10,924	9,728	943	213	9,533	6,795	448	2,720
40—50	13,893	7,047	6,846	288	121	6,201	3,299	558	3,426
50—60	8,602	4,237	4,365	151	60	3,473	1,191	613	3,114
60 and over	5,901	2,923	2,978	104	53	2,078	354	741	2,571

TABLE VIII.

Civil Condition by Age ror Selected Castes.

This table corresponds to table XIV of 1921.

2. The corresponding Provincial tables have been arranged to show the castes according to the prevalence of infant marriage. This has not been done in this table as an alphabetical arrangement facilitates references to any given caste if particulars are required, which would otherwise be difficult in the India table on account of the numbers tabulated.

3. Instead of merely reproducing provincial and state details by provinces and states severally, the details are shown by caste for India as a whole in so far as material has been supplied, the distinctive names under which allied castes have been shown in each province being retained for the provincial figures.

4. The castes tabulated are not inclusive but are selected as representative of various social tribal or occupational units. In column 3 a note will be found of any other table in which the caste in question also appears as a separate unit.

5. The statistics of any caste shown will be found to compare with the strength shown in Table XIV, but not in all cases with that in Table XVII, as material has not always been available in all provinces to compile for Civil Condition and Literacy up to the total strength of the caste.

6. All the Provinces and principal States and Agencies are represented in this table excep- the Andaman and Nicobar Islands, Aden and the Bombay States and Agencies, where no compilation of castes by Civil Condition was undertaken. Figures for Burma for certain selected races are given at the end of the table.

7. To economise in space other tables of this volume in which the castes detailed in this table also appear are represented in column 3 by small arabic instead of roman numerals.

Table VIII.—Civil Condition

Caste, Tribe or Race. 1	Province, State or Agency and Religion. 2	Also tabulated in: 3	Sex. 4	Population dealt with. 5	Unmarried. Total. 6	0—6. 7	7—13. 8	14—16. 9	17—23. 10	24—43. 11	44 & over. 12
1 AGRI	Bombay (Hindu)	**17**	**Males** ..	**119,063**	**57,938**	**25,986**	**20,694**	**5,460**	**4,114**	**1,447**	**237**
			Females ..	**117,182**	**42,530**	**25,952**	**14,575**	**676**	**1,044**	**240**	**43**
2 AMBALAVASI	....	**14,17**	**Males** ..	**8,743**	**5,325**	**1,724**	**1,386**	**546**	**840**	**706**	**123**
			Females ..	**8,623**	**3,521**	**1,576**	**1,237**	**371**	**222**	**96**	**19**
	Cochin (Hindu)	..	Males ..	4,538	2,864	882	755	295	471	402	59
			Females ..	4,673	1,958	842	678	225	143	56	14
	Travancore (Hindu)	..	Males ..	4,205	2,461	842	631	251	369	304	64
			Females ..	3,950	1,563	734	559	146	79	40	5
3 AMMAKODAGA	Coorg (Hindu)	..	**Males** ..	**336**	**202**	**55**	**52**	**30**	**40**	**24**	**1**
			Females ..	**330**	**166**	**64**	**61**	**16**	**25**	..	..
ARAYAN ..	....	**17**	**Males** ..	**15,330**	**8,911**	**3,188**	**2,770**	**1,068**	**1,393**	**464**	**28**
			Females ..	**14,624**	**7,078**	**3,215**	**2,631**	**732**	**395**	**78**	**27**
	Cochin (Hindu)	..	Males ..	3,457	2,008	651	595	247	395	116	4
			Females ..	3,117	1,450	666	525	176	74	7	2
	Travancore (Hindu)	..	Males ..	11,873	6,903	2,537	2,175	821	998	348	24
			Females ..	11,507	5,628	2,549	2,106	556	321	71	25
5 BAIDYA ..	....	**14,17**	**Males** ..	**61,052**	**33,802**	**10,413**	**9,993**	**4,273**	**5,997**	**2,879**	**247**
			Females ..	**56,104**	**24,097**	**10,812**	**9,374**	**2,492**	**936**	**422**	**61**
	Assam (Hindu)	..	Males ..	3,425	2,139	654	686	210	346	226	17
			Females ..	2,992	1,479	656	602	128	28	65	..
	Bengal (Hindu)	..	Males ..	57,627	31,663	9,759	9,307	4,063	5,651	2,653	230
			Females ..	53,112	22,618	10,156	8,772	2,364	908	357	61
BAIRAGI (Babaji Baishnab).	....	**14,17**	**Males**	**198,027**	**83,861**	**30,380**	**27,126**	**8,852**	**9,452**	**6,106**	**1,945**
			Females ..	**208,414**	**48,737**	**29,521**	**15,089**	**1,840**	**1,066**	**875**	**346**
	C. P. and Berar (Hindu).	..	Males ..	19,408	8,169	3,222	2,486	653	615	735	458
			Females ..	19,066	5,476	3,283	1,724	214	111	86	58
	Gwalior (Hindu)	..	Males ..	16,177	7,318	2,756	2,107	884	574	655	342
			Females ..	14,026	4,870	2,400	1,814	414	149	57	36
BAISHNAB..	Bengal (Hindu)	..	Males ..	162,442	68,374	24,402	22,533	7,315	8,263	4,716	1,145
			Females ..	175,322	38,391	23,838	11,551	1,212	806	732	252
BANJARA, etc.	....	**14,17,18**	**Males** ..	**344,788**	**166,623**	**62,660**	**48,379**	**22,920**	**17,625**	**9,240**	**5,799**
			Females ..	**325,911**	**131,407**	**63,308**	**42,302**	**12,027**	**9,423**	**2,878**	**1,469**
BANJARA ..	C. P. and Berar (Hindu and Tribal).	..	Males ..	76,660	37,833	16,822	12,372	3,355	2,920	1,308	1,056
			Females ..	75,388	28,763	16,713	9,196	1,354	751	506	243
	Mysore (Hindu)	..	Males ..	26,170	15,586	5,769	5,495	1,928	1,737	629	28
			Females ..	24,539	12,015	5,799	5,118	844	177	48	29
	C. P. and Berar (Muslim).	..	Males ..	58	35	10	14	4	6	1	..
			Females ..	55	26	17	7	2	..	..	..
LAMBADA..	Hyderabad (Tribal)	..	Males ..	153,856	72,176	23,101	19,222	11,664	9,095	5,345	3,749
			Females ..	146,610	60,118	24,181	17,972	7,246	7,868	1,879	972
LAMANI ..	Bombay ..	..	Males ..	18,937	11,202	4,840	3,747	1,133	879	493	110
			Females ..	17,923	8,797	5,029	3,255	360	70	70	13
LAMBANI ..	Mysore (Tribal)	..	Males ..	6,967	4,176	1,563	1,419	495	505	185	9
			Females ..	6,692	3,200	1,604	1,329	208	42	11	6
WANJARI ..	C. P. and Berar (Hindu).	..	Males ..	23,175	9,639	5,031	2,850	737	641	303	77
			Females ..	22,733	7,134	4,696	1,846	260	124	168	40
	Hyderabad (Hindu)	..	Males ..	38,965	15,976	5,524	3,260	3,604	1,842	976	770
			Females ..	31,971	11,354	5,269	3,579	1,753	391	196	166
BANIYA ..	....	**14,17**	**Males** ..	**487,553**	**240,826**	**82,128**	**72,866**	**25,824**	**26,772**	**24,717**	**8,519**
			Females ..	**429,629**	**150,067**	**80,833**	**58,165**	**7,556**	**1,959**	**1,078**	**476**
AGARWAL	Bengal (Hindu)	..	Males ..	10,855	4,336	1,335	1,247	615	674	402	63
			Females ..	7,441	2,469	1,289	960	136	57	27	..
	Delhi.. (Hindu)	..	Males ..	14,704	6,648	2,020	1,959	807	982	708	172
			Females ..	10,679	3,889	1,945	1,572	255	81	26	10
	Delhi.. (Jain)	..	Males ..	1,603	740	271	233	107	71	48	10
			Females ..	1,449	546	246	231	54	12	2	1
	Punjab Hindu	..	Males ..	187,699	101,377	33,551	30,186	10,521	11,153	11,848	4,118
			Females ..	159,421	63,533	32,449	25,171	4,475	1,030	303	105
	Punjab (Jain)	..	Males ..	12,683	6,386	2,322	2,065	747	583	524	145
			Females ..	11,538	4,679	2,311	1,887	371	68	33	9
	Rajputana (All-Religions).	..	Males ..	45,623	22,764	8,194	7,392	2,091	1,753	2,236	1,098
			Females ..	45,651	14,670	8,461	5,780	216	107	62	44
BANIYA ..	C. P. and Berar (All Religions).	..	Males ..	122,156	54,731	20,466	16,816	5,739	6,145	4,392	1,173
			Females ..	111,505	33,922	20,047	11,958	845	308	512	252
	Gwalior (Hindu)	..	Males ..	48,011	21,182	6,862	5,853	2,687	2,352	2,534	894
			Females ..	39,739	11,928	7,105	4,251	300	148	83	41
	Baroda (Hindu and Jain).	..	Males ..	12,011	6,047	1,878	1,893	663	849	557	207
			Females ..	10,954	3,742	1,806	1,666	188	73	8	1
DISAWAL	Baroda (Hindu and Jain).	..	Males ..	3,691	1,823	595	565	182	232	167	82
			Females ..	3,524	996	512	447	33	3	1	..
KAPOL ..	Baroda (Hindu and Jain).	..	Males ..	1,334	823	253	235	106	116	84	29
			Females ..	1,211	498	232	232	32	1	..	1
KHADAYATA	Baroda (Hindu and Jain).	..	Males ..	2,034	929	307	301	100	114	72	35
			Females ..	1,829	613	342	260	9	2	..	..
LAD ..	Baroda (Hindu and Jain).	..	Males ..	4,110	2,096	684	637	225	299	177	74
			Females ..	3,688	1,234	632	547	47	5	1	2

by age for selected castes.

Married. Total. 13	0—6. 14	7—13. 15	14—16. 16	17—23. 17	24—43. 18	44 & over. 19	Widowed. Total. 20	0—6. 21	7—13. 22	14—16. 23	17—23. 24	24—43. 25	44 & over. 26	
56,689	157	769	1,320	8,429	32,082	13,932	4,436	2	126	129	98	1,276	2,805	1
59,979	199	3,692	5,385	13,815	30,758	6,130	14,673	4	45	65	907	4,410	9,242	
2,997	..	1	5	136	1,629	1,226	421	..	..	..	6	121	294	2
3,393	..	22	181	765	1,833	592	1,709	..	..	8	59	468	1,174	
1,456	..	..	2	53	784	617	218	..	..	..	3	66	149	
1,702	..	6	74	377	936	309	1,013	..	..	3	44	303	663	
1,541	..	1	3	83	845	609	203	..	..	..	3	55	145	
1,691	..	16	107	388	897	283	696	..	..	5	15	165	511	
114	..	..	..	6	68	40	20	..	..	..	..	9	11	3
115	..	..	..	25	78	12	49	..	..	..	2	11	36	
5,854	..	2	8	400	3,500	1,944	565	..	..	1	14	177	373	4
5,938	..	10	204	1,472	3,379	873	1,608	..	..	6	50	434	1,118	
1,299	..	..	..	59	769	471	150	..	..	..	3	58	89	
1,282	..	..	37	311	749	185	385	..	..	1	13	98	273	
4,555	..	2	8	341	2,731	1,473	415	..	..	1	11	119	284	
4,656	..	10	167	1,161	2,630	688	1,223	..	..	5	37	336	845	
24,740	214	560	817	2,331	12,334	8,484	2,510	1	23	35	209	675	1,567	5
23,167	189	988	1,965	6,096	10,447	3,482	8,840	16	48	196	513	2,847	5,220	
1,169	..	2	14	49	597	507	117	..	..	..	2	29	86	
1,052	1	14	68	274	574	121	461	..	2	2	16	157	284	
23,571	214	558	803	2,282	11,737	7,977	2,393	1	23	35	207	646	1,481	
22,115	188	974	1,897	5,822	9,873	3,361	8,379	16	46	194	497	2,690	4,936	
98,935	638	2,673	3,507	13,030	48,946	30,191	15,181	36	100	210	807	4,881	9,147	6
100,083	1,402	11,256	9,994	23,332	39,913	14,186	59,594	106	432	756	3,268	24,520	30,512	
9,900	110	513	523	1,506	4,784	2,464	1,339	5	17	15	64	442	796	
10,154	196	1,025	880	2,180	4,558	1,315	3,436	4	13	14	88	935	2,382	
7,196	142	338	524	1,164	3,317	1,711	1,663	7	16	39	118	590	893	
6,745	196	593	781	1,727	2,601	847	2,411	11	35	69	175	918	1,203	
81,889	386	1,822	2,460	10,360	40,845	26,016	12,179	24	67	156	625	3,849	7,458	
83,184	1,010	9,638	8,333	19,425	32,754	12,024	53,747	91	384	673	3,005	22,667	26,927	
153,936	1,541	7,027	8,932	26,312	71,231	38,893	24,229	174	477	582	1,280	7,241	14,475	7
152,888	8,727	13,157	16,593	30,828	63,940	24,643	41,616	192	593	1,060	1,935	12,746	25,090	
35,046	359	1,503	1,907	5,646	17,586	8,045	3,781	7	75	78	284	1,136	2,201	
36,795	484	3,290	4,017	9,003	15,355	4,646	9,830	20	84	191	498	2,935	6,102	
9,543	2	4	35	446	6,299	2,757	1,041	..	..	2	28	351	660	
9,825	2	98	517	2,469	5,794	945	2,699	..	1	6	46	904	1,742	
21	..	..	..	4	15	2	2	..	..	..	..	..	2	
21	..	1	1	9	8	2	8	..	..	..	..	1	7	
69,166	982	3,857	5,328	13,787	28,740	16,472	12,514	91	214	226	565	4,064	7,354	
67,541	2,424	6,095	7,566	11,966	26,202	13,288	18,951	100	320	564	956	6,017	10,994	
7,175	66	113	199	666	4,302	1,829	560	2	4	5	11	147	391	
7,410	73	202	646	1,797	3,973	719	1,716	1	4	7	28	556	1,120	
2,564	..	1	5	146	1,671	741	227	..	1	..	4	73	149	
2,681	1	28	140	745	1,491	276	811	..		1	16	294	500	
11,829	119	1,060	758	1,908	5,274	2,710	1,707	32	97	107	181	483	807	
12,910	586	1,892	1,477	2,710	4,937	1,308	2,689	28	40	38	97	707	1,779	
18,592	13	489	700	3,709	7,344	6,337	4,397	42	86	164	207	987	2,911	
15,705	157	1,551	2,229	2,129	6,180	3,459	4,912	43	144	253	294	1,332	2,846	
200,546	591	3,819	8,225	36,536	103,004	48,371	46,181	62	149	326	1,485	14,429	29,730	8
196,521	1,384	10,136	20,621	52,264	88,532	23,584	83,041	50	228	585	2,837	28,949	50,392	
5,855	19	115	238	1,009	3,037	1,437	664	..	3	10	45	255	351	
3,782	27	201	512	978	1,709	355	1,190	1	4	62	90	450	583	
6,593	2	23	140	1,101	3,933	1,394	1,463	..	2	4	48	548	861	
5,117	5	63	381	1,351	2,673	644	1,673	..	1	9	42	560	1,061	
718	..	2	11	119	410	176	145	..	..	1	3	42	99	
713	1	8	61	178	359	106	190	..	..	2	5	55	128	
67,685	27	603	2,607	13,557	35,532	15,359	18,637	4	21	59	494	5,888	12,171	
68,410	253	1,875	6,396	19,310	31,970	8,606	27,478	10	32	112	951	9,853	16,520	
4,905	2	39	180	1,008	2,563	1,113	1,392		3	2	34	475	878	
4,957	2	93	420	1,392	2,378	672	1,902	..	3	4	65	731	1,099	
18,409	38	376	950	3,583	8,763	4,699	4,450	1	10	20	96	1,260	3,063	
21,417	64	1,127	2,383	5,332	9,603	2,908	9,564	7	23	53	334	3,461	5,686	
58,348	398	1,928	2,136	9,643	30,373	13,870	9,077	35	64	104	364	2,848	5,662	
55,122	918	4,982	6,308	13,760	23,940	5,214	22,461	20	100	194	774	7,783	13,590	
20,230	100	674	1,565	3,720	9,320	4,851	6,599	21	44	115	304	2,174	3,941	
18,991	109	1,498	2,557	4,719	7,541	2,567	8,820	11	56	122	303	2,729	5,599	
4,884	..	17	142	735	2,581	1,409	1,080	..	..	2	34	275	769	
4,689	1	76	440	1,352	2,162	658	2,523	1	4	12	79	877	1,550	
1,497	4	4	31	202	749	507	371	..	1	2	10	74	284	
1,507	..	47	161	427	687	185	1,021	..	2	3	29	338	649	
403	..	..	2	37	206	158	108	..	..	..	..	26	82	
446	..	1	31	123	220	71	267	..	..	..	7	91	169	
920	..	9	35	188	444	244	185	..	..	1	7	46	131	
875	1	32	118	246	361	117	341	..	..	..	8	114	219	
1,654	..	5	34	318	833	464	360	..	..	1	6	106	247	
1,701	..	41	182	462	712	304	753	..	..	3	27	288	435	

Table VIII.—Civil Condition

Caste, Tribe or Race. 1	Province, State or Agency and Religion 2	Also tabulated in: 3	Sex. 4	Population dealt with. 5	Unmarried. Total. 6	0—6. 7	7—13. 8	14—16. 9	17—23. 10	24—43. 11	44 & over. 12
8 **BANIYA**—*concld.*											
PORWAD ..	Baroda (Hindu and Jain).	..	Males ..	4,106	2,053	626	639	240	297	181	70
		..	Females ..	3,761	1,195	560	532	89	10	1	3
SHRIMALI ..	Baroda (Hindu and Jain).	..	Males ..	16,933	8,891	2,764	2,845	994	1,152	787	349
		..	Females ..	17,239	6,153	2,896	2,671	506	54	19	7
9 **BAURI** ..	..	14,17,18	**Males** ..	**199,902**	**89,804**	**38,796**	**31,584**	**8,797**	**7,301**	**3,066**	**260**
		..	**Females** ..	**206,081**	**61,802**	**38,339**	**20,320**	**2,016**	**698**	**347**	**82**
BAURI	Bengal (Hindu)	..	Males ..	164,205	71,095	30,624	25,262	6,870	5,761	2,420	158
		..	Females ..	167,033	45,200	29,966	14,242	609	215	135	33
BAVURI	Madras (Hindu)	..	Males ..	19,062	9,748	4,504	3,380	1,059	681	108	16
		..	Females ..	23,748	9,207	4,633	3,329	750	326	146	23
BAWARIYA	Delhi (Hindu)	..	Males ..	23	13	4	4	2	3	..	..
		..	Females ..	9	1	..	1	..	..	..	..
	(Punjab) (Hindu)	..	Males ..	8,420	4,619	1,989	1,497	460	434	203	36
		..	Females ..	7,625	3,540	1,887	1,328	225	62	29	9
	(Punjab) (Sikh)	..	Males ..	8,192	4,329	1,675	1,441	406	422	335	50
		..	Females ..	7,666	3,854	1,853	1,420	432	95	37	17
10 **BHANGI** ..	..	14,17	**Males** ..	**349,937**	**159,913**	**70,414**	**53,654**	**15,059**	**11,626**	**7,530**	**1,630**
		..	**Females** ..	**318,110**	**112,744**	**68,821**	**36,539**	**3,909**	**1,734**	**1,343**	**398**
	Bombay (Hindu)	..	Males ..	19,013	6,986	3,340	2,294	577	399	264	112
		..	Females ..	18,415	5,035	3,231	1,355	255	104	68	22
	United Provinces (All-Religions).	..	Males ..	265,530	122,534	53,634	40,529	11,659	9,141	6,258	1,313
		..	Females ..	238,078	85,540	52,471	27,588	2,718	1,306	1,126	331
	Baroda (Hindu)	..	Males ..	15,867	6,478	3,165	2,336	485	385	93	14
		..	Females ..	15,151	4,452	2,838	1,428	160	17	6	3
	Central India (Hindu).	..	Males ..	13,018	6,131	2,591	2,132	599	495	275	39
		..	Females ..	12,268	4,322	2,520	1,526	151	67	44	14
	Rajputana (All-Religions)	..	Males ..	19,945	9,356	4,209	3,224	852	579	374	118
		..	Females ..	18,631	6,748	4,179	2,219	206	68	61	15
	Western India States (Hindu).	..	Males ..	16,564	8,428	3,475	3,139	887	627	266	34
		..	Females ..	15,567	6,647	3,582	2,423	419	172	38	13
11 **BHAR**	United Provinces (All-Religions).	17	**Males**	**232,658**	**90,583**	**47,685**	**29,720**	**5,410**	**4,086**	**2,926**	**756**
			Females ..	**229,086**	**71,403**	**49,389**	**18,839**	**1,628**	**586**	**624**	**337**
12 **BHARBHUNJA** ..	United Provinces (All-Religions).	14,17	**Males** ..	**152,326**	**65,349**	**26,854**	**20,524**	**6,423**	**5,589**	**4,714**	**1,245**
		..	**Females** ..	**134,084**	**44,300**	**26,339**	**14,565**	**1,681**	**849**	**554**	**312**
13 **BHAT** ..	..	14,17	**Males** ..	**60,376**	**28,011**	**10,653**	**8,252**	**2,849**	**2,633**	**2,773**	**851**
		..	**Females** ..	**61,189**	**19,514**	**11,649**	**6,060**	**886**	**410**	**341**	**168**
	United Provinces (All-Religions).	..	Males ..	50,854	24,364	9,408	7,067	2,373	2,244	2,493	779
		..	Females ..	53,441	16,949	9,841	5,532	773	357	306	140
	Hyderabad (Hindu) ..		Males ..	9,522	3,647	1,245	1,185	476	389	280	72
			Females ..	7,748	2,565	1,808	528	113	53	35	28
14 **BHIL**	..	14,17,18	**Males** ..	**359,337**	**181,098**	**79,705**	**65,385**	**18,078**	**12,453**	**3,866**	**1,611**
		..	**Females** ..	**352,484**	**157,761**	**88,216**	**55,062**	**9,876**	**3,092**	**1,185**	**330**
	Bombay (Hindu)	..	Males ..	136,869	66,514	29,675	23,573	6,719	4,386	1,024	1,137
		..	Females ..	134,320	59,827	34,303	18,929	4,525	1,418	559	93
	C. P. and Berar (All Religions).	..	Males ..	12,568	5,085	2,497	1,994	360	169	48	17
		..	Females ..	12,425	3,891	2,531	1,325	14	11	9	1
	Baroda (Hindu and Tribal).	..	Males ..	27,789	13,295	5,982	4,660	1,347	1,018	254	34
		..	Females ..	26,753	11,564	6,660	4,026	696	151	26	5
	Gwalior (Hindu)	..	Males ..	39,430	16,491	6,989	5,450	1,820	1,427	658	147
		..	Females ..	38,340	14,331	8,877	4,745	422	140	69	78
	Hyderabad (Tribal) ..	..	Males ..	7,551	3,261	1,240	1,309	287	243	143	39
		..	Females ..	7,501	2,322	1,145	724	255	93	64	41
	Rajputana (Hindu Tribal and Christian).	..	Males ..	135,130	76,452	33,322	28,399	7,545	5,210	1,739	237
		..	Females ..	133,145	65,826	34,700	25,313	3,964	1,279	458	112
15 **BHILALA** ..	..	17,18	**Males** ..	**26,382**	**12,493**	**4,729**	**4,418**	**1,233**	**1,366**	**637**	**110**
		.	**Females** ..	**25,585**	**10,946**	**6,073**	**4,153**	**400**	**209**	**74**	**37**
	C. P. and Berar (Hindu).	..	Males ..	8,177	3,602	1,502	1,329	359	302	98	12
		..	Females ..	7,654	2,460	1,568	851	14	10	14	3
	Gwalior (Hindu)	..	Males ..	18,205	8,891	3,227	3,089	874	1,064	539	98
		..	Females ..	17,931	8,486	4,505	3,302	386	199	60	34
16 **BOHRA** (Vohora)	..	14,17	**Males** ..	**66,095**	**31,649**	**11,380**	**10,479**	**3,246**	**4,181**	**1,609**	**754**
		..	**Females** ..	**62,392**	**23,765**	**10,664**	**8,687**	**2,460**	**1,377**	**444**	**133**
	Bombay (Muslim)	..	Males ..	45,856	21,081	7,587	6,754	2,056	2,853	1,166	665
		..	Females ..	40,887	15,024	6,759	5,341	1,546	900	369	109
	C. P. and Berar (Muslim).	..	Males ..	1,206	777	164	263	155	162	30	3
		..	Females ..	1,407	678	286	250	83	51	7	1
	Baroda (Muslim)	..	Males ..	13,752	7,030	2,693	2,447	712	824	285	69
		..	Females ..	14,603	5,715	2,633	2,178	580	271	41	12
	Western India States (Muslim).	..	Males ..	5,281	2,761	936	1,015	323	342	128	17
			Females ..	5,495	2,348	986	918	251	155	27	11
17 **BRAHMAN** ..	..	14,17	**Males** ..	**7,165,796**	**3,479,568**	**1,155,304**	**1,041,443**	**377,485**	**436,066**	**359,863**	**109,407**
		..	**Females** ..	**6,461,876**	**2,033,967**	**1,125,813**	**752,841**	**93,857**	**32,099**	**21,002**	**8,355**
ANAVALA ..	Baroda (Hindu)	..	Males ..	6,137	3,239	873	1,023	371	430	348	194
		..	Females ..	5,681	1,843	868	863	102	8	..	2

by age for selected castes—*contd.*

Married.							Widowed.							
Total. 13	0—6. 14	7—13. 15	14—16. 16	17—23. 17	24—43. 18	44 & over. 19	Total. 20	0—6. 21	7—13. 22	14—16. 23	17—23. 24	24—43. 25	44 & over. 26	
1,659	..	6	30	270	817	536	394	..	..	2	11	96	285	
1,634	1	23	131	472	772	235	932	..	..	3	19	318	592	
6,786	1	18	124	1,046	3,443	2,154	1,256	1	1	3	29	316	906	
7,160	2	69	540	2,162	3,445	942	3,926	..	3	6	104	1,301	2,512	
102,528	**305**	**1,855**	**3,295**	**14,833**	**57,557**	**24,683**	**7,570**	**3**	**20**	**44**	**465**	**2,804**	**4,234**	9
107,145	**679**	**10,386**	**10,794**	**26,254**	**48,013**	**11,019**	**37,134**	**34**	**267**	**504**	**2,012**	**14,613**	**19,704**	
86,848	283	1,645	2,962	12,608	48,943	20,407	6,262	2	15	38	410	2,458	3,339	
89,385	601	9,841	9,630	21,668	38,912	8,733	32,448	32	256	474	1,847	12,965	16,874	
8,995	16	118	145	1,116	5,691	2,509	319	1	4	2	15	68	229	
11,136	62	342	700	2,985	5,818	1,229	3,405	2	9	17	102	1,274	2,001	
10	..	1	2	1	5	1	..	..	.	..	..	..	..	
6	..	..	..	..	5	1	2	..	.	..	..	..	2	
3,341	6	73	106	515	1,807	834	460	..	1	1	28	148	282	
3,407	15	159	303	865	1,599	466	678	..	2	11	28	223	414	
3,334	..	18	80	593	1,711	932	529	..	..	3	12	130	384	
3,211	1	44	161	736	1,679	590	601	..	..	2	35	151	413	
164,567	**1,230**	**8,034**	**10,443**	**27,963**	**83,525**	**33,372**	**25,457**	**57**	**304**	**596**	**2,044**	**9,067**	**13,389**	10
168,386	**1,775**	**14,308**	**17,567**	**38,178**	**78,832**	**17,726**	**36,980**	**63**	**249**	**372**	**1,132**	**11,331**	**23,833**	
10,876	386	1,418	877	1,675	4,427	2,093	1,151	17	64	44	180	345	501	
11,176	620	1,964	1,027	2,323	4,040	1,202	2,204	13	39	21	89	665	1,377	
122,347	574	4,823	7,551	21,019	63,876	24,504	20,649	23	176	458	1,545	7,543	10,904	
125,152	721	9,462	13,158	28,232	60,364	13,215	27,386	37	169	292	834	8,338	17,716	
8,583	65	716	620	1,596	3,690	1,896	806	5	27	21	74	231	448	
8,789	122	1,139	880	2,127	3,711	810	1,916	4	17	8	42	566	1,273	
6,126	49	273	340	920	3,325	1,219	761	6	7	13	44	297	394	
6,170	76	441	663	1,489	2,996	505	1,776	3	8	16	57	613	1,079	
9,227	87	552	675	1,564	4,532	1,817	1,362	5	22	37	146	418	734	
9,763	119	919	1,212	2,257	4,289	967	2,120	5	12	22	66	687	1,328	
7,408	69	252	380	1,189	3,675	1,843	728	1	8	23	55	233	408	
7,336	117	383	627	1,750	3,432	1,027	1,584	1	4	13	44	462	1,060	
127,100	**3,191**	**14,250**	**11,097**	**18,506**	**54,969**	**25,087**	**14,975**	**85**	**320**	**328**	**823**	**4,730**	**8,639**	11
129,955	**3,551**	**19,583**	**12,180**	**23,634**	**56,141**	**14,866**	**27,728**	**82**	**356**	**370**	**687**	**8,184**	**18,049**	
72,623	**751**	**3,844**	**4,245**	**11,130**	**37,381**	**15,272**	**14,354**	**35**	**144**	**220**	**828**	**5,298**	**7,829**	12
71,033	**955**	**6,517**	**6,779**	**13,975**	**34,394**	**8,413**	**18,751**	**37**	**126**	**184**	**623**	**5,597**	**12,184**	
26,502	**387**	**1,595**	**1,728**	**3,810**	**12,038**	**6,944**	**5,863**	**24**	**68**	**111**	**404**	**1,810**	**3,446**	13
30,216	**463**	**2,519**	**2,824**	**6,447**	**13,794**	**4,169**	**11,459**	**40**	**79**	**147**	**459**	**3,689**	**7,045**	
21,711	328	1,274	1,285	3,100	10,357	5,367	4,779	24	57	77	264	1,586	2,771	
25,728	401	2,185	2,460	5,368	12,016	3,358	10,764	40	73	128	406	3,514	6,603	
4,791	59	321	443	710	1,681	1,577	1,084	..	11	34	140	224	675	
4,488	62	334	424	1,079	1,778	811	695	..	6	19	53	175	442	
166,350	**574**	**3,508**	**7,273**	**28,957**	**85,367**	**40,672**	**11,839**	**20**	**52**	**128**	**660**	**4,202**	**6,827**	14
163,729	**706**	**8,701**	**17,371**	**41,141**	**76,106**	**19,704**	**30,994**	**33**	**126**	**277**	**832**	**8,809**	**20,917**	
66,555	196	1,033	2,001	12,063	35,850	15,412	3,800	1	6	32	205	1,436	2,120	
62,371	318	3,454	6,316	15,821	29,079	7,383	12,122	8	39	123	374	3,611	7,967	
6,864	17	188	394	1,223	3,718	1,324	619	.	5	3	18	242	351	
7,001	42	810	759	1,724	3,163	503	1,533	3	11	21	58	541	899	
13,389	5	82	295	2,232	7,003	3,772	1,105	2	1	8	63	338	693	
13,134	3	283	956	3,434	6,517	1,941	2,055	3	6	10	41	443	1,552	
21,150	143	825	1,436	3,949	9,149	5,648	1,789	16	20	37	128	675	913	
20,381	203	1,207	2,940	5,243	9,084	1,704	3,628	12	29	56	138	1,328	2,065	
4,039	208	278	302	584	1,590	1,077	251	1	8	9	14	78	141	
4,093	119	582	470	1,045	1,164	713	1,086	7	17	14	69	296	683	
54,353	5	1,102	2,845	8,906	28,057	13,438	4,325	..	12	39	232	1,433	2,609	
56,749	21	2,365	5,930	13,874	27,099	7,460	10,570	..	24	53	152	2,590	7,751	
12,778	**112**	**485**	**868**	**2,491**	**6,656**	**2,166**	**1,111**	**2**	**2**	**6**	**52**	**395**	**654**	15
11,528	**68**	**636**	**1,066**	**2,783**	**5,877**	**1,098**	**3,111**	**9**	**25**	**40**	**70**	**1,023**	**1,944**	
4,010	12	60	105	652	2,266	915	565	1	..	3	18	206	337	
3,973	4	336	458	967	1,888	320	1,221	1	4	14	28	439	735	
8,768	100	425	763	1,839	4,390	1,251	546	1	2	3	34	189	317	
7,555	64	300	608	1,816	3,989	778	1,890	8	21	26	42	584	1,209	
30,420	**403**	**1,343**	**1,226**	**4,228**	**14,270**	**8,950**	**4,026**	**9**	**39**	**27**	**152**	**1,148**	**2,651**	16
31,066	**755**	**1,823**	**1,921**	**7,486**	**14,069**	**5,012**	**7,561**	**13**	**66**	**122**	**315**	**1,801**	**5,244**	
21,978	377	1,060	1,024	3,138	10,242	6,137	2,797	6	27	20	119	815	1,810	
21,073	721	1,503	1,356	4,941	9,115	3,437	4,790	11	58	115	249	1,175	3,182	
375	6	7	16	32	165	149	54	..	..	..	1	20	33	
582	..	11	19	170	311	71	147	..	..	1	1	25	120	
5,927	15	174	156	821	2,857	1,904	795	3	12	5	18	217	540	
6,954	24	263	407	1,724	3,463	1,073	1,934	2	8	5	49	417	1,453	
2,140	5	102	30	237	1,006	760	380	..	..	2	14	96	268	
2,457	10	46	139	651	1,180	431	690	..	..	1	16	184	489	
3,116,365	**15,776**	**74,196**	**114,438**	**427,195**	**1,623,342**	**861,418**	**569,863**	**843**	**2,880**	**5,390**	**18,997**	**169,283**	**372,470**	17
3,031,480	**21,249**	**218,002**	**303,279**	**715,544**	**1,380,393**	**393,013**	**1,396,429**	**1,707**	**7,739**	**14,698**	**61,679**	**487,673**	**822,938**	
2,381	1	17	37	357	1,230	739	517	..	1	1	5	111	399	
2.618	1	66	211	692	1,248	400	1,220	..	2	4	43	435	736	

Table VIII.—Civil Condition

Caste, Tribe or Race. 1	Province, State or Agency and Religion. 2	Also tabulated in: 3	Sex. 4	Population dealt with. 5	Unmarried. Total. 6	0—6. 7	7—13. 8	14—16. 9	17—23. 10	24—43. 11	44 & over. 12
BRAHMAN—*contd.*											
AUDICH ..	Bombay (Hindu)	..	Males ..	14,488	6,004	1,786	1,965	681	766	563	243
		..	Females ..	13,204	3,639	1,713	1,403	218	124	117	64
	Baroda (Hindu)	..	Males ..	22,909	11,260	3,547	3,544	1,188	1,523	1,014	444
		..	Females ..	22,313	6,333	3,312	2,787	208	18	5	3
	Western India States (Hindu).	..	Males ..	40,547	20,776	7,142	7,009	2,575	2,505	1,164	381
		..	Females ..	39,602	13,988	7,077	5,885	715	208	79	24
CHITPAWAN, KOKANASTH and KONKANI	Bombay (Hindu)	..	Males ..	35,339	20,637	7,497	5,042	2,427	3,901	1,514	256
		..	Females ..	33,600	14,001	6,157	5,456	1,360	449	546	33
	Baroda (Hindu)	..	Males ..	1,911	1,127	279	278	158	280	113	19
		..	Females ..	1,628	619	282	251	72	12	2	..
	Cochin (Hindu)	..	Males ..	4,828	2,587	881	806	326	388	141	45
		..	Females ..	4,833	1,686	909	747	14	10	4	2
DESHASTH ..	Bombay (Hindu)	..	Males ..	120,226	64,072	21,238	18,782	7,444	10,520	4,925	1,163
		..	Females ..	107,440	39,784	20,909	15,848	2,163	526	265	73
	Baroda (Hindu)	..	Males ..	3,058	1,714	430	428	223	401	180	52
		..	Females ..	2,655	958	435	424	89	8	2	..
GAUD SARASWAT	Bombay (Hindu)	..	Males ..	18,891	10,908	3,618	3,473	1,314	1,700	681	122
		..	Females ..	18,997	7,663	3,497	3,243	688	165	51	19
KANARESE ..	Coorg (Hindu)	..	Males ..	685	376	83	112	48	89	41	3
		..	Females ..	573	209	90	105	12	1	1	..
	Madras (Hindu)	..	Males ..	52,920	26,518	9,256	8,237	3,057	4,026	1,508	434
		..	Females ..	53,722	16,843	9,420	6,798	322	149	115	39
KHEDWAL ..	Baroda (Hindu)	..	Males ..	2,069	1,081	356	338	110	117	96	64
		..	Females ..	1,923	535	281	240	13	1	..	..
MALAYALA ..	Madras (Hindu)	..	Males ..	14,158	6,954	2,103	1,743	770	1,407	799	132
		..	Females ..	12,175	4,825	2,132	1,438	425	427	270	133
	Cochin (Hindu)	..	Males ..	3,663	1,922	526	481	256	336	249	74
		..	Females ..	3,500	1,305	509	459	158	136	41	2
	Travancore *(Hindu).	..	Males ..	7,498	3,518	1,219	908	401	566	312	112
		..	Females ..	6,433	2,336	1,138	890	178	78	39	13
MEWADA ..	Baroda (Hindu)	..	Males	2,696	1,344	382	414	134	187	155	72
			Females ..	2,379	664	381	254	24	5	..	..
MODH ..	Baroda (Hindu)	..	Males ..	4,459	2,181	705	653	212	267	242	102
			Females ..	4,580	1,266	704	503	54	4	..	1
NAGAR ..	Baroda (Hindu)	..	Males ..	4,017	2,203	632	668	239	350	226	88
			Females ..	4,079	1,317	593	588	105	30	1	..
ORIYA ..	Madras (Hindu)	..	Males ..	71,846	32,859	13,759	11,623	3,882	2,676	724	195
			Females ..	79,281	20,035	13,948	5,308	275	189	244	71
TAMIL ..	Madras (Hindu)	..	Males ..	243,007	114,994	42,210	36,601	12,984	17,136	4,917	1,146
		..	Females ..	251,714	77,817	43,663	30,925	1,770	838	428	193
	Cochin (Hindu)	..	Males ..	10,884	6,327	2,318	2,173	770	829	207	30
		..	Females ..	10,870	4,161	2,297	1,775	70	12	5	2
TAPODHAN ..	Baroda (Hindu)	..	Males ..	3,038	1,402	555	501	152	127	51	16
		..	Females ..	3,032	850	530	295	18	3	2	2
TELUGU ..	Madras (Hindu)	..	Males ..	230,273	98,617	36,612	31,757	10,694	10,953	5,998	2,603
		..	Females ..	241,729	58,861	38,527	18,347	875	513	361	238
BRAHMANS Unspecified	Assam (Hindu)	..	Males ..	86,557	46,340	15,769	14,084	5,017	7,390	3,568	512
		..	Females ..	70,625	26,076	15,298	9,556	557	254	287	124
	Bengal (Hindu)	..	Males ..	788,513	385,807	126,068	116,312	44,397	65,016	30,479	3,535
		..	Females ..	667,667	226,938	122,796	86,789	10,439	3,877	2,158	879
	Bihar and Orissa (Hindu).	..	Males ..	1,069,759	488,664	167,269	161,792	51,108	54,244	44,551	9,700
		..	Females ..	1,031,528	283,573	165,847	105,587	7,278	2,570	1,771	520
	Central Provinces and Berar (All Religions)		Males ..	277,936	131,768	43,905	39,236	14,311	19,184	12,188	2,944
			Females ..	239,829	78,905	43,478	30,108	3,214	1,119	789	197
	Delhi (Hindu)	..	Males ..	30,524	14,342	3,949	3,678	1,778	2,561	1,992	384
		..	Females ..	19,686	7,116	3,759	2,652	497	145	56	7
	N.-W. F. Province (All Religions)	..	Males ..	10,723	5,258	1,314	1,188	557	1,041	914	244
		..	Females ..	6,477	2,569	1,256	843	233	170	52	15
	Punjab (Hindu)	..	Males ..	576,735	310,015	93,450	87,744	35,329	40,728	38,739	14,025
		..	Females ..	474,647	173,153	89,491	67,284	11,460	3,212	1,275	431
	Punjab (Sikh)	..	Males ..	3,911	2,122	600	504	222	314	348	134
		..	Females ..	2,653	1,054	493	373	101	42	29	16
	United Provinces (All Religions)	..	Males ..	2,420,848	1,190,338	386,916	344,057	119,522	128,462	156,106	55,275
		..	Females ..	2,135,117	664,257	373,153	241,066	30,356	8,884	7,890	2,908
	Baroda (Hindu)	..	Males ..	13,743	6,582	1,789	1,727	638	1,104	965	359
		..	Females ..	11,215	3,411	1,745	1,414	198	44	7	3
	Central India (Hindu)		Males ..	243,207	116,770	38,221	34,270	11,979	13,294	14,898	4,108
		..	Females ..	223,362	64,733	37,368	23,500	1,840	810	988	227
	Gwalior (Hindu)	..	Males ..	166,237	77,295	25,885	20,984	8,630	8,626	9,550	3,620
		..	Females ..	129,812	41,302	23,801	14,102	1,876	648	534	341
	Hyderabad (Hindu)	..	Males ..	196,654	77,259	28,649	20,877	12,593	7,483	5,276	2,381
		..	Females ..	179,814	60,727	24,335	18,039	11,195	4,120	1,807	1,231
	Jammu and Kashmir (Hindu).	..	Males ..	†94,931	50,990	16,556	13,680	5,758	7,278	5,889	1,829
		..	Females ..	†90,390	32,352	15,926	12,431	2,520	1,073	290	112
	Travancore (Hindu)	..	Males ..	27,233	13,813	5,135	4,334	1,621	1,968	635	120
		..	Females ..	26,908	9,603	[illegible]	3,928	208	[illegible]	[illegible]	[illegible]

by age for selected castes—*contd.*

Married.							Widowed.						
Total. 13	0—6. 14	7—13. 15	14—16. 16	17—23. 17	24—43. 18	44 & over. 19	Total. 20	0—6. 21	7—13. 22	14—16. 23	7—23. 24	24—43. 25	44 & over 26
7,114	95	201	364	926	3,484	2,044	1,370	10	16	33	9	361	891
6,719	99	558	780	1,550	2,790	942	2,846	14	53	57	[illegible]	915	1,618
9,656	5	96	227	1,374	4,851	3,103	1,993	4	5	5	40	452	1,487
9,998	11	571	1,119	2,769	4,238	1,290	5,982	4	9	24	244	2,052	3,649
16,604	37	313	524	2,373	7,961	5,396	3,167	4	11	22	118	728	2,284
17,903	133	964	1,737	4,424	7,510	3,135	7,711	3	11	52	333	2,588	4,724
12,621	63	99	238	925	6,879	4,417	2,081	2	23	29	32	380	1,615
12,549	25	141	821	3,414	6,167	1,981	7,050	4	10	23	290	2,478	4,245
645	..	1	2	15	363	264	139	..	..	..	1	25	113
629	..	2	37	185	327	78	380	..	..	..	10	133	237
2,046	..	..	6	160	1,053	827	195	..	..	..	1	34	160
2,171	1	46	249	561	1,023	291	976	..	1	2	29	275	669
47,019	164	408	556	4,618	26,372	14,901	9,135	2	8	29	143	1,900	7,053
44,811	192	1,648	4,784	12,623	20,007	5,557	22,845	9	60	145	1,034	8,292	13,305
1,022	1	..	1	45	580	395	322	..	..	..	1	74	247
1,012	1	4	80	279	522	126	685	..	1	1	28	220	435
6,974	20	31	31	367	3,698	2,827	1,009	1	1	..	8	175	824
7,406	20	87	497	1,936	3,804	1,062	3,928	1	4	9	144	1,335	2,435
254	..	1	..	18	167	68	55	..	..	..	1	18	36
213	..	5	28	70	93	17	151	..	..	..	5	65	81
23,491	25	43	171	2,392	12,935	7,925	2,911	..	3	..	43	575	2,290
24,437	41	1,324	2,842	6,498	10,622	3,110	12,442	2	16	77	531	3,999	7,817
795	1	12	26	132	370	254	193	..	..	..	2	39	152
905	8	92	102	207	384	112	483	..	1	6	21	159	296
6,696	..	14	14	515	3,559	2,594	508	..	..	..	14	128	366
5,032	..	199	393	1,176	2,437	827	2,318	..	10	43	122	608	1,535
1,640	..	..	..	92	801	747	101	..	..	..	..	28	73
1,401	..	4	43	246	801	307	794	..	..	..	13	175	606
3,706	..	3	15	312	1,848	1,528	274	..	..	..	4	72	198
2,722	..	42	166	639	1,355	520	1,375	..	2	5	29	378	961
1,095	..	14	38	168	502	373	257	..	..	..	3	51	203
1,044	2	100	122	247	426	147	671	..	1	5	19	226	420
1,846	..	13	47	264	899	623	432	2	..	2	8	98	322
2,021	5	114	205	536	911	250	1,293	..	2	2	39	443	807
1,443	..	7	17	129	688	602	371	..	1	..	3	58	309
1,583	5	62	131	421	726	238	1,179	..	3	9	45	396	726
36,591	96	412	1,123	6,109	18,961	9,890	2,396	..	11	13	62	475	1,835
39,929	215	5,897	4,054	10,032	15,920	3,811	19,317	15	123	201	,171	6,944	10,863
117,682	13	349	1,149	12,177	64,795	39,199	10,331	..	4	4	105	1,654	8,564
118,747	96	5,755	11,566	29,768	55,102	16,460	55,150	2	71	223	1,776	15,588	37,490
4,200	..	1	7	251	2,097	1,844	357	..	..	..	7	49	301
4,976	..	150	530	1,151	2,283	862	1,733	1	..	10	65	453	1,204
1,471	4	42	79	268	697	381	165	..	4	2	5	44	110
1,598	9	184	201	416	635	153	584	..	1	4	15	168	396
118,433	144	1,755	4,197	18,444	60,183	33,710	13,223	6	22	79	392	3,123	9,601
117,584	776	16,187	13,706	28,062	45,904	12,949	65,284	39	276	715	3,805	20,623	39,826
36,205	13	330	418	3,490	21,380	10,574	4,012	1	31	42	127	1,242	2,569
31,542	39	2,624	3,718	9,290	13,413	2,458	13,007	6	61	154	832	5,005	6,949
363,069	2,244	6,186	8,832	45,908	200,292	99,607	39,637	190	289	864	1,829	12,017	24,448
307,521	3,019	23,868	34,141	84,262	128,566	33,665	133,208	179	917	2,038	9,104	50,772	70,198
503,895	3,087	14,458	20,643	72,570	259,520	133,617	77,200	118	377	735	2,583	23,434	49,953
498,236	4,415	49,002	46,978	111,852	227,112	58.877	249,719	369	2,033	2,964	12,069	93,105	139,179
126,319	607	2,506	3,560	17,790	69,949	31,907	19,849	35	150	109	650	6,141	12,764
111,010	976	7,405	10,903	28,692	50,980	12,048	49,914	30	298	517	2,145	17,744	29,180
13,448	5	70	389	2,145	8,415	2,424	2,734	..	3	12	104	1,088	1,527
9,482	2	209	805	2,789	4,811	866	3,088	..	1	23	115	1,079	1,870
4,587	..	118	212	768	2,384	1,105	878	..	1	9	69	341	458
2,980	..	63	379	781	1,331	426	928	..	8	1	19	312	588
209,773	108	1,752	4,767	28,529	113,028	61,589	56,947	8	39	169	1,348	16,758	38,595
207,642	447	9,283	18,087	51,804	99,870	28,151	93,852	23	193	555	3,220	30,735	59,126
1,419	1	3	23	192	758	442	370	..	..	..	4	105	261
1,220	4	30	81	264	608	233	379	..	..	..	4	114	261
1,000,250	7,457	33,820	49,484	144,711	502,368	262,410	230,260	306	1,319	2,215	7,629	71,057	147,734
1,009,149	8,046	62,733	91,746	220,182	488,410	138,032	461,711	658	2,357	4,356	15,791	157,099	281,450
5,837	28	30	99	818	3,139	1,723	1,324	1	2	3	27	372	919
5,042	4	183	467	1,396	2,377	615	2,762	1	3	11	87	910	1,750
106,675	590	5,733	7,474	17,404	52,724	22,750	19,762	49	271	252	819	6,517	11,854
106,149	1,179	10,353	11,594	23,618	49,071	10,334	52,480	88	341	674	2,503	21,297	27,577
69,304	511	2,631	5,111	13,075	28,991	18,985	19,638	62	100	179	523	6,954	11,820
60,309	666	4,922	7,254	15,073	24,692	7,702	28,201	139	180	346	674	9,721	17,141
100,482	144	374	1,008	9,252	56,538	33,166	18,913	23	82	223	1,164	5,509	11,912
99,526	368	4,337	14,603	17,057	37,738	25,423	19.561	90	439	663	1,908	6,536	9,925
36,311	..	874	827	4,017	18,419	12,174	7,630	..	15	80	334	2,422	4,779
39,693	..	1,339	4,670	10,482	18,098	5,104	18,345	..	44	231	759	6,420	10,891
12,523	..	12	47	878	6,806	4,780	897	..	..	4	10	182	701
12,607	..	375	1,230	2,896	6,082	2,024	4,698	..	3	23	118	1,244	3,310

Table VIII.—Civil Condition

Caste, Tribe or Race.	Province, State or Agency and Religion.	Also tabulated in :	Sex.	Population dealt with.	Unmarried.						
					Total.	0—6.	7—13.	14—16.	17—23.	24—43.	44 & over.
1	2	3	4	5	6	7	8	9	10	11	12
BRAHMAN—*concld.*											
	Mysore (Hindu)		Males	126,542	66,751	23,018	21,298	8,164	10,656	3,030	585
			Females	118,621	42,975	23,974	18,246	493	135	89	38
	Rajputana (Hindu)		Males	112,196	52,834	18,804	17,119	5,445	5,237	4,567	1,662
			Females	107,582	33,685	18,450	12,091	1,464	983	326	371
18 **BRAHMBHAT** (including barot).	Baroda (Hindu and Jain).	14,17	**Males**	**7,362**	**3,690**	**1,220**	**1,107**	**343**	**437**	**394**	**189**
			Females	**7,219**	**1,990**	**1,171**	**713**	**97**	**4**	**5**	..
19 **BRAHUI**	Baluchistan (Muslim).	17,18	**Males**	**2,112**	**1,122**	**428**	**487**	**95**	**80**	**28**	**4**
			Females	**1,806**	**798**	**495**	**231**	**34**	**30**	**4**	**4**
20 **CHAMAR**	....	14,17	**Males**	**5,870,160**	**2,433,959**	**1,166,007**	**812,302**	**200,171**	**144,915**	**88,219**	**22,345**
			Females	**5,675,795**	**1,814,470**	**1,178,949**	**539,652**	**49,297**	**22,921**	**18,085**	**5,566**
CHAMAR	Bihar and Orissa (Hindu).		Males	612,875	221,144	122,609	73,049	11,557	8,465	4,346	1,118
			Females	673,986	184,572	128,109	49,727	3,633	1,616	1,188	299
	C. P. and Berar (All Religions).		Males	305,693	116,965	61,521	38,209	9,227	5,199	2,096	713
			Females	309,999	94,786	61,835	25,966	3,380	1,649	1,363	598
	Delhi (Hindu)		Males	23,174	8,698	4,053	3,099	704	446	354	42
			Females	19,437	6,242	4,163	1,843	109	70	47	10
	Delhi (Ad-Dharmi)		Males	246	69	33	26	8	..	..	2
			Females	193	51	33	18	..	..	..	..
	Delhi (Christian)		Males	1,388	563	300	206	37	10	6	4
			Females	1,356	464	297	143	7	4	10	3
	N. W. F. Province (All Religions)		Males	1,749	922	327	253	137	106	72	27
			Females	1,169	595	245	138	55	62	76	19
	Punjab (Hindu)		Males	366,739	174,821	70,309	60,953	18,415	14,362	8,508	2,274
			Females	318,224	115,226	68,798	40,671	3,958	1,053	592	154
	Punjab (Ad-Dharmi)		Males	139,641	61,376	27,126	20,848	4,093	4,082	4,196	1,031
			Females	116,708	39,182	24,751	10,965	845	1,316	977	328
	Punjab (Sikh)		Males	85,446	43,152	16,102	13,990	4,909	4,297	2,957	897
			Females	70,271	27,993	15,491	10,266	1,690	398	91	57
	United Provinces (All Religions)		Males	3,225,936	1,287,325	641,401	415,089	98,388	70,158	49,985	12,304
			Females	3,086,257	941,466	643,409	257,743	18,884	9,170	9,107	3,153
	Baroda (Hindu)		Males	21,005	9,611	4,210	3,804	997	498	78	24
			Females	21,797	7,316	4,073	2,806	382	48	7	.
	Central India (Hindu).		Males	258,924	106,423	49,911	38,702	9,724	,243	2,339	504
			Females	254,637	79,815	50,145	24,731	1,694	892	2,009	344
	Gwalior (Hindu)		Males	212,626	92,510	38,783	30,395	10,718	6,877	4,010	1,727
			Females	203,324	72,892	44,560	24,216	2,069	1,183	547	317
	Jammu and Kashmir (Hindu)		Males	21,672	10,808	4,109	3,393	1,192	1,242	628	244
			Females	19,517	7,501	4,112	2,660	569	125	31	4
	Rajputana (All Religions)		Males	203,584	90,957	41,328	34,141	8,590	4,556	1,909	433
			Females	193,061	66,365	42,347	22,136	1,285	383	184	30
CHAKKILIYAN	Madras (Hindu)		Males	303,687	170,305	65,928	62,730	18,161	17,148	5,787	551
			Females	303,088	141,968	68,702	57,270	9,809	4,509	1,469	209
HAMBHAR	Bombay (Hindu)		Males	61,220	26,508	13,044	9,139	2,022	1,348	652	303
			Females	60,205	18,614	12,928	4,696	336	291	336	27
	Western India States (Hindu).		Males	24,555	11,802	4,913	4,276	1,292	878	296	147
			Females	22,566	9,422	4,951	3,657	592	152	51	19
21 **CHENCHU**	..	14,17,18	**Males**	**5,256**	**2,594**	**1,053**	**826**	**289**	**263**	**128**	**35**
			Females	**5,086**	**2,157**	**1,049**	**616**	**180**	**170**	**97**	**45**
	Madras (Tribal)		Males	4,166	2,143	866	680	227	245	104	21
			Females	3,912	1,729	874	491	130	131	76	27
	Hyderabad (Tribal)		Males	1,090	451	187	146	62	18	24	14
			Females	1,174	428	175	125	50	39	21	18
22 **CHETTI**	Travancore (Hindu)	14,17	**Males**	**8,665**	**4,854**	**1,585**	**1,394**	**546**	**875**	**429**	**25**
			Females	**8,757**	**3,694**	**1,741**	**1,324**	**385**	**183**	**52**	**9**
23 **CHODHRA**	..	14,17,18	**Males**	**41,482**	**21,744**	**8,426**	**7,448**	**2,404**	**2,407**	**923**	**136**
			Females	**39,801**	**18,772**	**8,683**	**6,788**	**1,876**	**1,017**	**354**	**54**
	Bombay (Hindu)		Males	21,530	10,831	4,265	3,871	1,220	1,076	329	70
			Females	20,967	9,612	4,430	3,593	938	463	164	24
	Baroda (Hindu and Tribal).		Males	19,952	10,913	4,161	3,577	1,184	1,331	594	66
			Females	18,834	9,160	4,253	3,195	938	554	190	30
24 **CHUHRA**	..	14,17	**Males**	**381,989**	**205,094**	**78,680**	**67,269**	**22,302**	**21,811**	**12,586**	**2,446**
			Females	**317,577**	**139,927**	**74,147**	**50,376**	**9,814**	**3,477**	**1,673**	**440**
	Delhi (Hindu)		Males	9,987	4,376	1,920	1,429	341	381	272	33
			Females	7,918	3,003	1,843	973	110	57	19	1
	Delhi (Muslim)		Males	174	66	23	25	7	9	1	1
			Females	171	65	39	23	1	1	1	..
	Delhi (Christians)		Males	1,449	661	323	224	44	39	26	5
			Females	1,404	472	311	136	16	4	5	..
	N. W. F. Province (All Religions)		Males	6,380	3,007	777	605	374	668	532	51
			Females	2,905	1,093	525	931	109	30	25	13
	Punjab (Hindu)		Males	200,293	104,530	41,040	35,144	11,192	10,159	5,827	1,168
			Females	167,931	72,543	39,160	26,497	4,328	1,544	782	232
	Punjab (Ad-Dharmi)		Males	47,315	26,984	10,033	8,680	2,945	2,862	2,135	329
			Females	39,233	18,303	9,413	6,897	1,202	439	284	68
	Punjab (Sikh)		Males	85,481	48,465	17,792	15,722	5,579	5,907	2,782	683
			Females	71,860	32,010	16,240	11,576	2,908	937	266	83
	Punjab (Muslim)		Males	11,886	6,734	2,737	2,053	781	642	444	77
			Females	10,264	5,054	2,525	1,721	524	190	82	12

by age for selected castes—*contd.*

Married.							Widowed.							
Total. 13	0—6. 14	7—13. 15	14—16. 16	17—23. 17	24—43. 18	44 & over. 19	Total. 20	0—6. 21	7—13. 22	14—16. 23	17—23. 24	24—43. 25	44 & over. 26	
52,721	1	33	159	5,702	30,553	16,273	7,070	..	..	5	55	1,426	5,584	
52,054	6	3,156	6,980	14,815	21,295	5,802	23,592	1	37	178	1,140	7,811	14,425	
48,122	311	1,434	2,516	7,515	23,105	13,241	11,240	19	61	270	665	3,066	7,159	
49,310	438	3,918	5,239	12,389	20,698	6,628	24,587	29	167	347	1,191	8,821	14,032	
3,053	..	**56**	**102**	**419**	**1,494**	**982**	**619**	**2**	**7**	**5**	**13**	**144**	**448**	18
4,343	**20**	**290**	**310**	**879**	**1,437**	**407**	**1,886**	..	**7**	**11**	**82**	**603**	**1,183**	
928	**1**	**8**	**20**	**81**	**501**	**317**	**62**	..	..	**3**	**7**	**21**	**31**	19
911	..	**15**	**75**	**153**	**542**	**126**	**97**	..	**1**	**2**	**1**	**21**	**72**	
3,071,102	**42,249**	**238,316**	**216,783**	**479,510**	**1,488,854**	**605,390**	**365,099**	**1,029**	**6,186**	**8,346**	**21,942**	**126,743**	**200,853**	20
3,128,906	**56,814**	**372,338**	**317,654**	**623,676**	**1,430.749**	**327,675**	**732,419**	**1,837**	**7,201**	**8,353**	**19,864**	**228,805**	**466,359**	
365,700	9,346	46,622	27,094	51,446	162,029	69,163	26,031	196	1,069	853	1,722	8,432	13,759	
396,010	15,199	58,814	35,085	72,747	172,518	41,647	93,404	461	1,716	1,229	2,850	30,300	56,848	
177,090	4,127	16,285	11,821	29,648	79,249	35,960	11,638	25	183	237	796	3,844	6,553	
177,404	5,148	22,850	17,829	37,114	73,783	20,680	37,809	118	339	449	1,091	11,549	24,263	
12,583	9	732	1,062	2,487	6,497	1,796	1,893	..	17	47	132	780	917	
11,314	11	1,152	1,535	2,767	5,050	799	1,881	..	9	18	37	688	1,129	
166	..	6	6	34	88	32	11	..	..	..	2	4	5	
133	..	8	19	34	63	9	9	..	..	..	..	2	7	
727	1	40	53	144	367	122	98	..	3	..	11	32	52	
769	2	79	97	185	338	68	123	..	4	..	1	46	72	
712	..	6	41	141	373	151	115	..	3	10	12	47	43	
482	..	8	63	124	231	56	92	..	..	..	6	31	55	
162,536	191	5,830	9,885	29,361	82,890	34,379	29,382	3	160	372	1,386	9,923	17,538	
166,142	626	15,303	19,928	39,596	74,716	15,973	36,856	10	145	232	728	11,469	24,272	
66,416	239	5,976	5,500	10,342	28,370	15,989	11,849	3	61	116	396	3,642	7,631	
66,033	622	9,690	7,560	13,412	24,968	9,781	11,493	8	57	156	457	2,328	8,487	
34,465	30	838	1,877	6,032	16,810	8,878	7,829	4	27	59	248	2,363	5,128	
35,070	52	1,915	3,561	8,269	16,214	5,059	7,208	2	13	29	90	1,519	5,555	
1,722,231	25,281	140,938	128,653	268,264	837,485	321,610	216,380	634	4,027	5,487	14,554	78,251	113,427	
1,737.173	29,949	215,051	177,888	332,888	805,279	176,118	407,618	979	4,097	4,762	10,658	123,848	263,274	
10,463	35	476	691	1,783	,902	2,576	931	4	30	17	28	254	598	
11,525	110	1,126	1,385	2,355	5,492	1,057	2,956	2	22	26	44	852	2,010	
139,836	1,081	8,442	11,174	24,567	69,408	25,164	12,665	32	257	395	863	4,616	6,502	
139,549	2,481	17,045	16,772	29,657	62,247	11,347	35,273	73	325	413	970	13,380	20,112	
99,862	1,393	5,418	8,874	20,101	46,536	17,540	20,254	112	192	504	829	6,687	11,930	
100,195	1,081	10,961	12,942	21,276	42,080	11,855	30,237	150	204	596	1,272	10,309	17,706	
9,365	6	138	255	1,243	5,075	2,648	1,499	..	20	14	67	452	946	
9,411	1	369	1,061	2,173	4,328	1,479	2,605	.	9	53	96	876	1,571	
99,937	228	4,105	6,784	16,133	52,387	20,300	12,690	12	93	174	496	3,996	7,919	
102,859	503	10,389	12,313	21,775	47,740	10,139	23,837	16	129	202	460	7,829	15,201	
125,203	32	255	749	11,183	76,255	37,729	8,179	..	5	8	234	2,461	5,471	
130,405	39	1,511	5,453	29,894	76,870	16,638	30,715	1	35	98	795	10,786	19,000	
32,200	172	1,863	1,681	4,692	15,781	8,011	2,512	1	33	38	95	670	1,675	
33,809	753	5,369	3,202	6,998	14,071	3,416	7,782	9	90	79	229	2,254	5,121	
11,610	78	346	583	1,909	5,352	3,342	1,143	3	6	15	71	289	759	
10,623	237	698	961	2,412	4,761	1,554	2,521	8	7	11	80	739	1,676	
2,372	**8**	**33**	**82**	**342**	**1,268**	**639**	**290**	.	..	**2**	**22**	**109**	**157**	21
2,366	**14**	**118**	**249**	**605**	**1,091**	**289**	**563**	**1**	**6**	**26**	**53**	**203**	**274**	
1,853	3	21	61	268	1,003	497	170	..	..	1	20	69	80	
1,823	4	64	157	490	924	184	360	1	1	9	16	137	196	
519	5	12	21	74	265	142	120	..	.	1	2	40	77	
543	10	54	92	115	167	105	203	..	5	17	37	66	78	
3,518	..	**1**	**14**	**245**	**2,038**	**1,220**	**293**	..	..	..	**8**	**80**	**205**	22
3,696	..	**28**	**195**	**957**	**1,936**	**580**	**1,367**	..	**1**	**7**	**39**	**376**	**944**	
17,277	**56**	**100**	**127**	**1,929**	**9,846**	**5,219**	**2,461**	..	**1**	**10**	**120**	**763**	**1,567**	23
17,713	**69**	**124**	**563**	**3,889**	**9,716**	**3,352**	**3,316**	**7**	**20**	**17**	**108**	**814**	**2,350**	
9,351	54	98	94	1,119	5,166	2,820	1,348	..	1	8	68	399	872	
9,532	63	98	335	1,999	5,122	1,915	1,823	1	1	9	84	446	1,282	
7,926	2	2	33	810	4,680	2,399	1,113	..	..	2	52	364	695	
8,181	6	26	228	1,890	4,594	1,437	1,493	6	19	8	24	368	1,068	
149,019	**176**	**,657**	**6,341**	**24,698**	**78,874**	**35,273**	**27,876**	**9**	**121**	**254**	**1,303**	**9,546**	**16,643**	24
148,684	**422**	**7,364**	**13,060**	**36,279**	**72,198**	**19,361**	**28,966**	**6**	**77**	**103**	**578**	**8,129**	**20,073**	
4,897	5	248	311	932	2,627	774	714	..	4	13	59	299	339	
4,258	19	349	452	1,123	1,990	325	657	..	3	1	22	228	403	
97	..	2	3	14	62	16	11	..	..	..	1	6	4	
90	..	5	10	20	49	6	16	..	..	..	1	7	8	
653	6	84	74	112	242	135	135	..	3	1	6	46	79	
808	..	125	121	159	335	68	124	..	..	..	2	49	73	
2,830	..	135	128	557	1,333	677	543	..	1	13	32	262	235	
1,441	..	68	149	354	690	180	371	..	2	1	5	158	205	
80,199	144	2,403	4,060	13,610	42,050	17,932	15,564	5	89	171	741	5,492	9,066	
80,057	321	5,027	7,566	19,279	38,620	9,244	15,331	5	47	70	324	4,719	10,166	
17,121	11	323	532	2,750	8,912	4,593	3,210	..	6	22	115	932	2,135	
17,785	32	494	1,509	4,124	8,645	2,981	3,145	1	3	15	48	719	2,359	
31,454	7	271	870	4,933	17,104	8,269	5,562	4	11	22	251	1,671	3,603	
32,774	30	903	2,364	8,631	16,294	4,552	7,076	..	15	10	100	1,664	5,287	
4,375	1	28	130	584	2,545	1,087	777	..	..	3	38	278	458	
4,288	1	88	319	835	2,239	806	922	..	3	3	30	242	644	

Table VIII.—Civil Condition

Caste, Tribe or Race. 1	Province, State or Agency and Religion. 2	Also tabulated in : 3	Sex. 4	Population dealt with. 5	Unmarried. Total. 6	0—6. 7	7—13. 8	14—16. 9	17—23. 10	24—43. 11	44 & over. 12
CHUHRA—*concld.*											
	Punjab (Christian)	..	Males ..	19,024	10,271	4,035	3,387	1,039	1,144	567	99
		..	Females ..	15,891	7,384	4,091	2,162	616	275	209	31
25 **DARZI** ..	....	14,17	**Males** ..	**166,963**	**75,121**	**29,594**	**24,948**	**8,255**	**6,820**	**4,024**	**1,480**
		..	**Females** ..	**158,577**	**55,525**	**30,888**	**18,579**	**3,575**	**1,259**	**800**	**424**
BHAVSAR AND CHIPPA.	Baroda (Hindu and Jain).	..	Males ..	2,934	1,246	425	472	123	125	75	26
		..	Females ..	2,932	802	455	288	33	17	4	5
CHHIMBA ..	Punjab (Hindu)	..	Males ..	11,338	5,670	1,883	1,686	635	670	578	218
		..	Females ..	9,623	3,662	2,025	1,291	284	38	16	8
	Punjab (Sikh)	..	Males ..	9,182	4,840	1,531	1,316	613	551	582	247
		..	Females ..	7,559	2,892	1,468	1,035	238	64	69	18
	Punjab (Muslim)	..	Males ..	28,696	14,962	5,908	4,782	1,560	1,581	899	232
		..	Females ..	24,710	10,636	5,595	3,676	777	387	167	34
DARZI ..	Bombay (Hindu)*	..	Males ..	16,636	7,555	3,298	2,617	798	548	242	52
		..	Females ..	16,239	5,212	3,314	1,699	102	39	52	6
	C. P. and Berar (All Religions).	..	Males ..	26,210	10,498	4,639	3,635	986	782	368	88
		..	Females ..	25,019	8,966	4,597	2,142	132	43	35	17
	Baroda (Hindu and Jain).	..	Males ..	7,541	3,274	1,480	1,166	296	222	103	7
		..	Females ..	8,197	2,316	1,342	851	82	38	2	1
	Hyderabad (Hindu)†	..	Males ..	32,220	11,231	3,697	3,690	1,639	939	753	513
		..	Females ..	31,411	10,840	5,591	3,069	1,286	380	291	223
	Mysore (Hindu) ..	..	Males ..	10,488	5,899	2,249	1,992	725	742	170	21
		..	Females ..	10,039	4,338	2,362	1,761	144	47	19	5
	Western India States (Hindu).	..	Males ..	21,718	9,946	4,484	3,592	880	660	254	76
		..	Females ..	22,848	7,861	4,139	2,767	497	206	145	107
26 **DHOBI** ..	....	14,17	**Males** ..	**793,880**	**346,386**	**143,282**	**115,060**	**37,316**	**29,608**	**17,203**	**3,917**
		..	**Females** ..	**745,409**	**247,469**	**142,349**	**79,163**	**15,666**	**5,664**	**3,415**	**1,212**
DHOBI ..	Bombay (Hindu)‡	..	Males ..	13,387	6,349	2,598	2,176	565	610	322	78
		..	Females ..	13,125	4,186	2,423	1,283	254	170	52	4
	C. P. and Berar (All Religions).	..	Males ..	92,245	33,962	17,843	11,368	2,345	1,387	800	219
		..	Females ..	95,361	26,443	18,189	7,143	526	277	209	99
	Delhi (Hindu)	..	Males ..	1,805	794	304	286	84	67	46	7
		..	Females ..	1,367	534	324	172	25	9	4	..
	Delhi (Muslim)	..	Males ..	578	260	102	74	33	37	14	..
		..	Females ..	444	178	105	61	6	1	4	1
	Punjab (Hindu)	..	Males ..	5,824	2,699	1,123	860	261	247	173	35
		..	Females ..	4,608	1,832	1,049	651	91	19	17	5
	Punjab (Muslim)	..	Males ..	87,947	47,378	18,197	14,804	4,920	5,357	3,320	780
		..	Females ..	74,097	32,235	16,817	11,333	2,287	1,065	500	233
	United Provinces (All Religions).	..	Males ..	401,747	171,190	78,248	57,350	15,099	10,878	7,932	1,683
		..	Females ..	374,412	122,250	77,091	37,866	3,638	1,650	1,499	506
	Central India (Hindu).	..	Males ..	27,423	11,425	5,114	3,879	1,109	771	449	103
		..	Females ..	26,823	8,202	5,041	2,609	223	134	154	41
	Hyderabad (Hindu)§	..	Males ..	138,790	58,889	14,312	20,036	11,503	8,527	3,577	934
		..	Females ..	130,702	40,823	16,120	14,109	7,580	1,851	869	294
	Western India States (Hindu).	..	Males ..	2,274	1,162	471	467	111	87	25	1
		..	Females ..	2,300	925	496	358	48	12	11	..
VANNAN ..	Travancore (Hindu).	..	Males ..	6,770	3,666	1,437	1,115	381	515	194	24
		..	Females ..	6,663	2,971	1,415	1,071	269	163	38	15
VELUTHADA-NAYAP.	Travancore (Hindu)	..	Males ..	7,331	4,177	1,809	1,228	357	553	182	48
		..	Females ..	7,547	3,226	1,580	1,219	284	118	20	5
VELUTTEDAN	Cochin (Hindu) ..	..	Males ..	1,816	1,053	386	310	144	152	60	1
		..	Females ..	2,106	847	349	306	102	68	17	5
VETTUVAN ..	Cochin (Hindu) ..	..	Males ..	5,943	3,382	1,338	1,107	404	420	109	4
		..	Females ..	5,854	2,817	1,350	982	333	127	21	4
27 **DOM**	....	14,17	**Males** ..	**187,445**	**73,593**	**31,745**	**24,337**	**7,296**	**5,733**	**3,120**	**1,362**
		..	**Females** ..	**178,529**	**50,647**	**31,351**	**14,458**	**2,293**	**1,045**	**821**	**679**
BANSPHOR OR BASOR.	C. P. and Berar (All Religions).	..	Males ..	16,142	7,448	3,430	2,575	698	448	228	69
		..	Females ..	15,590	5,257	3,174	1,886	140	33	19	5
	Central India (Hindu).	..	Males ..	22,282	8,960	4,055	3,094	855	527	292	137
		..	Females ..	21,005	6,659	4,104	2,012	230	85	105	123
BURUD ..	Hyderabad (Hindu)‖	..	Males ..	19,054	6,241	1,763	1,356	1,053	988	542	539
		..	Females ..	15,723	4,881	1,840	1,246	888	362	266	279
DOM ..	Bengal (Hindu) ..	..	Males ..	71,279	27,951	11,705	9,857	2,656	2,348	1,145	240
		..	Females ..	68,783	16,156	11,142	4,178	373	217	173	73
	United Provinces .. (All Religions).	..	Males ..	58,688	22,993	10,792	7,455	2,034	1,422	913	377
		..	Females ..	57,428	17,694	11,091	5,136	662	348	258	199
28 **DOSADH (DUSADH).** ..	United Provinces (Hindu).	14,17	**Males** ..	**36,902**	**14,988**	**7,233**	**5,079**	**1,139**	**863**	**534**	**140**
		..	**Females** ..	**36,620**	**11,783**	**7,296**	**3,721**	**458**	**145**	**136**	**27**
29 **ELUTHASSAN** ..	Cochin (Hindu) ..	17	**Males**	**9,026**	**5,079**	**1,863**	**1,542**	**649**	**828**	**185**	**12**
			Females	**9,510**	**4,150**	**1,839**	**1,544**	**490**	**218**	**51**	**8**
30 **GADARIA** ..	..	14,17	**Males** ..	**1,063,238**	**463,015**	**191,865**	**152,936**	**47,822**	**40,794**	**25,227**	**4,371**
			Females ..	**987,967**	**321,633**	**193,121**	**108,606**	**11,372**	**4,099**	**3,554**	**881**
BHARWAD (BHARUD & DHANGAR).	Bombay (Hindu)	..	Males ..	74,079	29,205	12,919	10,077	2,827	2,052	1,048	282
		..	Females ..	69,790	18,372	12,267	5,190	454	198	168	95
	Baroda (Hindu) ..	..	Males	33,130	11,458	5,720	3,516	1,030	697	398	97
		..	Females	31,248	7,929	4,857	2,554	380	124	9	5
	Western India States (Hindu).	..	Males ..	88,258	33,908	15,675	11,023	2,959	1,995	1,915	341
		..	Females ..	82,248	25,378	15,177	7,906	1,114	350	799	32

*Including Shimpi, Sai and Mirai. †Including Shimpi. ‡Including Parit Agasa and Madival. §Including Chakala. ‖ Including Medari.

by age for selected castes—*contd.*

Married. Total. 13	0—6. 14	7—13. 15	14—16. 16	17—23. 17	24—43. 18	44 & over. 19	Widowed. Total. 20	0—6. 21	7—13. 22	14—16. 23	17—23. 24	24—43. 25	44 & over. 26	
7,393	2	163	233	1,206	3,999	1,790	1,360	..	7	9	60	560	724	
7,183	19	305	570	1,754	3,336	1,199	1,324	..	4	3	46	343	928	
77,738	**353**	**2,331**	**3,521**	**13,049**	**37,180**	**21,304**	**14,104**	**23**	**98**	**327**	**912**	**3,814**	**8,930**	**25**
80,244	**1,355**	**7,884**	**8,484**	**18,162**	**33,728**	**10,631**	**22,808**	**59**	**175**	**233**	**898**	**6,797**	**14,646**	
1,431	3	68	82	304	590	384	257	..	..	1	11	71	174	
1,501	11	144	163	329	650	204	629	1	1	5	14	188	420	
4,221	3	110	180	759	2,040	1,129	1,447	..	9	11	63	399	965	
4,661	15	335	489	1,156	1,985	681	1,300	1	3	4	25	302	965	
3,393	6	90	132	502	1,600	1,063	949	..		3	57	209	679	
3,754	8	178	333	844	1,606	785	913	..		1	12	173	726	
11,438	6	175	357	1,816	5,754	3,330	2,296	2	9	14	88	653	1,530	
11,420	15	494	935	2,430	5,686	1,860	2,654	..	2	8	67	675	1,902	
8,184	39	190	394	1,445	4,183	1,933	897	1	4	3	43	274	572	
8,274	101	931	943	2,211	3,471	617	2,753	2	13	17	92	932	1,697	
14,178	86	525	798	2,450	6,919	3,400	1,534	2	15	8	92	484	933	
13,955	228	1,797	1,506	3,212	5,852	1,360	4,098	5	27	31	109	1,222	2,704	
3,755	6	216	208	683	1,643	999	512	2	14	3	12	127	354	
4,460	36	447	481	1,046	1,915	535	1,421	1	4	10	33	390	983	
16,574	156	554	827	2,586	7,378	5,073	4,415	11	31	269	468	1,193	2,443	
16,489	482	2,181	1,857	2,928	6,388	2,653	4,082	34	74	105	297	1,296	2,276	
4,198	1	7	19	508	2,469	1,194	391	..	..	..	9	90	292	
4,310	..	168	552	1,283	1,902	405	1,391	..	1	12	49	491	838	
10,366	47	396	524	1,996	4,604	2,799	1,406	5	15	15	69	314	988	
11,420	459	1,209	1,225	2,723	4,273	1,531	3,567	15	49	40	200	1,128	2,135	
390,845	**3,940**	**22,713**	**24,608**	**63,446**	**187,876**	**88,262**	**56,649**	**142**	**779**	**1,025**	**4,209**	**18,582**	**31,912**	**26**
401,301	**6,110**	**41,979**	**41,547**	**84,374**	**177,780**	**49,601**	**96,549**	**271**	**899**	**1,163**	**3,517**	**29,659**	**61,040**	
6,315	24	225	257	998	3,325	1,486	723	2	3	1	17	198	502	
6,573	100	889	709	1,466	2,865	544	2,366	..	15	26	79	832	1,414	
54,068	854	4,482	3,680	9,041	24,552	11,459	4,215	44	68	66	242	1,350	2,445	
55,394	1,629	8,400	5,000	11,766	22,673	5,926	13,524	37	117	119	385	3,975	8,891	
891	..	15	26	153	542	155	120		..	2	10	51	57	
718	1	33	63	187	373	61	115	..	..	..	4	26	85	
279	..	4	12	59	153	51	39	..	..	..	1	13	25	
234	2	17	25	60	108	22	32	..	..	..	..	11	21	
2,614	1	41	135	478	1,474	485	511	..	1	5	34	190	281	
2,264	5	113	227	587	1,134	198	512	..	4	6	15	169	318	
33,491	26	446	974	4,638	17,620	9,787	7,078	2	16	33	283	2,383	4,361	
34,160	58	1,073	2,427	7,661	17,275	5,666	7,702	5	10	34	183	2,014	5,456	
200,746	2,121	13,299	13,712	31,947	100,091	39,576	29,811	59	375	448	1,666	10,534	16,729	
204,271	2,804	21,164	20,360	40,892	95,319	23,732	47,891	94	440	526	1,395	13,939	31,497	
14,288	112	768	1,040	2,437	7,150	2,781	1,710	3	36	37	109	651	874	
14,478	188	1,674	1,574	3,113	6,645	1,284	4,143	1	28	41	138	1,383	2,552	
68,470	797	3,422	4,718	12,786	27,277	19,470	11,431	31	279	428	1,813	2,899	5,981	
72,810	1,313	8,564	10,721	15,895	25,842	10,475	17,069	133	283	397	1,195	6,422	8,639	
975	5	7	30	192	552	189	137	1	1	3	8	35	89	
1,011	10	35	107	283	453	123	364	1	..	..	8	120	235	
2,800	..	4	14	284	1,581	917	304	..	..	1	15	106	182	
2,949	..	13	121	759	1,587	469	743	..	1	7	31	176	528	
2,877	..	..	4	182	1,734	957	277	..	..	..	1	81	195	
3,327	..	..	104	895	1,683	645	994	..		2	21	215	756	
669	..	..	1	42	374	252	94	..	..	..	..	28	66	
769	..	3	35	197	412	122	490	..		3	25	192	270	
2,362	..	..	5	209	1,451	697	199	..	..	1	10	63	125	
2,433	..	1	74	613	1,411	334	604	..	1	2	38	185	378	
101,549	**1,142**	**5,458**	**6,053**	**16,958**	**51,103**	**20,835**	**12,303**	**45**	**224**	**427**	**1,006**	**4,279**	**6,322**	**27**
99,704	**2,118**	**12,120**	**10,211**	**22,141**	**43,467**	**9,647**	**28,178**	**46**	**305**	**485**	**1,358**	**10,222**	**15,762**	
8,074	66	290	380	1,513	4,294	1,531	620	..	6	19	40	246	309	
8,274	44	651	907	2,064	4,002	606	2,059	1	13	25	75	751	1,194	
12,037	150	875	991	2,201	5,652	2,168	1,285	3	22	60	137	453	610	
11,715	221	1,317	1,249	2,497	5,310	1,121	2,631	6	31	50	116	917	1,511	
10,539	193	348	777	2,620	4,282	2,319	2,274	11	46	142	189	721	1,165	
8,713	375	763	1,004	2,561	2,940	1,070	2,129	5	44	42	150	706	1,182	
39,552	287	1,414	1,538	5,733	21,947	8,633	3,776	9	62	74	277	1,438	1,916	
38,626	830	5,320	3,678	8,931	16,833	3,034	14,001	12	140	237	737	5,581	7,294	
31,347	446	2,531	2,367	4,891	14,928	6,184	4,348	22	88	132	363	1,421	2,322	
32,376	648	4,069	3,373	6,088	14,382	3,816	7,358	27	77	131	280	2,267	4,581	
19,491	**351**	**1,537**	**1,509**	**2,896**	**8,990**	**4,208**	**2,423**	**2**	**35**	**75**	**123**	**840**	**1,323**	**28**
19,547	**413**	**2,112**	**1,834**	**3,779**	**8,816**	**2,593**	**5,290**	**1**	**95**	**114**	**185**	**1,606**	**3,280**	
3,631	**..**	**..**	**4**	**238**	**2,130**	**1,259**	**316**	**..**	**..**	**..**	**19**	**87**	**210**	**29**
3,750	**..**	**10**	**160**	**902**	**2,127**	**551**	**1,610**	**..**	**..**	**11**	**90**	**466**	**1,043**	
519,931	**4,631**	**31,329**	**32,415**	**76,862**	**260,200**	**114,494**	**80,292**	**228**	**908**	**1,353**	**3,928**	**27,084**	**46,791**	**30**
517,123	**7,817**	**55,810**	**53,700**	**112,436**	**231,667**	**55,693**	**149,211**	**322**	**982**	**1,430**	**4,850**	**47,828**	**93,799**	
39,921	722	2,768	2,578	5,745	18,253	9,855	4,953	45	91	122	334	1,344	3,017	
39,751	1,388	6,350	4,024	8,415	15,558	4,016	11,667	84	163	168	600	3,700	6,952	
19,054	200	1,975	1,813	3,725	7,500	3,841	2,618	3	92	81	161	783	1,498	
19,413	440	2,700	2,335	4,363	7,313	2,262	3,906	12	49	21	58	807	2,959	
47,607	906	5,093	4,301	8,446	18,774	10,087	6,743	36	139	134	389	2,155	3,890	
[illegible]	[illegible]	[illegible]	[illegible]	9,695	17,507	6,229	9,963	23	44	69	331	2,365	[illegible]	

Table VIII.—Civil Condition

Caste, Tribe or Race. 1	Province, State or Agency and Religion. 2	Also tabulated in: 3	Sex. 4	Population dealt with. 5	Unmarried. Total. 6	0—6. 7	7—13. 8	14—16. 9	17—23. 10	24—43. 11	44 & over. 12
GADARIA—*concld.*											
GADARIA	United Provinces (All Religions).		Males	535,958	221,073	98,555	72,969	20,090	14,911	12,045	2,503
			Females	483,589	152,220	98,825	46,047	3,544	1,662	1,676	466
	Gwalior (Hindu)		Males	45,433	18,844	7,508	6,155	2,030	1,447	1,180	524
			Females	42,308	16,123	9,930	5,231	457	275	183	47
KURUBA (*Kurub*).	Bombay (Hindu)		Males	62,214	26,358	11,602	8,926	2,599	2,529	618	84
			Females	60,153	16,777	10,523	5,398	400	267	134	55
	Coorg (Hindu)		Males	3,710	1,900	638	528	199	307	220	8
			Females	3,157	1,335	594	481	140	92	26	2
	Mysore (Hindu)		Males	218,058	119,072	38,803	39,341	15,953	16,695	7,749	531
			Females	213,269	82,595	40,477	35,442	4,835	1,114	549	178
	Mysore (Tribal)		Males	2,398	1,197	445	401	135	161	54	1
			Females	2,205	904	471	357	48	17	10	1
31 **GIRASIA**	Rajputana (Hindu & Tribal).	14,17,18	**Males**	**8,249**	**4,604**	**2,127**	**1,622**	**440**	**296**	**101**	**18**
			Females	**7,755**	**3,664**	**1,972**	**1,334**	**255**	**80**	**20**	**3**
32 **GHASI (Ghasia)**	C. P. & Berar (All Religions).	14,17	**Males**	**16,015**	**6,626**	**3,177**	**2,439**	**416**	**322**	**225**	**47**
			Females	**17,894**	**5,633**	**3,346**	**1,874**	**191**	**102**	**101**	**19**
33 **GOND**	..	14,17,18	**Males**	**1,161,214**	**517,549**	**232,436**	**172,357**	**52,948**	**36,321**	**18,495**	**4,992**
			Females	**1,213,180**	**428,169**	**238,831**	**142,907**	**25,936**	**11,140**	**7,612**	**1,743**
	C. P. & Berar (Hindu).		Males	504,710	213,372	100,397	73,795	19,273	12,623	5,911	1,373
			Females	531,963	176,705	105,496	57,026	7,900	3,084	2,309	890
	C. P. & Berar (Tribal).		Males	599,456	277,152	122,556	91,069	28,914	21,551	10,038	3,024
			Females	624,985	230,898	127,600	79,010	14,442	5,959	3,349	538
	Hyderabad (Tribal).		Males	57,048	27,025	9,483	7,493	4,761	2,147	2,546	595
			Females	56,232	20,566	5,735	6,871	3,594	2,097	1,954	315
34 **GUJAR**	..	14,17,18	**Males**	**1,112,724**	**566,227**	**207,910**	**184,112**	**61,400**	**56,957**	**45,196**	**10,652**
			Females	**925,968**	**348,620**	**198,436**	**121,129**	**18,156**	**6,439**	**3,673**	**787**
	Delhi (Hindu)		Males	8,525	4,222	1,340	1,258	523	547	503	51
			Females	5,766	2,039	1,209	726	78	15	10	1
	Delhi (Muslim)		Males	276	120	8	38	20	40	14	..
			Females	55	17	13	4	..	..	..	..
	N.-W. F. Province (All Religions).		Males	66,223	39,079	13,061	12,804	4,872	4,471	2,888	983
			Females	55,287	24,220	13,026	8,298	1,508	604	621	163
	Punjab (Hindu)		Males	96,208	48,866	16,372	15,225	5,488	5,689	4,926	1,166
			Females	74,231	24,903	14,679	8,730	1,195	224	68	7
	Punjab (Sikh)		Males	1,253	588	215	171	45	59	74	24
			Females	1,068	331	203	97	11	5	13	2
	Punjab (Muslim)		Males	283,585	144,958	53,047	47,592	15,200	14,665	11,982	2,472
			Females	237,762	95,065	53,067	33,076	5,369	2,335	968	250
	United Provinces (All Religions).		Males	206,458	105,661	36,279	32,062	11,115	10,679	11,900	3,626
			Females	162,224	57,367	32,989	19,737	2,564	727	1,222	128
	Central India (Hindu).		Males	45,453	18,444	7,198	6,318	1,742	1,558	1,344	284
			Females	39,249	11,028	7,049	3,555	227	92	82	23
	Gwalior (Hindu)		Males	60,816	28,231	10,410	9,088	3,176	2,618	2,232	707
			Females	58,498	22,145	12,748	7,384	1,480	344	117	72
	Jammu & Kashmir (Muslim).		Males	216,958	114,989	46,546	38,292	12,691	11,507	5,455	498
			Females	185,823	78,033	42,239	28,203	5,154	1,886	437	114
	Rajputana (Hindu)		Males	126,969	61,069	23,434	21,264	6,528	5,124	3,878	841
			Females	106,005	33,472	21,214	11,319	570	207	135	27
35 **HALWAI**	United Province (All Religions).	14,17	**Males**	**49,383**	**20,467**	**8,274**	**6,795**	**2,016**	**1,750**	**1,287**	**345**
			Females	**42,071**	**13,865**	**8,084**	**4,499**	**585**	**337**	**228**	**132**
36 **IDIGA**	Mysore (Hindu)	14,17	**Males**	**50,076**	**28,455**	**7,618**	**8,635**	**3,913**	**4,833**	**3,263**	**193**
			Females	**44,593**	**17,766**	**7,778**	**8,070**	**1,363**	**380**	**138**	**37**
37 **ILUVAN**	..	14,17	**Males**	**565,731**	**338,847**	**125,086**	**102,853**	**38,538**	**50,907**	**19,628**	**1,835**
			Females	**580,731**	**283,003**	**125,417**	**99,297**	**32,660**	**19,126**	**5,374**	**1,129**
	Cochin (Hindu)		Males	132,875	78,333	28,661	24,691	10,049	11,676	3,078	178
			Females	143,774	68,888	28,643	24,092	9,058	5,596	1,306	193
	Travancore (Hindu)		Males	432,906	260,514	96,425	78,162	28,489	39,231	16,550	1,657
			Females	436,957	214,115	96,774	75,205	23,602	13,530	4,068	936
38 **JAT**	....	14,17,18	**Males**	**4,443,163**	**2,394,500**	**819,369**	**734,317**	**246,665**	**279,668**	**250,312**	**64,169**
			Females	**3,578,146**	**1,454,199**	**764,095**	**525,855**	**94,524**	**45,166**	**19,394**	**5,165**
	Ajmer-Merwara (All Religions).		Males	15,919	5,880	2,576	1,714	454	560	468	108
			Females	14,073	3,396	2,430	920	35	3	8	..
	Delhi (Hindu)		Males	27,779	12,878	4,735	4,257	1,279	1,133	1,196	278
			Females	22,730	7,874	4,447	3,033	261	63	59	11
	Delhi Sikh		Males	1,122	524	95	70	74	150	127	8
			Females	395	146	77	51	10	6	2	..
	Delhi (Muslim)		Males	767	356	121	95	35	54	46	5
			Females	478	179	105	60	7	3	3	1
	N. W. F. Province (All Religions).		Males	44,369	23,832	6,324	6,245	3,784	4,544	2,752	183
			Females	31,958	14,512	7,229	4,538	1,277	922	428	118
	Punjab (Hindu)		Males	547,351	270,044	95,995	85,673	27,619	27,257	24,379	9,121
			Females	444,958	159,077	90,827	59,006	6,853	1,522	691	178
	Punjab (Sikh)		Males	1,213,819	673,526	201,878	195,121	70,889	84,607	88,712	32,319
			Females	919,333	366,736	178,399	138,758	30,923	12,786	4,506	1,364
	Punjab (Muslim)		Males	1,604,250	918,823	329,085	289,175	88,455	112,272	89,173	10,663
			Females	1,336,569	607,773	310,991	218,100	40,790	24,462	11,099	2,331
	United Provinces [illegible]		**Males**	**456,325**	**229,751**	**79,808**	**68,680**	**25,216**	**23,672**	**25,587**	[illegible]
			Females	**354,069**	**135,723**	**74,896**	**47,618**	[illegible]	[illegible]	[illegible]	[illegible]

by age for selected castes—*contd.*

Married.							Widowed.							
Total. 13	0—6. 14	7—13. 15	14—16. 16	17—23. 17	24—43. 18	44 & over. 19	Total. 20	0—6. 21	7—13. 22	14—16. 23	17—23. 24	24—43 25	44 & over. 26	
269,071	2,353	18,571	19,838	44,159	133,150	51,000	45,814	83	453	772	2,377	16,543	25,586	
265,031	2,802	29,556	28,984	54,465	120,983	28,241	66,338	107	434	807	1,906	19,782	43,302	
22,365	159	1,340	1,817	4,718	10,071	4,260	4,224	43	43	160	201	1,437	2,340	
20,917	364	2,374	2,713	4,508	8,075	2,883	5,268	66	73	110	396	1,767	2,856	
31,798	288	1,527	1,798	4,137	16,572	7,476	4,058	18	89	77	254	1,409	2,211	
31,994	1,152	4,856	3,068	6,550	13,788	2,580	11,382	29	171	124	439	4,157	6,462	
1,571	1	1	3	75	1,014	477	239	..	..	..	1	130	108	
1,536	..	12	30	343	1,003	148	286	1	1	1	11	104	168	
87,433	2	54	265	5,782	54,142	27,188	11,553	..	1	7	207	3,250	8,088	
90,494	14	3,163	7,423	23,808	46,850	9,236	40,180	..	47	128	1,096	15,068	23,841	
1,111	..	..	2	75	724	310	90	..	..	..	4	33	53	
1,080	..	22	81	289	590	98	221	..	..	2	13	78	128	
3,426	25	51	131	428	1,768	1,023	219	..	3	3	10	69	134	31
3,682	30	126	282	810	1,845	589	409	4	1	3	9	55	337	
8,772	156	514	499	1,268	4,339	1,996	617	14	5	5	85	205	308	32
9,985	294	844	785	2,016	4,595	1,451	2,276	12	23	28	94	629	1,490	
591,400	5,321	23,130	27,400	82,875	304,044	148,630	52,265	144	468	828	2,825	17,877	30,123	33
618,471	7,779	43,078	51,335	132,582	300,667	83,030	166,540	239	875	1,518	4,129	44,641	115,133	
269,861	2,416	13,197	13,376	38,143	136,165	66,564	21,477	54	219	295	1,395	7,412	12,102	
281,024	3,761	24,084	24,351	59,721	131,888	37,219	74,234	124	400	752	1,941	20,013	51,004	
295,865	2,370	8,806	11,828	41,222	158,213	73,426	26,439	53	126	193	960	9,170	15,937	
313,516	3,406	17,299	24,712	68,727	158,902	40,470	80,571	95	324	400	1,658	22,219	55,875	
25,674	535	1,127	2,196	3,510	9,666	8,640	4,349	37	123	340	470	1,295	2,084	
23,931	612	1,695	2,272	4,134	9,877	5,341	11,735	20	151	366	530	2,409	8,259	
460,387	1,106	14,038	21,190	64,078	242,714	117,261	86,110	81	431	757	3,276	28,365	53,200	34
465,874	2,337	33,569	44,596	100,849	221,862	62,661	111,474	165	505	807	2,930	32,170	74,847	
3,552	3	90	114	657	2,013	675	751	..	6	11	26	295	413	
3,018	10	185	334	762	1,451	276	709	..	..	4	24	249	432	
141	..	3	12	27	87	12	15	..	..	..	1	10	4	
32	..	2	4	9	16	1	6	..	..	..	1	3	2	
23,962	..	96	599	2,460	13,094	7,713	3,182	..	2	25	187	1,043	1,925	
25,566	..	279	2,135	4,747	13,962	4,443	5,501	..	7	39	136	1,727	3,592	
38,517	79	1,409	1,845	6,000	19,675	9,509	8,825	1	36	54	305	2,750	5,679	
39,049	147	3,829	3,825	8,222	18,178	4,848	10,279	1	42	65	203	2,820	7,148	
538	1	32	31	62	221	191	127	..	..	.	1	34	92	
601	2	74	47	99	258	121	136	..	1	..	2	25	108	
115,138	161	3,168	4,298	14,908	60,357	32,246	23,489	2	89	117	564	6,892	15,825	
116,497	604	9,214	9,654	23,945	54,553	18,527	26,200	12	94	113	474	6,246	19,261	
83,058	277	3,092	4,892	13,500	42,678	18,619	17,739	17	84	186	821	5,978	10,653	
82,320	496	5,289	7,615	18,644	39,771	10,505	22,537	26	82	99	542	6,879	14,909	
23,437	163	1,401	1,599	3,738	11,597	4,939	3,572	30	47	62	211	1,277	1,945	
22,306	318	2,953	2,558	4,931	9,486	2,060	5,915	7	42	55	184	1,949	3,678	
26,003	248	1,180	2,141	3,900	12,326	6,208	6,582	28	97	107	239	2,516	3,595	
26,494	374	2,298	3,462	6,095	10,064	4,201	9,859	113	94	144	294	3,836	5,378	
89,918	3	1,374	2,457	10,903	50,968	24,213	12,051	..	18	105	611	4,307	7,010	
92,290	28	3,035	8,804	22,121	46,640	11,662	15,500	..	44	188	867	4,233	10,168	
56,123	171	2,193	3,202	7,923	29,698	12,936	9,777	3	52	90	310	3,263	6,059	
57,701	358	6,411	6,158	11,274	27,483	6,017	14,832	6	99	100	253	4,203	10,171	
24,118	328	1,218	1,671	3,896	11,555	5,450	4,798	20	79	79	266	1,721	2,633	35
22,477	364	2,191	2,200	4,815	9,694	3,213	5,729	23	70	73	230	1,548	3,785	
18,828	..	17	63	1,128	12,746	4,874	2,793	..	..	3	31	1,215	1,544	36
17,577	..	561	1,648	5,005	9,204	1,159	9,250	..	12	59	398	4,156	4,625	
211,526	..	61	448	14,703	125,072	71,242	15,408	..	1	19	633	4,480	10,275	37
221,330	..	461	6,992	53,601	125,335	34,941	76,398	..	19	256	2,941	22,883	50,299	
50,366	..	5	88	3,623	29,515	17,135	4,176	..	..	4	181	1,187	2,804	
54,132	..	98	1,409	12,593	31,852	8,180	20,754	..	2	80	889	6,743	13,040	
161,160	..	56	360	11,080	95,557	54,107	11,232	..	1	15	452	3,293	7,471	
167,198	..	363	5,583	41,008	93,483	26,761	55,644	..	17	176	2,052	16,140	37,259	
1,698,938	3,390	35,080	60,642	237,890	875,333	486,603	349,725	97	910	1,939	10,188	101,446	235,145	38
1,768,119	5,969	84,620	129,111	373,263	842,104	273,052	415,328	175	892	2,112	7,857	98,402	306,390	
8,556	171	832	600	1,621	3,833	1,499	1,483	5	36	32	69	504	837	
8,324	383	1,220	847	1,786	3,372	716	2,353	9	23	20	41	673	1,587	
12,080	10	562	943	2,275	5,992	2,298	2,821	..	4	28	136	978	1,675	
12,271	24	1,113	1,565	2,782	5,417	1,370	2,585	..	2	6	38	728	1,811	
556	..	1	2	118	368	67	42	..	..	..	1	21	20	
229	..	2	16	74	118	19	20	..	..	..	..	5	15	
355	..	11	12	66	198	68	56	..	..	1	1	18	36	
254	..	21	30	53	118	32	45	..	..	..	..	12	33	
17,864	..	48	517	2,827	9,591	4,881	2,673	..	1	25	143	1,174	1,330	
13,537	..	128	706	2,972	7,560	2,171	3,909	..	2	25	200	1,294	2,388	
225,087	270	9,809	15,613	41,007	107,133	51,255	52,220	14	272	407	2,003	16,720	32,804	
230,474	857	20,330	25,829	52,825	102,530	28,103	55,407	15	123	180	838	15,216	39,035	
436,231	151	4,739	11,471	59,529	214,965	145,376	104,062	21	138	302	1,988	25,032	76,581	
438,345	476	13,825	28,458	93,302	213,755	88,529	114,252	25	109	269	1,195	21,219	91,435	
588,540	565	5,262	8,993	60,973	327,567	185,180	96,887	22	126	237	2,095	28,889	65,518	
598,152	1,228	17,221	30,872	127,429	323,863	97,539	130,644	35	177	360	2,216	31,008	96,848	
180,467	410	4,212	8,398	30,786	95,821	40,840	46,107	13	137	343	1,673	16,000	27,941	
173,317	319	8,091	15,235	39,245	85,398	25,029	45,029	30	107	633	1,427	11,571	31,261	

Table VIII.—Civil Condition

Caste, Tribe or Race. 1	Province, State or Agency and Religion. 2	Also tabulated in : 3	Sex. 4	Population dealt with. 5	Unmarried. Total. 6	0—6. 7	7—13. 8	14—16. 9	17—23. 10	24—43. 11	44 & over. 12
JAT—*concld.*											
	Central India (Hindu)		Males ..	15,215	6,255	2,331	2,028	688	646	475	87
			Females ..	12,887	3,666	2,156	1,284	122	42	44	18
	Jammu and Kashmir (Hindu) ..		Males ..	12,287	6,380	2,379	2,067	674	685	458	117
			Females ..	11,084	4,304	2,305	1,652	249	66	23	9
	Jammu and Kashmir (Muslim) ..		Males ..	62,227	33,857	12,794	10,967	3,917	3,701	2,187	291
			Females ..	57,856	23,309	12,684	8,057	1,720	645	179	24
	Rajputana (all Religions). ..		Males ..	441,733	212,394	81,248	68,225	23,581	20,387	14,752	4,201
			Females ..	371,756	127,504	77,549	42,778	4,282	1,517	1,062	316
39 KACHHI ..	.	14,17	**Males ..**	**468,894**	**206,927**	**88,746**	**67,107**	**21,124**	**15,290**	**12,047**	**2,613**
			Females ..	**412,209**	**139,228**	**88,932**	**42,441**	**3,779**	**1,710**	**1,586**	**780**
KACHHI ..	United Provinces (All Religions). ..		Males ..	372,760	165,627	71,021	53,618	13,888	12,146	9,891	2,063
			Females ..	328,575	108,767	70,252	33,104	2,666	1,030	1,219	496
	Gwalior (Hindu) ..		Males ..	91,891	39,664	16,990	12,905	4,108	3,039	2,092	530
			Females ..	79,723	29,451	18,041	8,977	1,105	678	366	284
KACHHIA ..	Baroda (Hindu and Jain).		Males ..	4,243	1,636	735	584	128	105	64	20
			Females ..	3,911	1,010	639	360	8	2	1	..
40 KAHAR *BHOI, DHIMAR, JHINWAR OR JHIWAR.*	.. ..	14,17	**Males ..**	**1,067,872**	**476,498**	**197,212**	**154,605**	**51,901**	**39,999**	**24,514**	**8,267**
			Females ..	**995,842**	**338,452**	**196,126**	**114,306**	**15,609**	**6,762**	**4,056**	**1,593**
BHOI ..	Hyderabad (Hindu) ..		Males ..	141,869	53,329	16,347	14,188	10,082	6,669	3,242	2,801
			Females ..	143,404	39,811	16,652	14,924	4,024	2,596	1,126	489
DHIMAR ..	C. P. and Berar (All Religions). ..		Males ..	161,064	68,216	33,105	23,450	5,891	3,929	1,404	437
			Females ..	161,754	51,646	32,779	16,616	1,388	458	305	100
JHIWAR (JHINWAR)	Delhi (Hindu) ..		Males ..	7,875	3,151	982	883	392	466	382	46
			Females ..	4,779	1,700	955	624	77	30	10	4
	Punjab (Hindu) ..		Males ..	68,171	34,592	12,776	11,098	3,842	3,507	2,591	778
			Females ..	56,911	22,417	12,058	8,247	1,461	418	179	54
	Punjab (Sikh) ..		Males ..	29,365	16,065	5,906	5,301	1,637	1,571	1,199	451
			Females ..	25,846	10,853	5,646	4,111	710	267	89	30
	Punjab (Muslim)		Males ..	50,952	27,523	10,680	9,106	2,874	2,888	1,558	417
			Females ..	43,776	19,595	10,006	7,261	1,445	574	249	60
KAHAR ..	C. P. and Berar (Hindu). ..		Males ..	6,510	2,950	1,314	1,146	281	157	46	6
			Females ..	6,477	2,218	1,504	681	20	7	3	3
	United Provinces (All Religions). ..		Males ..	602,066	270,672	116,102	89,433	26,902	20,812	14,092	3,331
			Females ..	552,895	190,212	116,526	61,842	6,484	2,412	2,095	853
41 KALAR ..	..	14	**Males ..**	**574,096**	**262,388**	**105,055**	**75,344**	**28,953**	**31,550**	**16,153**	**5,333**
			Females ..	**581,767**	**206,990**	**107,723**	**72,106**	**15,649**	**8,382**	**2,431**	**699**
KALAR	Central Provinces & Berar (All Religions).		Males ..	108,656	41,872	20,161	13,974	3,501	2,464	1,361	411
			Females ..	110,512	31,608	20,721	9,168	878	381	323	137
KALAL .. (*Eddiga Goundla*)	Hyderabad (Hindu) ..		Males ..	220,637	86,116	40,426	17,359	10,226	8,688	5,111	4,306
			Females ..	206,199	68,539	41,782	19,911	3,935	1,753	796	362
Kallan (Kalan)	Madras (Hindu) ..		Males ..	244,803	134,400	44,468	44,011	15,226	20,398	9,681	616
			Females ..	265,056	106,843	45,220	43,027	10,836	6,248	1,312	200
42 KANIYAN	..	14,17	**Males ..**	**9,855**	**5,772**	**1,997**	**1,666**	**656**	**980**	**402**	**71**
			Females ..	**9,638**	**4,581**	**1,873**	**1,543**	**573**	**387**	**164**	**41**
	Cochin (Hindu) ..		Males ..	1,950	1,152	384	321	157	216	67	7
			Females ..	1,891	885	318	285	128	114	35	5
	Travancore (Hindu) ..		Males ..	7,905	4,620	1,613	1,345	499	764	335	64
			Females ..	7,747	3,696	1,555	1,258	445	273	129	36
43 KATKARI ..	Bombay (Hindu)	17,18	**Males ..**	**16,499**	**7,660**	**3,533**	**2,757**	**606**	**565**	**168**	**31**
			Females ..	**15,522**	**6,054**	**3,782**	**1,976**	**185**	**63**	**37**	**11**
44 KAYASTHA	..	14,17	**Males ..**	**1,307,738**	**665,653**	**215,541**	**198,277**	**74,937**	**106,456**	**59,794**	**10,648**
			Females ..	**1,160,896**	**407,247**	**212,585**	**161,404**	**21,677**	**6,881**	**3,527**	**1,173**
	Bengal (Hindu) ..		Males ..	819,902	422,398	139,167	127,468	47,254	72,515	33,080	2,914
			Females ..	738,540	254,865	136,150	101,512	10,961	3,660	1,942	640
	Bihar and Orissa (Hindu). ..		Males ..	161,988	78,397	26,107	25,134	8,026	9,782	7,305	2,043
			Females ..	149,155	51,349	26,612	20,671	2,910	721	337	98
	Central Provinces & Berar (All Religions).		Males ..	20,333	10,572	3,436	3,151	1,205	1,736	920	124
			Females ..	18,496	6,903	3,502	2,657	454	156	86	48
	Delhi (Hindu) ..		Males ..	5,970	3,471	1,082	959	359	583	443	45
			Females ..	4,599	2,178	1,015	877	201	68	15	2
	United Provinces (All Religions).		Males ..	260,826	131,395	39,736	36,368	15,494	18,934	15,876	4,987
			Females ..	217,831	80,542	39,297	31,210	6,592	2,061	1,035	347
	Central India (Hindu).		Males ..	19,853	10,095	3,126	2,890	1,168	1,411	1,224	276
			Females ..	17,215	5,739	2,939	2,262	348	114	63	13
	Gwalior (Hindu) ..		Males ..	18,866	9,325	2,887	2,307	1,431	1,495	946	259
			Females ..	15,060	5,671	3,070	2,215	211	101	49	25
45 KHATIK ..	..	14,17	**Males ..**	**115,015**	**50,701**	**22,436**	**17,103**	**4,662**	**3,881**	**2,519**	**600**
			Females ..	**104,038**	**36,817**	**22,391**	**11,704**	**1,159**	**548**	**703**	**312**
	Delhi (Hindu) ..		Males ..	2,127	832	325	257	98	76	62	14
			Females ..	1,395	482	308	146	16	8	4	..
	United Provinces (All Religions).		Males ..	112,888	49,869	22,111	16,846	4,564	3,305	2,457	586
			Females ..	102,643	36,335	22,083	11,558	1,143	540	699	312

by age for selected castes—*contd.*

Married.							Widowed.							
Total. 13	0—6. 14	7—13. 15	14—16. 16	17—23. 17	24—43. 18	44 & over. 19	Total. 20	0—6. 21	7—13. 22	14—16. 23	17—23. 24	24—43. 25	44 & over. 26	
7,651	59	325	424	1,297	3,945	1,601	1,309	4	10	21	93	489	692	
6,757	87	739	694	1,601	2,908	728	2,464	5	19	25	83	824	1,508	
5,052	..	127	147	444	2,557	1,777	855	..	..	3	25	229	598	
5,339	..	258	744	1,124	2,461	752	1,141	..	7	14	28	429	963	
23,711	..	350	779	3,627	12,022	6,933	4,659	..	5	19	174	1,794	2,667	
27,307	..	683	2,001	6,912	14,027	3,684	7,240	..	16	44	178	1,865	5,137	
192,788	1,754	8,802	12,743	33,320	91,341	44,828	36,551	18	181	521	1,787	9,598	24,446	
193,813	2,595	20,989	22,114	43,158	80,577	24,380	50,439	56	307	536	1,613	13,558	34,369	
221,342	**1,050**	**7,691**	**13,990**	**37,502**	**117,693**	**43,416**	**40,625**	**80**	**312**	**630**	**1,959**	**15,289**	**22,355**	**39**
212,666	**1,290**	**17,194**	**25,139**	**47,447**	**101,208**	**20,388**	**60,315**	**141**	**437**	**772**	**1,957**	**19,844**	**37,164**	
175,053	643	5,666	10,551	28,952	95,379	33,862	32,080	24	196	444	1,720	12,051	17,645	
172,181	843	13,543	19,950	38,039	84,379	15,427	47,627	33	274	534	1,550	15,603	29,633	
44,066	402	1,899	3,291	8,155	21,292	9,027	8,161	55	114	184	218	3,119	4,471	
38,233	430	3,409	4,943	8,910	15,875	4,666	12,039	108	159	235	394	4,094	7,049	
2,223	5	126	148	395	1,022	527	384	1	2	2	21	119	239	
2,252	17	242	246	498	954	295	649	..	4	3	13	147	482	
500,738	**3,303**	**21,438**	**27,320**	**76,689**	**250,778**	**121,210**	**90,636**	**216**	**790**	**1,377**	**4,798**	**30,712**	**52,743**	**40**
516,848	**5,083**	**42,970**	**51,404**	**109,572**	**236,632**	**71,187**	**140,542**	**354**	**1,103**	**1,658**	**3,892**	**41,667**	**91,868**	
68,528	339	2,864	4,280	8,517	27,657	24,871	20,012	119	293	483	1,057	5,515	12,545	
75,509	623	6,579	7,949	14,301	27,255	18,802	28,084	170	369	579	649	8,243	18,074	
85,354	736	4,271	4,596	13,683	42,748	19,320	7,494	25	99	141	354	2,474	4,401	
88,309	1,514	9,962	9,134	19,312	39,463	8,924	21,799	31	132	220	639	6,953	13,824	
3,941	3	31	120	658	2,498	631	783	..	1	4	59	412	307	
2,557	1	75	249	692	1,299	241	522	..	1	..	18	161	342	
26,582	22	556	1,001	4,231	13,947	6,825	6,997	1	13	37	256	2,244	4,446	
27,479	52	1,831	2,710	6,422	12,803	3,661	7,015	..	13	31	148	1,920	4,903	
10,707	9	113	377	1,773	5,211	3,224	2,593	..	13	9	120	739	1,712	
12,136	5	388	939	2,841	5,808	2,155	2,857	..	4	20	33	595	2,205	
19,007	27	396	623	2,848	9,643	5,470	4,422	..	11	19	159	1,220	3,013	
20,208	88	877	1,546	4,794	9,458	3,445	3,973	..	7	15	79	895	2,977	
3,274	4	69	152	573	1,786	690	286	..	1	1	14	127	143	
3,376	35	315	377	790	1,573	286	883	2	4	4	28	251	594	
283,345	2,163	13,138	16,171	44,406	147,288	60,179	48,049	71	359	683	2,779	17,981	26,176	
287,274	2,765	22,943	28,500	60,420	138,973	33,673	75,409	151	573	789	2,298	22,649	48,949	
279,649	**2,156**	**10,563**	**13,004**	**34,252**	**138,372**	**81,302**	**32,059**	**113**	**323**	**516**	**1,327**	**10,667**	**19,113**	**41**
276,617	**4,127**	**23,969**	**22,742**	**56,086**	**136,220**	**33,473**	**98,160**	**380**	**673**	**1,031**	**3,305**	**32,855**	**59,916**	
61,167	841	4,303	3,819	10,023	28,464	13,717	5,617	39	70	80	267	1,906	3,255	
62,234	1,482	8,391	5,862	13,124	26,405	6,970	16,670	40	110	192	497	4,860	10,971	
118,654	1,292	6,106	8,897	18,110	49,208	35,041	15,867	74	252	430	797	5,193	9,121	
104,057	2,607	14,974	13,949	17,631	43,040	11,856	33,603	337	552	789	1,761	10,999	19,165	
99,828	23	154	288	6,119	60,700	32,544	10,575	..	1	6	263	3,568	6,737	
110,326	38	604	2,931	25,331	66,775	14,647	47,887	3	11	50	1,047	16,996	29,780	
3,778	..	**2**	**10**	**269**	**2,099**	**1,398**	**305**	..	..	..	**12**	**79**	**214**	**42**
3,752	..	**19**	**136**	**860**	**2,026**	**711**	**1,305**	..	**1**	**7**	**59**	**382**	**856**	
725	..	..	..	49	375	301	73	..	..	..	..	19	54	
694	..	..	12	146	398	138	312	..	..	1	1	96	201	
3,053	..	2	10	220	1,724	1,097	232	..	..	..	1	60	160	
3,058	..	19	124	714	1,628	573	993	..	1	6	45	286	655	
8,356	**35**	**107**	**125**	**984**	**5,141**	**1,964**	**483**	..	..	**5**	**27**	**194**	**257**	**43**
8,119	**117**	**364**	**497**	**1,951**	**4,496**	**694**	**1,349**	**6**	**3**	**5**	**68**	**479**	**788**	
564,308	**3,561**	**12,262**	**16,302**	**60,237**	**301,615**	**170,331**	**77,777**	**246**	**678**	**1,223**	**3,986**	**22,884**	**48,760**	**44**
523,752	**5,556**	**26,742**	**51,634**	**136,602**	**238,677**	**64,541**	**229,897**	**358**	**1,155**	**2,785**	**12,505**	**82,374**	**130,720**	
362,785	2,097	7,741	9,505	35,955	193,896	113,591	34,719	177	489	720	2,233	10,110	20,990	
335,863	2,949	19,253	37,930	93,785	144,410	37,536	147,812	230	829	2,051	9,631	55,637	79,434	
71,253	425	1,977	2,485	8,525	36,984	20,857	12,338	15	59	128	481	3,472	8,183	
65,799	676	2,944	4,896	14,849	33,257	9,177	32,007	41	140	168	1,099	10,848	19,711	
8,471	59	119	190	962	4,910	2,231	1,290	..	..	7	28	441	814	
8,024	71	336	695	2,040	3,954	928	3,569	8	14	31	156	1,225	2,135	
2,140	..	5	17	169	1,423	526	359	..	1	..	12	130	216	
1,953	..	16	92	533	1,120	192	468	..	..	3	5	159	301	
104,278	902	2,136	3,309	12,707	56,001	29,223	25,153	49	108	309	1,033	7,684	15,970	
97,683	1,712	3,461	6,798	22,071	49,126	14,515	39,606	48	128	450	1,261	12,359	25,360	
7,923	**50**	**104**	**211**	**953**	**4,373**	**2,232**	**1,835**	**3**	**3**	**7**	**102**	**617**	**1,103**	
7,642	**69**	**372**	**614**	**1,795**	**3,831**	**961**	**3,834**	**2**	**17**	**28**	**181**	**1,313**	**2,293**	
7,458	**28**	**180**	**585**	**966**	**4,028**	**1,671**	**2,083**	**2**	**18**	**52**	**97**	**430**	**1,484**	
6,788	**79**	**360**	**609**	**1,529**	**2,979**	**1,232**	**2,601**	**29**	**27**	**54**	**172**	**833**	**1,486**	
55,961	**621**	**3,027**	**3,731**	**9,214**	**27,937**	**11,431**	**8,353**	**13**	**136**	**212**	**572**	**2,796**	**4,624**	**45**
54,471	**663**	**5,431**	**6,073**	**11,561**	**24,781**	**5,962**	**12,750**	**10**	**130**	**205**	**459**	**3,661**	**8,285**	
1,158	**1**	**26**	**46**	**230**	**710**	**145**	**137**	..	..	**1**	**14**	**64**	**58**	
808	**4**	**44**	**115**	**222**	**369**	**54**	**105**	..	..	**1**	**4**	**35**	**65**	
54,803	**620**	**3,001**	**3,685**	**8,984**	**27,227**	**11,286**	**8,216**	**13**	**136**	**211**	**558**	**2,732**	**4,566**	
53,663	**659**	**5,387**	**5,958**	**11,339**	**24,412**	**5,908**	**12,645**	**10**	**130**	**204**	**455**	**3,626**	**8,220**	

Table VIII.—Civil Condition

Caste, Tribe or Race. 1	Province, State or Agency and Religion. 2	Also tabulated in : 3	Sex. 4	Population dealt with. 5	Unmarried. Total. 6	0—6. 7	7—13. 8	14—16. 9	17—23. 10	24—43. 11	44 & over. 12
46 KHATRI	..	**14,17**	**Males**	**322,510**	**180,248**	**56,986**	**49,939**	**19,936**	**28,188**	**20,052**	**5,147**
			Females	**262,216**	**112,532**	**53,973**	**43,069**	**9,651**	**3,688**	**1,645**	**506**
	Delhi (Hindu)		Males	7,989	3,873	1,227	1,163	438	668	318	59
			Females	5,791	2,334	1,210	861	178	68	17	..
	Delhi (Sikh)		Males	316	149	54	39	14	30	12	..
			Females	181	93	47	33	7	3	3	..
	N. W. F. Province (All-Religions).		Males	19,947	10,295	3,072	2,625	1,165	1,839	1,285	309
			Females	15,099	6,207	3,016	2,188	456	387	121	39
	Punjab (Hindu)		Males	254,289	144,374	45,145	40,039	16,146	22,690	16,236	4,118
			Females	206,562	89,287	42,482	34,487	7,753	2,802	1,339	424
	Punjab (Sikh)		Males	28,715	15,786	5,580	4,644	1,554	2,000	1,546	462
			Females	25,281	10,880	5,337	4,044	984	341	139	35
	Jammu and Kashmir (Hindu).		Males	11,254	5,771	1,908	1,429	619	961	655	199
			Females	9,302	3,731	1,881	1,456	273	87	26	8
47 KODAGA	Coorg (Hindu)		**Males**	**20,752**	**13,097**	**3,680**	**4,124**	**1,452**	**2,380**	**1,394**	**67**
			Females	**20,274**	**10,524**	**3,585**	**4,036**	**1,408**	**1,356**	**119**	**20**
48 KOMATI (Komti)	..	**14,17**	**Males**	**382,618**	**162,944**	**58,959**	**48,899**	**20,940**	**19,025**	**11,551**	**3,570**
			Females	**358,853**	**101,167**	**55,979**	**32,408**	**7,047**	**1,839**	**1,689**	**2,205**
	C. P. and Berar (Hindu).		Males	1,719	723	284	229	74	53	64	19
			Females	1,827	423	299	118	2	..	3	1
	Coorg (Hindu)		Males	100	49	15	17	5	8	4	..
			Females	111	43	26	16	1	..	..	..
	Madras (Hindu)		Males	217,367	97,914	33,986	31,055	11,877	12,219	7,034	1,743
			Females	211,436	59,637	33,342	18,665	2,950	1,183	1,362	2,135
	Hyderabad (Hindu)		Males	163,432	64,258	24,674	17,598	8,984	6,745	4,449	1,808
			Females	145,479	41,064	22,312	13,609	4,094	656	324	69
49 KONDH	Madras (Tribal)	**17,78**	**Males**	**171,416**	**73,732**	**30,542**	**25,333**	**9,168**	**8,560**	**4,408**	**721**
			Females	**175,821**	**68,124**	**31,006**	**23,026**	**7,122**	**4,046**	**2,044**	**880**
50 KOYA	Hyderabad (Tribal)	**17,18**	**Males**	18,217	7,976	1,524	2,604	**1,260**	970	842	**776**
			Females	15,421	4,769	2,149	1,010	**1,053**	233	196	**128**
51 KUMHAR (Kumbhar, Kumbara, Kumara).	..	**14,17**	**Males**	**1,096,910**	**485,389**	**210,733**	**158,755**	**45,340**	**39,021**	**25,004**	**6,036**
			Females	**1,001,510**	**343,300**	**207,407**	**109,373**	**14,606**	**6,703**	**3,996**	**1,215**
	Bombay (Hindu)		Males	12,393	6,015	2,537	2,221	561	475	198	23
			Females	12,814	3,896	2,472	1,287	50	57	24	6
	Central Provinces and Berar (All-Religions).		Males	66,320	25,489	12,590	8,485	2,072	1,441	761	140
			Females	64,991	19,683	12,805	5,843	592	226	139	78
	Delhi (Hindu)		Males	5,125	2,084	891	718	216	138	99	22
			Females	4,134	1,424	876	482	32	21	12	1
	Delhi (Muslim)		Males	54	22	9	7	..	2	3	1
			Females	38	13	8	5	..	..	..	..
	Punjab (Hindu)		Males	84,616	41,235	15,877	14,101	4,611	3,745	2,225	676
			Females	72,297	26,532	15,322	9,431	1,215	347	173	44
	Punjab (Sikh)		Males	17,206	9,518	3,415	3,156	1,029	1,042	649	227
			Females	14,032	5,799	2,844	2,255	469	149	56	26
	Punjab (Muslim)		Males	228,843	125,537	48,206	40,862	12,813	13,421	8,516	1,719
			Females	194,587	86,677	45,582	30,360	6,190	2,899	1,387	259
	United Provinces (All-Religions).		Males	405,884	158,129	75,742	50,093	12,927	9,799	7,733	1,835
			Females	376,755	113,342	75,312	31,859	3,077	1,441	1,246	407
	Baroda (Hindu and Jain).		Males	25,787	9,875	4,846	3,341	823	562	258	45
			Females	25,209	7,094	4,595	2,231	236	24	4	4
	Gwalior (Hindu)		Males	32,836	13,243	6,230	4,067	1,260	972	518	196
			Females	29,649	10,070	6,642	2,816	323	129	93	67
	Hyderabad (Hindu)		Males	80,919	31,976	14,225	9,564	3,239	2,484	1,758	706
			Females	73,229	23,162	14,142	6,494	826	828	625	247
	Mysore (Hindu)		Males	24,824	13,554	4,323	4,517	1,732	2,010	898	74
			Females	23,833	9,430	4,551	4,066	592	137	50	34
	Rajputana (All Religions).		Males	47,571	21,138	9,401	7,661	1,906	1,236	752	182
			Females	44,842	14,055	9,549	4,264	155	39	41	7
	Western India States (Hindu).		Males	64,532	27,574	12,441	9,962	2,651	1,694	636	190
			Females	65,100	22,123	12,707	7,980	849	406	146	35
52 KUNBI	..	**14,17**	**Males**	**3,090,644**	**1,133,283**	**492,860**	**353,658**	**110,183**	**77,779**	**74,204**	**24,599**
			Females	**2,894,893**	**753,531**	**474,583**	**228,587**	**23,862**	**14,274**	**8,532**	**8,693**
AJNA	Baroda (Anjana Chaudhari) (Hindu).		Males	19,683	7,341	2,981	2,328	699	678	525	**130**
			Females	18,776	4,661	2,871	1,444	119	214	8	**5**
GADVA PATIDAR	Baroda (Hindu and Jain).		Males	110,832	41,574	21,298	13,362	2,580	2,555	1,457	**322**
			Females	108,275	28,474	18,864	8,096	1,231	244	18	**21**
KAPU	Hyderabad (Hindu)		Males	490,183	190,620	57,807	65,165	34,080	15,448	12,258	**5,262**
			Females	452,737	136,317	65,621	54,887	6,251	5,326	2,923	**1,309**
KUNBI including REWA and LEWA KUNBI.	Western India States (Hindu).		Males	319,061	111,599	55,491	35,745	7,928	6,388	4,542	**1,505**
			Females	306,666	84,394	52,570	25,332	3,825	2,133	376	158
KUNBI	Bombay (Hindu)		Males	114,824	42,840	14,004	13,447	4,299	4,788	4,652	**1,650**
			Females	96,4[illegible]	22,586	12,464	7,179	1,295	619	610	**491**

by age for selected castes—*contd.*

Married.							Widowed.							
Total. 13	0—6. 14	7—13. 15	14—16. 16	17—23. 17	24—43. 18	44 & over. 19	Total. 20	0—6. 21	7—13. 22	14—16. 23	17—23. 24	24—43. 25	44 & over. 26	
120,280	**48**	**832**	**1,543**	**13,196**	**67,995**	**36,666**	**21,982**	**5**	**29**	**114**	**588**	**6,539**	**14,707**	**46**
111,163	**86**	**1,872**	**6,914**	**26,858**	**58,684**	**16,749**	**38,521**	**7**	**50**	**122**	**878**	**11,396**	**26,068**	
3,626	..	17	44	488	2,343	734	490	..	..	3	17	181	289	
2,829	1	25	211	734	1,545	313	628	..	1	1	18	188	420	
161	..	1	7	38	96	19	6	..	..	..	1	2	3	
80	..	..	6	31	37	6	8	..	..	..	2	2	4	
8,245	..	36	269	1,255	4,161	2,524	1,407	..	14	48	128	467	750	
7,010	..	227	701	1,817	3,235	1,030	1,882	..	4	11	79	598	1,190	
92,748	43	423	951	9,827	53,334	28,170	17,167	5	11	35	356	5,066	11,694	
86,083	69	1,304	5,005	20,872	45,993	12,846	31,192	6	40	74	627	9,176	21,269	
10,829	5	54	197	1,205	5,504	3,864	2,100	..	3	18	72	514	1,493	
11,125	16	255	671	2,403	5,729	2,051	3,276	1	3	5	53	911	2,303	
4,671	..	301	75	383	2,557	1,355	812	..	1	10	14	309	478	
4,036	..	61	320	1,001	2,145	509	1,535	..	2	31	99	521	882	
6,708	**1**	**9**	**7**	**203**	**4,102**	**2,386**	**947**	..	..	..	**6**	**339**	**602**	**47**
6,888	**6**	**6**	**39**	**1,385**	**4,407**	**1,045**	**2,862**	**1**	**2**	**3**	**30**	**953**	**1,873**	
190,072	**2,172**	**8,457**	**12,914**	**36,899**	**78,613**	**51,017**	**29,602**	**60**	**230**	**567**	**1,568**	**8,810**	**18,367**	**48**
176,701	**3,510**	**24,564**	**22,657**	**38,538**	**62,077**	**25.355**	**80,985**	**308**	**1,254**	**1,614**	**7,321**	**27,795**	**42,693**	
861	2	13	43	140	444	219	135	..	1	1	2	38	93	
831	6	128	110	201	307	79	573	..	2	6	34	202	329	
46	..	1	1	6	29	9	5	..	..	..	..	1	4	
51	..	4	9	19	17	2	17	..	..	..	1	4	12	
106,164	228	1,604	3,928	15,666	54,764	29,974	13,289	1	49	169	690	3,747	8,633	
104,537	265	11,750	10,868	26,225	41,107	14,322	47,262	30	260	694	3,614	16,383	26,281	
83,001	1,942	6,839	8,942	21,087	23,376	20,815	16,173	59	180	397	876	5,024	9,637	
71,282	3,239	12,682	11,670	12,093	20.646	10,952	33,133	278	992	914	3,672	11.206	16,071	
84,730	**706**	**1,592**	**3,410**	**10,035**	**49,633**	**19,299**	**7,954**	**47**	**123**	**342**	**848**	**2,973**	**3,621**	**49**
88,182	**1,493**	**3,466**	**6,400**	**19,433**	**46,065**	**11,325**	**19,515**	**374**	**456**	**679**	**1,548**	**7,274**	**9,184**	
8,592	**7**	**506**	**689**	**1,709**	**3,337**	**2,344**	**1,619**	**39**	**146**	**82**	**177**	**393**	**812**	**50**
8,228	**96**	**869**	**969**	**1.398**	**2,683**	**2,213**	**2,424**	**9**	**81**	**61**	**188**	**620**	**1,465**	
530,769	**5,075**	**31,371**	**33,740**	**83,841**	**254,969**	**121,773**	**80,752**	**170**	**870**	**1,227**	**3,895**	**25,799**	**48,791**	**51**
525,640	**6,819**	**53,099**	**51,936**	**110,101**	**234,601**	**69,084**	**132,570**	**291**	**1,078**	**1,403**	**3,957**	**37,243**	**88,598**	
5,710	21	103	162	633	2,948	1,843	668	..	1	3	37	144	483	
6,563	34	770	656	1,293	3,001	809	2,355	3	22	16	78	743	1,493	
37,392	518	2,735	2,622	6,213	17,665	7,639	3,439	14	96	48	237	1,120	1,924	
36,134	913	4,896	3,459	7,941	15,173	3,752	9,174	15	82	85	266	2,740	5.986	
2,585	..	74	179	492	1,406	434	456	..	2	6	19	161	268	
2,310	5	154	277	572	1,071	231	400	..	..	4	12	110	274	
28	..	2	4	1	15	6	4	..	..	..	..	2	2	
21	1	5	1	..	12	2	4	.	..	..	..	1	3	
36,357	23	857	1,953	6,559	18,487	8,478	7,024	3	18	50	286	2,170	4,497	
36,580	94	2,765	3,983	9,167	16,109	4,432	9,185	6	21	41	195	2,483	6,439	
6,314	10	74	241	980	3,126	1,883	1,374	..	3	12	55	381	923	
6,482	2	195	488	1,395	3,094	1,308	1,751	1	2	5	74	322	1,347	
87,145	134	1,034	2,314	11,669	46,247	25,747	16,161	8	22	139	531	4,956	10,505	
88,572	158	3,213	6,145	19,991	44,779	14,286	19,338	3	25	58	414	4,675	14,163	
216,101	2,802	18,523	16,619	35,236	101,517	41,404	31,654	61	461	647	1,902	11,136	17,447	
212,111	3,692	26,637	21,890	41,077	94,161	24,654	51,302	129	534	691	1,582	14,753	33,613	
14,049	93	1,240	1,165	2,720	5,594	3,237	1,863	7	59	40	70	549	1,138	
14,589	218	2,042	1,636	3,225	5,829	1,639	3,526	9	20	20	50	815	2,612	
16,261	155	976	1,339	2,909	7,052	3,830	3,332	24	85	109	169	1,374	1,571	
15,469	210	1,461	1,540	3,166	6,425	2,667	4,110	39	79	111	159	1,348	2,374	
42,875	956	2,543	3,135	5,624	19,267	11,350	6,068	29	48	65	187	1,395	4,344	
37,442	807	3,760	4,334	6,758	15,049	6,734	12,625	67	239	253	607	3,532	7,927	
10,106	..	7	32	720	6,303	3,044	1,164	.	..	..	8	357	799	
10,180	2	413	907	2,656	5,217	985	4,223	..	7	22	139	1,650	2,405	
23,387	62	899	1,647	3,929	11,691	5,159	3,046	1	23	24	79	829	2,090	
24,711	135	3,067	2,933	4,957	11,053	2,566	6,076	..	25	32	96	1,712	4,204	
32,459	301	2,304	2,328	6,156	13,651	7,719	4,499	23	52	84	315	1,225	2,800	
34,476	548	3,721	3,687	7,903	13,628	4,989	8,501	12	22	65	285	2,359	5,758	
1,694,698	**37,031**	**155,684**	**134,372**	**265,496**	**722,482**	**379,633**	**262,663**	**2,182**	**5,609**	**5,985**	**14,211**	**82,974**	**151,729**	**52**
1,677,812	**57,484**	**254,423**	**171,098**	**319,021**	**658,842**	**216,944**	**463,550**	**1,841**	**6,764**	**6,759**	**16,048**	**139,503**	**292 635**	
10,854	90	956	840	2,004	4,697	2,267	1,488	2	65	25	68	405	923	
10,721	209	1,622	1,366	2,174	4,171	1,179	3,394	9	38	32	45	961	2,309	
58,966	59	5,412	5,879	10,309	24,891	12,416	10,292	5	585	381	497	2,898	5,926	
63,054	146	11,869	7,704	13,290	23,647	6,398	16,747	18	371	196	319	4,997	10,846	
252,443	3,760	12,840	22,840	34,872	108,548	69,583	47,120	1,154	1,435	1,676	3,304	11,658	27,893	
238,055	4,515	33,723	30,778	42,452	83,192	43,395	78,365	527	1,402	1,676	4,298	26,019	44,443	
184,112	10,714	25,279	17,642	33,661	64,730	32,086	23,350	195	302	425	1,232	8,387	12,809	
189,267	14,051	30,494	20,366	39,052	62,512	22,792	33,005	75	254	319	1,404	9,800	21,153	
60,104	**1,453**	**4,263**	**4,049**	**10,649**	**23,775**	**15,915**	**11,880**	**132**	**233**	**242**	**635**	**3,214**	**7,424**	
55,921	**2,436**	**7,294**	**5,391**	**11,950**	**21,432**	**7,418**	**17,926**	**160**	**294**	**411**	**855**	**4,997**	**11,209**	

Table VIII.—Civil Conditio[n]

Caste, Tribe or Race. 1	Province, State or Agency and Religion. 2	Also tabulated in : 3	Sex. 4	Population dealt with. 5	Unmarried. Total. 6	0—6. 7	7—13. 8	14—16. 9	17—23. 10	24—43. 11	44 & over 12
KUNBI—*concld.*											
	Central Provinces & Berar (All-Religions)	..	Males	649,839	218,036	111,718	74,288	14,839	9,251	5,930	2,010
			Females	623,217	139,015	100,756	32,529	2,057	2,022	1,276	375
KURMI	Central Provinces and Berar (Hindu)	..	Males	155,021	56,348	28,373	17,832	4,205	3,528	1,909	501
			Females	159,483	42,062	29,539	11,214	597	342	229	141
	United Provinces (All Religions).	..	Males	915,857	337,932	149,235	92,348	25,652	26,053	34,601	10,043
			Females	840,357	213,335	144,589	57,919	5,307	2,363	2,317	840
	Central India (Hindu).	..	Males	105,117	35,454	16,385	10,421	3,075	2,469	2,603	501
			Females	100,075	23,595	16,014	6,542	384	206	262	187
	Hyderabad (Hindu)	..	Males	89,646	37,447	15,801	11,439	7,115	1,344	898	850
			Females	83,672	28,833	13,630	12,046	1,732	697	498	230
LEWA PATIDAR	Baroda (Hindu and Jain).	..	Males	120,581	54,092	19,767	17,283	5,111	5,277	4,829	1,825
			Females	105,202	30,259	17,665	11,399	1,064	108	15	8
53 **LABBAI** ..	..	14,17	**Males**	**171,255**	**99,503**	**36,675**	**33,503**	**9,574**	**14,209**	**5,125**	**417**
			Females	**193,153**	**79,603**	**36,749**	**32,581**	**6,510**	**2,763**	**816**	**184**
	Coorg (Muslim)..	..	Males	126	62	15	13	9	12	13	..
			Females	92	31	14	13	3	1	..	..
	Madras (Muslim)	..	Males	163,223	95,135	35,705	32,308	9,032	13,169	4,524	397
			Females	188,670	77,553	35,764	31,729	6,362	2,723	800	175
	Mysore (Muslim) ..	..	Males	7,906	4,306	955	1,182	533	1,028	588	20
			Females	4,391	2,019	971	839	145	39	16	9
54 **LINGAYAT** (Virshaiv).	..	..	**Males**	**991,218**	**513,979**	**160,357**	**165,377**	**79,964**	**65,224**	**35,998**	**6,959**
			Females	**966,306**	**376,800**	**163,361**	**154,263**	**38,358**	**10,880**	**6,362**	**3,576**
	Bombay Hindu ..	..	Males	191,772	92,869	33,302	29,203	11,422	12,019	6,283	640
			Females	183,209	59,716	31,952	21,758	3,452	1,072	1,012	470
	Coorg (Hindu) ..	..	Males	2,250	1,357	279	424	173	237	230	14
			Females	2,818	1,134	385	562	138	35	12	2
	Hyderabad (Hindu)	..	Males	397,604	194,467	57,434	66,300	38,233	16,799	11,075	4,626
			Females	391,235	163,150	59,665	64,557	24,293	7,458	4,485	2,692
	Mysore (Hindu) ..	..	Males	390,652	220,181	67,399	67,914	29,566	35,532	18,126	1,644
			Females	380,150	148,746	69,353	65,896	10,144	2,160	801	392
	Travancore (Hindu)	..	Males	8,940	5,105	1,943	1,536	570	737	284	35
			Females	8,894	4,054	2,006	1,490	331	155	52	20
55 **LODHA (LODHI)**	..	14,17	**Males**	**788,589**	**336,001**	**147,995**	**109,640**	**29,988**	**24,957**	**19,409**	**4,012**
			Females	**720,986**	**229,549**	**145,425**	**72,224**	**6,891**	**2,822**	**1,673**	**514**
	Central Provinces and Bera (All Religionrs).	..	Males	158,675	68,795	30,470	23,209	6,704	5,015	2,800	597
			Females	159,902	48,657	30,170	16,543	1,388	301	193	62
	United Provinces (All Religions).	..	Males	581,011	246,119	108,779	79,943	20,941	18,085	15,229	3,142
			Females	518,214	167,626	107,054	51,633	4,866	2,332	1,337	404
	Gwalior (Hindu) ..	..	Males	48,903	21,087	8,746	6,488	2,343	1,857	1,380	273
			Females	42,870	13,266	8,201	4,048	637	189	143	48
56 **LOHANA, ARORA, etc.**	..	14,17	**Males**	**751,673**	**405,024**	**136,545**	**123,220**	**51,239**	**52,873**	**34,953**	**6,194**
			Females	**654,518**	**270,465**	**135,537**	**102,228**	**20,775**	**6,983**	**4,185**	**757**
ARORA ..	N.-W. F. Province (All Religions).	..	Males	34,576	19,297	6,813	5,761	1,984	2,687	1,681	371
			Females	26,826	11,906	5,974	4,349	890	388	250	55
	Punjab (Hindu)	..	Males	352,791	192,349	67,577	58,662	21,032	24,902	16,871	3,305
			Females	306,057	132,819	66,454	51,062	9,010	3,339	2,477	477
	Punjab (Sikh)	..	Males	59,934	33,435	12,270	10,625	3,625	3,880	2,261	774
			Females	50,779	23,031	11,594	8,835	1,703	546	272	81
	Jammu and Kashmir (Hindu).	..	Males	1,032	469	164	77	52	89	62	25
			Females	776	317	148	139	18	9	3	..
LOHANA ..	Bombay (Hindu) (including Amits)	..	Males	246,243	129,851	38,963	37,872	20,843	18,185	12,585	1,403
			Females	213,115	80,714	40,585	28,579	8,009	2,340	1,075	126
	Baroda (Hindu) ..	..	Males	6,941	3,498	1,327	1,267	408	368	102	26
			Females	6,629	2,400	1,225	1,075	93	4	1	2
	Western India States (Hindu).	..	Males	50,156	26,125	9,431	8,956	3,295	2,762	1,391	290
			Females	50,336	19,278	9,557	8,189	1,052	357	107	16
57 **MAHAR** ..	..	14,17	**Males**	**1,710,718**	**734,297**	**313,142**	**243,136**	**79,832**	**59,864**	**28,812**	**9,511**
			Females	**1,712,698**	**551,343**	**315,963**	**168,992**	**36,234**	**16,058**	**9,404**	**4,692**
DHED and VANKER.	Bombay (Hindu)	..	Males	55,703	18,717	9,041	6,398	1,455	1,093	556	174
			Females	57,234	13,611	8,584	3,852	635	239	248	53
	Baroda (Hindu) ..	..	Males	53,285	22,069	10,458	8,228	1,936	1,097	311	39
			Females	54,703	15,846	9,945	5,266	526	88	13	8
	Hyderabad (Adi-Hindu).	..	Males	552,632	245,597	83,166	69,378	37,290	31,623	17,775	6,365
			Females	523,907	175,467	82,997	52,512	22,930	8,948	5,322	2,758
	Western India States (Hindu).	..	Males	108,558	53,418	21,025	20,070	6,369	4,130	1,431	393
			Females	105,618	44,091	22,816	17,087	2,802	879	386	121
HOLEYA ..	Coorg (Hindu) ..	..	Males	185	90	24	26	10	22	7	1
			Females	135	63	22	25	3	7	5	1
	Madras (Hindu) ..	..	Males	22,115	13,056	4,858	4,747	1,522	1,260	617	52
			Females	27,452	10,936	5,061	4,504	868	306	163	34
MAHAR (*Mehra*)	Bombay (Hindu)	..	Males	271,719	119,401	56,426	43,466	9,599	6,467	2,343	1,100
			Females	282,208	88,315	56,297	24,413	2,384	2,749	1,560	912
	Central Provinces and Berar (Hindu), Muslim and Tribal)	..	Males	646,152	261,762	128,084	90,754	21,633	14,166	5,767	1,358
			Females	661,200	202,909	130,191	61,300	6,086	2,820	1,707	805

by age for selected castes—*contd.*

Married. Total. 13	0—6. 14	7—13. 15	14—16. 16	17—23. 17	24—43. 18	44 & over. 19	Widowed. Total. 20	0—6. 21	7—13. 22	14—16. 23	17—23. 24	24—43. 25	44 & over. 26	
388,032	3,478	32,749	27,988	62,514	162,793	98,510	43,771	222	1,016	865	1,951	12,766	26,951	
386,356	15,060	70,110	35,857	73,276	144,869	47,184	97,846	329	1,425	1,453	2,773	25,759	66,107	
90,066	1,725	8,259	6,181	15,267	40,893	17,741	8,607	45	123	135	649	3,136	4,519	
92,328	2,870	13,055	8,71[illegible]	20,083	38,062	9,543	25,093	82	256	169	645	7,768	16,173	
491,846	13,493	54,589	38,389	71,044	219,950	94,381	86,079	250	1,348	1,571	4,642	31,803	46,465	
484,288	14,504	67,034	44,852	85,453	215,611	56,834	142,734	393	2,009	1,810	4,314	44,869	89,339	
61,397	1,917	7,286	5,225	9,498	27,020	10,451	8,266	47	195	189	506	3,019	4,310	
60,959	2,764	9,737	6,095	11,417	25,539	5,407	15,521	81	300	197	436	5,406	9,101	
41,164	273	2,054	2,622	5,581	19,772	10,862	11,035	114	236	397	470	2,919	6,899	
39,231	503	4,439	4,35[illegible]	6,421	15,241	8,272	15,608	144	338	419	565	4,222	9,920	
55,714	69	1,997	2,717	10,097	25,413	15,421	10,775	16	71	52	257	2,769	7,610	
57,632	426	5,046	5,619	13,453	24,566	8,522	17,311	23	77	77	394	4,705	12,035	
67,453	18	136	278	4,817	39,393	22,811	4,299	..	1	40	170	1,310	2,778	53
81,389	38	943	5,188	23,046	43,442	8,732	32,161	2	27	79	825	10,730	20,498	
60	..	..	..	3	41	16	4	..	..	..	..	2	2	
39	..	1	3	12	20	3	22	..	..	..	3	9	10	
63,995	18	136	275	4,628	37,208	21,730	4,093	..	1	40	168	1,253	2,631	
79,490	38	908	5,010	22,502	42,456	8,576	31,627	2	27	77	803	10,558	20,160	
3,398	..	..	3	186	2,144	1,065	202	..	..	..	2	55	145	
1,860	..	34	175	532	966	153	512	..	..	2	19	163	328	
404,125	2,645	8,613	10,194	36,863	221,128	124,682	73,114	179	385	557	1,721	19,291	50,981	54
404,565	6,671	28,821	88,990	93,496	184,093	52,494	184,941	418	1,013	1,853	7,033	66,708	107,911	
82,660	513	1,643	2,329	9,714	48,996	19,465	16,243	27	90	87	581	5,180	10,278	
80,316	1,295	8,795	9,155	19,066	35,368	6,637	43,177	66	422	686	2,264	16,190	23,549	
708	3	2	..	29	471	203	185	..	..	..	1	83	101	
912	1	6	70	303	482	50	772	..	..	3	38	361	370	
171,127	2,125	6,902	7,497	17,847	79,548	57,208	32,010	152	292	457	904	6,996	23,209	
169,566	5,357	15,375	16,763	30,683	71,620	29,768	58,519	351	505	834	1,785	17,872	37,172	
146,077	4	61	351	8,960	90,114	46,587	24,394	..	3	13	225	6,963	17,190	
150,040	18	4,620	12,806	42,453	74,698	15,445	81,364	1	86	326	2,902	31,992	46,057	
3,553	..	5	17	313	1,999	1,219	282	..	..	..	10	69	203	
3,731	..	25	196	991	1,925	594	1,109	..	..	9	44	293	763	
392,237	2,092	20,257	25,561	63,318	205,203	75,806	60,351	67	478	884	3,484	23,187	32,251	55
382,579	3,155	36,065	40,119	81,074	182,686	39,480	108,858	173	670	1,673	3,806	35,014	67,522	
81,906	681	4,744	4,673	13,893	41,468	16,447	7,974	24	48	85	346	2,822	4,649	
84.137	1,099	8,867	7,984	19,198	38,425	8,564	27,108	34	125	196	737	9,271	16,745	
286,534	1,300	14,626	19,209	45,191	151,347	54,861	48,358	23	379	697	2,791	18,552	25,916	
275,438	1,716	25,004	29,334	56,499	134,136	28,749	75,150	104	486	1,393	2,900	23,290	46,977	
23,797	111	887	1,679	4,234	12,388	4,498	4,019	20	51	102	347	1,813	1,686	
23,004	340	2,194	2,801	5,377	10,125	2,167	6,600	35	59	84	169	2,453	3,800	
296,803	214	3,086	7,448	36,993	174,001	75,061	49,846	22	56	249	2,776	16,457	30,286	56
295,633	338	6,223	19,424	76,525	148,284	44,839	88,420	22	116	288	2,256	29,544	56,194	
13,003	..	109	146	1,488	7,623	3,637	2,276	..	7	25	106	869	1,269	
11,218	..	154	690	3,091	6,098	1,185	3,702	..	5	13	112	1,420	2,152	
137,189	59	703	1,717	15,984	77,958	40,768	23,253	5	19	51	548	7,059	15,571	
132,314	161	2,944	8,852	32,379	69,832	18,146	40,924	10	63	97	925	12,757	27,072	
22,513	14	202	424	3,266	11,646	6,961	3,986	2	5	15	105	1,051	2,808	
22,105	25	435	1,297	5,359	11,347	3,642	5,643	3	7	18	152	1,490	3,973	
475	..	87	4	34	214	136	88	..	..	..	2	25	61	
340	..	6	17	68	190	59	119	..	1	..	..	51	67	
99,574	93	1,535	4,443	12,420	65,516	15,567	16,818	9	16	125	1,908	6,694	8,066	
104,125	90	1,950	6,235	29,380	49,585	16,885	28,276	6	30	72	600	10,724	16,844	
3,045	4	48	95	523	1,432	943	398	1	1	2	8	110	276	
3,128	5	94	293	844	1,421	471	1,101	..	..	3	31	340	727	
21,004	44	402	619	3,278	9,612	7,049	3,027	5	8	31	99	649	2,235	
22,403	57	640	2,040	5,404	9,811	4,451	8,655	3	10	85	436	2,762	5,359	
874,302	9,244	49,355	58,471	132,985	408,433	215,814	102,119	928	2,468	7,271	11,932	29,438	50,082	57
904,321	19,115	98,133	95,496	192,576	378,157	120,844	257,034	1,344	4,324	8,742	12,840	73,205	156,579	
32,710	783	3,063	2,184	4,966	13,284	8,430	4,276	30	95	112	289	1,398	2,352	
36,031	1,541	5,268	3,498	7,559	13,550	4,615	7,592	66	136	161	287	2,305	4,637	
28,246	92	1,840	2,155	4,887	12,190	7,082	2,970	8	84	63	185	813	1,817	
31,374	344	3,986	3,529	6,511	13,520	3,484	7,483	11	79	75	100	1,888	5,330	
258,584	3,087	14,807	21,460	36,347	117,412	65,471	48,451	658	1,624	6,213	8,777	13,106	18,073	
255,150	5,244	17,205	29,577	53,215	102,239	47,670	93,290	537	2,343	6,593	7,894	25,780	50,143	
48,179	561	1,578	3,407	8,539	22,680	11,414	6,961	28	85	103	729	2,796	3,220	
49,459	648	2,230	4,299	10,953	23,567	7,762	12,068	11	35	94	601	3,451	7,876	
86	..	..	..	5	65	16	9	..	..	..	..	5	4	
59	..	1	..	22	28	8	13	..	..	..	1	7	5	
8,252	8	18	16	366	5,028	2,816	807	..	2	..	11	274	520	
10,822	6	158	575	2,316	6,592	1,175	5,694	..	8	19	123	1,860	3,684	
142,211	1,249	7,198	8,147	22,380	70,047	33,190	10,107	27	122	198	557	2,798	6,405	
152,292	3,529	21,863	16,459	32,690	63,020	14,731	41,601	115	552	825	1,332	13,120	25,657	
355,862	3,464	20,839	21,087	55,458	167,641	87,373	28,528	177	456	582	1,384	8,243	17,686	
369,026	7,803	47,408	37,545	79,293	155,589	41,388	89,265	604	1,171	975	2,500	24,780	59,235	

Table VIII.—Civil Condition

Caste, Tribe or Race.	Province, State or Agency and Religion.	Also tabulated in :	Sex.	Population dealt with.	Unmarried. Total.	0—6.	7—13.	14—16.	17—23.	24—43.	44 & over.
1	2	3	4	5	6	7	8	9	10	11	12
MAHAR—*concld.*											
	Central Provinces and Berar (Christians).	..	Males ..	369	187	60	69	18	6	5	29
			Females ..	241	105	50	33	..	22	..	..
58 *MALI* (*Malakar*).	..	14,17	Males ..	534,120	200,146	97,492	66,695	17,179	10,589	6,417	1,774
			Females ..	519,669	146,922	95,520	41,202	5,566	2,417	1,621	596
	Ajmer-Merwara (All Religions).	..	Males ..	7,680	2,970	1,326	1,011	264	227	110	32
			Females ..	6,983	1,778	1,210	536	24	3	4	1
	Bombay (Hindu)	..	Males ..	33,552	15,551	7,025	5,571	1,501	1,102	296	56
			Females ..	33,826	11,386	6,959	3,306	518	452	129	22
	Central Provinces and Berar (All Religions).	..	Males ..	313,186	105,124	56,935	35,532	6,007	3,864	2,123	663
			Females ..	313,383	76,752	55,208	17,928	1,726	[illegible]	657	296
	Delhi (Hindu) ..	..	Males ..	3,381	1,245	417	378	153	158	130	9
			Females ..	2,376	756	440	276	29	7	4	..
	United Provinces (All Religions)	..	Males	95,729	41,859	17,106	13,756	4,512	3,392	2,442	651
			Females ..	85,151	29,356	17,174	10,313	1,074	389	328	78
	Central India. (Hindu).	..	Males ..	23,144	9,581	3,882	3,400	1,027	784	380	108
			Females ..	21,766	6,683	3,898	2,182	157	190	216	40
	Hyderabad (Hindu)	..	Males ..	51,611	20,807	9,622	5,931	3,406	851	761	236
			Females ..	50,997	18,172	9,598	5,870	1,895	394	25[illegible]	156
	Western India States (Hindu).	..	Males ..	5,837	3,009	1,179	1,116	309	211	175	19
			Females ..	5,187	2,039	1,033	791	143	45	24	3
59 **MALLAH** ..	United Provinces (All Religions).	14,17	**Males** ..	**145,091**	**64,679**	**30,663**	**22,292**	**5,356**	**3,405**	**2,379**	**584**
			Females ..	**152,873**	**50,483**	**32,237**	**15,591**	**1,363**	**549**	**559**	**184**
60 **MAPPILLA** (Moplah). ..	Coorg (Muslim) ..	14,17	**Males** ..	**6,051**	**3,260**	**464**	**642**	**477**	**942**	**725**	**10**
			Females ..	**2,753**	**1,060**	**433**	**469**	**107**	**34**	**16**	**1**
61 **MARATHA** ..	..	14,17	**Males** ..	**1,113,226**	**483,176**	**185,552**	**142,608**	**67,090**	**50,595**	**27,367**	**9,964**
			Females ..	**1,117,623**	**355,293**	**190,534**	**104,925**	**40,503**	**9,190**	**7,246**	**2,895**
	Bombay (Hindu)	.. *	Males ..	170,293	90,484	38,745	33,696	7,952	6,390	3,296	405
			Females ..	194,975	69,212	37,213	22,612	8,393	484	400	110
	Central Provinces and Berar (Hindu).	..	Males ..	145,576	54,953	24,150	18,850	5,028	4,132	2,293	500
			Females	141,613	36,007	22,577	10,808	1,174	701	487	260
	Baroda (Hindu) ..	..	Males ..	6,756	3,350	1,080	973	356	677	235	29
			Females ..	5,399	1,795	928	706	111	38	8	4
	Gwalior (Hindu) ..	..	Males ..	7,823	3,451	1,003	943	414	678	333	80
			Females ..	6,328	2,029	1,070	720	97	67	61	14
	Hyderabad (Hindu).	..	Males ..	751,082	313,516	115,017	82,606	51,322	35,847	19,880	8,844
			Females ..	740,476	234,892	123,170	65,112	30,183	7,750	6,207	2,470
	Mysore (Hindu) ..	..	Males ..	31,696	17,422	5,557	5,540	2,018	2,871	1,330	106
			Females ..	28,832	11,358	5,576	4,967	545	150	83	37
62 **MEGH**	..	14,17	**Males** ..	**1,041,229**	**492,841**	**154,157**	**154,919**	**82,340**	**53,493**	**36,088**	**11,844**
			Females ..	**1,033,712**	**393,053**	**174,957**	**124,659**	**40,945**	**22,086**	**20,287**	**10,119**
MADIGA ..	Bombay (Hindu)	..	Males ..	51,999	25,748	9,968	8,343	2,584	2,437	1,964	452
			Females ..	53,720	22,227	9,633	5,070	901	1,437	3,678	1,508
	Central Provinces and Berar (All Religions).	..	Males ..	2,973	1,234	553	420	114	79	57	11
			Females ..	2,499	816	539	210	36	24	4	3
	Coorg (Hindu) ..	..	Males ..	122	82	25	16	10	5	6	..
			Females ..	95	45	13	26	1	5	..	..
	Madras (Hindu) ..	..	Males ..	309,876	165,035	62,068	55,207	18,137	18,423	9,882	1,318
			Females ..	302,535	118,396	63,803	42,191	4,965	2,809	3,703	925
	Hyderabad (Adi-Hindu).	..†	Males ..	639,197	282,495	75,447	85,404	59,625	30,094	22,371	9,554
			Females ..	641,895	240,180	94,834	72,851	34,342	17,686	12,809	7,658
MEGH ..	Jammu and Kashmir (Hindu).	..	Males ..	37,062	18,267	6,096	5,529	1,870	2,455	1,808	509
			Females ..	32,968	11,389	6,135	4,311	700	125	93	25
63 **MIRASI** ..	Punjab (Muslim) ..	17	**Males** ..	**129,147**	**71,560**	**25,791**	**22,052**	**7,688**	**8,951**	**5,833**	**1,245**
			Females ..	**112,513**	**49,920**	**24,964**	**17,660**	**4,020**	**2,094**	**850**	**332**
64 **MOMIN** ..	..	14,17	**Males** ..	**1,271,801**	**570,739**	**246,998**	**186,140**	**54,942**	**47,706**	**28,167**	**6,786**
			Females ..	**1,142,448**	**410,609**	**235,359**	**137,651**	**19,133**	**9,833**	**6,532**	**2,101**
BAFINDA ..	Jammu and Kashmir (Muslim).	..	Males ..	17,679	9,403	3,567	3,138	1,099	1,034	465	100
			Females ..	16,193	6,643	3,525	2,418	454	138	54	54
JOLAHA (*JULAHA*).	Delhi (Hindu) ..	..	Males ..	4,958	1,957	811	617	182	206	127	14
			Females ..	3,658	1,160	730	353	40	19	16	2
	Delhi (Muslims) ..	..	Males ..	494	222	63	83	16	31	26	3
			Females ..	366	133	77	48	4	4	..	..
	Punjab (Hindu) ..	..	Males ..	27,560	12,870	4,580	3,993	1,599	1,464	997	237
			Females ..	23,593	7,779	4,405	2,801	296	207	59	11
	Punjab (Sikh) ..	..	Males ..	1,978	861	319	284	86	75	73	24
			Females ..	1,662	522	285	198	23	9	5	2
	Punjab (Muslims) ..	..	Males ..	331,748	179,225	67,052	56,444	19,774	20,241	13,105	2,609
			Females ..	280,831	124,974	64,002	45,079	9,265	4,152	1,945	531
	United Provinces (All Religions).	..	Males ..	523,916	222,095	103,907	73,983	18,207	15,095	8,727	2,176
			Females ..	481,287	160,459	99,682	48,602	5,326	3,302	2,995	552
	Central India (Muslim).	..	Males ..	3,689	1,237	571	380	123	105	45	13
			Females ..	3,627	1,050	575	297	97	44	36	1

by age for selected castes—*contd.*

Married.							Widowed.							
Total. 13	0—6. 14	7—13. 15	14—16. 16	17—23. 17	24—43. 18	44 & over. 19	Total. 20	0—6. 21	7—13. 22	14—16. 23	17—23. 24	24—43. 25	44 & over. 26	
172	..	12	15	37	86	22	10	..	..	..		5	5	
108	..	14	14	17	52	11	28	..	..	..	2	14	12	
295,187	3,448	22,621	21,046	45,923	133,819	68,330	38,787	181	527	836	2,006	12,451	22,786	58
296,074	8,743	43,301	29,203	57,746	119,819	37,262	76,673	232	803	1,447	2,189	21,230	50,772	
4,200	38	248	273	710	2,080	851	510	2	10	..	18	175	305	
3,957	133	571	401	853	1,655	344	1,248	2	5	6	15	408	812	
16,418	60	358	583	2,221	8,919	4,277	1,583	..	3	7	69	483	1,021	
17,231	140	2,219	1,771	3,646	7,706	1,749	5,209	4	31	44	151	1,762	3,217	
189,532	2,169	18,534	14,348	29,375	81,657	43,449	18,530	143	372	480	944	5,953	10,638	
190,746	6,711	33,068	17,591	36,451	73,888	23,037	45,885	179	529	485	1,238	12,015	31,439	
1,792	2	25	72	407	981	305	344	..	1	3	30	156	154	
1,317	..	45	150	328	668	126	303	..	..	2	3	95	203	
44,827	431	1,772	2,688	7,090	22,642	10,204	9,043	14	69	171	529	3,215	5,045	
43,588	421	3,227	4,047	9,010	21,569	5,314	12,207	22	76	600	310	3,406	7,793	
11,816	69	373	749	1,901	6,226	2,498	1,747	5	32	16	105	613	976	
11,254	99	1,203	1,221	2,627	5,120	984	3,829	2	19	59	124	1,296	2,329	
24,054	658	1,192	2,181	3,674	10,233	6,116	6,750	17	38	155	295	1,770	4,475	
25,443	1,211	2,760	3,765	4,252	8,086	5,369	7,382	23	140	248	329	2,055	4,587	
2,548	21	119	152	545	1,081	630	280	..	2	4	16	86	172	
2,538	28	208	257	579	1,127	339	610	..	3	3	19	193	392	
71,321	944	4,630	4,600	10,983	35,515	14,649	9,091	40	118	246	454	3,003	5,230	59
80,246	1,301	7,893	7,599	16,088	38,639	8,726	22,144	71	235	309	669	6,868	13,992	
2,664	..	..	3	131	1,949	581	127	..	..	..	5	80	42	60
1,316	1	19	81	396	725	94	377	..	..	6	24	153	194	
551,612	3,463	22,912	33,540	68,229	280,833	142,635	78,438	780	1,365	2,307	3,026	25,939	45,021	61
594,428	16,506	65,027	70,958	114,783	252,296	74,858	167,902	1,075	1,805	2,554	6,712	51,791	103,965	
72,996	131	669	1,405	7,190	37,257	26,344	6,813	14	35	32	94	1,229	5,409	
96,310	281	5,960	9,669	19,478	49,458	11,464	29,453	121	153	202	820	8,754	19,403	
80,258	542	4,500	4,689	13,263	36,461	20,803	10,365	27	136	226	512	3,411	6,053	
80,382	2,879	11,494	8,431	17,999	30,550	9,029	25,224	46	244	208	992	7,656	16,078	
2,973	1	4	22	365	1,887	694	433	..	..	1	13	160	259	
2,283	1	53	204	725	1,155	145	1,321	..	3	3	44	445	826	
3,511	29	98	205	692	1,632	855	861	1	3	19	28	329	481	
2,920	59	264	256	669	1,196	476	1,379	5	9	15	51	449	850	
379,343	2,760	17,632	27,159	45,939	195,726	90,127	58,223	738	1,191	2,028	2,354	20,225	31,687	
400,255	13,285	46,881	51,260	72,516	163,823	52,490	105,329	903	1,393	2,100	4,625	32,574	63,734	
12,531	..	9	60	780	7,870	3,812	1,743	..	..	1	25	585	1,132	
12,278	1	375	1,138	3,396	6,114	1,254	5,196	..	3	26	180	1,913	3,074	
461,694	3,502	11,700	21,936	61,408	230,457	132,691	86,694	1,222	2,132	4,448	7,653	25,420	45,819	62
484,119	5,327	36,287	59,768	108,070	199,764	74,903	156,540	1,586	4,494	8,248	11,258	52,657	78,297	
22,724	191	948	930	2,726	12,869	5,060	3,527	15	46	51	171	1,254	1,990	
23,846	904	3,471	2,072	4,781	10,407	2,211	7,647	14	94	115	343	3,039	4,042	
1,602	18	51	100	233	883	317	137	..	..	11	7	46	73	
1,411	22	186	143	344	632	84	272	1	7	4	10	94	156	
56	..	..	..	5	40	11	4	..	..	..	..	3	1	
35	..	..	3	9	21	2	15	..	..	..	..	8	7	
129,938	210	1,401	2,205	13,317	77,270	35,535	14,903	8	75	97	399	4,844	9,480	
135,752	857	9,725	11,998	34,112	66,822	12,238	48,387	21	847	473	2,199	19,407	25,440	
291,814	3,080	9,207	18,384	43,365	130,774	87,004	64,888	1,199	2,003	4,262	6,916	18,266	32,242	
306,936	3,542	22,437	43,906	64,811	113,868	58,372	94,779	1,550	3,535	7,566	8,450	28,423	45,255	
15,560	3	93	317	1,762	8,621	4,764	3,235	..	8	27	160	1,007	2,033	
16,139	2	468	1,646	4,013	8,014	1,996	5,440	..	11	90	256	1,686	3,397	
47,824	37	514	1,155	6,072	25,302	14,744	9,763	2	23	61	465	3,060	6,152	63
50,128	134	1,259	2,981	11,303	25,763	8,688	12,465	1	22	54	312	3,074	9,002	
601,921	6,018	31,075	32,804	97,900	287,152	146,972	99,141	604	1,102	1,641	5,000	33,525	57,269	64
594,704	9,911	59,505	59,410	129,008	265,345	71,525	137,135	324	1,256	2,020	4,503	38,324	90,708	
7,274	..	116	220	919	4,125	1,894	1,002	..	3	17	40	325	617	
7,824	..	249	729	2,055	3,791	1,000	1,726	..	22	15	32	503	1,154	
2,638	..	102	133	520	1,461	422	363	1	..	1	24	179	158	
2,136	4	143	292	532	984	181	362	..	..	3	8	121	230	
220	..	3	11	30	122	54	52	..	..	1	5	26	20	
206	1	14	20	45	106	20	27	..	..	..	..	14	13	
12,477	23	180	391	1,727	6,496	3,660	2,213	1	4	6	82	695	1,425	
12,191	33	871	1,348	2,927	5,639	1,373	3,623	1	13	22	95	1,103	2,389	
896	..	31	45	136	412	272	221	..	1	..	10	64	146	
931	2	75	75	223	383	173	209	..	..	..	4	29	176	
124,479	76	1,491	3,075	16,386	65,826	37,625	28,044	2	37	108	1,212	8,399	18,286	
126,587	244	4,564	8,800	28,883	63,675	20,421	29,270	10	53	101	627	7,070	21,409	
260,769	3,771	20,260	17,467	40,730	120,788	57,753	41,052	387	637	908	2,419	14,143	22,558	
267,906	5,785	31,541	25,340	54,771	118,907	31,562	52,922	126	501	710	1,417	13,776	36,392	
2,105	17	207	188	365	924	404	347	1	6	20	61	104	155	
2,077	32	328	277	404	785	251	500	..	25	18	66	148	243	

Table VIII.—Civil Condition

Caste, Tribe or Race. 1	Province, State or Agency and Religion. 2	Also tabulated in. 3	Sex. 4	Population dealt with. 5	Unmarried. Total. 6	0—6. 7	7—13. 8	14—16. 9	17—23. 10	24—43. 11	44 & over. 12
MOMIN—*contd.*											
JULAHI (Sale Dewang).	Hyderabad (Hindu).	..	Males ..	211,803	79,223	38,499	23,105	8,458	4,674	3,107	1,380
			Females ..	195,078	66,792	35,820	25,408	2,347	1,300	1,144	773
MOMNA ..	Baroda (Muslim)	..	Males ..	6,862	3,014	1,389	1,094	258	202	64	7
			Females ..	6,967	2,658	1,332	918	184	220	1	3
MUMIN (Jolaha).	Bengal (Muslim) ..	..	Males ..	141,114	60,632	26,240	23,019	5,140	4,579	1,431	223
			Females ..	129,186	38,439	24,926	11,529	1,097	438	277	172
65 **NAIBRAHAMAN, etc.**	..	14,17	**Males ..**	**1,008,945**	**455,577**	**182,106**	**148,121**	**48,679**	**41,849**	**27,840**	**6,982**
			Females ..	**911,274**	**310,316**	**180,657**	**102,074**	**13,982**	**7,167**	**4,567**	**1,869**
AMBATTAM ..	Cochin (Hindu) ..	..	Males ..	776	451	172	128	51	72	25	
			Females ..	794	331	149	130	31	15	6	..
HAJJAM ..	Bombay (Hindu)	*	Males ..	15,623	7,238	2,840	2,628	753	684	299	34
			Females ..	15,626	4,858	2,816	1,463	86	212	153	128
	Hyderabad (Hindu)	..	Males ..	83,855	37,406	13,098	11,807	5,881	4,426	1,549	645
			Females ..	75,890	25,752	14,111	7,400	1,817	1,428	710	286
	Western India States (Hindu).	..	Males ..	22,100	10,127	4,259	3,629	1,060	822	296	61
			Females ..	21,747	7,905	4,471	2,977	325	90	38	4
NAI	C. P. and Berar (All Religions).	..	Males ..	66,804	26,334	12,479	9,100	2,205	1,657	744	149
			Females ..	66,452	18,796	12,214	5,909	367	188	93	25
	Delhi (Hindu)	..	Males ..	3,115	1,294	509	438	145	120	68	14
			Females ..	1,318	444	252	131	36	13	9	3
	Delhi (Muslim) ..	..	Males ..	450	186	52	58	27	34	12	3
			Females ..	357	130	84	40	6	..	..	..
	Punjab (Hindu)	..	Males ..	55,634	27,541	9,582	8,762	3,077	2,991	2,315	814
			Females ..	45,506	16,581	9,033	6,210	917	254	98	69
	Punjab (Sikh)	..	Males ..	21,741	11,832	3,718	3,448	1,262	1,394	1,478	532
			Females ..	17,416	7,097	3,464	2,680	632	191	92	38
	Punjab (Muslim)	..	Males ..	127,164	67,388	25,096	21,170	7,149	7,838	5,158	977
			Females ..	108,691	48,103	24,829	16,611	3,708	1,877	830	248
	United Provinces (All Religions)	..	Males ..	475,856	209,394	86,822	68,803	21,251	16,825	12,713	2,980
			Females	430,601	142,325	85,714	46,775	4,918	2,289	1,857	772
	Central India (Hindu).	..	Males ..	48,916	20,348	8,449	6,883	2,070	1,658	1,084	204
			Females ..	45,548	13,582	8,331	4,445	287	161	250	108
	Gwalior (Hindu)	..	Males ..	28,877	12,604	4,708	4,093	1,479	1,277	767	280
			Females ..	25,496	8,272	4,925	2,462	376	251	168	90
NAU ..	United Provinces (Muslim).	..	Males ..	44,231	17,816	7,937	5,143	1,738	1,563	1,184	251
			Females ..	41,619	12,316	7,850	3,540	383	185	260	98
VALAND ..	Baroda (Hindu, Jain and Tribal).	..	Males ..	13,803	5,618	2,385	2,031	531	488	148	35
			Females ..	14,213	3,824	2,414	1,301	93	13	3	..
66 **NAMASUDRA** ..	..	14,17	**Males ..**	**1,139,311**	**538,268**	**198,483**	**183,711**	**58,539**	**66,008**	**28,715**	**2,812**
			Females ..	**1,094,566**	**324,451**	**211,218**	**101,353**	**5,107**	**2,544**	**3,194**	**1,035**
	Assam (Hindu) ..	..	Males ..	71,925	35,973	10,321	10,834	4,195	6,092	3,999	532
			Females ..	67,016	18,447	11,924	5,908	193	175	128	119
	Bengal (Hindu) ..	..	Males ..	1,067,386	502,295	188,162	172,877	54,344	59,916	24,716	2,280
			Females ..	1,027,550	306,004	199,294	95,445	4,914	2,369	3,066	916
67 **NAYAR (Nair)**	..	14,17	**Males ..**	**756,298**	**462,707**	**156,103**	**125,801**	**50,334**	**77,955**	**47,167**	**5,347**
			Females ..	**793,646**	**351,992**	**154,346**	**121,998**	**37,047**	**26,283**	**10,398**	**1,920**
	Coorg (Hindu) ..	..	Males ..	1,100	539	24	39	35	191	238	12
			Females ..	178	74	32	26	11	4	1	..
	Madras (Hindu) ..	..	Males ..	257,819	155,996	47,503	42,351	17,574	28,389	18,530	1,649
			Females ..	279,799	113,943	47,312	40,440	12,046	8,907	4,389	849
	Cochin (Hindu) ..	..	Males ..	66,225	42,868	14,125	11,714	4,829	7,090	4,546	564
			Females ..	76,412	33,850	13,736	11,485	4,083	3,293	1,132	121
	Travancore (Hindu)	..	Males ..	431,154	263,304	94,451	71,697	27,896	42,285	23,853	3,122
			Females ..	437,257	204,125	93,266	70,047	20,907	14,079	4,876	950
68 **OD, etc.** ..	..	14,17	**Males ..**	**176,991**	**88,346**	**33,546**	**28,918**	**10,725**	**9,918**	**4,538**	**701**
			Females ..	**170,858**	**65,612**	**31,098**	**26,343**	**5,670**	**1,409**	**794**	**208**
BELDAR ..	C. P. and Berar (All Religions).	..	Males ..	2,691	1,150	475	429	106	94	39	7
			Females	2,824	819	529	252	17	4	13	4
VADDA (*Vodda and Waddar*).	Bombay (Hindu)	..	Males ..	16,737	8,653	3,542	2,916	950	825	381	39
			Females ..	16,221	6,230	3,497	2,323	260	72	60	18
	C. P. and Berar (Hindu).	..	Males ..	2,951	1,409	765	444	88	79	29	4
			Females ..	3,467	1,376	821	446	35	23	31	20
	Hyderabad (Hindu)	..	Males ..	70,085	30,629	12,915	9,584	3,718	2,700	1,219	493
			Females ..	67,997	23,607	9,884	8,912	3,363	771	485	192
	Mysore (Hindu) ..	..	Males ..	84,527	46,505	15,849	15,545	5,863	6,220	2,870	158
			Females ..	80,349	33,580	16,367	14,410	1,995	539	205	64
ORAON	..	14,17,18	**Males ..**	**265,109**	**134,534**	**68,495**	**47,073**	**10,711**	**6,355**	**1,542**	**358**
			Females ..	**274,743**	**118,832**	**69,602**	**39,134**	**6,162**	**2,463**	**1,135**	**336**
	B. and O. (Hindu)	..	Males ..	79,412	37,358	21,080	13,018	1,911	925	347	77
			Females ..	84,352	31,474	19,914	10,053	875	330	227	75
	B. and O. (Christian)	..	Males ..	56,226	31,643	13,790	10,977	3,731	2,699	401	45
			Females ..	57,096	28,675	14,298	9,926	2,782	1,206	403	60
	B. and O. (Tribal)	..	Males ..	78,875	36,935	19,088	13,658	2,522	1,197	364	106
			Females ..	84,139	33,775	20,799	10,884	1,363	476	184	69

* Including Nhavi and Nadig.

by age for selected castes—*contd.*

Married.							Widowed.							
Total. 13	0—6. 14	7—13. 15	14—16. 16	17—23. 17	24—43. 18	44 & over. 19	Total. 20	0—6. 21	7—13. 22	14—16. 23	17—23. 24	24—43. 25	44 & over. 26	
112,426	1,313	4,969	7,713	24,757	45,961	27,713	20,154	198	363	477	730	7,472	10,914	
98,909	2,104	10,663	13,739	19,346	41,674	11,383	29,377	113	326	845	1,174	9,088	17,831	
3,416	27	177	209	592	1,565	846	432	2	6	7	12	138	267	
3,567	29	295	341	1,264	1,110	528	742	3	2	..	90	77	570	
75,221	791	3,539	3,352	11,738	39,472	16,329	5,261	12	45	96	405	1,980	2,723	
72,370	1,677	10,762	8,449	18,558	28,291	4,633	18,377	71	314	306	990	6,395	10,301	
472,939	4,497	24,028	27,420	78,113	231,716	107,165	80,429	198	741	1,113	4,285	27,354	46,738	65
476,211	7,133	44,281	46,285	100,443	217,737	60,332	124,747	332	946	1,448	4,194	36,535	81,292	
292	..	..	..	35	161	96	33	..	..	..	1	11	21	
351	..	3	26	84	198	40	112	..	..	1	6	42	63	
7,370	41	261	318	1,119	3,722	1,909	1,015	1	12	11	36	336	619	
7,926	104	827	857	1,746	3,550	842	2,842	5	32	27	129	894	1,755	
40,978	776	2,445	3,385	8,526	15,900	9,946	5,471	51	73	122	340	1,618	3,267	
41,024	1,483	6,283	5,771	7,049	13,758	6,680	9,114	73	158	388	692	2,973	4,830	
10,498	80	468	595	1,998	4,857	2,500	1,475	6	18	33	106	402	910	
11,024	182	986	1,107	2,675	4,546	1,528	2,818	6	16	30	157	871	1,738	
36,935	491	2,364	2,089	6,486	18,037	7,468	3,535	12	35	62	244	1,217	1,965	
37,181	741	4,575	3,477	8,254	16,359	3,775	10,475	15	58	73	273	3,178	6,878	
1,549	1	31	81	323	856	257	272	..	1	1	11	103	156	
695	2	36	79	190	312	76	179	..	..	..	1	66	112	
234	..	5	20	32	125	52	30	..	..	..	1	14	15	
197	..	6	14	41	120	16	30	..	..	..	1	5	24	
22,209	14	432	1,078	3,829	10,997	5,859	5,884	1	13	27	203	1,834	3,806	
22,538	60	1,497	2,237	5,497	10,360	2,887	6,387	1	28	15	138	1,821	4,384	
7,773	3	69	269	1,245	3,680	2,507	2,136	..	2	18	92	552	1,472	
8,195	5	227	608	1,794	3,898	1,663	2,124	..	..	6	39	457	1,622	
49,522	39	712	1,313	6,840	26,066	14,552	10,254	2	31	54	377	3,265	6,525	
49,501	126	1,773	3,423	11,144	24,858	8,177	11,087	..	21	52	282	2,553	8,179	
226,973	2,145	12,439	13,957	36,260	115,140	47,032	39,489	78	416	617	2,352	14,043	21,983	
228,164	2,858	19,901	21,473	47,706	109,544	26,682	60,112	139	400	572	1,858	17,760	39,383	
24,958	169	1,198	1,552	4,173	12,895	4,971	3,610	6	46	71	212	1,407	1,868	
24,389	348	2,586	2,580	5,434	11,243	2,198	7,577	19	59	90	228	2,613	4,568	
13,147	93	538	845	2,347	6,491	2,833	3,126	21	37	47	96	1,114	1,811	
12,984	185	1,135	1,567	2,833	5,403	1,861	4,240	50	119	164	252	1,276	2,379	
23,388	625	2,698	1,451	3,519	9,664	5,431	3,027	15	33	36	163	1,168	1,612	
24,107	951	3,531	2,136	4,087	10,296	3,106	5,196	19	37	23	94	1,314	3,709	
7,113	20	368	467	1,381	3,125	1,752	1,072	5	24	14	51	270	708	
7,935	88	915	930	1,909	3,292	801	2,454	5	18	7	44	712	1,668	
537,794	3,855	13,847	14,899	75,844	280,610	148,739	63,249	491	1,836	1,471	2,391	18,945	38,115	66
530,111	7,401	74,721	70,079	138,188	199,656	40,066	240,004	400	1,924	3,672	18,638	99,062	116,308	
31,734	22	120	702	3,455	17,821	9,614	4,218	4	44	90	297	1,332	2,451	
31,428	42	2,815	4,309	9,523	13,091	1,648	17,141	3	91	256	815	7,399	8,577	
506,060	3,833	13,727	14,197	72,389	262,789	139,125	59,031	487	1,792	1,381	2,094	17,613	35,664	
498,683	7,359	71,906	65,770	128,665	186,565	38,418	222,863	397	1,833	3,416	17,823	91,663	107,731	
266,918	2	98	486	11,595	149,765	104,972	26,673	..	8	25	642	8,347	17,651	67
294,006	5	1,292	12,587	69,107	161,264	49,751	147,648	..	65	739	5,815	45,210	95,819	
505	..	1	1	16	368	119	56	..	..	..	..	36	20	
86	..	2	3	19	54	8	18	..	..	1	1	7	9	
90,345	2	33	140	2,954	49,742	37,474	11,478	..	8	17	330	4,128	6,995	
100,183	5	600	4,982	23,362	54,974	16,260	65,673	..	54	525	2,920	21,814	40,360	
20,559	..	2	17	558	11,691	8,291	2,798	..	..	..	25	847	1,926	
26,015	..	65	876	5,766	14,953	4,355	16,547	..	5	54	754	5,656	10,078	
155,509	..	62	328	8,067	87,964	59,088	12,341	..	..	8	287	3,336	8,710	
167,722	..	625	6,726	39,960	91,283	29,128	65,410	..	6	159	2,140	17,733	45,372	
77,692	1,159	2,855	3,126	8,841	40,433	21,278	10,953	61	264	344	772	3,602	5,910	
78,628	1,049	4,734	8,140	18,176	36,659	9,870	26,618	63	369	523	1,366	8,904	15,393	68
1,412	2	55	51	240	748	316	129	..	1	3	6	42	77	
1,480	8	182	151	355	659	125	525	..	5	..	22	177	321	
7,217	62	204	222	810	4,294	1,625	867	8	10	7	29	272	541	
7,373	95	553	775	1,846	3,623	481	2,618	7	13	24	91	949	1,534	
1,422	18	101	85	235	687	296	120	1	3	5	15	33	63	
1,736	23	311	212	381	605	204	355	..	10	13	34	90	208	
33,474	1,077	2,478	2,660	5,387	13,660	8,212	5,982	52	248	328	652	2,027	2,675	
32,478	919	2,873	4,405	6,457	12,369	5,455	11,912	56	331	430	886	3,729	6,480	
34,167	..	17	108	2,169	21,044	10,829	3,855	..	2	1	70	1,228	2,554	
35,561	4	815	2,597	9,137	19,403	3,605	11,208	..	10	56	333	3,959	6,850	
118,141	1,075	4,038	5,948	17,672	62,973	26,435	12,434	26	57	165	567	4,449	7,170	69
125,158	1,189	7,571	10,510	24,969	62,038	18,881	30,753	68	141	239	859	9,737	19,709	
37,642	382	1,864	2,554	5,958	18,826	8,058	4,412	14	16	61	236	1,667	2,418	
41,795	383	3,470	3,994	7,181	20,090	6,677	11,083	32	70	97	367	3,657	6,860	
22,492	142	236	360	2,987	13,172	5,595	2,091	2	1	2	55	703	1,328	
23,044	180	332	1,111	5,168	12,290	3,963	5,377	9	6	17	106	1,672	3,567	
37,412	200	1,563	2,410	5,962	18,940	8,337	4,528	8	33	69	200	1,624	2,594	
39,578	242	3,135	3,701	7,974	18,940	5,586	10,786	27	55	84	293	3,493	6,834	

Table VIII.—Civil Condition

	Caste, Tribe or Race. 1	Province, State or Agency and Religion. 2	Also tabulated in. 3	Sex. 4	Population dealt with. 5	Unmarried. Total. 6	0—6. 7	7—13. 8	14—16. 9	17—23. 10	24—43. 11	44 & over. 12
	ORAON—*contd.*											
		C. P. and Berar. (Christian) ..		Males ..	24,047	13,964	6,737	4,777	1,434	868	137	11
				Females ..	23,470	11,794	6,696	4,176	647	219	51	5
		C. P. and Berar. (Tribals) ..		Males ..	26,549	14,634	7,800	4,643	1,113	666	293	119
				Females ..	25,686	13,114	7,895	4,095	495	232	270	127
70	**PANIKA, PAN Pankha, etc).**	C. P. and Berar (All Religions).	**14,17**	**Males ..**	**83,374**	**30,195**	**15,773**	**10,030**	**1,958**	**1,277**	**952**	**205**
				Females ..	**89,626**	**24,047**	**16,099**	**6,494**	**708**	**401**	**219**	**126**
71	**PARAIYAN (Parayan).**	..	**14,17**	**Males ..**	**616,033**	**337,463**	**122,482**	**116,192**	**38,332**	**44,286**	**14,739**	**1,432**
				Females ..	**643,868**	**271,162**	**128,744**	**104,985**	**21,898**	**11,340**	**3,564**	**631**
		Coorg (Hindu) ..		Males ..	184	88	22	24	10	22	10	..
				Females ..	156	56	28	20	4	3	1	..
		Madras (Hindu) ..		Males ..	543,691	298,288	108,872	103,916	33,534	38,127	12,652	1,187
				Females ..	573,506	238,917	115,043	93,279	18,031	8,982	3,068	514
		Travancore. (Hindu). ..		Males ..	36,230	19,183	6,563	6,002	2,413	2,964	1,092	149
				Females ..	34,454	15,518	6,560	5,689	1,898	1,051	257	63
		Travancore. (Christian) ..		Males ..	35,928	19,904	7,025	6,250	2,375	3,173	985	96
				Females ..	35,752	16,671	7,113	5,997	1,965	1,304	238	54
72	**PARAYAN**	Travancore (Hindu).	**14,17**	**Males ..**	**6,724**	**3,816**	**1,493**	**1,237**	**449**	**460**	**158**	**19**
				Females ..	**6,878**	**3,179**	**1,460**	**1,126**	**322**	**205**	**54**	**12**
73	**PATHAN**	..	..	**Males ..**	**1,327,775**	**700,716**	**246,216**	**217,317**	**74,533**	**92,898**	**59,929**	**9,823**
				Females ..	**1,147,565**	**476,974**	**240,224**	**164,981**	**35,207**	**19,871**	**12,523**	**4,168**
		Baluchistan (Muslim). ..		Males ..	1,025	592	156	169	56	102	94	15
				Females ..	731	337	138	155	27	9	6	2
		Delhi (Muslim) ..		Males ..	16,041	7,977	2,199	2,216	893	1,592	984	93
				Females ..	10,346	4,281	2,138	1,691	288	110	50	4
		N.-W. F. Province (Muslim). ..		Males ..	491,585	284,412	96,448	88,439	29,933	38,410	26,226	4,956
				Females ..	425,045	200,631	92,847	68,467	16,641	11,697	7,917	3,062
		Punjab (Muslim) ..		Males ..	190,923	106,340	34,686	31,326	11,339	16,219	11,245	1,525
				Females ..	154,479	67,962	33,753	23,770	5,802	2,978	1,360	299
		United Provinces (Muslim). ..		Males ..	579,291	273,516	103,499	86,307	29,273	32,200	19,182	3,055
				Females ..	515,095	185,081	102,138	63,423	11,038	4,625	3,090	767
		Baroda (Muslim) ..		Males ..	8,702	4,384	1,435	1,305	449	705	437	53
				Females ..	7,182	2,690	1,371	1,014	230	58	14	3
		Jammu and Kashmir .. (Muslim).		Males ..	10,554	5,851	1,985	1,928	605	740	527	66
				Females ..	8,734	3,924	1,994	1,383	341	178	18	10
		Mysore (Muslim) ..		Males ..	29,654	17,644	5,808	5,627	1,985	2,930	1,234	60
				Females ..	25,953	12,068	5,845	5,078	840	216	68	21
74	**PINJARA (Pinjari).**	..	**14,17**	**Males ..**	**7,838**	**4,172**	**1,575**	**1,342**	**466**	**521**	**253**	**15**
				Females ..	**7,557**	**3,020**	**1,529**	**1,236**	**182**	**54**	**15**	**4**
		Baroda (Muslim) ..		Males ..	2,380	1,068	481	367	99	88	26	7
				Females ..	2,384	760	419	278	47	14	1	1
		Mysore (Muslim) ..		Males ..	5,458	3,104	1,094	975	367	433	227	8
				Females ..	5,173	2,260	1,110	958	135	40	14	3
75	**PRABHU**	..	**14,17**	**Males ..**	**10,450**	**6,062**	**1,764**	**1,737**	**725**	**1,208**	**597**	**31**
				Females ..	**9,223**	**4,661**	**1,847**	**1,601**	**684**	**428**	**77**	**24**
		Bombay (Hindu) ..		Males ..	8,688	4,897	1,433	1,409	590	946	497	22
				Females ..	7,495	3,745	1,488	1,259	541	361	74	22
		Baroda (Hindu) ..		Males ..	1,762	1,165	331	328	135	262	100	9
				Females ..	1,728	916	359	342	143	67	3	2
76	**REBARI**	Rajputana (Hindu and Muslim).	**14,17**	**Males ..**	**57,022**	**26,856**	**10,506**	**9,188**	**3,344**	**2,473**	**1,130**	**215**
				Females ..	**53,332**	**18,107**	**10,427**	**6,210**	**895**	**330**	**194**	**51**
77	**RAJPUT**	..	**14,17**	**Males ..**	**4,951,465**	**2,513,751**	**835,596**	**758,867**	**270,211**	**300,641**	**271,917**	**76,519**
				Females ..	**4,297,692**	**1,483,754**	**800,595**	**534,196**	**84,921**	**35,581**	**21,421**	**7,040**
		Ajmer-Merwara (Hindu). ..		Males ..	9,687	4,637	1,418	1,306	476	745	480	212
				Females ..	7,586	2,267	1,283	843	83	29	22	7
		Bihar and Orissa (Hindu). ..		Males ..	729,105	357,035	113,959	112,201	31,827	39,509	48,162	11,377
				Females ..	659,823	199,303	107,781	77,328	8,377	2,931	2,069	817
		Central Provinces and Berar (All Religions). ..		Males ..	258,231	106,632	44,702	34,134	10,231	9,820	6,273	1,472
				Females ..	247,856	71,538	43,757	23,495	2,545	870	635	236
		Delhi (Hindu) ..		Males ..	19,652	8,322	2,422	2,152	1,034	1,480	1,138	96
				Females ..	11,012	3,858	2,156	1,390	184	77	42	9
		Delhi (Sikh) ..		Males ..	117	47	14	13	2	8	7	3
				Females ..	69	25	11	12	2	..	..	..
		Delhi (Muslim) ..		Males ..	3,622	1,476	439	374	138	307	199	19
				Females ..	2,114	753	412	268	47	17	7	2
		Punjab (Hindu) ..		Males ..	322,692	168,673	50,262	47,687	19,390	25,153	20,171	6,010
				Females ..	254,682	90,899	46,524	33,414	5,946	2,805	1,692	518
		Punjab (Sikh) ..		Males ..	27,933	15,228	6,083	4,068	2,235	1,536	986	270
				Females ..	21,661	9,498	5,313	3,173	623	261	109	19
		Punjab (Muslim) ..		Males ..	917,462	519,215	182,430	159,666	57,825	68,947	43,449	6,898
				Females ..	801,070	360,548	179,245	128,286	29,929	14,526	7,208	1,354
		United Provinces (All Religions). ..		**Males ..**	**2,013,289**	**998,638**	**321,991**	**296,978**	**108,402**	**112,366**	**119,277**	**39,624**
				Females ..	**1,743,647**	**557,362**	**315,327**	**198,239**	**25,675**	**9,564**	**6,109**	**2,449**
		Baroda (Hindu) ..		**Males ..**	**49,661**	**22,441**	**8,418**	**7,404**	**2,286**	**2,404**	**1,538**	**391**
				Females ..	**45,144**	**13,589**	**7,729**	**5,137**	**623**	**64**	**27**	**9**

by age for selected castes—*contd.*

Married.							Widowed.							
Total. 13	0—6. 14	7—13. 15	14—16. 16	17—23. 17	24—43. 18	44 & over. 19	Total. 20	0—6. 21	7—13. 22	14—16. 23	17—23. 24	24—43. 25	44 & over. 26	
9,432	..	31	143	1,301	5,849	2,108	651	..	..	3	34	210	404	
9,708	..	42	635	2,302	5,362	1,367	1,968	..	..	11	45	509	1,403	
11,163	351	344	481	1,464	6,186	2,337	752	2	7	30	42	245	426	
11,033	384	592	1,069	2,344	5,356	1,288	1,539	..	10	30	48	406	1,045	
49,204	**823**	**3,951**	**3,004**	**7,393**	**22,108**	**11,925**	**3,975**	**28**	**57**	**99**	**304**	**1,525**	**1,962**	70
52,279	**1,468**	**5,901**	**4,199**	**9,986**	**23,063**	**7,657**	**13,300**	**35**	**130**	**76**	**322**	**3,285**	**9,452**	
257,425	**36**	**372**	**1,077**	**19,703**	**156,443**	**79,789**	**21,145**	..	**11**	**16**	**451**	**6,161**	**14,506**	71
280,923	**92**	**3,235**	**12,756**	**70,551**	**160,298**	**33,991**	**91,783**	**6**	**61**	**194**	**2,207**	**32,376**	**56,939**	
85	..	..	..	5	68	12	11	..	..	..	1	7	3	
84	..	..	2	16	62	4	16	..	..	..	2	8	6	
227,058	36	347	949	17,482	137,341	70,903	18,345	..	10	11	334	5,265	12,725	
250,462	92	3,140	11,911	62,232	143,527	29,560	84,127	6	59	180	1,977	30,125	51,780	
15,551	..	20	86	1,146	9,692	4,607	1,496	..	1	2	82	467	944	
15,390	..	50	482	4,425	8,145	2,288	3,546	..	2	9	129	1,040	2,366	
14,731	..	5	42	1,075	9,342	4,267	1,293	..	..	3	34	422	834	
14,987	..	45	361	3,878	8,564	2,139	4,094	..	..	5	99	1,203	2,787	
2,676	..	**4**	**18**	**237**	**1,535**	**882**	**232**	..	..	**1**	**14**	**68**	**149**	72
2,808	..	**6**	**136**	**673**	**1,521**	**472**	**891**	..	..	**7**	**31**	**243**	**610**	
544,045	**3,114**	**14,318**	**15,645**	**59,766**	**291,153**	**160,049**	**83,014**	**220**	**696**	**1,096**	**4,361**	**28,669**	**47,972**	73
527,732	**4,014**	**23,095**	**35,641**	**111,428**	**276,854**	**76,700**	**142,859**	**165**	**389**	**1,130**	**4,139**	**41,099**	**95,937**	
381	..	1	3	29	243	105	52	..	..	1	1	27	23	
337	..	2	15	89	212	19	57	..	..	..	1	16	40	
7,087	2	42	156	969	4,116	1,802	977	..	6	5	44	436	486	
5,161	3	154	390	1,272	2,764	578	904	..	1	1	20	226	656	
179,940	..	838	2,824	16,643	101,056	58,579	27,233	..	314	606	1,572	10,082	14,659	
176,499	..	2,409	9,130	37,191	100,009	27,760	47,915	..	47	479	1,901	15,606	29,882	
72,639	42	359	930	7,379	40,530	23,399	11,944	1	13	47	425	4,032	7,426	
68,589	71	1,317	3,493	15,416	37,128	11,164	17,928	..	24	60	415	4,711	12,718	
265,021	3,064	13,011	11,551	33,231	134,016	70,148	40,754	218	360	432	2,278	13,419	24,047	
259,162	3,934	18,899	21,251	52,648	127,242	35,188	70,852	164	310	527	1,650	18,978	49,223	
3,672	5	16	45	479	2,060	1,067	646	1	..	4	14	228	399	
3,209	3	74	221	878	1,676	363	1,283	1	3	8	37	367	867	
4,177	1	44	113	479	2,405	1,135	526	..	3	1	17	201	304	
4,038	3	104	292	957	2,155	527	772	..	..	42	28	219	483	
11,128	..	7	23	557	6,727	3,814	882	..	..	..	10	244	628	
10,737	..	136	849	2,977	5,674	1,101	3,148	..	4	13	87	976	2,068	
3,308	..	**58**	**70**	**366**	**1,822**	**992**	**358**	..	**2**	**1**	**5**	**101**	**249**	74
3,486	**10**	**139**	**288**	**894**	**1,749**	**406**	**1,051**	..	**3**	**8**	**27**	**349**	**664**	
1,170	..	55	59	221	541	294	142	..	2	1	3	33	103	
1,248	10	82	110	340	547	159	376	..	2	6	3	100	265	
2,138	..	3	11	145	1,281	698	216	..	..	..	2	68	146	
2,238	..	57	178	554	1,202	247	675	..	1	2	24	249	399	
4,024	**6**	**50**	**105**	**212**	**2,653**	**998**	**364**	..	**1**	**3**	**9**	**92**	**259**	75
3,452	**26**	**42**	**158**	**970**	**1,790**	**466**	**1,110**	**9**	**8**	**10**	**39**	**395**	**649**	
3,500	6	50	102	194	2,356	792	291	..	1	3	9	82	196	
2,875	26	42	138	818	1,475	376	875	9	8	9	33	298	518	
524	..	..	3	18	297	206	73	..	..	..	..	10	63	
577	..	..	20	152	315	90	235	..	..	1	6	97	131	
26,128	**317**	**1,427**	**1,746**	**4,080**	**12,502**	**6,056**	**4,038**	**8**	**38**	**80**	**193**	**1,118**	**2,601**	76
26,253	**661**	**2,710**	**2,716**	**5,964**	**10,896**	**3,306**	**8,972**	**12**	**32**	**77**	**282**	**2,879**	**5,690**	
2,069,641	**9,675**	**53,819**	**78,561**	**282,978**	**1,071,802**	**572,806**	**368,073**	**599**	**2,141**	**3,984**	**13,494**	**111,304**	**236,551**	77
2,035,279	**13,731**	**124,620**	**171,560**	**459,960**	**993,981**	**271,418**	**778,659**	**1,015**	**4,018**	**7,545**	**26,519**	**255,133**	**484,429**	
4,455	19	56	94	679	2,602	1,005	595	1	1	5	18	170	400	
3,687	29	180	326	1,041	1,817	294	1,632	3	4	7	55	541	1,022	
317,293	2,091	10,531	14,111	41,994	160,025	88,541	54,777	173	474	706	1,938	17,230	34,256	
303,244	3,336	20,979	23,797	65,129	148,597	41,406	157,276	249	1,021	1,255	6,080	55,540	93,131	
136,658	1,160	8,281	7,923	22,204	65,982	31,108	14,941	31	132	154	639	4,885	9,100	
133,466	2,193	15,544	13,418	29,341	57,951	15,019	42,852	46	333	498	1,433	13,394	27,148	
9,770	2	123	319	1,710	6,068	1,548	1,560	..	2	10	93	683	772	
5,953	4	261	611	1,644	2,893	540	1,201	..	3	7	30	407	754	
63	..	..	4	13	38	8	7	..	..	..	..	5	2	
39	..	4	3	10	18	4	5	..	..	..	1	2	2	
1,891	1	35	52	355	1,153	295	255	..	1	2	20	127	105	
1,166	2	69	107	283	580	125	195	..	..	2	3	52	138	
127,903	58	1,008	2,574	15,572	69,310	39,381	26,116	..	23	97	714	8,289	16,993	
117,736	198	6,089	10,631	29,268	56,404	15,146	46,047	2	102	266	1,460	14,619	29,598	
11,040	6	45	238	2,384	4,935	3,432	1,665	2	5	5	39	545	1,069	
10,110	6	181	607	2,120	5,752	1,444	2,053	..	2	7	50	441	1,553	
341,330	309	3,143	6,389	36,248	188,735	106,506	56,917	8	137	236	1,772	16,040	38,724	
346,145	707	13,630	21,963	78,355	180,491	50,999	94,377	22	140	298	1,936	25,654	66,327	
851,843	4,493	23,903	35,900	123,103	435,281	229,163	162,808	290	1,066	2,124	6,051	48,646	104,631	
857,622	4,952	52,904	73,477	191,341	421,770	113,178	328,663	420	1,479	3,772	11,035	109,766	202,191	
24,049	21	573	1,096	4,140	12,096	6,123	3,171	5	21	15	102	886	2,142	
23,058	82	1,603	2,696	5,437	10,590	2,650	8,497	1	31	65	246	2,679	5,475	

Table VIII.—Civil Condition

Caste, Tribe or Race. 1	Province, State or Agency and Religion. 2	Also tabulated in. 3	Sex. 4	Population dealt with. 5	Unmarried. Total. 6	0—6. 7	7—13. 8	14—16. 9	17—23. 10	24—43. 11	44 & over. 12
RAJPUT—*contd.*	Central India (Hindu)		Males	114,723	54,766	18,520	17,536	6,047	6,089	5,325	1,249
			Females	103,552	33,876	18,080	12,122	1,724	745	890	315
	Gwalior (Hindu)		Males	66,304	31,223	10,792	8,624	3,319	3,861	3,163	1,464
			Females	49,207	16,166	8,021	5,085	1,234	916	543	367
	Hyderabad (Hindu)		Males	46,256	20,096	9,305	5,409	2,481	1,362	1,101	438
			Females	42,178	14,635	8,711	4,154	792	344	481	153
	Jammu and Kashmir (Hindu)		Males	34,177	19,689	5,660	5,012	2,102	3,074	3,132	709
			Females	25,759	8,246	4,022	2,882	739	274	264	65
	Jammu and Kashmir (Muslim)		Males	101,875	56,817	22,069	18,443	6,540	6,596	2,772	397
			Females	93,574	40,737	21,237	14,500	3,315	1,136	397	152
	Rajputana (Hindu)		Males	236,679	128,816	37,112	37,860	15,826	17,384	14,744	5,890
			Females	188,758	60,454	30,986	23,868	3,083	1,022	926	569
78 **SANTAL**		**14,17,18**	**Males**	**1,194,527**	**595,177**	**251,081**	**210,426**	**55,518**	**50,694**	**24,011**	**3,447**
			Females	**1,192,397**	**496,489**	**269,839**	**171,876**	**28,944**	**17,903**	**6,702**	**1,225**
	Bengal (Hindu)		Males	219,315	105,521	40,602	35,367	10,101	10,566	7,044	1,841
			Females	214,187	82,173	45,220	28,909	4,462	2,357	879	346
	Bengal (Tribal)		Males	176,802	86,789	36,695	30,168	7,786	8,217	3,352	571
			Females	175,576	71,127	38,848	24,677	3,960	2,693	845	104
	Bengal (Christian)		Males	5,477	2,924	1,029	1,056	314	350	157	18
			Females	5,277	2,575	1,037	1,053	247	157	73	8
	Bihar and Orissa (Hindu)		Males	247,799	130,215	53,406	44,570	14,088	12,516	5,195	440
			Females	248,615	107,560	57,346	36,485	6,867	4,764	1,797	301
	Bihar and Orissa (Christian)		Males	6,012	3,279	1,267	1,131	377	374	130	..
			Females	5,959	2,906	1,164	1,143	343	183	67	6
	Bihar and Orissa (Tribal)		Males	539,122	266,449	118,082	98,134	22,852	18,671	8,133	577
			Females	542,783	230,148	126,224	79,609	13,065	7,749	3,041	460
79 **SAWARA, etc.**		**14,17,18**	**Males**	**182,961**	**87,335**	**37,136**	**29,158**	**9,245**	**7,210**	**3,748**	**838**
			Females	**186,359**	**76,623**	**39,840**	**25,706**	**5,373**	**3,351**	**1,735**	**618**
SAHAR (Saharia).	Gwalior (Hindu)		Males	37,204	18,384	8,055	6,897	1,660	1,123	523	126
			Females	36,333	15,354	9,236	5,251	489	184	126	68
SAORA	Madras (Tribal)		Males	104,631	50,657	20,625	15,756	5,723	4,986	2,925	642
			Females	107,150	45,695	21,791	14,815	4,215	2,941	1,462	471
SAWARA	C. P. & Berar (Hindu).		Males	41,126	18,294	8,456	6,505	1,862	1,101	300	70
			Females	42,876	15,574	8,813	5,640	669	226	147	79
80 **SAYYAD**		**14,17**	**Males**	**526,564**	**277,022**	**97,639**	**87,742**	**29,994**	**38,106**	**20,261**	**3,280**
			Females	**465,432**	**191,774**	**93,738**	**68,113**	**16,069**	**8,445**	**4,173**	**1,236**
	Bengal (Muslim)		Males	86,300	40,333	15,586	14,390	3,855	4,519	1,742	241
			Females	76,605	25,499	14,372	8,971	1,196	475	313	172
	Delhi (Muslim)		Males	10,504	5,616	1,596	1,700	635	1,055	540	90
			Females	7,753	3,396	1,650	1,286	316	97	35	12
	N.-W. F. Province (Muslim).		Males	42,834	24,970	8,878	7,847	2,811	3,107	1,969	358
			Females	39,478	18,655	8,696	6,294	1,618	1,034	762	251
	Punjab (Muslim)		Males	157,818	86,947	29,769	26,305	9,346	12,528	7,699	1,300
			Females	135,484	59,523	28,033	20,872	5,517	3,179	1,443	479
	United Provinces (Muslim).		Males	164,335	82,259	29,173	25,497	9,112	11,386	6,024	1,067
			Females	147,839	58,564	27,963	20,418	5,408	3,068	1,468	239
	Baroda (Muslim)		Males	4,952	2,552	852	805	314	397	155	29
			Females	4,638	1,734	821	636	194	72	10	1
	Jammu & Kashmir (Muslim).		Males	20,675	11,481	4,257	3,805	1,370	1,340	612	97
			Females	19,051	8,453	4,480	2,981	699	212	62	19
	Mysore (Muslim)		Males	39,146	22,864	7,528	7,393	2,551	3,774	1,520	98
			Females	34,584	15,950	7,723	6,655	1,121	308	80	63
81 **SHAHA**	Bengal (Hindu)	**17**	**Males**	**215,375**	**99,871**	**35,541**	**32,167**	**11,393**	**13,926**	**5,837**	**1,007**
			Females	**204,636**	**62,841**	**36,090**	**22,128**	**2,772**	**1,040**	**569**	**242**
82 **TAGA**		**14,17**	**Males**	**76,198**	**39,489**	**12,878**	**10,661**	**4,320**	**4,528**	**4,895**	**2,207**
			Females	**61,400**	**22,477**	**11,992**	**8,058**	**1,481**	**588**	**262**	**96**
	Delhi (Hindu)		Males	576	327	103	81	39	51	40	13
			Females	467	180	92	64	21	3	..	..
	Delhi (Muslim)		Males	1,834	866	380	304	81	66	29	6
			Females	1,568	574	364	178	23	5	2	2
	United Provinces (All religions).		Males	73,788	38,296	12,395	10,276	4,200	4,411	4,826	2,188
			Females	59,365	21,723	11,536	7,816	1,437	580	260	94
83 **TANTI (Tatwa)**		**17,17**	**Males**	**307,755**	**108,669**	**54,644**	**34,048**	**7,526**	**7,772**	**3,943**	**736**
			Females	**325,733**	**79,832**	**53,499**	**21,916**	**2,437**	**1,049**	**833**	**98**
	Assam (Hindu)		Males	29,846	13,780	6,114	3,981	1,187	1,332	1,114	52
			Females	28,132	10,998	6,154	3,497	737	372	218	20
	Bihar & Orissa (Hindu).		Males	277,909	94,889	48,530	30,067	6,339	6,440	2,829	684
			Females	297,601	68,834	47,345	18,419	1,700	677	615	78
84 **TELI, etc.**		**14,17**	**Males**	**3,383,388**	**1,545,366**	**646,988**	**500,700**	**147,162**	**161,920**	**76,493**	**12,103**
			Females	**3,311,662**	**1,151,039**	**648,302**	**395,502**	**59,783**	**29,409**	**13,808**	**4,235**
GHANCHI	Bombay (Hindu)		Males	7,984	2,555	1,063	837	184	333	126	12
			Females	6,877	1,578	940	489	53	55	31	10
	Baroda (Hindu)		Males	7,325	2,816	1,304	954	219	187	118	34
			Females	6,975	1,920	1,174	691	53	..	1	1
	Baroda (Muslim)		Males	3,903	1,684	747	515	166	181	62	13
			Females	3,523	1,152	623	394	76	54	4	1

by age for selected castes—*contd.*

Married.							Widowed.							
Total. 13	0—6. 14	7—13. 15	14—16. 16	17—23. 17	24—43. 18	44 & over. 19	Total. 20	0—6. 21	7—13. 22	14—16. 23	17—23. 24	24—43. 25	44 & over. 26	
50,924	302	1,368	2,448	8,201	26,911	11,694	9,033	16	62	157	538	3,227	5,033	
48,519	749	3,915	4,905	11,642	22,653	4,655	21,157	31	107	196	1,037	8,168	11,618	
27,511	227	1,024	2,097	5,805	12,006	6,352	7,570	22	109	148	300	2,493	4,498	
23,138	375	1,875	2,745	5,333	8,938	3,872	9,903	84	205	317	566	3,352	5,379	
22,920	299	1,225	1,469	3,257	10,304	6,366	3,240	44	44	121	166	859	2,006	
21,153	364	2,059	3,047	4,853	7,167	3,663	6,390	38	94	180	369	1,500	4,209	
11,933	..	210	111	988	6,198	4,426	2,555	..	2	8	123	748	1,674	
11,949	..	431	1,257	2,966	5,369	1,926	5,564	..	295	109	306	1,728	3,126	
40,228	..	710	968	4,801	22,988	10,761	4,830	..	11	24	160	1,638	2,997	
43,064	4	812	3,599	10,553	22,994	5,102	9,773	..	64	63	262	2,796	6,588	
89,830	687	1,584	2,768	11,524	47,170	26,097	18,033	7	51	172	821	4,833	12,149	
85,230	730	4,084	8,380	20,644	39,997	11,395	43,074	119	138	503	1,650	14,494	26,170	
554,650	**4,223**	**17,138**	**20,337**	**73,597**	**306,935**	**132,420**	**44,700**	**80**	**293**	**954**	**3,394**	**17,031**	**22,898**	78
550,119	**4,682**	**23,155**	**46,800**	**126,666**	**274,276**	**69,540**	**145,789**	**327**	**1,129**	**2,369**	**8,202**	**48,440**	**85,322**	
103,226	755	4,735	3,198	12,964	55,504	26,070	10,568	37	78	302	1,263	4,086	4,802	
102,665	706	5,772	8,555	25,458	51,591	10,583	29,349	93	218	662	2,066	10,317	15,993	
83,669	541	1,678	2,314	10,039	47,512	21,585	6,344	6	23	113	462	2,371	3,369	
80,673	931	3,992	6,178	20,074	40,009	9,489	23,776	59	244	467	1,721	7,794	13,491	
2,305	8	27	41	195	1,388	646	248	..	1	1	11	119	116	
2,150	13	61	132	519	1,168	257	552	..	6	3	35	215	293	
110,367	572	2,411	3,338	15,480	63,884	24,682	7,217	3	27	91	467	2,830	3,799	
107,818	498	4,700	10,608	26,431	54,366	11,215	33,237	50	172	375	1,601	11,640	19,399	
2,568	20	74	63	292	1,445	674	165	..	..	1	8	81	75	
2,475	6	52	106	496	1,412	403	578	..	..	2	20	183	373	
252,515	2,327	8,213	11,383	34,627	137,202	58,763	20,158	34	164	446	1,183	7,594	10,737	
254,338	2,528	13,578	21,221	53,688	125,730	37,593	58,297	125	489	860	2,759	18,291	35,773	
87,796	**1,058**	**2,648**	**4,869**	**13,600**	**45,436**	**20,185**	**7,830**	**15**	**41**	**194**	**674**	**2,926**	**3,980**	79
89,761	**1,337**	**5,086**	**8,894**	**21,227**	**41,670**	**11,547**	**19,975**	**74**	**174**	**380**	**1,194**	**7,481**	**10,672**	
17,428	251	641	1,172	3,519	9,009	2,836	1,392	3	5	14	55	541	774	
17,578	388	1,602	2,735	4,783	6,788	1,282	3,401	44	36	57	105	1,282	1,877	
49,156	496	1,278	2,587	6,547	25,974	12,274	4,818	6	33	165	531	1,806	2,277	
50,041	780	2,033	4,155	11,473	24,495	7,105	11,414	24	122	279	907	4,252	5,830	
21,212	311	729	1,110	3,534	10,453	5,075	1,620	6	3	15	88	579	929	
22,142	169	1,451	2,004	4,971	10,387	3,160	5,160	6	16	44	182	1,947	2,965	
219,027	**1,119**	**3,980**	**5,633**	**24,822**	**117,749**	**65,724**	**30,515**	**79**	**119**	**214**	**1,120**	**9,701**	**19,282**	80
212,103	**1,614**	**9,348**	**15,575**	**50,642**	**106,123**	**28,801**	**61,555**	**59**	**206**	**422**	**1,967**	**18,154**	**40,747**	
43,297	414	1,536	2,069	6,239	22,378	10,661	2,670	4	23	47	171	981	1,444	
40,106	1,039	4,397	4,549	10,792	15,888	3,441	11,000	36	84	162	620	3,915	6,183	
4,345	1	16	76	422	2,636	1,194	543	1	1	2	23	209	307	
3,541	1	51	213	937	1,922	417	816	..	1	1	12	204	598	
15,670	..	87	285	1,647	8,748	4,903	2,194	..	5	32	144	802	1,211	
16,263	..	173	969	3,504	8,899	2,718	4,560	..	8	30	180	1,578	2,764	
59,925	44	385	1,129	6,698	32,227	19,442	10,946	3	13	24	317	3,519	7,070	
58,294	42	1,216	3,303	13,303	31,233	9,197	17,667	3	14	64	374	4,632	12,580	
70,417	659	1,877	1,902	7,745	36,617	21,617	11,659	71	75	97	417	3,355	7,644	
68,839	529	3,172	4,709	15,325	34,712	10,392	20,436	20	93	141	583	5,562	14,037	
2,043	..	5	11	268	1,134	625	357	..	1	1	3	122	230	
1,999	..	71	129	574	969	256	905	..	3	..	23	288	591	
8,252	1	69	134	1,012	4,871	2,165	942	..	..	10	30	328	574	
8,730	1	103	568	2,247	4,945	866	1,868	..	2	16	64	558	1,228	
15,078	..	5	27	791	9,138	5,117	1,204	..	1	1	15	385	802	
14,331	2	165	1,135	3,960	7,555	1,514	4,303	..	1	8	111	1,417	2,766	
101,988	**995**	**3,337**	**4,551**	**13,426**	**48,859**	**30,820**	**13,516**	**80**	**142**	**267**	**793**	**4,196**	**8,029**	81
101,580	**1,735**	**10,886**	**12,777**	**27,165**	**38,782**	**10,235**	**40,215**	**130**	**501**	**867**	**3,012**	**15,160**	**20,545**	
29,264	**69**	**862**	**1,157**	**4,789**	**14,694**	**7,693**	**7,445**	**5**	**19**	**47**	**218**	**2,022**	**5,134**	82
28,387	**88**	**1,304**	**2,411**	**6,807**	**13,756**	**4,021**	**10,536**	**7**	**28**	**94**	**355**	**3,467**	**6,585**	
205	..	1	6	29	116	53	44	..	..	..	1	10	33	
185	..	7	17	48	91	22	102	..	..	1	3	43	55	
828	2	33	41	116	444	192	140	..	3	5	3	47	82	
809	10	85	88	187	356	83	185	..	2	1	8	51	123	
28,231	67	828	1,110	4,644	14,134	7,448	7,261	5	16	42	214	1,965	5,019	
27,393	78	1,212	2,306	6,572	13,309	3,916	10,249	7	26	92	344	3,373	6,407	
182,399	**4,159**	**21,034**	**10,495**	**21,938**	**85,406**	**39,367**	**16,687**	**129**	**715**	**588**	**1,194**	**6,014**	**8,047**	83
190,412	**7,866**	**28,197**	**14,817**	**35,179**	**84,628**	**19,725**	**55,489**	**298**	**1,136**	**625**	**1,677**	**18,984**	**32,769**	
13,774	..	75	143	938	9,406	3,212	2,292	2	7	20	186	1,243	834	
13,714	5	195	644	3,090	8,586	1,194	3,420	..	5	22	140	1,632	1,621	
168,625	4,159	20,959	10,352	21,000	76,000	36,155	14,395	127	708	568	1,008	4,771	7,213	
176,698	7,861	28,002	14,173	32,089	76,042	18,531	52,069	298	1,131	603	1,537	17,352	31,148	
1,661,704	**16,052**	**96,327**	**78,949**	**209,400**	**837,886**	**423,090**	**176,318**	**453**	**2,140**	**2,175**	**8,343**	**57,353**	**105,854**	84
1,680,794	**29,481**	**160,330**	**133,683**	**376,810**	**777,082**	**198,408**	**479,829**	**634**	**3,128**	**3,180**	**12,943**	**152,333**	**307,611**	
4,979	93	586	383	652	2,298	967	450	1	2	3	13	147	284	
4,304	141	668	377	786	1,846	486	995	3	4	17	27	287	657	
4,049	10	296	327	800	1,725	891	460	1	3	4	20	132	300	
3,966	21	450	416	985	1,609	485	1,089	2	5	..	17	308	757	
1,955	11	113	99	365	849	518	264	..	3	2	7	68	184	
1,891	21	187	177	424	840	242	480	2	2	2	9	117	348	

Table VIII.—Civil Condition

Caste, Tribe or Race. 1	Province, State or Agency and Religion. 2	Also tabulated in. 3	Sex. 4	Population dealt with. 5	Unmarried. Total. 6	0—6. 7	7—13. 8	14—16. 9	17—23. 10	24—43. 11	44 & over. 12
TELI—*contd.* ..	Western India States (Hindu).	..	Males ..	1,999	885	353	309	82	77	37	27
			Females ..	1,934	639	400	202	25	11	1	..
	Bihar & Orissa (Hindu).	..	Males ..	531,797	194,405	99,432	66,823	11,869	9,282	5,783	1,216
			Females ..	528,336	145,362	97,673	41,220	2,999	1,971	1,093	406
	Bombay (Hindu)	..	Males ..	22,252	9,828	4,461	3,603	858	657	225	24
			Females ..	22,743	6,744	4,477	1,907	157	105	89	9
	C. P. & Berar (All Religions).	..	Males ..	501,952	165,527	97,770	51,910	8,115	4,433	2,481	818
			Females ..	520,929	126,585	93,626	28,051	1,849	1,331	1,304	424
	Delhi (Hindu)	..	Males ..	832	320	117	102	25	50	25	1
			Females ..	625	200	108	84	5	2	1	..
	Delhi (Muslim)	..	Males ..	1,054	463	194	144	41	47	31	6
			Females ..	798	287	159	107	16	4	1	..
	Punjab (Muslim)	..	Males ..	184,552	99,077	37,036	31,894	11,089	10,910	6,859	1,289
			Females ..	153,743	67,404	35,185	24,475	4,441	2,214	784	305
	United Provinces (All Religions).	..	Males ..	526,374	215,667	95,321	71,520	18,727	15,080	12,065	2,954
			Females ..	479,184	151,845	95,913	47,394	4,233	1,798	1,858	649
	Central India (Hindu).	..	Males ..	70,958	26,935	13,139	8,577	2,079	1,686	1,175	279
			Females ..	68,705	18,943	12,830	5,111	333	225	362	82
	Hyderabad (Hindu)	..	Males ..	38,773	15,282	7,618	4,160	1,360	1,046	833	265
			Females ..	34,382	11,531	7,516	2,736	710	296	157	116
Vaniyan ..	Madras (Hindu)	..	Males ..	1,472,257	803,301	286,099	257,260	91,618	116,870	46,317	5,137
			Females ..	1,471,757	611,904	295,267	240,753	44,383	21,211	8,073	2,217
	Travancore (Hindu)	..	Males ..	11,376	6,621	2,334	2,092	730	1,081	356	28
			Females ..	11,151	4,945	2,411	1,888	450	132	49	15
85 **THANDAPULAYAN.**	Travancore (Hindu)	18	**Males** ..	**386**	**204**	**100**	**56**	**18**	**25**	**3**	**2**
			Females ..	**409**	**189**	**92**	**65**	**20**	**11**	**1**	..
86 **TODA** ..	Madras (Tribal)	14,17,18	**Males** ..	**340**	**125**	**33**	**22**	**16**	**28**	**24**	**2**
			Females ..	**257**	**60**	**37**	**21**	**1**	..	**1**	..
87 **VISWABRAHMAN and others.**	—	14,17	**Males** ..	**2,525,211**	**1,186,290**	**454,841**	**379,683**	**125,535**	**126,422**	**80,083**	**19,726**
			Females ..	**2,285,643**	**812,963**	**445,065**	**237,860**	**44,725**	**20,513**	**10,943**	**3,857**
VISWA BRAHMAN.	Madras (Hindu)	..	Males ..	449,331	228,612	77,870	72,775	24,683	34,354	16,053	2,877
			Females ..	448,633	159,811	76,954	61,031	12,392	6,242	2,246	946
	Hyderabad (Hindu)	..	Males ..	14,293	5,615	2,086	2,288	541	410	171	119
			Females ..	12,449	4,846	2,563	1,561	650	52	20	..
VISWAKARMA	Mysore (Hindu)	..	Males ..	74,370	49,765	12,424	12,898	5,258	6,670	3,233	282
			Females ..	69,299	26,767	12,756	11,879	1,531	388	171	42
Carpenters— *BADHAI (Barhai).*	C. P. & Berar (All Religions).	..	Males ..	58,097	22,087	9,972	7,857	1,976	1,341	784	157
			Females ..	53,893	14,687	9,957	4,180	223	169	102	56
	United Provinces (All Religions).	..	Males ..	315,369	138,786	54,770	44,529	14,144	12,309	10,208	2,826
			Females ..	275,800	92,631	54,793	31,180	3,370	1,641	1,276	371
KHATI ..	Rajputana (Hindu)	..	Males ..	40,980	19,000	7,720	6,664	1,914	1,354	1,034	314
			Females ..	38,947	12,052	7,683	3,931	203	117	82	36
SUTAR ..	Bombay (Hindu)	..	Males ..	17,665	9,144	3,530	3,218	988	1,020	342	46
			Females ..	17,372	6,329	3,454	2,378	176	146	153	22
	Baroda (Hindu)	..	Males ..	12,412	5,222	2,207	1,803	527	395	167	123
			Females ..	11,863	3,185	1,906	1,190	75	7	6	1
(*BADE WADLA*)	Hyderabad (Hindu)	..	Males ..	58,274	22,711	8,327	7,074	2,947	2,233	1,347	783
			Females ..	52,076	17,643	9,145	5,685	1,248	778	569	218
	W. I. S. Agency	..	Males ..	25,592	11,883	5,033	4,414	1,187	888	311	50
			Females ..	25,476	9,043	4,956	3,503	346	129	90	19
TARKHAN ..	Delhi (Hindu)	..	Males ..	2,240	929	363	307	117	84	46	12
			Females ..	1,806	638	345	256	19	7	9	2
	Delhi (Sikh)	..	Males ..	738	275	98	68	28	45	33	3
			Females ..	385	154	88	52	8	3	3	..
	Delhi (Muslim)	..	Males ..	214	79	26	27	8	10	7	1
			Females ..	105	33	18	15	..	..	..	..
	Punjab (Hindu)	..	Males ..	78,979	39,552	14,287	12,940	4,376	3,828	3,130	991
			Females ..	67,748	24,355	13,898	8,992	1,001	272	144	48
	Punjab (Sikh)	..	Males ..	87,891	46,833	16,005	14,427	4,798	5,324	4,820	1,459
			Females ..	70,555	28,357	14,345	10,793	2,124	662	288	145
	Punjab (Muslim)	..	Males ..	188,299	102,389	38,789	32,463	10,926	11,715	7,255	1,241
			Females ..	158,530	71,022	36,497	25,211	4,918	2,855	1,220	321
	Jammu and Kashmir (Muslim).		Males ..	7,616	3,993	1,526	1,202	410	500	247	108
			Females ..	6,789	2,914	1,589	947	233	118	24	3
Goldsmiths— *SONAR (Sunar, Soni).*	Bombay (Hindu) (Soni Daivadnya Brahman).	..	Males ..	17,795	8,677	3,648	3,188	755	752	282	52
			Females ..	17,726	5,492	3,289	1,846	190	125	25	17
	C. P. & Berar (Hindu).	..	Males ..	72,550	30,527	13,701	10,272	2,839	2,295	1,209	211
			Females ..	69,991	20,000	12,887	6,327	373	179	150	84
	Punjab (Hindu)	..	Males ..	53,763	28,682	10,127	9,053	3,090	3,351	2,333	728
			Females ..	45,263	18,365	9,378	7,076	1,262	391	203	55
	Punjab (Sikh)	..	Males ..	13,683	7,656	2,751	2,388	740	807	723	247
			Females ..	11,683	5,003	2,471	1,925	378	118	85	26
	Punjab (Muslim)	..	Males ..	17,440	9,699	3,711	2,919	1,014	1,180	681	194
			Females ..	14,954	6,914	3,514	2,326	578	311	136	49
	United Provinces (All Religions).	..	Males ..	147,184	66,686	24,238	20,484	7,193	6,984	6,160	1,672
			Females ..	124,870	43,167	24,566	15,243	1,964	621	552	221

by age for selected castes—*contd.*

Married. Total. 13	0—6. 14	7—13. 15	14—16. 16	17—23. 17	24—43. 18	44 & over. 19	Widowed. Total. 20	0—6. 21	7—13. 22	14—16. 23	17—23. 24	24—43 25	44 & over. 26	
970	9	84	76	155	429	217	144	10	16	14	7	33	64	
1,011	27	122	99	238	396	129	284	..	..	3	3	87	191	
305,827	5,287	31,599	20,724	45,086	141,783	61,348	31,565	168	735	627	1,832	11,530	16,673	
303,606	9,723	45,984	25,995	58,548	131,656	31,700	79,368	237	1,347	915	2,180	25,414	49,275	
11,478	80	674	701	1,672	5,462	2,889	946	3	12	7	27	268	629	
12,373	283	1,841	1,178	2,630	5,198	1,243	3,626	5	27	28	83	1,075	2,408	
312,864	6,180	37,095	25,627	49,981	129,285	64,696	23,561	92	440	442	1,291	7,308	13,988	
324,384	13,348	58,319	29,300	62,498	124,561	36,358	69,960	159	612	420	1,516	17,648	49,605	
421	..	7	14	87	250	63	91	..	..	..	2	51	38	
357	1	14	42	102	159	39	68	..	..	..	3	22	43	
476	1	24	35	83	234	99	115	..	1	3	6	46	59	
442	5	39	63	102	195	38	69	..	1	..	1	20	47	
70,783	82	1,308	2,590	11,521	36,286	18,996	14,692	6	40	74	485	4,702	9,385	
70,655	181	3,753	5,603	16,506	33,631	10,981	15,684	7	43	57	294	3,826	11,457	
267,657	2,914	18,427	19,013	42,375	131,702	53,226	43,050	121	650	664	2,535	16,294	22,786	
262,952	3,563	29,052	26,577	53,900	120,326	29,534	64,387	127	628	682	1,873	18,524	42,553	
39,348	672	3,592	2,970	6,278	18,750	7,086	4,675	17	105	156	349	1,722	2,326	
39,290	1,122	5,648	4,223	7,997	17,092	3,208	10,472	36	135	117	285	3,467	6,432	
20,533	615	1,205	1,524	3,017	8,883	5,289	2,958	33	93	99	278	896	1,559	
17,976	806	2,156	2,264	3,317	5,951	3,482	4,875	47	137	149	273	1,350	2,919	
615,939	98	1,316	4,861	47,069	357,416	205,179	53,017	1	40	80	1,481	14,068	37,347	
632,984	239	12,081	42,152	167,510	331,166	79,836	226,869	9	187	790	6,332	79,739	139,812	
4,425	..	1	5	259	2,534	1,626	330	..	..	..	10	88	232	
4,603	..	16	217	1,267	2,456	647	1,603	..	..	..	47	449	1,107	
182	..	..	**2**	**14**	**100**	**66**	..	..	..	..	..	..	..	85
191	..	**1**	**8**	**55**	**90**	**37**	**29**	..	..	..	**1**	**13**	**15**	
182	..	**4**	**6**	**14**	**96**	**62**	**33**	..	..	**1**	**3**	**17**	**12**	86
166	**7**	**11**	**9**	**28**	**87**	**24**	**31**	**2**	**1**	..	**1**	**9**	**18**	
1,144,279	**7,487**	**40,315**	**53,644**	**166,226**	**573,084**	**303,523**	**194,642**	**368**	**1,951**	**2,972**	**8,300**	**64,563**	**116,488**	87
1,129,857	**12,165**	**89,854**	**104,602**	**254,699**	**514,144**	**154,393**	**342,823**	**563**	**2,352**	**3,872**	**13,462**	**105,709**	**216,865**	
197,454	859	2,597	4,886	21,080	106,759	61,273	23,265	24	221	368	945	6,937	14,770	
201,730	1,808	11,763	15,057	51,795	96,037	25,270	87,092	58	427	933	4,534	31,463	49,677	
7,374	17	180	249	674	4,111	2,143	1,304	4	41	58	34	333	834	
5,530	16	423	677	877	2,399	1,138	2,073	11	191	144	135	282	1,310	
29,540	..	16	98	1,990	18,034	9,402	4,065	..	2	1	60	1,275	2,727	
29,387	6	1,100	2,817	7,808	14,921	2,735	13,145	..	15	66	534	5,226	7,304	
31,907	207	1,573	1,796	5,058	15,311	7,962	4,103	7	473	367	196	1,093	1,967	
30,907	598	4,485	2,987	6,423	13,212	3,202	8,299	16	66	68	218	2,288	5,643	
147,892	974	6,146	8,078	23,029	76,334	33,331	28,691	21	211	366	1,418	10,342	16,333	
143,552	1,365	10,505	13,951	30,488	68,743	18,500	39,617	47	302	369	1,197	11,589	26,113	
18,972	111	718	1,103	3,078	9,265	4,697	3,008	..	25	54	146	934	1,849	
20,864	203	2,263	2,366	4,426	9,057	2,549	6,031	7	41	62	226	1,676	4,019	
7,812	5	161	187	884	4,245	2,330	709	..	..	3	17	171	518	
8,165	34	694	796	1,931	3,849	861	2,878	1	19	31	123	953	1,751	
6,435	11	254	396	1,171	2,944	1,659	755	2	10	7	26	185	525	
6,648	149	698	740	1,561	2,740	760	2,030	4	63	14	27	545	1,377	
29,478	383	1,710	2,600	4,932	11,047	8,806	6,085	40	73	105	225	2,269	3,373	
26,544	510	3,621	4,031	4,594	8,521	5,267	7,889	55	150	231	593	2,657	4,203	
12,279	111	614	730	2,341	5,370	3,113	1,430	4	14	23	71	400	918	
13,013	239	1,159	1,273	3,275	5,312	1,755	3,420	6	13	42	129	1,004	2,226	
1,100	1	35	73	187	597	207	211	..	2	2	12	74	121	
971	2	59	117	242	432	119	197	..	..	1	3	52	141	
439	..	1	6	111	272	49	24	..	..	..	2	11	11	
223	..	1	13	78	119	12	8	..	..	..	..	2	6	
118	..	4	10	23	58	23	17	..	..	..	1	7	9	
59	1	3	5	9	31	10	13	..	..	..	1	3	9	
31,664	37	786	1,548	5,302	15,692	8,299	7,763	..	24	48	298	2,301	5,092	
34,792	120	2,654	3,767	8,129	15,686	4,436	8,601	..	15	42	175	2,318	6,051	
33,184	16	355	1,246	5,448	15,892	10,227	7,874	1	8	36	217	2,118	5,494	
34,734	43	1,006	2,639	8,051	16,082	6,913	7,464	2	1	18	148	1,602	5,693	
71,145	55	733	1,583	9,363	37,520	21,891	14,765	..	10	61	401	5,154	9,139	
71,381	96	2,376	4,527	16,995	35,340	12,047	16,127	2	43	68	426	3,960	11,628	
3,150	1	29	75	368	1,896	781	473	..	2	1	19	162	289	
3,149	..	89	267	747	1,595	451	726	..	2	6	25	201	492	
8,348	36	338	443	1,323	4,059	2,149	770	..	1	1	34	209	525	
8,907	151	1,193	909	2,051	3,791	812	3,327	1	14	26	106	1,048	2,132	
38,012	368	1,629	1,930	6,612	18,325	9,148	4,011	8	41	101	211	1,403	2,247	
38,288	760	4,941	3,933	8,880	15,586	4,188	11,703	12	69	95	391	3,680	7,456	
20,767	25	349	693	3,193	10,600	5,907	4,314	..	10	22	138	1,342	2,802	
20,554	27	940	1,773	5,214	9,469	3,131	6,344	..	14	30	173	1,829	4,298	
5,073	2	66	166	837	2,514	1,488	954	..	1	2	46	234	671	
5,331	7	184	392	1,330	2,53[illegible]	881	1,349	..	5	6	18	333	987	
6,587	5	75	255	932	3,511	1,809	1,154	..	1	6	65	382	700	
6,586	13	190	487	1,614	3,187	1,095	1,454	..	4	6	42	387	1,015	
66,713	611	2,571	3,566	10,966	33,573	15,426	13,785	43	109	197	616	4,983	7,837	
62,639	721	4,648	6,213	14,004	29,002	8,051	19,064	35	148	316	819	6,018	11,728	

Table VIII.—Civil Condition

Caste, Tribe or Race. 1	Province, State or Agency and Religion. 2	Also tabulated in. 3	Sex. 4	Population dealt with. 5	Unmarried. Total. 6	0—6. 7	7—13. 8	14—16. 9	17—23. 10	24—43. 11	44 & over. 12
VISWABRAHMAN and others—*concld.*											
Goldsmiths—concld.											
	Hyderabad (Hindu) ..		Males ..	72,550	26,088	12,748	7,482	2,613	1,947	1,027	271
			Females ..	65,341	23,523	13,675	6,623	1,352	1,027	671	175
SONI ..	Baroda (Hindu) ..		Males ..	6,283	3,014	1,086	1,004	308	355	195	66
			Females ..	5,862	1,826	976	776	65	4	5	..
	Western India States (Hindu). ..		Males ..	16,214	8,380	3,151	2,864	953	895	350	167
			Females ..	16,411	6,330	3,169	2,567	402	122	43	27
Bla[illegible]ksmiths— *[illegible]OHAR* ..	C. P. and Berar (All Religions). ..		Males ..	102,194	42,079	19,938	14,156	3,635	2,657	1,290	403
			Females ..	101,109	31,740	20,287	9,725	865	371	365	127
	Punjab (Hindu) ..		Males ..	39,902	19,746	6,865	6,324	2,195	2,230	1,702	430
			Females ..	34,561	12,325	6,787	4,435	681	228	148	46
	Punjab (Sikh) ..		Males ..	8,805	4,670	1,597	1,472	589	434	418	160
			Females ..	7,655	3,007	1,516	1,103	267	70	31	20
	Punjab (Muslim) ..		Males ..	130,333	70,395	26,711	22,752	7,646	7,732	4,413	1,141
			Females ..	111,243	48,907	25,666	17,299	3,520	1,455	699	268
	United Provinces (All Religions). ..		Males ..	313,347	130,315	56,783	40,837	11,910	10,106	8,671	2,008
			Females ..	277,840	90,819	54,956	30,500	2,8[illegible]	1,148	1,030	342
	Baroda (Hindu) ..		Males ..	10,407	4,503	1,970	1,629	427	314	147	16
			Females ..	10,619	2,945	1,793	1,073	65	12	2	..
	Hyderabad (Hindu) ..		Males ..	51,365	20,179	8,163	5,753	3,638	1,397	912	316
			Females ..	42,095	12,458	6,419	4,195	1,089	425	246	84
Coppersmiths— *KASAR* ..	Hyderabad .. (Hindu). ..		Males ..	19,036	7,119	2,620	2,152	1,162	506	382	297
			Females ..	16,694	5,675	2,769	2,037	314	320	149	86
88 **YADAVA** ..	.. ..	**14,17**	**Males** .	**6,213,572**	**2,558,965**	**1,107,116**	**827,254**	**231,045**	**208,919**	**154,469**	**30,162**
			Females ..	**5,890,914**	**1,802,563**	**1,084,996**	**575,175**	**76,975**	**35,156**	**21,855**	**8,406**
AHIR ..	C. P. and Berar (Hindu). ..		Males ..	404,826	161,937	80,977	54,306	12,295	8,574	4,734	1,051
			Females ..	408,709	126,168	80,667	38,270	4,054	1,87[illegible]	989	311
	C. P. and Berar (Tribal). ..		Males ..	2,164	1,027	458	320	105	[illegible]	44	10
			Females ..	2,395	834	472	272	50	28	10	2
	Delhi (Hindu) ..		Males ..	7,723	3,441	1,250	1,070	344	369	338	70
			Females ..	5,316	1,959	1,100	735	92	18	12	2
	Punjab (Hindu) ..		Males ..	120,103	62,512	22,787	20,632	6,917	5,970	4,770	1,436
			Females ..	97,409	38,356	21,493	14,962	1,619	213	54	15
	Punjab (Muslim) ..		Males ..	1,248	685	236	202	59	111	68	9
			Females ..	1,060	510	219	171	53	28	32	7
	United Provinces (All Religions). ..		Males ..	2,056,549	835,188	366,257	259,425	69,413	61,828	64,968	13,297
			Females ..	1,840,239	538,159	354,724	155,827	13,143	5,648	6,030	2,787
	Central India (Hindu). ..		Males ..	121,675	50,697	21,220	17,489	4,846	3,989	2,741	412
			Females ..	111,202	33,642	20,751	10,849	749	424	689	180
	Gwalior (H[illegible]ndu) ..		Males ..	70,208	33,812	12,832	11,435	3,788	2,830	1,961	966
			Females ..	60,474	20,526	11,788	6,944	1,068	292	257	177
	Rajputana (All Relig[illegible]s). ..		Males ..	38,820	20,628	6,427	6,600	2,655	3,061	1,636	249
			Females ..	32,460	13,748	6,570	5,493	1,270	338	65	12
GAURA (Gauda)	Bihar and Orissa (Hindu). ..		Males ..	124,303	64,197	22,586	20,481	8,218	9,870	2,790	252
			Females ..	139,967	44,866	23,471	17,330	2,976	774	273	42
	Coorg (H[illegible]u) ..		Males ..	7,388	4,233	1,175	1,223	452	846	510	27
			Females ..	6,628	3,184	1,260	1,209	418	258	27	12
GOALA (Gopa) (Yadava).	Bihar and Orissa (Hindu). ..		Males ..	1,765,379	634,811	315,266	217,900	38,201	33,149	25,679	4,616
			Females ..	1,689,762	457,279	307,257	131,780	10,148	4,535	2,822	737
GOLA	.. Coorg (Hindu) ..		Males ..	289	158	44	48	17	28	20	1
			Females ..	231	94	39	44	8	2	1	..
	Madras (Hindu) ..		Males ..	400,006	193,789	70,273	60,776	22,631	22,873	14,561	2,675
			Females ..	406,473	133,167	70,440	47,402	8,165	3,594	2,469	1,097
	Mysore (Hindu) ..		Males ..	88,561	49,733	16,586	15,552	6,158	6,278	4,859	300
			Females ..	85,640	34,407	16,236	14,688	2,494	684	223	82
GOLAR ..	Central Provinces and Berar (Hindu). ..		Males ..	1,038	225	170	35	9	2	8	1
			Females ..	1,130	153	140	10	1	1	1	..
GOWARI ..	Central Provinces and Berar (All Religions). ..		Males ..	82,082	32,163	15,267	11,835	2,720	1,647	552	142
			Females ..	81,473	24,740	14,932	8,120	902	419	300	67
IDAYAN ..	Travan[illegible]ore (Hindu) ..		Males ..	4,072	2,230	790	649	251	368	165	7
			Females ..	4,385	1,612	734	641	172	54	8	3
YADAVA ..	Madras (Hindu) ..		Males ..	445,674	236,316	78,491	74,518	26,838	35,773	18,656	2,040
			Females ..	459,021	171,165	80,290	68,838	13,213	6,220	2,019	585
	Hyderabad (Hindu) ..		Males ..	471,464	171,183	74,024	52,758	25,128	11,263	5,409	2,601
			Females ..	456,940	157,994	72,413	51,590	16,380	9,749	5,574	2,288
89 **KACHIN** ..	Burma (All Religions).	**17,18**	**Males** ..	**71,647**	**41,436**	**10,861**	**12,061**	**5,807**	**6,909**	**5,306**	**492**
			Females ..	**72,273**	**35,370**	**10,940**	**11,143**	**4,461**	**5,100**	**3,220**	**506**
90 **KAREN** (**Pwo** and **Sgaw**).	Burma (All Religoins).	**14,17, 18**	**Males** ..	**406,027**	**246,350**	**79,203**	**71,179**	**26,029**	**38,409**	**27,478**	**4,052**
			Females ..	**408,308**	**234,893**	**81,374**	**69,771**	**24,484**	**35,427**	**19,594**	**4,243**
91 **MON** ..	Burma (All Religoins).	**14,18**	**Males** ..	**165,161**	**100,761**	**35,297**	**31,367**	**11,294**	**14,933**	**6,497**	**1,373**
			Females ..	**162,092**	**91,994**	**35,704**	**28,420**	**10,389**	**11,702**	**4,694**	**1,085**
92 **SHAN** ..	Burma (All Religions).	**14,17**	**Males** ..	**313,668**	**167,445**	**56,355**	**49,536**	**17,393**	**25,625**	**16,340**	**2,196**
			Females ..	**310,094**	**141,311**	**57,095**	**48,757**	**15,273**	**12,921**	**6,028**	**1,237**

by age for selected castes—concld.

Married. Total. 13	0—6. 14	7—13. 15	14—16. 16	17—23. 17	24—43. 18	44 & over. 19	Widowed. Total. 20	0—6. 21	7—13. 22	14—16. 23	17—23. 24	24—43. 25	44 & over. 26	
38,553	650	2,759	3,268	7,739	13,255	10,882	7,909	35	40	247	358	2,855	4,374	
32,230	1,006	4,731	4,582	6,078	10,231	5,602	9,588	60	168	326	692	3,235	5,107	
2,786	2	24	97	510	1,434	719	483	2	1	2	11	151	316	
2,833	5	148	320	812	1,250	298	1,203	1	3	9	41	358	791	
6,834	39	107	172	1,208	3,325	1,983	1,000	3	8	14	40	249	6,861	
7,575	89	215	694	2,105	3,248	1,224	2,506	2	6	27	108	822	1,541	
55,420	617	2,807	3,009	8,857	27,329	12,801	4,695	23	72	59	228	1,676	2,637	
55,332	922	6,325	5,257	11,673	24,979	6,176	14,037	25	111	132	375	3,880	9,514	
16,676	26	345	681	2,491	8,659	4,474	3,480	1	12	20	147	1,138	2,162	
17,424	55	1,361	1,736	3,817	8,398	2,057	4,812	1	17	24	97	1,317	3,356	
3,266	..	71	182	553	1,427	1,033	869	..	3	4	19	219	624	
3,818	4	138	328	831	1,776	741	830	..	2	2	16	170	640	
50,478	38	815	1,614	7,492	26,375	14,144	9,460	4	35	43	387	2,839	6,152	
51,170	125	2,158	3,789	11,929	24,926	8,243	11,166	5	18	53	253	2,667	8,170	
155,216	1,761	10,454	10,642	23,830	75,627	32,902	27,816	94	384	431	1,442	10,566	14,899	
149,662	2,086	16,077	14,565	30,211	68,608	18,115	37,359	144	267	441	1,166	10,700	24,641	
5,297	5	306	320	957	2,343	1,366	607	3	11	6	32	158	397	
5,761	51	601	649	1,348	2,403	709	1,913	3	12	12	27	545	1,314	
24,390	324	959	1,245	2,694	11,577	7,591	6,796	40	93	246	299	1,691	4,427	
21,854	680	2,333	2,077	4,493	7,357	4,914	7,783	54	128	231	513	2,157	4,700	
9,920	190	728	697	993	3,804	3,508	1,997	9	13	71	139	702	1,063	
8,244	273	772	868	880	3,320	2,131	2,775	11	18	41	131	742	1,832	
3,175,267	**44,854**	**250,193**	**199,383**	**436,441**	**1,529,859**	**714,537**	**479,340**	**2,081**	**8,866**	**11,465**	**26,817**	**165,323**	**264,788**	88
3,149,483	**71,059**	**389,818**	**289,750**	**607,076**	**1,419,533**	**392,197**	**933,863**	**3,195**	**13,460**	**14,709**	**36,075**	**302,929**	**568,500**	
222,428	2,671	16,689	14,620	35,631	106,847	45,970	20,461	113	254	441	1,441	7,677	10,535	
226,391	5,528	26,826	22,002	47,595	98,765	25,675	56,150	120	345	452	1,589	16,378	37,266	
1,046	2	21	32	113	585	293	91	..	..	..	3	31	57	
1,211	2	42	85	225	691	166	350	..	..	..	4	90	256	
3,486	1	82	203	703	1,930	567	796	..	..	10	37	288	461	
2,725	..	108	269	721	1,334	293	632	..	2	3	12	198	417	
46,127	19	724	2,167	7,854	24,663	10,700	11,464	1	18	60	305	3,321	7,759	
46,925	69	2,192	4,742	11,311	22,220	6,391	12,128	3	14	29	217	3,255	8,610	
445	..	2	10	84	214	135	118	..	..	..	3	35	80	
450	2	4	10	93	247	94	100	..	..	1	5	25	69	
1,047,524	16,437	96,892	76,214	151,949	498,707	207,325	173,837	426	2,210	2,795	7,736	62,925	97,745	
1,029,508	18,176	132,437	102,814	189,350	472,301	114,430	272,572	643	3,024	3,413	7,682	80,144	177,666	
62,732	462	3,844	4,626	9,812	32,169	11,819	8,246	13	112	155	468	3,259	4,239	
60,952	1,358	7,021	6,527	12,667	28,019	5,360	16,608	51	155	198	476	5,889	9,839	
29,604	160	1,540	1,875	5,493	14,276	6,260	6,792	55	205	241	383	2,358	3,550	
29,714	442	2,248	3,613	7,878	12,652	2,881	10,234	69	253	202	359	3,071	6,280	
14,175	22	74	194	1,740	8,446	3,699	4,017	..	3	2	47	1,294	2,671	
14,819	20	142	735	3,555	8,121	2,246	3,893	2	2	8	60	1,003	2,818	
54,978	15	673	1,887	5,486	31,470	15,447	5,128	1	75	164	203	1,355	3,330	
62,859	47	3,597	4,360	16,485	32,141	6,229	32,242	3	134	409	778	11,970	18,948	
2,773	..	7	8	116	1,815	827	382	..	..	1	8	152	221	
2,550	2	7	41	644	1,600	256	894	..	1	..	11	304	578	
1,007,020	18,484	107,238	68,107	140,284	465,361	207,546	123,548	745	2,903	2,327	6,691	44,447	66,435	
976,282	32,206	142,391	83,678	171,288	430,543	116,176	256,201	1,250	4,643	3,277	8,276	81,291	157,464	
104	..	..	..	6	69	29	27	..	..	..	..	13	14	
90	..	2	4	24	53	7	47	..	..	..	1	14	32	
182,615	1,752	5,932	7,949	21,847	94,635	50,500	23,602	55	191	568	1,511	7,258	14,019	
191,473	4,258	17,232	17,808	45,112	85,353	21,710	81,833	87	624	1,207	4,444	31,399	44,072	
33.916	2	18	109	1,751	20,726	11,310	4,912	..	5	8	43	1,295	3,561	
35,259	6	817	2,376	8,852	18,960	4,248	15,974	..	18	80	619	5,958	9,299	
751	31	158	61	99	301	101	62	2	3	1	..	20	36	
750	94	154	64	131	262	45	227	2	5	3	1	78	138	
45,273	324	1,872	2,568	7,026	21,228	12,255	4,646	18	43	65	243	1,206	3,071	
45,446	767	5,309	4,502	9,328	19,395	6,145	11,287	62	181	138	382	3,029	7,495	
1,670	..	2	1	110	974	583	172	..	..	..	2	52	118	
1,801	..	6	93	472	958	272	972	..	..	1	30	304	637	
188,178	100	801	1,367	13,669	108,067	64,174	21,180	2	10	27	513	5,650	14,978	
196,854	321	5,444	10,862	48,392	106,328	25,507	91,002	13	148	544	2,918	32,771	54,608	
230,422	4,372	13,624	17,385	32,668	97,376	64,997	69,859	650	2,834	4,600	7,180	22,687	31,908	
223,424	7,761	23,839	25,165	32,953	79,640	54,066	75,522	890	3,911	4,744	8,211	25,758	32,008	
27,550	..	**9**	**256**	**2,148**	**17,021**	**8,116**	**2,661**	..	**1**	**8**	**102**	**1,241**	**1,309**	89
29,864	..	**10**	**638**	**5,651**	**19,241**	**4,324**	**13,039**	..	..	**37**	**385**	**4,359**	**8,258**	
141,569	..	**18**	**194**	**8,251**	**84,699**	**48,407**	**18,108**	..	..	**9**	**238**	**5,362**	**12,499**	90
141,882	..	**5**	**774**	**20,663**	**86,792**	**33,648**	**31,533**	..	..	**60**	**897**	**8,201**	**22,375**	
58,420	..	..	**42**	**4,666**	**33,467**	**20,245**	**5,980**	..	..	..	**180**	**1,541**	**4,269**	91
58,967	..	**2**	**209**	**10,571**	**33,566**	**14,619**	**11,131**	..	..	**8**	**605**	**2,740**	**7,778**	
119,476	..	**2**	**284**	**8,824**	**71,776**	**38,590**	**26,747**	..	..	**62**	**2,013**	**11,634**	**13,038**	92
121,140	..	**11**	**3,496**	**26,785**	**70,636**	**20,212**	**47,643**	..	**3**	**597**	**4,225**	**13,681**	**29,137**	

TABLE IX.

Infirmities.

1. This table, which corresponds to Table XII of the 1921 Census, is divided into two parts. Part I shows the general distribution by Provinces and States of the total number of persons recorded as suffering from each infirmity, while Part II shows the corresponding details by age of those persons for India as a whole and for the Provinces and States scheduled in Part I.

2. Insanity, deaf-muteness, blindness and leprosy were recorded at the census as infirmities throughout India, except in those areas referred to on page 1 of this volume, where the population was estimated, and in the Trans-Frontier Posts in the Tribal Areas of the North-West Frontier Province. In addition to these returns 14,709 persons (8,424 males and 6,285 females) were also recorded in Travancore State as afflicted with elephantiasis, but are excluded from the figures shown against that unit in both Parts I and II of this table. 'Blind' was defined for enumeration purposes as totally blind in both eyes.

3. Persons returned as suffering from more than one infirmity have been treated as single persons for columns 2, 3 and 4, but the entries have been reiterated as if for separate individuals in the appropriate columns for each infirmity from which they suffered at the time of record. The figures in columns 2—4, therefore, do not correspond with the aggregate of the figures in columns 5—16, as the latter exceed the former by the total of multiple infirmity cases returned by the respective Provinces and States as shown in the statement at the end of the table.

4. There is much concealment of infirmities and the figures must be treated with the greatest reserve. Their significance is comparative, not absolute.

5. Age groups under which no returns have been received are omitted.

Table IX.—Infirmities—

Province, State or Agency. 1	Population afflicted. Persons. 2	Population afflicted. Males. 3	Population afflicted. Females. 4	Insane. Persons. 5	Insane. Males. 6	Insane. Females. 7
INDIA.	**1,095,678**	**601,402**	**494,276**	**120,304**	**74,002**	**46,302**
Provinces.	**874,634**	**486,741**	**387,893**	**98,449**	**60,424**	**38,025**
1 Ajmer-Merwara	2,807	1,386	1,421	217	145	72
2. Andaman and Nicobar Islands	26	17	9	7	6	1
3. Assam	25,960	15,080	10,880	5,037	2,929	2,108
4. Baluchistan (*Districts and Administered Territories*)	1,266	819	447	186	138	48
5. Bengal	113,431	68,235	45,196	21,705	12,650	9,055
6. Bihar and Orissa	98,869	57,237	41,632	8,264	5,416	2,848
Bihar	*62,315*	*36,053*	*26,262*	*3,981*	*2,506*	*1,475*
Orissa	*15,585*	*9,756*	*5,829*	*1,457*	*939*	*518*
Chota Nagpur	*20.969*	*11,428*	*9.541*	*2.826*	*1,971*	*855*
7. Bombay	78,553	44,547	34,006	10,911	7,065	3,846
Bombay Presidency	*62,369*	*34,518*	*27,851*	*8,351*	*5,350*	*3,001*
Sind	*16,054*	*9,930*	*6,124*	*2,546*	*1,706*	*840*
Aden	*130*	*99*	*31*	*14*	*9*	*5*
8. Burma	68,264	36,589	31,675	12,902	7,373	5,529
9. Central Provinces and Berar	71,224	34,704	36,520	4,526	2,844	1,682
Central Provinces	*52,446*	*24,422*	*28,024*	*3,266*	*2,088*	*1,178*
Berar	*18,778*	*10,282*	*8,496*	*1,260*	*756*	*504*
10. Coorg	248	136	112	31	13	18
11. Delhi	898	512	386	89	60	29
12. Madras	133,421	76,623	56,798	15,394	8,957	6,437
13. North-West Frontier Province (*Districts and Administered Territories*).	4,984	3,091	1,893	741	543	198
14. Punjab	82,091	46,616	35,475	7,220	4,853	2,367
15. United Provinces of Agra and Oudh	192,592	101,149	91,443	11,219	7,432	3,787
Agra	*131,152*	*69,799*	*61,353*	*8,257*	*5,523*	*2,734*
Oudh	*61,440*	*31,350*	*30,090*	*2,962*	*1,909*	*1,053*
States and Agencies.	**221,044**	**114,661**	**106,383**	**21,855**	**13,578**	**8,277**
16. Assam States	1,546	860	686	389	209	180
17. Baluchistan States	1,478	893	585	235	157	78
18. Baroda State	11,146	4,944	6,202	1,373	816	557
19. Bengal States	2,176	1,298	878	697	396	301
20. Bihar and Orissa States	12,279	6,657	5,622	781	486	295
21. Bombay States	12,546	6,992	5,554	1,734	1,091	64
22. Central India Agency	18,025	8,366	9,659	1,549	966	583
23. Central Provinces States	6,913	3,314	3,599	507	317	190
24. Gwalior State	8,593	3,728	4,865	453	292	161
25. Hyderabad State	22,196	12,656	9,540	2,200	1,337	863
26. Jammu and Kashmir State	14,781	8,600	6,181	1,424	952	472
27. Madras States Agency	15,559	9,404	6,155	2,877	1,607	1,270
Cochin State	*3,459*	*1,949*	*1,510*	*637*	*358*	*279*
Travancore State	*10,910*	*6,744*	*4,166*	*2,068*	*1,151*	*917*
Other Madras States	*1,190*	*711*	*479*	*172*	*98*	*74*
28. Mysore State	12,954	7,358	5,596	1,782	1,050	732
29. Punjab States	2,140	1,221	919	131	97	34
30. Punjab States Agency	15,548	8,936	6,612	988	669	319
31. Rajputana Agency	37,886	17,787	20,099	2,590	1,727	863
32. Sikkim State	202	111	91	5	3	2
33. United Provinces States	3,675	1,918	1,757	322	204	118
34. Western India States Agency	21,401	9,618	11,783	1,818	1,202	616

Part I.—Distribution by Provinces and States.

Deaf-Mutes.			Blind.			Lepers.			
Persons. 8	Males. 9	Females. 10	Persons. 11	Males. 12	Females. 13	Persons. 14	Males. 15	Females. 16	
230,895	**137,680**	**93,215**	**601,370**	**284,741**	**316,629**	**147,911**	**107,892**	**40,019**	
190,592	113,977	76,615	462,805	221,552	241,253	126,867	93,281	33,586	
410	261	149	2,162	968	1,194	18	12	6	1
8	6	2	9	4	5	2	1	1	2
6,780	3,859	2,921	9,222	4,556	4,666	5,164	3,864	1,300	3
278	204	74	781	458	323	24	20	4	4
35,437	21,301	14,136	36,740	19,834	16,906	20,845	15,290	5,555	5
24,003	14,709	9,294	47,754	23,018	24,736	19,329	14,408	4,921	6
16,841	*10,323*	*6,518*	*32,246*	*15,755*	*16,491*	*9,457*	*7,614*	*1,843*	
2,670	*1,726*	*944*	*5,596*	*2,805*	*2,791*	*5,924*	*4,328*	*1,596*	
4,492	*2,660*	*1,832*	*9,912*	*4,458*	*5,454*	*3,948*	*2,466*	*1,482*	
17,376	10,984	6,392	41,154	20,124	21,030	9,112	6,374	2,738	7
12,253	*7,380*	*4,873*	*32,957*	*15,638*	*17,319*	*8,808*	*6,150*	*2,658*	
5,108	*3,591*	*1,517*	*8,123*	*4,436*	*3,687*	*277*	*197*	*80*	
15	*13*	*2*	*74*	*50*	*24*	*27*	*27*	..	
16,967	9,115	7,852	27,727	12,751	14,976	11,127	7,607	3,520	8
12,703	7,550	5,153	42,924	17,201	25,723	11,506	7,341	4,165	9
8,626	*5,165*	*3,461*	*33,458*	*12,885*	*20,573*	*7,344*	*4,415*	*2,929*	
4,077	*2,385*	*1,692*	*9,466*	*4,316*	*5,150*	*4,162*	*2,926*	*1,236*	
101	55	46	100	58	42	17	11	6	10
148	104	44	656	342	314	9	8	1	11
33,308	18,741	14,567	51,881	24,258	27,623	33,127	24,842	8,285	12
1,597	1,074	523	2,463	1,351	1,112	249	164	85	13
16,161	10,258	5,903	57,254	30,405	26,849	1,853	1,326	527	14
25,315	15,756	9,559	141,978	66,224	75,754	14,485	12,013	2,472	15
16,884	*10,652*	*6,232*	*97,060*	*46,332*	*50,728*	*9,182*	*7,453*	*1,729*	
8,431	*5,104*	*3,327*	*44,918*	*19,892*	*25,026*	*5,303*	*4,560*	*743*	
40,303	**23,703**	**16,600**	**138,565**	**63,189**	**75,376**	**21,044**	**14,611**	**6,433**	
198	125	73	704	358	346	256	168	88	16
304	192	112	914	525	389	27	21	6	17
1,266	694	572	8,033	3,090	4,943	575	393	182	18
428	259	169	659	337	322	409	316	93	19
2,472	1,439	1,033	5,578	2,501	3,077	3,465	2,240	1,225	20
3,173	1,845	1,328	5,990	2,895	3,095	1,649	1,161	488	21
1,896	1,078	818	13,657	5,643	8,014	1,084	760	324	22
1,267	711	556	4,147	1,686	2,461	1,013	610	403	23
1,306	739	567	6,409	2,425	3,984	425	272	153	24
3,742	2,209	1,533	12,516	6,480	6,036	3,738	2,630	1,108	25
5,787	3,481	2,306	5,699	2,888	2,811	2,026	1,381	645	26
3,799	2,291	1,508	5,184	2,785	2,399	3,728	2,739	989	27
488	*283*	*205*	*1,595*	*758*	*837*	*745*	*553*	*192*	
2,883	*1,760*	*1,123*	*3,191*	*1,810*	*1,381*	*2,789*	*2,037*	*752*	
428	*248*	*180*	*398*	*217*	*181*	*194*	*149*	*45*	
3,950	2,254	1,696	6,553	3,556	2,997	733	536	197	28
835	465	370	955	503	452	227	162	65	29
2,536	1,624	912	11,464	6,233	5,231	687	491	196	30
3,126	1,896	1,230	31,627	13,782	17,845	543	382	161	31
164	89	75	26	14	12	7	5	2	32
428	271	157	2,641	1,222	1,419	304	235	69	33
3,626	2,041	1,585	15,809	6,266	9,543	148	109	39	34

Table IX.—Infirmities—Part II—Distribution by Age.

Age.	Population afflicted.			Insane.		Deaf-Mutes.		Blind.		Lepers.	
	Persons.	Males.	Females.	Males.	Females.	Males.	Females.	Males.	Females.	Males.	Females.
1	2	3	4	5	6	7	8	9	10	11	12
India.											
Total	**1,095,678**	**601,402**	**494,276**	**74,002**	**46,302**	**137,680**	**93,215**	**284,741**	**316,629**	**107,892**	**40,019**
0—1	2,138	1,187	951	28	26	240	221	878	669	43	35
1—2	3,159	1,738	1,421	69	54	389	380	1,241	941	48	51
2—3	5,305	2,897	2,408	157	124	967	885	1,703	1,342	85	68
3—4	8,061	4,563	3,498	277	213	2,144	1,680	2,087	1,558	86	68
4—5	11,145	6,336	4,809	538	415	3,150	2,379	2,534	1,909	169	144
Total 0—5	*29,808*	*16,721*	*13,087*	*1,069*	*832*	*6,890*	*5,545*	*8,443*	*6,419*	*431*	*366*
5—10	61,734	36,834	24,900	4,121	2,665	18,089	12,222	13,443	9,167	1,473	1,036
10—15	68,289	41,088	27,201	5,449	3,614	18,976	12,470	14,359	9,708	2,611	1,600
15—20	67,573	40,476	27,097	6,971	4,615	15,123	9,960	13,375	9,872	5,335	2,819
20—25	72,603	43,970	28,633	8,022	4,845	14,721	9,551	14,228	11,064	7,277	3,316
25—30	77,196	46,891	30,305	9,313	5,019	12,592	8,267	14,343	13,198	10,876	3,968
30—35	77,842	47,115	30,727	9,271	4,862	11,051	7,219	14,236	14,435	12,758	4,325
35—40	80,022	46,964	33,058	8,014	4,569	8,795	5,669	16,142	18,357	14,230	4,590
40—45	78,883	45,319	33,564	6,772	4,201	7,546	4,991	17,310	20,097	13,868	4,379
45—50	80,111	43,422	36,689	4,750	3,289	5,934	3,966	20,830	25,655	12,079	3,895
50—55	75,749	39,750	35,999	3,646	2,660	4,842	3,356	21,363	26,720	10,030	3,348
55—60	80,297	38,330	41,967	2,307	1,843	3,739	2,795	25,825	35,009	6,568	2,403
60—65	77,669	36,405	41,264	1,831	1,406	3,348	2,501	26,168	35,470	5,175	1,973
65—70	53,582	25,151	28,431	901	743	1,974	1,470	20,031	25,442	2,316	859
70 and over	111,696	51,342	60,354	1,294	1,022	3,685	3,051	43,705	55,323	2,825	1,133
Age Unspecified	2,624	1,624	1,000	271	117	375	182	940	693	40	9
Ajmer-Merwara.											
Total	**2,807**	**1,386**	**1,421**	**145**	**72**	**261**	**149**	**968**	**1,194**	**12**	**6**
1—2	5	2	3	..	..	1	1	1	2	..	..
2—3	7	3	4	..	..	1	2	2	2	..	..
3—4	11	6	5	..	..	2	2	4	3	..	..
4—5	18	9	9	1	2	3	2	5	5	..	..
Total 0—5	*11*	*20*	*21*	*1*	*2*	*7*	*7*	*12*	*12*	..	..
5—10	95	56	39	8	5	15	10	33	23	..	1
10—15	112	69	43	12	5	19	12	37	26	1	..
15—20	123	81	42	19	5	21	9	39	28	2	..
20—25	133	87	46	22	4	20	9	45	32	..	1
25—30	127	76	51	18	6	20	10	38	35	..	..
30—35	127	71	56	16	7	22	9	32	40	1	..
35—40	190	90	100	13	8	23	10	52	81	2	1
40—45	218	105	113	11	8	22	11	70	94	2	..
45—50	263	133	130	11	7	20	11	101	111	1	1
50—55	249	125	124	7	6	19	8	99	109	..	1
55—60	321	140	181	2	4	18	12	118	164	2	1
60—65	310	126	184	1	3	14	12	111	169	..	..
65—70	180	79	101	1	1	7	7	70	93	1	..
70 and over	318	128	190	3	1	14	12	111	177	..	..
Andaman and Nicobar Islands.											
Total	**26**	**17**	**9**	**6**	**1**	**6**	**2**	**4**	**5**	**1**	**1**
5—10	2	2	..	2	..	..	..	..	..	..	..
10—15	1	..	1	..	..	..	..	..	1	..	..
15—20	2	1	1	..	..	..	..	1	1	..	..
25—30	1	1	..	1	..	..	..	..	..	..	..
30—35	2	1	1	..	..	1	..	..	..	..	1
35—40	5	5	..	2	..	2	..	..	..	1	..
40—45	2	1	1	..	..	1	1	..	..	..	..
45—50	3	2	1	1	..	..	1	1	..	..	..
50—55	1	..	1	..	1	..	..	..	..	..	..
60—65	4	2	2	..	..	1	..	1	2	..	..
65—70	2	1	1	..	..	..	..	1	1	..	..
70 and over	1	1	..	..	..	1	..	..	..	..	..

Table IX.—Infirmities—Part II—Distribution by Age—*continued.*

Age.	Population afflicted.			Insane.		Deaf-Mutes.		Blind.		Lepers.	
	Persons.	Males.	Females.	Males.	Females.	Males.	Females.	Males.	Females.	Males.	Females.
1	2	3	4	5	6	7	8	9	10	11	12
					***Assam.**						
Total	***27,506**	**15,940**	**11,566**	**3,138**	**2,288**	**3,984**	**2,994**	**4,914**	**5,012**	**4,032**	**1,388**
0—1	42	23	19	..	..	1	2	23	16	..	1
1—2	87	42	45	2	2	12	17	26	25	2	2
2—3	185	87	98	3	6	44	56	37	36	3	2
3—4	301	158	143	10	9	98	91	46	39	4	4
4—5	359	202	157	18	12	134	104	50	35	8	8
Total 0—5	*974*	*512*	*462*	*33*	*29*	*289*	*270*	*182*	*151*	*17*	*17*
5—10	1,978	1,175	803	133	100	733	506	243	164	81	48
10—15	2,074	1,195	879	161	153	695	509	238	163	117	67
15—20	1,890	1,036	854	224	212	444	370	210	176	175	111
20—25	1,974	1,149	825	284	222	420	311	216	188	239	115
25—30	2,285	1,407	878	417	274	343	238	227	222	428	153
30—35	2,321	1,438	883	445	282	290	207	218	237	496	166
35—40	2,256	1,395	861	393	237	214	177	261	301	539	157
40—45	2,145	1,307	838	337	215	172	146	296	339	509	145
45—50	1,965	1,151	814	229	187	133	79	385	432	411	124
50—55	1,798	1,040	758	189	153	105	59	396	439	355	110
55—60	1,585	845	740	118	84	56	46	424	545	250	67
60—65	1,372	712	660	80	66	45	36	406	508	183	52
65—70	808	434	374	39	34	15	13	302	308	81	22
70 and over	2,081	1,144	937	56	40	30	27	910	839	151	34
					***Baluchistan.**						
Total	***2,744**	**1,712**	**1,032**	**295**	**126**	**396**	**186**	**983**	**712**	**41**	**10**
2—3	1	1	..	..	..	1	..	..	..	..	..
4—5	1	1	..	1	..	..	..	..	..	..	..
Total 0—5	*2*	*2*	..	*1*	..	*1*	..	..	..	..	..
5—10	4	3	1	1	..	1	..	2	1	..	..
10—15	7	6	1	1	..	2	1	3	..	..	..
15—20	7	6	1	2	..	3	1	..	..	1	..
20—25	9	7	2	3	1	2	..	2	1	..	..
25—30	14	10	4	3	2	3	..	4	2	..	..
30—35	15	9	6	2	2	2	1	5	3	..	..
35—40	12	9	3	3	3	1	..	5	..	..	..
40—45	10	9	1	5	1	2	..	2	..	..	..
45—50	8	8	..	3	..	1	..	4	..	..	..
50—55	6	4	2	..	..	2	..	2	1	..	1
55—60	7	6	1	..	..	1	..	5	1	..	..
60—65	7	5	2	..	..	..	..	5	2	..	..
65—70	3	..	3	..	..	..	..	..	3	..	..
70 and over	9	4	5	..	..	..	1	4	5	..	..
Age Unspecified	2,624	1,624	1,000	271	117	375	182	940	693	40	9
					Bengal.						
Total	**113,431**	**68,235**	**45,196**	**12,650**	**9,055**	**21,301**	**14,136**	**19,834**	**16,906**	**15,290**	**5,555**
0—1	172	112	60	5	2	21	21	77	33	9	4
1—2	283	159	124	10	11	57	50	89	56	7	7
2—3	614	353	261	26	25	183	143	136	89	11	5
3—4	1,179	681	498	65	52	442	336	171	107	13	10
4—5	1,548	889	659	95	74	607	461	185	114	18	16
Total 0—5	*3,796*	*2,194*	*1,602*	*201*	*164*	*1,310*	*1,011*	*658*	*399*	*58*	*42*
5—10	8,834	5,413	3,421	788	511	3,403	2,220	1,102	611	209	125
10—15	9,363	5,723	3,640	991	696	3,307	2,145	1,157	657	367	199
15—20	9,013	5,316	3,697	1,247	957	2,341	1,692	1,034	714	785	389
20—25	9,694	5,866	3,828	1,488	1,018	2,258	1,607	1,083	770	1,123	476
25—30	9,994	6,320	3,674	1,635	1,037	1,940	1,297	1,045	781	1,771	599
30—35	9,811	6,330	3,481	1,587	1,018	1,739	1,064	1,061	780	2,014	654
35—40	8,936	5,745	3,191	1,369	927	1,238	745	1,111	901	2,085	647
40—45	8,197	5,197	3,000	1,128	805	1,016	629	1,161	999	1,950	593
45—50	7,240	4,369	2,871	711	587	768	478	1,372	1,288	1,569	540
50—55	6,514	3,792	2,722	553	488	621	401	1,391	1,369	1,263	481
55—60	5,761	3,152	2,609	339	318	417	287	1,657	1,701	768	316
60—65	5,197	2,793	2,404	266	246	358	226	1,602	1,707	594	240
65—70	3,470	1,878	1,592	151	114	220	117	1,209	1,272	307	108
70 and over	7,611	4,147	3,464	196	169	365	217	3,191	2,957	427	146

* The entries under Assam and Baluchistan are inclusive of details for their respective states. Details by age are not available from the Tribal Areas of Baluchistan.

Table IX.—Infirmities—Part II—Distribution by Age—*continued.*

Age.	Population afflicted.			Insane.		Deaf-Mutes.		Blind.		Lepers.	
	Persons.	Males.	Females.	Males.	Females.	Males.	Females.	Males.	Females.	Males.	Females.
1	2	3	4	5	6	7	8	9	10	11	12
Bihar and Orissa.											
Total	**98,869**	**57,237**	**41,632**	**5,416**	**2,848**	**14,709**	**9,294**	**23,018**	**24,736**	**14,408**	**4,921**
0—1	403	202	201	3	4	83	106	113	87	3	4
1—2	535	289	246	6	2	111	117	169	122	3	5
2—3	707	381	326	7	4	137	144	228	169	10	10
3—4	961	557	404	12	5	254	189	284	204	8	7
4—5	1,271	757	514	34	22	372	242	329	230	25	23
Total 0—5	*3,877*	*2,186*	*1,691*	*62*	*37*	*957*	*798*	*1,123*	*812*	*49*	*49*
5—10	6,580	4,114	2,466	206	111	2,043	1,222	1,725	1,037	172	109
10—15	6,966	4,395	2,571	284	155	2,124	1,260	1,722	995	297	181
15—20	6,448	3,931	2,517	361	210	1,638	1,026	1,352	946	613	348
20—25	7,010	4,318	2,692	433	250	1,648	966	1,420	1,091	846	394
25—30	7,780	4,829	2,951	654	313	1,446	852	1,387	1,342	1,367	451
30—35	7,857	4,839	3,018	722	325	1,187	772	1,312	1,423	1,649	509
35—40	7,810	4,806	3,004	673	325	894	576	1,351	1,544	1,909	568
40—45	7,648	4,767	2,881	618	286	802	475	1,418	1,571	1,945	559
45—50	7,186	4,343	2,843	461	237	572	357	1,563	1,769	1,763	497
50—55	6,356	3,659	2,697	355	210	412	280	1,469	1,790	1,440	425
55—60	6,141	3,051	3,090	196	149	306	236	1,595	2,381	965	331
60—65	5,723	2,782	2,941	148	112	296	202	1,618	2,379	738	256
65—70	3,732	1,800	1,932	73	57	179	97	1,250	1,700	301	92
70 and over	7,755	3,417	4,338	170	71	205	175	2,713	3,956	354	152
***Bombay.**											
Total	***78,553**	**44,547**	**34,006**	**7,065**	**3,846**	**10,984**	**6,392**	**20,124**	**21,030**	**6,374**	**2,738**
0—1	134	69	65	3	1	6	7	55	56	5	1
1—2	219	117	102	12	4	23	22	81	72	1	4
2—3	361	205	156	20	16	65	51	118	85	2	4
3—4	543	323	220	27	25	141	99	150	95	5	1
4—5	829	482	347	45	42	208	152	218	144	11	9
Total 0—5	*2,086*	*1,196*	*890*	*107*	*88*	*443*	*331*	*622*	*452*	*24*	*19*
5—10	4,337	2,644	1,693	422	281	1,266	745	877	604	79	63
10—15	4,945	3,038	1,907	600	425	1,355	731	931	652	152	99
15—20	4,942	3,075	1,867	710	502	1,063	557	967	644	335	164
20—25	5,441	3,397	2,044	792	493	1,094	595	1,030	749	481	207
25—30	5,704	3,596	2,108	907	415	1,011	557	1,002	856	676	280
30—35	5,769	3,660	2,109	892	361	925	513	1,040	906	803	329
35—40	5,788	3,575	2,213	763	305	775	426	1,166	1,109	871	373
40—45	5,529	3,280	2,249	635	292	648	367	1,182	1,245	815	345
45—50	5,658	3,057	2,601	432	246	550	348	1,395	1,723	680	284
50—55	5,312	2,824	2,488	319	174	477	273	1,474	1,825	554	216
55—60	5,749	2,850	2,899	179	106	402	263	1,888	2,388	381	142
60—65	5,616	2,710	2,906	131	73	346	245	1,948	2,478	285	110
65—70	3,772	1,847	1,925	59	39	210	138	1,456	1,696	122	52
70 and over	7,905	3,798	4,107	117	46	419	303	3,146	3,703	116	55
Burma.											
Total	68,264	36,589	31,675	7,373	5,529	9,115	7,852	12,751	14,976	7,607	3,520
0—1	59	29	30	1	1	6	8	21	21	1	..
1—2	117	60	57	6	6	18	17	34	34	2	..
2—3	212	113	99	11	13	48	39	48	43	6	4
3—4	354	192	162	21	21	99	85	66	50	8	7
4—5	435	240	195	28	23	130	114	75	51	9	8
Total 0—5	*1,177*	*634*	*543*	*67*	*64*	*301*	*263*	*244*	*199*	*26*	*19*
5—10	2,877	1,615	1,262	220	183	861	708	387	277	161	102
10—15	3,608	2,030	1,578	332	275	980	817	420	315	317	181
15—20	4,909	2,783	2,126	624	490	993	855	492	419	699	379
20—25	5,311	3,062	2,249	731	546	954	822	550	464	858	437
25—30	5,769	3,467	2,302	928	602	798	723	666	544	1,100	452
30—35	5,713	3,499	2,214	968	589	724	639	712	595	1,113	405
35—40	5,534	3,296	2,238	900	566	648	544	858	821	909	319
40—45	5,354	3,083	2,271	809	555	599	515	907	910	788	304
45—50	4,905	2,601	2,304	546	461	494	402	1,030	1,204	548	253
50—55	4,832	2,450	2,382	443	413	448	369	1,139	1,397	433	216
55—60	4,810	2,256	2,554	304	294	344	322	1,344	1,793	274	158
60—65	4,424	2,017	2,407	248	226	318	279	1,253	1,786	210	129
65—70	3,197	1,373	1,824	111	110	223	193	962	1,456	84	72
70 and over	5,844	2,423	3,421	142	155	430	401	1,787	2,796	87	94

*Including Aden.

Table IX.—Infirmities—Part II—Distribution by Age—*continued.*

Age.	Population afflicted.			Insane.		Deaf-Mutes.		Blind.		Lepers.	
	Persons.	Males.	Females.	Males.	Females.	Males.	Females.	Males.	Females.	Males.	Females.
1	2	3	4	5	6	7	8	9	10	11	12
Central Provinces and Berar.											
Total	**71,224**	**34,704**	**36,520**	**2,844**	**1,682**	**7,550**	**5,153**	**17,201**	**25,723**	**7,341**	**4,165**
0—1	148	82	66	..	2	12	6	68	52	2	6
1—2	209	119	90	2	1	12	11	101	71	5	7
2—3	277	159	118	5	2	32	28	120	84	4	5
3—4	405	238	167	11	5	82	60	138	98	7	5
4—5	515	299	216	16	11	115	85	161	114	11	9
Total 0—5	*1,554*	*897*	*657*	*34*	*21*	*253*	*190*	*588*	*419*	*29*	*32*
5—10	2,961	1,772	1,189	164	110	699	471	827	532	100	88
10—15	3,337	2,015	1,322	230	162	770	474	864	553	169	145
15—20	3,363	2,004	1,359	266	186	658	369	781	592	316	223
20—25	3,697	2,206	1,491	314	188	651	374	824	689	437	251
25—30	4,172	2,420	1,752	381	174	635	377	782	908	640	305
30—35	4,608	2,556	2,052	369	170	624	390	782	1,097	796	413
35—40	5,404	2,763	2,641	297	169	534	377	987	1,562	955	550
40—45	5,607	2,831	2,776	249	145	484	341	1,140	1,777	971	523
45—50	6,043	2,906	3,137	181	104	456	303	1,400	2,283	887	458
50—55	5,572	2,597	2,975	139	76	390	264	1,374	2,272	711	375
55—60	6,265	2,598	3,667	88	53	371	298	1,649	3,039	502	295
60—65	6,004	2,378	3,626	70	48	348	285	1,576	3,059	396	248
65—70	3,915	1,471	2,444	27	27	201	174	1,058	2,150	196	104
70 and over	8,722	3,290	5,432	35	49	476	466	2,569	4,791	236	155
Coorg.											
Total	**248**	**136**	**112**	**13**	**18**	**55**	**46**	**58**	**42**	**11**	**6**
3—4	1	..	1	..	..	..	..	..	1	..	..
4—5	4	1	3	1	..	..	2	..	1	..	..
Total 0—5	*5*	*1*	*4*	*1*	..	..	*2*	..	*2*	..	..
5—10	18	9	9	1	1	7	6	2	2	..	..
10—15	29	18	11	2	1	8	7	7	2	1	1
15—20	31	20	11	1	2	11	5	8	3	..	1
20—25	28	19	9	1	1	11	4	6	3	1	1
25—30	22	9	13	..	3	6	6	2	4	1	..
30—35	24	9	15	1	4	5	6	2	4	1	1
35—40	15	8	7	1	3	2	2	3	2	2	..
40—45	11	6	5	2	..	2	3	2	2	..	..
45—50	16	8	8	1	1	1	3	5	3	1	1
50—55	16	9	7	1	1	1	2	6	3	1	1
55—60	11	8	3	1	..	1	..	5	3	1	..
60—65	9	5	4	..	1	..	..	4	3	1	..
65—70	6	3	3	..	..	..	..	3	3	..	..
70 and over	7	4	3	..	..	..	..	3	3	1	..
Delhi.											
Total.	**898**	**512**	**386**	**60**	**29**	**104**	**44**	**342**	**314**	**8**	**1**
0—1	1	1	..	..	..	..	..	1	..	..	..
1—2	4	3	1	1	..	1	..	1	1	..	..
2—3	2	1	1	..	..	..	..	1	1	..	..
3—4	4	2	2	..	..	..	1	2	1	..	..
4—5	14	7	7	1	..	3	3	3	4	..	..
Total 0—5	*25*	*14*	*11*	*2*	..	*4*	*4*	*8*	*7*	..	..
5—10	45	26	19	5	3	8	5	13	11	..	..
10—15	46	33	13	7	3	11	4	15	6	..	..
15—20	43	32	11	4	2	11	1	17	8	..	..
20—25	56	38	18	6	3	12	3	19	12	1	..
25—30	49	31	18	6	5	11	3	13	10	1	..
30—35	50	32	18	6	3	11	3	15	12	1	..
35—40	58	31	27	5	2	9	4	17	20	..	1
40—45	57	27	30	4	4	5	1	17	26	1	..
45—50	67	34	33	7	2	6	3	20	28	1	..
50—55	69	35	34	4	1	4	2	26	32	1	..
55—60	84	38	46	..	..	4	4	32	42	2	..
60—65	77	36	41	1	..	3	5	33	36	..	..
65—70	53	35	18	2	..	2	..	31	18	..	..
70 and over	119	70	49	1	1	3	2	66	46	..	..

Table IX.—Infirmities—Part II—Distribution by Age—*continued.*

Age.	Population afflicted.			Insane.		Deaf-Mutes.		Blind.		Lepers.	
	Persons.	Males.	Females.	Males.	Females.	Males.	Females.	Males.	Females.	Males.	Females.
1	2	3	4	5	6	7	8	9	10	11	12
Madras.											
Total	**133,421**	**76,623**	**56,798**	**8,957**	**6,437**	**13,741**	**14,567**	**24,258**	**27,623**	**24,842**	**8,235**
0—1	165	95	70	2	3	11	9	75	50	7	8
1—2	252	142	110	4	5	38	29	90	66	10	10
2—3	536	288	248	19	14	142	125	112	98	16	12
3—4	870	475	395	19	23	313	260	132	106	11	6
4—5	1,258	679	579	38	40	451	386	174	133	20	22
Total 0—5	*3,081*	*1,679*	*1,402*	*82*	*85*	*955*	*809*	*583*	*453*	*64*	*58*
5—10	8,036	4,567	3,469	403	304	2,819	2,192	1,072	757	296	234
10—15	9,115	5,233	3,882	535	437	2,956	2,209	1,169	902	593	351
15—20	9,415	5,474	3,941	760	594	2,221	1,708	1,143	1,051	1,366	599
20—25	10,349	6,136	4,213	972	676	2,161	1,712	1,197	1,106	1,827	732
25—30	11,070	6,861	4,209	1,234	741	1,805	1,439	1,205	1,173	2,631	866
30—35	11,098	7,109	3,989	1,261	713	1,550	1,175	1,224	1,202	3,087	904
35—40	11,182	7,194	3,988	1,062	696	1,191	838	1,476	1,514	3,483	946
40—45	10,455	6,622	3,833	864	635	958	718	1,544	1,580	3,268	904
45—50	9,332	5,577	3,755	597	458	660	521	1,652	1,975	2,678	808
50—55	8,443	4,815	3,628	466	378	498	408	1,702	2,154	2,154	693
55—60	8,152	4,112	4,040	279	277	337	293	2,133	2,984	1,369	489
60—65	7,545	3,719	3,826	202	204	264	234	2,193	3,015	1,061	379
65—70	5,291	2,569	2,722	108	99	148	118	1,842	2,357	478	151
70 and over	10,857	4,956	5,901	132	140	218	193	4,123	5,400	487	171
North-West Frontier Province. *(Districts and Administered Territories.)*											
Total	**4,984**	**3,091**	**1,893**	**543**	**198**	**1,074**	**523**	**1,351**	**1,112**	**164**	**85**
0—1	12	5	7	..	1	1	1	4	5	..	..
1—2	22	15	7	2	1	3	1	10	4	..	1
2—3	43	22	21	1	2	10	5	11	12	..	2
3—4	46	29	17	1	..	19	9	9	6	1	3
4—5	95	58	37	8	6	29	18	16	10	6	4
Total 0—5	*218*	*129*	*89*	*12*	*10*	*62*	*34*	*50*	*37*	*7*	*10*
5—10	407	269	138	51	19	139	69	75	45	13	10
10—15	444	301	143	65	21	150	67	77	49	19	7
15—20	383	255	128	69	24	106	46	67	51	18	11
20—25	370	241	129	66	25	92	41	73	54	15	12
25—30	368	241	127	62	24	90	48	77	53	14	4
30—35	352	235	117	57	18	88	41	75	53	15	6
35—40	310	199	111	40	12	75	26	73	68	11	6
40—45	305	186	119	37	11	58	30	85	74	9	4
45—50	322	182	140	30	13	45	32	97	91	11	4
50—55	298	165	133	25	11	42	23	89	97	9	4
55—60	300	167	133	13	6	31	17	117	110	9	2
60—65	267	152	115	7	3	28	16	111	95	6	2
65—70	164	93	71	4	..	18	6	70	64	2	1
70 and over	476	276	200	5	1	50	27	215	171	6	2
Punjab.											
Total	**82,091**	**46,616**	**35,475**	**4,853**	**2,367**	**10,258**	**5,903**	**30,405**	**26,849**	**1,326**	**527**
0—1	111	66	45	2	..	14	7	47	36	4	2
1—2	186	97	89	5	7	25	22	66	59	3	3
2—3	355	193	162	17	6	60	66	114	87	5	6
3—4	518	295	223	13	4	145	112	137	104	1	3
4—5	876	501	375	56	50	243	177	194	142	14	13
Total 0—5	*2,046*	*1,152*	*894*	*93*	*67*	*487*	*384*	*558*	*428*	*27*	*27*
5—10	4,870	2,892	1,978	400	219	1,379	893	1,101	864	44	32
10—15	5,302	3,213	2,089	515	247	1,260	899	1,213	934	52	26
15—20	4,575	2,892	1,683	539	259	1,173	640	1,138	750	72	43
20—25	4,632	2,954	1,678	528	255	1,129	589	1,233	789	76	55
25—30	4,400	2,752	1,648	530	225	930	488	1,212	892	100	56
30—35	4,226	2,623	1,603	505	213	810	424	1,191	917	124	53
35—40	4,220	2,498	1,722	449	196	625	319	1,279	1,170	157	49
40—45	4,355	2,502	1,853	398	180	527	268	1,452	1,368	135	48
45—50	5,240	2,832	2,408	289	143	419	223	1,964	2,014	174	38
50—55	5,244	2,748	2,496	205	116	329	176	2,073	2,180	151	27
55—60	6,377	3,393	2,984	131	93	292	147	2,908	2,723	70	29
60—65	6,666	3,583	3,083	106	62	252	134	3,168	2,867	62	24
65—70	5,801	3,142	2,659	57	37	142	100	2,914	2,519	37	14
70 and over	14,137	7,440	6,697	108	55	504	219	7,001	6,434	45	6

Table IX.—Infirmities—Part II—Distribution by Age—*continued.*

Age.	Population afflicted.			Insane.		Deaf-Mutes.		Blind.		Lepers.	
	Persons.	Males.	Females.	Males.	Females.	Males.	Females.	Males.	Females.	Males.	Females.
1	2	3	4	5	6	7	8	9	10	11	12
United Provinces of Agra and Oudh.											
Total	**192,592**	**101,149**	**91,443**	**7,432**	**3,787**	**15,756**	**9,559**	**66,224**	**75,754**	**12,013**	**2,472**
0—1	546	303	243	9	6	50	31	239	204	5	2
1—2	668	375	293	7	5	48	44	320	243	2	1
2—3	990	546	444	19	14	91	94	429	334	7	2
3—4	1,341	743	598	37	23	197	175	509	400	4	..
4—5	1,537	864	673	53	38	266	215	53[illegible]	421	11	3
Total 0—5	*5,082*	*2,831*	*2,251*	*125*	*86*	*652*	*559*	*2,034*	*1,602*	*29*	*8*
5—10	8,934	5,378	3,556	450	271	1,819	1,189	3,074	2,074	60	40
10—15	9,885	6,139	3,746	615	344	2,122	1,233	3,327	2,131	94	56
15—20	9,438	5,921	3,517	747	372	1,908	942	3,050	2,107	252	100
20—25	10,519	6,467	4,052	839	389	1,853	938	3,367	2,582	428	147
25—30	11,657	6,756	4,901	911	392	1,543	866	3,537	3,434	781	216
30—35	12,084	6,846	5,238	914	379	1,296	768	3,572	3,850	1,073	243
35—40	13,719	7,470	6,249	776	359	1,027	651	4,132	4,968	1,567	281
40—45	14,268	7,686	6,582	642	330	927	553	4,422	5,432	1,715	276
45—50	16,292	8,455	7,837	457	263	706	448	5,509	6,855	1,799	280
50—55	15,749	7,933	7,816	326	213	537	387	5,531	6,967	1,552	259
55—60	17,072	7,862	9,210	239	134	394	314	6,174	8,554	1,064	210
60—65	16,156	7,333	8,823	203	105	342	268	5,999	8.287	811	167
65—70	10,981	4,942	6,039	89	63	216	168	4,280	5.729	370	81
70 and over	20,756	9,130	11,626	99	87	414	275	8,216	11,182	418	108
Baroda State.											
Total	**11,146**	**4,944**	**6,202**	**816**	**557**	**694**	**572**	**3,090**	**4,943**	**393**	**182**
0—1	11	7	4	..	..	..	..	7	3	..	1
1—2	16	11	5	..	..	2	1	8	3	1	2
2—3	21	13	8	..	1	4	1	9	5	1	1
3—4	46	28	18	6	6	10	6	15	12	2	1
4—5	72	44	28	4	2	11	10	27	19	2	
Total 0—5	*166*	*103*	*63*	*10*	*9*	*27*	*18*	*66*	*42*	*6*	*5*
5—10	441	265	176	59	32	83	62	118	78	12	4
10—15	511	307	204	90	46	100	71	115	85	15	8
15—20	503	318	185	105	56	86	55	110	71	24	11
20—25	506	332	174	108	53	81	46	119	68	27	8
25—30	463	276	187	96	48	58	37	96	93	29	11
30—35	489	251	238	88	54	46	41	82	127	37	18
35—40	577	245	332	68	57	35	32	101	221	43	25
40—45	621	246	375	53	56	29	30	123	265	44	27
45—50	796	289	507	47	46	29	34	174	409	38	22
50—55	827	311	516	34	35	29	28	212	435	37	16
55—60	1,124	425	699	26	21	30	28	343	644	28	9
60—65	1,213	455	758	18	18	26	29	391	706	22	8
65—70	913	369	544	8	9	14	22	337	511	12	6
70 and over	1,996	752	1,244	6	17	21	39	703	1,188	19	4
Bengal States.											
Total	**2,176**	**1,298**	**878**	**396**	**301**	**259**	**169**	**337**	**322**	**316**	**93**
0—1	8	7	1	..	..	..	..	7	1	..	..
1—2	7	4	3	..	..	..	2	3	1	1	..
2—3	7	4	3	..	..	1	1	3	2	..	..
3—4	23	14	9	4	2	5	3	5	3	1	1
4—5	32	20	12	7	4	8	5	5	2	..	1
Total 0—5	*77*	*49*	*28*	*11*	*6*	*14*	*11*	*23*	*9*	*2*	*2*
5—10	164	103	61	45	27	39	20	17	12	4	2
10—15	175	105	70	47	37	39	18	13	12	8	4
15—20	161	93	68	36	33	32	17	14	14	12	5
20—25	191	114	77	38	35	37	18	20	19	19	6
25—30	211	130	81	50	40	27	12	19	20	35	9
30—35	200	130	70	50	33	24	8	18	17	38	12
35—40	180	113	67	32	24	17	8	24	23	42	13
40—45	166	106	60	25	19	12	8	26	25	43	8
45—50	145	95	50	21	11	8	5	27	28	40	6
50—55	121	78	4[illegible]	15	9	4	3	28	27	31	6
55—60	101	51	50	5	7	2	4	29	33	15	6
60—65	97	46	51	8	9	1	2	25	34	12	6
65—70	63	28	35	7	4	1	11	14	18	6	3
70 and over	124	57	67	6	7	2	24	40	31	9	5

Table IX.—Infirmities—Part II—Distribution by Age—*continued.*

Age.	Population afflicted.			Insane.		Deaf-Mutes.		Blind.		Lepers.	
	Persons.	Males.	Females.	Males.	Females.	Males.	Females.	Males.	Females.	Males.	Females.
1	2	3	4	5	6	7	8	9	10	11	12
Bihar and Orissa States.											
Total	**12,279**	**6,657**	**5,622**	**486**	**295**	**1,439**	**1,033**	**2,501**	**3,077**	**2,240**	**1,225**
0—1	38	17	21	..	..	..	..	16	20	1	1
1—2	65	34	31	..	..	..	3	32	27	2	1
2—3	109	61	48	..	..	17	15	40	30	4	3
3—4	150	87	63	2	1	40	29	40	30	6	4
4—5	178	98	80	4	2	48	38	41	36	6	4
Total 0—5	*540*	*297*	*343*	*6*	*3*	*105*	*85*	*169*	*143*	*19*	*13*
5—10	910	520	390	34	20	228	168	216	171	42	34
10—15	962	539	423	43	28	216	158	216	172	66	65
15—20	957	523	434	57	29	157	117	180	173	130	115
20—25	968	544	424	59	29	144	98	180	181	161	116
25—30	1,071	621	450	59	37	124	80	166	201	272	132
30—35	1,085	647	438	64	35	110	69	166	199	308	135
35—40	1,059	617	442	49	30	89	57	176	214	303	142
40—45	973	556	417	37	29	69	50	162	202	290	136
45—50	825	456	369	24	19	56	40	152	203	224	107
50—55	686	370	316	19	13	48	35	136	183	168	85
55—60	637	296	341	13	7	32	23	149	255	102	56
60—65	609	267	342	10	8	29	22	144	264	84	51
65—70	311	129	182	5	5	10	10	83	148	31	19
70 and over	686	275	411	7	3	22	21	206	368	40	19
Bombay States.											
Total	**12,546**	**6,992**	**5,554**	**1,091**	**643**	**1,845**	**1,328**	**2,895**	**3,095**	**1,161**	**488**
0—1	25	18	7	1	1	11	4	6	1	..	1
1—2	34	20	14	..	..	4	2	15	9	1	3
2—3	62	37	25	1	1	10	6	23	18	3	..
3—4	100	56	44	6	3	23	15	26	25	1	1
4—5	158	92	66	18	9	35	26	35	30	4	1
Total 0—5	*379*	*223*	*156*	*26*	*14*	*83*	*53*	*105*	*83*	*9*	*6*
5—10	734	428	306	86	51	168	143	153	95	21	17
10—15	862	514	348	116	67	213	149	147	104	38	28
15—20	773	456	317	123	64	173	115	123	98	37	40
20—25	809	503	306	135	67	176	108	135	100	57	31
25—30	859	539	320	131	63	149	113	133	102	126	42
30—35	865	498	367	117	66	141	101	119	147	121	53
35—40	875	532	343	93	58	133	70	151	157	155	58
40—45	928	517	411	81	60	118	97	171	208	147	46
45—50	889	477	412	60	43	114	65	173	251	130	53
50—55	925	500	425	46	28	102	85	223	268	129	44
55—60	862	407	455	29	25	73	62	238	343	67	25
60—65	966	500	466	27	17	83	62	313	366	77	21
65—70	575	285	290	9	12	33	30	220	238	23	10
70 and over	1,245	613	632	12	8	86	75	491	535	24	14
Central India Agency.											
Total	**18,025**	**8,366**	**9,659**	**966**	**583**	**1,078**	**818**	**5,643**	**8,014**	**760**	**324**
0—1	43	25	18	2	..	6	2	17	16	..	..
1—2	62	35	27		2	2	2	33	24	..	..
2—3	99	61	38	3	1	7	5	51	32	..	..
3—4	118	63	55	4	5	14	11	44	39	1	..
4—5	273	148	125	10	15	51	43	86	68	1	..
Total 0—5	*595*	*332*	*263*	*19*	*23*	*80*	*63*	*231*	*179*	*2*	..
5—10	981	580	401	75	45	178	106	315	250	15	6
10—15	944	562	382	80	53	122	79	338	244	29	11
15—20	1,121	654	467	123	73	129	112	380	268	34	22
20—25	979	585	394	121	46	118	78	326	259	33	17
25—30	1,096	582	514	134	56	86	72	315	360	58	32
30—35	1,011	519	492	108	57	67	57	264	364	86	21
35—40	1,389	617	772	90	56	67	52	370	617	95	54
40—45	1,223	519	704	59	40	52	37	327	582	84	49
45—50	1,590	679	911	48	34	52	44	483	803	101	34
50—55	1,256	555	701	37	27	27	24	405	631	79	23
55—60	1,772	667	1,105	32	29	35	28	544	1,028	62	25
60—65	1,328	496	832	11	14	23	18	421	797	45	9
65—70	925	340	585	13	11	11	17	305	551	13	8
70 and over	1,815	679	1,136	16	19	21	31	619	1,081	24	13

Table IX.—Infirmities—Part II—Distribution by Age—*continued.*

Age.	Population afflicted.			Insane.		Deaf-Mutes.		Blind.		Lepers.	
	Persons.	Males.	Females.	Males.	Females.	Males.	Females.	Males.	Females.	Males.	Females.
1	2	3	4	5	6	7	8	9	10	11	12
Central Provinces States.											
Total	**6,913**	**3,314**	**3,599**	**317**	**190**	**711**	**556**	**1,686**	**1,461**	**610**	**403**
0—1	17	9	8	..	..	..	..	8	7	1	1
1—2	19	12	7	..	..	..	..	11	7	1	..
2—3	42	21	21	..	..	7	6	12	14	2	1
3—4	76	41	35	1	1	22	15	17	17	1	2
4—5	97	57	40	2	3	31	19	21	15	3	3
Total 0—5	*251*	*140*	*111*	*3*	*4*	*60*	*40*	*69*	*60*	*8*	*7*
5—10	501	277	224	25	26	127	90	108	85	17	23
10—15	524	284	240	33	28	110	93	116	91	25	28
15—20	407	227	180	28	17	76	73	88	70	37	20
20—25	399	236	163	30	18	75	57	86	69	46	21
25—30	444	267	177	39	14	66	38	97	92	65	35
30—35	441	251	190	38	12	54	35	93	106	68	38
35—40	471	250	221	31	10	39	29	108	148	74	34
40—45	498	256	242	28	13	33	27	124	169	72	35
45—50	512	242	270	22	11	20	23	138	189	63	48
50—55	461	199	262	15	9	16	19	117	193	51	43
55—60	517	190	327	9	8	13	11	136	279	33	29
60—65	481	173	308	7	7	9	10	131	269	26	23
65—70	296	94	202	4	5	4	5	76	182	10	10
70 and over	710	228	482	5	8	9	6	199	459	15	9
Gwalior State.											
Total	**8,593**	**3,728**	**4,865**	**292**	**161**	**739**	**567**	**2,425**	**3,984**	**272**	**153**
0—1	17	8	9	..	..	..	..	8	9	..	..
1—2	18	10	8	..	..	1	1	9	7	..	..
2—3	19	11	8	..	..	1	2	10	6	..	..
3—4	36	21	15	..	..	3	3	18	12	..	..
4—5	59	31	28	2	1	9	7	20	19	..	1
Tatal 0—5	*149*	*81*	*68*	*2*	*1*	*14*	*13*	*65*	*53*	..	*1*
5—10	248	133	115	14	8	47	33	69	69	3	5
10—15	251	147	104	18	8	52	29	71	65	6	2
15—20	283	152	131	22	14	47	29	70	83	13	5
20—25	303	156	147	28	13	50	32	64	99	14	3
25—30	360	166	194	23	13	50	41	78	132	15	8
30—35	441	196	245	21	10	51	43	104	181	20	11
35—40	545	247	298	26	14	59	39	135	232	27	13
40—45	590	253	337	28	16	57	35	141	272	27	14
45—50	717	300	417	29	13	60	45	183	344	28	15
50—55	793	340	453	19	10	59	43	232	383	30	17
55—60	1,082	440	642	16	10	64	46	330	568	30	18
60—65	1,120	443	677	20	11	53	54	343	592	27	20
65—70	753	311	442	14	13	34	33	244	385	19	11
70 and over	958	363	595	12	7	42	52	296	526	13	10
Hyderabad State.											
Total	**22,196**	**12,656**	**9,540**	**1,337**	**863**	**2,209**	**1,533**	**6,480**	**6,036**	**2,630**	**1,108**
0—1	13	9	4	..	..	..	..	9	4	..	..
1—2	65	43	22	5	4	4	2	34	16	..	..
2—3	122	62	60	3	3	10	5	46	46	3	6
3—4	190	108	82	8	11	23	23	73	43	4	5
4—5	263	151	112	25	8	50	21	70	79	6	4
Total 0—5	*653*	*373*	*280*	*41*	*26*	*87*	*51*	*232*	*188*	*13*	*15*
5—10	1,189	688	501	86	55	169	119	382	305	51	22
10—15	1,457	828	629	111	79	194	148	442	356	81	46
15—20	1,585	934	651	142	88	205	117	468	384	119	62
20—25	1,765	1,047	718	149	96	197	132	489	397	212	93
25—30	1,820	1,129	691	175	98	201	129	529	376	224	88
30—35	1,855	1,054	801	134	95	178	147	473	443	269	116
35—40	1,471	850	621	106	59	145	85	369	381	230	96
40—45	1,916	1,119	797	120	76	173	131	482	456	344	134
45—50	1,374	818	556	68	34	122	71	384	358	244	93
50—55	1,671	946	725	66	33	136	103	480	483	264	106
55—60	955	538	417	25	23	75	46	308	311	130	37
60—65	1,724	913	811	55	35	132	93	512	586	214	97
65—70	781	424	357	29	28	59	49	250	240	86	40
70 and over	1,980	995	985	30	38	136	112	680	772	149	63

Table IX.—Infirmities—Part II—Distribution by Age—*continued.*

Age.	Population afflicted.			Insane.		Deaf-Mutes.		Blind.		Lepers.	
	Persons.	Males.	Females.	Males.	Females.	Males.	Females.	Males.	Females.	Males.	Females.
1	2	3	4	5	6	7	8	9	10	11	12
Jammu and Kashmir State.											
Total	**14,781**	**8,600**	**6,181**	**952**	**472**	**3,481**	**2,306**	**2,888**	**2,811**	**1,381**	**645**
0—1	20	11	9	..	..	4	5	6	3	1	1
1—2	46	24	22	1	..	10	11	10	8	3	3
2—3	108	61	47	4	1	36	29	15	12	6	5
3—4	166	97	69	7	3	68	51	18	12	5	5
4—5	206	115	91	9	8	84	62	19	17	6	6
Total 0—5	*546*	*308*	*238*	*21*	*12*	*202*	*158*	*68*	*52*	*21*	*20*
5—10	1,212	697	515	58	46	495	347	119	98	34	30
10—15	1,393	797	596	77	52	534	397	144	119	53	34
15—20	1,365	771	594	113	60	448	349	147	137	74	51
20—25	1,406	821	585	127	64	439	303	169	159	97	64
25—30	1,236	772	464	124	51	333	198	181	149	143	71
30—35	1,140	721	419	117	46	271	152	183	151	160	74
35—40	1,030	626	404	86	37	205	111	183	186	159	73
40—45	841	515	326	67	33	158	79	158	158	136	57
45—50	772	469	303	54	22	110	57	182	182	127	44
50—55	664	390	274	42	14	78	44	172	180	101	36
55—60	697	379	318	22	11	57	37	214	247	89	26
60—65	671	364	307	19	10	49	31	223	243	78	25
65—70	439	239	200	8	5	23	12	179	174	31	12
70 and over	1,369	731	638	17	9	79	31	566	576	78	28
Madras States Agency.											
Total	**15,559**	**9,404**	**6,155**	**1,607**	**1,270**	**2,291**	**1,508**	**2,785**	**2,399**	**2,739**	**989**
0—1	19	12	7	..	..	3	2	8	4	1	1
1—2	35	19	16	..	1	5	6	12	8	2	1
2—3	66	39	27	2	..	20	15	16	13	2	
3—4	108	62	46	2	1	42	28	17	15	1	2
4—5	140	82	58	3	2	55	34	20	18	4	4
Total 0—5	*368*	*214*	*154*	*7*	*4*	*125*	*85*	*73*	*58*	*10*	*8*
5—10	870	535	335	26	21	337	188	138	105	35	22
10—15	1,060	642	418	43	34	356	221	175	120	68	43
15—20	1,203	725	478	98	72	286	183	204	140	141	84
20—25	1,245	765	480	149	89	239	150	204	153	177	88
25—30	1,338	867	521	225	127	190	141	210	162	244	94
30—35	1,453	926	527	245	155	183	124	201	155	298	93
35—40	1,405	905	500	204	157	160	104	186	146	356	93
40—45	1,333	839	494	173	156	137	92	191	152	340	94
45—50	1,204	708	496	128	154	87	64	186	181	307	98
50—55	1,098	646	452	101	118	65	61	188	177	293	97
55—60	886	526	360	82	66	44	38	198	184	202	73
60—65	769	437	332	62	53	36	26	197	198	142	56
65—70	462	259	203	27	27	20	12	152	145	60	19
70 and over	815	410	405	37	37	26	19	282	323	66	27
(i) Cochin State.											
Total	**3,459**	**1,949**	**1,510**	**358**	**279**	**283**	**205**	**758**	**837**	**553**	**192**
0—1	5	4	1	..	..	1	..	3	1	..	..
1—2	7	4	3	..	1	1	1	3	1	..	..
2—3	10	7	3	2	...	3	1	1	2	1	..
3—4	17	10	7	1	..	6	3	3	4	..	..
4—5	27	16	11	1	..	8	4	6	6	1	1
Total 0—5	*66*	*41*	*25*	*4*	*1*	*19*	*9*	*16*	*14*	*2*	*1*
5—10	160	94	66	4	3	48	29	37	30	5	4
10—15	196	113	83	6	6	48	30	47	39	12	8
15—20	240	143	97	23	16	34	23	52	40	34	18
20—25	259	160	99	33	20	29	24	56	38	42	17
25—30	288	182	106	49	22	18	19	59	49	56	17
30—35	302	185	117	55	36	20	17	48	48	62	16
35—40	301	179	122	49	41	18	17	45	49	67	15
40—45	299	179	120	45	38	15	13	52	51	68	18
45—50	278	150	128	27	36	11	7	55	67	57	19
50—55	249	139	110	18	22	11	7	59	63	52	18
55—60	223	118	105	15	12	4	5	58	73	41	15
60—65	208	95	113	15	11	4	4	48	87	28	12
65—70	133	57	76	7	5	3	1	39	65	8	5
70 and over	257	114	143	8	10	1		87	124	19	9

Table IX.—Infirmities—Part II—Distribution by Age—*continued.*

Age.	Population afflicted.			Insane.		Deaf-Mutes.		Blind.		Lepers.	
	Persons.	Males.	Females.	Males.	Females.	Males.	Females.	Males.	Females.	Males.	Females.
1	2	3	4	5	6	7	8	9	10	11	12
(ii) Travancore State.											
Total	**10,910**	**6,744**	**4,166**	**1,151**	**917**	**1,760**	**1,123**	**1,810**	**1,381**	**2,037**	**752**
0—1	13	8	5	..	..	2	1	5	3	1	1
1—2	27	14	13	..	..	4	5	8	7	2	1
2—3	53	30	23	..	..	16	14	14	10	1	
3—4	85	49	36	1	1	33	23	14	11	1	1
4—5	103	61	42	2	2	42	25	14	12	3	3
Total 0—5	*281*	*162*	*119*	*3*	*3*	*97*	*68*	*55*	*43*	*8*	*6*
5—10	627	390	237	21	14	246	139	95	67	29	18
10—15	764	470	294	31	25	265	159	122	76	52	34
15—20	873	529	344	68	51	218	132	143	98	103	64
20—25	905	557	348	105	61	189	112	138	109	129	66
25—30	998	629	369	166	94	153	105	135	102	177	69
30—35	1,044	666	378	172	109	144	94	139	100	212	75
35—40	1,004	651	353	144	107	121	77	124	93	263	76
40—45	932	598	334	119	109	108	67	121	86	251	72
45—50	842	507	335	90	110	66	51	116	97	235	77
50—55	772	467	305	80	93	48	44	113	97	226	72
55—60	598	367	231	59	52	35	27	123	100	150	53
60—65	511	313	198	45	41	30	20	130	96	108	41
65—70	296	181	115	20	21	15	11	96	70	50	13
70 and over	463	257	206	28	27	25	17	160	147	44	16
(iii) Other Madras States.											
Total	**1,190**	**711**	**479**	**98**	**74**	**248**	**180**	**217**	**181**	**149**	**45**
0—1	1	..	1	..	..	..	1	..	..	..	..
1—2	1	1		..	..	..	..	1	..	..	..
2—3	3	2	1	..	..	1	..	1	1	..	..
3—4	6	3	3	..	..	3	2	..	..	..	1
4—5	10	5	5	..	..	5	5	..	..	..	..
Total 0—5	*21*	*11*	*10*	..	..	*9*	*8*	*2*	*1*	..	*1*
5—10	83	51	32	1	4	43	20	6	8	1	..
10—15	100	59	41	6	3	43	32	6	5		1
15—20	90	53	37	7	5	34	28	9	2	4	2
20—25	81	48	33	11	8	21	14	10	6	6	5
25—30	102	56	46	10	11	19	17	16	11	11	8
30—35	107	75	32	18	10	19	13	14	7	24	2
35—40	100	75	25	11	9	21	10	17	4	26	2
40—45	102	62	40	9	9	14	12	18	15	21	4
45—50	84	51	33	11	8	10	6	15	17	15	2
50—55	77	40	37	3	3	6	10	16	17	15	7
55—60	65	41	24	8	2	5	6	17	11	11	5
60—65	50	29	21	2	1	2	2	19	15	6	3
65—70	33	21	12	..	1	2		17	10	2	1
70 and over	95	39	56	1	..	..	2	35	52	3	2
Mysore State.											
Total	**12,954**	**7,358**	**5,596**	**1,050**	**732**	**2,254**	**1,696**	**3,556**	**2,997**	**536**	**197**
0—1	27	14	13	..	2	3	3	10	8	1	..
1—2	41	25	16	4	..	4	2	16	13	1	1
2—3	65	31	34	..	2	14	14	17	18	..	..
3—4	112	64	48	3	..	35	28	28	20	..	..
4—5	219	126	93	10	7	70	54	44	30	3	2
Total 0—5	*464*	*260*	*204*	*17*	*11*	*126*	*101*	*115*	*89*	*5*	*3*
5—10	1,211	680	531	69	61	364	297	242	174	9	4
10—15	1,313	737	576	94	77	365	301	272	197	10	2
15—20	1,116	636	480	115	76	268	206	242	191	20	10
20—25	1,106	643	463	123	69	250	187	248	195	26	15
25—30	1,056	597	459	131	78	196	163	231	200	41	24
30—35	1,003	579	424	135	75	176	126	215	199	55	25
35—40	899	556	343	111	74	152	79	226	172	74	20
40—45	806	485	321	82	66	114	69	217	168	73	19
45—50	703	407	296	52	43	75	46	215	189	65	19
50—55	603	340	263	39	30	55	38	200	182	46	14
55—60	628	331	297	30	32	43	25	219	223	40	17
60—65	603	308	295	21	20	35	23	219	237	34	15
65—70	468	245	223	12	10	17	16	198	191	18	9
70 and over	975	554	421	19	10	18	19	497	390	20	2

Table IX.—Infirmities—Part II—Distribution by Age—*continued.*

Age.	Population afflicted.			Insane.		Deaf-Mutes.		Blind.		Lepers.	
	Persons.	Males.	Females.	Males.	Females.	Males.	Females.	Males.	Females.	Males.	Females.
1	2	3	4	5	6	7	8	9	10	11	12
Punjab States.											
Total	**2,140**	**1,221**	**919**	**97**	**34**	**465**	**370**	**503**	**452**	**162**	**65**
1—2	1	1	..	..	..	..	..	1	..	..	..
2—3	11	5	6	3	..	..	4	3	2	..	..
3—4	6	3	3	..	..	3	3	..	..	..	..
4—5	27	16	11	..	1	8	8	8	2	..	..
Total 0—5	*45*	*25*	*20*	*3*	*1*	*11*	*15*	*12*	*4*	..	..
5—10	124	78	46	8	..	56	37	13	7	2	2
10—15	171	98	73	8	3	69	56	17	13	4	2
15—20	160	81	79	11	4	43	61	20	10	7	4
20—25	146	79	67	12	3	37	48	17	13	14	3
25—30	154	96	58	11	3	51	36	19	16	16	3
30—35	133	79	54	9	1	39	34	17	13	14	6
35—40	137	83	54	8	4	34	21	20	18	21	11
40—45	113	73	40	3	3	31	13	21	17	18	7
45—50	149	83	66	6	5	30	19	29	32	20	10
50—55	116	70	46	6	1	17	6	30	31	17	8
55—60	137	77	60	4	1	13	8	47	48	13	3
60—65	149	83	66	5	1	13	7	55	56	10	2
65—70	122	69	53	3	1	8	4	55	46	3	2
70 and over	284	147	137	..	3	13	5	131	128	3	2
Punjab States Agency.											
Total	**15,548**	**8,936**	**6,612**	**669**	**319**	**1,624**	**912**	**6,238**	**5,231**	**491**	**196**
0—1	19	10	9	..	1	2	2	8	6	..	..
1—2	27	16	11	..	..	2	4	14	7	..	..
2—3	51	30	21	4	..	10	8	18	14	..	..
3—4	74	46	28	7	1	18	10	22	17	1	..
4—5	146	84	62	12	6	35	21	39	37	..	1
Total 0—5	*317*	*186*	*131*	*23*	*8*	*67*	*45*	*101*	*81*	*1*	*1*
5—10	749	456	293	68	37	187	105	201	148	4	6
10—15	804	502	302	74	37	192	104	231	159	11	7
15—20	774	497	277	76	32	161	91	242	155	26	5
20—25	808	518	290	76	30	169	88	249	166	30	7
25—30	778	477	301	63	25	138	81	233	183	48	16
30—35	731	449	282	55	20	117	61	227	183	51	18
35—40	849	511	338	57	32	107	62	288	226	66	20
40—45	844	490	354	40	25	77	59	321	253	53	19
45—50	1,082	598	484	42	24	83	45	418	393	64	25
50—55	1,087	606	481	30	11	79	36	438	411	65	25
55—60	1,407	761	646	22	11	68	30	646	591	30	17
60—65	1,422	753	669	16	7	51	26	673	625	17	14
65—70	1,176	643	533	10	10	43	18	585	497	8	9
70 and over	2,720	1,489	1,231	17	10	85	31	1,380	1,160	17	7
Rajputana Agency.											
Total	**37,886**	**17,787**	**20,099**	**1,727**	**863**	**1,896**	**1,230**	**13,782**	**17,845**	**382**	**161**
0—1	49	31	18	..	2	4	..	25	15	2	1
1—2	77	41	36	1	1	3	8	36	27	1	..
2—3	128	61	67	3	6	6	11	52	50	..	..
3—4	164	87	77	4	5	19	10	63	61	1	1
4—5	273	146	127	26	16	35	30	84	79	1	2
Total 0—5	*691*	*366*	*325*	*34*	*30*	*67*	*59*	*260*	*232*	*5*	*4*
5—10	1,362	824	538	125	70	194	118	499	346	6	4
10—15	1,463	914	549	147	72	209	123	549	349	9	5
15—20	1,433	896	537	189	92	196	88	497	344	14	13
20—25	1,531	939	592	203	87	190	92	531	401	15	12
25—30	1,642	932	710	201	87	162	92	538	519	31	12
30—35	1,623	872	751	181	67	143	81	517	590	31	13
35—40	2,141	1,010	1,131	166	83	143	86	653	935	48	27
49—45	2,258	1,013	1,245	132	72	118	80	718	1,072	45	21
45—50	2,937	1,306	1,631	109	71	114	79	1,021	1,463	62	18
50—55	2,990	1,341	1,649	82	46	93	66	1,116	1,529	50	8
55—60	4,245	1,735	2,510	59	33	77	59	1,567	2,409	32	9
60—65	4,461	1,777	2,684	51	25	65	63	1,642	2,587	19	9
65—70	3,114	1,338	1,776	14	11	40	41	1,276	1,722	8	2
70 and over	5,995	2,524	3,471	34	17	85	103	2.398	3,347	7	4

Table IX.—Infirmities—Part II—Distribution by Age—*concluded.*

Sikkim State.

Age.	Population afflicted.			Insane.		Deaf-Mutes.		Blind.		Lepers.	
	Persons.	Males.	Females.	Males.	Females.	Males.	Females.	Males.	Females.	Males.	Females.
1	2	3	4	5	6	7	8	9	10	11	12
Total	**202**	**111**	**91**	**3**	**2**	**89**	**75**	**14**	**12**	**5**	**2**
0—1	1	1	..	..	..	..	..	1	..	..	..
1—2	2	1	1	..	..	1	1	..	..	..	..
2—3	3	1	2	..	..	1	2	..	..	..	..
3—4	7	3	4	..	..	2	4	1	..	..	..
4—5	8	4	4	..	..	4	4	..	..	..	..
Total 0—5	*21*	*10*	*11*	..	..	*8*	*11*	*2*	..	..	..
5—10	34	19	15	..	1	18	13	1	1	..	..
10—15	33	20	13	..	..	17	12	2	1	1	..
15—20	28	17	11	..	..	16	11	..	..	1	..
20—25	21	12	9	..	..	12	9	..	..	..	..
25—30	13	6	7	1	..	4	6	..	1	1	..
30—35	10	5	5	..	1	5	4	..	..	..	..
35—40	4	2	2	..	..	2	2	..	..	..	..
40—45	5	2	3	..	..	2	2	..	..	..	1
45—50	5	3	2	..	..	1	1	1	1	1	..
50—55	4	3	1	..	..	1	..	1	1	1	..
55—60	9	5	4	1	..	2	2	2	1	..	1
60—65	3	1	2	..	..	..	2	1	..	..	..
65—70	1		1	..	..	..	..	..	1	..	..
70 and over	11	6	5	1	..	1	..	4	5	..	

United Provinces States.

Age.	Persons.	Males.	Females.	Insane Males.	Insane Females.	Deaf-Mutes Males.	Deaf-Mutes Females.	Blind Males.	Blind Females.	Lepers Males.	Lepers Females.
Total	**3,675**	**1,918**	**1,757**	**204**	**118**	**271**	**157**	**1,222**	**1,419**	**235**	**69**
0—1	14	8	6	..	..	1	2	7	4	..	..
1—2	16	8	8	1	1	..	..	7	7	..	..
2—3	23	9	14	2	2	1	4	6	8	..	..
3—4	25	16	9	2	1	3	3	11	5	..	..
4—5	29	16	13	3	2	5	4	9	7	..	..
Total 0—5	*107*	*57*	*50*	*8*	*6*	*10*	*13*	*40*	*31*	..	..
5—10	197	124	73	20	12	37	21	68	41	1	..
10—15	212	134	78	20	15	39	17	73	45	4	2
15—20	198	117	81	21	16	27	17	65	47	7	1
20—25	211	135	76	22	16	23	16	79	42	12	2
25—30	215	128	87	25	12	27	13	65	56	11	6
30—35	208	123	85	28	8	27	12	53	60	15	5
35—40	225	128	97	17	10	18	13	66	68	29	7
40—45	219	116	103	10	10	16	9	62	76	29	8
45—50	254	141	113	12	2	18	7	79	95	32	9
50—55	259	148	111	11	2	14	4	90	97	33	9
55—60	298	134	164	4	5	4	5	98	144	28	10
60—65	317	126	191	4	2	4	5	101	177	18	7
65—70	273	110	163	1	1	3	2	101	158	5	2
70 and over	482	197	285	1	1	4	3	182	282	11	1

Western India States Agency.

Age.	Persons.	Males.	Females.	Insane Males.	Insane Females.	Deaf-Mutes Males.	Deaf-Mutes Females.	Blind Males.	Blind Females.	Lepers Males.	Lepers Females.
Total	**21,401**	**9,618**	**11,783**	**1,202**	**616**	**2,041**	**1,585**	**6,266**	**9,543**	**109**	**39**
0—1	24	13	11	..	..	1	3	12	8	..	..
1—2	41	14	27	..	1	2	4	12	22	..	..
2—3	79	38	41	4	5	8	4	26	32	..	..
3—4	126	68	58	5	6	22	19	41	33	..	..
4—5	205	117	88	8	9	50	32	59	47	..	..
Total 0—5	*475*	*250*	*225*	*17*	*21*	*83*	*62*	*150*	*142*	..	..
5—10	829	492	337	69	35	170	119	251	180	2	3
10—15	920	550	370	98	54	190	126	258	190	4	..
15—20	924	552	372	139	74	182	98	226	197	5	3
20—25	986	594	392	163	59	179	118	247	213	5	2
25—30	978	530	448	138	54	149	111	236	280	7	3
30—35	1,097	558	539	136	43	145	112	263	381	14	3
35—40	1,326	588	738	124	56	132	124	315	552	17	6
40—45	1,388	605	783	95	60	127	115	368	605	15	3
45—50	1,617	693	924	72	48	124	112	487	758	10	6
50—55	1,729	711	1,018	52	33	124	109	524	874	11	2
55—60	2,305	890	1,415	39	36	133	104	708	1,273	10	2
60—65	2,359	910	1,449	34	20	124	86	749	1,340	3	3
65—70	1,535	601	934	16	10	73	57	508	866	4	1
70 and over	2,933	1,094	1,839	10	13	106	132	976	1,692	2	2

Particulars of persons suffering from more than one infirmity.

Province or State.	Sex.	Insane and deaf-mute.	Insane and blind.	Insane and leper.	Deaf-mute and blind.	Deaf-mute and leper.	Blind and leper.	Insane, deaf-mute and blind.	Insane, blind and leper.	Blind, deaf-mute and leper.	Insane, deaf-mute and leper.	Insane, blind, deaf-mute and leper.
Total	**Males**	**1,445**	**215**	**76**	**611**	**133**	**304**	**46**	**3**	**5**	**6**	**3**
	Females	**891**	**186**	**33**	**461**	**103**	**147**	**23**	**1**	**4**	**3**	**2**
Assam	Males	80	5	2	11	9	21	..	..	..	..	..
	Females	83	14	..	9	2	8	..		..	..	..
Baluchistan	Males	1	2	..	..	..	..	..	..	..	..	..
	Females	1	..	..	1	..	..	..	..	..	..	..
Bengal	Males	545	49	25	109	27	63	9	..	4	3	..
	Females	317	28	6	70	8	22	3	..	1	2	..
Bihar and Orissa	Males	142	21	12	73	22	48	..	1	..	..	1
	Females	57	13	3	58	21	21	..	..	1	..	..
Burma	Males	150	17	3	68	7	8	2	..	..	..	..
	Females	106	6	1	74	5	8	1	..	..	..	..
Central Provinces and Berar.	Males	86	12	6	74	17	43	2	..	..	..	..
	Females	65	18	4	77	7	43	..	..	..	..	..
Coorg	Males	1	..	..	..	..	..	..	..	..	..	..
	Females	..	..	..	..	..	..	..	..	..	..	..
Delhi	Males	..	..	..	2	..	..	..	..	..	..	..
	Females	1	..	..	1	..	..	..	..	..	..	..
Madras	Males	68	12	5	38	11	40	..	..	1	..	..
	Females	51	16	1	27	4	12	1	..	1	..	..
North-West Frontier Province.	Males	22	6	..	5	3	1	2	..	..	..	..
	Females	12	5	..	1	4	1	..	1	..	..	..
Punjab	Males	116	28	17	85	17	7	16	2	..	2	1
	Females	76	38	12	50	7	6	10	..	1	1	2
United Provinces	Males	116	33	2	72	1	43	10	..	..	..	1
	Females	51	19	1	44	1	7	6	..	..	..	..
Baroda State	Males	30	1	..	7	..	3	3	..	..	1	..
	Females	18	8	..	20	2	2	1	..	..	..	..
Central India Agency	Males	28	16	1	23	1	8	2	..	..	..	..
	Females	28	14	..	..	31	5	1	..	..	..	..
Jammu and Kashmir State.	Males	34	8	1	28	16	15	..	..	..	..	..
	Females	10	2	3	18	9	11	..	..	..	..	..
Cochin State.	Males	..	1	1	..	..	1	..	..	..	..	..
	Females	1	..	..	..	1	1	..	..	..	..	..
Travancore State	Males	4	..	1	8	1	..	..	..	..	..	..
	Females	2	1	..	4	..	..	..	..	..	..	..
Mysore State	Males	22	4	..	8	1	3	..	..	..	..	..
	Females	12	4	2	7	1	..	..	..	..	..	..

NOTE.—The figures in this statement include the States attached to each Province, but those for Madras exclude Cochin and Travancore; separate details for which have been given.

In the Bombay Presidency, inclusive of Aden, and the Western India States Agency, no record of dual infirmities was kept, while in the Provinces and States not shown in the above list no instances of double infirmities were returned.

TABLE X.

Occupation or Means of Livelihood.

The general scheme of classification in this table follows that of Table XVII of the 1921 Census, but a few minor alterations, involving an increase by four in the number of occupational groups, have been carried out where the classification appeared incomplete or defective. The details and effect of these changes will be found in Chapter VIII of the Report Volume.

2. The table is divided into three parts. Part I contains a general summary by occupation for India, for British Territory and for States and Agencies; Part II gives the distribution in detail for the total enumerated population of each Province and State. The estimated population referred to on the fly-leaf to Table I of Ahmadabad in the Bombay Presidency of East Manglun in Burma and of the Agencies and Tribal Areas in the North-West Frontier Province has been omitted from both parts I and II of this table. Part III gives corresponding details for selected cities; in this part occupational groups with no entries against them have been omitted.

3. The treatment of dependants is not the same as in 1921. No attempt has been made to distribute persons wholly dependent according to their dependency on various occupational groups; but those dependants who by working full or part time help to augment the family income have been detailed according to the actual occupation by which their assistance is given. The system of classification followed was not entirely consistent in all States and Provinces, necessitating reclassification in some groups as a consequence of which discrepancies will be found between the figures in this table for groups 159 and 160 and those in the tables of Baroda, Cochin and Jammu and Kashmir States.

4. The figures under the columns for total following any occupation include persons following occupations as subsidiary to their principal occupation, so that the figures include as separate items a certain number of different occupations followed by single individuals to a maximum of two occupations per individual.

5. Persons undergoing sentence of rigorous imprisonment have been treated as working dependants wherever separate figures were available, and so entered against group 192; all other classes of prisoners have been entered in the principal occupation column against the same group, but have been excluded from the total for earners and included among non-working dependants in the heading to Part I of this table. This system was followed in the cases of Baluchistan, Bengal, Bihar and Orissa, the Central Provinces, Cochin, Delhi, Mysore, Travancore and the United Provinces. Elsewhere those undergoing simple have not been distinguished from those undergoing rigorous imprisonment.

6. The figures of 12,069 female earners, 2,364 female working dependants and 42 females following the occupation as subsidiary were shown in Bombay under group 17, Forest officers, rangers, guards, etc; as they relate to the Thana district where members of primitive tribes are numerous, they probably represent collectors of forest produce and have accordingly been reclassified for the India Table under group 19, leading to discrepancy between the India and the Bombay tables in the two groups mentioned.

Table X.—Occupation or Means of Liveli

India.

	Persons.	Males.	Females.
Total earners.	125,270,827*	97,415,536*	27,855,291*
Total working dependants.	28,615,063	7,644,575	20,070,488
Total non-working dependants.	196,643,667	75,560,501	121,083,166
Total population.	350,529,557	180,620,612	169,908,945

British

Total earners.
Total working dependants.
Total non-working dependants.
Total population.

Group Number.	Occupation.	India: Total following occupation.	India: As principal occupation. Males.	India: As principal occupation. Females.	India: As working dependants. Males.	India: As working dependants. Females.	India: As subsidiary to other occupation. Males.	India: As subsidiary to other occupation. Females.	British: Total following occupation	British: As principal occupation. Males.	British: As principal occupation. Females.
1	2	3	4	5	6	7	8	9	10	11	12
	Classes A, B, C and D.	168,830,114*	97,441,758*	27,859,229*	7,644,575	20,970,488	11,355,836	3,558,228	127,430,983*	76,080,280*	21,543,576*
	A.—PRODUCTION OF RAW MATERIALS.	111,164,586	68,892,510	18,629,322	5,808,075	10,310,532	6,328,003	1,196,139	83,858,169	54,271,385	14,486,989
	I.—EXPLOITATION OF ANIMALS AND VEGETATION.	110,760,324	68,644,794	18,552,896	5,796,208	10,300,541	6,281,157	1,184,728	83,548,715	54,076,988	14,425,084
	I. Pasture and Agriculture.	109,730,788	68,013,477	18,424,419	5,749,708	10,266,543	6,111,348	1,165,293	82,730,599	53,561,757	14,325,721
	(a) Cultivation ..	103,438,875	64,810,557	17,446,668	4,809,319	9,906,828	5,417,120	1,048,383	78,545,253	51,336,797	13,606,632
1	Non-cultivating proprietors taking rent in money or kind.	4,150,758	2,269,662	707,610	150,155	129,964	810,935	82,432	3,129,691	1,738,955	534,553
2	Estate Agents and Managers of owners.	69,833	54,199	7,312	1,952	377	5,881	112	37,330	27,616	5,759
3	Estate Agents and Managers of Government.	10,614	7,021	1,800	1,049	68	623	53	4,856	2,736	1,771
4	Rent Collectors, clerks, etc.	189,003	145,527	2,784	3,557	1,613	35,231	291	166,984	130,099	2,644
5	Cultivating owners ..	28,397,214	21,315,383	2,303,527	1,153,760	2,233,430	1,225,333	165,781	20,700,003	16,467,593	1,695,574
6	Tenant cultivators ..	36,238,654	25,564,656	4,276,698	1,331,493	3,001,057	1,747,539	317,211	28,539,412	20,069,519	3,443,784
7	Agricultural labourers ..	33,523,423	14,990,473	9,934,884	2,119,993	4,434,869	1,568,124	475,080	25,190,964	12,477,125	7,716,573
8	Cultivators of jhum, taungya and shifting areas.	859,376	463,636	212,053	47,360	105,450	23,454	7,423	776,013	423,154	205,974
	(b) Cultivation of special crops, fruit, etc. (Planters, managers, clerks and labourers).	1,907,126	960,151	599,113	43,780	55,174	209,896	39,012	1,421,463	738,521	488,568
9	Cinchona	2,227	1,180	956	42	1	48	..	2,227	1,180	956
10	Coconut	203,323	89,237	36,991	9,696	3,505	55,655	8,239	14,882	6,770	556
11	Coffee	55,163	33,657	17,139	571	676	2,615	505	23,220	14,297	6,534
12	Ganja	1,164	77	3	1	..	1,049	34	1,158	74	2
13	Pan-Vine	106,176	61,352	9,570	3,847	3,237	26,126	2,044	79,672	48,583	6,866
14	Rubber	19,008	14,933	2,910	323	263	556	23	10,041	7,715	1,634
15	Tea	1,069,250	548,639	449,265	6,812	15,616	38,121	10,797	994,368	507,032	416,510
16	Market gardeners, flower and fruit growers.	450,815	211,076	82,279	22,488	31,876	85,726	17,370	295,895	152,870	55,510
	(c) Forestry	412,631	193,489	70,871	19,554	26,578	87,417	14,722	275,013	128,271	49,465
17	Forest officers, rangers, guards, etc.	47,626	40,168	897	972	315	5,143	131	33,693	28,240	840
18	Wood cutters and charcoal burners	240,668	118,124	27,767	14,497	12,765	60,220	7,295	154,355	77,346	16,091
19	Collectors of forest produce	120,437	34,003	41,432	3,715	13,246	20,940	7,101	85,566	22,426	32,080
20	Collectors of lac ..	3,900	1,194	775	370	252	1,114	195	1,399	259	454
	(d) Stock raising ..	3,911,335	2,039,979	303,649	875,280	275,993	356,977	59,457	2,474,128	1,354,800	179,297
21	Cattle and buffalo breeders and keepers.	1,078,468	513,581	82,193	308,498	70,537	90,949	12,710	734,803	344,564	46,145
22	Breeders of transport animals	43,249	32,641	758	3,870	341	5,549	90	23,461	20,002	392
23	Herdsmen, shepherds and breeders of other animals.	2,789,618	1,493,757	220,698	562,912	205,115	260,479	46,657	1,715,864	990,234	132,760
	(e) Raising of small animals and insects.	60,821	9,301	4,118	1,775	1,970	39,938	3,719	14,742	3,368	1,759
24	Birds, bees, etc. ..	7,350	3,737	657	809	789	1,152	206	3,295	1,519	311
25	Silkworms	19,017	2,389	1,968	480	825	12,585	770	3,288	359	858
26	Lac cultivation ..	34,454	3,175	1,493	486	356	26,201	2,743	8,159	1,490	590
	2. Fishing and Hunting ..	1,029,536	631,317	128,477	46,500	33,998	169,809	19,435	818,116	515,231	99,363
27	Fishing and Pearling ..	967,880	601,126	120,864	37,815	30,945	161,288	15,842	801,745	504,612	98,204
28	Hunting	61,656	30,191	7,613	8,685	3,053	8,521	3,593	16,371	10,619	1,159
	II.—EXPLOITATION OF MINERALS.	404,262	247,716	76,426	11,867	9,991	46,851	11,411	309,454	194,397	61,905
	3. Metallic Minerals ..	54,462	36,776	9,852	952	799	4,331	1,752	28,866	20,224	5,117
29	Gold	12,241	10,745	585	25	146	520	220	556	116	55
30	Iron	12,056	4,688	3,891	244	201	2,228	804	236	164	38
31	Lead, silver and zinc ..	9,312	8,464	322	61	104	349	12	9,210	8,418	301
32	Manganese	14,132	7,546	4,711	149	127	916	683	12,716	6,610	4,451
33	Tin and wolfram ..	4,967	4,007	145	419	209	177	10	4,940	3,984	141
34	Other metallic minerals ..	1,754	1,326	198	54	12	141	23	1,208	932	131
	4. Non-Metallic Minerals ..	349,800	210,940	66,574	10,915	9,192	42,520	9,659	280,588	174,173	56,788
35	Coal	204,852	120,369	45,453	4,505	4,504	23,853	6,168	176,923	109,134	41,612
36	Petroleum	28,002	26,613	500	321	110	443	15	27,996	26,607	500
37	Building materials (including stone, materials for cement manufacture and clays).	50,388	31,232	7,938	4,118	2,324	4,140	636	20,155	13,476	3,626
38	Mica	12,713	4,821	2,822	102	124	4,213	631	12,357	4,644	2,798
39	Precious and semi-precious stones.	7,515	4,581	646	679	670	923	16	7,241	4,411	570
40	Salt, saltpetre and other saline substances.	43,615	21,292	9,075	965	1,413	8,716	2,154	33,780	14,241	7,586
41	Other non-metallic minerals	2,715	2,032	140	225	47	232	39	2,136	1,660	96

* Includes 3,116 earners (2,521 males 595 female)

hood—Part I—General Table for India.

Territory. Persons.	Territory. Males.	Territory. Females.		States and Agencies. Persons.	States and Agencies. Males.	States and Agencies. Females.
97,598,132*	76,056,944*	21,541,188*	Total earners.	27,672,695	21,358,592	6,314,103
18,718,936	4,600,132	14,118,804	Total working dependants.	9,896,127	3,044,443	6,851,684
155,114,481	59,233,881	95,880,600	Total non-working dependants.	41,529,186	16,326,620	25,202,566
271,431,549	139,890,957	131,540,592	Total population.	79,098,008	40,729,655	38,368,353

As working dependants. Males.	As working dependants. Females.	As subsidiary to other occupation. Males.	As subsidiary to other occupation. Females.	Total following occupation.	As principal occupation. Males.	As principal occupation. Females.	As working dependants. Males.	As working dependants. Females.	As subsidiary to other occupation. Males.	As subsidiary to other occupation. Females.	Group Number.
13	14	15	16	17	18	19	20	21	22	23	24
4,600,132	**14,118,804**	**8,406,023**	**2,682,168**	**41,399,131**	**21,361,478**	**6,315,653**	**3,044,443**	**6,851,684**	**2,949,813**	**876,060**	
3,540,315	**6,152,044**	**4,604,423**	**803,013**	**27,306,417**	**14,621,125**	**4,142,333**	**2,267,760**	**4,158,488**	**1,723,585**	**393,126**	
3,536,879	**6,148,819**	**4,566,562**	**794,383**	**27,211,609**	**14,567,806**	**4,127,812**	**2,259,329**	**4,151,722**	**1,714,595**	**390,345**	
3,511,550	**6,127,350**	**4,420,954**	**783,267**	**27,000,189**	**14,451,720**	**4,098,698**	**2,238,158**	**4,139,193**	**1,690,394**	**382,026**	
2,924,541	**5,947,772**	**4,007,769**	**721,742**	**24,893,622**	**13,473,760**	**3,840,036**	**1,884,778**	**3,959,056**	**1,409,351**	**326,641**	
66,604	60,197	679,520	49,862	1,021,067	530,707	173,057	83,551	69,767	131,415	32,570	1
697	316	2,878	64	32,503	26,583	1,553	1,255	61	3,003	48	2
85	68	145	51	5,758	4,285	29	964	..	478	2	3
1,769	1,569	30,716	187	22,019	15,428	140	1,788	44	4,515	104	4
517,284	1,178,013	748,549	92,990	7,697,211	4,847,790	607,953	636,476	1,055,417	476,784	72,791	5
1,008,849	2,494,264	1,280,524	242,472	7,699,242	5,495,137	832,914	322,644	506,793	467,015	74,739	6
1,289,763	2,133,305	1,244,599	329,599	8,332,459	2,513,348	2,218,311	830,230	2,301,564	323,525	145,481	7
39,490	80,040	20,838	6,517	83,363	40,482	6,079	7,870	25,410	2,616	906	8
23,781	**36,090**	**112,032**	**22,471**	**485,663**	**221,630**	**110,545**	**19,999**	**19,084**	**97,864**	**16,541**	
42	1	48	..	..	..	..	..	..	..	..	9
3,418	2,925	1,018	195	188,441	82,467	36,435	6,278	580	54,637	8,044	10
453	364	1,342	230	31,943	19,360	10,605	118	312	1,273	275	11
1	..	1,049	32	6	3	1	..	..	..	2	12
1,757	2,059	19,116	1,291	26,504	12,769	2,704	2,090	1,178	7,010	753	13
226	183	271	12	8,967	7,218	1,276	97	80	285	11	14
6,706	15,502	37,892	10,726	74,882	41,607	32,755	106	114	229	71	15
11,178	15,056	51,296	9,985	154,920	58,206	26,769	11,310	16,820	34,430	7,385	16
10,251	**14,589**	**63,437**	**9,000**	**137,618**	**65,218**	**21,406**	**9,303**	**11,989**	**23,980**	**5,722**	
709	127	3,653	124	13,933	11,928	57	263	188	1,490	7	17
7,018	4,968	44,585	4,347	86,313	40,778	11,676	7,479	7,797	15,635	2,948	18
2,521	9,470	14,600	4,469	34,871	11,577	9,352	1,194	3,776	6,340	2,632	19
3	24	599	60	2,501	935	321	367	228	515	135	20
552,266	**128,133**	**230,513**	**29,119**	**1,437,207**	**685,179**	**124,352**	**323,014**	**147,860**	**126,464**	**30,338**	
243,057	37,069	57,379	6,589	343,665	169,017	36,048	65,441	33,468	33,570	6,121	21
967	111	1,939	50	19,788	12,639	366	2,903	230	3,610	40	22
308,242	90,953	171,195	22,480	1,073,754	503,523	87,938	254,570	114,162	89,284	24,177	23
711	**766**	**7,203**	**935**	**46,079**	**5,933**	**2,359**	**1,064**	**1,204**	**32,735**	**2,784**	
323	461	581	100	4,055	2,218	346	486	328	571	106	24
57	241	1,579	194	15,729	2,030	1,110	423	584	11,006	576	25
331	64	5,043	641	26,295	1,685	903	155	292	21,158	2,102	26
25,329	**21,469**	**145,608**	**11,116**	**211,420**	**116,086**	**29,114**	**21,171**	**12,529**	**24,201**	**8,319**	
24,596	21,136	142,226	10,971	166,135	96,514	22,660	13,219	9,809	19,062	4,871	27
733	333	3,382	145	45,285	19,572	6,454	7,952	2,720	5,139	3,448	28
8,436	**3,225**	**37,861**	**8,630**	**94,808**	**53,319**	**14,521**	**8,431**	**6,766**	**8,990**	**2,781**	
525	**419**	**1,687**	**894**	**25,596**	**16,552**	**4,735**	**427**	**380**	**2,644**	**858**	
4	37	174	170	11,685	10,629	530	21	109	346	50	29
10	..	13	11	11,820	4,524	3,853	234	201	2,215	793	30
45	96	338	12	102	46	21	16	8	11	..	31
40	75	871	669	1,416	936	260	109	52	45	14	32
419	209	177	10	27	23	4	..	..	..	..	33
7	2	114	22	546	394	67	47	10	27	1	34
2,911	**2,806**	**36,174**	**7,736**	**69,212**	**36,767**	**9,786**	**8,004**	**6,386**	**6,346**	**1,923**	
750	463	20,264	4,700	27,929	11,235	3,841	3,755	4,041	3,589	1,468	35
321	110	443	15	6	6	..	..	..	..	..	36
376	432	2,014	231	30,233	17,756	4,312	3,742	1,892	2,126	405	37
55	48	4,188	624	356	177	24	47	76	25	7	38
678	670	897	15	274	170	76	1	..	26	1	39
536	1,061	8,243	2,113	9,835	7,051	1,489	429	352	473	41	40
195	22	125	38	579	372	44	30	25	107	1	41

whose occupations were not returned.

Table X.— Occupation or Means of Liveli

Group Number.	Occupation.	India.									
		Total following occupation.	As principal occupation.		As working dependants.		As subsidiary to other occupation.		Total following occupation	As principal occupation.	
			Males.	Females.	Males.	Females.	Males.	Females.		Males.	Females.
1	2	3	4	5	6	7	8	9	10	11	12
	B.—PREPARATION AND SUPPLY OF MATERIAL SUBSTANCES.	**29,639,471**	**17,784,556**	**5,161,789**	**897,785**	**1,762,826**	**3,413,706**	**618,809**	**22,128,162**	**13,646,995**	**3,880,535**
	III.—INDUSTRY. ..	**17,523,982**	**10,289,607**	**3,263,788**	**507,920**	**1,290,638**	**1,825,355**	**346,674**	**13,282,292**	**7,949,501**	**2,504,110**
	5. Textiles	**4,511,520**	**2,408,391**	**853,248**	**123,020**	**717,477**	**277,561**	**131,823**	**3,399,104**	**1,902,214**	**602,613**
42	Cotton ginning, cleaning and pressing.	282,847	185,253	48,831	10,713	12,408	21,844	3,798	214,321	147,987	34,887
43	Cotton spinning, sizing and weaving.	3,173,906	1,678,453	540,297	82,814	582,009	189,205	101,128	2,466,635	1,329,239	399,052
44	Jute pressing, spinning and weaving.	283,372	235,308	35,407	496	1,242	9,488	1,431	282,204	234,735	35,226
45	Rope, twine, string and other fibres	375,966	107,881	142,244	14,115	65,594	30,526	15,606	175,376	52,932	75,202
46	Wool carding, spining and weaving	128,608	57,926	28,767	6,008	16,646	16,111	3,150	69,307	33,313	19,328
47	Silk spinning and weaving ..	123,536	53,148	28,175	3,875	29,323	3,661	5,354	108,370	46,776	24,784
48	Hair (horse-hair) etc.	1,832	714	193	33	580	236	76	1,094	364	46
49	Dying, bleaching, printing, preparation and sponging of textiles.	109,699	73,798	19,366	3,983	6,623	5,238	691	64,315	46,559	9,819
50	Lace, crepe, embroideries, fringes, etc., and insufficiently described textile industries.	31,754	15,910	9,968	983	3,052	1,252	589	17,482	10,309	4,269
	6. Hides, skins and hard materials from the animal kingdom.	**359,863**	**250,911**	**32,998**	**14,993**	**13,172**	**43,329**	**4,460**	**235,111**	**168,212**	**22,188**
51	Working in leather	347,928	241,908	31,488	14,607	12,941	42,566	4,418	225,671	161,055	20,845
52	Furriers and persons occupied with feathers and bristles, brush makers.	1,372	1,011	179	61	60	54	7	1,002	745	163
53	Bone, ivory, horn, shell, etc., workers (except buttons).	10,563	7,992	1,331	325	171	709	35	8,438	6.412	1,180
	7. Wood	**1,972,565**	**1,231,128**	**264,616**	**58,291**	**77,688**	**299,201**	**41,641**	**1,476,781**	**941,512**	**187,110**
54	Sawyers	112,678	83,138	1,957	2,942	546	23,914	181	81,689	58,523	1,677
55	Carpenters, turners and joiners, etc.	1,081,755	847,241	16,503	34,345	6,876	173,898	2,892	829,451	656,216	11,095
56	Basket makers and other industries of woody materials, including leaves, and thatchers and builders working with bamboo, reeds, or similar materials.	778,132	300,749	246,156	21,004	70,266	101,389	38,568	565,641	226,773	174,338
	8. Metals	**845,420**	**628,169**	**37,787**	**31,466**	**15,648**	**126,696**	**5,654**	**630,012**	**481,497**	**22,276**
57	Smelting, forging and rolling of iron and other metals.	33,486	28,465	3,588	250	194	750	239	30,252	26,106	3,501
58	Makers of arms, guns, etc. ..	6,278	5,016	231	192	50	766	23	4,728	3,768	144
59	Blacksmiths, other workers in iron, makers of implements.	657,249	474,194	25,504	24,887	13,156	115,012	4,496	493,888	363,865	14,508
60	Workers in brass, copper and bell metal.	106,246	83,946	7,014	4,575	1,924	8,005	782	67,773	57,883	3,015
61	Workers in other metals (except precious metals).	39,200	34,058	1,262	1,432	260	2,078	110	30,965	27,819	948
62	Workers in mints, die-sinkers, etc.	2,961	2,490	188	130	64	85	4	2,406	2,056	160
	9. Ceramics	**1,196,437**	**692,698**	**225,038**	**34,861**	**72,233**	**150,291**	**21,316**	**882,103**	**521,311**	**165,696**
63	Potters and makers of earthenware	1,021,378	569,061	200,233	31,567	68,362	132,690	19,465	732,881	414,832	144,254
64	Brick and tile makers	133,689	97,019	16,988	2,651	2,866	12,757	1,408	110,873	81,788	14,089
65	Other workers in Ceramics ..	41,370	26,618	7,817	643	1,005	4,844	443	38,349	24,691	7,358
	10. Chemical products properly so called and analogous.	**735,207**	**384,467**	**167,123**	**16,318**	**35,396**	**114,398**	**17,505**	**596,973**	**311,805**	**141,629**
66	Manufacture of matches, fireworks and other explosives.	18,436	12,808	3,509	377	657	1,006	79	13,283	9,499	2,795
67	Manufacture of aerated and mineral waters and ice.	8,804	7,646	520	213	58	346	21	6,886	6,125	407
68	Manufacture and refining of vegetable oils.	674,951	340,252	158,912	15,236	33,629	109,901	17,021	548,085	274,826	135,451
69	Manufacture and refining of mineral oils.	12,198	10,607	869	85	322	253	62	11,654	10,164	840
70	Others	20,818	13,154	3,313	407	730	2,892	322	17,065	11,191	2,136
	11. Food Industries	**1,665,447**	**678,643**	**671,515**	**27,638**	**99,199**	**136,724**	**51,728**	**1,407,816**	**568,538**	**582,384**
71	Rice pounders and huskers and flour grinders.	600,120	99,854	407,011	2,822	46,777	15,257	28,399	521,673	89,770	355,780
72	Grain parchers, etc.	328,796	100,872	154,926	3,858	20,365	34,440	14,335	287,426	90,382	134,430
73	Butchers	117,058	95,837	7,756	3,402	1,546	7,820	697	92,108	77,421	5,758
74	Makers of sugar, molasses and gur	51,495	19,061	13,577	376	8,035	8,244	2,202	44,422	17,148	12,017
75	Sweetmeat and condiment makers	125,017	84,693	23,026	2,734	3,526	9,741	1,297	92,259	65,292	14,163
76	Toddy drawers	237,914	167,308	8,557	8,525	2,525	49,969	1,030	192,645	134,055	7,858
77	Brewers and distillers ..	6,562	3,555	1,344	665	389	484	125	1,790	884	639
78	Manufacturers of Tobacco ..	147,197	74,507	44,995	4,187	12,723	7,763	3,022	130,390	64,876	42,081
79	Manufacturers of Opium ..	273	186	32	5	17	29	4	127	82	12
80	Manufacturers of Ganja ..	331	222	63	24	1	21	..	171	113	46
81	Others	50,684	32,548	10,228	1,040	3,295	2,956	617	44,805	28,515	9,600
	12. Industries of dress and the toilet.	**3,915,956**	**2,426,264**	**635,081**	**139,330**	**180,149**	**480,736**	**54,396**	**2,905,241**	**1,836,487**	**496,770**
82	Boot, shoe, sandal and clog makers	852,317	622,848	49,736	35,147	32,456	105,311	6,819	562,482	438,017	29,082
83	Tailors, milliners, dress makers and darners.	718,754	470,883	113,083	22,233	42,165	59,143	11,247	515,170	346,169	82,683
84	Embroiderers, hat makers and makers of other articles of wear.	28,236	15,089	6,267	795	3,322	2,184	579	20,470	11,644	4,443
85	Washing and cleaning	1,262,662	587,223	372,057	50,636	84,412	139,498	28,836	989,343	477,163	300,824
86	Barbers, hair dressers and wigmakers.	1,026,571	715,146	85,542	30,184	16,349	173,208	6,142	804,207	556,080	75,412
87	Other industries connected with the toilet.	27,416	15,075	8,396	335	1,445	1,392	773	13,569	7,414	4,326

hood—Part I—General Table for India—*contd.*

British Territory.				States and Agencies.							
As working dependants.		As subsidiary to other occupation.		Total following occupation.	As principal occupation.		As working dependants.		As subsidiary to other occupation.		Group Number.
Males.	Females.	Males.	Females.		Males.	Females.	Males.	Females.	Males.	Females.	
13	14	15	16	17	18	19	20	21	22	23	24
430,477	1,144,710	2,602,488	422,957	7,511,309	4,137,561	1,281,254	467,308	618,116	811,218	195,852	
276,650	904,757	1,396,481	250,793	4,241,690	2,340,106	759,678	231,270	385,881	428,874	95,881	
64,262	543,893	186,001	100,121	1,112,416	506,177	250,635	58,758	173,584	91,560	31,702	
6,620	7,161	15,513	2,153	68,526	37,266	13,944	4,093	5,247	6,331	1,645	42
47,950	477,943	129,438	83,013	707,271	349,214	141,245	34,864	104,066	59,767	18,115	43
473	1,164	9,204	1,402	1,168	573	181	23	78	284	29	44
2,924	19,096	18,554	6,668	200,590	54,949	67,042	11,191	46,498	11,972	8,938	45
1,519	6,937	7,100	1,110	59,301	24,613	9,439	4,489	9,709	9,011	2,040	46
2,860	26,843	2,113	4,994	15,166	6,372	3,391	1,015	2,480	1,548	360	47
1	539	84	60	738	350	147	32	41	152	16	48
1,314	3,010	3,212	401	45,384	27,239	9,547	2,669	3,613	2,026	290	49
601	1,200	783	320	14,272	5,601	5,699	382	1,852	469	269	50
8,472	5,496	27,414	3,329	124,752	82,699	10,810	6,521	7,676	15,915	1,131	
8,323	5,396	26,765	3,287	122,257	80,853	10,643	6,284	7,545	15,801	1,131	51
13	33	41	7	370	266	16	48	27	13	..	52
136	67	608	35	2,125	1,580	151	189	104	101	..	53
35,543	48,684	237,622	26,310	495,784	289,616	77,506	22,748	29,004	61,579	15,331	
1,551	270	19,566	102	30,989	24,615	280	1,391	276	4,348	79	54
20,208	2,799	138,050	1,083	252,304	191,025	5,408	14,137	4,077	35,848	1,809	55
13,784	45,615	80,006	25,125	212,491	73,976	71,818	7,220	24,651	21,383	13,443	56
15,695	6,952	100,623	2,969	215,408	146,672	15,511	15,771	8,696	26,073	2,685	
84	80	251	230	3,234	2,359	87	166	114	499	9	57
122	29	646	19	1,550	1,248	87	70	21	120	4	58
13,502	6,231	93,236	2,546	163,361	110,329	10,996	11,385	6,925	21,776	1,950	59
1,433	451	4,883	108	38,473	26,063	3,999	3,142	1,473	3,122	674	60
463	99	1,573	63	8,235	6,239	314	969	161	505	47	61
91	62	34	3	555	434	28	39	2	51	1	62
20,203	40,059	119,501	15,333	314,334	171,387	59,342	14,658	32,174	30,790	5,983	
17,967	37,796	104,209	13,823	288,497	154,229	55,979	13,600	30,566	28,481	5,642	63
1,801	1,432	10,641	1,122	22,816	15,231	2,899	850	1,434	2,116	286	64
435	831	4,651	388	3,021	1,927	464	208	174	193	55	65
10,081	24,421	94,962	14,125	138,234	72,662	25,494	6,287	10,975	19,436	3,380	
139	342	473	35	5,153	3,309	714	238	315	533	44	66
61	9	282	2	1,918	1,521	113	152	49	64	19	67
9,570	23,258	91,234	13,746	126,866	65,426	23,461	5,666	10,371	18,667	3,275	68
63	295	238	54	544	443	29	22	27	15	8	69
198	517	2,735	288	3,753	1,963	1,177	209	213	157	34	70
18,195	78,894	117,222	42,583	257,631	110,105	89,131	9,443	20,305	19,502	9,145	
2,341	38,447	13,145	22,190	78,447	10,084	51,231	481	8,330	2,112	6,209	71
3,494	15,962	30,347	12,811	41,370	10,490	20,496	364	4,403	4,093	1,524	72
1,652	757	6,041	479	24,950	18,416	1,998	1,750	789	1,779	218	73
302	4,932	7,901	2,122	7,073	1,913	1,560	74	3,103	343	80	74
1,515	2,571	7,847	871	32,758	19,401	8,863	1,219	955	1,894	426	75
5,183	1,713	42,973	863	45,269	33,253	699	3,342	812	6,996	167	76
26	89	96	56	4,772	2,671	705	639	300	388	69	77
2,909	11,556	6,314	2,654	16,807	9,631	2,914	1,278	1,167	1,449	368	78
1	1	27	4	146	104	20	4	16	2	..	79
8	..	4	..	160	109	17	16	1	17	..	80
764	2,866	2,527	533	5,879	4,033	628	276	429	429	84	81
67,814	104,553	364,049	35,568	1,010,715	589,777	138,311	71,516	75,596	116,687	18,828	
17,432	13,751	61,924	2,276	289,835	184,831	20,654	17,715	18,705	43,387	4,543	82
10,704	24,610	43,975	7,029	203,584	124,714	30,400	11,529	17,535	15,168	4,218	83
369	1,609	1,990	415	7,766	3,445	1,824	426	1,713	194	161	84
21,802	54,119	114,015	21,420	273,319	110,060	71,233	28,834	30,293	23,483	7,416	85
17,387	9,888	141,400	4,040	222,364	159,066	10,130	12,797	6,461	31,808	2,102	86
120	576	745	388	13,847	7,661	4,070	215	869	647	385	87

Table X.—Occupation or Means of Liveli[hood]

Group Number.	Occupation.	India. Total following occupation.	As principal occupation. Males.	As principal occupation. Females.	As working dependants. Males.	As working dependants. Females.	As subsidiary to other occupation. Males.	As subsidiary to other occupation. Females.	British Total following occupation.	As principal occupation. Males.	As principal occupation. Females.
1	2	3	4	5	6	7	8	9	10	11	12
	B.—PREPARATION AND SUPPLY OF MATERIAL SUBSTANCES—contd.										
	III.—INDUSTRY—concld.										
	13. Furniture Industries ..	**23,895**	**16,545**	**3,171**	**435**	**858**	**2,498**	**388**	**19,723**	**13,409**	**2,833**
88	Cabinet makers, carriage painters, etc.	18,461	14,027	1,884	367	554	1,335	294	15,215	11,406	1,773
89	Upholsterers, tent-makers, etc. ..	5,434	2,518	1,287	68	304	1,163	94	4,508	2,003	1,060
	14. Building Industries ..	**692,932**	**511,640**	**74,614**	**16,704**	**15,569**	**68,146**	**6,259**	**470,746**	**362,748**	**44,836**
90	Lime burners, cement workers, excavators and well sinkers, stone cutters and dressers; Brick layers and masons; Builders, (other than buildings made of bamboo or similar materials), painters, decorators of houses, tilers, plumbers, etc.	692,932	511,640	74,614	16,704	15,569	68,146	6,259	470,746	362,748	44,336
	15. Construction of means of transport.	**33,302**	**27,432**	**467**	**1,167**	**99**	**4,099**	**38**	**25,583**	**21,787**	**879**
91	Persons engaged in making, assembling or repairing motor vehicles or cycles.	14,172	12,806	190	358	16	801	1	11,607	10,696	174
92	Carriage, cart, palki, etc. makers, and wheelwrights.	8,888	6,492	154	623	55	1,537	27	4,601	3,616	96
93	Ship, boat, aeroplane builders ..	10,242	8,134	123	186	28	1,761	10	9,375	7,475	109
	16. Production and transmission of physical force.	**24,907**	**21,232**	**2,221**	**171**	**26**	**1,233**	**24**	**18,869**	**16,280**	**2,197**
94	Heat, light, electricity, motive power, etc., Gas works and electric light and power. ..	24,907	21,232	2,221	171	26	1,233	24	18,869	16,280	2,197
	17. Miscellaneous and undefined Industries.	**1,546,531**	**1,012,087**	**295,909**	**43,526**	**63,124**	**120,443**	**11,442**	**1,214,230**	**803,701**	**233,699**
95	Printers, engravers, book binders, etc.	52,805	50,368	598	719	89	993	38	[illegible]	43,132	487
96	Makers of musical instruments ..	8,798	6,979	385	371	115	931	17	6,348	5,303	153
97	Makers of clocks and surgical or scientific instruments, etc.	9,430	8,704	65	142	17	501	1	7,457	6,970	59
98	Makers of jewellery and ornaments.	690,258	542,650	20,549	23,133	9,691	90,602	3,633	524,832	420,837	10,686
99	Other miscellaneous and undefined industries (toy making, taxidermy, etc.).	53,551	33,686	10,574	1,166	2,624	4,388	1,113	38,141	25,360	6,937
.00	Scavenging	731,689	369,700	263,738	17,995	50,588	23,028	6,640	592,817	302,099	215,377
	IV.—TRANSPORT.	**2,778,520**	**1,991,686**	**171,184**	**107,512**	**71,024**	**403,499**	**33,615**	**2,055,195**	**1,577,984**	**99,309**
	18. Transport by air	**330**	**295**	**11**	..	..	**24**	..	**309**	**275**	**11**
.01	Persons concerned with aerodromes and aeroplanes.	330	295	11	..	..	24	..	309	275	11
	19. Transport by water ..	**401,237**	**338,081**	**10,398**	**10,614**	**2,881**	**38,230**	**1,033**	**338,754**	**291,272**	**8,628**
102	Ship owners, boat-owners and their employees, officers, mariners, etc. Ships brokers, boatmen and towmen.	306,254	261,696	3,204	6,343	692	34,022	297	267,374	229,895	2,752
103	Persons (other than labourers) employed in harbours, docks, rivers and canals, including pilots.	35,720	33,217	749	664	59	1,023	8	28,928	27,078	624
104	Labourers employed on harbours, docks, rivers and canals.	59,263	43,168	6,445	3,607	2,130	3,185	728	42,452	34,299	5,252
	20. Transport by road ..	**1,610,809**	**1,008,431**	**132,443**	**74,649**	**43,904**	**331,945**	**19,437**	**1,164,233**	**771,004**	**78,680**
105	Persons (other than labourers) employed on the construction and maintenance of roads and bridges.	21,963	18,796	694	588	106	1,695	84	16,118	14,034	456
106	Labourers employed on roads and bridges.	498,460	249,270	103,489	36,363	34,850	59,334	15,154	282,514	160,017	59,524
107	Owners, managers and employees (excluding personal servants) connected with mechanically driven vehicles (including trams).	88,822	80,643	998	1,538	646	4,741	256	72,628	67,858	358
108	Owners, managers and employees (excluding personal servants) connected with other vehicles.	606,594	372,382	6,564	23,013	3,222	199,308	2,105	479,267	294,932	3,564
109	Palki, etc. bearers and owners ..	80,805	52,951	1,927	1,878	746	22,836	467	70,291	46,001	1,640
110	Pack elephant, camel, mule, ass and bullock owners and drivers.	149,921	105,381	3,890	6,947	2,031	30,861	811	107,206	79,408	1,617
111	Porters and messengers ..	164,244	129,008	14,881	4,322	2,303	13,170	560	136,209	108,754	11,521
	21. Transport by rail	**676,889**	**563,859**	**27,624**	**20,517**	**24,131**	**27,719**	**13,039**	**481,181**	**450,435**	**11,358**
112	Railway employees of all kinds other than porters and coolies.	361,377	342,219	4,181	3,210	696	10,950	121	301,274	287,595	3,622
113	Labourers employed on railway construction and maintenance and coolies and porters employed on railway premises.	315,512	221,640	23,443	17,307	23,435	16,769	12,918	179,907	162,840	7,736
	22. Post Office, Telegraph and Telephone services.	**89,255**	**81,020**	**708**	**1,732**	**108**	**5,581**	**106**	**70,718**	**64,998**	**632**
114	Post Office, Telegraph and Telephone services.	89,255	81,020	708	1,732	108	5,581	106	70,718	64,998	632

hood—Part I—General Table for India—*contd.*

Territory.				States and Agencies.							
As working dependants.		As subsidiary to other occupation.		Total following occupation.	As principal occupation.		As working dependants.		As subsidiary to other occupation.		Group Number.
Males.	Females.	Males.	Females.		Males.	Females.	Males.	Females.	Males.	Females.	
13	14	15	16	17	18	19	20	21	22	23	24
274	607	2,255	345	4,172	3,136	338	161	251	243	43	
225	389	1,143	279	3,246	2,621	111	142	165	192	15	88
49	218	1,112	66	926	515	227	19	86	51	28	89
8,140	7,483	44,981	3,058	222,186	148,892	30,278	8,564	8,086	23,165	3,201	
8,140	7,483	44,981	3,058	222,186	148,892	30,278	8,564	8,086	23,165	3,201	90
355	44	3,001	17	7,719	5,645	88	812	55	1,098	21	
147	5	585	..	2,565	2,110	16	211	11	216	1	91
93	16	772	8	4,287	2,876	58	530	39	765	19	92
115	23	1,644	9	867	659	14	71	5	117	1	93
68	23	280	21	6,038	4,952	24	103	3	953	3	
68	23	280	21	6,038	4,952	24	103	3	953	3	94
27,598	43,648	98,570	7,014	332,301	208,386	62,210	15,928	19,476	21,873	4,428	
342	50	604	20	8,170	7,236	111	377	39	389	18	95
223	59	598	12	2,450	1,676	232	148	56	333	5	96
41	17	369	1	1,973	1,734	6	101	..	132	..	97
12,898	4,457	75,053	901	165,426	121,813	9,863	10,235	5,234	15,549	2,732	98
682	1,122	3,356	684	15,410	8,326	3,637	484	1,502	1,032	429	99
13,412	37,943	18,590	5,396	138,872	67,601	48,361	4,583	12,645	4,438	1,244	100
35,817	11,303	319,951	10,831	723,325	413,702	71,875	71,695	59,721	83,548	22,784	
..	..	23	..	21	20	..	..	..	1	..	
..	..	23	..	21	20	..	..	..	1	..	101
5,949	1,528	30,954	423	62,483	46,809	1,770	4,665	1,353	7,276	610	
4,891	423	29,178	235	38,880	31,801	452	1,452	269	4,844	62	102
558	31	631	6	6,792	6,139	125	106	28	392	2	103
500	1,074	1,145	182	16,811	8,869	1,193	3,107	1,056	2,040	546	104
27,003	9,047	268,550	9,949	446,576	237,427	53,763	47,646	34,357	63,395	9,488	
229	62	1,261	76	5,845	4,762	238	359	44	434	8	105
4,543	5,151	45,972	7,307	215,946	89,253	43,965	31,820	29,699	13,362	7,847	106
954	48	3,322	88	16,194	12,785	640	584	598	1,419	168	107
13,597	1,147	164,484	1,543	127,327	77,450	3,000	9,416	2,075	34,824	562	108
479	330	21,648	193	10,514	6,950	287	1,399	416	1,188	274	109
4,393	803	20,732	253	42,715	25,973	2,273	2,554	1,228	10,129	558	110
2,808	1,506	11,131	489	28,035	20,254	3,360	1,514	797	2,039	71	111
2,261	659	16,114	354	195,708	113,424	16,266	18,256	23,472	11,605	12,685	
1,063	223	8,720	51	60,103	54,624	559	2,147	473	2,230	70	112
1,198	436	7,394	303	135,605	58,800	15,707	16,109	22,999	9,375	12,615	113
604	69	4,310	105	18,537	16,022	76	1,128	39	1,271	1	
604	69	4,310	105	18,537	16,022	76	1,128	39	1,271	1	114

Table X.—Occupation or Means of Liveli

Group Number.	Occupation.	India. Total following occupation.	India. As principal occupation. Males.	India. As principal occupation. Females.	India. As working dependants. Males.	India. As working dependants. Females.	India. As subsidiary to other occupation. Males.	India. As subsidiary to other occupation. Females.	British. Total following ocupation.	British. As principal occupation. Males.	British. As principal occupation. Females.
1	2	3	4	5	6	7	8	9	10	11	12
	B.—PREPARATION AND SUPPLY OF MATERIAL SUBSTANCES—contd.										
	V. TRADE	**9,336,969**	**5,503,263**	**1,726,817**	**282,353**	**401,164**	**1,184,852**	**238,520**	**6,790,675**	**4,119,510**	**1,277,116**
	23. Banks, establishments of credit, exchange and insurance.	**482,850**	**279,492**	**33,235**	**13,247**	**3,508**	**145,462**	**7,906**	**331,512**	**187,180**	**22,090**
115	Bank managers, money lenders, exchange and insurance agents, money changers and brokers and their employees.	482,850	279,492	33,235	13,247	3,508	145,462	7,906	331,512	187,180	22,090
	24. Brokerage Commission and export.	**71,194**	**61,308**	**1,099**	**1,136**	**405**	**7,121**	**125**	**56,054**	**48,871**	**868**
116	Brokers, Commission Agents, commercial travellers, Warehouse owners and employees.	71,194	61,308	1,099	1,136	405	7,121	125	56,054	48,871	868
	25. Trade in textiles	**526,690**	**390,616**	**35,229**	**20,699**	**12,358**	**63,863**	**3,925**	**390,057**	**298,299**	**25,382**
117	Trade in piece-goods, wool, cotton, silk, hair and other textiles.	526,690	390,616	35,229	20,699	12,358	63,863	3,925	390,057	298,299	25,382
	26. Trade in skins, leather and furs	**102,386**	**77,690**	**5,437**	**3,514**	**2,157**	**12,810**	**778**	**80,372**	**64,054**	**3,452**
118	Trade in skins, leather, furs, feathers, horn, etc., and in the articles made from these.	102,386	77,690	5,437	3,514	2,157	12,810	778	80,372	64,054	3,452
	27. Trade in wood	**197,302**	**88,942**	**35,754**	**5,116**	**9,442**	**40,576**	**17,472**	**157,630**	**67,158**	**28,585**
119	Trade in wood (not firewood) ..	122,646	60,771	19,638	3,125	3,057	23,001	13,054	100,595	46,368	16,845
120	Trade in barks	4,350	2,605	710	141	356	420	118	2,042	1,427	218
121	Trade in bamboos and canes ..	45,959	19,054	8,611	1,242	3,078	12,654	1,320	36,906	14,901	6,566
122	Trade in thatches and other forest produce.	24,347	6,512	6,795	608	2,951	4,501	2,980	18,087	4,462	4,956
	28. Trade in metals	**29,702**	**23,145**	**2,069**	**958**	**1,032**	**2,308**	**190**	**20,208**	**16,717**	**1,258**
123	Trade in metals, machinery, knives, fools, etc.	29,702	23,145	2,069	958	1,032	2,308	190	20,208	16,717	1,258
	29. Trade in pottery, bricks and tiles.	**53,539**	**24,043**	**13,116**	**2,069**	**7,260**	**4,869**	**2,182**	**31,701**	**17,550**	**6,881**
124	Trade in pottery, bricks and tiles.	53,539	24,043	13,116	2,069	7,260	4,869	2,182	31,701	17,550	6,881
	30. Trade in Chemical products ..	**74,655**	**45,474**	**13,410**	**1,043**	**2,737**	**9,807**	**2,184**	**63,994**	**38,705**	**11,905**
125	Drugs, dyes, paints, petroleum, .. explosives, etc.	74,655	45,474	13,410	1,043	2,737	9,807	2,184	63,994	38,705	11,905
	31. Hotels, cafes, restaurants, etc.	**547,226**	**308,715**	**116,867**	**26,923**	**37,312**	**41,864**	**15,545**	**285,093**	**186,170**	**59,244**
126	Vendors of wine, liquors, aerated waters and ice.	298,291	144,533	65,840	21,728	23,394	31,001	11,795	74,594	48,502	14,588
127	Owners and managers of hotels cook shops, sarais, etc. (and employees).	159,557	122,643	21,991	3,791	3,358	6,551	1,223	130,153	101,627	17,468
128	Hawkers of drink and food-stuffs.	89,378	41,539	29,036	1,404	10,560	4,312	2,527	80,346	36,041	27,188
	32. Other trade in food-stuffs. ...	**4,525,554**	**2,413,640**	**1,100,999**	**101,626**	**220,655**	**564,073**	**124,561**	**3,573,625**	**1,926,890**	**883,182**
129	Grain and pulse dealers. ..	1,035,612	644,912	189,041	28,493	29,105	125,630	18,431	804,454	505,631	150,780
130	Dealers in sweetmeats, sugar and spices.	400,234	234,435	90,686	11,266	21,728	34,461	7,658	301,721	176,689	72,897
131	Dealers in dairy produce, eggs and poultry.	589,923	217,269	197,233	12,639	46,354	86,786	29,642	451,129	182,436	145,110
132	Dealers in animals for food. ..	33,035	22,460	3,453	1,104	730	4,998	340	23,477	16,302	2,155
133	Dealers in fodder for animals. ..	178,013	53,516	77,030	2,646	8,741	22,163	13,917	108,951	37,830	45,964
134	Dealers in other food-stuffs. ..	2,146,742	1,143,538	523,794	41,372	109,398	275,581	53,053	1,778,838	936,072	450,452
135	Dealers in tobacco.	130,313	87,850	19,435	3,832	4,518	13,175	1,503	97,201	65,295	15,579
136	Dealers in opium.	6,571	5,460	168	147	48	737	11	4,207	3,508	115
137	Dealers in ganja.	5,061	4,200	159	127	33	536	6	3,647	3,127	130
	33. Trade in clothing and toilet articles.	**123,483**	**94,217**	**9,875**	**4,300**	**3,736**	**10,108**	**1,247**	**82,900**	**65,406**	**6,519**
138	Trade in ready made clothing and other articles of dress and the toilet (hats, umbrellas, socks, ready made shoes, perfumes, etc.)	123,483	94,217	9,875	4,300	3,736	10,108	1,247	82,900	65,406	6,519
	34. Trade in furniture	**69,848**	**45,855**	**7,834**	**1,631**	**5,754**	**7,358**	**1,416**	**55,905**	**37,611**	**6,088**
139	Trade in furniture, carpets, curtains and bedding.	18,966	11,726	3,121	544	705	2,390	480	14,182	8,674	2,529
140	Hardware, cooking utensils, porcelain, crockery, glassware, bottles, articles for gardening, etc.	50,882	34,129	4,713	1,087	5,049	4,968	936	41,723	28,937	3,559
	35. Trade in building materials ..	**25,749**	**15,478**	**4,797**	**1,161**	**967**	**2,697**	**649**	**14,057**	**8,449**	**2,668**
141	Trade in building materials (other than bricks, tiles and woody materials).	25,749	15,478	4,797	1,161	967	2,697	649	14,057	8,449	2,668

hood—Part I—General Table for India—*contd.*

Territory.				States and Agencies.							
As working dependants.		As subsidiary to other occupation.		Total following occupation.	As principal occupation.		As working dependants.		As subsidiary to other occupation.		Group Number.
Males.	Females.	Males.	Females.		Males.	Females.	Males.	Females.	Males.	Females.	
13	14	15	16	17	18	19	20	21	22	23	24
118,010	228,650	886,056	161,333	2,546,294	1,383,753	449,701	164,343	172,514	298,796	77,187	
7,421	1,516	107,253	6,052	151,338	92,312	11,145	5,826	1,992	38,209	1,854	
7,421	1,516	107,253	6,052	151,338	92,312	11,145	5,826	1,992	38,209	1,854	115
659	376	5,190	90	15,140	12,437	231	477	29	1,931	35	
659	376	5,190	90	15,140	12,437	231	477	29	1,931	35	116
7,748	5,465	50,862	2,301	136,633	92,317	9,847	12,951	6,893	13,001	1,624	
7,748	5,465	50,862	2,301	136,633	92,317	9,847	12,951	6,893	13,001	1,624	117
1,588	489	10,374	465	22,014	13,636	1,985	1,976	1,668	2,436	313	
1,538	489	10,374	465	22,014	13,636	1,985	1,976	1,668	2,436	313	118
2,927	7,122	35,893	15,945	39,672	21,784	7,169	2,189	2,320	4,683	1,527	
1,853	2,397	20,469	12,663	22,051	14,403	2,793	1,272	660	2,532	391	119
31	103	238	25	2,308	1,178	492	110	253	182	93	120
703	2,266	11,351	1,119	9,053	4,153	2,045	539	812	1,303	201	121
340	2,356	3,835	2,138	6,260	2,050	1,839	268	595	666	842	122
304	329	1,519	81	9,494	6,428	811	654	703	789	109	
304	329	1,519	81	9,494	6,428	811	654	703	789	109	123
691	2,088	3,736	755	21,838	6,493	6,235	1,378	5,172	1,133	1,427	
691	2,088	3,736	755	21,838	6,493	6,235	1,378	5,172	1,133	1,427	124
802	2,538	8,173	1,871	10,661	6,769	1,505	241	199	1,634	313	
802	2,538	8,173	1,871	10,661	6,769	1,505	241	199	1,634	313	125
4,376	14,000	16,850	4,453	262,133	122,545	57,623	22,547	23,312	25,014	11,092	
911	1,364	8,018	1,211	223,697	96,031	51,252	20,817	22,030	22,983	10,584	126
2,462	2,753	5,042	801	29,404	21,016	4,523	1,329	605	1,509	422	127
1,003	9,883	3,790	2,441	9,032	5,498	1,848	401	677	522	86	128
53,712	156,095	457,729	96,017	951,929	486,750	217,817	47,914	64,560	106,344	28,544	
11,733	18,349	103,728	14,233	231,158	139,281	38,261	16,760	10,756	21,902	4,198	129
6,053	13,693	27,016	5,373	98,513	57,746	17,789	5,213	8,035	7,445	2,285	130
6,022	21,176	74,798	21,587	138,794	34,833	52,123	6,617	25,178	11,988	8,055	131
683	489	3,678	170	9,608	6,158	1,298	421	241	1,320	170	132
1,546	5,490	9,428	8,693	69,062	15,686	31,066	1,100	3,251	12,735	5,224	133
25,855	93,451	228,178	44,830	367,904	207,466	73,342	15,517	15,947	47,409	8,223	134
1,726	3,418	10,065	1,118	33,112	22,555	3,856	2,106	1,100	3,110	385	135
71	21	481	11	2,364	1,952	53	76	27	256	136	
23	8	357	2	1,414	1,073	29	104	25	179	4	137
1,437	1,827	6,865	846	40,583	28,811	3,356	2,863	1,909	3,243	401	
1,437	1,827	6,865	846	40,583	28,811	3,356	2,863	1,909	3,243	401	138
811	4,344	6,173	878	13,943	8,244	1,746	820	1,410	1,185	538	
204	606	1,877	292	4,784	3,052	592	340	99	513	188	139
607	3,738	4,296	586	9,159	5,192	1,154	480	1,311	672	350	140
143	406	1,861	530	11,692	7,029	2,129	1,018	561	836	119	
143	406	1,861	530	11,692	7,029	2,129	1,018	561	836	119	141

Table X.—Occupation or Means of Liveli

Group Number.	Occupation.	India. Total following occupation.	As principal occupation. Males.	Females.	As working dependants. Males.	Females.	As subsidiary to other occupation. Males.	Females.	British Total following occupation.	As principal occupation. Males.	Females.
1	2	3	4	5	6	7	8	9	10	11	12
	B.—PREPARATION AND SUPPLY OF MATERIAL SUBSTANCES—concld.										
	V.—Trade—concld.										
	36. Trade in means of transport	**142,257**	**101,064**	**3,621**	**4,373**	**1,462**	**30,856**	**881**	**98,883**	**70,513**	**2,701**
142	Dealers and hirers in mechanical transport, motors, cycles, etc.	8,843	7,752	62	367	13	639	10	5,355	5,012	39
143	Dealers and hirers in other carriages, carts, boats, etc.	35,580	23,570	881	1,942	681	8,258	248	17,145	11,024	288
144	Dealers and hirers of elephants, camels, horses, cattle, asses, mules, etc.	97,834	69,742	2,678	2,064	768	21,959	623	76,383	54,477	2,374
	37. Trade in fuel	**371,203**	**117,877**	**129,020**	**11,599**	**34,060**	**49,189**	**29,458**	**232,013**	**77,988**	**82,550**
145	Dealers in fire-wood, charcoal, coal, cowdung, etc.	371,203	117,877	129,020	11,599	34,060	49,189	29,458	232,013	77,988	82,550
	38. Trade in articles, of luxury and those pertaining to letters and the arts and sciences.	**244,821**	**157,511**	**43,479**	**7,232**	**12,375**	**19,912**	**4,312**	**180,321**	**122,076**	**32,721**
146	Dealers in precious stones, jewellery (real and imitation), clocks, optical instruments, etc.	42,230	35,345	2,090	1,491	473	2,646	185	30,609	25,907	1,808
147	Dealers in common bangles, bead necklaces, fans, small articles, toys, hunting and fishing tackle, flowers, etc.	150,307	79,432	38,939	4,107	11,705	12,259	3,865	106,133	59,856	28,650
148	Publishers, book-sellers, stationers, dealers in music, pictures, musical instruments and curiosities.	52,284	42,734	2,450	1,634	197	5,007	262	43,579	36,313	2,268
	39. Trade of other sorts ..	**1,748,510**	**1,258,196**	**170,976**	**75,726**	**45,944**	**171,979**	**25,689**	**1,136,350**	**885,873**	**101,022**
149	Dealers in rags, stable refuse, etc.	26,027	18,200	3,521	774	966	2,317	249	11,274	9,151	995
150	General store keepers and shop keepers otherwise unspecified.	1,595,968	1,154,972	152,794	69,125	42,770	153,027	23,280	1,057,931	828,748	92,452
151	Itinerant traders, pedlars, and hawkers (of other than food, etc.).	59,230	41,833	8,917	1,381	1,079	4,290	1,730	47,659	35,975	6,447
152	Other trades (including farmers of pounds, tolls, and markets).	67,285	43,191	5,744	4,446	1,129	12,345	430	19,486	11,999	1,128
	C—PUBLIC ADMINISTRATION AND LIBERAL ARTS.	**4,819,452**	**3,550,388**	**299,808**	**233,066**	**63,637**	**643,496**	**29,057**	**3,324,290**	**2,464,778**	**198,963**
	VI.—PUBLIC FORCE	**941,323**	**820,153**	**3,762**	**14,300**	**3,259**	**99,267**	**582**	**609,152**	**535,038**	**1,930**
	40. Army	**330,648**	**309,794**	**1,096**	**5,016**	**632**	**13,926**	**184**	**180,052**	**171,225**	**684**
153	Army (Imperial).	228,314	216,972	674	764	14	9,748	142	178,184	169,450	644
154	Army (Indian States).	102,334	92,822	422	4,252	618	4,178	42	1,868	1,775	40
	41. Navy	**1,399**	**1,384**	**8**	**6**	..	**1**	..	**1,365**	**1,352**	**8**
155	Navy.	1,399	1,384	8	6	..	1	..	1,365	1,352	8
	42. Air Force	**1,875**	**1,834**	**4**	**4**	**21**	**12**	..	**1,826**	**1,787**	**4**
156	Air Force.	1,875	1,834	4	4	21	12	..	1,826	1,787	4
	43. Police	**607,401**	**507,141**	**2,654**	**9,274**	**2,606**	**85,328**	**398**	**425,909**	**360,674**	**1,234**
157	Police.	323,817	303,225	1,060	4,543	802	14,134	53	224,996	213,438	444
158	Village watchmen.	283,584	203,916	1,594	4,731	1,804	71,194	345	200,913	147,236	790
	VII.—PUBLIC ADMINISTRATION	**1,153,963**	**932,017**	**25,734**	**30,724**	**6,809**	**156,373**	**2,306**	**713,638**	**596,357**	**13,708**
	44. Public Administration	**1,153,963**	**932,017**	**25,734**	**30,724**	**6,809**	**156,373**	**2,306**	**713,638**	**596,357**	**13,708**
159	Service of the State.	387,578	358,836	3,421	4,489	408	20,265	159	352,563	328,355	2,955
160	Service of Indian and Foreign States.	279,563	236,114	6,334	14,442	2,801	19,593	279	16,250	13,200	124
161	Municipal and other local (not village) service.	151,060	131,212	9,239	3,191	1,375	5,657	386	123,462	112,128	6,299
162	Village officials and servants other than watchmen.	335,762	205,855	6,740	8,602	2,225	110,858	1,482	221,363	142,674	4,330
	VIII.—PROFESSIONS AND LIBERAL ARTS.	**2,724,166**	**1,798,218**	**270,312**	**188,042**	**53,569**	**387,856**	**26,169**	**2,001,500**	**1,332,383**	**183,325**
	45. Religion	**1,247,528**	**746,640**	**85,691**	**160,523**	**34,040**	**209,418**	**11,216**	**848,564**	**498,186**	**43,085**
163	Priests, ministers, etc. ..	807,160	479,257	45,240	103,273	16,836	154,091	8,463	611,091	367,334	28,516
164	Monks, nuns, religious mendicants.	231,730	130,968	23,748	46,807	13,865	15,416	926	117,056	51,838	5,053
165	Other religious workers. ..	58,873	38,668	5,386	3,483	1,736	9,074	526	33,897	22,746	3,073
166	Servants in religious edifices, burial and burning grounds, pilgrim conductors, circumcisers, etc.	149,765	97,747	11,317	6,960	1,603	30,837	1,301	86,520	56,268	6,443
	46. Law	**143,441**	**130,370**	**388**	**2,221**	**110**	**10,289**	**63**	**117,265**	**108,456**	**261**
167	Lawyers of all kinds, including Qazis, Law Agents and Mukhtiars.	75,000	68,737	270	1,338	93	4,517	45	60,641	56,661	167
168	Lawyers' clerks, petition writers, etc.	68,441	61,633	118	883	17	5,772	18	56,624	51,795	94
	47. Medicine	**369,483**	**217,581**	**86,963**	**4,955**	**9,082**	**42,930**	**7,972**	**304,749**	**181,906**	**72,464**
169	Registered medical practitioners including oculists	89,068	74.205	3,691	1,206	289	9,558	119	79.691	67,154	3,027

hood—Part I—General Table for India—*contd.*

Territory.				States and Agencies.							
As working dependants.		As subsidiary to other occupation.		Total following occupation.	As principal occupation.		As working dependants.		As subsidiary to other occupation.		Group Number.
Males.	Females.	Males.	Females.		Males.	Females.	Males.	Females.	Males.	Females.	
13	14	15	16	17	18	19	20	21	22	23	24
1,592	435	23,028	614	43,374	30,551	920	2,781	1,027	7,828	267	
67	3	226	8	3,488	2,740	23	300	10	413	2	142
448	32	5,255	98	18,435	12,546	593	1,494	649	3,003	150	143
1,077	400	17,547	508	21,451	15,265	304	987	368	4,412	115	144
4,303	17,022	31,589	18,561	139,190	39,889	46,470	7,296	17,038	17,600	10,897	
4,303	17,022	31,589	18,561	139,190	39,889	46,470	7,296	17,038	17,600	10,897	145
2,951	4,364	15,528	2,681	64,500	35,435	10,758	4,281	8,011	4,384	1,631	
555	238	1,924	177	11,621	9,438	282	936	235	722	8	146
1,948	4,028	9,396	2,255	44,174	19,576	10,289	2,159	7,677	2,863	1,610	147
448	98	4,208	249	8,705	6,421	187	1,186	99	799	13	148
26,595	10,234	103,433	9,193	612,160	372,323	69,954	49,131	35,710	68,546	16,496	
186	178	728	36	14,753	9,049	2,526	588	788	1,589	213	149
23,559	9,317	95,576	8,279	538,037	326,224	60,342	45,566	33.453	57.451	15,001	150
499	595	3,359	784	11,571	5,858	2,470	882	484	931	946	151
2,351	144	3,770	94	47,799	31,192	4,616	2,095	985	8,575	336	152
156,237	29,343	456,834	18,135	1,495,162	1,085,610	100,845	76,829	34,294	186,662	10,922	
2,999	378	68,554	253	332,171	285,115	1,832	11,301	2,881	30,713	329	
297	24	7,679	143	150,596	138,569	412	4,719	608	6,247	41	
289	1	7,659	141	50,130	47,522	30	475	13	2,089	1	153
8	23	20	1,2	100,466	91,047	382	4,244	595	4,158	40	154
4	..	1	..	34	32	..	2	..	..	..	
4	..	1	..	34	32	..	2	..	..	..	155
3	21	11	..	49	47	..	1	..	1	..	
3	21	11	..	49	47	..	1	..	1	..	156
2,695	333	60,863	110	181,492	146,467	1,420	6,579	2,273	24,465	288	
651	38	10,395	30	98,821	89,787	616	3,892	764	3,739	23	157
2,044	295	50,468	80	82,671	56,680	804	2,687	1,509	20,726	265	158
7,394	2,158	93,006	1,015	440,325	335,660	12,026	23,330	4,651	63,367	1,291	
7,394	2,158	93,006	1,015	440,325	335,660	12,026	23,330	4,651	63,367	1,291	
2,801	363	17,975	114	35,015	30,481	466	1,688	45	2,290	45	159
135	84	2,699	8	263,313	222,914	6,210	14,307	2,717	16,894	271	160
953	207	3,729	143	27,598	19,084	2,940	2,238	1,168	1,928	240	161
3,505	1,504	68,603	747	114,399	63,181	2,410	5,097	721	42,255	735	162
145,844	26,807	295,274	16,867	722,666	464,835	86,987	42,198	26,762	92,582	9,302	
132,344	16,601	152,539	5,809	398,964	248,454	42,606	28,179	17,439	56,879	5,407	
82,119	4,479	124,159	4,484	196,069	111,923	16,724	21,154	12,357	29,932	3,979	163
43,573	10,744	5,589	259	114,674	79,130	18,695	3,234	3,121	9,827	667	164
1,583	657	5,599	239	24,976	15,922	2,313	1,900	1,079	3,475	287	165
5,069	721	17,192	827	63,245	41,479	4,874	1,891	882	13,645	474	166
626	93	7,768	61	26,176	21,914	127	1,595	17	2,521	2	
239	76	3 454	44	14,359	12,076	103	1,099	17	1,063	1	167
387	17	4,314	17	11,817	9,838	24	496	..	1,458	1	168
2,455	5,824	35,522	6,578	64,734	35,675	14,499	2,500	3,258	7,408	1,394	
646	153	8,625	86	9,377	7,051	664	560	136	933	33	169

Table X.—Occupation or Means of Liveli

	Occupation.	India. Total following occupation.	As principal occupation. Males.	As principal occupation. Females.	As working dependants. Males.	As working dependants. Females.	As subsidiary to other occupation. Males.	As subsidiary to other occupation. Females.	British Total following occupation.	British As principal occupation. Males.	British As principal occupation. Females.
1	2	3	4	5	6	7	8	9	10	11	12
	C.—PUBLIC ADMINISTRATION AND LIBERAL ARTS—concld.										
	VIII.—Professions and Liberal arts—concld.										
170	Other persons practising the healing arts without being registered.	141,005	101,839	4,693	2,430	1,088	30,358	597	113,555	82,089	3,959
171	Dentists.	4,022	3,362	168	100	33	349	10	3,486	2,966	153
172	Midwives, vaccinators, compounders, nurses, masseurs, etc.	131,003	34,369	78,241	1,186	7,668	2,301	7,238	104,506	26,600	65,176
173	Veterinary surgeons.	4,385	3,806	170	33	4	364	8	3,511	3,097	149
	48. Instruction	**554,778**	**435,160**	**54,803**	**8,079**	**3,610**	**51,532**	**1,594**	**446,114**	**351,750**	**42,605**
174	Professors and teachers of all kinds.	513,818	400,268	51,895	7,281	3,405	49,458	1,511	413,696	323,271	40,601
175	Clerks and servants connected with education.	40,960	34,892	2,908	798	205	2,074	83	32,418	28,479	2,004
	49. Letters, arts and sciences (other than 44).	**408,936**	**268,467**	**42,467**	**12,264**	**6,727**	**73,687**	**5,324**	**284,808**	**193,085**	**24,910**
176	Public scribes, stenographers, etc.	4,669	3,465	572	176	11	437	8	3,631	2,739	531
177	Architects, surveyors, engineers and their employees (not being state servants).	12,492	10,055	116	890	1	1,424	6	9,447	7,718	106
178	Authors, editors journalists and photographers.	10,977	9,303	183	594	119	724	54	6,963	6,360	129
179	Artists, sculptors and image makers.	18,399	14,211	818	1,027	429	1,846	68	12,285	9,752	391
180	Scientists (astronomers, botanists, etc.)	2,312	1,913	113	100	20	154	12	1,664	1,401	74
181	Horoscope casters, astrologers, fortune tellers, wizards, witches and mediums.	37,778	23,681	2,926	1,886	794	7,083	1,408	22,288	15,133	1,096
182	Musicians (composers and performers other than military), actors, dancers, etc.	280,499	173,070	34,093	6,113	4,647	59,206	3,370	199,951	126,324	20,076
183	Managers and employees of places of public entertainments, race courses, societies, clubs.	16,508	14,507	724	471	102	659	45	12,466	11,483	538
184	Conjurors, acrobats, recitors, exhibitors of curiosities and wild animals, etc.	25,302	18,262	2,922	1,007	604	2,154	353	16,113	12,175	1,969
	D.—MISCELLANEOUS ..	**23,203,489**	**7,211,783**	**3,767,715**	**705,649**	**8,833,493**	**970,626**	**1,714,223**	**18,117,246**	**5,694,601**	**2,976,494**
	IX.—PERSONS LIVING ON THEIR INCOME.	**280,955**	**160,664**	**39,318**	**8,165**	**7,727**	**61,591**	**3,490**	**196,432**	**114,277**	**24,752**
	50. Persons living principally on their income.	**280,955**	**160,664**	**39,318**	**8,165**	**7,727**	**61,591**	**3,490**	**196,432**	**114,277**	**24,752**
185	Proprietors (other than of agricultural land) fund and scholarship-holders and pensioners.	280,955	160,664	39,318	8,165	7,727	61,591	3,490	196,432	114,277	24,752
	X.—DOMESTIC SERVICE ..	**12,674,110**	**1,805,006**	**886,991**	**289,481**	**7,916,799**	**242,433**	**1,533,400**	**10,021,969**	**1,301,433**	**658,230**
	51. Domestic service	**12,674,110**	**1,805,006**	**886,991**	**289,481**	**7,916,799**	**242,433**	**1,533,400**	**10,021,969**	**1,301,433**	**658,230**
186	Private motor-drivers and cleaners.	71,212	60,800	1,387	2,385	3,697	2,778	165	44,641	41,855	538
187	Other domestic service	12,602,898	1,744,206	885,604	287,096	7,913,102	239,655	1,533,235	9,977,328	1,259,578	657,692
	XI.—INSUFFICIENTLY DESCRIBED OCCUPATIONS.	**8,499,689**	**4,387,728**	**2,407,527**	**211,510**	**771,877**	**570,208**	**150,839**	**6,658,033**	**3,678,765**	**1,977,898**
	52. General terms which do not indicate a definite occupation.	**8,499,689**	**4,387,728**	**2,407,527**	**211,510**	**771,877**	**570,208**	**150,839**	**6,658,033**	**3,678,765**	**1,977,898**
188	Manufacturers, businessmen and contractors otherwise unspecified.	136,674	105,433	7,710	3,935	3,305	14,745	1,546	95,900	79,617	3,769
189	Cashiers, accountants, book-keepers, clerks and other employees in unspecified offices and warehouses and shops.	802,857	690,113	35,795	9,961	6,472	57,524	2,992	711,788	617,252	31,981
190	Mechanics otherwise unspecified ..	41,844	36,262	2,648	988	756	1,118	72	34,617	30,735	2,112
191	Labourers and workmen otherwise unspecified.	7,518,314	3,555,920	2,361,374	196,626	761,344	496,821	146,229	5,815,728	2,951,161	1,940,036
	XII.—UNPRODUCTIVE ..	**1,748,735**	**858,385**	**433,879**	**196,493**	**137,090**	**96,394**	**26,494**	**1,240,812**	**600,126**	**315,614**
	53. Inmates of Jails, Asylums and Almshouses.	**176,366**	**26,222**	**3,938**	**141,271**	**4,697**	**203**	**35**	**148,959**	**23,336**	**2,388**
192	Inmates of jails, asylums and Alms houses.	176,366	26,222	3,938	141,271	4,697	203	35	148,959	23,336	2,388
	54. Beggars, vagrants, prostitutes	**1,469,698**	**811,216**	**418,084**	**53,224**	**68,455**	**92,942**	**25,777**	**1,001,256**	**561,445**	**303,875**
193	Beggars and vagrants.	1,397,162	806,725	361,083	51,904	62,227	92,696	22,527	947,280	558,540	256,732
194	Procurers and prostitutes. ..	72,536	4,491	57,001	1,320	6,228	246	3,250	53,976	2,905	47,143
	55. Other unclassified non-productive industries.	**102,671**	**20,947**	**11,857**	**1,998**	**63,938**	**3,249**	**682**	**90,597**	**15,345**	**9,351**
195	Other unclassified non-productive industries.	102,671	20,947	11,857	1,998	63,938	3,249	682	90,597	15,345	9,351

hood—Part I—General Table for India—*concld.*

Territory.				States and Agencies.						
As working dependants.		As subsidiary to other occupation.		Total following occupation.	As principal occupation.		As working dependants.		As subsidiary to other occupation.	
Males.	Females.	Males.	Females.		Males.	Females.	Males.	Females.	Males.	Females.
13	14	15	16	17	18	19	20	21	22	23
1,438	952	24,651	466	27,450	19,750	734	992	136	5,707	131
57	23	277	10	536	396	15	43	10	72	..
297	4,693	1,724	6,016	26,497	7,769	13,065	889	2,975	577	1,222
17	3	245		874	709	21	16	1	119	8
4,768	1,988	44,096	907	108,664	83,410	12,198	3,311	1,622	7,436	687
4,452	1,933	42,572	867	100,122	76,997	11,294	2,829	1,472	6,886	644
316	55	1,524	40	8,542	6,413	904	482	150	550	43
5,651	2,301	55,349	3,512	124,128	75,382	17,557	6,613	4,426	18,338	1,812
52		307	2	1,038	726	41	124	11	130	6
537	1	1,079	6	3,045	2,337	10	353	..	345	..
84	14	374	2	4,014	2,943	54	519	105	350	52
439	245	1,439	19	6,114	4,459	427	588	184	407	49
53	20	112	4	648	512	39	47	..	42	8
331	230	4,453	1,045	15,490	8,548	1,830	1,555	564	2,630	363
3,686	1,535	46,116	2,214	80,548	46,746	14,017	2,427	3,112	13,090	1,156
82	19	328	16	4,042	3,024	186	389	83	331	29
387	237	1,141	204	9,189	6,087	953	620	367	1,013	149
473,103	6,792,707	742,278	1,438,063	5,086,243	1,517,182	791,221	232,546	2,040,786	228,348	276,160
3,817	2,912	48,456	2,218	84,523	46,387	14,566	4,348	4,815	13,135	1,272
3,817	2,912	48,456	2,218	84,523	46,387	14,566	4,348	4,815	13,135	1,272
3,817	2,912	48,456	2,218	84,523	46,387	14,566	4,348	4,815	13,135	1,272
187,886	6,389,090	177,244	1,308,086	2,652,141	503,573	228,761	101,595	1,527,709	65,189	225,314
187,886	6,389,090	177,244	1,308,086	2,652,141	503,573	228,761	101,595	1,527,709	65,189	225,314
319	47	1,853	29	26,571	18,945	849	2,066	3,650	925	136
187,567	6,389,043	175,391	1,308,057	2,625,570	484,628	227,912	99,529	1,524,059	64,264	225,178
128,793	300,255	457,964	114,358	1,841,656	708,963	429,629	82,717	471,622	112,244	36,481
128,793	300,255	457,964	114,358	1,841,656	708,963	429,629	82,717	471,622	112,244	36,481
1,218	265	10,724	307	40,774	25,816	3,941	2,717	3,040	4,021	1,239
5,574	4,739	49,648	2,594	91,069	72,861	3,814	4,387	1,733	7,876	398
180	705	824	61	7,227	5,527	536	808	51	294	11
121,821	294,546	396,768	111,396	1,702,586	604,759	421,338	74,805	466,798	100,053	34,833
152,607	100,450	58,614	13,401	507,923	258,259	118,265	43,886	36,640	37,780	13,093
120,440	2,643	12[illegible]	23	27,407	2,886	1,550	20,831	2,054	74	12
120,440	2,643	129	23	27,407	2,886	1,550	20,831	2,054	74	12
31,354	34,866	56,75[illegible]	12,964	468,442	249,771	114,20[illegible]	21,870	33,589	36,190	12,813
30,774	33,567	56,639	11,028	449,882	248,185	104,351	21,130	28,660	36,057	11,499
580	1,299	113	1,936	18,560	1,586	9,858	740	4,929	133	1,314
813	62,941	1,733	414	12,074	5,602	2,506	1,185	997	1,516	268
813	62,941	1,733	414	12,074	5,602	2,506	1,185	997	1,516	268

Table X.—Occupation or Means of Liveli

Province, State or Agency.	Total population.	Total earners principal occupation. Males.	Total earners principal occupation. Females.	Total working dependants. Males.	Total working dependants. Females.
	2	3	4	5	6
INDIA	**350,529,557**	**97,441,758***	**27,859,229***	**7,644,575**	**20,970,488**
Provinces	**271,431,549**	**76,080,280***	**21,543,576***	**4,600,132**	**14,118,804**
1 Ajmer-Merwara	560,292	175,671	31,433	16,469	69,951
2 Andamans and Nicobars	29,463	13,933	325	3,654	3,023
3 Assam	8,622,251	2,399,646	500,719	398,600	577,793
4 Baluchistan (*Districts and Administered Territories*).	463,508	166,913	2,297	6,882	7,196
5 Bengal	50,114,002	12,216,716	1,539,908	305,497	358,340
6 Bihar and Orissa	37,677,576	10,652,262	4,419,236	220,623	256,168
7 Bombay (*including Aden*) .. .	21,854,866*	5,902,090*	1,466,666*	459,233	682,908
Aden	*51,478*	*22,972*	*1,016*	*1,048*	*341*
8 Burma	14,647,497	3,778,336	1,417,187	473,435	542,079
9 Central Provinces and Berar ..	15,507,723	4,502,880	2,272,254	358,448	1,125,561
10 Coorg	163,327	62,345	22,228	1,778	25,322
11 Delhi	636,246	221,737	19,213	10,102	17,636
12 Madras	46,740,107	12,752,777	5,150,029	924,235	7,077.449
13 North-West Frontier Province (*Districts and Administered Territories*).	2,425,076	735,649	25,010	72,432	24,877
14 Punjab	23,580,852	6,487,009	441,538	789,776	607,935
15 United Provinces of Agra and Oudh	48,408,763	16,012,316	4,235,533	558,968	2,742,566
States and Agencies ..	**79,098,008**	**21,361,478**	**6,315,653**	**3,044,443**	**6,851,684**
16 Assam States	625,606	135,047	63,178	30,649	75,077
17 Baluchistan States	405,109	125,612	2,443	4,000	4,219
18 Baroda State	2,443,007	711,565	247,396	44,612	206,902
19 Bengal States	973,336	239,766	21,397	8,456	13,999
20 Bihar and Orissa States	4,652,007	1,285,997	559,110	84,510	137,722
21 Bombay States	4,468,396	1,086,317	252,588	162,955	306,669
22 Central India Agency	6,632,790	2,092,190	999,325	116,346	176,950
23 Central Provinces States	2,483,214	612,898	164,010	161,069	306,091
24 Gwalior State	3,523,070	1,209,935	325,766	69,463	131,689
25 Hyderabad State	14,436,148	3,262,208	1,561,674	987,432	991,220
26 Jammu and Kashmir State ..	3,646,243	752,104	56,045	221,997	895,159
27 Madras States Agency	6,754,484	1,560,594	571,069	180,727	1,000,724
Cochin State	*1,205,016*	*311,666*	*155,060*	*7,974*	*139,351*
Travancore State	*5,095,973*	*1,117,454*	*360,772*	*161,739*	*768,167*
Other Madras States	*453,495*	*131,474*	*55,237*	*11,014*	*93,206*
28 Mysore State	6,557,302	1,937,129	413,405	126,295	509.925
29 North-West Frontier Province (*Agencies and Tribal Areas*).	46,451	41,402	20	61	..
30 Punjab States	437,787	124,161	9,152	36,204	97,607
31 Punjab States Agency	4,472,218	1,367,987	85,903	202,787	243,116
32 Rajputana Agency	11,225,712	3,457,237	747,473	396,874	1,323,679
33 Sikkim State	109,808	37,611	33,736	930	953
34 United Provinces States	1,206,070	391,942	78,381	11,511	128,255
35 Western India States Agency ..	3,999,250	929,776	123,582	197,565	301,728

*Include 3,116 earners (2,521 males and 595 females) whose occupations were not returned.

hood—Part II—Provincial Distribution.

Total non-working dependants.		Total earners with subsidiary occupation.		*Class A.*—Production of Raw Materials. Total *Class A.* Total earners Principal occupation.		Total working dependants.		Total following occupation as subsidiary to other.		
Males.	Females.	Males.	Females.	Males.	Females.	Males.	Females.	Males.	Females.	
7	8	9	10	11	12	13	14	15	16	
75,534,279	**121,079,228**	**11,355,836**	**3,558,228**	**68,892,510**	**18,629,322**	**5,808,075**	**10,310,532**	**6,328,008**	**1,196,139**	
59,210,545	**95,878,212**	**8,406,023**	**2,682,168**	**54,271,385**	**14,486,989**	**3,540,315**	**6,152,044**	**4,604,423**	**803,013**	
103,941	162,827	21,911	2,442	88,355	15,268	14,599	65,751	12,087	1,396	1
2,115	6,413	517	10	4,851	114	3,368	2,972	113	5	2
1,738,960	3,006,533	432,789	83,682	2,085,554	441,421	377,232	364,062	276,071	59,045	3
96,209	184,011	48,168	289	92,632	362	6,153	5,321	35,123	110	4
13,519,485	22,174,056	1,081,915	104,601	8,822,500	793,130	233,043	50,862	680,367	32,673	5
7,921,253	14,208,034	1,317,258	247,595	8,577,374	3,236,152	181,287	171,073	589,346	117,337	6
5,143,906	8,200,063	359,348	85,032	3,681,243	1,078,980	354,251	487,341	229,097	58,356	7
8,325	*17,776*	*299*	*22*	*962*	*124*	*15*	*31*	*175*	*11*	
3,228,905	5,207,555	336,609	115,587	2,820,778	1,025,530	293,112	221,441	165,973	31,240	8
2,900,490	4,348,090	427,081	122,039	3,432,509	1,914,978	321,217	1,011,748	232,020	74,994	9
26,452	25,202	5,433	8,122	44,394	15,756	512	154	1,568	247	10
137,658	229,900	10,152	443	40,380	3,846	8,515	14,594	5,580	293	11
9,405,987	11,429,630	1,255,432	1,423,653	8,258,182	3,054,246	587,024	703,829	514,440	85,104	12
507,737	1,059,371	54,641	491	437,238	11,727	56,878	23,000	28,459	181	13
5,603,725	9,650,869	602,300	29,856	3,718,644	178,185	650,305	497,951	369,598	15,377	14
8,873,722	15,985,658	2,452,469	458,326	12,166,751	2,717,294	452,819	),531,945	1,464,581	326,655	15
16,323,734	**25,201,016**	**2,949,813**	**876,060**	**14,621,125**	**4,142,333**	**2,267,760**	**4,158,488**	**1,723,585**	**393,126**	
141,231	180,424	24,908	16,554	113,137	47,049	28,797	55,619	16,697	9,584	16
88,798	180,037	24,733	117	107,147	331	3,762	•834	20,306	36	17
501,640	730,892	59,823	6,428	472,290	162,450	34,407	188,746	29,458	3,134	18
267,940	421,778	18,170	1,205	205,441	9,692	7,762	8,797	11,905	836	19
917,915	1,666,753	216,363	48,249	1,097,511	370,133	79,323	109,116	115,733	28,136	20
1,039,351	1,620,516	89,404	17,131	803,942	194,893	140,314	259,232	48,883	8,779	21
.,196,902	2,051,077	257,022	33,266	1,510,707	797,047	103,411	160,243	134,733	17,911	22
461,418	777,728	42,810	8,169	525,684	133,107	151,908	277,526	20,855	5,795	23
587,633	1,198,584	156,452	28,692	876,117	229,759	51,635	106,492	91,338	13,764	24
3,120,370	4,513,244	616,751	348,984	1,850,887	982,131	512,243	558,945	342,188	199,300	25
964,237	756,701	194,795	21,397	569,068	21,701	203,024	24,660	153,669	13,726	26
1,631,711	1,809,659	387,518	251,395	872,063	324.599	112,219	39,330	282,678	31,408	27
270,173	*320,792*	*53,611*	*46,152*	*159,632*	*89,852*	*3,753*	*3,489*	*30,213*	*4,941*	
1,285,880	*1,401,961*	*307,639*	*185,314*	*623,326*	*198,674*	*100,550*	*22,028*	*241,183*	*24,007*	
75,658	*86,906*	*26,268*	*19,929*	*89,105*	*36,068*	*7,916*	*13,813*	*11,282*	*2,460*	
1,290,539	2,280,009	222,912	20,199	1,461,138	255,026	111,751	461,685	75,563	8,331	28
3,172	1,796	3,798	..	2,307	..	5	..	1,115	..	29
68,925	101,738	16,199	426	99,525	6,363	34,965	95,968	6,064	269	30
880,620	1,691,805	169,638	6,061	932,815	52,294	181,810	225,620	111,320	4,363	31
2,030,917	3,269,532	385,396	56,169	2,259,669	406,300	367,559	1,232,253	229,112	39,817	32
17,284	19,294	1,753	2,428	35,595	33,260	566	389	926	1,765	33
214,718	381,263	34,032	6,669	324,963	53,000	8,605	121,999	17,815	4,846	34
898,413	1,548,186	27,336	2,521	501,119	63,198	133,694	231,534	13,227	1,326	35

Table X.—Occupation or Means of Liveli

Class A.—Production of Raw

Sub-Class I.—Exploitation of

Province, State or Agency.	Total *Sub-Class I.* Total earners principal occupation. Males.	Females.	Total working dependants. Males.	Females.	Total following occupation as subsidiary to other. Males.	Females.	Total — Total earners principal occupation. Males.	Females.
1	17	18	19	20	21	22	23	24
INDIA	**68,644,794**	**18,552,896**	**5,796,208**	**10,300,541**	**6,281,157**	**1,184,728**	**68,013,477**	**18,424,419**
Provinces	**54,076,958**	**14,425,084**	**3,536,879**	**6,148,819**	**4,566,562**	**794,383**	**53,561,757**	**14,325,721**
1 Ajmer-Merwara	87,735	15,195	14,598	65,750	11,988	1,395	87,723	15,188
2 Andamans and Nicobars	4,851	114	3,368	2,972	113	5	4,785	114
3 Assam	2,070,810	440,473	376,808	364,025	275,615	59,029	2,036,034	439,606
4 Baluchistan (*Districts and Administered Territories*).	92,168	362	6,153	5,321	35,120	110	92,167	362
5 Bengal	8,797,343	775,666	232,812	50,640	679,208	32,313	8,638,122	749,490
6 Bihar and Orissa	8,497,464	3,210,362	180,805	170,835	562,274	110,987	8,454,135	3,201,108
7 Bombay (*including Aden*)	3,675,246	1,075,814	354,067	487,011	226,295	57,825	3,626,589	1,063,144
Aden	*935*	*124*	*15*	*31*	*175*	*11*	*340*	*122*
8 Burma	2,785,711	1,023,724	291,806	220,115	163,754	30,850	2,735,322	1,017,997
9 Central Provinces and Berar ..	3,418,557	1,907,067	321,084	1,011,476	230,884	74,205	3,379,183	1,900,986
10 Coorg	44,394	15,756	512	154	1,568	247	44,367	15,751
11 Delhi	39,809	3,836	8,515	14,594	5,566	293	39,633	3,834
12 Madras	8,249,251	3,051,257	586,812	703,649	512,581	84,976	8,130,795	3,016,279
13 North-West Frontier Province (*Districts and Administered Territories*).	437,121	11,727	56,877	23,000	28,445	181	436,853	11,726
14 Punjab	3,714,085	177,579	650,077	497,920	369,457	15,376	3,710,182	177,535
15 United Provinces of Agra and Oudh	12,162,443	2,716,152	452,585	2,531,357	1,463,694	326,591	12,14[illegible],367	2,712,601
States and Agencies ..	**14,567,806**	**4,127,812**	**2,259,329**	**4,151,722**	**1,714,595**	**390,345**	**14,451,720**	**4,098,698**
16 Assam States	113,067	46,877	28,669	55,617	16,672	9,584	111,851	45,661
17 Baluchistan States	107,063	331	3,762	334	20,297	36	104,836	325
18 Baroda State	470,978	161,807	34,394	188,734	29,425	3,133	469,736	161,078
19 Bengal States	205,441	9,692	7,762	8,797	11,905	836	204,710	9,690
20 Bihar and Orissa States	1,090,178	364,535	79,158	109,018	112,936	27,088	1,084,972	363,524
21 Bombay States	803,441	194,779	140,225	259,203	48,779	8,777	801,242	194,351
22 Central India Agency	1,507,943	796,371	103,400	160,181	134,255	17,874	1,504,174	795,986
23 Central Provinces States	525,562	133,046	151,900	277,432	20,809	5,774	523,922	132,832
24 Gwalior State	874,530	229,122	51,495	106,377	90,779	13,701	874,105	229,070
25 Hyderabad State	1,837,462	979,181	505,218	553,687	338,751	197,770	1,785,442	958,011
26 Jammu and Kashmir State ..	568,245	21,667	203,009	24,439	153,612	13,700	566,946	21,620
27 Madras States Agency	869,140	324,042	11[illegible],062	39,279	282,608	31,404	829,320	320,655
Cochin State	*159,622*	*89,845*	*3,753*	*3,489*	*30,165*	*4,941*	*151,450*	*88,999*
Travancore State	*621,047*	*198,330*	*100,402*	*21,998*	*241,183*	*24,007*	*589,400*	*195,790*
Other Madras States	*88,471*	*35,867*	*7,907*	*13,792*	*11,260*	*2,456*	*88,470*	*35,866*
28 Mysore State	1,449,860	254,599	111,742	461,683	75,014	8,325	1,448,872	254,486
29 North-West Frontier Province (*Agencies and Tribal Areas*).	2,307	..	5	..	1,115	..	2,307	..
30 Punjab States	99,449	6,362	34,961	95,967	6,054	269	99,403	6,36[illegible]
31 Punjab States Agency	932,514	52,285	181,782	225,579	111,278	4,363	931,473	52,255
32 Rajputana Agency	2,253,724	404,418	367,550	1,232,109	228,430	39,789	2,253,483	404,411
33 Sikkim State	35,595	33,260	566	389	926	1,765	35,395	33,260
34 United Provinces States	324,766	52,867	8,602	121,967	17,815	4,837	324,023	52,820
35 Western India States Agency ..	496,541	62,571	133,067	230,930	13,135	1,320	495,308	62,302

hood—Part II—Provincial Distribution—*contd.*

Materials—*contd.*

Animals and Vegetation.

Order 1.—Pasture and Agriculture.

Order 1.				Total *Sub-Order* 1 (*a*) Cultivation.						
Total working dependants.		Total following occupation as subsidiary to other.		Total earners principal occupation.		Total working dependants.		Total following occupation as subsidiary to other.		
Males.	Females.	Males.	Females.	Males.	Females.	Males.	Females.	Males.	Females.	
25	26	27	28	29	30	31	32	33	34	
5,749,708	**10,266,543**	**6,111,348**	**1,165,293**	**64,810,557**	**17,446,668**	**4,809,319**	**9,906,828**	**5,417,120**	**1,048,383**	
3,511,550	**6,127,350**	**4,420,954**	**783,267**	**51,336,797**	**13,606,632**	**2,924,541**	**5,947,772**	**4,007,769**	**721,742**	
14,598	65,750	11,984	1,395	82,571	14,687	11,567	64,417	11,051	1,333	**1**
3,368	2,972	105	5	1,519	53	40	104	68	2	**2**
371,653	363,380	235,382	58,824	1,680,879	151,642	268,556	344,788	186,125	47,236	**3**
6,153	5,321	35,119	110	82,766	286	3,393	4,825	15,959	51	**4**
230,733	46,435	655,242	29,931	8,393,877	632,152	182,778	44,431	633,653	28,751	**5**
179,941	170,346	534,620	109,379	8,310,190	3,176,200	144,311	164,282	499,385	106,054	**6**
350,103	481,732	221,327	55,002	3,450,907	1,023,251	277,905	463,263	205,118	51,665	**7**
4	*31*	*168*	*11*	*187*	*65*	*4*	*11*	*167*	*11*	
287,912	219,169	148,125	30,143	2,597,901	973,092	246,934	191,208	65,468	16,809	**8**
319,262	1,009,812	219,500	72,780	3,804,436	1,884,331	270,919	998,030	197,092	68,944	**9**
512	137	1,566	247	35,437	11,207	224	114	1,271	208	**10**
8,515	14,594	5,566	293	33,830	3,573	8,085	14,564	4,894	292	**11**
581,055	696,276	499,786	84,024	7,774,536	2,939,302	431,083	649,939	448,730	78,322	**12**
56,874	23,000	28,386	181	431,920	11,678	56,262	22,980	27,888	177	**13**
649,848	497,867	368,459	15,375	3,541,523	172,409	602,027	494,839	352,760	15,127	**14**
451,023	2,530,559	1,455,787	325,578	11,714,505	2,612,769	420,457	2,489,988	1,358,307	306,761	**15**
2,238,158	**4,139,193**	**1,690,394**	**382,026**	**13,473,760**	**3,840,036**	**1,884,778**	**3,959,056**	**1,409,351**	**326,641**	
28,511	55,310	16,278	9,524	104,755	41,755	24,752	53,705	8,355	8,280	**16**
5,741	315	20,008	35	89,723	240	2,332	135	8,241	13	**17**
34,369	188,708	29,303	3,133	449,001	154,793	30,411	182,084	25,032	2,666	**18**
7,751	8,797	11,647	836	200,995	7,120	7,036	8,687	11,510	804	**19**
79,073	108,847	109,331	26,927	1,030,408	348,819	53,397	102,867	90,173	26,005	**20**
140,118	258,768	48,196	8,500	770,029	190,537	122,249	252,312	42,256	7,342	**21**
103,287	160,134	130,171	17,777	1,419,224	780,207	65,984	150,397	103,971	14,019	**22**
151,638	277,116	19,983	5,766	496,348	129,504	141,465	270,585	15,996	5,542	**23**
51,484	106,343	90,627	13,677	839,674	223,663	42,864	104,649	82,412	12,226	**24**
489,090	543,524	328,821	190,439	1,558,371	877,074	427,798	473,700	290,629	162,095	**25**
202,961	24,322	153,391	13,627	539,064	19,802	174,358	18,163	149,712	12,536	**26**
108,255	38,732	280,238	31,144	674,112	250,890	89,189	34,853	204,771	21,645	**27**
3,632	*3,319*	*29,027*	*4,758*	*123,407*	*82,735*	*1,954*	*3,085*	*16,762*	*3,604*	
96,716	*21,622*	*239,993*	*23,930*	*464,081*	*132,711*	*85,059*	*20,582*	*177,680*	*15,669*	
7,907	*13,791*	*11,218*	*2,456*	*86,624*	*35,444*	*2,176*	*11,186*	*10,329*	*2,372*	
111,693	461,649	74,055	8,299	1,384,483	232,412	53,093	441,808	42,528	5,847	**28**
5	..	1,115	..	2,307	..	5	..	1,115	..	**29**
34,958	95,967	6,036	269	96,652	6,220	33,345	95,208	5,415	251	**30**
181,752	225,571	111,150	4,363	899,469	51,249	167,470	220,303	108,820	4,108	**31**
367,545	1,232,107	228,395	39,788	2,122,624	385,358	324,364	1,209,695	190,700	35,987	**32**
566	389	926	1,765	34,267	32,970	26	8	407	1,565	**33**
8,594	121,962	17,688	4,837	319,000	50,235	6,961	119,377	16,185	4,673	**34**
132,767	230,632	13,035	1,320	443,254	57,188	117,679	220,520	11,123	1,037	**35**

Table X.—Occupation or Means of Liveli

Class A.—Production of Raw

Sub-Class I—Exploitation of Animals and

Order 1.—Pasture and Agriculture

Sub-Order 1. (a)

Province, State or Agency.	*Group 1.*—Non-cultivating proprietors taking rent in money or kind.						*Group 2.*—Estate	
	Total earners principal occupation.		Total working dependants.		Total following occupation as subsidiary to other.		Total earners principal occupation.	
	Males.	Females.	Males.	Females.	Males.	Females.	Males.	Females.
1	35	36	37	38	39	40	41	42
INDIA	**2,269,662**	**707,610**	**150,155**	**129,964**	**810,935**	**82,432**	**54,199**	**7,312**
Provinces	**1,738,955**	**534,553**	**66,604**	**60,197**	**679,520**	**49,862**	**27,616**	**5,759**
1 Ajmer-Merwara	2,408	638	..	..	1,452	71	645	89
2 Andamans and Nicobars	..	..	..	..	..	..	..	..
3 Assam	18,802	3,580	755	287	17,347	680	140	..
4 Baluchistan (*Districts and Administered Territories*).	4,003	195	..	..	12,739	39	9	..
5 Bengal	451,684	164,663	8,172	4,047	145,683	9,506	1,081	39
6 Bihar and Orissa	89,788	16,552	1,140	1,458	47,933	2,147	1,027	8
7 Bombay (*including Aden*)	146,159	26,267	4,629	3,237	28,783	3,104	10,070	3,813
Aden	*99*	*47*	..	..	..	..	..	..
8 Burma	37,120	29,448	1,725	1,919	4,058	755	10	..
9 Central Provinces and Berar ..	43,385	9,139	991	503	21,445	1,441	149	2
10 Coorg	1,542	815	9	4	412	5	..	..
11 Delhi	1,394	283	11	28	1,713	129	2	..
12 Madras	381,472	151,484	13,401	14,872	51,939	4,254	7,793	613
13 North-West Frontier Province (*Districts and Administered Territories*).	32,997	3,625	3,969	883	12,352	123	..	..
14 Punjab	102,531	54,301	17,583	6,639	114,483	5,264	1,782	5
15 United Provinces of Agra and Oudh	335,670	73,563	14,219	26,320	219,181	22,344	4,908	1,190
States and Agencies ..	**530,707**	**173,057**	**83,551**	**69,767**	**131,415**	**32,570**	**26,583**	**1,553**
16 Assam States	1,619	807	118	156	429	47	..	..
17 Baluchistan States	7,219	96	..	..	1,720	9	..	..
18 Baroda State	11,908	8,823	..	..	5,663	295	282	..
19 Bengal States	3,545	1,706	14	3	1,892	63	24	..
20 Bihar and Orissa States	8,272	2,718	11	27	2,185	163	21	10
21 Bombay States	22,225	6,097	709	1,010	4,587	984	865	2
22 Central India Agency	12,025	1,934	77	46	3,428	108	186	..
23 Central Provinces States	1,314	217	22	2,495	340	9	2	..
24 Gwalior State	38,699	4,685	975	998	7,891	844	24	2
25 Hyderabad State	228,280	90,417	68,419	53,577	49,534	23,222	4,367	2
26 Jammu and Kashmir State ..	24,688	4,411	10,368	4,570	5,693	2,515	7	2
27 Madras States Agency	14,333	14,440	364	163	7,010	1,208	1,790	28
Cochin State	*4,070*	*3,220*	*14*	*7*	*1,226*	*207*	*470*	*7*
Travancore State	*7,861*	*10,133*	*285*	*96*	*4,256*	*887*	*1,318*	*21*
Other Madras States	*2,402*	*1,087*	*65*	*60*	*1,528*	*114*	*2*	..
28 Mysore State	27,240	16,034	337	4,503	5,977	275	103	19
29 North-West Frontier Province (*Agencies and Tribal Areas*).	1,600	..	1	..	252	..	..	..
30 Punjab States	1,027	835	14	16	1,705	151	2	..
31 Punjab States Agency	34,815	11,259	1,257	396	20,193	1,820	391	..
32 Rajputana Agency	58,144	4,583	..	..	9,113	233	17,117	1,468
33 Sikkim State	6	30	..	..	1	1	..	..
34 United Provinces States	2,753	1,005	283	674	3,002	592	41	..
35 Western India States Agency ..	30,995	2,960	582	1,133	800	31	1,361	20

hood.—Part II.—Provincial Distribution—*contd.*

Materials—*contd.*

Vegetation—*contd.*

—*contd.*

Cultivation.

Agents and Managers of Owners.				Group 3.—Estate Agents and Managers of Government.						
Total working dependants.		Total following occupation as subsidiary to other.		Total earners principal occupation.		Total working dependants.		Total following occupation as subsidiary to other.		
Males.	Females.	Males.	Females.	Males.	Females.	Males.	Females.	Males.	Females.	
43	44	45	46	47	48	49	50	51	52	
1,952	**377**	**5,881**	**112**	**7,021**	**1,800**	**1,049**	**68**	**623**	**53**	
697	**316**	**2,878**	**64**	**2,736**	**1,771**	**85**	**68**	**146**	**51**	
..	..	66	1	29	..	..	..	1	..	1
..	..	..	..	..	..	..	..	..	..	2
3	..	96	..	32	..	..	..	9	..	3
..	..	1	..	2	..	..	..	..	..	4
3	..	173	..	91	..	..	..	8	..	5
1	..	726	4	230	2	..	..	84	6	6
144	124	82	10	33	1,751	...	15	..	45	7
..	..	..	..	3	..	..	..	..	..	
..	..	3	..	193	..	..	..	..	..	8
10	..	33	..	199	8	..	5	11	..	9
..	..	..	..	..	..	..	..	..	..	10
..	..	..	..	1	..	..	..	..	..	11
283	191	812	43	1,005	10	85	48	16	..	12
..	..	..	..	6	..	..	...	3	..	13
182	..	108	..	97	..	..	..	4	..	14
71	1	778	6	818	..	..	..	9	..	15
1,255	**61**	**3,003**	**48**	**4,285**	**29**	**964**	..	**478**	**2**	
..	..	..	..	..	..	..	..	..	..	16
..	..	..	..	..	..	..	..	..	..	17
..	..	13	..	17	..	..	..	..	..	18
1	..	8	..	1	..	..	..	..	..	19
..	..	4	..	19	..	..	..	4	..	20
224	..	776		12	..	...	..	..	—	21
..	..	14	..	120	..	..	..	2	..	22
..	..	..	..	5	..	..	..	..	..	23
..	..	192	..	..	..	..	..	..	..	24
979	26	731	..	3,596	..	962	..	389	..	25
...	15	1	11	..	..	..	..	..	..	26
21	7	182	8	165	..	..	..	60	2	27
10	*1*	*151*	*6*	*74*	..	..	...	*47*	*2*	
11	*6*	*31*	*2*	*91*	..	..	...	*13*	...	
...	...	...	..	..	..	..	..	..	..	
6	—	59	..	1	..	..	..	1	...	28
...	—	...	..	..	..	..	...	..	...	29
—	..	1	..	..	..	..	...	..	..	30
12	9	19	..	66	..	1	..	15	..	31
—	—	987	29	268	25	..	...	7	—	32
...	—	—	..	..	..	..	..	—	—	33
—	—	—	..	..	..	..	—	—	—	34
12	4	16	—	15	4	1	—	..	..	35

Table X.—Occupation or Means of Liveli

Class A.—Production of Raw Materials

Sub-Class I.—Exploitation of

Order I.—Pasture and

Sub-Order 1 (a).—

	Province, State or Agency.	*Group 4.*—Rent collectors, clerks, etc.						*Group 5.*—	
		Total earners principal occupation.		Total working dependants.		Total following occupation as subsidiary to other.		Total earners principal occupation.	
		Males.	Females.	Males.	Females.	Males.	Females.	Males.	Females.
	1	53	54	55	56	57	58	59	60
	INDIA	**145,527**	**2,784**	**3,557**	**1,613**	**35,231**	**291**	**21,315,383**	**2,303,527**
	Provinces	**130,099**	**2,644**	**1,769**	**1,569**	**30,716**	**187**	**16,467,593**	**1,695,574**
1	Ajmer-Merwara	6	10	..	..	1	1	34,682	781
2	Andmans and Nicobars	6	..	..	..	..	..	358	28
3	Assam	2,804	19	98	11	1,208	18	926,547	70,541
4	Baluchistan .. .. .. (*Districts and Administered Territories.*)	15	..	..	..	..	..	56,033	2
5	Bengal	42,384	163	328	8	8,411	9	4,866,924	216,830
6	Bihar and Orissa	18,133	667	241	3	9,560	103	291,002	39,471
7	Bombay (*including Aden*)	2,914	399	311	161	131	23	757,233	77,012
	Aden	*9*	*4*	..	..	..	..	*20*	*13*
8	Burma	3,560	9	47	7	47	..	844,126	274,285
9	Central Provinces and Berar ..	6,993	178	60	5	876	13	1,707,248	288,105
10	Coorg	..	..	..	..	..	..	21,648	3,707
11	Delhi	12	..	..	..	..	..	17,593	666
12	Madras	10,773	966	378	1,318	564	2	3,928,480	571,819
13	North-West Frontier Province .. (*Districts and Administered Territories.*)	80	..	..	..	..	..	216,189	4,911
14	Punjab	463	..	18	..	19	..	1,707,744	54,454
15	United Provinces of Agra and Oudh	41,956	233	288	56	9,899	18	1,091,786	92,962
	States and Agencies ..	**15,428**	**140**	**1,788**	**44**	**4,515**	**104**	**4,847,790**	**607,953**
16	Assam States	8	..	..	..	1	..	69,293	28,763
17	Baluchistan States	..	..	..	..	..	..	48,496	28
18	Baroda State	185	..	..	..	14	..	292,478	27,674
19	Bengal States	459	..	4	..	67	..	123,550	3,085
20	Bihar and Orissa States	1,452	1	5	..	641	1	34,142	3,560
21	Bombay States	15	..	..	..	..	..	248,606	32,744
22	Central India Agency	557	13	1	..	1,015	11	163,794	33,080
23	Central Provinces States	219	5	..	..	5	..	349,206	31,149
24	Gwalior State	10	1	..	..	..	..	146,091	20,078
25	Hyderabad State	7,409	..	1,753	..	1,169	..	570,863	210,786
26	Jammu and Kashmir State ..	192	..	1	..	15	..	315,471	8,580
27	Madras States Agency	597	3	2	25	155	41	338,067	77,637
	Cochin State	*597*	*3*	*2*	*25*	*155*	*41*	*18,454*	*4,617*
	Travancore State	..	..	..	..	..	..	*255,401*	*57,885*
	Other Madras States	..	..	..	..	..	..	*64,212*	*15,135*
28	Mysore State	51	13	..	2	3	4	1,083,605	75,334
29	North-West Frontier Province (*Agencies and Tribal Areas*).	..	..	..	..	..	..	286	..
30	Punjab States	1	..	..	..	..	..	74,311	3,047
31	Punjab States Agency	642	..	22	17	12	..	532,749	26,977
32	Rajputana Agency	696	15	..	..	1,319	46	258,107	10,333
33	Sikkim State	..	..	..	..	..	..	14,555	3,539
34	United Provinces States	2,817	84	..	..	68	1	108,452	8,189
35	Western India States Agency ..	118	5	..	..	31	..	75,668	3,370

hood.—Part II.—Provincial Distribution—*contd.*

of Raw—*contd.*

Animals and Vegetation—*contd.*

Agriculture—*contd.*

Cultivation—*contd.*

Cultivating Owners. | *Group 6.*—Tenant cultivators.

Total working dependants. Males.	Total working dependants. Females.	Total following occupation as subsidiary to other. Males.	Total following occupation as subsidiary to other. Females.	Group 6.—Tenant cultivators. Total earners principal occupation. Males.	Total earners principal occupation. Females.	Total working dependants. Males.	Total working dependants. Females.	Total following occupation as subsidiary to other. Males.	Total following occupation as subsidiary to other. Females.	
61	62	63	64	65	66	67	68	69	70	
1,153,760	**2,233,430**	**1,225,333**	**165,781**	**25,564,656**	**4,276,698**	**1,331,493**	**3,001,057**	**1,747,539**	**317,211**	
517,284	**1,178,013**	**748,549**	**92,990**	**20,069,519**	**3,443,784**	**1,008,849**	**2,494,264**	**1,280,524**	**242,472**	
	..	2,628	25	29,609	941	..	..	4,887	45	1
1	..	14	..	950	24	36	104	26	2	2
22,371	59,430	65,873	26,733	571,796	24,858	5,172	2,934	89,948	15,857	3
..	..	588	2	20,650	9	55	..	1,912	2	4
..	..	223,565	10,654	782,180	33,474	..	..	55,798	1,642	5
4,224	2,207	26,326	1,277	6,129,665	1,778,433	65,241	94,507	205,174	31,570	6
22,066	21,688	30,696	3,634	1,006,580	97,550	38,573	17,729	64,845	9,337	7
4	*11*	*167*	*11*	..	..	..	..	..	..	
82,784	46,641	22,368	5,180	535,695	154,546	41,853	17,622	6,666	899	8
170,522	553,216	73,386	19,307	90,136	20,419	3,532	7,286	16,004	889	9
23	7	222	2	1,119	42	71	5	18	2	10
1	3	173	8	7,261	229	7,808	13,360	1,295	44	11
68,244	81,499	107,713	9,761	1,184,147	155,875	44,682	34,310	93,139	6,038	12
4,833	1,343	4,986	9	147,915	2,227	30,775	16,484	7,794	32	13
103,850	45,995	58,522	2,382	1,128,014	1,29,449	452,268	417,461	126,682	2,940	14
38,365	365,984	131,489	14,016	8,433,802	1,145,708	318,783	1,872,462	606,336	173,173	15
636,476	**1,055,417**	**476,784**	**72,791**	**5,495,137**	**832,914**	**322,644**	**506,793**	**467,015**	**74,739**	
11,485	21,271	2,623	2,289	11,369	5,561	1,843	3,384	914	1,907	16
..	..	1,047	1	30,255	1	35	2	4,767	2	17
24,854	164,086	7,843	610	55,715	6,408	5,557	17,998	4,683	287	18
..	..	6,008	294	15,266	186	–	..	831	21	19
424	96	1,746	91	676,369	90,402	3,980	3,832	33,143	12,357	20
4,435	6,380	7,208	876	311,372	40,560	12,960	25,405	10,791	700	21
3,524	3,623	6,972	382	833,117	230,539	39,920	90,739	50,327	3,375	22
123,890	225,251	12,370	4,881	14,961	677	1,033	9,688	754	8	23
2,839	2,430	14,398	1,217	556,415	118,229	18,435	33,205	41,160	4,892	24
146,099	128,084	101,773	2,586	264,521	112,856	69,812	54,705	50,174	22,914	25
102,032	4,375	87,636	4,278	187,233	6,024	61,503	8,000	54,642	4,671	26
58,581	17,492	138,967	12,440	85,977	13,101	13,157	1,990	28,056	1,315	27
244	*98*	*3,622*	*428*	*39,433*	*8,905*	*599*	*543*	*5,922*	*402*	
57,178	*8,152*	*132,027*	*11,166*	*38,146*	*2,224*	*12,457*	*522*	*20,525*	*588*	
1,159	*9,242*	*3,318*	*846*	*8,398*	*1,972*	*101*	*925*	*1,609*	*325*	
25,646	232,090	14,898	541	130,368	13,306	7,375	44,055	7,036	514	28
..	..	765	..	222	..	4	..	98	..	29
5,607	14,952	589	9	14,924	561	27,407	79,729	2,397	73	30
119,410	135,083	54,107	1,440	220,813	3,672	41,191	80,635	24,828	494	31
..	..	14,101	516	1,616,712	121,742	..	..	139,959	17,531	32
..	..	210	222	19,535	29,293	..	..	193	1,339	33
918	88,880	1,598	79	185,012	26,893	4,103	24,858	8,537	2,232	34
6,732	11,324	1,925	39	264.981	12,903	14,329	28,568	3,725	107	35

Table X.—Occupation or Means of Liveli

Class A.—Production

Sub-Class I.—Exploitation

Order 1.—Pasture and

Sub-Order 1 (a).—Cultivation—*concld.*

Province, State or Agency.	*Group 7.*—Agricultural Labourers. Total earners principal occupation. Males.	Total earners principal occupation. Females.	Total working dependants. Males.	Total working dependants. Females.	Total following occupation as subsidiary to other. Males.	Total following occupation as subsidiary to other. Females.	*Group 8.*—Cultivators Total earners principal occupation. Males.	Total earners principal occupation. Females.
1	71	72	73	74	75	76	77	78
INDIA	**14,990,473**	**9,934,884**	**2,119,993**	**4,434,869**	**1,568,124**	**475,080**	**463,636**	**212,053**
Provinces	**12,477,125**	**7,716,573**	**1,289,763**	**2,133,305**	**1,244,599**	**329,599**	**423,154**	**205,974**
1 Ajmer-Merwara	15,192	12,228	11,567	64,417	2,016	1,190	..	..
2 Andamans and Nicobars	205	1	3	..	28	..	..	..
3 Assam	52,137	3,094	233,211	237,290	9,710	1,278	108,621	49,550
4 Baluchistan .. .. .. (*District and Administered Territories*).	2,054	80	3,338	4,825	719	8	..	..
5 Bengal	2,241,853	215,882	173,619	36,989	199,566	6,895	7,680	1,101
6 Bihar and Orissa	1,780,344	1,341,067	73,463	66,107	209,576	70,947	1	..
7 Bombay (*including Aden*)	1,527,916	816,459	212,182	420,309	80,581	35,512	2	..
Aden	*56*	*1*	..	..	..	..	..	..
8 Burma	912,608	379,645	94,755	101,322	16,819	7,141	264,589	135,159
9 Central Provinces and Berar ..	1,356,326	1,566,480	95,804	437,015	85,337	47,304	..	..
10 Coorg	11,128	6,643	121	98	619	199	..	..
11 Delhi	7,567	2,395	265	1,173	1,713	111	..	..
12 Madras	2,218,605	2,038,371	297,893	509,581	191,605	57,256	42,261	20,164
13 North-West Frontier Province .. (*Districts and Administered Territories.*)	34,733	915	16,685	4,270	2,753	13	..	..
14 Punjab	510,892	34,200	28,126	24,744	52,942	4,541	..	..
15 United Provinces of Agra and Oudh	1,805,565	1,299,113	48,731	225,165	390,615	97,204	..	..
States and Agencies ..	**2,513,348**	**2,218,311**	**830,230**	**2,301,564**	**323,525**	**145,481**	**40,482**	**6,079**
16 Assam States	2,039	2,055	4,669	8,842	3,707	3,461	20,427	4,569
17 Baluchistan States	3,753	115	2,297	133	707	1	..	..
18 Baroda State	88,416	111,888	..	..	6,816	1,474	..	..
19 Bengal States	40,656	761	5,802	3,377	1,161	107	17,494	1,382
20 Bihar and Orissa States	310,005	252,088	48,977	98,912	52,450	13,393	128	40
21 Bombay States	186,707	111,133	103,915	219,515	18,893	4,782	227	1
22 Central India Agency	407,635	514,573	22,454	55,985	42,033	10,136	1,790	68
23 Central Provinces States	130,641	97,456	16,520	33,151	2,527	644	..	..
24 Gwalior State	98,435	80,668	20,615	68,016	18,771	5,273	..	..
25 Hyderabad State	479,335	463,013	139,774	237,308	86,859	73,373	..	..
26 Jammu and Kashmir State ..	11,066	780	452	1,161	1,522	1,059	407	5
27 Madras States Agency	233,174	145,667	17,062	15,173	30,333	6,629	9	14
Cochin State	*60,309*	*65,983*	*1,085*	*2,411*	*5,639*	*2,518*	..	..
Travancore State	*161,255*	*62,434*	*15,126*	*11,803*	*20,820*	*3,024*	*9*	*14*
Other Madras States	*11,610*	*17,250*	*851*	*959*	*3,874*	*1,087*	..	..
28 Mysore State	143,115	127,706	19,729	161,158	14,554	4,513	..	..
29 North-West Frontier Province .. (*Agencies and Tribal Areas.*)	199	..	..	..	..	..	..	..
30 Punjab States	6,387	1,777	317	511	723	18	..	..
31 Punjab States Agency	109,993	9,341	5,577	4,163	9,646	354	..	..
32 Rajputana Agency	171,580	247,192	324,364	1,209,695	25,214	17,632	..	..
33 Sikkim State	171	108	26	8	3	3	..	..
34 United Provinces States	19,925	14,064	1,657	4,965	2,980	1,769	..	..
35 Western India States Agency ..	70,116	37,926	96,023	179,491	4,626	860	..	..

hood—Part II—Provincial Distribution—*contd.*

of Raw Materials—*contd.*

of Animals and Vegetation—*contd.*

Agriculture—*contd.*

of jhum, taungya and shifting areas.

Total Sub-Order 1 (b).—Cultivation of special crops, fruit, etc. (planters, managers, clerks and labourers).

Total working dependants.		Total following occupation as subsidiary to other.		Total earners principal occupation.		Total working dependants.		Total following occupation as subsidiary to others.		
Males.	Females.	Males.	Females.	Males.	Females.	Males.	Females.	Males.	Females.	
79	80	81	82	83	84	85	86	87	88	
47,360	**105,450**	**23,454**	**7,423**	**960,151**	**599,113**	**43,780**	**55,174**	**209,896**	**39,012**	
39,490	**80,040**	**20,838**	**6,517**	**738,521**	**488,568**	**23,781**	**36,090**	**112,032**	**22,471**	
..	..	..	..	378	20	3	1	15	..	1
..	..	..	..	2,334	61	3,326	2,868	7	2	2
6,946	44,836	1,934	2,670	338,821	287,253	4,	13,202	36,105	10,909	3
..	..	..	..	822	..	[illegible]		24	..	4
656	3,387	449	45	173,079	112,674	1,474	431	11,051	296	5
1	..	6	..	9,095	3,746	577	118	6,437	333	6
..	..	..	..	11,249	2,582	579	730	1,105	153	7
..	..	..	..	*35*	*47*	..	*20*	*1*	..	
25,770	23,697	15,507	2,834	70,993	32,146	6,575	8,923	30,435	6,013	8
..	..	..	..	8,931	2,548	1,003	2,071	4,975	1.258	9
..	..	..	..	8,341	4,531	26	17	203	38	10
..	..	..	..	3,943	143	10	11	12	..	11
6,117	8,120	2,942	968	83,080	34,015	4,641	6,090	9,423	689	12
..	..	..	..	512	8	5	6	60	..	13
..	..	..	..	6,250	838	142	65	567	10	14
..	..	..	..	20,684	8,003	746	1,557	11,613	2,770	15
7,870	**25,410**	**2,616**	**906**	**221,630**	**110,545**	**19,999**	**19,084**	**97,864**	**16,541**	
6,637	20,052	681	576	4,983	3,517	1,155	710	6,506	952	16
..	..	..	..	40	..	..	5	12	..	17
..	..	..	..	1,179	332	78	285	163	32	18
1,215	5,307	1,543	319	3,009	2,555	18	27	53	30	19
..	..	..	..	563	226	3	1	9	1	20
6	2	1	..	1,506	403	68	168	298	183	21
8	4	180	7	8,376	3,003	164	323	3,866	402	22
..	..	..	..	953	325	567	898	970	31	23
..	..	..	..	1,018	91	28	24	200	154	24
..	..	..	..	20,500	14,992	7,374	13,611	4,801	4,865	25
2	42	203	2	886	176	35	45	357	246	26
2	3	8	2	138,727	67,977	8,822	910	71,941	9,087	27
..	..	..	..	*19,935*	*5,439*	*282*	*61*	*10,976*	*966*	
2	*3*	*8*	*2*	*118,665*	*62,525*	*8,538*	*849*	*60,918*	*8,121*	
..	..	..	..	*127*	*13*	*2*	..	*47*	..	
..	..	..	..	32,190	15,025	668	859	7,889	489	28
..	..	..	..	..	..	..	..	..	..	29
..	..	..	..	190	..	4	..	32	..	30
..	..	..	..	505	1	9	31	49	5	31
..	..	..	..	2,888	1,218	19	188	28[illegible]	29	32
..	..	..	..	14	..	..	1	4	..	33
..	..	..	..	317	375	33	424	21[illegible]	21	34
..	..	..	..	3,786	329	954	574	219	14	35

Table X.—Occupation or Means of Liveli

Province, State or Agency.	*Class A.*—Production / *Sub-Class I.*—Exploitation / *Order 1.*—Pasture and / *Sub-Order 1 (b).*—Cultivation of / *Group 9.*—Cinchona. Total earners principal occupation. Males.	Females.	Total working dependants. Males.	Females.	Total following occupataion as subsidiary to other. Males.	Females.	Total earners principal occupation. Males.	Females.
1	89	90	91	92	93	94	95	96
INDIA	**1,180**	**956**	**42**	**1**	**48**	..	**89,237**	**36,991**
Provinces	1,180	956	42	1	48	..	6,770	556
1 Ajmer-Merwara	..	..	..	..	..	..	..	..
2 Andamans and Nicobars	..	..	..	..	..	..	2,266	61
3 Assam	..	..	..	..	..	..	..	..
4 Baluchistan (*Districts and Administered Territories*).	..	..	..	..	..	..	..	..
5 Bengal	328	348	25	..	9	..	13	..
6 Bihar and Orissa	3	..	2	..	..	..	37	1
7 Bombay (*including Aden*) ..	77	..	..	..	..	..	24	1
Aden	..	..	..	..	..	..	..	..
8 Burma	456	195	..	1	..	..	57	15
9 Central Provinces and Berar ..	..	..	..	..	..	..	83	2
10 Coorg	..	..	..	..	..	..	..	..
11 Delhi	..	..	..	..	..	..	..	..
12 Madras	316	413	15	..	39	..	4,290	476
13 North-West Frontier Province (*Districts and Administered Territories*). ..	..	..	..	..	..	..	..	..
14 Punjab	..	..	..	..	..	..	..	..
15 United Provinces of Agra and Oudh	..	..	..	..	..	..	..	..
States and Agencies ..	..	..	..	..		..	82,467	36,435
16 Assam States	..	..	..	..	..	..	..	..
17 Baluchistan States	..	..	..	..	..	..	..	..
18 Baroda State	..	..	..	..	..	..	..	..
19 Bengal States	..	..	..	..	..	..	..	..
20 Bihar and Orissa States	..	..	..	..	..	..	..	..
21 Bombay States	..	..	..	..	..	..	179	19
22 Central India Agency	..	..	..	..	..	..	..	..
23 Central Provinces States	..	..	..	..	..	..	..	..
24 Gwalior State	..	..	..	..	..	..	..	.
25 Hyderabad State	..	..	..	..	..	..	..	..
26 Jammu and Kashmir State ..	..	..	..	..	..	..	..	..
27 Madras State Agency ..	..	..	..	..	..	..	82,278	36,415
Cochin State	..	..	..	..	..	..	*13,312*	*3,328*
Travancore State	..	..	..	..	..	..	*68,966*	*33,087*
Other Madras States ..	..	..	..	..	..	..	..	..
28 Mysore State	..	..	..	..	..	..	..	..
29 North-West Frontier Province (*Agencies and Tribal Areas*). ..	..	..	..	..	..	..	10	1
30 Punjab States	..	..	..	..	..	..	..	..
31 Punjab States Agency	..	..	..	..	..	..	..	..
32 Rajputana Agency	..	..	..	..	..	..	..	..
33 Sikkim State	..	..	..	..	..	..	..	..
34 United Provinces States	..	..	..	..	..	..	..	..
35 Western India States Agency ..	..	..	..	..	..	..	..	..

hood—Part II—Provincial Distribution—*contd.*

of Raw Materials—*contd.*

of Animals and Vegetation—*contd.*

Agriculture—*contd.*

special crops, fruit, etc. (Planters, managers, clerks and labourers)—*contd.*

Group 10.—Coconut. / *Group 11.*—Coffee.

Group 10: Total working dependants, Males	Group 10: Total working dependants, Females	Group 10: Total following occupation as subsidiary to other, Males	Group 10: Total following occupation as subsidiary to other, Females	Group 11: Total earners principal occupation, Males	
97	98	99	100	101	
9,696	**3,505**	**55,655**	**8,239**	**33,657**	
3,418	**2,925**	**1,018**	**195**	**14,297**	
..	..	..	..	..	1
3,326	2,868	7	2	4	2
..	..	..	..	1	3
..	..	..	..	..	4
..	..	5	..	1	5
2	..	234	2	1	6
3	..	..	..	14	7
..	..	..	..	*8*	
14	1	48	8	62	8
..	..	45	..	41	9
..	..	..	..	8,146	10
..	..	..	..	..	11
73	56	679	183	6,027	12
..	..	..	..	..	13
..	..	..	..	..	14
..	..	..	..	..	15
6,278	**580**	**54,637**	**8,044**	**19,360**	
..	..	..	..	6	16
..	..	..	..	..	17
..	..	..	..	..	18
..	..	..	..	..	19
..	..	..	..	..	20
2	13	14	1	..	21
..	..	..	..	..	22
..	..	..	..	..	23
..	..	..	..	..	24
..	..	..	..	..	25
..	..	..	..	..	26
6,276	567	54,621	8,043	387	27
95	*14*	*4,055*	*480*	*329*	
6,181	*553*	*50,566*	*7,563*	*58*	
..	..	..	..	..	
..	..	2	..	18,967	28
..	..	..	..	..	29
..	..	..	..	..	30
..	..	..	..	..	31
..	..	..	..	..	32
..	..	..	..	..	33
..	..	..	..	..	34
..	..	..	..	..	35

Group 11: Total earners principal occupation, Females	Group 11: Total working dependants, Males	Group 11: Total working dependants, Females	Group 11: Total following occupation as subsidiary to other, Males	Group 11: Total following occupation as subsidiary to other, Females	
102	103	104	105	106	
17,139	**571**	**676**	**2,615**	**505**	
6,534	**453**	**364**	**1,342**	**230**	
..	..	..	..	..	1
..	..	..	..	..	2
2	1	..	5	..	3
..	..	..	..	..	4
1	..	..	..	..	5
..	..	..	..	..	6
51	..	21	..	..	7
47	..	*20*	..	..	
31	27	22	444	183	8
21	..	..	..	..	9
4,391	25	17	201	38	10
..	..	..	..	..	11
2,037	400	04	692	9	12
..	..	..	..	..	13
..	..	..	..	..	14
..	..	..	..	..	15
10,605	**118**	**312**	**1,273**	**275**	
7	3	9	8	1	16
..	..	..	..	..	17
..	..	..	..	..	18
..	..	..	..	..	19
..	..	..	..	..	20
..	..	..	..	..	21
..	..	..	..	..	22
..	..	..	..	..	23
..	..	..	..	..	24
..	..	..	..	..	25
..	..	3	..	1	26
229	35	8	85	24	27
177	*4*	..	..	..	
52	*31*	*8*	*85*	*24*	
..	..	..	..	..	
10,369	80	292	1,180	249	28
..	..	..	..	..	29
..	..	..	..	..	30
..	..	..	..	..	31
..	..	..	..	..	32
..	..	..	..	..	33
..	..	..	..	..	34
..	..	..	..	..	35

Table X.—Occupation or Means of Liveli

Class A.—Production

Sub-Class I.—Exploitation

Order 1.—Pasture and

Sub-Order 1 (b).—Cultivation of

	Province, State or Agency.	*Group 12.*—Ganja. Total earners principal occupation. Males.	Females.	Total working dependants. Males.	Females.	Total following occupation as subsidiary to other. Males.	Females.	Total earners principal occupation. Males.	Females.
	1	107	108	109	110	111	112	113	114
	INDIA	**77**	**3**	**1**	..	**1,049**	**34**	**61,352**	**9,570**
	Provinces	74	2	1	..	1,049	32	48,583	6,866
1	Ajmer-Merwara	..	..	..	..	..	..	..	..
2	Andamans and Nicobars	..	..	..	..	..	..	..	..
3	Assam	4	..	..	..	2	..	2,522	915
4	Baluchistan (*Districts and Administered Territories*).	..	..	..	..	..	..	..	..
5	Bengal	37	1	1	..	1,044	32	26,916	775
6	Bihar and Orissa	..	..	..	..	..	..	1,179	76
7	Bombay (*including Aden*)	..	..	..	..	..	..	94	..
	Aden	..	..	..	..	..	..	..	..
8	Burma	..	..	..	..	..	..	7,902	3,663
9	Central Provinces and Berar	25	..	..	..	..	..	1,818	866
10	Coorg	..	..	..	..	..	..	2	..
11	Delhi	..	..	..	..	..	..	..	..
12	Madras	8	1	..	..	3	..	7,914	517
13	North-West Frontier Province (*Districts and Administered Territories*).	..	..	..	..	..	..	..	..
14	Punjab	..	..	..	..	..	..	..	..
15	United Provinces of Agra and Oudh	..	..	..	..	..	..	236	54
	States and Agencies	3	1	..	..	..	2	12,769	2,704
16	Assam States	..	..	..	..	..	..	2,260	570
17	Baluchistan States	..	..	..	..	..	..	..	..
18	Baroda State	..	..	..	..	..	..	40	..
19	Bengal States	..	..	..	..	..	..	46	..
20	Bihar and Orissa States	..	..	..	..	..	..	1	..
21	Bombay States	..	..	..	..	..	..	1	..
22	Central India Agency	..	..	..	..	..	..	2,641	936
23	Central Provinces States	..	..	..	..	..	..	22	..
24	Gwalior State	..	..	..	..	..	..	..	..
25	Hyderabad State	..	..	..	..	..	..	1,794	638
26	Jammu and Kashmir State	..	..	..	..	..	..	..	..
27	Madras States Agency	..	..	..	..	..	2	4,605	400
	Cochin State	..	..	..	..	..	*2*	*1,508*	*315*
	Travancore State	..	..	..	..	..	..	*3,037*	*83*
	Other Madras States	..	..	..	..	..	..	*60*	*2*
28	Mysore State	1	1	..	..	..	..	845	64
29	North-West Frontier Province (*Agencies and Tribal Areas*).	..	..	..	..	..	..	..	..
30	Punjab States	..	..	..	..	..	..	..	..
31	Punjab States Agency	..	..	..	..	..	..	..	..
32	Rajputana Agency	..	..	..	..	..	..	512	96
33	Sikkim State	..	..	..	..	..	..	..	..
34	United Provinces States	..	..	..	..	..	..	..	..
35	Western India States Agency	..	..	..	..	..	..	2	..

hood—Part II—Provincial Distribution—*contd.*

of Raw Materials—*contd.*

of Animals and Vegetation—*contd.*

Agriculture—*contd.*

special crops, fruit, etc. (Planters, managers, clerks and labourers)—*contd.*

Group 13.—Pan-Vine.				*Group 14.*—Rubber.						
Total working dependants.		Total following occupation as subsidiary to other.		Total earners principal occupation.		Total working dependants.		Total following occupation as subsidiary to other.		
Males.	Females.	Males.	Females.	Males.	Females.	Males.	Females.	Males.	Females.	
115	116	117	118	119	120	121	122	123	124	
3,847	**3,237**	**26,126**	**2,044**	**14,933**	**2,910**	**323**	**263**	**556**	**23**	
1,757	**2,059**	**19,116**	**1,291**	**7,715**	**1,634**	**226**	**183**	**271**	**12**	
..	..	..	..	..	..	..	..	..	..	1
..	..	..	..	..	..	..	..	..	—	2
72	133	1,186	165	..	..	..	..	..	..	3
..	..	..	..	..	..	..	..	..	..	4
458	15	8,170	134	4	..	..	..	4	..	5
180	10	1,206	50	..	..	..	..	..	..	6
10	..	5	..	13	..	..	..	..	..	7
—	..	..	..	..	..	..	..	..	..	
705	1,151	5,104	868	5,232	1,229	225	180	213	11	8
148	598	364	44	..	1	—	..	—	—	9
..	..	..	..	29	15	..	..	..	..	10
..	..	..	..	..	..	..	..	..	..	11
175	95	2,998	30	2,437	389	1	3	54	1	12
..	..	..	..	..	..	..	..	..	..	13
..	..	..	..	..	..	..	..	..	..	14
9	57	83	..	..	..	..	..	..	..	15
2,090	**1,178**	**7,010**	**753**	**7,218**	**1,276**	**97**	**80**	**285**	**11**	
185	208	661	270	..	..	..	..	..	..	16
..	..	..	..	—	..	..	..	..	..	17
13	..	..	..	..	..	..	..	..	..	18
..	..	2	..	..	..	..	..	..	..	19
..	..	1	..	..	..	..	..	..	..	20
..	..	..	..	4	..	1	..	..	..	21
60	42	300	27	..	..	..	..	..	..	22
4	1	2	..	..	..	..	..	..	..	23
..	..	..	..	..	..	..	..	..	..	24
779	853	504	321	..	..	..	..	..	..	25
..	..	..	..	..	..	..	..	..	..	26
1,026	57	4,908	133	7,299	1,276	96	89	285	11	27
63	*13*	*1,699*	*110*	*1,222*	*338*	*1*	*1*	*19*	..	
961	*44*	*3,170*	*23*	*5,987*	*938*	*95*	*79*	*266*	*11*	
2	..	*39*	..	..	..	..	..	..	..	
17	8	626	2	5	..	..	..	..	..	28
..	..	..	..	..	..	..	..	..	..	29
..	..	..	..	..	..	..	..	..	..	30
..	..	..	..	..	..	..	..	—	..	31
	..	..	..	..	..	..	..	..	..	32
..	..	..	..	..	..	..	..	..	..	33
..	..	..	..	..	..	..	..	..	..	34
..	..	..	..	..	..	..	..	..	..	35

Table X.—Occupation or Mens of Liveli

Province, State or Agency.	Class A.—Production; Sub-Class I.—Exploitation of; Order 1.—Pasture and; Sub-Order 1 (b).—Cultivation of; Group 15.—Tea. Total earners principal occupation. Males.	Females.	Total working dependants. Males.	Females.	Total following occupation as subsidiary to other. Males.	Females.	Group 16.—Market. Total earners principal occupation. Males.	Females.
1	125	126	127	128	129	130	131	132
INDIA	**548,639**	**449,265**	**6,812**	**15,616**	**38,121**	**10,797**	**211,076**	**82,279**
Provinces	**507,032**	**416,510**	**6,706**	**15,502**	**37,892**	**10,726**	**152,870**	**55,510**
1 Ajmer-Merwara	..	1	..	—	—	—	378	19
2 Andamans and Nicobars	..	..	..	—	—	—	64	..
3 Assam	333,979	285,585	4,479	12,828	33,613	9,992	2,315	751
4 Baluchistan (*Districts and Administered Territories*).	..	..	..	..	..	..	822	..
5 Bengal	140,635	111,344	968	416	1,527	92	5,145	205
6 Bihar and Orissa	235	223	3	2	100	30	7,640	3,446
7 Bombay (*including Aden*)	31	2	..	..	2	—	10,996	2,528
Aden	..	..	..	..	..	..	*27*	..
8 Burma	2,040	1,367	1,109	2,213	2,285	601	55,244	25,646
9 Central Provinces and Berar ..	194	7	..	..	49	..	6,770	1,651
10 Coorg	146	124	..	..	..	..	18	1
11 Delhi	..	..	..	..	..	..	3,943	143
12 Madras	28,790*	17,377*	119	23*	180	11	33,307	12,805
13 North-West Frontier Province (*Districts and Administered Territories*).	..	..	..	..	..	..	512	8
14 Punjab	948	473	28	20	125	..	5,302	365
15 United Provinces of Agra and Oudh	34	7	..	..	11	—	20,414	7,942
States and Agencies ..	**41,607**	**32,755**	**106**	**114**	**229**	**71**	**58,206**	**26,769**
16 Assam States	..	..	..	..	—	—	2,717	2,940
17 Baluchistan States	..	..	..	..	—	—	40	..
18 Baroda State	..	..	..	..	—	—	1,139	332
19 Bengal States	2,902	2,555	18	27	44	30	61	..
20 Bihar and Orissa States	15	1	1	..	4	—	547	225
21 Bombay States	..	..	..	..	..	..	1,322	384
22 Central India Agency	..	..	..	..	..	—	5,735	2,067
23 Central Provinces States	19	5	..	..	1	—	912	320
24 Gwalior State	..	..	..	..	..	..	1,018	91
25 Hyderabad State	..	..	..	..	..	..	18,706	14,354
26 Jammu and Kashmir State ..	..	..	..	..	..	..	886	176
27 Madras States Agency	37,411	28,047	86	65	179	35	6,837	1,610
Cochin State	*998*	*539*	*2*	..	*67*	*1*	*2,566*	*742*
Travancore State	*36,404*	*27,507*	*84*	*65*	*112*	*13*	*4,213*	*958*
Other Madras States	*9*	*1*	..	..	—	..	*58*	*10*
28 Mysore State	1,257	2,146	1	22	..	6	11,105	2,444
29 North-West Frontier Province (*Agencies and Tribal Areas*).	..	..	..	..	..	..	..	..
30 Punjab States	..	..	..	..	..	..	190	..
31 Punjab States Agency	3	..	..	..	1	..	502	1
32 Rajputana Agency	..	..	..	..	..	..	2,376	1,122
33 Sikkim State	..	..	..	..	..	..	14	—
34 United Provinces States	..	..	..	..	..	..	317	375
35 Western India States Agency ..	—	1	..	..	..	—	3,782	328

* Include persons employed on coffee and unspecified plantations.

hood—Part II—Provincial Distribution—*contd.*

of Raw Materials—*contd.*

Animals and Vegetation—*contd.*

Agriculture—*contd.*

special crops, fruit, etc. (Planters, managers, clerks and labourers)—*concld.*

gardeners, flower and fruit growers.

Total Sub-Order 1 (c).—Forestry.

Total working dependants.		Total following occupation as subsidiary to other.		Total earners principal occupation.		Total working dependants.		Total following occupation as subsidiary to other.		
Males.	Females.	Males.	Females.	Males.	Females.	Males.	Females.	Males.	Females.	
133	134	135	136	137	138	139	140	141	142	
22,488	**31,876**	**85,726**	**17,370**	**193,489**	**70,871**	**19,554**	**26,578**	**87,417**	**14,722**	
11,178	15,056	51,296	9,985	128,271	49,465	10,251	14,589	63,437	9,000	
3	1	15	..	290	53	3	1	20	3	1
..	..	..	..	862	..	..	..	30	1	2
116	241	1,299	752	2,593	102	253	100	3,667	84	3
6	..	24	..	261	1	337	55	95	..	4
22	..	292	38	5,869	173	23	94	1,539	16	5
390	106	4,897	251	4,756	2,803	124	442	3,226	1,016	6
566	709	1,098	153	15,711	19,972	895	4,507	3,477	1,637	7
..	..	*1*	..	*78*	*2*	..	..	..	..	
4,495	5,355	22,341	4,342	39,246	5,554	4,799	3,129	35,665	3,154	8
855	1,473	4,517	1,214	9,723	3,370	355	1,034	4,608	1,022	9
1	..	2	..	250	1	..	..	58	..	10
10	11	12	..	558	75	11	1	2	..	11
3,858	5,609	4,778	455	19,958	6,622	2,273	3,040	6,539	1,241	12
5	6	60	..	232	11	22	2	59	1	13
114	45	442	10	13,384	1,116	884	738	1,190	20	14
737	1,500	11,519	2,770	14,578	9,612	272	1,446	3,262	805	15
11,310	16,820	34,430	7,385	65,218	21,406	9,303	11,989	23,980	5,722	
967	493	5,837	681	135	112	160	84	547	23	16
..	5	12	..	203	35	3	..	39	..	17
65	285	163	32	1,816	84	168	18	2,272	8	18
..	..	7	..	231	..	2	..	28	2	19
2	1	4	1	2,085	858	27	353	813	440	20
65	155	284	182	2,901	307	407	269	2,369	390	21
104	281	3,566	375	7,920	4,408	209	649	5,698	1,098	22
563	897	967	31	1,252	479	117	304	475	36	23
28	24	200	154	1,644	1,406	139	352	404	153	24
6,595	12,758	4,297	4,544	22,947	5,080	6,451	4,864	5,263	1,263	25
35	42	357	245	1,489	3	26	4	359	3	26
1,303	133	11,863	839	6,327	662	159	50	1,393	162	27
117	*33*	*5,136*	*373*	*2,584*	*419*	*20*	*24*	*733*	*133*	
1,186	*100*	*6,719*	*466*	*3,639*	*243*	*139*	*26*	*508*	*92*	
..	..	*8*	..	*104*	..	..	..	*92*	..	
570	537	6,081	232	2,749	1,094	268	1,126	1,019	484	28
..	..	..	..	..	..	..	..	..	..	29
4	..	32	..	348	12	19	3	250	..	30
9	31	48	5	1,082	64	78	74	405	2	31
13	170	277	29	6,060	5,095	327	1,185	2,372	1,677	32
	1	4	..	637	70	10	11	15	9	33
33	424	212	21	1,295	156	45	61	78	..	34
954	574	219	14	4,097	1,481	688	2,582	181	32	35

Table X.—Occupation or Means of Liveli

Class A.—Production of

Sub-Class I.—Exploitation

Order 1.—Pasture and

Sub-Order 1 (c).—Forestry

	Province, State or Agency.	Group 17.—Forest officers, rangers, guards, etc.						Group 18.—Wood cutters	
		Total earners principal occupation.		Total working dependants.		Total following occupation as subsidiary to other.		Total earners principal occupation.	
		Males.	Females.	Males.	Females.	Males.	Females.	Males.	Females.
	1	143	144	145	146	147	148	149	150
	INDIA	**40,168**	**897**	**972**	**315**	**5,143**	**131**	**118,124**	**27,767**
	Provinces	**28,240**	**840**	**709**	**127**	**3,653**	**124**	**77,346**	**16,091**
1	Ajmer-Merwara	120	1	..	..	7	..	150	19
2	Andamans and Nicobars	361	..	..	..	1	..	1	..
3	Assam	1,004	..	39	..	231	..	1,126	72
4	Baluchistan (*Districts and Administered Territories*).	67	..	..	..	5	..	194	1
5	Bengal	1,149	71	1	2	306	13	4,563	98
6	Bihar and Orissa	616	16	2	..	315	2	3,333	2,003
7	Bombay (*including Aden*)	2,692	404	195	67	105	..	11,775	5,106
	Aden	..	..	..	..	..	..	*78*	*2*
8	Burma	6,385	54	154	6	389	2	24,636	2,111
9	Central Provinces and Berar ..	4,811	170	67	31	547	96	2,697	233
10	Coorg	119	..	..	..	22	..	131	1
11	Delhi	71	..	1	..	2	..	164	2
12	Madras	4,985	114	131	19	649	10	13,021	3,763
13	North-West Frontier Province (*Districts and Administered Territories*).	42	..	..	..	15	..	153	7
14	Punjab	2,885	10	71	2	245	1	9,452	611
15	United Provinces of Agra and Oudh	2,933	..	48	..	814	..	5,950	2,064
	States and Agencies ..	**11,928**	**57**	**263**	**188**	**1,490**	**7**	**40,778**	**11,676**
16	Assam States	1	..	..	..	..	..	123	112
17	Baluchistan States	2	..	..	..	..	..	195	34
18	Baroda State	325	..	4	..	15	..	1,452	75
19	Bengal States	105	..	1	..	23	1	126	..
20	Bihar and Orissa States	777	1	1	..	169	..	918	665
21	Bombay States	537	1	9	..	18	..	1,912	210
22	Central India Agency	2,326	9	3	1	180	..	1,808	1,072
23	Central Provinces States	525	8	2	..	22	..	344	81
24	Gwalior State	162	..	1	..	12	..	254	360
25	Hyderabad State	453	..	137	..	17	..	21,181	4,669
26	Jammu and Kashmir State ..	1,171	2	7	..	315	1	318	1
27	Madras States Agency	968	..	..	..	43	..	4,756	313
	Cochin State	*284*	..	..	..	*10*	..	*1,890*	*82*
	Travancore State	*604*	..	..	..	*24*	..	*2,842*	*231*
	Other Madras States	*80*	..	..	..	*9*	..	*24*	..
28	Mysore State	1,470	23	5	5	187	2	574	149
29	North-West Frontier Province (*Agencies and Tribal Areas*). ..	..	..	..	..	..	..	..	..
30	Punjab States	164	..	12	..	206	..	138	12
31	Punjab States Agency	627	..	7	..	162	..	327	46
32	Rajputana Agency	1,105	1	10	..	55	1	1,964	2,538
33	Sikkim State	595	..	7	..	1	2	14	64
34	United Provinces States	38	..	..	..	61	..	1,240	156
35	Western India States Agency ..	637	12	57	182	4	..	3,134	1,119

hood—Part II—Provincial Distribution—*contd.*

of Raw Materials—*contd.*

of Animals and Vegetation—*contd.*

Agriculture—*contd.*

—*contd.*

and charcoal burners.				*Group 19.*—Collectors of forest produce.						
Total working dependants.		Total following occupation as subsidiary to other.		Total earners principal occupation.		Total working dependants.		Total following occupation as subsidiary to other.		
Males.	Females.	Males.	Females.	Males.	Females.	Males.	Females.	Males.	Females.	
151	152	153	154	155	156	157	158	159	160	
14,497	**12,765**	**60,220**	**7,295**	**34,003**	**41,432**	**3,715**	**13,246**	**20,940**	**7,101**	
7,018	**4,968**	**44,585**	**4,347**	**22,426**	**32,080**	**2,521**	**9,470**	**14,600**	**4,469**	
3	1	12	3	20	33	..	..	1	..	1
..	..	..	..	500	—	..	..	29	1	2
80	66	2,659	56	463	30	134	34	777	28	3
337	55	90	—	..	..	..	..	..	..	4
21	92	1,210	3	116	4	..	—	6	..	5
63	221	2,570	952	727	754	59	221	307	51	6
617	1,572	3,253	1,215	1,215	14,462	83	2,868	119	422	7
..	—	—	—	—	..	—	—	..	..	
3,152	652	25,201	1,041	8,152	3,380	1,491	2,469	9,682	2,111	8
133	141	2,723	130	2,191	2,875	155	858	1,186	758	9
..	..	36	..	—	—	..	..	..	..	10
..	..	..	..	323	73	10	1	..	..	11
1,795	1,547	5,002	479	1,952	2,745	347	1,474	888	752	12
22	1	44	1	37	4	..	1	—	..	13
721	179	800	8	1,037	495	92	557	142	11	14
74	441	985	459	5,693	7,225	150	987	1,463	335	15
7,479	**7,797**	**15,635**	**2,948**	**11,577**	**9,352**	**1,194**	**3,776**	**6,340**	**2,632**	
153	84	516	23	11	..	7	..	31	..	16
2	..	30	—	6	1	1	..	9	..	17
163	18	2,247	4	32	8	1	—	10	4	18
1	..	5	1	—	..	..	—	..	..	19
15	268	440	352	380	183	9	85	151	37	20
323	142	2,232	145	452	67	75	74	119	244	21
46	47	1,750	365	3,536	3,256	151	587	3,587	666	22
28	93	214	3	358	385	87	211	183	26	23
8	41	113	20	1,282	1,046	130	311	279	133	24
5,784	4,474	4,864	1,106	703	208	174	229	160	88	25
19	4	44	2	—	..	..	..	—	..	26
114	32	1,151	70	603	349	45	18	197	92	27
10	*6*	*622*	*42*	*410*	*337*	*10*	*18*	*99*	*91*	
104	*26*	*448*	*28*	*193*	*12*	*35*	..	*96*	*1*	
..	..	*81*	—	..	..	..	..	*2*	—	
10	34	204	6	698	920	253	1,087	627	476	28
..	..	—	—	—	..	..	..	—	—	29
3	3	40	—	46	..	4	..	4	—	30
27	23	231	1	128	18	44	51	12	1	21
123	297	1,374	812	2,984	2,555	194	388	943	864	32
3	10	8	6	28	6	..	1	6	1	33
45	61	13	—	17	..	..	..	4	—	34
[illegible]	2,166	159	32	313	350	19	234	18	—	35

Table X.—Occupation or Means of Liveli

Class A.—Production

Sub-Class I.—Exploitation

Order 1.—Pasture and

Province, State or Agency.	*Sub-Order 1 (c).*—Forestry—*concld.* *Group 20.*—Collectors of lac. Total earners principal occupation. Males.	Females.	Total working dependants. Males.	Females.	Total following occupation as subsidiary to other. Males.	Females.	*Total Sub-order 1 (d)* Total earners principal occupation Males.	Females.
1	161	162	163	164	165	166	167	168
INDIA	**1,194**	**775**	**370**	**252**	**1,114**	**195**	**2,039,979**	**303,649**
Provinces	**259**	**454**	**3**	**24**	**599**	**60**	**1,354,800**	**179,297**
1 Ajmer-Merwara	..	..	..	..	..	..	4,483	428
2 Andamans and Nicobars	..	..	..	..	..	..	70	..
3 Assam	..	..	..	..	..	..	13,573	581
4 Baluchistan (*Districts and Administered Territories*).	..	..	..	..	..	..	8,317	75
5 Bengal	41	..	1	..	17	..	65,098	4,015
6 Bihar and Orissa	80	30	..	..	34	11	129,451	18,218
7 Bombay (*including Aden*)	29	..	..	..	..	..	148,574	17,337
Aden	..	..	..	..	..	..	*40*	*8*
8 Burma	73	9	2	2	393	..	26,547	6,756
9 Central Provinces and Berar ..	24	92	..	4	152	38	155,396	10,322
10 Coorg	..	..	..	..	..	..	339	12
11 Delhi	..	..	..	..	..	..	1,302	43
12 Madras	..	..	..	..	..	..	252,426	36,099
13 North-West Frontier Province (*Districts and Administered Territories*).	..	..	..	..	..	..	4,189	29
14 Punjab	10	..	..	..	3	..	148,977	3,168
15 United Provinces of Agra and Oudh	2	323	..	18	..	11	396,058	82,214
States and Agencies ..	**935**	**321**	**367**	**228**	**515**	**135**	**685,179**	**124,352**
16 Assam States	..	..	..	..	..	..	1,961	274
17 Baluchistan States	..	..	..	..	..	..	14,870	50
18 Baroda State	7	1	..	..	..	..	17,696	5,866
19 Bengal States	..	..	..	..	..	..	475	15
20 Bihar and Orissa States	10	9	2	..	53	51	51,613	13,424
21 Bombay States	..	29	..	53	..	1	26,802	3,104
22 Central India Agency	250	71	9	14	181	7	67,998	7,671
23 Central Provinces States	25	5	..	..	56	7	25,129	2,477
24 Gwalior State	6	..	..	..	..	..	31,761	3,910
25 Hyderabad State	610	203	356	161	222	69	180,863	60,349
26 Jammu and Kashmir State ..	..	..	..	..	..	..	25,408	1,629
27 Madras States Agency	..	..	..	..	2	..	9,678	1,116
Cochin State	..	..	..	..	*2*	..	*5,521*	*404*
Travancore State	..	..	..	..	..	..	*2,542*	*303*
Other Madras States	..	..	..	..	..	..	*1,615*	*409*
28 Mysore State	7	2	..	..	1	..	28,145	5,079
29 North-West Frontier Province (*Agencies and Tribal Areas*).	..	..	..	..	..	..	..	..
30 Punjab States	..	..	..	..	..	..	2,213	129
31 Punjab States Agency	..	..	..	..	..	..	30,417	941
32 Rajputana Agency	7	1	..	..	..	..	121,910	12,740
33 Sikkim State	..	..	..	..	..	..	677	220
34 United Provinces States	..	..	..	..	..	..	3,411	2,054
35 Western India States Agency ..	13	..	..	..	..	..	44,152	3,304

hood—Part II—Provincial Distribution—*contd.*

of Raw Materials—*contd.*

of Animals and Vegetation—*contd.*

Agriculture—*contd.*

Sub-Order 1 (d).—Stock raising.

Stock raising. Total working dependants. Males.	Stock raising. Total working dependants. Females.	Stock raising. Total following occupation as subsidiary to other. Males.	Stock raising. Total following occupation as subsidiary to other. Females.	*Group 21.*—Cattle and buffalo breeders and keepers. Total earners principal occupation. Males.	Total earners principal occupation. Females.	Total working dependants. Males.	Total working dependants. Females.	Total following occupation as subsidiary to other. Males.	Total following occupation as subsidiary to other. Females.	
169	170	171	172	173	174	175	176	177	178	
875,280	**275,993**	**356,977**	**59,457**	**513,581**	**82,193**	**308,498**	**70,537**	**90,949**	**12,710**	
552,266	**128,133**	**230,513**	**29,119**	**344,564**	**46,145**	**243,057**	**37,069**	**57,379**	**6,589**	
3,025	1,331	898	59	290	4	551	24	93	1	1
2	..	..	..	70	..	2	..	..	..	2
97,850	5,213	6,815	278	13,464	570	97,684	5,197	6,796	278	3
2,417	441	19,041	59	277	27	..	..	880	1	4
46,456	1,425	8,260	766	19,602	2,583	9,200	741	2,934	508	5
34,915	5,495	23,640	1,892	43,523	8,069	8,529	2,878	10,433	877	6
70,724	13,228	11,627	1,547	110,675	12,180	60,266	9,699	8,565	1,300	7
	..	..	..	*34*	*4*	..	..	..	..	
29,361	15,424	16,258	4,002	11,937	2,038	1,175	839	6,839	582	8
46,979	8,663	12,008	1,318	31,536	4,878	5,904	4,735	5,560	896	9
262	6	34	1	339	12	259	6	34	1	10
409	18	658	1	234	5	1	..	23	..	11
142,941	37,086	34,379	3,740	85,346	13,641	55,418	12,279	12,098	2,016	12
585	12	379	3	3,981	19	579	12	359	1	13
46,792	2,223	13,917	218	19,505	923	3,447	523	1,765	59	14
29,548	37,568	82,599	15,235	3,785	1,196	42	136	1,000	69	15
323,014	**147,860**	**126,464**	**30,338**	**169,017**	**36,048**	**65,441**	**33,468**	**33,570**	**6,121**	
2,444	811	295	199	1,924	270	2,365	754	273	136	16
1,406	175	11,716	22	853	5	203	84	1,662	..	17
3,712	6,311	1,811	427	5,882	4,590	714	2,682	1,198	377	18
695	83	56	..	188	10	480	83	2	..	19
25,631	5,570	5,780	211	3,643	10,328	2,598	1,522	605	30	20
17,394	6,019	3,273	585	19,531	2,019	14,587	4,763	2,603	271	21
36,882	8,660	8,902	570	9,179	842	1,730	271	792	83	22
9,476	5,184	1,903	107	14,435	1,978	5,788	3,668	1,462	90	23
8,453	1,318	7,611	1,143	5,686	459	1,226	250	1,482	43	24
46,874	50,792	27,482	22,049	22,751	9,404	7,388	7,816	4,421	2,969	25
28,518	6,109	2,883	841	6,389	428	6,972	647	1,203	240	26
9,987	2,916	2,016	246	3,708	394	3,035	228	879	133	27
1,376	*149*	*556*	*55*	*1,967*	*152*	*477*	*42*	*381*	*40*	
2,882	*162*	*710*	*107*	*1,691*	*222*	*2,484*	*144*	*498*	*85*	
5,729	*2,605*	*750*	*84*	*50*	*20*	*74*	*42*	..	*8*	
57,391	17,550	12,258	1,006	53	28	..	..	17	3	28
..	..	..	..	..	..	..	..	..	..	29
1,590	756	339	18	22	3	..	1	5	14	30
14,195	5,163	1,876	248	11,276	359	2,093	1,490	495	3	31
42,835	21,039	35,040	2,095	42,157	2,453	9,011	4,100	15,495	1,455	32
530	369	500	191	4	..	..	..	1	..	33
1,555	2,100	1,213	143	..	105	..	..	..	42	34
13,446	6,955	1,510	237	21,336	2,373	7,251	5,109	975	232	35

Table X.—Occupation or Means of Liveli

Class A.—Production

Sub-Class I.—Exploitation

Order I.—Pasture and

Sub-Order 1(d).—Stock raising—concld.

Province, State or Agency.	Group 22.—Breeders of transport animals. Total earners principal occupation. Males.	Females.	Total working dependants. Males.	Females.	Total following occupation as subsidiary to other. Males.	Females.	Total earners principal occupation. Males.	Females.
1	179	180	181	182	183	184	185	186
INDIA	**32,641**	**758**	**3,870**	**341**	**5,549**	**90**	**1,493,757**	**220,698**
Provinces	**20,002**	**392**	**967**	**111**	**1,939**	**50**	**990,234**	**132,760**
1 Ajmer-Merwara	100	1	13	14	38	2	4,093	423
2 Andamans and Nicobars	..	..	..	..	..	..	..	..
3 Assam	15	..	..	..	2	..	94	11
4 Baluchistan (*Districts and Administered Territories*).	619	..	..	..	204	35	7,421	48
5 Bengal	30	..	..	..	13	..	45,466	1,432
6 Bihar and Orissa	63	..	..	..	58	..	85,865	10,149
7 Bombay (*including Aden*)	3,545	150	178	40	161	..	34,354	5,007
Aden	*1*	..	..	..	..	..	*5*	*4*
8 Burma	182	21	47	9	106	5	14,428	4,697
9 Central Provinces and Berar ..	126	3	11	7	4	..	123,734	5,441
10 Coorg	..	..	..	..	..	..	..	..
11 Delhi	1	..	..	..	..	..	1,067	38
12 Madras	602	3	88	14	35	..	166,478	22,455
13 North-West Frontier Province (*Districts and Administered Territories*).	1	1	..	..	..	..	207	9
14 Punjab	14,328	213	630	20	1,087	8	115,144	2,032
15 United Provinces of Agra and Oudh	390	..	..	7	231	..	391,883	81,018
States and Agencies ..	**12,639**	**366**	**2,903**	**230**	**3,610**	**40**	**503,523**	**87,938**
16 Assam States	..	..	..	..	..	..	37	4
17 Baluchistan States	667	8	7	..	1,577	3	13,350	37
18 Baroda State	1,292	4	116	16	115	5	10,522	1,272
19 Bengal States	..	..	..	..	..	..	287	5
20 Bihar and Orissa States	1	..	..	..	1	..	47,969	3,096
21 Bombay States	1,554	129	841	28	176	9	5,717	956
22 Central India Agency	64	1	..	..	7	..	58,755	6,828
23 Central Provinces States	22	..	..	..	..	..	10,672	499
24 Gwalior State	1	..	..	..	..	..	26,074	3,451
25 Hyderabad State	1,431	11	542	1	726	..	156,681	50,934
26 Jammu and Kashmir State ..	279	1	15	..	71	16	18,740	1,200
27 Madras States Agency	156	..	55	..	29	..	5,814	722
Cochin State	*5*	..	*1*	..	..	..	*3,549*	*252*
Travancore State	*151*	..	*54*	..	*27*	..	*700*	*81*
Other Madras States	..	..	..	..	*2*	..	*1,565*	*389*
28 Mysore State	29	..	..	2	1	..	28,063	5,051
29 North-West Frontier Province (*Agencies and Tribal Areas*).	..	..	..	..	..	..	..	..
30 Punjab States	..	..	..	..	..	..	2,191	126
31 Punjab States Agency	3,566	128	635	91	371	..	15,575	454
32 Rajputana Agency	3,100	64	575	83	502	7	76,653	10,223
33 Sikkim State	..	..	..	..	..	..	673	220
34 United Provinces States	..	..	..	..	..	..	3,411	1,949
35 Western India States Agency ..	477	20	117	9	34	..	22,339	911

hood.—Part II.—Provincial Distribution—*contd.*

of Raw Materials—*contd.*

of Animals and Vegetation—*contd.*

Agriculture—*contd.*

Group 23.—Herdsmen, shepherds and breeders of other animals.				*Total Sub-Order 1(e).*—Raising of small animals and insects.						
Total working dependants.		Total following occupation as subsidiary to other.		Total earners principal occupation.		Total working dependants.		Total following occupation as subsidiary to other.		
Males.	Females.	Males.	Females.	Males.	Females.	Males.	Females.	Males.	Females.	
187	188	189	190	191	192	193	194	195	196	
562,912	**205,115**	**260,479**	**46,657**	**9,301**	**4,118**	**1,775**	**1,970**	**39,938**	**3,719**	
308,242	**90,953**	**171,195**	**22,480**	**3,368**	**1,759**	**711**	**766**	**7,203**	**935**	
2,461	1,293	767	56	1	..	..	..	..	..	1
..	..	..	..	..	..	..	..	..	..	2
166	16	17	..	168	28	326	77	2,670	317	3
2,417	441	17,957	23	1	..	..	..	..	..	4
37,256	684	5,313	258	199	476	2	54	739	102	5
26,386	2,617	13,149	1,015	643	141	14	9	1,932	84	6
10,280	3,489	2,901	247	148	2	..	4	..	..	7
..	..	..	..	..	..	..	..	..	..	
28,139	14,576	9,313	,415	635	449	243	485	299	165	8
41,064	3,921	6,444	422	697	415	6	14	817	228	9
3	..	..	..	..	..	..	..	..	..	10
408	18	635	1	..	..	..	..	..	..	11
87,435	24,793	22,246	1,724	786	241	117	121	715	32	12
6	..	20	2	..	..		..		..	13
42,715	1,680	11,065	151	48	4	3	2	25	..	14
29,506	37,425	81,368	15,166	42	3		..	6	7	15
254,670	**114,162**	**89,284**	**24,177**	**5,933**	**2,359**	**1,064**	**1,204**	**32,735**	**2,784**	
79	57	22	63	17	3	..	..	575	70	16
1,196	91	8,477	19	..	..	..	..	..	..	17
2,882	3,613	498	45	44	3	..	10	25	..	18
215	..	54	..	..	..	..	..	..	..	19
23,033	4,048	5,174	181	303	197	15	56	12,556	270	20
1,966	1,228	494	305	4	..	..	..	..	..	21
35,152	8,389	8,103	487	656	697	48	105	7,734	1,748	22
3,688	1,516	441	17	240	47	13	145	639	50	23
7,227	1,068	6,129	1,100	8	..	..	..	..	1	24
38,944	42,975	22,335	19,080	2,761	516	593	557	646	167	25
21,531	5,462	1,609	585	99	10	24	1	80	1	26
6,897	2,688	1,108	113	476	10	98	3	117	4	27
898	*107*	*175*	*15*	*3*	*2*	..	..	..	..	
344	*18*	*185*	*22*	*473*	*8*	*98*	*3*	*117*	*4*	
5,655	*2,563*	*748*	*76*	..	..	..	..	..	..	
57,391	17,528	12,240	1,003	1,305	876	273	326	10,361	473	28
..	..	..	..	..	..	..	..	..	..	29
1,590	755	334	4	..	..	..	..	..	..	30
11,467	3,582	1,010	245	..	..	..	..	..	..	31
33,249	16,856	19,043	633	1	..	..	..	..	..	32
530	369	499	191	..	..	..	..	..	..	33
1,555	2,100	1,213	101	..	..	..	..	..	..	34
6,078	1,837	501	5	19	..	..	1	2	..	35

Table X.—Occupation or Means of Liveli

Class A.—Production of Raw

Sub-Class I.—Exploitation of

Order 1.—Pasture and Agricul

Sub-Order 1(e).—Raising of

Province, State or Agency.	*Group 24.*—Birds, bees, etc. Total earners principal occupation.		Total working dependants.		Total following occupation as subsidiary to other.		Total earners principal occupation.	
	Males.	Females.	Males.	Females.	Males.	Females.	Males.	Females.
1	197	198	199	200	201	202	203	204
INDIA.	**3,737**	**657**	**809**	**789**	**1,152**	**206**	**2,389**	**1,968**
Provinces	**1,519**	**311**	**323**	**461**	**581**	**100**	**359**	**858**
1 Ajmer-Merwara	1	..	..	..	..	..	..	..
2 Andamans and Nicobars	..	..	..	..	..	..	..	..
3 Assam	20	9	2	1	28	5	19	..
4 Baluchistan (*Districts and Administered Territories*).	1	..	..	..	..	..	..	..
5 Bengal	2	..	..	..	..	..	196	476
6 Bihar and Orissa	9	2	..	..	5	1	17	11
7 Bombay (*including Aden*) ..	26	..	..	..	..	..	37	..
Aden	..	..	..	..	..	..	..	..
8 Burma	625	222	243	441	274	81	5	201
9 Central Provinces and Berar ..	57	2	3	..	102	..	..	..
10 Coorg	..	..	..	..	..	..	..	..
11 Delhi	..	..	..	..	..	..	..	..
12 Madras	701	71	72	17	141	6	85	170
13 North-West Frontier Province (*Districts and Administered Territories.*)	..	..	..	..	..	..	..	..
14 Punjab	48	4	3	2	25	..	..	
15 United Provinces of Agra and Oudh	29	1	..	..	6	7	..	..
States and Agencies ..	**2,218**	**346**	**486**	**328**	**571**	**106**	**2,030**	**1,110**
16 **Assam States**	10	..	..	..	5	..	..	..
17 **Baluchistan States**	..	..	..	..	..	..	..	..
18 **Baroda State**	44	3	..	10	25	..	..	..
19 **Bengal States**	..	..	..	..	..	..	..	..
20 **Bihar and Orissa States**	3	2	4	..	..	9	6	99
21 **Bombay States**	..	..	..	..	..	..	4	..
22 **Central India Agency**	25	..	1	..	..	..	..	..
23 **Central Provinces States**	..	..	..	..	..	..	..	4
24 **Gwalior State**	8	..	..	..	..	1	..	..
25 **Hyderabad State**	1,651	319	383	314	421	92	615	133
26 **Jammu and Kashmir State** ..	..	10	..	..	..	..	99	..
27 **Madras States Agency**	462	8	98	3	117	4	14	2
Cochin State	*3*	..	..	..	..	..	..	*2*
Travancore State	*459*	*8*	*98*	*3*	*117*	*4*	*14*	..
Other MadrasStates	..	..	..	..	..	..	..	..
28 **Mysore State**	1	4	..	..	1	..	1,288	872
29 **North-West Frontier Province (*Agencies and Tribal Areas.*)** ..	..	..	..	..	..	..	..	..
30 **Punjab States**	..	..	..	..	..	..	..	..
31 **Punjab States Agency**	..	..	..	..	..	..	..	..
32 **Rajputana Agency**	1	..	..	..	..	..	..	..
33 **Sikkim State**	..	..	..	..	..	..	..	..
34 **United Provinces States**	..	..	..	..	..	..	..	..
35 **Western India States Agency** ..	13	..	..	1	2	..	4	..

hood—Part II—Provincial Distribution—*contd.*

Materials—*contd.*

Animals and Vegetation—*contd.*

ture—*concld.*

small animals and insects—*concld.*

Group 25.—Silkworms.				*Group 26.*—Lac cultivation.						
Total working dependants.		Total following occupation as subsidiary to other.		Total earners principal occupation.		Total working dependants.		Total following occupation as subsidiary to other.		
Males.	Females.	Males.	Females.	Males.	Females.	Males.	Females.	Males.	Females.	
205	206	207	208	209	210	211	212	213	214	
480	**825**	**12,585**	**770**	**3,175**	**1,493**	**486**	**356**	**26,201**	**2,743**	
57	**241**	**1,579**	**194**	**1,490**	**590**	**331**	**64**	**5,043**	**641**	
..	..	..	..	..	..	..	..	..	..	1
..	..	..	..	..	..	..	..	..	..	2
10	38	214	4	129	19	314	38	2,428	308	3
..	..	..	..	..	..	..	..	..	..	4
2	54	736	102	1	..	..	..	3	..	5
..	1	41	7	617	128	14	8	1,886	76	6
..	..	..	..	85	2	..	4	..	..	7
..	..	..	..	..	..	..	..	..	..	
..	44	14	55	5	26	..	..	11	29	8
..	..	..	..	640	413	3	14	715	228	9
..	..	..	..	..	..	..	..	..	..	10
..	..	..	..	..	..	..	..	..	..	11
45	104	574	26	..	..	..	..	..	..	12
..	..	..	..	..	..	..	..	..	..	13
..	..	..	..	..	..	..	..	..	..	14
..	..	..	..	13	2	..	..	..	..	15
423	**584**	**11,006**	**576**	**1,685**	**903**	**155**	**292**	**21,158**	**2,102**	
..	..	..	..	7	3	..	..	570	70	16
..	..	..	..	..	..	..	..	..	..	17
..	..	..	..	..	..	..	..	..	..	18
..	..	..	..	..	..	..	..	..	..	19
..	54	414	66	294	96	11	2	12,142	195	20
..	..	..	..	..	..	..	..	..	..	21
..	..	..	..	631	697	47	105	7,734	1,748	22
..	32	..	..	240	43	13	113	639	50	23
..	..	..	..	..	..	..	..	..	..	24
126	171	152	36	495	64	84	72	73	39	25
24	1	80	1	..	..	..	..	..	..	26
..	..	..	..	..	..	..	..	..	..	27
..	..	..	..	..	..	..	..	..	..	
..	..	..	..	..	..	..	..	..	..	
..	..	..	..	..	..	..	..	..	..	
273	326	10,360	473	16	..	..	..	..	..	28
..	..	..	..	..	..	..	..	..	..	29
..	..	..	..	..	..	..	..	..	..	30
..	..	..	..	..	..	..	..	..	..	31
..	..	..	..	..	..	..	..	..	..	32
..	..	..	..	..	..	..	..	..	..	33
..	..	..	..	..	..	..	..	..	..	34
..	..	..	..	2	..	..	..	..	..	35

Table X.—Occupation or Means of Liveli

Class A.—Production of Raw

Sub-Class I.—Exploitation of

Order 2.—Fishing and

	Province, State or Agency.	*Total Order 2.*—Fishing and Hunting.							
		Total earners principal occupation.		Total working dependants.		Total following occupation as subsidiary to other.		Total earners principal occupation.	
		Males.	Females.	Males.	Females.	Males.	Females.	Males.	Females
	1	215	216	217	218	219	220	221	222
	INDIA.	**631,317**	**128,477**	**46,500**	**33,998**	**169,809**	**19,435**	**601,126**	**120,864**
	Provinces	**515,231**	**99,363**	**25,329**	**21,469**	**145,608**	**11,116**	**504,612**	**98,204**
1	Ajmer-Merwara	12	7	..	..	4	..	..	..
2	Andamans and Nicobars	66	..	..	..	8	..	66	..
3	Assam	34,776	867	5,155	645	40,233	205	34,584	841
4	Baluchistan (*Districts and Administered Territories*).	1	..	..	..	1	..	1	..
5	Bengal	159,221	26,176	2,079	4,205	23,966	2,382	158,624	26,123
6	Bihar and Orissa	43,329	9,254	864	489	27,654	1,608	42,108	9,100
7	Bombay (*including Aden*)	48,657	12,670	3,964	5,279	4,968	2,823	47,805	12,310
	Aden	*595*	*2*	*11*	..	*7*	..	*595*	*2*
8	Burma	50,389	5,727	3,894	946	15,629	707	49,855	5,726
9	Central Provinces and Berar ..	39,374	6,081	1,822	1,664	11,384	1,425	36,006	5,804
10	Coorg	27	5	..	17	2	..	27	5
11	Delhi	176	2	..	..	..	..	95	2
12	Madras	118,456	34,978	5,757	7,373	12,795	952	117,467	34,812
13	North-West Frontier Province (*Districts and Administered Territories*).	268	1	3	..	59	..	261	1
14	Punjab	3,903	44	229	53	998	1	3,296	12
15	United Provinces of Agra and Oudh	16,576	3,551	1,562	798	7,907	1,013	14,417	3,468
	States and Agencies ..	**116,086**	**29,114**	**21,171**	**12,529**	**24,201**	**8,319**	**96,514**	**22,660**
16	Assam States	1,216	1,216	158	307	394	60	1,215	1,216
17	Baluchistan States	2,227	6	21	19	289	1	2,224	6
18	Baroda State	1,242	729	25	26	122	..	1,230	729
19	Bengal States	731	2	11	..	258	..	727	2
20	Bihar and Orissa States	5,206	1,011	85	171	3,605	161	5,143	1,010
21	Bombay States	2,199	428	107	435	583	277	2,067	359
22	Central India Agency	3,769	385	113	47	4,084	97	3,496	338
23	Central Provinces States	1,640	214	262	316	826	8	1,516	211
24	Gwalior State	425	52	11	34	152	24	390	45
25	Hyderabad State	52,020	21,170	16,128	10,163	9,930	7,331	33,578	14,864
26	Jammu and Kashmir State ..	1,299	47	48	117	221	73	1,241	47
27	Madras States Agency	39,820	3,387	3,807	547	2,370	260	39,700	3,386
	Cochin State	*8,172*	*846*	*121*	*170*	*1,138*	*183*	*8,155*	*846*
	Travancore State	*31,647*	*2,540*	*3,686*	*376*	*1,190*	*77*	*31,545*	*2,540*
	Other Madras States	*1*	*1*	..	*1*	*42*	..	..	..
28	Mysore State	988	113	49	34	959	26	896	100
29	North-West Frontier Province (*Agencies and Tribal Areas*).	..	..	..	..	..	..	..	..
30	Punjab States	46	1	3	..	18	..	25	..
31	Punjab States Agency	1,041	30	30	8	128	..	990	30
32	Rajputana Agency	241	7	5	2	35		173	2
33	Sikkim State	..	..	..	..	..	..	..	..
34	United Provinces States	743	47	8	5	127	..	710	46
35	Western India States Agency ..	1,233	269	300	298	100	..	1,193	269

hood—Part II—Provincial Distribution—*contd.*

Materials—*contd.*

Animals and Vegetation—*concld.*

Hunting.

Group 27.—Fishing and Pearling.				*Group 28.*—Hunting.						
Total working dependants.		Total following occupation as subsidiary to other.		Total earners principal occupation.		Total working dependants.		Total following occupation as subsidiary to other.		
Males.	Females.	Males.	Females.	Males.	Females.	Males.	Females.	Males.	Females.	
223	224	225	226	227	228	229	230	231	232	
37,815	**30,945**	**161,288**	**15,842**	**30,191**	**7,613**	**8,685**	**3,053**	**8,521**	**3,593**	
24,596	**21,136**	**142,226**	**10,971**	**10,619**	**1,159**	**733**	**333**	**3,382**	**145**	
..	..	2	..	12	7	..	..	2	..	1
..	..	8	..	..	..	..	..	..	..	2
5,145	641	39,862	205	192	26	10	4	371	..	3
..	..	..	..	..	..	..	..	1	..	4
2,078	4,205	23,885	2,379	597	53	1	..	81	3	5
859	489	26,856	1,559	1,221	154	5	..	798	49	6
3,910	5,071	4,775	2,800	852	360	54	208	193	23	7
11	..	*7*	..	..	..	..	..	..	..	
3,804	946	15,530	706	534	1	90	..	99	1	8
1,402	1,557	10,360	1,383	3,368	277	420	107	1,024	42	9
..	17	2	..	..	..	..	..	..	..	10
..	..	..	..	81	..	..	..	..	..	11
5,657	7,359	12,513	928	989	166	100	14	282	24	12
3	..	56	..	7	..	..	..	3	..	13
206	53	843	1	607	32	23	..	155	..	14
1,532	798	7,534	1,010	2,159	83	30	..	373	3	15
13,219	**9,809**	**19,062**	**4,871**	**19,572**	**6,454**	**7,952**	**2,720**	**5,139**	**3,448**	
158	307	390	60	1	..	..	..	4	..	16
21	19	289	1	3	..	..	..	..	..	17
25	26	118	..	12	..	..	..	4	..	18
11	..	252	..	4	..	..	..	6	..	19
85	171	3,521	161	63	1	..	..	84	..	20
106	435	582	229	132	69	1	..	1	48	21
105	46	4,030	96	273	47	8	1	54	1	22
259	290	737	7	124	3	3	26	89	1	23
11	34	139	17	35	7	..	..	13	7	24
8,228	7,473	5,365	3,951	18,442	6,306	7,900	2,690	4,565	3,380	25
48	117	199	73	58	..	..	..	22	..	26
3,769	547	2,153	260	120	1	28	..	217	..	27
120	*170*	*1,088*	*183*	*17*	..	*1*	..	*50*	..	
3,659	*376*	*1,033*	*77*	*102*	..	*27*	..	*157*	..	
..	*1*	*32*	..	*1*	*1*	..	..	*10*	..	
48	33	887	16	92	13	1	1	72	10	28
..	..	..	..	..	..	..	..	..	..	29
3	..	18	..	21	1	..	..	..	..	30
30	8	128	..	51	..	..	..	..	..	31
5	2	27	..	68	5	..	..	8	1	32
..	..	..	..	..	..	..	..	..	..	33
1	5	127	..	33	1	7	..	..	..	34
296	**296**	**100**	..	**40**	..	**4**	**2**	..	..	35

Table X.—Occupation or Means of Liveli

Class A.—Production of Raw

Sub-Class II.—Exploitation of

	Province, State or Agency.	Total *Sub-Class II.*—Exploitation of Minerals.							
		Total earners principal occupation.		Total working dependants.		Total following occupation as subsidiary to other.		Total earners principal occupation.	
		Males.	Females.	Males.	Females.	Males.	Females.	Males.	Females.
	1	233	234	235	236	237	238	239	240
	INDIA	**247,716**	**76,426**	**11,867**	**9,991**	**46,851**	**11,411**	**36,776**	**9,852**
	Provinces	**194,397**	**61,905**	**3,436**	**3,225**	**37,861**	**8,630**	**20,224**	**5,117**
1	Ajmer-Merwara	620	73	1	1	99	1	2	1
2	Andamans and Nicobars	..	..	..	..	..	..	..	..
3	Assam	14,744	948	424	37	456	16	1	..
4	Baluchistan (*Districts and Administered Territories*).	464	..	..	..	3	..	175	..
5	Bengal	25,157	17,464	231	222	1,159	360	695	16
6	Bihar and Orissa	79,910	25,790	482	238	27,072	6,350	836	289
7	Bombay (*including Aden*)	5,997	3,166	184	330	2,802	531	1,119	31
	Aden	*27*		..	..	..	..	*9*	..
8	Burma	35,067	1,806	1,306	1,326	2,219	390	11,653	323
9	Central Provinces and Berar ..	13,952	7,911	133	272	1,136	789	5,558	4,426
10	Coorg	..	..	..	..	..	..	..	..
11	Delhi	571	10	..	..	14		..	..
12	Madras	8,931	2,989	212	180	1,859	128	175	27
13	North-West Frontier Province (*Districts and Administered Territories*).	117	..	1	..	14	..	..	..
14	Punjab	4,559	606	228	31	141	1	10	4
15	United Provinces of Agra and Oudh	4,308	1,142	234	588	887	64	..	..
	States and Agencies ..	**53,319**	**14,521**	**8,431**	**6,766**	**8,990**	**2,781**	**16,552**	**4,735**
16	Assam States	70	172	128	2	25	..	..	..
17	Baluchistan States	84	..	..	..	9	..	1	..
18	Baroda State	1,312	643	13	12	33	1	..	..
19	Bengal States	..	..	..	..	..	..	..	..
20	Bihar and Orissa States	7,333	5,598	165	98	2,797	1,048	4,072	4,030
21	Bombay States	501	114	89	29	104	2	77	17
22	Central India Agency	2,764	676	11	62	478	37	60	16
23	Central Provinces States	122	61	8	94	46	21	86	43
24	Gwalior State	1,587	637	140	115	559	63	..	..
25	Hyderabad State	13,425	2,950	7,025	5,258	3,437	1,530	385	38
26	Jammu and Kashmir State ..	823	34	15	221	57	26	36	5
27	Madras States Agency	2,923	557	157	51	70	4	783	218
	Cochin State	*10*	*12*	..	.	*48*	..	..	..
	Travancore State	*2,279*	*344*	*148*	*30*	..	..	*395*	*62*
	Other Madras States	*634*	*201*	*9*	*21*	*22*	*4*	*488*	*156*
28	Mysore State	11,278	427	9	2	549	6	10,936	349
29	North-West Frontier Province (*Agencies and Tribal Areas*).	..	..	..	..	..	..	..	..
30	Punjab States	76	1	4	1	10	..	1	..
31	Punjab States Agency	301	9	28	41	42	..	..	..
32	Rajputana Agency	5,945	1,882	9	144	682	28	..	..
33	Sikkim State	..	..	..	..	..	..	..	..
34	United Provinces States	197	133	3	32	..	9	..	..
35	Western India States Agency ..	4,578	627	627	604	92	6	115	19

hood—Part II—Provincial Distribution—*contd.*

Materials—*contd.*

Minerals.

Order 3.—Metallic Minerals.

Total *Order 3.*—Metalic Minerals.				*Group 29.*—Gold.						
Total working dependants.		Total following occupation as subsidiary to other.		Total earners principal occupation.		Total working dependants.		Total following occupation as subsidiary to other.		
Males.	Females.	Males.	Females.	Males.	Females.	Males.	Females.	Males.	Females.	
241	242	243	244	245	246	247	248	249	250	
952	**799**	**4,331**	**1,752**	**10,745**	**585**	**25**	**146**	**520**	**220**	
525	419	1,687	894	116	5[illegible]	4	37	174	170	
..	..	..	..	..	..	..	..	..	..	1
..	..	..	..	..	..	..	..	..	..	2
..	..	3	..	..	..	..	..	..	..	3
..	..	..	..	..	..	..	..	..	..	4
3	7	81	..	..	2	..	..	..	..	5
218	36	311	43	1	19	..	..	5	..	6
..	37	385	..	12	..	..	..	..	..	7
..	..	..	..	..	..	..	..	..	..	
58	246	403	180	58	19	1	21	161	168	8
43	87	312	671	18	15	3	16	6	2	9
..	..	..	..	..	..	..	..	..	..	10
..	..	..	..	..	..	..	..	..	..	11
..	6	191	..	25	..	..	..	1	..	12
..	..	..	..	..	..	..	..	..	..	13
3	..	1	..	2	..	..	..	1	..	14
..	..	..	..	..	..	..	..	..	..	15
427	380	2,644	858	10,629	530	21	109	346	50	
..	..	..	..	..	..	..	..	..	..	16
..	..	5	..	..	..	..	..	..	..	17
..	..	..	..	..	..	..	..	..	..	18
..	..	..	..	..	..	..	..	..	..	19
106	49	2,167	830	20	174	..	10	15	28	20
8	1	6	1	32	..	..	..	1	..	21
..	51	48	..	..	..	..	..	1	..	22
8	93	44	21	61	36	7	87	41	21	23
..	..	..	..	..	..	..	..	..	..	24
222	132	22	1	..	..	..	..	..	..	25
12	12	28	1	19	5	4	12	17	1	26
53	30	21	4	..	..	..	..	2	..	27
..	..	*2*	..	..	..	..	..	2	..	
44	*9*	..		..	..	..	..	..	..	
9	*21*	*19*	*4*	..	..	..	..	..	..	
8	..	291	..	10,460	315	2	..	257	..	28
..	..	..	..	..	..	..	..	..	..	29
..	..	..	..	1	..	..	..	..	..	30
..	..	11	..	..	..	..	..	11	..	31
..	..	..	..	..	..	..	..	..	..	32
..	..	..	..	..	..	..	..	..	..	33
..	..	..	..	..	..	..	..	..	..	34
10	12	1	..	36	..	8		..	..	35

Table X.—Occupation or Means of Liveli

Class A.—Production of Raw

Sub-Class II.—Exploitation

Order 3.—Metallic

Province, State or Agency.	Group 30.—Iron. Total earners principal occupation. Males.	Females.	Total working dependants. Males.	Females.	Total following occupation as subsidiary to other. Males.	Females.	Total earners principal occupation. Males.	Females.
1	251	252	253	254	255	256	257	258
INDIA	**4,688**	**3,891**	**244**	**201**	**2,228**	**804**	**8,464**	**322**
Provinces	**164**	**38**	**10**	..	**13**	**11**	**8,418**	**301**
1 Ajmer-Merwara	..	..	..	..	..	..	..	..
2 Andamans and Nicobars	..	..	..	..	..	..	..	..
3 Assam	..	..	..	..	..	..	..	..
4 Baluchistan (*Districts and Administered Territories*).	..	..	..	..	..	..	..	..
5 Bengal	..	..	..	..	..	..	..	..
6 Bihar and Orissa	108	38	10	..	5	11	143	105
7 Bombay (*including Aden*)	40	..	..	..	8	..	20	12
Aden	..	..	..	..	..	..	..	..
8 Burma	..	..	..	..	..	..	8,254	184
9 Central Provinces and Berar	7	..	..	..	..	..	..	..
10 Coorg	..	..	..	..	..	..	..	..
11 Delhi	..	..	..	..	..	..	..	..
12 Madras	9	..	..	..	..	..	..	..
13 North-West Frontier Province (*Districts and Administered Territories*).	..	..	..	..	..	..	..	..
14 Punjab	..	..	..	..	..	..	..	..
15 United Provinces of Agra and Oudh	..	..	..	..	..	..	..	..
States and Agencies	**4,524**	**3,853**	**234**	**201**	**2,215**	**793**	**46**	**21**
16 Assam States	..	..	..	..	..	..	..	..
17 Baluchistan States	..	..	..	..	..	..	..	..
18 Baroda State	..	..	..	..	..	..	..	..
19 Bengal States	..	..	..	..	..	..	..	..
20 Bihar and Orissa States	3,711	3,765	6	12	2,123	792	..	..
21 Bombay States	..	..	..	..	..	..	18	12
22 Central India Agency	60	16	..	51	47	..	..	..
23 Central Provinces States	2	7	1	6	3	..	..	..
24 Gwalior State	..	..	..	..	..	..	..	..
25 Hyderabad State	385	38	222	132	22	1	..	..
26 Jammu and Kashmir State	..	..	..	..	..	..	11	..
27 Madras States Agency	..	..	..	..	..	..	..	..
Cochin State	..	..	..	..	..	..	..	..
Travancore State	..	..	..	..	..	..	..	..
Other Madras States	..	..	..	..	..	..	..	..
28 Mysore State	354	27	5	..	20	..	..	..
29 North-West Frontier Province (*Agencies and Tribal Areas*).	..	..	..	..	..	..	..	..
30 Punjab States	..	..	..	..	..	..	..	..
31 Punjab States Agency	..	..	..	..	..	..	..	..
32 Rajputana Agency	..	..	..	..	..	..	..	..
33 Sikkim State	..	..	..	..	..	..	..	..
34 United Provinces States	..	..	..	..	..	..	..	..
35 Western India States Agency	12	..	..	..	..	..	17	9

hood—Part II—Provincal Distribution—*contd.*

Materials—*contd.*

of Minerals—*contd.*

Minerals—*contd.*

Group 31.—Lead, silver and zinc.				*Group 32.*—Manganese.						
Total working dependants.		Total following occupation as subsidiary to other.		Total earners principal occupation.		Total working dependants.		Total following occupation as subsidiary to other.		
Males.	Females.	Males.	Females.	Males.	Females.	Males.	Females.	Males.	Females.	
259	260	261	262	263	264	265	266	267	268	
61	**104**	**349**	**12**	**7,546**	**4,711**	**149**	**127**	**916**	**683**	
45	**96**	**338**	**12**	**6,610**	**4,451**	**40**	**75**	**871**	**669**	
..	..	..	..	..	..	..	..	..	..	**1**
..	..	..	..	..	..	..	..	..	..	**2**
..	..	3	..	..	..	..	..	..	..	**3**
..	..	..	..	..	..	..	..	..	..	**4**
..	..	..	..	..	..	..	..	..	..	**5**
..	7	243	9	..	..	..	..	..	..	**6**
..	37	..	..	946	18	..	..	377	..	**7**
..	..	..	..	..	..	..	..	..	..	
45	52	92	3	..	..	..	..	..	..	**8**
..	..	..	..	5,532	4,411	40	69	304	669	**9**
..	..	..	..	..	..	..	..	..	..	**10**
..	..	..	..	..	..	..	..	..	..	**11**
..	..	..	..	132	22	..	6	190	..	**12**
..	..	..	..	..	..	..	..	..	..	**13**
..	..	..	..	..	..	..	..	..	..	**14**
..	..	..	..	..	..	..	..	..	..	**15**
16	**8**	**11**	..	**936**	**260**	**109**	**52**	**45**	**14**	
..	..	..	..	..	..	..	..	..	..	**16**
..	..	..	..	..	..	..	..	..	..	**17**
..	..	..	..	..	..	..	..	..	..	**18**
..	..	..	..	..	..	..	..	..	..	**19**
..	..	..	..	341	91	100	27	26	10	**20**
6	..	..	..	..	..	..	..	..	..	**21**
..	..	..	..	..	..	..	..	..	..	**22**
..	..	..	..	..	..	..	..	..	..	**23**
..	..	..	..	..	..	..	..	..	..	**24**
..	..	..	..	..	..	..	..	..	..	**25**
8	..	11	..	..	..	..	..	..	..	**26**
..	..	..	..	488	156	9	21	19	4	**27**
..	..	..	..	..	..	..	..	..	..	
..	..	..	..	..	..	..	..	..	..	
..	..	..	..	*488*	*156*	*9*	*21*	*19*	*4*	
..	..	..	..	60	3	..	..	..	..	**28**
..	..	..	..	..	..	..	..	..	..	**29**
..	..	..	..	..	..	..	..	..	..	**30**
..	..	..	..	..	..	..	..	..	..	**31**
..	..	..	..	..	..	..	..	..	..	**32**
..	..	..	..	..	..	..	..	..	..	**33**
..	..	..	..	..	..	..	..	..	..	**34**
2	8	..	..	47	10	..	..	..	..	**35**

Table X.—Occupation or Means of Liveli

Class A.—Production of Raw

Sub-Class II.—Exploitation of

Order 3.—Metallic Minerals—*concld.*

Province, State or Agency.	*Group 33.*—Tin and wolfram.							
	Total earners principal occupation.		Total working dependants.		Total following occupation as subsidiary to other.		Total earners principal occupation.	
	Males.	Females.	Males.	Females.	Males.	Females.	Males.	Females.
1	269	270	271	272	273	274	275	276
INDIA	**4,007**	**145**	**419**	**209**	**177**	**10**	**1,326**	**198**
Provinces	**3,984**	**141**	**419**	**209**	**177**	**10**	**932**	**131**
1 Ajmer-Merwara	..	..	..	..	..	..	2	1
2 Andamans and Nicobars	..	..	..	..	..	..	..	..
3 Assam	..	..	..	..	..	..	..	..
4 Baluchistan (*Districts and Administered Territorries*).	..	..	..	..	..	..	175	..
5 Bengal	492	14	..	7	26	..	203	..
6 Bihar and Orissa	145	2	208	29	1	1	439	125
7 Bombay (*including Aden*)	51	..	..	..	..	..	50	1
Aden	..	..	..	..	..	..	*9*	..
8 Burma	3,296	120	211	173	150	9	45	..
9 Central Provinces and Berar	..	..	..	..	..	..	1	..
10 Coorg	..	..	..	..	..	..	..	..
11 Delhi	..	..	..	..	..	..	..	..
12 Madras	..	5	..	..	..	..	9	..
13 North-West Frontier Province (*Districts and Administered Territorries*).	..	..	..	..	..	..	..	..
14 Punjab	..	..	..	..	..	..	8	4
15 United Provinces of Agra and Oudh	..	..	..	..	..	..	..	..
States and Agencies	**23**	**4**	..	..	..	..	**394**	**67**
16 Assam States	..	..	..	..	..	..	..	..
17 Baluchistan States	..	..	..	..	..	..	1	..
18 Baroda State	..	..	..	..	..	..	..	..
19 Bengal States	..	..	..	..	..	..	..	..
20 Bihar and Orissa States	..	..	..	..	..	..	..	..
21 Bombay States	2	..	..	..	..	..	25	5
22 Central India Agency	..	..	..	..	..	..	..	..
23 Central Provinces States	..	..	..	..	..	..	23	..
24 Gwalior State	..	..	..	..	..	..	..	..
25 Hyderabad State	..	..	..	..	..	..	..	..
26 Jammu and Kashmir State	4	..	..	..	..	..	2	..
27 Madras States Agency	..	..	..	..	..	..	295	62
Cochin State	..	..	..	..	..	..	..	..
Travancore State	..	..	..	..	..	..	*295*	*62*
Other Madras States	..	..	..	..	..	..	..	..
28 Mysore State	17	4	..	..	..	..	45	..
29 North-West Frontier Province (*Agencies and Tribal Areas*).	..	..	..	..	..	..	..	..
30 Punjab States	..	..	..	..	..	..	..	..
31 Punjab States Agency	..	..	..	..	..	..	..	..
32 Rajputana Agency	..	..	..	..	..	..	..	..
33 Sikkim State	..	..	..	..	..	..	..	..
34 United Provinces States	..	..	..	..	..	..	..	..
35 Western India State Agency	..	..	..	..	..	..	3	..

hood—Part II—Provinicial Distribution—*contd.*

Materials—*contd.*

Minerals—*contd.*

Group 34.—Other metallic minerals.				*Order 4.*—Non-Metallic Minerals. *Total Order 4.*—Non-Metallic Minerals.						
Total working dependants.		Total following occupation as subsidiary to other.		Total earners principal occupation.		Total working dependants.		Total following occupation as subsidiary to other.		
Males.	Females.	Males.	Females.	Males.	Females.	Males.	Females.	Males.	Females.	
277	278	279	280	281	282	283	284	285	286	
54	**12**	**141**	**23**	**210,940**	**66,574**	**10,915**	**9,192**	**42,520**	**9,659**	
7	**2**	**114**	**22**	**174,173**	**56,788**	**2,911**	**2,806**	**36,174**	**7,736**	
..	..	..	..	618	72	1	1	99	1	1
..	..	..	..	..	..	..	..	..	..	2
..	..	..	..	14,743	948	424	37	453	16	3
..	..	..	..	289	..	..	..	3	..	4
3	..	55	..	24,462	17,448	228	215	1,078	360	5
..	..	57	22	79,074	25,501	264	202	26,761	6,307	6
..	..	..	..	4,878	3,135	184	293	2,417	531	7
..	..	..	..	*18*	..	..	..	..	..	
1	..	..	..	23,414	1,483	1,048	1,080	1,816	210	8
..	2	2	..	8,394	3,485	90	185	824	118	9
..	..	..	..	..	..	..	..	..	..	10
..	..	..	..	571	10	..	..	14	..	11
..	..	..	..	8,756	2,962	212	174	1,668	128	12
..	..	..	..	117	..	1	..	14	..	13
3	..	..	..	4,549	602	225	31	140	1	14
..	..	..	..	4,308	1,142	234	588	887	64	15
47	**10**	**27**	**1**	**36,767**	**9,786**	**8,004**	**6,386**	**6,346**	**1,923**	
..	..	..	..	70	172	128	2	25	..	16
..	..	5	..	83	..	..	..	4	..	17
..	..	..	..	1,312	643	13	12	33	1	18
..	..	..	..	..	..	..	..	..	..	19
..	..	3	..	3,261	1,568	59	49	630	218	20
2	1	5	1	424	97	81	28	98	1	21
..	..	..	..	2,704	660	11	11	430	37	22
..	..	..	..	36	18	..	1	2	..	23
..	..	..	..	1,587	637	140	115	559	63	24
..	..	..	..	13,040	2,912	6,803	5,126	3,415	1,529	25
..	..	..	..	787	29	3	209	29	25	26
44	9	..	..	2,140	339	104	21	49	..	27
..	..	..	..	*10*	*12*	..	..	*46*	..	
44	*9*	..	..	*1,984*	*282*	*104*	*21*	..	..	
..	..	..	..	*146*	*45*	..	..	*3*	..	
1	..	14	..	342	78	1	2	258	6	28
..	..	..	..	..	..	..	..	..	..	29
..	..	..	..	75	1	4	1	10	..	30
..	..	..	..	301	9	28	41	31	..	31
..	..	..	..	5,945	1,882	9	144	682	28	32
..	..	..	..	..	..	..	..	..	..	33
..	..	..	..	197	133	3	32	..	9	34
..	..	..	..	4,463	608	617	592	91	6	35

Table X.—Occupation or Means of Liveli

Class A.—Production of Raw

Sub-Class II.—Exploitation of

Order 4.—Non-Metallic

Province, State or Agency.	*Group 35.*—Coal. Total earners principal occupation. Males.	Females.	Total working dependants. Males.	Females.	Total following occupation as subsidiary to other. Males.	Females.	Total earners principal occupation. Males.	Females.
1	287	288	289	290	291	292	293	294
INDIA	**120,369**	**45,453**	**4,505**	**4,504**	**23,853**	**6,168**	**26,613**	**500**
Provinces	**109,134**	**41,612**	**750**	**463**	**20,264**	**4,700**	**26,607**	**500**
1 Ajmer-Merwara	21	..	..	..	7	..	..	..
2 Andamans and Nicobars	..	..	..	..	..	..	..	..
3 Assam	6,363	681	237	31	120	4	8,377	264
4 Baluchistan (*Districts and Administered Territories*).	289	..	..	..	1	..	..	..
5 Bengal	24,294	17,430	228	214	1,076	360	12	4
6 Bihar and Orissa	73,194	21,445	250	168	18,465	4,278	1	..
7 Bombay (*including Aden*) ..	30	6	..	..	..	..	..	2
Aden	*14*	..	..	..	..	..	..	..
8 Burma	..	..	..	..	..	..	17,154	230
9 Central Provinces and Berar ..	4,728	2,050	32	50	565	58	..	..
10 Coorg	..	..	..	..	..	..	..	..
11 Delhi	..	..	..	..	..	..	..	..
12 Madras	23	..	..	..	2	..	4	..
13 North-West Frontier Province (*Districts and Administered Territories*).	..	..	..	..	..	..	..	..
14 Punjab	92	..	3	..	28	..	1,059	..
15 United Provinces of Agra and Oudh	100	..	..	..	..	..	..	..
States and Agencies ..	**11,235**	**3,841**	**3,755**	**4,041**	**3,589**	**1,468**	**6**	..
16 Assam States	13	..	..	..	15	..	..	..
17 Baluchistan States	7	..	..	..	..	..	..	..
18 Baroda State	..	..	..	..	..	..	..	..
19 Bengal States	..	..	..	..	..	..	..	..
20 Bihar and Orissa States	2,752	1,330	57	26	292	49	..	..
21 Bombay States	..	..	..	..	..	..	..	..
22 Central India Agency	1,581	258	1	1	126	..	..	..
23 Central Provinces States	13	18	..	1	..	..	..	..
24 Gwalior State	..	..	..	..	..	..	..	..
25 Hyderabad State	6,832	2,230	3,696	4,013	3,146	1,419	..	..
26 Jammu and Kashmir State ..	..	..	..	..	..	..	1	..
27 Madras States Agency	..	..	..	..	..	..	..	..
Cochin State	..	..	..	..	..	..	..	..
Travancore State	..	..	..	..	..	..	..	..
Other Madras States	..	..	..	..	..	..	..	..
28 Mysore State	..	..	..	..	..	..	..	..
29 North-West Frontier Province (*Agencies and Tribal Areas*).	..	..	..	..	..	..	..	..
30 Punjab States	15	1	1	..	8	..	..	..
31 Punjab States Agency	..	..	..	..	..	..	..	..
32 Rajputana Agency	12	4	..	..	..	..	2	..
33 Sikkim State	..	..	..	..	..	..	..	..
34 United Provinces States	..	..	..	..	..	..	..	..
35 Western India States Agency ..	10	..	..	..	2	..	3	..

hood—Part II—Provincial Distribution—*contd.*

Materials—*contd.*

Minerals—*contd.*

Minerals—*contd.*

Group 36.—Petroleum. Total working dependants. Males.	Females.	Total following occupation as subsidiary to other. Males.	Females.	Group 37.—Building materials (including stone, materials for cement manufacture and clays). Total earners principal occupation. Males.	Females.	Total working dependants. Males.	Females.	Total following occupation as subsidiary to other. Males.	Females.	
295	296	297	298	299	300	301	302	303	304	
321	**110**	**443**	**15**	**31,232**	**7,938**	**4,118**	**2,324**	**4,140**	**636**	
321	110	443	15	13,476	3,626	376	432	2,014	231	
..	..	1	..	581	72	1	1	91	1	1
..	..	..	..	..	..	..	..	..	..	2
187	4	321	12	..	..	..	..	..	..	3
..	..	..	..	..	..	..	..	..	..	4
..	1	..	..	..	.	..	..	..	..	5
..	..	..	..	59	16	..	2	52	11	6
..	3	..	..	574	174	71	108	41	3	7
..	..	..	..	*2*	..	..	..	..	..	
117	102	111	3	1,298	294	89	39	420	83	8
..	..	..	..	3,449	1,435	57	135	244	60	9
..	..	..	..	..	..	..	..	..	..	10
..	..	..	..	532	..	..	..	..	..	11
..	..	..	..	5,714	1,401	157	103	1,024	70	12
..	..	..	..	..	..	..	..	..	..	13
17	..	10	..	..	..	..	..	..	..	14
..	..	..	..	1,269	284	1	44	142	3	15
..	..	..	..	17,756	4,312	3,742	1,892	2,126	405	
..	..	..	..	34	..	4	..	8	..	16
..	..	..	..	..	..	..	..	..	..	17
..	..	..	..	931	388	8	12	33	1	18
..	..	..	..	..	..	..	..	..	..	19
..	..	..	..	506	238	2	23	338	155	20
..	..	..	..	392	92	77	28	92	1	21
..	..	..	..	879	296	6	10	203	35	22
..	..	..	..	23	..	..	..	2	..	23
..	..	..	..	1,363	589	111	114	548	60	24
..	..	..	..	5,657	648	2,977	1,033	246	102	25
..	..	..	..	752	29	3	209	25	25	26
..	..	..	..	1,759	307	78	21	49	..	27
..	..	..	..	*10*	*12*	..	..	*46*	..	
..	..	..	..	*1,603*	*250*	*78*	*21*	..	..	
..	..	..	..	*146*	*45*	..	..	*3*	..	
..	..	..	..	49	..	..	..	7	..	28
..	..	..	..	..	..	..	..	..	..	29
..	..	..	..	1	..	..	..	..	..	30
..	..	..	..	..	..	..	..	..	..	31
..	..	..	..	2,199	1,294	8	70	510	26	32
..	..	..	..	..	..	..	..	..	..	33
..	..	..	..	..	..	..	..	..	..	34
..	..	..	..	3,211	431	468	372	65	..	35

Table X.—Occupation or Means of Liveli

Class A.—Production of Raw

Sub-Class II.—Exploitation of

Order 4.—Non-Metallic

Province, State or Agency.	*Group 38.*—Mica. Total earners principal occupation. Males.	Females.	Total working dependants. Males.	Females.	Total following occupation as subsidiary to other. Males.	Females.	Total earners principal occupation. Males.	Females.
1	305	306	307	308	309	310	311	312
INDIA	**4,821**	**2,822**	**102**	**124**	**4,213**	**631**	**4,581**	**646**
Provinces	**4,644**	**2,798**	**55**	**48**	**4,188**	**624**	**4,411**	**570**
1 Ajmer-Merwara	16	..	..	..	..	..	..	..
2 Andamans and Nicobars	..	..	..	..	..	..	..	..
3 Assam	..	..	..	..	..	..	..	3
4 Baluchistan (*Districts and Administered Territories*).	..	..	..	..	..	..	..	..
5 Bengal	6	4	..	..	1	..	3	..
6 Bihar and Orissa	2,987	1,570	1	4	3,979	600	35	..
7 Bombay (*including Aden*)	39	..	2	..	9	..	32	1
Aden	..	..	..	..	..	..	..	..
8 Burma	..	..	..	..	..	..	4,271	566
9 Central Provinces and Berar ..	..	..	..	..	..	..	..	..
10 Coorg	..	..	..	..	..	..	..	..
11 Delhi	..	..	..	..	..	..	..	..
12 Madras	1,596	1,224	52	44	199	24	34	..
13 North-West Frontier Province (*Districts and Administered Territories*).	..	..	..	..	..	..	36	..
14 Punjab	..	..	..	..	..	..	..	..
15 United Provinces of Agra and Oudh	..	..	..	..	..	..	..	..
States and Agencies ..	**177**	**24**	**47**	**76**	**25**	**7**	**170**	**76**
16 Assam States	..	..	..	..	..	..	..	..
17 Baluchistan States	..	..	..	..	..	..	..	..
18 Baroda State	..	..	..	..	..	..	..	..
19 Bengal States	..	..	..	..	..	..	..	..
20 Bihar and Orissa States	..	..	..	..	..	..	..	..
21 Bombay States	..	..	..	..	..	..	..	..
22 Central India Agency	..	..	..	..	..	..	141	76
23 Central Provinces States	..	..	..	..	..	..	..	..
24 Gwalior State	..	5	..	..	..	..	..	..
25 Hyderabad State	153	11	47	36	20	7	..	..
26 Jammu and Kashmir State ..	5	..	..	..	3	..	29	..
27 Madras States Agency	..	..	..	..	..	..	..	..
Cochin State	..	..	..	..	..	..	..	..
Travancore State	..	..	..	..	..	..	..	..
Other Madras States	..	..	..	..	..	..	..	..
28 Mysore State	..	..	..	..	..	..	..	..
29 North-West Frontier Province (*Agencies and Tribal Areas*).	..	..	..	..	..	..	..	..
30 Punjab States	..	..	..	..	..	..	..	..
31 Punjab States Agency	..	..	..	..	..	..	..	..
32 Rajputana Agency	16	..	..	..	2	..	..	..
33 Sikkim State	..	..	..	..	..	..	..	..
34 United Provinces States	..	..	..	..	..	..	..	..
35 Western India States Agency ..	3	8	..	40	..	..	..	..

hood—Part II—Provincial Distribution—*contd.*

Materials—*contd.*

Minerals—*contd.*

Minerals—*contd.*

Group 39.—Precious and semi-precious stones.				*Group 40.*—Salt, saltpetre and other saline substances.						
Total working dependants.		Total following occupation as subsidiary to other.		Total earners principal occupation.		Total working dependants.		Total following occupation as subsidiary to other.		
Males.	Females.	Males.	Females.	Males.	Females.	Males.	Females.	Males.	Females.	
313	314	315	316	317	318	319	320	321	322	
679	**670**	**923**	**16**	**21,292**	**9,075**	**965**	**1,413**	**8,716**	**2,154**	
678	670	897	15	14,241	7,586	536	1,061	8,243	2,113	
..	..	..	..	..	..	..	..	..	..	1
..	..	..	..	..	..	..	..	..	..	2
..	2	7	..	3	..	..	..	5	..	3
..	..	..	..	..		..	..	2	..	4
..	..	..	..	147	..	..	..	1	..	5
..	..	24	..	2,779	2,469	13	28	4,211	1,418	6
..	..	..	..	4,159	2,951	84	182	2,365	490	7
..	..	..	..	*2*	..	..	..	..	..	
678	668	853	15	691	393	164	271	432	109	8
..	..	..		11	..	..	..	..	..	9
..	..	..	..	..		..	..	..	..	10
..	..	..	..	3	..	..	..	..	..	11
..	..	..	..	1,385	322	3	14	443	34	12
..	..	13	..	81	..	1	..	1	..	13
..	..	..	..	2,043	543	38	22	38	1	14
..	..	..	..	2,939	908	233	544	745	61	15
1	..	**26**	**1**	**7,051**	**1,489**	**429**	**352**	**473**	**41**	
..	..	..	..	23	172	124	2	2	..	16
..	..	..	..	76	..	..	..	4	..	17
..	..	..	..	381	255	5	..	..	..	18
..	..	..	..	..	..	..	..	..	..	19
..	..	..	..	3	..	..	..	..	14	20
..	..	1	..	31	5	3	..	5	..	21
1	..	24	1	8	2	..	..	..	..	22
..	..	..	..	..	..	..	..	..	..	23
..	..	..	..	129	43	9	1	11	3	24
..	..	..	..	398	23	83	44	3	1	25
..	..	1	..	..	..	..	..	..	..	26
..	..	..	..	381	32	26	..	..	..	27
..	..	..	..	..	..	..	..	..	..	
..	..	..	..	*381*	*32*	*26*	..	..	..	
..	..	..	..	..	..	..	..	..	..	
..	..	..	..	293	78	1	2	251	6	28
..	..	..	..	..	..	..	..	..	..	29
..	..	..	..	..	..	..	..	..	..	30
..	..	..	..	283	3	28	40	18		31
..	..	..	..	3,693	584	1	74	155	2	32
..	..	..	..	..	..	..	..	..	..	33
..	..	..	..	197	133	3	32		9	34
..	..	..	..	1,155	159	146	157	24	6	35

Table X.—Occupation or Means of Liveli

Province, State or Agency.	Class A.—Production of Raw Materials—concld. Sub-Class II.—Exploitation of Minerals—concld. Order 4.—Non-Metallic Minerals—concld. Group 41.—Other non-metallic minerals. Total earners principal occupation.		Total working dependants.		Total following occupation as subsidiary to other.		Total. Class B— Total earners principal occupation.	
	Males.	Females.	Males.	Females.	Males.	Females.	Males.	Females.
1	323	324	325	326	327	328	329	330
INDIA	**2,032**	**140**	**225**	**47**	**232**	**39**	**17,784,556**	**5,161,789**
Provinces	**1,660**	**96**	**195**	**22**	**125**	**38**	**13,646,995**	**3,880,535**
1 Ajmer-Merwara	..	..	..	..	..	..	57,872	9,742
2 Andamans and Nicobars	..	..	..	..	..	..	2,716	10
3 Assam	..	..	..	..	..	..	201,344	33,876
4 Baluchistan (*Districts and Administered Territories*).	..	..	..	..	..	..	36,273	1,037
5 Bengal	..	10	..	..	..	..	2,008,413	411,316
6 Bihar and Orissa	19	1	..	..	30	..	1,056,897	593,541
7 Bombay (*including Aden*)	44	1	27	..	2	38	1,348,677	208,234
Aden	..	..	..	..	..	..	*12,481*	*480*
8 Burma	..	..	..	..	..	..	744,486	360,398
9 Central Provinces and Berar ..	206	..	1	..	15	..	738,196	233,118
10 Coorg	..	..	..	..	..	..	7,337	943
11 Delhi	36	10	..	..	14	..	118,672	9,034
12 Madras	..	15	..	13	.	..	2,580,822	762,055
13 North-West Frontier Province (*Districts and Administered Territories*).	..	..	..	..	..	..	176,152	5,922
14 Punjab	1,355	59	167	9	64	..	1,916,531	181,567
15 United Provinces of Agra and Oudh	..	..	..	..	..	..	2,652,607	1,069,742
States and Agencies ..	**372**	**44**	**30**	**25**	**107**		**4,137,561**	**1,281,254**
16 Assam States	..	..	..	..	..	..	11,461	13,702
17 Baluchistan States	..	..	..	..	..	..	11,618	1,772
18 Baroda State	..	..	..	..	..	..	150,850	34,908
19 Bengal States	..	..	..	..	..	..	16,887	7,704
20 Bihar and Orissa States	..	..	..	..	..	..	122,763	142,630
21 Bombay States	1	..	1	..	..	..	156,956	27,681
22 Central India Agency	95	28	3	..	77	1	335,997	99,224
23 Central Provinces States	..	..	..	..	..	..	59,691	19,730
24 Gwalior State	95	..	20	..	..	..	183,576	42,108
25 Hyderabad State	..	..	..	..	..	..	899,824	350,220
26 Jammu and Kashmir States ..	..	..	..	..	..	..	103,978	10,584
27 Madras State Agency	..	..	..	..	..	..	457,273	185,421
Cochin State	..	..	..	..	..	..	106,467	49,698
Travancore State	..	..	..	..	..	..	325,488	128,374
Other Madras States	..	..	..	..	..	..	25,318	7,349
28 Mysore State	..	..	..	..	..	..	270,977	80,717
29 North-West Frontier Province (*Agencies and Tribal Areas*).	..	..	..	..	..	..	4,215	20
30 Punjab States	59	..	3	1	2	..	17,126	1,844
31 Punjab States Agency	18	6	..	1	13	..	275,074	22,447
32 Rajputana Agency	23	..	..	..	15	..	748,004	198,327
33 Sikkim State	..	..	..	..	..	..	1,493	343
34 United Provinces States	..	..	..		..		43,259	17,165
35 Western India States Agency ..	81	10	3	23	..	..	266,539	24,707

hood—Part II—Provincial Distribution—*contd.*

Class B.—Preparation and Supply of Material Substances.

Preparation and Supply of Material Substances.				Total *Sub-Class III.*—Industry.						
Total working dependants.		Total following occupation as subsidiary to other.		Total earners principal occupation.		Total working dependants.		Total following occupation as subsidiary to other.		
Males.	Females.	Males.	Females.	Males.	Females.	Males.	Females.	Males.	Females.	
331	332	333	334	335	336	337	338	339	340	
897,785	**1,762,826**	**3,413,706**	**618,809**	**10,289,607**	**3,263,788**	**507,920**	**1,290,638**	**1,825,355**	**346,674**	
430,477	**1,144,710**	**2,602,488**	**422,957**	**7,949,501**	**2,504,110**	**276,650**	**904,757**	**1,396,481**	**250,793**	
935	2,975	6,283	726	27,620	6,622	648	2,482	3,214	368	1
16	11	323	4	1,059	9	14	7	250	3	2
12,028	207,266	119,387	22,339	65,790	19,458	5,872	201,360	42,512	19,654	3
302	1,865	10,468	143	12,762	713	154	1,807	1,144	99	4
24,168	32,209	263,761	22,913	970,102	263,898	12,080	22,993	102,444	11,468	5
12,746	46,519	479,889	83,397	623,405	365,935	8,824	32,481	289,017	42,355	6
53,584	63,451	84,297	12,484	786,543	147,865	34,124	46,925	44,885	7,462	7
372	*142*	*84*	*10*	*3,238*	*316*	*189*	*131*	*33*	*7*	
40,466	298,329	153,057	83,381	290,503	139,029	18,896	215,948	60,343	61,782	8
27,672	85,932	149,624	39,185	447,204	128,282	19,213	61,986	73,287	16,260	9
104	26	2,591	169	3,180	628	40	19	984	140	10
866	2,772	2,286	79	63,828	7,186	643	2,392	1,097	64	11
92,476	148,832	464,494	30,139	1,605,974	482,398	66,101	115,236	226,253	29,952	12
5,754	975	11,564	80	99,224	5,300	3,469	749	4,788	43	13
99,878	92,028	147,403	10,739	1,247,594	163,666	69,638	85,858	87,584	9,794	14
59,482	161,520	707,061	87,179	1,704,713	773,121	36,934	114,514	458,679	51,349	15
467,308	**618,116**	**811,218**	**195,852**	**2,340,106**	**759,678**	**231,270**	**385,881**	**428,874**	**95,881**	
1,068	18,926	5,756	5,877	5,450	8,004	546	17,469	1,190	3,652	16
191	3,883	3,819	77	4,297	1,689	101	3,872	830	64	17
8,976	17,854	16,359	1,570	88,649	22,682	4,897	13,432	8,168	1,046	18
383	5,069	3,462	195	4,445	3,593	192	4,505	887	79	19
3,382	24,988	69,438	16,851	85,866	89,131	1,762	19,465	43,104	10,282	20
9,530	16,896	23,189	4,729	98,501	19,379	6,559	12,929	13,576	2,575	21
5,078	6,783	81,995	9,722	218,433	62,298	3,142	4,268	42,736	3,536	22
8,393	27,140	17,681	2,191	40,854	10,713	6,634	20,759	12,006	662	23
8,001	11,981	35,987	7,165	122,071	28,017	5,033	8,390	19,581	3,738	24
301,941	262,169	188,603	100,054	359,044	140,729	124,053	91,381	76,531	37,763	25
3,221	6,394	25,101	5,941	69,411	6,435	2,250	5,449	15,963	4,589	26
34,429	65,604	69,751	20,174	251,975	141,100	23,623	60,710	32,544	16,691	27
1,847	6,381	16,136	4,826	59,073	41,306	1,386	6,070	6,814	3,927	
32,168	58,705	44,378	14,787	179,224	95,644	21,977	54,231	22,126	12,484	
414	518	9,237	561	13,678	4,150	260	409	3,604	280	
7,780	34,952	99,593	6,815	160,360	40,786	5,493	28,947	55,535	3,281	28
3	..	1,055	..	2,013	20	2	..	329	..	29
830	1,343	6,030	110	11,436	1,378	592	1,163	4,108	87	30
14,064	12,356	38,347	1,059	169,710	19,426	9,581	11,567	26,278	816	31
16,989	66,767	105,793	10,889	476,276	135,760	12,073	57,089	64,161	5,913	32
10	1	446	112	383	70	1	–	246	49	33
1,713	4,300	10,235	1,551	25,703	11,594	971	2,616	7,479	623	34
41,326	30,710	8,578	770	145,229	16,874	23,765	21,870	3,622	435	35

Table X.—Occupation or Means of Liveli

Class B.—Preparation and Supply

Sub-Class III.—

	Province, State or Agency.	Total *Order 5.*—Textiles.							
		Total earners principal occupation.		Total working dependants.		Total following occupation as subsidiary to other.		Total earners principal occupation.	
		Males.	Females.	Males.	Females.	Males.	Females.	Males.	Females.
		341	342	343	344	345	346	347	348
	INDIA ..	**2,408,391**	**853,248**	**123,020**	**717,477**	**277,561**	**131,823**	**185,253**	**48,831**
	Provinces	1,902,214	602,613	64,262	543,893	186,001	100,121	147,987	34,887
1	Ajmer-Merwara	4,438	1,702	138	830	401	107	514	171
2	Andamans and Nicobars	1	4	..	1	221	..		1
3	Assam	2,028	8,760	1,849	194,957	2,777	17,588	176	169
4	Baluchistan (*Districts and Administered Territories*).	319	36	2	4	86	8	8	..
5	Bengal	369,836	69,790	4,584	7,535	25,731	2,489	4,737	440
6	Bihar and Orissa	91,988	47,744	1,853	7,047	43,930	6,153	1,728	1,366
7	Bombay (*including Aden*)	296,606	70,276	10,324	25,647	7,445	1,908	53,756	7,885
	Aden	*305*	*102*	*8*	*30*	*3*	*5*	..	..
8	Burma	7,402	54,813	2,399	168,594	1,337	50,260	61	338
9	Central Provinces and Berar ..	109,899	32,292	6,271	32,461	14,162	3,245	13,109	5,664
10	Coorg	61	9	..	..	4	1	..	
11	Delhi	10,672	876	26	336	260	16	684	19
12	Madras	398,910	144,704	15,163	42,038	30,242	8,116	16,989	7,586
13	North-West Frontier Province (*Districts and Administered Territories*).	14,292	1,424	426	212	447	9	2,075	302
14	Punjab	270,687	43,749	15,117	28,621	20,497	4,128	27,901	2,691
15	United Provinces of Agra and Oudh	325,080	126,434	6,110	35,610	38,461	6,093	26,299	8,255
	States and Agencies ..	506,177	250,635	58,758	173,584	91,560	31,702	37,266	13,944
16	Assam States	146	6,860	144	16,835	54	3,151		
17	Baluchistan States	335	160	31	1,209	147	33	..	..
18	Baroda State	25,360	12,194	287	832	1,519	549	5,864	2,456
19	Bengal States	261	1,071	112	4,433	66	27	12	..
20	Bihar and Orissa States	31,219	21,278	674	7,192	12,988	1,934	125	47
21	Bombay States	27,223	9,758	1,664	6,285	2,028	741	1,282	236
22	Central India Agency	31,871	10,194	347	838	5,390	582	3,810	1,321
23	Central Provinces States ..	13,093	2,175	2,886	9,606	4,483	134	18	3
24	Gwalior State	28,324	4,957	890	1,834	2,932	698	2,066	440
25	Hyderabad State	99,427	43,852	29,466	21,318	18,962	9,931	7,059	4,188
26	Jammu and Kashmir State ..	10,052	2,177	618	3,460	2,639	2,326	293	97
27	Madras States Agency	54,528	65,058	10,430	43,112	10,591	8,150	7	1
	Cochin State	*13,196*	*22,141*	*911*	*4,573*	*1,753*	*1,308*	*2*	*1*
	Travancore State	*40,168*	*42,508*	*9,482*	*38,432*	*8,460*	*6,795*		..
	Other Madras States	*1,164*	*409*	*37*	*107*	*378*	*47*	*5*	
28	Mysore State	34,442	12,553	1,456	13,240	10,032	1,008	361	168
29	North-West Frontier Province (*Agencies and Tribal Areas*).	6?	1	..	..	80	..	..	..
30	Punjab States	2,042	388	117	491	893	34	266	7
31	Punjab States Agency	31,309	3,379	1,499	3,229	4,561	203	3,400	79
32	Rajputana Agency	82,398	47,151	3,640	30,254	12,158	1,928	9,552	3,934
33	Sikkim State	2	20	..	..	2	30	..	
34	United Provinces States	4,754	1,168	230	173	1,394	69	618	238
35	Western India States Agency ..	29,328	6,241	4,267	9,243	641	174	2,533	729

hood.—Part II.—Provincial Distribution—*contd.*

of Material Substances—*contd.*

Industry—*contd.*

Order 5.—Textiles.

Group 42.—Cotton ginning, cleaning and pressing.				*Group 43.*—Cotton spinning, sizing and weaving.						
Total working dependants.		Total following occupation as subsidiary to other.		Total earners principal occupation.		Total working dependants.		Total following occupation as subsidiary to other.		
Males.	Females.	Males.	Females.	Males.	Females.	Males.	Females.	Males.	Females.	
349	350	351	352	353	354	355	356	357	358	
10,713	**12,408**	**21,844**	**3,798**	**1,678,453**	**540,297**	**82,814**	**582,009**	**189,205**	**101,128**	
6,620	**7,161**	**15,513**	**2,153**	**1,329,239**	**399,052**	**47,950**	**477,943**	**129,438**	**83,018**	
1	76	74	9	3,112	1,118	50	596	312	94	1
..	..	..	..	..	..	..	..	..	..	2
..	..	10	6	1,104	7,580	1,672	192,036	2,201	17,348	3
..	..	2	..	96	..	..	..	10	1	4
1	73	533	3	127,692	30,394	4,116	4,879	18,006	1,711	5
10	41	644	174	81,427	37,420	1,687	5,668	37,849	3,406	6
3,007	1,363	872	118	207,854	47,705	4,716	17,582	3,249	776	7
..	..	..	..	*119*	*11*	*8*	..	*2*	..	
4	309	6	233	2,568	40,091	1,459	144,637	791	45,346	8
151	580	1,413	442	86,310	22,811	5,423	29,021	10,624	2,248	9
..	..	..	..	54	9	..	..	2	..	10
2	..	54	1	9,131	625	21	173	194	12	11
1,189	1,668	1,180	288	333,611	82,953	12,627	28,513	22,279	4,901	12
16	3	44	1	8,373	829	384	167	382	7	13
1,338	1,226	4,566	121	214,381	36,671	12,346	24,991	12,514	3,674	14
901	1,822	6,115	757	253,526	90,846	3,449	29,680	21,025	3,489	15
4,093	**5,247**	**6,331**	**1,645**	**349,214**	**141,245**	**34,864**	**104,066**	**59,767**	**18,115**	
..	..	..	..	132	6,190	140	16,680	51	3,035	16
..	..	..	..	127	1	..	..	28	..	17
..	..	680	347	16,584	8,301	126	218	624	163	18
..	..	..	..	112	1,061	112	4,432	47	27	19
..	5	1	..	30,301	20,179	563	6,962	12,592	,674	20
90	77	324	..	20,746	5,932	1,168	4,262	998	436	21
27	59	734	129	23,602	6,877	259	555	2,954	327	22
..	..	1	2	12,620	1,893	2,802	9,340	4,331	109	23
86	117	289	80	22,994	3,787	711	1,305	2,164	549	24
3,195	3,333	2,014	840	73,949	34,692	18,990	13,941	13,353	7,693	25
13	10	101	4	4,911	1,512	222	1,050	1,953	1,451	26
2	..	43	1	15,831	3,162	1,787	976	1,912	244	27
2	..	43	1	3,918	1,938	110	133	175	50	
..	..	..	..	11,117	1,046	1,651	822	1,412	176	
..	..	..	..	796	178	26	21	325	18	
3	..	35	42	23,568	6,804	1,049	8,156	3,876	439	28
..	..	..	..	63	1	..	..	80	..	29
..	1	82	..	1,440	343	62	420	377	33	30
184	13	651	5	24,429	2,484	1,195	2,937	3,327	184	31
184	1,181	1,282	189	57,854	34,215	2,687	26,795	9,478	1,585	32
..	..	..	..	2	13	..	..	2	12	33
27	66	29	1	3,744	686	198	71	1,296	23	34
282	385	65	5	16,205	3,112	2,793	5,966	324	131	35

Table X.—Occupation or Means of Liveli

Class B.—Preparation and

Sub-Class III.-

Order 5.—

	Province, State or Agency.	*Group 44.*—Jute pressing, spinning and weaving. Total earners principal occupation. Males.	Females.	Total working dependants. Males.	Females.	Total following occupation as subsidiary to other. Males.	Females.	*Group 45.*—Rope, Total earners principal occupation. Males.	Females.
	1	359	360	361	362	363	364	365	366
	INDIA	**235,308**	**35,407**	**496**	**1,242**	**9,488**	**1,431**	**107,881**	**142,244**
	Provinces	**234,735**	**35,226**	**473**	**1,164**	**9,204**	**1,402**	**52,932**	**75,202**
1	Ajmer-Merwara	1	9	..	15	..	..	40	37
2	Andamans and Nicobars ..	..	..	..	..	..	..	1	3
3	Assam	501	88	6	48	111	9	116	748
4	Baluchistan (*Districts and Administered Territories*).	..	..	..	..	..	..	4	..
5	Bengal	229,151	31,785	293	338	5,548	182	2,260	5,536
6	Bihar and Orissa	1,424	1,468	7	335	2,741	1,036	1,015	4,294
7	Bombay (*including Aden*)	103	306	2	30	14	45	16,839	5,848
	Aden	*1*	..	.	*30*	*1*	..	*24*	*87*
8	Burma	..	..	..	..	..	..	793	796
9	Central Provinces and Berar ..	471	329	23	148	188	58	1,224	751
10	Coorg	..	..	..	..	..	..	3	..
11	Delhi	14	..	..	..	.	..	11	5
12	Madras	1,577	469	69	116	346	54	7,559	40,106
13	North-West Frontier Province (*Districts and Administered Territories*).	31	20	..	..	2	..	208	233
14	Punjab	932	223	73	106	158	1	9,785	1,760
15	United Provinces of Agra and Oudh	530	529	..	28	96	17	13,074	15,085
	States and Agencies ..	**573**	**181**	**23**	**78**	**284**	**29**	**54,949**	**67,042**
16	Assam States	..	..	..	..	..	..	9	10
17	Baluchistan States	..	16	1	15	..	..	73	10
18	Baroda State	..	..	..	..	..	..	117	265
19	Bengal States	129	7	..	..	18	..	1	..
20	Bihar and Orissa States	23	62	1	..	43	11	240	411
21	Bombay States	..	..	..	..	..	..	3,085	2,350
22	Central India Agency	140	44	6	16	125	10	263	257
23	Central Provinces States	64	2	3	26	53	3	130	100
24	Gwalior State	..	..	..	..	..	.	43	40
25	Hyderabad State	..	..	..	..	..	..	5,455	1,908
26	Jammu and Kashmir State ..	8	4	..	1	2	2	83	1
27	Madras States Agency	3	..	..	..	..	..	38,129	58,833
	Cochin State	..	..	..	..	..	..	*9,247*	*20,190*
	Taravancore State	..	..	..	..	..	..	*28,825*	*38,598*
	Other Madras States	*3*	..	..	..	..	..	*57*	*45*
28	Mysore State	28	3	1	5	12	3	632	579
29	North-West Frontier Province (*Agencies and Tribal Areas*).	..	..	..	..	..	..	..	..
30	Punjab States	6	..	..	1	5	..	80	3
31	Punjab States Agency	2	..	4	..	1	..	1,146	421
32	Rajputana Agency	137	34	4	..	25	..	1,718	1,161
33	Sikkim State	..	..	.	..	..	..	..	..
34	United Provinces States	..	..	..	..	..	..	53	47
35	Western India States Agency ..	33	0	3	14	..	..	3 692	646

hood.—Part II.—Provincial Distribution—*contd.*

Supply of Material Substances—*contd.*

Industry—*contd.*

Textiles—*contd.*

twine, string and other fibres.				*Group 46.*—Wool carding, spinning and weaving.						
Total working dependants.		Total following occupation as subsidiary to other.		Total earners principal occupation.		Total working dependants.		Total following occupation as subsidiary to other.		
Males.	Females.	Males.	Females.	Males.	Females.	Males.	Females.	Males.	Females.	
367	368	369	370	371	372	373	374	375	376	
14,115	**65,594**	**30,526**	**15,606**	**57,926**	**28,767**	**6,008**	**16,646**	**16,111**	**3,150**	
2,924	**19,096**	**18,554**	**6,668**	**33,313**	**19,328**	**1,519**	**6,937**	**7,100**	**1,110**	
..	30	6	2	137	238	5	24	2	2	1
..	1	221	..	..	..	..	..	..	..	2
68	1,915	334	193	1	..	..	1	..	..	3
..	..	..	..	149	34	2	4	72	3	4
134	1,501	662	415	688	73	2	..	41	..	5
97	943	878	1,288	3,142	1,236	30	33	1,190	131	6
1,097	1,825	2,045	591	7,879	5,624	710	3,239	830	210	7
..	..	..	*1*	..	..	..	..	..	..	
141	661	242	100	..	..	..	..	..	..	8
71	387	585	164	1,565	1,086	148	981	944	164	9
..	..	1	..	3	..	..	..	..	1	10
1	2	..	..	62	25	..	4	3	..	11
534	8,747	3,983	2,145	6,468	3,878	144	971	1,446	315	12
6	14	..	..	605	..	..	4	..	..	13
563	1,344	2,164	260	1,756	711	48	210	124	15	14
212	1,726	7,433	1,510	10,858	6,423	430	1,466	2,448	269	15
11,191	**46,498**	**11,972**	**8,938**	**24,613**	**9,439**	**4,489**	**9,709**	**9,011**	**2,040**	
4	7	3	17	..	..	..	..	..	..	16
..	..	87	4	124	133	30	1,194	30	29	17
5	119	35	11	387	61	5	6	36	1	18
..	1	1	..	..	..	..	..	..	..	19
..	58	15	13	..	3	..	..	1	..	20
216	1,248	464	246	1,269	800	138	331	78	57	21
8	14	136	43	1,351	735	18	56	1,254	59	22
16	30	29	1	137	145	29	108	48	15	23
..	19	17	1	383	114	8	38	241	..	24
1,797	1,446	1,007	514	9,151	2,045	3,461	1,639	1,686	633	25
..	..	20	..	745	194	147	1,443	182	752	26
8,604	42,009	8,544	7,877	32	131	4	9	24	28	27
796	4,440	1,527	1,257	28	11	3	..	7	..	
7,808	37,568	7,009	6,619	..	..	..	..	..	..	
..	1	8	1	4	120	1	9	17	28	
38	200	552	145	5,831	2,841	249	3,194	4,590	341	28
..	..	..	..	..	..	..	..	..	..	29
25	61	24	..	175	24	30	6	289	1	30
26	102	111	1	56	71	12	29	299	13	31
99	231	759	52	1,236	905	41	286	202	28	32
..	..	..	..	..	7	..	..	..	18	33
..	..	45	1	280	62	5	3	24	44	34
353	953	123	12	3,456	1,168	312	1,367	27	21	35

Table X.—Occupation or Means of Liveli

Class B.—Preparation and

Sub-Class III.—

Order 5.—

Province, State or Agency.	*Group 47.*—Silk spinning and weaving. Total earners principal occupation. Males.	Females.	Total working dependants. Males.	Females.	Total following occupation as subsidiary to other. Males.	Females.	*Group 48.*—Hair Total earners principal occupation. Males.	Females.
1	377	378	379	380	381	382	383	384
INDIA	**53,148**	**28,175**	**3,875**	**29,323**	**3,661**	**5,354**	**714**	**193**
Provinces	**46,776**	**24,784**	**2,860**	**26,843**	**2,113**	**4,994**	**364**	**46**
1 Ajmer-Merwara	2	2	..	..	..	..	..	..
2 Andamans and Nicobars	..	..	..	..	..	..	..	..
3 Assam	101	163	103	937	120	32	..	..
4 Baluchistan (*Districts and Admistered Territories*).	7	..	..	..	1	..	..	..
5 Bengal	3,624	1,002	22	174	748	72	254	39
6 Bihar and Orissa	1,055	860	..	..	25	23	4	..
7 Bombay (*including Aden*)	2,869	1,628	244	1,036	226	58	23	..
Aden	..	..	..	..	..	..	..	..
8 Burma	3,713	13,567	786	22,970	292	4,580	..	..
9 Central Provinces and Berar	3,962	864	307	604	104	20	20	3
10 Coorg	1	..	..	..	1	..	..	..
11 Delhi	41	7	..	1	..	..	1	..
12 Madras	26,325	5,489	485	988	582	207	36	3
13 North-West Frontier Province (*Districts and Administered Territories*).	267	..	..	..	..	..	..	..
14 Punjab	939	222	12	22	8	2	..	..
15 United Provinces of Agra and Oudh	3,870	980	901	111	6	..	26	1
States and Agencies ..	**6,372**	**3,391**	**1,015**	**2,480**	**1,548**	**360**	**350**	**147**
16 Assam States	..	13	..	4	..	3	..	..
17 Baluchistan States	..	..	..	..	..	..	..	..
18 Baroda State	313	158	24	87	24	6	..	1
19 Bengal States	..	..	..	..	..	..	..	..
20 Bihar and Orissa States	528	564	110	163	336	236	..	..
21 Bombay States	117	255	1	93	34	1	..	..
22 Central India Agency	..	..	..	..	..	..	..	..
23 Central Provinces States	81	6	33	82	20	1	..	..
24 Gwalior State	..	..	..	..	..	..	..	..
25 Hyderabad State	881	375	552	348	141	84	72	16
26 Jammu and Kashmir State ..	322	4	152	1	49	1	7	..
27 Madras States Agency	319	66	19	76	18	..	..	..
Cochin State	..	..	..	..	..	..	..	..
Travancore State	*55*	*2*	*10*	*2*	*16*	..	..	..
Other Madras States	*264*	*64*	*9*	*74*	*2*	..	..	..
28 Mysore State	3,435	,899	106	1,560	924	28	1	..
29 North-West Frontier Province (*Agencies and Tribal Areas*).	..	..	..	..	..	..	..	..
30 Punjab States	..	..	..	..	..	..	..	..
31 Punjab States Agency	28	2	1	1	..	..	..	..
32 Rajputana Agency	1	1	..	..	..	..	197	130
33 Sikkim State	..	..	..	..	..	..	..	..
34 United Provinces States	..	..	..	..	..	..	..	..
35 Western India States Agency ..	347	48	17	65	2	..	73	..

hood.—Part II.—Provincial Distribution—*contd.*

Supply of Material Substances—*contd.*

Industry—*contd.*

Textiles—*contd.*

(horse-hair), etc.				*Group 49.*—Dyeing, bleaching, printing, preparation and sponging of textiles.						
Total working dependants.		Total following occupation as subsidiary to other.		Total earners principal occupation.		Total working dependants.		Total following occupation as subsidiary to other.		
Males.	Females.	Males.	Females.	Males.	Females.	Males.	Females.	Males.	Females.	
385	386	387	388	389	390	391	392	393	394	
33	**580**	**236**	**76**	**73,798**	**19,366**	**3,983**	**6,623**	**5,238**	**691**	
1	**539**	**84**	**60**	**46,559**	**9,819**	**1,314**	**3,010**	**3,212**	**401**	
..	..	..	..	120	82	2	69	1	..	1
..	..	..	..	..	..	..	..	..	..	2
..	..	..	..	19	..	..	..	1	..	3
..	..	..	..	55		..	..	1	..	4
1	534	15	44	313	117	5	2	23	4	5
..	..	40	16	2,169	1,027	20	27	558	79	6
..	..	..	..	4,175	732	134	242	176	94	7
..	..	..	..	160	2	..	..	..	..	
..	..	..	..	267	21	9	17	6	1	8
..	2	..	..	2,761	557	128	447	198	89	9
..	..	..	..	..	..	..	..	..	..	10
..	..	..	..	426	21	1	17	9	..	11
..	2	27	..	5,754	2,921	111	795	363	43	12
..	..	..	..	2,577	35	20	23	19	1	13
..	..	..	..	14,624	1,251	736	676	952	52	14
..	1	2	..	13,299	3,053	148	695	905	38	15
32	**41**	**152**	**16**	**27,239**	**9,547**	**2,669**	**3,613**	**2,026**	**290**	
..	..	..	..	1	..	..	..	..	..	16
..	..	..	..	11	..	..	..	2	..	17
..	..	..	..	1,934	273	117	273	92	9	18
..	..	..	..	6	1	..	..	..	..	19
..	..	..	..	2	11	..	4	..	..	20
..	..	..	..	656	184	46	270	126	1	21
..	..	2	..	2,642	879	29	124	178	14	22
..	..	..	..	18	4	2	1	1	2	23
..	..	..	..	2,774	545	84	351	173	51	24
26	30	36	11	2,483	480	1,261	462	641	124	25
1	..	1	..	396	19	27	..	85	14	26
..	..	..	..	163	2	11	2	49	..	27
..	..	..	..	..	..	..	..	*1*	..	
..	..	..	..	*128*	..	*10*	..	*23*	..	
..	..	..	..	*35*	*2*	*1*	*2*	*25*	..	
..	..	..	..	240	106	2	51	18	6	28
..	..	..	..	..	..	..	..	..	..	29
..	..	..	..	74	9	..	2	116	..	30
..	..	..	..	1,980	165	55	87	172	..	31
5	11	113	5	11,089	6,413	558	1,566	275	68	32
..	..	..	..	..	..	..	..	..	..	33
..	..	..	..	41	..	..	..	..	..	34
..	..	..	..	2,729	456	477	420	98	1	35

Table X.—Occupation or Means of Liveli

Class B.—Preparation

Sub-Class III.—

Province, State or Agency.	*Order 5.*—Textiles—*concld.* *Group 50.*—Lace, crepe, embroideries, fringes, etc., and insufficiently described textile industries. Total earners principal occupation.		Total working dependants.		Total following occupation as subsidiary to other.		*Order 6.*—Hides, Total *Order 6.*— Total earners principal occupation.	
	Males.	Females.	Males.	Females.	Males.	Females.	Males.	Females.
1	395	396	397	398	399	400	401	402
INDIA	**15,910**	**9,968**	**983**	**3,052**	**1,252**	**589**	**250,911**	**32,998**
Provinces	**10,309**	**4,269**	**601**	**1,200**	**783**	**320**	**168,212**	**22,188**
1 Ajmer-Merwara	512	45	80	20	6	..	2,570	115
2 Andamans and Nicobars	..	..	..	..	..	..	4	..
3 Assam	5	12	..	20	..	..	693	17
4 Baluchistan (*Districts and Administered Territories*).	..	..	..	..	..	4	18	..
5 Bengal	1,117	404	10	34	155	58	11,301	438
6 Bihar and Orissa	24	73	2	..	5	..	3,084	1,100
7 Bombay (*including Aden*) ..	3,108	548	414	330	33	16	13,269	2,764
Aden	*1*	*2*	..	..	..	*4*	*39*	*1*
8 Burma	..	..	..	..	..	..	346	32
9 Central Provinces and Berar ..	477	227	20	291	106	60	14,093	2,331
10 Coorg	..	..	..	..	..	..	2	..
11 Delhi	352	174	1	139	..	3	621	42
12 Madras	591	1,299	4	238	36	163	38,176	1,556
13 North-West Frontier Province (*Districts and Administered Territories*).	156	5	..	1	..	..	610	8
14 Punjab	369	220	1	46	11	3	11,134	232
15 United Provinces of Agra and Oudh	3,598	1,262	69	81	431	13	72,291	13,553
States and Agencies ..	**5,601**	**5,699**	**382**	**1,852**	**469**	**269**	**82,699**	**10,810**
16 Assam States	4	647	..	144	..	96	2	..
17 Baluchistan States	..	..	..	..	..	..	9	8
18 Baroda State	161	679	10	129	28	12	5,237	335
19 Bengal States	1	2	..	..	..	..	144	5
20 Bihar and Orissa States	..	1	..	..	..	..	44	78
21 Bombay States	68	1	5	4	4	..	3,255	125
22 Central India Agency	63	81	..	14	7	..	4,778	1,039
23 Central Provinces States	25	22	1	19	..	1	633	39
24 Gwalior State	64	31	1	4	48	17	5,552	1,764
25 Hyderabad State	377	148	184	119	84	32	5,507	1,097
26 Jammu and Kashmir State ..	3,287	346	56	955	246	102	4,616	306
27 Madras States Agency	44	2,863	3	40	1	..	780	12
Cochin State	*1*	*1*	..	..	..	..	*464*	*12*
Travancore State	*43*	*2,862*	*3*	*40*	..	..	*310*	..
Other Madras States	..	..	..	..	*1*	..	*6*	..
28 Mysore State	346	153	8	74	25	4	3,111	347
29 North-West Frontier Province (*Agencies and Tribal Areas*). ..	..	..	..	..	..	..	..	..
30 Punjab States	1	2	..	..	..	..	110	1
31 Punjab States Agency	268	157	22	60	..	..	2,683	922
32 Rajputana Agency	614	358	62	184	24	1	32,922	3,827
33 Sikkim State	..	..	..	..	..	..	..	..
34 United Provinces States	18	135	..	33	..	..	372	70
35 Western India States Agency ..	260	73	30	73	2	4	12,944	835

hood.—Part II.—Provincial Distribution—*contd.*

and Supply of Material Substances—*contd.*

Industry—*contd.*

skins and hard materials from the animal kingdom.

Hides, skins and hard materials from the animal kingdom. *Group 51.*—Working in leather.

Total working dependants.		Total following occupation as subsidiary to other.		Total earners principal occupation.		Total working dependants.		Total following occupation as subsidiary to others.		
Males.	Females.	Males.	Females.	Males.	Females.	Males.	Females.	Males.	Females.	
403	404	405	406	407	408	409	410	411	412	
14,993	**13,172**	**43,329**	**4,460**	**241,908**	**31,488**	**14,607**	**12,941**	**42,566**	**4,418**	
8,472	**5,496**	**27,414**	**3,329**	**161,055**	**20,845**	**8,323**	**5,396**	**26,765**	**3,287**	
76	128	676	36	2,560	101	76	124	672	36	1
..	..	..	..	..	..	..	..	..	..	2
54	13	274	5	664	17	53	13	270	?	3
4	2	..	..	15	..	4	2	..	..	4
137	10	1,424	35	7,879	280	121	7	1,148	26	5
39	63	1,444	312	2,631	950	13	56	1,303	297	6
980	873	1,108	189	12,566	2,584	959	839	1,059	189	7
..	..	*2*	..	*39*	*1*	..	..	*2*	..	
19	40	5	1	279	32	17	40	4	1	8
521	1,268	1,493	212	13,985	2,256	520	1,264	1,463	203	9
..	..	..	..	2	..	..	..	..	..	10
8	15	13	..	569	41	8	15	13	..	11
788	133	5,969	267	36,762	1,449	708	125	5,922	267	12
3	..	5	..	603	8	3	..	4	..	13
799	163	1,029	28	11,080	232	799	160	1,023	28	14
5,044	2,788	13,974	2,244	71,460	12,895	5,042	2,751	13,884	2,238	15
6,521	**7,676**	**15,915**	**1,131**	**80,853**	**10,643**	**6,284**	**7,545**	**15,801**	**1,131**	
1	..	6	..	2	..	1	..	6	..	16
..	3	..	..	9	8	..	3	..	..	17
452	2,012	1,059	59	5,119	333	443	2,012	1,059	59	18
1	..	29	..	143	5	1	..	23	..	19
..	12	16	32	22	50	..	12	2	32	20
300	420	395	9	3,247	125	300	420	395	9	21
73	138	1,242	73	4,715	1,030	73	138	1,236	73	22
58	71	158	9	633	39	58	71	158	9	23
224	483	1,463	134	5,550	1,764	223	483	1,462	134	24
2,817	779	1,451	225	5,229	1,069	2,690	741	1,421	225	25
76	120	1,497	377	4,533	304	76	107	1,483	377	26
76	3	83	1	689	12	76	3	78	1	27
9	..	*34*	*1*	*457*	*12*	*9*	..	*31*	*1*	
67	*3*	*29*	..	*226*	..	*67*	*3*	*27*	..	
..	..	*20*	..	*6*	..	..	..	*20*	..	
48	8	1,193	29	3,092	344	47	8	1,188	29	28
..	..	..	..	..	..	..	..	..	..	29
..	..	4	..	110	1	..	..	4	..	30
429	519	129	3	2,670	922	427	516	29	3	31
608	2,061	6,709	172	32,312	3,733	583	1,984	6,679	172	32
..	..	..	..	..	..	..	..	..	..	33
13	25	83	..	339	70	11	25	83	..	34
1,345	1,022	398	8	12,439	834	1,275	1,022	395	8	35

Table X.—Occupation or Means of Liveli

Class B.—Preparation and

Sub-Class III.—

Order 6.—Hides, skins and hard materials from the animal

Province, State or Agency.	*Group 52.*—Furriers and persons occupied with feathers, and bristles ; brush makers.						*Group 53.*—Bone, ivory,	
	Total earners principal occupation.		Total working dependants.		Total following occupation as subsidiary to other.		Total earners principal occupation.	
	Males.	Females.	Males.	Females.	Males.	Females.	Males.	Females.
1	413	414	415	416	417	418	419	420
INDIA	**1,011**	**179**	**61**	**60**	**54**	**7**	**7,992**	**1,331**
Provinces	**745**	**163**	**13**	**33**	**41**	**7**	**6,412**	**1,180**
1 Ajmer-Merwara	..	..	..	..	..	..	10	14
2 Andamans and Nicobars	..	..	..	..	..	..	4	..
3 Assam	..	..	..	..	..	..	29	..
4 Baluchistan (*Districts and Administered Territories*).	3	..	..	..	..	..	..	..
5 Bengal	15	2	..	..	..	..	3,407	156
6 Bihar and Orissa	28	..	..	..	38	..	425	150
7 Bombay (*including Aden*) ..	561	94	13	33	1	..	142	86
Aden	..	..	..	..	..	..	..	..
8 Burma	6	..	..	..	..	..	61	..
9 Central Provinces and Berar ..	20	63	..	..	..	4	88	12
10 Coorg	..	..	..	..	..	..	..	..
11 Delhi	21	1	..	..	..	..	31	..
12 Madras	10	1	..	..	2	..	1,404	106
13 North-West Frontier Province (*Districts and Administered Territories*).	..	..	..	..	..	..	7	..
14 Punjab	1	..	..	..	..	..	53	..
15 United Provinces of Agra and Oudh	80	2	..	..	..	3	751	656
States and Agencies ..	**266**	**16**	**48**	**27**	**13**	..	**1,580**	**151**
16 Assam States	..	..	..	..	..	..	..	..
17 Baluchistan States	..	..	..	..	..	..	..	..
18 Baroda State	2	..	..	..	..	..	116	2
19 Bengal States	..	..	..	..	..	..	1	..
20 Bihar and Orissa States	..	..	..	..	..	..	22	28
21 Bombay States	..	..	..	..	..	..	8	..
22 Central India Agency	55	7	..	..	3	..	8	2
23 Central Provinces States	..	..	..	..	..	..	..	..
24 Gwalior State	..	..	..	..	..	..	2	..
25 Hyderabad State	78	7	45	14	3	..	200	21
26 Jammu and Kashmir State ..	66	2	..	13	7	..	17	..
27 Madras States Agency	2	..	..	..	..	..	89	..
Cochin State	..	..	..	..	..	..	7	..
Travancore State	2	..	..	..	..	..	*82*	..
Other Madras States	..	..	..	..	..	..	..	..
28 Mysore State	6	..	..	..	..	..	13	3
29 North-West Frontier Province (*Agencies and Tribal Areas*).	..	..	..	..	..	..	..	..
30 Punjab States	..	..	..	..	..	..	..	..
31 Punjab States Agency	..	..	..	..	..	..	13	..
32 Rajputana Agency	9	..	..	..	..	..	601	94
33 Sikkim State	..	..	..	..	..	..	..	..
34 United Provinces States	..	..	..	..	..	..	33	..
35 Western India States Agency ..	48	..	3	..	..	..	457	1

hood.—Part II.—Provincial Distribution—*contd.*

Supply of Material Substances—*contd.*

Industry—*contd.*

kingdom—*concld.*

horn, shell, etc., workers (except buttons).

Order 7.—Wood.

Total *Order 7.*—Wood.

Total working dependants.		Total following occupation as subsidiary to other.		Total earners principal occupation.		Total working dependants.		Total following occupation as subsidiary to other.		
Males.	Females.	Males.	Females.	Males.	Females.	Males.	Females.	Males.	Females.	
421	422	423	424	425	426	427	428	429	430	
325	**171**	**709**	**35**	**1,231,128**	**264,616**	**58,291**	**77,688**	**299,201**	**41,641**	
136	**67**	**608**	**35**	**941,512**	**187,110**	**35,543**	**48,684**	**237,622**	**26,310**	
..	4	4	..	2,599	181	53	49	589	61	**1**
..	..	..	..	448	1	14	..	17	..	**2**
1	..	4	3	22,196	1,609	1,714	1,843	21,098	479	**3**
..	..	..	..	589	146	111	372	302	82	**4**
16	3	276	9	116,771	17,215	1,997	3,139	20,665	1,149	**5**
26	7	103	15	71,962	36,999	1,205	2,889	31,893	5,089	**6**
	1	48	..	82,005	10,742	4,527	4,389	8,129	1,135	**7**
..	..	..	..	452	68	70	48	10	..	
2	..	1	..	69,839	11,845	6,385	13,992	30,997	4,448	**8**
1	4	30	5	54,300	17,748	1,624	4,622	11,421	3,119	**9**
..	..	..	..	679	149	5	2	211	120	**10**
..	..	..	..	3,780	96	50	45	68	..	**11**
80	8	45	..	197,236	62,132	7,337	11,636	33,454	7,695	**12**
..	..	1	..	11,531	1,296	552	61	1,321	7	**13**
..	3	6	..	153,667	5,204	7,714	3,055	12,486	191	**14**
2	37	90	3	153,910	21,747	2,253	2,590	65,571	2,735	**15**
189	**104**	**101**	..	**289,616**	**77,506**	**22,748**	**29,004**	**61,579**	**15,331**	
..	..	..	..	2,222	103	187	71	760	291	**16**
..	..	..	..	909	1,160	33	2,144	181	18	**17**
9	..	..	..	11,025	991	683	594	1,165	137	**18**
..	..	6	..	933	30	24	3	236	3	**19**
..	..	14	..	10,118	14,336	153	3,087	6,723	2,873	**20**
..	..	..	..	15,939	2,399	1,046	1,612	3,899	671	**21**
..	..	3	..	33,264	12,328	528	836	6,111	741	**22**
..	..	..	..	5,316	1,397	524	1,503	1,172	103	**23**
1	..	1	..	12,033	2,933	515	886	2,451	466	**24**
82	24	27	..	28,383	9,985	8,831	5,630	6,723	2,852	**25**
..	..	7	..	9,399	525	277	37	2,910	337	**26**
..	..	5	..	50,636	19,252	3,711	7,348	6,519	5,337	**27**
..	..	*3*	..	*14,251*	*7,814*	*154*	*788*	*1,503*	*1,820*	
..	..	*2*	..	*34,292*	*10,967*	*3,469*	*6,525*	*4,531*	*3,446*	
..	..	..	..	*2,093*	*471*	*88*	*35*	*485*	*71*	
1	..	5	..	17,123	4,705	392	1,478	6,007	425	**28**
..	..	..	..	148	..	..	..	50	..	**29**
..	..	..	..	1,605	63	88	73	744	33	**30**
2	3	..	..	22,443	626	1,732	421	4,490	28	**31**
25	77	30	..	49,452	5,696	1,223	2,077	10,068	926	**32**
..	..	..	..	86	1	..	..	56	1	**33**
2	..	..	..	1,926	293	63	151	888	9	**34**
67	..	3	..	16,656	683	2,7[illegible]8	1,053	426	80	**35**

Table X.—Occupation or Means of Liveli

Class B.—Preparation and

Sub-Class III.—

Order 7.—

Province, State or Agency.	*Group 54.*—Sawyers.						*Group 55.*—Carpenters,	
	Total earners principal occupation.		Total working dependants.		Total following occupation as subsidiary to other.		Total earners principal occupation.	
	Males.	Females.	Males.	Females.	Males.	Females.	Males.	Females.
1	431	432	433	434	435	436	437	438
INDIA	**83,138**	**1,957**	**2,942**	**546**	**23,914**	**181**	**847,241**	**16,503**
Provinces	**58,523**	**1,677**	**1,551**	**270**	**19,566**	**102**	**656,216**	**11,095**
1 Ajmer-Merwara	35	1	..	..	12	..	2,227	12
2 Andamans and Nicobars	19	..	..	..	11	..	422	..
3 Assam	6,172	360	195	24	4,455	7	10,469	61
4 Baluchistan (*Districts and Administered Territories*).	47	..	..	..	..	..	207	..
5 Bengal	6,099	27	67	..	1,280	2	76,276	503
6 Bihar and Orissa	332	42	4	1	406	1	39,372	2,531
7 Bombay (*including Aden*) ..	3,974	564	193	129	779	26	66,986	1,797
Aden	*2*		..	..	..	..	*435*	..
8 Burma	20,017	377	831	100	7,423	36	34,516	250
9 Central Provinces and Berar ..	2,792	220	13	7	854	17	33,614	263
10 Coorg	69	..	..	..	19	..	387	..
11 Delhi	254	..	..	..	..	..	2,999	10
12 Madras	13,684	59	167	2	3,002	11	128,387	1,485
13 North-West Frontier Province (*Districts and Administered Territories*).	187	..	2	..	369	..	10,850	542
14 Punjab	1,998	17	66	6	105	1	132,797	1,732
15 United Provinces of Agra and Oudh	2,844	10	13	1	851	1	116,707	1,809
States and Agencies ..	**24,615**	**280**	**1,391**	**276**	**4,348**	**79**	**191,025**	**5,408**
16 Assam States	113	..	..	..	56	..	1,863	4
17 Baluchistan States	..	..	..	..	..	..	752	..
18 Baroda State	1,020	18	7	..	93	..	8,395	6
19 Bengal States	92	..	..	..	8	..	679	1
20 Bihar and Orissa States	380	2	..	..	495	1	2,228	73
21 Bombay States	306	3	84	7	1,235	..	11,314	161
22 Central India Agency	228	5	2	..	147	..	17,801	291
23 Central Provinces States	394	12	16	40	50	..	865	3
24 Gwalior State	3	..	..	..	..	..	8,604	352
25 Hyderabad State	908	39	337	123	113	3	18,964	3,223
26 Jammu and Kashmir State ..	1,691	24	27	2	374	4	5,678	31
27 Madras States Agency	13,040	6	446	..	1,201	..	28,195	151
Cochin State	*3,263*	*6*	*14*	..	*291*	..	*7,645*	*38*
Travancore State	*9,690*	..	*432*	..	*887*	..	*18,893*	*104*
Other Madras States	*87*	..	..	..	*23*	..	*1,657*	*9*
28 Mysore State	1,481	3	8	..	271	..	11,225	57
29 North-West Frontier Province (*Agencies and Tribal Areas*). ..	..	..	..	..	..	..	148	..
30 Punjab States	146	16	17	57	97	..	1,121	2
31 Punjab States Agency	2,809	..	307	..	80	..	15,653	240
32 Rajputana Agency	1,122	121	32	4	66	1	42,104	557
33 Sikkim State	10	..	..	..	23	..	76	..
34 United Provinces States	..	1	..	..	..	..	1,311	16
35 Western India States Agency ..	872	30	108	43	39	70	14,049	240

hood.—Part II.—Provincial Distribution—*contd.*

Supply of Material Substances—*contd.*

Industry—*contd.*

Wood—*concld.*

turners and joiners, etc.				*Group 56.*—Basket makers and other industries of woody materials, including leaves, and thatchers and builders working with bamboo, reeds or similar materials.						
Total working dependants.		Total following occupation as subsidiary to other.		Total earners principal occupation.		Total working dependants.		Total following occupation as subsidiary to other.		
Males.	Females.	Males.	Females.	Males.	Females.	Males.	Females.	Males.	Females.	
439	440	441	442	443	444	445	446	447	448	
34,345	**6,876**	**173,898**	**2,892**	**300,749**	**246,156**	**21,004**	**70,266**	**101,389**	**38,568**	
20,208	**2,799**	**138,050**	**1,083**	**226,773**	**174,338**	**13,784**	**45,615**	**80,006**	**25,125**	
42	1	341	2	337	168	13	48	236	59	**1**
..	..	6	..	7	1	14	..	..	..	**2**
562	38	6,619	10	5,555	1,188	957	1,781	10,024	462	**3**
3	..	96	..	335	146	108	372	206	82	**4**
953	33	10,586	73	34,396	16,685	977	3,106	8,199	1,074	**5**
539	81	19,610	356	32,258	34,426	662	2,807	11,877	4,732	**6**
3,530	578	5,986	173	11,045	8,381	804	3,682	1,364	936	**7**
69	..	*10*	..	*15*	*68*	*1*	*48*	..	..	
1,269	216	5,984	25	15,306	11,218	4,285	13,676	17,590	4,387	**8**
700	207	5,362	65	17,894	17,165	911	4,408	5,205	3,037	**9**
5	..	60	..	223	149	..	2	132	120	**10**
44	2	29	..	527	86	6	43	39	..	**11**
3,722	475	18,441	151	55,165	60,583	3,448	11,159	12,011	7,533	**12**
529	20	888	2	494	754	21	41	64	5	**13**
6,802	655	10,117	38	18,872	3,455	846	2,394	2,264	152	**14**
1,508	493	53,925	188	34,359	19,928	732	2,096	10,795	2,546	**15**
14,137	**4,077**	**35,848**	**1,809**	**73,976**	**71,818**	**7,220**	**24,651**	**21,383**	**13,443**	
95	2	320	2	246	99	92	69	384	289	**16**
7	..	132	..	157	1,160	26	2,144	49	18	**17**
526	55	780	..	1,610	967	150	539	292	137	**18**
23	..	129	..	162	29	1	3	99	3	**19**
19	..	3,016	23	7,510	14,261	134	3,087	5,212	2,849	**20**
559	144	1,738	41	4,319	2,235	403	1,461	926	630	**21**
283	28	3,381	24	15,235	12,032	243	808	2,583	717	**22**
27	20	158	1	4,057	1,382	481	1,443	964	102	**23**
334	81	1,738	157	3,426	2,581	181	805	713	309	**24**
5,743	2,758	4,603	1,422	8,511	6,723	2,751	2,749	2,007	1,427	**25**
207	2	1,830	5	2,030	470	43	33	706	328	**26**
1,739	37	1,397	12	9,401	19,095	1,526	7,311	3,921	5,325	**27**
89	*9*	*225*	*1*	*3,343*	*7,770*	*51*	*779*	*987*	*1,819*	
1,582	*28*	*874*	*7*	*5,709*	*10,863*	*1,455*	*6,497*	*2,770*	*3,439*	
68	..	*298*	*4*	*349*	*462*	*20*	*35*	*164*	*67*	
170	64	3,697	20	4,417	4,645	214	1,414	2,039	405	**28**
..	..	50	..	..	..	..	..	..	..	**29**
48	1	426	..	338	45	23	15	221	33	**30**
1,147	228	4,010	11	3,981	386	278	193	400	17	**31**
897	488	7,413	82	6,226	5,018	294	1,585	2,589	843	**32**
..	..	33	1	..	1	..	..	..	..	**33**
34	2	678	4	615	276	29	149	210	5	**34**
2,279	167	319	4	1,735	413	351	843	68	6	**35**

Table X.—Occupation or Means of Liveli

Class B.—Preparation and

Sub-Class III.—

	Province, State or Agency.	Total Order 8.—Metals.						Group 57.—Smelting, forging	
		Total earners principal occupation.		Total working dependants.		Total following occupation as subsidiary to other.		Total earners principal occupation.	
		Males.	Females.	Males.	Females.	Males.	Females.	Males.	Females.
	1	449	450	451	452	453	454	455	456
	INDIA	**628,169**	**37,787**	**31,466**	**15,648**	**126,696**	**5,654**	**28,465**	**3,588**
	Provinces	**481,497**	**22,276**	**15,695**	**6,952**	**100,623**	**2,969**	**26,106**	**3,501**
1	Ajmer-Merwara	1,437	144	29	32	92	2	2	..
2	Andamans and Nicobars	38	..	..	..	..	..	..	..
3	Assam	5,057	33	198	61	2,364	5	6	..
4	Baluchistan (*Districts and Administered Territories*).	1,601	..	12	3	145	..	..	..
5	Bengal	48,843	1,159	445	50	5,053	232	1,728	8
6	Bihar and Orissa	65,638	8,683	1,147	1,285	20,521	1,658	20,054	2,944
7	Bombay (*including Aden*) ..	34,553	1,838	1,755	509	2,125	170	1,002	110
	Aden	*189*	*2*	*2*	..	*4*	..	..	..
8	Burma	20,186	419	745	232	2,237	32	835	..
9	Central Provinces and Berar ..	36,763	2,538	1,747	1,905	5,180	312	596	109
10	Coorg	209	3	1	..	102	..	..	..
11	Delhi	3,933	57	29	7	16	..	49	..
12	Madras	76,451	2,833	2,592	961	9,693	131	1,583	328
13	North-West Frontier Province (*Districts and Administered Territories*).	9,708	50	251	17	371	..	..	..
14	Punjab	75,517	1,028	4,102	622	4,665	35	47	..
15	United Provinces of Agra and Oudh	101,563	3,491	2,642	1,268	48,059	392	204	2
	States and Agencies ..	**146,672**	**15,511**	**15,771**	**8,696**	**26,073**	**2,685**	**2,359**	**87**
16	Assam States	273	45	29	6	49	3	..	..
17	Baluchistan States	888	..	9	2	33	..	..	..
18	Baroda State	4,728	83	356	309	438	2	51	..
19	Bengal States	216	2	1	..	63	..	..	..
20	Bihar and Orissa States	11,476	3,753	304	728	3,196	239	28	15
21	Bombay States	4,675	265	267	232	649	37	27	4
22	Central India Agency	15,113	1,464	272	172	2,975	52	82	3
23	Central Provinces States	6,704	457	1,105	2,430	1,110	14	191	52
24	Gwalior State	5,252	736	221	329	1,562	87	..	..
25	Hyderabad State	22,346	6,485	7,827	3,190	5,474	2,019	139	2
26	Jammu and Kashmir State ..	4,013	33	192	3	1,319	10	910	2
27	Madras States Agency	16,779	481	1,384	192	844	40	80	..
	Cochin State	*3,873*	*348*	*47*	*31*	*85*	*12*	*29*	..
	Travancore State	*11,871*	*129*	*1,332*	*161*	*571*	*28*	..	..
	Other Madras States	*1,035*	*4*	*5*	..	*188*	..	*1*	..
28	Mysore State	8,556	125	152	65	2,626	7	255	4
29	North-West Frontier Province (*Agencies and Tribal Areas*). ..	152	..	..	..	31	..	..	..
30	Punjab States	891	6	78	21	442	..	..	..
31	Punjab States Agency	10,719	50	724	89	1,977	6	310	2
32	Rajputana Agency	21,006	1,279	428	693	2,169	155	175	1
33	Sikkim State	41	6	1	..	80	2	..	..
34	United Provinces States	1,997	57	119	70	726	5	..	..
35	Western India States Agency ..	10,847	184	2,302	165	310	7	161	2

hood.—Part II.—Provincial Distribution—*contd.*

Supply of Material Substances—*contd.*

Industry—*contd.*

Order 8.—Metals.

and rolling of iron and other metals.				*Group 58.*—Makers of arms, guns, etc.						
Total working dependants.		Total following occupation as subsidiary to other.		Total earners principal occupation.		Total working dependants.		Total following occupation as subsidiary to other.		
Males.	Females.	Males.	Females.	Males.	Females.	Males.	Females.	Males.	Females.	
457	458	459	460	461	462	463	464	665	466	
250	**194**	**750**	**239**	**5,016**	**231**	**192**	**50**	**766**	**23**	
84	**80**	**251**	**230**	**3,768**	**144**	**122**	**29**	**646**	**19**	
..	..	..	..	9	..	1	..	1	..	1
..	..	..	..	..	..	..	..	..	..	2
..	..	8	..	22	..	2	..	8	..	3
..	..	..	..	483	..	..	..	..	..	4
..	..	68	..	253	18	..	..	15	..	5
7	1	104	222	403	37	..	..	296	13	6
15	53	11	6	164	18	7	..	4	1	7
..	..	..	..	..	..	..	..	..	..	
3	..	1	..	27	..	..	..	..	..	8
32	9	23	2	1,833	65	109	1	9	5	9
..	..	..	..	..	..	..	..	2	..	10
..	..	..	..	2	..	..	..	..	..	11
27	17	36	..	27	..	..	..	7	..	12
..	..	..	..	..	..	..	..	..	..	13
..	..	..	..	75	6	2	..	12	..	14
..	..	..	..	470	..	1	28	292	..	15
166	**114**	**499**	**9**	**1,248**	**87**	**70**	**21**	**120**	**4**	
..	..	..	..	..	..	..	..	..	..	16
..	..	..	..	4	..	..	..	..	..	17
..	..	15	..	21	..	5	1	..	..	18
..	..	..	..	..	..	..	..	..	..	19
..	..	20	6	..	..	..	..	..	..	20
..	13	1	..	10	1	..	7	..	..	21
..	5	15	1	185	18	2	..	25	..	22
47	58	54	..	1	..	..	..	..	..	23
..	..	..	..	41	..	3	..	27	..	24
53	3	21	..	55	..	31	..	8	..	25
21	..	285	1	30	..	3	..	2	..	26
..	..	11	..	..	..	..	..	..	..	27
..	..	*11*	..	..	..	..	..	..	..	
..	..	..	..	..	..	..	..	..	..	
..	..	..	..	..	..	..	..	..	..	
3	14	24	1	24	..	..	..	10	..	28
..	..	..	..	..	..	..	..	..	..	29
..	..	..	..	..	..	..	..	4	..	30
11	15	9	..	3	..	..	..	1	..	31
9	6	27	..	738	64	3	13	42	3	32
..	..	..	..	..	..	..	..	..	..	33
..	..	..	..	1	..	..	..	..	..	34
22	..	17	..	135	4	23	..	1	1	35

Table X.—Occupation or Means of Liveli

Province, State or Agency.		*Class B.*—Preparation and / *Sub-Class III.*— / *Order 8.*— / *Group 59.*—Blacksmiths, other workers in iron, makers of implements.						*Group 60.*—Workers in brass,	
		Total earners principal occupation.		Total working dependants.		Total following occupation as subsidiary to other.		Total earners principal occupation.	
		Males.	Females.	Males.	Females.	Males.	Females.	Males.	Females.
	1	467	468	469	470	471	472	473	474
	INDIA	**474,194**	**25,504**	**24,887**	**13,156**	**115,012**	**4,496**	**83,946**	**7,014**
	Provinces	**363,865**	**14,508**	**13,502**	**6,231**	**93,236**	**2,546**	**57,883**	**3,015**
1	Ajmer-Merwara	1,241	118	24	30	74	1	105	25
2	Andamans and Nicobars	32	..	..	..	..	..	6	..
3	Assam	3,164	15	144	11	1,831	..	1,655	18
4	Baluchistan (*Districts and Administered Territories*).	990	..	12	3	142	..	59	..
5	Bengal	37,216	921	374	42	3,842	218	6,319	173
6	Bihar and Orissa	34,396	4,384	926	1,183	18,348	1,363	10,366	1,199
7	Bombay (*including Aden*)	20,929	1,192	1,211	376	1,642	137	6,644	211
	Aden	*118*	*2*	*2*	..	*4*	..	*32*	..
8	Burma	9,880	227	571	211	2,081	27	727	75
9	Central Provinces and Berar	29,446	1,930	1,352	1,708	4,726	274	3,467	280
10	Coorg	144	2	..	..	86	..	45	1
11	Delhi	2,403	28	25	4	11	..	728	5
12	Madras	57,853	1,721	2,172	835	8,682	116	11,661	556
13	North-West Frontier Province (*Districts and Administered Territories*).	9,170	48	250	17	354	..	161	..
14	Punjab	70,245	980	3,950	620	4,501	29	3,486	35
15	United Provinces of Agra and Oudh	86,756	2,942	2,491	1,191	46,916	381	12,454	437
	States and Agencies	**110,329**	**10,996**	**11,385**	**6,925**	**21,776**	**1,950**	**26,063**	**3,999**
16	Assam States	262	38	27	6	46	3	8	7
17	Baluchistan States	836	..	8	2	27	..	..	..
18	Baroda State	3,807	75	276	300	409	2	695	3
19	Bengal States	176	1	1	..	52	..	19	..
20	Bihar and Orissa States	8,658	3,272	259	681	2,690	222	2,787	464
21	Bombay States	3,828	156	246	194	614	32	708	83
22	Central India Agency	11,998	1,042	233	141	2,761	40	2,035	315
23	Central Provinces States	5,558	195	981	2,100	877	11	864	168
24	Gwalior State	4,094	603	168	306	963	20	778	129
25	Hyderabad State	13,817	3,879	4,801	2,192	3,808	1,425	7,439	2,514
26	Jammu and Kashmir State	2,356	12	155	1	1,000	8	706	5
27	Madras States Agency	11,618	315	1,237	180	720	16	3,988	147
	Cochin States	*2,532*	*227*	*35*	*30*	*49*	*7*	*957*	*118*
	Travancore State	*8,392*	*86*	*1,198*	*150*	*497*	*9*	*2,775*	*28*
	Other Madras States	*604*	*2*	*4*	..	*174*	..	*256*	*1*
28	Mysore State	6,244	81	[illegible]	42	2,351	5	923	21
29	North-West Frontier Province (*Agencies and Tribal Areas*).	152	..	..	..	31	..	..	..
30	Punjab States	856	6	78	21	433	..	18	..
31	Punjab States Agency	8,643	45	686	69	1,922	5	1,215	3
32	Rajputana Agency	17,665	1,095	273	468	2,018	152	2,042	88
33	Sikkim State	32	1	1	..	80	1	9	5
34	United Provinces States	1,957	42	119	68	714	5	39	15
35	Western India States Agency	7,772	138	1,705	154	260	3	1,790	32

hood.—Part II.—Provincial Distribution—*contd.*

Supply of Material Substances—*contd.*

Industry—*contd.*

Metals—*contd.*

copper and bell metal.				*Group 61.*—Workers in other metals (except precious metals).						
Total working dependants.		Total following occupation as subsidiary to other.		Total earners principal occupation.		Total working dependants.		Total following occupation as subsidiary to other.		
Males.	Females.	Males.	Females.	Males.	Females.	Males.	Females.	Males.	Females.	
475	476	477	478	479	480	481	482	483	484	
4,575	**1,924**	**8,005**	**782**	**34,058**	**1,262**	**1,432**	**260**	**2,078**	**110**	
1,433	**451**	**4,883**	**108**	**27,819**	**948**	**463**	**99**	**1,573**	**63**	
3	2	3	1	80	1	1	..	14	..	1
..	..	..	..	..	..	..	..	..	..	2
46	50	485	5	210	..	6	..	32	..	3
..	..	2	..	69	..	..	..	1	..	4
50	6	697	12	3,239	39	21	2	430	2	5
205	65	1,672	50	417	119	9	36	101	10	6
332	10	254	7	3,970	155	100	8	182	16	7
..	..	..	..	*39*	..	..	..	..	..	
69	11	19	3	8,711	117	102	10	136	2	8
219	168	233	15	1,420	152	34	19	189	16	9
..	..	13	..	20	..	1	..	1	..	10
..	..	1	..	749	24	4	3	4	..	11
269	96	634	2	5,327	228	124	13	334	13	12
..	..	..	..	377	2	1	..	17	..	13
101	..	76	6	1,658	7	49	2	76	..	14
139	43	794	7	1,572	104	11	6	56	4	15
3,142	**1,473**	**3,122**	**674**	**6,239**	**314**	**969**	**161**	**505**	**47**	
2	..	3	..	3	..	..	..	..	..	16
..	..	..	..	48	..	1	..	6	..	17
65	6	12	..	152	5	10	2	2	..	18
..	..	10	..	21	1	..	..	1	..	19
45	47	486	11	3	..	..	..	..	..	20
20	8	31	5	102	21	1	10	2	..	21
26	24	105	8	812	86	11	2	69	3	22
72	240	145	3	90	42	5	32	34	..	23
47	23	572	67	339	4	3	..	..	..	24
2,496	892	1,423	556	765	90	410	102	195	38	25
13	1	30	..	9	..	..	..	2	..	26
113	10	52	22	1,080	19	34	2	61	2	27
9	*1*	*10*	*4*	*354*	*3*	*3*	..	*15*	*1*	
103	*9*	*36*	*18*	*242*	*15*	*31*	*2*	*38*	*1*	
1	..	*6*	..	*84*	*1*	..	..	*8*	..	
13	..	118	..	1,022	19	5	9	94	1	28
..	..	..	..	..	..	..	..	..	..	29
..	..	5	..	17	..	..	..	..	..	30
21	5	26	1	548	..	6	..	19	..	31
140	206	67	..	299	19	3	..	14	..	32
..	..	..	1	..	..	..	..	..	..	33
..	..	12	..	..	..	..	2	..	..	34
[illegible]	[illegible]	25	..	929	8	480	..	6	3	35

Table X.—Occupation or Means of Liveli

Class B.—Preparation and

Sub-Class III.—

Province, State or Agency.	*Order 8.*—Metals—*concld.* *Group 62.*—Workers in mints, die-sinkers, etc. Total earners principal occupation.		Total working dependants.		Total following occupation as subsidiary to other.		*Total Order 9.*— Total earners principal occupation.	
	Males.	Females.	Males.	Females.	Males.	Females.	Males.	Females.
1	485	486	487	488	489	490	491	492
INDIA	**2,490**	**188**	**130**	**64**	**85**	**4**	**692,698**	**225,038**
Provinces	**2,056**	**160**	**91**	**62**	**34**	**3**	**521,311**	**165,696**
1 Ajmer-Merwara	..	..	..	..	..	..	1,601	586
2 Andamans and Nicobars	..	..	..	..	..	..	3	..
3 Assam	..	..	..	..	..	..	3,627	1,278
4 Baluchistan (*Districts and Administered Territories*).	..	..	..	..	..	..	400	32
5 Bengal	88	..	..	..	1	..	63,395	13,417
6 Bihar and Orissa	2	..	..	..	..	..	59,477	36,924
7 Bombay (*including Aden*)	1,844	152	90	62	32	3	39,294	9,768
Aden	..	..	..	..	..	..	*10*	*2*
8 Burma	6	..	..	..	..	..	4,613	5,040
9 Central Provinces and Berar ..	1	2	1	..	..	..	23,366	10,796
10 Coorg	..	..	..	..	..	..	131	119
11 Delhi	2	..	..	..	..	..	3,580	656
12 Madras	..	..	..	..	..	..	74,902	25,641
13 North-West Frontier Province (*Districts and Administered Territories*). ..	..	..	..	..	..	.	9,691	121
14 Punjab	6	..	..	..	..	..	106,698	4,457
15 United Provinces of Agra and Oudh	107	6	..	..	1	..	130,533	56,861
States and Agencies ..	**434**	**28**	**39**	**2**	**51**	**1**	**171,387**	**59,342**
16 Assam States	..	..	..	..	..	..	240	160
17 Baluchistan States	..	..	..	..	..	..	154	..
18 Baroda State	2	..	..	..	..	..	7,022	1,474
19 Bengal States	..	..	..	..	..	..	294	87
20 Bihar and Orissa States	..	2	..	..	..	..	8,214	6,546
21 Bombay States	..	..	..	..	1	..	8,783	1,813
22 Central India Agency	1	..	..	..	..	..	19,429	9,130
23 Central Provinces States	..	..	..	..	..	..	2,654	949
24 Gwalior State	..	..	..	..	..	..	9,788	2,961
25 Hyderabad State	131	..	36	1	19	..	20,233	10,845
26 Jammu and Kashmir State ..	2	14	..	1	..	1	3,705	473
27 Madras States Agency	63	..	..	..	..	..	8,897	4,972
Cochin State	*1*	..	..	..	..	..	*1,865*	*1,230*
Travancore State	*62*	..	..	..	..	..	*5,945*	*2,416*
Other Madras States	..	..	..	..	..	..	*1,087*	*1,326*
28 Mysore State	88	..	..	..	29	..	7,395	4,355
29 North-West Frontier Province (*Agencies and Tribal Areas*). ..	..	..	..	..	..	..	3	..
30 Punjab States	..	..	..	..	..	..	523	24
31 Punjab States Agency	..	..	..	..	..	..	12,245	299
32 Rajputana Agency	87	12	..	..	1	..	46,482	12,842
33 Sikkim State	..	..	..	..	..	..	9	..
34 United Provinces States	..	..	..	..	..	..	2,207	865
35 Western India States Agency ..	60	..	3	..	1	..	13,110	1,547

hood—Part II.—Provincial Distribution—*contd.*

Supply of Material Substances—*contd.*

Industry—*contd.*

Ceramics.				*Order 9.—Ceramics.* *Group 63.*—Potters and makers of earthenware.						
Total working dependants.		Total following occupation as subsidiary to other.		Total earners principal occupation.		Total working dependants.		Total following occupation as subsidiary to other.		
Males.	Females.	Males.	Females.	Males.	Females.	Males.	Females.	Males.	Females.	
493	494	495	496	497	498	499	500	501	502	
34,861	**72,233**	**150,291**	**21,316**	**569,061**	**200,233**	**31,567**	**68,362**	**132,690**	**19,465**	
20,203	**40,059**	**119,501**	**15,333**	**414,832**	**144,254**	**17,967**	**37,796**	**104,209**	**13,823**	
109	419	277	37	1,382	577	100	419	238	37	1
..	..	..	..	2	..	..	..	...	—	2
377	2,582	2,820	180	2,000	1,162	314	2,561	1,911	173	3
..	..	195	..	69	12	..	..	4	..	4
762	1,248	8,929	774	34,193	7,961	559	900	4,530	421	5
1,111	2,227	30,170	5,186	55,338	35,381	1,106	2,220	28,782	4,931	6
2,373	4,009	2,791	660	30,650	8,649	2,097	3,796	2,595	652	7
7	..	..	..	*7*	*2*	*7*	..	..	..	
553	3,256	974	1,115	2,499	4,710	437	3,160	587	1,061	8
1,372	5,575	3,802	1,009	17,175	8,030	1,207	5,038	2,871	729	9
2	9	68	2	130	119	2	9	68	2	10
90	203	106	..	1,675	334	62	193	22	..	11
3,883	6,891	13,763	1,176	68,025	24,771	3,805	6,842	12,698	1,123	12
158	78	182	1	4,191	73	152	76	135	1	13
6,393	2,574	6,113	115	85,466	2,793	5,473	2,370	4,328	83	14
3,020	10,988	49,311	5,078	112,037	49,682	2,653	10,212	45,440	4,610	15
14,658	**32,174**	**30,790**	**5,983**	**154,229**	**55,979**	**13,600**	**30,566**	**28,481**	**5,642**	
4	294	16	12	76	160	..	294	6	12	16
..	12	22	..	151	..	..	10	18	..	17
896	4,495	1,348	71	4,907	1,069	693	3,747	885	46	18
8	13	40	..	165	68	5	13	10	..	19
213	852	5,369	263	7,916	6,409	210	831	5,307	259	20
887	1,627	1,423	280	7,318	1,720	847	1,513	1,242	272	21
336	538	3,183	441	17,666	8,374	304	464	2,901	340	22
637	2,176	1,167	78	2,312	825	622	2,140	1,067	75	23
530	1,090	1,325	254	9,136	2,722	500	1,049	1,249	207	24
5,379	7,476	3,837	2,800	18,190	10,353	4,897	7,146	3,247	2,707	25
67	133	1,289	622	3,485	470	65	131	1,275	620	26
641	501	689	294	5,160	4,400	616	495	457	246	27
16	*21*	*69*	*33*	*1,157*	*986*	*13*	*16*	*35*	*4*	
593	*348*	*91*	*177*	*3,052*	*2,196*	*571*	*348*	*42*	*177*	
32	*132*	*529*	*84*	*951*	*1,218*	*32*	*131*	*380*	*65*	
436	2,742	4,027	351	7,120	4,254	436	2,742	3,986	348	28
..	..	85	..	3	..	..	..	85	—	29
16	33	101	...	484	24	16	33	99	—	30
663	450	1,200	14	10,895	238	590	328	1,090	12	31
1,243	5,226	5,137	445	45,301	12,599	1,228	5,187	5,068	442	32
..	...	...	..	9	..	..	..	..	..	33
91	272	330	23	1,850	823	91	266	313	23	34
9,611	4,244	202	35	12,085	1,471	2,480	4,177	176	33	35

Table X.—Occupation or Means of Liveli

Class B.—Preparation and

Sub-Class III.—

Order 9.—Ceramics—*concld.*

	Province, State or Agency.	*Group 64.*—Brick and tile makers. Total earners principal occupation. Males.	Total earners principal occupation. Females.	Total working dependants. Males.	Total working dependants. Females.	Total following occupation as subsidiary to other. Males.	Total following occupation as subsidiary to other. Females.	*Group 65.*—Other workers. Total earners principal occupation. Males.	Total earners principal occupation. Females.
	1	503	504	505	506	507	508	509	510
	INDIA	**97.019**	**16.988**	**2,651**	**2,866**	**12,757**	**1,408**	**26,618**	**7,817**
	Provinces	**81,788**	**14,089**	**1,801**	**1,432**	**10,641**	**1,122**	**24,691**	**7,353**
1	Ajmer-Merwara	2	8	..	..	..	..	217	1
2	Andamans and Nicobars	..	..	..	..	..	..	1	..
3	Assam	1,397	84	29	13	704	4	230	32
4	Baluchistan (*Districts and Administered Territories*).	307	20	..	..	191	..	24	..
5	Bengal	17,862	3,538	52	29	1,907	226	11,340	1,918
6	Bihar and Orissa	3,724	1,325	5	5	1,257	235	415	218
7	Bombay (*including Aden*)	7,627	866	238	157	168	7	1,017	253
	Aden	*3*	..	..	..	..	..	..	..
8	Burma	1,768	301	88	84	371	54	346	29
9	Central Provinces and Berar ..	5,278	2,390	159	517	923	279	913	376
10	Coorg	1	..	..	..	..	..	..	..
11	Delhi	1,824	315	28	10	84	..	81	7
12	Madras	6,505	856	70	37	1,036	53	372	14
13	North-West Frontier Province .. (*Districts and Administered Territories*).	5,497	48	6	2	47	..	3	..
14	Punjab	19,973	1,556	896	138	1,660	31	1,259	108
15	United Provinces of Agra and Oudh	10,023	2,782	230	440	2,293	233	8,473	4,397
	States and Agencies ..	**15,231**	**2,899**	**850**	**1,434**	**2,116**	**286**	**1,927**	**464**
16	Assam States	127	..	..	..	3	..	37	..
17	Baluchistan States	3	..	..	2	4	..	..	..
18	Baroda State	1,966	362	183	707	434	25	149	43
19	Bengal States	13	19	..	..	..	..	116	..
20	Bihar and Orissa States	298	135	3	21	59	4	..	2
21	Bombay States	1,426	91	39	113	181	8	39	2
22	Central India Agency	1,385	646	22	73	246	96	378	110
23	Central Provinces States	304	116	15	14	100	3	38	8
24	Gwalior State	294	113	11	22	75	2	358	126
25	Hyderabad State	1,656	472	362	291	513	90	387	20
26	Jammu and Kashmir State ..	201	..	2	..	13	2	19	3
27	Madras States Agenep	3,671	606	24	3	230	48	66	66
	Cochin State	*646*	*186*	*2*	*2*	*32*	*29*	*62*	*58*
	Travancore State	*2,893*	*220*	*22*	..	*49*	..	..	..
	Other Madras States	*132*	*100*	..	*1*	*149*	*19*	*4*	*8*
28	Mysore State	269	101	..	..	38	3	6	..
29	North-West Frontier Province (*Agencies and Tribal Areas*).	..	..	..	..	..	..	..	..
30	Pun)ab States	38	..	..	..	2	..	1	..
31	Punjab States Agency	1,127	49	59	93	108	2	223	12
32	Rajputana Agency	1,135	224	13	35	69	3	46	19
33	Sikkim State	..	..	..	..	..	..	..	..
34	United Provinces States	335	..	..	..	17	..	22	42
35	Western India States Agency ..	983	65	117	60	24	..	42	1

hood—Part II.—Provincial Distribution—*contd.*

Supply of Material Substances—*contd.*

Industry—*contd.*

in ceramics.				*Order 10.*—Chemical products properly so-called and analogous. Total *Order 10.*—Chemical products properly so-called and analogous.						
Total working dependants.		Total following occupation as subsidiary to other.		Total earners principal occupation.		Total working dependants.		Total following occupation as subsidiary to other.		
Males.	Females.	Males.	Females.	Males.	Females.	Males.	Females.	Males.	Females.	
511	512	513	514	515	516	517	518	519	520	
643	**1,005**	**4,844**	**443**	**384,467**	**167,123**	**16,318**	**35,396**	**114,398**	**17,505**	
435	831	4,651	388	311,805	141,629	10,031	24,421	94,962	14,125	
9	..	39	..	711	182	27	73	143	9	1
..	..	..	..	107	..	—	..	3	—	2
34	8	205	3	943	39	33	26	751	11	3
..	..	—	—	242	..	1	..	22	—	4
151	319	2,492	127	35,422	2,335	358	89	3,938	175	5
..	2	131	20	41,840	30,975	507	1,009	22,747	5,546	6
38	56	28	1	15,500	4,846	979	1,406	2,244	368	7
..	..	..	..	*73*	*2*	*1*	..	*1*	..	
28	12	16	..	15,204	2,422	350	544	2,353	198	8
6	20	8	1	8,256	4,122	461	1,958	2,963	624	9
..	..	..	..	18	..	2	..	6	2	10
..	..	..	..	796	29	4	13	4	..	11
8	12	29	..	29,718	8,028	1,379	2,791	4,828	417	12
..	..	..	..	2,685	31	103	11	256	..	13
24	66	125	1	37,847	1,452	2,383	1,022	3,700	53	14
137	336	1,578	35	122,516	87,168	3,444	15,479	51,004	6,722	15
208	**174**	**193**	**55**	**72,662**	**25,494**	**6,287**	**10,975**	**19,436**	**3,380**	
4	..	7	..	24	6	..	1	..	2	16
..	..	..	..	50	..	..	..	59	..	17
20	41	29	..	2,453	560	343	925	226	55	18
3	..	30	..	65	..	1	..	55	..	19
..	..	3	..	2,794	4,051	48	664	3,485	349	20
1	1	..	..	1,871	623	195	396	175	28	21
10	1	36	5	8,693	4,418	145	307	3,705	459	22
..	22	..	..	846	1,087	440	1,235	798	74	23
19	19	1	45	7,080	1,413	272	439	1,434	220	24
120	39	77	3	8,076	3,905	2,690	4,135	1,440	1,741	25
..	2	1	..	2,414	113	87	40	1,013	87	26
1	3	2	..	11,841	2,689	689	296	1,133	68	27
1	*3*	*2*	—	*3,264*	*408*	*64*	*53*	*384*	*31*	
..	..	..	—	*8,470*	*2,276*	*621*	*243*	*724*	*36*	
..	..	..	—	*107*	*5*	*4*	—	*25*	*1*	
..	..	3	..	2,031	680	138	619	2,000	76	28
..	..	..	..	..	..	..	—	—	..	29
..	..	..	..	287	24	11	14	64	..	30
14	29	2	..	4,167	225	180	194	831	9	31
2	4	..	..	14,033	2,586	281	840	2,416	125	32
..	..	..	..	..	..	—	..	..	..	33
—	6	..	..	2,014	2,541	10	469	367	81	34
14	7	2	2	3,923	56	66	40	235	6	35

Table X.—Occupation or Means of Liveli…

Province, State or Agency.	Class B.—Preparation and … Sub-Class III.— Order 10.—Chemical products properly so-called. Group 66.—Manufacture of matches, fire-works and other explosives. Total earners principal occupation.		Total working dependants.		Total following occupation as subsidiary to other.		Group 67.—Manufacture … Total earners principal occupation.	
	Males.	Females.	Males.	Females.	Males.	Females.	Males.	Females.
1	521	522	523	524	525	526	527	528
INDIA ..	**12,808**	**3,509**	**377**	**657**	**1,006**	**79**	**7,646**	**520**
Provinces	**9,499**	**2,795**	**139**	**342**	**473**	**35**	**6,125**	**407**
1 Ajmer-Merwara	5	..	..	3	1	..	36	2
2 Andamans and Nicobars	103	..	..	..	..	..	2	..
3 Assam	236	..	6	..	21	..	19	..
4 Baluchistan (*Districts and Administered Territories*).	..	..	..	..	..	..	28	..
5 Bengal	1,022	54	3	..	84	5	493	10
6 Bihar and Orissa	195	21	..	..	41	..	33	..
7 Bombay (*including Aden*)	2,861	1,391	53	255	35	2	1,158	39
Aden	..	..	..	..	..	..	*3*	..
8 Burma	1,619	1,123	21	59	6	17	786	4
9 Central Provinces and Berar ..	287	43	4	8	44	..	65	..
10 Coorg	..	..	..	..	..	..	8	..
11 Delhi	14	..		..	..	..	113	2
12 Madras	676	124	7	9	65	2	1,479	29
13 North-West Frontier Province (*Districts and Administered Territories*). ..	107	4	..	..	..	..	234	..
14 Punjab	905	3	33	2	71	..	769	6
15 United Provinces of Agra and Oudh	1,469	32	12	6	105	9	902	315
States and Agencies ..	**3,309**	**714**	**238**	**315**	**533**	**44**	**1,521**	**113**
16 Assam States	..	..	..	..	..	..	2	..
17 Baluchistan States	..	..	..	..	..	..	..	..
18 Baroda State	471	236	17	46	1	10	101	..
19 Bengal States	53	..	..	..	1	..	..	..
20 Bihar and Orissa States	5	2	..	..	7	..	3	29
21 Bombay States	295	109	24	124	11	..	70	..
22 Central India Agency	450	113	1	7	80	6	53	2
23 Central Provinces States	5	..	3	..	..	..	5	..
24 Gwalior State	400	56	7	51	137	11	147	4
25 Hyderabad State	218	37	104	54	29	9	147	11
26 Jammu and Kashmir State ..	81	2	1	..	15	2	7	..
27 Madras States Agency	573	118	47	1	73	6	336	..
Cochin State	*324*	*101*	*3*	*1*	*21*	*5*	*101*	..
Travancore State	*227*	*17*	*42*	..	*50*	*1*	*235*	..
Other Madras States	*22*	..	*2*	..	*2*	..	..	..
28 Mysore State	91	6	5	..	86	..	145	2
29 North-West Frontier Province (*Agencies and Tribal Areas*). ..	..	..	..	..	..	..	..	..
30 Punjab States	21	..	1	..	6	..	10	..
31 Punjab States Agency	122	1	10	13	15	..	144	..
32 Rajputana Agency	428	34	12	19	72	..	111	2
33 Sikkim State	..	..	..	..	..	..	..	
34 United Provinces States	2	..	..	..	..	..	52	16
35 Western India States Agency ..	94	..	6	..	..	..	188	7

hood—Part II.—Provincial Distribution.—*contd.*

Supply of Material Substances—*contd.*

Industry—*contd.*

and analogous—*contd.*

of aerated and mineral waters and ice. | *Group 68.*—Manufacture and refining of vegetable oils.

Total working dependants.		Total following occupation as subsidiary to other.		Total earners principal occupation.		Total working dependants.		Total following occupation as subsidiary to other.		
Males.	Females.	Males.	Females.	Males.	Females.	Males.	Females.	Males.	Females.	
529	530	531	532	533	534	535	536	537	538	
213	**58**	**346**	**21**	**340,252**	**158,912**	**15,236**	**33,629**	**109,901**	**17,021**	
61	**9**	**282**	**2**	**274,826**	**135,451**	**9,570**	**23,258**	**91,234**	**13,746**	
..	..	..	..	641	178	26	65	139	9	1
..	..	3	..	1	..	..	..	..	..	2
..	..	6	..	668	38	27	25	723	9	3
..	..	..	..	13	..	..	..	14	..	4
1	..	48	..	31,334	2,152	346	89	3,692	158	5
..	..	3	..	38,570	29,732	440	957	20,976	5,358	6
20	4	64	1	10,366	3,384	900	1,139	2,143	365	7
1	..	..	..	*68*	*2*	..	..	*1*	..	
2	1	6	..	4,042	791	258	159	1,905	137	8
..	..	4	..	6,122	3,260	407	1,570	2,671	531	9
2	..	2	..	10	..	..	..	3	2	10
..	..	..	..	422	24	4	13	4	..	11
9	2	109	1	26,344	7,675	1,341	2,777	4,399	412	12
..	..	..	..	2,095	20	93	10	233	..	13
23	..	24	..	35,211	1,432	2,318	1,006	3,548	53	14
4	2	13	..	118,987	86,765	3,410	15,448	50,784	6,712	15
152	**49**	**64**	**19**	**65,426**	**23,461**	**5,666**	**10,371**	**18,667**	**3,275**	
..	..	..	..	2	..	..	..	..	..	16
..	..	..	..	50	..	..	..	59	..	17
3	..	6	..	1,807	321	323	879	218	45	18
..	..	..	..	12	..	1	..	54	..	19
..	..	1	13	2,783	4,015	48	663	3,477	335	20
12	..		..	1,449	272	152	255	156	18	21
..	..	4	..	7,753	4,118	141	298	3,560	451	22
..	..	6	..	609	836	437	1,233	789	67	23
..	..	5	5	6,528	1,343	265	388	1,292	204	24
38	18	20	..	7,272	3,596	2,406	3,915	1,328	1,720	25
..	..	..	..	2,316	100	86	30	998	77	26
52	1	1	..	10,332	2,552	535	269	1,046	62	27
..	*1*	*1*	..	*2,505*	*303*	*61*	*39*	*354*	*26*	
52	..	..	..	*7,758*	*2,245*	*472*	*330*	*669*	*35*	
..	..	..	..	*69*	*4*	*2*	..	*23*	*1*	
1	..	15	..	1,748	660	132	619	1,899	76	28
..	..	..	..	..	..	..	..	..	..	29
2	..	..	..	254	24	8	14	57	..	30
10	..	..	..	3,872	224	160	181	815	9	31
1	..	3	..	13,254	2,530	268	820	2,330	125	32
..	..	..	..	..	..	..	..	..	..	33
2	4	..	..	1,960	2,525	103	465	367	81	34
31	26	3	1	3,425	345	601	342	222	5	35

Table X.—Occupation or Means of Liveli

Class B.—Preparation and Supply of

Sub-Class III.—Industry

Order 10.—Chemical products properly so-called and

Province, State or Agency.	*Group 69.*—Manufacture and refining of mineral oils. Total earners principal occupation. Males.	Females.	Total working dependants. Males.	Females.	Total following occupation as subsidiary to others. Males.	Females.	*Group* Total earners principal occupation. Males.	Females.
1	539	540	541	542	543	544	545	546
INDIA ..	**10,607**	**869**	**85**	**322**	**253**	**62**	**13,154**	**3,313**
Provinces ..	**10,164**	**840**	**63**	**295**	**238**	**54**	**11,191**	**2,136**
1 **Ajmer-Merwara**	1	1	..	2	..	..	28	1
2 **Andamans and Nicobars**	..	..	..	..	..	..	1	..
3 **Assam**	..	..	..	..	..	..	20	1
4 Baluchistan (*Districts and Administered Territories*).	..	..	..	..	..	..	201	..
5 Bengal	125	4	5	..	22	3	2,448	115
6 Bihar and Orissa	158	314	..	9	28	27	2,884	908
7 Bombay (*including Aden*)	474	5	2	7	2	..	641	27
Aden		..	..	..	..	..	*2*	..
8 Burma	8,405	155	7	22	3	..	352	349
9 Central Provinces and Berar ..	888	355	47	255	125	24	894	464
10 Coorg	..	..	..	..	..	..	..	..
11 Delhi	12	..	..	..	..	..	235	3
12 Madras	61	6	2	..	38	..	1,158	194
13 North-West Frontier Province (*Districts and Administered Territories*). ..	..	..	..	..	..	..	249	7
14 Punjab	2	..	..	..	..	..	960	11
15 United Provinces of Agra and Oudh	38	..	..	..	20	..	1,120	56
States and Agencies ..	443	29	22	27	15	8	1,963	1,177
16 Assam States	..	..	..	..	..	..	20	6
17 Baluchistan States	..	..	..	..	..	..	..	..
18 Baroda State	..	..	..	..	..	..	74	3
19 Bengal States	..	..	..	..	..	..	..	..
20 Bihar and Orissa States	..	..	..	..	..	..	3	5
21 Bombay States	45	..	7	1	4	..	12	247
22 Central India Agency	..	..	..	..	..	..	437	185
23 Central Provinces States	..	..	..	..	..	..	227	251
24 Gwalior State	..	..	..	..	..	..	5	10
25 Hyderabad State	84	10	15	16	5	..	355	251
26 Jammu and Kashmir State ..	2	11	..	10	..	8	8	..
27 Madras States Agency	295	4	..	..	6	..	305	15
Cochin State	*295*	*4*	..	..	*6*	..	*39*	..
Travancore State	..	..	..	..	..	..	*250*	*14*
Other Madras States	..	..	..	..	..	..	*16*	*1*
28 Mysore State	..	..	..	..	..	..	47	12
29 North-West Frontier Province (*Agencies and Tribal Areas*).	..	..	..	..	..	..	..	..
30 Punjab States	..	..	..	..	..	..	2	..
31 Punjab States Agency	3	..	..	..	..	..	26	..
32 Rajputana Agency	3	4	..	..	..	..	237	16
33 Sikkim State	..	..	..	..	..	..	..	..
34 United Provinces States ..	..	..	..	..	..	..	..	..
35 Western India States Agency ..	11	..	..	..	..	..	205	176

hood—Part II.—Provincial Distribution—*contd.*

Material Substances—*contd.*

—*contd.*

analogous—*concld.* | *Order 11.*—Food Industries.

70.—Others. | Total *Order 11.*—Food Industries.

Total working dependants.		Total following occupation as subsidiary to other.		Total earners principal occupation.		Total working dependants.		Total following occupation as subsidiary to other.		
Males.	Females.	Males.	Females.	Males.	Females.	Males.	Females.	Males.	Females.	
547	548	549	550	551	552	553	554	555	556	
407	**730**	**2,892**	**322**	**678,643**	**671,515**	**27,638**	**99,199**	**136,724**	**51,728**	
198	517	2,735	288	568,538	582,384	18,195	78,894	117,222	42,583	
1	3	3	..	1,044	629	8	56	107	21	1
..	..	..	..	21	..	..	..	1	..	2
..	1	1	2	3,375	5,988	211	1,314	592	1,139	3
1	..	8	..	1,397	18	..	..	99	2	4
3	..	92	9	35,989	132,240	465	7,836	6,353	5,521	5
67	43	1,699	161	48,743	105,731	628	12,163	20,337	7,474	6
4	1	..	..	26,035	7,929	1,051	1,424	2,348	1,047	7
..	..	..	..	*346*	*49*	*13*	*7*	*4*	*2*	
62	303	433	44	76,222	43,173	3,676	18,436	14,589	4,165	8
3	125	119	69	35,334	27,011	1,392	2,910	6,439	3,731	9
..	..	1	..	619	60	6	..	126	2	10
..	..	..	..	3,977	229	8	15	84	9	11
20	3	217	2	145,855	58,475	5,130	12,419	34,006	4,513	12
10	1	23	..	8,889	861	404	58	486	9	13
9	14	57	..	48,503	20,228	1,792	5,555	4,434	2,098	14
18	23	82	1	132,535	179,812	3,424	16,708	27,221	12,852	15
209	213	157	34	110,105	89,131	9,443	20,305	19,502	9,145	
..	1	..	2	210	423	11	116	81	57	16
.	..	..	..	173	203	12	20	71	8	17
..	..	1	.	3 226	1,851	200	370	421	74	18
..	..	..	..	173	2 271	9	40	6	15	19
..	i	..	1	5,100	26,926	120	5,055	2,999	3,956	20
..	16	4	10	1,691	432	102	90	677	304	21
3	2	61	2	6,632	4,186	75	236	787	262	22
..	2	3	7	3,413	2,798	203	2,052	538	97	23
..	..	..	..	2,996	2,628	86	693	329	618	24
127	132	58	12	13,057	4,155	4,259	3,429	2,537	930	25
..	..	..	..	4,639	219	109	35	748	132	26
55	25	7	..	31,790	26,397	2,337	4,960	5,676	1,805	27
..	*12*	*2*	..	*5,807*	*2,847*	*29*	*245*	*1,563*	*501*	
55	*13*	*5*	..	*25,274*	*23,876*	*2,303*	*4,714*	*3,960*	*1,300*	
..	..	..	..	*709*	*74*	*5*	*1*	*153*	*4*	
..	..	..	..	7,276	2,369	198	401	1,624	226	28
..	..	..	..	180	..	..	..	80	..	29
..	..	1	..	623	136	12	27	340	13	30
..	..	1	..	8,170	1,612	198	350	1,066	109	31
..	1	11	..	13,175	6,929	561	783	1,012	338	32
..	..	..	..	7	..	..	..	..	..	33
..	..	..	..	2,345	2,799	64	424	29,311	.	34
24	33	10	..	6,229	2,397	887	1,224	217	87	35

Table X.—Occupation or Means of Liveli

Province, State or Agency.	*Class B.*—Preparation and Supply of — *Sub-Class III.*—Industries — *Order 11.*—Food — *Group 71.*—Rice pounders and huskers and flour grinders. Total earners principal occupation.		Total working dependants.		Total following occupation as subsidiary to other.		*Group 72.*—Grain — Total earners principal occupation.	
	Males.	Females.	Males.	Females.	Males.	Females.	Males.	Females.
1	557	558	559	560	561	562	563	564
INDIA	**99,854**	**407,011**	**2,822**	**46,777**	**15,257**	**28,399**	**100,872**	**154,926**
Provinces	89,770	355,780	2,341	38,447	13,145	22,190	90,382	134,430
1 Ajmer-Merwara	100	262	2	5	60	18	49	19
2 Andamans and Nicobars	..	..	..	..	..	..	..	..
3 Assam	394	4,826	105	889	61	919	354	850
4 Baluchistan (*Districts and Administered Territories*).	130	18	..	..	53	2	21	..
5 Bengal	9,663	123,890	104	7,172	1,168	5,027	1,511	6,450
6 Bihar and Orissa	2,897	52,052	189	9,234	6,052	3,653	15,245	47,974
7 Bombay (*including Aden*)	1,861	2,487	82	623	170	738	1,611	1,198
Aden	..	..	..	..	..	..	..	*1*
8 Burma	43,473	13,985	1,042	4,790	1,282	1,303	..	..
9 Central Provinces and Berar	1,813	3,788	60	428	400	445	1,812	4,884
10 Coorg	2	28	..	..	24	..	38	29
11 Delhi	652	168	..	9	1	8	150	19
12 Madras	12,012	32,909	394	5,782	1,422	2,748	1,481	4,126
13 North-West Frontier Province (*Districts and Administered Territories*).	2,496	678	27	18	98	4	1,301	90
14 Punjab	5,826	10,087	144	1,611	1,428	1,011	5,609	4,791
15 United Provinces of Agra and Oudh	8,451	110,602	192	7,886	926	6,314	61,200	64,000
States and Agencies	**10,084**	**51,231**	**481**	**8,330**	**2,112**	**6,209**	**10,490**	**20,496**
16 Assam States	..	71	1	34	..	4	3	..
17 Baluchistan States	21	168	..	14	3	3	56	35
18 Baroda State	637	1,373	42	237	16	31	186	51
19 Bengal States	24	2,248	5	40	..	13	7	15
20 Bihar and Orissa States	301	11,631	9	3,033	157	3,096	4,556	15,193
21 Bombay States	92	212	13	39	11	155	53	25
22 Central India Agency	443	2,757	16	100	57	176	946	873
23 Central Provinces States	1,096	730	1	515	11	4	760	1,758
24 Gwalior State	225	2,333	14	645	157	410	361	172
25 Hyderabad State	451	583	193	536	73	128	38	102
26 Jammu and Kashmir State	1,582	148	45	7	423	54	91	35
27 Madras States Agency	1,034	17,846	37	1,647	116	1,626	15	9
Cochin State	*128*	*2,164*	*2*	*178*	*27*	*463*	*15*	*7*
Travancore State	*849*	*15,672*	*35*	*1,469*	*75*	*1,163*	..	..
Other Madras States	*57*	*10*	..	..	*14*	..	..	*2*
28 Mysore State	465	1,164	10	68	122	64	279	99
29 North-West Frontier Province (*Agencies and Tribal Areas*).	..	..	..	..	..	..	..	..
30 Punjab States	467	123	5	10	295	11	39	12
31 Punjab States Agency	2,292	831	29	92	562	48	927	649
32 Rajputana Agency	754	5,635	29	389	94	302	1,053	314
33 Sikkim State	..	..	..	..	..	..	..	..
34 United Provinces States	104	1,533	..	117	..	41	1,064	1,041
35 Western India States Agency	96	1,845	32	807	15	43	56	113

hood—Part II—Provincial Distribution—*contd.*

Material Substances—*contd.*

—contd.

Industries—*contd.*

parchers, etc. — *Group 73.*—Butchers.

Total working dependants. Males.	Total working dependants. Females.	Total following occupation as subsidiary to other. Males.	Total following occupation as subsidiary to other. Females.	Total earners principal occupation. Males.	Total earners principal occupation. Females.	Total working dependants. Males.	Total working dependants. Females.	Total following occupation as subsidiary to other. Males.	Total following occupation as subsidiary to other. Females.	
565	566	567	568	569	570	571	572	573	574	
3,858	**20,365**	**34,440**	**14,335**	**95,837**	**7,756**	**3,402**	**1,546**	**7,820**	**697**	
3,494	**15,962**	**30,347**	**12,811**	**77,421**	**5,758**	**1,652**	**757**	**6,041**	**479**	
1	6	3	..	290	7	..	4	4	..	1
..	..	..	..	10	..	..	..	..	..	2
13	374	108	181	157	..	1	..	49	..	3
..	..	..	..	367	..	..	..	38	..	4
66	542	434	401	3,428	119	14	29	168	..	5
228	2,805	9,268	3,508	4,274	799	31	16	596	63	6
76	325	159	69	8,463	2,037	425	232	573	151	7
..	..	..	..	*124*	..	*4*	..	*1*	..	
..	..	..	..	753	17	14	3	29	..	8
150	1,247	1,872	1,485	2,454	254	72	37	171	11	9
1	..	10	2	41	2	..	..	..	..	10
2	6	1	1	1,354	8	..	..	5	..	11
42	140	331	104	8,871	543	105	157	823	14	12
39	20	46	4	3,059	55	324	6	267	1	13
443	2,380	935	917	13,543	89	474	38	586	..	14
2,433	8,099	17,180	6,139	30,357	1,828	192	235	2,732	239	15
364	**4,403**	**4,093**	**1,524**	**18,416**	**1,998**	**1,750**	**789**	**1,779**	**218**	
..	..	..	..	48	..	..	..	68	..	16
..	..	35	5	63	..	..	..	33	..	17
20	36	2	1	391	9	25	9	2	..	18
..	..	..	2	34	..	..	..	..	..	19
109	2,021	2,759	860	10	..	..	..	3	..	20
..	1	18	75	377	16	16	2	41	6	21
15	75	266	60	852	63	1	..	16	1	22
62	1,414	414	88	17	4	1	..	..	..	23
14	31	79	191	378	5	1		3	2	24
12	93	1	25	4,902	1,232	1,437	615	757	185	25
2	15	13	58	1,330	5	24	7	103	6	26
..	1	..	..	630	54	10	..	83	4	27
..	..	..	..	*33*	..	..	..	*13*	..	
..	..	..	..	*315*	*1*	*6*	..	*22*	..	
..	*1*	..	..	*282*	*53*	*4*	..	*48*	*4*	
2	5	38	17	1,386	25	4	..	29	..	28
..	..	..	..	121	..	..	..	..	..	29
..	17	10	2	43	1	..	..	1	..	30
64	248	233	53	1,467	3	26	..	75	..	31
16	189	92	13	5,028	537	83	104	400	14	32
..	..	..	..	3	..	..	..	..	..	33
48	218	133	73	537	20	2	..	154	..	34
..	39	..	1	799	24	120	52	11	.	35

Table X.—Occupation or Means of Liveli

Class B.—Preparation and Supply of

Sub-Class III.—Industry

Order 11.—Food

	Province, State or Agency.	*Group 74.*—Makers of sugar, molasses and gur.						*Group 75.*—Sweetmeat	
		Total earners principal occupation.		Total working dependants.		Total following occupation as subsidiary to other.		Total earners principal occupation.	
		Males.	Females.	Males.	Females.	Males.	Females.	Males.	Females.
	1	575	576	577	578	579	580	581	582
	INDIA	**19,061**	**13,577**	**376**	**8,035**	**8,244**	**2,202**	**84,693**	**23,026**
	Provinces	**17,148**	**12,017**	**302**	**4,932**	**7,901**	**2,122**	**65,292**	**14,163**
1	Ajmer-Merwara	..	2	..	..	..	..	312	15
2	Andamans and Nicobars	..	..	..	..	..	..	1	..
3	Assam	6	5	1	3	57	12	1,803	129
4	Baluchistan (*Districts and Administered Territories*).	..	..	..	..	..	..	247	..
5	Bengal	1,944	66	22	1	2,005	15	5,833	318
6	Bihar and Orissa	1,028	98	1	..	151	8	6,807	2,143
7	Bombay (*including Aden*)	971	101	19	8	314	28	5,287	634
	Aden	*6*	*5*	..	..	..	..	*9*	..
8	Burma .. — — —	1,430	8,006	85	3,783	552	1,628	1,772	3,450
9	Central Provinces and Berar ..	29	4	—	2	13	—	2,323	186
10	Coorg	..	—	—	..	..	—	—	—
11	Delhi	149	3	..	—	44	—	992	1
12	Madras	3,767	3,677	142	1,124	1,039	427	7,843	4,749
13	North-West Frontier Province (*Districts and Administered Territories*).	120	..	..	..	1	..	507	..
14	Punjab	764	..	20	—	216	—	11,724	44
15	United Provinces of Agra and Oudh	6,940	55	12	11	3,509	4	19,841	2,494
	States and Agencies ..	**1,913**	**1,560**	**74**	**3,103**	**343**	**80**	**19,401**	**8,863**
16	Assam States	43	..	..	..	..	..	..	..
17	Baluchistan States	..	..	..	..	..	..	16	..
18	Baroda State	106	18	..	..	1	..	398	27
19	Bengal States	..	..	..	..	..	..	66	2
20	Bihar and Orissa States	3	1	..	..	..	..	28	23
21	Bombay States	9	..	..	..	..	..	274	32
22	Central India Agency	34	4	..	6	27	1	3,387	298
23	Central Provinces States	..	..	..	..	..	..	202	41
24	Gwalior State	..	..	..	..	..	..	1,874	77
25	Hyderabad State	202	104	41	100	26	16	1,156	647
26	Jammu and Kashmir State ..	2	..	..	..	..	..	577	11
27	Madras States Agency	701	1,405	15	2,989	30	63	1,817	7,321
	Cochin State	..	..	..	..	*3*	..	*588*	*642*
	Travancore State	*701*	*1,405*	*15*	*2,989*	*27*	*63*	*1,217*	*6,675*
	Other Madras States	..	..	..	..	..	..	*12*	*4*
28	Mysore State —	85	3	..	1	226	..	165	20
29	North-West Frontier Province (*Agencies and Tribal Areas*).	..	..	..	..	..	..	..	..
30	Punjab States	1	..	..	..	4	..	33	..
31	Punjab States Agency	391	..	17	..	16	..	1,886	8
32	Rajputana Agency	78	..	..	..	12	..	4,766	140
33	Sikkim State	..	..	..	..	..	..	..	..
34	United Provinces States	..	3	..	5	..	..	593	174
35	Western India States Agency ..	258	22	1	2	1	..	2,163	42

hood—Part II.—Provincial Distribution—*contd.*

Material Substances—*contd.*

—*contd.*

Industries—*contd.*

and condiment makers.				*Group 76.*—Toddy drawers.						
Total working dependants.		Total following occupation as subsidiary to other.		Total earners principal occupation.		Total working dependants.		Total following occupation as subsidiary to other.		
Males.	Females.	Males.	Females.	Males.	Females.	Males.	Females.	Males.	Females.	
583	584	585	586	587	588	589	590	591	592	
2,734	**3,526**	**9,741**	**1,297**	**167,308**	**8,557**	**8,525**	**2,525**	**49,969**	**1,030**	
1,515	**2,571**	**7,847**	**871**	**134,055**	**7,858**	**5,183**	**1,713**	**42,973**	**863**	
3	**8**	**9**	..	..	..	..	..	..	..	1
..	..	..	..	..	..	..	..	..	..	2
46	**33**	**233**	**10**	**20**	..	..	..	..	..	3
..	..	**2**	..	..	..	..	..	..	..	4
79	2	1,252	3	383	11	2	..	293	..	5
62	33	896	98	13,983	1,176	47	36	2,602	53	6
101	103	395	9	2,139	46	77	2	447	8	7
..	..	..	..	..	..	..	..	..	..	
214	1,633	655	440	22,723	534	1,956	468	10,644	109	8
44	54	188	9	194	4	1	2	4	..	9
..	..	..	..	517	..	3	..	92	..	10
4	..	23	..	..	..	..	..	..	..	11
256	340	947	209	92,747	5,834	2,955	1,106	28,871	675	12
..	..	..	..	..	..	..	..	..	..	13
333	1	643	..	..	..	..	..	..	..	14
373	364	2,604	93	1,349	253	142	99	20	18	15
1,219	955	1,394	426	33,253	699	3,342	812	6,996	167	
..	..	..	..	..	..	..	..	..	..	16
..	..	..	..	..	..	..	..	..	..	17
34	36	24	35	83	..	..	1	268	–	18
3	..	1	..	..	..	..	.	..	..	19
..	1	11	..	14	..	..	..	5	..	20
12	13	486	59	596	2	23	..	84	1	21
28	22	233	8	6	..	..	..	..	..	22
7	24	11	..	2	..	..	..	..	..	23
45	9	75	..	2	..	..	..	..	..	24
390	626	276	225	3,529	621	1,422	772	850	158	25
22	3	95	2	60	..	..	..	7	..	26
63	122	145	93	26,246	36	1,864	25	4,958	4	27
9	*42*	*59*	*34*	*4,500*	*34*	*14*	*25*	*1,432*	*4*	
54	*80*	*86*	*59*	*21,396*	..	*11,850*	..	*3,438*	..	
..	..	..	..	*350*	*2*	..	..	*88*	..	
..	4	51	..	2,613	19	33	..	821	4	28
..	..	..	..	..	..	..	..	..	..	29
3	..	9	..	..	..	..	..	..	..	30
30	..	152	..	77	..	..	..	..	..	31
105	11	279	4	..	..	..	..	..	..	32
..	..	..	..	..	..	..	..	..	..	33
14	70	6	..	23	21	..	14	..	..	34
463	14	40	..	2	..	..	..	3	..	35

Table X.—Occupation or Means of Liveli

Class B.—Preparation and Supply of

Sub-Class III.—Industry

Order 11.—Food

Province, State or Agency.	*Group 77.*—Brewers and distillers.						*Group 78.*—Manufacturers	
	Total earners principal occupation.		Total working dependants.		Total following occupation as subsidiary to other.		Total earners principal occupation.	
	Males.	Females.	Males.	Females.	Males.	Females.	Males.	Females.
1	593	594	595	596	597	598	599	600
INDIA	**3,555**	**1,344**	**665**	**389**	**484**	**125**	**74,507**	**44,995**
Provinces	**884**	**639**	**26**	**89**	**96**	**56**	**64,876**	**42,081**
1 Ajmer-Merwara	3	..	..	..	..	..	225	320
2 Andamans and Nicobars	..	..	..	..	..	..	3	..
3 Assam	13	150	..	4	4	16	9	3
4 Baluchistan (*Districts and Administered Territories*).	49	..	..	..	..	..	..	..
5 Bengal	25	1	..	..	4	..	9,746	1,324
6 Bihar and Orissa	93	8	..	..	20	..	4,292	1,465
7 Bombay (*including Aden*) ..	39	179	..	1	1	..	3,726	680
Aden	*7*	..	..	..	..	..	*67*	*1*
8 Burma	292	184	14	61	49	13	1,743	15,092
9 Central Provinces and Berar ..	16	4	..	1	3	..	26,459	17,733
10 Coorg	..	..	..	..	..	..	1	1
11 Delhi	11	..	..	..	..	..	47	2
12 Madras	145	88	3	16	6	8	17,105	5,202
13 North-West Frontier Province (*Districts and Administered Territories*).	19	..	..	..	..	..	213	1
14 Punjab	148	..	9	..	8	..	515	172
15 United Provinces of Agra and Oudh	31	25	..	6	1	19	792	86
States and Agencies ..	**2,671**	**705**	**639**	**300**	**388**	**69**	**9,631**	**2,914**
16 Assam States	86	330	9	80	9	45	..	..
17 Baluchistan States	..	..	..	..	..	..	..	..
18 Baroda State	70	27	..	..	5	..	940	323
19 Bengal States	1	..	..	..	..	..	9	6
20 Bihar and Orissa States	54	..	..	..	13	..	130	26
21 Bombay States	7	36	1	..	1	..	152	60
22 Central India Agency	271	65	5	17	115	4	645	114
23 Central Provinces States	377	31	117	53	75	4	957	228
24 Gwalior State	..	..	..	..	..	..	27	41
25 Hyderabad State	546	68	153	68	72	7	2,080	788
26 Jammu and Kashmir State ..	10	.	2	..	2	..	51	..
27 Madras States Agency	187	65	29	11	61	8	842	28
Cochin State	..	..	..	..	*2*	..	*529*	..
Travancore State	*187*	*65*	*29*	*11*	*59*	*8*	*305*	*25*
Other Madras States	..	..	..	..	..	..	*8*	*3*
28 Mysore State	27	2	..	..	..	..	1,800	971
29 North-West Frontier Province (*Agencies and Tribal Areas*).	..	..	..	..	..	..	..	..
30 Punjab States	4	..	1	..	..	..	1	..
31 Punjab States Agency	94	..	..	..	..	..	..	..
32 Rajputana Agency	912	80	317	71	35	1	427	139
33 Sikkim State	4	..	..	..	..	..		..
34 United Provinces States	..	..	..	..	..	..	7	..
35 Western India States Agency ..	21	1	5	..	..	..	1,561	190

hood—Part II—Provincial Distribution—*contd.*

Material Substances—*contd.*

—contd.

Industries—*contd.*

of Tobacco.				*Group 79.*—Manufacturers of Opium.						
Total working dependants.		Total following occupation as subsidiary to others.		Total earners principal occupation.		Total working dependants.		Total following occupation as subsidiary to other.		
Males.	Females.	Males.	Females.	Males.	Females.	Males.	Females.	Males.	Females.	
601	602	603	604	605	606	607	608	609	610	
4,187	**12,723**	**7,763**	**3,022**	**186**	**32**	**5**	**17**	**29**	**4**	
2,909	**11,556**	**6,314**	**2,654**	**82**	**12**	**1**	**1**	**27**	**4**	
2	32	29	3	..	..	..	1	..	..	**1**
..	..	..	..	..	..	..	..	..	..	**2**
..	1	2	..	..	..	..	..	..	..	**3**
..	..	..	..	..	..	..	..	..	..	**4**
155	80	799	74	38	..	..	..	..	..	**5**
65	39	716	87	26	7	..	..	21	4	**6**
246	102	227	27	16	5	1	..	..	..	**7**
7	..	*1*	..	..	..	..	..	..	..	
150	6,527	382	402	..	..	..	..	..	..	**8**
1,060	1,079	3,721	1,767	..	..	..	..	..	..	**9**
..	..	..	..	..	..	..	..	..	..	**10**
..	..	..	..	..	..	..	..	..	..	**11**
1,206	3,689	401	291	..	..	..	..	..	..	**12**
..	..	..	..	..	..	..	..	..	..	**13**
24	5	23	2	..	..	..	..	..	..	**14**
1	2	14	1	2	..	..	..	6	..	**15**
1,278	**1,167**	**1,449**	**368**	**104**	**20**	**4**	**16**	**2**	..	
..	..	..	..	..	..	..	..	..	..	**16**
..	..	..	..	..	..	..	..	..	..	**17**
40	39	55	7	4	..	..	..	..	..	**18**
..	..	..	..	..	..	..	..	..	..	**19**
2	..	48	..	..	..	..	..	..	..	**20**
30	32	14	8	..	1	..	3	..	..	**21**
6	15	72	7	1	..	..	..	..	..	**22**
13	30	27	1	..	..	..	..	..	..	**23**
..	8	15	15	..	..	..	..	..	..	**24**
588	608	479	185	..	..	..	..	..	..	**25**
..	..	6	..	18	..	..	..	..	..	**26**
205	45	219	3	..	..	..	..	..	..	**27**
2	..	*27*	..	..	..	..	..	..	..	
202	*45*	*189*	*3*	..	..	..	..	..	..	
1	..	*3*	..	..	..	..	..	..	..	
149	321	332	139	..	..	..	..	..	..	**28**
..	..	..	..	..	..	..	..	..	..	**29**
..	..	2	..	..	..	..	..	..	..	**30**
..	..	..	..	..	..	..	..	..	..	**31**
11	19	35	3	8	..	..	..	..	..	**32**
..	..	..	..	..	..	..	..	..	..	**33**
..	..	..	..	..	..	..	..	..	..	**34**
234	50	145	..	73	19	4	13	2	..	**35**

Table X.—Occupation or Means of Liveli

Class B.—Preparation and Supply of

Sub-Class III.—Industry

Order 11.—Food

Province, State or Agency.	*Group 80.*—Manufacturers of Ganja. Total earners principal occupation. Males.	Females.	Total working dependants. Males.	Females.	Total following occupation as subsidiary to other. Males.	Females.	*Group 81.*— Total earners principal occupation. Males.	Females.
1	611	612	613	614	615	616	617	618
INDIA ..	**222**	**63**	**24**	**1**	**21**	..	**32,548**	**10,228**
Provinces ..	**113**	**46**	**8**	..	**4**	..	**28,515**	**9,600**
1 Ajmer-Merwara	..	..	..	..	..	..	65	4
2 Andamans and Nicobars ..	..	..	..	..	..	..	7	..
3 Assam	..	..	..	..	..	..	619	25
4 Baluchistan (*Districts and Administered Territories*).	..	..	..	..	..	..	583	..
5 Bengal	1	..	..	..	..	..	3,417	61
6 Bihar and Orissa	10	2	..	..	2	..	88	7
7 Bombay (*including Aden*)	85	44	8	..	2	..	1,837	518
Aden	..	..	..	..	..	..	*133*	*42*
8 Burma	..	..	..	..	..	..	[illegible]	1,905
9 Central Provinces and Berar ..	..	..	..	..	..	..	234	154
10 Coorg	..	..	..	..	..	..	20	..
11 Delhi	..	..	..	..	..	..	622	28
12 Madras	..	..	..	..	..	..	1,884	1,347
13 North-West Frontier Province (*Districts and Administered Territories*).	17	..	..	..	..	..	1,157	37
14 Punjab	..	..	..	..	..	..	10,374	5,045
15 United Provinces of Agra and Oudh	..	..	..	..	..	..	3,572	469
States and Agencies ..	**109**	**17**	**16**	**1**	**17**	..	**4,033**	**628**
16 Assam States	..	..	..	..	..	..	30	22
17 Baluchistan States	..	..	..	..	..	..	17	..
18 Baroda State	..	..	..	..	..	..	411	23
19 Bengal States	..	..	..	..	..	..	32	..
20 Bihar and Orissa States	..	..	..	..	..	..	4	52
21 Bombay States	33	..	7	..	15	..	98	48
22 Central India Agency	..	..	..	..	..	..	47	12
23 Central Provinces States	..	..	..	..	..	..	2	6
24 Gwalior State	..	..	..	..	..	..	129	..
25 Hyderabad State	67	2	9	..	..	..	86	8
26 Jammu and Kashmir State ..	..	5	..	..	..	..	918	15
27 Madras States Agency	..	..	..	..	..	..	318	33
Cochin State	..	..	..	..	..	..	*14*	..
Travancore State	..	..	..	..	..	..	*304*	*33*
Other Madras States	..	..	..	..	..	..	..	..
28 Mysore State	..	..	..	..	..	..	456	66
29 North-West Frontier Province (*Agencies and Tribal Areas*).	..	..	..	..	..	..	59	..
30 Punjab States	..	..	..	..	..	..	35	..
31 Punjab States Agency	..	..	..	..	..	..	1,034	121
32 Rajputana Agency	6	8	..	..	2	..	143	76
33 Sikkim State	..	..	..	..	..	..	..	..
34 United Provinces States	..	..	..	..	..	..	17	7
35 Western India States Agency ..	3	2	..	1	..	..	197	139

hood—Part II—Provincial Distribution—*contd.*

Material Substances—*contd.*

—*contd.*

Industries—*concld.*

others.

Order 12—Industries of dress and the toilet.

Total *Order 12*.—Industries of dress and the toilet.

Total working dependants.		Total following occupation as subsidiary to other.		Total earners principal occupation.		Total working dependants.		Total following occupation as subsidiary to other.		
Males.	Females.	Males.	Females.	Males.	Females.	Males.	Females.	Males.	Females.	
619	620	621	622	623	624	625	626	627	628	
1,040	**3,295**	**2,956**	**617**	**2,426,264**	**635,081**	**139,330**	**180,149**	**480,736**	**54,396**	
764	**2,866**	**2,527**	**533**	**1,836,487**	**496,770**	**67,814**	**104,553**	**364,049**	**35,568**	
..	..	2	..	6,088	1,156	90	372	606	57	1
..	..	1	..	234	4	..	6	7	3	2
45	10	78	1	13,569	930	770	489	6,146	220	3
..	..	6	..	2,568	78	15	1,413	69	7	4
23	10	230	1	152,255	14,410	2,194	2,156	19,196	798	5
5	..	13	..	162,123	80,054	1,793	5,344	70,319	8,786	6
16	28	60	17	152,151	20,101	7,095	5,524	11,087	1,128	7
2	*7*	*2*	*2*	*598*	*67*	*61*	*26*	*4*	..	
201	1,171	996	270	44,240	18,928	2,789	10,381	4,597	1,441	8
5	60	67	14	101,136	19,599	3,874	9,493	19,455	2,968	9
2	..	..	..	760	235	12	5	329	11	10
2	..	10	..	16,428	1,508	152	698	321	9	11
27	65	166	37	387,082	149,479	21,067	30,506	65,134	6,058	12
14	5	74	..	27,583	840	1,366	235	1,447	10	13
345	1,511	595	168	341,400	20,034	18,422	13,972	23,404	1,212	14
79	6	229	25	428,870	169,414	8,175	23,959	141,932	12,860	15
276	**429**	**429**	**84**	**589,777**	**138,311**	**71,516**	**75,596**	**116,687**	**18,828**	
1	2	4	8	913	315	92	102	81	120	16
12	6	..	..	756	131	11	479	142	2	17
39	12	48	..	15,242	2,684	1,022	3,257	1,094	59	18
1	..	5	..	1,380	30	24	..	161	7	19
..	..	3	..	10,795	7,945	203	1,075	6,180	306	20
..	..	7	—	20,507	2,603	1,479	1,302	3,149	415	21
4	1	1	5	69,134	10,702	930	800	15,978	501	22
2	16	..	..	5,429	1,300	597	1,520	2,172	134	23
12	..	..	..	38,029	6,696	1,720	1,827	6,697	989	24
14	11	3	1	125,804	48,006	51,674	36,136	28,495	2,905	25
14	3	99	12	25,953	2,320	732	1,571	3,928	610	26
114	120	64	4	32,959	17,715	2,123	3,893	3,401	763	27
2	..	..	..	*4,723*	*4,944*	*65*	*210*	*561*	*152*	
112	*120*	*64*	*4*	*25,244*	*11,352*	*2,009*	*3,551*	*1,844*	*557*	
..	..	..	..	*2,992*	*1,419*	*49*	*132*	*996*	*54*	
..	2	5	2	30,199	6,308	1,502	8,918	14,219	645	28
..	..	80	..	760	2	2	..	..	..	29
3	..	19	..	3,054	157	199	257	1,109	[illegible]	30
32	10	28	8	50,493	2,112	2,474	2,285	8,365	208	31
..	..	63	1	123,134	24,976	2,248	8,909	18,064	804	32
..	..	..	..	124	39	..	..	70	15	33
..	..	..	..	7,540	2,329	238	993	2,833	320	34
28	246	..	43	27,572	1,941	4,246	2,272	549	21	35

Table X.—Occupation or Means of Liveli

Class B.—Preparation and Supply of

Sub-Class III.—Industry

Order 12.—Industries of

	Province, State or Agency.	*Group 82.*—Boot, shoe, sandal and clog makers.						*Group 83.*—Tailors,	
		Total earners principal occupation.		Total working dependants.		Total following occupation as subsidiary to others.		Total earners principal occupation.	
	1	Males. 629	Females. 630	Males. 631	Females. 632	Males. 633	Females. 634	Males. 635	Females. 636
	INDIA	**622,848**	**49,736**	**35,147**	**32,456**	**105,311**	**6,819**	**470,883**	**113,083**
	Provinces	**438,017**	**29,082**	**17,432**	**13,751**	**61,924**	**2,276**	**346,169**	**82,683**
1	Ajmer-Merwara	1,281	102	36	34	164	23	1,364	392
2	Andamans and Nicobars	16	..	..	..	..	..	77	3
3	Assam	1,111	40	54	17	420	4	5,913	318
4	Baluchistan (*Districts and Administered Territories*).	633	1	..	..	30	..	1,004	15
5	Bengal	21,315	1,511	290	63	1,295	17	40,313	2,508
6	Bihar and Orissa	29,484	6,117	281	85	9,290	578	22,102	8,009
7	Bombay (*including Aden*). ..	43,743	4,076	1,837	883	4,071	196	42,630	7,653
	Aden	*76*	..	*2*	..	..	..	*246*	*45*
8	Burma	5,507	983	540	664	671	29	22,259	14,612
9	Central Provinces and Berar ..	22,039	2,010	774	1,846	5,368	504	21,821	4,305
10	Coorg	22	1	3	..	28	..	235	18
11	Delhi	5,629	594	20	348	136	7	3,145	215
12	Madras	75,084	2,601	1,757	665	18,986	258	39,527	7,352
13	North-West Frontier Province (*Districts and Administered Territories*).	10,656	113	494	103	458	1	4,847	489
14	Punjab	167,345	5,198	10,201	7,722	12,239	428	51,240	9,282
15	United Provinces of Agra and Oudh	54,152	5,735	1,145	1,321	8,768	231	89,692	27,512
	States and Agencies ..	**184,831**	**20,654**	**17,715**	**18,705**	**43,387**	**4,543**	**124,714**	**30,400**
16	Assam States	57	7	4	..	2	..	708	304
17	Baluchistan States	484	..	3	..	78	..	95	8
18	Baroda State	2,646	114	239	669	120	3	4,970	2,076
19	Bengal States	101	1	..	..	4	..	351	2
20	Bihar and Orissa States	587	175	..	62	2	..	392	61
21	Bombay States	5,882	590	232	91	899	39	5,546	945
22	Central India Agency	26,711	2,517	357	179	7,830	121	12,804	2,696
23	Central Provinces States	1,560	144	251	415	676	4	742	83
24	Gwalior State	15,446	1,261	725	366	3,128	344	5,419	1,407
25	Hyderabad State	40,841	8,871	12,435	11,467	11,724	3,376	18,923	8,365
26	Jammu and Kashmir State ..	2,637	188	92	197	953	229	16,514	1,877
27	Madras States Agency	625	15	16	1	285	4	6,815	1,060
	Cochin State	..	..	..	..	*18*	*3*	*1,279*	*197*
	Travancore State	*224*	*11*	*15*	..	*21*	..	*4,275*	*850*
	Other Madras States	*401*	*4*	*1*	*1*	*196*	*1*	*261*	*13*
28	Mysore State	3,727	121	46	5	1,727	24	8,792	1,432
29	North-West Frontier Province (*Agencies and Tribal Areas*). ..	94	..	..	..	..	..	236	2
30	Punjab States	1,744	42	132	121	658	4	499	27
31	Punjab States Agency	27,959	892	1,389	1,734	6,185	168	9,191	558
32	Rajputana Agency	48,126	5,612	976	3,252	8,788	227	21,549	8,097
33	Sikkim State	18	..	..	..	1	..	91	38
34	United Provinces States	933	22	58	33	260	..	1,632	416
35	Western India States Agency ..	4,653	82	760	113	117	..	10,395	946

hood—Part II—Provincial Distribution—*contd.*

Material Substances—*contd.*

—*contd.*

dress and the toilet.

milliners, dress-makers and darners.				*Group 84.*—Embroiderers, hat makers and makers of other articles of wear.						
Total working dependants.		Total following occupation as subsidiary to other.		Total earners principal occupation.		Total working dependants.		Total following occupation as subsidiary to other.		
Males.	Females.	Males.	Females.	Males.	Females.	Males.	Females.	Males.	Females.	
637	638	639	640	641	642	643	644	645	646	
22,233	**42,165**	**59,143**	**11,247**	**15,089**	**6,267**	**795**	**3,322**	**2,184**	**579**	
10,704	**24,610**	**43,975**	**7,029**	**11,644**	**4,443**	**369**	**1,609**	**1,990**	**415**	
20	95	49	10	12	9	..	4	1	..	**1**
..	6	4	1	..	1	..	..	1	2	**2**
322	321	1,459	105	273	83	7	36	83	38	**3**
15	1,404	10	1	8	21	..	8	..	3	**4**
601	149	2,700	147	2,288	285	8	332	290	66	**5**
114	132	5,182	889	273	116	..	24	119	24	**6**
2,176	2,582	1,922	366	469	620	11	157	5	29	**7**
42	*25*	*4*	..	*7*	*4*	..	*1*	..	..	
1,670	8,957	2,501	1,191	2,671	1,379	289	503	1,182	189	**8**
961	2,409	2,519	460	469	59	20	281	61	3	**9**
7	..	151	2	1	..	..	..	1	..	**10**
28	25	86	1	2,552	122	4	1	..	..	**11**
1,319	1,374	3,479	440	561	523	4	160	133	9	**12**
177	88	422	8	597	72	..	3	3	..	**13**
2,202	2,479	3,852	444	1,058	267	25	81	43	42	**14**
1,092	4,589	19,639	2,964	412	886	1	19	68	10	**15**
11,529	**[illegible]**	**15,168**	**4,218**	**3,445**	**1,824**	**426**	**1,713**	**194**	**164**	
87	89	77	120	20	..	..	..	..	..	**16**
1	76	12	1	6	115	5	396	1	1	**17**
374	2,085	209	49	45	..	..	..	2	..	**18**
2	..	30	..	4	..	..	..	1	..	**19**
1	18	19	..	1	..	..	..	..	..	**20**
405	885	617	76	4	..	..	..	..	..	**21**
214	243	1,478	95	234	134	3	28	10	1	**22**
47	115	75	6	7	..	..	..	..	..	**23**
231	380	1,222	306	6	7	..	2	..	..	**24**
6,348	17,218	3,727	2,669	709	235	282	273	52	118	**25**
444	1,097	1,428	237	1,856	106	53	219	65	21	**26**
418	696	566	234	164	51	5	33	23	..	**27**
29	*49*	*148*	*51*	*63*	*9*	..	*1*	*16*	..	
390	*647*	*388*	*181*	*83*	*42*	*5*	*32*	*4*	..	
2	..	*30*	*2*	*18*	..	..	..	*3*	..	
271	488	1,231	110	98	80	4	96	5	6	**28**
2	..	..	..	..	..	..	..	..	..	**29**
39	33	206	..	4	9	2	21	1	..	**30**
462	219	743	16	40	6	9	2	..	..	**31**
336	1,930	2,146	236	135	982	25	436	28	12	**32**
..	..	67	15	..	..	..	..	..	..	**33**
47	554	1,226	32	17	5	..	..	..	..	**34**
1,800	1,429	89	16	95	94	38	207	6	..	**35**

Table X.—Occupation or Means of Liveli

Class B.—Preparation and Supply of

Sub-Class III.—Industry

Order 12.—Industries of dress and

Province, State or Agency.	*Group 85.*—Washing and cleaning. Total earners principal occupation.		Total working dependants.		Total following occupation as subsidiary to other.		*Group 86.*—Barbers, hair Total earners principal occupation.	
	Males.	Females.	Males.	Females.	Males.	Females.	Males.	Females.
1	647	648	649	650	651	652	653	654
INDIA	**587,223**	**372,057**	**50,636**	**84,412**	**139,498**	**28,836**	**715,146**	**85,542**
Provinces	**477,163**	**300,824**	**21,802**	**54,119**	**114,015**	**21,420**	**556,080**	**75,412**
1 Ajmer-Merwara	672	331	8	96	84	16	1,754	40
2 Andamans and Nicobars	80	..	..	..	..	..	61	..
3 Assam	1,939	479	101	110	1,228	71	4,316	10
4 Baluchistan (*Districts and Administered Territories*).	441	40	..	1	20	3	479	1
5 Bengal	30,306	7,000	572	1,430	4,110	352	57,704	2,975
6 Bihar and Orissa	45,019	43,085	629	4,010	21,356	5,463	64,769	21,461
7 Bombay (*including Aden*) ..	22,911	6,762	939	1,627	1,058	445	39,728	609
Aden	*156*	*17*	*11*	..	..	..	*117*	*1*
8 Burma	9,018	1,860	220	247	99	29	4,637	58
9 Central Provinces and Berar ..	17,491	12,058	910	4,714	4,709	1,858	38,938	469
10 Coorg	364	214	2	5	81	9	138	2
11 Delhi	2,509	465	20	71	10	..	2,539	110
12 Madras	180,963	136,516	13,657	27,560	24,648	5,239	90,159	1,898
13 North-West Frontier Province (*Districts and Administered Territories*).	4,434	137	235	32	160	..	6,995	29
14 Punjab	41,697	2,720	1,558	975	1,746	124	79,789	2,551
15 United Provinces of Agra and Oudh	119,319	89,157	2,951	13,241	51,706	7,811	164,074	45,199
States and Agencies ..	**110,060**	**71,233**	**28,834**	**30,293**	**25,483**	**7,416**	**159,066**	**10,130**
16 Assam States	44	4	1	1	..	..	64	..
17 Baluchistan States	55	8	2	7	7	..	115	..
18 Baroda State	919	430	87	410	20	3	6,662	64
19 Bengal States	155	23	1	..	5	7	769	4
20 Bihar and Orissa States	5,584	7,297	102	958	3,189	273	4,201	317
21 Bombay States	2,261	858	256	295	381	116	6,779	70
22 Central India Agency	8,438	4,904	98	318	1,898	273	20,627	209
23 Central Provinces States	1,174	829	143	919	662	111	1,868	51
24 Gwalior State	6,331	3,698	285	1,011	976	319	10,823	315
25 Hyderabad State	44,030	26,492	25,274	12,918	7,950	5,193	21,021	4,023
26 Jammu and Kashmir State ..	1,177	124	12	22	236	102	3,733	13
27 Madras States Agency	12,874	14,734	1,046	2,850	1,033	373	13,456	1,345
Cochin State	*1,604*	*4,222*	*28*	*148*	*117*	*68*	*1,756*	*516*
Travancore State	*9,831*	*9,123*	*989*	*2,577*	*636*	*260*	*10,831*	*1,326*
Other Madras States	*4,391*	*1,389*	*29*	*125*	*280*	*46*	*869*	*3*
28 Mysore State	10,648	4,396	925	8,280	7,212	471	6,729	16
29 North-West Frontier Province (*Agencies and Tribal Areas*)	269	..	..	..	..	..	161	..
30 Punjab States	222	39	9	15	47	..	585	40
31 Punjab States Agency	4,355	431	96	151	209	8	8,942	225
32 Rajputana Agency	7,860	4,960	246	1,413	963	132	38,854	2,246
33 Sikkim State	7	1	..	..	..	..	8	..
34 United Provinces States	2,342	1,421	53	277	693	34	2,566	462
35 Western India States Agency ..	1,315	584	198	448	2	..	11,103	230

hood—Part II—Provincial Distribution—*contd.*

Material Substances—*contd.*

—*contd.*

the toilet—*concld.*

dressers and wig-makers.				*Group 87.*—Other industries connected with the toilet.						
Total working dependants.		Total following occupation as subsidiary to other.		Total earners principal occupation.		Total working dependants.		Total following occupation as subsidiary to other.		
Males.	Females.	Males.	Females.	Males.	Females.	Males.	Females.	Males.	Females.	
655	656	657	658	659	660	661	662	663	664	
30,184	**16,349**	**173,208**	**6,142**	**15,075**	**8,396**	**335**	**1,445**	**1,392**	**773**	
17,387	**9,888**	**141,400**	**4,040**	**7,414**	**4,326**	**120**	**576**	**745**	**388**	
3	26	285	2	1,005	282	23	117	23	6	1
..	..	2	..	..	..	..	..	..	..	2
286	5	2,955	2	17	..	..	..	1	..	3
..	..	9	..	3	..	..	..	..	..	4
722	175	10,766	199	329	131	1	7	35	17	5
756	1,073	31,228	1,767	476	1,266	13	20	144	65	6
2,086	173	3,996	41	2,670	381	46	102	35	51	7
6	..	..	..	*2*	..	..	..	..	..	
59	4	64	1	148	36	11	6	80	2	8
1,203	127	6,713	77	378	698	6	116	85	66	9
..	..	68	..	..	..	..	..	..	..	10
80	253	89	1	54	2	..	..	..	..	11
4,318	566	17,672	51	788	589	12	181	216	61	12
460	9	404	1	54	..	..	..	..	..	13
4,432	2,715	5,513	174	271	16	4	..	11	..	14
2,982	4,762	61,636	1,724	1,221	925	4	27	115	120	15
12,797	**6,461**	**31,808**	**2,102**	**7,661**	**4,070**	**215**	**869**	**647**	**385**	
..	..	1	..	20	..	..	12	1	..	16
..	..	44	..	1	..	..	..	..	..	17
322	93	743	4	..	..	..	..	..	..	18
21	..	121	..	..	..	..	..	..	..	19
100	31	2,887	32	30	95	..	6	83	1	20
586	31	1,252	14	35	140	..	..	..	170	21
252	14	4,736	9	320	242	6	18	26	2	22
143	35	733	11	78	193	13	36	26	2	23
479	65	1,371	20	4	8	..	3	..	..	24
7,300	4,236	5,016	1,549	280	20	35	24	26	..	25
125	29	1,243	5	36	12	6	7	3	16	26
638	309	1,522	141	25	10	..	4	99	10	27
11	*12*	*246*	*23*	*21*	..	..	..	*16*	*7*	
610	*295*	*795*	*116*	..	..	..	..	..	..	
17	*2*	*481*	*2*	*4*	*10*	..	*4*	*6*	*3*	
246	1	3,989	..	205	263	10	48	55	34	28
..	..	..	..	..	..	..	..	..	..	29
17	67	197	..	..	..	..	..	..	..	30
518	178	1,228	16	6	..	..	1	..	..	31
520	1,178	5,734	47	6,610	3,079	145	700	405	150	32
..	..	2	..	..	..	..	..	..	..	33
80	121	654	254	..	3	..	8	..	..	34
1,450	73	335	..	11	5	..	2	..	..	35

Table X.—Occupation or Means of Liveli

Class B.—Preparation and Supply of

Sub-Class III.—Industry

Order 13.—

Province, State or Agency.	Total *Order 13.*—Furniture Industries.						*Group 88.*—Cabinet-makers,	
	Total earners principal occupation.		Total working dependants.		Total following occupation as subsidiary to other.		Total earners principal occupation.	
	Males.	Females.	Males.	Females.	Males.	Females.	Males.	Females.
1	665	666	667	668	669	670	671	672
INDIA	**16,545**	**3,171**	**435**	**858**	**2,498**	**388**	**14,027**	**1,884**
Provinces	**13,409**	**2,833**	**274**	**607**	**2,255**	**345**	**11,406**	**1,773**
1 Ajmer-Merwara	49	..	2	..	..	..	46	..
2 Andamans and Nicobars	..	..	..	..	..	..	..	..
3 Assam	124	2	1	..	13	..	45	2
4 Baluchistan .. .. .. (*Districts and Administered Territories*).	567	..	..	..	9	..	566	..
5 Bengal	2,155	691	4	54	116	24	1,834	304
6 Bihar and Orissa	61	165	..	..	11	18	45	136
7 Bombay (*including Aden*) ..	2,811	1,320	125	396	193	255	2,480	1,204
Aden	*12*	*2*	..	..	..	..	*3*	..
8 Burma	862	78	5	41	16	3	830	13
9 Central Provinces and Berar ..	2,579	170	73	78	1,560	18	2,398	19
10 Coorg	..	..	..	..	..	..	..	..
11 Delhi	361	1	..	..	..	..	357	1
12 Madras	1,071	19	35	..	186	12	922	12
13 North-West Frontier Province .. (*Districts and Administered Territories*).	250	..	2	1	4	1	202	..
14 Punjab	1,008	45	17	9	8	..	420	33
15 United Provinces of Agra and Oudh	1,511	342	10	28	139	14	1,261	49
States and Agencies ..	**3,136**	**338**	**161**	**251**	**243**	**43**	**2,621**	**111**
16 Assam States	..	29	..	7	..	14	..	..
17 Baluchistan States	3	12	..	3	..	2	3	..
18 Baroda State	222	35	5	57	21	8	166	1
19 Bengal States	1	..	..	..	..	..	1	..
20 Bihar and Orissa States	..	..	..	..	..	..	..	..
21 Bombay States	33	5	..	..	5	..	33	..
22 Central India Agency	311	91	5	1	16	..	73	..
23 Central Provinces States	151	17	10	21	8	..	140	1
24 Gwalior State	76	15	1	13	12	..	75	15
25 Hyderabad State	550	22	126	54	69	..	495	20
26 Jammu and Kashmir State ..	64	11	..	4	7	7	62	10
27 Madras States Agency	172	1	1	..	38	..	172	1
Cochin State	*124*	*1*	*1*	..	*16*	..	*124*	*1*
Travancore State	*48*	..	..	..	*10*	..	*48*	..
Other Madras States	..	..	..	..	*12*	..	..	..
28 Mysore State	164	6	1	5	23	..	59	..
29 North-West Frontier Province (*Agencies and Tribal Areas.*) ..	..	..	..	..	..	..	..	..
30 Punjab States	1	..	..	..	..	..	1	..
31 Punjab States Agency	19	..	..	..	..	..	19	..
32 Rajputana Agency	1,130	59	..	11	40	6	1,101	55
33 Sikkim State	..	..	..	..	..	..	..	..
34 United Provinces States	28	..	..	..	..	..	23	..
35 Western India States Agency ..	211	35	12	75	4	2	198	8

hood—Part II—Provincial Distribution—*contd.*

Material Substances—*contd.*

—*contd.*

Furniture Industries.

	carriage painters, etc.				Group 89.—Upholsterers, tent-makers, etc.						
	Total working dependants.		Total following occupation as subsidiary to other.		Total earners principal occupation.		Total working dependants.		Total following occupation as subsidiary to other.		
	Males.	Females.	Males.	Females.	Males.	Females.	Males.	Females.	Males.	Females.	
	673	674	675	676	677	678	679	680	681	682	
	367	**554**	**1,335**	**294**	**2,518**	**1,287**	**68**	**304**	**1,163**	**94**	
	225	**389**	**1,143**	**279**	**2,003**	**1,060**	**49**	**218**	**1,112**	**66**	
	2	..	..	..	3	..	..	..	..	..	1
	..	..	..	..	..	..	..	..	..	..	2
	1	..	9	..	79	..	..	..	4	..	3
	..	..	9	..	1	..	..	..	..	..	4
	4	10	98	9	321	387	..	44	18	15	5
	..	..	3	17	16	29	..	..	8	1	6
	117	327	140	252	331	116	8	69	53	3	7
	..	..	..	..	*9*	*2*	..	..	..	..	
	5	17	14	1	32	65	..	24	2	2	8
	53	5	623	..	181	151	20	73	937	18	9
	..	..	..	..	..	..	..	..	..	..	10
	..	..	..	..	4	..	..	..	..	..	11
	26	..	125	..	149	7	9	..	61	12	12
	..	..	3	..	48	..	2	1	1	1	13
	17	9	8	..	588	12	..	..	..	..	14
	..	21	111	..	250	293	10	7	28	14	15
	142	**165**	**192**	**15**	**515**	**227**	**19**	**86**	**51**	**28**	
	..	..	..	..	..	29	..	7	..	14	16
	..	..	..	..	..	12	..	3	..	2	17
	3	6	9	..	56	34	2	51	12	8	18
	..	..	..	..	..	..	..	..	..	..	19
	..	..	..	..	..	..	..	..	..	..	20
	..	..	5	..	..	5	..	..	..	..	21
	1	..	7	..	238	91	4	1	9	..	22
	10	21	7	..	11	16	..	..	1	..	23
	1	13	12	..	1	..	..	..	..	..	24
	120	50	69	4	55	2	6	4	..	..	25
	..	4	7	7	2	1	..	..	..	..	26
	1	..	38	..	..	..	..	..	..	..	27
	1	..	*16*	..	..	..	..	..	..	..	
	..	..	*10*	..	..	..	..	..	..	..	
	..	..	*12*	..	..	..	..	..	..	..	
	..	..	8	..	105	6	1	5	15	..	28
	..	..	..	..	..	..	..	..	..	..	29
	..	..	..	..	..	..	..	..	..	..	30
	..	..	..	..	..	..	..	..	..	..	31
	..	11	30	4	29	4	..	..	10	2	32
	..	..	..	..	..	..	..	..	..	..	33
	..	..	..	..	5	..	..	..	..	..	34
	6	60	..	..	13	27	6	15	4	2	35

Table X.—Occupation or Means of Liveli

Class B.—Preparation and Supply of

Sub-Class III.—Industry

Order 14.—Building

Total *Order 14.*—Building Industries.

Province, State or Agency.	Total earners principal occupation.		Total working dependants.		Total following occupation as subsidiary to other.		Total earners principal occupation.	
	Males.	Females.	Males.	Females.	Males.	Females.	Males.	Females.
1	683	684	685	686	687	688	689	690
INDIA	**511,640**	**74,614**	**16,704**	**15,569**	**68,146**	**6,259**	**511,640**	**74,614**
Provinces	**362,748**	**44,336**	**8,140**	**7,483**	**44,981**	**3,058**	**362,748**	**44,336**
1 Ajmer-Merwara	3,033	718	10	50	222	18	3,033	718
2 Andamans and Nicobars	39	..	..	..	1	..	39	..
3 Assam	4,474	124	87	21	1,344	5	4,474	124
4 Baluchistan .. .. .. (*Districts and Administered Territories.*)	1,619	15	..	..	169	..	1,619	15
5 Bengal	49,551	4,092	366	71	3,032	107	49,551	4,092
6 Bihar and Orissa	21,638	5,172	70	40	5,916	922	21,638	5,172
7 Bombay (*including Aden*)	54,148	6,114	1,811	1,081	4,091	303	54,148	6,114
Aden	*398*	..	*12*	*1*	*2*	..	*398*	..
8 Burma	12,023	707	317	109	1,330	69	12,023	707
9 Central Provinces and Berar ..	22,023	5,415	492	850	2,887	516	22,023	5,415
10 Coorg	238	22	..	..	42	..	238	22
11 Delhi	8,179	539	23	52	107	18	8,179	539
12 Madras	108,615	18,013	3,799	3,930	16,935	1,010	108,615	18,013
13 North-West Frontier Province .. (*Districts and Administered Territories*).	6,354	27	44	10	85	2	6,354	27
14 Punjab	33,459	591	789	150	2,503	20	33,459	591
15 United Provinces of Agra and Oudh	37,355	2,787	332	1,119	5,417	68	37,355	2,787
States and Agencies ..	**148,892**	**30,278**	**8,564**	**8,086**	**23,165**	**3,201**	**148,892**	**30,278**
16 Assam States	428	1	11	..	87	..	428	1
17 Baluchistan States	405	1	3	..	150	1	405	1
18 Baroda State	5,525	463	89	95	556	4	5,525	463
19 Bengal States	301	20	1	..	9	..	301	20
20 Bihar and Orissa States	1,089	2,102	15	544	744	257	1,089	2,102
21 Bombay States	5,589	486	198	148	608	14	5,589	486
22 Central India Agency	8,893	2,920	103	89	1,358	135	8,893	2,920
23 Central Provinces States	685	93	3	15	37	5	685	93
24 Gwalior State	4,097	394	185	127	730	80	4,097	394
25 Hyderabad State	10,641	2,807	3,466	3,421	2,443	1,477	10,641	2,807
26 Jammu and Kashmir State ..	610	25	25	2	83	4	610	25
27 Madras States Agency	25,574	1,563	936	150	2,596	176	25,574	1,563
Cochin State	*7,542*	*596*	*44*	*46*	*677*	*43*	*7,542*	*596*
Travancore State	*15,389*	*654*	*879*	*102*	*1,251*	*114*	*15,389*	*654*
Other Madras States	*2,643*	*313*	*13*	*2*	*668*	*19*	*2,643*	*313*
28 Mysore State	27,102	6,806	515	1,218	8,504	453	27,102	6,806
29 North-West Frontier Province .. (*Agencies and Tribal Areas.*)	28	..	..	..	2	..	28	..
30 Punjab States	653	19	15	11	216	1	653	19
31 Punjab States Agency	6,169	73	199	3	537	..	6,169	73
32 Rajputana Agency	39,882	11,571	370	1,367	4,069	587	39,882	11,571
33 Sikkim State	49	..	..	..	20	..	49	..
34 United Provinces States	431	7	..	..	134	1	431	7
35 Western India States Agency ..	10,741	927	2,430	896	282	6	10,741	927

hood—Part II—Provincial Distribution—*contd.*

Material Substances—*contd.*

—*contd.*

Industries. *Order 15.*—Construction of means of transport.

Group 90.—Lime burners, cement workers ; excavators and well sinkers ; stone cutters and dressers ; brick layers and masons ; builders (other than buildings made of bamboo or similar materials), painters, decorators of houses, tilers, plumbers, etc.

Total *Order 15.*—Construction of means of transport.

Total working dependants.		Total following occupation as subsidiary to other.		Total earners principal occupation.		Total working dependants.		Total following occupation as subsidiary to other.		
Males.	Females.	Males.	Females.	Males.	Females.	Males.	Females.	Males.	Females.	
691	692	693	694	695	696	697	698	699	700	
16,704	**15,569**	**68,146**	**6,259**	**27,432**	**467**	**1,167**	**99**	**4,099**	**38**	
8,140	**7,483**	**44,981**	**3,058**	**21,787**	**379**	**355**	**44**	**3,001**	**17**	
10	50	222	18	10	..	..	3	1	..	1
..	..	1	..	12	..	..	..	..	..	2
87	21	1,344	5	906	..	75	1	1,043	4	3
..	..	169	..	109	..	..	..	2	..	4
366	71	3,932	107	5,252	21	19	..	812	1	5
70	40	5,916	922	519	5	2	..	136	..	6
1,811	1,081	4,091	303	1,818	149	15	1	12	1	7
12	*1*	*2*	..	*35*	..	..	..	..	..	
317	109	1,330	69	6,364	49	143	24	684	8	8
492	850	2,887	516	623	76	11	4	71	1	9
..	..	42	..	66	..	8	..	1	..	10
23	52	107	18	312	1	..	..	1	..	11
3,799	3,930	16,935	1,010	3,399	24	50	5	184	2	12
44	10	85	2	365	..	5	..	15	..	13
789	150	2,503	20	965	..	18	1	15	..	14
332	1,119	5,417	68	1,067	54	9	5	24	..	15
8,564	**8,086**	**23,165**	**3,201**	**5,645**	**88**	**812**	**55**	**1,098**	**21**	
11	..	87	..	50	1	3	..	25	..	16
3	..	150	1	..	..	..	..	1	..	17
89	95	556	4	169	..	7	..	31	..	18
1	..	9	..	28	..	..	..	..	..	19
15	544	744	257	58	..	..	..	76	..	20
198	148	608	14	40	11	1	11	2	..	21
103	89	1,358	135	124	3	9	1	11	1	22
3	15	37	5	21	..	..	1	10	..	23
185	127	730	80	9	..	..	..	45	..	24
3,466	3,421	2,443	1,477	2,085	38	586	37	411	9	25
25	2	83	4	8	..	..	..	..	..	26
936	150	2,596	176	1,140	3	113	2	162	2	27
44	*46*	*677*	*43*	*79*	..	*1*	..	..	*30*	
879	*102*	*1,251*	*114*	*1,024*	*3*	*111*	*2*	*131*	*2*	
13	*2*	*668*	*19*	*37*	..	*1*	..	*1*	..	
515	1,218	8,504	453	937	8	12	..	287	7	28
..	..	2	..	..	..	..	..	..	..	29
15	11	216	1	1	..	..	..	..	..	30
199	3	537	..	362	..	15	..	4	..	31
370	1,367	4,069	587	176	20	..	3	28	1	32
..	..	20	..	3	..	..	..	..	..	33
..	..	134	1	..	3	..	..	..	..	34
2,430	896	282	6	434	1	66	..	5	1	35

Table X.—Occupation or Means of Liveli

Class B.—Preparation and Supply of

Sub-Class III.—Industry

Order 15.—Construction of

Province, State or Agency.	*Group 91.*—Persons engaged in making, assembling or repairing motor vehicles or cycles. Total earners principal occupation.		Total working dependants.		Total following occupation as subsidiary to other.		*Group 92.*—Carriage, cart, Total earners principal occupation.	
	Males.	Females.	Males.	Females.	Males.	Females.	Males.	Females.
1	701	702	703	704	705	706	707	708
INDIA	**12,806**	**190**	**358**	**16**	**801**	**1**	**6,492**	**154**
Provinces	**10,696**	**174**	**147**	**5**	**585**	..	**3,616**	**96**
1 Ajmer-Merwara	10	..	..	3	1	..	..	..
2 Andamans and Nicobars	12	..	..	..	..	..	..	..
3 Assam	533	..	13	..	55	..	201	..
4 Baluchistan (*Districts and Administered Territories*).	109	..	..	..	2	..	..	..
5 Bengal	1,705	1	3	..	256	..	1,142	10
6 Bihar and Orissa	359	1	2	..	80	..	152	4
7 Bombay Presidency (*including Aden*)	1,381	106	15	..	11	..	43	21
Aden	*27*	..	..	..	..	..	*7*	..
8 Burma	1,452	8	45	..	26	..	1,102	25
9 Central Provinces and Berar ..	321	55	6	1	37	..	139	21
10 Coorg	6	..	..	..	..	..	60	..
11 Delhi	296	1	..	..	1	..	16	..
12 Madras	2,449	1	33	1	67	..	568	15
13 North-West Frontier Province (*Districts and Administered Territories*).	243	..	5	..	12	..	102	..
14 Punjab	927	..	16	..	13	..	24	..
15 United Provinces of Agra and Oudh	893	1	9	..	24	..	67	..
States and Agencies ..	**2,110**	**16**	**211**	**11**	**216**	**1**	**2,876**	**58**
16 Assam States	22	..	..	..	..	..	19	1
17 Baluchistan States	..	..	..	..	..	..	..	..
18 Baroda State	105	..	1	..	4	..	49	..
19 Bengal States	12	..	..	..	..	..	15	..
20 Bihar and Orissa States	25	..	..	..	5	..	29	..
21 Bombay States	39	9	1	10	2	..	1	..
22 Central India Agency	118	1	8	..	3	..	6	2
23 Central Provinces States	7	..	..	..	..	..	14	..
24 Gwalior State	9	..	..	..	..	..	..	..
25 Hyderabad State	697	..	175	..	161	..	1,388	38
26 Jammu and Kashmir State ..	8	..	..	..	..	..	..	..
27 Madras States Agency ..	303	..	10	..	18	..	246	3
Cochin State	*36*	..	..	..	*8*	..	*32*	..
Travancore State	*230*	..	*9*	..	*9*	..	*214*	*3*
Other Madras States	*37*	..	*1*	..	*1*	..	..	..
28 Mysore State	484	..	3	..	18	..	451	8
29 North-West Frontier Province (*Agencies and Tribal Areas*).	..	..	..	..	..	..	..	..
30 Punjab States	1	..	..	..	..	..	..	..
31 Punjab States Agency	98	..	2	..	2	..	264	..
32 Rajputana Agency	92	3	..	..	1	1	70	5
33 Sikkim State	..	..	..	..	..	..	3	..
34 United Provinces States	..	3	..	..	..	..	..	..
35 Western India States Agency ..	96	..	11	..	..	..	321	1

hood—Part II—Provincial Distribution—*contd.*

Material Substances—*contd.*

—*contd.*

means of transport—*concld.*

etc. makers and wheel-wrights. | *Group 93.*—**Ship, boat, aeroplane builders.**

Total working dependants.		Total following occupation as subsidiary to other.		Total earners principal occupation.		Total working dependants.		Total following occupation as subsidiary to other.		
Males.	Females.	Males.	Females.	Males.	Females.	Males.	Females.	Males.	Females.	
709	710	711	712	713	714	715	716	717	718	
623	**55**	**1,537**	**27**	**8,134**	**123**	**186**	**28**	**1,761**	**10**	
93	16	772	8	7,475	109	115	23	1,644	9	
..	..	..	..	..	..	..	..	..	..	1
..	..	..	..	..	..	..	..	..	..	2
4	..	47	..	172	..	58	1	941	4	3
..	..	..	..	..	..	..	..	..	..	4
6	..	176	..	2,405	10	10	..	380	1	5
..	..	54	..	8	..	..	..	2	..	6
..	..	..	..	394	22	..	..	1	1	7
..	..	..	..	*1*	..	..	..	..	..	
54	8	410	5	3,810	16	44	16	248	3	8
2	3	17	1	163	..	3	..	17	..	9
8	..	1	..	..	..	..	..	..	..	10
..	..	..	..	..	..	..	..	..	..	11
17	4	62	2	382	8	..	..	55	..	12
..	..	3	..	20	..	..	..	..	..	13
2	1	2	..	14	..	..	..	..	..	14
..	..	..	..	107	53	..	5	..	..	15
530	39	765	19	659	14	71	5	117		
3	..	5	..	9	..	..	..	20	..	16
..	..	..	..	..	..	..	..	1	..	17
4	..	15	..	15	..	2	..	12	..	18
..	..	..	..	1	..	..	..	..	..	19
..	..	71	..	4	..	..	..	..	..	20
..	..	..	..	..	2	..	1	..	..	21
1	..	8	..	..	..	..	1	..		22
..	1	10	..	..	..	..	..	..		23
..	..	45	..	..	..	..	..	..		24
411	37	250	9	..	..	..	..	..	..	25
..	..	..	..	..	..	..	..	..	..	26
34	1	65	2	591	..	69	1	79	..	27
1	..	*18*	..	*11*	..	..	..	*4*	..	
33	*1*	*47*	*2*	*580*	..	*69*	*1*	*76*	..	
..	..	..	..	..	..	..	..	..	..	
9	..	267	7	2	..	..	..	2	..	28
..	..	..	..	..	..	..	..			29
..	..	..	..	..	..	..	..	..	..	30
13	..	2	..	..	..	..	..		..	31
..	..	27	..	14	12	..	2	..	..	32
..	..	..	..		..	..	..	..		33
..	..	..	..	..	..	..	..			34
55	..	..	1	22	..	..	..	3	..	35

Table X.—Occupation or Means of Liveli

Class B.—Preparation and supply

Sub-Class III.—Industry

Province, State or Agency.	Total *Order 16.*—Production and transmission of physical force.						*Order 16.*—Production — *Group 94.*—Heat, light, electricity	
	Total earners principal occupation.		Total working dependants.		Total following occupation as subsidiary to other.		Total earners principal occupation.	
	Males.	Females.	Males.	Females.	Males.	Females.	Males.	Females.
1	719	720	721	722	723	724	725	726
INDIA	**21.232**	**2,221**	**171**	**26**	**1,233**	**24**	**21,232**	**2,221**
Provinces	**16,280**	**2,197**	**68**	**23**	**280**	**21**	**16,280**	**2,197**
1 Ajmer-Merwara	74	..	..	..	4	..	74	..
2 Andamans and Nicobars	7	..	..	..	..	..	7	..
3 Assam	192	..	2	..	9	..	192	..
4 Baluchistan (*Districts and Administered Territories*).	191	..	..	..	..	..	191	..
5 Bengal	3,314	2	1	..	70	..	3,314	2
6 Bihar and Orissa	350	6	2	..	33	..	350	6
7 Bombay (*including Aden*)	2,063	2,013	7	22	10	9	2,063	2,013
Aden	*60*	..	..	..	..	..	*60*	..
8 Burma	2,524	8	26	..	23	..	2,524	8
9 Central Provinces and Berar	415	6	2	..	7	1	415	6
10 Coorg	..	..	..	..	..	..	..	..
11 Delhi	806	4	1	..	..	..	806	4
12 Madras	3,025	107	5	..	70	11	3,025	107
13 North-West Frontier Province (*Districts and Administered Territories.*)	146	..	1	..	7	..	146	..
14 Punjab	1,959	6	19	1	37	..	1,959	6
15 United Provinces of Agra and Oudh	1,214	45	2	..	10	..	1,214	45
States and Agencies	**4,952**	**24**	**103**	**3**	**953**	**3**	**4,952**	**24**
16 Assam States	10	..	..	..	..	..	10	..
17 Baluchistan States	3	..	..	..	..	..	3	..
18 Baroda State	250	10	..	..	2	..	250	10
19 Bengal States	12	..	..	..	..	..	12	..
20 Bihar and Orissa States	45	..	..	..	..	..	45	..
21 Bombay States	64	..	..	..	..	2	64	..
22 Central India Agency	593	4	4	..	17	..	593	4
23 Central Provinces States	21	..	..	..	1	..	21	..
24 Gwalior State	11	..	..	..	32	..	11	..
25 Hyderabad State	214	..	29	3	21	..	214	..
26 Jammu and Kashmir State	53	..	..	..	8	..	53	..
27 Madras States Agency	257	1	1	..	13	..	257	1
Cochin State	*22*	..	..	..	*5*	..	*22*	..
Travancore State	*174*	*1*	*1*	..	*6*	..	*174*	*1*
Other Madras States	*61*	..	..	..	*2*	..	*61*	
28 Mysore State	869	2	6	..	7	..	869	2
29 North-West Frontier Province (*Agencies and Tribal Areas.*)	5	..	..	..	..	..	5	
30 Punjab States	24	..	..	..	4	..	24	..
31 Punjab States Agency	912	..	1	..	827	..	912	..
32 Rajputana Agency	1,159	5	17	..	21	1	1,159	5
33 Sikkim State	5	..	..	..	..	..	5	..
34 United Provinces States	77	..	..	..	..	..	77	..
35 Western India States Agency	368	2	45	..	..	..	368	2

hood—Part II—Provincial Distribution—*contd.*

of Material Substances—*contd.*

—contd.

and transmission of physical force. | *Order 17.*—Miscellaneous and undefined Industries.

motive power, etc., gas works and electric light and power. | Total *Order 17.*—Miscellaneous and undefined Industries.

Total working dependents.		Total following occupation as subsidiary to other.		Total earners principal occupation.		Total working dependants.		Total following occupation as subsidiary to other.		
Males.	Females.	Males.	Females.	Males.	Females.	Males.	Females.	Males.	Females.	
727	728	729	730	731	732	733	734	735	736	
171	**26**	**1,233**	**24**	**1,012,087**	**2,95,909**	**43,526**	**63,124**	**120,443**	**11,442**	
63	23	280	21	803,701	233,699	27,598	43,648	98,570	7,014	
..	..	4	..	3,966	1,209	104	470	96	20	1
..	..	..	..	145	..	..	..	..	..	2
2	..	9	..	8,611	678	501	53	3,281	18	3
..	..	..	..	3,142	388	9	13	46	..	4
1	..	70	..	76,018	8,088	748	805	6,825	163	5
2	..	33	..	55,982	12,377	467	414	41,560	1,211	6
7	22	10	9	66,290	10,005	3,082	1,644	3,302	289	7
..	..	..	..	*721*	*21*	*15*	*19*	*3*	..	
26	..	23	..	30,678	1,515	1,489	299	1,201	42	8
2	..	7	1	38,417	6,178	1,373	862	3,847	504	9
..	..	..	..	397	31	4	3	95	2	10
1	..	..	..	10,383	3,148	252	1,008	117	12	11
5	..	70	11	141,534	11,387	1,873	3,926	11,789	544	12
1	..	7	..	7,120	642	154	66	162	4	13
19	1	37	..	164,750	66,640	12,073	30,113	8,693	1,914	14
2	..	10	..	196,268	111,413	2,469	3,972	17,556	2,291	15
103	**3**	**953**	**3**	**208,386**	**62,210**	**15,928**	**19,476**	**21,873**	**4,428**	
..	..	..	..	932	61	64	37	31	2	16
..	..	..	..	612	14	2	..	24	..	17
..	..	2	..	8,190	2,002	557	486	288	28	18
..	..	..	..	637	77	11	16	222	27	19
..	..	..	..	4,914	2,116	32	256	1,328	73	20
..	..	..	2	8,831	854	420	806	566	74	21
4	..	17	..	9,598	5,819	315	312	1,963	289	22
..	..	1	..	1,888	401	171	129	352	14	23
..	..	32	..	8,824	3,520	389	669	569	192	24
29	3	21	..	22,721	9,532	6,903	5,773	4,668	2,870	25
..	..	8	..	3,885	233	67	44	522	77	26
1	..	13	..	16,622	2,556	1,181	258	799	55	27
..	..	*5*	..	*3,863*	*965*	*45*	*103*	*134*	*26*	
1	..	*6*	..	*11,015*	*1,462*	*1,110*	*150*	*518*	*29*	
..	..	*2*	..	*1,744*	*129*	*26*	..	*147*	..	
6	..	7	..	21,155	2,522	637	253	4,986	54	28
..	..	..	..	674	17	..	..	1	..	29
..	..	4	..	1,622	560	56	236	191	2	30
1	..	827	..	20,019	10,128	1,467	4,027	2,291	236	31
17	..	21		51,327	18,819	1,454	4,863	2,270	425	32
..	..	..	..	57	4	..	..	18	1	33
..	..	..	..	2,012	1,462	48	39	431	1	34
45	..	..	..	13,866	1,513	2,154	1,275	353	8	35

Table X.—Occupation or Means of Liveli

Province, State or Agency.	Class B—Preparation and Supply; Sub-Class III.—Industry; Order 17.—Miscellaneous and unde-; Group 95.—Printers, engravers, book-binders, etc. — Total earners principal occupation. Males.	Females.	Total working dependants. Males.	Females.	Total following occupation as subsidiary to other. Males.	Females.	Group 96.—Makers of musical — Total earners principal occupation. Males.	Females.
1	737	738	739	740	741	742	743	744
INDIA	**50,368**	**598**	**719**	**89**	**993**	**38**	**6,979**	**385**
Provinces	**43,132**	**487**	**342**	**50**	**604**	**20**	**5,303**	**153**
1 Ajmer-Merwara	274	44	4	..	4	..	3	..
2 Andamans and Nicobars	27	..	..	..	..	..	..	..
3 Assam	379	3	17	..	60	..	91	2
4 Baluchistan (*Districts and Administered Territories*).	65	..	..	..	..	..	..	..
5 Bengal	13,891	57	3	1	175	4	1,945	8
6 Bihar and Orissa ...	365	5	4	..	48	..	836	36
7 Bombay (*including Aden*) ..	5,006	155	117	43	45	..	1,077	30
Aden	12	..	..	..	..	..	..	..
8 Burma	4,285	63	48	1	17	4	102	4
9 Central Provinces and Berar ..	1,129	36	3	1	23	12	383	59
10 Coorg	5	..	..	..	1	..	..	..
11 Delhi	1,052	5	1	..	..	..	27	..
12 Madras	9,576	44	99	2	123	..	299	1
13 North-West Frontier Province (*Districts and Administered Territories*).	364	..	..	..	7	..	28	..
14 Punjab	3,328	9	6	..	56	..	150	..
15 United Provinces of Agra and Oudh	3,386	66	40	2	45	..	362	12
States and Agencies ..	**7,236**	**111**	**377**	**39**	**389**	**18**	**1,676**	**232**
16 Assam States	153	2	..	..	..	..	6	..
17 Baluchistan States	..	..	..	..	..	..	..	..
18 Baroda State	558	..	8	..	9	..	64	2
19 Bengal States	70	..	3	..	7	..	7	..
20 Bihar and Orissa States	69	..	..	..	4	1	199	18
21 Bombay States	71	4	6	7	2	..	95	..
22 Central India Agency	391	5	..	..	22	..	14	..
23 Central Provinces States	15	..	..	..	3	..	246	..
24 Gwalior State	333	1	..	..	..	..	23	174
25 Hyderabad State	653	..	184	..	157	..	75	..
26 Jammu and Kashmir State ..	26	..	..	..	1	..	4	..
27 Madras States Agency	2,286	28	68	..	110	16	84	22
Cochin State	*643*	*2*	*9*	..	*35*	..	*5*	..
Travancore State	*1,580*	*26*	*59*	..	*73*	*16*	*79*	*22*
Other Madras States	*63*	..	..	..	*2*	..	..	..
28 Mysore State	1,336	17	13	30	49	..	78	..
29 North-West Frontier Province (*Agencies and Tribal Areas*).	..	..	..	..	..	..	..	..
30 Punjab States	21	..	..	..	2	..	..	..
31 Punjab States Agency	159	..	14	..	5	..	25	..
32 Rajputana Agency	342	46	6	..	15	..	26	3
33 Sikkim State	6	..	..	..	1	..	..	..
34 United Provinces States	..	..	..	..	..	..	..	..
35 Western India States Agency ...	747	8	75	2	2	1	730	13

hood—Part II—Provincial Distribution—*contd.*

of Material Substances—*contd.*

—*contd.*

fined Industries.—*contd.*

instruments. | *Group 97*.—Makers of clocks and surgical or scientific instruments, etc.

Total working dependants. Males.	Total working dependants. Females.	Total following occupation as subsidiary to other. Males.	Total following occupation as subsidiary to other. Females.	Total earners principal occupation. Males.	Total earners principal occupation. Females.	Total working dependants. Males.	Total working dependants. Females.	Total following occupation as subsidiary to other. Males.	Total following occupation as subsidiary to other. Females.	
745	746	747	748	749	750	751	752	753	754	
871	**115**	**931**	**17**	**8,704**	**65**	**142**	**17**	**501**	**1**	
223	**59**	**598**	**12**	**6,970**	**59**	**41**	**17**	**369**	**1**	
..	..	1	..	69	1	..	..	5	..	1
..	..	..	..	1	..	..	..	..	..	2
4	..	51	..	91	..	1	..	34	..	3
..	..	..	..	39	..	..	..	..	..	4
11	1	133	5	871	34	..	16	49	..	5
18	20	208	5	202	..	1	..	22	..	6
123	..	68	..	883	8	9	1	50	..	7
..	..	..	..	*24*	..	..	..	..	..	
2	..	13	..	621	1	12	..	29	..	8
23	31	99	2	257	1	1	..	14	1	9
..	..	..	..	4	..	1	..	..	..	10
..	..	..	..	279	..	..	..	..	..	11
33	7	20	..	930	6	3	..	114	..	12
..	..	..	..	142	1	1	..	6	..	13
1	..	..	..	1,494	..	12	..	30	..	14
3	..	5	..	1,087	7	..	..	16	..	15
148	**56**	**333**	**5**	**1,734**	**6**	**101**	..	**132**	..	
1	..	2	..	11	..	3	..	1	..	16
..	..	..	..	..	..	..	..	..	..	17
3	..	10	..	112	..	3	..	8	..	18
1	..	..	..	15	..	..	..	1	..	19
..	..	91	2	2	..	..	..	..	..	20
7	..	14	..	31	..	..	..	3	..	21
..	..	38	1	128	2	..	..	14	..	22
9	1	101	..	10	..	1	..	1	..	23
2	48	25	..	40	2	2	..	2	..	24
16	..	15	..	504	..	79	..	33	..	25
..	..	..	..	61	..	..	..	4	..	26
22	..	11	2	206	..	2	..	12	..	27
..	..	*1*	..	*187*	..	..	..	*7*	..	
22	..	*6*	*2*	*9*	..	*2*	..	*3*	..	
..	..	*4*	..	*10*	..	..	..	*2*	..	
..	..	13	..	120	..	..	..	17	..	28
..	..	..	..	2	..	..	..	..	..	29
..	..	..	..	5	..	1	..	..	..	30
..	..	..	..	186	..	1	..	15	..	31
..	..	3	..	207	2	4	..	14	..	32
..	..	..	..	..	..	..	..	..	..	33
..	..	..	..	7	..	..	..	..	..	34
87	7	10	..	87	..	5	..	7	..	35

Table X.—Occupation or Means of Liveli

Class B.—Preparation and Supply

Sub-Class III.—Industry

Order 17.—Miscellaneous and unde-

Province, State or Agency.	*Group 98.*—Makers of jewellery and ornaments. Total earners principal occupation. Males.	Females.	Total working dependants. Males.	Females.	Total following occupation as subsidiary to other. Males.	Females.	*Group 99.*—Other miscellaneous. Total earners principal occupation. Males.	Females.
1	755	756	757	758	759	760	761	762
INDIA	**542,650**	**20,549**	**23,133**	**9,691**	**90,602**	**3,633**	**33,686**	**10,574**
Provinces	**420,837**	**10,686**	**12,898**	**4,457**	**75,053**	**901**	**25,360**	**6,937**
1 Ajmer-Merwara	1,374	23	34	22	37	..	231	69
2 Andamans and Nicobars	12	..	..	..	..	..	..	..
3 Assam	5,960	28	452	9	2,676	7	125	17
4 Baluchistan (*Districts and Administered Territories*).	345	..	1	..	20	..	14	..
5 Bengal	42,256	1,648	541	11	5,564	41	1,148	750
6 Bihar and Orissa	40,398	1,934	378	111	39,390	286	5,319	2,435
7 Bombay (*including Aden*)	35,726	718	1,732	130	2,376	43	6,876	1,848
Aden	*111*	..	..	..	..	..	*6*	*3*
8 Burma	18,466	677	1,328	113	1,070	26	209	164
9 Central Provinces and Berar	28,623	568	1,199	151	3,398	92	1,300	290
10 Coorg	340	6	3	1	93	..	1	..
11 Delhi	2,273	48	19	1	3	..	645	29
12 Madras	115,730	2,139	4,281	3,329	9,088	76	565	103
13 North-West Frontier Province (*Districts and Administered Territories*).	3,001	41	94	12	115	..	15	..
14 Punjab	46,162	512	1,780	91	1,756	24	5,094	572
15 United Provinces of Agra and Oudh	80,171	2,344	1,056	476	9,467	306	3,818	660
States and Agencies	**121,813**	**9,863**	**10,235**	**5,234**	**15,549**	**2,732**	**8,326**	**3,637**
16 Assam States	532	53	55	36	19	2	6	..
17 Baluchistan States	397	..	2	..	18	..	1	..
18 Baroda State	3,804	25	415	34	52	1	126	2
19 Bengal States	368	5	7	..	210	..	..	2
20 Bihar and Orissa States	3,923	142	31	21	1,195	31	20	1
21 Bombay States	6,453	206	213	62	405	21	863	279
22 Central India Agency	11,080	281	199	16	987	50	1,786	832
23 Central Provinces States	1,270	61	148	52	229	8	72	31
24 Gwalior State	3,083	109	106	36	246	50	102	15
25 Hyderabad State	16,414	7,263	5,009	4,132	3,970	2,508	1,084	963
26 Jammu and Kashmir State	3,350	19	42	3	453	..	48	21
27 Madras States Agency	12,815	124	1,068	139	576	4	425	341
Cochin State	*2,769*	*67*	*34*	*5*	*65*	*1*	*92*	*336*
Travancore State	*8,523*	*48*	*1,009*	*134*	*379*	*3*	*332*	*5*
Other Madras States	*1,523*	*9*	*25*	..	*132*	..	*1*	..
28 Mysore State	16,285	277	604	157	4,791	29	246	101
29 North-West Frontier Province (*Agencies and Tribal Areas.*)	57	..	..	..	..	..	..	..
30 Punjab States	520	..	30	3	119	1	8	1
31 Punjab States Agency	6,783	79	488	15	548	3	167	11
32 Rajputana Agency	25,049	1,160	506	421	1,086	23	3,359	1,035
33 Sikkim State	18	2	..	..	17	1	..	..
34 United Provinces States	990	22	9	4	402	..	..	..
35 Western India States Agency	8,622	35	1,303	103	226	..	13	2

hood—Part II—Provincial Distribution—*contd.*

of Material Substances—*contd.*

—*concld.*

fined Industries—*concld.*

and undefined industries (toy-making, taxidermy, etc.)				*Group 100.*—Scavenging.						
Total working dependants.		Total following occupation as subsidiary to other.		Total earners principal occupation.		Total working dependants.		Total following occupation as subsidiary to other.		
Males.	Females.	Males.	Females.	Males.	Females.	Males.	Females.	Males.	Females.	
763	764	765	766	767	768	769	770	771	772	
1,166	**2,624**	**4,388**	**1,113**	**369,700**	**263,738**	**17,995**	**50,588**	**23,028**	**6,640**	
682	**1,122**	**3,356**	**684**	**302,099**	**215,377**	**13,412**	**37,943**	**18,590**	**5,396**	
7	34	8	6	2,015	1,072	59	414	41	14	1
..	..	..	..	105	..	..	..	..	..	2
9	7	154	..	1,965	628	18	37	306	11	3
..	..	25	..	2,679	388	8	13	1	..	4
118	143	311	47	15,907	5,591	70	633	593	66	5
39	68	1,142	239	8,862	7,967	27	215	750	681	6
175	313	564	148	16,722	7,246	926	1,157	199	98	7
1	..	1	..	568	18	14	19	2	..	
16	127	10	10	6,995	606	83	58	62	2	8
28	161	112	184	6,725	5,224	119	518	201	213	9
	..	..	..	47	25	..	2	1	2	10
1	2	..	..	6,107	3,066	231	1,005	114	12	11
50	15	453	1	14,434	9,094	407	573	1,991	467	12
2	..	6	..	3,570	600	57	54	28	4	13
148	183	283	26	108,522	65,547	10,126	29,839	6,568	1,864	14
89	69	288	23	107,444	108,323	1,281	3,425	7,735	1,962	15
484	**1,502**	**1,032**	**429**	**67,601**	**48,361**	**4,583**	**12,645**	**4,438**	**1,244**	
5	..	3	..	224	6	..	1	6	..	16
..	..	2	..	214	14	..	..	4	..	17
2	..	23	2	3,526	1,973	126	452	186	25	18
..	..	..	..	177	70	..	16	4	27	19
..	..	1	..	701	1,955	1	235	37	39	20
3	71	91	49	1,318	365	191	666	51	4	21
34	50	510	52	6,199	4,699	82	246	392	186	22
10	2	3	..	275	309	3	74	15	6	23
6	2	12	2	5,243	3,219	273	583	284	140	24
293	890	125	280	3,991	1,306	1,322	751	368	82	25
..	..	12	19	396	193	25	41	52	58	26
13	97	75	10	806	2,041	8	17	15	23	27
2	*85*	*25*	*10*	*167*	*560*	..	*13*	*1*	*15*	
11	*12*	*50*	..	*492*	*1,361*	*7*	*4*	*7*	*8*	
..	..	..	..	*147*	*120*	*1*	..	*7*	..	
5	11	8	6	3,090	2,127	15	55	108	19	28
..	..	..	..	615	17	..	..	1	..	29
..	.	3	..	1,668	559	25	233	67	1	30
7	9	8	..	12,699	10,038	957	4,003	1,715	233	31
106	360	156	9	22,344	16,573	832	4,084	996	393	32
..	..	..	..	33	2	..	..	..	..	33
..	..	..	..	1,015	1,440	39	35	29	1	34
..	10	..	..	3,667	1,455	684	1,153	108	7	35

Table X.—Occupation or Means of Liveli

Class B.—Preparation and Supply

Sub-Class IV.—Trans-

Province, State or Agency.	Total *Sub-Class IV.*—Transport. Total earners principal occupation. Males.	Females.	Total working dependants. Males.	Females.	Total following occupation as subsidiary to other. Males.	Females.	Total *Order 18.*—Trans- Total earners principal occupation. Males.	Females.
1	773	774	775	776	777	778	779	780
INDIA ..	**1,991,686**	**171,184**	**107,512**	**71,024**	**403,499**	**33,615**	**295**	**11**
Provinces ..	**1,577,984**	**99,309**	**35,817**	**11,303**	**319,951**	**10,831**	**275**	**11**
1 Ajmer-Merwara ..	14,348	390	27	19	764	4	..	..
2 Andamans and Nicobars	980	..	..	1	25	—	..	—
3 Assam ..	47,865	2,159	1,497	225	24,987	512	..	..
4 Baluchistan (*Districts and Administered Territories*).	14,575	294	73	4	2,002	34	40	..
5 Bengal ..	264,249	12,171	2,217	294	32,549	1,874	102	5
6 Bihar and Orissa ..	99,019	12,959	478	433	42,411	2,236	..	..
7 Bombay (*including Aden*)	182,244	11,248	4,891	2,169	11,189	637	40	6
Aden	*5,923*	*8*	*115*	*4*	*15*	—	*1*	—
8 Burma ..	198,606	9,911	10,778	2,760	51,893	1,523	57	..
9 Central Provinces and Berar	81,814	11,033	1,385	1,105	14,970	838	..	—
10 Coorg ..	1,502	11	26	2	892	5	—	—
11 Delhi ..	20,829	695	70	77	591	4	29	—
12 Madras	251,063	31,188	6,883	3,092	82,370	2,448	..	—
13 North-West Frontier Province (*Districts and Administered Territories*).	17,719	75	587	22	3,286	14	—	—
14 Punjab ..	190,574	2,354	5,232	838	14,752	139	7	—
15 United Provinces of Agra and Oudh	192,597	4,821	1,673	262	37,270	563	—	..
States and Agencies	**413,702**	**71,875**	**71,695**	**59,721**	**83,548**	**22,784**	**20**	—
16 Assam States ..	2,514	390	214	110	1,256	343	—	—
17 Baluchistan States ..	2,876	56	82	4	2,170	11	—	—
18 Baroda State ..	13,083	2,335	250	195	1,465	36	—	—
19 Bengal States ..	3,802	131	27	392	308	—	—	—
20 Bihar and Orissa States ..	11,238	7,256	761	1,516	3,996	309	..	—
21 Bombay States ..	9,268	325	399	341	2,259	271	..	..
22 Central India Agency	23,860	2,296	338	130	9,630	214	..	..
23 Central Provinces States ..	5,803	1,724	738	763	1,274	167	..	..
24 Gwalior State ..	6,859	617	195	129	2,051	131	..	..
25 Hyderabad State ..	146,588	48,047	59,750	51,811	23,800	20,782	..	..
26 Jammu and Kashmir State	8,468	455	388	74	1,817	60	4	..
27 Madras States Agency ..	50,559	1,243	2,466	263	8,719	89	..	..
Cochin State ..	*13,919*	*545*	*120*	*10*	*2,294*	*31*	..	—
Travancore State ..	*34,552*	*540*	*2,287*	*249*	*3,888*	*50*	—	—
Other Madras States ..	*2,088*	*158*	*59*	*4*	*2,537*	*8*	—	—
28 Mysore State ..	22,383	1,834	564	427	14,287	150	..	—
29 North-West Frontier Province (*Agencies and Tribal Areas*).	1,108	..	—	—	12	—	—	—
30 Punjab States ..	1,303	22	37	86	576	4	..	—
31 Punjab States Agency ..	24,983	364	474	94	2,398	25	..	—
32 Rajputana Agency ..	47,127	3,061	441	475	6,712	137	16	—
33 Sikkim State ..	404	103	3	1	120	49	..	—
34 United Provinces States ..	2,407	110	61	..	164	..	..	..
35 Western India States Agency	29,069	1,506	4,507	2,910	534	6	..	—

hood—Part II—Provincial Distribution—*contd.*

of Material Substances—*contd.*

port.

Order 18.—Transport by air.

port by air.				*Group 101.*—Persons concerned with aerodromes and æroplanes.						
Total working dependants.		Total following occupation as subsidiary to other.		Total earners principal occupation.		Total working dependants.		Total following occupation as subsidiary to other.		
Males.	Females.	Males.	Females.	Males.	Females.	Males.	Females.	Males.	Females.	
781	782	783	784	785	786	787	788	789	790	
..	..	**24**	..	**295**	**11**	..	..	**24**	..	
..	..	**23**	..	**275**	**11**	..	..	**23**	..	
..	..	..	..	..	..	..	..	..	..	1
..	..	..	..	..	..	..	..	..	..	2
..	..	..	..	..	..	..	..	..	..	3
..	..	..	..	40	..	..	..	..	..	4
..	..	22	..	102		..	..	22	..	5
..	..	..	..	..	..	..	..	..	..	6
..	..	..	..	40		..	..	..	..	7
..	..	..	..	*1*	..	..	..	..	..	
..	..	1	..	57	..	..	..	1	..	8
..	..	..	..	..	..	..	..	..	..	9
..	..	..	..	..	..	..	..	..	..	10
..	..	..	..	29	..	..	..	..	..	11
..	..	..	..	..		..	..	..	..	12
..	..	..	..	..	..	..	..	..	..	13
..	..	..	..	7	..	..	..	..	..	14
..	..	..	..	..	..	..	..	..	..	15
..	..	1	..	20	..	..	..	1	..	
..	..	..	..	..	..	..	..	..	..	16
..	..	..	..	..	..	..	..	..	..	17
..	..	..	..	..	..	..	..	..	..	18
..	..	..	..	..	..	..	..	..	..	19
..	..	..	..	..	..	..	..	..	..	20
..	..	..	..	..	..	..	..	..	..	21
..	..	..	..	..	..	..	..	..	..	22
..	..	..	..	..	..	..	..	..	..	23
..	..	..	..	..	..	..	..	..	..	24
..	..	..	..	..	..	..	..	..	..	25
..	..	..	..		..	..	..	..	..	26
..	..	..	..	..	..	..	..	..	..	27
..	..	..	..	..	..	..	..	..	..	
..	..	..	..	..	..	..	..	..	..	
..	..	..	..	..	..	..	..	..	..	
..	..	..	..	..	..	..	..	..	..	28
..	..	..	..	..	..	..	..	..	..	29
..	..	..	..	..	..	..	..	..	..	30
..	..	..	..	..	..	..	..	..	..	31
..	..	1	..	16	..	..	..	1	..	32
..	..	..	..	..	..	..	..	..		33
..	..	..	..	..	..	..	..	..	..	34
..	..	..	..	..	..	..	..	..	..	35

Table X.—Occupation or Means of Liveli

Class B.—Preparation and Supply

Sub-Class IV.—Transport

Order 19.—Transport by

Province, State or Agency.	Total *Order 19.*—Transport by water.						*Group 102.*—Ship-owners,	
	Total earners principal occupation.		Total working dependants.		Total following occupation as subsidiary to other.		Total earners principal occupation.	
	Males.	Females.	Males.	Females.	Males.	Females.	Males.	Females.
1	791	792	793	794	795	796	797	798
INDIA	**338,081**	**10,398**	**10,614**	**2,881**	**38,230**	**1,033**	**261,696**	**3,204**
Provinces	**291,272**	**8,628**	**5,949**	**1,528**	**30,954**	**423**	**229,895**	**2,752**
1 Ajmer-Merwara	3	..	..	..	..	..	2	..
2 Andamans and Nicobars	582	..	..	..	4	..	569	..
3 Assam	12,247	11	644	4	6,908	15	11,877	11
4 Baluchistan (*Districts and Administered Territories*).	..	..	..	..	..	..	..	..
5 Bengal	81,046	245	882	5	7,992	57	76,994	207
6 Bihar and Orissa	8,600	478	104	90	2,797	49	8,316	477
7 Bombay (*including Aden*) ..	57,424	3,866	1,600	1,057	2,550	93	33,361	584
Aden	*4,335*	*5*	*32*	*4*	*7*	..	*2,938*	*5*
8 Burma	70,506	1,277	1,757	135	5,356	67	62,202	658
9 Central Provinces and Berar ..	2,774	1,003	29	13	453	79	621	12
10 Coorg	2	..	..	..	..	..	2	..
11 Delhi	336	..	1	..	5	..	93	..
12 Madras	28,778	732	298	41	2,197	3	23,663	125
13 North-West Frontier Province (*Districts and Administered Territories*).	904	2	25	..	20	1	622	2
14 Punjab	12,526	193	421	58	670	5	3,003	15
15 United Provinces of Agra and Oudh	15,544	821	188	125	2,002	54	8,570	661
States and Agencies ..	**46,809**	**1,770**	**4,665**	**1,353**	**7,276**	**610**	**31,801**	**452**
16 Assam States	40	..	1	..	176	..	40	..
17 Baluchistan States	81	..	..	..	4	..	81	..
18 Baroda State	943	11	26	2	73	..	708	2
19 Bengal States	295	..	1	..	39	..	295	..
20 Bihar and Orissa States	2,597	15	6	2	1,060	3	2,595	15
21 Bombay States	2,291	13	36	168	151	2	1,642	13
22 Central India Agency	445	36	6	2	220	1	389	34
23 Central Provinces States	145	..	34	..	18	..	115	..
24 Gwalior State	54	1	..	..	77	5	45	1
25 Hyderabad State	5,410	624	2,987	981	1,285	526	..	..
26 Jammu and Kashmir State ..	3,743	184	221	71	1,152	42	3,098	180
27 Madras States Agency	16,934	158	1,054	8	2,088	11	15,900	159
Cochin State	*4,545*	*9*	*58*	*1*	*782*	*5*	*4,119*	*9*
Travancore State	*12,389*	*149*	*996*	*7*	*1,306*	*6*	*11,781*	*147*
Other Madras States	..	..	..	..	..	..	..	..
28 Mysore State	748	403	28	17	269	17	151	2
29 North-West Frontier Province (*Agencies and Tribal Areas*).	..	..	..	..	..	..	..	..
30 Punjab States	42	..	3	..	5	..	7	..
31 Punjab States Agency	3,526	34	12	.	480	3	340	9
32 Rajputana Agency	501	..	1	..	109	..	213	..
33 Sikkim State	..	1	..	..	..	..	..	1
34 United Provinces States	321	..	6	..	1	..	205	..
35 Western India States Agency ..	8,693	290	243	102	69	..	5,8[illegible]	39

hood—Part II—Provincial Distribution—*contd.*

of Material Substances—*contd.*

—*contd.*

water—*contd.*

boat-owners and their employees, officers, mariners, etc., ships brokers, boatmen and tow men.				Group 103.—Persons (other than labourers) employed in harbours, docks, rivers and canals, including pilots.						
Total working dependants.		Total following occupation as subsidiary to other.		Total earners principal occupation.		Total working dependants.		Total following occupation as subsidiary to other.		
Males.	Females.	Males.	Females.	Males.	Females.	Males.	Females.	Males.	Females.	
799	800	801	802	803	804	805	806	807	808	
6,343	**692**	**34,022**	**297**	**33,217**	**749**	**664**	**59**	**1,023**	**8**	
4,891	**423**	**29,178**	**235**	**27,078**	**624**	**558**	**31**	**631**	**6**	
..	..	..	..	1	..	..	..	..	..	1
..	..	4	..	..	..	..	..	..	..	2
644	4	6,900	15	112	..	..	..	5	..	3
..	..	..	..	..	..	..	..	..	..	4
879	5	7,977	56	2,139	38	3	..	8	1	5
104	90	2,754	49	193	..	..	..	19	..	6
856	78	2,204	7	7,726	503	413	27	72	1	7
32	*4*	*7*	..	*930*	..	..	..	..	..	
1,698	116	5,158	54	913	4	6	..	12	..	8
20	5	254	2	905	69	5	4	36	3	9
..	..	..	..	..	..	..	..	..	..	10
..	..	..	..	239	..	1	..	5	..	11
212	1	2,114	2	1,554	6	46	..	9	1	12
25	..	19	1	80	..	..	..	1	..	13
293	..	381	..	7,492	4	61	..	112	..	14
160	124	1,413	49	5,724	..	23	..	352	..	15
1,452	**269**	**4,844**	**62**	**6,139**	**125**	**106**	**28**	**392**	**2**	
1	..	176	..	..	..	..	..	..	..	16
..	..	4	..	..	..	..	..	..	..	17
26	2	35	..	162	..	..	..	..	..	18
1	..	39	..	..	..	..	..	..	..	19
6	2	1,060	3	2	..	..	..	..	..	20
4	167	140	2	491	..	30	1	10	..	21
6	..	216	1	40	..	..	1	4	..	22
34	..	16	..	30	..	..	..	2	..	23
..	..	56	5	..	..	..	..	21	..	24
..	..	..	..	..	..	..	..	..	..	25
208	71	1,024	42	236	..	..	..	75	..	26
1,012	8	1,815	9	511	..	17	..	159	2	27
57	*1*	*573*	*3*	*241*	..	..	..	*139*	*2*	
955	*7*	*1,242*	*6*	*270*	..	*17*	..	*20*	..	
..	..	..	..	..	..	..	..	..	..	
3	..	81		10	..	..	..	9	..	28
..	..	..	..	..	..	..	..	..	..	29
3	..	1	..	23	..	..	..	4	..	30
6	..	42	..	2,841	..	6	..	77	..	31
..	..	82	..	288	..	1	..	27	..	32
..	..	..	..	..	..	..	..	..	..	33
6	..	1	..	18	..	..	..	..	..	34
136	19	56	..	1,487	125	52	26	4	..	35

Table X.—Occupation or Means of Liveli

Province, State or Agency.	Class B.—Preparation and Supply — Sub-Class IV.—Transport — Order 19.—Transport by water—concld. — Group 104.—Labourers employed on harbours, docks, rivers and canals. — Total earners principal occupation.		Total working dependants.		Total following occupation as subsidiary to other.		Total Order 20.—Transport — Total earners principal occupation.	
	Males.	Females.	Males.	Females.	Males.	Females.	Males.	Females.
1	809	810	811	812	813	814	815	816
INDIA	**43,168**	**6,445**	**3,607**	**2,130**	**3,185**	**728**	**1,008,431**	**132,443**
Provinces	**34,299**	**5,252**	**500**	**1,074**	**1,145**	**182**	**771,004**	**78,680**
1 Ajmer-Merwara	..	..	..	..	..	..	2,319	319
2 Andamans and Nicobars	13	..	..	..	..	..	376	..
3 Assam	258	..	..	..	3	..	21,782	1,529
4 Baluchistan (*Districts and Administered Territories*).	..	..	..	..	..	..	7,739	294
5 Bengal	1,913	..	..	..	7	..	105,424	10,019
6 Bihar and Orissa	91	1	..	..	24	..	57,733	11,611
7 Bombay (*including Aden*) ..	16,337	2,779	331	952	274	85	50.259	3,971
Aden	*467*	..	..	..	..	..	*1,464*	*3*
8 Burma	7,391	615	53	19	186	13	96,354	7,737
9 Central Provinces and Berar ..	1,248	922	4	4	163	74	43,642	8,282
10 Coorg	..	..	..	..	..	..	1,442	7
11 Delhi	4	..	..	..	..	..	10,421	671
12 Madras	3,561	601	40	40	74	..	157,659	29,373
13 North-West Frontier Province (*Districts and Administered Territories*).	202	..	..	..	..	..	13,584	63
14 Punjab	2,031	174	67	58	177	5	96,761	1,628
15 United Provinces of Agra and Oudh	1,250	160	5	1	237	5	105,509	3,176
States and Agencies ..	**8,869**	**1,193**	**3,107**	**1,056**	**2,040**	**546**	**237,427**	**53,763**
16 Assam States	..	..	..	..	..	..	2,371	390
17 Baluchistan States	..	..	..	..	..	..	2,634	56
18 Baroda State	73	9	..	..	38	..	4,524	2,043
19 Bengal States	..	..	..	..	..	..	3,049	129
20 Bihar and Orissa States	..	..	..	..	..	..	6,735	6,936
21 Bombay States	158	..	2	..	1	..	4,804	270
22 Central India Agency	16	2	..	1	..	..	14,831	2,109
23 Central Provinces States	..	..	..	..	..	..	4,373	1,427
24 Gwalior State	9	..	..	..	..	..	4,247	420
25 Hyderabad State	5,410	624	2,987	981	1,285	526	95,793	33,642
26 Jammu and Kashmir State	409	4	13	..	53	..	3,828	270
27 Madras States Agency	423	2	25	..	114	..	28,574	788
Cochin State	*185*	..	*1*	..	*70*	..	*8,346*	*372*
Travancore State	*338*	*2*	*24*	..	*44*	..	*18,575*	*321*
Other Madras States	..	..	..	..	..	..	*1,653*	*95*
28 Mysore State	587	401	25	17	179	17	13,382	1,195
29 North-West Frontier Province (*Agencies and Tribal Areas*).	..	..	..	..	..	..	869	..
30 Punjab States	12	..	..	..	..	..	926	21
31 Punjab States Agency	345	25	..	..	361	3	10,101	313
32 Rajputana Agency	..	..	..	..	..	..	23,969	2,429
33 Sikkim State	..	..	..	..	..	..	350	102
34 United Provinces States	8	..	..	..	..	..	1,800	109
35 Western India States Agency ..	1,319	126	55	57	9	..	10,267	1,114

hood—Part II—Provincial Distribution—*contd.*

of Material Substances—*contd.*

—*contd.*

Order 20.—Transport by road.

by road.				*Group 105.*—Persons (other than labourers) employed on the construction and maintenance of roads and bridges.						
Total working dependants.		Total following occupation as subsidiary to other.		Total earners principal occupation.		Total working dependants.		Total following occupation as subsidiary to other.		
Males.	Females.	Males.	Females.	Males.	Females.	Males.	Females.	Males.	Females.	
817	818	819	820	821	822	823	824	825	826	
74,649	**43,904**	**331,945**	**19,437**	**18,796**	**694**	**588**	**106**	**1,695**	**84**	
27,003	9,047	268,550	9,949	14,034	456	229	62	1,261	76	
	13	640	3	35	..	..	..	9	..	1
..	1	19	..	6	..	..	..	..	..	2
715	190	16,657	494	840	4	6	..	246	..	3
73	4	1,979	34	60	..	..	..	..	..	4
1,218	285	22,553	1,779	350	10	77	..	63	2	5
307	308	33,315	2,121	181	54	..	..	30	14	6
2,473	703	7,481	430	1,747	5	4	1	45	..	7
73	..	*8*	..	*42*	..	..	..	..	..	
8,883	2,535	46,310	1,448	3,500	42	35	17	116	..	8
1,133	1,053	13,498	619	2,736	148	19	28	211	36	
26	1	868	..	8	..	..	..	..	..	10
67	77	565	4	53	1	..	..	1	..	11
6,199	2,984	76,724	2,405	1,658	160	22	12	264	24	12
540	19	2,980	12	545	1	8	..	77	..	13
3,931	737	12,314	133	1,942	26	56	4	176	..	14
1,430	137	32,647	467	373	5	2	..	23	..	15
47,646	34,857	63,395	9,488	4,762	238	359	44	434	8	
213	109	1,078	343	156	1	7	..	..	..	16
82	4	2,161	11	3	..	..	..	..	..	17
219	193	1,273	36	9	..	..	..	..	..	18
25	392	240	..	4	..	..	..	2	..	19
645	1,489	2,397	288	46	..	..	..	10	..	20
318	158	2,050	268	80	..	..	..	2	..	21
310	126	9,187	200	283	7	3	1	56	..	22
669	763	1,234	126	147	4	..	2	3	..	23
174	87	1,901	126	26	..	..	1	..	..	24
38,963	27,568	13,021	7,657	1,068	37	319	20	108	2	25
162	1	528	18	571	2	..	..	38	..	26
1,345	242	6,426	67	1,069	2	18	..	66	..	27
60	*7*	*1,443*	*26*	*143*	..	*2*	..	*35*	..	
1,226	*231*	*2,487*	*34*	*819*	*2*	*16*	..	*26*	..	
59	*4*	*2,496*	*7*	*107*	..	..	..	*5*	..	
517	400	13,468	133	294	78	3	1	120	4	28
..	..	12	..	16	..	..	..	..	..	29
25	86	386	4	4	..	..	..	11	..	30
332	94	1,477	22	640	..	9	13	5	..	31
399	421	5,932	134	169	73	..	3	12	..	32
3	1	108	49	4	..	..	..	1	..	33
55	..	149	..	34	..	..	..	..	..	34
3,190	2,723	367	6	139	34	..	3	..	..	35

Table X.—Occupation or Means of Liveli

Province, State or Agency.	Class B.—Preparation and Supply; Sub-Class IV.—Transport—; Order 20.—Transport; Group 106.—Labourers employed on roads and bridges. Total earners principal occupation. Males.	Females.	Total working dependants. Males.	Females.	Total following occupation as subsidiary to other. Males.	Females.	Group 107.—Owners, Total earners principal occupation. Males.	Females.
	827	828	829	830	831	832	833	834
INDIA	**249,270**	**103,489**	**36,363**	**34,850**	**59,334**	**15,154**	**80,643**	**998**
Provinces	**160,017**	**59,524**	**4,543**	**5,151**	**45,972**	**7,307**	**67,858**	**358**
1 Ajmer-Merwara	330	293	1	7	107	3	28	..
2 Andamans and Nicobars	2	..	..	..	..	..	90	..
3 Assam	12,238	1,304	237	126	9,104	251	1,789	..
4 Baluchistan (*Districts and Administered Territories*).	807	..	2	..	137	..	41	..
5 Bengal	38,738	9,064	527	270	8,551	1,693	8,275	29
6 Bihar and Orissa	12,510	8,043	88	200	9,251	1,919	2,819	15
7 Bombay (*including Aden*)	3,860	1,460	235	106	429	156	11,439	166
Aden	*41*	..	..	..	..	..	*570*	..
8 Burma	25,982	3,060	1,270	1,094	5,682	483	10,873	78
9 Central Provinces and Berar ..	7,465	5,768	225	875	1,266	448	4,713	5
10 Coorg	218	1	1	1	37	..	220	5
11 Delhi	1,518	523	7	62	11	2	385	1
12 Madras	43,629	28,356	1,830	2,322	10,040	1,998	14,205	56
13 North-West Frontier Province, (*Districts and Administered Territories*).	1,094	26	25	6	243	1	1,619	..
14 Punjab	6,600	605	44	73	449	8	6,748	3
15 United Provinces of Agra and Oudh	5,026	1,018	51	9	665	345	4,614	..
States and Agencies ..	**89,253**	**43,965**	**31,820**	**29,699**	**13,362**	**7,847**	**12,785**	**640**
16 Assam States	1,087	313	139	80	629	126	424	..
17 Baluchistan States	30	..	..	..	3	..	3	..
18 Baroda State	81	68	..	..	7	..	467	9
19 Bengal States	2,422	129	21	392	78	..	..	..
20 Bihar and Orissa States	5,692	6,920	630	1,489	697	282	60	1
21 Bombay States	828	160	48	58	59	10	986	..
22 Central India Agency	3,123	1,731	53	93	595	127	415	2
23 Central Provinces States	2,508	1,406	598	745	564	125	131	..
24 Gwalior State	1,718	141	34	16	191	107	351	189
25 Hyderabad State	54,140	29,493	27,260	23,646	8,227	6,833	1,597	380
26 Jammu and Kashmir State ..	1,419	242	82	..	186	4	2	..
27 Madras States Agency	7,607	538	435	215	842	50	5,679	47
Cochin State	*1,080*	*167*	*7*	*2*	*162*	*19*	*1,334*	*30*
Travancore State	*6,199*	*280*	*420*	*209*	*666*	*27*	*4,227*	*17*
Other Madras States	*328*	*91*	*8*	*4*	*14*	*4*	*118*	..
28 Mysore State	1,815	1,075	65	390	818	117	1,056	4
29 North-West Frontier Province (*Agencies and Tribal Areas*).	149	..	..	..	..	..	231	..
30 Punjab States	283	4	10	8	75	..	23	..
31 Punjab States Agency	608	21	18	18	100	..	809	..
32 Rajputana Agency	3,114	1,221	36	102	208	17	237	7
33 Sikkim State	286	101	3	1	81	49	1	..
34 United Provinces States	142	63	4	..	..	..	25	..
35 Western India States Agency ..	2,201	339	2,384	2,446	2	..	288	1

hood—Part II—Provincial Distribution—*contd.*

of Material Substances—*contd.*

contd.

by road —*contd.*

managers and employees (excluding personal servants) connected with mechanically driven vehicles (including trams).				*Group 108.*—Owners, managers and employees (excluding personal servants) connected with other vehicles.						
Total working dependants.		Total following occupation as subsidiary to other.		Total earners principal occupation.		Total working dependants.		Total following occupation as subsidiary to other.		
Males.	Females.	Males.	Females.	Males.	Females.	Males.	Females.	Males.	Females.	
835	836	837	838	839	840	841	842	843	844	
1,538	**646**	**4,741**	**256**	**372,382**	**6,564**	**23,013**	**3,222**	**199,308**	**2,105**	
954	**48**	**3,322**	**88**	**294,932**	**3,564**	**13,597**	**1,147**	**164,484**	**1,543**	
..	..	2	..	963	10	5	4	436	..	1
..	..	..	..	134	..	..	1	19	..	2
25	..	152	1	5,904	219	378	63	5,365	242	3
..	..	3	..	643	..	..	..	29	..	4
..	..	19	6	28,159	46	441	6	9,617	4	5
11	35	763	2	15,977	159	119	19	8,406	65	6
134	8	109	9	14,922	118	741	20	2,369	5	7
37	..	*5*	..	*382*	..	*3*	..	*3*	..	
459	3	188	4	32,001	1,141	5,747	292	38,906	821	8
70	..	157	..	16,397	174	330	37	9,832	78	9
..	..	24	..	949	..	25	..	793	..	10
..	..	..	..	4,177	34	20	4	354	..	11
110	2	1,159	66	78,945	481	3,817	636	61,452	277	12
25	..	96	..	4,969	7	183	5	990	4	13
98	..	459	..	21,732	53	766	..	2,379	1	14
22	..	191	..	69,060	1,122	1,025	60	23,537	46	15
584	**598**	**1,419**	**168**	**77,450**	**3,000**	**9,416**	**2,075**	**34,824**	**562**	
20	..	8	..	575	63	43	26	400	10	16
..	..	..	..	3	..	..	..	3	..	17
4	..	11	..	1,327	..	..	..	54	..	18
..	..	..	..	317	..	3	..	111	..	19
..	..	9	..	921	13	15	..	1,634	6	20
19	2	431	1	2,599	15	250	37	1,432	114	21
3	..	46	..	8,141	143	188	9	7,600	68	22
1	..	4	..	1,036	12	54	9	505	..	23
5	18	2	..	1,894	74	115	45	1,572	16	24
405	556	469	163	25,100	2,399	6,971	1,896	2,387	307	25
..	..	..	..	578	..	1	..	23	1	26
116	22	252	4	12,148	48	735	..	4,806	7	27
7	..	*74*	..	*3,856*	*23*	*19*	..	*713*	*1*	
107	*22*	*170*	*4*	*7,222*	*22*	*667*	..	*1,624*	*3*	
2	..	*8*	..	*1,070*	*3*	*49*	..	*2,469*	*3*	
7	..	137	..	10,120	37	436	9	12,349	12	28
..	..	12	..	..	..	..	..	..	..	29
1	..	4	..	112	..	3	..	24	..	30
2	..	15	..	2,797	34	128	..	403	..	31
..	..	16	..	5,139	50	41	9	1,203	16	32
..	..	..	..	21	..	..	..	7	..	33
..	..	..	..	828	46	51	..	105	..	34
1	..	3	..	3,794	66	382	35	206	..	35

Table X.—Occupation or Means of Liveli

Class B.—Preparation and Supply

Sub-Class IV.—

20.—Transport by

	Province, State or Agency.	*Group 109.*—Palki, etc. bearers, and owners. Total earners principal occupation.		Total working dependants.		Total following occupation as subsidiary to other.		*Group 110.*—Pack elephant, Total earners principal occupation.	
		Males.	Females.	Males.	Females.	Males.	Females.	Males.	Females.
	1	845	846	847	848	849	850	851	852
	INDIA	**52,951**	**1,927**	**1,878**	**746**	**22,836**	**467**	**105,381**	**3,890**
	Provinces	**46,001**	**1,640**	**479**	**330**	**21,648**	**193**	**79,403**	**1,617**
1	Ajmer-Merwara	26	..	..	..	2	..	255	12
2	Andamans and Nicobars	..	..	..	..	..	..	127	..
3	Assam	679	..	59	..	1,684	..	89	..
4	Baluchistan (*Districts and Administered Territories*).	1	..	..	..	..	..	1,636	71
5	Bengal	20,264	93	131	..	3,850	5	147	1
6	Bihar and Orissa	9,449	69	61	36	12,107	17	7,696	182
7	Bombay (*including Aden*)	145	1,419	2	294	7	168	11,312	440
	Aden	*6*	..	..	..	..	..	*105*	*3*
8	Burma	4,658	5	19	..	27	..	932	13
9	Central Provinces and Berar ..	254	1	12	..	163	1	1,107	83
10	Coorg	..	..	..	..	..	..	1	..
11	Delhi	1,180	..	..	..	..	..	573	30
12	Madras	1,892	7	7	..	637	1	3,133	11
13	North-West Frontier Province (*Districts and Administered Territories*).	133	..	..	..	2	..	5,120	18
14	Punjab	1,226	22	49	..	71	..	39,400	584
15	United Provinces of Agra and Oudh	6,094	24	139	..	3,098	1	7,880	172
	States and Agencies ..	**6,950**	**287**	**1,399**	**416**	**1,188**	**274**	**25,973**	**2,273**
16	Assam States	90	13	4	3	41	207	20	..
17	Baluchistan States	..	..	..	..	..	..	2,124	16
18	Baroda State	..	..	..	..	..	..	891	91
19	Bengal States	111	..	..	..	16	..	76	..
20	Bihar and Orissa States	5	1	..	..	47	..	5	..
21	Bombay States	7	..	..	..	1	..	280	95
22	Central India Agency	85	2	..	..	31	..	1,298	171
23	Central Provinces States	14	..	..	..	39	..	253	3
24	Gwalior State	69	..	..	..	..	..	121	15
25	Hyderabad State	5,802	254	1,367	410	812	65	4,115	1,010
26	Jammu and Kashmir State ..	..	..	..	..	..	..	1,257	26
27	Madras States Agency	142	7	18	3	100	2	274	1
	Cochin State	*125*	*7*	*2*	*3*	*99*	*2*	*176*	..
	Travancore State	*10*	..	*16*	..	*1*	..	*98*	..
	Other Madras States	*7*	..	..	..	..	..	..	*1*
28	Mysore State	3	1	..	..	3	..	78	..
29	North-West Frontier Province (*Agencies and Tribal Areas*). ..	..	..	..	..	..	..	473	..
30	Punjab States	9	..	..	..	3	..	372	3
31	Punjab States Agency	35	..	..	..	31	..	2,586	171
32	Rajputana Agency	95	1	10	..	11	..	10,131	653
33	Sikkim State	1	..	..	..	..	..	18	..
34	United Provinces States	341	..	..	..	36	..	42	..
35	Western India States Agency ..	141	8	..	..	17	..	1,559	18

hood—Part II—Provincial Distribution—*contd.*

of Material Substances—*contd.*

Transport—*contd.*

road—*concld.*

camel, mule, ass and bullock owners and drivers. *Group 111.*—Porters and messengers.

Total working dependants. Males.	Total working dependants. Females.	Total following occupation as subsidiary to other. Males.	Total following occupation as subsidiary to other. Females.	Total earners principal occupation. Males.	Total earners principal occupation. Females.	Total working dependants. Males.	Total working dependants. Females.	Total following occupation as subsidiary to other. Males.	Total following occupation as subsidiary to other. Females.	
853	854	855	856	857	858	859	860	861	862	
6,947	**2,031**	**30,861**	**811**	**129,008**	**14,881**	**4,322**	**2,303**	**13,170**	**560**	
4,393	**803**	**20,732**	**253**	**108,754**	**11,521**	**2,808**	**1,506**	**11,131**	**489**	
..	1	66	..	682	4	2	1	18	..	**1**
--	--	..	..	17	..	..	..	..	..	**2**
6	..	..	..	243	2	4	1	37	..	**3**
59	1	810	16	4,551	223	12	3	1,000	18	**4**
5	..	9	1	9,491	776	37	9	444	68	**5**
10	6	1,754	32	9,101	3,086	18	12	1,004	72	**6**
1,311	231	4,471	77	6,834	363	46	43	51	15	**7**
..	..	..	..	*318*	..	*33*	..	..	..	
242	3	540	4	18,408	3,398	1,111	1,126	851	136	**8**
77	22	425	4	10,970	2,103	400	91	1,444	52	**9**
..	..	..	..	46	1	..	..	14	..	**10**
38	11	170	2	2,535	82	2	..	29	..	**11**
284	2	1,737	2	14,197	302	129	10	1,435	37	**12**
296	7	1,557	7	104	11	3	1	15	..	**13**
2,003	507	6,216	75	19,113	335	915	153	2,564	49	**14**
62	12	2,908	33	12,462	835	129	56	2,225	42	**15**
2,554	**1,228**	**10,129**	**558**	**20,254**	**3,360**	**1,514**	**797**	**2,039**	**71**	
..	..	..	..	19	..	..	..	..	..	**16**
82	4	2,098	11	471	40	..	..	57	..	**17**
209	191	1,164	3	1,749	1,875	6	2	37	33	**18**
..	..	1	..	119	..	1	..	32	..	**19**
..	..	..	..	6	1	..	..	..	..	**20**
1	61	123	143	24	..	..	..	2	..	**21**
60	20	800	3	1,486	53	3	3	59	2	**22**
16	7	71	1	284	2	..	..	48	..	**23**
20	7	136	3	68	.	..	..	..	..	**24**
1,456	698	682	284	3,971	69	1,185	342	336	3	**25**
79	1	280	13	1	..	..	..	1	..	**26**
1	..	137	--	1,655	145	22	2	223	4	**27**
1	..	*137*	..	*1,632*	*145*	*22*	*2*	*223*	*4*	
--	..	..	--	..	..	..	..	..	..	
--	..	..	..	*23*	..	..	..	..	..	
6	..	41	..	16	..	..	--	..	--	**28**
--	--	--	--	..	..	..	--	..	..	**29**
5	..	161	..	123	14	6	78	108	4	**30**
66	17	219	..	2,626	87	109	46	704	22	**31**
291	209	4,153	97	5,084	424	21	98	329	2	**32**
--	..	9	--	19	1	--	..	10		**33**
--	--	--	--	388	--	--	..	8		**34**
262	13	54	..	2,145	648	161	226	85	1	**35**

Table X.—Occupation or Means of Liveli

Class B.—Preparation and Supply

Sub-Class IV.—Transport

Order 21.—Transport

Province, State or Agency	Total *Order 21.*—Transport by rail						*Group 112.*—Railway	
	Total earners principal occupation.		Total working dependants.		Total following occupation as subsidiary to other.		Total earners principal occupation.	
	Males.	Females.	Males.	Females.	Males.	Females.	Males.	Females.
1	863	864	865	866	867	868	869	870
INDIA ..	**563,859**	**27,624**	**20,517**	**24,131**	**27,719**	**13,039**	**342,219**	**4,181**
Provinces	**450,435**	**11,358**	**2,261**	**659**	**16,114**	**354**	**287,595**	**3,622**
1 Ajmer-Merwara	11,685	70	19	6	114	1	9,738	53
2 Andamans and Nicobars	..	..	..	..	..	..	..	..
3 Assam	11,442	619	91	31	1,066	2	5,800	12
4 Baluchistan (*Districts and Administered Territories*).	6,345	..	..	..	23	..	3,112	..
5 Bengal	37,045	1,869	105	4	1,313	37	38,596	618
6 Bihar and Orissa	30,714	850	65	35	5,812	61	18,813	153
7 Bombay (*including Aden*).. ..	66,971	3,100	612	347	970	22	44,664	1,158
Aden	*39*	..	*1*	..	..	..	*31*	..
8 Burma	26,811	745	117	90	183	8	14,002	77
9 Central Provinces and Berar ..	32,608	1,740	208	39	918	140	17,173	412
10 Coorg	12	..	..	..	2	..	12	..
11 Delhi	8,457	19	2	..	18	..	6,199	16
12 Madras	54,046	1,014	339	67	2,344	39	32,709	175
13 North-West Frontier Province (*Districts and Administered Territories*).	2,296	8	18	2	232	1	1,927	7
14 Punjab	71,235	509	685	38	1,223	1	44,345	267
15 United Provinces of Agra and Oudh	60,768	815	..	..	1,896	42	50,505	674
States and Agencies ..	**113,424**	**16,266**	**18,256**	**23,472**	**11,605**	**12,685**	**54,624**	**559**
16 Assam States	..	..	..	..	..	..	..	..
17 Baluchistan States	40	..	..	..	..	..	5	..
18 Baroda State	6,738	281	5	..	93	..	2,756	..
19 Bengal States	302	2	1	..	13	..	169	..
20 Bihar and Orissa States	1,653	305	6	25	471	18	987	44
21 Bombay States	1,659	41	43	15	40	..	1,091	11
22 Central India Agency .. .	7,428	147	21	..	171	13	4,042	9
23 Central Provinces States	1,083	297	8	..	17	41	311	..
24 Gwalior State	2,084	196	18	42	70	..	1,201	52
25 Hyderabad State	42,795	13,766	16,909	23,228	9,089	12,599	7,976	188
26 Jammu and Kashmir State ..	52	1	1	2	25	..	31	1
27 Madras States Agency	2,940	279	45	11	76	11	537	6
Cochin State	*738*	*163*	*1*	..	*22*	..	*187*	*2*
Travancore State	*1,886*	*56*	*44*	*11*	*25*	*10*	*181*	..
Other Madras States	*316*	*60*	..	..	*29*	*1*	*169*	*4*
28 Mysore State	6,651	221	18	10	390	..	4,907	44
29 North-West Frontier Province (*Agencies and Tribal Areas*).	107	..	..	..	..	..	84	..
30 Punjab States	235	1	3	..	113	..	170	1
31 Punjab States Agency	10,478	17	127	..	361	..	7,562	1
32 Rajputana Agency	20,700	610	40	54	632	3	16,593	158
33 Sikkim State	5	..	..		..	..	4	..
34 United Provinces States	179	1	..		10	..	125	1
35 Western India States Agency ..	8,295	101	1,011	85	34	..	6,073	43

hood—Part II—Provincial Distribution—*contd.*

of Material Substances—*contd.*

contd.

by rail.

employees of all kinds other than porters and coolies.				*Group 113.*—Labourers employed on railway construction and maintenance and coolies and porters employed on railway premises.						
Total working dependants.		Total following occupation as subsidiary to other.		Total earners principal occupation.		Total working dependants.		Total following occupation as subsidiary to other.		
Males.	Females.	Males.	Females.	Males.	Females.	Males.	Females.	Males.	Females.	
871	872	873	874	875	876	877	878	879	880	
3,210	**696**	**10,950**	**121**	**221,640**	**23,443**	**17,307**	**23,435**	**16,769**	**12,918**	
1,063	**223**	**8,720**	**51**	**162,840**	**7,736**	**1,198**	**436**	**7,394**	**303**	
17	5	79	..	1,947	17	2	1	35	1	1
..	..	..	..	..	..	..	..	..	..	2
69	..	475	..	5,642	607	22	31	591	2	3
..	..	4	..	3,233	..	..	..	19	..	4
33	1	771	5	28,449	1,251	72	3	542	32	5
41	12	2,487	18	11,901	697	24	23	3,325	43	6
322	124	629	8	22,307	1,942	290	223	341	14	7
1	..	..	..	*8*	..	..	..	..	..	
16	1	41	..	12,809	668	101	89	142	8	8
146	9	362	10	15,435	1,328	62	30	556	130	9
..	..	2	..	..	..	..	..	..	..	10
1	..	10	..	2,258	3	1	..	8	..	11
156	41	1,162	6	21,337	839	183	26	1,182	33	12
18	2	193	1	369	1	..	..	39	..	13
244	28	790	1	26,890	242	441	10	433	..	14
..	..	1,715	2	10,263	141	..	..	181	40	15
2,147	**473**	**2,230**	**70**	**58,800**	**15,707**	**16,109**	**22,999**	**9,375**	**12,615**	
..	..	..	..	..	..	..	..	..	..	16
..	..	..	..	35	..	..	..	..	..	17
1	..	28	..	3,982	281	4	..	65	..	18
..	..	7	..	133	2	1	..	6	..	19
5	2	386	2	666	261	1	23	85	16	20
28	13	29	..	568	30	15	2	11	..	21
9	..	68	13	3,386	138	12	.	103	..	22
8	..	13	..	772	297	..	..	4	41	23
17	41	34	..	883	144	1	1	36	..	24
1,167	352	642	54	34,819	13,578	15,742	22,876	8,447	12,545	25
1	2	21	..	21	..	..	..	4	..	26
..	..	12	..	2,403	273	45	11	63	11	27
.	..	*10*	..	*551*	*161*	*1*	..	*12*	..	
..	..	..	..	*1,705*	*56*	*44*	*11*	*25*	*10*	
..		*3*	..	*147*	*55*	..	..	*96*	*1*	
16	4	262	..	1,744	177	2	6	128	..	28
..	..	..	..	23	..	..	..	..	..	29
..	..	91	..	65	..	3	..	22	..	30
72	..	85	..	2,916	16	55	..	276	..	31
29	51	523	1	4,107	452	11	3	109	..	32
..	..	..	..	1	..	..	..	..	..	33
..	..	10	..	54	..	..	..	..	..	34
794	8	18	..	2,222	58	217	77	1	...	35

Table X.—Occupation or Means of Liveli

Class B.—Preparation and Supply

Sub-Class IV.—Transport—*concld.*

Order 22.—Post Office,

Province, State or Agency.	Total *Order 22.*—Post Office, Telegraph and Telephone Services. Total earners principal occupation. Males.	Females.	Total working dependants. Males.	Females.	Total following occupation as subsidiary to other. Males.	Females.	*Group 114.*—Post Office, Total earners principal occupation. Males.	Females.
	881	882	883	884	885	886	887	888
INDIA	**81,020**	**708**	**1,732**	**108**	**5,581**	**106**	**81,020**	**708**
Provinces	**64,998**	**632**	**604**	**69**	**4,310**	**105**	**64,998**	**632**
1 Ajmer-Merwara	341	1	..	..	10	..	341	1
2 Andamans and Nicobars	22	..	..	..	2	..	22	..
3 Assam	2,394	..	47	..	356	1	2,394	..
4 Baluchistan (*Districts and Administered Territories*).	451	..	..	..	..	..	451	..
5 Bengal	10,632	33	12	..	669	1	10,632	33
6 Bihar and Orissa	1,972	20	2	..	487	5	1,972	20
7 Bombay (*including Aden*)	7,550	305	206	62	188	92	7,550	305
Aden	*84*	..	*9*	..	..	..	*84*	..
8 Burma	4,878	152	21	..	43	..	4,878	152
9 Central Provinces and Berar	2,790	8	15	..	101	..	2,790	8
10 Coorg	46	4	..	1	22	5	46	4
11 Delhi	1,586	5	..	..	3	..	1,586	5
12 Madras	10,580	69	47	..	1,105	1	10,580	69
13 North-West Frontier Province (*Districts and Administered Territories*).	935	2	4	1	54	..	935	2
14 Punjab	10,045	24	195	5	545	..	1,045	24
15 United Provinces of Agra and Oudh	10,776	9	55	..	725	..	10,776	9
States and Agencies	**16,022**	**76**	**1,128**	**39**	**1,271**	**1**	**6,022**	**76**
16 Assam States	103	..	..	1	2	..	103	..
17 Baluchistan States	121	..	..	..	5	..	121	..
18 Baroda State	878	..	..	..	26	..	878	..
19 Bengal States	156	..	..	..	16	..	156	..
20 Bihar and Orissa States	253	..	104	..	68	..	253	..
21 Bombay States	514	1	2	..	18	1	514	1
22 Central India Agency	1,156	4	1	2	52	..	1,156	4
23 Central Provinces States	202	..	27	..	5	..	202	..
24 Gwalior State	474	..	3	..	3	..	474	..
25 Hyderabad State	2,590	15	891	34	405	..	2,590	15
26 Jammu and Kashmir State	841	..	4	..	112	..	841	..
27 Madras States Agency	2,111	18	22	2	129	..	2,111	18
Cochin State	*290*	*1*	*1*	*2*	*47*	..	*90*	*1*
Travancore State	*1,702*	*14*	*21*	..	*70*	..	*1,702*	*14*
Other Madras States	*119*	*3*	..	..	*12*	..	*119*	*3*
28 Mysore State	1,602	15	1	..	160	..	1,602	15
29 North-West Frontier Province (*Agencies and Tribal Areas*).	132	..	..	..	..	..	132	..
30 Punjab States	100	..	6	..	72	..	100	..
31 Punjab States Agency	878	..	3	..	80	..	878	..
32 Rajputana Agency	1,941	22	1	..	38	..	1,941	22
33 Sikkim State	49	..	..	..	12	..	49	..
34 United Provinces States	107	..	..	..	4	..	107	..
35 Western India States Agency	1,814	1	63	..	64	..	1,814	1

hood—Part II—Provincial Distribution—*contd.*

of Material Substances—*contd.*

Telegraph and Telephone Services. — Telegraph and Telephone Services. Total working dependants. Males.	Females.	Total following occupation as subsidiary to other. Males.	Females.	*Sub-Class V.*—Trade. — Total *Sub-Class V.*—Trade. Total earners principal occupation. Males.	Females.	Total working dependants. Males.	Females.	Total following occupation as subsidiary to other. Males.	Females.	
889	890	891	892	893	894	895	896	897	898	
1,732	**108**	**5,581**	**106**	**5,503,263**	**1,726,817**	**282,353**	**401,164**	**1,184,852**	**238,520**	
604	**69**	**4,310**	**105**	**4,119,510**	**1,277,116**	**118,010**	**228,650**	**886,056**	**161,333**	
..	..	10	..	15,904	2,730	260	474	2,305	354	1
..	..	2	..	677	1	2	3	48	1	2
47	..	356	1	87,689	12,259	4,659	5,681	51,888	2,173	3
..	..	..	..	8,936	30	75	54	7,322	10	4
12	..	669	1	774,062	135,247	9,871	8,922	128,768	9,571	5
2	..	487	5	334,473	214,647	3,444	13,605	148,461	38,806	6
206	62	188	92	379,890	49,121	14,569	14,357	28,223	4,385	7
9	..	..	..	*3,320*	*156*	*68*	*7*	*36*	*3*	
21	..	43	..	255,377	211,458	10,792	79,621	40,821	20,076	8
15	..	101	..	209,178	93,803	7,074	22,841	61,367	22,087	9
..	1	22	5	2,655	304	38	5	715	24	10
..	..	3	..	34,015	1,153	153	303	598	11	11
47	..	1,105	1	723,785	248,469	19,492	30,504	155,871	27,739	12
4	1	54	..	59,209	547	1,698	204	3,490	23	13
195	5	545	..	478,363	15,547	25,008	5,332	45,067	806	14
55	..	725	..	755,297	291,800	20,875	46,744	211,112	35,267	15
1,128	**39**	**1,271**	**1**	**1,383,753**	**449,701**	**164,343**	**172,514**	**298,796**	**77,187**	
..	1	2	..	3,497	5,308	308	1,347	3,310	1,882	16
..	..	5	..	4,445	27	8	7	819	2	17
..	..	26	..	49,118	9,891	3,829	4,227	6,726	488	18
..	..	16	..	8,640	3,980	164	172	2,267	116	19
104	..	68	..	25,659	46,243	859	4,007	22,338	6,260	20
2	..	18	..	49,187	7,977	2,572	3,626	7,354	1,883	21
1	2	52	..	93,704	34,630	1,598	2,385	29,629	5,972	22
27	..	5	..	13,034	7,293	1,021	5,618	4,401	1,362	23
3	..	3	..	54,646	13,474	2,773	3,462	14,355	3,296	24
891	34	405	..	394,192	161,444	118,138	118,977	88,272	41,509	25
4	..	112	..	26,099	3,694	583	871	7,321	1,292	26
22	2	129	..	154,739	43,078	8,340	4,631	28,488	3,394	27
1	*2*	*47*	..	*33,475*	*7,847*	*341*	*301*	*7,028*	*868*	
21	..	*70*	..	*111,712*	*32,190*	*7,904*	*4,225*	*18,364*	*2,253*	
..	..	*12*	..	*9,552*	*3,041*	*95*	*105*	*3,096*	*273*	
1	..	160	..	88,234	38,097	1,723	5,578	29,771	3,384	28
..	..	..	..	1,094	..	1	..	714		29
6	..	72	..	4,387	444	201	94	1,346	19	30
3	..	80	..	80,381	2,657	4,009	695	9,671	218	31
1	..	38	..	224,601	59,506	4,475	9,203	34,920	4,839	32
..	..	12	..	706	170	6	..	80	14	33
..	..	4	..	15,149	5,461	681	1,684	2,592	928	34
..	..	64	..	92,241	6,327	13,054	5,930	4,422	329	35

Table X.—Occupation or Means of Liveli

Class B.—Preparation and

Sub-Class V.—

Order 23.—Banks,

Province, State or Agency.	Total *Order 23.*—Banks, establishments of credit, exchange and insurance.						*Group 115.*—Bank	
	Total earners principal occupation.		Total working dependants.		Total following occupation as subsidiary to other.		Total earners principal occupation.	
	Males.	Females.	Males.	Females.	Males.	Females.	Males.	Females.
1	899	900	901	902	903	904	905	906
INDIA	**279,492**	**33,235**	**13,247**	**3,508**	**145,462**	**7,906**	**279,492**	**33,235**
Provinces	**187,180**	**22,090**	**7,421**	**1,516**	**107,253**	**6,052**	**187,180**	**22,090**
1 Ajmer-Merwara	1,718	85	37	9	573	7	1,718	85
2 Andamans and Nicobars ..	3	..	—	..	..	..	3	—
3 Assam	2,155	287	63	16	1,789	87	2,155	287
4 Baluchistan (*Districts and Administered Territories*).	100	—	..	—	12	..	100	..
5 Bengal .. — — —	44,267	4,185	486	146	11,138	557	44,267	4,185
6 Bihar and Orissa	6,713	636	113	72	10,720	347	6,713	636
7 Bombay (*including Aden*)	15,268	1,267	392	179	3,654	132	15,268	1,267
Aden — — —	*49*	—	*2*	—	*3*	*1*	*49*	—
8 Burma	9,312	1,266	200	136	1,827	523	9,312	1,266
9 Central Provinces and Berar ..	19,480	1,152	432	86	8,043	398	19,480	1,152
10 Coorg	15	1	..	..	107	..	15	1
11 Delhi	1,349	34	13	1	225	—	1,349	34
12 Madras	24,752	7,864	387	524	21,467	2,028	24,752	7,864
13 North-West Frontier Province (*Districts and Administered Territories*).	1,118	12	17	1	248	..	1,118	12
14 Punjab	30,923	1,191	4,661	88	11,513	86	30,923	1,191
15 United Provinces of Agra and Oudh	30,007	4,110	620	258	35,937	1,887	30,007	4,110
States and Agencies ..	**92,312**	**11,145**	**5,826**	**1,992**	**38,209**	**1,854**	**92,312**	**11,145**
16 Assam States	64	22	1	3	16	16	64	22
17 Baluchistan States	..	..	..	..	..	..	..	—
18 Baroda State	5,477	585	340	15	1,866	55	5,477	585
19 Bengal States	681	26	2	..	197	1	681	26
20 Bihar and Orissa States	341	31	9	3	976	26	341	31
21 Bombay States	3,043	479	201	225	877	199	3,043	479
22 Central India Agency	6,716	619	146	182	6,633	156	6,716	619
23 Central Provinces States	748	59	25	9	214	13	748	59
24 Gwalior State	3,365	429	296	51	2,955	189	3,365	429
25 Hyderabad State	14,069	2,036	2,985	755	2,207	291	14,069	2,036
26 Jammu and Kashmir State ..	2,026	128	39	..	1,039	70	2,026	128
27 Madras States Agency	7,038	1,974	98	26	2,592	367	7,088	1,974
Cochin State	*1,619*	*856*	*11*	*2*	*991*	*181*	*1,619*	*856*
Travancore State	*2,160*	*667*	*78*	*14*	*995*	*175*	*2,160*	*667*
Other Madras States	*3,259*	*451*	*9*	*10*	*606*	*11*	*3,259*	*451*
28 Mysore State	3,439	724	43	39	5,993	252	3,439	724
29 North-West Frontier Province (*Agencies and Tribal Areas*). ..	..	..	..	..	..	..	..	—
30 Punjab States	347	26	13	..	291	2	347	26
31 Punjab States Agency	5,392	243	575	20	2,468	33	5,392	243
32 Rajputana Agency	32,218	2,100	551	460	8,488	139	32,218	2,100
33 Sikkim State	2	2	..	..	5	..	2	2
34 United Provinces States	265	19	..	..	126	1	265	19
35 Western India States Agency ..	7,081	1,643	502	204	1,266	44	7,081	1,643

hood—Part II—Provincial Distribution—*contd.*

Supply of Material Substances—*contd.*

Trade—*contd.*

establishments of credit, exchange and insurance. | *Order 24.*—Brokerage, Commission and Export.

managers, money lenders, exchange and insurance agents, money changers and brokers and their employees.				Total *Order 24.*—Brokerage, Commission and Export.						
Total working dependants.		Total following occupation as subsidiary to other.		Total earners principal occupation.		Total working dependants.		Total following occupation as subsidiary to other.		
Males.	Females.	Males.	Females.	Males.	Females.	Males.	Females.	Males.	Females.	
907	908	909	910	911	912	913	914	915	916	
13,247	**3,508**	**145,462**	**7,906**	**61,308**	**1,099**	**1,136**	**405**	**7,121**	**125**	
7,421	1,516	107,253	6,052	48,871	868	659	376	5,190	90	
37	9	573	7	434	..	..	..	17	..	1
..	..	..	..	2	..	..	..	2	..	2
63	16	1,789	87	141	4	7	..	83	2	3
..	..	12	..	175	..	..	..	10	..	4
486	146	11,138	557	8,848	207	32	..	685	32	5
113	72	10,720	347	562	230	15	5	241	..	6
392	179	3,654	132	9,850	124	116	353	376	6	7
2	..	*3*	*1*	*316*	*26*	*8*	*2*	*9*	..	
200	136	1,827	523	2,184	56	26	3	193	3	8
432	86	8,043	398	3,047	83	71	1	651	2	9
..	..	107	..	85	2	1	..	36	..	10
13	1	225	..	765	4	..	..	1	..	11
387	524	21,467	2,028	8,589	78	78	6	1,543	11	12
17	1	248	..	896	3	15	..	81	..	13
4,661	88	11,513	86	8,193	21	293	6	288	..	14
620	258	35,937	1,887	5,100	56	5	2	983	..	15
5,826	1,992	38,209	1,854	12,437	231	477	29	1,931	35	
1	3	16	16	2	..	..	..	1	..	16
..	..	..	..	25	..	..	..	6	..	17
340	15	1,866	55	645	..	12	..	127	..	18
2	..	197	1	4	6	..	..	..	1	19
9	3	976	26	120	6	..	2	26	1	20
201	225	877	199	171	4	8	3	22	..	21
146	182	6,633	156	1,456	26	9	..	248	10	22
25	9	214	13	198	1	..	..	20	..	23
296	51	2,955	189	726	1	28	1	545	22	24
2,985	755	2,207	291	1,137	84	166	20	129	..	25
39	..	1,039	70	81	1	..	..	10	..	26
98	26	2,592	367	534	27	7	..	127	..	27
11	*2*	*991*	*181*	*94*	*22*	..	..	*32*	..	
78	*14*	*995*	*175*	*378*	*5*	*5*	..	*64*	..	
9	*10*	*606*	*11*	*62*	..	*2*	..	*31*	..	
43	39	5,993	252	1,141	6	3	..	188	1	28
..	..	..	..	9	..	..	..	..	..	29
13	..	291	2	117	..	1	..	6	..	30
575	20	2,468	33	1,617	3	48	..	52	..	31
551	460	8,488	139	2,939	26	48	2	270	..	32
..	..	5	..	10	..	..	..	..	..	33
..	..	126	1	25	21	..	..	..	..	34
502	204	1,266	44	1,480	19	147	1	154	..	35

Table X.—Occupation or Means of Liveli

Class B.—Preparation and

Sub-Class V.—

Province, State or Agency.	*Order 24.*—Brokerage, Commission and Export—*concld.* *Group 116.*—Brokers, commission agents, commercial travellers, ware-house owners and employees. Total earners principal occupation.		Total working dependants.		Total following occupation as subsidiary to other.		Total earners principal occupation.	
	Males.	Females.	Males.	Females.	Males.	Females.	Males.	Females.
1	917	918	919	920	921	922	923	924
INDIA	**61,308**	**1,099**	**1,136**	**405**	**7,121**	**125**	**390,616**	**35,229**
Provinces	**48,871**	**868**	**659**	**376**	**5,190**	**90**	**298,299**	**25,382**
1 Ajmer-Merwara	434	..	..	..	17	..	1,779	55
2 Andamans and Nicobars	2	..	..	..	2	..	2	..
3 Assam	141	4	7	..	83	2	3,296	199
4 Baluchistan (*Districts and Administered Territories*).	175	..	..	..	10	..	1,603	2
5 Bengal	8,848	207	32	..	685	32	56,504	5,308
6 Bihar and Orissa	562	230	15	5	241	..	13,682	2,687
7 Bombay (*including Aden*)	9,850	124	116	353	376	6	16,466	514
Aden	*316*	*26*	*8*	*2*	*9*	..	*112*	*6*
8 Burma	2,184	56	26	3	193	3	13,202	4,261
9 Central Provinces and Berar ..	3,047	83	71	1	651	2	20,676	1,419
10 Coorg	85	2	1	..	36	..	156	1
11 Delhi	765	4	..	..	1	..	4,641	52
12 Madras	8,589	78	78	6	1,543	11	64,100	7,671
13 North-West Frontier Province (*Districts and Administered Territories*).	896	3	15	..	81	..	3,683	29
14 Punjab	8,193	21	293	6	288	..	44,955	610
15 United Provinces of Agra and Oudh	5,100	56	5	2	983	34	53,554	2,574
States and Agencies ..	**12,437**	**231**	**477**	**29**	**1,931**	**35**	**92,317**	**9,847**
16 Assam States	2	..	..	..	1	..	801	1,300
17 Baluchistan States	25	..	..	..	6	..	717	..
18 Baroda State	645	..	12	..	127	..	5,397	55
19 Bengal States	4	6	..	..	..	1	489	13
20 Bihar and Orissa States	120	6	..	2	26	1	2,933	491
21 Bombay States	171	4	8	3	22	..	1,893	56
22 Central India Agency	1,456	26	9	..	248	10	7,518	302
23 Central Provinces States	198	1	..	..	20	..	1,014	150
24 Gwalior State	726	1	28	1	545	22	2,767	101
25 Hyderabad State	1,137	84	166	20	129	..	20,025	5,725
26 Jammu and Kashmir State ..	81	1	..	..	10	..	2,045	21
27 Madras States Agency	534	27	7	..	117	..	5,183	130
Cochin State	*84*	*22*	..	..	*32*	..	*1,916*	*65*
Travancore State	*378*	*5*	*5*	..	*64*	..	*3,154*	*46*
Other Madras States ..	*62*	..	*2*	..	*31*	..	*113*	*19*
28 Mysore State	1,141	6	3	..	188	1	7,302	593
29 North-West Frontier Province (*Agencies and Tribal Areas*).	9	..	..	..	..	..	53	..
30 Punjab States	117	..	1	..	6	..	275	..
31 Punjab States Agency	1,617	3	48	..	52	..	5,063	25
32 Rajputana Agency	2,939	26	48	2	270	..	15,411	445
33 Sikkim State	10	..	..	..	..	..	117	5
34 United Provinces States	25	21	..	..	..	..	1,466	363
35 Western India States Agency ..	1,480	19	147	1	154	..	11,848	72

hood—Part II—Provincial Distribution—*contd.*

Supply of Material Substances—*contd.*

Trade—*contd.*

Order 25.—Trade in textiles.

Total *Order 25*—Trade in textiles.				117.—Trade in piece-goods, wool, cotton, silk, hair and other textiles.						
Total working dependants.		Total following occupation as subsidiary to other.		Total earners principal occupation.		Total working dependants.		Total following occupation as subsidiary to other.		
Males.	Females.	Males.	Females.	Males.	Females.	Males.	Females.	Males.	Females.	
925	926	927	928	929	930	931	932	933	934	
20,699	**12,358**	**63,863**	**3,925**	**390,616**	**35,229**	**20,699**	**12,358**	**63,863**	**3,925**	
7,748	**5,465**	**50,862**	**2,301**	**298,299**	**25,382**	**7,748**	**5,465**	**50,862**	**2,301**	
8	6	71	3	1,779	55	8	6	71	3	1
..	..	..	..	2	..	..	..	..	..	2
149	17	1,750	17	3,296	199	149	17	1,750	17	3
39	..	633	6	1,603	2	39	..	633	6	4
506	810	13,996	481	56,504	5,308	506	810	13,996	481	5
93	324	4,278	264	13,682	2,687	93	324	4,278	264	6
650	297	926	47	16,466	514	650	297	926	47	7
1	..	*1*	..	*112*	*6*	*1*	..	*1*	..	
403	918	883	219	13,202	4,261	403	918	883	219	8
592	752	4,695	411	20,676	1,419	592	752	4,695	411	9
13	..	36	1	156	1	13	..	36	1	10
5	3	6	1	4,641	52	5	3	6	1	11
2,279	1,614	10,231	309	64,100	7,671	2,279	1,614	10,231	309	12
171	16	114	..	3,683	29	171	16	114	..	13
2,118	162	2,923	75	44,955	610	2,118	162	2,923	75	14
722	546	10,320	467	53,554	2,574	722	546	10,320	467	15
12,951	**6,893**	**13,001**	**1,624**	**92,317**	**9,847**	**12,951**	**6,893**	**13,001**	**1,624**	
53	257	117	133	801	1,300	53	257	117	133	16
2	..	49	..	717	..	2	..	49	..	17
409	16	463	1	5,397	55	409	16	463	1	18
..	..	44	2	489	13	..	..	44	2	19
47	33	1,322	66	2,933	491	47	33	1,322	66	20
121	48	301	2	1,893	56	121	48	301	2	21
64	14	1,022	18	7,518	302	64	14	1,022	18	22
104	235	369	16	1,014	150	104	235	369	16	23
93	23	214	90	2,767	101	93	23	214	90	24
7,123	5,690	3,379	1,005	20,025	5,725	7,123	5,690	3,379	1,005	25
25	..	396	10	2,041	21	25	..	396	10	26
219	47	1,087	97	5,183	130	219	47	1,087	97	27
19	*41*	*465*	*25*	*1,916*	*65*	*19*	*41*	*465*	*25*	
160	*6*	*537*	..	*3,154*	*46*	*160*	*6*	*537*	..	
40	..	*85*	*72*	*113*	*19*	*40*	..	*85*	*72*	
93	195	1,803	83	7,302	593	93	195	1,803	83	28
..	..	1	..	53	..	..	..	1	..	29
17	..	129	..	275	..	17	..	129	..	30
248	5	558	5	5,063	25	248	5	558	5	31
250	219	709	49	15,411	445	250	219	709	49	32
..	..	13	..	117	5	..	..	13	..	33
17	2	92	47	1,466	363	17	2	92	47	34
4,066	109	933	..	11,848	72	4,066	109	933	..	35

Table X.—Occupation or Means of Liveli

Class B.—Preparation and

Sub-Class V.—

Order 26.—Trade

Province, State or Agency.	Total *Order 26.*—Trade in skins, leather and furs.						*Group 118.*—Trade in skins, from	
	Total earners principal occupation.		Total working dependants.		Total following occupation as subsidiary to other.		Total earners principal occupation.	
	Males.	Females.	Males.	Females.	Males.	Females.	Males.	Females.
	935	936	937	938	939	940	941	942
INDIA	**77,690**	**5,437**	**3,514**	**2,157**	**12,810**	**778**	**77,690**	**5,437**
Provinces	**64,054**	**3,452**	**1,538**	**489**	**10,374**	**465**	**64,054**	**3,452**
1 Ajmer-Merwara	163	13	...	...	13	6	163	13
2 Andamans and Nicobars	3	..	..	..	..	..	3	..
3 Assam	1,690	21	107	33	925	17	1,690	21
4 Baluchistan (*Districts and Administered Territories*).	55	...	...	..	27	..	55	...
5 Bengal	22,706	821	206	15	2,874	31	22,706	821
6 Bihar and Orissa	4,468	1,057	36	84	2,246	261	4,468	1,057
7 Bombay (*including Aden*) ..	5,741	342	222	83	731	44	5,741	342
Aden	*37*	*1*	..	..	..	..	*37*	*1*
8 Burma	679	95	12	44	83	6	679	95
9 Central Provinces and Berar ...	2,179	342	26	137	383	27	2,179	342
10 Coorg	9	..	..	..	3	..	9	...
11 Delhi	249	3	..	..	..	..	249	3
12 Madras	12,594	511	158	59	2,161	65	12,594	511
13 North-West Frontier Province (*Districts and Administered Territories*).	242	5	8	2	44	..	242	5
14 Punjab	9,176	66	486	23	492	..	9,176	66
15 United Provinces of Agra and Oudh	4,100	176	277	9	392	8	4,100	176
States and Agencies ...	**13,636**	**1,985**	**1,976**	**1,668**	**2,436**	**313**	**13,636**	**1,985**
16 Assam States	3	2	..	..	..	2	3	2
17 Baluchistan States	12	..	..	..	7	..	12	..
18 Baroda State	137	25	3	..	81	1	137	25
19 Bengal States	708	11	2	..	136	..	708	11
20 Bihar and Orissa States	207	23	32	8	6	..	207	23
21 Bombay States	312	9	23	3	52	..	312	9
22 Central India Agency	609	87	1	..	155	8	609	87
23 Central Provinces States	94	26	5	29	40	...	94	26
24 Gwalior State	285	36	22	4	3	6	285	36
25 Hyderabad State	3,893	1,567	1,717	1,488	960	288	3,893	1,567
26 Jammu and Kashmir State ..	417	5	..	..	55	1	417	5
27 Madras States Agency	526	1	17	1	175	2	526	1
Cochin State	*171*	*1*	*2*	..	*19*	*1*	*171*	*1*
Travancore State	*218*	..	*10*	..	*22*	..	*218*	..
Other Madras States	*137*	..	*5*	*1*	*134*	*1*	*137*	..
28 Mysore State	1,213	9	9	1	426	4	1,213	9
29 North-West Frontier Province (*Agencies and Tribal Areas*).	..	..	..	..	..	..	..	..
30 Punjab States	37	..	..	..	1	..	37	..
31 Punjab States Agency	1,346	40	48	..	81	..	1,346	40
32 Rajputana Agency	2,933	93	22	106	252	1	2,933	93
33 Sikkim State	..	..	..	..	..	..	...	...
34 United Provinces States	..	..	..	..	..	..	..	..
35 Western India States Agency ..	904	51	75	28	6	..	904	51

hood—Part II—Provincial Distribution—*contd.*

Supply of Material Substances—*contd.*

Trade—*contd.*

in skins, leather and furs. | *Order 27.*—Trade in wood.

leather, furs, feathers, horn, etc., and the articles made these. | Total *Order 27.*—Trade in wood.

Total working dependants. Males.	Total working dependants. Females.	Total following occupation as subsidiary to other. Males.	Total following occupation as subsidiary to other. Females.	Total earners principal occupation. Males.	Total earners principal occupation. Females.	Total working dependants. Males.	Total working dependants. Females.	Total following occupation as subsidiary to other. Males.	Total following occupation as subsidiary to other. Females.	
943	944	945	946	947	948	949	950	951	952	
3,514	**2,157**	**12,810**	**778**	**88,942**	**35,754**	**5,116**	**9,442**	**40,576**	**17,472**	
1,538	**489**	**10,374**	**465**	**67,158**	**28,585**	**2,927**	**7,122**	**35,893**	**15,945**	
..	..	13	6	68	11	..	..	5	..	1
..	..	..	..	2	..	..	..	..	..	2
107	33	925	17	2,553	85	238	13	6,871	46	3
..	..	27	..	18	..	..	..	1	..	4
206	15	2,874	31	11,506	5,186	116	479	4,066	1,172	5
36	84	2,246	261	4,811	4,994	420	491	10,406	9,691	6
222	83	731	44	2,397	1,463	74	1,371	237	46	7
..	..	..	..	*2*	..	..	..	*1*	..	
12	44	83	6	9,227	3,158	455	2,084	4,352	1,168	8
26	137	383	27	8,312	8,760	372	1,325	5,565	3,012	9
..	..	3	..	5	1	..	..	15	..	10
..	..	..	..	221	6	1	..	3	..	11
158	59	2,161	65	12,208	2,788	976	1,093	2,937	611	12
8	2	44	..	1,230	10	46	1	182	..	13
486	23	492	..	9,154	337	204	111	714	41	14
277	9	392	8	5,446	1,78[illegible]	25	154	539	158	15
1,976	**1,668**	**2,436**	**313**	**21,784**	**7,169**	**2,189**	**2,320**	**4,683**	**1,527**	
..	..	..	2	107	8	3	1	179	6	16
..	..	7	..	..	..	..	..	..	..	17
3	..	81	1	537	21	26	..	44	..	18
2	..	136	..	560	41	73	28	54	1	19
32	8	6	..	751	924	122	125	901	182	20
23	3	52	..	331	124	22	56	34	30	21
1	..	155	8	1,035	369	8	19	380	100	22
5	29	40	..	318	406	18	72	139	599	23
22	4	3	6	334	1	61	..	..	..	24
1,717	1,488	960	288	4,541	1,303	1,496	1,464	972	306	25
..	..	55	1	662	89	3	8	149	96	26
17	1	175	2	8,487	2,526	204	109	698	103	27
2	..	*19*	*1*	*634*	*71*	*6*	*3*	*184*	*7*	
10	..	*22*	..	*7,756*	*2,377*	*197*	*97*	*462*	*94*	
5	*1*	*134*	*4*	*97*	*78*	*1*	*9*	*52*	*2*	
9	1	426	4	878	304	6	19	153	21	28
..	..	..	..	13	..	..	..	228	..	29
..	..	1	..	51	2	12	15	25	..	30
48	..	81	..	1,100	209	46	93	288	25	31
22	106	252	1	874	650	10	70	408	52	32
..	..	..	..	..	1	..	..	..	1	33
..	..	..	..	267	2	..	..	6	..	34
75	28	6	..	938	189	79	241	25	5	35

Table X.—Occupation or Means of Liveli

Class B.—Preparation and

Sub-Class V.—

Order 27.—

Province, State or Agency.	*Group 119.*—Trade in wood (not fire-wood).						*Group 120.*—Trade	
	Total earners principal occupation.		Total working dependants.		Total following occupation as subsidiary to other.		Total earners principal occupation.	
	Males.	Females.	Males.	Females.	Males.	Females.	Males.	Females.
1	953	954	955	956	957	958	959	960
INDIA	**60,771**	**19,638**	**3,125**	**3,057**	**23,001**	**13,054**	**2,605**	**710**
Provinces	**46,368**	**16,845**	**1,853**	**2,397**	**20,469**	**12,663**	**1,427**	**218**
1 Ajmer-Merwara	58	..	..	..	5	..	..	..
2 Andamans and Nicobars	2	..	..	..	..	..	..	..
3 Assam	1,259	25	58	4	1,110	12	7	..
4 Baluchistan (*Districts and Administered Territories*).	18	..	..	..	1	..	..	..
5 Bengal	9,439	3,400	96	197	2,569	409	70	40
6 Bihar and Orissa	3,938	4,120	397	451	9,877	9,608	456	31
7 Bombay (*including Aden*)	1,501	133	55	2	192	6	86	53
Aden	*1*	.	..	..	*1*	..	..	..
8 Burma	4,243	211	45	19	353	14	8	18
9 Central Provinces and Berar ..	4,638	6,447	231	722	3,620	2,353	12	6
10 Coorg	4	..	..	..	8	..	..	..
11 Delhi	198	3	1	..	3	..	..	..
12 Madras	8,740	1,220	753	854	1,649	193	601	70
13 North-West Frontier Province (*Districts and Administered Territories*).	1,034	9	31	1	157	..	145	..
14 Punjab	7,017	259	171	70	572	41	37	..
15 United Provinces of Agra and Oudh	4,279	1,018	15	77	353	27	5	..
States and Agencies ..	**14,403**	**2,793**	**1,272**	**660**	**2,532**	**391**	**1,178**	**492**
16 Assam States	86	3	3	..	119	1	..	..
17 Baluchistan States	..	..	..	..	..	..	..	..
18 Baroda State	474	..	26	..	34	..	..	..
19 Bengal States	199	8	1	..	15	1	..	..
20 Bihar and Orissa States	209	38	2	..	414	22	..	..
21 Bombay States	152	5	17	2	24	21	1	5
22 Central India Agency	668	66	7	8	239	72	1	..
23 Central Provinces States	180	171	..	14	73	121	7	..
24 Gwalior State	327	1	60	..	..	..	..	..
25 Hyderabad State	2,134	279	1,018	448	587	71	660	324
26 Jammu and Kashmir State ..	505	65	3	4	89	40	..	..
27 Madras States Agency	7,290	1,704	43	1	259	9	18	5
Cochin State ..	*388*	*2*	3	..	*108*	*5*	*4*	*3*
Travancore State	*6,813*	*1,692*	*40*	*1*	*117*	*3*	*14*	*2*
Other Madras States	*89*	*10*	..	..	*34*	*1*	..	..
28 Mysore State	253	160	..	9	29	4	422	53
29 North-West Frontier Province (*Agencies and Tribal Areas*).	13	..	..	..	228	..	..	..
30 Punjab States	50	2	12	15	25	..	..	..
31 Punjab States Agency	768	186	37	54	93	23	..	3
32 Rajputana Agency	186	15	..	8	283	..	31	102
33 Sikkim State	..	1	..	..	..	1	..	..
34 United Provinces States	267	2	..	..	6	..	..	..
35 Western India States Agency ..	642	87	43	97	15	5	38	..

hood—Part II—Provincial Distribution—*contd.*

Supply of Material Substances—*contd.*

Trade—*contd.*

Trade in wood—*contd.*

in barks.				*Group 121.*—Trade in bamboos and canes.						
Total working dependants.		Total following occupation as subsidiary to other.		Total earners principal occupation.		Total working dependants.		Total following occupation as subsidiary to other.		
Males.	Females.	Males.	Females.	Males.	Females.	Males.	Females.	Males.	Females.	
961	962	963	964	965	966	967	968	969	970	
141	**356**	**420**	**118**	**19,054**	**8,611**	**1,242**	**3,078**	**12,654**	**1,320**	
31	**103**	**238**	**25**	**14,901**	**6,566**	**703**	**2,266**	**11,351**	**1,119**	
..	..	..	..	10	..	..	..	..	..	**1**
..	..	..	..	..	..	..	..	..	..	**2**
..	..	2	..	758	55	139	9	4,095	30	**3**
..	..	..	..	..	..	..	..	..	..	**4**
..	..	..	..	1,693	534	17	17	1,411	120	**5**
..	1	50	7	378	733	23	27	339	65	**6**
4	10	24	11	368	1,126	13	1,237	10	29	**7**
..	..	..	..	..	..	..	..	..	..	
..	9	1	2	3,379	888	271	352	2,508	200	**8**
..	76	8	4	3,210	1,600	132	350	1,771	206	**9**
..	..	..	..	1	1	..	..	7	..	**10**
..	..	..	..	11	..	..	—	—	..	**11**
12	7	129	1	2,076	1,013	81	164	952	405	**12**
15	..	24	..	51	1	..	—	1	—	**13**
..	..	..	..	2,080	76	24	37	141	..	**14**
..	..	..	..	886	539	3	73	116	64	**15**
110	**253**	**182**	**93**	**4,153**	**2,045**	**539**	**812**	**1,303**	**201**	
..	..	..	..	21	5	..	1	60	5	**16**
..	..	..	..	..	..	..	..	..	..	**17**
..	..	..	..	48	2	..	..	1	—	**18**
..	..	..	..	361	30	72	28	39	..	**19**
..	..	..	..	484	729	120	121	397	65	**20**
1	..	..	..	159	107	4	49	10	9	**21**
..	..	..	..	211	192	1	11	103	24	**22**
..	..	..	..	96	75	14	44	5	—	**23**
..	..	..	..	7	..	1	..	..	—	**24**
97	**249**	**92**	**79**	**1,228**	**309**	**234**	**471**	**229**	**83**	**25**
..	..	..	..	..	1	..	..	..	1	**26**
1	..	3	1	424	87	63	16	140	8	**27**
..	..	*1*	*1*	*130*	*56*	*1*	*3*	*55*	*1*	
1	..	*1*	..	*289*	*31*	*62*	*13*	*85*	*7*	
..	..	*1*	..	*5*	..	..	..	..	..	
3	**3**	**81**	**10**	**100**	**66**	**3**	**3**	**33**	**3**	**28**
..	..	..	..	..	..	..	..	..	..	**29**
..	..	..	..	1	..	..	..	..	..	**30**
..	..	..	1	331	15	9	39	195	1	**31**
..	..	6	2	603	421	3	18	90	2	**32**
..	..	..	..	..	..	..	..	..	..	**33**
..	..	..	..	..	..	..	..	..	..	**34**
8	1	..	..	79	6	15	11	1	—	**35**

Table X.—Occupation or Means of Liveli

Class B.—Preparation and

Sub-Class V.—

Province, State or Agency.	*Order 27.*—Trade in wood—*concld.* *Group 122.*—Trade in thatches and other forest produce. Total earners principal occupation.		Total working dependants.		Total following occupation as subsidiary to other.		Total earners principal occupation.	
	Males.	Females.	Males.	Females.	Males.	Females.	Males.	Females.
1	971	972	973	974	975	976	977	978
INDIA	**6,512**	**6,795**	**608**	**2,951**	**4,501**	**2,980**	**23,145**	**2,069**
Provinces	4,462	4,956	340	2,356	3,835	2,138	16,717	1,258
1 Ajmer-Merwara	..	11	..	..	..	..	19	..
2 Andamans and Nicobars ..	..	..	..	..	..	..	..	..
3 Assam	529	5	41	..	1,664	4	564	19
4 Baluchistan (*Districts and Administered Territories*).	..	..	..	..	..	..	18	..
5 Bengal	304	1,212	3	265	86	643	2,029	41
6 Bihar and Orissa	39	110	..	12	140	11	444	100
7 Bombay (*including Aden*) ..	442	151	2	122	11	..	1,474	32
Aden	*1*	..	..	..	..	..	*5*	..
8 Burma	1,597	2,041	139	1,704	1,490	952	2,213	149
9 Central Provinces and Berar ..	452	707	9	177	166	449	1,110	56
10 Coorg	..	..	..	..	..	..	32	1
11 Delhi	12	3	..	..	..	..	255	2
12 Madras	791	485	130	68	207	12	3,711	113
13 North-West Frontier Province (*Districts and Administered Territories*).	..	..	..	..	..	..	262	1
14 Punjab	20	2	9	4	1	..	2,853	601
15 United Provinces of Agra and Oudh	276	229	7	4	70	67	1,733	143
States and Agencies ..	2,050	1,839	268	595	666	842	6,428	811
16 Assam States	..	..	..	..	..	..	2	1
17 Baluchistan States	..	..	..	..	..	..	..	..
18 Baroda State	15	19	..	..	9	..	924	19
19 Bengal States	..	3	..	..	..	..	36	3
20 Bihar and Orissa States	58	157	..	4	90	95	134	123
21 Bombay States	19	7	..	5	..	..	179	1
22 Central India Agency	155	111	..	..	38	4	601	46
23 Central Provinces States	35	160	4	14	61	478	133	7
24 Gwalior State	..	..	..	..	..	..	116	1
25 Hyderabad State	519	391	147	296	64	73	1,438	509
26 Jammu and Kashmir State ..	157	23	..	4	60	55	19	..
27 Madras States Agency	755	730	97	92	296	85	787	15
Cochin State	*112*	*10*	*2*	..	*20*	..	*236*	*8*
Travancore State	*640*	*652*	*94*	*83*	*259*	*84*	*542*	*7*
Other Madras States	*3*	*68*	*1*	*9*	*17*	*1*	*9*	..
28 Mysore State	103	25	..	4	10	4	545	20
29 North-West Frontier Province (*Agencies and Tribal Areas*).	..	..	..	..	..	..	..	..
30 Punjab States	..	..	..	..	..	..	14	2
31 Punjab States Agency	1	5	..	..	..	..	323	25
32 Rajputana Agency	54	112	7	44	29	48	680	18
33 Sikkim State	..	..	..	..	..	..	1	..
34 United Provinces States	..	..	..	..	..	..	67	20
35 Western India States Agency ..	179	96	13	132	9	..	429	1

hood—Part II—Provincial Distribution.—*contd.*

Supply of Material Substances—*contd.*

Trade—*contd.*

Total *Order 28.*—Trade in Metals.				*Order 28.*—Trade in Metals. *Group 123.*—Trade in metals, machinery, knives, tools, etc.						
Total working dependants.		Total following occupation as subsidiary to other.		Total earners principal occupation.		Total working dependants.		Total following occupation as subsidiary to other.		
Males.	Females	Males.	Females.	Males.	Females.	Males.	Females.	Males.	Females.	
979	980	981	982	983	984	985	986	987	988	
958	**1,032**	**2,308**	**190**	**23,145**	**2,069**	**958**	**1,032**	**2,308**	**190**	
304	**329**	**1,519**	**81**	**16,717**	**1,258**	**304**	**329**	**1,519**	**81**	
..	..	..	..	19	..	..	..	..	..	1
..	..	..	..	..	..	..	..	..	..	2
10	1	175	4	564	19	10	1	175	4	3
..	..	..	..	18	..	..	..	..	..	4
33	1	124	1	2,029	41	33	1	124	1	5
9	..	156	17	444	100	9	..	156	17	6
22	32	27	..	1,474	32	22	32	27	..	7
..	..	..	..	*5*	..	..	..	..	..	
57	40	192	5	2,213	149	57	40	192	5	8
19	6	175	9	1,110	56	19	6	175	9	9
..	..	10	..	32	1	..	..	10	..	10
5	..	..	..	255	2	5	..	..	..	11
41	10	361	12	3,711	113	41	10	361	12	12
..	..	1	..	262	1	..	..	1	..	13
104	210	211	33	2,853	601	104	210	211	33	14
4	29	87	..	1,733	143	4	29	87	..	15
654	**703**	**789**	**109**	**6,428**	**811**	**654**	**703**	**789**	**109**	
..	1	13	2	2	1	..	1	13	2	16
..	..	..	..	..	..	..	..	..	..	17
74	1	16	..	924	19	74	1	16	..	18
..	..	1	..	36	3	..	..	1	..	19
29	..	33	..	134	123	29	..	33	..	20
..	..	..	..	179	1	..	..	..	..	21
3	1	69	..	601	46	3	1	69	..	22
..	248	1	..	133	7	..	248	1	..	23
..	..	127	4	116	1	..	..	127	4	24
449	428	188	78	1,438	509	449	428	188	78	25
..	..	..	..	19	..	..	..	..	..	26
30	1	91	19	787	15	30	1	91	19	27
..	*1*	*44*	..	*236*	*9*	—	*1*	*44*	—	
30	..	*47*	*19*	*542*	*7*	*30*	—	*47*	*19*	
..	..	..	..	*9*	..	..	—	—	—	
33	1	102	1	545	20	33	1	102	1	28
..	..	..	..	..	..	..	..	..	..	29
..	3	2	..	14	2	..	3	2	—	30
17	8	79	3	323	25	17	8	79	3	31
7	3	67	2	680	18	7	3	67	2	32
..	..	..	..	1	..	..	..	..	—	33
..	8	..	..	67	20	..	8	..	—	34
2	..	..	..	29	1	12	—	..	—	35

Table X.—Occupation or Means of Liveli

Class B.—Preparation and

Sub-Class V.—

Order 29.—

Province, State or Agency.	Total *Order 29*.—Trade in pottery, bricks and tiles. Total earners principal occupation. Males.	Females.	Total working dependants. Males.	Females.	Total following occupation as subsidiary to other. Males.	Females.	*Group 124*.—Trade in Total earners principal occupation. Males.	Females.
1	989	990	991	992	993	994	995	996
INDIA ..	**24,043**	**13,116**	**2,069**	**7,260**	**4,869**	**2,182**	**24,043**	**13,116**
Provinces	**17,550**	**6,881**	**691**	**2,088**	**3,736**	**755**	**17,550**	**6,881**
1 Ajmer-Merwara	..	24	..	4	..	..	..	24
2 Andamans and Nicobars	..	..	..	..	..	..	..	..
3 Assam	155	18	..	8	133	4	155	18
4 Baluchistan (*Districts and Administered Territories*).	9	..	..	..	..	..	9	..
5 Bengal	6,081	2,004	176	1,031	1,039	178	6,081	2,004
6 Bihar and Orissa	1,169	1,536	52	164	1,149	217	1,169	1,536
7 Bombay (*including Aden*)	772	336	6	47	22	19	772	336
Aden	*1*	..	..	..	..	..	*1*	..
8 Burma	95	51	2	1	10	..	95	51
9 Central Provinces and Berar ..	2,022	1,144	77	498	272	84	2,022	1,144
10 Coorg	..	..	..	..	..	..	..	..
11 Delhi	175	4	..	..	..	..	175	4
12 Madras	3,213	1,449	133	222	733	243	3,213	1,449
13 North-West Frontier Province (*Districts and Administered Territories*).	408	..	..	..	1	..	408	..
14 Punjab	2,201	252	223	106	361	4	2,201	252
15 United Provinces of Agra and Oudh	1,250	63	22	7	16	6	1,250	63
States and Agencies ..	**6,493**	**6,235**	**1,378**	**5,172**	**1,133**	**1,427**	**6,493**	**6,235**
16 Assam States	19	..	1	..	..	..	19	..
17 Baluchistan States	11	..	..	..	..	..	11	..
18 Baroda State	42	49	1	11	4	..	42	49
19 Bengal States	31	20	..	..	4	..	31	20
20 Bihar and Orissa States	14	114	2	14	166	11	14	114
21 Bombay States	12	4	..	..	..	..	12	4
22 Central India Agency	558	908	3	32	72	44	558	908
23 Central Provinces States	26	4	..	13	1	..	26	4
24 Gwalior State	..	..	..	..	..	..	..	..
25 Hyderabad State	4,205	4,739	1,247	4,971	548	1,339	4,205	4,739
26 Jammu and Kashmir State ..	38	2	..	..	3	..	38	2
27 Madras States Agency	901	249	72	34	206	28	901	249
Cochin State	*179*	*157*	..	*17*	*33*	*19*	*179*	*157*
Travancore State	*709*	*89*	*72*	*16*	*136*	*5*	*709*	*89*
Other Madras States	*13*	*3*	..	*1*	*37*	*4*	*13*	*3*
28 Mysore State	100	36	6	33	62	2	100	36
29 North-West Frontier Province (*Agencies and Tribal Areas*).	..	..	..	..	..	..	..	..
30 Punjab States	1	..	..	..	..	..	1	..
31 Punjab States Agency	212	7	15	17	61	..	212	7
32 Rajputana Agency	184	100	11	12	6	1	184	100
33 Sikkim State	..	..	..	..	..	..	..	..
34 United Provinces States	..	..	..	..	..	..	..	..
35 Western India States Agency ..	139	3	20	35	..	2	139	3

hood—Part II—Provincial Distribution—*contd.*

Supply of Material Substances—*contd.*

Trade—*contd.*

Trade in pottery, bricks and tiles.				*Order 30.*—Trade in chemical products.						
pottery, bricks and tiles.				Total *Order 30.*—Trade in chemical products.						
Total working dependants.		Total following occupation as subsidiary to other.		Total earners principal occupation.		Total working dependants.		Total following occupation as subsidiary to other.		
Males.	Females.	Males.	Females.	Males.	Females.	Males.	Females.	Males.	Females.	
997	998	999	1000	1001	1002	1003	1004	1005	1006	
2,069	**7,260**	**4,869**	**2,182**	**45,474**	**13,410**	**1,043**	**2,737**	**9,807**	**2,184**	
691	2,088	3,736	755	38,705	11,905	802	2,538	8,173	1,871	
..	4	..	..	70	4	..	2	3	..	1
..	..	..	..	..	..	..	..	..	..	2
..	8	133	4	568	50	34	6	238	14	3
..	..	..	..	84	3	..	..	13	..	4
176	1,031	1,039	178	3,561	164	27	5	520	7	5
52	164	1,149	217	2,715	384	9	11	1,203	56	6
6	47	22	19	1,758	243	35	50	45	3	7
..	..	..	..	*17*	*1*	..	..	*1*	..	
2	1	10	..	4,552	959	161	218	927	52	8
77	498	272	84	10,356	8,338	358	2,169	3,668	1,588	9
..	..	..	..	4	..	..	..	..	..	10
..	..	..	..	379	6	..	..	1	..	11
133	222	733	243	4,208	1,000	37	41	482	62	12
..	..	1	..	130	1	..	..	3	..	13
223	106	361	4	5,142	40	100	2	191	..	14
22	7	16	6	5,178	713	41	34	879	89	15
1,378	**5,172**	**1,133**	**1,427**	**6,769**	**1,505**	**241**	**199**	**1,634**	**313**	
1	..	..	..	35	3	4	1	186	..	16
..	..	..	..	2	..	1	..	30	..	17
1	11	4	..	361	7	14	..	18	1	18
..	..	4	..	67	4	..	..	10	..	19
2	14	166	11	197	189	..	..	261	6	20
..	..	..	..	147	85	5	6	23	28	21
3	32	72	44	1,316	440	18	9	420	225	22
..	13	1	..	324	153	8	80	111	8	23
..	..	..	..	177	6	3	15	1	..	24
1,247	4,971	548	1,339	736	34	103	26	47	..	25
..	..	3	..	29	2	..	..	20	3	26
72	34	206	28	1,506	270	56	43	196	17	27
..	*17*	*33*	*19*	*620*	*26*	*5*	*3*	*70*	*2*	
72	*16*	*136*	*5*	*876*	*241*	*51*	*39*	*109*	*15*	
..	*1*	*37*	*4*	*10*	*3*	..	*1*	*17*	—	
6	33	62	2	227	30	3	7	52	1	28
..	..	..	..	..	..	..	—	..	..	29
..	..	..	..	21	..	..	..	5	—	30
15	17	61	..	509	2	3	..	10	—	31
11	12	6	1	756	255	5	11	239	16	32
..	..	..	..	..	..	..	..	..	..	33
..	..	..	..	63	38	..	..	..	8	34
20	35	..	2	206	7	13	1	5	..	35

Table X.—Occupation or Means of Liveli

Class B.—Preparation and

Sub-Class V.—Trade

Order 30.—Trade in chemical products—*concld.*

Province, State or Agency.	*Group 125.*—Drugs, dyes, paints, petroleum, explosives, etc.						Total *Order 31.*—Hotels,	
	Total earners principal occupation.		Total working dependants.		Total following occupation as subsidiary to other.		Total earners principal occupation.	
	Males.	Females.	Males.	Females.	Males.	Females.	Males.	Females.
1	1007	1008	1009	1010	1011	1012	1013	1014
INDIA	**45,474**	**13,410**	**1,043**	**2,737**	**9,807**	**2,184**	**308,715**	**116,867**
Provinces	**38,705**	**11,905**	**802**	**2,538**	**8,173**	**1,871**	**186,170**	**59,244**
1 Ajmer-Merwara	70	4	..	2	3	..	719	35
2 Andamans and Nicobars	..	..	..	..	..	..	50	..
3 Assam	568	50	34	6	238	14	1,694	184
4 Baluchistan (*Districts and Administered Territories*).	84	3	..	..	13	..	496	6
5 Bengal	3,561	164	27	5	520	7	13,194	1,017
6 Bihar and Orissa	2,715	384	9	11	1,203	56	13,956	10,512
7 Bombay (*including Aden*)	1,758	243	35	50	45	3	29,216	2,740
Aden	*17*	*1*	..	..	*1*	..	*246*	*14*
8 Burma	4,552	959	161	218	927	52	36,787	26,126
9 Central Provinces and Berar ..	10,356	8,338	358	2,169	3,668	1,588	4,869	393
10 Coorg	4	..	..	..	..	..	272	29
11 Delhi	379	6	..	..	1	..	1,738	62
12 Madras	4,208	1,000	37	41	482	62	52,118	16,498
13 North-West Frontier Province (*Districts and Administered Territories*).	130	1	..	..	3	..	3,100	6
14 Punjab	5,142	40	100	2	191	..	11,176	106
15 United Provinces of Agra and Oudh	5,178	713	41	34	879	89	16,785	1,530
States and Agencies ..	**6,769**	**1,505**	**241**	**199**	**1,634**	**313**	**122,545**	**57,623**
16 Assam States	35	3	4	1	186	..	26	197
17 Baluchistan States	2	..	1	..	30	..	88	..
18 Baroda State	361	7	14	..	18	1	3,347	201
19 Bengal States	67	4	..	..	10	..	80	1
20 Bihar and Orissa States	197	189	..	..	261	6	1,781	336
21 Bombay States	147	85	5	6	23	28	1,961	195
22 Central India Agency	1,316	440	18	9	420	225	2,856	266
23 Central Provinces States . ..	324	133	8	80	11	8	629	138
24 Gwalior State	177	6	3	15	1	..	1,098	107
25 Hyderabad State	736	34	103	26	47	..	76,798	45,451
26 Jammu and Kashmir State ..	29	2	..	..	20	3	1,494	112
27 Madras States Agency	1,406	270	56	43	196	17	13,549	8,330
Cochin State	*620*	*26*	*5*	*3*	*70*	*2*	*4,339*	*652*
Travancore State	*876*	*241*	*51*	*39*	*109*	*15*	*8,556*	*7,438*
Other Madras States	*10*	*3*	..	*1*	*17*	..	*654*	*240*
28 Mysore State	227	30	3	7	52	1	6,730	1,378
29 North-West Frontier Province (*Agencies and Tribal Areas*).	..	..	..	..	..	..	..	..
30 Punjab States	21	..	..	..	5	..	94	1
31 Punjab States Agency	509	2	3	..	10	..	1,355	5
32 Rajputana Agency	756	255	5	11	239	16	6,029	586
33 Sikkim State	..	..	..	..	..	..	136	93
34 United Provinces States	63	38	..	..	..	8	510	57
35 Western India States Agency ..	296	7	18	1	5	..	3,984	16

hood—Part II—Provincial Distribution—*contd.*

Supply of Material Substances—*contd.*

—*contd.*

Order 31.—Hotels, cafés, restaurants, etc.

cafés, restaurants, etc.				*Group 126.*—Vendors of wine, liquors, aerated waters and ice.						
Total working dependants.		Total following occupation as subsidiary to other.		Total earners principal occupation.		Total working dependants.		Total following occupation as subsidiary to other.		
Males.	Females.	Males.	Females.	Males.	Females.	Males.	Females.	Males.	Females.	
1015	1016	1017	1018	1019	1020	1021	1022	1023	1024	
26,923	**37,312**	**41,864**	**15,545**	**144,533**	**65,840**	**21,728**	**23,394**	**31,001**	**11,795**	
4,376	**14,000**	**16,850**	**4,453**	**48,502**	**14,588**	**911**	**1,364**	**8,018**	**1,211**	
3	7	28	3	237	23	3	7	20	1	1
..	..	..	..	3	..	..	..	..	..	2
26	61	252	31	323	76	5	1	49	5	3
..	..	11	..	49	..	..	..	2	..	4
77	16	947	20	4,128	399	43	9	576	17	5
53	149	3,509	785	12,739	9,497	45	86	3,133	620	6
1,151	451	1,048	112	3,476	230	232	40	207	13	7
13	*1*	*2*	..	*16*	*1*	..	..	*1*	..	
1,366	10,588	2,632	2,413	4,036	267	145	132	185	23	8
82	77	551	70	1,751	102	43	15	302	12	9
4	1	35	1	86	2	..	..	20	..	10
2	..	—	..	325	15	1	..	..	..	11
1,310	2,008	5,446	679	11,011	3,093	163	434	2,781	318	12
13	..	16	..	742	1	..	..	4	..	13
100	1	509	1	3,275	11	50	..	139	1	14
189	641	1,866	338	6,321	872	181	640	600	201	15
22,547	**23,312**	**25,014**	**11,092**	**96,031**	**51,252**	**20,817**	**22,030**	**22,983**	**10,584**	
4	45	6	60	18	161	4	36	4	6	16
..	..	..	..	27	—	..	..	..	..	17
166	85	331	3	780	69	48	39	222	2	18
1	..	3	..	36	..	..	..	..	..	19
57	23	1,073	96	1,754	334	57	23	1,063	95	20
123	46	318	83	1,025	55	83	29	208	9	21
24	9	491	22	1,665	200	18	9	425	19	22
53	378	201	9	582	130	50	378	199	8	23
40	21	282	2	542	67	22	18	150	1	24
21,049	21,795	19,944	10,636	74,133	44,641	20,305	21,062	19,255	10,371	25
15	57	86	25	86	..	..	1	6	..	26
409	284	835	53	6,835	4,846	96	67	406	29	27
50	*10*	*426*	*20*	*884*	*94*	*13*	*3*	*145*	*10*	
348	*270*	*325*	*26*	*5,812*	*4,735*	*77*	*62*	*203*	*16*	
11	*4*	*84*	*7*	*139*	*17*	*6*	*2*	*58*	*3*	
95	109	739	63	2,239	203	34	24	538	19	28
..	..	..	..	..	..	..	..	..	..	29
..	..	21	1	62	1	..	..	11	1	30
17	..	79	1	815	2	15	..	68	1	31
86	422	502	28	4,467	479	50	328	399	21	32
5	..	19	7	41	8	..	—	..	..	33
3	8	23	2	165	35	3	8	2	1	34
400	30	66	1	759	21	32	8	7	..	35

Table X.—Occupation or Means of Liveli

Class B.—Preparation and

Sub-Class V.—Trade

Order 31.—Hotels, cafés,

Province, State or Agency.	*Group 172.*—Owners and managers of hotels, cook shops, sarais, etc. (and employees). Total earners principal occupation.		Total working dependants.		Total following occupation as subsidiary to other.		*Group 128.*—Hawkers. Total earners principal occupation.	
	Males.	Females.	Males.	Females.	Males.	Females.	Males.	Females.
1	1025	1026	1027	1028	1029	1030	1031	1032
INDIA	**122,643**	**21,991**	**3,791**	**3,358**	**6,551**	**1,223**	**41,539**	**29,036**
Provinces	101,627	17,468	2,462	2,753	5,042	801	36,041	27,188
1 Ajmer-Merwara	172	9	..	..	5	..	310	3
2 Andamans and Nicobars	47	..	..	..	..	..	..	..
3 Assam	1,294	96	21	57	153	21	77	12
4 Baluchistan (*Districts and Administered Territories*).	323	5	..	..	4	..	124	1
5 Bengal	8,867	603	34	7	356	3	199	15
6 Bihar and Orissa	1,078	971	4	59	352	163	139	44
7 Bombay (*including Aden*)	23,672	2,308	824	253	707	73	2,0[illegible]8	202
Aden	*616*	*6*	*5*	..	*1*	..	*214*	*7*
8 Burma	16,558	2,831	410	917	697	189	16,193	23,028
9 Central Provinces and Berar ..	2,879	221	38	51	224	47	239	70
10 Coorg	161	10	4	1	14	..	25	17
11 Delhi	449	19	1	..	..	..	964	28
12 Madras	37,610	10,056	1,099	1,407	2,127	304	3,497	3,349
13 North-West Frontier Province .. (*Districts and Administered Territories*).	2,079	4	6	..	10	..	279	1
14 Punjab	2,205	75	13	..	227	..	5,696	20
15 United Provinces of Agra and Oudh	4,233	260	8	1	166	1	6,231	398
States and Agencies ..	**21,016**	**4,523**	**1,329**	**605**	**1,509**	**422**	**5,498**	**1,848**
16 Assam States	8	33	..	7	2	54	..	3
17 Baluchistan States	21	..	..	..	..	..	40	..
18 Baroda State	2,301	76	109	41	95	1	266	56
19 Bengal States	42	1	1	..	2	..	2	..
20 Bihar and Orissa States	27	2	..	..	10	1	..	..
21 Bombay States	888	111	38	17	98	73	48	29
22 Central India Agency	599	35	3	..	30	1	592	31
23 Central Provinces States	47	8	3	..	2	1	..	..
24 Gwalior State	109	1	1	..	54	1	447	39
25 Hyderabad State	1,815	373	512	271	467	208	850	437
26 Jammu and Kashmir State ..	1,175	106	14	56	58	23	233	6
27 Madras States Agency	6,216	2,957	235	52	393	20	498	527
Cochin State	*3,352*	*542*	*32*	*1*	*267*	*10*	*103*	*16*
Travancore State	*2,351*	*2,194*	*198*	*51*	*100*	*6*	*393*	*509*
Other Madras States	*513*	*221*	*5*	*2*	*26*	*4*	*2*	*2*
28 Mysore State	4,179	548	61	49	163	25	312	627
29 North-West Frontier Province .. (*Agencies and Tribal Areas*).	..	..	..	..	..	..	..	..
30 Punjab States	24	..	..	..	8	..	8	..
31 Punjab States Agency	402	3	1	..	8	..	138	..
32 Rajputana Agency	380	87	6	93	63	6	1,182	20
33 Sikkim State	95	85	5	..	19	7	..	..
34 United Provinces States	56	4	..	..	..	..	289	18
35 Western India States Agency ..	2,632	93	340	17	37	1	593	55

hood—Part II—Provincial Distribution—*contd.*

Supply of Material Substances—*contd.*

—*contd.*

restaurants, etc.—*concld.* | *Order 32.*—Other trade in food stuffs.

of drink and food stuffs. | Total *Order 32.*—Other trade in food stuffs.

Total working dependants.		Total following occupation as subsidiary to other.		Total earners principal occupation.		Total working dependants.		Total following occupation as subsidiary to other.		
Males.	Females.	Males.	Females.	Males.	Females.	Males.	Females.	Males.	Females.	
1033	1034	1035	1036	1037	1038	1039	1040	1041	1042	
1,404	**10,560**	**4,312**	**2,527**	**2,413,640**	**1,100,999**	**101,626**	**220,655**	**564,073**	**124,561**	
1,003	9,883	3,790	2,441	1,926,890	883,182	53,712	156,095	457,729	96,017	
..	..	3	2	6,831	1,078	141	172	966	89	1
..	..	..	..	137	..	2	1	21	..	2
..	3	50	5	50,681	9,309	2,858	4,649	29,966	1,572	3
..	..	5	..	1,914	12	8	..	430	3	4
..	..	15	..	389,736	100,320	4,812	5,573	71,329	5,902	5
4	4	24	2	147,572	135,885	1,439	8,361	79,208	19,107	6
95	158	134	26	111,965	22,730	5,182	4,934	9,746	2,104	7
8	*1*	..	..	*763*	*77*	*14*	*2*	*8*	*1*	
811	9,539	1,750	2,201	140,348	162,399	6,787	62,280	23,108	14,571	8
1	11	25	11	97,439	58,484	3,768	14,761	28,753	13,018	9
..	..	1	1	1,548	199	17	3	358	8	10
..	..	..	..	9,090	538	19	123	193	8	11
48	167	538	57	310,745	142,724	6,616	11,142	60,035	11,611	12
7	..	2	..	13,631	160	467	56	1,176	12	13
37	1	143	..	130,885	7,652	4,432	3,189	11,048	326	14
..	..	1,100	136	514,368	241,692	17,164	40,851	141,392	27,686	15
401	677	522	86	486,750	217,817	47,914	64,560	106,344	28,544	
..	2	..	..	1,494	3,195	171	902	2,292	1,099	16
..	..	..	..	886	22	5	7	115	..	17
9	5	14	..	23,487	8,097	2,079	3,701	2,704	322	18
..	..	1	..	4,407	3,689	61	134	1,533	89	19
..	..	..	..	14,875	34,708	300	3,113	14,900	4,124	20
2	..	7	1	11,767	1,725	758	1,251	1,404	660	21
3	..	36	2	48,937	24,683	846	1,717	15,898	4,221	22
..	..	..	..	6,513	4,237	519	1,965	2,260	355	23
17	3	78	..	19,529	7,200	952	2,001	5,387	1,752	24
232	462	222	57	79,830	37,616	28,407	34,097	15,990	8,106	25
1	..	22	2	8,510	2,837	284	120	2,064	414	26
78	163	36	4	79,199	24,408	4,844	3,528	15,420	2,186	27
5	*6*	*14*	..	*15,416*	*4,939*	*170*	*189*	*2,891*	*412*	
73	*157*	*22*	*4*	*60,608*	*17,754*	*4,658*	*3,279*	*11,346*	*1,635*	
..	..	..	..	*3,175*	*1,715*	*16*	*60*	*1,183*	*139*	
..	36	38	19	23,210	19,387	505	2,376	7,369	1,676	28
..	..	..	..	152	..	..	..	..	..	29
..	..	2	..	780	369	34	61	216	11	30
1	..	3	..	17,934	1,413	760	279	1,638	106	31
30	1	40	1	101,612	37,915	2,255	5,111	13,898	2,423	32
..	..	..	..	151	25	1	..	4	1	33
..	..	21	..	10,960	4,224	603	1,557	2,165	862	34
28	5	2	..	32,517	2,067	4,530	2,640	1,087	137	35

Table X.—Occupation or Means of Liveli

Class B.—Preparation and Supply

Sub-Class V.—Trade

Order 32.—Other trade

Province, State or Agency.	*Group 129.*—Grain and pulse dealers.						*Group 130.*—Dealers	
	Total earners principal occupation.		Total working dependants.		Total following occupation as subsidiary to other.		Total earners principal occupation.	
	Males.	Females.	Males.	Females.	Males.	Females.	Males.	Females.
1	1043	1044	1045	1046	1047	1048	1049	1050
INDIA	**644,912**	**189,041**	**28,493**	**29,105**	**125,630**	**18,431**	**234,435**	**90,686**
Provinces	**505,631**	**150,780**	**11,733**	**18,349**	**103,728**	**14,233**	**176,689**	**72,897**
1 Ajmer-Merwara	476	54	..	1	11	3	348	10
2 Andamans and Nicobars	..	..	..	..	..	..	31	..
3 Assam	8,758	3,194	291	895	5,971	646	2,474	267
4 Baluchistan (*Districts and Administered Territories*).	76	..	..	..	22	..	9	..
5 Bengal	62,269	28,542	872	1,050	13,001	1,122	31,801	4,454
6 Bihar and Orissa	33,049	15,773	155	1,005	12,118	1,727	17,027	5,476
7 Bombay (*including Aden*)	19,251	1,652	866	204	1,092	137	19,375	1,998
Aden	*16*	*7*	..	..	..	..	*158*	*4*
8 Burma	19,693	6,879	509	2,648	5,185	1,038	9,923	20,679
9 Central Provinces and Berar ..	14,673	12,535	363	2,068	4,103	1,644	6,602	1,691
10 Coorg	222	25	..	..	66	2	1,053	86
11 Delhi	906	8	4	..	1	..	665	22
12 Madras	52,123	22,142	1,392	2,162	8,928	1,003	31,544	28,146
13 North-West Frontier Province (*Districts and Administered Territories*).	6,271	65	325	24	593	2	1,944	9
14 Punjab	27,917	204	1,297	76	1,732	8	11,455	27
15 United Provinces of Agra and Oudh	259,947	59,707	5,659	8,216	50,905	6,901	42,438	10,032
States and Agencies ..	**139,281**	**38,261**	**16,760**	**10,756**	**21,902**	**4,198**	**57,746**	**17,789**
16 Assam States	411	824	13	258	129	77	234	189
17 Baluchistan States	375	5	..	..	9	..	19	1
18 Baroda State	10,978	493	1,095	614	1,064	16	6,343	4,614
19 Bengal States	778	2,608	2	60	200	47	350	161
20 Bihar and Orissa States	3,045	14,215	66	298	3,466	1,887	649	285
21 Bombay States	1,958	64	146	92	541	2	5,759	718
22 Central India Agency	16,958	3,169	222	169	2,925	135	3,141	1,088
23 Central Provinces States	1,453	1,138	121	203	366	101	223	226
24 Gwalior State	1,890	105	99	12	239	19	652	47
25 Hyderabad State	35,256	7,274	12,068	8,428	6,109	1,446	3,505	2,455
26 Jammu and Kashmir State ..	3,161	2,516	34	2	918	17	1,266	32
27 Madras States Agency	8,238	2,438	193	190	1,703	185	16,429	4,779
Cochin State	*5,732*	*913*	*41*	*26*	*934*	*47*	*3,115*	*1,767*
Travancore State	*2,346*	*1,422*	*152*	*163*	*517*	*137*	*13,234*	*2,955*
Other Madras States	*160*	*103*	..	*1*	*252*	*1*	*80*	*57*
28 Mysore State	6,326	1,272	71	39	1,224	79	2,249	617
29 North-West Frontier Province (*Agencies and Tribal Areas.*) ..	72	..	..	..	..	..	61	..
30 Punjab States	70	..	2	..	7	..	129	..
31 Punjab States Agency	8,543	78	447	3	245	2	1,975	53
32 Rajputana Agency	19,357	516	366	61	1,255	10	4,908	938
33 Sikkim State	..	..	..	..	..	..	17	1
34 United Provinces States	5,758	1,294	82	279	979	118	1,320	951
35 Western India States Agency ..	14,654	252	1,733	48	523	57	8,517	6

hood—Part II—Provincial Distribution—*contd.*

of Material Substances—*contd.*

—*contd.*

in food stuffs—*contd.*

in sweetmeats, sugar and spices.				*Group 131.*—Dealers in dairy produce, eggs and poultry.						
Total working dependants.		Total following occupation as subsidiary to other.		Total earners principal occupation.		Total working dependants.		Total following occupation as subsidiary to other.		
Males.	Females.	Males.	Females.	Males.	Females.	Males.	Females.	Males.	Females.	
1051	1052	1053	1054	1055	1056	1057	1058	1059	1060	
11,266	**21,728**	**34,461**	**7,658**	**217,269**	**197,233**	**12,639**	**46,354**	**86,786**	**29,642**	
6,053	**13,693**	**27,016**	**5,373**	**182,436**	**145,110**	**6,022**	**21,176**	**74,798**	**21,587**	
2	2	14	..	500	215	1	40	351	11	**1**
..	...	...	...	89	...	2	1	21	..	**2**
174	36	1,300	78	3,867	195	157	53	2,945	71	**3**
—	—	—	—	425	3	...	..	53	3	**4**
306	109	5,216	196	46,724	14,212	398	677	10,776	1,167	**5**
81	243	4,244	337	25,229	50,360	266	3,538	21,178	9,316	**6**
832	417	664	102	9,672	2,299	528	566	1,203	457	**7**
10	..	*2*	...	*56*	*39*	*4*	*2*	*1*	..	
437	8,101	1,546	1,983	1,998	426	32	90	214	29	**8**
163	360	1,047	355	5,082	4,472	180	1,268	2,020	692	**9**
13	1	226	5	49	28	1	1	8	..	**10**
1	3	22	...	2,061	55	10	3	129	3	**11**
931	1,884	4,651	1,152	11,221	17,214	284	1,384	2,918	2,071	**12**
58	14	109	6	1,417	37	73	15	400	2	**13**
337	5	542	1	17,150	964	476	546	4,127	94	**14**
2,718	2,518	7,435	1,158	56,952	54,630	3,614	12,994	28,455	7,671	**15**
5,213	**8,035**	**7,445**	**2,285**	**34,833**	**52,123**	**6,617**	**25,178**	**11,988**	**8,055**	
85	80	577	332	100	33	10	19	110	19	**16**
...	...	...	—	33	2	5	6	22	..	**17**
439	2,199	496	73	1,490	2,356	122	638	699	214	**18**
3	3	20	6	319	61	8	..	71	7	**19**
9	25	313	8	323	4,675	8	832	561	144	**20**
327	907	208	55	188	239	37	35	114	262	**21**
104	133	525	55	3,390	4,085	65	402	2,293	454	**22**
8	61	58	5	329	76	12	6	111	9	**23**
10	1	14	—	2,210	809	134	319	1,301	360	**24**
1,246	2,734	672	798	15,577	25,214	5,871	19,866	3,960	5,078	**25**
13	1	283	6	671	117	17	9	156	267	**26**
1,149	518	2,543	368	2,228	1,968	114	144	568	276	**27**
45	*57*	*350*	*95*	*625*	*782*	*19*	*33*	*155*	*108*	
1,103	*456*	*2,165*	*267*	*1,466*	*858*	*95*	*96*	*339*	*141*	
1	*5*	*28*	*6*	*137*	*328*	..	*15*	*74*	*27*	
50	34	780	50	2,186	8,607	58	912	686	82	**28**
..	..	..	..	19	..	..	..	..	..	**29**
2	..	26	..	145	61	22	21	118	9	**30**
41	1	175	6	1,495	70	42	18	315	15	**31**
25	155	301	104	3,061	2,928	43	537	689	109	**32**
..	..	..	..	..	...	..	..	1	..	**33**
275	448	202	366	221	190	8	1	124	..	**34**
1,427	735	252	53	848	632	41	1,413	89	10	**35**

Table X.—Occupation or Means of Liveli

Class B.—Preparation and Supply

Sub-Class V.—Trade

Order 32.—Other trade

Province, State or Agency.	*Group 132.*—Dealers in animals for food.						*Group 133.*—Dealers	
	Total earners principal occupation.		Total working dependants.		Total following occupation as subsidiary to other.		Total earners principal occupation.	
	Males.	Females.	Males.	Females.	Males.	Females.	Males.	Females.
1	1061	1062	1063	1064	1065	1066	1067	1068
INDIA	**22,460**	**3,453**	**1,104**	**730**	**4,998**	**340**	**53,516**	**77,030**
Provinces ..	**16,302**	**2,155**	**683**	**489**	**3,678**	**170**	**37,830**	**45,964**
1 Ajmer-Merwara	308	1	1	..	14	1	137	77
2 Andamans and Nicobars	6	..	..	..	..	..	..	..
3 Assam	54	1	3	4	102	1	75	12
4 Baluchistan (*Districts and Administered Territories*).	103	1	..	..	229	..	50	..
5 Bengal	849	53	23	2	229	9	1,006	388
6 Bihar and Orissa	496	43	1	1	337	4	1,034	2,315
7 Bombay (*including Aden*)	966	166	29	93	65	4	4,047	3,398
Aden	*18*	*3*	..	..	..	..	*22*	..
8 Burma	2,921	1,341	150	361	442	69	484	328
9 Central Provinces and Berar ..	535	73	7	5	88	58	3,410	10,421
10 Coorg	..	..	..	..	..	..	..	..
11 Delhi	312	..	..	..	..	..	349	137
12 Madras	5,319	342	342	16	1,607	20	3,030	4,632
13 North-West Frontier Province (*Districts and Administered Territories*).	215	..	..	..	12	..	2,144	34
14 Punjab	2,429	21	120	2	405	4	4,869	1,567
15 United Provinces of Agra and Oudh	1,789	113	7	5	148	..	17,195	22,655
States and Agencies ..	**6,158**	**1,298**	**421**	**241**	**1,320**	**170**	**15,686**	**31,066**
16 Assam States	18	35	1	13	12	4	5	4
17 Baluchistan States	94	..	..	..	27	..	4	..
18 Baroda State	134	7	3	..	5	4	200	167
19 Bengal States	113	..	..	..	11	..	22	..
20 Bihar and Orissa States	10	..	..	..	..	..	223	221
21 Bombay States	55	..	..	..	3	..	280	60
22 Central India Agency	274	71	2	3	146	11	2,860	5,526
23 Central Provinces States	5	1	..	..	6	..	453	126
24 Gwalior State	..	..	..	..	181	37	2,321	2,396
25 Hyderabad State	1,516	114	363	153	93	47	765	80
26 Jammu and Kashmir State ..	106	..	3	..	12	1	286	74
27 Madras States Agency	1,659	714	22	40	256	34	1,108	3,525
Cochin State	*1,390*	*694*	*17*	*49*	*192*	*30*	*175*	*146*
Travancore State	*164*	*3*	*5*	..	*30*	..	*917*	*3,316*
Other Madras States	*105*	*17*	..	*1*	*34*	*4*	*16*	*63*
28 Mysore State	434	162	5	11	190	29	234	1,204
29 North-West Frontier Province (*Agencies and Tribal Areas*).	..	..	..	..	..	..	..	..
30 Punjab States	3	..	..	..	..	..	223	233
31 Punjab States Agency	291	..	10	..	197	..	295	49
32 Rajputana Agency	1,315	189	5	7	178	3	5,752	17,083
33 Sikkim State	..	..	..	..	..	..	2	..
34 United Provinces States	26	5	..	1	..	..	169	155
35 Western India States Agency ..	105	..	7	3	3	..	484	163

hood—Part II—Provincial Distribution—*contd.*

of Material Substances—*contd.*

—*contd.*

in food stuffs—*contd.*

in fodder for animals. | *Group 134.*—Dealers in other food stuffs.

Total working dependants. Males.	Total working dependants. Females.	Total following occupation as subsidiary to other. Males.	Total following occupation as subsidiary to other. Females.	Total earners principal occupation. Males.	Total earners principal occupation. Females.	Total working dependants. Males.	Total working dependants. Females.	Total following occupation as subsidiary to other. Males.	Total following occupation as subsidiary to other. Females.	
1069	1070	1071	1072	1073	1074	1075	1076	1077	1078	
2,646	**8,741**	**22,163**	**13,917**	**1,143,538**	**523,794**	**41,372**	**109,398**	**275,587**	**53,053**	
1,546	**5,490**	**9,428**	**8,693**	**936,072**	**450,452**	**25,855**	**93,451**	**228,178**	**44,830**	
..	2	33	30	4,809	712	130	126	528	43	1
..	..	..	..	11	..	..	..	..	..	2
4	6	10	11	33,979	5,583	2,155	3,609	19,039	757	3
..	..	6	..	1,085	8	8	..	116	..	4
24	72	286	4	236,691	52,058	3,078	3,659	40,224	3,361	5
25	193	367	560	68,024	61,029	864	3,342	39,688	7,064	6
481	490	642	620	50,352	10,062	1,968	2,761	5,562	704	7
..	..	..	..	*397*	*10*	..	..	*4*	*1*	
32	157	110	26	101,436	127,568	5,376	48,981	14,674	11,033	8
236	1,543	1,986	5,153	61,722	27,916	2,524	9,131	18,067	4,927	9
..	..	..	..	183	51	2	1	42	1	10
..	87	5	1	4,631	316	4	30	35	4	11
188	547	633	588	183,768	67,845	3,173	4,913	38,655	6,611	12
1	1	17	2	854	15	8	2	34	..	13
223	523	585	38	65,062	4,859	1,967	2,037	3,588	180	14
332	1,869	4,748	1,660	123,465	92,430	4,598	14,859	47,926	10,145	15
1,100	**3,251**	**12,735**	**5,224**	**207,466**	**73,342**	**15,517**	**15,947**	**47,409**	**8,223**	
1	7	16	..	692	2,023	56	504	1,436	628	16
..	..	..	..	332	14	..	1	57	..	17
10	27	31	4	1,470	236	242	148	146	7	18
..	..	4	..	2,639	851	48	71	1,093	29	19
..	75	231	54	10,445	15,235	213	1,877	10,197	2,027	20
136	26	11	135	3,177	591	94	175	486	203	21
144	372	4,375	2,439	20,541	10,474	293	623	5,218	1,109	22
27	24	118	48	3,476	2,346	330	1,584	1,429	183	23
192	543	801	489	12,175	3,830	504	1,122	2,748	845	24
254	49	142	3	16,860	1,602	6,931	2,152	3,956	490	25
13	13	27	62	2,802	96	204	95	640	60	26
157	614	344	601	44,801	9,754	3,158	2,009	9,679	695	27
1	*1*	*97*	*48*	*3,790*	*626*	*44*	*23*	*1,089*	*84*	
154	*613*	*214*	*538*	*38,489*	*7,986*	*3,101*	*1,948*	*7,896*	*525*	
2	..	*33*	*15*	*2,522*	*1,142*	*13*	*38*	*694*	*86*	
32	180	55	207	9,517	7,097	201	1,100	3,818	460	28
..	..	..	..	..	..	..	..	..	..	29
3	..	12	2	193	75	5	40	51	..	30
19	29	51	5	4,753	1,160	200	228	630	78	31
42	1,185	6,455	1,161	65,068	16,011	1,765	3,127	4,857	1,035	32
1	..	1	..	132	24	..	..	2	1	33
1	12	44	14	3,263	1,594	232	816	806	359	34
68	95	17	..	5,130	329	1,041	275	160	14	35

Table X.—Occupation or Means of Liveli

Class B.—Preparation and Supply

Sub-Class V.—Trade.

32.—Other trade

Province, State or Agency.	*Group 135.*—Dealers in tobacco. Total earners principal occupation. Males.	Total earners principal occupation. Females.	Total working dependants. Males.	Total working dependants. Females.	Total following occupation as subsidiary to other. Males.	Total following occupation as subsidiary to other. Females.	*Group 136.*— Total earners principal occupation. Males.	Total earners principal occupation. Females.
1	1079	1080	1081	1082	1083	1084	1085	1086
INDIA	**87,850**	**19,435**	**3,832**	**4,518**	**13,175**	**1,503**	**5,460**	**168**
Provinces	**65,295**	**15,579**	**1,726**	**3,418**	**10,065**	**1,118**	**3,508**	**115**
1 Ajmer-Merwara	233	9	6	1	8	1	20	..
2 Andamans and Nicobars	..	..	..	..	..	..	..	..
3 Assam	915	56	61	46	466	8	378	..
4 Baluchistan (*Districts and Administered Territories.*)	160	..	..	..	3	..	2	..
5 Bengal	8,761	575	109	4	1,482	40	549	20
6 Bihar and Orissa	2,350	841	44	39	1,194	98	59	5
7 Bombay (*including Aden*)	7,473	3,129	465	390	483	80	479	14
Aden	*96*	*14*	..	..	*1*	..	..	..
8 Burma	3,502	5,149	218	1,935	893	393	391	29
9 Central Provinces and Berar ..	4,808	1,350	279	380	1,259	188	332	9
10 Coorg	41	9	1	..	16	..	..	..
11 Delhi	160	..	..	..	1	..	6	..
12 Madras	23,187	2,392	296	236	2,531	166	268	7
13 North-West Frontier Province (*Districts and Administered Territories*).	176	..	2	..	7	..	509	..
14 Punjab	1,631	10	11	..	42	1	334	..
15 United Provinces of Agra and Oudh	11,898	2,059	234	387	1,680	143	381	31
States and Agencies ..	**22,555**	**3,856**	**2,106**	**1,100**	**3,110**	**385**	**1,952**	**53**
16 Assam States	32	87	5	21	12	39	2	..
17 Baluchistan States	26	..	..	..	..	..	..	..
18 Baroda State	2,721	218	161	72	230	4	133	5
19 Bengal States	152	8	..	..	131	..	13	..
20 Bihar and Orissa States	113	72	4	6	68	1	48	1
21 Bombay States	297	52	12	16	34	3	48	1
22 Central India Agency	1,514	260	15	15	311	17	89	3
23 Central Provinces States	509	322	20	85	151	9	47	2
24 Gwalior State	49	4	1	2	72	2	20	3
25 Hyderabad State	5,684	877	1,565	678	1,020	244	272	..
26 Jammu and Kashmir State ..	213	2	..	..	27	1	3	..
27 Madras States Agency	4,616	1,229	34	3	313	27	80	..
Cochin State	*558*	*11*	*3*	..	*65*	..	*23*	..
Travancore State	*3,905*	*1,213*	*31*	*3*	*180*	*27*	*57*	..
Other Madras States	*153*	*5*	..	..	*68*	..	..	..
28 Mysore State	2,217	421	88	100	604	29	9	4
29 North-West Frontier Province (*Agencies and Tribal Areas*).	..	..	..	..	..	..	..	..
30 Punjab States	7	..	..	..	..	..	9	..
31 Punjab States Agency	314	3	1	..	7	..	268	..
32 Rajputana Agency	1,253	209	5	31	83	1	810	34
33 Sikkim State	..	..	..	..	..	..	..	..
34 United Provinces States	194	35	5	..	10	5	4	..
35 **Western India States Agency** ..	2,741	57	190	71	37	3	97	..

hood—Part II—Provincial Distribution—*contd.*

of Material Substances—*contd.*

—*concld.*

in food stuffs—*concld.*

Dealers in opium.				*Group 137.*—Dealers in ganja.						
Total working dependants.		Total following occupation as subsidiary to other.		Total earners principal occupation.		Total working. dependants.		Total following occupation as subsidiary to other.		
Males.	Females.	Males.	Females.	Males.	Females.	Males.	Females.	Males.	Females.	
1087	1088	1089	1090	1091	1092	1093	1094	1095	1096	
147	**48**	**737**	**11**	**4,200**	**159**	**127**	**33**	**536**	**6**	
71	**21**	**481**	**11**	**3,127**	**130**	**23**	**8**	**357**	**2**	
1	..	7	..	..	..	..	..	..	..	1
..	..	..	..	..	..	..	..	..	..	2
12	..	95	..	181	1	1	..	38	..	3
..	..	1	..	4	..	..	..	..	..	4
1	..	84	2	1,086	18	1	..	31	1	5
..	..	26	..	304	43	3	..	56	1	6
8	*12*	*29*	..	*350*	*12*	*5*	*1*	*6*	..	7
..	..	..	..	..	..	..	..	..	..	
33	7	44	..	..	..	..	..	..	..	8
7	2	75	1	275	17	9	4	108	..	9
..	..	..	..	..	..	..	..	..	..	10
..	..	..	..	..	..	..	..	..	..	11
8	..	65	..	285	4	2	..	47	..	12
..	..	4	..	301	..	..	..	..	..	13
..	..	25	..	38	..	1	..	2	..	14
1	..	26	8	303	35	1	3	69	..	15
76	**27**	**256**	..	**1,073**	**29**	**104**	**25**	**179**	**4**	
..	..	..	..	..	..	..	..	..	..	16
..	..	..	..	3	..	..	..	..	..	17
6	3	27	..	18	1	1	..	6	..	18
..	..	1	..	21	..	..	..	2	..	19
..	..	18	..	19	4	..	..	46	3	20
6	..	7	..	5	..	..	..	..	..	21
..	..	24	..	170	7	1	..	81	1	22
1	2	14	..	18	..	..	..	7	..	23
1	..	22	..	212	6	11	2	9	..	24
36	18	26	..	395	..	73	19	12	..	25
..	..	1	..	2	..	..	..	..	..	26
17	..	9	..	40	1	..	..	5	..	27
..	..	*6*	..	*8*	..	..	..	*3*	..	
17	..	*3*	..	*30*	*1*	..	..	*2*	..	
..	..	..	..	*2*	..	..	..	..	..	
..	..	2	..	38	3	..	..	10	..	28
..	..	..	..	..	..	..	..	..	..	29
..	..	2	..	1	..	..	..	..	..	30
..	..	18	..	..	..	..	..	..	..	31
4	4	79	..	88	7	..	4	1	..	32
..	..	..	..	..	..	..	..	..	..	33
..	..	..	..	5	..	..	..	..	..	34
5	..	6	..	38	..	18	..	..	..	35

Table X.—Occupation or Means of Liveli

Class B.—Preparation and Supply

Sub-Class V.—Trade

Order 33.—Trade

Province, State or Agency.	Total *Order 33.*—Trade in clothing and toilet articles.						*Group 138.*—Trade in ready-made	
	Total earners principal occupation.		Total working dependants.		Total following occupation as subsidiary to other.		Total earners principal occupation.	
	Males.	Females.	Males.	Females.	Males.	Females.	Males.	Females.
1	1097	1098	1099	1100	1101	1102	1103	1104
INDIA	**94,217**	**9,875**	**4,300**	**3,736**	**10,108**	**1,247**	**94,217**	**9,875**
Provinces	*65,406	6,519	1,437	1,827	6,865	846	65,406	6,519
1 Ajmer-Merwara	468	37	7	20	16	4	468	37
2 Andamans and Nicobars	..	..	..	..	..	..	..	..
3 Assam	6,660	411	200	70	694	28	6,660	411
4 Baluchistan (*Districts and Administered Territories*).	431	2	..	..	13	..	431	2
5 Bengal	7,210	205	82	2	714	5	7,210	205
6 Bihar and Orissa	2,656	1,077	20	9	565	219	2,656	1,077
7 Bombay (*including Aden*)	7,075	313	138	525	559	77	7,075	313
Aden	*19*	*2*	..	..	..	..	*19*	*2*
8 Burma	2,019	1,051	65	276	391	68	2,019	1,051
9 Central Provinces and Berar ..	5,465	722	184	162	748	78	5,465	722
10 Coorg	6	..	..	..	1	..	6	..
11 Delhi	2,083	45	7	8	2	..	2,083	45
12 Madras	11,692	894	117	72	1,674	90	11,692	894
13 North-West Frontier Province (*Districts and Administered Territories.*)	1,749	13	2	1	36	..	1,749	13
14 Punjab	7,523	82	325	24	497	4	7,523	82
15 United Provinces of Agra and Oudh	10,369	1,667	290	658	955	273	10,369	1,667
States and Agencies ..	28,811	3,356	2,863	1,909	3,243	401	28,811	3,356
16 Assam States	52	126	2	21	14	83	52	126
17 Baluchistan States	111	3	..	..	1	..	111	3
18 Baroda State	193	12	16	3	5	..	193	12
19 Bengal States	49	13	..	..	2	..	49	13
20 Bihar and Orissa States	858	267	6	33	353	12	858	267
21 Bombay States	166	4	7	..	8	..	166	4
22 Central India Agency	3,249	337	24	9	320	6	3,249	337
23 Central Provinces States	46	109	4	12	27	2	46	109
24 Gwalior State	1,351	11	29	..	6	30	1,351	11
25 Hyderabad State	8,269	1,484	2,303	1,418	1,161	250	8,269	1,484
26 Jammu and Kashmir State ..	875	7	1	..	67	1	875	7
27 Madras States Agency	755	48	22	5	197	7	755	48
Cochin State	*99*	*25*	*1*	*3*	*29*	*1*	*99*	*25*
Travancore State	*234*	*17*	*21*	*2*	*56*	*3*	*234*	*17*
Other Madras States	*422*	*6*	..	..	*112*	*3*	*422*	*6*
28 Mysore State	788	348	32	57	99	3	788	348
29 North-West Frontier Province (*Agencies and Tribal Areas*).	13	..	..	..	198	..	13	..
30 Punjab States	150	5	2	..	68	2	150	5
31 Punjab States Agency	1,287	16	31	..	59	..	1,287	16
32 Rajputana Agency	9,860	386	218	327	572	5	9,860	386
33 Sikkim State	1	..	..	..	..	..	1	..
34 United Provinces States	254	165	12	10	25	..	254	165
35 Western India States Agency ..	484	15	154	14	61	..	484	15

hood—Part II—Provincial Distribution—*contd.*

of Material Substances—*contd.*

—*contd.*

in clothing and toilet articles. | *Order 34.*—Trade in furniture.

clothing and other articles of dress and the toilet (hats, umbrellas, socks, ready-made shoes, perfumes, etc.). | Total *Order 34.*—Trade in furniture.

Total working dependants.		Total following occupation as subsidiary to other.		Total earners principal occupation.		Total working dependants.		Total following occupation as subsidiary to other.		
Males.	Females.	Males.	Females.	Males.	Females.	Males.	Females.	Males.	Females.	
1105	1106	1107	1108	1109	1110	1111	1112	1113	1114	
4,300	**3,736**	**10,108**	**1,247**	**45,855**	**7,834**	**1,631**	**5,754**	**7,358**	**1,416**	
1,437	**1,827**	**6,865**	**846**	**37,611**	**6,088**	**811**	**4,344**	**6,173**	**878**	
7	20	16	4	97	21	..	4	3	3	1
..	..	..	..	3	..	..	..	..	..	2
200	70	694	28	2,323	371	124	290	1,429	105	3
..	..	13	..	75	..	..	..	3	..	4
82	2	714	5	10,482	1,190	241	142	1,122	38	5
20	9	565	219	1,448	264	6	13	407	50	6
138	525	559	77	1,904	214	69	38	71	11	7
..	..	..	..	*5*	*5*	..	..	*1*	..	
65	276	391	68	3,758	2,143	188	838	1,101	283	8
184	162	748	78	3,109	705	42	326	535	113	9
..	..	1	..	15	4	..	..	11	..	10
7	8	2	..	307	2	..	..	1	..	11
117	72	1,674	90	5,289	613	61	2,652	1,075	254	12
2	1	36	..	686	1	..	..	1	..	13
325	24	497	4	2,401	51	57	13	31	..	14
290	658	955	273	5,714	509	23	28	383	21	15
2,863	**1,909**	**3,243**	**401**	**8,244**	**1,746**	**820**	**1,410**	**1,185**	**538**	
2	21	14	83	76	63	5	12	6	78	16
..	..	1	..	3	..	..	..	51	..	17
16	3	5	..	364	24	6	4	1	18	18
..	..	2	..	136	4	..	..	18	..	19
6	33	353	12	71	85	..	1	20	28	20
7	..	8	..	142	9	..	..	4	..	21
24	9	320	6	492	129	..	3	49	21	22
4	12	27	2	327	109	32	240	138	23	23
29	..	6	30	4	2	..	..	..	..	24
2,303	1,418	1,161	250	2,436	711	677	1,094	350	299	25
1	..	67	1	305	3	1	..	28	4	26
22	5	197	7	1,376	314	68	19	223	57	27
1	*3*	*29*	*1*	*373*	*166*	*6*	*1*	*84*	*35*	
21	*2*	*56*	*3*	*941*	*141*	*61*	*18*	*137*	*20*	
..	..	*112*	*3*	*62*	*7*	*1*	..	*2*	*2*	
32	57	99	3	716	18	..	..	79	2	28
..	..	198	..	..	..	..	..	..	..	29
2	..	68	2	45	1	..	..	42	..	30
31	..	59	..	300	20	..	10	54	..	31
218	327	572		907	248	9	15	22	8	32
..	..	..	..	..	1	..	..	..	..	33
12	10	25	..	167	1	2	..	..	..	34
154	14	61	..	377	4	20	12	..	..	35

Table X.—Occupation or Means of Liveli

Class B.—Preparation and Supply

Sub-Class V.—

Order 34.—Trade in furniture—*concld.*

	Province, State or Agency.	*Group 139.*—Trade in furniture, carpets, curtains and bedding.							
		Total earners principal occupation.		Total working dependants.		Total following occupation as subsidiary to other.		Total earners principal occupation.	
		Males.	Females.	Males.	Females.	Males.	Females.	Males.	Females.
	1	1115	1116	1117	1118	1119	1120	1121	1122
	INDIA	**11,726**	**3,121**	**544**	**705**	**2,390**	**480**	**34,129**	**4,713**
	Provinces	8,674	2,529	204	606	1,877	292	28,937	3,559
1	Ajmer-Merwara	74	8	..	4	3	1	23	13
2	Andamans and Nicobars	3	..	..	..	..	..	..	..
3	Assam	280	19	24	18	186	21	2,043	352
4	Baluchistan (*Districts and Administered Territories*).	28	..	..	..	3	..	47	..
5	Bengal	1,035	542	3	44	217	27	9,447	648
6	Bihar and Orissa	270	119	..	9	102	16	1,178	145
7	Bombay (*including Aden*)	592	67	7	11	30	6	1,312	147
	Aden	*4*	*5*	..	..	*1*	..	*1*	..
8	Burma	1,323	994	113	412	566	147	2,435	1,149
9	Central Provinces and Berar ..	433	127	4	15	125	10	2,676	578
10	Coorg	..	..	..	..	..	..	15	4
11	Delhi	212	2	..	..	1	..	95	..
12	Madras	1,204	238	17	57	306	63	4,085	375
13	North-West Frontier Province (*Districts and Administered Territories*).	334	1	..	..	..	..	352	..
14	Punjab	849	27	25	8	12	..	1,552	24
15	United Provinces of Agra and Oudh	2,037	385	11	28	326	1	3,677	124
	States and Agencies ..	3,052	592	340	99	513	188	5,192	1,154
16	Assam States	1	37	..	3	1	76	75	26
17	Baluchistan States	3	..	..	..	51	..	..	..
18	Baroda State	126	6	4	2	1	18	238	18
19	Bengal States	..	1	..	..	..	..	136	3
20	Bihar and Orissa States	4	75	..	..	4	22	67	10
21	Bombay States	18	..	..	..	1	..	124	9
22	Central India Agency	57	10	..	..	19	2	435	119
23	Central Provinces States	29	21	1	..	9	3	298	88
24	Gwalior State	..	..	..	..	..	..	4	2
25	Hyderabad State	1,117	95	273	63	167	12	1,319	616
26	Jammu and Kashmir State ..	233	..	1	..	25	..	72	3
27	Madras States Agency	819	255	56	18	155	52	557	59
	Cochin State	*178*	*111*	*2*	..	*32*	*31*	*195*	*55*
	Travancore State	*634*	*139*	*53*	*18*	*121*	*20*	*307*	*2*
	Other Madras States	*7*	*5*	*1*	..	*2*	*1*	*55*	*2*
28	Mysore State	161	..	..	..	13	1	555	18
29	North-West Frontier Province (*Agencies and Tribal Areas*).	..	..	..	..	..	..	..	..
30	Punjab States	15	..	..	..	..	..	30	1
31	Punjab States Agency	96	20	..	10	27	..	204	..
32	Rajputana Agency	107	72	1	2	40	2	800	176
33	Sikkim State	..	..	..	..	..	..	..	1
34	United Provinces States	153	..	..	..	..	..	14	1
35	Western India States Agency ..	113	..	4	1	..	..	264	4

hood—Part II—Provincial Distribution—*contd.*

of Material Substances—*contd.*

Trade—*contd.*

Group 140.—Hardware, cooking utensils, porcelain, crockery, glassware, bottles, articles for gardening, etc.				*Order 35.*—Trade in building materials. Total *Order 35.*—Trade in building materials.						
Total working dependants.		Total following occupation as subsidiary to other.		Total earners principal occupation.		Total working dependants.		Total following occupation as subsidiary to other.		
Males.	Females.	Males.	Females.	Males.	Females.	Males.	Females.	Males.	Females.	
1123	1124	1125	1126	1127	1128	1129	1130	1131	1132	
1,087	**5,049**	**4,968**	**936**	**15,478**	**4,797**	**1,161**	**967**	**2,697**	**649**	
607	**3,738**	**4,296**	**586**	**8,449**	**2,668**	**143**	**406**	**1,861**	**530**	
..	..	..	2	6	..	1	1	10	..	1
..	..	..	..	1	..	..	..	..	..	2
100	272	1,243	84	385	9	18	11	265	..	3
..	..	..	..	4	..	..	..	..	..	4
238	98	905	11	2,482	457	15	30	458	55	5
6	4	305	34	267	262	12	10	193	154	6
62	27	41	5	185	12	3	2	7	1	7
..	..	..	..	*12*	..	..	..	..	..	
75	426	535	136	363	110	13	34	74	11	8
38	311	410	103	511	70	15	22	67	19	9
..	..	11	..	1	1	..	..	2	..	10
..	..	..	..	173	4	..	..	..	..	11
44	2,595	769	191	2,248	1,646	50	258	735	283	12
..	..	1	..	404	..	..	..	..	..	13
32	5	19	..	640	11	16	32	12	..	14
12	..	57	20	779	86	..	6	38	7	15
480	**1,311**	**672**	**350**	**7,029**	**2,129**	**1,018**	**561**	**836**	**119**	
5	9	5	2	14	1	..	..	11	..	16
..	..	..	..	..	..	..	..	..	..	17
2	2	..	..	347	34	51	16	8	..	18
..	..	18	..	98	30	5	..	64	2	19
..	1	16	6	5	11	..	..	2	..	20
..	..	3	..	4		..	..	..	..	21
..	3	30	19	441	97	7	1	41	2	22
31	240	129	20	12	9	1	8	9	1	23
..	..	..	..	13	..	..	2	1	..	24
404	1,031	183	287	2,614	122	890	336	242		
..	..	3	4	16	..	..	..	2	..	26
12	1	68	5	2,086	1,117	16	8	155	2	27
4	*1*	*52*	*4*	*303*	*48*	*11*	*4*	*26*	..	
8	..	*16*	..	*1,679*	*988*	..	..	..	..	
..	..	..	*1*	*104*	*81*	*5*	*4*	*129*	*2*	
..	..	66	1	485	427	12	107	259	36	28
..	..	..	..	..	..	..	..	..	..	29
..	..	42	..	14	..	..	..	2	..	30
..	..	27	..	230	7	12	2	6	..	31
8	13	82	6	465	257	7	43	34	18	32
..	..	..	..	..	..	..	..	..	..	33
2	..	..	..	..	..	..	..	..	..	34
16	11	..	..	185	17	17	38	..	..	35

Table X.—Occupation or Means of Liveli

Class B.—Preparation and Supply

Sub-Class V.—

Order 35.—Trade in building materials—*concld.*

Group 141.—Trade in building materials (other than bricks, tiles and woody materials).

Province, State or Agency.	Total earners principal occupation.		Total working dependants.		Total following occupation as subsidiary to other.		Total earners principal occupation.	
	Males.	Females.	Males.	Females.	Males.	Females.	Males.	Females
1	1133	1134	1135	1136	1137	1138	1139	1140
INDIA	**15,478**	**4,797**	**1,161**	**967**	**2,697**	**649**	**101,064**	**3,621**
Provinces	**8,449**	**2,668**	**143**	**406**	**1,861**	**530**	**70,513**	**2,701**
1 Ajmer-Merwara	6	..	1	1	10	..	597	7
2 Andamans and Nicobars	1	..	..	..	..	..	..	..
3 Assam	385	9	18	11	265	..	998	84
4 Baluchistan (*Districts and Administered Territories*).	4	..	..	..	..	..	288	2
5 Bengal	2,482	457	15	30	458	55	5,436	386
6 Bihar and Orissa	267	262	12	10	193	154	2,978	193
7 Bombay (*including Aden*)	185	12	3	2	7	1	7,213	171
Aden	*12*	..	..	..	..	..	*14*	..
8 Burma	363	110	13	34	74	11	3,874	1,126
9 Central Provinces and Berar	511	70	15	22	67	19	2,761	107
10 Coorg	1	1	..	..	2	..	19	..
11 Delhi	173	4	..	..	..	..	531	3
12 Madras	2,248	1,646	50	258	735	283	9,574	265
13 North-West Frontier Province (*Districts and Administered Territories.*)	404	..	..	..	..	..	680	14
14 Punjab	640	11	16	32	12	..	10,290	26
15 United Provinces of Agra and Oudh	779	86	..	6	38	7	25,274	317
States and Agencies	**7,029**	**2,129**	**1,018**	**561**	**836**	**119**	**30,551**	**920**
16 Assam States	14	1	..	..	11	..	138	4
17 Baluchistan States	..	..	..	..	..	..	41	..
18 Baroda State	347	34	51	16	8	..	1,923	8
19 Bengal States	98	30	5	..	64	2	26	4
20 Bihar and Orissa States	5	11	..	..	2	..	22	25
21 Bombay States	4	..	..	..	..	..	295	4
22 Central India Agency	441	97	7	1	41	2	1,308	33
23 Central Provinces States	12	9	1	8	9	1	137	4
24 Gwalior State	13	..	..	2	1	..	498	1
25 Hyderabad State	2,614	122	890	336	242	58	7,689	503
26 Jammu and Kashmir State	16	..	..	..	2	..	2,294	31
27 Madras States Agency	2,086	1,117	16	8	155	2	2,234	26
Cochin State	*303*	*48*	*11*	*4*	*26*	..	*889*	*12*
Travancore State	*1,679*	*988*	..	..	..	..	*1,300*	*14*
Other Madras States	*104*	*81*	*5*	*4*	*129*	*2*	*45*	..
28 Mysore State	485	427	12	107	259	36	1,493	48
29 North-West Frontier Province (*Agencies and Tribal Areas*).	..	..	..	..	..	..	..	..
30 Punjab States	14	..	..	..	2	..	213	..
31 Punjab States Agency	230	7	12	2	6	..	2,893	9
32 Rajputana Agency	465	257	7	43	34	18	6,166	208
33 Sikkim State	..	..	..	..	..	..	4	..
34 United Provinces States	..	..	..	..	..	..	39	..
35 Western India State Agency	185	17	17	38	..	..	3,138	2

hood—Part II—Provincial Distribution—*contd.*

of Material Substances—*contd.*

Trade—*contd.*

Order 36.—Trade in means of transport.

Total *Order 36.*—Trade in means of transport.				*Group 142.*—Dealers and hirers, in mechanical transport, motors, cycles, etc.						
Total working dependants.		Total following occupation as subsidiary to other.		Total earners principal occupation.		Total working dependants.		Total following occupation as subsidiary to other.		
Males.	Females.	Males.	Females.	Males.	Females.	Males.	Females.	Males.	Females.	
1141	1142	1143	1144	1145	1146	1147	1148	1149	1150	
4,373	**1,462**	**30,856**	**881**	**7,752**	**62**	**367**	**13**	**639**	**10**	
1,592	**435**	**23,028**	**614**	**5,012**	**39**	**67**	**3**	**226**	**8**	
..	..	163	1	27	..	..	..	..	..	1
..	..	..	..	..	..	..	..	..	..	2
27	..	1,334	13	81	1	..	..	4	..	3
1	..	5,344	..	42	..	..	..	1	..	4
70	2	1,648	60	416	..	2	..	19	..	5
6	2	1,779	42	72	..	..	..	4	..	6
333	25	2,349	97	923	7	12	1	11	..	7
3	..	..	..	*3*	..	..	..	..	..	
172	128	1,311	135	708	16	4	1	12	1	8
22	62	969	186	312	7	..	1	16	7	9
..	..	3	..	1	..	..	..	3	..	10
8	1	13	..	190	1	..	..	1	..	11
499	18	3,847	51	879	3	38	..	83	..	12
9	3	158	..	209	..	1	..	1	..	13
314	74	1,475	14	479	3	8	..	5	..	14
131	115	2,635	15	673	1	2	..	66	..	15
2,781	**1,027**	**7,828**	**267**	**2,740**	**23**	**300**	**10**	**413**	**2**	
3	..	119	..	5	..	..	..	1	..	16
..	..	464	1	..	..	..	..	..	..	17
50	62	400	..	167	..	4	..	12	..	18
..	..	21	12	..	..	..	..	..	..	19
..	..	25	..	1	..	..	..	..	..	20
156	284	431	1	25	..	..	..	1	..	21
10	2	469	7	137	..	..	..	10	..	22
..	1	111	3	4	..	..	..	..	..	23
26	..	403	54	..	..	..	..	4	..	24
2,086	544	1,041	167	1,008	8	277	10	206	2	25
54	3	354	4	523	..	10	..	80	..	26
97	1	1,026	8	85	1	1	..	45	..	27
5	..	*326*	*3*	*18*	..	..	..	*38*	..	
91	*1*	*540*	*1*	*61*	*1*	*1*	..	*4*	..	
1	..	*160*	*4*	*6*	..	..	..	*3*	..	
15	108	963	7	200	..	..	..	7	..	28
..	..	..	..	..	..	..	..	..	..	29
..	1	73	..	1	..	..	..	1	..	30
44	..	375	1	177	..	..	..	4	..	31
81	7	1,271	1	209	14	..	..	42	..	32
..	..	..	..	..	..	..	..	..	..	33
..	..	14	..	6	..	..	..	..	..	34
156	14	68	1	201	..	2	..	..	..	35

Table X.—Occupation or Means of Liveli

Class B.—Preparation and Supply

Sub-Class V.—

Order 36.—Trade in means of

	Province, State or Agency.	*Group 143.*—Dealers and hirers in other carriages, carts, boats, etc.						*Group 144.*— Dealers and hirers	
		Total earners principal occupation.		Total working dependants.		Total following occupation as subsidiary to other.		Total earners principal occupation.	
		Males.	Females.	Males.	Females.	Males.	Females.	Males.	Females.
	1	1151	1152	1153	1154	1155	1156	1157	1158
	INDIA	**23,570**	**881**	**1,942**	**681**	**8,258**	**248**	**69,742**	**2,678**
	Provinces	**11,024**	**288**	**448**	**32**	**5,255**	**98**	**54,477**	**2,374**
1	Ajmer-Merwara	369	1	..	..	144	..	201	6
2	Andamans and Nicobars	..	..	..	..	..	..	..	..
3	Assam	355	1	10	1	577	3	562	82
4	Baluchistan (*Districts and Administered Territories*).	..	..	..	..	..	..	246	2
5	Bengal	274	5	1	..	62	..	4,746	381
6	Bihar and Orissa	303	4	..	1	550	..	2,603	189
7	Bombay (*including Aden*)	4,300	85	297	16	2,294	81	1,990	79
	Aden	*9*	..	..	..	..	..	*2*	..
8	Burma	390	74	16	8	186	9	2,776	1,036
9	Central Provinces and Berar ..	29	2	..	3	6	..	2,420	98
10	Coorg	..	..	..	..	..	..	18	..
11	Delhi	6	..	..	..	..	..	335	2
12	Madras	3,376	13	111	2	1,296	5	5,319	249
13	North-West Frontier Province (*Districts and Administered Territories.*)	115	..	..	..	..	..	356	14
14	Punjab	214	..	5	..	34	..	9,597	23
15	United Provinces of Agra and Oudh	1,293	103	8	1	106	..	23,308	213
	States and Agencies ..	**12,546**	**593**	**1,494**	**649**	**3,003**	**150**	**15,265**	**304**
16	Assam States	18	..	..	..	3	..	115	4
17	Baluchistan States ..	..	..	..	..	..	..	41	..
18	Baroda State	247	1	2	..	290	..	1,509	7
19	Bengal States	1	..	..	..	..	..	25	4
20	Bihar and Orissa States	10	25	..	..	2	..	11	..
21	Bombay States	102	..	13	141	389	..	168	4
22	Central India Agency	214	..	4	..	77	..	957	33
23	Central Provinces States	..	..	..	..	..	..	133	4
24	Gwalior State	6	..	..	..	2	..	492	1
25	Hyderabad State	4,696	437	1,316	484	595	145	1,985	58
26	Jammu and Kashmir State ..	615	1	1	..	34	..	1,156	30
27	Madras States Agency	707	13	24	1	301	4	1,442	12
	Cochin State	*288*	*3*	*2*	..	*185*	*3*	*583*	*9*
	Travancore State	*418*	*10*	*22*	*1*	*116*	*1*	*821*	*3*
	Other Madras States	*1*	..	..	..	..	..	*38*	..
28	Mysore State	324	1	8	5	191	1	969	47
29	North-West Frontier Province (*Agencies and Tribal Areas*).	..	..	..	..	..	..	..	..
30	Punjab States	..	..	..	..	1	..	212	..
31	Punjab States Agency .. .	592	..	9	..	48	..	2,124	9
32	Rajputana Agency	3,305	112	62	5	879	..	2,661	82
33	Sikkim State	..	..	..	..	..	..	4	..
34	United Provinces States	6	..	..	..	..	..	27	..
35	Western India States Agency ..	1,703	3	55	13	191	..	1,234	9

hood—Part II—Provincial Distribution—*contd.*

of Material Substances—*contd.*

Trade—*contd.*

transport—*concld.* of elephants, camels, horses, cattle, asses, mules, etc.				*Order 37.*—Trade in fuel. Total *Order 37.*—Trade in fuel.						
Total working dependants.		Total following occupation as subsidiary to other.		Total earners principal occupation.		Total working dependants.		Total following occupation as subsidiary to other.		
Males.	Females.	Males.	Females.	Males.	Females.	Males.	Females.	Males.	Females.	
1159	1160	1161	1162	1163	1164	1165	1166	1167	1168	
2,064	**768**	**21,959**	**623**	**117,877**	**129,020**	**11,599**	**34,060**	**49,189**	**29,458**	
1,077	**400**	**17,547**	**508**	**77,988**	**82,550**	**4,303**	**17,022**	**31,589**	**18,561**	
..	..	19	1	937	1,236	22	191	364	234	1
..	..	..	..	..	..	..	..	..	..	2
17	4	753	10	1,047	425	122	289	1,701	114	3
1	..	5,343	..	432	..	26	54	478	..	4
67	2	1,567	60	10,162	3,760	62	290	2,601	431	5
6	1	1,225	42	6,572	21,527	211	3,062	4,085	4,321	6
24	8	44	16	7,369	6,441	761	2,643	1,541	725	7
3	..	..	..	*15*	*9*	*1*	*2*	*3*	..	
152	119	1,113	125	4,673	1,304	298	552	2,457	332	8
22	58	947	179	3,081	4,921	208	1,110	2,876	2,454	9
..	..	..	..	1	..	..	..	..	..	10
8	1	12	..	939	154	21	142	80	2	11
350	16	2,468	46	17,035	19,862	1,958	6,522	8,663	7,098	12
8	3	157	..	316	49	7	7	114	2	13
301	74	1,436	14	5,559	1,101	208	242	647	44	14
121	114	2,463	15	19,865	21,770	399	1,918	5,982	2,804	15
987	**368**	**4,412**	**115**	**39,889**	**46,470**	**7,296**	**17,038**	**17,600**	**10,897**	
3	..	115	..	95	96	19	67	276	372	16
..	..	464	1	27	2	..	..	3	1	17
44	62	98	..	645	466	33	83	158	69	18
..	..	21	12	115	62	2	10	19	2	19
..	..	23	..	2,259	8,222	22	556	1,871	1,609	20
143	143	41	1	1,026	498	49	508	49	510	21
6	2	382	7	2,423	3,152	73	230	1,845	1,017	22
..	1	111	3	401	793	85	1,957	413	296	23
26	..	397	54	2,176	2,984	192	701	796	720	24
493	50	240	20	16,917	9,266	6,219	7,321	4,097	2,808	25
43	3	240	4	256	361	16	667	71	568	26
72	..	680	4	1,453	1,162	55	96	403	197	27
3	..	*103*	..	*543*	*251*	*7*	*7*	*30*	*106*	
68	..	*420*	..	*853*	*829*	*48*	*89*	*173*	*81*	
1	..	*157*	*4*	*57*	*82*	..	..	*150*	*10*	
7	103	765	6	2,210	3,802	133	1,011	1,445	543	28
..	..	..	..	..	..	..	..	..	..	29
..	1	71	..	9	6	..	3	3	..	30
35	..	323	1	456	80	34	87	35	8	31
22	2	350	1	8,038	13,843	149	1,880	6,011	2,052	32
..	..	..	..	14	2	..	..	1	1	33
..	..	14	..	330	436	24	63	28	5	34
93	1	77	1	1,039	1,237	191	1,798	76	119	35

Table X.—Occupation or Means of Liveli

Class B.—Preparation and Supply

Sub-Class V.—

Province, State or Agency.	*Order 37.*—Trade in fuel—*concld.* *Group 145*—Dealers in firewood, charcoal, coal, cowdung, etc. Total earners principal occupation. Males.	Females.	Total working dependants. Males.	Females.	Total following occupation as subsidiary to other. Males.	Females.	Total earners principal occupation. Males.	Females.
1	1169	1170	1171	1172	1173	1174	1175	1176
INDIA	**117,877**	**129,020**	**11,599**	**34,060**	**49,189**	**29,458**	**157,511**	**43,479**
Provinces	**77,988**	**82,550**	**4,303**	**17,022**	**31,589**	**18,561**	**122,076**	**32,721**
1 Ajmer-Merwara	937	1,236	22	191	364	234	374	52
2 Andamans and Nicobars	..	..	..	..	..	..	..	..
3 Assam	1,047	425	122	289	1,701	114	6,088	467
4 Baluchistan (*Districts and Administered Territories*).	432	..	26	54	478	..	66	..
5 Bengal	10,162	3,760	62	290	2,601	431	36,161	2,478
6 Bihar and Orissa	6,572	21,527	211	3,062	4,085	4,321	8,271	4,739
7 Bombay (*including Aden*)	7,369	6,441	761	2,643	1,541	725	10,273	3,055
Aden	*15*	*9*	*1*	*2*	*3*	..	*73*	..
8 Burma	4,673	1,304	298	552	2,457	332	4,328	1,380
9 Central Provinces and Berar	3,081	4,921	208	1,110	2,876	2,454	11,092	4,623
10 Coorg	1	..	..	..	..	..	65	28
11 Delhi	939	154	21	142	80	2	749	44
12 Madras	17,035	19,862	1,958	6,522	8,663	7,098	21,192	5,253
13 North-West Frontier Province (*Districts and Administered Territories*).	316	49	7	7	114	2	1,055	..
14 Punjab	5,559	1,101	208	242	647	44	4,132	307
15 United Provinces of Agra and Oudh	19,865	21,770	399	1,918	5,982	2,804	18,230	10,295
States and Agencies	**39,889**	**46,470**	**7,296**	**17,038**	**17,600**	**10,897**	**35,435**	**10,758**
16 Assam States	95	96	19	67	276	372	229	88
17 Baluchistan States	27	2	..	..	3	1	..	..
18 Baroda State	645	466	33	83	158	69	1,434	69
19 Bengal States	115	62	2	10	19	2	326	28
20 Bihar and Orissa States	2,259	8,222	22	556	1,871	1,609	737	207
21 Bombay States	1,026	498	49	508	49	510	1,134	88
22 Central India Agency	2,423	3,152	73	230	1,845	1,017	3,729	1,646
23 Central Provinces States	401	793	85	1,957	413	296	456	532
24 Gwalior State	2,176	2,984	192	701	796	720	3,064	804
25 Hyderabad State	16,917	9,266	6,219	7,321	4,097	2,808	8,444	4,669
26 Jammu and Kashmir State	256	361	16	667	71	568	152	6
27 Madras States Agency	1,453	1,162	55	96	403	197	1,998	99
Cochin State	*543*	*251*	*7*	*7*	*80*	*106*	*387*	*20*
Travancore State	*853*	*829*	*48*	*89*	*173*	*81*	*1,372*	*36*
Other Madras States	*57*	*82*	..	..	*150*	*10*	*248*	*43*
28 Mysore State	2,210	3,802	133	1,011	1,445	543	3,591	1,220
29 North-West Frontier Province (*Agencies and Tribal Areas.*)	..	..	..	..	..	..	..	..
30 Punjab States	9	6	..	3	3	..	67	12
31 Punjab States Agency	456	80	34	87	35	8	955	91
32 Rajputana Agency	8,038	13,843	149	1,880	6,011	2,052	7,470	1,074
33 Sikkim State	14	2	..	..	1	1	..	..
34 United Provinces States	330	436	24	63	28	5	237	94
35 Western India States Agency	1,039	1,237	191	1,798	76	119	1,412	31

hood—Part II—Provincial Distribution—*contd.*

of Material Substances—*contd.*

Trade—*contd.*

Order 38.—Trade in articles of luxury and those pertaining to letters and the arts and sciences.

Total *Order 38.*—Trade in articles of luxury, etc.				146.—Dealers in precious stones, jewellery (real and imitation), clocks, optical instruments, etc.						
Total working dependants.		Total following occupation as subsidiary to other.		Total earners principal occupation.		Total working dependants.		Total following occupation as subsidiary to other.		
Males.	Females.	Males.	Females.	Males.	Females.	Males.	Females.	Males.	Females.	
1177	1178	1179	1180	1181	1182	1183	1184	1185	1186	
7,232	**12,375**	**19,912**	**4,312**	**35,345**	**2,090**	**1,491**	**473**	**2,646**	**185**	
2,951	**4,364**	**15,528**	**2,681**	**25,907**	**1,808**	**555**	**238**	**1,924**	**177**	
5	9	9	2	158	..	..	..	..	..	1
..	..	..	..	..	..	..	..	..	..	2
220	103	1,852	32	236	11	20	..	96	2	3
..	..	..	..	12	..	..	..	..	..	4
299	53	3,145	298	9,763	139	170	7	634	8	5
79	157	2,181	453	688	86	..	12	85	6	6
368	717	744	634	2,710	500	151	88	107	130	7
..	..	..	..	*6*	..	..	..	..	..	
96	377	261	45	2,981	565	47	84	135	10	8
331	969	1,448	404	1,993	253	64	24	245	11	9
1	1	21	7	5	..	..	..	..	..	10
1	19	2	..	20	2	..	..	..	..	11
831	744	3,105	353	5,145	186	92	21	499	9	12
6	..	2	1	301	..	..	..	..	..	13
86	236	190	10	152	..	3	..	8	..	14
628	979	2,568	442	1,743	66	8	2	115	1	15
4,281	**8,011**	**4,384**	**1,631**	**9,438**	**282**	**936**	**235**	**722**	**8**	
30	13	39	5	..	6	..	..	..	2	16
..	..	..	..	..	..	..	..	..	..	17
106	50	53	9	647	1	36	..	26	..	18
6	..	33	4	17	..	3	..	3	..	19
137	83	151	78	252	4	56	..	33	..	20
16	24	163	3	25	1	..	..	6	..	21
44	83	390	60	915	20	6	..	68	1	22
26	226	61	22	47	1	..	..	3	..	23
104	206	154	25	1,211	14	45	..	30	..	24
3,382	6,336	1,594	1,273	2,049	144	700	209	285	3	25
2	1	14	9	69	..	..	..	5	..	26
102	5	286	34	453	6	9	..	34	..	27
	1	*37*	*28*	*141*	*1*	*1*	..	*16*	..	
96	..	*109*	*5*	*246*	*1*	*8*	..	*14*	..	
1	*4*	*140*	*1*	*66*	*4*	..	..	*4*	..	
87	667	946	88	721	62	16	2	95	..	28
..	..	..	..	..	..	..	..	..	..	29
1	7	4	..	1	..	..	..	..	..	30
23	56	114	2	127	..	..	..	..	..	31
51	225	331	16	2,346	22	20	24	119	1	32
.	..	..	..	..	..	..	..	..	..	33
2	26	23	2	57	..	..	..	..	..	34
162	3	23	1	501	1	45	..	15	1	35

Table X.—Occupation or Means of Liveli

Class B.—Preparation and Supply

Sub-Class V.—

Order 38.—Trade in articles of luxury and those pertaining to letters

	Province, State or Agency.	*Group 147.*—Dealers in common bangles, bead necklaces, fans, small articles, toys, hunting and fishing tackle, flowers, etc.						*Group 148.*—Publishers, book-	
		Total earners principal occupation.		Total working dependants.		Total following occupation as subsidiary to other.		Total earners principal occupation.	
		Males.	Females.	Males.	Females.	Males.	Females.	Males.	Females.
	1	1187	1188	1189	1190	1191	1192	1193	1194
	INDIA	**79,432**	**38,939**	**4,107**	**11,705**	**12,259**	**3,865**	**42,734**	**2,450**
	Provinces	59,856	28,650	1,948	4,028	9,396	2,255	36,313	2,263
1	Ajmer-Merwara	170	50	5	8	7	2	46	2
2	Andamans and Nicobars	..	..	..	..	..	..	..	..
3	Assam	2,862	281	44	80	320	7	2,990	175
4	Baluchistan (*Districts and Administered Territories*).	7	..	..	..	..	..	47	..
5	Bengal	3,868	987	26	10	491	102	22,530	1,352
6	Bihar and Orissa	5,976	4,395	71	126	1,850	425	1,607	258
7	Bombay (*including Aden*)	5,438	2,426	156	625	561	497	2,125	129
	Aden	*62*	..	..	..	..	..	*5*	..
8	Burma	536	719	26	282	73	32	811	96
9	Central Provinces and Berar	8,432	4,315	246	942	1,095	391	667	55
10	Coorg	31	25	1	1	19	7	29	3
11	Delhi	429	38	1	19	..	..	300	4
12	Madras	14,241	4,931	702	722	2,484	340	1,806	136
13	North-West Frontier Province (*Districts and Administered Territories*).	213	..	..	..	..	1	541	..
14	Punjab	2,284	305	51	236	86	10	1,696	2
15	United Provinces of Agra and Oudh	15,369	10,178	619	977	2,410	441	1,118	51
	States and Agencies	19,576	10,289	2,159	7,677	2,863	1,610	6,421	187
16	Assam States	47	21	15	3	29	..	182	61
17	Baluchistan States	..	..	..	..	..	..	..	..
18	Baroda State	575	67	54	50	23	9	212	1
19	Bengal States	11	8	..	..	3	..	298	20
20	Bihar and Orissa States	324	200	81	82	88	78	161	3
21	Bombay States	933	84	11	22	156	3	176	3
22	Central India Agency	2,603	1,610	37	83	307	59	211	16
23	Central Provinces States	390	531	26	223	44	22	19	..
24	Gwalior State	1,819	790	59	206	123	25	34	..
25	Hyderabad State	3,318	4,464	1,642	6,048	706	1,266	3,077	61
26	Jammu and Kashmir State	59	6	2	1	4	9	24	..
27	Madras States Agency	457	88	26	5	181	32	1,088	5
	Cochin State	*29*	*18*	*2*	*1*	*15*	*28*	*208*	*1*
	Travancore State	*258*	*31*	*23*	..	*31*	*3*	*868*	*4*
	Other Madras States	*170*	*39*	*1*	*4*	*135*	*1*	*12*	..
28	Mysore State	2,670	1,147	68	665	843	88	200	11
29	North-West Frontier Province (*Agencies and Tribal Areas*).	..	..	..	..	..	..	..	..
30	Punjab States	65	12	1	7	3	..	1	..
31	Punjab States Agency	700	91	23	56	113	2	128	..
32	Rajputana Agency	4,949	1,049	27	200	205	15	175	3
33	Sikkim State	..	..	..	..	..	..	..	..
34	United Provinces States	180	94	2	26	28	2	..	..
35	Western India States Agency	476	27	85	..	7	..	435	3

hood—Part II—Provincial Distribution—*contd.*

of Material Substances—*contd.*

Trade—*contd.*

and the arts and sciences—*concld.* / *Order 39.*—Trade of other sorts.

sellers, stationers, dealers in music, pictures, musical instruments and curiosities.				Total *Order 39.*—Trade of other sorts.						
Total working dependants.		Total following occupation as subsidiary to other.		Total earners principal occupation.		Total working dependants.		Total following occupation as subsidiary to other.		
Males.	Females.	Males.	Females.	Males.	Females.	Males.	Females.	Males.	Females.	
1195	1196	1197	1198	1199	1200	1201	1202	1203	1204	
1,634	**197**	**5,007**	**262**	**1,258,196**	**170,976**	**75,726**	**45,944**	**171,979**	**25,689**	
448	**98**	**4,268**	**249**	**885,873**	**101,022**	**26,595**	**10,234**	**103,433**	**9,193**	
..	1	2	..	1,624	72	36	49	64	2	1
..	..	..	..	474	1	..	2	25	1	2
156	23	1,436	23	6,691	316	456	109	2,431	87	3
..	..	..	..	3,168	3	1	..	347	1	4
103	36	2,020	188	143,697	7,518	2,631	327	12,362	303	5
8	19	246	22	116,189	28,564	871	691	26,135	2,822	6
61	4	76	7	150,964	9,124	5,047	2,610	6,140	327	7
..	..	..	..	*1,034*	*15*	*26*	..	*7*	*1*	
23	11	53	3	17,763	5,824	491	1,104	1,019	242	8
21	3	108	2	13,669	2,484	475	378	1,968	214	9
..	..	2	..	422	37	2	..	77	7	10
..	..	2	..	10,371	190	71	6	71	..	11
37	1	122	4	160,517	39,240	3,961	3,519	31,376	3,979	12
6	..	2	..	29,619	243	937	117	1,313	8	13
32	..	96	..	193,160	3,093	11,281	813	13,965	168	14
1	..	43	..	37,545	4,313	335	509	6,140	1,032	15
1,186	**99**	**799**	**13**	**372,323**	**69,954**	**49,131**	**35,710**	**68,546**	**16,496**	
15	10	10	3	340	202	12	24	35	26	16
..	..	..	..	2,522	..	..	..	93	..	17
16	..	4	..	3,858	219	443	180	447	9	18
3	..	27	4	827	25	12	..	128	2	19
..	1	30	..	354	481	96	13	252	21	20
5	2	1	..	26,604	4,692	1,083	1,172	3,673	367	21
1	..	15	..	10,460	1,490	318	74	1,127	55	22
..	3	14	..	1,658	576	141	145	286	15	23
..	..	1	..	19,143	1,790	927	437	3,481	402	24
1,040	79	603	4	141,151	45,625	37,839	31,194	35,423	14,605	25
..	..	5	..	6,880	89	143	15	2,963	87	26
67	..	71	2	72,127	2,382	2,024	424	4,771	217	27
2	..	*6*	..	*5,666*	*528*	*43*	*19*	*1,291*	*28*	
65	..	*64*	*2*	*20,376*	*1,541*	*1,978*	*394*	*3,306*	*174*	
..	..	*1*	..	*1,085*	*313*	*3*	*11*	*174*	*15*	
3	..	8	..	34,166	9,747	648	848	9,093	601	28
..	..	..	..	854	..	1	..	287	..	29
..	..	1	..	2,152	20	121	4	458	3	30
..	..	1	..	39,409	462	2,088	118	3,714	34	31
4	1	7	..	28,059	1,302	712	290	1,740	28	32
..	..	..	..	270	41	..	..	38	4	33
..	..	..	..	499	21	18	10	85	1	34
32	3	1	..	25,990	790	2,505	762	459	19	35

Table X.—Occupation or Means of Liveli

Class B.—Preparation and Supply of

Sub-Class V.—

Order 39.—Trade of other

Province, State or Agency.	*Group 149.*—Dealers in rags, stable refuse, etc. — Total earners principal occupation. Males.	Females.	Total working dependants. Males.	Females.	Total following occupation as subsidiary to other. Males.	Females.	*Group 150.*—General — Total earners principal occupation. Males.	Females.
1	1205	1206	1207	1208	1209	1210	1211	1212
INDIA	**18,200**	**3,521**	**774**	**966**	**2,317**	**249**	**1,154,972**	**152,794**
Provinces	9,151	995	186	178	728	36	828,748	92,452
1 Ajmer-Merwara	..	..	..	..	9	..	1,594	68
2 Andamans and Nicobars	..	..	..	..	..	..	473	1
3 Assam	..	..	..	..	1	..	6,165	286
4 Baluchistan (*Districts and Administered Territories*).	..	..	..	..	..	..	3,127	3
5 Bengal	51	12	..	..	6	..	135,326	6,990
6 Bihar and Orissa	3	..	..	..	..	..	112,292	27,434
7 Bombay (*including Aden*)	7,850	630	169	90	629	26	130,117	7,514
Aden	..	..	..	..	..	..	*729*	*5*
8 Burma	3	2	..	..	..	..	16,822	5,219
9 Central Provinces and Berar	6	22	..	38	2	2	12,135	1,808
10 Coorg	..	..	..	..	..	..	416	37
11 Delhi	13	..	..	..	..	..	10,238	188
12 Madras	319	326	7	50	44	7	157,281	38,284
13 North-West Frontier Province (*Districts and Administered Territories*).	246	..	..	..	1	..	28,953	243
14 Punjab	319	1	10	..	18	1	188,763	3,058
15 United Provinces of Agra and Oudh	341	2	..	..	18	..	25,046	1,319
States and Agencies	9,049	2,526	588	788	1,589	213	326,224	60,342
16 Assam States	..	..	..	..	..	..	340	202
17 Baluchistan States	..	..	..	..	..	..	2,522	..
18 Baroda State	74	19	5	4	..	2	2,841	185
19 Bengal States	..	..	..	..	..	..	743	19
20 Bihar and Orissa States	..	..	..	..	..	..	342	475
21 Bombay States	8,261	2,318	206	601	1,425	184	18,132	2,286
22 Central India Agency	34	10	12	1	..	..	10,085	1,410
23 Central Provinces States	..	..	..	..	..	..	1,400	434
24 Gwalior State	..	2	..	..	77	..	17,668	1,788
25 Hyderabad State	528	103	357	108	48	20	138,379	43,755
26 Jammu and Kashmir State	12	1	..	..	26	..	6,042	88
27 Madras States Agency	19	..	2	..	3	4	14,560	1,452
Cochin State	*3*	..	*2*	..	*3*	*4*	*4,990*	*442*
Travancore State	..	..	..	..	..	..	*8,556*	*698*
Other Madras States	*16*	..	..	..	..	..	*1,014*	*312*
28 Mysore State	15	53	4	13	2	2	19,980	5,820
29 North-West Frontier Province (*Agencies and Tribal Areas*).	..	..	..	..	..	..	854	..
30 Punjab States	..	..	..	..	..	..	2,141	19
31 Punjab States Agency	9	..	..	..	..	..	39,153	445
32 Rajputana Agency	50	..	..	..	7	1	25,516	1,166
33 Sikkim State	..	..	..	..	..	..	270	41
34 United Provinces States	..	..	..	..	..	..	471	20
35 Western India States Agency	47	20	2	61	1	..	24,78[illegible]	[illegible]

hood—Part II—Provincial Distribution—*contd.*

Material Substances—*contd.*

Trade—*contd.*

sorts—*contd.*

store-keepers and shop-keepers otherwise unspecified.				*Group 151.*—Itinerant traders, pedlars, and hawkers (of other than food, etc.)						
Total working dependants.		Total following occupation as subsidiary to other.		Total earners principal occupation.		Total working dependants.		Total following occupation as subsidiary to other.		
Males.	Females.	Males.	Females.	Males.	Females.	Males.	Females.	Males.	Females.	
1213	1214	1215	1216	1217	1218	1219	1220	1221	1222	
69,125	**42,770**	**153,027**	**23,280**	**41,833**	**8,917**	**1,381**	**1,079**	**4,290**	**1,730**	
23,559	**9,317**	**95,576**	**8,279**	**35,975**	**6,447**	**499**	**595**	**3,359**	**784**	
36	47	52	2	5	2	..	2	..	..	1
..	2	25	1	1	..	..	..	..	..	2
427	103	2,153	85	16	19	..	5	2	1	3
1	..	341	1	36	..	..	..	5	..	4
2,602	319	11,940	291	7,333	464	22	7	165	10	5
835	649	24,753	2,702	1,316	722	8	6	176	50	
4,692	2,460	4,995	284	9,584	892	100	28	415	8	7
25	..	*7*	..	*304*	*10*	*1*	..	..	*1*	
436	952	802	140	840	600	54	151	206	102	8
440	244	1,512	187	824	378	21	43	266	15	9
2	..	75	7	..	..	..	..	..	..	10
71	6	71	..	110	2	..	..	..	..	11
3,887	3,444	30,846	3,952	1,398	382	28	14	77	18	12
936	117	1,298	8	302	..	..	..	..	..	13
9,015	801	12,599	167	2,834	31	110	12	122	..	14
179	173	4,114	452	11,376	2,955	156	327	1,925	580	15
45,566	**33,453**	**57,451**	**15,001**	**5,858**	**2,470**	**882**	**484**	**931**	**946**	
12	24	34	26	..	..	..	..	..	..	16
..	..	93	..	..	..	..	..	..	..	17
428	175	412	7	872	15	7	1	25	..	18
12	..	116	1	1	..	..	..	..	..	19
96	13	250	21	5	6	..	..	2	..	20
854	551	2,098	183	92	84	15	15	147	..	21
302	66	1,108	50	73	24	1	..	5	1	22
131	119	254	12	230	139	10	26	27	3	23
878	437	3,403	402	5	..	..	..	..	..	24
36,500	30,700	34,904	13,705	1,646	1,745	721	360	400	878	25
110	15	1,305	87	36	..	..	..	4	..	26
778	146	2,598	101	271	22	..	..	15	..	27
36	*16*	*1,162*	*18*	*271*	*22*	..	..	*15*	..	
739	*119*	*1,280*	*68*	..	..	..	..	..	..	
3	*11*	*156*	*15*	..	..	..	..	..	..	
285	243	4,293	328	253	288	3	57	224	63	28
1	..	287	..	..	..	..	..	..	..	29
121	4	450	3	5	1	..	..	6	..	30
2,086	118	3,696	33	167	17	..	..	14	1	31
622	276	1,615	27	1,627	115	79	6	45	..	32
..	..	38	4	..	..	..	..	..	..	33
18	9	70	1	24	1	..	1	15	..	34
2,332	557	427	10	551	13	46	18	2	..	35

Table X.—Occupation or Means of Liveli

Province, State or Agency.	*Class B.*—Preparation and Supply of Material Substances—*concld.* *Sub-Class V*—Trade—*concld.* *Order 39.*—Trade of other sorts—*concld.* *Group 152.*—Other traders (including farmers of pounds, tools and markets).						*Class C.*—Public	
	Total earners principal occupation.		Total working dependants.		Total following occupation as subsidiary to other.		Total earners principal occupation.	
	Males.	Females.	Males.	Females.	Males.	Females.	Males.	Females.
1	1223	1224	1225	1226	1227	1228	1229	1230
INDIA	**43,191**	**5,744**	**4,446**	**1,129**	**12,345**	**430**	**3,550,388**	**299,808**
Provinces	**11,999**	**1,128**	**2,351**	**144**	**3,770**	**94**	**2,464,778**	**198,963**
1 Ajmer-Merwara	25	2	..	..	3	..	12,896	1,370
2 Andamans and Nicobars	..	..	..	..	..	..	1,651	20
3 Assam	510	11	29	1	275	1	54,011	2,233
4 Baluchistan (*Districts and Administered Territories*).	5	..	..	..	1	..	29,373	266
5 Bengal	987	52	7	1	251	2	363,293	19,977
6 Bihar and Orissa	2,578	408	28	36	1,206	70	164,531	23,163
7 Bombay (*including Aden*)	3,413	88	86	32	101	9	304,132	24,377
Aden	*1*	..	..	..	..	..	*1,903*	*51*
8 Burma	98	3	1	1	11	..	133,145	12,279
9 Central Provinces and Berar ..	704	276	14	53	188	10	141,325	13,384
10 Coorg	6	..	..	..	2	..	1,350	100
11 Delhi	10	..	..	..	..	..	21,685	1,031
12 Madras	1,519	248	39	11	409	2	466,566	38,089
13 North-West Frontier Province (*Districts and Administered Territories*).	118	..	1	..	14	..	69,041	988
14 Punjab	1,244	3	2,146	..	1,226	..	313,711	17,353
15 United Provinces of Agra and Oudh	782	37	..	9	83	..	388,068	44,333
States and Agencies ..	**31,192**	**4,616**	**2,095**	**985**	**8,575**	**336**	**1,085,610**	**100,845**
16 Assam States	..	..	..	..	1	..	5,308	269
17 Baluchistan States	..	..	..	..	..	..	4,383	36
18 Baroda State	71	..	3	..	10	..	51,866	3,284
19 Bengal States	83	6	..	..	12	1	5,684	118
20 Bihar and Orissa States	7	..	..	..	..	..	23,460	1,150
21 Bombay States	119	4	8	5	3	..	41,277	2,752
22 Central India Agency	268	46	3	7	14	4	101,111	5,827
23 Central Provinces States	28	3	..	..	5	..	11,366	673
24 Gwalior State	1,470	..	49	..	1	..	49,320	2,864
25 Hyderabad State	598	22	261	26	71	2	163,197	23,826
26 Jammu and Kashmir State ..	790	..	33	..	1,628	..	34,270	1,205
27 Madras States Agency	12,277	908	1,244	278	2,155	112	93,922	9,674
Cochin State	*402*	*64*	*5*	*3*	*111*	*6*	*19,533*	*2,823*
Travancore State	*11,820*	*843*	*1,239*	*275*	*2,026*	*106*	*68,212*	*6,556*
Other Madras States	*55*	*1*	..	..	*18*	..	*6,171*	*295*
28 Mysore State	13,918	3,586	356	535	4,574	208	79,891	5,157
29 North-West Frontier Province (*Agencies and Tribal Areas*).	..	..	..	..	..	..	33,831	..
30 Punjab States	6	..	..	..	2	..	3,223	196
31 Punjab States Agency	80	..	2	..	4	..	64,172	3,049
32 Rajputana Agency	866	21	11	8	73	..	232,450	35,425
33 Sikkim State	..	..	..	..	..	..	232	10
34 United Provinces States	4	..	..	..	..	..	9,673	1,150
35 Western India States Agency ..	607	20	125	126	22	9	76,974	4,180

hood—Part II—Provincial Distribution—*contd.*

Administration and Liberal Arts.

Total *Class C.*—Public Administration and Liberal Arts.				Sub-Class VI.—Public Force. Total *Sub-Class VI.*—Public Force.						
Total working dependants.		Total following occupation as subsidiary to other.		Total earners principal occupation.		Total working dependants.		Total following occupation as subsidiary to other.		
Males.	Females.	Males.	Females.	Males.	Females.	Males.	Females.	Males.	Females.	
1231	1232	1233	1234	1235	1236	1237	1238	1239	1240	
233,066	**63,637**	**643,496**	**29,057**	**820,153**	**3,762**	**14,300**	**3,259**	**99,267**	**582**	
156,237	**29,343**	**456,834**	**18,135**	**535,038**	**1,930**	**2,999**	**378**	**68,554**	**253**	
186	362	1,423	52	3,869	14	1	..	66	1	1
..	2	38	1	767	..	..	..	18	..	2
2,313	349	21,204	244	9,863	.	152	..	3,225	1	3
..	7	1,205	5	24,061	..	..	..	135	1	4
2,993	1,053	55,507	1,278	57,449	30	[illegible]	27	11,538	..	5
2,419	1,133	93,640	3,791	27,814	1	11	..	16,435	..	6
7,725	3,640	23,737	1,314	60,151	1,451	460	112	2,628	198	7
38	*9*	*9*	..	*1,258*	..	..	..	..	..	
117,870	11,279	15,321	354	30,784	4	28	..	86	1	8
2,103	1,515	25,248	1,534	40,018	226	329	210	4,424	36	9
10	3	640	2	180	..	..	..	18	..	10
29	37	1,358	23	7,760	..	1	..	851	..	11
7,934	3,635	99,379	3,862	55,177	30	501	8	5,686	1	12
637	69	7,363	82	39,833	28	111	1	3,722	7	13
6,603	2,497	37,395	982	81,824	37	776	3	6,380	4	14
5,415	3,762	73,376	4,611	95,488	109	338	17	13,342	3	15
76,829	**34,294**	**186,662**	**10,922**	**285,115**	**1,832**	**11,301**	**2,881**	**30,713**	**329**	
369	71	614	26	1,077	..	3	..	23	..	16
1	2	214	2	1,797	..	..	..	..	..	17
526	198	7,031	118	13,998	..	23	..	2,123	..	18
53	7	2,028	10	1,331	..	2	..	785	..	19
217	91	19,516	138	8,869	..	17	..	4,691	..	20
1,920	822	5,842	382	4,754	38	76	83	275	1	21
588	301	17,359	583	33,533	71	61	2	3,182	8	22
197	57	2,824	36	3,931	35	15	8	993	6	23
1,375	358	6,500	351	16,296	..	454	..	1,780	..	24
57,978	22,126	24,126	6,015	39,421	1,209	9,510	2,457	2,340	151	25
381	89	9,571	377	9,087	12	33	2	2,915	2	26
2,009	866	13,208	559	5,466	..	1	..	185	..	27
169	*137*	*2,785*	*135*	*1,026*	..	*1*	..	*29*	..	
1,804	*709*	*8,256*	*376*	*3,860*	..	..	..	*71*	..	
36	*20*	*2,167*	*48*	*580*	..	..	..	*35*	..	
727	375	33,054	769	16,694	309	73	49	4,050	149	28
50	..	1,120	..	32,795	..	45	..	1,001	..	29
134	58	2,727	15	736	..	8	..	380	..	30
1,380	1,387	10,863	208	20,120	1	115	..	2,187	1	31
2,632	5,314	24,584	1,266	55,376	106	301	262	3,236	8	32
8	3	258	4	53	..	..	..	19	..	33
189	408	2,612	15	2,522	..	2	2	172	—	34
6,095	1,761	2,611	48	17,259	51	562	16	426	3	35

Table X.—Occupation or Means of Liveli

Class C.—Public Administration and

Sub-Class VI.—Public

Order 40.—

Province, State or Agency.	Total *Order 40.*—Army.						*Group 153.*—Army	
	Total earners principal occupation.		Total working dependants.		Total following occupation as subsidiary to other.		Total earners principal occupation.	
	Males.	Females.	Males.	Females.	Males.	Females.	Males.	Females.
1	1241	1242	1243	1244	1245	1246	1247	1248
INDIA	**309,794**	**1,096**	**5,016**	**632**	**13,926**	**184**	**216,972**	**674**
Provinces	**171,225**	**684**	**297**	**24**	**7,679**	**143**	**169,450**	**644**
1 Ajmer-Merwara	2,237	10	1	..	17	..	2,203	10
2 Andamans and Nicobars	122	..	..	..	..	..	111	..
3 Assam	1,836	..	..	..	..	..	1,836	..
4 Baluchistan (*Districts and Administered Territories*).	19,179	..	..	..	5	..	19,178	..
5 Bengal	2,616	..	3	1	23	..	2,541	..
6 Bihar and Orissa	1,025	1	..	..	8	..	1,003	1
7 Bombay (*including Aden*)	18,986	605	52	22	14	136	18,743	565
Aden	*481*	..	..	..	..	..	*477*	..
8 Burma	5,215	1	2	..	6	..	5,215	1
9 Central Provinces and Berar ..	3,685	31	..	..	8	..	3,684	31
10 Coorg	2	..	..	..	..	..	2	..
11 Delhi	5,262	..	..	..	736	..	5,243	..
12 Madras	4,631	..	11	..	48	..	4,574	..
13 North-West Frontier Province (*Districts and Administered Territories*).	31,101	27	63	1	2,595	7	30,957	27
Punjab	40,727	9	159	..	1,682	..	39,816	9
United Provinces of Agra and Oudh	34,601	..	6	..	2,537	..	34,344	..
States and Agencies ..	**138,569**	**412**	**4,719**	**608**	**6,247**	**41**	**47,522**	**30**
16 Assam States	96	..	..	..	..	..	..	..
17 Baluchistan States	945	..	..	..	..	..	420	..
18 Baroda State	4,156	..	..	..	..	..	541	..
19 Bengal States	344	..	..	..	17	..	..	..
20 Bihar and Orissa States	..	..	..	..	..	..	..	..
21 Bombay States	216	..	2	..	21	..	125	..
22 Central India Agency	14,927	7	5	..	387	..	2,441	4
23 Central Provinces States	..	..	..	..	..	..	..	
24 Gwalior State	9,024	..	281	..	37	..	615	..
25 Hyderabad State	20,418	353	4,235	602	1,426	39	3,651	5
Jammu and Kashmir State ..	5,599	9	15	..	1,731	1	829	..
Madras States Agency	1,942	..	1	..	33	..	50	..
Cochin State	*81*	..	*1*	..	..	..	*4*	..
Travancore State	*1,726*	..	..	..	*32*	..	*46*	..
Other Madras States	*135*	..	..	..	*1*	..	..	..
28 Mysore State	6,925	20	5	1	12	..	4,324	18
29 North-West Frontier Province (*Agencies and Tribal Areas*).	32,792	..	45	..	999	..	32,792	..
30 Punjab States	214	..	3	..	83	..		
31 Punjab States Agency	9,034	..	63	..	769		356	..
32 Rajputana Agency	28,351	23	63	..	608	1	1,362	3
33 Sikkim State	2	..	..	..	..	..	2	..
34 United Provinces States	1,807	..	..	..	91	..	..	..
35 Western India States Agency ..	1,777	..	1	5	33	..	14	..

hood—Part II—Provincial Distribution—*contd.*

Liberal Arts—*contd.*

Force—*contd.*

Army.

(Imperial).				*Group 154.*—Army (Indian States).						
Total working dependants.		Total following occupation as subsidiary to other.		Total earners principal occupation.		Total working dependants.		Total following occupation as subsidiary to other.		
Males.	Females.	Males.	Females.	Males.	Females.	Males.	Females.	Males.	Females.	
1249	1250	1251	1252	1253	1254	1255	1256	1257	1258	
764	**14**	**9,748**	**142**	**92,822**	**422**	**4,252**	**618**	**4,178**	**42**	
289	**1**	**7,659**	**141**	**1,775**	**40**	**8**	**23**	**20**	**2**	
..	..	10	..	34	..	1	..	7	..	1
..	..	..	..	11	..	..	..	..	..	2
..	..	..	..	..	..	..	..	..	..	3
..	..	5	..	1	..	..	..	..	..	4
3	..	23	..	75	..	..	1	..	..	5
..	..	6	..	22	..	..	..	2	..	6
51	..	13	134	243	40	1	22	1	2	7
..	..	..	..	*4*	..	..	..	..	..	
2	..	6	..	..	..	..	..	..	..	8
..	..	8	..	1	..	..	..	..	..	9
..	..	..	..	..	..	..	..	..	..	10
..	..	736	..	19	..	..	..	..	..	11
11	..	48	..	57	..	..	..	..	..	12
59	1	2,585	7	144	..	4	..	10	..	13
157	..	1,682	..	911	..	2	..	..	..	14
6	..	2,537	..	257	..	..	..	..	..	15
475	**13**	**2,089**	**1**	**91,047**	**382**	**4,244**	**595**	**4,158**	**40**	
..	..	..	..	96	..	..	..	..	..	16
..	..	..	..	525	..	..	..	..	..	17
..	..	..	..	3,615	..	..	..	..	..	18
..	..	..	..	344	..	..	..	17	..	19
..	..	..	..	..	..	..	..	..	..	20
2	..	13	..	91	..	..	..	8	..	21
4	..	3	..	12,486	3	1	..	384	..	22
..	..	..	..	..	..	..	..	..	..	23
..	..	..	..	8,409	..	281	..	37	..	24
413	12	17	..	16,767	348	3,822	590	1,409	39	25
..	..	1,006	1	4,770	9	15	..	725	..	26
..	..	7	..	1,892	..	1	..	26	..	27
..	..	..	..	*77*	..	*1*	..	..	..	
..	..	*7*	..	*1,680*	..	..	..	*25*	..	
..	..	..	..	*135*	..	..	..	*1*	..	
..	1	..	..	2,601	2	5	..	12	..	28
45	..	999	..	..	..	..	..	..	..	29
..	..	..	..	214	..	3	..	83	..	30
8	..	..	..	8,678	..	55	..	769	..	31
3	..	44	..	26,989	20	60	..	564	1	32
..	..	..	..	..	..	..	..	..	..	33
..	..	..	..	1,807	..	..	..	91	..	34
..	..	..	..	1,763	..	1	5	33	..	35

Table X.—Occupation or Means of Liveli

Class C.—Public Administration and

Sub-Class VI.—Public

Order 41.—

	Province, State or Agency.	Total *Order 41.*—Navy.						*Group 155.*—	
		Total earners principal occupation.		Total working dependants.		Total following occupation as subsidiary to other.		Total earners principal occupation.	
		Males.	Females.	Males.	Females.	Males.	Females.	Males.	Females.
	1	1259	1260	1261	1262	1263	1264	1265	1266
	INDIA	**1,384**	**8**	**6**	..	**1**	..	**1,384**	**8**
	Provinces	1,352	8	4	..	1	..	1,352	8
1	Ajmer-Merwara	..	3	..	..	..	..	..	3
2	Andamans and Nicobars	..	..	..	..	..	..	..	..
3	Assam	..	..	..	..	..	..	..	..
4	Baluchistan (*Districts and Administered Territories*).	..	..	..	..	..	..	..	..
5	Bengal	16	..	..	..	..	..	16	..
6	Bihar and Orissa	..	..	..	..	..	..	..	..
7	Bombay (*including Aden*)	1,314	4	4	..	..	..	1,314	4
	Aden	..	..	..	..	..	..	..	..
8	Burma	..	..	..	..	..	..	..	..
9	Central Provinces and Berar ..	..	..	..	..	..	..	..	..
10	Coorg	..	..	..	..	..	..	..	..
11	Delhi	..	..	..	..	..	..	..	..
12	Madras	15	..	..	..	..	..	15	..
13	North-West Frontier Province (*Districts and Administered Territories*).	7	1	..	..	1	..	7	1
14	Punjab	..	..				..	..	..
15	United Provinces of Agra and Oudh	..	..	..	..	..	..	..	..
	States and Agencies ..	32	..	2	..	..	..	32	..
16	Assam States	..	..	..	..	..	..	..	..
17	Baluchistan States	..	..	..	..	..	..	..	..
18	Baroda State	..	..	..	..	..	..	..	..
19	Bengal States	..	..	..	..	..	..	..	..
20	Bihar and Orissa States	..	..	..	..	..	..	..	..
21	Bombay States	4	..	2	..	..	..	4	..
22	Central India Agency	..	..	..	..	..	..	..	..
23	Central Provinces States	..	..	..	..	..	..	..	..
24	Gwalior State	..	..	..	..	..	..	..	..
25	Hyderabad State	..	..	..	..	..	..	..	..
26	Jammu and Kashmir State ..	..	..	..	..	..	..	..	..
27	Madras States Agency	..	..	..	..	..	..	..	..
	Cochin State	..	..	..	..	..	..	..	..
	Travancore State	..	..	..	..	..	..	..	..
	Other Madras States	..	..	..	..	..	..	..	..
28	Mysore State	..	..	..	..	..	..	..	..
29	North-West Frontier Province (*Agencies and Tribal Areas*).	..	..	..	..	..	..	..	..
30	Punjab States	..	..	..	..	..	..	..	..
31	Punjab States Agency	..	..	..	..	..	..	..	..
32	Rajputana Agency	2	..	..	..	..	..	2	..
33	Sikkim State	..	..	..	..	..	..	..	..
34	United Provinces States	..	..	..	..	..	..	..	..
35	Western India States Agency ..	26	..	..	..	..	..	96	..

hood—Part II—Provincial Distribution—*contd.*

Liberal Arts—*contd.*

Force—*contd.*

Navy.				*Order 42.*—Air Force						
Navy.				Total *Order 42.*—Air Force.						
Total working dependants.		Total following occupation as subsidiary to other.		Total earners principal occupation.		Total working dependants.		Total following occupation as subsidiary to other.		
Males.	Females.	Males.	Females.	Males.	Females.	Males.	Females.	Males.	Females.	
1267	1268	1269	1270	1271	1272	1273	1274	1275	1276	
6	..	**1**	..	**1,834**	**4**	**4**	**21**	**12**	..	
4	..	1	..	1,787	4	3	21	11	..	
..	..	..	..	..	..	..	..	..	..	1
..	..	..	..	..	..	..	..	..	..	2
..	..	..	..	..	..	..	..	..	..	3
..	..	..	..	161	..	..	..	..	..	4
..	..	..	..	15	..	..	..	7	..	5
..	..	..	..	..	..	..	..	..	..	6
4	..	..	..	1,013	4	3	21	..	..	7
..	..	..	..	*245*	..	..	..	..	..	
..	..	..	..	..	..	..	..	..	..	8
..	..	..	..	4	..	..	..	..	..	9
..	..	..	..	..	..	..	..	..	..	10
..	..	..	..	21	..	..	..	..	..	11
..	..	..	..	..	..	..	..	..	..	12
..	..	1	..	435	..	..	..	..	..	13
..	..	..	..	136	..	..	..	4	..	14
..	..	..	..	2	..	..	..	..	..	15
2	..	..	..	47	..	1	..	1	..	
..	..	..	..	..	..	..	..	..	..	16
..	..	..	..	..	..	..	..	..	..	17
..	..	..	..	..	..	..	..	..	..	18
..	..	..	..	..	..	..	..	..	..	19
..	..	..	..	..	..	..	..	..	..	20
2	..	..	..	..	..	..	..	..	..	21
..	..	..	..	..	..	..	..	..	..	22
..	..	..	..	..	..	..	..	..	..	23
..	..	..	..	..	..	..	..	..	..	24
..	..	..	..	..	..	..	..	..	..	25
..	..	..	..	..	..	..	..	..	..	26
..	..	..	..	..	..	..	..	..	..	27
..	..	..	..	..	..	..	..	..	..	
..	..	..	..	..	..	..	..	..	..	
..	..	..	..	..	..	..	..	..	..	
..	..	..	..	1	..	..	..	..	..	28
..	..	..	..	..	..	..	..	..	..	29
..	..	..	..	..	..	..	..	..	..	30
..	..	..	..	1	..	..	..	..	..	31
..	..	..	..	1	..	..	..	..	..	32
..	..	..	..	..	..	..	..	..	..	33
..	..	..	..	..	..	..	..	..	..	34
..	..	..	..	44	..	1	..	1	..	35

Table X.—Occupation or Means of Liveli

Class C.—Public Administration

Sub-Class VI.—Public

Province, State or Agency.	*Order 42.*—Air Force—*concld.* *Group 156.*—Air Force. Total earners principal occupation. Males.	Females.	Total working dependants. Males.	Females.	Total following occupation as subsidiary to other. Males.	Females.	Total earners principal occupation. Males.	Females.
1	1277	1278	1279	1280	1281	1282	1283	1284
INDIA	**1,834**	**4**	**4**	**21**	**12**	..	**507,141**	**2,654**
Provinces	**1,787**	**4**	**3**	**21**	**11**	..	**360,674**	**1,234**
1 Ajmer-Merwara	..	..	..	..	..	..	1,632	1
2 Andamans and Nicobars	..	..	..	..	..	..	645	..
3 Assam	..	..	..	..	..	..	8,027	..
4 Baluchistan (*Districts and Administered Territories*).	161	..	..	..	..	..	4,721	..
5 Bengal	15	..	..	..	7	..	54,802	30
6 Bihar and Orissa	..	..	..	..	..	..	26,789	..
7 Bombay (*including Aden*)	1,013	4	3	21	..	..	38,838	838
Aden	*245*	..	..	..	..	..	*532*	..
8 Burma	..	..	..	..	..	..	25,569	3
9 Central Provinces and Berar ..	4	..	..	..	..	..	36,329	195
10 Coorg	..	..	..	..	..	..	178	..
11 Delhi	21	..	..	..	..	..	2,477	..
12 Madras	..	..	..	..	..	..	50,531	30
13 North-West Frontier Province (*Districts and Administered Territories*). ..	435	..	..	..	..	..	8,290	..
14 Punjab	136	..	..	..	4	..	40,961	28
15 United Provinces of Agra and Oudh	2	..	..	..	..	..	60,885	109
States and Agencies ..	**47**	..	**1**	..	**1**	..	**146,467**	**1,420**
16 Assam States	..	..	..	..	..	..	981	..
17 Baluchistan States	..	..	..	..	..	..	852	..
18 Baroda State	..	..	..	..	..	..	9,842	..
19 Bengal States	..	..	..	..	..	..	987	..
20 Bihar and Orissa States	..	..	..	..	..	..	8,869	..
21 Bombay States	..	..	..	..	..	..	4,534	38
22 Central India Agency	..	..	..	..	..	..	18,606	64
23 Central Provinces States	..	..	..	..	..	..	3,931	35
24 Gwalior State	..	..	..	..	..	..	7,272	..
25 Hyderabad State..	..	..	..	..	..	..	19,003	856
26 Jammu and Kashmir State ..	..	..	..	..	..	..	3,488	3
27 Madras States Agency	..	..	..	..	..	..	3,524	..
Cochin State	..	..	..	..	..	..	*945*	..
Travancore State	..	..	..	..	..	..	*2,134*	..
Other Madras States	..	..	..	..	..	..	*445*	..
28 Mysore State	1	..	..	..	..	..	9,768	289
29 North-West Frontier Province (*Agencies and Tribal Areas*). ..	..	..	..	..	..	..	3	..
30 Punjab States	..	..	..	..	..	..	522	..
31 Punjab States Agency	1	..	..	..	..	..	11,085	1
32 Rajputana Agency	1	..	..	..	..	..	27,022	83
33 Sikkim State	..	..	..	..	..	..	51	..
34 United Provinces State	..	..	..	..	..	..	715	..
35 Western India States Agency ..	44	..	1	..	1	..	15,412	51

hood—Part II—Provincial Distribution—*contd.*

and Liberal Arts—*contd.*

Force—*contd.*

Order 43.—Police.

Total *Order 43.*—Police.				*Group 157.*—Police.						
Total working dependants.		Total following occupation as subsidiary to other.		Total earners principal occupation.		Total working dependants.		Total following occupation as subsidiary to other.		
Males.	Females.	Males.	Females.	Males.	Females.	Males.	Females.	Males.	Females.	
1285	1286	1287	1288	1289	1290	1291	1292	1293	1294	
9,274	**2,606**	**85,328**	**398**	**303,225**	**1,060**	**4,543**	**802**	**14,134**	**53**	
2,695	**333**	**60,863**	**110**	**213,438**	**444**	**651**	**38**	**10,395**	**30**	
..	..	49	1	1,576	1	..	..	8	1	1
..	..	18	..	636	..	..	..	..	..	2
152	..	3,225	1	8,672	..	8	..	72	..	3
..	..	130	1	4,715	..	..	..	124	1	4
188	26	11,508	..	21,309	..	16	..	662	..	5
111	..	16,427	..	11,332	..	32	..	2,207	..	6
401	69	2,614	62	28,867	427	176	36	888	27	7
..	..	..	..	*528*	..	..	..	..	..	
26	..	80	1	25,569	3	26	..	80	1	8
329	210	4,416	36	12,099	1	19	2	160	..	9
..	..	18	..	178	..	..	..	18	..	10
1	..	115	..	2,334	..	..	..	9	..	11
490	8	5,638	1	30,862	..	188	..	789	..	12
48	..	1,126	..	5,908	..	29	..	772	..	13
617	3	4,694	4	22,095	12	157	..	716	..	14
332	17	10,805	3	39,286	..	..	..	3,890	..	15
6,579	**2,273**	**24,465**	**288**	**89,787**	**616**	**3,892**	**764**	**3,739**	**23**	
3	..	23	..	894	..	1	..	..	..	16
..	..	..	..	851	..	..	..	..	..	17
23	..	2,123	..	4,544	..	..	..	53	..	18
2	..	768	..	486	..	..	..	28	..	19
17	..	4,691	..	3,865	..	1	..	314	..	20
72	83	254	1	4,090	8	63	..	156	..	21
56	2	2,795	8	11,703	7	6	..	397	..	22
15	8	993	6	1,228	..	7	..	43	..	23
173	..	1,743	..	3,571	..	33	..	312	..	24
5,275	1,855	914	112	12,079	562	3,392	741	327	23	25
18	2	1,184	1	2,568	..	6	2	814	..	26
..	..	102	..	3,460	..	..	..	72	..	27
..	..	*29*	..	*924*	..	..	..	*29*	..	
..	..	*39*	..	*2,134*	..	..	..	*39*	..	
..	..	*34*	..	*402*	..	..	..	*4*	..	
68	48	4,038	149	6,825	..	..	..	120	..	28
..	..	2	..	3	..	..	..	2	..	29
5	..	297	..	376	..	2	..	139	..	30
52	..	1,418	1	6,543	..	24	..	311	..	31
238	262	2,628	7	16,352	11	35	16	513	..	32
..	..	19	..	32	..	..	..	13	..	33
2	2	81	..	28	..	..	..	2	..	34
560	11	392	3	10,289	28	322	5	123	..	35

Table X.—Occupation or Means of Liveli

Class C.—Public Administration

	Province, State or Agency.	*Sub-Class VI.*—Public Force—*concld.* *Order 43.*—Police—*concld.* *Group 158.*—Village watchmen. Total earners principal occupation.		Total working dependants.		Total following occupation as subsidiary to other.		Total earners principal occupation.	
		Males.	Females.	Males.	Females.	Males.	Females.	Males.	Females.
	1	1295	1296	1297	1298	1299	1300	1301	1302
	INDIA	**203,916**	**1,594**	**4,731**	**1,804**	**71,194**	**345**	**932,017**	**25,734**
	Provinces	**147,236**	**790**	**2,044**	**295**	**50,468**	**80**	**596,357**	**13,708**
1	Ajmer-Merwara	56	..	..	..	41	..	2,406	58
2	Andamans and Nicobars	9	..	..	..	18	..	720	..
3	Assam	1,355	..	144	..	3,153	1	9,034	101
4	Baluchistan (*Districts and Administered Territories*).	6	..	..	..	6	..	2,358	1
5	Bengal	33,493	30	172	26	10,846	..	48,887	358
6	Bihar and Orissa	15,457	..	79	..	14,220	..	13,414	305
7	Bombay (*including Aden*)	9,971	411	225	33	1,726	35	120,683	7,650
	Aden	*4*	..	..	..	..	..	*220*	*1*
8	Burma	..	..	..	..	..	..	44,150	323
9	Central Provinces and Berar ..	24,230	194	310	208	4,256	36	38,506	1,945
10	Coorg	..	..	..	..	..	..	350	3
11	Delhi	143	..	1	..	106	..	7,220	42
12	Madras	19,669	30	302	8	4,849	1	145,739	1,551
13	North-West Frontier Province (*Districts and Administered Territories*).	2,382	..	19	..	354	..	9,721	147
14	Punjab	18,866	16	460	3	3,978	4	76,912	531
15	United Provinces of Agra and Oudh	21,599	109	332	17	6,915	3	76,257	693
	States and Agencies ..	**56,680**	**804**	**2,687**	**1,509**	**20,726**	**265**	**335,660**	**12,026**
16	Assam States	87	..	2	..	23	..	1,433	19
17	Baluchistan States	1	..	..	..	..	..	1,335	..
18	Baroda State	5,298	..	23	..	2,070	..	12,022	359
19	Bengal States	501	..	2	..	740	..	957	8
20	Bihar and Orissa States	5,004	..	16	..	4,377	..	3,069	77
21	Bombay States	444	30	9	83	98	1	20,476	883
22	Central India Agency	6,903	57	50	2	2,398	8	39,882	1,269
23	Central Provinces States	2,703	35	8	8	950	6	3,307	134
24	Gwalior State	3,701	..	140	..	1,431	..	15,405	120
25	Hyderabad State	6,924	294	1,883	1,114	587	89	58,465	3,331
26	Jammu and Kashmir State ..	920	3	12	..	370	1	12,611	389
27	Madras States Agency	64	..	..	..	30	..	23,234	498
	Cochin State	*21*	..	..	..	..	..	*4,617*	*37*
	Travancore State	..	..	..	..	..	..	*16,272*	*412*
	Other Madras States	*43*	..	..	..	*30*	..	*2,345*	*49*
28	Mysore State	2,943	289	68	48	3,918	149	31,772	883
29	North-West Frontier Province (*Agencies and Tribal Areas*).	..	..	..	..	..	..	966	..
30	Punjab States	146	..	3	..	158	..	910	4
31	Punjab States Agency	4,542	1	28	..	1,107	1	16,721	424
32	Rajputana Agency	10,670	72	203	246	2,115	7	62,088	2,644
33	Sikkim State	19	..	..	..	6	..	82	1
34	United Provinces States	687	..	2	2	79	..	3,291	..
35	Western India States Agency ..	5,123	23	233	6	269	3	27,634	983

hood—Part II—Provincial Distribution—*contd.*

and Liberal Arts—*contd.*

Sub-Class VII.—Public Administration.

Total *Sub-Class VII.*—Public Administration.				Total *Order 44.*—Public Administration.						
Total working dependants.		Total following occupation as subsidiary to other.		Total earners principal occupation.		Total working dependants.		Total following occupation as subsidiary to other.		
Males.	Females.	Males.	Females.	Males.	Females.	Males.	Females.	Males.	Females.	
1303	1304	1305	1306	1307	1308	1309	1310	1311	1312	
30,724	**6,809**	**156,373**	**2,306**	**932,017**	**25,734**	**30,724**	**6,809**	**156,373**	**2,306**	
7,394	**2,158**	**93,006**	**1,015**	**596,357**	**13,708**	**7,394**	**2,158**	**93,006**	**1,015**	
12	26	397	3	2,406	58	12	26	397	3	1
..	..	14	..	720	..	..	..	14	..	2
128	2	3,511	2	9,034	101	128	2	3,511	2	3
..	..	432	1	2,358	1	..	..	432	1	4
81	3	2,558	2	48,887	358	81	3	2,558	2	5
322	174	3,595	37	13,414	305	322	174	3,595	37	6
2,549	1,439	13,894	595	120,683	7,650	2,549	1,439	13,894	595	7
21	..	*2*	..	*220*	*1*	*21*	..	*2*	..	
329	65	7,748	7	44,150	323	329	65	7,748	7	8
327	134	6,584	53	38,506	1,945	327	134	6,584	53	9
1	..	306	..	350	3	1	..	306	..	10
..	..	328	..	7,220	42	..	..	328	..	11
1,644	230	29,985	203	145,739	1,551	1,644	230	29,985	203	12
143	1	1,727	38	9,721	147	143	1	1,727	38	13
969	56	14,535	44	76,912	531	969	56	14,535	44	14
889	28	7,392	30	76,257	693	889	28	7,392	30	15
23,330	**4,651**	**63,367**	**1,291**	**335,660**	**12,026**	**23,330**	**4,651**	**63,367**	**1,291**	
2	..	51	..	1,433	19	2	..	51	..	16
..	..	6	..	1,335	..	..	..	6	..	17
4	29	2,436	13	12,022	359	4	29	2,436	13	18
3	..	96	1	957	8	3	..	96	1	19
24	..	5,471	14	3,069	77	24	..	5,471	14	20
458	249	3,122	123	20,476	883	458	249	3,122	123	21
138	55	6,515	115	39,882	1,269	138	55	6,515	115	22
25	..	391	..	3,307	134	25	..	391	..	23
253	4	480	16	15,405	120	253	4	480	16	24
20,198	3,625	7,220	236	58,465	3,331	20,198	3,625	7,220	236	25
94	39	2,961	91	12,611	389	94	39	2,961	91	26
10	1	2,052	41	23,234	498	10	1	2,052	41	27
10	*1*	*251*	*2*	*4,617*	*37*	*10*	*1*	*251*	*2*	
..	..	*1,004*	*24*	*16,272*	*412*	..	..	*1,004*	*24*	
..	..	*797*	*15*	*2,345*	*49*	..	..	*797*	*15*	
145	101	18,624	453	31,772	883	145	101	18,624	453	28
..	..	119	..	966	..	..	..	119	..	29
28	6	1,181	2	910	4	28	6	1,181	2	30
151	4	4,690	66	16,721	424	151	4	4,690	66	31
209	226	6,313	101	62,088	2,644	209	226	6,313	101	32
..	..	62	1	82	1	..	..	62	1	33
16	..	601	..	3,291	..	16	..	601	..	34
1,572	312	976	18	27,634	983	1,572	312	76	18	35

Table X.—Occupation or Means of Liveli

Province, State or Agency.		Class C.—Public Administration — Sub-Class VII.—Publio — Order 44.—Public — Group 159.—Service of the State. Total earners principal occupation. Males.	Females.	Total working dependants. Males.	Females.	Total following occupation as subsidiary to other. Males.	Females.	Group 160.—Service of — Total earners principal occupation. Males.	Females.
	1	1313	1314	1315	1316	1317	1318	1319	1320
	INDIA	**358,836**	**3,421**	**4,489**	**408**	**20,265**	**159**	**236,114**	**6,334**
	Provinces	**328,355**	**2,955**	**2,801**	**363**	**17,975**	**114**	**13,200**	**124**
1	Ajmer-Merwara	957	42	1	25	14	2	693	..
2	Andamans and Nicobars	651	..	..	..	5	..	..	..
3	Assam	6,824	11	37	2	788	..	2	..
4	Baluchistan (*Districts and Administered Territories.*)	1,894	1	..	..	4	..	29	..
5	Bengal	38,547	129	27	2	1,650	2	35	..
6	Bihar and Orissa	11,293	209	43	172	2,404	32	224	12
7	Bombay (*including Aden*)	58,346	1,117	978	47	3,368	29	1,409	59
	Aden	*115*	*1*	*1*	..	..	..	*3*	..
8	Burma	17,919	78	115	5	95	..	7,079	32
9	Central Provinces and Berar	23,942	382	171	57	1,071	10	217	10
10	Coorg	285	2	1	..	78	..		..
11	Delhi	5,865	24	..	..	21	..	94	1
12	Madras	68,581	304	459	37	3,285	4	759	8
13	North-West Frontier Province (*Districts and Administered Territories*).	7,998	113	55	1	951	32	12	..
14	Punjab	49,986	286	563	6	1,302	3	252	..
15	United Provinces of Agra and Oudh	35,267	257	351	9	2,939	..	2,395	2
	States and Agencies	**30,481**	**466**	**1,688**	**45**	**2,290**	**45**	**222,914**	**6,210**
16	Assam States	717	..	..	..	6	..	665	18
17	Baluchistan States	159	..	..	..	..	..	1,132	..
18	Baroda State	2	..	..	..	..	..	9,266	8
19	Bengal States	62	2	..	..	6	..	807	4
20	Bihar and Orissa States	400	..	10	..	5	..	1,852	24
21	Bombay States	12,923	181	208	20	1,347	43	3,859	380
22	Central India Agency	1,014	30	2	1	11	..	28,791	671
23	Central Provinces States	134	2	..	..	14	..	2,552	100
24	Gwalior State	60	..	..	..	..	..	15,083	103
25	Hyderabad State	1,279	19	544	6	29	..	28,540	1,179
26	Jammu and Kashmir State	9	..	..	..	..	..	11,955	320
27	Madras States Agency	94	..	..	..	8	..	18,023	454
	Cochin State	*1*	..	..	..	..	..	*3,476*	*20*
	Travancore State	*64*	..	..	..	..	..	*13,159*	*412*
	Other Madras States	*29*	..	..	..	*8*	..	*1,388*	*22*
28	Mysore State	262	13	..	..	17	1	19,958	325
29	North-West Frontier Province (*Agencies and Tribal Areas*).	938	..	..	..	119	..	..	..
30	Punjab States	6	..	..	..	..	..	698	4
31	Punjab States Agency	17	..	..	..	5	..	12,934	276
32	Rajputana Agency	514	30	3	2	54	1	51,696	1,823
33	Sikkim State	62	1	..	..	13	..	1	..
34	United Provinces States	11	..	..	..	..	..	2,593	..
35	Western India States Agency	11,818	188	921	16	656	..	12,509	521

hood—Part II—Provincial Distribution—*contd.*

and Liberal Arts—*contd.*

Administration—*contd.*

Administration—*contd.*

Indian and Foreign States.				*Group 161.*—Municipal and other local (not village) service.						
Total working dependants.		Total following occupation as subsidiary to other.		Total earners principal occupation.		Total working dependants.		Total following occupation as subsidiary to other.		
Males.	Females.	Males.	Females.	Males.	Females.	Males.	Females.	Males.	Females.	
1321	1322	1323	1324	1325	1326	1327	1328	1329	1330	
14,442	**2,801**	**19,593**	**279**	**131,212**	**9,239**	**3,191**	**1,375**	**5,657**	**386**	
135	**84**	**2,699**	**8**	**112,128**	**6,299**	**953**	**207**	**3,729**	**146**	
7	..	103	..	417	9	1	..	8	..	1
..	..	..	..	19	..	..	..	..	..	2
..	..	..	..	841	84	5	..	162	1	3
..	..	1	..	329	..	..	..	8	..	4
..	..	3	..	9,234	212	40	..	452	..	5
5	1	91	3	814	54	234	..	109	..	6
38	31	36	3	35,306	2,732	183	82	244	44	7
..	..	..	..	*102*	..	*20*	..	*2*	..	
79	52	1,945	1	12,784	201	54	7	356	2	8
..	..	6	..	7,132	1,521	79	73	229	24	9
..	..	..	..	30	1	..	..	5	..	10
..	..	..	..	1,150	17	..	..	5	..	11
..	..	61	1	14,640	890	106	5	819	4	12
..	..	..	..	656	32	7	..	34	6	13
1	..	37	..	14,803	217	164	35	380	37	14
5	..	416	..	13,973	329	80	5	918	28	15
14,307	**2,717**	**16,894**	**271**	**19,084**	**2,940**	**2,238**	**1,168**	**1,928**	**240**	
1	..	28	..	23	1	..	..	2	..	16
..	..	1	..	37	..	..	..	1	..	17
..	..	929	..	965	164	..	..	15	..	18
2	..	72	1	60	2	..	..	3	..	19
13	..	3,389	..	10	..	..	..	3	..	20
156	151	262	6	367	12	2	6	15	..	21
62	14	1,278	27	1,422	208	..	5	54	22	22
24	..	102	..	148	32	..	..	6	..	23
223	1	477	4	262	17	30	3	3	12	24
13,156	2,255	2,504	53	6,905	1,334	2,123	1,084	1,329	142	25
80	39	2,769	75	433	68	1	..	16	14	26
10	1	822	25	1,370	41	..	..	181	4	27
10	*1*	*118*	*1*	*373*	*16*	..	..	*57*	*1*	
..	..	*672*	*24*	*884*	..	..	..	*52*	..	
..	..	*32*	..	*113*	*25*	..	..	*72*	*3*	
..	..	506	2	2,065	31	..	..	72	3	28
..	..	..	..	23	..	..	..	..	..	29
20	6	327	..	88	..	..	..	10	..	30
131	3	812	22	1,176	139	2	..	78	..	31
114	76	2,312	39	2,436	644	1	10	129	37	32
..	..	..	..	6	..	..	..	2	..	33
15	..	158	..	93	..	..	..	..	..	34
300	171	146	17	1,195	247	79	60	9	..	35

Table X.—Occupation or Means of Liveli

Class C.—Public Administration

Province, State or Agency.	*Sub-Class VII.*—Public Administration—*concld.* *Order 44.*—Public Administration—*concld.* *Group 162.*—Village officials and servants other than watchmen. Total earners principal occupation.		Total working dependants.		Total following occupation as subsidiary to other.		Total earners principal occupation.	
	Males.	Females.	Males.	Females.	Males.	Females.	Males.	Females.
1	1331	1332	1333	1334	1335	1336	1337	1338
INDIA	**205,855**	**6,740**	**8,602**	**2,225**	**110,858**	**1,482**	**1,798,218**	**270,312**
Provinces	**142,674**	**4,330**	**3,505**	**1,504**	**68,603**	**747**	**1,333,383**	**183,325**
1 Ajmer-Merwara	339	7	3	1	272	1	6,621	1,298
2 Andamans and Nicobars	50	..	..	..	9	..	164	20
3 Assam	1,367	6	86	..	2,561	1	35,114	2,132
4 Baluchistan (*Districts and Administered Territories*).	106	..	..	..	419	1	2,954	265
5 Bengal	1,071	17	14	1	453	..	256,957	19,589
6 Bihar and Orissa	1,083	30	40	1	991	2	123,303	22,857
7 Bombay (*including Aden*)	25,622	3,742	1,350	1,279	10,246	519	123,298	15,276
Aden	..	..	..	..	..	..	*425*	*50*
8 Burma	6,368	12	81	1	5,352	4	58,211	11,952
9 Central Provinces and Berar ..	7,215	32	77	4	5,278	19	62,801	11,213
10 Coorg	35	..	..	..	223	..	820	97
11 Delhi	111	..	..	..	302	..	6,705	989
12 Madras	61,759	349	1,079	188	25,820	194	265,650	36,508
13 North-West Frontier Province (*Districts and Administered Territories*).	1,055	2	81	..	742	..	19,487	813
14 Punjab	11,871	28	241	15	12,816	4	154,975	16,785
15 United Provinces of Agra and Oudh	24,822	105	453	14	3,119	2	216,323	43,531
States and Agencies ..	**63,181**	**2,410**	**5,097**	**721**	**42,255**	**735**	**464,835**	**86,987**
16 Assam States	28	..	1	..	15	..	2,798	250
17 Baluchistan States	7	..	..	..	4	..	1,251	36
18 Baroda State	1,789	187	4	29	1,492	13	25,846	2,925
19 Bengal States	28	..	1	..	15	..	3,396	110
20 Bihar and Orissa States	807	53	1	..	2,074	14	11,522	1,073
21 Bombay States	3,327	310	92	72	1,498	74	16,047	1,831
22 Central India Agency	8,655	360	74	35	5,172	66	27,696	4,487
23 Central Provinces States	473	..	1	..	269	..	4,128	504
24 Gwalior State	..	..	..	..	..	..	17,619	2,744
25 Hyderabad State	21,741	799	4,375	280	3,358	41	68,311	19,286
26 Jammu and Kashmir State ..	214	1	13	..	176	2	12,572	804
27 Madras States Agency	3,747	3	..	..	1,041	12	65,222	9,176
Cochin State	*767*	*1*	..	..	*76*	..	*13,890*	*2,786*
Travancore State	*2,165*	..	..	..	*280*	..	*48,080*	*6,144*
Other Madras States	*815*	*2*	..	..	*685*	*12*	*3,252*	*246*
28 Mysore State	9,487	514	145	101	18,029	447	31,425	3,965
29 North-West Frontier Province (*Agencies and Tribal Areas*).	5	..	..	..	..	..	70	..
30 Punjab States	118	..	8	..	844	2	1,577	192
31 Punjab States Agency	2,594	9	18	1	3,795	38	27,331	2,624
32 Rajputana Agency	7,442	147	91	138	3,818	24	114,986	32,675
33 Sikkim State	13	..		..	47	1	97	9
34 United Provinces States	594	..	1	..	443	..	3,860	1,150
35 Western India States Agency ..	2,112	27	272	65	165	1	32,081	3,146

hood—Part II—Provincial Distribution—*contd.*

and Liberal Arts—*contd.*

Sub-Class VIII.—Professions and Liberal Arts.

Total *Sub-Class VIII.*—Professions and Liberal Arts.				*Order 45.*—Religion. Total *Order 45.*—Religion.						
Total working dependants.		Total following occupation as subsidiary to other.		Total earners principal occupation.		Total working dependants.		Total following occupation as subsidiary to other.		
Males.	Females.	Males.	Females.	Males.	Females.	Males.	Females.	Males.	Females.	
1339	1340	1341	1342	1343	1344	1345	1346	1347	1348	
188,042	**53,569**	**387,856**	**26,169**	**746,640**	**85,691**	**160,523**	**34,040**	**209,418**	**11,216**	
145,844	**26,807**	**295,274**	**16,867**	**498,186**	**43,085**	**132,344**	**16,601**	**152,539**	**5,809**	
173	336	960	48	3,020	357	110	132	610	23	1
..	2	6	1	15	..	..	..	1	..	2
2,033	347	14,468	241	14,804	754	1,392	115	6,661	108	3
..	7	638	3	1,634	11	..	..	586	3	4
2,721	1,023	41,411	1,276	77,063	2,889	857	86	12,528	290	5
1,986	959	73,610	3,754	65,911	7,590	1,138	609	46,912	1,748	6
4,716	2,089	7,215	521	44,694	4,367	2,661	1,070	3,370	225	7
17	*9*	*7*	..	*72*	*15*	*2*	*3*	..	..	
117,513	11,214	7,487	346	2,615	182	115,748	9,735	291	3	8
1,447	1,171	14,240	1,445	20,213	1,858	685	210	5,001	150	9
9	3	316	2	293	16	8	3	127	1	10
28	37	179	23	1,639	89	16	28	152	21	11
5,789	3,397	63,708	3,658	76,039	4,678	2,368	701	25,432	543	12
383	67	1,914	37	12,418	114	275	42	1,473	7	13
4,858	2,438	16,480	934	71,199	4,267	3,445	1,126	11,215	367	14
4,188	3,717	52,642	4,578	106,629	15,913	3,641	2,744	38,180	2,320	15
42,198	**26,762**	**92,582**	**9,302**	**248,454**	**42,606**	**28,179**	**17,439**	**56,879**	**5,407**	
364	71	540	26	1,023	50	238	52	181	5	16
1	2	208	2	847	6	..	..	185	..	17
499	169	2,472	105	13,042	1,768	404	165	1,749	86	18
48	7	1,147	9	1,394	23	32	7	372	2	19
176	91	9,354	124	5,723	699	119	22	5,523	39	20
1,386	490	2,445	258	6,492	993	933	228	1,328	139	21
389	244	7,662	460	12,354	770	226	43	4,960	71	22
157	49	1,440	30	1,380	89	59	27	522	10	23
668	354	4,240	335	9,871	529	404	67	2,695	146	24
28,270	16,044	14,566	5,628	39,087	11,288	18,998	10,649	8,892	3,741	25
254	48	3,695	284	7,962	473	154	33	2,535	164	26
1,998	865	11,021	518	19,327	2,963	993	75	3,471	206	27
158	*136*	*2,505*	*133*	*3,466*	*695*	*88*	*82*	*698*	*48*	
1,804	*709*	*7,181*	*352*	*14,750*	*2,254*	*875*	*665*	*2,073*	*153*	
36	*20*	*1,335*	*33*	*1,111*	*14*	*30*	*4*	*700*	*5*	
509	225	10,380	167	8,246	417	333	61	6,100	81	28
5	..	..	..	65	..	..	..	..	..	29
98	52	1,166	13	758	53	50	15	689	9	30
1,114	1,383	3,986	141	17,538	1,602	934	1,265	3,082	87	31
2,122	4,826	15,035	1,157	83,600	18,347	1,630	2,720	12,308	596	32
8	3	177	3	56	4	8	3	163	2	33
171	406	1,839	15	1,783	793	95	234	1,252	3	34
3,961	1,433	1,209	27	17,906	1,739	2,569	1,097	872	20	35

Table X.—Occupation or Means of Liveli

Class C.—Public Administration

Sub-Class VIII.—Professions

Order 45.—

Province, State or Agency.	*Group 163.*—Priests, ministers, etc.						*Group 164.*—Monks,	
	Total earners principal occupation.		Total working dependants.		Total following occupation as subsidiary to other.		Total earners principal occupation.	
	Males.	Females.	Males.	Females.	Males.	Females.	Males.	Females.
1	1349	1350	1351	1352	1353	1354	1355	1356
INDIA	**479,257**	**45,240**	**103,273**	**16,836**	**154,091**	**8,463**	**130,968**	**23,748**
Provinces	**367,334**	**28,516**	**82,119**	**4,479**	**124,159**	**4,484**	**51,838**	**5,053**
1 Ajmer-Merwara	635	42	18	10	115	..	1,665	241
2 Andamans and Nicobars	8	..	..	..	..	..	3	..
3 Assam	11,363	293	1,170	28	5,296	36	567	295
4 Baluchistan (*Districts and Administered Territories*).	1,370	6	..	..	564	3	80	..
5 Bengal	75,168	2,666	843	84	12,384	278	745	142
6 Bihar and Orissa	57,576	6,843	955	580	40,113	1,650	1,987	537
7 Bombay (*including Aden*)	7,386	682	352	73	503	18	28,738	2,948
Aden	*35*	*2*	*1*	..	..	..	..	*5*
8 Burma	705	48	71,365	7	71	1	7	58
9 Central Provinces and Berar ..	13,106	1,054	353	74	2,668	55	1,628	372
10 Coorg	41	..	2	..	18	..	2	..
11 Delhi	906	45	14	27	143	19	5	2
12 Madras	46,747	1,296	1,494	426	16,790	115	2,271	154
13 North-West Frontier Province (*Districts and Administered Territories*). ..	212	..	..	..	..	..	11,458	106
14 Punjab	49,954	2,895	1,942	730	8,180	270	2,283	127
15 United Provinces of Agra and Oudh	102,157	12,646	3,611	2,440	37,314	2,039	399	71
States and Agencies ..	**111,923**	**16,724**	**21,154**	**12,357**	**29,932**	**3,979**	**79,130**	**18,695**
16 Assam States	882	29	189	20	155	1	1	19
17 Baluchistan States	682	5	..	..	162	..	45	..
18 Baroda State	1,274	58	12	1	142	7	8,460	1,441
19 Bengal States	1,377	22	32	7	353	1	..	..
20 Bihar and Orissa States	3,480	639	88	19	2,870	25	1	..
21 Bombay States	1,717	253	146	71	371	41	2,903	343
22 Central India Agency	8,125	428	94	23	3,607	45	818	118
23 Central Provinces States	106	21	..	3	57	..	376	51
24 Gwalior State	5,145	306	195	46	965	29	4,094	222
25 Hyderabad State	35,573	10,150	18,129	10,066	8,308	3,606	382	40
26 Jammu and Kashmir State ..	3,994	173	105	12	1,025	45	1,005	106
27 Madras States Agency	6,433	8	422	7	1,497	1	79	191
Cochin State	*1,252*	*8*	*20*	*7*	*285*	*1*	*31*	*13*
Travancore State	*4,913*	..	*398*	..	*1,156*	..	*45*	*178*
Other Madras States	*268*	..	*4*	..	*56*	..	*3*	..
28 Mysore State	3,026	75	112	8	1,913	10	271	52
29 North-West Frontier Province (*Agencies and Tribal Areas*).	..	..	..	..	..	..	65	..
30 Punjab States	540	40	25	9	411	5	26	7
31 Punjab States Agency	13,379	1,461	835	1,246	2,050	65	1,211	15
32 Rajputana Agency	23,522	2,752	600	695	4,771	93	48,850	14,667
33 Sikkim State	23	2	..	1	9	1	32	1
34 United Provinces States	1,704	275	88	48	1,251	3	..	..
35 Western India States Agency ..	941	27	82	75	15	1	10,511	1,422

hood—Part II—Provincial Distribution—*contd.*

and Liberal Arts—*contd.*

and Liberal Arts—*contd.*

Religion—*contd.*

nuns, religious mendicants.				*Group 165.*—Other religious workers.						
Total working dependants.		Total following occupation as subsidiary to other.		Total earners principal occupation.		Total working dependants.		Total following occupation as subsidiary to other.		
Males.	Females.	Males.	Females.	Males.	Females.	Males.	Females.	Males.	Females.	
1357	1358	1359	1360	1361	1362	1363	1364	1365	1366	
46,807	**13,865**	**15,416**	**926**	**38,668**	**5,386**	**3,483**	**1,736**	**9,074**	**526**	
43,573	**10,744**	**5,589**	**259**	**22,746**	**3,073**	**1,583**	**657**	**5,599**	**239**	
85	105	411	14	241	38	4	11	48	2	1
..	..	..	..	1	..	..	..	1	..	2
57	31	216	19	2,155	141	110	35	829	51	3
..	..	2	..	11	..	..	..	..	..	4
11	1	46	..	327	15	..	..	44	..	
48	8	286	7	856	102	48	5	713	28	6
1,708	821	2,140	163	3,415	362	227	121	402	26	7
..	*3*	..	..	*12*	..	..	..	..	..	
41,075	9,606	..	2	1,216	65	713	12	210	..	8
28	37	267	40	3,171	280	152	61	1,476	36	9
1	..	..	..	2	..	..	1	1	..	10
..	..	..	..	208	28	2	..	6	..	11
257	41	565	2	4,344	595	84	30	1,247	39	12
272	39	1,422	7	306	3	3	2	49	..	13
29	53	169	4	4,728	541	215	263	387	42	14
2	2	65	1	1,765	903	25	116	186	15	15
3,234	**3,121**	**9,827**	**667**	**15,922**	**313**	**1,900**	**1,079**	**3,475**	**287**	
..	21	..	4	139	2	49	11	26	..	16
..	..	..	..	..	..	..	..	..	..	17
286	130	1,090	58	453	15	8	4	46	..	18
..	..	1	..	3	..	..	..	..	..	19
..	..	1	..	113	23	1	..	64	1	20
294	90	361	25	814	40	399	26	137	9	21
30	8	263	8	549	76	12	1	92	1	22
3	3	61	..	839	14	50	20	389	10	23
182	21	1,719	117	18	1	..	..	11	..	24
59	18	33	..	1,072	400	181	111	227	10	25
18	11	345	60	2,282	188	24	9	898	56	26
82	258	53	41	2,298	307	104	336	501	57	27
11	*4*	*38*	*5*	*602*	*86*	*17*	*3*	*132*	*11*	
71	*254*	*15*	*36*	*1,666*	*221*	*87*	*333*	*366*	*46*	
	..	..	..	*30*	..	..	..	*3*	..	
14	1	136	1	283	57	5	2	164	2	28
..	..	..	..	..	..	..	..	..	.	29
2	2	6	2	32	2	3	1	1	..	30
23	1	70	..	295	9	4	..	27	1	31
891	1,673	4,942	333	2,847	521	95	310	741	139	32
8	2	152	1	1	1	..	..	2	..	33
..	..	..	..	25	517	7	186	..	..	34
1,342	882	594	17	3,859	140	958	62	149	1	35

Table X.—Occupation or Means of Liveli

Class C.—Public Administration

Sub-Class VIII.—Professions

Order 45.—Religion.—*concld.*

	Province, State or Agency.	*Group 166.*—Servants in religious edifices, burial and burning grounds, pilgrim conductors, circumcisers, etc. Total earners principal occupation.		Total working dependants.		Total following occupation as subsidiary to other.		Total earners principal occupation.	
		Males.	Females.	Males.	Females.	Males.	Females.	Males.	Females.
	1	1367	1368	1369	1370	1371	1372	1373	1374
	INDIA	**97,747**	**11,317**	**6,960**	**1,603**	**30,837**	**1,301**	**130,370**	**388**
	Provinces	**56,268**	**6,443**	**5,069**	**721**	**17,192**	**827**	**108,456**	**261**
1	Ajmer-Merwara	479	36	3	6	36	7	227	2
2	Andamans and Nicobars	3	..	..	..	..	..	6	..
3	Assam	719	25	55	21	320	2	2,590	..
4	Baluchistan (*Districts and Administered Territories*).	173	5	..	..	20	..	52	..
5	Bengal	823	66	3	1	54	12	30,561	7
6	Bihar and Orissa	5,492	108	87	16	5,800	63	8,028	33
7	Bombay (*including Aden*)	5,155	375	374	55	325	18	7,952	39
	Aden	*25*	*8*	*1*	..	..	..	*132*	..
8	Burma	687	11	2,595	110	10	..	4,397	25
9	Central Provinces and Berar	2,308	152	152	38	590	19	4,357	68
10	Coorg	248	16	5	2	108	1	27	..
11	Delhi	520	14	..	1	3	2	447	..
12	Madras	22,677	2,633	533	204	6,830	387	18,201	26
13	North-West Frontier Province (*Districts and Administered Territories*).	442	5	..	1	2	..	517	35
14	Punjab	14,234	704	1,259	80	2,479	51	8,941	..
15	United Provinces of Agra and Oudh	2,308	2,293	3	186	615	265	22,153	26
	States and Agencies	**41,479**	**4,874**	**1,891**	**882**	**13,645**	**474**	**21,914**	**27**
16	Assam States	1	..	..	..	..	..	59	..
17	Baluchistan States	120	1	..	..	23	..	9	..
18	Baroda State	2,855	254	98	30	471	21	875	..
19	Bengal States	14	1	..	..	18	1	217	..
20	Bihar and Orissa States	2,129	37	30	3	2,588	13	46	..
21	Bombay States	1,058	357	94	41	459	64	1,102	14
22	Central India Agency	2,862	148	90	11	998	17	1,116	..
23	Central Provinces States	59	3	6	1	15	..	121	..
24	Gwalior State	614	..	27	..	..	..	822	1
25	Hyderabad State	2,060	698	629	454	324	125	4,372	88
26	Jammu and Kashmir State	681	6	7	1	267	3	566	1
27	Madras States Agency	10,517	2,457	385	150	1,420	107	6,631	10
	Cochin State	*1,581*	*588*	*40*	*68*	*243*	*31*	*822*	..
	Travancore State	*8,126*	*1,855*	*319*	*78*	*536*	*71*	*5,568*	*10*
	Other Madras States	*810*	*14*	*26*	*4*	*641*	*5*	*241*	..
28	Mysore State	4,666	233	202	50	3,887	68	1,140	6
29	North-West Frontier Province (*Agencies and Tribal Areas*).	..	..	..	..	..	..	..	..
30	Punjab States	160	4	20	3	271	2	67	..
31	Punjab States Agency	2,653	117	72	18	935	21	1,121	..
32	Rajputana Agency	8,381	407	44	42	1,854	31	2,127	7
33	Sikkim State	..	..	..	..	..	..	2	..
34	United Provinces States	54	1	..	..	1	..	160	..
35	Western India States Agency	2,595	150	187	78	114	1	1,361	..

hood—Part II—Provincial Distribution—*contd.*

and Liberal Arts—*contd.*

and Liberal Arts—*contd.*

Order 46—Law.

Total *Order 46*—Law. Total working dependants. Males.	Females.	Total following occupation as subsidiary to other. Males.	Females.	*Group 167.*—Lawyers of all kinds, including qazis, law agents and mukhtiars. Total earners principal occupation. Males.	Females.	Total working dependants. Males.	Females.	Total following occupation as subsidiary to other. Males.	Females.	
1375	1376	1377	1378	1379	1380	1381	1382	1383	1384	
2,221	**110**	**10,289**	**63**	**68,737**	**270**	**1,338**	**93**	**4,517**	**45**	
626	**93**	**7,768**	**61**	**56,661**	**167**	**239**	**76**	**3,454**	**44**	
..	..	8	..	91	..	..	..	4	..	1
..	..	..	..	1	..	..	..	..	..	2
49	..	616	..	987	..	..	..	90	..	3
..	..	..	..	8	..	..	..	..	..	4
32	14	1,734	..	17,017	4	16	..	788	..	5
22	..	1,573	13	5,170	3	3	..	826	..	6
116	1	338	30	5,429	33	84	1	155	30	7
2	..	*2*	..	*56*	..	*1*	..	*1*	..	
35	2	71	..	2,290	13	7	1	23	..	8
61	72	724	14	2,617	67	47	70	521	13	9
..	..	6	..	18	..	..	..	..	..	10
..	..	..	..	269	..	..	..	..	..	11
151	..	1,467	3	7,602	1	5	..	402	..	12
4	..	35	..	218	26	2	..	24	..	13
98	..	311	..	4,735	..	48	..	178	..	14
58	4	885	1	10,209	20	27	4	443	1	15
1,595	**17**	**2,521**	**2**	**12,076**	**103**	**1,099**	**17**	**1,063**	**1**	
..	..	..	..	19	..	..	..	..	..	16
..	..	1	..	4	..	..	..	..	..	17
2	..	29	..	361	..	..	..	7	..	18
4	..	47	..	128	..	1	..	40	..	19
..	..	19	..	40	..	..	..	13	..	20
21	2	92	..	648	5	8	2	33	..	21
8	..	76	1	697	..	5	..	39	1	22
12	..	18	..	74	..	..	..	10	..	23
9	..	62	..	344	1	3	..	22	..	24
1,135	15	617	..	3,870	88	977	15	561	..	25
12	..	139	..	121	1	2	..	38	..	26
512	..	1,099	..	1,986	1	..	..	158	..	27
2	..	*107*	..	*242*	..	..	..	*46*	..	
212	..	*983*	..	*1,625*	*1*	..	..	*112*	..	
1	..	*9*	..	*119*	..	..	..	..	..	
1	..	95	1	797	..	..	..	58	..	28
..	..	..	..	..	..	..	..	..	..	29
2	..	33	..	23	..	..	..	15	..	30
8	..	78	..	470	..	3	..	13	..	31
6	..	81	..	1,379	7	..	..	47	..	32
..	..	1	..	2	..	..	..	1	..	33
	..	8	..	77	..	..	..	..	..	34
160		26	..	1,036	..	100	..	8	..	35

Table X.—Occupation or Means of Liveli

Class C.—Public Administration

Sub-Class VIII.—Professions

Order 46.—Law—*concld.*

Province, State or Agency.	*Group 168.*—Lawyers' clerks, petition-writers, etc.							
	Total earners principal occupation.		Total working dependants.		Total following occupation as subsidiary to other.		Total earners principal occupation.	
	Males.	Females.	Males.	Females.	Males.	Females.	Males.	Females.
1	1385	1386	1387	1388	1389	1390	1391	1392
INDIA	**61,633**	**118**	**883**	**17**	**5,772**	**18**	**217,581**	**86,963**
Provinces	**51,795**	**94**	**387**	**17**	**4,314**	**17**	**181,906**	**72,464**
1 Ajmer-Merwara	136	2	..	..	4	..	415	306
2 Andamans and Nicobars	5	..	..	..	..	..	68	8
3 Assam	1,603	..	49	..	526	..	5,887	550
4 Baluchistan (*Districts and Administered Territories*).	44	..	..	..	..	..	589	187
5 Bengal	13,544	3	16	14	946	..	56,090	10,818
6 Bihar and Orissa	2,858	30	19	..	747	13	6,847	11,739
7 Bombay (*including Aden*)	2,523	6	32	..	183	..	12,565	4,354
Aden	*76*	..	*1*	..	*1*	..	*58*	*21*
8 Burma	2,107	12	28	1	48	..	21,826	5,527
9 Central Provinces and Berar ..	1,740	1	14	2	203	1	4,699	5,991
10 Coorg	9	..	..	..	6	..	129	22
11 Delhi	178	..	..	..	..	..	1,148	465
12 Madras	10,599	25	146	..	1,065	3	35,666	9,769
13 North-West Frontier Province (*Districts and Administered Territories*).	299	9	2	..	11	..	2,770	302
14 Punjab	4,206	..	50	..	133	..	18,342	7,002
15 United Provinces of Agra and Oudh	11,944	6	31	..	442	..	14,865	15,424
States and Agencies ..	**9,838**	**24**	**496**	..	**1,458**	**1**	**35,675**	**14,499**
16 Assam States	40	..	..	..	..	..	515	103
17 Baluchistan States		..	..	..	1	..	66	30
18 Baroda State	514	..	2	..	22	..	1,273	320
19 Bengal States	89	..	3	..	7	..	591	37
20 Bihar and Orissa States	6	..	..	..	6	..	564	97
21 Bombay States	454	9	13	..	59	..	1,254	155
22 Central India Agency	419	..	3	..	37	..	2,224	1,523
23 Central Provinces States	47	..	12	..	8	..	290	237
24 Gwalior State	478	..	6	..	40	..	951	924
25 Hyderabad State	502	..	158	..	56	..	5,624	2,526
26 Jammu and Kashmir State ..	445	..	10	..	101	..	997	116
27 Madras States Agency	4,645	9	215	..	941	..	9,692	1,244
Cochin State	*580*	..	*2*	..	*61*	..	*2,361*	*451*
Travancore State	*3,943*	*9*	*212*	..	*871*	..	*6,945*	*643*
Other Madras States	*122*	..	*1*	..	*9*	..	*386*	*150*
28 Mysore State	343	6	1	..	37	1	3,525	1,338
29 North-West Frontier Province (*Agencies and Tribal Areas*).	—	—	..	..	..	..	4	..
30 Punjab States	44	..	2	..	18	..	154	69
31 Punjab States Agency	651	..	5	..	65	..	2,362	556
32 Rajputana Agency	748	..	6	..	34	..	3,055	4,779
33 Sikkim State	..	..	..	..	..	..	10	2
34 United Provinces States	83	..	..	..	8	..	147	15
35 Western India States Agency ..	325	..	60	..	18	..	2,377	428

*Combined figures for groups 169 and 170 have been given here as there is no Act

hood—Part II—Provincial Distribution—*contd.*

and Liberal Arts—*contd.*

and Liberal Arts—*contd.*

Total *Order 47.*—Medicine. Total working dependants. Males.	Females.	Total following occupation as subsidiary to other. Males.	Females.	*Order 47.*—Medicine. *Group 169.*—Registered medical practitioners including oculists. Total earners principal occupation. Males.	Females.	Total working dependants. Males.	Females.	Total following occupation as subsidiary to other. Males.	Females.	
1393	1394	1395	1396	1397	1398	1399	1400	1401	1402	
4,955	**9,082**	**42,930**	**7,972**	**74,205**	**3,691**	**1,206**	**289**	**9,558**	**119**	
2,455	**5,824**	**35,522**	**6,578**	**67,154**	**3,027**	**646**	**153**	**8,625**	**86**	
1	17	28	10	101	9	..	1	4	1	1
..	2	3	1	16	..	..	..	..	..	2
111	160	2,251	68	1,707	22	13	..	207	1	3
..	..	20	..	166	5	..	..	..	..	4
315	516	10,121	703	28,706	544	141	6	4,769	23	5
41	212	2,904	1,699	3,222	212	14	..	717	20	6
326	649	494	145	7,284	518	209	21	146	7	7
1	*2*	..	..	*20*	*2*	*1*	*1*	..	..	
726	1,013	4,735	272	1,274	42	1	1	2	..	8
38	719	822	1,152	901	75	2	..	75	1	9
..	..	16	..	19	..	..	..	2	..	10
..	1	2	..	414	67	..	..	..	..	11
582	1,270	10,199	698	7,961	671	114	72	1,470	20	12
10	8	99	27	1,361	10	..	1	40	1	13
235	860	1,703	429	9,050	387	109	43	820	6	14
70	397	2,125	1,374	4,972	465	43	8	373	6	15
2,500	**3,258**	**7,408**	**1,394**	**7,051**	**664**	**560**	**136**	**933**	**33**	
45	13	190	6	69	1	1	..	11	1	16
..	2	5	1	11	..	..	..	..	..	17
13	..	99	18	881*	22*	13*	..	96*	..	18
2	..	333	5	203	..	2	..	114	..	19
17	1	664	13	90	2	..	..	16	..	20
63	46	134	15	983	38	59	..	104	2	21
10	79	286	213	459	34	1	..	15	..	22
1	7	55	9	67	3	..	..	14	..	23
22	179	272	66	128	3	13	..	6	..	24
1,793	2,014	1,263	640	1,270	291	452	130	237	22	25
6	8	160	35	267	9	3	1	48	1	26
390	69	2,360	87	456	39	..	..	78	1	27
21	*28*	*507*	*38*	*208*	*15*	..	..	*77*	*1*	
367	*25*	*1,624*	*32*	*225*	*22*	..	..	..	..	
2	*16*	*229*	*17*	*23*	*2*	..	..	*1*	..	
20	66	840	51	520	54	2	..	22	3	28
..	..	..	..	..	..	..	..	..	..	29
4	10	126	4	24	..	1	..	6	..	30
29	62	308	45	586	31	9	..	114	..	31
15	484	219	180	436	82	..	3	19	3	32
..	..	4	1	6	..	..	..	3	..	33
1	1	20	1	28	4	..	..	1	..	34
69	217	70	4	567	51	4	2	20	..	35

regarding the registration of medical practitioners in Baroda State.

M8CC

Table X.—Occupation or Means of Liveli

Class C.—Public Administration

Sub-Class VIII.—Professions

Order 47.—

Province, State or Agency.	Group 170.—Other persons practising the healing arts without being registered. Total earners principal occupation.		Total working dependants.		Total following occupation as subsidiary to other.		Total earners principal occupation.	
1	Males. 1403	Females. 1404	Males. 1405	Females. 1406	Males. 1407	Females. 1408	Males. 1409	Females. 1410
INDIA	**101,839**	**4,693**	**2,430**	**1,088**	**30,358**	**597**	**3,362**	**168**
Provinces	**82,089**	**3,959**	**1,438**	**952**	**24,651**	**466**	**2,966**	**153**
1 Ajmer-Merwara	144	4	..	..	13	1	4	..
2 Andamans and Nicobars	..	..	..	..	..	..	..	..
3 Assam	2,826	135	89	52	1,935	32	9	..
4 Baluchistan (*Districts and Administered Territories*).	89	12	..	..	13	..	9	2
5 Bengal	21,367	773	149	21	4,918	79	1,116	28
6 Bihar and Orissa	2,101	148	19	9	1,746	31	71	1
7 Bombay (*including Aden*)	2,817	179	44	8	262	5	200	55
Aden	*4*	*2*	..	..	..	..	*3*	..
8 Burma	15,280	190	565	31	4,422	21	382	51
9 Central Provinces and Berar ..	1,896	176	22	13	605	20	20	3
10 Coorg	69	5	..	..	10	..	..	..
11 Delhi	297	1	..	..	2	..	33	1
12 Madras	23,714	1,937	442	791	8,448	237	98	..
13 North-West Frontier Province (*Districts and Administered Territories*).	313	3	8	2	55	..	38	..
14 Punjab	5,001	116	81	13	709	4	363	9
15 United Provinces of Agra and Oudh	6,175	280	19	12	1,513	36	623	3
States and Agencies ..	**19,750**	**734**	**992**	**136**	**5,707**	**131**	**396**	**15**
16 Assam States	383	14	44	1	178	..	2	1
17 Baluchistan States	14	1	..	2	4	..	..	..
18 Baroda State	..	..	..	..	..	..	27	..
19 Bengal States	339	3	..	..	215	1	24	..
20 Bihar and Orissa States	232	3	2	..	560	2	..	..
21 Bombay States	119	10	2	..	26	..	..	..
22 Central India Agency	603	173	6	10	236	62	11	1
23 Central Provinces States	91	3	1	1	37	..	..	..
24 Gwalior State	567	..	2	..	221	..	..	..
25 Hyderabad State	3,060	242	517	76	691	24	110	9
26 Jammu and Kashmir State ..	382	14	2	1	82	5	19	1
27 Madras States Agency	8,438	168	363	17	2,206	20	85	1
Cochin State	*1,936*	*55*	*19*	*7*	*420*	*7*	*2*	..
Travancore State	*6,199*	*94*	*342*	*9*	*1,565*	*12*	*81*	*1*
Other Madras States	*303*	*19*	*2*	*1*	*221*	*1*	*2*	..
28 Mysore State	1,689	66	11	15	778	14	34	1
29 North-West Frontier Province (*Agencies and Tribal Areas*).	..	..	..	..	..	..	..	..
30 Punjab States	79	..	2	..	106	1	..	..
31 Punjab States Agency	1,243	2	16	..	168	..	38	..
32 Rajputana Agency	1,265	18	11	11	150	1	30	1
33 Sikkim State	..	..	..	..	..	..	..	..
34 United Provinces States	106	..	1	..	17	..	..	..
35 Western India States Agency ..	1,140	17	12	2	32	1	16	..

hood—Part II—Provincial Distribution—*contd.*

and Liberal Arts—*contd.*

and Liberal Arts—*contd.*

Medicine—*contd.*

Group 171.—Dentists.				***Group 172.***—Midwives, vaccinators, compounders, nurses, masseurs, etc.						
Total working dependants.		Total following occupation as subsidiary to other.		Total earners principal occupation.		Total working dependants.		Total following occupation as subsidiary to other.		
Males.	Females.	Males.	Females.	Males.	Females.	Males.	Females.	Males.	Females.	
1411	1412	1413	1414	1415	1416	1417	1418	1419	1420	
100	**33**	**349**	**10**	**34,369**	**78,241**	**1,186**	**7,668**	**2,301**	**7,238**	
57	**23**	**217**	**10**	**26,600**	**65,176**	**297**	**4,693**	**1,724**	**6,016**	
..	..	1	..	162	291	1	14	10	8	**1**
..	..	..	..	49	8	..	2	3	1	**2**
..	..	..	..	1,251	393	8	108	96	35	**3**
..	..	..	..	257	168	..	..	6	..	**4**
2	..	49	2	4,369	9,412	17	488	277	599	**5**
..	..	7	..	1,113	11,361	7	203	381	1,648	**6**
47	7	60	1	1,952	3,540	26	613	18	132	**7**
..	..	..	..	*29*	*17*	..	*1*	..	..	
6	16	9	2	4,656	5,244	154	965	300	249	**8**
..	..	2	5	1,458	5,734	13	706	139	1,126	**9**
..	..	..	..	39	17	..	..	4	..	**10**
..	..	..	..	400	396	..	1	..	..	**11**
2	..	..	..	3,750	7,157	24	407	244	441	**12**
..	..	..	..	1,006	289	2	5	4	26	**13**
..	..	12	..	3,716	6,490	41	804	156	419	**14**
..	..	137	..	2,422	14,676	4	377	86	1,332	**15**
43	**10**	**72**	..	**7,769**	**13,065**	**889**	**2,975**	**577**	**1,222**	
..	..	..	..	47	87	..	12	1	5	**16**
..	..	..	..	38	29	..	..	1	1	**17**
..	..	3	..	340	298	..	..	..	18	**18**
..	..	3	..	19	34	..	..	1	4	**19**
..	..	..	..	198	92	15	1	55	11	**20**
..	..	2	..	140	107	2	46	1	13	**21**
..	..	1	..	1,040	1,314	3	69	20	151	**22**
..	..	..	..	122	231	..	6	4	9	**23**
..	..	..	..	215	918	7	179	15	66	**24**
27	..	17	..	1,112	1,984	784	1,808	315	594	**25**
..	..	2	..	313	89	..	5	25	24	**26**
15	2	22	..	677	1,036	12	50	31	66	**27**
..	..	*1*	..	*199*	*381*	*2*	*21*	*7*	*30*	
15	*2*	*21*	..	*421*	*526*	*10*	*14*	*24*	*20*	
..	..	..	..	*57*	*129*	..	*15*	..	*16*	
..	..	7	..	1,027	1,204	5	51	23	33	**28**
..	..	..	..	4	..	..	..	..	..	**29**
..	..	..	..	48	69	1	10	13	3	**30**
..	..	12	..	477	523	4	62	14	45	**31**
..	..	3	..	1,292	4,677	4	470	46	174	**32**
..	..	..	..	4	2	..	..	1	1	**33**
..	..	..	..	13	11	..	1	2	1	**34**
1	8	..	..	643	360	52	205	..	3	**35**

Table X.—Occupation or Means of Liveli

Class C.—Public Administration

Sub-Class VIII.—Professions

Province, State or Agency.	*Order 47.*—Medicine—*concld.* *Group 173.*—Veterinary Surgeons. Total earners principal occupation. Males.	Females.	Total working dependants. Males.	Females.	Total following occupation as subsidiary to other. Males.	Females.	Total earners principal occupation. Males.	Females.
1	1421	1422	1423	1424	1425	1426	1427	1428
INDIA ..	**3,806**	**170**	**33**	**4**	**364**	**8**	**435,160**	**54,803**
Provinces	3,097	149	17	3	245	..	351,750	42,605
1 Ajmer-Merwara	4	2	..	2	..	..	1,043	229
2 Andamans and Nicobars	3	..	..	..	..	..	63	12
3 Assam	94	..	1	..	13	..	9,351	732
4 Baluchistan (*Districts and Administered Territories*).	68	..	..	..	1	..	355	54
5 Bengal	532	61	6	1	108	..	67,929	4,829
6 Bihar and Orissa	340	17	1	..	53	..	25,681	1,310
7 Bombay (*including Aden*) ..	312	62	..	..	8	..	35,476	4,863
Aden	*2*	..	..	..	..	..	*115*	*11*
8 Burma	234	..	..	..	2	..	15,551	4,664
9 Central Provinces and Berar ..	424	3	1	..	1	..	15,887	1,748
10 Coorg	2	..	..	..	..	..	296	44
11 Delhi	4	..	..	..	..	..	1,850	275
12 Madras	143	4	..	..	37	..	97,414	16,257
13 North-West Frontier Province (*Districts and Administred Territories*).	52	..	..	..	..	..	1,754	249
14 Punjab	212	..	4	..	6	..	31,474	3,755
15 United Provinces of Agra and Oudh	673	..	4	..	16	..	47,626	3,584
States and Agencies ..	709	21	16	1	119	8	83,410	12,198
16 **Assam States**	14	..	..	..	..	..	705	67
17 **Baluchistan States**	3	..	..	..	..	..	42	..
18 **Baroda State**	25	..	..	..	..	..	7,944	723
19 **Bengal States**	6	..	..	..	..	..	696	19
20 **Bihar and Orissa States**	44	..	..	..	33	..	3,486	134
21 **Bombay States**	12	..	..	..	1	..	3,385	372
22 **Central India Agency**	111	1	..	..	14	..	4,871	470
23 **Central Provinces States**	10	..	..	..	..	..	1,162	91
24 **Gwalior State**	41	3	..	..	30	..	1,534	156
25 **Hyderabad State**	72	..	13	..	3	..	6,794	2,064
26 **Jammu and Kashmir State** ..	16	3	1	1	3	5	1,887	175
27 **Madras States Agency**	36	..	..	..	23	..	21,931	4582
Cochin State	*16*	..	..	..	*2*	..	*4,774*	*1,408*
Travancore State	*19*	..	..	..	*14*	..	*16,332*	*2,117*
Other Madras States	*1*	..	..	..	*7*	..	*825*	*57*
28 **Mysore State**	255	13	2	..	10	1	13,665	1,811
29 **North-West Frontier Province** (*Agencies and Tribal Areas*).	..	..	..	..	..	..	..	..
30 **Punjab States**	3	..	..	..	1	..	219	16
31 **Punjab States Agency**	18	..	..	..	..	..	2,732	197
32 **Rajputana Agency**	32	1	..	..	1	2	5,776	437
33 **Sikkim State**	..	..	..	..	..	..	20	3
34 **United Provinces States**	..	..	..	..	..	..	544	34
35 **Western India States Agency** ..	11	..	..	..	..	..	6,017	[illegible]

hood—Part II—Provincial Distribution—*contd.*

and Liberal Arts—*contd.*

and Liberal Arts—*contd.*

Total *Order 48*— Instruction. Total working dependants. Males. 1429	Females. 1430	Total following occupation as subsidiary to other. Males. 1431	Females. 1432	*Order 48*.—Instruction. *Group 174*.—Professors and teachers of all kinds. Total earners principal occupation. Males. 1433	Females. 1434	Total working dependants. Males. 1435	Females. 1436	Total following occupation as subsidiary to other. Males. 1437	Females. 1438	
8,079	**3,610**	**51,532**	**1,594**	**400,268**	**51,895**	**7,281**	**3,405**	**49,458**	**1,511**	
4,768	**1,988**	**44,096**	**907**	**323,271**	**40,601**	**4,452**	**1,933**	**42,572**	**867**	
7	13	27	..	846	218	3	8	26	..	1
..	..	2	..	50	12	..	..	2	..	2
254	47	2,917	46	8,897	621	251	37	2,871	39	3
..	..	6	..	303	48	..	..	6	..	4
648	200	11,252	242	67,026	4,783	628	200	11,083	242	5
380	52	8,216	65	20,522	1,227	376	48	7,975	65	6
678	172	1,068	67	32,023	4,628	642	156	1,044	67	7
10	*4*	*5*	..	*110*	*11*	*10*	*4*	*5*	..	
250	193	278	20	14,462	4,630	239	189	271	20	8
175	24	714	26	15,200	1,559	160	21	676	21	9
1	..	67	1	292	44	1	..	67	1	10
4	..	21	2	1,529	241	4	..	21	2	11
1,704	1,044	13,498	288	94,172	15,696	1,529	1,037	13,273	267	12
45	5	221	3	1,673	230	44	4	213	3	13
429	169	1,230	36	29,592	3,438	422	166	1,198	34	14
193	69	4,579	111	36,684	3,226	153	67	3,846	106	15
3,311	**1,622**	**7,436**	**687**	**76,997**	**11,294**	**2,829**	**1,472**	**6,886**	**644**	
6	3	34	14	682	64	6	3	30	14	16
..	..	..	1	36	..	..	..	..	1	17
..	..	176	1	7,210	561	..	..	117	..	18
2	..	172	1	696	19	2	..	172	1	19
21	..	817	4	3,388	112	21	..	793	3	20
78	37	247	42	3,292	370	77	37	235	42	21
16	2	270	4	4,363	382	15	1	254	4	22
2	..	92	..	1,124	79	2	..	91	..	23
86	1	207	2	1,529	156	86	1	204	2	24
2,200	1,437	1,107	374	5,833	1,986	1,771	1,307	1,007	353	25
44	4	331	43	1,450	121	19	4	213	25	26
14	7	2,069	187	20,883	4,492	14	5	2,008	186	27
14	*7*	*405*	*31*	*4,323*	*1,374*	*14*	*5*	*387*	*31*	
..	..	*1,605*	*155*	*14,746*	*3,065*	..	..	*1,563*	*154*	
..	..	*59*	*1*	*814*	*53*	..	..	*58*	*1*	
47	49	1,211	8	12,415	1,548	40	37	1,101	7	28
..	..	..	..	..	..	..	..	..	..	29
18	1	107	..	195	15	18	1	96	..	30
12	1	190	1	2,465	180	12	1	176	1	31
90	15	295	5	5,130	368	90	15	281	5	32
..	..	5	..	20	3	..	..	5	..	33
14	..	30	..	451	34	14	..	30	..	34
661	85	76	..	5,835	804	642	60	73	..	35

Table X.—Occupation or Means of Liveli

Class C.—Public Administration

Sub-Class VIII.—Professions and Liberal

Order 48.—Instruction—*concld.*

Group 175.—Clerks and servants connected with education.

Province, State or Agency.		Total earners principal occupation.		Total working dependants.		Total following occupation as subsidiary to other.		Total earners principal occupation.	
		Males.	Females.	Males.	Females.	Males.	Females.	Males.	Females.
	1	1439	1440	1441	1442	1443	1444	1445	1446
	INDIA.	**34,892**	**2,908**	**798**	**205**	**2,074**	**83**	**268,467**	**42,467**
	Provinces	**28,479**	**2,004**	**316**	**55**	**1,524**	**40**	**193,085**	**24,910**
1	Ajmer-Merwara	197	11	4	5	1	..	1,916	404
2	Andamans and Nicobars	13	..	..	..	..	..	12	..
3	Assam	454	111	3	10	46	7	2,482	96
4	Baluchistan (*Districts and Administered Territories*).	52	6	..	..	..	..	324	13
5	Bengal	903	46	20	..	169	..	25,314	1,046
6	Bihar and Orissa	5,159	83	4	4	241	..	16,836	2,185
7	Bombay (*including Aden*)	3,453	235	36	16	24	..	22,611	1,653
	Aden	*5*	..	..	..	..	..	*48*	*3*
8	Burma	1,089	34	11	4	7	..	13,822	1,554
9	Central Provinces and Berar	687	189	15	3	38	5	17,645	1,548
10	Coorg	4	..	..	..	..	..	75	15
11	Delhi	321	34	..		..	..	1,621	160
12	Madras	3,242	561	175	7	225	21	38,330	5,778
13	North-West Frontier Province (*Districts and Administered Territories*).	81	19	1	1	8	..	2,028	113
14	Punjab	1,882	317	7	3	32	2	25,019	1,761
15	United Provinces of Agra and Oudh	10,942	358	40	2	733	5	25,050	8,584
	States and Agencies	**6,413**	**904**	**482**	**150**	**550**	**43**	**75,382**	**17,557**
16	Assam States	23	3	..	..	4		496	30
17	Baluchistan States	6	..	..	..	..	..	287	..
18	Baroda State	734	162	..	..	59	1	2,712	114
19	Bengal States	..	..	..	..	..	..	498	31
20	Bihar and Orissa States	98	22	..	..	24	1	1,703	143
21	Bombay States	93	2	1	..	12	..	3,814	297
22	Central India Agency	508	88	1	1	16	..	7,131	1,724
23	Central Provinces States	38	12	..	..	1	..	1,175	87
24	Gwalior State	5	..	..	..	3	..	4,441	1,134
25	Hyderabad State	961	78	429	130	100	21	9,434	3,320
26	Jammu and Kashmir State	437	54	25	..	118	18	1,160	39
27	Madras States Agency	1,048	90	..	2	61	1	7,641	377
	Cochin State	*451*	*34*	..	*2*	*18*	..	*2,467*	*232*
	Travancore State	*586*	*52*	..	..	*42*	*1*	*4,485*	*120*
	Other Madras States	*11*	*4*	..	..	*1*	..	*689*	*25*
28	Mysore State	1,250	263	7	12	110	1	4,849	393
29	North-West Frontier Province (*Agencies and Tribal Areas*)	..	..	..	..	..	..	1	..
30	Punjab States	24	1	..	..	11	..	379	54
31	Punjab States Agency	267	17	..	..	14	..	3,578	269
32	Rajputana Agency	646	69	..	..	14	..	20,428	[illegible],105
33	Sikkim State	..	..	..	..	..	..	9	..
34	United Provinces States	93	..	..	..	..	..	1,226	308
35	Western India States Agency	[illegible]	[illegible]	[illegible]	[illegible]	[illegible]		[illegible]	[illegible]

hood—Part II—Provincial Distribution—*contd.*

and Liberal Arts—*contd.*

Arts—*contd.*

Order 49.—Letters, Arts and Sciences (other than 44).

Total *Order 49*—Letters arts and sciences (other than 44): Total working dependants. Males.	Total working dependants. Females.	Total following occupation as subsidiary to other. Males.	Total following occupation as subsidiary to other. Females.	*Group 176.*—Public scribes, stenographers, etc.: Total earners principal occupation. Males.	Total earners principal occupation. Females.	Total working dependants. Males.	Total working dependants. Females.	Total following occupation as subsidiary to other. Males.	Total following occupation as subsidiary to other. Females.	
1447	1448	1449	1450	1451	1452	1453	1454	1455	1456	
12,264	**6,727**	**73,687**	**5,324**	**3,465**	**572**	**176**	**11**	**437**	**8**	
5,651	**2,301**	**55,349**	**3,512**	**2,739**	**531**	**52**	..	**307**	**2**	
55	174	287	15	26	3	..	..	4	..	1
..	..	..	..	2	..	..	..	..	..	2
227	25	2,023	19	12	..	..	..	..	..	3
..	7	26	..	19	..	..	..	1	..	4
869	207	5,776	41	709	189	1	..	20	1	5
405	86	14,005	229	168	1	1	..	105	..	6
935	197	1,945	54	366	107	..	..	..	..	7
2	..	..	..	*1*	..	..	..	..	..	
754	271	2,112	51	273	128	34	..	62	1	8
488	146	6,979	103	13	..	..	..	1	..	9
..	..	100	..	..	..	..	..	..	..	10
8	8	4	..	69	35	..	..	..	..	11
984	382	13,112	2,126	477	43	..	..	34	..	12
49	12	86	..	172	..	4	..	21	..	13
651	283	2,021	102	408	10	12	..	59	..	14
226	503	6,873	772	25	15	..	..	..	..	15
6,613	**4,426**	**18,338**	**1,812**	**726**	**41**	**124**	**11**	**130**	**6**	
75	3	135	1	3	..	..	..	..	..	16
1	..	17	..	..	..	..	..	..	..	17
80	4	419	..	..	..	..	..	..	..	18
8	..	223	1	3	..	..	..	7	..	19
19	68	2,331	68	10	..	..	..	11	..	20
291	177	644	62	54	..	2	..	8	..	21
129	120	2,070	171	1	..	..	..	1	..	22
83	15	753	11	..	..	..	..	..	..	23
147	107	1,004	121	..	..	..	..	..	..	24
4,144	1,929	2,687	873	276	14	117	10	52	3	25
38	3	530	42	19	4	1	..	2	1	26
386	88	2,022	38	174	..	..	..	39	..	27
33	*19*	*788*	*16*	*134*	..	..	..	*38*	..	
350	*19*	*896*	*12*	*40*	..	..	..	*1*	..	
3	..	*338*	*10*	..	..	..	..	..	..	
108	49	2,134	26	89	23	1	..	8	2	28
5	..	..	..	..	..	..	..	..	..	29
24	26	211	..	5	..	..	..	..	..	30
131	55	328	8	25	..	..	..	..	..	31
381	1,607	2,132	376	53	..	..	..	2	..	32
..	..	4	..	..	..	..	..	..	..	33
61	171	529	11	..	..	..	..	..	..	34
502	54	165	3	14	..	3	1	..	..	35

Table X.—Occupation or Means of Liveli

Class C—Public Administration

Sub-Class VIII—Professions and

Order 49.—Letters, Arts and Sciences

Province, State or Agency.		Group 177.—Architects, surveyors, engineers, and their employees (not being State servants).						Group 178.—Authors, editors,	
		Total earners principal occupation.		Total working dependants.		Total following occupation as subsidiary to other.		Total earners principal occupation.	
		Males.	Females.	Males.	Females.	Males.	Females.	Males.	Females.
1		1457	1458	1459	1460	1461	1462	1463	1464
	INDIA ..	**10,055**	**116**	**890**	**1**	**1,424**	**6**	**9,303**	**183**
	Provinces	**7,718**	**106**	**537**	**1**	**1,079**	**6**	**6,360**	**129**
1	Ajmer-Merwara	57	..	1	..	2	..	32	..
2	Andamans and Nicobars	4	..	..	..	..	..	2	..
3	Assam	328	1	2	..	41	..	100	..
4	Baluchistan (*Districts and Administered Territories*).	3	..	..	..	..	..	26	..
5	Bengal	1,651	48	514	..	557	4	606	9
6	Bihar and Orissa	1,053	1	11	..	368	2	342	43
7	Bombay (*including Aden*)	2,020	52	7	..	10	..	1,144	17
	Aden	*13*	..	..	..	..	..	*7*	..
8	Burma	43	..	..	..	..	..	869	23
9	Central Provinces and Berar ..	209	3	..	..	15	..	172	8
10	Coorg	2	..	..	..	..	..	3	..
11	Delhi	85	..	..	..	..	..	207	..
12	Madras	1,077	1	1	1	41	..	1,101	15
13	North-West Frontier Province (*Districts and Administered Territories*).	223	..	..	..	..	..	149	..
14	Punjab	530	..	1	..	11	..	663	..
15	United Provinces of Agra and Oudh	433	..	..	..	34	..	944	14
	States and Agencies ..	**2,337**	**10**	**353**	..	**345**	..	**2,943**	**54**
16	Assam States	27	..	..	..	2	..	3	..
17	Baluchistan States	..	..	..	..	..	..	10	..
18	Baroda State	48	..	..	..	..	..	158	..
19	Bengal States	58	..	..	..	1	..	6	..
20	Bihar and Orissa States	610	2	1	..	220	..	4	..
21	Bombay States	42	..	11	..	..	..	73	27
22	Central India Agency	49	2	..	..	2	..	103	..
23	Central Provinces States	5	..	..	..	..	..	..	..
24	Gwalior State	71	..	..	..	2	..	124	8
25	Hyderabad State	334	..	105	..	29	..	1,273	12
26	Jammu and Kashmir State ..	25	..	..	..	7	..	29	..
27	Madras States Agency	541	2	38	..	39	..	342	1
	Cochin State	*77*	..	..	..	*3*	..	*67*	..
	Travancore State	*456*	*2*	*38*	..	*36*	..	*257*	*1*
	Other Madras States	*8*	..	.	..	..	..	*18*	..
28	Mysore State	113	..	..	..	6	..	299	4
29	North-West Frontier Province (*Agencies and Tribal Areas*).	..	..	..	..	..	..	1	..
30	Punjab States	3	..	..	..	..	..	2	..
31	Punjab States Agency	114	..	1	..	18	..	19	..
32	Rajputana Agency	126	3	..	..	16	..	282	2
33	Sikkim State	3	..	..	2	2	..	1	..
34	United Provinces States	6	..	..	..	1	..	..	.
35	Western India States Agency ..	162	1	197	..	..			..

hood—Part II—Provincial Distribution—*contd.*

and Liberal Arts—*contd.*

Liberal Arts—*contd.*

(other than 44) —*contd.*

journalists and photographers.				*Group 179.*—Artists, sculptors and image-makers.						
Total working dependants.		Total following occupation as subsidiary to other.		Total earners principal occupation.		Total working dependants.		Total following occupation as subsidiary to other.		
Males.	Females.	Males.	Females.	Males.	Females.	Males.	Females.	Males.	Females.	
1465	1466	1467	1468	1469	1470	1471	1472	1473	1474	
594	**119**	**724**	**54**	**14,211**	**818**	**1,027**	**429**	**1,846**	**68**	
84	14	374	2	9,752	391	439	245	1,439	19	
..	6	1	..	45	2	..	..	3	..	1
..	..	..	..	..	..	..	..	..	..	2
..	..	51	..	54	1	9	..	19	1	3
..	..	..	..	2	..	..	..	..	..	4
2	..	71	..	1,930	64	39	145	109	4	5
10	6	26	..	130	55	..	..	71	6	6
2	..	33	..	1,190	20	107	..	34	1	7
1	..	..	..	..	..	..	..	..	..	
27	..	61	1	1,783	53	175	16	809	4	8
7	..	21	1	489	53	6	29	84	..	9
..	..	1	..	..	..	..	..	..	..	10
..	..	..	..	141	2	..	..	2	..	11
29	2	86	..	1,436	84	6	21	169	3	12
..	..	4	..	101	..	..	..	..	..	13
6	..	4	..	2,034	22	27	30	124	..	14
1	..	15	..	417	35	70	4	15	..	15
510	**105**	**350**	**52**	**4,459**	**427**	**588**	**184**	**407**	**49**	
1	..	..	..	55	..	1	..	1	..	16
1	..	..	..	..	..	..	..	..	..	17
..	..	3	..	64	..	5	..	1	..	18
..	..	2	..	11	..	..	..	29	..	19
..	..	4	..	91	6	4	2	35	2	20
14	98	10	49	1,302	35	100	5	17	..	21
2	..	18	..	131	6	12	11	19	1	22
..	..	1	..	57	1	..	..	4	..	23
3	2	69	1	13	..	..	..	8	..	24
469	5	152	..	980	110	411	119	156	40	25
2	..	1	..	..	..	..	..	..	..	26
5	..	45	2	191	..	7	1	35	2	27
..	..	*24*	*1*	*65*	..	*2*	..	*20*	*2*	
5	..	*19*	*1*	*123*	..	*5*	*1*	*13*	..	
..	..	*2*	..	*3*	..	..	..	*2*	..	
2	..	20	..	290	10	4	3	48	4	28
5	..	..	..	..	..	..	..	..	..	29
1	..	1	..	34	..	1	..	1	..	30
..	..	1	..	333	..	1	..	1	..	31
1	..	17	..	856	257	25	38	48	..	32
..	..	..	..	5	..	..	..	2	..	33
..	..	..	..	..	..	..	..	..	..	34
4	..	6	..	46	2	17	5	2	..	35

Table X.—Occupation or Means of Liveli

Class C.—Public Administration and

Sub-Class VIII.—Professions

Order 49.—Letters, Arts and

	Province, State or Agency.	*Group 180.*—Scientists (astronomers, botanists, etc.) Total earners principal occupation. Males.		Total working dependants. Males.	Females.	Total following occupation as subsidiary to other. Males.	Females.	*Group 181.*—Horoscope casters, Total earners principal occupation. Males.	Females.
		Males.	Females.	Males.	Females.	Males.	Females.	Males.	Females.
	1	1475	1476	1477	1478	1479	1480	1481	1482
	INDIA ..	**1,913**	**113**	**100**	**20**	**154**	**12**	**23,681**	**2,926**
	Provinces	**1,401**	**74**	**53**	**20**	**112**	**4**	**15,133**	**1,096**
1	Ajmer-Merwara	..	..	..	..	..	..	108	53
2	Andamans and Nicobars	..	..	..	..	..	..	..	..
3	Assam	45	..	..	..	14	..	334	2
4	Baluchistan (*Districts and Administered Territories*).	3	..	..	..	..	..	14	..
5	Bengal	15	..	..	..	1	..	1,760	40
6	Bihar and Orissa	2	..	..	..	6	..	431	58
7	Bombay (*including Aden*)	244	13	31	20	7	2	1,380	115
	Aden	..	..	..	..	..	..	..	*1*
8	Burma	..	..	..	..	..	..	1,557	306
9	Central Provinces and Berar ..	44	9	..	..	1	..	521	117
10	Coorg	..	..	..	..	..	..	20	1
11	Delhi	28	..	..	..	..	..	116	..
12	Madras	859	52	22	..	72	2	7,783	394
13	North-West Frontier Province (*Districts and Administered Territories*).	60	..	..	..	6	..	30	..
14	Punjab	94	..	..	..	5	..	879	3
15	United Provinces of Agra and Oudh	7	..	..	..	..	..	200	7
	States and Agencies ..	**512**	**39**	**47**	..	**42**	**8**	**8,548**	**1,830**
16	Assam States	..	..	..	..	..	..	21	..
17	Baluchistan States	..	..	..	..	..	..	..	..
18	Baroda State	..	..	..	..	..	..	242	..
19	Bengal States	..	..	..	..	..	..	19	..
20	Bihar and Orissa States	2	..	..	..	..	..	146	1
21	Bombay States	..	..	..	..	..	..	166	25
22	Central India Agency	1	..	..	..	..	..	231	1
23	Central Provinces States	..	..	..	..	..	8	69	..
24	Gwalior State	..	..	..	..	..	..	60	19
25	Hyderabad State	128	..	36	..	19	..	2,947	1,600
26	Jammu and Kashmir State ..	3	..	..	..	..	..	16	..
27	Madras States Agency	15	9	..	..	4	..	2,438	102
	Cochin State	*8*	*9*	..	..	*4*	..	*705*	*63*
	Travancore State	*7*	..	..	..	..	..	*1,407*	*32*
	Other Madras States	..	..	..	..	..	..	*126*	*7*
28	Mysore State	48	23	5	..	2	..	388	43
29	North-West Frontier Province (*Agencies and Tribal Areas*)	..	..	..	..	..	..	..	..
30	Punjab States	..	..	..	..	..	..	17	..
31	Punjab States Agency	29	2	..	..	..	..	302	..
32	Rajputana Agency	69	..	1	..	5	..	920	39
33	Sikkim State	..	..	..	..	..	..	..	..
34	United Provinces States	..	..	..	..	..	..	..	..
35	Western India States Agency ..	217	5	5	..	12	..	566	..

hood.—Part II—Provincial Distribution—*contd.*

Liberal Arts—*contd.*

and Liberal Arts—*contd.*

Sciences (other than 44)—*contd.*

astrologers, fortune-tellers, wizards, witches and mediums. *Group 182.*—Musicians (composers and performers, other than military), actors, dancers, etc.

Total working dependants.		Total following occupation as subsidiary to other.		Total earners principal occupation.		Total working dependants.		Total following occupation as subsidiary to other.		
Males.	Females.	Males.	Females.	Males.	Females.	Males.	Females.	Males.	Females.	
1483	1484	1485	1486	1487	1488	1489	1490	1491	1492	
1,886	**794**	**7,083**	**1,408**	**173,070**	**34,093**	**6,113**	**4,647**	**59,206**	**3,370**	
331	**230**	**4,453**	**1,045**	**126,324**	**20,076**	**3,686**	**1,535**	**46,116**	**2,214**	
..	30	12	..	1,464	328	54	138	236	15	1
..	..	..	..	..	..	..	..	..	..	2
24	3	186	1	1,181	47	189	9	1,626	11	3
..	..	..	..	138	11	..	7	23	..	4
11	1	184	..	17,376	531	280	24	4,710	32	5
11	2	692	7	13,913	1,927	371	78	12,618	207	6
26	3	70	..	10,387	997	687	138	1,682	46	7
..	..	..	..	*7*	..	*1*	..	..	--	
65	100	292	28	5,774	902	355	147	622	11	8
6	35	196	4	15,207	1,240	447	72	6,616	93	9
..	.	19	..	46	14	..	..	77	..	10
1	..	1	..	772	104	2	8	1	..	11
186	55	2,758	1,004	22,838	4,565	680	283	9,677	978	12
..	..	..	..	304	32	14	11	19	..	13
1	..	27	..	16,455	1,461	486	225	1,599	84	14
..	1	16	1	20,469	7,917	121	395	6,610	737	15
1,555	**564**	**2,630**	**363**	**46,746**	**14,017**	**2,427**	**3,112**	**13,090**	**1,156**	
3	..	12	..	379	30	70	3	120	1	16
..	..	1	..	264	..	..	..	16	..	17
..	..	23	..	1,185	59	69	4	339	..	18
..	..	4	..	375	1	7	..	176	..	19
2	1	190	..	738	132	12	65	1,850	66	20
37	5	7	1	1,942	200	99	68	478	12	21
5	..	47	..	5,860	1,650	104	103	1,904	166	22
2	..	112	..	1,010	77	65	15	636	3	23
1	3	..	..	3,520	1,064	135	99	925	120	24
1,304	537	1,034	341	1,822	1,151	906	903	769	355	25
1	..	1	..	757	23	14	3	334	19	26
129	7	760	15	3,478	226	196	23	1,060	19	27
4	*1*	*279*	*9*	*1,293*	*145*	*26*	*18*	*406*	*4*	
124	*6*	*374*	*6*	*1,669*	*65*	*168*	*5*	*430*	*5*	
1	..	*107*	--	*516*	*16*	*2*	..	*224*	*10*	
2	8	249	6	2,157	126	57	2	1,568	8	28
..	..	..	..	..	..	..	..	..	..	29
2	1	38	..	272	51	19	25	170	..	30
..	..	13	..	2,327	246	115	55	280	4	31
5	1	121	..	16,726	8,670	307	1,557	1,822	371	32
..	..	..	..	..	..	..	..	..	..	33
..	..	..	..	1,214	196	60	152	528	11	34
62	1	18	..	2,720	115	192	35	115	1	35

Table X.—Occupation or Means of Liveli

Class C.—Public Administration and

Sub-Class VIII.—Professions

Order 49.—Letters, Arts and Sciences

Province, State or Agency.	*Group 183.*—Managers and employees of places of public entertainment, race courses, societies, clubs.						*Group 184.*—Conjurors,	
	Total earers principal occupation.		Total working dependants.		Total following occupation as subsidiary to other.		Total earners principal occupation.	
	Males.	Females.	Males.	Females.	Males.	Females.	Males.	Females.
1	1493	1494	1495	1496	1497	1498	1499	1500
INDIA.	**14,507**	**724**	**471**	**102**	**659**	**45**	**18,262**	**2,922**
Provinces	**11,483**	**538**	**82**	**19**	**328**	**16**	**12,175**	**1,969**
1 Ajmer-Merwara	78	3	..	..	3	..	106	15
2 Andamans and Nicobars	4	..	..	..	..	..	..	..
3 Assam	148	—	3	..	41	..	280	45
4 Baluchistan (*Districts and Administered Territories*).	111	2	..	..	2	..	8	..
5 Bengal	561	4	1	..	22	..	706	161
6 Bihar and Orissa	134	7	..	..	10	..	663	93
7 Bombay (*including Aden*)	4,865	211	17	10	68	4	1,015	121
Aden	*20*	*2*	..	..	..	..	..	..
8 Burma	2,882	98	36	3	67	4	641	44
9 Central Provinces and Berar ..	410	57	6	..	30	5	580	61
10 Coorg	1	..	..	..	..	..	3	..
11 Delhi	162	9	..	..	..	—	41	10
12 Madras .. .. .. —	1,283	112	19	2	74	3	1,476	512
13 North-West Frontier Province (*Districts and Administered Territories*).	51	..	..	..	..	..	938	81
14 Punjab	153	19	..	4	3	..	3,803	246
15 United Provinces of Agra and Oudh	640	16	..	..	8	..	1,915	580
States and Agencies ..	**3,024**	**186**	**389**	**83**	**331**	**29**	**6,087**	**953**
16 Assam States	2	..	..	..	..	..	6	..
17 Baluchistan States	11	..	..	..	..	..	2	..
18 Baroda State	762	41	..	..	33	..	253	14
19 Bengal States	1	..	..	..	..	..	25	30
20 Bihar and Orissa States	2	..	..	..	..		100	2
21 Bombay States	99	..	14	..	7	..	136	10
22 Central India Agency	159	12	..	5	5	1	596	53
23 Central Provinces States	..	..	15	..	..	..	34	9
24 Gwalior State	6	..	..	..	..	..	647	43
25 Hyderabad State	623	10	322	37	114	5	1,051	423
26 Jammu and Kashmir State ..	41	10	..	..	7	19	270	2
27 Madras States Agency	86	..	..	..	9	..	376	37
Cochin State	*59*	..	..	..	*9*	..	*59*	*15*
Travancore State	*25*	..	..	..	..	..	*301*	*20*
Other Madras States	*2*	..	..	..	..	..	*16*	*2*
28 Mysore State	831	75	17	27	126	4	634	89
29 North-West Frontier Province (*Agencies and Tribal Areas*).	..	..	..	..	..	..	..	..
30 Punjab States	4	1	..	..	..	..	42	2
31 Punjab States Agency	18	1	..	..	..	..	411	20
32 Rajputana Agency	301	30	18	8	28	..	1,095	104
33 Sikkim State	..	..	..	..	..	..	..	..
34 United Provinces States	..	..	..	..	..	..	6	112
35 Western India States Agency ..	78	6	3	6	2	..	402	2

hood.—Part II.—Provincial Distribution—*contd.*

Liberal Arts—*concld.*

and Liberal Arts—*concld.*

(Other than 44)—*concld.*

acrobats, reciters, exhibitors of curiosities and wild animals, etc.

Class D.—Miscellaneous.

Total *Class D.*—Miscellaneous.

Total working dependants.		Total following occupation as subsidiary to other.		Total earners principal occupation.		Total working dependants.		Total following occupation as subsidiary to other.		
Males.	Females.	Males.	Females.	Males.	Females.	Males.	Females.	Males.	Females.	
1501	1502	1503	1504	1505	1506	1507	1508	1509	1510	
1,007	**604**	**2,154**	**353**	**7,211,783**	**3,767,715**	**705,349**	**8,833,493**	**970,626**	**1,714,223**	
387	237	1,141	204	5,694,601	2,976,494	473,103	6,792,707	742,278	1,433,063	
..	..	26	..	16,548	5,053	749	863	2,118	268	1
..	..	..	..	4,715	181	270	38	43	..	2
..	13	45	6	58,737	23,189	7,027	6,116	16,127	2,054	3
..	..	..	..	8,635	632	427	3	1,372	31	4
21	37	102	..	1,022,510	315,485	45,293	274,216	82,280	47,737	5
1	..	109	7	853,460	566,380	24,171	37,443	154,383	43,070	6
58	26	41	1	565,517	154,480	43,673	128,476	22,217	12,878	7
..	..	..	..	*7,626*	*361*	*623*	*159*	*31*	*1*	
62	5	199	2	79,927	18,980	21,987	11,030	2,258	612	8
16	10	15	..	190,850	110,774	7,456	26,366	20,189	6,326	9
..	..	3	..	9,264	5,429	1,152	25,139	634	7,704	10
5	..	..	..	41,000	5,302	692	233	928	48	11
41	18	201	136	1,447,207	1,295,639	236,801	6,221,153	177,119	1,274,548	12
31	1	36	..	53,218	6,373	9,163	833	7,255	148	13
118	24	189	18	538,123	64,433	32,990	15,459	47,904	2,758	14
34	103	175	34	804,890	404,164	41,252	45,339	207,451	39,881	15
620	**367**	**1,013**	**49**	**1,517,182**	**791,221**	**232,546**	**2,040,786**	**228,348**	**276,160**	
..	..	..	..	5,141	2,158	415	461	1,841	1,067	16
..	..	..	..	2,464	304	46	..	394	2	17
6	..	20	..	36,559	46,754	703	104	6,975	1,606	18
1	..	4	1	11,754	3,883	258	126	775	164	19
..	..	21	..	42,263	45,197	1,588	3,527	11,676	3,124	20
14	1	117	..	84,142	27,262	11,191	29,719	11,490	3,241	21
6	1	74	3	144,375	97,227	7,269	9,623	22,935	5,050	22
1	..	..	..	16,157	10,500	571	1,368	1,450	147	23
8	3	..	..	100,922	51,035	8,452	12,858	22,627	7,412	24
474	318	362	129	348,300	205,497	115,270	147,980	61,834	43,615	25
20	..	178	3	44,788	22,555	15,371	864,016	6,454	1,353	26
11	7	31	..	137,336	51,375	32,070	894,924	21,881	199,254	27
1	..	*5*	..	*26,034*	*12,682*	*2,205*	*129,344*	*4,477*	*36,250*	
10	*7*	*23*	..	*100,428*	*27,168*	*27,217*	*686,725*	*13,822*	*146,144*	
..	..	*3*	..	*10,874*	*11,525*	*2,648*	*78,855*	*3,582*	*16,860*	
20	9	107	2	125,123	72,505	6,037	12,913	14,702	4,284	28
..	..	..	..	1,049	..	3	..	508	..	29
1	..	1	..	4,287	749	275	238	1,378	32	30
14	..	15	4	95,926	8,113	5,533	3,753	9,108	431	31
24	3	73	5	217,114	107,421	9,694	19,345	25,907	4,197	32
..	..	..	..	291	123	346	560	123	547	33
1	19	..	..	14,047	7,066	1,004	1,548	3,370	257	34
19	6	10	2	85,144	31,497	16,450	37,723	2,920	37	35

Table X.—Occupation or Means of Liveli

Class D.—

Sub-Class IX.—

Province, State or Agency.	Total *Sub-Class IX.*—Persons living on their income. Total earners principal occupation. Males.	Females.	Total working dependants. Males.	Females.	Total following occupation as subsidiary to other. Males.	Females.	Total *Order 50.*—Persons living. Total earners principal occupation. Males.	Females.
1	1511	1512	1513	1514	1515	1516	1517	1518
INDIA	**160,664**	**39,318**	**8,165**	**7,727**	**61,591**	**3,490**	**160,664**	**39,318**
Provinces	**114,277**	**24,752**	**3,817**	**2,912**	**48,456**	**2,218**	**114,277**	**24,752**
1 Ajmer-Merwara	534	155	11	42	555	14	534	155
2 Andamans and Nicobars	8	3	..	1	1	..	8	3
3 Assam	1,141	152	42	44	667	13	1,141	152
4 Baluchistan (*Districts and Administered Territories*).	375	29	..	..	723	2	375	29
5 Bengal	20,288	4,174	189	295	2,418	262	20,288	4,174
6 Bihar and Orissa	1,338	351	24	17	825	29	1,338	351
7 Bombay (*including Aden*) ..	19,327	2,160	1,125	448	2,202	254	19,327	2,160
Aden	*104*	*3*	*6*	*1*	*5*	..	*104*	*3*
8 Burma	5,365	1,618	82	102	869	165	5,365	1,618
9 Central Provinces and Berar ..	4,283	674	81	372	420	40	4,283	674
10 Coorg	33	4	1	..	65	..	33	4
11 Delhi	1,358	413	26	67	432	19	1,358	413
12 Madras	17,466	7,240	472	703	3,735	361	17,466	7,240
13 North-West Frontier Province (*Districts and Administered Territories*).	2,053	154	46	46	2,002	37	2,053	154
14 Punjab	21,618	3,008	1,718	775	23,999	481	21,618	3,008
15 United Provinces of Agra and Oudh	19,090	4,617	..	..	9,543	541	19,090	4,617
States and Agencies ..	**46,387**	**14,566**	**4,348**	**4,815**	**13,135**	**1,272**	**46,387**	**14,566**
16 Assam States	170	19	3	1	2	..	170	19
17 Baluchistan States	479	3	..	..	68	..	479	3
18 Baroda State	3,484	2,421	..	..	892	86	3,484	2,421
19 Bengal States	244	66	4	1	38	2	244	66
20 Bihar and Orissa States	122	64	1	5	72	8	122	64
21 Bombay States	1,743	149	413	155	2,196	163	1,74	149
22 Central India Agency	3,867	1,340	37	24	423	40	3,867	1,340
23 Central Provinces States	64	22	2	..	7	..	64	22
24 Gwalior State	786	405	33	26	454	35	786	405
25 Hyderabad State	12,012	3,341	3,135	3,205	830	278	12,012	3,341
26 Jammu and Kashmir State ..	1,967	100	110	495	787	56	1,967	100
27 Madras States Agency	4,153	1,626	153	39	1,742	373	4,153	1,626
Cochin State	*1,495*	*1,172*	*29*	*10*	*1,087*	*336*	*1,495*	*1,172*
Travancore State	*2,369*	*411*	*78*	*23*	*583*	*35*	*2,369*	*411*
Other Madras States	*289*	*43*	*46*	*6*	*72*	*2*	*289*	*43*
28 Mysore State	5,909	1,187	16	55	820	39	5,909	1,187
29 North-West Frontier Province (*Agencies and Tribal Areas*).	..	..	..	..	..		..	..
30 Punjab States	183	40	8	14	422	23	183	40
31 Punjab States Agency	5,065	628	251	107	3,233	70	5,065	628
32 Rajputana Agency	3,888	1,474	124	285	1,034	78	3,888	1,474
33 Sikkim State	45	4	..	..	4	..	45	4
34 United Provinces States	86	61	..	..	30	2	86	61
35 Western India States Agency ..	2,120	1,616	58	403	81	19	2,120	1616

hood—Part II—Provincial Distribution—*contd.*

Miscellaneous—*contd.*

Persons living on their income.

Order 50.—**Persons living principally on their income.**

principally on their income.				*Group 185.*—**Proprietors (other than of agricultural land) fund and scholarships holders and pensioners.**						
Total working dependants.		Total following occupation as subsidiary to other.		Total earners principal occupation.		Total working dependants.		Total following occupation as subsidiary to other.		
Males.	Females.	Males.	Females.	Males.	Females.	Males.	Females.	Males.	Females.	
1519	1520	1521	1522	1523	1524	1525	1526	1527	1528	
8,165	**7,727**	**61,591**	**3,490**	**160,664**	**39,318**	**8,165**	**7,727**	**61,591**	**3,490**	
3,817	**2,912**	**48,456**	**2,218**	**114,277**	**24,752**	**3,817**	**2,912**	**48,456**	**2,218**	
11	42	555	14	534	155	11	42	555	14	1
..	1	1	..	8	3	..	1	1	..	2
42	44	667	13	1,141	152	42	44	667	13	3
..	..	723	2	375	29	..	..	723	2	4
189	295	2,418	262	20,288	4,174	189	295	2,418	262	5
24	17	825	29	1,338	351	24	17	825	29	6
1,125	448	2,202	254	19,327	2,160	1,125	448	2,202	254	7
6	*1*	*5*	..	*104*	*3*	*6*	*1*	*5*	..	
82	102	869	165	5,365	1,618	82	102	869	165	8
81	372	420	40	4,283	674	81	372	420	40	9
1	..	65	..	33	4	1	..	65	..	10
26	67	432	19	1,358	413	26	67	432	19	11
472	703	3,735	361	17,466	7,240	472	703	3,735	361	12
46	46	2,002	37	2,053	154	46	46	2,002	37	13
1,718	775	23,999	481	21,618	3,008	1,718	775	23,999	481	14
..	..	9,543	541	19,090	4,617	..	..	9,543	541	15
4,348	**4,815**	**13,135**	**1,272**	**46,387**	**14,566**	**4,348**	**4,815**	**13,135**	**1,272**	
3	1	2	..	170	19	3	1	2	..	16
..	..	68	..	479	3	..	..	68	..	17
..	..	892	86	3,484	2,421	..	..	892	86	18
4	1	38	2	244	66	4	1	38	2	19
1	5	72	8	122	64	1	5	72	8	20
413	155	2,196	163	1,743	149	413	155	2,196	163	21
37	24	423	40	3,867	1,340	37	24	423	40	22
2	..	7	..	64	22	2	..	7	..	23
33	26	454	35	786	405	33	26	454	35	24
3,135	3,205	830	278	12,012	3,341	3,135	3,205	830	278	25
110	495	787	56	1,967	100	110	495	787	56	26
153	39	1,742	373	4,153	1,626	153	39	1,742	373	27
29	*10*	*1,087*	*336*	*1,495*	*1,172*	*29*	*10*	*1,087*	*336*	
78	*23*	*583*	*35*	*2,369*	*411*	*78*	*23*	*583*	*35*	
46	*6*	*72*	*2*	*289*	*43*	*46*	*6*	*72*	*2*	
16	55	820	39	5,909	1,187	16	55	820	39	28
..	..	..	..	..	..	..	..	..	..	29
8	14	422	23	183	40	8	14	422	23	30
251	107	3,233	70	5,065	628	251	107	3,233	70	31
124	285	1,034	78	3,888	1,474	124	285	1,034	78	32
..	..	4	..	45	4	..	..	4	..	33
..	..	30	2	86	61	..	..	30	2	34
58	403	81	19	2,120	1,616	58	403	81	19	35

Table X.—Occupation or Means of Liveli

Class D.—

Sub-Class X.—Domestic

Province, State or Agency.	Total *Sub Class X.*—Domestic Service. Total earners principal occupation. Males.	Females.	Total working dependants. Males.	Females.	Total following occupation as subsidiary to other. Males.	Females.	Total earners principal occupation. Males.	Females.
1	1529	1530	1531	1532	1533	1534	1535	1536
INDIA	**1,805,006**	**886,991**	**289,481**	**7,916,799**	**242,433**	**1,533,400**	**1,805,006**	**886,991**
Provinces	**1,301,433**	**658,230**	**187,886**	**6,389,090**	**177,244**	**1,308,086**	**1,301,433**	**658,230**
1 Ajmer-Merwara	4,400	1,255	18	358	131	35	4,400	1,255
2 Andamans and Nicobars	736	29	3	37	4	..	736	29
3 Assam	22,123	3,297	2,295	3,440	2,279	264	22,123	3,297
4 Baluchistan (*Districts and Administered Territories*).	6,247	192	..	..	150	7	6,247	192
5 Bengal	358,045	155,343	25,998	264,610	28,201	42,497	358,045	155,343
6 Bihar and Orissa	82,211	63,712	5,179	28,544	23,798	8,961	82,211	63,712
7 Bombay (*including Aden*)	122,824	29,051	4,991	26,630	3,446	5,286	122,824	29,051
Aden	*2,753*	*219*	*379*	*151*	*5*	..	*2,753*	*219*
8 Burma	33,507	7,628	1,094	2,460	114	52	33,507	7,628
9 Central Provinces and Berar	54,471	29,369	1,448	10,031	5,214	1,972	54,471	29,369
10 Coorg	1,104	541	1,054	25,024	313	7,697	1,104	541
11 Delhi	21,694	2,055	29	49	70	8	21,694	2,055
12 Madras	102,931	164,439	134,661	6,007,755	52,951	1,227,588	102,931	164,439
13 North-West Frontier Province (*Districts and Administered Territories*).	9,813	1,907	924	159	2,303	37	9,813	1,907
14 Punjab	191,889	27,237	6,298	8,507	7,056	1,207	191,889	27,237
15 United Provinces of Agra and Oudh	289,438	172,175	3,894	11,486	51,214	12,475	289,438	172,175
States and Agencies	**503,573**	**228,761**	**101,595**	**1,527,709**	**65,189**	**225,314**	**503,573**	**228,761**
16 Assam States	2,038	307	63	174	14	38	2,038	307
17 Baluchistan States	937	111	..	..	134	..	937	111
18 Baroda State	5,397	2,517	2	..	231	72	5,397	2,517
19 Bengal States	4,966	621	28	104	309	122	4,966	621
20 Bihar and Orissa States	11,882	14,443	93	824	1,294	325	11,882	14,443
21 Bombay States	16,518	4,931	2,317	4,007	1,035	1,278	16,518	4,931
22 Central India Agency	37,164	16,092	416	1,105	4,541	1,049	37,164	16,092
23 Central Provinces States	6,696	5,398	95	802	544	78	6,696	5,398
24 Gwalior State	21,279	5,736	673	1,068	1,942	1,034	21,279	5,736
25 Hyderabad State	214,425	112,347	65,016	82,791	37,876	21,888	214,425	112,347
26 Jammu and Kashmir State	20,403	13,314	8,413	531,770	2,329	258	20,403	13,314
27 Madras States Agency	14,000	17,899	18,972	888,639	5,179	196,443	14800	17,899
Cochin State	*4,241*	*6,763*	*1,194*	*128,635*	*804*	*35,363*	*4,241*	*6,763*
Travancore State	*8,480*	*10,448*	*15,634*	*681,716*	*3,521*	*144,735*	*8,480*	*10,448*
Other Madras States	*2,079*	*688*	*2,144*	*78,288*	*854*	*16,345*	*2,079*	*688*
28 Mysore State	32,088	6,898	1,909	6,029	1,351	1,194	32,088	6,898
29 North-West Frontier Province (*Agencies and Tribal Areas*).	118	..	3	..	192	..	118	..
30 Punjab States	1,833	362	62	135	484	5	1,833	362
31 Punjab States Agency	27,075	2,609	938	1,589	2,243	128	27,075	2,609
32 Rajputana Agency	61,061	19,544	889	5,292	4,274	816	61,061	19,544
33 Sikkim State	186	108	338	557	73	540	186	108
34 United Provinces States	5,394	3,121	94	677	847	36	5,394	3,121
35 Western India States Agency	19,313	2,403	1,274	2,146	297	10	19,313	2,403

hood.—Part II.—Provincial Distribution—*contd.*

Miscellaneous—*contd.*

Service.

Order 51—Domestic Service.

Total *Order 51.*—Domestic.				*Group 186.* Private Motor drivers and cleaners.						
Total working dependants.		Total following occupation as subsidiary to other.		Total earners principal occupation.		Total working dependants.		Total following occupation as subsidiary to other.		
Males.	Females.	Males.	Females.	Males.	Females.	Males.	Females.	Males.	Females.	
1537	1538	1539	1540	1541	1542	1543	1544	1545	1546	
289,481	**7,916,799**	**242,433**	**1,533,400**	**60,800**	**1,387**	**2,385**	**3,697**	**2,778**	**165**	
187,886	**6,389,090**	**177,244**	**1,308,086**	**41,855**	**538**	**319**	**47**	**1,853**	**29**	
18	358	131	35	239	1	..	..	3	..	1
3	37	4	..	..	..	..	..	..	..	2
2,295	3,440	2,279	264	659	..	12	..	69	..	3
..	..	150	7	450	..	..	..	21	..	4
25,998	264,610	28,201	42,497	7,258	173	20	..	293	4	5
5,179	28,544	23,798	8,961	1,873	23	17	..	307	1	6
4,991	26,630	3,446	5,286	7,184	310	109	47	229	24	7
379	151	5	..	47	1	..	..	..	..	
1,094	2,460	114	52	1,928	..	7	..	26	..	8
1,448	10,031	5,214	1,972	265	4	2	..	9	..	9
1,054	25,024	313	7,697	14	..	..	..	2	..	10
29	49	70	8	1,503	..	4	..	1	..	11
134,661	6,007,755	52,951	1,227,588	11,080	23	106	..	565	..	12
924	159	2,303	37	431	3	8	..	15	..	13
6,298	8,507	7,056	1,207	3,372	1	34	..	128	..	14
3,894	11,486	51,214	12,475	5,599	..	..	..	185	..	15
101,595	**1,527,709**	**65,189**	**225,314**	**18,945**	**849**	**2,066**	**3,650**	**925**	**136**	
63	174	14	38	14	..	..	..	..	..	16
..	..	134	..	11	..	..	..	..	..	17
2	..	231	72	370	..	2	..	9	..	18
28	104	309	122	91	..	2	..	1	..	19
93	824	1,294	325	139	..	..	..	38	..	20
2,317	4,007	1,035	1,278	491	617	24	38	11	35	21
416	1,105	4,541	1,049	1,125	..	7	..	34	..	22
95	802	544	78	153	6	..	..	54	..	23
673	1,068	1,942	1,034	689	2	20	..	3	..	24
65,016	82,791	37,876	21,888	4,326	95	1,415	86	429	36	25
8,413	531,770	2,329	258	2,144	42	363	3,526	183	65	26
18,972	888,639	5,179	196,443	2,888	..	138	..	26	..	27
1,194	*128,635*	*804*	*35,363*	*252*	..	*14*	..	*5*	..	
15,634	*681,716*	*3,521*	*144,735*	*1,996*	..	*123*		..	..	
2,144	*78,288*	*854*	*16,345*	*640*	..	*1*	..	*21*	..	
1,909	6,029	1,351	1,194	3,399	77	14	..	90	..	28
3	..	192	..	11	..	..	..	..	..	29
62	135	484	5	28	..	..	..	..	..	30
938	1,589	2,243	128	272	..	1	..	12	..	31
889	5,292	4,274	816	1,430	3	4	..	24	..	32
338	557	73	540	4	1	..	..	2	..	33
94	677	847	36	..	..	..	..	..	..	34
1,274	2,146	297	10	1,360	6	76	..	9	..	35

Table X.—Occupation or Means of Liveli

Class D.—

Province, State or Agency.	Sub-Class X.—Domestic service—concld. Order 51.—Domestic service—concld. Group 187.—Other domestic service. Total earners principal occupation. Males.	Females.	Total working dependants. Males.	Females.	Total following occupation as subsidiary to other. Males.	Females.	Total Sub-Class XI.—Insuffi Total earners principal occupation. Males.	Females.
1	1547	1548	1549	1550	1551	1552	1553	1554
INDIA	**1,744,206**	**885,604**	**287,096**	**7,913,102**	**239,655**	**1,533,235**	**4,387,728**	**2,407,527**
Provinces	**1,259,578**	**657,692**	**187,567**	**6,389,043**	**175,391**	**1,308,057**	**3,678,765**	**1,977,898**
1 Ajmer-Merwara	4,161	1,254	18	358	128	35	8,347	3,041
2 Andamans and Nicobars	736	29	3	37	4	..	3,970	148
3 Assam	21,464	3,297	2,283	3,440	2,210	264	24,255	636
4 Baluchistan (*Districts and Administered Territories*).	5,797	192	..	..	129	7	846	4
5 Bengal	350,787	155,170	25,978	264,610	27,908	42,493	555,840	56,035
6 Bihar and Orissa	80,338	63,689	5,162	28,544	23,491	8,960	726,654	474,731
7 Bombay (*including Aden*)	115,640	28,741	4,882	26,583	3,217	5,262	357,227	93,644
Aden	*2,706*	*218*	*379*	*151*	*5*	..	*4,573*	*10*
8 Burma	31,579	7,628	1,087	2,460	88	52	40,856	9,531
9 Central Provinces and Berar ..	54,206	29,365	1,446	10,031	5,205	1,972	90,118	62,520
10 Coorg	1,090	541	1,054	25,024	311	7,697	7,983	4,832
11 Delhi	20,191	2,055	25	49	69	8	16,046	2,246
12 Madras	91,851	164,416	134,555	6,007,755	52,386	1,227,588	1,252,180	1,070,046
13 North-West Frontier Province (*Districts and Administered Territories*).	9,382	1,904	916	159	2,288	37	36,433	3,485
14 Punjab	188,517	27,236	6,264	8,507	6,928	1,207	180,731	15,259
15 United Provinces of Agra and Oudh	283,839	172,175	3,894	11,486	51,029	12,475	377,279	176,008
States and Agencies ..	**484,628**	**227,912**	**99,529**	**1,524,059**	**64,264**	**225,178**	**708,963**	**429,629**
16 Assam States	2,024	307	63	174	14	38	2,834	1,732
17 Baluchistan States	926	111	..	..	134	..	37	..
18 Baroda State	5,027	2,517	..	..	222	72	24,471	40,573
19 Bengal States	4,875	621	26	104	308	122	4,070	206
20 Bihar and Orissa States	11,743	14,443	93	824	1,256	325	21,336	24,741
21 Bombay States	16,027	4,314	2,293	3,969	1,024	1,243	54,746	16,817
22 Central India Agency	36,039	16,092	409	1,105	4,507	1,049	75,147	69,225
23 Central Provinces States	6,543	5,392	95	802	490	78	4,995	3,162
24 Gwalior State	20,590	5,734	653	1,068	1,939	1,034	64,060	40,719
25 Hyderabad State	210,099	112,252	63,601	82,705	37,447	21,852	65,879	35,987
26 Jammu and Kashmir State ..	18,259	13,272	8,050	528,244	2,146	193	13,684	6,592
27 Madras States Agency	11,912	17,899	18,834	888,639	5,153	196,443	115,741	29,980
Cochin State	*3,989*	*6,763*	*1,180*	*128,635*	*799*	*35,363*	*20,158*	*4,687*
Travancore State	*6,484*	*10,448*	*15,511*	*681,716*	*3,621*	*144,735*	*87,549*	*15,232*
Other Madras States	*1,439*	*688*	*2,143*	*78,288*	*833*	*16,345*	*8,034*	*10,061*
28 Mysore State	28,689	6,821	1,895	6,029	1,261	1,194	76,658	57,218
29 North-West Frontier Province (*Agencies and Tribal Areas*).	107	..	3	..	192	..	902	..
30 Punjab States	1,805	362	62	135	484	5	1,034	98
31 Punjab States Agency	26,803	2,609	937	1,589	2,231	128	34,606	1,634
32 Rajputana Agency	59,631	19,541	885	5,292	4,250	816	97,535	73,536
33 Sikkim State	182	107	338	557	71	540	48	3
34 United Provinces States	5,394	3,121	94	677	847	36	6,863	3,073
35 Western India States Agency ..	17,953	2,397	1,198	2,146	288	10	44,317	24,333

hood—Part II—Provincial Distribution—*contd.*

Miscellaneous—*contd.*

Sub-Class XI.—Insufficiently described occupations.

ciently described occupations.				*Order 52.*—General terms which do not indicate a definite occupation. *Total Order 52.*—General terms, which do not indicate a definite occupation.						
Total working dependants.		Total following occupation as subsidiary to other.		Total earners principal occupation.		Total working dependants.		Total following occupation as subsidiary to other.		
Males.	Females.	Males.	Females.	Males.	Females.	Males.	Females.	Males.	Females.	
1555	1556	1557	1558	1559	1560	1561	1562	1563	1564	
211,510	**771,877**	**570,208**	**150,839**	**4,387,728**	**2,407,527**	**211,510**	**771,877**	**570,208**	**150,839**	
128,793	**300,255**	**457,964**	**114,358**	**3,678,765**	**1,977,898**	**128,793**	**300,255**	**457,964**	**114,358**	
101	286	883	105	8,347	3,041	101	286	883	105	1
..	..	37	..	3,970	148	..	..	37	..	2
1,129	827	11,203	855	24,255	6,368	1,129	827	11,203	855	3
2	..	194	1	846	4	2	..	194	1	4
3,483	7,280	47,258	3,319	555,840	56,035	3,483	7,280	47,258	3,319	5
7,408	8,037	122,516	33,163	726,654	474,731	7,408	8,037	122,516	33,163	6
16,127	32,814	12,094	5,771	357,227	93,644	16,127	32,814	12,094	5,771	7
222	*4*	*17*	*1*	*4,373*	*10*	*222*	*4*	*17*	*1*	
2,180	2,354	1,232	390	40,856	9,531	2,180	2,354	1,232	390	8
3,247	14,347	9,222	3,264	90,118	62,520	3,247	14,347	9,222	3,264	9
94	113	246	5	7,983	4,832	94	113	246	5	10
55	97	384	21	16,046	2,246	55	97	384	21	11
79,289	202,180	114,787	44,414	1,252,180	1,070,046	79,289	202,180	114,787	44,414	12
2,272	430	2,610	64	36,433	3,485	2,272	430	2,610	64	13
4,754	1,981	8,670	444	180,731	15,259	4,754	1,981	8,670	444	14
8,652	29,509	126,628	22,542	377,279	176,008	8,652	29,509	126,628	22.542	16
82,717	**471,622**	**112,244**	**36,481**	**708,963**	**429,629**	**82,717**	**471,622**	**112,244**	**36,481**	
183	272	1,824	1,029	2,834	1,732	183	272	1,824	1,029	16
1	..	17	..	37	..	1	..	17	..	17
69	9	5,601	1,376	24,471	40,573	69	9	5,601	1,376	18
15	4	297	4	4,070	206	15	4	297	4	19
691	2,377	9,736	2,698	21,336	24,741	691	2,377	9,736	2,698	20
6,931	23,595	6,796	1,316	54,746	16,817	6,931	23,595	6,796	1,316	21
3,122	7,726	12,089	3,343	75,147	69,225	3,122	7,726	12,089	3,343	22
142	364	518	38	4,995	3,162	142	364	518	38	23
5,140	10,810	16,957	5,913	64,060	40,719	5,140	10,810	16,957	5,913	24
31,027	38,122	12,743	12,258	65,879	35,987	31,027	38,122	12,743	12,258	25
5,561	331,182	2,128	698	13,684	6,592	5,561	331,182	2,128	698	26
11,314	5,409	14,646	2,242	115,741	29,880	11,314	5,409	14,646	2,242	27
319	*316*	*2,490*	*445*	*20,158*	*4,687*	*319*	*316*	*2,490*	*445*	
10,697	*4,604*	*9,579*	*1,316*	*87,549*	*15,232*	*10,697*	*4,604*	*9,579*	*1,316*	
298	*489*	*2,577*	*481*	*8,034*	*10,061*	*298*	*489*	*2,577*	*481*	
3,537	6,737	10,748	2,533	76,658	57,218	3,537	6,737	10,748	2,533	28
..	..	316	..	902	..	..	..	316	..	29
45	15	378	2	1,034	98	45	15	378	2	30
696	1,236	1,670	154	34,606	1,634	696	1,236	1,670	154	31
2,552	11,015	11,754	2,370	97,535	73,536	2,552	11,015	11,754	2,370	32
1	2	42	7	48	3	1	2	42	7	33
380	635	2,263	194	6,863	3,073	380	635	2,263	194	34
11,310	32,112	1,721	306	44,317	24,333	11,310	32,112	1,721	306	35

Table X.—Occupation or Means of Liveli

Class D.—Miscellaneous—

Sub-Class XI.—Insufficiently described occupations.—

Order 52.—General terms which do not indicate a

Province, State or Agency.	*Group 188.*—Manufacturers, business men and contractors otherwise unspecified.						*Group 189.*—Cashiers,	
	Total earners principal occupation.		Total working dependants.		Total following occupation as subsidiary to other.		Total earners principal occupation.	
	Males.	Females.	Males.	Females.	Males.	Females.	Males.	Females.
1	1565	1566	1567	1568	1569	1570	1571	1572
INDIA	**105,433**	**7,710**	**3,935**	**3,305**	**14,745**	**1,546**	**690,113**	**35,795**
Provinces	**79,617**	**3,769**	**1,218**	**265**	**10,724**	**307**	**617,252**	**31,981**
1 Ajmer-Merwara	213	3	4	..	16	..	4,186	88
2 Andamans and Nicobars	33	..	..	..	15	..	18	..
3 Assam	1,787	19	72	1	761	2	4,661	56
4 Baluchistan (*Districts and Administered Territories.*)	361	..	1	..	65	1	471	4
5 Bengal	6,715	69	6	1	541	5	194,457	4,296
6 Bihar and Orissa	11,201	1,302	32	83	2,164	142	185,609	20,819
7 Bombay (*including Aden*)	12,054	405	163	11	383	..	90,504	4,661
Aden	*209*	..	*7*	*4*	*2*	..	*959*	*2*
8 Burma	1,469	18	40	4	52	..	6,570	59
9 Central Provinces and Berar ..	2,102	100	69	16	261	11	8,175	644
10 Coorg	124	..	3	..	25	..	408	2
11 Delhi	709	3	..	1	8	..	6,782	46
12 Madras	21,610	1,762	517	140	3,760	143	92,354	1,165
13 North-West Frontier Province (*Districts and Admintistered Territories*).	4,490	55	77	7	533	3	816	..
14 Punjab	9,297	33	158	1	455	..	8,511	96
15 United Provinces of Agra and Oudh	7,452	..	76	..	1,685	..	13,730	45
States and Agencies ..	**25,816**	**3,941**	**2,717**	**3,040**	**4,021**	**1,239**	**72,861**	**3,814**
16 Assam States	**186**	**2**	**1**	..	**3**	..	**107**	**9**
17 Baluchistan States	**35**	..	..	..	**11**	..	**1**	..
18 Baroda State	**619**	..	**32**	..	**63**	..	**1,424**	**6**
19 Bengal States	**220**	..	..	..	**15**	..	**1,481**	**51**
20 Bihar and Orissa States	**480**	**14**	**37**	**1**	**179**	**60**	**353**	**81**
21 Bombay States	**668**	**28**	**35**	**3**	**41**	..	**21,713**	**1,622**
22 Central India Agency	**1,041**	**33**	**23**	**2**	**197**	..	**5,992**	**193**
23 Central Provinces States	**198**	**3**	**1**	..	**72**	..	**1,002**	**4**
24 Gwalior State	**3,016**	**746**	**65**	**366**	**636**	**15**	**9,695**	**666**
25 Hyderabad State	**7,069**	**1,337**	**2,129**	**1,550**	**1,021**	**1,148**	**3,516**	**242**
26 Jammu and Kashmir State ..	**1,738**	**15**	**1**	**5**	**578**	**5**	**497**	**7**
27 Madras States Agency	**2,593**	**18**	**52**	..	**374**	**1**	**7,585**	**94**
Cochin State	***956***	..	***1***	..	***98***	***1***	***2,656***	***35***
Travancore State	***1,533***	***15***	***50***	..	***232***	..	***5,028***	***46***
Other Madras States	***104***	***3***	***1***	..	***44***	..	***901***	***13***
28 Mysore State	**2,986**	**74**	**14**	**9**	**454**	**4**	**6,549**	**337**
29 North-West Frontier Province (*Agencies and Tribal Areas*).	**31**	..	..	..	..	..	..	..
30 Punjab States	**28**	..	**1**	..	**18**	..	**212**	**4**
31 Punjab States Agency	**1,670**	**33**	**32**	**3**	**154**	..	**745**	..
32 Rajputana Agency	**1,700**	**37**	**82**	**11**	**163**	**1**	**8,849**	**493**
33 Sikkim State	**3**	..	**1**	..	**1**	..	**28**	..
34 United Provinces States	**133**	..	**1**	..	**18**	..	**156**	..
35 Western India States Agency ..	**1,402**	**1,601**	**195**	**1,090**	**23**	**5**	**2,956**	**5**

hood—Part II—Provincial Distribution—*contd.*

concld.

contd.

definite occupation—*contd.*

accountants, book-keepers, clerks and other employees unspecified in offices and warehouses and shops.				*Group 190.*—Mechanics otherwise unspecified.						
Total working dependants.		Total following occupation as subsidiary to other.		Total earners principal occupation.		Total working dependants.		Total following occupation as subsidiary to other.		
Males.	Females.	Males.	Females.	Males.	Females.	Males.	Females.	Males.	Females.	
1573	1574	1575	1576	1577	1578	1579	1580	1581	1582	
9,961	**6,472**	**57,524**	**2,992**	**36,262**	**2,648**	**988**	**756**	**1,118**	**72**	
5,574	**4,739**	**49,648**	**2,594**	**30,735**	**2,112**	**180**	**705**	**824**	**61**	
57	5	697	1	558	2	..	..	1	..	1
..	..	..	..	131	..	..	..	6	..	2
255	36	919	1	205	..	21	..	29	..	3
..	..	128	..	14	..	1	..	1	..	4
1,402	3,838	9,832	1,030	9,023	13	..	..	66	..	5
1,033	416	30,836	1,410	2,807	37	4	7	308	4	6
1,500	330	1,186	50	6,380	2,018	75	697	116	50	7
88	..	*8*	*1*	*329*	..	*63*	..	*3*		
89	5	109	..	1,001	..	13	..	24	..	8
143	23	474	56	930	4	6	1	21	..	9
10	..	94	..	8	..	..	..	..	..	10
..	..	6	..	682	..	..	..	..	..	11
935	83	4,285	39	7,577	22	48	..	217	7	12
..	..	4	..	26	..	..	..	3	..	13
109	3	135	1	751	16	2	..	4	..	14
41	..	943	6	642	..	10	..	28	..	15
4,387	**1,733**	**7,876**	**398**	**5,527**	**536**	**808**	**51**	**294**	**11**	
1	..	..	..	60	..	..	..	..	..	16
1	..	6	..	1	..	..	..	..	..	17
37	9	66	3	122	..	..	..	14	..	18
12	1	136	..	4	..	..	..	..	..	19
12	15	170	30	52	..	..	..	..	..	20
765	1,350	1,646	67	201	13	220	20	1	..	21
162	24	424	6	689	292	4	..	29	..	22
11	2	225	..	35	..	..	..	1	..	23
390	63	3,659	152	13	106	..	30	..	..	24
1,353	120	292	26	1,021	..	354	..	69	..	25
302	..	83	..	120	..	199	..	35	9	26
173	6	433	46	463	1	6	..	23	..	27
27	..	*206*	*14*	*454*	*1*	*5*	..	*23*	..	
134	*5*	*214*	*31*	*4*	..	..	..	..	..	
12	*1*	*13*	*1*	*5*	..	*1*	..	..	..	
24	114	212	7	1,753	66	6	..	61	2	28
..	..	..	..	..	..	..	..	..	..	29
4	..	57	..	2	..	..	..	11	..	30
7	..	64	..	625	2	7	..	43	..	31
129	26	221	61	218	48	..	..	7	..	32
..	..	4	..	..	2	..	..	..	..	33
7	..	90	..	..	..	..	..	..	..	34
997	3	88	..	148	6	12	1	..	..	35

Table X.—Occupation or Means of Liveli

Class D.—Miscellaneous—

	Province, State or Agency.	*Sub-Class XI.*—Insufficiently described occupations—*concld.* *Order 52.*—General terms which do not indicate a definite occupation—*concld.* *Group 191.*—Labourers and workmen otherwise unspecified.						Total *Sub-Class XII.*—Un	
		Total earners principal occupation.		Total working dependants.		Total following occupation as subsidiary to other.		Total earners principal occupation.	
		Males.	Females.	Males.	Females.	Males.	Females.	Males.	Females.
	1	1583	1584	1585	1586	1587	1588	1589	1590
	INDIA	**3,555,920**	**2,361,374**	**196,626**	**761,344**	**496,821**	**146,229**	**858,385**	**433,879**
	Provinces	**2,951,161**	**1,940,036**	**121,821**	**294,546**	**396,768**	**111,396**	**600,126**	**315,614**
1	Ajmer-Merwara	3,390	2,948	40	281	169	104	3,267	602
2	Andamans and Nicobars	3,788	148	..	..	16	..	1	1
3	Assam	17,602	6,293	781	790	9,494	852	11,218	13,372
4	Baluchistan (*Districts and Administered Territories.*)	..	..	..	..	..	..	1,167	407
5	Bengal	345,645	51,657	2,075	3,441	36,819	2,284	88,337	99,933
6	Bihar and Orissa	527,037	452,573	6,339	7,531	89,208	31,607	43,257	27,586
7	Bombay (*including Aden*)	248,289	86,560	14,389	31,776	10,409	5,671	66,139	29,625
	Aden	*3,076*	*8*	*64*	..	*4*	..	*186*	*129*
8	Burma	31,816	9,454	2,038	2,345	1,047	390	199	203
9	Central Provinces and Berar ..	78,911	61,772	3,029	14,307	8,466	3,197	41,978	18,211
10	Coorg	7,443	4,830	81	113	127	5	144	52
11	Delhi	7,873	2,197	55	96	370	21	1,902	588
12	Madras	1,130,639	1,067,097	77,789	201,957	106,525	44,225	74,630	53,914
13	North-West Frontier Province (*Districts and Administered Territories.*)	31,101	3,430	2,195	423	2,070	61	4,919	827
14	Punjab	162,172	15,114	4,485	1,977	8,076	443	143,885	18,929
15	United Provinces of Agra and Oudh	355,455	175,963	8,525	29,509	123,972	22,536	119,083	51,364
	States and Agencies ..	**604,759**	**421,338**	**74,805**	**466,798**	**100,053**	**34,833**	**258,259**	**118,265**
16	Assam States	2,481	1,721	181	272	1,821	1,029	99	100
17	Baluchistan States	..	..	..	..	..	..	1,011	190
18	Baroda State	22,306	40,567	..	..	5,458	1,373	3,207	1,243
19	Bengal States	2,365	155	3	3	146	4	2,474	2,990
20	Bihar and Orissa States	20,451	24,646	642	2,361	9,387	2,608	8,923	5,949
21	Bombay States	32,164	15,154	5,911	22,222	5,108	1,249	11,135	5,365
22	Central India Agency	67,425	68,707	2,933	7,700	11,439	3,337	28,197	10,570
23	Central Provinces States	3,760	3,155	130	362	220	38	4,402	1,918
24	Gwalior State	51,336	39,201	4,685	10,351	12,662	5,746	14,797	4,175
25	Hyderabad State	54,273	34,408	27,191	36,452	11,361	11,084	55,984	53,822
26	Jammu and Kashmir State ..	11,329	6,570	5,044	331,177	1,432	684	8,734	2,549
27	Madras States Agency	105,100	29,867	11,083	5,403	13,816	1,195	2,642	1,870
	Cochin State	*16,092*	*4,651*	*286*	*316*	*2,163*	*430*	*140*	*60*
	Travancore State	*81,984*	*15,171*	*10,513*	*4,599*	*9,133*	*1,285*	*2,030*	*1,077*
	Other Madras States	*7,024*	*10,045*	*284*	*488*	*2,520*	*480*	*472*	*733*
28	Mysore State	65,370	56,741	3,493	6,614	10,021	2,520	10,468	7,202
29	North-West Frontier Province (*Agencies and Tribal Areas*).	871	..	..	..	316	..	29	..
30	Punjab States	792	94	40	15	292	2	1,237	249
31	Punjab States Agency	31,566	1,599	650	1,233	1,409	154	29,180	3,242
32	Rajputana Agency	86,768	72,958	2 341	10,978	11,363	2,308	54,630	12,867
33	Sikkim State	17	1	..	2	37	7	12	8
34	United Provinces States	6,574	3,073	372	635	2,155	194	1,704	811
35	Western India States Agency ..	39,811	22,721	10,106	31,018	1,610	301	19,394	3,145

hood—Part II—Provincial Distribution—*contd.*

contd.

productive.		Sub-Class XII.—Unproductive.		Total *Order 53.*—Inmates of jails, asylums and alms houses.						
Total working dependants.		Total following occupation as subsidiary to other.		Total earners principal occupation.		Total working dependants.		Total following occupation as subsidiary to other.		
Males.	Females.	Males.	Females.	Males.	Females.	Males.	Females.	Males.	Females.	
1591	1592	1593	1594	1595	1596	1597	1598	1599	1600	
196,493	**137,090**	**96,394**	**26,494**	**26,222**	**3,938**	**141,271**	**4,697**	**203**	**35**	
152,607	**100,450**	**58,614**	**13,401**	**23,336**	**2,388**	**120,440**	**2,643**	**129**	**28**	
619	177	549	114	..	..	462	17	..	..	1
267	..	1	..	..	..	265	..	..	..	2
3,561	1,805	1,978	922	..	..	2,930	41	..	..	3
425	3	305	21	159	1	425	3	..	..	4
15,623	2,031	4,403	1,659	6,014	25	14,322	165	..	..	5
11,560	845	7,244	917	4,248	1,005	10,470	249	..	..	6
21,430	68,584	4,475	1,567	2,541	350	15,955	380	111	23	7
16	*3*	*4*	..	*4*	..	..	..	..	..	
18,631	6,114	43	5	..	..	13,041	220	..	..	8
2,680	1,616	5,333	1,050	1,563	114	1,664	21	..	..	9
3	2	10	2	..	..	..	..	..	..	10
582	20	42	..	379	2	554	2	..	..	11
22,379	10,515	5,646	2,185	..	..	14,716	1,032	..	..	12
5,921	198	340	10	239	3	5,757	52	18	..	13
20,220	4,196	8,179	626	..	..	12,950	84	..	..	14
28,706	4,344	20,066	4,323	8,193	888	26,929	377	..	..	15
43,886	**36,640**	**37,780**	**13,093**	**2,886**	**1,550**	**20,831**	**2,054**	**74**	**12**	
166	14	1	..	..	..	145	..	..	..	16
45	..	175	2	120	..	45	..	..	..	17
632	95	251	72	..	..	632	80	..	..	18
211	17	131	36	131	1	205	..	..	..	19
803	321	574	93	191	13	765	54	..	..	20
1,530	1,962	1,463	484	579	421	277	133	37	12	21
3,694	768	5,882	618	..	..	2,782	93	..	..	22
332	202	381	31	100	3	186	1	..	..	23
2,606	954	3,274	430	..	..	1,605	302	2	..	24
16,092	23,862	10,385	9,191	..	..	3,877	665	..	..	25
1,287	569	1,210	341	9	789	782	12	1	..	26
1,631	837	314	196	716	169	694	37	7	..	27
663	*383*	*96*	*106*	*47*	..	*160*	*12*	7	..	
808	*382*	*139*	*58*	*669*	*169*	*420*	*6*	..	..	
160	*72*	*79*	*22*	..	..	*114*	*19*	..	..	
575	92	1,783	518	507	17	570	16	..	..	28
..	..	..	..	..	..	..	..	..	..	29
160	74	94	2	..	..	82	3	..	..	30
3,648	821	1,962	79	..	..	2,468	82	..	..	31
6,129	2,753	8,845	933	8	..	4,740	198	27	..	32
7	**1**	**4**	..	**3**	..	**7**	..	..	..	33
530	236	230	25	112	5	441	3	..	..	34
,808	3,062	821	42	410	132	528	375	..	..	35

Table X.—Occupation or Means of Liveli

Class D.—Miscellaneous.—

Sub-Class XII.—Unpro-

Province, State or Agency.	*Order 53.* Inmates of jails, asylums and almshouses—*concld.* *Group 192.* Inmates of jails, asylums and alms houses. Total earners principal occupation.		Total working dependants.		Total following occupation as subsidiary to other.		Total *Order 54.*—Beggars, Total earners principal occupation.	
	Males.	Females.	Males.	Females.	Males.	Females.	Males.	Females.
1	1601	1602	1603	1604	1605	1606	1607	1608
INDIA.	**26,222**	**3,938**	**141,271**	**4,697**	**203**	**35**	**811,216**	**418,084**
Provinces	**23,336**	**2,388**	**120,440**	**2,643**	**129**	**23**	**561,445**	**303,875**
1 Ajmer-Merwara	..	..	462	17	..	..	3,243	602
2 Andamans and Nicobars	7,139*	148*	265	..	..	..	..	1
3 Assam	..	..	2,930	41	..	..	11,215	13,372
4 Baluchistan (*Districts and Administered Territories*).	159	1	425	3	..	..	1,008	406
5 Bengal	6,014	25	14,322	165	..	..	82,193	99,904
6 Bihar and Orissa	4,248	1,005	10,470	249	..	..	38,733	26,567
7 Bombay Presidency (*including Aden*)	2,541	350	15,955	380	111	23	49,590	20,164
Aden	*4*	..	..	..	..	..	*124*	*127*
8 Burma	..	..	13,041	220	..	..	15	143
9 Central Provinces and Berar ..	1,563	114	1,664	21	..	..	40,282	18,097
10 Coorg	..	..	..	..	..	..	144	52
11 Delhi	379	2	554	2	..	..	1,501	585
12 Madras	..	..	14,716	1,032	..	..	74,258	53,764
13 North-West Frontier Province (*Districts and Administered Territories*).	239	3	5,757	52	18	..	4,663	824
14 Punjab	..	..	12,950	84	..	..	143,726	18,918
15 United Provinces of Agra and Oudh	8,193	888	26,929	377	..	..	110,874	50,476
States and Agencies ..	**2,886**	**1,550**	**20,831**	**2,054**	**74**	**12**	**249,771**	**114,209**
16 Assam States	..	..	145	..	..	..	97	100
17 Baluchistan States	120	..	45	..	..	..	891	190
18 Baroda State	..	..	632	80	..	..	3,085	1,193
19 Bengal States	131	1	205	..	..	..	2,343	2,989
20 Bihar and Orissa States	191	13	765	54	..	..	8,718	5,936
21 Bombay States	579	421	277	133	37	12	8,418	3,577
22 Central India Agency	..	..	2,782	93	..	..	28,070	10,569
23 Central Provinces States	100	3	186	1	..	..	4,300	1,915
24 Gwalior State	..	..	1,605	302	2	..	14,796	4,171
25 Hyderabad State	..	..	3,877	665	..	..	54,103	52,950
26 Jammu and Kashmir State ..	9	789	782	12	1	..	8,716	1,758
27 Madras States Agency	716	169	694	37	7	..	1,926	1,695
Cochin State	*47*	..	*160*	*12*	*7*	..	*93*	*54*
Travancore State	*669*	*169*	*420*	*6*	..	..	*1,361*	*908*
Other Madras States	..	..	*114*	*19*	..	..	*472*	*733*
28 Mysore State	507	17	570	16	..	..	9,828	7,148
29 North-West Frontier Province (*Agencies and Tribal Areas*).	..	..	..	..	..	..	29	..
30 Punjab States	..	..	82	3	..	..	1,237	249
31 Punjab States Agency	..	..	2,468	82	..	..	29,171	3,242
32 Rajputana Agency	8	..	4,740	198	27	..	53,780	12,732
33 Sikkim State	3	..	7	..	..	..	9	8
34 United Provinces States	112	5	441	3	..	..	1,592	806
35 Western India States Agency ..	410	132	528	375	..	..	18,662	2,981

*Relate to convicts who receive pay and whose labour is productive. The figures are excluded from the order,

hood—Part II—Provincial Distribution—*contd.*

contd.

ductive.—*contd.*

Order 54.—Beggars, vagrants, prostitutes.

Vagrants, prostitutes.				*Group 193.*—Beggars and vagrants.						
Total Working dependants.		Total following occupation as subsidiary to other.		Total earners principal occupation.		Total working dependants.		Total following occupation as subsidiary to other.		
Males.	Females.	Males.	Females.	Males.	Females.	Males.	Females.	Males.	Females.	
1609	1610	1611	1612	1613	1614	1615	1616	1617	1618	
53,224	**68,455**	**92,942**	**25,777**	**806,725**	**361,083**	**51,904**	**62,227**	**92,696**	**22,527**	
31,354	**34,866**	**56,752**	**12,964**	**558,540**	**256,732**	**30,774**	**33,567**	**56,639**	**11,028**	
157	160	549	114	3,243	566	157	160	549	114	1
1	..	..	..	..	1	1	..	..	..	2
631	1,764	1,965	922	11,215	12,833	631	1,763	1,965	919	3
..	..	305	21	991	271	..	..	305	21	4
1,301	1,866	4,376	1,659	82,193	76,075	1,301	1,845	4,376	1,229	5
1,088	596	6,996	915	38,651	24,782	1,088	587	6,961	713	6
4,825	5,297	3,052	1,148	47,337	13,828	4,271	4,692	3,029	835	7
10	*1*	*4*	..	*118*	*42*	*10*	..	..	..	
5,558	5,885	3	..	..	..	5,558	5,885	3	..	8
999	1,590	5,332	1,050	40,207	16,701	997	1,560	5,330	996	9
3	2	10	2	144	52	3	2	10	2	10
28	18	42	..	1,488	273	28	17	42	..	11
7,558	9,463	5,594	2,174	74,160	45,972	7,543	9,169	5,551	1,673	12
164	146	292	10	4,617	696	163	143	284	10	13
7,264	4,112	8,170	626	143,531	17,999	7,261	4,101	8,168	604	14
1,777	3,967	20,066	4,323	110,763	46,683	1,772	3,643	20,066	3,912	15
21,870	**33,589**	**36,190**	**12,813**	**248,185**	**104,351**	**21,130**	**28,660**	**36,057**	**11,499**	
21	14	1	..	97	100	21	14	1	..	16
..	..	175	2	891	190	..	..	175	2	17
..	..	242	72	3,085	1,138	..	..	242	72	18
6	17	131	36	2,343	2,781	6	17	131	30	19
38	267	573	93	8,717	5,854	38	266	573	83	20
1,061	1,406	906	353	8,350	2,243	1,020	1,180	905	240	21
911	675	5,857	614	28,064	10,183	911	671	5,853	534	22
146	201	381	31	4,298	1,890	146	201	381	31	23
1,001	652	3,117	430	14,756	4,033	993	636	3,113	367	24
11,279	22,657	9,767	9,139	52,889	48,154	10,594	18,058	9,686	8,402	25
504	557	1,208	341	8,529	1,485	501	557	1,207	338	26
937	800	253	108	1,926	1,245	937	794	253	91	27
503	*371*	*35*	*18*	*93*	*54*	*503*	*371*	*35*	*18*	
388	*371*	*139*	*58*	*1,361*	*908*	*388*	*376*	*139*	*58*	
46	*53*	*79*	*32*	*472*	*283*	*46*	*47*	*79*	*15*	
1	70	1,762	518	9,804	5,560	..	..	1,730	278	28
..	..	..	..	29	..	..	..	..	..	29
76	71	88	2	1,237	249	76	70	83	2	30
1,180	739	1,939	79	29,142	3,033	1,180	737	1,938	71	31
1,376	2,655	8,737	928	53,770	12,545	1,376	2,553	8,733	891	32
..	1	4	..	9	8	..	1	4	..	33
89	233	230	25	1,592	737	89	233	230	25	34
3,244	2,674	819	42	18,657	2,923	3,242	2,672	819	42	35

sub-class and class totals as these persons have already been shown as earners against the occupation they pursue.

Table X.—Occupation or Means of Liveli

Class D.—Miscellaneous—

Sub-Class XII.—Unproductive—

Province, State or Agency.	*Order 54.*—Beggars, vagrants, prostitutes, etc.—*concld.* *Group 194.*—Procurers and prostitutes. Total earners principal occupation.		Total working dependants		Total following occupation as subsidiary to other.		Total *Order 55.*—Other Total earners principal occupation.	
	Males.	Females.	Males	Females.	Males.	Females.	Males.	Females.
1	1619	1620	1621	1622	1623	1624	1625	1626
INDIA	**4,491**	**57,001**	**1,320**	**6,228**	**246**	**3,250**	**20,947**	**11,857**
Provinces	**2,905**	**47,143**	**580**	**1,299**	**113**	**1,936**	**15,345**	**9,351**
1 Ajmer-Merwara	..	36	..	..	..	..	24	..
2 Andamans and Nicobars	..	..	..	..	..	..	1	..
3 Assam	..	539	..	1	..	3	3	..
4 Baluchistan (*Districts and Administered Territories*).	17	135	..	..	..	..	..	..
5 Bengal	..	23,829	..	21	..	430	130	4
6 Bihar and Orissa	82	1,785	..	9	35	202	276	14
7 Bombay (*including Aden*)	2,253	6,336	554	605	23	313	14,008	9,111
Aden	*6*	*85*	..	*1*	*4*	..	*68*	*2*
8 Burma	15	143	..	..	..	..	184	60
9 Central Provinces and Berar	75	1,396	2	30	2	54	133	..
10 Coorg	..	..	..	..	..	..	..	..
11 Delhi	13	312	..	1	..	..	22	1
12 Madras	98	7,792	15	294	43	501	372	150
13 North-West Frontier Province (*Districts and Administered Territories*).	46	128	1	3	8	..	17	..
14 Punjab	195	919	3	11	2	22	159	11
15 United Provinces of Agra and Oudh	111	3,793	5	324	..	411	16	..
States and Agencies	**1,586**	**9,858**	**740**	**4,929**	**133**	**1,314**	**5,602**	**2,506**
16 Assam States	..	..	..	..	..	..	2	..
17 Baluchistan States	..	..	..	..	..	..	..	..
18 Baroda State	..	55	..	..	..	..	122	50
19 Bengal States	..	208	..	..	..	6	..	..
20 Bihar and Orissa States	1	82	..	1	..	10	14	..
21 Bombay States	68	1,334	41	226	1	113	2,138	1,367
22 Central India Agency	6	386	..	4	4	80	127	1
23 Central Provinces States	2	25	..	..	..	..	2	..
24 Gwalior State	40	138	8	16	4	63	1	4
25 Hyderabad State	1,214	4,796	685	4,599	81	737	1,881	872
26 Jammu and Kashmir State	187	273	3	..	1	3	9	2
27 Madras States Agency	..	450	..	6	..	17	..	6
Cochin State	..	..	..	..	..	..	..	6
Travancore State	..	..	..	..	..	..	..	..
Other Madras States	..	*450*	..	*6*	..	*17*	..	..
28 Mysore State	24	1,588	1	70	32	240	133	37
29 North-West Frontier Province (*Agencies and Tribal Areas*).	..	..	..	..	..	..	..	..
30 Punjab States	..	..	..	1	5	..	..	..
31 Punjab States Agency	29	209	..	2	1	8	9	..
32 Rajputana Agency	10	187	..	2	4	37	842	135
33 Sikkim State	..	..	..	..	..	..	..	..
34 United Provinces States	..	69	..	..	..	..	..	..
35 Western India States Agency	5	58	2	2	..	..	322	32

hood—Part II—Provincial Distribution—*concld.*

concld.

concld.

Order 55.—Other unclassified non-productive industries.

unclassified non-productive industries. | *Group 195.*—Other unclassified non-productive industries.

Total Working dependants. Males.	Total Working dependants. Females.	Total following occupation as subsidiary to other. Males.	Total following occupation as subsidiary to other. Females.	Total earners principal occupation. Males.	Total earners principal occupation. Females.	Total working dependants. Males.	Total working dependants. Females.	Total following occupation as subsidiary to other. Males.	Total following occupation as subsidiary to other. Females.	
1627	1628	1629	1630	1631	1632	1633	1634	1635	1636	
1,998	**63,938**	**3,249**	**682**	**20,947**	**11,857**	**1,998**	**63,938**	**3,249**	**682**	
813	**62,941**	**1,733**	**414**	**15,345**	**9,351**	**813**	**62,941**	**1,733**	**414**	
..	..	..	..	24	..	..	..	..	..	1
1	..	1	..	1	..	1	..	1	..	2
..	..	13	..	3	..	..	..	13	..	3
..	..	..	..	..	..	..	..	..	..	4
..	..	27	..	130	4	..	..	27	..	5
2	..	248	2	276	14	2	..	248	2	6
650	62,907	1,312	396	14,008	9,111	650	62,907	1,312	396	7
6	*2*	..	..	*68*	*2*	*6*	*2*	..	..	
32	9	40	5	184	60	32	9	40	5	8
17	5	1	..	133	..	17	5	1	..	9
..	..	..	..	..	..	..	..	..	..	10
..	..	..	..	22	1	..	..	..	..	11
105	20	52	11	372	150	105	20	52	11	12
..	..	30	..	17	..	..	..	30	..	13
6	..	9	..	159	11	6	..	9	..	14
..	..	..	..	16	..	..	..	..	..	15
1,185	**997**	**1,516**	**268**	**5,602**	**2,506**	**1,185**	**997**	**1,516**	**268**	
..	..	..	..	2	..	..	..	..	..	16
..	..	..	..	..	..	..	..	..	..	17
..	15	9	..	122	50	..	15	9	..	18
..	..	..	..	..	..	..	..	..	..	19
..	..	1	..	14	..	..	..	1	..	20
192	423	520	119	2,138	1,367	192	423	520	119	21
1	..	25	4	127	1	1	..	25	4	22
..	..	..	..	2	..	..	..	..	..	23
..	..	155	..	1	4	..	..	155	..	24
936	540	618	52	1,881	872	936	540	618	52	25
1	..	1	..	9	2	1	..	1	..	26
..	..	54	88	..	6	..	..	54	88	27
..	..	*54*	*88*	..	*6*	..	..	*54*	*88*	
..	..	..	..	..	..	..	..	..	..	
..	..	..	..	..	..	..	..	..	..	
4	6	21	..	133	37	4	6	21	..	28
..	..	..	..	..	..	..	..	..	..	29
2	..	6	..	..	..	2	..	3	..	30
..	..	23	..	9	..	..	..	23	..	31
13	..	81	5	842	135	13	..	81	5	32
..	..	..	..	..	..	..	..	..	..	33
..	..	..	..	..	..	..	..	..	..	34
36	13	2	..	322	32	36	13	2	..	35

Table X.—Occupation or Means of

Group No.	Occupation.	Amritsar. Population. 264,840 Non-working Dependants. 166,091		Bombay. Population. 1,161,383 Non-working Dependants. 595,480		Calcutta including Howrah. Population. 1,421,607 Non-working Dependants. 730,866		Cawnpore. Population. 243,755 Non-working Dependants. 139,643		Delhi (excluding New Delhi and Cant., Population. 365,527 Non-working Dependants. 219,943	
		Earners.	Working Dependants.	Earners.	Working Dependants.	Earners.	Working Dependants.	Earners.	Working Dependants.	Earners.	Working Dependants.
	1	2	3	4	5	6	7	8	9	10	11
	Total of all Classes	**97,060**	**1,689**	**563,042***	**2,861**	**686,717**	**4,024**	**103,486**	**626**	**145,004**	**580**
	Class A.—Production of Raw-Materials.	**7,781**	**423**	**11,767**	**154**	**18,397**	**57**	**5,910**	**7**	**7,074**	**37**
	Sub-Class I.—Explcitation of Animals and Vegetation.	**7,775**	**423**	**10,690**	**154**	**18,024**	**57**	**5,910**	**7**	**6,710**	**37**
	Order 1.—Pasture and Agriculture	**7,764**	**423**	**8,237**	**154**	**16,320**	**52**	**5,664**	**7**	**3,587**	**37**
	Sub-order 1(a).—Cultivation ..	**5,755**	**358**	**2,577**	**154**	**14,212**	**52**	**4,735**	**7**	**3,793**	**22**
1	Non-cultivating proprietors taking rent in money or kind.	445	77	1,472	154	8,748	4	529	1	915	6
2	Estate Agents and Managers of owners.	..	..	68	..	37	..	112	..	1	..
3	Estate Agents and Managers of Government.	..	..	11	..	4	..	4	..	..	..
4	Rent Collectors, clerks, etc. ..	9	..	13	..	1,613	..	43	..	4	..
5	Cultivating owners	1,200	2	411	..	2,088	..	802	..	742	..
6	Tenant cultivators	3,138	279	94	..	454	..	1,287	..	996	11
7	Agricultural labourers	963	..	508	..	1,268	48	1,958	6	1,135	5
8	Cultivators of jhum, taungya and shifting areas.	..	..	..	..	..	..	..	..	..	..
	Sub-order 1(b).—Cultivation of special crops, fruit, etc.										
	(Planters, managers, clerks and labourers).	**228**	..	**2,118**	..	**1,461**	..	**274**	..	**2,147**	**9**
9	Cinchona	..	..	75	..	..	..	..	..	..	..
10	Coconut	..	..	2	..	..	..	..	..	..	..
11	Coffee	..	..	6	..	..	..	..	..	..	..
13	Pan-Vine	..	..	21	..	120	..	..	..	..	..
14	Rubber	..	..	13	..	..	..	..	..	..	..
15	Tea	..	..	30	..	32	..	..	..	..	..
16	Market gardeners, flower and fruit growers.	228	..	1,971	..	1,309	..	274	..	2,147	9
	Sub-order 1(c).—Forestry ..	**625**	**22**	**319**	..	**325**	..	**127**	..	**441**	..
17	Forest officers, rangers, guards, etc.	132	..	15	..	100	..	5	..	5	..
18	Wood cutters and charcoal burners	458	3	218	..	152	..	109	..	79	..
19	Collectors of forest produce ..	25	19	80	..	73	..	13	..	357	..
20	Collectors of lac	10	..	6	..	..	..	..	..	..	..
	Sub-order 1(d).—Stock raising ..	**1,156**	**43**	**3,176**	..	**321**	..	**528**	..	**206**	**6**
21	Cattle and buffalo breeders and keepers.	293	..	3,156	..	169	..	4	..	112	..
22	Breeders of transport animals ..	..	..	12	..	13	..	..	..	..	..
23	Herdsmen, shepherds and breeders of other animals.	863	43	8	..	139	..	524	..	94	6
	Sub-order 1(e).—Raising of small animals and insects.	..	..	**47**	..	**1**	..	..	..	..	..
24	Birds, bees, etc.	..	..	1	..	..	..	..	..	..	..
25	Silkworms	..	..	..	..	..	..	..	..	..	..
26	Lac cultivation	..	..	46	..	1	..	..	..	..	..
	Order 2.—Fishing and Hunting ..	**11**	..	**2,453**	..	**1,704**	**5**	**246**	..	**123**	..
27	Fishing and Pearling	11	..	2,451	..	1,695	5	218	..	53	..
28	Hunting	..	..	2	..	9	..	28	..	70	..
	Sub-Class II.—Exploitation of Minerals.	**6**	..	**1,077**	..	**373**	..	..	..	**364**	..
	Order 3.—Metallic Minerals ..	..	..	**86**	..	..	..	..	..	..	..
29	Gold	..	..	..	..	..	..	..	..	..	..
30	Iron	..	..	1	..	..	..	..	..	..	..
31	Lead, Silver and Zinc	..	..	..	..	..	..	..	..	..	..
32	Manganese	..	..	..	..	..	..	..	..	..	..
33	Tin and wolfram	..	..	43	..	..	..	..	..	..	..
34	Other metallic minerals ..	..	..	42	..	..	..	..	..	..	..
	Order 4.—Non-Metallic Minerals	**6**	..	**991**	..	**373**	..	..	..	**364**	..
35	Coal	..	..	22	..	370	..	..	..	..	..
36	Petroleum	..	..	..	..	..	..	..	..	..	..
37	Building materials (including stone, materials for cement manufacture and clays.	..	..	302	..	..	..	..	..	353	..
38	Mica	..	..	..	..	2	..	..	..	..	..
39	Precious and semi-precious stones	..	..	..	..	..	..	..	..	..	..
40	Salt, saltpetre and other saline substances.	6	..	666	..	1	..	..	..	2	..
41	Other non-metallic minerals ..	..	..	1	..	..	..	..	..	9	..
	Class B.—Preparation and Supply of Material Substances.	**61,289**	**916**	**312,014**	**1,887**	**305,816**	**200**	**81,275**	**81**	**96,179**	**422**

* Includes 3,116 earners whose occupations were not returned.

Livelihood—Part III—Cities.

Hyderabad (Deccan).		Karachi.		Lahore.		Madras.		Poona.†		Rangoon.		
Population. 466,894		Population. 263,565		Population. 429,747		Population. 647,230		Population. 256,003		Population. 400,415		
Non-working Dependants. 175,752		*Non-working Dependants.* 180,283		*Non-working Dependants.* 248,735		*Non-working Dependants.* 325,331		*Non-working Dependants.* 176,683		*Non-working Dependants.* 174,438		Group. No.
Earners.	Working Depen-dants.	Earners.	Working Depen-dants.	Earners.	Working Depen-dants.	Earners.	Working Depen-dants.	Earners.	Working Depen-dants.	Earners.	Working Depen-dants.	
12	13	14	15	16	17	18	19	20	21	22	23	
195,346	**95,796**	**75,918**	**7,364**	**176,228**	**4,784**	**224,824**	**97,075**	**77,195**	**2,125**	**219,055**	**6,922**	
17,617	**14,084**	**3,794**	**424**	**17,156**	**337**	**13,448**	**90**	**6,462**	**478**	**4,312**	**46**	
17,373	**14,084**	**3,500**	**424**	**17,065**	**337**	**13,404**	**90**	**6,462**	**478**	**4,254**	**46**	
16,989	**13,178**	**3,040**	**416**	**16,944**	**337**	**10,793**	**90**	**6,308**	**476**	**3,993**	**44**	
9,408	**5,582**	**2,330**	**416**	**14,425**	**289**	**6,955**	**42**	**4,618**	**440**	**1,750**	**34**	
4,270	1,720	1,777	258	4,721	44	2,735	13	414	44	437	8	1
591	402	45	..	35	..	..	..	..	..	10	..	2
255	237	..	..	..	..	6	..	..	..	13	..	3
1,769	712	69	145	..	..	11	..	79	..	68	..	4
695	500	329	13	3,794	104	1,935	29	419	7	325	10	5
902	328	..	..	3,400	114	1,337	..	33	..	426	2	6
926	1,683	110	..	2,475	27	931	..	3.673	389	470	14	7
..	..	..	..	..	..	..	..	..	..	1	..	8
1,502	**1,422**	**568**	..	**763**	**27**	**2,010**	**1**	**1,141**	**26**	**684**	**4**	
..	..	..	..	..	..	..	..	..	..	..	..	9
..	..	..	..	..	..	..	..	..	..	1	..	10
..	..	..	..	..	..	..	..	..	..	..	..	11
47	65	..	..	..	..	1	..	..	..	17	..	13
..	..	..	..	..	..	..	..	..	..	33	..	14
..	..	..	..	..	..	2	..	..	..	..	..	15
1,455	1,357	568	..	763	27	2,007	1	1,141	26	633	4	16
1,012	**1,278**	..	..	**290**	..	**202**	**2**	**115**	**1**	**400**	..	
123	21	..	..	218	..	5	..	7	..	205	..	17
731	1,100	..	..	52	..	65	..	107	1	73	..	18
89	79	..	..	20	..	132	2	1	..	122	..	19
69	78	..	..	..	..	..	..	..	..	..	..	20
4,948	**4,782**	**142**	..	**1,454**	**21**	**1,624**	**44**	**434**	**9**	**1,053**	**4**	
3,286	**3,823**	**80**	..	**358**	**2**	**1,555**	**32**	**363**	**9**	**939**	..	**21**
400	263	58	..	489	5	..	..	..	..	6	..	22
1,262	696	4	..	607	14	69	12	71	..	108	4	23
119	**114**	..	..	**12**	..	**2**	**1**	..	..	**106**	**2**	
91	67	..	..	12	..	2	1	..	..	106	2	24
21	31	..	..	..	..	..	..	..	..	..	..	25
7	16	..	..	..	..	..	..	..	..	..	..	26
384	**906**	**460**	**8**	**121**	..	**2,611**	..	**154**	**2**	**261**	**2**	
230	603	411	8	108	..	2,604	..	147	2	261	2	27
154	303	49	..	13	..	7	..	7	..	..	..	28
244	..	**294**	..	**91**	..	**44**	..	..	..	**58**	..	
17	..	..	..	..	..	**2**	..	..	..	**38**	..	
..	..	..	..	..	..	2	..	..	..	4	..	29
17	..	..	..	..	..	..	..	..	..	..	..	30
..	..	..	..	..	..	..	..	..	..	24	..	31
..	..	..	..	..	..	..	..	..	..	..	..	32
..	..	..	..	..	..	..	..	..	..	4	..	33
..	..	..	..	..	..	..	..	..	..	6	..	34
227	..	**294**	..	**91**	..	**42**	..	..	..	**20**	..	
46	..	..	..	..	..	8	..	..	..	..	..	35
..	..	..	..	..	..	..	..	..	..	4	..	36
171	..	..	..	..	..	..	..	..	..	12	..	37
7	..	..	..	..	..	1	..	..	..	..	..	38
..	..	..	..	..	..	33	..	..	..	4	..	39
3	..	294	..	91	..	..	..	..	..	..	..	40
..	..	..	..	..	..	..	..	..	..	..	..	41
71,453	**30,628**	**36,046**	**4,098**	**99,578**	**745**	**109,730**	**625**	**28,717**	**711**	**166,978**	**633**	

Table X.—Occupation or Means of

Group No.	Occupation.	Amritsar.		Bombay.		Calcutta including Howrah.		Cawnpore.		Delhi (excluding New Delhi and Cant).	
		Earners.	Working Depen-dants.	Earners.	Working Depen-dants.	Earners.	Working Depen-dants.	Earners.	Working Depen-dants.	Earners.	Working Depen-dants.
	1	2	3	4	5	6	7	8	9	10	11
	Class B.—Preparation and Supply of Material Substances—*contd.*										
	Sub-Class III.—Industry ..	**30,314**	**501**	**176,312**	**21**	**133,347**	**107**	**35,321**	**29**	**50,604**	**319**
	Order 5.—Textiles	**6,782**	**180**	**116,533**	**1**	**33,373**	**3**	**12,001**	**24**	**10,233**	**14**
42	Cotton ginning, cleaning and pressing.	47	..	1,875	..	267	..	130	12	570	..
43	Cotton spinning, sizing and weaving.	4,504	102	113,084	1	1,757	..	11,528	12	8,703	11
44	Jute pressing, spinning and weaving.	..	..	77	..	30,926	3	11	..	14	..
45	Rope, twine, string and other fibres.	11	56	82	..	121	..	22	..	13	..
46	Wool carding, spinning and weaving.	638	..	24	..	14	..	8	..	59	..
47	Silk spinning and weaving ..	346	..	11	..	14	..	..	..	48	..
48	Hair (horse-hair), etc.	..	..	1	..	5	..	..	..	1	..
49	Dying, bleaching, printing, preparation and sponging of textiles.	1,153	22	934	..	139	..	301	..	349	1
50	Lace, crepe, enbroideries, fringes, etc., and insufficiently described textile industries.	83	..	445	..	130	..	1	..	476	2
	Order 6.—Hides, skins and hard Materials from the animal kingdom.	**195**	**5**	**1,354**	..	**70**	..	**2,782**	..	**586**	**10**
51	Working in leather	183	5	772	..	70	..	2,743	..	534	10
52	Furriers and persons occupied with feathers, and bristles; brush makers.	..	..	517	..	..	..	4	..	21	..
53	Bone, ivory, horn, shell, etc., workers (except buttons).	12	..	65	..	..	..	35	..	31	..
	Order 7.—Wood	**2,863**	**70**	**6,418**	..	**12,079**	..	**1,208**	..	**2,816**	**11**
54	Sawyers	417	..	72	..	302	..	..	..	254	..
55	Carpenters, turners and joiners, etc.	2,144	70	5,863	..	9,646	..	1,146	..	2,102	1
56	Basket makers and other industries of woody materials, including leaves and thatchers and builders working with bomboo, reeds or similar materials.	302	..	483	.	2,131	:	62	..	460	10
	Order 8.—Metals	**2,858**	**12**	**3,213**	..	**3,719**	..	**1,487**	..	**3,428**	**17**
57	Smelting, forging and rolling of iron and other metals.	..	..	76	..	176	..	5	..	49	..
58	Makers of arms, guns etc. ..	..	..	65	..	76	..	..	..	2	..
59	Blacksmiths, other workers in iron, makers of implements.	2,473	12	1,409	..	2,730	..	1,221	..	1,946	10
60	Workers in brass, copper and bell metal.	226	..	282	..	244	..	227	..	682	..
61	Workers in other metals (except precious metals).	159	..	1,330	..	417	..	16	..	747	7
62	Workers in mints, die-sinkers, etc.	..	..	51	..	76	..	18	..	2	..
	Order 9.—Ceramics	**473**	**5**	**667**	..	**1,214**	..	**968**	..	**884**	..
63	Potters and makers of earthenware	395	2	486	..	447	..	838	..	772	..
64	Brick and tile makers	69	3	116	..	454	..	130	..	40	..
65	Other workers in ceramics ..	9	..	65	..	313	..	..	..	72	..
	Order 10.—Chemical products properly so called and analogous.	**745**	**8**	**439**	..	**1,483**	..	**1,441**	..	**502**	**2**
66	Manufacture of matches, fireworks and other explosives.	44	..	96	..	584	..	7	..	12	..
67	Manufacture of aerated and mineral waters and ice.	11	..	71	..	94	..	28	..	85	..
68	Manufacture and refining of vegetable oils.	462	8	16	..	475	..	1,386	..	158	2
69	Manufacture and refining of mineral oils.	..	..	16	..	..	..	..	..	12	..
70	Others	228	..	240	..	330	..	20	..	235	..
	Order 11.—Food Industries ..	**2,442**	**37**	**3,098**	**11**	**7,847**	**12**	**2,709**	..	**3,634**	**3**
71	Rice pounders and huskers and flour grinders.	26	..	52	..	1,452	..	1,005	..	675	1
72	Grain parchers, etc.	17	..	286	..	30	..	326	..	111	..
73	Butchers.	650	..	967	10	1,256	4	762	..	1,240	..
74	Makers of sugar, molasses and gur.	1	..	17	..	205	..	3	..	2	..
75	Sweetmeat and condiment makers.	648	6	533	..	668	..	596	..	923	..
76	Toddy drawers.	..	..	420	..	11	..	..	..	..	..
77	Brewers and distillers	52	4	2	..	..	..	..	..	..	..
78	Manufacturers of tobacco. ..	..	.	323	1	3,647	8	12	..	11	..
80	Manufacturers of ganja. ..	..	..	54	..	..	..	..	..	47	..
81	Others	1,048	27	444	..	[illegible]	..	5	..	625	2

Livelihood—Part III—Cities—*contd.*

Hyderabad (Deccan).		Karachi.		Lahore.		Madras.		Poona.		Rangoon.		
Earners.	Working Dependants.	Earners.	Working Dependants.	Earners.	Working Dependants.	Earners.	Working Dependants.	Earners.	Working Dependants.	Earners.	Working Dependants.	Group No.
12	13	14	15	16	17	18	19	20	21	22	23	
19,977	**8,470**	**13,932**	**1,783**	**40,421**	**587**	**52,670**	**423**	**16,392**	**383**	**70,090**	**359**	
1,091	**979**	**1,238**	**96**	**3,695**	**63**	**8,015**	**160**	**1,553**	**132**	**269**	**14**	
152	160	247	58	390	4	22	..	..	..	..	..	42
272	205	378	14	2,229	36	7,041	157	661	72	37	14	43
..	..	..	..	25	..	4	..	..	..	..	..	44
58	43	..	..	36	..	47	3	173	..	195	..	45
21	9	..	..	72	1	..	..	51	..	..	..	46
62	44	..	..	396	..	288	..	569	00	..	..	47
6	26	..	..	..	..	..	..	..	..	..	..	48
398	352	153	10	411	22	273	..	99	..	37	..	49
122	140	460	14	136	..	340	..	..	..	..	..	50
288	**147**	**902**	**68**	**702**	..	**180**	..	**57**	..	**123**	..	
235	84	823	68	689	..	169	..	57	..	88	..	51
44	43	79	..	..	..	11	..	..	..	5	..	52
9	20	..	..	13	..	..	..	..	..	30	..	53
2,258	**741**	**1,902**	**395**	**5,095**	**57**	**4,943**	**10**	**1,815**	**58**	**10,689**	**17**	
116	207	..	..	25	..	117	..	155	..	5,635	2	54
1,073	217	1,902	395	4,573	56	4,450	10	1,370	48	4,853	14	55
1,069	317	..	..	497	1	376	..	290	10	201	1	56
1,067	**471**	**781**	..	**3,764**	**30**	**2,472**	**4**	**624**	**29**	**2,035**	**4**	
17	17	..	..	35	..	8	..	..	..	765	1	57
12	10	56	..	..	..	19	..	..	..	7	..	58
608	265	725	..	3,356	25	1,579	4	275	27	755	1	59
211	97	..	..	265	5	261	..	168	2	45	2	60
88	45	..	..	108	..	605	..	181	..	459	..	61
131	37	..	..	..	..	..	..	..	..	4	..	62
529	**233**	**90**	..	**2,048**	**43**	**388**	**15**	**480**	**11**	**180**	**2**	
314	60	4	..	1,110	31	347	12	444	11	64	1	63
152	62	86	..	827	11	1	..	36	..	32	1	64
63	111	..	..	111	1	40	3	..	..	84	..	65
200	**133**	**903**	**7**	**807**	**12**	**226**	..	**65**	**1**	**3,941**	**15**	
80	84	..	..	3	..	16	..	16	..	1,742	14	66
71	30	716	7	343	5	136	..	25	..	564	..	67
37	16	50	..	383	7	20	..	24	1	584	1	68
10	3	17	..	..	..	..	..	..	..	902	..	69
2	..	120	..	78	..	54	..	..	..	89	..	70
3,681	**1,321**	**1,284**	**59**	**2,390**	**10**	**7,711**	**100**	**1,560**	**17**	**22,436**	**191**	
47	178	..	..	75	..	286	..	23	..	17,556	14	71
17	21	..	..	69	..	1,147	6	44	..	..	..	72
960	160	256	4	749	2	758	..	318	1	236	..	73
115	34	56	2	136	1	1	..	83	..	..	..	74
581	244	231	..	895	..	115	..	444	..	111	..	75
213	45	..	..	..	..	1,097	..	65	..	2	..	76
294	90	8	..	..	..	1	..	..	..	1	..	77
1,410	640	312	53	..	..	3,764	93	186	10	3,254	177	78
16	3	..	..	..	..	..	..	..	..	..	..	80
28	6	421	..	466	7	542	1	397	6	1,276	..	81

Table X.—Occupation or Means of

Group No.	Occupation.	Amritsar. Earners.	Amritsar. Working Dependants.	Bombay. Earners.	Bombay. Working Dependants.	Calcutta including Howrah. Earners.	Calcutta including Howrah. Working Dependants.	Cawnpore. Earners.	Cawnpore. Working Dependants.	Delhi (excluding New Delhi and Cant.) Earners.	Delhi (excluding New Delhi and Cant.) Working Dependants.
	1	2	3	4	5	6	7	8	9	10	11
	Class B.—Preparation and Supply of Material substances—*contd.*										
	Sub-Class III—Industry—*concld.*										
	Order 12.—Industries of dress and the toilet.	7,645	148	24,778	1	30,283	84	7,302	4	13,509	201
82	Boot, shoe, sandal and clog makers.	2,042	24	3,671	1	8,982	5	1,796	1	4,548	126
83	Tailors, milliners, dress makers and darners.	3,358	66	11,661	..	8,846	74	2,255	1	2,553	28
84	Embroiderers, hat-makers and makers of other articles of wear.	159	..	185	..	736	..	5	..	2,663	5
85	Washing and cleaning ..	1,359	43	5,588	..	7,478	5	1,641	2	2,140	35
86	Barbers, hair-dressers and wig-makers.	712	15	3,068	..	4,241	..	1,557	..	1,563	7
87	Other industries connected with the toilet.	15	..	605	..	..	..	48	..	42	..
	Order 13.—Furniture industries	597	..	1,179	..	1,423	..	64	..	353	..
88	Cabinet-makers, carriage painters, etc.	..	..	1,038	..	1,398	..	64	..	351	..
89	Upholsterers, tent-makers, etc. ..	597	..	141	..	25	..	..	..	2	..
	Order 14.—Building industries ..	1,015	13	3,371	..	13,539	..	652	..	6,073	15
90	Lime burners, cement workers; excavaters and well sinkers; stone cutters and dressers; brick layers and masons; builders (other than buildings made of bamboo or similar materials), painters, decorators of houses, tilers, plumbers, etc.	1,015	13	3,371	..	13,539	..	652	..	6,073	15
	Order 15.—Construction of means of transport.	87	..	771	..	1,933	..	200	1	260	..
91	Persons engaged in making, assembling or repairing motor vehicles or cycles.	87	..	583	..	1,105	..	200	1	251	..
92	Carriage, cart, palki, etc. makers, and wheel-wrights.	..	..	26	..	117	..	..	..	9	..
93	Ship, boat, aeroplane builders ..	..	..	162	..	711	..	..	..	..	..
	Order 16.—Production and transmission of physical force.	129	..	1,205	..	2,642	..	48	..	556	..
94	Heat, light, electricity, motive power, etc., gas works and electric light and power.	129	..	1,205	..	2,642	..	48	..	556	..
	Order 17.—Miscellaneous and undefined Industries.	4,483	23	13,286	8	23,742	8	4,459	..	7,770	46
95	Printers, engravers, book binders, etc.	416	..	2,171	..	10,777	..	338	..	983	1
96	Makers of musical instruments. ..	[illegible]	..	614	..	590	..	..	..	27	..
97	Makers of clocks and surgical or scientific instruments, etc.	[illegible]	..	300	..	463	..	42	..	269	..
98	Makers of jewellery and ornaments.	[illegible]	[illegible]	2,316	..	3,693	..	901	..	2,025	..
99	Other miscellaneous and undefined industries (toy-making, taxidermy, etc.).	[illegible]	[illegible]	[illegible]	..	43	..	32	..	660	2
100	Scavenging	2,108	9	5,996	8	8,176	8	3,146	..	3,806	43
	Sub-Class IV.—Transport ..	5,471	1	50,[illegible]28	..	62,900	56	5,323	..	16,268	67
	Order 18.—Transport by air ..	..	..	45	..	..	..	..	..	14	..
101	Persons concerned with aerodromes and aeroplanes.	..	..	45	..	..	..	..	..	14	..
	Order 19.—Transport by water ..	342	..	20,996	..	22,440	34	282	..	124	..
102	Ship-owners, boat-owners and their employees, officers, mariners, etc. Ships brokers, boatmen and towmen.	..	..	14,199	..	19,352	34	228	..	9	..
103	Persons (other than labourers) employed in harbours, docks, rivers and canals, including pilots.	342	..	1,531	..	1,755	..	54	..	113	..
104	Labourers employed on harbours, docks, rivers and canals.	..	..	5,266	..	1,333	..	..	..	2	..
	Order 20.—Transport by Road ..	2,597	1	14,977	..	26,448	4	2,814	..	8,834	67
105	Persons (other than labourers) employed on the construction and maintenance of roads and bridges.	15	1	522	..	1	..	..	..	28	..
106	Labourers employed on roads and bridges.	106	..	700	..	2,959	..	..	..	1,334	64
107	Owners, managers and employees (excluding personal servants) connected with mechanically driven vehicles (including trams).	595	..	5,302	..	7,836	..	137	..	351	..
108	Owners, managers and employees (excluding personal servants) connected with other vehicles.	1,616	..	3,465	..	9,236	..	2,125	..	3,632	3
109	Palki, etc., bearers and owners ..	..	..	21	..	1,289	..	..	..	1,160	..
110	Pack elephant, camel, mule, ass and bullock, owners and drivers.	105	..	14	..	5	..	24	..	132	..
111	Porters and messengers ..	160	..	4,953	..	5,122	4	528	..	2,197	..

Livelihood—Part III—Cities—*contd.*

Hyderabad (Deccan).		Karachi[a]		Lahore.		Madras.		Poona.		Rangoon.		
Earners.	Working Dependants.	Earners.	Working Dependants.	Earners.	Working Dependants.	Earners.	Working Dependants.	Earners.	Working Dependants.	Earners.	Working Dependants.	Group No.
12	13	14	15	16	17	18	19	20	21	22	23	
6,238	2,641	2,699	482	8,799	183	8,933	65	4,073	68	10,552	80	
1,490	583	63	41	2,710	70	682	..	806	20	1,190	3	82
1,456	559	991	128	1,914	31	3,734	3	1,558	25	4,445	70	83
71	18	19	..	19	..	232	1	283	15	491	2	84
1,587	706	1,058	236	1,848	32	2,635	55	686	6	5,012	5	85
1,605	760	568	77	2,308	50	1,624	6	740	2	1,407	..	86
29	15	..	..	..	..	26	..	..	..	7	..	87
99	44	140	8	51	..	240	..	88	..	557	1	
85	36	140	8	51	..	192	..	88	..	551	1	88
14	8	..	..	..	..	48	..	..	..	6	..	89
903	268	958	103	1,727	11	4,818	14	2,111	32	5,046	2	
903	268	958	103	1,727	11	4,818	14	2,111	32	5,046	2	90
713	201	..	..	292	..	399	1	260	..	4,133	7	
391	87	..	..	280	..	385	1	257	..	793	6	91
322	114	..	..	..	..	12	..	..	..	102	..	92
..	..	..	..	3	..	2	..	3	..	3,238	1	93
168	29	74	..	843	11	1,120	2	60	..	1,594	4	
168	29	74	..	843	11	1,120	2	60	..	1,594	4	94
2,742	1,262	2,961	565	10,208	167	13,225	52	3,646	35	8,535	22	
376	105	421	4	1,602	..	5,142	34	169	..	3,249	2	95
29	8	..	..	30	..	21	..	4	..	45	..	96
397	39	13	..	690	9	236	..	87	..	157	..	97
529	290	354	86	973	12	4,730	17	498	15	2,255	13	98
452	311	68	..	331	5	106	..	1,633	14	73	3	99
959	509	2,105	475	6,582	141	2,990	1	1,255	6	2,756	4	100
23,942	8,824	9,785	355	31,185	6	22,202	11	3,447	..	43,202	42	
..	..	..	..	..	..	..	..	..	..	..	..	
..	..	..	..	..	..	..	..	..	..	..	..	101
140	47	4,074	145	707	..	4,238	3	..	..	21,894	18	
..	..	2,698	41	4	..	1,061	..	..	..	17,170	18	102
..	..	778	50	641	..	1,115	..	..	..	181	..	103
140	47	598	54	62	..	2,062	3	..	..	4,543	..	104
16,496	5,826	2,058	65	6,943	1	11,296	3	886	..	15,323	23	
269	112	197	..	237	..	303	..	2	..	799	2	105
5,883	2,108	..	..	593	..	1,038	..	6	..	652	..	106
131	63	413	..	450	..	2,166	4	287	..	3,541	15	107
6,709	2,177	1,254	65	3,856	..	3,181	1	66	..	1,847	1	108
453	383	..	..	217	..	1,276	..	..	..	2,709	..	100
49	20	..	..	651	..	..	..	500	..	..	..	110
3,002	963	194	..	939	1	3,332	3	25	..	5,775	5	111

Table X.—Occupation or Means of

Group No.	Occupation.	Amritsar. Earners.	Amritsar. Working Dependants.	Bombay. Earners.	Bombay. Working Dependants.	Calcutta including Howrah. Earners.	Calcutta including Howrah. Working Dependants.	Cawnpore. Earners.	Cawnpore. Working Dependants.	Delhi (excluding New Delhi and Cant.) Earners.	Delhi (excluding New Delhi and Cant.) Working Dependants.
	1	2	3	4	5	6	7	8	9	10	11
	Class B.—Preperation and Supply of Material substances—*contd.*										
	Sub-Class IV—Transport—*concld.*										
	Order 21.—Transport by rail	2,076	..	13,344	..	10,540	18	2,082	..	6,493	..
112	Railway employees of all kinds other than porters and coolies.	1,552	..	10,152	..	7,992	..	1,875	..	4,867	..
113	Labourers employed on railway construction and maintenance and coolies and porters employed on railway premises.	524	..	3,192	..	2,548	18	207	..	1,626	..
	Order 22.—Post Office, Telegraph and Telephone services.	456	..	1,366	..	3,472	.	145	..	803	..
114	Post Office, Telegraph and Telephone services.	456	..	1,366	..	3,472	..	145	..	803	..
	Sub-Class V.—Trade	25,504	414	84,974	1,866	109,569	37	20,631	52	29,307	36
	Order 23.—Banks, establishments of credit, exchange and insurance.	1,030	..	3,672	..	2,934	..	826	..	1,005	..
115	Bank managers, money lenders, exchange and insurance agents, money changers and brokers and their employees.	1,030	..	3,672	..	2,934	..	826	..	1,005	..
	Order 24.—Brokerage Commission and export.	2,103	109	4,851	348	5,501	—	240	..	717	..
116	Brokers, commission agents, commercial travellers, warehouse owners and employees.	2,103	109	4,851	348	5,501	..	240	..	717	..
	Order 25.—Trade in textiles	4,655	34	992	..	5,041	—	3,993	..	4,504	5
117	Trade in piece-goods, wool, cotton, silk, hair and other textiles.	4,655	34	992	..	5,041	..	3,993	..	4,504	5
	Order 26.—Trade in skins, leather and furs.	826	22	91	..	1,119	..	329	..	239	..
118	Trade in skins, leather, furs, feathers, horn, etc., and the articles made from these.	826	22	91	..	1,119	..	329	..	239	..
	Order 27.—Trade in wood	425	..	346	..	872	..	69	..	212	..
119	Trade in wood (not fire-wood)	403	..	146	..	770	..	26	..	186	..
120	Trade in barks	..	..	38	..	37	..	..	..	..	..
121	Trade in bamboos and canes	22	..	29	..	44	..	4	..	11	..
122	Trade in thatches and other forest produce.	..	..	133	..	21	..	39	..	15	..
	Order 28.—Trade in metals	422	1	385	..	590	..	49	..	239	—
123	Trade in metals, machinery, knives, tools, etc.	422	1	385	..	590	..	49	..	239	—
	Order 29.—Trade in pottery, bricks and tiles.	3	..	73	..	130	..	21	—	179	—
124	Trade in pottery, bricks and tiles	3	..	73	..	130	..	21	..	179	—
	Order 30.—Trade in chemical products.	261	..	629	—	482	..	292	..	338	—
125	Drugs, dyes, paints, petroleum, explosives, etc.	261	..	629	..	482	..	292	..	338	..
	Order 31.—Hotels, cafes, restaurants, etc.	2,195	15	10,183	1	4,487	5	527	—	1,675	..
126	Vendors of wine, liquors, aerated waters and ice.	66	..	664	..	384	5	97	..	329	—
127	Owners and Managers of hotels, cook shops, sarais, etc. (and employees).	44	..	9,080	1	4,100	..	172	..	398	..
128	Hawkers of drink and food stuffs.	2,085	15	439	..	3	..	258	..	948	—
	Order 32.—Other trade in food stuffs.	8,341	115	12,549	6	35,357	24	10,229	46	7,732	19
129	Grain and pulse dealers	2,731	110	820	..	3,231	1	2,025	..	668	..
130	Dealers in sweetmeats, sugar and spices.	361	..	1,899	..	3,001	14	905	18	460	..
131	Dealers in dairy product, eggs, and poultry.	1,753	1	3,049	..	4,863	..	872	4	1,490	6
132	Dealers in animals for food.	83	..	22	..	153	..	34	..	307	..
133	Dealers in fodder for animals.	145	..	51	..	351	..	386	..	152	..
134	Dealers in other food stuffs.	3,209	4	2,768	5	22,113	9	5,231	24	4,511	13
135	Dealers in tobacco.	58	..	3,749	..	928	..	776	..	139	..
136	Dealers in opium.	1	..	27	..	110	..	..	..	5	..
137	Dealers in ganja.	..	..	164	1	607	..	..	..	..	..
	Order 33.—Trade in clothing and toilet articles.	464	1	1,775	372	2,137	..	92	..	1,985	2
138	Trade in ready made clothing and other articles of dress and the toilet (hats, umbrellas, socks, ready made shoes, prefumes, etc.)	464	1	1,775	372	2,137	..	92	..	1,985	2

Livelihood—Part III—Cities—*contd.*

Hyderabad (Deccan).		Karachi.		Lahore.		Madras.		Poona.		Rangoon.		Group No.
Earners.	Working Dependants.	Earners.	Working Dependants.	Earners.	Working Dependants.	Earners.	Working Dependants.	Earners.	Working Dependants.	Earners.	Working Dependants.	
12	13	14	15	16	17	18	19	20	21	22	23	
6,665	**2,853**	**3,011**	**19**	**22,517**	**1**	**5,456**	**..**	**2,432**	**..**	**4,397**	**1**	
4,709	422	2,374	..	14,628	1	4,169	..	1,131	..	3,063	1	112
1,956	2,431	637	19	7,889	..	1,287	..	1,301	..	1,334	..	113
641	**98**	**642**	**126**	**1,018**	**4**	**1,212**	**..**	**129**	**..**	**1,588**	**..**	
641	98	642	126	1,018	4	1,212	..	129	..	1,588	..	114
27,534	**13,334**	**12,329**	**1,960**	**27,967**	**152**	**34,858**	**191**	**8,878**	**328**	**53,686**	**232**	
1,366	**609**	**2,029**	**24**	**1,396**	**19**	**1,974**	**8**	**567**	**22**	**2,541**	**..**	
1,366	609	2,029	24	1,396	19	1,974	8	567	22	2,541	..	115
945	**163**	**761**	**17**	**880**	**1**	**1,173**	**1**	**145**	**..**	**1,125**	**2**	
945	163	761	17	880	1	1,173	1	145	..	1,125	2	116
1,556	**603**	**45**	**4**	**1,696**	**..**	**2,445**	**..**	**582**	**2**	**4,174**	**40**	
1,556	603	45	4	1,696	..	2,445	..	582	2	4,174	40	117
479	**276**	**606**	**6**	**469**	**..**	**288**	**..**	**78**	**..**	**139**	**2**	
479	276	606	6	469	..	288	..	78	..	139	2	118
2,195	**1,345**	**23**	**64**	**487**	**..**	**373**	**2**	**116**	**..**	**1,562**	**1**	
1,183	829	..	..	311	..	269	2	76	..	1,359	..	119
270	73	..	..	..	..	..	..	4	..	..	..	120
647	325	23	64	171	..	103	..	36	..	150	1	121
95	118	..	..	5	..	1	..	..	..	53	..	122
290	**116**	**14**	**..**	**178**	**1**	**363**	**1**	**3**	**..**	**946**	**1**	
290	116	14	..	178	1	363	1	3	..	946	1	123
466	**435**	**285**	**..**	**81**	**3**	**25**	**..**	**1**	**..**	**33**	**..**	
466	435	285	..	81	3	25	..	1	..	33	..	124
377	**76**	**..**	**..**	**663**	**..**	**702**	**..**	**64**	**..**	**1,773**	**..**	
377	76	..	..	663	..	702	..	64	..	1,773	..	125
2,761	**1,097**	**2,202**	**293**	**2,406**	**11**	**2,724**	**3**	**2,008**	**19**	**10,091**	**54**	
1,897	794	273	..	583	8	483	..	72	11	1,094	1	126
653	234	1,926	293	827	..	2,204	3	1,898	8	5,971	15	127
211	69	3	..	996	3	37	..	38	..	3,026	38	128
6,807	**2,589**	**3,448**	**342**	**8,768**	**45**	**12,278**	**145**	**3,083**	**108**	**20,666**	**96**	
2,951	548	22	..	1,268	..	1,832	..	245	3	5,067	9	129
766	450	626	2	2,136	19	1,265	8	81	..	1,187	9	130
1,059	943	459	12	1,872	..	2,143	6	728	48	598	..	131
404	115	..	..	89	..	123	..	9	..	493	3	132
236	61	1,177	32	633	..	30	..	24	..	91	..	133
140	63	593	147	2,408	26	6,225	131	1,863	57	12,322	70	134
990	306	346	149	309	..	638	..	54	..	851	5	135
135	45	206	..	52	..	21	..	28	..	57	..	136
126	58	19	..	1	..	1	..	51	..	..	..	137
1,302	**454**	**146**	**..**	**463**	**17**	**220**	**1**	**80**	**..**	**661**	**3**	
1,302	454	146	..	463	17	220	1	80	..	661	3	138

Table X.—Occupation or Means of

Group No.	Occupation.	Amritsar. Earners.	Amritsar. Working Dependants.	Bombay. Earners.	Bombay. Working Dependants.	Calcutta including Howrah. Earners.	Calcutta including Howrah. Working Dependants.	Cawnpore. Earners.	Cawnpore. Working Dependants.	Delhi (excluding New Delhi and Cant.) Earners.	Delhi (excluding New Delhi and Cant.) Working Dependants.
	1	2	3	4	5	6	7	8	9	10	11
	Class B.—Preparation and supply of material substances—*concld.*										
	Sub-Class V.—Trade—*concld.*										
	Order 34.—Trade in furniture ..	91	..	373	..	829	..	239	..	304	..
139	Trade in furniture, carpets, curtains and bedding.	44	..	225	..	238	..	83	..	209	..
140	Hardware, cooking utensils, porcelain, crockery, glassware, bottles, articles for gardening, etc.	47	..	148	..	591	..	156	..	95	..
	Order 35.—Trade in building materials.	15	4	12	..	169	..	20	..	163	..
141	Trade in building materials (other than bricks, tiles and woody materials).	15	4	12	..	169	..	20	..	163	..
	Order 36.—Trade in means of transport.	56	..	384	..	279	..	572	..	295	..
142	Dealers and hirers, in machanical transport, motors, cycles, etc.	14	..	151	..	163	..	92	..	182	..
143	Dealers and hirers in other carriages, carts, boats, etc.	..	..	184	..	12	..	432	..	6	..
144	Dealers and hirers of elephants, camels, horses, cattle, asses, mules, etc.	42	..	49	..	104	..	48	..	107	..
	Order 37.—Trade in fuel ..	352	13	532	8	1,979	..	1,269	..	645	..
145	Dealers in firewood, charcoal, coal, cowdung, etc.	352	13	532	8	1,979	..	1,269	..	645	..
	Order 38.—Trade in articles of luxury and those pertaining to letters and the arts and sciences.	180	3	970	..	5,122	..	307	6	682	..
146	Dealers in precious stones, jewellery (real and imitation), clocks, optical instruments, etc.	..	..	394	..	1,361	..	27	..	21	..
147	Dealers in common bangles, bead necklaces, fans, small articles, toys, hunting and fishing tackle, flowers, etc.	87	3	334	..	237	..	206	6	361	..
148	Publishers, book-sellers, stationers, dealers in music, pictures, musical instruments and curiosities.	93	..	242	..	3,524	..	74	..	300	..
	Order 39.—Trade of other sorts.	4,085	97	47,157	1,131	42,541	8	1,557	..	8,393	1
149	Dealers in rags, stable refuse, etc.	27	..	15	..	..	..	..	..	13	..
150	General store-keepers and shopkeepers otherwise unspecified.	3,695	97	37,722	1,129	36,791	8	1,109	..	8,282	1
151	Itinerant traders, pedlars and hawkers (of other than food, etc.)	361	..	7,601	2	5,734	..	421	..	89	..
152	Other traders (including farmers of pounds, tools and markets).	2	..	1,819	..	16	..	27	..	9	..
	Class C.—Public Administration and Liberal Arts.	7,863	1	61,302	13	60,264	1	8,629	3	11,476	22
	Sub-Class VI.—Public Force ..	1,547	..	9,042	..	7,330	..	3,369	..	2,863	..
	Order 40.—Army	423	..	3,053	..	1,754	..	1,453	..	1,255	..
153	Army (Imperial)	423	..	2,991	..	1,754	..	1,384	..	1,255	..
154	Army (Indian States)	..	..	62	..	..	..	69	..	..	..
	Order 41.—Navy	..	..	674	..	9	..	..	..	..	..
155	Navy	..	..	674	..	9	..	..	..	..	..
	Order 42.—Air Force	..	..	16	..	3	..	..	..	2	..
156	Air Force	..	..	16	..	3	..	..	..	2	..
	Order 43.—Police	1,124	..	5,299	..	5,564	..	1,916	..	1,606	..
157	Police	1,124	..	4,166	..	5,520	..	917	..	1,606	..
158	Village Watchmen	..	..	1,133	..	44	..	999	..	..	..
	Sub-Class VII.—Public Administration.	1,910	..	32,284	2	20,811	..	1,680	..	2,999	..
	Order 44.—Public Administration	1,910	..	32,284	2	20,811	..	1,680	..	2,999	..
159	Service of the State	1,297	..	5,053	1	14,135	..	1,081	..	1,958	..
160	Service of Indian and Foreign States.	..	..	164	..	..	..	..	..	65	..
161	Municipal and other local (not village) Service.	590	..	26,847	1	6,672	..	558	..	964	..
162	Village officials and servants other than watchmen.	23	..	220	..	4	..	41	..	12	..
	Sub-class VIII.—Professions and Liberal Arts.	4,406	1	19,976	11	32,123	1	3,580	3	5,614	22
	Order 45.—Religion	984	..	2,795	5	6,277	1	1,531	..	1,230	18
163	Priests, ministers, etc. ..	709	..	1,155	..	5,654	1	1,529	..	630	18
164	Monks, nuns, religious mendicants.	..	..	836	5	330	..	1	..	3	..
165	Other religious workers ..	273	..	165	..	4	..	..	..	169	..
166	Servants in religious edifices, burial and burning grounds, pilgrim conductors, circumcisers, etc.	2	..	639	..	289	..	1	..	428	..

Livelihood—Part III—Cities—*contd.*

Hyderabad (Deccan). Earners.	Hyderabad (Deccan). Working Dependants.	Karachi. Earners.	Karachi. Working Dependants.	Lahore. Earners.	Lahore. Working Dependants.	Madras. Earners.	Madras. Working Dependants.	Poona. Earners.	Poona. Working Dependants.	Rangoon. Earners.	Rangoon. Working Dependants.	Group No.
12	13	14	15	16	17	18	19	20	21	22	23	
656	128	68	3	999	..	824	..	238	..	1,396		
417	63	..	..	330	..	57	..	49	..	199	..	139
239	65	68	3	669	..	767	..	189	..	1,197	..	140
258	102	..	..	363	..	53	..	..	..	149	..	
258	102	..	..	363	..	53	..	..	..	149	..	141
912	302	529	87	186	..	107	..	453	..	652	1	
347	98	392	6	151	..	53	..	69	..	518	1	142
536	170	137	81	..	..	44	..	374	..	75	..	143
29	34	..	..	35	..	10	..	10	..	59	..	144
832	754	..	..	359	..	868	13	295	165	2,151	15	
832	754	..	..	359	..	868	13	295	165	2,151	15	145
4,216	2,155	19	..	815	10	1,597	6	340	..	1,746	6	
1,025	401	..	..	70	..	608	..	43	..	802	1	146
604	883	19	..	205	3	679	6	233	..	384	4	147
2,587	871	..	..	540	7	310	..	64	..	560	1	148
2,116	2,130	2,154	1,120	7,758	45	8,844	11	825	12	3,881	11	
65	55	..	..	18	..	..	..	498	1	1	..	149
1,544	1,837	2,050	1,118	7,721	45	8,513	11	327	11	3,469	6	150
394	162	104	2	19	..	277	..	..	..	379	5	151
113	76	..	..	..	..	54	..	..	..	32	..	152
47,758	18,036	14,423	269	31,666	82	25,246	83	19,312	180	23,255	3,250	
17,506	2,988	5,452	34	8,415	5	3,709	..	7,783	..	2,885	..	
13,106	1,562	4,315	34	5,570	..	1,076	..	6,292	..	445	..	
1,900	326	4,197	34	4,717	..	1,065	..	6,292	..	445	..	153
11,206	1,236	118	..	853	..	11	..	..	..	..	..	154
..	..	..	..	..	..	5	..	..	..	..	..	
..	..	..	..	..	..	5	..	..	..	..	..	155
..	..	720	..	18	..	..	..	..	..	..	..	
..	..	720	..	18	..	..	..	..	..	..	..	156
4,400	1,426	417	..	2,827	5	2,628	..	1,491	..	2,440	..	
4,164	1,330	417	..	2,827	5	2,628	..	1,232	..	2,440	..	157
236	96	..	..	..	..	..	..	259	..	..	..	158
16,994	8,361	3,479	1	14,439	8	8,269	1	6,742	167	9,967	2	
16,994	8,361	3,479	1	14,439	8	8,269	1	6,742	167	9,967	2	
1,209	525	3,120	..	12,461	..	6,337	1	5,974	162	3,073	1	159
14,237	6,985	..	..	159	..	4	..	7	..	17	..	160
1,430	805	359	1	1,790	6	1,878	..	546	..	6,868	1	161
118	46	..	..	29	2	50	..	215	5	9	..	162
13,258	6,687	5,492	234	8,812	69	13,268	82	4,787	13	10,403	3,248	
2,166	1,271	880	70	1,666	12	1,531	53	791	6	539	3,232	
1,238	728	347	..	949	8	888	..	102	2	240	2,284	163
153	54	517	70	10	..	68	..	390	3	8	911	164
388	212	..	..	311	4	65	..	25	..	91	6	165
387	277	16	..	396	..	510	53	4	1	200	31	166

Table X.—Occupation or Means of

	Amritsar.		Bombay.		Calcutta including Howrah.		Cawnpore.		Delhi (excluding New Delhi and Cant.)	
	Earners.	Working dependants.	Earners.	Working dependants.	Earners.	Working dependants.	Earners.	Working dependants.	Earners.	Working dependants.
1	2	3	4	5	6	7	8	9	10	11
Class C.—Public Administration and Liberal Arts—*concld.*										
Sub-Class VIII.—Professions and Liberal Arts—*concld.*										
Order 46.—Law	**519**	..	**1,731**	**1**	**9,256**	..	**369**	..	**383**	..
167 Lawyers of all kinds, including Qazis, Law Agents and Mukhtiars.	399	..	1,619	1	5,274	..	180	..	229	..
168 Lawyers' clerks, petition-writers, etc.	120	..	112	..	3,982	..	189	..	154	..
Order 47.—Medicine	**962**	..	**3,764**	**4**	**7,546**	..	**413**	..	**1,073**	**1**
169 Registered medical practitioners including oculists.	506	..	1,755	..	2,941	..	58	..	353	..
170 Other persons practising the healing arts without being registered.	267	..	208	..	1,443	..	121	..	273	..
171 Dentists	41	..	73	4	616	..	26	..	32	..
172 Midwives, Vaccinators, compounders, nurses, masseurs, etc.	145	..	1,684	..	2,524	..	167	..	413	1
173 Veterinary Surgeons	3	..	44	..	22	..	41	..	2	..
Order 48.—Instruction ..	**1,209**	**1**	**3,937**	..	**6,095**	..	**944**	..	**1,469**	**3**
174 Professors and teachers of all kinds	1,052	..	2,994	..	5,952	..	555	..	1,201	3
175 Clerks and servants connected with education.	157	1	943	..	143	..	389	..	268	..
Order 49.—Letters arts and sciences (other than 44).	**732**	..	**7,749**	**1**	**2,949**	..	**323**	**3**	**1,459**	..
176 Public scribes, stenographers, etc.	34	..	287	..	478	..	5	..	61	..
177 Architects, surveyors, engineers, and their employees (not being State servants).	40	..	195	..	151	..	..	..	78	..
178 Authors, editors, journalists and photographers.	29	..	393	..	307	..	28	..	175	..
179 Artists, sculptors and image-makers.	77	..	533	..	934	..	14	..	127	..
180 Scientists (astronomers, botanists, etc.).	..	..	82	..	2	..	..	..	22	..
181 Horoscope casters, astrologers, fortune-tellers, wizards, witches and mediums.	97	..	623	..	82	..	..	..	110	..
182 Musicians (composers and performers other than military) actors, dancers, etc.	444	..	1,142	..	917	..	234	3	745	..
183 Managers and employees of places of public entertainments, race courses, societies, clubs.	..	..	4,347	1	52	..	41	..	110	..
184 Conjurors, acrobats, recitors, exhibitors of curiosities and wild animals, etc.	11	..	147	..	26	..	1	..	31	..
Class D.—Miscellaneous ..	**20,127**	**349**	**174,843**	**807**	**302,240**	**3,766**	**27,672**	**535**	**30,275**	**99**
Sub-Class IX.—Persons living on their income.	**483**	**1**	**1,854**	**1**	**12,310**	..	**2,036**	..	**1,417**	**48**
Order 50.—Persons living principally on their income.	**483**	**1**	**1,854**	**1**	**12,310**	..	**2,036**	..	**1,417**	**48**
185 Proprietors (other than of agricultural land), fund and scholarships holders and pensioners.	483	1	1,854	1	12,310	..	2,036	..	1,417	48
Sub-Class X.—Domestic Service ..	**7,802**	**5**	**40,259**	**38**	**104,797**	**44**	**10,282**	..	**16,810**	**34**
Order 51.—Domestic Service ..	**7,802**	**5**	**40,259**	**38**	**104,797**	**44**	**10,282**	..	**16,810**	**34**
186 Private motor-drivers and cleaners	48	..	1,404	..	2,530	..	564	..	915	..
187 Other domestic service ..	7,754	5	38,855	38	102,267	44	9,718	..	15,895	34
Sub-Class XI.—Insufficiently described occupations.	**10,057**	**20**	**125,995**	**5**	**172,799**	**7**	**14,471**	**46**	**10,668**	**7**
Order 52.—General terms which do not indicate a definite occupation	**10,057**	**20**	**125,995**	**5**	**172,799**	**7**	**14,471**	**46**	**10,668**	**7**
188 Manufacturers, business men and contractors otherwise unspecified.	335	..	6,630	1	3,577	..	423	..	523	..
189 Cashiers, accountants, book-keepers, clerks and other employees in unspecified offices and warehouses and shops.	740	..	52,424	4	92,646	2	1,360	..	5,662	..
190 Mechanics otherwise unspecified ..	27	..	4,985	..	7,300	..	..	..	47	..
191 Labourers and workmen otherwise unspecified.	8,955	20	61,956	..	69,276	5	12,688	46	4,436	7
Sub-Class XII.—Unproductive ..	**1,785**	**323**	**6,735**	**763**	**12,334**	**3,715**	**883**	**489**	**1,380**	**10**
Order 53.—Inmates of jails, asylums and alms houses.	..	**318**	**208**	**752**	**791**	**3,715**	**315**	**489**	..	..
192 Inmates of jails, asylums and alms houses.	..	318	208	752	791	3,715	315	489	..	..
Order 54.—Beggars, vagrants, prostitutes.	**1,783**	**5**	**6,164**	**11**	**11,527**	..	**568**	..	**1,358**	**10**
193 Beggars and vagrants	1,771	5	5,014	11	3,624	..	551	..	1,034	9
194 Procurers and prostitutes	12	..	1,150	..	7,903	..	17	..	324	1
Order 55.—Other unclassified non-productive industries.	**2**	..	**363**	..	**16**	..	..	..	**22**	..
195 Other unclassified non-productive industries.	2	..	363	..	16	..	..	..	22	..

Livelihood—III—Cities—*concld.*

Hyderabad (Deccan). Earners.	Hyderabad (Deccan). Working Dependants.	Karachi. Earners.	Karachi. Working Dependants.	Lahore. Earners.	Lahore. Working Dependants.	Madras. Earners.	Madras. Working Dependants.	Poona. Earners.	Poona. Working Dependants.	Rangoon. Earners.	Rangoon. Working Dependants.	Group No.
12	13	14	15	16	17	18	19	20	21	22	23	
721	**248**	**920**	**3**	**1,454**	**11**	**1,428**	..	**317**	..	**949**	**1**	
549	184	218	..	905	8	1,296	..	231	..	334	..	167
172	64	702	3	549	3	132	..	86	..	615	1	168
3,253	**1,704**	**1,829**	**61**	**1,801**	**23**	**2,921**	**9**	**491**	**2**	**2,488**	**5**	
1,266	495	1,664	18	833	13	960	2	61	..	534	..	169
868	167	37	9	88	..	445	..	31	..	489	2	170
81	24	26	..	270	..	28	..	9	..	125	1	171
993	1,005	102	34	585	10	1,475	7	388	2	1,325	2	172
45	13	..	..	25	..	13	..	2	..	15	..	173
2,700	**1,568**	**752**	**78**	**1,789**	**21**	**4,712**	**13**	**2,222**	**5**	**2,622**	**4**	
2,312	1,239	693	78	1,281	20	4,596	13	1,311	5	2,117	4	174
388	329	59	..	508	1	116	..	911	..	505	..	175
4,418	**1,896**	**1,111**	**22**	**2,102**	**2**	**2,676**	**7**	**966**	..	**3,805**	**6**	
197	106	..	..	117	..	235	..	1	..	245	..	176
304	102	137	..	326	..	232	..	468	..	24	..	177
1,108	444	192	..	347	..	449	3	50	..	375	..	178
244	78	261	..	307	..	136	..	4	..	141	3	179
106	32	7	..	80	..	15	..	..	..	..	..	180
970	397	10	..	202	..	180	..	2	..	162	..	181
575	195	456	22	682	2	1,031	4	363	..	907	2	182
537	331	..	..	9	..	365	..	68	..	1,916	1	183
377	211	48	..	32	..	33	..	10	..	35	..	184
58,518	**33,048**	**21,655**	**2,573**	**27,833**	**3,620**	**76,400**	**96,277**	**22,704**	**756**	**24,510**	**2,993**	
8,451	**3,314**	**710**	**5**	**1,909**	**77**	**5,316**	**147**	**1,772**	**66**	**1,649**	**7**	
8,451	**3,314**	**710**	**5**	**1,909**	**77**	**5,316**	**147**	**1,772**	**66**	**1,649**	**7**	
8,451	3,314	710	5	1,909	77	5,316	147	1,772	66	1,649	7	185
29,169	**13,136**	**3,259**	**74**	**13,683**	**40**	**17,072**	**93,459**	**6,001**	**410**	**15,940**	**58**	
29,169	**13,136**	**3,259**	**74**	**13,683**	**40**	**17,072**	**93,459**	**6,001**	**410**	**15,940**	**58**	
2,520	1,133	3	..	749	4	2,476	..	638	1	1,493	1	186
26,649	12,003	3,256	74	12,934	36	14,596	93,459	5,363	409	14,447	57	187
13,313	**11,268**	**15,482**	**1,876**	**10,177**	**69**	**51,628**	**88**	**9,398**	**208**	**6,860**	**6**	
13,313	**11,268**	**15,482**	**1,876**	**10,177**	**69**	**51,628**	**88**	**9,398**	**208**	**6,860**	**6**	
2,622	1,373	1,017	64	1,544	4	1,448	..	62	..	159	..	188
2,187	784	444	7	1,960	..	18,166	10	955	10	825	1	189
145	210	84	..	205	..	4,030	..	2	..	375	3	190
8,359	8,901	13,937	1,805	6,468	65	27,984	78	8,379	198	5,501	2	191
7,585	**5,330**	**2,204**	**618**	**2,064**	**3,434**	**2,384**	**2,583**	**5,533**	**72**	**61**	**2,922**	
..	**1,440**	**725**	**2**	..	**3,408**	..	**2,577**	..	..	..	**2,820**	
..	1,440	725	2	..	3,408	..	2,577	..	..	..	2,320	192
6,074	**3,241**	**1,479**	..	**2,064**	**26**	**2,371**	**6**	**823**	**4**	**11**	**602**	
5,256	2,802	741	..	1,858	25	1,578	6	816	4	..	602	193
818	439	738	..	206	1	793	..	7	..	11	..	194
1,511	**649**	..	**616**	..	..	**13**	..	**4,710**	**68**	**50**	..	
1,511	649	..	616	..	..	13	..	4,710	68	50	..	195

TABLE XI.

Occupations of Selected Castes, Tribes or Races.

Part I of this table corresponds to Part I of Table XVI of 1911, a table which was not compiled for India in 1921 ; this time also its compilation was optional but a few figures are here presented as indicating the extent to which traditional occupations are being abandoned. Part II corresponds to Part II of Table XXI of 1921. The occupations are arranged in both parts of this table under twelve main heads corresponding to the sub-classes of the scheme of classification adopted for Table X.

2. The totals in columns 2, 3 and 4 of Part II will be found to correspond with the respective totals for the Provinces (British Territory *plus* States) and States as given in Table XIX of this volume. The aggregates for India do not correspond in the two tables as the figures for the Andamans and Nicobars, Coorg and the Western India States Agency, where the table was not compiled, have been omitted from this table, while those for Madras relate only to Madras City, Chingleput and the Nilgiris. A further discrepancy occurs in the figures for Europeans owing to the omission of ten non-Christian Europeans in Baluchistan. The figures for the Punjab include those for the Punjab States Agency.

3. The figures in columns 5—28 for both Europeans and Anglo-Indians do not in every case add up to the figures in column 2, the discrepancies being due to the omission in certain cases of the occupational details for working dependants. In the units against wh ch the aggregates of the figures in columns 5—28 agree with the figures in column 2 no working dependants were returned.

Table XI.—Occupations of Selected Castes,

Caste, Tribe or Race.	Province, State or Agency with alternative castes.	Traditional occupation.	Population dealt with. Earners and working dependants. Males.	Females.	Non-working dependants. Both sexes.
1	2	3	4	5	6
1 BARHAI ..	BIHAR AND ORISSA, CENTRAL PROVINCES, UNITED PROVINCES; includes *Sutar* returned from BARODA, BOMBAY and the WESTERN INDIA STATES, and *Tarkhan* from DELHI, JAMMU AND KASHMIR and the PUNJAB.	Carpenters	626,534	133,526	1,192,889
2 BHANGI .	BARODA, BOMBAY, UNITED PROVINCES, WESTERN INDIA STATES, includes *Chuhra* from DELHI, JAMMU AND KASHMIR, NORTH-WEST FRONTIER PROVINCE and the PUNJAB, and *Mehtar* from the CENTRAL PROVINCES.	Scavengers	355,305	200,524	526,771
3 BHAT, etc. ..	UNITED PROVINCES; includes *Brahmbhat* and *Barod* from BARODA.	Heralds and Genealogists ..	37,965	12,221	68,690
4 CHAMAR ..	BENGAL, BIHAR AND ORISSA, CENTRAL PROVINCES, DELHI, JAMMU AND KASHMIR, NORTH WEST FRONTIER PROVINCE, PUNJAB and the UNITED PROVINCES; includes *Chambhar*, *Muchi*, *Mochigar* and *Sochi* returned in BOMBAY and the WESTERN INDIA STATES.	Skinners and Tanners ..	3,098,705	1,976,602	4,395,253
5 DARZI ..	BARODA, CENTRAL PROVINCES, JAMMU AND KASHMIR and the UNITED PROVINCES; includes *Darji*, *Shimpi*, *Sai*, *Marai*, returned in BOMBAY and the WESTERN INDIA STATES.	Tailors	149,516	62,843	259,608
6 DHOBI ..	BENGAL, BIHAR AND ORISSA, CENTRAL PROVINCES, DELHI, PUNJAB, UNITED PROVINCES; includes *Parit*, *Agasa*, *Madiwal* returned in BOMBAY and the WESTERN INDIA STATES, and *Velluttedan* in COCHIN, also *vannan* and *Veluttadanayar* in TRAVANCORE.	Washermen	608,750	342,308	950,822
7 GUJAR ..	NORTH-WEST FRONTIER PROVINCE, UNITED PROVINCES; includes *Gujjar* returned in DELHI, JAMMU AND KASHMIR and the PUNJAB.	Herdsmen	532,926	179,140	886,984
8 JAT	DELHI, JAMMU AND KASHMIR, NORTH-WEST FRONTIER PROVINCE, PUNJAB, UNITED PROVINCES; includes *Jatt* in BALUCHISTAN.	Cultivators	2,388,860	299,131	4,356,283
9 JHINWAR, etc.	Includes *Dhimar* and *Kahar* returned in the CENTRAL PROVINCES; *Jhiwar* in DELHI, JAMMU AND KASHMIR and the PUNJAB, and *Kahar* in the UNITED PROVINCES.	Palki-bearers, etc. ..	598,856	334,512	859,932
10 KHATIK ..	DELHI; UNITED PROVINCES ..	Pig-breeders	73,430	30,152	115,471
11 KHATRI ..	DELHI, JAMMU AND KASHMIR, NORTH-WEST FRONTIER PROVINCE, PUNJAB; includes *Khattri* in the UNITED PROVINCES.	Traders	172,777	12,396	392,806

Tribes or Races.

Caste, Tribe or Race.	Province, State or Agency with alternative castes.	Traditional occupation.	Population dealt with. Earners and working dependants. Males.	Population dealt with. Earners and working dependants. Females.	Population dealt with. Non-working dependants. Both sexes.
1	2	3	4	5	6
12 **KUMHAR**	Bihar and Orissa, Central Provinces, Delhi, Jammu and Kashmir, Punjab, United Provinces; includes *Kumbhar* returned in Baroda, Bombay and the Western India States, also *Kusavan* in Cochin.	Potters	651,320	343,980	1,048,132
13 **KURMI**, etc.	Central Provinces, United Provinces; includes *Kunbi* in the Central Provinces, and also *Kadvia Patidar* and *Lewa Patidar* in Baroda.	Cultivators	1,298,133	760,447	1,730,079
14 **LOHAR**, etc.	Central Provinces, Jammu and Kashmir, Punjab, United Provinces; includes *Luhar* in Baroda, *Kamar* in Bengal, and Bihar and Orissa and *Luhar* and *Kammar* in Bombay and the Western India States.	Blacksmiths	570,994	192,488	1,044,678
15 **MOMIN**	Includes *Juloha* in Delhi, the Punjab and the United Provinces, *Jolaha* in Bengal, and Bihar and Orissa, and *Bafinda* in Jammu and Kashmir.	Weavers	899,947	334,446	1,730,334
16 **MALI**	Central Provinces, Delhi	Gardeners	205,707	155,231	271,385
17 **NAI**	Central Provinces, Delhi, Punjab and the United Provinces; includes *Hajjam* in Jammu and Kashmir and Bihar and Orissa and also, *Napit* and *Naibrahman* in the latter unit. *Hajam, Nhair, Nadig, Napit* in Bombay and the Western India States, *Napit* in Bengal, *Ambattan* in Cochin, *Valand* in Baroda, *Velakkattalavan* in Cochin, and *Velakkathiranayar* in Travancore.	Barbers	788,930	290,299	1,427,245
18 **NAT**	United Provinces	Acrobats	19,457	12,075	26,707
19 **OD**, etc.	Bombay, Western India States; includes *Beldar* and *Waddar* in the Central Provinces, and *Vaddar* in Bombay and the Western India States.	Earth workers.	32,752	17,868	71,816
20 **PINJARA**	Baroda	Cotton carders	1,343	655	2,766
21 **SANSI** ..	.. Delhi, Punjab; includes *Sansia* in the United Provinces.	Vagabonds and pilferers	8,118	2,546	17,114
22 **SONAR**, etc.	Bombay, United Provinces and the Western India States; includes *Soni* in Baroda, *Sunar* in the Central Provinces and the Punjab, *Soni* and *Aksali* in Bombay and the Western India States and *Panditattan* in Cochin.	Goldsmiths	228,771	45,363	461,809
23 **TANTI and KOSHTI.**	Bihar and Orissa, Bombay and the Central Provinces.	Weavers	273,517	153,827	446,305
24 **TELI and GHANCHI.**	Baroda, Bombay, Bihar and Orissa, Central Provinces, Delhi, Jammu, and Kashmir, Punjab, United Provinces, Western India States; includes *Vaniyan* in Travancore.	Oil pressers	1,174,514	609,274	1,982,340

Table XI.—Occupations of Selected Castes,

Caste, Tribe or Race.	Traditional occupation.	Earners and working dependants.		Number of earners whose caste tradition occupation was returned their: Principal means of livelihood.		Subsidiary means of livelihood.	
		Males.	Females.	Males.	Females.	Males.	Females.
1	2	3	4	5	6	7	8
1 BARHAI ..	.. Carpenters	626,534	133,526	329,066	7,110	67,630	1,290
2 BHANGI ..	.. Scavengers	355,305	200,524	179,108	131,875	7,219	3,116
3 BHAT ..	.. Heralds and Genealogists ..	37,965	12,221	2,851	1,020	583	94
4 CHAMAR	.. Skinners and Tanners	3,098,705	1,976,602	324,775	61,422	70,266	19,611
5 DARZI ..	.. Tailors	149,516	62,843	98,207	25,480	11,429	4,546
6 DHOBI ..	.. Washermen	608,750	342,308	268,857	167,842	79,997	13,634
7 GUJAR ..	.. Herdsmen	532,926	179,140	261,239	7,891	11,063	1,299
8 JAT ..	.. Cultivators	2,388,860	299,131	1,700,639	52,849	72,775	4,927
9 JHINWAR	.. Palki-bearers, etc.	598,856	334,512	141,580	110,919	26,558	6,909
10 KHATIK	.. Pig-breeders	73,430	30,152	14,641	7,617	2,231	613
11 KHATRI	.. Traders	172,777	12,396	91,448	1,544	2,346	122
12 KUMHAR	.. Potters	651,320	343,980	256,533	112,490	85,210	17,881
13 KURMI ..	.. Cultivators	1,298,133	760,447	1,033,830	302,117	24,339	9,354
14 LOHAR, etc.	.. Blacksmiths	570,994	192,488	256,462	13,991	62,171	2,997
15 MOMIN ..	.. Weavers	899,947	334,446	346,569	63,087	43,432	7,818
16 MALI ..	.. Gardeners	205,707	155,231	8,614	6,447	6,536	1,930
17 NAI ..	.. Barbers	788,930	290,299	417,246	85,306	100,663	5,688
18 NAT ..	.. Acrobats	19,457	12,075	..	..	..	..
19 OD, etc. ..	.. Earth workers	32,752	17,868	18,402	4,937	975	907
20 PINJARA	.. Cotton carders	1,343	655	179	89	24	6
21 SANSI ..	.. Vagabonds and pilferers ..	8,118	2,546	267	135	3	14
22 SONAR, etc.	.. Goldsmiths	228,771	45,363	160,494	5,762	15,612	1,007
23 TANTI and KOSHTI	Weavers	273,517	153,827	84,520	28,051	15,640	7,467
24 TELI and GHANCHI	Oil pressers	1,174,514	609,274	236,693	146,772	84,244	16,660

Tribes or Races—Part I—Selected Castes—*contd.*

Number of earners returning their traditional occupation as their principal means of livelihood who had some subsidary occupation.		Recorded principal occupation of earners.								
		I. Exploitation of Animals and vegetation.		II. Exploitation of Minerals.		III. Industry.		IV. Transport.		
Males.	Females.	Males.	Females.	Males.	Females.	Males.	Females.	Males.	Females.	
9	10	11	12	13	14	15	16	17	18	
93,099	4,171	225,721	57,579	1,441	253	11,966	4,552	3,764	141	1
36,965	15,110	108,570	10,268	786	186	11,342	2,982	4,424	417	2
687	99	26,132	5,192	67	1	594	397	592	24	3
106,131	19,683	2,326,420	1,232,519	14,486	7,529	82,255	68,351	35,245	6,175	4
41,274	6,439	31,027	7,700	75	122	3,153	991	525	29	5
65,699	23,656	271,268	74,613	809	640	11,135	3,252	4,361	198	6
31,223	2,281	142,547	11,526	438	85	2,759	1,173	6,069	139	7
175,195	4,572	137,426	10,001	1,382	137	31,964	5,060	27,445	165	8
21,254	11,150	354,834	89,162	1,644	302	17,643	18,048	12,043	825	9
2,056	808	42,707	8,992	134	18	3,074	2,118	1,987	158	10
9,743	254	16,610	1,102	296	23	9,778	1,510	9,053	37	11
92,688	31,503	305,393	85,494	1,773	439	13,473	3,494	12,050	824	12
77,767	15,323	120,879	93,109	864	205	14,219	8,046	7,901	393	13
72,416	5,440	215,489	52,525	2,390	971	26,975	4,058	4,356	222	14
37,694	3,906	385,724	134,616	5,824	2,357	39,371	10,282	12,557	344	15
1,057	999	164,122	84,701	179	96	3,136	467	1,420	90	16
110,881	9,829	275,485	75,679	1,179	427	12,518	3,607	3,797	301	17
..	..	9,471	2,563	86	5	440	297	157	19	18
17,012	4,385	6,671	2,712	317	77	1,460	352	353	150	19
30	11	159	72	1	..	117	8	55	1	20
15	80	3,753	238	32	9	221	30	49	16	21
53,416	1,924	37,904	15,274	237	14	4,231	1,359	1,142	86	22
27,120	8,284	141,624	63,291	1,779	2,185	5,031	3,727	2,351	364	23
56,711	15,610	714,030	221,896	3,158	1,247	29,514	7,485	17,357	942	24

Table XI.—Occupations of Selected Castes,

Caste, Tribe or Race.	Traditional occupation.	V. Trade. Males.	V. Trade. Females.	VI. Public Force. Males.	VI. Public Force. Females.
1	2	19	20	21	22
1 BARHAI, etc.	Carpenters	4,406	960	614	3
2 BHANGI	Scavengers	3,082	422	2,846	14
3 BHAT, etc.	Heralds and Genealogists	1,706	156	204	..
4 CHAMAR	Skinners and Tanners	20,979	25,107	2,399	7
5 DARZI	Tailors	5,940	529	206	2
6 DHOBI	Washermen	4,971	899	646	10
7 GUJAR	Herdsmen	3,600	339	2,837	1
8 JAT	Cultivators	15,708	941	19,744	..
9 JHINWAR, etc.	Palki-bearers, etc.	18,377	16,851	1,162	40
10 KHATIK	Pig-breeders	4,001	922	424	..
11 KHATRI	Traders	83	1	3,193	..
12 KUMHAR	Potters	7,821	2,581	371	2
13 KURMI, etc.	Cultivators	13,854	3,937	863	4
14 LOHAR, etc.	Blacksmiths	7,902	1,733	848	7
15 MOMIN	Weavers	26,635	3,638	1,585	1
16 MALI	Gardeners	3,190	1,639	187	2
17 NAI	Barbers	8,605	1,447	1,032	8
18 NAT	Acrobats	683	213	..	..
19 OD, etc.	Earth workers	456	231	23	..
20 PINJARA	Cotton carders	536	132	26	..
21 SANSI	Vagabonds and pilferers	246	105	1	..
22 SONAR, etc.	Goldsmiths	5,473	990	325	2
23 TANTI and KOSHTI.	Weavers	4,598	1,479	256	3
24 TELI and HANCHI.	Oil pressers	56,639	13,283	1,597	36

Tribes or Races—Part I—Selected Castes—*concld.*

Recorded principal occupation of earners—*concld.*

VII. Public Administration.		VIII. Professions and Liberal Arts.		IX. Persons living on their income.		X. Domestic Service.		XI. Insufficiently described occupations.		XII. Unproductive.		
Males.	Females.	Males.	Females.	Males.	Females.	Males.	Females	Males.	Females.	Males.	Females.	
23	24	25	26	27	28	29	30	31	32	33	34	
866	11	2,128	365	604	349	2,671	1,122	9,453	5,562	1,224	526	1
2,264	183	3,435	6,009	443	81	8,119	1,993	10,780	4,206	2,235	972	2
313	..	922	109	112	66	600	150	532	234	1,977	1,136	3
2,285	86	4,546	5,484	3,321	821	23,936	11,999	124,960	99,787	7,064	4,491	4
555	14	881	198	261	115	1,060	441	1,446	783	340	203	5
966	19	2,004	515	921	340	4,166	1,527	8,359	3,429	1,459	1,096	6
1,726	9	1,824	171	587	115	5,873	326	6,011	484	1,863	368	7
11,964	38	15,491	808	5,083	875	16,961	1,443	32,332	3,776	11,915	1,261	8
2,425	74	3,107	800	778	198	6,003	2,221	14,735	5,895	1,214	703	9
153	..	266	230	69	41	1,325	197	1,439	546	494	238	10
7,544	51	6,569	483	3,954	471	9,531	506	6,372	533	831	127	11
722	80	1,366	267	618	382	3,037	1,539	10,780	8,307	848	547	12
4,348	34	5,185	214	843	503	8,002	3,095	12,219	8,288	1,643	763	13
806	24	2,645	327	764	381	3,952	2,427	7,493	4,257	1,049	889	14
2,257	65	6,546	817	1,092	545	14,141	3,735	23,669	11,692	2,945	1,491	15
584	13	861	93	66	24	1,779	434	2,252	1,309	398	195	16
2,214	47	7,555	940	1,583	493	10,784	19,507	10,038	7,988	1,542	1,138	17
15	..	1,523	1,178	130	118	116	77	840	309	5,158	5,532	18
83	5	146	34	5	45	83	249	2,222	2,089	253	78	19
16	..	75	6	3	1	18	17	57	71	..	1	20
27	..	71	10	2	1	155	1	362	72	2,338	1,069	21
975	11	1,527	249	360	252	1,559	1,047	1,897	1,370	612	248	22
698	12	1,096	221	111	298	2,601	756	17,641	15,441	615	410	23
2.248	62	3,803	690	1,623	773	8,683	2,106	22,337	10,816	2,188	1,357	24

Table XI.—Occupations of Selected Castes, Tribes or Races—Part II—

Province, State or Agency.	Population dealt with.			Principal							
	Earners and working dependants.		Non-working dependants.	I. Exploitation of Animals and Vegetation.		II. Exploitation of Minerals.		III. Industry.		IV. Transport.	
	Males.	Females.	Both Sexes.	Males.	Females.	Males.	Females.	Males.	Females.	Males.	Females.
1	2	3	4	5	6	7	8	9	10	11	12
Europeans (including Armenians)	**90,608**	**8,313**	**62,399**	**3,069**	**123**	**1,435**	**22**	**4,080**	**267**	**6,758**	**217**
1 Ajmer-Merwara	1,104	72	500	..	..	..	..	4	..	151	..
2 Assam	2,123	168	1,071	1,431	4	170	1	27	1	66	..
3 Baluchistan	3,344	91	1,589	2	..	2	..	23	1	55	..
4 Bengal	8,539	1,403	13,088	432	32	190	..	1,975	51	820	70
5 Bihar and Orissa	2,904	378	3,107	117	11	227	7	415	13	553	6
6 Bombay (*excluding Aden*) ..	11,550	1,266	11,882	129	13	53	..	175	27	1,198	32
7 Burma..	6,587	703	4,361	313	7	549	8	642	15	1,402	15
8 Central Provinces and Berar ..	3,584	362	1,704	36	2	26	..	133	18	196	4
9 Delhi	2,487	269	1,550	..	..	..	..	141	28	105	13
10 Madras	3,923	658	3,179	214	26	3	..	110	28	487	17
11 North-West Frontier Province ..	9,724	109	1,743	2	1	..	..	..	..	4	..
12 Punjab	12,329	807	6,963	29	6	29	6	90	50	561	27
13 United Provinces of Agra and Oudh	15,490	1,165	6,846	94	16	..	..	192	14	796	26
14 Baroda State	73	22	40	..	..	..	..	2	..	35	2
15 Central India Agency	1,611	116	750	..	..	1	..	8	2	55	1
16 Cochin State	47	27	38	17	..	..	..	9	1	1	..
17 Gwalior State	41	10	60	..	..	..	..	6	..	13	..
18 Hyderabad State	1,917	20	690	2	..	13	..	13	2	5	..
19 Jammu and Kashmir State ..	71	54	73	2	..	..	..	6	7	..	..
20 Mysore State	2,488	406	2,517	86	3	165	..	74	6	72	4
21 Rajputana Agency	346	57	529	1	..	5	..	13	1	178	..
22 Sikkim State	4	4	..	..	..	..	..	..	2	..	..
23 Travancore State	322	146	119	162	2	2	..	22	..	5	..
Anglo-Indians	**32,440**	**9,285**	**82,351**	**990**	**221**	**550**	**20**	**3,312**	**640**	**10,407**	**429**
1 Ajmer-Merwara	326	41	865	..	..	..	..	1	1	283	..
2 Assam	224	41	385	15	4	4	..	3	..	129	2
3 Baluchistan	101	12	266	..	..	..	..	6	..	66	..
4 Bengal	6,141	1,603	19,829	91	41	114	2	734	18	1,680	161
5 Bihar and Orisa	1,775	285	4,578	64	20	52	1	216	15	1,049	13
6 Bombay (*excluding Aden*) ..	5,384	1,022	9,760	251	50	22	..	206	44	1,865	49
7 Burma..	4,679	1,299	13,222	190	21	147	4	638	56	1,316	82
8 Central Provinces and Berar ..	1,214	739	3,112	20	5	14	..	76	4	686	5
9 Delhi	332	63	615	..	..	..	..	17	17	48	4
10 Madras	4,108	1,387	9,541	118	34	..	..	772	286	859	14
11 North-West Frontier Province ..	57	6	98	..	..	..	..	1	..	14	..
12 Punjab	1,403	214	2,008	11	..	9	1	52	7	387	4
13 United Provinces of Agra and Oudh	2,485	638	8,149	110	19	..	..	155	35	1,211	39
14 Baroda State	22	3	38	..	..	..	..	..	..	11	..
15 Central India Agency	208	35	493	4	..	..	..	7	..	124	2
16 Cochin State	377	325	1,015	57	11	..	..	177	23	25	..
17 Gwalior State	47	13	71	..	..	..	..	8	..	14	..
18 Hyderabad State	1,499	654	1,217	11	..	17	12	22	32	150	42
19 Jammu and Kashmir State ..	42	32	49	..	..	..	..	1	4	..	..
20 Mysore State	1,551	708	6,050	12	3	171	..	170	45	262	9
21 Rajputana Agency	224	22	582	1	1	..	..	5	..	178	1
22 Sikkim State	1	..	1	..	..	..	..	..	..	..	..
23 Travancore State	240	143	407	35	12	..	..	45	3	50	2

Europeans and Allied Races and Anglo-Indians.

occupation of earners.

V. Trade.		VI. Public Force.		VII. Public Administration.		VIII. Professions and Liberal Arts.		IX. Persons living on their income.		X. Domestic Service.		XI. Insufficiently described occupation.		XII. Unproductive.		
Males.	Females.	Males.	Females.	Males.	Females.	Males.	Females.	Males.	Females.	Males.	Females.	Males.	Females.	Males.	Females.	
13	14	15	16	17	18	19	20	21	22	23	24	25	26	27	28	
3,507	**575**	**59,692**	**40**	**3,972**	**452**	**4,012**	**5,089**	**1,057**	**480**	**439**	**445**	**2,106**	**217**	**29**	**72**	
10	..	871	..	6	..	50	70	7	..	1	1	4	1	..	..	1
44	6	82	..	66	..	142	112	27	3	..	..	7	..	..	..	2
12	5	3,158	..	27	..	56	75	7	1	2	9	..	..	..	..	3
748	158	1,455	10	505	38	459	680	105	33	197	85	1,361	126	6	45	4
57	5	975	..	132	16	225	270	32	12	3	8	150	18	..	1	5
543	145	7,928	14	881	157	492	746	57	53	53	49	41	16	..	14	6
698	58	1,793	..	359	6	488	480	133	24	6	25	183	5	1	..	7
25	3	2,250	2	666	8	133	257	42	17	54	11	16	6	..	..	8
220	20	1,640	..	235	21	142	112	2	21	2	54	..	..	..	..	9
627	72	1,909	..	73	..	367	400	69	58	..	24	47	21	17	12	10
5	2	9,637	5	47	14	9	73	3	..	17	12	..	..	..	..	11
167	26	10,256	9	519	72	473	504	62	27	34	65	63	8	..	..	12
186	46	13,165	..	233	101	506	751	149	109	26	79	136	5	4	..	13
5	..	16	..	6	..	7	17	1	..	1	3	..	..	..	..	14
10	2	1,413	..	33	5	61	101	10	1	14	4	5	..	..	..	15
..	..	1	..	3	..	12	13	2	1	..	1	..	..	..	..	16
1	..	10	..	2	..	4	9	2	..	2	1	1	..	..	..	17
35	1	1,749	..	67	2	20	2	5	..	..	..	2	..	..	..	18
10	2	4	..	14	7	9	28	11	7	13	3	2	..	..	..	19
81	23	1,309	..	58	2	231	250	320	106	11	1	80	11	1	..	20
4	1	66	..	33	3	33	43	8	..	2	9	3	..	..	..	21
..	..	..	..	2	..	2	1	..	..	..	..	..	..	..	..	22
19	..	5	..	5	..	91	95	3	7	1	1	5	..	..	..	23
2,929	**588**	**-,736**	**11**	**3,208**	**354**	**2,618**	**3,541**	**1,542**	**624**	**951**	**614**	**2,626**	**533**	**128**	**172**	
11	2	1	..	..	..	12	33	11	..	1	2	6	3	..	..	1
5	1	..	..	36	..	10	23	16	3	1	1	3	..	..	..	2
3	1	10	..	6	..	7	9	..	..	1	2	2	..	..	..	3
717	109	110	..	403	80	348	549	153	62	205	109	1,516	345	10	26	4
10	1	27	..	72	12	52	155	47	12	6	19	178	25	1	1	5
608	51	353	..	944	52	595	501	165	53	237	134	138	58	..	30	6
553	151	157	..	725	50	422	797	250	47	51	41	179	18	..	..	7
17	5	38	3	116	16	67	133	57	7	87	12	29	9	..	1	8
81	1	67	..	48	11	65	18	2	5	4	7	..	..	..	..	9
419	192	66	..	201	..	302	348	287	183	..	53	132	..	73	69	10
2	..	15	1	17	4	2	1	..	..	6	..	..	..	..	..	11
78	16	321	6	240	15	157	129	31	7	25	25	40	1	..	1	12
150	13	110	..	130	18	313	349	134	82	16	65	112	5	2	..	13
3	..	2	..	3	..	..	3	1	..	1	..	..	..	..	..	14
7	..	8	..	21	3	11	23	8	6	14	..	4	1	..	..	15
29	3	3	..	9	..	23	42	14	4	2	6	29	..	..	..	16
2	..	2	..	2	..	2	5	1	..	4	4	12	4	..	..	17
135	12	402	1	112	83	44	32	25	9	204	114	13	48	42	43	18
..	1	5	..	12	6	4	14	..	1	18	..	..	..	..	..	19
88	29	36	..	66	3	163	341	332	136	57	18	190	15	..	1	20
2	..	2	..	12	..	13	19	1	..	7	1	3	..	..	..	21
..	..	..	..	1	..	..	..	..	..	..	..	..	..	..	..	22
9	..	1	..	32	1	6	17	7	7	4	1	40	1	..	..	23

TABLE XII.

Unemployment of Educated Persons.

See Part I, Chapter IX.

TABLE XIII.

Literacy by Religion and Age.

The general arrangement of this Table corresponds with that of Table VII of this volume. The sort for Literacy in Burma and in the Andamans and Nicobars having been similar to that for Civil Condition.

2. The population dealt with in this Table is identical to that detailed in Table VII with the exception that the total population of Baluchistan is detailed here the remarks in paragraphs 3 and 4 of the introductory note to that Table are otherwise relevant. The discrepancy between the figures for Aryas and Brahmos in this Table and in Table VII is due to the omission of details for these sects from Travancore State.

3. The figures for general literacy (*i.e.*, those in columns 5—7) are inclusive of the figures for literacy in English. No person below the age of five has been treated as literate for any column.

4. Separate statistics for Indian Christians, who are also included in the body of the Table under the head Christians, are given in the statement below :—

Literacy among Indian Christians.

Province, State or Agency.	Total number of Indian Christians.		Literate.		Illiterate.		Literate in English.	
	Males.	Females.	Males.	Females.	Males.	Females.	Males.	Females.
Ajmer-Merwara	2,086	1,953	1,332	1,190	754	763	757	468
Assam	121,264	123,927	26,030	10,758	95,234	113,169	4,072	1,039
Baluchistan	1,635	1,021	372	193	1,263	828	231	165
Bihar and Orissa	199,910	203,798	21,374	10,091	178,536	193,707	6,240	2,306
Bombay	157,188	132,751	48,506	22,524	108,434	110,189	26,962	12,856
Central Provinces and Berar ..	21,645	22,129	8,632	7,497	13,013	14,632	3,736	2,634
Coorg	1,895	1,308	696	196	1,199	1,112	266	31
Delhi	6,037	5,636	1,371	1,277	4,666	4,359	923	615
Madras	866,683	885,988	192,894	96,266	673,789	789,722	52,366	25.345
North-West Frontier Province	2,991	1,771	1,180	251	1,811	1,520	235	75
Punjab	215,527	180,102	12,864	8,749	202,663	171,353	6,569	5,067
United Provinces of Agra and Oudh.	89,706	83,371	13,767	12,184	75,939	71,187	8,990	8,254
Baroda	3,735	3,329	1,583	708	2,152	2,621	366	184
Central India	3,728	3,488	1,522	1,237	2,206	2,251	785	648
Cochin	165,317	167,724	78,968	53,780	86,349	113,944	Not	available.
Gwalior	465	491	220	243	245	248	94	114
Hyderabad	74,988	70,397	10,695	5,483	64,293	64,914	4,231	2,121
Jammu and Kashmir ..	1,100	842	188	120	912	722	84	57
Mysore	38,239	35,579	13,322	6,938	24,917	28,641	Not	available.
Rajputana	2,149	1,872	959	631	1,190	1,241	422	252
Travancore	814,029	789,069	308,577	162,656	505,452	626,413	27,046	9,253
Western India States ..	463	267	277	124	186	143	109	43

NOTE.—These statistics were not compiled in the Andamans and Nicobars, Bengal, Burma and Sikkim, but the total number of Indian Christians in all Provinces and States is 5,991,000 (3,039,000 males and 2,952,000 females) in round figures.

Table XIII.—Summary

Province, State or Agency.	Total Population aged 5 years and over. Persons.	Males.	Females.
1	2	3	4
INDIA	**296,301,570**	**153,778,322**	**142,523,248**
Provinces.	**230,063,148**	**119,393,242**	**110,669,906**
1. Ajmer-Merwara	475,237	253,805	221,432
2. Andamans and Nicobars	24,335	17,073	7,262
3. Assam	7,138,614	3,803,651	3,334,963
4. Baluchistan (*Districts and Administered Territories*).	101,026*	76,275	24,751
5. Bengal	42,328,283	22,194,423	20,133,860
6. Bihar and Orissa	32,074,981	16,060,433	16,014,548
Bihar	*21,973,676*	*11,067,940*	*10,905,736*
Orissa	*4,595,653*	*2,201,284*	*2,394,369*
Chota Nagpur	*5,505,652*	*2,791,209*	*2,714,443*
7. Bombay (*including Aden*)	8,600,450	9,884,477	8,715,973
Bombay	15,257,209	7,975,725	7,281,484
Sind	*3,295,957*	*1,878,563*	*1,417,394*
Aden	*47,284*	*30,189*	*17,095*
8. Burma	12,629,244	6,490,556	6,138,688
9. Central Provinces and Berar	13,083,574	6,573,656	6,509,918
Central Provinces	*10,168,827*	*5,071,568*	*5,097,259*
Berar	*2,914,747*	*1,502,088*	*1,412,659*
10. Coorg	143,805	80,907	62,898
11. Delhi	548,540	325,019	223,521
12. Madras	39,960,507	19,750,011	20,210,496
13. North-West Frontier Province (*Districts and Administered Territories*).	2,038,357	1,120,146	918,211
14. Punjab	19,840,303	10,971,332	8,868,971
15. United Provinces	41,075,892	21,791,478	19,284,414
Agra	*30,154,917*	*16,090,094*	*14,064,823*
Oudh	*10,920,975*	*5,701,384*	*5,219,591*
States and Agencies.	**66,238,422**	**34,385,080**	**31,853,342**
16. Assam States	513,066	251,413	261,653
17. Baluchistan States	6,008*	5,601	407
18. Baroda State	2,079,931	1,074,298	1,005,633
19. Bengal States	816,499	439,134	377,365
20. Bihar and Orissa States	3,858,944	1,900,845	1,958,099
21. Bombay States	3,757,062	1,940,143	1,816,919
22. Central India Agency	5,633,090	2,917,439	2,715,651
23. Central Provinces States	2,032,273	1,015,148	1,017,125
24. Gwalior State	3,014,056	1,611,408	1,402,648
25. Hyderabad State	12,007,929	6,211,181	5,796,748
26. Jammu and Kashmir State	3,066,701	1,646,407	1,420,294
27. Madras States Agency	5,627,196	2,807,253	2,819,943
Cochin State	*1,006,919*	*490,387*	*516,532*
Travancore State	*4,218,731*	*2,124,222*	*2,094,509*
Other Madras States	*401,546*	*192,644*	*208,902*
28. Mysore State	5,627,342	2,898,109	2,729,233
29. North-West Frontier Province (*Agencies and Tribal Areas*).	45,701	44,258	1,443
30. Punjab States	380,515	201,109	179,406
31. Punjab States Agency	3,789,879	2,104,525	1,685,354
32. Rajputana Agency	9,490,373	5,021,931	4,468,442
33. Sikkim State	92,651	47,296	45,355
34. United Provinces States	1,022,878	528,372	494,506
35. Western India States Agency	3,376,328	1,719,210	1,657,118

* Excludes the illiterate population who were

figures of Literacy.

Literate. Persons.	Literate. Males.	Literate. Females.	Illiterate. Persons.	Illiterate. Males	Illiterate. Females.	Literate in English. Persons.	Literate in English. Males.	Literate in English. Females.
5	6	7	8	9	10	11	12	13
28,138,856	**23,969,751**	**4,169,105**	**268,162,714**	**129,808,571**	**138,354,143**	**3,651,350**	**3,253,467**	**397,883**
22,730,421	**19,481,077**	**3,249,344**	**207,332,727**	**99,912,165**	**107,420,562**	**3,129,005**	**2,788,653**	**340,352**
59,261	51,478	7,783	415,976	202,327	213,649	12,900	11,334	1,566
4,149	3,815	334	20,186	13,258	6,928	961	875	86
666,316	591,690	74,626	6,472,298	3,211,961	3,260,337	89,603	84,873	4,730
35,844	31,986	3,858	65,182	44,289	20,893	11,462	9,939	1,523
4,693,713	4,033,262	660,451	37,634,570	18,161,161	19,473,409	1,058,978	960,396	98,582
1,703,866	1,574,506	129,360	30,371,115	14,485,927	15,885,188	169,934	157,149	12,785
1,117,559	*1,037,024*	*80,535*	*20,856,117*	*10,030,916*	*10,825,201*	*107,198*	*99,662*	*7,536*
539,353	*334,920*	*24,433*	*4,236,300*	*1,866,364*	*2,369,936*	*25,228*	*24,036*	*1,192*
226,954	*202,562*	*24,392*	*5,278,698*	*2,588,647*	*2,690,051*	*37,508*	*33,451*	*4,057*
2,011,970	1,737,813	274,157	16,588,480	8,146,664	8,441,816	374,182	316,003	58,179
1,773,666	1,529,650	244,016	13,483,543	6,446,075	7,037,468	324,713	272,698	52,015
229,719	*200,360*	*29,359*	*3,066,238*	*1,678,203*	*1,388,035*	*46,127*	*40,440*	*5,687*
8,585	*7,803*	*782*	*38,699*	*22,386*	*16,313*	*3,342*	*2,865*	*477*
4,646,088	3,635,790	1,010,298	7,983,156	2,854,766	5,128,390	161,690	130,976	30,714
867,765	790,981	76,784	12,215,809	5,782,675	6,433,134	91,273	81,964	9,309
613,847	*556,224*	*57,623*	*9,554,980*	*4,515,344*	*5,039,636*	*69,608*	*61,445*	*8,153*
253,918	*234,757*	*19,161*	*2,660,829*	*1,267,331*	*1,393,498*	*21,665*	*20,519*	*1,156*
25,336	19,892	5,444	118,469	61,015	57,454	3,982	3,279	703
89,472	73,377	16,095	459,068	251,642	207,426	33,185	29,105	4,080
4,318,880	3,706,975	611,905	35,641,627	16.043,036	19,598,591	579,364	508,309	71,055
100,366	89,058	11,308	1,937,991	1,031,088	906,903	25,717	23,921	1,796
1,247,757	1,097,044	150,713	18,592,546	9,874,288	8,718,258	249,607	230,390	19,217
2,259,638	2,043,410	216,228	38,816,254	19,748,068	19,068,186	266,167	240,140	26,027
1,837,106	*1,656,503*	*180,603*	*28,317,811*	*14,433,591*	*13,884,220*	*213,374*	*191,922*	*21,452*
422,532	*386,907*	*35,625*	*10,498,443*	*5,314,477*	*5,183,966*	*52,793*	*48,218*	*4,575*
5,408,435	**4,488,674**	**919,761**	**60,829,987**	**29,896,406**	**30,933,581**	**522,345**	**464,814**	**57,531**
31,182	24,675	6,507	481,884	226,738	255,146	5,232	4,516	716
4,931	4,849	82	1,077	752	325	126	124	2
434,734	355,067	79,667	1,645,197	719,231	925,966	32,022	30,218	1,804
49,568	45,512	4,056	766,931	393,622	373,309	6,829	6,271	558
149,228	139,505	9,723	3,709,716	1,761,340	1,948,376	8,767	8,493	274
266,074	238,052	28,022	3,490,988	1,702,091	1,788,897	23,823	22,520	1,303
294,117	268,545	25,572	5,338,973	2,648,894	2,690,079	29,663	26,918	2,745
45,663	42,498	3,165	1,986,6[illegible]	972,650	1,013,960	2,363	2,14[illegible]	223
141,342	126,147	15,195	2,872,714	1,485,261	1,387,453	13,614	12,717	897
595,633	527,594	68,039	11,412,296	5,683.587	5,728,709	72,846	65,329	7,517
123,885	114,807	9,078	2,942,816	1,531,600	1,411,216	19,469	18,660	809
1,605,803	1,136,061	469,742	4,021,39[illegible]	1,671,192	2,350,201	21,604	97,835	23,769
339,214	*225,425*	*113,789*	*667,705*	*264,962*	*402,743*	*36,975*	*28,533*	*8,442*
1,217,924	*866,313*	*351,611*	*3,000,807*	*1,257,909*	*1,742,898*	*80,651*	*65,500*	*15,151*
48,665	*44,323*	*4,342*	*352,881*	*148,321*	*204,560*	*3,978*	*3,802*	*176*
594,526	504,440	90,086	5,032,816	2,393,669	2,639,147	91,460	78,419	13,041
17,072	16,968	104	28,629	27,290	1,339	5,798	5,790	8
15,870	14,791	1,079	364,645	186,318	178,327	1,681	1,564	117
158,315	146,907	11,408	3,631,564	1,957,618	1,673,946	17,810	17,049	761
406,146	380,888	25,258	9,084,227	4,641,043	4,443,184	29,796	28,133	1,663
3,277	3,127	150	89,374	44,169	45,205	279	267	12
49,720	47,649	2,071	973,158	480,723	492,435	2,769	2,683	86
421,349	350,592	70,757	2,954,979	1,368,618	1,586,361	36,394	35,168	1,226

recorded by age.

Table XIII.—Literacy by Religion and Age—Part I—General Tab'-

Age and Religion.	Population. Total. Persons.	Total. Males.	Total. Females.	Literate. Persons.	Literate. Males.	Literate. Females.	Illiterate. Persons.	Illiterate. Males.	Illiterate. Females.	Literate in English. Persons.	Literate in English. Males.	Literate in English. Females.
1	2	3	4	5	6	7	8	9	10	11	12	13
All Religions	**350,517,086**	**180,613,801**	**169,903,285**	**28,138,856**	**23,969,751**	**4,169,105**	**322,378,230**	**156,644,050**	**165,734,180**	**3,651,350**	**3,253,467**	**397,883**
0—5	53,465,289	26,434,734	27,030,555	..	..	..	53,465,289	26,434,734	27,030,555	..	..	..
5—10	45,506,909	23,796,001	21,710,908	1,828,388	1,398,952	429,436	43,678,521	22,397,049	21,281,472	157,703	124,569	33,134
10—15	40,634,216	21,572,694	19,061,522	3,005,563	2,361,633	643,930	37,628,653	19,211,061	18,417,592	336,291	278,352	57,939
15—20	31,937,792	16,040,278	15,897,514	3,835,901	3,131,605	704,296	28,101,891	12,908,673	15,193,218	612,860	538,508	74,352
20 and over	178,215,112	92,361,877	85,853,235	19,461,463	17,070,089	2,391,374	158,753,649	75,291,788	83,461,861	2,544,386	2,311,928	232,458
Age unspecified	757,768	408,217	349,551	7,541	7,472	69	750,227	400,745	349,482	110	110	..

Table XIII.—Literacy by Religion and Age—Part I-A—General Table for India proper.

Age and Religion.	Total. Persons.	Total. Males.	Total. Females.	Literate. Persons.	Literate. Males.	Literate. Females.	Illiterate. Persons.	Illiterate. Males.	Illiterate. Females.	Literate in English. Persons.	Literate in English. Males.	Literate in English. Females.
All Religions	**335,869,589**	**173,133,125**	**162,736,464**	**23,492,768**	**20,333,961**	**3,158,807**	**312,376,821**	**152,799,164**	**159,577,657**	**3,489,660**	**3,122,491**	**367,169**
0—5	51,447,036	25,444,614	26,002,422	..	..	..	51,447,036	25,444,614	26,002,422	..	..	..
5—10	43,705,947	22,887,591	20,818,356	1,530,204	1,192,789	337,415	42,175,743	21,694,802	20,480,941	148,596	118,560	30,036
10—15	38,973,209	20,727,071	18,246,138	2,548,741	2,036,467	512,274	36,424,468	18,690,604	17,733,864	320,018	267,104	52,914
15—20	30,525,177	15,346,901	15,178,276	3,256,234	2,703,099	553,135	27,268,943	12,643,802	14,625,141	587,351	518,821	68,530
20 and over	170,460,452	88,318,731	82,141,721	16,150,048	14,394,134	1,755,914	154,310,404	73,924,597	80,385,807	2,433,585	2,217,896	215,689
Age unspecified	757,768	408,217	349,551	7,541	7,472	69	750,227	400,745	349,482	110	110	..
Hindu	**238,614,268**	**122,181,055**	**116,433,213**	**17,103,992**	**15,045,350**	**2,058,642**	**221,510,276**	**107,135,705**	**114,374,571**	**2,289,414**	**2,137,036**	**152,378**
0—5	35,727,673	17,606,196	18,121,477	..	..	..	35,727,673	17,606,196	18,121,477	..	..	..
5—10	30,449,951	15,870,748	14,579,203	1,094,421	874,310	220,111	29,355,530	14,996,438	14,359,092	90,307	76,621	13,686
10—15	27,358,875	14,522,361	12,836,514	1,846,940	1,511,806	335,134	25,511,935	13,010,555	12,501,380	207,440	181,851	25,589
15—20	21,536,107	10,863,103	10,673,004	2,361,009	2,000,436	360,573	19,175,098	8,862,667	10,312,431	388,617	357,015	31,602
20 and over	123,526,047	63,310,126	60,215,921	11,798,362	10,655,573	1,142,789	111,727,685	52,654,553	59,073,132	1,603,039	1,521,538	81,501
Age unspecified	15,615	8,521	7,094	3,260	3,225	35	12,355	5,296	7,059	11	11	..
Arya	***955,523***	***529,350***	***426,173***	***140,659***	***113,233***	***27,426***	***814,864***	***416,117***	***398,747***	***38,267***	***35,892***	***2,375***
0—5	*143,864*	*73,788*	*70,076*	..	..	..	*143,864*	*73,788*	*70,076*	..	..	..
5—10	*115,899*	*62,913*	*52,986*	*9,663*	*6,801*	*2,862*	*106,236*	*56,112*	*50,124*	*1,261*	*1,027*	*234*
10—15	*111,789*	*62,464*	*49,325*	*17,456*	*12,832*	*4,624*	*94,333*	*49,632*	*44,701*	*3,600*	*3,175*	*425*
15—20	*98,210*	*55,185*	*43,025*	*22,819*	*17,850*	*4,969*	*75,391*	*37,335*	*38,056*	*7,870*	*7,329*	*541*
20 and over	*485,718*	*274,965*	*210,753*	*90,712*	*75,741*	*14,971*	*395,006*	*199,224*	*195,782*	*25,536*	*24,361*	*1,175*
Age unspecified	*43*	*35*	*8*	*9*	*9*	..	*34*	*26*	*8*	..	..	..
Brahmo	***4,429***	***2,466***	***1,963***	***2,782***	***1,698***	***1,084***	***1,647***	***768***	***879***	***1,697***	***1,152***	***545***
0—5	*447*	*211*	*236*	..	..	..	*447*	*211*	*236*	..	..	..
5—10	*436*	*235*	*201*	*250*	*147*	*103*	*186*	*88*	*98*	*85*	*58*	*27*
10—15	*593*	*343*	*250*	*426*	*263*	*163*	*167*	*80*	*87*	*211*	*139*	*72*
15—20	*579*	*335*	*244*	*469*	*271*	*198*	*110*	*64*	*46*	*328*	*194*	*134*
20 and over	*2,372*	*1,340*	*1,032*	*1,636*	*1,016*	*620*	*736*	*324*	*412*	*1,073*	*761*	*312*
Age unspecified	*2*	*2*	..	*1*	*1*	..	*1*	*1*	..	..	..	..
Sikh	**4,324,215**	**2,424,064**	**1,900,151**	**335,274**	**288,902**	**46,372**	**3,988,941**	**2,135,162**	**1,853,779**	**55,642**	**52,368**	**3,274**
0—5	646,172	335,187	310,985	..	..	..	646,172	335,187	310,985	..	..	..
5—10	548,075	300,445	247,630	15,697	11,829	3,868	532,378	288,616	243,762	1,662	1,390	272
10—15	513,305	287,855	225,450	32,113	25,275	6,838	481,192	262,580	218,612	5,385	4,826	559
15—20	408,447	233,074	175,373	50,441	41,703	8,738	358,006	191,371	166,635	12,374	11,545	829
20 and over	2,207,731	1,267,177	940,554	237,001	201,073	26,928	1,970,730	1,057,104	913,626	36,220	34,606	1,614
Age unspecified	485	326	159	22	22		463	304	159	1	1	..

M8CC

Jain	**1,251,340**	**644,611**	**606,729**	**380,881**	**325,889**	**54,992**	**870,459**	**318,722**	**551,737**	**33,034**	**31,970**	**1,064**
0—5	171,239	85,002	86,237	..	..	..	171,239	85,002	86,237	..	..	..
5—10	148,714	76,876	71,838	25,526	19,238	6,288	123,188	57,638	65,550	1,236	1,141	95
10—15	139,315	73,407	65,908	41,300	31,809	9,491	98,015	41,598	56,417	3,295	3,136	159
15—20	117,648	61,277	56,371	51,575	41,777	9,798	66,073	19,500	46,573	6,643	6,383	260
20 and over	674,424	348,049	326,375	262,480	233,065	29,415	411,944	114,984	296,960	21,860	21,310	550
Buddhist	**435,857**	**224,232**	**211,625**	**33,205**	**29,110**	**4,095**	**402,652**	**195,122**	**207,530**	**4,388**	**3,927**	**461**
0—5	68,091	34,136	33,955	..	..	..	68,091	34,136	33,955	..	..	..
5—10	57,284	29,835	27,449	1,452	1,106	346	55,832	28,729	27,103	222	177	45
10—15	50,581	26,217	24,364	2,250	1,814	436	48,331	24,403	23,928	392	324	68
15—20	40,455	19,821	20,634	3,560	2,956	604	36,895	16,865	20,030	725	646	79
20 and over	219,446	114,223	105,223	25,943	23,234	2,709	193,503	90,989	102,514	3,049	2,780	269
Zoroastrian	**109,329**	**56,366**	**52,963**	**79,143**	**43,664**	**35,479**	**30,186**	**12,702**	**17,484**	**50,402**	**33,033**	**17,369**
0—5	9,335	4,723	4,612	..	..	..	9,335	4,723	4,612	..	..	..
5—10	10,069	5,208	4,861	4,500	2,410	2,090	5,569	2,798	2,771	1,847	1,012	835
10—15	10,339	5,349	4,990	6,689	3,536	3,153	3,650	1,813	1,837	3,456	1,916	1,540
15—20	10,009	5,066	4,943	8,485	4,412	4,073	1,524	654	870	6,018	3,507	2,511
20 and over	69,577	36,020	33,557	59,469	33,306	26,163	10,108	2,714	7,394	39,081	26,598	12,483
Muslim	**77,085,896**	**40,498,470**	**36,587,426**	**4,100,529**	**3,642,143**	**458,386**	**72,985,367**	**36,856,327**	**36,129,040**	**587,797**	**554,596**	**33,201**
0—5	12,415,995	6,193,283	6,222,712	..	..	..	12,415,995	6,193,283	6,222,712	..	..	..
5—10	10,556,081	5,613,744	4,942,337	269,686	215,908	53,778	10,286,395	5,397,836	4,888,559	27,152	23,861	3,291
10—15	9,216,115	4,945,085	4,271,030	431,312	353,033	78,279	8,784,803	4,592,052	4,192,751	56,261	50,679	5,582
15—20	7,137,399	3,546,893	3,590,506	556,468	473,916	82,552	6,580,931	3,072,977	3,507,954	99,426	92,241	7,185
20 and over	37,018,641	19,800,098	17,218,543	2,838,804	2,595,061	243,743	34,179,837	17,205,037	16,974,800	404,860	387,717	17,143
Age unspecified ..	741,665	399,367	342,298	4,259	4,225	34	737,406	395,142	342,264	98	98	..
Christian	**5,964,002**	**3,054,583**	**2,909,419**	**1,396,331**	**904,507**	**491,824**	**4,567,671**	**2,150,076**	**2,417,595**	**459,516**	**302,041**	**157,475**
0—5	963,456	481,463	481,993	..	..	..	963,456	481,463	481,993	..	..	..
5—10	797,527	407,149	390,378	114,667	64,694	49,973	682,860	342,455	340,405	25,732	14,049	11,683
10—15	726,950	372,967	353,983	181,432	103,695	77,737	545,518	269,272	276,246	43,079	23,839	19,240
15—20	576,366	287,778	288,588	215,894	130,545	85,349	360,472	157,233	203,239	72,253	46,465	25,788
20 and over	2,899,700	1,505,223	1,394,477	884,338	605,573	278,765	2,015,362	899,650	1,115,712	381,452	217,688	100,764
Age unspceified ..	3	3		..	..	..	3	3	..	..	..	..
Jewish	**22,923**	**11,825**	**11,098**	**8,262**	**5,033**	**3,229**	**14,661**	**6,792**	**7,869**	**5,238**	**3,605**	**1,633**
0—5	3,052	1,502	1,550	..	..	..	3,052	1,502	1,550	..	..	..
5—10	2,881	1,431	1,450	637	329	308	2,244	1,102	1,142	280	168	112
10—15	2,711	1,373	1,338	828	427	401	1,883	946	937	380	230	150
15—20	2,403	1,227	1,176	1,078	611	467	1,325	616	709	644	417	227
20 and over	11,876	6,292	5,584	5,719	3,666	2,053	6,157	2,626	3,531	3,934	2,790	1,144
Tribal	**7,611,803**	**3,788,282**	**3,823,521**	**44,351**	**39,648**	**4,703**	**7,567,452**	**3,748,634**	**3,818,818**	**2,270**	**2,130**	**140**
0—5	1,369,387	665,946	703,441	..	..	..	1,369,387	665,946	703,441	..	..	..
5—10	1,073,850	548,731	525,119	3,183	2,618	565	1,070,667	546,113	524,554	112	104	8
10—15	898,473	461,194	437,279	4,961	4,298	66[illegible]	893,512	456,896	436,616	214	200	14
15—20	655,179	306,242	348,937	6,416	5,623	79[illegible]	648,763	300,619	348,144	394	371	23
20 and over	3,614,914	1,806,169	1,808,745	29,791	27,109	2,682	3,585,123	1,779,060	1,806,063	1,550	1,455	95
Others	**422,013**	**230,752**	**191,261**	**6,651**	**5,900**	**751**	**415,362**	**224,852**	**190,510**	**998**	**910**	**88**
0—5	69,028	35,364	33,664	..	..	..	69,028	35,364	33,664	..	..	..
5—10	9,10[illegible]	[illegible]2,100	27,006	375	307	6[illegible]	58,731	31,793	26,938	31	27	4
10—15		[illegible]	24,403	726	631	95	53,824	29,516	24,308	63	60	3
15—20	39,246	21,273	17,973	1,040	905	135	38,206	20,368	17,838	145	129	16
20 and over	200,083	111,868	88,215	4,510	4,057	453	195,573	107,811	87,762	759	694	65

Literacy by Religion and Age—Part I-B—General Table for Burma.

Age and Religion.	Total. Persons.	Total. Males.	Total. Females.	Literate. Persons.	Literate. Males.	Literate. Females.	Illiterate. Persons.	Illiterate. Males.	Illiterate. Females.	Literate in English. Persons.	Literate in English. Males.	Literate in English. Females.
1	2	3	4	5	6	7	8	9	10	11	12	13
All Races	**14,647,497**	**7,480,676**	**7,166,821**	**4,646,088**	**3,635,790**	**1,010,298**	**10,001,409**	**3,844,886**	**6,156,523**	**161,690**	**130,976**	**30,714**
0—5	2,018,253	990,120	1,028,133	..	..	..	2,018,253	990,120	1,028,133	..	..	..
5—10	1,800,962	908,410	892,552	298,184	206,163	92,021	1,502,778	702,247	800,531	9,107	6,009	3,098
10—15	1,661,007	845,623	815,384	456,822	325,166	131,656	1,204,185	520,457	683,728	16,273	11,248	5,025
15—20	1,412,615	693,377	719,238	579,667	428,506	151,161	832,948	264,871	568,077	25,509	19,687	5,822
20 and over	7,754,660	4,043,146	3,711,514	3,311,415	2,675,955	635,460	4,443,245	1,367,191	3,076,054	110,801	94,032	16,769
Burmese	**8,596,031**	**4,202,079**	**4,393,952**	**3,394,712**	**2,601,198**	**793,514**	**5,201,319**	**1,600,881**	**3,600,438**	**60,112**	**51,202**	**8,910**
0—5	1,182,068	575,092	606,976	..	..	..	1,182,068	575,092	606,976	..	..	..
5—10	1,083,371	541,455	541,916	232,368	160,083	72,285	851,003	381,372	469,631	3,411	2,440	971
10—15	1,003,788	503,384	500,404	351,274	248,430	102,844	652,514	254,954	397,560	6,878	5,101	1,777
15—20	825,525	386,671	438,854	427,372	310,747	116,625	398,153	75,924	322,229	11,062	9,031	2,031
20 and over	4,501,279	2,195,477	2,305,802	2,383,698	1,881,938	501,760	2,117,581	313,539	1,804,042	38,761	34,630	4,131
Other Indigenous Races	**4,623,991**	**2,307,725**	**2,316,266**	**849,137**	**690,348**	**158,789**	**3,774,854**	**1,617,377**	**2,157,477**	**22,210**	**16,679**	**5,531**
0—5	676,231	334,262	341,969	..	..	..	676,231	334,262	341,969	..	..	..
5—10	580,410	293,005	287,405	47,974	34,283	13,691	532,436	258,722	273,714	1,329	889	440
10—15	529,345	268,674	260,671	78,667	58,026	20,641	450,678	210,648	240,030	2,641	1,775	866
15—20	442,823	209,458	233,365	106,173	80,777	25,396	336,650	128,681	207,969	4,329	3,032	1,297
20 and over	2,395,182	1,202,326	1,192,856	616,323	517,262	99,061	1,778,859	685,064	1,093,795	13,911	10,983	2,928
Chinese	**193,594**	**127,049**	**66,545**	**61,718**	**52,173**	**9,545**	**131,876**	**74,876**	**57,000**	**5,954**	**5,018**	**936**
0—5	22,630	12,013	10,617	..	..	..	22,630	12,013	10,617	..	..	..
5—10	20,379	11,106	9,273	3,066	2,010	1,056	17,313	9,096	8,217	368	245	123
10—15	18,904	10,639	8,265	4,742	3,193	1,549	14,162	7,446	6,716	709	486	223
15—20	18,245	11,902	6,343	6,913	5,315	1,598	11,332	6,587	4,745	1,063	846	217
20 and over	113,436	81,389	32,047	46,997	41,655	5,342	66,439	39,734	26,705	3,814	3,441	373
Indian Hindus	**565,609**	**425,389**	**140,220**	**148,143**	**135,525**	**12,618**	**417,466**	**289,864**	**127,602**	**23,249**	**21,145**	**2,104**
0—5	48,397	24,303	24,094	..	..	..	48,397	24,303	24,094	..	..	..
5—10	40,154	22,646	17,508	4,645	3,334	1,311	35,509	19,312	16,197	1,082	740	342
10—15	38,668	24,136	14,532	7,419	5,716	1,703	31,249	18,420	12,829	1,686	1,238	448
15—20	57,078	42,856	14,222	16,258	14,185	2,073	40,820	28,671	12,149	2,810	2,420	390
20 and over	381,312	311,448	69,864	119,821	112,290	7,531	261,491	199,158	62,333	17,671	16,747	924
Indian Muslims	**396,594**	**271,514**	**125,080**	**98,384**	**92,276**	**6,108**	**298,210**	**179,238**	**118,972**	**10,366**	**9,991**	**375**
0—5	47,431	23,682	23,749	..	..	..	47,431	23,682	23,749	..	..	..
5—10	40,941	22,185	18,756	3,046	2,366	680	37,895	19,819	18,076	260	224	36
10—15	38,086	22,281	15,805	4,856	3,959	897	33,230	18,322	14,908	491	428	63
15—20	41,993	28,718	13,275	10,793	9,746	1,047	31,200	18,972	12,228	1,159	1,073	86
20 and over	228 143	174,648	53,495	79,689	76,205	3,484	148,454	98,443	50,011	8,456	8,266	190
Other Indians	**55,622**	**37,008**	**18,614**	**23,111**	**18,153**	**4,958**	**32,511**	**18,855**	**13,656**	**8,850**	**6,800**	**2,050**
0—5	6,415	3,149	3,266	..	..	..	6,415	3,149	3,266	..	..	..
5—10	5,404	2,906	2,498	1,325	780	545	4,079	2,126	1,953	538	321	217
10—15	5,026	2,865	2,161	1,868	1,159	709	3,158	1,706	1,452	838	517	321
15—20	5,565	3,594	1,971	2,849	2,040	809	2,716	1,554	1,162	1,166	794	372
20 and over	33,212	24,494	8,718	17,069	14,174	2,895	16,143	10,320	5,823	6,308	5,168	1,140
Indo-Burman Races	**182,166**	**90,307**	**91,859**	**43,693**	**29,956**	**13,737**	**138,473**	**60,351**	**78,122**	**6,171**	**5,512**	**659**
0—5	31,351	15,705	15,646	..	..	..	31,351	15,705	15,646	..	..	..
5—10	26,929	13,405	13,524	3,770	2,316	1,454	23,159	11,089	12,070	344	268	76
10—15	23,975	12,037	11,938	5,428	3,406	2,022	18,547	8,631	9,916	665	531	134
15—20	18,119	8,370	9,749	6,208	3,971	2,237	11,911	4,399	7,512	1,007	867	140
20 and over	81,792	40,790	41,002	28,287	20,263	8,024	53,505	20,527	32,978	4,155	3,846	309

Others	**33,890**	**19,605**	**14,285**	**27,190**	**16,161**	**11,029**	**6,700**	**3,444**	**3,256**	**24,778**	**14,629**	**10,149**
0—5	3,730	1,914	1,816	—	..	..	3,730	1,914	1,816	..	..	..
5—10	3,374	1,702	1,672	1,990	991	999	1,384	711	673	1,775	882	893
10—15	3,215	1,607	1,608	2,568	1,277	1,291	647	330	317	2,365	1,172	1,193
15—20	3,267	1,808	1,459	3,101	1,725	1,376	166	83	83	2,913	1,624	1,289
20 and over	20,304	12,574	7,730	19,531	12,168	7,363	773	406	367	17,725	10,951	6,774

Table XIII.—Literacy by Religion and Age—Part II—By Provinces and States.

Ajmer-Merwara.

All Religions	**560,292**	**296,081**	**264,211**	**59,261**	**51,478**	**7,783**	**501,031**	**244,603**	**256,428**	**12,900**	**11,334**	**1,566**
0—5	85,055	42,276	42,779	..	..	..	85,055	42,276	42,779	..	..	..
5—10	68,572	36,408	32,164	3,857	3,017	840	64,715	33,391	31,324	540	408	132
10—15	63,558	34,404	29,154	6,007	4,802	1,205	57,551	29,602	27,949	1,100	894	206
15—20	55,704	29,565	26,139	8,129	6,864	1,265	47,575	22,701	24,874	2,152	1,901	251
20 and over	287,403	153,428	133,975	41,268	36,795	4,473	246,135	116,633	129,502	9,108	8,131	977

Andaman and Nicobar Islands.

All Religions	**27,943**	**18,885**	**9,058**	**4,149**	**3,815**	**334**	**23,794**	**15,070**	**8,724**	**961**	**875**	**86**
0—5	3,608	1,812	1,796	..	..	..	3,608	1,812	1,796	..	..	..
5—10	2,409	1,324	1,085	60	40	20	2,349	1,284	1,065	15	10	5
10—15	1,995	1,116	879	190	143	47	1,805	973	832	53	43	10
15—20	1,918	1,147	771	268	215	53	1,650	932	718	112	102	10
20 and over	18,013	13,486	4,527	3,631	3,417	214	14,382	10,069	4,313	781	720	61

Assam (*inclusive of Assam States*).

All Religions	**9,247,857**	**4,844,133**	**4,403,724**	**697,498**	**661,365**	**81,133**	**8,550,359**	**4,227,768**	**4,322,591**	**94,835**	**89,389**	**5,446**
0—5	1,596,177	789,069	807,108	..	..	..	1,596,177	789,069	807,108	..	..	..
5—10	1,249,517	653,574	595,943	51,990	41,072	10,918	1,197,527	612,502	585,025	2,978	2,477	501
10—15	1,056,778	555,922	500,856	77,733	62,749	14,984	979,045	493,173	485,872	7,416	6,509	907
15—20	850,665	403,581	447,084	91,083	76,189	14,894	759,582	327,392	432,190	15,052	13,952	1,100
20 and over	4,494,720	2,441,987	2,052,733	476,692	436,355	40,337	4,018,028	2,005,632	2,012,396	69,389	66,451	2,938
Hindu	**5,204,650**	**2,751,657**	**2,452,993**	**482,354**	**432,102**	**50,252**	**4,722,296**	**2,319,555**	**2,402,741**	**67,941**	**65,244**	**2,697**
0—5	865,791	429,587	436,204	..	..	..	865,791	429,587	436,204	..	..	..
5—10	674,444	351,440	323,004	35,110	28,285	6,825	639,334	323,155	316,179	2,038	1,712	326
10—15	568,907	299,155	269,752	52,488	43,101	9,387	516,419	256,054	260,365	5,225	4,634	591
15—20	464,386	226,088	238,298	61,771	52,912	8,859	402,615	173,176	229,439	10,869	10,244	625
20 and over	2,631,122	1,445,387	1,185,735	332,985	307,804	25,181	2,298,137	1,137,583	1,160,554	49,809	48,654	1,155
Muslim	**2,780,514**	**1,461,762**	**1,318,752**	**156,650**	**139,290**	**17,360**	**2,623,864**	**1,322,472**	**1,301,392**	**16,897**	**16,309**	**588**
0—5	499,633	245,617	254,016	..	..	..	499,633	245,617	254,016	..	..	..
5—10	405,758	216,128	189,630	13,664	10,618	3,046	392,094	205,510	186,584	659	592	67
10—15	345,938	184,848	161,090	19,290	15,578	3,712	326,648	169,270	157,378	1,566	1,441	125
15—20	272,957	125,589	147,368	19,939	16,723	3,216	253,018	108,866	144,152	2,794	2,647	147
20 and over	1,256,228	689,580	566,648	103,757	96,371	7,386	1,152,471	593,209	559,262	11,878	11,629	246
Tribal	**992,390**	**493,755**	**498,635**	**14,094**	**12,538**	**1,556**	**978,296**	**481,217**	**497,079**	**956**	**900**	**56**
0—5	185,517	91,467	94,050	..	..	—	185,517	91,467	94,050	..	—	—
5—10	132,624	67,434	65,190	761	600	161	131,863	66,834	65,029	22	17	5
10—15	109,025	55,153	53,872	1,312	1,077	235	107,713	54,076	53,637	68	59	9
15—20	86,077	39,102	46,975	2,142	1,832	310	83,935	37,270	46,665	163	150	13
20 and over	479,147	240,5992	38,548	9,879	9,029	850	469,268	231,570	237,698	703	674	29

Table XIII.—Literacy by Religion and Age—Part II—By Provinces and States—*contd.*

Age and Religion. 1	Total. Persons. 2	Total. Males. 3	Total. Females. 4	Literate. Persons. 5	Literate. Males. 6	Literate. Females. 7	Illiterate. Persons. 8	Illiterate. Males. 9	Illiterate. Females. 10	Literate in English. Persons. 11	Literate in English. Males. 12	Literate in English. Females. 13
Baluchistan (*inclusive of Baluchistan States*).												
All Religions	**868,617**	**488,414**	**380,203**	**40,775**	**36,835**	**3,940**	**827,842**	**451,579**	**376,263**	**11,588**	**10,063**	**1,525**
0—5	11,356	5,793	5,563	..	..	..	11,356	5,793	5,563	..	..	..
5—10	8,484	4,682	3,802	1,290	871	419	7,194	3,811	3,383	354	222	132
10—15	7,764	4,539	3,225	1,904	1,357	547	5,860	3,182	2,678	583	421	162
15—20	14,260	10,686	3,574	5,386	4,813	573	8,874	5,873	3,001	1,619	1,473	146
20 and over	68,985	54,497	14,488	24,654	22,322	2,332	44,331	32,175	12,156	8,922	7,837	1,085
Age unspecified	757,768	408,217	349,551	7,541	7,472	69	750,227	400,745	349,482	110	110	..
Bengal.												
All Religions	**50,114,002**	**26,041,698**	**24,072,304**	**4,693,713**	**4,033,262**	**660,451**	**45,420,289**	**22,008,436**	**23,411,853**	**1,058,978**	**960,396**	**98,582**
0—5	7,785,719	3,847,275	3,938,444	..	..	..	7,785,719	3,847,275	3,938,444	..	..	..
5—10	6,726,769	3,563,257	3,163,512	340,766	264,394	76,372	6,386,003	3,298,863	3,087,140	62,527	52,244	10,283
10—15	5,903,139	3,117,274	2,785,865	500,943	398,160	102,783	5.402,196	2,719,114	2,683,082	112,926	96,629	16,297
15—20	4,825,066	2,281,751	2,543,315	608,500	502,436	106,064	4,216,566	1,779.315	2,437,251	165,555	148,165	17,390
20 and over	24,873,309	13,232,141	11,641,168	3,243,504	2,868,272	375,232	21,629,805	10,363,869	11,265,936	717.970	663,358	54,612
Muslim	**27,497,624**	**14,200,142**	**13,297,482**	**1,572,607**	**1,383,814**	**188,793**	**25,925,017**	**12,816,328**	**13,108,689**	**263,847**	**245,348**	**18,499**
0—5	4,603,626	2,269,507	2,334,119	..	..	..	4,603,626	2.269,507	2,334,119	..	..	..
5—10	3,953,395	2,089,461	1,863,934	115,308	90,183	25,125	3,838,087	1,999,278	1,838,809	16,525	14,497	2,028
10—15	3,421,242	1,796,341	1,624,901	165,470	131,511	33,959	3,255,772	1,664,830	1,590,942	30,037	26,576	3,461
15—20	2,663,891	1,220,182	1,443,709	197,182	162,793	34,389	2,466,709	1,057,389	1,409,320	42,421	38,397	4,024
20 and over	12,855,470	6,824,651	6,030,819	1,094,647	999,327	95,320	11,760,823	5,825,324	5,935,499	174,864	165,878	8,986
Hindu	**21,570,407**	**11,299,914**	**10,270,493**	**3,013,687**	**2,575,897**	**437,790**	**18,556,720**	**8,724,017**	**9,832,703**	**736,671**	**678,855**	**57,816**
0—5	3,010,639	1,493,395	1,517,244	..	..	..	3,010,639	1,493,395	1,517,244	..	..	..
5—10	2,631,341	1,400,316	1,231,025	217,732	169,567	48,165	2,413,609	1,230,749	1,182,860	41,769	35,402	6,367
10—15	2,359,554	1,257,707	1,101,847	324,849	260,076	64,773	2,034,705	997,631	1,037,074	77,085	66,717	10,368
15—20	2,065,205	1,015,875	1,049,330	398,112	331,104	67,008	1,667,093	684.771	982,322	115,816	105,313	10,503
20 and over	11,503,668	6,132,621	5,371,047	2,072,994	1,815,150	257,844	9,430,674	4,317,471	5,113,203	502,001	471,423	30,578
Tribal	**528,037**	**268,757**	**259,280**	**3,874**	**3,069**	**805**	**524,163**	**265,688**	**258,475**	**208**	**196**	**12**
0—5	90,995	43,866	47,129	..	..	..	90,995	43,866	47,129	..	..	..
5—10	74,844	38,210	36,634	262	203	59	74,582	38,007	36,575	11	11	..
10—15	61,641	31,470	30,171	354	275	79	61,287	31,195	30,092	21	20	1
15—20	45,653	20,633	25,020	464	352	112	45,189	20,281	24,908	40	37	3
20 and over	254,904	134,578	120,326	2,794	2,239	555	252,110	132,339	119,771	136	128	8
Bihar and Orissa.												
All Religions	**37,677,576**	**18,794,138**	**18,883,438**	**1,703,866**	**1,574,506**	**129,360**	**35,973,710**	**17,219,632**	**18,754,078**	**169,934**	**157,149**	**12,785**
0—5	5,602,595	2,733,705	2,868,890	..	..	..	5,602,595	2,733,705	2,868,890	..	..	..
5—10	5,073,200	2,642,921	2,430,279	110,519	96,529	13,990	4,962,681	2,546,392	2,416,289	7,309	6,162	1,147
10—15	4,346,269	2,302,350	2,043,919	171,010	152,408	18,602	4,175,259	2,149,942	2,025,317	14,633	12,968	1,665
15—20	3,184,908	1,563,970	1,620,938	209,745	190,275	19,470	2,975,163	1,373,695	1,601,468	25,814	23,919	1,895
20 and over	19,470,604	9,551,192	9,919,412	1,212,592	1,135,294	77,298	18,258,012	8,415,898	9,842,114	122,178	114,100	8,078
Hindu	**31,011,474**	**15,493,257**	**15,518,217**	**1,452,130**	**1,357,929**	**94,201**	**29,559,344**	**14,135,328**	**15,424,016**	**127,566**	**121,586**	**5,980**
0—5	4,513,741	2,202,748	2,310,993	..	..	..	4,513,741	2,302,748	2,310,993	..	..	..
5—10	4,099,789	2,139,192	1,960,597	91,461	81,690	9,771	4,008,328	2,057,502	1,950,826	5,083	4,532	551
10—15	3,532,662	1,876,406	1,655,956	142,974	129,874	13,100	3,389,388	1,746,532	1,642,856	10,616	9,769	847
15—20	2,619,681	1,294,711	1,324,970	178,334	164,148	14,186	2,441,347	1,130,563	1,310,784	19,561	18,600	961
20 and over	16,245,901	7,980,200	8,265,701	1,039,361	982,217	57,144	15,206,540	6,997,983	8,208,557	92,306	88,685	3,621

Tribal	**2,048,809**	**1,011,522**	**1,037,287**	**11,834**	**10,563**	**1,271**	**2,036,975**	**1,000,959**	**1,036,016**	**721**	**692**	**29**
0—5	362,146	176,028	186,118	..	..	..	362,146	176,028	186,118	..	..	..
5—10	303,082	155,073	148,009	1,010	833	177	302,072	154,240	147,832	58	57	1
10—15	254,468	130,784	123,684	1,485	1,313	172	252,983	129,471	123,512	91	89	2
15—20	177,446	83,539	93,907	1,614	1,462	152	175,832	82,077	93,755	127	121	6
20 and over	951,667	466,098	485,569	7,725	6,955	770	943,942	459,143	484,799	445	425	2

Bombay. *

All Religions	**21,801,745**	**11,471,543**	**10,330,202**	**2,003,385**	**1,730,010**	**273,375**	**19,798,360**	**9,741,533**	**10,056,827**	**370,840**	**318,138**	**57,702**
0—5	3,248,579	1,617,255	1,631,324	..	..	..	3,248,579	1,617,255	1,631,324	..	..	..
5—10	2,819,745	1,486,771	1,332,974	127,262	99,394	27,868	2,692,483	1,387,377	1,305,106	11,155	7,618	3,537
10—15	2,476,229	1,331,194	1,145,035	211,253	168,834	42,419	2,264,976	1,162,360	1,102,616	25,100	18,529	6,571
15—20	1,951,538	1,002,201	949,337	279,783	232,850	46,933	1,671,755	769,351	902,404	56,247	46,067	10,180
20 and over	11,305,654	6,034,122	5,271,532	1,385,087	1,228,932	156,155	9,920,567	4,805,190	5,115,377	278,338	240,924	37,414
Hindu	**16,616,819**	**8,606,594**	**8,010,225**	**1,483,319**	**1,310,401**	**172,918**	**15,133,500**	**7,296,193**	**7,837,307**	**209,274**	**194,603**	**14,671**
0—5	2,492,274	1,233,764	1,258,510	..	..	..	2,492,274	1,233,764	1,258,510	..	..	..
5—10	2,156,820	1,123,360	1,033,460	95,907	76,816	19,091	2,060,913	1,046,544	1,014,369	4,429	3,588	841
10—15	1,909,166	1,010,748	898,418	161,796	132,383	29,413	1,747,370	878,365	869,005	13,048	10,929	2,119
15—20	1,492,973	751,488	741,485	211,589	179,790	31,799	1,281,384	571,698	709,686	33,756	30,196	3,560
20 and over	8,565,586	4,487,234	4,078,352	1,014,027	921,412	92,615	7,551,559	3,565,822	3,985,737	158,041	149,890	8,151
Muslim	**4,414,048**	**2,447,438**	**1,966,610**	**279,182**	**253,129**	**26,053**	**4,134,866**	**2,194,309**	**1,940,557**	**31,735**	**30,092**	**1,643**
0—5	653,738	332,418	321,320	..	..	..	653,738	332,418	321,320	..	..	..
5—10	570,644	315,716	254,928	16,506	13,516	2,990	554,138	302,200	251,938	777	617	160
10—15	480,678	275,043	205,635	26,624	22,289	4,335	454,054	252,754	201,300	1,885	1,755	130
15—20	383,406	210,242	173,164	36,867	32,396	4,471	346,539	177,846	168,693	5,091	4,711	380
20 and over	2,325,582	1,314,019	1,011,563	199,185	184,928	14,257	2,126,397	1,129,091	997,306	23,982	23,009	973
Jain	**199,808**	**109,633**	**90,175**	**60,680**	**52,332**	**8,348**	**139,128**	**57,301**	**81,827**	**7,624**	**7,371**	**253**
0—5	25,790	12,777	13,013	..	..	..	25,790	12,777	13,013	..	..	..
5—10	23,601	12,316	11,285	3,794	2,800	994	19,807	9,516	10,291	262	245	17
10—15	22,438	12,122	10,316	6,165	4,713	1,452	16,273	7,409	8,864	653	616	37
15—20	19,401	10,849	8,552	8,245	6,731	1,514	11,156	4,118	7,038	1,285	1,223	62
20 and over	108,578	61,569	47,009	12,476	38,088	4,388	66,102	23,481	42,621	5,424	5,287	137
Zoroastrian (Parsi)	**†89,199**	**46,166**	**43,033**	**64,607**	**35,859**	**28,748**	**24,590**	**10,307**	**14,283**	**42,306**	**27,718**	**14,588**
0—5	7,171	3,602	3,569	..	..	..	7,171	3,602	3,569	..	..	..
5—10	8,098	4,200	3,898	3,483	1,890	1,593	4,615	2,310	2,305	1,420	799	621
10—15	8,452	4,426	4,026	5,335	2,872	2,463	3,117	1,554	1,563	2,784	1,585	1,199
15—20	8,227	4,246	3,981	6,938	3,695	3,243	1,289	551	738	5,011	2,943	2,068
20 and over	57,249	29,692	27,557	48,851	27,402	21,449	8,398	2,290	6,108	33,091	22,391	10,700

Aden.

All Religions	**51,456**	**32,325**	**19,131**	**8,585**	**7,803**	**782**	**42,871**	**24,522**	**18,349**	**3,342**	**2,865**	**477**
0—5	4,172	2,136	2,036	..	..	..	4,172	2,136	2,036	..	..	..
5—10	4,848	2,593	2,255	157	104	53	4,691	2,489	2,202	62	33	29
10—15	4,456	2,875	1,581	524	446	78	3,932	2,429	1,503	139	95	44
15—20	4,876	3,007	1,869	799	689	110	4,077	2,318	1,759	304	244	60
20 and over	33,104	21,714	11,390	7,105	6,564	541	25,999	15,150	10,849	2,837	2,493	344

* Excluding Aden.

† Includes 2 females for whom these details were not available.

TABLE XIII.—Literacy by Religion and Age—Part II—By Provinces and States—*contd.*

Age and Religion.	Population. Total.			Literate.			Illiterate.			Literate in English.		
	Persons.	Males.	Females.	Persons.	Males.	Females.	Persons.	Males.	Females.	Persons.	Males.	Females.
1	2	3	4	5	6	7	8	9	10	11	12	13
Central Provinces and Berar.												
All Religions	**15,507,723**	**7,761,818**	**7,745,905**	**867,765**	**790,981**	**76,784**	**14,639,958**	**6,970,837**	**7,669,121**	**91,273**	**81,964**	**9,309**
0—5	2,424,149	1,188,162	1,235,987	..	..	..	2,424,149	1,188,162	1,235,987	..	..	..
5—10	1,958,964	998,119	960,845	58,237	48,740	9,497	1,900,727	949,379	951,348	3,512	2,626	886
10—15	1,755,245	903,256	851,989	94,332	81,338	12,994	1,660,913	821,918	838,995	7,574	6,242	1,332
15—20	1,398,959	683,585	715,374	125,708	112,266	13,442	1,273,251	571,319	701,932	15,288	13,582	1,706
20 and over	7,970,406	3,988,696	3,981,710	589,488	548,637	40,851	7,380,918	3,440,059	3,940,859	64,899	59,514	5,385
Hindu	**13,338,223**	**6,671,326**	**6,666,897**	**717,668**	**665,184**	**52,484**	**12,620,555**	**6,006,142**	**6,614,413**	**62,239**	**59,221**	**3,018**
0—5	2,075,275	1,017,955	1,057,320	..	..	..	2,075,275	1,017,955	1,057,320	..	..	..
5—10	1,681,203	856,644	824,559	47,207	40,569	6,638	1,633,996	816,075	817,921	1,662	1,436	226
10—15	1,510,768	777,552	733,216	77,823	68,776	9,047	1,432,945	708,776	724,169	4,941	4,479	462
15—20	1,201,358	587,223	614,135	103,821	94,742	9,079	1,097,537	492,481	605,056	10,782	10,097	685
20 and over	6,869,619	3,431,952	3,437,667	488,817	461,097	27,720	6,380,802	2,970,855	3,409,947	44,854	43,209	1,645
Tribal	**1,351,615**	**660,755**	**690,860**	**6,769**	**6,444**	**325**	**1,344,846**	**654,311**	**690,535**	**115**	**113**	**2**
0—5	222,507	107,787	114,720	..	..	..	222,507	107,787	114,720	..	..	..
5—10	171,381	86,730	84,651	459	431	28	170,922	86,299	84,623	3	3	..
10—15	149,696	76,082	73,614	766	722	44	148,930	75,360	73,570	9	8	1
15—20	119,035	55,405	63,630	935	877	58	118,100	54,528	63,572	21	20	1
20 and over	688,996	334,751	354,245	4,609	4,414	195	684,387	330,337	354,050	82	82	..
Muslim	**682,854**	**358,900**	**323,954**	**90,515**	**80,973**	**9,542**	**592,339**	**277,927**	**314,412**	**11,004**	**10,703**	**301**
0—5	107,067	52,829	54,238	..	..	..	107,067	52,829	54,238	..	..	..
5—10	90,157	46,468	43,689	6,298	5,194	1,104	83,859	41,274	42,585	545	520	25
10—15	79,458	41,711	37,747	9,579	8,041	1,538	69,879	33,670	36,209	894	857	37
15—20	64,620	33,613	31,007	13,089	11,304	1,785	51,531	22,309	29,222	1,764	1,704	60
20 and over	341,552	184,279	157,273	61,549	56,434	5,115	280,003	127,845	152,158	7,801	7,622	179
Coorg.												
All Religions	**163,327**	**90,575**	**72,752**	**25,336**	**19,892**	**5,444**	**137,991**	**70,683**	**67,308**	**3,982**	**3,279**	**703**
0—5	19,522	9,668	9,854	..	..	..	19,522	9,668	9,854	..	..	..
5—10	18,616	9,527	9,089	1,531	1,025	506	17,085	8,502	8,583	159	99	60
10—15	18,954	9,993	8,961	2,622	1,777	845	16,332	8,216	8,116	387	266	121
15—20	16,639	9,129	7,510	3,527	2,499	1,028	13,112	6,630	6,482	688	524	164
20 and over	89,596	52,258	37,338	17,656	14,591	3,065	71,940	37,667	34,273	2,748	2,390	358
Delhi.												
ll Religions	**636,246**	**369,497**	**266,749**	**89,472**	**73,377**	**16,095**	**546,774**	**296,120**	**250,654**	**33,185**	**29,105**	**4,086**
0—5	87,706	44,478	43,228	..	..	..	87,706	44,478	43,228	..	..	..
5—10	72,429	39,366	33,063	4,575	3,124	1,451	67,854	36,242	31,612	932	637	295
10—15	71,057	39,683	31,374	7,986	5,758	2,228	63,071	33,925	29,146	2,073	1,609	464
15—20	68,674	39,707	28,967	12,698	10,077	2,621	55,976	29,630	26,346	5,060	4,411	649
20 and over	336,380	206,263	130,117	64,213	54,418	9,795	272,167	151,845	120,322	25,120	22,448	2,672

Madras.

All Religions	**46,740,107**	**23,082,999**	**23,657,108**	**4,318,880**	**3,706,975**	**611,905**	**42,421,227**	**19,376,024**	**23,045,203**	**579,364**	**508,309**	**71,055**
0— 5	6,779,600	3,332,988	3,446,612	..	..	..	6,779,600	3,332,988	3,446,612	..	..	..
5—10	6,010,063	3,031,434	2,978,629	253,083	193,053	60,030	5,756,980	2,838,381	2,918,599	24,344	18,575	5,769
10—15	5,422,941	2,777,955	2,644,986	432,871	336,526	96,345	4,990,070	2,441,429	2,548,641	53,347	42,962	10,385
15—20	4,177,902	2,008,379	2,169,523	583,392	473,505	109,887	3,594,510	1,534,874	2,059,636	100,291	86,154	14,137
20 and over	24,349,601	11,932,243	12,417,358	3,049,534	2,703,891	345,643	21,300,067	9,228,352	12,071,715	401,382	360,618	40,764
Hindu	**41,277,410**	**20,380,283**	**20,897,127**	**3,642,343**	**3,173,642**	**468,701**	**37,635,067**	**17,206,641**	**20,428,426**	**435,268**	**406,715**	**28,553**
0— 5	5,935,319	2,913,771	3,021,548	..	..	..	5,935,319	2,913,771	3,021,548	..	..	..
5—10	5,271,868	2,656,440	2,615,428	208,271	162,624	45,647	5,063,597	2,493,816	2,569,781	16,705	14,114	2,591
10—15	4,754,569	2,437,571	2,316,998	358,261	284,511	73,750	4,396,308	2,153,060	2,243,248	38,712	33,974	4,738
15—20	3,664,287	1,766,949	1,897,338	486,826	402,147	84,679	3,177,461	1,364,802	1,812,659	75,867	69,626	6,241
20 and over	21,651,367	10,605,552	11,045,815	2,588,985	2,324,360	264,625	19,062,382	8,281,192	10,781,190	303,984	289,001	14,983
Muslim	**3,305,938**	**1,631,716**	**1,674,222**	**343,528**	**313,810**	**29,718**	**2,962,410**	**1,317,906**	**1,644,504**	**32,269**	**30,835**	**1,434**
0— 5	519,443	259,412	260,031	..	..	..	519,443	259,412	260,031	..	..	..
5—10	451,417	230,328	221,089	18,046	14,828	3,218	433,371	215,500	217,871	1,060	901	159
10—15	412,029	210,018	202,011	32,010	26,925	5,085	380,019	183,093	196,926	2,461	2,226	235
15—20	315,493	147,883	167,610	46,060	40,550	5,510	269,433	107,333	162,100	5,261	4,959	302
20 and over	1,607,556	784,075	823,481	247,412	231,507	15,905	1,360,144	552,568	807,576	23,487	22,749	738
Christian	**1,774,299**	**878,513**	**895,786**	**320,052**	**208,154**	**111,898**	**1,454,247**	**670,359**	**783,888**	**110,106**	**69,268**	**40,838**
0— 5	265,464	130,888	134,576	..	..	..	265,464	130,888	134,576	..	..	..
5—10	236,353	118,[illegible]	117,391	26,084	15,101	10,983	210,269	103,861	106,408	6,485	3,495	2,990
10—15	214,586	108,719	105,867	41,412	24,157	17,255	173,174	84,562	88,612	12,013	6,634	5,379
15—20	165,443	78,511	86,932	48,577	29,176	19,401	117,866	49,335	67,531	18,857	11,295	7,562
20 and over	892,453	441,433	451,020	203,979	139,720	64,259	688,474	301,713	386,761	72,751	47,844	24,907

Punjab.

All Religions	**23,580,852**	**12,880,510**	**10,700,342**	**1,247,757**	**1,097,044**	**150,713**	**22,333,095**	**11,783,466**	**10,549,629**	**249,607**	**230,390**	**19,217**
0— 5	3,740,549	1,909,178	1,831,371	..	..	..	3,740,549	1,909,178	1,831,371	..	..	..
5—10	3,143,832	[illegible],691,328	1,452,504	64,051	50,810	13,241	3,079,781	1,640,518	1,439,263	7,089	5,759	1,330
10—15	2,851,094	1,571,550	1,279,544	131,389	108,112	23,277	2,719,705	1,463,438	1,256,267	20,996	18,522	2,474
15—20	2,190,257	1,203,432	986,825	198,402	169,647	28,755	1,991,855	1,033,785	958,070	50,197	46,499	3,698
20 and over	11,655,120	6,505,022	5,150,098	853,915	768,475	85,440	10,801,205	5,736,547	5,064,658	171,325	159,610	11,715
Muslim	**13,332,460**	**7,241,612**	**6,090,848**	**393,659**	**353,305**	**40,354**	**12,938,801**	**6,888,307**	**6,050,494**	**81,341**	**76,334**	**5,007**
0— 5	2,184,488	1,113,879	1,070,609	..	..	..	2,184,488	1,113,879	1,070,609	..	..	..
5—10	1,822,654	978,898	843,756	22,965	19,444	3,521	1,799,689	959,454	840,235	2,511	2,184	327
10—15	1,610,827	887,055	723,772	46,645	40,424	6,221	1,564,182	846,631	717,551	6,964	6,317	647
15—20	1,210,478	659,280	551,198	67,746	59,896	7,850	1,142,732	599,384	543,348	16,312	15,238	1,074
20 and over	6,504,013	3,602,500	2,901,513	256,303	233,541	22,762	6,247,710	3,368,959	2,878,751	55,554	52,595	2,959
Hindu	**6,328,588**	**3,465,534**	**2,863,054**	**556,636**	**494,710**	**61,926**	**5,771,952**	**2,970,824**	**2,801,128**	**101,905**	**97,311**	**4,594**
0— 5	950,275	481,960	468,315	..	..	..	950,275	481,960	468,315	..	..	..
5—10	806,808	430,878	375,930	26,022	20,342	5,680	780,786	410,536	370,250	2,188	1,902	286
10—15	765,555	419,127	346,428	54,146	44,199	9,947	711,409	374,928	336,481	7,916	7,275	641
15—20	617,594	340,821	276,773	84,720	72,697	12,023	532,874	268,124	264,750	20,169	19,139	1,030
20 and over	3,188,356	1,792,748	1,395,608	391,748	357,472	34,276	2,796,608	1,435,276	1,361,332	71,632	68,995	2,637
Sikh	**3,064,144**	**1,703,584**	**1,360,560**	**247,313**	**211,828**	**35,485**	**2,816,831**	**1,491,756**	**1,325,075**	**42,180**	**39,833**	**2,347**
0— 5	462,939	240,647	222,292	..	..	..	462,939	240,647	222,292	..	..	..
5—10	395,365	217,179	178,186	12,270	9,346	2,924	383,095	207,833	175,262	1,253	1,079	174
10—15	366,576	205,771	160,805	25,886	20,527	5,359	340,690	185,244	155,446	4,348	3,964	384
15—20	280,813	158,524	122,289	38,030	31,260	6,770	242,783	127,264	115,519	9,852	9,246	606
20 nd aover	1,558,451	881,463	676,988	171,127	150,695	20,432	1,387,324	730,768	656,556	26,727	25,544	1,183

Table XIII.—Literacy by Religion and Age—Part II—By Provinces and States—*contd.*

Age and Religion.	Total.			Population Literate.			Illiterate.			Literate in English.		
	Persons.	Males.	Females.	Persons.	Males.	Females.	Persons.	Males.	Females.	Persons.	Males.	Females.
1	2	3	4	5	6	7	8	9	10	11	12	13
North-West Frontier Province. (*Districts and Administered Territories*).												
All Religions	**2,425,076**	**1,315,818**	**1,109,258**	**100,366**	**89,058**	**11,308**	**2,324,710**	**1,226,760**	**1,097,950**	**25,717**	**23,921**	**1,796**
0—5	386,719	195,672	191,047	..	..	..	386,719	195,672	191,047	..	..	..
5—10	334,706	183,669	151,037	5,267	4,102	1,165	329,439	179,567	149,872	709	552	157
10—15	288,425	163,622	124,803	8,880	7,230	1,650	279,545	156,392	123,153	1,529	1,351	178
15—20	215,504	117,251	98,253	15,365	13,367	1,998	200,139	103,884	96,255	4,063	3,861	202
20 and over	1,199,722	655,604	544 118	70,854	64,359	6,495	1,128,868	591,245	537,623	19,416	18,157	1,259
Muslim	**2,227,303**	**1,196,120**	**1,031,183**	**44,496**	**42,110**	**2,386**	**2,182,807**	**1,154,010**	**1,028,797**	**9,122**	**8.909**	**213**
0—5	358,736	181,479	177,257	..	..	..	358,736	181,479	177,257	..	..	..
5—10	312,253	171,728	140,525	2,640	2,386	254	309,613	169,342	140,271	231	207	24
10—15	268,655	152,709	115,946	4,598	4,205	393	264,057	148,504	115,553	677	638	39
15—20	193,848	103,440	90,408	7,088	6,636	452	186,760	96,804	89,956	1,766	1,721	45
20 and over	1,093,811	586,764	507,047	30,170	28,883	1,287	1,063,641	557,881	505,760	6,448	6,343	105
United Provinces of Agra and Oudh.												
All Religions	**48,408,763**	**25,445,006**	**22,963,757**	**2,259,638**	**2,043,410**	**216,228**	**46,149,125**	**23,401,596**	**22,747,529**	**266,167**	**240,140**	**26,027**
0—5	7,332,871	3,653,528	3,679,343	..	..	..	7,332,871	3,653,528	3,679,343	..	..	..
5—10	6,044,830	3,246,268	2,798,562	139,971	119,466	20,505	5,904,859	3,126,802	2,778,057	11,187	9,021	2,166
10—15	5,461,379	3,008,463	2,452,916	246,328	214,601	31,727	5,215,051	2,793,862	2,421,189	23,251	20,023	3,228
15—20	4,317,976	2,303,535	2,014,441	312,286	276,783	35,503	4,005,690	2,026,752	1,978,938	44,555	40,636	3,919
20 and over	25,251,707	13,233,212	12,018,495	1,561,053	1,432,560	128,493	23,690,654	11,800,652	11,890,002	187,174	170,460	16,714
Hindu	**40,905,586**	**21,488,425**	**19,417,161**	**1,823,849**	**1,676,893**	**146,956**	**39,081,737**	**19,811,532**	**19,270,205**	**171,904**	**162,601**	**9,303**
0—5	6,156,237	3,064,001	3,092,236	..	..	..	6,156,237	3,064,001	3,092,236	..	..	..
5—10	5,065,415	2,722,556	2,342,859	112,675	98,625	14,050	4,952,740	2,623,931	2,328,809	6,621	5,817	804
10—15	4,598,142	2,542,701	2,055,441	200,788	178,932	21,856	4,397,354	2,363,769	2,033,585	15,430	14,149	1,281
15—20	3,628,131	1,940,138	1,687,993	250,402	226,082	24,320	3,377,729	1,714,056	1,663,673	29,309	27,732	1,577
20 and over	21,457,661	11,219,029	10,238,632	1,259,984	1,173,254	86,730	20,197,677	10,045,775	10,151,902	120,544	114,903	5,641
Muslim	**7,181,927**	**3,780,453**	**3,401,474**	**357,674**	**311,569**	**46,105**	**6,824,253**	**3,468,884**	**3,355,369**	**49,392**	**47,740**	**1,652**
0—5	1,129,361	565,389	563,972	..	..	..	1,129,361	565,389	563,972	..	..	..
5—10	941,075	503,226	437,849	21,691	17,650	4,041	919,384	485,576	433,808	1,886	1,735	151
10—15	828,100	446,690	381,410	37,695	31,034	6,661	790,405	415,656	374,749	4,000	3,747	253
15—20	657,155	344,912	312,243	50,717	42,694	8,023	606,438	302,218	304,220	8,179	7,823	356
20 and over	3,626,236	1,920,236	1,706,000	247,571	220,191	27,380	3,378,665	1,700,045	1,678,620	35,327	34,435	892
Christian	**205,009**	**111,650**	**93,359**	**50,286**	**31,454**	**18,832**	**154,723**	**80,196**	**74,527**	**40,437**	**25,820**	**14,617**
0—5	30,734	15,593	15,141	..	..	..	30,734	15,593	15,141	..	..	..
5—10	24,842	13,167	11,675	3,988	1,976	2,012	20,854	11,191	9,663	2,458	1,288	1,170
10—15	22,574	12,153	10,421	5,333	2,682	2,651	17,241	9,471	7,770	3,437	1,791	1,646
15—20	21,424	12.138	9,286	7,557	5,042	2,515	13,867	7,096	6,771	6,275	4,359	1,916
20 and over	105,435	58,599	46,836	33,408	21,754	11,654	72,027	36,845	35,182	28,267	18,382	9,885
Baroda State.												
All Religions	**2,443,007**	**1,257,817**	**1,185,190**	**434,734**	**355,067**	**79,667**	**2,008,273**	**902,750**	**1,105,523**	**32,022**	**30,218**	**1,804**
0—5	363,076	183,519	179,557	..	..	..	363,076	183,519	179,557	..	..	..
5—10	304,213	160,033	144,180	36,065	25,194	10,871	268,148	134,839	133,309	644	535	109
10—15	288,872	152,007	136,865	63,865	45,794	18,071	225,007	106,213	118,794	2,876	2,564	312
15—20	241,691	122,832	118,859	75,204	57,718	17,486	166,487	65,114	101,373	7,596	7,099	497
20 and over	1,245,155	639,426	605,729	259,600	226,361	33,239	985,555	413,065	572,490	20,906	20,020	886

Bengal States.

All Religions	**973,336**	**516,162**	**457,174**	**49,568**	**45,512**	**4,056**	**923,768**	**470,650**	**453,118**	**6,829**	**6,271**	**558**
0— 5	156,837	77,028	79,809	..	..	..	156,837	77,028	79,809	..	..	..
5—10	133,701	70,045	63,656	2,558	2,119	439	131,143	67,926	63,217	403	334	69
10—15	114,576	60,265	54,311	4,275	3,584	691	110,301	56,681	53,620	772	656	116
15—20	92,712	43,630	49,082	6,783	6,015	768	85,929	37,615	48,314	1,189	1,055	134
20 and over	475,510	265,194	210,316	35,952	33,794	2,158	439,558	231,400	208,158	4,465	4,226	239

Bihar and Orissa States.

All Religions	**4,652,007**	**2,288,422**	**2,363,585**	**149,228**	**139,505**	**9,723**	**4,502,779**	**2,148,917**	**2,353,862**	**8,767**	**8,493**	**274**
0— 5	793,063	387,577	405,486	..	..	..	793,063	387,577	405,486	..	..	..
5—10	639,001	324,669	314,332	10,286	9,056	1,230	628,715	315,613	313,102	171	161	10
10—15	547,101	283,004	264,097	15,592	13,922	1,670	531,509	269,082	262,427	493	475	18
15—20	407,132	194,563	212,569	18,133	16,664	1,469	388,999	177,899	211,100	1,337	1,297	40
20 and over	2,265,710	1,098,609	1,167,101	105,217	99,863	5,354	2,160,493	998,746	1,161,747	6,766	6,560	206
Hindu	**4,194,878**	**2,063,008**	**2,131,870**	**143,732**	**134,660**	**9,072**	**4,051,146**	**1,928,348**	**2,122,798**	**8,034**	**7,885**	**149**
0— 5	707,653	345,748	361,905	..	..	..	707,653	345,748	361,905	..	..	..
5—10	571,638	290,538	281,100	9,932	8,768	1,164	561,706	281,770	279,936	154	147	7
10—15	490,788	254,366	236,422	15,005	13,434	1,571	475,783	240,932	234,851	459	445	14
15—20	367,686	176,296	191,390	17,345	15,983	1,362	350,341	160,313	190,028	1,247	1,222	25
20 and over	2,057,113	996,060	1,061,053	101,450	96,475	4,975	1,955,663	899,585	1,056,078	6,174	6,071	103
Tribal	**360,600**	**176,918**	**183,682**	**765**	**729**	**36**	**359,835**	**176,189**	**183,646**	**24**	**22**	**2**
0— 5	68,106	33,200	34,906	..	..		68,106	33,200	34,906	..	..	..
5—10	53,055	26,808	26,247	60	57	3	52,995	26,751	26,244	1	1	..
10—15	43,761	22,205	21,556	87	82	5	43,674	22,123	21,551	2	2	..
15—20	30,585	14,076	16,509	108	103	5	30,477	13,973	16,504	5	5	..
20 and over	165,093	80,629	84,464	510	487	23	164,583	80,142	84,441	16	14	2

Bombay States.

All Religions	**4,459,944**	**2,284,451**	**2,175,493**	**266,074**	**238,052**	**28,022**	**4,193,870**	**2,046,399**	**2,147,471**	**23,823**	**22,520**	**1,303**
0— 5	702,882	344,308	358,574	..	..		702,882	344,308	358,574		..	..
5—10	624,925	326,142	298,783	18,801	15,608	3,193	606,124	310,534	295,590	525	439	86
10—15	549,465	293,940	255,525	31,929	27,026	4,903	517,536	266,914	250,622	1,930	1,711	219
15—20	389,923	200,085	189,838	39,464	34,362	5,102	350,459	165,723	184,736	5,119	4,813	306
20 and over	2,192,749	1,119,976	1,072,773	175,880	161,056	14,824	2,016,869	958,920	1,057,949	16,249	15,557	692
Hindu	**3,920,786**	**1,998,198**	**1,922,588**	**215,380**	**193,778**	**21,602**	**3,705,406**	**1,804,420**	**1,900,986**	**19,823**	**19,056**	**767**
0— 5	617,800	302,404	315,396	..	..	..	617,800	302,404	315,396			..
5—10	552,415	287,165	265,250	15,327	12,859	2,468	537,088	274,306	262,782	393	344	49
10—15	487,324	259,310	228,014	26,141	22,322	3,819	461,183	236,988	224,195	1,549	1,413	136
15—20	342,012	174,623	167,389	31,973	27,936	4,037	310,039	146,687	163,352	4,251	4,041	210
20 and over	1,921,235	974,696	946,539	141,939	130,661	11,278	1,779,296	844,035	935,261	13,630	13,258	372
Muslim	**414,921**	**221,578**	**193,343**	**28,696**	**26,098**	**2,598**	**386,225**	**195,480**	**190,745**	**1,521**	**1,491**	**30**
0— 5	65,782	32,877	32,905	..	..	..	65,782	32,877	32,905		..	..
5—10	56,871	30,682	26,189	1,811	1,528	283	55,060	29,154	25,906	43	41	2
10—15	48,137	26,904	21,233	3,056	2,626	430	45,081	24,278	20,803	136	133	3
15—20	36,602	19,545	17,057	4,155	3,731	424	32,447	15,814	16,633	331	325	6
20 and over	207,529	111,570	95,959	19,674	18,213	1,461	187,855	93,357	94,498	1,011	922	19

Table XIII.—Liter cy by Religion and Age—Part II—By Provinces and States—*contd*

Age and Religion	Total.			Population Literate.			Illiterate.			Literate in English.		
	Persons.	Males.	Females.	Persons.	Males.	Females.	Persons.	Males.	Females.	Persons.	Males.	Females.
1	2	3	4	5	6	7	8	9	10	11	12	13
Central India Agency.												
All Religions	**6,632,790**	**3,405,438**	**3,227,352**	**294,117**	**268,545**	**25,572**	**6,338,673**	**3,136,893**	**3,201,780**	**29,663**	**26,918**	**2,745**
0—5	999,700	487,999	511,701	..	..	..	999,700	487,999	511,701	..	..	..
5—10	862,419	450,538	411,881	18,426	15,580	2,846	843,993	434,958	409,035	944	710	234
10—15	794,585	423,984	370,601	29,814	25,945	3,869	764,771	398,039	366,732	2,232	1,836	396
15—20	626,772	321,416	305,356	40,126	35,978	4,148	586,646	285,438	301,208	5,338	4,843	495
20 and over	3,349,314	1,721,501	1,627,813	205,751	191,042	14,709	3,143,563	1,530,459	1,613,104	21,149	19,529	1,620
Hindu	**5,852,204**	**3,002,203**	**2,850,001**	**231,914**	**214,992**	**16,922**	**5,620,290**	**2,787,211**	**2,833,079**	**19,632**	**18,654**	**978**
0—5	873,623	427,401	446,222	..	..	..	873,623	427,401	446,222	..	..	..
5—10	756,762	396,033	360,729	14,328	12,466	1,862	742,434	383,567	358,867	530	458	72
10—15	700,590	374,221	326,369	23,779	21,202	2,577	676,811	353,019	323,792	1,465	1,304	161
15—20	555,142	284,705	270,437	31,731	28,987	2,744	523,411	255,718	267,693	3,730	3,505	225
20 and over	2,966,087	1,519,843	1,446,244	162,076	152,337	9,739	2,804,011	1,367,506	1,436,505	13,907	13,387	520
Muslim	**376,637**	**198,346**	**178,291**	**38,176**	**33,951**	**4,225**	**338,461**	**164,395**	**174,066**	**4,131**	**3,977**	**154**
0—5	54,994	26,722	28,272	..	..	...	54,994	26,722	28,272	..	..	..
5—10	48,134	25,186	22,948	2,455	1,986	469	45,679	23,200	22,479	110	96	14
10—15	43,703	23,339	20,364	3,643	3,006	637	40,060	20,333	19,727	258	235	23
15—20	35,206	18,390	16,816	5,120	4,388	732	30,086	14,002	16,084	642	608	34
20 and over	194,600	104,709	89,891	26,958	24,571	2,387	167,642	80,138	87,504	3,121	3,038	83
Tribal	**340,752**	**170,828**	**169,924**	**265**	**251**	**14**	**340,487**	**170,577**	**169,910**	**6**	**5**	**1**
0—5	62,834	29,774	33,060	..	..	..	62,834	29,774	33,060	..	..	..
5—10	50,511	25,755	24,756	13	10	3	50,498	25,745	24,753	..	..	..
10—15	43,742	22,964	20,778	20	18	2	43,722	22,946	20,776	..	..	..
15—20	30,169	14,811	15,358	31	29	2	30,138	14,782	15,356	1	1	..
20 and over	153,496	77,524	75,972	201	194	7	153,295	77,330	75,965	5	4	1
Central Provinces States.												
All Religions	**2,483,214**	**1,235,385**	**1,247,829**	**45,663**	**42,498**	**3,165**	**2,437,551**	**1,192,887**	**1,244,664**	**2,363**	**2,140**	**223**
0—5	450,941	220,237	230,704	..	..	..	450,941	220,237	230,704	..	..	..
5—10	344,941	177,276	167,665	2,122	1,825	297	342,819	175,451	167,368	65	52	13
10—15	284,259	148,637	135,622	4,028	3,572	456	280,231	145,065	135,166	161	146	15
15—20	200,754	95,536	105,218	6,471	5,942	529	194,283	89,594	104,689	374	334	40
20 and over	1,202,319	593,699	608,620	33,042	31,159	1,883	1,169,277	562,540	606,737	1,763	1,608	155
Hindu	**1,788,401**	**886,123**	**902,278**	**39,143**	**36,924**	**2,219**	**1,749,258**	**849,199**	**900,059**	**1,554**	**1,548**	**6**
0—5	312,733	152,179	160,554	..	..	..	312,733	152,179	160,554	..	..	..
5—10	243,829	125,474	118,355	1,749	1,557	192	242,080	123,917	118,163	33	32	1
10—15	203,897	107,110	96,787	3,365	3,057	308	200,532	104,053	96,479	109	108	1
15—20	145,469	69,643	75,826	5,491	5,120	371	139,978	64,523	75,455	256	255	1
20 and over	882,473	431,717	450,756	28,538	27,190	1,348	853,935	404,527	449,408	1,156	1,153	3
Tribal	**617,599**	**310,156**	**307,443**	**761**	**736**	**25**	**616,838**	**309,420**	**307,418**	**5**	**5**	..
0—5	123,219	60,657	62,562	..	..	—	123,219	60,657	62,562	—	..	..
5—10	90,125	46,069	44,056	41	40	1	90,084	46,029	44,055	..	..	..
10—15	71,240	36,662	34,578	71	70	1	71,169	36,592	34,577	2	2	..
15—20	48,738	22,673	26,065	103	99	4	48,635	22,574	26,061	1	1	..
20 and over	284,277	144,095	140,182	546	527	19	283,731	143,568	140,163	2	2	..

Muslim	**23,254**	**11,733**	**11,521**	**3,065**	**2,754**	**311**	**20,189**	**8,979**	**11,210**	**275**	**267**	**8**
0—5	3,409	1,617	1,792	..	..	..	3,409	1,617	1,792	..	..	..
5—10	2,809	1,470	1,339	176	135	41	2,633	1,335	1,298	8	6	2
10—15	2,446	1,298	1,148	269	221	48	2,177	1,077	1,100	12	12	..
15—20	2,073	1,007	1,066	384	348	36	1,689	659	1,030	33	33	..
20 and over	12,517	6,341	6,176	2,236	2,050	186	10,281	4,291	5,999	222	216	6

Gwalior State.

All Religions	**3,523,070**	**1,867,031**	**1,656,039**	**141,342**	**126,147**	**15,195**	**3,381,728**	**1,740,884**	**1,640,844**	**13,614**	**12,717**	**897**
0—5	509,014	255,623	253,391	..	..	..	509,014	255,623	253,391	..	..	..
5—10	448,541	239,108	209,433	8,834	7,420	1,414	439,707	231,688	208,019	453	400	53
10—15	431,207	233,911	197,296	14,697	12,671	2,026	416,510	221,240	195,270	1,073	971	102
15—20	352,983	186,671	166,312	19,083	16,723	2,360	333,900	169,948	163,952	2,044	1,899	145
20 and over	1,781,325	951,718	829,607	98,728	89,333	9,395	1,682,597	862,385	820,212	10,044	9,447	597
Hindu	**3,271,576**	**1,732,247**	**1,539,329**	**113,753**	**102,395**	**11,358**	**3,157,823**	**1,629,852**	**1,527,971**	**10,638**	**10,196**	**492**
0—5	473,031	237,686	235,345	..	..	..	473,031	237,686	235,345	..	..	..
5—10	417,747	222,857	194,890	7,054	6,005	1,049	410,693	216,852	193,841	325	304	21
10—15	402,041	218,279	183,762	12,080	10,532	1,548	389,961	207,747	182,214	849	788	61
15—20	328,566	173,755	154,811	15,600	13,804	1,796	312,966	159,951	153,015	1,656	1,576	80
20 and over	1,650,191	879,670	770,521	79,019	72,054	6,965	1,571,172	807,616	763,556	7,858	7,528	330
Muslim	**204,297**	**109,412**	**94,885**	**16,927**	**14,716**	**2,211**	**187,370**	**94,696**	**92,674**	**1,800**	**1,676**	**124**
0—5	29,839	14,861	14,978	..	..	..	29,839	14,861	14,978	..	..	..
5—10	25,459	13,430	12,029	971	789	182	24,488	12,641	11,847	48	43	5
10—15	23,920	12,769	11,151	1,535	1,275	260	22,385	11,494	10,891	112	103	9
15—20	20,078	10,613	9,465	2,164	1,845	319	17,914	8,768	9,146	221	204	17
20 and over	105,001	57,739	47,262	12,257	10,807	1,450	92,744	46,932	45,812	1,419	1,326	93
Jain	**45,079**	**24,238**	**20,841**	**9,627**	**8,480**	**1,147**	**35,452**	**15,758**	**19,694**	**558**	**535**	**23**
0—5	5,827	2,930	2,897	..	..	..	5,827	2,930	2,897	..	..	..
5—10	5,099	2,695	2,404	694	576	118	4,405	2,119	2,286	31	30	1
10—15	5,022	2,746	2,276	962	812	150	4,060	1,934	2,126	59	58	1
15—20	4,147	2,225	1,922	1,204	1,022	182	2,943	1,203	1,740	93	91	2
20 and over	24,984	13,642	11,342	6,767	6,070	697	18,217	7,572	10,645	375	356	19

Hyderabad State.

All Religions	**14,436,148**	**7,370,010**	**7,066,138**	**595,633**	**527,594**	**68,039**	**13,840,515**	**6,842,416**	**6,998,099**	**72,846**	**65,329**	**7,517**
0—5	2,428,219	1,158,829	1,269,390	..	..	..	2,428,219	1,158,829	1,269,390	..	..	..
5—10	1,758,013	914,853	843,160	42,835	35,327	7,508	1,715,178	879,526	835,652	3,704	2,869	835
10—15	1,575,481	827,213	748,268	68,163	58,801	9,362	1,507,318	768,412	738,906	7,640	6,445	1,195
15—20	1,294,390	638,789	655,601	100,258	87,279	12,979	1,194,132	551,510	642,622	12,303	10,955	1,348
20 and over	7,380,045	3,830,326	3,549,719	384,377	346,187	38,190	6,995,668	3,484,139	3,511,529	49,199	45,060	4,139
Hindu	**12,176,727**	**6,203,053**	**5,973,674**	**405,614**	**367,794**	**37,820**	**11,771,113**	**5,835,259**	**5,935,854**	**40,200**	**37,894**	**2,306**
0—5	2,040,424	969,363	1,071,061	..	..	..	2,040,424	969,363	1,071,061	..	..	..
5—10	1,477,030	767,967	709,063	28,389	24,284	4,105	1,448,641	743,683	704,958	1,300	1,065	235
10—15	1,328,885	697,366	631,519	47,078	42,339	4,739	1,281,807	655,027	626,780	3,766	3,399	367
15—20	1,085,375	532,860	552,515	72,043	64,472	7,571	1,013,332	468,388	544,944	6,714	6,276	438
20 and over	6,245,013	3,235,497	3,009,516	258,104	236,699	21,405	5,986,909	2,998,798	2,988,111	28,420	27,154	1,266
Muslim	**1,534,666**	**791,435**	**743,231**	**158,859**	**137,410**	**21,449**	**1,375,807**	**654,025**	**721,782**	**19,275**	**17,982**	**1,293**
0—5	248,998	122,035	126,963	..	..	..	248,998	122,035	126,963	..	..	..
5—10	182,954	95,048	87,906	10,320	7,932	2,388	172,634	87,116	85,518	381	737	144
10—15	164,680	86,439	78,241	16,141	12,877	3,264	148,539	73,562	74,977	2,131	1,883	248
15—20	147,168	75,384	71,784	23,436	19,539	3,897	123,732	55,845	67,387	3,442	3,163	279
20 and over	790,866	412,529	378,337	108,962	97,062	11,900	681,904	315,467	366,437	12,821	12,199	629

Table XIII.—Literacy by Religion and Age—Part II—By Provinces and States—*contd.*

Age and Religion.	Population: Total. Persons.	Total. Males.	Total. Females.	Literate. Persons.	Literate. Males.	Literate. Females.	Illiterate. Persons.	Illiterate. Males.	Illiterate. Females.	Literate in English. Persons.	Literate in English. Males.	Literate in English. Females.
1	2	3	4	5	6	7	8	9	10	11	12	13
Hyderabad State.—*concluded.*												
Tribal	**544,789**	**280,584**	**264,205**	**2,672**	**2,171**	**501**	**542,117**	**278,413**	**263,704**	**124**	**96**	**28**
0—5	109,675	53,077	56,598	..	..	..	109,675	53,077	56,598	..	..	..
5—10	77,228	40,809	36,419	373	252	121	76,855	40,557	36,298	11	11	..
10—15	62,465	32,760	29,705	474	369	105	61,991	32,391	29,600	15	15	..
15—20	45,095	21,798	23,297	514	395	119	44,581	21,403	23,178	15	15	..
20 and over	250,326	132,140	118,186	1,311	1,155	156	249,015	130,985	118,030	83	55	28
Jammu and Kashmir State.												
All Religions	**3,646,243**	**1,938,338**	**1,707,905**	**123,885**	**114,807**	**9,078**	**3,522,358**	**1,823,531**	**1,698,827**	**19,469**	**18,660**	**809**
0—5	579,542	291,931	287,611	..	..	..	579,542	291,931	287,611	..	..	..
5—10	469,120	253,182	215,938	5,573	4,523	1,050	463,547	248,659	214,888	658	601	57
10—15	429,988	234,021	195,967	10,459	8,908	1,551	419,529	225,113	194,416	1,642	1,533	109
15—20	350,597	178,694	171,903	17,489	15,837	1,652	333,108	162,857	170,251	3,901	3,735	166
20 and over	1,816,996	980,510	836,486	90,364	85,539	4,825	1,726,632	894,971	831,661	13,268	12,791	477
Muslim	**2,817,636**	**1,497,252**	**1,320,384**	**45,619**	**43,454**	**2,165**	**2,772,017**	**1,453,798**	**1,318,219**	**4,168**	**4,045**	**123**
0—5	459,985	232,278	227,707	..	..	..	459,985	232,278	227,707	..	..	..
5—10	372,408	201,588	170,820	2,002	1,765	237	370,406	199,823	170,583	134	122	12
10—15	339,907	185,953	153,954	3,951	3,575	376	335,956	182,378	153,578	376	355	21
15—20	273,180	139,253	133,927	6,791	6,381	410	266,389	132,872	133,517	1,064	1,026	38
20 and over	1,372,156	738,180	633,976	32,875	31,733	1,142	1,339,281	706,447	632,834	2,594	2,542	52
Hindu	**736,222**	**393,699**	**342,523**	**69,806**	**63,681**	**5,625**	**666,916**	**330,018**	**336,898**	**14,202**	**13,754**	**448**
0—5	105,463	52,618	52,845	..	..	..	105,463	52,618	52,845	..	..	..
5—10	85,225	45,535	39,690	3,131	2,445	686	82,094	43,090	39,004	481	447	34
10—15	79,796	42,696	37,100	5,754	4,762	992	74,042	37,934	36,108	1,173	1,099	74
15—20	69,295	35,540	33,755	9,591	8,560	1,031	59,704	26,980	32,724	2,639	2,541	98
20 and over	396,443	217,310	179,133	50,830	47,914	2,916	345,613	169,396	176,217	9,909	9,667	242
Sikh	**50,662**	**26,457**	**24,205**	**6,458**	**5,555**	**903**	**44,204**	**20,902**	**23,302**	**660**	**622**	**38**
0—5	9,239	4,651	4,588	..	..	..	9,239	4,651	4,588	..	..	..
5—10	7,087	3,856	3,231	350	258	92	6,737	3,598	3,139	21	18	3
10—15	6,224	3,359	2,865	625	482	143	5,599	2,877	2,722	65	58	7
15—20	4,730	2,236	2,494	917	751	166	3,813	1,485	2,328	149	137	12
20 and over	23,382	12,355	11,027	4,566	4,064	502	18,816	8,291	10,525	425	409	16
Cochin State.												
All Religions	**1,205,016**	**589,813**	**615,203**	**339,214**	**225,425**	**113,789**	**865,802**	**364,388**	**501,414**	**36,975**	**28,533**	**8,442**
0—5	198,097	99,426	98,671	..	..	..	198,097	99,426	98,671	..	..	..
5—10	156,302	79,218	77,084	35,648	20,897	14,751	120,654	58,321	62,333	1,240	820	420
10—15	148,115	74,869	73,246	55,029	32,844	22,185	93,086	42,025	51,061	4,207	2,867	1,340
15—20	117,905	55,964	61,941	52,038	32,166	19,872	65,867	23,798	42,069	8,774	6,259	2,515
20 and over	584,597	280,336	304,261	196,499	139,518	56,981	388,098	140,818	247,280	22,754	18,587	4,167
Hindu	**780,484**	**377,933**	**402,551**	**192,320**	**134,962**	**57,358**	**588,164**	**242,971**	**345,193**	**23,193**	**18,822**	**4,371**
0—5	125,961	62,937	63,024	..	..	..	125,961	62,937	63,024	..	..	..
5—10	98,770	50,177	48,593	20,043	12,422	7,621	78,727	37,755	40,972	793	563	230
10—15	93,838	47,514	46,324	30,902	19,548	11,354	62,936	27,966	34,970	2,611	1,906	705
15—20	75,492	35,365	40,127	29,000	19,030	9,970	46,492	16,335	30,157	5,345	4,055	1,290
20 and over	386,423	181,940	204,483	112,375	83,962	28,413	274,048	97,978	176,070	14,444	12,298	2,146

istian	**334,870**	**166,195**	**168,675**	**134,137**	**79,705**	**54,432**	**200,733**	**86,490**	**114,243**	**13,032**	**9,041**	**3,991**
0— 5	57,195	28,841	28,354	—	—		57,195	28,841	28,354	..	..	..
5—10	45,410	22,819	22,591	14,325	7,599	6,726	31,085	15,220	15,865	423	241	182
10—15	42,883	21,490	21,393	22,145	11,883	10,262	20,738	9,607	11,131	1,517	899	618
15—20	33,305	16,139	17,166	21,172	11,636	9,536	12,133	4,503	7,630	3,248	2,041	1,207
20 and over	156,077	76,906	79,171	76,495	48,587	27,908	79,582	28,319	51,263	7,844	5,860	1,984
islim	**87,902**	**44,794**	**43,108**	**12,041**	**10,294**	**1,747**	**75,861**	**34,500**	**41,361**	**602**	**574**	**28**
0— 5	14,691	7,510	7,181	..	..	..	14,691	7,510	7,181	..	..	..
5—10	11,905	6,110	5,795	1,205	834	371	10,700	5,276	5,424	18	13	5
10—15	11,191	5,766	5,425	1,885	1,358	527	9,306	4,408	4,898	64	55	9
15—20	8,945	4,386	4,559	1,772	1,450	322	7,173	2,936	4,237	149	143	6
20 and over	41,170	21,022	20,148	7,179	6,652	527	33,991	14,370	19,621	371	363	8

Travancore State.

All Religions	**5,095,973**	**2,565,073**	**2,530,900**	**1,217,924**	**866,313**	**351,611**	**3,878,049**	**1,698,760**	**2,179,289**	**80,651**	**65,500**	**15,151**
0— 5	877,242	440,851	436,391	—	—	..	877,242	440,851	436,391	..	..	..
5—10	673,095	341,345	331,750	93,951	56,526	37,425	579,144	281,819	294,325	2,653	1,772	881
10—15	617,939	313,728	304,211	159,412	98,484	60,928	453,527	215,244	243,283	7,552	5,254	2,298
15—20	487,912	238,499	249,413	194,671	126,411	68,260	293,241	112,088	181,153	16,861	12,830	4,031
20 and over	2,439,785	1,230,650	1,209,135	769,890	584,892	184,998	1,669,895	645,758	1,024,137	53,585	45,644	7,941
Hindu	**3,134,888**	**1,567,925**	**1,566,963**	**703,440**	**519,200**	**184,240**	**2,431,448**	**1,048,725**	**1,382,723**	**41,704**	**36,199**	**5,505**
0— 5	531,742	266,491	265,251	..	..	..	531,742	266,491	265,251	..	..	..
5—10	402,939	204,082	198,857	52,392	32,514	19,878	350,547	171,558	178,979	1,331	967	364
10—15	370,245	187,834	182,411	89,002	56,698	32,304	281,243	131,136	150,107	3,675	2,783	892
15—20	296,862	143,821	153,041	110,245	74,031	36,214	186,617	69,790	116,827	8,387	6,816	1,571
20 and over	1,533,100	765,697	767,403	451,801	355,957	95,844	1,081,299	409,740	671,559	28,311	25,633	2,678
Christian	**1,604,475**	**814,833**	**789,642**	**472,357**	**309,276**	**163,081**	**1,132,118**	**505,557**	**626,561**	**37,296**	**27,692**	**9,604**
0— 5	282,178	142,209	139,969	..	..	..	282,178	142,209	139,969	..	..	..
5—10	220,826	111,984	108,842	39,072	22,035	17,037	181,754	89,949	91,805	1,282	768	514
10—15	202,417	102,621	99,796	65,950	38,121	27,829	136,467	64,500	71,967	3,760	2,361	1,399
15—20	156,122	77,329	78,793	78,145	46,883	31,262	77,977	30,446	47,531	8,117	5,673	2,444
20 and over	742,932	380,690	362,242	289,190	202,237	86,953	453,742	178,453	275,289	24,137	18,890	5,247
Muslim	**355,274**	**180,555**	**172,719**	**41,907**	**37,661**	**4,246**	**311,367**	**142,894**	**168,473**	**1,608**	**1,571**	**37**
0— 5	62,879	31,932	30,947	..	..	..	62,879	31,932	30,947	..	..	..
5—10	48,924	25,056	23,868	2,466	1,962	504	46,458	23,094	23,364	39	37	2
10—15	44,897	23,078	21,819	4,429	3,643	786	40,468	19,435	21,033	112	107	5
15—20	34,606	17,194	17,412	6,245	5,469	776	28,361	11,725	16,636	348	333	15
20 and over	161,968	83,295	78,673	28,767	26,587	2,180	133,201	56,708	76,493	1,109	1,094	15

Madras States (*exclusive of Cochin and Travancore*).

All Religions	**453,495**	**218,146**	**235,349**	**48,665**	**44,323**	**4,342**	**404,830**	**173,823**	**231,007**	**3,978**	**3,802**	**176**
0— 5	51,949	25,502	26,447	..	..	..	51,949	25,502	26,447	..	..	..
5—10	59,246	29,285	29,961	1,314	1,037	277	57,932	28,248	29,684	53	39	14
10—15	51,296	26,255	25,041	5,224	4,469	755	46,072	21,786	24,286	387	347	40
15—20	39,925	19,886	20,039	5,648	4,872	776	34,277	15,014	19,263	686	651	35
20 and over	251,079	117,218	133,861	36,479	33,945	2,534	214,600	83,273	131,327	2,852	2,765	87

Table XIII.—Literacy by Religion and Age—Part II—By Provinces and States—*contd.*

Age and Religion.	Total.			Population Literate.			Illiterate.			Literate in English.		
	Persons.	Males.	Females.	Persons.	Males.	Females.	Persons.	Males.	Females.	Persons.	Males.	Females.
1	2	3	4	5	6	7	8	9	10	11	12	13
Mysore State.												
All Religions	**6,557,302**	**3,353,963**	**3,203,339**	**594,526**	**504,440**	**90,086**	**5,962,776**	**2,849,523**	**3,113,253**	**91,460**	**78,419**	**13,041**
0—5	929,960	455,854	474,106	..	..	..	929,960	455,854	474,106	..	..	..
5—10	882,466	440,978	441,488	25,834	18,237	7,597	856,632	422,741	433,891	1,466	875	591
10—15	814,673	420,275	394,398	82,395	64,157	18,238	732,278	356,118	376,160	10,083	7,841	2,242
15—20	602,622	305,621	297,001	78,955	62,754	16,201	523,667	242,867	280,800	16,621	14,047	2,574
20 and over	3,327,581	1,731,235	1,596,346	407,242	359,292	48,050	2,920,239	1,371,943	1,548,296	63,290	55,656	7,634
Hindu	**6,015,880**	**3,066,332**	**2,949,548**	**487,827**	**426,697**	**61,130**	**5,528,053**	**2,639,635**	**2,888,418**	**65,149**	**60,253**	**4,896**
0—5	847,548	415,109	432,439	..	..	..	847,548	415,109	432,439	..	..	..
5—10	807,003	402,406	404,597	21,268	15,653	5,615	785,735	386,753	398,982	655	472	183
10—15	746,570	384,525	362,045	68,752	55,618	13,134	677,818	328,907	348,911	7,306	6,217	1,089
15—20	550,128	278,191	271,937	64,975	53,560	11,415	485,153	224,631	260,522	12,701	11,559	1,142
20 and over	3,064,631	1,586,101	1,478,530	332,832	301,866	30,966	2,731,799	1,284,235	1,447,564	44,487	42,005	2,482
Muslim	**398,628**	**213,381**	**185,247**	**67,332**	**51,876**	**15,456**	**331,296**	**161,505**	**169,791**	**6,711**	**6,174**	**537**
0—5	61,921	30,436	31,485	..	..	..	61,921	30,436	31,485	..	..	..
5—10	57,145	29,284	27,861	2,778	1,633	1,145	54,367	27,651	26,716	81	48	33
10—15	50,954	26,955	23,999	8,820	5,761	3,059	42,134	21,194	20,940	656	538	118
15—20	38,074	20,184	17,890	8,743	6,134	2,609	29,331	14,050	15,281	1,125	1,003	122
20 and over	190,534	106,522	84,012	46,991	38,348	8,643	143,543	68,174	75,369	4,849	4,585	264
Christian	**87,538**	**45,164**	**42,374**	**31,286**	**18,935**	**12,351**	**56,252**	**26,229**	**30,023**	**18,552**	**11,116**	**7,436**
0—5	12,449	6,339	6,110	..	..	..	12,449	6,339	6,110	..	..	..
5—10	10,904	5,520	5,384	1,485	731	754	9,419	4,789	4,630	714	347	367
10—15	10,345	5,180	5,165	3,750	1,956	1,794	6,595	3,224	3,371	2,015	1,009	1,006
15—20	9,134	4,490	4,644	4,143	2,175	1,968	4,991	2,315	2,676	2,603	1,322	1,281
20 and over	44,706	23,635	21,071	21,908	14,073	7,835	22,798	9,562	13,236	13,220	8,438	4,782
North-West Frontier Province. (*Agencies and Tribal Areas*).												
All Religions	**46,451**	**44,635**	**1,816**	**17,072**	**16,968**	**104**	**29,379**	**27,667**	**1,712**	**5,798**	**5,790**	**8**
0—5	750	377	373	..	..	..	750	377	373	..	..	..
5—10	641	368	273	63	53	10	578	315	263	2	2	..
10—15	778	562	216	140	126	14	638	436	202	14	13	1
15—20	8,791	8,607	184	3,190	3,171	19	5,601	5,436	165	943	942	1
20 and over	35,491	34,721	770	13,679	13,618	61	21,812	21,103	709	4,839	4,833	6
Punjab States.												
All Religions	**437,787**	**229,290**	**208,497**	**15,870**	**14,791**	**1,079**	**421,917**	**214,499**	**207,418**	**1,681**	**1,564**	**117**
0—5	57,272	28,181	29,091	..	..	..	57,272	28,181	29,091	..	..	..
5—10	50,210	25,975	24,235	514	440	74	49,696	25,535	24,161	31	26	5
10—15	47,466	25,198	22,268	1,100	979	121	46,366	24,219	22,147	118	111	7
15—20	39,635	20,436	19,199	1,901	1,727	174	37,734	18,709	19,025	310	294	16
20 and over	243,204	129,500	113,704	12,355	11,645	710	230,849	117,855	112,994	1,222	1,133	89

Punjab States Agency.

All Religions	**4,472,218**	**2,451,394**	**2,020,824**	**158,315**	**146,907**	**11,408**	**4,313,903**	**2,304,487**	**2,009,416**	**17,810**	**17,049**	**761**
0—5	682,339	346,869	335,470	..	—		682,339	346,869	335,470	..	..	..
5—10	571,280	307,758	263,522	5,055	4,166	889	566,225	303,592	262,633	329	291	38
10—15	529,591	291,950	237,641	11,071	9,464	1,607	518,520	282,486	236,034	1,219	1,123	96
15—20	427,034	233,003	194,031	21,055	18,933	2,122	405,979	214,070	191,909	3,431	3,285	146
20 and over	2,261,974	1,271,814	990,160	121,134	114,344	6,790	2,140,840	1,157,470	983,370	12,831	12,350	481
Hindu	**1,887,249**	**1,020,180**	**867,069**	**92,100**	**86,621**	**5,479**	**1,795,149**	**933,559**	**861,590**	**9,573**	**9,361**	**212**
0—5	277,535	139,385	138,150	..	..	..	277,535	139,385	138,150	..	..	..
5—10	235,874	125,146	110,728	2,641	2,187	454	233,233	122,959	110,274	183	174	9
10—15	221,824	120,469	101,355	6,034	5,230	804	215,790	115,239	100,551	677	649	28
15—20	182,974	98,464	84,510	11,996	11,000	996	170,978	87,464	83,514	1,758	1,713	45
20 and over	969,042	536,716	432,326	71,429	68,204	3,225	897,613	468,512	429,101	6,955	6,825	130
Muslim	**1,556,591**	**852,700**	**703,891**	**26,414**	**24,381**	**2,033**	**1,530,177**	**828,319**	**701,858**	**4,372**	**4,238**	**134**
0—5	255,242	130,269	124,973	..	..	.	255,242	130,269	124,973	..	..	..
5—10	208,758	113,764	94,994	1,114	950	164	207,644	112,814	94,830	64	57	7
10—15	184,358	102,750	81,608	2,282	1,995	287	182,076	100,755	81,321	245	229	16
15—20	141,694	76,037	65,657	4,079	3,697	382	137,615	72,340	65,275	910	885	25
20 and over	766,539	429,880	336,659	18,939	17,739	1,200	747,600	412,141	335,459	3,153	3,067	86
Sikh	**996,626**	**561,238**	**435,388**	**37,291**	**33,799**	**3,492**	**959,335**	**527,439**	**431,896**	**3,133**	**2,962**	**171**
0—5	144,459	74,579	69,880	..	..	—	144,459	74,579	69,880	..	..	..
5—10	122,618	66,697	55,921	1,210	964	246	121,408	65,733	55,675	54	45	9
10—15	119,507	66,614	52,893	2,587	2,114	473	116,920	64,500	52,420	242	214	28
15—20	99,260	56,856	42,404	4,676	3,994	682	94,584	52,862	41,722	680	634	46
20 and over	510,782	296,492	214,290	28,818	26,727	2,091	481,964	269,765	212,199	2,157	2,069	88

Rajputana Agency.

All Religions	**11,225,712**	**5,885,028**	**5,340,684**	**106,146**	**380,888**	**25,258**	**10,819,566**	**5,504,140**	**5,315,426**	**29,796**	**28,133**	**1,663**
0—5	1,735,339	863,097	872,242	—	..	..	1,735,339	863,097	872,242	..	..	..
5—10	1,472,995	783,824	689,171	0,205	18,073	2,132	1,452,790	765,751	687,039	1,354	1,230	124
10—15	1,364,988	745,362	619,626	35,295	32,077	3,218	1,329,693	713,285	616,408	2,815	2,616	199
15—20	1,064,302	563,456	500,846	52,173	48,270	3,903	1,012,129	515,186	496,943	5,159	4,910	249
20 and over	5,588,088	2,929,289	2,658,799	298,473	282,468	16,005	5,289,615	2,646,821	2,642,794	20,468	19,377	1,091
Hindu	**9,578,805**	**5,029,620**	**4,549,185**	**233,749**	**267,405**	**16,344**	**9,295,056**	**4,762,215**	**4,532,841**	**21,513**	**20,888**	**625**
0—5	1,471,889	732,294	739,595	—	..	..	1,471,889	732,294	739,595	..	..	..
5—10	1,251,331	667,306	584,025	13,844	12,487	1,357	1,237,487	654,819	582,668	905	864	41
10—15	1,165,093	638,395	526,698	24,702	22,616	2,086	1,140,391	615,779	524,612	2,057	1,965	92
15—20	909,809	[illegible]	426,368	37,022	34,411	2,611	872,787	449,030	423,757	3,902	3,787	115
20 and over	4,780,683	[illegible]	2,227,499	208,181	197,891	10,290	4,572,502	2,310,293	2,262,209	14,649	14,272	377
Muslim	**1,069,325**	**[illegible]**	**503,363**	**37,341**	**34,241**	**3,100**	**1,031,984**	**531,721**	**500,263**	**3,245**	**3,163**	**82**
0—5	170,008	84,827	85,181	—	..	..	170,008	84,827	85,181	..	—	—
5—10	142,809	75,807	67,002	1,807	1,541	266	141,002	74,266	66,736	115	113	2
10—15	129,681	70,234	59,447	3,046	2,625	421	126,635	67,609	59,026	241	227	14
15—20	101,322	53,427	47,895	4,697	4,225	472	96,625	49,202	47,423	482	468	14
20 and over	525,505	281,667	243,838	27,791	25,850	1,941	497,714	255,817	241,897	2,407	2,355	52
Jain	**300,748**	**146,004**	**154,744**	**80,082**	**75,820**	**4,262**	**220,666**	**70,184**	**150,482**	**2,593**	**2,530**	**63**
0—5	42,026	21,019	21,007	..	..	..	42,026	21,019	21,007	..	..	..
5—10	35,634	18,234	17,400	4,153	3,800	353	31,481	14,434	17,047	145	141	4
10—15	32,455	16,684	15,771	7,045	6,526	519	25,410	10,158	15,252	295	291	4
15—20	27,053	13,036	14,017	9,842	9,234	608	17,211	3,802	13,409	483	472	11
20 and over	163,580	77,031	86,549	59,042	56,260	2,782	104,538	20,771	83,767	1,670	1,626	44

Table XIII.—Literacy by Religion and Age—Part II—By Provinces and States—*concld.*

Age and Religion.	Total.			Population Literate.			Illiterate.			Literate in English.		
1	Persons. 2	Males. 3	Females. 4	Persons. 5	Males. 6	Females. 7	Persons. 8	Males. 9	Females. 10	Persons. 11	Males. 12	Females. 13
Sikkim State.												
All Religions	**109,808**	**55,825**	**53,983**	**3,277**	**3,127**	**150**	**106,531**	**52,698**	**53,833**	**279**	**267**	**12**
0—5	17,157	8,529	8,628	..	..	..	17,157	8,529	8,628	..	..	..
5—10	14,457	7,336	7,121	60	50	10	14,397	7,286	7,111	6	6	..
10—15	13,296	6,919	6,377	122	111	11	13,174	6,808	6,366	14	13	1
15—20	10,727	5,463	5,264	342	324	18	10,385	5,139	5,246	42	40	2
20 and over	54,171	27,578	26,593	2,753	2,642	111	51,418	24,936	26,482	217	208	9
United Provinces States.												
All Religions	**1,206,070**	**618,171**	**587,899**	**49,720**	**47,649**	**2,071**	**1,156,350**	**570,522**	**585,828**	**2,769**	**2,683**	**86**
0—5	183,192	89,799	93,393	..	..	..	183,192	89,799	93,393	..	..	..
5—10	151,173	78,371	72,802	3,085	2,860	225	148,088	75,511	72,577	132	121	11
10—15	133,477	71,946	61,531	5,064	4,740	324	128,413	67,206	61,207	299	290	9
15—20	110,523	55,662	54,861	6,119	5,780	339	104,404	49,882	54,522	481	473	8
20 and over	627,705	322,393	305,312	35,452	34,269	1,183	592,253	288,124	304,129	1,857	1,799	58
Hindu	**950,724**	**482,153**	**468,571**	**42,851**	**41,260**	**1,591**	**907,873**	**440,893**	**466,980**	**2,185**	**2,131**	**54**
0—5	143,094	70,005	73,089	..	..	..	143,094	70,005	73,089	..	..	..
5—10	119,195	61,336	57,859	2,813	2,628	185	116,382	58,708	57,674	112	102	10
10—15	105,144	56,391	48,753	4,561	4,295	266	100,583	52,096	48,487	247	239	8
15—20	86,646	43,079	43,567	5,293	5,025	268	81,353	38,054	43,299	389	382	7
20 and over	496,645	251,342	245,303	30,184	29,312	872	466,461	222,030	244,431	1,437	1,408	29
Muslim	**252,131**	**134,325**	**117,806**	**6,724**	**6,283**	**441**	**245,407**	**128,042**	**117,365**	**507**	**497**	**10**
0—5	39,548	19,529	20,019	..	..	..	39,548	19,529	20,019	..	..	..
5—10	31,571	16,824	14,747	259	224	35	31,312	16,600	14,712	16	16	..
10—15	27,994	15,380	12,614	497	439	58	27,497	14,941	12,556	49	48	1
15—20	23,588	12,436	11,152	817	748	69	22,771	11,688	11,083	87	86	1
20 and over	129,430	70,156	59,274	5,151	4,872	279	124,279	65,284	58,995	355	347	8
Western India States Agency.												
All Religions	**3,998,416**	**2,025,293**	**1,973,123**	**421,349**	**350,592**	**70,757**	**3,577,067**	**1,674,701**	**1,902,366**	**36,394**	**35,168**	**1,226**
0—5	622,088	306,083	316,005	—	—	..	622,088	306,083	316,005	..	..	..
5—10	552,224	286,046	266,178	36,359	28,057	8,302	515,865	257,989	257,876	891	834	57
10—15	506,773	268,829	237,944	57,095	44,552	12,543	449,678	224,277	225,401	3,384	3,229	155
15—20	384,001	197,162	186,839	62,060	49,698	12,362	321,941	147,464	174,477	7,845	7,570	275
20 and over	1,933,330	967,173	966,157	265,835	228,285	37,550	1,667,495	738,888	928,607	24,274	23,535	739

Table XIII.—Literacy by Religion and Age—Part III—Cities.

Age and Religion.	Population Total. Persons.	Total. Males.	Total. Females.	Literate. Persons.	Literate. Males.	Literate. Females.	Illiterate. Persons.	Illiterate. Males.	Illiterate. Females.	Literate in English. Persons.	Literate in English. Males.	Literate in English. Females.
1	2	3	4	5	6	7	8	9	10	11	12	13
Calcutta.												
All Religions	**1,196,734**	**814,948**	**381,786**	**473,589**	**362,558**	**111,031**	**723,145**	**452,390**	**270,755**	**227,858**	**190,620**	**37,238**
0—5	101,427	52,998	48,429	..	..	..	101,427	52,998	48,429	..	..	..
5—10	95,388	53,498	41,890	30,523	18,618	11,905	64,865	34,880	29,985	12,960	9,252	3,708
10—15	98,301	58,547	39,754	42,665	27,033	15,632	55,636	31,514	24,122	20,589	15,069	5,520
15—20	128,230	88,480	39,750	61,850	46,022	15,828	66,380	42,458	23,922	32,115	26,397	5,718
20 and over	773,388	561,425	211,963	338,551	270,885	67,666	434,837	290,540	144,297	162,194	139,902	22,292
Bombay.												
All Religions	***1,161,383**	**747,381**	**414,002**	**280,923**	**217,770**	**63,153**	**880,164**	**529,355**	**350,809**	**134,916**	**106,240**	**28,676**
0—5	103,338	53,506	49,832	..	..	..	103,338	53,506	49,832	..	..	..
5—10	93,921	53,713	40,208	11,792	7,418	4,374	82,129	46,295	35,834	4,172	2,516	1,656
10—15	86,031	50,852	35,179	18,081	11,773	6,308	67,950	39,079	28,871	7,341	4,749	2,592
15—20	115,323	67,890	47,433	31,137	22,050	9,087	84,186	45,840	38,346	15,696	11,256	4,440
20 and over	762,474	521,164	241,310	219,913	176,529	43,384	542,561	344,635	197,926	107,707	87,719	19,988
Madras.												
All Religions	**647,230**	**341,223**	**306,007**	**199,870**	**147,872**	**51,998**	**447,360**	**193,351**	**254,009**	**96,357**	**77,682**	**18,675**
0—5	74,686	37,516	37,352	..	..	..	74,868	37,516	37,352	..	..	..
5—10	69,561	35,600	33,961	11,173	6,941	4,232	58,388	28,659	29,729	4,251	2,812	1,439
10—15	66,083	33,863	32,220	18,272	11,493	6,779	47,811	22,370	25,441	8,038	5,543	2,495
15—20	67,539	33,738	33,801	28,494	19,535	8,959	39,045	14,203	24,842	15,301	11,768	3,533
20 and over	369,179	200,506	168,673	141,931	109,903	32,028	227,248	90,603	136,645	68,767	57,559	11,208
Agra.												
All Religions	**229,764**	**127,736**	**102,028**	**32,599**	**27,321**	**5,278**	**197,165**	**100,415**	**96,750**	**9,649**	**8,208**	**1,441**
0—5	33,972	17,122	16,850	..	..	..	33,972	17,122	16,850	..	..	..
5—10	27,113	15,103	12,010	1,670	1,153	517	25,443	13,950	11,493	463	287	176
10—15	25,387	14,054	11,333	3,254	2,465	789	22,133	11,589	10,544	914	670	244
15—20	23,940	12,890	11,050	5,687	4,716	971	18,253	8,174	10,079	1,741	1,503	238
20 and over	119,352	68,567	50,785	21,988	18,987	3,001	97,364	49,580	47,784	6,531	5,748	783
Ajmer.												
All Religions	**119,524**	**66,014**	**53,510**	**26,310**	**21,251**	**5,059**	**93,214**	**44,763**	**48,451**	**9,223**	**7,937**	**1,286**
0—5	16,452	8,142	8,310	..	..	..	16,452	8,142	8,310	..	..	..
5—10	13,218	7,097	6,121	1,721	1,203	518	11,497	5,894	5,603	415	303	112
10—15	12,731	6,940	5,791	2,663	1,916	747	10,068	5,024	5,044	808	635	173
15—20	12,966	7,059	5,907	3,754	2,928	826	9,212	4,131	5,081	1,459	1,257	202
20 and over	64,157	36,776	27,381	18,172	15,204	2,968	45,985	21,572	24,413	6,541	5,742	799

*Includes 296 persons (256 males and 40 females) for whom these details were not available.

Table XIII.—Literacy by Religion and Age—Part III—Cities—*contd.*

Age and Religion.	Population. Total.			Literate.			Illiterate.			Literate in English.		
	Persons.	Males.	Females.	Persons.	Males.	Females.	Persons.	Males.	Females.	Persons.	Males.	Females.
1	2	3	4	5	6	7	8	9	10	11	12	13
Allahabad.												
All Religions	**183,914**	**104,162**	**79,752**	**46,734**	**36,165**	**10,569**	**137,180**	**67,997**	**69,183**	20,969	**17,484**	**3,485**
0—5	24,002	12,145	11,857	..	..	..	24,002	12,145	11,857	..	..	..
5—10	20,479	10,984	9,495	3,320	2,191	1,129	17,159	8,793	8,366	1,232	859	373
10—15	18,860	10,427	8,433	4,964	3,416	1,548	13,896	7,011	6,885	2,113	1,574	539
15—20	18,222	10,588	7,634	6,687	5,332	1,355	11,535	5,256	6,279	3,616	3,130	486
20 and over	102,351	60,018	42,333	31,763	25,226	6,537	70,588	34,792	35,796	14,908	11,921	2,087
Amritsar.												
All Religions	**264,840**	**158,985**	**105,855**	**39,937**	**32,643**	**7,294**	**224,903**	**126,342**	**98,561**	12,288	**10,485**	**1,803**
0—5	34,839	17,654	17,185	..	..	..	34,839	17,654	17,185	..	..	..
5—10	30,983	16,916	14,067	1,947	1,451	496	29,036	15,465	13,571	322	226	96
10—15	29,729	17,122	12,607	4,011	3,090	921	25,718	14,032	11,686	896	652	154
15—20	27,850	17,546	10,304	6,509	5,128	1,381	21,341	12,418	8,923	2,082	1,745	337
20 and over	141,439	89,747	51,692	27,470	22,974	4,496	113,969	66,773	47,196	9,078	7,862	1,216
Bangalore.												
All Religions	**172,357**	**91,680**	**80,677**	**52,509**	**39,314**	**13,195**	**119,848**	**52,366**	**67,482**	19,900	**16,914**	**2,986**
0—5	24,270	11,982	12,288	..	..	..	24,270	11,982	12,288	..	..	..
5—10	20,870	10,564	10,306	3,006	1,746	1,260	17,864	8,818	9,046	381	245	136
10—15	19,553	10,185	9,368	6,837	4,391	2,446	12,716	5,794	6,922	2,265	1,675	590
15—20	18,870	10,165	8,705	8,224	5,831	2,393	10,646	4,334	6,312	3,958	3,283	675
20 and over	88,794	48,784	40,010	34,442	27,346	7,096	54,352	21,438	32,914	13,296	11,711	1,585
Bangalore Civil and Military Station.												
All Religions	**134,113**	**69,409**	**64,704**	**37,265**	**26,000**	**11,265**	**96,848**	**43,409**	**53,439**	19,109	**13,369**	**5,740**
0—5	19,015	9,473	9,542	..	..	..	19,015	9,473	9,542	..	..	..
5—10	16,938	8,658	8,280	1,302	691	611	15,636	7,967	7,669	514	266	248
10—15	15,595	7,875	7,720	4,045	2,319	1,726	11,550	5,556	5,994	2,041	1,246	795
15—20	13,742	6,839	6,903	5,045	3,105	1,940	8,697	3,734	4,963	2,745	1,806	939
20 and over	68,823	36,564	32,259	26,873	19,885	6,988	41,950	16,679	25,271	13,809	10,051	3,758
Bareilly.												
All Religions	**144,031**	**79,389**	**64,642**	**22,050**	**18,035**	**4,015**	**121,981**	**61,354**	**60,627**	**2,910**	**2,498**	**412**
0—5	21,094	10,533	10,561	..	..	..	21,094	10,533	10,561	..	..	..
5—10	17,353	9,247	8,106	1,337	994	343	16,016	8,253	7,763	113	93	20
10—15	15,546	8,541	7,005	2,305	1,679	626	13,241	6,862	6,379	269	220	49
15—20	14,266	7,997	6,269	2,976	2,273	703	11,290	5,724	5,566	554	471	83
20 and over	75,772	43,071	32,701	15,432	13,089	2,343	60,340	29,982	30,358	1,974	1,714	260

Baroda.												
All Religions	**112,860**	**62,744**	**50,116**	**40,336**	**31,129**	**9,207**	**72,524**	**31,615**	**40,909**	**10,221**	**9,222**	**999**
0—5	13,986	7,177	6,809	..	..	..	13,986	7,177	6,809	..	..	..
5—10	11,326	6,132	5,194	2,965	1,971	994	8,361	4,161	4,200	230	167	63
10—15	11,368	6,240	5,128	4,877	3,246	1,631	6,491	2,994	3,497	870	678	192
15—20	12,757	7,219	5,538	6,618	4,809	1,809	6,139	2,410	3,729	2,347	2,061	286
20 and over	63,423	35,976	27,447	25,876	21,103	4,773	37,547	14,873	22,674	6,774	6,316	458
Benares.												
All Religions	**205,315**	**114,551**	**90,764**	**41,859**	**34,334**	**7,525**	**163,456**	**80,217**	**83,239**	**12,140**	**10,722**	**1,418**
0—5	24,526	12,386	12,140	..	..	..	24,526	12,386	12,140	..	..	..
5—10	22,196	11,977	10,219	2,639	1,832	807	19,557	10,145	9,412	637	464	173
10—15	20,965	11,682	9,283	4,102	3,030	1,072	16,863	8,652	8,211	1,194	938	256
15—20	19,681	11,409	8,272	5,319	4,434	885	14,362	6,975	7,387	1,755	1,544	211
20 and over	117.947	67.097	50,850	29,799	25,038	4.761	88,148	42,059	46,089	8,554	7,776	778
Cawnpore.												
All Religions	**243,755**	**143,872**	**99,883**	**39,770**	**33,581**	**6,189**	**203,985**	**110,291**	**93,694**	**12,524**	**10,724**	**1,800**
0—5	27,136	13,733	13,403	..	..	..	27,136	13,733	13,403	..	..	..
5—10	23,906	13,407	10,499	2,297	1,425	872	21,609	11,982	9,627	480	328	152
10—15	22.112	12,834	9,278	3,221	2,475	746	18,891	10,359	8,532	909	706	203
15—20	23,034	13,219	9,815	5,088	3,984	1,104	17,946	9,235	8,711	1,757	1,489	268
20 and over	147,567	90,679	56,888	29,164	25,697	3,467	118,403	64,982	53,421	9,378	8,201	1,177
Dacca.												
All Religions	**138,518**	**79,365**	**59,153**	**50,717**	**35,265**	**15,452**	**87,801**	**44,100**	**43,701**	**22,166**	**18,214**	**3,952**
0—5	18,394	9,072	9,322	..	..	..	18,394	9,072	9,322	..	..	..
5—10	16,207	8,917	7,290	4,611	3,703	1,908	11,596	6,214	5,382	1,617	1,076	541
10—15	15,174	8,471	6,703	6,205	3,539	2,666	8,969	4,932	4,037	2,544	1,670	874
15—20	15,074	8,739	6,335	7,724	5,006	2,718	7,350	3,733	3,617	3,965	3,100	865
20 and over	73,669	44,166	29,503	32,177	24,017	8,160	41,492	20,149	21,343	14,040	12,368	1,672
***Delhi.**												
All Religions	**365,527**	**215,778**	**149,749**	**60,765**	**50,177**	**10,588**	**304,762**	**165,601**	**139,161**	**20,578**	**18,647**	**1,931**
0—5	47,722	24,219	23,503	..	..	..	47,722	24,219	23,503	..	..	..
5—10	40,105	21,941	18,164	3,143	2,193	950	36,962	19,748	17,214	486	358	128
10—15	38,916	21,963	16,953	5,445	3,919	1,526	33,471	18,044	15,427	1,218	1,006	212
15—20	39,433	23,187	16,246	8,265	6,527	1,738	31,168	16,660	14,508	3,032	2,737	295
20 and over	199,351	124,468	74,883	43,912	37,538	6,374	155,439	86,930	68,509	15,842	14,546	1,296
Howrah.												
All Religions	**224,873**	**145,120**	**79,753**	**72,569**	**55,013**	**17,556**	**152,304**	**90,107**	**62,197**	**25,718**	**22,898**	**2,820**
0—5	21,199	11,133	10,066	..	..	..	21,199	11,133	10,066	..	..	..
5—10	18,963	10,665	8,298	5,607	3,624	1,983	13,356	7,041	6,315	1,784	1,463	321
10—15	19,643	11,028	8,615	7,147	4,691	2,456	12,496	6,337	6,159	2,699	2,238	461
15—20	23,654	14,699	8,955	8,764	6,261	2,503	14,890	8,438	6,452	3,365	2,893	472
20 and over	141,414	97,595	43,819	51,051	40,437	10,614	90,363	57,158	33,205	17,870	16,304	1,566

*Excludes New Delhi and Cantonment.

Table XIII.—Literacy by Religion and Age—Part III—Cities—*contd.*

Age and Religion.	Total.			Population Literate.			Illiterate.			Literate in English.		
	Persons.	Males.	Females.	Persons.	Males.	Females.	Persons.	Males.	Females.	Persons.	Males.	Females.
1	2	3	4	5	6	7	8	9	10	11	12	13
Jaipur.												
All Religions	**144,179**	**77,933**	**66,246**	**19,168**	**17,024**	**2,144**	**125,011**	**60,909**	**64,102**	**3,334**	**3,061**	**273**
0—5	17,253	8,698	8,555	..	..	..	17,253	8,698	8,555	..	..	..
5—10	14,663	7,889	6,774	917	728	189	13,746	7,161	6,585	147	119	28
10—15	14,256	7,711	6,545	1,483	1,232	251	12,773	6,479	6,294	299	258	41
15—20	14,136	7,543	6,593	2,351	2,053	298	11,785	5,490	6,295	589	546	43
20 and over	83,871	46,092	37,779	14,417	13,011	1,406	69,454	33,081	36,373	2,299	2,138	161
Jubbulpore.												
All Religions	**124,382**	**69,258**	**55,124**	**30,745**	**24,714**	**6,031**	**93,637**	**44,544**	**49,093**	**10,555**	**8,802**	**1,753**
0—5	17,666	8,659	9,007	..	..	..	17,666	8,659	9,007	..	..	..
5—10	13,574	7,284	6,290	2,436	1,662	774	11,138	5,622	5,516	560	373	187
10—15	12,578	6,943	5,635	3,276	2,339	937	9,302	4,604	4,698	891	642	249
15—20	12,986	7,239	5,747	4,555	3,567	988	8,431	3,672	4,759	1,620	1,344	276
20 and over	67,578	39,133	28,445	20,478	17,146	3,332	47,100	21,987	25,113	7,484	6,443	1,041
Karachi.												
All Religions	**263,565**	**156,120**	**107,445**	**56,880**	**44,651**	**12,229**	**206,685**	**111,469**	**95,216**	**25,139**	**21,365**	**3,774**
0—10	65,364	33,626	31,738	3,652	2,296	1,356	61,712	31,330	30,382	785	535	250
10—15	25,960	14,481	11,479	4,984	3,290	1,694	20,976	11,191	9,785	1,535	1,101	434
15—20	27,011	15,952	11,059	8,169	6,151	2,018	18,842	9,801	9,041	4,042	3,373	669
20 and over	145,230	92,061	53,169	40,075	32,914	7,161	105,155	57,147	46,008	18,777	16,356	2,421
Lahore.												
All Religions	**429,747**	**274,587**	**155,160**	**100,885**	**81,631**	**19,254**	**328,862**	**192,956**	**135,906**	**42,916**	**37,438**	**5,478**
0—5	54,737	29,190	25,547	..	..	..	54,737	29,190	25,547	..	..	..
5—10	43,583	23,707	19,876	5,133	3,219	1,914	38,450	20,488	17,962	1,008	623	385
10—15	42,660	24,618	18,042	9,337	6,348	2,989	33,323	18,270	15,053	2,678	1,957	721
15—20	52,093	34,748	17,345	16,357	13,144	3,213	35,736	21,604	14,132	7,798	6,880	918
20 and over	236,674	162,324	74,350	70,058	58,920	11,138	166,616	103,404	63,212	31,432	27,978	3,454
Lucknow.												
All Religions	**274,659**	**159,458**	**115,201**	**47,216**	**40,402**	**6,814**	**227,443**	**119,056**	**108,387**	**21,839**	**18,936**	**2,903**
0—5	29,596	15,010	14,586	..	..	..	29,596	15,010	14,586	..	..	..
5—10	27,967	15,054	12,913	2,048	1,505	543	25,919	13,549	12,370	714	522	192
10—15	26,183	14,695	11,488	3,437	2,609	828	22,746	12,086	10,660	1,303	1,005	298
15—20	27,195	16,294	10,901	6,582	5,493	1,089	20,613	10,801	9,812	3,422	2,992	430
20 and over	163,718	98,405	65,313	35,149	30,795	4,354	128,569	67,610	60,959	16,400	14,417	1,983
Madura.												
All Religions	**182,018**	**91,676**	**90,342**	**49,118**	**40,664**	**8,454**	**132,900**	**51,012**	**81,888**	**11,996**	**10,401**	**1,595**
0—5	23,350	11,460	11,890	..	..	..	23,350	11,460	11,890	..	..	..
5—10	20,618	10,402	10,216	2,878	2,111	767	17,740	8,291	9,449	463	342	121
10—15	19,524	10,036	9,488	4,833	3,521	1,312	14,691	6,515	8,176	1,069	813	256
15—20	18,026	9,124	8,902	6,947	5,387	1,560	11,079	3,737	7,342	2,162	1,810	352
20 and over	100,500	50,654	49,846	34,460	29,645	4,815	66,040	21,009	45,031	8,302	7,436	866

Mandalay (*Municipality*).

All Religions	134,950	69,849	65,101	74,579	49,167	25,412	60,371	20,682	39,669	6,526	4,932	1,594
0—5	13,338	6,524	6,814	..	..	...	13,338	6,524	6,814	..	..	..
5—10	13,523	6,750	6,773	5,554	3,428	2,126	7,969	3,322	4,647	572	362	210
10—15	13,204	6,709	6,495	7,513	4,620	2,893	5,691	2,089	3,602	944	624	320
15—20	13,572	7,148	6,424	9,129	5,765	3,364	4,443	1,383	3,060	1,197	881	316
20 and over	81,313	42,718	38,595	52,383	35,354	17,029	28,930	7,364	21,566	3,813	3,065	748

Moradabad.

All Religions	110,562	61,346	49,216	16,267	12,585	3,682	94,295	48,761	45,534	4,602	3,995	607
0—5	17,348	8,689	8,659	..	..	..	17,348	8,689	8,659	..	..	..
5—10	13,224	7,001	6,223	1,111	751	360	12,113	6,250	5,863	201	157	44
10—15	12,183	6,495	5,688	1,818	1,234	584	10,365	5,261	5,104	433	332	101
15—20	11,661	6,389	5,272	2,400	1,812	588	9,261	4,577	4,684	754	636	118
20 and over	56,146	32,772	23,374	10,938	8,788	2,150	45,208	23,984	21,224	3,214	2,870	344

Multan.

All Religions	119,457	68,119	51,338	15,301	13,596	1,705	104,156	54,523	49,633	5,035	4,640	395
0—5	15,509	7,770	7,739	..	..	..	15,509	7,770	7,739	..	..	..
5—10	13,820	7,554	6,266	712	568	144	13,108	6,986	6,122	110	77	33
10—15	13,200	7,436	5,764	1,452	1,208	244	11,748	6,228	5,520	315	263	52
15—20	12,748	7,340	5,408	2,618	2,323	295	10,130	5,017	5,113	1,017	952	65
20 and over	64,180	38,019	26,161	10,519	9,497	1,022	53,661	28,522	25,139	3,593	3,348	245

Mysore.

All Religions	107,142	56,772	50,370	32,595	23,858	8,737	74,547	32,914	41,633	12,093	10,688	1,405
0—5	13,759	6,821	6,938	..	..	..	13,759	6,821	6,938	..	..	..
5—10	13,695	7,091	6,604	1,969	1,177	792	11,726	5,914	5,812	152	89	63
10—15	13,024	6,947	6,077	4,936	3,281	1,655	8,088	3,666	4,422	1,486	1,204	282
15—20	11,036	5,975	5,061	5,068	3,611	1,457	5,968	2,364	3,604	2,410	2,098	312
20 and over	55,628	29,938	25,690	20,622	15,789	4,833	35,006	14,149	20,857	8,045	7,297	748

Nagpur.

All Religions	215,165	116,403	98,762	46,840	35,807	11,033	168,325	80,596	87,729	16,912	14,068	2,844
0—5	28,206	14,140	14,066	..	..	..	28,206	14,140	14,066	..	..	..
5—10	24,545	12,792	11,753	3,932	2,649	1,283	20,613	10,143	10,470	871	578	293
10—15	23,167	12,345	10,822	5,726	4,127	1,599	17,441	8,218	9,223	1,473	1,111	362
15—20	22,531	11,971	10,560	7,495	5,659	1,836	15,036	6,312	8,724	2,985	2,480	505
20 and over	116,716	65,155	51,561	29,687	23,372	6,315	87,029	41,783	45,246	11,583	9,899	1,684

Patna.

All Religions	159,690	92,238	67,452	33,921	28,138	5,783	125,769	64,100	61,669	13,230	11,285	1,945
0—5	18,259	9,176	9,083	..	..	..	18,259	9,176	9,083	..	..	..
5—10	17,434	9,617	7,817	2,355	1,670	685	15,079	7,947	7,132	675	427	248
10—15	17,326	10,031	7,295	3,484	2,586	898	13,842	7,445	6,397	1,208	859	349
15—20	16,931	10,457	6,474	5,051	4,209	842	11,880	6,248	5,632	2,369	2,063	306
20 and over	89,740	52,957	36,783	23,031	19,673	3,358	66,709	33,284	33,425	8,978	7,936	1,042

Table XIII.—Literacy by Religion and Age—Part III—Cities—*concld.*

Age and Religion.	Total.			Population Literate.			Illiterate.			Literate in English.		
	Persons.	Males.	Females.	Persons.	Males.	Females.	Persons.	Males.	Females.	Persons.	Males.	Females.
1	2	3	4	5	6	7	8	9	10	11	12	13
Poona.												
All Religions	**162,901**	**86,784**	**76,117**	**51,826**	**39,609**	**12,217**	**111,075**	**47,175**	**63,900**	**19,507**	**16,844**	**2,663**
0—10	39,095	20,026	19,069	3,703	2,703	1,000	35,392	17,323	18,069	649	472	177
10—15	17,544	9,519	8,025	6,709	4,340	2,369	10,835	5,179	5,656	1,821	1,372	449
15—20	18,015	9,682	8,333	8,705	6,221	2,484	9,310	3,461	5,849	4,212	3,532	680
20 and over	88,247	47,557	40,690	32,709	26,345	6,364	55,538	21,212	34,326	12,825	11,468	1,357
Rangoon.												
All Religions	**400,415**	**271,063**	**129,352**	**187,733**	**138,665**	**49,068**	**212,682**	**132,398**	**80,284**	**55,682**	**43,579**	**12,103**
0—5	30,611	15,191	15,420	..	..	..	30,611	15,191	15,420	..	..	..
5—10	30,036	15,928	14,108	8,538	5,095	3,443	21,498	10,833	10,665	2,784	1,713	1,071
10—15	31,037	17,352	13,685	13,995	8,581	5,414	17,042	8,771	8,271	4,927	3,165	1,762
15—20	43,775	29,555	14,220	24,603	17,164	7,439	19,172	12,391	6,781	8,305	6,151	2,154
20 and over	264,956	193,037	71,919	140,597	107,825	32,772	124,359	85,212	39,147	39,666	32,550	7,116
Salem.												
All Religions	**102,179**	**51,786**	**50,393**	**21,174**	**17,537**	**3,637**	**81,005**	**34,249**	**46,756**	**5,160**	**4,707**	**453**
0—5	15,929	7,899	8,030	..	..	..	15,929	7,899	8,030	..	..	..
5—10	13,376	6,829	6,547	1,376	1,015	361	12,000	5,814	6,186	229	195	34
10—15	11,977	6,113	5,864	2,350	1,755	595	9,627	4,258	5,269	535	472	63
15—20	10,098	4,963	5,135	3,160	2,475	685	6,938	2,488	4,450	951	861	90
20 and over	50,799	25,982	24,817	14,288	12,292	1,996	36,511	13,690	22,821	3,445	3,179	266
Sholapur.												
All Religions	**135,574**	**72,079**	**63,495**	**21,389**	**18,334**	**3,055**	**114,185**	**53,745**	**60,440**	**4,394**	**4,000**	**394**
0—10	35,184	17,937	17,247	1,637	1,356	281	33,547	16,581	16,966	83	68	15
10—15	14,965	7,836	7,129	2,572	2,093	479	12,393	5,743	6,650	337	273	64
15—20	14,660	7,464	7,196	3,380	2,729	651	11,280	4,735	6,545	793	697	96
20 and over	70,765	38,842	31,923	13,800	12,156	1,644	56,965	26,686	30,279	3,181	2,962	219
Srinagar.												
All Religions	**173,573**	**94,793**	**78,780**	**17,575**	**16,480**	**1,095**	**155,998**	**78,313**	**77,685**	**8,263**	**7,989**	**274**
0—5	22,878	11,569	11,309	..	..	..	22,878	11,569	11,309	..	..	..
5—10	22,147	11,502	10,645	952	775	177	21,195	10,727	10,468	295	269	26
10—15	20,688	11,021	9,667	1,714	1,475	239	18,974	9,546	9,428	759	722	37
15—20	18,656	10,114	8,542	2,723	2,533	190	15,933	7,581	8,352	1,728	1,690	38
20 and over	89,204	50,587	38,617	12,186	11,697	489	77,018	38,890	38,128	5,481	5,308	173
Trichinopoly.												
All Religions	**142,843**	**72,997**	**69,846**	**45,955**	**35,370**	**10,585**	**96,888**	**37,627**	**59,261**	**15,130**	**13,005**	**2,125**
0—5	16,899	8,278	8,621	..	..	..	16,899	8,278	8,621	..	..	..
5—10	16,241	8,136	8,105	3,286	2,188	1,098	12,955	5,948	7,007	850	608	242
10—15	15,879	7,978	7,901	4,983	3,276	1,707	10,896	4,702	6,194	1,543	1,144	399
15—20	15,745	8,289	7,456	6,988	5,091	1,897	8,757	3,198	5,559	2,912	2,463	449
20 and over	78,079	40,316	37,763	30,698	24,815	5,883	47,381	15,501	31,880	9,825	8,790	1,035

TABLE XIV

Literacy by Selected Castes.

This Table, which corresponds to table IX of 1921, deals exclusively with the population **aged 7 years and over.**

2. The castes selected will generally be found in Provincial Tables arranged according to the proportion of literate persons returned in each. Here they have been arranged alphabetically to facilitate reference, as in Table VIII.

3. The remarks in paragraphs 3, 4 and 5 of the fly-leaf to Table VIII apply to this table also. Paragraph 6 is also rèlevant, except that here the Andaman and Nicobar Islands are also represented.

4. To economise in space other tables of this volume in which the castes detailed in this table also appear are represented in col. 3 by small arabic instead of Roman numerals.

Table XIV.—Literacy by Selected Castes.

	Caste, Tribe or Race.	Province, State or Agency and Religion.	Also tabulated in Table :	Total.			Literate.			Illiterate.			Literate in English.		
				Persons.	Males.	Females.	Persons.	Males	Females.	Persons.	Males.	Females.	Persons.	Males.	Females.
	1	2	3	4	5	6	7	8	9	10	11	12	13	14	15
1	**AGAMUDAIYAN** (Agamudia).	...	17	**421,199**	**200,823**	**220,376**	**48,948**	**47,269**	**1,679**	**372,251**	**153,554**	**218,697**	**2,044**	**1,969**	**75**
	AGAMUDAIYAN KALLAN (KALAN)	Cochin (Hindu)	..	211	99	112	34	31	3	177	68	109	1	1	..
		Madras (Hindu) ..	..	420,107	200,312	219,795	48,712	47,062	1,650	371,395	153,250	218,145	2,043	1,968	75
		Cochin (Hindu)	..	881	412	469	202	176	26	679	236	443	..	..	..
2	**AHOM**	Assam (Hindu) ..	17,18	**186,215**	**98,167**	**88,048**	**25,406**	**24,174**	**1,232**	**160,809**	**73,993**	**86,816**	**4,489**	**4,431**	**58**
3	**AMBALAVASI** ..	..	8,17	**14,066**	**7,019**	**7,047**	**9,610**	**5,786**	**3,824**	**4,456**	**1,233**	**3,223**	**1,545**	**1,281**	**264**
		Cochin (Hindu) ..	..	7,487	3,656	3,831	5,454	3,148	2,306	2,033	508	1,525	1,099	866	233
		Travancore (Hindu) ..	..	6,579	3,363	3,216	4,156	2,638	1,518	2,423	725	1,698	446	415	31
4	**ARAIN**	..	17	**1,057,206**	**587,614**	**469,592**	**36,325**	**32,379**	**3,946**	**1,020,881**	**555,235**	**465,646**	**6,907**	**6,488**	**419**
		Punjab (Muslim) ..	..	1,038,928	577,253	461,675	36,005	32,082	3,923	1,002,923	545,171	457,752	6,889	6,470	419
		Jammu and Kashmir (Muslim).	..	18,278	10,361	7,917	320	297	23	17,958	10,064	7,894	18	18	..
5	**ARAKH**	United Provinces (Hindu.)	17	**68,972**	**35,575**	**33,397**	**405**	**396**	**9**	**68,567**	**35,179**	**33,388**	**3**	**3**	..
6	**AWAN**	..	..	**649,291**	**354,290**	**295,001**	**24,540**	**22,274**	**2,266**	**624,751**	**332,016**	**292,735**	**4,652**	**4,299**	**353**
		N.-W. F. Province (Muslim)	..	225,598	126,060	99,538	9,496	8,467	1,029	216,102	117,593	98,509	2,392	2,107	285
		Punjab (Muslim) ..	..	423,693	228,230	195,463	15,044	13,807	1,237	408,649	214,423	194,226	2,260	2,192	68
7	**BABHAN** (Bhumihar-Brahman)	Bihar and Orissa (Hindu) ..	17,18	**722,561**	**384,187**	**338,374**	**97,973**	**89,646**	**8,327**	**624,588**	**294,541**	**330,047**	**5,615**	**5,504**	**111**
8	**BAIDYA**	..	8,17	**95,511**	**50,424**	**45,087**	**61,323**	**39,422**	**21,901**	**34,188**	**11,002**	**23,186**	**32,812**	**26,621**	**6,191**
		Assam (Hindu)	..	5,106	2,771	2,335	3,943	2,405	1,538	1,163	366	797	1,585	1,389	196
		Bengal (Hindu)	..	90,405	47,653	42,752	57,380	37,017	20,363	33,025	10,636	22,389	31,227	25,232	5,995
9	**BAIRAGI** (Babaji, Baishnab).	..	8.17	**344,358**	**166,973**	**177,385**	**49,918**	**43,976**	**5,942**	**294,440**	**122,997**	**171,443**	**6,332**	**5,811**	**521**
		Bengal (Hindu)	..	288,013	137,630	150,383	44,633	39,089	5,544	243,380	98,541	144,839	6,258	5,737	521
		C. P. and Berar (Hindu) ..	..	31,654	16,071	15,583	4,377	4,048	329	27,277	12,023	15,254	47	47	..
		Gwalior (Hindu) ..	..	24,691	13,272	11,419	908	839	69	23,783	12,433	11,350	27	27	..
10	**BAKKARWAL** ..	Jammu and Kashmir (Muslim).	..	**4,040**	**2,173**	**1,867**	**38**	**38**	..	**4,002**	**2,135**	**1,867**	..	..	..
11	**BALAI** (Balhai).	..	17	**292,151**	**147,697**	**144,454**	**2,066**	**2,029**	**37**	**290,085**	**145,668**	**144,417**	**43**	**40**	
		Ajmer Merwara (Hindu and Muslim).	..	15,941	8,169	7,772	370	362	8	15,571	7,807	7,764	28	28	..
		C. P. and Berar (All Religions).	..	44,078	22,138	21,940	561	554	7	43,517	21,584	21,933	3	..	3
		Central India (Hindu) ..	..	153,297	76,959	76,338	987	974	13	152,310	75,985	76,325	11	11	..
		Gwalior (Hindu) ..	..	78,835	40,431	38,404	148	139	9	78,687	40,292	38,395	1	1	..
12	**BALUCH** (Biloch) ..	..	17,18	**1,378,571**	**761,118**	**617,453**	**15,239**	**14,517**	**722**	**1,363,332**	**746,601**	**616,731**	**1,217**	**1,190**	**27**
		Baluchistan (Muslim) ..	..	765,094	415,937	349,157	6,117	5,987	130	758,977	409,950	349,027	445	438	7
		Bombay (Muslim) ..	..	124,376	74,108	50,268	2,319	2,107	212	122,057	72,001	50,056	135	132	3
		Punjab (Muslim) ..	..	489,101	271,073	218,028	6,803	6,423	380	482,298	264,650	217,648	637	620	17

13	**BANJARA, ETC.** ..	..	8,17,18	**572,078**	**298,327**	**273,751**	**6,462**	**6,034**	**428**	**565,616**	**292,293**	**273,323**	**148**	**144**	**4**
	BANJARA ..	C. P. and Berar (Hindu and Tribal.	..	117,643	59,472	58,171	1,441	1,355	86	116,202	58,117	58,085	31	31	..
		C. P. and Berar (Muslim)	..	86	48	38	1	1	..	85	47	38	..	..	..
		Central India (Hindu) ..	..	32,981	17,914	15,067	220	215	5	32,761	17,699	15,062	..	..	..
		Mysore { (Hindu) ..	..	39,137	20,399	18,738	381	353	28	38,756	20,046	18,710	9	9	..
		Mysore { (Tribal) ..	..	10,491	5,404	5,087	105	99	6	10,386	5,305	5,081	4	4	..
	LAMANI ..	Bombay (Hindu)	..	26,849	14,029	12,820	133	129	4	26,716	13,900	12,816	9	9	..
	LAMBADA ..	Hyderabad (Tribal) ..	..	249,587	129,682	119,905	1,674	1,560	114	247,913	128,122	119,791	23	19	4
	WANJARI ..	C. P. and Berar (Hindu) ..	..	35,416	17,993	17,423	1,339	1,279	60	34,077	16,714	17,363	37	37	..
		Hyderabad (Hindu) ..	..	59,888	33,386	26,502	1,168	1,043	125	58,720	32,343	26,377	35	35	..
14	**BANIYA**	..	8,17	**942,744**	**499,544**	**443,200**	**301,514**	**271,647**	**29,867**	**641,230**	**227,897**	**413,333**	**25,587**	**24,885**	**702**
	AGARWAL (*Agar-Wala*).	Bengal (Hindu) ..	..	15,625	9,501	6,124	5,378	4,663	715	10,247	4,838	5,409	1,007	947	60
		Delhi { (Hindu) ..	..	21,411	12,682	8,729	7,773	6,817	956	13,638	5,865	7,773	1,815	1,759	56
		Delhi { (Jain) ..	..	2,534	1,332	1,202	983	791	192	1,551	541	1,010	260	243	17
		Punjab { (Hindu) ..	..	280,826	154,117	126,709	78,888	74,770	4,118	201,938	79,347	122,591	7,151	6,940	211
		Punjab { (Jain) ..	..	19,584	10,359	9,225	6,298	5,744	554	13,286	4,615	8,671	768	751	17
		Central India (Hindu and Jain).	..	18,899	10,238	8,661	6,829	6,352	477	12,070	3,886	8,184	709	685	24
		Rajputana (All Religions)	..	74,509	37,390	37,119	19,616	18,914	702	54,893	18,476	36,417	775	764	11
	BANIYA ..	C. P. and Berar (All Religions) ..	..	191,777	101,257	90,520	67,197	60,540	6,657	124,580	40,717	83,863	4,779	4,682	97
		Gwalior (Hindu) ..	..	73,542	41,028	32,514	12,781	10,809	1,972	60,761	30,219	30,542	1,000	961	39
		Cochin (Hindu)	..	129	66	63	64	46	18	65	20	45	7	7	..
		Baroda (Hindu and Jain)	..	19,279	10,133	9,146	11,934	8,949	2,985	7,345	1,184	6,161	1,718	1,681	37
		Central India (Hindu and Jain).	..	9,123	4,424	4,699	1,258	1,209	49	7,865	3,215	4,650	46	45	1
	DISAWAL ..	Baroda (Hindu and Jain)	..	6,104	3,092	3,012	3,693	2,774	919	2,411	318	2,093	653	648	5
	GAHOI	Central India (Hindu) ..	..	12,217	6,393	5,824	3,087	3,000	87	9,130	3,393	5,737	34	34	..
	KAPOL	Baroda (Hindu and Jain).	..	2,060	1,081	979	1,362	972	390	698	109	589	210	202	8
	KESAR	Central India (Hindu) ..	..	11,547	5,662	5,885	1,554	1,468	86	9,993	4,194	5,799	32	32	..
	KHADAYATA ..	Baroda (Hindu and Jain)	..	3,213	1,727	1,486	2,003	1,576	427	1,210	151	1,059	352	346	6
	LAD	Baroda (Hindu and Jain)	..	6,482	3,426	3,056	3,947	3,082	865	2,535	344	2,191	772	768	4
	MAHESRI ..	Central India (Hindu) ..	..	8,449	4,546	3,903	3,506	3,241	265	4,943	1,305	3,638	235	230	5
	OSWAL	Central India (Hindu and Jain).	..	2,525	1,387	1,138	890	826	64	1,635	561	1,074	66	64	2
		Rajputana (Hindu and Jain)	..	119,143	57,446	61,697	38,858	37,264	1,594	80,285	20,182	60,103	1,061	1,025	36
	PORWAL (*Porwad*).	Baroda (Hindu and Jain)	..	6,680	3,480	3,200	4,076	3,015	1,061	2,604	465	2,139	510	496	14
		Central India (Hindu and Jain).	..	8,578	4,610	3,968	2,701	2,577	124	5,877	2,033	3,844	93	90	3
	SHRIMALI ..	Baroda (Hindu and Jain)	..	28,508	14,167	14,341	16,838	12,248	4,590	11,670	1,919	9,751	1,534	1,485	49
15	**BAURI**	..	8,17,18	**606,283**	**297,572**	**308,711**	**5,412**	**4,616**	**796**	**600,871**	**292,956**	**307,915**	**184**	**180**	**4**
	BAURI	Bengal (Hindu) ..	..	269,730	133,296	136,434	2,548	1,906	642	267,182	131,390	135,792	128	126	2
		Bihar and Orissa (Hindu)..	..	266,429	130,211	136,218	1,937	1,846	91	264,492	128,365	136,127	41	40	1
	BAVURI ..	Madras (Hindu) ..	..	33,592	14,541	19,051	589	571	18	33,003	13,970	19,033	..	..	..
	BAWARIA ..	Delhi (Hindu)	..	28	19	9	1	1	..	27	18	9	..	..	..
		Punjab { (Hindu) ..	..	12,148	6,425	5,723	150	124	26	11,998	6,301	5,697	11	11	..
		Punjab { (Sikh) ..	..	12,329	6,517	5,812	164	147	17	12,165	6,370	5,795	3	3	..
		United Provinces (Hindu)	..	12,027	6,563	5,464	23	21	2	12,004	6,542	5,462	1	..	1

Table XIV.—Literacy by Selected Castes—*contd.*

Caste, Tribe or Race.	Province, State or Agency and Religion :	Also tabulated in Table :	Total.			Literate.			Illiterate.			Literate in English.		
			Persons.	Males.	Females.	Persons.	Males.	Females.	Persons.	Males.	Females.	Persons.	Males.	Females.
1	2	3	4	5	6	7	8	9	10	11	12	13	14	15
19 **BHANGI**	..	8,17	**540,861**	**286,169**	**254,692**	**5,840**	**5,361**	**479**	**535,021**	**280,808**	**254,213**	**201**	**160**	**41**
BHANGI ..	Bombay (Hindu)	..	29,821	15,270	14,551	810	770	40	29,011	14,500	14,511	1	1	..
	United Provinces (All Religions).	..	396,148	211,299	184,849	2,353	2,194	159	393,795	209,105	184,690	169	129	40
	Baroda (Hindu) ..	..	24,819	12,632	12,187	1,396	1,212	184	23,423	11,420	12,003	6	6	..
	Central India (Hindu) ..	..	20,041	10,372	9,669	318	308	10	19,723	10,064	9,659	11	11	..
	Rajputana (All Religions)	..	29,972	15,644	14,328	217	166	51	29,755	15,478	14,277	11	11	..
	Western India States (Hindu).	..	24,886	13,019	11,867	211	207	4	24,675	12,812	11,863	..	..	..
MEHTAR ..	C. P. and Berar (All Religions).	..	15,174	7,933	7,241	535	504	31	14,639	7,429	7,210	3	2	1
17 **BARBHUNJA** ..	United Provinces (All Religions).	8,17	**231,439**	**124,686**	**106,753**	**6,500**	**6,312**	**188**	**224,939**	**118,374**	**106,565**	**148**	**141**	**7**
18 **BHAT** ..	..	8,17	**98,349**	**49,312**	**49,037**	**8,401**	**7,607**	**794**	**89,948**	**41,705**	**48,243**	**402**	**382**	**20**
	United Provinces (All Religions).	..	84,253	41,094	43,159	6,188	5,733	455	78,065	35,361	42,704	346	329	17
	Hyderabad (Hindu) ..	..	14,096	8,218	5,878	2,213	1,874	339	11,883	6,344	5,539	56	53	3
19 **BHIL**	..	8,17,18	**542,587**	**279,049**	**263,538**	**3,350**	**3,191**	**159**	**539,237**	**275,858**	**263,379**	**21**	**20**	**1**
	Bombay (Hindu)	..	206,688	106,997	99,691	1,115	1,096	19	205,573	105,901	99,672	13	13	..
	C. P. and Berar (All Religions).	..	19,903	10,054	9,849	58	58	..	19,845	9,996	9,849	..	..	..
	United Provinces (Hindu).	..	20	11	9	..	..	..	20	11	9	..	..	..
	Baroda (Hindu and Tribal)	..	41,887	21,800	20,087	1,917	1,785	132	39,970	20,015	19,955	3	3	..
	Gwalior (Hindu) ..	..	61,530	32,282	29,248	152	147	5	61,378	32,135	29,243	2	2	..
	Hyderabad (Tribal) ..	..	12,332	6,102	6,230	15	15	..	12,317	6,087	6,230	..	..	..
	Rajputana (Hindu Tribal and Christians).	..	200,227	101,803	98,424	93	90	3	200,134	101,713	98,421	3	2	1
20 **BHUINYA** (Bhuinyar Bhuiya, Bhumia). ..	..	17,18	**529,172**	**260,624**	**268,548**	**3,401**	**3,269**	**132**	**525,771**	**257,355**	**268,416**	**78**	**75**	**3**
	Bihar and Orissa (Hindu)..	..	499,587	246,433	253,154	3,288	3,166	122	496,299	243,267	253,032	78	75	3
	C. P. and Berar (Hindu)..	..	23,333	11,108	12,225	102	93	9	23,231	11,015	12,216	..	..	..
	C. P. and Berar (Tribal)..	..	6,252	3,083	3,169	11	10	1	6,241	3,073	3,168	..	..	..
21 **BOHRN** (Vohora) ..	..	8,17	**105,263**	**54,303**	**50,960**	**37,678**	**31,960**	**5,718**	**67,585**	**22,343**	**45,242**	**3,998**	**3,838**	**160**
	Bombay (Muslim) ..	..	71,282	37,886	33,396	23,696	21,140	2,556	47,586	16,746	30,840	3,175	3,043	132
	C. P. and Berar (Muslim)	..	2,157	1,036	1,121	1,178	806	372	979	230	749	231	226	5
	Baroda (Muslim) ..	..	22,985	11,041	11,944	9,238	7,060	2,178	13 747	3,981	9,766	376	360	16
	Western India States (Muslim).	..	8,839	4,340	4,499	3,566	2,954	612	5,273	1,386	3,887	216	209	7
22 **BRAHMAN** ..	..	8,17	**11,309,225**	**5,995,251**	**5,313,974**	**3,127,112**	**2,617,130**	**509,982**	**8,182,113**	**3,378,121**	**4,803,992**	**688,957**	**643,062**	**45,895**
ANAVALA ..	Baroda (Hindu) ..	..	10,075	5,263	4,812	6,306	4,584	1,722	3,769	679	3,090	1,088	1,072	16

M8CC

AUDICH ..	Bombay (Hindu)	23,975	12,597	11,378	12,417	9,374	3,043	11,558	3,223	8,335	2,137	2,049	88
	Baroda (Hindu)	38,339	19,353	18,986	18,766	14,420	4,346	19,573	4,933	14,640	2,471	2,437	34
	Western India States (Hindu). ..	65,753	33,364	32,389	27,316	24,256	6,060	38,437	12,108	26,329	4,420	4,265	155
CHITPAWAN, KOKANASTHA AND KONKANI.	Bombay (Hindu)	55,191	27,777	27,414	30,469	21,398	9,071	24,722	6,379	18,343	10,115	8,713	1,402
	Baroda (Hindu)	2,978	1,632	1,346	2,256	1,552	704	722	80	642	975	911	64
	Cochin (Hindu)	7,870	3,947	3,923	3,541	2,853	688	4,329	1,094	3,235	1,174	1,105	69
DESHASTHA ..	Bombay (Hindu)	185,152	98,822	86,330	97,327	79,912	17,415	87,825	18,910	68,915	26,698	25,271	1,427
	Baroda (Hindu)	4,846	2,627	2,219	3,419	2,434	985	1,427	193	1,234	1,285	1,198	87
EMBRAN ..	Cochin (Hindu)	1,342	853	489	705	562	143	637	291	346	57	53	4
GAUDA	Cochin (Hindu)	526	320	206	104	87	17	422	233	189	26	22	4
GAUD SARASWAT	Bombay (Hindu)	30,731	15,252	15,479	14,018	11,081	2,937	16,713	4,171	12,542	2,882	2,685	197
KANARESE ..	Coorg (Hindu)	1,085	602	483	662	497	165	423	105	318	212	190	22
	Madras (Hindu)	87,898	43,639	44,259	43,320	33,765	9,555	44,578	9,874	34,704	13,256	12,601	655
KHEDAWAL ..	Baroda (Hindu)	3,346	1,712	1,634	1,928	1,445	483	1,418	267	1,151	376	376	..
MALAYALA ..	Coorg (Hindu)	21	13	8	11	9	2	10	4	6	1	1	..
	Madras (Hindu)	22,098	12,055	10,043	12,597	9,135	3,462	9,501	2,920	6,581	2,245	2,082	163
	Cochin (Hindu)	6,128	3,137	2,991	4,148	2,670	1,478	1,980	467	1,513	297	294	3
	Travancore (Hindu)*	11,574	6,279	5,295	7,093	4,853	2,240	4,481	1,426	3,055	571	556	15
MEWADA ..	Baroda (Hindu)	4,310	2,314	1,996	2,087	1,738	349	2,223	576	1,647	227	226	1
MODH	Baroda (Hindu)	7,623	3,752	3,871	3,872	2,927	945	3,751	825	2,926	512	500	12
NAGAR	Baroda (Hindu)	6,866	3,385	3,481	4,568	2,942	1,626	2,298	443	1,855	1,405	1,293	112
ORIYA	Madras (Hindu)	123,094	57,991	65,103	37,936	33,876	4,060	85,158	24,115	61,043	4,718	4,548	170
TAMIL	Coorg (Hindu)	88	42	46	64	38	26	24	4	20	28	22	6
	Madras (Hindu)	408,737	200,784	207,953	255,792	175,831	79,961	152,945	24,953	127,992	96,281	89,856	6,425
	Cochin (Hindu)	17,138	8,566	8,572	11,757	7,442	4,315	5,381	1,124	4,257	4,532	4,233	299
TAPODHAN ..	Baroda (Hindu)	4,972	2,479	2,493	1,758	1,401	357	3,214	1,078	2,136	151	151	..
TELUGU ..	Coorg (Hindu)	9	8	1	7	6	1	2	2	..	5	5	..
	Madras (Hindu)	395,898	193,511	202,387	202,494	153,323	49,171	193,404	40,188	153,216	60,060	57,846	2,214
	Cochin (Hindu)	46	25	21	36	23	13	10	2	8	19	18	1
BRAHMAN, (UNSPECIFIED.)	Assam (Hindu)	126,056	70,774	55,282	61,696	50,993	10,703	64,360	19,781	44,579	14,275	13,728	547
	Bengal (Hindu)	1,201,684	660,011	541,673	542,832	425,765	117,067	658,852	234,246	424,606	208,573	190,601	17,972
	Bihar and Orissa (Hindu).. ..	1,760,182	899,285	860,897	343,686	319,863	23,823	1,416,496	579,422	837,074	34,691	33,327	1,364
	C. P. and Berar (All Religions). ..	428,734	233,389	195,345	159,514	135,679	23,835	269,220	97,710	171,510	33,411	31,398	2,013
	Delhi (Hindu)	42,495	26,570	15,925	13,606	11,389	2,217	28,889	15,181	13,708	5,458	4,948	510
	N.-W. F. Province (All Religions). ..	14,630	9,409	5,221	6,014	4,878	1,136	8,616	4,531	4,085	1,029	969	60
	Punjab (Hindu)	867,855	483,169	384,686	141,864	129,189	12,675	725,991	353,980	372,011	22,531	21,763	768
	Punjab (Sikh)	5,466	3,310	2,156	1,604	1,302	302	3,862	2,008	1,854	278	253	25
	United Provinces (All Religions). ..	3,779,429	2,026,169	1,753,260	637,825	593,905	43,920	3,141,604	1,432,264	1,709,340	52,788	49,412	3,376
	Baroda (Hindu)	21,390	11,925	9,465	11,825	9,045	2,780	9,565	2,880	6,685	1,964	1,842	122
	Central India (Hindu)	389,074	204,347	184,727	59,053	54,094	4,959	330,021	150,253	179,768	6,837	6,481	356
	Gwalior (Hindu)	244,985	139,779	105,206	32,515	27,472	5,043	212,470	112,307	100,163	4,899	4,723	176
	Hyderabad (Hindu)	322,859	167,838	155,021	129,957	117,663	12,294	192,902	50,175	142,727	12,921	11,890	1,031
	Jammu and Kashmir (Hindu)† ..	152,839	78,375	74,464	14,875	13,326	1,549	137,964	65,049	72,915	1,893	1,727	166
	Cochin (Hindu)	213	117	96	119	90	29	94	27	67	54	52	2
	Travancore (Hindu)	43,735	22,098	21,637	26,431	17,946	8,485	17,304	4,152	13,152	8,226	7,766	460
	Mysore (Hindu)	198,163	103,523	94,640	113,633	81,044	32,589	84,530	22,479	62,051	38,319	35,053	3,266
	Rajputana (Hindu)	181,727	93,062	88,665	23,289	22,053	1,236	158,438	71,009	87,429	2,586	2,550	36

* Includes Namputiri and Potti.

† Excludes figures for Mohyals.

Table XIV.—Literacy by Selected Castes—*contd.*

	Caste, Tribe or Race.	Province, State or Agency and Religion.	Also tabulated in Table:	Total.			Literate.			Illiterate.			Literate in English.		
				Persons.	Males.	Females.	Persons.	Males.	Females.	Persons.	Males.	Females.	Persons.	Males.	Females.
	1	2	3	4	5	6	7	8	9	10	11	12	13	14	15
23	**BRAHMBHAT** (including Barot).	Baroda (Hindu and Jain)	**8,17**	**12,168**	**6,140**	**6,028**	**4,020**	**3,482**	**538**	**8,148**	**2,658**	**5,490**	**272**	**271**	**1**
24	**CHAMAR**	..	**8,17**	**9,109,526**	**4,665,974**	**4,443,552**	**47,695**	**44,886**	**2,809**	**9,061,831**	**4,621,088**	**4,440,743**	**1,529**	**1,411**	**118**
	CHAKKILIYAN ..	Madras (Hindu)	..	472,073	237,727	234,346	3,627	3,335	292	468,446	234,392	234,054	108	105	3
		Cochin (Hindu)	..	683	363	320	19	12	7	664	351	313	1	..	1
	CHAMAR	Bihar and Orissa (Hindu)..	..	1,019,100	484,658	534,442	5,460	5,075	385	1,013,640	479,583	534,057	113	109	4
		C. P. and Berar (All Religions).	..	482,918	240,020	242,898	3,937	3,795	142	478,981	236,225	242,756	71	70	1
		Delhi (Hindu)	..	34,375	19,112	15,263	389	374	15	33,986	18,738	15,248	28	27	1
		Delhi (Ad-Dharmi) ..	..	373	213	160	5	5	..	368	208	160	..	..	..
		Delhi (Christian) ..	..	2,144	1,087	1,057	16	15	1	2,128	1,072	1,056	..	..	..
		N.-W. F. Province (All Religions).	..	2,346	1,422	924	41	41	..	2,305	1,381	924	3	3	..
		Punjab (Hindu) ..	..	545,026	296,236	248,790	2,769	2,536	233	542,257	293,700	248,557	257	255	2
		Punjab (Ad-Dharmi) ..	..	203,600	112,273	91,327	2,647	2,500	147	200,953	109,773	91,180	63	58	5
		Punjab (Sikh)	..	124,036	69,310	54,726	1,686	1,634	52	122,350	67,676	54,674	35	34	1
		United Provinces (All Religions).	..	4,970,540	2,558,620	2,411,920	16,571	15,739	832	4,953,969	2,542,881	2,411,088	618	530	88
		Baroda (Hindu) ..	.	34,368	16,756	17,612	2,450	2,210	240	31,918	14,546	17,372	13	13	..
		Central India (Hindu) ..	..	409,838	207,900	201,938	776	753	23	409,062	207,147	201,915	16	16	..
		Gwalior (Hindu) ..	..	329,871	172,338	157,533	906	817	89	328,965	171,521	157,444	13	12	1
		Jammu and Kashmir (Hindu).	..	32,961	17,557	15,404	152	143	9	32,809	17,414	15,395	4	4	..
		Rajputana (All Religions)	..	312,211	162,016	150,195	741	703	38	311,470	161,313	150,157	6	6	..
	CHAMBHAR ..	Bombay (Hindu) ..	..	94,518	48,003	46,515	2,757	2,614	143	91,761	45,389	46,372	152	141	11
		Western India States (Hindu)	..	36,931	19,561	17,370	2,655	2,500	155	34,276	17,061	17,215	26	26	..
	SAMAGARA ..	Coorg (Hindu)	..	5	4	1	..	..	..	5	4	1	..	..	..
		Madras (Hindu) ..	..	1,609	798	811	91	85	6	1,518	713	805	2	2	..
25	**CHENCHU**	.	**8,17,18**	**8,217**	**4,195**	**4,022**	**78**	**46**	**32**	**8,139**	**4,149**	**3,990**	**5**	**5**	..
		Madras (Tribal) ..	..	6,330	3,297	3,033	70	38	32	6,260	3,259	3,001	5	5	..
		Mysore (Tribal)	..	1,887	898	989	8	8	..	1,879	890	989	..	..	..
26	**CHETTI**	..	**8,17**	**18,302**	**8,966**	**9,336**	**4,918**	**4,008**	**910**	**13,384**	**4,958**	**8,426**	**326**	**312**	**14**
		Cochin (Hindu) ..	..	4,206	1,886	2,320	761	632	129	3,445	1,254	2,191	65	63	2
		Travancore (Hindu) ..	..	14,096	7,080	7,016	4,157	3,376	781	9,939	3,704	6,235	261	249	12
27	**CHODHRA**	..	**8,17,18**	**64,042**	**33,000**	**31,042**	**2,650**	**2,443**	**207**	**61,392**	**30,557**	**30,835**	**14**	**14**	..
		Bombay (Hindu) ..	..	33,684	17,211	16,473	564	542	22	33,120	16,669	16,451	3	3	..
		Baroda (Hindu and Tribal)	..	30,358	15,789	14,569	2,086	1,901	185	28,272	13,888	14,384	11	11	..
28	**CHUHRA**	..	**8 17**	**546,126**	**303,124**	**243,002**	**5,056**	**4,331**	**725**	**541,070**	**298,793**	**242,277**	**552**	**151**	**101**
		Delhi (Hindu) ..	..	14,118	8,062	6,056	248	234	14	13,870	7,828	6,042	19	18	..
		Delhi (Muslim) ..	..	283	151	132	3	3	..	280	148	132	1	1	..
		Delhi (Christian) ..	..	2,213	1,120	1,093	3	3	..	2,210	1,117	1,093	.	..	..

		N.-W. F. Province (All Religions).	..	7,983	5,603	2,380	406	380	26	7,577	5,223	2,354	26	22	4
		Punjab (Hindu) ..	..	287,549	159,104	128,445	2,374	1,977	397	285,175	157,127	128,048	274	236	38
		Punjab (Ad-Dharmi) ..	..	67,058	37,271	29,787	364	334	30	66,694	36,937	29,757	12	12	..
		Punjab (Sikh) ..	..	123,268	67,678	55,590	1,107	997	110	122,161	66,681	55,480	48	46	2
		Punjab (Muslim) ..	..	16,886	9,148	7,738	105	55	50	16,781	9,093	7,688	26	10	16
		Punjab (Christian) ..	..	26,768	14,987	11,781	446	348	98	26,322	14,639	11,683	146	106	40
29	**DARZI** ..	..	..	**469,291**	**250,177**	**219,114**	**44,230**	**39,933**	**4,297**	**425,061**	**210,244**	**214,817**	**2,124**	**2,040**	**84**
	BHAVASAR or CHHIPPA.	Baroda (Hindu and Jain)	8,17	4,971	2,506	2,465	2,232	1,810	422	2,739	696	2,043	114	111	3
	CHHIMBA ..	Punjab (Hindu) ..	..	17,034	9,452	7,582	685	643	42	16,349	8,809	7,540	59	55	4
		Punjab (Sikh) ..	..	13,728	7,645	6,083	1,285	1,173	112	12,443	6,472	5,971	73	69	4
		Punjab (Muslim) ..	..	41,880	22,780	19,100	848	805	43	41,032	21,975	19,057	87	87	..
	DARZI	Bombay (Hindu)* ..	..	26,120	13,298	12,822	7,722	7,100	622	18,398	6,198	12,200	615	571	44
		C. P. and Berar (All Religions).	..	41,672	21,483	20,189	7,680	7,244	436	33,992	14,239	19,753	313	311	2
		United Provinces (Hindu and Muslim).	..	206,023	113,184	92,839	6,001	5,656	345	200,022	107,528	92,494	165	159	6
		Baroda (Hindu and Jain)	..	12,871	6,053	6,818	3,724	2,910	814	9,147	3,143	6,004	49	48	1
		Hyderabad (Hindu)† ..	..	53,660	28,356	25,304	3,038	2,865	173	50,622	25,491	25,131	121	114	7
		Mysore (Hindu) ..	..	15,915	8,238	7,677	3,973	3,559	414	11,942	4,679	7,263	336	324	12
		Western India States (Hindu)	..	35,417	17,182	18,235	7,042	6,168	874	28,375	11,014	17,361	192	191	1
30	**DEVANGA** ..	..	17	**50,317**	**25,564**	**24,753**	**9,469**	**8,775**	**694**	**40,848**	**16,789**	**24,059**	**422**	**393**	**29**
		Cochin (Hindu) ..	..	2,559	1,268	1,291	521	471	50	2,038	797	1,241	31	29	2
		Mysore (Hindu) ..	..	47,758	24,296	23,462	8,948	8,304	644	38,810	15,992	22,818	391	364	27
31	**DHOBI** (Dhoba), etc.	..	8,17	**1,611,232**	**830,595**	**780,637**	**27,220**	**24,024**	**3,196**	**1,584,012**	**806,571**	**777,441**	**922**	**804**	**118**
	DHOBI	Bihar and Orissa (Hindu)..	..	344,330	172,575	171,755	5,336	5,036	300	338,994	167,539	171,455	87	85	2
		Bombay (Hindu).‡ ..	..	21,365	10,763	10,602	1,214	1,098	116	20,151	9,665	10,486	77	74	3
		C. P. and Berar (All Religions).	..	149,010	73,504	75,506	4,827	4,588	239	144,183	68,916	75,267	95	93	2
		Delhi (Hindu) ..	..	2,543	1,501	1,042	37	33	4	2,506	1,468	1,038	3	3	..
		Delhi (Muslim) ..	..	813	476	337	19	18	1	794	458	336	..	..	..
		Punjab (Hindu) ..	..	8,254	4,700	3,554	188	157	31	8,066	4,543	3,523	22	19	3
		Punjab (Muslim) ..	..	126,939	69,722	57,217	2,722	2,463	259	124,217	67,259	56,958	253	220	33
		United Provinces (All Religions).	..	615,742	321,319	294,423	2,324	2,135	189	613,418	319,184	294,234	116	71	45
		Central India (Hindu) ..	..	43,787	22,194	21,593	452	440	12	43,335	21,754	21,581	13	13	..
		Hyderabad (Hindu) ..	..	236,786	123,650	113,136	2,084	1,989	95	234,702	121,661	113,041	81	79	2
		Western India States (Hindu)	..	3,590	1,797	1,793	304	265	39	3,286	1,532	1,754	9	9	..
	VANNAN	Cochin (Hindu)	..	376	191	185	22	20	2	354	171	183	..	..	..
		Travancore (Hindu) ..	..	10,581	5,333	5,248	2,047	1,586	461	8,534	3,747	4,787	41	37	4
	VELUTHADANAYAR	Travancore (Hindu) ..	..	11,489	5,522	5,967	3,324	2,392	932	8,165	3,130	5,035	55	42	13
	VELUTTEDAN ..	Cochin (Hindu) ..	..	3,187	1,430	1,757	989	674	315	2,198	756	1,442	44	38	6
	VETTUVAN ..	Madras (Hindu) ..	..	23,331	11,313	12,018	831	740	91	22,500	10,573	11,927	16	14	2
		Cochin (Hindu) ..	..	9,109	4,605	4,504	500	390	110	8,609	4,215	4,394	10	7	3
32	**DHOR** (Dohor) ..	C. P. and Berar (Hindu) ..	17	**2,245**	**1,155**	**1,090**	**61**	**60**	**1**	**2,184**	**1,095**	**1,089**	..	..	..
33	**DOM** (Dum) ..	..	8,17	**532,470**	**270,671**	**261,799**	**4,867**	**4,279**	**588**	**527,603**	**266,392**	**261,211**	**270**	**247**	**23**
	BANSPHOR or BASOR	C. P. and Berar (All Religions).	..	25,017	12,646	12,371	200	198	2	24,817	12,448	12,369	1	1	..

* Including Shimpi, Sai. and Mirai.

† Including Shimpi.

‡ Including Parit, Agasa and Madival.

Table XIV.—Literacy by Selected Castes—*contd.*

Caste Tribe or Race.	Province, State or Agency and Religion.	Also tabulated in Table :	Total. Persons.	Total. Males.	Total. Females.	Literate. Persons.	Literate. Males.	Literate. Females.	Illiterate. Persons.	Illiterate. Males.	Illiterate. Females.	Literate in English. Persons.	Literate in English. Males.	Literate in English. Females.
1	2	3	4	5	6	7	8	9	10	11	12	13	14	15
DOM (Dum)—*contd.* *BANSPHOR or BASOR* —concld.	Central India (Hindu) ..	..	**34,748**	18,074	16,674	45	43	2	34,703	18,031	16,672	3	3	..
BURUD	Hyderabad (Hindu) ..	..	**30,590**	17,087	13,503	351	323	28	30,239	16,764	13,475	14	14	..
DOM	Bengal (Hindu) ..	..	**116,077**	59,278	56,799	2,779	2,333	446	113,298	56,945	56,353	211	193	18
	Bihar and Orissa (Hindu)	..	**227,675**	113,502	114,173	909	825	84	226,766	112,677	114,089	30	25	5
	Bihar and Orissa (Muslim)	..	**5**	5	..	..	..	..	5	5	..	..	..	..
	C. P. and Berar (Hindu) ..	..	**5,263**	2,651	2,612	109	105	4	5,154	2,546	2,608	..	..	..
	United Provinces (All Religions).	..	**93,095**	47,428	45,667	474	452	22	92,621	46,976	45,645	11	11	..
34 **DOSADH** (Dusadh) ..	..	**8,17**	**1,102,150**	**541,168**	**560,982**	**7,129**	**6,754**	**375**	**1,095,021**	**534,414**	**560,607**	**219**	**213**	**6**
	Bihar and Orissa (Hindu) ..	..	1,043,958	511,877	532,081	6,675	6,305	370	1,037,283	505,572	531,711	206	200	6
	United Provinces (Hindu).	..	58,192	29,291	28,901	454	449	5	57,738	28,842	28,896	13	13	..
35 **DUBLA**, etc. ..	..	**17,18**	**96,738**	**48,997**	**47,741**	**2,883**	**2,539**	**344**	**93,855**	**46,458**	**47,397**	**12**	**12**	..
DUBLA	Bombay (Hindu) ..	..	46,384	23,492	22,892	803	762	41	45,581	22,730	22,851	2	2	..
	Baroda (Hindu and Tribal)	..	9,939	4,975	4,964	549	471	78	9,390	4,504	4,886	3	3	..
TALAVIA ..	Baroda (Hindu and Tribal)	..	40,415	20,530	19,885	1,531	1,306	225	38,884	19,224	19,660	7	7	..
36 **FAQIR**	..	**17**	**569,125**	**312,617**	**256,508**	**15,587**	**14,873**	**714**	**553,538**	**297,744**	**255,794**	**568**	**560**	**8**
	Punjab (Hindu) ..	..	19,506	13,232	6,274	3,089	2,917	172	16,417	10,315	6,102	140	140	..
	Punjab (Sikh) ..	..	4,029	2,940	1,089	1,232	1,165	67	2,797	1,775	1,022	29	29	..
	Punjab (Muslim) ..	..	199,647	110,481	89,166	3,478	3,353	125	196,169	107,128	89,041	160	157	3
	United Provinces (All Religions).	..	340,647	183,130	157,517	6,817	6,567	250	333,830	176,563	157,267	214	209	5
	Baroda (Muslim) ..	..	5,296	2,834	2,462	971	871	100	4,325	1,963	2,362	25	25	..
37 **GADARIA**	.. ..	**8,17**	**1,653,221**	**866,514**	**786,707**	**24,649**	**23,449**	**1,200**	**1,628,572**	**843,065**	**785,507**	**1,040**	**954**	**86**
BHARWAD (*Bharud and Dhangar*).	Bombay (Hindu) ..	..	116,444	60,393	56,051	2,646	2,503	143	113,798	57,890	55,908	42	42	..
	Baroda (Hindu) ..	..	53,146	27,207	25,939	1,437	1,223	214	51,709	25,984	25,725	13	13	..
	Western India States (Hindu).	.	137,032	71,641	65,391	725	677	48	136,307	70,964	65,343	18	18	..
GADARIA ..	United Provinces (All Religions).	..	816,822	434,967	381,855	4,837	4,568	269	811,985	430,399	381,586	318	239	79
	Gwalior (Hindu) ..	..	69,671	37,723	31,948	257	232	25	69,414	37,491	31,923	16	16	..
KURUBA (*KURUB*)	Bombay (Hindu) ..	..	98,755	50,306	48,449	1,922	1,875	47	96,833	48,431	48,402	16	16	..
	Coorg (Hindu)	..	5,633	3,071	2,562	27	23	4	5,606	3,048	2,558	1	1	..
	Mysore (Hindu) ..	..	352,031	179,253	172,778	12,775	12,325	450	339,256	166,928	172,328	613	606	7
	Mysore (Tribal) ..	..	3,687	1,953	1,734	23	23	..	3,664	1,930	1,734	3	3	..
38 **GADDI**	U. P. (All Religions) ..	**17**	**67,197**	**36,712**	**30,485**	**600**	**502**	**98**	**66,597**	**36,210**	**30,387**	**53**	**14**	**39**
39 **GANDA**	C. P. and Berar (All Religions).	**17**	**135,486**	**65,413**	**70,073**	**1,159**	**1,115**	**44**	**134,327**	**64,298**	**70,029**	..	..	..
40 **GARO**	Assam (Tribal)	**17**	**101,329**	**50,502**	**50,827**	**565**	**505**	**60**	**100,764**	**49,997**	**50,767**	**36**	**32**	**4**

41	GHASI (Ghasia) ..	..	8,17	98,360	48,118	50,242	921	839	82	97,439	47,279	50,160	39	36	3
		Bihar and Orissa (Hindu)..	..	66,556	32,970	33,586	587	514	73	65,969	32,456	33,513	39	36	3
		C. P. and Berar (All Religions).	..	26,910	12,668	14,242	242	233	9	26,668	12,435	14,233	..	..	..
		Madras (Hindu) ..	..	4,894	2,480	2,414	92	92	..	4,802	2,388	2,414	..	..	..
42	GHUSURIA	Bihar and Orissa (Hindu)..	17	1,617	706	911	5	5	.	1,612	701	911	..	..	..
43	GOND	..	8,17,18	1,889,644	923,313	966,331	16,134	15,157	977	1,873,510	908,156	965,354	394	351	43
		C. P. and Berar. (Hindu) ..	..	824,425	401,843	422,582	10,303	9,669	634	814,122	392,174	421,948	260	240	20
		C. P. and Berar. (Tribal) ..	..	968,361	474,477	493,884	5,200	5,031	169	963,161	469,446	493,715	49	48	1
		Hyderabad (Tribal) ..	..	96,858	46,993	49,865	631	457	174	96,227	46,536	49,691	85	63	22
44	GOSAI (Gosavi, Atit, Gosain).	..	17	177,810	97,921	79,889	15,125	14,145	980	162,685	83,776	78,909	418	409	9
		C. P. and Berar (All Religions).	..	17,619	8,860	8,759	2,174	2,011	163	15,445	6,849	8,596	52	50	2
		United Provinces (All Religions).	..	121,366	65,621	55,745	5,644	5,447	197	115,722	60,174	55,548	186	182	4
		Baroda (Hindu)* ..	..	14,629	8,612	6,017	4,500	4,036	464	10,129	4,576	5,553	119	119	..
		Hyderabad (Hindu) ..	..	24,196	14,828	9,368	2,807	2,651	156	21,389	12,177	9,212	61	58	3
45	GUJAR	..	8,17,18	1,628,657	903,627	725,030	23,681	22,487	1,194	1,604,976	881,140	723,836	2,098	2,028	70
		Delhi (Hindu) ..	..	11,729	7,182	4,547	261	260	1	11,468	6,922	4,546	34	34	..
		Delhi (Muslim) ..	..	310	268	42	42	42	..	268	226	42	8	8	..
		N. W. F. Province (All Religions).	..	95,423	53,162	42,261	932	855	78	94,490	52,307	42,183	147	125	22
		Punjab (Hindu) ..	..	139,160	79,756	59,404	1,594	1,514	80	137,566	78,242	59,324	132	132	..
		Punjab (Sikh) ..	..	1,900	1,037	863	55	53	2	1,845	984	861	6	6	..
		Punjab (Muslim) ..	..	414,454	230,375	184,079	9,509	8,903	606	404,945	221,472	183,473	1,358	1,320	38
		United Provinces (All Religions).	..	298,598	169,885	128,713	5,488	5,264	224	293,110	164,621	128,489	230	225	5
		Central India (Hindu) ..	..	69,937	38,062	31,875	1,925	1,886	39	68,012	36,176	31,836	38	38	
		Gwalior (Hindu) ..	..	95,393	50,130	45,263	652	602	50	94,741	49,528	45,213	33	29	4
		Jammu and Kashmir (Muslim).	..	313,965	170,409	143,556	2,307	2,234	73	311,658	168,175	143,483	78	78	..
		Rajputana (Hindu) ..	..	187,788	103,361	84,427	915	874	41	186,873	102,487	84,386	34	33	1
46	HABURA	United Provinces (Hindu)	17	1,446	836	610	30	28	2	1,416	808	608	..	..	..
47	HALVAKKIVAKKAL	Bombay (Hindu) ..	..	18,506	9,835	8,671	80	78	2	18,426	9,757	8,669	.	..	..
48	HALWAI	United Provinces (All Religions).	8,17	74,361	40,761	33,600	7,699	7,365	334	66,662	33,396	33,266	283	280	3
49	HARI (Haddi) ..	..	17	110,960	54,728	56,232	1,239	1,196	43	109,721	53,532	56,189	17	17	..
		Bihar and Orissa (Hindu)	..	97,185	48,377	48,808	961	924	37	96,224	47,453	48,771	10	10	..
		Madras (Hindu) ..	..	13,775	6,351	7,424	278	272	6	13,497	6,079	7,418	7	7	..
50	IDIGA, ETC.	..	8,17	79,548	42,589	36,959	3,478	3,333	145	76,070	39,256	36,814	85	84	1
	IDIGA	Mysore (Hindu) ..	..	79,273	42,458	36,815	3,477	3,332	145	75,796	39,126	36,670	85	84	1
	IRIKA ..	Bihar and Orissa (Hindu)..	..	275	131	144	1	1	..	274	130	144	..	..	..
51	ILUVAN	..	8	896,009	440,695	455,314	242,513	188,499	54,014	653,496	252,196	401,300	7,798	6,275	1,523
		Cochin (Hindu) ..	..	219,345	104,214	115,131	57,466	44,704	12,762	161,879	59,510	102,369	2,597	2,138	459
		Travancore (Hindu) ..	..	676,664	336,481	340,183	185,047	143,795	41,252	491,617	192,686	298,931	5,201	4,137	1,064

* Includes figures for Bava.

Table XIV.—Literacy by Selected Castes—*contd.*

	Caste, Tribe or Race.	Province, State or Agency and Religion.	Also tabulated in Table:	Total. Persons.	Total. Males.	Total. Females.	Literate. Persons.	Literate. Males.	Literate. Females.	Illiterate. Persons.	Illiterate. Males.	Illiterate. Females.	Literate in English. Persons.	Literate in English. Males.	Literate in English. Females.
	1	2	3	4	5	6	7	8	9	10	11	12	13	14	15
52	**JAT** ..	..	8,17,18	**6,505,371**	**3,662,534**	**2,842,837**	**213,626**	**195,870**	**17,756**	**6,291,745**	**3,466,664**	**2,825,081**	**26,388**	**25,641**	**747**
		Ajmer-Merwara (All Religions).	..	24,418	13,167	11,251	820	791	29	23,598	12,376	11,222	85	82	3
		Baluchistan (All Religions)	..	77,157	42,227	34,930	318	318	..	76,839	41,909	34,930	6	6	..
		Delhi (Hindu) ..	..	41,293	23,034	18,259	2,293	2,230	63	39,000	20,804	18,196	561	560	1
		Delhi (Sikh) ..	..	1,345	1,027	318	761	668	93	584	359	225	255	235	20
		Delhi (Muslim) ..	..	1,019	646	373	101	90	11	918	556	362	37	34	3
		N.-W. F. Province (All Religions).	..	62,774	38,045	24,729	4,122	4,034	88	58,652	34,011	24,641	514	513	1
		Punjab (Hindu) ..	..	804,331	451,072	353,259	16,915	16,121	794	787,416	434,951	352,465	2,288	2,215	73
		Punjab (Sikh) ..	..	1,752,202	1,011,769	740,433	101,455	90,412	11,043	1,650,747	921,357	729,390	12,269	11,939	330
		Punjab (Muslim) ..	..	2,298,893	1,274,578	1,024,315	47,241	44,010	3,231	2,251,652	1,230,568	1,021,084	6,919	6,708	211
		United Provinces (All Religions).	..	654,918	376,094	278,824	32,539	30,418	2,121	622,379	345,676	276,703	2,770	2,669	101
		Central India (Hindu) ..	..	23,460	12,821	10,639	1,079	1,047	32	22,381	11,774	10,607	45	45	..
		Jammu and Kashmir (Hindu) ..	..	18,687	9,908	8,779	286	276	10	18,401	9,632	8,769	15	15	..
		Jammu and Kashmir (Muslim) ..	..	94,605	49,433	45,172	1,124	1,085	39	93,481	48,348	45,133	69	68	1
		Rajputana (All Religions)	..	650,269	358,713	291,556	4,572	4,370	202	645,697	354,343	291,354	555	552	3
53	**JUGI** (Jogi, Yogi) ..	.. ..	17	**371,811**	**193,607**	**178,204**	**52,921**	**47,270**	**5,651**	**318,890**	**146,337**	**172,553**	**7,243**	**6,760**	**483**
	YOGI	Assam (Hindu)	..	60,265	31,939	28,326	9,237	8,496	741	51,028	23,443	27,585	363	357	6
	JOGI (*Jugi*) ..	Bengal (Hindu)	..	311,546	161,668	149,878	43,684	38,774	4,910	267,862	122,894	144,968	6,880	6,403	477
54	**KACHHI** (Kachhia) ..	..	8,17	**700,864**	**379,018**	**321,846**	**11,006**	**10,051**	**955**	**689,858**	**368,967**	**320,891**	**381**	**373**	**8**
		United Provinces (All Religions).	..	558,519	301,072	257,447	6,366	5,860	506	552,153	295,212	256,941	241	240	1
		Gwalior (Hindu) ..	..	135,588	74,444	61,144	1,925	1,852	73	133,663	72,592	61,071	32	28	4
		Baroda (Hindu and Jain)	..	6,757	3,502	3,255	2,715	2,339	376	4,042	1,163	2,879	108	105	3
55	**KAHAR, ETC.** ..		8,17	**1,661,420**	**867,141**	**794,279**	**21,323**	**19,989**	**1,334**	**1,640,097**	**847,152**	**792,945**	**1,182**	**1,076**	**106**
	BHOI	Hyderabad (Hindu) ..	..	251,023	125,064	125,959	1,515	1,450	65	249,508	123,614	125,894	54	47	7
	DHIMAR ..	C. P. and Berar (All Religions).	..	254,628	127,198	127,430	4,412	4,139	273	250,216	123,059	127,157	144	121	23
	JHIWAR (*Jhinwar*).	Delhi (Hindu)	..	10,713	6,890	3,823	555	434	121	10,158	6,456	3,702	52	48	4
		Punjab (Hindu) ..	..	100,173	55,372	44,801	2,183	2,023	160	97,990	53,349	44,641	221	218	3
		Punjab (Sikh) ..	..	43,645	23,450	20,195	2,071	1,918	153	41,574	21,532	20,042	133	132	1
		Punjab (Muslim) ..	..	73,927	40,245	33,682	1,110	1,029	81	72,817	39,216	33,601	127	115	12
	KAHAR	C. P. and Berar (Hindu) ..	..	10,128	5,192	4,936	229	229	..	9,899	4,963	4,936	6	6	..
		United Provinces (All Religions).	..	917,183	483,730	433,453	9,248	8,767	481	907,935	474,963	432,972	445	389	56
56	**KALAR, ETC.** ..	..	8,17	**719,615**	**373,822**	**345,793**	**47,551**	**44,990**	**2,561**	**672,064**	**328,832**	**343,232**	**1,829**	**1,693**	**136**
	KALAR (*Kallar*)	C. P. and Berar (All Religions).	..	175,884	87,615	88,269	16,677	15,809	868	159,207	71,806	87,401	710	611	99

	KALWAR (*Kalal*)	United Provinces (All Religions).	..	203,413	107,362	96,051	23,716	22,701	1,015	179,697	84,661	95,036	880	850	30
		Hyderabad (Hindu) ..	..	340,318	178,845	161,473	7,158	6,480	678	333,160	172,365	160,795	239	232	7
57	**KALINJI** ..	.. Madras (Hindu) ..	**17**	**32,813**	**13,409**	**19,404**	**1,132**	**1,072**	**60**	**31,681**	**12,337**	**19,344**	**26**	**22**	**4**
58	**KANIYAN** ..	.. ..	**8,17**	**15,623**	**7,858**	**7,765**	**7,736**	**5,601**	**2,135**	**7,887**	**2,257**	**5,630**	**126**	**114**	**12**
		Cochin (Hindu)	..	3,139	1,566	1,573	2,058	1,265	793	1,081	301	780	53	49	4
		Travancore (Hindu) ..	..	12,484	6,292	6,192	5,678	4,336	1,342	6,806	1,956	4,850	73	65	8
59	**KANJAR** ..	.. ..	..	**18,856**	**10,114**	**8,742**	**422**	**404**	**18**	**18,434**	**9,710**	**8,724**	**40**	**30**	**10**
		Bihar and Orissa (Hindu)..	..	2,064	1,058	1,006	277	274	3	1,787	784	1,003	29	28	1
		United Provinces (All Religions).	..	16,792	9,056	7,736	145	130	15	16,647	8,926	7,721	11	2	9
60	**KANAKKAN** ..	.. ..	**17**	**27,907**	**13,576**	**14,331**	**1,430**	**1,211**	**219**	**26,477**	**12,365**	**14,112**	**25**	**22**	**3**
		Madras (Hindu) ..	..	17,622	8,468	9,154	375	338	37	17,247	8,130	9,117	14	14	..
		Cochin (Hindu) ..	..	10,285	5,108	5,177	1,055	873	182	9,230	4,235	4,995	11	8	3
61	**KAYASTHA** (Kaet) ..	..	**8,17**	**2,045,098**	**1,095,851**	**949,247**	**846,730**	**665,122**	**181,608**	**1,198,368**	**430,729**	**767,639**	**292,828**	**264,980**	**27,848**
		Bengal (Hindu) ..	..	1,277,672	678,461	599,211	512,699	387,425	125,274	764,973	291,036	473,937	207,078	185,894	21,184
		Bihar and Orissa (Hindu)..	..	267,584	140,635	126,949	100,140	85,120	15,020	167,444	55,515	111,929	27,446	25,498	1,948
		C. P. and Berar (All Religions).	..	31,753	16,838	14,915	14,789	12,021	2,768	16,964	4,817	12,147	4,153	3,833	320
		Delhi (Hindu)	..	8,472	4,888	3,584	4,864	3,438	1,426	3,608	1,450	2,158	2,887	2,555	332
		United Provinces (All Religions).	..	396,913	220,139	176,774	188,342	154,636	33,706	208,571	65,503	143,068	47,036	43,239	3,797
		Central India (Hindu) ..	..	30,879	16,674	14,205	12,703	11,101	1,602	18,176	5,573	12,603	1,912	1,833	79
		Gwalior (Hindu) ..	..	27,831	15,949	11,882	11,588	10,071	1,517	16,243	5,878	10,365	1,549	1,418	131
		Hyderabad (Hindu) ..	..	3,994	2,267	1,727	1,605	1,310	295	2,389	957	1,432	767	710	57
62	**KEWAT** ..	.. ..	**17**	**444,190**	**226,528**	**217,662**	**1,976**	**1,948**	**28**	**442,214**	**224,580**	**217,634**	**25**	**25**	..
		C. P. and Berar (Hindu) ..	..	9,713	4,938	4,775	89	86	3	9,624	4,852	4,772	2	2	..
		United Provinces (All Religions).	..	434,477	221,590	212,887	1,887	1,862	25	432,590	219,728	212,862	23	23	..
63	**KHATIK** ..	.. ..	**8,17**	**174,483**	**92,705**	**81,778**	**2,245**	**2,128**	**117**	**172,238**	**90,577**	**81,661**	**145**	**133**	**12**
		C. P. and Berar (Hindu)	..	1,564	760	804	93	84	9	1,471	676	795	3	3	..
		Delhi (Hindu) ..	..	2,884	1,801	1,083	75	69	6	2,809	1,732	1,077	10	10	..
		United Provinces (All Religions).	..	170,035	90,144	79,891	2,077	1,975	102	167,958	88,169	79,789	132	120	12
64	**KHATRI** ..	.. ..	**8,17**	**477,392**	**267,552**	**209,840**	**147,033**	**120,536**	**26,497**	**330,359**	**147,016**	**183,343**	**37,604**	**35,325**	**2,279**
		Delhi (Hindu) ..	..	11,342	6,762	4,580	4,917	3,867	1,050	6,425	2,895	3,530	2,406	2,207	199
		Delhi (Sikh) ..	..	396	262	134	200	159	41	196	103	93	110	105	5
		N.-W. F. Province (All Religions).	..	28,958	16,875	12,083	11,619	8,698	2,921	17,339	8,177	9,162	2,373	1,983	390
		Punjab (Hindu) ..	..	373,101	209,096	164,005	108,937	91,407	17,530	264,164	117,689	146,475	28,333	26,983	1,350
		Punjab (Sikh) ..	..	43,057	23,130	19,927	13,868	10,407	3,461	29,189	12,723	16,466	2,871	2,666	205
		Hyderabad (Hindu) ..	..	3,771	2,081	1,690	1,015	839	176	2,756	1,242	1,514	226	208	18
		Jammu and Kashmir (Hindu)	.	16,767	9,346	7,421	6,477	5,159	1,318	10,290	4,187	6,103	1,285	1,173	112
65	**KIRAR** (Kir)	.. Gwalior (Hindu) ..	**17**	**60,894**	**33,430**	**27,464**	**453**	**442**	**11**	**60,441**	**32,988**	**27,453**	**24**	**22**	**2**
66	**KOL** ..	.. ..	**8,17**	**122,695**	**60,538**	**62,157**	**301**	**290**	**11**	**122,394**	**60,248**	**62,146**	**7**	**7**	..
		C. P. and Berar (Hindu)	..	48,500	23,669	24,831	216	208	8	48,284	23,461	24,823	3	3	..
		C. P. and Berar (Tribal)	..	10,813	5,606	5,207	6	6	..	10,807	5,600	5,207	..	..	..
		United Provinces (Hindu)	..	63,382	31,263	32,119	79	76	3	63,303	31,187	32,116	4	4	..

Table XIV.—Literacy by Selected Castes—*contd.*

	Caste, Tribe or Race.	Province, State or Agency and Religion.	Also tabulated in Table:	Total.			Literate.			Illiterate.			Literate in English.		
				Persons.	Males.	Females.	Persons.	Males.	Females.	Persons.	Males.	Females.	Persons.	Males.	Females
	1	2	3	4	5	6	7	8	9	10	11	12	13	14	15
67	**KOLI** (Kohli and Dagi).	..	**17,18**	**362,318**	**192,321**	**169,997**	**4,905**	**4,700**	**205**	**357,413**	**187,621**	**169,792**	**149**	**146**	**3**
		C. P. and Berar (Hindu) ..	..	30,512	15,706	14,806	1,877	1,850	27	28,635	13,856	14,779	18	18	..
		Delhi (Hindu) ..	..	5,738	3,580	2,158	330	324	6	5,408	3,256	2,152	12	12	..
		Punjab (Hindu) ..	..	149,086	78,221	70,865	762	726	36	148,324	77,495	70,829	60	58	2
		Central India (Hindu) ..	..	73,848	37,229	36,619	768	750	18	73,080	36,479	36,601	46	45	1
		Gwalior (Hindu) ..	..	61,002	34,015	26,987	524	480	44	60,478	33,535	26,943	13	13	..
		Hyderabad (Hindu) ..	..	42,132	23,570	18,562	644	570	74	41,488	23,000	18,488	..	..	..
68	**KOMATI** (Komti) ..	..	**8,17**	**620,483**	**321,427**	**299,056**	**163,075**	**148,882**	**14,193**	**457,408**	**172,545**	**284,863**	**8,028**	**7,630**	**398**
		C. P. and Berar (Hindu) ..	..	2,955	1,433	1,522	974	941	33	1,981	492	1,489	63	63	..
		Coorg (Hindu) ..	..	170	85	85	74	57	17	96	28	68	11	9	2
		Madras (Hindu) ..	..	360,951	183,152	177,799	124,629	112,550	12,079	236,322	70,602	165,720	6,724	6,492	232
		Hyderabad (Hindu) ..	..	256,407	136,757	119,650	37,398	35,334	2,064	219,009	101,423	117,586	1,230	1,066	164
69	**KORI**	..	**17**	**767,549**	**394,368**	**373,181**	**8,511**	**8,256**	**255**	**759,038**	**386,112**	**372,926**	**668**	**645**	**23**
		C. P. and Berar (Hindu) ..	..	23,280	11,711	11,569	1,010	964	46	22,270	10,747	11,523	42	42	..
		United Provinces (All Religions).	..	744,269	382,657	361,612	7,501	7,292	209	736,768	375,365	361,403	626	603	23
70	**KORAVA** (Koracha, Korama).	..	**17**	**23,712**	**12,276**	**11,436**	**582**	**561**	**21**	**23,130**	**11,715**	**11,415**	**16**	**16**	..
	KORAMA ..	Coorg (Hindu) ..	..	106	57	49	10	10	..	96	47	49	1	1	..
		Mysore (Hindu) ..	..	11,026	5,599	5,427	229	221	8	10,797	5,378	5,419	3	3	..
		Mysore (Tribal) ..	..	2,839	1,476	1,363	71	68	3	2,768	1,408	1,360	..	..	..
	KORACHA ..	Mysore (Hindu) ..	..	8,279	4,365	3,914	257	247	10	8,022	4,118	3,904	12	12	..
		Mysore (Tribal) ..	..	1,462	779	683	15	15	..	1,447	764	683	..	..	..
71	**KORWA** (Korku) ..	..	**17,18**	**110,285**	**55,204**	**55,081**	**214**	**200**	**14**	**110,071**	**55,004**	**55,067**	**8**	**8**	..
	KORKU ..	C. P and Berar (Hindu)	..	57,177	28,818	28,359	106	100	6	57,071	28,718	28,353	8	8	..
	KORWA ..	C. P and Berar (Tribal).	..	52,686	26,186	26,500	77	73	4	52,609	26,113	26,496	..	..	..
		United Provinces (All Religions).	..	422	200	222	31	27	4	391	173	218	..	..	..
72	**KUDIYA**	..	**17,18**	**3,374**	**1,713**	**1,661**	**19**	**15**	**4**	**3,355**	**1,698**	**1,657**	..	..	..
		Coorg (Hindu) ..	..	436	218	218	..	..	..	436	218	218	..	..	..
		Madras (Hindu) ..	..	2,938	1,495	1,443	19	15	4	2,919	1,480	1,439	..	..	..
73	**KUDUMI CHETTI** ..	..	..	**20,385**	**10,545**	**9,840**	**2,632**	**2,427**	**205**	**17,753**	**8,118**	**9,635**	**83**	**79**	**4**
		Cochin (Hindu) ..	..	12,811	6,598	6,213	1,869	1,718	151	10,942	4,880	6,062	63	60	3
		Travancore (Hindu) ..	..	7,574	3,947	3,627	763	709	54	6,811	3,238	3,573	20	19	1
74	**KUMHAR** (Kumbhar, Kumbara, Kumara).	..	**8,17**	**1,679,698**	**886,865**	**792,833**	**34,170**	**31,182**	**2,988**	**1,645,528**	**855,683**	**789,845**	**1,370**	**1,310**	**60**

	KUMHAR (*Kumbhar, Kumbara, Kumara*).	Bombay (Hindu) ..	..	20,140	9,835	10,305	581	564	17	19,559	9,271	10,288	12	12	..
		C.P. and Berar (All Religions.)	..	104,456	53,198	51,258	4,034	3,847	187	100,422	49,351	51,071	93	90	3
		Delhi (Hindu) ..	..	7,487	4,234	3,253	172	155	17	7,315	4,079	3,236	12	12	..
		Delhi (Muslim) ..	..	74	45	29	9	8	1	65	37	28	3	3	..
		Punjab (Hindu) ..	..	125,588	68,713	56,875	1,673	1,551	122	123,915	67,162	56,753	163	158	5
		Punjab (Sikh) ..	..	24,966	13,781	11,185	839	764	75	24,127	13,017	11,110	76	75	1
		Punjab (Muslim) ..	..	329,339	180,495	148,844	3,512	3,255	257	325,827	177,240	148,587	319	312	7
		United Provinces (All Religions)	..	624,901	327,279	297,622	3,906	3,728	178	620,995	323,551	297,444	206	181	25
		Baroda (Hindu and Jain)	..	41,228	20,841	20,387	6,727	5,755	972	34,501	15,086	19,415	84	83	1
		Gwalior (Hindu) ..	..	49,185	26,427	22,758	264	229	35	48,921	26,198	22,723	9	9	..
		Hyderabad (Hindu) ..	..	123,922	65,709	58,213	1,600	1,466	134	122,322	64,243	58,079	133	123	10
		Mysore (Hindu) ..	..	39,781	20,501	19,280	2,092	1,998	94	37,689	18,503	19,186	46	42	4
		Rajputana (All Religions)	..	73,258	38,107	35,151	440	431	9	72,818	37,676	35,142	30	30	..
		Western India States (Hindu)	..	103,600	51,767	51,833	6,586	5,973	613	97,014	45,794	51,220	148	147	1
	KUSAVAN ..	Cochin (Hindu)	..	2,594	1,348	1,246	107	94	13	2,487	1,254	1,233	..	..	..
		Travancore (Hindu) ..	..	9,179	4,585	4,594	1,628	1,364	264	7,551	3,221	4,330	36	33	3
75	**KUNBI** ..	.. ..	**8,17**	**6,128,440**	**3,162,572**	**2,965,868**	**434,733**	**398,850**	**35,883**	**5,693,767**	**2,763,722**	**2,929,985**	**22,319**	**21,740**	**579**
	AJNA (*Anjna*) ..	Baroda (Hindu) ..	..	32,297	16,610	15,687	4,644	4,294	350	27,653	12,316	15,337	65	65	..
	KADVA PATIDAR	Baroda (Hindu and Jain)	..	178,717	89,470	89,247	38,705	34,626	4,079	140,012	54,844	85,168	644	633	11
	KAPU	Hyderabad (Hindu) ..	..	809,536	427,462	382,074	30,299	27,304	2,995	779,237	400,158	379,079	2,400	2,126	274
	KUNBI	Bombay (Hindu) ..	..	180,608	99,235	81,373	56,571	49,905	6,666	124,037	49,330	74,707	3,431	3,384	47
		C. P. and Berar (All Religions).	..	1,041,493	534,421	507,072	79,361	76,988	2,373	962,132	457,433	504,699	2,837	2,733	104
		Western India States (Hindu)*	..	492,631	252,661	239,970	27,235	26,256	979	465,396	226,405	238,991	4,166	4,153	13
	KURMI	Bihar and Orissa (Hindu)..	..	1,208,884	604,001	604,883	58,912	56,329	2,583	1,149,972	547,672	602,300	2,377	2,347	30
		C. P. and Berar (Hindu) ..	..	251,870	124,878	126,992	15,993	15,535	458	235,877	109,343	126,534	342	341	1
		United Provinces (All Religions).	..	1,433,750	752,879	680,871	41,772	40,834	938	1,391,978	712,045	679,933	1,284	1,262	22
		Central India (Hindu) ..	..	167,984	86,768	81,216	4,992	4,905	87	162,992	81,863	81,129	54	54	..
		Hyderabad (Hindu) ..	..	142,853	73,458	69,395	2,062	1,908	154	140,791	71,550	69,241	46	36	10
	LEWA PATIDAR	Baroda (Hindu and Jain)	..	187,817	100,729	87,088	74,187	59,966	14,221	113,630	40,763	72,867	4,673	4,606	67
76	**LABBAI**	..	**8,17**	**290,926**	**134,562**	**156,364**	**63,627**	**59,030**	**4,597**	**227,299**	**75,532**	**151,767**	**3,345**	**3,247**	**98**
		Coorg (Muslim)	..	189	111	78	50	41	9	139	70	69	1	1	..
		Madras (Muslim) ..	..	280,366	127,500	152,866	59,978	55,827	4,151	220,388	71,673	148,715	3,150	3,054	96
		Mysore (Muslim) ..	..	10,371	6,951	3,420	3,599	3,162	437	6,772	3,789	2,983	194	192	2
77	**LALBEGI**	..	**17**	**132**	**76**	**56**	**2**	**2**	..	**130**	**74**	**56**	..	..	..
		Bihar and Orissa (Hindu)	..	86	48	38	1	1	..	85	47	38	..	..	..
		Bihar and Orissa (Muslim)	..	46	28	18	1	1	..	45	27	18	..	..	..
78	**LODHA (Lodhi)**	..	**8,17**	**1,210,668**	**638,435**	**572,233**	**23,346**	**22,651**	**695**	**1,187,322**	**615,784**	**571,538**	**374**	**357**	**17**
		C. P. and Berar (All Religions).	..	256,099	127,500	128,599	11,425	11,019	406	244,674	116,481	128,193	156	151	5
		United Provinces (All Religions).	..	880,249	470,909	409,340	11,345	11,072	273	868,904	459,837	409,067	181	170	11
		Gwalior (Hindu) ..	..	74,320	40,026	34,294	576	560	16	73,744	39,466	34,278	37	36	1

*Including Rewa and Lewa Kunbi.

Table XIV.—Literacy by Selected Castes—*contd.*

Caste, Tribe or Race.	Province, State or Agency and Religion.	Also tabulated in Table :	Total.			Literate.			Illiterate.			Literate in English.		
			Persons.	Males.	Femaless.	Persons.	Males.	Females.	Persons.	Males.	Females.	Persons.	Males.	Females.
1	2	3	4	5	6	7	8	9	10	11	12	13	14	15
9 **LOHANA**, etc.	..	8,17	1,148,376	622,849	525,527	301,507	262,439	39,068	846,869	360,410	486,459	37,254	35,611	1,643
ARORA	Baluchistan (Hindu) ..	..	16,359	8,825	7,534	3,884	3,777	107	12,475	5,048	7,427	35	35	..
	N.-W. F. Province (All Religions).	..	48,615	27,763	20,852	13,031	10,890	2,141	35,584	16,873	18,711	2,408	2,237	171
LOHANA	Punjab (Hindu) ..	—	524,582	285,150	239,432	115,048	101,935	13,113	409,534	183,215	226,319	12,248	11,629	619
	Punjab (Sikh) ..	..	86,805	47,648	39,157	24,041	19,338	4,703	62,764	28,310	34,454	3,022	2,836	186
	Bombay (Hindu)* ..	..	379,612	207,178	172,434	110,160	97,414	12,746	269,452	109,764	159,688	16,801	16,372	429
	Baroda (Hindu) ..	..	11,008	5,609	5,399	5,375	4,375	1,000	5,633	1,234	4,399	357	352	5
	Western India States (Hindu).	..	81,395	40,676	40,719	29,968	24,710	5,258	51,427	15,966	35,461	2,383	2,150	233
80 **LUSHEI**	.. ..	17,18	87,169	40,647	46,522	12,016	10,586	1,430	75,153	30,061	45,092	695	651	44
	Assam (Tribal) ..	..	42,171	20,868	21,303	3,110	3,017	93	39,061	17,851	21,210	75	74	1
	Assam (Christian) ..	..	44,998	19,779	25,219	8,906	7,569	1,337	36,092	12,210	23,882	620	577	43
81 **MAHAR**, etc. —	.. ..	8,17	2,763,680	1,387,404	1,376,276	66,507	61,061	5,446	2,697,173	1,326,343	1,370,830	2,397	2,331	66
DHED and VANKAR	Bombay (Hindu) ..	..	92,892	45,849	47,043	4,908	4,547	361	87,984	41,302	46,682	45	45	..
	Baroda (Hindu) ..	..	87,130	42,727	44,403	10,871	8,930	1,941	76,259	33,797	42,462	108	106	2
	Hyderabad (Adi-Hindu) ..	..	900,850	465,721	435,129	6,102	5,303	799	894,748	460,418	434,330	361	331	30
	Western India States (Hindu).	..	169,087	86,944	82,143	1,578	1,501	77	167,509	85,443	82,066	5	5	..
HOLEYA	Coorg (Hindu)	..	274	161	113	2	2	..	272	159	113	1	1	..
MAHAR (*Mehra*) ..	Madras (Hindu) ..	..	39,634	17,249	22,385	134	127	7	39,500	17,122	22,378	1	1	..
	Bombay (Hindu) ..	..	436,284	214,017	222,267	12,761	11,836	925	423,523	202,181	221,342	705	689	16
	C. P. and Berar (Hindu, Muslim and Tribal)	..	1,037,029	514,427	522,602	30,053	28,725	1,328	1,006,976	485,702	521,274	1,153	1,139	14
	C. P. and Berar (Christian)	..	500	309	191	98	90	8	402	219	183	18	14	4
82 **MAHISHYA** (Chasi-kaibartta)	Bengal (Hindu) .. —	17	1,957,303	1,005,837	951,466	363,552	326,001	37,551	1,593,751	679,836	913,915	49,336	47,499	1,837
83 **MALAYAN** (Malayarayan). ..	.. ..	17,18	4,920	2,543	2,377	58	56	2	4,862	2,487	2,375	..	..	..
	Cochin (Hindu)	..	2,574	1,349	1,225	17	16	1	2,557	1,333	1,224	..	..	..
	Travancore (Hindu and Tribal).	..	2,346	1,194	1,152	41	40	1	2,305	1,154	1,151	..	..	..
84 **MALI** (Malakar) ..	.. ..	8,17	848,173	432,999	415,174	36,370	34,834	1,536	811,803	398,165	413,638	2,377	2,311	66
	Ajmer-Merwara (All Religions).	..	11,952	6,314	5,638	585	564	21	11,367	5,750	5,617	61	60	1
	Bombay (Hindu) ..	..	53,190	26,467	26,723	4,613	4,329	284	48,577	22,138	26,439	1,070	1,033	37
	C. P. and Berar (All Religions)	..	505,224	253,939	251,285	24,056	23,392	664	481,168	230,547	250,621	919	909	10
	Delhi (Hindu)	..	4,898	2,962	1,936	173	165	8	4,725	2,797	1,928	29	29	..
	United Provinces (All Religions).	..	145,712	78,178	67,534	3,091	2,943	148	142,621	75,235	67,386	130	127	3
	Central India (Hindu) ..	..	36,955	19,188	17,767	1,218	1,171	47	35,737	18,017	17,720	55	51	4
	Hyderabad (Hindu) ..	..	81,479	41,314	40,165	1,728	1,548	180	79,751	39,766	39,985	1	1	..
	Western India States (Hindu).	..	8,763	4,637	4,126	906	722	184	7,857	3,915	3,942	112	101	11

85	**MALLAH**	..	8,17	**586,074**	**284,352**	**301,722**	**5,630**	**5,453**	**177**	**580,444**	**278,899**	**301,545**	**115**	**114**	**1**
		Bihar and Orissa (Hindu) ..	..	353,366	170,908	182,458	3,088	2,946	142	350,278	167,962	182,316	59	58	1
		United Provinces (All Religions).	..	232,708	113,444	119,264	2,542	2,507	35	230,166	110,937	119,229	56	56	..
86	**MANG**	..	17	**188,515**	**94,362**	**94,153**	**2,580**	**2,314**	**266**	**185,935**	**92,048**	**93,887**	**146**	**145**	**1**
		Bombay (Hindu) ..	..	114,795	57,775	57,020	1,808	1,572	236	112,987	56,203	56,784	128	127	1
		C. P. & Berar (All Religons)	..	73,720	36,587	37,133	772	742	30	72,948	35,845	37,103	18	18	..
87	**MAPPILLA, etc.** ..	..	8,17	**52,970**	**28,450**	**24,520**	**8,058**	**7,009**	**1,049**	**44,912**	**21,441**	**23,471**	**255**	**239**	**16**
	JONAKAN (*Jonagan*)	Cochin (Muslim) ..	..	45,064	22,863	22,201	7,039	6,049	990	38,025	16,814	21,211	228	219	9
	MOPPILLA ..	Coorg (Muslim)	..	7,906	5,587	2,319	1,019	960	59	6,887	4,627	2,260	27	20	7
88	**MARATHA**		8,17	**2,092,858**	**1,092,524**	**1,000,334**	**98,161**	**88,520**	**9,641**	**1,994,697**	**1,004,004**	**990,693**	**14,433**	**13,617**	**816**
		Bombay (Hindu)† ..	..	548,515	300,404	248,111	31,017	27,985	3,032	517,498	272,419	245,079	7,439	7,008	431
		C. P. & Berar (Hindu)‡ ..	..	236,968	120,857	116,111	30,790	28,519	2,271	206,178	92,338	113,840	2,524	2,443	81
		Baroda (Hindu) ..	..	10,145	5,675	4,470	3,904	3,049	855	6,241	2,626	3,615	887	807	80
		Gwalior (Hindu) ..	..	11,984	6,790	5,194	4,027	3,482	545	7,957	3,308	4,649	805	769	36
		Hyderabad (Hindu) ..	..	1,235,685	632,567	603,118	21,087	18,873	2,214	1,214,598	613,694	600,904	1,643	1,525	118
		Cochin (Hindu)	..	167	92	75	83	67	16	84	25	59	35	34	1
		Mysore (Hindu) ..	..	49,394	26,139	23,255	7,253	6,545	708	42,141	19,594	22,547	1,100	1,031	69
89	**MEGH, etc.**		8,17	**1,734,190**	**882,348**	**851,842**	**9,889**	**8,786**	**1,103**	**1,724,301**	**873,562**	**850,739**	**576**	**526**	**50**
	MADIGA	Bombay (Hindu) ..	..	84,994	41,825	43,169	557	513	44	84,437	41,312	43,125	30	29	1
		C. P. & Berar (All Religions)	..	4,339	2,402	1,937	29	29	..	4,310	2,373	1,937	9	9	..
		Coorg (Hindu)	..	179	97	82	81	43	38	98	54	44	..	..	..
		Madras (Hindu) ..	..	485,444	247,590	237,854	2,489	2,160	329	482,955	245,430	237,525	95	87	8
		Hyderabad (Adi-Hindu)§ ..	..	1,101,440	559,471	541,969	6,270	5,618	652	1,095,170	553,853	541,317	403	365	38
	MEGH	Jammu and Kashmir (Hindu).	..	57,794	30,963	26,831	463	423	40	57,331	30,540	26,791	39	36	3
90	**MEO**	.. ..	17,18	**614,532**	**331,268**	**283,264**	**3,946**	**3,817**	**129**	**610,586**	**327,451**	**283,135**	**156**	**149**	**7**
	MENA (*Mina*) ..	Gwalior (Hindu) ..	..	54,195	28,732	25,463	286	280	6	53,909	28,452	25,457	5	5	..
		Rajputana (All Religions)	..	303,168	161,327	141,841	1,603	1,553	50	301,565	159,774	141,791	25	24	1
	MEO	Delhi (Muslim)	..	4,264	2,513	1,751	143	131	12	4,121	2,382	1,739	26	24	2
		Punjab (Muslim) ..	..	98,353	53,555	44,798	1,152	1,140	12	97,201	52,415	44,786	59	58	1
		United Provinces (All Religions).	..	23,626	13,856	9,770	373	325	48	23,253	13,531	9,722	38	35	3
		Rajputana (Hindu and Muslim)	..	130,926	71,285	59,641	389	388	1	130,537	70,897	59,640	3	3	..
91	**MERAT**	Ajmer-Merwara (Muslim)	18	**19,894**	**10,747**	**9,147**	**491**	**486**	**5**	**19,403**	**10,261**	**9,142**	**8**	**8**	..
92	**MOCHI (Muchi)** ..	..	17	**399,803**	**220,284**	**179,519**	**7,537**	**6,773**	**764**	**392,266**	**213,511**	**178,755**	**385**	**381**	**4**
		Bihar and Orissa (Hindu) ..	..	17,715	9,199	8,516	224	215	9	17,491	8,984	8,507	6	6	..
		Coorg (Hindu) ..	..	16	7	9	..	..	.	16	7	9	..	..	..
		Madras (Hindu) ..	..	1,468	704	764	75	75	..	1,393	629	764	5	5	..
		Punjab (Hindu) ..	..	3,843	2,660	1,183	160	148	12	3,683	2,512	1,171	19	19	..
		Punjab (Muslim) ..	..	361,075	199,178	161,897	4,202	3,943	259	356,873	195,235	161,638	304	301	3
		United Provinces (All Religions).	..	7,143	4,192	2,951	301	274	27	6,842	3,918	2,924	21	21	..
		Baroda (Hindu and Jain)	..	8,543	4,344	4,199	2,575	2,118	457	5,968	2,226	3,742	30	29	1

* Including Amits. † Including Kunbis of Satara and Ratnagiri. ‡ Includes 3 Christians (1 male and 2 females). § Including Chamar, Mang and Mochi.

Table XIV.—Literacy by Selected Castes—*contd.*

Caste, Tribe or Race.	Province, State or Agency and Religion.	Also tabulated in Table :	Total.			Literate.			Illiterate.			Literate in English.		
			Persons.	Males.	Females.	Persons.	Males.	Females.	Persons.	Males.	Females.	Persons.	Males.	Females.
1	2	3	4	5	6	7	8	9	10	11	12	13	14	15
93 **MOMIN**, ..	..	8,17	**2,661,625**	**1,378,497**	**1,283,128**	**91,809**	**81,110**	**10,699**	**2,569,816**	**1,297,387**	**1,272,429**	**6,644**	**5,866**	**778**
JOLAHA (*Julaha*)	Bihar and Orissa (Muslim)	..	773,370	374,428	398,942	28,187	24,974	3,213	745,183	349,454	395,729	1,517	1,481	36
	Delhi (Hindu) ..	..	7,070	4,146	2,924	437	417	20	6,633	3,729	2,904	6	6	..
	Delhi (Muslim) ..	..	719	431	288	19	19	..	700	412	288	4	4	..
	Punjab (Hindu) ..	..	42,110	22,956	19,154	608	576	32	41,502	22,380	19,122	43	41	2
	Punjab (Sikh) ..	..	3,034	1,659	1,375	211	200	11	2,823	1,459	1,364	..	..	..
	Punjab (Muslim) ..	..	481,193	264,618	216,575	9,216	8,546	670	471,977	256,072	215,905	804	782	22
	United Provinces (All Religions).	..	791,545	415,851	375,694	24,641	22,654	1,987	766,904	393,197	373,707	1,018	983	35
	Central India (Muslim) ..	..	6,120	3,100	3,020	204	198	6	5,916	2,902	3,014	4	4	..
JULAHI ..	Hyderabad (Hindu) ..	..	328,834	171,793	157,041	7,562	7,043	519	321,272	164,750	156,522	169	157	12
MOMNA ..	Baroda (Muslim) ..	..	11,047	5,444	5,603	1,482	1,357	125	9,565	4,087	5,478	24	24	..
MUMIN (*Jolaha*)	Bengal (Muslim) ..	..	216,583	114,071	102,512	19,242	15,126	4,116	197,341	98,945	98,396	3,055	2,384	671
94 **MUNDA**	..	17,18	**353,616**	**173,607**	**180,009**	**9,877**	**7,924**	**1,953**	**343,739**	**165,683**	**178,056**	**1,408**	**1,266**	**142**
	Bihar and Orissa (Hindu)	..	102,692	50,404	52,288	1,786	1,652	134	100,906	48,752	52,154	28	28	..
	Bihar and Orissa (Tribal)	..	167,347	81,406	85,941	1,045	874	171	166,302	80,532	85,770	52	51	1
	Bihar and Orissa (Christian)	..	83,577	41,797	41,780	7,046	5,398	1,648	76,531	36,399	40,132	1,328	1,187	141
95 **NADIYAL** (Kaibartta) ..	Assam (Hindu) ..	**17**	**72,412**	**38,388**	**34,024**	**7,600**	**7,032**	**568**	**64,812**	**31,356**	**33,456**	**750**	**725**	**25**
96 **NAIBRAHMAN** ..		8,17	**1,582,827**	**841,638**	**741,189**	**55,453**	**51,613**	**3,840**	**1,527,374**	**790,025**	**737,349**	**2,757**	**2,681**	**76**
AMBATTAN ..	Cochin (Hindu)	..	1,249	604	645	373	248	125	876	356	520	24	21	3
HAJJAM ..	Bombay (Hindu)* ..	..	25,442	12,741	12,701	3,057	2,799	258	22,385	9,942	12,443	153	151	2
	Hyderabad (Hindu) ..	..	130,153	69,930	60,223	2,441	2,312	129	127,712	67,618	60,094	141	125	16
	Western India States (Hindu)	..	34,843	17,755	17,088	3,289	3,008	281	31,554	14,747	16,807	117	115	2
NAI	C. P. and Berar (All Religions).	..	107,304	53,822	53,482	7,495	7,134	361	99,809	46,688	53,121	245	237	8
	Delhi (Hindu) ..	..	3,669	2,605	1,064	274	254	20	3,395	2,351	1,044	37	36	1
	Delhi (Muslim) ..	..	671	398	273	32	29	3	639	369	270	6	6	..
	Punjab (Hindu) ..	..	82,449	46,037	36,412	2,892	2,711	181	79,557	43,326	36,231	360	356	4
	Punjab (Sikh) ..	..	31,967	18,020	13,947	1,939	1,796	143	30,028	16,224	13,804	160	157	3
	Punjab (Muslim) ..	..	185,763	102,027	83,736	3,799	3,534	265	181,964	98,493	83,471	331	322	9
	United Provinces (All Religions).	..	728,701	386,811	341,890	15,703	14,976	727	712,998	371,835	341,163	637	624	13
	Central India (Hindu) ..	..	77,142	40,292	36,850	2,405	2,305	100	74,737	37,987	36,750	88	88	..
	Gwalior (Hindu) ..	..	44,391	24,055	20,336	1,039	993	46	43,352	23,062	20,290	50	48	2
NAU	United Provinces (Muslim)	..	68,453	35,654	32,799	2,216	2,100	116	66,237	33,554	32,683	142	135	7
NAYINDA ..	Mysore (Hindu) ..	..	37,531	19,494	18,037	3,252	3,063	189	34,279	16,431	17,848	138	132	6
VALAND ..	Baroda (Hindu) ..	..	23,099	11,393	11,706	5,247	4,351	896	17,852	7,042	10,810	128	128	..
97 **AMASUDRA** ..	..	8,17	**1,812,029**	**936,482**	**875,547**	**145,402**	**132,608**	**12,794**	**1,666,627**	**803,874**	**862,753**	**20,552**	**19,788**	**764**
	Assam (Hindu)	..	116,625	61,578	55,047	6,386	6,128	258	110,239	55,450	54,789	180	180	..
	Bengal (Hindu)	..	1,695,404	874,904	820,500	139,016	126,480	12,536	1,556,388	748,424	807,964	20,372	19,608	764

98	**NAT**		17	**60,433**	**29,385**	**31,048**	**482**	**424**	**58**	**59,951**	**28,961**	**30,990**	**72**	**72**	..
		Bihar and Orissa (Hindu)..	..	7,578	3,700	3,878	95	86	9	7,483	3,614	3,869	..	..	..
		United Provinces (All Religions).	..	52,855	25,685	27,170	387	338	49	52,468	25,347	27,121	72	72	..
99	**NAYADI**	..	17,18	**539**	**271**	**268**	**21**	**18**	**3**	**518**	**253**	**265**	**1**	**1**	..
		Madras (Hindu) ..	..	413	209	204	14	11	3	399	198	201	1	1	..
		Cochin (Hindu)	..	126	62	64	7	7	..	119	55	64	..	..	..
100	**NAYAR** (Nair) ..		8,17	**1,239,488**	**600,193**	**639,295**	**538,225**	**362,096**	**176,129**	**701,263**	**238,097**	**463,166**	**50,324**	**41,577**	**8,747**
		Coorg (Hindu)	..	1,222	1,076	146	281	273	8	941	803	138	15	13	2
		Madras (Hindu) ..	..	442,796	210,314	232,482	165,743	116,061	49,682	277,053	94,253	182,800	20,686	18,225	2,461
		Cochin (Hindu)	..	114,776	52,100	62,676	63,978	37,634	26,344	50,798	14,466	36,332	11,017	8,028	2,989
		Travancore (Hindu) ..	..	680,694	336,703	343,991	308,223	208,128	100,095	372,471	128,575	243,896	18,606	15,311	3,295
101	**NICOBARESE** ..	Andamans and Nicobars (Christian and Tribal)	17,18	**7,595**	**4,006**	**3,589**	**31**	**26**	**5**	**7,564**	**3,980**	**3,584**	**9**	**8**	**1**
102	**NUNIYA** (Luniya) ..	United Provinces (All Religions).	17	**368,914**	**187,522**	**181,392**	**3,931**	**3,868**	**63**	**364,983**	**183,654**	**181,329**	**114**	**113**	**1**
103	**OD**, etc. ..	.. ..	8,17	**315,942**	**160,174**	**155,768**	**2,855**	**2,669**	**186**	**313,087**	**157,505**	**155,582**	**103**	**98**	**5**
	BELDAR ..	C. P. and Berar (Hindu) ..	..	4,501	2,214	2,287	302	289	13	4,199	1,925	2,274	17	17	..
		United Provinces (All Religions).	..	35,069	17,949	17,120	211	211	..	34,858	17,738	17,120	23	23	..
	VADDA (*Vodda*, *Waddar*).	Bombay (Hindu) ..	..	25,747	13,125	12,622	335	271	64	25,412	12,854	12,558	6	5	1
		C. P. and Berar (Hindu)	..	4,790	2,167	2,623	12	11	1	4,778	2,156	2,622	1	1	..
		Hyderabad (Hindu) ..	..	113,179	56,041	57,138	604	551	53	112,575	55,490	57,085	6	6	..
		Mysore (Hindu) ..	..	132,656	68,678	63,978	1,391	1,336	55	131,265	67,342	63,923	50	46	4
104	**ORAON**	..	8,17,18	**494,125**	**243,149**	**250,976**	**11,455**	**8,599**	**2,856**	**482,670**	**234,550**	**248,120**	**1,346**	**1,108**	**238**
		Bihar and Orissa (Hindu)	..	132,565	63,174	69,391	1,352	1,155	197	131,213	62,019	69,194	29	28	1
		Bihar and Orissa (Tribal)	..	164,145	80,099	84,046	1,672	1,095	577	162,473	79,004	83,469	101	98	3
		Bihar and Orissa (Christian)	..	92,255	45,898	46,357	7,217	5,211	2,006	85,038	40,687	44,351	1,208	974	234
		C. P. and Berar (Hindu and Tribal).	..	71,076	36,668	34,408	276	271	5	70,800	36,397	34,403	1	1	..
		C. P. and Berar (Christian)	..	34,084	17,310	16,774	938	867	71	33,146	16,443	16,703	7	7	..
105	**PANIKA** (Pan, Pank, Pankha, etc).	....	8,17	**492,988**	**240,390**	**252,598**	**7,322**	**7,146**	**176**	**485,666**	**233,244**	**252,422**	**34**	**34**	..
		Bihar and Orissa (Hindu)..	..	354,214	173,640	180,574	4,027	3,940	87	350,187	169,700	180,487	15	15	..
		C. P. and Berar (All Religions).	..	138,774	66,750	72,024	3,295	3,206	89	135,479	63,544	71,935	19	19	..
106	**PARAIYAN** (Parayan)	..	8,17	**1,017,853**	**498,164**	**519,689**	**31,455**	**28,141**	**3,314**	**986,398**	**470,023**	**516,375**	**1,365**	**1,227**	**138**
		Coorg (Hindu)	..	290	162	128	5	4	1	285	158	127	..	..	..
		Madras (Hindu) ..	..	893,148	434,783	458,365	19,295	18,418	877	873,853	416,365	457,488	741	702	39
		Cochin (Hindu)† ..	..	9,312	4,649	4,663	295	259	36	9,017	4,390	4,627	5	5	..
		Tavancore (Hindu)	..	57,561	29,667	27,894	2,830	2,577	253	54,731	27,090	27,641	61	60	1
		Tavancore (Christian)	..	57,542	28,903	28,639	9,030	6,883	2,147	48,512	22,020	26,492	558	460	98
107	**PARAVAN**	..	8,17	**11,326**	**5,565**	**5,761**	**1,728**	**1,479**	**249**	**9,598**	**4,086**	**5,512**	**31**	**30**	**1**
		Madras (Hindu) ..	..	677	334	343	2	2	..	675	332	343	..	..	..
		Travancore (Hindu) ..	..	10,649	5,231	5,418	1,726	1,477	249	8,923	3,754	5,169	31	30	1

*Including Nhavi and Nadig.

†Including Tamil Parayans.

Table XIV.—Literacy by Selected Castes—*contd.*

	Caste, Tribe or Race.	Province, State or Agency and Religion.	Also tabulated in Table :	Total.			Literate.			Illiterate.			Literate in English.		
				Persons.	Males.	Females.	Persons.	Males.	Females.	Persons.	Males.	Females.	Persons.	Males.	Females.
	1	2	3	4	5	6	7	8	9	10	11	12	13	14	15
108	**PARDHI**	Hyderabad (Tribal) ..	17,18	**5,992**	**3,223**	**2,769**	**128**	**95**	**33**	**5,864**	**3,128**	**2,736**	..	..	..
109	**PASI**	..	17	**1,292,911**	**664,379**	**628,532**	**4,667**	**4,416**	**251**	**1,288,244**	**659,963**	**628,281**	**171**	**167**	**4**
		Bihar and Orissa (Hindu)	..	136,106	69,287	66,819	1,922	1,766	156	134,184	67,521	66,663	75	74	1
		United Provinces (All-Religions).	..	1,156,805	595,092	561,713	2,745	2,650	95	1,154,060	592,442	561,618	96	93	3
110	**PINJARA** (Penja, Pinara).	..	8,17	**12,281**	**6,263**	**6,018**	**1,747**	**1,553**	**194**	**10,534**	**4,710**	**5,824**	**33**	**32**	**1**
		Baroda (Muslim) ..	..	3,854	1,899	1,955	1,150	991	159	2,704	908	1,796	19	19	..
		Mysore (Muslim) ..	..	8,427	4,364	4,063	597	562	35	7,830	3,802	4,028	14	13	1
111	**PRABHU**	..	8,17	**16,021**	**8,680**	**7,341**	**10,683**	**6,724**	**3,959**	**5,338**	**1,956**	**3,382**	**5,558**	**4,717**	**841**
		Bombay (Hindu) ..	..	13,221	7,249	5,972	8,517	5,442	3,075	4,704	1,807	2,897	4,518	3,832	686
		Baroda (Hindu) ..	..	2,800	1,431	1,369	2,166	1,282	884	634	149	485	1,040	885	155
112	**PULAIYAN**	..	17	**374,085**	**186,176**	**187,909**	**27,099**	**21,350**	**5,749**	**346,986**	**164,826**	**182,160**	**563**	**459**	**104**
		Madras (Hindu) ..	..	18,852	8,064	10,788	358	296	62	18,494	7,768	10,726	5	5	..
		Cochin (Hindu)	..	64,418	31,290	33,128	3,423	2,855	568	60,995	28,435	32,560	49	43	6
		Travancore (Hindu) ..	..	164,562	82,318	82,244	6,778	5,702	1,076	157,784	76,616	81,168	69	54	15
		Travancore (Christian)	..	126,253	64,504	61,749	16,540	12,497	4,043	109,713	52,007	57,706	440	357	83
113	**REBARI**	Rajputana (Hindu and Muslim)	8,17	**88,423**	**46,191**	**42,232**	**278**	**258**	**20**	**88,145**	**45,933**	**42,212**	**30**	**30**	..
114	**RAJPUT**	..	8,17	**7,605,704**	**4,112,399**	**3,493,305**	**676,361**	**631,146**	**45,215**	**6,929,343**	**3,481,253**	**3,448,090**	**57,310**	**55,590**	**1,720**
		Ajmer-Merwara (Hindu) ..	..	14,520	8,249	6,271	3,042	2,611	431	11,478	5,638	5,840	607	591	16
		Bihar and Orissa (Hindu)..	..	994,110	523,702	470,408	119,572	113,560	6,012	874,538	410,142	464,396	8,303	8,156	147
		C. P. and Berar (All-Religions)	..	414,198	212,338	201,860	47,315	44,380	2,935	366,883	167,958	198,925	3,637	3,509	128
		Delhi (Hindu) ..	..	26,080	17,228	8,852	3,508	3,235	273	22,572	13,993	8,579	846	820	26
		Delhi (Sikh) ..	..	161	103	58	49	41	8	112	62	50	27	23	4
		Delhi (Muslim) ..	..	4,882	3,182	1,700	781	682	99	4,101	2,500	1,601	251	240	11
		Punjab (Hindu) ..	..	480,330	272,372	207,958	39,378	36,126	3,252	440,952	236,246	204,706	5,768	5,608	160
		Punjab (Sikh) ..	..	38,184	21,842	16,342	5,226	4,267	959	32,958	17,575	15,383	881	821	60
		Punjab (Muslim) ..	..	1,355,811	734,715	621,096	56,589	51,542	5,047	1,299,222	683,173	616,049	11,465	10,956	509
		United Provinces (All-Religions).	..	3,109,463	1,686,515	1,422,948	327,914	308,157	19,757	2,781,549	1,378,358	1,403,191	20,475	19,929	546
		Baroda (Hindu) ..	..	78,549	41,217	37,332	15,151	13,371	1,780	63,398	27,846	35,552	318	314	4
		Central India (Hindu) ..	..	180,577	95,885	84,692	17,749	15,964	1,785	162,828	79,921	82,907	1,084	1,042	42
		Gwalior (Hindu) ..	..	95,990	55,263	40,727	7,400	6,931	419	88,590	48,282	40,308	314	305	9
		Jammu and Kashmir. (Hindu) ..	..	50,254	28,517	21,737	5,613	5,275	338	44,641	23,242	21,399	654	642	12
		Jammu and Kashmir. (Muslim) ..	..	152,139	79,806	72,333	4,707	4,405	302	147,432	75,401	72,031	352	346	6
		Cochin (Hindu)	..	41	18	23	10	8	2	31	10	21	4	4	..
		Rajputana Hindu) ..	..	355,796	198,873	156,923	15,732	14,001	1,731	340,064	184,872	155,192	1,935	1,897	38
	RAJPUT KANET	Punjab (Hindu) ..	..	250,262	130,380	119,882	6,367	6,282	85	243,895	124,098	119,797	389	387	2
		Punjab (Buddhist) ..	..	4,357	2,194	2,163	258	258	..	4,099	1,936	2,163	..	..	.
115	**SAINI**		17	**197,454**	**109,260**	**88,194**	**7,829**	**7,272**	**557**	**189,625**	**101,988**	**87,637**	**1,177**	**1,166**	**11**
		Punjab (Hindu) ..	..	60,367	33,779	26,588	2,251	2,145	106	58,116	31,634	26,482	408	404	4
		Punjab (Sikh) ..	..	66,215	35,926	30,289	4,728	4,319	409	61,487	31,607	29,880	732	726	6

MSCC

		United Provinces (All Religions).	...	70,872	39,555	31,317	850	808	42	70,022	38,747	31,275	37	36	1
116	**SANSI**		17,18	**21,519**	**11,928**	**9,591**	**232**	**206**	**26**	**21,287**	**11,722**	**9,565**	**11**	**11**	
		Delhi (Hindu)	..	192	102	90	..	..	..	192	102	90	..	..	...
		Punjab (Hindu)	..	20,616	11,505	9,111	219	194	25	20,397	11,311	9,086	6	6	..
		United Provinces (Hindu)	..	600	260	340	12	11	1	588	249	339	4	4	..
		Jammu & Kashmir (Tribal)	..	111	61	50	1	1	..	110	60	50	1	1	..
117	**SANTAL**	..	8,17,18	**1,934,088**	**979,460**	**954,628**	**14,585**	**11,951**	**2,634**	**1,919,503**	**967,509**	**951,994**	**840**	**757**	**83**
		Bengal (Hindu)	..	346,089	177,921	168,168	2,659	2,189	470	343,430	175,732	167,698	128	122	6
		Bengal (Tribal)	..	275,298	139,560	135,738	1,661	1,362	299	273,637	138,198	135,439	89	88	1
		Bengal (Christian)	..	8,667	4,440	4,227	1,366	832	534	7,301	3,608	3,693	..	..	..
		Bihar and Orissa. (Hindu)	..	448,494	226 701	221,793	2,878	2,702	176	445,616	223,999	221,617	94	90	4
		Bihar and Orissa. (Tribal)	..	846,026	426,113	419,913	3,675	3,433	242	842,351	422,680	419,671	91	86	5
		Bihar and Orissa. (Christian)	..	9,514	4,725	4,789	2,346	1,433	913	7,168	3,292	3,876	438	371	67
118	**SAWARA**, etc.	..	8,17,18	**464,425**	**229,622**	**234,803**	**2,865**	**2,640**	**225**	**461,560**	**226,982**	**234,578**	**20**	**20**	...
	SAHAR (*Saheria*)	United Provinces (Hindu)	..	10,540	5,350	5,190	7	7	..	10,533	5,343	5,190	..	..	..
		Gwalior (Hindu)	..	55,560	28,895	26,665	16	15	1	55,544	28,880	26,664	..	..	..
	SAORA	Madras (Tribal)	..	168,059	83,504	84,555	709	630	79	167,350	82,874	84,476	3	3	..
	SAVARA (*Sawara*)	Bihar and Orissa (Hindu)	..	164,025	79,520	84,505	1,482	1,442	40	162,543	78,078	84,465	6	6	..
		C. P. and Berar (Hindu)	..	66,241	32,353	33,888	651	546	105	65,590	31,807	33,783	11	11	..
119	**SAYYAD**	..	8	**788,737**	**422,437**	**366,300**	**153,642**	**127,607**	**26,035**	**635,095**	**294,830**	**840,265**	**33,033**	**31,007**	**2,026**
		Baluchistan (Muslim)	..	21,976	11,127	10,849	587	578	9	21,389	10,549	10,840	40	40	..
		Bengal (Muslim)	..	131,454	70,296	61,158	35,864	28,809	7,055	95,590	41,487	54,103	9,903	8,875	1,028
		Delhi (Muslim)	..	15,008	8,906	6,102	4,386	3,588	798	10,622	5,318	5,304	1,375	1,302	73
		N.-W. F. Province (Muslim)	..	64,738	33,956	30,782	4,012	3,703	309	60,726	30,253	30,473	1,104	1,016	88
		Punjab (Muslim)	..	235,408	128,002	107,406	31,213	27,693	3,520	204,195	100,309	103,886	6,459	6,183	276
		United Provinces (Muslim)	..	253,759	134,432	119,327	61,442	51,024	10,418	192,317	83,408	108,909	12,461	12,027	434
		Baroda (Muslim)	..	7,917	4,100	3,817	2,759	2,285	474	5,158	1,815	3,343	219	209	10
		Mysore (Muslim)	..	58,477	31,618	26,859	13,379	9,927	3,452	45,098	21,691	23,407	1,472	1,355	117
120	**SHEIKH**	..	..	**1,756,272**	**967,346**	**788,926**	**212,343**	**184,055**	**28,288**	**1,543,929**	**783,291**	**760,638**	**45,213**	**43,766**	**1,447**
		Delhi (Muslim)	..	96,459	57,691	38,768	12,824	10,837	1,987	83,635	46,854	36,781	2,946	2,798	148
		Punjab (Muslim)	..	328,710	186,755	141,955	43,103	36,934	6,169	285,607	149,821	135,786	10,792	10,178	614
		United Provinces (Muslim)	..	1,286,846	699,077	587,769	149,687	130,471	19,216	1,137,159	568,606	568,553	30,983	30,320	663
		Baroda (Muslim)	..	21,570	11,608	9,962	5,527	4,846	681	16,043	6,762	9,281	290	286	4
		Jammu & Kashmir (Muslim)	..	22,687	12,215	10,472	1,202	967	235	21,485	11,248	10,237	202	184	18
121	**TAGA**	...	8,17	**112,559**	**63,246**	**49,313**	**7,231**	**6,829**	**402**	**105,328**	**56,417**	**48,911**	**567**	**562**	**5**
		Delhi (Hindu)	..	848	473	375	75	75	..	773	398	375	54	54	..
		Delhi (Muslim)	..	2,646	1,452	1,194	54	54	..	2,592	1,398	1,194	5	5	..
		United Provinces (All Religions).	..	109,065	61,321	47,744	7,102	6,700	402	101,963	54,621	47,342	508	503	5
122	**TELAGA**	...	17	**1,355,456**	**649,111**	**706,345**	**66,344**	**57,593**	**8,751**	**1,289,112**	**591,518**	**697,594**	**9,398**	**9,017**	**381**
		Coorg (Hindu)	..	234	122	112	37	32	5	197	90	107	..	..	..
		Madras (Hindu)	..	575,154	283,042	292,112	49,365	42,176	7,189	525,789	240,866	284,923	6,464	6,218	246
		Hyderabad (Hindu)	..	780,068	365,947	414,121	16,942	15,385	1,557	763,126	350,562	412,564	2,934	2,799	135
123	**TANTI**	Assam (Hindu)	8,17	**45,703**	**23,730**	**21,973**	**946**	**910**	**36**	**44,757**	**22,820**	**21,937**	**39**	**36**	**3**

Table XIV.—Literacy by Selected Castes—*contd.*

	Caste, Tribe or Race.	Province, State or Agency and Religion.	Also tabulated in Table :	Total. Persons.	Total. Males.	Total. Females.	Literate. Persons.	Literate. Males.	Literate. Females.	Illiterate. Persons.	Illiterate. Males.	Illiterate. Females.	Literate in English. Persons.	Literate in English. Males.	Literate in English. Females.
	1	2	3	4	5	6	7	8	9	10	11	12	13	14	15
124	**TELI** ..	..	**8,17**	**5,528,256**	**2,806,867**	**2,721,389**	**336,940**	**321,352**	**15,588**	**5,191,316**	**2,485,515**	**2,705,801**	**13,727**	**13,599**	**128**
	GHANCHI ..	Bombay (Hindu) ..	..	12,620	6,827	5,793	5,213	4,578	635	7,407	2,249	5,158	317	316	1
		Baroda (Hindu) ..	..	11,788	6,010	5,778	4,785	4,137	648	7,003	1,873	5,130	138	137	1
		Baroda (Muslim) ..	..	6,022	3,145	,2,877	1,849	1,566	283	4,173	1,579	2,594	76	76	..
		Western India States (Hindu)	..	3,134	1,627	1,507	674	650	24	2,460	977	1,483	17	16	1
	TELI ..	Bihar and Orissa (Hindu)..	..	977,135	489,125	488,010	58,050	55,905	2,145	919,085	433,220	485,865	1,789	1,748	41
		Bombay (Hindu) ..	..	35,686	17,708	17,978	2,693	2,639	54	32,993	15,069	17,924	73	72	1
		C. P. and Berar (All Religions).	..	811,706	397,910	413,796	42,247	40,814	1,433	769,459	357,096	412,363	900	884	16
		Delhi (Hindu) ..	..	1,231	715	516	48	43	5	1,183	672	511	13	13	..
		Delhi (Muslim) ..	..	1,493	859	634	19	17	2	1,474	842	632	1	1	..
		Punjab (Muslim) ..	..	265,798	147,428	118,370	3,720	3,469	251	262,078	143,959	118,119	366	357	9
		United Provinces (All Religions).	..	807,599	428,018	379,581	19,094	18,425	669	788,505	409,593	378,912	430	420	10
		Central India (Hindu) ..	..	111,847	57,130	54,717	3,368	3,280	88	108,479	53,850	54,629	52	49	3
		Gwalior (Hindu) ..	..	44,877	24,399	20,478	856	713	143	44,021	23,686	20,335	27	25	2
		Hyderabad (Hindu) ..	..	56,520	30,507	26,013	3,619	3,468	151	52,901	27,039	25,862	129	116	13
	VANIYAN ..	Madras (Hindu) ..	..	2,362,301	1,186,059	1,176,242	186,657	178,229	8,428	2,175,644	1,007,830	1,167,814	9,194	9,193	1
		Cochin (Hindu) ..	..	717	358	359	243	220	23	474	138	336	27	27	..
		Travancore (Hindu) ..	..	17,782	9,042	8,740	3,805	3,199	606	13,977	5,843	8,134	178	149	29
125	**TODA** ..	Madras (Tribal)	**8,17,18**	**518**	**307**	**211**	**24**	**16**	**8**	**494**	**291**	**203**	**9**	**7**	**2**
126	**ULLATAN** ..	..	**17,18**	**806**	**389**	**417**	**37**	**21**	**16**	**769**	**368**	**401**	..	..	..
		Cochin (Hindu) ..	..	630	311	319	28	17	11	602	294	308	..	..	..
		Travancore (Christian) ..	..	176	78	98	9	4	5	167	74	93	..	..	..
127	**VAGHRI** (Waghri) ..	..	**17**	**69,681**	**37,049**	**32,632**	**1,080**	**974**	**106**	**68,601**	**36,075**	**32,526**	**9**	**9**	..
		Bombay (Hindu) ..	..	22,558	12,060	10,498	164	158	6	22,394	11,902	10,492	2	2	..
		Baroda (Hindu) ..	..	27,566	14,568	12,998	641	551	90	26,925	14,017	12,908	4	4	..
		Western India States (Hindu)	..	19,557	10,421	9,136	275	265	10	19,282	10,156	9,126	3	3	..
128	**VALAIYAN** (Valan)	..	**17**	**25,515**	**13,153**	**12,362**	**5,396**	**4,461**	**935**	**20,119**	**8,692**	**11,427**	**181**	**140**	**41**
		Cochin (Hindu) ..	..	9,029	4,651	4,378	2,774	2,142	632	6,255	2,509	3,746	152	120	32
		Travancore (Hindu) ..	..	16,486	8,502	7,984	2,622	2,319	303	13,864	6,183	7,681	29	20	9
129	**VELAN** ..	..	**17**	**21,492**	**10,524**	**10,968**	**5,660**	**4,664**	**996**	**15,832**	**5,860**	**9,972**	**37**	**30**	**7**
		Cochin (Hindu) ..	..	8,745	4,162	4,583	2,513	2,159	354	6,232	2,003	4,229	28	25	3
		Travancore (Hindu) ..	..	12,747	6,362	6,385	3,147	2,505	642	9,600	3,857	5,743	9	5	4
130	**VELLALA** (Vellalan)	..	**17**	**59,973**	**30,208**	**29,765**	**23,654**	**18,294**	**5,360**	**36,319**	**11,914**	**24,405**	**4,306**	**3,791**	**515**
		Hyderabad (Hindu) ..	..	3,461	1,813	1,648	2,048	1,611	437	1,413	202	1,211	1,387	1,089	298
		Travancore (Hindu) ..	..	56,512	28,395	28,117	21,606	16,683	4,923	34,906	11,712	23,194	2,919	2,702	217
131	**VILKURUP** ..	Cochin (Hindu) ...	**17**	**1,447**	**659**	**788**	**373**	**283**	**90**	**1,074**	**376**	**698**	**1**	**1**	..

	Caste	Area													
132	**VISWABRAHMAN** ..	.. ..	**8,17**	**3,658,685**	**1,927,301**	**1,731,384**	**416,233**	**379,012**	**37,221**	**3,242,452**	**1,548,289**	**1,694,163**	**17,166**	**16,554**	**612**
	VISWABRAHMAN	Coorg (Hindu)	..	103	58	45	18	18	..	85	40	45	..	..	..
		Madras (Hindu) ..	..	740,391	370,578	369,813	135,395	124,912	10,483	604,996	245,666	359,330	5,308	5,088	220
		Hyderabad (Hindu) ..	..	22,045	12,186	9,859	2,130	2,025	105	19,915	10,161	9,754	70	69	1
	VISWAKARMA ..	Mysore (Hindu) ..	..	118,483	61,946	56,537	20,756	19,503	1,253	97,727	42,443	55,284	552	532	20
	Carpenters														
	BADHAI (*Barhai*)	C. P. and Berar (All Religions).	..	91,233	47,911	43,322	9,774	9,470	304	81,459	38,441	43,018	248	243	5
	KHATI	Rajputana (All Religions)	..	64,203	33,149	31,054	1,156	1,137	19	63,047	32,012	31,035	189	188	1
	SUTAR (*Sutradhar*).	Bombay (Hindu) ..	..	28,013	14,130	13,883	2,092	1,988	104	25,921	12,142	13,779	39	35	4
		Baroda (Hindu) ..	..	19,996	10,192	9,804	6,856	5,773	1,083	13,140	4,419	8,721	149	148	1
	(*Bade Waddla*) ..	Hyderabad (Hindu) ..	..	91,890	49,524	42,366	3,142	2,745	397	88,748	46,779	41,969	49	48	1
		Western India States (Hindu). ..	..	40,719	20,444	20,275	8,028	7,267	761	32,691	13,177	19,514	437	436	1
	TARKHAN .	Delhi .. (Hindu) ..	..	3,335	1,876	1,459	242	225	17	3,093	1,651	1,442	27	27	..
		Delhi .. (Sikh) ..	..	937	640	297	422	345	77	515	295	220	100	97	3
		Delhi .. (Muslim) ..	..	274	188	86	20	16	4	254	172	82	..	..	..
		Punjab .. (Hindu) ..	..	118,385	64,655	53,730	3,042	2,903	139	115,343	61,752	53,591	266	261	5
		Punjab .. (Sikh) ..	..	128,034	71,869	56,165	11,924	10,665	1,259	116,110	61,204	54,906	1,809	1,755	54
	Goldsmiths.	Punjab .. (Muslim) ..	..	271,390	149,455	121,935	6,978	6,381	597	264,412	143,074	121,338	722	707	15
	SONAR (*Soni*, *Sunar*, *Surnakar*).	Bombay (Hindu)* ..	..	28,396	14,111	14,285	6,559	6,176	383	21,837	7,935	13,902	255	245	10
		C. P. and Berar (Hindu) ..	..	114,805	58,473	56,332	25,724	24,322	1,402	89,081	34,151	54,930	905	896	9
		Punjab (Hindu) ..	..	79,469	43,611	35,858	10,212	9,439	773	69,257	34,172	35,085	686	678	8
		Punjab (Sikh) ..	..	20,135	10,930	9,205	2,924	2,648	276	17,211	8,282	8,929	230	229	1
		Punjab (Muslim) ..	..	25,151	13,724	11,427	1,457	1,326	131	23,694	12,398	11,296	135	117	18
		United Provinces (All Religions).	..	221,840	122,292	99,548	30,555	28,754	1,801	191,285	93,538	97,747	1,141	1,083	58
	SONI	Baroda (Hindu) ..	..	10,073	5,193	4,880	5,206	4,213	993	4,867	980	3,887	137	135	2
		Hyderabad (Hindu) ..	..	109,717	59,117	50,600	12,166	11,180	986	97,551	47,937	49,614	161	130	31
		Western India States (Hindu). ..	..	26,172	13,021	13,151	9,882	8,272	1,610	16,290	4,749	11,541	504	498	6
	Blacksmiths.														
	KAMMALAN ..	Cochin (Hindu)	..	36,122	17,488	18,634	10,708	8,936	1,772	25,414	8,552	16,862	157	143	14
		Travancore (Hindu) ..	..	162,323	81,538	80,785	44,555	36,843	7,712	117,768	44,695	73,073	641	576	65
	LOHAR	Central Provinces and Berar (All Religions).	..	161,491	81,616	79.875	12,325	11,988	337	149,166	69,628	79,538	206	199	7
		Punjab .. (Hindu) ..	..	60,728	33,010	27,718	1,152	1,085	67	59,576	31,925	27,651	69	69	..
		Punjab .. (Sikh) ..	..	13,343	7,208	6,135	1,048	936	112	12.295	6,272	6,023	79	77	2
		Punjab .. (Muslim) ..	..	189,027	103,580	85,447	5,709	5,245	464	183,318	98,335	84,983	668	639	29
		United Provinces (All Religions).	..	475,363	254,709	220,654	11,967	11,633	234	463.396	243,076	220,320	562	554	8
		Baroda (Hindu) ..	..	17,201	8,429	8.772	4,737	3,993	744	12,464	4,436	8,028	75	72	3
		Hyderabad (Hindu) ..	..	77,780	42,838	34,942	4,618	4,368	250	73,162	38,470	34,692	163	156	7
	PANCHAL ..	Hyderabad (Hindu) ..	..	60,260	31,395	28,865	1,643	1,323	320	5[illegible],617	30,072	28,545	299	297	2
	Coppersmiths.														
	KASAR	Hyderabad (Hindu) ..	..	29,858	16,217	13,641	1,111	959	152	28,747	15,258	13,489	128	127	1

*Including Daivadnya Brahman.

M8CC

Table XIV.—Literacy by Selected Castes—*concld.*

	Caste, Tribe or Race.	Province, State or Agency and Religion.	Also tabulated in Table :	Total.			Literate.			Illiterate.			Literate in English.		
				Persons.	Males.	Females.	Persons.	Males.	Females.	Persons.	Males.	Females.	Persons.	Males.	Females.
	1	2	3	4	5	6	7	8	9	10	11	12	13	14	15
33	**YADAVA**	—	8,17	**10,687,106**	**5,519,371**	**5,167,735**	**227,493**	**215,248**	**12,245**	**10,459,613**	**5,304,123**	**5,155,490**	**13,364**	**12,821**	**543**
	AHAR	United Provinces (Hindu)	..	341,794	187,204	154,590	2,664	2,542	122	339,130	184,662	154,468	132	125	7
	AHIR	C. P. and Berar. (Hindu) ..	..	643,459	321,065	322,394	11,166	10,570	596	632,293	310,495	321,798	404	396	8
		C. P. and Berar. (Tribal) ..	..	3,625	1,704	1,921	10	10	..	3,615	1,694	1,921	1	1	..
		Delhi (Hindu) ..	..	10,688	6,472	4,216	598	566	32	10,090	5,906	4,184	121	121	..
		Punjab (Hindu) ..	..	173,140	97,296	75,844	3,109	2,934	175	170,031	94,362	75,669	480	473	7
		Punjab (Muslim) ..	..	1,851	1,012	839	58	52	6	1,793	960	833	10	9	1
		United Provinces (All Religions).	..	3,140,125	1,673,429	1,466,696	34,509	33,504	1,005	3,105,616	1,639,925	1,465,691	1,319	1,296	23
		Central India (Hindu) ..	..	189,022	99,980	89,042	2,754	2,687	67	186,268	97,293	88,975	121	119	2
		Gwalior (Hindu) ..	..	105,336	57,161	48,175	1,068	1,015	51	104,270	56,146	48,124	33	33	..
		Rajputana (All Religions)	..	58,239	32,371	25,868	468	456	12	57,771	31,915	25,856	8	8	..
	GAURA (*Gauda*) ..	Bihar and Orissa (Hindu)	..	773,688	375,015	398,673	19,630	18,770	860	754,058	356,245	397,813	500	496	4
		Coorg (Hindu)	..	11,579	6,213	5,366	2,115	1,877	238	9,464	4,336	5,128	158	154	4
	GOALA	Bihar and Orissa (Hindu)*	..	2,779,933	1,430,884	1,349,049	55,464	52,959	2,505	2,724,469	1,377,925	1,346,544	2,492	2,455	37
	GOLA (*Golla, Gollaru*).	Coorg (Hindu)	..	437	245	192	65	59	6	372	186	186	2	2	..
		Madras (Hindu) ..	..	659,614	327,926	331,688	15,768	14,728	1,040	643,846	313,198	330,648	1,329	1,301	28
		Mysore (Hindu) ..	..	141,371	71,973	69,398	4,668	4,384	284	136,703	67,589	69,114	336	319	17
	GOWARI ..	C. P. and Berar (All Religions).	..	132,185	66,473	65,712	1,864	1,738	126	130,321	64,735	65,586	76	46	30
	IDAIYAN ..	Cochin (Hindu)	..	311	163	148	116	77	39	195	86	109	23	21	2
		Travancore (Hindu) ..	..	6,933	3,282	3,651	1,310	1,144	166	5,623	2,138	3,485	96	95	1
	YADAVAN ..	Coorg (Hindu)	..	4	4	..	1	1	..	3	3	..	..	..	..
		Madras (Hindu	..	745,478	367,081	378,397	63,004	58,741	4,263	682,474	308,340	374,134	5,275	4,963	312
		Hyderabad (Hindu) ..	..	768,294	392,418	375,876	7,086	6,434	652	761,208	385,984	375,224	448	388	60
134	**ARAKAN MAHOMEDAN**	Burma (Muslim) ..	..	**36,222**	**18,558**	**17,664**	**2,887**	**2,490**	**397**	**33,335**	**16,068**	**17,267**	**529**	**511**	**18**
135	**CHIN**	Burma (All Religions) ..	17,18	**130,789**	**63,563**	**67,226**	**1,906**	**1,897**	**9**	**128,883**	**61,666**	**67,217**	**81**	**81**	..
136	**KAREN** (Pwo & Sgaw) ..	Burma (All Religions) ..	8,17,18	**653,758**	**326,824**	**326,934**	**158,245**	**111,284**	**46,961**	**495,513**	**215,540**	**279,973**	**5,008**	**3,308**	**1,700**
137	**MON**	Burma (All Religions) ..	8,17,18	**256,252**	**129,864**	**126,388**	**74,934**	**59,316**	**15,618**	**181,318**	**70,548**	**110,770**	**1,328**	**1,101**	**227**
138	**SHAN**	Burma (All Religions) ..	8,17	**510,312**	**257,313**	**252,999**	**58,820**	**55,330**	**3,490**	**451,492**	**201,983**	**249,509**	**551**	**477**	**74**

*Including Ahir, Gopa and Yadava.

TABLE XV.

Language.

(1) This table which corresponds to table X of 1921 has on this occasion been tabulated in two parts.

(2) Part I shows details of the linguistic distribution of the inhabitants enumerated in each Province, State or Agency according to mother-tongue. The languages have been arranged according to a revised classification based on Sir George Grierson's revised scheme of Indian Languages. Languages which were grouped together under the head 'Other Languages' in many of the provincial returns, have here been reclassified as far as the details available permitted. Hindustani, under which term the returns of both Urdu and Hindi as spoken languages were amalgamated for census purposes, has been reclassified here as Western Hindi, Eastern Hindi or Bihari.

(3) Part II is intended to show the extent to which subsidiary languages are in practical use in addition to the mother-tongue of the speakers. The statistics in this part are not the result of a complete enumeration but of returns limited to those areas in which concurrent vernaculars were found to exist.

(4) The summary below gives the total number of persons recorded under the principal groups of the general scheme of classification followed for Part I :—

	Persons.	Males.	Females.
Population	*350,529,557*	*180,620,612*	*169,908,945*
A.—*Vernaculars of India*	*349,887,527*	*180,214,643*	*169,672,884*
Austric Family	*5,342,708*	*2,675,837*	*2,666,87*[illegible]
Austronesian Sub-Family	6,542	3,307	3,235
Austroasiatic Sub-Family	5,336,166	2,672,530	2,663,636
Tibeto-Chinese Family	*14,010,496*	*6,109,046*	*7,101,450*
Tibeto-Burman Sub-Family	12,982,840	6,392,133	6,590,707
Tai Chinese Sub-Family	1,027,656	516,913	510,743
Karen Family	*1,341,331*	*669,216*	*672,115*
Man Family	*947*	*502*	*445*
Dravidian Family	*71,644,787*	*35,847,723*	*35,797,064*
Indo-European Family	*257,492,805*	*134,082,997*	*123,409,808*
Unclassed Languages	*54,453*	*29,322*	*25,131*
B.—*Vernaculars of other Asiatic countries and Africa*	*302,324*	*197,655*	*104,669*
Indo-European Family (Aryan Sub-Family)	39,224	25,359	13,865
Tibeto-Chinese Family (Tai Chinese Sub-Family)	185,822	124,284	61,538
Semitic Family	59,954	37,052	22,902
Hamitic Family	5,039	2,946	2,093
Mongolian Family	11,943	7,806	4,137
Malayo-Polynesian Family	342	208	134
C.—*European Languages*	*339,706*	*208,314*	*131,392*
Indo-European Family	339,66	208,290	131,370
Mongolian Family	13	3	10
European Languages unspecified	33	21	12

Table XV.—Language—Part I—Mother Tongue.

	Province, State or Agency.	Population.			A.-Vernaculars of India.			Austric Family. Total Austric Family.			Austric Family. Austronesian Sub-Family. Indonesian Branch. Malay Group Total.		
		Persons.	Males.	Females.	Persons.	Males.	Females.	Persons.	Males.	Females.	Persons.	Males.	Females.
	1	2	3	4	5	6	7	8	9	10	11	12	13
	INDIA	**350,529,557**	**180,620,612**	**169,908,945**	**349,887,527**	**180,214,643**	**169,672,884**	**5,342,708**	**2,675,837**	**2,666,871**	**6,542**	**3,307**	**3,235**
	Provinces	**271,431,571**	**139,890,978**	**131,540,593**	**270,847,508**	**139,521,746**	**131,325,762**	**4,420,341**	**2,222,025**	**2,198,316**	**6,541**	**3,306**	**3,235**
1	Ajmer-Merwara	560,292	296,081	264,211	557,076	293,970	263,106	7	3	4	..	..	..
2	Andaman and Nicobar Islands	29,463	9,702	9,761	28,833	19,158	9,675	9,958	5,178	4,780	..	..	..
3	Assam	8,622,251	4,537,206	4,085,045	8,617,689	4,533,967	4,083,722	401,622	208,503	193,119	11	4	7
4	Baluchistan (*Districts and Administered Territories.*)	463,508	270,004	193,504	453,046	262,532	190,514	..	..	..	..	..	..
5	Bengal	50,114,002	26,041,698	24,072,304	50,054,389	26,006,318	24,048,071	893,484	452,325	441,159	..	..	..
6	Bihar and Orissa	37,677,576	18,794,138	18,883,438	37,663,896	18,786,523	18,877,373	2,240,860	1,117,138	1,123,722	..	..	..
7	Bombay (*including Aden*)	21,854,866	11,505,229	10,349,637	21,719,578	11,420,307	10,299,271	..	..	..	..	..	..
	Aden	*51,478*	*32,345*	*19,133*	*8,602*	*5,454*	*3,148*	..	..	..	..	..	..
8	Burma	14,647,497	7,480,676	7,166,821	14,438,457	7,344,350	7,094,107	487,686	245,674	242,012	6,368	3,232	3,136
9	Central Provinces and Berar	15,507,723	7,761,818	7,745,905	15,494,952	7,753,857	7,741,095	155,557	77,870	77,687	..	..	..
10	Coorg	163,327	90,575	72,752	162,998	90,393	72,605	..	..	..	..	..	..
11	Delhi	636,246	369,497	266,749	630,883	366,055	264,828	..	..	..	..	..	..
12	Madras	46,740,107	23,082,999	23,657,108	46,691,908	23,058,028	23,633,880	231,143	115,323	115,820	141	61	80
13	North-West Frontier Province (*Districts and Administered Territories.*)	2,425,076	1,315,818	1,109,258	2,411,053	1,305,726	1,105,327	2	2	..	..	..	..
14	Punjab	23,580,852	12,880,510	10,700,342	23,550,110	12,859,650	10,690,460	1	..	1	..	..	..
15	United Provinces of Agra and Oudh	48,408,785	25,445,027	22,963,758	*48,372,640	25,420,912	22,951,728	21	9	12	21	9	12
	States and Agencies	**79,097,986**	**40,729,634**	**38,368,352**	**79,040,019**	**40,692,897**	**38,347,122**	**922,367**	**453,812**	**468,555**	**1**	**1**	..
16	Assam	625,606	306,927	318,679	625,258	306,713	318,545	153,629	74,446	79,183	..	..	..
17	Baluchistan States	405,109	218,410	186,699	404,989	218,339	186,650	..	..	..	..	..	..
18	Baroda State	2,443,007	1,257,817	1,185,190	2,442,610	1,257,543	1,185,067	..	..	..	..	..	..
19	Bengal States	973,336	516,162	457,174	973,226	516,082	457,144	2,832	1,618	1,214	..	..	..
20	Bihar and Orissa States	4,652,007	2,288,422	2,363,585	4,651,757	2,288,261	2,363,496	733,657	361,586	372,071	..	..	..
21	Bombay States	4,468,396	2,288,623	2,179,773	4,467,547	2,288,105	2,179,442	..	..	..	..	..	..
22	Central India Agency	6,632,790	3,405,438	3,227,352	6,628,790	3,402,777	3,226,013	4,157	2,067	2,090	..	..	..
23	Central Provinces States	2,483,214	1,235,385	1,247,829	2,482,798	1,235,162	1,247,636	28,091	14,094	13,997	..	..	..
24	Gwalior State	3,523,070	1,867,031	1,656,039	3,522,381	1,866,526	1,655,855	..	..	..	..	..	..
25	Hyderabad State	14,436,148	7,370,010	7,066,138	14,418,592	7,357,573	7,061,019	..	..	..	..	..	..
26	Jammu and Kashmir State	3,646,243	1 938,338	1,707,905	3,645,508	1,937,905	1,707,603	..	..	..	..	..	..
27	Madras States Agency	6,754,484	3,373,032	3,381,452	6,748,157	3,369,574	3,378,583	1	1	..	1	1	..
	Cochin State	*1,205,016*	*589,813*	*615,203*	*1,203,731*	*589,200*	*614,531*	..	..	..	..	..	..
	Travancore State	*5,095,973*	*2,565,073*	*2,530,900*	*5,091,006*	*2,562,273*	*2,528,733*	..	..	..	..	..	..
	Other Madras States	*453,495*	*218,146*	*235,349*	*453,420*	*218,101*	*235,319*	1	1	..	1	1	..
28	Mysore State	6,557,302	3,353,963	3,203,339	6,541,837	3,345,943	3,195,894	..	..	..	..	..	..
29	North-West Frontier Province (*Agencies and Tribal Areas*)	46,451	44,635	1,816	42,287	40,624	1,663	..	..	..	..	..	..
30	Punjab States	437,787	229,290	208,497	437,696	229,260	208,436	..	..	..	..	..	..
31	Punjab States Agency	4,472,218	2,451,394	2,020,824	4,471,571	2,450,956	2,020,615	..	..	..	..	..	..
32	Rajputana Agency	11,225,712	5,885,028	5,340,684	11,223,676	5,883,892	5,339,784	..	..	..	..	..	..
33	Sikkim States	109,808	55,825	53,983	109,769	55,804	53,965	..	..	..	..	..	..
34	United Provinces States	1,206,048	618,150	587,898	1,206,007	618,130	587,877	..	..	..	..	..	..
35	Western India States Agency	3,999,250	2,025,754	1,973,496	3,995,563	2,023,728	1,971,835	..	..	..	..	..	..

* Includes 3 males enumerated in the U. P. States for whom separate details according to language were not available.

Table XV.—Language—Part I—Mother Tongue—*contd.*

Province, State or Agency.	Austric Family—*contd.* Austronesian Sub-Family. Indonesian Branch. Malay Group—*concld.* Malay. Persons.	Males.	Females.	Salon. Persons.	Males.	Females.	Austroasiatic Sub-Family. Mon-Khmer Branch. Austroasiatic Sub-Family Total. Persons.	Males.	Females.	Mon-Khmer Branch Total. Persons.	Males.	Females.	Mon Group. Talaing. Persons.	Males.	Females.
1	14	15	16	17	18	19	20	21	22	23	24	25	26	27	28
INDIA	**4,634**	**2,397**	**2,237**	**1,908**	**910**	**998**	**5,336,166**	**2,672,530**	**2,663,636**	**726,578**	**362,253**	**364,325**	**305,294**	**154,058**	**151,236**
Provinces	4,633	2,396	2,237	1,908	910	998	4,413,800	2,218,719	2,195,081	572,829	287,746	285,083	305,294	154,058	151,236
1 Ajmer-Merwara ..	..	..	..	..	..	..	7	3	4	..	..	..	..	..	..
2 Andaman and Nicobar Islands.	..	..	..	..	..	..	9,958	5,178	4,780	9,885	5,108	4,777	..	..	..
3 Assam	11	4	7	..	..	..	401,611	208,499	193,112	80,278	39,278	41,000	..	..	..
4 Baluchistan .. .. (*Districts and Administered Territories.*)	..	..	..	..	..	..	..	..	..	..	..	..	..	..	..
5 Bengal	..	..	..	..	..	..	893,484	452,325	441,159	1,336	914	422	..	..	..
6 Bihar and Orissa ..	..	..	..	..	..	..	2,240,860	1,117,138	1,123,722	10	3	7	..	..	..
7 Bombay (*including Aden*)	..	..	..	..	..	..	..	..	..	..	..	..	..	..	..
Aden	..	..	..	..	..	..	..	..	..	..	..	..	..	..	..
8 Burma	4,460	2,322	2,138	1,908	910	998	481,318	242,442	238,876	481,318	242,442	238,876	305,294	154,058	151,236
9 Central Provinces and Berar	..	..	..	..	..	..	155,557	77,870	77,687	..	..	..	..	..	..
10 Coorg	..	..	..	..	..	..	..	..	..	..	..	..	..	..	..
11 Delhi	..	..	..	..	..	..	..	..	..	..	..	..	..	..	..
12 Madras	141	61	80	..	..	..	231,002	115,262	115,740	..	..	..	..	..	..
13 North-West Frontier Province. (*Districts and Administered Territories.*)	..	..	..	..	..	..	2	2	..	1	1	..	..	..	..
14 Punjab	..	..	..	..	..	..	1	..	1	1	..	1	..	..	..
15 United Provinces of Agra and Oudh.	21	9	12	..	..	..	..	..	..	..	..	..	..	..	..
States and Agencies ..	1	1	..	..	..	..	922,366	453,811	468,555	153,749	74,507	79,242	..	..	..
16 Assam States ..	..	..	..	..	..	..	153,629	74,446	79,183	153,626	74,444	79,182	..	..	..
17 Baluchistan States ..	..	..	..	..	..	..	..	..	..	..	..	..	..	..	..
18 Baroda State ..	..	..	..	..	..	..	..	..	..	..	..	..	..	..	..
19 Bengal States ..	..	..	..	..	..	..	2,832	1,618	1,214	121	61	60	..	..	..
20 Bihar and Orissa States ..	..	..	..	..	..	..	733,657	361,586	372,071	2	2	..	..	..	..
21 Bombay States ..	..	..	..	..	..	..	..	..	..	..	..	..	..	..	..
22 Central India Agency ..	..	..	..	..	..	..	4,157	2,067	2,090	..	..	..	..	..	..
23 Central Provinces States ..	..	..	..	..	..	..	28,091	14,094	13,997	..	..	..	..	..	..
24 Gwalior State ..	..	..	..	..	..	..	..	..	..	..	..	..	..	..	..
25 Hyderabad State ..	..	..	..	..	..	..	..	..	..	..	..	..	..	..	..
26 Jammu and Kashmir State	..	..	..	..	..	..	..	..	..	..	..	..	..	..	..
27 Madras States Agency ..	1	1	..	..	..	..	..	..	..	..	..	..	..	..	..
Cochin State	..	..	..	..	..	..	..	..	..	..	..	..	..	..	..
Travancore State ..	..	..	..	..	..	..	..	..	..	..	..	..	..	..	..
Other Madras States ..	*1*	*1*	..	..	..	..	..	..	..	..	..	..	..	..	..
28 Mysore State ..	..	..	..	..	..	..	..	..	..	..	..	..	..	..	..
29 North-West Frontier Province. (*Agencies and Tribal Areas.*)	..	..	..	..	..	..	..	..	..	..	..	..	..	..	..
30 Punjab States ..	..	..	..	..	..	..	..	..	..	..	..	..	..	..	..
31 Punjab States Agency ..	..	..	..	..	..	..	..	..	..	..	..	..	..	..	..
32 Rajputana Agency ..	..	..	..	..	..	..	..	..	..	..	..	..	..	..	..
33 Sikkim State ..	..	..	..	..	..	..	..	..	..	..	..	..	..	..	..
34 United Provinces States	..	..	..	..	..	..	..	..	..	..	..	..	..	..	..
35 Western India States Agency.	..	..	..	..	..	..	..	..	..	..	..	..	..	..	..

Table XV.—Language—Part I—Mother Tongue—*contd.*

Austric Family—*contd.*

Austroasiatic Sub-Family—*contd.*

Mon-Khmer Branch—*concld.*

Palaung-Wa Group.

Province, State or Agency.	Palaung-Wa Group Total.			Wa.			Danaw.			Khamuk.			Yang (unspecified).			Yanglam.		
	Persons.	Males.	Females.	Persons.	Males.	Females.	Persons.	Males.	Females.	Persons.	Males.	Females.	Persons.	Males.	Females.	Persons.	Males.	Females.
1	29	30	31	32	33	34	35	36	37	38	39	40	41	42	43	44	45	46
INDIA ..	**177,012**	**88,963**	**88,049**	**22,142**	**11,401**	**10,741**	**1,159**	**582**	**577**	**191**	**190**	**1**	**3,151**	**1,410**	**1,741**	**10,725**	**5,485**	**5,240**
Provinces ..	176,914	88,917	87,997	22,142	11,401	10,741	1,159	582	577	191	190	1	3,151	1,410	1,741	10,725	5,485	5,240
Assam	32	32	..	..	..	..	..	..	..	..	..	..	..	..	..	..	..	..
Bengal	858	501	357	..	..	..	..	..	..	..	..	..	..	..	..	..	..	..
Burma	176,024	88,384	87,640	22,142	11,401	10,741	1,159	582	577	191	190	1	3,151	1,410	1,741	10,725	5,485	5,240
States ..	98	46	52	..	..	..	..	..	..	..	..	..	..	..	..	..	..	..
Bengal States ..	98	46	52	..	..	..	..	..	..	..	..	..	..	..	..	..	..	..

Province, State or Agency.	Mon-Khmer Branch—*concld.* Palaung-Wa Group—*concld.* Palaung and Pale.			Khasi Group. Khasi.			Nicobar Group. Nicobarese.			Munda Branch. Munda Branch Total.		
	Persons.	Males.	Females.	Persons.	Males.	Females.	Persons.	Males.	Females.	Persons.	Males.	Females.
1	47	48	49	50	51	52	53	54	55	56	57	58
INDIA	**139,644**	**69,895**	**69,749**	**234,387**	**114,124**	**120,263**	**9,885**	**5,108**	**4,777**	**4,609,588**	**2,310,277**	**2,299,311**
Provinces	139,546	69,849	69,697	80,736	39,663	41,073	9,885	5,108	4,777	3,840,971	1,930,973	1,909,998
Ajmer-Merwara	..	..	..	..	..	..	..	..	..	7	3	4
Andaman and Nicobar Islands ..	..	..	..	..	..	..	9,885	5,108	4,777	73	70	3
Assam	32	32	..	80,246	39,246	41,000	..	..	..	321,333	169,221	152,112
Bengal	858	501	357	478	413	65	..	..	..	892,148	451,411	440,737
Bihar and Orissa	..	..	..	10	3	7	..	..	..	2,240,850	1,117,135	1,123,715
Burma	138,656	69,316	69,340	..	..	..	..	..	..	..	..	..
Central Provinces and Berar ..	..	..	..	..	..	..	..	..	..	155,557	77,870	77,687
Madras	..	..	..	..	..	..	..	..	..	231,002	115,262	115,740
North-West Frontier Province (*Districts and Administered Territories*). ..	..	..	..	1	1	..	..	..	..	1	1	..
Punjab	..	..	..	1	..	1	..	..	..	..	..	..
States and Agencies.	98	46	52	153,651	74,461	79,190	..	..	..	768,617	379,304	389,313
Assam States	..	..	..	153,626	74,444	79,182	..	..	..	3	2	1
Bengal States	98	46	52	23	15	8	..	..	..	2,711	1,557	1,154
Bihar and Orissa States	..	..	..	2	2	..	..	..	..	733,655	361,584	372,071
Central India Agency	..	..	..	..	..	..	..	..	..	4,157	2,067	2,090
Central Provinces States	..	..	..	..	..	..	..	..	..	28,091	14,094	13,997

Table XV.—Language—Part I—Mother Tongue—*contd.*

Austric Family—*contd.*

Austroasiatic Sub-Family—*contd.*

Munda Branch—*contd.*

	Province, State or Agency.	Kherwari (Santali, Mundari, Ho, etc.) Persons.	Males.	Females.	Korku. Persons.	Males.	Females.	Kharia. Persons.	Males.	Females.	Juang. Persons.	Males.	Females.	Sawara. Persons.	Males.	Females.	Gadaba. Persons.	Males.	Females.
	1	59	60	61	62	63	64	65	66	67	68	69	70	71	72	73	74	75	76
	INDIA ..	**4,031,970**	**2,018,143**	**2,013,827**	**169,728**	**85,213**	**84,515**	**152,018**	**78,792**	**73,226**	**14,583**	**7,066**	**7,517**	**194,947**	**97,898**	**97,049**	**44,371**	**22,128**	**22,243**
	Provinces ..	3,337,749	1,675,420	1,662,329	156,580	78,520	78,060	106,063	56,314	49,749	5	4	1	194,947	97,898	97,049	43,667	21,788	21,879
1	Ajmer-Merwara ..	7	3	4	..	..	..	..	..	..	..	..	..	..	..	..	..	..	..
2	Andaman and Nicobar Islands.	..	..	..	..	..	..	..	..	..	..	..	..	..	..	..	..	..	..
3	Assam	293,893	154,519	139,374	3,742	2,028	1,714	4,358	7,433	6,925	..	..	..	9,340	5,241	4,099	..	..	..
4	Baluchistan ..	..	..	..	..	..	..	..	..	..	..	..	..	..	..	..	..	..	..
	(Districts and Administered Territories).																		
5	Bengal	877,206	442,332	434,874	..	..	..	14,815	8,970	5,845	..	..	..	..	..	..	..	..	..
6	Bihar and Orissa ..	2,165,105	1,077,824	1,087,281	..	..	..	75,695	39,269	36,426	5	4	1	45	38	7	..	..	..
8	Burma	..	..	..	..	..	..	..	..	..	..	..	..	..	..	..	..	..	..
9	Central Provinces and Berar.	1,525	737	788	152,838	76,492	76,346	1,194	641	553	..	..	..	..	..	..	..	..	..
10	Coorg	..	..	..	..	..	..	..	..	..	..	..	..	..	..	..	..	..	..
11	Delhi	..	..	..	..	..	..	..	..	..	..	..	..	..	..	..	..	..	..
12	Madras	13	5	8	..	..	..	..	..	..	..	..	..	185,562	92,619	92,943	43,667	21,788	21,879
13	North-West Frontier Province.	..	..	..	..	..	..	1	1	..	..	..	..	..	..	..	..	..	..
	(Districts and Administered Territories).																		
14	Punjab	..	..	..	..	..	..	..	..	..	..	..	..	..	..	..	..	..	..
15	United Provinces of Agra and Oudh.	..	..	..	..	..	..	..	..	..	..	..	..	..	..	..	..	..	..
	States and Agencies ..	694,221	342,723	351,498	13,148	6,693	6,455	45,955	22,478	23,477	14,578	7,062	7,516	..	..	..	704	340	364
16	Assam States ..	3	2	1	..	..	..	..	..	..	..	..	..	..	..	..	..	..	..
17	Baluchistan States ..	..	..	..	..	..	..	..	..	..	..	..	..	..	..	..	..	..	..
18	Baroda State ..	..	..	..	..	..	..	..	..	..	..	..	..	..	..	..	..	..	..
19	Bengal States ..	2,623	1,509	1,114	..	..	..	88	48	40	..	..	..	..	..	..	..	..	..
20	Bihar and Orissa States	680,840	335,860	344,980	..	..	..	37,985	18,543	19,442	14,578	7,062	7,516	..	..	..	..	..	..
21	Bombay States ..	..	..	..	..	..	..	..	..	..	..	..	..	..	..	..	252	119	133
22	Central India Agency	146	86	60	4,011	1,981	2,030	..	..	..	..	..	..	..	..	..	..	..	..
23	Central Provinces States	10,609	5,266	5,343	9,137	4,712	4,425	7,882	3,887	3,995	..	..	..	..	..	..	452	221	23

Table XV.—Language—Part I—Mother Tongue—*contd.*

Province, State or Agency.	Austric-Family—*concld.* Austroasiatic Sub-Family—*concld.* Munda Branch—*concld.* Munda (unspecified)			Tibeto-Chinese Family. Tibeto-Chinese Family Total.			Tibeto-Burman Sub-Family. Tibeto-Burman Sub-Family Total.			Tibeto-Himalayan Branch Total.			Tibetan Group. Tibetan Group Total.			Bhotia of Tibet or Tibetan.		
	Persons.	Males.	Females.	Persons.	Males.	Females.	Persons.	Males.	Females.	Persons.	Males.	Females.	Persons.	Males.	Females.	Persons.	Males.	Females
1	77	78	79	80	81	82	83	84	85	86	87	88	89	90	91	92	93	94
INDIA ..	**1,971**	**1,037**	**934**	**14,010,496**	**8,909,046**	**7,101,450**	**12,982,840**	**6,392,133**	**6,590,707**	**468,499**	**235,342**	**233,157**	**252,063**	**127,012**	**125,051**	**9,799**	**5,444**	**4,355**
Provinces ..	1,960	1,029	931	13,085,636	6,451,779	6,633,857	12,057,980	5,934,866	6,123,114	183,591	93,677	89,914	50,970	26,934	24,036	5,281	3,170	2,111
1 Ajmer-Merwara ..	..	..	..	..	..	..	..	..	..	..	..	..	..	..	..	..	..	..
2 Andaman and Nicobar Islands.	73	70	3	2,745	2,315	430	2,745	2,315	430	..	..	..	..	..	..	..	..	..
3 Assam ..	..	..	..	1,179,609	594,971	584,638	1,173,896	591,942	581,954	6,277	4,121	2,156	1,898	1,445	453	782	539	243
4 Baluchistan (*Districts and Administered Territories.*)	..	..	..	597	595	2	597	595	2	597	595	2	29	29	..	21	21	..
5 Bengal ..	127	109	18	338,269	171,951	166,318	338,269	171,951	166,318	141,783	71,019	70,764	14,520	7,727	6,793	2,867	1,552	1,315
6 Bihar and Orissa ..	..	..	..	42	22	20	42	22	20	25	16	9	19	11	8	..	..	..
7 Bombay (*including Aden*).	..	..	..	18	4	14	18	4	14	..	..	..	..	..	..	..	..	..
Aden ..	..	..	..	*1*	*1*	..	*1*	*1*	..	..	..	..	..	..	..	..	..	..
8 Burma ..	..	..	..	11,528,938	5,663,675	5,865,263	10,507,029	5,149,825	5,357,204	..	..	..	..	..	..	..	..	..
9 Central Provinces and Berar.	..	..	..	..	..	..	..	..	..	..	..	..	..	..	..	..	..	..
10 Coorg ..	..	..	..	..	..	..	..	..	..	..	..	..	..	..	..	..	..	..
11 Delhi ..	..	..	..	140	91	49	140	91	49	121	77	44	66	45	21	66	45	21
12 Madras ..	1,760	850	910	134	112	22	134	112	22	..	..	..	..	..	..	..	..	..
13 North-West Frontier Province. (*Districts and Administered Territories.*)	..	..	..	61	56	5	27	22	5	18	18	..	18	18	..	4	4	..
14 Punjab ..	..	..	..	30,955	15,696	15,259	30,955	15,696	15,259	30,781	15,619	15,162	30,431	15,447	14,984	1,541	1,009	532
15 United Provinces of Agra and Oudh.	..	..	..	4,128	2,291	1,837	4,128	2,291	1,837	3,989	2,212	1,777	3,989	2,212	1,777	..	..	..
States and Agencies.	11	8	3	924,860	457,267	467,593	924,860	457,267	467,593	284,908	141,665	143,243	201,093	100,078	101,015	4,518	2,274	2,244
16 Assam States ..	..	..	..	448,403	216,773	231,630	448,403	216,773	231,630	544	372	172	17	23	24	8	5	3
17 Baluchistan States ..	..	..	..	..	..	..	..	..	..	..	..	..	..	..	..	..	..	..
18 Baroda State ..	..	..	..	13	6	7	13	6	7	..	..	..	..	..	..	..	..	..
19 Bengal States ..	..	..	..	194,110	100,343	93,767	194,110	100,343	93,767	2,104	1,193	911	2	2	..	..	..	..
20 Bihar and Orissa States	..	..	..	..	..	..	..	..	..	..	..	..	..	..	..	..	..	..
21 Bombay States ..	..	..	..	..	..	..	..	..	..	..	..	..	..	..	..	..	..	..
22 Central India Agency	..	..	..	13	8	5	13	8	5	2	..	2	2	..	2	..	..	..
23 Central Provinces States	11	8	3	..	..	..	..	..	..	..	..	..	..	..	..	..	..	..
24 Gwalior State ..	..	..	..	..	..	..	..	..	..	..	..	..	..	..	..	..	..	..
25 Hyderabad State ..	..	..	..	20	16	1	20	16	4	..	..	..	..	..	..	..	..	..
26 Jammu and Kashmir State.	..	..	..	179,867	89,333	90,534	179,867	89,333	90,534	179,862	89,332	90,530	179,683	89,214	90,469	208	116	92
27 Madras States Agency	..	..	..	..	..	..	..	..	..	..	..	..	..	..	..	..	..	..
28 Mysore State ..	..	..	..	39	34	5	39	34	5	36	32	4	1	..	1	1	..	1
29 North-West Frontier Province. (*Agencies and Tribal Areas.*)	..	..	..	..	..	..	..	..	..	..	..	..	..	..	..	..	..	..
30 Punjab States ..	..	..	..	29,615	13,770	15,845	29,615	13,770	15,845	29,615	13,770	15,845	3,595	1,758	1,837	3,595	1,758	1,837
31 Punjab States Agency	..	..	..	2,689	1,546	1,143	2,689	1,546	1,143	2,667	1,536	1,131	2,622	1,511	1,111	136	94	42
32 Rajputana Agency ..	..	..	..	5	5	..	5	5	..	..	..	..	..	..	..	..	..	..
33 Sikkim State ..	..	..	..	70,067	35,421	34,646	70,067	35,421	34,646	70,067	35,421	34,646	15,130	7,561	7,569	570	301	269
34 United Provinces States	..	..	..	11	9	2	11	9	2	11	9	2	11	9	2	..	..	..
35 Western India States Agency.	..	..	..	8	3	5	8	3	5	..	..	..	..	..	..	..	..	..

Table XV.—Language—Part I—Mother Tongue—*contd.*

Tibeto-Chinese Family—*contd.*
Tibeto-Burman Sub-Family—*contd.*
Tibeto-Himalayan Branch—*contd.*
Tibetan Group—*concld.*

Province, State or Agency.	Bhotia of Baltistan or Balti.			Bhotia of Ladakh or Ladakhi.			Bhotia of Sharpa.			Bhotia of Bhutan or Lhoke.			Bhotia of Sikkim.			Bhotia (Others).		
	Persons.	Males.	Females.	Persons.	Males.	Females.	Persons.	Males.	Females.	Persons.	Males.	Females.	Persons.	Males.	Females.	Persons.	Males.	Females.
1	95	96	97	98	99	100	101	102	103	104	105	106	107	108	109	110	111	112
INDIA ..	**137,914**	**68,467**	**69,447**	**41,444**	**20,571**	**20,873**	**11,677**	**6,235**	**5,442**	**2,819**	**1,792**	**1,027**	**11,108**	**5,611**	**5,497**	**37,302**	**18,892**	**18,410**
Provinces ..	..	..	..	14	14	..	8,173	4,534	3,639	2,637	1,684	953	194	138	56	34,671	17,394	17,277
3 Assam ..	..	..	..	..	..	..	..	..	..	1,116	906	210	..	..	..	..	..	..
4 Baluchistan (*Districts and Administered Territories.*) ..	..	..	..	..	..	..	6	6	..	..	..	..	2	2	..	..	..	..
5 Bengal ..	..	..	..	..	..	..	8,167	4,528	3,639	1,521	778	743	192	136	56	1,773	733	1,040
6 Bihar and Orissa ..	..	..	..	..	..	..	..	..	..	..	..	..	..	..	..	19	11	8
13 North-West Frontier Province. (*Districts and Administered Territories.*)	..	..	..	14	14	..	..	..	..	..	..	..	..	..	..	..	..	..
14 Punjab ..	..	..	..	..	..	..	..	..	..	..	..	..	..	..	..	28,890	14,438	14,452
15 United Provinces of Agra and Oudh.	..	..	..	..	..	..	..	..	..	..	..	..	..	..	..	3,989	2,212	1,777
States and Agencies.	137,914	68,467	69,447	41,430	20,557	20,873	3,504	1,701	1,803	182	108	74	10,914	5,473	5,441	2,631	1,498	1,133
16 Assam States ..	..	..	..	..	..	..	..	..	..	39	18	21	..	..	..	..	..	..
19 Bengal States ..	..	..	..	..	..	..	..	..	..	..	..	..	..	..	..	2	2	..
22 Central India Agency	..	..	..	..	..	..	..	..	..	..	..	..	2	..	2	..	..	..
26 Jammu and Kashmir State.	137,914	68,467	69,447	41,418	20,546	20,872	..	..	..	6	5	1	..	..	..	137	80	57
31 Punjab States Agency	..	..	..	12	11	1	..	..	..	..	..	..	..	..	..	2,474	1,406	1,068
33 Sikkim State ..	..	..	..	..	..	..	3,504	1,701	1,803	137	85	52	10,912	5,473	5,439	7	1	6
34 United Provinces States	..	..	..	..	..	..	..	..	..	..	..	..	..	..	..	11	9	2

Province, State or Agency.	Pronominalized Himalayan Group Total.			Pronominalized Himalayan Group. Kanauri.			Kanashi.			Kiranti.			Non-Pronominalized Himalayan Group Total.			Non-Pronominalized Himalayan Group. Gurung.		
	Persons.	Males.	Females.	Persons.	Males.	Females.	Persons.	Males.	Females.	Persons.	Males.	Females.	Persons.	Males.	Females.	Persons.	Males.	Females.
1	113	114	115	116	117	118	119	120	121	122	123	124	125	126	127	128	129	130
INDIA ..	**113,952**	**56,028**	**57,924**	**26,122**	**12,071**	**14,051**	**348**	**170**	**178**	**87,482**	**43,787**	**43,695**	**102,484**	**52,302**	**50,182**	**3,609**	**1,861**	**1,748**
Provinces ..	58,896	29,404	29,492	57	34	23	348	170	178	58,491	29,200	29,291	73,725	37,339	36,386	2,986	1,606	1,380
3 Assam ..	1,289	700	589	..	..	..	..	..	..	1,289	700	589	3,090	1,976	1,114	711	468	243
4 Baluchistan (*Districts and Administered Territories.*)	488	488	..	..	..	..	..	..	..	488	488	..	80	78	2	16	16	..
5 Bengal ..	56,714	28,012	28,702	..	..	..	..	..	..	56,714	28,012	28,702	70,549	35,280	35,269	2,259	1,122	1,137
6 Bihar and Orissa ..	..	..	..	..	..	..	..	..	..	..	..	..	6	5	1	..	..	..
11 Delhi ..	55	32	23	55	32	23	..	..	..	..	..	..	..	..	..	..	..	..
14 Punjab ..	350	172	178	2	2	..	348	170	178	..	..	..	..	..	..	..	..	..
States and Agencies ..	55,056	26,624	28,432	26,065	12,037	14,028	..	..	..	28,991	14,587	14,404	28,759	14,963	13,796	623	255	368
16 Assam States ..	167	119	48	..	..	..	..	..	..	167	119	48	330	230	100	51	37	14
19 Bengal States ..	..	..	..	..	..	..	..	..	..	..	..	..	2,102	1,191	911	494	211	283
26 Jammu and Kashmir State.	179	118	61	..	..	..	..	..	..	179	118	61	..	..	..	..	..	..
28 Mysore State ..	..	..	..	..	..	..	..	..	..	..	..	..	35	32	3	..	..	..
30 Punjab States ..	26,020	12,012	14,008	26,020	12,012	14,008	..	..	..	..	..	..	..	..	..	..	..	..
31 Punjab States Agency	45	25	20	45	25	20	..	..	..	..	..	..	..	..	..	..	..	..
33 Sikkim State ..	28,645	14,350	14,295	..	..	..	..	..	..	28,645	14,350	14,295	26,292	13,510	12,782	78	7	71

Table XV.—Language—Part I—Mother Tongue—*contd.*

Tibeto-Chinese Family—*contd.*

Tibeto-Burman Sub-Family—*contd.*

Tibeto-Himalayan Branch—*contd.*

Non-Pronominalized Himalayan Group—*contd.*

	Province, State or Agency.	Murmi.			Sunwar.			Magari.			Newari.			Rong or Lepcha.			Kami.		
		Persons.	Males.	Females.	Persons.	Males.	Females.	Persons.	Males.	Females.	Persons.	Males.	Females.	Persons.	Males.	Females.	Persons.	Males.	Females.
	1	131	132	133	134	135	136	137	138	139	140	141	142	143	144	145	146	147	148
	INDIA ..	**42,673**	**21,926**	**20,747**	**3,433**	**1,683**	**1,750**	**17,478**	**8,683**	**8,795**	**9,666**	**5,325**	**4,341**	**25,151**	**12,655**	**12,496**	**175**	**23**	**152**
	Provinces ..	**34,084**	**17,383**	**16,701**	**2,754**	**1,335**	**1,419**	**14,450**	**6,991**	**7,459**	**7,341**	**4,011**	**3,330**	11,945	5,994	5,951	**148**	**7**	**141**
3	Assam ..	28	16	12	..	..	..	2,207	1,408	799	144	84	60	..	..	..	..	..	..
4	Baluchistan (*Districts and Administered Territories.*) ..	..	..	..	38	38	..	24	24	..	..	..	..	2	..	2	..	..	..
5	Bengal	34,053	17,365	16,688	2,716	1,297	1,419	12,216	5,556	6,660	7,197	3,927	3,270	11,943	5,994	5,949	148	7	141
6	Bihar and Orissa	3	2	1	..	..	..	3	3	..	..	..	..	..	..	..	..	..	..
	States and Agencies.	**8,589**	**4,543**	**4,046**	**679**	**348**	**331**	**3,028**	**1,692**	**1,336**	**2,325**	**1,314**	**1,011**	13,206	6,661	6,545	27	16	11
16	Assam States ..	..	..	..	..	..	..	247	173	74	32	20	12	..	..	..	..	..	..
19	Bengal States ..	1,607	979	628	..	..	..	1	1	..	..	..	..	..	..	..	..	..	..
28	Mysore State ..	..	..	..	..	..	..	..	..	..	35	32	3	..	..	..	..	..	..
33	Sikkim State ..	6,982	3,564	3,418	679	348	331	2,780	1,518	1,262	2,258	1,262	996	13,206	6,661	6,545	27	16	11

		Tibeto-Himalayan Branch—*concld.* Non-Pronominalized Himalayan Group—*concld.* Manjhi.			North Assam Branch. North Assam Branch Total.			Aka.			Abor.			Dafla.			Mishmi.		
		Persons.	Males.	Females.	Persons.	Males.	Females.	Persons.	Males.	Females.	Persons.	Males.	Females.	Persons.	Males.	Females.	Persons.	Males.	Females.
	1	149	150	151	152	153	154	155	156	157	158	159	160	161	162	163	164	165	166
	INDIA ..	**299**	**146**	**153**	**17,843**	**9,092**	**8,751**	**33**	**28**	**5**	**13,880**	**6,846**	**7,034**	**1,644**	**931**	**713**	**2,286**	**1,287**	**999**
	Provinces ..	17	12	5	17,837	9,091	8,746	33	28	5	13,874	6,845	7,029	1,644	931	713	2,286	1,287	999
3	Assam	..	..	..	17,836	9,090	8,746	33	28	5	13,874	6,845	7,029	1,644	931	713	2,285	1,286	999
5	Bengal	17	12	5	..	..	..	..	..	..	..	..	..	..	..	..	..	..	..
13	North-West Frontier Province (*Districts and Administered Territories.*)	..	..	..	1	1	..	..	..	..	..	..	..	..	..	..	1	1	..
	States and Agencies .	282	134	148	6	1	5	..	..	..	6	1	5	..	..	..	..	..	..
16	Assam States ..	..	..	..	6	1	5	..	..	..	6	1	5	..	..	..	..	..	..
33	Sikkim State ..	282	134	148	..	..	..	..	..	..	..	..	..	..	..	..	..	..	..

Table XV.—Language—Part I—Mother Tongue—*concld.*

Tibeto-Chinese Family—*contd.*
Tibeto-Burman Sub-Family—*contd.*
Assam-Burmese Branch.
Bara or Bodo Group.

Province, State or Agency.	Assam-Burmese Branch Total.			Bara or Bodo Group Total.			Garo.			Rabha.			Chutiya.			Koch.		
	Persons.	Males.	Females.	Persons.	Males.	Females.	Persons.	Males.	Females.	Persons.	Males.	Females.	Persons.	Males.	Females.	Persons.	Males.	Females.
1	167	168	169	170	171	172	173	174	175	176	177	178	179	180	181	182	183	184
INDIA ..	**12,478,611**	**6,136,706**	**6,341,905**	**911,210**	**465,768**	**445,442**	**230,674**	**117,214**	**113,460**	**27,008**	**13,463**	**13,545**	**4,317**	**2,246**	**2,071**	**9,552**	**4,897**	**4,655**
Provinces ..	**11,838,665**	**5,821,105**	**6,017,560**	**749,350**	**379,429**	**369,921**	**221,595**	**112,340**	**109,255**	**27,004**	**13,462**	**13,542**	**4,317**	**2,246**	**2,071**	**9,211**	**4,665**	**4,546**
2 Andaman and Nicobar Islands.	2,745	2,315	430	..	..	..	..	..	..	..	..	..	..	..	..	..	..	..
3 Assam	1,149,783	578,731	571,052	655,188	331,865	323,323	187,266	94,514	92,752	27,004	13,462	13,542	4,315	2,244	2,071	1,370	678	692
5 Bengal	192,693	97,192	95,501	94,135	47,538	46,597	34,327	17,825	16,502	..	..	..	..	..	..	7,818	3,964	3,854
6 Bihar and Orissa ..	17	6	11	..	..	..	..	..	..	..	..	..	..	..	..	..	..	..
7 Bombay (*including Aden*)	18	4	14	..	..	..	..	..	..	..	..	..	..	..	..	..	..	..
Aden	*1*	*1*	..	..	..	..	..	..	..	..	..	..	..	..	..	..	..	..
8 Burma	10,492,935	5,142,572	5,350,363	..	..	..	..	..	..	..	..	..	..	..	..	..	..	..
1 Delhi	19	14	5	..	..	..	..	..	..	..	..	..	..	..	..	..	..	..
2 Madras	134	112	22	25	25	..	..	..	..	..	..	..	2	2	..	23	23	..
3 North-West Frontier Province (*Districts and Administered Territories.*)	8	3	5	..	..	..	..	..	..	..	..	..	..	..	..	..	..	..
4 Punjab	174	77	97	..	..	..	..	..	..	..	..	..	..	..	..	..	..	..
5 United Provinces of Agra and Oudh.	139	79	60	2	1	1	2	1	1	..	..	..	..	..	..	..	..	..
States and Agencies	**639,946**	**315,601**	**324,345**	**161,860**	**86,339**	**75,521**	**9,079**	**4,874**	**4,205**	**4**	**1**	**3**	..	..	..	**341**	**232**	**109**
6 Assam States ..	447,853	216,400	231,453	9,123	4,576	4,547	5,214	2,563	2,651	2	..	2	..	..	..	..	..	..
8 Baroda State ..	13	6	7	..	..	..	..	..	..	..	..	..	..	..	..	..	..	..
9 Bengal States ..	192,006	99,150	92,856	152,735	81,762	70,973	3,865	2,311	1,554	..	..	..	..	..	..	341	232	109
2 Central India Agency	11	8	3	..	..	..	..	..	..	..	..	..	..	..	..	..	..	..
5 Hyderabad State ..	20	16	4	..	..	..	..	..	..	..	..	..	..	..	..	..	..	..
6 Jammu and Kashmir State.		1	4	2	1	1	..	..	..	2	1	1	..	..	..	..	..	..
8 Mysore State ..	3	2	1	..	..	..	..	..	..	..	..	..	..	..	..	..	..	..
1 Punjab States Agency	22	10	12	..	..	..	..	..	..	..	..	..	..	..	..	..	..	..
2 Rajputana Agency	5	5	..	..	..	..	..	..	..	..	..	..	..	..	..	..	..	..
5 Western India States Agency.	8	3	5	..	..	..	..	..	..	..	..	..	..	..	..	..	..	..

Province, State or Agency.	Bara or Bodo Group—*concld.*												Mikir Language.			Naga Group.		
	Bara Bodo or Plains Kachari.			Dimasa or Hills Kachari.			Lalung.			Tipura (Mrung).			Mikir.			Naga Group Total.		
	Persons.	Males.	Females.	Persons.	Males.	Females.	Persons.	Males.	Females.	Persons.	Males.	Females.	Persons.	Males.	Females.	Persons.	Males.	Females.
1	185	186	187	188	189	190	191	192	193	194	195	196	197	198	199	200	201	202
INDIA ..	**291,376**	**148,280**	**143,096**	**14,680**	**7,439**	**7,241**	**9,017**	**4,280**	**4,737**	**198,129**	**103,768**	**94,361**	**126,457**	**64,181**	**62,276**	**349,111**	**173,345**	**175,766**
Provinces ..	**290,935**	**148,054**	**142,881**	**14,680**	**7,439**	**7,241**	**8,673**	**4,089**	**4,584**	**49,510**	**24,481**	**25,029**	**123,425**	**62,653**	**60,772**	**273,059**	**136,937**	**136,122**
Assam	282,372	143,418	138,954	14,680	7,439	7,241	8,673	4,089	4,584	6,083	3,368	2,715	123,425	62,653	60,772	268,858	134,792	134,066
Bengal	8,563	4,636	3,927	..	..	..	..	..	..	43,427	21,113	22,314	..	..	..	..	..	..
Burma	..	..	..	..	..	..	..	..	..	..	..	..	..	..	..	4,201	2,145	2,056
States and Agencies	**441**	**226**	**215**	..	..	..	**344**	**191**	**153**	**148,619**	**79,287**	**69,332**	**3,032**	**1,528**	**1,504**	**76,052**	**36,408**	**39,644**
Assam States ..	210	126	84	..	..	..	344	191	153	321	168	153	3,032	1,528	1,504	76,052	36,408	39,644
Bengal States ..	231	100	131	..	..	..	..	..	..	148,298	79,119	69,179	..	..	..	..	..	..

Table XV.—Language—Part I—Mother Tongue—*contd.*

Tibeto-Chinese Family—*contd.*
Tibeto-Burmese Sub-Family—*contd.*
Assam-Burmese Branch—*contd.*
Naga Group—*contd.*

Province, State or Agency.	Naga-Bodo Sub-Group: Naga-Bodo Sub-Group Total. Persons.	Males.	Females.	Kachha Naga. Persons.	Males.	Females.	Kabui. Persons.	Males.	Females.	Others. Persons.	Males.	Females.	Western Naga Sub-Group: Western Naga Sub-Group Total. Persons.	Males.	Females.	Angami. Persons.	Males.	Females.
1	203	204	205	206	207	208	209	210	211	212	213	214	215	216	217	218	219	220
INDIA ..	**40,864**	**19,622**	**21,242**	**7,282**	**3,746**	**3,536**	**18,475**	**8,664**	**9,811**	**15,107**	**7,422**	**7,685**	**93,369**	**47,136**	**46,233**	**43,666**	**22,203**	**21,463**
Provinces ..	12,530	6,191	6,339	..	..	..	33	17	16	12,497	6,174	6,323	92,804	46,817	45,987	43,120	21,903	21,217
3 Assam ..	12,530	6,191	6,339	..	..	..	33	17	16	12,497	6,174	6,323	92,804	46,817	45,987	43,120	21,903	21,217
States and Agencies ..	28,334	13,431	14,903	7,282	3,536	3,746	18,442	8,647	9,795	2,610	1,248	1,362	565	319	246	546	300	246
16 Assam States ..	28,334	13,431	14,903	7,282	3,536	3,746	18,442	8,647	9,795	2,610	1,248	1,362	565	319	246	546	300	246

Province, State or Agency.	Western Naga Sub-Group.—*concld.* Kezhama. Persons.	Males.	Females.	Sema. Persons.	Males.	Females.	Rengma (all branches). Persons.	Males.	Females.	Central Naga Sub-Group: Central Naga Sub-Group Total. Persons.	Males.	Females.	Ao.* Persons.	Males.	Females.	Lhota. Persons.	Males.	Females.
1	221	222	223	224	225	226	227	228	229	230	231	232	233	234	235	236	237	238
INDIA ..	**5,288**	**2,879**	**2,409**	**38,146**	**18,937**	**19,209**	**6,269**	**3,117**	**3,152**	**55,733**	**26,474**	**29,259**	**33,117**	**15,325**	**17,792**	**18,254**	**8,970**	**9,284**
Provinces ..	5,286	2,877	2,409	38,129	18,920	19,209	6,269	3,117	3,152	55,728	26,472	29,256	33,117	15,325	17,792	18,249	8,968	9,281
3 Assam ..	5,286	2,877	2,409	38,129	18,920	19,209	6,269	3,117	3,152	55,728	26,472	29,256	33,117	15,325	17,792	18,249	8,968	9,281
States and Agencies ..	2	2	..	17	17	..	..	..	..	5	2	3	..	..	..	5	2	3
16 Assam States ..	2	2	..	17	17	..	..	..	..	5	2	3	..	..	..	5	2	3

*Chungli and Mongsen.

Province, State or Agency.	Central Naga Sub-Group—*concld.* Sangtam. Persons.	Males.	Females.	Eastern Naga Sub-Group: Eastern Naga Sub-Group Total. Persons.	Males.	Females.	Konyak. Persons.	Males.	Females.	Rangpang. Persons.	Males.	Females.	Other Eastern Naga Languages. Persons.	Males.	Females.	Naga Kuki Sub-Group: Naga Kuki Sub-Group Total. Persons.	Males.	Females.
1	239	240	241	242	243	244	245	246	247	248	249	250	251	252	253	254	255	256
INDIA ..	**4,362**	**2,179**	**2,183**	**102,815**	**52,590**	**50,225**	**9,478**	**4,562**	**4,916**	**11,072**	**5,710**	**5,362**	**82,265**	**42,318**	**39,947**	**48,429**	**23,340**	**25,089**
Provinces ..	4,362	2,179	2,183	102,808	52,585	50,223	9,471	4,557	4,914	11,072	5,710	5,362	82,265	42,318	39,947	1,313	713	600
3 Assam ..	4,362	2,179	2,183	102,808	52,585	50,223	9,471	4,557	4,914	11,072	5,710	5,362	82,265	42,318	39,947	1,271	685	586
8 Burma ..	..	..	..	..	..	..	..	..	..	..	..	..	..	..	..	42	28	14
States and Agencies ..	..	..	..	7	5	2	7	5	2	..	..	..	..	..	..	47,116	22,627	24,489
16 Assam States ..	..	..	..	7	5	2	7	5	2	..	..	..	..	..	..	47,116	22,627	24,489

Province, State or Agency.	Naga Group—*concld.*: Naga Kuki Sub-Group—*concld.* Memi (Mao). Persons.	Males.	Females.	Tangkhul. Persons.	Males.	Females.	Other or unspecified Naga Languages. Persons.	Males.	Females.	Kuki-Chin Group: Kuki-Chin Group Total. Persons.	Males.	Females.	Maring. Persons.	Males.	Females.	Kathe (Ponna) including Meithei (Manipuri). Persons.	Males.	Females.
1	257	258	259	260	261	262	263	264	265	266	267	268	269	270	271	272	273	274
INDIA ..	**19,287**	**9,620**	**9,667**	**29,142**	**13,720**	**15,422**	**7,901**	**4,183**	**3,718**	**972,886**	**475,643**	**497,243**	**4,251**	**2,111**	**2,140**	**391,903**	**192,217**	**199,686**
Provinces ..	1,250	672	578	63	41	22	7,876	4,159	3,717	575,833	285,067	290,766	34	21	13	93,034	49,129	43,905
3 Assam ..	1,250	672	578	21	13	8	3,717	2,042	1,675	222,658	110,388	112,270	34	21	13	88,914	46,905	42,009
5 Bengal ..	..	..	..	..	..	..	..	..	..	8,360	4,228	4,132	..	..	..	344	237	107
6 Bihar and Orissa ..	..	..	..	..	..	..	..	..	..	8	..	8	..	..	..	..	..	..
8 Burma ..	..	..	..	42	28	14	4,159	2,117	2,042	344,792	170,444	174,348	..	..	..	3,764	1,982	1,782
12 Madras ..	..	..	..	..	..	..	..	..	..	3	2	1	..	..	..	..	..	..
15 United Provinces of Agra and Oudh.	..	..	..	..	..	..	..	..	..	12	5	7	..	..	..	12	5	7
States and Agencies	18,037	8,948	9,089	29,079	13,679	15,400	25	24	1	397,053	190,576	206,477	4,217	2,090	2,127	298,869	143,088	155,781
16 Assam States ..	18,037	8,948	9,089	29,079	13,679	15,400	25	24	1	362,645	175,396	187,249	4,217	2,090	2,127	279,333	134,740	144,593
19 Bengal States ..	..	..	..	..	..	..	..	..	..	34,408	15,180	19,228	..	..	..	19,536	8,348	11,188

Table XV.—Language—Part I—Mother Tongue—*contd.*

Tibeto-Chinese Family—*contd.*
Tibeto-Burman Sub-Family—*contd.*
Assam-Burmese Branch—*contd.*
Kuki Chin Group—*contd.*

Old Kuki Sub-Group.

Province, State or Agency.	Old Kuki Sub-Group Total. Persons.	Males.	Females.	Aimol. Persons.	Males.	Females.	Anal. Persons	Males.	Females.	Chiru. Persons.	Males.	Females.	Hallam. Persons.	Males.	Females.	Kolreng (Koireng). Persons.	Males.	Females.
1	275	276	277	278	279	280	281	282	283	284	285	286	287	288	289	290	291	292
INDIA	**53,261**	**25,228**	**28,033**	**511**	**265**	**246**	**3,314**	**1,636**	**1,678**	**1,269**	**568**	**701**	**10,867**	**5,027**	**5,840**	**521**	**258**	**263**
Provinces	**20,141**	**9,378**	**10,763**	..	..	..	..	..	..	..	..	..	**497**	**252**	**245**	..	..	..
Assam	19,907	9,237	10,670	..	..	..	..	..	..	..	..	..	497	252	245	..	..	..
Burma	234	141	93	..	..	..	..	..	..	..	..	..	..	..	..	..	..	..
States and Agencies	**33,120**	**15,850**	**17,270**	**511**	**265**	**246**	**3,314**	**1,636**	**1,678**	**1,269**	**568**	**701**	**10,370**	**4,775**	**5,595**	**521**	**258**	**263**
Assam States	22,750	11,075	11,675	511	265	246	3,314	1,636	1,678	1,269	568	701	..	..	..	521	258	263
Bengal States	10,370	4,775	5,595	..	..	..	..	..	..	..	..	..	10,370	4,775	5,595	..	..	..

Old Kuki Sub-Group—*concld.* / Northern Chin Sub-Group.

Province, State or Agency.	Kom. Persons.	Males.	Females.	Mhar. Persons.	Males.	Females.	Rangkhol (Hranchal). Persons.	Males.	Females.	Others. Persons.	Males.	Females.	Northern Chin Sub-Group Total. Persons.	Males.	Females.	Paite. Persons.	Males.	Females.
1	293	294	295	296	297	298	299	300	301	302	303	304	305	306	307	308	309	310
INDIA	**2,662**	**1,292**	**1,370**	**21,583**	**10,025**	**11,558**	**1,745**	**860**	**885**	**10,789**	**5,297**	**5,492**	**128,808**	**62,780**	**66,028**	**14,674**	**7,420**	**7,254**
Provinces	..	..	..	**15,940**	**7,290**	**8,650**	**1,745**	**860**	**885**	**1,959**	**976**	**983**	**73,173**	**35,663**	**37,510**	**6,634**	**3,336**	**3,298**
3 Assam	..	..	..	15,940	7,290	8,650	1,745	860	885	1,725	835	890	26,473	12,692	13,781	6 634	3,336	3,298
5 Bihar and Orissa	..	..	..	..	..	..	..	..	..	..	..	..	8	..	8	..	..	..
3 Burma	..	..	..	..	..	..	..	..	..	234	141	93	46,692	22,971	23,721	..	..	..
States and Agencies	**2,662**	**1,292**	**1,370**	**5,643**	**2,735**	**2,908**	..	..	..	**8,830**	**4,321**	**4,509**	**55,635**	**27,117**	**28,518**	**8,040**	**4,084**	**3,956**
Assam States	2,662	1,292	1,370	5,643	2,735	2,908	..	..	..	8,830	4,321	4,509	55,635	27,117	28,518	8,040	4,084	3,956

Northern Chin Sub-Group—*concld.* / Central Chin Sub-Group.

Province, State or Agency.	Ralte. Persons.	Males.	Females.	Siyin. Persons.	Males.	Females.	Sokte. Persons.	Males.	Females.	Thado. Persons.	Males.	Females.	Central Chin Sub-Group Total. Persons.	Males.	Females.	Banjogi. Persons.	Males.	Females.
1	311	312	313	314	315	316	317	318	319	320	321	322	323	324	325	326	327	328
INDIA	**16,163**	**7,527**	**8,636**	**3,506**	**1,669**	**1,837**	**37,643**	**18,595**	**19,048**	**56,822**	**27,569**	**29,253**	**127,309**	**60,538**	**66,771**	**810**	**430**	**380**
Provinces	**16,047**	**7,476**	**8,571**	**3,506**	**1,669**	**1,837**	**36,866**	**18,229**	**18,637**	**10,120**	**4,953**	**5,167**	**124,943**	**59,300**	**65,643**	810	430	380
3 Assam	16,047	7,476	8,571	..	..	..	..	..	..	3,792	1,880	1,912	67,329	31,683	35,646	..	..	..
5 Bengal	..	..	..	..	..	..	..	..	..	..	..	..	1,471	736	735	810	430	380
5 Bihar and Orissa	..	..	..	..	..	..	..	..	..	8	..	8	..	..	..	..	..	..
3 Burma	..	..	..	3,506	1,669	1,837	36,866	18,229	18,637	6,320	3,073	3,247	56,143	26,881	29,262	..	..	..
States and Agencies	**116**	**51**	**65**	..	..	..	**777**	**366**	**411**	**46,702**	**22,616**	**24,086**	**2,366**	**1,238**	**1,128**	..	..	..
5 Assam States	116	51	65	..	..	..	777	366	411	46,702	22,616	24,086	366	197	169	..	..	..
9 Bengal States	..	..	..	..	..	..	..	..	..	..	..	..	2,000	1,041	959	..	..	..

Central Chin Sub-Group—*concld.* / Southern Chin Sub-Group.

Province, State or Agency.	Lai. Persons.	Males.	Females.	Lakher. Persons.	Males.	Females.	Lushei. Persons.	Males.	Females.	Pankhu. Persons.	Males.	Females.	Tashon. Persons.	Males.	Females.	Southern Chin Sub-Group Total. Persons.	Males.	Females.
1	329	330	331	332	333	334	335	336	337	338	339	340	341	342	343	344	345	346
INDIA	**39,646**	**19,121**	**20,525**	**6,250**	**3,036**	**3,214**	**60,471**	**28,453**	**32,018**	**83**	**31**	**52**	**20,049**	**9,467**	**10,582**	**66,288**	**32,733**	**33,555**
Provinces	**39,646**	**19,121**	**20,525**	**6,250**	**3,036**	**3,214**	**58,105**	**27,215**	**30,890**	**83**	**31**	**52**	**20,049**	**9,467**	**10,582**	**66,288**	**32,733**	**33,555**
3 Assam	..	..	..	6,186	3,004	3,182	57,231	26,820	30,411	..	..	..	3,912	1,859	2,053	..	..	..
5 Bengal	..	..	..	..	..	..	578	275	303	83	31	52	..	..	..	3,374	1,455	1,919
8 Burma	39,646	19,121	20,525	64	32	32	296	120	176	..	..	..	16,137	7,608	8,529	62,914	31,278	31,636
States and Agencies	..	..	..	..	..	..	**2,366**	**1,238**	**1,128**	..	..	..	..	..	..	..	..	..
6 Assam States	..	..	..	..	..	..	366	197	169	..	..	..	..	..	..	..	..	..
9 Bengal States	..	..	..	..	..	..	2,000	1,041	959	..	..	..	..	..	..	..	..	..

Table XV.—Language—Part I—Mother Tongue—*contd.*

Tibeto-Chinese Family—*contd.*

Tibeto-Burman Sub-Family—*contd.*

Assam Burmese Branch—*contd.*

Kuki-Chin Group—*concld.*

Province, State or Agency.	Southern Chin Sub-Group—*concld.* Chinbok.			Chinbon.			Khyang (Sho).			Khami (Kumi).			Yindu.			Unclassed Chin Languages Sub-Group. Unclassed Chin Languages Sub-Group Total.		
	Persons.	Males.	Females.	Persons.	Males.	Females.	Persons.	Males.	Females.	Persons.	Males.	Females.	Persons.	Males.	Females.	Persons.	Males.	Females.
1	347	348	349	350	351	352	353	354	355	356	357	358	359	360	361	362	363	364
INDIA ..	**20,195**	**9,913**	**10,282**	**10,268**	**5,089**	**5,179**	**2,825**	**1,276**	**1,549**	**32,991**	**16,449**	**16,522**	**9**	**6**	**3**	**69,998**	**34,807**	**35,191**
Provinces ..	20,195	9,913	10,282	10,268	5,089	5,179	2,825	1,276	1,549	32,991	16,449	16,522	9	6	3	68,966	34,470	34,496
5 Bengal.. ..	..	..	..	..	..	..	1,265	479	786	2,109	976	1,113	..	..	..	863	610	253
8 Burma.. ..	20,195	9,913	10,282	10,268	5,089	5,179	1,560	797	763	30,882	15,473	15,409	9	6	3	68,100	33,858	34,242
12 Madras ..	..	..	..	..	..	..	..	..	..	..	..	..	..	..	..	3	2	1
States and Agencies	..	..	..	..	..	..	..	..	..	..	..	..	..	..	..	1,032	337	695
19 Bengal States ..	..	..	..	..	..	..	..	..	..	..	..	..	..	..	..	1,032	337	695

Unclassed Chin Languages Sub-Group—*concld.*

	Ánu.			Chuanggyi.			Kaukadan.			Lawtú.			Ledu.			Matu.		
	Persons.	Males.	Females.	Persons.	Males.	Females.	Persons.	Males.	Females.	Persons.	Males.	Females.	Persons.	Males.	Females.	Persons.	Males.	Females.
1	365	366	367	368	369	370	371	372	373	374	375	376	377	378	379	380	381	382
INDIA ..	**3**	**2**	**1**	**32**	**16**	**16**	**294**	**137**	**157**	**9,725**	**4,626**	**5,099**	**1,719**	**863**	**856**	**154**	**82**	**72**
Provinces ..	3	2	1	32	16	16	294	137	157	9,725	4,626	5,099	1,719	863	856	154	82	72
8 Burma.. ..	..	..	..	32	16	16	294	137	157	9,725	4,626	5,099	1,719	863	856	154	82	72
12 Madras ..	3	2	1	..	..	..	..	..	..	..	..	..	..	..	..	..	..	..

	Ngorn.			Zongtu.			Saingbaung.			Shentang.			Sittu.			Taman.		
	Persons.	Males.	Females.	Persons.	Males.	Females.	Persons.	Males.	Females.	Persons.	Males.	Females.	Persons.	Males.	Females.	Persons.	Males.	Females.
1	383	384	385	386	387	388	389	390	391	392	393	394	395	396	397	398	399	400
INDIA ..	**5,808**	**2,727**	**3,081**	**13,048**	**6,429**	**6,619**	**8,031**	**4,273**	**3,758**	**7,324**	**3,615**	**3,709**	**4,282**	**2,343**	**1,939**	**9,228**	**4,614**	**4,614**
Provinces ..	5,808	2,727	3,081	12,016	6,092	5,924	8,031	4,273	3,758	7,324	3,615	3,709	4,282	2,343	1,939	9,228	4,614	4,614
5 Bengal.. ..	..	..	..	863	610	453	..	..	..	..	..	..	..	..	..	..	..	..
8 Burma.. ..	5,808	2,727	3,081	11,153	5,482	5,671	8,031	4,273	3,758	7,324	3,615	3,709	4,282	2,343	1,939	9,228	4,614	4,614
States and Agencies	..	..	..	1,032	337	695	..	..	..	..	..	..	..	..	..	..	..	..
19 Bengal States ..	..	..	..	1,032	337	695	..	..	..	..	..	..	..	..	..	..	..	..

Kuki Chin Group—*concld.*

	Unclassed Chin Languages Sub-Group—*concld.* Yo.			Yotun.			Other or unspecified Chin Sub-Group.			Other or unspecified Kuki Sub-Group			Kachin Group. Kachin.		
	Persons.	Males.	Females.	Persons.	Males.	Females.	Persons.	Males.	Females.	Persons.	Males.	Females.	Persons.	Males.	Females.
1	401	402	403	404	405	406	407	408	409	410	411	412	413	414	415
INDIA ..	**1,365**	**674**	**691**	**8,985**	**4,406**	**4,579**	**121,136**	**60,268**	**60,868**	**9,932**	**4,961**	**4,971**	**156,980**	**75,728**	**81,252**
Provinces ..	1,365	674	691	8,985	4,406	4,579	121,136	60,268	60,868	8,118	4,105	4,013	156,980	75,728	81,252
3 Assam ..	..	..	..	..	..	..	14,191	6,935	7,256	5,810	2,915	2,895	3,042	1,659	1,383
5 Bengal.. ..	..	..	..	..	..	..	..	..	..	2,308	1,190	1,118	1	1	..
8 Burma.. ..	1,365	674	691	8,985	4,406	4,579	106,945	53,333	53,612	..	..	..	153,897	74,051	79,846
15 United Provinces of Agra and Oudh.	..	..	..	..	..	..	..	..	..	..	..	..	40	17	23
States and Agencies	..	..	..	..	..	..	..	..	..	1,814	856	958	..	..	..
16 Assam States ..	..	..	..	..	..	..	..	..	..	344	177	167	..	..	..
19 Bengal States ..	..	..	..	..	..	..	..	..	..	1,470	679	791	..	..	..

Table XV.—Language—Part I—Mother Tongue—*contd.*

Tibeto-Chinese Family—*contd.*
Tibeto-Burman Sub-Family—*contd.*
Assam Burmese Branch—*contd.*
Burma Group.

Province, State or Agency.	Burma Group Total. Persons.	Males.	Females.	Burmese. Persons.	Males.	Females.	Arakanese. Persons.	Males.	Females.	Taungyo. Persons.	Males.	Females.	Intha. Persons.	Males.	Females.	Danu. Persons.	Males.	Females.
1	416	417	418	419	420	421	422	423	424	425	426	427	428	429	430	431	432	433
INDIA ..	**9,960,394**	**4,881,329**	**5,079,065**	**8,853,538**	**4,331,535**	**4,522,003**	**308,544**	**156,097**	**152,447**	**22,261**	**11,046**	**11,215**	**56,829**	**28,001**	**28,828**	**60,966**	**31,090**	**29,876**
Provinces ..	9,955,413	4,879,051	5,076,362	8,853,420	4,331,465	4,521,955	303,681	153,889	149,792	22,261	11,046	11,215	56,829	28,001	28,828	60,966	31,090	29,876
2 Andaman and Nicobar Islands.	2,745	2,315	430	2,745	2,315	430	..	..	..	..	..	..	..	..	..	..	..	..
3 Assam	37	27	10	37	27	10	..	..	..	..	..	..	..	..	..	..	..	..
5 Bengal	90,197	45,425	44,772	8,506	4,892	3,614	81,691	40,533	41,158	..	..	..	..	..	..	..	..	..
6 Bihar and Orissa	9	6	3	9	6	3	..	..	..	..	..	..	..	..	..	..	..	..
7 Bombay (*including Aden*).	18	4	14	18	4	14	..	..		..	..	..	..	..	..	..	..	..
Aden ..	*1*	*1*	..	*1*	*1*	..	..	..	..	..	..	..	..	..	..	—	..	—
8 Burma	9,862,015	4,831,039	5,030,976	8,841,760	4,324,033	4,517,727	221,945	113,311	108,634	22,261	11,046	11,215	56,829	28,001	28,828	60,966	31,090	29,876
11 Delhi	19	14	5	19	14	5	..	..	..	..	..	..	..	..	..	..	..	..
12 Madras ..	106	85	21	61	40	21	45	45	..	..	..	..	..	..	..	..	..	..
13 North-West Frontier Province (*Districts and Administered Territories.*)	8	3	5	6	1	5	..	..	..	..	..	..	..	..	..	..	..	..
14 Punjab	174	77	97	174	77	97	..	—	..	..	..	..	..	..	..	..	—	—
15 United Provinces of Agra and Oudh.	85	56	29	85	56	29	—	..	..	..	..	..	..	..	..	—	—	—
States and Agencies	**4,981**	**2,278**	**2,703**	**118**	**70**	**48**	**4,863**	**2,208**	**2,655**	..	..	..	..	..	..	..	..	..
16 Assam States ..	33	20	13	33	20	13	..	..	..	..	..	..	..	..	..	..	—	..
18 Baroda State ..	13	6	7	13	6	7	..	..	..	..	..	..	..	..	..	..	..	..
19 Bengal States ..	4,863	2,208	2,655	..	..	..	4,863	2,208	2,655	..	..	..	..	..	..	..	..	..
22 Central India Agency	11	8	3	11	8	3	..	..	..	..	..	..	..	..	..	..	..	..
28 Hyderabad State ..	20	16	4	20	16	4	..	..	..	..	..	..	..	..	..	..	..	..
26 Jammu and Kashmir State.	3	..	3	3	..	3	..	..	..	..	..	..	..	..	..	..	..	..
28 Mysore State ..	3	2	1	3	2	1	..	..	..	..	..	..	..	..	..	..	..	..
31 Punjab States Agency	22	10	12	22	10	12	..	..	..	..	..	..	..	..	..	..	..	..
32 Rajputana Agency ..	5	5	..	5	5	..	..	..	..	..	..	..	..	..	..	..	..	..
35 Western India States Agency.	8	3	5	8	3	5	..	..	..	..	..	..	..	..	..	..	..	..

	Maru. Persons.	Males.	Females.	Tavoyan. Persons.	Males.	Females.	Chaungtha. Persons.	Males.	Females.	Maingtha. Persons.	Males.	Females.	Atsi. Persons.	Males.	Females.	Yaw. Persons.	Males.	Females.
1	434	435	436	437	438	439	440	441	442	443	444	445	446	447	448	449	450	451
INDIA ..	**17,447**	**8,393**	**9,054**	**159,174**	**78,692**	**80,482**	**34,626**	**17,346**	**17,280**	**487**	**319**	**168**	**5,295**	**2,485**	**2,810**	**877**	**484**	**393**
Provinces ..	17,447	8,393	9,054	159,174	78,692	80,482	34,626	17,346	17,280	487	319	169	5,295	2,485	2,810	877	484	393
8 Burma	17,447	8,393	9,054	159,174	78,692	80,482	34,625	17,345	17,280	487	319	168	5,294	2,484	2,810	877	484	393
13 North-West Frontier Province (*Districts and Administered Territories.*)	..	..	..	..	..	..	1	1	..	..	..	..	1	1	..	..	..	..

Burma Group—*concld.* / Lolo-Muhso Group.

	Merguese. Persons.	Males.	Females.	Yanbye. Persons.	Males.	Females.	Lashi. Persons.	Males.	Females.	Lolo-Muhso Group Total. Persons.	Males.	Females.	Lahu. Persons.	Males.	Females.	Lisaw. Persons.	Males.	Females.
1	452	453	454	455	456	457	458	459	460	461	462	463	464	465	466	467	468	469
INDIA ..	**101,144**	**51,134**	**50,010**	**326,642**	**158,597**	**168,045**	**12,564**	**6,110**	**6,454**	**93,731**	**48,302**	**45,429**	**26,864**	**13,666**	**13,198**	**19,698**	**9,885**	**9,813**
Provinces	101,144	51,134	50,010	326,642	158,597	168,045	12,564	6,110	6,454	93,731	48,302	45,429	26,864	13,666	13,198	19,698	9,885	9,813
8 **Burma**	101,144	51,134	50,010	326,642	158,597	168,045	12,561	6,110	6,454	93,731	48,302	45,429	26,864	13,666	13,198	19,698	9,885	9,813

Table XV.—Language—Part I—Mother Tongue—*contd.*

Tibeto-Chinese Family—*contd.*
Tibeto-Burman Sub-Family—*contd.*
Assam Burmese Branch—*contd.*
Lolo-Muhso Group—*concld.*

Province, State or Agency.	Hpun. Persons.	Hpun. Males.	Hpun. Females.	Nung. Persons.	Nung. Males.	Nung. Females.	Kwi. Persons.	Kwi. Males.	Kwi. Females.	Akha. Persons.	Akha. Males.	Akha. Females.	Ako. Persons.	Ako. Males.	Ako. Females.	Pyin. Persons.	Pyin. Males.	Pyin. Females.
1	470	471	472	473	474	475	476	477	478	479	480	481	482	483	484	485	486	487
INDIA ..	**679**	**343**	**336**	**101**	**65**	**36**	**3,839**	**1,962**	**1,877**	**40,407**	**21,261**	**19,146**	**1,343**	**680**	**663**	**800**	**440**	**360**
Provinces ..	679	343	336	101	65	36	3,839	1,962	1,877	40,407	21,261	19,146	1,343	680	663	800	440	360
8 Burma	679	343	336	101	65	36	3,839	1,962	1,877	40,407	21,261	19,146	1,343	680	663	800	440	360

Sak (Lui) Group.

Province, State or Agency.	Sak (Lui) Group Total. Persons.	Sak (Lui) Group Total. Males.	Sak (Lui) Group Total. Females.	Kadu. Persons	Kadu. Males.	Kadu. Females.	Ganan. Persons.	Ganan. Males.	Ganan. Females.	Sak. Persons.	Sak. Males.	Sak. Females.	Daingnet. Persons.	Daingnet. Males.	Daingnet. Females.
1	488	489	490	491	492	493	494	495	496	497	498	499	500	501	502
INDIA ..	**34,299**	**16,591**	**17,708**	**20,305**	**9,962**	**10,343**	**7,144**	**3,168**	**3,976**	**691**	**350**	**341**	**6,159**	**3,111**	**3,048**
Provinces ..	34,299	16,591	17,708	20,305	9,962	10,343	7,144	3,168	3,976	691	350	341	6,159	3,111	3,048
8 Burma	34,299	16,591	17,708	20,305	9,962	10,343	7,144	3,168	3,976	691	350	341	6,159	3,111	3,048

Tibeto-Burman Sub-Family—*concld.*
Unclassed.
Mro Group.
Mro (Mru).

Tai Chinese Sub-Family.
Tai Branch.
Tai Group.

Province, State or Agency.	Mro (Mru). Persons.	Mro (Mru). Males.	Mro (Mru). Females.	Tai Group Total. Persons.	Tai Group Total. Males.	Tai Group Total. Females.	Lao. Persons.	Lao. Males.	Lao. Females.	Lu. Persons.	Lu. Males.	Lu. Females.
1	503	504	505	506	507	508	509	510	511	512	513	514
INDIA ..	**17,887**	**10,993**	**6,894**	**1,027,656**	**516,913**	**510,743**	**7,163**	**3,524**	**3,639**	**30,031**	**14,971**	**15,060**
Provinces ..	17,887	10,993	6,894	1,027,656	516,913	510,743	7,163	3,524	3,639	30,031	14,971	15,060
3 Assam	..	..	..	5,713	3,029	2,684	..	..	..	..	..	..
5 Bengal	3,793	3,740	53	..	..	..	..	..	..	..	..	..
8 Burma	14,094	7,253	6,841	1,021,909	513,850	508,059	7,163	3,524	3,639	30,031	14,971	15,060
13 North-West Frontier Province (*Districts and Administered Territories.*)	..	..	..	34	34	..	..	..	..	..	..	..

Tai Group—*contd.*

Province, State or Agency.	Khün. Persons.	Khün. Males.	Khün. Females.	Daye. Persons.	Daye. Males.	Daye. Females.	Khamti. Persons	Khamti. Males.	Khamti. Females.	Shangale. Persons.	Shangale. Males.	Shangale. Females.	Shan-Tayok. Persons.	Shan-Tayok. Males.	Shan-Tayok. Females.	Shan-Bama. Persons.	Shan-Bama. Males.	Shan-Bama. Females.
1	515	516	517	518	519	520	521	522	523	524	525	526	527	528	529	530	531	532
INDIA ..	**31,234**	**15,593**	**15,641**	**698**	**361**	**337**	**4,995**	**2,642**	**2,353**	**914,379**	**459,089**	**455,290**	**18,270**	**9,827**	**8,443**	**7,735**	**4,047**	**3,688**
Provinces ..	31,234	15,593	15,641	698	361	337	4,995	2,642	2,353	914,379	459,089	455,290	18,270	9,827	8,443	7,735	4,047	3,688
3 Assam	..	..	..	..	..	..	3,858	2,097	1,761	..	..	..	..	..	..	..	..	..
8 Burma	31,234	15,593	15,641	698	361	337	1,103	511	592	914,379*	459,089	455,290	18,270	9,827	8,443	7,735	4,047	3,688
13 North-West Frontier Province (*Districts and Administered Territories.*)	..	..	..	..	..	..	34	34	..	..	..	..	..	..	..	..	..	..

* Includes Shangyi.

Table XV.—Language—Part I—Mother Tongue—*contd.*

Tibeto-Chinese Family—*concld.*
Tai-Chinese Sub-Family—*concld.*
Tai Branch—*concld.*
Tai Group—*concld.*

Karen Family.
Karen Group.

Province, State or Agency.	Shan (unspecified).* Persons.	Males.	Females.	Siamese. Persons.	Males.	Females.	Karen Group Total Persons.	Males.	Females.	Monnepwa. Persons.	Males.	Females.	Bwe. Persons.	Males.	Females.
1	533	534	535	536	537	538	539	540	541	542	543	544	545	546	547
INDIA ..	**4,503**	**2,315**	**2,188**	**8,648**	**4,544**	**4,104**	**1,341,331**	**669,216**	**672,115**	**2,126**	**1,080**	**1,046**	**6,227**	**3,136**	**3,091**
Provinces ..	4,503	2,315	2,188	8,648	4,544	4,104	1,341,331	669,216	672,115	2,126	1,080	1,046	6,227	3,136	3,091
2 Andaman and Nicobar Islands.	..	..	..	..	..	..	263	133	130	..	..	..	..	..	..
3 Assam ..	1,855	932	923	..	..	..	..	..	..	..	..	..	..	..	..
8 Burma.. ..	2,648	1,383	1,265	8,648	4,544	4,104	1,341,066	669,081	671,985	2,126	1,080	1,046	6,227	3,136	3,091
15 United Provinces of Agra and Oudh.	..	..	..	..	..	..	2	2	..	..	..	..	..	..	..

* Includes Aitonia, Phakial, etc.

Karen Family—*contd.*
Karen Group—*contd.*

Province, State or Agency.	Karenbyu. Persons.	Males.	Females.	Brek. Persons.	Males.	Females.	Sgaw. Persons.	Males.	Females.	Paku. Persons.	Males.	Females.	Pwo. Persons.	Males.	Females.	Taungthu. Persons.	Males.	Females.
1	548	549	550	551	552	553	554	555	556	557	558	559	560	561	562	563	564	565
INDIA ..	**15,299**	**7,797**	**7,502**	**6,695**	**3,234**	**3,461**	**499,789**	**251,106**	**248,683**	**8,622**	**4,379**	**4,243**	**473,722**	**236,105**	**237,617**	**222,714**	**111,107**	**111,607**
Provinces ..	15,299	7,797	7,502	6,695	3,234	3,461	499,789	251,106	248,683	8,622	4,379	4,243	473,722	236,105	237,617	222,714	111,107	111,607
8 Burma.. ..	15,299	7,797	7,502	6,695	3,234	3,461	499,789	251,106	248,683	8,620	4,377	4,243	473,722	236,105	237,617	222,714	111,107	111,607
15 United Provinces of Agra and Oudh.	..	..	..	..	..	..	..	..	..	2	2	..	..	..	..	..	..	..

Karen Family—*concld.*
Karen Group—*concld.*

Province, State or Agency.	Padaung. Persons.	Males.	Females.	Yinbaw. Persons.	Males.	Females.	Gheko. Persons.	Males.	Females.	Karenni. Persons.	Males.	Females.	Zayein. Persons.	Males.	Females.	Karen (unspecified). Persons.	Males.	Females.
1	566	567	568	569	570	571	572	573	574	575	576	577	578	579	580	581	582	583
INDIA ..	**16,485**	**8,409**	**8,076**	**2,922**	**1,472**	**1,450**	**4,075**	**1,997**	**2,078**	**31,556**	**14,742**	**16,814**	**3,737**	**2,008**	**1,729**	**47,362**	**22,644**	**24,718**
Provinces ..	16,485	8,409	8,076	2,922	1,472	1,450	4,075	1,997	2,078	31,556	14,742	16,814	3,737	2,008	1,729	47,362	22,644	24,718
2 Andaman and Nicobar Islands.	..	..	..	..	..	..	..	..	..	..	..	..	..	..	..	263	133	130
8 Burma.. ..	16,485	8,409	8,076	2,922	1,472	1,450	4,075	1,997	2,078	31,556	14,742	16,814	3,737	2,008	1,729	47,099	22,511	24,588

Man Family.
Man Group.

Province, State or Agency.	Man Family Total. Persons.	Males.	Females.	Man Group Total. Persons.	Males.	Females.	Miao. Persons.	Males.	Females.	Yao. Persons.	Males.	Females.
1	584	585	586	587	588	589	590	591	592	593	594	595
INDIA ..	**947**	**502**	**445**	**947**	**502**	**445**	**830**	**442**	**388**	**117**	**60**	**57**
Provinces ..	947	502	445	947	502	445	830	442	388	117	60	57
8 Burma.. ..	947	502	445	947	502	445	830	442	388	117	60	57

Table XV.—Language—Part I—Mother Tongue—*contd.*

	Province, State or Agency.	Dravidian Family.											
		Dravidian Family Total.			Dravida Group.								
					Dravida Group Total.			Tamil.			Malayalam.		
		Persons.	Males.	Females.	Persons.	Males.	Females.	Persons.	Males.	Females.	Persons.	Males.	Females.
	1	596	597	598	599	600	601	602	603	604	605	606	607
	INDIA	**71,644,787**	**35,847,723**	**35,797,064**	**41,454,593**	**20,644,277**	**20,810,316**	**20,411,652**	**10,072,718**	**10,338,934**	**9,137,615**	**4,532,736**	**4,604,87**
	Provinces ..	**48,462,359**	**24,106,718**	**24,355,641**	**27,615,112**	**13,652,857**	**13,962,255**	**18,797,830**	**9,260,563**	**9,537,267**	**3,779,202**	**1,854,656**	**1,924,54**
1	Ajmer-Merwara	439	258	181	324	192	132	315	185	130	5	4	1
2	Andaman and Nicobar Islands ..	3,595	2,462	1,133	3,020	2,026	994	769	535	234	2,073	1,333	740
3	Assam	140,765	74,873	65,892	2,185	1,221	964	2,041	1,153	888	62	36	26
4	Baluchistan (*Districts and Administered Territories*).	25,113	14,506	10,607	172	103	69	150	89	61	12	8	4
5	Bengal	225,930	121,363	104,567	6,296	3,560	2,736	5,869	3,239	2,630	305	245	60
6	Bihar and Orissa	660,492	321,855	338,637	3,669	2,294	1,375	3,219	1,930	1,289	394	330	64
7	Bombay (*including Aden*) ..	2,887,773	1,488,758	1,399,015	2,657,762	1,362,320	1,295,442	25,289	14,929	10,360	11,713	3,933	7,780
	Aden	*47*	*36*	*11*	*39*	*31*	*8*	*18*	*14*	*4*	..	..	..
8	Burma	357,220	254,646	102,574	196,580	130,163	66,417	184,107	118,659	65,448	12,218	11,343	875
9	Central Provinces and Berar ..	1,130,801	557,327	573,474	19,003	9,946	9,057	9,540	5,243	4,297	335	220	115
10	Coorg	154,644	85,705	68,939	151,976	84,255	67,721	3,013	1,756	1,257	24,940	16,488	8,452
11	Delhi	1,706	1,104	602	1,579	1,031	548	1,579	1,031	548	..	..	..
12	Madras	42,870,484	21,181,757	21,688,727	24,570,084	12,054,266	12,515,818	18,560,059	9,110,666	9,449,393	3,726,727	1,820,474	1,906,253
13	North-West Frontier Province (*Districts and Administered Territories*).	302	270	32	144	126	18	144	126	18	..	..	..
14	Punjab	944	472	472	819	404	415	797	397	400	22	7	15
15	United Provinces of Agra and Oudh	2,151	1,362	789	1,499	950	549	939	625	314	396	235	161
	States and Agencies ..	**23,182,428**	**11,741,005**	**11,441,423**	**13,839,481**	**6,991,420**	**6,848,061**	**1,613,822**	**812,155**	**801,667**	**5,358,413**	**2,678,080**	**2,680,333**
16	Assam States	75	48	27	65	40	25	65	40	25	..	..	..
17	Baluchistan States	102,580	55,374	47,206	..	..	..	..	..	..	..	..	..
18	Baroda State	784	487	297	422	269	153	133	80	53	112	78	34
19	Bengal States	2,489	1,820	669	..	..	..	..	..	..	..	..	..
20	Bihar and Orissa States	236,645	115,880	120,765	60	31	29	50	22	28	9	8	1
21	Bombay States	613,035	312,466	300,569	599,876	305,499	294,377	771	380	391	10	7	3
22	Central India Agency	357,843	180,518	177,325	2,898	1,351	1,547	2,746	1,269	1,477	14	11	3
23	Central Provinces States	485,856	245,002	240,854	228	116	112	214	108	106	..	..	..
24	Gwalior State	1,211	824	387	949	623	326	949	623	326	..	..	..
25	Hyderabad State	8,730,009	4,448,664	4,281,345	1,681,388	865,296	816,092	61,024	32,931	28,093	270	176	94
26	Jammu and Kashmir State ..	16	11	5	10	10	..	10	10	..	..	..	..
27	Madras States Agency	6,673,495	3,331,574	3,341,921	6,606,411	3,297,637	3,308,774	1,233,688	614,359	619,329	5,349,468	2,670,951	2,678,517
	Cochin State	*1,171,611*	*572,329*	*598,782*	*1,159,469*	*566,813*	*592,656*	*66,164*	*33,247*	*33,917*	*1,088,081*	*530,737*	*557,344*
	Travancore State	*5,064,323*	*2,548,590*	*2,515,733*	*5,054,468*	*2,543,457*	*2,511,011*	*788,455*	*400,635*	*387,820*	*4,260,860*	*2,139,812*	*2,121,048*
	Other Madras States	*437,561*	*210,155*	*227,406*	*492,474*	*187,367*	*205,107*	*379,069*	*180,477*	*198,592*	*527*	*402*	*125*
28	Mysore State	5,977,533	3,047,667	2,929,866	4,946,607	2,520,091	2,426,516	313,685	161,918	151,767	8,513	6,842	1,671
29	North-West Frontier Province (*Agencies and Tribal Areas.*) ..	329	329	..	223	223	..	223	223	..	..	..	..
30	Punjab States	12	7	5	12	7	5	12	7	5	..		..
31	Punjab States Agency	44	25	19	44	25	19	43	25	18	1	..	1
32	Rajputana Agency	248	154	94	141	102	39	131	98	33	4	1	3
33	Sikkim State	..	..	..	..	..	..	..	..	..	..	..	..
34	United Provinces States	2	2	..	2	2	..	2	2	..	..	..	..
35	Western India States Agency ..	222	[illegible]	69	145	98	47	76	60	16	12	6	6

Table XV.—Language—Part I—Mother Tongue—*contd.*

Dravidian Family—*contd.*

Dravida Group—*concld.*

Province, State or Agency. 1	Kanarese. Persons. 608	Kanarese. Males. 609	Kanarese. Females. 610	Kodagu or Coorgi. Persons. 611	Kodagu or Coorgi. Males. 612	Kodagu or Coorgi. Females. 613	Tulu. Persons. 614	Tulu. Males. 615	Tulu. Females. 616	Toda. Persons. 617	Toda. Males. 618	Toda. Females. 619	Kota. Persons 620	Kota. Males. 621	Kota. Females. 622
INDIA ..	**11,206,380**	**5,690,410**	**5,515,970**	**45,368**	**23,220**	**22,148**	**651,842**	**324,290**	**327,552**	**600**	**340**	**260**	**1,136**	**563**	**573**
Provinces ..	**4,388,683**	**2,220,274**	**2,168,409**	**44,920**	**22,923**	**21,997**	**602,741**	**293,538**	**309,203**	**600**	**340**	**260**	**1,136**	**563**	**573**
1 Ajmer-Merwara ..	4	3	1	..	..	..	..	..	..	..	..	..	..	..	..
2 Andaman and Nicobar Islands.	178	158	20	..	..	..	..	..	..	..	..	..	..	..	..
3 Assam	82	32	50	..	..	..	..	..	..	..	..	..	..	..	..
4 Baluchistan (*Districts and Administered Territories*).	10	6	4	..	..	..	..	..	..	..	..	..	..	..	..
5 Bengal	109	76	33	..	..	..	..	..	..	..	..	..	13	..	13
6 Bihar and Orissa ..	56	34	22	..	..	..	..	..	..	..	..	..	..	..	..
7 Bombay (*including Aden*).	2,598,349	1,331,226	1,267,123	..	..	..	22,411	12,232	10,179	..	..	..	..	..	..
Aden .. .	*21*	*17*	*4*	..	..	..	..	..	..	..	..	..	..	..	..
8 Burma	255	161	94	..	..	..	..	..	..	..	..	..	..	..	..
9 Central Provinces and Berar.	9,126	4,481	4,645	2	2	..	..	..	..	..	..	..	..	..	..
10 Coorg	65,163	34,310	30,853	44,585	22,667	21,918	14,275	9,034	5,241	..	..	..	..	..	..
11 Delhi	..	..	..	..	..	..	..	..	..	..	..	..	..	..	..
12 Madras	1,715,191	849,697	865,494	332	254	78	566,055	272,272	293,783	597	340	257	1,123	563	560
14 Punjab	..	..	..	..	..	..	..	..	..	..	..	..	..	..	..
15 United Provinces of Agra and Oudh.	160	90	70	1	..	1	..	..	..	3	..	3	..	..	..
States and Agencies	**6,817,697**	**3,470,136**	**3,347,561**	**448**	**297**	**151**	**49,101**	**30,752**	**18,349**	..	..	..	..	..	..
16 Assam States ..	..	..	..	..	..	..	..	..	..	..	..	..	..	..	..
17 Baluchistan States ..	..	..	..	..	..	..	..	..	..	..	..	..	..	..	..
18 Baroda State ..	177	111	66	..	..	..	..	..	..	..	..	..	..	..	..
19 Bengal States ..	..	..	..	..	..	..	..	..	..	..	..	..	..	..	..
20 Bihar and Orissa States	1	1	..	..	..	..	..	..	..	..	..	..	..	..	..
21 Bombay States ..	599,089	305,106	293,983	..	..	..	6	6	..	..	..	..	..	..	..
22 Central India Agency	138	71	67	..	..	..	..	..	..	..	..	..	..	..	..
23 Central Provinces States.	6	4	2	8	4	4	..	..	..	..	..	..	..	..	..
24 Gwalior State ..	..	..	..	..	..	..	..	..	..	..	..	..	..	..	..
25 Hyderabad State ..	1,620,094	832,189	787,905	..	..	..	..	..	..	..	..	..	..	..	..
26 Jammu and Kashmir State.	..	..	..	..	..	..	..	..	..	..	..	..	..	..	..
27 Madras States Agency	19,328	10,022	9,306	..	..	..	3,927	2,305	1,622	..	..	..	..	..	..
Cochin State ..	*4,493*	*2,387*	*2,106*	..	..	..	*731*	*442*	*289*	..	..	..	..	..	..
Travancore State	*1,957*	*1,147*	*810*	..	..	..	*3,196*	*1,863*	*1,333*	..	..	..	..	..	..
Other Madras States	*12,878*	*6,488*	*6,390*	..	..	..	..	..	..	..	..	..	..	..	..
28 Mysore State ..	4,578,801	2,322,597	2,256,204	440	293	147	45,168	28,441	16,727	..	..	..	..	..	..
29 North-West Frontier Province (*Agencies and Tribal Areas*).	..	..	..	..	..	..	..	..	..	..	..	..	..	..	..
30 Punjab States ..	..	..	..	..	..	..	..	..	..	..	..	..	..	..	..
31 Punjab States Agency	..	..	..	..	..	..	..	..	..	..	..	..	..	..	..
32 Rajputana Agency ..	6	3	3	..	..	..	..	..	..	..	..	..	..	..	..
33 Sikkim State ..	..	..	..	..	..	..	..	..	..	..	..	..	..	..	..
34 United Provinces States.	..	..	..	..	..	..	..	..	..	..	..	..	..	..	..
35 Western India States	57	32	25	..	..	..	..	..	..	..	..	..	..	..	..

Table XV.—Language—Part I—Mother Tongue—*contd.*

Dravidian Family—*contd.*

Intermediate Group.

	Province, State or Agency.	Intermediate Group Total.			Kurukh or Oraon.			Malto.			Gondi.			Kandhi or Kui.			Kolami.		
	1	Persons. 623	Males. 624	Females. 625	Persons. 626	Males. 627	Females 628	Persons. 629	Males. 630	Females. 631	Persons. 632	Males. 633	Females. 634	Persons. 635	Males. 636	Females. 637	Persons. 638	Males. 639	Females. 640
	INDIA ..	**3,609,418**	**1,797,388**	**1,812,030**	**1,037,142**	**520,549**	**516,593**	**70,761**	**35,143**	**35,618**	**1,864,878**	**926,099**	**938,779**	**585,109**	**287,602**	**297,507**	**29,187**	**15,740**	**13,447**
	Provinces ..	**2,475,577**	**1,228,049**	**1,247,528**	**757,227**	**379,691**	**377,536**	**70,713**	**35,122**	**35,591**	**1,095,642**	**538,813**	**556,829**	**500,590**	**246,505**	**254,085**	**29,064**	**15,663**	**13,401**
1	Ajmer-Merwara	1	..	1	..	..	..	..	..	..	..	..	..	1	..	1	..	..	..
2	Andaman and Nicobar Islands.	140	127	13	140	127	13	..	..	..	..	..	..	..	..	..	..	..	..
3	Assam	107,804	57,268	50,536	52,516	27,896	24,618	4	4	..	49,104	26,246	22,858	6,180	3,120	3,060	..	..	..
4	Baluchistan (*Districts and Administered Territories*).	..	..	..	..	..	..	..	..	..	..	..	..	..	..	..	..	..	..
5	Bengal	188,428	102,089	86,339	185,100	100,444	84,656	3,304	1,633	1,671	24	12	12	..	..	..	..	..	..
6	Bihar and Orissa ..	634,716	307,840	326,876	517,015	250,052	266,963	67,403	33,484	33,919	1,135	551	584	49,163	23,753	25,410	..	..	..
7	Bombay (*including Aden.*)	702	431	271	..	..	..	..	..	..	..	..	..	..	..	..	702	431	271
	Aden	..	..	..	..	..	..	..	..	..	..	..	..	..	..	..	..	..	..
8	Burma	..	..	..	..	..	..	..	..	..	..	..	..	..	..	..	..	..	..
9	Central Provinces and Berar.	981,405	480,153	501,252	2,456	1,170	1,286	..	..	..	950,587	463,751	486,836	..	..	..	28,362	15,232	13,130
10	Coorg	..	..	..	..	..	..	..	..	..	..	..	..	..	..	..	..	..	..
11	Delhi	1	..	1	..	..	..	..	..	..	1	..	1	..	..	..	..	..	..
12	Madras	562,376	280,138	282,238	..	..	..	..	..	..	94,789	48,251	46,538	445,246	219,632	225,614	..	..	..
13	North-West Frontier Province (*Districts and Administered Territories*).	..	..	..	..	..	..	..	..	..	..	..	..	..	..	..	..	..	..
14	Punjab	1	1	..	..	..	..	..	..	..	1	1	..	..	..	..	..	..	..
15	United Provinces of Agra and Oudh.	3	2	1	..	..	..	2	1	1	1	1	..	..	..	..	..	..	..
	States and Agencies ..	**1,133,841**	**569,339**	**564,502**	**279,915**	**140,858**	**139,057**	**48**	**21**	**27**	**769,236**	**387,286**	**381,950**	**84,519**	**41,097**	**43,422**	**123**	**77**	**46**
16	Assam States ..	..	..	..	..	..	..	..	..	..	..	..	..	..	..	..	..	..	..
17	Baluchistan States ..	..	..	..	..	..	..	..	..	..	..	..	..	..	..	..	..	..	..
18	Baroda State ..	..	..	..	..	..	..	..	..	..	..	..	..	..	..	..	..	..	..
19	Bengal States ..	570	323	247	570	323	247	..	..	..	..	..	..	..	..	..	..	..	..
20	Bihar and Orissa States	229,180	112,210	116,970	139,478	68,585	70,893	48	21	27	5,135	2,507	2,628	84,519	41,097	43,422	..	..	..
21	Bombay States ..	123	77	46	..	..	..	..	..	..	..	..	..	..	..	..	123	77	46
22	Central India Agency	354,098	178,698	175,400	..	..	..	..	..	..	354,098	178,698	175,400	..	..	..	..	..	..
23	Central Provinces States	473,591	238,932	234,659	139,867	71,950	67,917	..	..	..	333,724	166,982	166,742	..	..	..	..	..	..
24	Gwalior State ..	192	144	48	..	..	..	..	..	..	192	144	48	..	..	..	..	..	..
25	Hyderabad State ..	76,087	38,955	37,132	..	..	..	..	..	..	76,087	38,955	37,132	..	..	..	..	..	..
26	Jammu and Kashmir State.	..	..	..	..	..	..	..	..	..	..	..	..	..	..	..	..	..	..
27	Madras States Agency	..	..	..	..	..	..	..	..	..	..	..	..	..	..	..	..	..	..
	Cochin State ..	..	..	..	..	..	..	..	..	..	..	..	..	..	..	..	..	..	..
	Travancore State ..	..	..	..	..	..	..	..	..	..	..	..	..	..	..	..	..	..	..
	Other Madras States	..	..	..	..	..	..	..	..	..	..	..	..	..	..	..	..	..	..
28	Mysore State ..	..	..	..	..	..	..	..	..	..	..	..	..	..	..	..	..	..	..
29	North-West Frontier Province (*Agencies and Tribal Areas*).	..	..	..	..	..	..	..	..	..	..	..	..	..	..	..	..	..	..
30	Punjab States ..	..	..	..	..	..	..	..	..	..	..	..	..	..	..	..	..	..	..
31	Punjab States Agency	..	..	..	..	..	..	..	..	..	..	..	..	..	..	..	..	..	..
32	Rajputana Agency ..	..	..	..	..	..	..	..	..	..	..	..	..	..	..	..	..	..	..
33	Sikkim State ..	..	..	..	..	..	..	..	..	..	..	..	..	..	..	..	..	..	..
34	United Provinces States	..	..	..	..	..	..	..	..	..	..	..	..	..	..	..	..	..	..
35	Western India States Agency.	..	..	..	..	..	..	..	..	..	..	..	..	..	..	..	..	..	..

Table XV.—Language—Part I—Mother Tongue—*contd.*

	Province, State or Agency.	Dravidian Family—*concld.* Intermediate Group—*concld.* Others (Konda). Persons.	Males.	Females.	Andhra Language Group. Telugu. Persons.	Males.	Females.	North-Western Language. Brahui. Persons.	Males.	Females.	Indo-European Family. Indo-European Family. Aryan Sub-Family Total. Persons.	Males.	Females.	Eranian Branch. Eastern Group Total. Persons.	Males.	Females.
	1	641	642	643	644	645	646	647	648	649	650	651	652	653	654	655
	INDIA ..	**22,341**	**12,255**	**10,086**	**26,373,727**	**13,291,050**	**13,082,677**	**207,049**	**115,008**	**92,041**	**257,492,805**	**134,082,997**	**123,409,808**	**2,270,466**	**1,241,831**	**1,028,635**
	Provinces ..	**22,341**	**12,255**	**10,086**	**18,267,260**	**9,166,212**	**9,101,048**	**104,410**	**59,600**	**44,810**	**203,520,854**	**106,063,071**	**97,457,783**	**2,064,912**	**1,125,440**	**939,472**
1	Ajmer-Merwara ..	..	..	..	114	66	48	..	..	..	556,324	293,534	262,790	293	249	44
2	Andaman and Nicobar Islands.	..	..	..	435	309	126	..	..	..	11,851	8,597	2,984	470	400	70
3	Assam		..	..	30,776	16,384	14,392	..	..	..	6,895,693	3,655,620	3,240,073	2,433	2,175	258
4	Baluchistan (*Districts and Administered Territories*).	..	.	..	42	31	11	24,899	14,372	10,527	427,278	247,398	179,880	303,493	165,939	137,554
5	Bengal ..	..	..	..	31,206	15,714	15,492	..	..	..	48,596,706	25,260,679	23,336,027	3,998	3,757	241
6	Bihar and Orissa ..	..	..	..	22,107	11,721	10,386	..	..	..	34,761,899	17,347,229	17,414,670	1,536	1,358	178
7	Bombay (*including Aden*).	..	..	..	149,807	80,788	69,019	79,502	45,219	34,283	18,826,727	9,928,876	8,897,851	315,228	178,483	136,745
	Aden	..	..	..	*8*	*5*	*3*	..	..	..	*8,554*	*5,417*	*3,137*	*44*	*44*	..
8	Burma	..	..	..	160,640	124,483	36,157	..	..	..	722,600	510,772	211,828	2,091	1,587	504
9	Central Provinces and Berar.	..	..	..	130,393	67,228	63,165	..	..	..	14,204,539	7,116,681	7,087,858	2,263	1,896	367
10	Coorg	..	..	..	2,668	1,450	1,218	..	..	..	8,354	4,688	3,666	..	..	..
11	Delhi	..	..	..	126	73	53	..	..	..	629,037	364,860	264,177	1,476	1,119	357
12	Madras	22,341	12,255	10,086	17,738,024	8,847,353	8,890,671	..	..	..	3,590,129	1,760,834	1,829,295	225	208	17
13	North-West Frontier Province (*Districts and Administered Territories*).	..	..	..	158	144	14	..	..	..	2,410,688	1,305,398	1,105,290	1,279,478	677,435	602,043
14	Punjab	..	..	..	124	67	57	..	..	..	23,513,258	12,840,853	10,672,405	149,824	88,946	60,878
15	United Provinces of Agra and Oudh.	..	..	..	640	401	239	9	9	..	48,366,041	25,417,052	22,948,989	2,104	1,888	216
	States and Agencies	..	..	..	**8,106,467**	**4,124,838**	**3,981,629**	**102,639**	**55,408**	**47,231**	**53,971,951**	**28,019,926**	**25,952,025**	**205,554**	**116,391**	**89,163**
16	Assam States ..	..	..	..	10	8	2	..	..	..	23,151	15,446	7,705	69	65	4
17	Baluchistan States ..	..	..	..	..	..	..	102,580	55,374	47,206	302,350	162,932	139,418	175,878	94,634	81,244
18	Baroda State ..	..	..	..	362	218	144	..	..	..	2,441,692	1,256,982	1,184,710	535	431	104
19	Bengal States ..	..	..	..	1,919	1,497	422	..	..	..	773,795	412,301	361,494	86	86	..
20	Bihar and Orissa States	..	..	..	7,405	3,639	3,766	..	..	..	3,681,371	1,810,747	1,870,624	43	27	16
21	Bombay States ..	..	..	..	12,977	6,856	6,121	59	34	25	3,854,422	1,975,594	1,878,828	6,538	3,715	2,823
22	Central India Agency	..	..	..	847	469	378	..	..	..	6,264,373	3,218,955	3,045,418	1,083	775	308
23	Central Provinces States	..	..	..	12,037	5,954	6,083	..	..	..	1,968,839	976,059	992,780	49	39	10
24	Gwalior State ..	..	..	..	70	57	13	..	..	..	3,521,170	1,865,702	1,655,468	560	359	201
25	Hyderabad State ..	..	..	..	6,972,534	3,544,413	3,428,121	..	..	..	5,688,088	2,908,661	2,779,427	335	276	59
26	Jammu and Kashmir State.	..	..	..	6	1	5	..	..	..	3,439,448	1,833,829	1,605,619	4,020	2,363	1,657
27	Madras States Agency	..	..	..	67,084	33,937	33,147	..	..	..	74,535	37,911	36,624	3	3	..
	Cochin State ..	..	..	..	*12,142*	*6,016*	*6,126*	..	..	..	*32,107*	*16,360*	*15,747*	*3*	*3*	..
	Travancore State ..	..	..	..	*9,855*	*5,133*	*4,722*	..	..	..	*26,570*	*13,606*	*12,964*	..	..	..
	Other Madras States	..	..	..	*45,087*	*22,788*	*22,299*	..	..	..	*15,858*	*7,945*	*7,913*	..	..	..
28	Mysore State ..	..	..	..	1,030,926	527,576	503,350	..	..	..	564,234	298,225	266,009	77	64	13
29	North-West Frontier Province (*Agencies and Tribal Areas*).	..	..	..	106	106	..	..	..	..	41,958	40,295	1,663	11,013	10,060	953
30	Punjab States ..	..	..	..	..	..	..	..	..	..	408,069	215,483	192,586	306	301	5
31	Punjab States Agency	..	..	..	..	..	..	..	..	..	4,468,838	2,449,385	2,019,453	3,409	2,231	1,178
32	Rajputana Agency ..	..	..	..	107	52	55	..	..	..	11,214,657	5,879,363	5,335,294	776	521	255
33	Sikkim State ..	..	..	..	..	..	..	..	..	..	39,702	20,383	19,319	..	..	..
34	United Provinces States	..	..	..	..	..	..	..	..	..	1,205,994	618,119	587,875	34	33	1
35	Western India States Agency.	..	..	..	77	55	22	..	..	..	3,995,265	2,023,554	1,971,711	740	408	332

Table XV.—Language—Part I—Mother Tongue—*contd.*

Indo-European Family—*contd.*
Aryan Sub-Family—*contd.*

Province, State or Agency.	Eranian Branch—*concld.* Eastern Group—*concld.* Pashto. Persons.	Pashto. Males.	Pashto. Females.	Balochi. Persons.	Balochi. Males.	Balochi. Females.	Persian. Persons.	Persian. Males.	Persian. Females.	Other Eranian Languages. Persons.	Other Eranian Languages. Males.	Other Eranian Languages. Females.	Dardic Branch Total. Persons.	Dardic Branch Total. Males.	Dardic Branch Total. Females.
1	656	657	658	659	660	661	662	663	664	665	666	667	668	669	670
INDIA ..	**1,636,490**	**894,852**	**741,638**	**628,086**	**343,758**	**284,328**	**5,282**	**2,873**	**2,409**	**608**	**348**	**260**	**1,522,936**	**826,872**	**696,064**
Provinces ..	**1,615,054**	**877,699**	**737,355**	**449,752**	**247,687**	**202,065**	**106**	**54**	**52**	..	..	..	**22,331**	**16,337**	**5,994**
1 Ajmer-Merwara ..	289	245	44	4	4	..	..	..	..	..	..	..	27	14	13
2 Andaman and Nicobar Islands.	441	372	69	29	28	1	..	..	..	..	..	..	..	..	..
3 Assam	1,634	1,573	61	799	602	197	..	..	..	..	..	..	2	2	..
4 Baluchistan (*Districts and Administered Territories*).	206,293	112,788	93,505	97,094	53,097	43,997	106	54	52	..	..	..	201	133	68
5 Bengal	3,998	3,757	241	..	..	..	..	..	..	..	..	..	63	52	11
6 Bihar and Orissa ..	1,536	1,358	178	..	..	..	..	..	..	..	..	..	16	11	5
7 Bombay (*including Aden*)	23,497	18,394	5,103	291,731	160,089	131,642	..	..	..	..	..	..	..	..	..
Aden	*42*	*42*	..	*2*	*2*	..	..	..	..	..	..	..	..	..	..
8 Burma	2,003	1,510	493	88	77	11	..	..	..	..	..	..	38	31	7
9 Central Provinces and Berar	2,164	1,829	335	99	67	32	..	..	..	..	..	..	4	..	4
10 Coorg	..	..	..	..	..	..	..	..	..	..	..	..	..	..	..
11 Delhi	1,470	1,113	357	6	6	..	..	..	..	..	..	..	116	97	19
12 Madras	224	207	17	1	1	..	..	..	..	..	..	..	13	4	9
13 North-West Frontier Province (*Districts and Administered Territories*).	1,279,471	677,428	602,043	7	7	..	..	..	..	..	..	..	2,173	1,487	686
14 Punjab	90,020	55,312	34,708	59,804	33,634	26,170	..	..	..	..	..	..	19,493	14,360	5,133
15 United Provinces of Agra and Oudh.	2,014	1,813	201	90	75	15	..	..	..	..	..	..	185	146	39
States and Agencies ..	**21,436**	**17,153**	**4,283**	**178,334**	**96,071**	**82,263**	**5,176**	**2,819**	**2,357**	**608**	**348**	**260**	**1,500,605**	**810,535**	**690,070**
16 Assam States	69	65	4	..	..	..	..	..	..	..	..	..	..	..	..
17 Baluchistan States ..	888	507	381	169,863	91,339	78,524	5,127	2,788	2,339	..	..	..	..	..	..
18 Baroda State	267	239	28	219	161	58	49	31	18	..	..	..	3	3	..
19 Bengal States	86	86	..	..	..	..	..	..	..	..	..	..	..	..	..
20 Bihar and Orissa States ..	43	27	16	..	..	..	..	..	..	..	..	..	..	..	..
21 Bombay States ..	501	388	113	6,037	3,327	2,710	..	..	..	..	..	..	..	..	..
22 Central India Agency ..	854	624	230	229	151	78	..	..	..	..	..	..	46	24	22
23 Central Provinces States ..	49	39	10	..	..	..	..	..	..	..	..	..	..	..	..
24 Gwalior State	560	359	201	..	..	..	..	..	..	..	..	..	28	21	7
25 Hyderabad State ..	320	264	56	15	12	3	..	..	..	..	..	..	12	7	5
26 Jammu and Kashmir State	3,408	2,012	1,396	4	3	1	..	..	..	*608	348	260	1,497,683	808,367	689,316
27 Madras States Agency ..	3	3	..	..	..	..	..	..	..	..	..	..	..	..	..
Cochin State ..	*3*	*3*	..	..	..	..	..	..	..	..	..	..	..	..	..
Travancore State ..	..	..	..	..	..	..	..	..	..	..	..	..	..	..	..
Other Madras States ..	..	..	..	..	..	..	..	..	..	..	..	..	..	..	..
28 Mysore State	71	61	10	6	3	3	..	..	..	..	..	..	29	18	11
29 North-West Frontier Province (*Agencies and Tribal Areas*).	11,013	10,060	953	..	..	..	..	..	..	..	..	..	464	459	5
30 Punjab States	306	301	5	..	..	..	..	..	..	..	..	..	84	64	20
31 Punjab States Agency ..	2,228	1,573	655	1,181	658	523	..	..	..	..	..	..	2,245	1,565	680
32 Rajputana Agency ..	585	410	175	191	111	80	..	..	..	..	..	..	11	7	4
33 Sikkim State	..	..	..	..	..	..	..	..	..	..	..	..	..	..	..
34 United Provinces States	34	33	1	..	..	..	..	..	..	..	..	..	..	..	..
35 Western India States Agency.	151	102	49	589	306	283	..	..	..	..	..	..	..	..	..

*Includes Wakhi and Khoki.

Table XV.—Language—Part I—Mother Tongue—*contd.*

Indo-European Family—*contd.*
Aryan Sub-Family—*contd.*
Dardic Branch—*contd.*

Province, State or Agency.	Khowar Group. Khowar, Chitrali or Arniya. Persons.	Males.	Females.	Dard Group. Dard Group Total. Persons.	Males.	Females.	Shina. Persons.	Males.	Females.	Kashmiri. Persons.	Males.	Females.	Kohistani. Persons.	Males.	Females.	Kafir Group. Kafir Group Total. Persons.	Males.	Females.
1	671	672	673	674	675	676	677	678	679	680	681	682	683	684	685	686	687	688
INDIA	**6,956**	**3,667**	**3,289**	**1,509,741**	**820,018**	**689,723**	**68,199**	**35,787**	**32,412**	**1,438,021**	**782,508**	**655,513**	**3,521**	**1,723**	**1,798**	**6,239**	**3,187**	**3,052**
Provinces	3	3	..	22,328	16,334	5,994	..	..	..	21,944	16,218	5,726	384	116	268	..	..	..
1 Ajmer-Merwara	..	..	..	27	14	13	..	..	..	27	14	13	..	..	..	..	..	..
2 Andaman and Nicobar Islands.	..	..	..	..	..	..	..	..	..	..	..	..	..	..	..	..	..	..
3 Assam	..	..	..	2	2	..	..	..	..	2	2	..	..	..	..	..	..	..
4 Baluchistan (*Districts and Administered Territories.*)	..	..	..	201	133	68	..	..	..	201	133	68	..	..	..	..	..	..
5 Bengal	..	..	..	63	52	11	..	..	..	63	52	11	..	..	..	..	..	..
6 Bihar and Orissa	..	..	..	16	11	5	..	..	..	16	11	5	..	..	..	..	..	..
7 Bombay	..	..	..	..	..	..	..	..	..	..	..	..	..	..	..	..	..	..
Aden	..	..	..	..	..	..	..	..	..	..	..	..	..	..	..	..	..	..
8 Burma	..	..	..	38	31	7	..	..	..	38	31	7	..	..	..	..	..	..
9 Central Provinces and Berar	..	..	..	4	..	4	..	..	..	4	..	4	..	..	..	..	..	..
10 Coorg	..	..	..	..	..	..	..	..	..	..	..	..	..	..	..	..	..	..
11 Delhi	..	..	..	116	97	19	..	..	..	116	97	19	..	..	..	..	..	..
12 Madras	..	..	..	13	4	9	..	..	..	6	4	2	7	..	7	..	..	..
13 North-West Frontier Province (*Districts and Administered Territories.*)	..	..	..	2,173	1,487	686	..	..	..	1,796	1,371	425	377	116	261	..	..	..
14 Punjab	..	..	..	19,493	14,360	5,133	..	..	..	19,493	14,360	5,133	..	..	..	..	..	..
15 United Provinces of Agra and Oudh.	3	3	..	182	143	39	..	..	..	182	143	39	..	..	..	..	..	..
States and Agencies	6,953	3,664	3,289	1,487,413	803,684	683,729	68,199	35,787	32,412	1,416,077	766,290	649,787	3,137	1,607	1,530	6,239	3,187	3,052
16 Assam States	..	..	..	..	..	..	..	..	..	..	..	..	..	..	..	..	..	..
17 Baluchistan States	..	..	..	..	..	..	..	..	..	..	..	..	..	..	..	..	..	..
18 Baroda State	..	..	..	3	3	..	..	..	..	3	3	..	..	..	..	..	..	..
19 Bengal States	..	..	..	..	..	..	..	..	..	..	..	..	..	..	..	..	..	..
20 Bihar and Orissa States	..	..	..	..	..	..	..	..	..	..	..	..	..	..	..	..	..	..
21 Bombay States	..	..	..	..	..	..	..	..	..	..	..	..	..	..	..	..	..	..
22 Central India Agency	..	..	..	46	24	22	..	..	..	46	24	22	..	..	..	..	..	..
23 Central Provinces States	..	..	..	..	..	..	..	..	..	..	..	..	..	..	..	..	..	..
24 Gwalior State	..	..	..	28	21	7	..	..	..	28	21	7	..	..	..	..	..	..
25 Hyderabad State	..	..	..	12	7	5	..	..	..	12	7	5	..	..	..	..	..	..
26 Jammu and Kashmir State	6,953	3,664	3,289	1,484,491	801,516	682,975	68,199	35,787	32,412	1,413,166	764,133	649,033	3,126	1,596	1,530	6,239	3,187	3,052
27 Madras States Agency	..	..	..	..	..	..	..	..	..	..	..	..	..	..	..	..	..	..
Cochin State	..	..	..	..	..	..	..	..	..	..	..	..	..	..	..	..	..	..
Travancore State	..	..	..	..	..	..	..	..	..	..	..	..	..	..	..	..	..	..
Other Madras States	..	..	..	..	..	..	..	..	..	..	..	..	..	..	..	..	..	..
28 Mysore State	..	..	..	29	18	11	..	..	..	29	18	11	..	..	..	..	..	..
29 North-West Frontier Province (*Agencies and Tribal Areas*).	..	..	..	464	459	5	..	..	..	453	448	5	11	11	..	..	..	..
30 Punjab States	..	..	..	84	64	20	..	..	..	84	64	20	..	..	..	..	..	..
31 Punjab States Agency	..	..	..	2,245	1,565	680	..	..	..	2,245	1,565	680	..	..	..	..	..	..
32 Rajputana Agency	..	..	..	11	7	4	..	..	..	11	7	4	..	..	..	..	..	..
33 Sikkim State	..	..	..	..	..	..	..	..	..	..	..	..	..	..	..	..	..	..
34 United Provinces States	..	..	..	..	..	..	..	..	..	..	..	..	..	..	..	..	..	..
35 Western India States Agency	..	..	..	..	..	..	..	..	..	..	..	..	..	..	..	..	..	..

Table XV.—Language—Part-I—Mother Tongue—*contd.*

Indo-European Family—*contd.*

Aryan Sub-Family—*contd.*

No.	Province, State or Agency.	Dardic Branch—concld. Kafir Group—concld. Bashgali. Persons.	Males.	Females.	Other Kafir languages. Persons.	Males.	Females.	Indo-Aryan Branch. Indo-Aryan Branch Total. Persons.	Males.	Females.	Outer Sub-Branch. Sanskrit Sub-Branch. Sanskrit Group. Sanskrit. Persons.	Males.	Females.	Outer Sub-Branch Total. Persons	Males.	Females.	North-Western Group. North-Western Group Total. Persons.	Males.	Females.
	1	689	690	691	692	693	694	695	696	697	698	699	700	701	702	703	704	705	706
	INDIA	**7**	**6**	**1**	**6,232**	**3,181**	**3,051**	**253,699,403**	**132,014,294**	**121,685,109**	**1,181**	**774**	**407**	**128,521,941**	**65,678,762**	**62,843,179**	**12,572,198**	**6,803,070**	**5,769,128**
	Provinces	..	..	..	..	..	..	201,433,611	104,921,294	96,512,317	950	575	375	116,151,021	59,397,327	56,753,694	10,795,305	5,852,283	4,943,022
1	Ajmer-Merwara	..	..	..	..	..	..	556,004	293,271	262,733	3	1	2	1,519	883	636	131	80	51
2	Andaman and Nicobar Islands.	..	..	..	..	..	..	11,111	8,197	2,914	..	..	..	1,805	1,506	299	83	83	..
3	Assam	..	..	..	..	..	..	6,893,258	3,653,443	3,239,815	..	..	..	6,160,583	3,228,720	2,931,863	17	16	1
4	Baluchistan (*Districts and Administered Territories.*)	..	..	..	..	..	..	123,584	81,326	42,258	..	..	..	78,330	48,114	30,216	77,356	47,282	30,074
5	Bengal	..	..	..	..	..	..	48,592,645	25,256,870	23,335,775	..	..	..	46,553,907	23,909,277	22,644,630	504	380	124
6	Bihar and Orissa ..	..	..	..	..	..	..	34,760,347	17,345,860	17,414,487	..	..	..	34,721,257	17,321,583	17,399,674	334	229	105
7	Bombay (*including Aden*) ..	..	..	..	..	..	..	18,511,499	9,750,393	8,761,106	291	199	92	12,692,850	6,605,841	6,087,009	3,145,303	1,748,585	1,396,718
	Aden	..	..	..	..	..	..	*8,510*	*5,373*	*3,137*	*1*	*1*	..	*768*	*633*	*135*	*4*	*3*	*1*
8	Burma	..	..	..	..	..	..	720,471	509,154	211,317	..	..	..	440,751	301,996	138,755	431	343	88
9	Central Provinces and Berar	..	..	..	..	..	..	14,202,272	7,114,785	7,087,487	5	5	..	5,703,731	2,862,154	2,841,577	2,248	1,663	585
10	Coorg	..	..	..	..	..	..	8,354	4,688	3,666	..	..	..	3,908	2,239	1,669	..	..	..
11	Delhi	..	..	..	..	..	..	627,445	363,644	263,801	..	..	..	7,604	4,575	3,029	88	55	33
12	Madras	..	..	..	..	..	..	3,589,891	1,760,622	1,829,269	620	346	274	2,182,701	1,039,393	1,143,308	2,826	2,368	458
13	North-West Frontier Province. (*Districts and Administered Territories.*)	..	..	..	..	..	..	1,129,037	626,476	502,561	1	1	..	1,035,651	557,856	477,795	1,034,975	557,307	477,668
14	Punjab	..	..	..	..	..	..	23,343,941	12,737,547	10,606,394	21	15	6	6,534,167	3,495,827	3,038,340	6,530,619	3,493,609	3,037,010
15	United Provinces of Agra and Oudh.	..	..	..	..	..	..	48,363,752	25,415,018	22,948,734	9	8	1	32,257	17,363	14,894	390	283	107
	States and Agencies ..	**7**	**6**	**1**	**6,232**	**3,181**	**3,051**	**52,265,792**	**27,093,000**	**25,172,792**	**231**	**199**	**32**	**12,370,920**	**6,281,435**	**6,089,485**	**1,776,893**	**950,787**	**826,106**
16	Assam States ..	..	..	..	..	..	..	23,082	15,381	7,701	..	..	..	7,419	4,864	2,555	..	..	..
17	Baluchistan States ..	..	..	..	..	..	..	126,472	68,298	58,174	..	..	..	126,031	67,988	58,043	126,030	67,987	58,043
18	Baroda State ..	..	..	..	..	..	..	2,441,154	1,256,548	1,184,606	.	..	..	54,672	28,891	25,781	18,631	9,461	9,170
19	Bengal States ..	..	..	..	..	..	..	773,709	412,215	361,494	..	..	..	746,929	395,828	351,101	..	..	..
20	Bihar and Orissa States	..	..	..	..	..	..	3,681,328	1,810,720	1,870,608	..	..	..	3,675,672	1,807,805	1,867,867	5	5	..
21	Bombay States ..	..	..	..	..	..	..	3,847,884	1,971,879	1,876,005	..	..	..	2,007,120	1,023,503	983,617	219,342	120,633	98,709
22	Central India Agency	..	..	..	..	..	..	6,263,244	3,218,156	3,045,088	5	5	..	57,800	30,488	27,312	1,323	795	528
23	Central Provinces States ..	..	..	..	..	..	..	1,968,790	976,020	992,770	..	..	..	308,380	154,753	153,627	1	1	..
24	Gwalior State ..	..	..	..	..	..	..	3,520,582	1,865,322	1,655,260	95	81	14	43,132	24,134	18,998	21,355	11,936	9,419
25	Hyderabad State ..	..	..	..	..	..	..	5,687,714	2,908,378	2,779,363	96	86	10	3,787,847	1,917,181	1,870,666	764	495	269
26	Jammu and Kashmir State	7	6	1	6,232	3,181	3,051	1,937,745	1,023,099	914,646	2	2	..	96,284	50,725	45,559	96,192	50,662	45,530
27	Madras States Agency ..	..	..	..	..	..	..	74,532	37,908	36,624	23	19	4	49,431	25,009	24,422	961	502	459
	Cochin State ..	..	..	..	..	..	..	*32,104*	*16,357*	*15,747*	..	..	..	*28,277*	*14,323*	*13,954*	*714*	*386*	*328*
	Travancore State	..	..	..	..	..	..	*26,570*	*13,606*	*12,964*	*23*	*19*	*4*	*19,643*	*9,921*	*9,722*	*246*	*116*	*131*
	Other Madras States	..	..	..	..	..	..	*15,858*	*7,945*	*7,913*	..	..	..	*1,511*	*765*	*746*	..	..	..
28	Mysore State ..	..	..	..	..	..	..	546,128	298,143	265,985	..	..	..	109,730	58,045	51,685	517	283	234
29	North-West Frontier Province. (*Agencies and Tribal Areas.*)	..	..	..	..	..	..	30,481	29,776	705	..	..	..	1,988	1,860	128	1,783	1,655	128
30	Punjab States ..	..	..	..	..	..	..	407,679	215,118	192,561	..	..	..	75	41	34	..	..	..
31	Punjab States Agency ..	..	..	..	..	..	..	4,463,184	2,445,589	2,017,595	..	..	..	859,369	472,918	386,451	859,214	472,831	386,383
32	Rajputana Agency ..	..	..	..	..	..	..	11,213,870	5,878,835	5,335,035	1	1	..	18,544	9,368	9,176	12,840	7,165	5,675
33	Sikkim State ..	..	..	..	..	..	..	39,702	20,383	19,319	..	..	..	18	12	6	..	..	..
34	United Provinces States	..	..	..	..	..	..	1,205,690	618,086	587,874	..	..	..	311	273	38	..	..	..
35	Western India States Agency	..	..	..	..	..	..	3,994,525	2,023,146	1,971,379	9	5	4	420,168	207,749	212,419	417,935	206,376	211,559

Table XV.—Language—Part I—Mother Tongue—*contd.*

Indo-European Family—*contd.*

Aryan Sub-Family—*contd.*

Indo-Aryan Branch—*contd.*

Outer Sub-Branch—*contd.*

Province, State or Agency.	North-Western Group—*concld.*						Southern Group.					
	Lahnda or Western Punjabi.			Sindhi.			Southern Group Total.			Marathi.		
	Persons.	Males.	Females.	Persons.	Males.	Females.	Persons.	Males.	Females.	Persons.	Males.	Females.
1	707	708	709	710	711	712	713	714	715	716	717	718
INDIA	**8,566,051**	**4,603,498**	**3,962,553**	**4,006,147**	**2,199,572**	**1,806,575**	**21,361,393**	**10,816,947**	**10,544,446**	**20,889,658**	**10,572,782**	**10,316,876**
Provinces	**7,611,064**	**4,079,881**	**3,531,183**	**3,184,241**	**1,772,402**	**1,411,839**	**15,328,296**	**7,759,695**	**7,568,601**	**14,917,335**	**7,547,464**	**7,369,871**
1 Ajmer-Merwara	46	38	8	85	42	43	949	545	404	949	545	404
2 Andaman and Nicobar Islands ..	..	..	..	83	83	..	352	283	69	352	283	69
3 Assam	..	..	..	17	16	1	4,319	2,426	1,893	4,315	2,422	1,893
4 Baluchistan .. .. .. (*Districts and Administered Territories.*)	44,981	28,078	16,903	32,375	19,204	13,171	881	769	112	789	697	92
5 Bengal	..	..	..	504	380	124	3,160	1,941	1,219	3,005	1,843	1,162
6 Bihar and Orissa	..	..	..	334	229	105	1,300	713	587	1,300	713	587
7 Bombay (*including Aden*) ..	212	142	70	3,145,091	1,748,443	1,396,648	9,542,084	4,852,955	4,689,129	9,336,405	4,742,593	4,593,812
Aden	..	..	..	*4*	*3*	*1*	*108*	*276*	*132*	*203*	*105*	*98*
8 Burma	..	..	..	431	343	88	1,384	1,085	299	673	480	193
9 Central Provinces and Berar ..	328	173	155	1,920	1,490	430	5,432,747	2,728,546	2,704,201	5,432,265	2,728,270	2,703,995
10 Coorg	..	..	..	..	..	..	3,908	2,239	1,669	1,577	871	706
11 Delhi	3	..	3	85	55	30	850	494	356	850	494	356
12 Madras	2,210	1,970	240	616	398	218	330,769	164,130	166,639	129,398	64,781	64,617
13 North-West Frontier Province .. (*Districts and Administered Territories.*)	1,034,957	557,295	477,662	18	12	6	262	183	79	238	160	78
14 Punjab	6,528,325	3,492,185	3,036,140	2,294	1,424	870	935	717	218	935	717	218
15 United Provinces of Agra and Oudh.	2	..	2	388	283	105	4,396	2,669	1,727	4,284	2,595	1,689
States and Agencies ..	**954,987**	**523,617**	**431,370**	**821,906**	**427,170**	**394,736**	**6,033,097**	**3,057,252**	**2,975,845**	**5,972,323**	**3,025,318**	**2,947.005**
16 Assam States	..	..	..	..	..	..	2	1	1	2	1	1
17 Baluchistan States	6,398	3,428	2,970	119,632	64,559	55,073	1	1	..	..	..	..
18 Baroda State	18	5	13	18,613	9,456	9,157	35,841	19,278	16,563	35,578	19,110	16,468
19 Bengal States	..	..	..	..	..	..	1	..	1	1	..	1
20 Bihar and Orissa States	..	..	..	5	5	..	412	224	188	412	224	188
21 Bombay States	..	..	..	219,342	120,633	98,709	1,787,441	902,790	884,651	1,778,722	898,947	879,775
22 Central India Agency	667	424	243	656	371	285	55,001	28,921	26,080	54,539	28,678	25,861
23 Central Provinces States. ..	..	..	..	1	1	..	185,279	93,730	91,549	185,279	93,730	91,549
24 Gwalior State	..	..	..	21,355	11,936	9,419	21,535	12,060	9,475	21,535	12,060	9,475
25 Hyderabad State	..	..	..	764	495	269	3,786,831	1,916,544	1,870,287	3,786,639	1,916,460	1,870,179
26 Jammu and Kashmir State ..	96,183	50,654	45,529	9	8	1	26	22	4	25	21	4
27 Madras States Agency	..	..	..	961	502	459	48,279	24,326	23,953	13,752	6,880	6,872
Cochin State	..	..	..	*714*	*386*	*328*	*27,560*	*13,934*	*13,626*	*5,210*	*2,612*	*2,598*
Travancore State	..	..	..	*247*	*116*	*131*	*19,229*	*9,642*	*9,587*	*7,054*	*3,520*	*3,534*
Other Madras States	..	..	..	..	..	..	*1,490*	*750*	*740*	*1,488*	*748*	*740*
28 Mysore State	11	9	2	506	274	232	107,617	56,937	50,680	91,322	47,025	44,297
29 North-West Frontier Province .. (*Agencies and Tribal Areas.*)	1,783	1,655	128	..	..	..	184	181	..	182	182	..
30 Punjab States	..	..	..	..	..	..	**22**	**9**	**13**	**22**	**9**	**13**
31 Punjab States Agency	**849,927**	**467,442**	**382,485**	**9,287**	**5,389**	**3,898**	**16**	**10**	**6**	**16**	**10**	**6**
32 Rajputana Agency	..	..	..	**12,840**	**7,165**	**5,675**	**2,444**	**885**	**1,559**	**2,433**	**880**	**1,553**
33 Sikkim State	..	..	..	..	..	..	..	..	..	..	..	..
34 United Provinces States	..	..	..	..	..	..	**14**	**8**	**6**	**14**	**8**	**6**
35 Western India States Agency	..	..	..	**417,935**	**206,376**	**211,559**	**2,151**	**1,322**	**829**	**1,850**	**1,093**	**757**

Table XV.—Language—Part I—Mother Tongue—*contd.*

Indo-European Family—*contd.*
Aryan Sub-Family—*contd.*
Indo-Aryan Branch—*contd.*
Other Sub-Branch—*contd.*

Province, State or Agency.	Southern Group—*concld.*			Eastern Group.											
	Konkani.			Eastern Group Total.			Oriya.			Bihari.			Bengali.		
	Persons.	Males.	Females.	Persons.	Males.	Females.	Persons.	Males.	Females.	Persons.	Males.	Females.	Persons.	Males.	Females.
1	719	720	721	722	723	724	725	726	727	728	729	730	731	732	733
INDIA	**471,735**	**244,165**	**227,570**	**94,588,350**	**48,058,745**	**46,529,605**	**11,194,265**	**5,484,976**	**5,709,289**	**27,926,559**	**14,014,592**	**13,911,967**	**53,468,469**	**27,516,715**	**25,951,754**
Provinces	410,961	212,231	198,730	90,027,420	45,785,349	44,242,071	7,665,034	3,751,929	3,913,105	27,733,284	13,917,020	13,816,264	52,633,141	27,075,773	25,557,368
1 Ajmer-Merwara ..	..	..	..	439	258	181	1	1	..	2	2	..	435	254	181
2 Andaman and Nicobar Islands.	..	..	..	1,370	1,140	230	191	163	28	..	..	..	1,171	969	202
3 Assam	4	4	..	6,156,247	3,226,278	2,929,969	202,689	104,845	97,844	..	..	..	3,960,712	2,083,124	1,877,588
4 Baluchistan	92	72	20	93	63	30	..	..	..	..	..	..	93	63	30
(Districts and Administered Territories.)															
5 Bengal	155	98	57	46,550,243	23,906,956	22,643,287	154,331	121,610	32,721	679	338	341	46,393,802	23,783,892	22,609,910
6 Bihar and Orissa	..	..	..	34,719,623	17,320,641	17,398,982	5,136,195	2,467,513	2,668,682	27,731,601	13,916,017	13,815,584	1,851,797	937,090	914,707
7 Bombay (*including Aden*)	205,679	110,362	95,317	5,463	4,301	1,162	..	..	..	603*	389	214	4,654	3,721	933
Aden	*205*	*171*	*34*	*356*	*354*	*2*	..	..	..	..	..	..	*356*	*354*	*2*
8 Burma	711	605	106	438,936	300,568	138,368	60,682	57,247	3,435	57	44	13	376,994	242,415	134,579
9 Central Provinces and Berar	482	276	206	268,736	131,945	136,791	263,133	128,750	134,383	268	184	84	5,335	3,011	2,324
10 Coorg	2,331	1,368	963	..	..	..	..	..	..	..	..	..	..	..	..
11 Delhi	..	..	..	6,666	4,026	2,640	30	26	4	..	..	..	6,632	3,997	2,635
12 Madras	201,371	99,349	102,022	1,849,106	872,895	976,211	1,847,434	871,560	975,874	..	..	..	1,672	1,335	337
13 North-West Frontier Province.	24	23	1	414	366	48	..	..	..	..	..	..	414	366	48
(Districts and Administered Territories.)															
14 Punjab	..	..	..	2,613	1,501	1,112	106	56	50	..	..	..	2,497	1,440	1,057
15 United Provinces of Agra and Oudh.	112	74	38	27,471	14,411	13,060	242	158	84	74	46	28	26,933	14,096	12,837
States and Agencies ..	**60,774**	**31,934**	**28,840**	**4,560,930**	**2,273,396**	**2,287,534**	**3,529,231**	**1,733,047**	**1,796,184**	**193,275**	**97,572**	**95,703**	**835,328**	**440,942**	**394,386**
16 Assam States ..	..	..	..	7,417	4,863	2,554	48	29	19	..	..	..	5,651	3,936	1,715
17 Baluchistan States ..	1	1	..	..	..	..	..	..	..	..	..	..	..	..	..
18 Baroda State	263	168	95	200	152	48	7	6	1	..	..	..	193	146	47
19 Bengal States	..	..	..	746,928	395,828	351,100	5,523	3,446	2,077	..	..	..	740,086	391,461	348,625
20 Bihar and Orissa States..	..	..	..	3,675,255	1,807,576	1,867,679	3,399,610	1,668,064	1,731,546	189,854	96,355	93,499	85,790	43,156	42,634
21 Bombay States ..	8,719	3,843	4,876	337	80	257	..	..	..	267	61	206	17	9	8
22 Central India Agency ..	462	243	219	1,476	772	704	31	28	3	718	318	400	727	426	301
23 Central Provinces States ..	..	..	..	123,100	61,022	62,078	122,518	60,697	61,821	10	10	..	572	315	257
24 Gwalior State	..	..	..	242	138	104	..	..	..	..	..	..	242	138	104
25 Hyderabad State ..	192	84	108	252	142	110	55	35	20	..	..	..	195	105	90
26 Jammu and Kashmir State	1	1	..	66	41	25	..	..	..	..	..	..	66	41	25
27 Madras States Agency.	34,527	17,446	17,081	191	181	10	15	11	4	..	..	..	176	170	6
Cochin State ..	*22,350*	*11,322*	*11,028*	*3*	*3*	..	..	..	..	..	..	..	*3*	*3*	..
Travancore State ..	*12,175*	*6,122*	*6,053*	*167*	*163*	*4*	..	..	..	..	..	..	*167*	*163*	*4*
Other Madras States ..	*2*	*2*	..	*21*	*15*	*6*	*15*	*11*	*4*	..	..	..	*6*	*4*	*2*
28 Mysore State	16,295	9,912	6,383	1,596	825	771	1,388	709	679	1	1	..	207	115	92
29 North-West Frontier Province.	2	2	..	21	21	..	..	..	..	..	..	..	21	21	..
(Agencies and Tribal Areas.)															
30 Punjab States ..	..	..	..	53	32	21	21	9	12	..	..	..	32	23	9
31 Punjab States Agency ..	..	..	..	139	77	62	1	1	..	..	..	..	138	76	62
32 Rajputana Agency ..	11	5	6	3,260	1,318	1,942	14	12	2	2,425	827	1,598	818	476	342
33 Sikkim State	..	..	..	18	12	6	..	..	..	..	..	..	18	12	6
34 United Provinces States	..	..	..	297	265	32	..	..	..	..	..	..	297	265	32
35 Western India States Agency.	301	229	72	82	51	31	..	..	..	..	..	..	82	51	31

* Includes Hindustani.

Table XV.—Language—Part I—Mother Tongue—*contd.*

Indo-European Family—*contd.*
Aryan Sub-Family—*contd.*
Indo-Aryan Branch—*contd.*

Province, State or Agency.	Outer Sub-Branch—*concld.* Eastern Group—*concld.* Assamese.			Mediate Sub-Branch. Mediate Group. Eastern Hindi.			Inner Sub-Branch. Inner Sub-Branch Total.			Inner Sub-Branch. Central Group. Central Group Total.		
	Persons.	Males.	Females.	Persons.	Males.	Females.	Persons.	Males.	Females.	Persons.	Males.	Females.
1	734	735	736	737	738	739	740	741	742	743	744	745
INDIA ..	**1,999,057**	**1,042,462**	**956,595**	**7,867,103**	**4,210,310**	**3,656,793**	**117,309,178**	**62,124,448**	**55,184,730**	**114,556,746**	**60,652,042**	**53,904,704**
Provinces ..	1,995,961	1,040,627	955,334	5,463,602	3,017,571	2,446,031	79,818,038	42,505,821	37,312,217	78,666,945	41,871,403	36,795,542
1 Ajmer-Merwara ..	1	1	..	855	504	351	553,627	291,883	261,744	553,442	291,738	261,704
2 Andaman and Nicobar Islands.	8	8	..	..	..	..	9,306	6,691	2,615	9,300	6,685	2,615
3 Assam	1,992,846	1,038,309	954,537	587,234	334,233	253,001	145,441	90,490	54,951	21,609	15,361	6,248
4 Baluchistan .. (*Districts and Administered Territories*).	..	..	..	39	26	13	45,215	33,186	12,029	37,351	26,937	10,414
5 Bengal	1,431	1,116	315	1,612,016	1,084,709	527,307	426,722	262,884	163,838	293,571	191,351	102,220
6 Bihar and Orissa ..	30	21	9	..	..	..	39,090	24,277	14,813	31,679	19,295	12,384
7 Bombay (*including Aden*)	206	191	15	20,929	10,381	10,548	5,797,429	3,133,972	2,663,457	5,792,184	3,130,917	2,661,267
Aden	..	..	..	..	..	..	*7,741*	*4,739*	*3,002*	*7,741*	*4,739*	*3,002*
8 Burma	1,203	862	341	..	..	..	279,720	207,158	72,562	238,370	178,892	59,478
9 Central Provinces and Berar	..	..	..	3,239,030	1,585,999	1,653,031	5,259,506	2,666,627	2,592,879	5,258,720	2,666,134	2,592,586
10 Coorg	..	..	..	..	..	..	4,446	2,449	1,997	4,446	2,449	1,997
11 Delhi	4	3	1	..	..	..	619,841	359,069	260,772	618,039	357,647	260,392
12 Madras	..	..	..	3,278	1,568	1,710	1,403,292	719,315	683,977	1,403,102	719,185	683,917
13 North-West Frontier Province. (*Districts and Administered Territories*).	..	..	..	221	151	70	93,164	68,468	24,696	87,992	64,506	23,486
14 Punjab	10	5	5	..	..	..	16,809,753	9,241,705	7,568,048	16,016,674	8,826,956	7,189,718
15 United Provinces of Agra and Oudh.	222	111	111	..	..	..	48,331,486	25,397,647	22,933,839	48,300,466	25,373,350	22,927,116
States and Agencies ..	3,096	1,835	1,261	2,403,501	1,192,739	1,210,762	37,491,140	19,618,627	17,872,513	35,889,801	18,780,639	17,109,162
16 Assam States ..	1,718	898	820	2,607	1,654	951	13,056	8,861	4,195	706	483	223
17 Baluchistan States ..	..	..	..	..	..	..	441	310	131	404	273	131
18 Baroda State ..	..	..	..	3	3	..	2,386,479	1,227,654	1,158,825	2,386,327	1,227,529	1,158,798
19 Bengal States ..	1,319	921	398	23,276	14,014	9,262	3,504	2,373	1,131	2,508	1,799	709
20 Bihar and Orissa States ..	1	1	..	..	..	..	5,656	2,915	2,741	5,574	2,857	2,717
21 Bombay States ..	53	10	43	1,120	710	410	1,839,644	947,666	891,978	1,838,093	946,729	891,364
22 Central India Agency ..	..	..	..	1,490,431	745,909	744,522	4,715,008	2,441,754	2,273,254	4,714,652	2,441,487	2,273,165
23 Central Provinces States ..	..	..	..	868,727	421,184	447,543	791,683	400,083	391,600	791,524	400,007	391,517
24 Gwalior State	..	..	..	7,707	3,654	4,053	3,469,648	1,837,453	1,632,195	3,469,350	1,837,272	1,632,078
25 Hyderabad State ..	2	2	..	540	315	225	1,899,258	990,796	908,462	1,899,258	990,796	908,462
26 Jammu and Kashmir State	..	..	..	3	1	2	1,841,456	972,371	869,085	1,207,007	644,622	562,385
27 Madras States Agency ..	..	..	..	..	..	..	25,078	12,880	12,198	25,077	12,879	12,198
Cochin State ..	..	..	..	..	..	..	*3,827*	*2,034*	*1,793*	*3,827*	*2,034*	*1,793*
Travancore State ..	..	..	..	..	..	..	*6,904*	*3,666*	*3,238*	*6,903*	*3,665*	*3,238*
Other Madras States ..	..	..	..	..	..	..	*14,347*	*7,180*	*7,167*	*14,347*	*7,180*	*7,167*
28 Mysore State ..	..	..	..	6,915	3,909	3,006	447,483	236,189	211,294	447,473	236,186	211,287
29 North-West Frontier Province. (*Agencies and Tribal Areas.*)	..	..	..	7	7	..	28,486	27,909	577	23,309	22,732	577
30 Punjab States	..	..	..	..	..	..	407,604	215,077	192,527	143,258	77,969	65,289
31 Punjab States Agency ..	..	..	..	..	..	..	3,603,815	1,972,671	1,631,144	2,962,088	1,635,608	1,326,480
32 Rajputana Agency ..	3	3	..	1,715	1,007	708	11,193,610	5,868,459	5,325,151	11,192,931	5,867,963	5,324,968
33 Sikkim State ..	..	..	..	450	370	80	39,234	20,001	19,233	368	308	60
34 United Provinces States	..	..	..	..	..	..	1,205,649	617,813	587,836	1,205,602	617,788	587,814
35 Western India States Agency	..	..	..	..	..	..	3,574,348	1,815,392	1,758,956	3,574,292	1,815,352	1,758,940

Table XV.—Language—Part I—Mother Tongue—*contd.*

Indo-European Family—*contd.*
Aryan Sub-Family—*contd.*
Indo-Aryan Branch—*contd.*
Inner Sub-Branch—*contd.*
Central Group—*concld.*

	Province, State or Agency.	Western Hindi.			Rajasthani.			Gujarati.			Bhili.			Khandesi.		
		Persons.	Males.	Females.	Persons.	Males.	Females.	Persons.	Males.	Females.	Persons.	Males.	Females.	Persons.	Males.	Females.
	1	746	747	748	749	750	751	752	753	754	755	756	757	758	759	760
	INDIA	**71,547,071**	**37,743,130**	**33,803,941**	**13,897,896**	**7,271,204**	**6,626,692**	**10,849,984**	**5,610,012**	**5,239,972**	**2,189,531**	**1,110,410**	**1,079,121**	**233,010**	**118,252**	**114,758**
	Provinces ..	**60,348,239**	**31,854,631**	**28,493,608**	**1,619,771**	**865,151**	**754,620**	**3,635,598**	**1,921,675**	**1,713,923**	**403,491**	**203,491**	**200,000**	**222,207**	**112,796**	**109,411**
1	Ajmer-Merwara	122,848	67,097	55,751	427,691	222,725	204,966	1,626	969	657	20	16	4	1	..	1
2	Andaman and Nicobar Islands	6,929	4,814	2,115	..	..	..	139	122	17	..	..	..	..	..	..
3	Assam	..	..	..	15,854	11,376	4,478	2,033	1,138	895	448	269	179	..	..	..
4	Baluchistan .. .. (*Districts and Administered Territories.*)	16,939	12,521	4,418	524	323	201	615	405	210	..	..	..	..	..	..
5	Bengal	253,674	163,372	90,302	18,876	12,397	6,479	6,505	4,462	2,043	..	..	..	..	..	..
6	Bihar and Orissa	..	..	..	17,945	10,132	7,813	5,304	3,412	1,892	..	..	..	..	..	..
7	Bombay (*including Aden*) ..	1,399,277	804,949	594,328	293,422	167,957	125,465	3,426,127	1,805,811	1,620,316	372,160	187,749	184,411	222,168	112,771	109,397
	Aden	*4,946*	*2,893*	*2,053*	..	..	..	*2,618*	*1,702*	*916*	..	..	..	..	..	..
8	Burma	192,567	145,589	46,978	388	153	235	17,706	12,511	5,195	..	..	..	..	..	..
9	Central Provinces and Berar	4,825.293	2,432,735	2,392,558	336,648	178,179	158,469	56,249	32,686	23,563	30,732	15,383	15,349	38	25	13
10	Coorg	4,382	2,405	1,977	7	7	..	53	33	20	..	..	..	..	..	..
11	Delhi	586,967	336,827	250,140	6,730	3,796	2,934	833	535	298	..	..	..	..	..	..
12	Madras	1,237,523	635,599	601,924	53,784	28,116	25,668	111,770	55,456	56,314	25	14	11	..	..	..
13	North-West Frontier Province (*Districts and Administered Territories.*)	19,221	13,915	5,306	596	309	287	144	56	88	..	..	..	..	..	..
14	Punjab	3,431,393	1,893,670	1,537,723	428.894	218,515	210,379	2,382	1,640	742	4	3	1	..	..	..
15	United Provinces of Agra and Oudh.	48,251,226	25,341,138	22,910,088	18,412	11,166	7,246	4,112	2,439	1,673	102	57	45	..	..	..
	States and Agencies ..	**11,198,832**	**5,888,499**	**5,310,333**	**12,278,125**	**6,406,053**	**5,872,072**	**7,214,386**	**3,688,337**	**3,526,049**	**1,786,040**	**906,919**	**879,121**	**10,803**	**5,456**	**5,347**
16	Assam States	..	..	..	391	237	154	2	1	1	..	..	..	..	..	..
17	Baluchistan States ..	153	109	44	6	2	4	3	3	..	..	..	..	..	..	..
18	Baroda State	78,188	42,684	35,504	7,246	4,389	2,857	2,119,551	1,088.238	1,031,313	180,384*	91,427	88,957	38	12	26
19	Bengal States	1,692	1,177	515	698	528	170	89	71	18	..	..	..	..	..	..
20	Bihar and Orissa States ..	..	..	..	4,339	2,052	2,287	900	570	330	..	..	..	..	..	..
21	Bombay States	167,075	85,545	81,530	9,517	5,555	3,962	1,453,228	748,110	705,118	207,168	106,796	100,372	..	..	..
22	Central India Agency ..	2,405,677	1,253,929	1,151,748	1,646,881	850,226	796,655	63,292	33,071	30,221	584,014	296,018	287,996	10,680	5,402	5,278
23	Central Provinces States	780,168	393,842	386,326	9,900	5,243	4,657	1,062	662	400	24	14	10	..	..	..
24	Gwalior State	2,228,829	1,192,752	1,036,077	1,133,081	588,288	544,793	28,661	17,093	11,568	75,469	37,200	38,269	..	..	..
25	Hyderabad State ..	1,573,630	819,138	754,492	270,868	141,034	129,834	33,915	18,069	15,846	16,285	8,925	7,360	..	..	..
26	Jammu and Kashmir State	6,257	3,499	2,758	320,345	171,917	148,428	289	235	54	66	31	35	..	..	..
27	Madras States Agency ..	19,647	10,063	9,584	639	312	327	4.710	2,437	2,273	..	..	..	..	..	..
	Cochin State	*2,565*	*1,340*	*1,225*	*1*	*1*	..	*1,261*	*693*	*568*	..	..	..	..	..	..
	Travancore State ..	*4,552*	*2,426*	*2,126*	..	..	..	*2,275*	*1,175*	*1,100*	..	..	..	..	..	..
	Other Madras States ..	*12,530*	*6,297*	*6,233*	*638*	*311*	*327*	*1,174*	*569*	*605*	..	..	..	..	..	..
28	Mysore State	382,876	202,493	180,383	59,711	30,845	28,866	4,600	2,604	1,996	11	6	5	..	..	..
29	North-West Frontier Province (*Agencies and Tribal Areas.*)	4,521	4,436	85	..	..	..	93	93	..	..	..	..	..	..	..
30	Punjab States	97,185	52,422	44,763	44	23	21	7	3	4	..	..	..	..	..	..
31	Punjab States Agency ..	459,445	246,529	212,916	184,506	97,016	87,490	132	91	41	2,938	1,652	1,286	..	..	..
32	Rajputana Agency ..	1,721,186	926,351	794,835	8,606,659	4,496,024	4,110,635	20,064	9,971	10,093	719,640	364,830	354,810	85	42	43
33	Sikkim State	86	84	2	264	210	54	..	..	..	..	..	..	..	..	..
34	United Provinces States ..	1,205,101	617,474	587,627	8	7	1	2	2	..	..	..	..	..	..	..
35	Western India States Agency	67,116	35,972	31,144	23,022	12,145	10,877	3,483,786	1,767,013	1,716,773	41	20	21	..	..	..

* Includes Kathodi .. .. 428 Persons. 216 males, 212 females.
Varli .. .. 483 ,, 262 males, 221 females.
Vasavi .. .. 11,025 ,, 5,570 males, 5,455 females.

Table XV.—Language—Part I—Mother Tongue—*contd.*

Indo-European Family—*contd.*
Aryan Sub-Family—*contd.*
Indo-Aryan Branch—*concld.*
Inner Sub-Branch—*concld.*

	Province, State or Agency.	Central Group—*concld.* Panjabi. Persons.	Males.	Females.	Pahari Group. Pahari Group Total. Persons.	Males.	Females.	Central Pahari. Persons.	Males.	Females.	Eastern Pahari, Khas-Kura or Naipali. Persons.	Males.	Females.	Western Pahari. Persons.	Males.	Females.	Pahari (Unspecified). Persons.	Males.	Females.
	1	761	762	763	764	765	766	767	768	769	770	771	772	773	774	775	776	777	778
	INDIA	**15,839,254**	**8,799,034**	**7,040,220**	**2,752,432**	**1,472,406**	**1,280,026**	**7,170**	**6,180**	**990**	**412,951**	**251,266**	**161,685**	**2,325,916**	**1,211,008**	**1,114,908**	**6,395**	**3,952**	**2,443**
	Provinces	12,437,639	6,913,659	5,523,980	1,151,093	634,418	516,675	6,720	5,853	867	351,617	214,803	136,814	788,727	411,563	377,164	4,029	2,199	1,830
	Ajmer-Merwara	1,256	931	325	185	145	40	48	48	.	84	51	33	..	..	..	53	46	7
	Andaman and Nicobar Island.	2,232	1,749	483	6	6	..	..	..	..	2	2	..	..	..	..	4	4	..
	Assam	3,274	2,578	696	123,832	75,129	48,703	44	36	8	123,788	75,093	48,695	..	..	.	..	..	..
	Baluchistan	19,273	13,688	5,585	7,864	6,249	1,615	3,132	2,866	266	4,653	3,309	1,344	25	24	1	54	50	4
	(Districts and Administered Territories.)																		
	Bengal	14,516	11,120	3,396	133,151	71,533	61,618	..	..	..	133,151	71,533	61,618	..	..	..	..	..	..
	Bihar and Orissa	8,430	5,751	2,679	7,411	4,982	2,429	..	..	..	7,411	4,982	2,429	..	..	..	..	..	..
	Bombay (*including Aden*)	79,030	51,680	27,350	5,245	3,055	2,190	..	..	..	1,413	1,024	389	..	..	..	3,832	2,031	1,801
	Aden	*177*	*144*	*33*	..	..	..	..	..	..	..	..	..	..	..	..	..	..	..
	Burma	27,709	20,639	7,070	41,350	28,266	13,084	2,969	2,542	427	38,381	25,724	12,657	..	..	..	..	..	..
	Central Provinces and Berar	9,760	7,126	2,634	786	493	293	256	129	127	476	324	152	..	..	..	54	40	14
	Coorg	4	4	..	..	..	..	..	..	..	..	..	..	..	..	..	..	..	..
	Delhi	23,509	16,489	7,020	1,802	1,422	380	12	12	..	146	72	74	1,644	1,338	306	.	..	..
	Madras	..	..	..	190	130	60	..	..	..	190	130	60	..	..	..	..	..	..
	North-West Frontier Province.	68,031	50,226	17,805	5,172	3,962	1,210	..	..	..	5,140	3,934	1,206	..	..	..	32	28	4
	(Districts and Administered Territories.)																		
4	Punjab	12,154,001	6,713,128	5,440,873	793,079	414,749	378,330	259	220	39	5,762	4,328	1,434	787,058	410,201	376,857	..	..	..
5	United Provinces of Agra and Oudh.	26,614	18,550	8,064	31,020	24,297	6,723	..	..	..	31,020	24,297	6,723	..	..	..	..	..	..
	States and Agencies	3,401,615	1,885,375	1,516,240	1,601,339	837,988	763,351	450	327	123	61,334	36,463	24,871	1,537,189	799,445	737,744	2,366	1,753	613
6	Assam States	313	245	68	12,350	8,378	3,972	32	22	10	12,318	8,356	3,962	..	..	..	..	..	..
7	Baluchistan States	242	159	83	37	37	..	37	37	..	..	..	..	..	..	..	..	..	..
8	Baroda State	920	779	141	152	125	27	..	..	..	152*	125	27	..	..	..	..	..	..
9	Bengal States	29	23	6	996	574	422	..	..	..	996	574	422	..	..	..	..	..	..
0	Bihar and Orissa States	335	235	100	82	58	24	..	..	..	82	58	24	..	..	..	..	..	..
1	Bombay States	1,105	723	382	1,551	937	614	..	..	..	200	134	66	..	..	..	1,351	803	548
2	Central India Agency	4,108	2,841	1,267	356	267	89	132	95	37	224	172	52	..	..	..	..	..	..
3	Central Provinces States	370	246	124	159	76	83	..	..	..	159	76	83	..	..	..	..	..	..
4	Gwalior State	3,310	1,939	1,371	298	181	117	..	..	..	53	39	14	245	142	103	..	..	..
5	Hyderabad State	4,560	3,630	930	..	..	..	..	..	..	..	..	..	..	..	..	..	..	..
6	Jammu and Kashmir State	880,050	468,940	411,110	634,449	327,749	306,700	3	3	..	1,120	810	310	633,326	326,936	306,390	..	..	..
7	Madras States Agency	81	67	14	1	1	..	..	..	..	1	1	..	..	..	..	..	..	..
	Cochin State	..	..	..	..	..	..	..	..	..	..	..	..	..	..	..	..	..	..
	Travancore State	*76*	*64*	*12*	*1*	*1*	..	..	..	..	*1*	*1*	..	..	..	..	..	..	..
	Other Madras States	*5*	*3*	*2*	..	..	..	..	..	..	..	..	..	..	..	..	..	..	..
28	Mysore State	275	238	37	10	3	7	..	..	..	..	..	..	..	..	..	10	3	7
29	North-West Frontier Province.	18,695	18,203	492	5,177	5,177	..	..	..	..	4,591	4,591	..	..	..	..	586	586	..
	(Agencies and Tribal Areas.)																		
30	Punjab States	46,022	25,521	20,501	264,346	137,108	127,238	2	..	2	217	187	30	264,127	136,921	127,206	..	..	..
31	Punjab States Agency	2,315,067	1,290,320	1,024,747	641,727	337,063	304,664	193	123	70	2,043	1,494	549	639,491	335,446	304,045	..	..	..
32	Rajputana Agency	125,297†	70,745	54,552	679	496	183	51	47	4	245	120	125	..	..	..	333	329	54
33	Sikkim State	18	14	4	38,866	19,693	19,173	..	..	..	38,866	19,693	19,173	..	..	..	..	..	..
34	United Provinces States	491	305	186	47	25	22	..	..	..	47	25	22	..	..	..	..	..	..
35	Western India States Agency	327	202	125	56	40	16	..	..	..	20	8	12	..	..	..	36	32	4

*Includes Garhwali.

† Includes Western Punjabi.

Table XV.– Language—Part I—Mother Tongue—*contd.*

Unclassed Languages.

	Province, State or Agency.	Unclassed Languages Total. Persons.	Males.	Females.	Andamanese. Persons.	Males.	Females.	Gipsy Languages. Persons.	Males.	Females.	Others (Indian unspecified or Language not returned). Persons.	Males.	Females.	B.—Vernaculars of other Asiatic countries and Africa. Total. Persons.	Males.	Females.
	1	779	780	781	782	783	784	785	786	787	788	789	790	791	792	793
	INDIA	**54,453**	**29,322**	**25,131**	**466**	**251**	**215**	**25,999**	**13,079**	**12,920**	**1,912**	**1,314**	**598**	**302,324**	**197,655**	**104,669**
	Provinces	16,040	8,435	7,605	466	251	215	13,845	6,989	6,856	1,729	1,195	534	287,701	188,922	98,779
1	Ajmer-Merwara	306	175	131	..	..	..	306	175	131	..	..	..	54	36	18
2	Andaman and Nicobar Islands	691	473	218	466	251	215	..	..	..	225	222	3	329	316	13
3	Assam	..	..	..	..	..	..	..	..	..	..	..	..	872	697	175
4	Baluchistan (*Districts and Administered Territories.*)	58	33	25	..	..	..	58	33	25	..	..	..	4,967	3,415	1,552
5	Bengal	..	..	..	..	..	..	..	..	..	..	..	..	9,693	6,995	2,698
6	Bihar and Orissa	603	279	324	..	..	..	603	279	324	..	..	..	376	274	102
7	Bombay (*including Aden*)	5,060	2,669	2,391	..	..	..	3,563	1,699	1,864	1,497	970	527	70,632	45,829	24,803
	Aden	..	..	..	..	..	..	..	..	..	..	..	..	*40,768*	*25,231*	*15,537*
8	Burma	..	..	..	..	..	..	..	..	..	..	..	..	181,145	120,257	60,888
9	Central Provinces and Berar	4,055	1,979	2,076	..	..	..	4,048	1,976	2,072	7	3	4	1,156	749	407
10	Coorg	..	..	..	..	..	..	..	..	..	..	..	..	19	11	8
11	Delhi	..	..	..	..	..	..	..	..	..	..	..	..	162	114	48
12	Madras	18	2	16	..	..	..	18	2	16	..	..	..	6,730	3,516	3,214
13	North-West Frontier Province (*Districts and Administered Territories.*)	..	..	..	..	..	..	..	..	..	..	..	..	6,122	3,664	2,458
14	Punjab	4,952	2,629	2,323	..	..	..	4,952	2,629	2,323	..	..	..	4,662	2,538	2,124
15	United Provinces of Agra and Oudh.	297	196	101	..	..	..	297	196	101	..	..	..	782*	511	271
					Burushaski.											
	States and Agencies	38,413	20,887	17,526	26,076	14,678	11,398	12,154	6,090	6.064	183	119	64	14,623	8,733	5,890
16	Assam States	..	..	..	..	..	..	..	..	..	..	..	..	25	21	4
17	Baluchistan States	59	33	26	..	..	..	59	33	26	..	..	..	112	64	48
18	Baroda State	121	68	53	..	..	..	121	68	53	..	..	..	147	116	31
19	Bengal States	..	..	..	..	..	..	..	..	..	..	..	..	94	71	23
20	Bihar and Orissa States	84	48	36	..	..	..	84	48	36	..	..	..	49	34	15
21	Bombay States	90	45	45	..	..	..	90	45	45	..	..	..	400	240	160
22	Central India Agency	2,404	1,229	1,175	..	..	..	2,404	1,229	1,175	..	..	..	513	281	232
23	Central Provinces States	12	7	5	..	..	..	11	6	5	1	1	..	17	8	9
24	Gwalior State	..	..	..	..	..	..	..	..	..	..	..	..	445	340	105
25	Hyderabad State	475	232	243	..	..	..	421	202	219	54	30	24	3,486	2,110	1,376
26	Jammu and Kashmir State	26,177	14,732	11,445	26,076	14,678	11,398	101	51	47	..	..	..	400	285	115
27	Madras States Agency	126	88	38	..	..	..	..	..	..	126	88	38	4,136	2,281	1,855
	Cochin State	*13*	*11*	*2*	..	..	..	..	..	..	*13*	*11*	*2*	*515*	*273*	*242*
	Travancore State	*113*	*77*	*36*	..	..	..	..	..	..	*113*	*77*	*36*	*3,596*	*1,993*	*1,603*
	Other Madras States	..	..	..	..	..	..	..	..	..	..	..	..	*25*	*15*	*10*
28	Mysore State	31	17	14	..	..	..	31	17	14	..	..	..	1,095	783	312
29	North-West Frontier Province (*Agencies and Tribal Areas.*)	..	..	..	..	..	..	..	..	..	..	..	..	350	210	140
30	Punjab States	..	..	..	..	..	..	..	..	..	..	..	..	12	3	9
31	Punjab States Agency	..	..	..	..	..	..	..	..	..	..	..	..	202	173	29
32	Rajputana Agency	8,766	4,370	4,396	..	..	..	8,766	4,370	4,396	..	..	..	127	86	41
33	Sikkim State	..	..	..	..	..	..	..	..	..	..	..	..	29	17	12
34	United Provinces States	..	..	..	..	..	..	..	..	..	..	..	..	3	3	..
35	Western India States Agency.	68	18	50	..	..	..	66	18	48	2	..	2	2,981	1,607	1,374

* Includes 4 persons (3 males and 1 female) enumerated in the United Provinces States.

Table XV.—Language—Part I—Mother Tongue—*contd*

Indo-European Family.
Aryan-Sub-Family.

Province, State or Agency.	Indo-European Family. Aryan Sub-Family Total. Persons.	Males.	Females.	Indo-Aryan Branch. Southern Group. Outer Sub-Branch. Southern Group Total. Persons.	Males.	Females.	Sinhalese. Persons.	Males.	Females.	Eranian Branch. Eranian Branch Total. Persons	Males.	Females.	Persian Group. Persian. Persons.	Males.	Females.
1	794	795	796	797	798	799	800	801	802	803	804	805	806	807	808
INDIA	**39,224**	**25,359**	**13,865**	**3,849**	**2,006**	**1,843**	**3,849**	**2,006**	**1,843**	**35,375**	**23,353**	**12,022**	**34,361**	**22,826**	**11,535**
Provinces	34,939	22,856	12,083	3,744	1,941	1,803	3,744	1,941	1,803	31,195	20,915	10,280	30,200	20,403	9,797
1 Ajmer-Merwara	19	16	3	1	1	..	1	1	..	18	15	3	18	15	3
2 Andaman and Nicobar Islands.	..	..	..	..	..	..	..	..	..	..	..	..	..	..	..
3 Assam	268	215	53	..	..	..	..	..	..	268	215	53	268	215	53
4 Baluchistan .. .. (*Districts and Administered Territories.*)	4,911	3,383	1,528	..	..	..	..	..	..	4,911	3,383	1,528	4,911	3,383	1,528
5 Bengal	1,754	1,106	648	25	25	..	25	25	..	1,729	1,081	648	1,029	753	276
6 Bihar and Orissa ..	172	133	39	..	..	..	..	..	..	172	133	39	87	83	4
7 Bombay (*including Aden*)	12,105	9,247	2,858	271	241	30	271	241	30	11,834	9,006	2,828	11,822	8,997	2,825
Aden	*57*	*40*	*17*	*6*	*6*	..	*6*	*6*	..	*51*	*34*	*17*	*50*	*33*	*17*
8 Burma	1,063	665	398	152	128	24	155	128	24	911	537	374	724	421	303
9 Central Provinces and Berar.	670	387	283	7	3	4	7	3	4	663	384	279	663	384	279
10 Coorg	..	..	..	..	..	..	..	..	..	..	..	..	..	..	..
11 Delhi	105	69	36	..	..	..	..	..	..	105	69	36	105	69	36
12 Madras	3,423	1,626	1,797	3,284	1,541	1,743	3,284	1,541	1,743	139	85	54	132	80	52
13 North-West Frontier Province (*Districts and Administered Territories*).	6,030	3,615	2,415	..	..	..	..	..	..	6,030	3,615	2,415	6,030	3,615	2,415
14 Punjab	3,833	2,009	1,824	1	1	..	1	1	..	3,832	2,008	1,824	3,832	2,008	1,824
15 United Provinces of Agra and Oudh.	586	385	201	3	1	2	3	1	2	583	384	199	579	380	199
States and Agencies ..	4,285	2,503	1,782	105	65	40	105	65	40	4,180	2,438	1,742	4,161	2,423	1,738
16 Assam States ..	..	..	..	..	..	..	..	..	..	..	..	..	..	..	..
17 Baluchistan States ..	110	62	48	..	..	..	..	..	..	110	62	48	109	61	48
18 Baroda State	1	1	..	1	1	..	1	1	..	..	..	..	..	..	..
19 Bengal States ..	87	64	23	..	..	..	..	..	..	87	64	23	87	64	23
20 Bihar and Orissa States	24	21	3	..	..	..	..	..	..	24	21	3	18	16	2
21 Bombay States ..	34	23	11	..	..	..	..	..	..	34	23	11	34	23	11
22 Central India Agency ..	216	126	90	..	..	..	..	..	..	216	126	90	216	126	90
23 Central Provinces States ..	7	3	4	..	..	..	..	..	..	7	3	4	7	3	4
24 Gwalior State	190	152	38	..	..	..	..	..	..	190	152	38	190	152	38
25 Hyderabad State ..	292	165	127	3	3	..	3	3	..	289	162	127	282	156	126
26 Jammu and Kashmir State. ..	296	196	100	..	..	..	..	..	..	296	196	100	296	196	100
27 Madras States Agency ..	103	75	28	62	34	28	62	34	28	41	41	..	41	41	..
Cochin State ..	*8*	*3*	*5*	*7*	*2*	*5*	*7*	*2*	*5*	*1*	*1*	..	*1*	*1*	..
Travancore State ..	*94*	*71*	*23*	*54*	*31*	*23*	*54*	*31*	*23*	*40*	*40*	..	*40*	*40*	..
Other Madras States ..	*1*	*1*	..	*1*	*1*	..	*1*	*1*	..	..	..	..	..	..	..
28 Mysore State ..	319	179	140	39	27	12	39	27	12	280	152	128	275	149	126
29 North-West Frontier Province (*Agencies and Tribal Areas.*)	350	210	140	..	..	..	..	..	..	350	210	140	350	210	140
30 Punjab States	11	3	8	..	..	..	..	..	..	11	3	8	11	3	8
31 Punjab States Agency ..	157	147	10	..	..	..	..	..	..	157	147	10	157	147	10
32 Rajputana Agency ..	99	71	28	..	..	..	..	..	..	99	71	28	99	71	28
33 Sikkim State ..	..	..	..	..	..	..	..	..	..	..	..	..	..	..	..
34 United Provinces States	3	3	..	..	..	..	..	..	..	3	3	..	3	3	..
35 Western India States Agency.	1,986	1,002	984	..	..	..	..	..	..	1,986	1,002	984	1,986	1,002	984

Table XV.—Language—Part I—Mother Tongue—*contd.*

Province, State or Agency.	Indo-European Family—*concld.* Arayn Sub-Family—*concld.* Eranian Branch—*concld.* Armenian Group. Armenian. Persons.	Males.	Females.	Tibeto-Chinese Family. Tai-Chinese Sub-Family. Tibeto-Chinese Family Total. Tai-Chinese Sub-Family Total. Persons.	Males.	Females.	Chinese Group. Chinese Group Total. Persons.	Males.	Females.	Yunnanese. Persons.	Males.	Females.
1	809	810	811	812	813	814	815	816	817	818	819	820
INDIA	**1,014**	**527**	**487**	**185,822**	**124,284**	**61,538**	**185,815**	**124,282**	**61,533**	**67,235**	**40,487**	**26,748**
Provinces .. .	995	512	483	185,673	124,184	61,489	185,666	124,182	61,484	67,235	40,487	26,748
1 Ajmer-Merwara	..	..	..	8	6	2	8	6	2	..	..	..
2 Andaman and Nicobar Islands ..	..	..	..	199	187	12	199	187	12	..	..	..
3 Assam	..	..	..	507	408	99	507	408	99	..	..	..
4 Baluchistan	..	..	..	40	21	19	40	21	19	..	..	..
Districts and Administered Territories.)												
5 Bengal	700	328	372	4,645	3,723	922	4,643	3,723	920	..	..	..
6 Bihar and Orissa	85	50	35	78	59	19	78	59	19	..	..	..
7 Bombay (*including Aden*) ..	12	9	3	1,524	1,024	500	1,524	1,024	500	..	..	..
Aden	*1*	*1*	..	*32*	*27*	*5*	*32*	*27*	*5*	..	..	..
8 Burma	187	116	71	178,324	118,507	59,817	178,324	118,507	59,817	67,235	40,487	26,748
9 Central Provinces and Berar ..	..	..	..	24	16	8	24	16	8	..	..	..
10 Coorg	..	..	..	..	..	..	..	..	..	..	..	..
11 Delhi	..	..	..	13	12	1	13	12	1	..	..	..
12 Madras	7	5	2	102	86	16	98	84	14	..	..	..
13 North-West Frontier Province (*Districts and Administered Territories*). ..	..	..	..	5	..	5	5	..	5	..	..	..
14 Punjab	..	..	..	124	87	37	123	87	36	..	..	..
15 United Provinces of Agra and Oudh	4	4	..	80	48	32	80	48	32	..	..	..
States and Agencies ..	**19**	**15**	**4**	**149**	**100**	**49**	**149**	**100**	**49**	..	..	..
16 Assam States	..	..	..	25	21	4	25	21	4	..	..	..
17 Baluchistan States	1	1	..	..	..	..	..	..	..	..	..	..
18 Baroda State	..	..	..	..	..	..	..	..	..	..	..	..
19 Bengal States	..	..	..	..	..	..	..	..	..	..	..	..
20 Bihar and Orissa States ..	6	5	1	..	..	..	..	..	..	..	..	..
21 Bombay States	..	..	..	6	..	6	6	..	6	..	..	..
22 Central India Agency	..	..	..	14	14	..	14	14	..	..	..	..
23 Central Provinces States	..	..	..	3	1	2	3	1	2	..	..	..
24 Gwalior State	..	..	..	..	..	..	..	..	..	..	..	..
25 Hyderabad State	7	6	1	12	8	4	12	8	4	..	..	..
26 Jammu and Kashmir State ..	..	..	..	3	2	1	3	2	1	..	..	..
27 Madras States Agency	..	..	..	4	4	..	4	4	..	..	..	..
Cochin State	..	..	..	*1*	*1*	..	*1*	*1*	..	..	..	..
Travancore State	..	..	..	*3*	*3*	..	*3*	*3*	..	..	..	..
Other Madras States	..	..	..	..	..	..	..	..	..	..	..	..
28 Mysore State	5	3	2	16	15	1	16	15	1	..	..	..
29 North-West Frontier Province (*Agencies and Tribal Areas*). ..	..	..	..	..	..	..	..	..	..	..	..	..
30 Punjab States	..	..	..	..	..	..	..	..	..	..	..	..
31 Punjab States Agency	..	..	..	37	18	19	37	18	19	..	..	..
32 Rajputana Agency	..	..	..	..	..	..	..	..	..	..	..	..
33 Sikkim State	..	..	..	26	14	12	26	14	12	..	..	..
34 United Provinces States	..	..	..	..	..	..	..	..	..	..	..	..
35 Western India States Agency ..	..	..	..	3	3	..	3	3	..	..	..	..

Table XV.—Language—Part I—Mother Tongue—*contd.*

Province, State or Agency.	Tibeto-Chinese Family—*concld.* Tai-Chinese Family—*concld.* Chinese Branch—*concld.* Chinese Group—*concld.* Other Chinese Languages.			Others (Anamese).			Tai Branch. Tai Group. Siamese.			Semitic Family. Semitic Family Total.			Arabic.		
	Persons.	Males.	Females.	Persons.	Males.	Females.	Persons.	Males.	Females.	Persons.	Males.	Females.	Persons.	Males.	Females.
1	821	822	823	824	825	826	827	828	829	830	831	832	833	834	835
INDIA	**118,572**	**83,792**	**34,780**	**8**	**3**	**5**	**7**	**2**	**5**	**59,954**	**37,052**	**22,902**	**54,788**	**34,374**	**20,414**
Provinces	**118,423**	**83,692**	**34,731**	**8**	**3**	**5**	**7**	**2**	**5**	**49,982**	**31,098**	**18,884**	**45,299**	**28,665**	**16,634**
1 Ajmer-Merwara	8	6	2	..	..	..	..	..	..	23	12	11	16	8	8
2 Andaman and Nicobar Islands ..	199	177	12	..	..	..	..	..	..	1	..	1	1	..	1
3 Assam	507	408	99	..	..	..	..	..	..	96	74	22	82	67	15
4 Baluchistan	40	21	19	..	..	..	..	..	..	9	5	4	9	5	4
(*Districts and Administered Territories.*)															
5 Bengal	4,643	3,723	920	..	..	..	2	..	2	2,743	1,751	992	1,535	1,148	387
6 Bihar and Orissa	78	59	19	..	..	..	..	..	..	126	82	44	123	81	42
7 Bombay (*including Aden*) ..	1,524	1,024	500	..	..	..	..	..	..	41,597	26,059	15,538	38,654	24,505	14,149
Aden	*32*	*27*	*5*	..	..	..	..	..	..	*36,154*	*22,668*	*13,486*	*33,483*	*21,272*	*12,211*
8 Burma	111,081	78,017	33,064	8	3	5	..	..	..	1,081	590	491	579	329	250
9 Central Provinces and Berar ..	24	16	8	..	..	..	..	..	..	441	333	108	440	333	107
10 Coorg	..	..	..	..	..	..	..	..	..	19	11	8	19	11	8
11 Delhi	13	12	1	..	..	..	..	..	..	33	25	8	33	25	8
12 Madras	98	84	14	..	..	..	4	2	2	3,038	1,674	1,364	3,035	1,672	1,363
13 North-West Frontier Province ..	5	..	5	..	..	..	..	..	..	24	14	10	24	14	10
(*Districts and Administered Territories.*)															
14 Punjab	123	87	36	..	..	..	1	..	1	668	419	249	667	419	248
15 United Provinces of Agra and Oudh	80	48	32	..	..	..	..	..	..	83	49	34	82	48	34
States and Agencies	**149**	**100**	**49**	..	..	..	..	..	..	**9,972**	**5,954**	**4,018**	**9,489**	**5,709**	**3,780**
16 Assam States	25	21	4	..	..	..	..	..	..	..	..	..	..	..	..
17 Baluchistan States	..	..	..	..	..	..	..	..	..	1	1	..	..	..	..
18 Baroda State	..	..	..	..	..	..	..	..	..	91	65	26	86	61	25
19 Bengal States	..	..	..	..	..	..	..	..	..	7	7	..	7	7	..
20 Bihar and Orissa States ..	..	..	..	..	..	..	..	..	..	25	13	12	25	13	12
21 Bombay States	6	..	6	..	..	..	..	..	..	348	213	135	192	144	48
22 Central India Agency	14	14	..	..	..	..	..	..	..	276	135	141	276	135	141
23 Central Provinces States	3	1	2	..	..	..	..	..	..	7	4	3	7	4	3
24 Gwalior State	..	..	..	..	..	..	..	..	..	255	188	67	255	188	67
25 Hyderabad State	12	8	4	..	..	..	..	..	..	3,172	1,932	1,240	3,172	1,932	1,240
26 Jammu and Kashmir State .	3	2	1	..	..	..	..	..	..	11	7	4	11	7	4
27 Madras States Agency	4	4	..	..	..	..	..	..	..	4,028	2,201	1,827	3,718	2,034	1,684
Cochin State .. .	*1*	*1*	..	..	..	..	..	..	..	*505*	*268*	*237*	*236*	*129*	*107*
Travancore State .. .	*3*	*3*	..	..	..	..	..	..	..	*3,499*	*1,919*	*1,580*	*3,458*	*1,891*	*1,567*
Other Madras States ..	..	..	..	..	..	..	..	..	..	*24*	*14*	*10*	*24*	*11*	*10*
28 Mysore State	16	15	1	..	..	..	..	..	..	755	586	169	746	584	162
29 North-West Frontier Province (*Agencies and Tribal Areas*).	..	..	..	..	..	..	..	..	..	..	..	..	..	..	..
30 Punjab States	..	..	..	..	..	..	..	..	..	1	..	1	1	..	1
31 Punjab States Agency	37	18	19	..	..	..	..	..	..	7	7	..	7	7	..
32 Rajputana Agency	..	..	..	..	..	..	..	..	..	17	10	7	16	9	7
33 Sikkim State	26	14	12	..	..	..	..	..	..	3	3	..	2	2	..
34 United Provinces States	..	..	..	..	..	..	..	..	..	..	..	..	..	..	..
35 Western India States Agency ..	3	3	..	..	..	..	..	..	..	968	582	386	968	582	386

Table XV.—Language—Part I—Mother Tongue—*contd.*

	Province, State or Agency.	Semitic Family—*concld.* Hebrew. Persons.	Hebrew. Males.	Hebrew. Females.	Maltese. Persons.	Maltese. Males.	Maltese. Females.	Syriac. Persons.	Syriac. Males.	Syriac. Females.	Hamitic Family. Hamitic Family Total. Persons.	Hamitic Family Total. Males.	Hamitic Family Total. Females.	Ethiopic Group. Ethiopic Group Total. Persons.	Ethiopic Group Total. Males.	Ethiopic Group Total. Females.
	1	836	837	838	839	840	841	842	843	844	845	846	847	848	849	850
	INDIA	**5,156**	**2,672**	**2,484**	**4**	**1**	**3**	**6**	**5**	**1**	**5,039***	**2,946**	**2,093**	**5,019**	**2,938**	**2,081**
	Provinces	4,678	2,432	2,246	4	1	3	1	..	1	5,014	2,928	2,086	5,006	2,925	2,081
1	Ajmer Merwara	7	4	3	..	..	..	..	..	..	2	..	2	2	..	2
2	Andaman and Nicobar Islands ..	..	..	..	..	..	..	..	..	..	..	..	..	..	..	..
3	Assam	14	7	7	..	..	..	..	..	..	..	..	..	..	..	..
4	Baluchistan (*Districts and Administered Territories*).	..	..	..	..	..	..	..	..	..	..	..	..	..	..	..
5	Bengal	1,208	603	605	..	..	..	..	..	..	1	..	1	..	..	..
6	Bihar and Orissa	3	1	2	..	..	..	..	..	..	..	..	..	..	..	..
7	**Bombay** (*including Aden*) ..	2,943	1,554	1,389	..	..	..	..	..	..	4,995	2,916	2,079	4,995	2,916	2,079
	Aden	*2,671*	*1,396*	*1,275*	..	..	..	..	..	..	*4,438*	*2,416*	*2,022*	*4,438*	*2,416*	*2,022*
8	Burma	498	260	238	4	1	3	..	..	..	9	9	..	9	9	..
9	Central Provinces and Berar ..	1	..	1	..	..	..	..	..	..	..	..	..	..	..	..
10	Coorg	..	..	..	..	..	..	..	..	..	..	..	..	..	..	..
11	Delhi	..	..	..	..	..	..	..	..	..	..	..	..	..	..	..
12	Madras	3	2	1	..	..	..	..	..	..	..	..	..	..	..	..
13	North-West Frontier Province (*Districts and Administered Territories*).	..	..	..	..	..	..	..	..	..	..	..	..	..	..	..
14	Punjab	..	..	..	..	..	..	1	..	1	7	3	4	..	..	..
15	United Provinces of Agra and Oudh	1	1	..	..	..	..	..	..	..	..	..	..	..	..	..
	States and Agencies ..	478	240	238	..	..	..	5	5	..	25	18	7	13	13	..
16	Assam States	..	..	..	..	..	..	..	..	..	..	..	..	..	..	..
17	Baluchistan States	1	1	..	..	..	..	..	..	..	..	..	..	..	..	..
18	Baroda State	5	4	1	..	..	..	..	..	..	9	5	4	..	..	..
19	Bengal States	..	..	..	..	..	..	..	..	..	..	..	..	..	..	..
20	Bihar and Orissa States ..	..	..	..	..	..	..	..	..	..	..	..	..	..	..	..
21	Bombay States	156	69	87	..	..	..	..	..	..	..	..	..	..	..	..
22	Central India Agency ..	..	..	..	..	..	..	..	..	..	1	1	..	1	1	..
23	Central Provinces States ..	..	..	..	..	..	..	..	..	..	..	..	..	..	..	..
24	Gwalior State	..	..	..	..	..	..	..	..	..	..	..	..	..	..	..
25	Hyderabad State	..	..	..	..	..	..	..	..	..	..	..	..	..	..	..
26	Jammu and Kashmir State ..	..	..	..	..	..	..	..	..	..	..	..	..	..	..	..
27	Madras States Agency ..	305	162	143	..	..	..	5	5	..	..	..	..	..	..	..
	Cochin State ..	*266*	*136*	*130*	..	..	..	*3*	*3*	..	..	..	..	..	..	..
	Travancore State ..	*39*	*26*	*13*	..	..	..	*2*	*2*	..	..	..	..	..	..	..
	Other Madras States ..	..	..	..	..	..	..	..	..	..	..	..	..	..	..	..
28	Mysore State	9	2	7	..	..	..	..	..	..	..	..	..	..	..	..
29	North-West Frontier Province (*Agencies and Tribal Areas*).	..	..	..	..	..	..	..	..	..	..	..	..	..	..	..
30	Punjab States	..	..	..	..	..	..	..	..	..	..	..	..	..	..	..
31	Punjab States Agency ..	..	..	..	..	..	..	..	..	..	..	..	..	..	..	..
32	Rajputana Agency	1	1	..	..	..	..	..	..	..	3	..	3	..	..	..
33	Sikkim State	1	1	..	..	..	..	..	..	..	..	..	..	..	..	..
34	United Provinces States ..	..	..	..	..	..	..	..	..	..	..	..	..	..	..	..
35	Western India States Agency	..	..	..	..	..	..	..	..	..	12	12	..	12	12	..

* Includes 20 persons (8 males and 12 females) who returned African as their mother tongue. Distribution :—

Serial No. 5 .. 1 female.
Serial No. 14 .. 3 males 4 females.
Serial No. 18 .. 5 males 4 females.
Serial No. 32 .. 3 females.

Table XV.—Language—Part I—Mother Tongue— *contd.*

Province, State or Agency.	Hamitic Family—*concld.* Ethiopic Group—*concld.* Somali.			Egyptian, Abyssinian and others.			Mongolian Family. Mongolian Family Total.			Ural-Altaic Group. Turkish.			Japanese Group. Japanese.		
	Persons.	Males.	Females.	Persons.	Males.	Females.	Persons.	Males.	Females.	Persons.	Males.	Females.	Persons.	Males.	Females.
1	851	852	853	854	855	856	857	858	859	860	861	862	863	864	865
INDIA	**4,522**	**2,476**	**2,046**	**497**	**462**	**35**	**11,943**	**7,806**	**4,137**	**7,630**	**4,596**	**3,034**	**4,304**	**3,206**	**1,098**
Provinces	4,521	2,475	2,046	485	450	35	11,757	7,649	4,108	7,502	4,487	3,015	4,246	3,158	1,088
Ajmer-Merwara	2	..	2	..	..	..	2	2	..	2	2	..	..	..	..
Andaman and Nicobar Islands ..	..	..	..	..	..	..	129	129	..	..	..	..	129	129	..
Assam	..	..	..	..	..	..	1	..	1	1	..	1	..	..	..
Baluchistan	..	..	..	..	..	..	7	6	1	7	6	1	..	..	..
(*Districts and Administered Territories.*)															
Bengal	..	..	..	..	..	..	550	415	135	3	..	3	547	415	132
Bombay (*including Aden*) ..	4,519	2,475	2,044	476	441	35	10,145	6,426	3,719	7,305	4,358	2,947	2,840	2,068	772
Aden	*4,438*	*2,416*	*2,022*	..	..	..	*85*	*80*	*5*	*13*	*9*	*4*	*72*	*71*	*1*
8 Burma	..	..	..	9	9	..	617	447	170	10	9	1	607	438	169
9 Central Provinces and Berar ..	..	..	..	..	..	..	21	13	8	4	2	2	8	7	1
11 Delhi	..	..	..	..	..	..	9	7	2	3	2	..	6	4	2
12 Madras	..	..	..	..	..	..	161	127	34	64	38	26	97	89	8
13 North-West Frontier Province ..	..	..	..	..	..	..	63	35	28	62	35	27	1	..	1
(*Districts and Administered Territories.*)															
14 Punjab	..	..	..	..	..	..	20	13	7	16	11	5	4	2	2
15 United Provinces of Agra and Oudh	..	..	..	..	..	..	32	29	3	25	23	2	7	6	1
States and Agencies ..	**1**	**1**	..	**12**	**12**	..	**186**	**157**	**29**	**128**	**109**	**19**	**58**	**48**	**10**
18 Baroda State	..	..	..	..	..	..	46	45	1	6	6	..	40	39	1
21 Bombay States	..	..	..	..	..	..	12	4	8	1	..	1	11	4	7
22 Central India Agency	1	1	..	..	..	..	6	5	1	6	5	1	..	..	..
25 Hyderabad State	..	..	..	..	..	..	10	5	5	9	4	5	1	1	..
26 Jammu and Kashmir State ..	..	..	..	..	..	..	86	80	6	86	80	6	..	..	..
27 Madras States Agency	..	..	..	..	..	..	1	1	..	..	..	..	1	1	..
Cochin State	..	..	..	..	..	..	*1*	*1*	..	..	..	..	*1*	*1*	..
28 Mysore State	..	..	..	..	..	..	5	3	2	..	..	..	5	3	2
Punjab States Agency	..	..	..	..	..	..	1	1	..	1	1	..	..	..	..
Rajputana Agency	..	..	..	..	..	..	7	5	2	7	5	2	..	..	..
Western India States Agency ..	..	..	..	12	12	..	12	8	4	12	8	4	..	..	..

Table XV.—Language—Part I—Mother Tongue—*contd.*

Province, State or Agency.	Mongolian Family—*concld.* Other Mongolian. Persons.	Males.	Females.	Malayo-Polynesian Family. Malayan Group. Malayan Group Total. Persons.	Males.	Females.	Tagalog and other Philippine Languages. Persons.	Males.	Females.	Javanese and other Malayan Languages. Persons.	Males.	Females.
1	866	867	868	869	870	871	872	873	874	875	876	877
INDIA	**9**	**4**	**5**	**342**	**208**	**134**	**48**	**38**	**10**	**294**	**170**	**124**
Provinces	**9**	**4**	**5**	**336**	**207**	**129**	**48**	**38**	**10**	**288**	**169**	**119**
2 Andaman and Nicobar Islands ..	..	..	..	..	..	..	..	..	..	..	..	..
5 Bengal	..	..	..	..	..	..	..	..	..	..	..	..
7 Bombay (*including Aden*) ..	..	..	..	266	157	109	..	..	..	266	157	109
Aden	..	..	..	*2*	..	*2*	..	..	..	*2*	..	*2*
8 Burma	..	..	..	51	39	12	48	38	10	3	1	2
9 Central Provinces and Berar ..	9	4	5	..	..	..	..	..	..	..	..	..
10 Coorg	..	..	..	..	..	..	..	..	..	..	..	..
11 Delhi	..	..	..	2	1	1	..	..	..	2	1	1
12 Madras	..	..	..	6	3	3	..	..	..	6*	3	3
13 North-West Frontier Province (*Districts and Administered Territories*) ..	..	..	..	..	..	..	..	..	..	..	..	..
14 Punjab	..	..	..	10	7	3	..	..	..	10	7	3
15 United Provinces of Agra and Oudh	..	..	..	1	..	1	..	..	..	1	..	1
States and Agencies ..	..	..	..	6	**1**	**5**	..	..	..	6	**1**	**5**
17 Baluchistan States	..	..	..	1	1	..	..	..	..	1	1	..
18 Baroda State	..	..	..	..	..	..	..	..	..	..	..	..
21 Bombay States	..	..	..	..	..	..	..	..	..	..	..	..
25 Hyderabad State	..	..	..	..	..	..	..	..	..	..	..	..
26 Jammu and Kashmir State ..	..	..	..	4	..	4	..	..	..	4	..	4
27 Madras States Agency	..	..		..	..	..	..	..	..	..	..	..
Cochin State	..	..	..	..	..	..	..	..	..	..	..	..
28 Mysore State	..	..	..	..	..	..	..	..	..	..	..	..
32 Rajputana Agency	..	..	..	1	..	1	..	..	..	1†	..	1

* Includes 2 males and 3 females who returned Kalade.

† Refers to one female for whom no language was returned.

Table XV.—Language—Part I—Mother Tongue—*contd.*

Province, State or Agency.	C.—European Languages.			C.—European Languages. Indo-European Family. Indo-European Family Total.			Greek Group. Greek (Romaic.)			Romance Group. Romance Group Total.			Romance Group. Italian.		
	Persons. 878	Males. 879	Females. 880	Persons. 881	Males. 882	Females. 883	Persons. 884	Males. 885	Females. 886	Persons. 887	Males. 888	Females. 889	Persons. 890	Males. 891	Females. 892
1															
INDIA	**339,706**	**208,314**	**131,392**	**339,660**	**208,290**	**131,370**	**352**	**234**	**118**	**15,430**	**9,210**	**6,220**	**1,239**	**905**	**334**
Provinces	**296,362**	**180,310**	**116,052**	**296,318**	**180,286**	**116,032**	**342**	**225**	**117**	**13,670**	**8,152**	**5,518**	**1,049**	**759**	**290**
1 Ajmer-Merwara	3,162	2,075	1,087	3,162	2,075	1,087	1	1	..	184	110	74	..	..	..
2 Andaman and Nicobar Islands ..	301	228	73	301	228	73	..	..	..	1	1	..	..	..	..
3 Assam	3,690	2,542	1,148	3,690	2,542	1,148	..	..	..	35	22	13	27	17	10
4 Baluchistan .. .. .. (*Districts and Administered Territories.*)	5,495	4,057	1,438	5,495	4,057	1,438	..	..	..	68	51	17	1	1	..
5 Bengal	49,920	28,385	21,535	49,910	28,382	21,528	68	25	43	661	408	253	286	236	50
6 Bihar and Orissa	13,304	7,341	5,963	13,304	7,341	5,963	7	7	..	232	132	100	81	40	41
7 Bombay (*including Aden*) ..	64,656	39,093	25,563	64,656	39,093	25,563	210	150	60	9,218	5,507	3,711	283	239	44
Aden	*2,108*	*1,660*	*448*	*2,108*	*1,660*	*448*	*83*	*55*	*28*	*471*	*370*	*101*	*189*	*177*	*12*
8 Burma	27,895	16,069	11,826	27,895	16,069	11,826	37	29	8	712	468	244	125	72	53
9 Central Provinces and Berar ..	11,615	7,212	4,403	11,614	7,212	4,402	5	3	2	407	205	202	2	1	1
10 Coorg	310	171	139	310	171	139	..	..	..	55	24	31	..	..	..
11 Delhi	5,201	3,328	1,873	5,201	3,328	1,873	1	1	..	63	46	17	8	4	4
12 Madras	41,469	21,455	20,014	41,436	21,434	20,002	9	8	1	1,647	913	734	167	96	71
13 North-West Frontier Province (*Districts and Administered Territories.*)	7,901	6,428	1,473	7,901	6,428	1,473	2	1	1	23	13	10	..	..	..
14 Punjab	26,080	18,322	7,758	26,080	18,322	7,758	..	..	..	142	97	45	20	17	3
15 United Provinces of Agra and Oudh	35,363*	23,604	11,759	35,363	23,604	11,759	2	..	2	222	155	67	49	36	13
States and Agencies	**43,344**	**28,004**	**15,340**	**43,342**	**28,004**	**15,338**	**10**	**9**	**1**	**1,760**	**1,058**	**702**	**190**	**146**	**44**
16 Assam	323	193	130	323	193	130	..	..	..	73	72	1	68	67	1
17 Baluchistan States	8	7	1	8	7	1	..	..	..	..	..	..	..	..	..
18 Baroda State	250	158	92	250	158	92	..	..	..	42	27	15	1	1	..
19 Bengal States	16	9	7	16	9	7	..	..	..	1	..	1	..	..	..
20 Bihar and Orissa States	201	127	74	201	127	74	..	..	..	17	12	5	..	..	..
21 Bombay States	449	278	171	449	278	171	..	..	..	138	105	33	..	..	..
22 Central India Agency	3,487	2,380	1,107	3,487	2,380	1,107	2	2	..	216	116	100	..	..	..
23 Central Provinces States	399	215	184	399	215	184	..	..	..	8	7	1	..	..	..
24 Gwalior State	244	165	79	244	165	79	..	..	..	14	14	..	..	..	..
25 Hyderabad State	14,070	10,327	3,743	14,070	10,327	3,743	7	6	1	204	125	79	42	23	19
26 Jammu and Kashmir State ..	335	148	187	335	148	187	..	..	..	19	6	13	5	..	5
27 Madras States Agency	2,191	1,177	1,014	2,191	1,177	1,014	..	..	..	254	161	93	16	7	9
Cochin State	*770*	*340*	*430*	*770*	*340*	*430*	..	..	..	*134*	*75*	*59*	*9*	..	*9*
Travancore State	*1,371*	*807*	*564*	*1,371*	*807*	*564*	..	..	..	*119*	*85*	*34*	*7*	*7*	..
Other Madras States	*50*	*30*	*20*	*50*	*30*	*20*	..	..	..	*1*	*1*	..	..	..	..
28 Mysore State	14,370	7,237	7,133	14,369	7,237	7,132	..	..	..	493	226	267	49	41	8
29 North-West Frontier Province (*Agencies and Tribal Areas.*)	3,814	3,801	13	3,814	3,801	13	..	..	..	..	..	..	..	..	..
30 Punjab States	79	27	52	79	27	52	..	..	..	3	..	3	..	..	..
31 Punjab States Agency	445	265	180	445	265	180	..	..	..	20	14	6	6	6	..
32 Rajputana Agency	1,909	1,050	859	1,909	1,050	859	1	1	..	61	39	22	3	1	2
33 Sikkim State	10	4	6	9	4	5	..	..	..	..	..	..	..	..	..
34 United Provinces States	38	17	21	38	17	21	..	..	..	..	..	..	..	..	..
35 Western India States Agency ..	706	419	287	706	419	287	..	..	..	197	134	63	..	..	..

* Includes 15 males enumerated in the U. P. States.

Table XV.—Language—Part I—Mother Tongue—*contd.*

	Province, State or Agency.	Indo-European Family—*contd.*																	
		Romance Group—*concld.*												Celtic Group.					
		French.			Spanish.			Protuguese.			Basque.			Celtic Group Total.			Welsh.		
		Persons.	Males.	Females.	Persons.	Males.	Females.	Persons.	Males.	Females.	Persons.	Males.	Females.	Persons.	Males.	Females.	Persons.	Males.	Females.
	1	893	894	895	896	897	898	899	900	901	902	903	904	905	906	907	908	909	910
	INDIA	**2,966**	**1,551**	**1,415**	**587**	**383**	**204**	**10,633**	**6,366**	**4,267**	**5**	**5**	..	**1,004**	**847**	**157**	**53**	**105**	**48**
	Provinces	2,648	1,407	1,241	534	340	194	9,438	5,645	3,793	1	1	..	933	794	139	125	86	39
1	Ajmer-Merwara	45	21	24	1	..	1	138	89	49	..	..	..	2	2	..	..	..	..
2	Andaman and Nicobar Islands ..	1	1	..	..	..	..	..	..	..	..	..	..	..	..	..	..	..	..
3	Assam	4	2	2	1	1	..	3	2	1	..	..	..	19	9	10	19	9	10
4	Baluchistan	9	4	5	3	3	..	55	43	12	..	..	..	25	18	7	9	9	..
	(*Districts and Administered Territories.*)																		
5	Bengal	191	67	124	46	43	3	138	62	76	..	..	..	25	17	8	8	6	2
6	Bihar and Orissa	79	44	35	7	7	..	64	40	24	1	1	..	67	33	34	37	19	18
7	Bombay (*including Aden*) ..	1,344	783	561	423	253	170	7,168	4,232	2,936	..	..	..	..	..	..	..	..	..
	Aden	*14*	*5*	*9*	*39*	*19*	*20*	*229*	*169*	*60*	..	..	..	..	..	..	..	..	..
8	Burma	179	102	77	13	4	9	395	290	105	..	..	..	..	..	..	..	..	..
9	Central Provinces and Berar ..	97	24	73	..	..	..	308	180	128	..	..	..	..	..	..	..	..	..
10	Coorg	5	1	4	..	..	..	50	23	27	..	..	..	1	1	..	..	..	..
11	Delhi	4	1	3	1	..	1	50	41	9	..	..	..	5	3	2	..	..	..
12	Madras	560	288	272	27	24	3	893	505	388	..	..	..	23	14	9	9	5	4
13	North-West Frontier Province ..	9	2	7	1	1	..	13	10	3	..	..	..	19	17	2	18	16	2
	(*Districts and Administered Territories.*)																		
14	Punjab	77	46	31	6	2	4	39	32	7	..	..	..	148	98	50	3	1	2
15	United Provinces of Agra and Oudh	44	21	23	5	2	3	124	96	28	..	..	..	599	582	17	22	21	1
	States and Agencies	318	144	174	53	43	10	1,195	721	474	4	4	..	71	53	18	28	19	9
16	Assam States	..	..	..	5	5	..	..	..	..	..	..	..	12	4	8	12	4	8
17	Baluchistan States	..	..	..	..	..	..	..	..	..	..	..	..	..	..	..	..	..	..
18	Baroda State	14	10	4	..	..	..	27	16	11	..	..	..	..	..	..	..	..	..
19	Bengal States	1	..	1	..	..	..	..	..	..	..	..	..	..	..	..	..	..	..
20	Bihar and Orissa States ..	7	5	2	..	..	..	10	7	3	..	..	..	..	..	..	..	..	..
21	Bombay States	16	12	4	..	..	..	122	93	29	..	..	..	..	..	..	..	..	..
22	Central India Agency	51	14	37	..	..	..	165	102	63	..	..	..	7	2	5	..	..	..
23	Central Provinces States	8	7	1	..	..	..	..	..	..	..	..	..	..	..	..	..	..	..
24	Gwalior State	..	..	..	..	..	..	14	14	..	..	..	..	..	..	..	..	..	..
25	Hyderabad State	64	44	20	6	6	..	92	52	40	..	..	..	23	22	1	6	6	..
26	Jammu and Kashmir State ..	11	6	5	2	..	2	1	..	1	..	..	..	1	1	..	..	..	..
27	Madras States Agency	3	2	1	29	29	..	202	119	83	4	4	..	6	5	1	1	1	..
	Cochin State	*1*	..	*1*	*6*	*6*	..	*114*	*65*	*49*	*4*	*4*	..	*1*	*1*	..	*1*	*1*	..
	Travancore State	*2*	*2*	..	*22*	*22*	..	*88*	*54*	*34*	..	..	..	*3*	*2*	*1*	..	..	..
	Other Madras States	..	..	..	*1*	*1*	..	..	..	..	..	..	..	*2*	*2*	..	..	..	..
28	Mysore State	127	38	89	11	3	8	306	144	162	..	..	..	13	10	3	8	7	1
29	North-West Frontier Province ..	..	..	..	..	..	..	..	..	..	..	..	..	1	1	..	1	1	..
	(*Agencies and Tribal Areas.*)																		
30	Punjab States	3	..	3	..	..	..	..	..	..	..	..	..	1	1	..	..	..	..
31	Punjab States Agency	2	1	1	..	..	..	12	7	5	..	..	..	..	..	..	..	..	..
32	Rajputana Agency	8	4	4	..	..	..	50	34	16	..	..	..	7	7	..	..	..	..
33	Sikkim State	..	..	..	..	..	..	..	..	..	..	..	..	..	..	..	..	..	..
34	United Provinces States	..	..	..	..	..	..	..	..	..	..	..	..	..	..	..	..	..	..
35	Western India States Agency ..	3	1	2	..	..	..	194	133	61	..	..	..	..	..	..	..	..	..

Table XV.—Language—Part I—Mother Tongue—*contd.*

Indo-European Family—*contd.*

Province, State or Agency.	Celtic Group—*concld.* Gaelic (Scotch). Persons.	Males.	Females.	Irish. Persons.	Males.	Females.	Balto-Slavonic Group. Slavonic (Russian, Polish and Others). Persons.	Males.	Females.	Teutonic Group. Teutonic Group Total. Persons.	Males.	Females.	English. Persons.	Males.	Females.
1	911	912	913	914	915	916	917	918	919	920	921	922	923	924	925
INDIA	**681**	**614**	**67**	**179**	**136**	**43**	**188**	**126**	**62**	**322,686**	**197,873**	**124,813**	**319,349**	**195,989**	**123,360**
Provinces	**671**	**607**	**64**	**137**	**101**	**36**	**178**	**120**	**58**	**281,195**	**170,995**	**110,200**	**278,033**	**169,186**	**108,847**
1 Ajmer-Merwara	2	2	..	..	..	..	1	..	1	2,974	1,962	1,012	2,972	1,962	1,010
2 Andaman and Nicobar Islands ..	..	..	..	..	..	..	..	..	..	300	227	73	298	225	73
3 Assam	..	..	..	..	..	..	2	2	..	3,634	2,509	1,125	3,615	2,500	1,115
4 Baluchistan .. .. .. (*Districts and Administered Territories.*)	..	..	..	16	9	7	..	..	..	5,402	3,988	1,414	5,396	3,986	1,410
5 Bengal	9	8	1	8	3	5	39	19	20	49,117	27,913	21,204	48,923	27,777	21,146
6 Bihar and Orissa	26	14	12	4	..	4	..	..	..	12,998	7,169	5,829	12,838	7,116	5,722
7 Bombay (*including Aden*) ..	..	..	..	..	..	..	73	45	28	55,155	33,391	21,764	53,429	32,386	21,043
Aden	..	..	..	..	..	..	*2*	..	*2*	*1,552*	*1,235*	*317*	*1,490*	*1,184*	*306*
8 Burma	..	..	..	..	..	..	51	45	6	27,095	15,527	11,568	26,866	15,328	11,538
9 Central Provinces and Berar ..	..	..	..	..	..	..	..	..	..	11,202	7,004	4,198	11,141	6,972	4,169
10 Coorg	..	..	..	1	1	..	..	..	..	254	146	108	254	146	108
11 Delhi	4	3	1	1	..	1	1	1	..	5,131	3,277	1,854	5,107	3,259	1,848
12 Madras	..	..	..	14	9	5	5	4	1	39,752	20,495	19,257	39,223	20,219	19,004
13 North-West Frontier Province .. (*Districts and Administered Territories.*)	..	..	..	1	1	..	..	..	..	7,857	6,397	1,460	7,853	6,397	1,456
14 Punjab	95	54	41	50	43	7	3	3	..	25,787	18,124	7,663	25,713	18,083	7,630
15 United Provinces of Agra and Oudh	535	526	9	42	35	7	3	1	2	34,537	22,866	11,671	34,405	22,830	11,575
States and Agencies	**10**	**7**	**3**	**33**	**27**	**6**	**10**	**6**	**4**	**41,491**	**26,878**	**14,613**	**41,316**	**26,803**	**14,513**
16 Assam States	..	..	..	..	..	..	..	..	..	[illegible]	117	121	237	117	120
17 Baluchistan States	..	..	..	..	..	..	..	..	..	[illegible]	7	1	8	7	1
18 Baroda State	..	..	..	..	..	..	1	..	1	207	131	76	201	128	73
19 Bengal States	..	..	..	..	..	..	..	..	..	15	9	6	9	6	3
20 Bihar and Orissa States	..	..	..	..	..	..	..	..	..	184	115	69	182	115	67
21 Bombay States	..	..	..	..	..	..	..	..	..	311	173	138	311	173	138
22 Central India Agency	3	1	2	4	1	3	..	..	..	3,262	2,260	1,002	3,253	2,257	996
23 Central Provinces States	..	..	..	..	..	..	..	..	..	391	208	183	388	205	183
24 Gwalior State	..	..	..	..	..	..	..	..	..	230	151	79	228	151	77
25 Hyderabad State	..	..	..	17	16	1	..	..	..	13,836	10,174	3,662	13,819	10,162	3,657
26 Jammu and Kashmir State ..	1	1	..	..	..	..	4	3	1	311	138	173	300	131	169
27 Madras States Agency	3	2	1	2	2	..	..	..	..	1,931	1,011	920	1,875	994	881
Cochin State	..	..	..	..	..	..	..	..	..	*635*	*264*	*371*	*631*	*264*	*367*
Travancore State	*3*	*2*	*1*	..	..	..	..	..	..	*1,249*	*720*	*529*	*1,199*	*704*	*495*
Other Madras States	..	..	..	*2*	*2*	..	..	..	..	*47*	*27*	*20*	*45*	*26*	*19*
28 Mysore State	..	..	..	5	3	2	1	..	1	13,862	7,001	6,861	13,825	6,987	6,838
29 North-West Frontier Province (*Agencies and Tribal Areas.*)	..	..	..	..	..	..	..	..	..	3,813	3,800	13	3,813	3,800	13
30 Punjab States	..	..	..	1	1	..	..	..	..	75	26	49	70	26	44
31 Punjab States Agency	..	..	..	..	..	..	3	3	..	422	248	174	421	247	174
32 Rajputana Agency	3	3	..	4	4	..	1	..	1	1,839	1,003	836	1,822	993	829
33 Sikkim State	..	..	..	..	..	..	..	..	..	9	4	5	9	4	5
34 United Provinces States ..	..	..	..	..	..	..	..	..	..	38	17	21	38	17	21
35 Western India States Agency ..	..	..	..	..	..	..	..	..	..	509	285	224	507	283	224

Table XV.—Language—Part I—Mother Tongue—*contd.*

Indo-European Family—*concld.*

Teutonic Group—*concld.*

	Province, State or Agency.	Dutch.			Flemish.			Norwegian.			Swedish.			Danish.			German.		
		Persons.	Males.	Females.	Persons.	Males.	Females.	Persons.	Males.	Females.	Persons.	Males.	Females.	Persons.	Males.	Females.	Persons.	Males.	Females.
	1	926	927	928	929	930	931	932	933	934	935	936	937	938	939	940	941	942	943
	INDIA	**845**	**512**	**333**	**153**	**79**	**74**	**71**	**44**	**27**	**263**	**146**	**117**	**187**	**57**	**80**	**1,867**	**1,046**	**821**
	Provinces	**834**	**505**	**329**	**134**	**64**	**70**	**68**	**43**	**25**	**257**	**143**	**114**	**114**	**47**	**67**	**1,755**	**1,007**	**748**
1	Ajmer-Merwara	..	..	..	..	..	..	..	..	..	..	..	..	1	..	1	1	..	1
2	Andaman and Nicobar Islands	..	..	..	..	..	..	..	..	..	1	1	..	..	..	..	1	1	..
3	Assam	..	..	..	..	..	..	1	..	1	11	5	6	3	1	2	4	3	1
4	Baluchistan (*Districts and Administered Territories.*)	..	..	..	..	..	..	..	..	..	..	..	..	2	1	1	4	1	3
5	Bengal	65	57	8	11	10	1	2	2	..	3	..	3	2	2	..	111	65	46
6	Bihar and Orissa	7	5	2	33	23	10	21	8	13	..	..	..	31	7	24	68	10	58
7	Bombay (*including Aden*)	547	300	247	..	..	..	..	..	..	76	45	31	2	..	2	1,101	660	441
	Aden	*12*	*7*	*5*	..	..	..	..	..	..	*1*	*1*	..	*2*	..	*2*	*47*	*43*	*4*
8	Burma	52	44	8	1	1	..	31	31	..	23	17	6	13	10	3	109	96	13
9	Central Provinces and Berar	1	..	1	..	..	..	..	..	..	24	8	16	..	..	..	36	24	12
10	Coorg	..	..	..	..	..	..	..	..	..	..	..	..	..	..	..	..	..	..
11	Delhi	..	..	..	..	..	..	..	..	..	..	..	..	2	1	1	22	17	5
12	Madras	152	96	56	45	9	36	1	1	..	82	49	33	56	24	32	193	97	96
13	North-West Frontier Province (*Districts and Administered Territories.*)	1	..	1	..	..	..	..	..	..	..	..	..	..	..	..	3	..	3
14	Punjab	1	..	1	42	21	21	3	..	3	1	..	1	1	1	..	26	19	7
15	United Provinces of Agra and Oudh	8	3	5	2	..	2	9	1	8	36	18	18	1	..	1	76	14	62
	States and Agencies	**11**	**7**	**4**	**19**	**15**	**4**	**3**	**1**	**2**	**7**	**3**	**4**	**23**	**10**	**13**	**112**	**39**	**73**
16	Assam States	..	..	..	..	..	..	..	..	..	..	..	..	..	..	..	1	..	1
17	Baluchistan States	..	..	..	..	..	..	..	..	..	..	..	..	..	..	..	..	..	..
18	Baroda State	6	3	3	..	..	..	..	..	..	..	..	..	..	..	..	..	..	..
19	Bengal States	..	..	..	..	..	..	..	..	..	6	3	3	..	..	..	..	..	..
20	Bihar and Orissa States	..	..	..	..	..	..	..	..	..	..	..	..	..	..	..	2	..	2
21	Bombay States	..	..	..	..	..	..	..	..	..	..	..	..	..	..	..	..	..	..
22	Central India Agency	..	..	..	..	..	..	..	..	..	..	..	..	..	..	..	9	3	6
23	Central Provinces States	..	..	..	3	3	..	..	..	..	..	..	..	..	..	..	..	..	..
24	Gwalior State	..	..	..	..	..	..	..	..	..	..	..	..	..	..	..	2	..	2
25	Hyderabad State	..	..	..	..	..	..	..	..	..	..	..	..	6	4	2	11	8	3
26	Jammu and Kashmir State	1	1	..	..	..	..	..	..	..	..	..	..	2	1	1	8	5	3
27	Madras States Agency	..	..	..	16	12	4	2	1	1	..	..	..	2	1	1	36	3	33
	Cochin State	..	..	..	*2*	..	*2*	..	..	..	..	..	..	..	..	..	*2*	..	*2*
	Travancore State	..	..	..	*14*	*12*	*2*	*2*	*1*	*1*	..	..	..	..	..	..	*34*	*3*	*31*
	Other Madras States	..	..	..	..	..	..	..	..	..	..	..	..	*2*	*1*	*1*	..	..	..
28	Mysore State	..	..	..	..	..	..	..	..	..	..	..	..	7	3	4	30	11	19
29	North-West Frontier Province (*Agencies and Tribal Areas.*)	..	..	..	..	..	..	..	..	..	..	..	..	..	..	..	..	..	..
30	Punjab States	..	..	..	..	..	..	1	..	1	1	..	1	..	..	..	3	..	3
31	Punjab States Agency	..	..	..	..	..	..	..	..	..	..	..	..	..	..	..	1	1	..
32	Rajputana Agency	2	1	1	..	..	..	..	..	..	..	..	..	6	1	5	9	8	1
33	Sikkim State	..	..	..	..	..	..	..	..	..	..	..	..	..	..	..	..	..	..
34	United Provinces States	..	..	..	..	..	..	..	..	..	..	..	..	..	..	..	..	..	..
35	Western India States Agency	2	2	..	..	..	..	..	..	..	..	..	..	..	..	..	..	..	..

Table XV.—Language—Part I—Mother Tongue—*concld.*

Province, State or Agency.	Mongolian Family. Mongolian Family Group Total. Persons.	Males.	Females.	Ural-Altaic Group. Esthonian. Persons.	Males.	Females.	Finnish. Persons.	Males.	Females.	Hungarian. Persons.	Males.	Females.	European Languages unspecified. Persons.	Males.	Females.
1	944	945	946	947	948	949	950	951	952	953	954	955	956	957	958
INDIA	**13**	**3**	**10**	**1**	**1**	..	**8**	..	**8**	**4**	**2**	**2**	**33**	**21**	**12**
Provinces	11	3	8	1	1	..	7	..	7	3	2	1	33	21	12
1 Ajmer-Merwara	..	..	..	..	..	..	..	..	..	..	..	..	..	..	..
2 Andaman and Nicobar Islands ..	..	..	..	..	..	..	..	..	..	..	..	..	..	..	..
3 Assam	..	..	..	..	..	..	..	..	..	..	..	..	..	..	..
4 Baluchistan .. .. .. (*Districts and Administered Territories.*)	..	..	..	..											
5 Bengal	10	3	7	1	1	..	6	..	6	3	2	1	..	..	..
6 Bihar and Orissa	..	..	..	..	..	..	..	..	..	..	..	..	..	..	..
7 Bombay (*including Aden*) ..	..	..	..	..	..	..	..	..	..	..	..	..	..	..	..
Aden	..	..	..	..	..	..	..	..	..	..	..	..	..	..	..
8 Burma	1	..	1	..	..	..	1	..	1	..	..	..	..	..	..
9 Central Provinces and Berar ..	..	..	..	..	..	..	..	..	..	..	..	..	..	..	..
10 Coorg	..	..	..	..	..	..	..	..	..	..	..	..	33	21	12
11 Delhi	..	..	..	..	..	..	..	..	..	..	..	..	..	..	..
12 Madras	..	..	..	..	..	..	..	..	..	..	..	..	..	..	..
13 North-West Frontier Provinc (*Districts and Administered Territories.*)	..	..	..	..	..	..	..	..	..	..	..	..	..	..	..
14 Punjab	..	..	..	..	..	..	..	..	..	..	..	..	..	..	..
15 United Provinces of Agra and Oudh	..	..	..	..	..	..	..	..	..	..	..	..	..	..	..
States and Agencies ..	2	..	2	..	..	..	1	..	1	1	..	1	..	..	..
16 Assam States	..	..	..	..	..	..	..	..	..	..	..	..	..	..	..
17 Baluchistan States	..	..	..	..	..	..	..	..	..	..	..	..	..	..	..
18 Baroda State	..	..	..	..	..	..	..	..	..	..	..	..	..	..	..
19 Bengal States	..	..	..	..	..	..	..	..	..	..	..	..	..	..	..
20 Bihar and Orissa States	..	..	..	..	..	..	..	..	..	..	..	..	..	..	..
21 Bombay States	..	..	..	..	..	..	..	..	..	..	..	..	..	..	..
22 Central India Agency	..	..	..	..	..	..	..	..	..	..	..	..	..	..	..
23 Central Provinces States	..	..	..	..	..	..	..	..	..	..	..	..	..	..	..
24 Gwalior State	..	..	..	..	..	..	..	..	..	..	..	..	..	..	..
25 Hyderabad State	..	..	..	..	..	..	..	..	..	..	..	..	..	..	..
26 Jammu and Kashmir State ..	..	..	..	..	..	..	..	..	..	..	..	..	..	..	..
27 Madras States Agency	..	..	..	..	..	..	..	..	..	..	..	..	..	..	..
Cochin State	..	..	..	..	..	..	..	..	..	..	..	..	..	..	..
Travancore State ..	..	..	..	..	..	..	..	..	..	..	..	..	..	..	..
Other Madras States ..	1	..	1	..	..	..	..	..	..	1	..	1	..	..	..
28 Mysore State	..	..	..	..	..	..	..	..	..	..	..	..	..	..	..
29 North-West Frontier Provinc (*Agencies and Tribal Areas.*)	..	..	..	..	..	..	..	..	..	..	..	..	..	..	..
30 Punjab States	..	..	..	..	..	..	..	..	..	..	..	..	..	..	..
31 Punjab States Agency	1	..	1	..	..	..	1	..	1	..	..	..	..	..	..
33 Sikkim State	..	..	..	..	..	..	..	..	..	..	..	..	..	..	..
34 United Provinces States	..	..	..	..	..	..	..	..	..	..	..	..	..	..	..
35 Western India States Agency ..	..	..	..	..	..	..	..	..	..	..	..	..	..	..	..

Table XV.—Language—Part II—Bilingualism.

Mother-Tongue. Language, and Province, State or Agency from which returned.	Total speakers.	Total Persons returned as speaking a language subsidiary to that shown in column 1.	Subsidiary Languages.
1	2	3	4
1. MON-KHMER BRANCH [Assam, Bengal and Burma.]	714,762	262,329	Burma Group (168,937), Tai (Shan) Group (90,927), Bengali (1,400), Other Tibeto Burman Languages (429), Assamese (319), Karen Group (295), Hindustani (21), Naipali (1).
KHASI [Assam and Bengal] ..	234,373	1,906	Bengali (1,400), Assamese (319), Tibeto-Burmese languages (165), Hindustani (21), Naipali (1).
2. KHERWARI [Bengal and Central Provinces.]	891,963	298,777	Bengali (273,402), Hindustani (33,333), Naipali (1,279), Oriya (994), Kurukh (65), Telugu (1).
3. KORKU [Central Provinces and Berar]	161,975	105,690	Hindustani (103,465), Marathi (2,044), Telugu (158), Gondi (23).
4. KHARIA [Bengal, Bihar and Orissa and Central Provinces.]	137,659	108,266	Hindustani (77,547), Oriya (28,687), Bengali (1,458), Naipali (460), Santali (118), Ho (25), Rai (6), Bhotia (3).
5. SAVARA [Madras]	185,562	71,448	Oriya (35,349), Telugu (34,567), Hill and Aboriginal (1,532).
6. GADABA [Madras]	43,667	31,886	Oriya (18,003), Telugu (13,803), Hill and Aboriginal (80).
7. BHOTIA [Bengal, United Provinces and Sikkim.]	33,652	21,023	Naipali (17,881), Hindustani (3,215), Rong (64), Bengal (3), Limbu (1).
8. KIRANTI [Bengal and Sikkim] ..	85,359	61,475	Naipali (60,071), Hindustani (300), Bengali (104), Bhotia (1), Rong (1).
9. GURUNG [Bengal and Sikkim] ..	2,831	1,891	Naipali (1,869), Hindustani (37).
10. MURMI [Bengal and Sikkim]	42,642	37,348	Naipali (37,198), Hindustani (167), Bhotia (1), Rai (1), Rong (1).
11. SUNWAR [Bengal and Sikkim] ..	3,395	3,202	Naipali (3,169), Hindustani (45).
12. MAGARI [Bengal and Sikkim] ..	14,997	12,336	Naipali (12,166), Hindustani (201), Bengali (1).
13. NEWARI [Bengal and Sikkim]	9,455	8,554	Naipali (8,539), Hindustani (63), Bengali (3), Rai (1).
14. RONG OR LEPCHA [Bengal and Sikkim]	25,149	16,805	Naipali (16,536), Bhotia (196), Hindustani (176), Limbu (2).
15. BARA OR BODO GROUP [Bengal] ..	246,870	20,572	Bengali (19,456), Hindustani (1,211), Arakanese (2).
16. KUKI-CHIN GROUP [Bengal]	36,606	4,152	Bengali (4,007), Arakanese (79), Hindustani (63), Naipali (2), Lushei (2).
17. BURMA GROUP [Bengal and Burma] ..	9,957,075	30,551	Tai (Shan) Group (16,536), Other Tibeto-Burmese Groups (4,501), Karen Group (3,488), Bengali (2,721), Mon Khmer Group (2,621), Burmese (511), Arakanese (80), Hindustani (17), Naipali (10), Khyang (8).
18. MRO [Bengal]	3,793	1	Bengali (1).
19. TAI GROUP [Burma]	1,021,909	247,781	Burma Group (240,185), Karen Group (5,230), Other Tibeto-Burmese Groups (1,393), Mon-Khmer Group (973).
20. KAREN GROUP [Burma]	1,341,066	782,832	Burma Group (763,897), Tai (Shan) Group (15,101), Mon Khmer Group (3,810), Other Tibeto-Burmese Groups (24).
21. TAMIL [Bengal, Bihar and Orissa, Madras, Hyderabad, Cochin, Travancore and Mysore.]	20,177,594	755,118	Telugu (359,161), Malayalam (222,999), Kanarese (124,209), Hindustani (43,089), English (4,796), Marathi (207), Saurasthri (160), Oriya (149), Bengali (127), Tulu (93), Hill and Aboriginal (74), Konkani (14), Banjari (11), Naipali (10), Mundari (5), Gujarati (1).
22. MALAYALAM [Bengal, Coorg, Madras Travancore and Cochin.]	9,101,440	183,829	Tamil (72,692), Tulu (59,370), English (29,342), Kanarese (7,321), Telugu (1,245), Hindustani (1,084), Coorgi (285), Konkani (28), Bengali (21), Oriya (5).
23. KANARESE [Bengal, Bombay, Coorg, Madras, Hyderabad, Cochin, Travancore and Mysore.]	11,196,103	1,378,517	Telugu (487,053), Tamil (463,005), Marathi (185,521), Hindustani (84,457), Tulu (38,015), Western Hind. (28,038), Konkani (15,457), Malayalam (13,953), Kodagu or Coorgi (1,342), English (566), Gujarati, (251), Banjari (228), Hill and Aboriginal (36), Oriya (15), Bengali (2) Yerava (1).
24. KODAGU OR COORGI [Coorg]	44,585	44,585	Kanarese (22,870), Malayalam (58), Tulu (19), Yerava (1).
25. TULU [Coorg, Madras, Cochin, Travancore and Mysore.]	629,425	99,987	Kanarese (81,850), Malayalam (8,361), Tamil (640), Kodagu or Coorgi (443), Hindustani (234), Telugu (88), Konkani (59), English (28), Marathi (11), Yerava (10).

Table XV.—Language—Part II—Bilingualism—*contd.*

Mother-Tongue. Language, and Province, State or Agency from which returned.	Total speakers.	Total Persons returned as speaking a language subsidiary to that shown in column 1.	Subsidiary Languages.
1	2	3	4
26. KURUKH OR ORAON [Bengal and Bihar and Orissa.]	984,486	620,889	Hindustani (469,785), Oriya (126,759), Bengali (18,723), Mundari (4,665), Naipali (928), Ho (311), Kherwari (7), Santali (6).
27. MALTO [Bengal and Bihar and Orissa] ..	70,755	9,732	Hindustani (6,407), Bengali (2,446), Santali (849), Oriya (30).
28. GONDI [Bengal, Bihar and Orissa, Central Provinces and Berar, Central India Agency and Hyderabad.]	1,720,790	867,574	Hindustani (495,823), Marathi (321,388), Telugu (21,592), Western Hindi (11,576), Eastern Hindi (10,053), Oriya (5,372), Rajasthani (1,432), Ho (195), Korku (130), Kanarese (12), Bengali (1).
29. KANDHI OR KUI [Bihar and Orissa and Madras.]	578,928	194,239	Oriya (145,117), Telugu (44,994), Hill and Aboriginal (4,120), Hindustani (8).
30. TELUGU [Bengal, Bihar and Orissa, Bombay, Central Provinces and Berar, Madras, Hyderabad, Cochin, Travancore and Mysore.]	26,176,411	3,575,685	Tamil (2,333,625), Kanarese (710,825), Hindustani (233,262), Marathi (144,148), Oriya (122,471), Malayalam (21,286), Hill and Aboriginal (4,232), Western Hindi (3,035), Gondi (1,243), Bengali (807), English (401), Gujarati (211), Tulu (66), Naipali (15), Arabic (5), Banjari (4), Saurashtri (2), Konkani (2).
31. BRAHUI [Baluchistan and Bombay] ..	207,040	48,585	Sindhi (31,198), Balochi (6,738), Western Hindi (5,319), Pashto (2,663), Dehwari (1,795), Persian (684), Unspecified Jagdali and Jatki (90), Lahnda (51), Kachchhi (35), Thareli or Dhatki (12).
32. PASHTO [Baluchistan, Bengal, North-West Frontier Province and Punjab.]	1,594,303	84,148	Lahnda (38,668), Panjabi (21,295), Hindustani (14,138), Brahui (2,399), English (2,095), Persian (2,013), Balochi (1,185), Unspecified Jagdali and Jatki (1,060), Arabic (578), Dehwari (184), Bengali (173), Gujari (139), Hindi (116), Kohistani (39), Western Pahari (17), Turkish (6).
33. BALOCHI [Baluchistan, Bombay and Punjab].	625,708	235,791	Sindhi (200,570), Lahnda (12,889), Brahui (16,904), Western Hindi (2,047), Pashto (1,562), Dehwari (941), Siraiki or Jatki (842), Persian (295), Unspecified Jagdali and Jatki (154), Gujarati (86), Hindustani (82), Marathi (13).
34. PERSIAN [Baluchistan]	5,233	2,487	Brahui (2,305), Western Hindi (163), Pash to (11), Sindhi (8).
35. SHINA [Jammu and Kashmir]	68,199	413	Panjabi (381), Kashmiri (28), Dogri (4).
36. KASHMIRI [North- West Frontier Province, Punjab and Jammu and Kashmir.]	1,437,237	23,916	Panjabi (15,018), Dogri (3,573), Hindustani (3,594), Western Pahari (1,245), Lahnda (358), Pashto (82), English (38), Persian (8).
37. KOHISTANI [North-West Frontier Province.]	388	184	Lahnda (87), Pashto (75), Panjabi (21), Persian (1).
38. LAHNDA OR WESTERN PUNJABI [Baluchistan, North-West Frontier Province, Punjab and Jammu and Kashmir].	2,069,186	180,460	Pashto (81,707), Balochi (61,018), Hindustani (21,469), Panjabi (8,960), English (2,900), Persian (1,935), Sindhi (1,276), Rajasthani (299), Arabic (196), Kohistani (156), Gujari (152), Unspecified Jagdali and Jatki (104), Brahui (97), Dogri (60), Naipali (47), Western Hindi (40), Kashmiri (36), Bengali (8).
39. SINDHI [Baluchistan, Bengal, Bombay, Baroda, Cochin, Rajputana Agency and Western India States Agency.]	3,967,042	173,009	Gujarati (108,333), Western Hindi (23,359), Siraiki (13,614), Balochi (11,540), English (9,259), Brahui (2,816), Panjabi (2,403), Marathi (2,013), Pashto (1,118), Malayalam (580), Lahnda (356), Persian (352), Hindustani (114), Rajasthani (86), Kanarese (62), Unspecified Jagdali and Jatki (26), Dehwari (14), Tamil (5), Naipali (2).
40. MARATHI [Bengal, Bombay, Central Provinces and Berar, Baroda, Central India Agency, Hyderabad and Cochin].	20,739,201	1,039,414	Hindustani (502,446), Kanarese (279,310), Telugu (63,583), Western Hindi (58,312), Gujarati (42,466), Khandeshi (23,144), Gondi (22,833), English (16,116), Malayalam (9,860), Oriya (9,348), Rajasthani (5,475), Konkani (3,393), Tamil (2,427), Tulu (520), Eastern Hindi (81), Bengali (40), Korku (24), Kachchhi (9).
41. KONKANI [Bombay, Madras, Cochin, Travancore and Mysore.]	466,386	252,598	Kanarese (111,548), Tulu (80,568), Malayalam (27,459), Marathi (13,609), English (11,133), Western Hindi (6,194), Hindustani (1,147), Gujarati (503), Tamil (427), Telugu (40).
42. ORIYA [Bengal, Bihar and Orissa, Central Provinces and Berar and Madras.]	10,928,759	351,163	Telugu (133,624), Hindustani (91,242), Ho (53,484), Bengali (37,476), Hill and Aboriginal (17,766), Marathi (10,917), Kandhi (5,278), Gondi (1,664), Mundari (886), Tamil (189), Kanarese (118), Naipali (8), Kurukh or Oraon, (5), Malayalam (5), Assamese (2), Kherwari (2).

Table XV.—Language—Part II—Bilingualism—*concld.*

Mother-Tongue. Language, and Province, State or Agency from which returned.	Mother-Tongue. Total speakers.	Total persons returned as speaking a language subsidiary to that shown in column 1.	Subsidiary Languages.
1	2	3	4
43. BENGALI [Assam, Bengal, Bihar and Orissa and Cochin.]	53,037,841	339,048	Hindustani (156,521), Oriya (88,043), Assamese (39,127), Santali (2,172), Kherwari (1,786), Arabic (1,759), Ho (565), Naipali (414), Mundari (334), Arakanese (315), Tibeto-Burmese Languages (192), Khasi (173), Koch (86), Kurukh (62), Burmese (23), Gujarati (19), Telugu (13), Panjabi (4), English (2), Tamil (2), Marathi (1), Rajasthani (1), Rong (1).
44. ASSAMESE [Assam and Bengal] ..	1,997,314	22,412	Bengali (20,752), Tibeto-Burmese Languages (1,581), Khasi (49), Hindustani (22), Naipali (2), Arakanese (1), Garo (1).
45. EASTERN HINDI [Bengal, Bihar and Orissa Central Provinces and Berar, Central India Agency and Sikkim.]	41,363,439	912,257	Marathi (376,809), Bengali (235,447), Oriya (217,003), Kherwari (18,526), Gondi (16,541), Western Hindi (16,131), Mundari (9,799), Santali (3,197), Kurukh or Oraon (4,143), Ho (3,061), Naipali (2,990), Telugu (2,458), Rajasthani (1,324), Korku (901), Arabic (401), Murmi (328), Panjabi (116), Assamese (60), Kharia (39), Gujarati (33), Tamil (31), Pashto (9), Magari (7), Bhotia (2), Sindhi (2), Burmese (1), Kanarese (1), Malayalam (1), Newari (1).
46. WESTERN HINDI [Baluchistan, Bombay, Delhi, Madras, North-West Frontier Province, Punjab, United Provinces, Baroda, Central India Agency, Gwalior, Hyderabad, Cochin, Travancore, Mysore and Western India States Agency].	63,627,043	1,273,600	Telugu (608,637), Kanarese (542,167), Marathi (308,946), Tamil (248,245), Gujarati (186,246), Panjabi (75,559), Rajasthani (62,428), Eastern Hindi (8,790), Konkani (6,952), Malayalam (6,568), English (4,678), Sindhi (4,574), Lahnda (3,223), Oriya (2,303), Pashto (2,520), Bhotia (1,316), Ahirani (1,192), Kachchhi (1,019), Bhili (899), Persian (817), Western Pahari (511), Tulu (468), Naipali (387), Haburi (76), Kashmiri (74), Arabic (23), Balochi (18), Brahui (11), Saurashtri (4), Unspecified Jagdali and Jatki (4), Bihari (3), Banjari (2), Hill and Aboriginal (1), Others (6).
47. RAJASTHANI [Bengal, Bombay, Delhi, Punjab, Central India Agency, Gwalior, Hyderabad, Mysore and Sikkim].	12,683,173	464,563	Western Hindi (157,968), Kanarese (81,557), Sindhi (54,177), Marathi (53,771), Telugu (50,852), Hindustani (34,391), Gujarati (15,341), Panjabi (8,325), Lahnda (3,131), Bhili (2,820), Bengali (2,121), Naipali (805), Thareli (326), Eastern Hindi (226), Kachchhi (52), Tamil (42), English (9), Tulu (1).
48. GUJARATI [Bengal, Bombay, Baroda, Central India Agency, Gwalior, Hyderabad, Cochin, Rajputana Agency and Western India States Agency].	10,633,861	256,415	Western Hindi (85,494), Kachchhi (53,277), Marathi (50,569), English (27,530), Rajasthani (20,491), Hindustani (8,284), Bhili (6,740), Kanarese (2,095), Malayalam (670), Sindhi (661), Telugu (224), Bengali (132), Eastern Hindi (49), Panjabi (19), Naipali (5), Tamil (4).
49. BHILI [Bombay, Baroda, Central India Agency, Central Provinces, Gwalior, Hyderabad and Rajputana Agency].	2,185,876	209,328	Gujarati (97,512), Marathi (57,846), Rajasthani (23,380), Hindustani (19,421), Western Hindi (7,026), Sindhi (2,548), Ahirani or Khandeshi (995).
50. KHANDESI [Bombay]	222,168	14,285	Marathi (13,523), Bhili (627), Western Hindi (76), Gujarati (59).
51. PUNJABI [Bengal, Bombay, Delhi, North-West Frontier Province, Punjab, Jammu and Kashmir, Rajputana Agency and Sikkim].	15,725,193	210,446	Hindustani (147,085), Kashmiri (13,593), Western Hindi (11,170), Lahnda (9,975), Sindhi (9,059), Pashto (6,487), Dogri (3,584), English (3,473), Western Pahari (2,976), Persian (891), Rajasthani (674), Marathi (545), Gujarati (365), Kohistani (237), Bengali (179), Siraiki (106), Arabic (94), Naipali (56), Kachchhi (16), Telugu (4), Others (52).
52. EASTERN PAHARI, KHAS-KURA OR NAIPALI [Bengal, North-West Frontier Province and Sikkim].	182,744	11,501	Hindustani (11,688), Bengali (1,017), Panjabi (872), Bhotia (208), Lahnda (207), Magari (177), Murmi (177), English (27), Rai (23), Kharia (10), Pashto (5), Newari (3), Assamese (2), Kurukh (2), Rajasthani (2), Rong (2), Others (2).
53. WESTERN PAHARI [Delhi, Punjab and Jammu and Kashmir].	2,325,646	23,986	Hindustani (8,020), Kashmiri (5,941), Panjabi (5,81[illegible]) Dogri (4,213).

TABLE XVI.

Religion.

This table corresponds with Table VI of the last Census and shows the distribution of the population by religion according to the province or state of enumeration.

2. The total population shown in this table is less than that in Table I owing to the omission of 2,308,221 persons (1,208,311 males and 1,099,910 females) for whom no particulars of religion were available, as the figures were not obtained by individual enumeration. The population thus omitted is as follows :—

	Persons.	Males.	Females.
(1) Bombay	75,735	30,674	45,061
(2) Burma	19,649	9,925	9,724
(3) North-West Frontier Province	2,212,837	1,167,712	1,045,125

Number (1) represents the estimated population of Ahmadabad believed to be almost entirely Hindu or Jain ; number (2) represents the estimated portion of the population of East Manglun in the Shan States and was probably either Tribal or Buddhist, while number (3) represents the population in the Agency and Tribal Areas of the North-West Frontier Province, and must be almost exclusively Muslim.

3. The term 'Brahmanic' has been used for those Hindus who were not returned as belonging to either the Arya Samaj or the Brahmo Samaj or to certain other reforming or segregative bodies, which have been shown together in 'Other Hindus'. These bodies consist of Deo-Samajists, Adi-Hindus, Adi-Dravidas, Adi-Karnatakas and such persons of the Satnami, Sanjogi, Kabirpanthi and Dadupanthi sects as returned themselves by these terms in place of the term Hindu. They include 1,479 persons (798 males, 681 females) who appear in the Bombay Table under 'Minor Religions'.

4. The statement below shows the number of persons tabulated as Jains and Buddhists who returned themselves as also Hindus :—

Province or State.	Jain.			Buddhist.		
	Persons.	Males.	Females.	Persons.	Males.	Females.
Bihar and Orissa	236	135	101	19	19	..
Central Provinces and Berar ..	3,800	2,043	1,757	26	16	10
Delhi	141	68	73	..	..	..
Punjab	7,623	4,035	3,588	..	..	..

In the Punjab 551 Hindus returned themselves as also Jain (526) or Buddhist (25), or Ad-Dharmi (7,287). They are included in the total of Other Hindus.

5. Sects of Christians, like those of Hindus and Muslims, have not been separately sorted, but collective figures for Roman Catholics, Syrians and Others, will be found in the statement at the end of this table.

6. Figures of Tribal Religion include 36 persons (32 males and 4 females) in Baluchistan who returned their religion as "Chuhra," and 134 persons (78 males and 56 females) returned as Sansi from Jammu and Kashmir State.

7. Details for the persons included under the head 'Minor Religions and Religion not Returned' are as follows :—

Province, State or Agency.	Total.			No Religion.			Indefinite Beliefs.			Chinese.			Remarks.
	Persons.	Males.	Females.	Persons.	Males.	Females.	Persons.	Males.	Females.	Persons.	Males.	Females.	
India ..	**571,187**	**329,014**	**242,173**	**153**	**79**	**74**	**940**	**576**	**364**	**150,240**	**99,174**	**51,066**	
Ajmer-Merwara ..	2	2	..	2	2	..	..	..	..	..	..	..	
Andamans and Nicobars	*148	139	9	..	..	..	..	..	..	111	103	8	*Includes Shintoists (males 36, female 1).
Assam	453	240	213	14	10	4	376	177	199	63	53	10	
Baluchistan ..	7	4	3	..	..	..	7	4	3	..	..	..	
Bengal	1,739	1,401	329	..	..	..	236	175	61	1,494	1,226	268	
Bihar and Orissa ..	†286	165	121	..	..	..	15	12	3	..	..	..	† Includes Kumbhipatias (153 males and 118 females).
Bombay Presidency	176	135	41	37	21	16	129	104	25	10	10	..	
Burma	‡148,909	98,932	50,877	..	..	..	40	18	22	148,551	97,773	50,778	‡Includes Shintoists (males 241, females 77)
Coorg ..	5	3	2	..	..	..	5	3	2	..	..	..	
Delhi	§439	246	193	..	..	..	..	..	..	..	..	..	
Madras	129	79	50	4	3	1	125	76	49	..	..	..	
Punjab (and Agency)	§418,789	228,509	190,280	..	..	..	..	..	..	..	..	..	§Ad-Dharmi.
United Provinces ..	3	3	..	..	..	..	3	3	..	..	..	..	
Travancore State ..	‖1	1	..	..	..	..	1	1	..	..	..	..	‖Siddhanar
Mysore State ..	106	51	55	95	42	53	..	..	..	11	9	2	
Rajputana Agency ..	1	1	..	1	1	..	..	..	..	..	..	..	
W. I. States Agency	3	3	..	..	..	..	3	3	..	..	..	..	

Note.—(a) Those shown as 'Chinese' were mostly returned as Confucians (23,713 males and 13,625 females), and the rest as Spirit (i.e., *Ancestor Worshippers (75,431 males and 37,424 females : from Burma) ; probably many Taoists are included under both these terms.*

(b) The term 'Indefinite Beliefs' includes the following terms :—

Agnostic, Ahimsa, Atheist, Christian Scientist, Deist, Free Thinker, Humanist, Monotheist, Rationalist, Sceptic, Spiritually Universal, Theosophist, Truth and "Freedom for India."

M8CC

Table XVI—

Province, State or Agency.	Population.			Brahmanic.		
	Persons.	Males.	Females.	Persons.	Males.	Females.
1	2	3	4	5	6	7
INDIA	**350,529,557**	**180,620,612**	**169.908,945**	**219,300,645**	**112,141,514**	**107,159,131**
Provinces	**271,431,549**	**139,890,957**	**131,540,592**	**161,869,166**	**82,697,843**	**79,171,323**
1. Ajmer-Merwara	560,292	296,081	264,211	431,907	226,412	205,495
2. Andaman and Nicobar Islands	29,463	19,702	9,761	7,528	5,410	2,118
Andaman Islands	*19,223*	*14,258*	*4,965*	*7,513*	*5,397*	*2,116*
Nicobar Islands	*10,240*	*5,444*	*4,796*	*15*	*13*	*2*
3. Assam	8,622,251	4,537,206	4,085,045	4,931,482	2,616,492	2,314,990
4. Baluchistan (*Districts and Administered Territories.*)	463,508	270,004	193,504	32,821	23,722	9,099
5. Bengal	50,114,002	26,041,698	24,072,304	6,576,764	3,367,891	3,208,873
6. Bihar and Orissa	37,677,576	18,794,138	18,883,438	30,987,158	15,480,344	15,506,814
Bihar	*25,727,500*	*12,896,660*	*12,830,840*	*21,091,077*	*10,603,473*	*10,487,604*
Orissa	*5,306,142*	*2,549,251*	*2,756,891*	*5,096,243*	*2,449,206*	*2,647,037*
Chota Nagpur	*6,643,934*	*3,348,227*	*3,295,707*	*4,799,838*	*2,427,665*	*2,372,173*
7. Bombay	21,854,866	11,505,229	10,349,637	16,607,609	8,601,900	8,005,709
Bombay Presidency	*17,916,318*	*9,291,930*	*8,624,388*	*15,601,259*	*8,040,097*	*7,561,162*
Sind	*3,887,070*	*2,180,954*	*1,706,116*	*1,004,765*	*560,782*	*443,983*
Aden	*51,478*	*32,345*	*19,133*	**1,585*	*1,021*	*564*
8. Burma	14,647,497	7,480,676	7,166,821	570,045	427,513	142,532
9. Central Provinces and Berar	15,507,723	7,761,818	7,745,905	13,336,372	6,670,278	6,666,094
Central Provinces	*12,065,885*	*6,002,239*	*6,063,646*	*10,270,485*	*5,106,632*	*5,163,853*
Berar	*3,441,838*	*1,759,579*	*1,682,259*	*3,065,887*	*1,563,646*	*1,502,241*
10. Coorg	163,327	90,575	72,752	146,006	79,558	66,448
11. Delhi	636,246	369,497	266,749	349,449	202,285	147,164
12. Madras	46,740,107	23,082,999	23,657,108	41,276,610	20,379,813	20,896,797
13. North-West Frontier Province (*Districts and Administered Territories.*)	2,425,076	1,315,818	1,109,258	135,198	80,481	54,717
14. Punjab	23,580,852	12,880,510	10,700,342	5,894,879	3,223,413	2,671,466
15. United Provinces of Agra and Oudh	48,408,763	25,445,006	22,963,757	40,585,338	21,312,331	19,273,007
Agra	*35,613,784*	*18,805,132*	*16,808,652*	*29,686,552*	*15,653,556*	*14,032,996*
Oudh	*12,794,979*	*6,639,874*	*6,155,105*	*10,898,786*	*5,658,775*	*5,240,011*
States and Agencies	**79,098,008**	**40,729,655**	**38,368,353**	**57,431,479**	**29,443,671**	**27,987,808**
16. Assam States	625,606	306,927	318,679	272,708	134,922	137,786
17. Baluchistan States	405,109	218,410	186,699	12,124	6,560	5,564
18. Baroda State	2,443,007	1,257,817	1,185,190	2,149,200	1,107,723	1,041,477
19. Bengal States	973,336	516,162	457,174	304,731	160,565	144,166
20. Bihar and Orissa States	4,652,007	2,288,422	2,363,585	4,194,837	2,062,993	2,131,844
21. Bombay States	4,468,396	2,288,623	2,179,773	3,921,041	1,998,350	1,922,691
22. Central India Agency	6,632,790	3,405,438	3,227,352	5,848,519	3,000,271	2,848,248
23. Central Provinces States	2,483,214	1,235,385	1,247,829	1,788,394	886,119	902,275
24. Gwalior State	3,523,070	1,867,031	1,656,039	3,255,977	1,724,311	1,531,666
25. Hyderabad State	14,436,148	7,370,010	7,066,138	9,699,615	4,948,408	4,751,207
26. Jammu and Kashmir State	3,646,243	1,938,338	1,707,905	642,273	343,349	298,924
27. Madras States Agency	6,754,484	3,373,032	3,381,452	4,323,099	2,141,780	2,181,319
Cochin State	*1,205,016*	*589,813*	*615,203*	*780,484*	*377,933*	*402,551*
Travancore State	*5,095,973*	*2,565,073*	*2,530,900*	*3,134,837*	*1,567,900*	*1,566,937*
Other Madras States	*453,495*	*218,146*	*235,349*	*407,778*	*195,947*	*211,831*
28. Mysore State	6,557,302	3,353,963	3,203,339	5,015,433	2,556,357	2,459,076
29. North-West Frontier Province (*Agencies and Tribal Areas.*)	46,451	44,635	1,816	-13,641	13,186	455
30. Punjab States	437,787	229,290	208,497	2,226,792	1,195,678	1,031,114
31. Punjab States Agency	4,472,218	2,451,394	2,020,824			
32. Rajputana Agency	11,225,712	5,885,028	5,340,684	9,567,234	5,023,365	4,543,869
33. Sikkim State	109,808	55,825	53,983	..	..	..
34. United Provinces States	1,206,070	618,171	587,899	949,643	481,518	468,125
35. Western India States Agency.	3,999,250	2,025,754	1,973,496	3,246,218	1,658,216	1,588,002

* Including persons of Non-Brahmanic Sects, if any.

Religion.

Hindus.												
Arya.			Brahmo.			Others.			Total Hindus.			
Persons.	Males.	Females.	Persons.	Males.	Females.	Persons.	Males.	Females.	Persons.	Males.	Females.	
8	9	10	11	12	13	14	15	16	17	18	19	
990,233	**547,964**	**442,269**	**5,378**	**3,166**	**2,212**	**18,898,884**	**9,923,656**	**8,975,228**	**239,195,140**	**122,616,300**	**116,578,840**	
828,244	**460,350**	**367,894**	**4,659**	**2,788**	**1,871**	**15,025,919**	**7,950,203**	**7,075,716**	**177,727,988**	**91,111,184**	**86,616,804**	
2,602	1,391	1,211	..	..	..	..	..	..	434,509	227,803	206,706	1
90	45	45	..	..	..	..	..	..	7,618	5,455	2,163	2
90	*45*	*45*	..	..	..	..	..	..	*7,603*	*5,442*	*2,161*	
..	..	..	..	..	..	..	..	..	*15*	*13*	*2*	
12	11	1	266	141	125	..	..	..	4,931,760	2,616,644	2,315,116	3
3,978	2,587	1,391	5	5	..	4,628	3,215	1,413	41,432	29,529	11,903	4
201	156	45	2,135	1,211	924	‖14,991,307	7,930,656	7,060,651	21,570,407	11,299,914	10,270,493	5
6,763	3,704	3,059	404	217	187	‡17,149	8,992	8,157	31,011,474	15,493,257	15,518,217	6
6,476	*3,541*	*2,935*	*187*	*109*	*78*	*17,149*	*8,992*	*8,157*	*21,114,889*	*10,616,115*	*10,498,774*	
15	*7*	*8*	*173*	*82*	*91*	..	..	..	*5,096,431*	*2,449,295*	*2,647,136*	
272	*156*	*116*	*44*	*26*	*18*	..	..	..	*4,800,154*	*2,427,847*	*2,372,307*	
11,951	6,680	5,271	182	113	69	1,479	798	681	16,621,221	8,609,491	8,011,730	7
1,555	*988*	*567*	*118*	*70*	*48*	..	..	..	*15,602,932*	*8,041,155*	*7,561,777*	
10,396	*5,692*	*4,704*	*64*	*43*	*21*	*1,479*	*798*	*681*	*1,016,704*	*567,315*	*449,389*	
..	..	..	..	..	..	..	..	..	*1,585*	*1,021*	*564*	
204	112	92	704	548	156	..	..	..	570,953	428,173	142,780	8
1,836	1,046	790	15	2	13	..	..	..	13,338,223	6,671,326	6,666,897	9
1,236	*722*	*514*	*15*	*2*	*13*	..	..	..	*10,271,736*	*5,107,356*	*5,164,380*	
600	*324*	*276*	..	..	..	..	..	..	*3,066,487*	*1,563,970*	*1,502,517*	
..	..	..	1	1	..	..	..	..	146,007	79,559	66,448	10
50,030	28,955	21,075	11	9	2	*373	210	163	399,863	231,459	168,404	11
122	64	58	631	376	255	7	4	3	41,277,370	20,380,257	20,897,113	12
7,779	3,877	3,902	..	..	..	..	..	..	142,977	84,358	58,619	13
425,997	237,692	188,305	162	98	64	**7,550	4,331	3,219	6,328,588	3,465,534	2,863,054	14
316,679	174,030	142,649	143	67	76	3,426	1,997	1,429	40,905,586	21,488,425	19,417,161	15
304,348	*167,124*	*137,224*	*142*	*67*	*75*	*3,370*	*1,956*	*1,414*	*29,994,412*	*15,822,703*	*14,171,709*	
12,331	*6,906*	*5,425*	*1*	..	*1*	*56*	*41*	*15*	*10,911,174*	*5,665,722*	*5,245,452*	
161,989	**87,614**	**74,375**	**719**	**378**	**341**	**3,872,965**	**1,973,453**	**1,899,512**	**61,467,152**	**31,505,116**	**29,962,036**	
..	..	..	182	91	91	..	..	..	272,890	135,013	137,877	16
78	55	23	2	2	..	45	34	11	12,249	6,651	5,598	17
2,801	1,589	1,212	70	37	33	..	..	..	2,152,071	1,109,349	1,042,722	18
..	..	..	30	17	13	336,901	178,789	158,112	641,662	339,371	302,291	19
..	..	..	41	15	26	..	..	..	4,194,878	2,063,008	2,131,870	20
21	11	10	..	..	..	26	15	11	3,921,088	1,998,376	1,922,712	21
3,097	1,620	1,477	66	33	33	522	279	243	5,852,204	3,002,203	2,850,001	22
6	3	3	1	1	..	..	..	..	1,788,401	886,123	902,278	23
1,308	688	620	..	..	..	14,291	7,248	7,043	3,271,576	1,732,247	1,539,329	24
3,700	1,896	1,804	182	98	84	*2,473,230	1,252,651	1,220,579	12,176,727	6,203,053	5,973,674	25
93,944	50,346	43,598	5	4	1	..	..	..	736,222	393,699	342,523	26
32	18	14	19	7	12	..	..	..	4,323,150	2,141,805	2,181,345	27
..	..	..	..	..	..	..	..	..	*780,484*	*377,933*	*402,551*	
32	*18*	*14*	*19*	*7*	*12*	..	..	..	*3,134,888*	*1,567,925*	*1,566,963*	
..	..	..	..	..	..	..	..	..	*407,778*	*195,947*	*211,831*	
45	36	9	76	41	35	§1,000,326	509,898	490,428	6,015,880	3,066,332	2,949,548	28
10	8	2	..	..	..	..	..	..	13,651	13,194	457	29
43,867	24,247	19,620	..	..	..	473	246	227	383,883	199,991	183,892	30
									1,887,249	1,020,180	867,069	31
11,471	6,196	5,275	44	32	12	†56	27	29	9,578,805	5,029,620	4,549,185	32
..	..	..	..	..	..	47,074	24,256	22,818	47,074	24,256	22,818	33
1,059	625	434	1	..	1	21	10	11	950,724	482,153	468,571	34
550	276	274	..	..	..	..	..	..	3,246,768	1,658,492	1,588,276	35

‡ Deo-Samajists. (Persons 16,624, males 8,749 and females 7,875) and Adi-Hindus (Persons 525, males 243 and females 282).

‖ Includes Adi-Dravidas (Persons 382, males 183 and females 199). § Adi-Karnataka. † Deo-Samajists. * Adi-Hindus.

**Includes 185 (106 Males & 79 females) Adi-Hindus.

Table XVI.—

Province, State or Agency.	Sikhs.			Jains.		
	Persons.	Males.	Females.	Persons.	Males.	Females.
1	20	21	22	23	24	25
INDIA	**4,335,771**	**2,432,449**	**1,903,322**	**1,252,105***	**645,097**	**607,008**
Provinces	**3,220,997**	**1,802,784**	**1,418,213**	**453,569**	**247,285**	**206,284**
1. Ajmer-Merwara	341	232	109	19,497	10,427	9,070
2. Andaman and Nicobar Islands	649	503	146	..	..	..
Andaman Islands	*649*	*503*	*146*	..	..	..
Nicobar Islands	..	..	..	..	..	..
3. Assam	2,497	1,740	757	2,636	2,000	636
4. Baluchistan (*Districts and Administered Territories*).	8,368	6,227	2,141	32	20	12
5. Bengal	7,320	5,414	1,906	9,167	6,571	2,596
Bihar and Orissa	5,653	3,622	2,031	3,734	2,058	1,676
Bihar	*1,736*	*1,012*	*724*	*1,856*	*1,006*	*850*
Orissa	*89*	*59*	*30*	*108*	*64*	*44*
Chota Nagpur	*3,828*	*2,551*	*1,277*	*1,770*	*988*	*782*
7. Bombay	20,893	13,081	7,812	200,015	109,763	90,252
Bombay Presidency	*2,378*	*1,874*	*504*	*198,670*	*109,006*	*89,664*
Sind	*18,505*	*11,202*	*7,303*	*1,144*	*633*	*511*
Aden	*10*	*5*	*5*	*201*	*124*	*77*
8. Burma	10,907	7,882	3,025	721	464	257
9. Central Provinces and Berar	4,241	2,828	1,413	77,895	40,333	37,562
Central Provinces	*3,788*	*2,566*	*1,222*	*57,493*	*29,773*	*27,720*
Berar	*453*	*262*	*191*	*20,402*	*10,560*	*9,842*
10. Coorg	..	..	..	83	43	40
11. Delhi	6,437	4,269	2,168	5,345	2,949	2,396
12. Madras	537	456	81	31,206	17,090	14,116
13. North-West Frontier Province (*Districts and Administered Territories.*)	42,510	26,284	16,226	..	..	..
14 Punjab	3,064,144	1,703,584	1,360,560	35,284	18,751	16,533
15. United Provinces of Agra and Oudh	46,500	26,662	19,838	67,954	36,816	31,138
Agra	*43,727*	*24,832*	*18,895*	*66,506*	*36,041*	*30,465*
Oudh	*2,773*	*1,830*	*943*	*1,448*	*775*	*673*
States and Agencies	**1,114,774**	**629,665**	**485,109**	**798,536**	**397,812**	**400,724**
16. Assam States	232	178	54	167	116	51
17. Baluchistan States	57	43	14	..	..	
18. Baroda State	521	453	68	48,408	24,570	23,838
19. Bengal States	14	4	10	502	400	102
20. Bihar and Orissa States	216	138	78	318	166	152
21. Bombay States	714	403	311	87,353	45,871	41,482
22. Central India Agency	1,426	911	515	50,268	26,635	23,633
23. Central Provinces States	279	175	104	1,960	1,083	877
24. Gwalior State	681	446	235	45,079	24,238	20,841
25. Hyderabad State	5,178	3,064	2,114	21,543	11,456	10,087
26. Jammu and Kashmir State	50,662	26,457	24,205	597	319	278
27. Madras States Agency	12	6	6	282	160	122
Cochin State	..	..	..	*210*	*118*	*92*
Travancore State	*12*	*6*	*6*	*41*	*21*	*20*
Other Madras States	..	..	..	*31*	*21*	*10*
28. Mysore State	100	63	37	29,613	15,920	13,693
29. North-West Frontier Province (*Agencies and Tribal Areas.*)	5,425	5,125	300	..	..	..
30. Punjab States	10,854	6,124	4,730	408	218	190
31. Punjab States Agency	996,626	561,238	435,388	7,448	3,993	3,455
32. Rajputana Agency	41,605	24,725	16,880	300,748	146,004	154,744
33. Sikkim State	..	..	..	2	2	..
34. United Provinces States	110	61	49	214	115	99
35. Western India States Agency.	62	51	11	203,626	96,546	107,080

* Includes 11,800 Jains (6,281 males and 5,519 females) who also returned themselves as Hindu, *vide Para.* 4 page 513.

Religion—*contd.*

Buddhists.			Zoroastrians.			Muslims.			
Persons.	Males.	Females.	Persons.	Males.	Females.	Persons.	Males.	Females.	
26	27	28	29	30	31	32		34	
12,786,806†	**6,314,999**	**6,471,807**	**109,752**	**56,626**	**53,126**	**77,677,545**	**40,867,320**	**36,810,225**	
12,693,089	**6,267,532**	**6,425,557**	**96,549**	**50,354**	**46,195**	**67,020,443**	**35,224,943**	**31,795,500**	
4	4	..	301	142	159	97,135	52,665	44,468	1
2,912	2,510	402	1	1	..	6,719	4,966	1,753	2
2,902	*2,502*	*400*	*1*	*1*	..	*6,434*	*4,722*	*1,712*	
10	*8*	*2*	..	..	..	*285*	*244*	*41*	
14,955	8,565	6,390	7	6	1	2,755,914	1,449,073	1,306,841	3
68	53	15	167	90	77	405,309	228,389	176,920	4
316,031	161,796	154,235	1,520	897	623	27,497,624	14,200,142	13,297,482	5
919	553	366	241	145	96	4,264,790	2,112,814	2,151,976	6
51	*37*	*14*	*48*	*25*	*23*	*3,689,954*	*1,819,928*	*1,870,026*	
396	*212*	*184*	*20*	*9*	*11*	*124,463*	*58,685*	*65,778*	
472	*304*	*168*	*173*	*111*	*62*	*450,373*	*234,201*	*216,172*	
2,204	1,724	480	89,544	46,414	43,130	4,456,897	2,474,400	1,982,497	7
2,048	*1,599*	*449*	*85,662*	*44,298*	*41,364*	*1,583,259*	*857,712*	*725,547*	
53	*28*	*25*	*3,537*	*1,868*	*1,669*	*2,830,800*	*1,589,735*	*1,241,065*	
103	*97*	*6*	*345*	*248*	*97*	*42,838*	*26,953*	*15,885*	
12,348,037	6,088,257	6,259,780	419	258	161	584,839	363,824	221,015	8
66	43	23	2,092	1,107	985	682,854	358,900	323,954	9
61	*39*	*22*	*1,849*	*969*	*880*	*383,174*	*201,352*	*181,822*	
5	*4*	*1*	*243*	*138*	*105*	*299,680*	*157,548*	*142,132*	
3	3	..	27	12	15	13,777	8,943	4,834	10
76	59	17	126	81	45	206,960	120,926	86,034	11
1,359	806	553	507	269	238	3,305,937	1,631,716	1,674,221	12
2	2	..	60	30	30	2,227,303	1,196,120	1,031,183	13
5,723	2,757	2,966	546	339	207	13,332,460	7,241,612	6,090,848	14
730	400	330	991	563	428	7,181,927	3,780,453	3,401,474	15
678	*375*	*303*	*855*	*484*	*371*	*5,318,077*	*2,818,828*	*2,499,249*	
52	*25*	*27*	*136*	*79*	*57*	*1,863,850*	*961,625*	*902,225*	
93,717	**47,467**	**46,250**	**13,203**	**6,272**	**6,931**	**10,657,102**	**5,642,377**	**5,014,725**	
90	57	33	2	1	1	24,600	12,689	11,911	16
..	..	..	..	..	..	392,784	211,700	181,084	17
43	42	1	7,127	3,071	4,056	182,630	93,759	88,871	18
14,532	7,606	6,926	..	..	..	312,476	166,615	145,861	19
1,376	682	694	23	14	9	19,516	10,298	9,218	20
4	2	2	1,468	799	669	414,931	221,586	193,345	21
13	13	..	976	506	470	376,637	198,346	178,291	22
3	1	2	17	12	5	23,254	11,733	11,521	23
..	..	..	239	96	143	204,297	109,412	94,885	24
52	26	26	1,784	937	847	1,534,666	791,435	743,231	25
38,724	19,287	19,437	5	3	2	2,817,636	1,497,252	1,320,384	26
160	98	62	16	12	4	467,396	238,052	229,344	27
96	*51*	*45*	*3*	*1*	*2*	*87,902*	*44,794*	*43,108*	
64	*47*	*17*	*13*	*11*	*2*	*353,274*	*180,555*	*172,719*	
..	..	..	..	..	..	*26,220*	*12,703*	*13,517*	
1,239	640	599	331	169	162	398,628	213,381	185,247	28
1	1	..	2	2	..	23,086	22,114	972	29
1,308	630	678	1	1	..	40,845	22,071	18,774	30
722	383	339	22	18	4	1,556,591	852,700	703,891	31
1	1	..	319	70	149	1,069,325	565,962	503,363	32
35,412	17,978	17,434	..	..	..	104	98	6	33
1	1	..	..	..	..	252,131	134,325	117,806	34
36	19	17	871	461	410	545,569	268,849	276,720	35

†Includes 45 Buddhists (35 Males and 10 Females) who also returned themselves as Hindus, *vide* para. 4 page 513.

Table XVI—

Province, State or Agency.	Christians.			Jews.		
	Persons.	Males.	Females.	Persons.	Males.	Females.
1	35	36	37	38	39	40
INDIA	**6,296,763**	**3,227,090**	**3,069,673**	**24,141**	**12,450**	**11,691**
Provinces	**3,866,660**	**1,993,009**	**1,873,651**	**21,206**	**11,002**	**10,204**
1. Ajmer-Merwara	6,947	4,000	2,947	49	29	20
2. Andaman and Nicobar Islands ..	1,461	984	477	..	..	..
Andaman Islands	*1,123*	*797*	*326*	..	..	..
Nicobar Islands	*338*	*187*	*151*	..	..	..
3. Assam	202,586	101,640	100,946	18	11	7
4. Baluchistan .. .. (*Districts and Administered Territories.*)	8,044	5,625	2,419	15	12	3
5. Bengal	180,299	95,849	84,450	1,867	957	910
6. Bihar and Orissa	341,894	170,128	171,766	24	15	9
Bihar	*30,593*	*15,477*	*15,116*	..	..	..
Orissa	*9,709*	*4,611*	*5,098*	*3*	*2*	*1*
Chota Nagpur	*301,592*	*150,040*	*151,552*	*21*	*13*	*8*
7. Bombay	317,042	176,310	140,732	17,739	9,190	8,549
Bombay Presidency	*299,664*	*165,025*	*134,639*	*12,603*	*6,546*	*6,057*
Sind	*15,133*	*9,523*	*5,610*	*985*	*509*	*476*
Aden	*2,245*	*1,762*	*483*	*4,151*	*2,135*	*2,016*
8. Burma	331,106	171,352	159,754	1,218	625	593
9. Central Provinces and Berar	50,584	26,438	24,146	153	88	65
Central Provinces	*45,189*	*23,673*	*21,516*	*132*	*78*	*54*
Berar	*5,395*	*2,765*	*2,630*	*21*	*10*	*11*
10. Coorg	3,425	2,012	1,413	..	..	..
11. Delhi	16,989	9,500	7,489	11	8	3
12. Madras	1,774,276	878,493	895,783	23	14	9
13. North-West Frontier Province .. (*Districts and Administered Territories*).	12,213	9,013	3,200	11	11	
14. Punjab	414,788	230,018	184,770	12	5	7
15. United Provinces of Agra and Oudh ..	205,006	111,647	93,359	66	37	29
Agra	*189,470*	*101,835*	*87,635*	*56*	*31*	*25*
Oudh	*15,536*	*9,812*	*5,724*	*10*	*6*	*4*
States and Agencies	**2,430,103**	**1,234,081**	**1,196,022**	**2,935**	**1,448**	**1,487**
16. Assam States	46,660	22,405	24,255	..	..	..
17. Baluchistan States	15	12	3	2	2	..
18. Baroda State	7,262	3,858	3,404	55	22	33
19. Bengal States	2,768	1,413	1,355	..	..	..
20. Bihar and Orissa States	74,832	37,057	37,775	..	..	..
21. Bombay States	16,006	7,960	8,046	929	450	479
22. Central India Agency	10,476	5,978	4,498	38	18	20
23. Central Provinces States	51,701	26,102	25,599	..	..	..
24. Gwalior State	1,198	592	606	..	..	..
25. Hyderabad State	151,382	79,444	71,938	27	11	16
26. Jammu and Kashmir State	2,263	1,243	1,020	..	..	..
27. Madras States Agency	1,958,811	990,503	968,308	1,749	884	865
Cochin State	*334,870*	*166,195*	*168,675*	*1,451*	*721*	*730*
Travancore State	*1,604,475*	*814,833*	*789,642*	*298*	*163*	*135*
Other Madras States	*19,466*	*9,475*	*9,991*	..	..	..
28. Mysore State	87,538	45,164	42,374	39	13	26
29. North-West Frontier Province .. (*Agencies and Tribal Areas.*)	4,286	4,199	87	..	..	..
30. Punjab States	206	100	106	..	..	..
31. Punjab States Agency	4,359	2,438	1,921	1	..	1
32. Rajputana Agency	5,778	3,107	2,671	38	18	20
33. Sikkim State	276	134	142	..	..	..
34. United Provinces States	2,890	1,516	1,374	..	..	..
35. Western India States Agency ..	1,396	856	540	57	30	27

Religion—*concld.*

Tribal Religions.			Minor Religions and Religion not returned.			
Persons.	Males.	Females.	Persons.	Males.	Females.	
41	42	43	44	45	46	
8,280,347	**4,119,267**	**4,161,080**	**571,187**	**329,014**	**242,173**	
5,779,709	**2,864,651**	**2,915,058**	**551,339**	**318,213**	**233,126**	
1,509	777	732	2	2	..	1
9,955	5,144	4,811	148	139	9	2
474	*255*	*219*	*37*	*36*	*1*	
9,481	*4,889*	*4,592*	*111*	*103*	*8*	
711,432	357,292	354,140	446	235	211	3
66	55	11	7	4	3	4
528,037	268,757	259,280	1,730	1,401	329	5
2,048,809	1,011,522	1,037,287	38	24	14	6
888,370	*443,057*	*445,313*	*3*	*3*	..	
74,891	*36,295*	*38,596*	*32*	*19*	*13*	
1,085,548	*532,170*	*553,378*	*3*	*2*	*1*	
129,135	64,721	64,414	176	135	41	7
128,931	*64,582*	*64,349*	*171*	*133*	*38*	
204	*139*	*65*	*5*	*2*	*3*	
..	..	..	..	..	..	
650,388	321,809	328,579	148,909	98,032	50,877	8
1,351,615	660,755	690,860	..	..	..	9
1,302,463	*636,433*	*666,030*	..	..	..	
49,152	*24,322*	*24,830*	..	..	..	
..	..	..	5	3	2	10
..	..	..	439	246	193	11
348,763	173,819	174,944	129	79	50	12
..	..	..	..	..	..	13
..	..	..	399,307	217,910	181,397	14
..	..	..	3	3	..	15
..	..	..	*3*	*3*		
..	..	..	..	..		
2,500,638	**1,254,616**	**1,246,022**	**19,848**	**10,801**	**9,047**	
280,958	136,463	144,495	7	5	2	16
2	2	..	..	..	..	17
44,890	22,693	22,197	..	..	..	18
1,382	753	629	..	..	..	19
360,600	176,918	183,682	248	141	107	20
25,903	13,176	12,727	..	..	..	21
340,752	170,828	169,924	..	..	..	22
617,599	310,156	307,443	..	..	..	23
..	..	..	..	..	..	24
544,789	280,584	264,205	..	..	..	25
134	78	56	..	..	..	26
2,907	1,511	1,396	1	1	..	27
..	..	..	..	..	..	
2,907	*1,511*	*1,396*	*1*	*1*		
..	..	..	..	..	..	
23,828	12,230	11,598	106	51	55	28
..	..	..	..	..	..	29
..	..	..	282	155	127	30
..	..	..	19,200	[illegible]	8,756	31
229,092	115,420	113,672	1	1	..	32
26,940	13,357	13,583	..	..	..	33
..	..	..	..	..	..	34
862	447	415	3	3	..	35

Territorial Distribution of Christians by Sect.

Province, State or Agency.	Total Christians.			Roman Catholic.			Romo-Syrian.			Other Syrian.			Others.		
	Persons.	Males.	Females.	Persons.	Males.	Females.	Persons.	Males.	Females.	Persons.	Males.	Females.	Persons.	Males.	Females.
1	2	3	4	5	6	7	8	9	10	11	12	13	14	15	16
INDIA ..	**6,296,763**	**3,227,090**	**3,069,673**	**2,113,659**	**1,075,036**	**1,038,623**	**654,939**	**330,063**	**324,876**	**525,607**	**266,267**	**259,340**	**3,002,558**	**1,555,724**	**1,446,834**
Provinces.	4,089,849	2,105,686	1,984,163	1,561,310	794,814	766,496	21,982	10,776	11,206	8,236	4,155	4,081	2,498,321	1,295,941	1,202,380
1. Ajmer-Merwara ..	6,947	4,000	2,947	2,051	1,199	852	..	..	..	..	..	..	4,896	2,801	2,095
2. Andamans and Nicobars	1,461	984	477	445	378	67	..	..	..	..	..	..	1,016	606	410
3. Assam	249,246	124,045	125,201	15,056	8,036	7,020	..	..	..	3	3	..	234,187	116,006	118,181
4. Baluchistan	8,059	5,637	2,422	1,511	1,025	486	..	..	..	1	1	..	6,547	4,611	1,936
5. Bengal	183,067	97,262	85,805	70,578	36,695	33,883	355	103	252	185	94	91	111,949	60,370	51,579
6. Bihar and Orissa ..	416,726	207,185	209,541	205,209	100,915	104,294	..	..	..	..	..	..	211,517	106,270	105,247
7. Bombay (*including Aden*)	333,048	184,270	148,778	196,124	109,915	86,209	358	287	71	420	270	150	136,146	73,798	62,348
8. Burma	331,106	171,352	159,754	89,678	47,009	42,669	..	..	..	3	1	2	241,425	124,342	117,083
9. Central Provinces and Berar	102,285	52,540	49,745	55,964	28,763	27,201	..	..	..	14	9	5	46,307	23,768	22,539
10. Coorg	3,425	2,012	1,413	2,808	1,686	1,122	..	..	..	16	14	2	601	312	289
11. Delhi	16,989	9,500	7,489	2,909	1,654	1,255	1	1	..	5	3	2	14,074	7,842	6,232
12. Madras ..	1,793,742	887,968	905,774	847,453	414,759	432,694	21,259	10,385	10,874	7,380	3,615	3,765	917,650	459,209	458,441
13. North-West Frontier Province.	16,499	13,212	3,287	1,578	1,214	364	..	..	..	..	..	..	14,921	11,998	2,923
14. Punjab	419,353	232,556	186,797	58,206	34,573	23,633	..	..	..	175	125	50	360,972	197,858	163,114
15. United Provinces of Agra and Oudh.	207,896	113,163	94,733	11,740	6,993	4,747	9	..	9	34	20	14	196,113	106,150	89,963
States and Agencies.	2,206,914	1,121,404	1,085,510	552,349	280,222	272,127	632,957	319,287	313,670	517,371	262,112	255,259	504,237	259,783	244,454
16. Baroda State ..	7,262	3,858	3,404	2,087	1,165	922	..	..	..	..	..	..	5,175	2,693	2,482
17. Central India Agency ..	10,476	5,978	4,498	4,349	2,234	2,115	..	..	..	5	2	3	6,122	3,742	2,380
18. Gwalior State ..	1,198	592	606	450	262	188	..	..	..	..	..	..	748	330	418
19. Hyderabad State ..	151,382	79,444	71,938	21,259	11,591	9,668	..	..	..	17	12	5	130,106	67,841	62,265
20. Jammu and Kashmir State	2,263	1,243	1,020	124	82	42	..	..	..	..	..	..	2,139	1,161	978
21. Cochin State ..	334,870	166,195	168,675	109,503	54,980	54,523	183,632	90,789	92,843	36,168	17,769	18,399	5,567	2,657	2,910
22. Travancore State ..	1,604,475	814,833	789,642	360,217	181,423	178,794	449,173	228,426	220,747	481,099	244,278	236,821	313,986	160,706	153,280
23. Mysore State ..	87,538	45,164	42,374	52,347	27,309	25,038	122	50	72	58	34	24	35,011	17,771	17,240
24. Rajputana Agency ..	5,778	3,107	2,671	1,465	823	642	..	..	..	..	..	..	4,313	2,284	2,029
25. Sikkim State ..	276	134	142	1	..	1	..	..	..	..	..	..	275	134	141
26. Western India States Agency	1,396	856	540	547	353	194	30	22	8	24	17	7	795	464	331
				Total Romanist ..		2,768,598	1,405,099	1,363,499	..	..	..	—	..	..	..

TABLE XVII.

Race, Caste or Tribe.

In tabulating caste the method followed in 1891 of tabulating as far as possible by traditional occupation has been followed in order to avoid the dispersion of closely connected castes involved in an alphabetical arrangement. Castes have been shown in consolidated figures as far as possible, and though variant names have generally been shown some purely local variants have disappeared in the process.

2 The castes shown are representative only and not a complete tabulation of the whole population, the total numbers covered by this table being 220,747,267. In the final summary all Hindus appear and Hindus alone are included, but the separate groups tabulated in the main table include Tribal and some Muslim groups, the basic principle followed having been first to give examples from all strata of the population corresponding in arrangement as far as possible to the occupation table (Table X), and secondly to include all castes which appear in more than one provincial table. The instructions for the compilation of caste were that all provinces should in the interests of economy compile figures only for such castes as the Local Government considered of sufficient importance. This has made it impossible to compile figures for all castes for all India. Castes and Tribes appearing in Tables VIII, XI, XIV, XVIII have been marked *, ||, † or § accordingly.

The figures of exterior castes in some cases differ slightly from those in Provincial Volumes on account of the exclusion here of certain doubtful cases.

Table XVII—Race, Tribe or Caste.

Group.	Description.	Names.	Persons.	Males.	Females.	Province, State or Agency where chiefly found.
I.	Primitive Tribes collecting forest produce (but generally speaking not, at any rate until recently, practising Agriculture).	..	**16,102**	**8,091**	**8,011**	
		Andamanese	461	251	210	Andaman Islands (460), B. & O. (1).
		Aranadan §	60	33	27	Madras (60).
		Chenchu * † §	10,342	5,256	5,086	Madras (8,078), Hyderabad (2,264).
		Kadan §	758	363	395	Madras (491), Cochin (267).
		Urali, Sholagar§, Hasala ..	4,481	2,188	2,293	Madras (3,325), Cochin (240), Travancore (916).
II.	Primitive Tribe, pastoral ..	**Toda* † §**	**597**	**340**	**257**	Madras (597).
III.	Tribes practising agriculture, hunting, fishing and industries (without effective differentiation of occupation), and nearly derived castes.	....	**26,718,640**	**13,441,212**	**13,277,428**	
1	South Indian group (all more or less Hinduised).	....	*98,776*	*50,130*	*48,646*	
		Eravallan§	541	271	270	Cochin (541).
		Kota§	1,121	562	559	Madras (1,121).
		Kudiya† §	4,046	2,045	2,001	Coorg (549), Madras (3,497).
		Kurichhan§	7,112	3,585	3,527	Madras (7,112).
		Kuruman§	12,028	6,310	5,718	Madras (12,028).
		Marratha§	34,593	17,327	17,266	Coorg (540), Madras (34,053).
		Mavilan§	1,341	799	542	Madras (1,341).
		Malasar§	5,101	2,405	2,696	Madras (5,101).
		Paniyan	32,410	16,560	15,850	Madras (32,410).
		Palliyan§	483	266	217	Travancore (483).
2	Bhil group (probably to be associated with 4 and 6 but otherwise generally Hinduised).	.. ..	*3,733,383*	*1,929,166*	*1,804,217*	
		Barela, Bhil* † §, Bhilala §, Dhanka, Mankar, Mavchi§ Pathia§, Rathia, Tadvi.	2,454,144	1,251,009	1,203,135	Bombay (852,253), Central India (653,263), Gwalior (125,026), Rajputana (655,647), Ajmer-Merwara (8,313). Central Provinces and Berar (46,231), United Provinces (28), Baroda (83,972), Hyderabad (15,052), Western India States (14,359).
		Girasia * §	29,232	15,212	14,020	Rajputana (29,231), Central India (1).
		Mina, Meo † §	1,110,479	589,910	520,569	Punjab (133,089), United Provinces (30,376), Central India (63,401), Gwalior (67,202), Rajputana (780,760), Ajmer-Merwara (8,017), Bombay (404), Central Provinces and Berar (8,128), Delhi (5,259), Western India States (13,843).
		Mer, Merat† §, ...	139,528	73,035	66,493	Ajmer-Merwara (108,588), Central India (52), Rajputana (30,888).
3	Koli group (possibly allied to 4 in origin, but speaking Aryanized languages and generally Hinduised as 2.)	....	*3,418,643*	*1,775,937*	*1,642,706*	
		Baria, Bhalia, Chodhra, * † § Gedia, Khant, .. Koli† §, Kotwal, Naikda§, Patelia§, Patanwadia. Thakarda, Talabda, Valvi§	3,418,643	1,775,937	1,642,706	Ajmer-Merwara (10,591) Bihar & Orissa (5,001) Bombay (1,988,265), Central Provinces and Berar (43,130), Punjab (182,235), Baroda (459,106), Gwalior (78,621), Hyderabad (52,472), Rajputana (91,405), Western India States (481,475), Delhi (6,934), Central India (19,408).
4	**Kol** group (Munda-speaking tribes and Hindi or Oriya-speaking derivative castes).	....	*7,283,743*	*3,622,103*	*3,661,640*	
		Asur§, Agariya§, Binjhia, Birjia§.	151,459	75,035	76,424	Bengal (763), Bihar and Orissa (75,182), United Provinces (69,141) Central India (6,373).
		Baiga§, Bhaina§, Binjhwar§, Bharia§, Bhumia†, Bhunjia, Bhuiya§, Ghatwar, Kadar (Bengal), **Khetawari§, Naiya, Pao.**	1,050,760	518,504	532,256	Bengal (51,553), Bihar and Orissa (725,199), Central Provinces and Berar (189,080), Central India (84,891), Rajputana (34), Sikkim (3).
		Birhor§	2,371	1,233	1,138	Bengal (21), Bihar and Orissa (2,350).
		Chero§	17,906	8,968	8,938	Bihar and Orissa (17,906).
		Gadaba§	48,154	23,758	24,396	Bihar and Orissa (277), Central Provinces and Berar (398), Madras (47,479).
		Ho§, Kol† §, Kharwar§, Kharia§, Mawasi, Bhogta Bhumij§, Munda† §, Kora.	2,315,276	1,146,722	1,168,554	Bengal (243,068), Bihar and Orissa (1,672,832), Central Provinces and Berar (104,822), United Provinces (76,848), Central India, (211,944), Rajputana (5,762).

Table XVII—Race, Tribe or Caste—*contd.*

Group.	Description.	Names.	Population. Persons.	Males.	Females.	Province, State or Agency where chiefly found.
		Juang§	15,024	7,332	7,692	Bihar and Orissa (15,024).
		Korku, Korwa † § ..	246,765	123,077	123,688	Bihar and Orissa (13,021), Central Provinces and Berar (203,192), Central India (30,046), United Provinces (504), Gwalior (2).
		Majhwar§, Majhi	23,414	12,050	11,364	Bengal (922), Central Provinces and Berar (19,110), Central India (3,044), Sikkim (338).
		Nagesia§	50,977	25,525	25,452	Bengal (2,291), Central Provinces and Berar (48,686).
		Parhaiya, Pahira	10,522	5,460	5,062	Bihar and Orissa (10,522).
		Santal*†, Saunta, Karmali§	2,524,472	1,265,087	1,259,385	Bengal (796,656), Bihar and Orissa (1,720,765), Central Provinces and Berar (7,051).
		*** †§ Sawara, Saonr, Savar, Saharia**	675,628	333,114	342,514	Bihar and Orissa (245,453), Central Provinces and Berar (86,028), Madras (211,781), United Provinces (14,113), Central India (22,338), Gwalior (76,219), Rajputana (19,696).
		Turi, Mahli	151,015	76,238	74,777	Bengal (36,608), Bihar and Orissa (114,407).
5	Oraon group (Dravidian speaking with Munda affinities; derived castes speak Hindi).	....	*1,943,929*	*978,220*	*965,709*	
		Bayar, Banmanu, Dhangar, Musahar.	811,746	408,433	403,313	Bengal (11,833), Bihar and Orissa (720,051), United Provinces (78,770), Central India (1,092).
		Maler, Mal-Paharia§ ..	110,849	56,268	54,581	Bengal (13,521), Bihar and Orissa (97,328)
		Oraon * † §	1,021,334	513,519	507,815	Bengal (228,140), Bihar and Orissa (637,111) Central Provinces and Berar (156,083).
6	Gond group (Dravidian-speaking tribes with Oriya or Hindi-speaking derivative castes).	....	*5,072,406*	*2,500,362*	*2,572,044*	
		Dhanwar§, Gond * † §, Kalota, Kamar†, §, Kawar,§ Kolam§, Kondh *,§ Konda Dora§ Koya§, *, Maria§, Muria§, Nagarchi§.	4,719,222	2,323,697	2,395,525	Andamans and Nicobars (90), Bengal (1,569), Bihar and Orissa (571,461), Bombay (562), Central Provinces and Berar (2,928,513), Madras (636,191), United Provinces (121,579), Central India (310,773), Gwalior (1,163), Hyderabad (146,918), Rajputana (403).
		Bhatra, Pardhan, Parja§ ..	353,184	176,665	176,519	Central Provinces and Berar (174,404), Madras (178,780).
7	Bodo group	....	*695,648*	*357,090*	*338,558*	
		Garo†, Hajong, Kachari,§ Mech§, Rabha.	695,648	357,090	338,558	Assam (621,735), Bengal (73,913).
8	Kuki-Chin group ..	**†, §**	*907,444*	*444,744*	*462,700*	
	Total Assam 536,385 ..	**Meithei**	330,545	162,022	168,523	Assam (324, 432), Burma (6,113).
	Total Bengal 22,065 ..	**Khami, Lakher, Banjogi** ..	39,530	19,592	19,938	Assam (6,105), Bengal (2,437), Burma (30,988).
	Total Burma 348,994 ..	**Lushei†§ Sokte, Thado,** ..	192,520	92,012	100,508	Assam (165,809), Bengal (3,036), Burma (23,675).
9	Mon-Khmer group ..	....	*418,766*	*206,563*	*212,203*	
		Khasi & Synteng ..	232,595	112,873	119,722	Andamans and Nicobars (65), Assam (232,530).
		Nicobarese † §	9,789	5,079	4,710	Andamans and Nicobars (9,789).
		Palaung§ & Others ..	165,917	83,328	82,589	Burma (165,917).
		Wa§	10,465	5,283	5,182	Burma (10,465).
10	Tai group	.. .. ..	*1,154,431*	*586,502*	*567,929*	
		Ahom † §	249,434	129,989	119,445	Assam (249,434).
		Khamti	4,793	2,462	2,331	Assam (3,672), Burma (1,121).
		Shan * †	900,204	454,051	446,153	Burma (900,204).
11	Others	....	*1,991,471*	*990,395*	*1,001,076*	
		Badaga §	43,075	21,819	21,256	Madras (43,075).
		Mro§	21,170	11,182	9,988	Bengal (7,404), Burma (13,766).
		Karen *,†,§	1,367,673	682,121	685,552	Burma (1,367,673).
		Naga§	272,529	133,693	138,836	Assam (268,303), Burma (4,2[illegible]4), Gwalior (2).
		Sak (Lui)	51,820	25,019	26,801	Burma (51,820).
		Salon	1,930	914	1,016	Burma (1,930).
		Singpho, Kachin * † § ..	156,253	75,359	80,894	Assam (2,908), Burma (153,345).
		Tharu, Bhoksa §	77,021	40,288	36,733	Bengal (482), Bihar and Orissa (37,338), United Provinces (39,201).

Table XVII—Race, Tribe or Caste—*contd.*

Group.	Description.	Names.	Population. Persons.	Males.	Females.	Province, State or Agency where chiefly found.
IV.	Land-owning and cultivating classes.	....	**62,981,007**	**32,826,510**	**30,154,497**	
1	Cultivating Brahmans ..	....	*1,251,139*	*661,491*	*589,648*	
		Babhan, Bhuinhar §, †	1,113,541	585,293	528,248	Bengal (847), Bihar and Orissa (895,602), Central Provinces and Berar (25,628). United Provinces (190,850), Central India (614).
		Taga* †	137,598	76,198	61,400	Delhi (4,445), United Provinces (133,153).
2	Rajput group	.. .. ..	*20,232,054*	*10,984,642*	*9,247,412*	
		Rajput *†	10,743,091	5,775,338	4,967,753	Bengal (156,978), Bihar and Orissa (1,412,440), Bombay (352,016), Central Provinces and Berar (506,087), Punjab (2,351,650), United Provinces (3,756,936), Baroda (94,893), Central India (388,942), Gwalior (393,076), Hyderabad (88,434), Jammu and Kashmir (256,020), Rajputana (669,516), Western India States (227,137).
		Jat * ‖ † §	8,377,819	4,637,135	3,740,684	Baluchistan (88,537), Delhi (53,277), North-West Frontier (76,327), Punjab (6,070,032), United Provinces (810,394), Jammu and Kashmir (149,073), Rajputana (1,042,153).
		Thakkar, Rathi, Rawat, Kanet † § Ghirath	714,503	369,574	344,929	Bombay (27,617), Punjab (564,250), Central India (5,000), Gwalior (16,397), Jammu and Kashmir (99,767), Rajputana (1,472).
		Daroga	187,582	94,008	93,574	Ajmer Merwara (10,182), Central India (296), Rajputana (177,104).
		Dangi	95,962	49,295	46,667	Central India (45,064), Rajputana (50,898)
		Sondhia	113,097	59,292	53,805	Central India (53,322), Gwalior (25,518), Rajputana (34,257).
3	Maratha group ..	.. ..	*17,195,169*	*8,761,062*	*8,434,107*	
		Maratha*, †	6,113,061	3,113,358	2,999,703	Bombay (4,229,331), Burma (594), Central Provinces and Berar (287,189), Baroda (12,165), Central India (15,976), Gwalior (14,151), Hyderabad (1,491,558), Cochin (107), Mysore (60,528), Rajputana (547), Western India States (915).
		Kanbi, Kunbi, Kurmi, Kurmi-kshattriya, Kapu, Kapewar, Raddi, Vakkaliga, Vellala * ‖ †	11,082,108	5,647,704	5,434,404	Andamans and Nicobar (679), Assam (26,331) Baluchistan (109), Bengal (194,652), Bihar and Orissa (1,452,724), Bombay (1,632,197). Central Provinces and Berar (1,608,995), Coorg (7,948), Delhi (560), Madras (200,790), United Provinces (1,885,946), Baroda (502,888), Central India (254,301), Gwalior (57,350), Hyderabad (1,120,723), Cochin (5,299), Travancore (71,641), Mysore (1,312,264), Rajputana (116,525), Sikkim (20), Western India States (630,166).
4	Others	..	*5,840,234*	*2,982,829*	*2,857,405*	
		Kalingi, Kalinji† ..	170,517	80,957	89,560	Madras (170,517).
		Bishnoi	70,461	37,337	33,124	Central India (588), Rajputana (69,873).
		Kolita	209,240	103,775	105,465	Bihar and Orissa (163,757), Central Provinces and Berar (45,483).
		Kisan	431,044	227,191	203,853	Bengal (2,659), Bihar and Orissa (98,585), United Provinces (329,800).
		Lodhi* †	1,742,470	910,540	831,930	Ajmer-Merwara (1,387), Andamans and Nicobars (44), Bengal (11,001), Central Provinces and Berar (318,577), Delhi (1,215), United Provinces (1,099,225) Central India (154,780), Gwalior (91,773), Hyderabad (6,908), Rajputana (57,560).
		Chasa, Raju	835,236	404,258	430,978	Bengal (56,778), Bihar and Orissa (778,313), Madras (145).
		Chasi Kaibartta (Mahisya)† ..	2,381,266	1,218,771	1,162,495	Bengal (2,381,266).
5	Cultivators and Watermen	.. ..	*4,170,928*	*2,112,698*	*2,058,230*	
		Kaibartta, Kewat † ..	1,813,278	908,487	904,791	Assam (165,702), Bengal (352,072), Bihar and Orissa (471,389), Central Provinces and Berar (197,035), Madras (40,855), United Provinces (550,162), Central India (36,063).
		Namasudra* †	2,265,476	1,156,316	1,109,160	Assam (170,519), Bengal (2,094,957).
		Patni	92,174	47,895	44,279	Assam (51,408), Bengal (40,766).
6	Cultivators and Agricultural Labourers.	.. ..	*4,670,649*	*2,339,518*	*2,331,131*	
		Halba, Mana	177,547	87,383	90,164	Central Provinces and Berar (177,547).
		Arakh, Pasi †	1,743,166	894,511	848,655	Ajmer-Merwara (49), Andamans and Nicobars (232), Baluchistan (228), Bengal (18,525), Bihar and Orissa (172,061), United Provinces (1,546,298), Central India (5,105), Gwalior (225), Rajputana (43).
		Bhar*, Rajbhar, Rajjhar, Rajwar.	630,708	315,860	314,848	Bengal (21,337), Bihar and Orissa (133,952), Central Provinces and Berar (10,477), United Provinces (464,942).
		Dhakar	162,188	83,901	78,287	Ajmer-Merwara (802), Central India (34,283) Gwalior (30,945), Rajputana (96,158).

Table XVII.—Race, Tribe or Caste—*contd.*

Group.	Description.	Names.	Population. Persons.	Males.	Females.	Province, State or Agency where chiefly found.
		Dhanuk§, Kandra ..	758,671	369,424	389,247	Ajmer-Merwara (1,680), Bengal (4,729), Bihar and Orissa (702,421), Central Provinces and Berar (6,894), Delhi (1,321), Central India (7,533), Gwalior (3,358), Rajputana (30,735).
		Dubla, Talavia † § ..	229,190	116,379	112,811	Bombay (150,439), Baroda (78,749), Western India States (2).
		Ghasia* †	141,850	70,350	71,500	Baluchistan (1), Bengal (5,640), Bihar and Orissa (76,320), Central Provinces and Berar (47,130), Madras (11,818), Central India (941).
		Kolgha §	2,105	1,049	1,056	Bombay (1,114), Baroda (991).
		Pallan	825,224	400,661	424,563	Madras (825,224).
7	Market gardeners, etc. ..	....	*7,540,179*	*3,951,055*	*3,589,124*	
		Arain, Kunjra, Koeri, Kachhi * †, Murao.	5,048,849	2,664,460	2,384,389	Andamans and Nicobars (112), Bengal (16,021), Bihar and Orissa (1,301,988), Delhi (3,334), North-West Frontier (6,550), Punjab (1,331,295), United Provinces (1,892,864), Baroda (8,155), Central India (226,963), Gwalior (173,695), Jammu and Kashmir (22,922), Rajputana (64,950).
		Saini, Mali * ‖ †, Phulmali, Malakar.	2,332,143	1,202,267	1,129,876	Ajmer-Merwara (14,663), Baluchistan (6,996), Bengal (79,084), Bihar and Orissa (167,148), Bombay (321,086), Central Provinces and Berar (626,569), Delhi (5,776), Madras (26,669), Punjab (250,948), United Provinces (270,829), Baroda (2,723), Central India (44,944), Gwalior (31,903), Hyderabad (102,608), Rajputana (369,173), Western India States (11,024).
		Kir, Kirar †	159,187	84,328	74,859	Ajmer-Merwara (1,184), Central India (39,765), Gwalior (78,561), Rajputana (39,677).
8	Pan-growers	....	*827,252*	*411,333*	*415,919*	
		Tamboli, Baraí	452,423	234,662	217,761	Bengal (195,139), United Provinces (212,732), Baroda (535), Central India (28,398), Gwalior (7,571), Rajputana (8,048).
		Labbai* †	374,829	176,671	198,158	Coorg (218), Madras (351,893), Travancore (10,421), Mysore (12,297).
9	Palm growers	....	*1,253,403*	*621,882*	*631,521*	
		Bhandari, Idiga* †, Iruvan, Siyal.	1,253,403	621,882	631,521	Bihar and Orissa (9,613), Madras (16), Baroda (265), Cochin (276,649), Mysore (94,669), Rajputana (17), Travancore (872,174).
V.	Pastoral Castes	....	**20,129,110**	**10,453,284**	**9,675,826**	
	Cattle herdsmen (A)					
1	Yadava group	**Ahar, Ahir, Gopi, Goshi, Goala, Golla, Gowari, Gaura, Kavundan, Idaiyan* †.**	*14,170,032*	*7,301,509*	*6,868,523*	Ajmer-Merwara (2,509), Andamans and Nicobars (416), Assam (56,398), Bengal (599,283), Bihar and Orissa (4,345,843), Bombay (66,397), Central Provinces and Berar (1,003,095), Coorg (14,541), Delhi (13,051), Madras (1,711,199), Punjab (221,933), United Provinces (4,323,958), Baroda (6,537), Central India (248,280), Gwalior (131,025), Hyderabad (928,404), Cochin (4,065), Travancore (8,457), Mysore (174,201), Rajputana (182,682), Western India States (127,758).
2	Others	....	*2,570,141*	*1,397,276*	*1,172,865*	
		Gujar* ‖ † §	2,430,669	1,323,538	1,107,131	Ajmer-Merwara (35,063), Bombay (620), Central Provinces and Berar (60,028), Delhi (14,625), North-West Frontier (121,510), Punjab (696,442), United Provinces (368,682), Central India (84,813), Gwalior (119,314), Jammu and Kashmir (402,781), Rajputana (526,791).
		Gopal, Gaddi†, Ghosi ..	139,472	73,738	65,734	Bombay (8,224), Madras (593), Punjab (3,853), United Provinces (83,759), Central India (15,777), Gwalior (8,616), Jammu and Kashmir (11,417), Rajputana (7,233).
	Other pastoral castes (B).					
3	Shepherds and goatherds (and weavers in wool).	....	*2,816,283*	*1,457,227*	*1,359,056*	
		Bharwad, Dhangar, Gadariya, Kuruba* †.	2,816,283	1,457,227	1,359,056	Baluchistan (46), Bengal (3,624), Bombay (842,468), Coorg (6,867), Delhi (2,423), United Provinces (1,019,547), Baroda (64,634), Central India (104,249), Gwalior (88,619), Mysore (435,930), Rajputana (77,370), Western India States (170,506).
4	Camelherds, etc. ..	....	*140,621*	*71,881*	*68,740*	
		ri* †	140,621	71,881	6 ,740	Ajmer-Merwara (2,396), Central India (618), Rajputana (137,607).

Table XVII.—Race, Tribe or Caste—*contd.*

Group.	Description.	Names.	Population. Persons.	Males.	Females.	Province, State or Agency where chiefly found.
5	Others (Pigkeepers, Goat-butchers, Vegetable-sellers and Tanners).	....	*431,230*	*225,010*	*206,220*	
		Tottiyan (Yenakolla, Yerragula)	1,855	947	908	Madras (1,659), Cochin (196).
		Khatik, Chik* ‖ † ..	412,620	215,731	196,889	Ajmer-Merwara (4,167), Baluchistan (19), Bengal (1,157), Central Provinces and Berar (20,406), Delhi (3,591), United Provinces, (215,531), Central India (10,678), Gwalior (15,800), Hyderabad (81,165), Jammu and Kashmir (579), Rajputana (59,527).
		Ghusuria†	1,846	805	1,041	Bihar and Orissa (1,846).
		Jogi	14,909	7,527	7,382	Mysore (14,909).
6	Miscellaneous Herdsmen and Drovers (nomads).		*803*	*381*	*422*	
		Kapariya	803	381	422	United Provinces (803).
VI.	Collectors of forest produce, professional hunters and fishermen.	....	**419,107**	**211,281**	**207,826**	
1	Catechu collectors ..	....	*140,503*	*70,895*	*69,608*	
		Katkari*, Khairwa, Khaira§	128,492	64,920	63,572	Bengal (38,287), Bombay (87,784), United Provinces (81), Baroda (551), Central India (393), Gwalior (1,395), Western India States (1).
		Kudubi§	12,011	5,975	6,036	Madras (12,011).
2	Hunters and Fowlers ..	....	*127,574*	*64,850*	*62,724*	
		Aheriya§	24,375	12,699	11,676	Ajmer-Merwara (87), United Provinces (23,084), Rajputana (1,204).
		Baheliya§	55,040	28,719	26,321	Bengal (4,449), United Provinces (48,447), Central India (2,144).
		Ullatan (Tracker) (64) † § ..	5,899	2,617	3,282	Cochin (778), Travancore (5,121).
		Vettuvan (64)§	41,444	20,418	21,026	Madras (28,325), Cochin (11,797), Travancore (1,322).
		Nayadi (300)†	816	397	419	Madras (520), Cochin (152), Travancore (144).
3	Fishermen	....	*151,030*	*75,536*	*75,494*	
		Gokha	48,622	23,660	24,962	Bihar and Orissa (48,622).
		Moger	773	345	428	Madras (773).
		Paravan * †	826	399	427	Madras (826).
		Valan (36) †	32,856	16,834	16,022	Cochin (11,684), Travancore (21,172).
		Arayan* †	33,574	17,212	16,362	Cochin (6,574), Travancore (27,000).
		Bagata §	34,379	17,086	17,293	Madras (34,379).
VII.	Miners, etc.	....	**1,325,878**	**677,248**	**648,630**	
1	Salt-makers	....	*283,821*	*145,122*	*138,699*	
		Kadupattan (Elluthassan)*	18,536	9,026	9,510	Cochin (18,536).
		Agri*	265,285	136,096	129,189	Bombay (265,285).
2	Saltpetre-diggers and Earth-workers.	....	*561,926*	*288,743*	*273,183*	
		Beldar, Bind, Nuniya, Od (Orh, Ottanaikan, Waddar)* ‖ †, Rehgar.	561,926	288,743	273,183	Ajmer-Merwara (22,604), Bengal (50,757), Bombay (121,002), Central Provinces and Berar (39,163), Delhi (7,183), Madras (3,236), Punjab (32,719), United Provinces (44,619), Baroda (2,028), Central India (6,246), Gwalior (476), Hyderabad (217,574), Jammu and Kashmir (2,812), Cochin (2,765), Rajputana (7,757), Western India States (985).
3	Miners	....	*480,131*	*243,383*	*236,748*	
		Saun§	480,131	243,383	236,748	United Provinces (473,682), Central India (6,449).
VIII.	Industrial	....	**41,867,646**	**21,434,722**	**20,432,924**	
1	Artizans	....	*7,735,393*	*4,035,408*	*3,699,985*	
		"Viswabrahman", Panchal or Kammalan (including Sonar, Aksali or Daivdan, Soni, Kansara, Thatera Barhai, Tarkhan, Sutar or Sutradhar, Lohar or Luvar, Saiat)* ‖ †.	7,735,393	4,035,408	3,699,985	Ajmer-Merwara (15,130), Andamans and Nicobars (28), Assam (12,575), Bengal (331,893), Bihar and Orissa (896,693), Bombay (502,057), Central Provinces and Berar (467,283), Coorg (128), Delhi (7,820), Madras (921,004) North-West Frontier (83,814), Punjab (1,161,151), United Provinces (1,472,600), Baroda (63,966), Central India (261,646), Gwalior (102,237), Hyderabad (474,047), Jammu and Kashmir (51,579), Cochin (45,546), vancore (209,068), Mysore (143,669), putana (370,527), Sikkim (4,828), stern India States (136,104).
1d		**Silpkar**	333,036	172,208	160,828	d Provinces (333,036).

Table XVII.—Race, Tribe or Caste—*contd.*

Group.	Description.	Names.	Population. Persons.	Males.	Females.	Province, State or Agency where chiefly found.
2	Ornament makers ..	....	*150,503*	*78,043*	*72,460*	
		Kachera, Lakhera, Manihar, Patwa.	150,503	78,043	72,460	United Provinces (109,743), Central India (12,006), Gwalior (5,186), Rajputana (23,568).
3	Tailors, Dyers, Calenders, etc.	....	*993,356*	*518,103*	*475,253*	
		"Tankkshatriya" (including Darzi, Shimpi, Chhippa, Bhavsar)* ‖ †.	926,274	482,454	443,820	Ajmer-Merwara (4,236), Bihar and Orissa (2,442), Bombay (132,022), Central Provinces and Berar (51,229), Delhi (295), Madras (188), North-West Frontier (2,193), Punjab (1,79,333), United Provinces (243,371), Baroda (21,639), Central India (42,592), Gwalior (32,248), Hyderabad (63,631), Jammu and Kashmir (2,667), Mysore (20,527), Rajputana (80,623), Western India States (47,038).
		Bandhera	1,107	525	582	Rajputana (1,107).
		Rangrez	58,044	31,065	26,979	Ajmer-Merwara (840), North-West Frontier (5,708), Central India (3,335), Gwalior (4,538), Hyderabad (26,751), Jammu and Kashmir (714), Rajputana (16,128).
		Damai	7,931	4,059	3,872	Bengal (6,065), Sikkim (1,866).
4	Cotton-carders	.. ..	*565,254*	*288,821*	*276,433*	
		Dhunia, Pinjara, Sarahira* ‖ †	565,254	288,821	276,433	Ajmer-Merwara (1,357), Bombay (23,102), North-West Frontier (12,557), Punjab (11,230), United Provinces (414,564), Baroda (4,764), Central India (34,504), Gwalior (13,608), Jammu and Kashmir (2,357), Mysore (10,631), Rajputana (26,388), Western India States (10,192).
5	Weavers	....	*7,348,295*	*3,761,748*	*3,586,547*	
		Devang, Kapali, Koshti ‖ †	921,201	475,573	445,628	Bengal (107,908), Bombay (101,092), Central Provinces and Berar (171,323), Madras (20,963), Central India (1,949), Gwalior (3,560), Hyderabad (452,049), Cochin (3,055), Mysore (59,302).
		Bhulia, Chadar, Sali, Tanti*‖†, Tatwa.	1,132,563	565,897	566,666	Bengal (330,518), Bihar and Orissa (689, 791), Bombay (75,442), Central Provinces and Berar (33,874), Central India (2,938).
		Tai	4,160	2,004	2,156	Baroda (4,160).
		Momin* ‖ †	3,122,100	1,610,094	1,512,006	Ajmer-Merwara (758), Baluchistan (31), Bengal (270,292), Bihar and Orissa (983,843), Bombay (35,092), Delhi (9,490), North-West Frontier (40,099), Punjab (672,243), United Provinces (1,005,203), Baroda (16,128), Central India (10,201), Gwalior (2,262), Jammu and Kashmir (33,912), Rajputana (17,087), Sikkim (8), Western India States (25,451).
		Balai†, Chaupal, Katia, Kori†, Jugi†.	2,165,953	1,107,048	1,058,905	Ajmer-Merwara (19,874), Andamans and Nicobars (47), Assam (83,922), Baluchistan (477), Bengal (384,634), Bihar and Orissa (2,737), Bombay (955), Central Provinces and Berar (137,284), United Provinces (923,546), Central India (284,418), Gwalior (97,828), Rajputana (230,231).
		Chaliyan (T.)	2,318	1,132	1,186	Cochin (2,318).
6	Weavers and Agricultural Labourers, Village Watchmen, etc.	....	*2,512,450*	*1,237,382*	*1,275,068*	
		Kaikolan	419,078	208,612	210,466	Madras (414,909), Cochin (3,714), Travancore (455).
		Pan* † §, Panka Ganda†, Paidi, Baraik.	1,241,322	608,663	632,659	Bengal (7,693), Bihar and Orissa (694,005), Central Provinces and Berar (402,753), Madras (110,056), Central India (26,815).
		Mala	852,050	420,107	431,943	Central Provinces and Berar (11,933), Madras (840,117).
7	Gunpowder and firework makers.	....	*19*	*3*	*16*	
		Golandaz	19	3	16	Rajputana (19).
8	Potters	....	*3,581,657*	*1,855,451*	*1,726,206*	
		Kumhar, Kusavan* ‖, †	3,580,143	1,854,685	1,725,458	Ajmer-Merwara (16,005), Baluchistan (109), Bengal (289,810), Bihar and Orissa (599,038), Bombay (168,068), Central Provinces and Berar (131,311), Delhi (9,352), North-West Frontier (23,202), Punjab (620,402), United Provinces (782,639), Baroda (55,119), Central India (99,022), Gwalior (62,485), Hyderabad (154,148), Jammu and Kashmir (17,721), Cochin (3,295), Travancore (12,377), Mysore (48,657), Rajputana (357,751), Western India States (129,632).
		Odan	1,514	766	748	Cochin (1,514).

Table XVII.—Race, Tribe or Caste—*contd.*

Group.	Description.	Names.	Population. Persons.	Males.	Females.	Province, State or Agency where chiefly found.
9	Furriers, Tanners, etc. ..	....	*16,455,487*	*8,400,221*	*8,055,266*	
		Mochi, Jingar, Dabgar ‖ †	1.026,405	553,019	473,386	Ajmer-Merwara (1,418), Assam (7,312), Baluchistan (388), Bengal (414,221), Bihar and Orissa (22,863), Bombay (5,587), Central Provinces and Berar (6,858), Coorg (20), Madras (1,842), North-West Frontier (26,759), Punjab (472,616), United Provinces (9,866), Baroda (11,559), Central India (3,718), Gwalior (3,517), Jammu and Kashmir (11,052,) Rajputana (14,118), Sikkim (19), Western India States (12,672).
		Sarki	3,677	2,045	1,632	Bengal (3,428), Sikkim (249).
		Chamar, Khalpa, Samagara*‖†	12,195,516	6,220,430	5,975,086	Ajmer-Merwara (15,915), Andamans and Nicobars (204), Baluchistan (22), Bengal (150,458), Bihar and Orissa (1,296,001), Bombay (303,296), Central Provinces and Berar (967,265), Coorg (5), Delhi (45,806), Madras (2,158), North-West Frontier (2,918), Punjab (1,102,465), United Provinces (6,312,193), Baroda (42,884), Central India (520,457), Gwalior (415,950), Jammu and Kashmir (41,220), Rajputana (930,128)*, Western India States (46,171).
		Chakkiiyan, Dhor* †. ..	671,926	338,635	333,291	Bombay (34,200), Central Provinces and Berar (6,732), Madras (613,392), Cochin (839), Travancore (6,328), Western India States (10,435).
		Semman	1,198	549	649	Madras (1,198).
		Mang, Megh, Meghwal, Madgi, Madiga* †.	2,556,765	1,285,543	1,271,222	Ajmer-Merwara (10), Bombay (384,069) Central Provinces and Berar (111,416) Coorg (217), Madras (616,717), Punjab (23,207), Baroda (37), Central India (2,625), Jammu and Kashmir (70,193), Hyderabad (1,281,092), Rajputana (23,273), Western India States (43,909).
10	Basket makers ..	....	*2,192,196*	*1,087,334*	*1,104,862*	
		Bellara	87	29	58	Madras (87).
		Godra, Godagali, Medar ..	2,926	1,453	1,473	Bihar and Orissa (1,553), Coorg (41), Madras (969), Travancore (363).
		Dom, Dombar, Bansphor, Dharkar, Dholi* †.	907,776	459,350	448,426	Ajmer-Merwara (5,418), Bengal (140,067), Bihar and Orissa (269,346), Bombay (13,227), Central Provinces and Berar (61,386), Madras (79,643), North-West Frontier (4), Punjab (37,541), United Provinces (116,116), Baroda (478), Central India (58,268), Gwalior (19,731), Hyderabad (34,777), Jammu and Kashmir (34,341), Rajputana (37,433).
		Koraga	4,042	1,874	2,168	Madras (4,042).
		Turi, Paraiyan (330) * † ..	1,277,365	624,628	652,737	Bombay (1,053), Coorg (340), Madras (1,117,754), Baroda (1,733), Cochin (11,914), Travancore (142,364), Rajputana (1), Western India States (2,206).
IX.	Transport	....	**5,490,613**	**2,812,993**	**2,677,620**	
1	Sailors, Boatmen, etc. ..	....	*945,558*	*468,405*	*477,153*	
		Kharva	50,607	26,752	23,855	Bombay (31,153), Baroda (6,699), Western India States (12,755).
		Mallah* †, **Goriya, Gonrhi** ..	894,951	441,653	453,298	Bengal (31,403), Bihar and Orissa (459,560), North-West Frontier (6,578), United Provinces (386,504), Central India (4,862), Gwalior (3,853), Rajputana (2,191).
2	Drivers of pack animals ..		*969,114*	*499,483*	*469,631*	
		Banjara, Lambadi, Labana, Lamani* † §.	951,022	489,485	461,537	Bihar and Orissa (5,878), Bombay (191,693), Central Provinces (204,213), Madras (420), North-West Frontier (8,279), Baroda (1,023), Central India (44,524), Gwalior (19,731), Hyderabad (371,402), Jammu and Kashmir (6,855), Mysore (64,368), Rajputana (32,313), Western India States (323).
		Thori	‡18,092	9,998	8,094	Ajmer-Merwara (2), Baroda (56), Central India (635), Rajputana (17,399).
3	Porters, Palki bearers, Boatmen (Vegetable sellers, Cultivators and Water-carriers).	....	*3,575,941*	*1,845,105*	*1,730,836*	
		Bhisti, Bhoi, Dhimar, Jhinwar, Kahar, Machhi, Tiyar * ‖ †.	3,575,941	1,845,105	1.730,836	Ajmer-Merwara (4,949), Andamans and Nicobars (130), Bengal (96,789), Bihar and Orissa (524,030), Bombay (110,688), Central Provinces and Berar (352,129), Delhi (12,720), North-West Frontier (5,285), Punjab (685,030), United Provinces (1,251,742), Baroda (10,613), Central India (123,708), Gwalior (45,885), Hyderabad (285,273), Jammu and Kashmir (12,316), Rajputana (50,393), Western India States (4,261).

‡ Includes Bambhi 84,420 Males and 78,445 Females.

Table XVII.—Race, Tribe or Caste—*contd.*

Group.	Description.	Names.	Population. Persons.	Males.	Females.	Province, State or Agency where chiefly found.
X.	Trade	....	**14,691,598**	**7,644,030**	**7,047,568**	
1	General Merchants and Traders.	....	*7,065,628*	*3,745,801*	*3,319,827*	
		Baniya* †, Bhatia, Chetti, * †, Khatri‖, Komati, Vaishya.	5,176,353	2,742,140	2,434,213	Ajmer-Merwara (32,249), Andamans and Nicobars (211), Baluchistan (4,522), Bengal (19,347), Bihar and Orissa (220,071), Bombay (313,874), Central Provinces and Berar (245,363), Coorg (211), Delhi (42,719), Madras (428,814), North-West Frontier (41,678), Punjab (895,275), United Provinces (1,310,151), Baroda (90,317), Central India (187,076), Gwalior (134,878), Hyderabad (397,504), Jammu and Kashmir (44,319), Cochin (22,281), Travancore (17,422), Mysore (44,235), Rajputana (610,783), Sikkim (174), Western India States (72,879).
		Bohra* †	212,752	110,943	101,809	Bombay (118,952), Burma (160), Central Provinces and Berar (7,926), Baroda (28,355), Central India (14,715), Gwalior (8,944), Cochin (74), Travancore (1,319), Rajputana (15,302), Western India States (17,005).
		Balija, Vadukan	40,613	22,119	18,494	Hyderabad (39,300), Cochin (1,313).
		Arora, Bhansali, Lohana* †	1,499,407	801,907	697,500	Baluchistan (23,516), Bombay (519,376), North-West Frontier (61,402), Punjab (775,734), Baroda (13,597), Jammu and Kashmir (3,548). Western India States (102,234).
		Memon	135,574	68,259	67,315	Bombay (42,958), Burma (3,855), Baroda (8,971), Cochin (684), Travancore (348), Western India States (78,758).
		Tarakan (T)	929	433	496	Cochin (929).
2	Others	....	*7,625,970*	*3,898,229*	*3,727,741*	
(a)	Corn-parchers		803,887	413,007	390,880	
		Bharbunja*, † Kandu ..	803,887	413,007	390,880	Bihar and Orissa (506,384), United Provinces (286,410), Baroda (410), Central India (5,371), Gwalior (1,669), Rajputana (3,643).
(b)	Sweetmeat-sellers	....	246,583	123,579	123,004	
		Halwai,* † Guria	246,583	123,579	123,004	Bihar and Orissa (153,961), United Provinces (91,454), Central India (956), Gwalior (7), Rajputana (205).
(c)	Oilmen	....	5,024,496	2,563,928	2,460,568	
		Tili	231,269	117,212	114,057	Assam (23,386), Bengal (207,883).
		Chakkan, Ganig, Ghanchi, Teli, Vaniyan* ‖ †.	4,793,227	2,446,716	2,346,511	Ajmer-Merwara (4,863), Andamans and Nicobars (98), Assam (17,278), Baluchistan (21), Bengal (295,306), Bihar and Orissa (1,210,496), Bombay (150,669), Central Provinces and Berar (1,022,881), Coorg (286), Delhi (3,309), Madras (226,405), North-West Frontier (7,179), Punjab (346,342), United Provinces (1,005,558), Baroda (21,744), Central India (141,542), Gwalior (57,233), Hyderabad (73,155), Jammu and Kashmir (15,843), Cochin (3,018), Travancore (23,188), Mysore (44,960), Rajputana (85,386), Sikkim (82), Western India States (36,385).
(d)	Certain Others	....	1,551,004	797,715	753,289	
		Kalar* †	1,017,179	524,039	493,140	Ajmer-Merwara (1,551), Bengal (13,540), Central Provinces and Berar (219,168), United Provinces (248,324), Baroda (1,606), Central India (47,957), Gwalior (15,225), Hyderabad (426,836), Rajputana (42,876), Sikkim (96).
		Shaha * Sunri	533,825	273,676	260,149	Bengal (497,119), Madras (36,704), Sikkim (2).
XI.	Professional	....	**45,071,791**	**23,154,100**	**21,917,691**	
1	Administrative and Ministerial.		*2,982,458*	*1,576,598*	*1,405,860*	
		Kayastha, Karan, Prabhu* †	2,946,228	1,558,939	1,387,289	Ajmer-Merwara (3,463), Andamans and Nicobars (185), Assam (135,590), Bengal (1,558,475), Bihar and Orissa (530,185), Bombay (38,926), Central Provinces and Berar (38,829), Delhi (10,571), Madras (46,490), United Provinces (478,657), Baroda (3,964), Central India (38,357), Gwalior (34,113) Hyderabad (4,895), Jammu and Kashmir (43), Rajputana (23,167), Sikkim, (11), Western India States (307).
		Kanakkan†	36,230	17,659	18,571	Madras (22,046), Cochin (14,184).

Table XVII.—Race, Tribe or Caste—*contd.*

Group.	Description.	Names.	Population. Persons.	Males.	Females.	Province, State or Agency where chiefly found.
2	Combatant (other than Rajput and Maratha).	....	*6,435,706*	*3,126,803*	*3,308,903*	
		Nayar* †	1,550,641	756,647	793,994	Andamans and Nicobars (29), Coorg (1,278), Madras (537,618), Cochin (143,208), Travancore (868,508).
		Bant	148,774	72,264	76,510	Coorg (1,369), Madras (147,405).
		Telaga	1,665,559	794,201	871,358	Coorg (280), Madras (699,089), Hyderabad (966,190).
		Khandait, Paik	1,060,587	510,197	550,390	Bengal (35,080), Bihar and Orissa (1,010,146), Central Provinces and Berar (4,712), Madras (7,716), Central India (1,288), Rajputana 1,645).
		Kallan* †, **Maravan** ..	948,630	460,659	487,971	Madras (932,871), Cochin (1,360), Travancore (14,399).
		Razu	69,979	34,820	35,159	Madras (69,979).
		Bedar, Boya	991,536	498,015	493,521	Bombay (206,883), Central Provinces and Berar (1,139), Coorg (443), Madras (545,066), Hyderabad (237,774), Cochin (231).
3	Village Watchmen (and field labourers).	.. ..	*1,627,790*	*806,763*	*821,027*	
		Ramoshi	58,715	30,168	28,547	Bombay (58,702), Central India (13).
		Bariki	3,695	1,765	1,930	Madras (3,695).
		Kotwar	28,635	14,153	14,482	United Provinces (64), Central India (28,571).
		Khangar, Dahayat ..	91,619	46,613	45,006	Ajmer-Merwara (2), Central Provinces and Berar (25,725), Madras (64), United Provinces (24,082), Central India (21,677), Gwalior (17,100), Rajputana (2,969).
		Dusadh* †	1,400,878	694,849	706,029	Bengal (36,420), Bihar and Orissa (1,290,936), United Provinces (73,522).
		Dandasi	44,248	19,215	25,033	Madras (44,248)
4	Other village servants (and agricultural labourers).	.. ..	*4,739,136*	*2,366,654*	*2,372,482*	
		Mahar, Mehra, Dhed, Vankar, Holiya, Pulayan (90) Cheruman* †	4,729,405	2,361,751	2,367,654	Ajmer-Merwara (31), Assam (5,424), Bengal (1,986), Bombay (1,264,104), Central Provinces and Berar (1,312,827), Coorg (407), Madras (296,359), Baroda (110,133), Central India (13,623), Gwalior (949), Hyderabad (1,076,539), Cochin (82,043), Travancore (365,150), Rajputana (25,384), Western India States (174,446).
		Sindhava	9,731	4,903	4,828	Baroda (9,731).
5	Heralds	.. .. ..	*307,274*	*156,790*	*150,[illegible]4*	
		Bhat, Brahmabhatt, Charan, Jasondhi.* ‖ †	307,274	156,790	150,484	Ajmer-Merwara (1,194), Bombay (21,891), United Provinces (104,295), Baroda (17,202), Central India (28,918) Gwalior (8,419), Hyderabad (17,270), Rajputana (75,554), Western India States (32,531).
6	Religious and Instructional	.. ....	*17,217,820*	*9,065,342*	*8,152,478*	
(a)	Priests	....	15,261,144	8,032,717	7,228,427	
		Brahman (all castes)* † ..	15,207,277	8,005,305	7,201,972	Ajmer-Merwara (27,670), Andamans and Nicobars (524), Assam (159,116), Baluchistan (3,703), Bengal (1,447,691), Bihar and Orissa (2,101,287), Bombay (914,757), Central Provinces and Berar (517,765), Coorg (1,407), Delhi (50,310), Madras (1,250,825), North-West Frontier (17,200), Punjab (1,058,598), United Provinces (4,5[illegible]5,965), Baroda (123,714), Central India (573,454), Gwalior (296,049) Hyderabad (376,468), Jammu and Kashmir (253,529), Cochin (41,324), Travancore (68,072), Mysore (245,163), Rajputana (899,942), Sikkim (8,560), Western India States (214,184).
		Kurukkal	319	158	161	Cochin (319).
		Gurao	31,459	16,199	15,260	Baroda (83), Central India (966), Hyderabad (30,410).
		Garoda	22,089	11,055	11,034	Baroda (7,796), Rajputana (8,699), Western India States (5,594).
(b)	Temple servants, etc. ..	.. .. ..	17,597	8,853	8,744	
		Ambalavasi* †	17,366	8,743	8,623	Cochin (9,211), Travancore (8,155).
		Mahabrahman	231	110	121	Rajputana (231).
	Ascetics and Mendicants ..	.. .. ..	1,896,225	1,002,587	893,638	
		Aghori	182	119	63	Central India (72), Gwalior (110).
		Bairagi*†	839,285	431,254	408,031	Bengal (337,771), Bombay (45,890), Central Provinces and Berar (80,717), Madras (376), United Provinces (148,285), Baroda (17,422), Central India (36,892), Gwalior (43,202), Hyderabad (30,583), Rajputana (29,648), Western India States (68,499).

Table XVII.—Race, Tribe or Caste—*contd.*

Group.	Description.	Names.	Population. Persons.	Males.	Females.	Province, State or Agency where chiefly found.
		Faqir†	820,577	442,640	377,937	Ajmer-Merwara (2,134), Central Provinces and Berar (10,524), Delhi (2,917), Punjab (287,445), United Provinces (430,911), Baroda (6,495), Central India (14,114), Gwalior (11,178) Rajputana (54,859).
		Jogi	111,596	59,505	52,091	Ajmer-Merwara (2,668), Bombay (1,457), Central India (12,499), Gwalior (11,051), Jammu and Kashmir (5,977), Rajputana (76,204), Western India States (1,740).
		Qalandar	390	214	176	Central India (16), Jammu and Kashmir (126), Rajputana (248).
		Sadhu	75,205	40,887	34,318	Ajmer-Merwara (5,622), Central India (1,088), Gwalior (136), Jammu and Kashmir (1,762), Rajputana (66,597).
		Sanyasi	4,022	2,922	1,100	Madras (68), Central India (714), Gwalior (1,103), Hyderabad (2,137).
		Swami	44,937	25,025	19,912	Rajputana (44,937).
		Udasi	31	21	10	Central India (15), Rajputana (16).
(*d*)	Medicinemen, Devil-dancers, etc.	....	42,854	21,185	21,669	
		Ojha	5,106	2,584	2,522	Central Provinces and Berar (5,106).
		Velan†	27,148	13,275	13,873	Cochin (10,895), Travancore (16,253).
		Malayan† §	3,185	1,645	1,540	Cochin (3,185).
		Panan (36)	7,415	3,681	3,734	Cochin (3,603), Travancore (3,812).
7	Astrologers	....	*98,390*	*49,095*	*49,295*	
		Joshi, Kaniyan* † ..	38,072	19,486	18,586	Bombay (7,920), Madras (1,470), Central India (2,857), Gwalior (6,330), Cochin (3,841), Travancore (15,652), Western India States (2).
		Valluvan	59,621	29,255	30,366	Madras (59,409), Cochin (212).
	Astrologers and Serpent priests.	**Pulluvan (30)**	697	354	343	Cochin (170), Travancore (527).
8	Medicine	....	*113,851*	*59,250*	*54,601*	
		Baidya* † .. .	110,739	57,627	53,112	Bengal (110,739).
		Vaid	3,112	1,623	1,489	Rajputana (3,112).
9	Barbers	....	*3,727,629*	*1,929,370*	*1,798,259*	
		Ambattan, Bhandari, Hajjam, Kelashi, Mhali, Nadig, Nai "Naibrahman", Napit, Nhavi, Pandithar Vellakattalavan* ‖ †.	3,725,850	1,928,528	1,797,322	Ajmer-Merwara (7,029), Assam (33,434), Baluchistan (125), Bengal (451,068), Bihar and Orissa (577,871), Bombay (175,818), Central Provinces and Berar (195,524), Delhi (5,246), Madras (360,301), North-West Frontier (27,242), Punjab (380,657), United Provinces (906,457), Baroda (29,164), Central India (95,949), Gwalior (54,819), Hyderabad (159,745), Jammu and Kashmir (37,623), Cochin (5,259), Travancore (742), Rajputana (166,096), Sikkim (17), Western India States (55,654).
		Vilkurup (32)†	1,779	842	937	Cochin (1,779).
10	Washermen	.. ..	*3,161,502*	*1,611,612*	*1,549,890*	
		Dhobi, Parit, Vannan, Veluttedan* ‖ †	3,161,428	1,611,572	1,549,856	Ajmer-Merwara (2,827), Assam (30,919), Baluchistan (749), Bengal (229,672), Bihar and Orissa (414,221), Bombay (79,423), Central Provinces and Berar (187,606), Coorg (1,397), Delhi (4,194), Madras (678,522), North-West Frontier (11,870), Punjab (175,557), United Provinces (776,159), Baroda (3,111), Central India (54,800), Gwalior (40,977), Hyderabad (269,492), Jammu and Kashmir (5,138), Cochin (4,365), Travancore (32,176), Mysore (109,490), Rajputana (43,832), Sikkim (6), Western India States (4,925).
		Puthirai-Vannan .. .	74	40	34	Madras (74).
11	Scavengers ..	....	*1,957,460*	*1,038,678*	*918,782*	
		Bhangi* ‖ †	797,599	419,569	378,030	Ajmer-Merwara (6,980), Bombay (94,950), United Provinces (503,608), Baroda (31,026), Gwalior (28,527), Rajputana (99,083), Western India States (33,425).
		Chuhra* ‖ †	721,981	395,050	326,931	Baluchistan (5,213), Delhi (21,138), North-West Frontier (9,285), Punjab (681,359), Jammu and Kashmir (4,986).
		Halalkhor ..	23,165	11,490	11,675	Bengal (876), Bihar and Orissa (22,289).
		Hari†	318,830	160,900	157,930	Assam (14,348), Bengal (146,735), Bihar and Orissa (115,613), Madras (42,134).
		Lalbegi† ..	5,145	3,593	1,552	Bengal (4,965), Bihar and Orissa (157), Sikkim (23).
		Mehtar ‖ †	88,723	47,126	41,597	Assam (2,364), Bengal (23,281), Central Provinces and Berar (32,182), Central India (30,893), Sikkim (3).
		Paki	2,017	950	1,067	Madras (2,017).

Table XVII.—Race, Tribe or Caste—*contd.*

Group.	Description.	Names.	Population. Persons.	Males.	Females.	Province, State or Agency where chiefly found.
12	Musicians, Dancers and Acrobats, Snake-Charmers, Palmists and Quack doctors.	....	*431,312*	*225,998*	*205,314*	
		Bajania	7,876	3,847	4,029	Bombay (1,626), United Provinces (34), Baroda (3,925), Rajputana (708), Western India States (1,583).
		Bahirupia	184	81	103	Bombay (110), Central India (20), Gwalior (17), Rajputana (37).
		Bazigar, Perna	2,734	1,424	1,310	Central India (743), Jammu and Kashmir (1,524), Rajputana (467).
		Dewar	2,813	1,278	1,535	Central Provinces and Berar (2,813).
		Dugla	9,523	5,121	4,402	Assam (9,523).
		Kakkalan	2,398	1,152	1,246	Cochin (732), Travancore (1,666).
		Kamad	25	10	15	Central India (25).
		Kela	9,493	4.637	4,856	Bihar and Orissa (9,493).
		Kolhati, Garudi	9,453	4,291	5,162	Bombay (8,625), Western India States (828).
		Makuria	2,389	1,168	1,221	Bihar and Orissa (2,389).
		Mangan	184	79	105	Bihar and Orissa (184).
		Mirasi*	283,637	151,345	132,292	Ajmer-Merwara (664), North-West Frontier (10,892), Punjab (244,726), Central India (1,136), Gwalior (1,170), Jammu and Kashmir (7,998), Rajputana (17,051).
		Nat ‖ †	100,603	51,565	49,038	Ajmer-Merwara (574), Baluchistan (227) Bengal (7,384), Bihar and Orissa (9,628) United Provinces (58,239), Central India (7,162), Gwalior (6,516), Jammu and Kashmir (25), Rajputana (10,848).
13	Agriculturists, Puppet showers, Watermen, Labourers and professional Criminals.	....	*1,981,201*	*989,653*	*991,548*	
		Bagdi, Bauri * † ..	1,671.481	834,759	836,722	Bengal (1,318,838), Bihar and Orissa (315,038), Rajputana (37,605).
		Bawaria§, Bavuri, Baori, Bagri, Vagri, Badhik* † .	309,720	154,894	154,826	Ajmer-Merwara (584), Bombay (62,221), Delhi (32), Madras (73,330), Punjab (32,527), United Provinces (17,323), Baroda (35,805), Central India (24,661), Gwalior (23,209), Jammu and Kashmir (3), Travancore (164), Rajputana (12,717), Western India States (27,144).
14	Criminals and Fowlers, Rope makers, Brush makers, etc.	.... ..	*290,262*	*151,494*	*138,768*	
		Beriya, Bhantu, Habura†, **Moghia, Sansi**‖ † §	91,271	47,505	43,766	Ajmer-Merwara (406), Bengal (7,263) Delhi (227), Punjab (33,228), United Provinces (15,200), Central India (10,984), Gwalior (9,884), Jammu and Kashmir (134), Rajputana (13,945).
		Bhamta, Uchlia, Ghantichor ..	7,457	3,715	3,742	Bombay (2,634), Central Provinces and Berar (4,336), Western India States (487).
		Kaikadi§, **Korava**†, **Yerukala tukuli), Kurar**	106,229	55,622	50,607	Bengal (631), Bombay (10,459), Central Provinces and Berar (2,211), Coorg (128), Madras (832), Central India (2,665), Gwalior (1,931), Hyderabad (69,158), Cochin (790), Mysore (17,124), Rajputana (300).
		Kan	34,002	17,865	16,137	Ajmer-Merwara (694), Bihar and Orissa (2,566), Central Provinces and Berar (1,301), United Provinces (24,126), Central India (1,147), Gwalior (402), Jammu and Kashmir (2), Rajputana (3,764).
		Pardhi§, **Phanse-Pardhi, Pardhi-Raj, Advichinchar**§, **Kuruvikkaran**†.	51,095	26,670	24,425	Bombay (15,244), Central Provinces and Berar (15,627), Delhi (274), Central India (3,988), Gwalior (2,366), Hyderabad (12,638), Western India States (958).
		Sanaurhiya	208	117	91	United Provinces (31), Central India (177).

Table XVII.—Race, Tribe or Caste—*contd.*

Group.	Description.	Names.	Population. Persons.	Males.	Females.	Province, State or Agency where chiefly found.
XII.	Domestic Servants	....	**132,460**	**67,979**	**64,481**	
		Bhuinmali	111,439	56,897	54,542	Assam (38,635), Bengal (72,804).
		Kudumi	21,021	11,082	9,939	Madras (11,411), Travancore (9,610).
XIII.	Racial groups containing various occupational castes or pursuits.	....	**2,190,936**	**1,213,837**	**977,099**	
		Baloch† §	1,333,215	731,988	601,227	Baluchistan (229,473), Bombay (435,439), Burma (64), North-West Frontier (37,199), Punjab (624,695), Baroda (1,011), Central India (115), Gwalior (24), Rajputana (628), Western India States (4,567).
		Bhotia	29,976	15,865	14,111	Bengal (14,783), Burma (1), Sikkim (15,192).
		Brahui* §	224,415	124,648	99,767	Baluchistan (152,588), Bombay (71,827).
		Feringhi (Goanese, East Indians, etc.).	997	764	233	Burma (801), Baroda (196).
		Jew	17,792	9,182	8,610	Ajmer-Merwara (49), Baluchistan (17), Bombay (14,517), Burma (1,261), North-West Frontier (11), United Provinces (66), Hyderabad (27), Cochin (1,451), Travancore (298), Rajputana (38), Western India States (57).
		(a) *White Jew.* ..	*144*	*62*	*82*	*Cochin (144).*
		(b) *Black Jew.*	*1,307*	*659*	*648*	*Cochin (1,307).*
		Makrani	23,014	12,493	10,521	Bombay (16,906), Baroda (639), Central India (613), Rajputana (1,320), Western India States (3,536).
		Mapilla* + ...	189,621	102,954	86,667	Burma (9,441), Coorg (8,804), Cochin (57,371), Travancore (114,005).
		Nepali (including Gurkha, Gharti, Gurung, etc.)	371,906	215,943	155,963	Assam (120,287), Baluchistan (5,029), Bengal (139,338), Burma (39,532), North-West Frontier (7,971), Baroda (91), Central India (487), Jammu and Kashmir (1,076), Rajputana (61), Sikkim (58,034).

Table XVII.—Race, Tribe or

1	Total Hindu Population. Persons. 2	Males. 3	Females. 4	Brahmans. Persons. 5	Males. 6	Females. 7
INDIA	*238,622,602	122,187,106	116,435,496	15,237,452	8,017,918	7,219,534
Provinces	*177,155,450	90,681,990	86,473,460	11,427,687	6,027,413	5,400,274
1. Ajmer-Merwara	434,509	227,803	206,706	27,657	15,028	12,629
2. Andamans and Nicobars	7,618	5,455	2,163	524	399	125
Andaman Islands	*7,603*	*5,442*	*2,161*	*524*	*399*	*125*
Nicobar Islands	*15*	*13*	*2*	..	..	..
3. Assam	4,931,760	2,616,644	2,315,116	158,518	87,451	71,067
4. Baluchistan (*Districts and Administered Territories*)	41,432	29,529	11,903	3,548	2,784	764
5. Bengal	21,570,407	11,299,914	10,270,493	1,438,177	778,343	659,834
6. Bihar and Orissa	31,011474	15,493,257	15,518,217	1 964,919	1,000,555	964,364
Bihar	*21,114,889*	*10,616,115*	*10,498,774*	*1,354,147*	*693,940*	*660,207*
Orissa	*5,096,431*	*2,449,295*	*2,647,136*	*428,549*	*209,111*	*219,438*
Chota Nagpur	*4,800,154*	*2,427,847*	*2,372,307*	*182,223*	*97,504*	*84,719*
7. Bombay (*excluding Aden*)]	16,619,636	8,608,470	8,011,166	782,405	422,876	359,529
Bombay Presidency	*15,602,932*	*8,041,155*	*7,561,777*	*756,932*	*407,649*	*349,283*
Sind	*1,016,704*	*567,315*	*449,389*	*25,473*	*15,227*	*10,246*
8. Central Provinces and Berar	13,338,223	6.671,326	6,666,897	493,792	265,066	228,726
Central Provinces	*10,271,736*	*5,107,356*	*5,164,380*	*390,464*	*207,848*	*182,616*
Berar	*3,066,487*	*1,563,970*	*1,502,517*	*103,328*	*57,218*	*46,110*
9. Coorg	146,007	79,559	66,448	2,723	1,472	1,251
10. Delhi	399,803	231,459	168,404	50,210	30,524	19,686
11. Madras	41.277,370	20,380,257	20,897,113	1,351,814	663,178	688,636
12. North-West Frontier Province (*Districts and Administered Territories*).	142,977	84,358	58,619	14,508	8,848	5,660
13. Punjab	6,328,588	3,465,534	2,863,054	766,796	422,561	344,235
14. United Provinces of Agra and Oudh	40,905,586	21,488,425	19,417,161	4,372,096	2,328,328	2,043,768
Agra	*29.994,412*	*15,822,703*	*14,171,709*	*3,069,754*	*1,644,378*	*1,425,376*
Oudh	*10,911,174*	*5,665,722*	*5,245,452*	*1,302,342*	*683,950*	*618,392*
States and Agencies	61,467,152	31,505,116	29,962,036	3,809,765	1,990,505	1,819,260
15. Assam States	272,890	135,013	137,877	598	413	185
16. Baluchistan States	12,249	6,651	5,598	155	103	52
17. Baroda State	2,152,071	1,109,349	1,042,722	123,714	64,161	59,553
18. Bengal States	641,662	339,371	302,291	9,465	5,865	3,600
19. Bihar and Orissa States	4,194,878	2,063,008	2,131,870	136,368	69,204	67,164
20. Bombay States	3,921,088	1,998,376	1,922,712	132,352	66,757	65,595
21. Central India Agency	5,852,204	3,002,203	2,850,001	573,454	300,732	272,722
22. Central Provinces States	1,788,401	886,123	902,278	23,953	12,859	11,094
23. Gwalior State	3,271.576	1,732,247	1,539,329	296,049	166,237	129,812
24. Hyderabad State	12,176,727	6,203,053	5,973,674	376,468	196,654	179,814
25. Jammu and Kashmir State	736,222	393,699	342,523	253,529	133,243	120,286
26. Madras States Agency	4,323,150	2,141,805	2,181,345	122,022	62,085	59,937
Cochin State	*780,484*	*377,933*	*402,551*	*41,324*	*21,013*	*20,311*
Travancore State	*3,134,888*	*1,567,925*	*1,566,963*	*68,072*	*34,731*	*33,341*
Other Madras States	*407,778*	*195,947*	*211,831*	*12,626*	*6,341*	*6,285*
27. Mysore State	6,105,880	3,066,332	2,949,548	245,163	126,542	118,621
28. North-West Frontier Province (*Agencies and Tribal Areas*).	13,651	13,194	457	773	740	33
29. Punjab States	383,883	199,991	183,892	50,027	26,604	23,423
30. Punjab States Agency	1,887,249	1,020,180	867,069	234,559	127,570	106,989
31. Rajputana Agency	9,578,805	5,029,620	4,549,185	854,575	441,990	412,585
32. Sikkim State	47,074	24,256	22,818	8,560	4,317	4,243
33. United Provinces States	950,724	482,153	468,571	153,797	75,887	77,910
34. Western India States Agency	3,246,768	1,658,492	1,588,276	214,184	108,542	105.642

* Excludes Aden and Burma where no caste table was prepared.

Caste—Summary Figures of Hindus.

Other Interior Castes.			Exterior Castes.			No Cases.			Caste not returned.			
Persons.	Males.	Females.	Persons.	Males.	Females.	Persons.	Males.	Females.	Persons.	Males.	Females.	
8	9	10	11	12	13	14	15	16	17	18	19	
171,190,624	‡	‡	**50,250,347**	**25,444,644**	**24,805,703**	**1,883,464**	‡	‡	**60,715**	**33,978**	**26,737**	
124,676,932	‡	‡	**39,137,405**	**19,805,074**	**19,332,331**	**1,869,619**	‡	‡	**43,807**	**25,013**	**18,794**	
329,492	173,169	156,323	76,816	39,300	37,516	..	..	..	544	306	238	1
6,492	4,647	1,845	512	364	148	90	45	45	..	..	..	2
6,477	*4,634*	*1,843*	*512*	*364*	*148*	*90*	*45*	*45*	..	..		
15	*13*	*2*	..	..	..	..	..	..	..	..	..	
2,941,717	1,561,542	1,380,175	1,829,009	966.004	863,005	2,516	1,647	869	..	..	..	3
32,182	22,769	9,413	5,702	3,976	1,726	..	..	..	..	..	..	4
11,395,599	5,937,695	5,457,904	6,899,809	3,565,083	3,334,726	1,809,015	1,002,597	806,418	27,807	16,196	11,611	5
23,255,950	11,655,002	11,600,948	5,760,071	2,821,884	2,938,187	23,791	12,670	11,121	†6,743	3,146	3,597	6
23,255,950	*11,655,002*	*11,600,948*	*3,982,983* *695,504* *1,081,584*	*1,946,135* *332,717* *543,032*	*2,036,848* *362,787* *538,552*	*23,287* *188* *316*	*12,399* *89* *182*	*10,888* *99* *134*	*6,743*	*3,146*	*3,597*	
14,086,807	7,299,463	6,789,344	1,750,424	886,131	864,293	..	..	..	..	..	..	7
13,195,127	*6,802,463*	*6,392,664*	*1,650,873*	*831.043*	*819,830*	..	..	..	..	..	..	
891,680	*497,000*	*394,680*	*99,551*	*55,088*	*44,463*	..	..	..	..	..	..	
9,912,520	4,962,197	4,950,323	2,927,343	1,441,577	1,485,766	4,568	2,486	2,082	..	..	..	8
7,625,695	*3,792,425*	*3,833,270*	*2,251,627*	*1,104,928*	*1,146,699*	*3,950*	*2,155*	*1,795*	..	..	..	
2,286,825	*1,169,772*	*1,117,053*	*675,716*	*336,649*	*339,067*	*618*	*331*	*287*	..		..	
118,481	63,872	54,609	24,803	14,215	10,588	..	..	..	..	..	..	9
275,674	159,739	115,935	72,883	40,526	32,357	1,096	670	426	..	..	..	10
32,687,758	‡	‡	7,234,104	3,558,003	3,676,101	3,694	‡	‡	..	..	..	11
122,971	‡	‡	5,463	3,735	1,733	30	‡	‡	..	..	..	12
4,326,847	2,374,805	1,952,042	1,228,180	663,754	564,426	6,765	4,414	2,351	..	..	..	13
25,184,442	13,344,247	11,840,195	11,322,281	5,800,522	5,521,759	18,054	9,963	8,091	8,713	5,365	3,348	14
19,058,011	*10,132,861*	*8,925,150*	*7,842,497*	*4,031,837*	*3,810,660*	*15,976*	*8,670*	*7,306*	*8,174*	*4,957*	*3,217*	
6,126,431	*3,211,386*	*2,915,045*	*3,479,784*	*1,768,685*	*1,711,099*	*2,078*	*1,293*	*785*	*539*	*408*	*131*	
46,513,692	**23,858,692**	**22,655,000**	**11,112,942**	**5,639,570**	**5,473,372**	**13,845**	**7,384**	**6,461**	**16,908**	**8,965**	**7,943**	
270,871	133,833	137,038	1,421	767	654	..	..	..	..	..	..	15
12,074	6,530	5,544	20	18	2	..	..	..	..	..	..	16
1,824,799	944,429	880,370	203,043	100,543	102,500	70	37	33	445	179	266	17
600,523	316,002	284,521	30,822	16,928	13,894	..	..	..	852	576	376	18
3,409.203	1,669,409	1,739,794	649,266	324,380	324,886	41	15	26	..	..	..	19
3,440,162	1,758,516	1,681,646	348,574	173,103	175,471	..	..	..	..	..	..	20
4,469,390	2,293,003	2,176,387	797,902	402,441	395,461	3,163	1,653	1,510	8,295	4,374	3921	21
1,511,579	748,322	763,257	252,732	124,871	127,861	137	71	66	..	..	..	22
2,296,100	1,215,760	1,080,340	678,119	349,562	328,557	1,308	688	620	..	..	..	23
9,318,589	4,749,165	4,569,424	2,473,230	1,252,651	1,220,579	[illegible],440	4,583	3,857	..	..	..	24
311,765	170,183	141,582	170,92[illegible]	90,273	80,655	..	..	..	..	..	..	25
2,239,916	1,100,334	1,139,582	1,955,446	976,398	979,048	66	38	28	5,700	2,950	2,750	26
612,171	*294,357*	*317,814*	*125,339*	*61,681*	*63,658*	*15*	*13*	*2*	*1,635*	*869*	*766*	
1,297,889	*647,599*	*650,290*	*1,764,811*	*883,489*	*881,322*	*51*	*25*	*26*	*4,065*	*2,081*	*1,984*	
329,856	*158,378*	*171,478*	*65,296*	*31,228*	*34,068*	..	..	..	..	..	..	
4,770,391	2,429,892	2,340,499	1,000,326	509,898	490,428	..	..	..	..	..	..	27
12,336	11,923	413	542	531	11	..	..	..	..	..	..	28
242,346	125,976	116,370	91,510	47,411	44,099	..	..	..	..	..	..	29
1,288,100	697,222	590,878	364,539	195,383	169,156	51	5	46	..	..	..	30
7,157,642	3,781,619	3,376,023	1,565,409	805,376	760,033	..	..	..	1,179	635	544	31
35,721	18,394	17,327	2,029	1,134	895	337	168	169	427	243	184	32
587,821	300,490	287,331	208,864	105,642	103,222	232	126	106	10	8	2	33
2,714,364	1,387,690	1,326,674	318,220	162,260	155,960	.	..	..	..	..	..	34

† Details by locality not available. ‡ Sex details not available.

TABLE XVIII.

Variation in Population of Selected Castes and Tribes.

Note :—The 1921 and 1891 figures for Bombay include those for the Western India States Agency also.

To economise in space, other tables of this volume in which the castes detailed in this table also appear are represented in colums 3 by small arabic instead of Roman numerals.

Table XVIII.—Variation in Population

Tribe or Caste.	Province, State or Agency and Religion.	Reference to Table.	Persons. 1931.	1921.	1911	1901.	1891.	1881.	Variation (Increase + 1921-1931.	1911-1921.	1901-1911.
1	2	3	4	5	6	7	8	9	10	11	12
1 **Advichinchar** ..	....	17	**28,840**	**17,408**	**17,896**	**1,103**	**358**	*	+11,432	—488	+6,793
(Pardhi, Phanse-Pardhi, Haran shikari, Chigarigar).	Bombay .. .. (Hindu)	..	15,244	12,240	16,534	262	358	..	+3,004	—4,294	+16,272
	Western India States (Hindu)	..	958	702	1,362	841	..	..	+256	—660	+521
Pardhi	Hyderabad .. (Hindu)	..	5,466	4,091	*	*	*	*	+1,375	..	..
	Do. .. (Tribal)	..	7,172	375	*	*	*	*	+6,797	..	..
2 **Agariya**	United Provinces .. (Hindu and Muslim).	17	(*a*) **69,141**	*	*	34,211	29,606	*		+34,930	
3 **Aheria**	United Provinces .. (Hindu)	17	**23,084**	*	**20,560**	**17,778**	**19,768**	*	+2,524		+2,782
4 **Ahom**	Assam .. .. (Hindu)	14,17	**249,434**	**215,885**	**197,444**	**178,049**	**153,528**	**179,314**	+33,549	+18,441	+19,395
5 **Andamanese** ..	Andamans and Nicobar, (Tribal) Islands.	14	**460**	**786**	**1,317**	**1,882**	*	*	—326	—531	—565
Coast tribes of Great Andamans.			90	209	455	625	*	*	—119	—246	—170
Jarawas ..	.... .. Do.	..	70	114	114	585	*	*	—44	..	—354
Sentinelese ..	.... .. Do.	..	50	117	117		*	*	—67	..	
Onges	.... . Do.	..	250	346	631	672	*	*	—96	—285	—41
6 **Andh**	....		**64,649**	**59,068**	**55,003**	**61,542**	**43,602**	**37,010**	+5,581	+4,055	—6,539
	Central Provinces and Berar. (Hindu)	.	58,549	52,434	52,378	39,679	43,602	37,010	+6,115	+56	+12,699
	Hyderabad .. (Hindu)	..	6,100	6,634	2,625	21,863	*	*	—534	+4,009	—19,238
7 **Aranadan** ..	Madras .. .. (Hindu and Tribal).	17	60	119	182	115	166	..	—59	—63	+67
8 **Asur**	..	17	**2,024**	**2,245**	**3,716**	**2,784**	**2,303**	..	—221	—1,471	+932
	Bihar and Orissa .. (Hindu)	..	1,077	611	333	457	*	..	+466	+278	—124
	Do. .. (Christian	..	308	559	284	21	*	..	—251	+275	+263
	Do. .. (Tribal)	..	639	1,075	3,099	2,306	*	..	—436	—2,024	+793
9 **Badaga**	Madras .. .. (Tribal)	17	**43,075**	**40,329**	**38,180**	**34,178**	**29,613**	**24,398**	+2,746	+2,149	+4,002
0 **Bagata**	Madras .. .. (Tribal)	17	**34,379**	**34,291**	**33,021**	**31,622**	**27,863**	..	+88	+1,270	+1,399
1 **Bahelia**	....	17	**48,447**	*	**38,795**	**40,699**	**33,955**	**67,360**	+9,652		—1,904
	United Provinces .. (Hindu)	..	45,458	*	34,211	37,845	32,121	67,360	+11,247		—3,634
	Do. .. (Muslim)	..	2,989	*	4,584	2,854	1,834	..	—1,595		+1,730
2 **Baiga**	....	17	**72,899**	**57,314**	**30,391**	**24,743**	**21,336**	**38,883**	+15,585	+26,923	+5,648
	Central Provinces and Berar. (Hindu)	..	14,288	3,652	1,887	24,743	21,336	38,883	+10,736	+1,665	+5,648
	Do. .. (Tribal)	..	22,798	24,026	28,504				—1,228	—4,478	
	Central India .. (Hindu)	..	30,914	26,461	*	*	*	*	+4,453	..	..
	Do .. (Tribal)	..	4,899	3,275	*	*	*	*	+1,624	..	..
3 **Balti**	Jammu and Kashmir (Muslim)	..	**47,326**	**124,760**	**72,439**	*	*	*	—77,434	+52,321	..
4 **Baloch (Biloch)** ..	....	14,17	**854,164**	**707,420**	**703,449**	**466,645**	**383,138**	**331,851**	+146,744	+3,971	+236,804
	Baluchistan .. (Muslim)	..	229,473	176,336	172,473	*	*	*	+53,137	+3,863	..
	Punjab .. .. (Muslim)	..	624,691	531,084	530,976	466,645	383,138	331,851	+93,607	+108	+64,331
5 **Banjara, etc.** ..	Hyderabad ..	8,14,17	**371,402**	**287,405**	316,083	172,578	*	*	+83,997	—28,678	+143,505
Banjari ..	.... (Hindu)	..	70,936	63,626	174,039	*	*	*	+7,310	—110,413	..
	.... .. (Tribal)	..	4,953	..	..	177	*	*		+4,776	
Lamani ..	.... .. (Tribal)	..	4,220	..	..	86,130	*	*		—81,910	
Lambadi ..	.... .. (Tribal)	..	291,293	223,779	142,044	86,271	*	*	+67,514	+81,735	+55,773
6 **Barwar**	United Provinces .. (Hindu)	..	(*c*)**4,318**	*	**5,007**	**5,955**	**5,706**	**5,711**	—689		—948
7 **Bathudi**	Bihar and Orissa .. (Hindu)	..	**73,891**	**59,167**	**54,414**	33,086	*	*	+14,724	+4,753	+21,328
8 **Bawaria**	....	8,14,17	**47,891**	**34,557**	**50,735**	29,750	28,526	22,402	+13,334	—16,178	+20,985
	Delhi .. .. (Hindu)	..	32	35	*	*	*	*	—3		
	Punjab .. .. (Hindu)	..	16,045	25,517	26,847	27,633	24,401	20,163	—9,472	—1,330	—786
	Do. .. .. (Sikh)	..	15,858	9,005	6,002	1,275	1,635	1,478	+6,853	+3,003	+4,727
	United Provinces .. (Hindu)	..	15,956	*	17,886	842	2,490	761	—1,930		+17,044
19 **Bhaina**	Central Provinces and Berar. (Hindu)	17	(*d*) **20,879**	**11,523**	**17,387**	**9,909**	**14,922**	*	+9,356	—5,864	+7,478
10 **Bharia Bhumia** ..	....	14,17	**681,165**	**630,862**	**714,960**	**652,499**	**529,249**	**29,529**	+50,303	—84,098	+62,461
	Central Provinces and Berar. (Hindu and Tribal).	..	55,341	52,052	51,006	33,561	49,194	29,529	+3,289	+1,046	+17,445
Bhuiya ..	Bihar and Orissa .. (Hindu)	..	621,062	578,427	663,280	609,989	442,844	*	+42,635	—84,853	+[illegible]3,291
	Do. (Christian).	..	36	20	197	..	..	*	+16	—177	+197
	Do. (Tribal)	..	4,726	363	477	8,949	37,211	*	+4 363	—114	—8,472

(*a*) Includes Muslims 1,097 (586 Males and 511 Females).

(*c*) Includes Muslims 4 (1 Male and 3 Females).

(*d*) Includes Tribals 4,043 (2,032 Males and 2,001 Females).

* Figures not available.

† Sex details not available.

of Selected Castes and Tribes.

Decrease—). 1891-1901.	1881-1891.	Net variation 1881-1931. (Increase +, Decrease—).	Males. 1931.	1921.	1911.	1901.	1891.	1881.	Females. 1931.	1921.	1911.	1901.	1891.	1881.	
13	14	15	16	17	18	19	20	21	22	23	24	25	26	27	
+745	..	..	14,959	7,995	9,994	561	182	*	13,881	9,413	7,902	542	176	*	1
—96	..	..	7,664	6,270	9,283	130	182	..	7,580	5,970	7,251	132	176	..	
..	..	..	485	313	711	431	..	..	473	389	651	410	..	..	
..	..	..	2,977	1,307	*	*	*	*	2,489	2,784	*	*	*	*	
..	..	..	3,833	105	*	*	*	*	3,339	270	*	*	*	*	
+4,605	..	..	34,271	*	*	16,388	14,705	*	34,870	*	*	17,823	14,901	*	2
—1,990	..	..	11,992	*	10,441	10,000	10,514	*	11,093	*	10,119	7,778	9,254	*	3
+24,521	+74,214	+70,120	129,989	112,400	101,961	90,808	78,842	91,485	119,445	103,485	95,483	87,241	74,686	87,829	4
..	..	..	250	414	628	1,036	*	*	210	372	689	846	*	*	5
..	..	..	38	104	221	335	*	*	52	105	234	290	*	*	
..	..	..	40	52	52 }	335	*	*	30	62	62 }	250	*	*	
..	..	..	25	54	54 }		*	*	25	63	63 }		*	*	
..	..	..	147	204	301	366	*	*	103	142	330	306	*	*	
+17,940	+6,592	+27,639	32,620	30,498	26,927	30,708	†	18,699	32,029	28,570	28,076	30,834	†	18,311	6
—3,923	+6,592	+21,539	29,820	25,827	25,563	19,318	†	18,699	28,729	26,607	26,815	20,361	†	18,311	
..	..	..	2,800	4,671	1,364	11,390	*	*	3,300	1,963	1,261	10,473	*		
—51	..	..	33	59	94	56	87	..	27	60	88	59	79		7
+481	..	..	1,159	1,124	1,822	1,418	1,170	..	865	1,121	1,894	1,366	1,133		8
..	..	..	599	294	150	241	*	..	478	317	183	216	*	..	
..	..	..	242	298	143	13	*	..	66	261	141	8	*	..	
..	..	..	318	532	1,529	1,164	*	..	321	543	1,570	1,142	*	..	
+4,565	+5,215	+18,677	21,819	20,097	18,898	16,561	14,892	12,253	21,256	20,232	19,282	17,617	14,721	12,145	9
+3,756	..	..	17,086	17,021	16,105	15,824	14,036	..	17,293	17,270	16,916	15,798	13,827	..	10
+6,744	—33,405	—18,913	25,491	*	20,651	20,652	17,648	34,654	22,956	*	18,144	20,047	16,307	32,706	11
+5,724	—35,239	—21,902	23,926	*	18,246	19,111	16,702	34,654	21,532	*	15,965	18,734	15,419	32,706	
+1,020	+1,834	+2,989	1,565	*	2,405	1,541	946	..	1,424	*	2,179	1,313	888	..	
+3,407	—17,547	+34,016	36,328	29,262	15,045	12,012	†	19,689	36,571	28,052	15,346	12,731	†	19,194	12
+3,407	—17,547	—1,797 {	7,046	1,654	935 }	12,012	†	19,689 {	7,242	1,898	952 }	12,731	†	19,194	
			11,389	12,042	14,110 }				11,409	11,984	14,394 }				
..	..	..	15,394	13,930	*	*	*	*	15,520	12,531	*	*	*	*	
..	..	..	2,499	1,636	*	*	*	*	2,400	1,639	*	*	*	*	
..	..	..	23,274	61,786	40,597	*	*	*	24,052	62,974	31,842	*	*	*	13
+83,507	+51,287	+522,318	466,391	386,657	382,632	252,617	†	179,179	387,773	320,763	320,817	214,028	†	152,672	14
..	..	..	124,848	97,375	93,819	*	*	*	104,625	78,961	78,654	*	*	*	
+83,507	+51,287	+292,840	341,543	289,282	288,813	252,617	†	179,179	283,148	241,802	242,163	214,028	†	152,672	
..	..	..	192,821	152,871	164,546	90,359	*	*	178,581	134,534	151,537	82,219	*	*	15
..	..	..	38,965	34,466	87,843	*	*	*	31,971	29,160	86,196	*	*	*	
..	..	..	2,938	..	..	92	*	*	2,015	..	..	85	*	*	
..	..	..	2,420	..	..	44,510	*	*	1,800	..	..	41,620	*	*	
..	..	..	148,498	118,405	76,703	45,757	*	*	142,795	105,374	65,341	40,514	*	*	
+249	—5	—1,393	2,092	*	2,292	2,977	2,700	2,392	2,226	*	2,715	2,978	3,006	3,319	16
..	..	..	36,516	29,056	27,611	16,368	*	*	37,375	30,111	26,803	16,718	*	*	17
+1,224	+6,124	+25,489	24,998	18,592	26,737	15,460	†	11,532	22,893	15,965	23,998	14,290	†	10,870	18
..	..	..	23	16	*	*	*	*	9	19	*	*	*	*	
+3,232	+4,238	—4,118	8,420	13,607	14,366	14,306	†	10,428	7,625	11,910	12,481	13,327	†	9,735	
—360	+157	+14,380	8,192	4,969	3,115	700	†	791	7,666	4,036	2,887	575	†	687	
—1,648	+1,729	+15,195	8,363	*	9,256	454	1,217	313	7,593	*	8,630	388	1,273	448	
—5,013	..	..	10,227	6,437	8,489	4,734	†	*	10,652	5,086	8,898	5,175	†	*	19
+123,250	+499,720	+651,636	332,778	309,273	347,395	312,979	†	14,406	348,387	321,589	367,565	339,520	†	15,123	20
—15,633	+19,665	+25,812	26,645	26,198	24,588	16,117	†	14,406	28,696	25,854	26,418	17,444	†	15,123	
+167,145	..	..	303,800	282,888	322,472	292,485	212,539	*	317,262	295,539	340,808	317,504	230,305	*	
..	..	..	19	8	99	..	..	*	17	12	98	..	..	*	
—28,262	..	..	2,314	179	236	4,377	19,488	*	2,412	184	241	4,572	17,723	*	

Table XVIII.—Variation in Population

Tribe or Caste.	Province, State or Agency and Religion.	Reference to Table.	Persons. 1931.	1921.	1911.	1901.	1891.	1881.	Variation (Increase +, 1921-1931.	1911-1921.	1901-1911.
1	2	3	4	5	6	7	8	9	10	11	12
21 Bhatra ..	.. Central Provinces and Berar.	17	**37,247**	*	*	*	**21,574**	*		**+15,673**	
	.. (Hindu)	..	650	*	*	*	*	*	..	..	..
	(Tribal)	..	36,597	*	*	*	*	*	..	..	..
22 Bhil, etc. ..	.. ....	8,14,17	**2,025,753**	**1,859,661**	**1,067,792**	**952 881**	**1,398,367**	**647,718**	**+166,092**	**+791,869**	**+114,911**
Bhil ..	.. Ajmer-Merwara (Hindu and Tribal).		8,313	6,812	6,509	5,325	7,752	6,549	+1,501	+303	+1,184
	Bombay .. .. (Hindu)	..	776,975	786,726	467,978	465,827	832,357	541,647	—9,751	+318,748	+2,151
	Central Provinces and Berar. (All religions).	..	30,325	24,865	27,785	28,416 (e)	28,195	41,868	+5,460	—2,920	—631
	United Provinces .. (Hindu)	..	28	*	*	279	190	*		—251	
	Baroda .. .. (Hindu)	..	53,235	23,569	24,755	..	38,920	24,913	+29,666	—1,186	—14,165
	Do. .. .. (Tribal)	..	1,307	20,098	17,081	37,650	20,621	31,777	—18,791	+3,017	—20,567
	Central India .. (Hindu)	..	144,836	49,305	*	*	*	*	+95,531	..	..
	Do. .. .. (Tribal)	..	218,288	288,832	*	*	*	*	—70,544	..	..
	Gwalior .. .. (Hindu)	..	86,571	2,463	10,478	..	*	*	+84,108	—8,015	..
	Do. .. .. (Tribal)	..	..	68,832	42,821	41,248	*	*	—68,832	+26,011	+1,573
	Hyderabad .. (Tribal)	..	15,052	13,723	9,921	9,554	*	*	+1,329	+3,802	+367
	Rajputana .. .. (Hindu)	..	457,509	103,589	63,004	9,245			+353,920	+40,585	+53,759
	Do. .. .. (Tribal)	..	198,005	445,937	385,903	330,541			—247,932	+60,034	+55,362
	Do. .. .. (Muslim)	..	..	4	3	..	470,332	*	—4	+1	+3
	Do. .. (Jain)	..	..	1	..	..			—1	+1	..
	Do. .. (Christian)	..	133	..	..	..			+133	..	..
	Western India States (Hindu and Tribal).	..	14,359	10,749	11,530	16,361	*	959	+3,610	—781	—4,831
Tadvi ..	.. Baroda .. .. (Hindu)	..	20,817	14,156	24	(f) 8,435	*	*	+6,661	+14,132	—8,412
23 Bhilala ..	.. ....	8,17	**232,230**	**196,457**	**1,563**	**17,145**	*	*	**+35,773**	**+194,894**	**—15,582**
	Central India .. (Hindu)	..	187,145	169,390	*	*	*	*	+17,755	..	..
	Do. .. (Tribal)	..	6,630	585	*	*	*	*	+6,045	..	..
	Gwalior .. .. (Tribal)	..	(g) 38,455	26,482	1,563	17,145	*	*	+11,973	+24,919	—15,582
24 Bhoksa ..	.. United Provinces .. (Hindu)	17	**7,618**	**7,610**	**6,637**	**5,064**	**1,208**	**5,664**	**+8**	**+973**	**+1,578**
25 Bhuinhar	.. ....	17	**25,628**	**11,990**	**27,620**	*	**2,970**	*	**+13,638**	**—15,630**	
	Central Provinces and Berar. (Hindu)	..	20,939	9,750	16,470	*	*	*	+11,189	—6,720	..
	Do. (Tribal)	..	4,689	2,240	11,150	*	*	*	+2,449	—8,910	..
26 Bhumij ..	.. ....	17	**274,018**	**240,229**	**272,667**	**244,586**	**238,455**	*	**+33,789**	**—32,438**	**+28,081**
	Bihar and Orissa .. (Hindu)	..	266,424	237,187	266,021	233,522	162,960	*	+29,237	—28,834	+32,499
	Do. .. (Tribal)	..	7,443	3,042	6,646	11,064	75,495	*	+4,401	—3,604	—4,418
	Do. .. (Christian).	..	151	..	..	..	..	..	..	..	..
27 Binjhwar, etc.	.. ..	17	**75,774**	**42,491**	**65,654**	**22,126**	**40,050**	*	**+33,283**	**—23,163**	**+43,528**
Bhurijia ..	Central Provinces and Berar. (Hindu)	..	3,318	6,376	6,921	3,086	6,187	*	—3,058	—545	+3,835
	Do. (Tribal)	..	5,195	..	..				+5,195	..	
Binjhwoor ..	Do. (Hindu)	..	61,581	35,191	52,862	19,040	33,863	*	+26,390	—17,671	+39,693
	Do. (Tribal)	..	5,680	924	5,871			..	+4,756	—4,947	
28 Birhor ..	.. ..	17	(h) **2,350**	**1,510**	**2,299**	**969**	**1,429**	*	**+840**	**—789**	**+1,330**
	Bihar and Orissa .. Hindu)	..	1,723	1,251	1,387	*	*	*	+472	—136	..
	Do. .. (Tribal)	..	626	259	912	*	*	*	+367	—653	..
29 Birjia ..	.. ....	17	**1,550**	*	**1,414**	**1,170**	*	*	**+136**		**+244**
	Bihar and Orissa .. (Hindu)	..	938	*	298	348	*	*	+640		—50
	Do. .. (Tribal)	..	612	*	1,116	822	*	*	—504		+294
30 Brahui ..	.. Baluchistan .. (Muslim)	8,17	**152,588**	**159,734**	**167,787**	*	*	*	**—7,146**	**—8,053**	..
31 Chakma ..	.. Bengal ..	..	**135 508**	**77,590**	(i) **58,672**	**49,718**	**42,556**	*	**+57,918**	**+18,918**	**+8,954**
	.. .. (Buddhist).	..	135,283	77,590	58,663	49,674	*	*	+57,693	+18,927	+8,989
	.. .. (Christian).	..	155	..	..	..	*	*	..	..	..
	.. .. (Hindu)	..	70	..	..	44	*	*		+26	
32 Chenchu ..	.. ..	8,14,17	**10,342**	**12,402**	**7,449**	**8,422**	**5,910**	**5,010**	**—2,060**	**+4,958**	**—973**
	Madras .. .. (Tribal)	..	8,078	6,281	7,449	7,163	5,910	5,010	+1,797	—1,168	+286
	Hyderabad .. (Tribal)	..	2,264	6,121	..	1,259	*	*	—3,857	+4,862	
33 Chero ..	.. Bihar and Orissa .. (Hindu)	17	**17,906**	*	**16,602**	**15,293**	**14,065**	*	**+1,304**		**1,309**
34 Chirimar	.. Delhi .. .. (Hindu and Muslim.	..	**274**	**263**	*	*	*	*	**+11**	..	..

*Figures not available.
†Sex details not available.
(e) Includes Muslims 9 (5 Males and 4 Females). (f) All Tribals. (g) All Hindus.

of Selected Castes and Tribes—*contd.*

Decrease—). 1891-1901. 13	1881-1891. 14	Net variation 1881-1931. (Increase +, Decrease—). 15	Males. 1931. 16	1921. 17	1911. 18	1901. 19	1891. 20	1881. 21	Females. 1931. 22	1921. 23	1911. 24	1901. 25	1891. 26	1881. 27	
	..	..	**18,658**	*	*	*	†	*	**18,589**	*	*	*	†	*	21
..	..	..	331	*		*	*	*	319	*	*	*	*	*	
..	..	..	18,327	*	*	*	*	*	18,270		*	*	*	*	
—445,486	**+750,654**	**+1,378,040**	**1,030,742**	**942,800**	**543,101**	**485,786**	†	**328,758**	**995,011**	**916,861**	**524,691**	**467,095**	†	**318,955**	22
—2,427	+1,203	+1,764	4,261	3,474	3,289	2,545	3,999	3,311	4,052	3,338	3,220	2,780	3,753	3,238	
—366,530	+290,710	+235,328	397,474	396,356	237,894	235,588	422,973	274,930	379,501	390,370	230,084	230,239	409,384	266,717	
+221	—13,673	—11,543	15,242	12,273	13,768	14,049	†	21,003	15,083	12,592	14,017	14,367	†	20,865	
+89	..	..	15	*	*	(e)48	117	*	13	*	*	(e) 231	73	*	
	+14,007	+28,322	27,158	12,257	12,441	..	20,044	12,963	26,077	11,312	12,314	..	18,876	11,950	
+17,029	—11,156	—30,470	631	10,235	8,681	19,392	10,472	16,047	676	9,863	8,400	18,258	10,149	15,730	
..	..	..	73,939	25,500	*	*	*	*	70,897	23,805	*	*	*	*	
..	..	..	109,666	144,854	*	*	*	*	108,622	143,978	*	*	*	*	
..	..	..	43,682	1,319	5,570	..	*	*	42,889	1,144	4,908	..	*	*	
..	..	..	..	35,010	20,968	21,514	*	*	..	33,822	21,853	19,734	*	*	
..	..	..	7,551	7,470	5,036	4,804	*	*	7,501	6,253	4,885	4,750	*	*	
			233,302	54,529	33,022	4,611			224,207	49,060	29,982	4,634			
			99,258	226,534	196,242	170,505			98,747	219,403	189,661	160,036			
—130,546	..	..	..	2	2	..	243,081	*	..	2	1	..	227,251	*	
			..	1	..	..			..	..	..	..			
			65	..	..	..			68	..	..	..			
+15,402		+13,400	7,730	5,719	6,181	8,441	*	504	6,629	5,030	5,349	7,920	*	455	
..	..	..	10,768	7,267	7	(f) 4,289	*	*	10,049	6,889	17	(f) 4,146	*	*	
..	..	..	**117,720**	**98,921**	**858**	**9,309**	*	*	**114,510**	**97,536**	**705**	**7,836**	*	*	23
..	..	..	94,926	85,395	*	*	*	*	92,219	83,995	*	*	*	*	
..	..	..	3,363	226	*	*	*	*	3,267	359	*	*	*	*	
..	..	..	(g) 19,431	13,300	858	9,309	*	*	(g) 19,024	13,182	705	7,836	*	*	
+3,856	**—4,456**	**+1,954**	**4,060**	**4,131**	**3,536**	**2,680**	**646**	**3,108**	**3,558**	**3,479**	**3,101**	**2,384**	**562**	**2,556**	24
+24,650	..	..	**13,031**	**6,281**	**14,126**	*	†	*	**12,547**	**5,709**	**13,494**	*	†	*	25
..	..	..	10,647	5,141	8,515	*	*	*	10,292	4,609	7,955	*	*	*	
..	..	..	2,434	1,140	5,611	*	*	*	2,255	1,100	5,539	*	*	*	
+6,131	..	..	**136,239**	**118,125**	**130,357**	**119,099**	**117,099**		**137,779**	**122,104**	**142,310**	**135,487**	**121,856**	*	26
+70,562	..	..	132,533	116,877	127,002	113,613	79,800	*	133,891	120,310	139,019	119,909	83,160	*	
—64,431	..	..	3,630	1,248	3,355	5,486	37,299	*	3,813	1,794	3,291	5,578	38,196	*	
..	..	..	76	..	..	..	..	..	75	..	..	..	..	..	
—17,924	..	..	**37,501**	**30,672**	**32,364**	**10,675**	†	*	**38,273**	**21,819**	**33,290**	**11,451**	†	*	27
—3,101	..	..	1,047	3,016	3,466	1,487	†	*	1,671	3,360	3,455	**1,599**	†	*	
			2,586	..	..				2,609	..	..				
—14,823	..	..	30,482	17,197	26,010	9,188	†	*	31,099	17,994	26,852	9,852	†	*	
			2,786	459	2,888				2,894	465	2,983				
—460	..	..	**1,217**	**749**	**1,084**	**485**	**743**	*	**1,133**	**761**	**1,215**	**484**	**686**	*	28
..	..	..	878	641	644	*	*	*	845	610	743	*	*	*	
..	..	..	338	108	440	*	*	*	288	151	472	*	*	*	
..	..	..	**796**	*	**647**	**549**	*	*	**754**	*	**767**	**621**	*	*	29
..	..	..	509	*	125	160	*	*	429	*	173	188	*	*	
..	..	..	287	*	522	389	*	*	325	*	594	433	*	*	
..	..	..	**83,528**	**88,961**	**93,095**	*	*	*	**69,060**	**70,773**	**74,69[illegible]**	*	*	*	30
+7,162	..	..	**72,016**	**40,801**	**31,014**	**26,425**	**22,789**	*	**63,492**	**36,789**	**27,658**	**23,293**	**19,767**	*	31
..	..	..	71,860	40,801	31,006	26,398	*	*	63,423	36,789	27,657	23,276	*	*	
..	..	..	100	..	..	..	*	*	55	..	..	..	*	*	
..	..	..	56	..	..	27	*	*	14	..		17	*	*	
+2,512	**+900**	**+5,332**	**5,256**	**7,027**	**3,768**	**4,115**	**3,037**	**2,580**	**5,086**	**5,375**	**3,681**	**4,307**	**2,873**	**2,430**	32
+1,253	+900	+3,068	4,166	3,335	3,768	3,713	3,037	2,580	3,912	2,946	3,681	3,450	2,873	2,430	
..	..	..	1,090	3,692	..	402	*	*	1,174	2,429	..	857	*	*	
+1,228	..	..	**8,968**	*	**8,239**	**7,717**	**6,976**	*	**8,938**	*	**8,363**	**7,576**	**8,089**	*	33
..	..	..	**133**	**133**	*	*	*	*	**141**	**130**	*	*	*	*	34

(*h*) Includes 1 Christian Male. (*i*) Includes Tribals 9 (8 Males and 1 Female).

Table XVIII.—Variation in Population

Tribe or Caste. 1	Province, State or Agency and Religion. 2	Reference to Table. 3	Persons. 1931. 4	1921. 5	1911. 6	1901. 7	1891. 8	1881. 9	Variation (Increase +. 1921-1931. 10	1911-1921 11	1901-1911. 12
35 **Chodhra, etc.** ..	....	8,14,17	**84,200**	**77,591**	**70,556**	**55,329**	**72,371**	**67,583**	**+6,609**	**+7,041**	**+15,221**
Chodhra ..	Bombay .. .. (Hindu)	..	45,282§	43,277	38,138	30,972	40,132	34,465	+2,005	+5,139	+ 7,166
	Baroda .. .. (Hindu)	..	29,736	1,315	11,709	..	26,646	5,527	+28,421	—10,394	—14,937
	Do. .. .. (Tribal)	..	9,050	31,526	19,657	23,324	2,850	26,690	—22,476	+11,869	—3,667
Valvi	Do. .. .. (Hindu)	..	101	..	565	..	2,428	115	—464		—1,863
	(Tribal)	..	31	1,473	481	1,033	315	786	—1,442	+992	—552
36 **Dhanak (Dhanka)** ..	....	17	**4,778**	**12,081**	**18,667**	**5,524**	**27,999**	**20,324**	**—7,303**	**—6,586**	**+13,143**
	Delhi .. .. (Hindu)	..	1,321	4,471	‡	‡	‡	‡	—3,150	..	..
	Baroda .. .. (Hindu)	..	3,457	6,289	2,033	..	27,840	20,291	—2,832	+4,256	—25,807
	Do .. .. (Tribal)	..	..	1,321	16,634	5,524	159	33	—1,321	—15,313	+11,110
37 **Dhanwar** ..	Central Provinces and Berar.	17	**23,955**	**16,766**	**18,637**	**10,815**	**12,403**	‡	**+7,189**	**—1,871**	**+7,822**
	Do. (Hindu)		19,343	13,701	14,257	‡	‡	‡	+5,642	—556	..
	.. (Tribal)	..	4,612	3,065	4,380	‡	‡	‡	+1,547	—1,315	..
38 **Dharhi, Kingharia and Pawaria.**	....	17	**13,989**	‡	‡	**15,118**	**14,806**	‡		—1,129	
	United Provinces of Agra and Oudh. (Hindu)		7,599	‡	‡	12,747	12,972	‡		—5,148	
	(Muslim)	..	6,390	‡	‡	2,371	1,834	‡		+4,019	
39 **Dubla and Talavia, etc.**	....	14,17	**227,632**	**197,983**	**189,444**	**141,850**	**151,300**	**151,255**	**+29,649**	**+8,539**	**+48,094**
Dubla and Talavia	Bombay .. .. (Hindu)	..	144,646‖	132,539	127,870	97,924	102,415	109,055	+12,107	+4,669	+29,946
	Baroda .. .. (Hindu)	..	65,218	42.270	46,496	12,551	48,869	41,607	+22,948	—4,226	+33,945
	Do. .. .. (Tribal)	..	241	9,564	4,127	28,492	16	593	—9,323	+5,437	—24,365
Vasawa ..	Do. .. .. (Hindu)	..	13,290	2,237	4,257	..	..	..	+11,053	—2,020	..
	Do. .. .. (Tribal)	..	4,237	11,373	6,694	2,383	..	..	—7,136	+5,679	+4,311
40 **Erakala***	Hyderabad .. (Tribal)	17	**53,045**	**30,385**	**2,013**	**33,449**	‡	‡	**+22,660**	**+28,372**	**—31,436**
41 **Eravalan**	Cochin .. .. (Hindu)	17	**541**	..	**503**	**292**	..	..	+41		+211
42 **Gadaba**	....	17	**48,154**	**53,770**	**45,115**	**41,124**	**34,133**	**31,587**	**—5,616**	**+8,655**	**+3,991**
	Bihar and Orissa .. (Hindu)	..	277	‡	‡	‡	177	‡		+100	
	Central Provinces and Berar. (All Religions)	..	398	..	..	729	555	‡		—331	
	Madras .. .. (Tribal)	..	47,479	53,770	45,115	40,395	33,401	31,587	—6,291	+8,655	+4,720
43 **Gamit or Gamta**	..		**71,239**	**64,573**	**59,507**	**45,763**	**52,019**	**39,553**	**+6,666**	**+5,066**	**+13,744**
	Bombay .. .. (Hindu)	..	11,933	12,599	9,892	7,126	10,404	8,412	—666	+2,707	+2,766
	Baroda .. .. (Hindu)	..	33,210	375	27,440	..	38,237	510	+32,835	—27,065	—10,797
	Do. .. .. (Tribal)	..	26,003	1,599	22,175	38,169	3,378	30,631	—25,596	+29,424	—15,994
	Western India States (Hindu)	..	93	‡	‡	468	‡	‡		—375	
44 **Gidhiya**	....		**377**	‡	‡	‡	**17**	‡			+360
	United Provinces .. (Hindu)	..	215	‡	‡	‡	17	‡			+198
	Do. .. (Muslim)	..	162	‡	‡	‡	‡	‡	..	..	..
45 **Girasia (Grassia)** ..	Rajputana	8,14,17	**29,234**	**24,910(j)**	**17,419**	**12,297**	**14,948**	‡	**+4,324**	**+7,491**	**+5,122**
	.. .. (Hindu)	..	20,976‖	24,877	16,268	5	‡	‡	—3,901	+8,609	+16,263
	.. .. (Tribal)	..	8,258	11	1,151	12,292	‡	‡	+8,247	—1,140	—11,141
46 **Gond**	....	8,14,17	**3,063,753**	**2,837,577**	**2,827,758**	**1,958,806**	**2,000.124**	**1,542,921**	**+226,176**	**+9,819**	**+868,952**
	Bihar and Orissa .. (Hindu)	..	255,022	209,302	208,023	‡	‡	‡	+45,720	+1,279	..
	Do. .. (Tribal)	..	708	24,853	25,673	‡	‡	‡	—24,145	—820	..
	Do. .. (Christian)	..	15	32	..	..	..	..	—17	..	..
	Bombay .. .. (Hindu)	..	562	..	..	542	856	..		+20	
	Central Provinces and Berar. (Hindu)	..	1,036,673	454,792	367,257				+581,881	+87,535	
	Do. .. (Tribal)	..	(k) 1,224,465	1,654,791	1,966,636	1,861,445	1,860,720	1,542,921	—430,326	—311,845	+472,448
	Madras .. .. (Tribal)	..	29,052	40,823	25,596	20,734	14,036	..	—11,771	+15,227	+4,862
	United Provinces .. (Hindu)	..	121,579	106,619	(m) 110,232	20,324	(l) 124,512	‡	+14,960	+3,613	+89,908
	Central India .. (Hindu)	..	208,339	160,522	‡	‡	‡	‡	+47,817	..	..
	Do. .. (Tribal)	..	74,058	86,964	‡	‡	‡	‡	—12,906	..	..
	Hyderabad .. (Tribal)	..	113,280	98,879	124,341	55,761	‡	‡	+14,401	—25,462	+68,580

*Excluding Kaikadi and Korwa.

†Sex details not available.

‡Figures not available.

§Includes 80 Males enumerated in the Western India States Agency.

‖Includes 2 Females enumerated in the Western India States Agency.

(j) Includes Muslims 22 (10 Males and 12 Females).

(k) Includes 20 Christians (9 Males and 11 Females) and 4 Muslims (3 Males and 1 Female).

of Selected Castes and Tribes—*contd.*

Decrease—). 1891-1901.	1881-1891.	Net variation 1881-1931. (Increase +, Decrease—).	Males. 1931.	1921.	1911.	1901.	1891.	1881.	Females. 1931.	1921.	1911.	1901.	1891.	1881.	
13	14	15	16	17	18	19	20	21	22	23	24	25	26	27	
−17,042	+4,788	+16,617	**42,492**	**39,928**	**35,897**	**27,879**	**36,635**	**34,012**	**41,708**	**37,6b3**	**34,653**	**27,450**	**35,736**	**33,571**	**35**
−9,160	+5,667	+10,817	22,466	22,307	19,276	15,540	20,214	17,276	22,816	20,970	18,862	15,432	19,918	17,189	
	+21,119	+24,209	15,411	646	6,083	..	13,603	2,919	14,325	669	5,626	..	13,043	2,608	
+20,474	−23,840	−17,640	4,541	16,234	10,016	11,829	1,464	13,327	4,509	15,292	9,641	11,495	1,386	13,363	
	+2,313	−14	58	..	268	..	1,200	58	43	..	297	..	1,228	57	
+718	−471	−755	16	741	254	510	154	432	15	732	227	523	16	354	
−22,475	+7,675	−15,546	**2,510**	**6,438**	**9,414**	**2,802**	**14,205**	**10,285**	**2,318**	**5,643**	**9,253**	**2,722**	**13,794**	**10,039**	**36**
..	..	..	705	2,532	‡	‡	‡	‡	616	1,939	‡	‡	‡	‡	
	+7,549	−16,834	1,805	3,227	958	..	14,119	10,265	1,652	3,062	1,075	..	13,721	10,026	
+5,365	+126	−33	..	679	8,456	2,802	86	20	..	642	8,178	2,722	73	13	
−1,588	..	..	**11,952**	**8,429**	**9,181**	**5,175**	†	‡	**12,003**	**8,337**	**9,456**	**5,640**	†	‡	**37**
..	..	..	9,635	6,831	7,074	‡	‡	‡	9,708	6,870	7,183	‡	‡	‡	
..	..	..	2,317	1,598	2,107	‡	‡	‡	2,295	1,467	2,273	‡	‡	‡	
+312	..	..	**7,023**	‡	‡	**7,596**	**7,487**	‡	**6,966**	‡	‡	**7,522**	**7,319**	‡	**38**
−225	..	..	3,870	‡	‡	6,328	6,554	‡	3,729	‡	‡	6,419	6,418	‡	
+537	..	..	3 153	‡	‡	1,268	933	‡	3,237	‡	‡	1,103	901	‡	
−9,950	+45	+76,377	**115,523**	**100,677**	**94,180**	**70,120**	**75,306**	**75,975**	**112,109**	**97,306**	**95,264**	**71,230**	**75,994**	**75,280**	**39**
−4,491	−6,640	+35,591	73,463	67,339	62,666	48,095	50,394	54,417	71,183	65,200	65,204	49,829	52,021	54,638	
−36,318	+7,262	+23,611	33,041	21,494	23,635	6,448	24,902	21,201	32,177	20,776	22,861	6,103	23,967	20,406	
+28,476	−577	−352	133	4,798	2,153	14,397	10	357	108	4,766	1,974	14,095	6	236	
..	..	..	6,734	1,161	2,214	..	..	..	6,556	1,076	2,043	..	..	..	
..	..	..	2,152	5,885	3,512	1,180	..	..	2,085	5,488	3,182	1,203	..	..	
..	..	..	**28,766**	**14,937**	**969**	**17,631**	‡	‡	**24,279**	**15,448**	**1,044**	**15,818**	‡	‡	**40**
..	..	..	**271**	..	**245**	**149**	..	..	**270**	..	**258**	**143**	..	..	**41**
+6,991	+2,546	+16,567	**23,758**	**27,495**	**23,011**	**20,831**	**16,796**	**16,045**	**24,396**	**26,275**	**22,104**	**20,293**	**16,782**	**15 542**	**42**
..	..	..	139	‡	‡	‡	89	‡	138	‡	‡	‡	88	‡	
+174	..	..	187	..	..	369	†	‡	211	..	..	360	†	‡	
+6,994	+1,814	+15,892	23,432	27,495	23,011	20,462	16,707	16,045	24,047	26,275	22,104	19,933	16,694	15,542	
−6,256	+12,466	+31,686	**36,386**	**32,947**	**30,120**	**23,125**	**26,281**	**20,173**	**34,853**	**31,626**	**29,387**	**22,638**	**25,738**	**19,380**	**43**
−3,278	+1,992	+3,521	6,117	6,343	4,860	3,591	5,212	4,159	5,816	6,256	5,032	3,535	5,192	4,253	
	+37,727	+32,700	17,084	196	13,871	..	19,394	296	16,126	179	13,569	..	18,843	214	
+34,791	−27,253	−4,628	13,155	26,408	11,389	19,291	1,675	15,718	12,848	25,191	10,786	18,878	1,703	14,913	
..	..	..	30	‡	‡	243	‡	‡	63	‡	‡	225	‡	‡	
	..	..	**206**	‡	‡	‡	**13**	‡	**171**	‡	‡	‡	**4**	‡	**44**
	..	..	137	‡	‡	‡	13	‡	78	‡	‡	‡	4	‡	
	..	..	69	‡	‡	‡	‡	‡	93	‡	‡	‡	‡	‡	
−2,651	..	..	**15,214**	**12,835**	**8,918**	**6,411**	**7,890**	‡	**14,020**	**12,075**	**8,501**	**5,886**	**7,058**	‡	**45**
..	..	..	10,830	12,814	8,331	1	‡	‡	10,146	12,063	7,937	4	‡	‡	
..	..	..	4,384	11	587	6,410	‡	‡	3,874	..	564	5,882	‡	‡	
−41,318	+457,203	+1,520,832	**1,503,026**	**1,384,916**	**1,383,490**	**948,649**	†	**766,550**	**1,560,727**	**1,452,661**	**1,444,268**	**1,010,157**	†	**776,371**	**46**
..	..	..	124,277	102,314	103,103	‡	‡	‡	130,745	106,988	104,920	‡	‡	‡	
..	..	..	418	12,315	12,544	‡	‡	‡	290	12,538	13,129	‡	‡	‡	
..	..	..	9	16	..	..	..	..	6	16	..	..	..	..	
−314	..	..	289	..	..	272	421	..	273	..	..	270	435	..	
+725	+317,799	+718,217	504,710 599,468	215,975 807,983	177,982 960,175	900,576	†	766,550	531,963 624,997	238,817 846,808	189,275 1,006,461	960,869	†	776,371	
+6,698	..	..	14,622	20,596	13,871	10,704	7,222	..	14,430	20,227	11,725	10,030	6,814	..	
−104,188	..	..	62,230	53,975	53,232	9,782	59,093	‡	59,349	52,644	57,000	10,542	65,419	‡	
..	..	..	103,481	80,110	‡	‡	‡	‡	104,858	80,412	‡	‡	‡	‡	
..	..	..	36,474	42,851	‡	‡	‡	‡	37,584	44,113	‡	‡	‡	‡	
..	..	..	57,048	48,781	62,583	27,315	‡	‡	56,232	50,098	61,758	28,446	‡	‡	

‖ Includes 3 Males enumerated in Ajmer-Merwara.

(*l*) Includes 8 Sikhs (4 Males and 4 Females).

(*m*) Includes Muslims 8 (2 Males and 6 Females).

Table XVIII.—Variation in Population

Tribe or Caste.	Province, State or Agency and Religion.	Reference to Table.	Persons. 1931.	1921.	1911.	1901.	1891.	1881.	Variation (Increase +, 1921-1931	1911-1921.	1901-1911.
1	2	3	4	5	6	7	8	9	10	11	12
47 **Gujar** ..	....	8,14,17	**1,111,513**	**1,001,767**	**923,025**	**611,263**	**599,528**	**538,867**	**+109,746**	**+78,742**	**+811,762**
	Delhi .. .. (All Religions)	..	14,625	13,041	†	†	†	†	+1,584	..	..
	Punjab .. .. (Hindu)	..	170,439	158,998	152,575	151,415	153,773	142,376	+11,441	+6,423	+1,160
	Do. .. .. (Muslim)	..	521,347	465,676	439,198	458,619	444,847	395,353	+55,671	+26,478	—19,421
	Do. .. .. (Sikh)	..	2,321	1,945	3,249	1,229	908	1,138	+376	—1,304	+2,020
	Jammu and Kashmir · (Muslim)	..	402,781	362,107	328,003	†	†	†	+40,674	+34,104	..
48 **Ho** ..	....	17	**523,158**	**441,424**	**420,179**	**383,206**	**329,973**	†	**+81,734**	**+21,245**	**+36,973**
	Bihar and Orissa .. (Hindu)	..	129,654	49,530	60,197	42,349	†	†	+80,124	—10,667	+17,848
	Do. .. (Tribal)	..	391,426	390,644	358,785	339,956	†	†	+782	+31,859	+18,829
	Do. .. (Christian),	..	2,078	1,250	1,197	901	†	†	+828	+53	+296
49 **Jat**	....	8,14,17	**6,345,700**	**5,694,884**	**5,108,917**	**4,883,300**	**4,499,489**	**4,223,282**	**+650,816**	**+585,967**	**+225,617**
	Baluchistan .. (Muslim)	..	82,689	66,982	78,400	†	†	†	+15,707	—11,418	..
	Delhi .. .. (All Religions)	..	53,277	47,620	†	†	†	†	+5,657	..	..
	Punjab .. .. (Hindu)	..	992,309	1,046,396	1,000,085	1,539,574	1,679,177	1,445,374	—54,087	+46,311	—539,489
	Do. .. .. (Sikh)	..	2,133,152	1,822,881	1,617,532	1,388,877	1,116,417	1,122,673	+310,271	+205,349	+228,655
	Do. .. .. (Muslim)	..	2,940,819	2,582,495	2,272,176	1,954,849	1,703,895	1,655,235	+358,324	+310,319	+317,327
	Jammu and Kashmir (Hindu)	..	23,371	25,861	25,194	†	†	†	—2,490	+667	..
	Do. (Muslim)	..	120,083	102,649	115,530	†	†	†	+17,434	—12,881	..
50 **Juang**	Bihar and Orissa ..	17	**15,024**	**10,454**	**12,823**	**11,159**	**9,173**	†	**+4,570**	**—2,369**	**+1,664**
	.. (Hindu)	..	7,887	2,542	1,306	1,848	†	†	+5,345	+1,236	—542
	.. (Tribal)	..	7,137	7,912	11,517	9,311	†	†	—775	—3,605	+2,206
51 **Kachari (including Mech).**	Assam	17	**215,696**	**193,962**	**191,773**	**180,511**	**.73,231**	**198,699**	**+21,734**	**+2,189**	**+11,262**
	.. .. (Hindu)	..	146,218	107,720	71,475	5,687	6,784	†	+38,498	+36,245	+65,788
	.. .. (Tribal)	..	66,180	86,242	120,298	174,824	166,447	†	—20,062	—34,056	—54,526
	.. .. (Christian).	..	3,298	†	†	..	..	..	..	..	..
52 **Kachin Group** ..	Burma .. .. (All Religions).	8,17	**153,345**	**146,845**	**162,374**	**64,742**	†	†	**+6,500**	**—15,529**	**+97,632**
53 **Kadan** ..	....	17	**758**	**996**	**1,238**	**1,099**	**1,134**	**594**	**—238**	**—242**	**+139**
	Madras (Hindu and Tribal)	..	491	722	791	789	913	594	—231	—69	+2
	Cochin .. (Hindu)	..	267	274	447	310	221	†	— 7	—173	+137
54 **Kaikadi**	Hyderabad ..	17	**12,798**	**24,794**	†	**4,216**	†	†	—11,996	+20,578	
	.. (Hindu)	..	9,986	24,794	†	†	†	†	—14,808	..	
	.. (Tribal)	..	2,812	†	†	4,216	†	†	—1,404		
55 **Kamar**	Central Provinces and Berar. (Hindu)	17 ..	**9,449**	†	**7,438**	**576**	**5,597**	†	+2.011		**+6,862**
	....		3,294	†	252	†	†	†	+3,042		..
	.. .. (Tribal)	..	6,155	†	7,186	†	†	†	—1,031		..
56 **Kamboh**	Punjab	..	**239,385**	**180,870**	**171,536**	**173,780**	**150,646**	**129,468**	**+58,515**	**+9,334**	**—2,244**
	.. (Hindu)	..	37,465	33,606	32,073	56,158	58,222	52,044	+3,859	+1,533	—24,085
	.. .. (Sikh)	..	98,737	64,194	67,912	41,292	34,148	27,497	+34,543	—3,718	+26,620
	.. .. (Muslim)	..	96,753	76,829	65,822	70,353	42,014	44,854	+19,924	+11,007	—4.531
57 **Kanet**	Punjab .. (All Religions).	17	**305,814**	**288,131**	**403,735**	**389,645**	**369,666**	**345,774**	**+17,683**	**—115,604**	**+14,090**
	.. .. (Hindu)	..	300,429	282,124	394,649	387,286	366,145	344,813	+18,305	—112,525	+7,363
	.. .. (Buddhist).	..	4,842	4,609	6,104	1,334	..	..	+233	—1,495	+4,770
58 **Kanikkaran (Including Malavelan).**	Travancore	17	**6,659**	**3,762**	**4,034**	**4,139**	†	†	**+2,897**	**—272**	**—105**
	.. (Hindu)	..	4,565	..	..	..	†	†	..	..	..
	.. .. (Tribal)	..	2,041	3,762	4,034	4,139	†	†	—1,721	—272	—105
	.. .. (Christian).	..	53	..		..	†	†	..	..	..
59 **Karen Group** ..	Burma .. (All Religions).	8,14,17	**1,367,673**	**1,220,356**	**1,099,048**	**904,424**	†	†	**+147,317**	**+121,308**	**+194,624**
60 **Karimpalan** ..	Madras .. (Hindu and Tribal).	..	**2,807**	**3,163**	**2,898**	**3,586**	**3,713**	**1,629**	**—356**	**+265**	**—688**
61 **Karmali**	Bihar and Orissa ..	17	**8,632**	†	**21,114**	†	†	†	—12,482		..
	.. (Hindu)	..	8,297	†	16,330	†	†	†	—8,033		
	.. (Christian)	..	32	†	..	†	†	†	..	..	..
	.. .. (Tribal)	..	303	†	4,784	†	†	†	—4,481		..
62 **Katkari, etc.** ..	....	8,17	**88,336**	**81,202**	**91,841**	**60,485**	**74,287**	**229**	**+7,134**	**—10,639**	**+31,356**
Katkari ..	Bombay .. (Hindu)	..	87,784	80,830	91,037	59 872	74,003	†	+6,954	—10,207	+31,165
	Western India States (Hindu)	..	1	..	282	..	..	..	—281		..
Kathodia ..	Baroda .. (Hindu and Tribal).	..	551	372	522	613	284	229	+179	—150	—91

* Sex details not available.
† Figures not available.

of Selected Castes and Tribes—*contd.*

Decrease—). 1891-1901.	1881-1891.	Net variation 1881-1931. (Increase +, Decrease—).	Males. 1931.	1921.	1911.	1901.	1891.	1881.	Females. 1931.	1921.	1911.	1901.	1891.	1881.	
13	14	15	16	17	18	19	20	21	22	23	24	25	26	27	
+11,735	**+60,661**	**+572,640**	**606,808**	**542,685**	**513,523**	**332,035**	*	**292,583**	**504,705**	**459,082**	**409,502**	**279,228**		**246,284**	**47**
..	..	..	8,804	7,553	†	†	†	†	5,821	5,488	†	†	†	†	
—2,358	+11,397	+28,063	96,208	89,567	86,393	84,213	*	79,612	74,231	69,431	66,182	67,202	*	62,764	
+13,772	+49,494	+125,994	283,585	253,424	241,397	247,128	*	212,290	237,762	212,252	197,801	211,491	*	183,063	
+321	—230	+1,183	1,253	1,137	1,935	694	*	681	1,068	808	1,314	535	*	457	
..	..	..	216,958	191,004	183,798	†	†	†	185,823	171,103	144,205	†	†	†	
+53,233	..	..	**253,713**	**214,109**	**203,494**	**187,189**	**162,632**	†	**269,445**	**227,315**	**216,685**	**196,017**	**167,341**	†	**48**
..	..	..	64,010	24,502	29,879	21,088	†	†	65,644	25,028	30,318	21,261	†	†	
..	..	..	188,711	189,015	173,008	165,675	†	†	202,715	201,629	185,777	174,281	†	†	
..	..	..	992	592	607	426	†	†	1,086	658	590	475	†	†	
+383,811	**+276,207**	**+2,122,418**	**3,515,881**	**3,192,335**	**2,886,969**	**2,705,355**	*	**2,347,631**	**2,829,819**	**2,502,549**	**2,221,948**	**2,177,945**	*	**1,875,651**	**49**
..	..	..	46,273	38,459	42,673	†	†	†	36,416	28,523	35,727	†	†	†	
..	..	..	29,674	26,616	†	†	†	†	23,603	21,004	†	†	†	†	
—139,603	+233,803	—453,065	547,351	586,332	564,128	859,465	*	806,125	444,958	460,064	435,957	680,109	*	639,249	
+272,460	—6,256	+1,010,479	1,213,819	1,056,297	950,215	790,167	*	641,058	919,333	766,584	667,317	598,710	*	481,615	
+250,954	+48,660	+1,285,584	1,604,250	1,418,775	1,257,450	1,055,723	*	900,448	1,336,569	1,163,720	1,014,726	899,126	*	754,787	
..	..	..	12,287	13,342	13,598	†	†	†	11,084	12,519	11,596	†	†	†	
..	..	..	62,227	52.514	58.905	†	†	†	57,856	50,135	56,625	†	†	†	
+1,986	..	..	**7,332**	**5,044**	**6,477**	**5,677**	**4,697**	†	**7,692**	**5,410**	**6,346**	**5,482**	**4,476**	†	**50**
..	..	..	3,855	1,221	616	952	†	†	4,032	1,321	690	896	†	†	
..	..	..	3,477	3,823	5,861	4,725	†	†	3,660	4,089	5,656	4,586	†	†	
+7,280	**—25,468**	**+16,997**	**110,841**	**98,645**	**94,281**	**87,268**	**85,638**	**98,870**	**104,855**	**95,317**	**97,492**	**93,243**	**87,592**	**99,829**	**51**
—1,097	..	..	*	*	*	*	*	†	*	*	*	*	*	†	
+8,377	..	..	*	*	*	*	*	†	*	*	*	*	*	†	
..	..	..	*	†	†	..	..	..	*	†	†	..	..	..	
..	..	..	**73,797**	**70,611**	**80,769**	**31,868**	†	†	**79,548**	**76,234**	**81,605**	**32,874**	†	†	**52**
—35	+540	+164	363	538	609	540	554	305	395	458	629	559	580	289	**53**
—124	+319	—103	215	390	399	379	460	305	276	332	392	410	453	289	
+89	..	..	148	148	210	161	94	†	119	126	237	149	127	†	
..	..	..	**6,134**	**12,642**	†	**2,173**	†	†	**6,664**	**12,152**	†	**2,043**	†	†	**54**
..	..	..	5,049	12,642	†	†	†	†	4,937	12,152	†	†	†	†	
..	..	..	1,085	†	†	2,173	†	†	1,727	†	†	2,043	†	†	
—5,021	..	..	**4,677**	†	**3,542**	**282**	*	†	**4,772**	†	**3,896**	**294**	*	†	**55**
..	..	..	1,627	†	110	†	†	†	1,667	†	142	†	†	†	
..	..	..	3,050	†	3,432	†	†	†	3,105	†	3,754	†	†	†	
+23,134	**+21,178**	**+109,917**	**129,391**	**97,394**	**94,165**	**93,333**	*	**69,832**	**109,994**	**83,476**	**77,371**	**80,447**	*	**59,636**	**56**
—2,064	+6,178	—14,579	20,593	18,586	17,559	30,423	*	28,240	16,872	15,020	14,514	25,735	*	23,804	
+7,144	+6,651	+71,240	52,610	34,619	37,109	22,290	*	14,953	46,127	29,575	30,803	19,002	*	12,544	
+28,339	—2,840	+51,899	52,670	40,759	36,582	37,465	*	23,848	44,083	36,070	29,240	32,888	*	21,006	
+19,979	**+23,892**	**—39,969**	**157,598**	**148,732**	**207,160**	**202,519**	*	**182,060**	**148,216**	**139,399**	**196,575**	**187,126**	*	**163,714**	**57**
+21,141	+21,332	—44,384	154,909	145,756	202,720	201,321	*	181,553	145,520	136,368	191,929	185,965	*	163,260	
..	..	..	2,403	2,274	2,903	655	..	..	2,439	2,335	3,201	679	.	..	
..	..	..	**3,525**	**1,967**	**2,166**	**2,124**	†	†	**3,134**	**1,795**	**1,868**	**2,015**	†	†	**58**
..	..	..	2,429	..	..	..	†	†	2,136	..	..	..	†	†	
..	..	..	1,071	1,967	2,166	2,124	†	†	970	1,795	1,868	2,015	†	†	
..	..	..	25	..	..	..	†	†	28	..	..	..	†	†	
..	..	..	**682,121**	**612,116**	**548,031**	**454,980**	†	†	**685,552**	**608,240**	**551,017**	**449,444**	†	†	**59**
—127	**+2,084**	**+1,178**	**1,502**	**1,651**	**1,362**	**1,857**	**1,893**	**841**	**1,305**	**1,512**	**1,536**	**1,729**	**1,820**	**788**	**60**
..	..	..	**4,852**	†	**10,680**	†	†	†	**3,780**	†	**10,434**	†	†	†	**61**
..	..	..	4,698	†	8,349	†	†	†	3,599	†	7,981	†	†	†	
..	..	..	7	†	..	†	†	†	25	†	..	†	†	†	
..	..	..	147	†	2,331	†	†	†	156	†	2,453	†	†	†	
—13,802	**+74,058**	**+88,107**	**45,131**	**41,423**	**45,803**	**29,695**	**37,266**	**118**	**43,205**	**39,779**	**46,038**	**30,790**	**37,021**	**111**	**62**
—14,131	..	..	44,851	41,229	45,400	29,402	37,121	†	42,933	39,601	45,637	30,470	36,882	†	
..	..	..	1	..	141	..	..	..	..	..	141	..	..	..	
+329	+55	+322	279	194	262	293	145	118	272	178	260	320	139	111	

Table XVIII.—Variation in Population

	Tribe or Caste.	Province, State or Agency and Religion.		Reference to Table.	Persons. 1931.	1921.	1911.	1901.	1891.	1881.	Variation (Increase +, 1921-1931.	1911-1921.	1901-1911.
	1	2		3	4	5	6	7	8	9	10	11	12
63	**Kattunayakan** ..	.. Madras	.. (Hindu and Tribal).	..	**1,581**	**4,017**	**2,475**	**2,486**	**1,085**	**1,418**	**—2,436**	**+1,542**	**—11**
64	**Kawar** ..	.. Central Provinces and Berar.	..	**17**	**287,156**	**222,067**	**229,412**	**118,246**	**123,585**	**73,822**	**+65,089**	**—7,345**	**+111,166**
		..	.. (Hindu)	..	275,965	221,674	200,875	†	†	†	+54,291	+20,799	..
		..	.. (Tribal)	..	11,191	393	28,537	†	†	†	+10,798	—28,144	..
45	**Khairwa**	.. United Provinces	.. (Hindu)	**17**	**81**	†	†	**25**	†	**81**		**+55**	
66	**Kharia** ..	.. Bihar and Orissa		**17**	**146,037**	**124,531**	**133,657**	**102,071**	**31,455**	†	**+21,506**	**—9,126**	**+31,586**
		..	.. (Hindu)	..	51,566	45,286	37,764	24,642	1,526	†	+6,280	+7,522	+13,122
		..	.. (Christian).	..	63,725	34,094	28,400	10,367	†	†	+29,631	+5,694	+18,033
		..	.. (Tribal)	..	30,746	45,151	67,493	62,033	26,929	†	—14,405	—22,342	+5,460
67	**Kharwar** (*a*)	.. Bihar and Orissa	.. (Hindu)	**17**	**63,124**	**58,772**	**53,331**	**41,925**	**41,787**	†	**+4,352**	**+5,441**	**+11,406**
68	**Khetauri** ..	.. Bihar and Orissa	.. (Hindu)	**17**	**26,787**(*b*)	**20,946**	**27,024**	**1,431**		†	**+5,841**	**—6,078**	**+25,593**
69	**Khyang** ..	.. Bengai ..		..	1,002	†	791	416	†	†	+211		+375
		..	.. (Hindu)	..	31	†	4	..	†	†	+27		..
		..	.. (Tribal)	..	14	†	328	..	†	†	—314		..
		..	.. (Buddhist).	..	957	†	459	416	†	†	+498		+43
70	**Kokna** ..	.. ....		..	**73,744**	**77,839**	**79,124**	**3,646**	**64,228**	**3,800**	**—4,095**	**—1,285**	**+75,478**
		Bombay	.. (Hindu)	..	65,792	71,077	72,673	†	58,615	†	—5,285	—1,596	+14,058
		Baroda	.. (Hindu)	..	6,449	893	1,906	..	5,590	414	+5,556	—1,013	—3,684
		Do.	.. (Tribal)	..	1,503	5,869	4,545	3,646	23	3,386	—4,366	+1,324	+899
71	**Kol** ..	..		**14,17**	**368,653**	**328,245**	**148,245**	**105,474**	**143,551**	**57,420**	**+40,408**	**+180,000**	**+42,771**
		Central Provinces and Berar.	(Hindu) ..		75,757	92,117	58,779	55,821	74,995	57,420	—16,360	+33,338	+26,777
		Do.	(Tribal	..	15,799	4,476	23,819				+11,323	—19,343	
		United Provinces	(Hindu)	..	76,848	68,941	65,647	49,653	68,556	†	+7,907	+3,294	+15,994
		Central India	.. (Hindu)	..	193,526	157,243	†	†	†	†	+36,283	..	..
		Do.	.. (Tribal)	..	6,723	5,468	†	†	†	†	+1,255	..	..
72	**Kolam** ..	.. Central Provinces and Berar.	..	**17**	**31,763**	**23,721**	**24,976**	**15,799**	**19,318**	**12,163**	**+8,042**	**—1,255**	**+9,172**
		..	.. (Hindu)	..	19,374	..	..	†	†	†	..		..
		..	.. (Tribal)	..	12,389	23,721	24,976	†	†	†	—11,332	—1,255	..
73	**Ko'gha** ..	.. Baroda	..	**17**	**991**	**857**	**692**	**570**	**2**	**198**	**+134**	**+165**	**+122**
		..	.. (Hindu)	..	798	2	25	..	..	179	+796	—23	..
		..	.. (Tribal)	..	193	855	667	570	2	19	+662	+188	+96
74	**Koli and Dagi**	.. ....		**14,17**	**2,347,640**	**2,233,114**	**2,212,202**	**2,253,393**	**2,307,054**	**1,777,697**	**+114,526**	**+20,912**	**—41,191**
		Bombay	.. (Hindu)	..	1,634,921	1,617,044	1,579,133	1,714,107	2,106,848	1,200,911	+17,877	+37,911	—134,974
		Central Provinces and Berar.	(Hindu)	..	(*p*) 43,130	41,049	36,146	28,038	32,628	30,398	+2,081	+4,903	+8,108
		Delhi	.. (Hindu and Muslim).	..	6,934	5,008	†	†	†	†	+1,926	..	
		Punjab	.. (Hindu)	..	181,370	163,750	169,948	153,866	167,578	78,471	+17,620	—6 198	+16,082
		Western India States	(Hindu)	..	481,285	406,263	426,975	357,382	†	467,917	+75,022	—20,712	+69,593
75	**Kondh, etc.**	.. ....		**8,17**	**741,078**	**698,668**	**750,289**	**680,313**	**702,538**	**307,427**	**+42,410**	**—51,621**	**+69,976**
	Jatapu ..	.. Madras	.. (Tribal)	..	78,132	81,844	92,520	75,718	81,152	63,337	—3,712	—10,676	+16,802
	Kond (Kandh, Khond).	Bihar and Orissa	.. (Hindu)	..	167,521	130,037	135,780	288,027	294,800	†	+37,484	—5,743	+14,802
		Do.	.. (Tribal)	..	148,188	157,218	167,049				—9,030	—9,831	
		Madras	.. (Tribal)	..	347,237	329,569	354,940	316,568	326,586	(*q*)244,090	+17,668	—25,371	+38,372
76	**Konda Dora**	.. Madras	.. (Tribal)	**17**	**85,952**	**65,466**	**89,775**	**88,715**	**81,063**	**19,705**	**+20 486**	**—24,309**	**+1,060**
77	**Korwa (Korku)**	.. ....		**14,17**	**237,847**	**185,553**	**200,077**	**152,003**	**141,244**	**110,951**	**+52,294**	**—14,524**	**+48,074**
	Korku ..	.. Central Provinces and Berar.	(Hindu)	..	94,549	46,553	84,781	127,729	130,615	110,951	+47,996	—38,228	+24,634
		Do.	.. (Tribal)	..	(*r*) 82,067	93,891	67,582				—11,824	+26,309	
		Central India	.. (Hindu)	..	12,467	6,998	†	†	†	†	+5,469	..	..
		Do.	.. (Tribal)	..	5,348	7,883	†	†	†	†	—2,535	..	..
	Korwa ..	.. Bihar and Orissa	.. (Hindu)	..	1,462	†	6,795	2,476	9,710	†	—5,333		+4,319
		Do.	.. (Tribal)	..	(*s*) 11,559	†	6,925	8,629			+4,634		—1,704
		Central Provinces and Berar.	(Hindu)	..	18,925	9,318	4,606	247	886	..	+9,607	+4,712	+33,747
		Do.	.. (Tribal)	..	(*t*) 7,651	11,154	29,388				—3,503	—18,234	
		United Provinces of Agra and Oudh.	(Hindu)	..	467	†	†	617	33	†		—150	
		Do.	.. (Jain)	..	37	†	†	..	..	†	..		
		Hyderabad	.. (Tribal)	..	3,315	9,756	†	12,305	†	†	—6,441	—2,549	
78	**Kota** ..	.. **Madras** ..	.. (Tribal)	**17**	**1,121**	**1,204**	**1,163**	**1,267**	**1,201**	**1,067**	**—83**	**+41**	**—104**
79	**Koya** ..	.. ....		**8,17**	**129,456**	**99,113**	**79,422**	**109,776**	**50,755**	**36,188**	**+30,343**	**+19,691**	**—30,354**
		Madras ..	.. (Tribal)	..	95,818	74,084	79,422	63,062	50,755	36,188	+21,734	—5,338	+16,360
		Hyderabad	.. (Tribal)	..	33,638	25,029	†	46,714	†	†	+8,609	—21,685	

(*a*) 1911-1891 figures include Tribal 110 and 2,961 Persons, respectively.
(*b*) Includes 14 Tribals (2 Males and 12 Females.)
(*r*) Includes 16 Christians (6 Males and 10 Females). (*s*) Includes 6 Christians (5 Males and 1 Female). (*t*) Includes 65 Christians (29 Males and 36 Females).
(*p*) Includes 1 Tribal Female.
(*q*) Sex not stated for 37,734 Persons.

of Selected Castes and Tribes—*contd.*

Decrease—). 1891-1901.	1881-1891.	Net variation 1881-1931. (Increase +, Decrease—).	Males. 1931.	1921.	1911.	1901.	1891.	1881.	Females. 1931.	1921.	1911.	1901.	1891.	1881.	
13	14	15	16	17	18	19	20	21	22	23	24	25	26	27	
+1,401	—333	+163	**750**	**1,911**	**1,311**	**1,674**	**542**	**756**	**831**	**2,106**	**1,164**	**812**	**543**	**662**	63
—5,339	+49,763	+213,334	**142,232**	**110,171**	**113,563**	**57,531**	*	**37,021**	**144,924**	**111,896**	**115,849**	**60,715**	*	**36,801**	64
..	..	..	136,538	109,926	99,134	†	†	†	139,427	111,748	101,741	†	†	†	
..	..	..	5,694	245	14,429	†	†	†	5,497	148	14,108	†	†	†	
—56		..	**44**	†	†	**13**	†	**40**	**37**	†	†	**12**	†	**41**	65
+70,616	..	..	**72,376**	**61,614**	**65,792**	**50,357**	**15,740**	†	**73,661**	**62,917**	**67,865**	**51,714**	**15,715**	†	66
+20,116	..	..	25,460	22,172	18,973	12,397	2,235	†	26,106	23,114	18,791	12,245	2,291	†	
..	..	..	31,350	17,050	13,985	5,132	†	†	32,375	17,044	14,415	5,235	†	†	
+35,104	..	..	15,566	22,392	32,834	30,390	13,505	†	15,180	22,759	34,659	31,643	13,424	†	
+138	..	..	**31,701**	**29,747**	**26,100**	**20,917**	**20,394**	†	**31,423**	**29,025**	**27,231**	**21,088**	**21,393**	†	67
..	..	..	**12,655**	**9,399**	**12,968**	**732**	†	†	**14,132**	**11,547**	**14,056**	**699**	†	†	68
..	..	..	518	†	353	206	†	†	484	†	438	210	†	†	69
..	..	..	24	†	4	..		†	7	†	..	..	†	†	
..	..	..	..	†	146	..	†	†	14	†	182	..	†	†	
..	..	..	494	†	203	206	†	†	463	†	256	210	†	†	
—60,582	+60,428	+69,944	**38,403**	**40,685**	**38,766**	**1,848**	**31,281**	**1.934**	**35,341**	**37,154**	**40,358**	**1,798**	**32,947**	**1,816**	70
		..	34,266	37,145	35,551	†	28,391	†	31,526	33,932	37,122	†	30,224	†	
..	+5,176	+6,035	3,364	440	977	..	2,879	209	3,085	453	929	..	2,711	205	
+3,623	—3,363	—1,883	773	3,100	2,238	1,848	11	1,775	730	2,769	2,307	1,798	12	1,611	
—38,077	+86,131	+311,233	**184,111**	**166,392**	**73,148**	**50,883**	*	**28,468**	**184,542**	**161,853**	**75,097**	**54,591**	*	**28,952**	71
—19,174	+17,575	+34,136	37,312	48,249	29,387	26,642	*	28,468	38,445	43,868	29,392	29,179	*	28,952	
			8,130	2,166	11,470				7,669	2,310	12,349				
—18,903	..	..	38,933	36,887	32,291	24,241	34,342	†	37,915	32,054	33,356	25,412	34,214	†	
..	..	..	96,326	76,361	†	†	†	†	97,200	80,882	†	†	†	†	
..	..	..	3,410	2,729	†	†	†	†	3,313	2,739	†	†	†	†	
—3,519	+7,155	+19,600	**15,987**	**11,925**	**12,331**	**7,735**	*	**6,118**	**15,776**	**11,796**	**12,645**	**8,064**	*	**6,045**	72
..	..	..	9,762	..	..	†	†	†	9,612	..	..	†	†	†	
..	..	..	6,225	11,925	12,331	†	†	†	6,164	11,796	12,645	†	†	†	
+568	—196	+793	**472**	**435**	**348**	**277**	**1**	**93**	**519**	**422**	**344**	**293**	**1**	**105**	73
—154	..	+619	373	2	16	..	..	84	425	..	9	..	..	95	
+568	—17	+174	99	433	332	277	1	9	94	422	335	293	1	10	
—53,661	+529,357	+569,948	**1,217,469**	**1,188,629**	**1,091,547**	**1,110,724**	*	**874,103**	**1,130,171**	**1,044,485**	**1,120,655**	**1,142,669**	*	**903,594**	74
—392,741	+905,937	+434,010	849,003	869,269	762,271	831,501	1,011,615	578,512	785,918	747,775	816,862	882,606	1,095,233	622,399	
—4,590	+2,230	+12,732	21,996	21,201	18,129	13,858		15,471	21,134	19,848	18,017	14,180	*	14,927	
..	..	..	4,201	3,040	†	†	†	†	2,733	1,968	†	†	†	†	
—13,712	+89,107	+102,899	94,043	84,415	87,711	79,828	*	40,450	87,327	79,335	82,237	74,038	*	38,021	
—110,535		+13,368	248,226	210,704	223,436	185,537	†	239,670	233,059	195,559	203,539	171,845	†	228,247	
—22,225	+395,111	+433,651	**363,231**	**343,478**	**369,604**	**211,823**	**358,478**	**142,480**	**377,847**	**355,190**	**380,785**	**338,490**	**344,060**	**127,204**	75
—5,434	+17,815	+14,795	39,287	39,135	44,952	37,972	41,300	32,525	38,845	42,709	47,568	37,746	39,852	30,812	
—6,773	..	..	80,706	62,723	66,129	142,488	146,526	†	86,815	67,314	69,651	145,539	148,274	†	
			71,822	76,581	81,919				76,366	80,637	85,130				
—10,018	+82,496	+103,147	171,416	165,039	176,504	161,363	170,652	109,955	175,821	164,530	178,436	155,205	155,934	96,392	
+7,652	+61,358	+66,247	**43,130**	**31,752**	**44.932**	**44,668**	**40.959**	**9,930**	**42,822**	**33,714**	**44,843**	**44,049**	**40,104**	**9,775**	76
+0,759	+30,293	+126,896	**119,112**	**93,306**	**99,521**	**74,618**	*	**56,391**	**118,735**	**92,247**	**100,556**	**77,385**	*	**54,560**	77
—2,886	+19,664	+65,665	47,454	23,276	42,251	62,807	*	56,391	47,095	23,277	42,530	64,922	*	54,560	
			40,773	45,864	33,308				41,294	48,027	34,274				
..	..	..	6,229	3,602	†	†	†	†	6,238	3,396	†	†	†	†	
..	..	..	2,080	4,135	†	†	†	†	2,668	3,748	†	†	†	†	
+1,395	..		781	†	3,309	1,204	4,912	†	681	†	3,486	1,272	4,798	†	
			5,738	†	3,491	4,294			5,821	†	3,434	4,335			
—639	..	..	9,384	4,541	2,276	114	*	..	9,541	4,777	2,330	133	*	..	
			3,679	5,386	14,886				3,972	5,768	14,502				
+584	..	..	222	†	†	238	16	†	245	†	†	379	17	†	
..	..	..	21	†	†	..	..	†	16	†	†	..	..	†	
..	..	..	2,151	6,502	†	5,961	†	†	1,164	3,254	†	6,344	†	†	
+66	+134	+54	**562**	**563**	**547**	**582**	**556**	**500**	**559**	**641**	**616**	**685**	**645**	**567**	78
+59,021	+14,567	+93,268	**65,871**	**50,893**	**39,316**	**56,226**	**26,093**	**18,412**	**63,585**	**48,220**	**40,106**	**53,550**	**24,662**	**17,776**	79
+12,307	+14,567	+59,630	47,654	36,434	39,316	31,857	26,093	18,412	48,164	37,650	40,106	31,205	24,662	17,776	
..	..	..	18,217	14,459	†	24,369	†	†	15,421	10,570	†	22,345	†	†	

*Sex details not available . † Figures not available.

Table XVIII.—Variation in Population

	Tribe or Caste.	Province, State or Agency and Religion.	Reference to Table.	Persons. 1931.	1921.	1911.	1901.	1891.	1881.	Variation (Increase +) 1921-1931.	1911-1921.	1901-1911.
	1	2	3	4	5	6	7	8	9	10	11	12
80	Kudiya	....	14,17	4,046	7,120	4,661	5,627	5,398	5,862	—3,074	+2,459	—966
		Coorg .. .. (Hindu and Tribal).		549	414	541	589	642	†	+135	—127	—48
		Madras .. .. (Hindu and Tribal).		3.497	6,706	4,120	5,038	4,756	5,862	—3,209	+2,586	—918
81	Kudubi	Do. .. .. (Hindu and Tribal).	17	12,011	7,285	10,366	10,350	10,657	4,173	+4,726	—3,081	+16
82	Kuki	....	17	16,592	6,133	5,563	9,170	6,295	†	+10,459	+570	—3,607
		Bengal .. .. (Hindu)	..	13,867	2,376	2,283	6,731	†	†	+11,491	+93	—4,448
		Do. .. .. (Tribal)	..	2,117	3,757	3,102	2,439	†	†	—1,640	+655	+663
		Do. .. .. (Buddhist)	..	..	..	178	..	†	†	..	..	..
		Do. .. .. (Christian)	..	608	..	..	..	†	†	..	..	..
83	Kuki, Chin ..	Burma .. .. (All Religions)	17	348,994	297,603	313,548	222,188	†	†	+51,391	—15,940	+91,355
84	Kurichchan ..	Madras .. (Hindu and Tribal).	17	7,112	7,465	9,722	9,642	9,876	7,887	—353	—2,257	+80
85	Kuruman ..	Madras .. (Hindu and Tribal).	17	10,447	10,988	9,772	10,092	16,857	3,675	—541	+1,216	—230
86	Lalung	Assam	..	43,448	41,033	39,219	§35,513	52,423	47,650	+2,415	+1,814	+3,706
		.. .. (Hindu)	..	31,179	3,354	496	..	798	†	+27,825	+2,858	—302
		.. .. (Tribal)	..	12,026	37,679	38,723	§35,513	51,625	†	—25,653	—1,044	+3,210
		.. .. (Christian)	..	243	..	..	..	..	..	..	..	..
87	Lasi	Baluchistan .. (Muslim	..	31,812	23,212	27,779	†	†	†	+8,600	—4,567	..
88	Lepcha	Bengal	..	25,780	18,690	18,874	19,451	(u) 15,507	†	+7,090	—184	—577
		.. .. (Hindu)	..	214	17	85	247	†	†	+197	—68	—162
		.. .. (Tribal)	..	522	..	3	41	†	†	+519		—38
		.. (Buddhist)	..	23,094	18,673	18,786	17,746	†	†	+4,421	—113	+1,040
		.. (Christain)	..	1,950	..	..	1,417	†	†		+533	
89	LoloMuhso Group ..	Burma .. (All Religions)		(v) 93,214	75,845	67,693	48,705	†	†	+17,369	+8,152	+18,988
90	Lushei	Bengal	17	3,036	†	59	135	1,229	†	+2,977		—76
		.. .. (Hindu)	..	752	†	59	135	†	†	+693		—76
		.. .. (Tribal)	..	25	†	..	..	†	†	..	..	..
		.. .. (Christian)	..	2,259	†	..	..	†	†	..	..	..
91	Mahtam	Punjab	..	64,004	94,325	81,805	82,719	56,982	50,313	—30,321	+12,520	—914
		.. .. (Hindu)	..	14,244	19,162	17,512	48,567	26,482	32,539	—4,918	+1,650	—31,055
		.. .. (Sikh)	..	36,347	63,322	50,056	19,176	17,536	8,047	—26,975	+13,266	+30,880
		.. .. (Muslim)	..	13,413	11,841	14,237	14,976	12,964	9,727	+1,572	—2,396	—739
92	Majhwar ..	Central Provinces and Berar.	17	19,110	10,199	14,210	†	†	†	+8,911	—4,011	..
		.. .. (Hindu)	..	18,940	9,854	9,849	†	†	†	+9,086	+5	..
		.. .. (Tribal)	..	170	345	4,361	†	†	†	+175	—4,016	..
93	Malapantaram ..	Travancore .. (Tribal)	..	(w) 187	57	104	51	..	..	+130	—47	+53
94	Malapulayan ..	Travancore .. (Hindu)	17	254	..	(x) 45	(x) 26	..	..	+209		+19
95	Malankudi .. (Vizhavan.)	Travancore .. (Hindu)	..	166	(x) 181	(x) 201	(x) 192	..	..	—15	—20	+9
96	Malasar-Malaurali	....	17	6,017	5,158	4,565	4,426	5,548	4,040	+859	+593	+139
	Malasar ..	Madras .. .. (Hindus and Tribal).		5,101 (y)	4,928	4,199	4,206	5,548	4,040	+173	+729	—7
	Mala-urali ..	Travancore .. (Tribal)	..	916	230	366	220	..	..	+686	—136	+146
97	Malay Group (z) ..	Burma .. (All Religions)	17	8,323	6,653	6,284	5,308	†	†	+1,670	+369	+976
98	Malayan and Malayarayan.	....	..	6,367	3,452	5,073	2,644	7,903	4,702	+2,915	—1,621	+2,429
	Malayan ..	Cochin .. .. (Hindu)	..	3,185	594	2,461	2,631	3,094	..	+2,591	—1,867	—170
	Malayarayan ..	Travancore .. (Hindu)	..	2,807	..	..	..	4,809	4,702		—2,002	
		Do. .. (Tribal)	..	120	2,858	2,612	13	..	..	—2,738	+246	+2,599
		Do. .. (Christian)	..	255	..	..	..	..	..	..	..	..
99	Mal Paharia ..	Bihar and Orissa ..	17(a)	37,437	39,972	38,553	25,628	17,068	†	—2,535	+1,419	+12,925
		.. .. (Hindu)	..	205	5,257	36,962	24,353	†	†	—5,052	—31,705	+12,609
		.. .. (Tribal)	..	37,170	34,715	1,591	1,275	†	†	+2,455	+33,124	+316
100	Man Group (b) ..	Burma .. (All Religions)	..	951	597	1,158	..	..	..	+354	—561	..
101	Mangrik ..	Jammu and Kashmir (Buddhist)	..	34,107	33,183	35,616	†	†	†	+924	—2,433	..
102	Maria	Central Provinces and Berar. ..	17	181,095	†	†	†	58,667	30,792	+122,428		
		.. .. (Hindu)	..	572	..	..	..	†	†	..	..	..
		.. .. (Tribal)	..	180,523	..	..	..	†	†	..	..	..
103	Marratha ..	..	..	34,593	34,359	35,898	33,808	28,305	28,114	+234	—1,539	+2,090
		Coorg .. ..(Hindu and Tribal)		540	1,710	1,476	2,457	2,384	†	—1,170	+234	—981
		Madras .. ..(Hindu and Tribal)		34,053	32,649	34,422	31.351	25,921	28,114	+1,404	—1,773	+3,071

(u) Sex not stated for 1,001 Persons. (v) Includes Lisaw (19,865), Lahn (27,184), Ako (1,343), Pyin (473), Kwi (3,837), Kaw (40,405) and Nung (107).
(w) Includes Hindus (10,061 Males and 39 Females).
† Figures not available.
* Sex details not available.
§ Sudden fall due to ravages of kala-azar.
(a) Includes 62 Christians (Males 33 and males 29).
(b) Includes Mia (831) and Yao (120).

of Selected Castes and Tribes—*contd.*

Decrease—).		Net variation 1881-1931. (Increase +, Decrease—).	Males.						Females.						
1891-1901.	1881-1891.		1931.	1921.	1911.	1901.	1891.	1881.	1931.	1921.	1911.	1901.	1891.	1881.	
13	14	15	16	17	18	19	20	21	22	23	24	25	26	27	
+229	—464	—1,816	2,045	3,762	2,311	2,826	2,731	2,942	2,001	3,358	2,350	2,301	2,667	2,920	80
—53	..	..	270	205	258	284	321	†	279	209	283	305	321	†	
+282	—1,106	—2,365	1,775	3,557	2,053	2,542	2,410	2,942	1,722	3,149	2,067	2,496	2,346	2,920	
—307	+6,484	+7,838	5,975	3,684	5,183	5,194	5,354	2,118	6,036	3,601	5,183	5,156	5,303	2,055	81
+2,875	..	..	8,898	2,997	2,787	4,623	3,060	†	7,694	3,136	2,776	4,547	3,235	†	82
..	..	..	7,535	1,242	1,142	3,404	†	†	6,332	1,134	1,141	3,327	†	†	
..	..	..	1,032	1,755	1,551	1,219	†	†	1,085	2,002	1,551	1,220	†	†	
..	..	..	..	..	94	..	†	†	..	..	84	..	†	†	
..	..	..	331	..	..	..	†	†	277	..	..	..	†	†	
..	..	..	172,473	148,525	154,586	110,290	†	†	176,521	149,078	158,957	111,898	†	†	83
—234	+1,989	—775	3,585	3,912	4,917	4,940	5,075	4,080	3,527	3,553	4,805	4,702	4,801	3,807	84
-6,765	+13,182	+6,772	5,560	5,763	5,180	5,416	8,994	1,801	4,887	5,225	4,592	4,676	7,863	1,874	85
-16,910	+4,773	—4,202	21,607	20,218	19,222	16,760	26,200	23,992	21,841	20,815	19,997	18,753	26,223	23,658	86
	..	..	*	*	*	..	*	†	*	*	*	..	*	†	
—16,112	..	..	*	*	*	*	*	†	*	*	*	*	*	†	
..	..	..	*	..	..	..		†	*	..	..	..	..	†	
..	..	..	16,635	12,365	14,857	†	†	†	15,177	10,847	12,922	†	†	†	87
+3,944	..	..	12,999	9,422	9,439	9,723	7,118	†	12,781	9,268	9,435	9,728	7,388	†	88
..	..	..	206	13	43	124	†	†	8	4	42	123	†	†	
..	..	..	274	..	2	22	†	†	248	..	1	19	†	†	
..	..	..	11,590	9,409	9,394	8,920	†	†	11,504	9,264	9,392	8,826	†	†	
..	..	..	929	..	..	657	†	†	1,021	..	..	760	†	†	
..	..	..	48,056	39,494	35,311	25,321	†	†	45,158	36,351	32,382	23,384	†	†	89
—1,094	..	..	1,465	†	24	62	587	†	1,571	†	35	73	642	†	90
..	..	..	355	†	24	62	†	†	397	†	35	73	†	†	
..	..	..	11	†			†	†	14	†	..	..	†	†	
..	..	..	1,099	†	..	..	†	†	1,160	†	..	..	†	†	
+25,737	+6,669	+13,691	34,167	50,032	43,602	43,921	*	26,989	29,837	44,293	38,203	38,798	*	23,324	91
+22,085	—6,057	—18,295	7,911	10,202	9,372	25,265	*	17,429	6,333	8,960	8,140	23,302	*	15,110	
+1,640	+9,489	+28,300	19,210	33,432	26,384	10,509	*	4,461	17,137	29,890	23,672	8,667	*	3,586	
+2,012	+3,237	+3,686	7,046	6,398	7,846	8,147	*	5,099	6,367	5,443	6,391	6,829	*	4,628	
..	..	..	9,805	5,524	7,196	†	†	†	9,305	4,675	7,014	†	†	†	92
..	..	..	9,720	5,332	4,969	†	†	†	9,220	4,522	4,880	†	†	†	
..	..	..	85	192	2,227	†	†	†	85	153	2,134	†	†	†	
..	..	..	110	34	59	31	..	..	77	23	45	20	..	..	93
..	..	..	125	..	17	14	..	..	129	..	28	12	..	..	94
..	..	..	81	72	98	97	..	..	85	109	103	95	..	..	95
—1,122	+1,508	+1,977	2,859	2,467	2 419	2,237	2,814	2,007	3,158	2,691	2,146	2,189	2,734	2,033	96
—1,342	+1,508	+1,061	2,405	2,338	2,250	2,131	2,814	2,007	2,696	2,590	1,949	2,075	2,734	2,033	
..	..	..	454	129	169	106	..	..	46	101	197	114	..	..	
..	..	..	4,219	3.144	3,336	3,065	†	†	4,104	3,509	2,948	2,243	†	†	97
—5,259	+3,201	+1,665	3,251	1,927	2,574	1,338	4,041	2,400	3,116	1,525	2,499	1,306	3,862	1,302	98
—463	..	..	1,645	441	1,280	1,330	1,543	..	1,540	153	1,181	1,301	1,551	..	
	+107	—1,895	1,427	..			2,498	2,400	1,380			..	2,311	2,302	
..	..	..	56	1,486	1,294	8	..	..	64	1,372	1,318	5	..	..	
..	..	..	123	..	..	..	..	..	132	..	..	..	..	..	
+8,560	..	..	18,729	20,214	19,068	12,266	8,349	†	18,708	19,758	19,485	13,362	8,719	*	99
..	..	..	112	2,921	18,303	11,610	†	†	93	2,336	18,659	12,743	†	†	
..	..	..	18,584	17,293	765	656	†	†	18,586	17,422	826	619	†	†	100
..	..	..	502	338	693	..	..	..	449	259	465	..	..	..	101
..	..	..	16,943	16,193	17,691	†	†	†	17,164	16,990	17,925	†	†	†	
..	+27,875	+150,303	90,668	†	†	†	*	15,543	90,427	†	†	†	*	15,249	102
..	..	..	325	..	..	..	†	†	247	..	..	..	†	†	
..	..	..	90,343	..	..	..	†	†	90,180	..	..	..	†	†	
+5,503	+191	+6,479	17,327	17,256	18,205	16,695	14,030	17,041	17,266	17,103	17,693	17,113	14,275	11,073	103
+73	..	..	360	1,101	1,438	1,431	1,388	†	180	609	38	1,026	996	†	
+5,430	—2,193	+5,939	16,967	16,155	16,767	15,264	12,642	17,041	17,086	16,494	17,655	16,087	13,279	11,073	

(x) All Tribal.
(y) Includes 846 Hindus (420 Males and 426 Females).
(z) Including Malaya (6,393 and Salon 1,930).

Table XVIII.—Variation in Population

Tribe or Caste. 1	Province, State or Agency and Religion. 2	Reference to Table. 3	Persons. 1931. 4	1921. 5	1911. 6	1901. 7	1891. 8	1881. 9	Variation (Increase + 1921-1931. 10	1911-1921. 11	1901-1911. 12
104 Mavillan	.. Madras (Hindu and Tribal)	17	1,341	1,737	2,517	2,148	2,590	2,915	—396	—780	+369
105 Mavchi	.. Baroda	17	919	479	989	879	1,889	450	+440	—510	+110
	.. .. (Hindu)	..	905	436	980	..	1,889	..	+469	—544	—909
	.. .. (Tribal)	..	14	43	9	879	..	450	—29	+34	—870
106 Mech	.. Bengal ..	17	(d) 9,984	10,777	20,730	24,418	26,618	*	—793	—9,953	—3,688
	.. .. (Hindu)	..	4,875	5,068	7,572	20,860	*	*	—193	—2,504	—13,288
	.. .. (Tribal)	..	2,561	5,709	12,878	3,558	*	*	—3,148	—7,169	+9,320
	.. .. (Christian)	..	2,541	..	280	..	*	*	+2,261		..
107 Meo (Mina)	....	14,17	809,903	700,037	731,189	671,767	656,986	116,992	+109,866	—31,152	+59,422
Meo ..	Delhi (Hindu and Muslim)		5,259	3,989	*	*	*	*	+1,270	..	..
	Punjab (Hindu and Muslim)		124,821	111,564	120,752	133,300	115,916	112,568	+13,257	—9,188	—12,548
Mina ..	Ajmer-Merwara (Hindu and Muslim).	..	5,252	3,939	4,223	64	4,648	4,424	+1,313	—284	+4,159
	Gwalior .. .. (Hindu)	..	67,202	60,128	46,943	..	*	*	+7,074	+13,185	..
	Do. .. .. (Tribal)	..	..	5,176	582	61,274	*	*	—5,176	+4,594	—60,692
	Rajputana .. .. (Hindu)	..	587,029	483,674	512,506	461,093	536,422	*	+103,355	—28,832	+51,413
	Do. .. .. (Muslim)	..	4	90	139	1	..	*	—86	—49	+138
	Do. .. .. (Tribal)	..	20,336	31,477	46,044	16,035	..	*	—11,141	—14,567	+30,009
108 Merat	....	14,17	28,733	19,430	20,008	9,112	14,723	14,114	+9,303	—578	+10,896
	Ajmer-Merwara .. (Muslim)	..	25,649	17,745	17,698	9,082	14,170	14,114	+7,904	+47	+8,616
	Rajputana .. (Muslim)	..	3,084	1,685	2,310	30	553	..	+1,399	—625	+2,280
109 Mikir	.. Assam ..	..	129,797	111,629	106,259	87,043‡	94,829	77,765	+18,168	+5,370	+19,216
	.. .. (Hindu)	..	31,283	10,977	736	..	504	*	+20,306	+10,241	+232
	.. .. (Tribal)	..	94,855	100,652	104,341	87,043	94,325	*	—5,797	—3,689	+17,298
	.. .. (Christian)	..	3,659	*	1,182	..	..	*	+2,477		..
110 Miri	Assam	..	85,038	68,725	57,792	46,720	37,430	25,636	+16,313	+10,933	+11,072
	.. .. (Hindu)	..	79,848	45,424	13,460	24,022	26,574	*	+34,424	+31,964	—10,562
	.. .. (Tribal)	..	5,152	23,301	44,332	22,698	10,856	*	—18,149	—21,031	+21,634
	.. .. (Christian)	..	38	..	..	..	..	*	..	..	..
111 Mon Group (e)	.. Burma (All Religions)	8,14	336,728	323,509	320,629	321,941	*	*	+13,219	+2,880	—1,312
112 Mro Group §	.. Burma (All Religions)	17	13,766	14,771	2,708	12,622	*	*	—1,005	+12,063	—9,914
113 Mro	Bengal ..	17	7,404	8,697	12,391	10,551	*	*	—1,293	—3,694	+1,840
	.. .. (Hindu)	..	68	..	1,109	9,800	*	*	—1,041		—8,691
	.. .. (Tribal)	..	8	8,697	11,238	..	*	*	—8,689	—2,541	..
	.. .. (Buddhist)	..	7,328	..	44	75	*	*	+7,284		—707
114 Muria	.. Central Provinces and Berar.	17	127,050	*	*	*	54,071	34	+72,979		
	.. (Hindu)	..	2,052	..	..	..	*	*	..	..	..
	.. (Tribal)	..	124,998	..	..	..	*	*	..	..	..
115 Munda	.. ..	14,17	658,450	559,662	558,200	416,905	333,464	*	+98,788	+1,462	+141,295
	Bengal .. .. (Hindu)	..	63,107	40,574	40,785	39,946			+22,533	—211	+839
	Do. .. .. (Tribal)	..	42,321	58,769	26,467	11,519			—16,448	+32,302	+14,948
	Do. .. .. (Buddhist)	..	1	..	..	..	11,154	*	..	..	..
	Do. .. .. (Christian)	..	3,257	..	..	68			+3,189		
	Bihar and Orissa .. (Hindu)	..	163,776	126,115	88,840	36,222	4,864	*	+37,661	+37,275	+52,618
	Do. .. .. (Christian)	..	133,506	93,814	80,508	56,447	*	*	+39,692	+13,306	+24,061
	Do. .. .. (Tribal)	..	252,482	240,390	321,600	272,703	317,446	*	+12,092	—81,210	+48,897
116 Murmi ..	.. Bengal	..	42,241	39,716	38,336	32,930	24,713‖	*	+2,525	+1,380	+5,406
	.. .. (Hindu)	..	706	679	1,559	2,277	*	*	+27	—880	—718
	.. .. (Tribal)	..	41	..	258	189	*	*	—217		+69
	.. (Buddhist)	..	41,491	39,037	36,519	30,331	*	*	+2,454	+2,518	+6,188
	(Christian)	..	3	..	..	133	*	*	—130		
117 Muthuvan	.. Travancore	..	1,301	257	379	808	1,077	..	+1,044	—122	—429
	.. (Hindu)	..	1,238	..	..	..	1,077	..	+161		
	.. (Tribal)	..	63	257	379	808	..	..	—194	—122	—429

(d) Includes 7 Buddhists (2 Males and 5 Females)

(e) All Talaings.

* Figures not available.

† Sex details not available.

‡ Sudden fall due to Kala-azar.

§ Mr. only.

‖ Six not stated for 1,288 Persons.

of Selected Castes and Tribes—*contd.*

Decrease—).		Net variation 1881-1931. (Increase +, Decrease—).	Males.						Females.						
1891-1901.	1881-1891.		1931.	1921.	1911.	1901.	1891.	1881.	1931	1921.	1911.	1901.	1891.	1881.	
13	14	15	16	17	18	19	20	21	22	23	24	25	26	27	
—442	—325	—1,574	799	930	1,363	1,143	1,399	1,521	542	807	1,154	1,005	1,191	1,394	10
—1,010	+1,439	+469	510	250	537	464	962	204	409	229	452	415	927	246	10
..		..	499	222	530	..	962	..	406	214	450	..	927	..	
+429		—436	11	28	7	464	..	204	3	15	2	415	..	246	
—2,200	..	..	5,423	5,828	10,860	13,014	13,834	*	4,561	4,949	9,870	11,404	12,784	*	10
..	..	..	2,746	2,720	3,867	11,082	*	*	2,129	2,348	3,705	9,778	*	*	
..	..	..	1,365	3,108	6,852	1,932	*	*	1,196	2,601	6,026	1,626	*	*	
..	..	..	1,310	..	141	..	*	*	1,231	..	139	..	*	*	
+14,781	+539,994	+692,911	428,796	374,460	387,351	351,491	†	61,697	381,107	325,577	343,838	320,276	†	55,295	10
..	..	..	3,008	2,247	*	*	*	*	2,251	1,742	*	*	*	*	
+17,384	+3,348	+12,253	67,146	60,515	64,119	69,218	†	58,959	57,675	51,049	56,633	64,082	†	53,609	
—4,584	+224	+828	3,017	2,258	2,442	14	2,731	2,738	2,235	1,681	1,781	50	1,917	1,686	
..	..	..	34,414	33,040	24,255	..	*	*	32,788	27,088	22,688	..	*	*	
..	..	..	..	2,664	330	30,613	*	*	..	2,512	252	30,661	*	*	
—75,329	..	..	310,782	257,413	272,411	243,102	286,593	*	276,247	226,261	240,095	217,991	249,829	*	
+1	..	..	3	32	64	1	..	*	1	58	75	..	..	*	
+16,035	..	..	10,426	16,291	23,730	8,543	..	*	9,910	15,186	22,314	7,492	..	*	
—5,611	+609	+14,619	15,294	10,411	10,967	4,876	8,649	8,532	13,439	9,019	9,041	4,236	6,074	5,582	10
—5,088	+56	+11,535	13,623	9,491	9,671	4,860	8,355	8,532	12,026	8,254	8,027	4,222	5,815	5,582	
—523	..	..	1,671	920	1,296	16	294	..	1,413	765	1,014	14	259	..	
—7,786	+17,064	+52,032	36,045	57,383	54,257	44,100	49,161	39,753	63,752	54,246	52,002	42,943	45,068	38,012	10
	..	..	†	†	†	..	†	*	†	†	†	..	†	*	
—7,282	..	..	†	†	†	†	†	*	†	†	†	..	†	*	
..	..	..	†	*	†	..	..	*	†	*	†	..	..	*	
+9,290	+11,794	+59,402	43,669	35,154	29,335	23,773	19,600	13,303	41,369	33,571	28,457	22,947	17,830	12,333	11
—2,552	..	..	†	†	†	†	†	*	†	†	†	†	†	*	
+11,842	..	..	†	†	†	†	†	*	†	†	†	†	†	*	
..	..	..	†	..	..	..	..	..	†	..	..	..	..	..	
..	..	..	170,142	163,830	159,235	162,529	*	*	166,586	159,679	161,394	159,412	*	*	1
..	..	..	7,248	7,520	1,342	5,931	*	*	6,518	7,251	1,366	6,691	*	*	1
..	..	..	3,934	4,713	6,339	5,394	*	*	3,470	3,984	6,052	5,157	*	*	1
..	..	..	43	..	582	5,086	*	*	25	..	527	4,714	*	*	
..	..	..	..	4,713	5,733	..	*	*	8	3,984	5,505	..	*	*	
..	..	..	3,891	..	24	308	*	*	3,437	..	20	443	*	*	
..	+54,037	..	63,482	*	*	*	†	18	63,568	*	*	*	†	16	1
	..	..	812	..	..	..	*	..	1,240	..	..	..	*	*	
..	..	..	62,670	..	..	..	*		62,328	..	..	..	*	*	
+83,441	..	..	326,875	282,515	276,202	207,661	164,733	*	331,575	277,147	281,998	209,244	168,731	*	1
			33,276	20,741	21,413	22,241	6,099	*	29,831	19,833	19,372	17,705	5,055	*	
			21,661	31,352	13,804	6,177			20,660	27,417	12,663	5,342			
+40,379	..	..	1	..	..	..			..	..	..	..			
	..	..	1,787	..	..	49			1,470	..	..	19			
..	..	..	80,212	66,078	42,937	18,191	2,422	*	83,564	60,037	45,903	18,031	2,442	*	
+31,358	..	..	66,435	46,679	39,898	28,001	*	*	67,071	47,135	40,610	28,446	*	*	
.. —44,743	..	..	123,503	117,665	158,150	133,002	156,212	*	128,979	122,725	163,450	139,701	161,234	*	
+8,217	..	..	21,434	20,189	19,556	16,460	11,926	*	20,807	19,527	18,780	16,470	11,499	*	
..	..	..	182	450	949	1,217	*	*	524	229	610	1,060	*	*	
..	..	..	25	..	132	97	*	*	16	..	126	92	*	*	
..	..	..	21,225	19,739	18,475	15,063	*	*	20,266	19,298	18,044	15,268	*	*	
..	..	..	2	..	..	83	*	*	1	..	..	50	*	*	
—269	..	..	649	122	195	409	545	..	652	135	184	399	532	..	
	..	..	623	..	..	..	545	..	615	..	..	..	532	..	
..	..	..	26	122	105	409	..	..	37	135	184	399	..	..	

Table XVIII.—Variation in Population

Tribe or Caste.	Province, State or Agency and Religion.	Reference to Table.	Persons. 1931.	1921.	1911.	1901.	1891.	1881.	Variation (Increase +, 1921-1931.	1911-1921.	1901-1911.
1	2	3	4	5	6	7	8	9	10	11	12
18 Naga ..	....	17	**139,965**	**132,668**	**128,457**	**77,052**	**59,055**	*	**+7,297**	**+4,211**	**+51,405**
Angami (Including Kezhama).	Assam ..	..	49,239	51,730	44,488‡	28,963	28,499	*	—2,491	+7,242	+15,525
	Do. (Tribal) ..	..	48,655	51,730	44,488	28,963	28,499	*	—3,075	+7,242	+15,525
	Do. (Christian) ..	..	584	*	..	..	..	*	..	..	..
Sema ..	.. ..	..	37,428	33,439	32,772‡	4,668	*	*	+3,989	+667	+28,104
	Do. (Tribal)	..	29,068	33,439	32,772	4,668	*	*	—4,371	+667	+28,104
	Do. (Christian) ..	..	8,360	*	*	..	*	*	..	..	..
Lhota ..	..	..	18,238	18,399	19,511	19,259	22,691	*	—161	—1,112	+252
	Do. (Tribal) ..	..	17,329	18,399	19,511	19,259	22,691	*	—1,070	—1,112	+252
	Do. (Christian) ..	..	909	*	..	..	*	*	..	..	..
Rengma ..	..	..	6,329	5,166	4,370	4,170	7,865	*	+1,163	+796	+200
	Do. (Tribal) ..	..	6,096	5,166	4,370	4,170	*	*	+930	+796	+200
	Do. (Christian) ..	..	233	*	..	..	*	*	..	..	..
Tangkhul	..	..	28,731	23,934‖	27,316	19,992	*	*	+4,797	—3,382	+7,324
	Do. (Tribal) ..	..	25,631	22,828	27,316	*	*	*	+2,803	—4,488	..
	Do. (Christian) ..	..	3,100	1,106¶	*	*	*	*	+1,994	..	..
19 Nagarchi ..	.. Central Provinces and Berar ..	17	**6,367**	..	**6,239**	..	**6,326**	..		**+128**	**—87**
	(Hindu) ..	..	4,745	..	6,239	..	*	..		—1,494	..
	(Tribal) ..	..	1,622	..	..	..	*	..	..	..	..
20 Nagesia ..	.. Central Provinces and Berar ..	17	(*g*) **48,686**	**14,792**	**44,165**	*	*	*	**+33,894**	**—29,373**	..
	(Hindu) ..	..	48,144	14,745	39,886	*	*	*	+33,399	—25,141	..
	(Tribal) ..	..	518	47	4,279	*	*	*	+471	—4,232	..
21 Nayakda ..	.. ..	17	**113,808**	**93,641**	**58,288**	**61,531**	**7?,479**	**33,533**	**+20,167**	**+35,353**	**—3,243**
	Bombay (Hindu)		101,954	84,969	48,258	54,561	65,863	26,289	+16,985	+36,711	—6,303
	Baroda (Hindu) ..	..	11,662	1,269	3,634	..	6,454	6,728	+10,393	—2,365	—2,820
	Do. (Tribal) ..	..	140	7,403	6,396	6,970	2,162	516	—7,263	+1,007	—574
	Western India States ..	..	52	*	*	*	*	*	..	..	..
22 Nayadi ..	.. ..	14,17	**296**	**301**	**292**	**240**	**123**	..	**—5**	**+9**	**+52**
	Cochin (Hindu) ..	..	152	119	220	215	123	..	+33	—101	+5
	Travancore (Hindu) ..	..	144	..	31	7	..	..		+113	+24
	Do. (Tribal) ..	..	..	182	41	18	..	..	..	+141	+23
123 Nicobarese	.. Andamans and Nicobars (Tribal and Christian).	14,17	**9,789**	**8,623**	**8,366**	**6,310**	*	*	**+1,166**	**+257**	**+2,056**
124 Oraon ..	.. ..	8,14,17	**1,021,355**	**842,906**	**835 994**	**557,843**	**444,716**	*	**+178,449**	**+6,912**	**+278,151**
	Bengal (Hindu) ..	..	136,427	64,677	84,457	110,550			+71,750	—19,780	—26,093
	Do. (Tribal) ..	..	83,792	137,765	80,880	7,675			—53,973	+56,885	+73,205
	Do. (Buddhist) ..	..	79	..	..	..	34,342		..	..	..
	Do. (Christian) ..	..	7,863	..	424	182				+7,439	+242
	Bihar and Orissa (Hindu) ..	..	222,152	96,148	52,482	42,218			+126,004	+43,666	+10,264
	Do. (Christian) ..	..	145,129	119,431	112,738	61,477	404,618	*	+25,698	+6,693	+51,261
	Do. (Tribal) ..	..	269,830	350,804	422,191	335,741			—80,974	—71,387	+86,450
	Central Provinces Berar (Hindu)	..	55,310	17,973	4,780	*			+37,337	+13,193	
	Do. (Tribal) ..	..	53,256	56,108	78 042	*	5,756	*	—2,852	—21,934	+ 77,066
	Do. (Christian)	..	47,517	*	*	*			..	..	
25 Pakhiwara	.. Punjab (Muslim) ..	..	**3,100**	**2,801**	**3,711**	**3,595**	**3,674**	**3,741**	**+299**	**—910**	**+116**
26 Palaung-Wa Group (*h*)	Burma (All Religions)	17	**176,382**	**156,703**	**175,940**	**86,846**	*	*	**+19,679**	**—19,237**	**+89,094**
27 Paliyan ..	.. Travancore (All Religions)	17	(*i*) **483**	(*j*) **289**	*	*	*	*	**+194**	..	..
28 Pano ..	.. Madras (Tribal) ..	..	**70,527**	**80,824**	**71,323**	**61,200**	**46,058**	**43,759** (*k*)	**—10,297**	**+9,501**	**+10,123**
29 Pardhan ..	.. Central Provinces & Berar	17	**119,555****	**95,818**	**118,630**	**14,382**	**83,654**	**60,279**	**+23,737**	**—22,812**	**+104,248**
	(Hindu) ..		63,743	20,007	25,170	*	*	*	+43,730	—5,163	..
	(Tribal)	..	55,811	75,811	93,460	*	*	*	—20,000	—17,649	..
30 Patelia—Patlia	.. ..	17	**19,952**	**31,271**	**13,859**	**10,199**	**15,235**	**10,042**	**—11,319**	**+17,412**	**+3,660**
Patelia ..	.. Bombay (Hindu)	..	544††	16,534	13,859	10,1?9	15,2351	0,042	—15,990	+2,675	+3,660
Patlia ..	.. Central India (Hindu)	..	8,268	14,737	*	*	*	*	—6,469	..	..
	Do. (Tribal)	..	11,140	..	*	*	*	*	..	..	..
31 Parja—Poroja	.. ..	17	**140,702**	**87,019**	**92,737**	**91,886**	**95,511**	*	**+53,683**	**—5,718**	**+851**
Parja‡‡ ..	Central Provinces and Berar (Hindu)		43		*	*		*			+4,111
	Do. (Tribal)		17,559	*	*	*	13,491				
Poroja ..	.. Madras (Tribal) ..	..	123,100	87,019	92,737	91,886	82,020	*	+36,081	—5,718	+851
32 Rawat ..	.. ..	17	**110,743**	**96,567**	**99,078**	**66,402**	**79,637**	**60,825**	**+14,176**	**—2,511**	**+32,676**
	Ajmer-Merwara (Hindu) ..	..	82,939	69,845	71,661	53,858	70,703	60,825	+13,094	—1,816	+17,803
	Rajputana (Hindu) ..	..	27,804	26,722	27,417	12,544	8,934	*	+1,082	—695	+14.873
33 Sak (Lui) Group(§§)	Burma (All Religious)	17	**51,820**	**49,726**	**12,756**	**39,935**	*	*	**+2,094**	**+36,970**	**—27,179**
34 Sansi	......	14,17	**29,375**	**17,666**	**24,439**	**27,595**	**26,506**	**19,929**	**+11,709**	**—6,773**	**—3,156**
Sansi ..	.. Delhi .. (Hindu) ..	..	227	264	*	*	*	*	—37	..	..
	Punjab .. (Hindu) ..	..	28,262	17,402	24,439	26,000	22,218	19,929	+10,860	—7,037	—1,561
Sansia ..	.. United Provinces (Hindu) ..	..	886	*	*	1,595	4,288	*		—709	

* Figures not available.
† Sex details not available.
‡ Sudden rise due to incorporation of new territory in the Naga Hills District.
§ Sex details not available.
‖ Sex details not available for 1,106 Persons.
¶ Deduced from Language Figure.
** Includes 1 Christian Female.
†† Incud:s 7 Persons (4 Males and 3 Females) enumerated in the Western India States Agency.
‡‡ Separate figures for previous censuses are not available as they were amalgamated with Gonds.
§§ Includes Kadu (36,400), Ganan (7,182), Sak (693), Daingnet (6,355) and Taman (1,190).

of Selected Castes and Tribes—*contd.*

Decrease—).		Net variation 1881-1931.	Males.						Females.						
1891-1901.	1881-1891.	(Increase +, Decrease—).	1931.	1921	1911.	1901.	1891.	1881.	1931.	1921.	1911.	1901.	1891.	1881.	
13	14	15	16	17	18	19	20	21	22	23	24	25	26	27	
+17,997	..	..	**69,151**	**64,941**	**63,244**	**37,818**	**29,854**	*	**70,814**	**66,621**	**65,213**	**59,234**	**29,201**	*	**118**
+464	..	..	25,013	26,498	22,588	14,729	14,568	*	24,226	25,232	21,900	14,234	13,931	*	
+464	..	..	§	§	§	§	§	*	§	§	§	§	§	*	
..	..	..	§	*	..	..	..	*	§	*	..	..	..	*	
..	..	..	18,630	16,474	16,325	2,457	*	*	18,798	16,965	16,447	2,211	*	*	
..	..	..	§	§	§	§	*	*	§	§	§	§	*	*	
..	..	..	§	*	*	..	*	*	§	*	*	..	*	*	
−3,432	..	..	8,957	8,824	9,448	9,026	11,443	*	9,281	9,575	10,063	10,233	11,248	*	
−3,432	..	..	§	§	§	§	§	*	§	§	§	§	§	*	
..	..	..	§	*	..	..	..	*	§	*	..	..	..	*	
−3,695	..	..	3,151	2,567	2,016	2,116	3,843	*	3,178	2,599	2,354	2,054	4,022	*	
..	..	..	§	§	§	§	*	*	§	§	§	§	*	*	
..	..	..	§	*	..	..	*	*	§	*	..	..	*	*	
..	..	..	13,400	10,578	12,867	9,490	*	*	15,331	12,250	14,449	10,502	*	*	
..	..	..	§	§	§	*	*	*	§	§	§	*	*	*	
..	..	..	§	§	*	*	*	*	§	§	*	*	*	*	
..	..	..	**3,239**	..	**2,991**	..	§	..	**3,128**	..	**3,248**	..	§	..	**119**
..	..	..	2,451	..	2,991	..	*	..	2,294	..	3,248	..	*	..	
..	..	..	788	..	..	..	*	..	834	..	..	..	*	..	
..	..	..	**24,196**	**7,194**	**22,207**	*	*	*	**24,490**	**7,598**	**21,958**	*	*	*	**120**
..	..	..	23,923	7,173	20,105	*	*	*	24,221	7,572	19,781	*	*	*	
..	..	..	258	21	2,102	*	*	*	260	26	2,177	*	*	*	
−12,948	**+40,946**	**+80,275**	**57,064**	**46,835**	**29,459**	**30,965**	**37,230**	**17,200**	**56,744**	**46,806**	**28,829**	**30,566**	**37,249**	**16,333**	**121**
−11,302	+39,574	+75,665	50,976	42,434	24,406	27,478	32,866	13,526	50,978	42,535	23,852	27,083	32,997	12,763	
	−274	+4,934	5,985	622	1,841	..	3,245	3,383	5,677	647	1,793	..	3,209	3,345	
+4,808	+1,646	−376	68	3,779	3,212	3,487	1,119	291	72	3,624	3,184	3,483	1,043	225	
..	..	..	35	*	*	*	*	*	17	*	*	*	*		
+117	..	..	**140**	**156**	**164**	**130**	**61**	..	**156**	**145**	**128**	**110**	**62**	..	**122**
+92	..	..	76	47	124	116	61	..	76	72	96	99	62	..	
..	..	..	64	..	18	3	..	..	80	..	13	4	..	..	
..	..	..	..	109	22	11	..	..	..	73	19	7	..	..	
..	..	..	**5,079**	**4,616**	**4,399**	**3,336**	*	*	**4,710**	**4,007**	**3,967**	**2,974**	*	*	**123**
+113 127	..	..	**513,537**	**419,791**	**414,031**	**276,635**	§	*	**507,818**	**423,115**	**421,963**	**281,208**	§	*	**124**
			73,287	34,529	45,243	63,153			63,140	30,148	39,214	47,397			
			44,612	70,061	43,820	3,922			39,180	67,704	37,060	3,753			
+84,065	..	..	79	..	..	..	19,340	*	..	..	..	..	15,002	*	
			4,116	..	314	123			3,747	..	110	59			
			108,358	48,660	26,309	22,147			113,794	47,488	26,173	20,071			
+34,818	..	..	72,123	59,204	55,594	30,280	193,328	*	73,006	60,227	57,144	31,197	211,290	*	
			131,947	169,476	200,964	157,010			137,883	181,328	221,227	178,731			
			27,887	9,112	2,397	*			27,423	8,861	2,383	*			
..	..	..	27,081	28,749	39,390	*	§	*	26,175	27,359	38,652	*	§	*	
			24,047	*	*	*			23,470	*	*	*			
−79	**−67**	**−641**	**1,748**	**1,529**	**2,111**	**1,872**	§	**2,009**	**1,352**	**1,272**	**1,600**	**1,723**	§	**1,732**	**125**
..	..	..	**88,611**	**78,674**	**88,978**	**44,531**	*	*	**87,771**	**78,029**	**83,962**	**42,315**	*	*	**126**
..	..	..	**266**	**155**	*	*	*	*	**217**	**134**	*	*	*	*	**127**
+15,142	**+2,299**	**+26,768**	**35,117**	**38,578**	**35,651**	**30,585**	**23,152**	**17,509**	**35,410**	**42,246**	**35,672**	**30,615**	**22,906**	**16,931**	**128**
−69,272	**+23,375**	**+59,276**	**58,310**	**48,222**	**57,711**	**7,147**	§	**29,904**	**61,245**	**47,596**	**60,919**	**7,235**	§	**30,375**	**129**
..	..	..	31,490	9,768	12,203	*	*	*	32,253	10,239	12,967	*	*	*	
..	..	..	26,820	38,454	45,508	*	*	*	28,991	37,357	47,952	*	*	*	
−5,036	**+5,193**	**+9,910**	**10,140**	**16,230**	**6,821**	**5,113**	**7,912**	**5,044**	**9,812**	**15,041**	**7,038**	**5,086**	**7,323**	**4,998**	**130**
−5,036	+5,193	−9,498	48	8,611	6,821	5,113	7,912	5,044	496	7,923	7,038	5,086	7,323	4,998	
..	..	..	4,280	7,619	*	*	*	*	3,988	7,118	*	*	*	*	
..	..	..	5,812	..	*	*	*	*	5,328	..	*	*	*	*	
−3,625	..	..	**70,089**	**44,464**	**47,792**	**47,029**	§	*	**70,613**	**42,555**	**44,945**	**44,857**	§	*	**131**
	..	..	23	*	*	*	§	*	20	*	*	*	§	*	
..	..	..	8,820	*	*	*			8,739	*	*	*			
+9,866	..	..	61,246	44,464	47,792	47,029	41,815	*	61,854	42,555	44,945	44,857	40,205	*	
−13,235	**+18,812**	**+49,918**	**57,714**	**51,636**	**52,585**	**36,121**	**42,203**	**33,309**	**53,029**	**44,931**	**46,493**	**30,281**	**37,434**	**27,516**	**132**
−16,845	+9,878	+22,114	43,362	37,078	37,877	29,681	37,469	33,309	39,577	32,767	33,784	24,177	33,234	27,516	
+3,610	..	..	14,352	14,558	14,708	6,440	4,734	*	13,452	12,164	12,709	6,104	4,200	*	
		..	**25,019**	**24,497**	**6,414**	**19,171**	*	*	**26,801**	**25,229**	**6,342**	**20,764**	*	*	**133**
+1,089	**+6,577**	**+9,446**	**16,088**	**10,276**	**13,451**	**14,925**	§	**10,850**	**13,287**	**7,390**	**10,988**	**12,670**	§	**9,079**	**134**
..	..	..	117	154	*	*	*	*	110	110	*	*	*	*	
+3,782	+2,289	+8,333	15,500	10,122	13,451	13,963	§	10,850	12,762	7,280	10,988	12,037	§	9,079	
−2,693	..	..	**471**	*	*	**962**	**2,333**	*	**415**	*	*	**633**	**1,955**	*	

(*g*) Includes 24 Christians (15 Males and 9 Females).
(*h*) Includes Wa (10,465), Danaw (1,157) Khamuk (194), Tai-Loi (11,856), Yang unspecified (420), Yanglam (10,867), Yangsek (2,677) and Palaung (138,746).
(*i*) Includes Hindus (Males 208 and Females 171), Tribal (Males 44 and Females 37) and Christians (Males 14 and Females 9).
(*j*) All Tribal.
(*k*) Sex not stated for 9,319 Persons.

Table XVIII.—Variation in Population

Tribe or Caste. 1	Province, State or Agency and Religion. 2	Reference to Table. 3	Persons. 1931. 4	1921. 5	1911. 6	1901. 7	1891. 8	1881. 9	Variation (Increase +, 1921-1931. 10	1911-1921. 11	1901-1911. 12
135 **Santal**	.. ..	**8,14,17**	**2,508,789**	**2,189,511**	**2,078,035**	**1,827,765**	**1.454,623**	‡	**+319,278**	**+111,476**	**+250,270**
	Bengal .. .. (Hindu) ..		433,502	158,383	165,328	150,488			+275,119	—6,945	+14,840
	Do. .. .. (Tribal) ..		352,386	553,657	504,092	377,927			—201,271	+49,565	+126,165
	Do. .. .. (Buddhist) ..		14	..	..	..	309,762	‡	..	..	..
	Do. .. .. (Christian) ..		10,754	..	1,269	1,003			+9,485		+266
	Bihar and Orissa .. (Hindu) ..		586,499	557,341	271,280	390,239			+29,155	+286,061	—118,959
	Do. .. .. (Christian) ..		13,279	8,367	7,896	7,928	1,144,861	‡	+4,912	+471	—32
	Do. .. .. (Tribal) ..		1,112,355	911,763	1,128,170	900,180			+200,592	—216,407	+227,990
136 **Saun**	United Provinces .. (Hindu)	**17**	**2,275**	‡	‡	**896**	**257**	**209**		**+1,379**	
137 **Saunta**	Central Provinces and Berar,	**17**	**7,051**	**3,942**	**10,403**	‡	**8**	‡	**+3,109**	**—6,461**	..
	(Hindu) ..		6,369	3,820	3,102	‡	8	‡	+2,549	+718	..
	(Tribal) ..		682	122	7,301				+560	—7,179	
138 **Sauria Paharia** ..	Bihar and Orissa ..	**17**	**59,891**	**55,600**	**62,734**	**47,066**	‡	‡	**+4.291**	**—7,134**	**+15,668**
	(Hindu) ..		112	145	5,424	11,377	‡	‡	—33	—5,279	—5,953
	(Christian) ..		449	482	407	..	‡	‡	—33	+75	+407
	(Tribal) ..		59,330	54,973	56,903	35,689	‡	‡	+4,357	—1,930	+21,214
139 **Savara, etc.** ..	....	**8,14,17**	**632.811**	**545,576**	**533,685**	**477,509**	**432,056**	**169,749**	**+87,235**	**+11,891**	**+56,176**
Saharia ..	United Provinces .. (Hindu) ..		14,113	‡	‡	7,559	‡	12,452	..	+6,554	..
	Gwalior .. .. (Hindu) ..		76,219	1,897	42,448	..	‡	‡	+74,322	—40,551	..
..	Do. .. .. (Tribal) ..		..	56,483	12,980	35,525	‡	‡	..	+43,503	—22,545
Saora ..	Madras .. .. (Tribal) ..		211,781	210,511	186,128	183,159	182,295	131,463	+1,270	+24,383	+2,969
Savar ..	Bihar and Orissa .. (Hindu) ..		244,648	189,897	204,458	212,138	203,115	‡	+54,751	—14,561	+5,810
	Do. .. (Tribal) ..		22	12,738	13,490				—12,716	—752	
Sawara or Saonr ..	Central Provinces and Berar. .. (Hindu) ..		84,971	74,050	74,181	39,128	46,646	25,834	+10,921	—131	+35,053
	Do. .. (Tribal) ..		1,057	..	..				..	..	
140 **Shin**	Jammu and Kashmir (Muslim) ..		**14,139**	**15,106**	**11,080**	‡	‡	‡	**—967**	**+4,026**	..
141 **Sholagar** ..	Madras .. .. (Tribal)	**17**	**2,957**	**2,776**	**1,944**	**5,727**	**2,793**	..	**+181**	**+832**	**—3,783**
142 **Tharu**	....	**17**	**69,403**	**61,751**	**63,639**	**51,431**	**53,352**	**27,172**	**+7,652**	**—1,888**	**+12,208**
	Bengal .. .. (Hindu) ..		425	‡	1,299	448	240	‡	—874		+851
	Do. .. .. (Tribal) ..		57	‡	18	64			+39		—46
	Bihar and Orissa .. (Hindu) ..		37,338	32,817	34,602	26,687	27,620		+4,521	—1,785	+7,915
	United Provinces .. (Hindu) ..		31,583	28,934	§27,720	‖24,232	25,492	‡	+2,649	+1,214	+3,488
143 **Thantapulayan** ..	Travancore .. (Hindu)	**8**	**795**	‡	‡	**15**	‡	‡	..	..	..
144 **Tipara**	Bengal		**203,069**	**153,921**	**130,025**	**101,508**	**90,306**	‡	**+49,148**	**+23,896**	**+28,517**
	(Hindu) ..		195,855	153,921	112,049	98,200			+41,934	+41,872	+13,849
	(Tribal) ..		7,076	..	16,984	216	90,306	‡		—9,908	+16,768
	(Buddhist) ..		135	..	992	3,092				—857	—2,100
	(Christian) ..		3	..	..	..			..	..	..
145 **Toda**	Madras .. (Tribal)	**8,14,17**	**597**	**640**	**748**	**607**	**739**	**689**	**—43**	**-108**	**—59**
146 **Toto**	Bengal		**334**	‡	**235**	**171**		‡		**+99**	**+64**
	(Hindu) ..		330	‡	104	..	‡	‡		+226	..
	(Tribal) ..		4	‡	131	171	‡	‡		—127	—40
147 **Ullatan** .. .. (Kocchuvelan).	....	**14,17**	**5,899**	**3,820**	**4,652**	**2,993**	**3,312**	**2,840**	**+2,079**	**—832**	**+1,659**
	Cochin .. .. (Hindu) ..		778	413	537	439	439	..	+365	—124	+98
	Travancore .. (Hindu) ..		4,824	2,912	3,974	2,393	2,873	2,840	+1,912	—1,062	+1,581
	Do. .. .. (Tribal) ..		77	495	141	161	..	..	—418	+354	—20
	Do. .. .. (Christian) ..		220	..	..	..	..	..	..	..	..
148 **Varli**	....	**17**	**206,919**	**177,596**	**190,835**	**152,303**	**168,631**	**63,184**	**+29,323**	**—13,239**	**+38,532**
	Bombay .. .. (Hindu) ..		206,551	177,391	190,237	151,693	167,250	63,184	+29,160	—12,846	+38,544
	Baroda .. .. (Hindu) ..		187	..	117	..	1,381	..	+70		—1,264
	Do. .. .. (Tribal) ..		181	205	481	610	..	..	—24	—276	—129
149 **Vetan** .. .. (Including Malavetan)	Travancore		**11,737**	**8,239**	**5,051**	**11,720**	**6,809**	**6,155**	**+3,498**	**+3,188**	**—6,669**
	(Hindu) ..		9,496	6,303	..	4,707	6,809	6,155	+3,193	+1,596	
	(Tribal) ..		241	1,936	5,051	7,013	..	..	—1,695	—3,115	—1,962
	(Christian) ..		2,000	..	..	..	..	..	..	..	..
150 **Vettuvan** .. (Cheruvetan).	Travancore	**8,14,17**	**1,322**	**1,321**	**1,486**	**1,085**	**87**	..	**+1**	**—165**	**+401**
	.. .. (Hindu) ..		1,251	1,148	1,482	1,081	87	..	+103	—334	+401
	.. .. (Tribal) ..		..	173	4	4	..	..	..	+169	..
	.. .. (Christian) ..		71	..	..	..	..	..	..	..	..
151 **Yakka**	Bengal		**1,015**	‡	**1,320***	**2,376**	**1,250**	‡	**—305**		**—1,056**
	(Hindu) ..		1,009	‡	1,309	2,363	1,250	‡	—300		—1,054
	(Buddhist) ..		6	‡	1	13			+5		—12
152 **Yashkun**	Jammu and Kashmir (Muslim) ..		**36,160**	**44,087**	**35,011**	‡	‡	‡	**—7,927**	**+9,076**	..

*Includes (Tribals 3 Males and 7 Females.)

† Sex details
‡ Figures not
§ Includes 1
‖ Includes 13

of Selected Castes and Tribes—*concld.*

Decrease—). 1891-1901.	1881-1891.	Net variation 1881-1931. (Increase +, Decrease—).	Males. 1931.	1921.	1911.	1901.	1891.	1881.	Females. 1931.	1921.	1911.	1901.	1891.	1881.
13	14	15	16	17	18	19	20	21	22	23	24	25	26	27
+373,142	..	..	1,256,709	1,092,171	1,032,976	909,649	724,848	‡	1,252,080	1,097,340	1,045,059	918,116	729,775	‡
			219,315	79,801	84,029	78,189			214,187	78,582	81,299	72,299		
			176,808	277,956	252,355	189,024			175,578	275,701	251,737	188,903		
+219,656	..	..	6	...	..	..	153,357	‡	8	..	..	..	156,405	‡
			5,477	..	675	538			5,277	..	594	465		
			293,807	276,289	131,243	193,078			292,692	281,052	140,037	197,161		
+153,486	..	..	6,754	4,185	3,850	3,814	571,491	‡	6,525	4,182	4,046	4,114	573,370	‡
			554,542	453,940	560,824	445,006			557,813	457,823	567,346	455,174		
+639	+48	+2,066	1,043	‡	‡	431	138	117	1,232	‡	‡	465	119	92
..	..	..	3,526	1,934	5,298	‡	†	‡	3,525	2,008	5,105	‡	†	‡
..	..	..	3,183	1,876	1,603	‡	†	‡	3 186	1,944	1,499	‡	†	‡
			343	58	3,695				339	64	3,606			
..	..	..	30,555	28,336	31,158	24,170	‡	‡	29,336	27,264	31,576	22,896	‡	‡
..	..	..	54	58	2,742	5,538	‡	‡	58	87	2,682	5,839	‡	‡
..	..	..	182	217	191	..	‡	‡	267	265	216	..	‡	‡
..	..	..	30,319	28,016	28,225	18,632	‡	‡	29,011	26,912	28,678	17,057	‡	‡
+45,453	+262,307	+463,062	311,230	268,477	263,125	239,447	†	87,066	321,581	277,099	270,560	238,062	†	82,683
—4,893		+1,661	7,122	‡	‡	4,115	‡	6,328	6,991	‡	‡	3,444	‡	6,124
..	..	..	38,745	1,168	21,945	..	‡	‡	37,474	729	20,503	..	‡	‡
..	..	..	..	28,540	6,804	20,455	‡	‡	..	27,943	6,176	15,070	‡	‡
+864	+50,832	+80,318	104,631	105,632	92,348	91,953	92,880	67,748	107,150	104,879	93,780	91,206	89,415	63,715
+9,023	..	..	118,568	90,690	99,222	104,069	100,179	‡	126,080	99,207	105,236	108,069	102,936	‡
			17	6,281	6,765				5	6,457	6,725			
—7.518	+20,812	+60,194	41,620	36,166	36,041	18,855	†	12,990	43,351	37,884	38,140	20,273	†	12,844
			527	..	..				530	..	..			
..	..	..	7,126	7,665	5,930	‡	‡	‡	7,013	7,441	5,150	‡	‡	‡
+2,934	..	..	1,400	1,300	981	2,829	1,398	..	1,557	1,476	963	2,898	1,395	..
—1,921	+26,180	+42,231	36,228	32,165	33,795	26,845	27,700	14,494	33,175	29,586	29,844	24,586	25,652	12,678
+272	..	..	326	‡	1,242	365	170	‡	99	‡	57	83	70	‡
			28	‡	11	64			29	‡	7	..		
—933	..	..	19,154	16,848	17,609	13,591	13,810	†	18.184	15,969	16,993	13,096	13,810	†
—1,260	—1,680	+4,411	16,720	15,317	14,933	12,825	13,720	14,494	14,863	13,617	12,787	11,407	11,772	12,678
..	..	..	386	‡	‡	9	‡	‡	409	‡	‡	6	‡	‡
+11,202	..	..	105,243	78,060	66,211	52,559	46,605	‡	97,826	75,861	63,814	48,949	43,701	‡
			101,448	78,060	56,979	50,685			94,407	75,861	55,070	47,515		
+11,202	..	..	3,715	..	8,717	126	46,605	‡	3,361	..	8,267	90	43,701	‡
			79	..	515	1,748			56	..	477	1,344		
			1	..	..	..			2	..	..	..		
+68	+50	—92	340	360	426	453	427	393	257	280	322	354	312	296
..	..	..	130	‡	125	72	‡	‡	204	‡	110	99	‡	‡
..	..	..	126	‡	56	..	‡	‡	204	‡	48	..	‡	‡
..	..	..	4	‡	69	72	‡	‡	..	‡	62	99	‡	‡
—319	+472	+3,059	2,617	1,815	2,458	1,497	1,681	1,413	3,282	2,005	2,194	1,496	1,631	1,427
..	..	..	375	211	261	211	208	..	403	202	276	228	231	..
—480	+33	+1,984	2,110	1,359	2,129	1,207	1,473	1,413	2,714	1,553	1,845	1,186	1,400	1,427
..	..	..	33	245	68	79	..	..	44	250	73	82	..	..
..	..	..	99	..	..	..	..	..	121	..	..	..	..	..
—16,328	+105,447	+143,735	105,421	89,511	94,628	75,331	83,147	30,940	101,498	88,085	96,207	76,972	85,484	32,244
—15,557	+104,066	+143,367	105,218	89,400	94,322	75,037	82,449	30,940	101,333	87,991	95,915	76,656	84,801	32,244
	..	..	112	..	52	..	698	..	75	..	65	..	683	..
..	..	..	91	111	254	294	..	..	90	94	227	316	..	..
+4,911	+654	+5,582	5,919	4,114	2,584	5,945	3,498	3,015	5,818	4,125	2,467	5,775	3,311	3,140
—2,102	+654	+3,341	4,770	3,101	..	2,403	3,498	3,015	4,726	3 202	..	2,304	3,311	3,140
..	..	..	124	1,013	2,584	3,542	..	..	117	923	2,467	3,471	..	..
..	..	..	1,025	..	..	..	..	..	975	..	..	..	..	..
+998	..	..	621	635	746	586	39	..	701	686	740	499	48	
+994	..	..	580	561	744	584	39	..	671	587	738	497	48	..
..	..	..	..	74	2	2	..	..	..	99	2	2	..	..
..	..	..	41	..	..	..	..	..	30	..	..	..	..	..
+1,126	..	..	438	‡	626	1,333	629	‡	577	‡	694	1,043	621	‡
+1,126	..	..	435	‡	622	1,326	629	‡	574	‡	687	1,037	621	†
			3	‡	1	7			3	‡	..	6		
..	..	..	19,091	23,373	17,965	‡	‡	‡	17,069	20,714	17,046	‡	‡	†

not available
available.
Muslim male.
Muslim males.

TABLE XIX.

Europeans and Allied Races and Anglo-Indians by Race and Age.

This table corresponds with Table XVI of 1921, and is divided into two parts—Part I of which shows details for the individual Provinces and States, and Part II for a selection of cities. Part A of both parts relates to Europeans, and is further sub-divided to show details for British subjects and others, while Part B relates to Anglo-Indians. Columns 2-4 show the total number of Europeans (with allied races) *plus* Anglo-Indians.

2. The age groups have been modified from the form which they took in 1921 to bring them more nearly into line with the groups adopted for other tables. Armenians have been included among Europeans and Allied Races as their numbers and importance do not justify separate treatment. The statement below shows their numbers where available, by the Province or State of enumeration :—

Province, State or Agency.	Persons.	Males.	Females.
INDIA	**1,313**	**671**	**642**
Baluchistan	1	..	1
Bengal	700	328	372
Bihar and Orissa	91	55	36
Burma	410	215	195
Central Provinces and Berar	1	..	1
Delhi	1	..	1
Madras	8	4	4
North-West Frontier Province	8	4	4
Punjab	4	2	2
United Provinces	57	36	21
Central India Agency	2	1	1
Hyderabad State	12	10	2
Jammu and Kashmir State	13	12	1
Mysore State	5	4	1

Note.—No Armenians were returned in the following units: Ajmer-Merwara, Assam, the Andamans and Nicobars, Baroda State, Cochin State, Coorg, Gwalior State, Rajputana Agency and Travancore State.

The figures against Bengal and Bihar and Orissa represent the number of persons enumerated therein who returned Armenian as their mother-tongue, and have been given here as separate figures were not extracted for Armenians in those units.

Table XIX.—Europeans and Allied Races and Anglo-

A.—European and Allied

(a) British

	Province, State or Agency.	Total.			All Ages.			0—13	
		Persons.	Males.	Females.	Persons.	Males.	Females.	Males.	Females.
	1	2	3	4	5	6	7	8	9
	INDIA	**306,529**	**188,583**	**117,946**	**155,555**	**110,137**	**45,418**	**11,905**	**10,094**
	Provinces	**271,092**	**166,441**	**104 651**	**139,840**	**98,284**	**41,556**	**11,099**	**9,248**
1	Ajmer-Merwara	2,908	1,914	994	1,524	1,172	352	94	94
2	Andaman and Nicobar Islands	311	240	71	214	180	34	8	8
3	Assam	3,671	2,525	1,146	2,961	2,093	868	150	176
4	Baluchistan .. .. (*Districts and Administered Territories*).	5,404	4,000	1,404	5,010	3,792	1,218	415	382
5	Bengal	50,587	28,665	21,922	20,895	13,110	7,785	2,027	1,233
6	Bihar and Orissa	12,782	7,140	5,642	5,572	3,386	2,186	496	491
	Bihar	*6,418*	*3,747*	*2,671*	*2,785*	*1,870*	*915*	*185*	*169*
	Orissa	*856*	*422*	*434*	*182*	*98*	*84*	*17*	*17*
	Chota Nagpur	*5,508*	*2,971*	*2,537*	*2,605*	*1,418*	*1,187*	*294*	*305*
7	Bombay	42,359	26,600	15,759	24,053	16,636	7,417	1,860	1,600
	Bombay Presidency	*32,204*	*19,532*	*12,672*	*16,542*	*11,226*	*5,316*	*1,155*	*1,113*
	Sind	*8,506*	*5,701*	*2,805*	*6,293*	*4,383*	*1,910*	*668*	*450*
	Aden	*1,649*	*1,367*	*282*	*1,218*	*1,027**	*191*	*37*	*37*
8	Burma	30,851	17,769	13,082	10,627	7,205	3,422	906	841
9	Central Provinces and Berar	10,313	6,474	3,839	5,075	3,782	1,293	980	345
	Central Provinces	*9,843*	*6,296*	*3,547*	*5,006*	*3,745*	*1,261*	*979*	*339*
	Berar	*470*	*178*	*292*	*69*	*37*	*32*	*1*	*6*
10	Coorg	222	117	105	122	69	53	11	9
11	Delhi	5,316	3,463	1,853	4,209	2,879	1,330	230	233
12	Madras	41,033	21,263	19,770	10,665	6,417	4,248	996	952
13	North-West Frontier Province .. .. (*Districts and Administered Territories*).	7,947	6,444	1,503	7,764	6,344	1,420	463	432
14	Punjab	22,644	16,411	6,233	19,106	14,358	4,748	1,290	1,296
15	United Provinces of Agra and Oudh ..	34,744	23,416	11,328	22,043	16,861	5,182	1,173	1,156
	Agra	*26,674*	*17,408*	*9,266*	*16,704*	*12,307*	*4,397*	*884*	*973*
	Oudh	*8,070*	*6,008*	*2,062*	*5,339*	*4,554*	*785*	*289*	*183*
	States and Agencies	**35,437**	**22,142**	**13,295**	**15,715**	**11,853**	**3,862**	**806**	**846**
16	Assam States	341	213	128	166	75	91	8	18
17	Baluchistan States	9	8	1	4	3	1	..	..
18	Baroda State	198	123	75	111	78	33	8	7
19	Bengal States	16	9	7	9	6	3	1	1
20	Bihar and Orissa States	245	142	103	103	57	46	11	5
21	Bombay States	154	87	67	78	43	35	1	3
22	Central India Agency	3,213	2,226	987	2,360	1,788	572	164	176
23	Central Provinces States	402	215	187	49	33	16	5	3
24	Gwalior State	242	127	115	101	54	47	7	7
25	Hyderabad State	5,997	4,456	1,541	1,853	1,760	93	29	12
26	Jammu and Kashmir State	321	143	178	151	69	82	2	4
27	Madras States Agency	3,244	1,704	1,540	539	343	196	30	41
	Cochin State	*1,829*	*878*	*951*	*72*	*38*	*34*	*5*	*8*
	Travancore State	*1,377*	*804*	*573*	*456*	*299*	*157*	*25*	*33*
	Other Madras States	*38*	*22*	*16*	*11*	*6*	*5*	...	..
28	Mysore State	13,720	6,925	6,795	4,907	2,929	1,978	375	419
29	North-West Frontier Province .. .. (*Agencies and Tribal Areas*).	3,790	3,777	13	3,779	3,772	7	1	1
30	Punjab States	54	25	29	34	18	16	4	1
31	Punjab States Agency	1,026	593	433	383	221	162	47	51
32	Rajputana Agency	1,760	960	800	856	463	393	99	85
33	Sikkim State	10	5	5	7	4	3	...	...
34	United Provinces States	29	11	18	18	7	11	2	1
35	Western India States Agency	666	393	273	207	130	77	12	11

* Includes 18 Males of unspecified age.

Indians by Race and Age. Part I—Details by Provinces and States.

Races (including Armenians).

Subjects.

14—16		17—23		24—33		34—43		44—53		54 and over.		
Males.	Females.	Males.	Females.	Males.	Females.	Males.	Females.	Males.	Females.	Males.	Females.	
10	11	12	13	14	15	16	17	18	19	20	21	
1,780	**1,949**	**25,129**	**4,556**	**40,650**	**10,531**	**16,071**	**9,240**	**9,470**	**4,956**	**5,114**	**4,092**	
1,621	**1,831**	**22,328**	**4,197**	**35,546**	**9,780**	**14,899**	**8,529**	**8,618**	**4,447**	**4,155**	**3,524**	
16	10	386	43	496	82	99	70	49	37	32	16	1
8	6	33	4	94	7	17	1	15	5	5	3	2
13	8	153	51	855	272	484	235	338	90	100	36	3
28	27	903	80	1,824	368	446	259	147	79	29	23	4
336	427	1,573	1,027	3,732	1,710	2,577	1,625	1,829	909	1,036	854	5
97	122	520	212	977	441	580	421	474	266	242	233	6
25	*42*	*394*	*68*	*684*	*189*	*240*	*193*	*217*	*123*	*125*	*131*	
2	*4*	*4*	*11*	*19*	*21*	*23*	*17*	*22*	*7*	*11*	*7*	
70	*76*	*122*	*133*	*274*	*231*	*317*	*211*	*235*	*136*	*106*	*95*	
275	248	3,509	776	5,518	1,792	3,372	1,686	1,462	821	622	494	7
219	*202*	*2,393*	*625*	*4,073*	*1,335*	*1,803*	*1,128*	*1,086*	*511*	*497*	*402*	
47	*43*	*782*	*139*	*1,075*	*393*	*1,407*	*501*	*304*	*296*	*100*	*88*	
9	*3*	*334*	*12*	*370*	*64*	*162*	*57*	*72*	*14*	*25*	*4*	
154	94	1,045	344	2,363	844	1,368	706	899	351	470	242	8
96	105	538	104	904	244	428	227	643	145	193	123	9
95	*105*	*535*	*101*	*893*	*236*	*419*	*219*	*636*	*142*	*188*	*119*	
1	...	*3*	*3*	*11*	*8*	*9*	*8*	*7*	*3*	*5*	*4*	
..	..	4	6	15	14	18	9	7	7	14	8	10
18	31	716	134	1,098	328	403	309	305	189	109	106	11
138	187	1,066	365	2,002	847	990	761	735	558	490	578	12
28	30	2,039	122	2,929	428	659	293	197	84	29	31	13
224	221	4,173	461	5,811	1,211	1,688	873	842	410	330	276	14
190	315	5,670	468	6,928	1,192	1,770	1,054	676	496	454	501	15
147	*216*	*3,984*	*407*	*4,872*	*1,013*	*1,466*	*895*	*579*	*426*	*375*	*467*	
43	*99*	*1,686*	*61*	*2,056*	*179*	*304*	*159*	*97*	*70*	*79*	*34*	
159	**118**	**2,801**	**359**	**5,104**	**751**	**1,172**	**711**	**852**	**509**	**959**	**568**	
4	1	10	4	10	15	12	16	13	20	18	17	16
..	..	..	..	2	1	1	..	..	...	...	...	17
2	1	10	4	22	5	12	8	10	8	14	..	18
..	..	..	..	1	..	1	..	1	2	2	..	19
..	..	2	6	11	12	12	12	15	5	6	6	20
..	1	9	5	14	10	2	6	11	6	6	4	21
20	9	483	40	849	136	149	123	83	57	40	31	22
2	..	1	3	3	4	7	3	8	2	7	1	23
3	2	5	7	12	5	10	10	11	9	6	7	24
18	6	82	10	1,061	27	153	11	170	15	247	12	25
1	..	6	4	10	24	19	23	19	12	12	15	26
1	2	47	16	123	44	75	55	42	21	25	17	27
..	*1*	*4*	*5*	*12*	*5*	*9*	*9*	*5*	*3*	*3*	*3*	
1	*1*	*42*	*10*	*111*	*38*	*64*	*44*	*35*	*17*	*21*	*14*	
..	..	*1*	*1*	..	*1*	*2*	*2*	*2*	*1*	*1*	..	
77	67	562	180	864	323	309	317	259	261	483	411	28
9	..	1,479	1	1,967	4	257	..	57	1	2	...	29
1	...	2	2	1	8	4	1	3	4	3	..	
5	5	23	20	45	23	43	27	30	26	28	10	33
15	23	59	50	82	80	74	75	90	49	44	31	32
...	...	...	2	...	..	..	1	3	..	1	..	33
...	..	..	...	1	6	2	3	1	1	1	..	34
1	1	21	5	26	24	30	20	26	10	14	6	35

Table XIX.—Europeans and Allied Races and Anglo-

A.—Europeans and Allied

(b)

Province, State or Agency.	All ages.			0—13		14—16	
	Persons.	Males.	Females.	Males.	Females.	Males.	Females.
1	22	23	24	25	26	27	28
INDIA	**12,579**	**7,199**	**5,380**	**855**	**831**	**198**	**178**
Provinces	**10,620**	**6,079**	**4,541**	**676**	**708**	**133**	**120**
1 Ajmer-Merwara	152	81	71	21	23	2	..
2 Andaman and Nicobar Islands	..	..	..	..	..	..	..
3 Assam	152	83	69	13	12	1	..
4 Baluchistan .. .. .. (*Districts and Administered Territories.*)	18	11	7	..	..	..	..
5 Bengal	2,119	1,373	746	133	143	28	32
6 Bihar and Orissa	683	359	324	47	67	6	5
Bihar	*192*	*75*	*117*	*16*	*16*	*1*	..
Orissa	*39*	*17*	*22*	*2*	*4*	*1*	..
Chota Nagpur	*452*	*267*	*185*	*29*	*47*	*4*	*5*
7 Bombay	2,148	1,394	754	145	136	24	17
Bombay Presidency	*1,486*	*927*	*559*	*71*	*95*	*15*	*13*
Sind	*283*	*164*	*119*	*52*	*27*	*4*	*3*
Aden	*379*	*303**	*76*	*22*	*14*	*5*	*1*
8 Burma	1,024	680	344	29	30	8	5
9 Central Provinces and Berar	498	217	281	38	36	6	8
Central Provinces	*406*	*182*	*224*	*36*	*27*	*6*	*7*
Berar	*92*	*35*	*57*	*2*	*9*	..	*1*
10 Coorg	16	4	12	..	5	..	..
11 Delhi	97	52	45	3	2	..	1
12 Madras	1,699	898	801	145	152	19	18
13 North-West Frontier Province .. .. (*Districts and Administered Territories*).	33	8	25	1	1	..	..
14 Punjab	543	228	315	30	47	3	8
15 United Provinces of Agra and Oudh ..	1,438	691	747	71	54	36	26
Agra	*641*	*322*	*319*	*30*	*32*	*10*	5
Oudh	*797*	*369*	*428*	*41*	*22*	*26*	*21*
States and Agencies	**1,959**	**1,120**	**839**	**179**	**123**	**65**	**58**
16 Assam States	83	78	5	—	—	1	—
17 Baluchistan States	2	2	..	..	..	..	..
18 Baroda State	24	8	16	1	1	..	..
19 Bengal States	7	3	4	2	1	..	..
20 Bihar and Orissa States	31	21	10	3	1	..	..
21 Bombay States	16	7	9	1	..	..	..
22 Central India Agency	117	48	69	6	7	1	2
23 Central Provinces States	28	17	11	2	1	..	..
24 Gwalior State	10	4	6	..	..	..	..
25 Hyderabad State	774	508	266	95	52	51	39
26 Jammu and Kashmir State	47	24	23	3	1	..	..
27 Madras States Agency	173	93	80	7	..	3	1
Cochin State	*40*	*20*	*20*	*2*	..	..	/
Travancore State	*131*	*72*	*59*	*5*	..	..	..
Other Madras States	*2*	*1*	*1*	..	..	*3*	..
28 Mysore State	504	215	289	40	48	4	13
29 North-West Frontier Province .. .. (*Agencies and Tribal Areas.*)	..	..	..	..	..	..	..
30 Punjab States	6	..	6	..	..	..	..
31 Punjab States Agency	27	23	4	3	..	1	..
32 Rajputana Agency	76	45	31	10	10	2	3
33 Sikkim State	1	..	1	..	..	..	..
34 United Provinces States	2	..	2	..	..	..	..
35 Western India States Agency	31	24	7	6	1	2	...

* Includes 2 Males of unspecified age.

Indians by Race and Age. Part I—Details by Provinces and States—*contd.*

Races (including Armenians)—*concld.*

Others.

17—23		24—33		34—43		44—53		54 and over.		
Males.	Females.	Males.	Females.	Males.	Females.	Males.	Females.	Males.	Females.	
29	30	31	32	33	34	35	36	37	38	
955	**463**	**1,854**	**1,385**	**1,495**	**1,286**	**1,074**	**678**	**766**	**559**	
796	**381**	**1,570**	**1,218**	**1,290**	**1,109**	**979**	**562**	**633**	**443**	
11	6	15	22	11	11	13	6	8	3	1
..	..	..	..	..	..	..	..	..	..	2
4	4	22	17	26	24	10	7	7	5	3
..	..	2	3	6	1	1	3	2	..	4
243	74	379	187	271	159	192	75	127	76	5
20	18	77	67	104	90	65	40	40	37	6
5	*4*	*18*	*22*	*21*	*35*	*10*	*19*	*4*	*21*	
..	..	*2*	*8*	*9*	*5*	*3*	*3*	..	*2*	
15	*14*	*57*	*37*	*74*	*50*	*52*	*18*	*36*	*14*	
156	77	442	229	310	158	207	92	108	45	7
108	*47*	*305*	*170*	*206*	*120*	*138*	*75*	*84*	*39*	
10	*20*	*35*	*34*	*33*	*23*	*22*	*8*	*8*	*4*	
38	*10*	*102*	*25*	*71*	*15*	*47*	*9*	*16*	*2*	
71	17	194	85	168	92	114	67	96	48	8
10	24	51	60	60	71	25	38	27	44	9
9	*21*	*47*	*50*	*41*	*51*	*20*	*29*	*23*	*39*	
1	*3*	*4*	*10*	*19*	*20*	*5*	*9*	*4*	*5*	
..	..	3	2	1	1	..	1	..	3	10
2	4	15	15	16	14	11	1	5	8	11
64	29	202	188	172	182	150	140	146	92	12
..	2	3	10	3	7	..	5	1	..	13
22	27	66	93	51	77	35	35	21	28	14
193	99	99	240	91	222	156	52	45	54	15
79	*16*	*72*	*103*	*40*	*75*	*53*	*45*	*38*	*43*	
114	*83*	*27*	*137*	*51*	*147*	*103*	*7*	*7*	*11*	
159	**82**	**284**	**167**	**205**	**177**	**95**	**116**	**133**	**116**	
26	..	33	..	13	4	3	..	2	1	16
..	..	..	..	2	..	..	..	..	..	17
..	..	2	1	4	9	1	5	..	..	18
..	..	..	2	1	1	..	..	..	..	19
3	2	8	1	2	3	3	1	2	2	20
..	..	2	3	..	6	3	..	1	..	21
6	1	12	8	10	22	4	13	9	16	22
..	1	2	6	5	1	6	2	2	..	23
1	..	..	1	2	2	..	1	1	2	24
87	51	129	49	88	33	26	24	32	18	25
..	..	4	5	6	9	6	4	5	4	26
12	6	37	37	13	22	14	10	7	4	27
2	*3*	*5*	*7*	*2*	*7*	*4*	*1*	*5*	*1*	
10	*3*	*32*	*30*	*11*	*15*	*9*	*8*	*2*	*3*	
..	..	..	..	..	..	*1*	*1*	..	..	
15	16	39	46	36	58	18	44	63	64	28
..	..	..	..	..	..	..	..	..	..	29
.	1	..	1	..	..	..	3	..	1	30
2	1	4	1	9	..	2	1	2	1	31
3	2		3	10	4	8	7	6	2	32
..	..	..	..	..	1	..	..	..	..	33
..	..	..	..	..	2	..	..	..	..	34
4	1	6	3	4	..	1	1	1	1	35

Table XIX.—Europeans and Allied Races and Anglo-

B.—Anglo-

Province, State or Agency.	All Ages.			0—3		4—6		7—13		14—
	Persons.	Males.	Females.	Males.	Females.	Males.	Females.	Males.	Females.	Males.
1	39	40	41	42	43	44	45	46	47	48
INDIA. ..	**138,395**	**71,247**	**67,148**	**6,317**	**5,977**	**5,409**	**4,943**	**11,921**	**11,433**	**5,234**
Provinces. ..	**120,632**	**62,078**	**58,554**	**5,509**	**5,219**	**4,733**	**4,352**	**10,504**	**10,147**	**4,567**
1 Ajmer-Merwara ..	1,232	661	571	58	62	48	53	124	102	52
2 Andaman and Nicobar Islands.	97	60	37	3	7	4	2	2	7	4
3 Assam	558	349	209	29	25	25	20	73	32	18
4 Baluchistan .. (*Districts and Administered Territories*).	376	197	179	21	21	24	17	41	37	13
5 Bengal	27,573	14,182	13,391	1,281	1,104	1,026	928	2,452	2,274	1,172
6 Bihar and Orissa ..	6,527	3,395	3,132	323	330	262	272	484	519	213
Bihar ..	*3,441*	*1,802*	*1,639*	*153*	*150*	*135*	*132*	*291*	*260*	*138*
Orissa ..	*635*	*307*	*328*	*22*	*23*	*23*	*19*	*54*	*102*	*29*
Chota Nagpur ..	*2,451*	*1,286*	*1,165*	*148*	*157*	*104*	*121*	*139*	*157*	*46*
7 Bombay	16,158	8,570	7,588	652	630	562	550	1,322	1,307	539
Bombay Presidency.	*14,176*	*7,379*	*6,797*	*548*	*536*	*476*	*480*	*1,175*	*1,178*	*494*
Sind	*1,930*	*1,154*	*776*	*99*	*91*	*83*	*68*	*144*	*128*	*45*
Aden	*52*	*37*	*15*	*5*	*3*	*3*	*2*	*3*	*1*	..
8 Burma	19,200	9,884	9,316	952	876	758	736	1,696	1,769	669
9 Central Provinces and Berar.	4,740	2,475	2,265	212	257	213	183	445	371	177
Central Provinces	*4,431*	*2,369*	*2,062*	*200*	*244*	*201*	*167*	*430*	*320*	*174*
Berar ..	*309*	*106*	*203*	*12*	*13*	*12*	*16*	*15*	*51*	*3*
10 Coorg	84	44	40	2	2	2	1	2	7	2
11 Delhi	1,010	532	478	39	47	48	28	70	73	18
12 Madras	28,669	13,948	14,721	1,235	1,255	1,119	1,045	2,561	2,578	1,064
13 North-West Frontier Province. (*Districts and Administered Territories*).	150	92	58	6	7	5	4	10	9	6
14 Punjab	2,995	1,825	1,170	176	143	135	112	257	169	134
15 United Provinces of Agra and Oudh.	11,263	5,864	5,399	520	453	502	401	965	893	486
Agra	*9,329*	*4,779*	*4,550*	*455*	*391*	*374*	*347*	*806*	*752*	*331*
Oudh	*1,934*	*1,085*	*849*	*65*	*62*	*128*	*54*	*159*	*141*	*155*
States and Agencies	**17,763**	**9,169**	**8,594**	**808**	**758**	**676**	**591**	**1,417**	**1,286**	**667**
16 Assam States ..	92	60	32	2	1	7	..	11	3	1
17 Baluchistan States ..	3	3	..	..	..	..	..	..	..	..
18 Baroda State ..	63	37	26	3	2	2	4	2	4	4
19 Bengal States ..	..	..	..	..	..	..	..	..	..	..
20 Bihar and Orissa States.	111	64	47	4	5	1	4	1	11	14
21 Bombay States ..	60	37	23	4	4	7	3	6	..	3
22 Central India Agency	736	390	346	45	33	28	41	53	45	12
23 Central Provinces States.	325	165	160	21	23	15	16	23	18	8
24 Gwalior State ..	131	69	62	8	8	9	10	7	10	2
25 Hyderabad State ..	3,370	2,188	1,182	115	97	116	75	140	99	119
26 Jammu and Kashmir State.	123	50	73	8	7	3	8	6	7	2
27 Madras States Agency	2,532	1,268	1,264	116	118	113	95	239	215	92
Cochin State ..	*1,717*	*820*	*897*	*90*	*88*	*82*	*74*	*157*	*154*	*68*
Travancore State	*790*	*433*	*357*	*26*	*26*	*31*	*21*	*79*	*61*	*24*
Other Madras States.	*25*	*15*	*10*	..	*4*	..	..	*3*	..	..
28 Mysore State ..	8,309	3,781	4,528	341	320	287	263	792	751	367
29 North-West Frontier Province (*Agencies and Tribal Areas*).	11	5	6	..	2	2	..	2	2	..
30 Punjab States ...	14	7	7	1	..	..	..	..	3	..
31 Punjab States Agency	616	349	267	68	63	29	18	35	28	16
32 Rajputana Agency ..	828	452	376	53	53	40	32	76	62	20
33 Sikkim State ..	2	1	1	..	..	..	..	..	..	.
34 United Provinces States.	9	4	5	..	1	1	1	..	..	.
35 Western India States Agency.	428	239	189	19	21	16	21	24	28	7

Indians by Race and Age. Part I—Details by Provinces and States—*concld.*

ndians.

16	17—19		20—29		30—39		40—49		50—59		60—69		70 and over.		
Females. 49	Males. 50	Females. 51	Males. 52	Females. 53	Males. 54	Females. 55	Males. 56	Females. 57	Males. 58	Females. 59	Males. 60	Females. 61	Males. 62	Females. 63	
5,202	**5,185**	**5,094**	**12,176**	**12,037**	**10,058**	**8,892**	**7,622**	**6,149**	**4,161**	**3,868**	**2,126**	**2,402**	**1,038**	**1,151**	
4,585	**4,492**	**4,369**	**10,675**	**10,620**	**8,914**	**7,880**	**6,617**	**5,194**	**3,523**	**3,231**	**1,711**	**2,008**	**833**	**949**	
46	57	38	136	92	83	84	62	52	23	20	11	17	7	5	1
..	5	1	19	9	6	5	12	2	4	4	1	..	..	..	2
15	22	19	58	41	64	28	33	12	13	7	11	9	3	1	3
9	4	5	23	36	40	30	24	16	6	5	1	2	..	1	4
1,154	995	1,006	2,511	2,426	1,928	1,752	1,479	1,189	766	828	371	444	201	286	5
198	236	212	591	544	536	473	439	274	198	168	77	108	36	34	6
110	*131*	*112*	*?81*	*279*	*247*	*249*	*231*	*160*	*122*	*101*	*47*	*64*	*26*	*22*	
30	*24*	*22*	*56*	*49*	*39*	*40*	*35*	*20*	*9*	*14*	*12*	*5*	*4*	*4*	
58	*81*	*78*	*254*	*216*	*250*	*184*	*173*	*94*	*67*	*53*	*18*	*39*	*6*	*8*	
590	707	640	1,667	1,493	1,485	1,130	944	675	397	335	192	173	103	65	7
534	*626*	*588*	*1,402*	*1,349*	*1,267*	*1,028*	*808*	*591*	*326*	*301*	*162*	*156*	*95*	*56*	
56	*80*	*52*	*257*	*140*	*209*	*101*	*133*	*81*	*66*	*34*	*30*	*16*	*8*	*9*	
..	*1*	..	*8*	*4*	*9*	*1*	*3*	*3*	*5*	..	..	*1*	..	..	
759	618	631	1,731	1,810	1,486	1,206	1,048	765	566	423	269	245	91	96	8
194	167	160	390	369	357	300	280	202	130	113	67	76	37	40	9
170	*165*	*148*	*383*	*341*	*335*	*269*	*260*	*187*	*122*	*108*	*62*	*70*	*37*	*38*	
24	*2*	*12*	*7*	*28*	*22*	*31*	*20*	*15*	*8*	*5*	*5*	*6*	..	*2*	
2	5	4	10	8	5	7	7	4	5	3	3	1	1	1	10
17	28	36	79	93	112	87	98	50	29	30	9	11	2	6	11
1,110	1,122	1,159	2,204	2,544	1,692	1,858	1,346	1,346	895	869	469	681	241	276	12
4	7	7	18	14	22	7	12	4	5	2	1	..	..	..	13
73	124	77	303	214	299	173	206	101	116	54	47	37	28	17	14
414	395	374	935	927	799	740	627	502	370	370	182	204	83	121	15
346	*297*	*310*	*754*	*765*	*684*	*618*	*532*	*431*	*313*	*319*	*163*	*165*	*70*	*106*	
68	*98*	*64*	*181*	*162*	*115*	*122*	*95*	*71*	*57*	*51*	*19*	*39*	*13*	*15*	
617	**698**	**725**	**1,501**	**1,417**	**1,144**	**1,012**	**1,005**	**955**	**638**	**637**	**415**	**394**	**205**	**202**	
3	3	2	7	5	9	5	5	5	11	2	1	6	3	..	16
..	..	..	2	..	1	..	..	..	..	..	..	..	..	..	17
1	3	3	9	4	6	4	6	1	2	3	..	..	..	..	18
..	..	..	..	..	..	..	..	..	..	..	..	..	..	..	19
2	7	4	11	7	13	8	6	2	4	3	3	1	..	..	20
..	5	4	4	3	5	5	2	3	1	1	..	..	..	..	21
25	21	25	60	61	80	64	57	23	21	15	11	12	2	2	22
7	13	14	35	35	31	15	10	20	7	4	2	4	..	4	23
..	..	3	9	7	17	11	8	4	5	4	2	1	2	4	24
74	224	123	545	222	306	134	397	192	120	81	78	60	28	25	25
1	..	6	5	7	11	10	9	6	5	9	..	11	1	1	26
90	89	104	144	190	153	159	131	138	101	82	57	43	33	30	27
68	*48*	*57*	*99*	*154*	*80*	*102*	*70*	*93*	*61*	*58*	*38*	*32*	*27*	*17*	
21	*41*	*46*	*44*	*34*	*70*	*55*	*56*	*45*	*37*	*24*	*19*	*11*	*6*	*13*	
1	..	*1*	*1*	*2*	*3*	*2*	*5*	..	*3*	..	..	..	..	..	
365	257	366	472	732	348	476	261	485	297	403	236	239	123	128	28
..	..	..	..	..	1	1	..	..	..	..	..	..	..	1	29
2	1	1	..	..	2	1	1	..	1	..	..	..	1	..	30
18	17	23	70	51	38	33	30	18	26	11	13	3	7	1	31
19	34	36	71	49	75	66	54	32	18	10	9	11	2	6	32
..	..	..	..	..	1	..	..	..	..	1	..	..	..	..	33
..	1	..	..	1	1	1	..	1	1	..	..	..	..	..	34
10	18	11	57	43	46	19	28	25	18	8	3	3	3	..	35

Table XIX.—Europeans and Allied Races and Anglo-

A.—Europeans and Allied

(a) British

	Cities. 1	Total. Persons. 2	Total. Males. 3	Total. Females. 4	All Ages. Persons. 5	All Ages. Males. 6	All Ages. Females. 7	0—13. Males. 8	0—13. Females. 9
1	Calcutta	32,850	18,271	14,579	14,324	8,921	5,403	954	767
2	Bombay	16,448	9,976	6,472	8,400	5,394	3,006	623	573
3	Madras	14,238	7,401	6,837	3,239	2,094	1,145	216	202
4	Agra	3,384	2,225	1,159	2,053	1,490	563	141	186
5	Ajmer	1,860	984	876	509	262	247	50	58
6	Allahabad	3,896	2,260	1,636	1,137	870	267	44	42
7	Amritsar	215	179	36	191	163	28	..	..
8	Bangalore	716	304	412	260	122	138	22	32
9	Bangalore Civil and Military Station	9,678	4,837	4,841	4,029	2,395	1,634	333	364
10	Bareilly	1,330	1,014	316	1,183	945	238	52	68
11	Benares	384	242	142	178	146	32	5	5
12	Cawnpore	2,548	1,727	821	2,042	1,498	544	150	156
13	Dacca	394	191	203	131	53	78	9	24
14	*Delhi	4,708	2,873	1,835	3,609	2,291	1,318	228	231
15	Gorakhpur	483	263	220	79	48	31	1	1
16	Howrah	2,041	1,104	937	796	432	364	72	81
17	Hyderabad	4,939	3,783	1,156	1,660	1,600	60	22	9
18	Jaipur	326	180	146	67	29	38	3	3
19	Jamshedpur	1,161	682	479	521	310	211	55	54
20	Jhansi	2,701	1,939	762	1,742	1,451	291	83	87
21	Jubbulpore	3,908	2,768	1,140	2,600	2,047	553	821	156
22	Lahore	6,090	4,347	1,743	4,907	3,488	1,419	224	385
23	Lucknow	5,886	4,396	1,490	3,647	3,183	464	173	101
24	Madura	803	430	373	97	60	37	14	10
25	Mandalay	1,737	1,005	732	590	414	176	61	35
26	Meerut	2,939	2,223	716	2,656	2,098	558	52	107
27	Moradabad	477	244	233	181	94	87	26	21
28	Nagpur	1,804	967	837	314	169	145	27	24
29	Patna	728	276	452	217	100	117	13	16
30	Poona*	4,979	3,240	1,739	3,459	2,595	864	164	178
31	Rangoon	14,403	7,966	6,437	3,931	2,537	1,394	259	304
32	Rawalpindi	3,775	2,797	978	3,100	2,476	624	163	130
33	Srinagar	184	73	111	93	38	55	2	3
34	Trichinopoly	1,353	613	740	161	97	64	16	12
35	Vizagapatam	1,019	546	473	215	115	100	20	18

* These refers to Greater Poona, *i.e.*, Poona Municipality, Poona Suburban, Poona and Kirkee Cantonments and Poona Taluka.

Indians by Race and Age. Part II—Details by Cities.

Races (including Armenians).

Subjects.

14—16.		17—23.		24—33.		34—43.		44—53.		54 and over.		
Males. 10	Females. 11	Males. 12	Females. 13	Males. 14	Females. 15	Males. 16	Females. 17	Males. 18	Females. 19	Males. 20	Females. 21	
235	288	1,246	769	2,645	1,183	1,798	1,137	1,307	642	736	617	1
127	96	789	377	1,683	776	1,180	659	719	303	273	222	2
13	21	336	115	777	290	370	257	273	150	109	110	3
8	43	421	49	691	105	133	92	59	37	37	51	4
10	8	27	34	48	52	51	47	44	32	32	16	5
14	7	307	18	305	82	118	80	48	20	34	18	6
35	7	25	6	40	12	63	3	..	..	..	..	7
2	3	6	7	26	29	27	31	14	22	25	14	8
74	63	527	156	757	251	188	243	146	197	370	360	9
4	7	327	15	435	72	91	50	24	15	12	11	10
..	..	37	2	76	8	19	10	6	4	3	3	11
25	22	466	59	590	135	153	94	69	46	45	32	12
1	4	2	11	13	12	11	17	14	7	3	3	13
14	31	497	133	776	326	370	305	298	188	108	104	14
1	..	1	..	11	11	12	10	16	6	6	3	15
17	15	44	48	95	85	107	71	69	36	28	28	16
18	5	24	8	998	18	134	3	161	8	243	9	17
..	2	2	4	4	10	8	6	3	8	9	5	18
4	9	22	29	71	46	79	43	63	21	16	9	19
12	19	658	21	524	73	116	56	36	23	22	12	20
81	74	60	47	253	70	205	101	509	46	118	59	21
44	68	855	149	1,549	315	412	248	308	169	96	85	22
30	72	1,191	32	1,481	109	199	94	62	42	47	14	23
..	2	3	4	16	8	11	7	13	6	3	..	24
12	1	66	18	128	47	71	40	44	24	32	11	25
15	51	752	63	910	162	325	138	34	32	10	5	26
4	2	2	8	22	15	18	21	21	10	1	10	27
2	6	5	14	32	28	34	30	49	27	20	16	28
3	9	1	9	13	16	25	31	38	28	7	8	29
46	26	870	114	1,055	224	229	186	121	90	110	46	30
45	34	315	124	746	342	588	322	411	163	173	105	31
24	12	887	43	1,018	216	277	153	73	45	34	25	32
..	..	2	4	4	14	8	12	13	10	9	12	33
1	2	7	8	22	17	26	12	22	9	3	4	34
5	8	14	13	19	15	27	22	19	16	11	8	35

* Includes figures for New Delhi.

Table XIX.—Europeans and Allied Races and Anglo-

A.—Europeans and Allied

(b)

	Cities.	All ages. Persons.	All ages. Males.	All ages. Females.	0—13 Males.	0—13 Females.	14—16 Males.	14—16 Females.
	1	22	23	24	25	26	27	28
1	Calcutta	1,663	1,104	559	115	118	26	32
2	Bombay	1,009	677	332	44	61	10	9
3	Madras	342	224	118	16	24	2	2
4	Agra	57	23	34	1	2	..	..
5	Ajmer	138	70	68	19	23	2	..
6	Allahabad	68	28	40	5	4	3	3
7	Amritsar	..	—	—	—	..	..	..
8	Bangalore	40	7	33	—	..	—	..
9	Bangalore Civil and Military Station	129	41	88	2	9	—	4
10	Bareilly	14	4	10	..	2	—	..
11	Benares	22	14	8	1	—	..	..
12	Cawnpore	13	7	6	—	..	..	..
13	Dacca	17	11	6	..	..	..	..
14	Delhi*	95	52	43	3	2	..	1
15	Gorakhpur	4	3	1	..	..	..	..
16	Howrah	27	18	9	1	1	..	..
17	Hyderabad	447	294	153	48	36	34	29
18	Jaipur	8	7	1	2	..	..	..
19	Jamshedpur	113	58	55	12	21	2	1
20	Jhansi	32	20	12	2	..	—	—
21	Jubbulpore	53	23	30	4	2	—	1
22	Lahore	146	63	83	12	16	..	4
23	Lucknow	714	336	378	32	8	26	21
24	Madura	52	25	27	5	..	..	..
25	Mandalay	55	21	34	3	1	..	..
26	Meerut	31	18	13	3	2	..	..
27	Moradabad	4	2	2	—	..	..	..
28	Nagpur	113	55	58	6	9	4	2
29	Patna	29	3	26	..	..	..	..
30	Poona	44	24	20	..	2	..	..
31	Rangoon	495	358	137	11	14	6	3
32	Rawalpindi	89	22	67	..	10	..	2
33	Srinagar	16	7	9	..	1	—	..
34	Trichinopoly	56	33	23	3	1	1	1
35	Vizagapatam	21	9	12	..	..	—	—

* Includes figures for New Delhi.

Indians by Race and Age. Part II—Details by Cities—*contd.*

Races (including Armenians)—*concld.*

Others.

17—23		24—33		34—43		44—53		54 and over.		
Males.	Females.	Males.	Females.	Males.	Females.	Males.	Females.	Males.	Females.	
29	30	31	32	33	34	35	36	37	38	
234	58	284	131	203	113	158	47	84	60	1
96	43	236	93	143	70	97	38	51	18	2
27	6	75	37	53	25	34	17	17	7	3
1	5	7	11	5	10	4	4	5	2	4
10	6	12	21	11	10	10	6	6	2	5
3	3	5	6	3	6	3	6	6	12	6
..	..	..	..	..	..	..	..	..	..	7
..	2	1	8	3	13	..	6	3	4	8
1	3	7	16	5	9	5	12	21	35	9
1	..	1	1	1	2	1	2	..	3	10
3	..	8	3	..	3	1	1	1	1	11
..	..	5	6	1	..	..	..	1	..	12
..	2	1	..	5	3	2	..	3	1	13
2	4	15	13	16	14	11	1	5	8	14
..	..	1	..	1	..	1	1	..	..	15
3	..	4	3	3	3	3	2	4	..	16
59	33	75	25	49	16	10	4	19	10	17
..	..	2	..	..	..	..	1	3	..	18
2	5	7	5	17	15	14	7	4	1	19
5	..	6	2	3	5	2	2	2	3	20
1	..	8	9	6	7	..	1	4	10	21
3	10	12	17	19	15	12	15	5	6	22
114	83	22	125	42	135	100	5	..	1	23
2	2	6	4	2	9	7	10	3	2	24
1	2	1	10	7	12	2	4	7	5	25
1	1	2	3	3	7	6	..	3	..	26
..	..	..	2	..	..	2	..	..	..	27
7	7	13	10	14	9	6	7	5	14	28
..	..	1	4	..	6	1	4	1	12	29
..	7	2	8	9	4	10	5	3	..	30
57	9	118	33	73	38	45	26	48	14	31
4	4	12	33	4	13	1	4	1	1	32
..	..	1	..	2	5	3	1	1	2	33
..	3	1	3	6	..	9	13	13	2	34
..	1	..	1	2	2	3	5	4	3	35

Table XIX.—Europeans and Allied Races and Anglo-

B.—Anglo-

	Cities.		All ages.			0—3.		4—6.		7—13.		14—
			Persons.	Males.	Females.	Males.	Females.	Males.	Females.	Males.	Females.	Males.
	1		39	40	41	42	43	44	45	46	47	48
1	Calcutta	..	16,863	8,246	8,617	680	630	537	495	1,345	1,357	590
2	Bombay	..	7,039	3,905	3,134	227	230	200	189	611	450	239
3	Madras	..	10,657	5,083	5,574	410	419	415	320	898	853	419
4	Agra ..	..	1,274	712	562	46	40	53	47	151	108	69
4	Ajmer ..	..	1,213	652	561	57	60	48	52	123	102	52
6	Allahabad	..	2,691	1,362	1,329	144	111	99	83	299	252	121
7	Amritsar	..	24	16	8	..	..	1	2	3	..	..
8	Bangalore	..	416	175	241	16	25	21	12	30	28	11
9	Bangalore Civil and Military Station.		5,520	2,401	3,119	169	174	168	144	588	518	293
10	Bareilly ..	..	133	65	68	7	7	6	2	10	4	2
11	Benares ..	..	184	82	102	16	14	10	13	8	12	1
12	Cawnpore	..	493	222	271	11	18	12	15	31	52	16
13	Dacca ..	..	246	127	119	13	10	9	12	22	41	15
14	Delhi* ..	..	1,004	530	474	39	47	48	28	70	72	17
15	Gorakhpur	..	400	212	188	22	24	21	15	30	26	9
16	Howrah .	..	1,218	654	564	60	65	51	42	120	62	34
17	Hyderabad	..	2,832	1,889	943	82	66	83	48	95	54	110
18	Jaipur ..	..	4	4	..	..	..	..	..	..	..	..
19	Jamshedpur	..	527	314	213	28	30	28	24	48	31	12
20	Jhansi ..	..	927	468	459	63	47	44	42	63	71	13
21	Jubbulpore	..	1,255	698	557	55	60	45	34	172	69	91
22	Lahore ..	..	1,037	796	241	70	12	44	31	104	22	61
23	Lucknow..	..	1,525	877	648	40	37	106	42	138	108	144
24	Madura ..	..	654	345	309	47	41	36	29	59	50	23
25	Mandalay	..	1,092	470	622	48	48	33	37	134	133	65
26	Meerut ..	..	252	107	145	9	8	8	7	11	14	8
27	Moradabad	..	292	148	144	3	1	4	3	27	21	21
28	Nagpur ..	..	1,377	743	634	71	70	59	51	155	111	58
29	Patna ..	..	482	173	309	25	20	13	19	17	92	7
30	Poona ..	..	1,476	621	855	32	52	44	65	83	188	39
31	Rangoon	..	9,977	5,071	4,906	462	397	352	340	807	841	333
32	Rawalpindi	..	586	299	287	37	47	24	22	38	37	1
33	Srinagar ..	..	75	28	47	2	1	1	3	4	5	..
34	Trichinopoly	..	1,136	483	653	40	46	43	24	92	170	23
35	Vizagapatam	..	783	422	361	17	22	24	27	89	60	52

Indians by Race and Age. Part II—Details by Cities—*concld.*

Indians.

-16.	17—19.		20—29.		30—39.		40—49.		50—59		60—69		70 and over.		
Females.	Males.	Females.	Males.	Females.	Males.	Females.	Males.	Females.	Males.	Females.	Males.	Females.	Males.	Females	
49	50	51	52	53	54	55	56	57	58	59	60	61	62	63	
763	626	660	1,497	1,631	1,178	1,133	886	808	490	602	255	311	162	227	1
157	325	295	819	750	772	567	441	266	169	131	85	71	17	28	2
422	369	492	869	1,075	576	714	441	505	382	391	213	259	91	124	3
63	57	44	114	97	96	68	58	36	31	31	17	22	20	6	4
46	56	38	136	91	79	80	60	52	23	19	11	17	7	4	5
98	67	83	178	208	167	184	135	113	88	104	51	60	13	33	6
1	3	..	2	4	4	..	..	1	3	..	..	..	..	..	7
14	9	29	27	50	18	35	18	27	16	10	6	7	3	4	8
269	132	226	257	479	170	319	138	342	199	327	182	208	105	113	9
5	4	5	8	14	9	8	12	12	6	8	..	2	1	1	10
5	5	9	14	19	9	7	7	11	6	11	3	1	3	..	11
25	20	26	44	53	33	32	26	27	20	17	6	2	3	4	12
19	7	8	25	11	12	5	15	10	5	1	3	2	1	..	13
17	28	36	79	93	112	86	97	48	29	30	9	11	2	6	14
9	16	11	38	28	38	36	18	22	10	6	6	5	4	6	15
31	55	50	111	124	126	71	62	62	20	32	11	19	4	6	16
58	201	106	507	189	259	103	360	172	97	70	72	54	23	23	17
..	..	..	1	..	2	..	..	..	..	..	..	..	1	..	18
7	24	15	64	42	55	38	37	15	14	3	3	7	1	1	19
27	27	34	86	83	79	77	49	33	25	25	14	13	5	7	20
72	43	37	94	87	66	72	69	55	29	38	17	19	17	14	21
14	65	18	154	42	137	46	82	29	45	13	19	9	15	5	22
57	85	52	151	133	83	86	68	54	40	37	15	29	7	13	23
20	27	25	50	54	41	43	41	20	13	16	7	10	1	1	24
60	44	34	77	85	80	61	48	40	24	17	14	5	3	2	25
8	9	8	19	18	15	14	13	25	8	27	4	8	3	8	26
37	15	14	33	32	17	13	18	11	4	6	4	3	2	3	27
49	53	47	107	99	92	87	80	66	45	26	16	18	7	10	28
38	9	26	19	54	35	31	29	13	13	7	6	7	—	2	29
102	39	70	119	145	82	80	63	79	43	40	15	29	62	5	30
356	322	345	990	1,029	792	696	547	445	289	249	127	155	47	53	31
17	22	21	62	62	50	39	31	24	16	10	5	6	1	2	32
1	..	5	3	5	7	5	7	4	3	7	—	10	1	1	33
90	43	59	88	102	52	74	44	40	36	26	13	13	9	9	34
22	34	21	69	62	57	47	31	54	32	16	9	22	8	8	35

Includes figures for New Delhi.

TABLE XX.

Summary Figures for Districts.

This table contains a summary of the detailed statistics in Tables I, II and XVI of Provincial Reports for the individual Districts or States in each Province, State or Agency. For more detailed information regarding these minor units reference should be made to the relevant Provincial Reports.

The figures for the Central India Agency include those for Khaniadhana State, political relations with which are conducted by the Resident at Gwalior.

Table XX.—Summary

District or State.	Area in square miles.	Population, 1931. Persons.	Males.	Females.	Population, 1921.	Percentage of variation. 1921-31.	1911-21.	Number of persons per square mile in 1931.	1921.
1	2	3	4	5	6	7	8	9	10
INDIA ..	**1,808,679**	**352,837,778**	**181,828,923**	**171,008,855**	**318,942,480**	**+10·6**	**+1·2**	**195**	**176**
AJMER-MERWARA.	**2,711**	**560,292**	**296,081**	**264,211**	**495,271**	+13·1	—1·2	207	183
ANDAMAN & NICOBAR ISLANDS	**3,143**	**29,463**	**19,702**	**9,761**	**27,086**	+8·8	+2·4	9	9
1 Andamans	2,508	19,223	14,258	4,965	17,814	+7·9	+1·0	8	7
2 Nicobars	635	10,240	5,444	4,796	9,272	+10·4	+5·1	16	15
ASSAM	**67,334**	**9,247,857**	**4,844,133**	**4,403,724**	**7,990,246**	+15·7	+13·2	137	119
British Territory	**55,014**	**8,622,251**	**4,537,206**	**4,085,045**	**7,459,128**	+15·6	+13·4	157	136
Surma Valley and Hill Division	*24,170*	*3,708,047*	*1,913,144*	*1,794,903*	*3,424,010*	*+8·3*	*+3·4*	*153*	*142*
1 Cachar	3,862	570,531	301,338	269,193	529,301	+7·8	+6·0	148	137
2 Sylhet	5,478	2,724,342	1,407,645	1,316,697	2,541,341	+7·2	+2·7	497	464
3 Khasia and Jaintia Hills ..	2,445	109,926	55,439	54,487	96,161	+14·3	—3·4	45	39
4 Naga Hills	4,293	178,844	89,536	89,308	158,801	+12·6	+6·6	42	37
5 Lushai Hills	8,092	124,404	59,186	65,218	98,406	+26·4	+7·9	15	12
Assam Valley Division ..	*27,084*	*4,855,711*	*2,592,144*	*2,263,567*	*3,990,203*	*+21·7*	*+22·9*	*179*	*147*
6 Goalpara	3,985	882,748	470,273	412,475	762,523	+15·8	+26·9	222	191
7 Kamrup	3,844	976,746	513,345	463,401	763,571	+27·9	+14·2	254	199
8 Darrang	2,842	584,817	317,103	267,714	477,188	+22·6	+27·0	206	168
9 Nowgong	3,896	562,581	298,585	263,996	398,007	+41·3	+31·9	144	102
10 Sibsagar	5,131	933,326	496,288	437,038	823,197	+13·4	+19·1	182	160
11 Lakhimpur	4,234	724,582	399,108	325,474	586,577	+23·5	+30·4	171	139
12 Garo Hills	3,152	190,911	97,442	93,469	179,140	+6·6	+12·7	61	57
Sadiya Frontier Tract ..	*3,200*	*53,345*	*28,686*	*24,659*	*41,249*	*+29·3*	*+122·5*	*17*	*13*
Balipara Frontier Tract ..	*560*	*5,148*	*3,232*	*1,916*	*3,666*	*+40·4*	*+324·8*	*9*	*7*
Assam States	**12,320**	**625,606**	**306,927**	**318,679**	**531,118**	+17·8	+10·2	51	43
1 Manipur	8,620	445,606	215,815	229,791	384,016	+16·0	+10·9	52	45
2 Khasi States	3,700	180,000	91,112	88,888	147,102	+22·4	+8·5	49	40
BALUCHISTAN ..	**134,638**	**868,617**	**488,414**	**380,203**	**799,625**	+8·6	—4·2	6	6
Districts and Administered Territories.	**54,228**	**463,508**	**270,004**	**193,504**	**420,648**	+10·2	+1·5	9	8
1 Quetta-Pishin	4,806	147,541	90,302	57,239	135,809	+8·6	+8·2	31	28
2 Loralai	7,525	86,087	47,936	38,151	82,473	+4·4	+2·1	11	11
3 Zhob	10,315	57,963	34,596	23,367	56,668	+2·3	—19·5	6	5
4 Bolan	359	4,688	3,466	1,222	4,874	—3·8	+69·2	13	14
5 Chagai	20,036	24,224	13,721	10,503	22,616	+7·1	+22·8	1	1
6 Sibi	11,187	143,005	79,983	63,022	118,208	+21·0	+1·5	13	11
Baluchistan States ..	**80,410**	**405,109**	**218,410**	**186,699**	**378,977**	+6·9	—9·8	5	5
1 Kalat	73,278	342,101	184,915	157,186	328,281	+4·2	—8·6	5	4
2 Las Bela	7,132	63,008	33,495	29,513	50,696	+24·3	—17·2	9	7
BENGAL.	**82,955**	**51,087,338**	**26,557,860**	**24,529,478**	**47,599,233**	+7·3	+2·8	616	574
British Territory. ..	**77,521**	**50,114,002**	**26,041,698**	**24,072,304**	**46,702,307**	+7·3	+2·7	646	602
Burdwan Division. ..	*13,984*	*8,647,189*	*4,452,882*	*4,194,307*	*8,050,642*	*+7·4*	*—4·9*	*618*	*576*
1 Burdwan..	2,705	1,575,699	814,891	760,808	1,434,771	+9·8	—6·5	583	530
2 Birbhum	1,699	947,554	472,687	474,867	851,725	+11·3	—9·4	558	501
3 Bankura	2,625	1,111,721	557,074	554,647	1,019,941	+9·0	—10·4	424	389
4 Midnapur	5,245	2,799,093	1,417,025	1,382,068	2,666,660	+5·0	—5·5	534	508
5 Hooghly	1,188	1,114,255	592,130	522,125	1,080,142	+3·2	—0·9	938	909
6 Howrah	522	1,098,867	599,075	499,792	997,403	+10·2	+5·7	2,105	1,911
Presidency Division ..	*17,853*	*10,108,229*	*5,475,366*	*4,632,863*	*9,446,124*	*+7·0*	*+0·3*	*566*	*529*
7 Twenty-four Parganas ..	5,257	2,713,874	1,464,953	1,248,921	2,458,792	+10·4	+7·5	516	468
8 Calcutta	33	1,196,734	814,948	381,786	1,077,264	+11·1	+3·3	36,265	32,644
9 Nadia	2,881	1,529,632	788,885	740,747	1,494,698	+2·3	—8·0	531	519
10 Murshidabad	2,091	1,370,677	683,483	687,194	1,224,181	+12·0	—9·0	656	585
11 Jessore	2,902	1,671,164	871,446	799,718	1,722,219	—3·0	—1·2	576	593
12 Khulna	4,689	1,626,148	851,651	774,497	1,468,970	+10·7	+6·7	347	313
Rajshahi Division ..	*19,163*	*10,668,066*	*5,549,437*	*5,118,629*	*10,387,046*	*+2·7*	*+2·1*	*557*	*542*
13 Rajshahi	2,609	1,429,018	741,295	687,723	1,497,338	—4·6	+1·0	548	574
14 Dinajpur	3,948	1,755,432	924,092	831,340	1,711,895	+2·5	+1·0	445	434
15 Jalpaiguri	2,932	983,357	533,819	449,538	936,269	+5·0	+3·7	335	319
16 Darjiling	1,212	319,635	170,131	149,504	282,748	+13·0	+6·5	264	233
17 Rangpur	3,496	2,594,785	1,356,594	1,238,191	2,503,215	+3·7	+5·1	742	716

Figures for Districts.

Distribution by Religion.										
Hindu.		Muslim.		Tribal.		Christian.		Others.		
Males. 11	Females. 12	Males. 13	Females. 14	Males. 15	Females. 16	Males. 17	Females. 18	Males. 19	Females. 20	
122,616,300	**116,578,840**	**40,867,320**	**36,810,225**	**4,119,267**	**4,161,080**	**3,227,090**	**3,069,673**	**9,790,635**	**9,289,127**	
227,803	**206,706**	**52,665**	**44,468**	**777**	**732**	4,000	**2,947**	**10,836**	**9,358**	
5,455	**2,163**	**4,966**	**1,753**	**5,144**	**4,811**	984	**477**	**3,153**	**557**	
5,442	2,161	4,722	1,712	255	219	797	326	3,042	547	1
13	2	244	41	4,889	4,592	187	151	111	10	2
2,751,657	**2,452,993**	**1,461,762**	**1,318,752**	**493,755**	**498,635**	**124,045**	**125,201**	**12,914**	**8,143**	
2,616,644	**2,315,116**	**1,449,073**	**1,306,841**	**357,292**	**354,140**	**101,640**	**100,946**	**12,557**	**8,002**	
779,541	*714,415*	*933,218*	*868,520*	*145,819*	*151,466*	*53,284*	*59,648*	*1,282*	*854*	
189,914	169,337	103,718	92,478	5,160	5,159	2,427	2,175	119	44	1
575,661	537,765	828,123	775,682	1,932	1,822	1,650	1,335	279	93	2
7,397	3,444	708	176	36,032	38,736	11,207	12,107	95	24	3
4,236	2,212	523	175	73,182	75,107	11,324	11,584	271	230	4
2,333	1,657	146	9	29,513	30,642	26,676	32,447	518	463	5
1,819,807	*1,588,184*	*515,217*	*438,082*	*199,357*	*190,491*	*47,970*	*40,953*	*9,793*	*5,857*	
208,376	177,530	205,386	182,323	45,912	43,477	9,796	8,740	803	405	6
370,688	339,307	128,785	111,637	9,946	9,547	3,034	2,549	892	361	7
246,546	209,110	37,529	29,974	23,469	20,901	8,453	7,263	1,106	466	8
172,664	153,052	95,597	82,165	27,094	26,000	2,615	2,428	615	351	9
445,670	395,378	24,916	18,991	16,744	15,290	7,152	6,079	1,806	1,300	10
360,774	300,946	17,541	8,408	7,998	6,763	8,356	6,508	4,439	2,849	11
15,089	12,861	5,463	4,584	68,194	68,513	8,564	7,386	132	125	12
14,809	*11,193*	*579*	*226*	*11,677*	*11,809*	*231*	*207*	*1,390*	*1,224*	
2,487	*1,324*	*59*	*13*	*439*	*374*	*155*	*138*	*92*	*67*	
135,013	**137,877**	**12,689**	**11,911**	**136,463**	**144,495**	**22,405**	**24,255**	**357**	**141**	
124,343	132,912	11,329	11,535	74,850	79,954	5,110	5,291	183	99	1
10,670	4,965	1,360	376	61,613	64,541	17,295	18,964	174	42	2
				Sikh.						
36,180	**17,501**	**440,089**	**358,004**	**6,270**	**2,155**	**5,637**	**2,422**	**238**	**121**	
29,529	**11,903**	**228,389**	**176,920**	**6,227**	**2,141**	**5,625**	**2,419**	**234**	**121**	
19,212	7,506	62,024	45,921	3,754	1,501	5,169	2,201	143	110	1
2,403	1,101	44,943	36,869	447	115	143	66	..	..	2
2,402	437	31,025	22,819	1,039	95	99	16	31	..	3
908	257	2,333	896	143	30	56	35	26	4	4
891	422	12,722	10,047	89	28	19	6	..	..	5
3,713	2,180	75,342	60,368	755	372	139	95	34	7	6
6,651	**5,598**	**211,700**	**181,084**	**43**	**14**	**12**	**3**	**4**	..	
5,841	4,965	179,027	152,207	31	11	12	3	4	..	1
810	633	32,673	28,877	12	3	..	..	..	..	2
				Tribal.						
11,639,285	**10,572,784**	**14,366,757**	**13,443,343**	**269,510**	**259,909**	**97,262**	**85,805**	**185,046**	**167,637**	
11,299,914	**10,270,493**	**14,200,142**	**13,297,482**	**268,757**	**259,280**	**95,849**	**84,450**	**177,036**	**160,599**	
3,684,470	*3,479,971*	*636,788*	*585,991*	*119,227*	*118,888*	*10,156*	*8,385*	*2,241*	*1,072*	
639,304	599,568	152,442	140,029	19,742	18,522	2,966	2,474	437	215	1
317,330	319,095	125,985	126,923	28,706	28,354	335	295	331	200	2
506,326	505,328	26,462	24,550	23,423	23,960	848	797	15	12	3
1,262,749	1,230,240	107,890	104,583	42,369	43,876	3,232	2,857	785	512	4
489,398	434,663	97,214	83,003	4,794	4,063	630	377	94	19	5
469,363	391,077	126,795	106,903	193	113	2,145	1,585	579	114	6
2,835,998	*2,343,129*	*2,551,004*	*2,220,161*	*30,892*	*27,770*	*44,544*	*36,729*	*12,928*	*5,074*	
945,206	797,181	487,774	425,459	19,891	17,060	11,103	8,860	979	361	7
547,846	274,447	229,311	81,844	327	99	26,243	21,241	11,221	4,155	8
294,404	279,642	488,911	456,004	234	211	5,225	4,817	111	73	9
294,703	294,848	378,983	382,599	9,058	9,049	169	229	570	469	10
326,807	307,423	543,840	491,531	325	316	471	448	3	..	11
427,032	389,588	422,185	382,724	1,057	1,035	1,333	1,134	44	16	12
1,961,798	*1,759,928*	*3,428,619*	*3,211,684*	*103,006*	*97,591*	*18,842*	*16,497*	*37,172*	*32,929*	
171,347	154,671	559,514	523,591	9,477	8,629	793	736	164	96	13
422,240	371,592	463,994	422,729	33,877	33,527	3,644	3,337	337	155	14
360,721	303,294	128,429	107,522	32,162	28,513	8,021	6,746	4,486	3,463	15
126,585	110,328	5,220	3,171	3,589	3,374	4,431	3,849	30,306	28,782	16
394,730	351,816	955,458	881,382	4,279	3,974	879	807	1,248	212	17

Table XX.—Summary

District or State.	Area in square miles.	Population, 1931.			Population, 1921.	Percentage of variation.		Number of persons per square mile in	
		Persons.	Males.	Females.		1921-31.	1911-21.	1931.	1921.
1	2	3	4	5	6	7	8	9	10
BENGAL—*concld.*									
18 Bogra	1,384	1,086,419	557,174	529,245	1,049,322	+3·5	+6·6	785	758
19 Pabna	1,818	1,445,654	739,027	706,627	1,393,850	+3·7	—2·7	795	767
20 Malda	1,764	1,053,766	527,305	526,461	1,012,409	+4·1	—1·3	597	574
Dacca Division. ..	*14,829*	*13,864,104*	*7,122,397*	*6,741,707*	*12,816,184*	*+8·2*	*+7·1*	*935*	*864*
21 Dacca	2,713	3,432,577	1,743,517	1,689,060	3,156,936	+8·7	+8·2	1,265	1,164
22 Maimansingh	6,237	5,130,262	2,667,194	2,463,068	4,837,219	+6·1	+6·9	823	776
23 Faridpur	2,356	2,362,215	1,206,348	1,155,867	2,219,250	+6·4	+4·8	1,003	942
24 Bakarganj	3,523	2,939,050	1,505,338	1,433,712	2,602,779	+12·9	+8·2	834	739
Chittagong Division. ..	*11,692*	*6,826,414*	*3,441,616*	*3,384,798*	*6,002,311*	*+13·7*	*+9·8*	*584*	*513*
25 Tippera	2,597	3,109,735	1,595,640	1,514,095	2,744,860	+13·3	+9·7	1,197	1,057
26 Noakhali	1,518	1,706,719	858,818	847,901	1,472,786	+15·9	+13·0	1,124	970
27 Chittagong	2,570	1,797,038	872,888	924,150	1,611,422	+11·5	+6·8	699	627
28 Chittagong Hill Tracts ..	5,007	212,922	114,270	98,652	173,243	+22·9	+12·6	43	35
Bengal States. ..	**5,434**	**973,336**	**516,162**	**457,174**	**896,926**	**+8·5**	**+9·0**	**179**	**165**
1 Cooch Behar	1,318	590,886	313,230	277,656	592,489	—0·3	—0·1	448	450
2 Tripura	4,116	382,450	202,932	179,518	304,437	+25·6	+32·6	93	74
Bihar and Orissa. ..	**111,702**	**42,329,583**	**21,082,560**	**21,247,023**	**37,955,087**	**+11·5**	**—1·2**	**379**	**340**
British Territory. ..	**83,054**	**37,677,576**	**18,794,138**	**18,883,438**	**33,995,418**	**+10·8**	**—1·4**	**454**	**409**
Patna Division. ..	*11,154*	*6,228,425*	*3,148,866*	*3,079,559*	*5,544,038*	*+12·3*	*—1·6*	*558*	*497*
1 Patna	2,068	1,846,474	956,124	890,350	1,576,879	+17·1	—2·0	893	763
2 Gaya	4,714	2,388,462	1,193,643	1,194,819	2,152,930	+10·9	—0·4	507	457
3 Shahabad	4,372	1,993,489	999,099	994,390	1,814,229	+9·9	—2·6	456	415
Tirhut Division. ..	*12,598*	*10,739,274*	*5,315,811*	*5,423,463*	*9,949,268*	*+7·9*	*—0·2*	*852*	*790*
4 Saran	2,683	2,486,468	1,220,049	1,266,419	2,339,953	+6·3	+2·2	927	872
5 Champaran	3,531	2,145,687	1,080,956	1,064,731	1,940,841	+10·6	+1·7	608	550
6 Muzaffarpur	3,036	2,941,025	1,443,847	1,497,178	2,754,945	+6·8	—3·2	969	907
7 Darbhanga	3,348	3,166,094	1,570,959	1,595,135	2,913,529	+8·7	—0·6	946	870
Bhagalpur Division ..	*18,583*	*8,759,801*	*4,431,983*	*4,327,818*	*7,880,211*	*+11·2*	*—3·2*	*471*	*424*
8 Monghyr	3,927	2,287,154	1,145,797	1,141,357	2,029,965	+12·7	—4·9	582	517
9 Bhagalpur	4,226	2,234,632	1,130,584	1,104,048	2,033,770	+9·9	—4·9	529	481
10 Purnea	4,972	2,186,543	1,129,681	1,056,862	2,021,568	+8·2	+1·8	440	407
11 Santal Parganas	5,458	2,051,472	1,025,921	1,025,551	1,794,908	+14·3	—4·5	376	329
Orissa Division. ..	*13,706*	*5,306,142*	*2,549,251*	*2,756,891*	*4,968,873*	*+6·8*	*—3·2*	*387*	*363*
12 Cuttack	3,654	2,176,707	1,028,134	1,148,573	2,064,678	+5·4	—2·1	596	565
13 Balasore	2,055	990,600	480,518	510,082	980,504	+1·0	—7·1	482	477
14 Angul	1,681	222,736	108,925	113,811	182,574	+22·0	—8·5	133	109
15 Puri	2,492	1,035,154	500,214	534,940	951,651	+8·8	—7·0	415	382
16 Sambalpur	3,824	880,945	431,460	449,485	789,466	+11·6	+6·1	230	206
Chota Nagpur Division ..	*27,013*	*6,643,934*	*3,348,227*	*3,295,707*	*5,653,028*	*+17·5*	*+0·9*	*246*	*209*
17 Hazaribagh	7,021	1,517,357	751,956	765,401	1,276,946	+18·8	—0·9	216	182
18 Ranchi	7,102	1,567,149	777,063	790,086	1,334,473	+17·4	—3·8	221	188
19 Palamau	4,916	818,736	409,778	408,958	733,394	+11·6	+6·6	167	149
20 Manbhum	4,095	1,810,890	940,009	870,881	1,548,777	+16·9	+0·1	442	378
21 Singhbhum	3,879	929,802	469,421	460,381	759,438	+22·4	+9·4	240	196
Bihar and Orissa States ..	**28,648**	**4,652,007**	**2,288,422**	**2,363,585**	**3,959,669**	**+17·5**	**+0·4**	**162**	**138**
Orissa Feudatory States ..	*28,046*	*4,465,385*	*2,196,691*	*2,268,694*	*3,807,172*	*+17·3*	*+0·3*	*159*	*136*
1 Athgarh	168	50,148	24,843	25,305	42,351	+18·4	—9·5	299	252
2 Talcher	399	69,702	34,674	35,028	51,015	+36·6	—22·9	175	128
3 Mayurbhanj	4,243	889,603	442,378	447,225	754,314	+17·9	+3·4	210	178
4 Nilgiri	278	68,594	34,117	34,477	65,222	+5·2	—5·1	247	235
5 Keonjhar	3,096	460,609	227,143	233,466	379,496	+21·4	+4·1	149	123
6 Pal-Lahara	452	27,974	13,835	14,139	23,789	+17·6	—7·4	62	53
7 Dhenkanal	1,463	284,326	136,646	147,680	233,691	+21·7	—13·5	194	160
8 Athmalik	730	64,272	32,287	31,985	59,749	+7·6	+11·1	88	82
9 Hindol	312	48,896	23,419	25,477	38,617	+26·6	—22·5	157	124
10 Narsinghpur	199	40,878	19,925	20,953	33,002	+23·9	—17·4	205	166
11 Baramba	134	46,688	22,596	24,092	38,630	+20·9	—6·8	348	288
12 Tigiria	46	24,822	12,141	12,681	19,534	+27·1	—15·9	540	425
13 Khandpara	244	77,929	37,281	40,648	64,289	+21·2	—12·9	319	263
14 Nayagarh	588	142,406	67,221	75,185	122,842	+15·9	—18·8	242	209
15 Ranpur	203	47,711	22,412	25,299	41,282	+15·6	—10·2	235	203

Figures for Districts—*contd.*

Distribution by Religion.										
Hindu.		Muslim.		Tribal.		Christian.		Others.		
Males. 11	Females. 12	Males. 13	Females. 14	Males. 15	Females. 16	Males. 17	Females. 18	Males. 19	Females. 20	
94,526	83,103	461,007	444,631	1,116	1,178	240	236	285	97	18
168,030	164,337	570,062	541,650	397	347	238	190	300	103	19
223,619	220,787	284,935	287,008	18,109	18,049	596	596	46	21	20
2,030,613	*1,928,257*	*5,055,847*	*4,777,442*	*9,002*	*8,840*	*20,405*	*21,041*	*6,530*	*6,127*	
568,529	556,364	1,168,390	1,125,006	2	..	6,542	7,668	54	22	21
619,114	555,214	2,033,595	1,893,957	8,739	8,655	5,586	5,178	160	64	22
426,748	420,316	775,462	731,695	260	184	3,868	3,669	10	3	23
416,222	396,363	1,078,400	1,026,784	1	1	4,409	4,526	6,306	6,038	24
787,035	*759,208*	*2,527,884*	*2,502,204*	*6,630*	*6,191*	*1,902*	*1,798*	*118,165*	*115,397*	
384,341	366,383	1,210,070	1,146,539	..	..	278	259	951	914	25
187,188	179,203	671,021	668,034	3	..	371	424	235	240	26
195,407	196,945	640,670	685,538	544	515	870	739	35,397	40,413	27
20,099	16,677	6,123	2,093	6,083	5,676	383	376	81,582	73,830	28
339,371	**302,291**	**166,615**	**145,861**	**753**	**629**	**1,413**	**1,355**	**8,010**	**7,038**	
201,513	178,560	110,468	98,288	753	629	95	77	401	102	1
137,858	123,731	56,147	47,573	..	..	1,318	1,278	7,609	6,936	2
17,556,265	**17,650,087**	**2,123,112**	**2,161,194**	**1,188,440**	**1,220,969**	**207,185**	**209,541**	**7,558**	**5,232**	
15,493,257	**15,518,217**	**2,112,814**	**2,151,976**	**1,011,522**	**1,037,287**	**170,128**	**171,766**	**6,417**	**4,192**	
2,852,459	*2,759,773*	*291,871*	*315,712*	*29*	*2*	*3,371*	*3,043*	*1,136*	*1,029*	
852,682	787,147	101,175	101,480	17	2	1,990	1,513	260	208	1
1,075,495	1,058,046	117,436	136,124	12	..	298	278	402	371	2
924,282	914,580	73,260	78,108	..	..	1,083	1,252	474	450	3
4,588,475	*4,650,216*	*724,206*	*770,162*	*259*	*233*	*2,730*	*2,803*	*141*	*49*	
1,072,048	1,104,936	147,703	161,302	1	..	282	178	15	3	4
903,010	884,264	175,988	178,247	252	233	1,681	1,974	25	13	5
1,258,489	1,290,517	184,852	206,239	6	..	481	406	19	16	6
1,354,928	1,370,499	215,663	224,374	..	..	286	245	82	17	7
3,175,181	*3,088,785*	*803,851*	*784,152*	*442,769*	*445,078*	*9,376*	*9,270*	*806*	*533*	
1,031,465	1,017,727	109,408	119,089	3,838	3,670	1,058	859	28	12	8
1,002,664	977,598	125,257	124,179	1,601	1,443	881	679	181	149	9
665,451	619,863	456,347	430,021	6,395	5,772	973	850	515	356	10
475,601	473,597	112,839	110,863	430,935	434,193	6,464	6,882	82	16	11
2,449,295	*2,647,136*	*58,685*	*65,778*	*36,295*	*38,596*	*4,611*	*5,098*	*365*	*283*	
996,424	1,110,406	29,965	36,139	272	166	1,222	1,651	251	211	12
457,943	486,738	15,661	16,074	6,220	6,576	685	690	9	4	13
80,344	83,319	176	117	28,249	30,224	156	151	..	..	14
488,555	522,524	10,875	11,643	..	..	768	768	16	5	15
426,029	444,149	2,008	1,805	1,554	1,630	1,780	1,838	89	63	16
2,427,847	*2,372,307*	*234,201*	*216,172*	*532,170*	*553,378*	*150,040*	*151,552*	*3,969*	*2,298*	
597,528	610,571	84,799	86,895	67,192	65,964	1,706	1,463	731	508	17
433,323	436,169	33,778	32,269	179,477	188,770	130,114	132,494	371	384	18
335,519	334,442	37,369	37,132	32,632	33,015	4,242	4,365	16	4	19
824,012	768,515	61,712	49,665	50,253	48,907	3,922	3,734	110	60	20
237,465	222,610	16,543	10,211	202,616	216,722	10,056	9,496	2,741	1,342	21
2,063,008	**2,121,870**	**10,298**	**9,218**	**176,918**	**183,682**	**37,057**	**37,775**	**1,141**	**1,040**	
1,999,547	*2,067,629*	*8,975*	*8,125*	*150,172*	*154,330*	*36,878*	*37,590*	*1,119*	*1,020*	
24,543	25,024	140	126	..	..	160	155	..	..	1
34,341	34,788	129	57	118	130	68	45	18	8	2
435,570	440,849	2,854	2,456	3,463	3,501	473	412	18	7	3
34,033	34,418	35	16	..	..	49	43	..	..	4
185,974	192,262	693	622	40,402	40,519	71	59	3	4	5
13,820	14,127	15	11	..	..	..	1	..	..	6
136,229	147,301	399	361	..	..	18	17	..	1	7
31,968	31,672	51	33	262	279	5	1	1	..	8
23,298	25,329	45	59	74	89	2	..	..	..	9
19,854	20,881	69	70	..	..	2	2	..	..	10
22,050	23,559	112	88	..	..	5	3	429	442	11
11,644	12,153	256	282	..	..	..	..	241	246	12
37,219	40,606	56	38	..	..	8	4	..	..	13
66,681	74,615	299	324	233	242	8	4	..	..	14
22,217	25,090	195	200	..	..	..	...	..	..	15

Table XX.—Summary

District or State. 1	Area in square miles. 2	Population, 1931. Persons. 3	Males. 4	Females. 5	Population, 1921. 6	Percentage of variation. 1921-31. 7	1911-21. 8	Number of persons per square mile in 1931. 9	1921. 10
Bihar and Orissa States—*concld.*									
16 Daspalla	568	43,402	20,896	22,506	34,509	+25·8	—39·5	76	61
17 Baud	1,264	135,248	67,070	68,178	124,411	+8·7	+9·7	107	98
18 Bamra	1,988	151,047	73,285	77,762	134,721	+12·1	—2·4	76	68
19 Rairakhol	833	35,710	17,727	17,983	31,225	+14·4	—1·6	43	37
20 Sonpur	906	237,920	117,067	120,853	226,751	+4·9	+5·1	263	250
21 Patna	2,399	566,924	280,305	286,619	494,456	+14·7	+21·0	236	206
22 Kalahandi	3,745	513,716	252,438	261,278	415,827	+23·5	—0·7	137	111
23 Gangpur	2,492	356,674	176,959	179,715	309,271	+15·3	+1·8	143	124
24 Bonai	1,296	80,186	40,026	40,160	68,178	+17·6	+16·9	62	53
Chota Nagpur States ..	*602*	*186,622*	*91,731*	*94,891*	*152,497*	*+22·4*	*+2·6*	*310*	*253*
25 Saraikela	449	143,525	70,990	72,535	115,192	+24·6	+4·9	320	257
26 Kharsawan	153	43,097	20,741	22,356	37,305	+15·5	—4·0	282	244
BOMBAY (*including Aden*) ..	**151,673**	**26,398,997**	**13,824,526**	**12,574,471**	**23,216,038**	**+13·7**	**—1·2**	**174**	**153**
British Territory (*excluding Aden*).	**123,599**	**21,879,123**	**11,503,558**	**10,375,565**	**19,291,719**	**+13·4**	**—1·8**	**177**	**156**
1 Bombay City	24	1,161,383	747,381	414,002	1,175,914	—1·2	+20·0	48,391	48,996
Northern Division.	*13,615*	*4,060,352*	*2,113,626*	*1,946,726*	*3,716,683*	*+9·2*	*+3·8*	*298*	*273*
2 Ahmadabad	3,846	*999,768	528,190	471,578	890,911	+12·2	+7·6	260	232
3 Broach	1,468	334,170	174,894	159,276	307,745	+8·6	+0·3	228	210
4 Kaira	1,620	741,650	395,104	346,546	710,982	+4·3	+2·8	458	439
5 Panch Mahals	1,608	454,526	236,622	217,904	374,860	+21·3	+16·1	283	233
6 Surat	1,651	693,613	348,283	345,330	674,351	+2·9	+3·1	420	408
7 Thana	3,422	836,625	430,533	406,092	757,834	+10·4	—2·7	244	221
Central Division ..	*38,553*	*7,372,637*	*3,764,586*	*3,608,051*	*6,214,036*	*+18·6*	*—4·6*	*191*	*161*
8 Ahmednagar	6,611	988,206	501,186	487,020	731,552	+35·1	—22·6	149	111
9 Khandesh, East	4,551	1,206,035	612,693	593,342	1,075,837	+12·1	+3·9	265	236
10 Khandesh, West	6,401	771,794	391,800	379,994	641,847	+20·2	+6·2	121	100
11 Nasik	5,882	1,000,048	508,865	491,183	832,576	+20·1	—0·8	170	142
12 Poona	5,332	1,169,798	601,013	568,785	1,009,033	+15·9	—5·8	219	189
13 Satara	5,053	1,179,712	592,303	587,409	1,024,720	+15·1	—5·1	233	203
14 Sholapur	4,569	877,520	453,509	424,011	743,549	+18·0	—3·4	192	163
15 Bombay Suburban District.	154	179,524	103,217	76,307	154,922	+15·9	+49·7	1,166	1,006
Southern Division ..	*25,029*	*5,397,681*	*2,697,011*	*2,700,670*	*4,905,709*	*+10·0*	*—3·1*	*216*	*196*
16 Belgaum	4,612	1,076,701	552,380	524,321	952,996	+13·0	+1·0	233	207
17 Bijapur	5,710	869,220	440,579	428,641	796,876	+9·1	—7·6	152	140
18 Dharwar	4,606	1,102,677	565,641	537,036	1,036,924	+6·3	+1·0	239	225
19 Kanara	3,946	417,835	214,085	203,750	401,727	+4·0	—6·6	106	102
20 Kolaba	2,166	628,721	315,017	313,704	562,942	+11·7	—5·2	290	260
21 Ratnagiri	3,989	1,302,527	609,309	693,218	1,154,244	+12·8	—4·0	327	289
Sind.	*46,378*	*3,887,070*	*2,180,954*	*1,706,116*	*3,279,377*	*+18·5*	*—6·7*	*84*	*71*
22 Hyderabad	4,417	662,924	371,788	291,136	573,450	+15·6	—6·3	150	130
23 Karachi..	11,107	650,240	369,873	280,367	542,065	+20·0	+3·9	59	49
24 Larkana	5,057	693,735	385,705	308,030	597,960	+16·0	—9·5	137	118
25 Nawabshah	3,888	496,612	279,032	217,580	418,660	+18·6	—6·6	128	108
26 Sukkur	5,608	623,779	349,312	274,467	510,292	+22·2	—11·0	111	91
27 Thar and Parkar	13,636	468,040	261,945	206,095	396,331	+18·1	—8·5	34	29
28 Upper Sind Frontier ..	2,665	291,740	163,299	128,441	240,619	+21·2	—8·5	109	90
Aden	**80**	**51,478**	**32,345**	**19,133**	**56,500**	**—8·9**	**+22·4**	**643**	**706**
Bombay States and Agencies	**27,994**	**4,468,396**	**2,288,623**	**2,179,773**	**3,867,819**	**+15·5**	**+0·1**	**160**	**138**
1 Cambay	350	87,761	46,851	40,910	71,762	+22·3	—1·2	251	205
2 Mahi Kantha Agency ..	3,124	518,164	263,398	254,766	450,478	+15·0	+9·2	166	144
Idar — ..	*1,668*	*262,660*	*131,927*	*130,733*	*226,351*	*+16·0*	*+11·6*	*157*	*136*
3 Rewa Kantha Agency ..	4,968	888,086	459,133	428,953	753,058	+17·9	+13·3	179	152
Rajpipla	*1,518*	*206,114*	*106,445*	*99,669*	*168,425*	*+22·4*	*+4·2*	*136*	*111*
4 Savantvadi	926	230,589	110,962	119,627	206,440	+11·7	—5·0	249	223
5 Southern Maratha States ..	6,253	1,648,248	841,856	806,392	1,442,088	+14·3	—1·6	264	231
Kolhapur	*3,217*	*957,137*	*490,336*	*466,801*	*833,726*	*+14·8*	*+0·3*	*298*	*259*
Sangli	*1,111*	*258,442*	*131,989*	*126,453*	*221,321*	*+16·8*	*—2·6*	*233*	*199*
6 Bhor	925	141,546	70,122	71,424	130,420	+8·5	—9·8	153	141
7 Other States	5,398	726,819	371,247	355,572	620,442	+17·1	—8·2	135	115
8 Khairpur (*Sind*)	6,050	227,183	125,054	102,129	193,131	+17·6	—13·7	38	32

* Statistics by religion of 924,033 persons only are available, the rest (75,735) were not enumerated by religion (*vide* paragraph 4 on fly leaf to

Figures for Districts—*contd.*

Distribution by Religion.										
Hindu.		Muslim.		Tribal.		Christian.		Others.		
Males. 11	Females. 12	Males. 13	Females. 14	Males. 15	Females. 16	Males. 17	Females. 18	Males. 19	Females. 20	
20,843	22,479	45	25	..	..	8	2	..	..	16
66,956	68,052	106	113	..	..	8	13	..	..	17
71,834	76,264	137	135	604	625	684	720	26	18	18
16,519	16,743	16	20	1,190	1,217	2	3	..	..	19
116,623	120,482	287	266	148	99	4	4	5	2	20
263,861	269,224	552	457	12,092	13,072	3,491	3,618	309	248	21
217,134	224,316	322	355	34,874	36,513	57	54	51	40	22
106,000	106,766	2,068	1,944	38,663	40,040	30,210	30,961	18	4	23
20,336	20,629	94	58	18,049	18,004	1,547	1,469	..	..	24
63,461	*64,241*	*1,323*	*1,093*	*26,746*	*29,352*	*179*	*185*	*22*	*20*	
48,787	48,719	1,029	805	21,006	22,847	153	158	15	6	25
14,674	15,522	294	288	5,740	6,505	26	27	7	14	26
10,607,867	**9,934,442**	**2,695,986**	**2,175,842**	**77,897**	**77,141**	184,270	**148,778**	**227,832**	**193,207**	
8,608,470	**8,011,166**	**2,447,447**	**1,966,612**	**64,721**	**64,414**	**174,548**	**140,249**	**177,698**	**148,063**	
505,588	284,273	143,918	65,328	2	..	51,466	29,262	46,407	35,139	1
1,738,539	*1,590,258*	*215,825*	*187,302*	*58,456*	*58,342*	*38,426*	*35,692*	*31,706*	*30,071*	
416,559	361,941	65,238	50,621	23	14	3,555	2,717	12,141	11,224	2
128,458	116,596	41,971	38,531	403	365	1,568	1,358	2,494	2,423	3
338,488	294,753	39,115	35,367	408	340	13,981	13,107	3,112	2,979	4
157,106	140,655	18,854	16,632	57,542	57,556	1,985	1,958	1,135	1,103	5
308,040	304,895	29,541	29,516	2	1	1,213	1,154	9,487	9,764	6
389,888	371,418	21,106	16,635	78	66	16,124	15,398	3,337	2,575	7
3,410,808	*3,294,407*	*246,141*	*219,202*	*6,122*	*6,007*	*53,153*	*48,056*	*48,362*	*40,379*	
448,136	438,016	26,283	24,339	345	323	18,292	17,166	8,130	7,176	8
540,079	525,562	65,478	61,624	496	476	1,201	1,039	5,439	4,641	9
363,082	353,714	20,606	18,998	4,373	4,299	874	760	2,865	2,223	10
469,617	456,807	29,774	26,635	821	867	3,579	2,791	5,074	4,083	11
549,928	528,535	31,066	23,931	48	28	10,393	8,813	9,578	7,478	12
559,579	556,943	21,978	20,787	..	..	1,370	1,297	9,376	8,382	13
409,690	383,744	37,700	34,783	1	..	1,678	1,682	4,440	3,802	14
70,697	51,086	13,256	8,105	38	14	15,766	14,508	3,460	2,594	15
2,386,220	*2,392,839*	*251,828*	*253,715*	2	..	*21,980*	*21,629*	*36,981*	*32,487*	
475,239	452,484	48,011	45,213	2	..	3,993	3,894	25,135	22,730	16
384,542	374,689	53,699	51,800	..	..	593	668	1,745	1,484	17
473,250	451,315	81,816	76,615	..	..	4,455	3,954	6,120	5,152	18
189,550	178,838	15,040	15,597	..	..	8,883	8,821	612	494	19
296,630	296,027	15,483	15,523	..	..	648	579	2,256	1,575	20
567,009	639,486	37,779	48,967	..	..	3,408	3,713	1,113	1,052	21
567,315	*449,389*	*1,589,735*	*1,241,065*	*139*	*65*	*9,523*	*5,610*	*14,242*	*9,987*	
109,696	89,104	260,130	200,790	..	..	483	288	1,479	954	22
95,762	66,354	260,607	205,178	115	57	8,307	4,845	5,082	3,933	23
62,614	51,760	322,234	255,665	24	8	88	32	745	565	24
63,411	52,490	213,874	163,872	..	..	75	55	1,672	1,163	25
97,040	80,449	248,484	191,664	..	..	480	347	3,308	2,007	26
121,710	97,140	138,349	107,615	..	..	74	38	1,812	1,302	27
17,082	12,092	146,057	116,281	..	..	16	5	144	63	28
1,021	**564**	**26,953**	**15,885**	..	..	1,762	**483**	**2,609**	**2,201**	
1,998,376	**1,922,712**	**221,586**	**193,345**	**13,176**	**12,727**	7,960	**8,046**	**47,525**	**42,943**	
39,603	34,194	5,377	4,918	..	..	170	87	1,701	1,711	1
243,228	234,856	11,083	10,586	4,000	4,165	321	378	4,766	4,781	2
124,510	*123,571*	*5,429*	*5,073*	..	..	*221*	*260*	*1,767*	*1,829*	
435,407	408,898	18,401	15,158	2,826	2,747	1,117	947	1,382	1,203	3
101,045	*95,325*	*4,330*	*3,525*	*33*	*39*	*484*	*346*	*553*	*434*	
105,763	113,623	2,356	2,674	4	4	2,780	3,288	59	38	4
748,500	720,142	53,163	50,096	13	2	3,295	3,161		32,991	5
443,033	*423,615*	*21,788*	*20,077*	..	..	*2,375*	*2,384*	*23,140*	*20,725*	
115,313	*111,114*	*9,826*	*9,295*	*13*	*2*	*411*	*350*	*6,426*	*5,692*	
69,003	70,428	798	760	..	..	25	12	296	224	6
336,381	321,142	26,225	26,759	6,333	5,809	241	165	2,067	1,697	7
20,491	19,429	104,183	82,394	..	..	11	8	369	298	8

Table D. Hence the details in columns 11-20, do not add up to the totals in columns 3-5.

Table XX.—Summary

District or State.	Area in square miles.	Population, 1931. Persons.	Males.	Females.	Population, 1921.	Percentage of variation. 1921-31.	1911-21.	Number of persons per square mile in 1931.	1921.
1	2	3	4	5	6	7	8	9	10
BURMA ..	**233,492**	***14,667,146**	**7,490,601**	**7,176,545**	**13,212,192**	**+11·0**	**+9·1**	**63**	**57**
Arakan Division. ..	*16,001*	*1,008,535*	*522,609*	*485,926*	*909,246*	*+10·9*	*+8·3*	*63*	*57*
1 Akyab	5,176	637,580	339,643	297,937	576,430	+10·6	+8·8	123	111
2 Hill District of Arakan ..	1,901	21,418	11,031	10,387	20,914	+2·4	—5·9	11	11
3 Kyaukpyu	4,767	220,292	107,729	112,563	199,873	+10·2	+8·1	46	42
4 Sandoway	4,157	129,245	64,206	65,039	112,029	+15·4	+9·0	31	27
Pegu Division ..	*13,799*	*2,549,637*	*1,375,268*	*1,174,369*	*2,310,379*	*+10·4*	*+10·7*	*185*	*167*
5 Rangoon City	77	400,415	271,063	129,352	345,621	+15·9	+16·6	5,200	4,489
6 Pegu	4,124	489,969	254,048	235,921	446,706	+9·7	+16·6	119	108
7 Tharrawaddy	2,815	508,319	252,548	255,771	492,429	+3·2	+13·6	181	175
8 Hanthawaddy	1,931	408,831	218,919	189,912	364,624	+12·1	+9·6	212	189
9 Insein	1,914	331,452	175,519	155,933	289,424	+14·5	+10·5	173	151
10 Prome	2,938	410,651	203,171	207,480	371,575	+10·5	—1·9	140	126
Irrawaddy Division ..	*13,460*	*2,334,774*	*1,199,758*	*1,135,016*	*2,030,044*	*+15·0*	*+8·6*	*173*	*151*
11 Bassein	4,145	571,043	292,029	279,014	489,473	+16·7	+11·0	138	118
12 Henzada	2,782	613,280	303,750	309,530	550,920	+11·3	+3·5	220	198
13 Myaungmya	2,815	444,784	235,655	209,129	370,551	+20·0	+10·7	158	132
14 Maubin	1,642	371,509	188,770	182,739	330,106	+12·5	+8·2	226	201
15 Pyapon	2,076	334,158	179,554	154,604	288,994	+15·6	+12·8	161	139
Tenasserim Division ..	*37,614*	*1,872,668*	*971,431*	*901,237*	*1,612,437*	*+16·1*	*+13·8*	*50*	*43*
16 Salween	2,582	53,186	27,990	25,196	49,028	+8·5	+8·0	21	19
17 Thaton	4,870	532,628	274,942	257,686	472,451	+12·7	+16·2	109	97
18 Amherst	7,410	516,233	270,677	245,556	417,910	+23·5	+13·6	70	56
19 Tavoy	5,390	179,964	92,637	87,327	156,786	+14·8	+15·9	33	29
20 Mergui	10,906	161,987	85,263	76,724	135,465	+19·6	+21·6	15	12
21 Toungoo	6,456	428,670	219,922	208,748	380,797	+12·6	+8·8	66	59
Magwe Division ..	*27,693*	*1,722,044*	*847,600*	*874,444*	1,560,283	*+10·4*	*+9·1*	*62*	*56*
22 Thayetmyo	4,642	274,177	135,565	138,612	255,406	+7·3	+2·9	59	55
23 Minbu	3,594	277,876	136,662	141,214	274,302	+1·3	+4·5	77	76
24 Magwe	3,724	499,573	250,783	248,790	425,926	+17·3	+17·0	134	114
25 Pakokku	5,356	499,181	241,137	258,044	465,771	+7·2	+13·7	93	87
26 Chin Hills	10,377	171,237	83,453	87,784	138,878	+23·3	—4·8	17	13
Mandalay Division ..	*12,504*	*1,696,332*	*836,894*	*859,438*	*1,551,718*	*+9·3*	*+5·8*	*136*	*124*
27 Mandalay	2,115	371,636	191,741	179,895	356,621	+4·2	+4·7	176	169
28 Kyaukse	1,245	151,320	74,880	76,440	142,677	+6·1	+0·8	122	115
29 Meiktila	2,238	309,999	147,171	162,828	289,897	+6·9	+3·3	139	130
30 Myingyan	2,710	472,557	228,784	243,773	439,334	+7·6	+10·8	174	162
31 Yamethin	4,196	390,820	194,318	196,502	323,189	+20·9	+5·5	93	77
Sagaing Division ..	*50,086*	*1,918,058*	*934,671*	*983,387*	*1,740,693*	*+10·2*	*+9·2*	*38*	*35*
32 Bhamo	4,146	121,193	59,984	61,209	112,960	+7·3	+4·8	29	27
33 Myitkyina	12,172	171,524	90,916	80,608	147,807	+16·0	+46·1	14	12
34 Shwebo	5,749	446,790	214,170	232,620	380,016	+17·6	+9·8	78	66
35 Sagaing	1,878	335,965	159,881	176,084	326,908	+2·8	+4·7	179	174
36 Katha	7,593	254,170	126,863	127,307	231,973	+9·6	+0·9	33	31
37 Lower Chindwin	3,681	383,434	178,543	204,891	354,148	+8·3	+8·5	104	96
38 Upper Chindwin	14,867	204,982	104,314	100,668	186,881	+9·7	+9·5	14	13
Eastern States ..	**62,335**	**1,565,098**	**802,370**	**762,728**	**1,497,392**	+4·5	+6·0	**25**	**24**
39 Northern Shan States ..	21,400	636,107	331,136	304,971	585,924	+8·6	+14·4	30	27
40 Southern Shan States ..	36,416	870,230	441,984	428,246	847,618	+2·7	+1·3	24	23
41 Karenni	4,519	58,761	29,250	29,511	63,850	—8·0	+0·3	13	14
CENTRAL PROVINCES AND BERAR.	**131,095**	**17,990,937**	**8,997,203**	**8,993,734**	**15,979,660**	+12·6	—0·3	**137**	**122**
British Territory ..	**99,920**	**15,507,723**	**7,761,818**	**7,745,905**	**13,912,760**	+11·5	—0·0	**155**	**139**
Jubbulpore Division ..	*18,956*	*2,463,466*	*1,240,655*	*1,222,811*	*2,296,508*	*+7·3*	*—5·2*	*130*	*121*
1 Saugor	3,964	544,589	280,385	264,204	528,380	+3·1	—2·4	137	133
2 Damoh	2,807	305,568	154,791	150,777	287,126	+6·4	—13·8	109	102
3 Jubbulpore	3,912	773,811	391,649	382,162	745,685	+3·8	—0·0	198	191
4 Mandla	5,057	445,766	221,359	224,407	386,446	+15·4	—4·6	88	76
5 Seoni	3,216	393,732	192,471	201,261	348,871	+12·9	—11·9	122	108

Statistics by Religion of 14,647,497 persons only are available, the rest (19,649) were

Figures for Districts—*contd.*

Distribution by Religion.										
Buddhist.		Muslim.		Tribal.		Christian.		Others.		
Males. 11	Females. 12	Males. 13	Females. 14	Males. 15	Females. 16	Males. 17	Females. 18	Males. 19	Females. 20	
6,088,257	**6,259,780**	**363,824**	**221,015**	**321,809**	**328,579**	**171,352**	**159,754**	**535,434**	**197,693**	
323,545	*330,154*	*140,276*	*115,193*	*40,654*	*37,692*	*1,033*	*851*	*17,101*	*2,036*	
170,099	167,562	132,976	109,405	20,826	19,039	255	143	15,487	1,788	1
1,386	1,178	88	20	9,404	9,125	10	6	143	58	2
94,038	101,114	3,736	2,958	9,070	8,301	104	108	781	82	3
58,022	60,300	3,476	2,810	1,354	1,227	664	594	690	108	4
1,001,435	*1,021,044*	*87,856*	*28,226*	*5,551*	*5,499*	*42,407*	*35,366*	*238,019*	*84,234*	
69,936	65,530	56,147	14,644	132	2	17,094	13,794	127,754	35,382	5
208,733	210,767	7,928	3,110	778	768	5,714	5,686	30,895	15,590	6
235,211	248,348	3,897	1,614	594	568	4,512	2,628	8,334	2,613	7
166,559	165,125	9,570	3,965	209	211	3,696	2,754	38,885	17,857	8
131,650	131,027	6,969	3,280	1,395	1,401	10,559	9,850	24,946	10,375	9
189,346	200,247	3,345	1,613	2,443	2,549	832	654	7,205	2,417	10
1,042,220	*1,052,950*	*34,928*	*10,869*	*1,766*	*1,904*	*52,854*	*52,837*	*67,990*	*16,456*	
247,527	251,955	8,228	3,165	376	385	19,647	20,091	16,251	3,418	11
284,713	297,274	3,764	2,062	484	494	7,654	7,871	7,135	1,829	12
195,197	190,874	12,071	3,079	689	556	12,302	11,789	15,396	2,831	13
168,194	171,777	4,683	1,583	159	408	6,905	7,347	8,829	1,624	14
146,589	141,070	6,182	980	58	61	6,346	5,739	20,379	6,754	15
797,225	*782,030*	*45,943*	*29,716*	*22,652*	*22,686*	*37,130*	*36,001*	*68,481*	*30,804*	
15,098	12,891	405	96	11,158	11,282	999	845	330	82	16
244,310	239,671	10,386	5,661	913	877	2,840	2,823	16,493	8,654	17
222,552	215,469	18,912	12,953•	3,332	3,377	4,648	4,737	21,233	9,020	18
82,292	82,287	1,934	1,117	893	832	2,310	2,177	5,208	914	19
62,713	61,152	7,849	6,702	1,768	1,588	4,964	4,497	7,969	2,785	20
170,260	170,560	6,457	3,187	4,588	4,730	21,369	20,922	17,248	9,349	21
726,470	*767,192*	*7,359*	*2,579*	*93,059*	*98,241*	*3,392*	*2,404*	*17,320*	*4,028*	
124,297	129,145	1,256	739	7,586	7,791	287	224	2,139	713	22
131,149	138,045	1,021	425	1,986	2,119	85	67	2,421	558	23
234,162	244,359	4,153	1,133	619	675	1,581	807	10,268	1,816	24
236,756	255,562	900	266	1,848	1,816	220	108	1,413	292	25
106	81	29	16	81,020	85,840	1,219	1,198	1,079	649	26
762,381	*812,776*	*29,414*	*23,961*	*2,544*	*1,679*	*7,699*	*6,012*	*34,856*	*15,010*	
149,491	154,985	14,053	10,403	870	117	5,508	4,176	21,819	10,214	27
69,383	72,130	3,712	3,588	1	..	306	322	1,478	400	28
141,447	159,298	2,609	2,322	..	..	274	227	2,841	981	29
225,525	242,545	914	431	3	..	221	163	2,121	634	30
176,535	183,818	8,126	7,217	1,670	1,562	1,390	1,124	6,597	2,781	31
821,642	*890,047*	*12,709*	*8,365*	*59,295*	*60,689*	*9,992*	*11,012*	*31,033*	*13,274*	
32,725	32,859	1,339	584	17,997	20,573	5,022	5,909	2,901	1,284	32
41,038	38,159	1,731	657	33,700	33,262	1,803	2,646	12,644	5,884	33
204,650	226,022	4,775	4,337	..	..	1,339	1,165	3,406	1,096	34
155,655	173,385	1,704	1,340	..	..	408	461	2,114	898	35
117,939	122,589	1,442	814	1,712	1,371	531	176	5,239	2,357	36
176,154	203,930	833	323	20	..	187	121	1,349	517	37
93,481	93,103	885	310	5,866	5,483	702	534	3,380	1,238	38
613,339	**603,587**	**5,339**	**2,106**	**96,288**	**100,189**	**16,845**	**15,271**	**60,634**	**31,851**	
225,049	220,712	2,961	728	39,362	42,980	3,624	3,304	50,215	27,523	39
379,616	374,860	2,158	1,305	43,114	40,743	8,075	7,247	9,021	4,091	40
8,674	8,015	220	73	[illegible]	16,466	5,146	4,720	1,398	237	41
Hindu.										
7,557,449	**7,569,175**	**370,633**	**335,475**	**970,911**	**998,303**	**52,540**	**49,745**	**45,670**	**41,036**	
6,671,326	**6,666,897**	**358,900**	**323,954**	**660,755**	**690,860**	**26,438**	**24,146**	**44,399**	**40,048**	
957,961	*939,022*	*57,676*	*51,572*	*200,073*	*210,438*	*6,401*	*4,904*	*18,544*	*16,875*	
247,101	233,020	13,655	12,091	9,583	9,832	994	936	9,052	8,325	1
134,626	131,082	5,439	5,077	10,555	10,776	325	178	3,846	3,664	2
350,708	346,647	25,763	21,851	6,405	6,856	4,494	3,203	4,279	3,605	3
118,713	119,221	3,667	3,199	98,123	101,187	410	400	446	400	4
106,813	109,052	9,152	9,354	75,407	81,787	178	187	921	881	5

estimated. Hence the details in columns 11-20 do not add up to the totals in columns 3-5.

Table XX.—Summary

District or State. 1	Area in square miles. 2	Population, 1931. Persons. 3	Males. 4	Females. 5	Population, 1921. 6	Percentage of variation. 1921-31. 7	1911-21. 8	Number of persons per square mile in 1931. 9	1921. 10
CENTRAL PROVINCES AND BERAR—*concld.*									
Nerbudda Division ..	*18,386*	*2,254,566*	*1,137,806*	*1,116,760*	*2,013,021*	*+12·0*	*—3·3*	*123*	*109*
6 Narsinghpur	1,978	321,481	161,417	160,064	315,162	+2·0	—3·2	163	159
7 Hoshangabad	3,693	486,630	248,226	238,404	445,733	+9·2	—2·5	132	121
8 Nimar	4,227	466,931	242,042	224,889	396,554	+17·7	+1·4	110	94
9 Betul	3,910	406,252	201,114	205,138	363,737	+11·7	—6·8	104	93
10 Chhindwara	4,578	573,272	285,007	288,265	491,835	+16·6	—4·9	125	107
Nagpur Division ..	*22,760*	*3,602,108*	*1,809,541*	*1,792,567*	*3,146,228*	*+14·5*	*+1·2*	*158*	*138*
11 Wardha	2,434	516,266	261 394	254,872	463,696	+11·3	+0·6	212	191
12 Nagpur	3,834	940,049	481,246	458,803	792,521	+18·6	+0·6	245	207
13 Chanda	9,312	759,695	381,204	373,491	660,630	+15·0	—2·0	82	71
14 Bhandara	3,623	824,496	408,799	415,697	717,747	+14·9	—2·5	228	198
15 Balaghat	3,557	561,602	276,898	284,704	511,634	+9·8	+4·7	158	144
Chhattisgarh Division	*22,051*	*3,745,745*	*1,814,237*	*1,931,508*	*3,381,687*	*+10·8*	*+7·5*	*170*	*153*
16 Raipur	9,717	1,527,573	739,950	787,623	1,392,768	+9·7	+4·2	157	143
17 Bilaspur	7,618	1,400,248	683,920	716,328	1,231,765	+13·7	+6·3	184	162
18 Drug	4,716	817,924	390,367	427,557	757,154	+8·0	+7·5	173	161
Berar Division ..	*17,767*	*3,441,838*	*1,759,579*	*1,682,259*	*3,075,316*	*+11·9*	*+0·6*	*194*	*173*
19 Amraoti	4,691	941,604	485,593	456,011	827,867	+13·7	—5·2	201	176
20 Akola	4,091	876,362	448,896	427,466	794,847	+10·3	+1·1	214	194
21 Buldana	3,766	766,584	388,966	377,618	703,643	+8·9	+4·4	204	187
22 Yeotmal	5,219	857,288	436,124	421,164	748,959	+14·5	+3·4	164	144
Central Provinces States..	**31,175**	**2,483,214**	**1,235,385**	**1,247,829**	**2,066,900**	**+20·1**	**—2·4**	**80**	**66**
1 Makrai	155	15,516	7,900	7,616	12,803	+21·2	—14·8	100	83
2 Bastar	13,062	524,721	263,248	261,473	464,407	+13·0	+7·2	40	36
3 Kanker	1,431	136,101	67,132	68,969	124,928	+8·9	—1·8	95	87
4 Nandgaon	871	182,380	87,886	94,494	147,906	+23·3	—11·6	209	170
5 Khairagarh	931	157,400	75,647	81,753	124,008	+26·9	—20·2	169	133
6 Chhuikhadan	153	31,668	15,238	16,430	26,122	+21·2	—16·1	207	171
7 Kawardha	798	72,820	35,098	37,722	61,783	+17·9	—20·4	91	77
8 Sakti	138	48,489	23,571	24,918	41,554	+16·7	+20·3	351	301
9 Raigarh	1,486	277,569	136,723	140,846	241,634	+14·9	+10·4	187	163
10 Sarangarh	540	128,967	62,443	66,524	117,781	+9·5	+15·4	239	218
11 Chang Bhakar	906	23,322	11,987	11,335	21,826	+6·9	—10·6	26	24
12 Korea	1,631	90,886	46,748	44,138	79,189	+14·8	+27·5	56	49
13 Surguja	6,055	501,939	254,923	247,016	377,679	+32·9	—11·9	83	62
14 Udaipur	1,055	97,738	49,425	48,313	71,124	+37·4	+9·7	93	67
15 Jashpur	1,963	193,698	97,416	96,282	154,156	+25·7	—11·6	99	79
COORG	**1,593**	**163,327**	**90,575**	**72,752**	**163,838**	**—0·3**	**—6·4**	**103**	**103**
DELHI	**573**	**636,246**	**369,497**	**266,749**	**488,452**	**+30·3**	**+18·0**	**1,110**	**852**
MADRAS	**152,975**	**53,494,591**	**26,456,031**	**27,038,560**	**47,779,297**	**+12·0**	**+3·4**	**350**	**312**
British Territory ..	***142,277**	**46,740,107**	**23,082,999**	**23,657,108**	**42,318,985**	**+10·4**	**+2·2**	**329**	**297**
1 Agency Division	19,869	1,763,765	879,303	884,462	1,514,406	+16·5	—4·0	89	76
2 Ganjam	4,799	2,053,381	941,187	1,112,194	1,835,562	+11·9	—1·9	428	382
3 Vizagapatam	4,575	2,442,950	1,191,218	1,251,732	2,213,826	+10·3	+2·0	534	484
4 Godavari..	4,905	2,903,109	1,430,816	1,472,293	2,522,305	+11·1	+4·0	592	514
5 Kistna	3,547	1,254,208	635,704	618,504	1,081,872	+15·9	+6·4	354	305
6 Guntur	5,757	2,035,660	1,028,993	1,006,667	1,809,574	+12·5	+6·6	354	314
7 Nellore	7,949	1,486,222	744,322	741,900	1,385,553	+7·3	+4·3	187	174
8 Cuddapah	5,919	949,397	483,914	465,483	887,929	+6·9	—0·7	160	150
9 Kurnool	7,581	1,024,961	520,238	504,723	914,890	+12·0	—2·2	135	121
10 Bellary	5,713	969,774	493,018	476,756	862,370	+12·5	—11·0	170	151
11 Anantapur	6,741	1,050,411	539,534	510,877	955,917	+9·9	—0·8	156	142
12 Madras	29	647,230	341,223	306,007	526,911	+22·8	+1·6	22,318	18,169
13 Chingleput	3,091	1,655,115	837,161	817,954	1,493,058	+10·9	+6·2	535	483
14 Chittoor	5,901	1,447,103	738,325	708,778	1,322,664	+9·4	+2·0	245	224
15 North Arcot	4,648	2,266,9[illegible]	1,131,610	1,135,379	2,002,087	+13·2	+5·2	488	431
16 Salem	7,058	2,433,972	1,211,743	1,222,229	2,135,799	+14·0	+3·4	345	303

* The area of each of the districts was taken by rounding the total of the taluka figures which in their turn were taken to the nearest

Figures for Districts—*contd.*

Distribution by Religion.										
Hindu.		Muslim.		Tribal.		Christian.		Others.		
Males. 11	Females. 12	Males. 13	Females. 14	Males. 15	Females. 16	Males. 17	Females. 18	Males. 19	Females. 20	
849,982	*824,830*	*59,203*	*53,821*	*217,699*	*228,126*	*4,879*	*4,554*	*6,043*	*5,429*	
133,214	131,019	5,802	5,602	20,845	22,045	175	119	1,381	1,279	6
210,899	202,404	12,368	11,107	22,567	22,883	1,196	1,005	1,196	1,005	7
193,412	179,171	26,839	24,086	17,659	17,770	2,486	2,442	1,646	1,420	8
136,689	138,404	3,644	3,393	59,642	62,241	418	428	721	672	9
175,768	173,832	10,550	9,633	96,986	103,187	604	560	1,099	1,053	10
1,603,730	*1,590,484*	*61,076*	*53,822*	*132,336*	*137,568*	*6,064*	*5,017*	*6,335*	*5,676*	
229,234	223,051	11,046	9,882	19,408	20,381	170	108	1,536	1,450	11
439,201	423,318	29,366	24,443	4,972	4,812	4,810	3,748	2,897	2,482	12
317,050	313,467	7,045	6,511	55,916	57,411	623	620	570	482	13
380,517	386,856	8,134	7,350	19,156	20,444	166	229	826	818	14
237,728	243,792	5,485	5,636	32,884	34,520	295	312	506	444	15
1,695,683	*1,810,044*	*23,397*	*22,607*	*86,325*	*89,898*	*6,329*	*7,041*	*2,503*	*1,918*	
679,436	724,443	10,251	9,741	45,954	49,439	2,980	3,000	1,329	1,000	16
637,289	669,610	9,495	9,178	34,231	34,441	2,459	2,757	446	342	17
378,958	415,991	3,651	3,688	6,140	6,018	890	1,284	728	576	18
1,563,970	*1,502,517*	*157,548*	*142,132*	*24,322*	*24,830*	*2,765*	*2,630*	*10,974*	*10,150*	
430,034	405,375	45,714	40,784	5,810	6,061	1,319	1,235	2,716	2,556	19
397,460	380,991	46,903	42,282	180	190	726	595	3,627	3,408	20
348,531	340,621	37,474	34,292	81	91	380	398	2,500	2,216	21
387,945	375,530	27,457	24,774	18,251	18,488	340	402	2,131	1,970	22
886,123	**902,278**	**11,733**	**11,521**	**310,156**	**307,443**	**26,102**	**25,599**	**1,271**	**988**	
5,045	4,947	514	513	2,311	2,127	..	1	30	28	1
79,871	78,954	988	979	181,390	180,530	920	953	79	57	2
30,302	31,484	353	321	36,385	37,077	13	11	79	76	3
85,044	91,767	1,268	1,244	915	890	163	221	496	372	4
74,016	80,117	1,177	1,226	..	..	209	218	245	192	5
14,770	15,884	383	474	5	..	1	..	79	72	6
34,470	37,037	512	571	50	44	2	5	64	65	7
23,255	24,608	210	190	89	09	6	6	11	5	8
135,651	139,833	891	852	..	..	68	75	113	86	9
62,224	66,319	165	165	..	..	49	40	5	..	10
3,671	3,338	45	28	8,271	7,969	..	..	..	..	11
13,437	12,186	592	464	32,709	31,484	7	4	3	..	12
219,891	212,922	3,625	3,410	31,327	30,633	13	16	67	35	13
40,887	39,872	134	137	8,404	8,304	..	..	..	.	14
63,589	63,010	876	947	8,300	8,276	24,651	24,049	..	..	15
79,559	**66,448**	**8,943**	**4,834**	..	..	**2,012**	**1,413**	**61**	**57**	
				Sikh.						
231,459	**168,404**	**120,926**	**86,034**	**4,269**	**2,168**	**9,500**	**7,489**	**3,343**	**2,654**	
				Tribal.						
22,522,062	**23,073,458**	**1,869,768**	**1,903,565**	**175,330**	**176,340**	**1,868,996**	**1,864,091**	**19,875**	**16,106**	
20,380,257	**20,897,113**	**1,631,716**	**1,674,221**	**173,819**	**174,944**	**878,493**	**895,783**	**18,714**	**15,047**	
705,541	707,842	2,899	2,611	154,577	157,776	16,276	16,224	10	9	1
923,313	1,096,036	2,849	2,636	13,620	12,140	1,352	1,339	53	43	2
1,168,068	1,229,406	11,740	11,944	5,206	4,672	6,182	5,700	22	10	3
1,361,227	1,401,188	26,101	26,178	98	103	43,118	44,755	272	69	4
551,147	538,376	32,228	30,779	44	49	52,040	49,249	245	51	5
827,075	812,759	80,956	76,690	13	25	120,672	117,100	277	93	6
659,836	657,584	51,960	51,232	..	..	32,512	33,081	14	3	7
401,118	387,074	64,175	60,306	..	..	18,573	18,094	48	9	8
407,752	397,280	74,791	70,770	..	..	37,598	36,657	97	16	9
434,332	423,093	54,191	49,613	..	..	3,561	3,552	934	498	10
484,967	458,801	50,515	48,439	..		3,431	3,115	621	522	11
273,661	246,500	38,341	31,690	..	..	27,271	26,843	1,950	974	12
796,101	780,036	19,503	17,501	..	..	20,750	19,976	807	441	13
691,261	665,123	41,704	38,344	..	..	5,344	5,301	16	10	14
1,037,383	1,040,839	67,593	68,442	..	..	21,788	21,329	4,846	4,769	15
1,167,762	1,180,563	32,091	29,791	..	..	11,832	11,835	58	40	16

decimal. Hence a difference of 3 in the provincial figure.

Table XX.—Summary

District or State.	Area in square miles.	Population, 1931. Persons.	Males.	Females.	Population, 1921.	Percentage of variation. 1921-31.	1911-21.	Number of per per square mile in 1931.	1921.
1	2	3	4	5	6	7	8	9	10
MADRAS—*concld.*									
17 Coimbatore	7,085	2,445,064	1,218,224	**1,226,840**	2,196,033	+11·3	+4·9	345	**310**
18 South Arcot	4,208	2,454,507	1,225,072	**1,229,435**	2,320,085	+5·8	—1·8	583	**551**
19 Tanjore	3,742	2,385,920	1,143,738	**1,242,182**	2,329,915	+2·4	—1·5	638	**623**
20 Trichinopoly	4,314	1,913,245	934,867	**978,378**	1,902,838	+0·5	+4·0	443	**441**
21 Madura	4,912	2,195,747	1,081,437	**1,114,310**	2,007,082	+9·4	+4·3	447	**409**
22 Ramnad	4,819	1,838,955	872,177	**966,778**	1,718,187	+7·0	+3·3	382	**357**
23 Tinnevelly	4,315	2,046,907	987.159	**1,059,748**	1,907,314	+7·3	+6·2	474	**442**
24 The Nilgiris	982	169,330	91,928	**77,402**	126,519	+33·8	+6·7	172	129
25 Malabar (*including Laccadives*)	5,794	3,533,944	1,716,138	**1,817,806**	3,098,871	+14·0	+2·8	610	535
26 South Kanara (*including Amindivis*).	4,021	1,372,241	663,950	708,291	1,247,368	+10·0	+4·4	341	310
Madras States ..	**10,698**	**6,754,484**	**3,373,032**	**3,381,452**	**5,460,312**	+23·7	+13·5	631	**510**
1 Cochin	1,480	1,205,016	589,813	615,203	979,080	+23·1	+6·6	814	662
2 Banganapalle	256	39,218	19,985	19,233	36,692	+6·9	—6·7	153	143
3 Pudukkottai	1,179	400,694	191,134	209,560	426,813	—6·1	+3·6	340	362
4 Sandur	158	13,583	7,027	6,556	11,665	+16·4	—13·8	86	74
5 Travancore	7,625	5,095,973	2,565,073	2,530,900	4,006,062	+27·2	+16·8	668	525
N.-W. F. PROVINCE ..	**36,356**	***4,684,364**	**2,528,165**	**2,156,199**	**5,076,476**	—7·7	+32·9	**129**	**140**
Districts and Administered Territories.	**13,518**	**2,425,076**	**1,315,818**	**1,109,258**	**2,251,340**	+7·7	+2·5	**179**	**167**
1 Hazara	3,009	670,117	358,193	311,924	622,349	+7·7	+3·2	223	207
2 Peshawar	2,637	974,321	538,146	436,175	907,367	+7·4	+4·9	369	344
3 Kohat	2,703	236,273	126,210	110,063	214,123	+10·3	—3·8	87	79
4 Bannu	1,698	270,301	145,163	125,138	246,734	+9·6	—1·3	159	145
5 Dera Ismail Khan ..	3,471	274,064	148,106	125,958	260,767	+5·1	+1·8	79	75
Agencies and Tribal Areas	**22,838**	**2,259,288**	**1,212,347**	**1,046,941**	**2,825,136**	—20·0	+74·2	**99**	**124**
Agencies ..	**18,302**	**1,430,776**	**766,362**	**664,414**	**1,485,582**	—3·7	+34·8	**78**	**81**
1 Malakand (Dir, Swat and Chitral).	11,383	902,075	465,470	436,605	865,860	+4·2	+50·2	79	76
2 Khyber	962	263,566	147,908	115,658	227,109	+16·1	+25·4	274	236
3 Kurram	739	63,352	35,395	27,957	103,142	—38·6	+4·5	86	140
4 North Waziristan .. .. } (a)	5,218	93,570	56,325	37,245	138,859	—32·6	—3·8	39	55
5 South Waziristan .. .. }		108,213	61,264	46,949	150,612	—28·2	+48·5		
Tribal Areas ..	**4,536**	**828,512**	**445,985**	**382,527**	**1,339,554**	**—38·2**	**+157·6**	**183**	**295**
Trans-border tribes under the political control of the Deputy Commissioner of—									
1 Hazara .. .. .. (b)	..	352,400	190,036	**162,364**	146,656	+140·3	+49·2	..	..
2 Peshawar .. .. (c)	2,299	305,410	162,510	**142,900**	1,034,015	—70·5	+330·4	133	450
3 Kohat .. .. .. (d)	1,493	128,900	70,200	**58,700**	116,600	+10·5	—19·0	86	78
4 Bannu .. .. .. (e)	..	22,160	11,916	**10,244**	11,034	+100·8	—38·3	..	..
5 Dera Ismail Khan .. (f)	744	19,642	11,323	8,319	31,249	—37·1	+59·4	26	42
PUNJAB. ..	**105,020**	**24,018,639**	**13,109,800**	**10,908,839**	**21,093,497**	**+13·9**	**+5·5**	**229**	**201**
British Territory ..	**99,200**	**23,580,852**	**12,880,510**	**10,700,342**	**20,685,478**	**+14·0**	**+5·7**	**238**	**209**
Ambala Division ..	*15,055*	*4,077,565*	*2,226,856*	*1,850,709*	*3,827,069*	*+6·5*	*+1·2*	*271*	*254*
1 Hissar	5,213	899,479	485,690	413,789	816,810	+10·1	+1·5	173	157
2 Rohtak	2,471	805,621	432,855	372,766	772,272	+4·3	+8·0	326	313
3 Gurgaon	2,263	740,163	398,513	341,650	682,361	+8·5	—6·6	327	302
4 Karnal	3,125	852,614	469,870	382,744	828,822	+2·9	+3·5	273	265
5 Ambala	1,882	742,962	416,471	326,491	681,477	+9·0	—1·4	395	362
6 Simla	101	36,786	23,517	13,269	45,327	—18·8	+17·9	364	449
Jullundur Division ..	*19,396*	*4,606,446*	*2,491,638*	*2,114,808*	*4,182,516*	*+10·1*	*+5·4*	*237*	*216*
7 Kangra	9,976	801,312	415,288	386,024	766,065	+4·6	—0·6	80	77

*Statistics by Religion of 2,471,527 persons are available the rest (2,212,837) were estimated. Hence the details in columns 11—20 do not work

(*a*) Includes Bhittanni.

(*b*) No separate area given.

(*c*) Includes—Buner 1,444 square miles.
Mohmand Territory 855 square miles.

(*d*) Orakzai tribal area.

(*e*) Included in Waziristan. *Vide* (*a*) above.

(*f*) Includes Shirani country 577 square miles.

Figures for Districts—*contd.*

Distribution by Religion.										
Hindu.		Muslim.		Tribal.		Christian.		Others.		
Males. 11	Females. 12	Males. 13	Females. 14	Males. 15	Females. 16	Males. 17	Females. 18	Males. 19	Females. 20	
1,164,569	1,177,098	29,335	27,029	..	..	24,184	22,656	136	57	17
1,147,980	1,153,533	38,486	37,564	..	..	36,103	35,904	2,503	2,434	18
1,034,852	1,113,166	64,213	81,407	..	..	44,347	47,311	326	298	19
848,689	888,416	35,851	36,655	..	..	50,056	53,252	271	55	20
994,944	1,026,392	44,948	45,639	..	..	41,513	42,256	32	23	21
775,651	844,092	49,990	71,261	..	..	46,515	51,414	21	11	22
826,029	872,921	53,428	66,907	..	..	107,687	119,917	15	3	23
70,996	60,057	6,697	4,261	261	17[illegible]	13,796	12,805	178	100	24
1,113,663	1,190,091	569,032	594,421	..	..	32,946	32,948	497	346	25
512,340	548,847	88,099	92,111	..	..	59,046	63,170	4,465	4,163	26
2,141,805	**2,181,345**	**238,052**	**229,344**	**1,511**	**1,396**	**990,503**	**968,308**	**1,161**	**1,059**	
377,933	402,551	44,794	43,108	..	..	166,195	168,675	891	869	1
14,927	14,249	4,308	4,282	..	..	748	702	2	..	2
175,281	192,259	7,159	8,035	..	..	8,694	9,266	..	..	3
5,739	5,323	1,236	1,200	..	..	33	23	19	10	4
1,567,925	1,566,963	180,555	172,719	1,511	1,396	814,833	789,642	249	180	5
				Sikh.						
97,552	**59,076**	**1,218,234**	**1,032,155**	**31,409**	**16,526**	**13,212**	**3,287**	**46**	**30**	
84,358	**58,619**	**1,196,120**	**1,031,183**	**26,284**	**16,226**	**9,013**	**3,200**	**43**	**30**	
15,461	9,799	338,082	298,712	4,393	3,237	256	176	1	..	1
26,501	15,820	489,650	409,033	15,211	9,060	6,742	2,232	42	30	2
8,504	4,889	114,487	103,958	2,292	957	927	259	..	..	3
14,528	11,653	126,671	111,003	3,278	2,204	686	278	..	..	4
19,364	16,458	127,230	108,477	1,110	768	402	255	..	..	5
13,194	**457**	**22,114**	**972**	**5,125**	**300**	**4,199**	**87**	**3**	..	
13,073	**457**	**20,549**	**962**	**5,116**	**300**	**4,186**	**87**	**3**	..	
1,121	143	1,436	236	272	52	99	31	..	..	1
5,995	9	5,193	30	2,883	..	2,381	25	..	..	2
336	269	3,016	611	252	240	78	30	..	..	3
{ 4,384	34	6,622	85	697	8	1,450	1	1	..	4
{ 1,237	2	4,282	..	1,012	..	178	..	2	..	5
121	..	**1,565**	**10**	**9**	..	**13**	..	..	..	
..	..	..	..	..	..		..	..	..	1
..	..	..	..	..	..	..	..	..	..	2
..	..	..	..	..	..	..	..	..	..	3
..	..	..	..	..	..	..	..	..	..	4
121	..	1,565	10	9	..	13	..	..	..	5
3,665,525	**3,046,946**	**7,263,683**	**6,109,622**	**1,709,703**	**1,365,290**	**230,118**	**184,876**	**240,766**	**202,105**	
3,465,534	**2,863,054**	**7,241,612**	**6,090,848**	**1,703,584**	**1,360,560**	**230,018**	**184,770**	**239,762**	**201,110**	
1,462,380	*1,210,835*	*610,770*	*519,628*	*129,860*	*99,648*	*9,643*	*7,884*	*14,203*	*12,714*	
315,578	267,842	135,840	117,944	30,542	24,627	583	524	3,147	2,852	1
353,935	302,028	72,820	65,060	328	268	2,452	2,355	3,320	3,055	2
266,641	226,533	129,479	112,878	281	219	730	733	1,382	1,287	3
313,117	252,169	141,372	118,358	9,692	7,236	806	663	4,883	4,318	4
195,270	151,441	126,913	103,924	88,485	67,070	4,284	2,857	1,459	1,199	5
17,839	10 822	4,346	1,464	532	228	788	752	12	3	6
857,486	*754,191*	*830,920*	*708,225*	*624,436*	*501,615*	*10,592*	*7,618*	*168,204*	*143,159*	
377,050	354,165	22,486	17,997	1,338	1,058	316	260	14,098	12,544	7

up to the totals in columns 3-5.

M8CC

Table XX.—Summary

	District or State.	Area in square miles.	Population, 1931. Persons.	Males.	Females.	Population, 1921.	Percentage of variation. 1921-31.	1911-21.	Number of persons per square mile in 1931.	1921.
	1	2	3	4	5	6	7	8	9	10
	PUNJAB—*concld.*									
8	Hoshiarpur	2,247	1,032,187	551,867	480,320	927,419	+11·3	+1·0	459	413
9	Jullundur	1,431	943,721	512,667	431,054	822,544	+14·7	+2·6	659	575
10	Ludhiana	1,452	672,494	375,560	296,934	567,622	+18·5	+9·8	463	391
11	Ferozepore	4,290	1,156,732	636,256	520,476	1,098,866	+5·3	+14·4	270	256
	Lahore Division ..	*12,353*	*5,879,075*	*3,277,661*	*2,601,414*	*5,047,437*	*+16·5*	*+6·6*	*476*	*409*
12	Lahore	2,682	1,378,570	794,389	584,181	1,129,839	+22·0	+13·0	514	421
13	Amritsar	1,593	1,117,120	621,040	496,080	929,374	+20·2	+5·5	701	583
14	Gurdaspur	1,889	970,898	531,935	438,963	852,192	+13·9	+1·8	514	451
15	Sialkot	1,578	979,617	537,301	442,316	877,867	+11·6	+0·7	621	556
16	Gujranwala	2,309	736,138	408,606	327,532	623,581	+18·1	+3·0	319	270
17	Sheikhupura	2,302	696,732	384,390	312,342	634,584	+9·8	+17·4	303	276
	Rawalpindi Division ..	*21,347*	*3,914,849*	*2,092,622*	*1,822,227*	*3,460,710*	*+13·1*	*+3·3*	*183*	*162*
18	Gujrat	2,250	922,427	498,336	424,091	824,046	+11·9	+4·6	410	366
19	Shahpur	4,789	821,490	445,836	375,654	719,918	+14·1	+11·6	172	150
20	Jhelum	2,773	541,076	282,714	258,362	477,068	+13·4	—6·7	195	172
21	Rawalpindi	2,023	634,357	342,771	291,586	569,224	+11·4	+3·9	314	281
22	Attock	4,117	583,960	306,949	277,011	512,249	+14·0	—1·4	142	124
23	Mianwali	5,395	411,539	216,016	195,523	358,205	+14·9	+4·9	76	66
	Multan Division ..	*31,049*	*5,102,917*	*2,791,733*	*2,311,184*	*4,167,746*	*+22·4*	*+11·4*	*164*	*134*
24	Montgomery	4,518	999,772	552,456	447,316	685,690	+45·8	+42·3	221	152
25	Lyallpur	3,224	1,151,351	630,749	520,602	957,881	+20·2	+16·2	357	297
26	Jhang	3,452	664,833	355,671	309,162	570,559	+16·5	+8·7	193	165
27	Multan	5,892	1,174,900	646,025	528,875	889,328	+32·1	+9·3	199	151
28	Muzaffargarh	6,052	591,375	320,674	270,701	568,478	+4·0	—0·2	98	94
29	Dera Ghazi Khan	5,325	491,044	269,341	221,703	469,052	+4·7	—6·2	92	88
	Biloch-Trans-Frontier Tract	2,586	29,642	16,817	12,825	26,758	+10·8	—6·4	11	10
	Punjab States ..	**5,820**	**437,787**	**229,290**	**208,497**	**408,019**	**+7·3**	**—1·0**	**75**	**70**
1	Dujana	91	28,216	14,537	13,679	25,833	+9·2	+1·4	310	284
2	Pataudi	52	18,873	9,922	8,951	18,097	+4·3	—7·4	363	348
3	Kalsia	188	59,848	33,306	26,542	57,371	+4·3	+2·6	318	305
4	Simla Hill States .. .	5,489	330,850	171,525	159,325	306,718	+7·9	—1·5	60	56
	UNITED PROVINCES OF AGRA AND OUDH.	**112,191**	**49,614,833**	**26,063,177**	**23,551,656**	**46,509,950**	**+6·7**	**—3·1**	**442**	**415**
	British Territory ..	**106,248**	**48,408,763**	**25,445,006**	**22,963,757**	**45,375,069**	**+6·7**	**—3·1**	**456**	**427**
	Agra	**82,094**	**35,613,784**	**18,805,132**	**16,808,652**	**33,208,427**	**+7·2**	**—3·0**	**434**	**405**
	Meerut Division ..	*9,180*	*4,907,632*	*2,675,930*	*2,231,702*	*4,508,582*	*+8·9*	*—2·5*	*535*	*491*
1	Dehra Dun	1,189	230,247	137,569	92,678	212,243	+8·5	+3·6	194	179
2	Saharanpur	2,133	1,043,920	573,810	470,110	937,471	+11·4	—5·0	489	440
3	Muzaffarnagar	1,654	894,662	489,306	405,356	793,983	+12·7	—1·6	541	480
4	Meerut	2,293	1,601,918	871,267	730,651	1,498,724	+6·9	—0·3	699	654
5	Bulandshahr	1,911	1,136,885	603,978	532,907	1,066,161	+6·6	—5·0	595	558
	Agra Division ..	*8,638*	*4,498,246*	*2,452,301*	*2,045,945*	*4,182,775*	*+7·5*	*—7·3*	*521*	*484*
6	Aligarh	1,947	1,171,745	636,037	535,708	1,061,745	+10·4	—8·9	602	545
7	Muttra	1,450	668,074	364,292	303,782	619,138	+7·9	—5·7	461	427
8	Agra	1,849	1,048,316	572,958	475,358	924,155	+13·4	—9·6	567	500
9	Mainpuri	1,674	749,633	412,600	337,033	748,027	+0·2	—6·2	448	447
10	Etah	1,718	860,478	466,414	394,064	829,710	+3·7	—4·8	501	483
	Rohilkhand Division ..	*10,786*	*5,556,105*	*2,991,787*	*2,564,318*	*5,215,941*	*+6·5*	*—8·0*	*515*	*484*
11	Bareilly	1,579	1,072,379	579,860	492,519	1,013,875	+5·8	—7·4	679	642
12	Bijnor	1,793	835,469	443,667	391,802	740,368	+12·8	—8·2	466	413
13	Budaun	2,010	1,010,180	546,519	463,661	975,397	+3·6	—7·5	503	485
14	Moradabad	2,289	1,284,108	687,850	596,258	1,198,739	+7·1	—5·1	561	524
15	Shahjahanpur	1,766	905,131	493,101	412,030	855,961	+5·7	—11·2	513	485
16	Pilibhit	1,349	448,838	240,790	208,048	431,601	+4·0	—11·5	333	320
	Allahabad Division ..	*10,189*	*5,016,352*	*2,691,877*	*2,324,475*	*4,778,820*	*+5·0*	*—3·0*	*492*	*469*
17	Farrukhabad	1,643	877,392	480,178	397,214	839,787	+4·5	—4·8	534	511
18	Etawah	1,689	746,005	413,071	332,934	733,532	+1·7	—3·5	442	434
19	Cawnpore	2,368	1,212,253	669,817	542,436	1,148,664	+5·5	+0·6	512	485
20	Fatehpur	1,642	688,789	361,406	327,383	652,392	+5·6	—3·6	419	397
21	Allahabad .	2,847	1,491,913	767,405	724,508	1,404,445	+6·2	—4·3	524	493

...gures for Districts—*contd.*

Distribution by Religion.										
Hindu.		Muslim.		Sikh.		Christian.		Others.		
Males. 11	Females. 12	Males. 13	Females. 14	Males. 15	Females. 16	Males. 17	Females. 18	Males. 19	Females. 20	
219,303	195,050	174,351	153,727	94,652	78,495	2,083	1,681	61,478	51,367	8
85,469	69,773	223,611	195,945	139,154	110,417	2,714	1,609	61,719	53,310	9
58,174	44,267	130,149	105,449	175,676	137,153	1,098	1,379	10,463	8,686	10
117,490	90,936	280,323	235,107	213,616	174,492	4,381	2,689	20,446	17,252	11
600,644	*451,174*	*1,888,696*	*1,521,988*	*618,925*	*489,828*	*155,085*	*126,869*	*14,311*	*11,555*	
159,112	99,607	464,043	351,777	137,580	106,724	32,107	24,990	1,547	1,083	12
101,185	73,207	290,387	234,289	219,788	180,163	8,862	7,757	818	664	13
136,160	113,244	268,771	224,445	99,724	78,747	23,702	19,541	3,578	2,986	14
111,853	94,512	333,637	275,996	53,996	40,959	36,579	29,786	1,236	1,033	15
52,201	40,561	287,794	233,549	41,075	30,520	26,940	22,424	596	478	16
40,133	30,013	244,064	201,932	66,762	52,715	26,895	22,371	6,536	5,311	17
184,481	*154,114*	*1,791,956*	*1,570,304*	*99,894*	*86,416*	*13,982*	*9,657*	*2,309*	*1,736*	
39,425	32,921	425,716	361,034	30,795	28,393	1,746	1,351	654	392	18
48,641	40,329	367,879	311,667	22,200	17,874	6,223	5,071	893	713	19
19,155	16,913	251,656	230,441	11,409	10,621	388	284	106	103	20
34,973	24,512	279,287	245,678	22,948	18,317	4,924	2,562	639	517	21
16,631	15,301	279,546	252,247	10,279	9,243	490	220	3	..	22
25,656	24,138	187,872	169,237	2,263	1,968	211	169	14	11	23
360,543	*292,740*	*2,119,270*	*1,770,703*	*230,469*	*183,053*	*40,716*	*32,742*	*40,735*	*31,946*	
69,445	51,219	381,956	315,586	82,261	65,894	9,618	7,627	9,176	6,990	24
71,357	51,269	389,159	331,837	117,039	94,352	24,899	20,619	28,295	22,525	25
52,999	49,925	297,801	255,052	4,551	3,925	267	227	53	33	26
98,646	78,456	515,218	427,719	23,241	16,212	5,780	4,144	3,140	2,344	27
38,284	34,293	279,319	233,946	2,938	2,349	133	113	..	..	28
29,706	27,511	239,106	193,805	439	321	19	12	71	54	29
106	67	16,711	12,758	..	..	..	..	..	..	
199,991	**183,892**	**22,071**	**18,774**	**6,124**	**4,730**	**100**	**106**	**1,004**	**995**	
11,650	10,697	2,883	2,980	1	..	3	2	..	..	1
8,227	7,369	1,640	1,528	1	..	2	1	52	53	2
16,085	12,465	11,843	9,954	5,121	3,914	14	8	243	201	3
164,029	153,361	5,705	4,312	1,001	816	81	95	709	741	4
21,970,578	**19,885,732**	**3,914,778**	**3,519,280**	**26,723**	**19,887**	**113,163**	**94,733**	**37,935**	**32,024**	
21,488,425	**19,417,161**	**3,780,453**	**3,401,474**	**26,662**	**19,838**	**111,647**	**93,359**	**37,819**	**31,925**	
15,822,703	**14,171,709**	**2,818,828**	**2,499,249**	**24,832**	**18,895**	**101,835**	**87,635**	**36,934**	**31,164**	
1,955,723	*1,626,761*	*668,919*	*562,643*	*7,675*	*4,853*	*26,271*	*22,769*	*17,342*	*14,676*	
112,728	76,887	20,724	13,063	931	545	2,886	1,934	300	249	1
375,061	304,862	192,651	160,517	1,624	864	2,014	1,642	2,460	2,225	2
339,529	277,898	138,813	118,262	749	446	5,436	4,719	4,779	4,031	3
645,475	543,504	203,207	169,247	4,093	2,764	9,320	7,589	9,172	7,547	4
482,930	423,610	113,524	101,554	278	234	6,615	6,885	631	624	5
2,151,708	*1,793,605*	*264,288*	*220,621*	*1,987*	*1,614*	*24,194*	*21,911*	*10,124*	*8,194*	
540,727	455,576	84,528	69,965	428	339	9,279	8,971	1,075	857	6
328,125	273,902	31,865	26,335	632	520	3,120	2,555	550	470	7
487,288	404,428	74,835	62,316	864	643	4,967	3,938	5,004	4,033	8
386,370	314,932	21,931	18,535	18	5	2,093	1,826	2,188	1,735	9
409,198	344,767	51,129	43,470	45	107	4,735	4,621	1,307	1,099	10
2,151,808	*1,819,779*	*793,865*	*764,896*	*13,780*	*11,775*	*31,288*	*27,024*	*1,046*	*844*	
415,168	348,884	156,806	137,225	258	140	7,577	6,227	51	43	11
274,780	240,080	165,686	148,370	1,333	1,655	1,327	1,232	541	465	12
442,561	372,124	95,578	84,158	68	60	8,206	7,255	106	64	13
410,181	349,747	253,075	225,772	12,051	9,865	12,211	10,625	332	249	14
414,906	342,980	77,159	68,161	28	28	998	847	10	14	15
194,212	165,964	45,561	41,210	42	27	969	838	6	9	16
2,372,863	*2,045,399*	*306,214*	*269,283*	*262*	*144*	*10,538*	*8,053*	*2,000*	*1,596*	
420,053	343,615	57,720	51,279	34	21	2,149	2,097	222	202	17
386,500	310,455	24,555	21,293	11	6	921	318	1,084	862	18
591,139	482,142	75,062	57,890	114	65	3,235	2,160	267	179	19
318,971	286,569	42,283	40,627	10	7	110	150	32	30	20
656,200	622,618	106,594	98,194	93	45	4,123	3,328	395	323	21

Table XX.—Summa

No.	District or State.	Area in square miles.	Population, 1931. Persons.	Males.	Females.	Population, 1921.	Percentage of variation. 1921-31.	1911-21.	Number of persons per square mile in 1931.	1921.
	1	2	3	4	5	6	7	8	9	10
	UNITED PROVINCES OF AGRA AND OUDH— *concld.*									
	Jhansi Division ..	*10,470*	*2,244,895*	*1,160,832*	*1,084,063*	*2,065,297*	*+8·7*	*—6·5*	*214*	***197***
22	Jhansi	3,619	690,413	357,551	332,862	606,499	+13·8	—10·9	191	**168**
23	Jalaun	1,549	426,022	223,326	202,696	405,439	+5·1	+0·2	275	**262**
24	Hamirpur	2,438	502,689	257,028	245,661	465,323	+8·0	—5·4	206	**191**
25	Banda	2,864	625,771	322,927	302,844	588,036	+6·4	—6·7	218	**205**
	Benares Division ..	*9,544*	*4,778,919*	*2,424,328*	*2,354,591*	*4,443,898*	*+7·5*	*—0·2*	*501*	***466***
26	Benares	1,093	1,016,378	525,030	491,348	952,031	+6·8	+1·6	930	**871**
27	Mirzapur	4,368	788,409	394,465	393,944	724,183	+8·9	—0·1	180	**166**
28	Jaunpur	1,550	1,236,071	612,908	623,163	1,155,105	+7·0	—0·1	797	**745**
29	Ghazipur	1,302	824,971	422,857	402,114	781,570	+5·6	—0·9	634	**600**
30	Ballia	1,231	913,090	469,068	444,022	831,009	+9·9	—1·7	742	**675**
	Gorakhpur Division ..	*9,565*	*7,217,162*	*3,695,749*	*3,521,413*	*6,720,715*	*+7·4*	*+3·0*	*755*	***703***
31	Gorakhpur	4,534	3,567,561	1,830,288	1,737,273	3,266,830	+9·2	+2·1	787	**721**
32	Basti	2,819	2,078,024	1,067,501	1,010,523	1,925,228	+7·9	+5·2	737	**683**
33	Azamgarh	2,212	1,571,577	797,960	773,617	1,528,657	+2·8	+2·4	710	**691**
	Kumaun Division ..	*13,722*	*1,394,473*	*712,328*	*682,145*	*1,292,399*	*+7·9*	*—2·7*	*102*	***94***
34	Naini Tal	2,721	277,286	162,337	114,949	276,875	+0·1	—14·4	102	**102**
35	Almora	5,389	583,302	292,004	291,298	530,338	+10·0	+0·9	108	**98**
36	Garhwal	5,612	533,885	257,987	275,898	485,186	+10·0	+1·2	95	**86**
	Oudh	**24,154**	**12,794,979**	**6,639,874**	**6,155,105**	12,166,642	+5·2	—3·1	530	**504**
	Lucknow Division ..	*12,040*	*5,856,543*	*3,114,469*	*2,742,074*	*5,567,241*	*+5·2*	*—5·8*	*486*	***462***
37	Lucknow	967	787,472	432,865	354,607	724,344	+8·7	—5·2	814	**749**
38	Unao	1,787	855,700	452,825	402,875	819,128	+4·5	—10·1	479	**458**
39	Rae Bareli	1,749	974,127	493,730	480,397	936,403	+4·0	—7·9	557	**535**
40	Sitapur	2,246	1,167,139	621,993	545,146	1,089,481	+7·1	—4·3	520	**485**
41	Hardoi	2,323	1,127,626	608,391	519,235	1,084,410	+4·0	—3·3	485	**467**
42	Kheri	2,968	944,479	504,665	439,814	913,475	+3·4	—4·8	318	**308**
	Fyzabad Division ..	*12,114*	*6,938,436*	*3,525,405*	*3,413,031*	*6,599,401*	*+5·1*	*—0·7*	*573*	***545***
43	Fyzabad	1,723	1,204,789	610,051	594,738	1,171,930	+2·8	+1·5	699	**680**
44	Gonda	2,842	1,576,003	806,532	769,471	1,473,389	+7·0	+4·3	555	**518**
45	Bahraich	2,639	1,136,348	592,716	543,632	1,065,377	+6·7	+1·7	431	**404**
46	Sultanpur	1,712	1,051,284	519,311	531,973	1,003,912	+4·7	—4·3	614	**586**
47	Partabgarh	1,442	906,233	441,992	464,241	855,130	+6·0	—5·0	628	**593**
48	Bara Banki	1,756	1,063,779	554,803	508,976	1,029,663	+3·3	—5·0	606	**586**
	United Provinces States ..	**5,943**	**1,206,070**	**618,171**	**587,899**	**1,134,881**	**+6·3**	**—4·6**	**203**	**191**
1	Benares	870	391,272	194,236	197,036	362,860	+7·8	+1·4	450	**417**
2	Rampur	893	465,225	250,618	214,607	453,607	+2·6	—14·6	521	**508**
3	Tehri-Garhwal	4,180	349,573	173,317	176,256	318,414	+9·8	+5·8	84	**76**
	BARODA STATE ..	8,164	2,443,007	1,257,817	1,185,190	2,126,522	+14·9	+4·6	299	**260**
	CENTRAL INDIA AGENCY	51,597	6,632,790	3,405,438	3,227,352	6,002,551	+10·5	—2·1	129	**116**
1	Indore	9,518	1,318,237	689,655	628,582	1,150,840	+14·5	+9·4	138	121
2	Bhopal	6,902	729,955	377,961	351,994	692,448	+5·4	—6·2	106	**100**
3	Rewa	13,000	1,587,445	795,381	792,064	1,401,524	+13·3	—7·5	122	**108**
4	Orchha	2,080	314,661	163,272	151,389	284,948	+10·4	—13·7	151	**137**
5	Datia	912	158,834	83,508	75,326	148,659	+6·8	—3·8	174	**163**
6	Dhar	1,784	243,430	123,775	119,655	229,771	+5·9	+19·8	136	**129**
7	Dewas, Senior	449	83,321	42,532	40,789	77,005	+8·2	+1·7	186	**172**
8	Dewas, Junior	419	70,513	36,183	34,330	66,998	+5·2	+5·3	168	**160**
9	Samthar	180	33,307	17,307	16,000	33,216	+0·3	+4·1	185	**185**
10	Jaora	602	100,166	51,582	48,584	85,778	+16·8	+3·9	166	**142**
11	Ratlam	693	107,321	55,086	52,235	85,489	+25·5	+3·6	155	**123**
12	Panna	2,596	212,130	108,133	103,997	197,600	+7·4	—13·7	82	**76**
13	Charkhari	880	120,351	62,086	58,265	123,405	—2·5	—6·9	137	**140**
14	Ajaigarh	802	85,895	44,220	41,675	84,790	+1·3	—2·6	107	**106**
15	Bijawar	973	115,852	60,333	55,519	111,723	+3·7	—10·8	119	**115**
16	Baoni	121	19,132	9,909	9,223	19,734	—3·1	—1·9	158	**163**
17	Chhatarpur	1,130	161,267	83,832	77,435	166,549	—3·2	—7·4	143	**147**
18	Sitamau	202	28,422	14,715	13,707	26,549	+7·1	+0·2	141	**131**
19	Sailana	279	35,223	17,950	17,273	27,165	+29·7	—5·0	126	**97**

Figures for Districts—*contd.*.

Distribution by Religion.										
Hindu.		Muslim.		Sikh.		Christian.		Others.		
Males. 11	Females. 12	Males. 13	Females. 14	Males. 15	Females. 16	Males. 17	Females. 18	Males. 19	Females. 20	
1,079,998	*1,010,292*	*71,376*	*66,209*	*356*	*141*	*3,240*	*2,020*	*5,862*	*5,401*	
327,309	308,114	21,484	17,920	334	123	2,920	1,608	5,504	5,097	22
208,351	188,515	14,822	14,061	7	6	63	51	83	63	23
240,416	228,936	16,413	16,382	5	4	137	286	57	53	24
303,922	284,727	18,657	17,846	10	8	120	75	218	188	25
2,217,079	*2,151,853*	*204,266*	*200,281*	*274*	*150*	*2,536*	*2,202*	*173*	*105*	
465,063	438,257	58,399	51,825	164	82	1,261	1,098	143	86	26
369,910	370,881	24,137	22,688	31	9	358	347	29	19	27
558,236	567,302	54,612	55,773	15	6	45	82	..	..	28
384,698	361,516	37,909	40,359	26	22	224	217	..	..	29
439,172	413,897	29,209	29,636	38	31	648	458	1		30
3,219,896	*3,068,535*	*474,174*	*451,412*	*157*	*134*	*1,484*	*1,305*	*38*	*27*	
1,636,597	1,554,874	192,370	181,222	39	41	1,251	1,114	31	22	31
881,677	834,615	185,688	175,801	36	9	95	93	5	5	32
701,622	679,046	96,116	94,389	82	84	138	98	2	..	33
673,628	*655,485*	*35,726*	*23,904*	*341*	*84*	*2,284*	*2,351*	*349*	*321*	
130,286	92,735	30,684	21,216	292	73	872	758	203	167	34
289,288	2 8,716	1,758	1,400	4	..	850	1,066	104	116	35
254,054	274,034	3,284	1,288	45	11	562	527	42	38	36
5,665,722	**5,245,452**	**961,625**	**902,225**	**1,830**	**943**	**9,812**	**5,724**	**885**	**761**	
2,688,283	*2,366,410*	*417,077*	*370,331*	*1,100*	*443*	*7,631*	*4,583*	*378*	*307*	
332,536	274,338	92,904	76,373	857	321	6,329	3,393	239	182	37
411,442	366,654	41,247	36,107	32	15	100	96	4	3	38
448,049	435,046	45,542	45,230	34	20	101	95	4	6	39
528,512	459,861	93,024	84,882	77	34	292	283	88	86	40
541,222	459,648	66,834	59,243	20	5	313	339	2	..	41
426,522	370,863	77,526	68,496	80	48	496	377	41	30	42
2,977,439	*2,879,042*	*544,548*	*531,894*	*730*	*500*	*2,181*	*1,141*	*507*	*454*	
540,850	527,487	67,707	66,799	100	44	1,369	385	25	23	43
663,071	629,848	142,987	139,148	63	35	379	416	32	24	44
463,743	424,742	128,179	118,354	512	395	226	106	56	35	45
459,421	467,844	59,823	64,052	24	13	37	60	6	4	46
392,068	411,881	49,793	52,228	9	1	85	88	37	43	47
458,286	417,240	96,059	91,313	22	12	85	86	351	325	48
482,153	**468,571**	**134,325**	**117,806**	**61**	49	**1,516**	**1,374**	**116**	**99**	
177,215	181,124	16,970	15,865	25	27	26	20	..	..	1
132,656	112,223	116,358	100,939	33	19	1,476	1,338	95	88	2
172,282	175,224	997	1,002	3	3	14	16	21	11	3
				Tribal.						
1,109,349	**1,042,722**	**93,759**	**88,871**	22,693	22,197	**3,858**	**3,404**	**28,158**	**27,996**	
3,002,203	**2,850,001**	**198,346**	**178,291**	**170,828**	**169,924**	**5,978**	**4,498**	**28,083**	**24,638**	
606,512	555,827	57,006	49,567	13,611	13,702	3,360	1,980	9,166	7,506	1
301,115	280,355	47,846	42,014	25,768	26,765	270	232	2,962	2,628	2
762,510	759,945	17,916	17,391	14,331	14,152	145	120	479	456	3
155,598	144,106	4,168	3,960	668	714	15	10	2,823	2,599	4
80,177	72,430	3,193	2,800	..	..	5	8	133	88	5
102,184	98,576	8,736	8,115	10,960	11,217	135	86	1,760	1,661	6
35,945	34,514	4,814	4,633	1,308	1 282	20	21	445	339	7
31,968	30,582	3,598	3,279	148	122	54	49	415	298	8
16,028	14,798	1,272	1,193	..	..	..	..	7	9	9
41,134	38,695	8,201	7,760	1,051	1,018	35	43	1,161	1,068	10
31,069	28,765	6,412	5,658	14,730	15,052	510	520	2,365	2,240	11
104,659	100,665	2,379	2,262	..	..	11	9	1,084	1,061	12
59,321	55,633	2,548	2,428	70	60	..	..	147	144	13
42,354	39,989	1,273	1,127	302	303	1	..	290	256	14
56,600	52,063	1,292	1,145	1,563	1,516	2	3	876	822	15
8,638	8,010	1,262	1,207	..	..	9	6	..	..	16
79,886	73,830	3,526	3,241	..	..	120	119	300	245	17
13,559	12,715	815	720	..	..	22	14	319	258	18
10,291	9,765	926	752	6,277	6,333	17	16	439	407	19

Table XX.—Summary

	District or State.	Area in square miles.	Population, 1931. Persons.	Males.	Females.	Population, 1921.	Percentage of variation. 1921-31.	1911-21.	Number of persons per square mile in 1931.	1921.
	1	2	3	4	5	6	7	8	9	10
	CENTRAL INDIA AGENCY —*concld.*									
20	Rajgarh	962	134,891	71,176	63,715	114,714	+17·6	—9·7	140	119
21	Narsinghgarh	734	113,873	59,554	54,319	101,426	+12·3	—7·7	155	138
22	Jhabua	1,336	145,522	74,129	71,393	123,932	+17·4	+11·4	109	93
23	Baraundha	218	16,071	8,443	7,628	15,912	+1·0	—6·3	74	73
24	Nagod	501	74,589	37,091	37,498	68,166	+9·4	—8·6	149	136
25	Maihar	407	68,991	34,101	34,890	66,540	+3·7	—9·0	170	163
26	Barwani	1,178	141,110	71,476	69,634	120,150	+17·4	+10·7	120	102
27	Ali Rajpur	836	101,963	52,342	49,621	89,364	+14·1	+23·3	122	107
28	Khilchipur	273	45,583	24,067	21,516	40,043	+13·8	—0·1	167	147
29	Other States	1,630	264,735	135,639	129,096	248,113	+6·7	—1·9	162	152
	COCHIN STATE :—(*See under Madras States.*)									
	GWALIOR STATE ..	**26,367**	**3,523,070**	**1,867,031**	**1,656,039**	**3,193,176**	**+10·3**	**—1·3**	**134**	**121**
	HYDERABAD STATE	**82,698**	**14,436,148**	**7,370,010**	**7,066,138**	**12,471,770**	**+15·8**	**—6·8**	**175**	**151**
1	Hyderabad City	53	466,894	247,623	219,271	404,187	+15·5	—19·4	8,809	7,626
2	Atraf-i-Balda	2,651	499,661	253,975	245,686	497,498	+0·4	—7·4	188	188
3	Warangal	7,944	1,117,693	575,819	541,874	925,041	+20·8	+2·2	141	116
4	Karimnagar	5,722	1,241,405	634,416	606,989	1,095,444	+13·3	—3·0	217	191
5	Adilabad	7,294	762,030	389,754	372,276	655,536	+16·2	+5·6	104	90
6	Medak	3,198	738,665	373,475	365,190	642,796	+14·9	—5·8	231	201
7	Nizamabad	3,265	623,225	313,556	309,669	499,765	+24·7	—11·7	191	153
8	Mahbubnagar	5,326	971,616	494,061	477,555	792,632	+22·6	+0·2	182	149
9	Nalgonda	6,049	1,133,409	580,897	552,512	948,301	+19·5	—8·4	187	157
10	Aurangabad	6,212	944,793	480,498	464,295	714,008	+32·3	—17·9	152	115
11	Bhir	4,132	633,690	325,396	308,294	467,616	+35·5	—24·8	153	113
12	Nander	3,771	722,081	367,170	354,911	671,019	+7·6	—3·9	191	178
13	Parbhani	5,125	853,760	434,777	418,983	765,787	+11·5	—1·7	167	149
14	Gulbarga..	6,975	1,225,008	621,687	603,321	1,095,753	+11·8	—7·9	176	157
15	Osmanabad	3,526	691,068	357,489	333,579	615,216	+12·3	—4·0	196	174
16	Raichur	6,630	937,535	473,161	464,374	880,420	+6·5	—7·4	141	133
17	Bidar	4,825	873,615	446,256	427,359	800,751	+9·1	—5·7	181	166
	JAMMU AND KASHMIR STATE	**84,516**	**3,646,243**	**1,938,338**	**1,707,905**	**3,320,518**	**+9·8**	**+5·1**	**43**	**39**
	Jammu Province (including jagirs).	*12,401*	*1,788,441*	*942,815*	*845,626*	*1,640,259*	*+9·0*	*+2·7*	*144*	*132*
1	Jammu	1,144	375,240	205,719	169,521	337,544	+11·2	+2·5	328	295
2	Kathua	1,022	161,232	85,993	75,239	154,209	+4·6	+1·6	158	151
3	Udhampur (*including Bhadrawah*). ..	5,074	273,668	143,514	130,154	245,255	+11·6	+1·7	54	48
4	Riasi	1,818	235,245	124,210	111,035	223,652	+5·2	+8·6	129	123
5	Mirpur	1,627	344,747	178,831	165,916	317,198	+8·7	—1·8	212	195
6	Chenani jagir	95	10,925	5,930	4,995	10,620	+2·9	+0·3	115	112
7	Poonch jagir	1,621	387,384	198,618	188,766	351,781	+10·1	+5·2	239	217
	Kashmir Province ..	*8,555*	*1,569,218*	*847,022*	*722,196*	*1,407,086*	*+11·5*	*+8·6*	*183*	*164*
8	Kashmir North	3,326	559,828	301,397	258,431	502,216	+11·5	+9·1	168	151
9	Kashmir South	2,822	771,943	419,190	352,753	688,761	+12·1	+7·7	274	244
10	Muzaffarabad	2,407	237,447	126,435	111,012	216,109	+9·9	+10·7	99	90
	Frontier Districts ..	*63,560*	*288,584*	*148,501*	*140,083*	*273,173*	*+5·6*	*+3·1*	*5*	*4*
11	Ladakh	45,762	192,138	96,259	95,879	183,476	+4·7	—1·7	4	4
12	Gilgit	3,118	31,902	17,752	14,150	28,706	+11·1	+19·8	10	9
13	Political Ilaqas	14,680	64,544	34,490	30,054	60,991	+5·8	+12·0	4	4
	MYSORE STATE. ..	**29,326**	**6,557,302**	**3,353,963**	**3,203,339**	**5,978,892**	**+9·7**	**+3·0**	**224**	**204**
1	Bangalore City	12	172,357	91,680	80,677	118,556	+45·4	+33·7	14,363	9,880
2	Bangalore District ..	2,922	908,056	461,905	446,151	788,379	+15·2	+3·8	311	270
3	Kolar Gold Fields (City) ..	30	85,103	45,051	40,052	87,682	—2·9	+4·7	2,837	2,923
4	Kolar District	3,161	763,934	389,262	374,672	704,657	+8·4	+1·2	242	223
5	Tumkur District	4,082	861,405	439,144	422,261	773,122	+11·4	+5·1	211	189
6	Mysore City	10	107,142	56,772	50,370	83,951	+27·6	+17·7	10,714	8,395
7	Mysore District	5,492	1,403,984	703,838	700,146	1,319,368	+6·4	+3·8	256	240
8	Chitaldrug District ..	4,149	656,569	336,786	319,783	574,179	+14·3	+1·8	158	138
9	Hassan District	2,635	596,937	300,746	296,191	583,960	+2·2	+0·6	227	222
10	Kadur District	2,771	347,715	184,389	163,326	333,538	+4·3	—1·5	125	120
11	Shimoga District ..	4,048	519,987	274,981	245,006	492,560	+5·6	—4·7	128	122
12	Civil and Military Station Bangalore.	14	134,113	69,409	64,704	118,940	+12·8	+18·0	9,580	8,496

Figures for Districts—*concld.*

Distribution by Religion.										
Hindu.		Muslim.		Tribal.		Christian.		Others.		
Males. 11	Females. 12	Males. 13	Females. 14	Males. 15	Females. 16	Males. 17	Females. 18	Males. 19	Females. 20	
				Sikh.						
1,020,180	**867,069**	**852,700**	**703,891**	**561,238**	**435,388**	**2,438**	**1,921**	**14,838**	**12,555**	
10,717	9,481	1,600	1,519	2	..	..	1	7	11	5
76,922	62,109	4,047	2,973	1,353	1,060	24	28	38	14	6
52,068	46,955	804	654	280	227	2	4	..	..	7
102,614	97,321	4,464	1,887	612	287	92	49	94	45	8
30,427	27,189	382	351	33	11	1	..	8	6	9
29,590	24,555	96,240	83,011	39,729	32,448	511	472	5,459	4,742	10
11,713	9,539	17,280	14,137	16,114	12,868	77	58	699	587	11
11,231	8,040	27,236	22,676	51,414	41,466	100	67	1,182	952	12
69,673	65,044	5,706	5,133	63	49	57	37	560	548	13
340,466	280,679	198,945	164,975	357,193	275,779	806	643	3,187	2,847	14
131,270	112,291	24,915	21,087	19,183	14,107	119	91	896	717	15
71,592	60,756	31,027	26,366	55,262	42,190	36	30	169	146	16
81,897	63,110	440,054	359,122	20,000	14,896	613	441	2,539	1,940	17
					Tribal.					
5,029,620	**4,549,185**	**565,962**	**503,363**	**115,420**	**113,672**	**107**	**2,671**	**170,919**	**171,793**	
2,099	1,399	512	288	..	..	84	56	58	36	1
388,017	337,067	76,471	65,107	..	..	160	138	36,505	32,753	2
28,551	23,218	12,502	9,614	815	629	–	..	474	452	3
962,012	869,429	93,234	83,629	1,653	1,588	386	300	52,627	61,124	4
696,380	655,649	28,346	25,487	48,061	46,483	293	186	34,104	31,921	5
59,925	60,533	3,300	3,210	46,313	47,017	98	107	2,347	2,256	6
17,004	17,123	453	401	..	..	..	..	297	286	7
21,124	20,223	2,045	1,869	13,534	13,213	33	34	2,255	2,209	8
107,797	106,248	3,838	3,844	..	..	4	3	2,841	2,969	9
101,044	92,741	3,561	2,977	..	..	272	231	6,798	8,904	10
1,256,918	1,126,386	112,338	102,243	1,349	1,250	795	763	15,667	14,066	11
39,506	36,757	3,467	3,130	324	312	8	7	1,189	1,044	12
1,314	1,232	56	53	..	..	..	..	75	60	13
290,088	259,278	104,110	92,350	..	..	48	31	2,015	1,831	14
211,278	178,445	50,308	43,746	..	..	346	279	1,393	1,159	15
130,354	105,575	8,903	7,939	64	34	21	42	1,155	899	16
72,578	60,181	3,914	3,387	..	..	7	9	230	219	17
50,705	45,929	4,377	4,181	..	..	31	19	1,405	1,243	18
135,975	126,705	22,993	21,241	1,789	1,736	30	13	3,614	3,264	19
105,482	96,847	5,398	4,894	3	2	21	8	2,197	1,870	20
325,624	303,792	24,531	22,537	1,515	1,4 8	470	444	2,916	2,567	21
25,845	24,428	1,305	1,236	..	..	..	1	757	661	22
24,256	**22,818**	**98**	**6**	**13,357**	**13,583**	**134**	**142**	**17,980**	**17,434**	
1,658,492	**1,588,276**	**268,849**	**276,720**	**447**	**415**	**856**	**540**	**97,110**	**107,545**	
1,272,169	1,223,656	228,451	234,890	425	399	617	356	79,893	90,642	1
162,262	*168,735*	*59,493*	*60,793*	*244*	*201*	*44*	*14*	*26,802*	*35,719*	
222,954	*210,171*	*52,462*	*52,502*	..	..	*93*	*57*	*3,357*	*3,556*	
166,392	*160,502*	*27,934*	*30,619*	*3*	*6*	*105*	*32*	*11,333*	*12,266*	
222,813	*210,447*	*21,985*	*20,761*	*18*	*48*	*160*	*117*	*12,180*	*11,745*	
84,139	*79,210*	*16,281*	*19,393*	...	...	*26*	*18*	*3,312*	*3,467*	
413,609	*394,591*	*50,296*	*50,822*	*160*	*144*	*189*	*118*	*22,909*	*23,889*	
127,337	120,930	9,967	9,411	18	16	50	35	7,472	7,232	2
163,125	155,026	25,705	28,160	4	..	175	142	4,676	4,718	3
95,861	88,664	4,726	4,259	..	..	14	7	5,069	4,953	4

APPENDIX I.

Fertility Tables.

1. These tables represent a compilation for India of the figures obtained by a special enquiry in the various Provinces and States, separate figures for which are given below the India totals.

2. The tables are self-explanatory and the matter is dealt with in Chapter V of the Report. They consist of the following :—

1. Sex of first-born.
2. Proportion of fertile and sterile marriages.
3. Average size of family correlated with age of wife at marriage.
4. Size of families by occupation of husbands.
5. Size of families by caste or religion and age of wife at marriage.
6. Duration of marriage correlated with caste or religion.

Table I.—Sex of First Born.

	Province, State or Agency. 1	Number of Females first born. 2	Number of Males first born. 3	Number of Females first born per 1,000 Males first born. 4	Number of slips examined. 5
	INDIA	**238,462**	**305,963**	**779**	**575,495**
1	Andaman and Nicobar Islands	364	416	875	907
2	Assam	2,884	3,284	879	6,466
3	Baluchistan	13,966	24,695	566	39,744
4	Baroda State	15,956	22,838	699	39,768
5	Bengal*	982	1,345	730	2,406
6	Bombay	66,756	82,637	808	157,906
7	Burma	500	653	766	1,153
8	Central India Agency	1,543	2,107	732	4,374
9	Central Provinces and Berar	9,336	11,747	795	21,643
10	Cochin State	14,275	15,451	924	33,471
11	Delhi	860	1,133	759	2,246
12	Gwalior State	710	978	726	1,688
13	Jammu and Kashmir State	5,702	9,661	590	15,714
14	Madras	17,862	20,249	882	42,658†
15	Mysore State	1,876	1,941	967	3,817
16	Punjab	72,432	92,163	786	173,432
17	Travancore State	8,416	9,790	862	18,456
18	Western India States Agency	4,042	4,875	829	9,646

* Completed marriages only. † Includes 495 slips where no indication of the sex of the first born was given.

Table II.—Proportion of Fertile and Sterile Marriages.

Province, State or Agency.	Age of wife at marriage.	Duration of Marriage years. 0—4 Fertile.	0—4 Sterile.	5—9 Fertile.	5—9 Sterile.	10—14 Fertile.	10—14 Sterile.	15 and over. Fertile.	15 and over. Sterile.
1	2	3	4	5	6	7	8	9	10
INDIA*	..	**164,491**	**71,502**	**213,807**	**41,930**	**214,696**	**27,433**	**444,161**	**26,513**
	0—12	1,588	1,592	5,933	1,188	11,792	645	26,767	604
	13—14	63,803	28,590	93,718	16,982	91,871	10,106	203,135	9,509
	15—19	81,610	34,427	92,905	19,473	87,890	13,509	165,421	12,917
	20—29	15,751	6,085	19,350	3,711	20,710	2,727	43,098	3,020
	30 and over	1,739	808	1,901	576	2,433	446	5,740	463
Nicobar Islands ..	All Ages	192	37	39	7	4	11	1	15
	0—14	16	2	2	..	1	..	..	..
	15—19	89	12	21	5	2	5	1	12
	20—29	82	21	16	4	1	6	..	3
	30 and over	5	2	..	..	..	..	..	..
Assam	All Ages†	691	231	1,412	68	1,380	19	2,631	34
	Under 13	35	33	164	23	189	5	457	7
	13—14	109	53	258	14	230	4	403	4
	15—19	368	113	697	22	729	6	1,348	18
	20—29	169	27	273	8	218	3	401	5
	30 and over	10	5	20	1	14	1	22	..
Baroda State	All Ages	3,983	5,379	30,163	4,010	33,346	1,157	124,721	2,479
	13—14	2,668	4,382	25,854	3,645	28,294	977	105,512	2,053
	15—19	968	854	3,519	286	4,065	114	15,026	261
	20—29	305	112	718	56	890	45	3,877	118
	30 and over	42	31	72	23	97	21	306	47

* Excludes Baluchistan, Bengal, Burma and the Andaman Islands.

† The difference of 54 between the total number of slips dealt with here and in Table I is due to the fact that marriage in which only one still-born child was born have been treated as sterile.

Table II.—Proportion of Fertile and Sterile Marriages—*concld.*

Province, State or Agency.	Age of wife at marriage.	Duration of Marriage years. 0—4 Fertile.	0—4 Sterile.	5—9 Fertile.	5—9 Sterile.	10—14 Fertile.	10—14 Sterile.	15 and over. Fertile.	15 and over. Sterile.
1	2	3	4	5	6	7	8	9	10
Bombay	**All Ages**	**117,951**	**39,955**	**97,144**	**26,602**	**73,418**	**18,932**	**52,916**	**14,770**
	0—14	51,738	15,867	44,792	9,501	34,614	6,907	26,126	4,762
	15—19	57,447	20,337	45,866	14,351	33,891	10,069	23,680	8,144
	20—29	7,865	3,283	5,874	2,388	4,442	1,737	2,830	1,652
	30 and over	901	468	612	362	471	219	280	212
Central India Agency ..	**All Ages**	**257***	**213**	**523**	**59**	**568**	**46**	**1,245**	**60**
	13—14	83	99	221	21	211	12	366	20
	15—19	132	99	233	25	277	26	672	24
	20—29	37	13	60	6	71	7	188	14
	30 and over	5	2	9	7	9	1	19	2
Central Provinces and Berar	**All Ages**	**1,824**	**221**	**4,466**	**133**	**6,698**	**136**	**8,077**	**88**
	Under 13	198	2	811	30	3,050	85	19	..
	13—14	629	85	1,734	48	1,809	25	3,405	44
	15—19	891	126	1,650	43	1,542	20	3,965	38
	20—29	96	8	250	12	279	5	532	6
	30 and over	10	..	21	..	18	1	66	..
Cochin State	**All Ages**	**3,337**	**2,505**	**5,311**	**433**	**5,315**	**205**	**15,959**	**406**
	0—12	45	159	258	58	523	27	2,718	66
	13—14	303	375	728	110	990	24	2,919	53
	15—19	2,115	1,565	3,264	178	2,862	86	7,919	188
	20—29	811	370	993	68	870	59	2,268	89
	30 and over	63	36	68	19	70	9	135	10
Delhi	**All Ages**	**144**	**136**	**400**	**64**	**428**	**22**	**1,021**	**31**
	0—12	7	26	63	28	82	8	284	13
	13—14	37	49	95	11	100	3	155	4
	15—19	79	51	198	24	200	9	417	13
	20—29	20	8	40	1	46	2	156	1
	30 and over	1	2	4	..	..	..	9	..
Gwalior State	**All Ages**	**748**	**1,109**	**2,643**	**694**	**3,665**	**300**	**9,547**	**363**
	0—12	154	584	1,028	466	1,828	202	5,518	207
	13—14	249	304	761	129	755	26	1,195	37
	15—19	268	176	693	73	862	42	2,217	77
	20—29	58	40	151	21	199	25	584	40
	30 and over	19	5	10	5	21	5	33	2
Jammu and Kashmir State	**All Ages**	**7,104**	**4,379**	**19,475**	**1,524**	**28,144**	**,061**	**70,408**	**1,502**
	13—14	1,216	1,546	4,144	469	7,374	209	17,230	280
	15—19	3,962	2,154	11,057	780	15,234	535	39,862	813
	20—29	1,703	572	3,811	222	4,825	259	11,452	326
	30 and over	223	107	463	53	711	58	1,864	83
Madras	**All Ages**	**4,064**	**1,834**	**8,188**	**778**	**8,298**	**547**	**18,101**	**848**
	13—14	1,573	913	3,913	429	3,859	264	8,120	414
	15—19	2,083	784	3,706	293	3,819	249	8,460	352
	20—29	354	118	539	48	595	30	1,453	76
	30 and over	54	19	30	8	25	4	68	6
Mysore State	**All Ages**	**493**	**106**	**1,188**	**43**	**1,172**	**26**	**1,994**	**35**
	13—14	237	52	679	24	683	13	1,226	12
	15—19	214	45	455	16	431	8	659	18
	20—29	38	8	53	2	57	5	104	4
	30 and over	4	1	1	1	1	..	5	1
Punjab	**All Ages**	**10,891**	**4,680**	**26,032**	**1,857**	**34,436**	**1,031**	**93,236**	**1,269**
	0—12	1,149	788	3,609	583	6,120	318	17,771	311
	13—14	2,286	1,195	5,906	435	7,754	215	17,721	191
	15—19	5,169	2,139	11,726	578	13,893	289	38,977	494
	20—29	2,022	498	4,327	205	5,742	130	15,884	211
	30 and over	265	60	464	56	927	79	2,883	62
Travancore State ..	**All Ages**	**6,990**	**6,893**	**12,538**	**1,440**	**13,178**	**571**	**41,034**	**728**
	13—14	1,012	2,218	3,392	619	3,982	182	17,630	284
	15—19	4,586	3,971	7,396	647	7,356	294	20,532	375
	20—29	1,307	666	1,675	160	1,798	93	2,858	69
	30 and over	85	38	75	14	42	2	14	..
Western India States Agency	**All Ages**	**5,822**	**3,824**	**4,285**	**4,218**	**4,646**	**3,369**	**3,270**	**3,885**
	0—14	1,647	1,450	1,239	1,527	1,215	1,245	1,037	1,351
	15—19	3,239	2,001	2,424	2,154	2,727	1,757	1,686	2,090
	20—29	884	341	570	510	677	321	511	406
	30 and over	52	32	52	27	27	46	36	38

* Slips in which duration of marriage life was not given have been omitted.

Table III.—Average Size of Family correlated with Age of Wife at Marriage.

Province, State or Agency.	All-Ages.					0—12					13—14				
	Number of families.	Number of children born alive.	Average observed.	Number of children surviving.	Average observed.	Number of families.	Number of children born alive.	Average observed.	Number of children surviving.	Average observed.	Number of families.	Number of children born alive.	Average observed.	Number of children surviving.	Average.
1	2	3	4	5	6	7	8	9	10	11	12	13	14	15	16
INDIA*	**568,628**	**2,368,172**	**4·2**	**1,661,448**	**2·9**	**40,729**	**154,120**	**3·8**	**112,127**	**2·8**	**191,783**	**809,891**	**4·2**	**552,345**	**2·9**
1 Andaman Islands	538	1,551	2·9	1,246	2·3	..	..	..	..	..	302	898	3·0	747	2·8
2 Assam	6,466	27,761	4·3	17,596	2·7	913	4,075	4·5	2,380	2·6	1,075	4,104	3·8	2,640	2·5
3 Baluchistan	39,744	163,001	4·1	108,949	2·7	..	..	..	..	..	8,127	31,087	3·8	20,303	2·6
4 Baroda State	39,768	226,456	5·7	136,795	3·4	..	..	..	..	..	30,915	177,469	5·7	106,887	3·5
5 Bombay	157,906	629,208	4·0	447,728	2·8	..	..	..	..	..	67,605†	264,340	3·9	183,315	2·7
6 Burma	1,153	4,309	3·7	2,549	2·2	4	16	4·0	7	1·8	60	222	3·7	126	2·1
7 Central India Agency	2,478	8,462	3·4	5,653	2·3	..	..	..	..	..	772	2,374	3·1	1,548	2·0
8 Central Provinces and Berar	21,643	84,610	3·9	58,743	2·7	4,195	15,348	3·7	10,476	2·5	7,869	31,494	4·0	20,730	2·6
9 Cochin State	33,471	125,878	3·8	92,458	2·8	3,854	17,126	4·4	12,776	3·3	5,502	22,177	4·0	16,682	3·0
10 Delhi	2,246	7,932	3·5	5,298	2·4	511	1,699	3·3	1,191	2·2	454	1,478	3·3	966	2·1
11 Gwalior State	1,802	11,317	6·3	6,400	3·6	603	3,819	6·3	2,170	3·6	195	1,214	6·2	750	3·9
12 Jammu and Kashmir State	12,374	70,416	5·6	47,469	3·8	..	..	..	..	..	1,815	11,460	6·3	7,635	4·2
13 Madras	42,658	142,554	3·3	103,698	2·4	..	..	..	..	..	19,485	63,157	3·2	46,087	2·4
14 Mysore State	4,847	20,937	4·3	14,976	3·1	..	..	..	..	..	2,825	11,341	4·0	8,172	2 9
15 Punjab	173,432	686,470	4·0	493,509	2·9	30,649	112,037	3·7	83,127	2·7	35,703	132,573	3·7	94,440	2·7
16 Travancore State	18,456	119,813	6·5	90,432	4·9	..	..	..	..	..	5,985	41,965	7·0	32,075	5·4
17 Western India States Agency	9,646	37,497	3·9	27,949	2·9	..	.	..	..	..	3,094†	12,538	4·1	9,242	3·0

* Details for Bengal have been excluded as this Table was not compiled in that unit in the above form.

† Includes wives married below the age of 13 years.

Table III.—Average Size of Family correlated with Age of Wife at Marriage—*concld.*

	Province, State or Agency	15—19.					20—29.					30 and over.				
		Number of families.	Number of children born alive.	Average observed.	Number of children surviving.	Average observed.	Number of families.	Number of children born alive.	Average observed.	Number of children surviving.	Average observed.	Number of families.	Number of children born alive.	Average observed.	Number of children surviving.	Average observed.
	1	17	18	19	20	21	22	23	24	25	26	27	28	29	30	31
	INDIA*	**249,874**	**1,022,209**	**4·1**	**726,118**	**2·9**	**75,758**	**328,181**	**4·3**	**232,804**	**3·1**	**10,484**	**53,771**	**5·1**	**38,054**	**3·6**
1	Andaman Islands	210	577	2·7	447	2·1	26	76	2·9	52	2·0	..	..	..	..	..
2	Assam	3,301	14,397	4·4	9,201	2·8	1,104	4,912	4·4	3,200	2·9	73	273	3·7	175	2·4
3	Baluchistan	17,555	71,765	4·1	46,987	2·7	12,365	52,034	4·2	36,450	2·9	1,697	8,115	4·8	5,209	3·1
4	Baroda State	5,819	33,982	5·8	20,807	3·6	2,586	13,429	5·2	8,250	3·2	448	1,576	3·5	851	1·9
5	Bombay	77,784	315,377	4·3	228,061	2·9	11,343	45,534	4·0	33,531	3·0	1,174	3,957	3·4	2,821	2·4
6	Burma	699	2,765	4·0	1,588	2·3	366	1,232	3·4	774	2·1	24	74	3·1	54	2·3
7	Central India Agency	1,272	4,414	3·5	2,949	2·3	387	1,505	3·9	1,063	2·7	47	169	3·6	93	2·0
8	Central Provinces and Berar	8,275	32,315	3·9	23,857	2·9	1,188	4,833	4·1	3,291	2·8	116	620	5·3	389	3·3
9	Cochin State	18,177	65,446	3·6	48,454	2·7	5,528	19,844	3·6	13,716	2·5	410	1,285	3·1	830	2·0
10	Delhi	991	3,553	3·6	2,339	2·4	274	1,140	4·2	760	2·8	16	62	3·9	42	2·6
11	Gwalior State	599	3,904	6·5	2,225	3·7	345	2,077	6·0	1,090	3·2	60	303	5·1	165	2·8
12	Jammu and Kashmir State	6,189	37,152	6·0	25,237	4·1	3,413	17,901	5·2	11,983	3·5	957	3,903	4·1	2,614	2·7
13	Madras	19,746	67,446	3·4	49,144	2·5	3,213	11,220	3·5	8,015	2·5	214	731	3·4	452	2·1
14	Mysore State	1,759	8,503	4·8	6,050	3·4	252	1,062	4·2	733	2·9	11	31	2·8	21	1·9
15	Punjab	73,265	281,360	3·8	199,529	2·7	29,019	129,318	4·5	93,261	3·2	4,796	31,182	6·5	23,152	4·8
16	Travancore State	8,993	58,778	6·5	44,046	4·9	3,124	17,786	5·7	13,291	4·3	354	1,284	3·6	1,020	2·9
17	Western India States Agency	5,240	20,475	3·9	15,197	2·9	1,225	4,278	3·5	3,344	2·7	87	206	2·4	166	1·9

* Details for Bengal have been excluded as this Table was not compiled in that unit in the above form.

Table IV.—Size of Families

Occupations.	India. Number of families examined.	Total number of children born alive.	Average per family.	Number of children surviving.	Proportion of surviving to total 1,000 born.	Andaman and Number of families examined.	Total number of children born alive.
1	2	3	4	5	6	7	8
Total of all classes	**408,161**	**1,740,399**	**4·3**	**1,213,457**	**697**	**845**	**2,782**
A.—Production of raw materials	**223,391**	**978,750**	**4 4**	**683,540**	**698**	**515**	**1,806**
Pasture and Agriculture	*213,025*	*911,655*	*4·3*	*631,841*	*693*	*515*	*1,806*
Cultivating owners	23,381	102,932	4·4	68,584	666	515	1,806
Agricultural labourers	13,421	57,691	4·3	40,507	702	..	..
Forestry	139	529	3·8	355	671	..	..
Stock raising	5,038	20,487	4·1	13,847	676	..	..
B.—Preparation and supply of material substances.	**92,323**	**387,301**	**4·2**	**266,963**	**689**	**145**	**429**
Industry	*48,203*	*201,825*	*4·2*	*138,608*	*687*	*74*	*232*
Textiles	5,670	20,835	3·7	15,237	731	..	..
Hides, skins and hard materials from the animal kingdom.	57	255	4·5	154	604	..	..
Wood	1,521	6,220	4·1	4,192	674	..	..
Sawyers, carpenters, turners and joiners, etc.	24,705	106,492	4·3	71,716	673 }		
Metals ..	688	2,628	3·8	1,756	668 }	63	179
Blacksmiths, other workers in iron, makers of implements, workers in brass, copper and bell metal.	959	3,674	3·8	2,582	703 }		
Ceramics	181	678	3·7	458	676	..	
Chemical products properly so called and analogous.	215	823	3·8	586	712	..	..
Food industries	983	4,269	4·3	3,043	713		..
Industries of the dress and the toilet	8,147	31,678	3·9	22,118	698	..	..
Building industries	1,117	4,506	3·8	3,053	678	..	..
Construction of means of transport	77	383	5·0	229	598	..	..
Production and transmission of physical force.	35	137	3·9	76	555	..	..
Miscellaneous and undefined industries	4,310	18,475	4·3	12,573	681	11	53
Scavenging	3,547	15,428	4·3	10,485	680	..	..
Transport	*4,077*	*14,893*	*3·7*	*10,245*	*688*	..	..
Transport by water	297	1,544	5·2	1,002	649	..	..
Transport by road	1,499	5,660	3·8	3,784	669	..	..
Transport by rail	451	1,577	3·5	1,122	711	..	..
Trade	*40,043*	*170,583*	*4·3*	*118,110*	*692*	*71*	*197*
C.—Public Administration and Liberal Arts	**34,453**	**139,219**	**4·0**	**99,701**	**716**	**103**	**319**
Public force	*2,671*	*10,464*	*3·9*	*7,108*	*679*	..	..
Army	1,543	5,486	3·6	3,999	729	..	..
Navy	..	..	..	..	..	..	..
Police	743	2,754	3·7	1,734	630	..	..
Public Administration	*19,232*	*74,688*	*3·9*	*53,842*	*721*	*103*	*319*
Professions and Liberal Arts	*12,550*	*54,067*	*4·3*	*38,751*	*719*	..	..
Religion	2,407	12,629	5·2	7,970	631	..	.
Law, medicine and instruction	7,360	27,412	3·7	20,824	760	..	..
D.—Miscellaneous	**57,994**	**235,129**	**4·1**	**163,253**	**694**	**82**	**228**
Persons living on their income	*3,407*	*17,054*	*5·0*	*12,146*	*712*	..	..
Domestic service	*6,401*	*24,068*	*3·8*	*16,526*	*687*	..	..
Insufficiently described occupations	*30,125*	*123,062*	*4·1*	*85,128*	*692*	*60*	*147*
Labourers and workmen otherwise unspecified	29,142	118,134	4·1	81,979	694	38	85
Unproductive	*14,585*	*58,668*	*4·0*	*41,692*	*711*	*22*	*81*
Inmates of jails, asylums alms houses, beggars and vagrants.	2,204	9,551	4·3	6,774	709	—	—
Other unclassified non-productive industries	58	326	5·6	204	626	..	—
Unemployed and occupations unspecified ..	15,517	60,061	3·9	41,797	696	22	81

by Occupation of Husband.

Nicobar Islands.			Assam.					Baluchistan.				
Average per family.	Number of children surviving.	Proportion of surviving to total 1,000 born.	Number of families examined.	Total Number of children born alive.	Average per family.	Number of children surviving.	Proportion of surviving to total 1,000 born.	Number of families examined.	Total number of children born alive.	Average per family.	Number of children surviving.	Proportion of surviving to total 1,000 born.
9	10	11	12	13	14	15	16	17	18	19	20	21
3·3	**2,133**	**767**	**6,466**	**27,761**	**4·3**	**17,596**	**634**	**39,744**	**163,001**	**4·1**	**108,949**	**668**
3·6	**1,404**	**777**	**5,985**	**25,696**	**4·3**	**16,033**	**624**	**33,385**	**139,575**	**4·2**	**93,407**	**669**
3·6	*1,404*	*777*	*5,985*	*25,696*	*4·3*	*16,033*	*624*	*33,368*	*139,522*	*4·2*	*93,356*	*669*
3·6	1,404	777	..	..	..	..	..	16,663	74,683	4·5	47,841	641
..	..	..	..	..	..	..	..	1,139	4,057	3·6	2,787	687
..	..	..	..	..	..	..	..	13	51	3·9	32	627
	..	..	..	..	..	..	..	2,788	11,127	4·0	7,744	696
2·9	**314**	**732**	..	..	..	..	..	**3,680**	**14,192**	**3·9**	**8,976**	**631**
3·1	*182*	*784*	..	..	..	..	..	*1,138*	*4,413*	*3·9*	*2,847*	*645*
..	..	..	..	..	..	..	..	43	174	4·0	129	741
..	..	..	..	..	..	..	..	..	..	..	..	..
..	..	..	..	..	..	..	..	161	644	4·0	433	672
..	..	..	..	..	..	..	..	130	512	3·9	361	705
2·8	145	810	..	..	..	..	..	177	742	4·2	483	651
..	..	..	..	..	..	..	..	169	713	4·2	461	647
..	..	..	..	..	..	..	..	36	127	3·5	78	614
..	..	..	..	..	..	..	..	23	74	3·2	61	824
..	..	..	..	..	..	..	..	114	451	4·0	279	619
..	..	..	..	..	..	..	..	282	1,040	3·7	638	613
..	..	..	..	..	..	..	..	45	167	3·7	88	527
..	..	..	..	..	..	..	..	..	..	..	..	..
..	..	..	..	..	..	..	..	..	..	..	..	..
4·8	37	698	..	..	..	..	..	230	894	3·9	583	652
..	..	..	..	..	..	..	..	129	469	3·6	309	662
..	..	..	..	..	..	..	..	*777*	*2,966*	*3·8*	*1,911*	*644*
..	..	..	..	..	..	..	..	37	278	7·5	149	536
..	..	..	..	..	..	..	..	532	2,023	3·8	1,320	652
..	..	..	..	..	..	..	..	194	619	3·2	415	670
2·8	*132*	*670*	..	..	..	..	..	*1,765*	*6,813*	*3·9*	*4,218*	*619*
3·1	**245**	**768**	..	..	..	..	..	**1,377**	**5,191**	**3·8**	**3,459**	**666**
..	..	..	..	..	..	..	..	*221*	*916*	*4·1*	*542*	*592*
..	..	..	..	..	..	..	..	44	148	3·4	104	703
..	..	..	..	..	..	..	..	..	..	..	..	..
..	..	..	..	..	..	..	..	177	768	4·3	438	570
3·1	*245*	*768*	..	..	..	..	..	*712*	*2,417*	*3·4*	*1,656*	*685*
..	..	..	..	..	..	..	..	*444*	*1,858*	*4·2*	*1,261*	*678*
..	..	..	..	..	..	..	..	303	1,287	4·2	850	660
..	..	..	..	..	..	..	..	47	193	4·1	146	756
2·7	**170**	**746**	**481**	**2,065**	**4·3**	**1,563**	**757**	**1,302**	**4,043**	**3·1**	**3,107**	**768**
..	..	..	..	..	..	..	..	*779*	*2,134*	*2·7*	*1,825*	*855*
..	..	..	..	..	..	..	..	*225*	*848*	*3·8*	*565*	*666*
2·5	*121*	*823*	*481*	*2,065*	*4·3*	*1,563*	*757*	*35*	*162*	*4·6*	*107*	*660*
2·2	68	800	481	2,065	4·3	1,563	757	..	..	..	..	..
3·7	***49***	***605***	..	..	..	..	..	*263*	*899*	*3·4*	*610*	*679*
..	..	..	..	..	..	..	..	..	..	..	..	..
..	..	..	..	..	..	..	..	263	899	3·4	610	679
3·7	49	605	..	..	..	..	..	..	..	..	..	..

Table IV.—Size of Families

Occupations.	Baroda State. Number of families examined.	Total number of children born alive.	Average per family.	Number of children surviving.	Proportion of surviving to total 1,000 born.	Bengal. Number of families examined.	Total number of children born alive.
1	22	23	24	25	26	27	28
Total of all classes	**39,768**	**226,456**	**5·7**	**136,795**	**604**	**2,406**	**14,501**
A.—Production of raw materials	**24,391**	**137,864**	**5·7**	**86,333**	**626**	**1,228**	**7,476**
Pasture and Agriculture	*24,391*	*137,864*	*5·7*	*86,333*	*626*	*1,209*	*7,379*
Cultivating owners	..	..	..	..	..	..	..
Agricultural labourers	1,399*	8,223	5·9	5,014	610	..	..
Forestry	..	..	..	..	..	..	..
Stock raising	836	3,950	5·8	2,228	564	..	..
B.—Preparation and supply of material substances.	**8,279**	**48,629**	**5·9**	**27,507**	**566**	**479**	**2,602**
Industry	*4,823*	*27,912*	*5·8*	*16,150*	*579*	*159*	*933*
Textiles	..	..	..	..	..	14	77
Hides, skins and hard materials from the animal kingdom.	..	..	..	..	..	19	98
Wood	..	..	..	..	..	11	77
Sawyers, carpenters, turners and joiners, etc.	4,602	26,666	5·8	15,453	580	..	..
Metals	..	..	..	..	..	15	104
Blacksmiths, other workers in iron, makers of implements, workers in brass, copper and bell metal.	..	..	..	..	..	..	..
Ceramics	..	..	..	..	..	..	..
Chemical products properly so called and analogous.	..	..	..	..	..	..	..
Food industries	..	..	..	..	..	..	
Industries of the dress and the toilet	..	..	..	..	..	..	..
Building industries	..	..	..	..	..	13	80
Construction of means of transport	..	..	..	..	..	..	..
Production and transmission of physical force.	..	..	..	..	..	..	..
Miscellaneous and undefined industries	221	1,246	5·6	697	559	87	497
Scavenging	221	1,246	5·6	697	559	..	..
Transport	*184*	*1,108*	*6·0*	*679*	*613*	*35*	*230*
Transport by water	97	614	6·3	391	637	3	9
Transport by road	87	494	5·7	288	583	13	75
Transport by rail	..	..	..	..	..	16	98
Trade	*3,272*	*19,609*	*6·0*	*10,678*	*544*	*281*	*1,439*
C.—Public Administration and Liberal Arts	**2,467**	**14,844**	**6·0**	**8,062**	**543**	**561**	**3,597**
Public Force	*320*	*1,809*	*5·7*	*1,112*	*615*	*18*	*115*
Army	..	..	..	..	..	..	..
Navy	..	..	..	..	..	..	..
Police	..	..	..	..	..	..	..
Public Administration	*913*	*5,509*	*6·0*	*2,806*	*509*	*299*	*1,812*
Professions and Liberal Arts	*1,234*	*7,526*	*6·1*	*4,144*	*551*	*244*	*1,670*
Religion	1,048	6,376	6·1	3,495	642	44	267
Law, medicine and instruction	151	937	6·2	547	584	194	1,372
D.—Miscellaneous	**4,631**	**25,119**	**5·4**	**14,893**	**593**	**138**	**826**
Persons living on their income	*239*	*1,337*	*5·6*	*724*	*542*	*53*	*357*
Domestic service	*178*	*836*	*4·7*	*502*	*600*	*27*	*143*
Insufficiently described occupations	*4,115*	*22,366*	*5·4*	*13,341*	*596*	..	..
Labourers and workmen otherwise unspecified	3,649	19,859	5·4	11,879	598	..	..
Unproductive	*99*	*580*	*5·9*	*326*	*562*	*58*	*326*
Inmates of jails, asylums alms-houses, beggars and vagrants.	90	517	5·7	288	557	..	..
Other unclassified non-productive industries	..	..	..	..	..	58	326
Unemployed and occupations unspecified	9	63	7·0	38	603	..	..

* Includes wood

† Returned as skilled (236), unskilled (417) others 84)

by Occupation of Husband—*contd.*

Average per family.	Number of children surviving.	Proportion of surviving to total 1,000 born.	Burma. Number of families examined.	Total number of children born alive.	Average per family.	Number of children surviving.	Proportion of surviving to total 1,000 born.	Central India Agency. Number of families examined.	Total number of children born alive.	Average per family.	Number of children surviving.	Proportion of surviving to total 1,000 born.
29	30	31	32	33	34	35	36	37	38	39	40	41
6·0	**9,531**	**657**	**1,153**	**4,309**	**3·7**	**2,549**	**592**	**4,362**	**15,416**	**3·5**	**9,790**	**635**
6·1	**4,820**	**645**	..	..	..	..	..	**154**	**509**	**3·3**	**298**	**585**
6·1	*4,756*	*644*	..	..	..	..	..	..	..	..	..	..
..	..	..	..	..	..	..	..	144	468	3·3	277	590
..	..	..	..	..	..	..	..	..	..	..	..	..
..	..	..	..	..	..	..	..	..	..	..	..	..
..	..	..	..	..	..	..	..	10	41	4·0	21	512
..	..	..	..	..	..	..	..	**307**	**1,223**	**4·0**	**771**	**630**
5·4	**1,642**	**631**	**170**	**760**	**4·5**	**426**	**561**	*156*	*517*	*3·3*	*312*	*603*
5·9	*565*	*606*	..	..	..	..	..	..	..	..	..	..
5·5	49	636	..	..	..	..	..	..	..	..	..	
5·2	54	551	..	..	..	..	..					
7·0	44	571	..	..	..	..	.. }	146	501	3·4	304	607
..	..	..	..	..	..	..	.. }					
6·9	68	654	..	..	..	..	.. }					
..	..	..	..	..	..	..	.. }					
..	..	..	..	..	..	..	..	..	..	..	..	..
..	..	..	..	..	..	..	..	..	..	..	..	..
..	..	..	..	..	..	..	..	..	..	..	..	..
..	..	..	..	..	..	..	..	..	..	..	..	..
6·2	41	512	..	..	..	..	..	..	..	..	..	..
..	..	..	..	..	..	..	..	..	..	..	..	..
..	..	..	..	..	..	..	..	..	..	..	..	..
5·7	309	622	..	..	..	..	..	10	16	1·6	8	500
..	..	..	..	..	..	..	..	10	16	1·6	8	500
5·9	*124*	*539*	..	..	..	..	..	*9*	*31*	*3·4*	*22*	*710*
3·0	3	333	..	..	..	..	..	..	..	..	..	..
5·8	36	480	..	..	..	..	..	9	31	3·4	22	710
6·1	64	653	..	..	..	..	..	..	..	..	..	..
5·1	*953*	*662*	*170*	*760*	*4·5*	*426*	*561*	*142*	*675*	*4·8*	*437*	*640*
6·4	**2,542**	**707**	**246**	**826**	**3·4**	**573**	**694**	**267**	**896**	**3·4**	**656**	**732**
6·4	*74*	*643*	..	..	..	..	..	*166*	*505*	*3·0*	*392*	*776*
..	..	..	..	..	..	..	..	134	492	3·0	387	787
..	..	..	..	..	..	..	..	..	..	..	..	..
..	..	..	..	..	..	..	..	2	13	6·5	5	385
6·1	*1,272*	*778*	*246*	*826*	*3·4*	*573*	*694*	*92*	*334*	*3·6*	*229*	*686*
6·8	*1,196*	*716*	..	..	..	..	..	*9*	*57*	*6·3*	*35*	*614*
6·1	169	633	..	..	..	..	..	2	8	4·0	6	750
7·1	1,001	730	..	..	..	..	..	7	49	7·0	29	592
6·0	**527**	**638**	**737**	**2,723**	**3·7**	**1,550**	**569**	**3,634**	**12,788**	**3·5**	**8,065**	**631**
6·7	*247*	*692*	..	..	..	..	..	*1*	*11*	*1·0*	*5*	*455*
5·3	*76*	*531*	..	..	..	..	..	*102*	*329*	*3·2*	*191*	*581*
..	..	..	..	..	..	..	..	*47*	*137*	*2·9*	*86*	*628*
..	..	..	..	..	..	..	..	45	136	3·0	86	632
5·6	*204*	*626*	*737*	*2,723*	*3·7*	*1,550*	*569*	*8*	*34*	*4·3*	*22*	*647*
..	..	..	..	..	..	..	..	..	..	..	..	..
5·6	204	626	..	..	..	..	..	..	..	..	..	..
..	..	..	737†	2,723	3·7	1,550	569	3,476	12,277	3·5	7,761	632

cutters, etc.

and have been classified accordingly as unspecified.

Table IV.—Size of Families

Occupations.	Central Provinces and Berar. Number of families examined.	Total number of children born alive.	Average per family.	Number of children surviving.	Proportion of surviving to total 1,000 born.	Cochin Number of families examined.	Total number of children born alive.
1	42	43	44	45	46	47	48
Total of all classes	**21,643**	**85,704**	**3·9**	**60,743**	**709**	**33,471**	**125,878**
A.—Production of raw materials	**10,984**	**43,749**	**4·1**	**29,820**	**682**	**8,086**	**31,594**
Pasture and Agriculture	*10,741*	*43,038*	*4·0*	*29,355*	*682*	*7,505*	*29,220*
Cultivating owners	..	..	..	..	..	5,048	19,722
Agricultural labourers	..	..	..	..	..	2,078	8,061
Forestry	65	256	3·9	186	727	61	222
Stock raising	155	528	3·4	415	786	10	27
B.—Preparation and supply of material substances.	**4,889**	**18,706**	**3·8**	**13,059**	**698**	**10,866**	**41,571**
Industry	*3,117*	*12,128*	*3·9*	*8,260*	*681*	*4,754*	*17,067*
Textiles	1,371	5,182	3·7	3,500	675	548	1,731
Hides, skins and hard materials from the animal kingdom.	..	..	..	..	..	38	157
Wood	..	..	..	..	..	1,196	4,510
Sawyers, carpenters, turners and joiners, etc.	305	1,230	4·0	888	722	1,055	3,898
Metals						350	1,281
Blacksmiths, other workers in iron, makers of implements, workers in brass, copper and bell metal.	404	1,598	3·9	1,145	717	323	1,184
Ceramics	..	..	..	..	..	145	551
Chemical products properly so called and analogous.	58	238	4·1	146	614	134	511
Food industries	58	278	4·8	180	650	811	3,540
Industries of dress and the toilet	138	438	3·1	303	692	557	1,905
Building industries	571	2,337	4·0	1,560	667	488	1,922
Construction of means of transport	77	383	4·9	229	598	..	..
Production and transmission of physical force.	35	137	3·9	76	555	..	..
Miscellaneous and undefined industries	100	307	3·0	233	759	487	1,859
Scavenging	..	..	..	..	..	23	94
Transport	*326*	*1,184*	*3·6*	*880*	*743*	*962*	*3,360*
Transport by water	..	..	..	..	..	137	526
Transport by road	97	356	3·6	264	742	739	2,548
Transport by rail	194	721	3·7	541	750	47	139
Trade	*1,446*	*5,394*	*3·7*	*3,919*	*727*	*5,150*	*20,244*
C.—Public Administration and Liberal Arts	**2,002**	**7,423**	**3·7**	**5,333**	**718**	**4,390**	**15,313**
Public Force	*328*	*1,187*	*3·6*	*747*	*629*	*237*	*788*
Army	..	..	..	..	..	1	2
Navy	..	..	..	..	..	..	..
Police	328	1,187	3·6	747	629	236	786
Public Administration	*941*	*3,498*	*3·7*	*2,529*	*723*	*1,265*	*4,530*
Professions and Liberal Arts	*733*	*2,738*	*3·7*	*2,059*	*751*	*2,888*	*9,995*
Religion	132	669	5·1	515	770	503	1,939
Law, medicine and instruction	514	1,664	3·2	1,292	777	2,178	7,255
D.—Miscellaneous	**3,768**	**15,826**	**4·2**	**12,531**	**792**	**10,129**	**37,400**
Persons living on their income	*56*	*337*	*6·0*	*225*	*674*	*504*	*2,003*
Domestic service	*1,532*	*5,261*	*3·4*	*3,765*	*716*	*1,085*	*4,143*
Insufficiently described occupations	*2,073*	*9,800*	*4·7*	*8,247*	*842*	*7,228*	*26,055*
Labourers and workmen otherwise unspecified	2,027	9,626	4·7	8,121	844	6,992	25,129
Unproductive	*107*	*428*	*3·9*	*294*	*687*	*1,312*	*5,199*
Inmates of jails, asylums, alms houses, beggars and vagrants.	107	428	3·9	294	687	19	61
Other unclassified non-productive industries	..	..	..	..	..	..	..
Unemployed and occupations unspecified	..	..	..	..	..	1,293	5,138

by occupation of Husband—*contd.*

State.			Delhi.					Gwalior State.				
Average per family.	Number of children surviving.	Proportion of surviving to total 1,000 born.	Number of families examined.	Total number of children born alive.	Average per family.	Total number of children surviving.	Proportion of surviving to total 1,000 born.	Number of families examined.	Total number of children born alive.	Average per family.	Number of children surviving.	Proportion of surviving to total 1,000 born.
49	50	51	52	53	54	55	56	57	58	59	60	61
3·8	**92,458**	**735**	**2,246**	**7,932**	**3·5**	**5,298**	**668**	**1,802**	**11,287**	**6·3**	**6,400**	**567**
3·9	**23,779**	**753**	**677**	**2,315**	**3·4**	**1,525**	**659**	**1,001**	**6,252**	**6·2**	**3,908**	**625**
3·9	22,087	756	677	2,315	3·4	1,525	659	984*	6,146	6·2	3,840	625
3·9	15,083	765	..	..	..	..	..	764	4,794	6·3	3,000	626
3·9	5,939	737	42	138	3·3	74	536	24	155	6·5	93	600
3·6	137	617	..	..	..	..	..	..	..	..	..	..
2·7	19	703	2	5	2·5	4	800	17	106	6·2	68	642
3·8	**30,747**	**740**	**405**	**1,240**	**3·1**	**773**	**623**	**326**	**2,177**	**6·7**	**1,086**	**499**
3·8	12,795	712	237	758	3·2	445	587	161	1,044	6·5	535	512
3·2	1,281	740	9	29	3·2	18	621	..	..	..	..	..
4·1	100	637	..	..	..	..	..	..	..	..	..	..
3·8	3,197	709	151	461	3·1	305	662	153	989	6·5	518	524
3·7	2,813	722	151	461	3·1	305	662	153	989	6·5	518	524
3·7	901	703	..	..	..	..	..	..	..	..	..	..
3·7	831	702	..	..	..	..	..	..	..	..	..	..
3·8	380	690	..	..	..	..	..	..	..	..	..	..
3·8	379	742	..	..	..	..	..	..	..	..	..	..
4·4	2,584	710	..	..	..	..	..	..	..	..	..	..
3·4	1,308	687	63	230	3·7	101	439	..	..	..	..	..
3·9	1,364	710	..	..	..	..	..	..	..	..	..	..
..	..	..	..	..	..	..	..	..	..	..	..	..
..	..	..	..	..	..	..	..	..	..	..	..	..
3·8	1,301	700	14	38	2·7	21	553	8	55	6·9	17	309
4·1	66	702	14	38	2·7	21	553	8	55	6·9	17	309
3·5	2,372	706	..	..	..	..	..	10	81	8·1	21	259
3·8	391	743	..	..	..	..	..	..	..	..	..	..
3·4	1,771	696	..	..	..	..	..	..	..	..	..	..
3·0	102	734	..	..	..	..	..	..	..	..	..	..
3·9	15,580	770	168†	482	2·9	328	680	155	1,052	6·8	530	504
3·5	**11,954**	**779**	**18**	**38**	**2·1**	**23**	**605**	**127**	**836**	**6·6**	**430**	**514**
3·3	546	692	2	4	2·0	4	1,000	13	69	5·3	36	522
2·0	2	1,000	2	4	2·0	4	1,000	..	..	..	..	..
..	..	..	..	..	..	..	..	..	..	..	..	..
3·3	544	692	..	..	..	..	..	..	..	..	..	..
3·6	3,506	774	..	..	..	..	..	57	400	7·0	206	515
3·5	7,902	789	16	34	2·1	19	559	57	367	6·4	188	512
3·8	1,408	726	..	..	..	..	..	46	284	6·2	138	486
3·3	5,875	809	16	34	2·1	19	559	11	83	7·6	50	602
3·7	**25,978**	**695**	**1,146**	**4,339**	**3·8**	**2,977**	**686**	**348**	**2,022**	**5·8**	**976**	**483**
4·0	1,529	763	..	..	..	..	..	9	60	6·7	29	483
3·8	2,995	723	597	2,573	4·3	1,714	666	198	1,227	6·2	562	458
3·6	17,447	670	211	756	3·6	537	710	91	490	5·4	252	514
3·6	16,774	668	211	756	3·6	537	710	61	317	5·2	169	533
4·0	4,007	771	338	1,010	3·0	726	719	50	245	4·9	133	543
3·2	40	656	1	5	5·0	2	400	17	85	5·0	51	600
..	..	..	..	..	..	..	..	..	..	..	..	..
4·0	**3,967**	**772**	**337**	**1,005**	**3·0**	**724**	**720**	**33**	**160**	**4·9**	**82**	**51**

*Includes rent collectors.

† Includes contractors and cashiers.

Table IV.—Size of Families by

Occupations.	Jammu and Kashmir State. Number of families examined.	Total number of children born alive.	Average per family.	Number of children surviving.	Proportion of surviving to total 1,000 born.	Madras. Number of families examined.	Total number of children born alive.	Average per family.	Number of children surviving.	Proportion of surviving to total 1,000 born.
1	62	63	64	65	66	67	68	69	70	71
Total of all classes ..	**15,164**	**88,811**	**5·8**	**61,106**	688	**42,658**	**140,390**	**3·4**	**102,083**	**727**
A.—Production of raw materials	**12,800**	**75,601**	**5·9**	**52,744**	**698**	**14,185**	**47,600**	**3·4**	**34,904**	**733**
Pasture and Agriculture	*12,800*	*75,601*	*5·9*	*52,744*	*698*	*14,185*	*47,600*	*3·4*	*34,904*	*733*
Cultivating owners	247	1,459	5·9	979	671	..	..	..	..	..
Agricultural labourers	85	525	6·1	255	486	..	..	..	..	..
Forestry	..	..	..	..	..	..	..	..	..	..
Stock raising	162	934	5·7	724	775	..	..	..	..	..
B.—Preparation and supply of material substances.	**1,425**	**7,839**	**5·5**	**5,090**	**649**	**10,878**	**35,635**	**3·3**	**25,452**	**714**
Industry	*878*	*4,660*	*5·3*	*3,040*	*652*	*4,547*	*15,084*	*3·3*	*10,679*	*707*
Textiles	..	..	..	..	..	..	..	..	..	..
Hides, skins and hard materials from the animal knigdom.	..	..	..	..	..	..	..	..	..	..
Wood	..	..	..	..	..	..	..	..	..	..
Sawyers, carpenters, turners and joiners, etc.	870	4,621	5·3	3,015	652	4,547	15,084	3·3	10,679	707
Metals	..	..	..	..	..	..	..	..	..	..
Blacksmiths, other workers in iron, makers of implements, workers in brass, copper and bell metal.	..	..	..	..	..	..	..	..	..	..
Ceramics	..	..	..	..	..	..	..	..	..	..
Chemical products properly so called and analogous.	..	..	..	..	..	..	..	..	..	..
Food industries	..	..	..	..	..	..	..	..	..	..
Industries of dress and the toilet	..	..	..	..	..	..	..	..	—	
Building industries	..	..	..	..	..	..	..	..	..	..
Construction of means of transport.	..	..	..	..	..	..	..	..	..	..
Production and transmission of physical force.	..	..	..	..	..	..	..	..	..	..
Miscellaneous and undefined industries.	8	39	4·8	25	641	..	..	..	..	..
Scavenging	8	39	4·8	25	641	..	..	..	..	..
Transport	*45*	*250*	*5·5*	*151*	*604*	*1,762*	*5,531*	*3·2*	*3,975*	*719*
Transport by water	23	117	5·1	68	581	..	..	..	..	..
Transport by road	22	133	6·0	83	624	..	..	..	..	..
Transport by rail	..	..	..	..	..	..	..	..	..	..
Trade	*502*	*2,929*	*5·8*	*1,899*	*648*	*4,629*	*15,020*	*3·2*	*10,798*	*719*
C.—Public Administration and Liberal Arts.	**439**	**2,530**	**5·8**	**1,472**	**582**	**10,082**	**32,021**	**3·2**	**24,021**	**750**
Public Force	*16*	*109*	*6·8*	*57*	*523*	*640*	*2,185*	*3·4*	*1,607*	*736*
Army	..	..	..	..	..	640*	2,185	3·4	1,607	736
Navy	..	..	..	..	..	..	..	..	..	..
Police	..	..	..	..	..	..	..	..	..	..
Public Administration	*130*	*725*	*5·5*	*466*	*643*	*7,471*	*23,864*	*3·2*	*17,898*	*750*
Professions and Liberal Arts ..	*293*	*1,696*	*5·8*	*949*	*560*	*1,971*	*5,972*	*3·0*	*4,516*	*756*
Religion	173	957	5·5	485	507	..	..	..	..	..
Law, medicine and instruction ..	29	149	5·1	97	651	1,971	5,972	3·0	4,513	756
D.—Miscellaneous	**500**	**2,841**	**5·7**	**1,800**	**634**	**7,513**	**25,134**	**3·3**	**17,706**	**705**
Persons living on their income ..	*103*	*543*	*5·2*	*342*	*630*	..	..	..	..	..
Domestic service	*50*	*307*	*6·1*	*192*	*625*	..		..	..	..
Insufficiently described occupations.	*114*	*688*	*6·0*	*468*	*680*	*6,351*	*20,836*	*3·3*	*14,734*	*707*
Labourers and workmen otherwise unspecified.	89	508	5·7	337	663	6,351	20,836	3·3	14,734	707
Unproductive	*233*	*1,303*	*5·5*	*798*	*612*	*1,162*	*4,298*	*3·7*	*2,972*	*692*
Inmates of jails, asylums, alms houses beggars and vagrants.	98	567	5·7	361	637	..	..	..	..	..
Other unclassified non-productive industries.	..	..	..		..	..	..	..	..	..
Unemployed and occupations unspecified.	135	736	5·4	437	594	1,162	4,298	3·7	2,972	692

* Including Police.

Occupation of Husband—*concld.*

Mysore State.					Punjab.					Travancore State.				
Number of families exa-mined.	Total number of children born alive.	Average per family.	Number of children surviv-ing.	Proportion of surviv-ing to total 1,000 born.	Number of families exa-mined.	Total number of children born alive.	Average per family.	Number of children surviv-ing.	Proportion of surviv-ing to total 1,000 born alive.	Number of families exa-mined.	Total number of children born.	Average per family.	Number of children surviv-ing.	Proportion of surviv-ing to total 1,000 born.
72	73	74	75	76	77	78	79	80	81	82	83	84	85	86
4,545	19,888	4·4	14,085	708	173,432	686,470	4·0	493,509	719	18,456	119,813	6·5	90,432	755
605	2,588	4·3	1,827	706	100,043	392,774	3·9	283,609	722	9,352	63,351	6·8	49,129	776
605	2,588	4·3	1,827	706	100,043	32,774	3·9	283,609	722	..	..	..	..	..
..	..	..	..	..	..	..	..	..	..	..	..	..	..	..
..	..	..	..	..	8,654	36,532	4·2	26,345	721	..	..	..	..	..
..	..	..	..	..	..	..	..	..	..	..	..	..	..	..
..	..	..	..	..	1,058	3,769	3·6	2,624	696	..	..	..	..	..
339	1,404	4·1	961	684	46,448	187,628	4·0	123,024	656	3,687	23,266	6·3	17,135	736
339	1,404	4·1	961	684	26,489	100,805	4·0	76,093	619	1,331	7,968	6·0	5,744	721
..	..	..	..	..	3,695	13,642	3·7	10,260	752	..	..	..	..	..
..	..	..	..	..	..	..	..	..	..	..	..	..	..	..
..	..	..	..	..	..	..	..	..	..	..	..	..	..	..
339	1,404	4·1	961	684	12,553	51,627	4·1	36,723	711	..	..	..	..	..
..	..	..	..	..	..	..	..	..	..	..	..	..	..	..
..	..	..	..	..	..	..	..	..	..	..	..	..	..	..
..	..	..	..	..	..	..	..	..	..	..	..	..	..	..
..	..	..	..	..	..	..	..	..	..	..	..	..	..	..
..	..	..	..	..	..	..	..	..	..	..	..	..	..	..
..	..	..	..	..	7,107	28,065	3·9	19,768	704	..	..	..	..	..
..	..	..	..	..	..	..	..	..	..	..	..	..	..	..
..	..	..	..	..	..	..	..	..	..	..	..	..	..	..
..	..	..	..	..	..	..	..	..	..	..	..	..	..	..
..	..	..	..	..	3,134	13,471	4·3	9,342	693	..	..	..	..	..
..	..	..	..	..	3,134	13,471	4·3	9,342	693	..	..	..	..	..
..	..	..	..	..	..	..	..	..	..	23	152	6·6	110	724
..	..	..	..	..	..	..	..	..	..	..	..	..	..	..
..	..	..	..	..	..	..	..	..	..	..	..	..	..	..
..	..	..	..	..	..	..	..	..	..	..	..	..	..	..
..	..	..	..	..	19,959†	80,823	4·0	56,931	704	2,333	15,146	6·5	11,281	744
3,001	13,600	4·5	9,730	715	7,304	29,104	4·0	21,348	734	2,009	12,681	6·1	9,853	777
54	210	3·9	146	695	638	2,445	3·8	1,749	715	18	122	6·8	96	787
54	210	3·9	146	695	638	2,445	3·8	1,749	715	..	..	..	..	..
..	..	..	..	..	..	..	..	..	..	..	..	..	..	..
..	..	..	..	..	..	..	..	..	..	..	..	..	..	..
1,431	6,685	4·7	4,881	730	4,424	16,955	3·8	12,347	728	1,148	6,814	5·9	5,228	767
1,516	6,705	4·4	4,703	701	2,242	9,704	4·3	7,252	747	903	5,745	6·4	4,529	788
156	842	5·4	504	599	..	..	..	..	..	..	..	..	..	..
..	..	..	..	..	2,242	9,704	4·3	7,252	747	..	..	..	..	..
600	2,296	3·8	1,567	683	19,637	76,964	3·9	55,528	721	3,348	20,515	6·1	14,315	698
..	..	..	..	..	..	..	..	..	..	1,663	10,272	6·2	7,220	703
497	1,881	3·8	1,267	674	1,886	6,398	3·4	4,602	719	24	122	5·1	95	779
103	415	4·0	300	723	7,557	29,035	3·8	20,933	721	1,659	10,110	6·1	6,992	692
103	415	4·0	300	723	7,557	29,035	3·8	20,933	721	1,538	9,367	6·1	6,478	692
..	..	..	..	..	10,194	41,531	4·1	29,993	722	2	11	5·5	8	727
..	..	..	..	..	1,872	7,888	4·2	5,738	727	..	..	..	..	..
..	..	..	..	..	..	..	..	..	..	..	..	..	..	..
..	..	..	..	..	8,322	33,643	4·0	24,255	721	..	..	..	..	..

† Includes contractors and cashiers.

Table V.—Size of Families by Community or Religion of Family.

Religion or Community.	Number of slips examined.	Total number of children born alive.	Average per family.	Number of children surviving.	Proportion of surviving to total 1,000 born.	Number of families with wife married at— 0—12.	13—14.	15—19.	20—30.	30 and over.
1	2	3	4	5	6	7	8	9	10	11
India										
Total ..	**528,864**	**2,242,711***	**4·2**	**1,569,983**	**700**	**41,950**	**172,286**	**229,408**	**72,471**	**10,321**
Hindu	302,403	1,291,923*	4·3	899,948	697	18,334	117,807	130,495	29,647	4,310
Brahman	7,875	40,599*	5·2	26,255	647	541	4,149	2,423	413	91
Other Interior Castes ..	21,624	106,732*	4·9	74,182	695	1,010	5,252	9,552	3,834	415
Kayastha	280	1,759*	6·3	1,166	663	14	116	120	22	8
Kurmi	316	1,409	4·5	805	571	7	199	92	16	2
Rajput	1,168	5,637	4·8	3,896	691	157	215	571	170	55
Viswakarma	174	879	5·1	558	635	4	65	76	22	7
Yadava	257	1,011	3·9	674	667	80	61	85	28	3
Nomadic Castes	199	662	3·3	431	651	72	27	74	22	*
Exterior Castes	35,349	149,302	4·2	104,217	698	870	13,100	16,838	4,112	429
Chamar	859	4,847	5·6	2,860	590	63	440	243	87	26
Sikh	23,391	96,550	4·1	68,982	714	3,872	4,713	10,633	3,655	518
Jain	1,739	7,240	4·2	5,044	697	38	867	765	65	4
Buddhist	617	2,357	3·8	1,916	813	..	32	221	281	83
Parsi	713	3,252	4·6	2,299	707	1	231	245	219	17
Jew	69	264	3·8	189	716	9	24	30	6	..
Muslim	141,526	577,778*	4·1	403,704	699	12,543	29,871	61,420	32,408	4,756
Christian	22,396	111,546	5·0	85,699	768	1,475	6,178	11,563	2,887	293
Tribal	9,640	48,415	5·0	30,918	639	689	3,340	3,629	1,778	182
Bhil	396	1,006	2·5	745	741	77	83	191	40	5
Other or unspecified	26,370	103,386†	3·9	71,284	689	4,989	9,223	10,407	1,525	158
Andaman and Nicobar Islands										
Total ..	**948†**	**2,781**	**2·9**	**2,100**	**755**	..	**324**	**300**	**259**	**43**
Hindu	290	926	3·2	691	746	..	150	79	46	15
Buddhist	52	138	2·7	111	804	..	14	18	18	2
Muslim	254	754	3·0	576	764	..	120	96	35	3
Christian	22	64	2·9	49	766	..	9	8	4	1
Tribal (Nicobarese)	311	829	2·7	627	756	..	20	94	154	21
Others	19	70	3·7	46	657	..	11	5	2	1
Assam										
Total ..	**6,466**	**27,761**	**4·3**	**17,956**	**634**	**913**	**1,075**	**3,301**	**1,104**	**73**
Tea Garden cooly Castes ..	2,198	7,540	3·4	5,184	688	401	598	1,096	102	1
Hill Tribes	4,268	20,221	4·7	12,412	614	512	477	2,205	1,002	72
Baluchistan										
Total ..	**39,744**	**163,001**	**4·1**	**108,949**	**668**	..	**8,130**	**17,537**	**12,369**	**1,708**
Hindu	1,688	5,954	3·5	3,840	645	..	884	576	203	25
Sikh	116	320	2·8	238	744	..	60	43	13	..
Muslim	37,894	156,553	4·1	104,752	669	..	7,163	16,906	12,143	1,682
Brahui (indigenous)	8,517	29,752	3·5	21,769	732	..	1,623	3,422	2,982	490
Pathan	6,502	35,445	5·5	19,304	545	..	1,169	3,214	1,874	245
Christian	46	174	3·8	119	684	.	23	12	10	1

* The discrepencies between the totals in column 3 and the sums of the constituent sub-totals in columns 7 to 11 are due to the omission in the latter columns of figures in the Andamans and Nicobars and in Bengal of families for which the details by age were absent or were at variance with the Indian group.

Table V.—Size of Families by Community or Religion of Family—*contd.*

Religion or Community.	Number of slips examined.	Total number of children born alive.	Average per family.	Number of children surviving.	Proportion of surviving to total 1,000 born.	Number of families with wife married at— 0—12.	13—14.	15—19.	20—30.	30 & over
1	2	3	4	5	6	7	8	9	10	11
Baroda State										
Total ..	**39,768**	**226,456**	**5·7**	**136,795**	**604**	...	**30,915**	**5,819**	**2,536**	**44**[illegible]
Hindu	32,638	186,167	6·7	111,308	607	..	26,288	4,238	1,803	30[illegible]
Brahman	2,520	14,923	5·9	8,011	537	..	2,125	289	96	1[illegible]
Bharwad	957	5,400	5·6	3,183	589	..	694	177	76	1[illegible]
Chunvalia	47	279	5·9	157	563	..	25	14	6	[illegible]
Valand	493	2,791	5·7	1,558	558	..	389	67	32	[illegible]
Bhangi	357	2,026	5·7	1,234	609	..	294	42	18	[illegible]
Vankar (Dhed)	1,904	10,860	5·7	6,762	623	..	1,472	271	131	3[illegible]
Chamar	479	2,745	5·7	1,570	572	..	387	64	26	[illegible]
Soni	231	1,533	6·6	791	516	..	198	21	11	[illegible]
Suthar	535	3,141	5·9	1,705	543	..	426	64	41	[illegible]
Luhar	373	2,066	5·5	1,108	536	..	290	61	19	[illegible]
Chodhra, Dhanka and Dhodia	1,095	6,082	5·6	3,757	618	..	537	344	194	2[illegible]
Bhil, Dhubea, Gamit Nayakda, Tadvi, Talavia.	3,158	18,470	5·8	12,092	655	..	2,159	649	298	5[illegible]
Muslim	2,494	13,940	5·6	8,446	606	..	1,715	513	215	5[illegible]
Pathan	97	536	5·5	322	601	..	65	25	4	[illegible]
Parsi	338	1,486	4·4	1,028	692	..	176	74	72	1[illegible]
Bengal						0–13	14–16	17–23	24 and over.	
Total ..	**2,406**	**14,501**	**6·0**	**9,531**	**657**	**910**	**816**	**385**	**295**	
Hindu	1,810	10,851	6·0	7,229	666	658	635	297	220	
Brahman	249	1,569	6·3	1,140	727	125	82	23	19	
Baidya	67	518	7·7	383	739	31	32	3	1	
Kayastha	241	1,479	6·1	1,031	697	110	104	19	8	
Other Hindus	1,253	7,285	5·8	4,675	642	392	417	252	192	
Muslim	528	3,242	6·1	2,023	624	240	162	69	57	
Others	68	408	6·0	279	684	12	19	19	18	
Bombay						0–12	13–14	15–19	20–30	30 & over
Total ..	**157,906**	**629,208**	**4·0**	**447,728**	**712**	..	**67,605***	**77,784**	**11,343**	**1,17**[illegible]
Hindu	141,348	563,693	4·0	401,276	712	..	61,083*	69,372	9,869	1,02[illegible]
Depressed	20,138	79,311	3·9	55,092	695	..	8,820*	9,614	1,529	17[illegible]
Sikh	7	17	2·4	17	1,000	..	2*	5	..	.
Jain	1,527	6,386	4·2	4,456	698	..	777*	687	59	[illegible]
Parsi	373	1,764	4·7	1,270	720	..	54*	171	147	[illegible]
Jews	7	41	5·9	28	683	..	2	4	1	..
Muslim	11,093	44,080	4·0	31,041	704	..	4,583*	5,530	859	12[illegible]
Christian	2,154	8,489	3·9	6,516	768	..	592*	1,258	293	1[illegible]
Others	1,397	4,738	3·4	3,124	659	..	512*	757	115	1[illegible]
Central India Agency										
Total ..	**4,380**	**15,223**	**3·5**	**8,373**	**550**	**1,225**	**1,045**	**1,484**	**523**	**10**[illegible]
Hindu	2,642	8,513	3·2	5,279	620	756	649	953	239	4[illegible]
Brahman	175	613	3·5	369	602	76	35	59	5	..
Other Interior Castes ..	904	3,122	3·5	1,823	584	237	262	262	123	2[illegible]
Balai	88	289	3·3	186	644	31	13	27	15	[illegible]
Bania	148	550	3·7	317	576	61	55	24	7	[illegible]
Bharud	94	303	3·2	176	581	13	33	27	18	[illegible]
Dangi	94	261	2·8	166	636	47	16	20	10	1
Dhakad	66	235	3·6	155	660	42	15	5	3	[illegible]
Mankar	111	428	3·9	252	589	21	22	53	12	[illegible]

* Denote families with wife married at age 0-14.

Table V.—Size of Families by Community or Religion of Family—*contd.*

Religion or Community.	Number of slips examined.	Total number of children born alive.	Average per family.	Number of children surviving.	Proportion of surviving to total 1,000 born.	Number of families with wife married at— 0—12.	13—14.	15—19.	20—30.	30 & over.
1	2	3	4	5	6	7	8	9	10	11
Central India Agency—*concld.*										
Hindu—*concld.*										
Mewali	77	249	3·2	185	743	26	18	26	5	2
Sirvi	168	565	3·4	301	533	33	44	69	20	2
Ahir	57	261	4·6	157	602	6	18	23	8	2
Gaoli (Gwal)	108	260	2·4	193	742	42	22	34	9	1
Kurmi	89	482	5·4	174	361	7	65	12	3	2
Rajput	259	795	3·1	599	753	94	54	89	15	7
Banjara	197	653	3·3	426	652	72	27	74	21	3
Chamar	101	382	3·8	217	568	24	13	54	8	2
Muslim	349	1,625	4·7	1,086	668	12	90	99	116	32
Tribal	744	2,386	3·2	1,757	736	164	144	314	109	13
Bhil	396	1,006	2·5	745	741	77	83	191	40	5
Others	1,041	3,685	3·5	996	270	390	245	309	79	18
entral Provinces and Berar										
Total ..	21,643	85,704	4·0	60,743	709	4,195	7,869	8,275	1,188	116
ochin State										
Total ..	33,471	125,878	3·8	92,458	735	3,854	5,502	18,177	5,528	410
Hindu	20,626	74,957	3·6	54,526	727	2,292	3,316	10,805	3,923	290
Brahman	1,724	6,222	3·6	4,888	786	369	542	729	73	11
Ullatan	3	17	5·7	10	588	1	..	1	1	..
Vetuvan	243	906	3·7	634	700	22	36	126	58	1
Pulayan	1,009	4,049	4·0	2,648	654	167	112	532	183	15
Iluvan	6,916	26,103	3·8	19,216	736	619	937	3,883	1,384	93
Kammalan	1,244	4,565	3·7	3,279	718	130	214	686	197	17
Nayar	5,474	19,076	3·9	13,867	727	381	725	2,871	1,383	114
Pandittattan	27	108	4·0	90	833	3	5	18	1	..
Tarakan	1	..	0·0	..	..	..	..	..	1	..
Other Hindus	336	1,182	3·5	745	630	58	50	174	51	3
Parsi	2	2	1·0	1	500	1	1	..	..	..
Jew	62	223	3·6	161	722	9	22	26	5	..
Muslim	1,919	8,006	4·2	5,636	704	265	362	962	298	32
Christian	10,862	42,690	3·9	32,134	753	1,287	1,801	6,384	1,302	88
Anglo-Indian	76	338	4·4	262	776	3	7	52	13	1
elhi										
Total ..	2,246	7,932	3·5	5,298	668	511	454	991	274	16
Hindu	1,833	6,246	3·4	4,241	679	432	378	802	209	12
Muslim	359	1,512	4·2	935	618	73	70	160	53	3
Others	54	174	3·2	122	701	6	6	29	12	1
walior State										
Total ..	1,802	11,317	6·2	6,400	566	603	196	599	353	51
Hindu	1,279	7,902	6·2	4,530	573	442	145	431	235	26
Brahman	257	1,577	6·1	795	504	96	25	81	49	6
Other Interior Castes ..	548	3,295	6·2	1,968	597	178	67	192	99	12
Ahir	67	372	5·6	250	672	32	5	19	11	..
Kayastha	39	280	7·2	135	482	14	6	16	3	..
Rajput	182	1,185	6·5	710	599	63	27	66	24	2
Sonar	13	78	6·0	35	449	4	1	2	5	1
Exterior Castes	109	688	6·3	364	530	42	11	32	23	1
Chamar	97	618	6·4	334	540	39	9	26	22	1
Muslim	194	1,309	6·8	655	500	54	13	50	66	11
Christian	2	7	3·5	6	857	..	..	1	1	..
Tribal	64	427	6·7	273	639	13	3	23	21	4
Bhil	27	180	6·7	109	606	4	1	6	12	4
Others	327	2,099	6·2	1,209	576	107	38	117	51	14

Table V.—Size of Families by Community or Religion of family—*concld.*

Religion or Community.	Number of slips examined.	Total number of children born alive.	Average per family.	Number of children surviving.	Proportion of surviving to total 1,000 born.	Number of families with wife married at— 0—12.	13—14.	15—19.	20—30.	30 & over.
1	2	3	4	5	6	7	8	9	10	11
Jammu and Kashmir State										
Total	**12,230**	**70,062**	**5·7**	**47,828**	**683**	..	**1,797**	**6,127**	**3,372**	**9[illegible]4**
Hindu	2,750	15,705	5·7	10,600	675	..	550	1,538	480	182
Brahman	837	4,924	5·9	3,287	668	..	180	458	140	5[illegible]
Other Interior Castes	1,169	6,766	5·8	4,502	665	..	219	677	216	57
Lohar and Tarkhan	93	533	5·7	330	619	..	16	54	17	6
Rajput	727	3,657	5·0	2,587	707	..	134	416	131	46
Nomadic Castes	2	9	4·5	5	556	..	..	..	1	1
Exterior Castes	302	1,767	5·9	1,204	681	..	59	163	46	34
Chamar	182	1,102	6·1	739	671	..	31	99	31	21
Sikh	213	1,359	6·4	915	673	..	25	130	51	7
Jain	3	22	7·3	12	546	..	1	1	1	..
Buddhist	565	2,219	3·9	1,805	813	..	18	203	263	81
Muslim	8,661	50,532	5·8	34,361	680	..	1,196	4,241	2,562	662
Bafinda	103	517	5·0	360	696	..	9	49	38	7
Christian	6	34	5·6	21	618	..	2	3	1	..
Others	32	191	6·0	114	597	..	5	11	14	2
Mysore State										
Total	**4,320**	**19,107**	**4·4**	**13,934**	**729**	..	**2,592**	**1,516**	**204**	**8**
Hindu	3,374	15,200	4·5	10,851	714	..	2,120	1,135	116	3
Brahman	1,414	7,096	5·0	5,082	716	..	925	476	13	..
Interior Castes	1,430	5,933	4·1	4,283	722	..	914	449	65	2
Vakkaliga	227	927	4·1	631	680	..	134	80	13	..
Viswakarma	68	268	3·9	193	720	..	48	20	..	..
Yadava	25	118	4·7	74	627	..	16	9	..	..
Exterior Castes	210	858	4·1	583	685	..	83	101	25	1
Jain	75	313	4·2	226	722	..	59	16	..	..
Muslim	558	2,345	4·2	1,823	777	..	333	190	34	1
Christian	262	1,079	4·1	909	842	..	55	153	51	3
Others	51	170	3·3	125	735	..	25	22	3	1
Punjab										
Total	**173,432**	**686,470**	**3·9**	**493,509**	**719**	**30,649**	**35,703**	**73,265**	**29,019**	**4,796**
Hindu	73,272	299,702	4·1	214,719	716	14,412	17,010	30,412	9,366	2,072
Ad-Dharmi	1,427	5,891	4·1	4,059	689	179	367	647	204	30
Sikh	23,055	94,854	4·1	67,812	715	3,872	4,626	10,455	3,591	511
Jain	134	519	3·9	350	674	38	30	61	5	..
Muslim	75,436	284,773	3·8	205,852	723	12,139	13,687	31,720	15,761	2,129
Christian	1,535	6,622	4·3	4,776	721	188	350	617	296	84
Travancore State										
Total	**18,456**	**119,813**	**6·5**	**90,432**	**755**	..	**5,985**	**8,993**	**3,124**	**354**
Hindu	10,058	6[illegible],954	6·2	45,301	731	..	2,456	5,346	2,023	233
Brahman	699	3,675	5·3	2,683	730	..	317	340	37	5
Other Interior Castes	7,187	44,010	6·1	31,994	727	..	1,652	3,838	1,525	172
Nayars	3,793	23,906	6·3	17,938	750	..	861	1,928	879	125
Exterior Castes	2,172	14,269	6·6	10,624	745	..	487	1,168	461	56
Iluvas	1,711	11,493	6·7	8,689	756	..	357	925	384	45
Muslim	942	5,819	6·2	4,153	714	..	226	522	178	16
Christian	7,456	52,040	7·0	40,978	790	..	3,303	3,125	923	105
Western India States Agency										
Total	**9,646**	**37,497**	**3·9**	**27,949**	**745**	..	***3,094**	**5,240**	**1,225**	**87**
Hindu	8,795	34,173	3·9	25,557	748	..	*2,778	4,808	1,135	74
Exterior Castes	1,463	5,453	3·7	4,171	765	..	*396	827	223	17
Muslim	845	3,288	3·9	2,365	719	..	*313	431	88	13
Christian	6	36	6·0	27	[illegible]	..	[illegible]			

Table VI.—Duration of Marriage correlated

Religion or Community of Husband.	Total. Number of slips examined.	Total. Number of children.	Total. Average per family.	Under 10 years. Number of families.	Under 10 years. Number of children.	Under 10 years. Average per family.	10 years. Number of families.	10 years. Number of children.	10 years. Average per family.
1	2	3	4	5	6	7	8	9	10
INDIA.									
Total ..	**899,783**	**3,477,211**	**3·9**	218,240	373,197	**1·7**	**47,931**	**148,153**	**3·1**
Hindu	509,257	2,002,396	3·9	125,179	207,513	1·7	26,042	75,362	2·9
Brahman	32,461	112,495	3·5	8,916	12,948	1·5	1,371	3,761	2·7
Other Interior Castes	83,309	316,527	3·8	21,778	30,074	1·4	3,847	10,247	2·7
Kayastha	706	2,722	3·9	167	237	1·4	27	67	2·5
Kurmi	316	1,409	4·5	90	177	2·0	20	62	3·1
Rajput	4,698	16,076	3·4	1,133	1,634	1·4	328	772	2·4
Viswakarma	1,847	6,461	3·5	473	710	1·5	140	382	2·7
Yadava	938	2,675	2·9	262	281	1·1	71	170	2·4
Nomadic Castes	197	653	3·3	71	104	1·5	14	30	2·1
Exterior Castes	36,761	144,678	3·9	9,823	17,117	1·7	2,255	7,055	3·1
Chamar	3,155	10,713	3·4	848	1,389	1·6	198	630	3·2
Sikh	25,740	105,185	4·1	6,419	12,220	1·9	1,471	4,27[illegible]	2·9
Jain	4,632	19,288	4·2	1,193	1,898	1·6	258	800	3·1
Buddhist	2,167	9,964	4·6	492	1,800	3·6	11	44	4·0
Parsi	1,127	4,823	4·3	170	299	1·8	40	120	3·0
Jew	7	41	5·9	2	6	3·0	1	10	10·0
Muslim	264,542	940,469	3·6	60,840	109,206	1·8	15,926	54,029	3·4
Christian	37,506	169,798	4·5	9,341	12,809	1·4	1,280	3,733	2·9
Tribal	28,155	116,407	4·1	6,612	11,548	1·8	1,228	3,579	2·9
Bhil	574	1,655	2·9	231	261	1·1	54	152	2·8
Others or unspecified	26,650	108,840	4·1	7,992	15,898	2·0	1,674	6,205	3·7
ASSAM.									
Total ..	**6,466**	**27,761**	**4·3**	2,402	4,489	**1·9**	**448**	**1,491**	**3·3**
Tea Garden cooly Castes	2,198	7,540	3·4	890	1,458	1·6	170	484	2·3
Hill tribes	4,268	20,221	4·7	1,512	3,031	2·0	278	1,007	3·6
BALUCHISTAN.									
Total ..	**39,744**	**163,001**	**4·1**	8,046	19,051	**2·4**	**3,660**	**11,492**	**3·1**
Hindu	1,688	5,954	3·5	456	787	1·7	163	483	3·0
Sikh	116	320	2·8	55	76	1·4	7	22	3·1
Muslim	37,894	156,553	4·1	7,516	18,143	2·4	3,486	10,980	3·1
Brahui (indigenous)	8,517	29,752	3·5	2,421	5,605	2·3	939	2,792	3·0
Pathan	6,502	35,445	5·5	1,632	4,348	2·7	506	2,190	4·3
Christian	46	174	3·8	19	45	2·4	4	7	1·8
BARODA STATE.									
Total ..	**205,238**	**829,700**	**4·0**	43,535	64,952	**1·5**	**6,035**	**15,627**	**2·6**
Hindu	166,110	668,268	4·0	35,121	51,322	1·5	4,648	10,989	2·4
Brahman	13,210	52,110	3·9	3,322	4,637	1·4	360	989	2·7
Vankar	9,476	39,630	4·2	1,789	2,383	1·3	244	601	2·5
Jain	2,844	11,894	4·2	625	687	1·1	92	248	2·7
Parsi	754	3,059	4·1	79	130	1·6	20	48	2·4
Muslim	12,695	50,341	2·4	2,975	4,560	1·5	438	1,213	2·8
Christian	251	1,163	4·6	54	96	1·8	5	15	3·0
Tribal	22,634	91,896	4·1	4,681	7,977	1·7	832	2,214	2·7
BENGAL.									
Total ..	**2,406**	***9,531**	**4·0**	**6**	**5**	**0·8**	62	235	**3·8**
Hindu	1,810	7,229	4·0	4	4	1·0	41	149	3·6
Brahman	249	1,140	4·6	..	..	..	2	13	6·5
Baidya	67	383	5·7	..	..	..	..	..	..
Kayastha	241	1,031	4·3	..	..	..	1	4	4·0
Muslim	528	2,023	3·8	1	1	1·0	19	78	4·1
Others	68	279	4·1	1	..	0·0	2	8	4·0

with Community or Religion of Family.

Duration of Marriage with present wife.

10—19			20—31			32 years.			33 and over.		
Number of families.	Number of children.	Average per family.	Number of familes.	Number of children.	Average per family.	Number of families.	Number of children.	Average per family.	Number of families.	Number of children	Average per family.
11	12	13	14	15	16	17	18	19	20	21	22
268,487	1,073,908	4·0	259,738	1,266,330	4·9	20,583	121,909	5·9	84,804	493,714	5·8
158,172	616,987	3·9	137,332	737,251	5·4	13,924	83,536	5·8	48,608	281,747	5·8
9,962	28,496	3·0	8,007	42,727	5·3	909	5,478	6·0	3,296	19,085	5·8
24,638	95,079	3·9	24,415	129,798	5·3	1,684	9,953	5·9	6,947	41,376	6·0
121	506	4·2	121	644	5·3	55	213	3·9	215	1,055	4·9
111	539	4·9	76	462	6·1	2	17	8·5	17	152	9·0
1,488	4,939	3·3	1,274	6,202	4·9	85	415	4·9	390	2,114	5·4
605	2,171	3·9	470	2,521	5·4	28	147	5·3	131	530	4·0
284	868	3·1	247	918	3·7	3	18	6·0	71	420	6·0
41	158	3·9	51	256	5·0	6	21	3·5	14	84	6·0
11,281	46,277	4·1	10,206	54,671	5·4	537	3,166	5·9	2,659	16,392	6·2
1,073	3,544	3·3	840	4,022	4·8	36	179	5·0	160	949	5·9
7,313	29,606	4·1	6,856	37,897	5·5	445	2,598	5·8	3,236	18,593	5·7
1,322	5,545	4·2	1,177	6,879	5·8	155	994	6·4	527	3,172	6·0
463	2,430	5·2	593	3,640	6·1	309	1,200	3·9	299	850	2·8
288	1,248	4·3	303	1,559	5·1	50	230	4·6	276	1,367	5·4
2	11	5·5	1	4	4·0	..	..	..	1	10	10·0
74,686	310,007	4·2	87,392	324,170	3·7	3,560	19,890	5·6	22,138	123,167	5·6
8,729	37,598	4·3	12,359	75,255	6·1	842	5,689	6·9	4,955	34,714	7·0
8,950	35,122	3·9	7,619	43,441	5·7	884	5,190	5·9	2,862	17,527	6·1
154	547	3·6	91	418	4·6	4	33	8·2	40	244	6·1
8,562	35,354	4·1	6,106	36,234	5·9	414	2,582	6·3	1,902	12,567	6·6
1,818	9,269	5·1	1,349	8,923	6·6	55	370	6·7	394	3,219	8·2
634	2,574	4·1	415	2,461	5·9	18	93	5·2	71	470	6·6
1,184	6,695	5·7	934	6,462	6·9	37	277	7·5	323	2,749	8·5
10,685	42,769	4·0	13,266	63,304	4·8	306	1,928	6·3	3,781	24,457	6·5
457	1,686	3·7	469	2,250	4·8	17	74	4·4	126	674	5·3
35	134	3·0	14	64	4·6	1	3	3·0	4	21	5·3
10,179	40,885	4·0	12,775	60,939	4·8	288	1,851	6·4	3,650	23,755	6·5
2,290	7,969	3·5	2,253	9,995	4·4	45	233	5·2	569	3,158	5·6
1,630	8,745	5·4	1,896	12,846	6·8	88	754	8·6	750	6,562	8·7
14	64	4·6	8	51	6·4	..	..	..	1	7	7·0
63,656	236,943	3·7	56,764	311,147	5·5	9,497	56,971	6·0	25,751	144,060	5·6
51,419	191,443	3·7	45,928	249,167	5·4	7,980	48,278	6·0	21,014	117,069	5·6
3,838	14,286	3·7	3,272	18,191	5·6	578	3,707	6·4	1,790	10,300	5·8
2,941	11,250	3·8	2,824	15,780	5·6	513	3,097	6·0	1,165	6,519	5·6
797	3,096	3·9	763	4,465	5·9	133	852	6·4	434	2,546	5·9
182	702	3·9	204	960	4·7	38	151	4·0	231	1,068	4·6
3,752	14,299	3·8	3,445	18,552	5·4	494	2,747	5·6	1,591	8,970	5·6
78	316	4·1	73	452	6·2	12	84	7·0	29	200	6·9
7,428	27,087	3·6	6,401	35,552	5·6	840	4,859	5·8	2,452	14,207	5·8
59	234	4·0	231	690	3·0	620	2,348	3·8	1,428	6,019	4·2
40	157	3·9	168	502	3·0	487	1,860	3·8	1,070	4,537	4·3
7	29	4·1	14	57	4·1	53	229	4·3	173	812	4·7
..	..	..	2	9	4·5	17	89	5·2	48	285	5·9
4	11	2·7	5	22	4·4	52	196	3·8	179	798	4·5
14	60	4·3	47	135	2·9	118	419	3·6	329	1,330	4·0
5	17	3·4	16	53	3·3	15	69	·6	29	132	4·5

Table VI.—Duration of Marriage correlated

Religion or Community of Husband.	Total. Number of slips examined.	Total. Number of children.	Total. Average per family.	Duration of Marriage: Under 10 years. Number of families.	Under 10 years. Number of children.	Under 10 years. Average per family.	10 years. Number of families.	10 years. Number of children.	10 years. Average per family.
1	2	3	4	5	6	7	8	9	10
BOMBAY.									
Total ..	**157,906**	**629,208**	**4·0**	**42,929**	**85,337**	**2·0**	**11,013**	**36,342**	**3·3**
Hindu	141,348	563,693	4·0	37,974	75,144	2·0	9,782	31,820	3·3
Exterior Castes	20,138	79,311	3·9	5,268	10,302	2·0	1,438	4,589	3·2
Sikh	7	17	2·4	5	9	1·8	..	..	..
Jain	1,527	6,386	4·2	475	1,043	2·2	149	496	3·3
Parsi	373	1,764	4·7	91	169	1·9	20	72	3·6
Jew	7	41	5·9	2	6	3·0	1	10	10·0
Muslim	11,093	44,080	4·0	3,208	6,433	2·0	764	2,752	3·6
Christian	2,154	8,489	3·9	681	1,512	2·2	187	697	3·7
Others	1,397	4,738	3·4	493	1,021	2·1	110	495	4·5
BURMA.									
Burmese	**1,153**	**4,309**	**3·7**	**720**	**1,680**	**2·3**	**75**	**328**	**4·4**
CENTRAL INDIA AGENCY.									
Total ..	**4,380**	**15,223**	**3·5**	**1,416**	**1,967**	**1·4**	**377**	**1,013**	**2·7**
Hindu	2,642	8,533	3·2	958	1,260	1·3	217	577	2·7
Brahman	175	613	3·5	61	59	1·0	5	11	2·2
Other Interior Castes	904	3,102	3·4	302	439	1·5	85	237	2·8
Balai	88	289	3·3	29	34	1·2	9	34	3·8
Bania	148	550	3·7	46	66	1·4	10	26	2·6
Bharud	94	303	3·2	30	37	1·2	8	22	2·8
Dangi	94	261	2·8	35	37	1·1	12	36	3·0
Dhakad	66	235	3·6	9	15	1·7	6	14	2·3
Mankar	111	428	3·9	34	58	1·7	11	32	2·9
Mewali	77	249	3·2	30	65	2·2	15	45	3·0
Sirvi	168	565	3·4	72	97	1·3	12	22	1·8
Ahir	57	261	4·6	12	18	1·5	5	15	3·0
Gaoli (Gwal)	108	260	2·4	48	49	1·0	9	24	2·7
Kurmi	89	482	5·4	20	46	2·3	5	17	3·4
Rajput	259	795	3·1	82	95	1·2	23	62	2·7
Banjara	197	653	3·3	71	104	1·5	14	30	2·1
Chamar	101	382	3·8	44	57	1·3	3	8	2·7
Muslim	349	1,625	4·7	87	159	1·8	23	71	3·1
Tribal	744	2,386	3·2	273	378	1·4	74	236	3·2
Bhil	396	1,006	2·5	179	213	1·2	41	114	2·8
Others	1,041	3,685	3·5	277	383	1·4	104	243	2·4
CENTRAL PROVINCES AND BERAR.									
Total ..	**21,643**	**87,778**	**4·1**	**5,892**	**11,473**	**1·9**	**1,286**	**3,942**	**3·1**
DELHI.									
Total ..	**2,246**	**7,932**	**3·5**	**744**	**1,067**	**1·4**	**151**	**419**	**2·8**
Hindu	1,833	6,246	3·4	604	799	1·3	124	333	2·7
Muslim	359	1,512	4·2	115	223	1·9	22	70	3·2
Others	54	174	3·2	25	45	1·8	5	16	3·2
GWALIOR STATE.									
Total ..	**17,319**	**60,526**	**3·5**	**4,832**	**5,720**	**1·2**	**1,193**	**2,935**	**2·5**
Hindu	14,911	52,088	3·5	4,090	4,759	1·2	1,017	2,511	2·5
Brahman	2,886	9,985	3·5	884	1,004	1·1	194	430	2·2
Other Interior Castes	9,508	33,308	3·5	2,724	3,176	1·2	638	1,615	2·5
Ahir	748	2,036	2 7	196	199	1·0	54	123	2·3
Kayastha	465	1,691	3·6	167	237	1·4	26	63	2·4
Rajput	1,504	5,814	3·9	317	353	1·1	76	177	2·3
Kumhar	132	616	4·7	17	27	1·6	10	24	2·4
Luhar, Sunar and Sutar ..	623	2,229	3·6	159	174	1·1	55	118	2·1
Exterior Castes	1,422	4,490	3·2	364	431	1·2	114	269	2·4
Chamar	1,293	4,049	3·1	316	363	1·2	101	233	2·3
Bhangi	129	441	3·4	48	68	1·4	13	36	2·8
Jain	37	113	3·1	15	19	1·3	..	..	..
Muslim	2,338	8,20[illegible]	3·5	717	922	1·3	174	419	2·4
Christian	33	11[illegible]	3·5	10	20	2·0	2	5	2·5
Tribal	509	1,904	3·7	146	162	1·1	44	122	2·8
Bhil	178	649	3·6	52	48	0·9	13	38	2·9

with Community or Religion of Family—*contd.*

vith present wife.

10—19			20—31			32 years.			33 and over.		
Number of families.	Number of children.	Average per family.	Number of familes.	Number of children.	Average per family.	Number of families.	Number of children.	Average per family.	Number of families.	Number of children.	Average per family.
11	12	13	14	15	16	17	18	19	20	21	22
50,787	**212,390**	**4·2**	**40,236**	**216,775**	**5·4**	**2,290**	**13,147**	**5·7**	**10,651**	**65,217**	**6·1**
45,581	190,458	4·2	36,321	195,489	5·4	2,066	11,700	5·7	9,624	59,082	6·1
6,516	26,926	4·1	5,224	27,300	5·2	245	1,429	5·8	1,447	8,765	6·1
2	8	4·0	..	..	..	..	..	..	..	..	..
449	2,109	4·7	360	2,119	5·9	17	110	6·5	77	509	6·6
106	546	5·2	99	599	6·0	12	79	6·6	45	299	6·6
2	11	5·5	1	4	4·0	..	..	..	1	10	10·0
3,497	14,907	4·3	2,751	14,782	5·4	158	1,011	6·4	715	4,195	5·9
654	2,673	4·1	482	2,713	5·6	25	153	6·1	125	741	5·9
496	1,678	3·4	222	1,069	4·8	12	94	7·8	64	381	6·0
269	**1,575**	**5·9**	**80**	**681**	**8·5**	**1**	**3**	**3·0**	**8**	**42**	**5·3**
1,205	**4,701**	**3·9**	**1,006**	**5,205**	**5·2**	**35**	**178**	**5·1**	**341**	**2,159**	**6·3**
652	2,367	3·6	576	2,926	5·1	21	95	4·5	218	1,308	6·0
45	165	3·7	37	225	6·1	1	6	6·0	26	147	5·7
224	829	3·7	228	1,180	5·2	10	57	5·7	55	360	6·5
19	75	3·9	28	134	4·8	1	4	4·0	2	8	4·0
42	166	4·0	37	213	5·8	2	17	8·5	11	62	5·6
24	70	2·9	26	127	4·9	1	5	5·0	5	42	8·4
22	74	3·4	19	94	4·9	2	10	5·0	4	10	2·
21	67	3·2	22	100	4·5	..	..	..	8	39	4·
26	102	3·9	29	130	4·5	1	10	10·0	10	96	9·6
17	62	3·6	15	77	5·1	..	..	..	..	..	..
36	142	3·9	36	220	6·1	1	1	1·0	11	83	7·
27	135	5·0	10	68	6·8	..	..	..	3	25	8·
24	50	2·1	18	69	3·8	..	..	..	9	68	7·
31	141	4·5	25	186	7·4	..	..	..	8	92	11·
59	179	3·0	56	244	4·4	3	3	1·0	36	212	5·
41	158	3·9	51	256	5·0	6	21	3·5	14	84	6·
22	107	4·9	24	163	6·8	..	..	..	8	47	5·
120	559	4·7	86	560	6·5	3	21	7·0	30	255	8·
221	896	4·1	120	504	4·2	4	29	7·3	52	343	6·
110	370	3·4	38	146	3·8	1	8	8·0	27	155	5·
322	1,249	3·9	262	1,361	5·2	8	41	5·1	68	408	6·
7,031	**28,944**	**4·1**	**5,350**	**29,610**	**5·5**	**364**	**2,315**	**6·4**	**1,720**	**11,494**	**6·**
672	**2,635**	**3·9**	**566**	**3,061**	**5·4**	**16**	**110**	**6·9**	**97**	**640**	**6·**
548	2,090	3·8	463	2,424	5·2	12	84	7·0	82	516	6·
108	476	4·4	98	609	6·2	4	26	6·5	12	108	9·
16	69	4·3	5	28	5·6	..	..	..	3	16	5·
5,003	**17,392**	**3·5**	**4,938**	**26,377**	**5·3**	**128**	**774**	**6·0**	**1,225**	**7,328**	**6·**
4,349	14,972	3·4	4,258	22,718	5·3	115	720	6·3	1,082	6,408	5·
803	2,806	3·5	738	4,321	5·9	27	133	4·9	240	1,291	5·
2,779	9,734	3·5	2,617	14,362	5·5	84	513	6·1	666	3,908	5·
226	651	2·9	211	722	3·4	2	14	7·0	59	327	5·
117	495	4·2	116	622	5·4	3	17	5·7	36	257	7·
444	1,575	3·6	502	2,745	5·8	15	95	5·3	150	869	5·
37	130	3·5	50	296	5·9	..	..	..	18	139	7·
170	618	3·6	190	1,017	5·6	3	24	8·0	46	224	4·
459	1,325	4·9	408	1,977	4·8	5	32	6·4	72	456	6·
428	1,189	2·8	378	1,819	4·8	5	32	6·4	65	413	6·
31	136	4·	30	158	5·3	..	..	..	7	43	6·
10	29	2·9	9	44	4·9	1	7	7·0	2	14	7·
634	2,357	3·7	664	3,587	5·4	12	47	4·0	137	877	6·
10	34	3·4	7	28	4·0	..	..	..	4	29	7·
117	444	3·8	164	923	5·6	3	25	8·3	35	228	6·
44	177	4·0	53	272	5·1	3	25	8·3	13	89	6·

Table VI.—Duration of Marriage correlated

Religion or Community of Husband.	Total.			Duration of Marriage — Under 10 years.			10 years.		
	Number of slips examined.	Number of children.	Average per family.	Number of families.	Number of children.	Average per family.	Number of families.	Number of children.	Average per family.
1	2	3	4	5	6	7	8	9	10
JAMMU AND KASHMIR STATE.									
Total ..	**151,816**	**479,477**	**3·2**	**33,498**	**53,252**	**1·6**	7,966	29,376	3·7
Hindu	31,608	99,423	3·1	8,667	15,016	1·7	1,963	5,362	2·7
Brahman	9,644	23,984	2·5	2,918	5,028	1·6	513	1,483	2·9
Other Interior Castes	16,050	55,442	3·5	4,219	7,302	1·7	1,046	2,706	2·6
Lohar and Tarkhan, etc.	1,156	3,964	3·4	293	499	1·7	76	227	3·0
Rajput	2,935	9,467	3·2	734	1,186	1·6	229	533	2·3
Exterior Castes	1,823	6,559	3·6	503	1,001	2·0	99	413	4·2
Chamar	1,761	6,282	3·6	488	969	1·9	94	389	4·1
Sikh	2,562	9,994	3·9	734	1,740	2·4	198	393	2·0
Jain	15	63	4·2	3	8	2·6	..	..	..
Buddhist	2,167	9,964	4·6	492	1,800	3·6	11	44	4·0
Muslim	115,380	359,716	3·1	23,566	34,592	1·5	5,793	23,576	4·1
Bafinda	1,062	3,837	3·6	260	451	1·7	92	247	2·7
Christian	84	317	3·8	36	96	2·7	1	1	1·0
MYSORE STATE.									
Total ..	**4,320**	**19,107**	**4·4**	**1,467**	**2,974**	**2·0**	**335**	**1,149**	**3·4**
Hindu	3,374	15,200	4·5	1,112	2,221	2·0	250	849	3·4
Brahman	1,414	7,096	5·0	430	898	2·1	95	341	3·6
Other Interior Castes	1,430	5,933	4·1	516	1,007	2·0	110	365	3·3
Vakkaliga	227	927	4·1	70	131	1·9	15	45	3·0
Viswakarma	68	268	3·9	21	37	1·8	9	37	4·1
Yadava	25	118	4·7	6	15	2·5	3	8	2·7
Exterior Castes	210	858	4·1	69	133	1·9	18	53	2·9
Jain	75	313	4·2	34	82	2·4	8	26	3·3
Muslim	558	2,345	4·2	214	449	2·1	53	180	3·4
Christian	262	1,079	4·1	88	189	2·1	17	69	4·1
Others	51	170	3·3	19	33	1·7	7	25	3·6
PUNJAB.									
Total ..	**173,432**	**686,470**	**3·9**	**43,215**	**80,993**	**1·9**	**10,452**	**29,721**	**2·8**
Hindu	73,272	299,702	4·1	17,291	29,360	1·7	4,394	12,223	2·8
Ad-Dharmi	1,427	5,891	4·1	447	763	1·7	90	281	3·1
Sikh	23,055	94,854	4·1	5,625	10,395	1·9	1,266	3,856	3·1
Jain	134	519	3·9	41	59	1·4	9	30	3·3
Muslim	75,436	284,773	3·8	19,811	40,093	2·0	4,732	13,437	2·8
Christian	1,535	6,622	4·3	447	1,086	2·4	51	175	3·4
TRAVANCORE STATE.									
Total ..	**102,068**	**419,691**	**4·1**	**27,119**	**34,206**	**1·3**	3,762	**10,346**	**2·8**
Hindu	61,866	241,887	3·9	16,687	21,301	1·3	2,385	6,533	2·7
Brahman	4,883	17,567	3·6	1,301	1,322	1·0	202	494	2·5
Other Interior Castes	45,379	176,795	3·9	12,148	15,654	1·3	1,704	4,663	2·7
Nayar	23,008	90,226	3·9	6,449	8,416	1·3	788	2,276	2·9
Exterior Castes	11,604	47,625	4·1	3,238	4,325	1·3	479	1,376	2·8
Ilavas	9,730	40,799	4·2	2,715	3,749	1·4	391	1,167	3·0
Muslim	7,067	26,004	3·7	2,428	3,150	1·3	364	1,049	2·9
Christian	33,135	151,802	4·6	8,004	9,755	1·2	1,013	2,764	2·7
WESTERN INDIA STATES AGENCY.									
Total ..	**9,646**	**37,497**	**3·9**	**2,419**	**6,031**	**2·5**	1,116	3,737	3·4
Hindu	8,795	34,173	3·9	2,215	5,540	2·5	1,058	3,533	3·3
Exterior Castes	1,463	5,453	3·7	337	868	2·6	104	347	3·3
Muslim	845	3,288	3·9	202	481	2·4	58	204	3·5
Christian	6	36	6·0	2	10	5·0	..	..	..

with Community or Religion of Family—*concld.*

with present wife.

10—19			20—31			32 years.			33 and over.		
Number of families.	Number of children.	Average per family.	Number of families.	Number of children.	Average per family.	Number of families.	Number of children.	Average per family.	Number of families.	Number of children.	Average per family.
11	12	13	14	15	16	17	18	19	20	21	22
48,375	173,216	4·6	**55,360**	**162,590**	**2·9**	**1,821**	**9,282**	**5·1**	**9,796**	**51,761**	**5·3**
10,865	30,322	2·8	7,646	35,280	4·6	512	2,661	5·2	1,955	10,782	5·5
3,408	3,728	1·9	2,114	9,633	4·6	146	783	5·4	545	3,329	6·1
5,409	19,589	3·6	4,099	18,934	4·6	243	1,291	5·3	1,034	5,620	5·4
415	1,456	3·5	263	1,355	5·2	25	123	4·9	84	304	3·6
985	3,185	3·2	716	3,213	4·5	67	317	4·7	204	1,033	5·1
648	2,364	3·6	454	2,145	4·7	31	147	4·7	88	496	5·6
623	2,248	3·6	438	2,040	4·6	31	147	4·7	87	489	5·6
849	3,147	3·7	586	3,449	5·7	27	195	7·3	168	1,070	6·3
5	21	4·2	4	10	2·5	1	5	5·0	2	19	9·5
463	2,430	5·2	593	3,640	6·1	309	1,200	3·9	299	850	2·8
31,157	137,136	4·4	46,526	120,181	2·6	970	5,210	5·4	7,368	39,021	5·3
359	1,374	3·8	244	1,288	5·3	32	148	4·6	75	329	4·4
36	160	4·4	5	30	6·0	2	11	5·5	4	19	4·8
1,424	7,043	4·9	**896**	**6,408**	**7·2**	**37**	**289**	**7·8**	**161**	**1,244**	**7·7**
1,097	5,453	5·0	745	5,361	7·2	33	250	7·6	137	1,066	7·8
464	2,447	5·3	340	2,717	8·0	13	99	7·6	72	594	8·3
475	2,243	4·7	264	1,829	6·9	16	124	7·8	49	365	7·4
80	398	5·0	51	276	5·4	2	17	8·5	9	60	6·7
20	97	4·9	17	95	5·6	..	..	..	1	2	2·0
7	32	4·6	8	59	7·4	1	4	4·0	..	..	..
51	236	4·6	65	385	5·9	1	6	6·0	6	45	7·5
23	133	5·8	10	72	7·2	..	..	..	..	..	..
185	940	5·1	87	635	7·3	3	27	9·0	16	114	7·1
103	455	4·4	46	299	6·5	1	12	12·0	7	55	7·9
16	62	3·9	8	41	5·1	..	..	..	1	9	9·0
53,657	217,284	4·1	**44,464**	**233,603**	**5·3**	**3,226**	**20,573**	**6·4**	**18,418**	**104,296**	**5·7**
23,747	99,116	4·2	19,017	104,373	5·5	1,392	10,178	7·3	7,431	44,452	6·0
409	1,818	4·4	315	1,967	6·2	13	83	6·4	153	979	6·4
6,427	26,317	4·1	6,256	34,384	5·5	417	2,400	5·8	3,064	17,502	5·7
38	157	4·1	31	169	5·5	3	20	6·7	12	84	7·0
22,956	89,499	3·9	18,809	92,643	4·9	1,390	7,814	5·6	7,738	41,287	5·3
489	2,195	4·5	351	2,034	5·8	24	161	6·7	173	971	5·6
26,383	**108,926**	**4·1**	**32,710**	**186,231**	**5·7**	**1,937**	**12,415**	**6·4**	**10,157**	**67,567**	**6·7**
17,227	69,626	4·0	19,417	105,925	5·5	1,059	6,515	6·2	5,019	31,987	6·3
1,347	5,035	3·7	1,492	7,583	5·1	91	521	5·7	450	2,612	5·8
12,724	51,097	4·0	14,323	77,359	5·4	749	4,576	6·1	3,731	23,336	6·3
6,610	27,253	4·1	7,021	38,625	5·5	359	2,249	6·3	1,781	11,407	6·4
3,156	13,494	4·3	3,602	20,983	5·8	219	1,408	6·4	910	6,039	6·6
2,678	11,725	4·4	3,016	17,933	6·0	165	1,092	6·6	765	5,133	6·7
1,814	7,620	4·2	1,907	10,663	5·6	100	632	6·3	454	2,890	6·4
7,342	31,680	4·3	11,386	69,643	6·1	778	5,268	6·8	4,612	32,692	7·1
2,463	**10,587**	**4·3**	**2,522**	**11,725**	**4·7**	**250**	**1,206**	**4·8**	**876**	**4,211**	**4·8**
2,190	9,297	4·3	2,324	10,836	4·7	230	1,121	4·9	778	3,846	4·9
429	1,825	4·3	429	1,718	4·0	36	144	4·0	128	551	4·3
270	1,269	4·7	197	884	4·5	20	85	4·3	98	365	
3	21	7·0	1	5	5·0	..	..	..	..	..	..

APPENDIX II.

Census of Indians on the High Seas.

An attempt was made at this census to enumerate Indians on the high seas through the agency of the port authorities at Aden, Bombay, Calcutta, Karachi, Madras and Rangoon. High Seas schedules were issued for some six months beforehand to all Masters of vessels shipping Indian crews for a period which was likely to cover the date of the Census of India, *viz.*, the 26th February 1931, to be returned by the Master from the first port of call after that date. All vessels which returned high seas schedules at the Port of Madras were found on examination to have been in Indian waters on the night of the census and were consequently treated as normal port or sea-going population and included in the Presidency totals. The population returned at the ports of Aden, Karachi and Bombay was included in the ordinary provincial population of Bombay and Aden, but such of the figures as were separately available have been again included here with the returns received in Rangoon and Calcutta, which have been tabulated separately in forms corresponding with certain tables of the Imperial series, and appear in this appendix arranged as follows :—

Table I.—Birthplace—Corresponds to Imperial Table VI.

Table II.—Age, Sex and Civil Condition by Religion—Corresponds to Imperial Table VII.

Table III.—Occupation—Corresponds to Imperial Table X.

Table IV.—Literacy by Religion and Age—Corresponds to Imperial Table XIII.

Table V.—Language—Corresponds to Imperial Table XV.

Part I.—Mother Tongue.

Part II.—Bilingualism.

Table VI.—Religion—Corresponds to Imperial Table XVI.

Table VII.—Race, Caste or Tribe—Corresponds to Imperial Table XVII.

Table I.—Birthplace.

Birthplace	Total. Persons.	Total. Males.	Total. Females.	Port of Aden. Persons.	Port of Aden. Males.	Port of Aden. Females.	Port of Bombay. Persons.	Port of Bombay. Males.	Port of Bombay. Females.	Port of Calcutta. Persons.	Port of Calcutta. Males.	Port of Calcutta. Females.	Port of Karachi. Persons.	Port of Karachi. Males.	Port of Karachi. Females.	Port of Rangoon. Persons.	Port of Rangoon. Males.	Port of Rangoon. Females.
1	2	3	4	5	6	7	8	9	10	11	12	13	14	15	16	17	18	19
Total Population ..	**12,540**	**12,418**	**122**	**1,234**	**1,209**	**25**	**612**	**548**	**64**	**9,781**	**9,749**	**32**	**141**	**141**	..	**772**	**771**	**1**
A.—Born in India ..	**12,500**	**12,380**	**120**	**1,231**	**1,208**	**23**	**612**	**548**	**64**	**9,747**	**9,715**	**32**	**141**	**141**	..	**769**	**768**	**1**
(a) Provinces ..	**11,765**	**11,692**	**73**	**950**	**930**	**20**	**350**	**330**	**20**	**9,592**	**9,560**	**32**	**121**	**121**	..	**752**	**751**	**1**
1. Assam	2,927	2,927	..	2	2	..	1	1	..	2,830	2,830	..	5	5	..	89	89	..
2. Bengal ..	6,805	6,790	15	245	244	1	5	5	..	5,972	5,958	14	68	68	..	515	515	..
3. Bihar and Orissa	258	258	..	2	2	..	..	..	..	231	231	..	..	..	..	25	25	..
4. Bombay ..	471	445	26	283	272	11	66	56	10	84	79	5	30	30	..	8	8	..
Aden ..	*3*	*3*	..	*3*	*3*	..	..	..	..	..	..	..	..	..	..	..	..	..
5. Burma ..	80	76	4	7	4	3	..	..	..	11	11	..	..	..	..	62	61	1
6. Central Provinces and Berar.	7	7	..	2	2	..	1	1	..	4	4	..	..	..	..	..	..	..
7. Delhi	5	5	..	..	..	..	1	1	..	4	4	..	..	..	..	..	..	..
8. Madras ..	172	168	4	44	42	2	10	10	..	83	81	2	1	1	..	34	34	..
9. North-West Frontier Province. (*Districts and Administered Territories*).	11	11	..	3	3	..	1	1	..	7	7	..	..	..	..	..	..	..
10. Punjab ..	421	400	21	129	127	2	196	186	10	72	63	9	16	16	..	8	8	..
11. United Provinces of Agra and Oudh.	608	605	3	233	232	1	69	69	..	294	292	2	1	1	..	11	11	..
(b) States and Agencies.	**60**	**57**	**3**	**26**	**23**	**3**	**19**	**19**	..	**9**	**9**	..	**3**	**3**	..	**3**	**3**	..
12. Baroda State ..	7	7	..	2	2	..	3	3	..	2	2	..	..	..	..	..	..	..
13. Bengal States ..	1	1	..	..	..	..	..	..	..	1	1	..	..	..	..	..	..	..
14. Bombay States	27	24	3	*23	20	3	*1	1	..	..	..	..	*3	3	..	..	..	..
15. Central India Agency.	5	5	..	1	1	..	4	4	..	..	..	..	..	..	..	..	..	..
16. Hyderabad State	12	12	..	..	..	..	11	11	..	..	..	..	..	..	..	1	1	..
17. Madras States Agency (Cochin State).	2	2	..	..	..	..	..	..	..	1	1	..	..	..	..	1	1	..
18. Mysore State ..	4	4	..	..	..	..	..	..	..	3	3	..	..	..	..	1	1	..
19. Punjab States .. (including agency).	1	1	..	..	..	..	..	..	..	1	1	..	..	..	..	..	..	..
20. Rajputana Agency.	1	1	..	..	..	..	..	..	..	1	1	..	..	..	..	..	..	..
(c) French and Portuguese Settlements.	**440**	**396**	**44**	**44**	**44**	..	**243**	**199**	**44**	**123**	**123**	..	**17**	**17**	..	**13**	**13**	..
(d) India unspecified	**235**	**235**	..	**211**	**211**	..	..	..	..	**23**	**23**	..	..	..	..	**1**	**1**	..
B.—Born in other Asiatic countries.	**37**	**37**	..	**1**	**1**	..	..	..	..	**33**	**33**	..	..	..	..	**3**	**3**	..
Within British Dominions.	**23**	**23**	..	..	..	..	..	..	..	**21**	**21**	..	..	..	..	**2**	**2**	..
21 Ceylon ..	22	22	..	..	..	..	..	..	..	20	20	..	..	..	..	2	2	..
22 Straits Settlements and Malaya.	1	1	..	..	..	..	..	..	..	1	1	..	..	..	..	..	..	..
Outside British Dominions.	**14**	**14**	..	**1**	**1**	..	..	..	..	**12**	**12**	..	..	..	..	**1**	**1**	..
23 Afghanistan ..	2	2	..	..	..	..	..	..	..	2	2	..	..	..	..	..	..	..
24. Arabia ..	4	4	..	..	..	..	..	..	..	3	3	..	..	..	..	1	1	..
25. China ..	6	6	..	..	..	..	..	..	..	6	6	..	..	..	..	..	..	..
26. Nepal ..	2	2	..	1	1	..	..	..	..	1	1	..	..	..	..	..	..	..
C.—Born in Europe (outside British Dominions).	**1**	**1**	..	..	..	..	..	..	..	1	1	..	..	..	..	..	..	..
27. Holland ..	1	1	..	..	..	..	..	..	..	1	1	..	..	..	..	..	..	..
D.—Born in Africa (outside British Dominions).	**2**	..	**2**	**2**	..	**2**	..	..	..	..	..	..	..	..	..	..	..	..
28. Egypt	2	..	2	2	..	2	..	..	..	..	..	..	..	..	..	..	..	..

*Including Western India States Agency.

Table II.—Age, Sex and Civil Condition by Religion.

Age and Religion.	Population.			Unmarried.			Married.			Widowed.		
	Persons.	Males.	Females.	Persons.	Males.	Females.	Persons.	Males.	Females.	Persons.	Males.	Females.
1	2	3	4	5	6	7	8	9	10	11	12	13
PORT OF CALCUTTA—												
All Religions ..	**9,781**	**9,749**	**32**	**3,023**	**3,016**	**7**	**6,566**	**6,548**	**18**	**192**	**185**	**7**
0—5 ..	9	8	1	9	8	1	..	..	..	..	..	..
5—10 ..	9	6	3	7	5	2	2	1	1	..	..	..
10—15 ..	18	15	3	14	12	2	4	3	1	..	..	..
15—20 ..	1,262	1,258	4	802	801	1	454	451	3	6	6	..
20—40 ..	7,055	7,043	12	2,122	2,121	1	4,827	4,818	9	106	104	2
40—60 ..	1,359	1,350	9	64	64	..	1,223	1,219	4	72	67	5
60 and over	69	69	...	5	5	..	56	56	..	8	8	..
Muslims ..	**9,060**	**9,045**	**15**	**2,838**	**2,832**	**6**	**6,073**	**6,066**	**7**	**149**	**147**	**2**
0—5 ..	5	4	1	5	4	1	..	..	..	..	..	..
5—10 ..	5	4	1	5	4	1	..	..	..	..	..	..
10—15 ..	14	12	2	11	9	2	3	3	..	..	..	..
15—20 ..	1,206	1,204	2	770	769	1	431	430	1	5	5	..
20—40 ..	6,597	6,591	6	1,990	1,989	1	4,517	4,512	5	90	90	..
40—60 ..	1,183	1,180	3	53	53	..	1,081	1,080	1	49	47	2
60 and over	50	50	..	4	4	..	41	41	..	5	5	..
Hindus ..	**402**	**387**	**15**	**92**	**91**	**1**	**275**	**265**	**10**	**35**	**31**	**4**
0—5 ..	4	4	...	4	4	..	..	..	..	..	..	..
5—10 ..	4	2	2	2	1	1	2	1	1	..	..	..
10—15 ..	3	2	1	2	2	..	1	..	1	..	..	..
15—20 ..	26	24	2	10	10	..	16	14	2	..	..	..
20—40 ..	254	250	4	65	65	..	179	176	3	10	9	1
40—60 ..	95	89	6	8	8	..	65	62	3	22	19	3
60 and over	16	16	..	1	1	..	12	12	..	3	3	..
Christians ..	**304**	**302**	**2**	**90**	**90**	..	**208**	**207**	**1**	**6**	**5**	**1**
10—15 ..	1	1	..	1	1	..	..	..	..	..	..	..
15—20 ..	28	28	..	21	21	..	7	7	..	..	..	..
20—40 ..	194	192	2	65	65	..	124	123	1	5	4	1
40—60 ..	78	78	..	3	3	..	74	74	..	1	1	..
60 and over	3	3	..	..	..	..	3	3	..	..	..	..
Others ..	**15**	**15**	..	**3**	**3**	..	**10**	**10**	..	**2**	**2**	..
15—20 ..	2	2	..	1	1	..	..	..	..	1	1	..
20—40 ..	10	10	..	2	2	..	7	7	..	1	1	..
40—60 ..	3	3	..	..	..	..	3	3	..	..	..	..
PORT OF RANGOON—												
All Religions ..	**772**	**771**	**1**	**357**	**356**	**1**	**393**	**393**	..	**22**	**22**	..
10—15 ..	1	1	..	1	1	..	..	..	..	..	..	..
15—20 ..	83	82	1	56	55	1	26	26	..	1	1	..
20—40 ..	612	612	..	291	291	..	305	305	..	16	16	..
40—60 ..	72	72	..	8	8	..	59	59	..	5	5	..
60 and over	4	4	..	1	1	..	3	3	..	..	..	..
Muslims ..	**675**	**675**	..	**312**	**312**	..	**343**	**343**	..	**20**	**20**	..
10—15 ..	1	1	..	1	1	..	..	..	..	..	..	..
15—20 ..	68	68	..	46	46	..	21	21	..	1	1	..
20—40 ..	541	541	..	257	257	..	270	270	..	14	14	..
40—60 ..	62	62	..	7	7	..	50	50	..	5	5	..
60 and over	3	3	..	1	1	..	2	2	..	..	..	...
Hindus ..	**38**	**38**	..	**14**	**14**	..	**22**	**22**	..	**2**	**2**	..
15—20 ..	5	5	..	2	2	..	3	3	..	..	..	..
20—40 ..	31	31	..	12	12	..	17	17	..	2	2	..
40—60 ..	2	2	..	..	..	..	2	2	..	..	..	..
Christians ..	**38**	**37**	**1**	**18**	**17**	**1**	20	20	..	..	..	..
15—20 ..	6	5	1	5	4	1	1	1	..	..	..	..
20—40 ..	23	23	..	12	12	..	11	11	..	..	..	..
40—60 ..	8	8	..	1	1	..	7	7	..	..	..	..
60 and over	1	1	..	..	..	..	1	1	..	..	..	..
Others ..	**21**	**21**	..	**13**	**13**	..	8	8	..	..	..	..
15—20 ..	4	4	..	3	3	..	1	1	..	..	..	..
20—40 ..	17	17	..	10	10	..	7	7	..	..	..	..

NOTE.—This table was not compiled for the sea-going population returned at the ports of Aden, Bombay and Karachi.

Table III.—Occupation.

(Total for Ports of Rangoon, Calcutta, Bombay, Karachi, Aden.)

Total Earners	11,519
Total non-working Dependants	1,021
Total population	12,540

Occupation.	Total following occupation.	As principal occupation.		As subsidiary to other occupation.	
		Males.	Females.	Males.	Females.
1	2	3	4	5	6
All Occupations	**14,010**	**11,427**	**92**	**2,491**	..
A.—Production of Raw Materials	**2,469**	**18**	**1**	**2,450**	..
I.—Exploitation of Animals and Vegetation	**2,469**	**18**	**1**	**2,450**	..
1. Pasture and Agriculture	**2,469**	**18**	**1**	**2,450**	..
(a) Cultivation	**2,469**	**18**	**1**	**2,450**	..
1. Non-cultivating proprietors taking rent in money or kind	6	3	..	3	..
5. Cultivating owners	4	3		..	..
6. Tenant Cultivators	2,264	6		2,258	..
7. Agricultural Labourers	195	6	..	189	..
B.—Preparation and Supply of Material Substances	**11,129**	**11,088**	**3**	**38**	..
III.—Industry	**176**	**162**	..	**14**	..
5. Textiles	**1**	..	..	**1**	..
45. Rope, twine, string and other fibres ..	1	..	..	1	..
7. Wood	**18**	**15**	..	**3**	..
55. Carpenters, turners and joiners, etc. ..	18	15	..	3	..
8. Metals	**2**	**1**	..	**1**	..
59. Blacksmiths, other workers in iron, makers of implements	2	1	..	1	..
10. Chemical products properly so-called and analogous	**1**	**1**	..	..	..
67. Manufacture of aerated and mineral waters and ice	1	1	..	..	..
11. Food Industries	**117**	**116**	..	**1**	..
73. Butchers	38	38	..	..	..
76. Toddy drawers	79	78	..	1	..
12. Industries of dress and the toilet ..	**28**	**22**	..	**6**	..
83. Tailors, milliners, dress makers and darners	14	8	..	6	..
85. Washing and cleaning	4	4	..	..	..
86. Barbers, hair-dressers and wig-makers ..	10	10	..	..	..
16. Production and transmission of physical force	**2**	**2**	..	..	..
94. Heat, light, electricity, motive power, etc., Gas works and electric light and power	2	2	..	..	..
17. Miscellaneous and undefined industries	**7**	**5**	..	**2**	..
95. Printers, engravers, book-binders, etc. ..	2	1	..	1	..
97. Makers of clocks and surgical or scientific instruments, etc.	1	..	..	1	..
100. Scavenging	4	4	..	..	..
IV.—Transport	**10,850**	**10,841**	..	**9**	..
19. Transport by Water	**10,849**	**10,841**	..	**8**	..
102. Ship owners, boat owners and their employees, officers, mariners, etc., ships brokers, boatmen and tow men ..	10,846	10,838	..	8	..
103. Persons (other than labourers) employed in harbours, docks, rivers and canals, including pilots	3	3	..	..	..
20. Transport by Road	**1**	..	..	**1**	..
108. Owners, managers and employees (excluding personal servants) connected with other vehicles	1	..	..	1	..

Table III.—Occupation—*concld.*

Occupation.	Total following occupation.	As principal occupation. Males.	As principal occupation. Females.	As subsidiary to other occupation. Males.	As subsidiary to other occupation. Females
1	2	3	4	5	6
V.—Trade	**103**	**85**	**3**	**15**	..
23. Banks, establishments of credit, exchange and insurance	**2**	**2**	..	..	..
115. Bank managers, money-lenders, exchange and insurance agents, money changers and brokers and their employees	2	2	..	..	..
24. Brokerage Commission and Export	**2**	..	..	2	..
116. Brokers, commission agents, commercial travellers, warehouse owners and employees	2	..	..	2	..
25. Trade in Textiles	**3**	**3**	..	..	..
117. Trade in piece-goods, wool, cotton, silk, hair and other textiles	3	3	..	..	..
31. Hotels, cafes, restaurants, etc. ..	**21**	**21**	..	..	..
127. Owners and managers of hotels cook-shops, sarais, etc. (and employees) ..	21	21	..	..	..
32. Other trade in food stuffs ..	28	25	3	..	..
129. Grain and pulse dealers	27	24	3	..	..
130. Dealers in sweetmeats, sugar and spices	1	1	..	..	..
38. Trade in articles of luxury and those pertaining to letters and the arts and sciences	**1**	..	..	1	..
146. Dealers in precious stones, jewellery (real and imitation), clocks, optical instruments, etc.	1	..	..	1	..
39. Trade of other sorts	**46**	**34**	..	**12**	..
150. General storekeepers and shopkeepers otherwise unspecified	28	16	..	12	..
152. Other trades (including farmers of pounds, tools and markets)	18	18	..	..	..
C.—Public Administration and Liberal Arts	**41**	**35**	**4**	**2**	..
VI.—Public Force	**18**	**18**	..	..	..
43. Police	**18**	**18**	..	..	..
157. Police	13	13	..	..	..
158. Village Watchmen	5	5	..	..	..
VII.—Public Administration	**3**	**3**	..	..	..
44. Public Administration	**3**	**3**	..	..	..
159. Service of the State	3	3	..	..	..
VIII.—Professions and Liberal Arts ..	**20**	**14**	4	2	..
47. Medicine	**15**	**11**	**4**	..	..
169. Registered medical practitioners including oculists	12	11	1	..	..
172. Midwives, Vaccinators, compounders nurses, masseurs, etc.	3	..	3	..	..
48. Instruction	**3**	**2**	..	**1**	..
174. Professors and Teachers of all kinds ..	3	2	..	1	..
49. Letters arts and sciences (other than 44)	**2**	**1**	..	**1**	..
177. Architects, surveyors, engineers and their employees (not being state servants)	1	1	..	..	..
179. Artists, sculptors and image makers ..	1	..	..	1	..
D.—Miscellaneous	**371**	**286**	**84**	**1**	..
X.—Domestic Service	**3**	**2**	..	**1**	..
51. Domestic Service	**3**	**2**	..	**1**	..
186. Private motor drivers and cleaners ..	**3**	2	..	1	..
XI.—Insufficiently described occupations	**368**	**284**	**84**	..	..
52. General terms which do not indicate a definite occupation	**368**	**284**	**84**	..	..
188. Manufacturers, businessmen and contractors otherwise unspecified ..	1	1	..	..	..
191. Labourers and workmen otherwise unspecified	367	283	84	..	..

Table IV.—Literacy by Religion and Age.

Name of Port and Religion.	Total population.			Literate.			Illiterate.			Literate in English.		
	Persons.	Males.	Females.	Persons.	Males.	Females.	Persons.	Males.	Females.	Persons.	Males.	Females.
1	2	3	4	5	6	7	8	9	10	11	12	13
Total	**12,540**	**12,418**	**122**	**3,734**	**3,666**	**68**	**8,806**	**8,752**	**54**	**107**	**107**	..
*Aden	1,234	1,209	25	468	450	18	766	759	7	Not available.		
*Bombay	612	548	64	251	203	48	361	345	16		Do.	
*Karachi	141	141	..	50	50	..	91	91	..		Do.	
Calcutta—												
All Religions ..	**9,781**	**9,749**	**32**	**2,727**	**2,726**	**1**	**7,054**	**7,023**	**31**	**75**	**75**	..
0—5 ..	9	8	1	..	..	..	9	8	1	..	..	..
5—10 ..	9	6	3	..	..	..	9	6	3	..	..	..
10—15 ..	18	15	3	2	2	..	16	13	3	..	..	..
15—20 ..	1,262	1,258	4	319	318	1	943	940	3	6	6	..
20 and over ..	8,483	8,462	21	2,406	2,406	..	6,077	6,056	21	69	69	..
Muslims	**9,060**	**9,045**	**15**	**2,467**	**2,467**	..	**6,593**	**6,578**	**15**	**35**	**35**	..
0—5 ..	5	4	1	..	..	..	5	4	1	..	..	..
5—10 ..	5	4	1	..	..	..	5	4	1	..	..	..
10—15 ..	14	12	2	2	2	..	12	10	2	..	..	..
15—20 ..	1,206	1,204	2	299	299	..	907	905	2	3	3	..
20 and over ..	7,830	7,821	9	2,166	2,166	..	5,664	5,655	9	32	32	..
Hindus	**402**	**387**	**15**	**101**	**100**	**1**	**301**	**287**	**14**	**7**	**7**	..
0—5 ..	4	4	..	..	..	..	4	4	..	..	..	..
5—10 ..	4	2	2	..	..	..	4	2	2	..	..	..
10—15 ..	3	2	1	..	..	..	3	2	1	..	..	..
15—20 ..	26	24	2	7	6	1	19	18	1	1	1	..
20 and over ..	365	355	10	94	94	..	271	261	10	6	6	..
Christians— ..	**304**	**302**	**2**	**152**	**152**	..	**152**	**150**	**2**	**33**	**33**	..
10—15 ..	1	1	..	..	..	..	1	1	..	..	..	..
15—20 ..	28	28	..	12	12	..	16	16	..	2	2	..
20 and over ..	275	273	2	140	140	..	135	133	2	31	31	..
Others	**15**	**15**	..	**7**	**7**	..	**8**	**8**	..	..	..	..
15—20 ..	2	2	..	1	1	..	1	1	..	..	..	..
20 and over ..	13	13	..	6	6	..	7	7	..	..	..	..
Rangoon—												
All Religions ..	**772**	**771**	**1**	**238**	**237**	**1**	**534**	**534**	..	**32**	**32**	..
10—15 ..	1	1	..	..	..	..	1	1	..	..	..	..
15—20 ..	83	82	1	30	29	1	53	53	..	2	2	..
20 and over ..	688	688	..	208	208	..	480	480	..	30	30	..
Muslims	**675**	**675**	..	**200**	**200**	..	**475**	**475**	..	**15**	**15**	..
10—15 ..	1	1	..	..	..	..	1	1	..	..	..	..
15—20 ..	68	68	..	21	21	..	47	47	..	..	..	..
20 and over ..	606	606	..	179	179	..	427	427	..	15	15	..
Hindus	**38**	**38**	..	**4**	**4**	..	**34**	**34**	..	**3**	**3**	..
15—20 ..	5	5	..	1	1	..	4	4	..	..	..	..
20 and over ..	33	33	..	3	3	..	30	30	..	3	3	..
Others	**59**	**58**	**1**	**34**	**33**	**1**	**25**	**25**	..	**14**	**14**	..
15—20 ..	10	9	1	8	7	1	2	2	..	2	2	..
20 and over ..	49	49	..	26	26	..	23	23	..	12	12	..

*Age details not available.

Table V.—Language—Part I—Mother Tongue.

Language.	Total.			Port of Calcutta.			Port of Rangoon.		
	Persons.	Males.	Females.	Persons.	Males.	Females.	Persons.	Males.	Females.
1	2	3	4	5	6	7	8	9	10
Total	**10,553**	**10,520**	**33**	**9,781**	**9,749**	**32**	**772**	**771**	**1**
A.—Languages of India	**10,448**	**10,415**	**33**	**9,687**	**9,655**	**32**	**761**	**760**	**1**
Austric Family	*2*	*2*	..	*2*	*2*	..	..	..	..
Khasi	2	2	..	2	2	..	..	..	..
Tibeto-Chinese Family	*42*	*41*	*1*	*4*	*4*	..	*38*	*37*	*1*
Burmese	42	41	1	4	4	..	38	37	1
Dravidian Family	*88*	*86*	*2*	*65*	*63*	*2*	*23*	*23*	..
Tamil	66	64	2	54	52	2	12	12	...
Malayalam	2	2	..	2	2	..	..	..	...
Kanarese	2	2	..	2	2	..	..	..	..
Telugu	18	18	..	7	7	..	11	11	...
Indo-European Family	*10,316*	*10,286*	*30*	*9,616*	*9,586*	*30*	*700*	*700*	..
Sindhi	10	10	..	10	10	..	..	..	...
Marathi	2	2	..	2	2	..	..	..	...
Konkani	132	132	..	121	121	..	11	11	...
Oriya	35	35	..	34	34	..	1	1	...
Bengali	7,805	7,805	..	7,295	7,295	..	510	510	..
Assamese	23	23	..	23	23	..	..	..	...
Eastern Hindi	2,197	2,180	17	2,023	2,006	17	174	174	...
Gujarati	47	45	2	47	45	2	..	..	...
Panjabi	65	54	11	61	50	11	4	4	...
B.—Vernaculars of other Asiatic Countries	**73**	**73**	..	**72**	**72**	..	**1**	**1**	...
Indo-European Family	*19*	*19*	..	*18*	*18*	..	*1*	*1*	..
Sinhalese	7	7	..	6	6	..	1	1	..
Persian	12	12	..	12	12	..	..	..	...
Tibeto-Chinese Family	*3*	*3*	..	*3*	*3*	..	..	..	..
Chinese	3	3	..	3	3	..	..	..	...
Semitic Family	*51*	*51*	..	*51*	*51*	..	..	..	..
Arabic	51	51	..	51	51	..	..	..	..
C.—European Languages	**32**	**32**	..	**22**	**22**	..	**10**	**10**	..
Indo-European Family	*32*	*32*	..	*22*	*22*	..	*10*	*10*	..
English	32	32	..	22	22	..	10	10	..

NOTE.—This table was not compiled for the sea-going population returned at the ports of Aden, Bombay and Karachi.

Table V.—Language—Part II—Bilingualism.

Mother tongue and subsidiary language.	Port of Calcutta. Males.	Port of Rangoon. Males.
Bengali—		
No subsidiary language ..	4,266	278
Any subsidiary language ..	3,029	232
Subsidiary language—		
Hindustani	2,126	216
Burmese	..	8
Arabic	629	3
English	274	5
Eastern Hindi—		
No subsidiary language ..	1,000*	157
Any subsidiary language ..	1,023	17
Subsidiary language—		
Bengali	766	9
Burmese	..	3
Tamil	1	..
Arabic	90	..
Persian	..	1
English	166	4
Assamese—		
No subsidiary language ..	4	..
Any subsidiary language ..	19	..
Subsidiary language—		
Hindustani	15	..
English	4	..
Khasi—		
No subsidiary language ..	..	..
Any subsidiary language ..	2	..
Subsidiary language, English	2	..
Oriya—		
No subsidiary language ..	21	..
Any subsidiary language ..	13	1
Subsidiary language—		
Bengali	1	..
Hindustani	12	1

Mother tongue and subsidiary language.	Port of Calcutta. Males.	Port of Rangoon. Males.
Burmese—		
No subsidiary language ..	1	18†
Any subsidiary language ..	3	20
Subsidiary language—		
Hindustani	2	20
Arakanese	1	..
Gujarati—		
No subsidiary language ..	5‡	..
Any subsidiary language ..	42	..
Subsidiary language—		
Hindustani	41	..
English	1	..
Kanarese—		
No subsidiary language ..	1	..
Any subsidiary language ..	1	..
Subsidiary language, English	1	..
Konkani—		
No subsidiary language ..	52§	5
Any subsidiary language ..	71	6
Subsidiary language—		
Hindustani	36	5
English	21	1
Portuguese	14	..
Panjabi—		
No subsidiary language ..	..	..
Any subsidiary language ..	..	4
Subsidiary language—		
Hindustani	..	3
Burmese	..	1
Tamil—		
No subsidiary language ..	34	6
Any subsidiary language ..	20	6
Subsidiary language—		
Bengali	2	..
Hindustani	16	5
Burmese	..	1
English	2‖	..

Mother tongue and subsidiary language.	Port of Calcutta. Males.	R
Telugu—		
No subsidiary language ..	6	
Any subsidiary language ..	1	
Subsidiary language—		
Hindustani	1	
Burmese	..	
Tamil	..	
Arabic—		
No subsidiary language ..	12	
Any subsidiary language ..	39	
Subsidiary language—		
Hindustani	17	
English	22	
Chinese—		
No subsidiary language ..	2	
Any subsidiary language ..	1	
Subsidiary language—		
Hindustani	1	
Persian—		
No subsidiary language ..	4	
Any subsidiary language ..	8	
Subsidiary language—		
Marathi	6	
English	2	
Sinhalese—		
No subsidiary language ..	..	
Any subsidiary language ..	..	
Subsidiary language—		
Hindustani	..	
English—		
No subsidiary language ..	10	
Any subsidiary language ..	12	
Subsidiary language—		
Hindustani	4	
Burmese	..	
Tamil	1	
Portuguese	7	

*Includes 17 Females. †Includes 1 Female. ‡Includes 2 Females.

§Includes two persons speaking Marathi as mother tongue.

‖Refers to two females who are also included against the number of males speaking any subsidiary language to mother tongue Tamil.

Table VI.—Religion.

Name of Port.	All Religions.			Hindus			Sikhs.			Buddhists.			Zoroastrians.			Muslims.			Christians.		
	Persons.	Males.	Females.	Persons.	Males.	Females.	Persons.	Males.	Females.	Persons.	Males.	Females.	Persons.	Males.	Females.	Persons.	Males.	Females.	Persons.	Males.	Females.
1	2	3	4	5	6	7	8	9	10	11	12	13	14	15	16	17	18	19	20	21	22
Total	**12,540**	**12,418**	**122**	**601**	**574**	**27**	**1**	**1**	..	**35**	**35**	..	**24**	**15**	**9**	**11,241**	**11,202**	**39**	**638**	**591**	**4**
1. Aden	1,234	1,209	25	134	124	10	1	1	..	..	..	..	6	5	1	1,021	1,007	14	72	72	.
2. Bombay ..	612	548	64	25	23	2	..	..	..	..	..	..	17	9	8	363	353	10	207	163	4
3. Calcutta ..	9,781	9,749	32	402	387	15	..	..	..	14	14	..	1	1	..	9,060	9,045	15	304	302	
4. Karachi ..	141	141	..	2	2	..	..	..	..	..	..	..	..	..	..	122	122	..	17	17	.
5. Rangoon ..	772	771	1	38	38	..	..	..	..	21	21	..	..	..	..	675	675	..	38	37	

Table VII.—Race, Caste or Tribe.

Caste and Religion.	Total.			Port of Aden.			Port of Bombay.			Port of Calcutta.			Port of Karachi.			Port of Rangoon.		
	Persons.	Males.	Females.	Persons.	Males.	Females.	Persons.	Males.	Females.	Persons.	Males.	Females.	Persons.	Males.	Females.	Persons.	Males.	Females.
1	2	3	4	5	6	7	8	9	10	11	12	13	14	15	16	17	18	19
Total ..	**12,540**	**12,418**	**122**	**1,234**	**1,209**	**25**	**612**	**548**	**64**	**9,781**	**9,749**	**32**	**141**	**141**	..	**772**	**771**	**1**
Muslims ..	**11,241**	**11,202**	**39**	**1,021**	**1,007**	**14**	**363**	**353**	**10**	**9,060**	**9,045**	**15**	**122**	**122**	..	**675**	**675**	..
Bohra ..	5	4	1	5	4	1	..	..	..	..	..	..	..	..	..	..	..	..
Pathan ..	108	108	..	2	2	..	106	106	..	..	..	..	..	..	..	..	..	..
Saiyad ..	18	18	..	..	..	..	..	..	..	18	18	..	..	..	..	..	..	..
Sheikh ..	487	487	..	267	267	..	176	176	..	..	..	..	44	44	..	..	..	..
Others or unspecified.	10,623	10,585	38	747	734	13	81	71	10	9,042	9,027	15	78	78	..	675	675	..
Hindus	**601**	**574**	**27**	**134**	**124**	**10**	**25**	**23**	**2**	**402**	**387**	**15**	**2**	**2**	..	**38**	**38**	..
Bagdi ..	1	1	..	..	..	..	..	..	..	1	1	..	..	..	..	..	..	..
Baidya ..	1	1	..	..	..	..	..	..	..	1	1	..	..	..	..	..	..	..
Bhaya ..	1	1	..	..	..	..	1	1	..	..	..	..	..	..	..	..	..	..
Brahman ..	8	7	1	3	2	1	1	1	..	4	4	..	..	..	..	..	..	..
Bania ..	8	5	3	7	4	3	1	1	..	..	..	..	..	..	..	..	..	..
Dhobi ..	2	2	..	..	..	..	..	..	..	2	2	..	..	..	..	..	..	..
Dom	1	1	..	..	..	..	..	..	..	1	1	..	..	..	..	..	..	..
Jogi	1	1	..	..	..	..	..	..	..	1	1	..	..	..	..	..	..	..
Kalu	1	1	..	..	..	..	..	..	..	..	..	..	..	..	..	1	1	..
Kamar ..	1	1	..	..	..	..	..	..	..	1	1	..	..	..	..	..	..	..
Kayastha ..	3	3	..	..	..	..	..	..	..	3	3	..	..	..	..	..	..	..
Kharva ..	50	50	..	50	50	..	..	..	..	..	..	..	..	..	..	..	..	..
Khatri ..	4	3	1	..	..	..	..	..	..	4	3	1	..	..	..	..	..	..
Koli	8	8	..	..	..	..	..	..	..	7	7	..	..	..	..	1	1	..
Korangi ..	4	4	..	..	..	..	..		..	4	4	..	..	..	..	..	..	..
Loona ..	1	1	..	..	..	..	..	..	..	1	1	..	..	..	..	..	..	..
Mahar ..	4	4	..	..	..	..	4	4	..	..	..	..	..	..	..	..	..	..
Maratha ..	9	9	..	..	..	..	9	9	..	..	..	..	..	..	..	..	..	..
Mehta ..	33	33	..	..	..	..	..	..	..	30	30	..	..	..	..	3	3	..
Napit.. ..	2	2	..	..	..	..	..	..	..	2	2	..	..	..	..	..	..	..
Patel ..	5	3	2	5	3	2	..	..	..	..	..	..	..	..	..	..	..	..
Rajput ..	6	6	..	..	..	..	..	..	..	6	6	..	..	..	..	..	..	..
Rewat ..	12	12	..	11	11	..	..	..	..	..	..	..	..	..	..	1	1	..
Rohatria ..	3	2	1	3	2	1	..	..	..	..	..	..	..	..	..	..	..	..
Talbaji ..	1	1	..	1	1	..	..	..	..	..	..	..	..	..	..	..	..	..
Others ..	431	412	19	54	51	3	9	7	2	334	320	14	2	2	..	32	32	..
Sikhs	**1**	**1**	..	**1**	**1**	..	..	..	..	..	..	..	..	..	..	..	..	..
Buddhists ..	**35**	**35**	..	..	..	..	..	..	..	**14**	**14**	..	..	..	..	**21**	**21**	..
Zoroastrians ..	**24**	**15**	**9**	**6**	**5**	**1**	**17**	**9**	**8**	**1**	**1**	..	..	..	..	..	..	..
Christians ..	**638**	**591**	**47**	**72**	**72**	..	**207**	**163**	**44**	**304**	**302**	**2**	**17**	**17**	..	**38**	**37**	**1**

APPENDIX III.

Persons of Indian Origin enumerated in various parts of the British Empire.

The tables below give details for persons of Indian Origin enumerated in various parts of the British Empire. Wherever possible the return of Birthplace, Religion, Civil Condition, Occupation and Age was made but in cases this return was partial, which accounts for the discrepancies between the figures under the several headings in the statements below.

2. The figures detailed in these statements are not in every case the result of enumerations in 1931 but of records over a period of about six years (*viz.*, 1926-31). The majority of the returns are, however, the result of census enumerations in 1931, and such as are not will be found dated in the column for designation on each statement.

APPENDIX

Statement showing details of persons of Indian origin enumerated in various parts

Colony or Protectorate.		Total.		Total British India.		Bombay.	Madras.	Bengal.	Assam.	United Provinces.	Central Provinces.
		Males.	Females.	Males.	Females.	Both Sexes.	Both Sexes.	Both Sexes.	Both Sexes.	Both Sexes.	Both Sexes.
1		2	3	4	5	6	7	8	9	10	11
Total	..	**813,143**	**491,257**	**72,371**	**13,687**	**9,275**	**64,583**	**5,583**	**965**	**503**	**115**
				312							
1. British Guiana ..	..	69,729	60,811	..	..	..	..	..	..	..	..
2. British Honduras (1930)	..	266	231	..	..	..	..	..	..	..	..
3. British Malaya ..	..	421,028	202,981	..	..	..	..	..	..	..	..
4. Ceylon (Colombo) ..	..	66,141	14,580	54,174	9,322	854	62,178	92	4	134	17
5. Cyprus ..	..	3	1	3	..	..	..	1	..	..	..
6. Egypt (1927) ..	..	623	198	..	..	..	..	..	..	..	..
7. England and Wales ..	..	6,844	285	5,971*	251	929	384†	2,229	757	273	73
8. Fanning Island ..		4	..	2	..	1	1	..	..	..	..
9. Gibraltar	..	56	..	56	..	56	..	..	..	..	..
0. Gilbert and Ellice Islands	..	1	..	1	..	..	..	1	..	..	..
1. Gold Coast Colony	..	56	..	54	..	52	1	..	..	..	..
2. Hong Kong ..	..	3,989	756	2,722	179	98	7	51	.	62	1
3. Irish Free State (1926)	..	919	1,070	..	..	..	..	..	..	..	..
4. Malta	..	38	5	..	..	..	..	..	..	..	..
5. Mauritius ..	..	139,668	129,202	3,260	1,672	816	1,541	2,575	..	..	..
6. Nigeria	..	32	..	..	..	..	..	..	..	..	..
17. North Borneo ..	..	843	363	357	52	18	114	13	..	3	..
18. Northern Ireland (1926)	..	485	518	..	..	..	..	..	..	..	..
19. Northern Rhodesia ..	..	139	32	108	11	103	13	..	..	..	..
20. Nyasaland ..	..	1,306	203	..	..	..	..	..	..	..	..
21. Palestine	..	34	26	..	..	..	..	..	..	..	..
22. Scotland	..	1,986	17	1,648	13	261	84	615	204	29	24
23. Seychelles	..	398	105	312		78	229	4	..	1	..
24. Sierra Leone ..	..	22	3	19	..	19	..	..	..	..	..
25. Somaliland ..	..	310	210	82	34	61	24	2	..	1	..
26. Soudan	..	368	157	..	..	..	..	..	.	..	..
27. Tanganyika ..	..	14,177	9,245	..	..	..	..	..	..	..	..
28. Tongan Islands ..	..	19	4	15	2	10	7	..	..	..	..
29. Trinidad and Tobago	..	73,704	64,963	..	..	..	..	..	..	..	..
30. Zanzibar	..	9,955	5,291	3,899	2,151	5,919	..	..	..	..	..

NOTE.—Except where stated the above figures are the result of enumerations in 1931.

* Includes 1 Male born in the Andaman and Nicobar Islands.

† Includes 2 Males born in Coorg.

(*a*) Hyderabad State.

(*b*) Details by States not available.

(*c*) 3,393 Persons (2,935 Males and 458 Females) in Tranvancore State ; 205 Persons (122 Males and 83 Females) in Mysore ; Western India States 658 Persons (621 Males and 37 Females) ; Gwalior 1 Male ; Cochin State 2,446 Persons (2,379 Males and 67 Females) ; Baroda State 9 Males ; Hyderabad 8 Persons (3 Males and 5 Females).

(*d*) 1 in Hyderabad and 1 in Baroda State.

III.

of the British Empire for the period 1926-31.

Born in: Central India Agency.	Punjab (including Agency).	Baluchistan.	North-West Frontier Province.	Burma.	Delhi.	Bihar and Orissa.	Rajputana and Ajmer-Merwara.	Principal Indian States.		Colony of Enumeration.		Elsewhere out of India.		India unspecified.		
Both Sexes.	Both Sexes.	Both Sexes.	Both Sexes.	Both Sexes.	Both Sexes.	Both Sexes.	Both Sexes.	Males.	Females.	Males.	Females.	Males.	Females	Males.	Females.	
12	13	14	15	16	17	18	19	20	21	22	23	24	25	26	27	
28	4,661	8	211	171	51	160	55	6,531	711	332,399	310,112	2,881	2,129	398,563	164,513	
								7		128		42		14		
..	..	..	..	..	..	..	..	..	..	54,836	51,617	446	405	14,447	8,789	1
..	..	..	..	..	..	..	..	..	..	202	206	25	19	39	6	2
..	..	..	..	..	..	..	..	..	..	68,394	63,111	..	..	352,634	139,870	3
6	132	..	15	1	16	44	3	(c) 6,070	650	4,812	4,356	307	81	778	171	4
..	2	..	..	..	..	..	..	..	..	..	..	..	1	..	..	5
..	..	..	..	..	..	..	..	..	..	116	102	42	22	465	74	6
21	1,088	8	152	135	29	106	37	(j) 252	21	..	..	..	..	621	13	7
..	..	..	..	..	..	..	..	..	..	1	..	1	..	..	..	8
..	..	..	..	..	..	..	..	..	..	..	..	..	..	..	..	9
..	..	..	..	..	..	..	..	..	..	..	..	..	..	..	..	10
..	1	..	..	..	..	..	..	..	..	..	..	..	..	2	..	11
1	2,649	..	16	2	3	3	8	(e) 73	3	401	460	35	26	758	88	12
..	..	..	..	..	..	..	..	..	..	..	..	..	..	919	1,070	13
..	..	..	..	..	..	..	..	..	..	..	1	1	1	37	3	14
..	..	..	..	..	..	..	..	..	..	134,967	126,843	144	87	1,297	600	15
..	..	..	..	..	..	..	..	..	..	..	..	..	..	32	..	16
..	253	..	3	1	1	..	3	(f) 20	2	270	277	35	14	161	18	17
..	..	..	..	..	..	..	..	..	..	..	..	..	..	485	518	18
..	3	..	..	..	..	..	..	(d) 2	..	6	9	17	12	6	..	19
..	..	..	..	..	..	..	..	..	..	49	47	5	3	1,252	153	20
..	..	..	..	..	..	..	..	..	..	7	7	2	4	25	15	21
..	374	..	25	32	2	7	4	(i) 29	1	..	..	..	...	(h) 309	3	22
..	..	..	..	..	..	..	.	(g) 7		128		42		14		23
..	..	..	..	..	..	..	..	..	..	1	..	2	3	..	..	24
..	..	..	..	..	..	..	..	(b) 84	34	105	90	39	52	..	..	25
..	28	..	..	..	..	..	..	..	..	31	33	21	19	316	105	26
..	..	..	..	..	..	..	..	..	..	3,849	3,754	1,086	991	9,242	4,500	27
..	..	..	..	..	..	..	..	(a) 1	..	1	2	2	..	..	..	28
..	..	..	..	..	..	..	..	..	..	58,734	56,212	232	234	14,738	8,517	29
..	131	..	..	..	..	..	..	..	..	5,617	2,985	439	155	..	..	30

(e) Kashmir State 12 Males balance Hyderabad State.

(f) Mysore State 3 Males; Baroda 4 Males and 1 Female; Cochin State 2 Males and 1 Female; Travancore State 9 Males; Jammu and Kashmir 1 Male; Western India States 1 Male.

(g) Baroda State 3; Mysore State 1; Travancore 1; Cochin 1; Western India States Agency 10.

(h) Includes certain persons who failed to make the return of birthplace.

(i) Gwalior 2 Males; Hyderabad 8 Males and 1 Female; Kashmir 14 Males; Mysore 5 Males.

(j) Baroda 8 Males; Gwalior 10 Males and 1 Female; Kashmir 38 Males; Hyderabad 154 Males and 17 Females; Mysore 41 Males and 3 Females Sikkim 1 Male.

APPENDIX

Statement showing details of persons of Indian origin enumerated in various parts

Colony or Protectorate.	Religion. Hindus. Males.	Hindus. Females.	Muslims. Males.	Muslims. Females.	Christians. Males.	Christians. Females.	Zoroastrians. Males.	Zoroastrians. Females.	Others. Males.	Others. Females.
1	28	29	30	31	32	33	34	35	36	37
Total .	587,858	370,992	123,044	63,876	59,644	41,279	366	273	21,643	7,551
	3,746		10,680		1,148			225	10	
1. British Guiana	51,630	44,712	11,549	10,240	5,885	5,310	43	27	622	522
2. British Honduras (1930) ..	20	2	1	..	236	229	..	..	9	..
3. British Malaya	333,960	175,242	47,962	8,544	22,699	13,915	..	..	16,407	5,280
4. Ceylon (Colombo)	38,721	7,422	13,952	3,251	10,901	3,097	100	77	2,467	733
5. Cyprus	..	..	3	1	..	..	..	..	..	..
6. Egypt (1927)	..	..	378	138	42	18	..	..	203	42
7. England and Wales	Information not available.									
8. Fanning Island	1	..	2	..	..	..	..	..	1	..
9. Gibraltar	55	..	1	..	..	..	..	..	..	..
10. Gilbert and Ellice Islands ..	..	..	..	..	1	..	..	..	..	..
11. Gold Coast Colony ..	54	..	1	..	1	..	..	..	..	..
12. Hong-Kong	1,494	164	2,168	395	3	1	45	18	279	178
13. Irish Free State (1926) ..	Information not available.									
14. Malta	38	5	..	..	..	..	..	..	..	..
15. Mauritius	105,454	96,778	26,069	24,564	7,504	7,584	6	3	635	273
16. Nigeria	28	..	1	..	..	..	..	..	3	..
17. North Borneo	260	88	557	252	25	23	..	..	1	..
18. Northern Ireland (1926) ..	Information not available.									
19. Northern Rhodesia	78	14	49	5	12	13	..	..	..	..
20. Neyasaland	373	72	859	107	27	12	2	2	45	10
21. Palestine	..	..	18	3	5	2	..	..	11	21
22. Scotland	Information not available.									
23. Seychelles	282 Persons		67 Persons		144 Persons		..	..	10 Persons	
24. Sierra Leone	18	..	3	3	1	..	.	..	..	..
25. Somaliland	86	45	177	147	18	3	12	4	17	11
26. Soudan	276	89	77	59	5	..	..	..	10	9
27. Tanganyika	5,162	2,600	8,131	6,259	116	52	35	17	733	317
28. Tongan Islands	16	4	2	..	1	..	..	..	..	..
29. Trinidad and Tobago ..	50,134	43,755	11,084	9,908	12,163	11,020	123	125	200	155
30. Zanzibar	3,464 Persons		10,553 Persons		1,004 Persons		225 Persons		..	..

Includes—
(*a*) 1 divorced.
(*b*) 2 males and 1,333 females divorced.
(*c*) 302 males and 272 females divorced.
(*d*) 20 males and 16 females divorced.
(*e*) 2 males divorced.

III—*contd.*

of the British Empire for the period 1926-31.

Civil Condition: Married Males 38	Married Females 39	Single Males 40	Single Females 41	Widowed Males 42	Widowed Females 43	Occupation: Commercial Males 44	Commercial Females 45	Agricultural Males 46	Agricultural Females 47	Industrial Males 48	Industrial Females 49	Indefinite Males 50	Indefinite Females 51	Non-Productive Males 52	Non-Productive Females 53	
285,367	207,788	239,496	164,889	9,932	20,081	87,792	9,607	270,707	114,453	41,202	5,454	186,253	44,649	216,349	311,183	
		268,515 M.+92,885 F.				211		73		21		46		152		
27,228	26,556	(f) 39,301	28,987	3,200	5,268	6,316	1,182	34,612	17,941	2,213	166	1,698	1,055	24,890	40,467	
77	59	182	157	7	15	5	1	46	1	11	1	79	3	125	225	2
152,513	110,096	268,515 Males		92,885 Females.		29,596	618	153,408	69,431	18,280	1,135	133,898	11,845	85,846	119,952	3
				Widowed or Divorced.												
31,745	7,404	33,194	5,710	1,202	1,466	32,391	5,866	499	235	7,134	2,582	25,867	5,801	250	96	4
2	1	1	..	..	..	1	..	..	..	2	..	..	..	..	1	5
Information not available						288	2	2	..	50	..	164	7	119	189	6
3,308	114	3,438	152	98	19	730	22	..	..	75	..	4,303	8	1,733*	258*	7
1	..	3	..	..	..	3	..	..	..	1	..	..	..	..	..	8
36	..	18	..	2	..	56	..	..	..	..	..	..	..	..	..	9
1	..	..	..	..	..	..	..	..	..	..	..	1	..	..	..	10
25	..	27	..	4	..	54	..	..	..	..	..	2	..	..	..	11
1,907	305	2,014	413	68	38	183	2	2	..	269	..	2,690	21	845	733	12
Information not available						43	15	46	22	117	27	306	165	407	841	13
23	2	15	3	..	..	36	..	..	..	..	..	..	..	2	5	14
48,942	49,648	(c) 85,045	67,340	4,236	11,018†	8,251	845	53,223	14,704	4,347	361	8,583	2,049	65,264	111,243	15
7	..	10	..	(15 Unclassified)		32	..	..	..	..	..	..	..	..	..	16
324	114	505	243	14	6	82	..	148	9	118	..	257	1	238	353	17
						Information not available.										18
84	15	51	17	4	..	91	..	11	..	5	..	..	..	32	32	19
771	133	(e) 518	67	17	3	1,072	..	12	..	40	..	9	1	173	202	20
18	12	16	12	..	2	8	9	3	..	13	6	2	1	8	10	21
1,134	9	811‡	6	41§	2	1,674	..	..	..	29	..	283	17	..	..	22
158	30	233	67	7	8	211 Persons		73 Persons		21 Persons		46 Persons		152 Persons		23
11	1	11	2	..	..	20	..	..	..	1	..	..	..	1	3	24
155	104	151	(a) 94	4	12	128	2	1	..	..	..	84	1	97	207	25
112	66	254	91	2	..	234	..	..	..	47	..	24	..	63	157	26
6,576	4,038	(d) 7,222	4,622	379	585	3,860	97	120	4	1,505	6	360	8	8,332	9,130	27
10	2	6	2	3	..	9	..	1	..	8	1	..	..	1	3	28
6,590	6,420	(g) 66,470	56,904	644	1,639	2,629	946	28,573	12,106	6,937	1,169	7,642	23,666	27,923	27,076	29
3,610	2,659	(b) 6,345 Males		2,632 Females.						Details not available.						

(f) 111 males and 109 females divorced.
(g) 16 males and 13 females divorced.
* Includes 106 children (70 boys and 36 girls) for whom no return of occupation was made.
† 2,641 persons (1,445 males and 1,196 females) for whom no return of Civil Condition was received.
‡ Includes 21 males whose Civil Condition was not stated.
§ Includes 2 divorced males.

APPENDIX III—*concld.*

Statement showing details of persons of Indian origin enumerated in various parts of the British Empire for the period 1926-31.

Colony or Protectorate.	Age.											
	0—10.		10—20.		20—40.		40—60.		60 and over.		Unspecified.	
	Males.	Females.	Males.	Females.	Males.	Females.	Males.	Females.	Males.	Females.	Males.	Females.
1	54	55	56	57	58	59	60	61	62	63	64	65
Total	**143,023**	**140,767**	**128,148**	**98,578**	**393,912**	**179,691**	**124,680**	**56,399**	**20,823**	**14,130**	**1,449**	**976**
1. British Guiana	19,360	19,063	13,105	12,767	21,173	18,314	13,553	8,785	2,361	1,733	177	149
2. British Honduras (1930) ..	89	91	57	53	60	57	42	18	16	11	2	1
3. British Malaya	57,172	56,619	52,053	36,064	247,519	91,545	58,038	16,124	6,246	2,629	..	..
4. Ceylon (Colombo)	3,771	3,562	10,869	2,508	39,361	5,888	10,883	2,092	1,251	529	6	1
5. Cyprus	..	..	..	..	1	1	2	..	..	..	..	..
6. Egypt (1927)	Information not available.											
7. England and Wales	39	17	281	57	5,583	155	858	46	83	10	..	..
8. Fanning Island	..	..	..	..	4	..	..	..	..	..	..	..
9. Gibralter	..	..	6	..	40	..	10	..	..	..	..	..
10. Gilbert and Ellice Islands ..	..	..	..	..	..	.	..	..	1	..	..	..
11. Gold Coast Colony	..	..	6	..	42	..	7	.	1	..	..	..
12. Hong Kong	232	257	473	134	2,842	284	409	68	33	13	..	..
13. Irish Free State (1926)	141	125	201	193	256	305	215	304	106	143	..	..
14. Malta	2	3	10	..	23	2	3	..	..	..	..	..
15. Mauritius	36,329	35,919	30,223	28,678	42,939	38,670	22,605	19,137	6,314	5,973	1,258	825
16. Nigeria	..	..	6	..	23	..	3	..	..	..	..	..
17. North Borneo	170	178	87	82	349	93	213	8	24	2	..	..
18. Northern Ireland (1926)	Information not available.											
19. Northern Rhodesia	11	13	9	5	77	13	38	1	4	..	..	..
20. Neyasaland	67	59	224	39	840	95	169	8	6	2	..	..
21. Palestine	4	5	1	8	16	6	12	6	1	1	..	..
22. Scotland	5	1	47	..	1,649	12	265	3	14	1	6	..
23. Seychelles	49	44	69	24	173	24	87	9	20	4	..	..
24. Sierra Leone	1	..	1	..	16	3	3	..	1	..	..	..
25. Somaliland	75	56	31	45	144	86	53	15	7	8	..	..
26. Soudan	46	62	70	9	189	85	58	1	5	..	..	..
27. Tanganyika	3,496	3,712	2,379	1,920	6,500	2,859	1,565	625	237	129	..	..
28. Tongan Islands..	1	2	1	..	15	2	2	..	..	..	..	..
29. Trinidad and Tobago	19,419	19,525	15,479	14,674	20,925	19,761	14,151	8,337	3,730	2,666	..	..
30. Zanzibar	2,544	1,454	2,460	1,318	3,153	1,431	1,436	812	362	276	..	..

APPENDIX IV.

Figures of Area and Population by Religion to the nearest thousand.

The statement below has been compiled on recent census figures in the form of Appendix I to Volume I of the Report of the Indian Statutory Commission, in order to show the population of provinces with Sind and Orissa as separate units.

2. The table includes under the Provinces only territory which is in British India (with the exception of Berar, which is included with the Central Provinces and as part of the total for Governors Provinces and for British India).

3. The estimated populations referred to in column 15 against Bombay represents the estimated population of Ahmedabad believed to be almost entirely Hindu and Jain, while those in the Agency and Tribal Areas of the North-West Frontier Province are almost exclusively Muslim.

APPENDIX IV.

Figures of Area and Population by Religion to the nearest thousand.

Province, State or Agency.	Area in Square miles.	Total Population.	Hindus.	Sikhs.	Jains.	Buddhists.	Zoroastrians.	Muslims.	Christians. European (and Allied Races).	Christians. Anglo-Indians.	Christians. Indians.	Tribal Religions.	Others.	Not enumerated by religion.
1	2	3	4	5	6	7	8	9	10	11	12	13	14	15
INDIA	**1,576,000**	**338,171,000**	**238,624,000**	**4,325,000**	**1,251,000**	**439,000**	**109,000**	**77,093,000**	**156,000**	**119,000**	**5,691,000**	**7,630,000**	**445,000**	**2,289,000**
I. British India	818,000	256,534,000	177,124,000	3,203,000	453,000	345,000	96,000	66,157,000	135,000	101,000	3,293,000	5,129,000	422,000	76,000
(a) Governors' Provinces	*801,000*	*255,008,000*	*176,127,000*	*3,195,000*	*428,000*	*342,000*	*96,000*	*65,706,000*	*127,000*	*99,000*	*3,273,000*	*5,118,000*	*421,000*	*76,000*
1. Assam	55,000	8,622,000	4,932,000	3,000	3,000	15,000	..	2,756,000	3,000	*	199,000	711,000	..	..
2. Bengal	78,000	50,114,000	21,570,000	7,000	9,000	316,000	2,000	27,498,000	23,000	28,000	129,000	528,000	4,000	..
3. Bihar	69,000	32,372,000	25,915,000	6,000	4,000	1,000	..	4,140,000	6,000	6,000	320,000	1,971,000	..	..
4. Bombay (*including Aden*) ..	77,000	18,044,000	15,604,000	3,000	199,000	2,000	86,000	1,626,000	18,000	14,000	270,000	129,000	17,000	76,000
5. Central Provinces and Berar ..	99,000	15,323,000	13,174,000	4,000	78,000	..	2,000	682,000	6,000	5,000	40,000	1,332,000	..	..
6. Madras	136,000	45,326,000	39,996,000	1,000	31,000	1,000	..	3,303,000	12,000	29,000	1,728,000	225,000	..	..
7. North-West Frontier Province ..	14,000	2,425,000	143,000	43,000	..	..	..	2,227,000	8,000	..	4,000	..	..	..
8. Orissa	22,000	6,905,000	6,541,000	..	..	..	..	129,000	..	1,000	15,000	219,000	..	..
9. Punjab	99,000	23,581,000	6,329,000	3,064,000	35,000	6,000	1,000	13,332,000	20,000	3,000	392,000	..	399,000	..
10. Sind	46,000	3,887,000	1,017,000	18,000	1,000	.	4,000	2,831,000	7,000	2,000	6,000	..	1,000	..
11. United Provinces of Agra and Oudh	106,000	48,409,000	40,906,000	46,000	68,000	1,000	1,000	7,182,000	24,000	11,000	170,000	..	..	..
(b) Chief Commissioners' Provinces ..	*17,000*	*1,526,000*	*997,000*	*8,000*	*25,000*	*3,000*	..	*451,000*	*8,000*	*2,000*	*20,000*	*11,000*	*1,000*	..
12. Baluchistan	9,000	137,000	9,000	1,000	..	..	..	126,000	1,000	..	..	..	..	..
13. Other Chief Commissioners' Provinces (*Delhi, Ajmer-Merwara, Coorg and the Andamans and Nicobars*).	8,000	1,389,000	988,000	7,000	25,000	3,000	..	325,000	7,000	2,000	20,000	11,000	1,000	..
II. Indian States†	690,000	79,052,000	61,453,000	1,110,000	798,000	94,000	13,000	10,634,000	13,000	18,000	2,395,000	2,501,000	23,000	..
III. Agencies and Tribal Areas ..	68,000	2,585,000	47,000	12,000	..	..	..	302,000	8,000	..	3,000	..	..	2,213,000
North-West Frontier Province ..	23,000	2,259,000	14,000	5,000	..	..	..	23,000	4,000	..	..	..	..	2,213,000
Baluchistan	45,000	326,000	33,000	7,000	..	..	..	279,000	4,000	..	3,000	..	..	..

* 558 Anglo-Indians have been omitted in the process of converting absolute figures to thousands.

† Includes :—

Baluchistan States	80,000	405,000	12,000	..	..	..	..	393,000	..	..	..	..	..	..

M8CC—31-7-33—2,200—GIPS